DATE DUE

DEMCO 38-296

AMERICAN NATIONAL BIOGRAPHY

AMERICAN
NATIONAL BIOGRAPHY

Published under the auspices of the
AMERICAN COUNCIL OF LEARNED SOCIETIES

General Editors

John A. Garraty

Mark C. Carnes

VOLUME 6

OXFORD UNIVERSITY PRESS

New York   1999   Oxford

OXFORD UNIVERSITY PRESS

Oxford   New York
Athens   Auckland   Bangkok   Bogotá
Buenos Aires   Calcutta   Cape Town   Chennai
Dar es Salaam   Delhi   Florence   Hong Kong   Istanbul
Karachi   Kuala Lumpur   Madrid   Melbourne   Mexico City
Mumbai   Nairobi   Paris   São Paulo   Singapore
Taipei   Tokyo   Toronto   Warsaw
and associated companies in
Berlin   Ibadan

Published by Oxford University Press, Inc.,
198 Madison Avenue, New York, New York 10016
http://www.oup-usa.org

Oxford is a registered trademark of Oxford University Press

Funding for this publication was provided in part by
the Andrew W. Mellon Foundation, the Rockefeller Foundation,
and the National Endowment for the Humanities,
a federal agency.

Library of Congress Cataloging-in-Publication Data

American national biography / general editors, John A. Garraty, Mark C. Carnes
p.   cm.
"Published under the auspices of the American Council of Learned Societies."
Includes bibliographical references and index.
1. United States—Biography—Dictionaries.   I. Garraty, John Arthur,
1920–   .   II. Carnes, Mark C. (Mark Christopher), 1950–   .
III. American Council of Learned Societies.
CT213.A68   1998   98-20826   920.073—dc21   CIP
ISBN 0-19-520635-5 (set)
ISBN 0-19-512785-4 (vol. 6)

Printing (last digit): 9 8 7 6 5 4 3 2 1

Printed in the United States of America
on acid-free paper

DAFORA, Asadata (4 Aug. 1890–4 Mar. 1965), singer, dancer, and choreographer, was born John Warner Dafora Horton in Freetown, Sierra Leone. Little is known about his parents, but both were a part of the prominent black elite in colonial society. Dafora's great-great-grandfather was the first black man to be knighted by Queen Victoria and the first black mayor of Sierra Leone. Dafora's parents, moreover, met in England, while his father was studying at Oxford and while his mother was studying the piano. Following this tradition of European schooling, Dafora received a British education at the local Wesleyan School in Freetown and went on to study music and dance in Italy and Germany.

Dafora's career took off after he moved to New York City in 1929, traveling with a troupe of African dancers from various tribes. His first years in New York were rather unremarkable, however, and there is little evidence of Dafora's impact on the theatrical scene during this period. But that soon changed with Dafora's production of *Kykunkor* in 1934, the theatrical event of the season. The show had languished until it received critical notice in the *New York Times* from John Martin, the dance critic, on 9 May 1934. After Martin's glowing account, 425 people appeared at the theater that evening, 200 of whom had to be turned away. The large crowds continued, forcing the show to move to a bigger theater at City College and eventually reopen in other venues around town as the show sold out from May to August, almost all of its unplanned run.

Kykunkor told the story of a tribal wedding ritual in West Africa in which a jealous rival of the groom employs Kykunkor, a witch woman, to cast a death spell on the groom, who is eventually saved from death by a witch doctor. Full of drama and celebration, the rather conventional story of love and jealousy gained its allure from witches, spells, and elaborate ceremonies. The story also served as a showpiece for vibrant group dances and pantomime solos, all accompanied by vigorous drumming and singing. Eighteen men and women, some African, some African American, in colorful costumes, dancing to live music, created quite a visual feast.

Many audience members viewed the production as a concert direct from the jungle. Leading artists and intellectuals of the time populated the audience, including George Gershwin, Sherwood Anderson, Theodore Dreiser, and Carl Van Vechten, seeking an authentic experience of "primitive" Africa. As the souvenir program following the production proclaimed, *Kykunkor* impressed even scientists and explorers as a rare, truthful vision of Africa. James Chapin, curator of the American Museum of Natural History, declared, "Never outside of Africa have I ever seen or heard anything so typically Ethiopian. . . . The drum rhythms and most of the singing rang so true as to carry me back to the dark continent."

Leading African Americans also praised the authenticity of *Kykunkor*. Premiering during the final years of the artistic fervor now known as the Harlem Renaissance, the production received the praise of the stringent critic Alain Locke. A prime promoter of the Harlem Renaissance, Locke saw in Dafora's *Kykunkor* true African art transplanted to America. He extolled its stylistic purity and its artistry, devoid of the baseness and vulgarity that he often criticized in the cultural forms of African Americans. According to Locke, this was "primitive" art at its best, undiluted and inspirational.

Much of the stamp of authenticity came from the prominence of African dancing in the production. Vastly different from the linear and tightly held backbones of ballet and even modern dance at this time, African dance was comprised of flat-footed stomping, isolated actions of the hips, torso, and shoulders in rhythmic patterns, and bodies bent forward from the waist on deeply bowed legs with protruding buttocks. Dancing barefoot to pounding drums was seen as an innate racial talent by many, so that *Kykunkor* reinforced common perceptions of dark-skinned peoples as being close to nature, animals, and the basic functions of living, including sex.

Dafora worked within these conceptions and excelled partly because of them. *Kykunkor* established him as the prime exponent of authentic African dance. He went on to work on the Negro Theatre Unit of the Works Progress Administration's Federal Theatre Project, choreographing Orson Welles's direction of a Haitian version of *Macbeth* in 1936. He then left the Federal Theatre Project to work on his next production, *Zunguru* (1938). *Zunguru* was similar to *Kykunkor* in its use of African ritual, music, and dance, but it never achieved the success of its predecessor. Dafora then choreographed dances for Paul Robeson's revival of *Emperor Jones* in 1939.

Most of Dafora's career rested on the spectacular success of *Kykunkor*, and he was never able to re-create that achievement on stage. In the early 1940s, however, he became a noted spokesperson for the African Academy of Arts and Research, founded in 1943. The academy's purpose was to foster interest in and support of African culture, and Dafora was one of its stars. He and his troupe played a prominent role in the very successful African festivals sponsored by the academy beginning in 1943. The first two festivals, in 1943 and 1945, even attracted the attendance of Eleanor Roosevelt, who was eager to show her support of cultural events promoting racial understanding.

Dafora went on tour around the United States with his troupe in 1946–1947. Appearing at all the leading African-American colleges, he carried through with his lifelong attempt to promote African culture. He had less and less opportunity to do so as he grew older, facing competition from younger dancers and choreographers such as Pearl Primus and Katherine Dunham who creatively combined African and Caribbean rituals with American theatrics. Dafora's African "authenticity" eventually led him to make an appearance at the Great Apes House at the New York Zoological Society in June 1949, an outward indication that his trademark authenticity had become a kind of cage, restricting his creativity and narrowly marking his talents.

In 1947 Dafora created *Batanga*, another dance-drama in the tradition of *Kykunkor*, but it received little praise. He languished in the 1950s, retreating from public view. Fed up with the United States, he went back to Sierra Leone in May 1960, returning only briefly to the United States in 1962 for health reasons. The following year he returned again to Sierra Leone. He died in Harlem, New York.

• Dafora's papers at the New York Public Library's Schomburg Center for Research in Black Culture provide the best insight into the vicissitudes of his career. Souvenir programs, reviews, and some correspondence detail his successes in the 1930s and 1940s. John O. Perpener, "The Seminal Years of Black Concert Dance" (Ph.D. diss., New York Univ., 1992), and Leah Creque-Harris, "The Representation of African Dance on the Concert Stage" (Ph.D. diss., Emory Univ., 1991), supply an introduction to Dafora. Lynne Fauley Emery, *Black Dance from 1619 to Today*, rev. ed. (1988), gives an overview of African Americans in dance with some attention to Dafora, as do Richard Long, *The Black Tradition in American Dance* (1989), and Edward Thorpe, *Black Dance* (1989).

JULIA L. FOULKES

DAFT, Leo (13 Nov. 1843–28 Mar. 1922), electrical engineer, was born in Birmingham, England, the son of Thomas B. Daft, a civil engineer, and Emma Matilda Sturges. His father started a firm to design greenhouses and conservatories, but when Leo was young, his father became a consulting engineer in London to large construction and shipbuilding firms. Leo attended local schools and Liverpool Collegiate School. When he was fifteen he became a draftsman in his father's office. He attended engineering lectures by William Pole at London University as a special student but did not seek a degree. Daft made drawings for Pole to use in his lectures. Through his father he became acquainted with electrical engineer Cromwell Fleetwood Varley, who advised him in electrical projects. Another of his father's friends, William Siemans, lent him electrical equipment. Daft's father provided laboratory space in the family home, where Daft carried out experiments with electricity, did other projects in physics, and delved into photography.

In about 1865, while serving as his father's agent in Liverpool on shipbuilding affairs, Daft presented a paper to the Liverpool Polytechnic Society on sheathing iron ships, in which he discussed the nature of the galvanic (electrical) effects of the different metals used for this purpose. There he also became acquainted with some Americans and decided in 1866 to make a career in the United States. He traveled to Louisville, Kentucky, where he was hired as an assistant engineer on the Mount Vernon extension of the Louisville and Nashville Railroad; after its completion he moved to New York City. His efforts to sell electric signaling equipment of his own manufacture were not successful, so in 1871 he set up a photography business in Troy, New York, which became fairly large and profitable. He sold the first print of one of his photographs of the Mohawk Valley for $300 (the print was seven feet wide and twenty inches high). In 1871 he married Katherine Anna Flansburgh of Albany, New York; they had four children.

Daft went to England in 1879 to settle his deceased father's estate. That year the first successful nonbattery electric locomotive was displayed at an industrial exhibition in Berlin, which led to increased interest in electric transportation. After returning to New York, Daft took a position with the New York Electric Light Company, which soon became the Daft Electric Company. The firm moved from New York to Greenville, New Jersey, in 1881 and later to Marion, New Jersey.

Daft's company in 1883 installed what was probably the first electric elevator in the world at the Garner Cotton Mills in Newburgh, New York. He continued to install electric elevators, and he also developed a power distribution system in New York City. A similar system that he built in Boston in 1884 was the first commercial complete central station for electrical distribution of power. At the Philadelphia Electrical Exhibition in 1884, Daft created an exhibit for the journal *Electrical World*, in which a daily newspaper was printed by electrotype, while the typesetting for the newspaper was being completed in New York. It was a popular attraction and drew attention to the capabilities of electrical power.

In 1883 Daft began research involving an electrically operated railroad. He was not the first: Thomas Davenport of Vermont had built a small one in 1834, and Robert Davidson of Scotland had built a large electric locomotive in 1838, which was destroyed by locomotive drivers and stokers who feared for their jobs. Trying out various types of traction, Daft created a system of two overhead wires in which the power was gathered by what he called a "troller" (from which the word "trolley" was derived). He built an electric locomotive, named *Ampere*, for the Saratoga and Mount McGregor Railroad and a short line at Coney Island, New York. In 1884 his company built an electric road in Baltimore, Maryland. The next year it provided electrical equipment for a branch of the Baltimore Union Passenger Railway Company, one of the first commercial lines to use electricity. This equipment continued to operate without breakdown for four years.

According to an anonymous biographer of Daft, "The four independent motors were of the single-reduction type, towing 16-foot trailers, and the regulation was series-parallel, the four spools of each motor being so connected to the controller without the use of idle resistance in any form" (*Cassier's Magazine*, p. 262). It was a successful demonstration of the power available in the electrical system to handle grades and curves. Daft named the electric cars *Morse* and *Faraday* in recognition of those pioneers in electricity. A later electric car that he built, the *Ben Franklin*, was used for some years on the Ninth Avenue Elevated Line in New York City.

Daft was a successful pioneer in the use of electricity for locomotion. His system of electric cars continued to be used into the 1880s by a number of small transit systems. At some later time he invented a process of vulcanizing rubber onto metal by electrochemical means, which was also used for many years. He was a charter member of the American Institute of Electrical Engineers. Daft never became a U.S. citizen. He died in Albany, New York.

• The New York Public Library has copies of stereographs taken by Daft. Two accounts of Daft's life and accomplishments were written before his death, but the authors are unidentified: "Leo Daft," *Electrical World*, 30 Mar. 1889, p. 184, and "Leo Daft: An Electric Railway Pioneer," *Cassier's Magazine* 21 (July 1901): 263–64. Histories of electric railroads that deal with Daft's contributions include Robert Post, "America's Electric Railway Beginnings: Trollers and Daft Dummies," *Southern California Quarterly* 69 (1987): 203–21, and Post, *Street Railways and the Growth of Los Angeles* (1989). An obituary is in the *Journal of the American Institute of Electrical Engineers* (May 1922).

ELIZABETH NOBLE SHOR

DAGG, John Leadley (13 Feb. 1794–11 June 1884), Baptist minister and educator, was born in a log cabin near Middleburg, Loudoun County, Virginia, the son of Robert Dagg, the saddler and postmaster of the village, and Sarah Davis. Poverty contributed in part to his limited formal education, which ended after six years. At fourteen he began to teach in a small school near Middleburg. Though lacking a college degree he had innate intellectual abilities evidenced by his mastery of Latin, Greek, and Hebrew. While studying by candlelight, however, he damaged his eyesight so severely that after 1823 he could read and write only with the assistance of others.

He was baptized in 1812 by the Ebenezer Baptist Church and in 1817 entered the Baptist ministry, serving as pastor at Dumfries and other small churches in Virginia until 1825. From 1825 to 1834 he served the much larger Fifth Baptist Church in Philadelphia. During this period he was active in the Triennial Convention, the earliest national organization of denominational life among Baptists. When problems with his throat compelled Dagg to leave a regular preaching position, he accepted the presidency of Haddington Institute, a theological school for Baptist ministers near Philadelphia. There he formally began teaching theology.

Dagg married twice. He and Fanny H. Thornton of Virginia were married in 1817; they had four children, including a son who followed his father into the ministry and also became a college president. In 1832, eight years after the death of his first wife, Dagg married a widow, Mrs. Mary Young Davis.

In 1836 Dagg was invited to assume the presidency of the Alabama Female Athenaeum in Tuscaloosa. During Dagg's years as president he became acquainted with Basil Manly, Sr., who, as president of the University of Alabama, conferred the D.D. degree upon Dagg in 1843. The following year he moved to Mercer University, then located in Penfield, Georgia, to serve as professor of theology. The next year he was elevated to the presidency. In 1845 Dagg joined Manly and other ministers in forming the Southern Baptist Convention, also assisting in writing the constitution of that body. During his years at Mercer Dagg wrote several essays, including "Origin and Authority of the Bible" (1853), a defense of the Bible's authority that later was incorporated into his *Manual for Theology* (1857). He was successful also in building the school's theological faculty, which became one of the strongest in the South before the Civil War.

Dagg retired from Mercer in 1856, then lived with relatives in Georgia until 1870 when he moved to Hayneville, Alabama, where he died. His retirement years were productive. Four books, published during these years extended his influence among Southern Baptists and established his reputation as the pioneer Baptist theologian in America. His *Manual of Theology*, a summary of theology for southern ministers, was followed in 1858 by *A Treatise on Church Order*, a presentation of church polity in Baptist churches. *The Elements of Moral Science*, in which he defends the institution of slavery, appeared in 1859, and *The Evidences of Christianity* was published in 1869. These books became texts in many Southern Baptist schools, rivaling or replacing others by northerner Francis Wayland, who defended abolition views. Aside from his defense of slavery, Dagg's theological position was a moderate Calvinism, typical of most Baptists in the early nineteenth century.

• J. L. Dagg, "Autobiography of John L. Dagg," is a rare manuscript housed at Mercer University in Macon, Ga. R. G. Gardner, "John Leadley Dagg," *Review and Expositor* 54 (1957): 246–63, is a well-researched introduction to his life. Also see R. G. Gardner, "John Leadley Dagg: Pioneer American Baptist Theologian" (Ph.D. diss., Duke Univ., 1957). Dagg's writings are available at the Historical Commission of the Southern Baptist Convention in Nashville, Tenn.

BRUCE L. SHELLEY

DAGGETT, Rollin Mallory (22 Feb. 1831–12 Nov. 1901), journalist, congressman, minister to Hawaii, and author, was born in Richville, New York, the son of Eunice White and Gardner Daggett, farmers. Daggett was the youngest of seven children, the other six being girls. After his mother's death in 1833, the family moved to Defiance, Ohio, in 1837. In 1849 Daggett became a printer, learning a trade which endowed him with an education and influenced his later choice of a journalistic career.

Gold in California lured him West in 1850. Daggett took the overland passage, traveling partly with wagon trains and partly alone on foot. He mined gold for the next two years, with moderate success. In 1852 he quit mining and moved to San Francisco, where he became a printer again. With J. Macdonough Foard, Daggett founded the *Golden Era*, one of the earliest literary journals of the West and also one of the most important, for it featured the contributions of such established or rising talents as Artemus Ward (Charles Farrar Browne), Dan De Quille, and Mark Twain. Daggett performed all sorts of functions for the magazine—from contributing fiction and editorials to soliciting subscriptions—before selling it in 1860.

Several months later, Daggett and several partners began publishing a newspaper, the San Francisco *Daily Evening Mirror*. The paper early became outspokenly Republican, and Daggett, who was both opinionated and courageous, enjoyed engaging the journal in controversies. He resigned, however, in 1861 and in 1862 moved to Virginia City, Nevada, where he began the most important phase of his life.

With a partner Daggett established a brokerage house. He also became active in politics and joined the Virginia City *Territorial Enterprise* as a reporter. The *Enterprise*, under its owners Joseph T. Goodman and Denis McCarthy, soon became one of the great newspapers of the Old West, employing some of the most distinguished writers and colorful free spirits of western journalism: Dan De Quille, Mark Twain, Alf Doten, James Townsend, and C. C. Goodwin. Daggett's pugnacious assaults on corruption and injustice undoubtedly helped create the paper's tradition of fearless honesty which influenced Twain. But when Goodman sold the *Enterprise* in 1874 to his political arch-enemy, the financier William Sharon, Daggett adapted easily to the reversal of the paper's political stance—from fierce independence to mouthpiece of its wealthy owner—and he served Sharon as an editorial writer and sometime editor.

Daggett was one of Twain's *Enterprise* friends with whom he kept in touch. In 1880, as congressman, Daggett aided Twain in his efforts to persuade Congress to establish copyright laws. Several years later, Twain reciprocated by helping Daggett publish his book on Hawaiian legends. Some indication of their cordial relationship can be seen in Twain's playful allusion to Daggett in the humorous sketch, "The Carson Fossil-Footprints" (1884).

Daggett remained with the *Enterprise* until 1879. Aspiring to literary fame, he wrote a good deal of verse and also collaborated with Joseph T. Goodman, his editor, on a five-act mystery play, *The Psychoscope* (1871), which was at least a generation ahead of its time in its use of realism.

In 1871, at the age of thirty-seven, Daggett married seventeen-year-old Maggie Curry. Two daughters and a son were born to them, but the son died in infancy and Maggie died of tuberculosis in 1877. In 1883 Daggett married Lizzie Hinds, a Seattle heiress thirty-one years younger than he. She died several years later without bearing him any children.

Daggett's devotion to the Republican party involved him in politics even while he continued to work for the *Enterprise*. He was elected in 1862 to the Nevada Territorial Council, on which he took strong pro-Union stands. Between 1867 and 1876 Daggett served as clerk of the United States Circuit and District Courts for Nevada. He was elected in 1876 as an elector for Nevada pledged to Rutherford B. Hayes.

In 1879 Daggett was elected to a two-year term as a Republican congressman from Nevada. While in Washington, he favored anti-railroad and anti-Chinese legislation. His record indicates that he routinely supported Nevada causes and that he cooperated closely with the "silver kings," especially Senior John Percival Jones and John Mackay, who dominated Nevada politics.

Daggett's 1881 bid for reelection ended in defeat, but he stayed in Washington to seek political preferment. His efforts were rewarded in 1882 when President Chester Arthur appointed him minister to the kingdom of Hawaii. He remained in that position until 1885.

In 1882 Daggett published his most notable work of fiction, *Braxton's Bar*, a novel set in the mining country. After his return from Hawaii, he published, with Hawaii's King David Kalakaua, *The Legends and Myths of Hawaii* (1888). The last years of Daggett's life were spent composing short works of prose and poetry for western magazines and newspapers. A bold and resourceful personality typifying the final stage of the settlement of the American frontier, Daggett filled his remarkable days with adventure, variety, and achievement. He died at his home in San Francisco.

• A short archival file of Daggett poems and memorabilia exists in the Bancroft Library of the University of California-Berkeley. The microfilm of the surviving issues of the Virginia City *Territorial Enterprise* contains the richest available store of Daggett's editorials and news stories, but as almost all of this material is unsigned, identification is a problem. The only biography of Daggett is Francis Phelps Weisenburger, *Idol of the West: The Fabulous Career of Rollin Mallory Daggett* (1965), which makes substantial use of official records and such papers as have been kept by his descendants. The best contemporary sources of anecdotes about Daggett can be found in Myron Angel's classic *History of Nevada* (1881; repr. 1958, 1973) and Charles C. Goodwin, *As I Remember Them* (1913). Recent short discussions of Daggett can be found in Ivan Benson, *Mark Twain's Western Years* (1966); Henry Nash Smith, ed. *Mark Twain of the Enterprise* (1957); Lawrence I. Berkove, "Life after Twain: The Later Careers of the *Enterprise* Staff," *Mark Twain Journal* 29, no. 1 (Spring 1991): 22–28; and Berkove's introduction to his edition of *The Psychoscope* (1993). An obituary appears in the Salt Lake City *Daily Tribune*, 24 Nov. 1901.

LAWRENCE I. BERKOVE

DAHL, Theodor Halvorson (2 Apr. 1845–18 Jan. 1923), Lutheran clergyman and church leader, was born in Baastad, Mellem Borgesyssel, Norway, the son of Halvor Thoreson Smaadal and Anne Maastad. After attending a Latin school in Christiania from 1862 to 1865 he emigrated to America. He attended Augustana Theological Seminary (located at that time in Paxton, Illinois), a school of the Scandinavian Augustana Lutheran church. He graduated with a C.T. (Candidatus Theologiae) in 1867 after two years of study. That year he was ordained to the ministry by T. N. Hasselquist, president of both the seminary and the synod, and he married Rebekka Oline Gjertsen; they had several children.

Dahl's career as a pastor began on the Minnesota frontier as a home missionary in the New London and Litchfield areas west of the Twin Cities (1867–1873). It continued in Green Bay, Wisconsin, and vicinity (1873–1881) and concluded in Stoughton, Wisconsin (1881–1902). Between 1867 and 1870 he was a member of the Scandinavian Augustana Synod. In 1870 he changed his affiliation to the Norwegian-Danish Lutheran Conference (1870–1890), serving as secretary from 1876 to 1881 and as president from 1881 to 1886. In 1890 Dahl became a member of the United Norwegian Lutheran church, for which he served as vice president (1894–1902) and president (1902–1917). In these church bodies he was a strongly committed, persistent advocate of the union of all Norwegian Lutheran church organizations.

In 1890 the United church was formed through the merger of the Norwegian-Danish Lutheran Conference, the Norwegian Augustana Synod, and the so-called Anti-Missourian Brotherhood. The Anti-Missourians were composed of pastors and congregations that had withdrawn from the Norwegian Synod as a result of differences concerning the doctrine of predestination (the "election to salvation" controversy). The unusual name derived from their objection to the influence of the Missouri Synod within the Norwegian Synod. In 1894 Dahl wrote a small book titled *Fred og Strid* ("peace and strife") that described the process of merger, celebrated its achievement, and condemned the conflict and tension that occurred within the denomination over the transfer of Augsberg Seminary in Minneapolis to the United church. (Dahl advocated a union of Norwegian church bodies on a confessional basis.)

The United church was the largest of the Norwegian-American Lutheran church bodies, occupying a middle position between the low-church, pietistic Hauge's Synod and the very conservative, doctrinally oriented Norwegian Synod. Representing a mediating position, the United church sought to be a bridge between the two. In its effort to be inclusive, the United church was somewhat similar to the Church of Norway. The United church provided primary leadership for the unification movement. In one of his annual reports Dahl succinctly expressed the church's purpose: "The cause of union has been on the program of the United church since its birth."

Dahl assumed the presidency of the United church in 1902 upon the death of Gjermund Hoyme, who had been its president since 1890. He had a distinguished career as the able, experienced leader of the church, which was a thriving and aggressively mission-minded body. Although in its home mission program it concentrated on outreach to Norwegian settlers who were moving northward and westward from the older areas of settlement, it also played a prominent role in city mission and welfare work. At the same time much effort was expended in support of a growing foreign mission enterprise. The church was heavily involved in education, supporting several church colleges and encouraging a burgeoning academy movement. Dahl was a gifted administrator and an effective leader in promoting and supporting these activities. He provided spiritual nurture and guidance for the church through his biblical preaching and through his reports and addresses at annual meetings and on other occasions.

In 1917 a second merger occurred and again Dahl played a key role. While he was president of the United church, the Norwegian Lutheran Church in America (NLCA) was formed, resulting from the union of the United church, the Norwegian Synod, and Hauge's Synod. It was particularly fitting that Dahl's presidency should culminate and conclude with the church union to which he had devoted so much time and energy. The United church was in existence for only twenty-seven years, and Dahl was its president for fifteen of those years. During the last six years of his life he was chaplain at Fairview Hospital in Minneapolis, and he died in that city.

• A valuable source of information on Dahl is an impressive memorial publication of the United church on the occasion of its twenty-fifth anniversary, N. C. Brun, ed., *Fra Ungdomsaar* (1915). Scattered references to Dahl are found in E. Clifford Nelson, *The Lutheran Church among Norwegian-Americans*, vol. 2 (1960), and J. A. Bergh, *Den norsk lutherske Kirkes Historie i Amerika* (1914). Basic biographical information is in O. M. Norlie, ed., *Norsk lutherske Prester i Amerika, 1843–1913* (1914), which was translated and revised by Rasmus Malmin, et al., as *Who's Who among Pastors in all the Norwegian Lutheran Synods in America, 1843–1927* (1928); O. N. Nelson, *History of the Scandinavians and Successful Scandinavians in the U.S.*, 2d ed. (1901); and J. C. Jensson Roseland, *American Lutheran Biographies* (1905).

EUGENE L. FEVOLD

DAHLBERG, Edward (22 July 1900–23 Feb. 1977), writer, was born in a charity ward in Boston, Massachusetts, the illegitimate son of Saul Gottdank, a barber, and Lizzie Dahlberg, a factory worker. The family went to Dallas, Texas, where Gottdank taught Lizzie barbering and then absconded with the family money. He came back twice more to do the same before leaving for good. Dahlberg hardly remembered the man himself, but the image of a father rejecting his son haunted his writing from first to last.

Dahlberg and his mother wandered up and down the midlands, finally settling in Kansas City, where she opened for business in the Star Lady Barbershop. Dahlberg's first novel, *Bottom Dogs*, published in England in 1929, describes these years as a sequence of harrowing mishaps in which his mother loses all her money to vicious lovers. But Dahlberg dates the start of his life from memories of this city, which he called "my Tarsus," alluding to St. Paul's beginnings in southern Turkey, near the Mediterranean, before his conversion to Christianity.

Dahlberg's preoccupation with his origins and the details of his growing up flow from a desire to mythologize the literal and to create parallels between a rootless American existence and the wealth of literary relation in classical literature and the Bible. As such, he was offended to read in D. H. Lawrence's foreword to *Bottom Dogs* a reference to naturalism, by which he inferred a literal-minded and self-pitying manner of writing.

Both *Bottom Dogs* and its sequel, *From Flushing to Calvary* (1932), continue the narrative of Dahlberg's early life to the time when one of his mother's lovers, Henry Smith, persuaded her to give him up to an orphanage. Dahlberg makes a searing account of his unhappy life in a Catholic orphanage in Kansas City and in the grim Dickensian world of the Jewish Orphan Asylum in Cleveland, where he languished from 1912 to 1917. After release he worked as a messenger in Cleveland and returned to his mother in Kansas City, where he was a drover in the stockyards. He had a short stint in the army in 1918 and then drifted west working odd jobs until he reached Los Angeles.

Dahlberg's real education began under the tutelage of a self-taught guru, Max Lewis, a resident of the Young Men's Christian Association, where Dahlberg was also billeted. He read the classics and the literature of revolt, Friedrich Nietzsche, Samuel Butler, Ralph Waldo Emerson, and the Romantics. In 1921 he enrolled at the University of California at Berkeley, taking courses in philosophy and anthropology; disillusioned with California ways, he migrated east two years later and finished college at Columbia University in New York City. Soon after, he was teaching high school and launching his writing career. His mother joined him in 1926 in a house near the Calvary Cemetery in Astoria, hence the title of his second autobiographical novel, *From Flushing to Calvary*.

Dahlberg left for Europe in 1926 after marrying Fanya Fass, from a well-to-do Cleveland family; they had no children. The couple lived in Paris, Monte Carlo, and Brussels, but the marriage broke down. Dahlberg drifted into the remaining literary circles of the modernist movement, which included Hart Crane, Ernest Hemingway's close friend Robert McAlmon, and Richard Aldington, a founder with Ezra Pound of imagist poetry. Dahlberg was soon recognized as a promising novelist when Edmund Wilson greeted the publication of *Bottom Dogs* as a work "of distinction."

In 1930 Dahlberg moved back to the United States to write for *Poetry*, the *Nation*, *Pagany*, the *New Republic*, and *New Masses*, the core of both the literary avant-garde journals and the socialist political reviews.

From Flushing to Calvary was completed by about 1931, and its last installment was published as *Kentucky Blue Grass Henry Smith* (1932). He was now a pivotal figure in literary New York and counted among his friends Sherwood Anderson and photographer Alfred Stieglitz. William Carlos Williams was another lasting influence, especially in Williams's historical essays published as *In the American Grain* (1925). In 1933 Dahlberg was in Berlin and had his own run-in with uniformed Nazis in a bar, which led to the writing of the first anti-Hitler novel in America, *Those Who Perish* (1934). A year later Dahlberg delivered his paper "Fascism and Writers" at the first meeting of the American Writers' Congress, which he had helped to organize.

By 1936 Dahlberg had renounced his early prose and socialist ties in New York and rusticated in a boardinghouse on Cape Ann, Massachusetts, looking for a new direction. He found it in a meeting with the young scholar and poet Charles Olson, who shared with Dahlberg his research on the connections between Melville's *Moby-Dick* and Shakespeare's *King Lear*. The relationship opened Dahlberg's eyes to the possibility of reinterpreting his own life through a much wider lens of literature and myth.

Dahlberg wrote a series of critical essays exposing the mythical and literary sources of American classics, which he called *Do These Bones Live* (1941), retitled *Can These Bones Live* in later editions. There and elsewhere Dahlberg established links between the American and the Mediterranean imagination. But his main purpose was to expose the isolation of the American in the New World, a place cut off from the civilizations of the past and stripped of the consolations of art and wisdom. He found evidence of suffering and loneliness in the major writers of the American renaissance and saw his own dilemma as a writer in the same terms. *The Flea of Sodom*, published in 1950, is a first attempt to read his personal life in New York from the mythological perspective developing in his critical writing. But *The Flea* is also a farewell to his old political convictions and the literary establishment of New York, which he castigated as a socialist coterie bent on excluding writers from other points of view.

In 1942 Dahlberg married Winifred Sheehan Moore; they had two sons. A crucial event in his life was the death of his mother four years later, ending a troubled but obsessive relationship that was the centerpiece of his ongoing autobiographical canon. Dahlberg now saw himself in terms of the biblical story of Abraham expelling his son Ishmael and his mother Hagar. His wanderings through America's "macadam deserts" paralleled the wanderings of Ishmael. After his divorce from Winifred Moore, Dahlberg married Rlene LaFleur Howell in 1950 and resumed his restless journeys between coasts and abroad.

Other books followed: *The Sorrows of Priapus* (1957), on the human sex drive, a subject that fascinated him from his own turbulent life with companions and wives, and *Truth Is More Sacred* (1961), an exchange of letters on literature with Herbert Read. The key text of his career, *Because I Was Flesh* (1964), brought to high finish the method of mythological narrative he had been developing for the past twenty-five years. The broad thematic approach of his critical writing and the self-scrutiny of his novels merged into a retelling of his life through a prose style that appropriated the synchronic techniques of the modernist long poem. T. S. Eliot, Pound, James Joyce, and Olson all had their influence in the making of this mythological account of an American wanderer looking for his true father.

Dahlberg had raised autobiography to a high art in *Because I Was Flesh*; a florid, erudite prose style, notable for its eccentric imagery and biblical resonance, found its true strength in the revamping of an Old Testament story of abandonment and self-making. Dahlberg not only retold the story in a new lyrical prose fraught with allusions to Hebrew and Greek mythology, but he transformed his own persona from the earlier novels into an archetypal voice suffering the pains of an impersonal culture at a transpersonal level. No longer is Lorrie Gilchrist, his protagonist of the early novels or the figurative "I" of later essays, deployed as the narrator, but a new voice appears as a mythopoeic emcee in the tradition of Eliot's Tiresias and Pound's Homeric narrator. *Because I Was Flesh* takes its place among the experimental classics of the century.

New critical essays followed in *Alms for Oblivion* (1964), as well as poetry, *Cipango's Hinder Door* (1966) and *The Leafless American* (1967). Paul Carroll edited a miscellany of Dahlberg's writings, *The Edward Dahlberg Reader*, in 1967, and in *The Carnal Myth* (1968), Dahlberg returned to the theme of sexuality in classical literature. In 1971 Dahlberg wrote a final version of his life in *The Confessions of Edward Dahlberg*, a breezy and caustic account of well-threshed materials. A symbolic chapter thirty-three is reserved for telling the bitter ending of his friendship with Olson, by far the most important man in his life.

In 1965 Dahlberg returned to his roots in Kansas City and taught briefly at the University of Missouri, where he completed a book of oracular instructions on the meaning of sloth, lust, loneliness, myth, and faith titled *Reasons of the Heart*. Celebrated as a man of letters among a wider audience in these years, Dahlberg experienced the fame and acceptance he had sought all his life. In 1967 a selection of his letters appeared under the title *Epitaphs of Our Times*. After a long life of travel and the disruptions of rocky marriages, Dahlberg married for a fourth time, in 1967, to Julia Lawlor and settled once more in New York City, where he died.

• Most of Dahlberg's papers are in the Humanities Research Center, University of Texas, Austin. *A Bibliography of Edward Dahlberg* was edited by Harold Billings (1971). Dahlberg's letters to Charles Olson are collected in *In Love, In Sorrow: The Complete Correspondence of Charles Olson and Edward Dahlberg*, ed. Paul Christensen (1990). The principal biography is Charles DeFanti, *The Wages of Expectation: A Biography of Edward Dahlberg* (1978). Fred Moramarco has written a full-length critical study of Dahlberg's prose, *Edward Dahlberg* (1972). Other glimpses into his writing life can be found in John Cech's *Charles Olson and Edward Dahlberg: A Portrait of a Friendship* (1982) and in Harold Billings's edition of *Edward Dahlberg: American Ishmael of Letters* (1968). A Festschrift was edited by Jonathan Williams as *Edward Dahlberg: A Tribute* (1970).

PAUL CHRISTENSEN

DAHLBERG, Edwin Theodore (27 Dec. 1892–6 Sept. 1986), pastor, was born in Fergus Falls, Minnesota, the son of Elof Dahlberg and Christine Ring, farmers. The youngest of four children, Dahlberg was raised on a Swedish Baptist farm until age ten, when the family moved to Minneapolis. He was baptized in the Olivet Baptist Church (now University Baptist Church) and graduated in 1914 from the University of Minnesota, where Rutledge Thornton Wiltbank, pastor of the Olivet Baptist Church and psychology professor at the university, inspired him to enter the ministry.

Intent on pursuing his newly chosen profession, Dahlberg soon enrolled at Rochester Theological Seminary in Rochester, New York, where he studied under Walter Rauschenbusch, "prophet of the social gospel." While in seminary Dahlberg also worked as Rauschenbusch's student secretary, joining the Fellowship of Reconciliation at Rauschenbusch's invitation. It was during this time that Dahlberg became a lifelong pacifist. Upon his graduation in 1917, Dahlberg wanted to refuse to register for the draft to witness to his pacifist convictions and to protest exemption for theological students. Dahlberg was eventually persuaded to register, however, and accepted an exemption only after his mother suffered a conveniently timed "heart attack." He later recounted the severe feelings of guilt and denial of Christian discipleship that such circumstances provoked in a sermon, "The Place of the Pacifist in Wartime," which he delivered at the First Baptist Church of Syracuse on the first anniversary of the bombing of Pearl Harbor.

Continuing at Rochester seminary, Dahlberg received his bachelor of divinity degree in 1918 and was ordained at the Olivet Baptist Church of Minneapolis in May 1918. He married Emilie Louise Loeffler in August of that same year; the couple had three children. From 1918 to 1921 he pastored the Baptist church in Potsdam, New York, also maintaining posts at two nearby preaching stations, one Presbyterian, one Baptist. From 1921 to 1931 he pastored the Maple Street Baptist Church of Buffalo, New York, raising funds for its new building. He then moved on to serve the First Baptist Church of St. Paul, Minnesota, for eight years. Robert Torbet, Carl Tiller, and Gordon Torgerson, members of his church youth group, later became denominational leaders. Dahlberg pastored the First Baptist Church in Syracuse, New York, from 1939 to 1950, developing a reputation as a noted preacher. While in Syracuse, Dahlberg also helped organize various Baptist organizations, including the Baptist Pacifist Fellowship in 1940. He was twice elected president of the Northern Baptist Convention, in 1946 and 1948, was a member of the Baptist World

Alliance Executive Committee from 1947 to 1955, and was a delegate to the constituting assembly of the World Council of Churches in Amsterdam in 1948. In addition to his work with these organizations, he was also a member of the Central Committee of the WCC from 1948 to 1954.

Dahlberg pastored the Delmar Baptist Church in St. Louis, Missouri, from 1950 to 1962, a position that ran concurrently with much of his time at the WCC. He attended the WCC Central Committee meeting in Lucknow, India, in 1952–1953 and WCC assemblies in Evanston, Illinois (1954) and New Delhi, India (1961). In 1955–1956 he was also president of the American Baptist Home Mission Society. Dahlberg, previously a participant in the Federal Council of Churches, was a delegate to the constituting assembly of the National Council of Churches of Christ in 1950, later serving the NCCC as president from 1957 to 1960.

Dahlberg was the first Baptist and the first active pastor to hold the post of NCCC president. He led the council during the Cold War period when John Foster Dulles had articulated the U.S. policy of massive retaliation, that is, any Soviet-bloc behavior that threatened vital interests of the West would result in a U.S. nuclear strike against the USSR. In his inaugural address to the council in 1958, Dahlberg challenged this U.S. policy, calling instead for one of massive reconciliation led by Christian churches. He said, "If we would concentrate on economic aid, the reduction of armaments, the exchange of visiting delegations . . . we would go far toward the reduction of those fears and tensions which now goad whole nations into a suicidal leap into the abyss of death" (*National Council Outlook* 8 [Jan. 1958]: 8). While in office Dahlberg urged admission of China to the United Nations, a position that drew sharp criticism from right-wing organizations. He also promoted the civil rights movement by refusing to hold meetings at establishments that did not permit black delegates to attend. He traveled on Christmas missions to American armed forces in Alaska (1957), Spain and Morocco (1958), and Taiwan and the Pacific islands (1959).

Because of his continuing efforts for peace and human rights, Dahlberg accumulated many accolades throughout his career. In 1961 he received the Gandhi Award from Promoting Enduring Peace, Inc. Colgate Rochester Divinity School established the annual Dahlberg Ecumenical Lectureship. From 1963 to 1966 Dahlberg also served as preacher-in-residence at Crozer Theological Seminary, and in 1964 American Baptists established a biennial peace prize in his name, with the initial prize being awarded to the Reverend Martin Luther King, Jr.

Even during the latter part of his life, Dahlberg continued to be ecumenically and internationally active, participating at age seventy-three in the Interfaith Peace Mission to Vietnam. Likewise, when he was ninety years old, he visited the Soviet Union with members of the Baptist Peace Fellowship of North America and spoke at a Baptist church in Moscow. In addition to his diplomatic interests Dahlberg also authored six books, several pamphlets, and many periodical articles, with his sermons appearing in several collections. In his free time, he was fond of hiking and mountain climbing; for thirty years, regardless of his schedule, he would spend an entire night each vacation in solitary prayer. After Dahlberg's first wife died in 1968, he married Viola Louise Palmiter in 1977. Dahlberg died at the Orangewood retirement community in Phoenix, Arizona.

Widely respected as a preacher, lecturer, and pastor, Dahlberg has been characterized as a minister who maintained a balance between a warmhearted faith in the Jesus of the New Testament and a social vision that made the gospel part of the contemporary scene. Such a balance is evident in his words, "The essential thing to my mind in the church today is that we must bring about a fusion of evangelism and social action." Dahlberg was involved both in sit-ins urging equal rights and in peace demonstrations opposing the Vietnam War. Opposed to nuclear weapons and the Cold War mentality, he called instead for a theology of peace, saying, "The answer to the war philosophy must ultimately be found in the conscience and ideology of religious men and women and the degree to which they address themselves to . . . justice, mercy and peace" (*Baptist Peace News*, Apr. 1970).

• Dahlberg's papers, including his sermons and scrapbooks, are at the American Baptist–Samuel Colgate Historical Library in Rochester, N.Y. Oral history interviews with Dahlberg made in 1955, 1973, and 1981 are also available there. His texts include *Youth and the Homes of Tomorrow* (1934), *Which Way for a Christian?* (1939), *Are You a Christian?* (1943), *The Book of Revival: A Popular Study of Paul's Letter to the Romans* (1947?), *This Is the Rim of East Asia* (1962), and *I Pick Up Hitchhikers* (1978). He also edited and contributed to *Herald of Evangel— 60 Years of American Christianity* (1965). Articles and sermons by Dahlberg appeared frequently in the *Baptist*, the *Standard*, and the *Watchman-Examiner*. For details concerning his relationship with Rauschenbusch, see John E. Skoglund, "Edwin Dahlberg in Conversation: Memories of Walter Rauschenbusch," *Foundations* 18 (Sept. 1975): 209–18. An obituary is in the *New York Times*, 9 Sept. 1986. For an additional tribute see Philip E. Jenks, "Edwin T. Dahlberg: The Good Neighbor," *American Baptist* 184 (Jan.–Feb. 1987): 14–15, 57.

JAMES R. LYNCH

DAHLEN, Bill (5 Jan. 1870–5 Dec. 1950), baseball player and manager, was born William Frederick Dahlen in Nelliston, New York, near Cooperstown, the son of a masonry contractor. His parents' names are unknown. He graduated from Fort Plain (N.Y.) High School and played baseball for two years at the Clinton (N.Y.) Liberal Institute. Dahlen joined the Cobleskill, New York, team in the New York State League in 1890. He played second base and made 137 hits in only 85 games for a .342 batting average. His excellent play caught the attention of a friend of Cap Anson, the manager of the Chicago Colts (later known as the Cubs) in the National League.

Dahlen made the 1891 Colts as the third baseman, although he did see time at shortstop and in the outfield. He was second on the Chicago team with nine home runs and third with 76 runs batted in. Dahlen batted .260 for the second-place Colts. The 5′9″, 175-pound Dahlen batted third in the order in 1891 and 1892 but usually batted lower in the order in later years. In 1892 he divided time between third base and shortstop for Chicago and raised his batting average to .291. Although a free swinger, Dahlen did not strike out excessively and drew more than 1,000 walks in his career. Not known as a power hitter, Dahlen sprayed the ball to all fields, and his speed allowed him to stretch singles into doubles and doubles into triples. Always a threat to steal a base, Dahlen pilfered a career-high 60 bases in 1892 and stole 30 or more bases in a season nine times.

In 1893 the right-handed Dahlen played mostly at shortstop and batted .301. The following year Anson again alternated him between shortstop and third base in what proved to be Dahlen's best season. He recorded career highs in batting average (.362), home runs (15), runs batted in (107), and runs scored (150). Dahlen also had an incredible streak of making hits in 70 of 71 games. After hitting safely in 42 straight games, he was held hitless on 7 August 1894 but then had hits in the next 28 games. From 1891 to 1896 Dahlen averaged an incredible 122.3 runs scored per season. From 1895 on he played shortstop almost exclusively. Dahlen had another tremendous year offensively in 1896 when he batted .352, scored 137 runs, and stole 51 bases. He hit .290 in 1897 despite missing two months after being badly spiked in a game.

Good-hitting shortstops are rare in baseball, and Dahlen was a fine hitter. However, to stay in the game as a shortstop a player must field the position well. Dahlen was one of the finest fielding shortstops of the nineteenth century. He had excellent range, great lateral mobility, and a strong, accurate arm. Using small, flimsy gloves in the deadball era, his error totals are high by modern standards. However, a century later Dahlen was still among the career leaders in assists, putouts, and chances at shortstop.

Dahlen was noted for his nasty temper and stubborn disposition. He argued with and agitated umpires, managers, and players. Anson once made him get off the train on a Colts road trip for arguing over a pass for the sleeper car. In the end his penchant for arguments cost him his job with Chicago, and his contract was transferred to the Brooklyn Superbas for the 1899 season. With Dahlen at shortstop, Ned Hanlon's Superbas won National League pennants in 1899 and 1900. On 12 December 1903 Dahlen was traded to John McGraw's New York Giants for journeyman pitcher John Cronin and 20-year-old shortstop Charlie Babb. In 1904 he led the league with 80 RBIs and was second in stolen bases with 47. With Dahlen at shortstop, the Giants won 106 games and a pennant, but no World Series was played owing to squabbles between the National and American leagues. In 1905 New York won 105 games and defeated the Philadelphia Athletics four games to one for the world championship. Dahlen was flawless at shortstop during the series but went hitless in 15 at-bats.

By 1907 Dahlen's batting average had fallen to .207. On 3 December 1907 the Giants packaged "Bad Bill" with catcher Frank Bowerman, outfielder George Browne, first baseman Dan McGann, and young reliever George Ferguson in a deal with the Boston Doves (later known as the Braves) for shortstop Al Bridwell, catcher Tom Needham, and first baseman Fred Tenney. Dahlen batted .239 as the Boston shortstop in 1908, his last season as an everyday player. The Doves released him after the 1909 season.

Charlie Ebbets decided to bring Dahlen back to Brooklyn to manage his team, which had finished 55½ games out of first place in 1909. Brooklyn improved a little under Dahlen's leadership, as the Superbas finished 40 games out in 1910. A new name, the Dodgers, and a new stadium in 1912, christened Ebbets Field, were insufficient to improve the team's standings. In four years as manager, Dahlen never led Brooklyn out of the second division of the league standings. He remained popular with the fans but was disliked by many of his own players, the umpires, and the sportswriters. He was suspended by the league president several times. On 20 April 1912 Dahlen got into a fistfight with umpire Cy Rigler. Ebbets fired Dahlen after the 1913 campaign in favor of Wilbert Robinson, one of John McGraw's coaches with the rival crosstown Giants.

Dahlen married Jeanette Hoglund in December 1903, and they had a daughter. After leaving the Dodgers he coached a semiprofessional baseball team in Brooklyn and worked as a bullpen attendant at Yankee Stadium. Dahlen also worked on the loading docks for a few years and owned a gas station. He died in Brooklyn.

During his playing career Dahlen played in 2,443 games and made 2,457 hits, 413 doubles, 163 triples, and 84 home runs. Dahlen scored 1,590 runs and drove in 1,233 runs. He stole 547 bases and had a career batting average of .272. His offensive numbers compare favorably with or exceed those of Hall of Fame shortstops Luis Aparacio, Luke Appling, Dave Bancroft, Joe Cronin, Rabbit Maranville, and Bobby Wallace. His fielding statistics are among the finest ever. Dahlen recorded 13,325 chances, 4,850 putouts, and 7,500 chances at shortstop. Among Hall of Fame shortstops, only Maranville had more putouts, and only Aparicio had more assists. No Hall of Fame shortstop handled more chances than Dahlen. As a manager Dahlen was less notable; he won 251 games and lost 355, with nine games ending in ties.

• The National Baseball Hall of Fame Library in Cooperstown, N.Y., has a file on Dahlen. Shorter biographies are found in the Society of American Baseball Research, *Nineteenth Century Stars* (1989); Michael Shatzkin, ed., *The Ballplayers* (1990); and Gene Karst and Martin Jones, Jr., *Who's Who in Professional Baseball* (1973). For the complete statistical data on Dahlen's playing career and major league managerial record, see Rick Wolff, ed., *The Baseball Encyclopedia*,

9th ed. (1993), and John Thorn et al., eds., *Total Baseball*, 5th ed. (1997). Obituaries are in the *Sporting News*, 11 Dec. 1950, and the *New York Times*, 6 Dec. 1950.

FRANK J. OLMSTED

DAHLGREN, John Adolphus Bernard (13 Nov. 1809–12 July 1870), naval officer, was born in Philadelphia, Pennsylvania, the son of Bernard Ulric Dahlgren, a merchant and diplomat, and Martha Rowan. Dahlgren received his early education at a Quaker school in Philadelphia. Because of his father's position as Swedish consul, the Dahlgrens were a well recognized and respected family. When the elder Dahlgren died suddenly in 1824, the family was left in financial difficulty. Though initially denied entrance, thanks to family connections in February 1826 Dahlgren was granted an appointment as a midshipman in the U.S. Navy. His first assignment was to the frigate *Macedonian* under Captain James Barron on the Brazil station. His second voyage was aboard the sloop *Ontario* (1829–1831) in the Mediterranean. After a period of shore duty in 1834, he was assigned to the Coast Survey. During his service with the Coast Survey (1834–1837), Dahlgren displayed considerable ability at mathematics. He was promoted to lieutenant 8 May 1837.

In the summer of 1837 Dahlgren became afflicted with a serious loss of vision. He requested leave from the department and went to Paris seeking help from French specialists. He returned to Washington in 1838 unimproved. In 1839 he married Mary C. Bunker; they had seven children. They retired to a farm in Bucks County, Pennsylvania, and remained there four years while Dahlgren struggled to regain his sight.

In May 1843, with his sight recovered, Dahlgren returned to active duty and moved his family to Wilmington, Delaware. He left them in November to sail aboard the *Cumberland*, bound for the Mediterranean station. He returned to Wilmington in November 1845, and after spending slightly more than a year on leave with his family, Dahlgren was ordered in January 1847 to report to Washington for duty with the Ordnance Department of the navy. Dahlgren so impressed his superiors that in August he was given direction of all ordnance matters at the Washington Navy Yard.

During his years at the Washington Navy Yard Dahlgren improved production methods and also introduced in 1850 his design for a new type of large cannon capable of withstanding the pressure required to fire heavy shot. Each Dahlgren Gun was cast with a uniform diameter so that the metal would cool evenly. The barrel was then machined to produce a thin muzzle and a thick breech, the latter being necessary to withstand the intense pressure produced by exploding powder. This method allowed the manufacture of large-caliber guns that were still light enough to be useful aboard ships. The shape of the guns was similar to that of the bottles in which soda was purchased, and so they were often called "soda-water guns." Dahlgren Guns became immensely popular and played a critical

role in arming navies in the United States and elsewhere.

Dahlgren was also responsible for the invention of a small, lightweight brass howitzer. This boat gun could be carried aboard small craft and was particularly useful in amphibious type landings. To demonstrate the advancements in ordnance made under his direction, in 1857 Dahlgren asked and was given command of the sloop of war *Plymouth*. He fitted it with his new guns and on 24 June 1857 left Washington bound on a training cruise. *Plymouth* returned home in November, having proved that large-caliber guns of the Dahlgren design could be safely fired aboard ship.

Dahlgren was at the Washington Navy Yard in April 1861 at the outbreak of the Civil War. The yard's commander Franklin Buchanan resigned to "go South," and Dahlgren was appointed to replace him. On 16 July 1862 he was promoted to captain, and two days later he took command of the Bureau of Ordnance. Dahlgren's reputation and his proximity to the White House often brought him in contact with President Abraham Lincoln, outside of the normal chain of command, which was looked upon with some suspicion by Dahlgren's peers. On 7 February 1863 he was promoted to rear admiral. Four months later, 24 June, Dahlgren was ordered to take command of the South Atlantic Blockading Squadron.

As commander of the Blockading Squadron, Dahlgren's chief goal was the capture of the port of Charleston. His predecessor, S. Francis Du Pont, had tried and failed in this attempt and was recalled as a result. During Dahlgren's command Charleston was kept under siege for almost two years. Pressed at sea by Dahlgren's forces and from the land side by Sherman's advancing army, the Confederates evacuated Charleston 17–18 February 1865. Dahlgren was ordered to transfer his command of the squadron 9 June, when the force was integrated with the Northern Blockading Squadron and returned to its prewar status as the Atlantic Squadron.

Dahlgren returned to Washington. His first wife having died (date unknown), on 2 August 1865 he married Madeleine Vinton Goddard (Sarah Madeleine V. Dahlgren), an author. They had three children. In September 1866 Dahlgren was ordered to take command of the South Pacific Squadron and left for his station on 1 December. He returned in July 1868 and was reassigned as chief of ordnance. In postwar Washington the bureau came under heavy criticism for lack of innovation. Feeling the pressure, Dahlgren asked to be reassigned. In August 1869 he was made commandant of the Washington Navy Yard, where he died.

• The Dahlgren papers are located at the Library of Congress. Dahlgren published two important works: *The System of Boat Armament in the United States Navy* (1852) and *Shells and Shell Guns* (1856). Published documents relating to the Civil War may be found in *The Official Records of the Union and Confederate Navies in the War of the Rebellion* (30 vols., 1894–1922); David K. Allison, "John A. Dahlgren: Innovator in Uniform," in *Captains of the Old Steam Navy: Makers of the American Naval Tradition, 1840–1880*, ed. James Bradford (1986); Madeleine Vinton Dahlgren, *Memoir of John A. Dahlgren* (1891); William M. Fowler, Jr., *Under Two Flags: The American Navy in the Civil War* (1990); and Clarence S. Peterson, *Admiral John A. Dahlgren, Father of U.S. Naval Ordnance* (1945).

WILLIAM M. FOWLER

DAHLGREN, Sarah Madeleine Vinton (13 July 1825–28 May 1898), author, was born in Gallipolis, Ohio, the daughter of Samuel Finley Vinton, a U.S. congressman, and Romaine Madeleine Bureau. Dahlgren was educated at Monsieur Picot's boarding school in Philadelphia and the Convent of Visitation in Georgetown in the District of Columbia. She married Daniel C. Goddard in 1846; Goddard was a lawyer and an assistant secretary of the Interior Department. They had two children. After Goddard died in 1851, Dahlgren returned to her father's house in Washington, D.C., and helped to support her family by writing and translating. In 1865 she married Rear Admiral John Adolphus Dahlgren of the U.S. Navy. They had three children before he died in 1870.

Dahlgren was strongly opposed to woman suffrage, and her 1871 pamphlet, *Thoughts on Female Suffrage*, emphasized that the franchise was a burden for women. Opponents of the issue used *Thoughts* before the committees of Congress. She was also an officer of the Anti-Woman Suffrage Society, formed in 1871. When petitioning the Senate Committee on Privileges and Elections, she claimed that she spoke for the "masses of silent women, whose silence does not give consent, but who, in most modest earnestness, deprecate having the political life forced upon them," apparently overlooking the fact that silence did not necessarily indicate support for Dahlgren's position. Neither side had communicated with the silent women and thus could not state with certainty how they felt.

Matilda Joslyn Gage, chair of the Committee of Arrangements for the National Woman Suffrage Association Convention, invited Dahlgren and her friends to the 1872 convention in Washington, D.C., in an effort to engage Dahlgren in a debate with Elizabeth Cady Stanton, the association's president, about woman suffrage:

As you [Dahlgren] have publicly expressed your opposition to woman's enfranchisement, not only through the papers, but also by a petition against it to Congress, we feel sure you will gladly accept our invitation and let us know your reason for the faith that is within you.

Dahlgren thanked Gage for the invitation but refused to participate in the debate. She explained

that in the very fact of soliciting us to "hold debate" on a public platform, on this or any other question, you entirely ignore the principle that ourselves and our friends seek to defend, viz., the preservation of female modesty.

The functions of men and women in the State as citizens are correlative and opposite. They cannot be made common without seriously impairing the public virtue.

Our men must be brave, and our women modest, if this country may hope to fulfill her true mission for humanity.

Dahlgren added that she had fully explicated her position against woman suffrage in her articles and suggested that Gage refer to these publications.

In a petition against woman suffrage addressed to the U.S. Senate, Dahlgren and her supporters listed the following points among the reasons they were against women having the right to vote: The Bible teaches that women have a different and "higher, sphere apart from public life"; women have a "full measure of duties, cares, and responsibilities" delegated to them, and they are "unwilling to bear other and heavier burdens"; it would "be adverse to the interests of the workingwomen of the country"; and the changes would increase the "discord in the existing marriage relation." Probably to Dahlgren's satisfaction, the woman suffrage amendment introduced into Congress in 1878 was overwhelmingly defeated.

Although she was against women voting and their participation in politics, Dahlgren was apparently comfortable with women being in certain leadership roles, as is evident in her service as president of the Ladies' Catholic Missionary Society and her involvement in the Washington Literary Society. In 1873 she was one of the founders of the Washington Literary Society and its first vice president. Moreover, her home was a gathering place for numerous literary friends.

In addition to her political writings, Dahlgren wrote novels (often using the pseudonym "Corinne" or "Cornelia"). Her works include *South Mountain Magic* (1882), a novel that deals with the beliefs of the descendants of German settlers in a Maryland community, and *A Washington Winter* (1883), a romance set in Washington. Dahlgren's novels were often serialized in popular magazines. A conservative, traditional Catholic perspective runs through her essays and novels.

Well versed in several languages, Dahlgren's translations include Charles-Forbes-René de Montalembert's *Pius IX and France* (1861), Don Juan Donoso Cortes's *An Essay on Catholicism, Authority and Order* (1862), and Adolphe de Chambrun's *The Executive Power in the United States: A Study of Constitutional Law* (1874). In the preface of *The Executive Power*, James A. Garfield (the future president) complimented Dahlgren on her translation skills: "The work has been done with so much grace that the reader discovers nothing in the style to indicate that it is a translation."

Dahlgren died in Washington. Her work provides valuable insight into a conservative woman's perspective on the issues of gender roles and women's rights.

• In addition to the titles mentioned above, Dahlgren's works include *Idealities* (1859), *Memoir of Ulric Dahlgren* (1872), *Etiquette of Social Life in Washington* (1873), *South Sea Sketches* (1881), *Memoir of John A. Dahlgren* (1882), *The Lost Name* (1886), and *The Woodley Lane Ghost and Other Stories* (1899).

Elizabeth Cady Stanton, Matilda J. Gage, and Susan B. Anthony, *History of Woman Suffrage* (1881), includes letters by and about Dahlgren. Dahlgren's petitions, "To the U.S. Senate against Woman Suffrage" and "Sherman-Dahlgren XVI. Amendment," are also in *History of Woman Suffrage.* Her obituary is in the *Washington Post*, 29 May 1898, and the *Washington Evening Star*, 30 May 1898.

SANDRA M. GRAYSON

DAILEY, Albert Preston (16 June 1938–26 June 1984), jazz pianist and composer, was born in Baltimore, Maryland. Little is known of his parents or early years except that he studied piano from an early age. At age fifteen Dailey became the house pianist at the Royal Theater in Baltimore, where he performed for four years. He studied piano and composition at Morgan State University from 1955 to 1956 and the Peabody Conservatory from 1956 to 1959.

During the early 1960s Dailey distinguished himself as a worthy jazz accompanist and member of a rhythm section. From 1960 to 1963 he toured with singer Damita Jo and learned vocal accompanimental style. He also led a trio at the Bohemian Caverns in Washington, D.C., from 1963 to 1964. Dailey moved to New York City in 1964. From 1964 to 1966 Dailey freelanced with notable jazz musicians such as drummer Roy Haynes, bassist Charles Mingus, vocalist Sarah Vaughan, saxophonist Hank Mobley, and trumpeter Art Farmer. Trumpeter Freddie Hubbard stated in Nat Hentoff's liner notes to Hubbard's 1966 album *Backlash*, which was Dailey's first recorded appearance, "I heard him with Art Farmer, and he was so good I wondered where he'd been."

Dailey continued to freelance during the latter part of the 1960s, gradually gaining wider recognition for his varied yet original style. Bebop bandleader and clarinetist Woody Herman hired Dailey to perform with his big band and used him for both the 1967 Monterey Jazz Festival and the live festival recording *Concerto for Herd.* During Dailey's tenure the Woody Herman orchestra was featured in a 1968 performance at the Royal Festival Hall in London. An audience member at the London concert, writer Richard Palmer, said of the performance, "Dailey produced a solo . . . breathtaking in its amalgam of sizzling power and masterly elegance."

Dailey was immersed in the rapidly evolving musical environment of New York City during the 1960s. His stylistic development reflected the richness and variety of this experience. He counted the traditional and early swing pianist Art Tatum and bop pianist Bud Powell as major influences, with Barry Harris and Tommy Flanagan as models for his hard bop piano style. Dailey showed an equal familiarity with blues, swing, bop, cool, and avant-garde genres and demonstrated a command over musical energy and melodic and harmonic vocabulary. He displayed his powerful technique and dexterity at the keyboard particularly in swing and bebop styles, with popular song ballads being the vehicle that best suited his exploratory style.

In 1968 Art Blakey invited Dailey to join the Jazz Messengers. Dailey remained with the group until 1969. In the early 1970s Dailey continued to lead a diverse freelance career, performing with vocalists Joe Williams and Betty Carter, the Thad Jones/Mel Lewis Big Band, and Modern Jazz Quartet vibraphonist Milt Jackson. Tenor saxophonist Sonny Rollins invited Dailey to become a member of his quartet in 1970. He performed off and on with the group until 1973.

Dailey recorded his first album as a leader, *The Day after the Dawn*, in 1972 for Columbia. Except for two tracks on the album, "September of My Years" and the "Theme from *Clockwork Orange*," all the works recorded were original compositions by Dailey, including notable works such as "Bittersweet Waltz" and "A Lady's Mistake." Among the side musicians who appeared on the album were bassist Richard Davis, bassist Percy Heath, and drummer Roy Haynes. The composition "Free Me!" was remarkable in that Dailey performed on every instrument used on the work—piano, electric piano, bass, drums, and synthesizer. In spite of wide critical acclaim, Columbia dropped Dailey from the label after this album.

In 1973 tenor saxophonist Stan Getz hired Dailey as his pianist. Dailey became a source of inspiration for Getz. In an interview with *Down Beat*'s Arnold Jay Smith, Getz stated, "I can sit and listen to Albert Dailey for extended periods of time. He invents every second." Dailey toured Europe with Getz in 1974. A July 1974 *New York Times* review of a concert in Avery Fisher Hall that featured the cool jazz–style Gerry Mulligan Quintet, the modal jazz–oriented Bill Evans Trio, and Getz's quartet specifically praised Dailey's unaccompanied solo as "effectively electrifying." On 21 May 1975 Dailey performed on the first album Getz recorded for Columbia, a Latin jazz date titled *The Best of Both Worlds.* Dailey also recorded on Getz's third album for Columbia, *The Master*, in October 1975; for commercial reasons the album was not released until 1983.

Dailey remained musically active apart from his association with Getz. In 1975 he composed a work for voices and electronic instruments titled "Africa Suite." Dailey also recorded *Summer Solstice* with saxophonist Azar Lawrence in 1975 alongside bassist Ron Carter. Dailey returned to Art Blakey's Jazz Messengers in 1973 and remained until 1976, participating in the 1976 album *Backgammon.* Dailey's sideman appearances in 1976 included albums by drummer Elvin Jones and saxophonist Lee Konitz. Avant-garde and free jazz saxophonist Archie Shepp used Dailey with bassist Reggie Workman and drummer Charles Persip for his 1977 album *Ballads for Trane*, a memorial tribute to John Coltrane. Dailey also appeared on trumpeter Dizzy Reece's January 1978 album *Manhattan Project.*

Dailey's July 1978 album *That Old Feeling*, recorded for the Steeplechase label, was his second album as leader. The album included bassist Buster Williams, who had previously performed with Art Blakey, and drummer Billy Hart, Getz's regular drummer for five years. They provided the framework for Dailey's mature imaginative style, demonstrated particularly in his treatments of the tracks "Lover Man," "Yesterdays," "That Old Feeling," and "Body and Soul." Dailey showed a variety of influences ranging across the gamut of pianists, such as pentatonic runs reminiscent of avant-garde pianist McCoy Tyner and jabbing left-hand punctuations similar to the funky hard bop style of Horace Silver. Dailey also demonstrated a penchant for grand improvised solo concluding sections in many of his tunes. Finally, Dailey's blazing treatment of "Body and Soul" at eighty-four bars to the minute commended his physical strength and technical dexterity as a pianist.

In January 1979 Dailey recorded both *The Heavy Hitter*, with rhythm-and-blues tenor saxophonist Eddie "Lockjaw" Davis, and *World of Trombones*, a nine-trombone jazz ensemble including Curtis Fuller and Steve Turre, with a rhythm section led by trombonist Slide Hampton. In February he recorded alongside fusion trumpeter Randy Brecker on alto saxophonist Bunky Green's *Places We've Never Been*. In July he recorded *Good Cookin'* with tenor saxophonist Junior Cook.

Getz and Dailey recorded a momentous album, *Poetry*, for Elektra in January 1980. On this album the duo beautifully presented seven bop and popular standards that ideally displayed the contrast of Getz's smooth, lyrical style with Dailey's jagged, responsive touch. Dailey recorded the final two works of the album as solo tracks. The interaction between the two musicians was acclaimed by *Jazz Journal International* critic Richard Palmer as "a dream duo." *Poetry* was released in 1984.

The year 1981 saw Dailey record his third album as leader, *Textures*, with bassist Rufus Reid, drummer Eddie Gladden, and tenor saxophonist Arthur Rhames. The album featured all original compositions by Dailey, including "Dailey Bread" and "Textures." As part of the New York Kool Jazz Festival, Dailey presented a recital in June at Carnegie Hall. His sideman appearances in 1981 included recordings with composer and tenor saxophonist Ricky Ford on *Tenor for the Times* and with tenor saxophonist Charlie Rouse on *Upper Manhattan Jazz Society*.

Dailey recorded as sideman for the remaining years of his life. The year 1982 saw him record *Things Unseen!* for saxophonist Bob Mover and *The Bash* for guitarist Bruce Forman. He rejoined Ricky Ford along with fusion guitarist Larry Coryell to record Ford's *Future's Gold* in February 1983. Dailey's final album appearance was with saxophonist Phil Woods on guitarist Jack Wilkins's 1984 album *Captain Blued*. Getz and Dailey performed a brief West Coast tour early in 1984 to promote the release of *Poetry*.

Dailey was on another tour in 1984 when he succumbed to pneumonia. He never completed the tour, and he died in Denver, Colorado. One source directly states that Dailey was an early victim of the AIDS epidemic; others merely state Dailey died of pneumonia or a respiratory infection. Dailey was survived by three children and one grandchild. There is little information regarding Dailey's marriage or children readily available to the public.

The point at which Dailey entered the musical establishment proved to be a pivotal time in the history of jazz. The palette of styles during the late 1950s ranged from hard bop, modal, cool, and Latin jazz to the beginning of avant-garde and free jazz, with straight-ahead bebop and swing as mainstream elements. Later developments such as fusion (the combination of rock and jazz) and post-bop styles further widened the possibilities for exploration. Within this context, Dailey's career surveyed the gamut of styles and combined them to form a unique voice in jazz piano.

• Ron Wynn's career synopsis in the *All Music Guide to Jazz*, 2d ed. (1996), is the most comprehensive to date, including a select discography for Dailey and a cross-listing of recordings on which Dailey appeared as a sideman. Additional biographical information appears in Mike Hennessey's liner notes to *That Old Feeling: Albert Dailey Trio* (SteepleChase SCCD 31107; re-release, 1995) and Michael Cuscuna's liner notes to *Textures: Albert Dailey* (Muse MR 5256; 1981). Information regarding Dailey's affiliation with Stan Getz exists in Donald L. Maggin, *Stan Getz: A Life in Jazz* (1996), and on Stan Getz's liner notes to the Getz/Dailey duo album *Poetry* (Elektra Musician 60730; 1984). A retrospective by Richard Palmer appears in *Jazz Journal International* 38 (Mar. 1985): 17–18. Substantial obituaries exist in the *New York Times*, 3 July 1984, and *Jazz Forum* 89 (1984). 23.

DAVID E. SPIES

DAILEY, Ulysses Grant (3 Aug. 1885–22 Apr. 1961), surgeon, was born in Donaldsonville, Louisiana, the son of Tony Hanna Dailey, a bartender, and Missouri Johnson, a teacher. His parents were then living in Fort Worth, Texas; Mrs. Dailey had returned to her mother's home to give birth. The Daileys visited Chicago, Illinois, several times, and Grant (as he preferred to be called) had some of his early schooling there. He was also educated in Donaldsonville, in the preparatory academy at Straight College (later Dillard University) in New Orleans, and at the Fort Worth High School. Brought up by his mother (the couple separated after a few years) in an atmosphere of books and music, Grant became a piano player.

While a student in Fort Worth, Dailey became the office boy for Ernest L. Stephens (who was white), a practicing physician and professor of materia medica in the medical department of Fort Worth University. Impressed by Dailey's seriousness, Stephens encouraged the young man's wide reading. When a typhoid epidemic struck the city, Stephens had Dailey visit his homebound patients to take temperatures and do similar tasks. With his increasing experience in medicine, Dailey decided to pursue this profession rather than music.

Dailey was accepted by the Northwestern University Medical School after several conversations with the dean, and enrolled in the fall of 1902. Despite being the youngest of the 150 students in his class and having to work to pay his way, he did well. The director of the anatomical laboratory hired him as an assistant and instructor for two years. Dailey received an M.D. in June 1906.

Dailey was then denied the opportunity, on the basis of his race, of spending two weeks at Mercy Hospital in Chicago doing obstetrics in the charity ward. Allen Kanavel, professor of clinical surgery at Northwestern University Medical School, wanted to take Dailey on as an assistant but could not do so for the same reason. In 1907 Provident Hospital, a black-run Chicago hospital, appointed Dailey gynecologist to their dispensary. In 1910 he became an associate surgeon, and from 1912 to 1926 he held the title of attending surgeon.

The major turning point in Dailey's medical career came in 1908 when Dr. Daniel Hale Williams of Provident Hospital invited Dailey to be his surgical assistant. Remaining in this capacity until 1912, Dailey learned much in the way of surgical technique from Williams. From 1916 to 1918 he also served as an instructor in clinical surgery at Northwestern, and from 1920 to 1926 he was an attending surgeon at Fort Dearborn Hospital. In 1912 and 1925 Dailey took two trips of several months each to Europe for postgraduate studies on surgical subjects.

In February 1916 Dailey married Eleanor Curtis, sister of Dr. Austin M. Curtis of Washington, D.C. Shortly after this Dailey suffered an almost fatal attack of tuberculosis and was ill for several months. Childless, the couple adopted five-year-old twins in 1924.

In 1926 Dailey purchased two large houses at Michigan Boulevard and Thirty-seventh Street and had them remodeled into the Dailey Hospital and Sanitarium, free from racial restrictions. Unhappily, one of his patients there was Daniel Hale Williams, of whom Dailey had to make a terminal diagnosis. The economic depression forced Dailey to close this institution in 1932. During its existence the hospital had provided affiliations for young black specialists and good care for black patients.

From Williams, Dailey had learned the importance of surgical clinics and educational lectures for black surgeons in the South. He frequently organized and took part in such endeavors at Meharry Medical College in Nashville, Tennessee, the John A. Andrew Clinical Society in Tuskeegee, Alabama, and other southern locations as well as in Washington, D.C., and New York.

In 1945 the American College of Surgeons elected Dailey a member (along with three other black surgeons). The only previous African-American members had been Dailey's mentor, Williams, a charter member in 1913, and Louis Tompkins Wright in 1943.

Dailey joined the National Medical Association (the black counterpart of the American Medical Association) in 1908 and remained a member for fifty-three years. Active at the annual meetings as a speaker and discussant, Dailey served as chairman of the Surgical Section in 1914 and gave the Oration in Surgery in 1940. In 1928 he began a four-year stint as chairman of the National Program Committee, and in 1932 he presented one of the association's first scientific exhibits (on sixty operations for goiter). As president of the association in 1915–1916, Dailey was the youngest president up to that time and the first from Chicago. However, his primary activity was with the *Journal of the National Medical Association*, on which he served as a member of the editorial board (1910–1943), associate editor (1943–1948), and editor (1948–1950). In 1950 he was named consulting editor. He also wrote several columns for the journal in which he alternated reviews of the literature with reports of his own work. The association honored him with its Distinguished Service Award in 1949.

In 1935 Dailey became a charter member of the International College of Surgeons. He served on the board of trustees, the editorial board, and as associate editor for the *Journal of the National Medical Association*. His major efforts for the college consisted of several extended trips to Pakistan, India, Japan, and other countries, during which he gave frequent surgical lectures and clinics and promoted local efforts for undergraduate and graduate medical education. A high point of his travels was a five-day visit with Albert Schweitzer in 1953 at Schweitzer's Forest Hospital in Lambaréné, Gabon.

Dailey's major surgical interests were the treatment of peptic ulcer (in which he initiated the technique of phrenic nerve crush in 1950) and the treatment of the thyroid. He spoke and wrote often on these, and other, topics both in the United States and abroad, and some sixty of his articles were published.

In 1952 Dailey retired from his position as chief of the surgical staff at Provident Hospital, and four years later he retired from active practice. He and his wife had purchased a house near Port-au-Prince in Haiti, a country they had often visited and enjoyed and for which he had served as honorary consul in Chicago for several years. However, after a few months of life on the island Dailey was forced by worsening health to sell their home and return to Chicago, where he died. Dailey became known for his careful and innovative surgery, widespread efforts as a teacher, active work in the United States and abroad for several surgical organizations, and for breaking ground for members of his race through his surgical endeavors.

• There is no major collection of Dailey's papers. The most thorough biography is Donald Preston, *The Scholar and the Scalpel* (1966). A summary of his life and career is found in William K. Beatty, "Ulysses Grant Dailey—Surgeon, Teacher, and Ambassador," *Proceedings of the Institute of Medicine of Chicago* 38 (1982): 140–51. Obituaries are in the *Chicago Daily Defender*, 24 Apr. 1961; and the *Chicago Tribune*, the *Chicago Sun Times*, the *Chicago American*, and the *New York Times*, all 23 Apr. 1961.

WILLIAM K. BEATTY

DAKIN, Henry Drysdale (12 Mar. 1880–10 Feb. 1952), biochemist, was born in Hampstead, London, England, the son of Thomas Burns Dakin, owner of a sugar refinery, and Sophia Stevens. In 1893 the family moved to Leeds, where the elder Dakin operated an iron and steel business. Dakin began his education at Merchant Taylor's School in London and continued at Leeds Modern Academy. In 1898 he entered Yorkshire College, a part of the federal Victoria University that later became the University of Leeds. He received his B.Sc. in 1901 and his D.Sc. in 1909. Before entering the college, Dakin was apprenticed for four years to the city analyst of Leeds, T. Fairley; in that position he carried out many determinations on constituents of foods, fertilizers, drinking water, gasworks byproducts, and even poisons and other forensic materials. He later attributed his breadth of interests and adeptness in laboratory operations to this training.

On arrival at the college, Dakin—already with a few analytical publications pending—worked under an organic chemist, Julius B. Cohen, on chlorination of benzene derivatives, serving as Cohen's laboratory demonstrator, editor, and tutor to other students. Dakin's prodigious output of research publication over the next three decades was already beginning: between the analytical work and the research with Cohen, he had about eighteen papers to his credit before he embarked on postgraduate research with other mentors.

An 1851 Exhibition research grant in 1902 allowed Dakin to work with S. G. Hedin at the Lister Institute in London, where he began the studies of enzyme action that would occupy him for the rest of his life and give him his nickname, "Zyme." He observed that enzymes of opposite optical rotations (known as enantiomeric forms) had different effects on the molecules on which they acted. He proposed that the first step in this action was a transient attachment of molecule to enzyme, dependent in some way on the three-dimensional configuration of the enzyme. This insight has stood the test of time.

From London Dakin went to Heidelberg to work with Albrecht Kossel on protamines, a class of proteins rich in the amino acid arginine; this led to the discovery of the enzyme arginase. Returning to the Lister in 1904, he continued work on enzymes and also synthesized epinephrine and allied compounds, relating their structure to physiological activity.

In 1905 there occurred an event that changed his life and enriched the new science of biochemistry in the United States. Christian A. Herter maintained his own research laboratory on the upper floors of his Madison Avenue residence in New York City, with a number of workers investigating aspects of medicine and physiology. He needed a chemist, and the Lister's director, C. J. Martin, recommended Dakin. By November 1905 the first of a series of papers on Dakin's most important work, oxidation of organic compounds in the animal body, was submitted from "the Laboratory of Christian A. Herter" to the *Journal of Biological Chemistry*—founded that year by Herter, who also acted as editor.

Over the next decade Dakin painstakingly demonstrated the steps in the biological oxidation of fatty acids, hydroxy acids, and amino acids and their expected products, using his in vitro equivalent of physiological oxidizing agents, mildly alkaline hydrogen peroxide. His occasional collaborator in these studies was a classmate from Leeds, Harold W. Dudley, who worked in Herter's laboratory in 1913 and 1914. Spinoffs from this work included clarification of the mechanism of oxidation of proteins and carbohydrates, end-group analyses for proteins, new solvent systems for extraction of protein hydrolyzates, and a new derivitization reagent for aldehydes and ketones, *p*-nitrophenylhydrazine, which is still used in organic analysis. Dakin summarized the oxidation work in *Oxidations and Reductions in the Animal Body* (1912; 2d ed., 1922).

This was not the only investigation that Dakin pursued during the period up to 1930. He continued his studies of enzymes, providing an ever-clearer picture of how they work; he determined the amino-acid contents of animal and vegetable proteins; and he investigated the chemical and physiological properties of optically active compounds. He did basic work in so many areas of the developing science of biochemistry that much of it is now taken for granted, and his name hardly ever appears in connection with it. During World War I his interest was diverted into a study of disinfectants for battlefield use; the result was Dakin's solution, a borate-buffered hypochlorite applied to wounds by an irrigation method worked out by the surgeon Alexis Carrel, and chloramine-T, a drinking-water disinfectant still used by campers.

In 1910 Christian Herter died, and Dakin took over both as laboratory director and journal editor at the request of Herter's widow, Susan Dows Herter. In 1916 he married her; they had no children. In 1918 the Dakins purchased a house in Scarborough-on-Hudson, thirty miles north of New York City, and set up a building behind it to serve as a laboratory. There Dakin worked alone for the remainder of his life, keeping in touch with the world of biochemistry only through journals, correspondence, and occasional visitors. He continued to publish through 1946. He died at home. Honors conferred on Dakin included fellowship in the Royal Society (1917), the French Legion of Honor for his war work, the Chemists' Club's Conné Medal, and the Royal Society's Davy Medal.

• Some of Dakin's correspondence is in the Max Bergmann Papers at the American Philosophical Society, Philadelphia. The most complete biographical treatment, with a full discussion of Dakin's work and a bibliography of his nearly 150 papers, is by Percival Hartley in *Obituary Notices of Fellows of the Royal Society* 8 (1952–1953): 129–48. See also two sketches by Hans T. Clarke: *Journal of the Chemical Society* (1952): 3319–24; and *Journal of Biological Chemistry* 198 (1952): 491–94. For a different slant on Dakin, with input from Herter's daughters, see Robert M. Hawthorne, Jr., "Henry Drysdale Dakin, Biochemist (1880–1952): The Option of Obscurity," *Perspectives in Biology and Medicine* 26 (1983): 553–66.

ROBERT M. HAWTHORNE JR.

DAKIN, James Harrison (24 Aug. 1806–13 May 1852), architect, was born in Northeast Township, Dutchess County, New York, the son of James Dakin (occupation unknown) and Lucy Harrison. He was a mentor to his younger brother, Charles Bingley Dakin, who also became an architect.

After learning the carpentry trade from his uncle, James Dakin moved to New York City, where he was apprenticed to Alexander Jackson Davis when the firm of Town and Davis, Architects, was formed in 1829. That year Dakin married Joanna (or Georgianna) Belcher; they had seven children, two of whom survived to adulthood. Dakin became a full partner by 1832, when the firm was renamed Town, Davis and Dakin, Architects. Dakin and Ithiel Town did most of the design for the main building of New York University in 1833, an influential collegiate Gothic work.

In 1833 Dakin left Town, Davis and Dakin to establish his own firm in New York. The following year he designed one of the finest buildings of his career, the Bank of Louisville in Kentucky, as well as the First Presbyterian Church in Troy, New York, done in the Greek revival style.

James's brother Charles, whom James had hired as a draftsman for Town, Davis and Dakin, moved to New Orleans in 1834. James followed in 1835, and the brothers formed Dakin and Dakin in New Orleans; Charles soon opened a branch office in Mobile, Alabama. Charles supervised the construction of the Government Street Presbyterian Church in Mobile from 1836 to 1837. In New Orleans James designed the Gothic-style St. Patrick's Church in 1838 and the State Arsenal in 1839. That year was a fateful one for James. Charles died near St. Gabriel, Louisiana, of an unknown cause, the Great Fire of Mobile destroyed much of the firm's incomplete work there, and the contract for St. Patrick's Church was lost in a dispute.

The disagreement centered around the construction methods used by Dakin for the partially completed church. A panel of arbitrators, headed by James Gallier, an Irish-English architect whom Dakin had hired in New York for Town, Davis and Dakin (and who, in 1834–1835, had been a partner of Charles), met to render a finding. Several other panelists, who were Irish-American builders and contractors, joined with Gallier to dismiss Dakin; they subsequently gave the job to Gallier. Dakin appealed the resulting court case and won in the Louisiana Supreme Court, but by the time of the judgment the church, which was owned by its Irish parishioners, was bankrupt as a result of the panic of 1837. Dakin was forced to declare bankruptcy in 1841, partially as a result of the St. Patrick's Church matter.

But he carried on, designing the Gayoso House Hotel in Memphis, Tennessee, in 1842 and the Medical College of Louisiana in 1843. By 1845 he had accepted as an apprentice Henry Howard, among the best of the next generation of Louisiana architects.

Dakin served briefly in the Mexican War in 1846, returning that same year to design the University of Louisiana, adjacent to the Medical College. The latter was absorbed by the university, and in later years the entire complex ultimately became Tulane University. After winning a competition in 1847 for the Louisiana State Capitol with a daring Gothic design, he moved to Baton Rouge, supervising construction of the capitol until 1850.

Dakin left the capitol job with only interior detailing unfinished to become the architect for the New Orleans Custom House. He found the original design by Alexander Thompson Wood unsatisfactory and proposed instead a freestanding, cast-iron frame and a central courtyard for air circulation. But a political and sociological dispute arose between Creole and Anglo-Saxon factions over the changes. To create the courtyard for air and ventilation, Dakin proposed moving the main banking room from the center to the Canal Street front. The Creoles of the French Quarter objected that that would give the Anglo-American sector across Canal Street a business advantage. Creole Democratic congressmen debated the change on the floor of Congress. Dakin, a friend of the Whig president, Zachary Taylor, was ousted after a heated hearing in which the great architect Isaiah Rogers sided with Dakin. He returned to Baton Rouge, where he completed the capitol interior. He died there after "a long and painful illness" (*New Orleans Daily Picayune*, 18 May 1852, p. 2).

Dakin's influence was disseminated in many ways. The location of his major buildings in highly visible places, like the Mississippi River levees in Baton Rouge, Memphis, and New Orleans—the river was the highway of the time—and the New York University campus in New York City helped draw attention to his highly imaginative designs and set lofty professional standards. Dakin also provided many engravings for Minard Lafever's architectural books, which became builders' handbooks all over America. Dakin had been honored in the 1830s by an invitation to become one of the founding members of the American Institution of Architects, forerunner of the American Institute of Architects. The spread of ideas on architecture and mutual support marked their activities. Among the imaginative architects who created the Gothic, Greek, and Egyptian revivals in America, James Dakin must be numbered in the forefront.

• Primary sources for James Dakin are limited and scattered. The best is the collection of some 230 original drawings at the New Orleans Public Library, Louisiana Department. Howard-Tilton Library at Tulane University has letters of Dakin and his mother. His Louisiana capitol diary is at Louisiana State University Library, Manuscripts Division. At Columbia University, Avery Library, are the financial records of Town, Davis and Dakin. These were all used for Arthur Scully, Jr., *James Dakin, Architect: His Career in New York and the South* (1973). A good overview of Dakin's partner Alexander Jackson Davis can be had from the show catalog of the Metropolitan Museum of Art, *Alexander Jackson Davis: American Architect, 1803–1892* (1992). Two indispensable articles are Jane B. Davies, "A. J. Davis' Projects for a Patent Office Building, 1832–1834," *Journal of the Society of Architectural Historians* 24 (1965): 229–51, and Glenn Patton, "Chapel in the Sky: Origins and Edifices of the University of the City of New York," *Architectural Review* 145 (1969): 177–

80. Kim Keister, "Capital Castle," *Historic Preservation*, May–June 1994, pp. 36–45, 93–95, and 98, provides excellent photographic coverage of the Louisiana State Capitol.

ARTHUR SCULLY, JR.

DALE, Alan (14 May 1861–21 May 1928), theater critic, was born Alfred J. Cohen in Birmingham, England. The names of his parents are not known. He was educated at King Edward's School in Birmingham and attended Oxford University, where he passed junior and senior local examinations. He married Carrie Livingston Frost in 1886; they had two children. He began a career in journalism and thirty years later recalled that "in the seventies and eighties, when the drama in England was at its lowest ebb, when wretched, ill-made adaptations from the French enlisted the services of cheap hacks, and poverty-stricken translators, drama criticism went under. Any fool wrote about the 'drama.' The newspaper selected their least valuable reporter, and sent him to the theatre" (1915, p. 164). His decision to emigrate to the United States in 1887 may have been influenced by those conditions.

Adopting the name Alan Dale (after the character Alan-a-Dale in the De Koven Opera Company's popular production of *Robin Hood*), he became drama critic for the *New York Evening World*. Dale quickly emerged as an iconoclast, eschewing the ponderous and sentimental approach to criticism that was the norm and substituting a breezy irreverence to the extent that some credited him as the originator of the Broadway "wise-crack." Although his "raspatory pen" exercised a salutary influence, it also encouraged what some saw as an excess of brashness and "cigar-store humor" among the next generation of drama critics, which included Heywood Broun, Percy Hammond, and George Jean Nathan. In his day, Dale was indisputably the most widely read and respected drama critic in the United States. However, he was probably also the first critic to be barred from a New York theater. Indeed, most producers at one time or another refused him admission to their productions. According to Marc Goodrich, "when his stinging quips got him into trouble on one paper, he simply adjusted his monocle and in his suave, well-mannered fashion shifted to another."

Dale left the *Evening World* in 1895 to work for William Randolph Hearst's *New York Journal* but spent most of his career, until his death, as drama critic for the *New York American*. While he maintained his celebrity, Dale's style mellowed somewhat at the *American*, and he even abandoned wearing his characteristic red necktie; his monocle gave way to horn-rimmed glasses. Dale's review of *The Easiest Way* by Eugene Walter (*New York American*, 20 Jan. 1909) exemplifies his style. The play, he wrote,

purported to sketch the familiar picture of the theatre-woman, struggling for her virtue amid the alleged temptations of Broadway—temptations that are popularly supposed to begin at the lobster-palace and end at the devil, but which last night began at the devil and ended at the lobster-palace. It did sketch this picture, with daubs of color, splashes of verity and a dazzling varnish of candor at which a sophisticated audience laughed last night, at which a less sophisticated audience might feel impelled to grieve.

In addition to numerous syndicated magazine articles, Dale published books of dramatic criticism, novels, and memoirs. His play, *The Madonna of the Future*, about a wealthy young woman who decides to have a child but not encumber herself with a husband, opened at the Broadhurst Theatre in January 1918. The *New York Times* reviewer praised the "brilliant dialogue" and reported the audience's initial shock but noted that, by the third act, "both ideas and situation are swallowed up, overwhelmed in a flood of repartee and paradox—vast surges of words, as someone has said, beating upon a little reef of ideas." Nevertheless, *The Madonna of the Future* became the target of a "clean play" drive and was closed for immorality.

As a widower, Dale lived during his last years with his sister in Bayside, Queens. He died suddenly, of a heart attack, during one of his annual visits to England to review the London theatrical scene.

• Among Dale's books are *Jonathan's Home* (1885), *A Marriage Below Zero* (1885), *An Eerie He and She* (1889), *Miss Innocence* (n.d.), *Familiar Chats with Queens of the Stage* (1890), *An Old Maid Kindled* (1890), *My Footlight Husband* (1893), *A Moral Busybody* (1894), *His Own Image* (1899), *A Girl Who Wrote* (1902), *Conscience on Ice* (1902), *Wanted A Cook* (1904), *The Great White Way* (1909), and *When A Man Commutes* (1918). Dale wrote about his own profession in "The Drama Critic," *The Theatre* 22 (Oct. 1915): 164–65, 199–200). The best source of information on Dale is an article by Marc Goodrich, "Those Who Sit in Judgment," the *Theatre* 46 (Oct. 1927): 40, 60. Other sources of data include *Who's Who in Music and Drama* (1914); *Who Was Who in America*, vol. 1: *1897–1942*; *Who Was Who in the Theatre, 1912–1976*; and Montrose J. Moses, ed., *The American Theatre as Seen by Its Critics, 1752–1934* (1934; repr. 1967). Reviews of Dale's play are in the *New York Times*, 29 Jan. 1918; *Bookman* 47 (1918): 75; and the *Dramatic Mirror* 78 (9 Feb. 1918): 5, 7. An obituary is in the *New York Times*, 22 May 1927, with follow-up notices on 23 May and 7 June.

FELICIA HARDISON LONDRÉ

DALE, Chester (3 May 1883–16 Dec. 1962), investment banker and art collector, was born in New York City, the son of Thomas W. Dale, a department store salesman, and Jane Roberts. Dale attended Peekskill Military Academy, but he left school when he was fourteen and began working as an office boy and runner on Wall Street. By 1904 he was an independent broker, and in 1909 he formed a partnership specializing in railroad mortgages and utility bonds with his friend William C. Langley. In 1911 Dale married Maud Murray a few weeks after she divorced his friend Frederick M. Thompson; they had no children.

Maud Dale was an amateur painter, and it was she who cultivated her husband's interest in art. In the first years of their marriage the couple collected American art, including works by Mary Cassatt, Benjamin West, Guy Pene du Bois, and their neighbor on East Nineteenth Street in New York City George Bellows

(Pene du Bois and Bellows both painted portraits of Dale). In the 1920s the Dales traveled to Europe and began buying art there, focusing on French paintings of the nineteenth and early twentieth centuries as well as on earlier works that seemed to prefigure modern developments in art. Always a shrewd businessman, Dale became a partner in the Galerie Georges Petit of Paris, a leading dealer in impressionist and postimpressionist art in the early 1930s; he thus gained an insider's knowledge of the market.

In 1928 the Dales' collection was shown at the Wildenstein Gallery in New York City, strengthening the growing taste for French and modern art in the United States. A catalog of the show, with an essay written by Maud Dale, sold out within three days. While his wife generally guided the selection of the work the Dales bought, Chester Dale enjoyed the challenge of finding and acquiring valuable artwork. He boasted that "no dealer ever *sold* me a picture—talked me into buying one, that is."

In 1935, with his fortune intact despite the Great Depression, Dale retired from W. C. Langley and Company. For the rest of his life, while staying in touch with the financial markets, he focused his energies on art collecting and museums. Dale served as a trustee on the boards of the Museum of Modern Art in New York (1929–1931), the Art Institute of Chicago (1943–1952), the Philadelphia Museum of Art (1943–1956), the Metropolitan Museum of Art (1952–1962), and the Washington, D.C., National Gallery of Art (1943–1955), where he was president of the board from 1955 until his death. Asserting that "a shroud has no pockets," Dale lent or donated much of his collection of more than seven hundred paintings, drawings, and lithographs, including work by Edouard Manet, Claude Monet, Auguste Renoir, Edgar Degas, Henri Toulouse-Lautrec, Paul Cézanne, Henri Matisse, Amedeo Modigliani, and Pablo Picasso. These works were often mobile; he lent pieces for long periods in the 1930s and 1940s to the Philadelphia Museum of Art and the Art Institute of Chicago. It was at the National Gallery of Art that Dale's collection finally came to rest in the early 1950s.

Dale continued to buy artwork even after his wife's death in 1953, but his best purchases had been made in the 1920s. In 1954 Dale married Mary Towar Bullard, who had been Maud Dale's secretary since 1928. "Chester-Dale," as both of his wives called him, was known for his encyclopedic memory and quick intuitive judgment, skills that he exercised both on Wall Street and in the art market. A former welterweight boxer and fire-fighting enthusiast (he was an honorary member of the New York City Fire Department), as well as a heavy drinker, Dale tended toward strong passions and a love of competition. Salvador Dali, from whom Dale bought two paintings, commented that "most collectors seek advice and wait; he falls in love with a picture and then he takes it."

Dale died in New York City. On his death the pieces he loved too much to lend during his lifetime were left to the National Gallery; he also gave the museum money for student fellowships and the general purchase fund. The stipulation in Dale's will that his collection had to be accepted in its entirety forced the National Gallery to change its policy of only holding the work of artists who had been dead at least twenty years. While there are several masterpieces in the Dale collection, such as Picasso's *Family of Saltimbanques* (1905), the collection also includes many works of lesser quality, especially among the nineteenth-century American paintings and the post-Picasso European works. Dale often chose paintings with explicitly sentimental appeal, like Renoir's 1870 *Girl with a Watering Can*. However, his collection of French paintings filled a significant gap in the National Gallery's collection, and many of the works he donated have become favorites of the museum's visitors.

Despite his minimal knowledge of art history and his uneven taste, as a businessman Dale understood the art world perfectly. Often buying at the bottom of the market, he was an important early collector of impressionist and postimpressionist French art.

• Some of Dale's unpublished correspondence, along with scrapbooks and other memorabilia, is in the Archives of American Art in Washington, D.C. Dale wrote "The Golden Century of French Art," *New York Times Magazine*, 17 May 1942. Geoffrey T. Hellman, "Custodian," *New Yorker*, 25 Oct. 1958, gives a sense of Dale's character and life; other articles about Dale and his collection include Henry McBride, "The Chester Dale Collection at New York," *Formes* (Apr. 1931); Murdock Pendleton, "Ambassador to Art," *Esquire*, Feb. 1938; Henry McBride, "Chesterdale's Way," *Art News*, Dec. 1952; Aline B. Saarinen, "New Regime at the National Gallery," *New York Times Magazine*, 6 May 1956; Neil MacNeil, "Chester Dale," *McCall's*, Nov. 1963; H. Lester Cooke, "A Plunger in the Market," *Art in America*, Apr. 1965; and "The Most Unlikely Collector," in John Walker, *Self-Portrait with Donors* (1969), and Walker, *National Gallery of Art, Washington, D.C.* (1963; rev. ed., 1976). Catalogs dealing specifically with the collection are Maud Dale, *Before Manet to Modigliani in the Chester Dale Collection* (1929); *Eighteenth and Nineteenth Century Paintings and Sculpture of the French School in the Chester Dale Collection* (1953; rev. ed., 1965); *Twentieth Century Paintings and Sculpture of the French School in the Chester Dale Collection* (1952; rev. ed., 1965); and *Paintings Other than French in the Chester Dale Collection* (1965), all published by the National Gallery. Alfred Frankfurter's "How Great Is the Dale Collection?" *Art News*, May 1965, is a somewhat critical evaluation of the collection. An obituary is in the *New York Times*, 18 Dec. 1962.

BETHANY NEUBAUER

DALE, Richard (6 Nov. 1756–26 Feb. 1826), naval officer, was born in Norfolk County, Virginia, the son of Winfield Dale and Ann Sutherland. His father had been a noted shipwright of the Portsmouth region, and in 1768 Dale, aged twelve years, joined the merchant marine. By 1775 he was rated as chief mate and commanded several vessels engaged in the West India trade. The following year Dale served as a lieutenant in the Virginia state navy until his capture by the British. During confinement at Norfolk, friends persuaded him to abandon the American cause, and he signed on as mate aboard a Loyalist tender. Dale received a severe wound fighting in this capacity, but he remained loyal to the British until captured by the American brig *Lexington* near Bermuda. The captain, John Barry, was so impressed by his youthful captive that he prevailed upon Dale to rejoin the American side. Accordingly, he obtained a midshipman's commission in the Continental navy in July 1776.

Dale remained aboard the *Lexington* and participated in several successful cruises until September 1777, when his vessel was captured by the *Alert*. Confined to Mill Prison, Plymouth, he made a daring escape in February 1778 but was recaptured in London. A year later Dale escaped again and arrived in France, where he joined the frigate *Bonhomme Richard* as first lieutenant under captain John Paul Jones. Dale commanded the gun deck during the famous victory over the British *Serapis* on 23 September 1779 and, despite severe wounds, led the boarding party. He remained with Jones on the *Alliance* in 1779–1780 and returned to America on board the *Ariel* in 1781. In June of that year he transferred to the frigate *Trumbull* and was wounded again during combat with the ship *Iris*. Dale concluded his revolutionary service in 1782 by commanding the privateer *Queen of France* for several months.

After the onset of peace, Dale resumed his merchant marine activities and partook of the flourishing China trade. In 1791 he married Dorothea Crathorne. (Two of their sons joined the navy and died in that service.) On 4 June 1794 Dale became the fourth of six captains commissioned by President George Washington to serve in the newly established naval establishment. When the threat of war with Algiers subsided, Congress canceled all naval construction, and Dale found himself without a command. He obtained a furlough in 1795 and captained the merchant ship *Ganges* on a voyage to Canton, China. Three years later maritime friction with France erupted into the Quasi-War and Dale was recalled to serve aboard the *Ganges*, which had been purchased and rearmed as a warship. Dale conducted several cruises between Long Island and the Virginia Capes in search of French privateers but encountered none. Shortly after he became embroiled in a seniority dispute with Captain Thomas Truxtun and threatened to resign. Navy Secretary Benjamin Stoddert tried to accommodate his desire to command and promised him a frigate when one became available, but Dale decided on an unpaid leave to pursue commercial activities. In 1799 he sailed for China as a privateer and took no further part in the war while command of the *Ganges* fell upon Captain Thomas Tingey.

By 1800 the issue of Dale's seniority had been resolved in his favor, and he was reinstated as the third-ranking captain. On 20 may 1801 he was appointed to command a squadron consisting of the frigates *President*, *Philadelphia*, and *Essex* and the schooner *Enterprise*. He then sailed to North Africa to bring an end to depredations against American commerce by the Barbary pirates. Dale arrived off of Gibraltar on 1 July and made several threatening demonstrations against

the ports of Tripoli, Tunis, and Algiers. On 1 August 1801 the *Enterprise* defeated a Tripolitan ship of similar size, at which point the pirates conspicuously avoided Dale's squadron and abandoned several vessels at Gibraltar. In March 1802 Dale was routinely relieved by Commodore Richard V. Morris and returned to the United States. Shortly after he resigned his commission and retired to Philadelphia. Dale remained active in social and political affairs, and during the War of 1812 he served on a committee designated for the city's protection. He died in Philadelphia.

Dale was a gallant and able naval officer. His ambitions were thwarted by the young nation's lack of naval assets, which in many instances had to be purchased from the civilian sector. He also exuded a stiff-necked recalcitrance toward matters of seniority. Dale's willingness to abandon the navy in wartime to pursue the lucrative China trade also appears self-serving but occurred when the government lacked the wherewithal to keep him employed. On balance, Dale served capably when given the opportunity.

• Dale's official correspondence is in Record Group 45, Captains' Letters, National Archives. Large collections of his personal papers are at the Historical Society of Pennsylvania and the American Philosophical Society, both in Philadelphia, and at the New-York Historical Society. Smaller caches exist at the Massachusetts Historical Society and at the Smith Naval Collection, Clements Library, University of Michigan. See also two edited works by Dudley W. Knox, *Naval Documents Related to the Quasi-War with France* (96 vols., 1935–1938) and *Documents Related to the United States Wars with the Barbary Pirates* (6 vols., 1939–1944), as well as the anonymous compilation "American Naval Affairs, 1798–1802," *New York Public Library Bulletin* 11 (1907): 411–19. Panegyrical sketches include "Life of Commodore Dale," *Port Folio* 3 (1814): 499–515; John H. Brown, *American Naval Heroes* (1899); and Bryan Hannon, *Three American Commodores* (1935).

JOHN C. FREDRIKSEN

DALE, Samuel (1772–23 May 1841), frontiersman, was born in Rockbridge County, Virginia, the son of Scotch-Irish parents whose names are unknown. Dale's parents migrated form the Carlisle area of Pennsylvania to the Shenandoah Valley shortly before Samuel, the first of nine children, was born. The family moved often. In 1775 they settled on the Clinch River on Virginia's remote southwestern frontier. At the end of the Revolution they moved to the Georgia frontier in Greene County. All of Samuel's formative years were spent on the Indian borderlands, where his earliest schooling was not in books but in the art of frontier survival and border warfare. In this regard was an adept student. He became a skilled woodsman whose abilities to navigate uncharted forests, slip undetected through hostile Indian country, and endure extraordinary hardships place him in the company of Daniel Boone, Simon Kenton, and a handful of heroic pioneers who opened the Old Southwest to white settlement.

In December 1792 both of Samuel's parents died within a week of one another, and thus he had to assume the responsibility of providing for his siblings, the youngest a mere infant. For a livelihood he turned to the only things he knew—hunting, farming, and fighting Indians. With the help of the other children he planted crops, hired a trustworthy older man to care for the family, and in 1793 joined a company of mounted soldiers raised to protect the Georgia settlers from the warring Creek Indians. For the next three years Dale served as a military scout and quickly gained renown for his prowess at scouting and fighting Indians. In 1796 the troop was disbanded, and Dale returned home with enough money to pay off the farm debt.

In the following years Dale earned a living doing a variety of things. He acquired a four-horse wagon and hauled freight in Savannah, Georgia, during the winter months when his animals were not needed on the farm. Successful at this, he outfitted a trading expedition to the Creek nation in 1799, bartering merchandise for hides, peltry, and cattle, which he sold on the seaboard. About this time a brisk emigration of white settlers into the newly organized Mississippi Territory commenced, and Dale put three wagon teams to work transporting emigrants through the Creek and Choctaw lands to the Tombigbee settlements. He then sold the return loads of Indian goods in Savannah. In 1803 he was guide for the commissioners who laid out a government road through lands in northwestern Georgia, where shortly he opened a trading post. In 1808 he moved closer to Georgia's Indian frontier, acquiring land in Jones County on which he built a mill. But milling was not to his liking, and he soon resumed trading and piloting settlers through Indian country.

In October 1811 Dale eavesdropped while the great Shawnee leader Tecumseh made an impassioned speech at Tuckabatchee urging the Creek nation to join his Indian confederation and halt the advance of white settlement. A militia captain, Dale was also present at the opening contest of the Creek Indian War, the Battle of Burnt Corn, on 27 July 1813. Seriously wounded in that engagement, he recovered to participate in one of the most celebrated fights of the war. In November 1813 he and a scouting party that included Jeremiah Austill, James Smith, and a slave named Caesar attacked a large war canoe filled with eleven Creek warriors descending the Alabama River near Randon's Creek in Monroe County. Caesar brought the attacking canoe alongside the Indian vessel and held it secure while Dale and his two friends fought the Indians with clubbed rifles. The fierce hand-to-hand combat lasted only a few short minutes. When it was over Dale and his party, with no serious injuries to themselves, had killed nine Indians in the bloody encounter, allowing only two to escape. During years of border warfare Dale, who was known to the Indians as "Big Sam" because of his physical stature and exceptional strength, had killed many Indians in hand-to-hand combat, but nothing contributed as much to his legendary fame as the canoe fight. A company of soldiers on the distant river bank, powerless to render assistance, witnessed the fight, and in retelling

the story the soldiers added greatly to Dale's Homeric reputation for skill and bravery in battle.

After the war Dale settled in Monroe County on the Alabama River, where he served as militia colonel and tax collector. In 1816 he was elected a delegate to the convention that divided the Mississippi Territory, and the following year he won election to the general assembly of the newly-created Alabama Territory. About this time he raised a company of volunteers to restore peace in neighboring Butler County, where a renegade group of Creeks led by Savannah Jack was stealing cattle and killing white settlers. After Alabama became a state, Dale continued his political service; between 1819 and 1830 he was elected eight times to represent Monroe in the Alabama legislature. Barely literate, he rarely spoke in the legislative debates and had no aptitude for politics. His fame as an Indian fighter and soldier, not his legislative accomplishments, explain his political popularity. In acknowledgement of his important role in wresting the country from the Indians, the Alabama legislature in 1821 conferred on Dale the rank of brigadier general. Three years later it made him a member of the small committee of dignitaries that escorted the marquis de Lafayette from Georgia to the Alabama capital at Cahaba. In 1831 the federal government commissioned him to remove the Choctaw Indians to their new homes along the Arkansas and Red rivers. Injured when his horse fell, Dale was compelled to give up his commission and return home to recuperate.

Choctaw removal opened new lands in Mississippi for white settlement. Always on the lookout for prime land, Dale, who in about 1830 had moved from Monroe to Perry County, Alabama, again moved in 1831 to Mississippi. From one of the departing Choctaws he purchased a reserve of two sections of land in what became Lauderdale County, where he established his plantation and spent the final years of his life. In 1836 he was elected Lauderdale County's first representative to the Mississippi legislature. Though he served for most of the decade, his legislative career in Mississippi was as undistinguished as it had been in Alabama. A taciturn, solitary man, Dale never married. He died at his plantation near Daleville, Mississippi.

• Because Dale was barely literate, he left no letters, journals, or diary for biographers to use in writing his life. Drawing upon Dale's spoken reminiscences, J. F. H. Clairborne published *Life and Times of General Sam Dale, the Mississippi Partisan* (1860), which is essentially autobiographical. Brief sketches of his life can be found in Thomas McAdory Owen, *History of Alabama and Dictionary of Alabama Biography* (4 vols., 1921), and Dunbar Rowland, *Mississippi* (3 vols., 1907). Contemporary accounts are in Albert James Pickett, *History of Alabama and Incidentally of Georgia and Mississippi from the Earliest Period* (1851); and A. B. Meek, *Romantic Passages in Southwestern History* (1857). Dale's activities in the Creek Indian War are detailed in H. S. Halbert and T. H. Ball, *The Creek War of 1813 and 1814* (1895), and more recently in Frank L. Owsley, *Struggle for the Gulf Borderlands,* the Creek War and the Battle of New Orleans, 1812–1815 (1981). An obituary is in the *Natchez Free Trader*, 15 June 1841.

CHARLES D. LOWERY

DALE, Sir Thomas (?–9 Aug. 1619), soldier, of unknown parentage, served as deputy governor and lord marshal of the Virginia settlement (1611–1616) and in that capacity was twice acting governor of the colony. Dale himself tells us almost all there is to know of his life before his involvement with the Virginia venture, writing to the states-general of the Netherlands in 1618 that he had "served this country about thirty years, first as a soldier and last as a captain." Taken at face value, this statement suggests that he was of the English yeomanry and was impressed or volunteered to serve as a common soldier in the earl of Leicester's expedition of 1588 to the Low Countries. He was, to judge from his subsequent career, able and ambitious, and England's military society was fluid. By 1594 he was serving as a captain in an English expedition in Ireland; subsequently he was in French service, then in 1599–1601 he was back in Ireland, serving with the earl of Essex. He seems to have escaped involvement in Essex's treason, but it is not until 1603 that we again find him with a military command, serving as a garrison captain in the Dutch town of Terthol. He was still in Dutch service when, in 1610–1611, he was recruited by the Virginia Company of London for service in Virginia.

The Virginia settlement had been established in 1607 under the auspices of the company. By 1609 it was obvious that the venture was failing. Disease, starvation, and Indian warfare had decimated the settlement; the leaders were perpetually bickering; no profits had been returned. As a consequence, the company turned to England's military establishment, particularly the English garrisons in the Netherlands, both as a model for the settlement and for leaders. In the course of his military career Dale had made friends and patrons of the powerful, including Sir Francis Vere (commander of the English troops in the Netherlands), Sir Thomas Gates (a fellow officer and patentee of the Virginia Company), the earl of Southhampton (eventually treasurer of the company), and Sir Robert Cecil (principal secretary to James I and a proponent of overseas settlements). Such friends had won him a knighthood in 1606, brought him to the attention of the company in 1610, and subsequently negotiated his temporary release from Dutch service. In March 1611, shortly after marrying Elizabeth Throckmorton, a distant relative of Vere's, he sailed for America.

Dale's commission named him "marshal"—defined in the military of the moment as an officer charged with military justice and the order of the camp—and third in command in Virginia after Thomas Lord De La Warr and Gates. In the absence of both of them, Dale assumed the governorship on his arrival in Jamestown in early June, surrendering it when Gates came in August. A quasi-military regime was already in place when Dale arrived, the confused egalitarianism of the first government having been replaced by drum-beat absolutism during De La Warr's brief sojourn in the colony as lord governor and captain general (April 1610–May 1611). Between them, Gates and Dale honed a system that required the settlers to "labour or else not eat, and be tied within the bounds of sharp laws and severe discipline." Together with William Strachey, they codified the laws and regulations of the colony and dispatched them to England to be published as the *Lawes Divine, Morall and Martiall* (1612). Although often attributed to Dale alone, even referred to by some as "Dale's Laws," the laws were actually a compendium of instructions from London and gubernatorial decrees dating back to 1609. Dale seems to have directly contributed only the "Instructions of the Marshal," a series of strictly military regulations based on the military codes used in the English and Dutch establishments in the Netherlands.

Strong leadership and stringent laws brought order to the infant settlement. The colony expanded, Dale leading half the settlers upriver to palisade the curls of the James River; subsequently he dispatched a group to found a fishing settlement, known as "Dale's Gift," on the eastern shore. Skirmishes with the Indians were almost constant, but in the spring of 1614, after Gates's departure and with Dale again serving as acting governor, the marshal combined military bravado with adroit diplomacy to bring about a tenuous peace. The year before, Pocahontas, daughter of the paramount Indian chief of the area, Powhatan, had been seized and brought to Jamestown. Dale determined to use the fortuitous event to his own advantage, and with 150 men he launched a series of shipborne raids against Indian villages along the Pamunkey River. Landing in front of Powhatan's own town, he paraded his men in battle array, and then offered a peace to be cemented by the marriage of Pocahontas to the Englishman John Rolfe. Powhatan agreed. The peace that followed lasted until the "Great Massacre" of 1622, when a quarter of the settlers were killed in a single day.

Dale left Virginia in 1616. In American history he is an interim figure, standing between the disastrous first entry of 1607 and the tobacco-based prosperity to come. He was part of a quasi-military experiment in colonization, and while that experiment succeeded to the extent of ensuring Virginia's continued existence, the colony Dale left displayed, as one historian has written, "the quiet primness of a corpse" (Prince, p. 362). Back in England, Dale called on his friends twice more, first to help him prosecute a yearlong suit against the states-general of the Netherlands for pay due him for the years during which he had been on leave from Dutch service and abroad in Virginia (£1,000), then to obtain the command of an East India Company expedition against the Dutch in the Far East. He won both back pay and the command, sailed for the east in February 1618, and died of a "languishing sickness" in India. He was survived by his wife but had no children.

• There is no collection of Dale papers; the few extant that are from and about him are scattered. Alexander Brown, *The Genesis of the United States* (1890), printed extracts of many but not always accurately, twisting meanings and even misquoting in order to support a romanticized version of Dale's early years and his recruitment by the Virginia Company. Walter F. Prince, "The First Criminal Code of Virginia," American Historical Association, *Annual Report, 1898* 1 (1899): 309–63, was long the standard interpretation, but David H. Flaherty's "Introduction" to *For the Colony in Virginea Britannia: Lawes Divine, Morall and Martiall* (1969) is a necessary corrective. The most extensive treatment of both Dale and the military regime are to be found in the following works by Darrett B. Rutman: "The Historian and the Marshal: A Note on the Background of Sir Thomas Dale," *Virginia Magazine of History and Biography* 68 (1960): 284–94; "The Virginia Company and Its Military Regime," in *The Old Dominion: Essays for Thomas Perkins Abernethy*, ed. Rutman (1964); and *A Militant New World, 1607–1640* (1979), pp. 125–231.

DARRETT B. RUTMAN

DALE, Thomas (1700–16 Sept. 1750), physician, jurist, and poet, was born in Hoxton, England, to a gentry family with medical interests. His parents' names are unknown. He attended Brasenose College, Oxford University, from 1717 to 1720 and in 1921 began study at the University of Leyden, from which he received a medical degree on 23 September 1723 for *Dissertatio medico-botanica inauguralis de Pareira Brava et Serapia officinarum*, which was published that same year. He established his medical practice in London. Dale's mastery of Dutch, German, French, classical Greek, and Latin enabled him to supplement his income with fees for translating medical texts. Mounting debt and familial opposition to his marriage prompted his removal to Charleston, South Carolina, in summer 1732. Dale's wife, Maria (maiden name unknown), died shortly after their arrival. They had no children.

Dale's credentials, sociable manner, and professional ability gained him immediate access to the highest levels of Carolina society. Governor Robert Johnson and Attorney General Charles Pinckney advanced his interest by arranging a marriage in 1733 with Mary Brewton, daughter of Charleston's foremost merchant, Miles Brewton. The couple had two sons, neither of whom lived to adulthood. Despite Dale's lack of legal education, Governor Johnson appointed him assistant justice in 1733. During the 1730s Dale became a fixture in the public life of Charleston. He served as steward of the St. George's Society, the private association charged with easing the assimilation of English immigrants into Carolina society, and he became a justice of the peace in 1737. He was an administrator of the slave detention workhouse and an overseer of the public markets. In 1739 he was elevated to a judgeship on the court of general sessions. Dale was a moving force in the creation of the colony's first insurance plan, which failed because of the devastations wrought by the great fire of 1740. He also served a term in 1749–1750 as an elected representative for St. Peters Parish in the royal assembly.

As a physician, Dale waged war against the multitude of uncredentialed practitioners who passed as doctors in Charleston. In 1735 he established a laboratory in the province, manufacturing medicines and distilling gin. The botanical interests displayed in his Leyden dissertation were reanimated by proximity to one of the richest collection areas in North America. He supplied his botanist uncle, Samuel Dale, with a steady stream of specimens. With the 1738 outbreak of smallpox in Carolina, Dale entered into a controversy with James Killpatrick (later Kirkpatrick) over the practice of inoculation and wrote two medical polemics, "The Case of Miss Mary Roche," published in the *South Carolina Gazette* on 2 November 1738, and the satirical "The Puff; or, A Proper Reply to Skimmington's Last Crudities," published in the *South Carolina Gazette* on 25 January 1739. Dale's animosity toward Killpatrick was as much political as medical. Killpatrick was a supporter of the Georgia colony, while Dale was a champion of Carolina's prerogatives.

During the 1730s Dale was the chief spokesman of the group of cosmopolitan wits who congregated in the Court Room of Shephard's (later Gordon's) Tavern. The group promoted the establishment of a theater in Charleston, sponsored public balls and concerts, instigated the jailing of the evangelist George Whitefield when he preached against dancing in Charleston, and satirized Whitefield when he was released. Several of Dale's poems have survived, including "Prologue to the Orphan . . . ," *South Carolina Gazette* (8 Feb. 1735), announcing the transit of arts to South Carolina; "Prologue Spoken to the Orphan . . . ," *South Carolina Gazette* (8 Feb. 1735); "Epilogue to the Orphan . . . ," *South Carolina Gazette* (22 Feb. 1735); "Epilogue to the Recruiting Officer," *Gentleman's Magazine* (6 May 1736), and his most widely published poem, "The Congratulation. Humbly Address'd to the Rev. Mr. Whitefield on His 68 Preachments in Forty Days, with the Great and Visible Effect of Meat and Money that Ensued Therefrom, &c," which appeared anonymously in the *South Carolina Gazette* (26 June 1740). Dale and Killpatrick were the finest poets in the Carolinas during the first half of the eighteenth century.

Dale survived three wives and two children. The memory of his second wife lives on in a Charleston ghost story; she haunts the Dale House on Church Street. His third wife was Anne Smith. His fourth wife, Hannah Simons, who survived him, presided over a tea table of female wits. Thomas Simons Dale, the sole surviving offspring of Dale's four marriages, became a notable physician in Scotland. Dale died in Charleston, South Carolina.

• Dale's letters of the 1730s to Rev. Thomas Birch survive in the Thomas Birch Papers, British Library, London. Personal information on Dale is in A. S. Salley, *Register of St. Philip's Parish, Charleston, 1720–1758* (1904). Dale's medical career is detailed in R. E. Seibels, "Thomas Dale M.D., of Charleston, S.C.," *Annals of Medical History* 3 (1931): 50–57. His legislative career is in Walter Edgar and N. Louise Bailey, *Biographical Directory of the South Carolina House of Represen-

tatives, vol. 2 (1977). His literary career is discussed in A. Franklin Parkes, "Thomas Dale," in *American Writers before 1800: A Biographical and Critical Dictionary*, vol. 2, ed. James Levernier and Douglas Wilmes (1983). See also the chapter titled "Gaining Admission" in David S. Shields, *Civil Tongues and Polite Letters in British America* (1997).

DAVID S. SHIELDS

DALEY, Arthur John (31 July 1904–3 Jan. 1974), sportswriter, was born in New York City, the son of Daniel M. Daley, a rope manufacturer, and Mary Greene. Educated in New York City's Catholic schools, Daley attended Fordham University where he played baseball until a hand injury turned him to writing. He became sports editor of the *Fordham Ram*. After graduating in 1926, he began what became his lifelong job with the *New York Times*. In the 1920s and 1930s he gained recognition as a reporter and writer. In December 1942 he replaced John Kiernan as writer of the "Sports of the Times" column "until further notice." The "further notice" lasted for more than thirty years until Daley's death. Originally, the feature appeared six days a week, and Daley eventually completed more than ten thousand columns.

In 1928 Daley married Betty Blake; they had four children. At the *Times* he covered sports ranging from auto and boat races to track and field. His trip to the Berlin Olympics in 1936 marked the first time the *New York Times* had assigned a sportswriter overseas. He was to cover four more Olympics. He visited the Kentucky Derby annually and wrote about leading personalities in sports as diverse as boxing and golf. As early as 1947 he predicted that professional basketball would become a major spectator event. He followed and promoted the rise of professional football, and he developed a close friendship with New York Giants' owner Jack Mara. After Daley's death, the National Football League established the Arthur J. Daley Award to honor annually its outstanding executive.

Despite his varied reporting interests, Daley left no doubt that baseball held first place in his heart. "It took me no time at all to learn that baseball provided better, richer and more fascinating material than all other sports combined." More than half of his "Sports of the Times" columns dealt with baseball. From January 1947 through November 1951 his columns explored game-fixing and the case of Shoeless Joe Jackson. Novelist Bernard Malamud later noted that these columns inspired him to write *The Natural* (1952).

Daley's direct style conveyed an air of detachment and dignity. Although shy and aloof, he was a capable interviewer, roaming stadiums bedecked in outlandish ties and carrying a clipboard for his notes. Athletes noted that he was adept at catching the right moment for his questions. He carefully prepared for his interviews, maintaining a sizable clipping file to assist in his research. His interests ranged from stars like Babe Ruth and Knute Rockne to the lowly New York Mets of 1962. He varied his columns, ranging from contemporary personalities to retrospectives on past stars. Daley disliked some sports figures, notably Curt Flood and Muhammad Ali, but most often he simply chose not to write about them. Daley enjoyed a wide audience, including President John F. Kennedy, who called himself an "avid reader."

Although most sports historians rank Daley below Red Smith as a stylist and commentator, Daley in 1956 became the first sportswriter to win a Pulitzer Prize. He also received the Grantland Rice Award in 1961, the Sportswriter of the Year Award in 1963, and the Football Writers Distinguished Service Award in 1970. Daley's favorite pieces were published in *Sports of the Times* (1959).

Besides his newspaper work, Daley wrote several books: *Times at Bat* (1950), *Knute Rockne: Football Wizard of Notre Dame* (1960), *Kings of the Home Run* (1962), *Pro Football's Hall of Fame* (1963), and *The Story of the Olympic Games*, with James Kiernan (1969). He also contributed many articles to magazines. Daley died in New York City.

• See the Arthur Daley File in the National Baseball Library, Cooperstown, N.Y. Of Daley's columns in the *New York Times*, see especially 22 Feb. and 8 May 1956; 8 Oct. 1961; and 4 and 6 Jan. 1974. For his place in sportswriting, see Randall Poe, "The Writing of Sports," *Sport Inside Out*, ed. David L. Vanderwerken and Spencer K. Wertz (1985); Ira Berkow, *Red: A Biography of Red Smith* (1986); and David Halberstam, *Summer of '49* (1989). An obituary appeared in the *New York Times*, 4 Jan. 1974.

JIM HARPER

DALEY, Richard Joseph (15 May 1902–20 Dec. 1976), mayor of Chicago, was born in a working-class neighborhood of Chicago, Illinois, the son of Michael Daley, a sheetmetal worker, and Lillian Dunne. He attended Catholic schools and after several long years of night school graduated from DePaul Law School in 1934.

Daley worked his way up through the Democratic party precinct and ward organization and made his first successful run for public office as a state representative in 1936. In June of that year he married Eleanor Guilfoyle; they had seven children, including a son, Richard, who later became mayor of Chicago. A devout Roman Catholic, Daley attended mass every morning.

Daley was elected to the Illinois senate first in 1936 as a write-in candidate after the GOP incumbent died unexpectedly during the campaign. In 1938 he switched back to the Democrats and was reelected to the senate, where he remained until 1946 when he suffered his only election defeat, as a candidate for Cook County sheriff. In 1949 Daley was picked by Governor Adlai Stevenson to become director of the Illinois Department of Finance. In that position he expanded his grasp of budgets and public finance. A year later Daley was elected clerk of Cook County, a post he held through 1955. His ascent to the mayor's office was made possible by Daley's election as chairman of the Cook County Democratic Central Committee in 1953. In 1955 he defeated two-term mayor Martin F. Kennelly in the Democratic primary, and in the general election he beat the Republican, Robert K. Merriam, by a comfortable margin.

During the next two decades Daley was reelected mayor every four years over a series of nominally nonpartisan but generally Republican contenders. The source of his power derived from his dual role as mayor and as party chairman. He ran a tightly controlled party structure and made maximum use of about 35,000 city workers and patronage employees to bring out the vote. Daley also won public support because he focused on the delivery of municipal services and gave substance to the Chicago slogan: "the city that works." He first attracted national attention as a political strategist for his important role in helping John F. Kennedy win the Democratic nomination and the presidential election in 1960. His reputation as a "president maker" soared, and for a few years thereafter all Democratic presidential aspirants dutifully sought out the "da mare's" blessing.

Dedicated to redeveloping his city, Daley encouraged the construction of downtown skyscrapers, including what was then the world's tallest building, the Sears tower; enlarged the world's busiest airport, O'Hare; and stimulated expressway expansion and improved rapid transit facilities. His administration set a rapid pace of urban renewal, the demolition of blighted areas, and the building of new public housing. As with all of his enterprises, he mixed politics and business. To those who scoffed at his efforts, his answer was that "good politics makes for good government." When reporters taunted him about the evils of the party machine, Daley snapped back, "Organization, not machine. Get that, organization, not machine."

The year 1968 was disastrous for the Daley legend, however. In the wake of the assassination of Martin Luther King, Jr., in April, a firestorm of arson, looting, and rioting swept through Chicago's black Westside. An outraged mayor issued an order that was spread across newspaper headlines and broadcast over television screens throughout the nation: "Shoot to kill any arsonist . . . with a Molotov cocktail in his hand." Daley's order provoked the wrath of the liberal news media, but the worst was yet to come. In August, during the 1968 Democratic National Convention, Chicago was the site of a week of antiwar turmoil and street violence by demonstrators and the police. A postconvention report labeled the disorder a "police riot" and placed responsibility on the mayor. In a flight of journalistic hyperbole, commentator Eric Sevareid compared that week in Chicago to the Russian invasion of Czechoslovakia. Daley's reputation was left in tatters, and for a few years thereafter several professional societies refused to hold their annual meetings and conferences in Chicago. Liberals predicted that he was finished as a political leader, and the lockout of Daley delegates by the George McGovern wing at the 1972 Democratic National Convention seemed to support that view.

Daley's travails continued in December 1969 when Democratic state's attorney Edward R. Hanrahan got

himself and the party into deep trouble during a police raid that resulted in the shooting to death of two black radicals who belonged to the Black Pathers. Then, in 1971, Chicago columnist Mike Royko, known for his mordant wit, published a wickedly clever and entertaining bestseller, *Boss: Richard J. Daley of Chicago*, which New York journalist Jimmy Breslin said did "more written damage to a man than perhaps anything I have ever read."

As the decade developed, the Daley administration was shaken by additional scandals that further undermined the machine. James R. Thompson, an ambitious and hard-working U.S. attorney (later governor of the state), secured indictments of fifty Chicago policemen, two district commanders, and a half dozen of Daley's close associates, including a former Democratic governor of the state, Otto Kerner, the mayor's council floor leader, and the mayor's speech writer; they all went to jail. Then, in May 1974 Daley suffered a stroke. He died two-and-a-half years later in Chicago.

Although evidence of venality tainted some of Daley's cronies, the mayor himself appeared to have remained free of corruption. Numerous clandestine investigations of the mayor by federal, state, and local watchdogs failed to turn up a single, solid charge of corruption against him. One notable exception was a lucrative insurance contract that was awarded to his son's firm. When criticized by an alderman, Daley exploded with rage, telling his critic-councilman to "kiss my ass" and asking, what had the world come to if a father could no longer help out his son?

In addition, stories of Daley's impending demise were greatly exaggerated, as the Daley political organization continued to win elections. Despite a decade-long campaign against him by civil rights leaders, he continued to keep a majority of black elected officials on his side of the aisle. He achieved this by granting enough patronage and favors to black elected officials to carry their support but never enough to alienate white supporters. His unprecedented election to a sixth term in 1975 showed that the Daley machine still had some muscle.

As mayor, Daley compiled an enviable record on the labor front, settling more than twenty major strikes by forcing agreements. The striking unions varied from the gravediggers to the public schoolteachers to the Lyric Opera Orchestra. Many of these conflicts were resolved because the mayor had appointed legions of his boyhood pals to various positions of power and because others had assumed the leadership of unions. Contributing to his success was the fact that Daley bought labor peace by giving municipal employees high wages and by allowing very few layoffs.

His success is especially noteworthy given that the times were not auspicious for urban political longevity. The ghetto riots, black power demands, and anti–urban renewal protests of the 1960s and 1970s contributed greatly to the defeat of many prominent urban leaders, including Detroit's "wonderboy" mayor, Jerome Cavanagh, photogenic limousine liberal John Lindsay of New York, the nation's first big city black mayor, Carl Stokes of Cleveland, and Sam Yorty of Los Angeles. Daley survived this career-killing era both because he managed a city that worked and because he brought a sense of stability to Chicago during a time of deep divisions and great upheavals. Daley projected and often lived up to the image of an in-charge leader who had a firm hand on the throttle. This was profoundly appealing to Chicago voters, who were heavily Catholic and "corporate" in social outlook, ethnic and blue-collar in occupation, conservative in their public manners, and deeply angered by what they saw as an ill-mannered generation of young radicals who ridiculed their parents' occupations, religion, politics, and life styles. Stability and order were what the electorate ordered, and that's what Daley delivered.

Less enviable was his verbal record. Daley stumbled through twenty years of mispronunciations, slurred word-endings, malapropisms, and side-splitting gaffes. In a soaring flight of rhetoric he once told an audience, "We must rise to high and higher platitudes" (meaning "plateaus"). Also, while touring a scientific exhibit, his honor was overheard to say, "It is amazing what they will do once the atom is harassed." In a moment of outrage he told newsmen, "The police are not here to create disorder; they are here to preserve disorder." In a moment of pique he said he would clarify something "for the enlightenment and edification and hallucination of the alderman from the fiftieth ward." He also earned poor marks for his unwillingness to reach out to the suburbs, his slow accommodation of blacks and Hispanics into the party, and his often stormy and tempestuous relationship with the news media.

The controversies and scandals of his tenure notwithstanding, opinion polls show that Daley was one of the dozen or so most effective mayors of the twentieth century. He kept the lid on political turmoil that elsewhere overturned one urban regime after another. He used the mayor's office to reform and modernize the police and fire departments. He presided over one of the largest downtown building booms in the city's history. He brought a major new campus of the University of Illinois into Chicago and expanded the world's busiest airport. Daley also made use of his ability as a budget manager and an expert on public finance to steer Chicago away from the shoals that bankrupted New York City and Cleveland.

A decade after Daley's death, a Gallup poll found that he was still popular with the electorate, as seven out of ten Chicagoans thought he had been a "good" mayor. A 1985 poll of experts, including historians, mayoral biographers, political scientists, and journalists who had studied and written extensively about mayors, ranked Daley as the best of Chicago's forty mayors who had served since 1837. "If Daley was more successful than other mayors," as state representative Woods Bowman observed, speaking at a 1977 conference at the University of Illinois at Chicago, "it was because he was more observant of detail, more canny in his analyses of political possibilities, and when compromise failed more powerful than his opponents."

• A small collection of Daley materials, including typed speech transcripts, 1955–1966, can be found in the Special Collections at the University of Illinois at Chicago library. For a knowledgeable life and death account of Daley, see Len O'Connor, *Clout: Mayor Daley and His City* (1975) and *Requiem: The Decline and Demise of Mayor Daley and His Era* (1977). For the Irish dimension, see Eugene Kennedy, *Himself: The Life and Times of Mayor Richard J. Daley* (1978). For the best works on how the Daley political machine functioned, see Milton Rakove, *Don't Make No Waves, Don't Back No Losers: An Insider's Analysis of the Daley Machine* (1975) and *We Don't Want Nobody Nobody Sent* (1979). For ranking Chicago's mayors, see Melvin G. Holli, "Mirror, Mirror on the Wall, Who Is the Greatest Mayor of Them All?" in *The Mayors: The Chicago Political Tradition*, ed. P. Green and M. Holli (1987; rev. ed., 1994), and "Daley to Daley," in *Restoration: Chicago Elects a New Daley*, ed. P. Green and M. Holli (1991). Obituaries are in the *Chicago Tribune* and the *Chicago Sun Times*, 21 and 22 Dec. 1976.

MELVIN G. HOLLI

DALHART, Vernon (6 Apr. 1883–14 Sept. 1948), country and popular singer, was born Marion Try Slaughter in rural Marion County in northeast Texas, the son of Robert Marion Slaughter, a local rancher, and Mary Jane Castleberry. During the time young Slaughter was growing up, the area was still very much a part of the Old West, with gunfights and cattle drives. When he was twelve Slaughter's father was killed in a knife fight with his brother-in-law, which resulted in the youngster's move to Dallas around 1896 with his mother. There he studied formally at the Dallas Conservatory of Music and began singing in public at the First Baptist Church. Before then, however, he had absorbed many of the genuine cowboy songs while on his father's ranch and had learned to play the jew's-harp and the harmonica.

By 1900 he had married Sadie Lee Moore-Livingston; they had one daughter. For reasons not entirely clear, he decided in 1910 to move to New York City to further his music career and to better support his young family. He worked at a piano warehouse, studied voice at night, and did freelance work as a church soloist and singer for funerals. His voice—a pleasant and flexible tenor—soon developed to where he was able to get roles in light opera, including runs of "Girl of the Golden West" and "H.M.S. Pinafore." Then in 1916 he saw an advertisement in a New York newspaper that wanted "singers for recording sessions." The advertiser was inventor Thomas A. Edison, who was just making the switch from cylinder records to flat discs and was looking for new singers. Dalhart went for the audition, and, noting that almost all the other singers were ones he knew from light opera, decided to audition with a vaudeville "dialect" song, "Can't Yo' Heah Me Callin,' Caroline." Edison smiled and said, "You are the man for me," and Dalhart's recording career was started.

During the next eight years, Slaughter became known as Vernon Dalhart—he took the stage name from two small towns in his native Texas—and became one of the most prolific record makers in the nation. Though his repertoire included everything from light opera to religious pieces, and from World War I topical songs to ersatz Scotch songs, his specialty became songs in southern dialect. "I never had to learn it," he explained later. "When you are born and brought up in the South, your only trouble is to talk any other way." Though he recorded extensively for Edison, by 1919 he was making an occasional record for Victor, and by 1921 he was also working for Columbia. Throughout the 1920s he would become the most prolific of the New York studio singers, eventually amassing a discography of more than 5,000 sides. With such constant work, he seldom had to resort to stage work or, after 1920, radio work to provide for his family.

By early 1924 many record companies were getting interested in a new type of music coming out of the South—what was then called "Old Time Music" or "Hill Country Music," which would eventually become "country music." Many of the authentic singers lived in the rural South and were not especially interested in coming to New York to record; record executives hit upon the idea of having Dalhart, a trained studio singer who could read a lead sheet, use his southern style to try his hand at these songs. In 1924 Dalhart was given a record of a song called "The Wreck on the Southern Old 97" and told to learn it; he did and made a successful recording for both Edison and Victor. As the "B" (or opposite) side, they chose a song that had been partly written by his cousin, fellow Texan Guy Massey, entitled "The Prisoner's Song." When Victor released the two in October 1924, the result was a runaway bestseller for the new record industry. Eventually it would sell more than one million copies—astounding for a time when there were relatively few Victrolas in the country—and become the first country record to do so.

During the next two years Dalhart followed this hit up with a rash of records of what were then called "event songs," ballads about current disasters or murders. They included "The Death of Floyd Collins" (about the cave explorer), "The Wreck of the Shenandoah" (an airship), "The John T. Scopes Trial" (about the evolution controversy), and "Little Mary Phagan" (about a Georgia murder). Often Dalhart recorded under false names when recording songs for Victor's rival labels (especially Columbia and OKeh), including Al Carver, Wolfe Ballard, Tobe Little, Jeff Calhoun, Mack Allen, and over 100 others. For months on end his records would account for seven or eight of a company's top ten selling "country" records. His success helped create the country music industry as we know it today, convincing the record companies that such songs had a definite sales appeal.

For much of this time, Dalhart worked with a young Kansas songwriter, singer, and guitarist named Carson J. Robison. Robison became a skilled writer of event songs but later was able to produce sentimental favorites like "My Blue Ridge Mountain Home" and the topical "Eleven Cent Cotton and Forty Cent Meat," both of which he recorded as duets with Dalhart. Robison split with Dalhart in 1928 and went on to a solo career on the radio and as a songwriter. The thousands of dollars in royalties that Dalhart made enabled him to buy a huge English Tudor home in fashionable Mamaroneck, New York, as well as a matched pair of Cadillacs. But his studio work began to wane in the late 1920s as more authentic singers like Jimmie Rodgers and Gene Autry came on the scene. To make matters worse, he lost much of his fortune in the stock market crash of 1929.

He continued to try to record through the 1930s but with little success. By 1942 he was out of the music business and working as a night watchman in Bridgeport, Connecticut, forgotten by all except a few fans. He died in Bridgeport and was buried there under a headstone that read simply "Marion T. Slaughter."

Today Dalhart is remembered as the nation's first really successful country music star and one of the most prolific makers of records in American history. Though his stiff, formal delivery had little appeal to modern audiences, and though he was often dismissed as an inauthentic "citybilly," he was a major force in the popularization of rural vernacular music.

• Useful sources on Dalhart are Walter Haden, "Vernon Dalhart," in *Stars of Country Music*, ed. Judith McCulloh and Bill C. Malone (1975), and Jim Walsh, "Favorite Pioneer Recording Artists: Vernon Dalhart," *Hobbies Magazine*, May–Dec. 1960.

CHARLES K. WOLFE

DALL, Caroline Wells Healey (22 June 1822–17 Dec. 1912), author and reformer, was born in Boston to Mark Healey, a merchant and conscientious Unitarian, and Caroline Foster. At her father's insistence, Caroline Healey was well educated by the standards of women's education of the time. She was trained at home by tutors and attended Joseph Hale Abbot's nearby school for girls. When Mark Healey experienced financial difficulties during the depression of 1837, Caroline's education enabled her to work as vice-principal of Miss English's School for Young Ladies in Georgetown, D.C., from 1842 until 1844.

Caroline Healey's interests as a young woman centered in the social and intellectual changes occurring in the Unitarian community. Confronted with urban growth and the determined proselytizing of evangelical denominations, Unitarians who once prided themselves on their reasonableness initiated benevolent efforts in the 1830s. Around 1840, Caroline participated in programs to assist Boston's working classes by teaching Sunday school at the West Church, operating a day nursery for working women, and acting as a religious visitor to private homes. In 1844 she married Charles Appleton Dall, a graduate of Harvard Divinity School who did similar work as a minister-at-large, first in St. Louis and, at the time of their marriage, in

Baltimore. Caroline Dall assisted her husband in his work.

During the same period, she was attracted to the transcendentalist ideas emerging within Unitarianism. In 1841, she had attended a series of conversations led by Margaret Fuller, and much later in her life she published a transcript of the discussions as *Margaret and Her Friends* (1895). In a reminiscence titled *Transcendentalism in New England* (1897), Dall professed her adherence to transcendentalist principles. Her writings of the 1840s suggest, however, that she was not immediately converted. Dall's first book, *Essays and Sketches* (1849), treated such standard Christian themes as the Lord's Supper and the Sabbath without allusion to the revolutionary transcendentalist concept of intuitive revelation. Perhaps like many religiously liberal young people, Dall was impressed by the intellectual energy of the transcendentalists but either failed to comprehend or did not altogether accept their philosophical ideas.

A cataclysmic event in Caroline Dall's personal life in 1855 seems to have initiated her most impressive period of intellectual growth. Charles Dall's physical and apparent mental instability had caused much mobility among pastorates during the first decade of the couple's marriage. Following his breakdown in Toronto, Canada, in 1854, Rev. Dall returned to Boston and then sailed alone for India the following year to serve as a Unitarian minister-at-large, a position he retained until his death in 1886. One friend attributed Caroline's decision to stay in Boston to a lack of financial resources and to the needs of her children, born in 1845 and 1849. Though she dutifully honored Dall's memory in the documents she collected in *Memorial to Charles Appleton Dall* (1902), Caroline's sudden conversion to women's rights in the mid-1850s must have been conditioned by the shock of finding herself responsible for two children in a society with few employment opportunities open to wives of the professional classes. She helped to organize women's rights conventions in 1855 and 1859 but turned increasingly to lecturing as a medium for airing her views on women, no doubt in part because of public speaking's financial rewards.

Dall's most important book, *The College, the Market, and the Court; or Woman's Relation to Education, Labor, and Law* (1867), began as a series of lectures delivered in Boston between 1859 and 1861. A plea for coeducation, economic opportunity, and equality under the law, *The College, the Market, and the Court* is notable for its social-scientific mode of analysis. Dall had a keen sense of the interdependency of social problems, the power of public opinion, and the utility of crosscultural comparisons. In light of her approach, it is not surprising that she was a founding member of the American Social Science Association in 1865 and served on its executive committee until 1905. Even so, secular and religious values continued to coexist in Dall's thinking, since she remained active in Sunday school work and preached in Unitarian pulpits.

Dall published several other works on women, including sketches of famous women in *Historical Pictures Retouched* (1860). Yet most of her later work was ephemeral in nature, such as a series of children's books titled *Patty Gray's Journey to the Cotton Islands* (1869–1870), a travel account of *My First Holiday; or, Letters Home from Colorado, Utah, and California* (1881), and *What We Really Know about Shakespeare* (1886). It is possible that as intellectual life became professionalized and as male-dominated universities increasingly monopolized serious thought, an informally educated and aging woman such as Caroline Dall was subtly pushed toward popular subjects. After 1879, Dall lived out the rest of her life with her son, William Healey Dall, in Washington, D.C., where he worked for the Smithsonian Institution.

Caroline Dall's life epitomizes the blend of opportunities and restrictions that educated women confronted in mid-nineteenth-century America. Influenced by Unitarianism, transcendentalism, and social science, Dall produced one penetrating study of women but had little chance to develop her intellectual talents fully or to pursue professional goals.

• The principal collections of Caroline Dall's papers are located in the Massachusetts Historical Society, Boston, and the Schlesinger Library, Radcliffe College. The most thorough source of biographical information is the entry by Stephen Nissenbaum in Edward James, ed., *Notable American Women*, vol. 1 (1971). On Dall's early life, see also her autobiography, *Alongside* (1900), and Barbara Welter, "The Merchant's Daughter. A Tale from Life," *New England Quarterly* 42 (1969): 3–22.

ANNE C. ROSE

DALL, Charles Henry Appleton (12 Feb. 1816–18 July 1886), Unitarian minister and missionary, was born in Baltimore, Maryland, the son of James Dall and Henrietta Austin, occupations unknown. At the age of eight he was sent to his father's family in Boston for an education. He graduated from Harvard College in 1837—along with Henry David Thoreau and Richard Henry Dana—and Harvard Divinity School in 1840. Dall became thoroughly imbued with the liberal Christian piety and social conscience of the moderate Unitarianism shaped by William Ellery Channing, and he identified closely with its institutions as distinguished from those of the more theologically conservative Congregationalism.

Dall was ordained an evangelist in St. Louis and served as a Unitarian "minister-at-large" there (1840–1842), in Baltimore (1843–1845), and in Portsmouth, New Hampshire (1846). He spent most of 1842 in England observing Unitarian churches and social reform efforts. Like most Protestant urban reformers of the period, Dall believed that the way to fight ignorance, idleness, and vice was through instruction, employment, and religion. He was more successful at promoting elementary, adult, and vocational schooling for the lower classes than he was in attracting others to Unitarianism or convincing them of the need to tackle unemployment.

Dall's position in the St. Louis church was terminated when the congregation decided it needed an assistant pastor instead of a minister-at-large. Dall had not impressed the congregation with his preaching ability and was not offered the new position. He moved on to brief pastorates in Needham, Massachusetts (1847–1849), and Toronto, Canada (1850 or 1851–1853 or 1854), both of which ended as a result of financial disagreements with parishioners; Dall believed that the Needham congregation also disapproved of both his assertion of ministerial authority and his reform activities.

In 1854, in poor health and seemingly without career options beyond the Unitarian ministry, Dall was back in the Boston area; there he learned that the American Unitarian Association (AUA) was opening a mission in Calcutta, India. In the 1820s the association had given nominal financial support to former Scottish Baptist missionary William Adam's efforts to organize European Unitarians in India and to attract Hindu intellectuals to liberal Christianity. (Adam later founded the Toronto church that Dall served in the 1850s.) An 1854 visit to India by American Unitarian Charles Brooks convinced the Christian Unitarians of the AUA that the time was ripe to spread liberal Christianity among Europeans and reform-minded Indians. Dall, with his strong Unitarian identity, fervent liberal piety, and long-standing interest in various forms of outreach, was a logical choice as the first (and only) American Unitarian foreign missionary.

Dall lived in Calcutta from the middle of 1855 until his death there, with visits to the United States in 1862, 1869, 1872, 1875, and 1882. His activities over the years included ministering to the European and American Unitarian congregation (organized as the Unitarian Society for the Propagation of the Gospel in India), founding and managing a variety of Sunday, poor boys', and girls' schools and the popular School of Useful Arts (1860), and reaching out to those non-Christians interested in a liberal form of Christianity.

His relations with high-caste Hindus brought Dall the most attention and controversy. British and American Unitarians had long hoped that the critical reappraisal of Hinduism and the interest in Christianity of Bengali reformers Ram Mohan Roy, members of the Brahmo Somaj ("congregation of *brahman*," organized by Roy in 1828 as a Hindu counterpart to Unitarianism), and midcentury Brahmo leader Keshab Chandra Sen would result in their adopting Unitarianism. Dall endeavored to lead Western-educated Indians away from a philosophical Hindu theism that appreciated Jesus of Nazareth as a universal moral teacher but used Christianity to strengthen rather than replace Hinduism toward an authentic liberal Christianity. He preached to his own congregation and in other Christian churches and schools, gave lectures on Christianity to Hindus (published in 1856 as *Some Gospel Principles*) and on the Brahmo Somaj to Christians, and published a range of religious literature. When Dall's efforts to convert and train Indian Unitarian leaders failed, after several promising candidates proved to be unreliable and self-serving, he formed the Rammohun Roy Society (1857, later the Hitoishini Association), for Brahmo Somaj members interested in studying Roy and Christianity. After Somaj leaders, irritated with his proselytizing, discouraged him from attending Somaj meetings, Dall took his most controversial step in 1871 when he actually joined the Hindu society, a move that elicited criticism from Brahmos and American Unitarians—both groups asking what a Christian missionary was doing in a Hindu society—but no converts. Dall's greatest contribution to Calcutta continued to be his schools, which flourished in his later years but were closed by his wife shortly after his death.

Dall had married Caroline Wells Healey, educator and friend of Transcendentalist Margaret Fuller, in 1844. She had helped him with his mission work in Baltimore, had published books on women's rights and, in Toronto, had written for women's journals and worked with fugitive slaves. The couple had been married, probably not happily, for a little more than ten years when he left for India and she remained in the United States with their two children. Their son, William Dall, became a prominent paleontologist.

Charles Dall held a unique position as the sole foreign missionary of an American church that over its history has preferred inter-religious conversation to active proselytizing. Along with those of other British and American missionaries, his lectures, publications, organizations, and schools helped to create an elite class of educated, English-speaking liberal Hindu leaders who were familiar with European culture and religion but were more inclined to reform than to reject traditional Indian religion. Although the original goal of his mission may have been the conversion of Hindus to liberal Christianity, Dall's unusual work in India was in fact a stage in the transition from traditional missions to the mutually respectful inter-religious dialogue of the twentieth century. As such it was a unique encounter of American and Indian intellectual traditions.

• Dall's college papers are in the Harvard University Archives; his letters to the AUA and his personal papers from both his American and Indian careers are in the Harvard Divinity School's Andover-Harvard Library. Various letters from India were published in the AUA *Quarterly Journal*, and Dall published occasional mission reports, including *Twenty-five Years: General Report of the India Mission, of the American Unitarian Association* (1880). While he was in Calcutta Dall also published *A Discourse Occasioned by the Death of Abbot Lawrence* (1855), *Lecture on Rajah Rammohun Roy* (1871), *The Theist's Creed* (1872), "The Brahmo Somaj of India led by Baboo Keshub Chunder Sen with Facts Historical and Personal," in *Brahmananda Keshub Chunder Sen*, ed. C. G. Banerjee, vol. 2 (1874), *The True Life* (1876), and *What Is Christianity? Sonship to God* (1883).

Early biographical treatments include John Healy Heywood, *Our Indian Mission and Our First Missionary* (1887); Henry Williams, *Memorials of the Class of 1837 of Harvard University* (1887); and Caroline Dall, ed., *Memorial to C. H. A. Dall* (1902). Spencer Lavan, *Unitarians and India:*

A Study in Encounter and Response (1977), describes and evaluates Dall's work in Calcutta and discusses its Indian and Unitarian contexts.

DALL, William Healey (21 Aug. 1845–27 Mar. 1927), natural historian, paleontologist, and malacologist, was born in Boston, Massachusetts, the son of Charles Henry Appleton Dall, a Unitarian missionary, and Caroline Wells Healey, the author of numerous publications on women's rights. Dall's father became a missionary to India in 1855, which limited the financial resources of his family and ultimately prevented Dall from attending college. Deeply influenced by Augustus A. Gould's handsomely illustrated *Report on the Invertebrata of Massachusetts* while still a young man, Dall developed a fascination with shells. The Mollusca became an abiding concern with him for the balance of his life. By the time he was seventeen, his interest and aptitude in natural history led to his being mentored by Gould, Harvard zoologist Louis Agassiz, and the faculty of the Museum of Comparative Zoology at Harvard University in the art of collecting and identifying mollusks and other fauna. Diligent and well organized, Dall began to obtain and prepare collections of diverse specimens of flora and fauna for Agassiz and the Smithsonian Institution. While in Boston, he also attended lectures on medicine and anatomy at Harvard.

Unable to find any career opportunities in Boston, Dall became in 1863 a clerk in the land office of the Illinois Central Railway in Chicago. There he became friends with Robert Kennicott and other Chicago naturalists. In his leisure time he studied specimens and collections in the museum of the Chicago Academy of Science. His interest in science and his growing knowledge of the methods of natural history led Kennicott to offer him in 1865 a position on the Western Union Telegraph Expedition, which was preparing to lay an intercontinental telegraph line through the Yukon and Alaska across the shallow Bering Straits to Siberia. Dall's participation in this venture ultimately made him the leading U.S. expert on the flora, fauna, peoples, and geography of Alaska. Before sailing for Russian America, Dall received training and instructions from zoologist Spencer Fullerton Baird at the Smithsonian Institution. Coming under Baird's kindly mentoring and patronage had a profound influence on Dall's career; he later acknowledged his debt to Baird, who became the first commissioner of the U.S. Commission of Fish and Fisheries in 1871 and secretary of the Smithsonian Institution in 1878, in his careful biography of him, *Spencer Fullerton Baird: A Biography* (1915).

Passing through California on his way north in the late spring of 1865, Dall became a member of the California Academy of Science and collected along the Pacific coast. He shipped more than 5,300 specimens, including mollusks, crustaceans, chitons, brachiopods, fish, birds, mammals, and regional flora, to the Smithsonian before he sailed for Alaska. By the end of Au-

gust, he had reached the Aleutians, where he dredged, collected, and made soundings, becoming the first American scientist to initiate systematic exploration of the marine fauna of that region. After visiting Siberia and collecting in that region, he returned from those northern waters in November 1865 with more than 5,100 individual specimens. With the death of Kennicott along the banks of the Yukon River in September 1866, the 21-year-old Dall was named the director of the scientific corps and became responsible for the first detailed examination of the interior of Alaska and its resources. Experiencing temperatures as low as 40 degrees below zero, he spent the fall and winter of 1866 in the small, native village of Nulato on the Yukon River, studying Indian and Eskimo linguistics, collecting specimens, and mapping much of that great river. When the successful laying of the second transatlantic cable brought to an end his responsibilities to Western Union, he spent the summer of 1867 obtaining more than 4,500 specimens for the Smithsonian.

Upon returning to Washington in December 1868, Dall devoted his time to preparing an account of his experiences in Alaska and developing an appraisal of the assets of that region, which had been acquired by the United States only a year earlier. The publication of Dall's *Alaska and Its Resources* (1870) provided Americans with the first detailed statement of the wealth and potential of Alaska and established his reputation as the nation's foremost expert on the region. Realizing that the vastness of that land required extensive investigations, Baird appointed Dall acting assistant to the Coast Survey, of which Baird was head, in 1871, and Dall began a coastal survey of the Aleutian Islands and Alaskan coastal waters. With a coastline greater than that of the nation's Atlantic, Gulf, and Pacific coasts combined, the task was enormous. Dall commanded vessels that surveyed those waters intermittently from 1872 to 1880. With U.S. commercial interest in Alaska growing, the need to address the dangers of navigation in those essentially uncharted waters became paramount. In 1874 Dall began to work on this problem and in 1883 published the *Pacific Coast Pilot, Coasts and Islands of Alaska*, the first major government guide to Alaskan waters and the basis for all future studies and publications of this nature prepared by the Coast and Geodetic Survey. From 1870 to 1884 Dall prepared more than 400 articles and papers in scientific journals such as the *Bulletin of the U.S. Fish Commission*, the *American Journal of Conchology*, and the *Bulletin of the Museum of Comparative Zoology*, among many others. In 1880 he married Annette Whitney; they had three children.

In 1884 Dall joined the recently created U.S. Geological Survey as a paleontologist and was assigned to work on mollusks at the U.S. National Museum. From the north tower of the Smithsonian Institution, he initiated his pioneering studies in the taxonomy of recent and fossil mollusks and was granted by the Smithsonian the title of honorary curator of the Division of Mollusks and Tertiary Fossils. Between 1890 and 1910 he traveled six times more to the Pacific

Northwest and Alaska to examine the geology and mollusks of that region. In 1899 he was one of the scientists who participated in the Harriman Alaska Expedition. Dedicated to the advancement of the study of mollusks, from 1893 to 1927 he held a professorship from the Wagner Free Institute of Science in Philadelphia, Pennsylvania. In this position he gave a series of annual lectures on some aspect of invertebrate paleontology. In 1891 he examined the Tertiary geology of Florida and in 1893 surveyed the same formations in Georgia. Always seeking to broaden the base of specimens available to malacologists, he acquired for the Smithsonian the extensive collection of mollusks gathered by the distinguished British conchologist J. Gwyn Jeffreys. From 1899 to 1915 Dall was honorary curator of the Bishop Museum in Honolulu, Hawaii, where he cataloged Andrew Garrett's collection of shells from the Pacific Islands. Dall retired from the USGS in 1923 but continued to work in his office until his death, in Washington, D.C.

Blessed with strong organizational skills, the capacity to initiate and complete a task, and the enthusiasm to maintain lasting professional ties with scientists throughout the world, Dall was a remarkably productive scientist. Writing in longhand, he authored more than 1,600 papers and made substantial contributions in diverse areas. Courageous in spirit and venturesome in his thinking, he was both an explorer and a scientist. His Alaskan studies provided the first substantial introduction to the fauna, geology, oceanography, and climatology of that distant region. A gifted taxonomist, he identified, classified, and named more than 5,400 genera, sub genera, and species of recent and fossil mollusks.

• Dall's extensive correspondence, logbooks, journals, and personal papers are preserved in the William Healey Dall Papers in the U.S. National Museum, Washington, D.C. Paul Bartsch et al. provide an introduction to his life and a bibliography of his works in "A Bibliography and Short Biographical Sketch of William Healey Dall," *Smithsonian Miscellaneous Collections* 104, no. 15 (1946): 1–96. Additional biographical and select bibliographical material is in W. P. Woodring's memoir of Dall in National Academy of Sciences, *Biographical Memoirs* 31 (1958): 92–113. A thorough analysis of his contributions in taxonomy is Kenneth J. Boss et al., *The Zoological Taxa of William Healey Dall* (1968). Morgan B. Sherwood's "William Healey Dall, Dean of Alaskan Experts" in his *Exploration of Alaska* (1965), pp. 36–56, contains a thoughtful analysis of Dall's contributions to Alaskan and North Pacific scholarship. See also Edward A. Herron, "William Healy Dall, Alaska Pioneer," *Natural History* 57 (Apr. 1948): 176–79, and C. Hart Merriam, "William Healey Dall," *Science*, 8 Apr. 1927, pp. 345–47.

PHILLIP DRENNON THOMAS

DALLAS, Alexander James (21 June 1759–16 Jan. 1817), lawyer and politician, was born in Kingston, Jamaica, the son of Dr. Robert Dallas, a native of Scotland, and his second wife Sarah (Cormack) Hewitt. When Alexander was about five, the family moved to Edinburgh and then to London. Dallas attended James Elphinston's academy where reasoning and the English language were stressed. Having completed these studies at about age eighteen, he intended to study law at the Inner Temple. Instead, due to family financial difficulties, he worked as a clerk and accountant in his uncle's London mercantile house until it closed in 1779. Dallas then turned to the study of literature. He married the sixteen-year-old Arabella Maria Smith in 1780; they eventually had nine children with six living to adulthood.

The young couple moved to Jamaica in 1781. Although an anticipated £7,000 inheritance from the estate of Dallas's father did not materialize, family connections allowed Dallas to be admitted to the bar. Jamaica proved unhealthy for Maria, and, having accumulated about $3,000 through inheritances, the couple settled in Philadelphia in June 1783. Since Pennsylvania required two years residency before one could practice law, Dallas worked as a clerk and studied law. He also became involved in theater work and joined the unsuccessful effort to have the ban on theatrical performances repealed.

Dallas was admitted to the bar in 1785, but his practice grew rather slowly over the next five years. He supplemented his income by skillfully editing William Spotswood's *Pennsylvania Herald* (1787–1788) and *Columbian Magazine* (1787–1789). As editor of the *Herald*, Dallas called for the creation of a more vigorous central government, but his candid reporting of the fight over the proposed Constitution caused Spotswood to drop him as editor. In this same period, Dallas expanded his legal knowledge when he began what became a long, useful career as a writer on legal subjects. In June 1790 he published the first of his carefully compiled and highly regarded *Reports of Cases Ruled and Adjudged in the Courts of Pennsylvania, Before and Since the Revolution*. In three additional volumes of *Reports of Cases* (1798, 1799, 1807), Dallas focused on decisions of the federal Circuit Court of Pennsylvania and the U.S. Supreme Court. He thus became the first reporter of Supreme Court decisions, and his volumes are still cited today.

Dallas's political career began in earnest in January 1791 when, at Governor Thomas Mifflin's request, he became Pennsylvania's secretary of the commonwealth. He held the post under Mifflin until 1799 and served Governor Thomas McKean in the same capacity until 1801. Dallas drafted most of Mifflin's state papers and, because of Mifflin's growing incapacity due to drinking, performed many of the duties of governor in the late 1790s. Dallas, who proclaimed monarchy a threat to republican governments, was a principal founder and penman of the Antifederalist, pro-France Philadelphia Democratic Society (1793) and of Pennsylvania's Democratic Republican party. In the 1790s he stoutly opposed Jay's treaty (*Features of Mr. Jay's Treaty* [1795]), called for a strict construction of the Constitution, attacked the idea that English common law could apply in the United States, and served as legal counsel for John Fries, the leader of the 1799 Fries Rebellion against the federal direct tax.

Nevertheless, Dallas believed in the sanctity of the legal profession, dressed in aristocratic style, wore his hair powdered, numbered many conservatives among his friends and, with Maria, became famous for hosting lavish entertainments. Not surprisingly, he belonged to the moderate wing of the Democratic Republican party. Counseling that grievances must be settled by the rule of law, he opposed the 1794 Whiskey Rebellion. And, although he steadfastly supported the national Republican party, by the early 1800s Dallas openly denounced the "tyranny" of Pennsylvania's radical Republicans. He especially disliked what he considered their disdain for the law and their attacks on men of wealth and talent. While commonwealth secretary, Dallas compiled and arranged for the publication of the *Laws of the Commonwealth of Pennsylvania* for 1700–1801 (4 vols., 1793–1801). He became U.S. district attorney for eastern Pennsylvania in 1801 and retained that post until 1814. As his fame and wealth grew (by 1814 he earned more than $20,000 a year), Dallas moved further right philosophically. In 1805, the year he helped found Pennsylvania's conservative Constitutional Republican party, Dallas argued for interpreting the Constitution broadly and for embracing English common law.

Dallas, whose important *An Exposition of the Causes and Character of the Late War with Great Britain* first appeared in 1815, backed the War of 1812. He helped Albert Gallatin, his good friend and secretary of the treasury, obtain financing for the war. Dallas himself became treasury secretary in October 1814 when the nation was virtually bankrupt. Although he held that post a mere two years, Dallas achieved much. Under his leadership, the Treasury Department was reorganized, the federal debt lowered, a surplus created, and the nation moved back to a specie payment system. Acting like a disciple of Alexander Hamilton (1755–1804), Dallas championed the creation of what became the Second Bank of the United States and obtained passage of a protective tariff that was, however, less protective than he desired. In addition, Dallas carried out James Monroe's plan for creating military outposts on the western frontier. From 14 March into December 1815, Dallas served as the acting secretary of war and ably oversaw the drastic peacetime reduction of the army. In 1815 he also functioned briefly as the temporary secretary of state.

Amid widespread praise, Dallas returned to private law practice in Philadelphia in the fall of 1816 and died there. His death was attributed to an attack of stomach gout. In addition to his other activities, Dallas became a member of Philadelphia's St. George's Society (1789) and its Hibernian Society (1794); he was elected to the American Philosophical Society (1791) and also elected a trustee of the University of Pennsylvania (1794). His principal biographer, Raymond Walters, Jr., struck the right note when he said that Dallas "holds a secure place as one of the first-rate men of secondary rank in the early days of the American republic."

• In addition to the publications already cited, Dallas produced many government documents, most notably his reports as secretary of the treasury. Many of his papers were apparently destroyed or discarded, and no principal Dallas manuscript collection exists. Important Dallas materials can be found in a wide range of archives including the Pennsylvania State Archives, Harrisburg; the National Archives; the Library of Congress; Girard College, Philadelphia; the American Philosophical Society; the Harvard Business School; and the New York Public Library. Various items appear in many collections of the Pennsylvania Historical Society, especially the George Mifflin Dallas Collection. But the richest source of manuscript materials relating to Dallas is contained within the Gallatin papers housed in the New-York Historical Society. Printed sources appear in the George Dallas work noted below; published papers of the leading political figures of the day; the Pennsylvania House and Senate Journals; the *Pennsylvania Archives*, 2d ser., 4; 4th ser., 3–4; 6th ser., 3–4; 9th ser., 1–3. The Genealogical Society of Pennsylvania holds a two-volume Dallas family history compiled in 1894, and the family genealogy appears in James Dallas, *History of the Family of Dallas* (1921). The *Port Folio* for March 1817 contains a valuable six-page "brief sketch" of Dallas's life; Arabella Maria Dallas's *Autobiographical Memoir for Her Children* (n.d.) is especially useful on the couple's early years together. George M. Dallas, *Life and Writings of A. J. Dallas* (1871), offers both a lengthy biography laced with excerpts from relevant documents and reprintings of Dallas papers including correspondence not otherwise available. The only modern biography is Raymond Walters, Jr., *Alexander James Dallas: Lawyer, Politician, Financier, 1759–1817* (1943).

JOHN K. ALEXANDER

DALLAS, George Mifflin (10 July 1792–31 Dec. 1864), vice president of the United States, senator, and diplomat, was born in Philadelphia, Pennsylvania, the son of Alexander James Dallas, a prominent lawyer and Democratic Republican politician, and Arabella Maria Smith. He graduated with highest honors from Princeton in 1810 and studied law with his father before his admission to the bar in 1813.

An aristocratic young man who enjoyed reading French and writing poetry, Dallas was also an ardent nationalist who longed to fight in the War of 1812. To deflect his son's military ambitions, Alexander Dallas secured his appointment in 1813 as private secretary to Albert Gallatin on a mission to Russia to seek the czar's mediation in the war. George Dallas traveled to Russia, England, and finally Belgium before being dispatched to the United States with a preliminary draft of the peace treaty in 1814.

Alexander Dallas, now secretary of the treasury, appointed his son to a minor post in his department. In 1816 George Dallas married Sophia Chew Nicklin, with whom he had eight children. That same year he began the practice of law in Philadelphia and became legal counsel for the new Second Bank of the United States (BUS), which his father had helped to create.

Upon his father's sudden death in 1817, Dallas began to play a larger role in Democratic Republican politics as a member of a faction, headed by Philadelphians, called the Family party. Although the group was not especially ideological, Dallas favored a protective tariff and felt that the divisive sectional issues surrounding the Missouri Compromise should be handled by denying Congress had the power to regulate slavery in the territories. He admired John C. Calhoun, then a nationalist, and hoped through Pennsylvania's alliance with Ohio and South Carolina to forestall further domination of the Democratic Republican party by Virginians. Although Dallas was defeated for the assembly in 1817, his faction was successful statewide, and he was appointed deputy attorney general for Philadelphia, serving until 1820.

Unable to stir popular enthusiasm for Calhoun, Dallas's faction belatedly switched to Jackson in 1824. When Jacksonians triumphed locally in 1828, Dallas was selected mayor of Philadelphia, interesting himself in street improvements and the founding of an orphan asylum. He served until April 1829, when the party's national triumph brought him appointment (thanks largely to Calhoun) as district attorney for the Eastern District of Pennsylvania. In 1831, when Isaac Barnard resigned from the U.S. Senate, Dallas was one of five candidates for his seat and won election on the eleventh ballot.

The two years Dallas spent in the Senate were enlivened by the bank war and the nullification crisis. Although an occasional critic of BUS president Nicholas Biddle, who supported a rival Pennsylvania faction, Dallas was a stockholder and director of the bank. Biddle expected Dallas to actively support its recharter by Congress. Dallas introduced the bank's memorials requesting recharter, defended the bank three times in debate, voted in favor of charter renewal, and voted to override the president's veto. Yet he understood the struggle's political motivation and felt he was being used in an effort to divide the Democratic party. As a result, his support for recharter was nominal rather than heartfelt, and it weakened him among the bank's supporters in Pennsylvania without endearing him to Jackson.

The tariff also presented problems. Popular in iron-producing Pennsylvania, the tariff was much less popular among Democrats elsewhere, especially South Carolina. Denying in lengthy speeches that South Carolina's economic woes were attributable to the tariff, Dallas supported the protective tariff of 1832 and Jackson's subsequent efforts to quash South Carolina's nullification of it. However, Dallas understood the party's need to compromise on the issue, although he voted against the 1833 compromise tariff. The breach between Calhoun and Jackson over nullification advanced the political prospects of Martin Van Buren of New York. Factional leaders seeking to block Van Buren's rise mentioned Dallas, among others, as a favorite son for Pennsylvanians to support in lieu of Van Buren. His judgment impaired by his own vanity, Dallas allowed himself to be used by others, fatally narrowing his own base of support.

Retiring from the Senate in 1833, Dallas was appointed state attorney general. In that position he undertook a well-publicized investigation of the management of the Eastern State Penitentiary. When a

Whig/Anti-Mason coalition won power in 1835, he left office and rallied Democrats around the issue of denying the Bank of the United States a state charter, thereby clearly assuming the antibank stance expected of Jacksonians. Economic elites in Philadelphia, including many of his acquaintances, condemned his stand. In 1837 Van Buren became president and offered his rival the post of minister to Russia, and Dallas accepted. He chiefly dealt with the interpretation of an 1824 treaty regarding the right of American ships to trade along the American Pacific coast north of 54° 40' N. Dallas eventually accepted Russia's interpretation of the treaty restricting trade. Bored with the empty social whirl of St. Petersburg, where he felt an outsider, Dallas resigned his post in 1839.

Upon his return to the United States, Dallas found James Buchanan, long his factional rival, the dominant figure in Pennsylvania politics. While practicing law, Dallas maintained an uneasy relationship with President Van Buren, privately questioning the president's decision to remove public monies from banks in reaction to the panic of 1837 and declining his offer of the attorney generalship in 1840.

Dallas's niece had married Robert J. Walker, a senator from Mississippi, and through him Dallas became interested in the 1840s in the acquisition of Texas. When the expansionist James K. Polk won the Democratic presidential nomination in 1844, his supporters sought a northerner from a large state for his running mate. Silas Wright of New York, a supporter of Van Buren (who had been denied the presidential nomination), was offered the vice presidency but refused. Walker then suggested Dallas because he was an expansionist, would be at least acceptable to Van Buren, and might reassure Pennsylvania Democrats concerned about low tariffs. Dallas, who was not present at the convention, was selected on the second ballot.

Dallas devoted himself to the campaign, reporting frequently to Polk on northern politics, advising him on issues (including the need to write a letter to reassure Pa. Democrats further on the tariff), and making sure that his own positions (on nativism, for instance) coincided with Polk's. (The party was actively pursuing naturalized voters and condemning nativism while trying not to offend the native-born Protestants who were the majority of party members.) After Polk's victory, Dallas was disappointed when the new president gave Buchanan the most important position in his cabinet and virtually ignored Dallas's suggestions on patronage matters. Presiding over the Senate, Dallas sought to arrange a compromise on the low Walker Tariff to make it acceptable to Pennsylvania but, when he could not do so, cast the deciding vote to pass the bill, justifying his decision as compatible with the 1844 party platform on which he and Polk had been elected. Dallas was hanged in effigy in Philadelphia, but he continued to hope he might succeed Polk in the White House. As his favorite issue, expansionism, became entangled with the issue of the extension of slavery into new territories, however, his prospects dimmed, and his name was mentioned for the presidency only by Democrats seeking to halt Buchanan's quest for the same post.

In 1849 Dallas returned to Philadelphia to practice law. Continuing to believe the Constitution did not permit Congress to legislate on territorial slavery, Dallas recommended a constitutional amendment deciding the issue one way or the other. He defended the Fugitive Slave Act of 1850 in an effort to show southerners that not all northerners opposed slavery. Dallas thought President Franklin Pierce, elected in 1852, was a poor leader but accepted the post of minister to Britain from him in 1856.

Dallas's urbane, dignified bearing, which had been a handicap in American politics, proved to be an asset in Britain. The British, after a prolonged period of rivalry, were interested in cooperating with the United States in the Western Hemisphere. Thus, even though the British minister in the United States, John Crampton, had just been expelled for recruiting American citizens for service in the Crimean War, Dallas was not similarly expelled. Instead, in October 1856 he and the British foreign secretary, Lord Clarendon, concluded the Dallas-Clarendon Convention, clarifying the responsibilities of both countries in Central America as described in the Clayton-Bulwer Treaty of 1850, which stated that neither country would colonize or dominate the isthmian area. The Mosquito Indians, over whom the British had claimed a protectorate, were to become part of Nicaragua, and the Bay Islands were recognized as part of Honduras. The latter provision was struck from the agreement in the U.S. Senate on the grounds that the islands had always been a part of Honduras and the treaty's wording implied U.S. approval of Britain's treaty with Honduras. The modified treaty was unacceptable to the British, and Buchanan, who had become president in 1857, decided to carry on further negotiations in Washington.

Although Buchanan kept Dallas in London, he gave him no real power. Nonetheless, Dallas was able to secure the Dallas-Malmesbury Memorandum, in which the British agreed that visiting ships flying the U.S. flag to ascertain whether they were slavers constituted illegal search.

Depressed by news of the breakup of the Democratic party, secession, and war, Dallas gladly turned over the legation to Charles Francis Adams in 1861 and returned to Philadelphia, where he died. Remarkable in none of his achievements, he represented the honorable norm for public servants of his generation.

• Dallas's papers are at the Historical Society of Pennsylvania, Philadelphia. Additional letters are at the University of Michigan Library, Temple University, and the Library of Congress. Diplomatic diaries and letters were published in Susan Dallas, ed., *Diary of George Mifflin Dallas, while United States Minister to Russia, 1837–1839, and to England, 1856–1861* (1892), and Julia Dallas, ed., *A Series of Letters from London Written during the Years 1856, '57, '58, '59, and '60* (1869). A biography is John M. Belohlavek, *George Mifflin Dallas: Jacksonian Patrician* (1977). On Pa. politics see Philip S. Klein, *Pennsylvania Politics (1817–1832)* (1940), and Charles M. Snyder, *The Jacksonian Heritage: Pennsylva-*

nia Politics, 1833–1848 (1958). On diplomacy see Sister Therese A. Donovan, "Difficulties of a Diplomat: George Mifflin Dallas in London," *Pennsylvania Magazine of History and Biography* 92 (1968): 421–40; and Mary W. Williams, *Anglo-American Isthmian Diplomacy, 1815–1915* (1916; repr. 1965). An obituary is in the *New York Times*, 1 Jan. 1865.

PHYLLIS F. FIELD

DALLENBACH, Karl M. (20 Oct. 1887–23 Dec. 1971), psychologist, was born in Champaign, Illinois, the son of John Dallenbach, a farmer and businessman, and Anna Mittendorf. The "M," Dallenbach always argued, was his entire middle name, since that was what was on his birth certificate. Dallenbach went to the University of Illinois with the intent to become an attorney. He was influenced to study psychology there by John Wallace Baird, a former student of Edward Bradford Titchener of Cornell University. Dallenbach received his B.A. in psychology from the University of Illinois in 1910 and went on a fellowship to the University of Pittsburgh, where he received his master's degree in psychology in 1911. Because of Baird's influence, Dallenbach did his doctoral work at Cornell University under Titchener, the head of the structuralist school of experimental psychology. Structuralism was the school of psychology that held that all complex experience could be reduced to simple, elementary experiences by means of a conscious process called introspection. Dallenbach received his Ph.D. in 1913 with a dissertation on the psychology of attention, the degree to which one can focus on one aspect of a complex experience and suppress other aspects. Titchener's influence on Dallenbach would last a lifetime. Also in 1913 Dallenbach married Margaret Douglas; they had three children.

Dallenbach spent two years on the psychology faculty at the University of Oregon and one year at Ohio State University before Titchener called him back to the faculty at Cornell in 1916. His academic career was interrupted by World War I, in which he was involved in the Psychological Testing Corps. After the war he returned to Cornell.

Using a loan against his birthright for funding, Dallenbach purchased the *American Journal of Psychology* in 1920 from G. Stanley Hall, who had founded the journal in 1887. He purchased it so that Titchener could be its sole editor, something Titchener had wanted for many years. Dallenbach became business manager of the journal that year and in 1925, when Titchener resigned the editorship, became its editor, a position he held or shared with others until 1968.

Dallenbach became a world authority on the psychology of attention in the 1910s and 1920s. In the 1920s Dallenbach conducted classic research in the effect of sleep versus activity on the retention of learned material. He demonstrated in his research with J. G. Jenkins that given the same interval between learning material and recalling it, activity will degrade the memory more than inactivity or sleep. This supported the interference theory of forgetting over the disuse theory. In the 1940s he also did some of the pioneering research in auditory localization research, demonstrating that the blind locate objects by sound echoes rather than some "sixth sense." He also did pioneering research in areas of temperature and vestibular senses.

During World War II, Dallenbach headed the psychological testing of recruits for the U.S. Army. After the war, he returned to Cornell, where he remained Sage Professor of Psychology until 1948. That year he left Cornell for the University of Texas, where he chaired the department of psychology until 1958. It was during his direction of the department that psychology at the University of Texas became a nationally recognized program. He continued teaching, researching, and editing until 1968, when he formally retired. He died in Austin, Texas.

Dallenbach influenced generations of experimental psychologists who gained their Ph.D.s under him. His research was prolific and many of his studies already mentioned are still cited as classics in the experimental psychological literature. He remained idealistic in his views of the purpose of higher education and the essential nature of experimental research in psychology.

• Dallenbach's papers are at Cornell University. Dallenbach wrote an autobiography, which is included in Edwin G. Boring and Gardner Lindzey, *A History of Psychology in Autobiography*, vol. 5 (1967), pp. 59–91. Two significant biographical articles on him are Rand B. Evans, "Karl M. Dallenbach: 1887–1971," *American Journal of Psychology* 85 (1972): 463–76, and Boring, "Karl M. Dallenbach," *American Journal of Psychology* 71 (1958): 1–40. A bibliography of Dallenbach's writings may be found in Margaret C. McGrade, "A Bibliography of the Writings of Karl M. Dallenbach," *American Journal of Psychology* 71 (1958): 41–44. An obituary is Rand B. Evans, "Karl M. Dallenbach: 1887–1971," *American Journal of Psychology* 85 (1972): 462–76.

RAND B. EVANS

DALLIN, Cyrus Edwin (22 Nov. 1861–14 Nov. 1944), sculptor, was born in Springville, Utah, the son of English immigrant settlers Thomas Dallin and Jane Hamer. In his youth Dallin played with Indian children from a nearby Ute encampment, and modeled animal figures with clay from the riverbanks. While working at his father's mine, he fashioned two portrait heads out of white clay that were exhibited at a fair in Salt Lake City. The portraits attracted the admiration of two wealthy miners who financed Dallin's 1880 trip to Boston, Massachusetts, where he became an apprentice to the sculptor Truman H. Bartlett, father of Paul Bartlett. In 1882 he opened his own studio in the city, and several years later he won a competition for an equestrian statue of Paul Revere, but because of financial problems it was not erected until 1940.

During this period Dallin's lifelong fascination with the American Indian began to manifest itself, and in 1888 his *The Indian Hunter* was awarded a gold medal at the American Art Association in New York City. In 1888 Dallin went to Paris and studied at the Académie Julian under Henri Michel Chapu, where he sculpted academic themes. After seeing Buffalo Bill Cody's "Wild West Show," he was inspired to make the equestrian *Signal of Peace* (Lincoln Park, Chicago, Ill.), for which one of the Indians in the troupe posed. This statue won honorable mention at the Paris Salon of 1890 and assured Dallin's fame in America when it was awarded a first-class medal at the World's Columbian Exposition in Chicago in 1893. In 1891 he married Vittoria Colonna Murray; they had three sons. Until 1894 they lived in Utah, where Dallin executed a number of commissions, including the figure of the Angel Moroni on the dome of the Mormon Temple. Although the sculptor executed works for the Mormons, he was a Unitarian. He returned to the East and taught modeling at the Drexel Institute in Philadelphia, Pennsylvania, from 1895 to 1896.

In June 1896 Dallin went back to Paris to perfect his technique and studied at the École des Beaux-Arts with Jean Dampt. His second equestrian Indian subject, the powerful *Medicine Man* (Fairmount Park, Philadelphia), won a silver medal at the Paris International Exposition of 1900. He returned to the United States that year and settled in Boston, where he taught at the Massachusetts State Normal Art School until 1941. Although his third equestrian statue *Protest* won a gold medal at the Louisiana Purchase Exposition in St. Louis, Missouri, in 1904, it was never cast into permanent material on a large scale. The last and best known of the four equestrian groups, *Appeal to the Great Spirit* (Museum of Fine Arts, Boston), was awarded a gold medal at the Paris Salon of 1909. Throughout the remainder of his long career Dallin produced many public and private commissions of various historical subjects such as the Puritan religious dissenter *Anne Hutchinson* (State House, Boston), *Sir Isaac Newton* (Library of Congress), and *Pioneer Women of Utah* (Springville, Utah); his last noteworthy Indian sculpture was *Massasoit* (Cole's Hill, Plymouth, Mass.), commissioned by the Improved Order of Red Men to commemorate the chief who greeted the Pilgrims. He was a charter member of the National Sculpture Society, the National Institute of Arts and Letters, and the Royal Society of Arts in London. An expert with the longbow, Dallin was national archery champion in 1915 and served as president of the National Archery Association in 1919. He died in Arlington Heights, Massachusetts.

Dallin worked in the conservative, naturalistic tradition of the Paris academies where he had studied. His fame rested on his success in capturing the heroic pathos and profound dignity of the American Indian. Although the sculptor's idealized imagery drew upon the "noble savage" tradition, his sympathy and sensitivity for the Indian was remarkable even in an era when racial antagonism had abated and the American Indian emerged as a romantic figure.

• A number of manuscripts and scrapbooks concerning Dallin's career are preserved at the Springville Museum of Art, Springville, Utah. The standard monograph on him, Rell G. Francis, *Cyrus E. Dallin: Let Justice Be Done* (1976), contains a selected bibliography and a list of his sculptures. For overviews and critical assessments, see Lorado Taft, *History of*

American Sculpture (1903), pp. 496–501, and Wayne Craven, *Sculpture in America* (1984), pp. 527–31. See also Anna Seaton-Schmidt, "An American Sculptor: Cyrus E. Dallin," *International Studio* 58 (1916): 109–14; William Howe Downes, "Cyrus E. Dallin, Sculptor," *Brush and Pencil* 5 (Oct. 1899): 1–18, reprinted with variations in *New England Magazine* 21 (Oct. 1899): 196–209; and the exhibition catalog by Kent Ahrens, *Cyrus E. Dallin, His Small Bronzes and Plasters* (1995). An obituary is in the *New York Times*, 15 Nov. 1944.

ROBERT WILSON TORCHIA

DALTON, Bob (13 May 1869–5 Oct. 1892), outlaw, was born Robert Rennick Dalton in Missouri (probably Cass County), the son of James Lewis Dalton, a farmer, horse breeder, and trader, and Adeline Lee Younger. His mother was a half-sister of Henry Younger, the father of the Younger brothers of James–Younger gang notoriety, and thus the Younger brothers and the Dalton boys shared the same grandfather, Charles Lee Younger. Four of the fifteen children born to Lewis and Adeline Dalton died violent deaths. The family lived in Cass, Bates, and Clay counties in western Missouri, an area plagued before, during, and after the Civil War by border conflicts and rampant outlawry. About 1882 the family moved to Coffeyville, Kansas, and shortly thereafter into Indian Territory near present-day Vinita, Oklahoma. While still an adolescent, Dalton followed his older brothers Frank and Gratton into law enforcement; all three brothers served as deputy U.S. marshals in Indian Territory. On 27 November 1887 Frank was killed while making an arrest. In August 1888, in Indian Territory near Coffeyville, Dalton, acting as a posseman under his brother Grat, shot and killed a suspected horsethief named Charles Montgomery. He was only nineteen years old when he was sworn in as a deputy U.S. marshal in January 1889. He was also employed as a detective for the Osage Indian Agency during this period. The first recorded incident of lawbreaking by any of the Dalton boys occurred on Christmas Day 1889, when Dalton and another brother, Emmett, allegedly "introduced whiskey into Indian Territory." Charges against Emmett were later dropped but Dalton was bound over for trial. He did not appear, his bonds were forfeited, and he never stood trial. In August 1890 Dalton, Emmett, and Grat were charged with horse stealing. Grat was jailed for a time, but eventually the charges were dropped. In a dispute over fees unpaid by the government, Dalton and Grat left the marshal's service about this time. Late in 1890 Dalton, Grat, and Emmett went to California to visit their brother Bill. When a Southern Pacific train was held up and robbed at Alila, California, on 6 February 1891, detectives focused their investigation on the Dalton brothers. Recognized as the leader of what officers were now calling the "Dalton gang," Dalton was described on a Southern Pacific Railroad reward poster as "about twenty-three . . . ; height, 6 ft. 1½ inches; well built and straight; light complexion, but florid and healthy looking; boyish beard and mustache; light hair and eyes; weight 180 to 190 lbs.; large, bony, long-fingered hands, showing no acquaintance with work; large nose and ears; white teeth; long sunburned neck, square features. . . . Is a good poker and card player; drinks whisky in moderation, but does not chew tobacco; smokes brown paper cigarettes occasionally." Dalton and his brothers Emmett, Grat, and Bill were indicted on 17 March 1891 and charged with train robbery and assault with intent to murder the express car messenger. Dalton and Emmett eluded the officers and escaped back to Indian Territory, but Grat and Bill were arrested. In separate trials at Visalia, Tulare County, Bill was acquitted but Grat was convicted of train robbery. At Grat's trial, eyewitnesses to the holdup were shown photographs of Dalton and identified him as one of the robbers.

Back in their familiar haunts, which had become Oklahoma Territory, Dalton and Emmett enlisted other desperadoes and began a campaign of outlawry that would make the Dalton gang as well known as the earlier James–Younger gang. Although various outlaws drifted in and out of the gang, Dalton remained the acknowledged leader. Emmett was at his side, as was Grat, who later broke jail in California and joined his brothers in Oklahoma. In May 1891 the gang held up a Santa Fe train at Wharton Station, Indian Territory; in September they struck a Missouri, Kansas, & Texas (MK&T) train at Lillietta Station, Indian Territory. In June 1892 they held up a Santa Fe train at Red Rock in the Cherokee Strip and the following month an MK&T express at Adair in Indian Territory.

Emboldened by these successful train holdups and the national publicity they had engendered, Dalton planned a double bank robbery that would top the exploits of the storied James–Younger gang. His targets were the C. M. Condon & Co. Bank and the First National Bank of Coffeyville, Kansas, a town in which the Daltons had lived and with which they were familiar. On the morning of 5 October 1892, the three Dalton brothers and two other outlaws rode into Coffeyville and simultaneously held up the employees of both banks. When an alarm was sounded by a passerby, a furious gun battle erupted. All five outlaws were struck by multiple bullets. Dalton, Grat, Bill Power, and Dick Broadwell were killed outright, and Emmett was seriously wounded. Four Coffeyville citizens, including the town marshal, were killed and three others wounded. Emmett survived and at a March 1893 trial was convicted of murder and sentenced to life in prison. He was later paroled and wrote two books recounting the experiences of the Daltons. Dalton and Grat were buried together in a Coffeyville cemetery not far from the gravesite of Frank, their slain lawman brother, as was their companion, Bill Power.

A well-built, handsome young man, Dalton undoubtedly possessed admirable qualities. He was temperate in his habits, staunchly loyal to his family, and fearless and bold to the point of recklessness. He started adult life as a peace officer and might have become one of the best had he been more fairly treated by the government that employed him. Although his great double bank robbery attempt at Coffeyville ended in disaster and resulted in the deaths of himself and seven others, it did ensure his place in the national memory as one of the most daring outlaws of the West.

• Ben Dalton, a law-abiding brother, recounted the history of his outlaw siblings in an interview in the *San Francisco Chronicle*, 27 Oct. 1892. *The Dalton Brothers and Their Astounding Career of Crime, by an Eyewitness*, published anonymously in 1892, contains many errors of fact. Emmett Dalton, with professional help, wrote two books on the outlaws, *Beyond the Law* (1918) and *When the Daltons Rode* (1931). Frank F. Latta, *Dalton Gang Days* (1976), deals primarily with the brothers' troubles in California. Nancy B. Samuelson, *The Dalton Gang Story* (1992), sets straight many previously published inaccuracies in the Dalton story and is the best source on the Dalton family.

ROBERT K. DEARMENT

DALTON, John Call, Jr. (2 Feb. 1825–12 Feb. 1889), physiologist and medical educator, was born in Chelmsford, Massachusetts, the son of John Call Dalton, a physician, and Julia Ann Spalding. Dalton graduated from Harvard College, his father's alma mater, in 1844, and he immediately entered Harvard Medical School, from which he earned his M.D. in 1847. During his medical school days, Dalton served as a house apothecary at Massachusetts General Hospital; after graduation, he continued his association with the hospital as a house surgeon.

In mid-nineteenth-century America young and ambitious physicians commonly traveled to Paris or London for postgraduate medical education. Encouraged by his former professors, Dalton traveled to Paris in 1850 to study physiology under the tutelage of Claude Bernard. Bernard was then earning fame for developing physiology as an experimental science independent of pathology and comparative anatomy and for the introduction into biological research of experimental techniques, especially vivisection. His year with Bernard was a turning point in Dalton's life; when he returned to Boston, he determined to pursue not the clinical practice of a physician but the laboratory research of a physiologist. Fulfilling this goal entailed medical instruction, not medical practice.

Dalton's first post on returning to Boston was a short stint as an instructor at the Boylston Medical School. Competition from the Harvard Medical School made the continued existence of Boylston tenuous at best, so in 1851 Dalton accepted the more secure offer of the chair of physiology at the Buffalo Medical College. In 1854 he became professor of pathology and physiology at the Vermont Medical College in Woodstock, Vermont. In 1855 he was elected chair of physiology at the New York College of Physicians and Surgeons (modern-day Columbia University School of Medicine). Between 1859 and 1864 he held a concurrent teaching appointment at the Long Island College Hospital; between 1861 and 1864 he served during the Civil War as an assistant surgeon in the Army Medical Corps. He resigned his chair in 1883, only to be selected the following year to succeed Alonzo Clark as president of the New York College of Physicians and Surgeons, a position he held until his

death. Dalton was active in several medical and scientific associations, including the National Academy of Sciences, the New York Academy of Medicine, and the New York Pathological Society.

Dalton's pedagogical style as well as his independent physiological research separated him from other medical school instructors of the time. He was the first American instructor of physiology to supplement didactic lectures with vivisectional demonstrations of physiological activities such as the heartbeat or the actions of poisons. Dalton's physiological preparations were elementary; nonetheless, they were a striking departure from the pedagogy of his day and marked him to his contemporaries as an innovative instructor and reformer of medical education. He published in 1859 the first edition of his popular *A Treatise of Human Physiology: Designed for the Use of Students and Practitioners of Medicine*, which eventually went to seven editions. In 1851 his essay on the corpus luteum had been awarded a prize by the American Medical Association; twenty years later he published "Sugar Formation in the Liver" (*Transactions of the New York Academy of Medicine*, 1871). Some physiologists had disputed Bernard's claims for the glycogenic function of the liver, but this latter piece corroborated Bernard's work on the topic, and many considered it to be Dalton's most significant scientific paper. But as the years went by, the demands of teaching, public lectures, writing, and the meager institutional and financial support for independent scientific research gave Dalton little time to pursue his physiological investigations. His peers—especially those who had been educated in Europe and considered pure research necessary for the advancement of scientific medicine in the United States—recognized that instead of teaching medical undergraduates, someone with Dalton's intelligence and training should have been free to pursue pure physiological research (Fye, p. 32).

Dalton's strong and vocal advocacy of vivisection as a necessary tool both for the improvement of medical education and for the advancement of physiology brought him into conflict during the 1860s and 1870s with Henry Bergh and the American Association for the Prevention of Cruelty to Animals. The association worked incessantly to sponsor legislation to ban vivisection. Although New York State eventually passed such laws, Dalton coordinated efforts to add amendments that excluded animal experimentation in universities or medical schools.

Significant attempts to improve U.S. medical education gained momentum in the 1880s, during the time when Dalton was president of the New York College of Physicians and Surgeons. He agreed with the reformers' agenda to improve medical education by substituting a graded curriculum for a loosely organized two-year curriculum and by augmenting lectures with laboratory instruction. For his part, he sought endowments for the construction of laboratories in all medical schools (although he concentrated his efforts at his own college). Although Dalton himself neither trained advanced students in physiology nor established a physiological research laboratory, he was among the reformers of medical education who thought the inclusion of basic sciences as taught in Europe crucial to the development of U.S. medicine. Dalton died at his home in New York City. He had never married.

In a memorial, his friend and colleague, Silas Weir Mitchell, Philadelphia physician and neurologist, wrote that Dalton was "America's first professional physiologist" ("Memoir of John Call Dalton, 1825–1889," *Biographical Memoirs of the National Academy of Sciences* 3 [1890]: 3). Other Dalton biographers have also echoed this claim, but modern scholarship tempers this assertion and would probably accord this accolade to others such as Henry Pickering Bowditch or H. Newell Martin. The evaluation of Dalton that endures, however, is that he made significant novel contributions to U.S. medical education and performed significantly original physiological research against staggering odds. These accomplishments place Dalton among the first rank of those who created American medical science.

• Recent scholarship on Dalton does not mention the existence of any Dalton manuscripts or papers. *John Call Dalton, M.D., U.S.V.* (privately printed, 1892), is his own account of his Civil War experience. Among his other books are *The Experimental Method in Medicine* (1882), *Topographical Anatomy of the Brain* (1885), *Physiology of the Cerebellum* (1886), and *A Treatise on Physiology and Hygiene for Schools, Families, and Colleges* (1868). In addition to these books he wrote several journal and magazine articles on topics such as the circulation of the blood, embryology, and microscopic anatomy. Dalton is the subject of a chapter in Bruce Fye, *The Development of American Physiology: Scientific Medicine in the Nineteenth Century* (1987); the book has a good bibliography. Although the following books do not mention Dalton specifically, they could aid the understanding of the medicine and science of his time: Kenneth Ludmerer, *Learning to Heal: The Development of American Medical Education* (1985); John Harley Warner, *The Therapeutic Perspective: Medical Practice, Knowledge, and Identity in America 1820–1885* (1986); and Frederic L. Holmes, *Claude Bernard and Animal Chemistry: The Emergence of a Scientist* (1974).

THOMAS P. GARIEPY

DALY, Arnold (22 Oct. 1875–13 Jan. 1927), actor, was born Peter Christopher Arnold Daly in Brooklyn, New York, the son of Joseph J. Daly, an importer of cabinet wood, and Mary Arnold. Upon his father's death in 1886 Daly left parochial school, having previously been expelled from four public schools. He then held a series of jobs, among them office boy to the theatrical producer Charles Frohman and callboy at the Lyceum Theatre. Daly began his acting career in 1892 as a bit player in a touring company that featured Fanny Rice, one of the popular stars of the day. He made his New York debut on 12 April 1895 as Chambers in an adaptation of Mark Twain's *Pudd'nhead Wilson*. In 1896–1897 he toured with the actor-dramatist William Gillette, playing Wilfred Varney in Gillette's *Secret Service* (1895). Daly then accompanied Gillette to London, where he made his English debut on 18 April

1898 as Henry Mackintosh in Gillette's *Too Much Johnson* (1894). Upon returning to New York in 1899, Daly appeared in several plays, most notably Clyde Fitch's *Barbara Frietchie* (1899), which starred Julia Marlowe. Daly married Mary Blythe, a fellow member of the company, in 1900. Subsequently twice divorced, they had one daughter. Between 1901 and 1903 Daly appeared in a number of unsuccessful plays, but he received much favorable response from critics.

In 1903 Daly began the work that ensured his lasting reputation, his productions of plays by George Bernard Shaw. Before 1903, only two of Shaw's plays had been presented in the United States: *Arms and the Man* in 1894 and *The Devil's Disciple* in 1897, both produced by Richard Mansfield. In 1898 Daly had become interested in Shaw's *Candida* (1895) and had made several unsuccessful attempts to interest producers in the play. In 1903 he presented the play himself, on a budget of $1350. At this time Daly entered into a partnership with the playwright and producer Winchell Smith, who served primarily as his business manager. Their production of *Candida* premiered at the Princess Theatre in New York on 9 December 1903, with Daly in the role of Marchbanks. Given 150 performances, the production was among Daly's major successes as an actor. The success of *Candida* also marked the beginning of Shaw's popularity in the United States. On 9 February 1904 Daly added to his repertoire Shaw's *The Man of Destiny* (1897), in which he played Napoleon. Later that year he took the two Shaw plays on tour, along with two one-act plays written by Daly, *A Trifle* and *The Suicide* (both 1904).

During the summer of 1904, Daly went to England to consult with Shaw, who not only gave Daly permission to produce others of his works but also wrote *How He Lied to Her Husband* (1904) especially for Daly, who premiered it on 26 September 1904 in New York. Shaw's *You Never Can Tell* (1899) was added to Daly's repertoire on 9 January 1905, and Shaw's *John Bull's Other Island* (1904) followed on 10 October 1905. Up to this time, Daly had received high critical praise for his Shavian productions, although the plays were controversial owing to their unconventional ideas. Serious problems for Daly began in October 1905 when he announced his intention to produce Shaw's *Mrs. Warren's Profession* (1898), a play which argues that many poor women are driven to prostitution by the wretched working conditions imposed on them by upright citizens. Anthony Comstock, New York's would-be censor of public morality, mounted a protest against the play, but Daly persisted. After one experimental performance in New Haven, Connecticut, on 27 October, the police forbade further performances there. Undeterred, Daly opened the play in New York on 30 October 1905, where anticipation was so intense that tickets, which at the box office cost $2, were reportedly selling on the street for as much as $30. Police commissioner William McAdoo, who attended the opening, not only closed the production after one performance but also arrested Daly, the house manager, and the entire cast. Only one of New York's numerous theater critics—John Corbin of the *Sun*—defended the production; the others were unanimous in their denunciations of the play as morally depraved. Shaw responded with a pamphlet, published in the United States with an introduction by Corbin, who wrote: "Before the production of the play all of the sensational papers, and some that pretend not to be sensational, used column upon column of their most prominent space to create an unwarranted expectation of something lewd, and after it used those same columns to falsify what actually happened. The denunciations of the play were as hysterical and hypocritical in proportion as the papers were yellow and foul." Although Daly and all those charged were cleared, the verdict did not come until July 1906 and was then virtually ignored by the press.

These events signaled a downward turn in Daly's fortunes. He became increasingly combative, a trait that often spoiled promising ventures. In April 1906, Smith withdrew from his partnership with Daly, who nevertheless produced *Arms and the Man* that same month and subsequently took it and his earlier Shaw successes on tour. In 1906 Daly was for a time under the management of the Shuberts, then a rising force in American theater, but, as was typical of Daly, he soon became dissatisfied and broke from them, leaving himself in serious financial difficulties. In late 1906 he appeared for the first time on the vaudeville stage, a recourse he often took thereafter in the absence of suitable theatrical engagements.

In the 1907–1908 season, Daly sought to implement a long cherished desire to establish a "theater of ideas," in which he could produce "artistically worthwhile plays, untrammeled by others' interference." On 15 October 1907 he opened his Theatre Antoine, named for André Antoine, the French pioneer of the modern theater, in New York. This venture, greeted with low attendance and open hostility from the press, soon closed. Subsequently, Daly alternated roles in the theater with appearances in vaudeville and in silent films. He also produced plays he admired whenever he could raise the money, but few of these efforts gained audience support. Among the foreign playwrights whose works he presented were Oscar Wilde, Paul Hervieu, and Hermann Bahr. From time to time he revived plays by Shaw who, having quarreled with Daly, apparently first in 1911 over Shaw's dissatisfaction with Daly's London production of *Arms and the Man*, was by 1915 seeking legal means to prevent Daly from producing his dramas. In 1917 Daly appeared briefly under the management of David Belasco, one of America's most successful producers and playwrights. He also performed occasionally in London in limited engagements. Despite his contentiousness throughout these later years, Daly was seldom out of work and enjoyed high critical status as an actor. In his *The Popular Theatre* (1918), George Jean Nathan states that Daly "is today doubtless the foremost actor on the native stage." Daly's last major role was as Marshal Bazaine in the Theatre Guild's 1926 production of Franz Werfel's *Juarez and Maximilian* (1925). Daly died in New York in a fire that swept his apartment building.

Daly is remembered primarily for his popularization of Shaw's plays in the United States between 1903 and 1905. He was convinced of the correctness of his own taste, even in the face of rejection by critics and public, and he persisted in what he considered a crusade against commercialism in the theater. His convictions underlie his attempt to establish a theater of ideas in the United States, even before the "little theater" movement in the United States arrived to champion modernism. His contributions were curtailed not only by censorship and public indifference to the kind of theater he favored, but also by his own combativeness, which often soured relationships with those who might have helped him achieve his goals.

• An Arnold Daly Scrapbook, containing photos, extensive newspaper and magazine clippings, and theater programs, is housed in the Locke collection of the Billy Rose Theatre Collection, New York Public Library for the Performing Arts at Lincoln Center. Many of Daly's own writings are included in his *The Dominant Male: Essays and Plays* (1921). The only biography of Daly is B. H. Goldsmith, *Arnold Daly* (1927). Response to the controversy over *Mrs. Warren's Profession* can be found in George Bernard Shaw, *The Author's Apology from Mrs. Warren's Profession* (1905), with an introduction, "The Tyranny of Police and Press," by John Corbin; and in all major New York newspapers, especially between late Oct. and Dec. 1905. Obituaries are in the *New York Times*, 14 Jan. 1927, and *Variety*, 19 Jan. 1927.

OSCAR G. BROCKETT

DALY, Augustin (20 July 1838–7 June 1899), theatrical manager and playwright, was born John Augustin Daly in Plymouth, North Carolina, the son of Captain Denis Daly, a sailor and owner of a lumber business, and Elizabeth Duffey. Captain Daly died when Augustin was only three, and, reduced in circumstances, his mother moved her family, first to Norfolk, Virginia, and then to New York City. There, Augustin and his elder brother Joseph Daly fell under the spell of the theater. The New York City public school he attended could not compete with theatricals for his attention, and his fitful formal education ended at age sixteen. He took a variety of clerkships at local concerns while spending every available moment attending professional productions and staging his own theatricals in his back yard. Unlike most stage-struck individuals, Daly never desired to act; he was always more fascinated by the challenge of producing plays.

Daly's true education took place attending Wallack's and Burton's Theatres, two of the leading repertory companies of the 1850s. Inspired by these examples, at age seventeen Daly rented the Brooklyn Museum for an evening to present the "Melville Troupe of Juvenile Comedians." He also began to churn out plays, which he audaciously offered to the day's leading stars, such as Joseph Jefferson (1829–1905) and Laura Keene.

Undeterred by the string of refusals, Daly nevertheless decided to supplement his struggling dramatic career with a try at journalism. He had been a reporter for the *Sunday Courier* only a few weeks when, at age twenty-one, he became its theater critic. For a decade Daly continued writing dramatic criticism, not only for the *Courier* but simultaneously for the *Sun*, *Express*, *Citizen*, and the *Times*. In an age generally unconcerned about conflicts of interest, Daly's role as critic did not prevent him from acting as press agent for Kate Bateman and the flamboyant Adah Isaacs Menken. These various endeavors gave him a wealth of theatrical experience that he later drew upon when managing his own company.

During these years Daly's playwriting career also began to flourish. His first triumph, *Leah the Forsaken* (1862) (an adaptation of the German play *Deborah*), was a sentimental potboiler well suited to Kate Bateman. His *Under the Gaslight* (1867) became one of the great melodramas on the nineteenth-century American stage, highlighted by a spectacular train effect and the oft-imitated rescue of the hero tied on the railroad tracks. His other plays included *A Flash of Lightning* (1868), *The Red Scarf* (1868), *The Undercurrent* (1888), and *Horizon* (1871), perhaps his best work (though not a commercial success). Daly also staged a number of loosely plotted, unabashedly lowbrow variety shows that became great hits.

Yet most of the plays Daly presented in his theaters were not original with him. He depended overwhelmingly on adaptations from popular novels, from successful German and French plays of the era, and from abridgements of Shakespeare. Daly dramatized ten novels over the course of his career, most notably *Divorce* (1871), based on Anthony Trollope's *He Knew He Was Right*, and *Pique* (1875), based on Florence Lean's *Her Lord and Master* and Victor Hugo's *Les Misérables*. As the years passed he relied even more heavily upon dramatic imports from Germany and France. He staged forty-two German plays, mainly simple-minded, morally unobjectionable, popular farces. French drama, which set the standard in the nineteenth-century western theater, provided another sixty-five adaptations, of which *Frou Frou* (1870) and *The Lottery of Love* (1888) had the longest initial runs. In each case Daly ensured that these foreign dramas assumed a distinctively American flavor, even giving most of them American settings.

Scholars have questioned Daly's heralded claim to have written many of his greatest productions. Marvin Felheim has pointed out the extent to which both his original plays and his adaptations were actually penned by others. The most important of these ghostwriters was Daly's brother Joseph. An attorney and judge, Joseph shared his brother's love of the theater. Joseph frequently wrote his brother's dramatic criticism when Augustin was out of town, and a silent collaboration ensued, with Joseph probably the senior author of the plays attributed to his more famous brother.

Augustin Daly's diminished authorial reputation, however, must not detract from his genuine theatrical achievements. Daly mastered all aspects of theater and was an important innovator, particularly in acting and directing, but also in lighting and scenery. His accomplishments as manager of the most successful theater company in American history remain impressive.

In 1869 Daly married Mary Duff, the daughter of a prominent theater owner. The same year he opened his first theater, the Fifth Avenue, and quickly made it the standard of theatrical excellence. His success resided partly in choosing effective plays to present, but even more so in their staging. To a degree not seen before on the American stage, Daly scrutinized every detail of production. Sitting in the fifth row of his theater during rehearsals, he demanded rereadings until they suited his taste. Although he occasionally brought in stars—an Edwin Booth, E. A. Sothern, or Adelaide Neilson—Daly's was a stock company based on ensemble acting: there were no stars, and every part, small or large, was assigned and defined by Daly. His dictatorial manner terrorized some performers and drove away others, yet he created a highly disciplined troupe that presented consistently higher quality performances than any other theater in the United States.

Daly's later productions also favored more natural, realistic treatments. Though nineteenth-century notions of realism and naturalism may strain modern definitions, Daly's company was widely lauded for advancing believable characterization. During Daly's 1880 European tour a Paris critic noted that "the propensity for naturalism shows itself in a thousand details. The fashion of entering, sitting, taking a chair, talking, taking leave, going out, coming in,—it is the usage of everyday life." Unfortunately, Daly suffered the fate of many pioneers. Becoming captive to his innovative stage directions, he failed to see that they later hardened into their own conventionality.

Daly not only controlled what was seen on his stage, but he extended his influence beyond the footlights. His actors had to abide by a strict code of behavior outside the theater, this to avoid any "Bohemian tendencies" that would reflect poorly on the troupe. He also had a great talent for enticing important theater critics such as William Winter and Edward Dithmar into becoming de facto shills of his theater. Those critics he could not control he barred from his house or even sought to have fired.

The first phase of Daly's managerial career lasted from 1869 until 1877, when, after surviving a devastating fire, two moves, and the panic of 1873, he was forced to sell his theater to pay his debts. Following a brief and unsuccessful attempt to recoup his theatrical fortunes in England, Daly returned to New York City and with the financial help of his father-in-law, theater owner John Duff, opened his renamed Daly's Theatre at Broadway and Thirtieth Street in 1879. For the next two decades Daly's remained the theater of choice among New York society and a necessary stop for visitors to the city.

Daly now assembled his most famous acting company—forty-four players in all—most eminently Ada Rehan, John Drew, (1853–1927), Anne Gilbert, and James Lewis. The company's signature was comedy, particularly the ever-popular German farces and French melodramas. Daly had produced Shakespeare in his early years as manager, and after a few years hiatus he returned to the Bard in the mid-1880s. These were lavish productions, *Twelfth Night*, *The Tempest*, and *The Taming of the Shrew*, earning the greatest acclaim. Daly considered Shakespeare's text no less inviolate than any other dramatist's, and the plays were not only bowdlerized for Victorian tastes (usually by critic William Winter), but entire scenes were removed, rearranged, or amalgamated for what Daly considered greater continuity. Increasingly, his productions of Shakespearean and other English classics such as Farquhar's *The Recruiting Officer* and Sheridan's *The School for Scandal* showcased the popular and loyal Ada Rehan, who remained with Daly over twenty years.

Daly's company functioned as a training school for actors at a time when formal dramatic instruction was in its infancy. Many future stars passed through Daly's company at some time in their career: Fanny Davenport, Otis Skinner, Clara Morris, Henrietta Crosman, John Drew, Henry Miller (1860–1926), and Blanche Bates among them. Players frequently acknowledged that Daly instilled in them both the fundamentals and the fine points of their profession.

Daly's ambitions were not bounded by the Atlantic. In 1884 his troupe became the first complete American company to cross the Atlantic. Two years later he added the Continent to his England visit, and in 1888, 1891, and 1897 he returned yet again to increasingly enthusiastic receptions. He also established a Daly's Theatre in London in 1893, though with mixed success.

Augustin Daly's entire life revolved about his passion for the theater. "He not only loved the theater ardently," wrote critic Brander Matthews, "he lived for it alone." The death of his two young sons from diphtheria within a few days of one another seemed to push him harder in his work. Tall and mustachioed, Daly cut a striking figure. He was not particularly convivial (though a founding member of The Players) and kept aloof even from his own troupe (Ada Rehan excepted). Though his theatrical sensibility was essentially melodramatic, he elevated standards of production above what the American theater had previously known. Daly died in Paris.

• The Augustin Daly Papers are in the Folger Shakespeare Library in Washington, D.C. Other materials are available at Amherst College's Daly Collection in Amherst, Mass., and the Billy Rose Theatre Collection of the New York Public Library in New York City. Daly's most important statement on the theater is an 1886 article in *The North American Review* entitled "The American Dramatist." In addition to his plays, he authored a biography of the eighteenth-century actress Peg Woffington, *Woffington: A Tribute to the Actress and the Woman* (1888). The best critical study of Daly is Marvin Felheim, *The Theater of Augustin Daly* (1956), but Joseph F. Daly, *The Life of Augustin Daly* (2 vols., 1917), contains more detail on his life and reprints many letters.

BENJAMIN MCARTHUR

DALY, Charles Patrick (31 Oct. 1816–19 Sept. 1899), jurist and author, was born in New York City, the son of Michael Daly, a carpenter and hotel manager, and Elizabeth (maiden name unknown). Daly attended a parochial school for a short time. Following the death of Daly's mother, his father remarried, and after his father's death, Daly was left in the care of his stepmother. At age thirteen he fled his home and settled briefly in Savannah, Georgia, working as an apprentice to a quillmaker. Within a year he left Savannah and went to sea for two years. Returning to New York City in 1832, he was apprenticed to a cabinetmaker. At night he educated himself through reading at the library of the Mechanic's and Tradesman's Society and participation in a literary society. In 1836 he exchanged the cabinetmaker's apprenticeship for one in a law office. He passed the New York bar examination in 1839 and became a junior partner in the same firm.

In addition to practicing law, Daly became active in the Democratic party and was elected to the sixty-sixth session of the New York Assembly in 1843. He was involved in the legislature's investigation of the administration of the Leake and Watts asylum trust, a controversial affair that increased his prominence substantially. Daly sponsored a bill to establish Central Park in New York City. He drafted another bill regarding reforms of the Court of Common Pleas, the unforeseen results of which would later affect his own career as a judge. His increased prominence led to an opportunity to run for a second term in the assembly and the offer of a congressional candidacy, both of which he declined. Governor William Bouck subsequently appointed Daly as a judge of the Court of Common Pleas of New York in 1844. Elected four times, Daly served as a judge from 1844 to 1885. He held the post of first judge from 1858 to 1871 and that of chief judge from 1871 until his retirement at the mandatory age of seventy in 1885. He married Maria Lydig in 1856; they had no children.

The most celebrated case to come before Judge Daly was that involving the alleged instigators of the Astor Place Riots of 1849. Upon their conviction for conspiracy, riot, and arson, Daly handed out relatively light sentences (although the leader was heavily penalized). His actions were equally assailed and praised in New York newspapers, but the case did establish important precedent related to the crime of riot under American law.

While on the bench Daly also remained very active in both local and national political affairs. The two most notable events with which he was associated were connected with the Civil War. In 1861 crew members of the Confederate privateer *Jefferson Davis* were placed on trial for piracy. The Confederate government threatened to execute Union prisoners in reprisal if the sailors were condemned as pirates. Daly advised Abraham Lincoln's cabinet to recharacterize the charges; the crew members were instead incarcerated as prisoners of war, and this policy became the rule for the rest of the Civil War. Daly likewise counseled the president's cabinet in the *Trent* affair of 1861, in which two Confederate emissaries, James Mason and John Slidell (a social acquaintance of the Dalys), were traveling on board a British-flagged vessel in international waters when the ship was seized by a Union warship and the delegates imprisoned. The action outraged the British government, leading some within it to press for reconsideration of Britain's neutral stance in the Civil War. Daly was prominent among those who counseled Lincoln and his cabinet to release Mason and Slidell on the joint bases of international law and political expediency. Following the Civil War, Daly devoted himself to the cases and administration of the Court of Common Pleas.

Former president Chester A. Arthur presided over the ceremonies for Judge Daly's retirement from the bench on 31 December 1885, an event also attended by David Dudley Field, James C. Carter, Elihu Root, F. R. Coudert, and John W. Sterling. Arthur commented that Daly's judicial career had been characterized by "love of truth and justice, courtesy and candor, wide and profound learning, strict impartiality and stainless integrity."

Daly's learning ranged far beyond the bench. He wrote on a wide variety of topics, including the history of law and the courts of New York, Jewish ethnography, Shakespearean drama, and geography. He joined the American Geographic Society in 1856 and served as its president from 1864 until his death. He gave frequent lectures on geographical subjects, assisted in the planning and fundraising for various expeditions, and met with a number of leading figures in the field of exploration. Daly also corresponded with King Leopold II of Belgium with regard to African exploration and suppression of the slave trade. After his retirement from the court, Daly was occupied chiefly with literary and geographical interests, as well as the maintenance of a small law practice. He died at Sag Harbor, New York.

• Daly's letters and papers are deposited in the New York Public Library. Additional papers are in the American Geographical Society archives and library, New York City, and those of the Friendly Sons of St. Patrick, also in the New York Public Library. Since Daly served as the official reporter for the Court of Common Pleas, the twenty-one volumes of *Daly's Reports* (1849–1885) provide case-related information. Works by Daly include *Historical Sketch of the Judicial Tribunals of New York from 1623 to 1846* (1855; also referred to as *History of the Court of Common Pleas for the City and County of New York*), *The Common Law: Its Origin, Sources, Nature, and Development, and What the State of New York has Done to Improve upon It* (1894), and *The Settlement of the Jews in North America*, ed. Max Kohler (1893). Daly published numerous pamphlets and articles, which are listed in the bibliography of Harold E. Hammond, *A Commoner's Judge: The Life and Times of Charles Patrick Daly* (1954). See also James W. Brooks, *History of the Court of Common Pleas of the City and County of New York* (1896), pp. 77–82, 159–200, 239–44; Alden Chester, ed., *Legal and Judicial History of New York* (1911), pp. 394–400; Theron G. Strong, *Landmarks of a Lawyer's Lifetime* (1914), p. 133; Max J. Kohler, *Charles P. Daly: A Tribute to His Memory* (1899); and *Green Bag*, Nov.

1894. Obituaries are in the *Bulletin of the American Geographical Society* 31 (1899): 398; *New York Times*, 20 Sept. 1899; and *American Hebrew*, 22 Sept. 1899.

BARRY T. RYAN

DALY, Marcus (5 Dec. 1841–12 Nov. 1900), copper magnate, was born near Ballyjamesduff, Ireland, the son of Luke Daly and Mary Coyle, poor peasant farmers. At age fifteen he emigrated to New York, where he worked at a variety of jobs before sailing in 1861 to California via the Panama route. Gaining experience in the mines of Calaveras and Grass Valley, he moved on to the Comstock Lode in Nevada, where he became a mine foreman for John W. Mackay. At the end of the 1860s he tried his hand briefly in the new Nevada boom camps of White Pine and Mineral Hill, then was hired by the Walker brothers, David, Joseph, Matthew, and Samuel, who were Salt Lake City bankers, to supervise their Utah properties, including the Emma and the Ophir mines. There he met Margaret Evans, whom he married in 1872. They had four children.

In 1876 the Walkers sent him to Butte, Montana, to inspect the Alice mine, which they and Daly subsequently purchased jointly and which Daly supervised. Daly soon sold his share and acquired an interest in the Anaconda, on the southeast side of Butte Hill, then bought the whole mine for $30,000. Turned down by the mercantile and banking firm Walker Brothers when he sought development capital, Daly successfully turned to a California triumvirate—Lloyd Tevis, George Hearst, and Ben Ali Haggin—that would become involved with a hundred western mines, including the Ontario in Utah and the Homestake in the Dakotas. With the trio's support, Daly bought up adjacent property and proceeded to develop the Anaconda as one of the world's great copper mines.

To help meet the new demand for copper on the brink of the age of electricity, in 1883 Daly built a huge new smelter on Warm Springs Creek, twenty-six miles west of Butte, and developed the town of Anaconda. Since the mines devoured timber on a huge scale and the smelter consumed vast amounts of wood and coal as fuel, with considerable foresight he acquired vast forest lands (often cutting illegally on the public domain), numerous sawmills, coal mines, coke facilities, dams, and power plants. When existing freight charges grew too high, Daly built his own railroad to haul ore and equipment between Butte and Anaconda.

From 1881 to the late 1890s Daly was general manager of the new Anaconda Copper Mining Company and owner of one-quarter of its shares. He actively brought top-level metallurgists and furnace men from Europe and scoured the West for miners and supervisors. He paid his men well, trained many in copper technology, knew them and their families on a personal basis, tended to their needs, and evoked a fierce loyalty on their part.

In 1891 Anaconda moved from a private operation controlled by the Hearst-Haggin-Tevis-Daly group to the incorporated Anaconda Mining Company, with shares traded on the international market. Four years later, it was reorganized and for a time European capitalists held nearly half of the stock. Daly became president of the new corporation in 1899. He was vital to consolidating various properties on Butte Hill with Anaconda and in the formation in 1899 of the gigantic Amalgamated Copper Company, backed by Standard Oil capital. Daly is believed to have sold his interest for some $39 million, but he remained as president. With his plant manager he designed a wholly new automated reduction works, which opened two years after his death.

Although never an active candidate for political office, Daly was a powerful force and his rivalry with fellow Democrat and copper king William A. Clark would dominate Montana politics for a dozen years. Behind the scenes, the two went after each other with unusual intensity and bitterness, with Daly's newspaper, the *Anaconda Standard*, which he had started in 1889, playing an important role. Both Daly and Clark dug deep into their own pockets to block the opposition, either with outright bribery or slightly more sophisticated chicanery. With a liberal use of whiskey and cigars, Daly's henchmen quietly passed the word to his employees, who generally delivered the vote Daly sought.

Beginning in 1888, when he undercut Clark's run for the territorial delegate post, Daly moved constantly to block the political ambitions of his dapper antagonist. With statehood, a legislature deadlocked along party lines sent two sets of senators, including Clark, to Washington, D.C., in 1889, but the Republican majority there rejected Clark and his fellow Democrat Martin Maginnis. In 1893, when the short term of one of the new senators expired, Clark was again a leading contender and liberally expended funds to buy votes; Daly responded in kind. After countless ballots, gridlock prevailed, no candidate was selected, and Montana for more than a year had but one senator. In 1894 the Clark-Daly feud again dominated the political scene, this time over location of the capital, an issue that had been hard fought but left unsettled two years earlier. Daly is reputed to have spent $500,000 promoting his beloved Anaconda fiefdom, while Clark laid out only slightly less before Helena was selected.

The battle of the two titans reached its climax in the 1899 legislative session, when Clark again sought a seat in the U.S. Senate. With bribery rampant, Clark was selected, but Daly helped finance a Senate committee investigation that recommended that Clark not be seated. Finally, in 1900, when Daly was on his deathbed, Clark achieved his senatorship.

Daly and his family lived on an estate in the Bitter Root Valley. He also developed a 22,000-acre horse farm near Hamilton, where he bred and trained fine racehorses, including the great Tammany and Montana, which carried his copper and green colors in top national and international competition. Daly died in his suite in the Hotel Netherland in New York City.

Daly was first of all an empire builder and a political manipulator. His life was cast in the best rags-to-riches tradition of Horatio Alger. Self-educated, the stocky, ruddy, blue-eyed Irishman who chewed tobacco and sometimes swore was at times modest, generous, and farsighted; he had an uncanny nose for ore and a talent for organization. At the same time, his political instincts were often primitive, shameless, and corrupt. Michael P. Malone, one of Daly's most perceptive critics, sums up his role, both positive and negative: "More than any other man, he built the mining industry of Montana. As much as any man, he defiled the political life of Montana" (p. 157).

• Daly papers are in the Montana Historical Society Archives and some letters are in the Wells, Fargo & Company Records at the Huntington (Calif.) Library. No adequate biography of Daly has yet been published. H. Minar Shoebotham, *Anaconda: Life of Marcus Daly the Copper King* (1956), William H. Hoover, *Marcus Daly (1841–1900)—and His Contributions to Anaconda* (1950), and Isaac F. Marcosson, *Anaconda* (1957), are all undocumented and uncritical. An excellent, well-balanced, and judicious account of the larger context of Daly's life, based on a broad use of sources, is Michael P. Malone, *The Battle for Butte: Mining and Politics on the Northern Frontier, 1864–1906* (1981). An obituary is in the *Anaconda Standard*, 13 Nov. 1900.

CLARK C. SPENCE

DALY, Reginald Aldworth (18 May 1871–19 Sept. 1957), geologist, was born on a farm near Napanee, Ontario, Canada, the son of Edward Daly, a tea merchant, and Jane Maria Jeffers. When the boy was five years old, the family moved into Napanee, where he attended the public schools and, he later said, had "a simple life in a small town, under the direction of parents with high standards of conduct."

Daly attended Victoria College in Toronto, Ontario (now part of the University of Toronto), where he became interested in geology through one of the professors. He received an A.B. in 1891, became an instructor in mathematics at the college for a year, and received an S.B. in 1892. He then entered Harvard University, where he earned an M.A. in geology in 1893, carried out field studies at Mount Ascutney, Vermont, and received a Ph.D. in geology in 1896.

Through a fellowship, Daly studied in Europe from 1896 to 1898, first at Heidelberg University in Germany, where he learned the techniques of thin-section analysis from mineralogist Karl Harry Ferdinand Rosenbusch. He spent the second year with François Antoine Alfred Lacroix, director of the mineralogy laboratory of the École de Hautes Études in Paris. During vacations he traveled widely in Europe and attended the Seventh International Geological Congress in Russia.

From 1898 to 1901 Daly was instructor in physiography at Harvard, and he offered a course in oceanography. He left Harvard in 1901 to work as a geologist for the Canadian International Boundary Commission along the Forty-ninth Parallel. In 1903 he married

Louise Porter Haskell; their only child died at three years of age.

Daly became professor of geology at Massachusetts Institute of Technology in 1907. In 1912 he returned to Harvard as Sturgis-Hooper Professor of Geology, a position he held until retirement in 1942. He was chairman of the geology department from 1912 until 1925. During World War I Daly went to France as chief librarian for the Young Men's Christian Association. In 1920 he became a citizen of the United States.

Daly devoted his summers to fieldwork in geology. The study of Mount Ascutney occupied him for several years, and the summary, "The Geology of Ascutney Mountain, Vermont," was published in 1903 as *United States Geological Survey Bulletin 209*. This mountain of distinct mineral assemblages cuts into totally different surrounding rock. Daly presented a theory of "magmatic stoping," in which he proposed that detached blocks of the original rock had sunk into underlying magma, where they were incorporated at great depth and temperature, and so altered the magma. He began compiling data on rock densities and melting temperatures.

His survey along the Canada–United States border, conducted during six field seasons, extended over an area 400 miles long, five to ten miles wide, across the Cascade Range and Rocky Mountains form Vancouver, British Columbia, to Alberta Province. Daly said of it, "Each traverse generally meant a more or less taxing mountain climb through brush or brulé. The geology could not be worked out in the detail which this mountain belt deserves." Birch noted that "Daly brought back some 1,500 rock specimens and studied 960 thin sections . . . He took some 1,300 photographs, sounded lakes, studied the stratigraphy, structure, petrology, economic geology, glacial geology, physiography." In addition to about twenty shorter papers, Daly summarized the work in a three-volume report, "Geology of the North American Cordillera at the 49th Parallel of Latitude" (*Geological Survey of Canada Memoir 38* [1912]). From this study he theorized on the nature of igneous rocks and in 1914 published a textbook, *Igneous Rocks and Their Origin*. Beginning with the simple definition of igneous rocks as intrusive granite and extrusive basalt, he established a classification of these rocks based on their mineral content. This required many analyses of chemical composition.

In later summers Daly carried out geologic studies in western Canada, Hawaii, Sweden, South Africa, and areas of the western and northeastern United States. He was especially interested in how igneous rocks from great depth become differentiated into a wide assortment of crystalline rocks. At first he favored the concept that liquid magma separated into materials of different composition. His former MIT student, Canadian geologist Norman Levi Bowen, from twenty years of laboratory studies of crystallization in rocks, concluded that crystallization itself was a primary cause of the separation into various rock types. Daly incorporated Bowen's 1928 summary (*Ev-*

olution of the Igneous Rocks) into his own revised textbook *Igneous Rocks and the Depths of the Earth* (1933).

Daly's interests were drawn to oceanic islands, originally to determine the differences between continental and oceanic rocks. In 1919 he mapped islands of American Samoa for a program of the Carnegie Institution of Washington. At various times he visited Hawaii, Ascension Island, and Saint Helena Island. He determined that the island rocks of the Atlantic and Pacific oceans were basalts that were nearly alike in composition. He observed from sea-floor charts and shorelines that on many widely separated islands appeared platforms at about 180-feet depth, and he proposed that this represented the depth of sea level at the time of maximum glaciation.

Daly rejected the idea that submarine canyons found along many coasts were drowned river valleys. He observed that their depths of several thousand feet were too great for sea level to have reached that point. In 1936 he proposed that these canyons had been sculptured by massive flows of sediment down the edge of the continental slope, an idea that was amplified by Dutch geophysicist Philip Henry Kuenen and especially by oceanographer Bruce Charles Heezen in the 1950s.

Daly's influence in geology was considerable. He theorized on the strength and elasticity of the earth's upper layers, the nature of the interior of the earth, and oceanic subjects. His books, based on lecture series, included *Changing World of the Ice Age* (1934), *Architecture of the Earth* (1938), and *Floor of the Ocean* (1942), as well as his graduate textbook, *Strength and Structure of the Earth* (1940). His ideas led to more accurate theories when improved techniques of chemistry, geophysics, and oceanography were developed.

Daly received the Hayden Medal of the Philadelphia Academy of Science, the Penrose Medal of the Geological Society of America (1935), the William Bowie Medal of the American Geophysical Union, and the Wollaston Medal of the Geological Society of London. He was elected to the National Academy of Sciences in 1925. He died in Cambridge, Massachusetts.

• Daly's papers are in the Harvard University Archives. In addition to the books already mentioned, he wrote about 150 papers. Biographical accounts are by Marland P. Billings in *Proceedings of Geological Society of America for 1958* (1959), pp. 115–122, and by Francis Birch in National Academy of Sciences, *Biographical Memoirs* 34 (1960): 31–64, with bibliography. Obituaries are in the *New York Times*, 20 Sept. 1957, and *Science*, 3 Jan. 1958.

ELIZABETH NOBLE SHOR

DALY, Thomas Augustine (28 May 1871–4 Oct. 1948), humorist, poet, and columnist, was born in Philadelphia, Pennsylvania, the son of John Anthony Daly and Anne Victoria Duckett, owners of the first Catholic bookstore in Philadelphia. He attended public schools and at age fourteen entered Villanova College, "majoring in cigarettes and baseball." Daly dropped out in 1889 and completed two more years at St. John's College (later Fordham University). In 1896 he married

Nannie Barrett and settled in the Germantown section of Philadelphia. A 1910 *American Magazine* article praised Daly's success as poet, businessman, and family man and included a photograph with the caption "Thomas A. Daly and Family: An Epic in Nine Cantos," referring to the couple and their seven children.

Like many humorist poets in early twentieth-century America, Daly gained an audience through the newspaper. From 1889 to 1891 he was a clerk at the *Philadelphia Record*, graduating to reporter and later, editorial writer. He became general manager of Philadelphia's *Catholic Standard and Times* in 1898 and, while establishing the country's most successful weekly Catholic newspaper, built a reputation as a humorist: "I started a little column in that paper of my own free will, for the double purpose of taking my mind off my business cares and of getting the paper quoted for its original humor. Both purposes were achieved" (Masson, p. 415).

Daly became best known for his Italian-American dialect, for which he had cultivated an ear while working as a grocery store clerk and later as a cub reporter in Philadelphia's crowded Italian neighborhoods. In one of his more popular poems, "Mia Carlotta," Daly writes, "Giuseppe, da barber, he maka da eye, / An' lika da steam engine puffa an' sigh, / For catcha Carlotta w'en she ees go by." According to Franklin P. Adams, "Unless you have heard this strong, sweet man recite [these poems] you haven't extracted their full meaning."

From more than ten years of writing humorous verse and jokes Daly earned membership in the American Press Humorists and, later, presidency of the organization in 1906 and 1907. In 1905 he began lecturing throughout the United States and Europe, and the following year he published his first book of verse. *Canzoni* includes humorist poetry in Italian and Irish dialect about the life of the inner-city immigrant, in addition to poems in black dialect and standard English. "What is most admirable throughout the volume," according to a *Catholic World* critic, "is the union of wit, humor, or sprightliness, as the case may be, with a genuine respect for all that is pure, sweet, tender, manly, and noble" (1906, pp. 547–48). The twelve editions that followed confirmed Daly's popularity. With *Carmina* in 1909 he focused on the aspirations of Italian and Irish immigrants to become Americans. An *Independent* reviewer wrote, "The ballads have point, pathos and human nature," and "are the sort of thing that you cut out of a newspaper and carry around in your pocket to read to appreciative friends until the clipping is worn out, and then you copy it, unless you know it by heart" (1909, p. 1084).

In *Songs of Wedlock* (1916), Daly writes on topics of popular interest such as the rewards of marriage and raising children. He expands on this theme in 1924 with *Herself and the Houseful*, "telling the story of twenty-five years of happy married life with 'herself.'" He targets a children's audience with *Little Polly's Poems* (1913) by writing in the voice of a child.

Despite, or rather owing to, his popular success, Daly (as one of the first comic poets who broke away from the British poetic tradition) was accused of being a "nonpoet" who was far too "sentimental." Thomas Masson, author of *Our American Humorists*, questions this accusation: "Why does sentimentality run riot in the movies? . . . Where any particular work is taken hold of by the public, be assured that there is something to it" (p. 398). While some critics condemned Daly's poetry as journalistic, others celebrated his choice of themes, mastery of the use of dialect for comic effect, and ability to write just as pleasing traditional poetry. According to critic Louis Untermeyer, "To become one of our great poets, he needs nothing more than more of T. A. Daly."

Meanwhile, Daly was being promoted in the newspaper field. From 1915 to 1918 he was associate editor of the *Philadelphia Evening Ledger*. When offered the same position by his first newspaper, the *Philadelphia Record*, he accepted and remained eleven years. In 1929 Daly joined the *Philadelphia Evening Bulletin*, writing the weekly column "Rhymes and Ripples" until his death.

Daly continued to publish collections of poetry. Of the *Selected Poems of T. A. Daly* (1936), Benét wrote, "'To a Thrush' is one of the most touching and beautiful." The poem was awarded second prize by *The Lyric Year* over 10,000 others in a contest for best poem representing current American poetry. Ted Robinson wrote of Daly's last book, *Late Lark Singing* (1946), "characteristic, witty, mostly light, is welcome, though it makes me melancholy. . . . one knows that the poet himself is neither downcast nor sentimental when he proclaims this as his valedictory volume. For his is not only an old-fashioned Muse, but an old-fashioned Faith. He is not one to shed tears over the prospect of retiring from his labors."

Daly earned his nickname "troubadour" because of his contribution of entertaining parodic verse for more than forty years and because he worked to the end of his life despite serious illness. After suffering a stroke on 14 August 1948, he dictated his last newspaper column to his two sons. He died seven weeks later in Philadelphia General Hospital.

• Early writings of Daly's are held in a special collection at Villanova University. For an illustration and complete list of his publications, see Patricia Owens Williams's article in the *American Humorists, 1800–1950* edition of the *Dictionary of Literary Biography*, vol. 11. Daly is mentioned as "comic poet" in Thomas L. Masson, *Our American Humorists* (1931), and in the second volume of the 1922 edition of *The American Writers* series by Howard Willard Cook. Also see Franklin P. Adams, "Interesting People: T. A. Daly," *American Magazine*, Oct. 1910, pp. 750–51, William Rose Benét, "The Phoenix Nest: Contemporary Poetry," *Saturday Review of Literature*, 29 Aug. 1936, p. 18, Harold T. Pulsifer, "Poetry of the Average Man," *The Outlook*, 1 Feb. 1913, pp. 259–62, Ted Robinson, "A Timeless Troubadour," *Saturday Review of Literature*, 23 Nov. 1946, p. 42, and Louis Untermeyer's review in the *New York Times*, 1 Dec. 1912. Numerous other reviews can be found in the *New York Times*, *Catholic World*, *The Independent*, and *Outlook*. An obituary is in the *New York Times*, 5 Oct. 1948.

BARBARA L. CICCARELLI

DALZELL, John (19 Apr. 1845–2 Oct. 1927), attorney and congressman, was born in New York City, the son of Samuel Dalzell, a Scotch-Irish immigrant and shoemaker, and Mary McDonnell. When John was two years old, his family moved to Pittsburgh, Pennsylvania, where he attended public school and the Western University of Pennsylvania (now the University of Pittsburgh). He left to attend Yale University, from which he received his B.A. in 1865. In 1867 he married Mary Louise Duff; they had five children.

Returning to Pittsburgh, Dalzell was admitted to the bar in 1867 and began to practice in the firm of John H. Hampton. This association led to a twenty-year partnership, and the firm, known as Hampton and Dalzell, served many Pennsylvania railroad companies and the Westinghouse companies. Elected to Congress in 1886, Dalzell continued his work on behalf of Westinghouse, though at a reduced caseload, after his election. Hampton and Dalzell dissolved in 1887, and Dalzell formed a new firm, Dalzell, Scott and Gordon, that same year.

Dalzell ran for Congress as a Republican, was elected to the Fiftieth Congress, and served from 1887 to 1913. He represented the Twenty-second Congressional District, which consisted primarily of the city of Pittsburgh and a few other townships and boroughs. After redistricting, he represented the more suburban Thirtieth Congressional District beginning in 1903. His wife was a source of great assistance to him in campaign matters and with constituents. Dalzell ran for the Senate in 1899 and in 1901, but he was defeated both times.

The years during which Dalzell served in Congress were turbulent, and the leadership of the House changed hands several times. The Democrats controlled the House during his first two years in Congress and also from 1891 to 1895. Dalzell served as chair of the Pacific Railroads Committee from 1889 to 1890, when the Republicans held the majority. He took on a more active role in House affairs after the Republicans regained the House in 1895, serving in both the Ways and Means Committee and the Rules Committee. He became chair of the Rules Committee in 1910.

Dalzell rose to prominence through his involvement with the Dingley Tariff Bill of 1897. Protectionist tariffs, which assessed additional duties on raw goods and materials, such as steel, glass, sugar, and cotton, were a subject of friction between Democrats and Republicans at that time. Democratic opponents of the tariffs linked them to high consumer prices and corporate monopolies and called for their reduction. Because the House and Senate had been unable to agree on a reform bill, a conference committee was established and Dalzell was appointed to it. The conference committee report, which he helped draft, was enacted and became known as the Dingley Tariff Act of 1897.

After the Dingley Tariff had been in effect for several years, some considered the duties imposed exorbitant, and opponents called for its revision. A bill was introduced in 1909 by Congressman Sereno Payne to reduce the rates of the existing tariff. The House passed a version of his bill, which brought the rates down significantly. However, the Senate, under the leadership of Senator Nelson W. Aldrich, added many protectionist amendments to the bill. Dalzell used the Rules Committee as a platform to call for the rejection of the Senate bill and the establishment of a conference committee. He served on the conference committee created to resolve the dispute and acted as a floor leader in support of the bill reported by the committee. Though it did reduce rates, many lawmakers continued to oppose the legislation, which they saw as still protectionist in character. The conference committee report was adopted after extensive debate. President William Howard Taft signed the bill, though he had earlier called for more significant reductions. Protectionist tariffs continued to be a bone of contention between Democrats and Republicans in the following years.

Following the debate on the tariff, Democrats and a group of insurgent Republicans launched a challenge to Speaker Joseph Cannon's authority in January 1910. During this revolt, Dalzell steadfastly supported his Republican leader. The insurgents achieved a small victory when the House passed a resolution providing for the election of members of a select committee to investigate a dispute between the Interior Department and the Forest Department. Appointment of committee members had previously been a privilege reserved for the Speaker.

This modest triumph encouraged the insurgents to challenge the Speaker more directly. Congressman George Norris offered a resolution in March that provided for the election of the members of the Rules Committee and the removal of the Speaker as chair of that committee. Dalzell, seeing the danger, moved that the resolution was not in order. What ensued over the next several days changed the way the House conducted business and altered the role of the Speaker. Speaker Cannon left Dalzell to act as Speaker pro tempore while he garnered votes and support in an effort to hold off the insurgents. The matter was unresolved for several days during extensive debate and a recess.

When the House reconvened, Cannon upheld Dalzell's motion that the resolution was out of order. The House overruled Cannon and approved Norris's resolution. Cannon then challenged the insurgents to remove him as Speaker of the House. An attempt was made but failed.

After this fight, Dalzell was elected to serve on the Rules Committee and was also elected chair. He served in this capacity only until 1911, when the Democrats assumed control. Dalzell left Congress following the 1912 general election, in which a deep division in the Republican party between conservatives and progressives contributed to the loss of the presidency that year. Dalzell retired from public life and moved to Washington, D.C., for several years. In 1925 he moved to Altadena, California, where he died.

Dalzell served in Congress during an era of reform. Though he was often in a position of resistance to reform, he played a significant role in the passage of two key tariff acts. He was also an able debater and formidable opponent to the insurgents.

• The Library of Congress holds the only known collection of Dalzell manuscripts. Dalzell's role in the fight against the House insurgents is covered in Blair Bolles, *Tyrant from Illinois* (1951). James Holt, *Congressional Insurgents and the Party System* (1967), also provides some important information on that conflict. Edward Kaplan, *Prelude to Trade Wars* (1994), discusses the controversy affiliated with both the Dingley Tariff Act and the Payne-Aldrich Tariff Act. Government Printing Office, *Comparison of the Tariffs of 1887 and 1909* (1910), provides a detailed list comparing the rates established under both tariff acts. Dalzell's obituary is in the *Pittsburgh Post Gazette*, 4 Oct. 1927.

LAURA RUNDELL

DAM, Carl Peter Henrik (21 Feb. 1895–17 Apr. 1976), biochemist, was born in Copenhagen, Denmark, the son of Emil Dam, a pharmaceutical chemist and writer of biographical and historical books, and Emilie Peterson, a teacher. Henrik Dam's early education was in Copenhagen. He then studied chemistry at the Polytechnic in Copenhagen and received his M.S. in 1920. For three years he served as chemistry instructor at the Royal School of Agriculture and Veterinary Medicine. In 1923 he became a biochemistry instructor at the physiology laboratory of the University of Copenhagen. Dam married Inger Olsen of Esrom, Denmark, in 1924; they had no children.

Dam spent the year of 1925 studying microchemical analysis at the University of Gratz in Austria with Fritz Pragel. On his return to Copenhagen, he was appointed assistant professor at the University of Copenhagen's Institute of Biochemistry, and the following year he was promoted to associate professor. In 1934 the university awarded him a Ph.D. for a dissertation that summarized his studies on the biological importance of sterols.

In the years 1928 to 1930, while studying cholesterol metabolism in chickens, Dam made his first important discovery concerning vitamin K when he noted that chicks newly hatched from eggs of mothers fed a cholesterol free diet had hemorrhages under their skins and their blood clotted slowly. Because he could not explain these phenomena on the basis of the lack of any known dietary factor, he postulated that the subcutaneous hemorrhages and slow clotting observed in these chicks was the result of a new experimental disease: a metabolic disturbance due to the absence of a hitherto unknown dietary factor. From 1932 until 1933 Dam, funded by a grant from the Rockefeller Foundation, pursued these dietary studies in collaboration with Rudolph Shoenheimer at the University of Freiburg in Germany. Two years later working in Zu-

rich, Switzerland, with Paul Karrer, Dam isolated a previously unknown dietary factor from the chlorophyll of green leaves and described the substance as a fat-soluble vitamin. Dam named the new dietary factor vitamin K after the first letter of the Scandinavian and German word for coagulation, *koagulation*, thus symbolizing the vitamin's ability to promote coagulation of the blood and prevent hemorrhage. Dam's further studies on the vitamin's role in blood clotting demonstrated that synthesis of another protein, prothrombin, necessary for initiating the events leading to blood clotting, was dependent on vitamin K. Edward A. Doisy at Saint Louis University determined the structure of vitamin K and showed that the animal and plant forms differed slightly in their chemical structure. In further studies on vitamin K, Dam found that intestinal bacteria produced the vitamin and that in most healthy people, therefore, bleeding disorders resulting from lack of vitamin K were rare. Dam's discovery of vitamin K revolutionized the treatment of many hemorrhagic disorders. This vitamin became particularly important in the prevention and control of hemorrhage in surgery and obstetrics.

In 1940 when the Nazis occupied Denmark, Dam was on a lecture tour in the United States, sponsored by the American Scandinavian Foundation. Because of the uncertainties of the fate of Denmark Dam remained in the United States and continued his work on vitamin K during 1941 at the Woods Hole Marine Biological Laboratory. He then spent three years at the University of Rochester as senior research associate. Dam shared the 1943 Nobel Prize for physiology and medicine with Edward A. Doisy. The regular award ceremony in Stockholm was suspended because of World War II, so Dam and Doisy received the award from the Swedish ambassador in New York City under the aegis of the Swedish American Foundation. In 1945 Dam joined the Rockefeller Institute as an associate member.

In 1946 Dam returned to Copenhagen's Polytechnic Institute, where he had been named professor of biochemistry and head of the biology department in absentia in 1941. There he continued research on vitamin K, vitamin E, fats, cholesterol, and gallstone formation. Dam served as director of the biological division of the Danish Fat Research Institute from 1956 until 1963. His chief recreational pleasure was travel. Dam died in Copenhagen. At his request news of his death was delayed for about a week to allow services to be private.

• For biographical information, see *Current Biographical Yearbook* (1949), pp. 134–36; *Modern Scientists and Engineers*, vol. 1 (1908), pp. 258–59; and *Nobel Prize Winners* (1987), pp. 243–45. An obituary is in the *New York Times*, 25 Apr. 1976.

DAVID Y. COOPER

D'AMATO, Cus (17 Jan. 1908–4 Nov. 1985), boxing coach and manager, was born Constantine D'Amato in the Bronx, New York, the son of Damiamo D'Amato and Elizabeth Rosato, Italian immigrants who had come to the United States in 1899. D'Amato's father worked as a coal and ice delivery man to support his large family of eight sons, only five of whom survived infancy. Cus D'Amato was the second youngest. His mother died before he entered school; consequently, D'Amato grew up on the streets, where his given name was abbreviated to Cus. There he acquired his father's love of pugilism and practiced it readily. D'Amato's father had been a wrestler, and one of his brothers boxed. By the age of twelve he had suffered a head injury in a fight with an adult that left him nearly blind in one eye. After dropping out of high school D'Amato worked briefly as a millworker and as a campaign worker in New York City mayor Fiorello La Guardia's political club, but his main interest remained boxing. He became a partner in a Manhattan gym in the 1930s, although his eye injury precluded any chance of a career as a boxer. The entrepreneurial venture was interrupted by military service; but upon his discharge from the army D'Amato resumed his less than lucrative business. He lived frugally, sleeping at the gym and allegedly being supported by his father.

In the 1940s he met Camille Ewald, who would become his lifelong companion even though they would never marry. During that time D'Amato began to train Rocky Graziano, the first of the boxing stars with whom he would become affiliated. D'Amato later attracted other troubled youths like Graziano to his tutelage. D'Amato developed the innovative and unconventional "peek-a-boo" style, which kept both hands in front of the body to defend against counterpunches. This departure from the traditional style of placing one foot and one arm forward would be associated with heavyweight champions Floyd Patterson and Mike Tyson; but D'Amato became best known as a guru of mental discipline. As a youth he had confronted his own fears by challenging a neighborhood bully. According to Jose Torres, one of D'Amato's protégés, the successful outcome of this challenge led D'Amato to believe that boxing was really "a contest of character and ingenuity. The boxer with more will, determination, desire, and intelligence is always the one who comes out the victor." It was a doctrine that the forceful D'Amato imposed on his fighters. Torres claimed that D'Amato did not advise fighters, but commanded them. Critics claimed that such training produced robotic boxers; but they also admitted that D'Amato's fighters had confidence, discipline, and control of their emotions.

Under D'Amato's guidance, Floyd Patterson, at age twenty-one became the youngest heavyweight champion in history in 1956. As Patterson's manager, D'Amato became involved in a controversial affair that altered boxing history. The International Boxing Club (IBC), an organization backed by gangsters, had monopolized championship bouts and boxers' contracts since the late 1940s, requiring that fights be held in New York City at Madison Square Garden, which it controlled. A federal antitrust suit, which lingered throughout the 1950s, eventually forced the disbandment of the IBC; but by that time D'Amato had effectively broken the monopoly. A shrewd, independent operator who was known as a maverick, D'Amato organized a championship tour after 1956 that removed Patterson's heavyweight title fights from New York City and from IBC influence. With the monopoly broken, independent promoters and cable television ventures fostered multimillion dollar bouts in the years that followed. However, D'Amato lived the rest of his life in a somewhat paranoid state, fearful of reprisal.

In 1959 D'Amato regained his manager's license on a technicality, after losing it when the government accused him of fraternizing with known hoodlums. Despite the victory he failed to renew his license and moved to Camille Ewald's home near Catskill, New York, in 1962. There he opened another gym, financed in part by his New York friends Jim Jacobs and Bill Cayton. Ewald's home would eventually serve as a halfway house for wayward youth. Under D'Amato's tutelage and his role as a surrogate father, boxing and strict discipline served as rehabilitation.

In addition to Torres, who became the world light heavyweight champion in 1965, D'Amato coached other champions, such as Wilfredo Benitez and Edwin Rosario. He preferred to develop young fighters whom he could infuse with his own brand of discipline. D'Amato never had a written contract with Torres, who claimed that D'Amato disdained money as a source of evil and never took even his own share of millions of dollars earned in the championship matches. Kevin Rooney, another D'Amato protégé, confirmed that his mentor eschewed riches; D'Amato believed that the boxer should be the primary recipient of any profits earned from a fight. In 1971 D'Amato declared bankruptcy.

In the 1970s D'Amato developed Rooney first as a boxer, then as a trainer who later became prominent in his own right. In December 1982 D'Amato became the legal guardian of 16-year-old Mike Tyson upon the death of Tyson's mother; Tyson had resided with D'Amato since age thirteen. Having moved Tyson from the Tryon School for Boys, a New York State correctional facility, D'Amato provided him with some social stability, channeled his aggressiveness, and groomed his natural abilities. However, he did not live to see Tyson knock out Trevor Berbick in 1986 and become the youngest heavyweight champion to that time. D'Amato had died in Mount Sinai Hospital in New York City, leaving no survivors.

• A small clipping file on D'Amato is at the International Boxing Hall of Fame, Canastota, N.Y. Information on his life is readily available in biographical works on Mike Tyson, such as Jose Torres, *Fire and Fear: The Inside Story of Mike Tyson* (1989). Montieth M. Illingworth presented a more critical portrayal in *Mike Tyson: Money, Myth, and Betrayal* (1991). More balanced but limited works include Phil Berger, *Blood Season: Tyson and the World of Boxing* (1988); and Peter Heller, *Bad Intentions: The Mike Tyson Story* (1989). Additional information is in Sam Andre and Nat Fleischer, *A Pictorial History of Boxing* (1987); Peter Heller, *In This Corner* (1973); Angus G. Garber III, *Boxing Legends* (1988);

Dave Anderson, *In the Corner: Great Boxing Trainers Talk about Their Art* (1991); and Hugh Mc Ilvanney, "Mighty Mike Shoulders A Heavy Task," *Sports Illustrated*, 24 Nov. 1986, pp. 38–44. An obituary is in the *New York Times*, 5 Nov. 1985. Phone conversations with Kevin Rooney, 21 Mar. and 5 Apr. 1995, and an undated follow-up letter clarified some of the mystery surrounding D'Amato's life and provided his family background.

GERALD R. GEMS

DAMERON, Tadd (21 Feb. 1917–8 Mar. 1965), arranger, bandleader, and composer, was born Tadley Ewing Peake Dameron in Cleveland, Ohio. Information on his parents is not available. Dameron attended Oberlin College and took premed courses before deciding to become a musician. His career began rather inauspiciously as a singer in 1938 with Freddy Webster's band. It then continued with several lesser-known groups that included Zach Whyte, Blanche Calloway (Cab's sister), and Vido Musso (Benny Goodman's former saxophonist). At the age of twenty-three, Dameron was hired by Harlan Leonard, an alumnus of Benny Moten's band who was then leading a band formed from the former Thamon Hayes Rockets. The Harlan Leonard Rockets thrived in Kansas City from the mid-1930s to the mid-1940s, along with the bands of Count Basie and Jay McShann. The Rockets' style was permeated with the blues and consisted of a swinging rhythm section and strong soloists. Dameron contributed several compositions that featured dense orchestrations, chromatic harmonies, unison lines, and strong swing concepts (including "A la Bridges" and "Dameron Stomp," both recorded by Leonard in 1940).

Dameron's arranging skills led to his writing "If You Could See Me Now" for Sarah Vaughan (1946, Musicraft 398). This was one of the first bebop ballads, developed from a Dizzy Gillespie cadenza performed on "Groovin' High." The composition became a featured tune for both Dameron and Vaughan, who was then a pianist and vocalist for the Eckstine band. Dameron composed the title song for Coleman Hawkins on *Half-Step Down, Please* (1947, Victor 20-3143). Dameron also wrote songs for Jimmie Lunceford, George Auld, and Dizzy Gillespie, including "Good Bait," "Our Delight," and "Soulphony," which Gillespie's bebop big band premiered at Carnegie Hall in 1948. Dameron's ability to harmonize, orchestrate, and expand the small-band bebop format into a creative vehicle for a progressive big band is especially evident on the singles "Good Bait" (1947, Victor 20-2878) and "Our Delight" (1947, Musicraft 399). He appeared as a sideman on Gillespie's 1945 recording of "Hot House" (Guild 1002), one of several compositions that became jazz standards.

Dameron made his performance debut as a bandleader with Babs Gonzales's Three Bips and a Bop in 1946–1947 at Minton's Playhouse in New York. Some of his compositions are based on contrafact, a common practice of bebop composers; for example, "Hot House" was a new bop melody fitted to the chords of Cole Porter's song "What Is This Thing Called Love?" Other pieces, however, such as "Lady Bird," feature atypical chord changes and harmonic rhythm.

In addition to being an arranger and composer of real talent, Dameron was considered a very capable pianist. He served as the leader of groups featuring some of the finest jazz musicians of his day. In September 1947 one of his bands featured Fats Navarro as its principal soloist. At the Royal Roost in 1948 Dameron played with Navarro, Allan Eager, Curley Russell, and Kenny Clarke; that year Wardell Gray also joined the Royal Roost group. This band recorded several of Dameron's compositions that became standards, including "The Chase," "The Squirrel," "Our Delight," and "Dameronia" (all 1947); and "Jahbero," "Lady Bird," and "Symphonette" (1948).

In May 1949 Dameron went with Miles Davis to the Paris Jazz Festival, and the two were involved in several unsuccessful American groups. Dameron lived in England for a while, scoring occasionally for Ted Heath's big band. When Dameron returned to the United States, he found work as a pianist and the director of Bull Moose Jackson's rhythm-and-blues band (1951–1952). In 1953 Dameron formed a band of his own, which included trumpeter Clifford Brown. He featured Brown (muted solo) on "Theme of No Repeat" on the *Arranger's Touch* album as well as on a short three-movement composition titled "Fontainebleau" (*Fontainebleau*, 1956, Prestige 7037). Dameron's drug addiction grew out of control, however, and led to his imprisonment in 1958. After three years he was released, but he did not become active again as a composer and musician. Dameron died of cancer in New York City.

Dameron is considered one of the most important composers and arrangers of the bebop era. Although he played "arranger's piano" (a la Gil Evans and Carla Bley), he was important nonetheless as a performer with his groups featuring Navarro, which made some of the finest recordings from the late 1940s. "Hot House" and "Lady Bird" in particular remain cornerstones of the bebop repertory. Through his writing, Dameron posthumously became a key figure in the revival of bebop that began to flourish under Wynton Marsalis and others in the 1980s.

• Articles that cover Dameron's influences, career, and contributions and include information on his unique approach to arranging and composing are J. Burns, "Tadd Dameron," *Jazz Journal* 20, no. 8 (1967): 20; J. Cook, "Tadd Dameron," *Jazz Monthly* 6, no. 1 (1960): 23; B. Coss, "Tadd's Back," *Down Beat* 29, no. 4 (1962): 18; M. Harrison, "Tadd Dameron," in *The New Grove Dictionary of Jazz* (1988); V. Wilmer, "The Magic Touch: A Swan-Song for Tadd Dameron," *Jazz Beat* 2, no. 5 (1965): 20; and H. Woodfin, "The Complete Originality of Tadd Dameron," *Jazz and Blues* 3, no. 1 (1973): 4. Considerable detail on Dameron's activities with Miles Davis appears in Jack Chambers, *Milestones*, vol. 1: *The Music and Times of Miles Davis to 1960* (1983).

EDDIE S. MEADOWS

DAMESHEK, William (22 May 1900–6 Oct. 1969), physician and hematologist, was born in Voronezh, Russia, the son of Isadore Dameshek, a hatmaker, and Bessie Muskin. Dameshek moved with his parents to the United States in 1903 and was raised in Medford, Massachusetts. His early education was in the Boston English High School, where he excelled and gained entrance to Harvard University. He joined the U.S. Army in 1918, and upon his discharge he enrolled in the Harvard Medical School, where he received his M.D. in 1923. In the same year Dameshek married Rose Thurman; the couple had one daughter.

Dameshek served a two-year internship in the Boston City Hospital, where he came into contact with Ralph C. Larrabee, initiating his interest in blood and its abnormalities. Upon completing his internship, Dameshek set up a clinical practice while continuing his association with Larrabee at the Boston City Hospital. He also helped teach a course on laboratory medicine at Tufts University from 1926 to 1927. Work with Larrabee resulted in Dameshek's first paper on a hematological subject, "The Reticulated Blood Cells—Their Clinical Significance" (*Boston Medical and Surgical Journal* 194 [1926]: 759–68).

Dameshek joined the staff of the Beth Israel Hospital in Brookline, Massachusetts, in 1928 and remained there as a hematologist for ten years. His work was primarily concerned with the hematology lab that he had established and directed. At the end of this period, he moved to the Joseph H. Pratt Diagnostic Hospital (later the New England Medical Center) in Boston. There Dameshek organized what became the Blood Research Laboratory. He also returned in 1939 to Tufts, where he was appointed first to the clinical chair and then to the full chair of medicine. He remained professor there until he reached retirement age in 1966. His last years were spent in New York City at the Mount Sinai Medical School, where he was a professor of medicine emeritus and attending hematologist.

Dameshek was first and foremost a clinician. His greatest strength lay in his management of patients with hematological disorders. His practice was immense and was comprised of patients from all over the world. Dameshek was also a teacher. His lectures were well thought out and clear, but he excelled in teaching on the wards. As he went from bed to bed, followed by a long train of medical students, interns, residents, and visiting physicians, he encouraged his patients and discussed their case histories. In these presentations, Dameshek, who thrived on controversy, postulated many theories of disease, some very controversial, with the goal of stimulating lively discussion and provoking thought.

Dameshek was a clear, concise writer and a fine editor. His several texts included *Hemolytic Syndromes* (1949), *The Hemorrhagic Disorders* (1955), and *Leukemia*, with Frederick W. Gunz (1958). His talents were exemplified in the journal he founded in 1946, *Blood*. Dameshek remained editor of this journal until his death.

One of Dameshek's early research contributions was his development of the bone marrow aspiration procedure for clinical diagnosis of hematological diseases. This procedure eventually led to the possibility of bone marrow transplantation. In 1938 he conceived of the idea of autoimmune diseases in the development of hematological disorders, and he worked out the pathogenesis of radiation-induced leukemia. His other research interests included agranulocytosis, hypersplenism, and Mediterranean anemia. In actuality, Dameshek spent only a small amount of time behind the laboratory bench. In hematology he is generally considered to have been a catalyst, who initiated questions and suggested ways for their solution. He often collaborated with his students on papers. His creativity stimulated his laboratory and spilled over into the medical community to such an extent that his ultimate contributions are difficult to assess.

Dameshek was an energetic man who had an enormous capacity for work and a forceful personality. Although these traits annoyed some, he had a large and loyal following, and even his adversaries were influenced by his ideas. With his enormous capacity for work, he was able to maintain an active practice, edit *Blood*, direct an active training program, engage in countless organizational activities, and maintain a travel itinerary that rivaled that of an international diplomat.

Dameshek believed in a universal community of man from the scientific as well as the humanistic standpoint. To this end he struggled to get permission for hematologists from communist countries to attend the 1956 meeting of the American Society of Hematology in Boston. This effort was exerted at a time when the atmosphere in the United States was not favorable for cultural and scientific interchange with communist countries. Dameshek's academic and financial support contributed to the advancement of hematology in Russia, South America, and Israel.

Dameshek died unexpectedly in New York City during open-heart surgery in an attempt to repair a dissecting aneurysm. At the time of his death, Dameshek still maintained an active practice, a full lecture schedule, and a training program. He is known as the "father of hematology."

• Biographical accounts include James Tullis, "Memoirs of William Dameshek 1900–1969," *Blood* 35 (1970): 1–2; Henry M. Strartton, "William Dameshek: A Personal Remembrance," *Blood* 35 (1970): 4–5; and F. W. Gunz, "William Dameshek 1900–1969," *Blood* 35 (1970): 577–82. A bibliography of his works from 1922 to 1960 is in *Blood* 15 (May 1960): 585–95 after "A Biographical Comment" by William H. Crosby. An obituary is in the *New York Times*, 7 Oct. 1969.

DAVID Y. COOPER

DAMIEN, Father (3 Jan. 1840–15 Apr. 1889), Roman Catholic priest, was born Joseph de Veuster in Tremeloo, Belgium, the son of François (also called Frans) de Veuster, a Flemish farmer, and Anne Catherine. His mother taught him a little at home, and he helped a local laborer who was both a blacksmith and a grave-digger. His father wanted him to become a merchant and sent him to an academy at Braine-le-Compt in the province of Hainault to learn French. But Joseph was eager to follow his brother Auguste, who after serving his novitiate in Paris was transferred to Louvain. In 1859 Joseph began to train there to become a lay brother. Calling himself Damien, he was transferred to the novitiate of Issy, near Paris, where he studied Latin and took vows of poverty, chastity, and obedience in 1860 as a brother of the Sacred Hearts of Jesus and Mary. He served and studied in Paris and Louvain. When his brother contracted typhus and was unable to fulfill his ambition to become a missionary in the Hawaiian Islands, Damien asked for and was given the assignment. He began his voyage from Bremerhaven in October 1863, went around Cape Horn, and docked at Honolulu in March 1864. In May he was ordained deacon and priest.

From 1864 until 1873 Father Damien served as a missionary priest on the island of Hawaii. He built chapels for his parishioners, first at Puna and then Kohala-Hamakua. In 1864, during the reign of Hawaiian King Kamehameha V, a leper colony on the island of Molokai was established and more than a hundred lepers were exiled there. The colony was poorly supplied and administered. The authorities naively believed that crippled lepers could raise their own food. The lepers, some of whom were nursed by spouses and relatives, combined horrible suffering and licentious behavior. A law requiring the police to identify and deport lepers from the other islands was not enforced. In 1873, however, a year after Kamehameha died, Lunalilo was elected king and ordered the authorities to find lepers and deport them. At a church function on the island of Maui in May, Damien heard his bishop, Louis Maigrêt, lament the fact that the lepers on Molokai had no priest. Damien instantly volunteered to go and sailed two hours later with a cargo of fifty newly identified lepers and some cattle. On the island, at Kalawao and Kalaupapa, he found two slovenly settlements between steep cliffs and the sea, with the inhabitants in rags and with little food, most of them badly infected, many huddled or lying helplessly together in damp, open huts. Damien counted a population of eight hundred, of whom 80 percent were ill. Within a few weeks he briefly revisited Honolulu to request lumber from the Board of Health and private donors. The authorities promptly ordered him to remain on Molokai and threatened him with imprisonment should he return to Honolulu. He replied that he would do as he deemed necessary, and soon the order was rescinded. He was a priest for the Catholics among the lepers but ministered to the spiritual and other needs of all, regardless of their religious beliefs. He quickly became plumber, carpenter, mason, nurse, physician, and undertaker.

Father Damien saw to the building of huts and houses for his patients, better sanitation facilities, a hospital, more chapels, and orphanages and schools. He constantly badgered officials for better and more regular supplies of food, clothes, blankets, and materials. He sought to convert non-Catholics, and with considerable success. He did all that he could to stamp out gambling, illegally manufactured liquor, and debauchery, including prostitution. A dramatic moment came when in 1881 Princess Liliuokalani visited the island. Moved to tears, she made Damien a knight of the Royal Order of Kalakaua, but the government remained parsimonious. Damien's mission gained strength, but he grew autocratic and crotchety. He could rarely get along with priests sent to aid him temporarily.

By the late 1880s Damien was grievously suffering from leprosy himself. It is uncertain when he contracted the disease. Beginning in 1864 in Honolulu, he heard confessions from lepers and visited their huts. He was in close contact with everyone on Molokai, bathed scores of ill and dying parishioners, amputated their rotting limbs without gloves, heard their confessions often even as they vomited on him, and buried hundreds of their corpses. He smoked a pipe—and shared it with his lepers—to fumigate their huts and his own clothes. By 1877 he first noted suspicious marks on his skin. In the early 1880s he began to experience foot pains and partial leg paralysis. He was described in 1884 as a vigorous 204-pound man, but only a year later he accidentally upset a kettle of boiling water on his foot and felt no pain. When word reached the outside world of his condition, expressions of sympathy and donations of money and goods poured in. Permanent helpers came. The assistant he was most fond of was Ira Barnes Dutton, known as Brother Joseph. A lay brother, he arrived in 1886 at Molokai—to remain and serve there until 1930. In 1888 Father Louis-Lambert Conrardy, Father Wendelin Moellers, and a contingent of Sisters of Charity joined the settlement and also survived him. Toward the end, Damien's face turned purplish, his nose swelled, his right ear grew misshapen, and his fingers became gnarled. Remaining as active as possible, at the last he discussed only two topics of concern to him—his many almost helpless orphans and his doubts concerning his own spiritual worth. His quiet death was an inspiration to all who witnessed it.

Repulsive rumors soon began to circulate about Damien. The worst emanated from the Reverend Charles McEwen Hyde, an affluent Presbyterian minister in Honolulu. He had visited Molokai in 1885 to help dedicate a Protestant church, met Damien there, and praised his work. Later, however, perhaps because of interchurch animosities, Hyde wrote a letter to a colleague (2 Aug. 1889), in which he violently criticized Damien. It was published, first in the *San Francisco Occident* (28 Aug.) and later in the *Sydney (Australia) Presbyterian* (26 Oct.). In it Hyde describes Damien as bigoted, coarse, dirty, and headstrong and adds that he contracted leprosy through impure relations with diseased women. Robert Louis Stevenson, unsuccessfully seeking health in the South Sea islands, visited Molokai a few weeks after Damien's death, conferred with Brother Joseph, and was impressed by Damien's work. In response to Hyde's letter, he published "An Open Letter to the Reverend Doctor Hyde of Honolulu," dated 25 February 1890, in the *Scots Observer* in May, denouncing Damien's detractor. Stevenson fully expected to be sued for libel, but Hyde contented himself with labeling Stevenson as a "bohemian crank . . . a negligible person whose opinion signified nothing." Inquiries by the bishop of Hawaii and Protestant authorities cleared Damien of all charges. His body was originally interred in Kalawao, Molokai, but in 1936 it was placed in his congregation chapel in Louvain. In 1995 Pope John Paul II beatified Damien—beatification being the last of several steps before sainthood in the Roman Catholic Church.

• Correspondence and other papers relating to Father Damien are in the archives of the Congregation of the Sacred Hearts in Rome and in Louvain, the archives of the Hawaii Catholic Mission at Honolulu, the Belgian Consul at Honolulu, the Notre Dame University archives, and the Library of Congress in Washington, D.C. Biographical studies are Charles Warren Stoddard, *The Lepers of Molokai* (1885; enl. ed., 1905), and *Father Damien: The Martyr of Molokai* (1901); Vital Jourdain, *Le Père Damien de Veuster . . .* (1931), trans. Francis Larken and Charles Davenport as *The Heart of Father Damien . . .* (1955; rev. ed., 1960); Charles J. Dutton, *The Samaritans of Molokai: The Lives of Father Damien and Brother Dutton among the Lepers* (1932); John Farrow, *Damien the Leper* (1937, partly fictitious); and Gavan Daws, *Holy Man: Father Damien of Molokai* (1973). Reginald Yzendoorn, *History of the Catholic Mission in the Hawaiian Islands* (1927), provides background information. Robert L. Gale, *Charles Warren Stoddard* (1977), and Roger Austen, *Genteel Pagan: The Double Life of Charles Warren Stoddard* (1991), discuss Stoddard's relationship to and written comments on Damien. The foreword to George L. McKay, *Father Damien: An Open Letter to the Reverend Doctor Hyde of Honolulu from Robert Louis Stevenson* (1968), provides details of the Hyde-Stevenson controversy, as does Ian Bell, *Dreams of Exile: Robert Louis Stevenson, a Biography* (1992).

ROBERT L. GALE

DAMON, Ralph Shepard (6 July 1897–4 Jan. 1956), airline executive, was born in Franklin, New Hampshire, the son of William Cotton Damon, a successful businessman, and Effie Ives. Damon earned a B.A. from Harvard University in 1918. He had planned to become an astronomer, but World War I first interrupted and then changed his plans. In the summer of 1918 he entered the U.S. Army Air Service and trained as a pilot. Although he saw no action in the war, when Damon mustered out of service in 1919 he sought employment in the infant aviation industry. Unsuccessful for a time, he worked in the construction industry. In 1922 he married Harriet Dudley Holcombe, and they eventually had four children.

Soon after his marriage Damon's fortunes changed. With the U.S. Postal Service developing a transcontinental airmail system, the aviation industry's fortunes rose, and Damon took a job as factory superintendent for the Curtiss Aeroplane and Motor Company in San Diego, California. Curtiss was building airmail aircraft at the time, but with Damon's assistance the firm turned to the making of airliners. Damon was a force

behind the design and construction of the "Condor," the first airliner with sleeping accommodations. Damon rose through the ranks of the Curtiss corporation, and in 1935, at age thirty-eight, he was named president of the company.

Damon presided over Curtiss until 1936, when the company, falling on hard times during the depression and losing airline contracts for airliners to the revolutionary Douglas DC series of transports, was forced to restructure. When this took place, Damon left Curtiss and accepted the position of vice president for operations with American Airlines. American Airlines, under the energetic leadership of C. R. Smith, had developed from its base in Texas into an air carrier of regional significance. Damon helped Smith build American into one of the "big four" national airlines along with TWA, United, and Eastern. During his tenure as operations director, Damon initiated flights into all the major East and West Coast cities.

In 1941 Damon left American Airlines to take the presidency of Republic Aviation Corporation. He apparently took this job at the behest of Under Secretary of War Robert Patterson and Chief of Staff of the Army Air Force Henry H. Arnold to speed up production of the P-47 "Thunderbolt" fighter. The Army Air Force had high hopes for the aircraft—it was durable, reliable, heavily armed, and armored, and though not fast it was not easily destroyed—but Republic was not producing them at the rate required to meet military requirements. Damon's task was to raise production levels to 450 P-47s per month. By 1943 he had succeeded, through the implementation of a series of production management changes, practices borrowed from the automotive industry, and the upgrading of equipment.

In 1943 Damon returned to American Airlines, at first as a vice president, and in 1945 he was elevated to the presidency in place of C. R. Smith, who became chair of the board. While the war was still going on, the airlines began to jockey for position and markets in the postwar world. Damon called for regulated competition for air carriers, both within the United States, where regulation had been in place since the Air Commerce Act of 1938, and in overseas markets. He particularly opposed the position of Juan Trippe, head of Pan American Airways, who urged U.S. licensing of a single carrier to operate internationally, one that could compete with subsidized foreign airlines. Trippe believed that Pan American should be the "chosen instrument" because it had long been involved in foreign operations, whereas other carriers had provided almost exclusively domestic service. Damon, however, recognized that such a monopoly would close lucrative foreign opportunities in the postwar world.

The controversy came to a climax early in May 1945, when the Senate Commerce Committee's subcommittee on aviation held hearings to help frame legislation. Testifying, Damon argued that contract service to wartime military operations around the globe had prepared U.S. airlines for foreign service, and he asked that all qualified carriers be allocated international routes on the same basis as they received domestic routes. Congress adopted this position, and the Civil Aeronautics Board, governing the U.S. airline industry, awarded Pan American, American, and TWA international routes. Even so, Pan American remained the dominant U.S. carrier operating internationally for the next three decades.

Damon's insertion of American Airlines into the international market at the end of World War II did not sit well with either C. R. Smith or Juan Trippe. In 1949 Smith and Trippe negotiated, without Damon's knowledge, the transfer of American's foreign operating subsidiary, American Overseas Airlines, to Pan American. Incensed that he had not been consulted, Damon resigned from American Airlines in December 1948, just before the transaction's effective date.

Damon was not unemployed for long; Howard Hughes asked him to take over the presidency of TWA early the next year. Hughes, chair of the board, was so eccentric even in the 1940s that he had difficulty keeping capable lieutenants. When Damon arrived, TWA had been without a president for eight months, but more important it had lost $18.6 million, and its stock had plummeted from $76 to $16 a share in the previous three years. The airline was overextended, poorly equipped, at a loss for leadership, and less than six months from bankruptcy. Damon commented after joining TWA, partly to boost morale, that "I've always had the good fortune to join a winning team just as it is starting to win." He knew his work was cut out for him: he had to fend off Hughes while returning TWA to solvency.

Damon immediately began restructuring the corporation, reducing liabilities, consolidating operations, reassessing the TWA route structure, and selling $4 million in common stock. He made 1949 a turnaround year for the airline, and when he was finished TWA was a smaller, less-ambitious organization, but it was not broke. He also transferred older, inefficient aircraft to shorter routes and raised the money to buy twelve new Martin 2-0-2 airliners and several modern Lockheed Constellations. By the end of 1949 Damon appeared to be a genius, as TWA reported a profit for the first time in more than three years.

TWA continued its recovery throughout the rest of Damon's presidency. Damon saw the coming of jet transportation and positioned TWA to take advantage of the sea change. Speaking to the Newcomen Society late in 1952 he said, "The jet age is on the horizon and [quoting Kipling] 'we are at the opening verse of the opening chapter of endless possibilities.'" Damon did not live to see this transformation, however. Always thin and frail-looking, Damon entered a hospital in Dallas in late 1955 and died of pneumonia not long thereafter in Mineola, New York.

Ralph Damon was a member of a fraternity of young men who rose to prominence in the new aviation industry between the two world wars. Each of them glimpsed something of the potential of aviation to change the way in which humanity lived and conducted its activities. While chasing that vision Damon

and his associates made personal fortunes. Damon helped to shape the airline industry and place it on the path it has followed since his death.

• There is no known collection of Damon's papers. Material by and about him can be found in scattered collections at the National Air and Space Museum, Smithsonian Institution, Washington, D.C.; at the American Airlines Corporate Archives in Dallas, Tex.; and at the Trans World Airlines Archives in Kansas City, Mo. Damon's speech to the Newcomen Society is available in "*TWA*": *Nearly Three Decades in the Air* (1952). For more information on his career see Robert W. Rummel, *Howard Hughes and TWA* (1991); and Robert J. Serling, *Eagle: The History of American Airlines* (1983) and *Howard Hughes' Airline: An Informal History of TWA* (1985). A report on his restructuring of TWA can be found in "Mr. Damon Begins to Move," *Fortune*, July 1949, pp. 65–67. An obituary is in the *New York Times*, 5 Jan. 1956.

ROGER D. LAUNIUS

DAMROSCH, Frank Heino (22 June 1859–22 Oct. 1937), music educator, was born in Breslau, now part of Poland, the son of Leopold Damrosch, a leading violinist and conductor in Europe and later in New York, and Helene von Heimburg, an opera singer in Weimar. As a boy, Frank, who was originally named Franz, for his godfather Franz Liszt, met Liszt, Richard Wagner, violinist Joseph Joachim, and pianist Clara Schumann. Even by German standards the family lived and breathed music, and all the children received thorough grounding in all areas of music.

In 1871 Leopold Damrosch accepted an offer to head New York City's Arion Society and emigrated with his family. The twelve-year-old Frank was enrolled in the New York public schools, subsequently completing his education at City College in 1874. At first, as a bit of a flight from his family, Damrosch did not pursue a musical career. He worked briefly as a broker on Wall Street, and in 1876 he moved west, settling in Denver. There his musical proclivities resurfaced. In Denver Damrosch found little of the musical life to which he was accustomed, so he went to work as a church organist and choral director. He organized several community singing societies and in 1884 became the supervisor of music for the Denver public schools.

When his father died suddenly of pneumonia in 1885, Damrosch returned to New York. His father had become a leading figure in the New York opera scene, and Damrosch, along with his younger brother Walter, took up many of his father's duties. Damrosch became chorus master of the Metropolitan Opera and established several singing societies in New York. From 1897 to 1905 he served as supervisor of music for the New York public school system and from 1898 to 1912 was conductor of the Oratorio Society. Damrosch always sought to maximize popular involvement in music. For children especially Damrosch believed involvement was a must so that music would become a lifetime joy and never a mere duty.

Damrosch's ambitions and strivings as a music educator achieved great success in 1905 when he secured a

$500,000 grant from investment banker James Loeb. Loeb's grant enabled him to establish the Institute of Musical Art in New York, which became the first truly world-class music school in the United States, due in large measure to Damrosch's tireless work. As its director, he secured top faculty for all positions and taught extensively himself in voice, composition, conducting, and theory. With his connections in the West as well as in New York, Damrosch was able to draw student talent from all over the country and from other nations. The institute merged with the Juilliard Graduate School in 1926, and Damrosch served as dean, working endlessly to maintain the school's pedagogical foundations, a goal he pursued into his retirement years until his death in New York City.

• The best book on the life and work of Frank Damrosch is George Martin, *The Damrosch Dynasty: America's First Family of Music* (1983); it covers the musical activities of the entire Damrosch family and connects the musical life of the family to broader social and historical trends. A more narrow but still narratively useful account of Damrosch's life can be found in Lucy Poate Stebbins, *Frank Damrosch* (1945). A good treatment of Damrosch's extensive work to promote musical and singing activities among the mass of people is L. P. Stebbins and R. P. Stebbins, *Frank Damrosch: Let the People Sing* (1945).

ALAN LEVY

DAMROSCH, Leopold (22 Oct. 1832–15 Feb. 1885), musician and conductor, was born in Posen, Prussia (now Poznań, Poland), the son of Heinrich Damrosch. Neither his father's occupation nor his mother's name is known. Like many middle-class Germans of the nineteenth century, Damrosch grew up in a music-loving family and received thorough musical training as part of his general education. Musical activity, however, was valued more as an avocation than as a profession, so his father objected when Damrosch expressed a desire to pursue music professionally. Damrosch reluctantly yielded to family pressures and halted his music studies. He completed Gymnasium training, embarked briefly on legal studies, and ultimately switched to medicine, completing a medical degree in 1854. Music continued to beckon, however, and within a year of earning his medical degree Damrosch left medicine for the violin. Consequently, the rift with his parents widened. Indeed, when Damrosch's famous son Walter was consulted about his father for an article in the *Dictionary of American Biography*, he confessed he had no idea what his grandfather's profession had been, so little did his father speak of him.

Within three years of his beginning musical studies and performances, Damrosch gained the notice of Franz Liszt, who appointed Damrosch concertmaster of his orchestra in Weimar, quite an achievement for a mere 24-year-old. That same year, 1861, Damrosch married singer Helene von Heimburg, with whom he had eight children. Some of the children did not survive, but two sons—Frank (named for his godfather, Franz Liszt) and Walter—became significant figures in twentieth-century American music.

In 1858 Damrosch became conductor of the Philharmonic Society of Breslau. There, in the tradition of the German kapellmeister, he became the organizer and leader of all things musical in the city. His years of success in Breslau earned him international fame, and in 1871 he was invited to New York to lead the prominent Arion Society of New York. Damrosch accepted the post and brought his family to the United States later that year. Once in New York, Damrosch plunged himself into the musical life of the city, as he had in Breslau. The steady immigration of Germans into New York since 1848 had established a demand for concert music making of high order, and Damrosch was among the early members of New York's German community to gain cultural and financial success.

Along with Theodore Thomas, Damrosch became a leading music entrepreneur and conductor in New York, and the two were keen rivals. In Germany, "classical" music was not the exclusive property of the wealthy; it was popular among all the people, and Damrosch saw no reason why this could not be the case in New York. A chief difference between New York and Breslau was that the latter had a wide range of established institutions through which people could gain access to concerts and to music education for their children. Thus Damrosch set out to create similar concert forums, musical organizations, singing societies, and schools. And he involved his children in these efforts. These organizations, including concert halls, outdoor concerts, and cafe ensembles, grew in popularity. Amidst these many flourishing musical activities, Damrosch founded the New York Symphony Society in 1878. For the next fifty years Damrosch and his son Walter led the New York Symphony. (In 1927 it merged with the Philharmonic.) Under Damrosch the Symphony quickly became a world-class orchestra.

In the nineteenth century a conflict grew between musicians who championed the moderns of the age—Berlioz, Liszt, Wagner—and those who favored the more traditional styles of Mozart, Beethoven, and such later figures as Mendelssohn and Schumann, all of whom tended to follow more traditional precepts of harmony and form. Such aesthetic conflict raged in most European musical centers, and Damrosch's and Thomas's aesthetic differences fueled a similar warfare in New York. The stakes were practical as well as aesthetic, for the favor of critics, concert hall managers, and audiences meant more frequent and higher-paying engagements. When Thomas and Damrosch encountered one another at a music shop in Union Square, the much larger and taller Thomas roared at Damrosch: "I want to tell you one thing; whoever crosses my path I crush." Thomas was the aesthetic conservative in the battle, Damrosch the modernist.

To the extent that such matters can be judged, Thomas won the symphony war against Damrosch. He was the more popular conductor in New York as well as in other musical centers such as Chicago and Cincinnati. Beyond the aesthetic points at issue, Damrosch's Jewish background aroused some enmity, though religion was never very important to him. One anti-Semitic critic, for instance, sneeringly labeled Damrosch a "Germanized Hebrew." Furthermore, Damrosch was less popular than Thomas with New York musicians, as he had a reputation for being capricious in temperament, patronizing in manner, and unpredictable in musical interpretations and tempi. Though no less stern, Thomas was the more temperamentally predictable and, not coincidentally, the more artistically pedestrian.

Doggedly championing the moderns, Damrosch played a most important role in introducing Wagnerian musical drama to American audiences. Before Damrosch's efforts, opera in the United States was predominantly Italian in language, repertory, and personnel. Damrosch staged the first full presentations of many of Wagner's operas at the Metropolitan Opera, persevering against many attacks from angry critics. By the mid-1880s Damrosch seemed ready to continue his popular and successful work as an opera and symphony conductor. But with Wagnerian suddenness and tragedy, Leopold Damrosch died of pneumonia in New York. He was only fifty-three. Damrosch's sons carried on their father's legacy with great success, Walter leading the New York Symphony and Frank heading the Institute of Musical Art.

• The best book on the Damrosch family is by George Martin, *The Damrosch Dynasty, America's First Family of Music* (1983). The work is encyclopedic with regard both to the musical and broader social history pertinent to the life and work of Leopold Damrosch and his sons. Walter Damrosch wrote *My Musical Life* (1923), in which he gives extensive coverage to his father's work. Another family member, Gretchen Damrosch Finletter, wrote *From the Top of the Stairs* (1946), a reminiscence of the family's musical life. On the operatic life of New York in the late nineteenth century, the best work is Joseph Horowitz, *Wagner Nights* (1994).

ALAN LEVY

DAMROSCH, Walter Johannes (30 Jan. 1862–22 Dec. 1950), conductor and composer, was born in Breslau, Prussia (now Wrocław, Poland), the son of Leopold Damrosch, a conductor, and Helene von Heimburg, an opera singer. His father, a converted Jew, and his mother had met in Weimar, where Leopold was concertmaster of the ducal court orchestra led by Franz Liszt and Helene was a leading singer of opera and lieder. Moving to Breslau in 1858 as chief of the Orchesterverein, Leopold soon became a conductor distinguished enough to attract the attention of such luminaries as Liszt, Peter Cornelius, Richard Wagner, Carl Tausig, Anton Rubinstein, Joseph Joachim, Hans von Bülow, and Clara Schumann, all of whom were Leopold's personal friends. It was into this milieu that Walter Johannes was born.

In 1871 Leopold was offered the position of director of the Arion Society, and the Damrosches immigrated to New York City. There Leopold established himself anew as a conductor of the Arion Society, the Oratorio Society, German opera at the Metropolitan, and occasionally the New York Philharmonic. He also founded the rival New York Symphony Society in 1878.

In this professional atmosphere young Walter not only absorbed the necessary musical skills but also learned the value of diplomacy. He played piano well enough to know the standard repertory and express it with conviction. He mastered all the techniques of score reading, tempo memory, and baton control necessary for the successful conductor. His affability, extraordinary good looks, and articulateness enhanced these prodigious musical skills. When his father became ill, the 23-year-old Walter was therefore ready to step in to take his place. Conducting both *Die Walküre* and *Tannhäuser* at the Metropolitan Opera, he launched himself on a career that would last for decades into the twentieth century. In turn, besides conducting at the Metropolitan, he directed the New York Symphony Orchestra (also known as the Symphony Society of New York) and the Oratorio Society (from 1885) and founded the Damrosch Opera Company (1895).

In the 1920s he conducted concerts on radio's "NBC Music Appreciation Hour," and he became music adviser to the National Broadcasting Company in 1927. As a composer Damrosch confined himself to operas, most of which not only were performed but also achieved some degree of critical success: *The Scarlet Letter* (Boston, 1896), *The Dove of Peace* (Philadelphia, 1912), *Cyrano de Bergerac* (Metropolitan, 1913), and *The Man without a Country* (Metropolitan, 1937). Damrosch himself admitted to the "overwhelming influence of Wagner," and even such a sympathetic observer as Giulio Gatti-Casazza, then manager of the Metropolitan Opera, which awarded a $10,000 prize and production to *Cyrano*, emphasized the quality of the critic William J. Henderson's libretto and of the singers' performances, rather than the music, though he did say in his *Memories of the Opera* (1941) that "Damrosch is a good musician with a good experience of the theatre."

Damrosch's greatest talent lay in his ability to organize and sustain large artistic projects by gaining the interest and financial support of wealthy patrons. He became a veritable arts adviser to Andrew Carnegie, the industrialist, who subsequently gave funds for the erection of Carnegie Hall and for a time was president and chief financier of both Damrosch's New York Symphony Orchestra and his Oratorio Society. Damrosch was responsible for the invitation to Tchaikovsky to conduct his own works for the opening of Carnegie Hall in 1891. It was through Carnegie that Damrosch gained entry into the world of society and politics. In 1890 he married Margaret Blaine, daughter of the Republican candidate for president in 1884, James G. Blaine. They had eight children, only four of whom survived to adulthood and one of whom, Gretchen Damrosch Finletter, wrote a book of reminiscences that shows Walter and Margaret to have had a sharing and coequal relationship in which, generally speaking, he would be allowed the last word on artistic affairs; she was the authority on politics.

When the New York Symphony Orchestra was reorganized in 1903, Damrosch persuaded Harry Harkness Flagler, scion of two famous oil families, to become its patron. As permanent conductor, Damrosch introduced Sunday afternoon concerts to New York and took the symphony to every part of the United States, often to cities where a symphony orchestra had never been heard before.

During the American participation in World War I, Damrosch was a cultural ambassador to France, where he conducted concerts in Paris and later organized a bandmasters' training school for General John J. Pershing. He set in motion a series of events that included the first tour of Europe by an American orchestra (the New York Symphony Orchestra) and the founding of the American Conservatory at Fontainebleau, where Nadia Boulanger would nurture a generation of young American composers.

Like his father, Damrosch introduced many significant pieces to the American public by such composers as Ralph Vaughan Williams (the *London* and *Pastoral* symphonies), Jean Sibelius (*Tapiola* and the Fourth Symphony), Maurice Ravel (*Daphnis et Chloë*), and Arthur Honegger (*Pacific 231*). He conducted the premieres of Ernest Bloch's symphonic poem *America*, George Gershwin's Concerto in F (which Damrosch had commissioned), and many other American works by composers such as George W. Chadwick, Henry K. Hadley, Daniel Gregory Mason, John Alden Carpenter, Deems Taylor, Edward Burlingame Hill, and Aaron Copland.

During his professional career, Damrosch had the misfortune to stand comparison with some of the finest conductors in the world who were induced to come to the United States: Anton Seidl, Gustav Mahler, Wilhelm Gericke, Karl Muck, and Arturo Toscanini. Furthermore, he inherited the baggage of his father's bitter rivalries, such as that with the conductor Theodore Thomas. As a result, his successes seemed automatically to inspire hostility among influential critics like Henry T. Finck, a longtime admirer of Thomas. Finck once wrote that while Seidl devoted "body and soul" to his conducting, Damrosch could direct both *Tristan* and *Die Meistersinger* on the same day and come off looking "cool as a cucumber."

Later opinion was not as harsh. In fact, even the sometimes querulous Virgil Thomson said in 1942 that Damrosch "got the loveliest sound out of the Philharmonic I have ever heard anybody get" (*The Musical Scene*, p. 42). Some observers found Damrosch's habit of making comments about the music he was about to conduct annoying. Like an evangelist, he used the force of his personality to try to make the inherent difficulties of his subject seem less onerous and even more exciting to first-time audiences and children. From 1928 to 1948, as the radio apostle of good music he did more to make the United States the locus of twentieth-century musical activity than any other figure save perhaps Leonard Bernstein. Damrosch died at his home on Manhattan's East Side.

Damrosch was lauded during his lifetime with decorations from the French, Italian, Belgian, and Spanish governments; the silver medal of the Worshipful Company of Musicians of London; and the gold medal of the National Institute of Arts and Letters. In 1922 several of his colleagues gave a concert to raise funds for the Walter Damrosch Fellowship in Music at the American Academy in Rome. Damrosch was president of the National Institute of Arts and Letters (1927–1929 and 1936–1941) and the American Academy of Arts and Letters (1941–1948), and he was the first president of the Musicians Emergency Fund (1933–1943).

In 1959 the city of New York established Damrosch Park in Lincoln Center on a 2.5-acre site next to the Metropolitan Opera House. It was dedicated to the "distinguished family of musicans"—Leopold, Frank, and Walter Damrosch, Clara Damrosch Mannes (Walter's younger sister), and her husband David Mannes, founders of the Mannes College of Music.

• Walter Damrosch's papers are in the Music Division, New York Public Library for the Performing Arts. Damrosch's autobiography, *My Musical Life* (1923; rev. ed., 1930), provides a selective factual account and should be read together with Lucy Poate Stebbins and Richard Poate Stebbins, *Frank Damrosch: Let the People Sing* (1945), for a more complete account of the family, especially its origins. Three doctoral dissertations deal largely with Damrosch's cultural and educational activities: Frederick Theodore Himmelein, "Walter Damrosch, a Cultural Biography" (Univ. of Virginia, 1972); William Ray Perryman, "Walter Damrosch: An Educational Force in American Music" (Indiana Univ., 1972); and M. Elaine Goodell, "Walter Damrosch and His Contributions to Music Education" (Catholic Univ. of America, 1973). For insight into his private life, see his daughter Gretchen Damrosch Finletter's *From the Top of the Stairs* (1946). W. J. Henderson, "Walter Damrosch," *Musical Quarterly* 18 (Jan. 1932): 1–8, is an objective but friendly evaluation written by the professional music critic who collaborated with Damrosch as his librettist for *Cyrano*. George Martin, *The Damrosch Dynasty: America's First Family of Music* (1983), provides a "kaleidoscopic . . . saga" of three generations of the Damrosches that helps place Walter's life in the context of his famous family.

VICTOR FELL YELLIN

DANA, Charles Anderson (8 Aug. 1819–17 Oct. 1897), newspaper editor, was born in Hinsdale, New Hampshire, the son of Anderson Dana, a farmer and small-time merchant, and Ann Dennison. Distantly related to the wealthy and prominent descendants of colonial settler Richard Dana, Charles Dana grew up keenly aware of his family's diminished social status. Poverty and the repeated business failures of his father would have a profound effect on the development of Dana's political ideology, leading him to attack wealth and privilege and to identify with the interests of the "producing classes."

Despite the difficulties of his boyhood, Dana gained admission to Harvard College in the fall of 1839. Financial problems continued to plague him, however, and he completed only one full year of college. (Although Dana never graduated from Harvard, in 1861 he was awarded an honorary bachelor of arts degree, as of the class of 1843.) It was in Cambridge that Dana met George Ripley, the Transcendentalist minister who established Brook Farm.

Dana joined Brook Farm in 1841. A farmer and a teacher in the Brook Farm school, Dana's nickname was "the professor." During the winter of 1842 Dana and several other Brook Farmers became interested in Fourierism, a French form of socialism. In 1845 the Brook Farmers began publishing the *Harbinger*, a weekly newspaper intended to advance the cause of Fourierism, and Dana became one of its leading contributors. As a Fourierist, Dana argued that workers and the reformers who had their partisan interests at heart should reorganize society along cooperative lines. Later, as powerful editor of the *New York Sun*, Dana would continue to be guided by this vision, despite the rapidly changing nature of American society.

In March 1846 a fire broke out at Brook Farm, and the nearly completed "phalanstery" building burned to the ground. Most of the inhabitants began to drift away; Dana accepted a fulltime job at the *New York Tribune*. Within a few weeks Dana and his new bride, Brook Farmer Eunice Macdaniel, moved to New York City. The couple would have four children.

In the spring of 1848 *Tribune* editor Horace Greeley sent Dana to Europe. Dana's letters from France and Germany, published in the *Tribune*, form an extraordinary record of the revolutionary events as told from a sympathetic American perspective. When Dana returned to New York in March 1849, Greeley created a new position for the thirty-year-old correspondent, managing editor. Charles Dana was managing editor of the *New York Tribune* for thirteen years. While it is Greeley's name that is generally associated with the Whig *Tribune* of the 1850s, Dana contributed far more to that paper than has been recognized. One of Dana's more memorable accomplishments was the acquisition of Karl Marx as a regular correspondent. In addition to his duties at the *Tribune*, Dana began two major literary projects during the 1850s, *The Household Book of Poetry* (1857) and the first volume of what eventually would become the sixteen-volume *American Cyclopaedia* (1858).

Dana and Greeley came to have sharp differences in the mid-1850s, differences that were fueled by what Greeley viewed as Dana's impetuous actions during the senior editor's frequent absences from New York. The secession crisis further deepened the rift between the two men. While Greeley believed that compromise was still possible even as the slaveholding states were threatening to secede, Dana, like most Republican radicals, felt that secession was unconstitutional and would lead to war. Following the firing on Fort Sumter and the secession of the upper South, the *Tribune*, at Dana's urging, proclaimed: "THE NATION'S WAR-CRY: Forward to Richmond!" When the untrained Union troops were defeated at the disastrous battle of Bull Run, the *Tribune* was widely blamed—and most

Tribune staffers believed that Greeley held Dana responsible.

Bull Run marked a turning point in Dana's life. Though Dana later claimed that his relations with the editor remained as "cordial as ever," on 27 March 1862 Greeley gave the stockholders notice that one or the other of them must leave the paper. Dana resigned, writing to a friend that he was "astounded" and suggesting that Greeley's vanity had been the real cause of his "expulsion." According to biographer James Harrison Wilson, Secretary of War Edwin Stanton asked Dana to enter the service of the War Department "at once" upon the announcement of his resignation, and Dana accepted.

In April 1863 Stanton appointed Dana to a special commission to investigate the pay service in the western armies. The new title was misleading; Stanton was actually sending Dana to Vicksburg, where he would be secretly charged with the task of spying on Major General Ulysses S. Grant, the controversial hero of Shiloh and Fort Donelson. Impressed with the quality of Dana's telegraphic dispatches, Stanton appointed him assistant secretary of war in the summer of 1863. Throughout the remainder of the war, Dana served an important role as mediator between General Grant, Secretary of War Stanton, and President Abraham Lincoln. Relaying the general's views and defending his actions when necessary, the erstwhile editor became not only a major player on the national stage but also a journalist of potentially great importance to the Republican party.

Dana's connections with the Republican party paid off when, at the end of the war, a group of Republican businessmen approached him with an offer to edit the *Chicago Republican*. Dana accepted their offer, and as editor of the *Republican* (1865–1866) experimented with a number of techniques that he would later use at the *New York Sun*. Short, pithy paragraphs, a deft editorial touch, and breezy humor dominated the *Republican* and gave Chicago readers a feisty alternative to the relatively staid *Chicago Tribune*. Dana left the *Chicago Republican* in May 1866 for reasons that have never been clear. Although Dana's friends later claimed that he left because of the stockholders' bad financial management of the paper, his enemies suggested that Dana was forced out because of his unseemly pursuit of a political appointment as collector of the Port of New York.

Despite his controversial departure from the *Chicago Republican*, Dana was nevertheless able to interest his wealthy Republican friends in speculating with him on another newspaper venture. When in 1867 Moses S. Beach offered to sell Dana the *New York Sun* for $175,000, he immediately accepted. Beach's package included an Associated Press franchise, $50,000 worth of new presses, a small job-printing office, and the good will of the *Sun*'s advertisers.

The *Sun* was a terrific bargain. The successful morning daily already had a large readership among those whom Dana described as the city's "mechanics and small merchants." One of New York's oldest newspapers, the *Sun* had been established in 1833 as the city's first "penny paper." Still, Charles Dana's purchase of the *Sun* surprised observers of the newspaper business, who wondered how Dana could reconcile the interests of his Republican stockholders with the views of the *Sun*'s readers, who were overwhelmingly Democratic. The answer became clear on 27 January 1868, when Dana published the prospectus of the *Sun*'s new management. By proclaiming that the *Sun* would "continue to be an independent newspaper, wearing the livery of no party," Dana suggested that he would use the familiar notion of "independence" as a strategy to keep both his readers and his stockholders happy.

Ever mindful of his preexisting working-class readership, Dana announced in October 1868 that the *Sun* would be "an uncompromising advocate of the laboring masses." The *Sun* provided extensive coverage of labor organizations, union meetings, and strikes. Reflecting a Fourierist emphasis on cooperation and self-help (the same values that Dana had espoused in the 1840s), the *Sun* advocated cooperative associations of workingmen that would build housing, establish reading rooms, and provide lectures and self-help programs. Dana also championed the interests of his readers by printing frequent reminders that city services, such as parks and public baths, should be made available to the producing classes on days and at hours when they were free to benefit from them.

Dana's claim of political "independence" should not obscure the consistent voice of the paper. There was a regularity of temperament—if not of ideology—in the *Sun* for the thirty years that Dana edited the paper. This regularity stemmed from the editor's sense of himself as an outsider, which accounted for both his identification with the immigrant working people of New York City and his increasing support for the Democratic party.

Although Dana continued to claim that the *Sun* was politically independent, it became consistently anti-Grant shortly after the president's inauguration in March 1869. Republican officials found the *Sun*'s attacks on the president and his cabinet to be particularly deplorable because they had anticipated that Dana would run his paper in the interest of their party.

At the height of its popularity, approximately 1870 to 1884, the *Sun* had the largest circulation of any morning daily in the city. Noted for its urbanity, its concise reporting, and its deft use of language, the *New York Sun* set standards for a generation of journalists—and invented one of the most widely quoted definitions of news: "When a dog bites a man, that is not news, but when a man bites a dog, that is news." Dana provided his readers with a dizzying array of information on politics, literature, and stories of general human interest. When a 1919 anniversary issue of the *Sun* looked back on Dana's achievements, it recalled that the editor had believed his readers would "enjoy a discourse upon the architecture of the tombs of the Pharaohs as much as [they] liked a description of the Tombs of Centre Street."

Charles Dana's editorial voice was central to the *Sun*'s success. From the time Dana bought the paper, according to one *Sun* reporter, "it may be truthfully said that Dana was the *Sun* and the *Sun* was Dana." This complete editorial control—which nineteenth-century Americans called "personal journalism"—worked as long as a newspaper remained profitable, and the *Sun* made money during the 1870s.

By 1884 Dana had reached the pinnacle of his professional career. Yet, to the astonishment of observers, Dana nearly threw it all away by bolting the Democratic party, launching a series of personal attacks on Democratic reform candidate Grover Cleveland, and putting the prestige of the *New York Sun* behind Greenback-Labor nominee Benjamin Butler, whom *Sun* reporter Edward P. Mitchell described as "standing on a platform of Greenback-Labor declarations which Dana would scarcely touch with tongs." At first glance, it is almost inconceivable that Dana could have opposed this particular nominee of the Democratic party. Dana favored nearly every plank of the 1884 Democratic platform. It was the candidate he could not stomach and for the most trivial of reasons. Cleveland had slighted the editor in 1882, during his tenure as New York's governor, and Dana could not forgive the insult.

It is hardly surprising that Dana's competition dismissed him as irresponsible. Dana failed to anticipate the defeat he risked by leaving the Democratic party because he failed to realize the strength of his readers' partisan allegiance. Moreover, Dana had no way of anticipating the competition of the *New York World*, a traditionally Democratic paper that Joseph Pulitzer bought and revitalized in October 1883 and for which the *Sun*'s abandoning of the Democratic candidate was an unforeseen boon.

Charles Dana was caught by surprise when the *Sun*'s daily circulation plummeted from 145,000 to 82,300 between 1884 and 1886. Because the *Sun* and the *World* competed for the same market of laborers, factory workers, and immigrants, *Sun* readers who had been repelled by Dana's bolt from the Democratic party found a ready haven in Pulitzer's *World*. In addition, Pulitzer used bold illustrations and alliterative headlines to draw in new readers. Beset by rumors that the *Sun*'s stockholders were unhappy with his management of the paper, Dana took the unprecedented step of mortgaging the *Sun* building to raise capital, probably to buy new presses. The *Sun*'s competition jumped upon the mortgage as evidence that the paper was tumbling toward ruin. When the *World* found out, it printed the mortgage in its entirety and thereafter referred to the paper as "the *Sun*, mortgaged."

Though the outlook for the *Sun* appeared dire by the mid-1880s, Dana was not about to surrender. In 1886 the editor abandoned the *Sun*'s traditional four-page length in order to compete with the eight-page *World*. Dana's gamble paid off; the *Sun*'s new length and more modern look stopped the decline in daily circulation. No longer willing to watch Pulitzer steal his readers out from under him, Dana reoriented his newspaper in the 1890s and appealed to a new audience. Aided in part by the changing configuration of the Democratic party, Dana reversed the *Sun*'s slide toward bankruptcy by silencing the voice of the *Sun* as the "uncompromising advocate" of the workingman.

After Pulitzer siphoned off so many of the *Sun*'s readers, Dana began to espouse views more in keeping with New York's Democratic "Swallowtails," those prominent merchants, bankers, and lawyers who directed the city's economy. As Dana began to defend the interests of the conservative Democrats, he also began to sell more newspapers. Circulation did not begin to approach that of Pulitzer's *World*, but the *Sun* achieved a remarkable recovery nonetheless.

The defection of working-class readers from the *Sun* to Pulitzer's *World* contributed to Dana's growing conservatism in the 1890s. Equally important, however, were the larger social and political currents that swept through the Democratic party, leaving no place for the Swallowtails who shared Dana's newfound conservative principles. When the Democratic party nominated William Jennings Bryan as its presidential candidate in 1896, Dana abandoned the party. In a landmark editorial published on 6 August Dana reversed nearly thirty years of tradition at the *Sun* and openly supported the Republican candidate, William McKinley. Given the alternative of Bryanism, the *Sun* became a Republican newspaper.

Charles A. Dana died in New York City the next year. Of all Dana's achievements, he had asked to be remembered for only one. The *Sun*'s announcement of his death was brief. It appeared the next day on page two, at the top of the editorial columns. It read exactly as he had instructed: "CHARLES ANDERSON DANA, Editor of THE SUN, died yesterday afternoon."

• Although there are miscellaneous collections of Dana's letters in a number of repositories, including the Library of Congress, the New York Public Library, the New-York Historical Society, the Boston Public Library, and the Massachusetts Historical Society, the best record of his ideas can be found in the pages of the *New York Sun*. For Dana's views on journalism, see Charles A. Dana, *The Art of Newspaper Making* (1895). The most recent biography of Dana is Janet E. Steele, *The Sun Shines for All: Journalism and Ideology in the Life of Charles A. Dana* (1993). Earlier biographies include Candace Stone, *Dana and the Sun* (1938), and James Harrison Wilson, *The Life of Charles A. Dana* (1907). For assessments of Dana's contribution to American journalism, see Edward P. Mitchell, *Memoirs of an Editor* (1924); Frank M. O'Brien, *The Story of the Sun, New York: 1833–1928* (1928); and Charles J. Rosebault, *When Dana Was the Sun* (1931).

JANET E. STEELE

DANA, Charles Loomis (25 Mar. 1852–12 Dec. 1935), neurologist, was born in Woodstock, Vermont, the son of Charitie Scott Loomis and Charles Dana, a prosperous merchant. He received his undergraduate degree from Dartmouth College in 1872, then studied medicine briefly at Dartmouth before moving to Washington, D.C. There he served for several years as secretary to Senator Justin S. Morrill of Vermont; in 1875 or 1876 he became the private secretary to Spencer Fullerton Baird at the Smithsonian Institution. He resumed his medical studies at Georgetown Medical College and at Columbian University Medical College, from which he received an M.D. in 1876. He was awarded a second M.D. by the College of Physicians and Surgeons (New York) a year later.

Dana then worked for two years at Bellevue Hospital under Austin Flint (1812–1886) and Edward G. Janeway before launching his own practice. To supplement his income he served for a time between 1879 and 1888 at Ellis Island and as an assistant surgeon in the United States Marine Hospital Corps. Under the influence of Flint, he became professor of physiology in 1880 at the New York Women's Medical College, holding that position until 1887. He began to publish original articles, mainly in the *Medical Record*, which he also helped to edit. In 1886 he became a fellow of the New York Academy of Medicine, in which he became a central figure as president (1905–1906), chair of the Public Health Relations Committee (1911–1928), and trustee (1906–1934).

Meanwhile, Dana's interest in neurology was sparked by his association with Edward C. Seguin, William A. Hammond, and especially George M. Beard, whose New York practice Dana covered during several summers. Dana joined the New York Neurological Society in 1881 and the American Neurological Association a year later, eventually serving as president of each. He held the post of professor of diseases of the mind and nervous system at the New York Post-Graduate Hospital and Medical School from 1884 to 1895, later serving on its board of directors. From 1902 until his retirement in 1934, he was professor of nervous diseases in the Cornell Medical School in New York City. He also served on the Board of Trustees of the New York Neurological Institute, resigning this post in 1925 in the belief that the institute's new affiliation with Columbia University created a conflict of interest for him.

In 1892 Dana published an influential *Text-Book of Nervous Diseases* that remained a classic through ten editions over a thirty-year period. In this text he attempted a thorough-going application of new ideas and experimental results from general pathology to the study of the nervous system. This distinguished his work from the earlier treatise by William A. Hammond, which was almost entirely grounded on clinical observations. However, he prefaced his work with the advice that "conduct is almost more important than technique in neurology." The sixth edition included chapters on psychiatry, which the author deleted in later editions. For Dana, unlike the American neurologists who had preceded him, the specialty of neurology was firmly centered on organic nervous disorders. In his later years, however, he enthusiastically recommended the study of medical psychology, and, after the First World War, he reincorporated this field into his textbook. Dana also became interested in what he called "economic neurology" and particularly in eugenics. His hundreds of articles in medical journals, published during an active career spanning over half a century, reported on clinical and pathological studies of a wide range of neurological diseases.

Dana married Lillian Gray Farlee in 1882. Only one of their three children survived, and Lillian Dana died in 1893. The neurologist immersed himself in his work and in a number of overlapping social and intellectual circles. He belonged to the Century and University Clubs, to the Sons of the American Revolution, the Loyal Legion, and the Society of Colonial Wars, in addition to his medical associations. He was highly regarded as a generous and loyal friend and as an inspiring teacher.

Dana was the founder (in 1898) and long-time leader of the Charaka Club, in which some of the most prominent physicians of the United States gathered to share literary and historical interests. His own medico-historical contributions centered on the classics, including pieces on "Horace on the Psychoses" and "the cult of Aesculapius." His literary monographs, published by the private Elm Tree Press established by his brothers, included a number of editions of works of Horace and a volume called *Poetry and the Doctors* (1916).

Dana came into public view as a medico-legal expert, beginning with the case of Charles J. Guiteau (Garfield's assassin), and as an active member of the State Charities Aid Association. He also wrote for the general public on health-related topics such as insanity, rest and play, and against prohibition. His articles appeared in the pages of such magazines as the *North American Review*, *Forum*, *Scribner's*, and *Science*. Dana revealed much of his attitude toward his profession in *The Peaks of Medical History* (1926), which emphasized the dynamic and social aspects of the practice of medicine. While he felt that few branches of medicine were yet sciences, he stressed that all were established on a scientific basis. In his own neurological work, Dana attempted to integrate these two facets of medicine, the social and the scientific.

He retired from practice in 1933 and died two years later in Harmon-on-Hudson, New York.

• The best account of Dana's life, including a bibliography of his publications, is [Smith Eli Jelliffe], "Charles Loomis Dana, M.D.," *Journal of Nervous and Mental Diseases* 83 (1936): 622–37. Essentially the same obituary notice, without the bibliography, appears in the *Transactions of the American Neurological Association* 62 (1936): 187–93.

BONNIE ELLEN BLUSTEIN

DANA, Francis (13 June 1743–25 Apr. 1811), public official, diplomat, and jurist, was born in Charlestown, Massachusetts, the son of Richard Dana, a lawyer, and Lydia Trowbridge. Francis entered Harvard College in 1758 and graduated in 1762. He received an M.A. from Harvard in 1765 at the same time that he was studying law in Cambridge with his uncle Edward Trowbridge. Dana was admitted to the Massachusetts bar in 1767 and became successful in his practice. In 1773 he married Elizabeth Ellery, daughter of William Ellery, a prominent resident of Newport, Rhode Island, and his first wife, Ann Remington. The couple had seven children, including the elder Richard Henry Dana.

Dana's expressed opposition to the restrictive policies of the British government in the 1760s helped win his election to the Massachusetts First Provincial Congress that met in October 1774. Dana, however, did not serve in this body, nor was he even in the colony when hostilities erupted at Lexington and Concord. On that momentous day in April 1775 he was in Newport, Rhode Island, preparing to sail to Britain hoping to settle matters involving his father's estate and to promote Anglo-American conciliation. Dana discussed the emerging conflict in America with several statesmen in London. He absorbed the liberal political philosophy of theorists such as Joseph Priestley and Richard Price, and he also became fully apprised of the uncompromising stance of the royal government with regard to the colonial rebellion. By the time of his return to America in the spring of 1776, he was convinced that the only course for the colonists was to declare their separation from Great Britain.

Dana devoted himself to government service for more than three years after the Declaration of Independence. Following his return from Britain, he was elected to the upper house (council) of the Massachusetts state legislature. He served in this body for four consecutive terms, distinguishing himself by his diligence and dedication, while simultaneously managing successful business and legal activities. Then in November 1777 he traveled to Philadelphia to serve in the Continental Congress, to which he had been elected by the Massachusetts General Court. There he initially worked as a member of the Board of War and the Marine Committee. More conspicuous, however, were Dana's activities as chairman of Congress's committee on military reorganization, which took him to a meeting with General George Washington in early 1778. The resultant proposals for a general restructuring of Continental army forces took several months to finalize but were eventually accepted by Congress. Later in 1778 Dana was part of a three-member congressional committee that rejected Lord North's peace proposals, which had been brought to America by the Carlisle Commission. While in Congress, he also signed the Articles of Confederation for Massachusetts, though he harbored doubts about the decentralized form of government that the articles provided. His disillusionment with the contentiousness, sectional divisiveness, and procrastination that prevailed in the Continental Congress finally prompted him to leave that body in August 1778 and return to Massachusetts. There he again was elected to the upper house of the state legislature.

Dana's most memorable work on behalf of the American cause occurred during the final phase of the Revolution. In October 1779 he learned that Congress was considering his selection as secretary to a projected American peace commission, an appointment that in fact he soon received. Dana sailed from Boston on 13 November 1779 with John Adams and Adams's son

John Quincy, and they arrived in Paris the following February after an overland journey from Spain. The confidence Adams had in him was evident in July 1780 when Adams left Dana in charge of his affairs while he traveled to Holland seeking a Dutch loan.

Apparently as a result of this same support from Adams, as well as from other influential New Englanders, on 19 December 1780 Dana was selected as minister of the United States to Russia. He received his congressional commission the following March; he then journeyed to Amsterdam, where he conferred with Adams and engaged thirteen-year-old John Quincy as his secretary. On 7 July 1781 he began a long journey to the court of Empress Catherine the Great at St. Petersburg. Arriving in the Russian capital the following month, Dana quickly discovered that he would be unsuccessful in his attempts to obtain recognition from Russia or its commitment to defending freedom of the seas or developing commercial ties. This frustrating situation was due in part to the fact that his conflicting instructions demanded that he subordinate any initiatives to the interests of the French minister in Russia. Dana's achievements in St. Petersburg were further limited by the unwillingness of Empress Catherine to alienate the British government by officially receiving him. Nevertheless, prior to his return to America in August 1783, Dana could claim a few successes from his mission: he had been able to establish some valuable diplomatic connections with John Adams and Benjamin Franklin, two of the American peace commissioners in Paris, and he also brought back well-researched information concerning trade possibilities in the Baltic.

Following his return to the postrevolutionary United States, Dana remained in government service. In May 1784 he took a seat in Congress, then meeting at Annapolis, Maryland, but he resigned the following January to return to Massachusetts. That same year Governor John Hancock appointed him an associate justice on the state Supreme Judicial Court. Dana was disappointed with the low remuneration he received, but his business and legal enterprises furnished him considerable wealth. He was appointed a delegate to the Annapolis Convention in 1786 and the Philadelphia Constitutional Convention in 1787, but ill health prevented his attendance at either gathering. He had recovered sufficiently by January 1788 to support the completed Constitution at his state's ratifying convention. Dana also served as a presidential elector for the Federalists, and he generally supported their political program in the following decade.

Dana's final public service was as chief justice of the Commonwealth of Massachusetts, a position to which he was appointed on 29 November 1791. He generally adopted a conservative approach while on the bench, upholding the principles of English Common Law and demanding that strict judicial procedures be followed in the courtroom. He supported the legality of the Alien and Sedition Acts and repeatedly lectured juries on alleged offenses committed by the Jeffersonians. Still, he declined opportunities to become a Federalist candidate for governor or to serve on the 1797 mediation committee that President Adams sent to France. His formal retirement from public life occurred on 7 May 1806, when he resigned from the court.

Dana spent his retirement years in a variety of intellectual activities. He authored articles for several publications, most notably the *Monthly Anthology*. His memberships in prominent organizations included the Society for Propagating the Gospel among Indians and Others in North America, the American Academy of Arts and Sciences, and the Society for the Promotion of Agriculture. Advanced age obliged him to decline election to the Harvard University overseers in 1810. He died in Cambridge, Massachusetts.

• The Massachusetts Historical Society is the best source for manuscript material relating to Dana. It holds the Dana Family Manuscripts and the related manuscript collections of John Adams, John Quincy Adams, and the Ellery Family Papers. Some other original documents relating to Dana's life can be found in Harvard University Library and Harvard University Archives, J. P. Morgan Library, American Antiquarian Society, National Archives, Library of Congress, and Historical Society of Pennsylvania. A full-length biography of Dana is William Cresson, *Francis Dana: A Puritan Diplomat at the Court of Catherine the Great* (1930). Of the short sketches of Dana's life, the most rewarding is in Clifford K. Shipton, *Biographical Sketches of Those Who Attended Harvard College in the Classes 1761–1763 (Sibley's Harvard Graduates)*, vol. 15 (1970), pp. 204–17. Other works that offer relevant details or documents include Elizabeth E. Dana, *The Dana Family in America* (1956), Francis Wharton, *The Revolutionary Diplomatic Correspondence of the United States*, vols. 1–6 (1884), Francis P. Renaut, *Les Relations Diplomatiques entre la Rusie et Les États Unis: La Mission Dana* (1923), Worthington C. Ford, ed., *Writings of John Quincy Adams*, vols. 1, 4 (1912, 1913), and Lyman H. Butterfield, ed., *Adams Family Correspondence*, vols. 1–2 (1963).

SHELDON S. COHEN

DANA, Freeman. *See* Taylor, Phoebe Atwood.

DANA, Israel Thorndike (6 June 1827–13 Apr. 1904), physician, was born in Marblehead, Massachusetts, the son of Samuel Dana, a Congregational pastor, and Henrietta Bridge. The product of a financially secure and learned family, Dana entered a two-year apprenticeship in a Boston counting house at the age of seventeen. In 1847 he began the study of medicine at Harvard, where he took his first, third, and fourth course of lectures and received an M.D. in 1850. His second course of lectures was taken at the College of Physicians and Surgeons in New York. After graduation he studied medicine for two years in Europe, principally in Dublin and Paris.

Upon returning from Europe, Dana found that the only physician in Marblehead had just died, and many urged him to open a practice in his hometown. But on the advice of a Dr. Pearson of Salem that Portland, Maine, was a city that "was bound to flourish," he moved there in 1852 and set up a successful practice. Dana had an aversion to specialized medicine, which he feared would be too disruptive to his first interest, general practice. As he became acknowledged as proficient in the treatment of heart and lung disorders, however, he gradually conceded that such specialization was good for the community-at-large. He was not involved in surgical pursuits except in a very limited fashion, preferring to leave that field to those with the expertise. In 1854 he married Carrie Jane Starr; they had nine children.

Dana was actively involved in the development of the medical profession almost from the beginning of his move to Portland. In 1856, along with Drs. William C. Robinson and Simon Fitch he founded the Portland Medical School for Preparatory Instruction, where he taught physiology, pathology, and practice. He was a founder of the Portland Dispensary for the treatment of the indigent of the city, which he supported financially, and encouraged others to support. The dispensary provided patients for the students at the medical school to study. In 1875 he was one of the founders of the Maine General Hospital, where he became senior attending physician. He also taught at the Medical School of Maine at Bowdoin College, starting in 1860 as professor of materia medica and therapeutics and then serving as professor of theory and practice, from 1862 to 1869 and 1880 to 1897; upon retirement he was elected professor emeritus. Dana was president of the Cumberland County Medical Association and the Maine Medical Association, a charter member of the Association of American Physicians, and an original member and first president of the Portland Clinical Society. During the Civil War he served briefly (1862) as a volunteer assistant surgeon in Armory Square Hospital in Washington, D.C. Dana was frequently consulted by colleagues and wrote papers and gave lectures on diseases of the heart and lungs.

Besides medicine, Dana's other lifelong commitment was to religion. He was a pillar of the State Street Orthodox Congregational Church of Portland from its founding in 1852 until his death. He helped found the YMCA chapter of Portland, served as superintendent of Sunday school for a number of years, was a student of theology, and was known to engage in impassioned yet reasoned debate on various religious subjects. It was not uncommon for him to pray fervently at the bedside of his more seriously ill patients. A year after the death of his first wife, he married Caroline Beck Lyman of Portland in 1876; they had one child. He was a member of the Portland Society of Natural History, and had a strong interest in the study of botany. Family summer vacations were usually two-week botanical expeditions in the White Mountains of New Hampshire. The last four to five years of his life were spent in forced retirement because of declining health, which was apparently precipitated by the sudden, unexpected death of his beloved son, Dr. William Lawrence Dana of Portland. Dana died in Portland.

Dana's contributions to medicine, especially in the training of doctors in virtually every aspect of the profession except surgical practice, place him in the vanguard of medical reform. Not only was he educated to a level of qualification that was beyond the norm in an age of quackery, but he took it upon himself to share his learning and experiences with new generations of physicians.

• There are no manuscript records by or about Dana. Dana's major writings appear in the *Transactions of the Maine Medical Association*: "Renewal or Restorative Principle in the Treatment of Disease," article no. 19 (1867): 120–27; "Defective Drainage and Sewerage as a Source of Disease," article no. 21 (1871): 132–47; "The Pathology of Pulmonary Phthisis," article no. 11 (1880); "The Treatment of Chronic Bright's Disease," article no. 52 (1885); "Apoplectiform Seizures: Diagnosis of Different Forms and Their Treatment," article no. 14 (1889); and "The Sequelae of Pneumonia," article no. 40 (1893). Obituaries appear in the *Bowdoin College Obituary Record* (1904): 281–83; *Men of Progress*, comp. Richard Herndon (1897), pp. 20–21; *Records of the Portland School for Medical Instruction, 1871–1904*, Maine Historical Society Collection #85; *Maine Physicians*, comp. James Spalding, Maine Historical Society Collection #513; *Maine Medical Society Transactions* (1904), pp. 194–96.

BRIAN C. LISTER

DANA, James Dwight (12 Feb. 1813–14 Apr. 1895), geologist, zoologist, and teacher, was born in Utica, New York, the son of James Dana, a businessman, and Harriet Dwight. His father was a descendant of Richard Dana who settled in Cambridge, Massachusetts, in 1640. Dana, a studious scholar, was educated in the Utica High School, where his interest in science appeared early and developed through hard work, talent, and intelligence, despite his father's disparagement of science as a career. Attracted to Yale College by Benjamin Silliman's reputation, he attended from 1830 to 1833, and after earning a B.A. he became a mathematics instructor of midshipmen in the navy. From a visit to the Mediterranean Sea on a naval vessel (1833–1834) came Dana's first geological publication, a letter to the *American Journal of Science* on the volcano of Mount Vesuvius (1835).

In 1836 Dana returned to New Haven, Connecticut, as an assistant in chemistry to Silliman. There he wrote *System of Mineralogy* (1837), perhaps his best-known work, which he kept revising throughout his life. He soon left to become the geologist and mineralogist of Charles Wilkes's exploring expedition to the South Seas, setting sail from New York on the USS *Peacock* in August 1838 and returning in June 1842, after circumnavigating the globe. The voyage was hazardous—there was a shipwreck off the coast of Oregon, an overland trek to San Francisco, visits to Australia and the Philippines, and a return home by way of the Cape of Good Hope. Like other naturalists of his day, Dana's oceangoing experiences set their mark on the course of his career. He was employed by the U.S. government for the next thirteen years studying and classifying the zoological and mineral specimens amassed on the trip. Some of this time was spent, unhappily, in Washington, D.C. ("a city where there are no books"), enmeshed in bureaucracy and red tape. From this project came three of his great works, *Report on Zoophytes* (1846), in which more than 200 new species were described, *Report on the Geology of the Pa-*

cific (1849), and *Report on Crustacea* (1852–1854), in which as many as 500 new species were listed. These were massive quarto volumes with numerous plates.

In June 1844 Dana married Henrietta Frances Silliman, third daughter of Benjamin Silliman. They settled in New Haven and had six children; four survived, of whom the eldest, Edward Salisbury Dana, became a mineralogist, professor of chemistry at Yale College, and an associate editor of the *American Journal of Science*. Dana's brother-in-law, Benjamin Silliman, Jr., was professor of chemistry at Yale. In 1846 Dana was appointed an associate editor of Benjamin Silliman's *American Journal of Science*, the most influential scientific publication of its time in the United States, and by 1851 he was in full control of the journal. He held the position for the rest of his life and was responsible for improving its quality. In 1850 he succeeded his father-in-law at Yale College, becoming in 1855 the professor of natural history (renamed "geology and mineralogy" in 1864). Dana, vigorous and influential in the affairs of the college, was involved in the growth of science at the college, and played a significant role in the establishment of the Sheffield Scientific School (a new department), a graduate school of science that conferred doctoral degrees, and the Peabody Museum of Natural History (1876), in which he built the mineral and geological collections.

Dana was a small but imposing man, modest and without guile, and an inspirational, dedicated teacher of geology who was greatly admired by his students. Raised in a devoutly Christian home, he held strong religious convictions throughout his life. Though he believed that Scripture was the word of an ever-present God, he preached that science had much to offer religion and that it could clarify the Bible. When science was vigorously attacked in the fundamentalist tract *The Six Days of Creation* by Lewis Tayler (1855), Dana wrote a detailed rebuttal in the theological journal *Bibliotheca Sacra* (1856–1857) denying that a conflict existed, aiming to delineate the separate roles of science and religion, with the hope of an accommodation of the two paths to Truth. As a devout Christian and a believer in Special Creation, it took fifteen years for him to accept the theory of evolution. Even so, he rejected Darwin's natural selection in favor of a directed, neo-Lamarckian explanation of how evolution takes place. He disagreed with naturalist Louis Agassiz, who believed in the separate creation of blacks and whites.

In the late 1850s Dana suffered a "nervous breakdown," presumably due to "incessant mental exertion," and after spending ten months in Europe with his wife, he returned to America in good health. In the 1860s he prepared his *Manual of Geology* (1862) and *Textbook of Geology* (1864), which became standard works that ran through several editions. His health broke down again in 1868 and in 1869–1870; his recovery was slow, requiring paleontologist O. C. Marsh to take over his lectures. Though his daily life was carefully regulated, by 1880 he was relieved of most duties, and by 1890 he was freed of all official responsibility. Throughout more than thirty years of undiagnosed, debilitating illness, a chronic invalid who could work only three hours each day, his mind remained fully clear and active, and the revision of his works and the production of new books remained vigorous, due, it was said, to his endurance and self-control. Throughout his years of illness, he gradually retreated from outside commitments. In 1872 his *Coral and Coral Islands* appeared and was revised in 1890. Having visited the Hawaiian Islands (1887), he published *Characteristics of Volcanoes* in 1890. The same year *Genesis and Science* appeared, and in 1891 he published *On the Four Rocks of the New Haven Region, with Walks and Drives about New Haven*. In 1895 he prepared the last of his manuals (geology).

Dana was the preeminent American geologist of his day, a major force in the professionalization of the science. He provided a structure for American geology and mineralogy, theorizing about larger problems such as the formation and stability of oceans and continents and the formation of mountains, which he erroneously believed was due to an uneven shrinking of the earth as it cooled. His work on the classification and nomenclature of minerals was of the greatest importance.

Dana was an associate of the "Lazzaroni" (of which Agassiz was a leading member), a self-appointed, highly political group dedicated to the elevation of scientific standards in the United States. Many honors fell to Dana, including membership in numerous scientific societies: the Royal Society of London; the Institute of France; the Royal Academies of Berlin, Vienna, and St. Petersburg; the Academy of Natural Sciences of Philadelphia; and the American Philosophical Society. He was president of the American Association for the Advancement of Science (1854–1855) and was a charter member of the National Academy of Sciences. He was the recipient of the Wollaston Medal of the Geological Society of London (1872) and the Copley Medal of the Royal Society of London (1877), and he was awarded the Walker Prize of the Boston Society of Natural History (1892). He died in New Haven, Connecticut.

• Dana's papers are in the Yale University Library manuscript collection. His life has been chronicled in Daniel C. Gilman, *The Life of James Dwight Dana* (1899); Michael L. Prendergast, *James Dwight Dana: The Life and Thought of an American Scientist (1978)*; and E. S. Dana, "James Dwight Dana," *American Journal of Science* 49 (1895): 328–56, which contains an almost complete bibliography of his father's work, nearly 300 books and papers. A considerable amount of information about Dana is scattered throughout Robert V. Bruce, *The Launching of Modern American Science, 1846–1876* (1987).

LEONARD WARREN

DANA, John Cotton (19 Aug. 1856–21 July 1929), librarian and museum director, was born in Woodstock, Vermont, the son of Charles Dana and Charitie Scott Loomis. His father ran a general store and raised his sons with a New England emphasis on education and reading. Throughout his life, Dana maintained strong ties with his birthplace.

Dana enrolled at Dartmouth in 1874, where he edited *The Aegis*, a humorous classbook, and compiled *Junior History of the Class of Seventy-eight, Dartmouth College* (1878) as class historian. After graduation (1878), he returned to Woodstock to study law but his health was undermined by tuberculosis. He went to Rico, Colorado, for the dry climate, and joined Frank Wadleigh Gove, a Dartmouth classmate, as a land and mineral surveyor in May 1880. Later that year, Dana was admitted to the Colorado bar but he worked primarily as a surveyor; he was a member of a surveying party that discovered the ruins of the cliff dwellers of the Mesa River in 1881.

Dana returned briefly to Woodstock in the spring of 1882 and then moved to New York City. He passed the New York State bar exam in May 1883 but was unable to find a legal position. Ill again, Dana left for Fergus Falls, Minnesota, in March 1884 and then moved to Ashby, Minnesota, where he practiced law and edited the local newspaper, the *Ashby Avalanche*.

Restless and unhappy, Dana returned to Colorado in September 1884 where he sold real estate in Colorado Springs. In the spring of 1885, he surveyed for the Colorado railroads and then moved in 1887 to Glenwood Springs to become a construction superintendent. He preached briefly there in a Unitarian church, where he met Adine Rowena Waggener. They were married on 15 November 1888; there were no children.

Dana's article, "The Public School," in the *Denver Arbitrator* (16 Feb. 1889), questioned the quality of public education and influenced the superintendent of the Denver school board to appoint (May 1889) Dana as first librarian of Denver School District No. 1 (later the Denver Public Library) and as secretary of the board of education. This library was created under a new state law allowing school boards to levy taxes to purchase library books for public use. Dana's library opened with about 2,000 volumes and three reading rooms, including one for women. He had no specific training for librarianship but immediately began publicizing the library and within the first six months it circulated over 6,000 volumes. Dana developed collections useful to Denver citizens, including business material and picture files; began, in conjunction with the Colorado Medical Association, a medical collection that later became the Denver Medical Library; opened reference shelves to the public; began a circulating picture collection (1891) for children that could be loaned to school classes; established a separate children's department (1894); and started museum collections and exhibits.

Although he was popular, Dana was personally attacked for acquiring "goldbug" literature when free silver was a dominant local cause, but he defended his right to stock and to circulate literature that presented both sides of this topic. Finally, Dana supported the Denver Mercantile Library when the local chamber of commerce attacked the school board for supporting it with tax funds.

Feeling he could accomplish more elsewhere, Dana went in 1898 to the City Library of Springfield, Massachusetts, a large, established library system with a collection of about 100,000 volumes but serious physical barriers to its easy use. Dana made the library a strong social force in the community and employed many of the procedures he had used successfully in Denver. With a $90,000 bequest for materials in economics and in the social sciences, he established the David Ames Wells Economic Library.

In four years, circulation increased 45 percent but problems arose for Dana over the art museum and the museum of natural history, which Dana wanted to run along with the library. This conflicted with a wealthy private collector and curator of the art museum with more traditional views. Dana was unhappy with his situation and when it did not improve, he resigned in 1901 to become librarian of the Free Public Library of Newark, New Jersey, in 1902.

Dana spent the rest of his life at Newark and made his most innovative and long-lasting impact on American librarianship by making the Newark library one of the most successful urban public libraries in the United States. The library opened branches throughout the city, perhaps the most notable of which was the business branch, which opened in 1904 in the Newark business district.

Three major developments marked Dana's career at Newark. The first was intense publicity to bring the library to people's attention. Through library publications and other publicity material, Dana advertised the library and its work as no other American librarian to that time had done. The American Library Association (ALA) named its public relations award for him. His second accomplishment was the establishment of the Newark Business Library in the business district to collect "everything we can find relating to business." Finally, Dana's career at Newark was highlighted by his museum development.

There were no museum facilities in Newark in 1902, for the city was culturally overshadowed by New York, and so Dana decided to exhibit American art (1903). In 1905, he opened a science museum on the library's fourth floor and founded the Newark Museum Association in 1909. He made the Newark Museum as popular as the library. To attract children, he established a junior museum in 1913 in the Newark Public Library with exhibitions labeled and designed to appeal to young people.

When World War I forced the closing of the branches in rented quarters, Dana proposed the use of city-owned buildings; he also saw the need for books for the armed services and was one of the "movers" in the ALA committee that organized book collections in various states. During the war hysteria Dana resisted attempts to remove German books from library shelves; he opposed censorship on the basis of anything except the best principles of book selection.

Dana was a prominent national figure with an active interest in library associations and organizations. In 1892 he began a long and often stormy relationship with the ALA. As its president (1896), Dana drew up a petition to establish a school library section to emphasize the importance of "appropriate book collections" to school boards. However, he soon became one of the ALA's severest critics, attacking the ALA leadership for not accomplishing as much for the library profession as Dana felt that it should. As examples, he used the ALA's refusal to incorporate the Special Libraries Association, its cumbersome direction of important matters, and its failure to bring its members together for the greater advancement of the organization.

Shortly after the formation of Newark's business branch, Dana contacted other special librarians, who suggested a national library association to serve their needs. At the ALA conference in Bretton Woods, New Hampshire, in 1909, Dana invited those interested persons to meet with him to form the Special Libraries Association; he was its first president. At the ALA Mackinac Island Conference the next year, Dana tried to incorporate the new association into the ALA; the failure of that move heightened Dana's dissatisfaction with the ALA.

Dana participated in civic activities to establish the library as a social force. At Newark he played an important role in the community, accomplishing much for the library and for the museum by using his political influence. He was a prolific writer who contributed frequently to newspapers, to periodicals, and to professional publications; he also published numerous pamphlets and broadsides. Much of his writing was designed to assist others to practice his developments. His published work ranges from 1889 (a note to *Library Journal* on the establishment of the Denver Public Library) to 1929 (the posthumously published "Libraries and Fiction").

Dana had other interests, including a lifelong one in printing, which he carried into his library career. He also used hand tools and maintained an extensive carpenter's shop, where he designed and built model boxes to carry and to display museum objects as well as a simple device to move display cases. He spent summers at Woodstock farming and served for two years on the executive committee of the Windsor County Fair.

Dana avoided personal publicity and declined honorary degrees from Dartmouth, Rutgers, and Princeton, but he prized a directorship in the Deutscher Werkbund and honorary membership in the Chinese Library Association. He had few close personal friends but was fondly known as the "First Citizen of Newark." Though his staff often found it difficult to keep up with his pace, they generally liked and appreciated him. From 1923 he was in poor health, and he died in New York. He was buried in Woodstock.

• The official papers of John Cotton Dana are in several repositories. The Newark Public Library has five, three-drawer metal cabinets with Dana material and library scrapbooks in its Special Collections Division as well as a Dana press and font. The Denver Public Library has three scrapbooks (1891–1897), clippings, correspondence, booklets, and typed copies of four Dana letters. The Springfield, Mass., City Library has file material and unpublished manuscripts. Dartmouth College Archives has Dana's college diary as a freshman (1874–1875). The American Library Association Archives at the University of Illinois at Urbana-Champaign has a small amount of Dana's correspondence and his personal folder (1891–1919). The Woodstock (Vt.) Historical Society, located on the Dana family homestead, has only secondary sources. A description of the house that was such an important part of Dana's life is in *Colonial Homes*, Feb. 1992, pp. 52–55, 119. For compilations of Dana's publications, see the works of Hazel A. Johnson and Beatrice Winser: "John Cotton Dana," *Library Quarterly* 7 (Jan. 1937): 50–98, *Librarian at Large; Selected Writings of John Cotton Dana* (1991), *Libraries: Addresses and Essays* (1916; repr. 1966), and *Publications Written or Edited by John Cotton Dana* (1917).

See also Jon Eldridge, "The John Cotton Dana Legacy: Promoting Libraries for Users," *Wilson Library Bulletin* 66 (Apr. 1992): 46–50, 134; Richard Grove, "Pioneers in American Museums: John Cotton Dana," *Museum News* 56 (May–June 1971): 32–39, 86–88; Chalmers Hadley, *John Cotton Dana: A Sketch* (1943); "John Cotton Dana: A Contemporary Appraisal of His Contributions and Lasting Influence on the Library and Museum Worlds 60 Years after His Death," *Art Library Journal* 15, no. 2 (1990): 5–9; Frank Kingdon, *John Cotton Dana; A Life* (1940); Barbara Lipton, "John Cotton Dana and the Newark Museum," *Museum Quarterly* 30 (Spring–Summer 1979): 1–58; and Marian M. Winser, "John Cotton Dana and the Special Libraries Association," *Special Libraries* 50 (May 1959): 208–11. An obituary is in the *New York Times*, 22 July 1929, and a tribute, "A Wise Leader and a Great Friend," is in *The Library* 3 (July–August 1929).

MARTIN J. MANNING

DANA, Richard (26 June 1700–17 May 1772), lawyer, justice of the peace, and resistance leader, was born in Cambridge, Massachusetts, the son of Daniel Dana, a selectman of Cambridge, and Naomi Croswell. Little is known of his early life. In 1718 he graduated from Harvard College, where his roommate was John Hancock, father of the famous patriot and in 1721 he was inoculated against smallpox. He then began to practice law in Marblehead, Massachusetts. The Massachusetts General Court appointed him notary public for the ports of Marblehead and Salem in 1733, a post he held until Marblehead elected him to the House of Representatives for one term, his only one, in 1738. In 1737 he married Lydia Trowbridge, the daughter of Thomas Trowbridge and sister of Judge Edmund Trowbridge of the prominent Cambridge family. The couple had nine children, one of whom was the revolutionary patriot and Massachusetts statesman Francis Dana. Richard Dana and Edmund Trowbridge remained lifelong friends although Trowbridge became a Loyalist during the Revolution.

In 1745, the year after Dana moved to Charlestown, Massachusetts, Governor William Shirley appointed him as a justice of the peace for Middlesex County. He lost that post in 1748, when he relocated to the South End of Boston, which remained his home for the rest of his life. He regained his justiceship in 1756. Meanwhile, Dana practiced law in Boston, where he was accorded great respect. Not only did the town use him for much of its legal business and entrust him with the important post of overseer of the poor, but he also frequently presided over the sometimes tempestuous town meetings. John Adams recorded and approved of his nickname, "Father Dana."

Dana was a bitter foe of Thomas Hutchinson and was considered the equal of Boston resistance leaders James Otis and Samuel Adams by his contemporaries. An example of his vehemence was an argument in which he "was all on fire, his face was inflated and empurpled, he thundered and lightened" in attacking Hutchinson, leaving his adversary Edmund Trowbridge "as pale as death" (William Ellery to Richard Henry Dana, 10 Mar. 1819, Dana Family Papers). Dana was a charter member of Boston's Sons of Liberty, which selected him out of all the town's justices of the peace to hear Stamp Master Andrew Oliver's forced oath of 17 December 1765 promising never to enforce the Stamp Act. Dana also served on the town committee that "investigated" the Boston Massacre of 5 March 1770. In this capacity he tried to show the world that innocent townspeople had been brutally murdered, while he conveniently ignored the fact that six beleaguered soldiers were taunted and pelted with snowballs, ice, and rocks by a large mob.

Dana died suddenly in Boston and was greatly mourned by the patriots. An obituary in the *Boston Gazette* of 1 June 1772 noted that "he was exemplary in Carefulness, Diligence, and Frugality, whereby he has left . . . a handsome Fortune. . . . HE HATED FLATTERY" and was "a most inveterate enemy to Luxury and Prodigality. . . . a passionate opposer of all those (even from the highest to the lowest, but especially the former) who in his Judgment were Enemies to the Civil and Religious Rights of his Country, and he very well understood what those Rights were."

• Some of Dana's papers may be found in the Dana Family Papers at the Massachusetts Historical Society in Boston. Clifford K. Shipton's sketch in *Sibley's Harvard Graduates*, vol. 6 (1942), pp. 236–39, incorporates what little material survives on Dana's life from scattered sources.

WILLIAM PENCAK

DANA, Richard Henry (15 Nov. 1787–2 Feb. 1879), essayist and poet, was born in Cambridge, Massachusetts, the son of Francis Dana, a lawyer and judge, and Elizabeth Ellery. Born into a socially prominent and affluent family, Dana was educated at Harvard, although his years there were framed by family tragedies. He entered the school in 1804, the year of the family's loss of much of its fortune due to unsound investments by an older brother. Next he was expelled from the university without a degree for taking part in a student rebellion in 1807, the year of his mother's death. He then studied law, first in Newport where he had lived with his maternal grandparents from age ten to fifteen, then in Baltimore, passing the bar in 1811. In an autobiographical sketch prepared for Rufus

Griswold in 1841, Dana attributed his unenthusiastic practice of the law to "feeble health and great constitutional sensitiveness," and he limited his practice after the first few years to representing relatives from England in their business transactions in the United States.

Instead of law, Dana devoted himself to literary pursuits—partly, he declared at mid-life, a reaction against the Lockeian rationalism he was exposed to at Harvard and partly through the influence of early-life friendships with the painter Washington Allston and with Edward Tyrell Channing, brother of the elder William Ellery Channing. In 1814 Dana helped establish the *North American Review*, assisting E. T. Channing in editing the journal in 1818. A review he wrote in 1819 of William Hazlitt's *Lectures on the English Poets* persuasively attacked the prevailing estimation of Alexander Pope as in the first rank of English poets, alienating him from most of his *Review* associates. In expressing a preference for "the great depth of the sentiment and the utter, beautiful simplicity of the language" of William Wordsworth over "the one unvarying note from the pipe of Pope" (Dana, vol. 2, pp. 261–62, 200), Dana committed himself to the Romantic idealism reflected in his later stories and verse.

All of Dana's fiction (four novellas whose melodramatic plots are dominated by heroes of Romantic sensibilities) was published in the *Idle Man*, a magazine he founded in New York in 1821, which folded for lack of readership in six months. The first two of his poems to be published appeared in 1825 in the *New York Review*, whose editor, William Cullen Bryant, Dana had befriended when he assisted in arranging for the publication of Bryant's "Thanatopsis" in 1817 in the *North American Review*. Despite sharp differences in their political and religious beliefs, Dana and Bryant remained close friends until Bryant's death in 1878.

A slim volume of Dana's poetry, *The Buccaneer and Other Poems*, was published in 1827. "The Buccaneer," a long narrative poem concerning the reappearance of a ghost ship after the massacre of its passengers, was one of the best-known American poems throughout the 1830s. Its use of the theme of retribution through a supernatural agent reveals the influence of Samuel Taylor Coleridge's *The Rime of the Ancient Mariner*. Dana's publications after that date are limited to a few poems and a handful of reviews and essays. In 1833 he published a volume containing his writings for the *Idle Man* and the score of poems he had written. In 1835 the last of his essays, "Law As Suited to Man," appeared in the *Biblical Repository and Quarterly Observer*. In 1850 he issued a two-volume edition of his complete poems, stories, essays, and reviews.

From 1839 to 1851 Dana lectured throughout the Northeast on William Shakespeare—sometimes presenting a course of eight lectures over a period of several weeks, other times a single lecture drawn from the course. The lectures were popular and were an important source of income for Dana during this period, but they were never published. His characterization of

Hamlet in Lecture 8 as "one of your introspective, meditative, moralizing, refined, sensitive beings, living in his own ideal, and shrinking from the actual" seems more accurate as a self-portrait than as one of Hamlet. Dana spent the remainder of his years in solitary study.

Like his friend Bryant, Dana was often referred to in his lifetime as a "patriarch" of American letters—having been somewhat influential in the formative years (1815–1835) of an American belles lettres tradition. His poetry and literary criticism displayed the strong influence of British sources. In a diary entry for 23 April 1850, marking the recent death of Wordsworth, Dana identifies Shakespeare, Wordsworth, and Coleridge as the three main influences on his life and thought. Entries in his diaries from 1844 through 1863 include hundreds of comments on and quotes from his readings of British authors from Geoffrey Chaucer to Robert Southey but virtually no entries on American writers. Unlike Bryant, Dana remained politically aloof and became increasingly conservative as he withdrew from public life. In 1851 he responded to an invitation to write for the antislavery publication the *Liberty Bell* by stating that there were important differences between his views and those of the abolitionists, that he was "an Old Tory" who had reservations about women taking part in public concerns and who had no faith in or liking for democracy.

Dana was married in 1813 to Ruth Charlotte Smith. They had four children before her death in 1822. One of their children was Richard Henry Dana, Jr., author of *Two Years before the Mast* (1840). Dana died at his residence in Boston.

• Dana's papers, including the manuscript of his lectures on Shakespeare and his diaries, are in the Dana Family Collection at the Massachusetts Historical Society. His *Poems and Prose Writings* (1850) was republished in 1970. George H. Whittemore's "Our Eldest Poet" appeared in the 9 Jan. and 16 Jan. 1879 issues of the Boston weekly *The Watchman* just before Dana's death. An important assessment after Dana's death is Richard Henry Stoddard, "Richard Henry Dana," *Harper's New Monthly Magazine*, Apr. 1879, pp. 769–76. Two unpublished doctoral dissertations on Dana are Doreen May Hunter, "Richard Henry Dana, Sr.: An American Romanticist" (Univ. of California, Berkeley, 1969), and George M. Weimer, "Richard Henry Dana, the Elder, Critic" (New York Univ., 1920).

JOSEPH FLIBBERT

DANA, Richard Henry, Jr. (1 Aug. 1815–6 Jan. 1882), lawyer and author, was born in Cambridge, Massachusetts, the son of Richard Henry Dana, Sr., a poet and journalist, and Ruth Charlotte Smith. After routine earlier schooling, Dana interrupted his attendance at Harvard College because of weakened eyesight aggravated by measles. In August 1834 he sailed from Boston as a common seaman on a five-month voyage around Cape Horn and on to California, where he then worked ashore mainly at collecting, storing, and curing hides. He returned home in September 1836, resumed his studies at Harvard, graduated with the class

of 1837, was confirmed in the Episcopal Cathedral Church of St. Paul, in Boston, and studied at Dane Law School, Harvard (1837–1840). He was admitted to the bar (1840) and began a lucrative private practice, largely in admiralty law.

Dana, a man of great energy, wrote *Two Years before the Mast* and taught elocution at Harvard while attending classes there. His book, published in 1840, was an immediate success in the United States and in England, and it permanently influenced works about the sea, making their authors both more realistic about and also more cognizant of the common sailor's plight. About thirty books with titles echoing Dana's were published by 1860. The most notable literary beneficiary was Herman Melville, who in Chapter 24 of *White-Jacket* (1850) calls *Two Years before the Mast* "unmatchable" and whose *Moby-Dick* (1851) shows several traces of its influence. Unfortunately, Dana sold all rights to his book for $250 to the Harper publishing firm, which netted some $50,000 on the narrative until the original copyright expired in 1869. Dana, however, was happy that the popularity of his book caused his law practice to flourish.

Two Years before the Mast, a many-faceted literary classic, appeals to juvenile readers and sensitive adults alike. It records an observant young man's twenty-five months at sea and in primitive California. The many details of seagoing life are presented engagingly. Even as the narrative portrays the maturing of a green hand into an experienced, daring sailor, it becomes an archetypal yarn about a youth who, like dozens of legendary heroes, steps over the home threshold into places of challenging danger, learns self-control afloat and ashore, wins out, and returns home mature and fundamentally changed.

In 1841 Dana married Sarah Watson in Hartford, Connecticut. (The couple eventually had six children, including Richard Henry Dana III, who married Henry Wadsworth Longfellow's daughter Edith.) The same year Dana published *The Seaman's Friend*, a popular handbook on seamanship, customs at sea, and the duties and rights of sailors, officers, and masters both at sea and on shore. At this time, Dana began to keep a journal that became a repository for almost daily comments (to 1860) on his personal and professional activities in and near Boston; sketches of persons, places, and events noted when he was briefly away from home; and accounts of his more extended vacations in England, France, and around the world.

In 1842 Dana began a successful career as a conservative public lecturer on topics relating to law, politics, and patriotism. Two years later he took on Francis Edward Parker, a well-connected Bostonian, as his law partner and gradually became involved in practical politics. In 1848 he attended the National Free-Soil Convention in Buffalo, to the displeasure of materialistic Bostonians; in 1851–1852 he defended persons accused of freeing Shadrach, a slave apprehended under terms of the Fugitive Slave Act of 1850, again agonizing well-to-do Bostonians. In 1853 Dana participated in the Massachusetts Constitutional Convention. Then in 1854, after unsuccessfully defending Anthony Burns, a more famous fugitive slave caught in Boston, he was attacked on the street at night by an ex-boxer hired by prosouthern elements. The thug hit Dana with an iron bar over his right eye and nearly killed him. Too much a theorist and a purist, Dana did not join the emerging Republican party in 1855, although he campaigned on the state level for office-seeking friends favoring Free-Soil policies and opposing Know-Nothing tactics. A signal honor occurred for Dana, also in 1855, when he was asked to become one of the original members of a Boston social gathering that two years later formally became the Saturday Club. Other members included scientist Louis Agassiz, writers Ralph Waldo Emerson, James Russell Lowell, and John Lothrop Motley, and literary critic Edwin Percy Whipple.

In 1856 Dana enjoyed a six-week summer vacation in England and France, during which he saw, for the first time in his life, many of the historic and literary shrines he had only read about and also dined with several influential figures in public life. A rather frenzied trip to Cuba in 1859 resulted in *To Cuba and Back* (1859), a charming but spotty and hastily written travel book that describes Havana, the socioeconomic, political, religious, and cultural life of Cuba, the arduous slave life on a sugar plantation owned by a rich friend, and even a bullfight. Dana seems not to have known how to relax. Overwork in the summer of 1859 caused him to suffer a fainting fit. When his physician ordered him to take another sea voyage, he did so—alone and with a vengeance. For 433 days he went around the world, stopping at Cuba, Panama, California, Hawaii, China, Japan, India, Arabia, Egypt, Greece, Italy, Switzerland, Germany, the Netherlands, and England and advancing his journal, by careful commentary on everything of significance, to its grand total of 600,000 words.

The following years saw Dana's greatest professional success, but also several humiliations. In 1861 President Abraham Lincoln appointed Dana to be U.S. district attorney for Massachusetts. He held this position for five years, the high point of which was his successful Supreme Court defense of the federal position concerning Civil War "Prize Cases"—that is, the legality of seizing enemy vessels by Union forces. Lincoln personally commended him. But in 1866, almost immediately after editing and publishing *Henry Wheaton's Elements of International Law*, Dana was sued for plagiarism by William Beach Lawrence, the previous editor of the book. The case dragged on until 1879, soured Dana's later years, and resulted in his being found guilty of "infringement" in some fourteen separate passages. Dana served two terms in the Massachusetts legislature representing Cambridge (1867–1869). During part of this time (1867–1868) he was retained by the law department of President Andrew Johnson's administration to recommend treatment of Jefferson F. Davis, the defeated president of the former Confederate states. Dana proposed dropping all charges of high treason against Davis, was successfully sup-

ported by fellow moderates, but lost popularity in the eyes of vengeful political radicals in Massachusetts. Not surprisingly, Dana, a moderate Republican, was defeated by Benjamin F. Butler (1818–1893), a radical and unprincipled Republican candidate, in their 1868 contest for election to the U.S. House of Representatives. Far sadder was Dana's being nominated in 1876 by President Ulysses S. Grant to be minister to England, only to have the coveted honor—and the dream of his life—blocked in the Senate by unscrupulous political and personal enemies, including Butler and also Pennsylvania's patronage senator Simon Cameron, who called Dana "one of those damn literary fellers." Others accused him of being a plagiarist, a high-priced attorney, and the kid-gloved "Duke of Cambridge."

Retiring from law in 1878, Dana spent his last years in France, Switzerland, and Italy, casually studying international law (in the unrealized hope of writing a definitive treatise on the subject) and sightseeing with his wife. He died in Rome.

• Unpublished material by and concerning Dana is in the Massachusetts Historical Society, Boston; the Longfellow House and the Women's Archives of Radcliffe College, Cambridge, Massachusetts; and the Library of Congress and the National Archives, Washington, D.C. Autobiographies by Dana are *An Autobiographical Sketch (1815–1842)*, ed. Robert F. Metzdorf (1953), and *The Journal of Richard Henry Dana, Jr.*, ed. Robert F. Lucid (3 vols., 1968). A bibliography of Dana's writings can be found in *Speeches in Stirring Times and Letters to a Son*, ed. Richard Henry Dana III (1910). See also Charles Francis Adams, *Richard Henry Dana: A Biography* (2 vols., 1890; rev. ed. 1891; repr. 1983), a standard nineteenth-century work, stressing Dana's moral, social, and professional virtues; Samuel Shapiro, *Richard Henry Dana, Jr.: 1815–1882* (1961), written with a political slant; and Robert L. Gale, *Richard Henry Dana, Jr.* (1969), emphasizing the literary quality of Dana's varied output.

ROBERT L. GALE

DANA, Samuel Luther (11 July 1795–11 Mar. 1868), chemist, was born in Amherst, New Hampshire, the son of Luther Dana, a merchant and sea captain, and Lucy Giddings. His elder brother was James Freeman Dana, the Harvard and Columbia chemist with whom he would collaborate in geological surveying. Both boys were educated at Phillips Academy, Exeter, New Hampshire, and Harvard University, where Samuel received his A.B. in 1813. After a stint in the law office of his uncle, Judge Samuel Dana of Charlestown, Massachusetts, he accepted a commission as a second lieutenant in the artillery and served from 1813 until the end of the War of 1812, in 1815. Thereafter he returned to Harvard, where he earned his M.D. from the medical school in 1818. From that year until 1826 he practiced medicine in Massachusetts, first in Gloucester and then in Waltham. At the beginning of this time he collaborated with his brother in a survey that was jointly published in the *Memoirs of the American Academy of Arts and Sciences* (1818), "Outlines of the Mineralogy and Geology of Boston and Its Vicinity, with a Geological Map." In 1820 he married Ann Theodora Willard, the daughter of Harvard's seventh president.

During the years of his medical practice in the country's fabric-producing center, Dana became more and more interested in the chemical aspects of textile manufacture, and in 1826 he constructed a factory in Waltham that made sulfuric acid and bleaching powder (calcium hypochlorite). In 1828 his wife died, and he married her sister Augusta. Dana had a total of four children. His firm merged with the Newton (Mass.) Chemical Company, and Dana remained with the company until 1833 as superintendent and chemist. In that year he visited Europe, observing textile production and publishing a paper on sulfuric acid manufacture. In 1834 he became chemist of the Merrimac Print Works in Lowell, Massachusetts, and introduced a number of changes that earned a worldwide reputation for Lowell textiles. His improvements included the "American system" of bleaching fabric before printing, and he made extensive studies of the use of madder, or turkey red, a dye obtained from the root of an Old World plant. Among other things, he found that the removal of traces of the mordant used in the dye printing process, carried out at the time with cow dung, could be accomplished with the active ingredient of the dung, sodium phosphate.

These investigations led to an interest in manures and their applications in agriculture. "Manures" was a term of broad application in the nineteenth century, referring not just to animal excreta but to composts and all forms of artificial plant foods. Dana informed himself about every aspect of the subject, in many cases through his own chemical research on manures, soils, irrigation, bone meals, and a variety of other topics of interest to agriculturalists. He presented his findings first as a series of lectures on chemistry as applied to agriculture, given before interested citizens of Lowell, then as the first of some five editions of *A Muck Manual, for Farmers* (1842; 5th ed., 1855). He defended the "homely title" of the volume in the preface to the fifth edition: "I shall not discredit my child by being ashamed of his name. It was good at the christening, and I trust will be thought respectable in manhood." In addition to the *Muck Manual*, Dana published his prize-winning "Essay on Manures" (1843), submitted to the Massachusetts Society for the Promotion of Agriculture. This paper was reprinted virtually unaltered in the second series of *Rural Hand Books* published by Saxton in 1856.

In his fifties Dana became interested in problems of lead in drinking water, arising principally from pipes in use at the time. The outcome of this interest was *Lead Diseases* (1848), a translation from the French of L. Tanquerel des Planches's treatise on the subject. He also took up the manufacture of oil from rosin and produced his usual technical advances in this area. Dana's journal publications were few over his lifetime, for he was a research employee of companies that preferred to withhold their trade secrets. Nonetheless, he had a strong effect on the textile printing industry and

was one of the pioneers of scientific agriculture in this country. To this latter end, like other agricultural chemists of his generation, he spent much of his time in his later years testing his ideas by actual farming. Dana died in Lowell, Massachusetts.

• W. J. Youmans, *Pioneers of Science in America*, contains an account of Dana. Dirk J. Struik, *Yankee Science in the Making* (1948), contains a short life of Dana and an excellent sketch of the Boston geological survey. Brief mention is in Edgar F. Smith, *Chemistry in America* (1914). An obituary notice is in the *American Journal of Science* (May 1868): 424–25.

ROBERT M. HAWTHORNE JR.

DANA, Samuel Whittelsey (13 Feb. 1760–21 July 1830), lawyer, congressman, and U.S. senator, was born in Wallingford, Connecticut, the son of James Dana, a staunchly "Old Light" Congregational minister, and Catherine Whittelsey. In 1775, at age fifteen, Samuel graduated with high honors from Yale College. Moving to the vibrant Connecticut River port of Middletown, an affluent center for the West Indies trade, Dana read law under Judge J. T. Hosmer. He joined the Connecticut bar in 1778 and connected himself to the wealthy, and decidedly Federalist, mercantile community around him. He enhanced his reputation with a brigadier generalship in the Connecticut militia. Dana served in the Connecticut Assembly from 1789 until late 1796, when voters in the Middletown district elected him to replace Uriah Tracy in Congress. After the resignation of James Hillhouse in 1810, the assembly transferred Dana to the U.S. Senate.

In 1820, near the end of Dana's career in national politics, John Quincy Adams described him as a "uniformly high-toned federalist," referring to the elitist assumptions about politics and society shared by most New England Federalists of Dana's generation. His public record was one of consistent ideological and sectional hostility toward Jeffersonian Republicanism. Like most Americans who experienced the Revolution, Dana despised monarchy and systems of hereditary ranking, but he still thought in hierarchical terms, with deference to merit expected of the common citizen. "When men are distinguished by their burdens," he observed on the House floor in 1798, "ought they not to be distinguished also by their privileges?" His classically conservative views assumed more systematic style in a pair of formal treatises: *Essay on Political Society* (1800) and *Specimen of Republican Institutions* (1802). The former work, his clearest statement of political philosophy, viewed society narrowly, as the combination of two major groups: "the rich, the few, the rulers" and "the poor, the many, the ruled." The *Essay* defined liberty, whose meaning was hotly debated in Dana's era, as "exemption from useless restraint."

For Dana, the crisis that led to the Alien and Sedition Acts in 1798 was a chance to refine the views published later and to help orchestrate a public policy based on Federalist political philosophy. Viewing immigrants as disruptive generally, Dana argued that laws to restrict "dangerous" aliens were rooted in the inherent power of government to preserve itself. Convinced that the ordinary public was fickle, corruptible, and susceptible to demagogues, civil liberty had to be construed tightly: the First Amendment provided no "license to injure others." The outspoken Republican congressman Matthew Lyon, prosecuted under the Sedition Act, was a "kernel of filth." Dana supported the anti-Jeffersonian Judiciary Act of 1801, protested the repeal of internal taxes that had protected importers while burdening landholders, and objected to the impeachment of Justice Samuel Chase.

A self-declared "statesman of the school of Washington," Dana deplored "party spirit," declaring it "an evil which perhaps time only will cure." But he stuck to Federalist positions, especially in foreign policy. He called for repeal of the 1778 alliance with the French who, under Napoleon in the 1790s, had "set at defiance every moral principle." The Louisiana Purchase drew his scorn as an over-extension of presidential power. He cursed Thomas Jefferson's embargo as an archaic, "old colonial" system, designed to hinder the "talents, enterprise, and integrity" of the merchant class and erode the patriotism of the community. For similar reasons, he opposed nonintercourse and, between 1806 and 1812, defined the Federalist strategy of arming merchantmen as an alternative to all-out war against Britain. Though in no respect a "war hawk," Dana still promoted defensive naval power, with frigates instead of "mere gunboats." His concern was to protect merchant vessels along the Atlantic coast; confrontation with the British on the open sea was another matter.

More politically cunning than many Federalists and less prominent than some, Dana opted for a path of survival after 1812 rather than flinging himself on a flaming pyre of archaic principles. As a member of the Senate, Dana voted against the declaration of war, but he played little direct role in Federalist dissent during that struggle. He steered clear of the Hartford Convention in 1814–1815, despite obvious philosophical sympathy with sentiments expressed there. After the war, his positions consistently mirrored sectional interest. Following the inclinations of Connecticut bankers, he recoiled from the Second Bank of the United States in 1816. The perceived threat to New England from rapid frontier growth contributed to his stands against the 1816 "Bonus Bill" for internal improvements and the Land Act of 1820, which ended an ill-advised credit system for public land sales. Against slavery on moral grounds and worried about disturbances to political harmony, he scorned the combined admission into the Union of Maine and Missouri in 1820 and urged a delay of statehood for the latter, noting "no occasion for haste" as long as "the people of Missouri were not in a state of suffering." Governmental retrenchment, a predictable concern after an expensive war, was the last major focus of Dana's Senate career, which ended, with little notice, in March 1821. For his life in public service, he had sacrificed the more extensive fortune he could have earned in private law practice. Before leaving Washington, he published *Observations on Public Principles and Characters* (1820), his political memoirs.

The Connecticut Republican landslide of 1818, putting Jeffersonians in lasting control of both legislative houses and the governorship, left Dana no chance of Senate reelection in 1820. He retreated to his law practice in Middletown, serving as mayor, beginning in 1822, and as chief judge of the Middlesex county court from 1825 until his death. Never marrying before age sixty-one, he took Mary Wyllys Pomeroy as his wife in July 1821; they had no children. Dana died in Middletown.

• The Beineke Library at Yale University contains a few scattered Dana letters and an unpublished essay on politics. His career in the House and Senate is best followed in Joseph Gales and William W. Seaton, comps., *Annals of Congress*, 2d sess., 8th Cong., 1797, through 2d sess., 16th Cong., 1821. Of particular value on the Federalists after 1800 is David Hackett Fischer, *The Revolution of American Conservatism: The Federalist Party in the Era of Jeffersonian Democracy* (1965), and Shaw Livermore, Jr., *The Twilight of Federalism: The Disintegration of the Federalist Party, 1815–1830* (1962). On Connecticut during the period of Dana's career, see Richard J. Purcell, *Connecticut in Transition, 1775–1818* (1963). An obituary is in the *Middletown Gazette*, 28 July 1830.

JOHN R. VAN ATTA

DANA, William Buck (26 Aug. 1829–10 Oct. 1910), publisher and entrepreneur, was born in Utica, New York, the son of James Dana, a hardware merchant, and Harriet Dwight. He was born into the local mercantile elite and into a family profoundly affected by contemporary religious revivals. Prior to graduating from Yale in 1851, Dana won election to Skull and Bones, and in his senior autograph book, a classmate prophetically praised his financial ability. Returning to Utica, he studied law with his father's counsel for a year and practiced successively with brother-in-law J. Wyman Jones and future brother-in-law N. Curtis White. Dana's dependence on class, kin, and friendship ties characterized his entire career. He prospered at law, learning management and, from clients, much about business. He also evidenced Utica's entrepreneurial spirit, becoming partner to a brother in an agricultural and seed warehouse and investing in the latter's screw company.

In 1861, two years after acquiring land for a residence in Englewood, New Jersey, which Jones was developing, Dana changed careers. Through Jones's influence he acquired *Hunt's Merchants' Magazine*, the country's leading business monthly, which had fallen on bad times. A year of mentoring from Isaac Smith Homans, Jr., editor of the *Banker's Magazine* and a Jones associate, and Dana's own skillful management brought success. The Civil War disrupted trade, increased production costs, and forced Dana to cut *Hunt's* from 144 to eighty pages per issue; nevertheless, Dana accumulated reserves from the profitable operation of the magazine.

Having seen the impact on Utica of the Erie Canal in the 1820s, the coming of the railroads in the 1830s, the formation of the first telegraph company, and the rise of manufacturing, Dana was sensitive to technological and economic change. He believed that the commercial impact of telegraphic and oceanic steamship communication and the restoration of the national union in 1865 would revive business. Forming a partnership with John G. Floyd, Jr., former law associate and brother of his wife, he published on 1 July 1865, in New York City, the initial edition of the nation's first weekly business newspaper, the *Commercial and Financial Chronicle*. Patterned after the London *Economist*, the *Chronicle*, in an era of press partisanship, pledged to be nonpartisan and independent. Anchored in Dana's Presbyterian morality, the constitutional law of Chancellor James Kent, and the free market economics of Francis Wayland (1796–1865), which he had studied at Yale, the paper advocated the principles of political economy, maintaining that the needs of the country's industrial and commercial interests were the only proper basis for public policy, and offered unrivaled comprehensiveness and accuracy. Following Wayland, Dana conceived of labor and capital as being properly involved in a harmonious relationship. Thus, he usually condemned strikes but, also, excesses on the part of capital in its relations with labor. In enabling businessmen to make informed decisions Dana intended not only to advocate correct principles, but to promote their operation as well. He promised much, and his thirty-two page weekly delivered.

The *Chronicle*, occupying a unique niche, flourished. At the end of 1870, it absorbed *Hunt's*. Subscribers at first numbered perhaps 4,500, increasing by 1910 to perhaps 17,000 of the country's most influential bankers, financiers, industrialists, and public officials. It also introduced special supplements that reported on the American Bankers' Association annual convention (1868), government and railroad securities (1875), electric railroads (1895), banking (1895), corporate securities (1903), and other subjects. The *Chronicle* averaged sixty pages weekly by 1910, the supplements (with up to three-fourths of its 500 yearly pages devoted to advertising) adding as many more. Offering supplements free to subscribers while keeping annual subscriptions at $10 throughout his life, Dana increased the value of his product and buttressed his market position. Core readership resided in the financial community: virtually every important bank in the country advertised in the *Chronicle*.

A gold Democrat, opponent of speculation, and proponent of economic orthodoxy, Dana made the *Chronicle* the nation's most authoritative business publication. As a consistent champion of a stable monetary system that reflected actual value, Dana opposed inflationary measures and could be found among those who condemned the Greenbackers and Populists. His paper, however, while taking positions on a wide range of politically charged economic and business issues, scrupulously adhered to its formally independent and nonpartisan stance. (Few persons outside his small circle of intimates knew that Dana was a Democrat.) Providing information for a key national audience, the *Chronicle* helped create a national marketplace. Its columns were, and remain for scholars, indispensable sources on the state of business during Dana's lifetime. When Floyd retired in 1894, the firm incorporated, with Dana as president and, initially, sole stockholder. He directed the paper until his death, although during his final years he transferred various stock holdings to corporate vice president and associate editor Jacob Seibert, Jr., and to treasurer and railroad affairs analyst Arnold Guyot Dana, who was his nephew. From 1871 to 1883 Dana also owned the Palisade Mountain House, a resort hotel in Englewood, and as many as 200 additional acres in the vicinity. Instrumental, with his protégé, William Outis Allison, in securing the separate incorporation of Englewood Cliffs in 1895, Dana held various borough offices, serving as mayor from 1903 to 1910.

Dana published two books: *Cotton from Seed to Loom* (1878) fixed him as an authority on the world cotton trade; *A Day for Rest and Worship* (1911) posthumously expressed his religious convictions. He and his wife, Katherine Floyd, whom he married in 1855, shared a striking love and intellectual partnership. The Danas adopted three children. In 1908, hoping for an heir to carry on the company, he adopted his grandson. He died in New York City, leaving an estate of some $2 million including the *Chronicle*, correctly termed by the publisher (11 Apr. 1939) as "at once his biography and his monument." This first American business weekly, taking advantage of modern communication, set the standard for all business journals to follow.

• Very little has been written about Dana. His personal papers are in two collections, one at the archives of the William Floyd Estate, a unit of Fire Island National Seashore, Mastic Beach, N.Y., the other (some unduplicated originals, many copies) in the possession of Douglas Steeples. Scattered items are in the Yale University Archives; items relating to Dana's New Jersey real estate holdings are in the Bergen County Administration Building, Hackensack, N.J.; Dana's estate records are in the Suffolk County Surrogate Court, Riverhead, N.Y.; a few letters are in the holdings of the Manuscript Division of the Library of Congress. Mary Ryan, *Cradle of the Middle Class: The Family in Oneida County, New York, 1790–1865* (1981), offers important background material, including some references to the Dana family. The only published material on Dana himself is Douglas Steeples, "Dana and the Chronicle," *Essays on Economic and Business History* 10 (1992): 152–67 and *Long Island Forum* 53 (1991): 27–35, and "Young Will Dana: The Education of an Entrepreneur," *Essays on Economic and Business History* 11 (1993): 326–43.

DOUGLAS STEEPLES

DANCY, John Campbell, Jr. (13 Apr. 1888–10 Sept. 1968), Detroit Urban League executive director, was born in Salisbury, North Carolina, the son of John C. Dancy, a public official, and Laura Coleman. Brought up with three siblings in a comfortable, educated, southern family, he embraced his father's commitment to the African Methodist Episcopal Zion church and Booker T. Washington's accommodationism. His father was a successful typesetter, schoolteacher, newspaper editor, county politician, collector of customs in Wilmington, North Carolina, and recorder of deeds in Washington, D.C. Young Dancy attended Livingstone College (grade school), Phillips Exeter Academy (prep school), and the University of Pennsylvania. He studied sociology and graduated in 1910 but shied from the Republican party politics that benefited his father. He wed Maude Bulkley in 1917, and after her death in 1931, he married Malinda Wells, who died in 1964. He had no children.

Initially, Dancy became principal of Smallwood Institute in Claremont, Virginia, and secretary of a Young Men's Christian Association in Norfolk, both black institutions. In 1916 he entered New York City to become secretary of the Big Brother Program, later remembering his assistance to a very young Countee Cullen, the Harlem Renaissance poet. There he also came in contact with Eugene K. Jones, executive secretary of the National Urban League, who influenced him to serve as industrial secretary of the metropolitan area. Two years later, Dancy took the helm of the Detroit Urban League, succeeding Forrester B. Washington, and concentrating on job opportunities for black city dwellers. He brought workers and employees together through a personal diplomacy that turned on accommodationism and an antiunion position, producing mostly unskilled jobs in a racist climate and boom-bust economy. He also managed to place some blacks in skilled industrial and white-collar positions, often breaking the color line in Detroit's private and public sectors. During World War II Dancy shelved his antiunion position when the United Automobile Workers began enrolling black members and permitting them leadership roles in some locals and in the international and defense production needs reduced the league's role as an employment agent.

Long before that occurred, however, Dancy also pushed the league into travelers' aid, recreation, education, health, and housing. He provided southern migrants entering Detroit with temporary lodging and employment possibilities. Beyond sponsoring community dances and athletic contests for school-age children year round, he conceived of the Green Pastures Camp for poor and working-class youngsters. He established a baby clinic and promoted National Negro Health Week throughout Detroit's black neighborhoods. He furthered scholarship assistance to promising students and supported construction of the Brewster Homes, the first government-funded units for black Detroiters. Dancy also emphasized social etiquette and cultural programs, opening community centers in east side and northwest areas. In all of these endeavors, he appealed to corporate sponsorship or, in the case of the clinics and housing project, municipal and federal support, respectively.

From 1918 through the Second World War, Dancy sought equal, albeit oftimes separate treatment for black residents. Each of his programs addressed an area in which blacks, particularly new arrivals, were excluded from vital opportunities and services. Like his father, who owed his most important federal appointments to Booker T. Washington, he endeavored to work through existing structures with philanthropic-minded and, in some cases, segregation-minded whites. Hence Dancy's temperament, conservatism, allies, and United Community Services–funding from individuals and influential businesses required a low profile in legal and militant protests, lest he risk the loss of income necessary to operate the Detroit Urban League. In the Ossian Sweet case (1925), which was litigated by the National Association for the Advancement of Colored People (NAACP), he helped raise defense funds for the noted black physician accused of shooting white rioters who had opposed his move into their neighborhood; Dancy testified at Sweet's trial as an expert on housing conditions in Detroit. But Dancy acted as an individual, not as a DUL official. More often he stood well beyond conflict, as in the Sojourner Truth Housing controversy (1942), which turned bloody before black defense workers and their families—under armed guard—occupied the federally funded units that whites had opposed being located in their neighborhood.

In the face of changing racial attitudes and increased black militancy, Dancy and the DUL still played an important, though less prominent, role in postwar race relations. Less protest-minded than most black and union leaders of the period, he maintained contact with entrepreneurs, philanthropists, and politicians, now openly embracing unionism and integration as each became increasingly acceptable to black workers and white benefactors, respectively. He continued to enlighten many white leaders on racial issues and to administer a larger, more bureaucratic league facing new socioeconomic and demographic realities created by an expanding black population.

For forty-two years Dancy assisted hundreds of blacks, migrants and residents alike, and articulated the aspirations of thousands more. He also aided and inspired the development of numerous individuals, including surgeon Remus Robinson, social worker Geraldine Bledsoe, and artist Hughie Lee-Smith. He served as black Detroit's advocate and conduit, often as its only voice or one of its very few voices on various official and private bodies such as the Detroit House of Correction and the American Red Cross, and he facilitated similar appointments of other prominent blacks. An elitist, Dancy practiced "moral guardianship" (Levine, p. 122); an architect, he advanced "community building strategies" (Thomas, p. 63).

In his autobiography, *Sand against the Wind* (1966), Dancy advocated developing "a climate of good human relations" as the key to racial progress. He stressed persuasion over provocation and civility over confrontation; he seemed every bit a member of W. E. B. Du Bois's talented tenth, yet he embraced Booker T. Washington's gradualism and deference, altering his accommodation—as did Washingtonians elsewhere in the North—to meet changing urban conditions and Urban League principles. Dancy's leadership style was soft spoken and dignified. Sincere and accomplished, though limited by his own class bias and cultural distance from rank-and-file blacks, he symbolized an era in race relations that had ended long before his death in Detroit but that had benefited from his life. He presented one of many black viewpoints, helped build a community, bolstered its working and middle classes, and cultivated its white allies, which collectively assisted the civil rights movement of another generation.

• Influences in Dancy's early life can be gleaned from his father's papers in the Carnegie Library, Livingstone College, Salisbury, N.C. Dancy's personal papers are scant, while those of the Detroit Urban League are extensive; both collections are a part of the Michigan Historical Collections (MHC), Bentley Historical Library, University of Michigan. Oral histories of Dancy exist in his own and in the Alex Baskin Collection (MHC). In *Sand against the Wind*, Dancy provides insights into his life and beliefs. He advanced the Urban League in occasional articles such as "The Negro People in Michigan," *Michigan History Magazine* 24 (Spring 1940): 221–40. Richard W. Thomas, *Life for Us Is What We Make It* (1992), contains the fullest account of Dancy's Detroit years from 1915 to 1945 and places it in the context of black community efforts. David Allan Levine, *Internal Combustion* (1976), discusses Dancy briefly and less favorably during the 1915–1926 period, while August Meier and Elliott Rudwick, *Black Detroit and the Rise of the UAW* (1979), touches on his labor position during the critical years of unionization, 1937 to 1943. Dominic J. Capeci, Jr., *Race Relations in Wartime Detroit* (1984), does the same for the Sojourner Truth Housing controversy of 1942. An obituary is in the *Michigan Chronicle*, 21 Sept. 1968.

DOMINIC J. CAPECI, JR.

DANDRIDGE, Dorothy (9 Nov. 1922–8 Sept. 1965), movie actress and singer, was born Dorothy Jean Dandridge in Cleveland, Ohio, the daughter of Cyril Dandridge, a Baptist minister, and Ruby Jean Butler, a movie and radio comedienne. Dorothy, a child entertainer, was in and out of school while her mother directed and choreographed her two children in a sister vaudeville act. The "Wonder Kids" performed in Cleveland's black Baptist churches and toured throughout the South for five years.

In the early 1930s Ruby, whose husband had left her just before Dorothy's birth, moved her family to the Watts section of Los Angeles, California, to further their careers in show business. The Wonder Kids recruited another girl, Etta Jones, and formed a singing group called the Dandridge Sisters. In 1937 the act was sold to Warner Bros. for a movie called *A Day at the Races*. The Dandridge Sisters also made appearances at the Cotton Club in Harlem, New York, and toured with Duke Ellington, Cab Calloway, and Jimmy Lunceford.

The outbreak of World War II interrupted the Dandridge Sisters' international tour and initiated their demise. Around this time Dorothy Dandridge met Harold Nicholas, who was one of the famous dancing Nicholas Brothers, and in 1942 they were married. In 1945 Dandridge's only child was born, and Harold immediately deserted his family because their child was severely brain damaged. In later years Dandridge teamed up with both Rose Kennedy and Jacqueline Kennedy Onassis in an effort to help the mentally challenged under the auspices of the Joseph P. Kennedy, Jr., Foundation.

Dandridge's first important film role was Queen of the Jungle in Columbia Pictures' *Tarzan's Peril* (1951). Dore Schary of MGM then hired Dandridge to play a compassionate black schoolteacher in *Bright Road*, costarring Harry Belafonte. During this time, Dandridge began her night club and concert engagements. In 1951 band leader Desi Arnaz agreed to temporarily employ Dandridge in his act at the Hollywood Mocombo. This appearance compelled Maurice Winnick, a British theatrical impresario, to offer Dandridge an engagement at the Cafe de Paris in London. The next year the Chase Hotel in St. Louis, Missouri, which had never employed a black performer to entertain in its dining room, booked her for an engagement. Dandridge informed the management that she would not perform unless blacks were allowed to obtain reservations and be permitted to use the main entrance. These conditions were agreed upon by the hotel management, and a table was reserved for black members of the National Association for the Advancement of Colored People on opening night.

The most memorable and award-winning screen performance for Dandridge was in the title role of *Carmen Jones* (1954) produced by Otto Preminger in association with 20th Century–Fox. *Carmen Jones* costarred Pearl Bailey and Belafonte. In 1955 Dandridge became the first black actor to be nominated for an Oscar in a starring role and the first black woman to take part in the Academy Awards show, presenting the Oscar for film editing. Dandridge also won a Golden Globe Award of Merit for Outstanding Achievement for the best performance by an actress in 1959. Dandridge's international acclaim led 20th Century–Fox to offer her a three-year contract that was the first and most ambitious offer given to a black performer by that studio. During the same year, Dandridge became the first black headliner to appear at the Waldorf-Astoria Hotel in New York City.

During the 1950s Dandridge starred in several films for 20th Century–Fox, Columbia Pictures, and foreign film companies. *Island in the Sun* (1957), with James Mason, Joan Fontaine, and Belafonte, was Hollywood's first major interracial film and was a box office success. In *Tamango* (1959), Dandridge portrayed an African slave in love with a white ship captain, played by Austrian actor Curt Jurgens. She costarred with Sidney Poitier in *Porgy and Bess* (1959). In addition to her film credits, Dandridge appeared on several television shows during the 1950s including "The Mike Douglas Show," "The Steve Allen Show," and "The Ed Sullivan Show." In November 1954 she also appeared on the cover of *Life* magazine, making history as the first black to do so.

In 1959 Dandridge married Jack Dennison (or Denison), a white restaurateur and night club owner; the marriage ended in divorce in 1962. In 1961 Dandridge costarred in a film with Trevor Howard, titled *Malaga*. Dandridge's last concert appearances included engagements in Puerto Rico and Tokyo. Her death was reported as the result of acute drug intoxication, an ingestion of the antidepressant Tofranil at her apartment in West Hollywood, California.

A retrospective article in the *Los Angeles Herald Examiner* lamented that Dandridge's passing meant "the ceasing of exquisite music . . . she walked in beauty . . . regal as a queen." In her lifetime Dandridge was named by a committee of photographers as one of the five most beautiful women in the world. She was an international celebrity who believed in breaking down barriers to achieve racial equality. Dandridge realized that a black male could become a big star without romantic roles, but a sexy black actress like herself was limited because the American public was not ready for interracial romance on the screen. On 20 February 1977 Dandridge, the first black leading lady, was posthumously inducted into the Black Filmmakers Hall of Fame at the annual Oscar Micheaux Awards presentation in Oakland, California. Vivian Dandridge, her sister, accepted the award. In December 1983 Belafonte, Poitier, and others petitioned to secure a star on the Hollywood Walk of Fame for Dandridge, a trailblazer for blacks in the American film industry.

• A clippings file on Dandridge is in the Billy Rose Theatre Collection at the New York Public Library for the Performing Arts, Lincoln Center. Dandridge wrote an autobiography, *Everything and Nothing: The Dorothy Dandridge Tragedy* (1970), with Earl Conrad. A book-length biography is Earl Mills, *Dorothy Dandridge* (1991). Reliable information about Dandridge's life and films is in Patrick Agan, *The Decline and Fall of the Love Goddesses* (1979); Donald Bogle, *Brown Sugar: Eighty Years of America's Black Female Superstars* (1980); and Lindsay Patterson, *Anthology of the American Negro in the Theatre: A Critical Approach* (1967). A useful article for considering Dandridge's image in the 1950s is in *Life*, Nov. 1954, pp. 87–90. An obituary is in the *New York Times*, 8 Sept. 1965.

SAMUEL CHRISTIAN

DANDRIDGE, Ray (31 Aug. 1913–12 Feb. 1994), baseball player, was born Raymond Emmitt Dandridge in Richmond, Virginia, the son of Archie Dandridge, a cigarette factory worker, and Alberta Thompson. The family moved to Buffalo, New York, when Ray was ten years of age. There he participated in various sports, especially Golden Glove boxing and high school football. The latter sport led to a knee injury that plagued him in his later career. At age twenty he played for the Richmond Paramount Giants against the Detroit Stars of the Negro National League. The Paramount Giants gave his father $25, and Ray, packing a straw suitcase, boarded the bus to play with the Stars. He hit only .211 as a rookie in the Negro National League, and at season's end, he said, the team had to pawn its bus to raise the money to send him home.

Moving to the Newark Dodgers in 1934, Dandridge concentrated on hitting line drives instead of home runs. As a result he blossomed offensively, batting .436. Meantime, veteran players such as Jud Wilson and Dick Lundy taught the bowlegged youngster how to charge ground balls. "Dandridge had plenty of guts," one old-time pitcher said. "Guys used to fake bunts to draw the third baseman in. Some wouldn't come in too close. Dandridge would." Laughed another old-timer: "You could drive a freight train between his legs, but you couldn't drive a baseball through them." Nicknamed "Hooks," "because he had a great pair of hands," Dandridge grew into one of the best infielders of all time as well as a good line-drive hitter. Those who saw him play have compared him to Hall of Fame third baseman Brooks Robinson, who later played with the Baltimore Orioles.

The *Baseball Encyclopedia*, based on exhaustive research of newspaper box scores, credits Dandridge with a .369 batting average in 1935. As a result of this performance, he was selected to play in the East-West all-star game and in Puerto Rico over the winter, on a black all-star team matched against white major leaguers.

The Newark Dodgers changed their name to the Eagles in 1936, and Dandridge batted .301 and .354 for the next two years. In 1937 George "Mule" Suttles, the all time Negro home run champion, joined the Eagles at first base. With Willie "Devil" Wells at shortstop, Dick Seay at second base, and Dandridge at third base, the Eagles boasted "a million-dollar infield." Clark Griffith, owner of the white Washington Senators of the American League, considered Dandridge and Wells to be better than any two infielders in the major leagues at that time. "Nothing could get through that little hole between us," Dandridge beamed.

Dandridge had one of his best years at bat in 1938, hitting .375. That year *New York Daily News* columnist Jimmy Powers urged the New York Giants to sign him and several other black stars, but integration was still nearly a decade away. In 1939, with Negro League payrolls depressed, Dandridge signed with Veracruz in the Mexican League and batted .346 and .367 the next two years, teaming with Wells and home-run champion Josh Gibson to win the pennant. The president of Mexico presented him with a trophy inscribed, "He came, he conquered."

From 1942 through 1944 Dandridge batted .310, .354, and .370. The wealthy Mexican baseball magnate Jorge Pascual named Dandridge player-manager of the Mexico City Reds in 1945; that season the Reds won the league pennant, while Dandridge batted .366 and hit in 29 consecutive games.

After Jackie Robinson joined the Dodgers in 1947, the Negro Leagues began folding. However, Mexican teams started to bid for both white and black stars, and several major leaguers accepted the offers. Against four former big league pitchers, Dandridge batted .455. Upset that the white players generally were paid more than he was, Dandridge decided to leave Mexico. But Pascual sent police to stop him, offer him

$10,000, and bring him back in a limousine. He also bought Dandridge a new house in Newark. The reconciled player rewarded the magnate by batting .373 in 1948 to lead the league.

Later in 1948 Cleveland Indians owner Bill Veeck wanted to sign Dandridge for the pennant drive. But because Veeck refused to pay a bonus, Dandridge chose to stay in Mexico for another year. When future Yankees pitcher Whitey Ford played in Mexico, Dandridge "hit him like he owned him," one player laughed. Years later Dandridge would reminisce on the TV show "Good Morning America," "I know Whitey Ford had one of the best curve balls. But I had one of the best bats!"

In 1949, while Dandridge was player-manager of the New York Cubans, a black team, the major league New York Giants saw him play at their stadium, the Polo Grounds. Impressed, the Giants signed him to a minor league contract and sent him to their top farm team in Minneapolis. "I was 35," Dandridge said, "but I told them I was 30."

Dandridge was a hit both with the fans and with his teammates. He stayed in white hotels everywhere but Louisville and Kansas City, where he boarded with black families. At first Dandridge played second base, then was shifted to third, where he made some spectacular plays. He also batted .362 and just missed winning the American Association batting title. Although Dandridge led Minneapolis to the league pennant that season, the Giants still did not promote him to the major leagues.

The next year, 1950, Dandridge batted .311 and was voted his league's most valuable player. Yet the Giants still refused to promote him, believing he was too old. Sal Maglie, who had known Dandridge in the Mexican League, was then a Giant pitcher. He reacted to the decision angrily, saying, "I know damn well we'd have won the pennant with Dandridge." Meantime, a rookie named Willie Mays reported to Minneapolis, and Dandridge took charge of him. "He was like a father to me," Mays said later. When the Giants needed help in their 1951 pennant drive, it was Mays who got the call, not Dandridge.

Dandridge played winter ball in Cuba from 1937 to 1952. In 1953 he was on the Sacramento and Oakland teams of the Pacific Coast League, batting .268. He ended his career at Bismarck, South Dakota, in 1955.

When Dandridge retired, his career batting averages were .326 in the Negro Leagues, .318 at Minneapolis, and .347 against barnstorming big leaguers. In 1987 he was elected to the National Baseball Hall of Fame by the Veterans' Committee.

After his playing days were over, Dandridge scouted briefly for the Giants, tended bar in Newark, and supervised a city recreation center. He died in Palm Bay, Florida.

• For further reading, see John B. Holway, *Blackball Stars* (1988); James Riley, *Dandy, Day and the Devil* (1987); Robert Peterson, *Only the Ball Was White* (1970); and James Overmayer, *Effa Manley and the Newark Eagles* (1994). Dandridge's career statistics are found in the *Baseball Encyclopedia* (1992), p. 2626. An obituary is in the *New York Times*, 14 Feb. 1994.

JOHN B. HOLWAY

DANDY, Walter Edward (6 Apr. 1886–19 Apr. 1946), physician and neurosurgeon, was born in Sedalia, Missouri, the son of John Dandy, a railroad engineer, and Rachel Kilpatrick. Dandy was raised in a fundamentalist sect, the Plymouth Brethren; as an adult he would give up these religious views as too strict. Dandy graduated as valedictorian of his high school class at the age of seventeen and went on to attend the University of Missouri at Columbia, where he was elected to Phi Beta Kappa and Sigma Xi, the national scientific honorary society, and graduated in 1907 as one of the "First Five."

Encouraged by his teachers, Dandy applied to the Johns Hopkins University Medical School and was admitted in 1907 with advanced standing as a second-year student. During his first summer vacation (1908), on a sternwheeler in the Upper Mississippi River, he studied the reproduction and artificial propagation of a commercial freshwater mussel species that was becoming extinct, thus getting an early start on his research career. At Johns Hopkins Dandy excelled in anatomy and surgery and during his junior year was one of the top ten students of his class. He continued his research, publishing his first paper in the *American Journal of Anatomy* in 1910 on the early development of a human embryo. He received an M.D. in 1910, graduating in the top quarter of his class. Dandy's anatomical accomplishments and drawing skills brought him to the attention of Harvey Cushing, a pioneer in neurosurgery at the university. Dandy stayed on in Baltimore, working with Cushing as a Hunterian Fellow studying pituitary gland function and the vascular anatomy of the dog and cat. Cushing's influence and newly developing skills in the then-embryonic field of neurological surgery led Dandy to choose this field for his career endeavors.

In 1912 Cushing was invited to Harvard University to assume the chair of surgery. Because strong personality differences with Dandy had developed, Cushing did not ask Dandy to accompany him to Harvard. Instead, Dandy accepted the invitation of Chairman of Surgery William Halsted to remain at Johns Hopkins as assistant resident surgeon.

With Kenneth D. Blackfan, a resident in pediatrics, Dandy did much to develop understanding of the causes of hydrocephalus, the accumulation of excess cerebrospinal fluid (CSF) in the brain. In turn, their studies provided greater insight into the circulation pathways, production, and resorption of CSF. By blocking an anatomical fluid pathway, the Aqueduct of Sylvius, in a dog, Blackfan and Dandy were able to reproduce the human condition, thus creating an animal model of hydrocephalus. They also injected dye into the CSF pathways of dogs and demonstrated various types of hydrocephalus. Dandy and Blackfan's classic publications "An Experimental and Clinical

Study of Internal Hydrocephalus" (*Journal of the American Medical Association* 61 [1913]: 2216–17) and "Internal Hydrocephalus: Second Paper" (*American Journal of Diseases of Children* 14 [1917]: 424–43) have remained landmarks in the diagnostic and pathological understanding of hydrocephalus.

Turning his power of invention to clinical medicine, Dandy recognized a common thread in two seemingly unrelated happenings: the previously reported serendipitous finding that air is found in the brain after a skull fracture and his own observation of a patient in the hospital who had an intestinal perforation that caused air under the diaphragm to be visible on an X ray. In 1917 Dandy devised a technique whereby air was introduced into the cerebrospinal fluid pathways via a catheter. This procedure of ventriculography, as it came to be called, for the first time made structures within the brain, both normal and abnormal, readily visible on X ray. In turn, it became possible to locate intracranial lesions with reasonable accuracy in the preoperative work-up of the surgical patient. This technique has proved to be one of the single greatest contributions to neurosurgery.

Equally innovative was another technique developed in 1918 by Dandy: pneumoencephalography, a method for removing cerebrospinal fluid from the brain and replacing it with air. By repositioning the patient, the air could be carried up into the ventricular system, which it outlined, improving X-ray visualization. Following up on this work, Dandy became interested in visualizing the internal anatomy of the ventricular system of the brain. A close associate, Howard A. Kelly, had developed a cystoscope for looking into the urinary bladder. In 1922 Dandy adapted this instrument for navigating throughout the ventricular system and rapidly became facile in its use. He used the ventriculoscope for diagnosis and tissue biopsy, removing blockages and excising a brain structure implicated in the causation of hydrocephalus.

As a result of these studies, Dandy was appointed associate professor of surgery in 1921 at the age of thirty-five; promotion to full professor (as clinical professor of neurosurgery) would follow in 1931. In 1924 he married Sadie Estelle Martin, a dietitian at Johns Hopkins Hospital; they had four children.

In 1923 Dandy designed and used the first postoperative recovery room, providing patients with close observation in that critical period immediately after brain or spine surgery. The three-bed unit he established was staffed around the clock by specially trained nurses. Postoperative patients were placed in a controlled environment where their breathing, fluid balance, mental status, and other functions were monitored so that deleterious changes could be quickly corrected. Dandy was also always attempting to improve operating room equipment. Working with the General Electric Company, he designed a headlight that would not blind the surgeon and yet would illuminate the surgical field. Frustrated by the design of the Gigli saw used to elevate the cranial bone flap, he offered a better design to a Swedish company. Saws meeting Dandy's specifications manufactured by Stille remained the best on the market seventy-five years after their introduction.

In 1925 Dandy described a novel surgical approach to the trigeminal nerve for relief of trigeminal neuralgia, the notoriously painful tic douloureux. Having observed that an artery or vein compressed a portion of the trigeminal nerve in many patients, he proposed a technique of surgical decompression. This was an important contribution as it reduced postoperative inflammation of the cornea and facial paralysis. For the treatment of glossopharyngeal neuralgia, in which severe pain occurs in the roof of the mouth and back of the throat, Dandy devised a technique analogous to the one he proposed for trigeminal neuralgia. Using a similar approach, in 1928 Dandy designed an operation for relief of Ménière's disease (intractable vertigo leading to hearing loss) in which he cut a portion of the eighth cranial nerve.

In 1921 Dandy made an important improvement in the surgical treatment of acoustic neuroma, or tumor of the acoustic nerve. Cushing had pioneered the so-called intracapsular approach for removal of such tumors, in which the surgeon left the tumor capsule behind, leading to frequent recurrence of tumor and re-operation. In the first in a series of seminal papers, Dandy described in 1921 a new technique for the removal of the tumor capsule along with the tumor; this more radical resection led to a substantial reduction of the long-term death rate due to acoustic neuroma. Publication of this report led to bitter and acrimonious exchanges between Dandy and Cushing. Cushing claimed that by stating results that were "too good" to be true, Dandy was misleading surgeons; Dandy had in addition failed even to mention Cushing's classic work on acoustic tumors published in 1917. A careful review of Dandy's work has shown this technique to be quite effective.

Dandy's surgical skills, his total knowledge of the anatomy of the brain and nearby structures, and his development of ventriculography allowed him to create surgical approaches to what were considered inaccessible regions of the brain, such as the so-called intraventricular compartments and the region of the pineal gland. In two important monographs, *Benign Tumors of the Third Ventricle of the Brain: Diagnosis and Treatment* (1933) and *Benign, Encapsulated Tumors in the Lateral Ventricles of the Brain: Diagnosis and Treatment* (1934), Dandy showed that intraventricular tumors could be surgically removed without causing more than minimal side effects.

In 1929 Dandy published a paper in the American Medical Association's *Archives of Surgery* on sciatica, a condition from which he himself suffered. The paper reported his clinical findings that sciatica commonly resulted from a rupture of an intervertebral disc and that when the disc was removed the pain and other symptoms resolved. Before Dandy's publication, the symptoms brought about by ruptured discs were thought to result from benign tumors of the disc rather than being recognized as a disc rupture. Although these findings were not appreciated at the time of publication, they have since been acknowledged as accurate.

In 1932 Dandy contributed one of the earliest monographs devoted solely to brain surgery, a section of Dean Lewis's *System of Surgery*. This work was beautifully illustrated with drawings by Dandy, Dorcas Hager, and Max Brodël, the eminent illustrator at Johns Hopkins. The 600-page text proved so popular and helpful to the neurosurgery profession that it was still in print in 1966, having helped at least three generations of neurosurgeons to learn their craft.

Still another pioneering contribution was Dandy's treatment of intracranial aneurysms. An aneurysm of an artery follows the weakening of its wall, and treatment of such a lesion was at that time considered extremely hazardous. Using skillful techniques, Dandy in 1938 designed some of the early surgical approaches and techniques for the treatment of aneurysms of the Circle of Willis, a vitally important circle of connected arteries at the base of the brain.

Dandy's final monograph was *Orbital Tumors: Results following the Transcranial Operative Attack* (1941). In this beautifully illustrated work on tumors of the orbit, the bony cage surrounding the eye, Dandy demonstrated a series of reliable approaches to tumors in still another region that had been previously considered inaccessible, thereby revolutionizing the treatment of such growths.

As a physician Dandy was known to be gruff but compassionate. He would treat the indigent free, even paying the costs of their hospital stays, and yet he would not hesitate to charge high fees to those who could afford them. Because of his outstanding reputation he was asked to operate on famous personalities and members of their families. He operated on Pulitzer Prize–winning author Margaret Mitchell, for a spinal cord tumor. In August 1940 Dandy was asked to travel to Mexico City to consult on the case of Leon Trotsky, the Russian revolutionary who had been attacked and severely injured. Unfortunately Trotsky died while Dandy was en route.

Dandy was a prolific writer, exquisitely competent surgeon, and hard worker. It was not uncommon for him to perform three to five operations in a single day, and he often worked as many as six days a week. Dandy's international reputation drew surgeons from around the world to observe his operations. In a little-known footnote to his career, Dandy designed, and received a patent for, the first protective baseball cap. He included a hard fiber or plastic liner inside the cap for cranial protection while the player was at bat. The original cap was designed in 1941 for Larry S. MacPhail of the Brooklyn Dodgers after Dandy heard of a St. Louis ball player who had been seriously injured after being hit in the head. One of these skull protectors remains on exhibit at the Baseball Hall of Fame in Cooperstown, New York.

Dandy can truly be called one of the great pioneers in American neurosurgery. After his death in Baltimore, an editorial obituary in the *Baltimore Sun*

characterized his contributions to the field as based on "the imaginative genius to conceive of new and startling techniques, courage to try them and skill—superb skill—to make them successful."

• The majority of Dandy's papers are at the Johns Hopkins University Archives, Baltimore, Md. There are also collections of his papers and archival material at the American Association of Neurological Surgeons, Park Ridge, Ill., and at Yale Medical School, New Haven, Conn. Dandy's most important publications in journals include "Ventriculography following the Injection of Air into the Cerebral Ventricles," *Annals of Surgery* 68 (1918): 5–11; "Röntgenography of the Brain after the Injection of Air into the Spinal Canal," *Annals of Surgery* 70 (1919): 397–403; "An Operation for the Total Extirpation of Tumors in the Cerebello-Pontine Angle: A Preliminary Report," *Johns Hopkins Hospital Bulletin* 33 (1922): 344–45; "Section of the Sensory Root of the Trigeminal Nerve at the Pons: Preliminary Report of the Operative Procedure," *Johns Hopkins Hospital Bulletin* 36 (1925): 105–6; "An Operation for the Total Removal of Cerebello+pontile (Acoustic) Tumors," *Surgery, Gynecology, and Obstetrics* 41 (1925): 129–48; "Ménière's Disease: Its Diagnosis and a Method of Treatment," *Archives of Surgery* 16 (1928): 1127–52; and "The Treatment of Trigeminal Neuralgia by the Cerbellar Route," *Annals of Surgery* 96 (1932): 787–95. Among Dandy's other published works, see especially "Surgery of the Brain," in *Practice of Surgery*, ed. D. Lewis, vol. 12 (1932); and *Intracranial Arterial Aneurysms* (1944).

The fullest treatment of Dandy's life and career is W. L. Fox, *Dandy of Johns Hopkins* (1984). See also the biographical sketches by E. Campbell in *Journal of Neurosurgery* 8 (1951): 249–92, and by A. E. Walker in *The Founders of Neurology*, ed. W. E. Haymaker and F. Schiller (1970). His contributions to neurosurgery are assessed in D. Fairman, "Evolution of Neurosurgery through Walter E. Dandy's Work," *Surgery* 19 (1946): 581–604. Obituaries are in *Surgery* 19 (1946): 577–79, *Annals of Surgery* 126 (1947): 113–15, and the *New York Times*, 20 Apr. 1946.

JAMES T. GOODRICH

DANE, Nathan (29 Dec. 1752–15 Feb. 1835), lawyer, legislator, and legal writer, was born in Ipswich, Massachusetts, the son of Daniel Dane and Abigail Burnham, prosperous farmers. Dane, one of twelve children, received a common school elementary education. He worked on his father's farm until he entered Harvard College at the unusual age of twenty-two. Dane's college career from 1774 to 1778 was interrupted by the American Revolution; he apparently performed militia service in Boston during the British siege of the city in 1775–1776. In his academic studies Dane displayed an aptitude for mathematics, which later bore fruit when, as a legislator, he took special interest in taxation, government finance, and census issues. Throughout his life Dane retained the studiousness that marked his college years.

After graduating from Harvard, Dane taught school in Beverly, Massachusetts, while reading law in the law office of Judge William Wetmore in Salem. Dane's simultaneous involvement in teaching school and in studying law contributed to his lifelong commitment to the promotion of legal education. He married Mary Brown, a widow, in November 1779; the union lasted for his lifetime, but there were no children.

Admitted to the bar in 1782, Dane practiced law in Beverly but frequently interrupted his legal career for public service. Between 1782 and 1785 he served in the Massachusetts House of Representatives. Then, from 1785 to 1789, he was elected as a delegate to the Congress of the Confederation. Dane proved to be a very active and productive delegate. He worked on many of the major committees of the Congress. His leadership was especially important during the summer of 1787, when many of the delegates from other states, including those from New England, left New York, then the seat of the federal government, to participate in the Constitutional Convention in Philadelphia, which had been called to revise the Articles of Confederation. Dane made an outstanding contribution in drafting and steering through the Congress the Northwest Ordinance of 1787, an organic document second only to the Constitution of the United States itself in its importance to the future development of the Republic. While the ideas behind the Ordinance's principal provisions were the product of many minds, the final version as enacted was chiefly the work of Nathan Dane. As John Quincy Adams later reported to Justice Joseph Story, "The Ordinance for the Northwestern Territory alone, entitles him [Dane] to the gratitude of this nation, and of posterity, as long as the Union shall last" (Johnson, p. 35). Dane introduced to the Ordinance the provision prohibiting slavery or involuntary servitude in the territory covered by the document. He favored the use of civilian over military authority in the Northwest Territory. He also supported the individual rights provisions contained in the Ordinance, which anticipated his advocacy of a federal Bill of Rights and also made him one of the nation's earliest civil libertarians.

Dane's position on the original Constitution has been a matter of historical dispute ever since James Madison linked Dane with Richard Henry Lee as an opponent of ratification. However, the complete historical record strongly suggests that Dane fully supported the work of the Philadelphia Convention. His key position in the Confederation Congress facilitated congressional authorization of the Convention in the first instance; it also gave Congress a role in transmitting the Constitution as adopted to the states for ratification and in finally declaring it to be in effect. Dane deeply believed that the Articles of Confederation lacked energy and that more power was necessary "before our complex machine of government can be compleated" (Johnson, p. 65). As his principal biographer has concluded, "At each stage of the Constitution's development, even through the establishment of the machinery of its execution, Dane supported the Federal Constitution" (Johnson, p. 72).

After his service in the Confederation Congress, Dane returned to his law practise in Beverly. During the decade of the 1790s he was elected to the Massachusetts Senate, where he served between 1793 and 1798. This would prove to be the end of Dane's legislative career because of the onset and steady progression of deafness, which made him increasingly unable to take part in legislative debates. His public service took a new form, however, for in 1795 he began work on a revision of Massachusetts law, a project that took nearly two decades but that bore fruit with the publication, in 1814, of the Revised Laws. Dane was one of three revisal commissioners, along with Joseph Story and William Prescott.

Dane would have one more highly visible political position. In 1814, in the midst of the War of 1812, a war that was particularly unpopular in New England, the Massachusetts House of Representatives sent a delegation of twelve men, including Dane, to Hartford, Connecticut. Extremely controversial in its time and much criticized by the Democratic-Republicans as a Federalist plan to break up the Union, the significance of the Hartford Convention has been the subject of dispute among historians ever since. One thing is clear, however; the Convention tainted all who participated in it, including Dane. While Dane always remained a strong Federalist, he would defend his participation in the Hartford Convention on the grounds that his presence added a note of moderation to its proceedings. As he explained to a friend at the time, "somebody must go to prevent mischief." Years later, Joseph Story reported that Dane had expressly "disclaimed any intention to promote any measures calculated to dissolve the Union" (quoted in Johnson, p. 92). Dane's biographer concludes that "before, during, and after the [Hartford] Convention, he remained loyal to the Union and to the Federal Constitution" (Johnson, p. 93).

In his remaining years, Dane turned his attentions to his writings and to legal education. A series of historical essays, which he called "A Moral and Political Survey of America," was never published. But his General Abridgement and Digest of American Laws, with Occasional Notes and Comments did appear in print in eight volumes in 1823 and 1824, with a ninth volume published in 1829 as an updated supplement. This pioneering work of legal scholarship was the product of forty years of prodigious study and reflection. The work was designed to aid lawyers and law students and was, in its form, the first legal textbook; it was encyclopedic rather than analytical or innovative. While the bulk of the sources used came from Massachusetts law, Dane wanted to give the book a national perspective "to show the spirit and principles of the laws of our several States" (Johnson, p. 103) and thereby contribute to the establishment of an American jurisprudence separate and apart from English law. While the General Abridgement was not the first American lawbook, it has earned Dane the title "Father of American Jurisprudence."

Through the profits derived from the success of the Abridgement, plus the income he received from shrewd investments in toll bridges, turnpikes, and the Bank of the United States, Dane was in a position to contribute substantial sums to various philanthropic enterprises. The most notable of these was his establishment of the Dane Professorship of Law at Harvard in 1829. For that purpose, Dane donated $15,000, on the condition that the first occupant of the position would be his old friend Justice Joseph Story. With Story as the first Dane Professor, Harvard soon became the foremost institution for legal education in the country.

Dane died in Beverly. While not a statesman of the first rank, Dane's role as the principal sponsor of the Northwest Ordinance marked him as one of the more important figures in America's founding generation. His work in compiling a comprehensive compendium of American law was a singular accomplishment. And his contribution to legal education had great importance for the advancement of the legal profession on a national scale. These genuine and substantial achievements, eclipsed as they were by those of his more illustrious contemporaries, should support a higher historical assessment of Dane's career than he has yet received.

• Dane's manuscript papers are held by the Library of Congress, the Beverly Historical Society, the Massachusetts Historical Society, and the Essex Institute of Salem. Many of Dane's letters were published in E. C. Burnett, ed., *Letters of Members of the Continental Congress* (8 vols., 1921–1936). Dane's "Moral and Political Survey of America" (unpublished) is held by the Wellesley College Library. Interesting references to Dane's relationship with Joseph Story are contained in R. Kent Newmyer, *Supreme Court Justice Joseph Story: Statesman of the Old Republic* (1985). The best modern treatment is Andrew J. Johnson, "The Life and Constitutional Thought of Nathan Dane" (Ph.D. diss., Indiana Univ., 1964).

GEORGE DARGO

DANENHOWER, John Wilson (30 Sept. 1849–20 Apr. 1887), naval officer and arctic explorer, was born in Chicago, Illinois, the son of William Washington Danenhower, a publisher and political activist; his mother's name is not known. After graduating from the U.S. Naval Academy in 1870, he served in Europe, the North Pacific, and at the U.S. Naval Observatory. In 1878 he suffered a mental breakdown and was confined for four months at the Government Hospital for the Insane in Washington, D.C. After his release he served on the *Vandalia*, escorting ex-President Ulysses S. Grant on a European tour. While abroad he learned of Lieutenant George W. De Long's proposed arctic expedition. This expedition was a joint venture of the U.S. Navy and the newspaper magnate James Gordon Bennett, and Danenhower used his family's political connections with Grant to secure an appointment as the expedition's navigation officer. He joined De Long in Le Havre, France, on the expedition's ship *Jeannette*.

During the voyage to the United States, Danenhower impressed De Long with his hard work and positive attitude. Although De Long learned about his hospitalization, Danenhower convinced De Long that he had completely recovered from his mental problems. Burdened by numerous other critical problems, De Long elected to retain Danenhower.

The *Jeannette* sailed from San Francisco on 8 July 1879, bound for the Bering Strait and the Arctic Ocean. Several prominent geographers believed that a warm current passed through the Bering Strait to create an open Arctic Ocean. Experts suggested that a possible polar continent north of Alaska and Siberia would permit overland travel to the North Pole. These academics ignored reports of Captain James Cook, who had sailed through the Bering Strait on his last expedition. Cook found that an icy ocean blocked his attempt to sail to the North Pole or through the Northeast and Northwest Passages.

In the Arctic Ocean, the ice soon beset the *Jeannette* north of Siberia, carrying the trapped vessel in a northwesterly direction. Danenhower performed his duties until December 1879, when he developed a severe eye inflammation. Surgeon James Ambler unsuccessfully tried drugs to treat the mysterious ailment. Danenhower finally confessed to Ambler the cause of his eye problem—syphilis. During January 1880, while the crew struggled to save the ship, Dr. Ambler performed surgery by candlelight on Danenhower's left eye. The patient endured his painful operation with great courage. He suffered through many months confined to his darkened cabin; his left eye useless and his right eye threatened. The ship and her captive crew spent a second winter icebound in the Arctic Ocean north of Siberia.

On 16 May 1881 a new island appeared on the horizon, which De Long named Henrietta after Bennett's mother. Soon they spotted a second new island, which they named Jeannette. De Long hoped that these islands would provide a safe harbor where they could repair the ship. Since Danenhower and Lieutenant Charles Winans Chipp, the executive officer, were disabled, De Long assigned Engineer George W. Melville to lead a party to Henrietta Island. After a difficult trip, Melville reported that the island was barren with no safe anchorage. The *Jeannette* drifted past the new islands, until 11 June, when the ice crushed the ship. De Long and his men quickly unloaded food and equipment onto the ice. Danenhower removed the bandages from his eyes so that he could save his navigational gear. The ship's loss stranded thirty-three men more than four hundred miles north of mainland Siberia. They had adequate food and clothing but faced a daunting journey hauling their lifeboats across the ice. Although Danenhower outranked Melville, De Long gave Melville command of Danenhower's boat. Danenhower resented receiving orders from a staff officer, but he willingly hauled the boat. Although Danenhower was a line officer, De Long relieved him from duties and gave Engineer Melville command of a working party. De Long considered Danenhower physically unfit for duty and resented the earlier failure to fully disclose his medical history. Subsequently, De Long placed Danenhower under Melville's command in one of the three small boats for the last leg of the journey to the mainland.

After forty days of backbreaking labor on the ice, the explorers discovered a large new island, which they named for their sponsor, Bennett. De Long claimed possession of the new island and spent nine days resting and exploring this newest U.S. territory. South of Bennett Island they reached open water and began the voyage to the mainland. De Long, Melville, and Chipp each commanded a small boat. As they approached the broad delta of the Lena River in mid-September, a gale separated the three boats. Chipp's boat disappeared and apparently sank. Danenhower's seamanship saved Melville's boat during the storm, and they landed on the east side of the delta. Making their way upriver, they encountered natives and reached a small village. De Long's party landed at the northern end of the delta. Short of food and confused by an erroneous map, they pushed south through a maze of freezing swamps. On 9 October De Long sent two men ahead to seek Russian settlements and attain help. The two men met natives who did not understand English. Critical days passed before Melville learned of their location and organized a rescue attempt. De Long and the rest of his men died around 30 October. Melville's rescue party reached the area on 9 November, but found only the expedition records. Deep snow prevented the discovery of De Long's final camp until the following spring. Meanwhile, Danenhower took five invalids to the Siberian town of Yakutsk, where they contacted the outside world. Danenhower learned that the U.S. Navy had promoted him to lieutenant in 1879. He arrived home in May 1882.

After his return, Danenhower published an account of the expedition, testified before a naval court of inquiry, and made a lecture tour. In 1885 he married Helen L. Sloan, the daughter of New York politician George B. Sloan; the couple had two children. Danenhower later served on the staff of the U.S. Naval Academy. On 11 April 1887, while commanding the training ship *Constellation*, his ship ran aground. Disturbed by the thought of a facing a court-martial, Danenhower committed suicide in Annapolis, Maryland.

Danenhower's ability as a writer and lecturer greatly exceeded his performance as an explorer. During most of his polar service he was an invalid, made no discoveries himself, and seriously burdened his associates. De Long probably intended to file charges against him for conduct unbecoming an officer. On the other hand, Danenhower's seamanship did save Melville's boat during the gale. Perhaps Danenhower's greatest legacy to polar exploration was his son, Sloan, who commanded the first submarine attempt to reach the North Pole in 1931.

• Expedition records, correspondence, and logbooks of the *Jeannette* Expedition are in Record Group 45 of the Naval Records Collection at the National Archives; additional material is at the U.S. Naval Academy. The inquiry proceedings were published as *Jeannette Inquiry. Before the Committee on Naval Affairs of the United States House of Representatives, Forty-Eighth Congress* (1884). Danenhower wrote an account of the *Jeannette* expedition, *Lieutenant Danenhower's Narrative of the Jeannette* (1882). His account also appeared in compilations such as Richard Perry, *The Jeannette: And a Narrative Encyclopaedia of Arctic Explorations* (1883); and Herman Dieck, *The Marvellous Wonders of the Polar World* (1885).

Other primary accounts are George W. Melville, *In the Lena Delta* (1884); Raymond L. Newcomb, *Our Lost Explorers: The Narrative of the Jeannette Expedition* (1882); Emma De Long, ed., *The Voyage of the Jeannette* (1884); and William H. Gilder, *Ice Pack and Tundra* (1883). Sir Hubert Wilkins, *Under the North Pole* (1931), contains a biographical sketch of Danenhower and his father. Some popular works on Danenhower and his expedition are Leonard F. Guttridge, *Icebound* (1986); A. A. Hoehling, *The Jeannette Expedition* (1967); and Edward Ellsberg, *Hell on Ice* (1938). De Long's wife Emma added her perspective in *Explorer's Wife* (1938). An obituary is in the *New York Times*, 21 Apr. 1887.

TED HECKATHORN

DANFORTH, Charles Haskell (30 Nov. 1883–10 Jan. 1969), anatomist, was born near Norway, Maine, the son of James Danforth and Mary File Haskell, farmers. He studied biology at Tufts College with the intention of becoming a naturalist and received his A.B. in 1908. After graduating he accepted an unexpected offer to teach anatomy at the Washington University School of Medicine in St. Louis, Missouri. He soon entered that school's graduate program and earned his A.M. in 1910 and his Ph.D. in anatomy in 1912 by making use of his skills as a naturalist. His dissertation on the anatomy of the Mississippi paddlefish occasioned many field trips to the muddy bottomlands of the Mississippi River and its tributaries in search of prime specimens for dissection.

Shortly after completing his graduate work, Danforth began to investigate the hereditary aspects of anatomy. In 1914 he became an associate at Washington University and married Florence Wenonah Garrison; they had three children. That year he published a study of a family with hereditary congenital cataract. This study was followed by investigations into other hereditary eye defects as well as the relationship between heredity and the conception of twins—all of which contributed to his promotion to associate professor of anatomy in 1916. The latter study was later expanded to consider the reasons why "identical" twins are not really identical, a phenomenon Danforth explained in terms of anatomical asymmetry: no single individual's right side is exactly like his or her left side, and since identical twins are formed from different sides of an ovum they are not exact duplicates of one another.

Danforth's growing interest in hereditary anatomy led him to undertake studies of the frequency of abnormally short "toes" in birds, a comparison of African-American twins whose hands had more than ten fingers, and hereditary and racial variation in the long thumb muscle of the human hand. In 1919 he took part in an anthropometric study of World War I veterans that measured the size and proportions of the body parts of more than 100,000 young men immediately before their discharge from the military in order to establish a basis for gauging changes in growth and development in the American male physique in future years. These studies led Danforth to consider the general genetic aspects of heredity, and in particular the frequency of mutation and the incidence of hereditary traits in humans. In 1921 he addressed the Second International Congress of Eugenics, offering the first estimate of the frequency of mutation rates of dominant human genes. Unfortunately, Danforth's pioneering efforts in this area faded into obscurity, and it was not until 1935 that his method for estimating mutation frequency was reinvented by the noted British geneticists J. B. S. Haldane and L. S. Penrose.

In 1922 Danforth accepted an offer to teach anatomy at Stanford University as an associate professor, and he was promoted to full professor the next year. Having begun a study of the hereditary aspects of human hair while at Washington University, over the next three years he investigated the abnormal growth and distribution of body hair—particularly the facial hair of white women. He published the results of these studies in *Hair with Special Reference to Hypertrichosis* (1925). Danforth also began to raise and develop a colony of mice for purposes of investigating mutations in a controlled environment. His work with this colony included studying the relationship between heredity and the abnormal occurrence of fatty tissue, the doubling of body parts, and the development of both male and female sex organs in an individual mouse.

Although Danforth continued to experiment with the mouse colony until his death, in 1927 he expanded his study of genetics and heredity by working with domestic fowl in such a way that led him into the field of endocrinology. He investigated the genetic causes of breed-specific and gender-specific plumage patterns by transplanting skin grafts between chicks of different breeds and genders. He discovered that in certain cases the development of the appropriate breed pattern was determined by the genetic makeup of the feather follicle, while the appropriate gender pattern was determined by the sex hormone secreted by the host bird. In certain other cases the feather follicle alone determined both breed and gender plumage patterns. This discovery led him to conclude that genes and hormones act "merely as regulators, or as necessary aids in creating for the protoplasm special conditions under which it may attain one or another of its inherent potentialities" (Allen, p. 348).

In 1938 Danforth became executive head of the Department of Anatomy, a position he held until his retirement in 1949. He was elected to the National Academy of Sciences in 1942. He served as vice president and chairman of the anthropology section of the American Association for the Advancement of Science in 1932 and as president of the association's Pacific Division in 1950–1951. He also served as second vice president of the American Association of Anatomists from 1936 to 1938, vice president of the Society for Experimental Biology and Medicine from 1941 to 1943, president of the Western Society of Naturalists from 1942 to 1944, and vice president of the American Society of Human Genetics in 1951–1952. Danforth edited the *American Journal of Physical Anthropology* from 1927 to 1942 and the *Anatomical Record* from 1928 to 1948, and he was a member of the editorial board of *Growth* from 1940 to 1949. He died in Palo Alto, California.

Danforth was not a "typical scientist." In a day when most researchers opted to specialize in increasingly narrow fields of endeavor, he chose instead to generalize by combining the skills and insights of a naturalist, an anatomist, an anthropologist, a geneticist, and an endocrinologist. Moreover, he considered himself to be a teacher first and foremost and refused to let his own research interests interfere with his responsibility of teaching anatomy. Nonetheless, his work with human heredity, the hair follicle, mouse genetics and mutation, and the role of genes and hormones in feather characterization contributed to a deeper understanding of the complex interactions among genes, hormones, and environment in determining the anatomical growth and development of an individual organism.

• Some of Danforth's letters can be found in the Leslie Clarence Dunn Papers in the American Philosophical Society's archives in Philadelphia, Pa. Some of his endocrinological research was published as "Relation of Genic and Endocrine Factors in Sex," in *Sex and Internal Secretions*, 2d ed., Edgar Allen (1939). A good biography, which includes a complete bibliography of Danforth's work, is Benjamin H. Willier, National Academy of Sciences, *Biographical Memoirs* 44 (1975): 1–56.

CHARLES W. CAREY, JR.

DANFORTH, Thomas (Nov. 1623–5 Nov. 1699), magistrate of Massachusetts, was born in Framlingham, Suffolk County, England, and was baptized on 20 November 1623, the son of Nicholas Danforth and Elizabeth (maiden name unknown). His father, a prosperous yeoman who was known as a patron of Puritan divines, decided to emigrate to Massachusetts shortly after the death of his wife in 1634. Nicholas Danforth died in 1638, committing his two sons, Thomas and an elder brother Samuel, to the care of the Reverend Thomas Shepard in Cambridge.

Little is known of Danforth's youth and education, but his career shows him to have been well read if not formally schooled. He was admitted to the status of freeman (voting citizenship) in Massachusetts on 10 May 1643 as a resident of Cambridge. In 1644 he married Mary Withington of Dorchester, Massachusetts. The couple had twelve children. A farmer and prosperous landowner, Danforth served his town both as a selectman and as town clerk on various occasions throughout his career. His first position in colonial government appears to have been recorder of deeds for Middlesex County, a post he held from 1652 until 1686.

In 1650 the overseers of Harvard College named Danforth treasurer of the college. His brother Samuel had graduated from the college in 1643 and was named one of the fellows when the General Court of the colony granted the college a formal charter in 1650. Danforth does not appear to have exercised the duties of treasurer until after President Henry Dunster's resignation in 1654, apparently because of Dunster's refusal to yield the control of the institution's finances that he had exerted prior to the charter. Danforth served continually thereafter as treasurer until 1669, when he became the college's steward, a post he held until 1682. This post, comparable to that of a steward on an English manor, was a position of considerable distinction. He was in charge of the day-to-day operations of the college, including the provision of food, fuel, and various other material goods. In 1654 he was also chosen clerk of the Harvard overseers. His friction with Dunster spilled over into their private lives and fueled several lawsuits between the two men.

Danforth deserves much of the credit for the college's survival and modest prosperity during the seventeenth century, though the sparsity of detailed records prevents a precise assessment. In a funeral elegy, his nephew John Danforth praised his contribution as steward and treasurer: "Charged and Discharged were the Quarter Bills, Drained not thy Stock, but with large Hundreds fills." John Danforth also praised his uncle as "A Bounteous Patron unto many a Plant In thy [Harvard's] fair Nursery, whose Means were scant," referring to the steward's practice of paying the fees for some poor students out of his own pocket.

Danforth's greater role in public life began when he was chosen to represent Cambridge as a deputy in the Massachusetts legislature, the General Court, in 1657. He was reelected the following year. In 1659 he was first chosen assistant and was annually reelected to the colony's upper house until 1679 when he was elected to the office of deputy governor. Danforth then served in this position until the surrender of the colony charter in 1686. As deputy governor he worked closely with Governor Simon Bradstreet, who sought to retain the traditional Puritan policies of the region against mounting criticism from the royal government. He also served the colony as president of the Province of Maine (1680–1686) and as one of the commissioners of the United Colonies of New England. In 1682 he was one of the men who prepared the instructions to the Massachusetts agents who were defending the charter in England. When that effort failed and the old charter government was replaced by the Dominion of New England, Danforth retired from public life.

Danforth was recognized as one of the leaders of the "popular" party in the Bay colony, though he was willing to take unpopular stands. He was a strong supporter of missionary efforts among American Indians, and the early Indian students at Harvard boarded with Danforth. During King Philip's War, when general sentiment against all Indians was at its height, he defended those converted Praying Indians who had remained loyal to the colonists. Similarly, in 1692 he made clear his opposition to the conduct of the witch trials in Salem. His nephew praised him as "like Nicodemus He was One, and stood like Him, stout Protestant alone Gainst a Committee [the judges] whose blind Indignation Condemn'd the Best Men of that Generation." "I've sometimes heard him say," wrote John Danforth, "that He had ever As lieve die by the Ax as by the Feaver; In a good cause and with a Conscience Good."

In 1689 Boston residents took advantage of news of England's Glorious Revolution to rid themselves of the Dominion of New England, their own version of Stuart despotism. Danforth was one of the members of the committee that succeeded in forcing the Dominion's governor-general, Sir Edmund Andros, to surrender his authority. Along with Bradstreet and other members of the old charter government, he resumed the posts which he had held following the last colony elections. Following the granting of a new royal charter in 1692 Governor William Phipps named Danforth an associate justice of the colony's superior court, and he served in that capacity from 1692 until his death.

Mary Danforth died in 1697. Danforth's brother Samuel became one of the leading ministers of the midcentury in New England. His election sermon in 1670 provided the phrase "Errand into the Wilderness" which Perry Miller used in the twentieth century to capture the essence of the spirit that brought the colonists to the New World.

Though not noted for any particular accomplishments, Danforth contributed significantly to the success of Harvard College during his years as an officer of the corporation. As was the case with Bradstreet, whose significance was much the same, Danforth's presence in the Massachusetts government provided a link with builders of the Bay colony such as John Winthrop and John Endecott, whom he had known and of whom he could speak with authority. He was a living witness to what had been the goals and principles of the founding generation and as such was an effective advocate for maintaining the old New England way at a time when it was threatened by economic and social changes that eventually undermined Puritanism.

• The records kept by Danforth as treasurer of Harvard College are in College Book 3, 1636–1779, in the Harvard College Archives, and are reprinted in the Colonial Society of Massachusetts, *Publications*, 15 (1925), pp. 172–332. There is neither a collection of Danforth's private correspondence nor any biography. John Danforth's elegy is printed with commentary in Harold S. Jantz, "A Funeral Elegy for Thomas Danforth, Treasurer of Harvard," *Harvard Library Bulletin* 1 (1947): 113–15. Aside from his treatment in standard reference sources, his activities can best be followed in political histories of the colony, in Samuel Eliot Morison, *Harvard College in the Seventeenth Century* (2 vols., 1936), and in Margery Somers Foster, *"Out of Small Beginnings . . . ": An Economic History of Harvard College in the Puritan Period* (1962).

FRANCIS J. BREMER

DANFORTH, William Henry (10 Sept. 1870–24 Dec. 1955), food industry executive, was born in Charleston, Missouri, the son of Albert Hampton Danforth, a general store proprietor and bank president, and Rebecca Lynn. An intelligent and responsible boy, he was sent to live alone and attend the Manual Training School in St. Louis, Missouri, at the age of fourteen. He was soon invited to stay with the family of a classmate, with whom he remained until his graduation in 1887. Although he was already drawn to a career in business—his senior class essay was entitled "A Commission Merchant"—he enrolled in Washington University in St. Louis, where from 1887 to 1892 he majored in engineering. Upon graduating, he found work as a salesman for a brick company, but, since the business was both seasonal and dependent on the economy, he found it unsatisfactory. Two older friends whom he had met at the Methodist church where he was active in Sunday school work, George Robinson and William Andrews, owned a retail feed store near the university and proposed that Danforth join them in producing formula horse and mule feed. Reasoning that horses had to eat all year and in bad times as well as good, he borrowed one-third of the $12,000 capital investment from his father and on 1 January 1894 formed the Robinson-Danforth Commission Company with them, serving as secretary-treasurer. In October of that year he married Adda Bush, with whom he had two children.

The firm created a blend of crushed oats and cracked corn that horses found more digestible than the whole grain commonly used, and it soon began producing special mixes for pigs, poultry, and cows as well. Marketed as Purina Feed, to emphasize the purity of the ingredients, the product sold well, and after seven months the three partners shared a first dividend of $2,912. Danforth's job was to keep the books, but he was active in every aspect of the work, from mixing and loading the grain to buying the ingredients and merchandising the feed. Within a year he became the company's principal buyer and star salesman, traveling to mills in Iowa, Minnesota, and Kansas and dealing with jobbers throughout the region. In March 1896 he was made the company's president when Robinson stepped down to become vice president, and on 26 May Danforth purchased Andrews's share when the third partner retired. The next day a tornado devastated St. Louis and completely demolished the Robinson-Danforth mill. As there was no tornado insurance at that time, the company was left with no assets, but Danforth, now the majority stockholder, secured a $25,000 bank loan with nothing but his reputation as security and had a new and larger mill built.

The company prospered and in 1898 expanded into the breakfast cereal business. Interested in nutrition since his youth, Danforth began buying cracked wheat from a miller in Kansas and packaging it as Purina Whole Wheat Cereal. A popular health-food advocate of the time, Dr. Everett Ralston, had recommended whole grains in his book *Life Building*, widely sold through the Ralston Health Clubs, which claimed 800,000 members. Ralston agreed to endorse the cereal on condition that his name be included in the company name, and in 1902 the Robinson-Danforth Company was renamed Ralston Purina. That same year it adopted its red and white checkerboard logo, one of the best-known trademarks in American business. Vigorously promoted at the 1904 St. Louis World's Fair, Ralston Purina's various products reached $1.25 million in sales that year. In 1926 the firm acquired the Ry-Krisp plant in Minnesota, the first of several nutrition-related food companies and other businesses it

was to purchase. When Ralston Purina went public in 1945, Danforth and his family owned 27 percent of the company's stock, then valued at $9 million.

Always active in church and charity work, Danforth interrupted his business career in 1918 to accept a position as general secretary of the Young Men's Christian Association with the army's Third Infantry Division in France, where he served for a year before returning to run Ralston Purina. His contagious enthusiasm, religious faith, and personal industry were an inspiration to his employees, whom he regarded with paternal affection. From 1919 he wrote an inspirational "Monday Morning Message" every week to be placed on the desks of all Purina executives and later sent to all employees and friends. He also promoted his moral views in a number of books, privately printed and distributed to "the Purina Family." The best known of these was *I Dare You!* (1931), which outlined his system of "Four-Fold Development: Think Tall, Stand Tall, Smile Tall, Live Tall," urging a balance of physical, mental, social, and religious growth.

Active in philanthropic and civic organizations, Danforth contributed generously to the church and to numerous youth programs. He served as the president of the Missouri State Sunday School Board and was a founder and director of the American Youth Foundation and the National Christmas Carols Association. He was also a director of the First National Bank of St. Louis, the St. Louis Union Trust Company, the New York Life Insurance Company, and the Illinois Terminal Railroad and a trustee of Berea College in Kentucky. In 1927 he established the Danforth Foundation, a national education philanthropy "dedicated to enhancing the humane dimensions of life" by granting fellowships and scholarships to college students and by building "meditation chapels" on college campuses and in hospitals. By 1995 the assets of the Danforth Foundation were valued at nearly $300 million, much of it in company stock.

Danforth turned the presidency of Ralston Purina over to his son Donald in 1932 but continued to participate in the business as chairman of the board. Still dynamic in his old age, he was regarded as a shrewd and sometimes dictatorial executive but a benevolent employer. By the time of his death in St. Louis, Missouri, the company he had started more than a half-century before was the largest producer of farm and pet feed in the United States.

• The authorized biography of Danforth is Gordon M. Philpott, *Daring Venture: The Life Story of William H. Danforth* (1960), and his business affairs are discussed in Michael Patrick Allen, *The Founding Fortunes: A New Anatomy of the Super-Rich Families in America* (1987). For a detailed account of the Ralston Purina Company, see "Cow Chow—and Wow," *Fortune*, Jan. 1947, pp. 86ff; R. H. Dean, "Tall Orders at Checkerboard Square," *Nation's Business*, Feb. 1972, pp. 98–99; and the company's centennial pamphlet *The Ralston Chronicle: 1894–1994* (1994). An obituary is in the *New York Times*, 25 Dec. 1955.

DENNIS WEPMAN

DANIEL, Annie Sturges (21 Sept. 1858–10 Aug. 1944), physician and public health reformer, was born in Buffalo, New York, the daughter of John M. Daniel, a coal and wood merchant, and Marinda Sturges. Both of her parents died while Annie was still a young child, and she was subsequently sent to Monticello, New York, to live with relatives. Curiosity about biology and anatomy led her to enroll in the Woman's Medical College of the New York Infirmary, where she specialized in obstetrics, gynecology, and pediatrics. After receiving her M.D. in 1879, she worked as a pharmacist at the infirmary for a year before serving her internship. In 1881 Daniel was placed as the physician in charge of the Out-Practice Department, also known as the Tenement House Service, of the New York Infirmary. Assigned to this department by Dr. Elizabeth Blackwell on a probationary basis, Daniel, after one year, was permanently named to the post.

The services of the department included staff visitations to the tenements on the East Side of New York City. Although some young middle-class physicians under her were shocked by the filth and overcrowding of the mostly immigrant populations in tenements, Daniel met the problems with a clearer view. While some thought the tenement dwellers "unresponsive," Daniel associated their ill health with insufficient food and clothing and unsanitary living conditions caused by their poverty. Daniel's vision into these problems provided a strong influence and model for many other young interns and set an example for future social service work.

The immigrant families were responsive to Daniel's patient care. She saw to their medical needs by always returning quickly to ill patients and taught women the basics of hygiene and proper dietary habits. Sometimes bringing a chicken on her visits, Daniel saw that the department supplied the necessities of food, fuel, and clothing and that at Thanksgiving and Christmas families had holiday dinners. During the winter, when the tenement apartments were chilly, she put quarters into gas meters to keep the families' rooms warm. Even when circumstances seemed hopeless, she never discouraged immigrant families and instead watched them improve their situations by rising out of poverty to do well over the years.

Training in Daniel's Out-Practice Department became so important that by 1889 it was included in the Woman's Medical College coursework requirements. Students accompanied her on visitation routes. Her expectations of students were high, and she demanded that reports be exact even to detailing tenement room dimensions and specifying the number of people occupying a room. Students had to learn to handle the tasks associated with the everyday events of the people living in tenements, such as arranging funerals, counteracting the effects of old-country superstitions to effectively treat patients with medicines, and teaching families how best to make the most of their meager salaries. In the 1890s Daniel's lecture coursework included a class on the "normal child" because she felt it necessary training to be able understand abnormal

children. Daniel published a summary of her first ten years in the Out-Practice in *Report of Out-Practice of the N.Y. Infirmary for Women and Children* (1891). Daniel later wrote a summary of the history of the Out-Practice, "A Cautious Experiment," which was serialized in the *Medical Woman's Journal* from May 1939 to December 1942.

Respect for Daniel came not only from students and the immigrants but from officials who came to her for advice. Her expertise won her an appointment to serve as an investigator for the New York State Tenement House Commission in 1884. Home manufacturing particularly disturbed her. Children, some as young as three, helped their mothers add to the family income by doing piecework. No regulations existed, and children worked long hours, confined in a foul and unsanitary atmosphere that Daniel believed caused "irreparable damage" to the brain and other health problems for the children. Her concerns led to her service on an 1892 congressional committee that looked into home sweatshop operations. She also testified on the effects of homework at an 1894 state tenement committee. She continued her drive to eliminate this type of labor, earning her the name "the Angel of the Lower East Side."

Cited as being the first woman to show the need for reform in tenements and in sweatshop practices, Daniel was also a spokesperson for change in prisons. In 1886, while serving as the attending physician to the Women's Prison Association of New York, she wrote a report on the conditions of women prisoners that was published the following year. Based on the report, three reforms were recommended, and in 1888 a law was passed providing for separate police stations for the detainment of women under arrest; two matrons to be attached to each station with charge of the female prisoners; and the separation of women and men prisoners.

During the depression, the Out-Practice was closely connected to social services in coordinating relief measures as Daniel had twice the number of visits to make and the Out-Practice infirmary had a 50 percent increase in the patient load. A 1934 study of 1,733 families completed by Daniel showed that the services of the department had become essential because none of the residents could have afforded any type of services by a physician. By the 1940s, when she retired, many of the concerns such as child labor and improved hygiene had been eliminated through legislation. Following her retirement she continued to act as a consultant to the hospital. Daniel, who never married, died in New York City.

Dedicated throughout her career to the cause of women and children, Daniel had been active in the suffrage movement and the Working Woman's Society. Her most concentrated efforts, however, were directed at the Out-Practice Department of which she was in charge for sixty years. Where others despaired of the immigrant's poor living conditions, she realized the potential to be had through education and care of her patients, and each day she walked a minimum of six miles to see them. Her innovative work among the tenement dwellers became an early model for the endeavors of settlement workers and social services.

• Daniel left no papers. Information on her work at the New York Infirmary is in its *Annual Reports*. Her articles include "The City's Health-Living Conditions," *Municipal Affairs* (June 1898), and "How Wearing Apparel Is Fashioned in the Tenements," *Charities*, 1 Apr. 1905, pp. 624–29. An interview conducted with her is printed in "Doctoring the Poor for 35 Years," *New York Times*, 6, 15 Mar. 1914. Other sources include William R. Stewart, *The Philanthropic Work of Josephine Shaw Lowell* (1911); The New York Infirmary, *The New York Infirmary: A Century of Devoted Service, 1854–1954* (1954); Esther Pohl Lovejoy, *Women Doctors of the World* (1957); S. Josephine Baker, *Fighting for Life* (1939; repr. 1974); and Regina Markell Morantz-Sanchez, *Sympathy and Science: Women Physicians in American Medicine* (1985). Obituaries are in the *New York Times*, 11 Aug. 1944, and *Medical Woman's Journal* (Sept. 1944).

MARILYN ELIZABETH PERRY

DANIEL, Charles (11 Aug. 1879–14 May 1971), art collector and gallery owner, was born in New York City, the middle of nine children. His father (whose name is unknown) was a coal miner in Germany before emigrating to the United States. In 1868 he met and married Daniel's mother, and together they opened a German restaurant in what is now Manhattan's Chelsea district. Daniel completed high school and went to work at his parents' restaurant until approximately 1900, when he opened a place of his own with his brother George. Located on the corner of 9th Avenue and 42d Street, the Daniel Saloon became a regular meeting place for young painters such as Glenn O. Coleman (whose family had a printing shop nearby), Max Kuehne, and Ernest Lawson. Through these artists, Daniel began to learn about contemporary painting, to visit the local exhibitions, and, eventually, to collect works of art. In 1910 Daniel visited Alfred Stieglitz's Little Galleries of the Photo-Secession (known as 291) to see an exhibition of Henri Matisse, but he came away with two paintings by John Marin. Daniel later credited this visit with Stieglitz for changing the direction of his collecting and the direction of his life.

When his brother complained that the artists were giving their saloon business a bad name, Daniel rented an office on 47th Street where artists could meet and show each other their work. The first public exhibition at the Daniel Studio was held in March 1912, presenting such painters as Kuehne, Lawson, Samuel Halpert, George Luks, Kathleen McEnery, and others. Daniel went back to Stieglitz with $1,200 to buy more of Marin's work, telling Stieglitz "that he wanted to buy them as a dealer, to make money, and also to become Marin's dealer regularly." In February 1913 the International Exhibition of Modern Art opened in Manhattan. Many of the artists Daniel collected and exhibited were dissatisfied with the Armory Show's emphasis on European art and complained bitterly about the lack of support that young, modern American artists received. Daniel decided to sell his half of the saloon to his brother and devote himself full time to promoting contemporary American art. The Daniel Gallery opened in the fall of 1913 in the front apartment of the top floor at 2 West 47th Street. Its first catalog described the gallery's goals: "It is dedicated to the younger painters of individuality and to the older who have kept alive an ideal through many years of work and endeavor. The aim of this Gallery is to encourage individuality and promote a more general appreciation of the finer thing in art." Rockwell Kent, then a promising painter and illustrator, helped with the interior decoration and designed a logo for the gallery. Man Ray, whose paintings Daniel was already buying, helped by designing and lettering the exhibition catalogs for the first season. A friend of Man Ray's, writer Alanson Hartpence, became Daniel's assistant and was responsible for bringing many of the most radical artists to the gallery. Elizabeth McCausland, a critic, described the gallery's opening: "There suddenly appeared a new champion of modern art in America, a dealer—Charles Daniel—to whom many of our leading artists pay grateful tribute."

For the next nineteen years, the Daniel Gallery exhibited and supported the work of young, mostly unknown artists. Although Stieglitz gained celebrity status for promoting modern artists, he actually supported very few and passed many on to Daniel. "Most of these painters were never hung in 291," wrote author and critic Alfred Kreymborg; "[I] eventually saw and followed their work in the principal descendant of the hornet's nest: The Daniel Gallery." Daniel gave Man Ray his first three one-man shows in 1915, 1916, and 1919. He also sent him a regular allowance so that Man Ray could devote himself to painting. Painters Charles Demuth, Peter Blume, and Preston Dickinson received their first exhibitions at the Daniel Gallery; Demuth was given eight one-man shows from 1914 to 1923. Avant-garde artists such as Stuart Davis and Stanton MacDonald-Wright could be seen at Daniel's before they achieved fame. The sculptor William Zorach wrote that Daniel was "a great influence on American art. The artists he took up, showed and promoted, were the advanced and the unknown who had no reputation and no place in the world to exhibit. . . . Charles Daniel had little knowledge of art and no confidence in himself, but he had what is more important, an instinct for the real in art and a belief in artists. When Daniel opened his gallery, Stieglitz said, 'Well, if saloonkeepers are going into art, America is certainly waking up.'"

Daniel sponsored trips for Blume, Marsden Hartley, and Preston Dickinson, among other painters. He exhibited dozens of female artists alongside men, including Elsie Driggs, Katherine Schmidt Shubert, Rosella Hartman, and Margarite Zorach. He showed prints and drawings as often as paintings, as well as photography, ceramics, wood carving, site-specific installations, and embroidery. By 1915 the Daniel Gallery was the leading venue for modern American art. As James Britton, a contemporary critic, remarked, "The storm center has shifted again and is back home at the Daniel Gallery, where it is welcomed with supreme good humor by that persistent believer and zealous propagandist—Mr. Charles Daniel. . . . Like a second *Daniel come to judgement* with a certainty of confidence, this *believer* has lined up his battery and fired and behold! The spattered remains of the critics . . . Oh, these *Danielites*!"

After the First World War, Daniel began exhibiting modern French, German, and Russian artists in addition to Americans. The first such show in 1922 featured Pablo Picasso, Juan Gris, and other cubist painters. The Japanese-American painter Yasuo Kuniyoshi was given eight solo exhibitions, and Kuniyoshi served as the gallery's photographer (as Man Ray had earlier). When the collector and benefactor Galka Scheyer wanted to organize an American tour of the "Blue Four" (Lyonel Feininger, Alexy Jawlensky, Wassily Kandinsky, and Paul Klee), she came to Daniel, who not only gave them a show in 1925 but also wrote the catalog himself.

In 1926 Daniel moved his gallery to Madison Avenue at 57th Street, where the art market was then centered. The critic Murdoch Pemberton commented on the move and on Daniel's continued independence: "He is a fortunate person who finds his lot in life so much to his liking that the crowd passes by him arousing no envy. We imagine that they could discontinue the elevator at 600 Madison Avenue, plug up the stairs and Daniel . . . would never notice it." However, Daniel's financial situation grew increasingly unstable with the death of his best customer Ferdinand Howald, the stock market crash of 1929, and the expanding competition for contemporary art. Besides a dozen new commercial galleries, Albert Gallatin's Gallery of Living Art opened in 1927, the Museum of Modern Art in 1929, and the Whitney Museum of American Art in 1931. In the fall of 1932 Daniel's paintings and other possessions were seized for nonpayment of rent, and the Daniel Gallery officially closed.

In 1946 Parke-Bernet Galleries exhibited and auctioned the Daniel Collection, those paintings found in his gallery when it was closed. Publicity for the sale spoke of the "late Charles L. Daniel," even though he was still alive and living on Horatio Street in Greenwich Village. Daniel later moved in with his sister and his nephew John Buckspies, where he lived penniless until his death at the age of ninety-two.

At the start of Daniel's career as a gallery owner, an editorial in *American Art News* commented: "He is the first art collector who has ever had the courage to invest his money in a gallery on faith in his ideals, and his action will no doubt find sincere appreciation." Without promoting himself, he championed young, unknown American artists who became some of the most celebrated of the twentieth century.

• The records of the Daniel Gallery were lost or destroyed, but an oral history is held in the Archives of American Art, Smithsonian Institution, reel no. 1343. An invaluable curatorial file with original notes is held by the Zabriskie Gallery, New York City, where an exhibition titled Charles Daniel and the Daniel Gallery was mounted in 1993. Elizabeth McCausland, "The Daniel Gallery and Modern American Art," *Magazine of Art* 44, no. 7 (Nov. 1951), served as the inspiration for the master's thesis by Julie Mellby, "A Record of Charles Daniel and the Daniel Gallery" (Hunter College of CCNY, 1993). Raphael Soyer's personal reminiscence is in the *American Art Journal* 3, no. 2 (Fall 1971). See also Herbert J. Seligmann, *Alfred Stieglitz Talking* (1966); Richard Lee Rubenfield, "Preston Dickinson: An American Modernist" (Ph.D. diss., Ohio State Univ., 1985); Alfred Kreymborg, *The Troubadour* (1925); William Zorach, *Art Is My Life* (1967); James Britton, "Daniel's Modernists," *American Art News*, 30 Oct. 1915; Murdoch Pemberton, "As We Like It," *Art News*, 23 Oct. 1926; "Daniel Collection at Parke-Bernet," *Art Digest*, 1 Mar. 1946; and "At the Galleries," *American Art News*, 20 Dec. 1913. An obituary is in the *New York Times*, 17 May 1971.

JULIE MELLBY

DANIEL, Daniel (6 June 1890–1 July 1981), sportswriter, was born Daniel Markowitz in New York City, the son of Morris Markowitz, a builder; his mother's name is unknown. The family moved to Springfield, Massachusetts, and Kansas City, Missouri, and then back to New York, where Daniel worked summer jobs at his father's construction sites. He attended several colleges, including the City College of New York, but graduated from none. Intending to become a doctor but not sure if he was too squeamish for medical science, he applied for a part-time job in the sports department of the *New York Herald* on New Year's Eve 1907, waited three hours for the editor to return to his desk, and was hired in the early morning hours.

Daniel made his first mark when he answered the office telephone one Thanksgiving morning and heard the reporter assigned to the Villanova-Fordham football game call in sick. He covered the game himself and battled a dense fog to write a story that earned his editor's praise. A few months later he got his first big break, an assignment to cover the Brooklyn Dodgers during spring training in Macon, Georgia. "The Brooklyn club carried me, for free," he recalled. "I got three dollars a day, or $21 a week. I was rich. I was famous. And I was done for insofar as anything but sports writing was concerned" (*Sporting News*, 19 Mar. 1958).

Over the next few years Daniel covered many sports, but he was drawn to his first love, baseball. Years later he remembered seeing his first major league game in 1902 when John McGraw became manager of the New York Giants. He recalled attending the first home game of the New York Highlanders (later the Yankees) in 1903 and a Labor Day doubleheader between the Giants and the St. Louis Cardinals. Daniel became a Giants fan and idolized McGraw: "To touch his uniform was like communing with the gods on high Olympus" (*Sporting News*, 31 Jan. 1935).

Daniel was working for the *New York Press* in 1913 for thirty dollars a week when sports editor Nat Fleischer assigned him to cover the football game in which the Carlisle Indians upset undefeated Dartmouth,

31–10. The managing editor liked his story so much that he gave its author his first byline, "By Daniel," since anti-Semitism prevented the use of "Marko-witz."

When the Federal League challenged the hegemony of the two established major leagues, the *Press* gave the Federals good coverage, and Daniel, as he was now known, often received inside information. Near the end of the 1915 season he received an anonymous telephone tip that the upstart league would go out of business and that the Giants would buy a pair of Federal League stars. Daniel wrote the story and after some initial disbelief, he was proved right. Daniel married Mollie Schron in 1918; they had twin daughters.

Daniel began covering the New York Yankees on a regular basis when he went to spring training in 1919 for the *New York Sun*. A teetotaler, he had trouble keeping up with other reporters who socialized nightly with Yankees co-owner Tillinghast Huston. Still, he beat his competitors to the story that the Yankees planned to open their home season on a Sunday, taking quick advantage of a new state law permitting Sunday baseball. One day, while sitting in the spring training sun, he heard manager Miller Huggins deflect criticism leveled by the team's other co-owner, Colonel Jacob Ruppert. "Colonel," said Huggins, uttering a retort that entered the baseball lexicon immediately, "the pitchers are ahead of the hitters."

Covering the Yankees became Daniel's steady occupation, and his affection for this team went far beyond the limits of objective journalism. Roger Kahn, in *The Era* (1993), called Daniel's prose "promotional copy," and Fred Lieb, another esteemed sportswriter, said, "Daniel climbed on board the Yankee bandwagon, and has chortled over Yank successes since" (*Sporting News*, 5 Mar. 1952). But Leonard Koppett was willing to forgive Daniel's excesses: "His opinions and whatever distortions they contained were unquestionably his own" (*Sporting News*, 25 July 1981). When Daniel selected a personal all-time all-star team in 1953, other writers were surprised that he picked Yankees at only three positions: Lou Gehrig at first base, Babe Ruth in the outfield, and Bill Dickey at catcher.

In 1922 Daniel helped Fleischer and several others found *The Ring*, boxing's most prestigious publication. He wrote for this monthly throughout his career, served as an associate editor, and was president of the Boxing Writers of America.

New York's daily newspapers endured a series of mergers, but Daniel was always able to land on his feet. In 1924 he became sports editor of the *World* (later the *World-Telegram*), and in 1932 he began to contribute regularly to the *Sporting News*, where he signed his work, "Dan Daniel." When he asked if his father had any objection to a legal name change, the reply was "Not at all. Markowitz isn't your real name anyway."

From his editorial positions, and especially after he began answering readers' questions in his Saturday column, "Ask Daniel," he developed a reputation as a foremost authority and earned the nickname "Mr.

Baseball." A standard pressbox joke when a reporter unearthed a tidbit of new information was for a colleague to remark, "Daniel had it yesterday." By the 1960s, when he stopped writing regularly, Daniel was one of his profession's most esteemed members, "the only baseball writer in the United States," in his own words, "who achieved every distinction that is possible for a baseball writer to attain." National chairman of the Baseball Writers' Association of America in 1957, he received that organization's highest honor, the J. G. Taylor Spink Award in August 1973. He died in Pompano Beach, Florida.

• Clipping files are held at the archives of the *Sporting News*, St. Louis, Mo., and at the National Baseball Library, Cooperstown, N.Y. An interview with Daniel is in Jerome Holtzman, *No Cheering in the Press Box* (1974). Obituaries are in the *New York Times*, 2 July 1981, and the *Sporting News*, 18 July 1981.

STEVEN P. GIETSCHIER

DANIEL, John Moncure (24 Oct. 1825–30 Mar. 1865), diplomat and editor, was born in Stafford County, Virginia, the son of John Moncure Daniel, a country doctor, and Elizabeth Mitchell. As a child, Daniel received a rigorous education from his father and was known as an insatiable bookworm. He was particularly fond of the writings of Joseph Addison, Jonathan Swift, and Sir Richard Steele. In 1840 he went to Richmond to live with his great-uncle, Justice Peter V. Daniel of the U.S. Supreme Court, whose devotion to slavery, states' rights, and southern social customs influenced his young nephew. After returning home briefly in 1843, Daniel spent a year in Fredericksburg studying law with Judge John Tayloe Lomax. Daniel's father died in 1845, and lacking sufficient funds to continue his studies, Daniel returned to Richmond, where he found work in the library of the Patrick Henry Society.

Perhaps to supplement his meager income, Daniel began submitting articles to the *Richmond Enquirer*. His career as a journalist progressed quickly. His sharp and lively prose earned him a position in 1846 as the coeditor of the *Southern Planter*, a monthly agricultural magazine, and before the year ended he became the sole editor. Under Daniel's stewardship the magazine expanded its readership and became more political in content. He left in May 1847 to join a new Democratic newspaper, the *Richmond Semi-Weekly Examiner*, as coeditor. By April 1848 he was the editor in chief and sole proprietor of the *Examiner*.

Daniel's aggressive editorial style made the *Examiner* one of the leading Democratic papers of the South. Although Richmond was a Whig stronghold at the time, Daniel launched a relentless crusade against Whig leaders in Richmond and their local newspaper, the *Richmond Whig*, which earned him many lifelong personal and political enemies. An observer in 1848 described him as "an electric battery, full charged, whose touches shocked the staid and lofty leaders in Virginia politics." Daniel extolled states' rights, slavery, and the cause of the Democratic party. He deeply admired John C. Calhoun and strove to make the *Examiner* Calhoun's organ in Virginia. He denounced bitterly the compromise plan of 1850, declaring that the North had "broken down the walls of the Southern city, and have yet to plunder it, to burn it, and to massacre its inhabitants" (*Examiner*, 17 Sept. 1850). Daniel's editorial style was meticulous and dictatorial. He unhesitatingly threw out paid advertisements to make room for long editorials, and he revised submissions at will. The columns of the *Examiner* were infused with his acerbic personality and brilliant invective.

In 1853 President Franklin Pierce appointed Daniel as chargé d'affaires to the court of Victor Emmanuel II in Turin, Italy. Daniel cared little for his official duties as an ambassador and spent much of his time traveling in Europe. He was alienated irrevocably from diplomatic society at the court when a letter he wrote ridiculing Turin court life was translated into Italian by one of his enemies and circulated in Italy. Despite numerous missteps and scandals, Daniel remained at his post until 1860, when the news of South Carolina's secession hastened his return home to resume the helm of the *Examiner*. He claimed that the departure of some southern states, although badly handled, compelled a unified southern secession, and he campaigned vehemently for Virginia to secede immediately.

At the outset of the Civil War, Daniel expressed confidence in Confederate president Jefferson Davis and advocated a strong central government and an aggressive military strategy. "No power in Executive hands can be too great, no discretion too absolute, at such moments as these. We need a dictator" (*Examiner*, 8 May 1861). He urged the adoption of conscription, traditionally unpopular in American culture, as the most judicious way to recruit soldiers from all classes of the population. By early 1862, frustrated with the "fatal paralysis" of the army and Davis's refusal to include him in his councils, Daniel turned against the administration with a vengeance. He began to attack Davis personally, accusing him of meddling excessively in military affairs, appointing unqualified cronies to his cabinet and to military posts, and in general mismanaging the war effort. Nothing but "the extinction of the dynasty of ignorant and imbecile politicians who have long monopolized place and power" would bring southern victory, Daniel claimed (*Examiner*, 15 Apr. 1862). One particularly biting attack on Confederate secretary of the treasury Edward A. Elmore in 1864 resulted in a duel—one of nine Daniel fought in his lifetime—in which Daniel was wounded in the foot. Like other harsh critics of the Confederate government, he distinguished between the Confederate administration and the cause of southern independence, to which he remained deeply committed.

Daniel, who never married, devoted his life to the *Examiner*, from which he derived a profit of at least $50,000 a year. Although he repeatedly exhorted Confederate citizens to sacrifice luxuries for the cause, he lived in a lavishly furnished two-bedroom apartment above the *Examiner* office and in a three-story brick house in Richmond. He twice served briefly in the Confederate army, as a major on the staff of General John B. Floyd in 1861 and as an aide to General Ambrose P. Hill in 1862. He was accompanied on both occasions by his slave cook and valet. "I hate pain, I cannot bear it, and yet I should like to be able to show an honorable scar in this cause," he confided to his assistant, George W. Bagby (Bagby, p. 64). A wound in the arm at Mechanicsville in the summer of 1862 gave Daniel sufficient cause to retire permanently from military service.

By the summer of 1864 Daniel despaired of a Confederate victory and lost much of his zeal for espousing the Confederate cause. In January 1865 he fell ill with pneumonia and suffered recurring bouts throughout the spring. In his final months he became convinced that the Confederacy was defeated and that the only reasonable course was Reconstruction on the best possible terms. He died in Richmond after weeks of severe illness, only days before the office of the *Examiner* was destroyed by fire as Confederate troops retreated from the city. Under Daniel's stewardship, the *Examiner* became the most widely read organ of discontent in the Confederacy. His outspoken criticism of the Davis administration epitomized the internal dissent that wracked the Confederacy, contributing to its ultimate defeat.

• No collection of Daniel's letters is available except his correspondence with the State Department while at Turin. He may have kept two diaries in his life, neither of which have come to light. The office of the *Examiner*, which may have contained many of Daniel's valuable papers, was destroyed in the Richmond fire of Apr. 1865. *The Richmond Examiner during the War* (1868) is a posthumous publication of selected *Examiner* editorials accompanied by a memoir written by his brother, Frederick S. Daniel. A biography, *The Life of Stonewall Jackson, from Official Papers, Contemporary Narratives, and Personal Acquaintance, by a Virginian* (1863; repr. 1864), is attributed to Daniel. Daniel's career is recounted in George W. Bagby, *John M. Daniel's Latch-Key* (1868; repr. 1884); R. W. Hughes, *Editors of the Past* (1897); Robert E. Cowart, "Thunder of the Confederacy" (unpublished ms., Robert E. Cowart Papers, Special Collections Department, Robert W. Woodruff Library, Emory University, Atlanta, Ga.); and Raymond K. Cooley, "John M. Daniel, Editor of the Richmond *Examiner* and Gadfly of the Confederacy" (M.A. thesis, Old Dominion Univ., 1973). Obituaries are in the *Examiner*, 31 Mar. 1865, and the *New York Times*, 7 Apr. 1865.

SUSAN WYLY-JONES

DANIEL, John Warwick (5 Sept. 1842–29 June 1910), Confederate soldier, legal scholar, and U.S. senator, was born in Lynchburg, Virginia, the son of William Daniel, Jr., a lawyer and judge, and Sarah Ann Warwick. He attended private schools in the Lynchburg area; after attending Lynchburg College from 1855 to 1859, he enrolled in a classical school administered by Dr. Gessner Harrison. When Virginia seceded from the Union in 1861, Daniel interrupted his education to enlist in the cavalry. He rose to major and fought in several battles, including Gettysburg. At the battle of the Wilderness in 1864 he received a wound that put him on crutches for the remainder of his life and earned him the sobriquet of the "Lame Lion of Lynchburg."

After fighting for the Confederacy, Daniel renewed his determination to become a member of the law profession. In 1866 he attended the University of Virginia for a year, then he entered a successful legal practice. He entered politics in 1869, when he was elected to the Virginia House of Delegates as a Conservative. That year he married Julia Elizabeth Murrell; they had five children. Also at this time Daniel published his first law text, *The Law and Practice of Attachment* (1869).

During the 1870s Daniel's political stature as a Conservative began to rise. He made several bids for a national political office but had to settle for state senator in 1875. While a state politician and legislator, he continued to establish himself as a lawyer and legal scholar. In 1876 he published *A Treatise on the Law of Negotiable Instruments*, which was later proclaimed to be one of the three greatest textbooks of Daniel's generation. He became one of the most prosperous and widely known members of the Virginia Bar Association.

In 1877 Daniel's statewide political reputation was enhanced when he unsuccessfully sought the Conservative nomination for governor as a so-called Funder, demanding that the Virginia state debt be fully honored, as opposed to the Readjuster faction, which agitated for a downward revision of the debt. The debt issue split the Conservative party, and Daniel became the leader of the Funder faction. By 1881 the Readjuster wing of the party had organized into a separate political party, and Daniel resigned his state senate seat and ran, once more unsuccessfully, as a Conservative/Funder nominee. With the statewide victory of the Readjusters in 1881, Daniel began to favor the renovation of the Conservative party, which was gaining widespread support across the state in both urban and rural areas for fear that Readjusterism in reality meant Republican/black rule in the future.

When the Conservative convention met in 1883, Daniel emerged as the favorite of the party, which was renamed the Democratic party. He played an important leadership role, both in and out of the convention, to construct a political organization that would successfully challenge the opposition and maintain Democratic control of the state for years to come. The changes in the political structure included the organization of election machinery, the creation of administrative boards with new powers, and the gerrymandering of congressional districts to favor the Democrats. As a result of the gerrymandering, Daniel was elected to Congress in 1884. In 1885 he attained his ultimate goal, the U.S. Senate, where he remained until 1910.

Daniel's success in the growth and development of the Virginia democracy and his rise to power in 1885 were owed to his statewide popularity, his organizational skills, his forceful personality, and his nostalgic vision of times past. With spellbinding oratory, he did much to establish and support the "cult" of the "Lost Cause," a romantic and sentimental version of the "Old South" that included defense of Southern secession, regard for the Confederate greats, and white supremacy. He convinced many Virginians that the Democratic party was the protector and guardian of the cult. In a speech dedicating a statue of Robert E. Lee, he pictured Lee as "the priest of the people" in "this age of ruthless competition for wealth and power." He often said to his audiences, "I am a Democrat because I am a white man and a Virginian."

Throughout his senatorial career, Daniel made every effort to control Virginia politics to ensure Democratic solidarity. With the rise of Populism and the third-party movement in Virginia in the late 1880s, he had to bow to political realities and support measures that would especially appeal to the agrarian debtor class, such as free silver, lower tariffs, and federal aid for southern schools and businesses. He also fought against electoral reforms for the same reasons.

Daniel was against the initiative and referendum. He opposed the Force Bill of 1890, an attempt to end corruption at the polls in the South. At the state convention in 1897 he was active in the defeat of the proposal for a direct primary system to nominate U.S. senators by popular vote, an issue that eventually led to a challenge by an independent faction for control of the state Democratic machine. He also took part in the state constitutional convention in 1902 as chairman of the Franchise Committee to draft a provision for the disfranchisement of black voters. He believed that this provision was needed to restore the political integrity of the state, in other words to eliminate the Republican party as a serious contender in Virginia politics.

Daniel was Virginia's first fifth-term senator. As a member of the minority party for most of his long tenure, he was ineligible for committee chairmanships and had little opportunity to initiate legislation. Even so, he took his position seriously and was known for his devotion to duty and his speaking ability. He served on several important committees, including Foreign Relations, Finance, and Appropriations. Even though he was considered a conservative, Daniel took a somewhat moderate position toward many of the domestic issues that came before the Senate. He urged passage of the federal eight-hour day, he supported the regulation of railroad labor and employment practices, and voted to regulate the railroads. In foreign affairs he approved of President William McKinley's decision to go to war against Spain, however, he joined the anti-imperialist faction in the Senate in opposition to annexation of the Philippines. He supported President Theodore Roosevelt's handling of the black soldiers riot in Brownsville, Texas, in 1906. He died in Lynchburg, Virginia.

Daniel is remembered for his political career. In his thirty years of public service, he emerged as a figurehead of the Confederate cult in Virginia and throughout the South. Overcoming intraparty strife in 1885, he won this significant election and became the principal founder of a unified, all embracing Virginia democracy, which stood the test of time.

• Daniel's papers are in the James Memorial Library, Lynchburg, Va.; the Alderman Library, University of Virginia, Charlottesville; and the Duke University Library, Durham, N.C. The collection at the Duke University Library contains the most revealing letters on Daniel's political career. See also Sylvia D. Vecellio, "John Warwick Daniel, Lame Lion of Lynchburg: Youth, Soldier, and Rising Politician, 1842–1885" (M.A. thesis, Univ. of Virginia, 1950); Richard B. Doss, "John Warwick Daniel: A Study in the Virginia Democracy" (Ph.D. diss., Univ. of Virginia, 1955); Allen W. Moger, *Virginia: Bourbonism to Byrd, 1870–1925* (1968); Raymond Pulley, *Old Virginia Restored, 1870–1930* (1968); and Edward Younger, ed., *The Governors of Virginia 1860–1978* (1982). Substantive obituaries are in *Harper's*, 9 July 1910, and *Review of Reviews*, 10 Aug. 1910.

THOMAS E. GAY, JR.

DANIEL, Peter Vivian (24 Apr. 1784–31 May 1860), lawyer, state official, and associate justice of the U.S. Supreme Court, was born at "Crow's Nest," in Stafford County, Virginia, the son of Travers Daniel, a planter, and Frances Moncure. His ancestors settled in Virginia early in the seventeenth century and founded a prominent gentry family. Daniel attended the College of New Jersey at Princeton for a time, but left in 1805 to read law in Richmond with Edmund Randolph, a former Virginia governor and U.S. attorney general. Daniel joined the Virginia bar in 1808 and within two years married his mentor's daughter, Lucy Randolph, with whom he had three children. The couple settled in Richmond but also spent much time at "Spring Farm," a plantation just outside the city that Daniel purchased from his father-in-law.

A staunch Jeffersonian Republican, Daniel adhered throughout his life to the political principles of states' rights and strict constructionism enunciated in the Virginia and Kentucky resolutions of 1798. With this affiliation and his later prominence in the Democratic party, Daniel never flourished at the Richmond bar, dominated as it was by Federalists and Whigs before the Civil War. Although he practiced law until his appointment to the bench many years later, Daniel early focused more of his energies on politics.

Despite meeting fellow attorney John Seddon in a duel over personal and professional matters in which his antagonist was fatally wounded, Daniel was able to generate enough local support to win election to the Virginia House of Delegates from Stafford County in 1808. He served rather inconspicuously for two terms, but two years later the general assembly elected him to a seat on the council of state, an advisory board designed to limit the power of the governor. In 1818 Daniel became presiding officer of that board and thus served in effect as Virginia's lieutenant governor until purged in 1835 by the Whig majority in the general assembly.

Daniel performed some of his most important public service as a member of the council, particularly in mobilizing Virginia during the War of 1812. Because the council also held limited appellate jurisdiction, he wrote some of his first legal opinions while lieutenant governor. He cast many of these opinions, even in the most mundane cases, in constitutional terms, evidence of his penchant for assuming a lofty theoretical position from which to heap disdain on those who might question either his beliefs or authority. At the same time he consistently championed the rights of criminal defendants. He not only advocated a softening of the criminal code of Virginia, but he also sought justice by ensuring a strict adherence to procedural rules, especially in cases involving African-American defendants.

As Daniel solidified his political standing in the 1830s, he joined the so-called Richmond Junto, a group of powerful Jacksonian Democrats who worked tirelessly to advance the cause of the national party in Virginia. Daniel took a prominent role in election efforts of both Andrew Jackson and Martin Van Buren. In return for his strong support of Jackson against the Bank of the United States, the president offered him the post of attorney general. But already uncomfortable with the "spoils system," Daniel politely declined the position, claiming as an excuse that the salary was insufficient for the work required. In 1836, however, following Daniel's reappointment to the council and the elevation of Virginian Philip P. Barbour to the U.S. Supreme Court, Daniel accepted Jackson's offer to become judge of the U.S. District Court for eastern Virginia.

When Barbour died suddenly in February 1841, President Van Buren seized the opportunity to nominate Daniel, his friend and political ally, to the unexpected opening on the court. Desperate to achieve his goal in the last troubled days of his administration, Van Buren ignored routine selection procedures and placed Daniel's name before Congress barely two days after Barbour's death. Angry Whig senators attempted to bury the nomination, but failed narrowly when they were unable to prevent a quorum at a midnight confirmation vote on 2–3 March 1841, just a day before Van Buren left office.

Daniel brought to the court a devotion to simple Jeffersonian agrarianism and an inveterate hatred of banks and corporations in general. Passionately committed to states' rights, state sovereignty, and limited government, he envisioned himself as a crusader against rising national power and economic consolidation and a defender of slavery. In a rapidly changing economic and social world, Daniel was doomed to fight a rearguard action against American progress and the irrepressible legal and constitutional developments that came with it. By the end of his eighteen years on the court, his voice was heard often in dissent.

When Daniel first ascended to the bench, he most often spoke for the court in cases involving land, equity, or procedural issues. On broader matters he consistently opposed the expansion of federal regulatory or jurisdictional authority and resisted the doctrine of federal exclusiveness under the commerce clause. In the *License Cases* (1847) and *Passenger Cases* (1849) he supported state regulation, and in *Pennsylvania v. Wheeling Bridge* (1851) he denied that the state had the power to bring an action on behalf of a local commercial interest.

Attempting to restrict the access of corporations to the federal courts, Daniel argued that corporations were artificial persons, not "citizens," and therefore unable to use the federal courts on the basis of diversity of citizenship, as in *Rundle v. Delaware and Raritan Canal Co.* (1852). His dissent in *Planters' Bank of Mississippi v. Sharp* (1848) opposed application of the contract clause to corporate charters, arguing that contracts remained subject to the police power of the states. In his only majority opinion on a contracts issue, *West River Bridge Co. v. Dix* (1849), Daniel wrote that a state must have the power of eminent domain to condemn any property for public use, even if the property was held by a corporation whose charter was viewed as creating contractual rights.

As he grew older, Daniel became increasingly bitter toward the North and northerners, in some measure as a response to intensified attacks on slavery. In *Prigg v. Pennsylvania* (1842), a case involving the federal fugitive slave statute and northern "personal liberty laws," he attacked the 1820 Missouri Compromise as unconstitutional and contended that Congress had no power to restrict slavery in the territories. Joining the majority in *Dred Scott v. Sanford* (1857), he went further than any other justice in declaring that freed black slaves, because they had originally been held as property, could not be citizens.

Daniel was devastated by his wife's death in 1847. He took comfort in his close relationship with his unmarried daughter, Elizabeth, and in his friendship with Chief Justice Roger B. Taney. He dreaded the long weeks and months away from his family while attending court in Washington or riding his circuit in Alabama and Mississippi. In 1853 he married Elizabeth Harris, the daughter of Dr. Thomas Harris of Philadelphia. The couple had two children before Daniel's much younger wife died tragically in January 1857. Broken in health and spirit, Daniel retired from the court at the end of the 1858–1859 term and died the following year in Richmond.

• A number of Daniel's letters from a family collection at the University of Virginia were edited by William D. Holt, Jr., and published in *Journal of Mississippi History* 4 (1942): 168–71, *West Virginia History* 3 (1941–1942): 267–74, and *Western Pennsylvania Historical Magazine* 24 (1941): 127–30. A revealing set of letters from Daniel to his daughter Elizabeth, written from Washington and while riding the judicial circuit, can be found in the Daniel family papers at the Virginia Historical Society in Richmond. John P. Frank, *Justice Daniel Dissenting: A Biography of Peter V. Daniel, 1784–1860* (1964), remains the fullest and best treatment of Daniel's life, but Lawrence Burnette, Jr., "Peter V. Daniel: Agrarian Justice," *Virginia Magazine of History and Biography* 62 (1954): 289–305, provides a valuable brief summary of his career. For an excellent assessment of Daniel as a justice, see Frank Otto Gatell, "Peter V. Daniel," in *The Justices of the United States Supreme Court, 1789–1978: Their Lives and Major Opinions,* ed. Leon Friedman and Fred L. Israel, vol. 1 (1980), pp. 795–814. An obituary is in the *Richmond Enquirer,* 1 June 1860.

E. LEE SHEPARD

DANIELS, Bebe (14 Jan. 1901–16 Mar. 1971), entertainer, was born Phyllis Bebe Daniels in Dallas, Texas, the daughter of Danny Daniels (Melville Daniel MacMeal), the actor-manager of a traveling stock theater company, and Phyllis Griffin, his leading lady. From birth Daniels was called "Bebe," which means baby in Spanish, reflecting her mother's Spanish ancestry. Daniels first appeared onstage when she was only ten weeks old, and she performed in her first Shakespearean production at the age of four. After her father left the family around 1907–1908, Daniels's mother took her to Los Angeles, California. She played child roles onstage until a new labor law was passed. In 1910 she made her silent film debut in *The Common Enemy.*

When she was fourteen, after having played children in many western films, Daniels succeeded in making herself look "older," and she won a contract with director Hal Roach. For Roach, she teamed with Harold Lloyd in nearly 300 knockabout, physically demanding one- and two-reel comedies. Daniels later wrote that when she was eighteen Lloyd asked her to marry him; she declined the offer. Her film persona evolved into the "good little bad girl" type. Having spent ten days in jail for a series of speeding tickets, Daniels made *The Speed Girl* in 1921, capitalizing on the well-reported incident. During this time Daniels was dating heavyweight champion Jack Dempsey. Strikingly beautiful, with dark brown eyes and blue-black hair, Daniels costarred with Rudolph Valentino in *Monsieur Beaucaire* (1924). Under contract at Paramount, she trailed only Gloria Swanson and Pola Negri in popularity. In 1924 she met Ben Lyon, a handsome leading man, and the two became romantically involved.

With the establishment of talking pictures, executives at Paramount did not feel confident that Daniels could make the transition to the new medium, for no apparent reason. Consequently she defiantly bought out her contract and moved to Radio-Keith-Orpheum in 1929, accepting a cut in her usual salary in exchange for a percentage of the gross, which proved lucrative for her. Although she lacked formal voice training, Daniels convinced the studio that she could sing, so that she could star in the film of the Broadway musical *Rio Rita.* The 1929 film was half in color and featured Daniels in white against pink and red backgrounds; it was one of the great successes of the first wave of movie musicals.

In 1930 Daniels and Lyon were married; they had two children. Daniels became a recording success; among her musical films was *42nd Street* (1933), which proved to be a classic. She sang and danced the title song, along with "You're Getting To Be a Habit With Me." Daniels made her last American film in 1935; by then she had made two musical films in Great Britain.

Between 1933 and 1939 Daniels and Lyon made theater tours throughout Britain; they also played in variety shows at the Palladium and became the first American stars to appear on BBC television. They made their first joint British film, *Not Wanted on Voy-*

age, which was well received there. Following the outbreak of World War II, Daniels and Lyon chose to remain in Britain. They appeared in a revue called *Haw Haw*, which opened in December 1939 and set the tone for their morale-boosting efforts on stage and radio during the war years.

Daniels began her British recording career with "Start the Day Right" and other numbers from *Haw Haw*. Her performance of songs by American expatriate Nat B. Ayer, such as "If You Were the Only Girl in the World," at the American Eagle Club were very well received there, which inspired Lyon's creation of "Hi, Gang!" a landmark radio program that ran weekly from 1940 until Lyon enlisted in the U.S. Army at the end of 1942. On the show, a fast-paced variety program, Daniels introduced such songs as "The White Cliffs of Dover" and "Tiggerty-Boo!" which became the British forces' "Thumbs-Up Song." Daniels and Lyon began broadcasting "Stars and Stripes" on the BBC North American Service, a program featuring interviews with American servicemen in Britain. Daniels and Lyon opened their London home to British and American servicemen, and they toured Britain, entertaining the forces of both nations. An American B-17 was named *Bebe's Boys*, a tribute to the esteem in which the troops held Daniels.

Daniels and Lyon appeared in the revue *Gangway*, which ran from December 1941 through the end of 1942. In the show, she sang "Night and Day" and "Blue Champagne" and delivered a comic lecture called "Can Woman Ever Replace the House?" In 1943 she played the title role in Cole Porter's *Panama Hattie*, a role she called her favorite. The show opened in London at the Picadilly, but a few days later the theater was destroyed in an air raid. The show was moved to the Adelphi, where it enjoyed a long run.

Following D day, Lyon, by then a lieutenant colonel in the Army Air Force, flew Daniels to Normandy. Six hundred yards behind the front lines, she recorded interviews with wounded American servicemen. In her joint autobiography with Lyon, *Life with the Lyons*, she writes that her broadcasts assured American civilians that "a war injury, even a major one, was not necessarily the end" and that "the cream of our Medical Corps extended right up to the front line" (p. 233). In 1946 Daniels was awarded the Medal of Freedom for her "unselfish interest in the welfare of American soldiers."

After three years in Hollywood, where Daniels produced a film, *The Fabulous Joe* (1947), she and Lyon returned to Britain in 1949. In 1950 they began their radio series "Life with the Lyons," which ran for thirteen years and was translated to stage, television, and film. Daniels, who wrote the scripts, played a slightly vague, sentimental version of herself. She also coauthored an Anglo-American cookbook during this period. Daniels and Lyon gave seven Royal Command Performances. Nearly forgotten in the United States, they had become household names in Great Britain. When she died in London, Lyon wrote, "She was not only my wife, she was my life." A lifelong celebrity, star of American silent films and pioneering film musicals as well as British variety, musical stage, radio, and television, Bebe Daniels was the sort of public personality who made audiences—including wartime servicemen—regard her as part of their families.

• Daniels and Lyon's joint autobiography, *Life with the Lyons* (1953), is notable for its unliterary quality, comprising essentially a collection of personal primary source material. Jill Allgood, *Bebe and Ben* (1975), provides details of Daniels's last two decades.

JAMES ROSS MOORE

DANIELS, Charles Meldrum (24 Mar. 1885–9 Aug. 1973), swimmer, was born in Dayton, Ohio. Nothing is known of his parentage or early education. His Olympic career began at the 1904 Games in St. Louis, Missouri, where he won three gold, one silver, and one bronze medal. The gold medals came for his performances in the 220-yard freestyle, the 440-yard freestyle, and on the winning 4 × 50-yard freestyle relay team; the silver medal was won in the 100-yard freestyle, behind Hungary's Zoltán von Halmay; and the bronze was earned in the 50-yard freestyle behind von Halmay and the American J. Scott Leary. Daniels also competed in the Intercalated Olympics of 1906 in Athens, where he won the 100-meter freestyle. He defended that title at the 1908 Olympics in London and added another bronze medal in the 4 × 200 meter freestyle relay.

Daniels's amazing record at the Amateur Athletic Union championships began in 1904 when he won the 220-yard and 440-yard national titles outdoors. He won three outdoor titles from 1905 through 1907, and he took four, the 100 yards, 220 yards, 440 yards, and one mile, in 1908. His career tapered off in 1909 and 1910 as he emphasized longer distances. Nevertheless, he took two outdoor national championships. Daniels proved just as dominant indoors, winning three titles in 1906 and consecutive titles from 1909 through 1911. He also captured two national championships in England and the 100-yard Amateur Swimming Association championship in both 1906 and 1907. He retired shortly after the 1911 AAU Indoor Championships.

Daniels likely set more world records than did any male swimmer. At the turn of the century, world records were recognized at myriad distances, giving him a crack at several records virtually every time he dove into a pool. His first world records were set on 13 February 1904 when he established marks for both 250 yards and 300 yards at Travers Island, New York. His last record was set on 28 March 1911 in Pittsburgh, when he swam 200 meters in 2:26.0. In between, he claimed more than ninety world marks. His most amazing performance came in two races swum two days apart in February 1907 in New York City. In the first, on 23 February, he set records at sixteen distance marks from 250 yards to 950 yards. Two days later, at specified points in a one-mile race, he set long-course outdoor world records over twelve distances.

Daniels's best career times were 54.8 seconds in the 100 yards at Chicago on 7 April 1910; 1:02.8 in the 100 meters at New York City on 5 April 1910; 2:26.0 in the 200 meters at Pittsburgh on 28 March 1911; 2:20.0 in the 220 yards at New York City on 22 February 1906; 3:57.6 in the 300 meters at New York on 4 March 1910; 5:54.2 in the 400 meters at Travers Island, New York, on 19 September 1908; 7:03.4 in the 500 meters/550 yards at New York on 23 February 1907; 11:44.8 in the 880 yards/800 meters at New York on 23 February 1907; and 23:40.7 in the one mile at New York on 25 February 1907.

Daniels, who was well known as a writer on swimming, produced several editions of the Spalding guides to swimming, and he later cowrote, with Louis Handley and Otto Wahle, *Speed Swimming*, the definite text of the early twentieth century. Daniels also won the bridge and squash championships of the New York Athletic Club, and he became a top amateur golfer, although he never won a major championship. He was known as a crack marksman. In 1909 he married Mrs. Florence Goodyear Wagner, heir to the Goodyear tire fortune. He started his own automobile sales business, and, after retiring from swimming, he spent the rest of his career managing his investments. He retired to Carmel, California, where he died.

The world's greatest swimmer from 1904 until 1911, Daniels profoundly influenced the development of American swimming by perfecting the Australian crawl, changing it slightly to be renamed the American crawl, and using it to win a record thirty-one AAU individual championships. He set world freestyle records at every distance from 25 yards to one mile, and incredibly he posted twenty-eight world records within a two-day period in 1908. Among American swimmers, his tally of eight Olympic medals has been bettered only by Mark Spitz.

• Information on Daniels's swimming career can be found in John Arlott, *The Oxford Companion to Sports and Games* (1976); Pat Besford, *The Encyclopedia of Swimming*, 2d ed. (1976); Lord Killanin and John Rodda, eds., *The Olympic Games, 1984*, 3d ed. (1983); and Bill Mallon and Ian Buchanan, *Quest for Gold: The Encyclopedia of American Olympians* (1984). A brief obituary is in the *San Francisco Chronicle*, 10 Aug. 1973.

BILL MALLON

DANIELS, Farrington (8 Mar. 1889–23 June 1972), physical chemist, was born in Minneapolis, Minnesota, the son of Franc Burchard Daniels, a superintendent with American Express, and Florence Louise Farrington. Daniels received a B.S. in 1910 and an M.S. in 1911 in chemistry from the University of Minnesota and a Ph.D. in physical chemistry in 1914 from Harvard University, where he studied under T. W. Richards. World War I prevented Daniels's acceptance of a traveling scholarship for study with Fritz Haber in Berlin; instead he accepted a position at Worcester Polytechnic Institute, where he remained until March 1918, when he volunteered for military service. Daniels was commissioned a first lieutenant in

the Chemical Warfare Service and spent the rest of the year working on nitrogen fixation and the elimination of fogging in gas masks. He worked in 1919–1920 at the Fixed Nitrogen Research Laboratory in Washington, D.C. In 1920 he joined the chemistry faculty at the University of Wisconsin in Madison. Daniels rose through the professional ranks at Wisconsin, serving as chairman of his department from 1952 until his retirement in 1959. He continued to maintain an active research program until his death, directing most of his later efforts to the promotion of solar energy. Daniels had married Olive Miriam Bell in 1917; they had four children.

The most prominent of Daniels's wide range of research areas were chemical kinetics, particularly of the nitrogen oxides; the applications of "appropriate technology," or the use of technology most suited to the situation; and the development of solar and other alternative energies. His kinetics researches, which he conducted from the 1920s to 1960, dealt largely with nitrogen fixation and the nitrogen oxides. In the early 1920s chemists were only beginning to understand the energy changes (thermodynamics) and the rates and mechanisms (kinetics) of chemical reactions. Daniels's classic 1921 study of nitrogen pentoxide established quantitatively its rate and mechanism of decomposition. His study also provided convincing evidence that contributed to the demise of the radiation hypothesis then current in kinetics. According to this hypothesis, infrared radiation from the walls of the container rather than intermolecular collisions provided the energy required to activate a reaction.

Daniels also investigated the photochemical decomposition of nitrogen pentoxide and later expanded these studies to measure the efficiency of photosynthesis in controlled laboratory experiments. His efficiencies were as high as 30 percent, whereas for the conversion of sunlight in agricultural crops they were only 0.2 percent per acre per year. These results pointed out the benefits of further photoconversion research.

Daniels's expertise in the kinetics of nitrogen oxides led to his pioneering studies on the applications of appropriate technology. Beginning in 1939 and continuing into the 1950s Daniels constructed several high-temperature regenerative (heat-exchanging) ceramic pebble-bed furnaces in which he combined atmospheric nitrogen and oxygen for the production of nitrate-containing fertilizers and explosives. He envisioned them as a cheaper, more practical alternative to, and a more appropriate technology than, the high-pressure Haber ammonia synthesis, especially in underdeveloped countries. The U.S. Army and the Food Machinery Company constructed a 40-ton per day demonstration plant in Kansas after the war, but its operation was not economical, and production ceased in September 1954.

Daniels's design of a gas-cooled nuclear reactor for peacetime energy production in the United States and in underdeveloped countries was a second project aimed at promoting appropriate technologies. While serving as director of the Manhattan Project's Metallurgical Laboratory at the University of Chicago from 1945 to mid-1946 Daniels used his experience with high-temperature ceramic furnaces to design a small (5–50 megawatt), helium gas–cooled reactor. The Atomic Energy Commission (AEC) awarded Daniels $3 million to construct an experimental reactor at Oak Ridge, Tennessee, but the Cold War was just beginning, and in 1947 the AEC canceled Daniels's proposed reactor in order to concentrate on the production of nuclear weapons. Its action ended the United States's opportunity to construct the world's first peacetime atomic power plant (built by the Soviet Union in 1954).

Daniels's nuclear research provided an opportunity to expand his longtime interest in kinetics to include radioactive decay in solids. Having observed the thermoluminescence (light emission upon heating) of quartz vessels previously exposed to radiation in a nuclear reactor, he investigated the glow curves of several hundred naturally occurring minerals and laboratory crystals. His research supported studies showing that thermoluminescence in laboratory-grown crystals occurred only after exposing them to X-rays or gamma rays, whereas the thermoluminescence of naturally occurring minerals resulted from their activation by small amounts of radioactive elements present as impurities. Daniels's work on thermoluminescence found application in geochemical studies including stratigraphy, age determinations of naturally thermoluminescent ores, and in recovering uranium from low-grade ores. In the early 1960s John Cameron, Daniels's colleague at the University of Wisconsin, used thermoluminescence radiation to develop a lithium fluoride dosimeter that measured clinical radiation and monitored human exposure to radiation.

For twenty-five years after the cancellation of his reactor project Daniels actively promoted solar energy. Like nuclear energy, solar energy was little developed in 1947, and Daniels believed it had even greater potential as an appropriate technology, especially in underdeveloped countries or geographic regions that received ample amounts of sunlight, such as Mexico, India, and many of the Pacific Ocean islands. His early solar research was both theoretical and applied; later he dealt more with practical applications of solar energy, particularly solar cooling, cooking, and distillation, each of which had comparatively low research and development costs and involved solar units that were relatively easy to construct and apply. In developing his solar apparatus Daniels showed a sensitivity to the traditions and cultures of different societies, as he recognized that the acceptance and use of solar units required a society to perceive them as appropriate to solving its problems or improving its quality of life. The user—as well as the inventor—has to value the technology. On-site testing and user construction from locally obtained materials are therefore crucial to successful long-term adoption. Despite the unforeseen technological difficulties and unsuspected sociological misunderstandings that sometimes arose, the search for appropriate technology remained the motivating force behind Daniels's solar program and his commitment to the development of solar energy.

Daniels was active in a number of societies, serving as president of the American Chemical Society (1953), the Geochemical Society (1958), the Solar Energy Society (1965–1967), and Sigma Xi (1965). He was associate director and then director of the Metallurgical Laboratory (1944–1946); chairman of the Board of Governors, Argonne National Laboratory (1945–1947); and was elected to the National Academy Sciences (1947) as well as its vice president (1957–1961). The ACS awarded him its highest honors: the Willard Gibbs Medal (1955), the Priestley Medal (1957), and the James Flack Norris Award (1957).

Daniels was the author or coauthor of 300 papers and several books, including *Mathematical Preparation for Physical Chemistry* (1928), the many editions of the textbooks *Physical Chemistry* (1931–1970) and *Experimental Physical Chemistry* (1929–1970), *Chemical Kinetics* (1937), *Challenge of Our Times* (1953), and the widely acclaimed *Direct Use of the Sun's Energy* (1964). He died in Madison, Wisconsin.

As a dedicated teacher and the author or coauthor of two widely used textbooks that went through many editions, Daniels was a major force in the scientific education of thousands of students. He had a genuine concern for the social implications of science and was a well-known spokesman for science, effectively promoting both as an officer in several scientific societies and through numerous lectures in the United States and abroad.

• Daniels's papers are in the archives of the University of Wisconsin's Memorial Library. They contain correspondence from numerous scientists, from his years as chairman of the chemistry department, and from his presidencies of the ACS and other scientific societies. A collection of Daniels's family correspondence is in the library of the Wisconsin Historical Society, Madison. There are also several boxes of his papers on solar energy in the Rockefeller Archive Center in North Tarrytown, N.Y. The most complete biography of Daniels, Olive Bell Daniels's privately printed *Farrington Daniels: Chemist and Prophet of the Solar Age* (1978), contains a complete listing of Daniels's papers and books. Copies of it are in the university's library and archives and in the possession of family members. For Daniels's work on nitrogen fixation see Anthony N. Stranges, "Farrington Daniels and the Wisconsin Process for Nitrogen Fixation," *Social Studies of Science* 22 (1992): 317–27. Obituaries include John E. Willard, "Farrington Daniels (1889–1972)," *Biographical Memoirs: Year Book of the American Philosophical Society* (1972), pp. 149–52, as well as the notice in the *New York Times*, 24 June 1972.

ANTHONY N. STRANGES

DANIELS, Jonathan (26 Apr. 1902–6 Nov. 1981), journalist, author, and government official, was born in Raleigh, North Carolina, the son of Josephus Daniels, a journalist, and Addie Worth Bagley. Daniels attended public schools in Raleigh until 1913 and then St. Albans School in Washington, D.C., when his father assumed the post of secretary of the navy. In 1921 he received a bachelor of arts degree in English from the

University of North Carolina (UNC) at Chapel Hill, where he served as editor of the campus paper and was a classmate of novelist Thomas Wolfe. The following year, he received his master's degree, also in English from UNC. During the summers, Daniels worked as a reporter for the *Raleigh News and Observer*, which his family owned and operated and of which his father was editor in chief.

In the summer after receiving his M.A., Daniels worked as a reporter for the *Louisville Times*. Josephus Daniels encouraged his son to further his education by attending law school, thinking a legal background would be helpful in the newspaper business. Daniels took his father's advice and enrolled at Columbia University, but he flunked out after the first year. Returning home, Daniels took a special summer course at UNC and passed the state bar examination (1923). He tried one case before definitely deciding on a career in the newspaper industry. "I defended my cook's son when he was charged with assaulting his wife. Got him off with the costs of court and quit while I was ahead," Daniels later said.

In 1923 Daniels married Elizabeth Bridgers of Raleigh, with whom he had one daughter. That same year he took his first permanent job as a sports editor for his father's paper. This began Daniels's long career in journalism, a career he would use over the next four decades to speak out on issues of the changing times, especially on race relations in the South.

In the mid-1920s Daniels familiarized himself with various aspects of the newspaper industry. He spent three years in Washington as the *News and Observer's* political correspondent. He then returned to Raleigh to work on his first novel, *Clash of Angels* (1930). The book, a satire, concerns the battle between the angels Lucifer and Jehovah, with the author challenging conventional religion and favoring Lucifer. The high praise given to *Clash of Angels* enabled Daniels to win a Guggenheim creative writing fellowship. Although he spent sixteen months in France, Italy, and Switzerland working on another novel, it was never published.

After the sudden death of his wife in 1929, Daniels left North Carolina for New York to become a staff writer for *Fortune* magazine. While in New York, he met Lucy Cathcart of South Carolina; they married in 1932 and eventually had three daughters. The same year, Daniels resumed his involvement with the family paper, this time as associate editor.

When his father accepted President Frankin D. Roosevelt's appointment as ambassador to Mexico in 1933, Daniels took over as editor of the *News and Observer*, a position he held until 1942. It was during this time that he first used the editorial page to air his views on race relations in the South, to his mind the issue of greatest concern for the region. Shortly after assuming command of the paper, he commented on several racial issues, including the unfair treatment blacks received in southern courts. According to biographer Charles W. Eagles, Daniels wrote with cautious irony to his father in July 1933, "I hope I am not making your paper too much of a colored boy's friend."

Though Daniels's views differed from those of his father, who, according to Eagles, saw no need to discuss race relations and accepted the segregation and subordination of African Americans, Josephus Daniels did not object to his son's editorials. Jonathan Daniels's dissent from not only his father's position, but the position of most white southerners of the early 1930s—though "mild" and sometimes "apologetic," says Eagles—nonetheless became a vehicle for racial reform in the South. In the following years, his thoughts would evolve as the transformation in southern race relations occurred and his editorials would reflect his changing ideas.

In addition to running the paper during his father's absence, Daniels wrote three books: *A Southerner Discovers the South* (1938), *A Southerner Discovers New England* (1940), and *Tar Heels: A Portrait of North Carolina* (1941). The first of these books, concerns, in part, the New Deal's effect on the Old South, which he welcomed as a challenge to outworn traditions and which gave impetus to his liberal views on race relations. He also wrote articles for many national magazines, including the *Saturday Evening Post*, *McCall's*, and *Harper's*.

At the beginning of World War II, Daniels's father returned to Raleigh and resumed command of the paper. Daniels, in turn, answered Roosevelt's call to become involved in the war effort and moved to Washington. Daniels had first met the future president when Roosevelt was serving as assistant secretary of the navy under Daniels's father's command. It was not until July 1941, however, that Daniels became politically involved with Roosevelt, having accepted Roosevelt's offer to be a member of the Voluntary Participation Committee of the Office of Civilian Defense (OCD). Eleanor Roosevelt headed the committee, while OCD itself was directed by Fiorello La Guardia, then mayor of New York City. According to Daniels in his book *White House Witness, 1942–1945* (1975), OCD was in a state of confusion because of Mayor La Guardia's divided duties and Mrs. Roosevelt's rank as first lady; soon after the attack on Pearl Harbor on 7 December 1941, both left office. Daniels assumed Mrs. Roosevelt's position. While at OCD, Daniels was involved in the recruitment of volunteers for various roles, including air-raid wardens and defense-bond salespeople. The Red Cross and other agencies, however, competed with OCD in these ventures, and to many OCD was "a useless appendage to the war effort" (*White House Witness*, p. 6), an opinion Daniels did not share. But as OCD fell into disarray, so Daniels was to recall, the president sent word that "under no circumstances was I to leave government. He had important work for me to do" (*White House Witness*, p. 15). He was appointed an administrative assistant to the president (1943–1945) and assumed tasks related to racial problems, overseas aviation, and discrimination in employment, among other duties.

In 1945 Daniels was appointed the president's press secretary. One of his first duties in this capacity was to select for release to the press and public pictures from

Roosevelt's meeting at Yalta with British prime minister Winston Churchill and Soviet premier Joseph Stalin. The president, then quite ill, appeared haggard and frail. Daniels chose "the least tragic pictures, those were sad enough" (*White House Witness*, p. 3). He was serving as press secretary when Roosevelt died on 12 April 1945.

Daniels soon resigned his position but remained in Washington at the request of President Harry S. Truman to help reorganize the presidential staff. The lasting friendship that developed between the two men led to Daniels's biography of Truman, *The Man of Independence* (1950).

In the spring of 1945 Daniels returned to Raleigh and worked part time on the newspaper, devoting much of his time to other writing. He became editor of the paper in January 1948 after the death of his father, but later that year he returned to Washington to help Truman with his reelection campaign. He relied on his managing editor at the *News and Observer* to see to the day-to-day operations of the newspaper's staff. After winning a full term as president, Truman appointed Daniels to the Public Advisory Board of the Economic Cooperative Administration and to the post of U.S. member of the United Nations Subcommittee on Prevention of Discrimination and Protection of Minorities.

At the end of the Truman administration, Daniels resumed more direct involvement in managing the *News and Observer*. He became, however, an inveterate writer of books. *The End of Innocence* (1954), his account of life in Washington during Woodrow Wilson's presidency, was based on his father's diaries. *The Time between the Wars: Armistice to Pearl Harbor* (1966), drawn from his own journals during his time in Roosevelt's administration, disclosed details of Roosevelt's love affair with Lucy Page Mercer, Eleanor Roosevelt's former social secretary.

Daniels continued to speak out on racial issues in the 1950s and 1960s. In March 1954, for example, he spoke before the National Urban League in New York City and said establishing equality between the races and moving "the American Negro from a second-class status" was of greatest national concern. Despite his longing for equality, however, Daniels did not want the Supreme Court decision in the pending school desegregation case, *Brown v. Board of Education*, "to wipe out school segregation in all the schools of the South. . . . I view that day with apprehension," Daniels said (Eagles, p. 155). He did not doubt that blacks and whites could coexist peacefully, but he feared that an end to separation could result both in fewer African-American teachers and in whites being less willing to pay taxes for quality schools. When the Supreme Court decided in May 1954 that "separate but equal" had no place in the public schools, Daniels urged southerners to face the court order with "composure and good sense" and "wisdom for which fear and anger are no substitutes" (Eagles, p. 169).

During the early 1960s, when civil-rights protests were increasingly frequent, Daniels's ongoing commentary on race relations led some of his readers to complain that other news was not getting fair coverage. Nonetheless, he continued to write on this topic and in his editorials repeatedly urged Congress to pass the 1964 Civil Rights Bill, which he called "symbolic in nature . . . of the Negro's aspirations and hopes" (Eagles, p. 226). President Lyndon B. Johnson signed the Civil Rights Act on 2 July 1964.

That same year, Daniels began to relinquish his editorial responsibilities to staff associates. In the late 1960s he and his wife moved permanently to Hilton Head, South Carolina, having first become regular visitors to the island in 1961. As editor emeritus, he continued to work for the *News and Observer* until his full retirement in 1968. Daniels became well known on Hilton Head, a resort town he had once considered one of "the winter islands of millionaires" and "irrelevant to the picture of the South." He cofounded the *Island Packet*, which became Hilton Head's local paper, and wrote a weekly column for it. After a period of declining health, Daniels died on Hilton Head.

From the time of the New Deal through the postwar civil-rights movement, Daniels spoke out on racial issues in editorials and other writings. According to Eagles, few other southern liberals espoused their views for as long a period. As heir apparent to his father and then, in his own right, editor in chief of the *Raleigh News and Observer*, he could voice his opinions with exceptional freedom. In serving two presidents, he could also further the cause of racial equity. In his twenty-one books and thousands of newspaper and magazine articles, he commented on the history and changing political, social, and economic structure of his beloved South. In his retirement he became a vocal opponent of development along the southeastern coast. Considered by his friend Vermont Royster, former editor of the *Wall Street Journal*, to be "a philosopher in spite of himself," Daniels once said, "if you don't try always to keep the jungle back, the jungle will engulf you" (*News and Observer*, 7 Nov. 1981).

• The personal papers of Jonathan Daniels are housed in the Southern Historical Collection at the University of North Carolina at Chapel Hill. In addition to the books mentioned in the text, he wrote *Frontier on the Potomac* (1946), *The Forest Is the Future* (1957), *Prince of Carpetbaggers* (1958), *Stonewall Jackson* (1959), *Mosby—The Gray Ghost of the Confederacy* (1959), *Robert E. Lee* (1960), *Thomas Wolfe, October Recollections* (1961), *The Devil's Backbone: The Story of the Natchez Trace* (1962), *They Will Be Heard: America's Crusading Newspaper Editors* (1964), *Washington Quadrille* (1968), *Ordeal of Ambition: Jefferson, Hamilton, Burr* (1970), *The Randolphs of Virginia* (1972), and *The Gentlemanly Serpent and Other Columns from a Newspaperman in Paradise* (1974). A good source of information on Daniels's personal background and views on race relations is Charles W. Eagles's *Jonathan Daniels and Race Relations: The Evolution of a Southern Liberal* (1982). A transcript of Eagles's interview with Daniels is on deposit in the Southern Historical Collection, UNC. Eagles's book also cites many of Daniels's editorials in the *Raleigh News and Observer*. The *New York Times* obituary, 7 Nov. 1981, contains some factual inaccuracies; a better source is the extensive article that ran in the *News and Observer* of the same date.

LISABETH G. SVENDSGAARD

DANIELS, Josephus (18 May 1862–15 Jan. 1948), publisher, secretary of the navy, and ambassador, was born in Washington, North Carolina, during a bombardment by Union gunboats, the son of Josephus Daniels, Sr., a shipbuilder, and Mary Cleaves Seabrook. His father refused to join the Confederate forces and died in 1865. His mother raised three sons by opening a millinery shop and served as the town's postmistress. She was later fired from the latter position because of her son's anti-Republican editorials.

From his earliest years on, Daniels was fascinated by what Oliver Wendell Holmes referred to as the "lead poisoning" of journalism. At age eighteen he quit the Wilson Collegiate Institute in Wilson, North Carolina, to edit the *Wilson Advance*, a weekly he later purchased in 1882 with the help of his mother, who mortgaged the family home for $2,000. Writing only local stories at first, he soon gained the courage to develop more hard-hitting material, and, after retaining a local judge to help, Daniels began writing the reform-minded editorials with which he was identified throughout his life. Although C. Vann Woodward described Daniels as a spokesperson for "Progressivism—For Whites Only," biographer Joseph L. Morrison warned against judging the racist talk and cruel cartoons that appeared in Daniels's newspapers by late twentieth-century standards. However irresponsible and demagogic the North Carolina white supremacy politics of the period may appear, Morrison believes Daniels played a role as an arbiter of political decency who helped materially to create a climate in which extremists could not flourish.

After becoming a partner in two other rural weeklies in Rocky Mount and Kingston, North Carolina, he was elected president of the North Carolina Press Association at age twenty-two. Stimulated by his coverage of the North Carolina courts, Daniels also studied law at the University of North Carolina and passed the bar exam in 1885. During that same year he and Walter H. Page bought controlling interest in the *Raleigh State Chronicle*. Page moved on to become editor of the *Atlantic Monthly* magazine, helped establish Doubleday and Company, and served as ambassador to Great Britain. Daniels also became more involved in politics and government, as well as starting another weekly, the *North Carolinian*. In 1888 he married Addie Worth Bagley. The couple had four sons, and a daughter who died in childhood.

Although he was awarded the position of state printer, his weekly newspapers were not successful. In 1893 Daniels accepted his first federal job in the Grover Cleveland administration. He served as chief clerk of the Department of the Interior. He remained in Washington from 1893 to 1895 before returning to Raleigh, where he had purchased the *News and Observer* in 1894.

Under Daniels's editorial leadership, the *News and Observer* became "an aggressive exponent of Democracy, free from factions and favoritism." Over the years Daniels crusaded to improve North Carolina through better hospitals, child-labor laws, and against exploitation by the railroads. He was also pro-union and opposed the sale of liquor. An active Methodist, Daniels believed that "a newspaper should be like a preacher—always upholding righteousness." He considered church news big news and said, "Anything to make folks better goes on page one-A." Despite efforts by advertisers and friends to intimidate him, he proclaimed, "I'll put everything in the paper that God Almighty allows to happen in the world." Not everyone appreciated his efforts as a crusading editor, and some nicknamed his newspaper the "Nuisance and Disturber." Morrison says that as Daniels became the dominant political editor of North Carolina he probably was "a more authentic spokesman for the New South" than either Henry Grady of Atlanta or Henry Watterson of Louisville.

Elizabeth Brown Dickey wrote that one reason for Daniels's involvement in politics was his strong belief in democracy. "Our only danger in discussing what is wrong with the world today is in failing to make democracy work," he said. "It can't work with party machines, county unit systems, labor unions, or monopolies running the country. The people themselves must be interested: democracy depends on the eternal vigilance of the common man."

A Democratic national committeeman from North Carolina for more than twenty years, Daniels was a great admirer of William Jennings Bryan, whom he supported in Bryan's three unsuccessful attempts for the presidency. Daniels was more successful in his support of Woodrow Wilson for president in 1912 and as a reward was named secretary of the navy in 1913. Assistant Secretary Franklin D. Roosevelt complemented Daniels's disarming country bumpkin appearance with skilled administrative abilities that made them a highly successful team. Daniels sought to reform the navy in the interests of the common man. He instituted a number of personnel reforms, such as requiring sea service for promotion, instituting compulsory schooling for poorly educated sailors, and improving the quality of the U.S. Naval Academy.

Among Daniels's other reforms were insisting that 100 sailors be admitted to the naval academy each year and setting up training schools for them. He fought the seniority system and signed an unpopular order in 1914 that banned beer, wine, and liquor aboard navy ships. Although he was the last of Wilson's cabinet ministers to vote to go to war in 1917, he became a leader in the fight against the enemy. He is given credit for engineering the "Bridge of Ships" in World War I, by which approximately 2 million doughboys sailed to Europe without the loss of a single life, despite the ever-present menace of enemy submarines. After the war he supported the League of Nations and never forgave the Republicans who blocked U.S. participation.

He felt the obstructionist tactic contributed to World War II.

In contrast to the fame he experienced during his early journalistic and political days in North Carolina and his period of national and even international influence, the period between the administrations of Presidents Warren Harding and Herbert Hoover is referred to as his "decade of obscurity." Daniels returned to his power base at the *News and Observer*. Unlike modern editors who attempt to maintain an aura of objectivity in their newspapers, Daniels actively campaigned for Roosevelt in Oregon, California, Nevada, Utah, Nebraska, and other states.

One of Roosevelt's first acts after winning the 1932 presidential election, enthusiastically backed by Daniels, was to appoint his former superior as ambassador to Mexico. This appointment was received coolly because of Daniels's role in the bloody American occupation at Veracruz in 1914, as well as his lack of experience in foreign service or fluency in Spanish. His homespun manner with the Mexican people and the value of his work combined to overcome such doubts, however. During the period 1933–1942 Daniels diligently implemented the Roosevelt Good Neighbor Doctrine and helped solidify friendly relations on both sides of the Rio Grande. His autobiography, *Shirt-Sleeve Diplomat* (1947), documents the things he saw and the people he met in both countries while emphasizing what was happening in Mexico in relation to officials, fellow diplomats, the Mexican people, and the American colony. Referring to himself as "foreign correspondent in Mexico," Daniels also describes an official mission to Europe, yearly visits to the United States, and trips to nearly every state in the Mexican Republic. Critics of Daniels said that although he was personally charming, he was soft-headed and perhaps a little senile, a weak and ineffectual idealist at a post that required tough-minded firmness. His own view of his mission was summed up in a single sentence in his letter of resignation. "I went to Mexico animated by a single purpose," he told President Roosevelt, "to incarnate your policy of the Good Neighbor." As a result, he believed, "the relations between Mexico and the United States are on the most sincerely friendly basis in their history."

After finishing his ambassadorial mission, Daniels returned again to the family-owned newspaper where he was an active "editor at eighty." Throughout the war years he continued to crusade and editorialize for the causes of public education and the state's Good Health Program and offer advice to President Roosevelt and his colleagues in journalism. In addition, he set about finishing the massive project of writing his autobiography, which would comprise five volumes and 2,700 pages.

In 1939 *Tar Heel Editor*, the first of the five volumes, was published. Daniels's son told him that the books were too long, to which Daniels jokingly responded that he wrote his books for quantity, not quality. "I want mine to be big enough to be useful as a deadly weapon," he joked. The foreword of *Tar Heel Editor* says that "it is believed that the pen pictures of the men of that period and the semibiographical accounts of everyday events and the unfolding of how people lived and what they thought in Eastern North Carolina in his youth and young manhood are typical of what went on in most communities in the South during the years after Reconstruction. The book, therefore, has more than local significance."

The second of his autobiographical volumes, *Editor in Politics* (1941), focuses on the Cleveland administration, in which he held a position in Washington; the rise of the Populist party; and an estimate of the leaders of the Fusion coalition and of the long and intimate friendship Daniels had with William Jennings Bryan. With copious extracts from his diary, Daniels chronicled *The Wilson Era: Years of Peace, 1910–1917* (1944) and *The Wilson Era: Years of War and After, 1917–1923* (1946), which include highlights in the political career of the former New Jersey governor and president, as well as reflections of Daniels's visits to France, England, Italy, Germany, Belgium, Holland, Luxembourg, and the World War I battlefields. They also examine the period of disillusionment following the refusal of the United States to take a seat in the League of Nations. The last of the five volumes, *Shirt Sleeve Diplomat*, records his experiences as an ambassador, as well as other events of the Roosevelt administration. In his review of the book, George Creel, a former journalist who gained international fame as chairman of the Committee on Public Information during World War I, was so enthusiastic about Daniels's ambassadorial role in Mexico that he likened it to Benjamin Franklin's in France.

Notwithstanding his involvement in government, Daniels remained active in journalism, particularly with the American Society of Newspaper Editors (ASNE), which held annual conferences in Washington, D.C. Daniels continued to remind fellow editors of the need for their watchdog institution to remain free of unnecessary governmental control. In the first postwar meeting of the ASNE in 1946, Daniels was instrumental in getting the society to postpone what he considered a too-hasty approval of the State Department's takeover of the functions of the Office of War Information. In remarks at the annual meeting, he observed that "government officials always think the policies they are carrying out are wise and they ought to disseminate them. If we make the mistake of not supporting a free press without a government censor the day may come that men will be in office who will send out news to suit the party or the politics they believe in."

Daniels responded positively to the report of the Hutchins Commission on a Free Responsible Press in 1947. Although the report was received by most newspaper editors with bitterness, Daniels editorialized, "The report truly points out the bias of owners who have large incomes is responsible for the loss of influence of the press as the tocsin of the people."

According to Morrison, "'The Old Man' preferred to act his own tocsin, not to hire syndicated columnists to sound his alarm bell." Such was his concern that the last time he attended an ASNE meeting was in the year before his death. On being recognized as "a grand old gentleman who gets younger every year," Daniels expressed concern that newspaper columnists flourished because editors were lazy. Despite his critical comments, however, the editors were warmed and cheered to have Josephus Daniels, "the dean of newspaper editors in America," there, full of the old twinkle and radiance.

On 18 May 1947, Daniels's birthday, newspapers all over the country printed a column by Drew Pearson honoring Daniels. Pearson wrote, "When the last surviving member of the Woodrow Wilson cabinet achieves the lusty age of eighty-five, and when on that birthday he still writes a daily editorial and keeps his sense of humor and his sane philosophy of life, and when he is just as great an inspiration to his neighbors and to his family and the nation as Josephus Daniels— then that's news."

The following January Daniels caught a cold, which led to the pneumonia that claimed his life in his home in Raleigh. Among the eulogistic tributes was one from the *Winston Salem Journal* that claimed that North Carolina was one of the most progressive states in the South because of Josephus Daniels and that his personality has influenced all America to some degree.

• Daniels's papers are in the Library of Congress, the University of North Carolina Historical Collection, and the files of the Raleigh *News and Observer*. He was one of the more prolific writers in journalism. Among the books with revealing journalistic and political insights on Daniels are E. David Cronon, *Editor in Politics* (1941) and *Josephus Daniels in Mexico* (1960); and *The Cabinet Diaries of Josephus Daniels, 1913–1921*, ed. Cronon (1963). A more recent biography is Joseph L. Morrison, *Josephus Daniels: The Small-d Democrat* (1966). An obituary is in the *New York Times*, 16 Jan. 1948.

ALF PRATTE

DANIELS, Mabel Wheeler (27 Nov. 1878–10 Mar. 1971), composer, was born in Swampscott, Massachusetts, the daughter of George Frank Daniels and Sarah Mariah Wheeler, members of Boston's Handel and Haydn Society chorus. Her father also served as president of the society for many years. At an early age Mabel showed musical talent, and she studied piano with several local teachers. By age ten she was composing little piano pieces, including "The Fairy Charm Waltz," which has been preserved. She also displayed literary interests, and while she attended the Girls' Latin School, a preparatory school in Boston, several of her short stories were published.

She entered Radcliffe College in 1896, studying harmony and counterpoint as well as literature. She was also active in musical programs, including the college glee club and campus operetta productions. She composed two operettas, *The Court of Hearts* and *Alice in Wonderland Continued*, which were performed in school productions. She graduated from Radcliffe magna cum laude in 1900.

Following graduation she continued her music education, studying composition and orchestration with George Chadwick in Boston. In 1903 she traveled to Germany and for two years, during the winter months, studied composition with Ludwig Thuille at the Königlichen Musikschule in Munich, returning to Boston during the summers. In 1905 her charming memoir of her musical experiences and travels in Germany, *An American Girl in Munich: Impressions of a Music Student*, was published.

In 1911 Daniels was appointed director of the Radcliffe Glee Club and composed many choral works for the group. That year the National Federation of Music Clubs awarded her prizes for her choral works *Eastern Song* and *The Voice of My Beloved*. Her first major work, *The Desolate City*, for baritone solo and orchestra, won the attention of Mrs. Edward MacDowell, director of the MacDowell Colony in New Hampshire. She arranged for the work to be performed at the colony's 1913 summer festival, and this began Daniels's long relationship with the artists' retreat, where she often composed during the summer months. In later years she joined the board of the Edward MacDowell Association.

In 1913 she was appointed to head the music program at Simmons College in Boston. She left this position in 1918 to devote herself primarily to composing. She served as president of the Radcliffe Musical Association from 1917 to 1919. Her inspiring work *Peace with a Sword*, for chorus and orchestra, was produced by the Handel and Haydn Society in Boston's Symphony Hall in 1917 and was published that year by A. P. Schmidt. A few years later Daniels revised the work, calling it *Peace in Liberty*, and the new edition was published by Schmidt in 1929.

The Wild Ride, a choral octavo for men's voices, won an award from the League of American Penwomen in 1926. Daniels composed *Exultate Deo* for mixed chorus and orchestra to celebrate Radcliffe College's fiftieth anniversary in 1929, and it was published that year by Schmidt. Her first major orchestral work was *Deep Forest* at the MacDowell Colony in 1931. It was first performed in a version for chamber orchestra in New York by Georges Barrère's Little Symphony, then rescored for full orchestra and performed by Nicolai Sokoloff, Serge Koussevitzky, Sir John Barbirolli, and other conductors. Another orchestral work, *Pirates' Island*, was performed by the Cleveland Orchestra in 1935, then selected by Ted Shawn for his ballet company.

Daniels's best-known work, *Song of Jael*, a cantata for mixed chorus, soprano, and orchestra, was first performed at the Worcester Festival in 1940. Other major works include *Songs of Elfland*, for women's chorus, soprano, flute, harp, strings, and percussion (1924); *Pastoral Ode*, for flute and strings (1940); *The Holy Star*, for mixed chorus and orchestra (1928); and *Three Observations for Three Woodwinds* (1943), plus a variety of choral octavos and songs with piano accompaniment. Her early works are stylistically representative of the European traditions of her teachers, incorporating long melodic lines in a Romantic idiom. Her music after the mid-1930s shows more daring harmonically and formally, with a bold use of dissonances and complex orchestral color.

Throughout her life Daniels maintained a close relationship with Radcliffe College, serving as a trustee in 1945 and receiving a citation by the school in 1954. At the dedication of the Radcliffe Graduate Center in 1966 she was honored, and several of her works were performed at the ceremony. The Mabel Daniels Beneficiary Fund was established for needy music students, and she often provided stipends to Radcliffe student composers. Daniels never married. She died in Cambridge, Massachusetts.

• Daniels's music manuscripts and papers are housed in Radcliffe College's Schlesinger Library on the History of Women in America and in the Boston Public Library. Other manuscripts and letters are at the New England Conservatory, Washington State University, and the University of Illinois Music Library. In *Modern Music Makers* (1952) Madeleine Goss presents a lively and intimate description of Daniels's career and music and provides a chronology of her life, a list of her major works, and a sample musical autograph. A more complete list of works is in Aaron I. Cohen, *International Encyclopedia of Women Composers*, 2d ed. (1987). David Ewen, *American Composers: A Biographical Dictionary* (1982), surveys her musical career and offers quotes from reviews of performances of her music. An obituary is in the *Boston Globe*, 11 Mar. 1971.

STEPHEN M. FRY

DANNAY, Frederic (20 Oct. 1905–3 Sept. 1982), writer and editor of mystery and detective novels and short stories, was born Daniel Nathan in Brooklyn, New York, the son of Meyer H. Nathan, a liquor dealer, and Dora Walerstein. After graduating from Boys' High School, Brooklyn, Dannay worked primarily as an advertising copywriter until he became a full-time fiction writer in 1931. He married three times: in 1926 to Mary Beck, with whom he had two children; in 1947 to Hilda Wiesenthal, with whom he had one child before her death in 1972; and in 1976 to Rose Koppel.

Dannay legally changed his name from Daniel Nathan, combining his first and last names and taking the given name of Frédéric Chopin, whom he admired. He is better known, however, as Ellery Queen, the pseudonym he shared with his cousin, Manfred Bennington Lee, and under which he wrote and edited the majority of his novels, stories, and collections.

An avid reader of detective fiction since childhood, Dannay often discussed with Lee the possibility that they should write their own novel in the style of the erudite mystery writer, S. S. Van Dine. In 1928, using the name Ellery Queen, the two entered *McClure's* magazine novel-writing contest and, to their surprise, won. Before the work came to print, however, and before Dannay and Lee received their $7,500 prize money, the magazine folded. Fortunately the cosponsor of the competition, publisher Frederick A. Stokes, stepped in and in 1929 published *The Roman Hat Mystery*, which promptly sold 8,000 copies and thereby launched both the character and the "author" Ellery Queen.

After quitting their respective jobs in 1931 to write full time, Dannay and Lee worked twelve-hour days in their respective New York homes, then met at a small office they called their "hideout," close to Fifth Avenue at an address unknown even to their wives. There the two claimed to compete rather than collaborate, sharing all elements of plotting and writing and continually attempting to outwit each other with unexpected turns in the plots they were hatching.

The cloak of secrecy extended to the identity of Queen and later to that of "Barnaby Ross" (the pseudonym under which they created their second detective hero, Drury Lane), which they took elaborate and theatrical measures to protect for as long as possible by appearing at publicity events in black masks. They even staged a lecture tour on which Queen and Ross would demonstrate their art, one suggesting the basis for a plot, the other complicating it, and the pair then solving the mystery for the audience's delectation.

The Ellery Queen books vary considerably in content. Many are in the familiar "hard-boiled" detective style, with locked rooms and deathbed clues half-uttered by dying victims. Such works are stunningly logical but frequently barren of human or social context. Some of the later novels, however, while containing many of the former elements, deal interestingly with human relationships, McCarthyite persecution, capital punishment, antiwar sentiments, and even, in a rather clumsy although not unsympathetic portrait, homosexuality. The character of Ellery Queen began as an upper-class pedant with a rather ostentatious vocabulary and a penchant for stilted idioms. As fashions changed, however, Queen's image warmed and his language mellowed to witty repartee. He developed and maintained an image as something of a philanderer, despite the fact that he was initially introduced as a married father of one son. Never accepting a fee for his detective work, Queen, like his authors, supposedly made his living writing detective fiction. His cases typically began from a random point or bizarre clue to a baffling, but never exotic, murder and were solved, in the style of Sherlock Holmes, by fastidious attention to detail and, as the character Queen once claimed, a process of "sheer, unassailable, incontrovertible logic."

Following an early embarrassment, when many in the medical profession complained about the lack of realism in the hospital setting of *The Dutch Shoe Mystery*, Dannay and Lee carefully researched the background information for each subsequent novel. Dannay fiercely resented the literary elitism of writers and critics who looked down their noses at detective fiction, and he firmly and prophetically maintained that literary critics would one day discover in mystery novels a valuable window to recent history.

Alone and with Lee, Dannay's book sales worldwide had exceeded 150 million by the early 1990s. Of his works, more than forty were Ellery Queen novels;

several appeared under the pen name of Barnaby Ross; one, an autobiographical novel, was written under Daniel Nathan; at least twenty were juvenile mysteries (written as Ellery Queen, Jr.); and he and Lee wrote more than a dozen short-story collections. After astute reprocessing and resale in different formats aimed at different segments of the market, an Ellery Queen novel often sold more than a million copies at a time when the average mystery novel sold three to five thousand.

Dannay, recovering from a serious car accident in late 1941, persuaded publisher Lawrence E. Spivak to start *Ellery Queen's Mystery Magazine*, which rapidly became the largest-selling mystery magazine in the world, promoting short fiction at a time when many writers, under pressure from the publishing industry at large, were turning to the more profitable novel format. Over the years the magazine published many stories by Nobel- and Pulitzer-prize-winning authors. It also provided a forum for less-established writers and for many authors such as Arthur Miller and Sinclair Lewis not usually thought of as crime writers. The magazine, together with Dannay's own extensive private collection of mystery and detective fiction, some of it extremely rare, furnished material for more than 100 anthologies that introduced and preserved both popular and more esoteric samples of mystery and detective fiction.

From 1938 to 1949 Dannay and Lee wrote a successful weekly radio mystery drama. It was played out before a studio audience of invited guests who were asked during the intermission to solve the mystery. In 1939, the pair collaborated on the radio program *Author! Author!* (in which Dannay and Lee appeared—as characters named "Ellery" and "Queen," respectively—and solved riddles and radio charades, in a variation of the quiz show format). They also wrote the scripts for the weekly program *The Adventures of Ellery Queen*, which ran successfully on CBS radio from 1938 to 1949. Of the three Ellery Queen television series (two in the 1950s and one in 1975–1976), none was actually written by Dannay and Lee, although some episodes drew from certain of their novels. The same is true of the thirteen Ellery Queen movies. The identity of Dannay and Lee as authors of the Ellery Queen series was revealed in *Publishers Weekly*, 10 Oct. 1936, and was widely known by 1940.

Dannay died in White Plains, New York, nine years after Lee. One of the most widely recognized crime writers in America, Dannay hated violence and claimed never even to have fired, much less owned, a gun. As half of Ellery Queen, the second most popular detective writer of all time (after Arthur Conan Doyle), Dannay repeatedly refused to succumb to publishers' interpretations of "popular taste." He believed the mystery story should always be "pure puzzle" and rejected many suggestions to embellish what for him and Lee had been a winning formula, saying, "If there's no love story in the puzzle, there's no love story." Francis M. Nevins, Jr., *Royal Bloodline: Ellery Queen, Author and Detective* (1973), suggests that

Dannay was primarily responsible for the development of concepts, themes, and plots, while Lee worked on expanding characters and incidents. The authors themselves, however, claimed to alternate in their responsibility for the various composition and writing tasks. While Dannay was the sole editor and collector for the magazines and anthologies, the one book he wrote alone, the autobiographical novel *The Golden Summer* (1953), written under the name Daniel Nathan, was a commercial failure.

• Dannay's manuscript collection is housed at Columbia University, while his personal collection of detective and mystery fiction, together with a small number of letters to him and a very few that he wrote himself, is housed at the Humanities Research Center, University of Texas, Austin. Among the most famous of Dannay's works as Ellery Queen are *The French Powder Mystery* (1930), *The Spanish Cape Mystery* (1935), *Inspector Queen's Own Case* (1956), *The House of Brass* (1968), and *A Fine and Private Place* (1971). *A Study in Terror* (1966), a novelization of a screenplay, was reprinted as *Sherlock Holmes versus Jack the Ripper*. As Barnaby Ross, Dannay is noted for *The Tragedy of X* (1932), *The Tragedy of Y* (1932), and *The Tragedy of Z* (1933), which were reissued under the name of Ellery Queen in 1940, 1941, and 1942, respectively. Under the name Ellery Queen, Jr., appeared *The Black Dog Mystery* (1941) and *The Purple Bird Mystery* (1966). Of several short story collections, *The Case Book of Ellery Queen* (1945) was a bestseller. Dannay co-authored more than a dozen plays, including (with Raymond Moore) *Danger, Men Working* (1936). He edited more than 100 anthologies including (with Lee until 1971, then alone) *The Queen's Awards* (later, *Ellery Queen's Awards*), and *Ellery Queen's International Casebook* (1964), a collection of true crime stories. Dannay's works of criticism include *The Detective Story: A Bibliography* (1942; repr. 1969), and *Queen's Quorum: A History of the Detective-Crime Short Story as Revealed by the 106 Most Important Books Published in This Field Since 1945* (1951; rev. ed., 1969). Among books about Ellery Queen, notable are A. Boucher's *Ellery Queen: A Double Profile* (1951), and *A Silver Anniversary Tribute to Ellery Queen from Authors, Critics, Editors, and Famous Fans* (1954). An obituary is in the *New York Times*, 5 Sept. 1982.

PETER E. MORGAN

DANZIG, Allison (27 Feb. 1898–27 Jan. 1987), sports journalist, was born in Waco, Texas, the son of German immigrants Morris Danzig, a timber merchant, and Ethel Harvith. His father moved the family to New York City in 1909, when he entered the knitting goods manufacturing business. Later the elder Danzig relocated his business to Albany, New York, where Allison excelled in scholastics and sports. Despite his height of 5'6" and weight of 117 pounds, he played quarterback on the Albany High School football team. Danzig also played baseball and competed in track and field. In 1917 he graduated from high school and won a Regents Scholarship to Cornell University.

Intending to pursue a career in journalism, Danzig majored in English and history at Cornell. As a freshman he entered a writing contest for a position on the editorial board of the *Cornell Sun*, the student newspaper. His chief competitor was E. B. White, who later became a leading writer for the *New Yorker* and a renowned stylist. The winner of the contest would be the contributor who filled the most space in the paper by the end of the spring semester. Although Danzig achieved that goal, White won the contest and the seat on the board. White later acknowledged, as Danzig then suspected, that his success resulted from fraternity politics, as one of his fraternity brothers was a member of the newspaper's editorial board.

In disgust over the outcome of the contest, Danzig left Cornell and enlisted in the U.S. Army. Stationed at Camp Grant, Illinois, during World War I, he earned the rank of second lieutenant. While awaiting orders to embark for France, Danzig and his entire unit fell ill to the influenza pandemic that swept through the camp. Discharged from the army in 1919 following the signing of the Armistice, he returned to Cornell and graduated with his class in 1921. In both 1919 and 1920 Danzig played on the Cornell varsity football team as a substitute halfback. Weighing only 125 pounds, he was one of the smallest, but most determined, players on the team.

After graduating from Cornell, Danzig joined the *Brooklyn Eagle* as a sports correspondent. He earned five dollars for his first story about a Long Island junior championship golf tournament. For the next two months, he remained on space rates, earning between eight and twelve dollars per week, writing about baseball, billiards, boxing, golf, football, and tennis. The turning point in Danzig's career came with his 1921 article on the New York Metropolitan Lawn Tennis Singles Championship, from which he earned his own byline and a promotion to full-time correspondent at a weekly salary of twenty-five dollars.

In 1923 Danzig married Dorothy Charlotte Chapman; they would have three children. That same year he joined the *New York Times* as its chief tennis correspondent and began a seasonal pattern of sports reporting that he maintained throughout his 45-year tenure at that paper. Each season saw Danzig shift his interest between several sports. After the conclusion of the outdoor tennis season, capped by the U.S. Lawn Tennis Association Championship in September, Danzig would turn his attention to college football. During the winter and early spring, he would write about indoor tennis, court tennis, racquets, and squash. As summer approached, Danzig would report on college rowing before returning to the outdoor lawn tennis tournaments. In 1932 he complemented his reporting repertoire by covering the Summer Olympic Games in Los Angeles, California. Danzig resumed his Olympic coverage in London, England, in 1948; in Helsinki, Finland, in 1952; in Melbourne, Australia, in 1956; and in Rome, Italy, in 1960. His stories provided an insightful look at the adaptation of the Olympics to the geopolitical realignments of the Cold War and the accommodation of the state-supported amateur teams of the Soviet Union and its satellites.

Danzig authored or edited, alone or in collaboration, nine sports books. His first, *The Racquet Game* (1930), marked the first book-length examination of court tennis, racquets, and squash and established

him as an authority on those sports. In 1948 Danzig coedited, with Peter Bradwein, *Sport's Golden Age: A Close-Up of the Fabulous Twenties*, a collection of essays by the leading sports journalists of the 1920s. He distinguished himself as an historian of college football with *The History of American Football* (1956) and *Oh, How They Played the Game: The Early Days of Football* (1971). Critics regarded the *History of Baseball: Its Great Players, Teams and Managers* (1959), coauthored with Joe Reichler, as the best account of the national pastime in fifty years. *The Fireside Book of Tennis* (1972), coedited with Peter Schwed, showcased the writing of the century's most outstanding tennis correspondents. His last book, *The Winning Gallery: Court Tennis Matches and Memories*, came in 1985.

Early in his career Danzig's reporting reflected the unrestrained enthusiasm of the "Gee Whiz" generation of sports journalists writing during the golden age of American sports. Relying on hyperbole and allusions to the classics, natural disaster, and war, he and other writers cast the sports heroes and heroines of the 1920s as unassailable superstars. Danzig, however, set himself apart from other tennis correspondents through authoritative analysis of strategy and technique. As his career progressed his writing became increasingly straightforward, underscoring his knowledge of the game and its players. Tennis correspondents and players alike consulted Danzig on every aspect of the game. In 1933 Danzig coined the term "Grand Slam" to collectively describe the Australian, French, British, and American tennis championships. Arguably the foremost tennis correspondent of the twentieth century, he retired from the *New York Times* in 1968. That same year Danzig became the first journalist inducted into the U.S. Lawn Tennis Hall of Fame (now International Tennis Hall of Fame) in Newport, Rhode Island. He died of a heart attack in Ridgewood, New Jersey.

• Biographical files on Danzig are located at the archives of the *New York Times*, New York City, and the International Tennis Hall of Fame and Museum, Newport, R.I. Other useful articles include Bud Collins, "Danzig's Strokes Were Elegant," *Boston Globe*, 9 July 1987; Joy Duckett, "A Fireside Chat with Allison Danzig," *World Tennis* 28 (May 1981): 40; and Barry Lorge, "Chronicler of the U.S. Championships," *Tennis Magazine*, Sept. 1987, pp. 107–8. For examinations of sports journalism during the 1920s, see Mark Inabinett, *Grantland Rice and His Heroes: The Sportswriter as Mythmaker in the 1920s* (1994); Benjamin G. Rader, *American Sports: From the Age of Folk Games to the Age of Spectators* (1983); and Robert Kilborn, "Sports Journalism in the 1920s: A Study of the Interdependence of the Daily Newspaper and the Sports Hero" (master's thesis, Michigan State Univ., 1972). An obituary is in the *New York Times*, 28 Jan. 1987.

ADAM R. HORNBUCKLE

DA PONTE, Lorenzo (10 Mar. 1749–17 Aug. 1838), poet, librettist, and libertine, was born Emanuele Conegliano in Ceneda (near Venice), Italy, the son of Geremia Conegliano, a tanner and dealer in leather, and Rachele Pincherle. Following the death of his wife in about 1754, Geremia Conegliano wished to marry a

Roman Catholic woman and so, together with his three living sons, converted from Judaism to Catholicism in 1763. As was customary at the time, the new converts took the surname of the current bishop of Ceneda, Monsignor Lorenzo Da Ponte, and Emanuele, the eldest son, took the prelate's first name. His conversion and the bishop's patronage enabled young Lorenzo to receive an excellent education, especially in the Latin and Italian languages, at the episcopal seminary in Ceneda and later at the seminary in the nearby town of Portugruaro. He progressed so rapidly that he became an instructor at the latter institution in 1770, professor of languages in 1771, and vice rector in 1772. He was ordained as a Roman Catholic priest in 1773, a career decision he was soon to regret.

Da Ponte abandoned his position at Portogruaro in the fall of 1773, reportedly in a fit of pique, and moved to Venice where he indulged in a life of idleness, gambling, and sexual dissipation. From 1774 to 1776 he taught at the seminary in Treviso; there he revealed a flair for teaching Italian literature and began to develop his talent as a poet. This interlude came to an end when the Venetian senate, after a hearing on some allegedly radical poems he had written for an academic ceremony, forbade him from ever again teaching in the Venetian republic. He then returned to a highly dissolute life in Venice. His activities provided the authorities with ample excuse to banish him in 1779 from the territory of the Venetian republic for fifteen years. In danger of arrest, he fled to the town of Gorizia, then part of the Austrian empire.

Sometime in late 1781, Da Ponte went to Vienna armed with a letter of introduction to Antonio Salieri, then composer to the Austrian imperial court. In the spring of 1783, Emperor Joseph II established a new Italian opera company to perform at the imperial theater. Though Da Ponte had never written an opera libretto and had no theatrical experience, he asked Salieri to recommend him for the position of poet to the Italian theater. Amazingly, he received the appointment, which carried with it direct access to the emperor. His first libretto, performed in December 1784 with music by Salieri, was a fiasco. However, his next effort, written for the Spanish composer Vicente Martín y Soler, was a great success at its premiere in January 1786. For the next five years, he wrote many librettos for the leading composers of Italian opera of the day and supervised their production at the Burgtheater in Vienna.

Da Ponte's chief claim to fame lies in the three opera librettos he wrote for Wolfgang Amadeus Mozart: *The Marriage of Figaro* (1786); *Don Giovanni* (1787); and *Così fan Tutte* (1790). Unfortunately, almost nothing is known of the exact nature or details of the collaboration between composer and poet, though Mozart is known to have been very demanding of his librettists. The libretto for *The Marriage of Figaro* was a condensation and adaptation of the famous French play of the same title by Pierre Augustin Caron de Beaumarchais, first performed in 1784. *Don Giovanni*, derived from a popular story based in turn upon a Spanish play of

1630 by Tirso de Molina, was written for performance in Prague where it, like *Figaro* previously, had a great success. The libretto for *Così fan Tutte* seems to have been an original creation by Da Ponte. The collaboration between Mozart and Da Ponte has come to be considered one of the great ones in operatic history, equaled perhaps only by that between Giuseppe Verdi and Arrigo Boito in the late nineteenth century.

Da Ponte's patron and friend, Emperor Joseph II, died in 1790. He did not get on well with the new emperor, Leopold II, who in 1791 dismissed him as court poet and forced him to leave Vienna. He then lived for a time in Trieste, where in 1792 he married Ann Celestine Ernestine Grahl, a young woman many years his junior. The exact nature of the ceremony is unclear, since Da Ponte was still officially a Catholic priest, but the marriage proved a lasting one and produced five children. The newlyweds eventually made their way to London where, after a year of poverty, Da Ponte became librettist to the King's Theatre in late 1793. He continued to write for that organization until 1804, but he also became increasingly involved in the management and fundraising efforts of the company, which plunged him into heavy indebtedness. His other ventures in bookselling and publishing only increased his financial problems. In April 1805 he was forced to immigrate to the United States to avoid imprisonment for debt. He arrived in Philadelphia on 4 June 1805.

The thirty-three years that Da Ponte spent in the United States proved anticlimactic. He tried various ways of earning a living but none proved wholly satisfactory. He became a grocer, first in New York City and then in Elizabethtown, New Jersey, until 1807. He then gave private lessons in Italian language and literature and later opened a private academy in New York. In 1811 he moved to Sunbury, Pennsylvania, where he again became a grocer. In 1819 he returned to New York where he once more privately taught Italian language and literature. In 1825 he was appointed professor of Italian literature at Columbia College (later Columbia University); he received no salary but was permitted to collect "reasonable" fees from anyone attending his lectures. Unfortunately, though he held this position until his death, he had few students. During this period he was also the proprietor of an Italian bookshop. To the end of his life he was a vigorous proselytizer for Italian culture in his adopted country.

In 1832–1833 Da Ponte persuaded an Italian impresario to bring a company of singers to New York and Philadelphia for a season of Italian opera; the venture was not a financial success and left Da Ponte in debt. Undaunted, he raised a large sum of money to build in New York the first building in the United States specifically designed as an opera house. The initial season of the house in 1833–1834 under Da Ponte's management lost money; he took no further part in the venture and the opera house burned down in 1839. Da Ponte died in New York City.

• Da Ponte published his memoirs in four volumes in Italian in New York between 1823 and 1827. An enlarged and corrected edition in three volumes appeared in 1829–1830. Two modern English translations appeared in 1929: *Memoirs of Lorenzo Da Ponte, Mozart's Librettist*, trans. and ed. L. A. Sheppard; and *Memoirs of Lorenzo Da Ponte*, trans. Elizabeth Abbott, ed. Arthur Livingston. Though the *Memoirs* are the major source for Da Ponte's long life, they are an often unreliable blend of fact and fantasy. A more recent and scholarly biography is Sheila Hodges, *Lorenzo Da Ponte: The Life and Times of Mozart's Librettist* (1985). An earlier and more lively life is April FitzLyon, *The Libertine Librettist: A Biography of Mozart's Librettist, Lorenzo da Ponte* (1955). For Da Ponte's operatic ventures in New York, see John Dizikes, *Opera in America: A Cultural History* (1993).

JOHN E. LITTLE

DARE, Virginia (18 Aug. 1587–?), the first child of English parents in the New World, was born on Roanoke Island in the colony of Virginia, now North Carolina, the daughter of Ananias Dare and Elenor (also spelled Ellinor, Eleanor, and Elyoner) White, Roanoke colony settlers. The facts of Virginia Dare's life are scant. Her mother left Plymouth, England, while pregnant with Virginia, on 8 May 1587 as one of the settlers in Sir Walter Raleigh's third attempt to establish an English colony in the New World. Virginia's maternal grandfather, the artist John White (fl. 1585–1593), was the colony's governor. In late July 1587 the colonists began to construct their settlement on Roanoke Island, and a few weeks later Virginia Dare was born. On 24 August Virginia was baptized, most likely by White. She was named Virginia, as White writes in his "Narrative of the 1587 Virginia Voyage," "because this childe was the first Christian borne in Virginia."

At the request of the other colonists, White returned to England for supplies and reinforcements on 27 August 1587. His was the last recorded contact between the Roanoke settlers and Europe. Detained in England, White could only return to Roanoke three years later. On his arrival he found none of the colonists, only the word "Croatoan" carved on both a tree and a doorpost, presumably a sign that the colonists had tried to move to the lands of a nearby Native-American tribe with whom they had become friends.

Virginia Dare's importance to American history rests mainly on the legends associated with the "Lost Colony." As the first child of English parents in the New World, she came to represent the aspirations of English colonization. That Elenor Dare sailed to Virginia while pregnant symbolized the English hopes for establishing a permanent settlement in the New World. From this same hope sprang a number of stories about "white Indians." Native Americans with European physical features or cultural practices, implying that the Roanoke colonists had intermixed with Native-American societies in and around the Virginia colony. The first of these reports appears in Captain John Smith's (1580–1631) *A True Relation* (1608), and such reports continued to be made until at least the publication of John Lawson's *A New Voyage to Carolina* (1709). William Strachey's *Historie of Travaile into Virginia Britannia* (c. 1612) mentions infor-

mation gathered from Native Americans about possible survivors of the Roanoke colony, including four men, two boys, and one young woman. Coming at a time when Virginia Dare would have been in her early twenties, if she were still alive, Strachey's report inevitably connected her with the rumored "white Indian" woman. In the nineteenth and twentieth centuries, Virginia Dare was revived as a literary character, serving in several pieces as the symbol for the blending of European and Native-American cultures. The best known of these works is Paul Green's outdoor drama *The Lost Colony* (1937), still produced every summer on Roanoke Island. The mystery surrounding Virginia Dare's life has made her a mythic symbol for English settlement in North America.

• The best work on the Roanoke voyages is David Beers Quinn, *Set Fair for Roanoke: Voyages and Colonies, 1584–1606* (1985). For information on the treatment of Virginia Dare in literature, see Robert D. Arner, "The Romance of Roanoke: Virginia Dare and the Lost Colony in American Literature," *Southern Literary Journal* 10 (Spring 1978): 5–45, revised and reprinted as *The Lost Colony in Literature* (1985).

E. THOMSON SHIELDS, JR.

DARGAN, Edmund S. (15 Apr. 1805–24 Nov. 1879), legislator and judge, was born near Wadesboro, in Montgomery County, North Carolina, the son of a Baptist minister, whose given name is unknown, and a woman whose maiden name was Lilly. Dargan's full middle name is listed in a number of sources as either Strother or Spawn. His father died when Dargan was very young. There was no adequate estate, and to earn a livelihood he became an agricultural laborer. Dargan was a self-educated young man who studied the law in typical nineteenth-century fashion, in the law office of a local practitioner in Wadesboro. After a year of study he was admitted in 1829 to the North Carolina bar. The following year he walked to Alabama, where he settled in Washington in Autauga County. He was admitted to the Alabama bar and served as a justice of the peace in Autauga County for a number of years.

Dargan moved to Montgomery in 1833 and married Roxana Brack. In 1841 he finally settled in Mobile, where he would spend most of his life. He never became an inordinately wealthy man, but he rose well above the relative economic modesty of his youth. After his admission to the bar he spent most of his life in the practice of law, and by 1860 he owned thirteen slaves and had an estate estimated at $80,000. His conduct in regard to slavery—even though he never ruled against the plantocracy as a judge—suggests some ambivalence. Although manumission was in considerable disfavor throughout the South during the 1850s, Dargan served in 1858 as a witness in a case involving an emancipation paid for by the slave himself.

Dargan served as a state circuit court judge in Mobile County in 1841 and 1842, just after he moved there. He had a brief tenure on the Alabama Supreme Court, first as an associate judge from 1847 to 1849, and then as the state's chief justice from 1849 to 1852.

His opinions reveal a man firmly committed to the ideas of liberal capitalism. He believed deeply in the laissez-faire contract doctrine, for instance, which was prevalent in nineteenth-century American law. In *Judge v. Wilkins* (1851), for example, he ruled that an inequality in a bargain was no evidence of fraud, and that agreements "profitable or unprofitable, are considerations not for courts of justice, but for the party himself." He was equally rigorous in holding that it was the terms of the contract itself that defined obligations. In *Sims & Jones v. Knox* (1850), for instance, he held that the parties had stipulated certain terms in the hire of a slave, and had omitted others, and that the court could not read in any by implication. However, the chance to frame legal doctrine as a judge did not hold Dargan's interest very long. He resigned from the state supreme court in 1852 and never again held a judicial office, although he practiced law in Mobile until his death there more than twenty years later.

Dargan, who appeared eccentric, even in his dress, to many of his contemporaries who knew him, rarely stayed in one political job for long. He served one term in the Alabama State Senate (1844), one year as mayor of Mobile, and then was elected to the U.S. House of Representatives as a Democrat in the Twenty-ninth Congress (Mar. 1845–Mar. 1847). He did not seek reelection, but the one term he served was propitious. He took a crucial part in the Oregon debate and sponsored the compromise whereby the United States gave up its claim of title to the territory up to fifty-four degrees forty minutes in favor of the forty-ninth parallel. The forty-ninth parallel became the final boundary settlement between the United States and British claims. He took no other prominent position on the outstanding issues that came before Congress during his short term, such as the acquisition of Texas.

Dargan surfaced again in the political forum in 1852 as part of a group of Mobile "fire-eaters"—men who were not unequivocal partisans, even though they generally adhered to the Democratic party. A fire-eating brand of southernism, however, had to wait to carry the day, and when it came in the secession winter, Dargan joined in support of secession in the Alabama convention. He then served a term in the Confederate Congress and once again declined to seek reelection. While in the congress he tended to strongly favor those means he considered necessary to uphold the independence of the South, such as the conscription of troops and the suspension of the writ of habeas corpus. He was a little more ambivalent on the issue of impressment of private property. In November 1862 he wrote to Jefferson Davis to inform him that the people in the countryside outside Mobile were afraid to bring produce into the city for fear of seizure by the government.

With the end of his term in the Confederate Congress in 1864, Dargan resumed the practice of law and never reentered the political realm. He played no distinct role in the Reconstruction of Alabama. It is not clear whether he actually argued the cases associated with his law firm, but there are numerous examples of cases involving the firm during the postwar years. One case, perhaps, can stand as an example of his later practice. *Carter's Heirs v. Carter's Admr's* (Jan. term, 1865) showed the kind of problem left after the end of slavery. Dargan's firm successfully argued against the validity of a last testament that involved giving a slave either his freedom or the privilege of being at-large and enjoying the fruits of his labor as if he were free. They claimed that Alabama law in 1861, the year of the testator's death, did not allow such loose rein over a slave. Dargan presented a good lawyerly argument to win the case despite himself having been a marginal party to the prospective emancipation of a slave in the late 1850s. Dargan, in any event, continued his devotion to the law until his death.

• A small but useful collection of Dargan's papers is in the Alabama Department of Archives and History, Montgomery. The papers are cataloged under the name Edmund Spawn Dargan, which is the way he appears in J. Mills Thorton III, *Politics and Power in a Slave Society: Alabama, 1800–1860* (1978). His service in the Confederate Congress can be followed in Thomas B. Alexander and Richard E. Beringer, *The Anatomy of the Confederate Congress: A Study of the Influences of Member Characteristics on Legislative Voting Behavior, 1861–1865* (1972). Very brief sketches of Dargan are in a number of biographical collections, but none more intimate than that of William Garrett, *Reminiscences of Public Men in Alabama, for Thirty Years* (1872).

THOMAS D. MORRIS

DARGAN, Olive Tilford (11 Jan. 1869–22 Jan. 1968), writer, was born on a farm near Litchfield, Kentucky, the daughter of Elisha Francis Tilford and Rebecca Day, schoolteachers. She grew up on a farm in the mountains, the real-life site of some of her fictions. By age fourteen, she was a one-room schoolteacher, instructing up to forty students of all ages in all subjects. Her omnivorous intellectual appetite fed her later works. She earned a two-year degree from George Peabody College for Teachers in Nashville, Tennessee, in 1888.

While briefly attending Radcliffe College in Cambridge, Massachusetts (1893–1894), she met a young Harvard poet, Pegram Dargan, whom she married in 1898. The couple lived variously on a farm in North Carolina, in England, and in New York City. They only had one child, who died soon after birth. In 1915 Pegram drowned at sea, and Olive Dargan thereafter lived an independent life, writing and tending her garden at her Asheville, North Carolina, home.

Dargan gained fame as a result of tragedy. Upon her husband's death, she memorialized her feelings for him in *The Cycle's Rim* (1916), a sequence of fifty-three sonnets, one more sonnet than weeks in a year. The fifty-third sonnet begins a new year and symbolizes everlasting renewal. Dargan's *Cycle's Rim* begins: "Deep lies thy body, jewel of the sea, / Locked down with wave upon wave. Pearl drift among / The coral towers, and yet not thee, not thee!" The sonnet cycle continues with its Browningesque syntax and sea-wave rhythm to evoke eternal symbols, such as spring, music, time, and love. The volume garnered prizes from the Southern Society of New York and from the North Carolina Literature and History Association.

In the teens and early twenties Dargan continued publishing verse, which appeared in such magazines as *Scribner's*, *Bookman*, *The Fugitive*, and *The Liberator*, and in 1924 she received the Belmont-Ward Fugitive prize.

Dargan also continued to write dramas, something she had taken up early in her married life. Readers today may find some of Dargan's characters to be stiff mouthpieces for ideas, but the critic Sylvia Jenkins Cook has remarked that Dargan's plays are her earliest social criticism. Dargan uses the device of displacing the action to another country to comment upon American mores. For example, in *The Journey*, a play from her collection *The Flutter of the Goldleaf* (1922, with Frederick Peterson), a Chinese woman kills herself when she realizes that her new husband is so infatuated with her that he has neglected his duty of leading political reformers.

In the late twenties Dargan questioned the worth of her writing and laid aside her pen. However, a highly publicized strike by textile workers in Gastonia, North Carolina, and the Crash of 1929 caused her to lift it again in the cause of the millworkers. Because Dargan feared that her poetry audience would disapprove of her working at an "inferior" craft (as fiction was then viewed), and because her protagonists worked in the communist and unionist causes, Dargan wrote her three socially critical novels under the pseudonym Fielding Burke.

The first novel, *Call Home the Heart* (1932; rev. ed., 1993), contrasted pre- and postindustrial mountain life. Dargan draws Ishmalee, the central character, as a feminist hero and spokeswoman for the environment. Ishmalee labors on her ancestral farm in the southern Appalachians six days a week. On the seventh she seeks secret places in the woods wherein she is renewed by her love of nature. Marriage breaks her cycle of work and rest and adds the burden of caring for children to that of tending the impoverished farm. At last, spiritually and physically exhausted, she escapes the mountain community with a lover and flees to a milltown. There, Ishmalee notices the poverty and chronic illness of the millworkers and joins the communist push to organize against the mills' owners. At the climax, Ishmalee cannot accept the communist doctrine of the social equality of whites and blacks, and she flees back to her mountain, where her husband has waited for her.

Edwin Seaver, reviewer for the *New Republic* (29 Jan. 1936), wrote, "What chiefly characterized *Call Home the Heart* was its lyrical idealism, its fine soil quality, its sense of the tragic. In other words, Fielding Burke carried over into her fiction the merits of Olive Dargan's poetry, and so contributed to the proletarian novel, whose direction was toward the didactic and the tendentious, elements of the soil and the native folk of which it was badly in need." Marxists of the period, however, objected to the novel's happy ending. To counter Marxist criticism, Dargan wrote a sequel, *A Stone Came Rolling* (1935), in which Ishmalee comes back down the mountain to dedicate her life to revolutionary causes. Cook notes that one of the main themes is that of the social utopia supplanting revealed religion. Dargan's final novel, about mineworkers, is *Sons of the Stranger* (1947).

Dargan returned to poetry with her 1958 publication of *The Spotted Hawk*. This book of verse, her most widely acclaimed volume, won North Carolina's Roanoke-Chowan award for excellence in literature. Her last volume was a collection of short fiction, *Innocent Bigamy* (1962). Dargan died in Asheville, North Carolina.

Dargan's best works are her poems, her short stories, and her first novel. Her poetry shows a wide range of styles and voices, from the densely packed and highly musical sonnet to the laconic character sketch in verse à la Sarah Orne Jewett or Robert Frost. Her short stories, such as those in *Highland Annals* (1925, repr. as *From My Highest Hill* in 1941), reflect a sharp naturalist's eye, an ear for dialogue, her concern for the worker's plight, and her admiration for strong, independent women. Her works were known and acclaimed mostly in the South; and as documents of the South as it became industrialized, Dargan's works can be enjoyed by the modern reader.

• Dargan's few papers are housed in the Southern Historical Collection at the University of North Carolina in Chapel Hill. In addition, the North Carolina Collection, also at Chapel Hill, has copies of her works and includes Virginia Terrell Lathrop's short typescript biography (25 Aug. 1959) and Jane and Thomas Polsky, "The Two Lives of Olive Tilford Dargan," *Southern Packet* 4 (4 June 1948): 1–4. No lengthy treatments of Dargan's works exist. For additional insights, see Robert Bain and Louis Rubin, *History of Southern Literature* (1985); Lina Mainiero, *American Women Writers: A Critical Reference Guide from Colonial Times to the Present*, vol. 1 (1979); Sylvia Jenkins Cook, *From Tobacco Road to Route 66* (1976); and Walter B. Rideout, *The Radical Novel in the United States* (1956).

Dargan's other book-length works include *The Pathflower, and Other Verses* (1904), *Lords and Lovers and Other Dramas* (1906), and *The Mortal Gods, and Other Plays* (1912).

M. CATHERINE DOWNS

DARIN, Bobby (14 May 1936–20 Dec. 1973), singer and songwriter, was born Walden Robert Cassotto in East Harlem, New York, the son of Vanina "Nina" Cassotto, who was eighteen years old, unmarried, and living on welfare at the time of Bobby's birth. The identity of his father was never revealed to him. To save the family from scandal, Nina's mother, Vivian "Polly" Cassotto, raised the baby as her own. Bobby grew up believing that his grandmother was his mother, while his real mother pretended to be his sister. He did not learn the truth until 1968, when he was thirty-two years old. The disclosure crushed him emotionally and physically. He told family and friends, "My whole life has been a lie" (Darin, p. 234). In 1942 Nina married Carmine "Charlie" Maffia, with whom she had three more children.

Bobby's later life was shaped by the illness that plagued him as a child. At age eight, he contracted rheumatic fever. He suffered four episodes of the debilitating disease before he was thirteen. These attacks caused extensive damage to his heart. Doctors told the family that Bobby would not live past the age of sixteen. The family coddled and pampered Bobby, a natural impulse, but one that proved destructive.

Treated like royalty throughout his youth, Darin developed into a cocky, arrogant young man. His sister Vivienne Walden later said, "Bobby was wonderful, but he thought the sun rose when he got up in the morning. He thought that everything existed for his pleasure or his need or his wants" (Darin, p. 13). He was also very ambitious, and with his sights set on a career in show business, he vowed to become a legend by the age of twenty-five.

After a semester spent studying drama at Hunter College, Darin dropped out to devote all of his energy to music. He held a variety of odd jobs and used his earnings to pay for demonstration records of his songs.

In his late teens, Darin dated singer Connie Francis, whose manager, George Scheck, was instrumental in launching Bobby's career. Scheck liked Darin's sound and, after advising him to change his name (reports of how "Darin" was selected vary widely), landed him a recording contract with Decca Records and an appearance on the television series "Stage Show."

Darin's first single, "Rock Island Line," flopped, as did the three follow-up singles he cut for Decca. When his one-year contract was up, Decca dropped him. He was signed by Atco Records and churned out three more singles, none of which garnered much notice.

Darin's fortunes changed in 1958, with the release of "Splish Splash," a novelty tune that he wrote in less than twenty minutes. The single sold more than 100,000 copies in three weeks, hitting number three on the music charts. Proving he was no one-hit wonder, he followed up with three more gold records, "Queen of the Hop" (1958), "Dream Lover" (1959), and "Mack the Knife" (1959). "Mack the Knife" earned Darin a Grammy Award, Best New Artist of 1959, and Best Male Vocal Performance.

What made Darin unique was not his singing voice, which has been described as "average," but rather his showmanship. His vitality and finger-snapping, hip-grinding style of delivery made him a popular nightclub attraction. His first nightclub engagement, in June 1959, was opening for comedian George Burns's Las Vegas act. Within a year, he was headlining at clubs in Las Vegas, New York, Los Angeles, and Washington, D.C.

While at the pinnacle of his music career, Darin decided to tackle another avenue of show business: motion-picture acting. He landed a supporting role in the Rock Hudson comedy *Come September* (1961), which also starred sixteen-year-old movie star Sandra Dee. Darin and Dee were married in 1960, shortly after filming was completed. They had one child.

The *Hollywood Reporter* offered the following assessment of Darin's film acting debut: "Something of a surprise, and a pleasant one, is Bobby Darin. [He] turns out to be a good native actor, handling his lines and role with agreeable finesse" (27 June 1961). He remained active in film throughout the 1960s, most notably in *Captain Newman, M.D.* (1963), for which he earned an Academy Award nomination.

In the late 1960s, Darin jettisoned his trademark tuxedo and his pop-rock singing style. Sporting sideburns and denim jeans, he attempted to launch a new image as a protest singer. Though he had one big hit during this period—"If I Were a Carpenter" (1966)—for the most part, his politically oriented folk songs were not well received. A long period of seclusion and self-reflection followed, during which Darin gave away most of his possessions and lived out of a trailer.

In 1971, reverting to the suave style that made him famous, Darin successfully revived his nightclub career. He said at the time, "Some people think I'm a fine actor, and I'm very happy about that. I have touched base as a songwriter. Some people feel I'm very equipped in that area, and I'm glad about that. But the thing that really is a super charging, super energetic source for me is doing nightclub performances." Darin was also popular with television audiences, starring in two variety series, "The Bobby Darin Amusement Company" (1972) and "The Bobby Darin Show" (1973).

With a recording contract at Motown Records and a $2 million Las Vegas nightclub deal, Darin was back at the top of his profession when he succumbed to heart disease. Divorced from Sandra Dee in 1967, Darin remarried in 1973 legal secretary Andrea Yeager. The marriage was short-lived, however, and Darin was divorced at the time of his death in Los Angeles.

Many of Darin's songs are still radio-station mainstays, and a testament to his enduring fame was his 1990 induction into the Rock and Roll Hall of Fame. Though the question of whether he achieved legendary status is debatable, he did succeed in becoming one of the most popular teen idols of the 1950s. His friend and mentor George Burns said of Bobby, "He sang great, he danced great, he moved good, he was a good actor, he had a great sense of humor. And it would be impossible for Bobby Darin to be anything different than a star."

• Dodd Darin, the son of Bobby Darin and Sandra Dee, authored a joint biography of his famous parents, *Dream Lovers: The Magnificent Shattered Lives of Bobby Darin and Sandra Dee* (1994). Two other full-length studies are: Al DiOrio, *Borrowed Time: The 37 Years of Bobby Darin* (1981), and Jeff Bleiel, *That's All: Bobby Darin on Record, Stage and Screen* (1993). Connie Francis wrote about her relationship with Darin in her autobiography, *Who's Sorry Now?* (1984). James Robert Parish and Michael R. Pitts, *Hollywood Songsters: A Biographical Dictionary* (1991), offers an extensive profile of Darin, including a filmography and album discography.

Notable newspaper and magazine profiles of the entertainer include: Charles Champlin, "Bobby Darin—A Confidence Game," *Los Angeles Times*, 21 Jan. 1966; Doris Klein, "Bobby Darin, Night Club Success, Still Waiting for Right Movie Role," *Hollywood Reporter*, 8 Dec. 1967; Edward Linn, "Little Singer with a Big Ego," *Saturday Evening Post*, 6 May 1961; Peer Oppenheimer, "Whatever Happened to Bobby Darin?" *Family Weekly*, 1 Sept. 1968; John L. Scott, "'New' Bobby Darin Retains Old Flair," *Los Angeles Times*, 10 Mar. 1966; "Look at Me," *Newsweek*, 9 Apr. 1962; and "Bobby's Back in Town," *TV Guide*, 26 Dec. 1956. Obituaries are in the *Hollywood Reporter*, the *Los Angeles Times*, and the *New York Times*, 21 Dec. 1973; *Variety*, 26 Dec. 1973; and *Newsweek* and *Time*, 31 Dec. 1973.

BRENDA SCOTT ROYCE

DARLEY, Felix Octavius Carr (23 June 1822–27 Mar. 1888), illustrator, was born in Philadelphia, Pennsylvania, the son of John Darley, an English comic actor, and Eleanora Westray, an actress. In Philadelphia, the Darleys were part of an extended family of actors associated with the Chestnut Street Theater. At age fourteen Darley was placed as a clerk apprentice for the Dispatch Transportation Line in Philadelphia but continued his hobby of copying old master engravings and contemporary illustrations by English artists such as Thomas Rowlandson and George Cruikshank. His passion for caricature and the sketching of Philadelphia street scenes brought him to the attention of the publisher Thomas Dunn English, who paid him for a few designs for the weekly newspaper *Saturday Museum*, which Edgar Allan Poe was then editing. Encouraged by his success, Darley left his clerkship in 1841 and secured a position as staff illustrator for *Graham's Lady's and Gentleman's Magazine*. His drawings also began to appear in *Godey's Magazine*, and in 1843 he sold to the *Dollar Newspaper* two drawings that later became vignettes for Poe's *The Gold Bug*. Darley's success was assured when in the late 1840s the Philadelphia publishers Carey & Hart commissioned him to create sketches for their Library of American Humorous Works. The first volume was published in 1846; over the next twenty-five years nearly 100 more volumes appeared, many of which were illustrated by Darley.

As an illustrator Darley worked in two ways. Most often he created sepia wash drawings that were then translated by engravers on wood or metal engraving plates. But he also employed a method of pure outline drawing that was reproduced by lithographers working on stone. This latter style of pure outline was influenced by the engravings of the English neoclassic sculptor John Flaxman and the German illustrator Moritz Retzsch. Darley's earliest illustrations, titled *Scenes in Indian Life: A Series of Original Designs Etched in Stone*, were done in this outline style. Sold by subscription in five installments beginning in April 1843, these etched lithographs were also reproduced in the *U.S. Democratic Review*, which had a reputation for publishing the best prints by Continental and British illustrators. For over forty years, according to John C. Ewers, "Darley's Indians were seen more often in widely read American books and magazines than were the Indian pictures of any other artist" (p. 98).

Impressed by Darley's work, the American Art Union commissioned him to create its annual gift engravings for subscribers. Between 1848 and 1851 he cre-

ated three projects for the Art Union. In 1848 he produced six etched lithographs to illustrate Washington Irving's *Rip Van Winkle*. Their popularity was such that Darley was invited the following year to create six more prints based on the author's *Legend of Sleepy Hollow*. These works, along with commissions to illustrate Francis Parkman's *The California and Oregon Trail: Being Sketches of Prairie and Rocky Mountain Life* in 1849 and Irving's *A History of New York* in 1850, established Darley as America's foremost illustrator.

Darley moved to New York in 1848. When he was elected to the National Academy of Design in 1853, he was regarded as the most popular illustrator in the country. In 1856 he received an important commission from the publisher James G. Gregory to illustrate the entire works of James Fenimore Cooper (*Cooper's Novels Illustrated by Darley* [32 vols., 1859–1861]), which were later published as *The Cooper Vignettes* (1862) "in a large folio volume of India proofs." Darley also illustrated works by Alfred Lord Tennyson (1865 and 1866); Henry Wadsworth Longfellow, notably his *Evangeline* (1867 and 1883); Charles Dickens (1878 and 1888); Nathaniel Hawthorne, *The Scarlet Letter* (1879); and Shakespeare (1884 and 1888).

In 1859 Darley married Jane Colburn of Cambridge, Massachusetts. They moved to Claymont, Delaware, where a family homestead existed and where he spent the rest of his life. They had no children. Darley continued to draw regularly for *Appleton's Magazine* and *Harper's*. He also made vignettes for bank notes and drawings that were made into prints, suitable for framing.

After the Civil War, Darley visited Europe, where his steel engraving *Dahlgren's Cavalry Charge at Fredericksburg* was exhibited at the Paris Exposition of 1867. Following his trip, he published *Sketches Abroad with Pen and Pencil* in 1868. Later, in 1876, he received further acclaim as America's preeminent illustrator at the 1876 Philadelphia Centennial. His last illustrations appeared in a book titled *Picturesque California and the Region West of the Rocky Mountains* (1888), edited by the naturalist John Muir, a work that also included five illustrations by Frederic Remington. Darley died in Claymont.

American book illustration can be said to have begun with Darley, who illustrated more than 300 books and countless magazine articles. He set the standard for design and the integration of image and text. The linear clarity and humorous charm of many of his drawings accounted for his success with the American public. His illustrations were known throughout America, and his influence was great; Winslow Homer, among many other artists, began his career trying to emulate Darley. Furthermore, Darley's illustrations of popular American novels and histories became an important way for Americans to visualize their past at a time when the United States was becoming a nation and stories of a common experience helped unite them.

• Examples of Darley's work can be found at the Delaware Art Museum, Wilmington; the Library of Congress; the Museum of Fine Arts, Boston; the New York Public Library; and Princeton University Library, Sinclair Hamilton Collection of Illustrated Books. The standard work on Darley remains Theodore Bolton, *The Book Illustrations of F. O. C. Darley* (1952), which first appeared in the *Proceedings of the American Antiquarian Society* 61 (Apr. 1951): 136–82. Frank Weitenkampf, "F. O. C. Darley, American Illustrator," *Art Quarterly* 10 (Spring 1947): 100–113, consulted Bolton's *American Book Illustrators* (1938) and provides a detailed analysis of the evolution of Darley's graphic style. An important addition to the literature on Darley is Anne Christine Hahler, ". . . *Illustrated by Darley": An Exhibition of Original Drawings* (1978), which updates Bolton's checklist. Sue W. Reed, "F. O. C. Darley's Outline Illustrations," in *The American Illustrated Book in the Nineteenth Century*, ed. W. R. Ward (1982), is an excellent discussion of Darley's indebtedness to the late eighteenth-century neoclassical work of the British draftsman John Flaxman. John C. Ewers, "Not Quite Redman: The Plains Indians Illustrations of Felix O. C. Darley," *American Art Journal* 3 (Fall 1971): 88–98, is an analysis by an ethnologist of Darley's various depictions of Indian life. Further assessments of Darley's accomplishments can be found in Theodore E. Stebbins, Jr., *American Master Drawings and Watercolors* (1977), and James C. Best, *American Popular Illustration, a Reference Guide* (1984).

SALLY WEBSTER

DARLING, Edward V. (23 Sept. 1890–28 July 1951), theater manager and agent, was born in Waterbury, Connecticut, the son of William J. Darling, a salesman, and his wife (name unknown). Darling's father moved his family to New York City near the turn of the century. His son, while still in his teens, studied shorthand and typing in the hope of becoming a secretary and office manager. Away from school, he spent many hours in the vaudeville houses of Manhattan, seeing as many shows daily as his free time and pocket money allowed.

In 1905 Eddie Darling's career plans and his avocational interest in vaudeville coincided when Edward F. Albee offered the fifteen-year-old a secretarial job in his office. Since 1885 the Maine-born Albee had been the partner of theater magnate Benjamin Franklin Keith, who with his precursor Tony Pastor had essentially created American vaudeville. Before Pastor opened his first Manhattan theater in 1881 and Keith opened a similar theater in Boston a few years later, theatrical entertainment for the family had been largely nonexistent in metropolitan areas. Apart from opera houses and plush theaters—both of which catered to what was then called "the carriage trade"—the staples of popular entertainment (comedy routines, popular songs, and the like) could be found chiefly in local beer halls.

By the time Darling joined the Keith organization as a secretary, Albee and Keith had already fashioned a chain of vaudeville theaters throughout the Northeast, giving urban America a form of family entertainment that would grow and prosper during the ensuing two decades. Although they had competitors, none matched the top-drawing talent that the "Keith cir-

cuit" (as the Keith-Albee enterprise was known in show business) presented daily in increasingly lavish theaters.

Within two years after his hiring, Darling became E. F. Albee's personal secretary. As Albee grew busier with the exponential growth of the Keith circuit, he began to rely on Darling to assist him with the talent bookings on which the business depended. By then Keith and Albee had fashioned the structure of the playbills for their larger theaters, which were known as "big-time vaudeville" in contrast to the lesser talent featured by some of their "small-time" competitors. Typically, the large Keith theaters featured two shows a day from Monday through Saturday (a matinee at the noon hour, followed by a second show at eight o'clock in the evening), with each show comprising nine individual "acts"—short performances by individual singers, dancers, acrobats, jugglers, comedians, and other performers.

The difficult tasks that Albee constantly faced were arranging the nine-act playbills so that each act would build and hold the audience's interest and determining which acts should play which theaters from one week to the next. As Albee delegated more responsibility to Darling, he soon discovered that the teenager possessed abilities that went well beyond the requirements of a personal stenographer. Not only did Darling have an instinctive sense of talent (the Keith circuit continuously auditioned new acts), he also had an unerring sense of the sequence in which each act should be presented for maximum effect.

Moreover, Darling had a prodigious memory, as the theatrical trade paper *Variety* documented in one of its frequent articles about him: "Quite a remarkable feat of memorizing was exhibited, impromptu, Monday last, by Eddie Darling when that young man, without reference to sheets, books or notes, recited, without a slip, the entire bills for next week in their running order in the seven big-time Keith vaudeville theaters he books" (5 Oct. 1917). As Albee and the other Keith executives also learned, Darling was an able negotiator—a vital talent given the egos and salary demands of such highly paid Broadway superstars as Nora Bayes, Eva Tanguay, Elsie Janis, and Harry Houdini, all of whom the young Darling dealt with almost weekly. His engaging, likable personality enabled him to resolve disputes during negotiations between the Keith management and its demanding stars and to mediate problems that occasionally arose among highly competitive performers.

The ingratiating manner that marked Darling's style as an executive, even more than the power that he exerted over the careers of all Keith artists, earned him the respect of vaudeville performers and their agents and made him one of the best-loved people in show business. "A presentation to Eddie Darling is underway by about sixty vaudeville artists," *Variety* reported in June 1917. "It is to be a testimonial of esteem for the rather youthful Darling in his exceedingly difficult position of booking the large B. F. Keith theaters. According to reports, neither Mr. Darling nor anyone connected with the Keith theaters has been consulted, the subscribing artists making it a personal tribute from themselves only."

As the growth of the motion picture industry gradually drew audiences away from vaudeville in the late 1920s, the scope of Darling's career and influence steadily narrowed. In 1930, with big-time vaudeville becoming a shadow of the massive organization of a quarter-century earlier, the forty-year-old Darling became an independent agent, dividing his time between New York and Hollywood. There his first-name familiarity with vaudeville greats—many of whom were sought by the Hollywood studios after Al Jolson's triumph in the pioneering sound film, *The Jazz Singer*—gave Darling an edge over other agents. But as the powerful Hollywood studios began to develop their own stars as sound-film technology steadily improved, Darling's usefulness to the industry lessened, and he returned permanently to New York City. He had essentially retired by the early 1940s, although he still maintained a small office not far from his residence on Manhattan's Park Avenue, where he died.

• Darling was the subject of numerous articles in *Variety* and *Billboard* between 1910 and 1925. See, for example, "Eddie Darling's Memory," *Variety*, 5 Oct. 1917; "An Eddie Darling Tribute," *Variety*, 15 June 1917; and *Billboard*, 18 June 1917. He is profiled in Abel Green and Joe Laurie, Jr., *Show Biz: From Vaude to Video* (1953), Bernard Sobel, *A Pictorial History of Vaudeville* (1961); and Marian Spitzer, *The Palace* (1969), which chronicles the playbills and stars of the most prestigious of the Keith theaters. He is mentioned in the autobiographies and biographies of some former Keith circuit stars. See, for example, Mae West, *Goodness Had Nothing to Do with It* (1959), and James A. Drake, *Rosa Ponselle: A Centenary Biography* (1997). An obituary is in the *New York Times*, 30 July 1951.

JAMES A. DRAKE

DARLING, Flora Adams (25 July 1840–6 Jan. 1910), author and founder of women's patriotic societies, was born in Lancaster, New Hampshire, the daughter of Harvey Adams, a carriage manufacturer, and his second wife, Nancy Dustin Rowell. Flora's family had no connection to the notable patriots of Revolutionary days. Her father's democratic ideals and views on history and politics were passed on to Flora, who received her formal education at Lancaster Academy.

Married on 12 March 1860 to Colonel Edward Irving Darling, a southerner and twenty-two years her senior, Darling settled in Louisiana with her husband and had one son. The couple traveled to England at the beginning of 1861 but came back to the United States following the start of the Civil War. Darling returned to her parents' home in New England until summoned to Richmond, Virginia, when her husband was wounded in February 1863. Wounded again during the battle for Franklin, Tennessee, Edward Darling died shortly thereafter. Although Darling said that her husband held the rank of general, this claim was never substantiated.

Following her husband's death, Darling was arrested in New Orleans as she tried to make her way back to her father's home. When she was arrested, her jewels, money, and Confederate bonds were confiscated and were not restored upon her release eight days later. She alleged that on her return trip to New York she was thrown down the ship's hatch and that her hand sustained permanent crippling injuries. Although she filed a claim with Congress, she did not receive the compensation of $5,683 until 1903. Before departing from Louisiana for Washington, D.C., where she became a government employee, Darling contracted malaria. In 1876 the illness recurred impairing both her hearing and her vision.

Hoping to supplement her income, Darling started a writing career in the 1880s by publishing *Mrs. Darling's Letters, Or Memories of the Civil War* (1883), a book that favored the South. Subsequent works *A Social Diplomat* (1889), *A Winning, Wayward Woman* (1889), and *Was It a Just Verdict?* (1890) followed a more autobiographical format. Her book *A War Episode, Or History of the Darling Claim vs. the United States* (1900), told of her lawsuit against the government to regain her possessions. In *A War Episode* she claimed she "was made an innocent victim" of circumstances "hard to explain, and much more hard to endure." She also contributed romantic short stories to a number of magazines and wrote poetry.

Darling's relationship with the Daughters of the American Revolution (DAR) was fraught with conflict. A society whose members were women with collateral descendancy from participants of the revolutionary war, the DAR began as a result of its exclusion from the Sons of the American Revolution during that group's 1890 convention. Although Darling asserted that she formed the society, her story never matched that of the other original founders. Apparently the society was already thought of and solicitation for members had begun when Darling took the initiative to send out a letter announcing the first meeting to begin the organization of the DAR in the fall of 1890. Seeking cohesiveness and harmony, the new society overlooked Darling's assertiveness. The group adopted colors and a motto, the motto being changed within a month at the request of Darling to "Home and Country." This was expanded to "God, Home and Country" in 1972. Members agreed that the DAR's official publication would be *Adams Magazine*, edited by Darling's nephew who revamped a previous publication to fit the society's needs.

Because of her hearing loss, Darling never sought high office but served as vice president in charge of organization, which required her to travel throughout the country to enlist new members. Almost immediately tensions arose between Darling and the DAR officers in Washington who already felt resentment about her bold calling of the first meeting. Although she was reported to be dedicated to her mission and enthusiastic with prospective members, Darling's unpredictability and erratic bookkeeping created chaos within the organization. When she ordered 10,000 application blanks, the board refused to pay. Darling retaliated by ignoring the board's decision to raise membership fees and continued to charge the old rates. Washington and New York newspapers published all the news about the DAR's problems, adding to an already stressful situation, and Darling aired her viewpoint in *Adams Magazine*.

Darling refused to acknowledge the DAR board's authority after it revised its constitution on 26 May 1891 and would not allow the society to use her name. The board responded by vacating her office. Darling resigned from the national society in August, asking that the DAR delete her name from its records. She turned *Adams Magazine* into the official paper for her new organization, the Daughters of the Revolution, founded on 20 August 1891, and used a seal on the cover that resembled the DAR symbol. The magazine was published until 1896. Membership in the Daughters of the Revolution was based on lineal descent rather than the DAR's collateral descent and favored a stronger state organization. On 8 January 1892 she started the Daughters of the United States of the War of 1812 and was named president-general. In 1901 Darling published *The Founding and Organization of the Daughters of the American Revolution and Daughters of the Revolution*, in which she claimed to be the founder of the DAR, a claim disputed by other histories.

In 1907 Darling published both a book of verses titled *1607–1907: Memories of Virginia* and *Senator's Daughter*. She became vice president of the Lamperti School of Music and founded the Edward Irving Darling Musical Society in honor of her son, a composer, who died in 1894. She attempted to educate Native American girls in the East, worked to have the government sponsor a cultural academic institution, and sold life insurance. She had earlier converted to Roman Catholicism. She died in New York City.

A controversial woman of many pursuits, Flora Darling moved the formation of women's patriotic organizations forward. Although not a suffragist or a women's rights advocate, and despite adversity and physical limitations, she persuaded women to band together into a social awareness fostered by their ancestry and patriotic concerns.

• Flora Darling's papers consist of more than 4,500 pieces, mainly letters, and are at the library of the College of William and Mary. Additional writings by Darling include *Senator Athens, C.S.A.* (1889) and *Helen Wadsworth* (1899). For additional information on the DAR and the DR, see Mary S. Lockwood and Emily Lee Sherwood, *Story of the Records, D.A.R.* (1906); Letitia Green Stevenson, *A Brief History of the D.A.R.* (1913); Wallace Evan Davies, *Patriotism on Parade* (1955); Martha Strayer, *The D.A.R.: An Informal History* (1958); and Ann Arnold Hunter, *A Century of Service: The Story of the D.A.R.* (1991). Obituaries appear in the *Evening Star* (Washington, D.C.), 6 Jan. 1910; the *New York Times* and the *Washington Post*, 7 Jan. 1910; and the *Bulletin of the U.S. Daughters of 1812*, Feb. 1910.

MARILYN ELIZABETH PERRY

DARLING, Jay Norwood (21 Oct. 1876–12 Feb. 1962), political cartoonist and conservationist, known as "Ding," was born in Norwood, Michigan, the son of the Reverend Marcellus Warner Darling, a public school administrator and Congregational minister, and Clara R. Woolson. Darling grew up from the age of ten in Sioux City, Iowa, a frontier community surrounded by prairie teeming with wildlife. He spent many days and nights hunting, fishing, camping, and horseback riding in the pristine natural bounty that provided what he described as the "pleasantest recollections" of his long and eventful life.

In 1896 he enrolled in Beloit College in Wisconsin. Near the end of his junior year, Darling was expelled, reportedly for publishing a series of yearbook cartoons that were unflattering to the college president and faculty. These cartoons were the first he signed "D'ing," a contraction of his surname.

After returning to Beloit and graduating in 1900, Darling was obliged to work and save money for tuition before enrolling in Rush Medical School in Chicago. He returned home and joined the *Sioux City Journal* as a reporter and photographer. When Darling once submitted a sketch in place of a missed photograph, the editor was sufficiently impressed to publish the work of the self-taught artist. Darling's dream of a medical career was soon displaced by his growing reputation as a cartoonist.

In 1906 Darling married Genevieve "Penny" Pendleton; they had two children. Soon thereafter he accepted an offer from the *Des Moines Register* and *Leader* to be the papers' political cartoonist. Subsequently he was approached by representatives of the *Baltimore Sun*, the *Milwaukee Journal*, the *Chicago Daily Examiner*, and the *Cleveland Leader*, among others.

In 1911 Darling accepted a position at the *New York Globe*, which offered a large circulation and a new syndication service. Although at the *Globe* he made friends with luminaries such as Edna Ferber, William Allen White, and Grantland Rice, Darling objected to the editorial restrictions imposed on him. "Iowans," he suggested to a friend, "think more to the square inch than New Yorkers to the square mile." Meanwhile, the management at the *Register* and *Leader*, which had never restricted Darling's freedom of expression, was eager to bring him back to Des Moines to help boost the papers' circulation.

Darling returned to the *Register* and *Leader* in 1913 and, except for his later federal service, remained with the papers (the *Leader* later became the *Des Moines Tribune*) until his retirement in 1949. Beginning in 1916 his work also appeared in the *New York Herald Tribune*, which syndicated it in more than a hundred daily newspapers. He won two Pulitzer Prizes (awarded in 1924 and 1943) for his political cartoons, many of which were devoted to federal agricultural policies and most of which reflected Darling's commitment to the Republican party and his suspicion of a powerful federal government. Other cartoons urged protection of waterfowl and conservation of forests and waterways.

Darling wrote, "All it takes to be a conservationist is to have been awake and a witness to what has happened to all our continental forests, soils, waters, minerals and wildlife in the last fifty or seventy-five years and he'll be a conservationist from fright!" (letter to Lynn Bogue Hunt, 27 Jan. 1944). He warned that "the topsoil which goes swirling by in our rivers at flood stage may look like mud to you, but it is beefsteak and potatoes, ham and eggs and homemade bread with jam on it" (letter to R. H. Musser, 19 June 1951). His widely distributed conservation cartoons and conspicuous leadership in efforts to shield the Iowa Conservation Commission from political interference were brought to the attention of President Franklin D. Roosevelt, a frequent subject of Darling's critical New Deal cartoons. In March 1934 an unlikely partnership was created when Roosevelt appointed Darling chief of the U.S. Bureau of Biological Survey—the forerunner of the Fish and Wildlife Service.

During his tenure, Darling enforced federal hunting laws energetically. He originated the Federal Duck Stamp Program to raise revenue for the purchase and protection of fragile wetlands and designed the first stamp in the series. The program to date has generated more than $475 million for the acquisition of more than four million acres of waterfowl habitat. He also designed the flying Canada goose symbol that marks every U.S. national wildlife refuge.

In spite of his distaste for the New Deal and his dislike of centralized authority, Darling did not hesitate to use the full force of the federal government to achieve his ecological ends. He persuaded Congress to appropriate significant new funding to expand the wildlife refuge system and instituted a nationwide program of cooperative wildlife research units that he had piloted at Iowa State College (now Iowa State University) in 1932.

By the time Darling had reorganized the Biological Survey, replaced much of its staff, and ensured its improved funding, he had also alienated much of the Washington, D.C., establishment. With capable leadership of the survey assured, Darling was eager to return to his cartooning career and to other environmental pursuits. He resigned as chief in November 1935 and soon afterward sought financial support from arms and ammunition manufacturers for a conservation consortium. The result was the National Wildlife Federation, formed to combat depredation of the environment by commercial interests. He served as the federation's president during its first three years. Darling resigned the position following an auto accident involving his son. He continued to fight, through his editorial cartoons and his personal support of environmental legislation, for wise stewardship of the nation's natural resources. He was especially active in efforts to introduce principles of conservation into elementary and secondary school curricula.

Darling wintered on Captiva Island, Florida, and for years worked to set aside fragile barrier island acreage on neighboring Sanibel Island as a refuge (established in 1945). In 1967 the resulting national wildlife refuge was renamed in his memory.

Darling was also an accomplished artist. Many of his original etchings—especially the one based on his illustration for the original duck stamp—are recognized as valuable works of wildlife art. That image, of a mallard duck and hen alighting on a marsh, has been reproduced on more than 124 million postage stamps and duck (revenue) stamps.

Although he won scores of awards in addition to his Pulitzer Prizes, including honorary doctorates, the Audubon Medal, the Roosevelt Medal, and the prestigious Hutchinson Award, the modest Darling likened his honors to "awarding medals to generals who lost all their wars" and described the granting of his second Pulitzer Prize as a mistake in judgment. He died in Des Moines.

Darling enjoyed extraordinary success in each of three careers—editorial cartoonist, wildlife artist, and conservationist. His greatest legacy is represented by the massive expansion of the nation's system of wildlife refuges. The J. N. "Ding" Darling Foundation, established after his death, continues to promote his principles and ideals through its support of conservation education and research.

• Darling's papers and original cartoons are held in the Department of Special Collections at the University of Iowa Library. The Cowles Library at Drake University in Des Moines houses proof prints of Darling's cartoons from the *Des Moines Register*. Darling wrote two books: *Ding Goes to Russia* (1932) and *The Cruise of the Bouncing Betsy: A Trailer Travelogue* (1937). Several anthologies of his cartoons were published in his lifetime; they include *As Ding Saw Hoover* (1954), *It Seems Like Only Yesterday* (1960), and *Ding's Half Century* (1962). Darling's life is portrayed in David L. Lendt, *Ding: The Life of Jay Norwood Darling* (1979), which includes a detailed bibliography. A catalog of his etchings and other works of art is in Amy N. Worthen, *The Prints of J. N. Darling* (1984). An obituary is in the *Des Moines Register*, 12 Feb. 1962.

DAVID L. LENDT

DARLINGTON, Philip Jackson, Jr. (14 Nov. 1904–16 Dec. 1983), zoologist, was born in Philadelphia, Pennsylvania, the son of Philip Jackson Darlington, an engineer. His mother, whose name is unknown, was a schoolteacher. His family moved when Darlington was young to Hartford, Connecticut, where he spent much of his childhood bird watching and collecting beetles. He entered Harvard College in 1922 to study botany and zoology and graduated with a B.A. in 1926. He received his M.S., also from Harvard, in 1927.

Darlington's graduate studies at Harvard were interrupted in 1928, when he had the chance, as an entomologist with the United Fruit Company, to travel to Santa Marta, Colombia. Returning to Harvard in 1929, he brought back with him an extensive collection of insects and 306 skins of birds, representing 237 species.

Darlington completed a Ph.D. at Harvard in 1931 and soon set off again to collect, this time to Australia. He returned to the United States two years later with 341 mammal specimens, which he gave to the Museum of Comparative Zoology at Harvard. Professionally, he became assistant curator of insects at the museum, a position that allowed him regular trips abroad.

One of Darlington's best known field trips, reported in the *New York Times* on 19 November 1934, was his climb to the summit of Mount La Hotte on the isle of Haiti. As the first zoologist to make this trip, he spent twenty-six days, including four days alone on the mountain, "cutting through the brush up to the peak and back. He was slowed by cold, rain and flooded rivers," reported the newspaper, which went on to quote Darlington:

The difficulty of my trip confirms La Hotte's bad reputation. . . . "It is said to be by all odds the hardest country in the whole island. Not one of the numerous ornithologists who worked Hispaniola has reached the summit, and only one (Beck) has been high enough to get the real mountain fauna. . . . [Swedish botanist] Ekman and [American botanist H. D.] Barker, botanizing, made three unsuccessful attempts to reach the summit of La Hotte before they finally succeeded. It was some very good advice from Barker plus good luck in choosing the right ridge that got me up. (p. 19)

When he returned to the United States, he brought with him hundreds of species of flightless mountain beetles that were to that point unknown, in addition to river-living beetles, new frogs, some reptiles, and six peripatus. A new genus of snakes was later named *Darlingtonia* in his honor. He had systematically chosen specimens from various altitudes. On subsequent collecting trips to the Sierra Maestra in Cuba he gathered many West Indian carabids, which became the subject of much of his work.

In 1940 Darlington was appointed fall curator of *Coleoptera* at the Museum of Comparative Zoology and soon after entered World War II as a first lieutenant in the Malaria Survey of the Army Sanitary Corps. He served in the Bismarcks, New Guinea, and the Philippines and finally retired from active duty with the rank of major in April 1944. On a field survey for malaria in New Guinea, Darlington had his arm severely injured in an attack by a crocodile while scaling the summit of Mount Wilhelm, the highest peak in the Bismarck Range. The animal dragged Darlington to the bottom of a jungle pool, where despite torn arms and crushed bones, the scientist managed to break free of its jaws, swim to land, and hike to a hospital. This, however, did not stop him from continuing to collect, even after he left active duty, specimens to take back to the Harvard museum. He eventually regained full use of his arms.

Darlington returned to the United States in 1944. In 1951 he was appointed curator of insects at the Harvard Museum of Comparative Zoology. As curator, Darlington spent much of his career criss-crossing the globe, even taking his family along at times. In 1956–1957 his wife, Elizabeth Koch, whom he had married in 1942, and Philip Frederick (his only child) spent eighteen months living out of a truck with him in the Australian outback. In 1962–1963 he made trips to Tierra del Fuego and the southernmost regions of South America. He was appointed in 1962 Alexander Agas-

siz Professor of Zoology, a position he held until his retirement in 1971.

Darlington was the author of more than 120 papers and three books: *Zoogeography: The Geographical Distribution of Animals* (1957), which won the Daniel Giraud Eliot Medal of the National Academy of Sciences in 1969, *Biogeography of the Southern End of the World: Distribution and History of Far-Southern Life and Land, with an Assessment of Continental Drift* (1965), and *Evolution for Naturalists: The Simple Principles and Complex Reality* (1980). Most of his writing dealt with the ecology and distribution of the *Carabidae*, but he also published on natural selection and biogeography.

In recognition of his work, Darlington was awarded two John Simon Guggenheim fellowships (1947 and 1957) and was elected to the American Academy of Arts and Sciences and the National Academy of Sciences in 1964. Darlington died in Cambridge, Massachusetts.

One of the world's leading insect taxonomists and zoological specimen collectors, Darlington is remembered for his work on the distribution and ecology of carabid beetles, his well-known studies of mimicry in beetles, and a revised theory of Old World tropical origin of the dominant vertebrates. George E. Ball, a fellow biologist, described Darlington as "independent in spirit and action, highly imaginative, a splendid embodiment of the 'Protestant work ethic,' with the ability and determination to express facts and ideas clearly and simply" (p. 1). Darlington "enjoyed field work, was a determined and superb collector, and an astute observer. . . . He [also] understood well the value of museum material, both for its traditional taxonomic use, and for the information that could be obtained and the inferences that could be made from it, about way of life of the species represented in the collections" (Ball, pp. 17–18).

• There are collections of Darlington papers at the Archives of the Museum of Comparative Zoology at Harvard University and at the University of New Hampshire. An unpublished account of the record-making ascent of Mount La Hotte in Haiti by Darlington himself is "Through Rural Haiti." The description in Wilson's memorial (below) is based on that manuscript. George E. Ball's 1985 celebratory volume, *Taxonomy, Phylogeny and Zoogeography of Beetles and Ants: A Volume Dedicated to the Memory of Philip Jackson Darlington, Jr. (1904–1983)*, evaluates his work and contributions to science and includes a biographical sketch by Frank M. Carpenter, who met Darlington in 1924. It also contains a bibliography of Darlington's works. The book itself is reviewed in *Systematic Zoology* 38, no. 1 (1989). A biographical sketch by E. O. Wilson appears in National Academy of Sciences, *Biographical Memoirs* 60 (1991): 32–44. For details on the crocodile attack, see two articles in the 31 Mar. 1944 evening edition of the *Boston Globe*, "Harvard Scientist Fights Crocodile with Bare Hands" and "'Had Episode with Crocodile,' Wife Reads."

MARIANNE FEDUNKIW STEVENS

DARLINGTON, William (28 Apr. 1782–23 Apr. 1863), physician, botanist, and author, was born in Chester County, Pennsylvania, the son of Edward Darlington, a farmer who also found time to serve in the Pennsylvania legislature, and Hannah Townsend. Wanting to escape the drudgery of farm work that had restricted his schooling to a few winter months each year, at age eighteen Darlington persuaded his father to pay the necessary fees for his apprenticeship to study medicine with John Vaughan in Wilmington, Delaware. In return, his father required that he give up his inheritance of a share of the family farm.

During Darlington's two and a half years with Vaughan he also revealed an aptitude for languages that later enabled him to master German and Spanish and to read both French and Latin. To complete his medical education Darlington attended lectures at the University of Pennsylvania during two winter terms and was awarded the M.D. in the spring of 1804. There he came under the influence of Benjamin Smith Barton, who fired his enthusiasm for botany, and he met William Baldwin, a fellow medical student, who nursed him through a serious illness. After completing his education, Darlington signed on as ship's surgeon on the *Bengal* for a voyage to Calcutta (years later his anonymous observations on that city were published in the *Analectic Magazine* [Apr.–May 1819]). This trip, which lasted a year, provided the finances needed for him to marry Catherine Lacey in 1808; they would have seven children. Money from the voyage also supported the establishment of his medical practice in West Chester, Pennsylvania, also in 1808.

As his medical practice became profitable, with the result that he could purchase a small farm for himself, Darlington turned to public endeavors of many sorts. He became a trustee of the West Chester Academy (forerunner of West Chester University); he served three months as a major of volunteers in the War of 1812 but never saw action; and, as a Democratic-Republican, was elected to the Fourteenth, Sixteenth, and Seventeenth Congresses. He reported on the debates in Congress to *Niles' Weekly Register*; during the debate leading to the Missouri Compromise, Darlington gave a speech comparing slavery, a disease of the body politic, with the devastation of the contagious disease smallpox. He published numerous anonymous newspaper essays on matters of public interest, which are known today only because of copies pasted into his scrapbooks.

After his service as a federal lawmaker, Darlington was appointed a visitor to the U.S. Military Academy at West Point, then served as prothonotary and clerk of the courts of Chester County until 1830, when he was elected president of the Bank of Chester County. He gave up the practice of medicine in 1834. For the remainder of his life, while overseeing the welfare of the bank, he devoted his attention to botany and education. With friends he founded the Chester County Cabinet of Natural Science in 1826. Lectures offered by Darlington and others brought in enough money for the cabinet to commission Thomas U. Walter to design a building for it, and it became, for a time, the most successful of the provincial natural history societies.

The cabinet's herbarium helped to provide material for the revision of Darlington's technical book, *Florula Cestrica* (1826), in which he gave brief descriptions of 735 native and naturalized plants in the vicinity of West Chester, where it was published; in its "Observations" he discussed many folk remedies. Arranged by the Linnaean system of classification, this material was much enlarged to cover all of Chester County and retitled *Flora Cestrica* (1837), which also had a second edition in 1853. Recognizing that he had become out of step with accepted botanical practice, Darlington rearranged his plants in natural families for the 1853 edition. His *Agricultural Botany* (1847)—by its subtitle "an enumeration of useful plants and weeds"—was written as a practical guide for the American farmer. With the German and Spanish names of plants removed and line drawings added, this book was republished in 1859 as *American Weeds and Useful Plants*.

Darlington's biographical books were the products of the last two decades of his life. The first was *Reliquiae Baldwinianae* (1843), edited to preserve the letters exchanged between William Baldwin and Henry Muhlenberg and to preserve Baldwin's letters to Darlington. Baldwin, whose life was cut short by tuberculosis while he was botanist on Stephen H. Long's expedition to the Rocky Mountains, had lived most of his days outdoors because of his illness; though he published little, he collected much, and he had been a major supplier of specimens to sedentary botanists like Muhlenberg, Darlington, and John Torrey. As Baldwin had collected in the footsteps of John and William Bartram in Florida, it was only natural that when a cache of Bartram papers was discovered, the letters were turned over to Darlington for publication. To these he added the papers of Humphry Marshall, cousin of John Bartram, who had also planted an early botanical garden, and issued them as *Memorials of John Bartram and Humphry Marshall . . .* (1849). In both books he wrote biographical sketches of the principals, long discursive footnotes to identify the most important persons mentioned, and included in the second an essay "Progress of Botany in North America."

"Those ancient manuscripts," he said of the Bartram papers, "were not only jumbled together in a chaotic mess, but were generally much injured by time," with the result that what appeared illegible to him he omitted. In both books he made elisions, though these are marked, and he omitted whole extant documents without giving any reason. Nevertheless, his work was a first step toward an understanding of the work of both John and William Bartram, and it helped to preserve their papers and those of other early American botanists. Darlington died in West Chester, Pennsylvania.

He was called the Nestor of American botany by Asa Gray, professor of natural history at Harvard, who helped to write the Latin inscription for Darlington's tombstone. He might with equal justice be called its Plutarch. It is true that his counsel was sought by a wide circle of correspondents, both in the United States and Europe, and that the local floras he published did set a standard for their time; but it has been his pioneering effort to record the lives of early botanists that has kept Darlington's memory alive for later generations.

• As an editor of the historically significant letters of other botanists, Darlington saw to the preservation of his own. The largest collection, at the New-York Historical Society, consists of nineteen volumes of correspondence, diaries, and notebooks, ten of the volumes being letters addressed to him. His letters to L. D. von Schweinitz are at the Academy of Natural Sciences of Philadelphia, to Charles Wilkins Short at the Filson Club History Society, to Increase Lapham at the State Historical Society of Wisconsin, to W. J. Hooker at the Kew Botanic Gardens, to Alexander Wilson at the University of Michigan, to George Englemann at the Missouri Botanical Garden, and to Asa Gray at the Herbarium Libraries of Harvard University. The University of Kansas has 300 letters sent to him by his wife and six of his notebooks; West Chester University has annotated books from his library and some of his correspondence; and the College of Physicians of Philadelphia has his notes on lectures by Benjamin Rush and Philip Syng Physick. Other papers of his are found at the Historical Society of Pennsylvania, the Free Library of Philadelphia, the Library of Congress, the American Philosophical Society, and the Linnaean Society of London.

Darlington had hoped his son would be his biographer, and he himself left several unfinished autobiographical manuscripts; but the most substantial biographical account is *That Magnificent Cestrian: Dr. William Darlington* (1985), an undocumented 87-page pamphlet by Dorothy I. Lansing. Joseph Ewan's introduction to the 1967 reprint of *Memorials of John Bartram . . .* (1849) and his introduction to the 1969 reprint of *Reliquiae Baldwinianae* place these books in their historical context. The biographical sketch in John W. Harshberger's *The Botanists of Philadelphia* (1899) derives mostly from Washington Townsend's contemporaneous *Memorial of Wm. Darlington* (1863). The most authoritative obituary is that of T. P. James in the *Proceedings of the American Philosophical Society* 9 (1863): 330–43.

CHARLES BOEWE

DARROW, Clarence (18 Apr. 1857–13 Mar. 1938), lawyer, orator, and author, was born Clarence Seward Darrow at Kinsman, in rural Ohio, the son of Amirus Darrow, a furniture maker and undertaker, and Emily Eddy. He initially attended local public schools and then, in 1873–1874, the preparatory department of Allegheny College; thereafter he taught school in Vernon, Ohio, for three years while concurrently studying law books. In 1877 he enrolled in the law department of the University of Michigan, at which he remained only one year. He then apprenticed at a law office in Youngstown and was admitted to the Ohio bar on oral examination at the age of twenty-one.

In April 1880 Darrow married Jessie Ohl, the daughter of a moderately prosperous local farmer, and set up law practice in Andover, Ohio, ten miles from his birthplace, where their only child was born. Although Darrow's practice was unremunerative, he gained a reputation for public speaking there, and the Darrows soon moved to Ashtabula, the county seat, where in 1885 he was elected without contest to the part-time position of borough city solicitor.

In Ashtabula, Darrow's intellectual horizons were widened by his reading of Henry George's *Progress and Poverty* and John Peter Altgeld's *Our Penal Machinery and Its Victims*. In 1887 he moved to Chicago by himself, sending for his family to join him there a few months later, and he remained based in Chicago for the rest of his life.

Initially lacking Chicago clients, Darrow threw himself into city politics. He at once sought out Altgeld, then a superior court judge, and the friendship that ensued became the closest of Darrow's life. By dint of Altgeld's favor, Darrow came to prominence in his newly adopted city. Altgeld, well connected politically, prevailed upon Mayor DeWitt Cregier to appoint Darrow successively as the city's special assessment attorney, assistant corporation counsel, and acting corporation counsel. When Cregier was defeated in 1891 and Darrow lost his job on the Chicago payroll, Altgeld continued to guide his protégé's career by persuading him in 1891 to accept a job in the law department of the Chicago & Northwestern Railway.

The Chicago & Northwestern was an indulgent and liberal employer, allowing Darrow to continue to advise Altgeld in his successful campaign to become governor of Illinois in 1892 and to practice law on the side while remaining on the railroad's payroll. Nevertheless, in 1894 Darrow resigned from his position with the railroad in order to defend American Railway Union president Eugene Debs in the anti-injunction proceedings brought against him by the federal government in the aftermath of the Pullman strike. These proceedings, which were finally dropped, brought Darrow to such prominence in Chicago that he secured endorsement in the third district of Illinois as the Democratic candidate for the House of Representatives. Over confident, he failed to campaign vigorously enough to win this election. (The only elective position he ever subsequently held was in the Illinois general assembly, in which he served briefly as an Independent representing the Seventeenth District in 1903.)

When Altgeld was defeated in 1896 for a second term as governor, he joined Darrow's law office. On Altgeld's death in 1902, Darrow gave a memorial address of which he was so proud that he reproduced it as an appendix to his autobiography.

Like Altgeld, Darrow disdained the routine work of the law and his attention wandered from his practice to such diversions as those available at Jane Addams's Hull-House and the Sunset Club, a debating society in which he was very active. His complete absorption in these activities caused his marriage to fail, and the Darrows were divorced in 1897. Cut free from the restraints of marriage, Darrow went to Oshkosh, Wisconsin, in 1898 to defend Thomas I. Kidd, an official of the Woodworkers' Union who, having organized a strike against the Paine Lumber Company, had been charged along with two others with conspiring to injure the company. Darrow saw this as a use of the machinery of criminal justice to oppress the working man, very much like the Pullman case. After he made a magnificent speech in favor of the right to strike, the jury acquitted Kidd. This case further enhanced Darrow's reputation as a friend of organized labor.

Darrow next gained major public attention in 1902 as an advocate for the United Mine Workers in the "Anthracite Arbitration" between the workers and coal mine owners of Pennsylvania before a commission appointed by President Theodore Roosevelt. In this proceeding, conducted without a jury, a more conciliatory Darrow appeared than in either the Debs or Kidd case. The results he obtained from the commission—including back-pay for some of the miners—impressed Samuel Gompers, President of the American Federation of Labor, a fact that was to bring Darrow much union business for the next eight years. In 1903 Darrow married a journalist, Ruby Hamerstrom; they had no children.

Upon his return to Chicago from the anthracite arbitration, Darrow entered into his last conventional law partnership, with Francis Wilson (later a federal judge) and Edgar Lee Masters, a lawyer-poet. It was to be an unhappy combination, in which Darrow's unilateral decisions were resented by the others, particularly Masters, who was both jealous of Darrow's fame and contemptuous of how it was obtained. The practice, never stable, broke up when Darrow departed from Chicago to undertake two major cases of significance: first, the 1908 defense of Big Bill Haywood (and others associated with the Western Federation of Miners) on a charge of murdering Idaho's governor, and second, the 1911 defense of the McNamara brothers, accused of dynamiting the *Los Angeles Times* building.

The Haywood trial, although conducted in the relatively inaccessible venue of Boise, received enormous publicity for its dramatic details and as the first trial to be covered by the press wire-services. The principal prosecution witness, Harry Orchard, admitted to having committed several murders himself but had turned state's evidence. Darrow attacked him with all his forensic might, and Haywood was acquitted.

In 1911 Darrow defended the McNamara brothers in Los Angeles against the charge that they had dynamited the *Los Angeles Times*, killing twenty-one people. He did so reluctantly and only at the urging of Samuel Gompers, among others. After being confronted with incontrovertible evidence of the brothers' guilt and pleading them guilty, so as to avert the possibility that they might be sentenced to death if convicted after a trial, Darrow himself was charged with, and tried twice for, attempted bribery of prospective jurors in the McNamara case. In Darrow's first prosecution the trial judge directed an acquittal, but the second trial (in which attempted bribery of a different juror was charged) resulted in a hung jury. Thus, although Darrow was never convicted, he was not acquitted either, and his reputation was severely damaged. It was Darrow's last case on behalf of organized labor.

Back in Chicago, his law partnership gone, his savings depleted by the expense of defending himself in Los Angeles (Gompers had refused him financial help from the AFL), and his reputation tarnished, Darrow eked out a living in criminal defense work of a mostly routine kind, although occasionally a noteworthy case came to him, such as the prosecution in 1926 of Frank Lloyd Wright, the architect, for violation of the Mann Act (prohibiting crossing state lines for immoral purposes). The federal indictment of Wright was dismissed in March 1927 after a number of Wright's prominent friends petitioned federal authorities.

World War I saw Darrow reemerge as a respected public figure. An undeviating supporter of the Allied cause and a strong advocate of American intervention from 1914 until the armistice, Darrow was active in war propaganda. His reputation rehabilitated, Darrow still had his two greatest triumphs—his defenses of Nathan Leopold and Richard Loeb and of John Thomas Scopes, for which he is remembered in print and film alike—yet to come.

Leopold and Loeb were two students who in 1924 had killed a schoolboy, Bobby Franks, who had lived in their Chicago neighborhood. On Darrow's advice they pleaded guilty of murdering their victim in order to avoid a jury trial. Darrow made a brilliant and successful plea in mitigation to save them from the death penalty. Public opinion was shocked by the result, because many people could not imagine any crime more deserving of capital punishment.

The Scopes trial, a 1925 prosecution of a schoolteacher under a Tennessee statute criminalizing the teaching of evolution, was very much a period piece, chiefly remarkable for the opportunity it gave Darrow to cross-examine his longtime foe, William Jennings Bryan. Scopes was convicted and fined $100.

Two cases taken by Darrow in the postwar period had racial undertones. In 1926 he twice defended Ossian Sweet, a black physician, together with his younger brother Henry, on charges of conspiracy to murder in Detroit. Sweet had moved into a white neighborhood, and when a hostile crowd had gathered outside his house, a shot fired from within it had killed a bystander. After the jury in the first trial hung, Sweet was retried and acquitted in the second one. In the last big case of Darrow's career, he defended in 1932 Thomas Massie, a white naval officer stationed in Hawaii, for having killed a Hawaiian whom he suspected of having raped his wife. Many of Darrow's admirers were shocked that he had accepted such a client, and in spite of Darrow's efforts Massie was convicted of manslaughter. Darrow's performance in this case may have revealed that his powers were waning, but his client's case had never been strong.

Although Darrow's last appearance as a trial lawyer was on Massie's behalf, he remained in the headlines as the chairman of the National Recovery Review Board, a position to which he was appointed in 1934 by President Franklin Delano Roosevelt. Darrow was opposed to the New Deal, and the board's report was unwelcome.

Darrow's final years were spent as an invalid, tended by his wife in the rented apartment on Chicago's Midway that they had shared for virtually their entire married life, and where he died. At a memorial service held at the Bond Chapel at the University of Chicago, Darrow's own eulogy of Altgeld, delivered nearly forty years before, was repeated as fitting its author just as well as its original subject.

Darrow's career inspired several theatrical, film, and television depictions. *Inherit the Wind*, by Jerome Lawrence and Robert E. Lee, dramatized the Scopes trial on Broadway in 1955 and was subsequently made into a film in which Spencer Tracy portrayed Darrow. *Compulsion*, by Meyer Levin (1956), depicted the Leopold and Loeb case in thinly disguised fiction and in 1960 was made into a movie of the same name starring Orson Welles as Darrow. In 1991 a television special titled "Darrow," starring Kevin Spacey, was made for American Playhouse and KCET-TV, the Los Angeles public television channel, and aired nationally.

Darrow's individualism makes his influence on his times difficult to assess, especially as he held formal political office only briefly. As an orator he was one of the first moderns, who repudiated the flowery rhetoric of the Victorian orators in favor of plain words, but as a lawyer, disinclined to collaborate with professional colleagues and impatient of tasks of law office management, he represented a small-practice tradition that was being eclipsed during his lifetime. His huge contemporary impact, like that of many trial lawyers, appears ephemeral in retrospect. Although he nursed literary ambitions, his writings (as distinct from his speeches) are relatively undistinguished; but at his best his oratory has rarely been equaled. Discussions of the film depictions of Darrow appear in Paul Bergman and Michael Asimov, *Reel Justice* (1996).

• Relatively few of Darrow's papers survive, but there are some in the Library of Congress and at the University of Chicago. A bibliography is Willard D. Hunsberger, *Clarence Darrow: A Bibliography* (1981). Arthur Weinberg edited a collection of Darrow's speeches and writings under the title *Attorney for the Damned* (1957) and another in collaboration with his wife Lila Weinberg, titled *Verdicts out of Court* (1963). A more recent compilation of speeches is Richard J. Jensen, *Clarence Darrow: The Creation of a Myth* (1992). Darrow wrote a fictionalized account of his childhood, *Farmington* (1904), and an autobiography, *The Story of My Life* (1932). He also published *Realism in Literature and Art* (1899), *Crime: Its Cause and Treatment* (1922), and assorted journalism. Biographies are Irving Stone, *Clarence Darrow for the Defense* (1941); Kevin Tierney, *Darrow: A Biography* (1979); and Arthur Weinberg and Lila Weinberg, *Clarence Darrow, a Sentimental Rebel* (1980). Geoffrey Cowan, *The People vs. Clarence Darrow* (1993), a detailed study of the bribery trials in Los Angeles, is interesting in concluding that Darrow was probably guilty as charged in these trials of 1911–1913.

KEVIN TIERNEY

DARROW, David (21 June 1750–27 June 1825), Shaker elder, was born in Norfolk, Connecticut, the son of Nathaniel Darrow and Rachel (maiden name unknown), farmers. Sometime during his youth the family moved westward across the Taconic Mountains into an area known as the "Yankee zone," a region

contested by both New York and the Massachusetts Bay Colony. By 1774 members of the Darrow family were living in the New Lebanon area on the road between Pittsfield, Massachusetts, and Albany, New York. Darrow married Prudence Mudge, the daughter of Jarvis Mudge, a mill owner; the couple had at least three children. One source states that Darrow "fought faithfully in the army of the Revolution and attained the rank of lieutenant" (White and Taylor, p. 45).

Darrow was one of the first American converts to the "Shaking Quakers," a small community of English sectarians who had come to America in 1774 led by the visionary Ann Lee. In the spring of 1780 Darrow and several others from the New Lebanon area visited the Shaker community at Niskeyuna, a site northwest of Albany, and found the sect's religious views and practices more attractive than those associated with the evangelical revivals they had been attending. Darrow confessed his sins and began a lifelong involvement with the Shakers. He and his wife Prudence, his parents, and his brother George and his wife were all listed on an early inventory of new members.

In July 1780 Darrow was arrested while driving a flock of sheep from New Lebanon to the community at Niskeyuna. Authorities accused him of treason: they thought he was aiding the British in the American War for Independence. He and several companions, who were opposed to war on religious grounds, were imprisoned in Albany with suspected Tories and prisoners of war. Tradition has it that Darrow and the others preached to large crowds from their prison cells. Darrow was paroled in November, thanks to the intervention of his father-in-law. In 1783 Darrow confronted a violent mob seeking to assault Ann Lee, who was visiting in New Lebanon. On that occasion he was resolute in his commitment to Shakerism despite hostility and persecution. Later in that decade, when the United Society of Believers in Christ's Second Appearing gathered into local communal societies, leaving their farms and homes, Darrow and his brother George deeded land to the Shaker community at New Lebanon, land on which the first meetinghouse was built in 1785.

Darrow's expanding responsibilities among the Shakers confirmed his rising stature in the society. He first served as a traveling missionary in New England, seeking converts and visiting those identified as Shakers. He then spent the winter of 1791–1792 in that capacity in Maine. In 1792 Joseph Meacham, the leader of the society's central ministry, appointed Darrow to the position of elder brother in the first family of the church at New Lebanon. Darrow's responsibilities included general supervision of the family members and special leadership of religious activities. He continued in this position until 1805, when he was chosen by Lucy Wright, Meacham's successor, to head up the new western settlement at Turtle Creek (later Union Village), three miles west of Lebanon in Warren County, Ohio. Darrow arrived in Ohio with two companions in the early summer where they joined the first three Shaker missionaries sent to the Ohio Valley.

In Ohio, Darrow became the undisputed leader of Shakerism in the West and the principal architect of its expansion and consolidation at several sites in Ohio, Kentucky, and for a time Indiana. Under his leadership Union Village became the hub and nerve center of western Shakerism. During his years as elder in the ministry at Union Village, Darrow supervised construction of the village proper and dealt with repeated outbursts of mob violence directed against the Shakers. When apostates absconded with the Believers' assets or brought suits against the village, Darrow went to court on behalf of the society. He presided over the missionary effort that produced hundreds of converts both at Union Village and at additional locations where other new villages were established. In March 1807 he and several companions visited the nearby Shawnee Indians in hopes of persuading them to accept the Believers' gospel. Darrow had a hand in the writing of the first major statement of Shaker theology, *The Testimony of Christ's Second Appearing Containing a General Statement of All Things Pertaining to the Faith and Practice of the Church of God in This Latter-day*, published in Lebanon, Ohio, in 1808. This publication became a manifesto and a continuing point of reference for generations of Shakers.

During the years of his leadership, Union Village grew to include nearly 600 Believers organized into five communal families. The Shakers at Union Village formally signed its first covenant on 15 January 1812. For more than fifteen years Darrow was assisted in the ministry by Eldress Ruth Farrington. Often members of the ministry traveled to the other villages to encourage new Believers or to deal with problems.

Although Darrow did not always agree with the decisions of the central ministry in New York, he remained loyal and obedient, regarding them as his superior, undesirous of a separate western variety of Shakerism. After an extended period of failing health, he died at Union Village. Known affectionately as "Father David," Darrow was eulogized at his funeral, attended by 500 Shakers, as the "foundation of the west" and as "the spiritual lead & protector of this people." Darrow was, in fact, the pivotal figure in the establishment of Shakerism in the Ohio Valley.

• Darrow's correspondence from Ohio, written to the eastern Shakers, can be found in the collections of Shaker papers in the Western Reserve Historical Society, Cleveland, Ohio, and in the Library of Congress. Darrow also signed the preface of *The Testimony of Christ's Second Appearing* along with Benjamin Seth Youngs, the principal author, and John Meacham. For detailed accounts of the role of Union Village in western Shakerism, see J. P. MacLean, *Shakers of Ohio: Fugitive Papers concerning the Shakers of Ohio, with Unpublished Manuscripts* (1907), and F. Gerald Ham, "Shakerism in the Old West" (Ph.D. diss., Univ. of Kentucky, 1962). Later Shakers viewed Darrow with great respect. See Anna White and Leila S. Taylor, *Shakerism: Its Meaning and Message* (1905). For the larger historical context surrounding Darrow's life among the Shakers, see Edward Deming Andrews, *The People Called Shakers: A Search for the Perfect Society* (1963), and Stephen J. Stein, *The Shaker Experience in America: A History of the United Society of Believers* (1992).

STEPHEN J. STEIN

DARROW, Karl Kelchner (26 Nov. 1891–7 June 1982), physicist and administrator, was born in Chicago, Illinois, the son of Edward Everett Darrow and Helen Kelchner, and a nephew of Clarence S. Darrow, the well-known trial lawyer. His parents' occupations are not known, but Karl Darrow was raised in comfortable surroundings. He received a broad education in literature and science, obtaining his B.S. from the University of Chicago in 1911, and then studied physics in Paris and Berlin between 1911 and 1912. He earned his doctorate in physics in 1917 under Robert A. Millikan, chairman of the Department of Physics at the University of Chicago.

Darrow spent most of his career in private industry. In 1917, just after receiving his Ph.D., Darrow became a research physicist at Western Electric. He transferred to the Bell Telephone Laboratories after its founding in 1925 and remained at Bell in northern New Jersey until his retirement in 1956. In 1943, at age fifty-one, Darrow married Elizabeth Marcy. The couple had no children.

Darrow's principal work at the Bell Telephone Laboratories involved not original scientific research, but appraising, synthesizing, and abstracting the works of other physicists including research in solid-state physics and quantum mechanics. The task was a critical one at a time when the number of publications in physics was rapidly expanding, creating a need for critical review articles. During his career Darrow wrote more than two hundred articles, many of which appeared in the *Bell System Technical Journal*. He also wrote several books and textbooks, including *Introduction to Contemporary Physics* (1926), *Electrical Phenomena in Gases* (1932), *The Renaissance of Physics* (1936), and *Atomic Energy* (1948). During summers, he was on occasion a visiting professor at Stanford, Chicago, and Columbia Universities, and he taught briefly as William Allen Neilson Professor at Smith College.

Darrow's major contribution to the development of American physics was his role in the American Physical Society (APS), in which he served as executive secretary from 1941 until 1967. Partly because of its contributions to the military during the Second World War, the discipline of physics expanded rapidly in the 1950s and 1960s, gaining prestige and influence. During Darrow's tenure the APS grew from four thousand to twenty-three thousand members. As executive secretary, Darrow was responsible for virtually all of the society's business, including management of its meetings. Darrow maintained the society's emphasis on research rather than social policy, and he introduced at society meetings a series of invited lectures intended to provide broad overviews on major research areas, an aid for physicists who found their own fields of research increasingly specialized.

Darrow received a number of honorary awards. He was made chevalier of the French Legion of Honor in 1951 for his contributions to scientific and cultural relations between France and the United States, and he received the Karl Taylor Compton Gold Medal of the American Institute of Physics, given for "high statesmanship in physics," in 1960. A formal, dryly humorous man, Darrow wrote in a lucid prose style easily identified by close associates and insisted that APS officials wear tuxedos to meeting banquets so members could recognize them. He died in New York.

• Letters to and from Darrow are in the Karl K. Darrow papers at the Niels Bohr Library of the American Institute of Physics. An oral history interview with Darrow by Henry Barton and W. J. King, made in 1964, is also available at the Niels Bohr Library. Darrow's career is briefly reviewed in John H. Van Vleck, "Karl Kelchner Darrow—Writer, Councilor and Secretary," *Physics Today*, Apr. 1967, pp. 23–26. Background on Darrow's work in the American Physical Society may be found in Melba Phillips, "The American Physical Society: A Survey of Its First Fifty Years," *American Journal of Physics* 58, no. 3 (1990): 219–30. An obituary by W. W. Havens, Jr., appears in *Physics Today*, Nov. 1982, pp. 83–84.

RONALD E. DOEL

DART, Isom (1848–3 Oct. 1900), black cowboy and rustler, also known as Ned Huddleston, was born in Arkansas. Dart's early life is an enigma. Biographical accounts give a lively "Wild West" picture of an itinerant cowboy and occasional gang member based on legend and folklore. What is known is that sometime in the mid-1880s, Dart settled in Brown's Hole, an isolated area where the borders of Colorado, Wyoming, and Utah meet. He worked initially for the Middlesex Land and Cattle Company but later found gainful employment on the Bassett Ranch.

Dart was adept at many practical trades, but his true calling was as a cowboy. His skill in handling horses and the use of the rope soon distinguished him as one of the best cowhands in the region. Dart's congenial personality also helped him gain acceptance in social circles. He became an adopted member of the Bassett family. In time he became quite knowledgeable about the people with whom he worked or who worked in the area, both honest and dishonest. Although a sociable man, he never married.

Dart's notoriety as a rustler mirrored his cultural surroundings. Brown's Hole was well known as an outlaws' hangout because of its rugged terrain and its distance from law enforcement centers. Even some resident ranchers, such as Elizabeth Bassett for whom Dart worked, were suspected of rustling the livestock of their neighbors.

Many remember Dart as but another resident cowboy who supplemented his income by rustling livestock and who was very good at it. To his credit, Dart tried to establish a legitimate ranch of his own. His personal property would always be meager compared with that of the large landowners, but he had some business savvy. However, some people did not believe that all his stock had been acquired legally. Surprisingly, public records reveal only a few concerted efforts to bring him to justice. From 1888 to 1890 Dart appeared in district court only five times in Sweetwater County, Wyoming, and Routt County, Colorado, on the charges of larceny, destruction of personal property, stealing horses, and illegally branding neat cattle. Unable to find either any credible evidence to the contrary or witnesses to testify against Dart, the Sweetwater County attorney dismissed all the charges.

An often reported story portrays Dart as an honest and, through inference, a forgiving man. In 1888 Sweetwater County deputy sheriff Elroy Philbrick sought out and arrested Dart. At one point during the long ride to Green River, the buckboard slipped off the road, and Philbrick was seriously injured. Dart came to his aid, took Philbrick to the hospital, and then turned himself over to the sheriff. At Dart's trial, Philbrick told the jury what Dart had done. As the story goes, the jury was so impressed by Dart's honesty and generosity that it ignored the evidence against him and rendered a verdict of not guilty.

In reality, after his cases were dismissed, Dart sued Philbrick for $5,000 in personal damages. At issue was Philbrick's authority to arrest Dart. Dart argued that he was in Routt County, Colorado, at the time of his apprehension and that Philbrick's warrant from Wyoming Territory was thus not applicable in Colorado. Only extradition proceedings could legally bring Dart to Sweetwater County from Colorado. Philbrick countered that he, Philbrick, may have been in Colorado, but he had a valid warrant for Dart's arrest anyway. Philbrick was found innocent. Dart's lawyer asked for a new trial, but none was held.

In Routt County, Dart was charged along with two other men with the theft and destruction of property. Dart was taken into custody and stood trial. Although found guilty, he apparently eluded punishment by escaping from jail.

By 1900 vigilante justice had come to the Brown's Hole area. Fed up with the continuing problem of rustlers, wealthy cattlemen hired Tom Horn, a notorious stock detective, to do their bidding. Horn mailed anonymous warnings to his intended victims, instructing them to leave the area or face the consequences. Horn's threats did not deter anyone. That summer Horn killed two of Dart's neighbors, Matt Rash and James McKnight.

Ten years had passed since Dart's last court appearance, but he was still under suspicion for rustling livestock. While walking outside his cabin, Dart was shot and died immediately. No one was charged with Dart's death, but most historians believe that Tom Horn killed Dart.

Isom Dart was well known for being a skilled cowboy and by all accounts relished that lifestyle. More importantly, his presence as a black cowboy was part of the cultural diversity characteristic of the American West, and his fate was but another example of how prominent cattlemen once brandished their influence.

• Civil and criminal case files involving Isom Dart are in the Wyoming State Archives and the Colorado State Archives. For a poignant look at his life in the Bassett family, see Grace McClure, *The Bassett Women* (1985). Biographical sketches do not always agree on specifics but are dramatic and sensational. See, for example, W. G. Tittsworth, *Outskirt Episodes* (1927); Cary Stiff, "Isom Dart," *Empire Magazine*, 13 July 1969, pp. 10–16; Sandy Wilson, "Horse Thief: Cattle Rustling and Legitimate Wrangling," *Wild West*, Feb. 1985, pp. 10–12, 16; and John Rolfe Burroughs, *Where the Old West Stayed Young* (1962). For the role of Tom Horn, see Dean F. Krakel, *The Saga of Tom Horn* (1954); Chip Carlson, *Tom Horn: "Killing Men Is My Specialty . . . "* (1991); and Charles Kelley, *The Outlaw Trail* (1959). An obituary is in the *Craig Courier*, 13 Oct. 1900.

CARL V. HALLBERG

DARTON, Nelson Horatio (17 Dec. 1865–28 Feb. 1948), geological mapper, groundwater specialist, and bibliographer, was born in Brooklyn, New York, the son of William Darton, Jr., a shipbuilder and civil engineer, and Caroline Matilda Thayer. Darton was a self-trained geologist who dropped out of public school before the age of thirteen to apprentice as a chemist in his uncle's business. He became a member of the American Chemical Society at age sixteen and shortly thereafter started his own business, selling distilled water. As a practical chemist he became interested in minerals and collected in New Jersey. By age seventeen, Darton had spoken before the New York Academy of Sciences and published his first paper. The conclusion he derived from fieldwork was that some of the rock strata in eastern New Jersey were ancient lava flows, a new concept at that time, but one that was immediately accepted.

Partly as a consequence of his growing interest in geology, Darton began a card catalog on geological references to the New York area. This attracted the attention of the geologist G. K. Gilbert, whom Darton further impressed during a local field trip. As a result, on 1 February 1886 Darton began work with the U.S. Geological Survey (USGS) and continued in federal service for more than fifty years. He was active, even after retirement, and three weeks before his death he lectured for half an hour to the Geological Society of Washington on the geology of the District of Columbia and vicinity; he was the last surviving original member of that society.

Darton's library efforts resulted in several publications and laid the foundations for the bibliography of North American geology, one of the most useful of USGS publications. After a few years working mainly on bibliographic activities for the Appalachian Division, Darton was assigned to fieldwork, but even during that earlier period he had mapped two quadrangles in Virginia; these published Folios of the USGS consist of maps covering one degree of latitude by one degree of longitude. In 1890 he investigated phosphate deposits in Florida and throughout his career both mapped and investigated nonmetalliferous economic deposits. The Florida trip whetted his appetite for studying the geology of the Atlantic Coastal Plain,

and, under the nominal direction of the more senior geologist W J "No Stop" McGee, he mapped these younger deposits in Virginia and Maryland. When the USGS had financial difficulties in 1892, he was transferred to the New York State Survey and compiled a geologic map of the state. This entailed considerable fieldwork in a short time. The basic geological structure he produced for the map—which was credited to McGee—remains unchanged.

Darton's work on potable water while he was a young chemist and his mapping on the Atlantic Coastal Plain led him into the practical field of investigating underground water sources, for these were free from surface contaminates and disease-causing organisms. By 1895 he was a specialist on artesian waters in the mid-Atlantic region, and shortly thereafter he was assigned to study water problems in the West. Darton began his investigations in the Black Hills of South Dakota and expanded into North Dakota, Nebraska, Kansas, Colorado, and Wyoming. Later in the seasons, when the weather was cold on the High Plains, he would transfer his activities to Arizona and New Mexico and continue fieldwork. To understand the groundwater, one had to understand the surface geology, and Darton became a master at rapidly grasping the essential features of stratigraphy and structure in a region.

Adequate topographic maps did not then exist for most places. Darton compiled his own maps on which to plot the geology he observed. He produced state maps of South Dakota and North Dakota; both his geologic maps and his topographic maps were published by the USGS, though some were long delayed. It was not uncommon for him to map 100 square miles a week using a buggy. With the aid of an automobile, he was able to cover up to 500 square miles a week in Texas. Granted, this was a broad-brush approach to geology, yet his mapping was remarkably accurate even by later standards.

Darton had assembled a fine corps of mappers in the USGS Hydrologic Branch, but a reorganization dissolved the group and on 1 July 1907 Darton transferred to the Technologic Branch, studying raw materials. In 1910, when this branch evolved into the Bureau of Mines, he joined that agency, working on the structure of the Pennsylvania anthracite field, but he was mainly concerned with coal mine safety; he also advised the Bureau of Reclamation on dam sites.

During July 1913 Darton returned to the USGS, and one of his first assignments was in West Texas and New Mexico investigating salt and potash deposits, which were critical during World War I, when foreign supplies of fertilizer were cut off. He also prepared a railroad guide to geology along the Santa Fe route, a USGS publication that was sold at newsstands. During this period he compiled state geologic maps of Arizona and New Mexico and began work in Texas. On leave from the USGS, he explored for oil in Central America, Baja California, and Venezuela. He studied water resources in Cuba and relationships of lava flows to human occupation in Mexico.

In 1935, by presidential order, his federal service was extended a year to age seventy-one. After retirement, he retained his office and continued working, among other activities investigating the geological history of nearby gravel deposits and the bedrock geology within the city of Washington, D.C. He was the author of more than 200 publications and maps. He published USGS Bulletins, Folios (more than any other geologist), professional papers, and water supply papers, as well as contributing to many professional journals. Between 5 and 10 percent of the conterminous United States was mapped by Darton. He is considered the consummate reconnaissance geologist of this country.

Darton married Lucy Lee Harris on 18 July 1891 and had one child before the marriage ended in divorce. He remarried on 3 November 1903 to Alice Wealdon Wasserbach, with whom he had two more children. Darton died in Chevy Chase, Maryland.

• Darton's notes from his fieldwork are at the U.S. Geological Survey office in Denver, Colo. The two best published memorials are Phillip B. King, "Memorial to Nelson Horatio Darton," *Proceedings of the Geological Society of America for 1948* (1949): 145–96, which contains both a portrait and a bibliography, and Watson H. Monroe, "Memorial: Nelson Horatio Darton (1865–1948)," *Bulletin of the American Association of Petroleum Geologists* 33 (1949): 116–23, which also provides a portrait. An obituary is in the *New York Times*, 4 Mar. 1948.

ELLIS L. YOCHELSON

DA SILVA, Howard (4 May 1909–16 Feb. 1986), actor, director, and playwright, was born Howard Silverblatt in Cleveland, Ohio, the son of Benjamin Silverblatt, a dress cutter, and Bertha Sohon. The family later moved to New York City and then to Pittsburgh, Pennsylvania. Da Silva completed his education with a year at the Carnegie Institute of Technology (1927–1928), supporting himself by working in the city's steel mills. He then hitchhiked to New York and became an apprentice in the Civic Repertory Company for a year's study. His debut as an actor in the company's 1929 production of *The Lower Depths* began a 55-year career that encompassed not only the stage—in drama, comedy, and musical comedy—but also films, radio, and television. Often Da Silva was active in several of these fields in a single year.

Da Silva remained with the Civic Repertory Company until 1934, playing some forty roles in their productions. In 1935 he went to the Cleveland Playhouse as an actor in three productions, and he directed two others for the People's Theater of Cleveland. In 1936 he made his first appearance in a film, *Once in a Blue Moon*. That same year he became a radio director for the Federal Theater of the Air, in charge of two weekly productions. In 1937 he appeared in *Golden Boy* on Broadway and was chosen by Orson Welles for the Federal Theater Project's production of *The Cradle Will Rock*. His role in the play as the labor organizer Larry Foreman allowed him to make use of his rich singing voice. Further appearances in the next few

years included playing Jack Armstrong in *Abe Lincoln in Illinois* (1938), a role he repeated in a 1940 film version. Between 1940 and 1942 he appeared in sixteen more films, including *Blues in the Night* (1941), *Sergeant York* (1941), and *Keeper of the Flame* (1942). He married Jane Taylor in 1941; the marriage ended in divorce in 1947.

In 1943 Da Silva came back to the New York stage in the historic American musical *Oklahoma!*, playing the dour farmhand, Jud. After its run of some 500 performances was over, he returned to Hollywood for more movie roles. For his performance as a stolid bartender in *Lost Weekend* (1945) he was nominated for an Academy Award, as he was for his playing of a sadistic sea captain in *Two Years before the Mast* (1946). Now in high demand as an expert character actor, Da Silva appeared in twelve more films between 1947 and 1951. He married Marjorie Nelson in 1950.

In 1951 the House Un-American Activities Committee (HUAC), investigating communism in the movie industry, subpoenaed Da Silva. The actor invoked his Fifth Amendment protection against self-incrimination and refused to answer the committee's questions. The committee questioned several witnesses about Da Silva's affiliations, but none identified him as a Communist, and only one (actor Sterling Hayden) admitted to having seen him at a meeting of Hollywood Communists. Under the circumstances, the committee did not pursue the matter further, but Da Silva soon became a target of anti-Communist pressure groups that intimidated film and television producers into blacklisting the actor. No new screen roles came his way, and even *Slaughter Trail*, a 1951 western completed but not released before Da Silva's HUAC appearance, was re-edited to eliminate the actor. He received no screen credit for his work on the picture; his scenes were reshot with Brian Donlevy in the role.

Da Silva returned to the theater, giving concert readings of Mark Twain, Anton Chekhov, and Sholom Alecheim in 1951–1952. In 1953 he was the star, director, and producer of *The World of Sholom Alecheim* on Broadway and on tour. He directed and appeared in productions at regional playhouses in New York and Pennsylvania in 1955 and 1956 and in Ohio in 1958. On Broadway in 1957, Da Silva directed *Tevya and His Daughters*, and he was recognized anew as a skilled actor in *Compulsion*: "Howard Da Silva is . . . excellent as the prosecution attorney—bold, loud, intelligent, realistic, vulgar in his pious tone," wrote the *New York Times* reviewer (25 Oct. 1957). The production of *Fiorello!* in 1959 brought him further success in the musical comedy field, playing a disarming rascal of a politician. The character's song "Little Tin Box," a hymn to graft, "perfectly expresses the festive cynicism of political humbug; and Howard Da Silva's corrosive voice suits it exactly" (*New York Times*, 24 Nov. 1959).

The 1960s saw Da Silva active as a director as well as an actor. Besides his off-Broadway work, which included directing two revivals of *The Cradle Will Rock*

(1960 and 1964), he had a major success with his direction of the comedy *Purlie Victorious* (1961), which ran for 261 performances. He appeared in a low-budget movie, *David and Lisa*, that proved to be a "sleeper" hit; his performance in the role of a psychiatrist brought him a nomination for the British Academy of Motion Picture Arts and Sciences Award. In 1965 he was the coauthor of *The Zulu and the Zayda*, a play on apartheid in South Africa. Two other film roles brought him back to the Hollywood studios in 1964 and 1966, and he appeared in a number of television series and specials during the decade. On stage, he played Claudius in *Hamlet* (1964) and the Archbishop in *The Unknown Soldier and His Wife* (1967). Another major success at the end of the decade was his appearance as Benjamin Franklin in the musical *1776* (1969). A reviewer enthused: "Mr. Da Silva has a voice as sweet as molasses and as mellow as rum, and his humor and good nature are a constant delight" (*New York Times*, 17 Mar. 1969). After his second marriage ended in divorce in 1960, he married Nancy Nutter in 1961. By his three marriages, he had five children.

The remaining years of his career saw Da Silva less active. He recreated his role in *1776* for the film version (1972). He was a guest artist at the Syracuse Repertory Theatre in 1972–1973. A final stage appearance came in *The Most Dangerous Man in America* (1976), a play he had co-written, at the Coconut Grove Playhouse in Florida. He repeated his role as Claudius in *Hamlet* for a television production (1975), and the same year he was seen on the TV screen as Mr. Peachum in *The Beggar's Opera* and as Khrushchev in *The Missiles of October*. For his supporting role in television's *Verna: USO Girl* (1978) he received an Emmy Award. His two last film appearances were in *Mommie Dearest* (1981) and *Garbo Talks* (1984). He died of lymphoma at his home in Ossining, New York.

At six-foot-two and 250 pounds, Da Silva had a commanding stage presence and a powerful voice. He was devoted to all aspects of theater; a *New York Times* article described him as a man who "discusses acting with the vigor and scholarship of a fanatic" (28 Sept. 1947). He had the energy to carry on several kinds of theatrical work at once; in 1963, for instance, he spent his days at rehearsals of *Cages*, an off-Broadway production he directed, then at night he played a leading role in the Broadway comedy *Dear Me, the Sky Is Falling*. How could he stand up to the physical and emotional drain? "Naturally," he told a reporter, "you have to be intensely interested in the theater, excited by it. And I still am" (*Newark Evening News*, 8 June 1963).

• Materials on the career of Da Silva are in the Billy Rose Theatre Collection at the New York Public Library for the Performing Arts, Lincoln Center. His article, "One Man's W.P.A. Experience," *New York Times*, 22 Dec. 1974, is informative. A list of his appearances and other creative work is in Monica O'Donnell Hubbard and Owen O'Donnell, eds., *Contemporary Theatre, Film and Television*, vol. 5 (1988). Details of his life as an actor are in Phil Koury, "Ex-Mill Hand," *New York Times*, 28 Sept. 1947; and Jack Gaver, "Actor Changes Pace," *Newark Evening News*, 8 June 1963. The issues of communism in Hollywood and blacklisting are treated in Victor Navasky, *Naming Names* (1980); John Cogley, *Report on Blacklisting* (2 vols., 1956); and Eric Bentley, *Thirty years of Treason: Excerpts from Hearings before the House Committee on Un-American Activities, 1938–1968* (1971). Obituaries are in the *New York Times*, 18 Feb. 1986; the *Washington Post*, 20 Feb. 1986; and *Variety*, 26 Feb. 1986.

WILLIAM STEPHENSON

DAUGHERTY, Harry Micajah (26 Jan. 1860–12 Oct. 1941), politician, was born in Washington Court House, Ohio, the son of John H. Daugherty, a farmer and merchant tailor, and Jane Draper. John Daugherty died of diphtheria when Harry was only four years of age, and Harry was weakened by the disease. The family struggled financially, and Harry learned to fend for himself, working in a series of odd jobs as a youth. Spurning his mother's desire for him to become a Methodist minister, Daugherty instead chose law as a profession. Though he had not attended college, Daugherty enrolled at Michigan Law School and graduated in 1881. In 1884 he married Lucy Walker, and they had one son and one daughter.

Upon returning from Michigan to Washington Court House, Daugherty took a position as a junior partner in a local law firm. He quickly became a prominent attorney and shifted from criminal cases to corporate law. As his law practice thrived, he began to dabble in local politics, serving as a city councilman (1886–1887), as chairman of the county central committee (1886), and as prosecuting attorney for Fayette County.

Daugherty was elected as a Republican to the Ohio House of Representatives in 1890 and served two tumultuous terms (1891–1895). Early in his second term, Daugherty became embroiled in a scandal. He stood accused of accepting "seven crisp $500 bills" in exchange for casting his vote in the house for U.S. senatorial candidate John Sherman. An investigation ensued but failed to discover any concrete evidence that directly implicated Daugherty. Nonetheless, the accusation effectively thwarted his ambitions to attain higher elective office.

Daugherty's lack of success did not curb his political activities. Over the next two decades, he remained active in Ohio politics, serving in a variety of posts, including Ohio chairman of William Howard Taft's failed presidential reelection bid in 1912. In these years, while also conducting a good deal of lobbying, Daugherty assiduously cultivated many prominent Ohio politicians, who increasingly turned to him for his organizational abilities and his keen knowledge of Ohio politics. One such politician was Warren G. Harding, an amiable conservative U.S. senator from Blooming Grove, Ohio, who had announced his intention to seek the Republican presidential nomination in 1920. His chances were slim, but thanks in part to Daugherty, Harding emerged as the GOP nominee. During the campaign Daugherty, who later in his memoirs exaggerated the role he played in Harding's rise to the presidency, served as Harding's campaign manager. Following his victory in 1920, the president-elect offered Daugherty as a reward the post of attorney general.

Daugherty was ill prepared to handle his new duties, and his tenure at the Justice Department was marked by incompetence and malfeasance. This was not, however, unexpected. Prior to assuming his duties, one observer acidly remarked, "It won't be long before Harry Daugherty is selling the sunshine off the steps of the capitol" (*The President Makers*, p. 223). The new attorney general stacked the department with Republican officials, who often proved both corrupt and woefully inept. As attorney general Daugherty exhibited a lack of political acumen and overall effectiveness. When railroad workers went on strike in 1922, he argued to the president that Communists were behind the strike, which was untrue, and urged Harding to take drastic action to crush the strikers. With Harding's approval, Daugherty obtained a sweeping injunction against union leaders, which proved to be acutely unpopular and politically damaging to the administration. Further adding to the general sense that Daugherty was not in control of his own department were his failed attempts to prosecute high level antitrust cases.

Daugherty's ineptitude was overshadowed by charges of corruption leveled at him personally. His name figured prominently in the scandals that engulfed the Harding administration. Daugherty, whose ethics had always been suspect, became known as one of the "Ohio Gang," a pejorative term for members of the administration who exploited their Ohio roots and personal connection to Harding to enrich themselves. Harding died in 1923 just as the scandals were coming to light, and the new president, Calvin Coolidge, deciding that the revelations leveled against the attorney general made him a political liability, demanded Daugherty's resignation in April 1924. Throughout all his travails, Daugherty defiantly maintained his innocence. He was twice indicted by a grand jury, but each time a jury acquitted him owing to lack of evidence—evidence that Daugherty had destroyed just before leaving the Justice Department. After the acquittals Daugherty returned to Ohio, where he resumed his law practice and worked on his memoirs, *The Inside Story of the Harding Tragedy* (1932). The work represented an unsuccessful attempt by the disgraced Daugherty to exonerate himself from the scandals that engulfed him and others members of the Harding administration. Daugherty died in Columbus, Ohio.

• Daugherty's papers are in the Manuscript Collections at the Ohio Historical Society in Columbus. James N. Giglio, *H. M. Daugherty and the Politics of Expediency* (1978), is a definitive full-length biography. On Daugherty's role in electing Harding, see Francis Russell, *The President Makers: From Mark Hanna to Joseph P. Kennedy* (1976). Eugene P. Trani and David L. Wilson, *The Presidency of Warren G. Harding* (1977), and Russell, *The Shadow of Blooming Grove: Warren G. Harding in His Times* (1968), discuss in length Harding's relationship with Daugherty. Charles L. Mee, Jr.,

The Ohio Gang: The World of Warren G. Harding (1981), is an excellent summation of the scandals. See also Randolph C. Downes, *The Rise of Warren Gamaliel Harding, 1865–1920* (1970). An obituary is in the *New York Times*, 13 Oct. 1941.

JUSTIN P. COFFEY

DAUGHERTY, Hugh Duffy (8 Sept. 1915–25 Sept. 1987), college football coach, was born in Emeigh, Pennsylvania, the son of Joseph Aloysius Daugherty, a miner and later a manager of a mine company store, and Elizabeth Nesbit Wilson. Daugherty's father moved the family to Barnesboro, Pennsylvania, to open his own clothing store. The business failed during a prolonged local coal strike, and Daugherty's father struggled for many years to pay off his debts. Daugherty began playing football at age eleven as a lineman with a local youth team, the "Alley Eleven."

On the Barnesboro High football team Daugherty played center, following two older brothers in that position. Daugherty's mother was determined that her children would gain college degrees, but the family's limited resources and debts meant that each had to work before attending college. After graduating from high school in 1932, he spent two years working in the Phillips-Jones shirt factory in Barnesboro and two years toiling in the coal mines at Arcadia, Pennsylvania. On Sundays he played semiprofessional football for the Barnes Athletic Club team.

In 1936 Daugherty entered Syracuse University on an academic scholarship and majored in finance. He played one year under head coach Vic Hansen and three years under head coach Ossie Solem and line coaches Clarence "Biggie" Munn and Charles "Bud" Wilkinson. In his sophomore year Daugherty became a starter at the guard position, but he suffered a cracked vertebra in the 1939 game against Michigan State. After recovering, he was elected co-captain of the Syracuse team in his senior year.

Upon graduating with a B.A. in business in 1940, Daugherty joined the U.S. Army and was commissioned a second lieutenant in late 1941. Before shipping overseas Daugherty met and married Frances Steccati in 1942; they had two children. Daugherty served twenty-six months in New Guinea with the 387th Port Battalion of the Army Transportation Corps and advanced to the rank of major. He was awarded the Bronze Star. After his return to the United States in the fall of 1945 and while recovering from a kidney operation, Daugherty coached football part time at Trinity Prep School in New York City.

In 1946 Munn, the new head coach at Syracuse, hired Daugherty as line coach. Daugherty followed Munn in 1947 to Michigan State, where, as the line coach, Daugherty spent seven seasons turning out offensive lines that the sportswriters admiringly called "Duffy's Toughies," Their success was due to a combination of conditioning, mental attitude, technique and execution of basic blocking skills and schemes, and the excellent recruitment of talent. Six of his linemen were named All-Americans. From the 1947 through the 1953 seasons Coach Munn's teams compiled a 54–9–2 record and claimed a national championship in 1952. After Michigan State won the Rose Bowl game in January 1954, Munn became the school's athletic director and named Daugherty as his successor.

In his first season as head football coach Daugherty's team had a 3–6 season record, winning only one Big Ten Conference game. In the 1955 season, however, his team went 9–1 and defeated the University of California at Los Angeles in the Rose Bowl. In 1955 Daugherty was elected collegiate Coach of the Year by the largest margin in the history of the poll of college coaches since its beginning in 1934. His teams were 7–2 in 1956 and 8–1 in 1957. After some lackluster seasons (including losing seasons in 1958 and 1964 and 5–4 records in 1959 and 1962), Daugherty's teams won consecutive national championships in 1965 and 1966, as his teams compiled 10–1 followed by 9–0–1 records and perfect Big Ten Conference records at 7–0–0. In his final six seasons at Michigan State, Daugherty's coaching record was 27–34–1, with only one winning season at 6–5 in 1971. In his 1974 autobiography Daugherty admitted that he should have left Michigan State five or six years earlier than he did and that such a move would have extended his coaching career by six or seven years beyond 1972, his last season. He stagnated as a coach at Michigan State because he could not recruit as effectively as he had done in earlier years.

Daugherty's reputation for success brought him head coaching job offers at the University of Texas in 1956, Southern California in 1960, and Notre Dame in 1963, as well as professional coaching job offers. In an era of many coaching martinets and remote, aloof coaching legends, Daugherty was a colorful, amiable, and witty personality who remained accessible to the press and who spoke to hundreds of banquet gatherings annually. He was known for his impish Irish humor, his illustrative stories, and his always quotable quips. He downplayed the preeminence of the coach, stressing instead the importance of talent and luck in winning.

Daugherty's success at Michigan State can be attributed to several factors. He enjoyed a close personal relationship with the university president, John Hannah, who supported the football program and saw successful football teams as important to the school's image and campus atmosphere. In the critical area of recruitment, Daugherty effectively located blue-chip athletes in areas such as Pennsylvania and western Massachusetts and even Hawaii, and he was the first collegiate coach to actively recruit black players out of the South. About half of his recruits came from out of state, reflecting the growing popularity of national recruitment in the 1960s. Daugherty himself recruited the most skilled players and used his charm, humor, and personableness to win over the parents of recruits. Daugherty also knew that his job as head coach was to win, to beat such traditional opponents as Michigan and Notre Dame and to post winning season records. He did not promote football as a character-building sport, as many coaches did, but honestly and directly acknowledged that he had been hired to win.

Daugherty utilized the complex multiple-offense system that previous head coach Munn had developed and made it work by careful game preparation, demanding conditioning, and minute emphasis on execution and timing. He simplified the teaching of the multiple-offense system so his linemen could learn their blocking assignments more quickly. He also developed multiple defensive alignments and formations that stressed players' reaction to the ball and protection of assigned areas. Daugherty published three articles in *Scholastic Coach*; coauthored with Clifford B. Wilson II *1st and Ten* (1961), which explained his additions to and variations of the multiple-offense system; and published *Defense Spartan Style* (1967), which explained the defensive alignments that brought such success in the 1965 and 1966 seasons. These defensive schemes emphasized two basic fronts of linemen and linebackers with a flexible four-deep secondary featuring a "rover" back. Michigan State teams were conditioned by tough and demanding drills and full-speed contact scrimmages, but Daugherty also allowed his players to call the coaches by their first names and knew when to relax his discipline and demanding system so that the game could still be fun for his players. The success of his football teams brought pride and a winning tradition to a school that underwent dramatic growth from an agricultural college to a major university in the 1950s and 1960s.

During his nineteen seasons as head coach at Michigan State, Daugherty compiled a 109-69-5 record, was the Football Writers of America Coach of the Year twice, and gained national top-ten rankings in seven seasons. He resigned after a 5–5–1 record in the 1972 season and was appointed assistant to the university's vice president in charge of development. In this position he handled fundraising and general public relations. In 1973 Daugherty began working for ABC Sports as a color commentator on college football telecasts with Chris Schenkel and Bud Wilkinson. As a television commentator, however, Daugherty did not prove to be as lively, funny, or insightful as he had been as a coach and popular banquet speaker, and ABC ended the contract after just two seasons.

In his retirement Daugherty lived in Santa Barbara, California, where he died. In 1984 he was elected as a coach to the National Football Foundation College Football Hall of Fame.

• The Hugh Duffy Daugherty Papers, covering 1947 to 1975, are located in the Michigan State University Archives and Historical Collections. The Voice Library at Michigan State University has seven voice recordings of Daugherty interviews and speeches. *Duffy: An Autobiography*, written with Dave Diles, was published in 1974. Articles on Daugherty's career as head coach include "Driving Man," *Time*, 8 Oct. 1956, pp. 66–75; William (Red) Gleason, "The Merry Maestro of Michigan State," *Saturday Evening Post*, 17 Nov. 1956, pp. 37, 156–158; and Gerald Holland, "'Duffy Will Think of Something,'" *Sports Illustrated*, 12 Nov. 1956, pp. 74–80. For one of Daugherty's star players' view of his coach, see

Bubba Smith and Hal DeWindt, *Kill, Bubba, Kill!* (1983). Merrin D. Hyman and Gordon S. White, Jr., *Big Ten Football: Its Life and Times, Great Coaches, Players and Games* (1977); Fred W. Stabley, *The Spartans: Michigan State Football*, 2nd ed. (1988); and Lynn Henning, *Spartan Seasons: The Triumphs and Turmoil of Michigan State Sports* (1987), are also essential sources. See also Beth L. Shapiro, "John Hannah and the Growth of Big-time Intercollegiate Athletics at Michigan State University," *Journal of Sport History* 10 (Winter 1983): 26–40. Obituaries are in the *Detroit Free Press, Detroit News*, and *Lansing State Journal*, 26 Sept. 1987.

DOUGLAS A. NOVERR

DAVEISS, Joseph Hamilton (4 Mar. 1774–8 Nov. 1811), lawyer, was born in Bedford County, Virginia, the son of Joseph Daveiss, a planter, and Jean Hamilton. In 1779 Daveiss moved with his parents to Danville, Kentucky, where Daveiss's father established a farm. Daveiss received no formal education until he was twelve, when he began a three-year course of study at private academies near Harrodsburg; he excelled as a student. At fifteen he returned to the farm to assist his father. He left three years later to fight Native Americans who were harassing Kentuckians north of the Ohio River. Upon his return to the farm, he read law with George Nicholas and in 1795 began a practice in Danville. Daveiss's practice flourished because of his knowledge of real property law, a useful specialty given the chaotic condition of Kentucky land titles.

President John Adams (1735–1826) appointed Daveiss federal district attorney for Kentucky in 1800, but Daveiss also continued his private practice. He appeared before the U.S. Supreme Court in August 1801 in the highly publicized case of *Mason v. Wilson*. At issue was title to approximately thirty thousand acres of valuable Kentucky land. He was the first lawyer from west of the Allegheny Mountains to appear before the Court, and despite the importance of the occasion, he argued the case dressed in the rough garb of a frontiersman. The brilliance of his oratory and logic outweighed any disadvantage in appearance; the Court ruled for his client. Daveiss gained fame and considerable wealth from the case. As was common in such cases, he received half of the disputed acreage as his fee.

In 1803 Daveiss married Ann Marshall, sister of Chief Justice John Marshall; they had no children. Three years later Daveiss initiated the most celebrated case he prosecuted as federal district attorney. In early 1806 he bombarded President Thomas Jefferson with letters detailing an alleged plot by Aaron Burr (1756–1836) to separate the western states and territories from the Union and to invade Mexico. Because Daveiss was an ardent Federalist and most of Burr's alleged co-conspirators were respected Republicans, Jefferson, himself a Republican, ignored the accusation. Seeking to expose what he believed to be a treasonous plot (and to enhance the depleted fortunes of the Federalist party in Kentucky), Daveiss in November asked Federal District Judge Harry Innes to convene a grand jury in Frankfort. Daveiss hoped that

Burr and others would be indicted for the high misdemeanor of plotting to invade Mexico. Because of the absence of crucial witnesses, a dearth of evidence, and the opposition of Judge Innes, Daveiss failed in two attempts to produce an indictment. In 1807 Jefferson removed Daveiss from office; shortly thereafter, Daveiss published a bitter attack on the president's conduct of the Burr affair.

Daveiss moved his law practice to Lexington in 1807. There he earned large fees in land title disputes. In the fall of 1811 he joined William Henry Harrison's military expedition against Native Americans in the Old Northwest. He was wounded on 7 November 1811 at the battle of Tippecanoe and died the next day. His fame as a lawyer and soldier prompted four states (Kentucky, Illinois, Indiana, and Missouri) to name counties in his honor.

• There is no collection of Daveiss's papers; some legal correspondence is among the papers of George Nicholas, Special Collections, University of Kentucky Library. An early sketch, R. Coleman, "Jo Daviess [*sic*] of Kentucky," *Harper's New Monthly Magazine*, Aug. 1860, pp. 341–56, is highly anecdotal. For a summary of Daveiss's efforts to expose the Burr conspiracy, see Milton Lomask, *Aaron Burr: The Conspiracy and Years of Exile, 1805–1836* (1982). Daveiss's argument in *Wilson v. Mason* is summarized in the report of the case, 1 Cranch 45 (1801).

ROBERT M. IRELAND

DAVENPORT, Benjamin Butler (1871?–7 Apr. 1958), playwright, actor, and theater manager, was born in New York City, the son of John L. Davenport, a water commissioner, and (probably) Delia Post. He may have been called John at birth. Butler later claimed to have been dedicated to his art from age six, when his mother gave him a toy theater, or from age eight, when he "caught a glimpse" of Edwin Booth and Helena Modjeska while visiting the theatrical mogul Charles Frohman's Stamford, Connecticut, home, which was near "Bramhall," the Davenports' estate. Little else is known of Davenport's childhood.

In his teens he apprenticed for a year with Augustin Daly's repertory company, playing bit parts and understudying "five actors, none of whom missed a single performance!" In the next few years of his brief professional acting career, while appearing with Frohman's company and with Henrietta Crosman in *Mr. Wilkinson's Widows* (c. 1891), young Davenport encountered Henry Irving, Ellen Terry, Sarah Bernhardt, Eleonora Duse, and other theater greats. They peopled the countless anecdotes a much older Davenport would tell to enchant his Free Theatre audiences.

A sudden decline in the family fortune interrupted his happy actor's life; to support his mother and sisters he was forced to work for "eight black years" in the real estate business. In April 1909 he reappeared in New York City's drama pages: apparently emulating Daly, the mentor of his teens, Davenport announced the building of a new playhouse on Sixty-third Street to house a repertory stock company producing modern American plays. Davenport was already writing plays at the time. But by November the building had stopped at the second story; Davenport's backer had abandoned him and the project.

In 1910 the Schuberts produced Davenport's *Keeping Up Appearances*, an autobiographical play about a family dominated by a cruel father; the production failed at the box office. Davenport favored the period's popular naturalist dramatic style and journalistic choice of themes, but his plays, dealing with white slavery and similar subjects, were closed by the police. He returned to Stamford and real estate; he also founded a small acting company to present his plays in a barn close to Bramhall.

Davenport often described his life as being controlled by voices commanding major changes and "miracles" that solved major crises. One morning in 1915, awakened with a start by a voice ordering, "Go to New York and get a theatre," he took the first train and advertised for a building to convert into a small playhouse. One of the replies brought him to 138 East Twenty-seventh Street near Lexington Avenue, close to his birthplace. The small building had housed the Knights of Columbus, Baptists, Spiritualists, and then an Armenian church; Davenport leased it and paid $300 for two months' rent, leaving himself with $3.17 for alterations. "Miraculously," the Cohan-Harris office saved him by paying $750 to option his play *The Depths of Purity*. The new Bramhall Playhouse's first presentation, on 2 April 1915, was *The Importance of Coming and Going*, written and directed by its leading actor, Butler Davenport.

The playhouse's first box office–supported years were lean. By 1923 Davenport's lease and his enterprise were about to expire together; he staged one of his gloomiest social-problem plays, *Difference in Gods: The Psychology of a Family in Four Acts*, leading to another miracle. In the audience was a wealthy couple from the West on the verge of divorce. They had been sent by a friend to this play, which dramatized and solved their problem. Reconciled and grateful, they gave Davenport $10,000, which he used as down payment to purchase his theater building.

Davenport then decided to dedicate his life "to spreading the idea that nobody should pay for theatre admissions. . . . We have free schools, free art museums, free symphony concerts and libraries. Why not theatres?" The Bramhall Playhouse closed and reopened on 17 January 1923 as the Davenport Theatre, "the First Free Theatre in the World," supported only by voluntary contributions. Except for a brief absence in 1928 to play *The Passing of the Third Floor Back* at Wallack's theater (his final commercial theater experience), Davenport was happily "at home" on East Twenty-seventh street for the rest of his life.

Mortgage payments became difficult during the depression, and by 1931 Davenport needed his greatest miracle. About to lose his theater "for the seventh time," he awoke "with the name of a wealthy gentleman burning in my brain. . . . I knew of him and he knew of me, though we had never spoken to each other." Davenport telephoned, met, and persuaded the gentleman to buy the theater for about $35,000, permanently freeing Davenport of mortgage worries.

Young volunteer student-actors filled the casts and crews of Davenport-directed plays, in which he often played leading roles. (He played Hamlet many times over the years; cast photos show Claudius, Gertrude, and Polonius looking young enough to be Hamlet's grandchildren.) The volunteers performed after work at full-time day jobs, then stayed for late-night rehearsals of new productions. Only Davenport and two cast members who doubled as stagehands were paid—one dollar a day. Davenport, who never married, lived above his theater in a memorabilia-filled apartment.

Production costs were paid from contributions collected in baskets during intermissions at which Davenport appeared, wrapped in Shakespearean toga, to spellbind audiences with twenty-minute chats on topics varying from memories of Booth, Modjeska, and Konstantin Stanislavsky to the evils of fascism.

Mayor Fiorello La Guardia stumbled on the theater while attending a nearby fire and sent Davenport a letter commending the Free Theatre's contribution to the city's culture. Its varied, constantly changing repertory regularly presented Shakespeare, Molière, and modern dramas by Henrik Ibsen, Anton Chekhov, Somerset Maugham, and Davenport himself. There were usually ten productions a year, four of them new to the company; each was rehearsed for three weeks. In 1935 Davenport estimated that he had already offered more than a hundred plays. With a few forced lapses into selling tickets, the Free Theatre continued into the 1940s.

Living by leasing his tiny theater to commercial productions, Davenport in his late eighties seemed to some merely an elderly theatrical eccentric. But long before, he had summed up his stagestruck life as the actor-manager of his own private "theatre of service," telling audiences each night, "I've been so tremendously rich—in everything but money!" Davenport died in New York City a few days after what would have been his theater's forty-third anniversary.

• There is little or no documentation of Davenport's early life: there is no birth certificate for a "Benjamin Butler" Davenport, but a John Davenport, "second child of John Davenport and Delia Post Davenport," was registered as born at 145 East Twenty-ninth Street on 15 May 1871. The address, the father's birthplace in Connecticut, and his employment as some sort of "water commissioner" seems consistent with what is known of B. B. Davenport's family and its political connections. A scrapbook in the Theatre Research Collection at the New York Public Library for the Performing Arts, Lincoln Center, contains photographs, a few yellowing clippings, and programs. The most extended treatments of Davenport's life in the theater are in two *New York Times* articles: "Hamlet Down Under," 7 Apr. 1935, on the occasion of the Davenport Free Theatre's twentieth anniversary, and "B. Davenport et Cie. Have an Anniversary," 31 Mar. 1940, celebrating the start of its twenty-sixth year. See also "The Davenport Free Theatre, El Primer Teátro Libre del Mundo," *Prometeo*, Oct. 1948, pp. 12–13. A short obituary appears in the *New York Times*, 8 Apr. 1958.

DANIEL KREMPEL

DAVENPORT, Charles Benedict (1 June 1866–18 Feb. 1944), geneticist, eugenicist, and science administrator, was born at his family's farm, "Davenport Ridge," near Stamford, Connecticut, where four generations of Davenports had lived, the son of Amzi Benedict Davenport, a real estate agent, and his second wife, Jane Joralemon Dimon. Because of the nature of his father's business, the family spent winters in Brooklyn. Davenport's mother, a religious skeptic and avid naturalist, helped cultivate these characteristics in her son. His father's stern and uncompromising Protestantism was also a strong influence, and young Charles was tutored at home where he could learn the values of discipline and hard work and also serve as janitor and errand boy for his father's business. Davenport developed a quiet, even taciturn demeanor, but from an early age he communicated voluminously in journals and diaries.

In 1879 Davenport entered Brooklyn Collegiate and Polytechnic Institute for his first formal education. There he struggled to reach the top of his class and in 1886 received a B.S. with honors. After working for most of the next year as a railroad rodman, Davenport defied his father and enrolled in Harvard College to study natural history. He received an A.B. in 1889 and a Ph.D. in zoology in 1892, both from Harvard. As a graduate student, Davenport worked under one of the great morphologists of the late nineteenth and early twentieth centuries, Edward L. Mark. Davenport's doctoral dissertation was a largely descriptive and morphological investigation of budding in several species of Bryozoans (small, sessile invertebraled currently called Entoprocta).

From 1892 to 1899 Davenport held an instructorship at Harvard. Rejecting the largely descriptive methodology of Mark, Davenport began more experimentally oriented work. At the same time he offered courses in "experimental morphology," which included subjects such as the physiology of development, regeneration, the causes of variation, and the effects of hybridization and selection. Two of his undergraduate students, William E. Castle and Walter B. Canon, went on to become important experimental biologists in their own right.

In 1984 Davenport married Gertrude Crotty, a graduate student at the predecessor of Radcliffe College and formerly an instructor in zoology at the University of Kansas; they had three children. A biologist in her own right, Crotty coauthored several papers with her husband. The couple remained in Cambridge until 1899, although in 1898 Davenport assumed directorship of the Brooklyn Academy of Arts and Sciences Biological Laboratory in Cold Spring Harbor, Long Island, a position he held until 1923.

In 1899 Davenport first met mathematics (and then eugenics) professor Karl Pearson and gentleman amateur Francis Galton in London and immediately became an enthusiastic supporter of their new statistical methods, or "biometrics" (the quantitative study of variation in organisms). Pearson and Galton invited Davenport to become a coeditor of their new journal, *Biometrika*, in 1901. Davenport's own book, *Statistical Methods with Special Reference to Biological Variation*, which went through four editions between 1899 and 1936, was a major vehicle for introducing quantitative and biometrical methods into biology in the United States. Throughout the remainder of his life, Davenport was a constant advocate of the biometrical approach.

In 1899 Charles Otis Whitman, head of the zoology department at the University of Chicago, invited Davenport to develop plans for a farm (to be associated with the Marine Biology Laboratory at Woods Hole, Mass.) to pursue studies on experimental breeding and the effects of selection on larger, agriculturally important animals. Rather than give up the idea when plans failed to materialize, Davenport quickly began negotiations with the newly organized Carnegie Institution of Washington to gain support for an independent research institute. After many delays, negotiations were completed in 1903, and the Station for Experimental Evolution in Cold Spring Harbor was opened in 1904 with Davenport as director.

The function of the Station for Experimental Evolution was to promote and coordinate research on problems relating to heredity and variation, using methods of hybridization, selection, and cytology. As one of the founders of the American Breeders Association in 1903, Davenport, along with his colleague Willet M. Hays of the U.S. Department of Agriculture, was keenly interested in how knowledge of heredity could be used to improve methods of plant and animal breeding. It was Davenport's aim to unite theoretical with practical knowledge and to use science as the basis for rationalizing breeding practices. Among the first staff members were George H. Shull, an important pioneer in the development of hybrid corn, and Albert F. Blakeslee, a plant cytologist who helped to establish the validity of the chromosome theory of heredity in plants. Later investigators included Milislav Demerec, Oscar Riddle, and E. C. MacDowell.

At first skeptical of the newly discovered (1900) Mendelian theory of heredity, Davenport eventually became one of its strongest supporters. His own work at the station involved breeding experiments with an extraordinarily wide range of animals, including snails, mice, houseflies, moths, sow (pill) bugs, trout, cats, chickens, and canaries. The results of most of these studies were inconclusive, but the experiments with chickens were highly successful and showed Davenport to be a first-rate breeder and geneticist. Unfortunately, as was characteristic of much of his work, he compiled results with such speed that the data was often unreliable, and his analysis lacked depth. Even so, by 1910 Davenport had become one of the leading spokesmen for the new Mendelian theory of heredity and the Station for Experimental Evolution, an increasingly important research institute.

In 1907 Davenport had become interested in the application of Mendel's principles to the problem of human heredity and published the first in a series of papers coauthored with his wife on the inheritance of eye, skin, and hair color, as well as hair form (curly, straight, etc.). Soon human genetics and its offshoot, eugenics, came to occupy most of Davenport's attention. In his *Eugenics* (1910), Davenport defined eugenics as "the science of human improvement by better breeding." The practice of eugenics involved both research and social action programs. The research program focused on determining what human traits—physical, physiological, and behavioral—were inherited and in what patterns. The social action program aimed to promote, through education and political lobbying, policies that would encourage those people with the "best heredity" to have a large number of offspring and discourage or prevent those with "poor heredity" (meaning usually those of lower socioeconomic groups or of nonwhite races) from having many, or any, children. For the remainder of his career, Davenport directed most of his attention toward eugenics research and the promotion of eugenical policies in many arenas.

In need of additional funds and staff to pursue eugenics work further, Davenport approached Mary Harriman, widow of E. H. Harriman, the founder of the Union Pacific Railroad, whose response was enthusiastic. Almost immediately she provided an annual appropriation of approximately $35,000. The Eugenics Record Office, as the new research facility was called, opened on 1 October 1910 at Cold Spring Harbor, with Harry H. Laughlin, a former instructor in agricultural breeding from Northeast Missouri State Normal School, as superintendent and Davenport as director. Davenport began a series of investigations into aspects of the inheritance of human personality and mental traits, and over the years he generated hundreds of papers and several books on the genetics of alcoholism, pellagra (later shown to be due to a vitamin deficiency), criminality, feeblemindedness, seafaringness, bad temper, intelligence, manic depression, and the biological effects of race crossing. In virtually all of these studies, while admitting that environmental influences played some role, Davenport emphasized, on the basis of flimsy and subjective data, the genetic component almost exclusively. From pedigree studies and family histories, he argued (incorrectly, as we now believe) that most such traits were determined by single Mendelian genes (either dominant or recessive). Davenport also supported, though did not usually engage in directly, Laughlin's more openly political activities, including testifying before Congress on behalf of the Johnson Act (the immigration restriction law of 1924), and facilitating numerous state laws authorizing compulsory sterilization of those deemed to be genetically inferior, which had been passed in thirty states by 1935.

Davenport's eugenics work was highly controversial and was often vigorously opposed by other geneticists. His prodigious writings brought considerable attention to the topic of eugenics, but his conclusions were often simplistic, increasingly out of touch with findings in genetics, and riddled with racial and class bias.

Only his most ardent admirers regarded it as truly scientific work.

During Davenport's tenure at Cold Spring Harbor, several reorganizations took place there. In 1918 the Carnegie Institution of Washington took over funding of the ERO with an additional handsome endowment from Mary Harriman. In 1921 the two institutions were combined as the Department of Genetics of the Carnegie Institution of Washington. Davenport retired from the directorship of the department in 1934, and the ERO, after a long decline that was sealed by the association of eugenics with Nazi race hygiene, officially closed on 31 December 1939.

Davenport was distinguished more for his continual enthusiasm for new subjects of research and his intense personal drive than for any particular scientific discovery. He was a persistent organizer and promoter of biology, work for which he received many honors. He was elected to the American Philosophical Society in 1907 and to the National Academy of Sciences in 1912. In addition to establishing the laboratories at Cold Spring Harbor, he was founder of the Eugenics Research Association and the Conservative Taxpayers League (Long Island). During World War I he was appointed a major in the Sanitary Corps and assigned to make biometrics measurements on recruits. He served as president or vice president of ten professional societies and was treasurer for the Sixth International Congress of Genetics, held in Ithaca, New York, in 1932 and president of the Third International Congress on Eugenics held in New York City, also in 1932. He received the Gold Medal of the National Institute of Social Science in 1923.

Although Davenport served as a scientific administrator throughout most of his career, he was not particularly effective in that role. His silent, almost secretive manner, his lack of humor, his inability to accept criticism and to coordinate the work of the various individuals serving under him, left the department directionless most of the time. His own prestigious research and writing and his considerable ability to garner funds were not enough to provide intellectual and organizational leadership to the diverse investigators working at Cold Spring Harbor. He was criticized for always responding to the event of the moment, thus never staying long enough with any one topic to bring it to a conclusion. True to this description, he died in Cold Spring Harbor of pneumonia contracted while working feverishly outdoors in mid-February to clean the skull of a whale washed ashore a few weeks before. He intended the skull as a major attraction for the town's whaling museum, of which he was curator and director.

• Davenport's scientific and personal papers are at the American Philosophical Society, Philadelphia, and contain a wealth of information about his early life as well as his scientific career. Two detailed biographical sketches are Oscar Riddle, National Academy of Sciences, *Biographical Memoirs* 25 (1948): 75–110, and E. C. MacDowell, *Bios* 17 (1946): 2–50, both of which contain a complete bibliography of Davenport's published work. A study by Charles Rosenberg in the *Bulletin of the History of Medicine* 35 (1961): 266–76, still remains one of the most insightful accounts of Davenport's early work in human genetics and eugenics. Garland Allen's study on the founding and history of the Eugenics Record Office in *Osiris* 2 (1986): 225–64, details Davenport's role in establishing an institutional base for the developing American eugenics movement. See also Lee Richard Hiltzkc, "The Brooklyn Institute of Arts and Sciences' Biological Laboratory, 1890–1924: A History" (Ph.D. diss., SUNY–Stonybrook, 1993). Additional references on eugenics and Davenport's work can be found in Allan Chase, *The Legacy of Malthus* (1977), and Mark Haller, *Eugenics: Hereditarian Attitudes in American Thought* (1963).

GARLAND E. ALLEN

DAVENPORT, Edward Loomis (15 Nov. 1815–1 Sept. 1877), stage actor, was born in Boston, Massachusetts, the son of Asher Davenport, a tavern keeper, and Demis Loomis. He attended Mayhew School in Boston and was employed as a hotel clerk and at the Exchange Coffee House in Boston. Davenport made his first stage appearance in 1836 at the Lion Theatre, or Brick Circus, in Providence, Rhode Island, as Parson Willdo in support of Junius Brutus Booth's Sir Giles Overreach in Philip Massinger's *A New Way to Pay Old Debts* (1632). Davenport subsequently played small roles in various stock companies, including the Tremont Theatre in Boston and the Walnut Street Theatre in Philadelphia. He made his first New York appearance on 9 August 1843 as Frederick Fitzallen in *He's Not A-Miss* in a company led by Mrs. Henry Hunt (later to be Mrs. John Drew).

After several seasons playing at the Bowery Theatre, at Niblo's Garden, and at the Boston Museum, Davenport was engaged as leading man for a company headed by Anna Cora Mowatt for a national tour in 1846–1847 and for tours of London and the English provinces from 1847 until 1850. He made his London debut on 5 January 1848 at the Princess's Theatre as Sir Thomas Clifford in Sheridan Knowles's *The Hunchback* (1832). Davenport remained in England for seven seasons (1847–1854), touring the provinces as an American tragedian and playing in support of such English stars as Gustavus Vaughan Brooke and William Charles Macready. In the season of 1850–1851 he was hired by Benjamin Webster, the manager of the Haymarket Theatre, to support Macready in his series of farewell engagements. Davenport won the admiration of London critics with his performances as Brutus, Laertes, Macduff, Iago, and Othello. Displaying his versatility, Davenport was also enthusiastically received in the rollicking comic role of William the Sailor in Douglas Jerrold's popular melodrama *Black-Eyed Susan* (1829). The *Times'* critic commented: "His hilarity is hearty and unaffected, his pathos is manly and genuine, and, as an additional quality, he looks the part to perfection."

While in England, Davenport married in 1849 a young English actress, Elizabeth "Fanny" Vining, the daughter of the London comedian Frederick Vining. The Davenports had seven children, all of whom pursued stage careers. Davenport's wife regularly acted with him until his retirement. After his death, she continued to act occasionally. Her last appearance was as Lady Macbeth at the Boston Globe Theatre in 1890.

In 1854 Davenport returned to the United States where for more than twenty years he sustained a successful career as a leading actor, playing in the major theaters of Boston, New York, and Philadelphia, and with many of the era's principal performers. In 1858, for example, he supported Charlotte Cushman in her series of farewell appearances.

Davenport occasionally ventured into theatrical management, at the Howard Athenaeum in Boston from 1859 to 1861 and the Chestnut Street Theatre in Philadelphia from 1870 until 1874. In the 1860s he toured successfully in combination with J. W. Wallack, Jr. From 1869 until 1871 he was a member of Augustin Daly's Fifth Avenue Theatre company. In the early 1870s he toured the South and New England with his own company, and in 1875 he was engaged to play Brutus, perhaps his finest Shakespearean role, in an elaborate revival of *Julius Caesar* mounted at Booth's Theatre in New York by the impresarios Henry Jarrett and Henry David Palmer. (The production was actually based on Edwin Booth's 1871 revival.) Also featured in this production were Lawrence Barrett as Cassius and Frank C. Bangs as Marc Antony. The production played for 103 performances in New York, a record run for a Shakespeare play. It then toured eastern cities for another 119 performances. Davenport's last appearance was on 5 March 1877 in the title role of W. S. Gilbert's *Dan'l Druce* (1876) at the Howard Athenaeum. He died at his home in Canton, Pennsylvania.

Davenport was among the more versatile actors of his era, equally adept at playing broad farcical characters, melodramatic villains, and tragic heroes. His career repertoire included not only Hamlet, Shylock, Macbeth, Richard III, Prospero, Cardinal Richelieu, Sir Lucius O'Trigger in Sheridan's *The Rivals* (1775), and Bill Sikes in a dramatic adaptation of Dickens's *Oliver Twist*, but he also played roles in sensational theatrical claptrap with such titles as *The Scalp Hunters* (1855) and *The Man with the Red Beard* (1857). Until it was eclipsed by Edwin Booth, Davenport's Hamlet was considered by many critics the finest of its day. Davenport's Sir Giles Overreach was also a forceful performance, equal to if not surpassing the performances of Edmund Kean and Junius Brutus Booth. Davenport himself counted Sir Giles among his favorite parts because of its "tremendous power and passion."

Although capable of projecting emotional energy and intensity and with an impressive physical appearance and a strong, melodious, if sometimes husky voice, Davenport had a reputation as "a master of histrionic technique and a precisionist rather than an overwhelmer in performance." Except for his portrayal of Sir Giles, which, over the years that he played him, became increasingly naturalistic and emotionally powerful, Davenport aimed for emotional restraint. A contemporary, Henry Dickinson Stone, observed that in Davenport's impersonations "calm judgment controls his impulses." (Ironically, the more vicious, vigorous, and horribly brilliant he made Sir Giles, the more audiences avoided it.) On balance, even his best roles were often judged cold or overly intellectual. William Winter complained that Davenport was "deficient in soul." This quality for Winter made even "his otherwise excellent Hamlet . . . as metallic as the rapier he carried."

Ultimately, Davenport's very versatility may have worked to his disadvantage. As Henry P. Goddard noted, his "versatility led people to doubt his greatness in the highest walks of tragedy to which most great actors confine themselves." Unwilling or unable to specialize but playing both great tragic heroes and vapid clowns, he, according to Goddard, "never won the popular recognition or the great pecuniary rewards that fell to . . . men of less genius."

• The most complete biography of Davenport is Edwin Francis Edgett's *Edward Loomis Davenport: A Biography* (1901; repr. 1970). Charles H. Shattuck illuminates Davenport's acting style in *Shakespeare on the American Stage: From the Hallams to Edwin Booth*, vol. 1 (1976), pp. 117–24. See also Henry P. Goddard, "Recollections of Edward L. Davenport," *Lippincott's Magazine*, Apr. 1878, pp. 463–66; Montrose J. Moses, *Famous Actor-Families in America* (1906; repr. 1968), pp. 227–49; Donald Mullin, ed., *Victorian Actors and Actresses in Review* (1983), pp. 149–53; Henry Dickinson Stone, *Personal Recollections of the Drama* (1873; repr 1969), pp. 121–22; William C. Young, *Famous Actors and Actresses on the American Stage: Documents of American Theater History* (1975); and Garff B. Wilson, *A History of American Acting* (1966), pp. 87–90. Obituaries appear in the *Clipper* (New York), 8 Sept. 1877, and the *New York Times*, 2 Sept. 1877.
DANIEL J. WATERMEIER

DAVENPORT, Eugene (20 June 1856–31 Mar. 1941), agricultural educator, was born near Woodland, Michigan, the son of George Martin Davenport and Esther Sutton, farmers. His parents were Universalists. He attended local schools, taught school briefly, and graduated from Michigan Agricultural College (later Michigan State University) with a B.S. in 1878. For ten years he helped his father operate the family farm. In 1881 he married Emma Jane Coats; they had one child who survived infancy.

Returning to Michigan State in 1888, Davenport served as assistant to Professor William J. Beal, a pioneer of the "new botany," read (on the advice of Manly Miles) the reports of John B. Lawes and Joseph H. Gilbert on agricultural experiments they carried out on plants and animals at Rothamsted, the Lawes family manor near St. Albans, England, and earned a master's degree in agriculture. From 1889 to 1891 Davenport was professor of practical agriculture and superintendent of the college farm.

In 1891 a wealthy Brazilian invited Davenport to establish an agricultural college at Piracicaba in the state of São Paulo. When the Michigan authorities refused a leave of absence, he resigned and went to Brazil. Finding São Paulo unprepared for this venture, Davenport departed in April 1892 for England, where he visited the oldest agricultural experiment station in the world at Rothamsted. He then farmed in Woodland, Michigan, until accepting an appointment at the University of Illinois in 1894.

Taking up his duties as dean of and professor in the College of Agriculture and as agriculturist of the Agricultural Experiment Station on 1 January 1895, Davenport found the College of Agriculture on the verge of extinction. When his proposals to revitalize the college met resistance from President Andrew S. Draper, Davenport, convinced that the farmers of the state would support him, took matters to the farmers without reference to university authorities. Efforts to form a new state farmers' organization were underway when Davenport became dean, and in 1895 a bill created the Illinois Farmers' Institute (IFI) as a public corporation whose purpose was to encourage useful education among the farmers and to develop the state's agricultural resources. A member of the institute's board of directors and chair of its committee on agricultural education, Davenport worked through the IFI to achieve his goals.

Davenport had given considerable thought to agricultural education, which he viewed as essential to the proper development of the rich natural resources of the state and nation. Strongly influenced by the theory of evolution, he maintained that when people struggled under equal conditions, the ultimate victor would be the group that had the better food supply. Since the final supremacy of the races depended primarily on agriculture, Anglo-Saxons were duty bound to foster an intelligent and progressive agriculture. The nation needed a new, universal education in the name of efficiency and culture. Students in a college of agriculture should devote equal time to agricultural studies, scientific studies, and elective studies of a liberal character. Davenport urged the division of agriculture into various specialties with a head in charge of each division. He wanted relations between the College of Agriculture and the Agricultural Experiment Station put on a sounder footing, and he stressed the college's need for equipment and its own building.

In 1898, when at last President Draper publicly stated his views on agricultural education, he recommended establishment of a high school that would take boys from the farm and give them a certificate at the end of two or three years of practical work. Draper looked backward, Davenport forward; in the ensuing struggle Davenport triumphed.

In 1899 the board of trustees requested $150,000 for an agricultural building, the governor endorsed the request, and the Farmers' Institute campaigned for the appropriation. Draper complained that Davenport had "run amuck among farmer politicians and political leaders in the State and against my constant advice" (letter to Lucy L. Flower, Draper Letterbooks, 27 Jan. 1899). The legislature not only passed the bill but also directed that half of the funds from the two Morrill Acts—the 1862 act providing the states funds for the establishment of land-grant colleges and the 1890 act providing an additional annual sum to each land-grant college—be devoted to teaching agriculture.

These advances inaugurated a new era for the College of Agriculture, an era marked by construction of an Agricultural Building, an expanded curriculum, more faculty, and an enrollment of more than 100 students, all by 1900. In that year the Department of Household Science was added to existing departments of animal husbandry, dairy husbandry, horticulture, and veterinary science. Davenport could now boast that Illinois had become one of the nation's foremost agricultural colleges.

Davenport had been professor of animal husbandry since March 1895, but in 1901, after a specialist in this field joined the faculty, his title was changed to professor of principles of variation and selection in domesticated animals and plants (thremmatology). He taught a course in applied evolution and directed theses.

After Davenport was named director of the Agricultural Experiment Station in 1896, he formed a number of advisory committees for the work, and in 1901 they combined to secure a law that provided state funds to conduct agricultural research in six areas. Davenport planned the lines of experiment in conference with station staff and the advisory committees, and highly significant work was conducted with corn and soils.

By late 1903 Davenport had accomplished the larger part of what he had come to Illinois to do. "The most significant thing that happened here during my administration," Draper later confessed, "was the development of the College of Agriculture, and I did all I could to prevent it" (Davenport, "Notable People I Have Known," p. 3). Thereafter Davenport was mainly occupied with the administration of teaching and of scientific research. In 1909–1910, when the Farmers' Institute and its auxiliary, the Association of Domestic Science, sought the removal of Isabel Bevier, head of the Department of Household Science, on the grounds that her department did not offer practical courses in homemaking, Davenport, who was beholden to these outside groups, requested her resignation. Standing her ground, Bevier retained her position.

Davenport served as vice president of the university from 1920 to 1922. In this capacity he headed a faculty committee to study the budget, and in 1921 a bill incorporating his committee's recommendations for a vastly increased biennial appropriation went through the legislature unanimously. Retiring in 1922, Davenport went back to the family farm in Michigan. In retirement he traveled in the West and Alaska, wrote, and in 1928–1929 returned to the university as assistant to President David Kinley for half a year to help ease the 1929 biennial appropriation bill through the general assembly.

Over the course of his career Davenport authored works on corn, milk and milk production, the market classes of horses, experiments with wheat, soil fertility investigations, and similar topics, most of which appeared as bulletins. His writings on agriculture include *The Study of Farm Animals* (1901–1902), *Principles of Breeding: A Treatise on Thremmatology* (1907),

The Development of the Natural Resources of the State (1908), *Domesticated Animals and Plants* (1910), *Twelve Studies in Agriculture* (1911), *The Farm* (1927), and, with Aretas Nolan, *Agricultural Arts* (1938). He wrote and spoke on industrial education, publishing articles, pamphlets, and books on the subject, notably *The Next Step in Agricultural Education* (1908) and *Education for Efficiency: A Discussion of Certain Phases of the Problem of Universal Education with Special Reference to Academic Ideals and Methods* (1909; rev. ed., 1914). His excursions to the Rocky Mountains yielded *Vacation on the Trail* (1923). He died at his home in Woodland.

Throughout his life Davenport embraced the dominant ideology of late nineteenth-century America. He was a Republican, a believer in free enterprise, a Congregationalist, a proponent of Anglo-Saxon supremacy, a patriot, and an advocate of traditional moral values. A prolific writer, he expressed himself with great clarity and vividness. His greatest achievement was in the field of agricultural education. Rescuing the College of Agriculture from oblivion, he made it into one of the best of its kind in the nation. "A great educator and scientist," his friend David Kinley wrote when Davenport retired, "his far-sighted vision of the agricultural needs and policy of the State and University have made him one of the outstanding figures in the Agriculture of the State and Nation." Davenport labored tirelessly to make vocational education part of secondary education, and to him the "greatest real victory" of his life was the introduction of courses in agriculture and domestic science into the public high schools of the country.

• The Eugene Davenport Papers, comprising 9.5 cubic feet in the University Archives, University of Illinois at Urbana-Champaign, include correspondence, manuscripts, publications, and a 578-page manuscript autobiography, "What One Life Has Seen," with an appendix titled "Notable People I Have Known" (with an index). Davenport also published autobiographical accounts in "A Son of the Timberlands" (*The Country Gentleman*, nine issues, Sept. 1925 to Sept. 1926) and *Timberland Times* (1950). A manuscript of the latter, with illustrations and a separate revised and enlarged appendix, is in the Rare Book and Special Collections Library, University of Illinois at Urbana-Champaign. Ruth Warrick, in consultation with Anna C. Glover, produced "A Bibliography of Writings Published and Unpublished, by and about Eugene Davenport" (typewritten, June 1954, in the Agricultural Library at the University of Illinois, Urbana-Champaign). Though incomplete, it includes published materials (with an index); comments in the *Prairie Farmer* (1938–1941); unpublished materials; writings about Dean Davenport; and radio and miscellaneous materials.

Sources that treat Davenport's career include Richard G. Moores, *Fields of Rich Toil: The Development of the University of Illinois College of Agriculture* (1970); Deborah Fitzgerald, *The Business of Breeding: Hybrid Corn in Illinois, 1890–1940* (1990); and John C. Hudson, *Making the Corn Belt: A Geographical History of Middle-Western Agriculture* (1994). An obituary is in the *New York Times*, 1 Apr. 1941.

WINTON U. SOLBERG

DAVENPORT, Fanny Lily Gypsy (10 Apr. 1850–26 Sept. 1898), actress, was born in London, England, the daughter of Edward Loomis Davenport, an American actor, and Fanny Elizabeth Vining Gill, a British actress. Fanny moved to Boston in 1854 with her family following her father's six successful years of acting in England. Her schooling was often interrupted by her family's theatrical touring, during which she performed in children's roles.

Davenport's first notable role in New York City was as King Charles II of Spain in *Faint Heart Never Won Fair Lady* on 14 February 1862 at Niblo's Garden Theatre. She continued to act with her father's company, appearing as Mrs. Mildmay in Tom Taylor's *Still Waters Run Deep* at the Tremont Theatre in Boston in 1864. That same year, she became the soubrette in a Louisville, Kentucky, stock company, appearing as Carline in the musical *The Black Crook*, by Charles Barras, the role that launched her career. From Louisville, she went to Louisa Lane Drew's Arch Street Theatre in Philadelphia. There she was seen and hired by John Augustin Daly, who had recently taken over management of the Fifth Avenue Theatre in New York City. Davenport opened successfully in New York City as Lady Gay Spanker in Dion Boucicault's *London Assurance* in 1869, with her father in the role of Sir Harcourt Courtly. During the nine years in which Davenport was leading lady with Daly's company, she performed in revivals, new plays, and Shakespearean plays. She excelled in such roles as Lady Gay Spanker and Lady Teazle in Richard Sheridan's *School for Scandal*.

Davenport startled audiences with her appearances as the tramp, Ruth Tredgett, in William S. Gilbert's *Charity* in 1874 when she concealed her beauty under the rags, dirt, and unkempt hair of the outcast and hopeless Tredgett. She displayed a dramatic presence that led Daly to create the role of Mabel Renfrew for her in *Pique*, one of Daly's great successes, which opened in 1876 and ran for 238 consecutive performances.

Davenport's success encouraged her to form a company and tour for several years, presenting an extensive and varied repertoire of comedies, tragedies, modern French plays, and plays by Shakespeare, including the *Taming of the Shrew*, in which she played Katherine to Edwin Booth's Petruchio.

Davenport married twice; first in 1879 to Edwin H. Price, a supporting actor in her company and later her business manager. They divorced in 1888. Less than a year later, Davenport married the leading man in her company, William Melbourne MacDowell, who had played opposite her for several years. They purchased a summer home in South Duxbury, Massachusetts, naming it "Melbourne Hall."

A significant turning point in Davenport's career occurred in 1883, when she obtained the American rights to *Fedora* by Victorien Sardou, which was being performed in Paris by Sarah Bernhardt. Her production was an immediate success, and for five years Davenport performed *Fedora* almost exclusively in the United States. In 1887 she secured the American rights to Sardou's *La Tosca*, followed by his *Cleopatra*, both of which Bernhardt had also performed. *Gismonda*, which opened in 1894, was the last of the Sardou/Bernhardt productions performed by Davenport, who reportedly paid $25,000 for the script. It was her most elaborate scenic production and remained part of Davenport's repertoire until her death. Davenport expanded her range by acting in these roles, which were more serious and emotionally demanding than many of her earlier roles.

Davenport's reputation rested primarily on her association with the four Sardou heroines she portrayed. "Miss Davenport's presence was well adapted to such roles; powerfully but well built, she added to her grace a marked beauty of feature. . . . she made her roles great through exertion, not through unconscious inspiration. Critics speak of her 'plastic demeanor,' of her well-simulated frenzies. She won by her extensive grasp of situation and movement, not by her quietude and repression" (Moses, p. 253). In 1897, after devoting thirteen years almost exclusively to productions of Sardou's melodramas, Davenport attempted a romantic drama about Joan of Arc, *Soldier of France* by Frances Aymar Mathews. It was an unfortunate choice, as the public could not accept the tall, matronly actress as the youthful Joan, and the production was a failure. She attempted to revive the Sardou plays to salvage the season despite ill health caused by her anxiety and exhaustion. Her last performance was in *Cleopatra* at the Grand Opera House in Chicago in March 1898, after which her illness forced her to end the season. She retired to Melbourne Hall, where she died later that year of a heart ailment and was buried in Forest Hills Cemetery, Boston.

During the early part of her career, Davenport's success relied upon her beauty, personality, and vivaciousness. William Winter described the young Davenport in *Vagrant Memories* (1915) as "a voluptuous beauty, radiant with youth and health, taut and trim of figure, having regular features, a fair complexion, golden hair, sparkling hazel eyes, and a voice as naturally musical and cheery as the fresh, incessant rippling flow of a summer brook" (p. 229). As she matured, her dramatic talent grew. She excelled as the strong, emotional characters Gismonda and La Tosca. According to Jay Benton in *Famous American Actors of To-day* (1896): "The varying phases of Sardou's Tuscan heroine seem almost as if created expressly for her. In the soft, languorous moments, in her cooing petulance, in the rage of jealousy, in her pleading fondness, in her terrible struggles, in the carrying out of her horrible revenge on Scarpia she was always excellent, and oftentimes great" (pp. 117–18). Davenport was an outstanding and successful actress and manager who introduced new plays and new translations to the United States as well as presenting elaborate productions of old plays. A shrewd business woman, she was also an actress not afraid to attempt unusual and demanding roles.

• The Performing Arts Library at Lincoln Center in New York City has Melbourne MacDowell's scrapbook and clippings. "Some Childish Memories," an account by Davenport of her childhood, appeared in *Lippincott's Magazine*, Oct. 1888, p. 42. Biographical material on Fanny Davenport can be found in Montrose Moses, *Famous Actor-Families in America* (1906); Frederick E. McKay and Charles E. L. Wingate, eds., *Famous American Actors of To-day* (1896); Amy Leslie [Lillie W. Brown], *Some Players: Personal Sketches* (1899); and "The Daring Davenports," *Greenbook Magazine*, Mar. 1913. Supplementary material appears in George C. D. Odell, *Annals of the New York Stage* (1939); John Ranken Towse, *Sixty Years of the Theater* (1916); Arthur Hornblow, *A History of the Theatre in America from Its Beginnings to the Present Time*, vol. 2 (1919); and Arthur Row, "Great Moments in Great Acting," *Poet Lore*, May–June 1918. Obituaries are in the *New York Clipper* and the *New York Dramatic Mirror*, 8 Oct. 1898.

SUSAN S. COLE

DAVENPORT, George (1783–4 July 1845), Indian trader and frontier townsite entrepreneur, was born in Lincolnshire, England. Nothing is presently known of his parentage or childhood, although he apparently enjoyed the equivalent of a good common-school education. At age seventeen he was placed with an uncle, a captain of a merchant vessel. In 1804 Davenport's ship visited New York, where he broke his leg and had to be left behind to recuperate.

In 1805 he joined the U.S. Army with the immediate rank of sergeant—evident testimony to his intelligence and maturity. He served with the First Infantry Regiment in the Sabine expedition on the Texas-Louisiana border (1806), the campaign against hostile Potawatomi in Illinois (1812), and the battle of Lundy's Lane in Canada and the siege of Fort Erie (both 1814). At the close of the War of 1812 he was discharged after ten years' honorable and sometimes hazardous service.

Davenport promptly found employment as agent of a government contractor charged with provisioning troops at a soon-to-be-established military post on the upper Mississippi River. In 1816 Davenport accompanied an army detachment in locating Fort Armstrong (present-day Rock Island Arsenal) on an isle above the mouth of the Rock River. In 1818 Davenport resigned his commissary agency to devote himself to various independent enterprises. But he would spend the rest of his life in a house and business complex near the fort. When the U.S. government later declared the entire island a military reservation and ejected other squatters, an act of Congress permitted Davenport to purchase his estate.

Rock Island lay within a riverside concentration of Sauk and Mesquakie (Fox) villages that had been pro-British in the recent war. Davenport's immigrant origins thus made him an immediate favorite with the local Indians, and he became known as "Saganosh" (Englishman) among the tribes on the upper Mississippi. Antoine LeClaire, a half-blood Potawatomi originally employed by Davenport as an interpreter, became a close friend and business partner. At least one of Davenport's sons grew up as a fluent Mesquakie speaker.

In 1817 Davenport entered the fur trade, first with the dangerously anti-American Winnebagos of northern Illinois and Wisconsin, who had not been visited by white traders in some time. This commerce, despite two serious attempts on his life, turned out very profitably. Within a few years Davenport—in direct competition with the powerful American Fur Company—began trading with the more accessible Sauk and Mesquakie. By the mid-1820s he not only operated three trading posts on the Rock River but five along the Mississippi. Four of these stood on the Iowa side, where Davenport and his largely French-Canadian employees bought winter-harvested furs and deerskins as well as quantities of feathers, beeswax, and deer tallow. Davenport's fifth Mississippi post, at the mouth of Illinois' Fever River, collected high-grade lead excavated and smelted by the natives at the Galena and Dubuque diggings. All these products converged on Davenport's Rock Island compound for repackaging and shipment south.

In 1824 Davenport took Russell Farnham as a partner. Two years later the American Fur Company bought them out; they became company employees, Davenport managing the trade north of the Iowa River and Farnham the south. Davenport continued in this capacity until native title to central Iowa had been extinguished. From 1838 to 1840 he served as Indian agent for the Sauk and Mesquakie and he helped negotiate the Iowa land cessions of 1837 and 1842.

By this point Davenport's attention had turned to various townsite speculations in and around what would ultimately become the highly urbanized "quad-cities area" (Rock Island and Moline, Illinois; Davenport and Bettendorf, Iowa). The first of these ventures was a preemption claim near the mouth of the Rock River on which stood the (temporarily) vacated village of the Sauk leader Black Hawk. When the Sauk reoccupied the village, Davenport urged them to join their brethren in Iowa and, during an audience with Andrew Jackson, unsuccessfully recommended that the president simply pay the recalcitrants to move. Davenport always thought that had his advice been taken, the resulting Black Hawk War (1832) would have been avoided. But its occurrence elevated Davenport to acting quartermaster general (organizing supplies for the troops) of Illinois volunteers with the rank of colonel, a title he retained for the rest of his life.

After the war Davenport and various other investors laid out the adjacent communities of Rock Island, Davenport (named for himself), LeClaire, and Port Byron. He subsequently joined Antoine LeClaire in platting Davenport's first and second residential additions. In the early 1840s he financed an addition to Moline. Davenport's ancillary interests also profited. He and LeClaire owned Davenport's first hotel, and in 1838 they established themselves as forwarding and commission merchants with the area's largest store. After steamboats entered the upper Mississippi, Davenport kept a wood yard from which their captains purchased fuel. A role in local politics helped enhance his entrepreneurial standing. When Rock Island County, Illinois, was organized, he served as one of its charter commissioners.

Nineteenth-century sources are understandably circumspect about Davenport's family life. He married Margaret Bowling Lewis, a widow with two children, in 1815. But his own two sons were born to his stepdaughter, Susan M. Lewis, and a daughter to one Catharine Prouit.

By the 1840s Davenport was wealthy. For many years his Greek revival mansion is said to have been the most elegant riverside residence above St. Louis. It was rumored that he kept large sums about the place, and in 1845 intruders wounded him so severely that he perished from loss of blood. A bounty hunter tracked down his murderers, three of whom were hanged.

Davenport's contemporary (and fellow immigrant) John Jacob Astor offers the model by which Indian-trade profits were most spectacularly translated into riches from urban real estate. In comparison, Davenport was a small operator. But he more aptly than Astor, perhaps, illustrates a classic entrepreneurial metamorphosis—western soldier into Indian trader into land speculator—that was realized, in whole or in part, by numberless nineteenth-century frontiersmen from the colonial Atlantic seaboard to the West Coast.

• Manuscript records of Colonel Davenport's activities as an Indian trader are in the microfilmed Davenport Family Collection, 1819–1923, State Historical Society of Iowa, Des Moines. The basic biographical account is Franc B. Wilkie, *Davenport Past and Present* (1858). For additional details, see especially William J. Petersen, ed., *The Annals of Iowa: Volume One—1863* (1964); Charles Negus, "The Early History of Iowa," *Annals of Iowa* 8 (1870): 297–309; D. W. Flagler, *A History of the Rock Island Arsenal* (1877); and William A. Meese, *Early Rock Island* (1905). Brief references to Davenport's private life appear in August P. Richter, *Geschichte der Stadt Davenport und des County Scott* (1917), and Gayle A. McCoy, *A Clearing in the Forest: The Story of Colonel George Davenport* (1980). For a report by the detective who brought Davenport's killers to justice, see Edward Bonney, *Banditti of the Prairies* (1850).

ROBERT R. DYKSTRA

DAVENPORT, Herbert Joseph (10 Aug. 1861–16 June 1931), economist, was born in Wilmington, Vermont, the son of Charles N. Davenport, a lawyer, and Louise Haynes. Both parents came from established New England families. Davenport invested his inheritance in real estate in South Dakota while in his early twenties but lost his fortune in the panic of 1893. He studied at the University of South Dakota (Ph.B., 1884), Harvard Law School (1884–1886), the University of Leipzig (1890), the École des Sciences Politiques of Paris (1890–1891), and the University of Chicago (Ph.D., 1898). Davenport's wide-ranging experience and his studies in many fields at several universities contributed to his eclecticism and nondoctrinaire qualities as well as to his relatively nonideological realism.

Davenport worked from 1899 to 1902 as a high school principal in Lincoln, Nebraska. He commenced a university career at the age of forty-one in the department of economics at the University of Chicago, where he taught from 1902 to 1908. Afterward he taught at the University of Missouri, where he was also head of the department from 1908 to 1914 and dean of the School of Commerce from 1914 to 1916, and finally at Cornell University from 1916 to 1929. In 1911 he married Harriet Crandall; they had two children. He served as president of the American Economic Association in 1920.

Intellectually, Davenport was one of the leading theorists of his period despite his iconoclasm. His work was suffused with tensions. He stressed a descriptive economics but held strong policy views. He advocated a realistic economics but emphasized careful definition and rigorous, coherent theorizing. He sought to exclude normative and psychological elements from economic theory, yet his specific, and sometimes narrow, definitions could be myopic and inward-turning. He searched for real causes of economic phenomena but incorporated both his own and imagined business conceptions and distinctions. By attempting to cleanse Austrian and Marshallian neoclassicism of their moralist and social functionalist features, thereby making them both more accessible and more acceptable, he contributed to the establishment of neoclassicist hegemony in the twentieth century. He contributed to the reformulation of microeconomics from an absolutist value theory to a relativist price theory that in others' hands became absolutist in its hold on the economic imagination as the exclusive focus of theory. Davenport was personally close to the heterodox Thorstein Veblen, but it seems that either he could not comprehend Veblen's emphasis on the importance of institutions for understanding the economic system or he felt that economics need not be so widely defined. While joining with Veblen in pursuit of a nonteleological, matter-of-fact economics, Davenport pursued the study of dynamics only so far, considerably short of the evolutionary program affirmed by Veblen.

Davenport stressed the economy as a process in which economic agents sought wealth and engaged in activities regulated by the price-cost mechanism and in which entrepreneurial opportunity-cost–based adjustments were central. Such a conception of economics excluded both the moralist and social functionalist interpretations, which he believed were rampant in the economics of his time. Davenport's conception emphasized both the simple mechanics of price (demand and supply without metaphysical embellishments)—and correlatively a theory of distribution based on price theory—and what he considered to be the realities of business practice. This approach enabled him to focus on certain features of capitalist economic organization and practice that, while not entirely novel, had hitherto not been either so central or so explicit: entrepreneurial calculations in a context of price formation, the importance of assuming competition, the capitalization element in the theory of interest, the interest rate as a monetary phenomenon, the multiple expansion and contraction of money, the role of reservation prices, the importance of unemployment, and so on. His inclusion of illegal activity, lobbying, litigation, and similar activities not usually considered within the ambit of economic theory somewhat represented a forerunner of modern public choice and rent-seeking theories. His work was an interesting amalgam of the ideas of J. Laurence Laughlin, Thorstein Veblen, Irving Fisher, and even the much-criticized Alfred Marshall and Henry George (1839–1897).

Davenport emphasized the practice of economics from the standpoint of price in a society dominated by the private, acquisitive point of view. He rejected the idea that economic theory should be the monopoly of reactionaries and a saccharine and smug, if subtle, defense of privilege, in favor of both a more positivist discipline and a more pluralistic society. Nevertheless, his conception of economics—coupled as it was with the neoclassicist quest for solutions that are determinate and in equilibrium as well as optimal, ostensibly in the search for scientific rigor—was later to result in a corpus of theory—mainstream neoclassical microeconomics—that could readily be used to affirm whatever is as what ought to be, as the optimal outcome. The limited radicalism of Davenport, for whom private gain did not necessarily equate with social welfare, and who could criticize business practice with the knowledge of both a businessman and a lawyer as well as an economist, later seemed to become an intrinsically conservative doctrine.

Frank Albert Fetter, in a review of Davenport's *Economics of Enterprise* (1913) in the June 1914 issue of the *Journal of Political Economy*, applauded Davenport's emphasis on the idea that "valuations in terms of private capital do not necessarily reflect production in a social sense," but Fetter also thought that Davenport would have scrapped "the whole existing structure of theoretical economics" more ruthlessly than Karl Marx. In 1927, however, in an essay on the present state of economic theory in the United States published in a Festschrift for Friedrich von Wieser, Fetter referred to Davenport's criticism of hedonistic psychology (and its ethical implications) as "mild." These disparate views illustrate the idea that valuative and comparative judgments often reflect more on a perspective than on the object of judgment itself.

Davenport did not have the stature of such economists as Irving Fisher, Frank W. Taussig, Edwin R. A. Seligman, or Fetter; nor did he establish a distinctive school. But he was a member of a loosely formed American psychological school whose members included Fisher, John Maurice Clark, and Fetter; and among those whom he influenced were Paul Homan and Morris Copeland. He died in New York City.

• Davenport was the author of a number of important and influential treatises in economic theory. These include, in ad-

dition to *Economics of Enterprise*, *Outlines of Economic Theory* (1896), published prior to his receiving the doctorate, and *Value and Distribution* (1908). *The Economics of Alfred Marshall* was published posthumously in 1935. A penetrating analysis of Davenport's ideas is presented in Joseph Dorfman, *The Economic Mind in American Civilization*, vol. 3 (1949), pp. 375–90. Frank Albert Fetter's essay, "Present State of Economic Theory in the United States of America," has been republished in *Research in the History of Economic Thought and Methodology*, archival supp., vol. 2 (1991), pp. 9–45. Informative obituary articles include those by Morris A. Copeland in the *Economic Journal* 41 (1931): 496–500, and by Paul T. Homan in the *American Economic Review* 21 (1931): 696–700.

WARREN J. SAMUELS

DAVENPORT, Ira Erastus (17 Sept. 1839–8 July 1911), and **William Henry Harrison Davenport** (1 Feb. 1841–1 July 1877), mediums and stage magicians, were born in Buffalo, New York, the sons of Ira Davenport, a police officer, and Virtue Honeysett. Following publicity about the Fox sisters and their spirit "rappings" of 1848, the two Davenport boys, encouraged by their parents, began experimenting with similar activities. They found that, while tied with heavy knots, they could cause musical instruments hung from the ceiling near them to produce sounds, like the seeming spirit trumpets and bells of the seance room. Their childhood presentations of such feats, reportedly under the direction of the spirit John King familiar to early Spiritualism, attracted attention in Buffalo. As their reputation spread, they were taken to New York City in 1855. Although their performances produced much comment, they were widely dismissed as the results of sleight of hand. Nonetheless, the Davenports improved their work and became very popular as performers, whether regarded as mediums or as entertainers. Their most famous act involved the use of a large cabinet or boxlike structure that had three doors across the front, which when open, fully exposed the interior. The cabinet had no inner partitions. Before a performance the cabinet would be carefully inspected by a local committee. Then the two brothers, seated on facing benches in the two outermost sections of the cabinet, would be tightly and elaborately bound with ropes by volunteers from the audience. Musical instruments would be placed on a bench in the middle section, apparently out of reach. Then the doors would be closed. Almost instantly in the midsection of the cabinet spirit hands would appear from behind a window in the door, and various musical instruments would begin to play, apparently without human agency. At the conclusion the two end doors would be opened to show the brothers still tied as before. At another stage of the performance, either before or after the music, the doors would be briefly closed. Then the brothers would walk out, one at a time, unbound; after the doors were closed briefly once more, they would open to show the brothers tied up again.

The cabinet performance, repeated countless times before large audiences, excited much controversy. In 1864 the brothers embarked on a four-year tour of Europe, accompanied during the first year by J. B. Ferguson, a southern preacher who lectured in conjunction with the performances and who was a strong believer in their spiritual nature. Of medium height, quite similar in appearance, handsome and bearded, the Davenport brothers generally made a good impression and left even the most sophisticated observers in their audiences puzzled and astounded. Only on a very few occasions were performances considered unsatisfactory. Early in their career, their powers largely failed them before an investigative committee of Harvard professors sponsored by the *Boston Courier*. In England in 1865, rowdy and obviously skeptical crowds stormed on stage in Liverpool, Huddersfield, and Leeds, causing the brothers to cancel the remainder of their British engagements.

After their return from Europe the brothers toured the United States until 1874, when they began a world tour. It ended with William's sudden death in Sydney, Australia. Afterward Ira retired to a farm in Mayville, New York, where he died. He was survived by three children. Ira had married Augusta Green in February 1862. She soon died, and in 1866, during the tour of Europe, he had married Louise Toulet in Paris. The following year, according to his father, William had married Matilda May in Königsberg, but according to magician Harry Houdini, who knew Ira in later years, the marriage was to Adah Isaacs Menken in Paris.

The Davenport brothers rarely publicly attributed the phenomena in their shows to supernatural agency; neither did they deny such an explanation, being content to let observers draw their own conclusions. Nonetheless their shows did much to promote the burgeoning Spiritualist movement, as many Spiritualists clearly saw them as demonstrations of the new forces they believed were emerging in the world. On the other hand, the repertoire of the modern professional magician also owes much to the brothers' mastery of the cabinet and the remarkable escape, and the Davenports undoubtedly led some observers to conclude that much alleged Spiritualist phenomena could be replicated by extremely skillful illusionists. Harry Houdini, the great escape artist and prominent skeptic of mediumship, broadly hinted in *A Magician among the Spirits* (1924) that toward the end of his life Ira had acknowledged to him that he had used trickery, but there is no other evidence of such a confession.

• Accessible material on the Davenports is in Slater Brown, *The Heyday of Spiritualism* (1970), and Arthur Conan Doyle, *A History of Spiritualism* (1926). *The Davenport Brothers* (1869), by Ira Davenport, their father, is interesting but not always reliable. Other important contemporary sources are T. L. Nichols, *A Biography of the Brothers Davenport* (1864) and *Supramundane Facts in the Life of Rev. J. B. Ferguson* (1865); and P. B. Randolph, *The Davenport Brothers* (1869). The Harvard investigation is reported in a pamphlet prepared by George Lunt, *Spiritualism Shown as It Is! Boston Courier Report . . .* (1859).

ROBERT S. ELLWOOD

DAVENPORT, James (1716–1757), revivalist and Presbyterian minister, was born in Stamford, Connecticut, the son of the Reverend John Davenport, a Congregationalist minister, and Elizabeth Morris Maltby. He graduated in 1732 from Yale College, where he was regarded as a prodigy. He was licensed to preach on 8 October 1735 and ordained to the ministry of the Congregational Church at Southold, Long Island, in 1738.

Two years later Davenport fell under the influence of George Whitefield, Gilbert Tennent, and the revivalist spirit. Believing himself called to be an itinerant evangelist, he addressed his congregation on the subject for twenty-four hours, resulting in his confinement to his room for several days. He began to journey through New England with Whitefield, who said of him "that he never knew one keep so close a walk with God." Davenport soon undertook evangelistic tours on his own, beginning with a small effort in Easthampton, followed by a greater one on the New England coast between Stonington and New Haven. His work was distinguished by unusual behavior. He claimed to be able to distinguish elect persons, whom he greeted as brethren, from the reprobate, whom he termed neighbors. He sang in the streets on the way to worship and preached sermons filled with emotional outbursts and denunciations of ministers and others who opposed his enthusiasm. The climax of the tour came in New Haven, where he incited the students at Yale against Thomas Clap, the rector of the college, and James Noyes, minister of New Haven's First Church. His efforts proved so disruptive that, in early 1742, the Connecticut General Assembly passed an "Act for Regulating Abuses and Correcting Disorders in Ecclesiastical Affairs," which stipulated that itinerant preachers could be treated as vagrants. Shortly afterward Stratford lodged a complaint against him. Davenport was arrested and brought to Hartford for trial, where he was judged not fully sane and deported under guard to Long Island.

Within a month he resumed his evangelistic travels, this time to Boston, where the ministers had already voted to deny him the use of their churches. Davenport took to the streets, violently denouncing the ministers as unconverted and reprobate. Arrested again, he was judged insane and removed to Long Island. The Southold church refused to dismiss Davenport but voted to censure him, not for enthusiasm, but for abandoning his pastoral responsibilities to the church. In March 1743 he journeyed to New London to lead a group of Separate Congregationalists in establishing a new church. He insisted that they renounce worldliness by burning wigs, fancy clothes and jewelry, and the books of religious leaders with whom he disagreed. His list of books to be burned included works by many of the most revered names among Puritans, including Sewell, Colman, and Increase Mather. The book burning cost him a great deal of his remaining public support.

After his return to Southold, Davenport suffered dismissal from his church, as well as a serious illness.

These personal setbacks, along with the earnest entreaties of two revivalist ministers, Eleazar Wheelock and Solomon Williams, were enough to convince him to desist. In July 1744 he published *Confessions and Retractions*, in which he repented of his excesses and confessed to having been led by a "false spirit." His revivalist career was over.

Davenport spent the remaining years of his life serving a series of New Side Presbyterian churches in New Jersey. His gradual rehabilitation among these moderate presbyterians led to his election as moderator of the New Side Synod in 1754. Controversial to the end, Davenport found himself fighting a petition for removal from his pulpit in the Presbyterian Church in Freehold, New Jersey, at the time of his death in Hopewell, New Jersey.

Davenport's revivalist career, marked by excess, posed a crisis for the Awakening in New England. His behavior became the example for those who feared the dangers of enthusiasm. Supporters of the revival took pains to separate themselves from him, while detractors of the movement insisted that he represented the logical consequence of revivalism. Leaders on both sides blamed him for the growing divisions among the churches in New England.

• The life and work of James Davenport are prominent in treatments of the Great Awakening in New England. Of particular value are Richard L. Bushman, ed., *The Great Awakening: Documents on the Revival of Religion, 1740–1745* (1970), and Alan Heimert and Perry Miller, eds., *The Great Awakening: Documents Illustrating the Crisis and Its Consequences* (1967). Harry S. Stout and Peter Onuf provide a more extended treatment in "James Davenport and the Great Awakening in New London," *Journal of American History* 70 (1983): 556–78. Early accounts of Davenport's life provide a glimpse of his reputation among Congregationalists and Presbyterians. An especially interesting analysis can be found in Joseph Tracy, *The Great Awakening: A History of the Revival of Religion in the Time of Edwards and Whitefield* (1841).

MICHAEL R. McCOY

DAVENPORT, John (Apr. 1597–15 Mar. 1670), Congregational Puritan clergyman, was born in Coventry, Warwickshire, England, the son of Henry Davenport, a merchant in that town, and Winifred Barneby. He matriculated at Merton College, Oxford, in 1613, having shortly before that time experienced a religious conversion. After two years he transferred to Magdalen, Oxford, but left the university before obtaining his degree in order to accept a chaplaincy at Hilton Castle, Durham. In 1619 he became curate at St. Lawrence Jewry in the city of London, where he became acquainted with the tenets of Puritanism. He earned a reputation as an inspiring preacher and was elected vicar of the London parish of St. Stephen's, Coleman Street, in 1624. The influence of prominent Puritan nobility was needed to persuade the bishop of London to approve the choice of Davenport, which was obtained because at this point he conformed to the liturgical practices of the church, believing that differences over such matters must be subordinated to the need

for a united Calvinist front against Catholicism and Arminianism. In 1625 he was awarded both the B.D. and M.A. degrees by Magdalen, Oxford. In that same year he garnered favorable notice for his efforts to minister to his congregation during a severe outbreak of the plague.

The spread of Anticalvinism in the church under Archbishop William Laud drove Davenport and other Puritans toward nonconformity, while the foreign policy of Charles I made them critics of the government as well. In 1625 Davenport helped organize the Feofees for the Purchase of Impropriations, a corporation that sought to spread Puritan influence by purchasing church livings and awarding them to zealous preachers. Together with his fellow trustees, Davenport was called before the Court of High Commission, and the enterprise was quashed. In 1627 he joined with Richard Sibbes, William Gouge, and Thomas Taylor in soliciting funds for the relief of Protestant refugees from the Thirty Years' War. In *A Royal Edict for Military Exercises* (1629), a sermon preached before the London Artillery Company, he urged English support for the cause of international Protestantism, which was threatened by the conflict on the Continent. Anticipating that he would eventually be silenced for his views, Davenport left England for the Netherlands in 1633.

The congregation of the English church in Amsterdam called him to assist the Reverend John Paget, but the call was blocked by Paget. In discussions and correspondence with John Cotton, Thomas Goodwin, and Thomas Hooker, Davenport had been moving toward advocacy of congregational powers, and the dispute with Paget revealed some of the tensions that would later result in the division of Puritans into Congregationalists and Presbyterians. Davenport's *Church Government and Church-Covenant Discussed* (1643) and *The Power of the Congregational Churches Asserted and Vindicated* (1672) contain statements of his position and his responses to Paget that circulated in manuscript in the 1630s. He briefly ministered to unofficial congregations in Amsterdam and Rotterdam but then secretly returned to England in 1636 to prepare to migrate to America.

Together with Theophilus Eaton, who would become the first governor of New Haven Colony in 1643, and other members of his former parish of St. Stephens, Davenport arrived in Boston, Massachusetts, in June 1637. His prominence in the English Puritan movement guaranteed him an important role in the colonies. He participated in the Cambridge Synod, the examination of the Antinomian Anne Hutchinson, and advised in the organization of Harvard College. In 1638 he founded the town and colony of Quinnipiac, later renamed New Haven, where Eaton and his supporters hoped to find commercial opportunities not available in Boston. The organization of New Haven reflected Davenport's belief in congregations rigorously restricted to the elect and in civil affairs strongly controlled by the godly.

Davenport closely followed the course of the Puritan Revolution in England. He was invited to sit in the

English Westminster Assembly, convened in 1643 to propose a reform of the national church, but chose to remain in New England and offer advice from afar. He was the spokesman for the colonial clergy in *An Answer of the Elders of Severall Churches in New England* (1643), which responded to queries from English brethren. He also authored a number of other tracts on church polity and saving faith that were published in England during the 1640s and 1650s. In all these efforts Davenport sought to promote Congregationalism and defend it against Presbyterian attacks from the right and sectarian criticism on the left.

Davenport supported New Haven's cooperation with Connecticut in seeking military assistance from the Protectorate in an effort to dislodge the Dutch from New Netherlands in 1654, but the expedition was canceled with the end of the first Anglo-Dutch War that spring. When the Cromwellian regime collapsed he was instrumental in providing refuge in the colonies for the proscribed regicides Edward Whalley and William Goffe. *The Saints Anchor-Hold, in All Storms and Tempests* (1661) was a series of sermons preached to the New Haven faithful urging them to maintain faith in their mission despite the restoration of the Stuart monarchy in England.

Davenport himself continued to cling tenaciously to the model of the New England Way created by his generation of founders. He unsuccessfully opposed the merger of New Haven into the more liberal Connecticut Colony in 1662. He was one of the foremost opponents of the liberalization of church membership known as the Half-Way Covenant. Upon the death of John Wilson (1591–1667), the conservative majority of the First Church of Boston invited Davenport to assume the vacant pastorship of that distinguished congregation. His efforts to gain release from the New Haven church led to acrimonious charges of deception, and his assumption of the Boston pastorate led to a split in that congregation. The formation of the Third (Old South) Church by the dissidents produced a major religious and political controversy in Massachusetts, with Davenport assuming a prominent role as defender of orthodoxy and tradition. His election sermon to the Massachusetts General Court in 1669 was a partisan call to return to the practices of the founders.

He had married Elizabeth Wooley, about whom little is known, in England prior to 1619. Their only child, John, Jr., was born and baptized on 15 April 1635 at The Hague, where Davenport had gone following his dispute with Paget in Amsterdam. He died of a paralytic stroke in Boston.

• Davenport manuscripts are in the Yale University Library. In addition to his publications listed above, Davenport was the author of *A Protestation . . . upon Occasion of a Pamphlet Entitled "A Just Complaint"* (1635), *The Profession of Faith of . . . Mr J D* (1642), *Church Government and Church Covenant Discussed* (1644), *The Knowledge of Christ Indispensably Required of All Men That Would Be Saved* (1653), *Another Essay for Investigation of the Truth* (1663), and *God's Call to His People to Turn unto Him* (1669). His correspondence has been published in Isabel M. Calder, *Letters of John Davenport, Pu-*

ritan Divine (1937); the introduction contains substantial biographical information, as does Calder, *The New Haven Colony* (1934; repr. 1962).

FRANCIS J. BREMER

DAVENPORT, Thomas (9 July 1802–6 July 1851), blacksmith and inventor, was born near Williamstown, Vermont, the son of Daniel Davenport and Hannah Rice, farmers. Eighth in a family of eleven children, Davenport had little formal schooling. The premature death of his father during the winter of 1812 from "spotted fever" left the family to fend for itself. At age fourteen Davenport was apprenticed to a Williamstown blacksmith. Under the terms of his indenture, he was allowed to attend school for six weeks every winter and was given room and board. Davenport completed his apprenticeship at the age of twenty-one and set up a smithy in Brandon, Vermont. He married Emily Goss, the daughter of a prosperous farmer, in 1827; they had two sons.

Around 1830, Davenport moved his shop to the nearby hamlet of Forestdale, Vermont. In 1833 he became aware of a powerful electromagnet, designed by American physicist Joseph Henry, that was used to separate ore at the Penfield and Hammond Iron Works in Crown Point, New York. Deeply impressed by the magnet's professed ability to "lift a common blacksmith's anvil," he set out to purchase one for his own experimentation. After a number of misadventures, Davenport, with the assistance of his brother Oliver, a peddler and tinkerer, succeeded in buying an electromagnet after all of the goods on Oliver's peddling cart had been auctioned off and his brother's horse traded for a poorer one. This horseshoe-shaped magnet, with arms about twelve inches long and about six inches apart, cost $75, a formidable sum for a blacksmith.

That night Thomas Davenport set to work inspecting his new purchase. His wife, Emily, recorded all of the details as he carefully deconstructed the electromagnet. After learning how the device was constructed, Davenport made another of soft iron, larger than the first. Davenport and his equally enthusiastic wife wound on the alternating layers of wire and of insulating silk, obtained from Emily's wedding gown, which she had torn into strips. This new electromagnet proved to be even stronger than the one they had purchased. Describing his thoughts at this juncture, Davenport wrote, "Like a flash of lightning the thought occurred to me that here was available power . . . ere long, this mysterious and invisible power will supersede steam."

By the summer of 1834 Davenport's experiments with electromagnets resulted in the development of a small electric "engine," or motor, built with the assistance of Orange Smalley, another Forestdale blacksmith who shared many of Davenport's scientific interests. The motor consisted of four electromagnets, two on opposite sides of a revolving disk, and two stationary ones, placed near the periphery of the revolving wheel. All four electromagnets were connected through a commutator to an electric battery. By July 1834 Davenport had succeeded in making his "engine" revolve at about thirty revolutions per minute. British scientist Michael Faraday's experiments in creating "electrical rotations" (1821), Joseph Henry's "philosophical toy" (1831), and William Sturgeon's "magnetic engines" (1832) had anticipated Davenport's work. Davenport's machine, with its spinning armature, however, embodied the same principles that would underlie direct current motors much later in the nineteenth century.

In December 1834 Davenport went with his invention to Middlebury College, hoping to obtain a professional opinion about its merit. A Professor Turner examined the motor and declared it "nothing less than a new motive power, an electro-magnetic engine." A second professor praised it as one of the greatest inventions of the nineteenth century. Davenport was told to have his invention patented immediately, and the professors offered to assist Davenport in preparing his papers for the patent application. With badly needed financial assistance provided by his friends, Davenport went to Washington, D.C., in 1835 to patent his motor. During the journey, he stopped to show his machine to prominent individuals at the Rensselaer Institute in Troy, New York; Princeton University; and the University of Pennsylvania in Philadelphia. When he reached the U.S. Patent Office in Washington, Davenport no longer had sufficient funds to pay for the patent application. In absolute discouragement, he returned to Forestdale.

Professor Amos Eaton, who had earlier seen Davenport's machine displayed at the Rensselaer Institute, convinced Davenport to demonstrate his motor at Troy on 14 October 1835. The demonstration had a successful outcome, enabling Davenport to obtain some additional financial assistance. He spent 1836 constructing and exhibiting miniature electrical machines in the hope of raising enough funds to patent his motor and go into manufacturing. One of Davenport's new creations was a circular electric railway, thirty-six inches in diameter, with the "electro-magnetic engine" mounted on the train itself. This was the predecessor of not only the toy electric train, but also the electric streetcar. With the money raised by this venture, Davenport was finally able to apply for a patent. However, Davenport's patent application and model were destroyed in the Patent Office fire of 15 December 1836. He immediately submitted a second application and model. On 25 February 1837 Davenport was issued Patent No. 132, for "Improvement in Propelling Machinery by Magnetism and Electro Magnetism."

Until 1843 Davenport attempted unsuccessfully to establish a market for his inventions. He set up a combination workshop and laboratory in New York City, where he worked to expand on his discoveries. Using printing presses run by battery-powered motors, he published the *Electro-Magnet and Mechanics Intelligencer* and *The Electro-Magnet*, said to be the world's first journals dealing with electrical matters. Unfortunately, after only a few issues, the undertaking failed, largely because of a lack of an economical, dependable source of electric power. With success eluding him at every turn, Davenport failed physically and returned to Brandon, Vermont, in about 1843. Retiring to a small farm near Salisbury, Vermont, he performed successful experiments with an electromagnetic player piano three years later. He died in Salisbury.

• Davenport's unfinished personal memoirs, which reveal the human side of the inventor, are in the archives of the Vermont Historical Society. Walter Rice Davenport, *Biography of Thomas Davenport: The "Brandon Blacksmith", Inventor of the Electric Motor* (1929), written by Davenport's nephew, often digresses into sentimental and nostalgic musings. Waldemar Kaempffert, *A Popular History of American Invention* (1924), and Franklin Leonard Pope, "The Inventors of the Electric Motor," *Electrical Engineer* (7 Jan. 1891–4 Feb. 1891), both provide essential information. Thomas Commerford Martin, *An Appreciation of Thomas Davenport* (1910), was written on the occasion of the Ninth Annual Meeting of the Vermont Electrical Association with the New England section of the National Electric Light Association on 28 Sept. 1910. For a good understanding of the technological context of Davenport's motor, refer to Harold Sharlin's chapter on "Applications of Electricity," in vol. 1 of *Technology in Western Civilization* (1967), ed. Melvin Kranzberg and Carroll W. Pursell, Jr.

DANIEL MARTIN DUMYCH

DAVEZAC, Auguste Genevieve Valentin (May 1780–15 Feb. 1851), politician and diplomat, was born in Aux Cayes, Saint-Domingue (now Haiti), the son of Jean Pierre Valentin Joseph D'Avezac, a wealthy planter, and Marie Rose Valentine D'Avezac de Castera. Sent to France by his father for education at the military college of La Flèche, he thus escaped the violence of revolution and slave insurrection that wracked his island home in the late 1790s. Early in the nineteenth century he migrated to Virginia, where he engaged briefly in the practice of medicine. He married Margaret Andrews of Accomac County in 1804, before moving on to New Orleans to join his mother and other family members, who had settled there after flight from Saint-Domingue. The number of his children is unknown. The marriage of his sister Louise to Edward Livingston in 1805 provided the relationship that largely determined the course of his public life thereafter. As was the custom in Louisiana at the time, he conformed to the usages of his new national attachment by abandoning the aristocratic form of his patronymic in favor of the republican "Davezac."

In the few months since his arrival in Louisiana from New York in 1804, Livingston had already established himself as one of the community's leading attorneys and political figures. He quickly won position as a principal protagonist of the Gallic community in New Orleans and in the process emerged as a major opponent of the bumbling governor, William C. C. Claiborne. Davezac became Livingston's chief lieutenant in all these enterprises, serving as his right-hand man not only in political activities but in the extensive land speculations that the New Yorker had undertaken in an attempt to rebuild his fortunes. At the same time, he studied law under Livingston's expert tutelage and won admission to the Louisiana bar in the early 1800s.

The British invasion of Louisiana in 1814 provided another opportunity for Davezac to establish claims on later political advancement. Livingston's leadership in bringing Andrew Jackson to New Orleans to defend the city gave him particular influence with the general, which he used to win Davezac appointment as personal aide to the commander with the rank of major, a title by which he would be known through the remainder of his life. During the New Orleans campaign Davezac's services proved invaluable to Jackson, not only as interpreter but also as an unofficial liaison between the general and the Gallic community, which was always suspect in the mind of the Tennessean. With his usual loyalty to those who served him faithfully, Jackson in the years ahead often gave testimony to Davezac's bravery and contributions to victory during the New Orleans campaign.

Livingston's election to Congress in 1822 removed him from New Orleans to Washington, leaving Davezac to act as his patron's principal agent in Louisiana. This involved him deeply in Livingston's land speculations in what became known as the Bastrop claims (dating back to the Spanish colonial period) in the northern part of the state and in the notorious complexities of the New Yorker's classic legal battles over title to the batture before New Orleans, the strip of valuable land built up by sediment from the Mississippi River in front of the city levees. Davezac also became prominent in his own right as a successful criminal defense attorney, famed for the theatrics of his courtroom performance and the florid style of his oratory. The same flamboyance characterized other aspects of his life as well; his open camaraderie with the pirate brothers Jean and Pierre Laffite and his frequent flirtation with debtors prison became regular grist for the gossip mills of the city. In the mid- and late 1820s he served briefly as a member of the state legislature and in the city council of New Orleans, where he figured as a fiery promoter of creole interests in opposition to those of the newer elements in the community. His adamant bias in favor of the original area of the city (now known as the French Quarter) contributed in large measure to disaffection in the "American" section of New Orleans, which led to division of the corporation into three independent municipalities in 1836.

When Jackson became president in 1829 and Livingston U.S. senator from Louisiana, Davezac won appointment as secretary of the American legation at The Hague in August of that year, a post that he held until named chargé d'affaires to the Netherlands in October 1831, a few months after Livingston's appointment as secretary of state. His tenure in that position lasted until July 1839, during which time he also undertook a mission to the Kingdom of the Two Sicilies, 1833–1834, in an unsuccessful attempt to negotiate a treaty of general commerce. On his return from Europe in 1839 he and his family relocated to New York, where Livingston had moved in 1835.

Davezac's diplomatic service proved essentially unsatisfactory and in many ways highly questionable, marked by failure to conform responsibly to instructions and eventually by extensive irregularity in his financial accounts. But his continued place in the affections of Jackson, his regular flow of correspondence to Martin Van Buren and James K. Polk, and his loyal service to the Democratic party as a member of Tammany Hall after 1839 and of the New York state legislature from 1843 to 1845, led Polk to appoint him in April 1845 to his old post as chargé d'affaires in the Netherlands. He served there until September 1850 and died in New York City shortly after his return from this last assignment.

• The largest body of Davezac correspondence is in the Edward Livingston Manuscript Collection at Princeton University, but many of his letters are also to be found in the papers of Andrew Jackson, Martin Van Buren, and James K. Polk in the Library of Congress. His only literary work is the unsigned eulogistic "Fragments of Unpublished Reminiscences of Edward Livingston," *United States Magazine and Democratic Review* 8 (1840): 366–84, written at the time of an attack on Livingston's memory by Henry Clay during the presidential campaign of that year. Davezac figures as well in Charles Havens Hunt, *The Life of Edward Livingston* (1864), and Louise L. Hunt, *Memoire of Mrs. Edward Livingston* (1886). Details of his difficulty in clearing accounts with the Department of State may be found in Records of the Fifth Auditor of the Treasury, Letterbook 3, RG 217, National Archives, and in letters to him from Secretary of State John Forsyth in 1836 and 1838 in the Livingston manuscripts.

JOSEPH G. TREGLE, JR.

DAVID, John Baptist Mary (4 June 1761–12 July 1841), Catholic bishop, writer, and founder of the Sisters of Charity of Nazareth, was born at Couëron in Brittany, France, the son of Jean David and Jeanne Audrain of prosperous peasant stock. Educated at the College of the Oratorians and Grand Seminary of Nantes and the Seminary of St. Sulpice in Paris, he entered in 1783 the Society of St. Sulpice, or Sulpicians, a body founded to conduct seminaries. On 24 September 1785 he was ordained a priest by the archbishop of Paris. He taught at the Minor Seminary of Angers from 1785 until 1790, when the French Revolution induced the Sulpicians to volunteer their services to the newly consecrated bishop of Baltimore, John Carroll.

On 28 March 1792 David arrived in Baltimore, Maryland, with the second band of Sulpicians chosen to complete the establishment of St. Mary's Seminary, begun in 1791, the first Catholic seminary in the United States. For his first eight years, however, David served as a missionary in southern Maryland, where he introduced retreats. He then spent two years at Georgetown College as a teacher of philosophy before he was called to St. Mary's Seminary to teach theology. There he also served as acting president of St. Mary's College (1810–1811) and ecclesiastical superior of the Sisters of Charity of Emmitsburg, Maryland (1809–1811). In the latter position he was often at odds with the mother superior, Elizabeth Seton, over matters of authority and organization.

David was persuaded by his friend Benedict Joseph Flaget, bishop-elect of Bardstown, Kentucky, to accompany him to his new diocese to open a seminary. The first Catholic seminary west of the Appalachians was lodged originally at St. Thomas Farm near Bardstown in 1811. The seminary was later relocated next to the new cathedral, completed in 1819. David, as director, teacher, and counselor, trained a remarkable body of missionary priests, including several future bishops. In December 1812 he also founded the Sisters of Charity of Nazareth. Recognizing the talents of the young Catherine Spalding, who was elected first superior by the sisters themselves, he soon left to her the day-to-day administrative affairs of the sisterhood but continued as ecclesiastical director.

Bishop Flaget, in an attempt to prevent David's being chosen bishop of another see, asked Rome to name him his coadjutor with right of succession. Appointed a bishop on 4 July 1817, David was raised to the episcopacy by Flaget in the cathedral of Bardstown on 15 August 1819. Townspeople, however, continued to call him "Father David." As coadjutor David proved a poor choice. Retiring, modest, ascetic, Flaget's senior by two years, he was increasingly beset by ill health and a paralyzing fear of responsibility. Though he occasionally served as a missionary to nearby congregations, the portly prelate spent most of his time at sedentary tasks. He was a musician, an organist, and a prolific writer. Among his devotional and apologetical works were *True Piety* (1814), *Compilation of Church Music and Hymns* (1815), *Vindication of the Catholic Doctrine, concerning the Use and Veneration of Images* (1821), *Address of the Rt. Rev. Bishop David, to His Brethren of Other Professions, on the Rule of Faith* (1822), *Defence of the Vindication of the Catholic Doctrine, concerning the Use and Veneration of Images* (1823), and *Catechism of Christian Doctrine* (1825).

On 25 August 1832, as the result of a misreading in Rome of Bishop Flaget's request for an administrative change that would have replaced David as coadjutor with a younger man, David himself was named bishop of Bardstown. His only official act as a bishop ordinary was to give over the administration of the diocese to Flaget until the mistake could be rectified by the latter's reinstatement. In October 1833, however, he did attend the Second Provincial Council of Catholic Bishops in Baltimore in Flaget's stead. When in 1834 another coadjutor (Guy Ignatius Chabrat, the first priest ordained from David's seminary) was granted Flaget, David defended the choice despite Chabrat's unpopularity because of his nationality and tactlessness. Apparent dissatisfaction with his spiritual direction also caused him in 1833 to resign his superiority of the Sisters of Charity, not without some bitterness.

David retired to "The Solitude," his residence near the cathedral, where he continued to preside at liturgical ceremonies and grace important events. When his death seemed imminent, Mother Catherine Spalding had him carried the four miles to the motherhouse at Nazareth, where he died.

• The principal part of David's correspondence is housed in the archives of the University of Notre Dame, the archdiocese of Baltimore, and the Sisters of Charity of Nazareth. His two biographies are Columba Fox, *The Life of the Right Reverend John Baptist Mary David (1761–1841), Bishop of Bardstown and Founder of the Sisters of Charity of Nazareth* (1925), and Charles Lemarié, *Mgr J.-B. David (1761–1841)* (1973). See also Joseph B. Code, *Dictionary of the American Hierarchy* (1964), and Clyde F. Crews, *An American Holy Land: A History of the Archdiocese of Louisville* (1987).

THOMAS W. SPALDING

DAVIDGE, John Beale (1768–23 Aug. 1829), surgeon, medical educator, and founder of the University of Maryland, was born in Annapolis, Maryland, the son of Henry Davidge, a captain in the British army, and Honor Howard. His father died while he was small, and his mother apprenticed him to a cabinetmaker, but Davidge was eventually able to pursue medical studies with the financial support of friends. He enrolled in St. John's College in Annapolis, where he received his M.A. in 1789. After graduation he studied medicine in Annapolis under James and William Murray. He continued his medical education, specializing in anatomical study, at the University of Edinburgh and the University of Glasgow, receiving his M.D. from the latter on 22 April 1793. Davidge married Wilhelmina Stuart, of the Firth of Solway, Scotland, in 1793; they had one son. After she died he married Rebecca Troup Polk, widow of Josiah Polk; they had three daughters.

Davidge practiced medicine for the next three years in Birmingham, England, before returning to the United States and settling in Baltimore, Maryland. He took an active public role in combating yellow fever during a severe epidemic in Baltimore in 1797. He discussed the disease in many newspaper accounts and published these views in *Treatise on Yellow Fever* (1798). He argued against treatment by bleeding, claiming that this method "called the medical mind back to the almost antiquated system of depletion." Davidge became one of the first attending physicians of the Baltimore General Dispensary on its formation in 1801. In 1802 he began offering private courses on anatomy, surgery, midwifery, and physiology. He was soon joined by two young physicians, James Cocke and John Shaw, and the three began offering a more extended course of lectures, with Davidge heading the department of anatomy and surgery. In 1805 he delivered the first annual oration before the Medical and Chirurgical Faculty of Maryland. For the accommodation of his department and lectures, Davidge financed the building of an anatomical theater, which was soon destroyed by an antidissectionist mob. However, with the support of his professional contemporaries, he secured legislative support for the founding of the College of Medicine of Maryland in 1807. After its founding, Davidge was appointed dean. The college's operation reflected Davidge's belief that each disease must be studied, cataloged, and treated as an individual entity. In 1812 the state legislature called for the College of Medicine of Maryland to annex itself to the other three colleges or faculties which, united in 1813, became known as the University of Maryland, with the College of Medicine of Maryland becoming the university's medical school. Davidge held the chair of anatomy from 1807 until his death and served as the school's dean for a number of years.

Davidge was a prolific writer. He published *Nosologia Methodica*, in Latin, the first edition in 1812 and the second edition in 1813, in which he devised a new classification of diseases which, according to contemporaries, surpassed the standard nosological work in both simplicity and convenience. *Physical Sketches* was published in two volumes in 1814 and 1816, and *Treatise on Amputation* in 1818. In the latter work Davidge detailed a new method of operation which he invented, called the "American." He also edited *Bancroft on Fevers* in 1821, and the *Baltimore Philosophical Journal and Review*, of which only one issue (1823) was published. Davidge pioneered several surgical methods and procedures, including amputations at the shoulder joint, ligation of the gluteal artery for an aneurysm, ligation of the carotid artery, and in 1823, a total resection (removal) of the parotid gland. Davidge did not purge for diarrhea and bleed for fevers, as was common practice, but rather bled for diarrhea and purged for fever, believing that "no two general actions can take place at the same time." He also believed that menstruation was a secretion of the uterus excited by ovarian irritation.

Davidge was a man of upright character and deep religious convictions and a learned scholar to whom ambitious men and pupils were devoted. His students called him "Father of the University." Davidge delivered lectures which, according to his colleague, Lunsford P. Yandell, "were models of simple elegance." In January 1829 Davidge was diagnosed with a sinus cancer; despite excruciating pain, he delivered lectures on his own symptoms and progress. He died at his house in Maryland. An anatomical theater at the University of Maryland, used as a medical history museum, was named after him.

• A small collection of Davidge's papers and writings is in the Historical-Special Collections, Health Sciences and Human Services Library, University of Maryland School of Medicine, Baltimore. Davidge's medical thesis was entitled *Dissertatio Physiologica de Causis Catameniorum* (1794). Eugene F. Cordell detailed Davidge's life in *American Medical Biographies* (1920) and discussed his activities in the formation of the University of Maryland in *Historical Sketch of the University of Maryland* (1891). George H. Callcott offers additional information on Davidge in *History of the University of Maryland* (1982).

PHILIP K. WILSON

DAVIDGE, William Pleater (17 Apr. 1814–7 Aug. 1888), actor, was born near Ludgate Hill, London, England. Little information has survived about his childhood and education; his parents' names are not known, but he described his father as a merchant. As a child Davidge became involved with amateur dramatics and chose the theater for his life's work. In his youth he played the minor role of James in *The Miller's Maid* at London's Drury Lane Theatre. He made his adult debut in Nottingham in 1836, playing Adam Winterton in *The Iron Chest*, a popular melodrama by George Colman the younger. That same year, Davidge appeared in London at the Queen's Theatre, winning great favor as Baron Oakland in *The Haunted Tower*. He continued to appear in such London theaters as the Victoria and toured the provinces, Ireland, and Scotland, learning the craft of acting. In 1842 he married Elizabeth Clark, with whom he had three children; they settled in Manchester. Davidge appeared as the Soothsayer in a command performance of Shakespeare's *Julius Caesar* with Charles Kean's company at Windsor Castle in the winter of 1849.

In 1850 E. A. Marshall offered Davidge a two-year engagement at the Broadway Theater in New York City to play principal old male roles, in competition with the popular William Burton. Davidge made his American debut on 19 August 1850 as Sir Peter Teazle in Sheridan's *The School for Scandal*. He later appeared as Caliban in Shakespeare's *The Tempest*. As a stock actor he supported many of the leading players of his time, including Edwin Forrest, Julia Dean, Mme Celeste, and Lola Montez. Davidge remained at the Broadway Theater until 1855, when he began touring the United States. He was associated with many theaters in New York City, acting in John Wood's company at the Olympic Theater in 1863–1864 and appearing with Edwin Booth in Shakespearean revivals at the Winter Garden Theater. He joined Augustin Daly's Fifth Avenue Theater company in 1869 and remained with the group until 1877. During the season of 1877–1878 he toured with a company supporting Fanny Davenport; the following season he acted Dick Deadeye in Gilbert and Sullivan's *H.M.S. Pinafore* at the Standard Theater in New York City. He rejoined Daly's company in 1879 but left again in 1880 to perform in the farcical play *All the Rage*, which was performed in many cities for the next three years. Davidge then supported Margaret Mather for a season. In November 1885 he joined the Madison Square Theater Company, remaining there until his death near Cheyenne, Wyoming Territory, en route to an engagement in San Francisco.

While never achieving stardom, Davidge was widely considered one of the best of the old school of English comedians, excelling in Shakespearean plays and the older English comedies. Critic Edward A. Dithmar noted in the *New York Times* (30 May 1886) that his "long face, prominent nose, highly expressive mouth; his ambling gait, all impress themselves with ludicrous effect upon the spectator." Dithmar considered Davidge "a grotesque Caliban, a delightful Touchstone, an irresistibly amusing Dogberry, a mild, placid, philosophical Sir Hugh, a ponderous Nick Bottom, a much-befuddled old Gobbo, [and] an unctuous, jovial Sir Toby." Other roles for which he won acclaim were Sir Peter Teazle, Old Hardy in Hannah Cowley's *The Belle's Stratagem*, Hardcastle or Tony Lumpkin in Goldsmith's *She Stoops to Conquer*, Mr. Croaker in Goldsmith's *The Good Natured Man*, and Jem Baggs in the farce *The Wandering Minstrel*. Davidge also appeared in musicals; most notable was his portrayal of Dick Deadeye in the first American performance of *H.M.S. Pinafore* in New York. He was said to have played more than 1,100 characters during his career.

Davidge wrote at least one play, *The Family Party*, which Daly promised to produce but never did; it was apparently never published. His autobiography, *Footlight Flashes*, describes theatrical conditions and practices in detail but supplies few details about the actor's life.

Davidge vigorously defended the theatrical profession against censure from a group of ministers, including Theodore L. Cuyler, with a pamphlet entitled *The Drama Defended*, published in 1859. The pamphlet remained in print for about thirty years. In it Davidge suggests that ministers acknowledge offenses committed by men of the cloth before attacking theater personnel. He further defends his profession by claiming that St. Paul had seen fit to include a verse from the Greek playwright Menander into Holy Scripture.

Davidge's theatrical reputation was that of a hardworking, gifted, and earnest man who strengthened his profession and advanced the cause of art. The *New York Mirror*, however, portrayed him as a hard man to know, describing him as an old curmudgeon who especially hated managers. Nonetheless, after his death the *New York Mirror*, the leading theatrical trade paper of the day, described him as a man who loved truth and honor before all else; who would rather starve than do another man wrong; who was vigilantly zealous in his duties as a citizen, actor, and father; and who early in life fixed a high standard of integrity to which he obstinately adhered, remaining honest and fearlessly outspoken.

• The Theatre Collection at the New York Public Library for the Performing Arts has clipping files on Davidge. In his autobiography, *Footlight Flashes* (1866), he gives very few details about his life. Edward A. Dithmar sums up Davidge's career in "Davidge's Half Century," *New York Times*, 30 May 1886. See also Laurence Hutton, *Plays and Players of This Century* (1875), for scattered references; Thomas Marshall, *Lives of the Most Celebrated Actors and Actresses* (1847); and Charles E. Wingate, *Shakespeare's Heroes on the Stage* (1896). Obituaries are in the *New York Times*, 8 Aug. 1888, and in the *New York Mirror*, 11 Aug. 1888.

STEPHEN M. ARCHER

DAVIDSON, Donald Grady (18 Aug. 1893–25 Apr. 1968), author and teacher, was born in Campbellsville, Tennessee, the son of William Bluford Davidson, a teacher and principal, and Elma Wells. The family followed the father—a cultivated man with a special interest in classical languages and literatures—from one small Tennessee community to another as he directed and taught at various schools. Family ties were close in this region, and the younger Davidson's mind was shaped not only by his scholarly father but also by his musically talented mother, his maternal grandmother—who lived with the family and told him tales of the Federal occupation of middle Tennessee—and a number of granduncles who were Confederate veterans. Davidson attended several excellent preparatory schools and in 1909 began studies at Vanderbilt University in Nashville. After one year there, however, he encountered financial difficulties, and left the university to work as a schoolteacher in Cedar Hill and Mooresville, Tennessee, until he had saved enough money to return to Vanderbilt in 1914. He continued to finance his education by teaching English and German at Wallace University School in Nashville even while taking classes. Studying under John Crowe Ransom and attending meetings at the home of Sidney Mttron Hirsch, Davidson began developing some of the friendships that would shape his intellectual life. World War I intervened first, however, leading him to Officer Candidate School in the summer of 1917—he received his bachelor's degree from Vanderbilt in absentia—and a commission as a second lieutenant in the U.S. Army. Promoted to first lieutenant in early 1918, he found time to wed Theresa Sherrer of Oberlin, Ohio, before being shipped to the western front. After seeing action in the Manheuelle woods—while carrying a packet of Ransom's poetry with him—he returned to the United States and was discharged in June 1919.

Settling in with his wife and newborn daughter, Davidson began shaping what would become his lifelong career. After a year spent teaching English at Kentucky Wesleyan College and working as a reporter, he became an instructor at Vanderbilt in 1920 and began working toward his master's degree. He renewed his friendship with Ransom and, returning to meetings of Hirsch's informal circle, soon began his association with new members Allen Tate and Robert Penn Warren. Those meetings had shifted from their earlier focus on philosophy and religion to poetry; by 1922 those members who most regularly and fruitfully produced verse, seeking a public forum in which to present their work, founded the literary magazine *The Fugitive*. Ransom was the senior member, Tate the intellect that had brought a modernist literary sensibility to the group, and young Warren the most powerful raw talent, but it was Davidson who became the day-to-day guiding force behind the magazine. Besides being a regular contributor of short verse, he served as editor in 1923 and contributed profoundly to the group cohesiveness and enthusiasm that made the venture work. As *The Literary Correspondence of Donald Davidson and Allen Tate* (1974) clearly reveals, he was always less the pure artistic intellect than the practical organizer who made things happen.

Nonetheless, Davidson remained interested in developing his own poetic gifts and published *An Outland Piper*, his first volume of verse, in 1924—the same year in which he received an assistant professorship at Vanderbilt. This early collection was markedly romantic and generally melancholy in tone, though some poems had a clear satirical sense that took the measure of such romanticism and many others showed evidence of a modernist literary aesthetic that suggested the influence of Tate. After the final issue of *The Fugitive* in December 1925, Davidson found more time to devote himself to his own work: *The Tall Men* (1927), a long, semiautobiographical poem that attempted to capture the vanishing southern tradition of his forebears. It was Davidson's single most ambitious poem, but it also suffered from the heavy-handed privileging of ideas over aesthetics that characterized much of his later work.

Taking time from his many ongoing activities—he edited the book page of the *Nashville Tennessean* from 1924 to 1930 and had been promoted to associate professor in 1929—Davidson used his ideas of a traditional society as the centerpiece for organizing a new project, perhaps his most enduring: the Agrarian symposium *I'll Take My Stand* (1930). Davidson had increasingly come to see the poet as a seer who speaks from the tradition of his people and, accordingly, as a sort of prophetic social critic. Just as he had been a leading voice in organizing the poetic efforts of the Fugitives, Davidson rallied his now scattered colleagues—and other contributors—to an outright prose condemnation of modern American culture and an accompanying defense of the traditional southern way of life. Davidson, along with Andrew Lytle, was distinctive in believing in the possibility of practical success for the Agrarian movement, whereas Tate, Ransom, and Warren saw it as a more abstract literary and cultural statement; whatever their later disagreements, however, it was largely Davidson's exhortation that brought Tate back into the fold and got the project under way.

Davidson's later writings reveal his continuing concern with Agrarian ideals at the expense of the aesthetic appeal that had marked the best work of the Fugitives. His polemical essays in *The Attack on Leviathan: Regionalism and Nationalism in the United States* (1938) and *Still Rebels, Still Yankees and Other Essays* (1957)—his best prose collection—are clear indictments of modern political and social trends. Similar themes characterize Davidson's later poems, such as "Lee in the Mountains," wherein the defeated general nobly walks in civilian clothes, "commanding in a dream where no flag flies," yet finally attaining a vision of "lost forsaken valor" reborn.

A full professor from 1937, Davidson remained busy—teaching as well as publishing more poetry, composition textbooks, and even prose pieces on the Tennessee River—in the last three decades of his life. Unlike most of the other Agrarians, he never abandoned his loyalty to the cause that they had famously espoused in *I'll Take My Stand*. Aside from summers teaching at Middlebury College in Vermont, he spent his remaining days at Vanderbilt, retiring from teaching as professor of English emeritus in 1964. He died in Nashville. While he may not have achieved the enduring literary reputation of his esteemed colleagues, Davidson was absolutely essential to the success of their group efforts. Without his practical and temperamental contributions, neither the Fugitives nor the Agrarians could have achieved the cohesiveness that assured their place in American literary history.

• The largest collection of Davidson's papers is at the Joint Universities Library in Nashville. A number of works on Davidson mingle biographical information with critical appraisal: Louise Cowan, *The Fugitive Group: A Literary History* (1959), remains the authoritative study of *The Fugitive* and Davidson's role in it; Louis Rubin, *The Wary Fugitives: Four Poets and the South* (1978), is an award-winning study by one of southern literature's most distinguished scholars and clearly places Davidson in relation to Allen Tate, John Crowe Ransom, and Robert Penn Warren. Thomas Daniel Young and M. Thomas Inge, *Donald Davidson: An Essay and a Bibliography* (1965), has an exhaustive bibliography of Davidson's writings through 1964; Young and Inge, *Donald Davidson* (1971), is a thorough critical study that supplements selections from the prior bibliography with all of Davidson's publications after 1964.

FARRELL O'GORMAN

DAVIDSON, George (9 May 1825–2 Dec. 1911), surveyor, geodesist, and astronomer, was born in Nottingham, England, the son of Thomas Davidson, and Janet Drummond. His family emigrated to Philadelphia when he was seven, and he attended its public schools. At Central High School, Alexander Bache, later a founder of the National Academy of Sciences, was his teacher and encouraged his interest in science. The school had a small telescope, and Davidson, who became a student assistant, learned to observe with it. He also measured and recorded daily the local magnetic field of the earth. A hard worker, he graduated as the valedictorian of his class in 1845. Bache had become superintendent of the U.S. Coast Survey in 1843, and Davidson joined the survey in Washington after finishing high school. He then spent several years in the South, learning field surveying on the job. In 1850, soon after the United States took over California from Mexico, Davidson was put in charge of the survey on the West Coast. Charts were badly needed, and he mapped harbors, headlands, and points all along the coast, from San Diego north to the Columbia River. The field work involved many hardships, which included frequent landings in small boats through the surf.

In 1857 Davidson was an expert witness in the "Limantour Claim" trial in San Francisco. José Y. Limantour held purported land grants, supposedly issued by Manuel Micheltorena, the Mexican governor of Alta California in the 1840s, covering a large area at the northern end of the San Francisco peninsula together with Angel, Yerba Buena, Alcatraz, and the Farallones Islands. If the grants were valid, all Americans living in San Francisco could be considered squatters, whose titles to land were worthless under the Treaty of Guadalupe Hidalgo. Davidson testified that the seals were counterfeits and the documents themselves invalid. The American court found in favor of the settlers, Limantour fled to Mexico, and Davidson became a local hero. In 1858 he married Ellinor Fauntleroy, the daughter of a former coast survey employee under whom he had worked in the South; they had three children. After the Civil War, Davidson was sent to Alaska in 1867 to make a quick survey while negotiations were still in progress between the United States and Russia for its purchase. In 1868 he returned to San Francisco, in charge of the survey on the Pacific Coast, a position he held for more than a quarter of a century.

Davidson was interested in astronomy; he took a telescope with him on his surveying trips and observed assiduously with it. He soon became convinced that the western mountains, with their thin, clear air, were much better sites for astronomical observatories than were the smoky, dirty, hazy cities in which they were then located. He published short papers to this effect in the Proceedings of the California Academy of Sciences and the U.S. Coast and Geodetic Survey Report in 1872. Active in the California Academy of Sciences, Davidson was its president from 1871 to 1887. During this period the academy was supported by many wealthy San Franciscans. One of them, the millionaire recluse James Lick, made an unsolicited gift of a site for a permanent home for the academy. Davidson called on Lick to thank him and on return visits awakened the lonely old man's interest in astronomy, with tales of the planets and stars, the rings of Saturn, and the mountains on the moon. Lick was enthralled, and Davidson persuaded him to leave his fortune to found a high-altitude observatory that would make his name famous throughout the world. In October 1873 Lick announced that he would spend $1 million to build an observatory in the Sierra Nevada at an elevation of 10,000 feet. In 1874 Lick set up a board of trust to carry out this and other charities.

As part of his duties with the coast survey, Davidson headed an expedition to Japan to observe and photograph a transit of Venus at the end of 1874. He combined it with a trip around the world and was gone for nearly two years. In Davidson's absence, Lick changed his mind about the location of the observatory, and it was built on 4,200-foot Mount Hamilton, just east of San Jose, its completion occurring twelve years after the "generous miser's" death in 1876. Davidson, who had evidently hoped to become the director of the observatory, had a falling out with Lick after his return from Japan and was never close to him again. But he had been key in persuading Lick to build the largest telescope in the world, a 36-inch refractor, on America's first mountaintop observatory. Davidson's participation in the founding and location of Lick Observatory was his most significant contribution to astronomy.

In 1879 Davidson built his own much smaller observatory, ironically on the low Holladay's Hill, in foggy San Francisco. There he had a 6.4-inch Clark refractor, with which he observed every clear night in the early evening or just before dawn. He liked to show students and public groups the stars at this, the first astronomical observatory built in California. In 1895 Davidson was abruptly dismissed from the Coast and Geodetic Survey at the age of seventy. Still full of life, he opened an office in downtown San Francisco as a consulting engineer. In 1897 William W. Duffield, the chief of the survey who had discharged Davidson, was himself turned out of office. Davidson campaigned vigorously for this post but did not get it. In 1897 Edward S. Holden, the first director of Lick Observatory, was forced to resign. Davidson immediately became a sentimental favorite to replace him, but the astronomers on the staff considered him a cranky old man with little up-to-date knowledge of their science. At an open meeting of the University of California Regents, James E. Keeler, a young astrophysicist and the first astronomer at Lick Observatory, was elected narrowly over Davidson to be director. Davidson claimed that he had been secretly offered a professorship if he would withdraw from the contest but had refused to do so. Immediately afterward he was named professor of geography at the University of California, a position he held until he retired in 1905. He died in San Francisco.

• Davidson's papers and correspondence are in the Bancroft Library of the University of California at Berkeley. One of his most interesting published papers is "Total Solar Eclipse of January 11, 1880 at Mt. Santa Lucia, 6,000 Ft. Elevation, California," *U.S. Coast and Geodetic Survey Reports*, Appendix no. 20 (1882) 463–68, especially since the University of California considered building an observatory at this location, now called Junipero Serra Peak, in the 1970s. A short biography by Charles B. Davenport, "George Davidson, 1825–1911," *Biographical Memoirs of the National Academy of Sciences* 18 (1937): 189–217, includes a partial bibliography of Davidson's papers and articles. His biography is Oscar Lewis, *George Davidson: Pioneer West Coast Scientist* (1954), which is supplemented from the astronomical side by W. W. Campbell, "The Astronomical Activities of Professor George Davidson," *Publications of the Astronomical Society of the Pacific* 26 (1914): 28–37. See also Donald E. Osterbrock, *James E. Keeler: Pioneer American Astrophysicist and the Early Development of American Astrophysics* (1984).

DONALD E. OSTERBROCK

DAVIDSON, James Wood (9 Mar. 1829–15 June 1905), journalist and educator, was born in Craven County, South Carolina, the son of Alexander Davidson and Sarah (maiden name unknown). Davidson's father was a planter in Craven County, later resurveyed and renamed Newberry, South Carolina. James was educated at South Carolina College at Columbia (later the University of South Carolina), and after graduating with distinction in 1852, he taught Greek and ancient languages in Winnsboro until 1859 and in Columbia until the beginning of the Civil War. Davidson was made adjutant of the Thirteenth Regiment of the South Carolina Volunteers under the command of Stonewall Jackson. His property and literary writings were destroyed during the war.

Returning to Columbia after the war, Davidson both taught and was a graduate student at the College of South Carolina until 1871. Because the pay was so poor for teachers, he turned to journalism and wrote for the *Charleston News* and the *New York Times*. He then set out on a career as an editor for newspapers in Washington, D.C., and New York. In 1869 he published *A School History of South Carolina*, which was later adopted as a public school textbook, and another book, *Living Writers of the South*, which later would receive acclaim as a work of great distinction. Davidson explained in his preface to the school history that his purpose was to be "as little as possible tinged with sectional feelings." *Living Writers of the South* was a unique view of regional writers, a new literary perspective at that time.

After moving to Washington in 1871, Davidson began gathering materials at the Library of Congress for a dictionary of southern authors. In 1873 he moved to New York, and during his eleven years there, Davidson was on the staff of the *Evening Post* as literary editor, drama editor, and art editor. From 1873 to 1878 he was also the American correspondent of the *London Standard*. During his years in New York he also wrote for American and foreign periodicals, and he worked as a correspondent in the educational department of a publishing house.

In 1883 Davidson married Josephine Allen, a widow who was a native of Bristol, England. They moved to South Florida on Lake Worth, north of Miami near Palm Beach, where he settled in April 1884 to write his dictionary of southern writers and to cultivate pineapples and other fruit. In 1885 he was elected to represent Dade County at the Florida Constitutional Convention. Davidson represented an immense area in the Lake Worth region that is now Palm Beach County.

In 1886 Davidson published a letter-writing handbook, *The Correspondent*. Shortly after, he moved to Washington, D.C., where he worked as a clerk for the U.S. Treasury and continued writing. During this period Davidson continued to research sources in the Library of Congress and to gather material about southern authors. He compiled the names of more than 3,000 southern authors with examples of their writing. Two years later he published *The Poetry of the Future* and the next year *Florida of Today*.

During most of his career Davidson worked on his lifetime project. By the time of his death in Florida he had collected 4,000 names for inclusion, but it is not known what became of Davidson's bibliography of southern authors.

Editor Lucian Lamar Knight described Davidson's writing: "His style as a writer is characterized by choice and elegant diction and by unusual vigor and penetration of thought." In 1897 Colonel John P. Thomas wrote of Davidson's efforts to preserve literature:

If ripe scholarship and high character, and deepest loyalty to the best sentiment of the south and the union; if rare attainments in the higher reaches of literature are wanted in educational establishments in South Carolina, these compose the dowry of Davidson, the architect of his own fortunes: and the State would be wise to call him back and get at his hands the benefit of his knowledge and his wisdom.

No one in the South was better equipped to compile a definitive collection of southern writers at the time than was Davidson, Thomas added. He considered Davidson to be a struggling man of letters.

Some authors have credited Davidson with discovering as far back as 1868 that southern writers had contributed as many as ten times more in literary works than had been recognized in the North.

Davidson was a scholar, a teacher, and a writer who served the Confederacy and found his property and literary research destroyed by the Civil War. During the postwar Reconstruction period the financial constraints he faced required him to combine his teaching and writing talents in Columbia, South Carolina, before moving on to Washington, D.C., New York, and Florida, where he wrote and edited works of literature, drama, and art, as well as researched and wrote about southern writers of the period.

• Correspondence of James Wood Davidson related to his work with the *Southern Literary Messenger* is in the Alderman Library at the University of Virginia. Several bibliographic reference sources include Davidson, among them Perry J. Ashley, "Newspaper Publishing in South Carolina: A Beginning Checklist," an unpublished collection. Another guide, Sharon G. Boardman, "South Carolina Newspapers on File in the Library of Congress, Washington, D.C.," was published in 1980. Both are available at the Thomas Cooper Library, Columbia, S.C. Other reference works of value include Winifred Gregory, *American Newspapers, 1821–1936* (1937); James B. Meriwether, ed., *South Carolina Journals and Journalists* (1974); John Hammond Moore, *Research Materials in South Carolina: A Guide* (1967); S. N. D. North, *History and Present Condition of the Newspaper and Periodical Press of the United States* (1884); and *Rowell's American Newspaper Directory*, absorbed by *N. W. Ayer & Son's Directory* in 1910. The University of Florida Library of Florida History includes J. B. Whitfield, comp., *Florida State Government: An Official Directory of the State Government* (1885). An obituary is in the South Carolina *State*, 8 July 1905.

JEAN CARVER CHANCE

DAVIDSON, Jo (30 Mar. 1883–2 Jan. 1952), sculptor, was born Joseph Davidson in New York City, the son of Jacob S. Davidson and Haya Getzoff, Russian Jewish immigrants. During his childhood Davidson lived in tenement housing on the Lower East Side. Through the combined industry of family members, the children were fed and educated. Davidson began to study art at the Art Students League, where he attended evening classes with George de Forest Brush, George Bridgman, and Bryson Burroughs. Around 1902 Davidson moved to New Haven, Connecticut, ostensibly to attend medical school at Yale University. More interested in art classes than medicine, however, Davidson soon discovered clay. By 1903 he had returned to New York City, where he worked as an assistant in the studio of sculptor Hermon Atkins MacNeil. Davidson continued to take classes at the Art Students League, and in 1906 he first exhibited a sculpture in the winter exhibition at the National Academy of Design. Davidson traveled to Paris in 1907 for further study. After three weeks in the atelier of academic sculptor Jean-Antoine Injalbert at the École des Beaux-Arts, Davidson left for the more bohemian world of his fellow American expatriate artists. It was during this time that he sculpted one of his most daring works, a bust of painter John Marin (1908, National Portrait Gallery, Smithsonian Institution), but for the most part, his style was traditional, formed on that of nineteenth-century French sculptors (such as Auguste Rodin) working in terra-cotta and bronze.

By 1910 Davidson had gained the patronage and friendship of Gertrude Vanderbilt Whitney. While Davidson was still in France, Whitney purchased his *Head of a Swiss Girl* (1909) and later found working space for him in New York near her own studio at 23 Macdougal Alley. Whitney remained a supporter of Davidson's work through commissions for portraits, purchases, and opportunities for exhibition. During these years Davidson established a lifelong pattern of peripatetic travel, most often in France, England, and the United States.

Davidson married Yvonne de Kerstrat, whom he met in France, in 1909; they had two sons. The family maintained a residence in Paris, where Yvonne became a fashionable dress designer. In 1926 Davidson purchased "Bécheron," an estate near Tours, which would be his primary studio and home until his death (with the exception of 1940–1945, years he spent at Stone Court Farm in Lahaska, Pennsylvania).

Davidson was given his first one-man show in 1910 at the New York Cooperative Society. This exhibition was followed by several others in New York and Chicago. By the time of his participation in the Armory Show in 1913, Davidson's work was well known. Although portrait sculpture was to become the most important and lucrative aspect of Davidson's oeuvre, his initial success was founded on a number of evocative bronze, marble, and terra-cotta male and female torsos. He continued for many years to make nude figures in the style of Rodin, but they received little critical attention.

In 1914 Davidson made a number of portrait busts in London, including a likeness of Joseph Conrad. In 1916 he persuaded President Woodrow Wilson to sit for a bust, and after the close of the First World War, Davidson created a group of sculptures of men associated with the Paris Peace Conference. These busts, which included portraits of General John J. Pershing, Marshal Ferdinand Foch, and Georges Clemenceau, were exhibited in 1920 in New York City as A Plastic History of the War. In 1923 he also made one of his best-known sculptures, a large seated statue of Gertrude Stein (National Portrait Gallery).

Davidson increasingly sought out subjects for his burgeoning "plastic history," although he worked on commission as well. Those who knew him admired his immense vitality and ability to befriend and sculpt the leading celebrities of any place he happened to be. Fellow artist Waldo Peirce characterized Davidson's Paris studio in 1923 as a "menagerie of busts of all the lime-lighters of the world." Davidson did not require lengthy sittings from his subjects. As he noted in his 1951 autobiography, "My approach to my subjects was very simple. I never had them pose but we just talked about everything in the world. . . . Sometimes [they] talked as if I was their confessor. As they talked I got an immediate insight" (pp. 86–87).

Davidson used his charm and *joie de vivre* not only to gain sitters and commissions but to promote his own career in the emerging world of the mass media and celebrity culture. He forged friendships with a number of journalists, who made sure that his work and visage were prominently displayed in newspapers and magazines, particularly in New York City. His massive square face, with its full beard and twinkling eyes, was to be found in articles on his work, in photographs that documented his sittings with famous subjects, in the society pages, and in cartoons published in the *New Yorker*; his name was even a clue in crossword puzzles. From around 1920 until his death Jo Davidson was a recognized celebrity in his own right, a designation that had more to do with his personality and self-promotion than with his gift for the fine arts. Sometimes other artists complained about Davidson's success. As George Biddle remarked in his diary in 1937, "All of us are exhausted by Jo's vitality, his conceit and complete lack of gray matter." But others understood Davidson's particular niche in the artistic world. His friend Guy Pène du Bois predicted as early as 1918 that "some time hence, people may believe that not to have been in Davidson's gallery of notables is not to have been a notable" ("Who's Who in Art: J. Davidson," *Evening Post Magazine*, 8 June 1918, p. 7).

Davidson's traditional busts, created in marble, bronze, or terra-cotta, carried honorific, even classical connotations at a time when photography, film, and caricature were emerging as the modern media of choice for celebrity portraiture. During his long career Davidson sculpted the heads of famous Americans such as John D. Rockefeller, Charles Lindbergh, Will Rogers, Ernie Pyle, Frank Sinatra, Helen Keller, Albert Einstein, and Dwight D. Eisenhower. He also made busts of liberal politicians and radical reformers, including Andrew Furuseth, Mother Jones, Robert La Follette, Lincoln Steffens, Franklin Delano Roosevelt, and Henry Wallace. Davidson sculpted a number of artists and literary figures, such as George Luks, Georgia O'Keeffe, and Robinson Jeffers, as well as a series of British authors done in 1929–1931 for Doubleday, Doran and Company.

In 1924 Davidson traveled with Robert La Follette to Russia, where Davidson made a series of busts of prominent Russians, all duly featured on the front page of the pictorial section of the *Washington Post*. He made a group of portraits of Spanish loyalists during the Spanish Civil War, which were exhibited at a benefit in New York in 1938 with a catalog written by Dorothy Parker and Ernest Hemingway. In 1941, to promote inter-American relations, Nelson Rockefeller arranged for Davidson to travel to South American nations to sculpt the heads of their presidents. This collection was exhibited at the National Gallery of Art in 1942. In the spring of 1941, while in Caracas, Venezuela, Davidson married a childhood friend, Florence Gertrude Lucius, whose acquaintance he had renewed after the death of Yvonne Davidson in 1934.

By the mid-1940s Davidson's humanitarian views and immense popularity led him to be a figurehead for a group known as the Independent Citizens' Committee of the Arts, Sciences and Professions, which supported the presidential candidacy of Henry Wallace in 1948. By 1950 Davidson had been branded a Communist, even though the *New York Times* commented after his death that "he was no politician and no profound economic philosopher" (3 Jan. 1952). Rather, Davidson was, and kept, "the best company in the world." In 1947 he described his great retrospective exhibition at the American Academy of Arts and Letters as "some 40 odd years of plastic history." Davidson's last project was to have been a number of portraits of Israeli leaders, including David Ben-Gurion and Golda Meir. He visited Israel in 1951 but did not live to complete the busts. Davidson died at Bécheron, in Saché, after a brief illness.

• Davidson's personal and professional correspondence, clippings, and files on many of his portrait commissions are contained in the Jo Davidson Papers, Manuscript Division, Library of Congress. The largest public collection of Davidson's work is owned by the National Portrait Gallery, Smithsonian Institution. A thorough account of Davidson's life and work is Janis Conner and Joel Rosenkranz, "Jo Davidson," *Rediscoveries in American Sculpture: Studio Works, 1893–1939* (1989), pp. 10–18. Much information may also be found in *Between Sittings: An Informal Autobiography of Jo Davidson* (1951), which is particularly good for understanding Davidson's gift for self-promotion. A lengthy obituary is in the *New York Times*, 3 Jan. 1952.

BRANDON BRAME FORTUNE

DAVIDSON, Lucretia Maria (27 Sept. 1808–27 Aug. 1825), and **Margaret Miller Davidson** (26 Mar. 1823–25 Nov. 1838), poets, were born in Plattsburgh, New York, the daughters of Oliver Davidson, a doctor, and Margaret Miller. Always frail and highly sensitive, Lucretia Davidson entered the Plattsburgh Academy at age four and began composing verse before she was taught to write. Periodically withdrawn from school lest assiduous studying make her ill—intellectual excitement was said to exhaust the delicate "constitution"—she eagerly read history, current fiction, and drama. Her father's income, however, was inadequate for a large family susceptible to illness. Because her mother was periodically bedridden by tuberculosis and other ailments, Lucretia, at fifteen, managed the household. Doubtful that the daughter of an impecunious family was entitled to spend time reading and writing, she quietly relinquished such pursuits until her mother encouraged her to write and study in moderation.

Moss Kent, a family friend, was so impressed by Lucretia's desire for knowledge that he offered to pay for her further education. In November 1824 she was sent to Emma Willard's female seminary in Troy, New York, where she learned painting and dancing and enthusiastically but compulsively studied French, geology, and composition. Her severe cold and depression that winter, treated with emetics and bloodletting, were attributed to mental overwork, homesickness, and the strain, for a modest girl, of public oral examinations. Her parents decided in the spring of 1825 that a change of climate might be beneficial, but Lucretia collapsed again after a few weeks at a boardingschool in Albany. Brought home to Plattsburgh with unmistakable symptoms of advanced tuberculosis, she wrote in bed, keeping her books nearby so that she could see them, and died a month later.

Selections from Lucretia's occasional and descriptive poems, paraphrases of scripture, and romantic narratives were published in *Amir Khan, and Other Poems* (1829) with an introductory biographical sketch by Samuel F. B. Morse. England's poet laureate Robert Southey recounted her history and quoted several of her poems as evidence of "precocious genius" (*Quarterly Review* [London] 41 [1829]: 292).

Although Lucretia has generally been regarded as a more original and versatile poet than Margaret, their reputations were intertwined. According to their mother, Lucretia's "poetic mantle" descended, "like a robe of light, on her infant sister." Margaret listened intently to Mrs. Davidson's recollections of Lucretia and vowed to "'fill her place'" (Irving, p. 13). At play she improvised dialogues and narratives about historical and fictitious characters. Educated at home by her mother, at age six she reportedly wrote verse impromptus and read the Bible as well as poetry by Milton, Thomson, Cowper, Scott, and Byron aloud with pleasure and appropriate expression. Margaret's poems are more obviously autobiographical than Lucretia's, her style more expansive. She wrote romantic narratives in verse and prose, paraphrases of biblical passages, reflections on mortality, and tributes to her mother.

The family moved several times within New York State in hopes of finding a more salubrious climate, but relocation, excursions, and medical treatments proved ineffectual. Margaret survived scarlet fever and a "liver complaint" but was diagnosed at twelve as hopelessly consumptive. When writing and studying were proscribed to prolong her life, the usually buoyant girl became restless and depressed. Allowed to return to her books and pen, she declared that she was well, but within a few weeks her lungs hemorrhaged. After Margaret died at Saratoga, her mother collected her papers, wrote an account of her life, and presented these manuscripts to Washington Irving, who quoted extensively from Mrs. Davidson's narrative in his *Biography and Poetical Remains of the Late Margaret Miller Davidson* (1841).

Lucretia and Margaret Davidson were posthumously acclaimed as ethereal spirits and prodigies. Widely noticed in literary periodicals of the early 1840s, their "poetical remains" went through twenty-six American editions by 1860. Commentators who were moved by the sisters' faith and filial devotion elevated them as exemplars of native genius, "native" meaning both "innate" and "American." Irving's biography of Margaret began by evoking Lucretia as "a lovely American girl" who early evinced "rare poetic excellence."

Ironically, literary nationalism was also a declared motive of the few antebellum reviewers who minimized the intrinsic merit of the Davidsons' poems. In 1841 Edgar Allan Poe stated in *Graham's Magazine*, "The name of Lucretia Davidson is familiar to all readers of Poetry"—but not for altogether legitimate reasons. He argued that deference to British opinion along with pity and esteem for the Davidsons had inflated American estimates of their poetry (*Complete Works of Edgar Allan Poe* [1902], vol. 20, p. 174). Editor-anthologist Rufus W. Griswold included the sisters in *The Poets and Poetry of America* (1842) and *The Female Poets of America* (1849). Observing that the "beauty of their characters" was justly appreciated, he remarked that the Davidsons were "not the most wonderful" native prodigies he could name. Since their later efforts showed no "advancement" over their earliest effusions, it was reasonable to conclude that they were incapable of becoming great poets (*Female Poets*, p. 152).

These measured assessments had no discernible effect on the Davidsons' popularity. Caroline May's *American Female Poets* (1848) apotheosized them as "twins in thought, feeling, loveliness, and purity" (p. 285). Laudatory sketches appeared in the *Ladies' Repository* in 1854 and 1866. Such tributes, like the biographies, appealed to the contemporary appetite for stories that promoted religion and morality while touching the heart.

Other cultural factors contributed to the sisters' fame. Pulmonary tuberculosis, the "Destroyer" of thousands of nineteenth-century Americans and Europeans, was idealized in literary culture as an expression of exquisite sensibility—if the victim was young, gifted, and white. When Irving, on meeting Margaret in 1833, learned that her "moral and physical constitution" closely resembled Lucretia's and that she was subject to the same "kindling of the imagination," he warned her mother to avoid "fostering her poetic vein" (p. 10). Most reviewers commented on the wisdom of nurturing a passion for literature in delicate children. There was a consensus that the Davidsons' early deaths were inevitable; the *North American Review* rationalized, "The fire of genius and susceptibility must burn, and must consume the delicate frame" (53 [1841]: 142).

The Davidsons' careers intersected with movements to reform medicine, hygiene, and formal education and with debates about woman's nature and prerogatives. While the social advantages of educating girls were widely recognized, there was general concern about feebleness and invalidism in women. In 1837 the *American Annals of Education* quoted from Dr. William Sweetser's book on tuberculosis: "There is such a thing . . . as *educating a child to death*." "Fe-

males," especially, "are unquestionably, too often overworked" (7: 15–16). Other medical treatises of the period warned against excessive "stimulation" of the brain, insisting that feelings and romantic fantasies must be disciplined and that schools should not strain children's intellect while restricting their physical activity.

Catharine Sedgwick argued that Lucretia Davidson was one of many privileged girls debilitated by conditions typical of boarding schools: overheated, chilly, or poorly ventilated rooms and insufficient outdoor exercise. America needed well-educated but healthy women. Because marriage was their "common destiny," preparation for competent, cheerful domesticity was a parental and daughterly duty (*Poetical Remains*, p. 60). Sarah J. Hale, an advocate of education for women, denied that rigorous schooling destroyed Lucretia, but she faulted Margaret's mother for allowing the child's "imagination" to develop "at the expense of her constitution when, by patient and prudent training, it might have been suppressed" (*Woman's Record*, 2d ed. [1855], p. 285).

Lucretia and Margaret Davidson wrote fluently for an audience of family and friends. With time and constructive criticism, Lucretia might have achieved distinction as a poet. Both sisters became famous in the mid-1800s because prominent authors who admired them related their lives and writings to timely issues: early religious instruction, literary nationalism, the value of domesticity, and reforms in medicine and formal education. The Davidsons are noteworthy for historians of literature, education, and medicine. The biographical and critical texts that embalmed them illuminate antebellum aesthetic standards while reflecting medical and popular assumptions about women's potentials.

• Rutgers University holds the Davidson family papers, described by Jeslyn Medoff in "Divine Children: The Davidson Sisters and Their Mother," *Journal of the Rutgers University Libraries* 46 (June 1984): 16–27. The most detailed biographies are the sketches by Catharine Sedgwick in *Poetical Remains of the Late Lucretia Maria Davidson* (1841) and Washington Irving in *Biography and Poetical Remains of the Late Margaret Miller Davidson* (1841). The cultural milieu is examined in Cheryl Walker, *The Nightingale's Burden: Women Poets and American Culture before 1900* (1982), and in Walker's anthology, *American Women Poets of the Nineteenth Century* (1992). Also useful are Elsie Lee West's editorial introduction and notes to Washington Irving, *Oliver Goldsmith: A Biography; Biography of the Late Margaret Miller Davidson* (1978).

Joseph F. Kett surveys American views of precocity from 1830 to 1930 in "Curing the Disease of Precocity," *American Journal of Sociology* 84, supp. (1978): S183–S211. Contemporary doctors' treatises on tuberculosis, education, and the health of young people include Amariah Brigham, "Consumption: Pulmonary Consumption and Means of Prevention," *Knickerbocker Magazine*, July 1836, pp. 1–12, and *Remarks on the Influence of Mental Cultivation and Mental Excitement upon Health*, 2d ed. (1833); and William Sweetser, *Mental Hygiene; or, An Examination of the Intellect and Passions . . . and Their Influence upon Health and Longevity*, 2d ed. (1850). Female invalidism is addressed in Brigham's prefaces to his *Remarks* and in Catharine Beecher, *Letters to the People on Health and Happiness* (1855).

MARY DE JONG

DAVIDSON, Margaret Miller. *See* Davidson, Lucretia Marie, and Margaret Miller Davidson.

DAVIDSON, Thomas (25 Oct. 1840–14 Sept. 1900), philosopher, was born in Old Deer, Aberdeenshire, Scotland, the son of Thomas Davidson and Mary Warrender, farmers. A remarkable student from an early age, Davidson attended King's College, Aberdeen, on scholarship and graduated in 1860, winning the class prize for his work in Greek. He taught for six years in Scotland and England, and while teaching he became engaged to Maye McCombie, daughter of the publisher of the *Aberdeen Free Press*. The young couple could not reconcile her devout Baptist beliefs and Davidson's heterodox religious views, and they broke off the engagement in 1865. Davidson disclosed to philosopher William James his "unhappy love affair in Scotland," indicating the role it played in his decision never to marry. In 1866 Davidson emigrated to Canada where he taught in London, Ontario. A teaching position brought him to St. Louis, Missouri, where he met William T. Harris, later U.S. commissioner of education; he sharpened his philosophical bent in a group that gathered around Harris, the St. Louis Hegelians.

Not one to be tied down for long in a conventional career, Davidson moved to Boston in 1873, where he joined a philosophical circle that included William James. He supported himself by lecturing, tutoring, and writing. His sharp critique of the teaching methods of Harvard's Greek department appeared in the *Atlantic Monthly* and may have cost him an appointment at that institution. As James observed, Davidson "became more and more unconventional and even developed a sort of antipathy to all regular academic life" (*McClure's Magazine*, May 1905, p. 6).

Davidson remained, nonetheless, a committed and peripatetic seeker of the truth. He traveled frequently to Europe, studying archaeology in Athens, and became something of a disciple of Catholic philosopher Cardinal Rosmini. He lived an ascetic life for six years in Domo d'Ossola, Italy, immersing himself in Rosmini's work, translating some of his writing, and producing his own critical study, *The Philosophical System of Antonio Rosmini-Serbati* (1882).

Following his years in Italy he lived briefly in England, becoming one of the founders of the Fellowship of the New Life, from which later sprang the Fabian Society. The mid-1880s found him back in the United States. In 1889 he established the Glenmore School of the Culture Sciences in the Adirondacks in upstate New York. Annually thereafter Davidson offered a "summer course of study" at Glenmore, where students and fellow scholars combined lectures, discussion, and physical activity. Davidson's intellectual breadth was remarkable, encompassing philosophy, religion, history, art, language, literature, ethics, economics, and politics. Notable philosophers and intellectuals, including John Dewey, W. T. Harris, William James, Hugo Münsterberg, and Stephen S. Wise, sojourned to Glenmore to share in the proceedings. He also exchanged ideas with Felix Adler and the followers of his Ethical Culture movement who summered at a nearby camp.

In the last two years of his life Davidson found the work and the disciples he craved. In a series of lectures, "Problems which the Nineteenth Century Hands on to the Twentieth," at the Educational Alliance (a settlement house on the Lower East Side of Manhattan), Davidson challenged his largely working-class, immigrant audience to take its education into its own hands: "If you will form a class, and fall to the work in dead earnest, I will come down and meet you once a week and teach you." He proceeded to offer weekly lectures to a group that soon numbered more than a hundred. He also led a smaller discussion class focusing on philosophy. When he went to Glenmore in the Adirondacks in the summer of 1899, he wrote a series of lengthy weekly letters to members of the class, who continued meeting in his absence to study history and philosophy. He invited several of the most promising of his Lower East Side students to join him and his colleagues for the summer course in the Adirondacks. There they read Plato, Dante in the original Italian, Goethe, and Tennyson and grappled with the meaning of life.

He challenged his students to share the knowledge they were acquiring by founding "a Breadwinners' College . . . which will teach men and women to become public-spirited, generously cultured, pure and high-minded, an institution which will help more than anything else to banish ignorance and moral poverty" (Knight, pp. 83–84). Davidson offered his vision of education as an alternative to the socialist perspective that was then very influential in immigrant Jewish circles. By the winter of 1899–1900 Davidson's class had become part of a larger effort in adult education spearheaded by a number of his Lower East Side followers.

Thomas Davidson died of cancer in Montreal. His followers at the Educational Alliance, nevertheless, threw themselves into the work of Breadwinners' College, expanding the evening program for working people from the Lower East Side. By 1902 its weekly attendance numbered 600; the next winter almost 800 were taking classes. Under the initial leadership of Morris Raphael Cohen, later a renowned philosopher and teacher at City College in his own right, the program continued for seventeen years. The original group that had studied under Davidson also formed the Thomas Davidson Society, which continued to meet for four decades. William James best summed up the meaning of Davidson's life:

In the example he set to us all of how, even in the midst of this intensely worldly social system of ours, in which each human interest is organized so collectively and so commercially, a single man may still be a knight-errant of the intellectual life, and preserve full freedom in the midst of sociability . . . Asking no man's permission, bowing the knee to no tribal idol, renouncing the conventional channels of recognition, he showed us how a life devoted to purely intellectual ends could be beautifully wholesome outwardly, and overflow with inner contentment. (*McClure's Magazine*, May 1905, p. 11)

• Davidson's papers, consisting primarily of correspondence, lectures, articles, and books, are at Sterling Memorial Library, Yale University. Two valuable collections of his writings and articles about him published shortly after his death are Charles M. Bakewell, ed., *The Education of the Wage-Earners* (1904), and William Knight, ed., *Memorials of Thomas Davidson, the Wandering Scholar* (1907). Useful reminiscences of Davidson include Bakewell, "A Democratic Philosopher and His Work," *International Journal of Ethics* 11 (July 1901): 440–54; Louis I. Dublin, "Thomas Davidson: Educator for Democracy," *American Scholar* 17 (Spring 1948): 201–11; and Morris R. Cohen, *A Dreamer's Journey: The Autobiography of Morris Raphael Cohen* (1949). An account of the work of Davidson's protégés after his death is in Cohen, "The Work of the Davidson Class," *American Hebrew*, 27 June 1902, pp. 157–59. On the relationship between Davidson and Cohen see Leonora Cohen Rosenfield, ed., *Portrait of a Philosopher: Morris R. Cohen in Life and Letters* (1962). More recent scholarship is in David A. Hollinger, *Morris R. Cohen and the Scientific Ideal* (1975), and Lewis S. Feuer, "The East Side Philosophers: William James and Thomas Davidson," *American Jewish History* 76 (Mar. 1987): 287–310.

THOMAS DUBLIN

DAVIE, William Richardson (20 June 1756–5 Nov. 1820), statesman and soldier, was born in Egremont, Cumberlandshire, England, the son of Archibald Davie, a manufacturer of damask fabric, and Mary Richardson. In 1763 he was brought by his father to Waxhaw, South Carolina, to be adopted by his mother's brother, the Reverend William Richardson, a Presbyterian clergyman. He was educated at an academy in Charlotte, North Carolina—Queen's Museum College. He then studied at Princeton, from which he graduated in 1776 with first honors. He subsequently studied law in Salisbury, North Carolina. Although he was licensed to practice law in 1780, his service in the revolutionary war deferred his becoming a jurist until 1782.

For three months in 1777–1778 Davie served in the Camden, South Carolina, area under General Allen Jones, whose daughter, Sarah, he married in 1782, and with whom he had six children.

In 1779 he served first as lieutenant, then captain, of a troop of cavalry. His responsibilities included clearing the territory around the Catawba River of the Tory loyalists who collaborated with the British troops. (North Carolina, in proportion to its population, had the largest number of Tories in the colonies.) Joining the forces of Casimir Pulaski, Davie received the commission of major. Seriously wounded while leading a charge at the Battle of Stono near Charleston, he was hospitalized for five months. After his recovery he resumed active duty, serving with such distinction that he was appointed colonel in September 1780.

South Carolina after the autumn of 1780 was entirely at the mercy of the British, while North Carolina lay open to attack. After the defeat of Thomas Sumter's troops, Davie led the only active corps operating in the region between Camden and Salisbury. Cornwallis marched on Charlotte, and Davie moved to successfully defend it. General Nathanael Greene appointed him commissary general for an army almost devoid of funds, which he, nonetheless, succeeded in supplying from January to May 1781.

Andrew Jackson served as a young soldier under Davie. One of Jackson's biographers writes that "so far as any man was General Jackson's model soldier, William Richardson Davie of North Carolina was the individual. He was swift but wary; bold in planning enterprises, but most cautious in execution; sleeplessly vigilant; untiringly active; one of those cool, quick men who apply master-wit to the art of war; who are good soldiers because they are earnest and clear-sighted men" (Parton, 1: 72).

After the war Davie settled in Halifax, on the Roanoke River, where he practiced law for the next fifteen years. In 1782 he defended three Tory officers against a charge of high treason. They were sentenced to death but then were pardoned by the governor, who exchanged them for American soldiers held by the British.

Davie was elected to serve nine sessions of the North Carolina House of Commons (1784–1798). He was an ardent conservative who naturally aligned with the Federalists. As a legislator he fought for a sound currency, opposing the printing of paper money with nothing to back it up. He advocated a lenient policy toward Loyalists who sought to regain confiscated property, but he was most often outvoted. He opposed the cession to the federal government of the lands that would later become Tennessee. (The cession finally took place in 1789.) In 1789 he introduced a bill for the founding of the University of North Carolina and subsequently drew up its charter, chose its location at Chapel Hill, laid its cornerstone, arranged for its endowment, appointed its faculty, and planned its curriculum.

Davie was a delegate to the Federal Constitutional Convention in Philadelphia in 1787. Here he cast North Carolina's vote for the Connecticut Compromise, which provided for one legislative house with two representatives from each state and another house in which each state would be represented in proportion to population. This was possibly the most important vote taken at the convention, paving the way for ratification of the Constitution by the states. Davie also seconded the proposal that the executive be removable by impeachment and conviction. Upon returning home, Davie fought hard for his state's ratification of the Constitution. He attended the ratification convention in 1788, where the majority voted neither to ratify nor reject, and the convention in 1789, where, because the Federalists held a majority, the Constitution was finally accepted.

In 1797 Davie was appointed commander of the state militia. He became a grand master of the Masons. In 1798 he was elected governor of North Carolina by the legislature. While governor he sought to place the choice of presidential electors in the hands of the legislature rather than by popular vote, so as to benefit the Federalists in the election of 1800. He failed in this effort, however. He also saw to the military preparedness of the state in the face of a possible French attack, investigated frauds in the land office, and arranged for the demarcation of disputed boundaries with Tennessee and South Carolina.

Davie did not serve long as governor; in 1799 President John Adams (1735–1826) appointed him as one of three delegates to negotiate a treaty with France, seeking indemnification of damages for each nation and its citizens, and pacts of amity and commerce. Napoleon met with the American delegates on 30 September 1800, and freedom of commerce between the two countries was agreed upon. In 1802 President Thomas Jefferson chose Davie to serve as commissioner representing the United States to arbitrate a treaty between North Carolina and the Tuscarora Indians. By its terms the Tuscaroras were allowed to extend former leases, as well as make new ones, on land they owned in North Carolina. On 12 July 1916 title would terminate, and these lands would revert to the state.

Defeated in his run for congressional office in 1803, Davie retired from politics to spend his remaining days on his estate, "Tivoli," in Lancaster County, South Carolina. There he served as the first president of the South Carolina Agricultural Society. In 1811 he was awarded the first doctorate of laws to be granted by the University of North Carolina, in recognition of his role as founding father of that institution. Although President James Madison asked him to serve as major general during the War of 1812, he preferred to farm his plantation until his death.

• By far the best treatment of Davie's life is Blackwell P. Robinson, *William R. Davie* (1957). The entry in *The National Cyclopaedia of American Biography* contains many discrepancies in dates. Also useful is F. W. Hubbard, "Life of W. R. Davie," in *The Library of American Biography*, ed. Jared Sparks, ser. 2, vol. 15 (1848). Information on his military and legal career can be found in W. J. Peele, ed., *Lives of Distinguished North Carolinians* (1898), and information on his military career is in James Parton, *Life of Andrew Jackson* vol. 1 (1860). Information on his role in the Federal Constitutional Convention is in William K. Boyd, *History of North Carolina, 1783–1860*, vol. 2 (1919). There are several collections of Davie's papers: the William R. Davie Papers (No. 1, 1779–1819; No. 2, 1758–1852) are in the Southern Historical Collection at the University of North Carolina at Chapel Hill; the William R. Davie Papers (1778–1817) are at the North Carolina Department of Archives and History, Raleigh.

RUTH ROSENBERG

DAVIES, A. Powell (5 June 1902–26 Sept. 1957), Unitarian clergyman, was born Arthur Powell Davies in Birkenhead, England, the son of Arthur Davies, a tin smelter, and Martha Powell, both natives of Wales. A business college graduate, Davies worked as a bookkeeper on the Liverpool docks and participated in the post–World War I strikes there before being selected by the first Labour Member of Parliament from that district to serve as his secretary in the House of Commons. In London Davies joined a Fabian debating society and met George Bernard Shaw, who, impressed with his ability to think on his feet while talking, urged Davies to enter politics. Davies had a religious commitment, however, and instead matriculated at Richmond College, then the University of London Methodist training school. After he graduated with a B.D. in 1925, he was ordained a deacon in the Wesleyan Methodist District in London, which assigned him to organize a new mission church in Becontree, a suburb of London (1925–1928). He married Muriel Hannah, daughter of a Methodist minister, in December 1927, and in May 1928 they emigrated to the United States, where he was assigned to two rural parishes in Maine. The couple would have two children. After briefly attending Boston University School of Theology, Davies was assigned to the Pine Street Church, Portland, where his preaching on controversial social and international questions soon made him a prominent spokesman for liberal causes.

Making an amiable shift to the Unitarian movement, in 1933 Davies was called to the Community Church of Summit, New Jersey, where he became active in the Metropolitan Liberal Ministers Association and before long was a recognized leader in the American Unitarian Association. As spokesperson for the younger insurgent ministers, he became intent on leading the Unitarian movement into what he viewed as more vital, dynamic expressions of liberal democratic, universalistic commitments. He chaired meetings held around the country that devised a platform called "The Faith behind Freedom," and his work as chairperson of the program for the 1934 continental Unitarian Annual Meetings brought him into a denominational leadership role. He was appointed to lead a commission to draft a new statement of faith, a role that made him the generally acknowledged leading spokesperson of modern Unitarianism.

Called, in 1944, to be senior minister of the prestigious All Souls Unitarian Church in Washington, D.C., Davies rapidly became recognized as one of the most influential preachers in the United States. His political skill emerged when he chaired the Emergency Conference on Civilian Control of Atomic Energy, a committee representing more than ninety national organizations, which successfully lobbied Congress to set up the Nuclear Energy Commission under civilian rather than military control. In the 1940s he worked to desegregate recreational facilities in the District of Columbia, beginning with the police boys' club in his own church, and he organized a boycott that led to the desegregation of restaurants in the district. At the end of the Second World War, he led a campaign to feed and clothe dislocated Europeans. *Time* magazine wrote of Davies, "In Washington, D.C., where many talk but few listen, spare, sharp-profiled Rev. A (for

Arthur) Powell Davies, 44, is a man who is heard" (4 Oct. 1946). He was a leading figure in the struggle for the separation of church and state, an advocate of birth control, a leading opponent of Senator Joseph R. McCarthy, and a founder of Americans for Democratic Action as a consortium of Anti-Communist liberal forces in America.

Davies carried his message to the nation beyond the pulpit as both a frequent speaker at university chapel services and as a contributing writer to such publications as the *New Republic*, the *Nation*, the *Progressive*, *Union Now*, the *New York Times Magazine* and *Book Review*, and the *Herald-Tribune Book Section* as well as various religious journals. His published books include *The Faith of an Unrepentant Liberal* (1946), *American Destiny* (1942), *America's Real Religion* (1949), *Meaning of the Dead Sea Scrolls* (1956), and *The Urge to Persecute* (1953), among others. He died of a pulmonary infarction—similar to a heart attack—in his study in Washington, D.C., just a few days after preaching, on 22 September, a widely quoted sermon condemning the federal government for not intervening in the Little Rock, Arkansas, school desegregation stalemate of September 1957. The day following his death President Dwight D. Eisenhower ordered federal marshals into Little Rock.

• Archival information can be found at the Meadville/Lombard Theological Library in Chicago and at the Unitarian Universalist archives, Harvard/Andover Library, Harvard Divinity School, Cambridge, Mass. For additional biographical information see George N. Marshall, *A. Powell Davies and His Times* (1990).

GEORGE N. MARSHALL

DAVIES, Arthur Bowen (26 Sept. 1862–24 Oct. 1928), artist, was born in Utica, New York, the son of David Thomas Davies, a lay preacher in the Methodist church, and Phoebe Loakes (also spelled Lokes). His British parents immigrated in 1856 to the United States. Interested in art since childhood, Arthur began his formal training at the age of fifteen with Dwight Williams, a local art teacher in Cazenovia, New York. In 1878, when the family moved to Chicago, Arthur continued his studies at the Chicago Academy of Design. He supported himself with a menial job at the Chicago Board of Trade. Within a year he contracted an illness, thought to be tuberculosis, and sought a cure in Colorado. By 1881, he was well enough to travel to Mexico, where he worked as a civil engineering draftsman and railroad surveyor. In 1883 Davies returned to Chicago and resumed art studies with Charles Corwin at the Art Institute of Chicago.

In order to pursue a career as an artist, Davies moved to New York City in 1886, where he enrolled in the Art Students' League, a progressive school attended by many prominent late-nineteenth- and twentieth-century artists. He earned a living as a freelance illustrator for such journals as *Century Magazine* and *St. Nicholas*.

In the early 1890s, Davies decided to focus his efforts on painting. His early works, primarily small, atmospheric landscapes in oil and watercolor, belonged to the late Romantic tradition typified by the twilight scenes of the American painter George Inness. In 1888 Davies began exhibiting his works at the American Art Galleries and the American Watercolor Society. That same year he met William Macbeth, one of the few New York dealers to specialize in contemporary American art. As Davies's first dealer, Macbeth would prove instrumental in furthering his career. Equally important was Davies's first encounter in 1888 with the works of French symbolist Pierre Puvis de Chavannes exhibited at the National Academy of Design. Puvis de Chavannes's classically ordered, idyllic paintings would exert a lingering influence throughout Davies's stylistic development.

During this formative artistic period, Davies courted Dr. Lucy Virginia Meriwether, the chief resident at the New York Infant Asylum. They were married in 1892. Her father enabled the newlyweds to purchase a farm in Congers, New York. Renaming the property "The Golden Bough," the idealistic couple planned to raise a family and to combine farming with their careers; they had two children. While his bride enjoyed country life and the success of her rural medical practice, Davies soon lost interest in farming and regretted his isolation. In 1893 he reestablished a studio in Manhattan, where he lived during the week. On weekends, he commuted to the farm. This arrangement, which led to the couple's eventual estrangement, continued until Davies's death.

During the 1890s, Davies consolidated his position as a respected New York artist. His works were exhibited at the prestigious National Academy of Design. After selling his first painting in 1893, he began to attract patrons such as Benjamin Altman, the typewriter manufacturer Henry Harper Benedict, and, somewhat later, Lizzie Bliss, whom he met in 1907. In 1895 Altman financed Davies's first trip to Europe. The following year William Macbeth presented the artist's first solo exhibition. In 1897 Davies again traveled abroad, this time as Macbeth's purchasing agent. On his European travels Davies studied a wide variety of artistic traditions, from the frescoes of Pompeii to the brooding, symbolist paintings of the Swiss artist Arnold Böcklin.

In his mature work, Davies fused these eclectic sources to create a pastoral dream world filled with graceful nymphs and unicorns. Such mysterious and enchanting imagery earned him recognition and awards, notably the Silver Medal at the 1901 Pan-American Exposition in Buffalo and the William A. Clark Prize (1916) at the Sixth Biennial Exhibition of the Corcoran Gallery of Art in Washington, D.C.

Neither Davies's professional success nor his idyllic artistic vision reflected the turmoil of his personal life. In 1902 the painter met a dancer, Edna Potter. Within a year, they were living together in Manhattan. Reluctant to dissolve his marriage, Davies, under the assumed name David A. Owen, led a double life, with Edna Potter as his common-law wife; they had one child. For the rest of his life, Davies concealed this relationship from all but his most intimate associates, creating in him the strain to which friends and biographers later attributed his reticence and distant, professorial demeanor.

The duality of Davies's personal life mirrored a dichotomy in his professional life. If Davies's friezelike compositions of ethereal figures in idyllic settings satisfied conservative tastes, his energetic activities as an exhibition organizer, collector, and patron helped undermine the academic tradition in American art. Davies befriended two of the principal leaders of the antiacademic trend in American art: Robert Henri, whom he met in 1900, and Alfred Stieglitz, a photographer and the proprietor of the vanguard gallery "291," whom Davies first met in 1907. In 1908 Davies joined Henri to challenge the restrictive exhibition policies of the National Academy of Design with the exhibition of "The Eight" at William Macbeth's. Through his participation in the controversial show, Davies assumed a leadership role in the emerging antiacademic Independent movement. He also helped arrange a nine-city tour for this exhibition of dissident artists. That organizational experience served him well when, in 1912, he was elected the second president of the newly formed Association of American Painters and Sculptors (AAPS). The association was founded to expand exhibition opportunities for progressive artists. Under Davies's skilled leadership, the AAPS mounted the 1913 Armory Show, in some ways the most significant exhibition ever organized in this country. Known officially as the International Exhibition of Modern Art, the display of some 1,300 works by European and American artists introduced avant-garde art to mass audiences at Manhattan's Sixty-Ninth Regiment Armory, the Art Institute of Chicago, and Boston's Copley Hall. Davies was primarily responsible for the international scope of the exhibition.

After the Armory Show Davies continued to promote the cause of modern art. In December 1913 he arranged an exhibition of forty works by American modernists at the Carnegie Institute in Pittsburgh. He then persuaded the New York dealer N. E. Montross to present a modified version of the show at his gallery in February 1914. The show subsequently toured to Detroit, Cincinnati, and Baltimore. Encouraging collectors to acquire modern art, Davies advised many of this country's earliest patrons of modern art, including Lizzie Bliss, Mrs. John D. Rockefeller, Sally Lewis, and John Quinn. He himself amassed a considerable art collection that reflected his eclectic tastes, ranging from ancient medallions to modern masterpieces by Constantin Brancusi and Pablo Picasso. Assuming the role of patron, Davies provided support for his fellow artists; for example, Marsden Hartley's 1912 European travels were financed in part by Davies.

Davies's involvement with modern art affected his stylistic evolution. In 1913 he began to organize his compositions within a network of cubist color planes. His most ambitious efforts in this vein were the mural-scale canvas *Dances* (1915, Detroit Institute of Arts) and a series of murals completed for Lizzie Bliss's mu-

sic rooms (now in the collection of the Munson-Williams-Proctor Institute, Utica). But recognizing the limited success of such cubist experiments, Davies reverted to his symbolist style of painting around 1917, although he continued to explore cubist compositions in printmaking. During this period, Davies also experimented with sculpture. A group of small-scale bronze sculptures and reliefs in *pâte verre* (glass paste) reflected his antiquarian interests and collecting habits. Under the influence of Gustavus Eisen's "inhalation theory," Davies began around 1922 to depict his figures at the climax of breathing. Davies believed that by adopting this device he would recapture the vitality of ancient art. Between 1924 and 1926 he completed his last major murals, a series commissioned by Mrs. John D. Rockefeller for International House on Riverside Drive in New York.

Davies died unrecognized in Florence while traveling with Edna Potter and their daughter. The resultant month's delay in the news of his death did not prevent the ultimate revelation of his secret life to his family and to the world. The subsequent dispersal of Davies's art collection at public auction in April 1929 probably lent impetus to the establishment of the Museum of Modern Art in New York later that year. In his dual career as an artist and patron, Davies fostered a network of private and institutional support for the growth of modern art in the United States.

• The principal body of the artist's papers is retained by the Davies family in Congers, New York. Significant correspondence from Davies may be found in the papers of William Macbeth, Walt Kuhn, Sally Lewis, and Frederick Newlin Price in the Archives of American Art, Smithsonian Institution. Important letters from Davies are also located in the Alfred Stieglitz Archive, Collection of American Literature, Beinecke Rare Book and Manuscript Library, Yale University, New Haven; in the John Quinn Memorial Collection of the New York Public Library, Astor, Lenox and Tilden Foundations; and in the Elmer MacRae Papers in the Hirshhorn Museum and Sculpture Garden, Smithsonian Institution, Washington, D.C. The two most useful studies of Davies's art are Joseph S. Czestochowski, *The Works of Arthur B. Davies* (1979), and Stephen S. Prokopoff et al., *Dream Vision: The Work of Arthur B. Davies* (1981). For Davies's role as a patron, see Judith Zilczer, "Arthur B. Davies: The Artist as Patron," *American Art Journal* 19, no. 3 (1987): 54–83. For his role in the Armory Show, see Milton W. Brown, *The Story of the Armory Show* (rev. ed., 1988). A concise but excellent biography of the artist is Brooks Wright, *The Artist and the Unicorn* (1978). Obituaries are in *Art News* 27, no. 12 (1928): 12; and *The Arts* 15, no. 2 (1929): 29–93.

JUDITH ZILCZER

DAVIES, Henry Eugene, Jr. (2 July 1836–6 Sept. 1894), soldier and public official, was born in New York City, the son of Henry Eugene Davies, a lawyer and judge, and Rebecca Tappan. A student at both Harvard and Williams College, he graduated from Columbia in 1857. Thereafter he practiced law in New York, where in 1858 he married Julia Rich. Whether they had any children is not known. At the outbreak of the Civil War, Davies's education and social position helped him gain a captaincy in a prominent New York regiment, the Duryée Zouaves (Fifth N.Y. Volunteer Infantry). Early in May 1861 he accompanied his outfit to Fort Monroe, Virginia, at the confluence of the Chesapeake Bay and the James River. In that early theater of the war, Davies supervised picket duty and conducted scouting expeditions within Major General Benjamin F. Butler's Department of Virginia. In the battle of Big Bethel, 10 June, the first land engagement in the eastern theater, Captain Davies led his company of red-trousered Zouaves in a spirited advance against the center of the Confederate line, only to be withdrawn by commanders too inexperienced to realize that victory was within reach.

Davies's baptism of battle revealed a capacity for higher command, but he grew tired of infantry service. He coveted a commission in the cavalry, for which his short stature and slender physique appeared to recommend him. Again, family and service connections served him well: on 1 August he was appointed a major in the Second New York (the "Harris Light") Cavalry, an outfit organized and led by his uncle, Colonel J. Mansfield Davies, with a comrade from the Duryée Zouaves, Lieutenant Colonel H. Judson Kilpatrick, as second in command. Dapper and soft-spoken (he was afflicted by a noticeable lisp), Davies soon developed a reputation as a strict disciplinarian and a stickler for military etiquette. His men considered him a "perfect gentleman," without hauteur or snobbishness.

For the first year and a half of its existence, the Second New York saw action in a succession of campaigns as part of the Army of the Potomac and, during the Second Bull Run (Second Manassas) campaign, in the Army of Virginia. More often than not, the regiment formed part of small, compact units of horsemen, usually attached to infantry commands. Often it was fragmented into battalions, squadrons, and companies for field service. In these campaigns, Davies comported himself ably and courageously, winning special notice for his handling of skirmisher units. The plaudits of his superiors enabled him to rise to lieutenant colonel, 6 December 1862, as Kilpatrick succeeded to regimental (and later brigade) command.

Rejoining his regiment in April 1863 after a long furlough, Davies learned that a new era had dawned. By order of the commander of the Army of the Potomac, Major General Joseph Hooker, the heretofore scattered troopers had been grouped into a large, powerful corps. Under its new chief, Major General George Stoneman, the corps set out on an expedition into the rear of Robert E. Lee's Army of Northern Virginia during the Chancellorsville campaign. Part of a column led by Colonel Kilpatrick, Davies's regiment destroyed strategic railroads, burned supply depots, and raided to the gates of Richmond before seeking refuge from pursuers on the Virginia Peninsula. The Second New York was not so successful during the second battle of Brandy Station, 9 June, where a sabre charge led by Davies went awry. Attacked in flank and rear by the horsemen of Major General J. E. B. Stuart, the New Yorkers were forced into a confused retreat.

Sent home on medical leave a week after the battle, Davies missed the rest of the Gettysburg campaign, but when draft riots swept New York in mid-July, he left his sickbed to help lead the city's mounted units against the mob.

Upon retaking the field in mid-August, Davies was promoted to colonel of his regiment. A little over a month later he was a brigadier general—one of the few nonprofessional soldiers to attain star rank in the cavalry in the East. One of Davies's sergeants noted that "no promotion was ever more fitly made." At the head of the First Brigade, Third Division, Cavalry Corps, he served with distinction in the series of post-Gettysburg engagements along the Rappahannock and Rapidan rivers, including Third Brandy Station (13 Sept.), Buckland Mills (19 Oct.), and Germanna Ford (18 Nov.).

In late November and early December Davies took part in the abortive Mine Run campaign, and three months later he returned to Richmond on an expedition led by Kilpatrick, designed to capture and sack the enemy capital. On 1 March 1864, when the raiders encountered unexpected resistance from Richmond's defense battalion, Davies persuaded his commander to attack a key sector of the works, an idea that might have opened the city to invasion. At the eleventh hour, however, a nervous Kilpatrick called off the assault and retreated, his mission unaccomplished.

At the outset of the 1864 campaign, the army's new mounted leader, Major General Philip H. Sheridan, placed Davies at the head of the First Brigade, Second Division, Cavalry Corps. Davies led the command in a succession of raids, skirmishes, and battles, including Todd's Tavern, the largest dismounted cavalry fight of the war (7 May); Yellow Tavern, where Stuart took a mortal wound (11 May); Haw's Shop (28 May); Trevilian Station (11–12 June); St. Mary's Church (24 June); and Second Deep Bottom (13–20 Aug.); as well as in the several engagements around Petersburg, including Reams's Station, the Vaughan Road, the Boydton Plank Road, and Jarratt's Station. He was wounded at Hatcher's Run on 6 February 1865. Davies capped his war service by seizing more than 200 supply wagons and 400 horses and mules at Paines's Crossroads, 5 April 1865, a critical loss that may have influenced Robert E. Lee to end his retreat from Petersburg and Richmond and surrender his army at Appomattox Court House.

Resigning from the army on 1 January 1866 as a major general, Davies returned to his law practice in Manhattan. Until 1869 he served as the city's public administrator and from 1869 until 1872 as assistant district attorney for the southern district of New York. Moving to the Hudson Valley late in life, he wrote a memoir, *Ten Days on the Plains* (1871; repr. 1985); a volume of genealogy, *A Genealogical and Biographical Monograph on the Family and Descendants of John Davies of Litchfield, Connecticut* (1895); and a well-crafted biography, *General Sheridan* (1895). He also published *General Statement of the System of Taxation Ex-*

isting in the City of New York, March 1, 1883 (1883). Davies died in Middleboro, Massachusetts.

Davies's Civil War record appears to speak for itself. He participated in dozens of engagements without a published word of censure. On the contrary, repeated praise from his superiors and steady promotions testify to a high level of leadership. A dissenting voice, however, comes from one of his regimental officers, Colonel Walter Raleigh Robbins of the First New Jersey Cavalry (a regiment in Davies's brigade), who scrutinized Davies in brigade command. Robbins concluded that Davies depended heavily on his subordinates in planning and executing tactics, realizing that he himself "lacked the faculty of knowing how to dispose of his forces in order to get the best results." Too often, when Davies made his own dispositions, things went wrong. An example cited by Robbins is the December 1864 engagement near Jarratt's Station, Virginia, when the general ordered Major Lucius M. Sargent, Jr., of the First Massachusetts to lead a mounted charge across broken ground against a trio of forts, each mounting three cannon. Before reaching its objective, the major's detachment was devastated by shrapnel and canister, most of its men being killed or wounded. As the mortally wounded Sargent was borne past Davies, he cursed the brigade commander for his disastrous tactics. Although the incident never made the official reports, the rank and file viewed it as another illustration of Davies's "usual incapacity."

• Since no body of his personal papers exists, one must recreate Davies's life and career from published sources. His campaign reports are available in various volumes of *The War of the Rebellion: A Compilation of the Official Records of the Union and Confederate Armies* (128 vols., 1880–1901). The operations of his commands can be traced in general works such as Charles D. Rhodes, *History of the Cavalry of the Army of the Potomac* (1900), and the first two volumes of Stephen Z. Starr's trilogy, *The Union Cavalry in the Civil War* (1979–1985). Davies's role in Kilpatrick's raid on Richmond is briefly told in Virgil Carrington Jones, *Eight Hours before Richmond* (1957), while his participation in the Appomattox campaign receives detailed treatment in Henry E. Tremain, *Last Hours of Sheridan's Cavalry* (1904). As for the memoirs of contemporaries, the *Personal Memoirs of P. H. Sheridan, General United States Army* (1888) presents a balanced, objective account of the general; while a favorable portrait of Davies emerges from Willard W. Glazier, *Three Years in the Federal Cavalry* (1870); and a much more critical view is expressed in Lilian Rea, ed., *War Record and Personal Experiences of Walter Raleigh Robbins, from April 22, 1861, to August 4, 1865* (1923).

EDWARD G. LONGACRE

DAVIES, John Vipond (13 Oct. 1862–4 Oct. 1939), civil engineer, was born in Swansea, Wales, the son of Andrew Davies, a physician, and Emily Vipond. He attended classes at the Wesleyan College, Taunton, England, and the University of London, but he received no degree. In 1880 he began as an apprentice to contracting engineers Parfitt & Jenkins in Cardiff, Wales. Although their specialty was structural work, they also built drydocks and engines. He next worked for several years as an assistant engineer engaged in construction at the Monmouthshire coal mines. To gain broader experience, in 1888 he served as a marine engineer on a voyage to Australia.

When Davies arrived in the United States in 1889, he was hired by Austin Corbin of the Philadelphia & Reading Railroad. Corbin had formed a subsidiary company at Mahanoy City, Pennsylvania, to take coal waste from the railroad's considerable mining interests and convert it into a usable and profitable form. Since about one-seventh of all coal mined ended as dust, the process Davies helped devise had considerable importance to the company. Coal particles along with a pitch binder were compacted under great pressure to produce coal briquettes that were manageable and that burned with an intensity equal to or better than lump coal.

After completing this project, Davies moved to New York City where he continued his association with Charles M. Jacobs, with whom he had worked on the coal reclamation project. First, he assisted Jacobs with plans to develop Corbin's Long Island Railroad as part of an overall rapid transit system; he then served as assistant chief engineer during the construction of the East River Gas Company tunnel project.

The ten-foot-diameter tunnel through the bed of the East River carried mains from the gas plant at Ravenswood, Queens, to Manhattan. Despite several delays, the subaqueous construction, which included excavating under Blackwell's Island, was the first successful bore under the city's extensive harbor. By relying on the safety provided by a tunnel shield and compressed air, work progressed relatively uneventfully and was completed in 1893.

Jacobs had opened a consulting engineering office in 1891; at the conclusion of the tunnel project he and Davies formed a professional partnership. The East River project established their specialty, and they became leading consultants, primarily in New York City, in subaqueous and foundation work. During the late 1890s Davies continued his association with the Long Island Railroad, overseeing the line's Atlantic Avenue improvement in Brooklyn and also serving as superintendent of their floating equipment. In 1895 Davies married Ruth Ramsey. The couple had three children.

The first large-scale project undertaken by Jacobs and Davies commenced in 1902 when they set about completing the moribund Hudson River railroad tunnel. Work on the "Old North" tunnel, which would link New York and New Jersey, had actually begun in 1874. But construction had progressed slowly, and with the onset of countless technical and financial problems, the work was finally abandoned in the 1890s. The tunnel's completion in 1904 was made possible only by solid financial backing and the sound engineering skills of Jacobs and Davies. Their method of pushing the riverbed silt aside rather than excavating it as the work progressed was new and became a much-copied technique in future subaqueous tunnel work. This was the first tunnel of any kind under the Hudson River; eventually it became part of the city's rapid transit system.

As general consulting civil engineers, the firm was occasionally called on to carry out projects other than tunnels. One of the most prominent of these undertakings was Hales Bar Dam near Chattanooga, Tennessee. It was to provide hydroelectric power for the Chattanooga and Tennessee River Power Company, and although construction began in 1905, unexpected geological faults and the withdrawal of contractors caused the work to be seriously delayed. In a demonstration of their versatility, Jacobs and Davies hired their own crews and assumed execution of the work in June 1910. The dam was successfully completed in 1913 and was put on line in 1914.

The firm of Jacobs and Davies was incorporated in 1909. In that same year Davies renewed his association with the Hudson and Manhattan Railroad Company. The firm undertook to extend the line's rails in New Jersey and beneath Manhattan. In time Davies not only became chief engineer of the Hudson and Manhattan but an officer and director of the company as well.

The engineering skills of Jacobs and Davies led to international projects that included tunnels for a hydroelectric project in Mexico and the rapid transit system in Paris. Work on another utility tunnel under the East River began in 1910. This ambitious project was in the area of Hell Gate and was carried out for the Astoria Light, Heat, and Power Company. When it was completed, gas manufactured on Long Island was brought into the city through the tunnel by way of two 72-inch-diameter castiron mains. At the same time this project was being carried out, the firm was providing engineering supervision of the excavation for the site of the New York Central Railroad's Grand Central Station in New York City.

In 1913 discussions took place regarding construction of a railroad tunnel through the Rocky Mountains at the Continental Divide. Davies was appointed to a three-member board of engineers that eventually oversaw the project.

In 1916 Jacobs retired and returned to his native Great Britain. Davies, however, maintained the organization under the same name and continued to serve as its president until his death.

The recommendations made by Davies and the board of engineers to the Denver Tunnel Commission regarding the location and profile of the Rocky Mountain tunnel were carried out, beginning in 1923. By the time the Moffat Tunnel was holed through in 1927, severe unexpected flooding had tested the engineering skills of all involved.

Davies was consultant on—and in some cases built—a number of other important projects. The broad spectrum of his work included design of a city water supply tunnel under the Detroit River, preliminary plans for railroad tunnels under the Hudson and East rivers for the Pennsylvania Railroad, proposals for tunnels in New Orleans and San Francisco, design and construction of intake and discharge tunnels for

the New York Edison Company, and membership on commissions in New York and New Jersey studying a Hudson River highway crossing.

Davies was a member of the American Society of Civil Engineers and a charter member of the American Institute of Consulting Engineers. He also belonged to the Institution of Civil Engineers, the American Institute of Mining and Metallurgical Engineers, and the United Engineering Societies. He was active in the Railroad Club of New York, the Engineers Club, and the Oakland Golf Club.

Davies was awarded the Telford Gold Medal in 1914 by England's Institution of Civil Engineering. The American Society of Civil Engineers honored him in 1913 with the Norman Gold Medal for his paper "Air Resistances to Trains in Tube Tunnels" and in 1917 with the Thomas Fitch Rowland Prize for his paper "The Astoria Tunnel under the East River for Gas Distribution in New York City." In 1930 the society presented him with its Fowler Professional Award. His writing was primarily technical and appeared in professional publications. He died at his home in Flushing, New York.

• Information on the life of Davies is scant and must be assembled from several sources. His comments on various projects appear as transcribed discussions in the American Society of Civil Engineers, *Transactions* (1915, 1916, 1919, 1920, 1921, 1931). His two award-winning articles in the *Transactions* (1912, 1916), clearly illustrate his engineering knowledge. Davies's skill as a historian of engineering is revealed in his "Progress in the Art of Tunneling," *Engineering News-Record* (1924). One of the most thorough sketches of his life, written by fellow tunnel expert James Forgie, is "Memoir of John Vipond Davies" in the American Society of Civil Engineers, *Transactions* (1940). An obituary is in the *New York Times*, 5 Oct. 1939.

WILLIAM E. WORTHINGTON, JR.

DAVIES, Joseph Edward (29 Nov. 1876–9 May 1958), lawyer, diplomat, and author, was born in Watertown, Wisconsin, the son of Edward Davies, a successful wagonmaker, and Rahel Paynter, a minister of the Welsh Congregationalist church. An outstanding high school and university student, Davies took an A.B. and an LL.B. at the University of Wisconsin and practiced law in his home county from 1902 to 1906. He married Emlen Knight in 1902; they had three children.

In 1906 Davies moved to Madison, where he became active as a trial lawyer and in state Democratic party politics. He played a leading role in winning the party's nomination and then the presidential race in Wisconsin for Woodrow Wilson in 1912. His reward was appointment as the first chairman of the newly created Federal Trade Commission in 1915. An opponent of monopolies but a strong believer that government should interfere as little as possible in a free-enterprise economy, Davies soon antagonized those in the party who wanted government to assert its new regulatory powers over business. Davies was a poor chairman, complained Louis Brandeis, because he "hated monopolies but loved bigness" when bigness "was the real curse." After little more than one year in office, his fellow commissioners managed to oust Davies from the chairmanship. Disappointed, Davies served briefly on the War Industries Board. In 1918 a new opportunity presented itself when the death of a U.S. senator from Wisconsin necessitated a special election. Davies ran strongly as his party's candidate, but he made the mistake of censuring Senator Robert M. La Follette (1855–1925), who opposed Wilson's internationalist policies and enjoyed wide-ranging support in his home state of Wisconsin. In a closely contested election, Davies lost by fewer than 5,000 votes to his Republican opponent.

Placing his political ambition on hold, Davies returned to the law and moved to Washington, D.C., in 1920, where he organized the law firm of Davies, Jones and Beebe. The three partners, all former trade commissioners, specialized in antitrust and international law and dispensed expensive advice to businesspeople worried about the legal niceties of their activities in the boom times of the 1920s. Davies himself made headlines when he won a record-breaking fee rumored to be in excess of $2 million for his performance as defense counsel in the Ford Tax Case of 1927–1928. Henry Ford (1863–1947) and some of his stockholders were being sued by the federal government for nonpayment of taxes, and Davies not only won a dismissal of the charges but also a handsome tax refund for his clients. In 1935 Davies made headlines of quite a different kind when he divorced his wife and married Marjorie Merriweather Post Hutton, heiress to the General Foods fortune and Washington socialite. They had no children.

Little more than a year later, the White House announced that Davies was to be the next ambassador to the Soviet Union. The prospect of sending the millionaire couple to the workers' state provoked some irreverent newspaper comments. As best he could, Davies defended himself against the charge that his political ambition, rekindled by a second marriage, and a generous contribution to President Franklin D. Roosevelt's reelection campaign were his only qualifications for the post in Moscow. He pointed out that in the 1920s he had acted as counsel to governments and businesses in Mexico, Peru, the Netherlands, Greece, and the Dominican Republic. He was not an inexperienced observer of the international scene, and the "boss" (as he affectionately called FDR) had given him a special mission to find out "the facts" about the Soviet Union. Davies did not tell reporters that he and Marjorie planned to be short-term tenants only in Moscow; they had been promised London.

This last unpublicized item of news might have lightened the atmosphere in the American embassy in Moscow, where the professional diplomats (George Kennan, Loy Henderson, and others) were in a mood of revolt when they heard of Davies's appointment. The end of 1936 was not an auspicious moment for an amateur to come to the Soviet Union to explain the brutal and bizarre events that were happening there. A

few weeks before Davies's arrival, Joseph Stalin staged the first show trial in Moscow and unleashed the full fury of the purges aimed at opponents of his regime. Stalin claimed to have uncovered a monstrous conspiracy between the "anti-Party bloc" of supporters of the exiled Leon Trotsky and the spy networks of hostile Western nations. The aim of this conspiracy was to destroy Soviet power. Isolated in the diplomatic village in Moscow, the American secretaries watched horrified as Stalin's purge machine plunged ruthlessly into the ranks of the party and beyond. Images of Stalin as paranoid and pathological played like lightning flashes in the American embassy's somber reporting of the bloodletting all around them. "We are witnessing," reported the American embassy, "the self-erasure of the power of the Soviet Union."

Patiently Davies listened to this indictment of the regime in Moscow by the secretaries, but his lawyer's instinct told him to reserve judgment until he had examined all the facts firsthand. A few months after his arrival, Davies undertook the first of a number of inspection trips into the agricultural and industrial heartland of the Soviet Union. The damage inflicted by Stalin was frightful, reported Davies, but there could be no doubt that the nation would survive this latest crisis in growth. The Soviet Union was simply one of the greatest physical forces for good or evil that existed in the world—it would not disappear.

Returning to the embassy in Moscow, Davies thought he knew why he and the professional diplomats differed so dramatically in their findings. The diplomats in the village had personal immunity against everything but their emotions. So "prolonged and incessant" were the "hammer blows" of the terror, recalled Kennan in his memoirs, that the "effect was never to leave me." Davies was understanding. Nevertheless, he reported to Washington that it would be foolish to write off the Soviet Union as unfit to be the ally of the Western democracies at a time when the Axis powers were preparing to fight a global war.

This was the message that Davies took home with him to Washington. Appointed to a second post in Brussels (1938) and then wartime committee work (1939–1941) in the State Department, Davies proclaimed loudly to anyone who would listen, "We must get Russia back before it is too late." No one appeared to pay any attention. His State Department colleagues condemned him for trying to appease Stalin who had shown his true colors when he signed a friendship pact with Adolf Hitler in August 1939. Davies's advocacy was an embarrassment to most; one person, however, responded promptly when Davies offered to write a popular account of what he had seen in the Soviet Union for the enlightenment of his fellow citizens. "Grand, go ahead, Joe," President Roosevelt replied, as the Red Army continued to amaze everyone with its heroic and sustained defense of the motherland. "I can't take communism nor can you but to cross this bridge I would hold hands with the Devil." Davies's *Mission to Moscow* (1941) appeared a few days after Japan's attack on Pearl Harbor, and its author became an instant pundit on the Soviet Union. His unshakable belief that the Soviet Union was destined to play a vital role in the defeat of the Axis powers was confirmed each day by reports from the eastern front.

Admitted to the inner circle of presidential advisers, Davies was sent by Roosevelt to meet with Stalin and help prepare for the Teheran Conference in 1943. In the last year of the war, President Harry S. Truman sent him to London to discuss plans for peacetime cooperation with Winston Churchill and then took him to Potsdam. In 1946 Davies was awarded the Medal for Merit, the nation's highest civilian award, to add to his Lenin Peace Medal. Davies undertook his last mission for the White House in 1951, when he attended an Organization of American States conference on nationalization issues.

From influence at the highest level of policy making to rejection was to be a short step for Davies as the Cold War intensified in the 1950s. These were not good years for him. His health was failing, his marriage was breaking up, and Davies saw his reputation collapse as the professionals who had scorned his views in the 1930s and 1940s took charge of making containment policy under Truman and Dwight D. Eisenhower. Davies died in Washington, D.C. The published tributes to him invariably concluded that he had been both naive and mistaken about the Soviet Union.

When he wrote *Mission to Moscow* in 1941, Davies set himself the task of explaining why he was right and the secretaries were wrong about the strength of the Soviet Union. He had been fortunate to escape the oppressive atmosphere of the diplomatic village in Moscow and to discover a nation whose resources—human and material—were vast enough to survive Stalin's purges and to defeat Hitler's armies. He rejected Western diplomatic reporting of the Soviet Union under Stalin as a self-destructive Asiatic despotism, an "evil empire" in the making. Historians today question whether the totalitarian model contrived by diplomats in the 1930s to explain the terror describes the larger nation created by Stalin. Davies was right about the strength of this nation when it was important to be right, and his insights still deserve attention.

• Davies's papers are at the Library of Congress and include diary entries, biographical notes, and an unpublished autobiography, "In the Days of Their Power and Glory." Richard H. Ullman, "The Davies Mission and United States–Soviet Union Relations 1937–1941," *World Politics* 9 (Jan. 1957): 220–39, is a trenchant Cold War period critique. Elizabeth K. MacLean, "Joseph E. Davies and Soviet-American Relations 1941–1943," *Diplomatic History* 4 (1980), helps to restore some balance. Keith Eagles, *Ambassador Joseph E. Davies and American-Soviet Relations, 1937–1941* (1985) and Elizabeth Kimball MacLean, *Joseph E. Davies; Envoy to the Soviets* (1992) are both full-length studies.

KEITH D. EAGLES

DAVIES, Marion (3 Jan. 1897–22 Sept. 1961), actress, was born Marion Cecilia Douras in Brooklyn, New York, the daughter of Bernard J. Douras, a lawyer, and Rose Reilly. Davies grew up in prosperous neigh-borhoods in Brooklyn, Manhattan, and, for two years, Chicago. She ended her academic education in 1913 by leaving the Convent of the Sacred Heart in Hastings-on-Hudson, New York, where she had boarded for three years. After training in tap and ballet, and with the encouragement of older sisters who already were performers, she began getting parts in musical revues. Like her three sisters she changed her name from Douras to Davies when she began her stage career.

In 1915 while in the revue *Stop! Look! Listen!* she began a relationship with newspaper publisher William Randolph Hearst, then fifty-two, that after an uncertain start and some troubled interludes lasted until his death in 1951. One of the most famous, and scandalous, couples of their era, Hearst and Davies never married. Millicent Willson, mother of Hearst's five children, refused his perhaps half-hearted requests for divorce; for years he continued to spend time with her. However, he found many ways to express his strong, often possessive commitment to Davies. By 1916 publicity from Hearst newspapers, later followed by Hearst's heavy investment in her professional training, enhanced the fame she already was winning among New York theater audiences. Her winsome beauty and ability to engage an audience helped her turn a persistent stammer into an asset.

In 1917 she appeared in her first movie, *Runaway, Romany*, and in 1919 Cosmopolitan Pictures, established by Hearst, released her first feature film, *Cecilia of the Pink Roses*. She soon took a role in the company's management, as Hearst began to transfer his filmmaking operations from New York, where Davies temporarily remained, to California. Despite some expensive failures, films such as *When Knighthood Was in Flower* (1922) and *Little Old New York* (1923) won her both popular and critical success, making her one of the highest-paid women in America. The heavy-handed financial and promotional backing of the Hearst empire sometimes diverted attention from her genuine comedic talent, as did Hearst's attempts to satisfy his fantasies by pushing her into inappropriate dramatic roles and overwrought costume epics. By late 1925 the palatial (more than 100 rooms) San Simeon, most extravagant of Hearst's and Davies's various residences, was ready for occupancy, and there they entertained the rich and famous in a manner recorded in numerous memoirs as well as in fiction and film.

Davies appeared in more than forty films, most released, in collaboration with either Cosmopolitan or Marion Davies Productions, by Paramount, Metro-Goldwyn-Mayer, or, for her final films, Warner Brothers. Despite a successful transition from silent to sound films, her career encountered various problems. Her drinking made her miss some assignments, her later films consistently lost money, and in part due to Hearst's preferences she continued to play innocent young heroines long after she was out of place in such roles. In 1937 she made her last movie. Davies invested her wealth wisely, mainly in real estate, and helped Hearst survive financial crises aggravated by his compulsive spending. She earned a reputation as one of the most generous benefactors in Hollywood, assisting many charitable causes, most notably a children's clinic in Los Angeles that bears her name. In 1951, soon after Hearst's death, Davies and merchant marine Captain Horace G. Brown entered into a sometime tempestuous marriage that lasted until her death in Hollywood.

A few of her films, such as *Quality Street* (1927) and *Show People* (1928), continue to receive respectful critical attention. However, by the end of her life she had become best known as the assumed inspiration for the Susan Alexander role in Orson Welles and Herman Mankiewicz's 1941 film *Citizen Kane*. Like Davies, Alexander was winsome and engaged in a notorious relationship with a wealthy newspaper publisher and public figure, although to satisfy Hollywood's production code the fictional character had to marry her paramour before she could live openly with him. Both Davies and Alexander became addicted to both alcohol and jigsaw puzzles and lived, sometimes with overbearing crowds of guests and sometimes in lonely isolation, on a vast estate of wild extravagance. But the differences were significant. Alexander was an opera singer rather than an actress, and she never brought pleasure to an audience. Davies did.

• The Library of the Academy of Motion Picture Arts and Sciences in Beverly Hills, Calif., has various pertinent materials, including clippings, photographs, production information for a few of her films, and some letters, including the Marion Davies–Hedda Hopper correspondence. For a biography and useful annotated list of Davies's films, see Fred Lawrence Guiles, *Marion Davies: A Biography* (1972). Her posthumously published memoir, *The Times We Had: Life with William Randolph Hearst* (1975), includes an apologetic foreword by Orson Welles. See also W. A. Swanberg, *Citizen Hearst: A Biography of William Randolph Hearst* (1961). An obituary is in the *New York Times*, 24 Sept. 1961.

GEORGE H. ROEDER, JR.

DAVIES, Samuel (3 Nov. 1723–4 Feb. 1761), Presbyterian minister, author, and educator, was born in the Welsh Tract in Pencader Hundred, New Castle County, Delaware, the son of David Davies (whose family name appears also as David and Davis) and Martha Thomas, farmers. After his mother shifted her allegiance from the Baptists to the Presbyterians, Davies enrolled at the classical academy conducted by the Reverend Samuel Blair at Fagg's Manor, Pennsylvania. Blair, one of America's best teachers of the mid-eighteenth century, trained Davies thoroughly in the classics, initiated him into the experiential piety of revivalistic Calvinism, and prepared him for the Presbyterian ministry. Shortly after Davies finished his study with Blair, he was licensed by the New Side (or revivalistic) Presbytery of New Castle on 30 July 1746. Later that year he married Sarah Kirkpatrick, who died giving birth on 15 September 1747.

On 19 February 1747 Davies was ordained by his presbytery as an evangelist to Virginia, a colony that at the time had almost no Dissenting Protestant minis-

ters. During the spring of 1747 Davies spent one month itinerating in Hanover County, Virginia, but not before obtaining a preaching license from the Virginia General Court. Tubercular symptoms forced him to break off his preaching tour. The next year, with health improved, Davies received another call from the scattered Dissenters of Hanover County and began a permanent ministry. Once again, however, he took the prudent step of obtaining a license in Williamsburg, this time from Governor William Gooch. On 4 October 1748, soon after settling in Virginia, Davies married Jane Holt, whose brother John later helped Davies publish sermons, poems, and political commentary. The Davies had six children, five of whom survived to adulthood. Oddly, only one of his children became a professing Christian.

Davies's career as a minister, though lasting little more than a decade and regularly complicated by ill health, was distinctive for its remarkable range. More than anyone else he was responsible for the growth of Presbyterianism in Virginia and much of the upper South. When he settled in Hanover County, a handful of Presbyterian families were scattered throughout Virginia north of the James River. When he departed in 1759, each of his seven preaching stations had become a full-fledged church, a presbytery had been organized for Virginia (established 30 Dec. 1755), nearly ten other ministers had joined him in the work, missionary activity had been carried out in the Carolinas, and the Presbyterians had won a substantial measure of de facto toleration from Virginia's Anglican establishment. Davies's success was due to his religious zeal, his political persistence, and his patriotic service.

As a New Side Presbyterian, Davies stressed the need for spiritual regeneration. His sermons effectively drove home the main themes of revivalistic Calvinism—the desperate condition of the soul without God, the generous freedom of divine grace in rescuing sinners, and the holy privilege of devoting a redeemed life to the service of God. Unlike some revivalist colleagues, however, Davies presented his message with rhetorical sophistication. A sermon from February 1757 on Christ as "the only foundation" well illustrated his skill. His listeners were asked, "Have you been formed into proper stones for this spiritual temple? Has God hewn you . . . by his word, and broken off whatever was rugged, irregular, and unfit to be compacted into the building? . . . Do you feel this divine architect daily carrying on this work in you, polishing you more and more into a resemblance of Christ?" (*Sermons* [1849 ed.], vol. 2, p. 39). Davies's combination of natural diction and affecting rhetoric had its profoundest effect in spreading the Christian faith, but it also influenced the style of political speech. The young Patrick Henry often heard Davies preach and later claimed to have been influenced by what he heard.

Davies succeeded in Virginia because of his political skill almost as much as his homiletical skill. As a Presbyterian he was suspect as a rival by some Anglican ministers and as a source of social disorder by the Virginia government. Davies sought to alleviate these anxieties by emphasizing the civilizing force of the religion he preached. He also argued that Presbyterians warranted protection under the Act of Toleration passed by Parliament in 1689. With these arguments, Davies and his Dissenting colleagues made some legal headway. But they achieved even more freedom for their churches when the Presbyterians took the lead in rousing the population during the French and Indian Wars. Davies was a particularly effective orator on behalf of Britain in the war with France, and official worries about the Presbyterians faded away rapidly after Davies's indispensable contribution to the war effort.

Davies also enjoyed a considerable reputation as a teacher. He prepared several young men for academies such as the one he had attended and also for the Presbyterians' College of New Jersey (later Princeton University). He was himself an avid reader of contemporary poetry and British moralists like Samuel Johnson, as well as of theology, and he eagerly assisted his parishioners in their efforts to secure books. The College of New Jersey bestowed the M.A. on Davies in September 1753, and from that point Davies's attachment to this institution grew steadily. From November 1753 to February 1755 he undertook a trip to Great Britain with Gilbert Tennent, another stalwart of New Side Presbyterianism, to raise money for the college. The two not only succeeded in securing at least £3,000 (which was used to move the college from Newark to Princeton and to construct Nassau Hall), but Davies was also able to promote the cause of religious freedom through personal interviews, secure patronage for several educational projects, and meet George Whitefield, John and Charles Wesley, and many other religious leaders.

Of all Davies's labors as a teacher, the most remarkable was solicitude for the education of African-American slaves and Native Americans. He was not a social radical and in fact owned at least one or two slaves himself. But he was a determined pioneer in training slaves to read, providing them with books, and urging them to become regular members of the church. A sermon from 1754, *The Duty of Christians to Propagate Their Religion among the Heathens, Earnestly Recommended to the Masters of Negro Slaves in Virginia*, defended African Americans as fully human, at least for religious and educational purposes. By 1755 Davies had baptized 100 slaves and regularly preached to 200 more.

Davies was also a considerable amateur poet. Like the Puritan Edward Taylor in New England, he often wrote hymns or poems related to the biblical texts that he used in his sermons. Through his wife's brother Davies published in 1752 a collection titled *Miscellaneous Poems, Chiefly on Divine Subjects*. In form the poems are respectable examples of neoclassical style; in substance they occasionally rise above conventional piety, as when in "Conjugal Love and Happiness" Davies likens his wife to a "noble Vine" who "Round the rough Trunk with loving Tendrils twine, / And blooms on high, a fair prolific Vine." Davies was the first Anglo-American to write a body of published hymnody, eighteen of which are extant, including at least one still found in some Protestant hymnbooks, "Great God of Wonders."

In August 1758 the trustees of the College of New Jersey, after having recently lost presidents Aaron Burr (1715–1757) and Jonathan Edwards (1703–1758) through death, asked Davies to become their head. He refused this first request, in large part because his parishioners could not countenance his departure. But when the trustees repeated their request, Davies agreed. He was in Princeton by July and, with characteristic energy, threw himself immediately into college business. He lived in Princeton only nineteen months before his death there, but it was long enough to show that, had he survived, he might have become the most notable American college president before the Revolution. At the College of New Jersey, Davies placed a new stress on oratory, strengthened the students' work in English composition, inventoried the library, encouraged Benjamin Rush (who became a notable patriot and reformer) to pursue a medical career, trained several postgraduates for the ministry, transformed commencement into a day-long spectacle of declamation and debate, himself wrote odes (on "Peace" and "Science") that were sung at his two commencements, and regularly urged the undergraduates to seek the New Birth. Worn out by his labors, Davies succumbed to pneumonia only one month after preaching a memorable sermon on the same text that Aaron Burr had chosen the first Sunday of the year of his demise, Jeremiah 28:16—"This year you shall die."

• A few of Davies's letters are preserved with the Benjamin Rush manuscripts at the Historical Society of Pennsylvania; a few other papers are in the Princeton University Library and the Presbyterian Historical Society (Philadelphia). Excellent editions of Davies's poetry are Louis Fitzgerald Benson, "The Hymns of President Davies," *Journal of the Presbyterian Historical Society* 2 (1903): 343–73, and Richard Beale Davis, ed., *Collected Poems of Samuel Davies* (1968). At least twenty-six of Davies's works were published in his lifetime and can be read in the Early American Imprint series. Many of Davies's sermons were printed in his own lifetime. After his death over eighty of them were published in a collected edition, *Sermons on Important Subjects*, that was reprinted under various titles for more than a century after his death. George William Pilcher edited the diary Davies wrote during his British trip, *The Reverend Samuel Davies Abroad* (1967), and also wrote a solid biography, *Samuel Davies: Apostle of Dissent in Colonial Virginia* (1971), as well as several important articles such as "Samuel Davies and the Instruction of Negroes in Virginia," *Virginia Magazine of Biography and History* 74 (1966): 293–300. Davies's Virginia career is examined in Wesley M. Gewehr, *The Great Awakening in Virginia, 1740–1790* (1930); Ernest Trice Thompson, *Presbyterians in the South*, vol. 1 (1963); and William Henry Foote, *Sketches of Virginia: Historical and Biographical* (1850). Foote transcribes many valuable documents. Alan Heimert, *Religion and the American Mind from the Great Awakening to the Revolution* (1966), is outstanding on the political implications of Davies's oratory. For his career at the College of New Jersey, see Thomas Jefferson Wertenbaker, *Princeton 1746–1896* (1946);

Douglas Sloan, *The Scottish Enlightenment and the American College Ideal* (1971); and James McLachlan, ed., *Princetonians 1748–1768: A Biographical Dictionary* (1976).

MARK A. NOLL

DAVIS, Adelle (25 Feb. 1904–31 May 1974), nutritionist and author, was born Daisie Adelle Davis on a farm in Lizton, Hendricks County, Indiana, the daughter of Charles Eugene Davis and Harriette McBroom. Ten days after Davis's birth, her mother became paralyzed, then died when the baby was seventeen months old. Davis later was said to have decided on a career in nutrition in reaction to having been malnourished as a baby when after her mother's death she was fed with a medicine dropper. The youngest of five daughters, Davis was raised by her father and an elderly aunt. She later dropped the name Daisie because of its association with farm animals. Despite the large family, she had a strict and lonely upbringing. As a child she worked on the farm and attended 4-H meetings.

After graduating from Lizton High School, Davis attended Purdue University beginning in 1923 and then transferred to the University of California at Berkeley two years later. She received her B.A. in dietetics, or household science, in 1927. After graduation she moved to New York and took dietetics training at Bellevue and Fordham hospitals, became a dietician for the Yonkers public schools, and was a consulting nutritionist for three obstetricians at the Judson Health Center in New York. In 1931 Davis moved back to California and became a consulting nutritionist for the Alameda County Health Clinic in Oakland and for the William E. Branch Clinic in Hollywood. She received her M.S. in biochemistry from the University of Southern California School of Medicine in 1939. Her private consulting practice, started around 1927–1928, continued until 1958.

In 1946 Davis married George Edward Leisey, an engineer and surveyor ten years her junior; they adopted two children. According to their marriage certificate, Davis had been married before. Davis and Leisey were divorced in 1953, and in 1960 Davis married Frank Vernon Sieglinger, a retired accountant and lawyer.

Early in her career Davis published two minor books, *Optimum Health* (privately printed in 1935) and *You Can Stay Well* (1939); she followed these with the high school textbook *Vitality through Planned Nutrition* (1942). Davis first became a public figure when her cookbook, *Let's Cook It Right*, was published in 1947. It was first revised in 1962. She dedicated it "to my daughter, Barbara, in the hope that her husband and children will not have to eat TV dinners." *Let's Cook It Right* is a nonthreatening introduction to healthful cooking. Davis stresses the use of natural foods and is particularly concerned with carcinogens and the importance of healthy food in preventing cancer. Recipes are uncomplicated and easy to follow, and Davis includes numerous variants for many recipes. Beginning *Let's Cook It Right* with a good introduction on nutrition, Davis includes chapters on meat, meat substitutes, leftovers, fish, eggs and cheese, vegetables, soups, salads, bread, and healthful desserts. *Let's Cook It Right* gives directions and advice in a concise, direct style. It became Davis's most successful book, free from the repetitions that plagued her other books.

In *Let's Have Healthy Children* (1951), Davis concentrates on diets for pregnant women. She stresses vitamin supplements and advocates breastfeeding. *Let's Eat Right to Keep Fit* (1954) was attacked by the medical profession for its declarations that diseases and abnormalities could be largely prevented by vitamin supplements. In this book Davis describes her own regimen and prescribes what the reader must eat to prevent illness.

Davis's most unconventional book is *Exploring Inner Space: Personal Experiences under LSD-25* (1961), published under the pseudonym of Jane Dunlap. In a flamboyant style, Davis describes her early experiments with LSD and her spiritual revelations and visions while under its influence. Despite medical reports about LSD's harm to the genes and the body, Davis speaks in favor of its benefits, contradicting her lifelong warnings about ingesting chemicals and carcinogens. In *Let's Get Well* (1965), she prescribes vitamins and diets for common illness and diseases. Using anecdotes, case histories, and personal testimonials, she builds her arguments for healthy eating and vitamin and mineral supplements. Davis's most controversial book, it advises taking heavy doses of vitamins, a practice that the American Medical Association has warned against because of potential toxicity.

With each new book Davis seemed to become both more popular and more controversial. She became a favorite on television and the lecture circuit while she was being subjected to increasing criticism from the medical establishment. Her readers and followers were true believers, and her manner and style were convincing and sincere. What Davis attempted to do in her books was to act as a self-styled authority between the medical industry and the lay nutritionist. She was able to take a vast amount of data and simplify it for the lay reader, but she has been accused of factual inaccuracies. On the other hand, she has been validated by professionals and colleagues and appreciated by readers, including W. C. Fields and Charles Laughton, whom she helped personally. She turned out to be right, for example, about the benefits of vitamin E in general and for preventing anemia in premature infants. Davis did more to make Americans aware of nutrition and their eating habits than any other health professional. During her lifetime, over ten million copies of her books were sold.

In 1973, at the peak of her popularity, Davis discovered that she had bone marrow cancer. This she blamed on having had "too many X-rays," and less than a year later she died at home in Palos Verdes Estates, California.

• Biographical information on Davis can be found in Jane Howard, "Earth Mother to the Foodists," *Life*, 22 Oct. 1971; "High Priestess of Nutrition," *Time*, 18 Dec. 1972; Daniel

Yergin, "Supernutritionist," *New York Times Magazine*, 20 May 1973; and John Poppy's interview with Davis in *Look*, 15 Dec. 1970. For critiques of her work see Ruth Baker, "Encounter with Adelle Davis," *Journal of Nutrition Education* 4 (Summer 1972): 92–94, and Edward H. Rynearson, "Americans Love Hogwash," *Nutrition Review* 1974 (July 1974): 1. See also Ronald M. Deutsch, *The New Nuts among the Berries* (1977). Obituaries are in the *New York Times*, 1 June 1974, and the *Washington Post*, 2 June 1974.

ANN RAYSON

DAVIS, Alexander Jackson (24 July 1803–14 Jan. 1892), architect, was born in New York City, the son of Cornelius Davis, a bookseller and editor of theological works, and Julia Jackson. Davis spent his early years in New Jersey and attended elementary school in upstate New York. In 1818 Davis went to Alexandria, Virginia, to learn the printing trade from a half-brother. His enthusiastic reading of romantic literature and acting in amateur theatrical productions stimulated his imagination and aroused his sense of drama.

From 1823 onward he lived mostly in New York City. Resolving to become a professional artist, he drew especially views of buildings there and in the Northeast, many of which were published as engravings and lithographs. One of the early American lithographic artists, he drew for Anthony Imbert in New York and William Pendleton in Boston; an expert delineator and watercolorist, he was one of the finest architectural renderers of his period. His temperament and early experience as an artist, rather than the usual background of a builder, gave Davis a visual approach to the aesthetics of architecture and the freedom to explore innovative ideas, forms, and styles.

Turning seriously to architecture, Davis drafted briefly for Josiah R. Brady. He studied in the libraries of Ithiel Town and the Boston Athenaeum, and began to create original designs. In January 1829 Davis designed James A. Hillhouse's country house at New Haven, and in February 1829 he became Town's partner. He remained in partnership with Town until May 1835 (with James H. Dakin for eighteen months), and again in 1842–1843. After Town, except for a year with Russell Warren in 1835–1836, he worked alone, without a clerk and with only an occasional draftsman. In 1836–1837 he and Thomas U. Walter led in forming the American Institution of Architects, which soon failed; twenty years later, Davis was an original trustee of the American Institute of Architects, an organization that has long survived.

Town & Davis produced outstanding civic, institutional, religious, commercial, and residential buildings of many types, from New England to New Orleans. Most were forceful, innovative versions of the Greek Revival, with deep porticoes, giant columns, and massive piers, as in the state capitols of Indiana (1831–1835) and North Carolina (1833–1840) and New York's Custom House (1833–1842) but the designs also explored Tuscan, Gothic, Egyptian, and Oriental styles. Throughout his career Davis's urban and institutional designs were usually based on the rational symmetry of classicism, even when their style was ostensibly Gothic, as at the Virginia Military Institute (1848–1861) and the House of Mansions in New York City (1858–1859, not extant). Many designs incorporated his precursory multistoried "Davisean" window, used in these buildings and at Davidson College, for example. Sometimes Davis brought features and decorative details from his rural designing into the urban scene, in such forms as bay and oriel windows, verandas, and bracketed eaves.

For rural settings, especially hilly landscapes, Davis introduced villas and cottages with the harmonizing irregularities and dramatic lines of romantic Gothic, Italianate, and Bracketed forms. In his book *Rural Residences* (issued 1838), he criticized "the bald and uninteresting aspect of our houses" and "the want of connexion [of the house] with its site." Inspired by English picturesque models, Davis's designs worked to overcome these deficiencies. Early examples were Robert Donaldson's gate houses in Annandale-on-Hudson, New York (1836, not extant; 1841), Henry Sheldon's Gothic cottage near Tarrytown, New York (1838–1840), William Paulding's "Knoll" near Tarrytown, New York (1838–1842; enlarged as "Lyndhurst," 1864–1867), Joel Rathbone's "Kenwood" near Albany, New York (1842–1849, not extant), and John M. Morehead's "Blandwood" in Greensboro, North Carolina (1844).

Davis's romantic country houses were first built along the Hudson Valley, but his ideas and patterns were widely disseminated in Andrew Jackson Downing's books and in the *Horticulturist*, publications on which Davis collaborated (1839–1850). In 1863 Robert Donaldson, for whom Davis designed the first American Gothic cottage, wrote to him: "*Downing stole your thunder* for a while, but I always . . . claimed for you the *seminal* ideas which have been so fruitful."

Of Davis's own designs for romantic villas and cottages, some hundred were executed (never exact duplicates) with irregularities and decorative features for harmony and interest in the rural scene. Several designs were for the romantically landscaped suburb Llewellyn Park, West Orange, New Jersey (in whose concept Davis probably shared with Llewellyn S. Haskell. Outstanding were his Gothic villas for Philip St. George Cocke (1845–1848), Henry K. Harral (1846–1850, not extant), and John J. Herrick (1855–1859, not extant), as well as his cottage villas for Henry Delamater (1844) and William J. Rotch (1845–1847?). Davis produced many villas of an "Americanized Italian" design, notably those for Haskell (1850–1852, not extant), Richard O. Morris (1851–1854), Richard Lathers (1851–1852, not extant), and Edwin C. Litchfield (1853–1858). For appropriate settings, a few country houses, like "Montgomery Place" (1841–1844, 1863–1864), were classical in style.

The Civil War drastically changed America and adversely affected Davis's career, although his postwar designs for Gothic Lyndhurst (1864–1865) and neoclassical Montgomery Place were the climax to his rural residential designs. In 1878 Davis closed his office, where he had usually both lived and worked. He joined his wife, Margaret Beale, whom he had married in 1853, and their two children. "Wildmont," his summer lodge overlooking Llewellyn Park, West Orange, New Jersey, was enlarged for year-round use, but it burned down in 1884, before the family could move there, and Davis died in a small house on its site.

Innovative and influential, Davis was a leader in bringing American architecture into the modern period, freeing it from past limitations and opening it to new forms and styles. Robert A. M. Stern has called Davis "a modern architect." He introduced styles new to America and invented the American Bracketed style. His designs broke open the boxlike American house form, with projections extending in every direction, bay and oriel windows reaching out, and verandas linking the house with the surrounding landscape. His interior planning was often unusual, moving toward open floor plans and space flow. Tempered by classical rationalism, Davis worked in the Romantic spirit of his day, with a deep love of nature that harmonized architecture and landscape, but his designs looked into the future.

• The major collections of Davis's drawings and papers are in the Metropolitan Museum of Art, Avery Architectural and Fine Arts Library at Columbia University, New-York Historical Society, New York Public Library, and Henry Francis du Pont Winterthur Museum, Winterthur, Del. In William Dunlap's *History of the Rise and Progress of the Arts of Design in America* (1834), the entry on Davis was edited from his draft. A survey of his life and work is in Amelia Peck, ed., *Alexander Jackson Davis, American Architect, 1803–1892* (1992), with a list of works and reproductions of many drawings; other drawings appear in [Jane B. Davies], *A. J. Davis and American Classicism* (1989). The entry on Davis in the *Macmillan Encyclopedia of Architects* (1982) has a long biographical account and a bibliography. Roger Hale Newton's *Town & Davis, Architects: Pioneers in American Revivalist Architecture, 1812–1870* (1942) is outdated. For Davis's relationship with Andrew Jackson Downing, see George B. Tatum, ed., *Prophet with Honor* (1989). For Davis's educational designs, see Paul Venable Turner, *Campus: An American Planning Tradition* (1984), and John V. Allcott, *The Campus at Chapel Hill* (1986); for his work in the South, see Mills Lane's series of books, *Architecture of the Old South* (1984–1996).

JANE B. DAVIES

DAVIS, Alice Brown (10 Sept. 1852–21 June 1935), Seminole leader and merchant, was born in Park Hill, Cherokee Nation (now in Cherokee County, Okla.), the daughter of John F. Brown, a physician, and Lucy Redbeard, a Seminole of the Panther clan (Kachaki). Her parents met while her father was employed as a contract physician for the federal government during the removal of most of the Seminoles from Florida to the Indian Territory in the 1840s. One of seven children, Alice was educated at home and also attended schools in the Cherokee Nation and the Presbyterian mission school near Wewoka.

Owing to a Seminole law at the time that forbade marriage to Americans, the family had to reside outside of the Seminole Nation and lived in Park Hill until the outbreak of the Civil War. During the war, the family lived in Fort Gibson and afterward moved to Greenhead Prairie (now in Pottawatomie County, Okla.). Her father died in 1867 as a result of overwork during a cholera epidemic, and her mother died shortly thereafter. Her oldest brother, John, then assumed responsibility for the family.

Alice married George R. Davis, a merchant's clerk, in 1874 in Okmulgee, Creek Nation (now in Okmulgee County, Okla.); they had eleven children. In 1882, they moved to the Seminole Nation and established a trading post and ranch at Arbeka in the northeast corner of the nation (now in Seminole County, Okla.). A post office was established there within the year, with George as postmaster. After George died in 1899, Alice continued to run the store, ranch, and post office.

Following the Civil War, the Brown family emerged as one of the most prominent in the Seminole Nation. Davis's older brother, John F. Brown, Jr., a successful merchant and rancher, was elected principal chief in 1885 and served until his death in 1919. Another brother, Andrew J. Brown, served as tribal treasurer during much of the late nineteenth century. Both were also Baptist ministers.

Davis entered public life in various capacities after John's election, often serving as an interpreter for Seminoles dealing with U.S. authorities and in federal courts and acting as disbursing agent for Union pensions to Seminole veterans of the Civil War. She participated in delegations to Mexico in 1903, 1905, and 1910 that unsuccessfully pressed Seminole claims to a land grant made to Seminole chief Kowakochi (Wildcat) by the Mexican government in the 1850s. She was also part of a missionary party from the Oklahoma Seminoles to the Florida Seminoles in 1909.

Davis taught at Emahaka Academy for Girls and Mekasukey Academy for Boys, tribal boarding schools, during the 1890s and early 1900s. She served as superintendent of Emahaka Academy from 1905 to 1906. During this period the U.S. government was extending its control over tribal affairs in preparation for the division of tribal lands among the Seminoles, formal dissolution of the Seminole government, and the admission of Oklahoma into the Union. Federal authorities questioned Davis's handling of finances at the school, and she turned it over to them in 1906.

In 1922, the government needed the signature of the Seminole principal chief on the deed of sale for the Emahaka Academy. Since the office had lapsed following John Brown's death, President Warren G. Harding appointed Davis to the office. Although her appointment drew protest from the Seminoles, who felt a man should hold the office, she was confirmed in the post. Her tenure, however, was brief. When she demanded compensation to the Seminoles for a portion of the Emahaka property lost owing to federal mismanagement, the secretary of the interior summarily dismissed her.

Despite her earlier financial success, allotment and the transition from an independent Seminole Nation to the new state of Oklahoma in 1907 proved an economic hardship for Davis, as for many prosperous Indians. Indian merchants began to face increased competition from white merchants, who previously were largely excluded by federal regulations, and Indian ranchers lost free access to extensive, tribally owned grazing lands and were restricted to their much smaller allotments or forced to rent pasturage from other landowners. Because of a chronic shortage of cash in the Indian Territory, most businesspeople there relied heavily on credit, and this undoubtedly contributed to the subsequent decline or failure of many Indian entrepreneurs such as Davis. By the end of her life, she was living in modest circumstances in Wewoka, Oklahoma, where she died.

A capable and assertive woman, Alice B. Davis enjoyed a long and varied career, exceptional for her times. A successful merchant and rancher as well as public servant, she displayed personal and public concern for her people and often aided the less fortunate. Recognized as an outstanding Native American and citizen of Oklahoma, Davis is commemorated by a bronze bust on display at the American Indian Hall of Fame in Anadarko, Oklahoma. A women's dormitory at the University of Oklahoma has also been named after her.

• Biographical information on Davis can be found in Carolyn Thomas Foreman, *Indian Women Chiefs* (1954) and "John Jumper," in *Chronicles of Oklahoma* (1951); Angie Debo, *The Road to Disappearance* (1941); Edwin C. McReynolds, *The Seminoles* (1957); and [Muriel H. Wright], "Seal of the Seminole Nation," in *Chronicles of Oklahoma* (1956), and "Unveiling the Sculptured Bronze of Alice Brown Davis," in *Chronicles of Oklahoma* (1965). Obituaries and accounts of her life are in the *Wewoka Times-Democrat*, 21, 23, and 24 June 1935, and the *Daily Oklahoman*, 22 June 1935.

RICHARD A. SATTLER

DAVIS, Andrew Jackson (11 Aug. 1826–13 Jan. 1910), prominent American Spiritualist and author, was born in Blooming Grove, New York, the son of Samuel Davis, an uneducated farmer, weaver, and shoemaker, and his wife (name unknown). Davis grew up in poverty and received little formal education. In 1841 he was apprenticed to a shoemaker in Poughkeepsie. There, after lectures by a phrenologist and mesmerist named Grimes had sparked enthusiasm for hypnotism, he met William Levingston, a local tailor who was interested in trance states. Levingston found that Davis was an extraordinarily adept subject. Davis soon was able to perform clairvoyance and medical diagnosis while in hypnotic trance, reportedly could read newspapers blindfolded, and saw human bodies as transparent, revealing their auras and inner anatomy.

In March 1844, waking from sleep the night following a hypnotic session, and not long after the death of his mother, Davis claimed to have had a visionary experience. Called by a voice like his mother's, he found himself speeding unhindered over the Catskill Mountains. He saw a flock of sheep in great confusion and brought them to order. He then received three myste-

rious figures. First, a diminutive personage handed him a scroll with the enigmatic words:

As they were, so they are:
As they are, so they will be!
Now do you believe it?

Davis opined that these lines compared the sheep to the human race, which is confused, as the sheep once were, and will be set to rights as the sheep are now. Crossing the Hudson River in his vision, he reached a graveyard. There, he met Galen, the great physician of antiquity, who gave him an elegant cane, or staff, of healing. Finally, the tall form of the eighteenth-century spiritual philosopher Emanuel Swedenborg appeared, promising that he would instruct and guide him. This presence is significant, for the life and thought of Davis—like that of Spiritualism generally—can be regarded as a combination of mesmerist practice and Swedenborgian doctrine.

Not long after this experience, Davis began delivering discourses on scientific, historical, and philosophical matters while in trance. His amanuensis was a Universalist minister named William Fishbough, and the small circle that attended the séances sometimes included Edgar Allan Poe, the Fourierist Albert Brisbane, and the utopian communalist Thomas Lake Harris. In 1847 Davis's trance revelations were published as *The Principles of Nature, Her Divine Revelations, and a Voice to Mankind*. Despite some eight hundred pages, this encyclopedic book created a sensation. It began with the creation of the world from "liquid fire," presented the history of human religion from a deistic perspective, and spoke of the spiritual constitution of humankind. The destiny of the soul was articulated in passages that acknowledge Swedenborg as precursor but depart from the Swede in such particulars as Davis's refusal to accept hell or the unique authority of the Christian Scriptures. The book favored the views of the French utopian Charles Fourier, denounced conventional religion, and in general exuded an ultraliberal spirit. Then, as later, the book's originality was much debated.

Davis published a magazine advancing his views, the *Univercolum and Spiritual Philosopher*, from 1847 to 1849. When mysterious rappings were announced at the home of the Fox sisters near Rochester, New York, in 1848, the phenomenon that ignited the Spiritualistic movement, Davis was quick to interpret them in terms of his philosophy and became a leading spokesman for the new faith.

Also in 1848, Davis married Catherine ("Katie") DeWolfe Dodge, a wealthy woman twenty years his senior and in poor health, whom he called his "Spirit-Sister." The union followed her much-publicized divorce. She died five years later, but Davis soon lost his inheritance in litigation and bad business ventures. In 1855 he married another divorcée, Mary Fenn Love, a prominent Spiritualist and worker for women's rights, who escaped her oppressive marriage by embracing Spiritualism and Davis.

Davis asserted that marriage is truly valid only between soul mates; those who find themselves in non-spiritual unions have the right and indeed the duty to seek divorce; genuine soul mates, when they come together, possess freedom to determine whether their conjugal partnership will be temporal or eternal. That view of love and marriage, highly controversial at the time, was tested in 1884 when Davis proceeded to divorce Mary on the grounds that he now realized they were not true soul mates. Although he defended this action at length in his autobiography, *Beyond the Valley* (1885), the divorce did much harm to his reputation. In 1885 he married Della E. Markham.

Between 1850 and 1855 Davis wrote his major work, *The Great Harmonia*, in five volumes. Its "Harmonial Philosophy" provided an intellectual understanding of the varied phenomena of Spiritualism. Beyond Spiritualist circles the book influenced radical social, educational, medical, and religious thought. At times, as in 1878, when he disassociated himself from Spiritualism to form the short-lived First Harmonial Associated of New York, Davis felt himself in tension with what he saw as the tendency of most Spiritualists to look for sensational séance room manifestations more than philosophical depth.

The Harmonial Philosophy could be considered an open naturalism. In contrast to the supernaturalism and salvationism of Christianity, Davis—who did not consider himself a Christian—viewed the spiritual realm as continuous with nature and governed by natural laws appropriate to its own character. He believed that after physical death spirits gravitate to a level that reflects the extent to which their lives have been in harmony with universal, divine law; they then progress through a series of six spheres above earth (the higher of which were called the Summerland) to greater and greater degrees of perfection. In the same way, the earth world was becoming better and better. Although critics may see Davis as insufficiently aware of the tenacious power of evil in human affairs, his views fitted the optimistic mood of radical thinkers of his day.

In 1863 Davis gave a lecture in New York in which he idyllically described the education of children in the Summerland in garden schools called Lyceums. His listeners were impressed enough to found such schools on earth, commencing the Lyceum movement in Spiritualism. The Lyceums were based on Davis's teaching that "a child is the repository of infinite possibilities. Enfolded in the human infant is the beautiful 'image' of an imperishable and perfect being." This educational method anticipated a great deal of later pedagogical theory in endeavoring to draw out a child's own potential rather than injecting knowledge and restricting development to predetermined channels.

In 1886 Davis took a degree from the United States Medical College in New York. He then moved to Boston, where he practiced medicine and operated a bookstore. He died in Boston.

Davis to a large extent created early Spiritualism's juxtaposition of Neoplatonist/Swedenborgian metaphysics, mesmeric trance, and radical/utopian thought on social issues such as marriage. Although little read today, his books and lectures had considerable influence in his time and provide important insights into the mid-nineteenth-century American experience.

• In addition to those already cited, Davis's major works include his autobiography, *The Magic Staff* (1857), and its sequel, *Beyond the Valley* (1855), and treatises such as *The Penetralia, Being Harmonial Answers* (1856), *The Harbinger of Health* (1861), and *A Stellar Key to the Summer Land* (1867). Important material is anthologized in Anon., *The Harmonial Philosophy: A Compendium and Digest of the Works of Andrew Jackson Davis* (1917). Though there is no full-length biography of Davis, information about him may be found in studies of the Spiritualist movement, such as Ann Braude, *Radical Spirits* (1989), Slater Brown, *The Heyday of Spiritualism* (1970), J. Stillson Judah, *The History and Philosophy of the Metaphysical Movements in America* (1967), and Geoffrey K. Nelson, *Spiritualism and Society* (1969). See also Robert W. Delp, "Andrew Jackson Davis and Spiritualism," in A. Wrobel, ed., *Pseudo-Science and Society in Nineteenth-Century America* (1987).

ROBERT S. ELLWOOD

DAVIS, Arthur Powell (9 Feb. 1861–7 Aug. 1933), hydrographer and engineer, was born near Decatur, Illinois, the son of John Davis, a livestock farmer, nurseryman, newspaper owner, and congressman, and Martha Ann Powell. When he was eleven years old, his family relocated to a farm close to Junction City, Kansas, where he graduated from high school. Davis entered the Kansas State Normal School (now Emporia State University) in Emporia, Kansas. After graduating, he moved to Washington, D.C., in 1882. He also joined the U.S. Geological Survey, then directed by his uncle John Wesley Powell, as an assistant topographer in 1882; in 1884 he was given a position as a topographer of the Rocky Mountain Division.

In 1888 Davis received a B.S. from the Corcoran Scientific School of Columbian College (now George Washington University). That year he was transferred to the Irrigation Survey, for which he selected and surveyed reservoir sites for two years. He married Elizabeth Brown, a part-time astronomical calculator who worked on the *American Ephemeris and Nautical Almanac*, in 1888; they had four daughters. He then became the head of topographic work for the Southwest Section of the U.S. Geological Survey. Appointed hydrographer in 1896, he was placed in charge of all U.S. Geological Survey stream gauging (measurements of stream flow) in 1896–1897. He was then assigned to the Isthmian Canal Commission as a hydrographer in charge of determining rainfall, stream flow, flood control, and other hydrographic conditions for both the Panama and Nicaraguan canal routes. After the U.S. Reclamation Service was established within the U.S. Geological Survey in 1903, Davis was appointed as assistant chief engineer. In 1907, when the Reclamation Service became an independent agency, he became its chief engineer in 1908 and, in 1914, its director. He was a member of a seven-man board of engineers in 1909 that reported on the feasibility and type of canal to be built in Panama; and in 1911, for the Russian government, he investigated irrigation possibilities in the Kara Kum Desert using the waters of the Amudarya River in Turkestan (along the border between Turkmenistan and Uzbekistan). From 1912 to 1917 Davis served as the vice president of the Joint Conference on Standard Specifications for Portland Cement, which promulgated the first uniform government specifications for portland cement. Meanwhile, in 1914 the American Red Cross sent Davis to the Honan, Anhwi, and Kiangsu provinces in China to survey and investigate the Huai River Conservancy Project. He studied the slides in the Culebra Cut of the Panama Canal in 1915 as a member of a National Academy of Sciences committee.

In 1920 the Reclamation Service, under Davis's direction, was ordered under the Kinkaid Act to study and report on the lower Colorado River and problems of flood protection for the Imperial Valley of California. In that same year and following the death of his first wife (1917), he married Marie McNaughton of Washington, D.C.; they had no children. Davis then served as technical consultant to the Colorado River Commission, established by Congress in 1921 to mediate the conflicting claims of the seven Colorado basin states to use of the river's water. In 1923 he was sent to London, England, as a technical adviser of the United States before the Pecuniary Claims Arbitration following the First World War. Davis also was the Lyman Lecturer on conservation of water resources at Yale University in 1922 and 1924.

Davis presided over dam construction and project development under the aegis of the U.S. Reclamation Service from 1902 to 1923. Under his supervision the service built more than 100 dams and projects to bring irrigation water to more than 3 million acres in sixteen western states. It reportedly created homes and jobs for 500,000 people. Davis was the first to propose construction of multipurpose dams, generating electricity as well as providing irrigation water and thus paying the cost of constructing irrigation projects. He also is generally credited with being the first to envision the Boulder Canyon Project (Hoover or Boulder Dam), for preparing its preliminary plans, and for locating the dam site. Under his administration and with his sponsorship, the technology of dam construction, tunnel driving, and aqueduct installation underwent exponential growth.

Notable structures completed under Davis's supervision include the six-mile-long Gunnison Tunnel in Colorado (1909); the four-mile-long Strawberry Tunnel in Utah; the Shoshone Dam (now Buffalo Bill) in Wyoming (highest in the world when completed in 1910); the Roosevelt Dam in Arizona (dedicated 1911); the Arrowrock Dam in Idaho (highest in the world when completed in 1915); and the Elephant Butte Dam in New Mexico (1916). Although many subsequent dams and projects somewhat overshadow those constructed under Davis's supervision, his work presaged the era of building large, multipurpose hydroelectric and irrigation dams in the United States during the middle twentieth century. Works built during his administration and subsequently by the Bureau of Reclamation became an essential foundation of the society and economy between the Rocky Mountains and the Pacific Ocean. The projects also irrevocably altered the western landscape and its environments.

Davis described many of the projects completed under his administration in *Irrigation Works Constructed by the United States Government* (1917). *Problems of Imperial Valley and Vicinity* (Senate Document 142, 67th Cong., 2d sess. 1922), a report mandated by the Kinkaid Act of 1920, gives special attention to flood control on the lower Colorado River and strongly recommends constructing the Boulder Canyon Project. Davis also authored *Irrigation Investigation in Arizona* (1898); *Hydrography of Nicaragua* (1899); *Elevation and Stadia Tables* (1901); *Hydrography of the American Isthmus* (1902); *Water Storage on Salt River, Arizona* (1903); and *Irrigation Engineering* (1919), written with Herbert M. Wilson.

Under Davis, the Reclamation Service continued to attract criticism because the settlers on the lands of the irrigation projects largely failed to meet the payments required to defray project costs. In addition, delay in completion of projects was chronic, and settlers complained that the service was not attentive to their needs. Finally, the service became embroiled in political conflicts between promoters of different projects and advocates of public and private power development. Although not responsible for many of the problems, Davis became the scapegoat, and in 1923 Hubert Work, the secretary of the interior, dismissed him by reorganizing the Reclamation Service as the Bureau of Reclamation and abolishing the position of director. Work justified his action by declaring that the chief executive of the Reclamation Service/Bureau should be a businessman rather than an engineer.

Davis's dismissal was denounced by professional engineering associations as an unwarranted intrusion of politics into scientific and technical affairs and as part of a crusade against public power generation on the part of private power companies. Threatened congressional investigation, however, did not materialize. Almost immediately after his dismissal, Davis became the chief engineer and general manager of the East Bay Municipal Utility District, which supplies domestic water to communities along the east side of San Francisco Bay. In the early 1930s he was a consultant to the Soviet government on irrigation in Turkestan and Transcaucasia, and in 1933 he was appointed as a consulting engineer in the Bureau of Reclamation. By this time, however, he was too ill to accept the appointment.

Davis was the vice president of the Washington Academy of Sciences in 1908 and the president of the American Society of Civil Engineers in 1920. He was an honorary member of the Washington Society of Engineers and the president of the society in 1907. He was a fellow of the American Geographical Society and a member of the American Philosophical Society and the American Academy of Political and Social Science. He was a member of the Commonwealth Club of San Francisco and of the Cosmos Club, founded by his uncle, John Wesley Powell, in Washington, D.C. Davis died in Oakland, California.

• Basic sources of information that address Davis's life and contributions include *Civil Engineering*, Sept. 1933, p. 538; Charles A. Bissell and F. E. Weymouth, "Arthur Powell Davis, Past President, American Society of Civil Engineers," *Transactions, American Society of Civil Engineers* 100 (1935): 1582–91; Doris Ostrander Dawdy, *Congress in Its Wisdom: The Bureau of Reclamation and the Public Interest* (1989); "Arthur Powell Davis, Boulder Dam Consultant, Dies," *Engineering News Record*, 10 Aug. 1933, p. 181; Albert R. Golze, *Reclamation in the United States* (1952); Gene M. Gressley, "Arthur Powell Davis, Reclamation and the West," *Agricultural History* 42 (July 1968): 241–57; and Kurt E. Peck, *Water for the West: The Bureau of Reclamation, 1902–1977* (1979). An obituary is in the *New York Times*, 8 Aug. 1933.
RALPH L. LANGENHEIM, JR.

DAVIS, Arthur Vining (30 May 1867–17 Nov. 1962), industrialist, financier, and philanthropist, was born in Sharon, Massachusetts, the son of Perley B. Davis, a Congregational minister, and Mary Vining. Educated in Hyde Park, Massachusetts, and at Roxbury Latin School in Boston, Davis enrolled at Amherst College and graduated in 1888 at the top of his class. He left for Pittsburgh, where Alfred Hunt, a metallurgist and former parishioner of Davis's father, hired him to help Charles Martin Hall, a research chemist. Hall had discovered an inexpensive method for electrolytically reducing alumina into aluminum, and he was trying to produce aluminum at the Pittsburgh Reduction Company's pilot plant. On Thanksgiving Day 1888 Hall and Davis poured the plant's first commercial-grade aluminum, and an industry was born. In 1896 Davis married Florence Holmes, who died in 1908; the couple had no children.

As Davis recalled, "While it was a great and wonderful thing to invent the process for making aluminum, it was a totally different . . . and infinitely more difficult problem to make aluminum commercially, and a still greater problem to utilize the aluminum when made." In order to create a market for the household use of aluminum, Davis churned out a raft of aluminum pots and pans and recruited college students to sell them across the country. As aluminum developed new uses—especially in aviation—production grew. The Pittsburgh Reduction Company, which in 1907 changed its name to the Aluminum Company of America, or Alcoa, grew as well. By lowering production costs and increasing output, Davis encouraged a sharp reduction in the price of aluminum over the years.

Davis's technical and managerial acumen allowed him to rise to the top of Alcoa. He had become a close assistant to Hunt and after Hunt's death in 1899 was promoted to general manager. In 1910 Davis replaced Richard Mellon as company president. In 1912 he married Elizabeth Hawkins Weiman; Davis had one stepdaughter as a result of this marriage.

Even before he became president, it was Davis who guided Alcoa's policies, and he was quick to implement Hunt's strategy of vertical integration. Alcoa soon controlled all stages of aluminum production, from bauxite supplies, to refineries, to the fabricating facilities where aluminum was turned into sheets, foil, tubing, cookware, and other products. Discouraging potential rivals was central to Alcoa's competitive gains: the company enjoyed economies of scale that made it unprofitable for others to enter the field. Davis once explained that at Alcoa "it was always our idea to carry on the business in such a manner that the inducement to go into the aluminum business would not be inordinately great." Davis also moved aggressively to dominate new markets for aluminum—such as in the aircraft and auto industries and in building and construction—and stressed company research to maintain Alcoa's lead in new technologies.

Davis increased Alcoa's foreign holdings as well, establishing hydroelectric power sources, smelters, foundries, and sales offices in Europe and Canada. It was in Canada in the mid-1920s that Davis realized perhaps his greatest social achievement, the creation of a model community for Alcoa families. The town, called "Arvida" after the first two letters of Davis's three names, was located in Quebec and featured houses on generous plots sold to company employees at affordable prices and low interest. The company also provided schools and police and fire service. Arvida earned widespread recognition as a successful example of a company-run community.

In a surprise 1928 move, Davis divested virtually all of Alcoa's foreign holdings, creating Aluminum Limited of Canada (now known as Alcan). Davis had concluded that the company could not effectively manage both American and European operations. He also wished to create top positions for his younger brother Edward and for Roy Hunt, Alfred Hunt's son, both of whom were vying to succeed Davis, who was contemplating retirement. Edward Davis became head of Aluminum Limited, Hunt stayed at Alcoa, and Davis became Alcoa's first chairman of the board.

During World War II, Davis, at this time in his seventies, worked with the federal government to help meet the immense Allied demand for aluminum. Alcoa's early assurances of a plentiful supply were quickly contravened by shortages in 1941, and the government had to step in to ensure adequate production. Davis spent most of the war in Washington, and between 1941 and 1943 he arranged for Alcoa to build and manage more than twenty new plants that would be owned and financed by the government. Alcoa devoted its wartime aluminum production almost entirely to military demands, especially for aircraft, shifting away from civilian markets, and thereby contributed to the decisive Allied air superiority. For his role in the successful aluminum production drive, Davis received the Presidential Certificate of Merit. During the war he also allowed the navy to recommission his yacht, the *Elda*, as a patrol boat.

The end of the war spelled the end of Alcoa's monopoly. Since 1911 the federal government had targeted Alcoa for antitrust legislation, and in 1937 its efforts culminated in an antitrust suit. Protective of the empire he had created, in 1938 the gritty Davis spent six straight weeks on the witness stand. He displayed a mastery of detail and manufacturing concepts as well as a keen memory of events that won him praise even from the prosecuting team. In 1942 a lower court judge acquitted Alcoa. But the government appealed the decision, and in 1945 Judge Learned Hand of the U.S. Second Circuit Court ruled Alcoa a monopoly not through intent but by virtue of market share. The early wartime shortages of aluminum bolstered the argument to dismantle Alcoa's absolute monopoly. Alcoa was blamed for the shortfalls, and the government was unwilling to risk again relying so heavily on one company to produce a strategic product. The final blow came in 1946, when the War Surplus Property Board decided to sell the aluminum facilities built for the war to Reynolds Metals and Kaiser Aluminum at cut-rate prices, thus creating two rivals for Alcoa and fostering competition in all phases of aluminum production.

Although he remained as Alcoa chairman until 1957, often visiting his office in Manhattan, Davis's full-time work with the company ended after the war. His enthusiasm may have been dampened by the demise of the monopoly he had been instrumental in creating. In 1946 Davis relocated to Florida. His second wife had died in 1933, and he took up residence with his secretary, Evelyn Mitchell, who provided companionship and business consultation. Although in his eighties, Davis had no plans to retire, and he soon amassed a second fortune in real estate. He purchased more than 120,000 acres in Florida, including one-eighth of Dade County; bought 30,000 acres on Eleutheu Island in the Bahamas, developing a resort there that became one of his favorite retreats in his last years; and owned 200,000 acres on Cuba's Isle of Pines. Davis's diverse properties included an ice cream plant, a cement plant, a furniture factory, and an airline. He also made business forays into cattle raising, chicken farming, and fruit canning.

Not all of Davis's enterprises were profitable. His first Miami business venture was a pineapple plantation, which lost money. His most spectacular failure was a Caribbean shipping concern, Three Bays Lines; Davis reportedly lost $7 million in this venture. But most of Davis's enterprises were lucrative, and in 1959 he gained more than 3 million shares of non-voting stock as partial payment for transferring over 90 percent of his real estate empire to the Arvida Corporation, a land company that he had formed. His business dealings created a boom in Florida's economy, and although he refused to estimate his wealth, Davis was unquestionably one of the richest men in the country, with a personal fortune of more than $350 million. At the age of ninety-five he supervised construction of a

new home in Coral Gables, a mansion that he called "Journey's End." His decision to build a new house so late in life reflected his energy and his continual belief that he had many years ahead of him.

Davis will be most strongly associated with his seventy years of service at Alcoa. At barely over five feet tall, he was sensitive about his stature and compensated with tough, truculent behavior and a booming voice that one journalist described as similar to "the rushing of a heavy freight train through a long tunnel." Imperious and temperamental, Davis felt no qualms about reprimanding subordinates in public. He suffered a heart attack in 1956, but he remained feisty even in old age. Up until his death in Miami, Davis could also easily indulge in his habit of drinking martinis by the pitcher. He bequeathed most of his wealth to the Arvida community and to trusts held by banks in Miami and Pittsburgh, used to create two Arthur Vining Davis Foundations.

Although blunt and brusque, Davis was a brilliant business leader. Through deft management, investment, and technological innovation, he was responsible for building Alcoa into a monopoly that endured for more than half a century, a remarkable achievement in the annals of industry. In so doing, he also helped to introduce aluminum to America and to the world; it was a product that quickly became standard in consumer and industrial use.

• Davis rarely granted interviews and left few personal papers; distrustful of reporters, he studiously shunned publicity. The Alcoa Corporation developed an eight-page essay on his life to coincide with the company's centennial (1988). Information on Davis can also be found in histories of Alcoa, including George D. Smith, *From Monopoly to Competition: The Transformation of Alcoa, 1888–1986* (1988). A standard earlier work is Charles Carr, *Alcoa: An American Enterprise* (1952). See also Junius Edwards, *The Immortal Woodshed: The Story of the Inventor Who Brought Aluminum to America* (1955), a biography of Charles Martin Hunt; Charlotte Muller, *Light Metals Monopoly* (1968); and Carlo Lamur, *The American Takeover: Industrial Emergence and Alcoa's Expansion in Guyana and Suriname, 1914–1921* (1985). The *Miami Herald* ran a long story on Davis's real estate activities, 11 Dec. 1955; *Fortune* magazine, Sept. 1956, also reported on these activities. Obituaries are in *Time*, 7 Dec. 1962, and the *Miami Herald*, *Miami News*, and *New York Times*, 18 Nov. 1962.

YANEK MIECZKOWSKI

DAVIS, Bancroft (29 Dec. 1822–27 Dec. 1907), jurist and diplomat, was born John Chandler Bancroft Davis in Worcester, Massachusetts, the son of John Davis (1761–1847), a congressman, senator, and three-time governor nicknamed "Honest John," and Eliza Davis, sister of historian George Bancroft. A member of the Harvard class of 1840, Davis was suspended in his senior year for unknown reasons but was nevertheless awarded his A.B. by Harvard in 1847. By that time he had already studied law, been admitted to the Massachusetts bar, opened an office in New York City, and published *The Massachusetts Justice* (1847), his first work in legal history. His father's prominence in the

Whig party and friendship with Abbott Lawrence led to his appointment, on 31 August 1849, as secretary of the American legation in London, where he acted at various times as chargé d'affaires and moved in literary circles. Resigning that position on 30 November 1852 to resume the practice of law, he was admitted to the New York bar in 1853 and entered the law firm of Judge William Kent (later Kent, Eaton & Davis). But he did not entirely relinquish his British ties. From 1854 to the outbreak of the Civil War he served as American correspondent for the *Times* of London. In 1857 he married Frederica Gore King, a granddaughter of Rufus King (1755–1827). The couple remained childless.

Ill health forced Davis to give up his law practice in 1862, to undergo medical treatment abroad, and to move to a farm near Newburgh, New York, in 1863. By 1868 he had recovered sufficiently to run for public office. Elected to the New York State Assembly as a Republican, he had barely taken his seat before applying for and then accepting appointment as first assistant secretary of state under his neighbor Hamilton Fish on 25 March 1869. President Ulysses S. Grant soon designated him as arbitrator of the dispute between Great Britain and Portugal over the status of Bulama, an island off the west coast of Africa. His report of 23 April 1870, recognizing Portugal's title to the territory, strengthened his expertise in international law. This expertise made him a logical choice to serve on a joint high commission appointed in the following year to arrange the settlement of the Anglo-American dispute over the so-called *Alabama* claims (arising from damages done during the Civil War to U.S. shipping by Confederate cruisers built in Great Britain). He was named the commission's American secretary, and participated in the drafting of the Treaty of Washington of 8 May 1871, which provided for an arbitration tribunal to meet at Geneva. He prepared the carefully annotated and highly regarded *Treaties and Conventions Concluded between the United States and Other Powers since July 4, 1776* (1873) in the same year.

Davis resigned his State Department post and was appointed the American agent before the arbitration tribunal, charged with preparing and presenting the American case. Together with Fish he was responsible for the aggressive tone of the American presentation and for the reintroduction into the proceedings of claims for compensation for indirect damages stemming from the alleged prolongation of the war by British actions. Such claims had prevented earlier agreement and came close to wrecking the arbitration process this time, but they may well have increased Great Britain's willingness to settle for actual damages. On 14 September 1872 the Geneva Tribunal awarded the United States $15.5 million, redefining the responsibilities of belligerents and neutrals in the process, and thus setting important precedents for future arbitration of international claims. Frank Warren Hackett, an American member of the Alabama Claims Commission, credited "the tact and stamina of Bancroft Davis" with rescuing the agreement from failure.

On 24 January 1873 Davis was reappointed assistant secretary of state and was named minister to Germany by President Grant in July 1874. In Berlin he succeeded his uncle, George Bancroft, at a time when U.S.-German relations were at their most serene. His major accomplishment was the compilation of a lengthy report on the glories of the Berlin Museum, with the recommendation that an institution like it be established in the United States. In accordance with custom, Davis resigned as minister at the beginning of a new administration, and President Rutherford B. Hayes named him to the U.S. Court of Claims in January 1878. That tribunal had been established in 1855 to adjudicate claims against the government. He returned to the State Department at President Chester A. Arthur's request in December 1881, in part to help the new secretary of state, Frederick T. Frelinghuysen, undo the aggressive Latin American policy of his predecessor, James G. Blaine. Invitations to a Pan-American conference that Blaine had extended were canceled, and the bungling and unpopular American attempt to mediate a settlement of the War of the Pacific among Chile, Bolivia, and Peru was halted.

Reappointed to the Court of Claims in June 1882, he resigned in November 1883 to become reporter of the U.S. Supreme Court, a position he retained for nineteen years. During that time he edited volumes 108–86 of the *U.S. Reports* and found time to write on a variety of mainly legal-historical subjects. His books on the committees of the Continental Congress concerned with admiralty cases and the *Alabama* claims, as well as his annotated edition of Samuel Freeman Miller's *Lectures on the Constitution of the United States*, stem from these years. He retired in 1902 but remained in Washington until his death.

Davis was always fascinated by the historical development of the law and, despite his earlier successes as lawyer, diplomat, and judge, probably found his true niche as Supreme Court reporter. He not only provided excellent annotation for the volumes he edited but also classified and arranged the historical material in the office of the Clerk of the Supreme Court, publishing much of it in the justly celebrated appendix to volume 131 of *U.S. Reports* (1888).

• The Bancroft Davis Papers are in the Library of Congress. There is no biography, although some biographical information appears in *Harvard Graduates' Magazine* (Mar. 1908); *Proceedings of the American Antiquarian Society* (Apr. 1908); and *Proceedings upon the Occasion of Presenting to the Court of Claims of the United States a Portrait of John Chandler Bancroft Davis* (1912). The most substantive obituaries are in the *New York Tribune* and the *Washington Post*, 28 Dec. 1907.

In addition to his public writings cited in the text above, Davis produced *The Case of the United States, to be laid before the Tribunal of Arbitration . . . at Geneva* (1871); *The Counter Case of the United States . . .* (1872); and *Notes upon the Treaties of the United States with Other Powers* (1873). His privately published writings not mentioned in the text include *Re-*

port upon the *Conditions and Sources of Business of the Illinois Central Railroad* (1855); *The Committees of the Continental Congress, Chosen to Determine Appeals from the Courts of Admiralty* (1888); *Mr. Fish and the Alabama Claims* (1893); and a pamphlet, *Origin of the Book of Common Prayer of the Protestant Episcopal Church in the United States of America* (1897). See also Carnegie Endowment for International Peace, *The Controversy over Neutral Rights between the United States and France, 1797–1800* (1917).

MANFRED JONAS

DAVIS, Benjamin Jefferson (27 May 1870–28 Oct. 1945), publisher and political figure, was born in Dawson, Georgia, the son of Mike Davis (who changed his name from Mike Haynes in 1868 or 1869) and Katherine Davis, farmers and ex-slaves. His formal education ended after the sixth grade, and Davis worked as a bricklayer and teacher before becoming a printer. He learned the trade while working for Tom W. Loyless, a white Dawson publisher and printer, and then opened his own printing business. He soon became a moderately wealthy man, living in a two-story, fifteen-room house while his siblings eked out their livings as sharecroppers. In 1898 he married Jimmie Willard Porter, a Dawson native who had been educated at Hampton and Tuskegee Institutes; they had a son and daughter.

In 1903 Davis began publishing the *Independent*, a black weekly newspaper that sold throughout Georgia and that within a year reported that its circulation had risen to 100,000. Although the paper consisted mostly of club, social, and church news as well as feature stories on new black-owned businesses, its scathing editorials condemning lynching, convict labor, and disfranchisement made Davis "the idol of the backwoods poor Negro farmers." Banned in many Georgia towns because of its militancy, the *Independent* thrived on the advertising dollars it attracted from Atlanta businesses and financial institutions, both white and black, after Davis relocated to that city in 1909.

Davis was a strong supporter of Booker T. Washington, who often contributed articles to the paper, and a detractor of Marcus Garvey and W. E. B. Du Bois, although all three men felt the sting of Davis's barbs when he felt they deserved them. As Du Bois noted, Davis was "a fearless and forceful man." In 1919, when a bundle of papers was returned from a small Georgia town with a threatening note attached to it, Davis drove there and personally handed out the papers while about 200 armed blacks and whites watched.

In Atlanta, Davis became a leader of the District Grand United Order of Odd Fellows, a black fraternal organization. Largely because of his influence, the Odd Fellows grew to 33,000 members by 1912 and became the wealthiest black fraternity in the South. In 1912 he helped oversee the development of the Odd Fellows Block in downtown Atlanta. The block formed the center of the city's black commercial and professional community, and the Odd Fellows Building, which housed the *Independent*'s new offices, was its crown jewel.

Davis was one of the wealthiest men in Atlanta; he owned three automobiles when most whites owned none, and he hired white people to buy his family's clothes in white stores so that his wife would not have to confront "Jim Crow." He once received the president of Liberia at his mansion, the site of many a lavish party. His wealth and status as a businessman propelled him into partisan politics, and he soon became a force in the Republican party. He attended every GOP national convention as a delegate from 1908 until his death.

In 1916 Davis appeared before the Platform Committee to advocate decreasing southern representation in Congress in direct proportion to black disfranchisement. He served as secretary of the Georgia Republican party for eighteen years and in 1925 became a member of the Republican National Committee. As a national committeeman during Calvin Coolidge's administration, Davis dispensed patronage, and appointments to all federal posts in Georgia required his personal approval. His son "used to view with sardonic pleasure the small-time [white] postmasters beating a path to my father's door . . . seeking favors of a Negro political boss."

Davis paid a high price for such power. Twice the Ku Klux Klan burned crosses on his lawn in protest of his political clout, and unknown assailants frequently threw rocks through his windows and slashed his tires. After his inauguration in 1928, Herbert Hoover set out to purge powerful blacks like Davis from positions of importance in the state Republican organizations of the South, particularly in Georgia, South Carolina, and Mississippi, in an effort to make the GOP more attractive to southern white voters. Rumors began circulating that Davis had sold federal positions to the highest bidder and that he had humiliated white applicants for such jobs.

In 1928 Davis was called before a U.S. Senate special committee investigating campaign expenditures. He was grilled for a week, primarily by Senator Walter George (D-Ga.), who got Davis to admit receiving $2,000 from Hoover to cover campaign expenses. When Davis could neither recall how he had spent the money nor produce any records or receipts, Hoover forced him to resign from the national committee.

Despite this embarrassment Davis retained a great deal of influence in the state party organization. He was very successful at recruiting black voters for the GOP, an important fact in Atlanta, where blacks could vote in municipal elections. He also served as president of the Young Men's Republican Club of Georgia at the age of seventy-three. But in 1944 Davis showed signs of abandoning the GOP, as so many other blacks had done following their effective removal from positions of importance in the state organizations. The national convention attempted to unseat Davis's "black and tan" delegation (comprising both black and white members) in favor of an all-white one. Davis, whose son, Benjamin, Jr., had just won election to the New York City Council as a Communist, made reference to that election when addressing the convention and threatened to lead the GOP's few remaining blacks into the Communist party if his delegation was not seated.

Davis stopped publishing the *Independent* in 1932, when its circulation had dropped to 27,000. Instead, he devoted himself to political, fraternal, and community work through the Odd Fellows, Young Men's Christian Association, Atlanta Community Chest, Masons, Elks, and Knights of Pythias. He became president of the Baptist Layman's League of Georgia and at the time of his death was editor of the *National Baptist Review*. He also lent assistance to his son's political career despite their obvious differences in philosophy. He died in Harlem while visiting his children.

• Davis figures prominently in Gerald Horne, *Black Liberation/Red Scare: Ben Davis [Jr.] and the Communist Party* (1994), his son's biography. The importance of the elder Davis's political role is assessed in Hanes Walton, Jr., *Black Republicans: The Politics of the Black and Tans* (1975). An obituary is in the *New York Times*, 29 Oct. 1945.

CHARLES W. CAREY, JR.

DAVIS, Benjamin Jefferson (8 Sept. 1903–22 Aug. 1964), Communist party leader, was born in Dawson, Georgia, the son of Benjamin Davis, Sr., a publisher and businessman, and Willa Porter. Davis was educated as a secondary-school student at Morehouse in Atlanta. He entered Amherst College in 1922 and graduated in 1925. At Amherst he starred on the football team and pursued lifelong interests in tennis and the violin. He then attended Harvard Law School, from which he graduated in 1928. He was a rarity—an African American from an affluent family in the Deep South; however, his wealth did not spare him from the indignities of racial segregation. While still a student at Amherst, he was arrested in Atlanta for sitting in the white section of a trolley car. Only the intervention of his influential father prevented him from being jailed. As he noted subsequently, it was the horror of Jim Crow—the complex of racial segregation, lynchings, and police brutality—that pushed him toward the political left.

After graduating from Harvard, Davis was well on his way to becoming a member of the black bourgeoisie. He worked for a period at a black-owned newspaper, the *Baltimore Afro-American*, and in Chicago with W. B. Ziff, who arranged advertising for the black press. He then returned to Georgia, where he passed the bar examination and opened a law practice.

At this point an incident occurred that led to Davis's joining the Communist party (CP). Angelo Herndon, a young Communist in Georgia, was arrested under a slave insurrection statute after leading a militant demonstration demanding relief for the poor. William Patterson, a black lawyer and Communist who led the International Labor Defense, recruited Davis to handle Herndon's case. Through discussions with his client, Davis decided to join the party in 1933.

As Davis was joining the CP, those African Americans who could vote were in the process of making a transition from voting for Republicans to voting for the Democratic party of Franklin D. Roosevelt. The GOP—particularly in the South, where Davis's father was a Republican leader—was pursuing a "lily-white" strategy that involved distancing itself from African Americans, who had been one of its staunchest bases of support; simultaneously, Roosevelt's "New Deal" promised relief from the ravages of the Great Depression.

Davis did not favor the Democrats, because in the South they continued to lift the banner of Jim Crow. His joining the CP was not unusual, given the times: many prominent African-American intellectuals of that era—Langston Hughes and Paul Robeson, for example—worked closely with the Communists, not least because theirs was one of the few political parties that stood firmly in favor of racial equality. Moreover, the Soviet Union and the Communist International, which it sponsored—unlike the United States and its European allies—stood firmly in favor of the decolonization of Africa. Davis felt that capitalism was inextricably tied to the slave trade, slavery, and racism itself, and that socialism was the true path to equality.

Davis handled the trial of Herndon, and after the case went to the U.S. Supreme Court, with another lawyer dealing with the appeal, his client was freed. Davis went on to serve as a lawyer in the case of the "Scottsboro Boys," African-American youths charged falsely with the rape of two white women. They too were eventually freed because of decisions by the high court—after many years and many appeals—but Alabama then retried and convicted them.

Threats on Davis's life and the CP's desire to provide a more prominent role for him led to his moving to New York City in the mid-1930s. There he worked as journalist and editor with a succession of Communist journals, including the *Harlem Liberator*, the *Negro Liberator*, and the *Daily Worker*. At that last paper, he worked closely with the budding novelist Richard Wright, with whom he shared a party cell; in this Communist organizational unit, Davis had the opportunity to comment on and shape some of Wright's earliest writings.

At its zenith during the 1930s, the Communist party in New York State had about twenty-seven thousand members, of whom about two thousand were African Americans. Davis played a key role in the founding of the National Negro Congress, which had been initiated by the Communists; for a while the NNC included leading members of the National Association for the Advancement of Colored People (NAACP), the labor leader A. Philip Randolph, and the Reverend Adam Clayton Powell, Jr.

Davis developed a close political relationship with Powell, a New York City councilman. When Powell moved on to represent Harlem in the U.S. House of Representatives, he anointed Davis as his successor. Davis was duly elected in 1943 and received a broad range of support, particularly from noted black artists and athletes such as Billie Holliday, Lena Horne, Joe Louis, Teddy Wilson, and Count Basie. He received such support for a number of reasons. There were his qualifications—lawyer, journalist, powerful orator, and organizer. There was also the fact that at this time both the Democrats—who were influenced heavily by white Southerners hostile to desegregation—and the Republicans were not attractive alternatives for African Americans. Moreover, in 1943 the United States was allied with the Soviet Union, which had led to a decline in anticommunism, a tendency that in any event was never strong among African Americans.

On the city council Davis fought for rent control, keeping transit fares low, and raising pay for teachers, among other measures. He received substantial support not only from African Americans but also from many Jewish Americans, who appreciated his support for the formation of the state of Israel and for trade unions. In 1945 he was reelected by an even larger margin of victory. By the time he ran for reelection in 1949, however, the political climate had changed dramatically. The wartime alliance with the USSR had ended, and in its place there was a Cold War internationally and a "Red Scare" domestically. Supporting a Communist now carried a heavy political price; simultaneously, many of Davis's African-American supporters were now being wooed by the Democratic administration of President Harry Truman.

During his race for the presidency in 1948, Truman was challenged from the left by Henry Wallace, nominated by the Progressive party. Because Wallace received the support of such African-American luminaries as Paul Robeson and W. E. B. Du Bois, there was fear among some Democrats that Truman's support from black voters would be eroded; in a close race this could mean victory for Republican candidate Thomas Dewey. Furthermore, Truman found it difficult to portray his nation as a paragon of human rights in its Cold War struggle with the Soviet Union when blacks were treated like third-class citizens. Those pressures led Truman to put forward a civil rights platform in 1948 that outstripped the efforts of his predecessors in the White House. The Democrats succeeded in helping to undermine electoral support for Wallace and for Davis. Not only was Davis defeated in his race for reelection to the city council in 1949; he was also tried and convicted, along with ten other Communist leaders, of violating the Smith Act, which made the teaching or propagation of Marxism-Leninism a crime. After the U.S. Supreme Court in 1951 upheld these convictions in *Dennis v. United States*, Davis was jailed in federal prison in Terre Haute, Indiana, from 1951 to 1955. While there, he filed suit against prison segregation; *Davis v. Brownell*, coming in the wake of the 1954 high court decision invalidating racial segregation in schools (*Brown v. Board of Education*), led directly to the curbing of segregation in federal prisons. After his release from prison, Davis married Nina Stamler, who also had ties to the organized left; they had one child, a daughter.

Davis's final years with the CP were filled with tumult. In 1956, in the wake of the Soviet intervention in Hungary, the revelations about Stalin's brutal rule aired at the Twentieth Congress of the Soviet Communist party, and the Suez War, turmoil erupted in the U.S. party. Davis was a leader of the "hardline" faction that resisted moves toward radical change spearheaded by "reformers." Some among the latter faction wanted the Communists to merge with other leftist parties and entities and become a "social democratic" organization, akin to the Socialist party of France; others did not want the party to be identified so closely with Moscow. There were those who disagreed with Davis's opposition to the actions of Israel, Britain, and France during the Suez War. Some felt that Davis's acceptance of the indictment of Stalin was not sufficiently enthusiastic; still others thought that Davis and his ideological allies should not have backed the Soviet intervention in Hungary. These internal party squabbles were exacerbated by the counterintelligence program of the Federal Bureau of Investigation that was designed, in part, to disrupt the party and ensure that it would play no role in the nascent civil rights movement.

When Martin Luther King, Jr., the Atlanta minister and civil rights activist, was stabbed by a crazed assailant in New York City in 1958, Davis rushed to the hospital and provided blood for him. The Davis-King tie led J. Edgar Hoover to increase the FBI's surveillance of the civil rights movement. But as the civil rights movement was blooming, the Communist party was weakening. Nevertheless, during the last years of his life Davis became a significant and frequent presence on college campuses, as students resisted bans on Communist speakers by inviting him to lecture. The struggle to invite Communists to speak on campus was a significant factor in generating the student activism of the 1960s, from the City College of New York to the University of California at Berkeley.

By the time Davis died in New York City, the party was a shadow of its former self. His life showed, however, that African Americans denied equality ineluctably would opt for more radical solutions, and this in turn helped to spur civil rights reforms. African slaves had been an early form of capital and a factor in the evolution of capitalism; that a descendant of African slaves became such a staunch opponent of capitalism was, in that sense, the closing of a historical circle.

• Davis's papers, including the unexpurgated version of his memoir, are at the Schomburg Center for Research in Black Culture of the New York Public Library. See also the published version of his memoir, *Communist Councilman from Harlem: Autobiographical Notes Written in a Federal Penitentiary* (1969). The most complete account of his life is Gerald Horne, *Black Liberation/Red Scare: Ben Davis and the Communist Party* (1994). On the Herndon case, see Angelo Herndon, *Let Me Live* (1937). On the Communist party, see William Z. Foster, *History of the Communist Party of the United States* (1968). Obituaries are in the *New York Times*, 24 Aug. 1967, and the *Worker*, 1 Sept. 1967.

GERALD HORNE

DAVIS, Benjamin Oliver, Sr. (28 May 1880–26 Nov. 1970), U.S. Army general, was born in Washington, D.C., the son of Louis Patrick Henry Davis, an Internal Revenue Service messenger, and Henrietta Stewart. Growing up in a middle-class section of Washington, D.C., Davis maintained that he was not conscious of the racial barriers around him. He first experienced racial segregation when he attended the M Street High School, one of Washington's segregated high schools; during his last year of high school he attended classes part time at Howard University. He also first became involved in the military while in high school, rising to the rank of captain in the High School Cadets. His record prompted his commission as a second lieutenant in the First Separate battalion, District of Columbia National Guard, a post he left in April 1898.

In 1898 Congress created ten new regiments, including four units for black Americans. In July 1898 Davis signed up and was made a first lieutenant in the Eighth U.S. Infantry Regiment, stationed in Chickamauga, Georgia. A year later the all-black unit was disbanded, and Davis was discharged from the army.

Following Davis's discharge, his father attempted to gain his son an appointment to West Point, but in the depth of the Jim Crow era, President William McKinley was unwilling to appoint a black man. Davis was disappointed but still desired a military career, so in June 1899 he reenlisted in the army. Assigned to Troop I, Ninth Cavalry, he was promoted to corporal and, in May 1901, to second lieutenant. His first posting was as a lieutenant in the Philippines, where he helped put down the Filipino insurgency.

In 1902 Davis married Elnora Dickerson, a lifelong friend. They had three children. Davis spent the next three years at Fort Washakie, Wyoming, where he was promoted to first lieutenant. In 1905 he was transferred from his combat unit to Wilberforce University, where he was a professor of military science and tactics. This assignment, which he held until 1909, irritated Davis because it appeared that the army did not want black American officers in a position of authority over white troops.

In 1909 Davis became the military attaché to Liberia, where he stayed until November 1911, when his poor health prompted him to request a transfer. He was given command of a machine gun platoon with the Ninth Cavalry, stationed in Wyoming. In 1915 Davis was again transferred to Wilberforce and was promoted to captain. The next year his wife died in childbirth. In 1919 Davis married Sadie Overton, a fellow Wilberforce teacher.

In 1917 Davis returned to the Philippines, where he remained until 1920, when he was transferred to the Tuskegee Institute in Alabama, a school for black students founded by Booker T. Washington in 1881, and promoted to lieutenant colonel. In 1924 he was attached to a battalion of the Ohio National Guard, in 1929 he was sent back to Wilberforce, and in 1930 he was promoted to full colonel, the highest rank received by a black American to that date. Assigned as a graveside escort to widows and mothers of servicemen who died in Europe during World War I, Davis performed this task admirably for two years, winning praise from the bereaved.

Davis spent more time at Tuskegee and Wilberforce, but in 1938 he became commander of the 369th New York National Guard. On 25 October 1940 President Franklin D. Roosevelt promoted Davis to brigadier general, the nation's first black general. This promotion came only days before the presidential election and was probably made to help sway the black vote. In January 1941 Davis received a command position over the Fourth Brigade, Second Cavalry Division, in Fort Riley, Kansas.

In June 1941 Davis, who had retired but was recalled to active duty shortly thereafter, began work in the inspector general's office as an adviser for matters pertaining to black soldiers. To improve morale he suggested desegregation of the front lines by placing black soldiers in infantry positions as they were needed, but he did not openly criticize segregation. He attributed much of the morale problem among black soldiers to white officers not winning the confidence of their men. In reports to the General Staff Davis stated that the black soldiers resented the segregation policy.

Over the course of the next two years (1942–1943) Davis was sent to several locations in Europe and the United States to study and report on racial problems. He made many suggestions, but most were ignored by the military. General Davis did win a few victories, including the assignment of black troops into combat, and he was a voice in the fight to desegregate Red Cross blood.

Davis retired from the army on 20 July 1948 in a public ceremony attended by President Harry S. Truman. Remaining active in his retirement, he joined several committees, including the American Battle Monuments Commission. Davis died in Great Lakes Naval Hospital in Chicago and was buried in Arlington National Cemetery. A pioneer, he broke through the army's color line and rose to the highest military rank then achieved by an African American.

• Davis's papers are in the possession of Mrs. James McLendon, Chicago, Ill. The best assessment of his life is Marvin Fletcher, *America's First Black General* (1989). Sources on Davis's military career include Fletcher, *The Black Soldier and Officer in the United States Army* (1974), and Jack D. Foner, *Blacks and the Military in American History* (1974). Davis is briefly mentioned in Richard M. Dalfiume, *Desegregation of the U.S. Armed Forces* (1969). Personal history and general information is in Ben Albert Richardson, *Great Black Americans*, 2d rev. ed. (1976); and Benjamin O. Davis, Jr., *Benjamin O. Davis, Jr., American: An Autobiography* (1991), by Davis's son. An obituary is in the *New York Times*, 27 Nov. 1970.

CRAIG J. REPKO

DAVIS, Bergen (31 Mar. 1869–30 June 1958), physicist, was born in Whitehouse, New Jersey, the son of John Davis and Catherine Marie Dilts, farmers. After completing the eighth grade he developed tuberculosis, which prevented him from attending high school, a deprivation he compensated for by reading many of the volumes in the nearby county library. He particularly enjoyed the scientific articles in *Chambers's Ency-*

clopedia and his brother's college physics textbooks; in order to understand the material more completely, he taught himself geometry and trigonometry. In 1888 he regained his health, and having sufficiently tutored himself, he began teaching at the district school he had attended as a child.

After matriculating at Rutgers College in 1891, Davis returned to teaching for a year in 1894 to earn enough money to complete his education; he received his B.S. degree in 1896. For the next three years he taught at New York City's School for the Deaf during the day and conducted experiments in the physics laboratory at Columbia University in the evening. In 1899 he enrolled at Columbia, where he concentrated on the measurement of the velocity and pressure of stationary sound waves. In the process he invented the sound mill, an apparatus that measures the amplitude of vibrating air. He received his A.M. and Ph.D. degrees from Columbia in 1900 and 1901, respectively.

After graduation Davis was awarded the two-year John Tyndall Fellowship, which he used to study the motion of ions, molecules with either a positive or negative charge, in a varying magnetic field. He did this work at Göttingen University in Germany and at Cambridge University in England. In 1903 he returned to Columbia as a tutor in physics. He devoted his research efforts there to investigating the electrical conductivity of ions and the amount of energy required to ionize a molecule in a gaseous state. In 1907 he was promoted to instructor and awarded the Ernest Kempton Adams Fellowship which he used to conduct experiments on the optical properties of the ether, a now-discredited substance that some scientists then believed to be the medium through which electromagnetic waves were transmitted. Davis was promoted to adjunct professor in 1909 and to associate professor in 1913, following a one-year leave of absence when he suffered a recurrence of tuberculosis.

In 1915 Davis offered additional verification for the emerging quantum theory of atomic structure by clearing up the discrepancies in an experiment involving ionized gaseous molecules, conducted the year before by the German physicists James Franck and Gustav Hertz. Although their experiment demonstrated for the first time that energy exists in atoms in discrete states or quanta, as originally suggested by the German physicist Max Planck, there were a number of ambiguities in their findings concerning the energy levels of ionization, and Davis was able to clarify these.

As a result of his work with ionization Davis was drawn to the study of X-rays, the part of the electromagnetic spectrum that can penetrate solids and ionize gases. Although X-rays had been discovered in 1895, no means for either generating or measuring them existed, so Davis's first task was to design and build the necessary equipment and to establish an X-ray research laboratory. The first practical application of X-ray technology soon followed: he used one of his new machines to search for contraband hidden in bales of cotton being shipped to Germany prior to the entry of the United States into World War I. He also addressed the wave-length energy distribution in the continuous X-ray spectrum, publishing the results in 1917.

In 1920, the year after his promotion to full professor, Davis demonstrated that the emission of X-rays, which result when an electron is driven out of either of the two innermost nuclear orbits (known as the K and L orbits), is a function of the amount of voltage applied to the atom. In 1922 Davis married Matie Pearl Clark, with whom he had no children. Over the next eight years he conducted several experiments concerning the fine structure, closely related wavelengths that appear on the same spectral line, of the K and L spectral lines for a number of metals that showed that some wavelengths were significantly thinner than predicted by classical mechanics.

Much of this work was made possible by the double-crystal spectrometer, an instrument Davis began working on in 1920 and perfected by 1929. Previous spectrometers allowed for the viewing and examination of X-ray wavelengths by diffracting them off a crystal prism into the lens of a telescope. After experimenting with a number of crystals, Davis discovered that by properly positioning the two unpolished halves of a carefully-cut piece of calcite, he could obtain a resolving power higher by a factor of ten than that of the single-crystal spectrometer. In 1929 he prepared the data on crystal gratings, an alternative method to the use of prisms for diffracting electromagnetic radiant energy, for the *International Critical Tables*. He retired in 1939; a heart attack the year before had left him permanently disabled. He died in New York City.

From 1923 to 1926 Davis was a member of the Physics Division of the National Research Council. In 1932 he was vice president of Section B of the American Association for the Advancement of Science; he was made an emeritus life member of that organization in 1949. For a number of years he served as an X-ray consultant to the staff of the Crocker Laboratory for Cancer Research, and in 1937 he became a member of its consulting board. He was a fellow of the American Physical Society and the American Optical Society, and a member of the National Academy of Sciences. In 1929 he was awarded a bronze medal by the Research Corporation of America.

Davis made two important contributions to the advancement of science. His work with ionized gases and K and L spectral lines contributed to the development of quantum theory and mechanics. His invention of the double-crystal spectrometer advanced the study of X-rays and contributed to the scientific understanding of electromagnetic radiation.

• Davis's papers are in the Columbia University Library. A biography, which includes a complete bibliography, is Harold W. Webb, "Bergen Davis," National Academy of Sciences, *Biographical Memoirs* 34 (1960): 65–82. Obituaries are in the *New York Times*, 2 July 1958, and *Science*, 2 Jan. 1959.

CHARLES W. CAREY, JR.

DAVIS, Bette (5 Apr. 1908–6 Oct. 1989), film, television, and stage actress, was born Ruth Elizabeth Davis in Lowell, Massachusetts, the daughter of Harlow Morrell Davis, a lawyer, and Ruth Favor, a writer, artist, and amateur photographer. According to biographical accounts, her father was cold and uncaring to both wife and children. Bette Davis's competitive spirit and fierce independence were rooted in her childhood. Known as Betty, she was an "ugly duckling" who craved attention and had her first audience at age six. Angered at being told to play outside while her mother entertained, she knocked on the door and made a solemn entrée. She marched in with a tray and placed it on a lace doily. The women screamed. It was a dead mouse. She smiled.

In 1915 Davis's parents separated. Ruth obtained a divorce in 1918, which alienated her family. Harlow, though a successful patent attorney, refused to provide child support. Ruth and her children began an eight-year odyssey that took them to Florida, New York, New Jersey, and Maine. Davis and her sister, Barbara (called Bobby), attended boarding schools while Ruth worked at various jobs in New York. (During her high school years, Davis changed the spelling of her first name after the example of Honoré de Balzac's *La Cousine Bette*.) Later, Davis took a series of summer jobs, including waitressing, to help her mother.

Davis credited her acting debut in a play at Crestalban Academy (Mass.) as Santa Claus. "I made a fiery entrance by getting too close to the candlelit tree." She sustained severe facial burns and was in pain for months. At Cushing Academy (Mass.) she found drama and dance coach mentors "who developed in me the grace of movement which served me so well." In 1925, the summer of her junior year, at a New Hampshire dance school Davis performed in *A Midsummer Night's Dream* under the direction of a New York actor, who told her mother she was a stage natural. But after graduation, Davis worked as a secretary. As a birthday treat, Ruth took her to Boston to see Henrik Ibsen's *The Wild Duck*, starring the extravagantly mannered Blanche Yurka. On her return home, Davis mimicked her and suddenly decided on a theatrical career.

She acted in stock company productions and studied with John Murray Anderson. In 1928 she appeared off Broadway with the Provincetown Players, then in a national tour of *The Wild Duck*. Her professional stage debut came in 1928 in George Cukor's production of *Broadway* in Rochester, New York. Davis debuted on Broadway in 1929 in *The Lady from the Sea*. A screen test for Samuel Goldwyn was a failure, but in 1930, after a play she was in closed on Broadway, she tested for Universal Studios and was offered a six-month contract.

Runty, fidgety, and, like Yurka, mannered to the point she parodied herself, with a voice that gasped as if it was a last breath and eyes that seemed to pop out, Davis defied the norms of Hollywood beauty represented by Greta Garbo and Jean Harlow. As a survivor in a business that could easily break one's spirits, she claimed that her strength came from her mother: "I owe her everything. Ruthie wasn't the typical show business mother. She overprotected and coddled me rather than pushing me into the spotlight." She debuted in *The Bad Sister* (1931) and soon made more appearances on screen. But her early screen persona proved so overpowering that audiences had no sympathy for her. She was dubbed "box office poison." Davis, however, felt that she was not the problem, but that it was the roles she was assigned instead.

Signed by Jack Warner of Warner Bros. in 1932 to a seven-year contract, Davis brought intelligence and wit to her films. She soon felt wasted "in junk," however, and complained vigorously. Two years and fifteen films into her contract, she netted her first triumph when she was loaned to RKO to portray the comely, illiterate waitress Mildred in *Of Human Bondage* (1934) opposite Leslie Howard. *Life* magazine declared, "Probably the best performance ever recorded on the screen by a U.S. actress." In spite of the great acclaim, she was not nominated for an Academy Award. Davis and others felt that Warner had punished her.

With the exception of *The Petrified Forest* (1936), Davis's films were in general no better than before. For the notoriously bad *Dangerous* (1935), in which she did everything but eat the scenery, Davis was not only nominated for an Academy Award but also won. She claimed it "was a consolation prize for not nominating me the year before."

In 1937 Davis did the unthinkable by refusing to perform in a film as mandated by her contract. Warner Bros. suspended her, leading to a lawsuit that Davis lost. She became resigned to working out her contract when suddenly Jack Warner developed faith in her potential. He paid her court costs, had screenplays tailored for her, and bought novels that both he and she thought right for her strong character. Although Davis tested for and claimed that she was offered the role of Scarlett O'Hara in *Gone with the Wind*, she turned down the opportunity because the suggestion that Errol Flynn play Rhett Butler was to her mind "a mistake."

Beginning with *Jezebel* (1938), for which she won her second Academy Award, Davis ushered in the era of the women's picture, turgid melodramas steeped in sentimentality. She schemed, seduced, suffered, and sacrificed her way into the hearts of millions and became the studio's top female star, establishing one of filmdom's preeminent careers. In each of the following four years, she was nominated for an Oscar for roles in *Dark Victory* (1939), *The Letter* (1940), *The Little Foxes* (1941), and *Now, Voyager* (1942). After notable performances in *Watch on the Rhine* and *Old Acquaintance* (both 1943), she received another Oscar nomination for her acting in *Mr. Skeffington* (1944). Her screen persona spilled over into her personal life. She divorced her first husband, Harmon Oscar Nelson, Jr., in 1938, having married him in 1932; her second husband, Arthur Farnsworth, whom she married in 1940, died in 1943; her third marriage, to William

Grant Sherry, ended in divorce after four years in 1949. Meanwhile, she had numerous affairs.

During the shooting of *Deception* (1946), strife again flared between Davis and Warner, and a near-fatal car crash took an emotional toll. Following the birth of her daughter in 1947, she spent a year away from the sound stage, but her next two pictures, made in 1948, floundered at the box office. On the set of *Beyond the Forest* (1949), problems developed between Davis and director King Vidor. She told Warner, "If you don't get another director, I want out of my contract!" The producer had papers drawn up and delivered within fifteen minutes. According to Vidor, as recorded by Davis biographer Charles Higgam, "She took the news after [seventeen] years at the studio . . . without carrying on . . . and did the rest of the picture like the pro she was. Suddenly, I saw the stuff she was made of."

From earning $10,000 a week, Davis was out of work. In 1950, in the midst of the collapse of her third marriage, she gave a superb performance in RKO's *Payment on Demand* (released in 1951). Darryl Zanuck, head of 20th Century–Fox, hired her to replace Claudette Colbert, who, because of a skiing injury, had to quit work on a film loosely based on the life of actress Elisabeth Bergner. The result was *All about Eve* (1950), for which Davis received an Oscar nomination and a New York Film Critics award. She also acquired another husband in 1950, her costar Gary Merrill, with whom she adopted two children; the couple divorced in 1960. Two years after her triumph in *All about Eve*, Davis received one last Oscar nomination for her performance in *The Star* (1952).

During her later years Davis continued to have to push for work, even placing a trade ad pleading for acting roles. This led to films of the macabre, TV movies and miniseries, guest spots on regular series of TV, and the stage. In the 1960s she scored popular successes in two especially ghoulish movies, *Whatever Happened to Baby Jane?* (1962), which costarred her old rival Joan Crawford, and *Hush Hush . . . Sweet Charlotte* (1964).

In spite of warnings about her interference, tardiness in past stage work, and insecurities, director Joshua Logan recruited Davis in 1974 for the stage musical *Miss Moffat*, adapted from the 1945 film *The Corn Is Green*, in which she had starred. It was her first stage appearance since 1961 in the Broadway production of Tennessee Williams's *Night of the Iguana*.

Although Logan admired Davis's ability to think for herself, as rehearsals progressed, he found her "deeply frightened of something that even she couldn't find words for." Her performances could vary from stirring to embarrassing. After several weeks she was forced to quit because of a pinched nerve, and the production folded at a total loss. A long list of producers, directors, and peers found her difficult, often monstrous. "I don't regret the dust I've kicked up," said Davis. "Any actor who doesn't dare to make an enemy should get out of the business. I worked for my career and I'll protect it as I would my children."

Late in her life Davis faced a number of problems in her private life. She was estranged from her daughter and adopted son. Stricken with breast cancer in 1983, she had a mastectomy, suffered strokes that altered her appearance, and broke her hip. She never gave up smoking several packs of cigarettes a day. She died in Paris en route home from being honored at a Spanish film festival.

• Davis's autobiographies, *The Lonely Life* (1962), with Sanford Dody, and *This 'n That* (1987), with Michael Herskowitz, are not excessively revealing or definitive, suffering from many omissions. Among numerous biographies, Charles Higham, *Bette: The Life of Bette Davis* (1981), and Lawrence J. Quirk, *Fasten Your Seat Belts: The Passionate Life of Bette Davis* (1990), are well researched. Barbara Leaming, *Bette Davis: A Biography* (1992), and James Spada, *More Than a Woman: An Intimate Biography of Bette Davis* (1993), are filled with juicy, fun gossip. The most detailed filmography appears in Whitney Stines, *Mother Goddam* (1974), which has a running commentary by Davis. Illustrated filmographies include Gene Ringgold, *The Films of Bette Davis* (1966), and Quirk, *Bette Davis: Her Films and Career* (1985). Other biographies and autobiographies, especially those of Brian Aherne, Mary Astor, Frank Capra, John Houston, and Josuha Logan, as well as several Hollywood anthologies, make extensive mention of Davis. Alexander Walker, *Bette Davis, a Celebration* (1986), is richly illustrated and detailed with an excellent filmography. Of interest because of the authors' relation to Davis are *My Mother's Keeper* (1985), by B. D. Hyman (Davis's daughter), and *Bette, Rita, and the Rest of My Life* (1988), by Gary Merrill. An obituary is in the *New York Times*, 8 Oct. 1989.

ELLIS NASSOUR

DAVIS, Blind John (7 Dec. 1913–12 Oct. 1985), blues pianist, was born John Henry Davis in Hattiesburg, Mississippi, the son of a speakeasy owner. Davis was blinded from a tetanus infection at the age of nine. As a boy he moved with his family to Chicago, where he began playing the piano professionally as a teenager for his father, who owned several speakeasies in the city. While his playing was based in the blues, Davis incorporated various American musical forms, including ragtime, New Orleans jazz, swing, and boogie-woogie. In the Chicago blues scene he became known for his versatility and for his clear, relaxed style.

In the 1930s and 1940s Davis earned a living as a regular session player for Lester Melrose's Blue Bird Records Label, the most popular blues label of the period. He recorded with many of Chicago's most prominent blues musicians, including Tampa Red, "Big Bill" Broonzy, and John Lee "Sonny Boy" Williamson. Davis performed on such classic recordings as Tampa Red's "It Hurts Me, Too," Williamson's "Whoo Doo," "Sloppy Drunk Blues," and "Western Union Man," and on Broonzy's "I Feel So Good."

While working for Blue Bird, Davis also led his own six-piece and seven-piece bands, which played in nightclubs, dance halls, and hotels, both in Chicago and across the United States. Davis's groups reflected the pianist's broad tastes, playing standard popular tunes and swing jazz as well as traditional blues.

Though best known as an accompanist and band leader, in 1938 and 1939 Davis made several solo recordings on the Vocalian label.

In 1952 Davis joined Broonzy on a performance tour in Europe, the first ever by blues musicians. Over the next twenty years Davis returned many times to Europe, where he developed a more loyal following than he could have had in the United States. During that period, when he was not touring, Davis often performed with drummer Judge Riley in Chicago nightclubs.

Davis released three LPs during his career, *Stomping on a Saturday Night* (Alligator Records), an album recorded in 1977 at Club Popular in Bonn, West Germany; *You Better Cut That Out*, which was released by Red Beans Records in 1985; and *Blind John Davis*, a collection of his 1938 and 1939 Vocalian recordings, which was released by Story of Blues.

Though not generally known for his work as a solo performer, Davis was nonetheless considered one of the most consistent, versatile, and skillful piano accompanists in the blues music industry of the twentieth century. His performances in Europe in the 1950s opened a new and vigorous market for blues musicians at a time when interest in the music was waning in the United States. Davis died in Chicago.

• There are several short biographical treatments of Blind John Davis in print, including Robert Santelli, *The Big Book of Blues: A Biographical Encyclopedia* (1993); Norbert Hess, "In Memoriam," *Blues Forum*, no. 19 (Feb. 1986): 18–21; and an obituary in *Living Blues*, no. 70 (1986): 45. See also Robert Palmer, "The Piano Blues of Blind John Davis," *New York Times*, 6 July 1979.

THADDEUS RUSSELL

DAVIS, Charles Henry (16 Jan. 1807–18 Feb. 1877), naval officer and hydrographer, was born in Boston, Massachusetts, the son of Daniel Davis, solicitor general of Massachusetts, and Lois Freeman, the sister of James Freeman, the first Unitarian minister in New England. Davis entered Harvard College in 1821 but left two years later to become a midshipman and did not complete his degree until 1841. From 1824 to 1840 Davis served in the Mediterranean, the Baltic, the West Indies, the South Atlantic, and the Pacific; made warm friends, including Samuel F. Du Pont; searched for mutineers; rounded Cape Horn four times; and nearly perished in a hurricane. In 1829 Davis ranked sixth among the thirty-nine midshipmen who passed their examination that year, and he was commissioned a lieutenant in 1834.

When on leave in Cambridge, Davis studied mathematics with Benjamin Peirce, preparing him for his future scientific pursuits. In 1842 he married Peirce's sister-in-law, Harriette Blake Mills, whose father was a U.S. senator; they had six children, four of whom lived past childhood. That same year Davis was appointed an assistant in the U.S. Coast Survey and in 1843 was in charge of the hydrography of the coast from Maine to Rhode Island. In trying to discern the laws of tidal action, Davis published two important

scientific articles, "A Memoir upon the Geological Action of the Tidal and Other Currents of the Ocean" (*Memoirs American Academy* 6 [1849]) and "The Law of Deposit of the Flood Tide" (*Smithsonian Contributions to Knowledge* 3 [1852]). The work of the Coast Survey made apparent the need for a national ephemeris. In July 1849 Davis began work on the *American Ephemeris and Nautical Almanac*, and its first well-received volume appeared in 1852. Davis's scholarship earned him additional friendships with Joseph Henry of the Smithsonian Institution and Alexander D. Bache of the Coast Survey as well as promotion to commander in 1854.

An assignment from 1856 to 1859 to the Pacific Squadron interrupted Davis's direction of the *Nautical Almanac*, but even while at sea he continued his scientific work. In 1857 he published his translation from Latin of Karl Friedrich Gauss's *Theory of the Motion of the Heavenly Bodies Moving about the Sun in Conic Sections*, adding an appendix to that classic work in mathematics and astronomy, originally published in 1809. While in the Pacific waters he translated from French and added his own notes to Charles Marie Philippes de Kerhallet's *General Examination of the Pacific Ocean*, originally published in 1851. Davis's translation, based on the second edition (1856), was first published in 1861 and became the standard book on navigating the Pacific.

When the Civil War came in 1861, Davis was in Cambridge directing the *Nautical Almanac*. Ordered to the Navy Department in Washington, he acted as the executive head of the Bureau of Detail, which assigned naval officers and purchased ships. He also served as the secretary of a confidential board of bureau chiefs to advise the secretary of the navy and was the secretary and author of the reports of the Blockade Board that planned naval and military operations on the Atlantic and Gulf coasts of the Confederacy.

On 18 September 1861 Davis was detached from his Washington duties to equip an expedition to capture Port Royal, South Carolina. He was made fleet captain and chief of staff of the South Atlantic Blockading Squadron under the command of his friend Du Pont. Despite a severe storm en route, the 7 November attack on Port Royal was successful, and Davis made a significant contribution with his extensive hydrographic knowledge. Du Pont recognized that, in addition to information, Davis possessed a keen, independent intellect and was unrestrained in expressing his thoughts and convictions. Davis was promoted to captain that same month. On 20 December he was in charge of closing the Charleston Harbor to Confederate traffic by sinking fifteen stone-filled wooden ships.

Returning to Washington in February 1862, Davis assumed command of the Mississippi River Flotilla from 9 May to October 1862. In that capacity, he earned his promotion to commodore on 16 July 1862 and rear admiral on 7 February 1863 by forcing the evacuation of Fort Pillow on 4 June 1862 and two days later destroying the Confederate River Defense Fleet at Memphis and receiving the surrender of that city.

Despite Davis's successes, Secretary of the Navy Gideon Welles replaced him with David Dixon Porter. "Davis," Welles thought, "is more of a scholar than sailor, . . . is an intelligent but not an energetic, driving, fighting officer, . . . is kind and affable, but has not the vim, dash . . . of Porter" (Beale and Brownsword, vol. 1, p. 158).

Welles believed that Davis's intellectual and administrative capabilities could best be utilized in the Navy Department, where from November 1862 to April 1865 Davis headed the Bureau of Navigation. He was largely responsible for the origin of that bureau, which included all the navy's scientific departments and its academy. As part of this new bureau, Davis created an independent Hydrographic Office. During these years he served on numerous boards, including the permanent commission with Henry and Bache that advised the department on all questions concerning science and art and suggested a National Academy of Sciences, which was established in 1863.

At the close of the Civil War, Davis left the Bureau of Navigation to return fully to science as the superintendent of the Naval Observatory. In 1866 he prepared a public document reviewing all the surveys of possible railway and canal routes connecting the Atlantic and Pacific oceans, which became the standard reference for early surveys and expeditions. From 1867 until 1869 Davis was ordered to sea as the commander in chief of the Brazil Station, and for three years, beginning in 1870, he was commander of the Norfolk Navy Yard, where as a Yankee in Virginia he felt as isolated as if he had been at sea. In 1874 Davis returned as superintendent of the Naval Observatory, where he prepared both its and the navy's display for the Philadelphia Centennial Exhibition. His edited *Narrative of the North Polar Expedition U.S. Ship "Polaris," Captain Charles Francis Hall* was published in 1876. He died in Washington, having worked at the Naval Observatory the previous day.

• The best source on Davis is Charles H. Davis, Jr., *The Life of Charles Henry Davis, Rear Admiral, 1807–1877* (1899). Also of interest is a memoir of Davis by one of his sons-in-law, Henry Cabot Lodge, *Early Memories* (1913). Many important references to Davis are in John D. Hayes, ed., *Samuel Francis Du Pont: A Selection from His Civil War Letters* (3 vols., 1969), and in Howard K. Beale and Alan W. Brownsword, eds., *Diary of Gideon Welles* (3 vols., 1960). A synopsis of his career and a few of his letters are in Robert Means Thompson and Richard Wainwright, eds., *Confidential Correspondence of Gustavus Vasa Fox, Assistant Secretary of the Navy, 1861–1865*, vol. 2 (1920). An obituary is in the *New York Times*, 19 Feb. 1877.

OLIVE HOOGENBOOM

DAVIS, Charles Henry, II (28 Aug. 1845–27 Dec. 1921), naval officer, was born in Cambridge, Massachusetts, the son of Rear Admiral Charles Henry Davis and Harriette Blake Mills. Davis was the scion of one of New England's oldest and most prominent families. His grandfather Daniel Davis had served as solic-

itor general of the Commonwealth of Massachusetts for thirty years, while his grandmother was the sister of the first Unitarian minister in the United States.

Davis's father, in addition to his regular naval duties, pursued a lifelong interest in astronomy, coauthored scientific works, and twice served as superintendent of the U.S. Naval Observatory. Davis in many ways emulated his father. Appointed acting midshipman on 29 November 1861, Davis missed active service in the Civil War. He was commissioned ensign on 1 November 1866, master one month later, lieutenant in 1869, and lieutenant commander in 1869. This meteoric rise meant that Davis spent most of his service in command ranks. His early rise to rank enabled him to pursue his personal interests to an unusual extent. Fleet Admiral Ernest J. King, who served under him as a junior officer, considered Davis a "queer fish." Davis, King remembered, "came to be what the British call[ed] 'the Owner' [of his merchant ship] and wanted to have his creature comforts" (archives of Naval War College). These tendencies became more pronounced after Davis reached flag rank. Few people dared to disturb the admiral when he was in his shipboard quarters, where he "was usually writing or sketching or even painting," unusual pursuits for naval officers of the period.

Davis's scientific interests blossomed during the decade 1876–1885 when he was engaged in astronomical work at the Naval Observatory and also headed expeditions to the west coast of Central and South America, Asia, and the Atlantic to determine precise longitudes of various ports through the use of submarine cables. Davis subsequently coauthored three Hydrographic Office publications of this work, *Telegraphic Determination of Longitudes* (1880, 1883, 1885), and individually through the Bureau of Navigation, Navy Scientific Paper No. 6, *Chronometer Rates as Affected by Changes of Temperature and Other Causes* (1877).

Promoted to commander in 1885, Davis served as chief intelligence officer (1889–1892) and superintendent of the Naval Observatory (1897–1902). Through his 1875 marriage to Louisa Quakenbush, Davis became a brother-in-law of Henry Cabot Lodge, a prominent Republican politician who frequently intervened to assist Davis's career. In Davis's temporary detachment from the Naval Observatory (Apr.–Nov. 1898) to command the converted cruiser *Dixie* during the war with Spain, it is difficult not to discern the influence of political connections. Similarly, a 1901 attempt by the secretary of the navy to send Davis to sea was canceled by President Theodore Roosevelt after an appeal by Lodge, who was one of Roosevelt's closest political associates.

In November 1902 Davis finally returned to sea in command of the battleship *Alabama*. Commissioned rear admiral on 24 August 1904, Davis assumed command of a battleship division and subsequently a battleship squadron of the Atlantic Fleet. This duty had but one interruption during Davis's final years of active service. From December 1904 to March 1905 he served as the U.S. commissioner in the international commission meeting in Paris to investigate the "Dogger Bank Incident," the ill-fated Russian Baltic Fleet's attack on the Hull fishing fleet as the Russians sailed toward their rendezvous with the Imperial Japanese Fleet at Tsushima.

Continuing political influence in Davis's career alienated a number of his peers and may well have prevented his appointment as commander in chief of the Atlantic Fleet; the position was offered to Rear Admiral Robley D. Evans in 1905. For the final two years of his active service, Davis functioned as second in command to the widely popular "Fighting Bob" Evans.

In January 1907, while Davis was in Guantanamo Bay, Cuba, a severe earthquake shook Jamaica. Rushing, with a battleship and a destroyer, to the aid of the victims, Davis dispensed with the usual naval courtesies including gun salutes to the British flag and to the governor of Jamaica, Sir Frank Swettenham. While such a course of action seemed reasonable under the circumstances, Swettenham, a man well known for his anti-American bias, took exception. He demanded a prompt American withdrawal even though the need for the American aid was abundantly apparent. Swettenham then dispatched an intemperate letter condemning as unwarranted Davis's intervention and in the process created an unseemly incident that was finally closed by Swettenham's removal from office.

In the final months of his service, Davis saw the American battleship fleet grow rapidly as ships authorized during the war with Spain entered service. The closest he came to his coveted appointment as commander in chief was a temporary one of about two weeks in May 1907 when Evans was ill. Davis retired on 28 August 1907 after forty-five years of service.

After his retirement from active duty, Davis served on the Perry Victory Centennial Commission in 1912. In his later years, he devoted much time to watercolor and oil painting, an activity in which he had regularly engaged while on active duty. He enjoyed some success, selling many pictures. He also mounted exhibitions in Washington and New York. He was, according to Rear Admiral Caspar F. Goodrich, a "seaman, navigator, astronomer, linguist, . . . a courtly, widely read and cultivated man of the world" (*Boston Transcript*, 28 Dec. 1921). Davis died in Washington, D.C.

In 1899 Davis published a biography of his father, *Life of Charles Henry Davis, Rear Admiral, 1807–1877.* "Notwithstanding the active and prominent life which Admiral Davis led, and his energy and dash as a naval commander," the son wrote of his father, "his tastes, especially in his later years, were much more those of a refined gentleman of literary leisure than of the active man of the world. He was little inclined to mingle in general society, but rather sought that of the cultivated few whose tastes were congenial with his own" (pp. 334–35). In this final assessment of his father, Davis unwittingly described himself.

• Some aspects of Davis's early life are mentioned in his biography of his father. A detailed summary of Davis's naval career is in William B. Cogar, *Dictionary of Admirals of the U.S. Navy*, vol. 2: *1901–1918* (1991), pp. 66–67. See also *Boston Transcript*, 28 Dec. 1921, for a eulogy by Rear Admiral Caspar F. Goodrich. *Science*, 24 Feb. 1922, and *Army and Navy Register*, 31 Dec. 1921, also contain obituaries.

JAMES R. RECKNER

DAVIS, Charles Henry Stanley (2 Mar. 1840–7 Nov. 1917), physician, philologist, and Orientalist, was born in Goshen, Connecticut, the son of Timothy Fisher Davis, a physician, and Moriva Hatch. Davis received his early education in the public school system of Meriden, Connecticut, and later through a private tutor, Dr. William Baker. In 1864 he entered the University of Maryland, where he began studies in medicine. He received an M.D. in 1866 from the University of the City of New York. He then undertook postgraduate work in Boston, Massachusetts, and during this period began the publication (1866) of the *Boston Medical Register*. In 1867 he joined his father in a successful private practice in Meriden for two years and then traveled abroad to complete further postgraduate studies in Europe. For several months he attended hospital practice in the cities of Paris and London. In 1869 he married Caroline Elizabeth Harris, with whom he had one son. The couple settled in Meriden, where Davis resumed a successful medical practice and remained for the rest of his career.

Davis became an active social, political, and medical leader in Connecticut. As one of the founders of the City Medical Society, he served for many years as its secretary. He also served as mayor of Meriden for two terms (1887–1888), declining a third one, and served in the state's house of representatives for three terms (1873, 1885, 1886). In addition he served on a number of local political committees and on the board of education. Davis was president of the local Savings and Loans Association. He was also the attending physician for the Curtis Home for Old Ladies and Orphans (1886–1908) and for the State School for Boys (1895–1900), while maintaining his active private practice.

During the period of his medical studies in New York City (1865–1866), Davis had entered into partnership with Charles H. Thomas, a successful medical publisher and well-known philologist and translator who had opened a bookstore that specialized in Oriental and classical books. Their association led to the formation of New York City's Philological Society. Davis undertook the study of languages, becoming proficient in Hebrew and Syriac, and later Arabic, Assyrian, ancient Egyptian, several old Persian tongues, and Celtic dialects. He became an ardent bibliophile and reader and eventually amassed a library of over 6,000 volumes with extensive holdings in Oriental languages and literature. He became a contributor at age eighteen to a literary column for the *New York Chronicle*, later the *Round Table*, and also the *Saturday Press*. In 1870 he produced his first major publication, *History of Wallingford, Conn, . . . including Meriden*. From 1887 to 1902 he was editor of *Biblia*, a journal of biblical and Oriental archaeology. He also coauthored a classic work titled *History of Ancient Egypt in the Light of Modern Discoveries* (1896). In 1894 he published an edition of *Egyptian Book of the Dead* that provided an English translation of the Louvre Papyrus and part of the Turin Papyrus. The breadth of Davis's career can be seen from other writings that he provided on *Greek and Roman Stoicism* (1903), *Grammar of the Old Persian Language* (1878), a translation of the Koran from Arabic into English, and a grammar of modern Irish language (1909). His last literary work was *Some of Life's Problems* (1914).

Among Davis's other publications are *Clergyman's Sore-Throat (Chronic Follicular Pharyngitis)* (1879), *The Voice as a Musical Instrument* (1879; repr. 1907), and *The Classification, Training, and Education of the Feeble-Minded, Imbecile and Idiotic Children* (1883). His other medical publications include *The Self-Cure of Consumption without Medicine* (1904) and *How to Be Successful as a Physician* (1905). Davis also published several articles in professional journals on sore throat consumption, and idiocy between 1879 and 1892. He became corresponding secretary to the Scientific Association and edited eight volumes of its *Transactions.* Davis died in the Connecticut State Hospital.

• A collection of correspondence and papers of Davis and his wife that includes letters, publications, manuscripts, and speeches are in the archives and manuscript collection of Yale University's Sterling Memorial Library.

JAMES T. GOODRICH

DAVIS, Clyde Brion (22 May 1894–19 July 1962), journalist and novelist, was born in Unadilla, Nebraska, the son of Charles N. Davis and Isabel Brion, shopkeepers. When Clyde was one year old the family moved to Chillicothe, Missouri, where Clyde's father operated a saw mill. Clyde attended high school in Kansas City, excelling in gymnastics and drawing. He dropped out of school at fourteen and worked for a time as a printer's apprentice, attending the Kansas City Art Institute at night. Eventually he got a job in the art department of the *Kansas City Star*. He also worked as a steamfitter's helper, a chimney sweep, a furnace repairman, a press-feeder, and an electrician.

Davis enlisted in the army at the outset of World War I, served in France, and gained valuable journalistic experience as a writer for the army newspaper. After returning from overseas in 1919 he took a job with the Burns Detective Agency and soon thereafter began a series of jobs (1919–1937) with several newspapers, including the *Denver Post*, the *Denver Rocky Mountain News*, the *Albuquerque Morning Journal*, the *San Francisco Examiner*, the *Seattle Post-Intelligencer*, and the *Buffalo Times*. In 1926 Davis married Martha Wirt; they had one son, David Brion, who went on to become a professor of history at Yale and win a Pulitzer Prize and a National Book Award.

After the publication of his first novel, *The Anointed* (1937), Davis briefly returned to journalism when he was sent to Europe as a reporter for a syndicate in 1941. Otherwise, except for two uneventful months in Hollywood as a screenwriter and two years as an associate editor for Rinehart & Company (the publisher of his work until the mid-1940s), he made his living exclusively as a novelist.

In many ways *The Anointed* set the standard for Davis's subsequent books, most of which are narrated by an ingratiatingly obtuse man driven by impossibly large ambitions. Davis's first novel is narrated by "Horseshoes" Harry Patterson, a sailor who is sustained by the belief that he is destined for great things. After many adventures at home and abroad, Harry's wanderlust is tamed by Marie, a librarian whom he plans to marry, and by his less than glamorous occupation as a grocery store clerk in San Francisco. The novel earned accolades from John Steinbeck and T. S. Stribling and provided the basis for the 1945 film *Adventure*, starring Clark Gable and Greer Garson and directed by Victor Fleming.

Davis next wrote *The Great American Novel* (1938). The protagonist is Homer Zigler, a newspaperman who believes he has "a sympathy for people and an ability for putting myself in the other fellow's shoes." He is therefore obsessively determined to write a novel that captures the wide range of American experience in the twentieth century. Although treated ironically, this ambition was undoubtedly shared by Davis himself, who recreated in his novel the life of America from 1906 to 1937.

Imperceptiveness is a comic flaw that characterizes many of Davis's self-deceived central characters, including his youthful protagonists. His next novel, *Northend Wildcats* (1938), a story about a youth gang in a small town at the turn of the century, featured such a character. Other books depicting youthful experience include *Jeremy Bell* (1947) and *North Woods Whammy* (1951). *Nebraska Coast* (1939) was something of a departure. Although the story is narrated by young Clint Macdougall, the central figure is the boy's strong, idealistic father Jack, who becomes a mayor and ultimately runs for Congress. Dedicated to Davis's own father, *Nebraska Coast* is characteristic of many Davis fictions: the impact of its romantic epic sweep is undermined by the author's careful attention to manners. Depicting the westward migration of a typical upstate New York family, Davis's slow-paced yarn downplays the inherent drama of frontier hardship brought on by severe winters, drought, and the threat of Indian attack, and instead emphasizes the commonplace activities of the time—especially canal-boating, train and steamboat travel, and buffalo hunting.

The 1940s were fruitful years for Davis. In 1940 two books appeared in rapid succession: *The Arkansas* and *Sullivan. Follow the Leader*, a satire of a war hero who becomes a businessman, was published in 1942. *The Rebellion of Leo McGuire* (1944) recounts the life of its antihero from his impoverished youth in Buffalo to his activities as a master burglar. McGuire hopes to transcend his dubious life of crime by putting his experiences down on paper; like so many of Davis's narrators, he believes his writings will constitute not only personal redemption but a genuine contribution to the betterment of the world.

Davis tapped his own experience for several other novels throughout the 1940s, including *The Stars Incline* (1946), which tells of a life in journalism; *Temper the Wind* (1948), about prizefighting; and most prominently, *Playtime Is Over* (1949). This last novel tells the story of Master Sergeant Stephen Fletcher Lewis, who has retired to a solitary existence in Arkansas and has begun to reminisce about his varied and often extraordinary adventures as a soldier of fortune.

The nonfiction *The Age of Indiscretion* (1950), ostensibly a memoir of Davis's life in Missouri at the turn of the century, is also an attack on modernist writers, particularly T. S. Eliot. To counter Eliot's sophisticated pessimism, Davis presents his own optimistic and often folksy cultural analysis. Davis rejects Eliot's claims of cultural decline by celebrating the achievements of contemporary America, asserting that "there is more happiness per capita today than in 1900."

Davis's spirited and straightforward populism remained his trademark for the rest of his career in such books as *Thudbury: An American Comedy* (1952), *The Newcomer* (1954), *Something for Nothing* (1956), *Unholy Uproar* (1957), *The Big Pink Kite* (1960), and *Shadow of a Tiger* (1963). Davis died in Salisbury, Connecticut.

Davis's novels received generally favorable reviews when they appeared, but since his death there has been virtually no scholarly interest in him. Perhaps this is not surprising since in his quest for authenticity Davis eschewed the fashionable trends and biases embraced by the literati. Instead he chose to tell his stories in a plain, unpretentious manner in an effort to truthfully explore the travails of ordinary men. But the results are uneven. His prose, while at times delightful—dryly humorous and sharply revealing of character nuance and historical reality—can also be tedious. Still, Davis may be linked to other American originals who sought to keep American writing in contact with the bounty of rich, raw experience that has frequently given birth to the greatest works of literature.

• Other important works by Davis include the nonfiction books *Illinois: Portrait of a Nation's Hub* (1956) and *New Prisons, New Men* (1945). Davis also edited *Eyes of Boyhood* (1953). His periodical publications include "Tips," *Atlantic Monthly*, Sept. 1946, pp. 126–27; "Horse Sense," *Atlantic Monthly*, Nov. 1946, pp. 120–22; and "Blueprints for the Novel," *Writer*, Mar. 1944, pp. 71–74. Herbert S. Gorman, *The Man with the Seeing Eye* (1946), is an important source, as is Steven G. Kellman, "The Self-Begetting Great American Novel: Clyde Brion Davis's Melding of Traditions," *Southwest Review* 62 (Winter 1977): 65–72.

THOMAS NEWHOUSE

DAVIS, David (9 Mar. 1815–26 June 1886), jurist, was born in Cecil County, Maryland, the son of David Davis, a physician, and Ann Mercer. After completing a course of study at Kenyon College in Gambier, Ohio, Davis read law in the office of Henry W. Bishop in Lenox, Massachusetts. At this time he also came under the influence of Judge William P. Walker, his future father-in-law. In 1835, after a year at the New Haven Law School, Davis headed to what was then the western frontier. He settled in Pekin, Illinois, where he opened a legal practice. After suffering the first of a lifelong series of bouts of malaria, he purchased the practice of another attorney, Jesse Fell, and moved to Bloomington, Illinois, which remained his home until his death.

While struggling to maintain a legal practice, Davis became involved in local politics. In 1840, as a member of the Whig party, he ran unsuccessfully for the state legislature. Five years later he won election to that body and quickly became an influential member. In 1847 he was elected to the state's Constitutional Convention, becoming noteworthy for his successful advocacy for the popular election of state court judges.

In 1848 Davis himself benefited from this change when he was elected judge of the Eighth Judicial Circuit of Illinois. He presided over this court for the next fourteen years (1848–1862). During this period Davis's friendship with Abraham Lincoln became close: Davis even allowed Lincoln to preside over his court in his absence. Both men continued their involvement in politics, and following the break-up of the Whig party in the 1850s over the slavery issue, both joined the newly created Republican party in 1856. Davis supported Lincoln's unsuccessful bid for the Senate against Stephen Douglas in 1858, and two years later, at the Republican convention in Chicago, it was Davis, who was instrumental in securing the presidential nomination for Lincoln. Following Lincoln's election Davis accompanied him to Washington and was rewarded with an appointment to investigate certain claims against the federal government involving General John C. Frémont.

Although many believed that Davis's relationship with Lincoln made an appointment to the Supreme Court inevitable, Davis himself was "diffident" about the matter, preferring a lower federal judgeship in the Midwest. At the time of Lincoln's election there were three vacancies on the Court, and Davis was Lincoln's third appointee, following Noah Swayne and Samuel Miller. Davis took his seat on the Supreme Court on 10 December 1862. Despite his misgivings about his qualifications to sit on the Court, it was his inability to avoid Washington politics that proved most frustrating for the new Justice. His political involvement and his desire to find positions for his friends were a constant drain on his time and energy.

During his fourteen-year tenure on the Court Davis participated in several notable decisions. That for which he is best remembered is the Court's 1866 ruling in *Ex parte Milligan*. In September 1862, President Lincoln had issued a proclamation suspending the writ of habeas corpus for civilian prisoners in the North under military authority. Such persons could be arrested for resisting the draft, obstructing volunteers, or other acts of disloyalty. Moreover, such individuals could be tried and punished by courts-martial or military commission. Lambdin P. Milligan, leader of the Sons of

Liberty, an Indiana Copperhead group opposed to the war, was tried and convicted by a military commission based on the proclamation. Overturning Milligan's conviction, Davis held that Lincoln's suspension of the writ of habeas corpus had been an unconstitutional usurpation of congressional authority and that the president had no authority to authorize the use of military courts except in case of controlling necessity. Although Davis received harsh criticism from Republicans for this decision, he believed it an important statement of civil liberties protection.

Aside from his opinion in *Milligan*, Davis was a consistent supporter of the Republican majority positions on the Supreme Court during and after Reconstruction. In the *Prize Cases* (1863), Davis and the Court upheld the position that citizens of the seceded states could be treated as wartime belligerents. Along with the majority, he refused to block the government's military program of reconstruction of the South in *Georgia v. Stanton* (1867), and the use of test oaths of loyalty for restoration of southerners' political rights. In the Legal Tender Cases (1870–1871), he supported the federal government's authority to issue paper notes as legal currency, and though generally favorable to business interests, he voted with the majority in upholding state business regulation in the landmark case *Munn v. Illinois* (1876).

Davis was active in Lincoln's successful reelection bid in 1864, but he was becoming increasingly concerned about Lincoln's position on slavery and the president's relationship to the radical faction of the Republican party. Davis had strongly opposed the Emancipation Proclamation, and although he eventually accepted the end of slavery in the South, following Lincoln's assassination Davis became increasingly frustrated with both President Johnson's ineptitude and the Radical Republicans' vindictiveness toward the South and the president. Indeed, the impeachment and trial of Johnson convinced Davis that he could no longer even consider himself a Republican.

Used to the bustle of politics, by 1870 Davis had become discontented with his relatively cloistered life on the Supreme Court. Moreover, his disgust with Grant and Republican party policies made him receptive to the possibility of reentering politics as a candidate for president. His flirtation with presidential politics was short-lived. Nominated by the Labor Reform Convention in Columbus, Ohio, in early 1872, he lost the Liberal Republican convention in Cincinnati later that year to Horace Greeley. During the contested election of 1876, it was assumed that Davis would serve as the "fifth justice" on the Electoral Commission Congress created to determine whether Hayes or Tilden had the electoral majority. However, while Congress debated the bill to create the commission, Democrats and independents in the Illinois legislature elected Davis to the U.S. Senate. Davis was surprised by his election but accepted the new position and resigned his seat on the Supreme Court. The final commission position was thus given to Republican justice Bradley, and Hayes was certified as president. Believing,

wrongly, that Davis would have supported Tilden, Democrats reviled the new senator. Davis served in the Senate for a single term, and as that body was evenly divided between Democrats and Republicans, Davis as an independent quickly became influential and was eventually elected president pro tem.

Davis's first wife, Sarah Woodruff, whom he had married in 1838 in Illinois, died in 1879. They had two surviving children. In 1883 he married Adeline Burr of Fayetteville, North Carolina. They lived in Bloomington until his death.

Davis was neither a brilliant thinker nor a charismatic leader. His judicial career, particularly his Supreme Court tenure, is remembered primarily for his opinion in the *Milligan* case. His fame rested largely on his association with Lincoln, which continued even after Lincoln's death as Davis served as administrator of his estate. Yet in an age when party politics mattered, Davis was an acknowledged master of party organization and electoral management.

• A collection of Davis's papers and letters is held by the Chicago Historical Society. A full biography is Willard L. King, *Lincoln's Manager: David Davis* (1960), which focuses on Davis's political career. For Davis's tenure on the Supreme Court, see Stanley Kutler, *Judicial Power and Reconstruction Politics* (1968); David M. Silver, *Lincoln's Supreme Court* (1956); and Charles Fairman, *Mr. Justice Miller and the Supreme Court, 1862–1890* (1939). For details of the 1876 election, see Charles Fairman, *Five Justices and the Electoral Commission of 1877*, Supplement to vol. 7, Holmes Devise History of the Supreme Court (1988). An obituary is in the *New York Times*, 27 June 1886.

ROBERT M. GOLDMAN

DAVIS, Dwight Filley (5 July 1879–28 Nov. 1945), tennis player and U.S. secretary of war, was born in St. Louis, Missouri, the son of John Tilden Davis, a dry goods merchant and banker, and Maria Jeanette Filley. The family's financial success and public-mindedness made it a leader on the St. Louis business, education, and social scenes. Following preparatory school at Smith Academy in St. Louis, Davis attended Harvard University, earning a Bachelor of Arts in 1900. While in college, he gained national prominence as a singles and doubles tennis player. In his junior and senior years he was the runner-up in the U.S. men's singles championship, and in those same two years and the year after he and his partner, Holcombe Ward, won the national doubles championship. In 1900 his name became forever associated with the sport when, after urging the establishment of international team competition, he donated a trophy, formerly called the International Lawn Tennis Challenge Trophy, which immediately became known as the Davis Cup. The award continued to be the symbol of international supremacy in team tennis. Davis was captain of the 1900 team and played on the 1902 team, both of which were victorious. This multinational competition significantly expanded worldwide interest in the sport.

Upon graduation, Davis returned to his hometown and entered law school at Washington University. In 1903 he earned an LL.D.; however, he never practiced law, choosing instead a life of public service, first locally, then nationally. In 1905 he married Helen Brooks; they had four children. Between 1903 and 1915 Davis served St. Louis in a variety of positions, including elected terms in the House of Delegates and Board of Freeholders, appointed terms on the boards of the public library, Museum of Fine Arts, and Public Improvement, and appointment to several commissions, including Public Baths, Public Recreation, Parks, and City Planning. Under his leadership, sports and recreational facilities were greatly expanded, and the city gained notoriety as the first municipality in the nation to provide public tennis courts. His accomplishments led to national attention and in 1908 to a term on the Executive Committee of the National Municipal League.

With the outbreak of World War I in 1914, Davis developed what was to remain a lifelong interest in military preparedness. In 1915 he participated in the first Plattsburg Training Camp, a summer camp that provided military education and training for civic and business leaders. In 1916–1917 he visited Europe as a member of the Rockefeller War Relief Commission, returning shortly before U.S. entrance into the conflict. He enlisted in the Missouri National Guard, and in August he received a commission as captain in the infantry. In May 1918 his unit, now part of the Thirty-fifth Division, set sail for France and in the fall of the year was actively engaged in the St.-Mihiel and Meuse-Argonne offensives. In the latter campaign Davis, then a major, earned the Distinguished Service Cross for extraordinary heroism. Before leaving the army, he was promoted to lieutenant colonel.

Upon returning to Missouri, Davis unsuccessfully sought the 1920 Republican nomination for the U.S. Senate. The following year President Warren Harding appointed him to the War Finance Corporation, which had the responsibility of promoting export trade. In 1923 Harding selected him as assistant secretary of war, a position he held until October 1925, when President Calvin Coolidge chose him as secretary of war to replace the ailing John W. Weeks. Davis, who was Coolidge's youngest cabinet member, remained in the post through the end of the administration in 1929.

During Davis's six years in the War Department, the U.S. Army struggled against a Congress and a public that showed little interest in military preparedness. In this period of shrinking budgets, the secretary proved to be an able administrator and effective spokesman for the department. Beyond the day-to-day operations, his primary contributions were in three areas: industrial mobilization, military aviation, and armored warfare.

As assistant secretary and secretary, Davis pushed, with moderate success, for a comprehensive industrial mobilization plan that would assure that the nation's industrial capacity could meet the army's procurement needs in the event of war. Unfortunately, the plan was not ready until 1930, the year after he left office. He did, however, in 1923 play a major role in the establishment of the Army Industrial College in Washington, D.C. That school trained many of the military procurement officers that later were in logistical leadership positions during World War II. His most newsworthy activities came between 1924 and 1926 and centered on the controversy between high-ranking army officers over the role of air power. He took a strong stand against the actions of the most outspoken air advocate, General William "Billy" Mitchell, and pressed for his 1925 court-martial. After being found guilty, Mitchell resigned rather than face suspension. Davis did, however, remain in relatively good stead with air advocates by supporting the recommendations of the president's Aircraft Board, headed by Dwight W. Morrow. The board opposed creating a separate air force, but it urged increasing emphasis on military aviation.

Davis's forward-looking position on aviation was matched by his vision of armored warfare. In 1927 he directed the General Staff to pursue the development of a small, mobilized force. Development of the units fell to tank advocate, Major Adna Romanza Chaffee, Jr., who in the next decade led the army toward a fully mechanized cavalry. Davis's performance in the War Department can best be described as steady and competent oversight of a lackluster department in a lackluster period for the nation's armed forces.

In 1929 President Herbert Hoover appointed Davis governor general of the Philippine Islands. In his new administrative post, Davis successfully promoted and implemented major road and harbor improvements, school reform, and laws that strengthened the economy. He also successfully avoided the trap of getting involved in local politics and the controversial issue of independence. In 1932, because of his wife's ill health, he resigned his position and returned home. Shortly thereafter his wife died. Four years later, in 1936, he married Pauline Morton Sabin, widow of the financier Charles Sabin and daughter of the former secretary of the navy Paul Morton.

From the time he left the Philippines until the outbreak of World War II, Davis traveled, pursued a tung oil business in Florida, and served as a member then chairman of the Brookings Institute. Although a vociferous critic of Franklin D. Roosevelt and the New Deal, he accepted the president's 1942 offer to be director general of the Army Specialist Corps, which provided commissions to highly skilled personnel who could not meet the army's physical standards. When the corps was absorbed by the Army Service Forces later that year, he was retained in an advisory capacity for the duration of the war, maintaining his rank of major general. He died in Washington, D.C., and was buried in Arlington National Cemetery.

• Davis left no personal papers. Several of his speeches are in contemporary magazines. His activities at the War Department and in the Philippines can best be tracked in the *New York Times*, 6 Mar. 1927, 8 Aug. 1928, and 18 May 1929. For information on his contributions to tennis and the Davis Cup, see United States Lawn Tennis Association, *Official Encyclopedia of Tennis* (1972). A good general account of War Department activities in the 1920s is in Allan R. Millett and Peter Maslowski, *For the Common Defense: A Military History of the United States* (1994). Davis's contributions in the realm of industrial mobilization are in Marvin A. Kreidberg and Merton G. Henry, *History of Military Mobilization in the United States Army, 1775–1945* (1955), and the air controversy is examined in Alfred F. Hurley, *Billy Mitchell: Crusader for Air Power* (1964). Obituaries are in the *New York Times* and the *Dallas Morning News*, 29 Nov. 1945.

KEITH D. McFARLAND

DAVIS, Eddie "Lockjaw" (2 Mar. 1922–3 Nov. 1986), tenor saxophonist, was born in New York City, the son of Eleanor (maiden name unknown). His father (name unknown) worked menial jobs and saw little of his family. Davis dated his admiration for musicians to a time when his older brother was a bouncer at the Savoy Ballroom and would let Eddie and his twin brother in for free. He decided drummers and saxophonists had the greatest fame and finest women; the drums being cumbersome, he bought a saxophone. Self-taught, he was playing at Monroe's Uptown House eight months later. He married Beatrice (maiden name unknown) around 1941; they had one daughter.

With the aim of eventually getting into the New York musicians' union via a transfer, Davis moved to Philadelphia, Pennsylvania, where he joined the local union and Jimmy Gorham's Kentuckians, a big band, in 1940 or 1941. In the summer of 1942 Gorham's band was at the Club Harlem in Atlantic City. That same year Cootie Williams heard Davis and Bud Powell in a group at the Club Caravan and hired them, along with three other sidemen, for his big band. They worked at the Savoy Ballroom in New York City before embarking on a six-month tour on the RKO theater circuit. In 1944 Davis quit Williams's orchestra in Los Angeles and returned to New York. He joined the big bands of Lucky Millinder (1944), Louis Armstrong (for four months, c. 1945), and Andy Kirk (1945–1946). In the meantime Davis began working with small modern jazz groups, initially in a quartet including Thelonious Monk. Davis disliked Monk's idiosyncratic piano accompaniments; later he maintained a firm intolerance for anything remotely connected to avant garde jazz performance.

At Davis's first session as a leader in May 1946, Savoy record producer Bod Shad named one of the performances *Lockjaw*, hence his nickname and the subsequent affectionate abbreviations "Lock" and "Jaws." He also was known as the Fox, for his shrewdness and wisdom. During a long stay at Minton's Playhouse from around 1947 to 1952, he led informal sessions. In addition to performing, he acted as the "policeman" on the bandstand, asking unqualified musicians not to play and asking fine musicians to stop, if they hogged the stage for too long. He took three- to four-week breaks from Minton's for other jobs and in 1951 toured for sixteen weeks with George Shearing and the All American All Stars.

In the summer of 1951 Davis made his first tenor saxophone and Hammond organ recordings with organist Bill Doggett, bassist Oscar Pettiford, and drummer Shadow Wilson. He joined Count Basie's big band in May 1952, staying to the end of July 1953, when he was replaced by Frank Foster. He said that he left because, under producer John Hammond's influence, Basie was featuring Paul Quinichette (imitating Lester Young) as the tenor saxophone soloist. Returning to the sax and organ combination, he worked with organist Doc Bagby (1954–1955) and then led a trio with organist Shirley Scott, beginning in February 1955. He rejoined Basie late in September 1957, touring Europe in the fall and then leaving at the New Year. He reactivated the trio, which was resident at Count Basie's club in Harlem from 4 February 1958 to 1 February 1959, and then toured. From this period came his (and Scott's) greatest series of albums, collectively called *The Eddie "Lockjaw" Davis Cookbook*.

Tiring of the sax and organ combination, Davis became co-leader of a quintet with saxophonist Johnny Griffin in 1960, recording the album *Tough Tenors* in November and a session at Minton's Playhouse in January 1961 (issued under various *Live . . .* titles). Albums apart from Griffin included *Trane Whistle*, which placed Davis's improvising in a big band setting (1960), and *Afro-Jaws*, a Latin jazz collection (1961). After two successful years the group began to lose money. Griffin immigrated to Europe in 1963 because of tax difficulties. Davis saw too many musicians growing old and still having to endure long hours and difficult travel to survive. Seeking an alternative, he withdrew from performance in June 1963 to act as a booking agent with Shaw Artists Corporation. In July 1964 he temporarily replaced Foster in Basie's group, pending the arrival of Sal Nistico. He briefly resumed his job as a booking agent but then became road manager for Basie in November 1964 and a few weeks later took a second salary as tenor saxophonist, replacing Nistico. John Shaw described Davis as "warm, outgoing: . . . a highly articulate conversationalist."

For the next decade Davis was in and out of Basie's band. Among his leaves of absence were an expansion of the two-tenor idea, in a tour of England with tenor saxophonists Ben Webster, Bud Freeman, Eddie Miller, and Alex Welsh in the spring of 1967; a period with Tommy Flanagan's trio in Los Angeles in November of that year; and work alongside Basie's orchestra as a member of the Jazz at the Philharmonic All Stars in June 1972. To take advantage of a lower tax rate, Davis made his home in Las Vegas, Nevada, from 1973 or 1974, although he was on the road performing most of the year. He toured internationally as a leader for another decade. Among his albums were *Swingin' Till the Girls Come Home* (1976), *Straight Ahead* (1976), and *The Heavy Hitter* (1979). He also co-led a group with Harry "Sweets" Edison from about 1975 to 1979; their albums included *Edison's Lights* (1976). In 1984 Davis was stricken by stomach cancer, and in his last year he performed only occasionally. He died in Culver City, California.

In a review of *The Heavy Hitter*, Shirley Klett wrote that "Jaws could be likened to Humphrey Bogart—a rough exterior with unexpected depths" (*Cadence* 6, no. 2 [Feb. 1980]: 17). His playing epitomized the "tough tenor" style: equally founded in swing, bop, gospel, and rhythm and blues, it combined gutsy timbres, hard driving rhythms, and emotive rhetorical gestures, with instrumental virtuosity, harmonic subtlety, and a sophisticated sense of melodic design.

• Interviews with Davis are by John Shaw, "Lockjaw Davis: A Musician Who Matters," *Jazz Journal* 23, no. 9 (Sept. 1970): 10–11; Valerie Wilmer, *Jazz People* (1970), pp. 31–40; Art Taylor, *Notes and Tones: Musician-to-Musician Interviews* (1977), pp. 83–91; Vern Montgomery, "Jaws Unlocks," *Jazz Journal International* 36, no. 7 (July 1983): 14–15; and Bob Rusch, "Eddie Lockjaw Davis," *Cadence* 14, no. 1 (Jan. 1988): 5–18, 64, and 14, no. 2 (Feb. 1988): 5–15, 20. Basie describes his relationship with Davis and admires his work as a road manager in Albert Murray, *Good Morning Blues: The Autobiography of Count Basie* (1985); a full and detailed chronology of their association may be extracted from Chris Sheridan, *Count Basie: A Bio-discography* (1986). An obituary is in the *San Francisco Examiner*, 5 Nov. 1986.

BARRY KERNFELD

DAVIS, Edmund Jackson (2 Oct. 1827–7 Feb. 1883), politician and governor of Texas, was born in St. Augustine, Florida, the son of William Godwin Davis, a land developer and attorney, and Mary Ann Channer. He received a common school education in Florida. In January 1848 he moved with his family to Galveston, Texas, where he worked as a clerk in the post office and read law. In 1849 he moved to Corpus Christi, Texas, where he continued his study of law and also clerked in a mercantile establishment. He passed the bar in 1849 and began practice in southern Texas. In 1858 he married Anne Elizabeth Britton, the daughter of a state senator. They had three children, one of whom died in infancy.

In 1853 Davis was elected district attorney at Brownsville. He served until 1856 when named judge of the state's Twelfth Judicial District. He held that position until 1861. At first a member of the Whig party, he became a Democrat in 1857, only to support Sam Houston in 1859 and 1861 against the regular wing of the party. He ran for the secession convention as a Unionist in 1861 but was defeated. After secession Davis refused to take an oath of loyalty to the Confederacy and his judicial position was vacated in April 1861.

Davis and other Unionists fled Texas in the spring of 1862. In Washington, D.C., he proposed arming Texas loyalists on the border, and in October 1862 he received a commission to raise a cavalry regiment that became the First Texas Cavalry, United States Volunteers. He was with his unit at the battle of Galveston in January 1863. In March 1863 he was captured on Mexican soil while bringing his family out of Texas but was released by Confederate authorities after protests by Mexico. He returned as a part of General Nathaniel Banks's expedition into southern Texas in

1863–1864. Promoted to brigadier general in November 1864, he commanded a cavalry division in Louisiana during the rest of the war.

Following the war Davis returned to Corpus Christi. He served in the Texas constitutional convention of 1866 but was not elected when he ran for the state senate in the general election that year. A critic of Presidential Reconstruction, he joined the Texas Republican party in 1867 and served as president of the constitutional convention of 1868–1869. In the convention he supported what became the Radical position, including an expansion of black political rights, restriction on the political power of ex-secessionists, and division of Texas into three states. In the election of 1869 he ran as the Radical candidate for governor against Andrew J. Hamilton and was elected.

Davis took office in the spring of 1870 and served until January 1874. As governor he supported legislation creating public schools, a state police force, and various agencies to support economic development. He favored limited state support for railroads but opposed the large-scale aid that was given. He gave general support for blacks in securing full civil rights. Opponents undermined his authority with charges that his administration was corrupt, wasteful, and despotic. In the state election of 1873 he was defeated by the Democratic candidate, Richard Coke. A crisis developed in the consequent change of government when the state supreme court ruled Coke's election illegal. Davis's attempt to enforce the court's decision brought him to a confrontation with Democratic leaders intent on ending Republican rule. Armed conflict was avoided only when Davis, unable to secure Federal support, stepped aside and allowed the Democrats to organize the new legislature and inaugurate Coke.

Davis then practiced law in Austin and continued to be the leader of the state Republican party until his death. He ran for governor in 1880 but was defeated by Oran M. Roberts. In 1882 he ran for Congress but was defeated by the Democratic candidate John Hancock. Although hated politically for his role in Reconstruction, even his enemies always considered Davis to be personally honest. He died in Austin.

• The James P. Newcomb Papers in the Barker Texas History Center, University of Texas at Austin, contain the best collection of Davis letters. A few letter presses from his administration exist in the Governor's Papers, Texas State Archives. See also Ronald N. Gray, "Edmund J. Davis: Radical Republican and Reconstruction Governor of Texas" (Ph.D. diss., Texas Tech Univ., 1976). For Davis during Reconstruction see Carl H. Moneyhon, *Republicanism in Reconstruction Texas* (1980).

CARL H. MONEYHON

DAVIS, Edwin Hamilton (22 Jan. 1811–15 May 1888), physician and archaeologist, was born in Hillsboro, Ohio, the son of Henry Davis and Avis Slocum. During his boyhood Davis became interested in numerous circular, square, and octagonal earthworks of the so-called Mound Builders culture in Ross County, Ohio. He continued his investigations of mounds while attending Kenyon College, graduating in 1833. His commencement address, "Antiquities of Ohio," was heard by Daniel Webster, who encouraged Davis to continue his mound investigations. In 1836 he assisted Charles Whittlesey, Ohio's topographic engineer, in his survey of various Indian mounds and sites in the state. Davis married Lucy Woodbridge in 1841; they had nine children, among them John Woodbridge Davis, who became a well-known civil engineer.

After graduating from Cincinnati Medical College in 1838 Davis practiced medicine in Chillicothe, Ohio, until 1850. In Chillicothe he met the newspaper editor Ephraim George Squier, with whom he began collaborative surveys of Indian mounds in the area. During Davis's time, archaeology was considered an interest rather than a vocation, and Davis and Squier personally funded their mound survey work. Their surveys, explorations, and excavations covered over 200 mounds and earthworks in south-central Ohio. Their efforts culminated in the first published work of the Smithsonian Institution, *Ancient Monuments of the Mississippi Valley Comprising the Results of Extensive Original Surveys and Explorations* (1848). This volume remains a classic in the early annals of Americanist archaeology and is the only record of some Ohio mounds that are no longer in existence. Davis moved to New York in 1850 to chair the department of materia medica and therapeutics at the New York Medical College and taught there until 1860. Some of his students became interested in archaeology, and he wrote of specimens that were sent to him by "my former students from Central and South America" (*Smithsonian Report* [1866], p. 370). In 1854 Davis delivered a series of lectures on archaeology at the Lowell Institute in Boston and later to various scientific societies in New York City.

In 1866 Davis approached Joseph Henry, the first secretary of the Smithsonian Institution, about organizing some of the artifact collections that he and Squier had made based upon an ethnological map created by Franz Waitz, a pioneer in psychological anthropology and early Americanist ethnology. His organization of the artifact collections at the Smithsonian reflected the influence of American Ethnological Society founder Albert Gallatin, German physiologist Carl Ludwig, American ethnologist and geologist George Gibbs, and American ethnologist Lewis Henry Morgan (author of *Ancient Society* [1877]) on ethnological knowledge of the time. During Squier's absence in Peru in 1864, Davis sold most of their collection for $10,000 to William Blackmore of London. After being sold many times the Davis and Squier collection finally ended up in the American Museum of Natural History in New York City. Davis died in New York City.

• Davis's "Report" in the *Smithsonian Report* (1866) is an excellent source for his archaeological activities. James B. Griffin provides a short biographical account of Davis's life and career in his introduction to Davis and Squier's *Ancient Monuments of the Mississippi Valley Comprising the Results of the Extensive Original Surveys and Explorations* (1848; repr.

1973). See also Terry A. Barnhart, "Of Mounds and Men: The Early Career of Ephraim George Squier" (Ph.D. diss., Miami Univ., 1989), which is the primary source of information on Squier's career. An obituary is in the *New York Times*, 16 May 1888.

DOUGLAS R. GIVENS

DAVIS, Elmer (13 Jan. 1890–18 May 1958), author, journalist, and radio commentator, was born Elmer Holmes Davis in Aurora, Indiana, the son of Elam H. Davis, a cashier for the First National Bank of Aurora, and Louise Severin, principal at the local high school. Described by a childhood friend as an avid reader, Davis began his long career with newspapers the summer after his freshman year in high school by obtaining a job as a printer's devil for the *Aurora Bulletin*. By 1906, when Davis entered Franklin College at age sixteen, he had received his first payment for a newspaper story—$25 from the *Indianapolis Star*. He continued his association with the *Star* through his college years, serving as its Franklin correspondent.

Graduating in 1910 with a bachelor of arts degree, Davis received a Rhodes scholarship to Oxford that same year. In 1911 he received a master's degree from Franklin College for courses completed while in residence. Described by his biographer Roger Burlingame as "a sort of financial hypochondriac," Davis managed to concoct a scheme whereby he obtained free passage overseas. He had the idea that if he could get all forty-eight scholarship winners on one ship, the company that owned the vessel might be willing to give him free passage. His scheme worked: he and the other scholarship winners sailed to Oxford aboard the *Haverford*, whose main cargo consisted of cattle.

Although Davis's time at Oxford was cut short owing to the illness and eventual death of his father, he managed to make frequent trips to the European continent, gathering information on politics and foreign affairs that served him well in coming years. During these travels he met Florence MacMillan of Mount Vernon, New York, whom he married in 1917; they had one daughter and one son. Returning to the United States in 1913, Davis found few job prospects in Aurora and took an editorial position with *Adventure* magazine in New York. A year later, the *New York Times* hired him as a reporter, a job he held for the next decade. During his *Times* career he covered a hodgepodge of stories, ranging from the 1923 championship boxing match in Shelby, Montana, to political conventions (for which he created the popular Hoosier political commentator Godfrey G. Gloom from Amity, Indiana) and religious rallies.

In December 1923 Davis left his secure job at the *Times* for the insecure career of a freelance writer. He wrote fiction and nonfiction for publications such as the *Saturday Review of Literature*, *New Republic*, and *Harper's*. He also continued to churn out popular novels—series begun in 1913 with *The Princess Cecilia*—and stories for popular magazines such as *Liberty Magazine* and *Collier's*. Enjoying success as a writer, Davis purchased a summer home in Mystic, Connecticut.

While he was writing a serialized mystery novel for the *Saturday Evening Post* in August 1939, Davis received a telephone call from Paul White, news department director for the Columbia Broadcasting System (CBS). White asked him to come to New York to fill in as a news analyst for the popular broadcaster H. V. Kaltenborn, who was on assignment in Europe. Davis had done occasional broadcasts and had earlier substituted for Kaltenborn. Leaving his mystery serial unfinished, Davis spent the next few weeks reporting on the European crisis, working as much as eighteen hours a day but actually broadcasting for no more than one hour a day.

Despite being older than most radio commentators, Davis became a hit with listeners. According to fellow broadcaster Edward R. Murrow, Davis managed to survive his years at Oxford "with accent and outlook unimpaired," and his midwestern accent helped endear him to the nationwide radio audience. The former Hoosier believed his success was due in part to the accidental advantage of having a voice sounding like "back home." Reviewing his career after his death, his former employer, the *Times*, gave other reasons: "News broadcasting in those days was heavily larded with pomposity and unction. Mr. Davis had neither. But he loved facts, unadorned facts, and he had an incisive, analytical mind" (19 May 1958).

Over the next few years Davis's reports of the war news became daily listening for millions. Murrow, fast becoming a celebrity through his broadcasts from wartime London, told Davis that he was proud to be working with him on CBS. "I have hopes that broadcasting is to become an adult means of communication at last," said Murrow. "I've spent a lot of time listening to broadcasts from many countries . . . and yours stand out as the best examples of fair, tough-minded, interesting talking I've heard" (Burlingame, p. 174). Davis's ability to reach out and seize the American public's attention was clearly evident in his March 1942 broadcast urging the federal government to create one organization responsible for coordinating war news. E. B. White, writing in the *New Yorker*'s "Talk of the Town" column, proclaimed, "Of the twelve steps we would like to see taken in this war without further delay, the first is the unification of the information bureaus and the appointment of Elmer Davis to head them up. Mr. Davis, on the air the other night, presented the best case for unification and the strongest indictment of the present mess. In our opinion not only is he right but he is the man to sit on the desk" (14 Mar. 1942, p. 13).

Davis, however, thought others might be more suitable for such a position; he wrote to presidential adviser Harry Hopkins to suggest Murrow, William L. Shirer, or Rex Stout as possible choices. President Franklin D. Roosevelt, however, selected the man he described as the broadcaster "with the funny voice. Elmer—Elmer something." On 13 June 1942 the government announced the creation of the Office of War Information, with Davis as its director. The new agency consolidated the functions of the Office of Facts and Figures, the Office of Government Reports, the Division of Information in the Office for Emergency Management, and the Foreign Information Service of the Office of Co-Ordinator of Information.

Davis presided over a federal agency with a budget that reached about $25 million. The agency's approximately 30,000 employees included newspaper editors, editorial writers, advertising experts, publicists, playwrights, poets, film directors, lawyers, anthropologists, sociologists, psychologists, and diplomats. Despite his lack of administrative experience, Davis managed to weld this disparate group into an effective information agency. The director spelled out his philosophy in signs posted in the OWI's offices in the Library of Congress, in the Social Security Building, and in the U.S. Information Building: "This is a people's war, and the people are entitled to know as much as possible about it."

Obtaining the information, however, proved to be a major headache for Davis. He had constant battles with armed forces officials regarding the release of war news to the public. Along with battling the military, Davis in his three and a half years in office also had to weather complaints from politicians that he was working to promote not the war, but Roosevelt and the New Deal; infighting among various OWI employees; and wild accusations that he was a Communist stooge. His continued efforts to acquaint the public with the war's progress lasted until September 1945, when, with World War II's end, the OWI ceased to exist. In announcing the agency's liquidation, President Harry Truman complimented Davis and his staff for their "outstanding contribution to victory." Freed from his OWI responsibilities, Davis returned to radio, offering news commentary for the American Broadcasting Company (ABC).

Davis may have left behind his wartime battles, but he was soon engaged in another struggle to inform the American public, a battle against the Communist "witch hunt" begun by Senator Joseph McCarthy. In a speech on 9 February 1950 in Wheeling, West Virginia, McCarthy proclaimed that he held in his hand a list consisting of 205 known Communists in the State Department. Although a special Senate committee found little or no evidence to back McCarthy's charges, the Korean War's outbreak in June 1950 helped to heighten American fears about the possibility of Communist-sponsored subversion in the United States.

McCarthy's later disproven charges created a climate of fear and suspicion and spawned a new term, McCarthyism. The hysteria prompted by the Wisconsin senator reached such a pitch that when Davis appealed for calm in one radio broadcast, arguing "we had better wait and see if the evidence justified conviction," an aggrieved listener wrote him, "We cannot wait for convictions; what we want is confessions."

Throughout the McCarthy years Davis, in his radio broadcasts and books like his 1954 bestseller *But We Were Born Free*, appealed to the better nature of the American citizen, becoming one of the strongest spokesmen for reason during those troubled times. "I regret that I have to mention McCarthy; I regret that he exists," Davis wrote. "But he does exist, and not to mention him would be as if people in a malarial country refused to mention the anopheles mosquito. (There is a quinine that can neutralize his [McCarthy's] venom; it is called courage. It does not seem to be widely distributed in the upper ranks of our government.)" (Burlingame, pp. 307–9). Davis's strong stance prompted letters of both praise and censure.

The firm grip McCarthy enjoyed on the American public came apart in the spring of 1954 with the Army-McCarthy hearings, which were televised nationally. Viewers perceived McCarthy as a villain, and on 2 December 1954 the Senate voted to censure him.

The battles Davis fought on behalf of freedom and fair play, although bloodless, had an impact on his health. He suffered a stroke in March 1958 and died in Washington, D.C., two months later. His obituary in the *Times* called him the "Mount Everest of commentators" and praised him for always sounding to his listeners like a "rational adult."

• The papers of the Office of War Information are in the National Archives and Records Administration in Washington, D.C. Davis's life and career are explored in Roger Burlingame's biography *Don't Let Them Scare You: The Life and Times of Elmer Davis* (1961) and in his *New York Times* obituary of 19 May 1958. Writings by Davis are collected in *By Elmer Davis* (1964), ed. Robert Lloyd Davis. For Davis's work as head of the OWI, see Allan M. Winkler, *The Politics of Propaganda: The Office of War Information, 1942–1945* (1978).

RAY BOOMHOWER

DAVIS, Ernie (14 Dec. 1939–18 May 1963), football player, was born in New Salem, Pennsylvania, a coal mining district. The names and occupations of his parents cannot be ascertained. He never knew his father, who left the family soon after his son's birth and subsequently died in an accident. His mother moved to Elmira, New York, leaving the one-year-old Ernie with his grandparents in nearby Uniontown, Pennsylvania. Ten years later Davis rejoined his mother in Elmira.

Davis's athletic career began at the Elmira Free Academy, where he starred in both basketball and football. He was named a *Scholastic Coach* magazine high school All-American in both sports in 1957–1958 but was recruited to play football by more than thirty-five schools, including Notre Dame. He chose to go to Syracuse University because of its proximity to Elmira and the intercession of an Elmira attorney and a Syracuse alumnus.

Davis led his freshman football team to an undefeated season in 1958. He then played three years of varsity football at Syracuse, during which time the team achieved a record of twenty wins and five losses. They beat Texas in the 1960 Cotton Bowl and Miami in the 1961 Liberty Bowl; the team had won the national championship in 1959. Davis, the leading rusher all three seasons, led the team in pass receiving in 1961, gained 3,414 all-purpose yards, and averaged 6.6 yards per carry in his career. His 15.7 yards per carry

in one game against West Virginia in 1959 and his seasonal average of 7.8 yards per carry remain Syracuse records. In the 1960–1961 seasons he gained more than 100 yards per game eleven times. Davis was chosen the outstanding player in both the Cotton and Liberty bowls.

Davis made All-American in 1960 and was chosen again in 1961 unanimously. His numerous honors included the 1961 Heisman Trophy, awarded annually to the outstanding college football player. Davis was the first African American to earn the Heisman, winning it in close balloting over fullback Bob Ferguson of Ohio State and his old boyhood friend from Uniontown, Sandy Stephens, who had gone on to star at the University of Minnesota.

Syracuse used the "winged T" formation with an unbalanced line. Davis would run from either the tailback or wingback position. At 6'2" and 205 pounds, he possessed, in the words of his coach Ben Schwartzwalder, that "rare combination of power and speed." Davis ran effectively off tackle, on reverses, and on power sweeps around end and proved to be an effective blocker and a sure-handed pass receiver. He had the ability to break open games with long gains, including his 87-yard run with a pass against Texas in the 1960 Cotton Bowl. Playing before the free substitution rule was introduced, Davis was an effective defensive back. He was often compared with Jim Brown, the 1956 Syracuse All-American who had become a star in the National Football League with the Cleveland Browns. Davis, in fact, broke ten of Brown's intercollegiate records. During his junior year, 1960–1961, Davis also played varsity basketball. He graduated from Syracuse in 1962 with a bachelor's degree in business administration and was honored by his classmates as a senior marshall at the commencement. A deeply religious man and a member of the Baptist church, he never married.

In 1962 Davis played in the East-West Shrine game, in an all-star game in June, and later that summer in the college all-star game against the Green Bay Packers. The first player chosen in that year's professional football draft, he was the focus of an intense bidding war between the NFL's Washington Redskins, the Buffalo Bills of the rival American Football League, and the Canadian Football League. Washington subsequently traded his NFL rights to the Cleveland Browns, which in December 1961 signed him to an $80,000 three-year contract.

Davis became ill with acute monocytic leukemia during practice for the college all-star game in 1962. He participated in preseason practice with the Browns and worked briefly as a sales trainee for the Pepsi-Cola Company, but he was too disabled to play professional football. His condition deteriorated that fall, and after one last visit to a Syracuse spring practice game in April he reentered a Cleveland hospital, where he died. Davis was buried in Elmira.

Although subjected to racial taunting from the earliest days of his career, Davis said after the racially charged Cotton Bowl game against Texas in 1960 that he never gave much thought to such issues. This passivity stood in sharp contrast to the militancy of some of his fellow African-American athletes later in that decade. In 1979 Davis was elected posthumously to the National Football Foundation College Hall of Fame.

• Some information on Davis's college career is in the files of the Syracuse University Sports Information Office, Syracuse, N.Y. The Texas Cotton Bowl incident is discussed in the *New York Times*, 2, 3, and 12 Jan. 1960. For his return to basketball at Syracuse in 1961, see the *New York Herald Tribune*, 1, Mar. 1961. For comment on his receiving the Heisman Trophy, see the *New York Times*, 29 Nov. and 7 Dec. 1961. For his plans to play professional football, see the *New York Herald Tribune*, 7 Dec. 1961, and the *New York Times*, 3, 5, and 10 Dec. 1961. Reports of his illness and prospects of playing for the Browns are in the *New York Times*, 6 and 7 Oct. 1962, and Paul Brown, with Jack Clary, *PB: The Paul Brown Story* (1979). For a contemporary student's memories, see Judy Adams, "Ernie Davis," *Daily Orange* (Syracuse Univ.), 1 June 1963. Also see Robert C. Gallagher, *Ernie Davis: The Elmira Express* (1983). Insights can be gleaned from John T. Brady, *The Heisman: A Symbol of Excellence* (1984); Steven Clark, *Fight against Time: Five Athletes—A Legacy of Courage* (1979); Ernie Davis and Bob August, "I'm Not Unlucky," *Saturday Evening Post*, 30 Mar. 1993, pp. 60–62; W. A. Nack, "A Life Cut Short," *Sports Illustrated*, 4 Sept. 1989, pp. 136–46; Bill Libby, *Heroes of the Heisman Trophy* (1973); *Official 1993 NCAA Football* (1993); "Pro Patient," *Newsweek*, 22 Oct. 1962, p. 76; Ken Rappoport, *The Syracuse Football Story* (1975), *1993 Syracuse Football Story* (1993); and A. Wright, "Ernie Davis: A Man of Courage," *Sports Illustrated*, 27 May 1963, pp. 24–25. Obituaries and commentary are in the *New York Times*, 19, 22, and 23 May 1963, the *Syracuse Herald Journal*, 18 May 1963, and the *Syracuse Post Standard*, 19 May 1963.

DANIEL R. GILBERT

DAVIS, Frances Elliott (28 Apr. 1882–2 May 1965), public health nurse, nurse-educator, and community advocate, was born in Shelby, North Carolina, the daughter of an unlawful interracial marriage between Darryl Elliott, a part African-American Cherokee sharecropper, and Emma (maiden name unknown), the daughter of a plantation owner and Methodist minister. Darryl Elliott fled the state early in Frances's life, leaving her to be raised by her mother. Both parents had died by 1887, after which Davis was raised in a succession of foster homes. At the age of twelve she was sent to Pittsburgh, Pennsylvania, where she lived under the guardianship of the Reverend Mr. Vickers. In the Vickers household she was regarded more as a domestic helper than a ward; consequently her early formal education was pursued on a sporadic basis. Determined to succeed, she possessed the intrepidity to upgrade her reading skills on her own.

In 1896, at the age of fourteen, Davis was granted permission by the Vickerses to seek outside employment and had the good fortune to have her services retained by the Joseph Allison Reed household. Taking an interest in Davis, the Reeds assumed the role of patrons and helped her to flee to Knoxville, Tennessee, two years later when the Vickerses demanded she re-

sign her position. The Reeds continued their sponsorship by financing her education to the end of normal school. By 1905 she had secured the prerequisites for normal school training at Knoxville College, from which she graduated in 1907 at the age of twenty-five, and, on the advice of Mrs. Reed, she undertook a teaching career to maintain her subsidized education.

Pursuing her early dream "to be a nurse and help little children," Davis worked one year at a hospital built at Knoxville College until she had to resign as a result of ill health. Temporarily, she assumed a teaching post in Henderson, North Carolina, instructing third and fourth graders at the Henderson Normal Institute. Having saved sufficient funds for the training program, Davis applied in 1910 to the Freedmen's Hospital Training School for Nurses in Washington, D.C. Anxious that her application not be denied on the basis of age, she changed her birth date from 1882 to 1889 and started her training at the age of twenty-seven years.

In 1913 the District of Columbia administered exams to the graduating students on the basis of their race, with the exam for the white nurses considered the more rigorous. Davis demanded a chance to write the other test and became the first African American in the district to write and pass the exam.

From 1913 to 1916 Davis held various positions, first as a private duty nurse, then in 1914 she accepted the position of nursing supervisor at Provident Hospital, an all-black hospital in Baltimore, Maryland. During the summers of 1916 and 1920 she acted as a camp nurse for a community-based camp for needy mothers and young children in the Washington, D.C., area. While at Provident, Davis made an application to the American Red Cross, where, under the tutelage of M. Adelaide Nutting, head of the nursing department, she became the first African American to attend its approved program at Teachers College, Columbia University. To compensate for her inexperience in the public and rural health areas she took a field placement in July 1917 at Lillian Wald's Henry Street Settlement House in New York City.

Completing her training, Davis was assigned by the American Red Cross Town and Country Nursing Service to Jackson, Tennessee, which had specifically requested the services of an African-American nurse. In addition to using her midwifery skills, she conducted preventive medicine classes in basic sanitation and prenatal care.

In April 1917, when the United States entered World War I, Davis's race precluded her from joining the Army Nurse Corps, which refused African-American applicants until after the war. While her white colleagues automatically were awarded their American Red Cross pins, allowing them to transfer to the corps, Davis's pin did not arrive until 2 July 1918 and was inscribed with a "1A." The letter *A* designated the wearer as "Negro," indicating that she was the first African-American Red Cross nurse. The *A* system remained in effect until 1949. Davis's involvement with the war effort was indirect in that she nursed soldiers in training at Chickamauga, Tennessee. Unfortunately that same year Davis succumbed to an influenza epidemic that left her heart permanently damaged.

Davis's talents as an educator, community-based nurse, and administrator were recognized, and for the remainder of her career her services were in constant demand. In 1919 while serving as director of nurses training at John A. Andrew Memorial Hospital in Tuskegee, Alabama, she accepted a proposal from Dunbar Hospital in Detroit, Michigan, that she be responsible for organizing the first training school for African-American nurses in Michigan. The following year, she also accepted a staff position with the Detroit Visiting Nurses Association, an affiliation that she would hold for many years.

In 1921 Davis took a leave of absence to marry William A. Davis, of Detroit, a professional musician who performed in a band as well as offering private lessons. Their only child was stillborn in 1922, and in 1923 Davis resumed her career. She returned to Dunbar determined to upgrade the training program for nurses. Although she was able to garner funding from Senator James Couzens, a Michigan philanthropist, hospital physicians refused to accept monies that would only benefit nurses. Disgusted with their tactics Davis resigned her position in March 1927. She left Dunbar to accept a position with the Child Welfare Division of the Detroit Health Department, where she directed prenatal, maternal, and child health clinics.

In 1929 Davis was awarded a Julius Rosenwald Fellowship for pursuit of a B.S. in nursing at her alma mater, Teachers College; however, she was forced to withdraw from the program as a result of ill health. When she and William returned to Michigan, they moved to Inkster, a predominantly African-American community outside of Detroit.

During the height of the depression Davis devoted her time to running a commissary at the Ford Motor plant that distributed food to the inhabitants of Inkster. She had also petitioned Henry Ford to act as a patron, in which capacity he paid the utility bills, provided clothing, and supplied the means for repairing homes. In return recipients were able to earn a wage through helping to improve the physical appearance of Inkster. She also organized projects that qualified youths for National Youth Administration grants, which also created a wage mechanism. In 1932 Davis resigned her position with the Detroit Health Department to devote her time to the commissary.

In 1935 Davis returned to work for the Visiting Nurses Association, where she remained for five years, while at the same time serving as a member on the Inkster school board. After leaving the VNA she established a day nursery in Inkster. This nursery was such a success that it attracted the attention of Eleanor Roosevelt, who demonstrated her support by soliciting funds for the center. In 1940 Davis left the day nursery center to assume a position at Eloise Hospital in Wayne County, Michigan, where she remained until 1951, when illness forced her to take a leave of absence. Once recuperated, she chose to remain at home to nurse her husband, who died in 1959.

Scheduled to be honored at the American Red Cross convention on 11 May 1965, Davis died on 2 May, in Mount Clemens, Michigan. Her Red Cross pin was presented to the convention officials to be entered into their historical collection.

• An excellent article on Davis is "Frances Elliott Davis," in *American Nursing: A Biographical Dictionary*, ed. Vern L. Bullough et al. (1988), pp. 76–77. Also see Darlene Clark Hine, *Black Women in White: Racial Conflict and Cooperation in the Nursing Profession, 1890–1950* (1989), pp. 134–36, and "Frances Reed [Elliott] Davis," in *Dictionary of American Nursing Biography*, ed. Martin Kaufman (1988), pp. 81–83. Reference to Davis's career with the American Red Cross is in M. Elizabeth Carnegie, *The Path We Tread: Blacks in Nursing Worldwide, 1854–1944* (1995).

M. DALYCE NEWBY

DAVIS, Francis Breese, Jr. (16 Sept. 1883–22 Dec. 1962), business executive, was born in Fort Edward, New York, the son of Francis Breese Davis and Ella Underwood, farmers. He graduated from the Sheffield Scientific School, Yale, in 1906 and in 1913 married Jean Reybold; the couple had one child.

Davis's first job was in the city engineer's office in New Haven, Connecticut. He also worked briefly for the Empire Engineering Corporation, constructing the Erie Barge Canal near Fort Edward. Between 1907 and 1909 he worked in the maintenance-of-way department of the Philadelphia, Baltimore, and Washington Railroad. In 1909 he joined the Du Pont Company as a construction engineer at Du Pont's Belin plant in Moosic, Pennsylvania.

At first Davis moved between different divisions, gaining experience of operations management as well as construction. Following the separation of the Atlas and Hercules explosive businesses from Du Pont in a 1912 antitrust settlement, Davis assisted Lammot du Pont in the black powder department as division superintendent of the sporting powder division. The wartime expansion of the explosives trade resulted in Davis being involved in the construction and commissioning of new Du Pont munitions factories in Virginia and Tennessee. Little information survives on the wartime period of Davis's career, but he emerged as a trusted manager who moved steadily away from technician's work toward administrative roles. He was appointed as a vice president of the Du Pont Chemical Company in 1919, a firm established to dispose of surplus plants and equipment acquired during the war. In 1921 he joined General Motors, of which the du Pont family had recently become a major stockholder. Davis was in a fairly junior position as assistant general manager of the Saginaw division. Two years later he returned to the main Du Pont organization as department manager of Du Pont's Pyralin division, which manufactured celluloid plastics and finished goods, including a compound used to line curtains inside automobiles. In 1925 Du Pont merged Davis's division with the newly acquired Viscoloid Company, and Davis became president of Du Pont Viscoloid. In 1925 he was also appointed president of the Celastic Corporation, a joint venture between Du Pont and U.S. Shoe Machinery. In addition Davis was chairman (1928) of the Pittsburgh Safety Glass Company (PSGC). Both Celastic and PSGC were paper corporations set up by Du Pont to develop new technologies.

Davis's major promotion and most notable business role began in 1929 when he replaced Charles Seger as chairman and president of the U.S. Rubber Company. Irénée du Pont and Pierre du Pont had established a sizable shareholding in U.S. Rubber through two private share-buying syndicates in 1927. The firm had been the largest American rubber manufacturer in the early 1900s but had been overtaken by Goodyear, Firestone, and Goodrich, losing market share steadily during the period from 1912 to 1928. Scrutiny of the firm's financial reports had convinced the du Ponts that profits could be increased by reducing inventories and indebtedness. U.S. Rubber's plantation investments, the largest of any American company, also were an attraction given the relatively high prices that had resulted from the British rubber restriction scheme in the mid-twenties, high prices that had resulted from British quotas on exports of rubber from their Southeast Asian colonies, then the main sources of supply. By the end of 1928 Irénée du Pont had decided that managerial changes were required. In January 1929 Davis was elected president and chairman of U.S. Rubber. He retired in 1949, though he remained on the finance committee until 1959 as well as an advisory director.

As Glenn D. Babcock, historian of U.S. Rubber, has shown, Davis applied the Du Pont style of management, embodied in Alfred P. Sloan's work at General Motors, to U.S. Rubber. Some plants were closed, finances were controlled tightly by U.S. Rubber treasurer William DeKrafft, and there was a degree of decentralization of management. Davis's strategy relied, in particular, on reviving the tire division. U.S. Rubber obtained a contract for half of General Motors's tire consumption between 1931 and 1941. In addition, U.S. Rubber built up major contracts with mass distributors, notably Montgomery Ward. The strategy of high-volume, low-cost contracts with large retailers had been pioneered by Goodyear, the leading tire manufacturer, in 1926 with a contract to supply all Sears tires. However, Davis was prepared to accept the low profit margins on such business in the belief that U.S. Rubber's costs could be reduced. The impact of the strategy was reflected dramatically in U.S. Rubber's market share. The firm accounted for 27 percent of the original equipment market in 1940 compared to 7 percent in 1929, and the firm's share of the renewal business expanded from 6.5 percent to 31 percent over the same period. In financial terms U.S. Rubber's long-term debt was reduced from $104.1 million in 1929 (far larger than that of any other tire firm) to $45 million (in line with the other major producers) by 1938 and to $27 million by 1945. Just as much as the more celebrated Sloan personified decen-

tralized management at General Motors, Davis embodied the Du Pont approach to management between the wars with its mix of close attention to financial performance and to the relationship between production and management: a decentralized administration with operating departments and service divisions under the tight central direction of financial matters. In his relative anonymity he was perhaps more representative than Sloan of the emerging managerial class in American business. Yet Davis's career was based on the du Pont family's confidence in his abilities and, in that sense, on their patronage.

Davis retired to a plantation at Yemassee, South Carolina. His interests included bird-watching, antiques, and the breeding of cattle and ponies as well as owning three General Motors dealerships in South Carolina. Davis died in Savannah, Georgia, and was buried in Wilmington, Delaware.

• There is little archival trace of Davis's activities or views. A few letters relating to Davis are in the Du Pont archives at the Hagley Museum and Library in Wilmington, as well as some material on his role at U.S. Rubber in the records relating to the Du Pont antitrust suit, *U.S. v. E. I. du Pont de Nemours and Co., et al.* The defense case includes an outline of the Du Pont principles of management and argues that Davis applied such principles without being "a pawn of the Du Ponts" or engaged in any illegal relationship with General Motors. A set of court records relating to the case are held in the Hagley Library, whose archives include some related correspondence, though little by Davis. The definitive account of Davis's business career is Glenn D. Babcock, *History of United States Rubber: A Case Study in Corporate Management* (1966). Unfortunately the corporate records on which Babcock's excellent study was based were destroyed. See also Daniel Nelson, *American Rubber Workers and Organized Labor, 1900–1941* (1988), and his "Managers and Non-Union workers: Union Avoidance Strategies in the 1930s," *Industrial and Labor Relations Review* 43, no. 1 (1989): 48–52. The context of Davis's career is summarized in Michael J. French, *The U.S. Tire Industry: A History* (1990) and his "Structural Change and Competition in the U.S. Tire Industry, 1920–1937," *Business History Review* 60 (Spring 1986): 28–54. An obituary is in the Wilmington *Evening Journal*, 24 Dec. 1962.

MICHAEL FRENCH

DAVIS, Garret (10 Sept. 1801–22 Sept. 1872), U.S. congressman and U.S. senator, was born in Mount Sterling, Kentucky, the son of Jeremiah Davis and his wife, whose maiden name was Garret. Davis's father was a blacksmith and also a legislator and local political leader, and his brother, Amos, served in Congress from 1833 to 1835. After being educated in local academies in and around Mount Sterling, he served as deputy circuit court clerk in Mount Sterling and Paris, Kentucky, where he also studied law. Davis began a law practice in Paris in 1823, and from 1833 to 1835 he served three terms in the state legislature.

In 1839 Davis began the first of four consecutive terms in the U.S. House of Representatives, representing one of the agricultural districts of Kentucky's prosperous Bluegrass region. In the House he championed the Whig party and the policies of his friend,

Henry Clay. He retired in 1847 to manage his large farm in Bourbon County and to practice law. His devotion to farming entitled him to be ranked among the leading agricultural experts in Kentucky. He declined the Whig party's nomination for lieutenant governor in 1848. As a delegate to the Kentucky constitutional convention of 1849, he failed to secure major restrictions against immigrant voting and to defeat the elective judiciary. Resigning as a delegate to the convention before its adjournment, he campaigned unsuccessfully for the rejection of the new constitution in the ensuing election. His staunch nativism made him a formative leader of the American party in Kentucky, and in 1856 he unsuccessfully sought that party's presidential nomination. Even his close friends in Kentucky regarded him as an unacceptable candidate because of his tendency to exaggerate the deficiencies of his perceived enemies, a characteristic that undermined his effectiveness throughout his political career.

In December 1861 Davis's passionate nature paid off when the Kentucky legislature elected him to the U.S. Senate, in part because of his energetic activities on behalf of the Union. In the spring of 1861 he had served as Abraham Lincoln's agent in the distribution of rifles to Union partisans in Kentucky. During the early stages of his senatorial career, he continued his spirited embrace of Lincoln and the Union. However, as the conflict grew more radical in nature and came to encompass emancipation as an objective, Davis, a slave owner, abandoned his commitment to the president and his policies. In early 1864 he introduced resolutions in the Senate that described Lincoln and his supporters as destroyers of the Constitution who were violating civil liberties, plundering the treasury, and perpetuating the spoils system. So intemperate were these resolutions that they nearly resulted in Davis's expulsion from the Senate. His bigotry and sarcasm also were in evidence when he offered an amendment to the proposed Thirteenth Amendment, which, if adopted, would have denied U.S. citizenship to African Americans and consolidated the states of New England into two states, East and West New England (the latter proposal doubtless being a tongue-in-cheek attempt to reduce the political power of a region of "radical" Yankees). He likewise strenuously opposed the involvement of the Union army in state elections, a growing controversy in his home state.

Following the war, Davis became an outspoken opponent of Reconstruction. In a speech opposing the Civil Rights Bill of 1866, he declared that if the bill became law he would feel compelled to regard himself as an enemy of the government and work for its destruction, an announcement that prompted certain residents of New York to renew the call for his removal from the Senate. In 1867 he joined the Democratic party, whose support enabled him to win reelection to the Senate. After unsuccessfully attempting to raise the rate on hemp imports, he opposed the Tariff of 1867 and expressed reservations about a bill to protect the property of married women in the District of Columbia. In 1867 he also proposed federal regulation of

interstate railroad rates and two years later, in support of the Louisville & Nashville Railroad, helped defeat a bill that would have authorized a railway through central Kentucky from Cincinnati to Tennessee. His death in Paris, Kentucky, cut short his second senatorial term and his efforts to elect Horace Greeley president.

In 1826 he married Rebecca Trimble, the daughter of Robert Trimble, later an associate justice of the U.S. Supreme Court. They had three children. Rebecca Davis died in 1842, and in 1845 Davis married Eliza Jane Elliott, the widow of a fellow lawyer from Paris.

• There is no significant collection of Davis's papers. For biographical sketches see H. Levin, *The Lawyers and Lawmakers of Kentucky* (1897), and J. M. Armstrong, ed., *The Biographical Encyclopaedia of Kentucky of the Dead and Living Men of the Nineteenth Century* (1878). Davis's congressional record can be traced in the relevant volumes of the *Congressional Globe* and the *Congressional Record*. An obituary is in the *New York Times*, 23 Sept. 1872.

ROBERT M. IRELAND

DAVIS, Gary D. (30 Apr. 1896–5 May 1972), guitarist and religious singer, was born in Laurens County, South Carolina, south of Spartanburg, the son of John Davis and Evelina (maiden name unknown), farmers. One of eight children, he grew up on a farm he later described as being so far out in the country "you couldn't hear a train whistle blow unless it was on a cloudy day." Partially blinded as a baby, Davis was placed in the care of his grandmother. He showed an aptitude for music as a boy, first playing harmonica and later, with his grandmother's help, constructing a guitar. When he was between the ages of seven and ten his mother gave him a guitar, and over the next several years he became proficient, possibly learning from a local musician, Craig Fowler, and an uncle. By age ten he was singing in a Baptist church and playing for local dances. In his teens Davis began adding blues to a repertoire that already included country dance tunes and religious songs.

Around 1910 Davis began working in Greenville with a local string band that included guitarist Willie Walker, a blind musician he greatly admired. In 1914 Davis entered the South Carolina School for the Deaf and the Blind but left after six months because he did not like the food—an example of the willful independence that characterized his life. Returning to Greenville, he resumed working with the string band, and in 1919 he married Mary Hendrix, a woman five years his senior. By 1926, when he showed up in Durham, North Carolina, he was single again, supposedly because Mary had jilted him for another blind musician, Joe Walker, Willie's brother.

After working as a street musician for several years, Davis, now completely blind, became increasingly focused on his religious convictions. He went to Washington, North Carolina, where he was ordained in the Free Baptist Connection Church, and he began traveling as a singing preacher on the religious revival circuit. Around 1933 he returned to work as a street singer in Durham, where he began playing with guitarist Blind Boy Fuller and George Washington, a guitar and washboard player also known as "Bull City Red," who doubled as Fuller's "lead boy." Through Fuller, Davis met James Baxter "J. B." Long, manager of the Durham United Dollar Store and a scout for American Record Company. When Long took Fuller to New York to make records in the summer of 1935, he took Davis and Bull City Red along. On 23 July, under the name "Blind Gary," Davis recorded two solo blues, "I'm Throwin' up My Hand" and "Cross and Evil Woman Blues," the only early examples of his blues repertoire. Several days later he recorded thirteen religious sides, twelve of which were issued. Paid a flat fifty dollars for the session, Davis later concluded that Long had shortchanged him, and tension between the two men precluded any further recording activity.

Throughout the 1930s and into 1940 Davis was listed on Durham welfare rolls, hiding his street singing to retain eligibility. Davis told suspicious caseworkers he was seldom home because he was preaching and was only interested in saving souls.

Always aware of his vulnerability to larceny, Davis routinely carried weapons, among them a large pocket knife. According to legend, an acquaintance once tried to snatch away a dollar bill that had just been placed in Davis's hand by a passerby. It was supposed to be a prank, but Davis instantly seized the prankster and stabbed him repeatedly until he collapsed, all the while thanking the Lord for delivering a thief and sinner into his hands.

In the late 1930s or early 1940s Davis married Annie Bell Wright, a woman from Wake County, North Carolina. He moved from Durham to Raleigh and in about 1940 moved to New York. He remained in the New York City and New Jersey areas for the rest of his life. In New York he was ordained again, becoming a minister of the Missionary Baptist Connection Church. Over the next two decades he became a familiar figure in Harlem, preaching and singing on the streets.

During the 1940s Davis reunited with harmonica player Sonny Terry and guitarist Brownie McGhee, with whom he had played in Durham. He also taught for a time at McGhee's Home of the Blues Music School in Harlem. Possibly through his friendship with Terry and McGhee, Davis came to the attention of the nascent folk revival movement in the 1950s. A flurry of New York recordings for Stinson in 1954, Riverside in 1956, and Folk Lyric in 1957 established his folk credentials, and in the 1960s Davis became a fixture on the coffeehouse and folk festival circuits. He excited audiences with his instrumental skills on guitar, banjo, and harmonica and even consented to perform secular material along with his large repertoire of religious songs. He recorded for Prestige, Folkways, Biograph, and other documentary labels up to 1971 and toured England several times to critical acclaim. Davis was also featured in several short films and in the 1970 documentary *Black Roots*.

Despite his revival fame, Davis remained close to his roots in the church, serving as an assistant pastor in the True Heart Baptist Church in the Bronx and retaining ties with other Baptist congregations and groups. Continuing to tour as a folk musician in the early 1970s, Davis suffered a fatal heart attack in Hammonton, New Jersey, on the way to a concert.

A Piedmont-style guitarist, Davis employed only two fingers (the thumb and index finger) in his picking technique but was nevertheless able to generate formidable speed and complexity. To complement his picking, he had great command of chord positions. As one fellow Durham area guitarist, Willie Trice, told interviewer Bill Phillips, "While you were playing one chord, Davis would play five."

Although Davis had the repertoire of a songster, he much preferred material with spiritual meaning. Critics dubbed his music "holy blues" because it blended sacred content with secular vocal and guitar stylings. While many traditional African-American artists performed blues-tinged religious songs—indeed, blues and gospel share a common heritage—Davis was singular for the complexity of his instrumental technique. Among the artists and followers of the folk revival, Davis was lionized for his instrumental pyrotechnics and his authenticity—a living street singer who had known legends like Blind Boy Fuller and Willie Walker. Davis also influenced other guitar technicians such as Ry Cooder and Stefan Grossman, and his songs have been reprised by artists ranging from Peter, Paul, and Mary to Taj Mahal to John Cephas.

• For additional biographical information, see Bruce Bastin, *Red River Blues: The Blues Tradition in the Southeast* (1986); Samuel Charters, *The Blues Makers* (1991); Sheldon Harris, *Blues Who's Who: A Biographical Dictionary of Blues Singers* (1989); and Bill Phillips, "Piedmont Country Blues," *Southern Exposure* 2, no. 1 (Spring/Summer 1974): 56–62. For an interview and discussion of his style and repertoire, see Stefan Grossman, *Rev. Gary Davis/Blues Guitar* (1974). For a discography, see Robert M. W. Dixon and John Godrich, *Blues and Gospel Records: 1902–1943* (1982), and Mike Leadbitter and Neil Slaven, *Blues Records, 1943–1970*, vol. 2 (1994). To hear Davis's early material, try *The Complete Early Recordings of Reverend Gary Davis*, Yazoo 2011. For an obituary, see "Rev. Gary D. Davis," *Living Blues*, no. 8 (Spring 1972): 6.

BILL MCCULLOCH
BARRY LEE PEARSON

DAVIS, George (1 Mar. 1820–23 Feb. 1896), lawyer, Confederate senator, and Confederate attorney general, was born in New Hanover (now Pender) County, North Carolina, the son of Thomas Frederick Davis, a prominent planter, and Sarah Isabella Eagles. He attended W. H. Harden's school in Pittsboro, was tutored at home, and at fourteen entered the University of North Carolina, graduating in 1838 at the head of his class. After reading law with his brother in Wilmington, he was admitted to the bar at age twenty and licensed statewide a year later.

Establishing his practice in Wilmington, the eloquent Davis soon built a solid reputation in the fields of corporate, criminal, and maritime law. In 1848 he became general counsel for the Wilmington and Weldon Railroad and remained with that company until it was absorbed by the Atlantic Coast Line, for which Davis held the same position until his death. He was also a director of the Bank of Wilmington. Davis's avocation was history, particularly of the Cape Fear region, where his family had lived for over a hundred years. He became a popular speaker on historical subjects, and his research in primary sources helped debunk a number of myths about colonial North Carolina. In November 1842 he married Mary A. Polk, with whom he had six children before her death in 1863.

Although he held no elective office before the Civil War, Davis was an active member of the Whig party. Generally conservative, he was a proponent of the national bank, the protective tariff, and territorial expansion. At the 1848 state convention he lost the gubernatorial nomination by only one vote, and his 1852 eulogy of Henry Clay further solidified his standing within the party.

With the demise of the Whigs, Davis aligned himself with the Constitutional Union party in 1860. He felt that secession was not the answer to the sectional conflict, and after Abraham Lincoln's election he continued to speak against immediate withdrawal from the Union. The state legislature chose Davis as one of five delegates to the Washington Peace Conference in early 1861, but he returned disillusioned with the "Black Republicans." In an address at Wilmington on 2 March he declared: "The division must be made on the line of slavery. The State must go with the South" (*Daily Wilmington Herald*, 4 Mar. 1861).

Even though Davis published a statement asking that he not be considered for a position in the Confederate Provisional Congress, he was chosen an at-large delegate. In September 1861 he was elected to the Confederate Senate on the twenty-fifth ballot. Davis chaired the Committee on Claims and was also appointed to the Buildings and Finance committees, where he was highly conservative on monetary matters. His nationalistic ideals carried over to the Confederacy, making him one of the Senate's staunchest supporters of Jefferson Davis's administration. Much of the legislation he introduced promoted a large and efficient army.

Since Davis drew only a two-year term, he had to stand for reelection in 1863 and lost to William A. Graham. As it turned out, however, he did not even serve until the end of the First Congress. After a three-month search for a replacement for Thomas H. Watts as attorney general, Jefferson Davis (no relation) offered the position to the North Carolinian, apparently at the urging of Graham and others. The appointment was generally praised, receiving the endorsement of four of the five Richmond newspapers.

Davis was unanimously confirmed by the Senate and took office in January 1864 as the Confederacy's fourth and final attorney general. He wrote seventy-four opinions. Although inconsistent at times, he was generally a strict constructionist and declared two state laws unconstitutional during his tenure. A fervent supporter of a supreme court while in the Senate, Davis as attorney general became increasingly convinced that the attorney general should not have the authority to overturn congressional acts approved by the president, even if an act were unconstitutional. Only once did he rule against a Confederate law.

Although Davis and the president were not always in agreement, Jefferson Davis felt that his attorney general was usually "right at last," and a friendship developed between the two men during the final year of the war. The president did not listen, however, when George Davis advised, after Robert E. Lee's surrender, that the Confederacy attain the best peace terms it could and hand out the remains of the treasury to the soldiers. By that time both men were in flight from Richmond along with other government leaders. Davis traveled with the presidential party as far as Charlotte, then resigned his position, the first cabinet member to do so. He left for Florida in the hope of securing passage to England. Captured at Key West, he was imprisoned at Fort Hamilton, New York, until paroled on 2 January 1866.

Returning to Wilmington, Davis began to rebuild his law practice. In May 1866 he married Monimia Fairfax, with whom he had at least two children. That same year he served as a delegate to the Philadelphia Convention, a meeting of moderate Republicans and Democrats. An outspoken critic of Reconstruction, he decried the 1868 constitution imposed on North Carolina and was a prime mover behind its reform seven years later. He admitted, though, that his "ambition went down with the banner of the South, and, like it, never rose again" (Sprunt, p. 20). Davis declined appointment as chief justice of the state supreme court in 1878, informing Governor Zebulon Vance that the position did not pay enough. He rendered his final significant public service in 1880, when he and Thomas Ruffin negotiated the sale of the state's interest in the Western North Carolina Railroad. In his final years Davis continued to practice law and gave occasional lectures on local history. He died at his home in Wilmington. Although Davis spent over fifty years as a prominent attorney and public servant in North Carolina, he is most often remembered as the final Confederate attorney general.

• Davis's papers are in the Southern Historical Collection at the University of North Carolina. Several of Davis's monographs are published in *A Memorial of the Hon. George Davis* (1896) and E. A. Alderman and J. C. Harris, eds., *Library of Southern Literature*, vol. 3 (1909). His eulogy of Jefferson Davis is in *In Memoriam: Wilmington's Tribute of Respect to Ex-President Davis* (1890). A letter from Davis on the flight from Richmond is in the *Southern Historical Society Papers* 5 (1878): 124–26. Rembert W. Patrick, ed., *The Opinions of the Confederate Attorneys General, 1861–1865* (1950), contains Davis's official reports. Patrick also has a good sketch of Davis in *Jefferson Davis and His Cabinet* (1944). Davis is the subject of several older works, including James Sprunt, *George Davis* (1919); Samuel A. Ashe, *George Davis, Attorney General of the Confederate States* (1916); and H. G. Connor, *George*

Davis (1911). Fletcher M. Green, "George Davis, North Carolina Whig and Confederate Statesman, 1820–1896," *North Carolina Historical Review* 23 (Oct. 1946): 449–70, contains references to many of Davis's short monographs. Obituaries are in the Wilmington *Morning Star*, 25 Feb. 1896, the Wilmington *Messenger*, 25 Feb. 1896, and the Wilmington *Weekly Tribune*, 28 Feb. 1896.

KENNETH H. WILLIAMS

DAVIS, George Stacey (23 Aug. 1870–17 Oct. 1940), baseball player and manager, was born in Cohoes, New York, the son of Abram Davis and Sarah Healy. Nothing is known of the circumstances of his family or the extent of his formal education. Davis's life in baseball began in 1889 with an Albany, New York, independent minor league team. In 1890 he became an outfielder with the Cleveland Spiders of the National League, where he played for three seasons with good but unremarkable performance. In 1893 Cleveland traded Davis to the New York Giants for future Hall of Famer Buck Ewing. The change worked out well for Davis and the Giants: during his ten seasons with the team, Davis batted over .300 nine times. In his first year with the Giants, Davis set several milestones that would endure both for the team and for the National League for many years. In a game against Philadelphia on 11 May, Davis became one of the first players to get five hits in five at bats, including a home run and a triple, to lead the team to a win. The following month against the Chicago Colts (the predecessor to the Cubs), Davis became the first player to hit a home run and a triple in the same inning; the feat was repeated only thirty-three years later by Bob Fothergill of the Detroit Tigers. The crowning achievement of Davis's first season with the Giants was a 33-game hitting streak, which was ended by Cleveland, his former team. The batting streak set a longstanding Giants' team record.

Davis's remarkable season in 1893 ingratiated him with Giants team owner Edward Talcott, which led to a better contract. As the 1894 season began, Davis was considered a Giants' star. That year Davis prepared a newspaper article offering batting advice for novices. The baseball historian Harold Seymour best described the content of this article: Davis declared that batters needed a "free and easy swing, standing up at the plate as though you mean business, and striding forward to meet the pitch." After all, he noted, "batting required plenty of nerve" (Seymour, p. 281). Davis also anticipated what late twentieth-century players achieved with video tape: he suggested that batters practice by observing their swing in front of a mirror in order to detect errors and enhance strengths.

The new owner of the Giants, Andrew Freedman, demonstrated his enthusiasm for Davis in 1895 when he selected him as the manager of the Giants, replacing Monte Ward. Ward was considered a good manager but was viewed with some trepidation because of his involvement in organizing the Player's League five years earlier. Still, Freedman's naming of the 24-year-old Davis as the new manager surprised many. The pressure of managing did not overwhelm his playing performance, as he batted .345 that year. In a 23–9 loss to the Phillies, he even mustered an impressive six hits.

Davis relinquished his managerial duties the following year. In 1897 he switched from third base to shortstop, a position he would play consistently for the rest of his tenure with the Giants and for most of his career. During that season, he led the National League with 134 runs batted in.

Davis served as the Giants' manager again during the 1900 and 1901 seasons. At the start of the 1901 season he previewed the pitches of Christy Mathewson, who would go on to become a significant force in the Giants' starting rotation. Mathewson called one of his pitches a "freak pitch." Davis, who had a reputation for being able to hit any pitch, swung futilely at Mathewson's pitch, which the manager labeled a "fadeaway." The term has stuck in baseball parlance, although the pitch became better known as a screwball.

In 1902, in an effort to soothe the volatile relationship between the National and American leagues, Freedman reluctantly sold Davis's contract to Chicago White Sox owner Charles Comiskey in 1902. Davis played the 1902 season and garnered significant fan support in Chicago. The following season, however, Davis petitioned National League president Harry Pulliam for permission to return to the Giants. Pulliam consented, and Davis became a Giant again early in the 1903 season, in violation of the peace treaty between the two leagues. American League president Ban Johnson threatened a renewed schism between the two leagues, while Comiskey acquired an injunction that prevented Davis from playing for the Giants only four games after his return to New York. On 20 July the National League directors voted that Davis could only play for Chicago. Davis sat out the rest of the 1903 season and rejoined the White Sox in 1904, remaining with them until the end of his major league career after the 1909 season. He helped the 1906 White Sox, known that season as the "hitless wonders," win the World Series with a .308 average.

Davis's impressive career numbers include in 2,377 games played, 2,688 hits, 1,435 runs batted in, and a lifetime batting average of .297. To some, his great talent for hitting was overshadowed by his independent attitude toward his contracts in 1903. That year he made several enemies in the baseball community, and it is probable that the events of that season prevented him from being elected to the National Baseball Hall of Fame.

Davis had minimal involvement with baseball after his last season with the White Sox. He served as a player-manager for Des Moines, Iowa, of the Western League in 1910, and he scouted for the New York Yankees in 1915 and for the St. Louis Browns in 1917. For a period of time he also sold automobiles. Davis married Jane Holden, though details of the marriage are not known. He died in Philadelphia.

• For an anecdotal view of Davis's career, see Harold Seymour, *Baseball: The Early Years* (1960), and Donald Honig, *Baseball America: The Heroes of the Game and the Times of Glory* (1985). The best-documented aspects of Davis's life are his baseball statistics, which are in Joseph L. Reichler, ed., *The Baseball Encyclopedia*, 6th ed. (1985), and James Charleton, ed., *The Baseball Chronology: The Complete History of the Most Important Events in the Game of Baseball* (1991).

PAUL WAYNE RODNEY

DAVIS, Harold Lenoir (18 Oct. 1894?–31 Oct. 1960), author and poet, was born in Rone's Mill, Oregon, the son of James Alexander Davis, a country schoolteacher, and Ruth Bridges. His family moved to Antelope, Oregon, in 1906. While there Harold worked as a typesetter, cowboy, sheepherder, and packer. He learned French, German, Spanish, Greek, and some Gaelic from the immigrants who were arriving in Oregon.

In 1908 his family moved to the Columbia River town of The Dalles in Oregon. From 1912 to 1916 he worked as deputy county assessor and deputy sheriff of Wasco County, Oregon, and in 1917 he did survey work for the United States General Land Office. In September 1918 he was drafted into the army; serving less than three months at Fort McDowell, California, in the Quartermaster Corps, he was given an honorable discharge in December 1918.

In 1919 Davis began writing poetry. Through poetry he wanted to record the rhythms of western life by capturing the flavor and vernacular of people and events he grew up with. He sent these poems to Harriet Monroe, whose *Poetry* magazine also published Robert Frost, T. S. Eliot, and E. E. Cummings. In 1919 his "Primapara" poems, published in the April issue of *Poetry*, won the Levinson Prize for poetry. Carl Sandburg called him the leading poet of the Northwest. Between 1920 and 1925 he published seventeen poems in *Poetry*. In 1926, along with James Stevens, he published an eight-page pamphlet, *Status Rerum: A Manifesto upon the Present Condition of Northwestern Literature*, which criticized the literary establishment for its romantic portrayals of the western experience. Their collaborative efforts included the stories "Occidental's Prodigal" (1928) and "Oleman Hattie" (1928), which were published in *Adventure*. (Stevens was listed as the author of these works.)

In 1928 Davis married Marion Lay, also a writer, and moved to Bainbridge Island, Washington. Here, Davis and Stevens had a radio show that featured music and folktales. Throughout his life Davis collected folksongs, which he played on the guitar and sang on the program.

In 1929, at the urging of H. L. Mencken, Davis wrote short stories and sketches, which Mencken published in *American Mercury*. This was the first prose fiction Davis published under his own name. The first story published was "Old Man Isbell's Wife" (1929). Delighted with his work, Mencken asked for more. Davis sent him "Back to the Land—Oregon, 1907" (1929), "A Town in Eastern Oregon" (1930), and

"Team Bells Woke Me" (1931). These sketches detailed the ups and downs of the Oregon homestead rushes.

In 1930 Davis moved to Arizona where he published the short stories "Flying Switch" and "Shiloh's Waters." That same year he returned to Bainbridge Island, Washington. In 1932 he received the Guggenheim Exchange Fellowship to Mexico, where he and his wife moved later that year. In 1933 he published the poems "New Birds" and "In Argos." Finding that writing poetry did not pay well, Davis decided to end his career as a poet.

Davis then turned his attention to writing prose. His first novel, *Honey in the Horn*, was published in 1935. In this novel Davis tried to capture the unique nature of Oregon valley residents once again without placing them in the popular romantic myths of the frontier. His characters grow spiritually as they experience the joys and sorrows of frontier life. In 1935 it won the Harper Novel Prize and in 1936 the Pulitzer Prize for fiction.

After residing in Mexico, Davis and his wife moved to Nashville, Tennessee, and lived there from 1935 to 1936. They also visited Baltimore and New York City before buying a ranch in Napa, California, in May 1937. After an apparently unhappy marriage, they divorced in 1942.

In 1939 Davis published the short stories "Open Winter" and "Homestead Orchard" and in 1941 "A Flock of Trouble." In 1942 Harper & Brothers published a collection of his poetry, *Proud Riders and Other Poems*. Over the next few years he published the novels *Harp of a Thousand Strings* (1947), *Beulah Land* (1949), *Winds of Morning* (1952), *The Distant Music* (1957), and short prose works, *Team Bells Woke Me* (1953) and *Kettle of Fire* (1959). These pieces also dealt with themes of the American frontier.

In 1953 Davis married Elizabeth Tonkin Martin del Campo in San Antonio, Texas. On 7 February 1954 a critical essay he had written for the *New York Times Book Review* about western writing, entitled "The Elusive Trail to the Old West," appeared. In it Davis argued that early western writers failed to universalize the experiences of their characters. He always strove to make his works universal and archetypal and felt it was the job of contemporary western authors to unify past and present and art and life. In January 1959 he wrote "Stock-Taking," a poem/essay that inventoried his poetic intent and showed his disapproval of the fads poets were favoring. He began a novel, tentatively entitled "Exit, Pursued by a Bear," which he never finished. Davis died in San Antonio.

Davis lived in an era of old mining towns and saw the changes that occurred in the New West of the Oregon region. Without glorifying the Old West, Davis sought in his poetry and fiction to preserve frontier values he found lacking in contemporary America. The West he knew from studying history and from his own experience did not fit into the romantic myths of the West that writers before him depicted. He personally saw the high hopes and dashed dreams of the characters he portrayed, and he saw the capacity for the human spirit to suffer loss and survive.

• Davis's papers and manuscripts are in the Humanities Research Center at the University of Texas at Austin. Other collections can be found at the University of Oregon Library and the Tennessee State Library and Archives. Valuable primary sources include the Harriet Monroe Collection of the Joseph Regenstein Library at the University of Chicago, the Library of the University of Washington in Seattle, the Douglas County Museum in Roseburg, Ore., the Charles Erskine Scott Wood Papers, dated from 1914–1942, and a letter to a Mr. Brumbaugh in the Bancroft Library at the University of California at Berkeley. Other collections of Davis's work include *The Selected Poems of H. L. Davis* (1978) and *H. L. Davis: Collected Essays and Short Stories* (1986). Robert Bain, *H. L. Davis* (1974), is a valuable biography that traces Davis's career and works; it also contains an extensive bibliography of primary and secondary sources. See also Paul T. Bryant, "H. L. Davis: Viable Uses for the Past," *Western American Literature* 3 (1968): 3–18, for a consideration of Davis's writing techniques.

ELIZABETH A. ARCHULETA
SUSAN E. GUNTER

DAVIS, Henry Gassaway (16 Nov. 1823–11 Mar. 1916), industrialist and U.S. senator, was born in Woodlawn, Baltimore County, Maryland, the son of Caleb Davis and Louise Warfield Brown. Davis's father, a construction contractor who worked for the Baltimore and Ohio Railroad, suffered debilitating financial reverses when Davis was young, and his mother supported the family by operating a girls' school.

After several years of farm work, in 1842 Davis went to work as a brakeman and conductor for the Baltimore and Ohio, rising to the position of station agent at Piedmont, Virginia, by 1853. In 1854 he opened a general store in Piedmont with his brothers, which by the eve of the Civil War had become the leading mercantile firm in the upper Potomac Valley. Davis married Katharine Anne Bantz in 1853; they had seven children.

A strong supporter of the Union, Davis grew prosperous from contracts to supply the government and railroads with mercantile goods and hardware and expanded into farming, banking, timbering, and coal mining. He bought property in Maryland, where he built a summer home and village called Deer Park. By 1871 he was the leading businessman and politician in the upper Potomac region and one of the richest men in West Virginia.

Entering politics during the Reconstruction era, Davis was elected to the West Virginia House of Delegates as a Union-Conservative in 1865 and to the state senate in 1868 and 1870. Opposing political restrictions on former Confederates, he helped lead the revived Democratic party to victory over the Republican founders of the state. With fellow industrialist Johnson Newlon Camden, he built the Democratic party in the state by establishing newspapers, cultivating editors, and providing funds for the party and for particular candidates.

In 1871 Davis became the first Democrat to represent West Virginia in the U.S. Senate, and in 1877 he was elected to a second term. In the Senate he chaired the Committee on Appropriations for two years and was an active member of the Special Committee on Transportation Routes to the Seaboard.

In 1875 Davis's daughter, Hallie, married Stephen Benton Elkins, and the two men became close business associates and political allies, even though Elkins, a former congressional representative of the territory of New Mexico, was a Republican. In 1881 they organized the West Virginia Central and Pittsburgh Railway Company with Davis serving as president. The following year they launched construction of the north-south line that ran from Piedmont to Elkins and passed through rich coal and timber regions in the mountains of eastern and central West Virginia. In 1902, after selling the West Virginia Central to a syndicate headed by George J. Gould, Davis and Elkins became the leading figures in another railroad, the Coal and Coke, which ran from the upper Monongahela region of Tygart's Valley westward via the Elk River to Charleston. Davis was active in the management of the Coal and Coke and its ancillary enterprises until 1912. Leading political figures of both parties were often investors in the Davis and Elkins enterprises.

In 1883, fearing defeat if he sought reelection, Davis announced his retirement from the Senate. In 1887, tired of the factional fights among West Virginia Democrats, disappointed that he had not received an appointment in Grover Cleveland's administration, and alarmed by the national party's flirtation with tariff reform, which he believed threatened the state's coal producers, Davis turned his back on the party he had helped to build in West Virginia and quietly supported Republicans on both the state and national levels. He invited his former Senate colleague Benjamin Harrison (1833–1901) of Indiana, a strong protectionist, to Deer Park in August 1887 and urged him to seek the Republican nomination for president. He also helped Elkins, who had been living in New York and Washington, to relocate to West Virginia and encouraged him to assume leadership of the state Republican party in the hope that a Republican victory in West Virginia would give Elkins a Senate seat from which to oppose attacks on the coal tariff. Although Democrats narrowly carried the state in 1888 as Harrison was elected president, Davis's apostasy helped to bring about a massive transformation of West Virginia politics. Despite some recovery by the Democrats in 1892, their long domination of the state soon came to an end and was replaced by an even longer era of Republican rule. The key event was the election of 1894, when Davis gave no assistance to Democrats and sent out the word to workers in his firms along the West Virginia Central that they should vote Republican. Meanwhile Elkins organized a sweeping Republican victory that led to his election by the legislature to the U.S. Senate. Davis took particular satisfaction in the defeat of Democratic congressman William Lyne Wilson, a leading national spokesman for tariff reform.

Remarkably, Davis remained a Democrat and was even able to recover his leadership in the party, because many of his Democratic rivals who had supported tariff reform bolted in 1896, when the party nominated William Jennings Bryan on a free silver platform. With the Republicans in the ascendancy in West Virginia, the benefits of leadership were meager, however, and Davis never realized his ambition to return to the Senate. In 1904 he attained some measure of the national standing he had sought when, at the age of eighty-one, he was the Democratic candidate for vice president.

Despite his long political career, Davis remained an inarticulate speaker, often appearing humorless and bland in public. He excelled in behind the scenes maneuvering and in developing ties with influential figures, often entertaining leading national politicians of both parties at his Deer Park summer home. In 1892 both he and Elkins built palatial homes at Elkins, and these later became part of Davis and Elkins College, a Presbyterian liberal arts institution that began operations in 1904 on land donated by its namesakes. Davis died in Washington at the home of his daughter.

• The Henry G. Davis Papers, a rich collection covering some fifty years of business and politics, are in the West Virginia and Regional History Collection, West Virginia University Library, Morgantown, W.Va. Charles M. Pepper, *The Life and Times of Henry Gassaway Davis* (1920), is a commemorative volume authorized by the Davis family and gives inadequate coverage of his career. Davis, his son-in-law Elkins, and his political ally Camden are all given critical attention in John Alexander Williams, *West Virginia and the Captains of Industry* (1976). An obituary is in the *New York Times*, 11 Mar. 1916.

JERRY BRUCE THOMAS

DAVIS, Henry Winter (16 Aug. 1817–30 Dec. 1865), congressman and author, was born in Annapolis, Maryland, the son of Reverend Henry Lyon Davis, the president of St. John's College and Episcopal pastor of St. Ann's Parish in Annapolis, and Jane Brown Winter. Davis was tutored at home, learning to read by the time he was four. His father moved to Wilmington, Delaware, in 1824 or 1825, after being fired from St. John's, because his Federalist principles clashed with those of Andrew Jackson's supporters. During that time, Davis lived with an aunt in Alexandria and attended Loring Woart's academy. When his parents returned to Maryland in 1827, Davis lived with them on a farm in Anne Arundel County. Along with his classical studies, hunting, and farming, he learned about slavery firsthand from his father's slaves, who, he later wrote, "habitually spoke of the days when God would deliver them."

In 1833 Davis entered Kenyon College in Ohio, graduating in 1837. His father died that same year, and although money was short, Davis refused to sell any of the family slaves to pay the $400 tuition at the University of Virginia Law School. Reflecting the declining profitability of keeping slaves in Maryland's exhausted tobacco fields, Davis acknowledged that "the swarm of black people . . . ate my father out of house and home."

Aided by an aunt's generosity, Davis studied in 1839 and 1840 at the University of Virginia and established a practice in Alexandria. In 1845 he married Constance Gardiner, whom he described as "most accomplished and charming." They had no children. When she died in 1849, Davis moved to Baltimore, where in 1857 he married Nancy Morris. The couple had two daughters.

Davis had been attracted to politics even as a college student. Ever mindful of his father's invocation "to beware of the follies of Jacksonism," he became a Whig. When that party collapsed after 1852, Davis joined the new Know Nothing party, which was especially powerful in Maryland. In 1855, 1857, 1859, and 1863 he was elected to Congress from Baltimore's Fourth District.

In Congress Davis earned a reputation as a compelling orator and a brilliant debater intent on opposing what he called "the agitation of slavery" and avoiding the divisive matters sweeping through Congress, such as the attempt to organize Kansas under the proslavery Lecompton constitution. Instead Davis focused on the agenda of his party, which sought to restrict the rapid influx of Catholic Irish and German immigrants. In his pamphlet *The Origin, Principles and Purposes of the American Party* (1852), he argued, "American Republicans alone are entitled to rule the American Republic."

Reelected to the Thirty-sixth Congress as a Know Nothing despite that party's waning power, Davis cast a crucial vote in the long struggle over the election of the Speaker of the House in the winter of 1859–1860. Yet his vote for the conservative Republican William Pennington was condemned by the Maryland legislature, one of whose members encouraged the appropriation of $500 to send Davis to Liberia. Undeterred in his effort to find a middle way between the North and South even as he despised the Democratic party as an organization of traitors, Davis supported the Unionist John Bell in the election of 1860. When southern states began seceding, Davis became a powerful voice in the antisecessionist movement in Maryland, and he tried to create an anti-Democratic coalition. "Smite fearlessly the Democratic party. The union will survive its fragments," said Davis as he argued that the election of Abraham Lincoln was not the threat that southerners described.

Denying any extremism, Davis declared that he did not wish the South to believe that the North was "full of John Browns, traitors to the Constitution, bent on servile insurrection, endeavoring to invade your state institutions." Some said that the charismatic Marylander might find a seat in President Lincoln's cabinet, though Davis had only joined the Republican party after the election of 1860. Instead Davis remained in Congress, offering compromise resolutions designed to resolve issues such as the return of fugitive slaves.

In 1861 Davis lost his congressional seat, in part because Baltimore's Union Republicans remembered his support of Bell in 1860. Reelected to Congress in 1863, he became chairman of the House Committee on Foreign Affairs. Davis supported emancipation by Congress but not by the executive, the recruitment of black soldiers, and a new constitution for Maryland that would free the state's slaves. Always a believer in the balance of powers among the judiciary, legislative, and executive branches, Davis emerged as a critic of Lincoln's wartime suspension of the writ of habeas corpus. He challenged emancipation by the president, which he considered a state matter.

His understanding of the importance of Congress led Davis, who was chairman of the Select Committee on the Rebellious States, to introduce a legislative plan for Reconstruction. Known as the Wade-Davis Bill, it was less lenient than Lincoln's plan in dealing with those who had aided the rebellion. In its final form, the Wade-Davis Bill required a majority, not one-tenth, of those enrolled after military resistance in a state ended to take an oath to support the U.S. Constitution before a convention could be called to reestablish a state government there.

The differences between Davis's bill and Lincoln's vaguer plans for reconstructing the Union suggested a growing conflict between Congress and the executive, which would continue in Andrew Johnson's administration. Davis's bill repudiated the Confederate war debt, disfranchised Confederates, and in general pointed the way for congressional programs in the late 1860s, such as the Fourteenth Amendment. Pocket-vetoed by the president, the Wade-Davis Bill became the Maryland congressman's legacy to those who opposed executive control of Reconstruction. It also led to a storm of protest in Maryland, making Davis's renomination impossible. Later Davis favored black voting, Lincoln's reelection, and the execution of Confederate president Jefferson Davis for treason.

Davis died of pneumonia in Baltimore. His greatest contribution to his state was his intractable opposition to secession and his support of emancipation as a Unionist. "In Maryland we are dull," he once said, "and cannot recognize the right of secession."

• A notable collection of Henry Winter Davis Papers is in the Maryland Historical Society, and a more important collection is in the Samuel F. Du Pont Papers in the Eleutherian Mills Historical Library in Greenville, Del. Davis himself was the author of several pamphlets and a book, *The War of Ormuzd and Ahriman* (1852). His autobiography is found in Bernard Steiner, *The Life of Henry Winter Davis* (1916). The most helpful biography is Gerald Henig, *Henry Winter Davis: Antebellum and Civil War Congressman from Maryland* (1973). See also James Creswell, *Oration on the Life and Character of Henry Winter Davis* (1866).

JEAN HARVEY BAKER

DAVIS, Jeff (6 May 1862–3 Jan. 1913), governor of Arkansas and U.S. senator, was born near Rocky Comfort, Arkansas, the son of Lewis W. Davis, a Baptist preacher and Confederate chaplain, and Elizabeth Phillips. He was named after the president of the Confederacy. In 1866 Lewis Davis was elected county and probate judge of Sevier County, but three years later the Davises resettled in Dover, Pope County. In 1873 the family moved to the railroad town of Russellville, where Lewis Davis became a successful attorney, a real estate agent, a newspaper editor, and a one-term state legislator. As the son of one of Russellville's most prosperous citizens, Jeff enjoyed a privileged adolescence. Educated in the local public schools, he spent two years at the University of Arkansas before transferring to the law department of Vanderbilt University in 1880. At Vanderbilt he completed the standard two-year law program in a single year, but the university refused to grant him a diploma, because he had failed to meet a residency requirement. In the summer of 1881 he gained admittance to the bar, but in the fall he returned to Tennessee to attend Cumberland University. In the spring of 1882, after he was finally granted his law degree, he became the junior partner in his father's firm.

In 1882 Davis married Ina MacKenzie; the marriage produced twelve children, eight of whom survived infancy. After his first wife's death in 1910, Davis married Leila Carter in 1911. They had no children.

Davis became involved in local politics in the mid-1880s and began his active political career in 1888, when he served as a Democratic presidential elector, stumping the state for Grover Cleveland, white supremacy, and "reform." In 1890 he ran successfully for district attorney and was reelected two years later. In 1896 he ran for Congress, challenging William L. Terry, a popular three-term congressman from Little Rock, but his hopes for the Democratic nomination ended with a disappointing showing at the Pope County convention. Following his loss to Terry, Davis became totally absorbed in the presidential campaign of William Jennings Bryan. As a presidential elector for the second time, he assumed the role of a political evangelist, entertaining the voters with spellbinding oratory and preaching the Bryanist gospel of free silver. Davis's performance in the 1896 campaign drew statewide attention, catapulting him to the state attorney generalship in 1898.

Davis's tenure as attorney general proved to be the most memorable in the state's history. By challenging the legality of the Kimbell State House Act, which provided for the construction of a new capitol on the site of the existing state penitentiary, and by rendering a highly controversial extraterritorial interpretation of the Rector Antitrust Act, he created a major political uproar. According to Davis, the Rector Act prohibited any trust from doing business in Arkansas—regardless of where the trust had been organized. To make his point, he filed suit against every fire-insurance company operating in the state, demanding their withdrawal from industrywide pricing agreements. The fire-insurance companies responded by threatening to cancel all existing policies, prompting outraged businesspeople to hold protest meetings across the state. Supported by the legislature, Davis refused to back down. He was later overruled by the state supreme court, ending the controversy legally, but politically the ruling simply stoked the fire. Styling himself a martyr, Davis took his case to the people in a whirlwind campaign for the governorship. Visiting virtually every county in the state, he conducted a one-man crusade against the "Yankee trusts" and their local collaborators. He declared:

The war is on, knife to knife, hilt to hilt, foot to foot, knee to knee, between the corporations of Arkansas and the people. . . . If I win this race I have got to win it from every railroad, every bank and two-thirds of the lawyers and most of the big politicians. But if I can get the plain people of the country to help me, God bless you, we will clean the thing out. (Dunaway, pp. 51–52)

Although ridiculed by the state press and branded a demagogue by his four opponents, Davis carried 74 of 75 counties in the 1900 Democratic primary, winning the most resounding political victory in Arkansas history to that time.

Davis's governorship, which lasted three terms (1901–1907), was marked by bitter factionalism and a series of controversies related to a style of politics known as "Jeff Davisism." Davis's mastery of political invective, his ruthless determination to gain control of the legislature and to create a statewide political machine, his struggle to oversee the building of a new state capitol and the reform of the state prison system, and his periodic battles with prohibitionists, ministers, and other members of what he called "the high-collared crowd" led to increasingly desperate attempts to drive him from power. Following a landslide victory in the 1902 primary, several political opponents accused him of public drunkenness and generally immoral behavior and had him expelled from the Second Baptist Church of Little Rock. In February 1903 legislative leaders, angered by his interference in state prison affairs and other alleged improprieties, brought impeachment proceedings against him. When the impeachment effort failed, Davis counterattacked with charges of persecution and emerged from the episode stronger than ever. In the 1904 primary he won 57.8 percent of the vote, and during his third term he finally gained control of the legislature, which approved several of his pet projects, including an extraterritorial antitrust law, the creation of a state reform school, and the reorganization of penitentiary management. During his last two years as governor Davis was at the peak of his power, but he devoted most of his efforts to a race for the Senate. Relying on a clever blend of personal charisma, folksy humor, class rhetoric, and white supremacist demagoguery, he defeated Senator James Berry, an aging one-legged Confederate veteran who had served in the Senate since 1885.

Davis promised that he would take Washington by storm, but his plans quickly went awry. To his dismay, the rough-and-tumble style of political combat that had proved so effective in Arkansas seemed strangely out of place in the Senate. Soon after his arrival in Washington, he introduced an antitrust bill and, to the amazement of his colleagues, delivered a long and impassioned harangue against "the malefactors of great wealth." The speech drew sharp criticism from the national press and several senators, who pointed out that senatorial etiquette proscribed long-winded speeches by new members. Davis claimed that his antitrust speech had "swept the cobwebs off the ceiling of the Senate chamber," but in truth he was bitterly disappointed by the Washington establishment's refusal to take him seriously. Although he later apologized for his intemperate rhetoric and his breach of etiquette, the press continued to portray him as a wild-eyed, backwoods buffoon, and Davis retreated into stony silence.

A deteriorating power base in state politics compounded Senator Davis's problems, and he spent the remainder of his career brooding about his lack of influence in Little Rock and Washington. In 1909 he gained some notoriety by introducing a bill prohibiting speculation in crop futures, but in 1910 his apparent collusion with East Arkansas land speculators during the so-called "sunk lands" affair tarnished his reform image and accelerated his political decline. During his final years in the Senate, he became increasingly absorbed in his family life and spent less and less time in Washington. In the 1912 senatorial primary, Davis fought off a stiff challenge from Representative Stephen Brundidge, and for a time his reelection seemed to rekindle his interest in public policy. His comeback was cut short by a fatal stroke in Little Rock, two months before the expiration of his first term. Davis's funeral was one of the largest in Little Rock history, as thousands of mourners paid their respects to early twentieth-century Arkansas's most engaging political folk hero.

Davis was a genuinely paradoxical figure who left an ambiguous legacy. Although he was a successful college-educated attorney, he sincerely and convincingly played the role of a hillbilly folk hero. Though deeply religious, he battled with preachers and prohibitionists throughout his career. Though passionately egalitarian, he became a ruthless political boss. He was a humanitarian reformer who tried to reform an inhumane penal system, but he was also a vicious Negrophobe who promoted black disfranchisement and defended lynching. He was an agrarian radical who dramatized and personalized the problems of downtrodden farmers, yet for the most part he practiced a politics of catharsis and symbolic action that inhibited radical change. He was an innovative politician who knew how to acquire and hold power, but his administrations produced more politics than government, more ritual than legislation.

• Davis left no personal papers, but two small collections of related material are at the University of Arkansas Library in Fayetteville. The best introduction to Davis is Charles Jacobson, *The Life Story of Jeff Davis: The Stormy Petrel of Arkansas Politics* (1925), an insider's account written by the governor's private secretary. L. S. Dunaway, ed., *Jeff Davis,*

Governor and United States Senator: His Life and Speeches (1913), is a useful and highly entertaining collection of speeches and personal reminiscences. The most comprehensive treatment of Davis's career is Raymond Arsenault, *The Wild Ass of the Ozarks: Jeff Davis and the Social Bases of Southern Politics* (1984). The best brief accounts of Davis's political activities are John Gould Fletcher, *Arkansas* (1947); Rupert Vance, "A Karl Marx for Hill Billies," *Social Forces* 9 (Dec. 1930): 180–90; Cal Ledbetter, Jr., "Jeff Davis and the Politics of Combat," *Arkansas Historical Quarterly* 33 (Spring 1974): 16–37; Richard L. Niswonger, "A Study of Southern Demagoguery: Jeff Davis of Arkansas," *Arkansas Historical Quarterly* 39 (Summer 1980): 114–24; Arsenault, "Governor Jeff Davis," in *The Governors of Arkansas: Essays in Political Biography*, ed. Timothy P. Donovan and Willard B. Gatewood (1981); and Annette Shelby, "Jeff Davis of Arkansas: 'Professional Man of the People,'" in *The Oratory of Southern Demagogues*, ed. Cal M. Logue and Howard Dorgan (1981). See also Paige E. Mulhollan, "The Issues of the Davis-Berry Senatorial Campaign in 1906," *Arkansas Historical Quarterly* 20 (Summer 1961): 118–26; Arsenault, "Charles Jacobson of Arkansas: A Jewish Politician in the Land of the Razorbacks, 1891–1915," in *Turn to the South: Essays on Southern Jewry* (1979); Niswonger, *Arkansas Democratic Politics, 1896–1920* (1990); John William Graves, *Town and Country: Race Relations in an Urban-Rural Context: Arkansas, 1865–1905* (1990); and Fon Louise Gordon, *Caste and Class: The Black Experience in Arkansas, 1880–1920* (1995). Obituaries are in the (Little Rock) *Arkansas Gazette* and the *New York Times*, both 3 Jan. 1913.

RAYMOND ARSENAULT

DAVIS, Jefferson (3 June 1808?–6 Dec. 1889), president of the Confederate States of America and U.S. senator, was born in Christian (later Todd) County, Kentucky, the tenth and last child of Samuel Emory Davis and Jane Cook, farmers. The year of his birth is uncertain; for many years Davis regarded 1807 as correct, but he later settled upon 1808.

Samuel Davis, a frontier farmer, owned a few slaves but was not wealthy. Seeking better lands in the Southwest, he moved his family to the Louisiana Territory when Jefferson was two or three and then to Woodville, Mississippi. Apparently Samuel Davis valued education, because he sent his youngest son at age eight to St. Thomas College, a Dominican school in Springfield, Kentucky. After two years there Jefferson returned to Mississippi and attended local academies. In 1823 he went to Transylvania University in Lexington, Kentucky, where he studied for a year.

Samuel Davis, an emotionally undemonstrative man, died in 1824. At this point, Jefferson's eldest brother, Joseph Emory Davis, became a major influence on his life. After practicing law in Natchez, Mississippi, Joseph had established a flourishing plantation on bottomland next to the Mississippi River in Warren County, Mississippi. He arranged an appointment to West Point for his youngest brother, who studied there from 1824 to 1828.

At West Point Davis's academic record was respectable but undistinguished; he graduated twenty-third in a class of thirty-three. More notable was his high-spirited behavior. He broke many regulations, accumulated numerous demerits, and faced a court-martial in the summer following his plebe year for visiting an off-limits tavern. Proud and unwilling to admit error, Davis based his defense at the court-martial on hairsplitting and technicalities and barely avoided dismissal. Strong-willed, he was as yet undisciplined, except in a ramrod-straight bearing that he adopted and maintained for the rest of his life.

After graduation, Davis served six and a half years as a lieutenant in the infantry, stationed in the West. He saw little or no action. He even missed most of the Black Hawk War in 1832, since he was on furlough when this brief conflict with the Sauk Indians broke out. Promotion came slowly in the small peacetime army, and soon Davis was looking for an alternate occupation. In 1833 he fell in love with Sarah Knox Taylor, the daughter of Lieutenant Colonel Zachary Taylor—the commandant at Fort Crawford, Wisconsin, where Davis was then stationed—who forbade a marriage for at least two years because he did not want his daughter to marry a military man. In 1835 the quick-tempered and contentious Davis faced a court-martial for insubordination after he failed to turn out on a rainy morning and adopted a haughty manner with a superior officer. The military court found Davis guilty of the specified behavior but refused to deem it a military offense. Dissatisfied with this verdict and with the army, Davis decided to resign. Convincing "Knoxie" Taylor that a summer in Mississippi would not be unhealthy, he married her on 17 June 1835.

Within three months his bride was dead, a victim of either malaria or yellow fever. Davis himself fell gravely ill also. Although he recovered physically, he had to face simultaneously a deep personal loss, the end of his military career, and probably feelings of guilt about Sarah's death that his proud and self-conscious nature would not allow him to admit. For several years he devoted himself to farming on his brother's plantations in Mississippi. Although both men regarded "Brierfield" as Jefferson Davis's plantation, Joseph Davis retained legal title to the land and continued to act in a fatherly role. He gave his younger brother a loan to buy slaves and advice on slave management. The brothers permitted their slaves a degree of responsibility and self-regulation that was unusual for the time. Reading widely and discussing public affairs with Joseph, Jefferson Davis formed strong states' rights, Democratic principles and developed ambitions for public office. He also cultivated a new public demeanor. Formal, serious, and cold in manner, he used formidable self-control to restrain outbursts of anger and self-righteousness.

In 1843 he ran, unsuccessfully, for the state legislature. The next year he campaigned extensively for the Democratic party while he courted Varina Howell, an intelligent woman from Natchez who was half his age. Initially she was not pleased with Davis's manner of "taking for granted that everybody agrees with him when he expresses an opinion," but he won her over. They were married in 1845, and in the same year Davis won election to Congress. The campaign was an exhausting one, during which he suffered the first of many viral infections of his left eye. These eventually caused blindness and recurrent facial pain, which by the mid-1850s occasionally incapacitated him. But now his political star was rising. Enamored of John C. Calhoun, Davis fought for strict states' rights positions but also aggressively favored territorial expansion.

After the war with Mexico began, he accepted an appointment, over Varina's objections, as colonel of the First Regiment of Mississippi Volunteers and hurried to Mexico. Davis's unit played a prominent role in the capture of Monterrey and then, in February 1847, took the lead in repelling an attack by Santa Anna at the battle of Buena Vista. Davis was wounded in the right foot during the latter engagement, but his exploits made him a military hero in Mississippi. For years to come he answered inquiries about the "V" formation in which his men met the Mexican cavalry charge, and he devoted much time and ink to countering any slight directed toward the valor of Mississippi's troops. His vigorous defense of his fellow Mississippians pleased the state's leaders, and in August 1847 he accepted appointment to the U.S. Senate.

Temporarily hobbled by crutches, but aggressive and combative, in Washington Davis was soon involved in the first of a half-dozen near duels that marked his political career, this one with Mississippi's other senator, Henry S. Foote. On the Senate floor Davis was outspoken and strongly expansionist. He favored annexing large amounts of Mexican territory and declared that the Gulf of Mexico belonged to the United States. He also began to speak in defense of slavery and southern interests in the territories. His harsh criticism of abolitionists and his insistent, energetic defense of what he viewed as southern rights soon made him a rising spokesman for his native region.

Throughout the 1850s Davis was determined and consistent in his stand on the territories. Following Calhoun's compact theory, Davis asserted that the territories belonged to all the states and that no decision to exclude slavery could be made before a territory became a state and assumed sovereign power. The South must be allowed "an experiment," an opportunity to see if slavery was suited to new territories. Although Davis granted that some territories might evolve into free states, he condemned any interference with southerners' right to take slavery into new lands and try to establish it there. On 18 July 1850 he further declared, "We claim that the Federal Government shall provide the means of enforcing our constitutional rights . . . within those Territories." His position did not change during the decade, although his expectation that slavery would be useful in mining or irrigated agriculture in the Southwest rapidly faded.

Davis's fierce opposition to the Compromise of 1850 earned him a reputation as a leading southern radical. He objected to the admission of California as a free state, declaring that southern rights had been denied since California never went through a territorial stage. Putting no trust in popular sovereignty, Davis argued that a real compromise would extend the Missouri Compromise line to the Pacific Ocean, "with the specific recognition of the right to hold slaves in the territory below that line." Mississippi's leaders favored southern protest through the Nashville Convention and called a state convention to consider resistance. By the time this convention met in 1850, however, it was clear that the South as a whole was ready to accept the compromise. To aid the Democratic party in an uphill contest in Mississippi in 1851, Davis resigned his Senate seat and ran for governor. His personal popularity made the contest close, but he lost and considered leaving politics.

In little more than a year, however, Davis returned to public life as secretary of war in the administration of Franklin Pierce. He proved a hardworking and competent secretary who stressed promotions on merit, better training, and expansions of the army's arsenals, fortifications, and size. Although he permitted a protracted and unseemly quarrel with General Winfield Scott to mar his record, he strengthened the army technologically by converting flintlock muskets to rifles and supporting experiments with breech-loading rifles and improved cannons. On grounds of national security he advocated a transcontinental railroad and was delighted when surveys suggested that a southern route was most feasible. In the administration generally Davis was an influential prosouthern voice. He shared the rest of the cabinet's interest in acquiring Cuba and arranged the meeting at which Stephen Douglas secured Pierce's support for the Kansas-Nebraska bill.

When Davis reentered the Senate in 1857, he resumed his advocacy of southern rights but showed a growing tendency to defend the South within the nation and through the Democratic party. He feared that abolitionists were trying to encircle the South and cut off slavery's expansion in order to begin its destruction. But as other southerners became more radical in their views, Davis sought solutions within the Union. His genuine feeling for the Union emerged most clearly in the summer of 1858 when he visited New England for reasons of health. His reception on this tour convinced him that there were many "true State Rights Democrats" in the North.

He did not, however, number Stephen Douglas among them. Although Davis hoped that a triumphant Democratic party would protect the South in the Union, he and other southerners were ready, after the Dred Scott decision, to insist upon their territorial rights. Douglas's views on popular sovereignty were unacceptable. In order to block Douglas from the Democratic presidential nomination, Davis in 1860 offered his resolutions on the "relations of states," which asserted that the federal government should protect southern rights in the territories. He did not expect Congress to pass a slave code, but his action focused attention on the issue and on Douglas.

That fall Davis hoped that the Democratic party might unite behind a candidate even if it could not agree on a platform. When these hopes failed, he supported John C. Breckinridge, but when election returns showed that Abraham Lincoln had won, Davis was not among those who favored immediate secession. Long after most of Mississippi's leaders were ready to secede, Davis supported cooperation by southern states. As a member of the Senate's Committee of Thirteen he offered to support the Crittenden Compromise if Republicans would do likewise. This moderation in the secession crisis helped make Davis an attractive choice for president of the Confederate States once the dissolution of the Union became a reality. His stands for southern rights were well known, but he did not alarm the Upper South. Davis accepted his election by the Montgomery convention with reluctance, for he would have preferred to serve the South as a general in command of Mississippi's troops.

To his formidable tasks as Confederate president Davis brought total dedication and a clear focus on the goal of independence. As chief executive Davis proved to be intelligent, adaptable, not bound by inappropriate tradition, determined, and persistent. In the pursuit of independence he helped bring remarkable changes to the South and marshaled its limited resources rather effectively against a more powerful opponent. Despite continuing health problems and the accidental death of his son Joseph, he worked exceedingly long hours. Keeping his contentious nature largely in check, he endured criticism that would have enraged almost anyone. Davis lacked some important skills, such as the ability to communicate with and inspire ordinary citizens, and his loyalty to some appointees was misplaced. But his performance during the war seems superior to that of any other prominent southern politician.

Davis built a powerful central government. He saw himself as a strict constructionist but never doubted that the Confederate Constitution gave him war powers that were necessary in the crisis. From the first he insisted that state troops come under the central government's control, and when four state governors sought the return of state-owned arms he declared in disgust that "if such was to be the course of the States . . . we had better make terms as soon as we could." Despite enormous local pressures, Davis insisted that "the idea of retaining in each State its own troops for its own defense" was a "fatal error. . . . Our safety—our very existence—depends on the complete blending of the military strength of all the States into one united body, to be used anywhere and everywhere as the exigencies of the contest may require."

After only one year of war he sought and obtained a power unprecedented in American history: conscription. The idea of compelling men to fight in the armies was anathema to some southerners and generated fierce protests from political leaders such as Governor Joseph Emerson Brown of Georgia. But Davis was convinced that the Confederacy could not survive without conscription, for, as Secretary of War James Seddon later admitted, "the spirit of volunteering had died out." Davis answered Brown's protests unflinchingly and argued for a Hamiltonian interpreta-

tion of the Constitution's "necessary and proper" clause. In another restriction of personal liberties Davis requested and obtained the suspension of the writ of habeas corpus on repeated occasions to deal with disloyalty in threatened areas. Although he scrupulously refrained from acting without congressional authority, he urged what he believed necessary even in the face of criticism.

Seeing that it was essential to control not only the South's manpower, but also its economy, Davis obtained through legislation extensive power over railroads and shipping. By these means he tried to ensure that foreign trade and the transportation system would serve the country's needs. Arguing that the Confederacy must become independent economically, Davis encouraged industries and used the government's power over exemptions and details to keep factories running. Thousands of government agents reached deep into local communities to collect food as tax-in-kind or procure a variety of valuable materials through impressment. The government set up salt works and salt mines and even seized the metal coils from distilleries to obtain copper. Eventually Davis's administration employed over 70,000 civilians and was larger, in proportion to population, than the U.S. government.

Davis's military training and his desire to command revealed themselves in hours of labor over the details of military planning and support. Davis did not, however, meddle with commanders in the field any more than Abraham Lincoln, who has seldom received the criticism leveled at Davis. His overall strategy of an "offensive defensive" was sound, given the South's resources and the political and social reality that the Confederacy had to defend its territory. He fully understood the importance of concentrating the South's forces at the points of greatest threat, rather than spreading them out in a perimeter defense, and he incessantly badgered reluctant generals and state leaders to transfer troops. His appointments, particularly in the western theater, were unwise and his confidence in some commanders a mistake in judgment. In retrospect it is clear that too little attention was given early in the war to the enormous western theater, but Davis's overall approach to departments was sensible.

Given its meager resources, the Confederacy bore up surprisingly well on the battlefield. Internal political and social problems, however, damaged morale and weakened the armies long before military defeat appeared inevitable. Davis faced serious discontent from both extremes of the white class system. To many planters the Confederacy represented a means of sheltering their lives from the changes threatened by the "Black Republicans." When the war brought great change, and the Confederate government itself impressed slaves, taxed crops, and destroyed cotton near enemy lines, planters reacted with surprise and outrage. They and their political allies who fulminated about states' rights may have been sincere, but they also were shortsighted and self-serving. Davis patiently answered criticisms and allowed legal challenges to his policies to be settled in state courts, which supported the Confederacy, but there was nothing he could do to remove planter discontent.

The common people of the Confederacy grew disaffected not for ideological reasons, but because their conditions of life became intolerable. Often they favored stronger government action if it would alleviate suffering. Impoverished soldiers' families also resented the privileges enjoyed by planters, particularly those related to the draft, such as the exemption of overseers and the ability of those with means to hire a substitute. The combination of poverty and resentment over a "rich man's war and a poor man's fight" nourished a growing stream of desertions from the Confederate ranks. To these problems Davis was largely insensitive. He allowed inequitable policies to become law, and later, when more perceptive officials such as Commissioner of Taxes Thompson Allen or Secretary of War James Seddon urged measures to alleviate distress, he concluded that resources were too limited to allow action. His neglect of the common people's suffering led directly to military weakness.

Davis's style of leadership also hampered his ability to counter problems of morale. Immersing himself in details of administration in Richmond, he chose to endure criticism rather than attempt to lead and inspire public opinion. He lacked Lincoln's ability to speak to the fears and hopes of ordinary people, and his occasional, hurried tours into the southern heartland accomplished little. Formidable though internal problems were, Davis's handling of them did not match his management of military affairs.

The Confederate president's flexibility on slavery and commitment to independence emerged clearly late in the war, when he proposed arming and freeing the South's slaves. It is likely that Davis considered this possibility earlier, but he had hoped to influence the 1864 northern elections and could not afford a well-publicized, divisive debate within the South. After Lincoln's reelection, however, he straightforwardly argued that slavery was less important than independence and that slaves would fight and deserved freedom as a reward. These proposals aroused enormous opposition, but as was usually the case, Davis won Congress's approval for most of his plan.

After the Civil War Davis was imprisoned for two years at Fortress Monroe in Hampton Roads. Despite damage to his health, he survived and carried himself through the postwar years as a defeated but unrepentant Confederate. He published two turgid volumes, collectively entitled *The Rise and Fall of the Confederate Government*, which repeated the obsolete compact theory of government and defended the South's right to secede. He headed a short-lived insurance company and a similarly unsuccessful British trading venture. With Varina he found some moments of rest and peace, but in 1872 and 1878 the last two of their four sons died. Only Varina and two daughters survived when Davis succumbed to pneumonia in New Orleans.

• An old but still useful edition of Davis's papers is Dunbar Rowland, ed., *Jefferson Davis: Constitutionalist; His Letters, Papers, and Speeches* (10 vols., 1923). A superior edition, *The Papers of Jefferson Davis* (1971–), is being published under the successive editorship of Haskell M. Monroe, Jr., James T. McIntosh, and Lynda L. Crist. Additional useful documents may be found in *The War of the Rebellion: A Compilation of the Official Records of the Union and Confederate Armies* (128 vols., 1880–1901). The best biographical study is William C. Davis, *Jefferson Davis: The Man and His Hour* (1991). Other biographies are Hudson Strode, *Jefferson Davis* (3 vols., 1955–1964), and Clement Eaton, *Jefferson Davis* (1977). See also Emory M. Thomas, *The Confederate Nation, 1861–1865* (1979), and Paul D. Escott, *After Secession: Jefferson Davis and the Failure of Confederate Nationalism* (1978).

PAUL D. ESCOTT

DAVIS, Jefferson Columbus (2 Mar. 1828–30 Nov. 1879), soldier, was born in Clark County, Indiana, the son of William Davis, a farmer, and Mary Drummond, both natives of Kentucky. In 1846, following the outbreak of the Mexican War, he enlisted in the Third Indiana Infantry and participated with it in the battle of Buena Vista (22–23 Feb. 1847). On 17 June 1848 he received a second lieutenant's commission in the regular army and was assigned to the First Artillery Regiment. In 1852 he became a first lieutenant, a rank he still held while serving as a member of the garrison of Fort Sumter when it was bombarded by the Confederates on 12–14 April 1861, initiating the Civil War.

In August 1861 Davis, now a captain, left the regular army on being appointed colonel of an Indiana volunteer regiment by Governor Oliver P. Morton of that state. Promoted to brigadier general in December 1861, he commanded a division at the battle of Pea Ridge in Arkansas (6–7 Mar. 1862) where he played a key role in securing the Union victory by his promptness and the skill with which he deployed his troops. What seemed to be a bright military future suddenly and permanently became clouded, however, by the most dramatic episode of Davis's career. Assigned, following further service as a division commander in Mississippi in the late spring of 1862, to the command of Major General William Nelson (1824–1862) in Louisville, Kentucky, he was so deeply offended by what he deemed to be an insulting reprimand from Nelson that on the morning of 29 September 1862, accompanied by Governor Morton, he went to Nelson's headquarters at the Galt House hotel. Finding Nelson in the lobby, he demanded "satisfaction" for the insult, and when Nelson responded by calling him an "insolent puppy," he threw a wadded-up calling card into Nelson's face. In turn Nelson, who weighed three hundred pounds, slapped Davis in the face and then went upstairs. While he was doing so, Davis procured a revolver and followed him. Hearing Davis, Nelson turned around and started toward him. "Not another step!" cried Davis, who then shot Nelson in the chest, mortally wounding him. Although placed under arrest, Davis was never court-martialed, perhaps because Nelson had forgiven him before dying, and thanks to Morton's political influence he soon received command of a division in the Army of the Cumberland. Nevertheless, his personal reputation was irreparably damaged.

As a division commander Davis took part and performed well in the battles of Stones River (31 Dec. 1862–1–2 Jan. 1863), Chickamauga (19–20 Sept. 1863), and Chattanooga (23–25 Nov. 1863). During the Atlanta campaign his division occupied Rome, Georgia, on 18 May 1864 and came closer than any other Federal unit to penetrating the Confederate defenses at the Battle of Kennesaw Mountain on 27 June. On 28 July, at Sherman's behest, Davis rose from a sick bed to lead his division in a flanking march, only to faint when he mounted his horse. Such zeal won Sherman's favor, with the result that on 24 August Davis became commander of the XIV Corps with the brevet rank of major general. He soon justified Sherman's confidence in him by carrying out the only successful major frontal attack of the Atlanta campaign when two divisions of his corps seized a vulnerable salient in the Confederate line at the second battle of Jonesboro (1 Sept.). He continued to command the XIV Corps capably during the March to the Sea (Nov.–Dec. 1864) and Sherman's campaign through the Carolinas (Feb.–Apr. 1865), but at war's end his official rank remained that of brigadier general of volunteers—a fact that he bitterly resented. Moreover, during the March to the Sea he stained his reputation further by another brutal act. On 8 December, after his corps crossed Ebeneezer Creek, he needlessly had the pontoon bridge removed, thereby stranding a large number of black refugees from slavery who were following his column. When pursuing Confederate cavalry approached, many of the blacks, fearful of being massacred, attempted to swim across the creek and drowned.

In 1866 Davis returned to the regular army with the rank of colonel in command of the Twenty-third Infantry Regiment. Two years later, following the acquisition of Alaska from Russia, his regiment occupied that territory, and in 1873 it took part in a campaign against the Modoc Indians in northern California and southern Oregon. The remainder of Davis's military career was uneventful, ending with his death while in Chicago. He was buried in Indianapolis, where he had resided with his wife, Mariette Woodson (Athon) Davis, when not on active duty.

Davis was an active, aggressive, and able officer. Judged solely by military criteria, his service and performance during the Civil War entitled him to the major generalcy he never acquired: he was one of the best division leaders in the Union army and proved to be a competent corps commander. On the other hand, as a person he was vain, vindictive, and—as his murder of Nelson and his callous treatment of the black refugees demonstrated—at times even vicious. Hence it is difficult to sympathize with his resentment at not obtaining promotion to higher rank. In sum, Davis the soldier deserves respect but not Davis the man.

• Davis wrote an autobiography that is available in typescript at the Indiana Historical Society, Indianapolis, but it is so brief and superficial as to be of little historical value. The best primary source on his Civil War activities, the most important phase of his career, is *The War of the Rebellion: A Compilation of the Official Records of the Union and Confederate Armies* (128 vols., 1880–1901), which contains his reports as well as correspondence by and about him. The *Official Records* should be supplemented, however, by Franz Sigel, "The Pea Ridge Campaign," *Battles and Leaders of the Civil War*, vol. 1 (1887), pp. 314–34; Peter Cozzens, *No Better Place to Die: The Battle of Stones River* (1990) and *This Terrible Sound: The Battle of Chickamauga* (1992); and Albert Castel, *Decision in the West: The Atlanta Campaign of 1864* (1992). For Davis's slaying of Nelson, the essential primary sources are Don Carlos Buell, "East Tennessee and the Campaign of Perryville," *Battles and Leaders of the Civil War*, vol. 3 (1887), pp. 42–44, and James B. Fry, *Military Miscellanies* (1889), pp. 486–505. On the incident at Ebeneezer Creek, see Joseph T. Glatthaar, *The March to the Sea and Beyond: Sherman's Troops in the Savannah and Carolinas Campaigns* (1985), p. 64 and citations.

ALBERT CASTEL

DAVIS, Jerome Dean (17 Jan. 1838–4 Nov. 1910), missionary and professor of theology, was born in Groton, New York, the son of Hope Davis, a farmer and schoolteacher, and Brooksy Woodbury. In 1861, while a student at Beloit College, he joined the Union army, reaching the rank of lieutenant colonel at the age of twenty-six. He reentered Beloit College in 1865 and graduated as salutatorian of his class in 1866. Upon graduation from Chicago Theological Seminary in 1869, he was appointed to serve a church in Cheyenne, Wyoming, by the Congregational Home Missionary Society. On 15 July of the same year, he was married to Sophia Strong, a first cousin of Josiah Strong. They had four children, all of whom became missionaries. With the completion of a church building in Cheyenne, Davis and his wife were accepted as missionaries of the American Board of Commissioners for Foreign Missions and arrived in Japan in 1871. It is noteworthy that prior to their departure for Japan they attended the annual meeting of the American Board in Salem, Massachusetts, where they met Joseph Hardy Neesima, a young Japanese student at Andover Seminary.

Situated in Kobe first, working with O. H. Gulick, D. C. Greene, and their families, Davis was soon involved in informal programs teaching English as well as the Bible because Christian missionaries were still banned from open proselytizing. With the loosening of governmental restrictions, Davis was able to organize a church in Sanda, north of Kobe, in 1875.

In December of the previous year Joseph Neesima, upon completion of his theological training at Andover Seminary and his ordination for the Christian ministry by the Congregational church, was appointed a corresponding member of the Japan Mission of the American Board. Neesima returned to Japan on 26 December 1874 with a plan to start a Christian college.

Davis was one of the first active participants in Neesima's attempt to start an educational program based upon Christian faith. Neesima gained valuable assistance from Yamamoto Kakuma, a counselor of Kyoto Prefecture, who offered a piece of his land for the proposed school, which was named Doshisha, or "One Purpose Company." Davis became the first foreign teacher, and the school opened on 29 November 1875 with eight students.

Davis was an essential part of the new faculty, teaching biblical studies, which were not officially approved by the government at first, as well as scientific subjects. He was also an effective coordinator and mediator between Neesima and missionaries of the American Board, whose understanding of the purpose and nature of the school at times did not agree with that of Neesima. The administration of the school was largely laid upon Davis while Neesima negotiated with the central government for full approval and recognition of Doshisha, which finally were given in March 1876.

Davis was not only Neesima's co-worker, but also his intimate friend. When Neesima married Yamamoto Kakuma's sister Yaye, the wedding service was held at Davis's residence and was conducted by Davis. Three days before that, Yaye was baptized by Davis, also at his house. Beyond this personal intimacy, Davis and Neesima had deep respect and appreciation for each other. Davis was always loyal to Neesima as the head of Doshisha, making constructive suggestions and taking important roles in administration and teaching.

By the middle of 1876 Neesima and Davis were joined on the faculty of theology by Dwight Whitney Learned and Wallace Taylor. A record dated 1878 indicates that Davis taught such subjects as mathematics, science, trigonometry, and algebra in addition to theology and ethics.

One of the significant events in Davis's career at Doshisha was his encounter with a group of young men who studied under Captain L. L. Janes, a teacher in a government institution in Kumamoto on the island of Kyushu. Though under pressure not to pursue any teaching of the Christian faith, Janes effectively conveyed biblical messages to young men who came mainly from a samurai background. Upon the conversion of forty of his students on 30 January 1876, Janes referred thirty of them to Davis for the specific purpose of Christian education. As the main administrator of the school, Davis dealt with these passionately religious and often boisterous young men with sensitive care and led them to academic and religious maturity in three years. They were not easy years, but Davis dealt with them patiently, and they became outstanding leaders in the Japanese church.

Davis also served as a prophetic voice for women's education in Japan. He persuaded the American Board to establish Kobe Women's College on 12 October 1875, with Eliza Talcott as the first principal. The Doshisha Girls' School was opened on 21 April 1877 at Davis's residence under the leadership of Yaye Neesima and Alice Jennette Starkweather.

Sophia Davis died in 1886, and in 1888 Davis married Frances Hooper of Worcester, Massachusetts, who was on the faculty of the Doshisha Girls' School in Kyoto.

The untimely death of Neesima on 23 January 1890 caused Davis great sorrow, but he remained a central figure at Doshisha until 1910, serving as a trustee and professor of systematic theology. His writings included *An Outline of Theology, The Concept of Atonement, The Outline of Christian Ethics*, all in Japanese, and *A Maker of New Japan: Rev. Joseph Hardy Neesima* (1890) in English.

He died in Oberlin, Ohio. His last words to his loved ones, spoken the day before his death, were, "I have no other message than my life; my life is my message to my children." Davis was an able scholar and committed evangelist who was indispensable in making Doshisha an outstanding Christian school and whose theological teaching and writing had a significant impact on theological thought in Japan.

• For further information see J. Merle Davis, *Davis—Soldier, Missionary* (1916).

ROBERT MIKIO FUKADA

DAVIS, John (13 Jan. 1787–19 Apr. 1854), lawyer and politician, was born in Northborough, Massachusetts, the son of Isaac Davis and Anna Brigham, farmers. Davis attended Yale College, graduating with high honors in 1812, after which he studied law in the office of Francis Blake, a prominent Worcester lawyer, and was admitted to the bar in 1815. After a short time in Spencer, Massachusetts, he settled in Worcester and established a successful law practice. In 1822 Davis married Eliza Bancroft, a sister of historian, Democratic politician, diplomat, and secretary of the navy George Bancroft. They had five sons, including John Chandler Bancroft Davis, who became a distinguished diplomat, and Horace Davis, who was a manufacturer, congressman from California, cofounder of Stanford University, and president of the University of California.

Davis began his political career as a Federalist, then moved into the National Republican party in the 1820s. A committed opponent of Andrew Jackson and Jacksonian Democracy, Davis supported John Quincy Adams in 1824 and won election to the U.S. House of Representatives. Thereafter he became a partisan of Henry Clay and associated himself with Abbott Lawrence, the wealthy and politically powerful leader of the Clay faction in Massachusetts, and the dominant manufacturing wing of the party. Davis's relationship with Lawrence and the manufacturers would bring him into direct conflict with Adams, with Daniel Webster, and eventually with the antislavery wing of the Massachusetts Whig party.

In Congress Davis distinguished himself as an unrelenting opponent of Jackson and a spokesman for conservative financial policies, especially protectionism. His speeches on the protective tariff and defense of the 1828 "Tariff of Abominations" were printed and widely circulated. He also was a leading opponent of Clay's compromise tariff of 1833, a posture that only momentarily strained his relations with Clay but did not diminish his support from Lawrence and Massachusetts textile manufacturers.

In 1833, at the urging of National Republican leaders, Davis resigned from Congress to campaign for governor of Massachusetts against Adams, the candidate of the Antimasonic party, and Marcus Morton, the perennial Democratic candidate. Adams had hoped to win National Republican support, but former Federalists and Masons in the National Republican party opposed Adams and chose Davis as their candidate. With the support of the popular outgoing governor, Levi Lincoln, Davis won a plurality of the votes but not an outright majority. The choice of governor then fell to the Massachusetts legislature. When Adams, fearing that Morton would draw the Antimasonic party into a coalition with the Democrats, withdrew in favor of Davis, Davis's election was assured. Davis was embarrassed when members of his party were unwilling to pay their political debt to the Antimasons, and he was unable to forge a National Republican–Antimason coalition against Jacksonian Democracy. Jackson's assault on the Bank of the United States was highly unpopular in Massachusetts and greatly contributed to Davis's reelection in 1834. By then the National Republican party had transformed itself into the anti-Jackson Whig party, with Davis as its titular leader in Massachusetts.

Davis essentially continued Lincoln's programs as governor and made no significant new initiatives. His attempt to secure a revision of the state constitution failed when western farmers prevented the assembly of a state constitutional convention. They feared that Davis was too closely associated with manufacturers in the eastern part of the state. Under Davis's sympathetic leadership, industry continued to flourish, and expansion of state transportation continued.

In 1835, after a close contest between Davis and Adams, the Massachusetts legislature chose Davis to replace retiring senator Nathaniel Silsbee in the U.S. Senate. Davis had the full support of manufacturing interests, Masons, and former Federalists, many of whom mistrusted Adams for his early defection from the Federalist party and advocacy of Antimasonry. Adams had led in the balloting until he announced support for Jackson's remonstrance against France, which was contrary to official Whig policy. Whigs in the Massachusetts Senate, partly at the urging of Webster, threw their support to Davis, whom the Democrats preferred to Adams as well. Webster expected Davis's friends to support his bid for the Whig presidential nomination in 1836.

In the Senate Davis resumed his role as a prominent conservative spokesman on financial and commercial issues. He also played a leading role in the conflict with Great Britain over the northeastern boundary. Davis was hostile to the British claims and insisted that the United States not relinquish any territory to Britain along the Maine–New Brunswick border. Although he supported Martin Van Buren's efforts to preserve American neutrality during the Canadian rebellions of 1838, he was aroused by a minor conflict in the Aroostook Valley and insisted that Britain had "invaded" the United States.

Davis remained in the Senate only until 1840, when at the insistence of the Massachusetts Whig hierarchy, he resigned to campaign again for governor. He won easily in the election of 1840, was reelected by a narrow margin in 1841, and was defeated in 1842, when the election went to the Democratic-controlled state legislature. His short term as governor produced no significant new legislation or programs but was notable in Davis's opposition and final grudging willingness to compromise on the Maine boundary issue.

Davis's defeat in Massachusetts stemmed from bitter divisions in the Massachusetts Whig party between the Webster faction and the faction of Lawrence, Davis, and Clay. Also at issue was Davis's conflict with Webster during the Webster-Ashburton negotiations. Webster, appointed secretary of state in 1841 by President William Henry Harrison, had refused to resign from the succeeding Tyler administration well after John Tyler had infuriated Whigs in general and Clay in particular. The Massachusetts Whig party officially denounced Tyler and, led by Lawrence, demanded Webster's resignation. Webster, insisting that he had to remain in office to complete his negotiations with Lord Ashburton over a number of Anglo-American issues, ultimately did resign in 1843. In retaliation for Davis's policy during the negotiations with Ashburton and deeply hostile to Massachusetts Whig leadership, Webster refused to campaign for Davis. Morton won a plurality of votes, and the Democratic legislature elected Morton to the governorship. Webster's continued opposition also caused Davis to decline the Whig gubernatorial nomination in 1843.

Davis's defeat in Massachusetts likely cost him a vice presidential nomination on the 1844 Clay ticket. In 1842 Webster attempted to block attempts by Lawrence and his allies to commit the state party to Clay's nomination for president in 1844. Lawrence not only overcame Webster's opposition but also secured the endorsement of Davis for vice president. Shortly afterward, Davis received a second endorsement at a Whig mass rally in Dayton, Ohio. The Whigs at their national convention in Baltimore, however, chose Theodore Freylinghuysen of New Jersey as their candidate for vice president. Clay was not persuaded that Davis had sufficient political power to overcome Webster's opposition in Massachusetts, which could cost him the state. In addition, Davis's caution on antislavery issues and lukewarm opposition to the annexation of Texas had not won him support from the growing antislavery Whig faction in Massachusetts and the Northeast. In contrast to the antislavery Whigs' emphasis on the moral evil of slavery and unqualified opposition to its extension by the annexation of Texas, Davis had emphasized political, economic, legal, and constitutional issues, a position common to textile manufacturing Whigs who did not want to antagonize their southern Whig allies. Restrained support for the antislavery Whigs on the Texas issue ended when abolitionists joined the antislavery movement and threatened to take over the anti-Texas movement.

Davis returned to political office in 1845. The Whigs had recaptured control of the Massachusetts legislature and governorship in 1844. In 1845, over Lawrence's opposition, the legislature elected Webster to the U.S. Senate to replace Rufus Choate, but when the other Massachusetts senator, Isaac C. Bates, died suddenly on 16 March, Lawrence's faction succeeded in electing Davis to replace him. Davis and Webster had not spoken to each other since 1842.

Davis was one of the two senators (along with John M. Clayton of Del.) who voted against the declaration of war against Mexico on 12 May 1846. On 12 August 1846 he spoke at such length in favor of the Wilmot Proviso, an amendment to a military appropriations bill that stipulated that no territory acquired from Mexico would be open to slavery, that the Senate had no time to vote. The bill had already passed the House. Davis later explained that he had intended to speak long enough to leave time only for a vote, which he thought would be positive. He doubted opponents of the proviso would refuse needed military appropriations and delay peace negotiations, and he claimed simply to have misjudged the time. Scholars remain divided on the plausibility of Davis's explanation and whether the bill would have passed had it come to a vote.

Whatever support Davis had gained from the antislavery Whigs, now known as "Conscience Whigs," for his nearly solitary opposition to the vote for war with Mexico he lost as a result of his Wilmot Proviso speech. Conscience Whigs accused him of willfully preventing a vote that would have divided northern and southern Whigs (now referred to as "Cotton Whigs") and would have threatened the close relations between Massachusetts cotton textile manufacturers and southern Whig planters. Davis made no attempt to appease the Conscience Whigs and thereafter promoted official Whig policy of a speedy peace with Mexico with no annexation of territory. In 1848 Conscience Whigs joined Webster's supporters in an unsuccessful attempt to prevent Davis's reelection.

Davis's hostility toward Webster and continued opposition to the expansion of slave territory determined his position on the bills that comprised the Compromise of 1850. Davis voted against the bills for the territorial organization of Utah and New Mexico, both of which were silent on the establishment of slavery during the territorial stage but allowed the territories to apply for statehood "with or without slavery as their constitution may prescribe." He also voted against the harsh Fugitive Slave Bill, which made it more difficult for northern states to avoid returning fugitive slaves to their southern owners, a bill that Webster insisted was necessary to preserve the Union. Davis supported the bills for the admission of California as a free state, the Texas–New Mexico boundary settlement and federal assumption of a substantial part of the Texas debt as compensation, and the abolition of the slave trade in the District of Columbia.

Davis's opposition to Webster continued after the passage of the compromise bills. He regarded Webster's support for the Compromise of 1850 as an attempt to appease the South and win southern Whig support for the presidential nomination, and he joined his fellow Cotton Whigs in securing the nomination for Winfield Scott in 1852. He campaigned actively for Scott in the election. Davis declined renomination for the Senate and retired from his seat on 3 March 1853.

Davis spent his remaining years in Worcester, where he served as president of the American Antiquarian Society. Known as "Honest John" for his integrity, he was a solid and reliable politician whose strength was his loyalty and pragmatism rather than his brilliance or imagination. He died in Worcester, Massachusetts.

• Davis's papers are in the American Antiquarian Society of Worcester, Mass. Information on Davis is in Arthur B. Darling, *Political Changes in Massachusetts, 1824–1828: A Study of Liberal Movements in Politics* (1925); Ronald P. Formisano, *The Transformation of Political Culture: Massachusetts Parties, 1790s–1840s* (1983); Kinley J. Brauer, *Cotton versus Conscience: Massachusetts Whig Politics and Southwestern Expansion, 1843–1848* (1967); and Martin B. Duberman, *Charles Francis Adams, 1807–1886* (1960).

KINLEY BRAUER

DAVIS, John Chandler Bancroft. *See* Davis, Bancroft.

DAVIS, John Wesley (16 Apr. 1799–22 Aug. 1859), physician and Indiana legislator, was born in New Holland, Pennsylvania, the son of the Reverend John Davis and Margaret Jones. The family later moved to Cumberland County, near Shippensburg, where John worked on the family farm, had brief apprenticeships with a clockmaker and a storekeeper, and then began the study of medicine in the office of George D. Fouke of Carlisle. As part of his medical study, Davis attended medical lectures at the University of Maryland in Baltimore during the winters of 1819–1820 and 1820–1821. In the fall of 1820 he married Ann Hoover of Shippensburg, with whom he had ten children. After graduating from medical school in April 1821, Davis began practicing medicine in Pennsylvania and then in Maryland, but he realized only a modest return. In 1823 he moved to Carlisle, Indiana, where he established a successful medical practice and soon entered public life.

His political career got off to an inauspicious start in 1828 when Davis was defeated in a race for the state senate. The next year, however, he was elected judge of the Sullivan County Probate Court, the first of a series of electoral and appointed offices Davis filled with great competence if not distinction. His career as a legislator began in 1831 when he was elected to the Indiana General Assembly, the first of what would eventually be six scattered terms. He was reelected without opposition in 1832 and soon found himself in the Speaker's chair. His studious background made him a fine parliamentarian; his demeanor and sense of fairness made him an attractive presiding officer. This demeanor, however, could be challenged by party loyalty. He once remarked to a persistent heckler, "My friend, to save you trouble and me annoyance, I will say now that I endorse everything the Democratic party ever has done, and everything that it ever will do."

Due to such loyalty, President Andrew Jackson appointed him to serve as one of the Indian treaty commissioners in negotiations with the Prairie Potawatomi in October 1832. These negotiations resulted in another large transfer of territory, the eventual removal of the Potawatomi, and additional recognition of Davis as a "Jackson man." Eventually he served four terms in the House of Representatives (the 24th, 26th, 28th, and 29th Congresses) and held the Speakership during the Twenty-ninth Congress, which dealt with the issues preliminary to and attendant to the war with Mexico in 1846 and 1847. In Congress, Davis supported continuation of the Cumberland, or National, Road; improvements to waterways in the Midwest; graduation (the gradual reduction of western land prices); and economy in the military. On slavery his stance was generally prosouthern, and he favored the American Colonization Society and its state subsidiaries.

Declining to seek reelection to Congress in 1846, Davis accepted an appointment from President James K. Polk to become the American commissioner to China. Davis returned home in 1850 and served again in the state legislature and as Speaker. In 1852 he was the presiding officer of the convention that nominated Franklin Pierce for the presidency. After his election, Pierce appointed Davis to the governorship of the Oregon Territory, where he served for slightly less than a year before returning to Indiana and eventually to another term in the state legislature. His final public service was his appointment in 1858 as a visitor to the U.S. Military Academy at West Point. Davis died the following year at his home in Carlisle, Indiana.

• A few of Davis's letters appear in *The John Tipton Papers*, ed. Nellie Armstrong Robertson and Dorothy Riker (3 vols., 1942), and in manuscript collections at the Indiana Historical Society Library and the Indiana State Library in Indianapolis. The most useful published sources on his life are Thomas J. Wolfe, *A History of Sullivan County, Indiana*, vol. 1 (1909), pp. 46–49, and William Wesley Woollen, *Biographical and Historical Sketches of Early Indiana* (1883), which includes a brief autobiographical account by Davis written in 1858 or 1859. Hope Bedford wrote a short thesis on his career, "John Wesley Davis" (master's Thesis, Butler Univ., 1930).

RALPH D. GRAY

DAVIS, John William (13 Apr. 1873–24 Mar. 1955), lawyer and Democratic presidential candidate, was born in Clarksburg, West Virginia, the son of John James Davis, a prominent attorney, Presbyterian elder, and former congressman, and Anna Kennedy. Davis earned both the A.B. (1892) and LL.B. (1895) at Washington and Lee University, where he also taught law for one year. In June 1899 he married Julia McDonald of Charles Town. Fourteen months later

she died after giving birth to a daughter, who survived. In 1912 he married Ellen Graham Bassel of Clarksburg; they had no children.

Meanwhile, Davis's practice with his father in Clarksburg flourished. His exceptional skill attracted corporations, and by 1910, when he won election to Congress, his clients included some of the most important railroad, mining, and lumber companies in the state. He was appointed to the Judiciary Committee, a rare distinction for a freshman.

Davis was conservative on issues such as woman suffrage and regulation of business but moderately liberal on others. He supported President Woodrow Wilson's New Freedom, especially tariff reform. He also sympathized with labor to a point. Unwilling, as he confided to his mother, "to go . . . [labor's] length and pull down the pillars of the temple" by abolishing the writ of injunction in labor disputes, he nevertheless drafted the restrictive injunction clause of the Clayton Antitrust Act of 1914. His speech on abuse of the writ, wrote Felix Frankfurter, was the "ablest" of the entire debate. Davis won further acclaim for his summation in the impeachment trial of federal judge Robert W. Archbald in 1912–1913.

Appointed solicitor general in 1913, Davis argued most of the more notable constitutional cases of the Progressive Era during a five-year tenure. In spite of a strong personal commitment to states' rights, he won rulings that overturned Oklahoma's antiblack "grandfather clause" on voting rights and declared Alabama's convict lease (peonage) system a form of involuntary servitude. He successfully defended federal authority to regulate interstate oil pipelines. He also won affirmation of the government's right, as exercised in the Adamson Act of 1916, to regulate railroad wages under limited conditions. Conversely, Davis lost the first child labor case (*Hammer v. Dagenhart*) and failed to persuade the Supreme Court that the U.S. Steel Corporation was a monopoly in restraint of trade. All told, he won forty-eight of the sixty-seven cases he argued orally. "Of all the persons who appeared before the Court in my time," said Justice Oliver Wendell Holmes, "there was never anybody more elegant, more clear, more concise or more logical than John W. Davis."

In September 1918, while en route to a German-American conference on prisoners of war in Switzerland, Davis was named ambassador to the Court of St. James's. Called temporarily to Paris in 1919 to draft a convention for the occupation of the Rhineland, he played an influential role in providing for civilian control of the occupying army over the vigorous opposition of Marshal Ferdinand Foch. Meanwhile Davis's dignity and grace, his sensitivity and fair-mindedness, earned him the esteem of the British establishment. Davis, said King George V, "was one of the most perfect gentlemen I have ever met." The British gave him their confidence to a surprising degree. (Except for a shipboard talk en route to England, President Wilson had no substantive communication whatever with Davis during his two and a half years as ambassador.) Davis eased tension somewhat between British and American representatives over Ireland and the aspirations of both groups in the oil fields of the Middle East.

In 1920 Davis refused to encourage a boomlet for his nomination for president. He returned to the United States in 1921 and became head of an eminent Wall Street law firm, later Davis Polk Wardwell. Among the firm's clientele was J. P. Morgan and Company. Four years later the prolonged deadlock imposed on the Democratic National Convention by the presidential aspirations of Senator William G. McAdoo of California and Governor Alfred E. Smith of New York enabled Davis to win his party's presidential nomination on the 103d ballot. He quite understood that the lingering resentment of Irish Americans and other ethnic groups opposed to the war and the peace settlement, as well as the prosperity under the Republican administrations of Presidents Warren G. Harding and Calvin Coolidge, made the nomination an empty honor. "Thanks," he said to a friend, "but you know what it's worth."

Conceiving it as his duty to hold the party together, Davis repressed his desire to call unequivocally for U.S. membership in the League of Nations and on the World Court. His mild denunciations of the Ku Klux Klan drove many Democrats to the Republicans, and his failure to present a progressive alternative to Coolidge drove others to the third-party candidate, Senator Robert M. La Follette of Wisconsin. The election returns gave Davis a little more than eight million popular votes to Coolidge's sixteen million and La Follette's almost five million.

In the divisive presidential campaign of Governor Smith against Secretary of Commerce Herbert Hoover, Davis spoke eloquently for Smith, a Catholic, and for the cause of religious freedom. He also gave nominal support to Franklin D. Roosevelt in 1932. Yet he opposed Roosevelt's domestic program almost from the beginning, and he soon joined Smith, the du Ponts, and other conservatives in organizing the anti–New Deal Liberty League. He further bored into the New Deal in a half dozen lawsuits, including one against the National Labor Relations Act. As he aged, Davis became increasingly intolerant of social and economic reform, and even as he supported the United Nations and most of the Truman-Eisenhower Cold War policies, he flailed Truman's Fair Deal. Mainly, however, he devoted himself to the practice of law.

Davis's legal philosophy was no less traditional than was his political philosophy. Although he was adaptable to a point, as his briefs and oral arguments demonstrated, he remained fervently attached to states' rights, strict constitutional construction, and stare decisis, the principle of basing judicial decisions on precedent. "Somewhere, sometime," he declared in arguing for "separate but equal" in the school segregation suit of 1954 (*Brown v. Board of Education*), "to every principle comes a moment of repose when it has been so often announced, so confidently relied upon,

so long continued, that it passes the limits of judicial discretion and distrust."

Davis further insisted that human and property rights were inseparable. Though he regarded himself as a Jeffersonian, his economic views were in fact Spencerian. He accepted the aggregation of great wealth as a function of the natural order, except as economic power was used to foster monopoly, and he consistently deplored steeply graduated income and inheritance taxes. His arguments against expansion of the commerce clause in the 1920s and 1930s reinforced these views. Conversely, Davis retained a mild civil libertarian strain to the end. He defended selective conscientious objection in a pro bono case in 1931, *U.S. v. Macintosh*, and he served as counsel to J. Robert Oppenheimer, accused of being a security risk, in 1954. Yet Davis never really lived up to his declaration in 1946 that the "supreme function" of lawyers was to be "sleepless sentinels on the ramparts of human liberty and there to sound the alarm whenever an enemy appears."

Davis's true distinction was as an appellate lawyer. He argued more cases—141—before the Supreme Court than any lawyer to that time. His greatest victory, *Youngstown Sheet & Tube Co. v. Sawyer*, came in 1952. President Truman's seizure of the steel industry, he averred in oral argument, was not only a usurpation of power without parallel in American annals, but "a reassertion of the kingly prerogative, the struggle against which illumines all the pages of Anglo-Saxon history." A modest man for all his eminence, Davis deemed his own achievements as relatively small: "I seem to have been caught at the skirt of great events without really quite influencing them." He died in Charleston, South Carolina.

• The John W. Davis Papers at Yale University include personal and professional correspondence from the early 1920s to Davis's death, a four-volume ambassadorial diary, a number of scrapbooks, and numerous photographs. They also include typescripts of Davis's disappointingly uninformative oral memoir (the original is in the Oral History Collection at Columbia University) and interviews with his family, friends, and associates. The papers of John James Davis and Julia McDonald Davis at West Virginia University are extremely useful for his early life. William H. Harbaugh, *Lawyer's Lawyer: The Life of John W. Davis* (1973), is a full-scale biography. Robert K. Murray, *The 103rd Ballot* (1976), describes the presidential campaign of 1924. Much insight into Davis can be gleaned from Julia Davis, *Legacy of Love* (1961). Also see her *The Embassy Girls* (1992). Julia Davis and Dolores A. Fleming, eds., *The Ambassadorial Diary of John W. Davis* (1993), includes virtually everything of importance in the original. An obituary is in the *New York Times*, 25 Mar. 1955.

WILLIAM H. HARBAUGH

DAVIS, Katharine Bement (15 Jan. 1860–10 Dec. 1935), social worker, prison reformer, and sex researcher, was born in Buffalo, New York, the daughter of Frances Bement and Oscar Bill Davis, a manager for the Bradstreet Company, precursor of Dun and Bradstreet, the credit rating firm. When her father suffered business reversals following the panic of 1873, Davis had to postpone plans for college and work as a public school teacher for ten years. She continued her studies independently and in 1890 entered Vassar College at the age of thirty, graduating two years later with honors.

Davis began her career in food chemistry and nutrition, influenced by Vassar graduate Ellen H. Richards, a pioneer in the field of domestic science. While pursuing graduate study in food chemistry at Columbia University in 1892–1893, Davis taught at Brooklyn Heights Seminary for Girls. In 1893 she was tapped to set up a model worker's home at the World's Columbian Exposition in Chicago. Her task was "to [im]personate a workingman's wife who has four children to care for and whose husband earns about $450 a year," the average worker's income at the time (letter to Edward Atkinson, 1 Apr. 1893, Massachusetts Historical Society). The experiment propelled Davis from domestic science into social work. She was offered a position as head resident of the St. Mary's Street College Settlement in Philadelphia. Following the example of Jane Addams's Hull-House, Davis instituted reading rooms, educational classes, and clubs for her largely immigrant and African-American neighbors. She also established model tenements. Once, when the city proved too slow in condemning a substandard boardinghouse, Davis took matters into her own hands and smashed all the windows.

In 1897 Davis left the settlement to begin doctoral work in political economy at the University of Chicago, where she studied with Thorstein Veblen and minored in the new field of sociology. She received her Ph.D., cum laude, in 1900.

Whether Davis wished to pursue an academic career is unclear, but discrimination against women in the academy largely precluded a university position, even at a time when few faculty members could boast a Ph.D. Of the first fifteen women doctorates graduated from the University of Chicago in the social sciences, not one received an academic appointment. Davis, on the advice of influential Boston philanthropist Josephine Shaw Lowell, took the New York civil service examination in preparation for an appointment as superintendent of the newly opened Reformatory for Women at Bedford Hills.

At the reformatory beginning in January 1901 Davis initiated a program emphasizing education and employment. The inmate population consisted primarily of women between the ages of sixteen and thirty, most convicted of relatively minor crimes such as drunkenness, vagrancy, prostitution, and petty larceny. Davis's work in political economy and sociology convinced her that women's crime generally resulted from low wages, inequality, and inadequate employment. She set out to expand women's options through classes and vocational training, and she put her charges to work outdoors landscaping and laying cement walkways on the reformatory grounds. Although it was common for men to learn trades in prison, up until Davis launched her experiment at Bedford Hills women inmates did little more than domestic tasks designed to prepare them for work as servants on their return to society.

Only when she was faced with overcrowding and recidivism did Davis temper her enthusiasm for rehabilitation by calling for separate facilities for "defectives," whom she deemed incorrigible. To develop a scientific way to predict an inmate's prospects for rehabilitation, Davis in 1910 hired a resident psychologist to administer tests to inmates.

Davis's conviction that scientific research should form the basis for prison sentencing led in 1912 to a joint enterprise with John D. Rockefeller, Jr. Rockefeller had become concerned with the problem of prostitution when he served on a special grand jury impaneled in 1910 to investigate commercialized vice in New York City. He put his enormous philanthropic clout behind research into social vice and crime, creating a Bureau of Social Hygiene in 1911. Impressed with Davis, whom he once described as "the cleverest woman I have ever met," he purchased land adjacent to Bedford Hills and in 1912 established a Laboratory of Social Hygiene where Davis could study female offenders.

During this period Davis gained international recognition for her emergency relief work in Messina, Sicily. When a severe earthquake occurred while Davis was on vacation in 1909, she joined relief workers, and her efforts won her medals from the Red Cross and from King Victor Emmanuel, as well as a commendation from the pope.

In 1914 Davis left Bedford Hills when reform mayor John Purroy Mitchel appointed her commissioner of corrections for New York City. Davis became the first woman to hold a cabinet-level position in the city's government. As commissioner she abolished striped uniforms for prisoners, developed a farm colony for boys in Orange County, and initiated a drug treatment center. She won praise in 1914 when she quelled a riot among male prisoners on Blackwell's Island. In 1915, after the press attacked conditions in the city's jails, a state commission set out to investigate Davis's leadership, which some complained was "too severe." The mayor and other prison reformers rallied to her defense, and Davis rode out the storm. She resigned as commissioner in 1915 to head the parole board after the passage of an indeterminate sentence law that she had actively supported. In 1917 Mayor Mitchel failed to win reelection, and Davis lost her position.

Davis moved immediately to the Rockefeller Bureau of Social Hygiene. Under her direction from 1917 to 1928, the bureau expanded its research into the broader fields of public health and social hygiene. During World War I Davis headed a subcommittee on women and girls under the auspices of the Commission on Training Camp Activities' Social Hygiene Division. Upon her return to the bureau in 1920, she undertook an ambitious study of female sexuality. *Factors in the Sex Life of Twenty-two Hundred Women* (1929) was a landmark work that showed that behaviors considered deviant—including masturbation, homosexual activity, and multiple sexual partners—were common among the college and club women who made up her sample.

The board of directors of the Bureau of Social Hygiene took a dim view of Davis's sex research and tried to limit the book's distribution. Even before its publication the board convinced Rockefeller to terminate Davis's appointment.

Davis retired in 1928 to Pacific Grove, California, where she lived with her two sisters, who, like Davis, had never married. She died in Pacific Grove.

• Some Davis papers may be found in the Bureau of Social Hygiene Collection, Rockefeller Archive Center, North Tarrytown, N.Y. One of Davis's published works is "Why They Failed to Marry," *Harper's Magazine*, Mar. 1928, pp. 460–69. A brief autobiographical treatment of her early life and education appears in "Three Score Years and Ten," *University of Chicago Magazine*, Dec. 1933, pp. 58–61, and a biographical piece is Jean Henry Large, "A Man's Job," *University of Chicago Magazine*, Jan. 1934, pp. 105–8. The best recent treatment of Davis can be found in Ellen Fitzpatrick, *Endless Crusade: Women Social Scientists and Progressive Reform* (1990). See also Estelle Freedman, *Their Sisters' Keepers* (1981); and Fitzpatrick, ed., *Katharine Bement Davis, Early 20th Century American Women, and the Study of Sex Behavior* (1987). Obituaries are in the *New York Times* and the *Herald Tribune*, both 11 Dec. 1935.

SARAH STAGE

DAVIS, Mary Evelyn Moore (12 Apr. 1852?–1 Jan. 1909), author, was born in Talladega, Alabama, the daughter of John Moore, a physician, and Marian Lucinda Crutchfield. (Some sources cite her year of birth as 1844.) At a young age she moved with her family to a plantation in Texas, where she was home schooled and became an avid reader of both French and Spanish literature. Little is known about her early family history, except that her father was descended from two prominent Puritan families in Massachusetts and that her maternal uncles reportedly fought on both sides during the Civil War. In 1874 she married Thomas Edward Davis, a former officer in the Confederate army and, at the time of their marriage, editor in chief of the *Houston Telegraph*. He later became editor in chief of the *New Orleans Daily Picayune*. Their marriage was childless, and Major Davis appears to have been quite supportive of his wife's literary efforts, as her poems and short stories were published in his newspapers.

Judging by the dates of publication given for her many works, Davis, who went by "Mollie," seems to have written prolifically throughout her adult life, apparently in spite of a chronic malady that kept her bedridden for long periods of time. Her first novel, *In War Times at La Rose Blanche* (1888), later was described as a "beautiful history of the life of the Southern people, who were left at home during the great struggle between the North and South." According to her obituary, many of the incidents in the novel were taken from Davis's own childhood, but because of the dearth of information regarding her early life, the text's autobiographical reliability is impossible to determine. The story, of the Civil War and its effect on

both the Euro-American and African-American inhabitants of a plantation located in Northeast Texas, is told from a particularly southern perspective.

Davis spent most of her adult life in New Orleans, where she became very familiar with the local Creole culture and helped to organize a variety of literary organizations. Her novels, short stories, and poetry are set predominantly in post–Civil War New Orleans. Her abundant use of the many dialects that were spoken in the Deep South in the late nineteenth and early twentieth centuries, coupled with her keen eye for physical description, qualify Davis as a regional writer of local color fiction. In his introduction to her short story "The Love-Stranche" for the *Library of Southern Literature*, William B. Smith wrote that "it is in the short story, that form of literature originated and perfected by the coryphaeus of Southern letters, that Mrs. Davis has perhaps achieved her most eminent success" (p. 1275). Several of her short stories were published in what Smith described as "the Northern monthlies" (*Harper's*, *Atlantic Monthly*). It is her novels, however, that seem to offer greater complexity for the modern reader.

The Queen's Garden (1900), a romance novel that tells the story of a Creole girl who travels from Texas to New Orleans to be reunited with her dead father's sister, contains extensive descriptions of the gardens found in the city's historic French Quarter. These descriptions serve as metaphors for the problem of determining racial identity in the intertwined blood lines of Creole culture. Davis's most complex novel, and the one that represents the fullest development of character to be found in her collected work, is *The Price of Silence* (1907), an examination of the aftermath of the Civil War and its effects on the upper classes of New Orleans Creole society as well as the cultures of both the North and South. One character, the grandson of a Union officer, speaks with a northern dialect. Davis's rendering of his speech patterns is not only well done; it is virtually unheard-of in the work of local color artists recognized as representative of the southern regions.

Davis's work is interesting because it intermingles seemingly disparate cultural perspectives and thereby offers varied readings of historical events that have tended to be understood only in "Yankee" terms. Her poem "Pere Dagobert" (1896), for example, describes the turn-of-the-century French, Catholic, Creole culture of New Orleans by incorporating both French and English descriptions of Dagobert, the leader of the city's French Catholic Capuchin monastery. Conversely, but with equal facility, a Creole patois is used in the poem "Throwing the Wanga" (1896) in order to depict the practice of voodoo in the city's African and Caribbean communities. In particular, the poem describes how one woman uses voodoo to win back "her man" from another woman who has cast a Wanga, or spell, over him.

Davis, who had a great interest in Texas as well as Louisiana, also wrote *Under Six Flags: The Story of Texas* (1897; repr. 1953), a southern version of the history of Texas in which the role of French colonial interests and the predominance of Catholicism in the newly established state of Texas are emphasized. Essentially a children's history of the settlement of Texas, *Under Six Flags* was used as a primary school textbook in the early years of the twentieth century. Another of Davis's books, *Under the Man-Fig* (1895), is set in a small Texas town. This historically based romance novel chronicles the state's development from the end of the Civil War until the beginning of the Spanish-American War in 1898.

Although considered local color literature, her writings are more diverse than the term denotes. Her effective overlapping of dialects and languages and her presentation of a southern perspective that acknowledges yet refuses to justify its difference from a northern perspective distinguish her prolific output. Unusual for the work of a southern writer is her emphasis on Catholicism. Also uncommon, for a woman writer of her period, is her examination of race relations. Davis died in New Orleans.

• The University of Texas at Austin houses archival materials on Davis, and some information on her is available through the Historical Society of New Orleans. Most of her poetic works that were published in periodicals were later published in collections, such as *Minding the Gap and Other Poems* (1867?), *Poems by Mollie E. Moore* (1869? or 1872?), and the posthumously published *Selected Poems by Mollie Moore Davis*, ed. Grace King (1927). Her short stories can largely be found in *An Elephant's Track, and Other Stories* (1897). The only critical work done on Davis can be found in William B. Smith's biographical essay in the *Library of Southern Literature* (1907–1913) and in C. W. Wilkinson, "The Broadening Stream: The Life and Literary Career of Mollie E. Moore Davis" (Ph.D. diss., Univ. of Illinois, 1947). Davis's obituary in the *Daily Picayune*, 2 Jan. 1909, which seems to rely heavily on Smith's essay, is the most complete source of information on the author and her work.

LESLIEE ANTONETTE

DAVIS, Mary Fenn Robinson (17 July 1824–18 July 1886), Spiritualist lecturer and women's rights advocate, was born in Clarendon, New York, the daughter of Chauncey Robinson and Damaris Fenn, farmers. She grew up in Randolph, New York, in a Baptist family. In 1846 she married Samuel G. Love, with whom she had two children. Both she and her husband found the Calvanist theology oppressive, however, and the bonds of marriage constricting. Two new movements that appeared during the next few years reflected their views and quickly gained their participation: Spiritualism and women's rights. Her contributions to Spiritualist periodicals began in 1850 with a poem, "To Our Spirit Guardian," published under the name "Mrs. S. G. Love" in the *Spirited Messenger* (12 Oct. 1850), and continued until her death. Her articles argued for greater autonomy for women and freer access to divorce, as well as addressing more general concerns of women's rights and Spiritualism. She served as vice president of the New York State Woman's Rights Convention of 1853, where she attracted attention for her address critiquing marriage and the

double standard, warning that "the chief evils of society" spring from "domestic uncongeniality." The following year she traveled to Indiana to obtain a divorce from Samuel Love. Shortly thereafter she married Andrew Jackson Davis, who shared her views about the immorality of loveless marriages. Davis, a prophet of American Spiritualism, was revered as a font of visionary wisdom by believers. Together, they devoted themselves to the promotion of the new faith and to keeping it closely tied to a program of women's rights, abolition, and social reform.

A more accomplished speaker than her husband, Davis frequently spoke on women's rights to large audiences at Spiritualist conventions. She added to the notoriety of the 1859 Rutland (Vt.) Free Convention by charging that the economic disabilities of women made marriage a form of prostitution. From 1860 to 1864 she and her husband published the *Herald of Progress*, a weekly devoted to Spiritualism and progressive reform. During these years New York City Spiritualists viewed her as "the presiding spirit" of their weekly Sunday meetings at Dodsworth Hall, where she opened each meeting, gave frequent lectures, and conducted "the Children's Lyceum," the Spiritualist Sunday school program she founded with her husband.

After the Civil War, Davis added woman suffrage to her reform concerns. She helped organize the New Jersey State Woman Suffrage Association in 1867, often serving as an officer both of the State Association and of the Orange (N.J.) Woman Suffrage Club. When the first women's literary club, Sorosis, began in New York City the following year, Davis was an avid participant, serving as vice president in 1873 and attempting to add concern for underprivileged women to the club's interests.

In 1876 Davis's daughter died giving birth to twins, and she withdrew from public life to care for her four young grandchildren. In 1885 her husband and co-worker of thirty years informed her that he had discovered his true "spiritual affinity" in another woman. The announcement cost him much of his reputation in reform circles, where his wife was as highly esteemed as he. Nevertheless, the sixty-year-old Davis, true to her principles, received the news with apparent equanimity and did not fight the ensuing divorce. She assumed her mother's maiden name, Fenn, and died a year and a half later at her son-in-law's home in West Orange, New Jersey.

• Most of Davis's own writing appears in Spiritualist periodicals such as *Banner of Light*, *Herald of Progress*, *Spiritual Age*, and *Spirit Messenger*, as well as in *National Anti-Slavery Standard* and *Ladies Own Magazine*. Davis also published two pamphlets: *Danger Signals: An Address on the Uses and Abuses of Modern Spiritualism* (1875) and *Death in the Light of Harmonial Philosophy* (1876). Biographical information is in the autobiographical works of Andrew Jackson Davis, *The Magic Staff* (1857), *Memoranda of Persons, Places, and Events* (1868), and *Beyond the Valley* (1885). Her women's rights activities can be followed in Paulina Wright Davis, *A History of the National Woman's Rights Movement* (1871), and E. C.

Stanton et al., *History of Woman Suffrage*, vols. 2 and 3 (1882–1886). See also Ann Braude, *Radical Spirits: Spiritualism and Women's Rights in Nineteenth-Century America* (1989), and Ernest Joseph Isaacs, *A History of Nineteenth-Century American Spiritualism as a Religious and Social Movement* (Ph.D. diss., Univ. of Wisconsin, 1975). Obituaries are in the *Banner of Light*, 31 July and 7 Aug. 1886; *Woman's Journal*, 24 July 1886; and *Light*, 21 Aug. 1886.

ANN D. BRAUDE

DAVIS, Miles (25 May 1926–28 Sept. 1991), jazz trumpeter and bandleader, was born Miles Dewey Davis III in Alton, Illinois, the son of Miles Dewey Davis, Jr., a dentist, and Cleota Henry. When Davis was one year old, the family moved to East St. Louis, Missouri, where his father practiced dental surgery and farmed, raising special breeds of hogs. They settled in a white neighborhood while Davis was in elementary school.

He took up trumpet at age thirteen, studying in school and taking private lessons from jazz trumpeter Elwood Buchanan and the first trumpeter with the St. Louis Symphony, Joseph Gustat. At age sixteen he began playing professionally, joining Eddie Randle's Blue Devils. He also played informally with trumpeter Clark Terry around 1942, before Terry was drafted. Around 1944 Davis began a relationship with Irene Birth, a dancer and fellow student at Lincoln High School. They had three children but never married; they separated permanently in 1950.

Davis finished school but missed his graduation to tour for two weeks with a swing combo in June 1944. Sitting in with singer Billy Eckstine's big band at the Riviera Club in St. Louis, he met trumpeter Dizzy Gillespie and alto saxophonist Charlie Parker. Davis joined Eckstine's band for its next engagement, in Chicago.

Early in 1945 Davis went to New York City to enroll at the Institute of Musical Art (later the Juilliard School of Music). His announced intention, to satisfy his parents, was to pursue classical studies; but a career in the racist culture of mid-century American symphony orchestras was an impossibility, and anyway he had no interest in classical music. His actual intention was to spend as much time as possible playing bebop with Parker (who became his roommate) and Gillespie while working on jazz trumpeting and piano harmony in the institute's practice rooms.

That fall Davis went home to tell his father that he was dropping out of the institute. Receiving encouragement, he returned to New York to play jazz professionally. He joined Parker's quintet at the Three Deuces nightclub in October 1945. The following month he continued with Parker at the Spotlite club and recorded with Parker for the Savoy label. He then formed a trio with pianist Sir Charles Thompson and drummer Connie Kay for an engagement at Minton's Playhouse in Harlem, where Parker, Gillespie, and others sat in, and he remained at Minton's with tenor saxophonist Coleman Hawkins's group. At this point Davis stopped sharing his apartment with Parker and instead roomed with the underrecorded and now legendary trumpeter Freddie Webster, whose beautiful tone and sense of melodic economy Davis reportedly emulated.

Home for Christmas, Davis joined alto saxophonist Benny Carter's big band at the Riviera and toured west with Carter. In Los Angeles he worked with Carter's small group while doubling after hours with Parker for jam sessions at the Finale club. In 1946 he made his first recordings with Parker for the Dial label, including "Yardbird Suite" and "Ornithology." After working with bassist Charles Mingus and tenor saxophonist Lucky Thompson, he joined Eckstine around September 1946. En route with the big band back to New York, he played with saxophonists Gene Ammons and Sonny Stitt in the first of what would later become annual Christmastime stopovers in Chicago, where his sister settled.

Eckstine's group disbanded in February 1947. Davis joined Gillespie's big band until April, when Parker formed a quintet with pianist Duke Jordan, bassist Tommy Potter, and drummer Max Roach. With the Three Deuces on Fifty-second Street and later the Royal Roost on Broadway serving as their home base, the quintet toured extensively and remained reasonably stable in light of Parker's notoriously irresponsible behavior. John Lewis, Tadd Dameron, and Al Haig took over the piano chair at various points, and Curley Russell temporarily replaced Potter. For Savoy in May 1947 the quintet recorded Davis's composition "Donna Lee," a dauntingly difficult but beautifully crafted melodic bop theme. Davis also made further sessions with Parker's group on Dial.

During this period Davis met arranger Gil Evans, who helped with questions about jazz harmony and supplied an arrangement of "Robbin's Nest" in exchange for permission to use "Donna Lee" in pianist Claude Thornhill's band. Davis subsequently became involved in a casual group of musicians who congregated at Evans's basement apartment, including Lewis and saxophonists Gerry Mulligan and Lee Konitz. Having become the partner of the leading bop musician, Parker, Davis was about to take the first of several path-breaking steps in his career, instigating a significant departure from bop: cool jazz. Evans's circle wanted to capture the understated sound of Thornhill's big band, but with its instrumentation pared down to trumpet, trombone, French horn, tuba, alto and baritone saxophones, piano, bass, and drums, and with a subtle balance drawn between big band arrangement and small combo improvisation. Davis was the key: " 'He took the initiative and put the theories to work,' Mulligan says. 'He called the rehearsals, hired the halls, called the players, and generally cracked the whip' " (Chambers, vol. 1, p. 99).

While at the Royal Roost, Davis secured two weeks for the nonet in September 1948. Their reception was uneventful, but after Davis and Roach quit Parker's quintet on 23 December 1948, the nonet made now-classic recordings for Capitol that were eventually collected and reissued under the rubric *Birth of the Cool*.

In addition to the import of the group's playing, Davis here recorded his first great solos on "Godchild," "Move" (both Jan. 1949), and his own composition "Boplicity" (Apr. 1949). Freed from the hectic pace of Parker's melodic world, Davis showed qualities of relaxation, swing, timbral beauty, and melodic nuance that became hallmarks of his personal style.

Davis returned to the Royal Roost as the featured soloist in Dameron's Big Ten for three weeks in February to March, and a Davis-Dameron quintet performed at the first Festival International de Jazz in Paris in early May 1949. After returning to New York, Davis became hooked on heroin, as had so many of his eminent colleagues, including Parker, Dameron, Mulligan, Ammons, Roach, saxophonists Stan Getz and Sonny Rollins, drummer Art Blakey, and trumpeter Fats Navarro. Writer Jack Chambers points out that the wonder is not that Davis became addicted, but that he had managed to avoid addiction for so long in this environment.

Davis and Getz co-led a sextet at the club Birdland in February 1950. While on tour once again with Eckstine in September 1950, Davis and Blakey were arrested in Los Angeles for drug possession. They were acquitted, but Davis had trouble finding steady work as a result of the negative publicity. He led a band accompanying singer Billie Holiday at the Hi-Note club in Chicago during the Christmas and New Year holidays. Back in New York, he recorded "Au Private" and "Star Eyes" with Parker on 17 January 1951. He held periodic engagements as a bandleader at Birdland and obscure, irregular jobs in other cities, and he made numerous recordings that were less than his best, before returning to his father's farm early in 1954, locking himself in his bedroom, and suffering through heroin withdrawal.

Going to Detroit, Davis worked at the Bluebird Inn with tenor saxophonist Billy Mitchell's band for a few months. In his autobiography he says that he resumed narcotic use; but the available drug was so diluted that it had little effect, and he soon stopped altogether. Returning to New York in the spring of 1954, he began to work out in a gymnasium, training as a boxer.

Over the next fifteen years the now-recovered Davis made a succession of consistently brilliant recordings. Such a sustained creative outburst is unparalleled in jazz, and in a concise overview, one can list only some of these tracks and albums and describe those that altered the course of jazz, without doing justice to the many sessions that are "merely" brilliant without being path-breaking. The first were done for the Prestige label in an affiliation that dated back to Davis's fallow period and that bore fruit with "Walkin'" (Apr. 1954), "Airegin," "Oleo," "But Not for Me," and "Doxy" with Rollins (June 1954) and "Bags' Groove" and "The Man I Love" with Thelonious Monk in a session at which the two men nearly came to blows but still managed to play their best (Dec. 1954). Percy Heath played bass and Kenny Clarke, drums, on all three sessions, with Horace Silver on piano in April and June and Milt Jackson, vibraphone, in December.

On the date with Rollins, Davis introduced the stemless harmon mute, producing a quietly brooding, intense, buzzing sound of such originality that any jazz trumpeter who subsequently used this device automatically evoked Davis's name. He used the stemless harmon mute to play "'Round about Midnight" in the course of an acclaimed cameo appearance with Monk's group at the Newport Jazz Festival in July 1955.

Davis then formed his first lasting quintet, with Rollins, pianist Red Garland, bassist Paul Chambers, and drummer Philly Joe Jones, for an engagement at the Café Bohemia in New York. Tenor saxophonist John Coltrane replaced Rollins for a fall tour of nightclubs, during which time Davis signed with Columbia Records while preparing to complete his obligations to Prestige.

A shrewd and successful businessman who became one of the few affluent African-American jazz musicians, Davis tolerated no compromise over fees. He was equally uncompromising about presentation, making it emphatically clear that he was a musician and not an entertainer. His public behavior became as cold as he could manage, and he became notorious for playing with his back to the audience, refusing to announce tune titles, and walking off the stage altogether. He temporarily disbanded the quintet early in 1956 to have an operation for a growth on his larynx. The irrepressibly contentious Davis then got into a shouting match too soon after surgery and permanently damaged his voice, which became a growly whisper that only added to his off-putting aura.

The quintet's hard bop albums include *'Round about Midnight* for Columbia (1955–1956) and *Cookin' with the Miles Davis Quintet, Relaxin' with the Miles Davis Quintet, Workin' with the Miles Davis Quintet*, and *Steamin' with the Miles Davis Quintet* for Prestige (all 1956). His four sidemen were addicted to heroin, and Jones and Coltrane were especially troublesome, their respectively exhilarating and audacious musical contributions being counterbalanced by their unreliability. Rollins twice replaced Coltrane (Oct. 1956 and Apr.–Sept. 1957); tenor saxophonist Bobby Jaspar (Sept. 1957) and alto saxophonist Cannonball Adderley (Oct. 1957) took over when Rollins formed his own group; and drummer Art Taylor (Apr.–Sept. 1957) and pianist Tommy Flanagan (Sept.–Oct. 1957) filled in for Jones and Garland. In November 1956 and November 1957 Davis traveled to Europe to perform as a soloist, and in the latter year he recorded the soundtrack for director Louis Malle's film *Ascenseur pour l'échafaud*. Later in his career he made many more fall tours to Europe.

During this period Davis initiated a series of orchestral projects with Evans. The first, *Miles Ahead* (May 1957), featured Davis playing flugelhorn (rather than trumpet) over a lush carpet of brass, reed, and rhythm section sounds. *Miles Ahead* and its companion albums constitute the most original and successful departure from the then-stolid conventions of big band writing.

Late in December Coltrane, having overcome his addiction, rejoined Davis, who now led a sextet, including Adderley, Garland, Chambers, and Jones. The group lasted for two years with few changes in personnel; pianists Bill Evans (Apr.–Nov. 1958) and Wynton Kelly (from Feb. 1959) took over for Garland, who formed his own trio, and the comparatively subdued drummer Jimmy Cobb replaced the fiery Jones, whose drug problems persisted. This sextet is regarded by many as the finest small group in the history of jazz.

New recordings included Davis's rare appearance as a sideman, on Adderley's *Somethin' Else* (Mar. 1958); the sextet's *Milestones* (Apr. 1958) and *Kind of Blue* (Mar.–Apr. 1959), with Evans displacing Kelly for most of the latter album; and the second orchestral project, *Porgy and Bess*, presenting Evans's interpretation of George Gershwin's opera with Davis's flugelhorn and muted trumpet functioning in place of vocalists (July–Aug. 1958). The title track of *Milestones*; "So What," "All Blues," and "Flamenco Sketches" from *Kind of Blue*; and portions of the Gershwin project exemplify another landmark in Davis's career, the establishment of a new style, modal jazz, in which the fast-moving chord progressions of bop and its derivatives cool jazz and hard bop gave way to slow-moving or even static harmonies.

In New York on 26 August 1959 Davis was harassed by a white policeman evidently for no reason other than Davis's being with a white woman. He resisted and was beaten severely. Legal actions were dropped after bargaining, but Davis, never one to take an offense lightly, was permanently scarred emotionally.

Adderley left to form his own band in September 1959, and Coltrane followed suit after a European tour from March to April 1960. In the interim Davis recorded his last significant collaboration with Evans, *Sketches of Spain*, which presented a reorchestration of Joachin Rodrigo's *Concierto de Aranjuez* and other Spanish-flavored themes, with Davis's flugelhorn and muted trumpet serving in place of a flamenco guitar. Over the next few years Davis tried to find a suitable saxophonist to replace Coltrane. Among those who passed through the band were Jimmie Heath, Stitt, and Hank Mobley, whom Davis paired with Coltrane for two tracks of the album *Some Day My Prince Will Come* (Mar. 1961).

On 21 December 1960 Davis married Frances Taylor, a dancer whose image graced his mid-1960s album covers. They had no children. Hand in hand with his fame, his Ferrari, his audaciousness, his affluence, his beautiful wife, and his seemingly endless string of extramarital affairs came Davis's "certification" as one of America's handsomest and sexiest men in 1961, when he was placed on the best-dressed list in *Gentlemen's Quarterly*.

After Kelly, Chambers, and Cobb quit to work as a trio at the end of 1962, a second quintet of historic import gradually took shape in the course of recording the album *Seven Steps to Heaven* (Apr.–May 1963). Tenor saxophonist George Coleman, pianist Herbie

Hancock, bassist Ron Carter, and drummer Tony Williams played together from the time of the album *Miles Davis in Europe* (July 1963) through a concert at Philharmonic Hall in New York preserved on *My Funny Valentine* and *"Four" and More* (Feb. 1964). The too-conservative Coleman was replaced by the too-radical free-jazz tenor saxophonist Sam Rivers, who found himself bored with Davis's music during their Japanese tour in the spring, before Davis found the right stylistic mix in saxophonist Wayne Shorter, who joined that summer. Proceeding from compositions that Shorter contributed to Davis's album *E.S.P.* (Jan. 1965), the quintet developed pieces in an offshoot of bop that came to be known as "time, no changes," emphasizing fast tempos and ambiguous chromatic harmony, and Hancock, Carter, and Williams formed perhaps the most flexibly interactive rhythm section ever heard in jazz.

In the mid-1980s Chambers revealed that Davis had for decades suppressed the fact that he had the congenital disease sickle-cell anemia, specific to African Americans. He fought the effects through hard exercise; hence his boxing. By the early 1960s he was in considerable pain, suffering from arthritis, and in the spring of 1965 he underwent a major operation to replace his left hip socket. He resumed his career in November, working at the Village Vanguard in New York before moving during the holidays to the Plugged Nickel in Chicago, where the band was recorded. On 31 January 1966 he was hospitalized for an inflamed liver. He took three more months off, stopped drinking, and then resumed touring nightclubs and college campuses. In June 1967 the quintet recorded the album *Nefertiti*, its title track presenting a novel approach whereby trumpet and saxophone become in effect the accompanists, playing the same melody over and over again, while the members of the rhythm section improvise.

Davis divorced Frances in February 1968. His most frequent companion at this time was actress Cicely Tyson, but in September 1968 he married soul singer Betty Mabry; they had no children, separated in 1969, and divorced in 1971. Among his many other woman friends was Marguerite Eskridge, with whom he had a son.

In 1967 Davis began to nudge his recordings toward rock music, a process that eventually resulted in two path-breaking jazz-rock albums of 1969, *In a Silent Way* and *Bitches Brew*, marking the conclusion of Davis's remarkable run of innovations in jazz. The turn also brought a sartorial change, with Davis discarding elegant business suits in favor of outfits with African and Native American themes. At this point he severed the link between his working band and his recording band. Carter and Hancock, then Williams, and finally Shorter left the quintet in 1969, and over the next several years Davis drew from a large pool of sidemen. Details are too complicated to enumerate here; a partial list affirms Davis's continuing extraordinary ear for young talent: reed player Bennie Maupin; saxophonists Steve Grossman, Gary Bartz, Dave Liebman,

Carlos Garnett, and Sonny Fortune; keyboard players Chick Corea, Joe Zawinul, and Keith Jarrett; electric guitarist John McLaughlin; bassists Miroslav Vitous, Dave Holland, and Michael Henderson; drummers Jack DeJohnette, Billy Cobham, and Al Foster; and percussionist Airto Moreira.

During the first half of the 1970s Davis was in semi-retirement, taking long vacations. On 1 October 1972 he crashed his Lamborghini and broke both ankles. After several months of rehabilitation he resumed performing; but he played electronic keyboard as often as trumpet, and sometimes he hardly performed at all. Chambers reports, "His arthritic hip kept him in constant pain and forced him to abandon his regimen in the gym. He had more run-ins with the police, leading to a variety of charges, including alleged narcotics and weapons offences. The abstinences of a few years earlier were replaced by indulgences. He drank more heavily, perhaps hoping to kill the pain, but succeeded only in aggravating a peptic ulcer. He began receiving injections of morphine in order to keep moving. And, in the end, he collapsed and stayed down for a long time" (Chambers, vol. 2, p. 234).

In 1975 the deterioration of Davis's joints obliged him to retire. He underwent another operation on his larynx, he was treated for a stomach ulcer and gallstones, and in December 1975 his hip was replaced. The retirement lasted five years, and characteristically he refused to disclose his health problems, leaving open the opportunity for wild speculations.

Davis recorded a new album in mid-1980 and early 1981, *The Man with the Horn*, and he resumed performing in the summer of 1981 with saxophonist Bill Evans (unrelated to the pianist of that name), electric guitarist Mike Stern, electric bassist Marcus Miller, Foster, and percussionist Mino Cinclu. Davis now presented a new public image, much more accessible, a legend in his own time. Tyson had resumed seeing him toward the end of his rehabilitation, and in November 1981 they married. They had no children and divorced in 1989.

In January 1982 Davis suffered a stroke that temporarily paralyzed his right hand. He took acupuncture treatments, stopped smoking and drinking, swam daily, and in April was able to resume touring. His international travels were again interrupted from November 1983 to June 1984 by another hip operation and pneumonia. By the mid-1980s he was obliged to take insulin shots for diabetes, and he had bronchial pneumonia early in 1989.

At year's end in 1982 Davis hired electric guitarist John Scofield, who was probably the finest soloist in his final bands. Other band members included, at various times, saxophonists Bob Berg, Branford Marsalis, and Kenny Garrett; electric guitarists Robben Ford and Joseph McCreary (known as Foley); and bassist Darryl Jones, together with several keyboard players (including Davis himself). Time and again reviews of their concerts were wildly enthusiastic. The reviewers often expected a reprise of Davis's droningly monotonous jazz-funk of the early 1970s, but instead received

much more. For reasons unknown the concurrent recordings are consistently disappointing. Some idea of the band's impact may be gleaned from the film *Music at Montreux*, made at the festival in Switzerland in July 1991, two months before Davis's death in Santa Monica, California. This movie was combined with the PBS film *Miles Ahead: The Music of Miles Davis* to make the documentary *Miles Davis: A Tribute* (1993).

Davis may have been a great jazz composer, but details are obscured by his working method, whereby it is impossible to ascertain what he appropriated from others and what he invented on his own. In any event his sidemen testified repeatedly to his oblique ways of teaching that less is more and silence in music is golden, and of cajoling them to play as they never had before. While leading his widely imitated combos and Evans's unique big band through innovations in cool jazz, modal jazz, orchestral jazz, "time, no changes," and jazz-rock ("I've changed music five or six times," he reports in his autobiography, p. 381), and while discovering dozens of young jazz greats and a new muted trumpet sound, Davis developed an utterly original approach to trumpet and flugelhorn melody, in which he was rivaled perhaps only by Holiday in his ability to bring unimagined depth to improvisation through the endlessly varied manipulation of fine nuances of pitch and rhythmic placement. Although Davis came to hate the word "jazz," asserting that it was a racist term, he belongs on any short list of the greatest jazz musicians.

• By far the finest historical account is Jack Chambers, *Milestones*, vol. 1: *The Music and Times of Miles Davis to 1960* (1983), and *Milestones*, vol. 2: *The Music and Times of Miles Davis since 1960* (1985), collected as *Milestones: The Music and Times of Miles Davis* (1989); unfortunately Chambers also felt obliged to supply commentary on almost all of Davis's recordings, a task for which he is severely unqualified. For excellent musical analysis, see Ian Carr, *Miles Davis: A Critical Biography* (1982). Davis himself, obviously operating with Chambers's work in hand, fleshes out his story with some additional factual detail and much characteristic hip talk and invective in a collaboration with Quincy Troupe, *Miles: The Autobiography* (1989). The finest periodical articles are collected in Bill Kirchner, ed., *The Miles Davis Reader* (1997). See also Michael James, *Miles Davis* (1961; repr. in Stanley Green, ed., *Kings of Jazz* [1978]). See also Barry Dean Kernfeld, "Adderley, Coltrane, and Davis at the Twilight of Bebop: The Search for Melodic Coherence" (Ph.D. diss., Cornell Univ., 1981); Jan Lohman, *The Sound of Miles Davis: The Discography: A Listing of Records and Tapes, 1945–1991* (1992); Gary Tomlinson, "Cultural Dialogics and Jazz: A White Historian Signifies," in *Disciplining Music: Musicology and Its Canons*, ed. Katherine Bergeron and Philip V. Bohlman (1992), pp. 64–94; and Thomas Owens, *Bebop: The Music and Its Players* (1995), pp. 113–27. An obituary is in the *New York Times*, 29 Sept. 1991.

BARRY KERNFELD

DAVIS, Nathan Smith (9 Jan. 1817–16 June 1904), physician and educator, was born in rural Chenango County, New York, the son of Dow Davis and Eleanor Smith, farmers. After attending his district school, Davis commenced reading for a medical career with a local doctor and graduated with an M.D. from the College of Physicians and Surgeons of the Western District of New York in Fairfield in 1837. While studying for his degree he earned enough at odd jobs "to buy me a small library of books and a pocket case of instruments to commence practice with" (Fishbein, p. 4).

For the next twelve years he practiced medicine throughout New York, moving to Binghamton in 1838. That year he married Anna Maria Parker; they had three children. Beginning in 1844, concerned about the meager preparation of many doctors, he urged that a national convention of physicians be called to deal with the low standards observed by medical schools and societies. Two years later, largely as a result of his persistence and initiative, an organizational meeting was held in New York City. Davis was appointed chairman of a committee to draw up reform proposals. In 1847 these proposals were adopted at Philadelphia, where steps were taken to effect a permanent organization. The name American Medical Association was decided upon at this meeting. That same year he moved to New York City and taught dissection at the College of Physicians and Surgeons. In 1849 he was called to Chicago to fill the chair of principles and practice of medicine at Rush Medical College.

Davis spent the rest of his life in Chicago, where he became a major builder of medical and civic institutions. In 1850 he played the dominant role in the founding of Mercy Hospital, the city's first. He led a movement to build an adequate sewage system and ensure a clean water supply. He broke with Rush Medical School over issues of standards and curriculum and in 1859 founded the Chicago Medical College, the first college to extend the course of medical study to three years and to grade the curriculum. President Charles W. Eliot later wrote that he had "mistakenly thought that the Harvard Medical School was the pioneer in these respects" (Eliot to N. S. Davis, Jr., 24 Aug. 1896, Medical Library, Northwestern University). In 1891 the school became an integral part of Northwestern University. Davis also took part in the organization of the Chicago and Illinois Medical Societies, the Chicago Academy of Sciences, Northwestern University, the Chicago Historical Society, and the Washingtonian Home for alcoholics. He was editor of the *Chicago Medical Journal* from 1855 to 1859, founded the *Chicago Medical Examiner* in 1860, and served as the first editor of the *Journal of the American Medical Association* from 1883 to 1889.

Davis was a person of stern conscience and humanitarian outlook. From his limited income (he never raised his standard fee of one dollar per office call) he gave generous support to a number of causes. Throughout his life he was active in behalf of temperance, public libraries, and relief for the poor. He looked to be literally a doctor of the Old School, with his slight build, shaggy hair, side whiskers, and swallow-tailed coat, which he wore until his death in Chicago. But, in fact, he was an important bridge between the prescientific era in American medicine and the advent of modern medicine.

• A small collection of Davis papers may be found in the library of the Northwestern University Medical School, as can the minutes of the faculty of the Chicago Medical College (1859–1891). Many of his published writings are collected in the John Crerar Collection, Illinois Institute of Technology. Among Davis's publications, the following are noteworthy: *Inaugural Address Delivered at the Opening of the Medical Department of Lind University* (1859); *History of Medical Education and Institutions in the United States* (1851); "A Brief History of the Chicago Medical Society from Its Origins to the End of Its First Half Century of Progress," *Chicago Medical Recorder* 11 (1901): 199–204; "A Brief History of Medical Journalism in Chicago to the End of the Nineteenth Century," *Clinical Review* 16 (1902): 468–71; and *Lectures on the Principles and Practice of Medicine* (1884). The only biography was written by I. N. Danforth, *Life of Nathan Smith Davis* (1907). His grandson, Nathan Smith Davis III, wrote an account of Davis's life for Morris Fishbein, ed., *A History of the American Medical Association 1847 to 1947* (1947). Sketches of Davis's career in Chicago are in Thomas N. Bonner, "Dr. Nathan Smith Davis and the Growth of Chicago Medicine 1850–1900," *Bulletin of the History of Medicine* 26 (1952): 360–74, and *Medicine in Chicago: A Chapter in the Social and Scientific Development of a City*, 2d ed. (1991).

THOMAS NEVILLE BONNER

DAVIS, Owen Gould (28 Jan. 1874–14 Oct. 1956), playwright, was born in Portland, Maine, the son of Owen Warren Davis, an iron manufacturer, and Abigail Augusta Gould. Davis attended the University of Tennessee and Harvard University, where he was better known as an athlete than as a literary figure. He left Harvard without a degree in 1893 and worked for a time as a mining engineer before turning to the popular theater as a career. In 1901 or 1902 he married actress Elizabeth Drury Breyer, whom he had met while working for a stock company in Rochester, New York. They had two sons, both of whom worked in the performing arts: Owen Davis, Jr., who drowned in Long Island Sound in 1949, was a stage and film actor; Donald Davis, a writer, collaborated on several plays with his father, and worked in television and film. Davis spent most of his working life in New York City.

Owen Davis claimed that he was the author of more than 300 plays during the course of his career. The actual number is unclear, however, because he sometimes wrote under pseudonyms. Brooks Atkinson, in *Broadway*, places the number at between 150 and 200. Davis's earliest plays were sensational melodramas, such as *In the Hands of the Enemy* (1902), *Nellie, the Beautiful Cloak Model* (1906), and *Convict 999* (1907), written for the cheap stock and touring companies common in the first decade of the century. Davis ground out dozens of formula scripts during this period, many of them for Al Woods, the producer of melodramas and other popular plays.

These early plays were "practically motion pictures," Davis wrote in his autobiography *I'd like to Do It Again* (1931), "as one of the first things I learned was that my plays must be written for an audience who, owing to the huge, uncarpeted, noisy theaters, couldn't always hear the words and who, a large percentage of them having only just landed in America, couldn't have understood them in any case." Davis claimed that, at the time, he "wrote for the eye rather than the ear and played out each emotion in action, depending on my dialogue only for the noble sentiments so dear to audiences of that class." The result of this early work was that Davis gained a reputation as a hack dramatist, a reputation that would never entirely be dispelled, even though Davis produced more serious work later in his career.

Davis's first script for a Broadway show was *The Battle of Port Arthur* (1908), a musical extravaganza at the Hippodrome, the huge Sixth Avenue spectacle house. The Hippodrome was operated at the time by the famous producers of light popular entertainment, Lee Shubert and J. J. Shubert, in whose Rochester, New York, stock company Davis had worked at the turn of the century. From 1908 until 1921, Davis wrote a mixed lot of comedies and melodramas, mostly for Broadway. Among the more successful were *The Family Cupboard* (1913) and *Forever After* (1918), produced by a Shubert associate, William A. Brady, and starring his daughter, the well-known actress Alice Brady. The Shubert brothers presented a number of Davis's shows, including *The Wishing Ring* (1910), *Those Who Walk in Darkness* (1919), *Page Mr. Cupid* (1920), and *The Detour* (1921).

With *The Detour* Davis revealed a significant, if only temporary, change in the direction of his work. The play, a realistic treatment of rural life, was influenced by Ibsen's dramas as well as those of Eugene O'Neill and other progressive American playwrights of the day. In *The History of the American Drama*, Arthur Hobson Quinn notes that in *The Detour*, Davis "tried to depict characters rather than mere types, and while the play did not succeed financially, it was recognized by the discriminating as being among the best of the season's products."

In 1922 Davis adapted Josef and Karel Capek's *The Insect Comedy* as *The World We Live In*, and the following year he wrote *Icebound*, produced by Sam Harris, which the reviewer for the *New York Times* called "a grim and nearly relentless play of the New England and the New Englanders that Owen Davis knows." *Icebound* won the 1923 Pulitzer Prize for drama, and Davis was subsequently elected to the National Institute of Arts and Letters. He became increasingly interested in copyright and censorship issues affecting dramatists, and in 1926 he helped to negotiate the minimum basic contract between the Dramatists Guild and the Managers Protective Association.

With the exception of *The Detour* and *Icebound*, Davis continued for the most part to write the kind of popular Broadway fare that had occupied him during the previous decade. Among his Broadway successes of the 1920s were *The Haunted House* (1924) and *Easy Come, Easy Go* (1925). Several of Davis's later plays were adaptations of stories or novels. Among them was the classic comedy, *The Nervous Wreck* (1923), which

would serve as the basis for the 1928 Eddie Cantor musical *Whoopee*, and the 1944 Danny Kaye film *Up in Arms*. In 1926 Davis adapted *The Great Gatsby* for the stage; in 1936, *The Good Earth* and *Ethan Frome* (both with his son Donald Davis); and in 1941, the popular *Mr. and Mrs. North*. In 1926 he collaborated with Fulton Oursler on *Sandalwood* and with S. N. Behrman on *The Man Who Forgot*. Davis was also active as a radio and screen writer, creating scripts for "The Gibson Family" radio series (1934) and two Will Rogers films, *They Had to See Paris* (1929) and *So This Is London* (1930).

Davis's last Broadway play, *No Way Out* (1944), was a failure, closing after only eight performances. Davis never returned to writing for the theater, although he continued to talk about creating "serious" work of the sort that had gained him the Pulitzer Prize. In fact, Davis's real talent was as a prolific writer of popular comedies and mysteries. During his last years he was plagued by failing health and increasingly poor eyesight. Davis died in New York City.

• Davis wrote two entertaining but not always accurate autobiographies, *I'd Like to Do It Again* (1931) and *My First Fifty Years in the Theatre* (1950). Biographical sketches appear in volumes 5 through 12 of *Who's Who in the Theatre*; *Twentieth Century Authors* (1950); and *The Oxford Companion to the American Theatre* (1992), among other reference works. For the reception of many of Davis's plays, see James M. Salem, *A Guide to Critical Reviews* (1973). Articles with useful information about Davis include Frank Rahill, "When Heaven Protected the Working Girl," *Theatre Arts* (Oct. 1954); Lewin Goff, "The Owen Davis–Al Woods Melodrama Factory," *Educational Theatre Journal* (Oct. 1959); and Barry B. Witham, "Owen Davis: America's Forgotten Playwright," *Players* (Oct.–Nov. 1970). Obituary notices appear in the *New York Times*, 15 Oct. 1956, and in *Variety*, 17 Oct. 1956.

BROOKS MCNAMARA

DAVIS, Paulina Kellogg Wright (7 Aug. 1813–24 Aug. 1876), abolitionist, suffragist, and educator, was born in Bloomfield, New York, the daughter of Captain Ebenezer Kellogg and Polly Saxton. In 1817 the family moved to an undeveloped area near Niagara Falls. Davis's enjoyment of the frontier's exhilirating freedom ended with the deaths of her parents. In 1820 she went to live with a strict orthodox Presbyterian aunt in LeRoy, New York, where she was educated and attended church regularly.

Under her aunt's influence, Davis joined the Presbyterian church. She embraced religion and was an outstanding participant at revival meetings. However, she suffered from thoughts of damnation and chafed at the church's hostility to outspoken women. Davis later recalled that she was not happy until, "I outgrew my early religious faith, and felt free to think and act from my own convictions." Though little is known about Davis's early education, she did develop a thirst for knowledge.

Davis planned to become a missionary, but was thwarted by the church's refusal to send single women to convert the heathen. An ardent suitor, Francis

Wright, convinced her that there were abundant heathen in Utica, including himself, and after five months of courtship they were married in 1833.

Wright shared Davis's passion for causes. He was a wealthy merchant from a prosperous family in Utica, and he joined his resources and executive ability with Paulina's managerial skills and enthusiasm. They were active in the Bethel Church until they resigned in protest of its proslavery stance. In 1842, when the antislavery activist Abby Kelley was their guest, they organized meetings around Utica and served on the executive committee of the Central New York Anti-Slavery Society.

In addition to abolitionism, the childless Wrights supported women's rights reforms. Although her husband prohibited her from public speaking, she joined forces with feminists such as Elizabeth Cady Stanton and Susan B. Anthony. She worked with Ernestine Rose on petitioning the New York state legislature in the late 1830s for married women's property rights and also studied women's health issues.

Her husband's death in 1845 left Davis desolate but wealthy and free to embark on a career as a lecturer. She moved to New York City to study medicine, and in 1846 she gave her first lectures in anatomy and physiology, for women only. She toured the eastern United States with a mannequin imported from Paris, to demonstrate the female physiognomy and to urge women to become physicians. The mannequin's unveiling shocked some women, but others embraced the cause and became pioneering doctors. Davis's new expertise led Abby Kelley to insist that she assist during the birth of her first child.

In the late 1840s Davis met widower Thomas Davis, an antislavery Democrat, in Providence, Rhode Island. Thomas Davis had immigrated to the United States from Ireland in 1817, and his first wife, Eliza Chace, was a close friend of Helen and William Lloyd Garrison. They were married in April 1849 and adopted two daughters. A successful jeweler, Thomas Davis was also public spirited, and he supported many of Paulina's causes, including women's equality in marriage. He served in the Rhode Island State Senate from 1845 to 1853 and then in the U.S. Congress from 1853 to 1855.

Paulina Davis discontinued her lectures on anatomy in 1850 and worked on the National Woman's Rights convention held that fall in Worcester, Massachusetts. Two years later at the 1852 convention Davis decided to launch the first women's magazine devoted to the "elevation of woman." With women's education her primary objective, Davis began editing *The Una*, named for a character in Edmund Spenser's *Faerie Queene*, in February 1853. The purpose was to "discuss the rights, sphere, duty and destiny of woman, fully and fearlessly." Davis was determined to provide a source for written dialogue between women on the subject of labor, marriage, suffrage, and schooling, and to demand that women enjoy more job opportunities and better pay. As she wrote in September 1853, "whoever can pay for himself and support himself will be free." She solicited articles from feminist and social scientist Caroline Healy Dall and other prominent women reformers. This entertaining and instructive periodical, infused with feminist mottoes from philosophers, provides a unique window on the world of women in the 1850s.

When Davis moved to Washington, D.C., with her husband in January 1854, she continued to edit the monthly paper. However, a year later she invited Dall to share editorial responsibilities, and the magazine's editorial office was transferred to Boston. Dall's commitment to making *The Una* a literary magazine clashed with Davis's vision of the magazine as an organ for reform. Within a year *The Una* collapsed. Yet Davis continued to agitate for women's rights. She broke with her old abolitionist friends and joined Elizabeth Cady Stanton to promote woman suffrage over enfranchisement for male African Americans. As she wrote in an 1854 editorial, "The harmony, unity, and oneness of the race, can not be secured while there is class legislation; while one half of humanity is cramped within a narrow sphere and governed by arbitrary power."

After returning to Providence from Washington, D.C., in 1855, the Davises lived in a spacious house, surrounded by an extensive lawn and grand old trees, one and a half miles from town. Here Paulina Davis resided as a sort of foreign princess in Providence. She was too serious for society women and too radical for the college community. "Nevertheless," wrote a friend, "she was a radiant figure in its circle of literary, artistic and reformatory people." Davis avoided isolation by importing artists and reformers. Visitors included the poet Walt Whitman, who enjoyed her hospitality, conversation, and free spirit.

Beginning in 1869 Davis made many of the arrangements for the twentieth anniversary meeting of the Woman Suffrage Movement held at the Apollo Hall in New York City in October 1870. In 1871 she published the proceedings as *The History of the National Woman's Rights Movement*.

In the 1860s and 1870s Davis traveled abroad with an adopted daughter and a niece. She met many prominent European reformers and indulged her love of art by studiously copying the paintings of great masters. She abandoned her artwork when she became crippled with arthritis during the 1870s.

Davis was a gracious but determined, daring but respected leader whose intelligence, dedication, organizational skills, and wealth enabled her to make a significant contribution to the cause of women's rights. Through the conventions she organized and through publications she informed people about ways to organize for much needed reforms. She died at home in Providence, Rhode Island, and was eulogized by Elizabeth Cady Stanton.

• Paulina Davis's speeches and letters are in the Vassar College Library. The best sources on Davis are Sherry Ceniza, "Walt Whitman and 'Woman under the New Dispensation': The Influence of Louisa Van Velsor Whitman, Abby Hills

Price, Paulina Wright Davis and Ernestine L. Rose on Whitman's Poetry and Prose" (Ph.D. diss., Univ. of Iowa, 1990); *The Letters of William Lloyd Garrison*, ed. Walter M. Merrill and Louis Ruchames (6 vols., 1971–1981); Dorothy Sterling, *Ahead of Her Time: Abby Kelley and the Politics of Antislavery* (1991); and Mary P. Ryan, *The Cradle of the Middle Class: The Family in Oneida County, New York, 1790–1865* (1981). An obituary is in the *New York Times*, 25 Aug. 1876.

SARAH HENRY LEDERMAN

DAVIS, Pauline Morton Sabin. *See* Sabin, Pauline Morton.

DAVIS, Raymond Cazallis (23 June 1836–10 June 1919), university librarian and pioneering teacher of bibliography, was born in Cushing, Maine, the son of George Davis, a sea captain, and Katherine (or Katharine) Young. From his early years he demonstrated an interest in reading and literature. A two-year journey with his father, 1849–1851, was to result in his only published book, *Reminiscences of a Voyage around the World* (1869). After preparatory schooling in New Hampshire, he entered the University of Michigan in 1855. His classmate and later patron, Claudius B. Grant, wrote of him: "It is no exaggeration to say that he was the most conspicuous member of that class. In height, fully six feet two inches, erect, manly bearing, with a kindly and intelligent face and withal of modest demeanor. He was at once recognized by us all as a young man of more than ordinary parts."

For the better part of his life Davis had health problems. Near the end of his sophomore year at Michigan he had a nervous breakdown that caused him to withdraw from the university, and for a full decade, 1857–1867, he was unable to engage in extended intellectual pursuits. During the summer of 1868 he received a letter from Grant, now becoming a power in state and university affairs, letting him know that an appointment as assistant university librarian was open to him. Davis accepted and assumed the position in October. From the start he was popular with students and was known as an effective librarian. After a lengthy dispute regarding finances between the librarian, Andrew Ten Brook, and the board of regents, Davis in 1872 was appointed librarian, beginning with the 1873–1874 academic year. But Davis, who evidently played no role in the matter, withdrew his acceptance of the position after much sympathy for Ten Brook developed. For the next five years he was "a sort of minute man for all kinds of calls," often related to the sea; but this time there was no recurrence of his earlier intellectual limitations. Meanwhile, support for Ten Brook withered, and in June 1877 he was fired. Grant, now a regent, wrote his friend offering him, at the age of forty-one, the post of librarian. This time Davis accepted.

Davis's major contribution to librarianship was his developing a credit course in bibliographic instruction. Praise for this pioneering endeavor is due as well to the Michigan Board of Regents, who, in an 1865 resolution, encouraged Davis to deliver a series of lectures on books and bibliography. In turn, this resolu-

tion in all probability descends from Emerson's declaration, made as early as 1847, that colleges should have a chair for "professors of books." Whereas Ten Brook made some short-lived efforts to comply with the regents' resolution, Davis took the mandate as integral to his function as librarian. At first he delivered a series of informal lectures covering the history of bibliography, practical advice for effective use of library resources, plus "Fiction—Its Place in a Course of Reading" and "Historical Novels." Though there was no precedent for these lectures, Davis went significantly further when, in 1883, he began to offer a one-hour elective credit course in bibliography. In a series of nineteen lectures he presented three divisions of the subject: historical; material or practical description of books; and intellectual, devoted to classification and discussion of superior books in seven principal fields. That Davis had a superior knowledge of the first division, historical bibliography, is demonstrated by his unpublished book, "From the Papyrus Roll to the Modern Book." At an 1886 conference of the American Library Association, Davis delivered a lengthy paper, later published in the *Library Journal* (Aug.–Sept. 1886), titled "Teaching Bibliography in Colleges." Davis's example was the basis for similar courses being offered at Cornell (1886) and at least four or five other academic institutions by 1892, beyond which point Davis's influence becomes more speculative. But there does appear to be a link between Davis's example and the expectation that graduate students in seminars—which were being introduced into graduate programs in the 1880s—acquire a proficiency in using library resources. After being designated librarian emeritus in 1905, Davis was appointed lecturer in bibliography, and his course was expanded to extend over two semesters.

Davis's tenure as librarian (1887–1905) fell within James B. Angell's great presidency (1871–1909), a period of major advancement in instruction and research. But funds for libraries' collections came directly from the legislature, to which Angell could not dictate. Leaving the major library functions in the hands of capable assistants, Davis—ever the bookman librarian—described his tenure as a "struggle for books." Unable to match its competitors numerically, the library was characterized as being of the "traditional type, administered by a scholar for scholars. . . . The book collection was exceptional but not in the least popular." The aptness the latter characterization was owing to the emphasis placed upon research and fulfillment of instructional requirements. Davis himself was conversant with the best literature of all eras. Pushing his energies to the limit, Davis spent his summers on the East Coast, restoring his strength and reading and studying for his course on bibliography. Until his marriage to Ellen Regal in 1880 he spent summers at Cushing, Maine, and then later at other ocean resorts.

Davis also described his tenure as librarian as "a struggle with books." The 1883 library, despite its multitier stack, its "seminary" and reading areas, was soon insufficient to meet service requirements because of inadequate space and staffing. Davis understood the situation and, during his final year, gave full support to Theodore Wesley Koch, his designated successor.

Despite his academic career's having been terminated by illness, he was adopted as a member of the class of 1859, and Michigan awarded him in 1881 an honorary master of arts degree. All along, and increasingly as the years went by, he was referred to as "Professor Davis." When he fully retired in 1914 he was appointed Professor George P. Williams Emeritus Professor. He died in Ann Arbor, Michigan.

• Davis's manuscript writings, including his "Autobiography; or, the Reminiscences of One More Distinguished for Length of Days Than for Greatness of Achievement," are located at the Michigan Historical Collections, University of Michigan, Ann Arbor. Davis's published "Annual Reports" and stories appearing in the generally excellent student newspapers are also important sources of information. The most complete assessment of Davis's life and career is John C. Abbott's *Raymond Cazallis Davis and the University of Michigan General Library, 1877–1905* (Ph.D. diss., Univ. of Michigan, 1957).

JOHN C. ABBOTT

DAVIS, Rebecca Blaine Harding (24 June 1831–29 Sept. 1910), writer, was born in Washington, Pennsylvania, the first child of Richard W. Harding, a businessman and city official, and Rachel Leet Wilson. Her English father emigrated from Ireland in about 1821; her well-educated mother came from one of Washington's leading families. At the time of Rebecca's birth, her parents were living in Big Spring (now Huntsville), Alabama, but moved to Wheeling, Virginia (now W. Va.), when she was about five years old. Educated by her mother, in 1845 Rebecca returned to her birthplace for her secondary education, graduating as valedictorian of her class at the Washington Female Seminary in 1848.

She returned to her family home in Wheeling, an expanding mill town on the Ohio River, where she helped with the house and her four younger siblings. She continued her education by studying German with her brother Wilson, a student at Washington College from 1850 to 1854. In the late 1850s she began writing for the *Wheeling Intelligencer*.

Publication of "Life in the Iron Mills" in the April 1861 issue of *Atlantic Monthly* brought Rebecca Harding instant fame and recognition as a promising new writer. Publication came within days of the beginning of the Civil War; in May Wheeling became the capital of "New Virginia" when the western counties of Virginia resisted secession and worked toward statehood. Here she witnessed both the fierce passions and the terrible brutality caused by the war.

"Life in the Iron Mills" is Davis's best-known, most frequently reprinted, and most artistically successful work. This tragic story of the Wheeling "iron puddler" (Furnace tender) Hugh Wolfe and his cousin Deb's botched effort to free him from a stifling life of heavy labor and poverty has become emblematic of American realism and naturalism.

James T. Fields, the *Atlantic* editor, urged the unknown writer to submit more; in October 1861 he began serial publication of "A Story of To-Day," republished in 1862 as *Margret Howth*. Artistically flawed as a result of Fields's insistence that Harding provide more "sunshine" in her dark picture of life in an Indiana industrial town, the novel nevertheless contains an important statement of Harding's realist creed. Defending her "crude and homely" story against idealized "New England idyls," Harding speaks directly to her reader: "You want something, in fact, to lift you out of this crowded, tobacco-stained commonplace, to kindle and chafe and glow in you. I want you to dig into this commonplace, this vulgar American life, and see what is in it. Sometimes I think it has a new and awful significance that we do not see." While negotiating with Fields about this story, Harding began her correspondence and friendship with his wife, Annie.

Harding's first publication also led to marriage. Reading "Life in the Iron Mills" prompted Lemuel Clarke Davis, then reading law in Philadelphia, to write to Harding, and soon he traveled to Wheeling to meet her. The next year, in June—despite the war— she traveled north, to New York, Boston, and Concord (where she stayed in the house of Nathaniel Hawthorne). On her return, she stopped for a week in Philadelphia, and when she reached Wheeling in late July she was engaged.

Through Clarke Davis, Rebecca began writing for *Peterson's*, a Philadelphia lady's magazine published by his friend Charles Peterson: her story, "The Murder of the Glen Ross," appeared in November and December 1861. Less prestigious than the *Atlantic*, *Peterson's* paid considerably better. Despite her agreement in 1862 to write exclusively for the *Atlantic* for the next year, she was soon publishing frequently in both magazines. Her *Atlantic* stories in these years tended to reflect the tensions of the war in a border state, whereas her *Peterson's* pieces (usually labeled "potboilers") often dealt with strange happenings, thefts, forgery, and the like.

Following their marriage in 1863, the Davises lived in Philadelphia, spending summers for twenty years at Point Pleasant, New Jersey. The first of their three children, Richard Harding Davis, was born in 1864.

For almost fifty years following her first publication, Davis continued to publish stories and articles focused on the commonplace in an ever-expanding number of periodicals, including *Scribner's*, *Lippincott's*, *Harper's Monthly*, children's magazines, religious publications, and the *Saturday Evening Post*. In 1869 Davis joined the staff of the *New York Tribune*; for twenty years she contributed articles and editorials on contemporary topics. In 1875 she began contributing to the *Independent*, a New York weekly. In all, her bibliography includes more than 500 separate entries; little attempt has been made to chronicle her newspaper writing.

Usually labeled a "pioneer American realist," Davis is difficult to classify. At times her work is bold and experimental; at others it seems trite and formulaic. Years before Stephen Crane and William Dean Howells, she combined her insistent focus on the "tough, practical reality" of "today"—often sordid, grim, and unhappy—with Christian sentimentalism and a Romantic interest in folk legends and the simplicity of the preindustrial natural landscape. Using place like a local colorist, she describes many different regions. Her subjects include racism, insane asylums, political scandal, lost heirs, thwarted love, prostitution, and the struggle of the artist. Many stories concern feminist questions of women's role (or "work" in Davis's parlance) in modern industrial society. Because a very antifeminist tract published in 1870, *Pro Aris et Focis* (For altar and hearth), was misattributed to Davis, her position on women's issues has been obscured.

Many critics have argued that Davis never fulfilled the promise of her first published story: she wrote too much, too fast. Corrupted by submission to editors' demands and her desire for commercial success, critics charge, she traded artistic integrity for "hackwork." However, new evaluations are in order: as post-modernist, post-structuralist, and feminist ways of reading replace earlier standards valuing form and control, what was labeled a "grotesque mixture" of realist and romantic elements in 1965 can now be reread as a strong and subversive challenge to traditional norms.

Davis died at the Mount Kisco, New York, estate of her son Richard.

• The Davis family papers in the Alderman Library of the University of Virginia include the major collection of Davis manuscripts; other items are in the Buffalo and Erie County Library, Buffalo, N.Y., and the Henry E. Huntington Library, San Marino, Calif. Book publications (all previously published in periodicals) include *Waiting for the Verdict* (1867), *Dallas Galbraith* (1868), *John Andross* (1874), *A Law Unto Herself* (1878), *Natasqua* (1886), *Kent Hampden* (1892), *Doctor Warrick's Daughters* (1896), and *Frances Waldeaux* (1897); *Silhouettes of American Life* (1892) collects thirteen of Davis's best stories. Jane Atteridge Rose, "A Bibliography of Fiction and Non-Fiction by Rebecca Harding Davis," *American Literary Realism* 22, no. 3 (1990): 67–85, lists 505 separate publications. Davis's autobiography, *Bits of Gossip* (1906), is a rich source of information. The best biographies are by Helen W. Shaeffer, "Rebecca Harding Davis, Pioneer Realist" (Ph.D. diss., Univ. of Pennsylvania, 1947), who interviewed people who had known Davis, and William Grayburn, "The Major Fiction of Rebecca Harding Davis" (Ph.D. diss., Pennsylvania State Univ., 1965), who offers extensive readings of selected writings and updates Shaeffer's list of Davis's publications. Tillie Olsen's impressionistic "Biographical Interpretation," in Olsen, ed., *Life in the Iron Mills and other Stories* (1972; repr. 1985), includes a substantial account of the life. Davis is the focus of four chapters of Gerald Langford's *The Richard Harding Years: A Biography of a Mother and Son* (1971). In *Rebecca Harding Davis and American Realism* (1991), Sharon Harris provides biographical information as background to her discussions of Davis's whole career. Philip B. Eppard, "Rebecca Harding Davis: A Misat-

tribution," *Papers of the Bibliographical Society of America* 69 (1975): 265–67, points out that Davis did not write *Pro Aris et Focis*. An obituary is in the *New York Times*, 30 Sept. 1910.

NANCY CRAIG SIMMONS

DAVIS, Richard Beale (3 June 1907–30 Mar. 1981), educator, was born in Accomack, Virginia, the son of Henry Woodhouse Davis, a Methodist minister, and Margaret Josephine Wills. After graduating from Randolph-Macon College (A.B., 1927), he taught at the McGuire University School (1927–1930) and Randolph-Macon Academy (1930–1932) before continuing his education at the University of Virginia. A student of historian James Southall Wilson, Davis received the A.M. in 1933 and the Ph.D. in 1936. Later that year he married Lois Camp Bullard; they had no children.

As an associate professor of English at Mary Washington College in 1936, Davis began his career in higher education as a teacher-researcher. From 1940 to 1946 he was an associate professor at the University of South Carolina, serving on military leave, from 1943 to 1946, in Louisiana as an officer in the U.S. Navy. In 1947 he moved to the University of Tennessee, Knoxville, beginning an association that lasted—even after his official retirement from teaching in 1977—for the remainder of his life. As chairman of the American literature curriculum there from 1947 to 1962, he was responsible for developing a program that ranked with those of the best state universities. In 1962 Davis was among the first professors to be named Alumni Distinguished Service Professor, the highest honor the Tennessee university system bestows on its faculty.

Fellowships and grants, lectureships, and memberships kept Davis in the mainstream of academia. He won two Guggenheim fellowships (1947, 1960–1961), a National Endowment for the Humanities senior fellowship (1974), a National Humanities Center fellowship (1979–1980), three American Philosophical Society grants (1951–1952, 1958, 1962), a Fulbright lectureship to Norway (1953–1954), and a U.S. Department of State–sponsored lectureship to India (1957). He also played leadership roles in the American Studies Association (executive committee, 1958–1961, 1968–1971), the Modern Language Association (among many others, chair, American Literature Group, 1975), the South Atlantic Modern Language Association (president, 1964–1965), the Southern Humanities Conference (chair, 1960), and the Society for the Study of Southern Literature (president, 1968–1970). He was a member of the American Antiquarian Society and the Virginia Historical Society.

Doing research for his 1955 biography of seventeenth-century author and sometime Virginia colonist George Sandys, Davis became acquainted with members of Britain's historic Sandys family and managed to gather a major collection of George Sandys's writings, now at the University of Virginia at his bequest. As an inveterate book reviewer of colonial and early Americana for the Phi Beta Kappa *Key* and other periodicals, and through judicious purchases of out-of-print and rare books and pamphlets, Davis amassed a personal "working library," as he called it, which in the 1970s was probably the best private collection of primary and secondary materials relating to the early South. Along with his desk and appropriate memorabilia, Davis bequeathed this library to Randolph-Macon College, where it remains intact as a research center.

Early in Davis's education he began to focus on the colonial South as a period and area rich in unexplored primary materials. The breadth and depth of his interest are reflected in "Spadework, American Literature, and the Southern Mind: Opportunities," his 1965 South Atlantic Modern Language Association presidential address. In this, he discussed the major tenet of his professional life—his belief that mature research into early southern culture would prove that the colonial and revolutionary South had a far greater role than had previously been recognized in the intellectual development of the nation. Finally numbering more than 100 books and articles, Davis's studies reached fruitful maturity in his *Intellectual Life in Jefferson's Virginia*, which won the first award of the American Association of State and Local History in 1963, and the 1,892-page, three-volume *Intellectual Life in the Colonial South, 1585–1763*, which received—among other honors—the National Book Award for history in 1979. At the time of his death in Knoxville, Tennessee, Davis was working on a continuation of this history, covering the revolutionary war years and exploring the southern roots of the early republic.

• A general review of Davis's academic achievements is "A Colloquium on the Present State of the Study of Early American Literature and the Contributions of Richard Beale Davis to this Study," which took place on 23 Apr. 1977, was edited from the transcript by Michael A. Lofaro, and published in *Tennessee Studies in Literature* 26 (1981): 1–47, a journal of which Davis had been a founding editor. See also J. A. Leo Lemay, ed., *Essays in Early Virginia Literature Honoring Richard Beale Davis* (1977), and James H. Justus, "Introduction," in *No Fairer Land: Studies in Southern Literature before 1900*, ed. J. Lasley Dameron and James W. Mathews (1986). An obituary is in the *Knoxville News-Sentinel*, 31 Mar. 1981.

BEN HARRIS MCCLARY

DAVIS, Richard Harding (18 Apr. 1864–11 Apr. 1916), foreign correspondent and author, was born in Philadelphia, Pennsylvania, the son of Rebecca Harding, a novelist, and Lemuel Clarke Davis, a newspaper editor. Davis's mother, once a promising writer, had turned to churning out potboilers to support her family, and Richard carried from childhood the burden of her frustrated ambitions.

There was no question that he would become a writer. An inattentive student, he drifted through various private academies and was fortunate to be accepted at Lehigh University in 1882. Although his grades placed him near the bottom of his class, he was already a well-developed personality, sporting the foppish wardrobe, complete with fawn-colored kid gloves and cane, that was to become his trademark. His refusal to submit to freshman hazing led to the abolition of the

custom at Lehigh and attracted the attention of the national press. In 1885 he made a tour of the southern states as a correspondent for the *Philadelphia Inquirer*, of which his father was an editor. Invited to withdraw from Lehigh because of poor grades, he studied briefly at Johns Hopkins University in Baltimore, then became a reporter for the *Philadelphia Press*.

In 1889 Davis moved on to Charles Dana's *New York Sun*. During his first full day on the job, he scored a coup, making a citizen's arrest of a notorious con artist who had mistaken him for a gullible tourist. Within a few months Davis turned from the reporter's beat to fiction, launching a series of short stories featuring man-about-town Cortlandt Van Bibber, whose harmless escapades and chivalrous deeds provided the *Sun*'s readers with a glimpse of upper-class manners and mores.

Davis had arrived on the scene at a time when journalism was coming to be seen as an exciting, even glamorous, profession. His novella, *Gallegher* (1890), the story of a newspaper copy boy who solves a murder, entranced critics and the public alike, inspiring numerous imitations. The popularity of Van Bibber and Gallegher was exceeded only by the celebrity of their creator. Charles Dana Gibson chose Davis as the model for the male counterpart of the Gibson girl, sealing his reputation as the 1890s ideal of American manhood. Pink-cheeked yet rugged, he combined a patina of European sophistication with a moral code that would not have embarrassed a Boy Scout.

A few months after *Gallegher*'s publication, Davis was appointed editor of the prestigious *Harper's Weekly*. His interest in his editorial duties proved fitful, but he used the post as a platform to establish himself as a foreign correspondent. Vivid description and acerbic, confident judgments were the hallmarks of Davis's reporting from abroad. He never doubted the superiority of Anglo-Saxon virtues, yet he was quick to admit that Anglo-Saxons, like everyone else, often failed to live up to them, criticizing the overseas English for insularity and condescension and Americans for their superficial values and infatuation with overnight success.

Davis's career as a war correspondent began with coverage of an abortive revolution in Honduras in 1893 and continued through the early stages of World War I. In between, he covered almost every international conflict of importance, including the Greco-Turkish War of 1897, the Boer War, and the Russo-Japanese War of 1904. He is best remembered for his reporting from Cuba. In 1897 he and artist Frederick Remington visited the island on behalf of the *New York Journal*, but Davis's attempt to join the Cuban insurgents was frustrated by the *Journal*'s premature publicity. A year later, when the United States declared war on Spain, Davis traveled with the Fifth Army as a representative of the *New York Herald* and *Harper's Weekly*.

An admirer of Theodore Roosevelt, Davis attached himself to the Rough Riders, covering (and taking part in) the unit's skirmish with Spanish troops at Las

Guasimas. His thrilling, if inaccurate, account of the Rough Riders' charge up Kettle (San Juan) Hill made Roosevelt a war hero. As he and other correspondents on the scene realized, the heroics of the battlefield stood in sharp contrast to the unpreparedness of the general staff. Davis thought it unpatriotic and bad for morale to discuss such matters while victory hung in the balance, but three days after the battle he penned a scathing exposé. The *Herald* withheld the article until after the signing of the armistice, and when it appeared it created a sensation, in part because such criticisms were not expected from a writer of Davis's relatively conservative views.

In between assignments abroad, Davis enjoyed a second career as an author of short stories and romantic novels. The latter typically featured a self-made American man who engages in deeds of derring-do in an exotic locale and is rescued from cynicism and certain amorphously defined temptations by the love of an intelligent, tomboyish American girl. *Soldiers of Fortune* (1897) was a tremendous commercial success and established the formula so firmly in the public mind that Davis felt trapped by his own facility. In *Captain Macklin* (1902) he attempted to move beyond clichés, creating a flawed protagonist and a plot that revealed the American government as capable of deception. He was devastated when reviewers and readers failed to recognize the work as a step forward.

Although Davis was often mentioned in the society pages as the escort of Ethel Barrymore, Maude Adams, heiress Helen Benedict, and others, these relationships were wholly platonic. Throughout his adult life, he suffered periodic bouts of paralyzing depression. Davis's letters contain only scattered hints of the nature of his distress; however, his extreme physical modesty and obsession with personal cleanliness were often noted by his contemporaries. The great love of his youth was the Princess Alix of Hesse, whom he had encountered only once, in passing, when they happened to tour the Acropolis on the same day. This infatuation from afar inspired his novel *The Princess Aline* (1895), and in 1896 he went to Moscow to report Alix's coronation as the Empress Alexandra of Russia.

Like the protagonist of *The Princess Aline*, Davis idealized women yet was consumed by anxiety that no particular woman was ideal enough to make him happy. While this conflict presented itself in an extreme form in his personal life, uncertainty about the changing role of women (which he favored, in principle) and shifting moral standards in general, combined with the fear that domesticity meant the end of personal self-development, were themes that struck a responsive chord with his public, both male and female.

In about 1898 Davis concluded that he had at last found the perfect mate in Cecil Clark, the daughter of family friends and an accomplished portrait painter and sportswoman. His decision to ask for her hand in marriage received international publicity when he hired a fourteen-year-old messenger to hand-carry his proposal from London to America in a race against the transatlantic mails. Clark accepted, with the proviso that she would not share her husband's bed. Davis interpreted this condition as an extension of bluestocking high-mindedness and was confident that Cecil would relent in time. They were married in May 1899. She was, however, a lesbian, and the marriage was never consummated.

The acquisition of an elegant if emotionally distant wife and a rural estate in Mount Kisco, New York, spurred Davis to augment his income by writing for the stage. Several of his plays were hits, including *The Dictator* (1904), a farce that opened on Broadway with John Barrymore as the male lead, and a musical, *The Yankee Tourist* (1907). But once again, Davis's attempts to tackle more ambitious material were little appreciated by reviewers. One of the highest-paid writers of his day, he was nevertheless perpetually on the brink of bankruptcy, and the fear of commercial failure constrained his efforts at experimentation.

By 1910 Davis had fallen in love with Bessie McCoy, a dancer known as "the Yama-Yama Girl" after her performance of a similarly named novelty number in the Broadway show *The Three Twins*. Only after the death of his mother, who had remained a dominant influence in his life, did he feel free to ask Cecil for a divorce, and he and Bessie were married in 1912. The summer of 1914 found Davis in Belgium, where he wrote a much-praised account of the Germans' entry into Brussels (*With the Allies* [1914]) and was briefly detained as a spy. His only child was born the following January—a joyful occasion overshadowed by recurring bouts of angina, misdiagnosed as indigestion. He died of a massive heart attack at "Crossroads Farm," his home near Mount Kisco.

Even at the height of his fame, Davis struck many of his contemporaries as an anachronism. Despite his self-conscious attempt to speak for youth, he remained trapped in an indeterminate sensibility, caught between the modern temperament and the genteel tradition. He was often criticized as a prig and a self-promoter, and for his tendency to write of war as a stimulating exercise for gentlemen. As the critic Philip Littell put it, an ideal day in the life of Richard Harding Davis consisted of "shrapnel, chivalry and sauce mousseline, and so to work the next morning." Davis did his best to live up to his own moral code and generally succeeded. A ferociously hard worker, he often extended himself to help colleagues and friends in need. Moreover, when not carried away by the enthusiasms of the moment, he was a reliable observer. An advocate of a standing army and by temperament pro-establishment, he was skeptical of imperial adventures, and his prejudices were generally subordinated to his sense of fair play.

Much of Davis's journalism and the best of the short stories, especially "The Reporter Who Made Himself King," "The Bar Sinister," and "The Deserter," are still worth reading; even the more dated novels are well paced and radiate with a suppressed eroticism that might profitably be studied by would-be authors of popular fiction. But it is Davis's style that has had a lasting impact on American letters. He made personal journalism an accepted literary genre, and as the prime exemplar of "muscular Christianity" defined a new and self-consciously masculine sensibility. Ernest Hemingway is Davis's most obvious heir, but others, including Frank Norris and Sinclair Lewis, acknowledged a debt to him. One can also discern his influence in the careers of Norman Mailer and Tom Wolfe.

• The bulk of Davis's papers are in the Barrett Collection of the Alderman Library at the University of Virginia. Other correspondence remains in the hands of the family and private collectors. Scribner's published an edition of Davis's collected works in 1916, but Henry Cole Quimby, *Richard Harding Davis: A Bibliography* (1924), lists many additional entries, including unsigned newspaper articles. *The Adventures and Letters of Richard Harding Davis* (1917), edited by his brother Charles, gives the flavor of Davis's opinions. Fairfax Davis Downey, *Richard Harding Davis: His Day* (1933), is informal in tone. More complete accounts of his life are in two more recent biographies: Gerald Langford, *The Richard Harding Davis Years* (1961), and Arthur Lubow, *The Reporter Who Would Be King* (1992). For a negative view on Davis see Philip Littell, "Richard the Lion-Harding," in *Book & Things* (1919).

JOYCE MILTON

DAVIS, Richard L. (24 Dec. 1864–25? Jan. 1900), African-American coal miner and officer of the United Mine Workers of America (UMWA), was born in Roanoke, Virginia. Little is known about his personal life, including the names of his parents and the size of his family. He obtained his early education in the Roanoke schools, which he attended during the winter months. At eight years of age he took a job in a local tobacco factory. After spending nine years in the tobacco industry, Davis became increasingly disgusted with the very low wages and unfavorable conditions on the job. In 1881 he migrated to southern West Virginia and took his first job as a coal miner in the newly opened Kanawha and New River coalfields. The following year he moved to Rendville, Ohio, a small mining town in the Hocking Valley region, southeast of Columbus. In Rendville, Davis married, supported a family, and worked until his death, from lung failure. Upon his death the UMWA paid special tribute to Davis, lamenting that the organization had lost a "staunch advocate" of the rights of workers.

Davis's coal mining career is well documented in the columns of the *United Mine Workers' Journal* (*UMWJ*) and the *National Labor Tribune* (*NLT*), a labor paper published in Pittsburgh, Pennsylvania. In 1891 Davis was elected to the executive board of the UMWA District Six (Ohio). He held the Ohio post for six years, and in 1896 and again in 1897 he was elected to the national executive board, the highest position held by an African American in the UMWA. Davis's influence was felt at the local, regional, and national levels. In 1892, for example, when owners sought to segregate one mine in Rendville, making it all black, at lower pay, and with poorer working conditions than before, Davis rallied black and white workers against the proposal; he firmly resisted the company's effort to divide workers along racial lines. In another instance,

Davis opposed the development of segregationist policies in Congo, Ohio. After calling attention to segregated housing, he observed a similar pattern in the mines and urged an end to such racial stratification.

He also used the labor press to strengthen the cause of labor solidarity across ethnic and racial lines. In numerous articles in the *UMWJ* and the *NLT*, he not only attacked the unjust policies of coal companies but also criticized rank-and-file white miners and their leaders for perpetuating racially discriminatory policies in the mines and unions. Although he consistently encouraged blacks to join the union (and at times severely criticized them for their reluctance), he placed their grievances squarely before white workers. He opposed exclusionary hiring practices, advocated the election of blacks to leadership positions in the union, and protested white miners' discriminatory attitudes and behavior toward black workers. On one occasion, Davis rebuked his white counterparts for referring to black men as "big buck niggers." "I assure anyone that I have more respect for a scab than I have for a person who refers to the negro in such way, and God knows the scab I utterly despise." Davis urged white workers not to play into the hands of operators by discriminating against blacks, exhorting them instead to organize against corporate exploitation and confront those who gained unequal benefits from the "sweat and blood" of fellow workers.

Although change occurred slowly, Davis was a tireless organizer and defender of workers' rights through the 1890s. He helped to establish new locals, strengthen existing ones, and advise miners during bitter industrial disputes in West Virginia, western Pennsylvania, and Alabama as well as Ohio. During his organizing efforts in West Virginia and Alabama, Davis faced threats on his life and had to flee. Sometimes, as a result of his organizing activities, he lost his job; his family faced deprivation, and he found it exceedingly difficult to push forward. In 1898, for example, operators refused to hire him, and, for its part, the UMWA rejected his bid for employment as a paid organizer. Davis nearly despaired: "I have been sandbagged; I have been stoned, and last of all deprived of the right to earn a livelihood for myself and family. . . . It makes me almost crazy to think of it." African-American miners decried Davis's treatment. As one black miner stated, "If he was a white man he would not be where he is—mark that—but being a negro he does not get the recognition he should have. . . . Such treatment will not tend to advance the interest of our union, but will retard its progress and cause colored men to look with suspicion upon it."

Still, despite the debilitating impact of racial injustice from within and from without the union, Davis retained his commitment to organized labor and influenced the U.S. labor movement at a pivotal moment in its history. Although blacks constituted less than 15 percent of the nation's 400,000 coal miners in 1900, thanks in part to the organizing activities of black miners like Davis, they made up 24 percent of the union's membership in the bituminous mines.

At a time when African Americans faced increasing restrictions on their civil rights, witnessed the meteoric rise of Booker T. Washington, and turned increasingly toward the ideology of racial solidarity and self-help, black and white workers joined the UMWA, an interracial union within the American Federation of Labor. Davis's life symbolized this complicated intertwining of workers' class and racial identities at the turn of the twentieth century. It also suggests how some Americans regarded their position in the political economy, how they used their union to foster working-class solidarity, and how they articulated an alternative ideology in the industrial age.

• The key primary sources for research on the life and career of Richard L. Davis are the *United Mine Workers Journal* (particularly 23 Apr. 1896 and 25 Jan. 1900) and the *National Labor Tribune*, (especially 13 Dec. 1890 through 14 Nov. 1891). For studies highlighting the class dimensions of Davis's career, see the pioneering essay by Herbert Gutman, "The Negro and the United Mine Workers of America: The Career and Letters of Richard L. Davis and Something of Their Meaning, 1890–1900," in Gutman, *Work, Culture, and Society in Industrializing America* (1977), and Stephen Brier, "The Career of Richard L. Davis Reconsidered: Unpublished Correspondence from the National Labor Tribune," *Labor History* 3 (Summer 1980): 420–29. For an emphasis on the racial aspects of Davis's life and labor, see Philip Foner, *Organized Labor and the Black Worker, 1619–1973* (1974). Two studies help to reconcile these divergent views: Ronald L. Lewis, *Black Coal Miners in America: Race Class and Communist Conflict 1780–1980* (1987), and Joe W. Trotter, Jr., *Coal, Class, and Color: Blacks in Southern West Virginia, 1915–32* (1990).

JOE W. TROTTER

DAVIS, Sammy, Jr. (8 Dec. 1925–16 May 1990), variety performer and entertainer, was born in Harlem, New York, the son of Sammy Davis, Sr., an African-American dancer, and Elvera "Baby" Sanchez, a Puerto Rican chorus girl, both in Will Mastin's *Holiday in Dixieland*, a vaudeville troupe. He lived with his paternal grandmother, Rosa B. Davis, whom he called "Mamma." After his sister was born in 1927, his parents separated.

Davis went on the road at age three with his father, performing with a Will Mastin vaudeville show, known then as an all-colored revue. The group came on between the main acts and served as just another anonymous comedy group to liven up the audience. Davis affectionately referred to Mastin as his uncle. The first show Mastin developed that included Davis was *Struttin' Hannah from Savannah*. When he was seven, he got the billing "Silent Sam, the Dancing Midget." He made his film debut as Rufus, a seven-year-old singer and dancer, in a 1933 film with Ethel Waters, *Rufus Jones for President*. Davis performed for about thirty years with his father and the man he called his uncle as the Will Mastin Trio. The act was originally conceived as a conventional flash dance act, with three men doing extremely intricate tap dancing at flying speed. They would run on, do their dancing, and then run off without connecting with the audience.

Davis developed the idea that they should add more variety to the act and add a human dimension, which became his famous impressions of other stars. Because of his career as a child star, he never received any formal education except occasional tutoring.

While performing in Detroit in 1941, Davis shared the billing with Frank Sinatra, then an up-and-coming young singer. They instantly became friends. Davis once said, "He is my friend, and he is to me one of the nicest human beings I have ever known in my life."

In 1942 Davis was drafted into the U.S. Army and sent to basic training for infantry at Fort Francis E. Warren in Cheyenne, Wyoming, to be in one of the first integrated units in U.S. military history. There he encountered racism at its worst when a group of white enlisted men painted him white after they saw him talking to a white female officer. That conversation had been about his joining the Special Services branch. He finally got the appointment and fulfilled his duty entertaining other soldiers.

When Davis got out of the army, the Mastin trio played Las Vegas, Nevada, at a time when hotels there barred them as guests because of their skin color. Davis met strong racial prejudice wherever he entertained in the United States, despite his obvious talent. When he went to see Frank Sinatra at the Copa Cabana Club in New York City, he was turned away. The next night Davis got in, and Sinatra took an interest in his career and in helping him break social barriers from then on.

Early in 1952, when Davis was the opening act at Ciro's in Hollywood, California, he dazzled the audience with his tap dance routine, jokes, impressions, dramatic songs, and ability to play every instrument in the orchestra. He was an overnight sensation, and his reputation quickly spread. Two years later Davis was recording songs for Decca, including "Hey There," "The Birth of the Blues," "That Old Black Magic," and "My Funny Valentine." Decca released *Starring Sammy Davis, Jr.* (1954), an album featuring his impressions of Dean Martin, Jimmy Durante, Johnny Ray, and Bing Crosby. In November 1954 Davis lost his left eye as a result of a traffic accident. For a while he wore an eye patch, but it was later replaced by an artificial eye. His first performance after the accident was in January 1955 at Ciro's in Los Angeles with the trio. Later that year, after studying with Max Nussbaum, the rabbi at Temple Israel Hollywood, he converted to Judaism.

In 1956 Davis played Fletcher Henderson in the film *The Benny Goodman Story*, which starred Steve Allen. That same year he played a character based on himself in the Broadway stage production of *Mr. Wonderful*, which also featured his father and Mastin. After it closed in February 1957, his father retired. The "Ed Sullivan Show" on CBS provided Davis with his first solo appearance on TV. That was followed by roles on "General Electric Theater," the "Steve Allen Show," and the "Dick Powell Show." He also recorded the album *Sammy Davis, Jr., Live at Town Hall* (1958), which provides a hint of the fast-paced shows for which he became so well known.

To direct attention away from his interracial affair with actress Kim Novak, Davis was married in Las Vegas in 1958 to Loray White, an African-American dancer. Harry Belafonte was his best man. The ill-fated marriage lasted three months.

In the 1950s and 1960s Davis moved in the fast lane with fellow celebrities Sinatra, Dean Martin, Peter Lawford, and Joey Bishop in a group known as the Rat Pack. They partied as hard as they entertained and became notorious for their wild escapades. The pinnacle of the Rat Pack's existence was the infamous "Summit at the Sands" in 1960 when they went to Las Vegas to shoot scenes for the caper film *Ocean's 11*, while simultaneously playing the Sands Hotel and Casino.

While traveling in Europe in 1960, Davis met Swedish actress May Britt. When they decided to marry that October, there was much controversy over the interracial wedding, so it was postponed until after the election of John F. Kennedy as president of the United States, a campaign in which the Rat Pack had been very active. Sinatra was best man at the wedding. During their eight-year marriage, which was burdened by hate mail, death threats, and bias against miscegenation, they had a daughter and adopted two sons. Kennedy waited until 1963 to invite Davis to the White House. When the president learned that May Britt would accompany her husband, he barred media photographers. Although the occasion was not widely publicized, it caused emotional pain to Davis and his family.

Davis's major film breakthrough came in 1959 when he played Sportin' Life in the screen adaptation of George Gershwin's *Porgy and Bess*. His next role was as the sailor Danny Johnson, with Eartha Kitt in *Anna Lucasta* (1959). Davis's second role in an opera film was the Street Singer in *Die Dreigroschenoper* (1963), a production of Kurt Weill and Bertolt Brecht's *Threepenny Opera* in the original German.

In 1964, in one of his most important stage roles, Davis played a boxer struggling to become successful in *Golden Boy*, a musical adaptation of Clifford Odets's 1930s play, which ran for two years in Britain and on Broadway in the United States. It included one of the first fully integrated casts, and in 1965 Davis was nominated for a Tony Award for best actor in a musical. Also in 1965 he made an excellent jazz recording, *Our Shining Hour*, with Count Basie and arrangement by Quincy Jones. In 1966 he starred in *A Man Called Adam*, filmed by his own company, Trace-Mark Productions, in New York City. That same year Davis did some of his finest recording work on an album called *Sounds of '66*, with the Buddy Rich Big Band. In 1969 he created the role of Big Daddy in the film version of the musical *Sweet Charity*, but by then his heavy drinking had begun to get serious. The assassinations of Dr. Martin Luther King and Robert Kennedy affected him deeply and caused his spirits to sink even lower.

In the 1960s and 1970s Davis appeared on many television shows, including "The Beverly Hillbillies," "Mod Squad," the "Tonight Show" (as substitute host for Johnny Carson), "Here's Lucy," "Make Room for Granddaddy," and "All in the Family." On "Rowan and Martin's Laugh-In" he created anew an old vaudeville routine, "Here Comes de Judge," and made the phrase "Here come da judge" a popular comedic statement. Regardless of his personal pain, he always wanted his audiences to laugh.

In 1970, two years after his divorce from May Britt, Davis married Altovise Gore, an African-American dancer whom he had met while doing a revival of *Golden Boy* in London. She and Davis adopted a son, and their marriage lasted until his death.

Davis joined the Republican party in 1972 and became a supporter of Richard Nixon. He traveled to Vietnam to entertain the troops fighting the war there and encouraged the idea of the festive party for former prisoners of war that Nixon held on the White House lawn on 24 May 1973, at which Davis, Bob Hope, and others entertained. After Davis entertained at a state dinner, he and his wife spent the night in the White House at the president's invitation. He later performed at the Republican National Convention in Miami Beach, Florida, and at a rally he hugged Nixon. The photograph of the embrace, which was disseminated across the nation, caused an uproar of criticism from African-American Democrats and from entertainers who felt that Davis had sold out to political forces hostile to the civil rights movement. Davis later explained that he had been so touched by Nixon's concern for his problems that he had hugged the president spontaneously. His career plummeted.

Among the songs for which Davis was best known—including "I've Got to Be Me," "The Birth of the Blues," and "Me and My Shadow" (recorded with Frank Sinatra)—none more closely reflected his own sense of vulnerability than "Mr. Bojangles." Ironically, its success certainly contributed to his being called "Mr. Entertainment." About an aging, down-on-his-luck dancer named Bojangles (not to be confused with the famous and successful tap dancer Bill "Bojangles" Robinson), the song had a powerful effect on Davis: "[It] spooked me. I had seen too many performers who'd slid from headlining to playing joints, then toilets, and finally beer halls. . . . The song was my own worst nightmare. I was afraid that was how I was going to end."

Davis's career was not at an end, however. He was able to return to the musical stage as Little Chap in *Stop the World . . . I Want to Get Off* at the New York State Theater in Lincoln Center in August 1978. Nor had he lost face in much of the African-American community. In 1979 *Ebony* magazine gave him a lifetime achievement award. His film credits in the 1980s included the box-office success *Cannonball Run* (1981) and the less-noticed *Heidi's Song* (1982), *Cannonball Run II* (1984), and *Moon over Parador* (1988). His last film, *Tap* (1989), which he felt was his best, featured Davis as a tired, old tap dancer.

Davis was a pioneer for African Americans in the entertainment field. He not only danced and sang, he also played bass, trumpet, vibraphone, piano, and percussion. He broke color barriers on the stage early in his career, and he challenged the restrictions on African Americans to be in the audience in places where he performed. His life told a story of persecution—at times intense—by white Americans who refused to accept him as their equal despite his immense talent and self-taught genius. Yet he never became bitter. He believed throughout his lifetime that if he worked hard enough and proved himself to others through his talent, that he could transcend racial prejudice. To a significant extent he did; his peers in the entertainment world—black and white alike—freely acknowledge his abilities.

To many, Davis was larger than life. He had a powerful, magnetic presence when he performed, with his fedora pulled down over one eye, his "conk" hairstyle, high-heeled black boots, expensive jewelry, and flashy costumes. But he will always be remembered for his exceptional talents. A singer of perfect pitch and rhythm, he was also an exceptional mimic, whose impressions of James Cagney and Charlie Chaplin were famous. His tap dancing made him an idol for many, including the young Gregory Hines, who later became a renowned tap dancer, actor, and entertainer.

Davis gained attention as well for his tireless philanthropic activities, which included the founding of the Sammy Davis Jr. National Liver Institute. A lifetime member of the National Association for the Advancement of Colored People, he was an ardent supporter of the civil rights movement, and in 1969 the NAACP awarded him the Spingarn Medal for his outstanding achievements. In 1987 President Ronald Reagan presented him the Kennedy Center Honor for his many humanitarian efforts and his long show-business career.

In a television tribute to Davis in 1989, the immensely popular entertainer Michael Jackson, a much younger star possessing a similar charisma, performed a song of his own that acknowledged his debt to Davis as a path-breaking model for black entertainers. Davis was not scheduled to perform because of ill health, but the emotion of the evening took over. He put on his tap shoes and did a tap improvisation with Gregory Hines, his heir apparent as a dancer. It was his last public appearance.

A heavy smoker who often appeared on TV lighting one cigarette after another, Davis died of throat cancer in Los Angeles, California. Davis may have done more than any other African American of his time to liberate black entertainers from the demeaning stereotypes based on the Stepin Fetchit character of an earlier era. As Quincy Jones wrote, "Sammy Davis Jr. did it all the way no one had done it before" (*Rolling Stone*, 28 June 1990). Davis the entertainer once said, "For as long as I can remember, Las Vegas has been my spiritual home." To commemorate his death, there were ten minutes of darkness on the entertainment strip in Las Vegas, a fact that speaks more to his achievement of his goals than anything else ever could.

• Davis wrote three autobiographies with Jane Boyar and Burt Boyar, *Yes I Can* (1965), *Hollywood in a Suitcase* (1980), and *Why Me?* (1989). A biography produced by the Arts and Entertainment cable network, *Sammy Davis, Jr.: Mr. Entertainment*, tells his life story in video (1994; 1996). Record albums not mentioned in the text include *Portrait of Sammy Davis, Jr.* (MGM [1972]), the original soundtrack of the movie *Porgy and Bess* (Columbia Records [1960; 1969]), and *Try a Little Tenderness* (Decca [1970; 1979]). He also performed on *The Incomparable Nat "King" Cole* (Warner Reprise Video [1992]) and with Frank Sinatra and Dean Martin (compact disc, [Jazz Hour, (1962); 1993]). He recorded more than twenty albums for the Capitol, Decca, Reprise, and Warner Bros. labels. Obituaries are in *Ebony*, July 1990; *Newsweek*, 28 May 1990; *Rolling Stone*, 28 June 1990; *U.S. News and World Report*, 28 May 1990; and the *New York Times*, 17 May 1990, among many other periodicals. The 4 June 1990 issue of *Jet* magazine is devoted to Davis and includes a list of his top twenty albums and singles.

CAROLYN L. QUIN

DAVIS, Samuel Post (4 Apr. 1850–17 Mar. 1918), journalist, author, and historian, was born in Branford, Connecticut, the son of the Reverend George R. Davis, an Episcopalian priest, and Sylvia Nichols. As Davis's father accepted different pulpits, the family moved to Ansonia, Connecticut; Newark, New Jersey; and Racine, Wisconsin. In Racine, Samuel attended the Racine College private school but apparently did not complete the secondary curriculum. He accompanied his parents when they subsequently moved to Brownsville, Nebraska, then to Nevada City, California, and finally to Carson City, Nevada.

Davis's journalistic career began in 1867 when he worked as a reporter on the *Brownsville (Nebr.) Advertiser*. He also reported for the *Omaha Herald*, the *Lincoln Statesman*, and the *St. Louis Republican*. After he was fired from the *Republican* for passing off fiction as news, he found employment on the *Chicago Times*, where he was encouraged to continue writing fiction when there was a dearth of genuine news. Davis worked for several newspapers in California when he moved there in 1872. In 1875 he moved to Virginia City, Nevada, where he reported for the *Evening Chronicle*. In 1879 Davis accepted a post on the *Carson City Morning Appeal*, managed by Nellie Verrill Mighels, the widow of its well-known proprietor and editor, Henry Rust Mighels. Within a year, Davis married Nellie Mighels, who had four children from her first marriage. Two more children were subsequently born to them. Davis became editor of the paper in 1880 and remained so for the next twenty years. Under Davis, the *Appeal* enhanced its record, already established by Mighels, of being respected for its integrity and its lively editorial style.

Davis was a well-liked journalist. From the time he arrived in 1875 on the Comstock, the mining region of western Nevada, he was known for his storytelling ability, his stock of anecdotes, and his sense of humor. Sometimes the target of good-natured banter, he gave back better than he received. One of his most famous and long-standing humorous inventions was the fictitious newspaper, the *Wabuska Mangler*. It began in 1889 as a private joke between Davis and Edward Payson Lovejoy, a former editor and resident of Wabuska, Nevada. Davis used the invention as an outlet for his humor; he pretended Lovejoy was the *Mangler*'s editor, ascribed ridiculous news stories to it, and disparaged its management and editorial policies. Other Nevada newspapers took an interest in the imaginary journal, quoted Davis's insults, and sometimes joined in the fun by pretending to take sides. The *Mangler* thus became a Comstock legend.

Under Davis, the *Appeal* strongly supported Nevada and Carson City interests. It did so as an independent organ and not as a mouthpiece of the Republican party, toward which it was inclined, or the miners' unions, with which it was sympathetic. Davis strongly supported the cause of free silver because the economy of Nevada depended heavily on it, but he also pressed for economic diversification and encouraged activities such as agriculture that might bring diversification about. He was an ethical journalist, fighting the power of the railroads and openly criticizing incompetence and corruption within his own party. In 1892 he was briefly jailed for refusing to name a secret source of information. In 1895, on the ground that the public had a right to know, he again used a secret source to report on a Carson City Mint investigation.

Davis made the *Appeal* a financially successful as well as respected newspaper. His vigorous but practical measures to energize the economy and improve the state won him continued support from advertisers. His campaign to popularize tree planting led to the state's adoption in 1887 of an Arbor Day. He helped popularize civic improvement measures. He was influential in bringing the famous and lucrative James Corbett-Bob Fitzsimmons prize fight to Carson City in 1897. The *Appeal* survived the depression of the 1890s as a forward-looking newspaper whose reportage and editorial opinions were highly regarded outside of Nevada as well as within.

A political dimension to his career opened in 1895, when Davis was appointed to the position of Nevada's deputy secretary of state. In 1898 he was elected on the Silver party ticket to the post of state controller, which he held until 1906. In this position he was instrumental in forcing an insurance company president who had contributed stockholders' money to the Republican party to resign and his company to return the money to the stockholders, and in requiring all insurance companies that did business with Nevada and California to pay casualty losses in full—a significant change from their previous intention of offering only partial payment. He also reorganized the state revenue system more equitably. From 1907 to 1913 he served as state industrial and publicity commissioner.

Davis's early penchant for literary activity developed on a series of fronts in the 1870s when he wrote and produced in Virginia City *The Bohemians' Blunder* (1877), a satirical play, and began sending short stories, poetry, and essays to the *Argonaut*. In the 1880s Davis began contributing frequently to western literary outlets such as the *Californian*, the *San Franciscan*, the *Overland Monthly*, and the *San Francisco Examiner* and *San Francisco Call* Sunday supplements. Over the years he wrote a number of poems, which show skill but limited talent, and many now-dated humorous sketches; he was most successful as a writer of fiction. His one anthology, *Short Stories* (1886), a collection of stories, sketches, and poems, contains some fine tales. Davis continued to write short stories for more than another decade, but some of his best work, though occasionally reprinted, has not yet been collected.

A major achievement of Davis was his editing of the two-volume *History of Nevada* (1913). Building on Myron Angel's *History of Nevada* (1881), Davis and other contributors added material that Angel missed as well as that which occurred after 1881. The two books are complementary and are recognized as indispensable sources of information about early Nevada. Davis loved Nevada and served it with distinction and integrity both as a journalist and as a political figure. His stories have yet to be properly evaluated. When they are, the best of them will be found good enough to last as minor literature.

• Collections of Davis material may be found in the Davis Family Papers in the library at the University of Nevada, Reno; the Nevada Historical Society, Reno; and in the Henry M. Yerington Papers, Bancroft Library, University of California at Berkeley. Several of Davis's early stories are reprinted in Duncan Emrich, *Comstock Bonanza* (1950). Anecdotal information about Davis may be found in works such as Ella Sterling Cummings, *The Story of the Files* (1893); Wells Drury, *An Editor on the Comstock Lode* (1936); Sylvia Crowell Stoddard, *Sam Knew Them When* (1996); and most histories of Nevada and Nevada journalism. He is mentioned a number of times in *The Journals of Alfred Doten, 1849–1903*, ed. Walter Van Tilburg Clark (1973). A good biography is Daniel Edward Small, "Sam Davis of *The Morning Appeal*" (M.A. thesis, Univ. of Nevada, 1978). Obituaries are in the *Carson City Daily Appeal* and the *Nevada State Journal*, both 18 Mar. 1918.

LAWRENCE I. BERKOVE

DAVIS, Stuart (7 Dec. 1892–24 June 1964), artist, was born in Philadelphia, Pennsylvania, the son of Edward Wyatt Davis, a newspaper art editor, and Helen Stuart Foulke, a sculptor. The Davis family moved to East Orange, New Jersey, in 1901. Davis attended East Orange High School, but he left in 1909 to study with Robert Henri at Henri's School of Art in New York. Through his association with Henri, Davis became acquainted with members of "The Eight," including John Sloan and George Luks. These socially conscious artists became the young painter's friends and mentors.

In 1910 Davis exhibited his work for the first time at the Exhibition of Independent Artists in New York City. Leaving the Henri school in 1912, he began contributing work to *The Masses*, a left-leaning journal that employed many prominent artists, including John Sloan, who was art director during much of Davis's tenure. Davis became a full staff member in 1913 and remained with *The Masses* until 1916, when he resigned over a disagreement about editorial policy. After he left *The Masses*, his work, which had been in a realist mode, became more abstract.

In 1913 Davis participated in the ground-breaking International Exhibition of Modern Art (known as the Armory Show) in New York City, exhibiting five watercolors, including the landscape *Servant Girls* (c. 1913), which depicts four workingwomen in a moment of leisure. Spending his summers first in Provincetown and later in Gloucester, Davis completed enough works for his first solo exhibition at the Sheridan Square Gallery in New York in 1917. The following year he was drafted and served as a cartographer in the U.S. Army Intelligence department. Returning to New York at the end of the war, Davis continued to paint in his abstract style and at the same time contributed drawings to magazines, including *The Dial* (1920–1923) and the *Little Review*. It was in the latter, in 1920, that a Davis drawing accompanied the "Nausicaa" section of James Joyce's *Ulysses*.

Davis began his Tobacco series in 1921. These were works based on cigarette packages and executed in a cubist style. He spent the summer of 1923 in Santa Fe, New Mexico, with his photographer brother Wyatt and John and Dolly Sloan. Davis's first museum exhibition, at the Newark Museum, opened in 1925. The next year, the Whitney Studio Club (later the Whitney Museum) presented a retrospective of the 34-year-old artist's career.

Edith Halpert, proprietor of New York's the Downtown Gallery, became Davis's dealer in 1927. Halpert presented eleven solo exhibitions of Davis's work in the course of their association. Davis began his Eggbeater series this same year. These still life paintings focusing on an eggbeater, an electric fan, and a rubber glove moved him away from the European cubist style and reflected his own development of abstraction. The Whitney's purchase of two of his paintings in 1928 provided Davis with the funds to go to Paris. Settling into a studio in Paris, he painted the city with a colorful palette and traditional perspectives. Critics found these works, such as *Place Pasdeloup* (1928, Whitney Museum of American Art), *Blue Café* (1928, Phillips Collection), and *Rue des Rats No. 2* (1929, Hirshhorn Museum and Sculpture Garden), "retrogressive" from his more formerly abstract Eggbeater series, but Davis later said that "the actuality was so interesting I found a desire to paint it just as it was" (quoted in Sims, p. 54).

While in Paris, Davis met Brooklyn native Bessie Chosak, whom he married in 1929. Returning to New York, the couple settled in Greenwich Village. For two years (1931–1932) Davis taught at the Art Students League. In 1932 Bessie contracted peritonitis after an abortion and died. In this same year, Davis was commissioned by the designer Donald Deskey to create a mural for the men's lounge at Radio City Music Hall. The mural, titled *Men without Women*, now in the collection of the Museum of Modern Art, has been interpreted by critic Rudi Blesh as a comment on Davis's own life as a recent widower.

As the depression worsened, Davis joined the government-sponsored relief program, the Public Works of Art Project, in 1933 and continued with its successor, the Federal Art Project, until 1939. During his time on the New Deal fine arts projects, Davis completed a number of murals as well as paintings and prints. Returning to his earlier social activism, Davis joined the Artists' Union in 1934 and was soon elected its president. In 1935 he became editor and a frequent contributor to the Artists' Union's magazine, *Art Front*. Davis also held offices in the American Artists Congress. In 1934 he met Roselle Springer; they married four years later and had one child.

After leaving the Federal Art Project, Davis taught at the New School for Social Research in New York and held that position until 1950. During the 1940s he participated in a number of exhibitions, including solo showings at the Downtown Gallery, a joint retrospective with Marsden Hartley at the Cincinnati Modern Art Society (1941), a group exhibition, "Artists for Victory," at the Metropolitan Museum of Art (1942), and "Portrait of America," an exhibition sponsored by the Pepsi-Cola company. Davis's entry, *The Terminal*, won first prize in the exhibition and was reproduced on 600,000 Pepsi-Cola calendars for 1945. In that same year the Museum of Modern Art mounted a major retrospective of Davis's work. Davis participated in the Container Corporation of America's art program, which reproduced his works in *Time Magazine* and *Fortune* in 1946.

Named by *Look* magazine as one of the United States' ten best artists in 1948, Davis, now in his mid-fifties, was one of the most familiar and respected painters in America. His popularity was based on a number of factors, one of which was that his work, though abstract, still retained recognizable forms. Furthermore, Davis's subject matter had an immediate appeal. His oft-quoted remark from 1945, "I am an American, born in Philadelphia of American stock. I studied art in America. I paint what I see in America, in other words, I paint the American scene . . . " (quoted in *Stuart Davis Memorial Exhibition*, p. 14), set him apart from the European and European-influenced artists of the mid-century.

Accolades and exhibitions flowed to Davis throughout the 1950s. He served as a visiting professor at Yale University in 1951; from 1954 to 1964 he was a member of the directing faculty at the Famous Artists School in Westport, Connecticut; in 1956 he was elected to the National Institute of Arts and Letters; and he won the Solomon R. Guggenheim Museum International Award twice, in 1958 and 1960. Major exhibitions included the First Bienal de São Paulo in 1951; the XXVI Biennale, Venice, in 1952; and a retrospective at the Walker Art Center in 1957. Davis died in New York City.

Davis's work during the last years of his life echoed the themes and preoccupations he depicted in his earlier years. Often using motifs or elements from previous drawings or paintings, he reworked these images into wholly new creations. Such later works as *Unfinished Business* (1962, the William H. Lane Collection), *Letter and His Ecol* (1962, Pennsylvania Academy of Fine Arts), and *Blips and Ifs* (1963–1964, Amon Carter Museum), though popular with the public, met with disdain from critics who disliked his vivid palette and pictorial abstraction. With the advent of the pop art movement of the early 1960s, however, a younger generation of artists and critics re-discovered Stuart Davis.

• Major collections of Davis's works are in the Phillips Collection (Washington, D.C.), the Museum of Modern Art (New York), the National Museum of American Art (Smithsonian Institution), the Whitney Museum of American Art, the Metropolitan Museum of Art, and the Detroit Institute of Arts. The Stuart Davis Papers are held by Harvard University Art Museums, Fogg Art Museum. Davis's scrapbooks and interviews are available at the Archives of American Art (Smithsonian Institution). Davis's writings have been edited by Diane Kelder in *Stuart Davis* (1971). *Stuart Davis* (1945) is a brief and sometimes inaccurate autobiography. An important source of biographical information is Karen Wilkin, *Stuart Davis* (1987). Lowery Stokes Sims, ed., *Stuart Davis: American Painter* (1991), is a catalog to accompany an exhibition at the Metropolitan Museum of Art and contains useful biographical information. Other sources include *Stuart Davis Memorial Exhibition, 1894–1964* (1965) and Jane Meyers, ed., *Stuart Davis: Graphic Work and Related Paintings with a Catalogue Raisonné of the Prints* (1986). An obituary is in the *New York Times*, 26 June 1964.

MARTIN R. KALFATOVIC

DAVIS, Thurston Noble (12 Oct. 1913–17 Sept. 1986), Jesuit priest and editor of *America*, was born in Philadelphia, Pennsylvania, the son of Noble T. Davis, a sales representative for the *Saturday Evening Post*, and Rose Mary Carey. As a child Davis moved from Kentucky to Georgia to Ohio as a result of his father's occupation, finally settling in Bloomfield, New Jersey. At the age of fourteen Davis commuted from Bloomfield to the Jesuit military high school, Xavier, in lower Manhattan. After high school (1931) he entered the Society of Jesus (Jesuits), receiving a B.A. in philosophy from Georgetown University in 1937 and theological education at the Jesuits' Woodstock College in Maryland between 1937 and 1942. He was ordained for the priesthood in 1942 and after two years of work in Jesuit educational institutions was sent to Harvard University where, studying under the classicist Werner Jaeger, he received his Ph.D. in the history of philosophy, defending his dissertation "Autarkeia: Historical Development of a Concept from Homer to Aristotle" (1947).

From 1947 to 1953 Davis was a professor and then dean of Fordham College at Fordham University in New York City. As dean, he inaugurated the honors program and the junior year abroad program, combined graduate and undergraduate facilities, and generally improved Fordham's academic quality.

Davis came to national prominence in American Catholicism in 1953 and 1954 when he became a contrib-

uting and then an associate editor of the Jesuit weekly magazine *America*. At the time, some Catholic liberals feared that Davis was sent to *America* to moderate the anti-McCarthyism of the former editor, Robert C. Hartnett, S.J. Such was not the case, however. Davis was no friend of McCarthyism, nor was he as conservative as some thought he might be. Although he abhorred communism, he criticized Catholic anti-Communists for their undemocratic tactics. "Unless communism is fought with clean democratic hands," he wrote, "we risk being infected by the very totalitarian poison we abhor."

In 1955 Davis was named editor in chief of *America*, and for the subsequent thirteen years of radical change and revolution in American society and in American Catholicism, he provided progressive leadership as an editor. Although he opposed the tactics of some peace activists during the 1960s, he asserted that the doctrine of the Incarnation meant that, for *America*, "Nothing, absolutely nothing, that concerns the good of the human person on any level of life should be outside our purview." From this perspective he opened *America* to a wide discussion of many of the controversial issues of the day: the war in Vietnam, racial justice, religious liberty, contraception, divorce and remarriage, poverty, and ecumenism. A passionate defender of freedom of the press, he told an international conference of Jesuit editors in 1960 that "without this essential freedom, there can be no authentic public opinion, for wherever the Catholic press or the press in general is muzzled, public opinion has no means of self-expression."

He also promoted frank expression of divergent Catholic opinions on a variety of social and political issues, believing that the free exchange of opinions was the most creative means for resolving societal problems. His editorial policy and his participation in the renewal of American Catholicism in the post–Vatican II era was governed by an attitude of Christian hope: "While we take full account of the Fall of Man and the weaknesses of human nature," he wrote, "we scorn fatalism, and we rest our resolute rejection of despair on the capacities of human free will elevated by divine grace and aided by the constant protection of divine Providence."

In 1964 he renovated an old New York City hotel and established there America House, a major center for national Jesuit initiatives in the 1960s and 1970s. At that house he founded in 1967 the John LaFarge Institute, which brought together leaders from many fields of study and from many religious traditions to discuss major religious, moral, social, and international issues. The following year he established the John Courtney Murray Forum to provide public lectures on issues relating to religious thought and common life in the United States. He directed the Forum for the rest of his life.

After leaving the editorship of *America* in 1968, he continued to work for the LaFarge Institute and the Murray Forum, but he also became from 1970 to 1978 a national consultant to the general secretary of the

United States Catholic Conference, a national civil corporation of the American Catholic Bishops. In that post he provided the bishops with advice on a host of issues relating to post–Vatican II ecclesiastical reforms and to the church's stand on public moral and social issues in American society.

Throughout his adult life Davis was urbane, cultured, and, though personally reserved, passionate about issues of justice. He was concerned, too, about young people, especially during the 1960s, and, though paternal in manner, he gave young Catholics a voice in *America* while counseling their elders to have patience with the "rebellious" sixties generation and with the so-called new breed in the church.

Davis was a voice of moderation at a time of ecclesiastical and social upheaval in American society. Within the Catholic church he provided a forum for the expression of diverse opinions and thereby diffused some of the potential for disintegrating conflict. Following in the twentieth-century *America* tradition, he also invited Catholics to address the major political issues of the day from a perspective of faith and justice. During the 1960s, however, his efforts made *America* Catholics self-consciously aware of the church's affirmative as well as reproving role in the development of what the Second Vatican Council called the modern world. Davis was a major transitional figure in American Catholicism, having experienced as an adult both the pre- and post–Vatican II church and society. He had sympathies for them both. Davis died at America House in New York City.

• Davis's letters and unpublished papers are located at America House in New York City and the Jesuit Archives at Georgetown University. There is no biography of Davis. R. A. Schroth, "What's on Your Minds?" *Commonweal*, 24 Oct. 1986, pp. 549–50, and "Thurston N. Davis, SJ (1913–1986)," *America*, 4 Oct. 1986, pp. 157–58, provide brief accounts of his life. An obituary is in the *New York Times*, 19 Sept. 1986.

PATRICK W. CAREY

DAVIS, Varina Anne Jefferson (27 June 1864–18 Sept. 1898), "the Daughter of the Confederacy" and author, was born in the Confederate White House in Richmond, Virginia, the daughter of Jefferson Davis, the president of the Confederate States of America, and Varina Anne Howell. During her father's two-year imprisonment after the war, while her older siblings were in Canada with their grandmother, "Winnie," as she was known, stayed in the South with her mother and even visited her father in his cell. Later admirers would emphasize her role as "the only ray of sunshine" for the first family of the Confederacy in their darkest days.

The Davis family faced a great deal of difficulty throughout Winnie's childhood, both because of the tensions of Reconstruction and because of her father's economic uncertainties. When Jefferson Davis was first freed from prison in 1867, the family spent several years in England. From 1870 to 1876 they lived in Memphis while Jefferson Davis worked as an executive in an insurance company that eventually folded.

In 1876, Davis enrolled in the Friedlander Institute, a Protestant girls' school in Karlsruhe, Germany; she stayed in Europe until 1881, rarely seeing her parents. In Germany she experienced spartan living conditions, while becoming relatively accomplished in German, French, art, and music. Returning to the South when she was seventeen, Davis was anxious to please her father but was also nervous about living in a culture that was no longer familiar to her. She spent much of her time at the new family home "Beauvoir" on the Mississippi gulf coast, but she also socialized frequently in New Orleans and elsewhere.

In 1886 Davis accompanied her father on his first major speaking tour since the Civil War. When he was too ill to appear at some of the stops the train made through the South, his daughter came out for him and greeted the crowd. When General John Gordon, a candidate for governor in Georgia, introduced her as "*the* Daughter of the Confederacy," the cheers this statement produced inspired Gordon and the press to repeat the phrase often. As people talked about how moving it was to see Winnie Davis, the idealization of her personal characteristics began. For the rest of her life, she was a favorite honored guest for countless Lost Cause events.

In the winter of 1886–1887 Davis visited family friends in the Northeast. While in Syracuse, New York, she met and fell in love with a young patent lawyer, Alfred Wilkinson. The relationship was apt to stimulate criticism in the South not only because Wilkinson was a northerner but also because his maternal grandfather was Samuel May, one of the leaders of the abolitionist movement.

Although Davis began suffering from anxiety and loss of appetite in 1888, she did publish two works that year, "Serpent Myths" in the February *North American Review* and a small book on the Irish patriot Robert Emmet, *An Irish Knight of the Nineteenth Century*. In September, soon after she had made another trip to the Northeast, Wilkinson traveled to Mississippi to ask Mr. and Mrs. Davis if he could marry their daughter. Both parents at first adamantly opposed the match, but Wilkinson's charm and their daughter's vow that she would love no one else wore down their resistance. After agreeing to keep the engagement secret, Davis returned to Syracuse for another visit.

Davis's chronic physical and emotional ailments increased so markedly in 1889 that she went to Europe in the fall with a distant cousin, the wife of Joseph Pulitzer, to try to calm her nerves. In December 1889, two months after her departure, Jefferson Davis died. The news overwhelmed Davis so much that she had a nervous breakdown, and her mother encouraged Wilkinson to go to Europe to help her. Although Davis at first stated she no longer wanted to consider marriage, she eventually relented, and her mother wrote a friend in March that they were engaged. Formal announcements followed in April in newspapers across the country. By the summer of 1890 Wilkinson and the

Davis family began receiving letters opposing the marriage of the Daughter of the Confederacy with a "Yankee," possibly including physical threats.

Lost Cause advocates have tended to proclaim that the marriage was called off so that Winnie Davis could honor the South and keep her father's name. The actual end to the engagement, however, developed after a fire in the summer of 1890 that destroyed the Wilkinson mansion in Syracuse and killed a servant. Wilkinson may have been at least partially responsible for the fire because he had left some extremely flammable benzene there. A New York *Times* article (7 Oct. 1890, p. 5) indicates as well that Varina Davis probably asked a friend to investigate his financial standing at this time.

In the early fall of 1890, Varina Davis and Winnie Davis questioned Wilkinson about both the fire and his economic status. Mrs. Davis apparently believed Wilkinson had lied to them when he said earlier that he had supported his mother and that he had enough money to provide for a wife. He, in turn, had incorrectly assumed that Davis had enough money to support herself. The same article in the New York *Times* declares that the engagement had been called off, suggesting that money was probably the primary cause. Southern newspapers, however, tended to blame Davis's poor health.

Although North-South conflicts had affected the relationship between Winnie Davis and Alfred Wilkinson, there is no reason to believe that they would not have married if they had had enough money and mutual trust. Davis never became engaged again, but she continued to lead an active social life.

Davis lived with her mother in New York City, where they both received retainers from the New York *World*. During this time Davis published a number of articles as well as two novels—in 1895 *The Veiled Doctor*, about the failed marriage of a doctor and a self-centered beauty, and in 1898 *A Romance of Summer Seas*, about the tensions caused by gossips on a cruise to Asia. She also went South for a number of Confederate commemorative events, where she shook hands until she had blisters. In 1895 she attended a reunion of the United Confederate Veterans at the Winnie Davis Auditorium in Houston, Texas. Although she reigned as Queen of Comus in the 1892 New Orleans Mardi Gras, most of her socializing was in the North.

In the spring of 1898, Davis made a trip to the Middle East, where she may have contracted a parasite. In July, at her mother's urging, she attended a Confederate reunion in Atlanta, where she became sicker. She recovered enough to attend a ball in early September but then died shortly thereafter of malarial gastritis in Narragansett Pier, Rhode Island. A special railroad car, with both northern and southern veterans as guards, took her body to Richmond, Virginia. A mile-long procession escorted her casket to the burial next to her father and brothers in Hollywood Cemetery. The Richmond chapter of the United Daughters of the Confederacy soon organized a movement to raise money for a graveside monument, which was unveiled on 10 November 1899.

The letters and resolutions that Davis's mother received reveal more than any other documents the extent to which Winnie Davis had become a southern symbol, almost the female counterpart to Robert E. Lee. The following excerpt from the resolution passed by the Pat Cleburne Camp, No. 222, of the United Confederate Veterans (found at the Eleanor S. Brockenbrough Library of the Museum of the Confederacy in Richmond, Virginia) is typical.

She was the embodiment of all that is great and noble in Southern womanhood and her life made her an exemplar for the women of all nations, and the uncrowned queen in the hearts of her own people. . . . as the Confederacy went down without a stain upon its honor, so its daughter, "Winnie" Davis, yielded up her bountiful life, with a name that will live in song and story, fadeless and pure.

Winnie Davis apparently had two identities, a private self involved in intellectual and social pleasures found most readily in the Northeast and her occasional transformation into the symbol of southern femininity as the Daughter of the Confederacy.

• Some letters by Winnie Davis and many references to her can be found in the collections of the papers of Jefferson Davis and his family at the Alabama Department of Archives and History; the Beauvoir Museum in Biloxi, Mississippi; the Historic New Orleans Collection; the Library of Congress; the Mississippi Department of Archives and History; Transylvania University; Tulane University; the University of Alabama; and the University of Georgia. There is also information in the Joseph Pulitzer Papers at Columbia University. Some useful, though often poorly edited, letters are in Jefferson Davis, *Private Letters* (1966), edited by Hudson Strode.

The publications of Varina Anne Jefferson Davis include "The American Girl Who Studies Abroad" in the *Ladies' Home Journal*, Feb. 1892, p. 99 and Mar. 1892, p. 6; "The Ante-Bellum Southern Woman," in *Confederate Veteran*, Mar. 1893, pp. 73–74; and "Jefferson Davis in Private Life," in the *New York Herald*, 11 Aug. 1895, sec. 4, pp. 1–2; as well as newspaper articles in the *New York World* and elsewhere, some of which may be unsigned.

The most complete discussion of Davis's life is in two articles by Suzanne T. Dolensky in *The Journal of Mississippi History*, "Varina Howell Davis, 1889 to 1906: The Years Alone" (May 1985) and "The Daughters of Jefferson Davis: A Study of Contrast" (Nov. 1989). Gaines Foster, *Ghosts of the Confederacy* (1987) illuminates the significance of Davis to supporters of the Lost Cause. Also helpful is Ishbel Ross, *First Lady of the South: The Life of Mrs. Jefferson Davis* (1958). Mary Craig Sinclair interviewed Varina Davis and various family friends about Winnie Davis; some of her findings are in the Upton Sinclair Papers at the University of Indiana, Bloomington, and in her autobiography, *Southern Belle* (1962). "Daughter of the Confederacy" by Craddock Goins in *The American Mercury* (1940) includes a number of factual errors. Numerous memorial resolutions and letters are at the Eleanor S. Brockenbrough Library at the Museum of the Confederacy, Richmond, Virginia. Among the articles around the time of her death are ones in the New York *Times*, 19–24 Sept. 1898; the Charleston *News and Courier*, 19–26 Sept. 1898; and *Confederate Veteran*, Oct. 1898.

CITA COOK

DAVIS, Varina Howell (7 May 1826–16 Oct. 1906), First Lady of the Confederacy, was born in Louisiana, the daughter of William Howell, a slaveowning planter, and Margaret Kempe. Raised in Mississippi, she obtained an unusually fine education for a white southern woman, attending an elite girls' academy in Philadelphia and studying at home with a private tutor. By the time she met her future husband, Jefferson Davis, in 1843, she was an articulate, spirited young woman, rather than the demure "lady" that most white southerners expected women in the planter class to be.

Davis, seventeen years her senior, was a rich planter and slaveowner. He was also a handsome, well-spoken man, and young Varina was attracted to him despite what she called his arrogant manner. For his part, Davis seems to have been drawn to her youth, beauty, and wit; a lonely widower, he was ready to remarry. The couple fell in love, but they did not have a tranquil courtship. Even in the early stages, the relationship was marked by misunderstanding and conflict. At one point, Howell asked Davis not to write to her anymore. Nevertheless they married in February 1845.

The early years of the Davis marriage were even more turbulent. The couple lived near Varina's brother-in-law Joseph E. Davis, who still controlled the disposition of Jefferson's property. Soon after the wedding, she learned that Joseph Davis had composed a will that prevented her from inheriting her husband's estate. She protested this inequity, but her husband told her to accept it. She soon became even more estranged from her husband when he left home to fight in the Mexican War without informing her in advance. When Davis returned in 1847, he was appointed to the U.S. Senate, and he was still so angry with his wife over the inheritance dispute that he left her in Mississippi for almost a year. It had become clear that he was an authoritative, traditional man who expected his wife to do as she was told, to assume a role she was far too well educated and too strong willed to play—that of a so-called lady.

Somehow the couple reconciled, and Varina Davis moved to Washington, D.C., where she lived for most of the next twelve years. She enjoyed life in the nation's capital and made many friends, including the famous diarist Mary Boykin Chesnut. Taking a keen interest in contemporary politics, she relished the intellectual stimulation of city life. The Davis marriage became somewhat more harmonious, and the couple had four children. Still, she and her husband continued to disagree about finances and household matters, and she never forgave her brother-in-law for cutting her out of the family fortune.

The secession crisis of 1860–1861 alarmed Varina Davis, as she did not wish to leave Washington and return to the South, telling her mother that the Confederacy did not have the resources to defeat the North. She apparently also had private doubts about slavery, for years later she wrote that it was absurd to fight a war to preserve it. When her husband became Confederate president, she went reluctantly to Richmond, where she became a controversial figure. Her direct manner put off many people who expected her to play a more sedate, "ladylike" role. Her opposition to secession does not seem to have been widely known, but her shrewd political remarks disturbed some politicians, who began to accuse her of manipulating the Confederate president. In fact, she had little influence over her husband, who made his own political and military decisions. She was relieved when the war ended in 1865, telling a friend that the past four years had been the worst of her life.

The immediate postwar years were also unhappy ones. Her husband was charged with treason and went to a federal prison for two years. When he was released in 1867, the family teetered on the brink of poverty. Jefferson Davis tried several business ventures in the United States and overseas, but all of them failed. The couple eventually moved to Memphis, and Varina Davis began to work part-time as a seamstress, gradually taking over the management of the household. In the late 1870s Jefferson Davis retired to a home on the Gulf Coast of Mississippi, which had been given to him by a family friend. His physical and mental health declined, and he died of pneumonia in 1889. Varina Davis then threw herself into the task of writing a book about her husband, a two-volume, 1,638-page biography. Published in 1890, its reverential tone is at odds with the reality of her married life. The book did not sell well, and the publisher went bankrupt.

Varina Davis then astonished white southerners by moving to Manhattan. She spent the last years of her life working as a journalist for the *New York World*, writing about contemporary and historical topics, making a clean break with the role of the "lady." This was probably the most rewarding phase in her life, and it highlights how restrictive sex roles could be for white women in both the Old and New South. After her death in New York City, she was buried in Richmond beside her husband.

• Varina Davis's papers are located in the Jefferson Davis Papers at Rice University. For information on her life, see *The Papers of Jefferson Davis*, ed. James T. McIntosh et al. (1971–), and Irvin Bell Wiley, *Confederate Women* (1975). On Davis's life in Richmond, see Eli N. Evans, *Judah P. Benjamin: The Jewish Confederate* (1988). A biographical summary is in *Portraits of American Women*, ed. G. J. Barker-Benfield and Catherine Clinton (1991). For an account of white southern women during the Civil War, see George C. Rable, *Civil Wars: Women and the Crisis of Southern Nationalism* (1989).

JOAN E. CASHIN

DAVIS, Watson (29 Apr. 1896–27 June 1967), science writer and editor, was born in Washington, D.C., the son of Charles Allan Davis, a high-school principal, and Maud Watson, a teacher. Davis attended George

Washington University, where he received a bachelor's degree in civil engineering in 1918 and a civil engineering degree in 1920. In 1919 he married Helen Augusta Miles, a fellow student and a chemist; they had two children.

Davis began his lifelong association with science in 1917 as an assistant engineer-physicist with the National Bureau of Standards. In 1920 he also became the part-time science editor for the *Washington Herald*, the first newspaper science editor in the United States. In 1921 a news agency to popularize science, Science Service, was launched in Washington by newspaper magnate E. W. Scripps and major American scientific organizations, and Davis applied successfully for the position of news editor of this fledgling venture. Under the direction of former chemistry professor and journalist Edwin E. Slosson, Science Service grew to be a great voice for the popularization of science in the United States, particularly through its weekly newsletter (later magazine) *Science News Letter* (later *Science News*). Davis left the National Bureau of Standards in 1922 to devote his energies full-time to Science Service, and in 1923 he became its managing editor. After Slosson's death in 1929, Davis became acting director. He was not finally named director until 1933, in part because some of Science Service's trustees wanted someone with a stronger scientific background.

Under Davis's guidance Science Service flourished. Its syndicated articles were purchased by more than 100 newspapers, and *Science News Letter* reached a circulation of 30,000 by 1940. Davis began a weekly national radio interview program on the Columbia Broadcasting System, *Adventures in Science*, which continued until 1959. He also wrote a monthly science column for *Current History* magazine from 1924 to 1932. He often spoke out on the benefits of science to the public; in the *Annals of the American Academy of Political and Social Science* (1942), he wrote, "If we as a people think clearly and scientifically, there is a chance that we can rescue this muddled world after all." In 1934 Davis was among the twelve founders of the National Association of Science Writers (president, 1942–1943). Helen Davis joined Science Service in 1940, helping with business matters, editing the popular magazine *Chemistry*, which Science Service published from 1944 to 1962, and writing a syndicated column on the history of science.

Beginning in the early 1940s Davis began to expand the syndicate's popularization activities into other areas, particularly targeting youth. The Science Clubs of America, organized in 1941, were supported with ideas and material. By early 1945 there were about 7,000 clubs with a membership of more than 150,000 children. Science Service sponsored the International Science Fair, which complemented the regional science fairs New York's American Institute had originally sponsored. Through the Science Talent Search, Science Service identified the nation's talented science students and invited the best of them to the Science Talent Institute in Washington to hear lectures by leading scientists.

Davis was also involved with activities outside Science Service. Foremost was his role in founding the American Documentation Institute (ADI) in 1937. ADI devoted its activities to innovations in the library sciences, emphasizing microfilm, a term Davis coined. He served as president from 1937 to 1947. Beginning in 1940 he was a member of the National Inventors Council of the Department of Commerce. He was also a trustee of George Washington University (1949–1961) and of Jackson Laboratory in Bar Harbor, Maine (1949–1967), a member of the executive board of the National Child Research Center, and a member of the board of the American Eugenics Society. He was a fellow of the American Institute and of the American Association for the Advancement of Science, and a member of numerous scientific, engineering, and journalism societies.

After World War II Davis was the absolute head of the Science Service. The board of trustees, never very active, became even less so, and none of the other staff members wielded any control. His autocratic manner and explosive temper, coupled with the low salaries and minimal benefits offered to workers, led to a steady exodus of staff. Until the 1950s, however, his steadfast devotion to science and its ideals and Science Service's profitability satisfied the trustees. During the 1950s the service's fortunes declined in the face of increasing competition from the growing number of science writers on newspaper staffs. The news service saw its sales decrease, the quality of *Science News Letter* fell, and the funding of the youth activities was insufficient. Davis took on contract work for the National Science Foundation (NSF) to help augment Science Service's finances.

By the late 1950s Davis's personal and professional fortunes both took a downturn. His wife died in 1957; he married Marion Shaw Mooney, a teacher, in 1958. His contract proposals to the NSF's "Public Understanding of Science" program, which the foundation actively solicited, were too poorly argued to be funded. Davis continued as head of the diminished Science Service until 1966, when he was forced to retire by the trustees. He died in Washington, D.C.

Davis helped make Science Service the most important institution for popularization between the world wars, and he helped train a generation of science writers. He was respected by scientists; after his death the chairman of the Atomic Energy Commission, Glenn T. Seaborg, said, "Watson Davis has done more for the popularization of science and the understanding of science by the general public than any other individual."

• Davis's papers are in the Smithsonian Institution Archives, Washington, D.C. Material is also in the National Association of Science Writers Papers in the Cornell University Library. Davis's popular books include *The Story of Copper* (1924), *Science Today* (1931), *The Advance of Science* (1934), *Science Picture Parade* (1940), and *The Century of Science* (1963). On Science Service and science journalism, see Hillier Krieghbaum, "American Newspaper Reporting of Science News," *Kansas State College Bulletin* (15 Aug. 1941);

David J. Rhees, "A New Voice for Science: Science Service Under Edwin E. Slosson, 1921–1929" (master's thesis, Univ. of North Carolina at Chapel Hill, 1979); Bruce V. Lewenstein, "Public Understanding of Science" in America, 1945–1965" (Ph.D. diss., Univ. of Pennsylvania, 1987); and George R. Ehrhardt, "Descendants of Prometheus: Popular Science Writing in the United States, 1915–1948" (Ph.D. diss., Duke Univ., 1993). Obituaries are in the *New York Times*, 28 June 1967; *Science News*, 8 July 1967; and *Chemical and Engineering News*, 10 July 1967.

GEORGE R. EHRHARDT

DAVIS, William Augustine (21 Sept. 1809–15 Jan. 1875), postal official, was born in Barren County, Kentucky, the son of Hardin Davis and Elizabeth Wynne, farmers. Following a childhood on his parents' farm, Davis journeyed at age fourteen to Charlottesville, Virginia, to prepare for admission to the University of Virginia. To help support himself while he was in school, Davis worked in the Charlottesville post office for his mother's brother, John Winn (family members spelled their name differently). Davis could hardly have guessed it at the time, but this stint in his uncle's office was the opening chapter of a half century of distinguished service in the American postal system, then the largest public agency in the United States.

Davis accepted a clerkship in the Richmond post office shortly before completing his degree and never graduated from the University of Virginia. This appointment was striking testimony to his growing reputation as a postal administrator. While it was not unknown in this period for postal officials to move from office to office, clerkships in large towns such as Richmond were hard to come by and avidly sought. During the next twenty-five years, Davis built on this reputation and acquired a special expertise in the area of mail distribution. He also secured the necessary income to marry Anne Hopkins of Richmond in 1843 and to raise a large family that eventually included eight children.

In the spring of 1855 Davis resigned the Richmond clerkship and moved his family to St. Joseph, Missouri. The following October, he was appointed postmaster of St. Joseph. Precisely how Davis obtained this office is something of a mystery. Conceivably, he knew that the position would become vacant before he left Richmond. Or it may have been a happy coincidence. In any event, by this time Davis's abilities had become well known not only to his official superiors in the postal bureaucracy, but also to the leading public men of Virginia, who were familiar with Davis's solid work in Richmond.

Davis's tenure as St. Joseph postmaster was greatly complicated by the establishment of a regularly scheduled stagecoach service between St. Joseph and California. Overnight, Davis found himself responsible for sorting virtually all of the mail that passed between the Atlantic seaboard and the West Coast. Further complicating his task was the fact that postal officials required the overland mail to depart for California a mere three hours after the arrival of the train bringing the mail from the East. As a consequence, Davis and

his staff confronted the formidable administrative challenge of sorting the mail in an extremely limited period of time. Proving equal to the challenge, he quickly devised a set of procedures that greatly facilitated the rapid sorting of the mail.

In 1861 Davis lost the St. Joseph postmastership in a political maneuver that was unrelated to his official work. After the presidential election of 1860, Abraham Lincoln's incoming administration awarded the St. Joseph postmastership to a loyal Republican. Since Davis was a Democrat, his dismissal was inevitable. Nevertheless, Davis's successor, John L. Bittinger, recognized the importance of Davis's work in coordinating the overland mail and kept Davis on as his chief clerk. In this capacity Davis made his most notable contribution to postal administration. Intent upon reducing the pressure upon himself and his staff, Davis secured official permission in July 1862 to introduce on-board mail sorting on a specially outfitted car on the Hannibal & St. Joseph Railroad. For a time, Davis rode the railway car himself. Though on-board mail sorting—or, as it would come to be called, railway mail—had been a standard postal procedure for several decades in Great Britain and Canada, it had not yet been adopted in a major way in the United States. Davis's experiment did much to popularize the procedure with his official superiors and, for this reason, he is sometimes called the "founder" of the railway mail service in the United States. In fact, however, the establishment of the railway mail service took almost a decade and was the work of many individuals, the most prominent of whom included George B. Armstrong of Chicago, who became general superintendent of the railway mail service in 1869.

Although Davis did much to impress his official superiors with the practicality of railway mail, he was not destined to figure prominently in its further expansion. While it is conceivable that Davis had no interest in rising further within the postal system, it is more likely that his advancement was blocked by his attachment to the Democratic party and his close ties with the South. For whatever reason, Davis remained in a variety of subordinate positions in the postal system until his death in St. Joseph. Ten years later, Congress officially acknowledged Davis's role in the origins of the railway mail service in its official history of the institution. A few years later, Davis's reputation received a further boost when Bittinger, Davis's official superior during the period of his mail-sorting experiment, published an even more adulatory account of Davis's official career.

• Davis's personal papers do not appear to have survived, though there is a small collection of material bearing on his career at the National Postal Museum, Smithsonian Institution. The most detailed sketch of his career can be found in a pamphlet written by John L. Bittinger, *The Railway Postal Service Originated by William A. Davis of St. Joseph, Missouri* (n.d.), a copy of which is at the National Postal Museum. For the official government account, see U.S. Post Office. *History of the Railway Mail Service*. 48th Cong., 2d sess., 1885, S. Ex. Doc. 40. Both include copious extracts from official correspondence. For a valuable short account, see George Gerard Tunell, *Railway Mail Service: An Historical Sketch* (1902).

RICHARD R. JOHN

DAVIS, William Morris (12 Feb. 1850–5 Feb. 1934), geologist, meteorologist, and geographer, was born in Philadelphia, Pennsylvania, the son of Edward Morris Davis, a businessman with interests in railroads, mines, and the textile trade, and Maria Mott. Davis was associated with the civic elite of Philadelphia on both sides of his family. His maternal grandmother was the abolitionist Lucretia Mott; Davis himself bore the name of his uncle, a prominent businessman who was elected to Congress when Davis was a boy. Raised as a Quaker, Davis withdrew from the Society of Friends when his father was expelled for enlisting in the Union army during the Civil War. Davis later became a Unitarian, although he continued to use Quaker plain language with family members to the end of his life.

An interest in natural history, stimulated by summers in the farmlands outside Philadelphia, led Davis to matriculate at the Lawrence Scientific School of Harvard University. He graduated in 1869 and stayed at Harvard for an additional year to earn a master's degree as a mining engineer. While at Harvard, Davis was introduced to formal geological study by Raphael Pumpelly, Josiah Dwight Whitney, and Nathaniel Southgate Shaler. Davis accompanied Pumpelly on a tour of the mining districts of the Lake Superior region during the summer of 1869 and helped Whitney conduct field work later that same season in the Rocky Mountains. Another teacher, Benjamin Gould, invited Davis to accompany him to Argentina in 1870 to organize an astronomical observatory. Davis stayed in Córdoba for two and a half years, assisting with astronomical observations and undertaking meteorological work. Unhappy with Gould's overbearing manner, Davis returned to Philadelphia, where he became a bookkeeper in his father's coal company. A spell at Shaler's geological camp in the Cumberland Gap during the summer of 1875, however, left him resolved to return to a career in science. The following spring he accepted Shaler's offer of an assistantship in Harvard's geology department.

At Harvard Davis won promotion to instructor after three years and the seasoning of a round-the-world trip, taken in 1877–1878 while on a leave of absence. He published little and had to struggle to interest his students in geology, physical geography, and meteorology. In 1882 Harvard's president, Charles W. Eliot, advised Davis that prospects for promotion were not good. The warning made a strong impression; as Davis later told a colleague, "I set to work and built a house and camped on the ground here, to fight it out" (Davis to Lawrence Martin, 14 May 1912, quoted in Chorley et al., p. 131). Commencing a lifelong regimen of research and writing, Davis turned out a profusion of articles on structural geology, especially the Triassic formations of the Connecticut River valley,

and an even larger volume of papers on meteorological topics. His interest in climate ultimately led to his publication of *Elementary Meteorology* (1894), a textbook widely used in colleges. Davis's industry and his growing national reputation led Eliot to advance Davis in 1885 to assistant professor and in 1890 to professor of physical geography.

Davis received notice in the 1880s for his work in geology and meteorology but became internationally known for research in physical geography. He entered the subject by way of the study of rivers—their classification, impact on landscapes, development over time, and responses to the uplift and subsidence of underlying land masses. The study of streams and rivers was important to many of the geologists whose work Davis had studied as a student and young instructor. John Wesley Powell, Clarence Dutton, and Grove Karl Gilbert had emphasized the ways in which water shaped the peculiar landscapes of the American West. Davis extended and developed this aspect of their work by examining the rivers of the better-watered districts of the East, by formulating certain ideal types of river systems, and by connecting these types together in a grand cycle of erosion.

First explicated in his 1889 paper on "The Rivers and Valleys of Pennsylvania," and reiterated and applied in scores of subsequent works, Davis's cycle commenced with an episode of uplift that exposed a region to the dissecting action of climate and culminated in the reduction of the region to a peneplain or "almost plain" that was nearly at base level, the level of the water into which the region's rivers flow. The intermediate forms that the land and river systems might assume, he suggested, depended on relief, the resistance of the rocks to erosion, the permeability of soils, rainfall, and other factors. Running water, in Davis's view, was generally the most important agent in molding landscapes, and he believed that rivers, like the landscapes they mold, develop through orderly stages. At the outset of an erosion cycle, rivers are shallow and imperfect agents of drainage, often emptying into lakes that form in depressions. With time, river channels deepen and tributary streams develop and capture more and more of the drain-water of the region. Lakes empty and waterfalls that resulted from local contrasts in the hardness of rock are worn back. Erosion sharpens the aboriginal divides separating drainage basins. As side-streams form their own valleys, the surface areas of the valley slopes increase, as does the efficiency of streams in transporting waste material. At maturity, the river system consists of headwater branches that continue to gnaw at uplands; the valley proper, which deepens and widens as the river entrenches itself and meanders; and the flood plain, where debris is deposited. As time passes and the river reduces relief within its basin, a kind of old age is approached. The erosion of mountainous uplands reduces rainfall, and the widening of valleys reduces the efficiency of drainage and waste movement. The river becomes more sluggish, tributaries dwindle in number, and the pace of change in landforms slows—until another episode of uplift may rejuvenate the rivers and initiate a new cycle.

Davis described his model of landscape evolution as "a scheme of the imagination" and frankly acknowledged that it idealized and simplified natural processes and forms. Such idealization, in his view, was necessary if the study of landforms was to move beyond bare description toward explanatory accounts of structure and development. Davis propagated this message with extraordinary energy and success. He demonstrated the power of his model by reconstructing the structure and history of particular districts, such as the coastal plain of New Jersey and the river valleys of northern France, and by analyzing the origins of structural features found in many landscapes, such as river terraces and meanders. He developed variations on his basic model to account for the peculiarities of landforms in arid climates, such as those of the American West and South Africa; in regions molded by glacial action, such as the Massif Central of France and the Tein Shan Mountains of central Asia; and in districts shaped by marine erosion, such as Cape Cod. Davis had a strong artistic sense; much of his influence derived from his ability to see the landscape in new ways and to describe what he saw in sketches and rich verbal descriptions. His lectures, abundantly illustrated with lantern slides and block diagrams, attracted broad attention. During trips to Europe and the American West, he enrolled scores of geologists and geographers in field expeditions that became seminars in the interpretation of landforms. By the turn of the century, Davis had become the unrivaled leader of physical geography, a field he preferred to call physiography and that has since come to be known as geomorphology.

In 1898 Davis was appointed Sturgis-Hooper Professor of geology at Harvard; he held the chair until his retirement in 1912. Davis extended his influence further by organizing in 1904 the Association of American Geographers and playing an active role in the Geological Society of America. He was an exchange professor at Berlin in 1908–1909 and at the Sorbonne in 1911–1912. After his retirement, Davis traveled extensively and taught at a half-dozen universities in the western states, including the University of California at Berkeley, Stanford, and the California Institute of Technology. He also took up research on the origins and development of coral formations—a subject that had earlier received attention from Charles Darwin and James Dwight Dana and had, more recently, been the subject of new interpretive work by Davis's successor in Harvard's Sturgis-Hooper chair, Reginald Daly. Davis summed up his work on this subject in *The Coral Reef Problem* (1928), a work that essentially endorsed the view of Darwin and Dana that barrier reefs and atolls are consequences of the slow subsidence of the sea floor beneath the upward-growing formations.

Davis married Ellen Bliss Warner of Springfield, Massachusetts, in 1879; they had three children. In 1914, a year after the death of his first wife, Davis married Mary Morrill Wyman of Cambridge, Massachu-

setts. After the death of his second wife in 1923, he married in 1928 Lucy L. Tennant of Milton, Massachusetts. He had no children with these two wives. Davis died in Pasadena, California, where he had made his home during his final years.

Davis's encyclopedic knowledge of the earth sciences as well as his prodigious energy, limpid prose, and incisive sketches commanded nearly universal respect. His evolutionary analyses of landform development reverberated powerfully with broader evolutionary themes that dominated much of the science of his era. European and American professional societies awarded him more than a dozen medals for his scholarship, and he received honorary degrees from institutions on three continents. At the same time, his supreme self-confidence, deductive style of thought, and impatience with those of more modest capabilities inspired fear among many of his pupils and antagonism among some colleagues. Although Davis had many students, none proved as creative as their master nor as deft at blending science and artistry. Geography, a field that Davis did much to promote, came more and more to treat landforms as matrices for human activities rather than as subjects of inquiry in their own right. Geology, a field in which Davis had his roots, ultimately turned away from Davis's qualitative approach to erosion and highly stylized accounts of geological change, although even critics of the Davisian system acknowledged the enduring appeal of Davis's masterful essays and powerful synthetic imagination.

• A large collection of Davis's papers is at the Houghton Library, Harvard University. Davis summarized his work on the Connecticut River valley in "The Triassic Formation of Connecticut," *U.S. Geological Survey, Annual Report, 1896–1897* 18, pt. 2 (1898): 1–192. His classic "The Rivers and Valleys of Pennsylvania" was published in *National Geographic Magazine* 1 (1889): 183–253. The fullest statement of Davis's views on the cycle of erosion appears in his *Die Erklärende Beschreibung der Landformen* (1912). Davis's student, Douglas W. Johnson, drew together twenty-six of his teacher's papers on geomorphology in *Geographical Essays* (1909; repr. 1954). Richard J. Chorley et al., *The History of the Study of Landforms; or, the Development of Geomorphology*, vol. 2, *The Life and Work of William Morris Davis* (1973), offers a full and fair treatment of Davis that is based on extensive research in unpublished papers and interviews with Davis's associates and family members. This work includes extensive quotations from his unpublished papers and a bibliography of his more than 600 articles and books. Briefer biographical treatments include A. P. Brigham, "William Morris Davis," *Geographen Kalender, Year 7* (1909): 1–73; Reginald A. Daly, "William Morris Davis, 1850–1934," National Academy of Sciences, *Biographical Memoirs* 23 (1945): 263–303; and Kirk Bryan, "William Morris Davis—Leader in Geomorphology and Geography," *Annals of the Association of American Geographers* 25 (1935): 23–31. Modern critical reviews of Davis's work include Sheldon Judson, "William Morris Davis—An Appraisal," *Zeitschrift für Geomorphologie* 4 (1960): 193–201; Charles G. Higgins, "Theories of Landscape Development: A Perspective," in *Theories of Landform Development*, ed. Wilton N. Melhorn and Ronald C. Flemal (1975); and, most important, Flemal, "The Attack on the Davisian System of Geomorphology: A Synopsis," *Journal of Geological Educa-*

tion 19 (1971): 3–13. Davis's methods are discussed in Gordon L. Davies, "Research by Debate: The Geomorphology of William Morris Davis," *History of Science* 13 (1975): 139–45. An obituary is in the *New York Times*, 7 Feb. 1934.

JOHN W. SERVOS

DAVIS, William Stearns (30 Apr. 1877–15 Feb. 1930), historian and novelist, was born in Amherst, Massachusetts, the son of William Vail Wilson Davis, a Congregational minister, and Frances Stearns, both from old New England stock. Davis stated that one of the strongest influences of his boyhood was his maternal grandfather's large library. William Augustus Stearns was president of Amherst College, Massachusetts, and Davis was born in his mansion. Because of the family's frequent moves when William Davis accepted calls to new parishes, the library became a constant in his education. One of his favorite boyhood occupations was to study world atlases, which he read while standing on a hassock at a library table.

The early years of Davis's education were guided by his father. Because of childhood illness he was confined at home from the ages of ten to eighteen. His time was spent in reading for entertainment and education. He also began to write stories to distract himself from his illness. After a full recovery, Davis attended Worcester (Mass.) Academy. He entered Harvard University, where he received his A.B. (1900), A.M. (1901), and Ph.D. (1905) in history. Davis's first academic post was as lecturer at Radcliffe College in 1904–1905. From there he moved to Beloit College, Wisconsin, where he was instructor and professor of history in 1906–1907. He accepted an appointment at Oberlin College in Ohio as associate professor of medieval and modern European history from 1907 to 1909. Davis ended his teaching career as professor of history at the University of Minnesota, where he taught from 1909 to 1927. He was an excellent teacher with the ability to put life into his lectures. In September 1911 he married Alice Williams Redfield; they had no children.

Although Davis contributed to history as a scholarly discipline, he was intrigued by the human side of history, which, at the time, was neglected by the discipline. Later in his career he became a defender of biographers and an opponent of debunkers of history. In 1917 he wrote that "it is the business of teachers of history to welcome every new set of facts about former happenings, and not to refuse them merely because they do not fit in with past notions." As a vehicle for expressing his view of history, he wrote historical fiction. After early attempts to write short stories set in various historical periods, Davis selected Rome in the time of Julius Caesar as the theme of his first successful historical novel. While still at Harvard, he wrote *A Friend of Caesar*, which was published in 1900. Best known during his lifetime for his fiction, he published eight more novels, *God Wills It* (1901), *Belshazzar* (1902), *A Victor of Salamis* (1907), *The Friar of Wittenberg* (1912), *The Beauty of the Purple* (1924), *The White Queen* (1925), *Gilman of Redford* (1927), and

The Whirlwind (1929). His fictional books were not classics in the genre of historical fiction, but they were accurate and maintained an interesting story line. Davis was deeply engrossed while writing a novel and entered what he referred to as a "dream world." He suffered from depression when one was finished, feeling then that "the bottom dropped out of existence." His last novel so devastated him that he vowed never to write another, but he relented and was plotting another novel before his death.

Davis also wrote several history texts. Titles include *An Outline History of the Roman Empire* (1909), *The Influence of Wealth in Imperial Rome* (1910), *Readings in Ancient History* (1913), *A Day in Old Athens* (1914), *A Medieval and Modern History* (1914), *The Roots of the War* (1918), *A History of France* (1918), *A Short History of the Near East* (1922), *Life on a Medieval Barony* (1923), and *Europe since Waterloo* (1926).

During World War I Davis was strongly anti-German and objected to the pacifist movement. In 1916 he wrote, "I see the leaders of the pacifist movement and the leaders of pro-Germanism in this country associated together in a proximity which gives absolute confirmation to surmises which we friends of the preparedness movement have long since taken as morally proved" (letter to Hamilton Holt, 2 Dec. 1916). As a result of his research he believed that the emergence of modern Germany was a threat to Western society. In 1917 he wrote, "there has never been anything like this before in the history of the world. It is in the completest sense of the word ILLEGAL" (letter to Dr. McKinnon, 15 Mar. 1917). This was a belief that he examined in *Roots of the War* (1918), which was one of his most widely read nonfiction books.

Davis was a member of the American Historical Society and Phi Beta Kappa. He enjoyed fishing and hiking. Davis resigned his position at the University of Minnesota in 1927 to devote his time to writing. He and his wife moved to Exeter, New Hampshire, where his brother, Harold S. Davis, lived. In New England Davis and his wife spent their summers on the shore at the cottage they named "Clam Rock Cottage," where they entertained friends and colleagues. He enjoyed boating and invited his guests for journeys along the coast in the family motorboat. Davis remained in Exeter until he contracted pneumonia after an operation and died at age fifty-three.

• Davis papers are in the University of Minnesota Archives. They include a few of his manuscripts and correspondence (1914–1930) that reflect his political interests. Biographical essays on David appear in *Twentieth Century Authors* (1942), and in Stanley J. Kunitz and Howard Haycraft, *Junior Book of Authors* (1940). See also "William Stearns Davis: Historical Novelist," *Wilson Bulletin* 4 (Jan. 1930): 192. Obituaries are in the *Minneapolis Journal*, 16 Feb. 1930, and the *Minnesota Daily*, 18 Feb. 1930.

PENELOPE KROSCH

DAVIS, Winnie. *See* Davis, Varina Anne Jefferson.

DAVISON, George Willets (25 Mar. 1872–16 June 1953), lawyer and banker, was born in Rockville Center, New York, the son of Robert Anthony Davison, a lawyer, and Emeline Sealy. Davison, a Methodist, attended Wesleyan University where his academic excellence earned him election to Phi Beta Kappa and graduation with honors in 1892. He earned an LL.B. in 1894 from New York University. He married Harriet Rice Baldwin the following year; they had two children who both died young.

Davison began his law career in 1894 when he was admitted to the New York State bar. He joined a law firm that year and then formed a partnership in 1896 emphasizing private corporate law, with the exception of three years (1897–1899) that he worked in the Queens County (N.Y.) district attorney's office. Having developed an interest in corporate finance, Davison moved into banking in 1912 when he became vice president of Central Trust Company of New York. Davison, who remained with the bank until he retired in 1939, actively sought to expand it both internally and through mergers. In 1918 Central Trust merged with Union Trust Company to form Central Union Trust Company, and Davison became president in 1919. A decade later he significantly increased the bank's size by negotiating a merger with Hanover National Bank. He served until 1933 as president and from 1933 to 1939 as board chairman of the new bank, Central Hanover Bank and Trust Company (now part of Chemical Bank).

Davison's firm ideas concerning the direction of individual commercial banks and the entire commercial banking system reflected a risk-averse banking philosophy and conservative economic stances. He believed that commercial banks should compete in providing better quality services rather than competing in prices because he feared that excessive price competition would lead to risky use of funds.

Davison's philosophy was reflected in his bank's conservative lending practices and its emphasis on providing trust services to its wealthier customers. Trust services involve banks managing, rather than owning, a portfolio of assets in a fiduciary capacity for an individual, the estate of a deceased person, or for corporations. Offering trust services provides a steady income for the bank with little risk but also with little potential for rapid expansion. Davison eschewed rapid growth, preferring to work closely with a small number of corporate customers and to remain highly liquid.

Davison's bank expanded its deposits by establishing an extensive network of correspondent banking relationships—involving the sale of bank services to other banks—rather than its own branches outside New York City. He believed that locally owned, independent banks that established correspondent relationships with larger banks served the needs of local communities better than did branch banking. Davison admitted that branch banking within a metropolitan area might benefit customers by providing them increased convenience; Central Hanover did have several branches

in commercial-industrial locations and in very high income neighborhoods but not in middle-class residential areas. He argued, however, that branch banking in small communities drained financial resources from smaller communities to larger cities, where banks' headquarters generally were located. He contended that the growth of correspondent banking relations safeguarded individualism in U.S. banking because the small bank could obtain from the larger correspondent bank services such as loan evaluation and trust operations, which could be too expensive for small banks to provide themselves, and still retain local control over banking operations. In Davison's view, branch banking would reduce local control and thus reduce the bank's concern for its local community. His views were controversial because many other experts at the time considered correspondent banking harmful to local communities by hindering competition and that branch banking brought beneficial competition into smaller markets.

Davison forcefully articulated his ideas and attempted to influence public policy. In 1929 he defended correspondent banking in his best-known speech, "The Evolution of Commercial Banking," to the American Bankers Association. In the same year he chaired a commission that studied New York State banking laws. In congressional testimony (1930–1931), he vigorously opposed any liberalization of regulations concerning branch banking. Davison also testified to Congress that he favored prohibiting bank trust departments from purchasing securities from their security affiliates because such practices could easily be abused. While he agreed that regulations should be placed on new acquisitions of security affiliates, he also contended that it would be too disruptive to require commercial banks to sell off their existing security affiliates.

Davison continued to contribute to public policy debates throughout the 1930s. As president of the New York Clearing House Association (1933–1935), he worked to restore confidence in banks to stem the banking crisis that peaked in early 1933; these discussions ultimately resulted in the Emergency Banking Act of 1933. As chair of the advisory committee to the Reconstruction Finance Corporation's New York Loan Agency, he represented New York bankers who were reluctant to use all the funds that they could raise for this governmental agency. He vigorously opposed the creation of the Federal Deposit Insurance Corporation because he thought governmental insurance of deposits would tempt banks to engage in risky activities. From 1933 to 1938 Davison served as a director of the New York Federal Reserve Bank.

Davison's main interests outside of banking were supporting Wesleyan University and collecting fine art and rare books. He served on Wesleyan's board of trustees for forty-one years (1912–1953) and as its chairman for fifteen years (1928–1943). He donated to Wesleyan a large collection of fine prints in 1938, the Davison Art Center in 1952, his collection of rare books that reflected his interest in English literature in

1952, and a $6 million bequest in 1953. Davison died in New York City.

Davison's career included success as both a lawyer and a banker. He brought prosperity to his bank through judicious mergers and his emphasis on risk-averse management of bank assets. He eloquently argued against too much centralization of banking. The turbulent banking crisis of the 1980s might have been avoided had bankers paid attention to Davison's concerns that deposit insurance combined with banks' too-rapid growth could lead to too many high-risk and low-quality loans.

• There are no known collections of his papers. Davison's ideas concerning banking can be found in his articles "Banking Evolution in America," *American Bankers Association Journal* 22 (Oct. 1929): 309–10, 391–92, 414–15; and "Concentration of Money Power Threatens Business Initiative," *Printers Ink Monthly* (Jan. 1930): 31–32, 92, 94; and in his testimony to the House Banking and Currency Committee, Hearings on Branch, Chain and Group Banking, 71st Cong., 2d sess., H.R. 141 (1930), and to the subcommittee of the Senate Banking and Currency Committee, Hearings on the Operations of the National and Federal Reserve Banking Systems, 71st Cong., 3d sess. (1931). Herman E. Krooss, *Executive Opinion: What Business Leaders Said and Thought on Economic Issues, 1920s–1960s* (1970), pp. 68, 127, 136–37, 376, briefly discusses Davison's economic ideas. Biographical information on Davison is in the *Wesleyan University Alumnus* (Aug. 1953) and the *Wesleyan Argus*, 7 Nov. 1953. Helen M. Burns, *The American Banking Community and New Deal Banking Reforms, 1933–35* (1974), discusses Davison's role in formulating the Emergency Banking Act of 1933. William S. Gray, *The Hanover Bank, 1831–1951* (1951), and Benjamin J. Klebaner, "The Manufacturers Hanover Decision and New York City Banking since 1945," *Revue Internationale D'Histoire De La Banque* (1986): 86–109, provide background concerning the development of the Hanover Bank. Obituaries are in the *New York Times*, 17 June 1953, and the *Wesleyan University Alumnus*, Aug. 1953.

ROBERT STANLEY HERREN

DAVISON, Gregory Caldwell (12 Aug. 1871–7 May 1935), naval officer and inventor, was born in Jefferson City, Missouri, the son of Alexander Caldwell Davison, a physician, and Sarah Pelot Eppes. In 1888 he was appointed to the U.S. Naval Academy at Annapolis, Maryland, and graduated with the class of 1892.

Davison began his naval career much as other midshipmen but soon became so competent in the field of naval technology that the course of his life was forever connected with communications, weapons, and ordnance. His first ship was the *San Francisco*. In 1894 he was commissioned as an ensign. Following this tour of duty, he was assigned for a short period aboard torpedo boats. In 1898 he married Alice Lydia Shepard, the daughter of a rear admiral. No record exists of any children. At the outbreak of the Spanish-American War in 1898, Davison was with the *Oneida*, which operated in Cuban waters during the conflict. He was promoted to lieutenant, junior grade, in March 1899. The next year he was placed in command of a succession of torpedo boats, obtaining a knowledge of these

craft and their roles. Also in 1900 he was promoted to lieutenant.

In 1901 Davison's career in naval technology was launched with what would normally have been a routine, mundane assignment. He was aboard the *New York* when the time arrived for an engine overhaul. Placed in charge of the task, he performed the astounding feat of bettering the speed of its original trial run. His technical reputation rising, he was selected to assist in an early wireless communications experiment aboard the *New York*, during which he assisted Guglielmo Marconi in ship-to-shore radio communications. Soon after this successful trial, the U.S. Navy began equipping its major combatants with the new radios.

By 1902 the mechanically talented Davison received an appropriate assignment that greatly benefited the navy and his career. Posted to the Bureau of Ordnance, he worked on improving British-designed torpedoes, using steam rather than compressed air. He was then assigned to command a torpedo boat and later the reserve torpedo boat fleet at the Norfolk, Virginia, navy yard. In 1904–1905 he commanded the torpedo boat destroyer *Paul Jones* on a Pacific cruise, during which he and his crew won two gunnery trophies, aided by a special gun sight called the "Davy Jones" that Davison had designed and constructed. Returning to the East Coast, he in 1905–1907 performed ordnance duties at the Naval Torpedo Station in Rhode Island. While there he improved the balanced turbine torpedo and was promoted to lieutenant commander in July 1906.

In December 1907, after fifteen years in the navy, Davison resigned his commission to pursue a more lucrative career in industry. Joining America's premier submarine manufacturer, the Electric Boat Company, as a vice president, he designed an improved steam generator for torpedoes and a recoilless aircraft gun. During World War I, with vastly expanded ordnance contracts pouring in from Washington, he became the chief engineer with the General Ordnance Company while also remaining with the Electric Boat Company. At General Ordnance he designed the Y-gun, a propelling mount for the delivery of depth charges, which became the standard fixture for all U.S. destroyers and submarine chasers.

In 1920 the U.S. Navy, following a series of tests and investigations, severely cut back its dependence on commercial ordnance companies, thereby diminishing Davison's utility to the Electric Boat Company. Even before World War I, navy officials charged with submarine construction had resented the company's high-handed methods, accusing it of failing to meet navy specifications and building its own patented designs. Additionally, navy ordnance officers claimed the company routinely pressured the navy into buying inferior products by arranging for congressional pressure to be exerted on the secretary of the navy and his assistants. These complaints received some corroboration when a German U-boat was examined and found to be technically far superior to the products of the

Electric Boat Company. As a result, the navy constructed and staffed its own submarine design and fabrication facilities. Although the Electric Boat Company continued to bid on and fulfill navy contracts for submarines, the designs the company used often originated with U.S. Navy employees and officers.

Davison resigned from the Electric Boat Company in 1922 to enter the oil business in Kentucky and West Virginia. After he left Electric Boat, he designed a mobile, light antiaircraft and field gun. He died in Lyme, Connecticut.

Davison's innovative designs advanced the U.S. Navy's capabilities in undersea and antisubmarine warfare. Ironically, had he stayed in the navy, he undoubtedly would have made an even greater contribution. When he resigned his commission and entered commercial industry, the navy was becoming increasingly dependent on private sector firms. The naval reaction to that dependence called for technologically gifted officers and personnel to design future weapons systems, an environment made to order for people of Davison's talent.

• Material relating to Davison is in the U.S. Navy Records, Bureau of Navigation, Records of Officers, National Archives and Records Administration. His career highlights are in U.S. Navy registers, 1892–1907. Davison's career is partially traced in L. R. Hamersly, *The Records of Living Officers of the U.S. Navy and Marine Corps*, 6th ed. (1898). The best study of the stormy relationship between the navy and the Electric Boat Company is in Gary F. Weir, *Building American Submarines, 1914–1940* (1991). An obituary is in the *New York Times*, 9 May 1935.

ROD PASCHALL

DAVISON, Henry Pomeroy (13 June 1867–6 May 1922), banker and chairman of the American National Red Cross War Council, was born in Troy, Pennsylvania, the son of George Bennett Davison, a merchant of farm implements, and Henrietta Bliss Pomeroy. Davison attended public school in Troy until 1882, when his grandmother provided money for him to attend Greylock Institute in Massachusetts. In the summers he worked as a schoolteacher, but once he completed his education he became a clerk in the Troy bank owned by his Pomeroy uncles.

Banking fascinated Davison, but he soon found his uncles' bank too restrictive. He went to New York City but could not find a job. In Bridgeport, Connecticut, he received the job of runner in the Pequonnock National Bank. Although he advanced to receiving teller, he still wanted to move to New York. Upon hearing of a new bank being organized there in 1891, Davison applied as a teller at Astor Place National Bank, and eventually he was hired.

While working at the Astor Place, Davison married Kate Trubee of Bridgeport in 1893; they had four children. In 1894 Davison became assistant cashier at Liberty National Bank. He moved up rapidly, becoming president in 1899 at the age of thirty-two. In 1902 First National Bank of New York offered Davison a position as vice president. Davison accepted because First National was much larger and more prestigious than Liberty National.

Davison's years at First National were extremely important in the history of American banking, and he played a significant role in events. One trend that had been developing since the 1890s was the growth of trust companies as competitors with banks. Trust companies could do almost anything a bank could do, and because they had more latitude in making loans and investments, and could keep lower reserves against deposits, many banks felt that trusts had unfair regulatory competitive advantages. Davison had the idea of organizing a trust company that would not compete with banks but would take care of transactions that law prohibited banks from doing, such as managing trust funds and other types of fiduciary work. The result was Bankers Trust Company, organized in March 1903. Davison mostly chose younger, less well-known bankers as its officers and directors. Davison himself became a director and chairman of the executive committee, positions he held until his death. Bankers Trust Company subsequently absorbed Mercantile Trust, Manhattan Trust, and Astor Trust, and by the time Davison died, Bankers Trust had nearly $400 million in total resources.

Davison also played an important part during the panic of 1907, which began when depositors of Knickerbocker Trust Company started a run. Many bankers and trust company officials feared the run would spread, and they asked J. Pierpont Morgan to stem the tide. The first concern was whether Knickerbocker Trust had sufficient assets to justify the large-scale loans that would be necessary to save it. Morgan asked his partner George Perkins to choose someone to head a committee to scan the books of Knickerbocker (and later other institutions). Perkins, who was a director of First National Bank, named Davison. Davison, in turn, chose men from Bankers Trust to help him. As panic spread across New York and the country, Davison and his colleagues from Bankers Trust played a pivotal role in deciding which institutions would receive loans and in what amounts, but Morgan arranged the loans. When the crisis was over, Morgan was praised in the press, but only bankers knew of Davison's role.

Davison's third contribution to American banking history resulted from his association with Senator Nelson Aldrich (R=R.I.). The panic of 1907 had led Congress to pass the Aldrich-Vreeland Act, which provided for the issuance of emergency currency and established the National Monetary Commission, chaired by Aldrich. The commission investigated banking conditions in the United States and abroad with the goal of designing banking and monetary reforms that might help avoid future panics. Aldrich wanted a practical banker's help and consulted Davison. When commission members went to Europe in 1908, Davison accompanied them to London, Paris, and Berlin for conversations with bankers. While abroad, Aldrich became convinced that American money needed to be based on more assets than just government bonds, and he began to see the advantages of central banking, in which one institution was a lender of last resort in times of stress. In subsequent months, Davison was one of four men who helped Aldrich draft his plan of monetary reform.

The Aldrich Plan called for a National Reserve Association with branches located across the nation. Local associations of banks would choose the staff of the branch offices. All national banks would become members of a reserve association and would deposit part of their reserves with a branch. In exchange, member banks would be able to rediscount their assets (that is, each bank could borrow money upon its assets from the branch). In this way the association would constitute a lender of last resort but could also act to stabilize money markets even in normal times. At the top of the system would be a national reserve board of forty-five men.

The Aldrich Plan never became law, in spite of efforts by Aldrich, Davison, and other bankers in New York and Chicago. The failure was mostly because the Democrats captured a majority in the House of Representatives in 1910 and refused to cooperate with leading Republicans like Aldrich. However, the Federal Reserve Act passed in 1913 was similar in many ways to the Aldrich Plan. Thus, Davison played a notable role in the creation of the most important monetary institution in the United States.

While the work of the National Monetary Commission was still underway, Davison received an offer to join J. P. Morgan & Co., the premier private banking house on Wall Street. Pierpont Morgan had been impressed by Davison's performance during the panic of 1907, and Davison became a Morgan partner on 1 January 1909. Within the firm all partners met every morning and discussed all business of the firm. Thus, any partner could have an impact on any transaction. However, each partner did have principal responsibility for certain jobs, and because Davison's biographer became a partner in 1911, historians have some idea of Davison's most important activities. One of these was to arrange for Guaranty Trust Company to merge with Morton Trust and Fifth Avenue Trust. Thomas F. Ryan was a major stockholder of all three, and the merger was his idea. Davison worked out the financial details and became a member of the board of directors of the largest trust in the United States and chairman of its executive committee. Now Davison had a leading role in two large trust companies.

In part because of these connections, Davison was called to testify before the Pujo Committee in the "Money Trust Investigation." The committee started from the premise that a money trust existed in which a few men controlled billions of dollars worth of companies. Several Morgan partners testified. All, including Davison, denied that a money trust existed but could not deny that partners of J. P. Morgan & Co. sat as directors for numerous banks, trust companies, railroads, and large industrial concerns. Still, Davison believed his testimony that no money trust existed, and he pointed out that just because interlocking director-ships existed did not mean that J. P. Morgan & Co. had absolute control of all those companies involved. In spite of Davison's best efforts, however, most Americans believed the Pujo investigation proved the existence of a money trust involving the Morgan firm.

Davison was also in charge of American lending in China. At the request of the State Department, several American banks had agreed to form a consortium to promote Chinese economic development to support the Open Door policy. This was a thankless task for Davison. Although some loans and a general currency reform were arranged, it took much patience. The consortium did not profit from its efforts, and in 1913 it abandoned the plan after the Woodrow Wilson administration rejected dollar diplomacy for China.

Another Davison job for J. P. Morgan & Co. related to British and French financial needs during World War I. From the beginning Davison was pro-Allies, and he became involved in underwriting British and French government securities for the American market. Davison also oversaw a line of credit that the firm extended to the British, which ran as high as $400 million. When the United States entered the war, the government took over the task of lending to the Allies, and Davison concentrated on having the Morgan firm repaid for its line of credit.

This is the one time in his career that his co-workers criticized Davison. Several times, members of the British government thought that Davison was too high-handed and stubborn with the Wilson administration. But Davison's actions caused no lasting breach between Britain and the U.S. government. Throughout the rest of his career, colleagues praised Davison for his humor, ability to avoid arguments between people at conferences, and gift for making loyal friends and allies.

These traits were especially useful to Davison when he became chairman of the American Red Cross War Council. When the United States entered World War I, Red Cross officials realized they would have to undertake a major effort to expand and raise funds. The directors convinced President Wilson, who was also president of the Red Cross, that he needed someone new to take charge during the emergency. Although Wilson did not really trust Wall Street bankers, Cleveland H. Dodge persuaded Wilson to make Davison chairman of the War Council in May 1917.

Davison's view of the Red Cross mission was expansive. He wanted to provide aid to the U.S. armed forces and help the Allies (civilian and military) as much as possible. To undertake so large a task would take an enormous amount of money. During the war about $400 million was raised for the American Red Cross. This financial success was largely due to Davison and his connections with wealthy businessmen. Davison's influence also aided the necessary bureaucratic expansion, since many of the new positions were filled by volunteers who left careers to serve at his request.

It is difficult to summarize the importance of the American Red Cross after U.S. entry into the war without minimizing its accomplishments. It provided army and navy personnel with medical supplies, sweaters, socks, hospital care, ambulance service, canteen service, assistance with family problems, Christmas packets, and much else. It provided some of the same aid to Allied soldiers and civilians, but in addition it helped refugees find acceptable housing and jobs or, if possible, return home and start anew. Davison described all this in his book, *The American Red Cross in the Great War* (1920), although he ignored his own role as the primary decision maker, a role the minutes of the War Council clearly reveal.

Although Wilson initially distrusted Davison, both shared an internationalist vision of the future in which the United States would take a leading role. After Davison and the other members of the War Council resigned on 28 February 1919, he had the president's support as he worked on the concept of expanding the worldwide role of the Red Cross in peacetime. He could not do this through the International Red Cross, because its charter allowed only for wartime activities. Ultimately, he helped to charter the League of Red Cross Societies in May 1919, becoming chairman of its board of governors.

Davison looked to the American Red Cross to provide financial support until the league could raise money from other national members, but there was significant reluctance among the Americans to accept Davison's plan for the league to take over relief activities in Europe. Eventually, Davison had to allow the league to concentrate on public health needs rather than relief.

Although Davison remained chairman of the league's board for the remainder of his life, his participation was limited after March 1920. He did not know it yet, but he was developing the brain tumor that would cost him his life. In his last two years, he kept up with the business of the Morgan firm and the League through letters and visits from friends, but his health was never good. He died, at the peak of his career, at his residence in Long Island, New York.

There is much to respect in Davison's life. He was a small-town boy made good. He was an accomplished banker and millionaire (his estate was valued between $2.5 and $5 million). He was a visionary who hoped to create a world where peace could be maintained. His personality was naturally happy, his family life was loving and stable, and he had many friends who mourned his passing. His biographer, Thomas Lamont, subtitled his book "The Record of a Useful Life," but this is too modest. A better choice would be "The Record of an Admirable Man." He accomplished much, both as a financier and as an administrator of the American Red Cross.

• The best single source on Davison is Thomas W. Lamont's biography, *Henry P. Davison: The Record of a Useful Life* (1933). Although essentially laudatory, this work disagrees with other sources only regarding the outcome of the Pujo investigation and the attitude of the British government toward Davison's services in World War I.

Other sources are also useful. On his business career, see the papers of Thomas W. Lamont (Harvard), Dwight Morrow (Amherst), George Perkins (Columbia), and Willard D. Straight (Cornell). See also Vincent P. Carosso, *The Morgans: Private International Bankers, 1854–1913* (1987), and Ron Chernow, *The House of Morgan* (1990). For the Chinese loan situation, see Charles Vevier, *The United States and China, 1906–1913: A Study of Finance and Diplomacy* (1955). For the attitude of the British government toward Davison and his services during the war, see Kathleen Burk, *Britain, America and the Sinews of War, 1914–1918* (1985). On the National Monetary Commission and the Aldrich Plan, see the papers of Nelson W. Aldrich (Library of Congress) and Frank A. Vanderlip (Columbia). See also Nelson W. Aldrich, *A Suggested Plan for Monetary Reform* (1911); Nathaniel W. Stephenson, *Nelson W. Aldrich* (1930); and Eugene Nelson White, *The Regulation and Reform of the American Banking System, 1900–1929* (1983).

For Davison's career with the Red Cross, see the records of the American Red Cross War Council (National Archives) and the unindexed papers of Davison (American National Red Cross Headquarters, Washington, D.C.). Also useful are the papers of Edward M. House (Yale), Woodrow Wilson (Library of Congress), the American National Red Cross (Hoover Institution on War, Revolution and Peace), and Foster Rhea Dulles, *The American Red Cross* (1950). For the founding of the League of Red Cross Societies, see the papers of the League of Red Cross Societies (Hoover Institution) and Clyde E. Buckingham, *For Humanity's Sake* (1964). In addition to *The American Red Cross in the Great War*, Davison also published some articles, which are indexed in *Reader's Guide to Periodical Literature*.

Davison's illness and death are fully reported in the *New York Times*, 7 May 1922, which also contains other information about him.

SUE C. PATRICK

DAVISON, Wild Bill (5 Jan. 1905–14 Nov. 1989), jazz cornetist, was born William Edward Davison in Defiance, Ohio, the son of Edward Davison, a railroad engineer, and Ann Kreps, a pianist and singer. In 1913, after his father left home, Davison and his mother moved in with his maternal grandparents. With the help of an older friend, he started playing mandolin at age eleven and then learned bugle while a member of the Boy Scouts, moving on to banjo and cornet two years later. One of the local bands he played with during 1919–1920 was the Ohio Lucky Seven, and while on a job with them in 1922 he first heard and met Bix Beiderbecke, an event that inspired him to concentrate on the cornet. After a stint playing mellophone and cornet with Rollin Potter's Peerless Players in Cincinnati in the spring of 1923, he joined the Chubb-Steinberg orchestra and made his first records in 1924 and 1925, playing cornet solos that clearly demonstrate his admiration for the lyrical, clear-toned Beiderbecke style.

In early 1926, following an engagement in New York City, Davison returned to Defiance and later joined the Seattle Harmony Kings for a job that took him to Chicago. In 1927 he joined the Benny Meroff orchestra and recorded with them in 1928 and 1929. His solos on "Smiling Skies" and "Talk Of The Town," recorded twelve months apart, display not only growing confidence but the increasing impact of Louis Armstrong's hotter, more driving style as well.

Because Meroff's theater pit band mainly provided specialty numbers and accompaniments to vaudeville acts, in his off-hours Davison sought out such young jazz musicians as clarinetist Frank Teschemacher, tenor saxophonist Bud Freeman, pianist Joe Sullivan, banjoist Eddie Condon, and drummer George Wettling, a clique already known for its innovative approach to hot playing. Besides working in Meroff's orchestra, between 1928 and 1931 Davison also freelanced with other commercial bands, but in early 1932 he and Teschemacher formed their own jazz-based big band.

In the early morning of 1 March 1932, the open-top convertible in which Davison was driving Teschemacher home was struck broadside at an intersection by a darkened taxi rushing through a red light. When Davison's car slammed into a tree, both musicians were thrown over the windshield and hood, with Teschemacher landing headfirst on the concrete curb. Davison escaped injury, and though officially cleared of any blame, on learning of Teschemacher's death several hours later, he reportedly said, "Now what am I going to do for a sax player?" To those who overheard it, the remark seemed to imply a callous self-interest, but Davison later claimed that his actual words were, "Now where the hell are we going to get another sax player to take *his* place?" Garbled repetition, however, led to his being ostracized by his colleagues and ultimately forced him to move to Milwaukee, where he lived in relative obscurity from 1933 to 1941. Although he made no commercial recordings during this period, his solo excerpts on privately made acetate discs offer proof that by this time all elements of his mature style had taken form, especially his unique growl, for which no precedent can be found in the playing of either Beiderbecke or Armstrong.

In 1939 Davison played briefly at Boston's Ken Club with clarinetist Pee Wee Russell and pianist Gene Schroeder, and in 1940, on his first recordings in over a decade, he was listed on the small Collector's Item label as "Wild" Bill Davison. To all indications, this was the first known use of that sobriquet in print. The grievance held against him for his presumed reaction to Teschemacher's death must have soothed somewhat over the years, for in the spring of 1941 Davison was hired to lead the band at Nick's, guitarist-promoter Condon's stronghold in Greenwich Village. During this engagement, along with Russell and trombonist George Brunies, he soon established himself as the top-ranking cornetist in the Condon camp. In 1943, after leading another band in Boston, he went into Jimmy Ryan's on 52d Street with a group that included clarinetist Rod Cless and pianist James P. Johnson. That same year he participated in a re-creation of the Original Dixieland Jazz Band for Katherine Dunham's *Tropical Revue* and made his first, and most important, recordings for the Commodore label. Using Russell, Brunies, Schroeder, Condon, Wettling, and bassist Bob Casey, on 27 November 1943 Davison recorded "That's A Plenty," "Panama," "Riverboat Shuffle," and "Muskrat Ramble." Two days later,

with the same personnel but under Brunies's nominal leadership, he recorded "Royal Garden Blues," "Ugly Child," "Tin Roof Blues," and "That Da Da Strain." The next day, with clarinetist Edmond Hall taking Russell's place, he returned to the studio to record "Clarinet Marmalade," "Original Dixieland One Step," "At The Jazz Band Ball," and "Baby, Won't You Please Come Home?" Although certainly not the first in the genre, these recordings, taken as a whole, helped spearhead a revival of interest in traditional small band improvised jazz, and they have been widely valued ever since.

Davison received his military draft notice a day or so before the first of these sessions, but he had time for two transcription dates for World Broadcasting Systems before reporting for duty. One reprised some of the Commodore titles, and the other was a tribute to the ODJB, but neither was licensed for commercial sale. In January and September 1945 Davison again recorded for Commodore, but his January 1946 date is especially notable for the presence of clarinetist Albert Nicholas. After his discharge from the army, presumably in late 1945, Davison worked briefly with pianist Art Hodes and then led his own small group in St. Louis before opening in New York on 20 December 1945 at Eddie Condon's new club, where he remained as featured player for many years. Besides making guest appearances at Stuyvesant Casino, Davison also played regularly in 1947 on the weekly "This Is Jazz" radio series and continued to record prolifically through the 1950s. The major part of Davison's activities during the 1950s centered around Condon and his hard-drinking circle of Prohibition-reared jazzmen, and while their riotous public behavior caused them little trouble in New York, it did arouse widespread press disapproval during their February 1957 tour of England.

After some time at the 400 Club in Los Angeles in 1959, Davison played with Chicago clarinetist Johnny Lane in the summer of 1961, went on tour with his own group in 1962, and appeared with the Salt City Six and the Surf Side Six in 1963. In the spring of 1964 he led a band at New York's Metropole and commenced a series of tours that ultimately took him to twenty-one countries over the next twenty-five years. While continuing to tour, in 1966 he began appearing annually at the Manassas Jazz Festival. In October 1971 he embarked on a 36-state tour with the Stars of Jazz, a Hodes-led sextet that included Condon and clarinetist Barney Bigard. In 1974 Davison made Denmark his home base for European tours, but five years later he settled in California. The last ten years of his life were dominated by tours, festivals, and honors. However, after a lifetime of heavy drinking, climaxed by a severe attack of bleeding ulcers, along with liver and lung ailments, Davison was forced into abstinence in 1984. There to provide him with moral support and stern but loving supervision was his fifth wife, the former film actress Anne Stewart, whom he had married in 1952 while working at Condon's. In 1986 the Davisons were crowned "Emperor and Empress of Jazz" at the Sacramento Jazz Festival, and following an appearance on Johnny Carson's "Tonight Show," he resumed his itinerary of world tours and festivals. Leaving no children, he died in Santa Barbara.

Wild Bill Davison was the most consistently inspired and inventive cornetist to come out of rough-and-tumble 1920s Chicago. To his early synthesis of the Beiderbecke and Armstrong styles, he added an entirely unique sound that could blend as easily with the unorthodox timbres of clarinetists Russell and Hall as it could with the more polished, Benny Goodman–like tone of Peanuts Hucko, in the 1950s a regular companion on the Condon bandstand. Equally at home with fast, ferociously heated stomps, slow blues, and lyrical ballads, in the space of a few beats he could jump from *sotto voce* grumbles in his lower register to heart-stopping, soaring shrieks in his upper, all the while maintaining a logical line of melodic continuity. One of the most prolific jazz recordings artists of his time, Davison can be heard at his best on the early Commodores, the 1945 and 1949 Blue Note sessions with Hodes and soprano saxophonist Sidney Bechet, the recordings from "This Is Jazz," and many of his own later albums.

• Little documentation exists on Davison's early years, and what is known comes from sketchy, sometimes contradictory interviews with Davison, his wife, and fellow musicians. Although it does contain a brief biographical section, Doug Armstrong, *Wild Bill Davison: A Celebration* (1991), is essentially a collection of photographs and memorabilia. More detailed accounts of the setting for Davison's formative years are in William Howland Kenney, *Chicago Jazz: A Cultural History, 1904–1930* (1993); Charles Edward Smith, "The Austin High Gang" in *Jazzmen*, ed. Frederic Ramsey, Jr., and C. E. Smith (1939); and Eddie Condon, *We Called It Music* (1947) and *Eddie Condon's Scrapbook of Jazz* (1973). An account of the circumstances leading to Davison's departure from Chicago is in Marty Grosz, "Notes" to the Time-Life Giants of Jazz album set, *Frank Teschemacher* (1982), while annotations of Davison's recordings for Commodore from 1943 through 1946 can be found in Dan Morgenstern's notes for Mosaic's *The Complete Commodore Jazz Recordings* (1990). Following Davison's death, *Jazzbeat* (Summer 1991) published several reminiscences and appreciations. The best discographical sources are Brian Rust, *Jazz Records, 1897–1942* (1982), and Walter Bruyninckx, *Traditional Jazz Discography, 1897–1988* (1989).

JACK SOHMER

DAVISSON, Clinton Joseph (22 Oct. 1881–1 Feb. 1958), physicist, was born in Bloomington, Illinois, the son of Joseph Davisson, a painter and paperhanger, and Mary Calvert. Davisson's sister described the home as "a happy congenial one—plenty of love but short on money." Davisson did not begin school until age seven, and he lost another year of schooling because of illness, graduating from Bloomington High School at age twenty. His high scholastic standing, especially in physics and mathematics, was achieved in spite of his frail health and the need to work nights at

the McLean County Telephone Company; it earned him a scholarship to the University of Chicago for the school year 1902–1903.

Davisson's first physics instructor at Chicago was Robert A. Millikan, who later (1923) received the Nobel Prize in physics for his determination of the fundamental charge of the electron and his research on the photoelectric effect. Davisson was impressed by Millikan's devotion to physics and to the teaching of physics; he was "delighted to find that physics was the concise, orderly science [he] had imagined it to be, and that a physicist could be so openly and earnestly concerned about such matters as colliding bodies."

But owing to lack of funds, Davisson was forced to leave Chicago at the end of his first year, and he returned to Bloomington to work for the McLean County Telephone Company. In January 1904 Millikan obtained a temporary position for Davisson as assistant in physics at Purdue University, and by June 1904 Davisson was able to return to the University of Chicago where he continued his studies until August 1905. Forced to leave a second time for lack of funds, Davisson again obtained a physics position upon Millikan's recommendation, this time at Princeton University where he served as a part-time instructor until 1910. In the meantime he was able to return to Chicago during the summers of 1906, 1907, and 1908, obtaining his B.S. there in August 1908.

Davisson continued his study of physics at Princeton and was again fortunate to come under the influence of an outstanding electron physicist, Owen W. Richardson, a visiting professor from England who later (1928) won the Nobel Prize in physics for his studies on the thermionic emission of electrons. Davisson later claimed that it was from both Millikan and Richardson that he caught "the physicist's point of view—his habit of mind—his way of looking at things," rather than from any courses that he took. Davisson followed both Millikan and Richardson into the field of electron physics, writing his Ph.D. dissertation on the positive ions emitted from alkaline metal salts, a topic that he later pursued in his professional studies. In August 1911, after having graduated from Princeton, Davisson married Richardson's sister, Charlotte Sara, who was visiting her brother from England; the couple had four children.

Davisson was appointed instructor in physics at the Carnegie Institute of Technology in Pittsburgh in the fall of 1911. He found the eighteen-hour teaching load rather heavy, leaving him little time for research. He also complained of the difficulty of obtaining adequate experimental equipment, and in six years at Carnegie he published only three short theoretical notes. One positive event during this period was his visit during the summer of 1913 to the Cavendish Laboratory in Cambridge, England, where he worked with Joseph John Thomson, winner of the 1906 Nobel Prize in physics for the discovery of the electron.

When the United States entered World War I, Davisson attempted to enlist in the military service but was turned down because of his frailty. He thereupon obtained a position in war-related research in the engineering department of the Western Electric Company in New York City, taking a leave of absence from Carnegie Tech. His work at Western Electric, the manufacturing arm of the American Telephone and Telegraph Company (AT&T), was in the field of telecommunications, supervising the development and testing of oxide-coated nickel filaments as a substitute for platinum filaments. Although the work was routine and frustrating, Davisson stayed on at Western Electric after the war in spite of Carnegie Tech's offer of a promotion to assistant professor.

Western Electric had a continuing interest in oxide-coated filaments because of the desire to supply AT&T with a reliable means of amplifying and relaying electronic signals over long distances. The "loading coils" then in use were clearly inadequate, and it appeared that the future lay in electronics. Davisson's supervisor, Harold D. Arnold, assigned Davisson to investigate the matter further.

Although this work was primarily commercially oriented, Davisson focused much of his attention on some of the fundamental questions that it raised. In 1920 he and a new assistant, Charles H. Kunsman, found that some of the electrons directed against a clean nickel target in a vacuum were "elastically scattered" or reflected by the target with no loss in energy. Thinking that these electrons might be used as a tool for learning something about the structure of the atoms that made up the target, a topic that was of great interest to physicists at that time, Davisson expanded the scope of these studies, including the investigation of materials other than nickel. He and Kunsman developed a series of experiments that lasted for about three years. Their efforts, although carried out with Davisson's characteristic attention to experimental detail and thorough theoretical analysis, yielded only mediocre results, and the project was dropped when Kunsman left Western Electric in late 1923. Davisson continued on with his other investigations on a variety of topics involving the fundamentals of thermionic emission under high vacuum.

One year later, joined by a new colleague, Lester H. Germer, Davisson attempted to reactivate the electron tube that had been standing idle since Kunsman left. On 5 February 1925, during the normal baking period designed to improve the vacuum, an accident occurred that changed fundamentally the nature of their investigation. The notebook entry simply states "Liquid air bottle broke and cracked the trap during the bombarding process. Secondary filament gone and target badly oxidized." After the tube had been repaired by a heating process that removed the oxide from the target, the new experiments revealed that the electrons were being scattered much differently than they had before; Davisson and Germer decided to open the tube to examine the nickel target more closely. They found that the heating process had fused the small crystals of nickel into larger crystals. They concluded that the new scattering data revealed the patterns of the crystalline arrangement of nickel atoms rather than the structure of the individual atoms themselves. To pursue this new line of investigation they prepared a target composed of a single crystal of nickel. By mid-1926, however, they had not achieved the results they were seeking.

At this time an event occurred that again changed the nature of the investigation. In 1926 Davisson and his wife made a trip to England to visit friends and relatives. Their trip coincided with the Oxford meeting of the British Association for the Advancement of Science, and Davisson brought along some of his new experimental results to show to physicists there. Inspired by the new theory of wave mechanics that had just been introduced by Louis de Broglie and Erwin Schroedinger, several of them thought Davisson's curious curves might be an indication that the electrons were being diffracted by the target atoms much as light is diffracted by finely ruled gratings. During his voyage home Davisson studied the new theory with great interest and began thinking of ways to test it.

After Davisson returned to New York, he and Germer developed and carried out an extensive series of experiments for that purpose. Indicative of the great interest shown in this project, Bell Telephone Laboratories (the new name given to the research division of Western Electric in 1925) assigned an additional person, Chester J. Calbick, to assist them. These experiments were completed by mid-1927 and led to the publication of two papers that established conclusively that electrons do indeed have wave properties and are not simply localized particles as had been previously thought.

Although their evidence for electron waves was convincing, Davisson and Germer spent the next few years extending their investigations, writing additional papers, and presenting numerous talks explaining their findings. In recognition of the fundamental nature of the discovery of electron diffraction, Davisson was awarded the Nobel Prize for physics in 1937, a prize he shared with George P. Thomson of England, who had achieved similar results in a very different manner at about the same time.

Having demonstrated that electrons have wave properties, Davisson turned his attention to the field of electron optics. He and Calbick made important contributions to the theory and construction of electron lenses, electron microscopes, and the finely focused electron beam tubes used to evaluate picture quality in early television tubes. He also published articles on the application of electron diffraction techniques to the study of metal surfaces, on x-ray reflection, and on the transverse Doppler effect. During World War II he worked on the theory and construction of various electronic devices, especially the magnetron and quartz crystal plates, for the armed forces. Davisson retired from Bell Labs in 1946 and spent his remaining years as a visiting professor at the University of Virginia in Charlottesville where he worked on problems concerned with the ultracentrifuge. He died in Charlottesville.

The discovery of electron diffraction by Davisson and Germer and its interpretation in terms of electron waves is one of the fundamental developments of twentieth-century physics. Davisson's investigations of thermionic emission yielded results of great practical value to AT&T and the electronics industry at large, and of fundamental importance to the field of theoretical electron physics. His contributions to numerous other fields of electron physics also had wide theoretical and practical applications. Perhaps as significant as the specific technical and scientific contributions that Davisson made, however, was the role he played in transforming Bell Labs, and by example some other modern industrial laboratories, into fundamental research centers. As a researcher, Davisson was notable for his attention to careful preparation, his devotion to detail, and his pursuit of thorough understanding.

• Davisson's papers are in the Library of Congress. The correspondence between Davisson and Richardson is found in the Owen W. Richardson Papers, Humanities Research Center, University of Texas at Austin, available on microfilm at the American Institute of Physics, New York City. Although many of Davisson's papers were lost when Bell Labs moved from New York City to New Jersey, the records of his experiments with Kunsman, Germer, Calbick, and others is recorded in the notebooks held by Bell Telephone Laboratories in Murray Hill, N.J. The most important paper announcing the discovery of electron diffraction is C. J. Davisson and L. H. Germer, "Diffraction of Electrons by a Crystal of Nickel," *Physical Review* 30 (Dec. 1927): 705–40, although the first public announcement of their results is "The Scattering of Electrons by a Single Crystal of Nickel," *Nature* 119 (16 Apr. 1927): 558–60. A valuable personal biography, written by a colleague at Bell Labs, is Mervin J. Kelly, *Biographical Memoirs, National Academy of Sciences* 36 (1962): 51–84; it contains a nearly complete bibliography of Davisson's published papers. A comprehensive study of the discovery of electron diffraction, including many personal details, is Richard K. Gehrenbeck, "C. J. Davisson, L. H. Germer, and the Discovery of Electron Diffraction" (Ph.D. diss., Univ. of Minnesota, 1973).

RICHARD K. GEHRENBECK

DAWES, Charles Gates (27 Aug. 1865–23 Apr. 1951), banker and vice president of the United States, was born in Marietta, Ohio, the son of General Rufus R. Dawes and Mary Beman Gates. His father served gallantly in the Civil War and later went into the lumber business and served one term in Congress. Dawes earned his B.A. (1884) and M.A. (1887) from Marietta College and his LL.B. (1886) from the Cincinnati Law School. In 1887 he moved to Lincoln, Nebraska, to practice law. He was an earnest opponent of the entrenched railroad powers, spending hours in court fighting discriminatory rail rates. His initial investments in real estate paid off, however, and he gradually became more sympathetic to conservative business views. For the rest of his life he would promote and defend the contribution of business and businessmen to the increasing wealth of the United States. He married Caro Blymyer of Cincinnati in 1889, and they had

two children. After their son drowned in 1912, the couple adopted two more children. Although conservative, Dawes was always willing to hear opposing viewpoints. In Lincoln, Dawes became lifelong friends with John J. Pershing and William Jennings Bryan and, despite Dawes's unwavering commitment to the Republican party, his respect for Bryan never diminished.

In the 1893 panic, Dawes suffered some financial reverses, from which he soon recovered, but he never forgot the lesson that a "ninety day note falls due." In 1894 he acquired manufactured gas plants in La Crosse, Wisconsin, and Evanston, Illinois, where he established his home. Dawes maintained strong family ties, bringing his three younger brothers, Beman G., Henry M., and Rufus C. Dawes, into his business enterprises. By the time he was thirty-five Dawes's shrewd business investments had made him wealthy.

Having known William McKinley from family connections in Ohio, Dawes corralled delegates for him in Illinois and then served as McKinley's western treasurer during the 1896 presidential campaign. Dawes's service was rewarded in 1897 with appointment as comptroller of the currency, from which he resigned in 1901 to run against Albert J. Hopkins for the Republican nomination for U.S. senator. After losing the nomination, he turned his attention from politics to banking as president of the new Central Trust Company of Illinois in 1902. During the next fifteen years he earned a national reputation in business circles speaking out on behalf of banking and trust reform. Dawes advocated insuring bank deposits, and during the trust-busting era of Theodore Roosevelt (1858–1919) he opposed condemning all corporations and trusts because of those few who abused the 1890 Sherman Anti-Trust Act.

In 1917 he obtained a commission as a major in the army, joining an engineering unit of the newly formed American Expeditionary Force (AEF). In France, Dawes's old friend Pershing tapped him to head the General Purchasing Board, established to coordinate the purchasing of supplies by army agents in Europe. Dawes performed in exemplary fashion, and through his work and that of his board the AEF obtained over ten million tons of supplies from war-torn Europe. He also served on the Military Board of Allied Supply, which coordinated purchasing among the Allies. After the war he remained in Europe as a brigadier general and served on the U.S. Liquidation Commission. His vigorous defense of army purchasing before a postwar congressional investigating committee earned him the nickname "Hell 'n Maria Dawes."

Back home, his banking position seemed too tame, and Dawes accepted Warren Harding's invitation in 1921 to become the first director of the Bureau of the Budget. A firm believer in balanced budgets, Dawes implemented Harding's election pledge to trim government expenditures wherever possible. Government purchasing requests were channeled through the Budget Bureau to reduce duplication and increase efficiency. During his year as budget director, Dawes cut expenditures by more than one-third. In 1922 he returned to Chicago and entered local politics, creating the staunchly patriotic Minutemen of the Constitution who opposed radicalism in organized labor.

Germany's inability to meet its reparations payments in 1922 prompted the creation in 1923 of a Committee of Experts of the Allied Reparations Commission to oversee a revision of the payments schedule. The commission, chaired by Dawes, devised a five-year plan to stabilize the German economy and established a more reasonable repayment scheme. For his work on the "Dawes Plan," he shared the 1925 Nobel Peace Prize with Sir J. Austen Chamberlain.

In 1924 Dawes was chosen to be Calvin Coolidge's running mate after Dawes's close friend and former Illinois governor, Frank O. Lowden, declined. While Coolidge stayed home, Dawes traveled thousands of miles campaigning against the Ku Klux Klan, the Democrats, and the radicalism of the Progressive candidate, Robert M. La Follette (1855–1925). Once elected, Dawes shocked the normally staid inaugural proceedings by demanding in his first speech that a limit be placed on Senate filibustering. His efforts to reform the Senate rules failed. Nonetheless, he worked diligently in the Senate fulfilling his obligations as presiding officer and, despite Coolidge's opposition, actively promoted passage of the McNary-Haugen farm relief bill. He also rallied Senate support for the 1928 Kellogg-Briand Peace Pact.

Dawes refused to seek nomination for president in 1928 and spent his first months out of office in 1929 serving on a private commission devoted to reorganizing the finances of the Dominican Republic. In June 1929 Herbert Hoover (1874–1964) appointed Dawes ambassador to Great Britain, where he served until January 1932. He participated in pre-conference negotiations for the 1930 London Naval Armaments Conference and served as a member of the U.S. delegation.

In January 1932 Hoover appointed Dawes to head the newly formed Reconstruction Finance Corporation (RFC), which loaned federal funds to shore up the nation's faltering economy. The pressing needs of his own struggling Chicago bank, however, required him to resign in June 1932 and return home. He reluctantly sought a large RFC loan to prop up the Central Republic Bank & Trust Company, which his bank became as the result of a merger. Although heavily criticized for this action, Dawes managed to stabilize Chicago banking during the grim days of 1932; his reorganized bank survived and eventually repaid its debt.

After 1932 and the election of Franklin D. Roosevelt as president, Dawes's active political career was over. He remained in Chicago, working at his bank and performing a variety of civic duties. He spoke out against American involvement in World War II but otherwise stayed out of the limelight. He died in Evanston.

Charles Dawes regarded service to community and country as one's highest calling. He matured in the age of big business, and as a self-made man he extolled the virtues of business in society. His gruff exterior masked a sentimental interior and a well-developed sense of humor. Although brusk, and sometimes profane, he was a good listener, charitable, and quietly religious. Six feet tall, thin, with brown eyes and hair, and seemingly always in a hurry, Dawes had little patience for long-winded speeches or endless meetings. In his own affairs he took control, whether in his bank, or on an international committee of banking experts, or with military officials. An amateur musician, he played the piano and flute and wrote the popular "Melody in A Major." Dawes served his country and the Republican party in positions of national and international importance. The influence of the successful businessman on government during the first third of the twentieth century is ably represented by Dawes's public career.

• Dawes's papers are in the Special Collections Department of Deering Library at Northwestern University. The Evanston Historical Society occupies his home in Evanston and contains some scrapbooks and other personal items. Record groups in the National Archives that contain relevant material include: Record Group 101, Office of the Comptroller of the Currency; Record Group 120, American Expeditionary Forces (World War I); Record Group 51, Bureau of the Budget; and Record Group 234, Reconstruction Finance Corporation. Dawes's published diaries include: *A Journal of the Great War* (1921); *The First Year of the Budget of the United States* (1923); *Notes as Vice President, 1928–1929* (1935); *A Journal of Reparations* (1939); *Journal as Ambassador to Great Britain* (1939); and *A Journal of the McKinley Years* (1950). His other publications include *The Banking System of the United States and Its Relation to the Money and Business of the Country* (1894), *Essays and Speeches* (1915), and *How Long Prosperity?* (1937). Two published journalistic accounts are Paul R. Leach, *That Man Dawes* (1930), and Bascom N. Timmons, *Portrait of an American* (1953). The best biography remains unpublished (a copy is at the Evanston Historical Society), John E. Pixton, Jr., "American Pilgrim: A Biography of Charles Gates Dawes" (1957).

EDWARD A. GOEDEKEN

DAWES, Henry Laurens (30 Oct. 1816–5 Feb. 1903), congressman and senator, was born in Cummington, Hampshire County, Massachusetts, the son of Mitchell Dawes and Mercy Burgess, farmers. He attended local schools and received private instruction before entering Yale College, from which he graduated in 1839. Dawes taught school for a few months and then wrote articles for the *Greenfield Gazette and Courier*, the *North Adams Transcript*, and the *Pittsfield Eagle*. While studying in the law school at Albany, New York, in 1840, he addressed crowds in support of William Henry Harrison for the presidency. After completing his law education in the office of Wells and Davis in Greenfield, Dawes was admitted to the Massachusetts bar in 1842. He began his practice in North Adams but soon relocated to Pittsfield. He also secured a faculty position at Ashfield Academy in Massachusetts, where he met Electa Allen Sanderson, daughter of the headmaster. They married in 1844 and raised three children.

Dawes's political career began in 1848 with his election to the lower house of the Massachusetts state legislature, where he served in 1848, 1849, and 1852. He was elected to one term in the state senate in 1850 and was a member of the state constitutional convention of 1853. For the next four years he held the position of U.S. district attorney for the western region of Massachusetts. During this time, Dawes helped organize the new Republican party in his state.

In 1857 Dawes was elected as a Republican to the U.S. House of Representatives, where he served until 1875. Recognized as a legislator of great ability, he earned a solid reputation for his parliamentary managerial style in committee hearings and for his skillful debating on the floor of the House. A strong defender of President Abraham Lincoln and the North at the time of the Civil War, he frequently visited Union troops in camps and hospitals. Dawes grew steadily in influence and power during his long tenure in office. He succeeded to the chairmanship of the Committee on Appropriations in 1869 and the Committee on Ways and Means in 1871, the two most important House committees. This combination endowed him with considerable power over legislation of all kinds, permitting him to curtail lavish government expenditures. He was also chairman of the Committee on Elections from 1861 to 1869.

During the turbulent post–Civil War period, Dawes was increasingly in the national spotlight. On the day following Lincoln's death, he conferred with the new president, Andrew Johnson, and pledged his support. He cautioned Republicans to follow the path of moderation and prudence. A party stalwart, Dawes wanted to preserve a solid Republican organization, believing that a strong nation depended upon Republican predominance. When Johnson vetoed the Freedmen's Bureau Bill in 1866, Dawes deplored the consequences of the veto on the Republican party. On 22 February he wrote to his wife that Congress was furious: "Madness rules the house and there is no reason at either end of the Avenue. The great fruits of war are to be lost or postponed for a generation." A month later, on 31 March, a disgusted Dawes reiterated his thoughts in another letter to his wife: "They [Radicals] can cry and howl and . . . alarm the country at the terrible crisis the President has involved us in, and he is fool enough, or wicked enough . . . to furnish them with material fuel for the flame, depriving every friend he has of the least ground upon which to stand and defend him."

Johnson's actions relating to Reconstruction measures pained Dawes considerably by 1866. Cognizant that a political alliance with Johnson was out of the question, Dawes refused to compromise his principles. Although he detested the extreme tactics of Radical Republicans, Dawes demanded stronger guarantees of southern loyalty and obedience than did the president, whom he claimed lacked statesmanship.

Dawes reluctantly severed his ties with the beleaguered chief executive.

Dawes's break with Johnson constituted but one phase in a House career that was noteworthy in several respects. A strong supporter of maintaining protective tariff schedules, especially for the textile industry, Dawes was viewed as the champion of New England manufacturers. Along with Representative John A. Bingham of Ohio, he sponsored the wool and woolen tariff of 1868. In addition to his protectionist stand, Dawes defended the National College for Deaf Mutes and the enlargement of the Hospital for the Insane in the nation's capital. Adopting the suggestion of Cleveland Abbe, a noted meteorologist, Dawes in 1869 endorsed the plan for the issuance of daily weather bulletins from all sections of the country, which led to the creation of the National Weather Service. Some contemporaries even referred to Dawes as the "father" of this weather bureau. In 1869 he sought the Speakership of the House of Representatives, but after lengthy consultations, he withdrew in favor of Representative James G. Blaine of Maine.

After eighteen years in the House, Dawes was elected in 1875 to the U.S. Senate, where he served continuously until his retirement in 1893. In his role as a senator from Massachusetts, Dawes, holding the seat once occupied by Charles Sumner, continued his support of tariff protection. A member of the Committee on Buildings and Grounds, he proposed legislation to complete the Washington Monument, which, owing to an absence of funds, had been left unfinished since before the Civil War. The structure was finally dedicated in 1885. As chairman of the Senate Committee on Indian Affairs, Dawes secured money for educational facilities on reservations and brought Native Americans under federal criminal laws.

Dawes is best remembered as the author of the Indian Emancipation Act of 1887, usually called the Dawes General Allotment (Severalty) Act. This measure was designed to assimilate Native Americans into the mainstream of American life and into the American political and economic systems. Reformers contended that reservations fostered indolence and perpetuated tribal customs that hindered assimilation with society. The Dawes Act provided for the dissolution of Native-American tribes as legal entities and the division of tribal lands among individual members and empowered the president to allot these lands within the reservations, contingent on tribal agreements. The government retained a probationary 25-year trust patent, designed to guard against the sale of the holdings to unscrupulous speculators, after which the individual would have full ownership and title to the land with a conferral of U.S. citizenship. The act provided 160 acres to each head of a family, 80 acres to each adult single person, and smaller amounts of land to others who would leave the reservation. President Grover Cleveland, whose encouragement helped to assure passage of the measure, signed and praised the Dawes Act.

Although the Dawes Act was an attempt to resolve the complex problems surrounding the status of Native-American tribes and lands and in its day was often compared to the Magna Carta and the Declaration of Independence, the measure was ultimately a failure, both in its endeavor to impose a different culture on Native Americans and in the multitude of legalities the law generated over the years. Although showing good intentions, the Dawes Act failed to free Native Americans from governmental dependency. It left millions of acres of land to the government for white settlement. Native American degradation continued; promises of a better education and life rang hollow. The butchery at the battle of Wounded Knee in 1890 demonstrated how meaningless were these intentions, which deprived Native Americans of their property and compelled them to farm on worthless land rather than hunt. Dawes had hoped that assistance would come from churches and philanthropic societies in a common effort with the government to improve the lives of Native Americans. Lacking such aid and with the nation determined to resist special concessions to Native Americans, the failure of the Dawes Act was not surprising. It was finally replaced by the Indian Reorganization Act of 1934 during the administration of President Franklin D. Roosevelt.

Troubled by hearing problems, Dawes retired from the Senate in 1893. With his simple tastes, dignified manners, and personal integrity, he endeared himself to friends and adversaries in Washington and Massachusetts. Senator George F. Hoar, a Massachusetts Republican, recorded in his autobiography that Dawes had proven himself capable of handling the duties and burdens of the offices entrusted to him by the people.

After his retirement from political life, Dawes lived uneventfully at his home in Pittsfield, Massachusetts, with his daughter. His mind was alert, and he maintained his interest in public affairs, remaining until the end a friend of Native Americans. From 1893 to 1903 he headed the Commission of the Five Civilized Tribes (Dawes commission) to negotiate for the voluntary abandonment of tribal relations from a group that had been exempted from the 1887 act. In this connection, he visited Indian Territory in 1895. Seven years later, President Theodore Roosevelt called upon the veteran statesman when he visited Pittsfield. Known as the "Sage of Pittsfield," Dawes died in his home city.

Dawes achieved national recognition as a politician during Reconstruction and the Gilded Age. Although not an eloquent orator, he quickly mastered issues and worked tirelessly in the committee room for the legislation he supported.

• The Henry L. Dawes Papers, including an incomplete biography by his daughter, are in the Manuscripts Division of the Library of Congress. A few letters are in the Massachusetts Historical Society in Boston, the Massachusetts State Library in Boston, and the New-York Historical Society in New York. The Oklahoma Historical Society in Oklahoma City has papers relating to the Dawes commission, and the Dawes Family Papers in the Oliver Wendell Holmes Library at Phillips Academy in Andover, Mass., contain valuable letters relating to personal and public affairs, congressional events, and legislation. Dawes published *The New Dogma of the South* (1860). The major study of Dawes is Fred H. Nicklason, "The Early Career of Henry L. Dawes, 1816–1871" (Ph.D. diss., Yale Univ., 1967). An excellent article is Steven J. Arcanti, "To Secure the Party: Henry L. Dawes and the Politics of Reconstruction," *Historical Journal of Western Massachusetts* 5 (1977): 33–45. George F. Hoar, *Autobiography of Seventy Years* (2 vols., 1903), contains material on Dawes's years in Congress. His endeavors on behalf of Native Americans are recounted in Anna L. Dawes, *The Indian as a Citizen* (1917); Charles C. Painter, *The Dawes Land in Severalty Bill and Indian Emancipation* (1887); and Loring Benson Priest, *Uncle Sam's Stepchildren: The Reformation of United States Indian Policy, 1865–1887* (1942). An obituary is in the *Boston Evening Transcript*, 5 Feb. 1903.

LEONARD SCHLUP

DAWES, Rufus Cutler (30 July 1867–8 Jan. 1940), utility executive and civic leader, was born in Marietta, Ohio, the son of Rufus R. Dawes, a businessman, and Mary Beman Gates. His family background included Marietta's founders, while his father acquired a sizable fortune in a series of business ventures that included railroad construction, contracting, and a rolling mill operation. Although the latter enterprise failed in the Panic of 1873, his father soon entered the wholesale lumber business, and young Dawes grew up amid wealth.

After receiving his early education in local schools, Dawes entered Marietta College, earning his A.B. in 1886 and his A.M. in 1889. In the latter year Dawes joined his father's firm and was successful enough to marry Helen Virginia Palmer of Washington Court House, Ohio, in 1893; they had seven children.

Dawes remained with his father until 1897, when, at the request of his older brother Charles (who had just been appointed comptroller of the currency by President McKinley), he assumed the management of gas plants in La Crosse, Wisconsin, and Evanston, Illinois. Charles Dawes, a successful lawyer and banker, had entered the utility business to reverse financial losses that he had suffered in the Panic of 1893. The natural gas industry was expanding because of improved technologies, which allowed the efficient transportation of gas over long distances, and increased demand from both consumers and industry. With his brothers Henry May and Beman Gates, Rufus Dawes incorporated Dawes Brothers in 1902. The firm, which later organized both the Metropolitan Gas and Electric Company and the Union Gas Company, was an industry pioneer, serving as a holding company for a nationwide chain of utility firms. Dawes became particularly active in developing the vast natural gas reserves in northern Louisiana. A Dawes subsidiary, the North Shore Gas Company, pioneered the use of high-pressure gas mains in its pipeline between Waukegan and Evanston, Illinois.

As his prominence in the business world grew, Dawes was increasingly called upon for public service.

He served as a member of the Illinois state pension laws commission (1918–1919) and in 1920 participated in that state's constitutional convention. Dawes's expertise in political and financial affairs proved extremely valuable when he again served his brother as chief of staff of assistants on the Committee of Experts of the Allied Reparations Commission. Formed in 1923, the commission was created to deal with the chaos brought on by the post–World War I collapse of the German economy. Racked by runaway inflation, Germany found itself unable to pay the onerous financial indemnification mandated by the Versailles Treaty. In the face of the threat of escalating political and economic turmoil, the Allied Reparations Commission led by Charles Dawes and Owen D. Young, devised a five-year plan, which was implemented in 1924 to allow Germany to stabilize its economy and renew reparations. Despite the importance of the "Dawes Plan," which earned Charles Dawes a share of the 1925 Nobel Peace Prize, and his yeoman efforts to bring about its completion, Rufus Dawes remained characteristically modest about his own role; his book on the subject, *The Dawes Plan in the Making* (1925), contained a total of two self-references.

While brother Charles went on to win the American vice presidency in 1924, Rufus Dawes returned to the United States and began disposing of Dawes Brothers' assets in 1926. All holdings were sold by 1929, and Dawes had assumed a prominent leadership role in the proposed Chicago World's Fair. In 1928 he had been named one of fourteen incorporators (as well as president) of A Century of Progress, a nonprofit corporation formed with the goal of producing a suitable celebration in time for Chicago's 1933 centennial. Backed by eighty of Chicago's leading citizens, the fair sought to display how the previous century's progress in technology applied to business. The exposition, financed entirely by local private contributions, concessionaire rentals, and the sale of exhibition space, received no government support whatsoever. Contained in twenty-nine modernistic buildings on a 424-acre site that had been reclaimed from Lake Michigan, the exposition also featured the first use of lighting as an integral part of architectural design. After opening on 27 May 1933, the exposition ran for two years and drew a total of 16 million visitors. Not insignificantly, the event also finished with several hundred thousand dollars in profits (one of very few such operations to do so).

With fair profits divided among five permanent local institutions, Dawes became president of the Museum of Science and Industry in 1934 and held that position until his death in Evanston. Although often overshadowed by his more illustrious brother, Dawes is remembered as a solid businessman who contributed materially to the successful implementation of the Dawes Plan, as well as for his profitable stewardship of the 1933 Chicago World's Fair.

• No collection of Dawes's papers appears to have survived. Although his brother Charles's books, *Journal of the McKinley Years* (1950), *Notes as Vice President* (1935), and *Journal as Ambassador to Great Britain* (1939), contain limited information on Rufus Dawes's life and career, the best secondary source remains Glenn A. Bishop, ed., *Chicago's Accomplishments and Leaders* (1932). An obituary is in the *New York Times*, 9 Jan. 1940.

EDWARD L. LACH, JR.

DAWES, William (6 Apr. 1745–25 Feb. 1799), Boston patriot, was born in Boston, Massachusetts, the son of William Dawes, a tailor, grocer, and goldsmith, and Lydia Boone. He became a wealthy tanner in Boston and married Mehitable May in 1768; they had seven children.

Dawes's family ties made it logical for him to become involved in the Boston resistance movement. His cousin, colonel of militia Thomas Dawes, was a patriot leader. The famous North End Caucus that organized protests met at William Dawes's house. Dawes's anti-British sentiment was undoubtedly augmented after his wife was propositioned by one British soldier and he caught another in the act of breaking into his house with intent to steal during the occupation of Boston. Dawes may have been responsible for removing the two three-pound ceremonial cannon of the Ancient and Honorable Artillery Company, to which he belonged, from Boston during the siege in 1774.

On 18 April 1775 Dawes disguised himself as a country bumpkin, perhaps an inebriated one, to pass unsuspected across the narrow "neck" that separated Boston from the mainland, which British soldiers guarded heavily during the siege. He carried the same written message as Paul Revere: "A large body of the King's troops (supposed to be a brigade of about 12[00], or 1500) were embarked in boats from Boston, and gone to land at Lechmere's Point." The British destination was Concord, where they hoped to arrest John Hancock and Samuel Adams for treason and seize munitions stored by the patriots.

Whereas Revere began his famous ride in Charlestown and passed through Medford, Dawes left the neck and rode through Brookline, Cambridge, and Menotomy (present-day Arlington), mostly along the main road, the present-day Massachusetts Avenue, escaping just before the British closed the neck to forestall intelligence of their march. Dawes and Revere successfully rendezvoused, as did a third messenger, Samuel Prescott, at Lexington. On his way from there to Concord, however, Revere was captured by a British patrol; the other men, following two hundred yards behind him, turned back. Dawes was then thrown from his horse and spent the night in an abandoned barn before going home. Only Prescott, who had unexpectedly joined the team—he was a native of Concord on the way home from courting a woman in Lexington—reached his destination. However, all three gave the alarm wherever they went, successfully rousing the country to muster at Concord to meet the advancing army.

Dawes may have fought at the battle of Bunker Hill. In 1777 he was appointed commissary for the Continental army at Worcester, Massachusetts, where he remained after the Revolution, opening a general store with his brother-in-law John Coolidge. From 1786 to 1787 he served as clerk of the Ancient and Honorable Artillery Company of Massachusetts after it was revived for the first time since 1775. In 1790 Dawes began selling his various properties in Boston and Worcester. After his first wife died in 1793, he married Lydia Gendall in 1795. Their daughter, Mehitable, was born in 1796 and published a hearsay memoir of her father's ride in 1875.

Dawes's final residence was Marlborough, Massachusetts. His health had declined after the war, and he died relatively young. His widow inherited a farm and mansion at Marlborough and a mansion in Boston that she sold for $6,400. Dawes's adherents have tried unsuccessfully to gain for him equal status with Paul Revere; some have gone to the extent of arguing erroneously that he completed the ride to Concord. Yet while he was by no means as indispensable to the cause as Revere—whose roles as a propagandist and courier to Philadelphia were *sui generis*—his courage in undertaking the same risky ride on the night of 18 April 1775 fully justifies the high esteem in which his fellow revolutionaries held him.

• C. Burr Dawes, *William Dawes: First Rider for Revolution* (1976), reprints most of the surviving documents relating to Dawes and relates what is known of his life amid a rambling account of the Revolution in Massachusetts. David Hackett Fischer, *Paul Revere's Ride* (1994), and H. W. Holland, *Wm. Dawes and His Ride with Paul Revere* (1878), are also useful.

WILLIAM PENCAK

DAWKINS, Henry (fl. c. 1753–c. 1786), copperplate engraver, was born in England and immigrated to America about 1753 or 1754. Nothing is known of his parentage, education, or training. We know his nationality only from an advertisement in the *Pennsylvania Journal and Weekly Advertiser*, 19 January 1758, in which he described himself as an "Engraver from London."

Apparently Dawkins first settled in New York, for his earliest dated work is a bookplate designed and engraved in 1754 for a lawyer of that city, John Burnet. In October 1755 Dawkins advertised in the *New-York Mercury* that he was established in his own business, having left Anthony Lamb, an instrument maker. Dawkins noted that he "engraves in all sorts of metals," suggesting that he produced not only copperplates for prints but perhaps nameplates for doors and ornamentation on scientific instruments, as he probably had for Anthony Lamb.

In 1757 Dawkins settled in Philadelphia and married Priscilla Wood; they had seven children. In Philadelphia, he assisted James Turner, a well-established engraver from Marblehead, Massachusetts. Turner engraved printing plates, watch and clock faces, and stamps for seals and bookbinders. Presumably Dawkins performed the same sorts of work.

Among Dawkins's notable engravings were a number of bookplates and advertisements for tradesmen and residents of New York and Philadelphia. These were executed in the decorative style known as rococo. Characteristic of this style were decorative cartouches, often asymmetrical in shape; spiky grasses and flowers projecting from shields bearing coats of arms of the owners of the bookplates; and shells and elegant mantling (foliated ornamentation). American engravers often copied these motifs directly from English examples; Dawkins was no exception. Among those who commissioned bookplates from him were Whitehead Hicks, Francis Hopkinson, Samuel Jones, Benjamin Kissam, John Crooke Ludlow, Jacob Roome, Samuel Stringer, William Sword, Josiah Short Vavasour, and Peter W. Yates. Typically, bookplates were not dated, so it is difficult to be precise about when they were commissioned. However, bookplate commissions were an important business for colonial engravers and can be used to establish the identities of eighteenth-century book collectors. Since the coats of arms were often created by the engravers, their use denotes aspirations toward gentility.

Engraved advertisements, commonly known as trade cards, were often very ornamental, featuring a cartouche with illustrations of the wares manufactured or sold by the tradesman. The trade card Dawkins engraved for Anthony Lamb (c. 1755), for example, features a portrait of Sir Isaac Newton and examples of the scientific instruments made by Lamb. The framework of the mantling of the trade card for Benjamin Harbeson, a coppersmith and manufacturer of pots and pans in Philadelphia, was directly copied from the English trade card for Henry Patten, a London razor maker.

Other important works by Dawkins include *A General Chart of All the Coast of the Province of Louisiana* (1760–1765); *Benjamin Lay* (c. 1760); views of the Pennsylvania Hospital (1761) and Nassau Hall at Princeton (1764); maps of Philadelphia (1762) and Pennsylvania (1770); *The Paxton Expedition*, a political print of 1764; and engravings for the *Transactions* of the American Philosophical Society (1771). *Liberty Triumphant; or, The Downfall of Oppression* (1774) is a political print dealing with the tea crisis that has been attributed to Dawkins. He was a prominent Freemason and engraved several certificates and meeting notices for the Masonic lodge in Philadelphia. His output as an engraver was significant both in quantity and quality.

By the end of 1775, Dawkins moved to New York. There he became associated with Isaac and Israel Young and others in a plot to counterfeit paper currency issued by the New York Colony. At the same time he was commissioned to engrave legitimate bills of credit. Young also engaged him to counterfeit Continental, Connecticut, and Massachusetts bills of credit. In May 1776 Dawkins was apprehended on Long Island. In July it was decreed that he would serve a jail sentence of an undetermined length. Because of transportation difficulties, he was jailed in White Plains, New York, instead of Albany. Although at that time many pieces of currency carried the legend "Death to

Counterfeiters," he was not executed for his crime. Conditions in prison were so inhospitable that he pleaded with the New York Committee of Safety for death. It is not known whether Dawkins was released from prison or escaped, but in 1777 he was back at work.

After his time in prison, Dawkins produced a limited amount of signed work, including seals for Connecticut and New York. The Connecticut seal appears on several broadsides published in 1777 and 1779. The work for New York included an officer's commission dated 1778. In 1780 Dawkins received payment from the Continental Congress for "engraving and altering the border and back pieces for striking the bills of credit of the United States." No additional knowledge of his work during or after the Revolution is known, although one writer suggests that he engraved bookplates in the early 1780s.

Dawkins's first wife died in 1770. A marriage license was issued to him and Mary McDowell on 3 April 1771, but the actual marriage was not recorded. No death notice of Dawkins has been located, but an advertisement in the 2 May 1786 issue of the *Freeman's Journal* notes the availability for purchase of "eight elegantly engraved copperplates, by Dawkins, little the worse for wear, containing the most approved copies for beginners, suitable for either copperplate Printers or Booksellers." This group of plates was possibly prepared for a penmanship book, but no copy is known to exist. The sale of these copperplates suggests the end of Dawkins's career and life.

Dawkins was one of the expert engravers whose talents were used to ornament the publications of his era. He brought to the colonies skills developed in London and knowledge of the rococo style that helped shape colonial taste for ornamentation. One of his trade cards has been called one of the "grandest of American advertising sheets." He was among the best and most versatile engravers of his generation. His reputation for excellence led to important commissions for maps and views that resulted in permanent records of the physical aspect of colonial America. Between the death of James Turner in 1759 and the American Revolution, Dawkins's elegant and precise work dominated the market for engravings in Philadelphia.

• Wilford P. Cole provided a complete account of the life and works of Dawkins in "Henry Dawkins, Engraver" (M.A. thesis, Univ. of Delaware, 1966). An article by Cole on the portrait of Benjamin Lay, "Henry Dawkins and the Quaker Comet," appeared in the *Winterthur Portfolio* 4 (1968). Additional information on the counterfeiting activities of Dawkins appears in John Broome, "The Counterfeiting Adventure of Henry Dawkins," *American Notes and Queries* 8 (Mar. 1950), and Stephen Decatur, "The Conflicting History of Henry Dawkins," *American Collector* 7 (Jan. 1939). Decatur's article reproduces several engravings by Dawkins. A listing of the engraved book illustrations and separately published prints of Dawkins is in the Catalogue of American Engravings, a machine-readable database at the American Antiquarian Society, Worcester, Mass. Several works by Dawkins are described in the Philadelphia Museum of Art's *Philadelphia:*

Three Centuries of American Art (1976) and in Morrison H. Heckscher and Leslie Greene Bowman, *American Rococo, 1750–1775* (1992). Edgar P. Richardson attributed *The Downfall of Oppression* to Dawkins in "Four American Political Prints," *American Art Journal* 6 (Nov. 1974). Richardson also wrote of Dawkins's political prints in "The Birth of Political Caricature," in *Philadelphia Printmaking*, ed. Robert F. Looney (1976).

GEORGIA BRADY BARNHILL

DAWSON, John (1762–31 Mar. 1814), statesman, was born in Caroline County, Virginia, the son of the Reverend Musgrave Dawson, an Anglican rector, and Mary Waugh. His father died in 1763, and his mother married Joseph Jones, a Fredericksburg lawyer, in 1779. John Dawson attended the College of William and Mary (of which his uncles, William and Thomas Dawson, had been president) and was admitted as a sophomore to Harvard College in May 1780. There he received private instruction in science and graduated in 1782. Three years later he began corresponding with James Madison, whom he probably met through his stepfather. Dawson represented Spotsylvania County in the Virginia House of Delegates, 1786–1787, 1787–1788, and 1789. He opposed the payment of prerevolutionary debts owed to British creditors but feared prodebtor legislation and paper money issued by the states. While Madison was attending the Confederation Congress during the autumn of 1787, Dawson kept him informed about the proceedings of the Virginia General Assembly and about public opinion on the recently drafted federal Constitution.

Dawson had also encountered James Monroe in the household of his stepfather, who was also Monroe's uncle and guardian. Dawson and Monroe became political colleagues in the state convention that met in Richmond to ratify the Constitution in June 1788. As the two delegates for Spotsylvania County, they opposed ratification. Like many anti-Federalists, Dawson criticized the Constitution's lack of a bill of rights. He feared that consolidation of the central government would lead to a standing army and insecurity of private property, but his opposition to the Constitution never affected his friendship with Madison, its leading architect.

The Virginia General Assembly elected Dawson to the last session of the Confederation Congress. He presented his credentials in New York on 1 December 1788, although the Confederation Congress last had a quorum in October. He congratulated Madison for sponsoring in the First Federal Congress the constitutional amendments that became the Bill of Rights. Despite his anti-Federalism, Dawson asked Madison to help him obtain various jobs in the new federal government, complaining that "I am really tir'd of the inactive station I am at present in" (*The Papers of James Madison*, vol. 13, p. 263).

Dawson studied law and in June 1789 was admitted to the bar in Fredericksburg. On 16 December the general assembly elected him to the Council of State. Like most anti-Federalists, Dawson became a Republican during the partisan realignment of the early 1790s. He opposed national and state banks and Hamilton's policy of the federal government's assumption of the states' revolutionary war debts. Like many Virginians, he was concerned about the location of the federal district, which as a result of the compromise of 1790 was located on the Potomac River in return for the southern states' acceptance of assumption. Like Madison, Dawson urged that the United States secure navigation rights to the Mississippi River—then controlled by Spain—which he recognized as crucial for the economic development of the South. As a presidential elector in 1793, he supported George Clinton in the balloting for vice president. He was pro-French and anti-British in foreign policy. He opposed the Jay Treaty of 1794 with Great Britain. After John Taylor of Caroline resigned from the U.S. Senate, Henry Tazewell defeated Dawson in the 1794 balloting in the general assembly to fill the vacancy. In the congressional election on 20 March 1797, Dawson defeated Thomas Posey in Madison's former district, composed of Spotsylvania, Orange, Louisa, and Madison counties. He took his seat on 15 May and served in the House of Representatives for the rest of his life.

Dawson opposed President John Adams's policy of confrontation with France and prosecution of the Quasi-War. He served on the committee that reported articles of impeachment against Senator William Blount of Tennessee for plotting to help the British seize Spanish Florida and Louisiana. On occasion during Adams's presidency, he met with Madison and Monroe to plan political strategy. In circular letters to his constituents in 1798, he denounced President Adams's handling of the XYZ affair and the Federalist-sponsored Alien and Sedition Acts. When a tie between Thomas Jefferson and Aaron Burr threw the presidential election into the House of Representatives, Dawson voted for Jefferson, helping to secure his victory.

In 1801 Dawson delivered the convention concluding the Quasi-War with France to Charles-Maurice de Talleyrand-Périgord, the French foreign minister, and was received, the American commercial agent reported, "with great politeness." He had told Secretary of State Madison, "My wishes are to obtain some information on the characters and views of the European nations from actual survey" (*The Papers of James Madison*, Secretary of State Series, vol. 1, p. 33). While in France, Dawson also met the marquis de Lafayette, who had been financially ruined during the French Revolution, and he subsequently sponsored legislation granting Lafayette federal lands that had been reserved for Continental army officers. During his European tour the Federalist press attacked him as effeminate. Unfazed by the innuendos, the voters in his district continued to return Dawson to Congress. In 1803 he sponsored the Twelfth Amendment, which provided for separate election of the president and vice president in order to prevent a recurrence of a tie such as had occurred between Jefferson and Burr.

Dawson applied unsuccessfully to Madison for territorial governorships in Mississippi and Louisiana.

He chaired the House of Representatives Committee on the District of Columbia, 1813–1814. As an aide to Major General Jacob Brown during the War of 1812, he traveled to the Great Lakes, where he developed tuberculosis. He died in Washington, D.C. Dawson was a leading figure in the politics and society of the early republic. Known as "Beau" because of his elegant dress and manners, he was a dashing and eligible bachelor in Fredericksburg (where he owned a house), Philadelphia, and Washington.

• A major collection of Dawson's correspondence is in the James Madison Papers at the Library of Congress; that correspondence is being published in *The Papers of James Madison*, ed. William T. Hutchinson et al., 20 vols. (1962–). A speech by Dawson in the Virginia ratifying convention was published in Merrill Jensen et al., eds., *The Documentary History of the Ratification of the Constitution*, vol. 10: *Ratification of the Constitution by the States: Virginia*, pt. 3 (1993), pp. 1488–95. Dawson's congressional speeches were published in *Debates and Proceedings in the Congress of the United States*, comp. Joseph Gales, Sr., et al. (42 vols., 1834–1856), generally known as the *Annals of Congress*. A biographical sketch of Dawson is in Charles C. Dawson, *A Collection of Family Records* (1874). An obituary is in the Washington, D.C., *Daily National Intelligencer*, the Republican party organ, 2 Apr. 1814.

THOMAS A. MASON

DAWSON, William (1704–20 July 1752), educator and poet, was born in Aspatia, Cumberland County, England, the son of William Dawson. His mother's name is not recorded. Although little is known about his parentage and circumstances, his family was comfortable enough to send him at age fifteen to Queen's College, Oxford. He received his B.A. in 1725 and his M.A. in 1728. After taking holy orders in 1729, Dawson emigrated to Williamsburg, perhaps at the instigation of William Stith, a Virginian from a wealthy and powerful family who was also a student at Queen's College and whose sister, Mary Randolph Stith, Dawson married sometime before 1734. Dawson served first as tutor, then as professor of moral philosophy at the College of William and Mary. Personable, talented, and well connected, Dawson won the approbation and support of James Blair, president of the college, commissary to the bishop of London, and powerful and irascible public figure. Through his own merit and Blair's support, he became chaplain of the House of Burgesses and rector of the choice James City parish, and upon Blair's death in 1743, succeeded him as commissary and as president of the college. Oxford awarded him a D.D. by diploma in 1747 in recognition of his achievements.

Dawson's tenure as president and commissary was a difficult one, as the Anglican church was increasingly pressured by charges of corruption and by inroads made into their parishes by dissenters strengthened by the Great Awakening. Dawson fought this pressure on two fronts, through his own work overseeing the education of ministers and through legal action, which attempted to keep dissenting ministers from preaching. He believed that ministers educated at home were far better and less prone to corruption than those sent over from England, and his career at the college was dedicated to improving homegrown clergy. The difficulties under which he labored are well represented in a letter from his lawyer, Benjamin Waller, himself a strong Anglican. Responding to Dawson's query about legal means of controlling the dissenters, he suggested that "the immoral & almost scandalous Lives" of some of the clergy "gives the Enemy too much Occasion of reproach" and continued: "If therefore the Heads of the Churches would join pious Examples to gentle & charitable Persuasions, those poor Souls who are led astray . . . would be more wrought upon than by Severity which they will call Persecution for Conscience Sake" (Isaac, pp. 156–57). Dawson himself seems to have been well suited to work for such change. Governor William Gooch wrote of him in 1739, "Mr. Dawson is a thorough Scholar, a good Christian, and Orthodox Preacher . . . in all respects fitted for Ecclesiastical Jurisdiction" (quoted in Hubbell, p. 34).

Besides distinguishing himself as a clergyman and educator, Dawson was an active and competent writer, authoring the first book of poetry printed in Virginia. *Poems on Several Occasions . . . by a Gentleman of Virginia*, published in October 1736 in Williamsburg by William Parks, is a collection of verses apparently written while he was a student at Oxford. He refers in his preface to the work as juvenalia, a classification supported by references in the poems to Oxford, student life, and the English landscape. Although the poems show little sophistication, they reveal Dawson's competence in imitating a variety of classical forms and show him proficient in the kind of witty converse that distinguished the eighteenth-century gentleman. The sixteen poems, which include a celebration of morning, love poems, and criticism of the contemporary stage, reflect the influence of the Cavalier poets, as well as Milton and Pope.

Dawson continued to write poetry, publishing in the colonial newspapers and at least one English magazine. The tradition of pseudonymous authorship makes recovery of Dawson's periodical poetry difficult, and only a few poems have been identified as unquestionably Dawson's: "To a Lady. On a Screen of Her Working" was printed in December 1736 in both the *Virginia Gazette* and the *London Magazine*; "The Wager," found in the *New York Gazette* (27 Mar. 1749), and "The Obedient Wives," in the *Pennsylvania Gazette* (29 Dec. 1737), are poems about the war of the sexes written for the amusement of his friends and widely reprinted throughout the colonies. Probably Dawson's also are elegies for Robert "King" Carter, in the *American Weekly Mercury* (14 Sep. 1732), and John Randolph, in the *Virginia Gazette* (8 Apr. 1737). Dawson died in Williamsburg.

William Dawson was a pivotal figure in the colony of Virginia at the time when the power of the Anglican church was beginning to be seriously challenged. He was also the first poet to have his work printed in Virginia, a southern colony whose contribution to an American literary identity is only beginning to be assessed, and one of the earliest published poets in America.

• Dawson's papers, containing letters and sermons, are in the Dawson collection in the Library of Congress. Also in the Library of Congress is the William and Mary Miscellany, a collection of Latin and English poems probably written by Dawson's students, though some may have been written by Dawson himself. George Washington's copy of *Poems on Several Occasions* is in the Boston Athenaeum. This copy has been reprinted twice, once in a limited edition in 1920, edited and introduced by Earl Gregg Swem; and once in 1930, edited and introduced by Ralph L. Rusk. At the time of these printings, Dawson had not yet been identified as the book's author. This determination was made in Harold L. Dean, "An Identification of the 'Gentleman of Virginia,'" *Papers of the Bibliographical Society of America* 31 (1937): 10–20. Important to understanding Dawson as a public figure are George M. Brydon, *Virginia's Mother Church* (1947–1952), and Daniel Mack Hockman, "The Dawson Brothers and the Virginia Commissariat, 1743–1760" (Ph.D. diss., Univ. of Illinois at Urbana-Champaign, 1975). For discussion of Dawson's literary importance, see Richard Beale Davis, *Intellectual Life in the Colonial South, 1585–1763* (1978), and Jay B. Hubbell, *The South in American Literature, 1607–1900* (1954). See also Rhys Isaac, *The Transformation of Virginia, 1740–1790* (1982), and J. A. Leo Lemay, *A Calendar of American Poetry in the Colonial Newspapers and Magazines and in Major English Magazines through 1765* (1972).

DAPHNE H. O'BRIEN

DAWSON, William Crosby (4 Jan. 1798–5 May 1856), representative and senator, was born in Greene County, Georgia, the son of George Dawson and Katie Ruth Marston Skidmore, farmers. As a youth, Dawson was given the best education available in the frontier community where his family lived. After studying with the Reverend Dr. Cumming, Dawson attended the county academy in Greensboro and then the University of Georgia, from which he graduated in 1816. He studied law for a year at the office of Thomas W. Cobb in Lexington before attending the famous Litchfield Law School in Connecticut. Graduating in 1818, Dawson returned to Greensboro and began practicing law. In 1819 he married Henrietta Mounger Wingfield. They had seven children before her death in 1850. Dawson became a highly regarded and successful lawyer in Greensboro. Although he earned his fame as a politician, he maintained a large and lucrative law practice throughout his career.

Dawson's political career began in 1822, when he was elected to the Georgia House of Representatives. In 1828 Dawson was appointed by the legislature to compile the statutes of Georgia, which he completed in 1831 with the publication of *Compilation of the Laws of the State of Georgia*. In 1834 Dawson was elected to the Georgia Senate and served for two terms. Already a popular legislator, he became a local military hero after raising a volunteer troop, the Greene County Volunteers, during hostilities with the Creeks and the Seminoles in 1836, and he received a special command from General Winfield Scott to defend Columbus, Georgia. As a result, Dawson was the only States'

Rights candidate in Georgia to win election to the U.S. House of Representatives in 1836. Twice reelected, Dawson became a prominent member of the emerging Georgia Whig party and was nominated in 1839 to be the Speaker of the House. In 1841 Georgia Whigs selected Dawson as their gubernatorial candidate, but he lost the election to Democrat Charles McDonald after Democrats criticized his vote in Congress for an increase in the duties on tea and coffee and his tacit support of Whig efforts to revive a national bank. Feeling he could no longer effectively represent his state after his decisive defeat, Dawson resigned his seat in Congress in November 1841 and returned to law. He remained an active participant in the Whig party in Georgia, however, attending state and national party conventions to support Henry Clay for the presidency in 1844. In 1845 a Whig governor awarded Dawson a coveted position on the bench of the Superior Court of the Ocmulgee Judicial Circuit, but he resigned after a year to resume his highly successful law practice.

Dawson returned to political office as a U.S. senator in March 1849 after a narrow victory over Democrat Walter T. Colquitt. In his six years in the Senate, Dawson became a nationally known politician. On familiar terms with Senate titans Clay and Daniel Webster, Dawson was an ardent supporter of Clay's compromise plan in 1850, a complex congressional agreement intended to resolve the sectional crisis over slavery in the territories. Dawson was a prominent member of the 1850 Georgia convention that drafted the famous Georgia Platform, which committed the state to the recent compromise but reserved secession as a last resort if Congress attempted further encroachments against slavery. As party allegiances broke down in Georgia over the compromise, Dawson became a leader of the Unionists who supported Howell Cobb for governor in 1851 on a procompromise platform. Like other southern Whigs, Dawson demanded that the Whig party platform accept the compromise as the definitive solution to the slavery question. In a Senate speech in April 1852, Dawson vowed to act with no party or candidate who did not accept "the *finality* of the compromise," an ultimatum that was repeated in Whig newspapers and conventions across the South. The nomination of General Scott over Millard Fillmore at the Whig national convention in 1852 was sufficient to drive most Georgia Whigs away from the party, but Dawson remained loyal to the national party and supported Scott in the presidential election. By 1854, however, Georgia Whigs had effectively dissolved ties with any national organization, and Dawson joined other southern Whigs in voting for the Kansas-Nebraska Act to repeal the Missouri Compromise line, a bill that northern Whigs opposed adamantly. During this time Dawson was also involved in the southern commercial convention movement, presiding over the 1853 convention in Baltimore and the 1854 convention in Charleston.

At the end of his term as senator in 1855, Dawson retired from political life to enjoy the comforts of home and family, particularly the companionship of his sec-

ond wife, Eliza M. Williams, whom he had married in 1854. They had no children. He continued to practice law in Greensboro until his sudden death there of bilious cholic. Dawson's funeral attracted a large crowd of mourners, including one hundred women of the Southern Masonic Female College, which Dawson had supported. A popular advocate and a respected politician for over thirty years, Dawson rose to national prominence as a leader of the Georgia Whig party and a defender of compromise in 1850. The county of Dawson, Georgia, organized in 1857, was named in his honor, as was the town of Dawson in Terrell County, Georgia.

• Dawson's papers are in the Robert W. Woodruff Library at Emory University in Atlanta, Ga. Dawson's career is described in Stephen F. Miller, *Bench and Bar of Georgia* (1858), which includes a eulogy prepared by Judge Eugenius A. Nisbet; William J. Northen, ed., *Men of Mark in Georgia* (1907–1912); Charles C. Dawson, *A Collection of Family Records* (1874); and Paul Murray, *The Whig Party in Georgia, 1825–1853* (1948). His role in the 1850 compromise debate is described in Richard H. Shryock, *Georgia and the Union of 1850* (1926). Dawson's involvement with the Commercial Convention movement is described in John G. Van Deusen, *The Ante-Bellum Southern Commercial Conventions* (1926). Obituaries are in the Milledgeville *Federal Union*, 13 May 1856, and the *New York Times*, 15 May 1856.

SUSAN WYLY-JONES

DAWSON, William Levi (26 Apr. 1886–9 Nov. 1970), congressman, was born in Albany, Georgia, the son of Levi Dawson, a barber, and Rebecca Kendrick. Dawson received his early education in Albany, then attended Fisk University in Nashville, Tennessee, receiving a bachelor's degree in 1909.

In 1912 Dawson joined thousands of other African Americans migrating to Chicago. Hoping to become one of the few black professionals in the city, Dawson enrolled at the Kent School of Law. In 1917, while still a law student, he interrupted his studies to volunteer for military service during World War I. He served as a first lieutenant with the 365th Infantry in France, where he was wounded in the shoulder and gassed during the Meuse-Argonne campaign.

After the war Dawson resumed his legal studies at Northwestern Law School and was admitted to the Illinois bar in 1920. Two years later he married Nellie Brown, with whom he had two children. Dawson practiced law until 1928 when he waged an unsuccessful campaign in the Republican primary against the incumbent white congressman Martin Madden, who represented the largely African-American First Congressional District in Chicago.

In 1933 Dawson campaigned successfully for a seat on the Chicago City Council. Then in 1938, at a time when most African Americans began switching their party allegiances to the Democrats, Dawson was nominated by the Republican party to run against Democrat Arthur Mitchell for the congressional seat for the First District. Dawson ran on an anti–New Deal platform and lost. A year later he also lost his city council seat to a Democrat.

Following Dawson's city council defeat, he was approached by Chicago Mayor Edward J. Kelly, a Democrat who was eager for an African American to lead the party in the city's largely black second ward. Dawson accepted Kelly's offer to be Democratic committeeman and soon established himself as Chicago's preeminent black Democratic leader, a position he held for the rest of his life.

Dawson quickly won favor with the Chicago Democratic organization by building an effective vote-producing machine in African-American neighborhoods. In 1942 he was elected to Congress from Chicago's First Congressional District, first defeating Earl Dickerson in the Democratic primary and then Republican candidate William King in the general election. When Dawson took his seat in 1943, he was the only African-American member of the House of Representatives.

As a member of Congress, Dawson sought to advance a limited civil rights agenda while maintaining that the United States was the best place "in all the world for our people." He called for an end to discrimination in defense industries, voted against regressive income tax measures, and testified before the House Judiciary Committee against the poll tax. In 1948 Dawson was selected to chair the Negro Division of the Democratic National Committee. Based on seniority, Dawson gained the chair of the House Committee on Governmental Operations (later renamed Government Operations) in 1949, becoming the first African-American chairman of a congressional committee.

A loyal Democrat, Dawson toed the party line on foreign policy, faithfully supporting measures to contain communism even during the controversial Vietnam War debate of the 1960s, when many black Democratic leaders broke with the Johnson administration. Throughout his congressional career, Dawson continued to control political patronage on Chicago's South Side and was the leading black member of the city's Democratic machine. He delivered huge blocks of votes for Democrats in municipal, state, and national elections. In 1955, for example, Dawson's four wards accounted for 40 percent of Richard J. Daley's winning margin in the Chicago mayoral election. Criticized by some civil rights activists for "selling out" his black constituency to a party that failed to challenge Jim Crow laws in the South or de facto segregation in the North, Dawson replied, "Where else but in the Democratic organization could a black man, whose ancestors were slaves, rise so high?"

During the 1960s Dawson came under increasing attack from civil rights activists, in part for his unwillingness to criticize the Democratic Party for acting too slowly against segregation and for his hostility toward civil rights leaders. When the Reverend Martin Luther King, Jr., initiated a campaign in Chicago in 1966 to challenge racial discrimination and poverty among the city's African-American population, Dawson denounced King as an "outside agent."

Dawson had fallen ill while campaigning in 1962 and never fully recovered his health. He died in Chicago.

Dawson served in Congress for twenty-seven years, longer than any African American to that point. As one of very few African Americans to serve in Congress before the victories of the civil rights movement, he maintained a steady but lonely voice against racial discrimination. Yet his career was paradoxical. As an unswervingly loyal member of a party that often forestalled civil rights advances, Dawson remained largely outside, and often hostile to, the leading black movements of his time.

• There are a number of short biographical treatments of Dawson, most notably Maurin Christopher, *America's Black Congressmen* (1971). See also William L. Clay, *Just Permanent Interests: Black Americans in Congress, 1870–1991* (1992), and Charles Stone, *Black Political Power in America*, rev. ed. (1970). An obituary is in the *New York Times*, 10 Nov. 1970.

THADDEUS RUSSELL

DAY, Albert (6 Oct. 1812–26 Apr. 1894), physician, temperance advocate, legislator, and leader in the treatment of inebriety, was born in Wells, Maine, the son of Nahum Day and Persis Weeks. Little is known about Day's family or his youth; his father died early, forcing Day to earn a living and save his studying for the evening.

Day's life's work in aid of the inebriate is said to have been inspired by the Washingtonian temperance movement of the 1840s, an early nineteenth-century secular revival focusing exclusively on the reform of habitual drunkards. Washingtonians pledged sobriety to one another in small groups in which former drinkers shared stories of their struggles against the bottle and vowed to help fellow members remain sober through companionship, moral support, and financial assistance. During the 1840s an estimated 600,000 people, mostly artisans and small businesspeople, joined the Washingtonians, making it one of the largest temperance movements of the nineteenth century.

Elected to the state legislature in 1856, Day quickly secured from the Commonwealth of Massachusetts a charter for the country's first inebriate asylum, the Washingtonian Home, incorporated in Boston in 1857. He served as its superintendent until 1867, operating it with both state and private funds. During this time he also earned his M.D. from Harvard Medical School (1866); he wished to complement the moral therapy offered at the Washingtonian Home with the scientific treatment of the inebriate's physical disabilities. Day managed the Washingtonian Home effectively, reforming thousands of habitual drunkards during his first nine years there.

In 1867 Day left Boston to become superintendent of the financially and politically troubled New York State Inebriate Asylum in Binghamton. During his brief tenure there, he championed institutional efforts to have patients seek treatment voluntarily rather than subjecting them to the enforced incarceration advocated by his predecessor, the asylum's founder, Joseph E. Turner. As with his patients at the Washingtonian Home, Day emphasized the reform and rebuilding of both spirit and mind. Although he enjoyed some therapeutic success in Binghamton, he grew tired of fending off the political assaults of the institution's trustees. In 1870 a fire broke out at the facility, and the trustees accused Day of arson. In response, Day resigned, returning to Massachusetts to establish the Greenwood Institute for inebriates. There he treated patients until 1873, when, coincidentally, he lost Greenwood to a fire. Two years later Day was asked to return to the Washingtonian Home and serve again as its superintendent. This he did until 1893, when he retired because of failing health, taking several of his recovering patients with him to his home in Melrose Highlands, Massachusetts, to continue their treatment. Day died there one year later.

Day was a founding member of the American Association for the Cure of Inebriates (AACI), established in 1870. He published articles on the nature of inebriety, the means of effecting cures, and the social and economic consequences of habitual drunkeness. He also addressed the issue of women's inebriety and remarked on the double standard society used to condemn women drinkers more than their male counterparts. His only monograph, *Methomania*, appeared in 1867 and achieved wide circulation. According to Thomas Crothers, editor of the *Quarterly Journal of Inebriety*, *Methomania* was "an excellent summary at the time of the facts of inebriety, and was a very useful influential work." Day was esteemed for his strong character, integrity, practical bent, and singular devotion to his inebriate charges.

In assessing Day's contributions to the field, Crothers remarked that although he was not regarded as "a great scholar or bold pioneer leader far in advance of his day and generation," Day nonetheless was an "eminently wise prudent man who sought rather to give shape and direction to events of the present," a man who translated the "half-theories" of inebriety research into "working principles, good for the present and valuable as stepping stones for the future." At the time of his death, Day had spent thirty-seven years in inebriate asylum work; he had provided medical care for more inebriates than any other individual in the United States, his patients numbering in the tens of thousands. Moreover, he had established what would become America's longest lived institution specifically for the medical treatment of inebriates, the Washingtonian Home, one of the few such institutions to survive Prohibition.

• There is no formal collection of Albert Day papers. Brief biographical sketches include Thomas Crothers, "The Late Dr. Albert Day: A Biographical Sketch," *Quarterly Journal of Inebriety* 18 (1896): 51–55; "Albert Day," in *The Standard Encyclopedia of the Alcohol Problem*, ed. Ernest Cherrington, vol. 2 (1924), p. 767; and Mark Lender, "Albert Day," in *Dictionary of American Temperance Biography: From Temperance Reform to Alcohol Research, the 1600s to the 1980s* (1984), pp. 128–29. On the Washingtonian movement, see Jack Blocker, *American Temperance Movements: Cycles of Reform* (1989); Jed Dannenbaum, *Drink and Disorder: Temperance Reform in Cincinnati from the Washington Revival to the WCTU* (1984); Robert Hampel, *Temperance and Prohibition*

in Massachusetts, 1813–1852 (1982); and Milton A. Maxwell, "The Washington Movement," *Quarterly Journal of Studies on Alcohol* 11 (Sept. 1950).

SARAH W. TRACY

DAY, Arthur Louis (30 Oct. 1869–2 Mar. 1960), geophysicist, was born in Brookfield, Massachusetts, the son of Daniel Putnam Day and Fannie Maria Hobbs. Little is known of his family or youth.

Day attended the Sheffield Scientific School of Yale University, earning an A.B. in 1892 and a Ph.D. in physics two years later. Immediately thereafter, the Sheffield Scientific School engaged Day as an instructor in physics. Day's youth and energy won the respect and affection of students, but he published nothing during the next three years. Eager both to improve his understanding of experimental technique and to earn credentials in research, Day traveled to Germany in 1897 and applied for an assistantship at the Physikalisch-Technische Reichsanstalt (PTR) in Charlottenburg. As Germany's leading center for the measurement of physical constants, the PTR did not often take in inexperienced foreign scientists, but Day's earnestness and willingness to work without salary impressed its director, Friedrich Kohlrausch. Day was granted an unpaid assistantship and put to work on a project to improve methods for measuring high temperatures. When his senior collaborator was disabled by illness, Day was appointed to the regular staff. Working with physicist Ludwig Holborn, Day subsequently used gas thermometers to establish a scale extending up to 1,150°C, thereby bettering the earlier limits of accurate measurement by more than 500°C. In 1900 he married Kohlrausch's daughter, Helene; they had four children.

Following their marriage, the Days moved to Washington, D.C., where Day was appointed physical geologist in the Division of Chemical and Physical Research of the U.S. Geological Survey. Under the supervision of George Ferdinand Becker, the division was equipping a laboratory to investigate the physical properties of igneous rocks at high temperatures. Such investigation, Becker believed, would shed light on a host of geological problems, including the mechanisms of volcanic and tectonic action, the genesis of minerals and ore deposits, and the nature of subterranean magmas. Research on rock-forming minerals in the vicinity of their melting points, however, called for experimental skills that few American scientists had. Day's experience in pyrometry and firsthand knowledge of the techniques of the PTR made him an ideal candidate to take charge of such a program. Important, too, was Day's skill at public speaking, which had been honed in the classrooms at Yale. Because of the distance of the laboratory's research from the economic concerns of the public and Congress, Becker felt the need for an associate who could both plan experiments and speak convincingly of the importance of geophysical research.

Although a physical geologist in name, Day had little knowledge of rocks or minerals. While waiting for pyrometric equipment to arrive from Europe, he explored the literature of geology and petrology. He also embarked on an ambitious program of reading in the literature of the new science of physical chemistry, much of which dealt with the behavior of solutions. Although the physical chemist generally dealt with dilute aqueous solutions and the petrologist with solutions of molten minerals, Day recognized that many of the principles and techniques applicable in one field could be applied to the other. In 1903 Day undertook to explore the thermal properties of the soda-lime feldspars, the most common mineral in the earth's crust, in collaboration with chemist Eugene T. Allen and petrologist Joseph P. Iddings. Their results, published in 1905, offered strong evidence that soda-lime feldspars were solid solutions forming a continuous isomorphous series—a finding that had the effect of firmly associating these feldspars with a large class of isomorphous mixtures that had been better studied by physical chemists. Day and Allen's paper set a new standard for research in experimental petrology. Unlike many earlier investigators, they had used chemically pure starting materials: laboratory-prepared samples of soda-lime feldspars. They had taken pains to fix temperatures of phase changes in their samples with all the precision that contemporary technology allowed. And they had discussed their results in light of recent work in physical chemistry. Similar laboratory studies of other minerals, Day believed, would create the knowledge necessary to explain how igneous rocks, in all their diversity, could arise from relatively homogeneous magmas of molten silicates.

In 1905 the Carnegie Institution of Washington authorized the construction of a laboratory for geophysical research. Although Becker had prepared many of the initial plans for this undertaking, the trustees of the Carnegie Institution selected Day as the laboratory's first director, in large part because he was more willing to adapt his research plans to the financial resources available.

Day served as director of the Geophysical Laboratory of the Carnegie Institution of Washington from his appointment in 1907 until his retirement in 1936. Under his management, the laboratory became the world's leading center for the study of igneous rocks and their constituent minerals. Working with collaborators, especially Allen, E. S. Shepherd, and Robert Sosman, Day extended his own research in pyrometry and experimental petrology. An excellent judge of talent, Day also brought to his laboratory other young co-workers including Norman Levi Bowen and L. H. Adams, who later made landmark contributions to the experimental study and theoretical interpretation of rock-forming minerals. Although experimental research was at the core of the geophysical laboratory's mission, Day also organized field work in volcanology and seismology, believing that controlled laboratory investigations and more traditional studies of natural phenomena should be mutually reinforcing enterprises. On Day's advice, the Carnegie Institution contributed to the construction of a volcano observatory

near Mount Kilauea, Hawaii, in 1911. Day was instrumental as well in securing the cooperation of many of the universities and colleges of California in developing a network of seismological research stations along the West Coast during the 1920s. Day's personal research on the geysers, fumeroles, and hot springs of California and the Yellowstone region, conducted during the 1920s and 1930s, were important contributions to the study of geothermal activity.

Day was not a prolific writer, but his contributions were of strategic value in the growth of geophysics and experimental petrology. His skillful management of the geophysical laboratory during its formative decades did much to bring the quantitative methods of physics and chemistry into the earth sciences. He also played a role in establishing scientific research in the American glass and ceramics industries when, during World War I, he took a leave of absence from the laboratory to take charge of production of high-quality glass for the War Industry Board. In 1918 he was named vice president in charge of manufacturing of the Corning Glass Works, a position that he retained until 1936. Day's ability was also recognized by his scientific colleagues, who elected him to the presidencies of the Philosophical Society of Washington in 1911, the Washington Academy of Sciences in 1924, and the Geological Society of America in 1938. He was home secretary of the National Academy of Sciences from 1913 to 1918 and vice president of the academy from 1933 to 1941.

Day's first marriage ended in divorce in 1931. In 1933 he married Ruth Sarah Easling of Corning, New York. Day died in Bethesda, Maryland.

• Some of Day's professional correspondence is at the offices of the Carnegie Institution of Washington in Washington, D.C. The George Ferdinand Becker Papers at the Library of Congress contain letters that are relevant to Day's appointment to the U.S. Geological Survey and his role in the organization of the Geophysical Laboratory of the Carnegie Institution. Robert B. Sosman, "Memorial to Arthur Louis Day (1869–1960), *Bulletin of the Geological Society of America* 75 (1964): 147–55, includes a bibliography of Day's writings. Useful, too, is Philip H. Abelson, "Arthur Louis Day," *Biographical Memoirs of the National Academy of Sciences* 47 (1975): 27–47. Day's work at the geophysical laboratory is discussed by John W. Servos, "To Explore the Borderland: The Foundation of the Geophysical Laboratory of the Carnegie Institution of Washington," *Historical Studies in the Physical Sciences* 14 (1983): 147–85, and H. S. Yoder, Jr., "Scientific Highlights of the Geophysical Laboratory, 1905–1989," in *Annual Report of the Director of the Geophysical Laboratory, 1988–1989* (1989), pp. 143–97.

JOHN W. SERVOS

DAY, Caroline Stewart Bond (18 Nov. 1889–5 May 1948), anthropologist and college teacher, was born in Montgomery, Alabama, the daughter of Georgia Fagain and Moses Stewart. She was a light-skinned mulatto of African-American, Native-American, and European descent. The Stewart family lived several years in Boston, Massachusetts, where Caroline attended public schools. After her father's death, Caroline and her mother moved to Tuskegee, Alabama, where Georgia Stewart taught school and married John Percy Bond, a life insurance executive. The couple had two children, and Caroline adopted Bond's name. She attended Tuskegee Institute and in 1912 earned a Bachelor of Arts degree from Atlanta University. She taught English at Alabama State College in Montgomery for a year and then worked for the Young Women's Christian Association (YWCA) in Montclair, New Jersey. In 1916 she began studying English and classical literature at Radcliffe College of Harvard University, earning a second bachelor's degree in 1919. At Radcliffe she impressed anthropology professor Earnest A. Hooton, who encouraged her to begin collecting the physiological and sociological data on the "almost inaccessible class of educated persons of mixed Negro and White descent" that eventually led to her graduate studies.

After World War I Caroline Bond took a semester off and worked in New York City as executive secretary of the Circle for Negro War Relief under the leadership of W. E. B. Du Bois. She also served as student secretary of the National Board of the YWCA. After graduating, she moved to Waco, Texas, and taught English at Paul Quinn College, where she served as dean of women, and then at Prairie View State College, where she was head of the English department. There she met and married Aaron Day, a chemistry teacher, in March 1920. He then became a salesman for the National Benefit Life Insurance Company, where his wife's stepfather also worked. From 1922 to 1929 Caroline Day taught English and drama at Atlanta University. Her essays, short stories, plays, children's stories, and poetry, published in magazines and anthologies, reflect her interest in the life and problems of blacks and mulattos. An article in *The Crisis* (Sept. 1925) discusses plays suitable for black student actors, and her autobiographical story "The Pink Hat" in *Opportunity* (Dec. 1926) describes a young woman's experience "passing" in white society.

In 1927 Earnest Hooton, Day's former teacher, received a grant from the Bureau of International Research of Harvard University and Radcliffe College, which allowed Day to continue her research. Although her work was interrupted by her rheumatic heart condition, she entered Harvard's graduate school of anthropology and earned a master of arts in 1930. The Harvard African Studies series *Varia Africana* published her master's thesis, *A Study of Some Negro-White Families in the United States* (1932). This study of mulatto families was the first of its kind in anthropology, treating sociological, genealogical, and physiological aspects of "Negro-White crosses."

In 1930 the Days moved to Washington, D.C. Unable to have children because of her weak heart, Caroline Day befriended and informally adopted a teenage boy. She taught English at Howard University, worked as a social worker and director of a D.C. settlement house in 1934, and was appointed general secretary of the Phillis Wheatley "Colored" YWCA in 1937. In 1935 Aaron Day was promoted to the head office of

the North Carolina Mutual Life Insurance Company, and in 1939 the family joined him in Durham, North Carolina. There Caroline Day began teaching English and drama at North Carolina College for Negroes (now North Carolina Central University). Poor health continued to limit her career, and except for occasional teaching and some unpublished writings, she spent the rest of her life with her family—gardening, reading, and attending club activities. She died in Durham from complications of her chronic heart condition.

Day came to her study of mixed-blood crosses from her experience as a mulatto. Proud of her mixed heritage, she also understood the handicaps facing blacks and the temptation to "pass for white" in a race-biased society. Her study involved people who, she said, were not "the types with which the public is familiar" nor "those used as literary material by the novelists and playwrights" of her day (*Study*, p. 3); rather she presented a "real cross-section of life among colored people of mixed blood in this country" (*Inventory*, p. 3). In reviewing her work in *The Crisis* (Mar. 1930), Day noted that intermarriage was a problem rarely written about because "few popular writers have dared attempt the subject and few scientists have had sufficient material at their disposal to warrant venturing conclusions" (p. 81). Focusing on the racial categories "Negro, Indian, and White," she documented not only the physiological characteristics—skin color, physical measurements, hair samples, and appearance—of 346 families (including 1,347 living individuals of a total of 2,537), but she also collected photographs, family stories, and information relating to their homes, occupations, salaries, religion, education, political connections, and sometimes their "passing" into white society. Collecting data was difficult because of what Day recognized as the "mystery and humiliation of illegitimacy" and the "fear of exposure" of families in the white community (*Study*, pp. 4–5). Hooton qualified the anthropometric conclusions of Day's study because of her limited sample, and others have criticized her methodology as unsophisticated; nevertheless, Day's findings and sociological observations are valuable to biographers, historians, genealogists, and anthropologists. Her data challenged stereotypes and refuted theories that miscegenation produced inferior types (*Study*, p. 106). Her stories of hardship and achievement demonstrate the strength and resiliency of black and mixed-race individuals. In dealing with the question of whether blacks should be absorbed into the white population, Day contended, "The grim joke of the whole matter is that for 150 years and more he has been absorbed and his descendants are constantly rubbing elbows in daily life with some of the very ones who are discussing them" (*Study*, p. 11).

• Day's papers are available at the Peabody Museum of Harvard University. The thirty-five boxes include correspondence, manuscripts, clippings, and the anthropometry forms, questionnaires, tables and guides used in her research, as well as family histories, genealogical charts, photographs, and hair samples of her subjects. The collection, disorganized and inaccessible for many years, was processed beginning in 1991. *Inventory of the Papers of Caroline Bond Day* (rev. 1996), gives a detailed catalog of the collection with the names of all subjects and a brief bibliography of related sources. Day's *A Study of Some Negro-White Families in the United States* (1932) was reprinted in 1970. Some of Day's work is available in Werner Sollers et al., *Blacks At Harvard: A Documentary History of African-American Experience at Harvard and Radcliffe* (1993). An obituary is in the *Durham Morning Herald*, 7 May 1948.

CAROL BAKER SAPORA

DAY, Clarence Shepard, Jr. (18 Nov. 1874–28 Dec. 1935), author, illustrator, and humorist, was born in New York City, the son of Clarence Shepard Day, a stockbroker, and Lavinia Elizabeth Stockwell. As the son of a prominent businessman, Day followed the "traditional route" for those in his social class. He was educated at St. Paul's School in Concord, New Hampshire, received a B.A. from Yale in 1896, and went to work with his father. Day, Sr., a governor of the New York Stock Exchange, presented Clarence with a seat on the exchange in 1897, and in 1898 the son became a partner at Clarence S. Day and Company.

Yet life as a stockbroker did not seem to suit, and when the Spanish-American War broke out in 1898, Day, a member of the naval reserve, enlisted. He served first as a seaman and later as a yeoman on the *Nahant*, a training ship stationed in New York Harbor. During this time he developed the crippling form of arthritis that would plague him for the rest of his life.

Day returned to the business world after he was mustered out in 1898, but in 1903 he was forced by his illness to retire. He attempted to recover his health in Arizona and Colorado in 1904–1905 and even bought a ranch in Colorado. Although he was unable to walk, Day had himself propped up on a pony and rode every day on his property. But by 1905 he had returned to New York City.

From 1905 to 1909 Day was the sole owner and publisher of the *Yale Alumni Weekly*. He also managed a glove business from his apartment overlooking Central Park and speculated in the stock market. By 1910 he had become a freelance writer; essays, short sketches, and poetry were published in *Harper's*, the *New Yorker*, the *Saturday Evening Post*, the *Yale Review*, and the *New Republic*. His short poems, illustrated by his own pen-and-ink drawings, were widely reprinted. Day also wrote introductions to and drew illustrations for the work of other authors. From 1915 to 1921 he worked as a book reviewer for the *Metropolitan*, a monthly magazine, and under the pseudonym B. H. Arkwright he wrote a financial column for the same magazine.

This Simian World (1920), Day's first published book, satirizes human nature and poses the question of what people would be like had they descended from a species other than primates. If, for example, our ancestors had been ants, we would be "good citizens," but without the vote. Day notes that "the ant is knowing and wise; but he doesn't know enough to take a vacation." If cats were our forebears, people would be "courteous and suave." Cleanliness would be terribly important, and vegetarians would not exist. The individual essays that comprise the book are humorous yet also provide insight into the human condition. Day's own drawings illustrate the text.

Alfred Knopf, Day's publisher, sent a copy of *This Simian World* to U.S. Supreme Court justice Oliver Wendell Holmes, who said that "in the garb of wit . . . it teaches many lessons we need to learn." Later Holmes told Dean Acheson that "there was more wisdom in its ninety-odd pages than all the other books of his library put together" (quoted in Knopf, p. 102).

Day's next book, *The Crow's Nest* (1921), later augmented and revised for posthumous publication as *After All* (1936), continued his comic insight into human nature. Included are parables such as "Humpty Dumpty and Adam," Day's irreverent version of the Fall. His drawings also enhance this volume.

These drawings are like cartoons and have been described as having a "grotesque impishness" (Yates, p. 233). Often he drew characters, such as a bumbler or a henpecked husband, with a face like his own. *Thoughts without Words* (1928) consists of drawings with only a few words that, "like flies," buzz "around each of the pictures" with pithy statements such as "A man convinced against his will / Is of the same opinion still."

In 1928 Day married Katherine Briggs Dodge, a librarian from Concord, Massachusetts. They had one daughter.

Although Day worked at his writing, he was unable to make a living from it and supplemented his income by speculating in the stock market. The crash of 1929 left him in severe financial straits and resulted in a move from an elaborate Riverside Drive apartment to "less distinguished quarters" (Schwartz, p. 113). Bedridden, his home was also his office and the center of his life.

Day's next book, *God and My Father* (1932), describes his boyhood memories of his father and was a critical success. The public was also impressed and enchanted by the strategy "mother" employed to finally get "father" baptized. *In the Green Mountain Country* (1934) is an eloquent description of the death and funeral of President Calvin Coolidge. *Scenes from the Mesozoic* (1935) uses prehistoric humans and animals to satirize modern life and society, effectively combining Day's illustrations and verse.

His most popular book, published the year he died, was, in fact, almost lost. *Life with Father* was collected from sketches published previously in the *New Yorker* and included an original introductory chapter as well as a concluding chapter. The new chapters were written by hand, and the previously published chapters were cut and pasted onto manuscript paper. There were no copies of the manuscript. After being sent to the publisher, it was mistakenly wrapped up with a much larger manuscript and forwarded to the printer, who extracted the large manuscript from the package and threw away Day's thin manuscript. At this point the author was dying, and the publisher could not bring himself to let Day know he had lost the only copy of *Life with Father*. Fortunately, the waste paper was traced to a mill in Massachusetts, and all but three pages were rescued as they were being fed into the hopper.

Life with Father is Day's major contribution to American letters. It was a Book-of-the-Month Club selection and was on the nonfiction bestseller list in both 1935 and 1936. At one point it was selling 1,000 copies a day. "Father" is portrayed as a loveable tyrant who "didn't know he was a tyrant," and "mother" is shown as a woman who knows how to handle him and is "particularly elusive when Father was trying to hammer her into shape." One of the funniest chapters is "The Noblest Instrument," describing Father's efforts to have Clarence become a musician. Neighbors, family, and the teacher, particularly, suffered as Clarence attempted to draw the bow across the strings. The image of the teacher attempting to comfort the violated violin shows Day's understated humor at its best.

The book also was the basis of a play, a film, and a television series. Adapted by Howard Lindsay and Russel Crouse, the play *Life with Father* (1940) had one of the longest runs in Broadway theatrical history. The film *Life with Father* (1947), produced by Warner Bros., was based on the play and starred William Powell as Father and Irene Dunn as Mother. An all-star cast included Elizabeth Taylor, Edmund Gwenn, and Zasu Pitts. The television series ran on CBS from 22 November 1953 to 5 July 1955 with Leon Ames as Father and Lurene Tuttle as Mother.

Despite being unable to even hold a pen except with the help of an elaborate pulley arrangement, Day never discussed or even acknowledged his illness. Friends would visit him at all hours of the day and night as he entertained in his bedroom. His sense of humor was never daunted by his pain, and the stories of his boyhood show an individual who was able to recreate the joys and problems of a family life with a charming but irrascible father and a carefree and illogical mother.

Day died in New York City of pneumonia and was buried at Woodlawn Cemetery. His final book, *Life with Mother* (1937), collected stories focusing on her particular foibles, was published posthumously. It, too, became a nonfiction bestseller.

Clarence Day was a popular author of magazine articles and books. His most successful book, *Life with Father* (1935), is valued not only for his delightful anecdotes about "father" and his attempts to organize his chaotic household, but also as a social history of upper-middle-class New York society. Despite suffering for most of his adult life from the pain of a disabling disease, Day is remembered for his joie de vivre and his wry sense of humor.

• Day's letters are at the Beinecke Rare Book and Manuscript Library, Yale University. A complete list of Day's books, including those he wrote introductions for and illustrated, is in Richard A. Schwartz, *Encyclopedia of American Humorists* (1988). Biographical and critical material on Day can be found in Stanley Kunitz, *Twentieth Century Authors* (1942) and the *National Cyclopaedia of American Biography* (1940). See also Norris W. Yates, *The American Humorist: Conscience of the Twentieth Century* (1964), and Richard A. Schwartz's chapter on Day in *American Humorists, 1800–1950* (1982). A particularly informative article by Day's publisher, Alfred A. Knopf, is "Publishing Clarence Day," *Yale University Library Gazette* 55 (Jan. 1981): 101–15. An obituary is in the *New York Times*, 29 Dec. 1935.

MARCIA B. DINNEEN

DAY, David Talbot (10 Sept. 1859–15 Apr. 1925), chemist and geologist, was born in East Rockport (now Lakewood), Ohio, the son of Willard Gibson Day, a Swedenborgian minister, and Caroline Cathcart. His family moved to Baltimore, Maryland, a few years later. There is little record of his early life, but he was an exhibitor at the U.S. Centennial Exposition in Philadelphia in 1876, at age seventeen. The official catalog of the exposition, however, lists no entry for Day, so the details of his participation are not clear.

Day majored in chemistry under Ira Remsen at Johns Hopkins University and received his A.B. in 1881. His summaries of manganese, chromium, and tungsten mineral resources appeared in the first volume of the *Mineral Resources of the United States* (1882), compiled by Albert Williams, Jr. As a special agent for the U.S. Geological Survey (USGS) from 1883 to 1885, he later included a wider variety of mineral resources in his reports.

Day continued graduate work in chemistry under Remsen, who at that time was building Johns Hopkins into the premier institution for graduate work in chemistry in the United States. Day received his Ph.D. in chemistry in 1884, with the dissertation "Changes Effected by Heat in the Constitution of Ethylene."

After spending 1884–1885 as a demonstrator of chemistry at the University of Maryland, in 1886 Day was appointed chief of the USGS statistical division in Washington, D.C. He compiled the mining statistics for the Eleventh U.S. Census in 1890, which supplied the first actual census of the U.S. mining industry. In 1900 the statistical division became the Mining and Mineral Resources Division, of which Day remained chief until 1907. He had married Elizabeth Eliot Keeler in 1886; they had two children.

At the time of Day's appointment, statistics of mineral production were obtained from secondary sources and were therefore of questionable value. He established the policy of close personal contact between the technical men at the USGS and the mineral producers. This required a level of trust not previously given to outsiders, because the data was mostly from confidential records. Day's skill and engaging personality inspired the trust that these statistics would be used with proper discretion.

From 1885 to 1905 Day compiled the USGS annual report *Mineral Resources of the United States*, which, because of his great rapport with people in the mining industry, came to be recognized as authoritative. His 1905 publication (with E. T. Richards) on the black-sand placers, a well-known source for gold and other important metals, of the Pacific Coast remained a primary reference on this subject at the end of the twentieth century.

Day was put in charge of petroleum exhibits at the Chicago World's Fair (1893), the Philadelphia Centennial (1899), and the Paris World's Fair (1900). In 1897 he was secretary on the Jury of Awards for the State of Tennessee Centennial. He was also appointed director of mining for the Cotton States and International Exposition (Atlanta, Ga., 1896), the Trans-Mississippi Exposition (Omaha, Neb., 1898), and the Buffalo (N.Y.) Exposition of 1901. For both the St. Louis (Mo.) Exposition (1904) and for the Louisiana Purchase Exposition in Bene Merenti, Austria, he was honorary chief of the department of mining and metallurgy. He was also honorary commissioner of mining at the Lewis and Clark Exposition (Portland, Or., 1905) and at the Jamestown (Va.) Exposition in 1907.

Day was awarded U.S. Patent No. 826,089 for the process of refining and purifying hydrocarbon oils on 17 July 1906. In 1907 he was appointed chemist in charge of petroleum investigations at the USGS, studying the economics of oil shale. In 1908 he began a systematic examination of all varieties of petroleum in the United States, which ultimately resulted in standardized procedures for petroleum analyses. He was the U.S. Commissioner at the International Commission for Petroleum Tests from 1907 to 1909, and continued to contribute to the publication of *Mineral Resources of the United States.*

In 1914 the U.S. Bureau of Mines established a Petroleum Division. Because Day's interest lay with technology rather than geology, he moved at that time from the USGS to the bureau to serve as a consulting chemist and to continue his studies on the fundamental nature of petroleum. His work on a cracking process for changing heavier oils into gasoline attracted wide attention. In fact, the first commercial cracking process was developed by chemists at Indiana Standard who, like Day, had graduated from Johns Hopkins.

Day was a pioneer in oil shale research in the United States. His collaborative work with Elmer Grant Woodruff of the USGS on the extensive oil shale deposits of northwestern Colorado and northeastern Utah in 1913 was the first survey and field extraction tests of such a region. Day remained at the Bureau of Mines until 1920, when he resigned from government service to continue his research on oil distillation. He moved to Santa Maria, California, where he erected a laboratory for oil shale distillation. Interest in development of oil shale deposits was keen at that time, because conventional oil supplies seemed to be waning. Later development of vast oil supplies in Texas, California, and Venezuela convinced Day that the need for oil shale development could be deferred.

Day's crowning publication achievement was the two-volume *Handbook of the Petroleum Industry* (1922), which he edited. This became a comprehensive reference in its day. Among the professional contributors to the publication were his son and a nephew.

Day was active in many technical societies throughout his long career. He joined the American Institute of Mining and Metallurgical Engineers in 1887 and was vice president in 1893 and 1900. The Geological Society of America elected him a fellow in 1891. He was a founding member of the Geological Society of Washington (D.C.) in 1893. Other memberships included the American Chemical Society, National Statistical Society, Society of Industrial Chemists, American Petroleum Institute, National Geographic Society, and Schweizische Geographische Gesellschaft (Geographical Society of Switzerland). He was editor in chief of the *Engineering and Mining-Press Journal* from 1901 to 1902 and served as president of the fuels section of the International Congress of Applied Chemistry in 1912. He also served without salary as secretary to the Joseph Austin Holmes Safety Association, a society for mining safety founded in honor of the first director of U.S. Bureau of Mines. Day died in Washington, D.C.

Day is regarded as the father of the Mineral Resources Division of the USGS, even though he was really a chemist rather than a geologist. His experiments on petroleum fractionation led to the identification method of adsorption chromatography, which contributed to the development of modern techniques of chromatography. Although an oil shale industry did not develop at the time, Day's oil shale investigations led him to recommend the designation of oil reserves in case of shortages. From his recommendations came the Naval Oil Reserves in the western United States, beginning with the first reserve at Elk Hills, California, on 2 September 1912. The reserves ensured that the United States would have sufficient fuel to supply its ships in a national emergency.

• A biographical sketch of Day appears in Eugene C. Robertson, *Centennial History of the Geological Society of Washington, 1893–1993* (1994), pp. 53–54. Information on the U.S. Centennial Exposition was obtained from a personal communication of Lee Stanley, archivist at the Philadelphia City Archives. Obituaries are Nelson H. Darton, "David Talbot Day," *Proceedings of the Geological Society of America for 1933* (1934): 185–92, which includes a bibliography of Day's publications; M. R. Campbell, "David Talbot Day," *Transactions of the American Institute of Mining and Metallurgical Engineers* (1925): 1371–73; and in *Engineering and Mining Journal-Press* (1925): 703; the *Washington Evening Star,* 16 Apr. 1925; and the *New York Times,* 17 Apr. 1925.

GRETCHEN LUEPKE

DAY, Dorothy (8 Nov. 1897–29 Nov. 1980), founder of the Catholic Worker movement and *Catholic Worker,* a monthly newspaper, was born in Brooklyn, New York, the daughter of John Day, a newspaperman, and Grace Satterlee. Her father was a frustrated novelist and horseracing writer whose work took the family to Oakland and Chicago. While in Chicago, Day won a scholarship to the University of Illinois in 1914. She dropped out after two years to return to New York with her family, but she had become a socialist in college and was soon estranged from her father. She lived on the Lower East Side, where she wrote for the *Call,* a socialist daily. There and at the *Masses,* an avant-garde magazine founded by Greenwich Village radicals, she developed a style of personal journalism concerned less with issues or ideologies than with the life experiences of the poor, the suffering, and the socially marginal. Day became well acquainted with many of the New York literary and artistic figures who were fomenting a cultural rebellion in the years just prior to America's entry into the First World War, including Floyd Dell, Eugene O'Neill, and Mike Gold. Day's romance with Gold—who became editor of the *Daily Worker*—inspired the legend that she was a member of the Communist party, a bit of folklore she did nothing to dispel.

After the war Day endured several disastrous personal relationships including a brief marriage (1920–1921) to Barkeley Tobey, a literary promoter; she lived in Europe, New Orleans, and Chicago, where she was arrested during a raid on an IWW rooming house suspected of harboring prostitutes. She also wrote a semi-autobiographical novel, *The Eleventh Virgin* (1924). In 1925 she moved to a beach house on Staten Island and entered into a common-law marriage with Forster Batterham, a fisherman and anarchist from an old southern family. Day gave birth to her only child in March 1926. Since having had an abortion earlier in the decade, Day had feared that she could not have a child; she was so moved by the event that she had her daughter, Tamar, baptized in the Catholic church in the hope that she would be spared the loneliness and doubt that Day herself had known for so long. Day and most of her biographers place Tamar's birth a full year later than when it actually occurred, thus shortening considerably the period of uncertainty that preceded Day's own entry into the church. In fact, she struggled for over eighteen months with a desire to reconcile her newfound interest in religion with her deep commitment to the militantly irreligious Batterham. She finally concluded that "no human creature could receive or contain so vast a flood of love and joy as I felt after the birth of my child" and chose to be baptized into the Roman Catholic church on 18 December 1927.

Over the next five years Day traveled widely on a variety of journalistic assignments for both Catholic and secular periodicals and tried her hand at screenwriting before returning to New York permanently in 1932. Discovering that many of her radical convictions had survived her conversion experience, she sought a vocation that would reconcile her spirituality with her fervor for social justice. A Catholic magazine editor sent Peter Maurin to see her, believing that she might know what to make of this strange Frenchman, a veteran of a failed Catholic agrarian movement who had been living in Canada since the early years of the century. He had wandered to New York around 1930 and attempted to indoctrinate influential Catholics with his back-to-the-land theories of "cult, culture, and cultivation," through which the presumed synthesis of medieval Christendom could be recreated. He convinced Day that her vocation was to publish a newspaper promoting his ideas, a blend of reactionary European Catholic theory and a gentler "personalist" ideology emphasizing the responsibility of individual Christians to remake the social order one act of mercy at a time.

Maurin soon became the symbol of the fledgling movement rather than its leader, as Day overshadowed him by shrewdly blending his agrarian utopianism with a more realistic advocacy of the unemployed and hungry. Where Maurin would say, in rejecting labor unions, "Strikes don't strike me," Day wrote a memorable story on workers who occupied the General Motors plant during a 1937 strike. Day was attracted to Maurin because he embodied the ideal of voluntary poverty that she identified with Catholicism, which offered solace from the bourgeois radicalism of her unhappy early adulthood. In this respect she resembled other disaffected rebels from bohemia, but in the depth of her commitment to her new faith she was unrivaled. Out of her own beliefs and the inspiration of Maurin she shaped a new Catholic ethos, rejecting both capitalism and communism in the name of a community in which all women and men were spiritually linked as members of the Mystical Body of Christ.

Day was influenced by the Catholic Social Doctrine first articulated in Pope Leo XIII's encyclical *Rerum Novarum* (1891) and then updated by Pius XI in *Quadregesimo Anno* (1931). The doctrine called for the redistribution of wealth and—while promoting the rights of private property—argued that workers had an inherent right to a just wage and a dignified life centered around the family and the church. The *Catholic Worker* introduced this tradition to thousands of American Catholics, but Day went well beyond the official doctrine in encouraging the laity to cultivate intimately personal relationships with Christ and to embrace the spirit of poverty and redemptive suffering.

She offered a powerful new mystique to many young Catholics who were beginning to question the authoritarian structure of the church. The Catholic Worker houses in New York and Chicago became the focal points of a romantic renewal of Catholic culture during the 1930s. European luminaries like Jacques and Raissa Maritain lent their blessing to the new movement, and the firm of Sheed & Ward published numerous books imbued with the spirit of holy poverty and the quest for Christian social justice. By the late 1930s Day was at the center of a spectacular Catholic renaissance: the *Catholic Worker*'s circulation exceeded 100,000, and houses of hospitality sprang up from coast to coast and in Europe and Australia. The official church, though wary at first, came to recognize the power of this lay-dominated movement, and prelates often paid tribute to Day for leading such a passionate example of Catholic action. Although she was occasionally accused of being soft on communism, Day was, by the end of the 1930s, the most prominent laywoman in the American church.

In the early 1940s the movement nearly collapsed as a result of Day's unwavering pacifism. Although in the 1930s Day had sometimes described her movement as "anarchist," the implications went unnoticed until scores of young Catholic Workers received draft notices in 1940 and 1941. Many of these young men were second-generation American Catholics intent on demonstrating their loyalty to the United States by serving in the armed forces when called. Day refused to compromise, and as a result several of the houses of hospitality closed, including the Chicago house, which was particularly adamant in its rejection of pacifism. A number of Catholic Workers sought conscientious objector status and served time in internment camps. Day, who never voted and never sought tax-exempt status for her movement, urged complete noncooperation with the selective service.

This crisis in the movement led Day toward a deeper interest in personal spirituality. Catholic Worker life in the 1940s centered around austere retreats such as those conducted at the movement's farm commune in Easton, Pennsylvania. The Easton retreats were led by several French-Canadian priests whose writings were branded as heretical by leading theologians. They were accused of a version of Jansenism, a French heresy of the Counter-Reformation that derogated the body and nature in the name of a mystical otherworldliness. The Catholic Worker retreats stressed the total mortification of the senses and the denunciation of the flesh. Day continued to defend the retreat masters even after they were silenced by church authorities and reassigned to remote locales. The retreats fostered in Day a much greater sense of her own spiritual authority and gave her a renewed conviction that political struggle must be subordinated to interior transformation.

In 1946 Day changed the title of her *Catholic Worker* column to "On Pilgrimage." Her distinctively personal essays relating spirituality to everyday life won her increasing admiration as a major religious writer. The aftermath of Hiroshima and Nagasaki partly vindicated her pacifism, and the Catholic Worker movement attracted a new generation of writers and thinkers often more sophisticated than those of the prewar generation. Michael Harrington lived in the New York house and wrote for the paper in the early 1950s, acquiring much of the data for *The Other America* (1962). Many of the new Catholic Workers were more interested in Day's preconversion life in bohemia than her religiosity, and almost in spite of herself Day saw the movement become part of the counterculture of Greenwich Village in the 1950s, as the separatism of the original movement grew outdated in an era of ecumenism. Day gained notoriety by participating in protests against New York City's mandatory air-raid drills, for which she was jailed. Poets of the Beat Generation read their works at the Friday evening discussion meetings that had been initiated "for the clarification of thought" by Maurin in the 1930s. The anarchist Ammon Hennacy fell in love with Day in the early 1950s, but Day remained celibate. An avowed anticlerical, Hennacy engaged in a one-man crusade against nuclear weapons that encouraged critiques of the church itself, which Day found excessive. She doggedly resisted the movement's gradual drift away from the institutional church.

Day's fervent devotion to the church caused her to appear out of step to many in the 1960s, precisely at the moment her social radicalism was embraced by many young people. The first draft card burners in the early 1960s were Catholic Workers. Prominent members of the Catholic Left—including the Trappist monk Thomas Merton—feared the Catholic Worker movement had lost its bearings. At the same time, Day was ambivalent about the reforms effected at the Second Vatican Council (1962–1965). While other prominent Catholic women clamored for revisions in the church's teachings regarding sexuality and birth control, Day worked intensively on her spiritual journals and defended the church against its critics on the left and right. During the 1970s she was slowed by age. She died in New York City.

Dorothy Day was an enormously charismatic woman who was compared by her followers to Greta Garbo and Joan of Arc. She was an imposing figure in austerely braided hair and secondhand clothing who inspired loyalty and occasionally fear in young Catholic Workers who stood in awe of her background and accomplishments. When she became a Catholic in 1927, the church in America operated largely within the boundaries of a defensive subculture, enjoying little influence in secular society. By the time of her death, it was a vital force in American life, and many Catholics credited Day and her movement with awakening them to a richer faith. Since Day originally envisioned the Catholic Worker movement as separatist, she was not pleased with changes in Catholic life that tended to make the faithful more comfortable in their dual identity as Catholics and Americans. But in creating a tradition of genuine radical Catholicism in America, she contributed profoundly to the religious life of the nation.

• The Dorothy Day–Catholic Worker Papers are located at Memorial Library, Marquette University, Milwaukee, Wis. Along with her autobiography, *The Long Loneliness* (1952), Day's major writings include *From Union Square to Rome* (1938), *House of Hospitality* (1939), and *Loaves and Fishes* (1963). Her spiritual journal is excerpted in William Miller, ed., *All Is Grace* (1987). Miller is also the author of *Dorothy Day: A Biography* (1982). The Catholic Worker movement is treated in Mel Piehl, *Breaking Bread: The Catholic Worker and the Origin of Catholic Radicalism in America* (1982), and Nancy L. Roberts, *Dorothy Day and the* Catholic Worker (1984). An interpretation of Day and the movement is offered in James Terence Fisher, *The Catholic Counterculture in America, 1933–1962* (1989). An obituary is in the *New York Times*, 1 Dec. 1980. See also David J. O'Brien, "The Pilgrimage of Dorothy Day," *Commonweal*, 19 Dec. 1980.

JAMES TERENCE FISHER

DAY, Edith (10 Apr. 1896–1 May 1971), actress, was born in Minneapolis, Minnesota, the daughter of Oscar Day, a theater critic, and Ella Mahla. Educated locally, Day made her dramatic debut with *Dancing Around* (1915) in St. Paul and was on Broadway by the age of twenty.

After *Pom-Pom* (1916), *Follow Me* (1916), and a 1917 tour of *His Little Widows*, Day starred in the aeronautical musical comedy *Going Up*, singing Louis Hirsch's hit song "The Tickle-Toe." The show ran until 1919. In 1918 Day married film producer Carle Carlton. They had no children.

For Carleton's companies Day appeared in three feature films, *The Grain of Dust* (1918), playing an unsympathetic moralist; *Romance of the Air* (1918), as the heroic lover of an American in France's flying Lafayette Escadrille; and *Children Not Wanted* (1920), as the wrongly accused heroine who rears her dead best friend's child.

In 1919 Carleton teamed with lyricist Joseph McCarthy to produce the McCarthy–Harry Tierney *Irene* for Broadway. Running 670 performances, *Irene* established a New York long-run record that stood for eighteen years. Day's character Irene O'Dare, one of the era's Cinderellas (others included Hirsch's *Mary* and Jerome Kern's *Sally*, both 1920), was an upholsterer's assistant sent to a Long Island mansion to mend cushions. Instantly smitten, the handsome young man of the house persuades a male couturier friend to hire Irene to pose as a socialite, modeling his latest creations. Unusually for its time, *Irene* made some calculated jibes at the manners of the rich. At an elegant party, Irene sings "Alice Blue Gown" and ends in the hero's arms. The song, named after Theodore Roosevelt's daughter's favorite color, became a classic popular song. At one point, there were seventeen road companies of *Irene*.

Musical historian Ethan Mordden wrote that *Irene*, with World War I behind it and the jazzy twenties stretching ahead, made Edith Day the heroine of the moment. He added, "Her style might have become *the* style, but Edith Day, like her predecessors, was primarily a singer . . . the new heroine needed rhythm, hotcha, pizazz."

Five months into the New York run of *Irene*, a coin toss gave Day the right to head the London company. When she sang "Alice Blue Gown" at the Theatre Royal, Drury Lane, on 7 April 1920, she "established her reputation in a single night." The next day, the *Tatler*'s theater critic wrote, "This radiant young American is . . . versatility itself, and has complete joie de vivre." The review added that she received "a reception seldom rivalled in the history of our stage." Day, whose marriage to Carlton was dissolved in 1920, married her London *Irene* costar Pat Somerset in 1921. They had one child, later killed in World War II. Their marriage was dissolved in 1923.

After *Irene*, Day remained in London, starring in the unsuccessful *Jenny* (1922). She returned to New York for *Orange Blossoms* (1922) and *Wildflower* (1923). *Wildflower* was the first hit show for composer Vincent Youmans and of all his musical scores the closest to operetta. His biographer, Gerald Bordman, wrote of the "robin-voiced" Day, "This wide eyed,

round faced, dark haired beauty . . . chose her roles carefully, refusing to become stereotyped." In *Wildflower*, which proved to be her last appearance on an American stage, she was a volatile Italian singing the infectious "Bambalina."

After Mary Ellis, the original star of the 1925 Rudolph Friml operetta *Rose Marie*, chose to return to straight drama, its lyricist Oscar Hammerstein II suggested Day for the lead role in the London production. *Rose Marie* opened at Drury Lane in 1925, and for the rest of the decade the Day-Hammerstein combination made London theatrical history with their versions of American originals. At Drury Lane there were 851 performances of *Rose Marie*, followed by 432 for Sigmund Romberg's *The Desert Song* (1927) and 350 for Kern's *Show Boat* (1928), the production that introduced Paul Robeson as Joe, singing "Ol' Man River." These shows also helped establish Sir Alfred Butt's Drury Lane Theatre as the home of spectacular musical plays, and Day became popularly known as "The Queen of Drury Lane."

Day's talents were particularly suited to the era's London stage; she could produce a mannered diction when necessary. Her flexible, colorful voice might have lacked complete range, but the British loved her specialty, the plucky traditional heroine, as well as her display of what London critics called "commitment." From 1925 on Day made London her home. Since Broadway "original cast" recordings, unlike their British counterparts, did not at this time exist, Day's recordings of all these shows (and London's *Irene*) carry historical importance.

In 1930 Day again starred at Drury Lane in the London premiere of another American Tierney-McCarthy show, *Rio Rita*, but the production did not succeed. At thirty-four her "type" was less in demand, and other American expatriates such as Ellis and Peggy Wood (operetta) and the stylish dancer Dorothy Dickson (musical comedy) were taking roles that might earlier have gone to Day. In 1931 Day formed a variety act singing show tunes with Robert Naylor, playing venues such as the Palladium. In the same year she began to appear on BBC radio on variety programs such as "Monday at Eight."

An original London musical, *Luana* (1932), was a failure. In 1936 Day starred in a revival of *The Desert Song*, and in 1943 she costarred with Britain's Evelyn Laye in Hammerstein and Romberg's London original *Sunny River*, an ambitious musical play (one of a legendary series of contemporary Hammerstein failures) set in New Orleans at the beginning of the nineteenth century. Day sang the title song, evoking "the strong movement and cheerfulness of the great [Mississippi] river flowing in the sunlight to the sea." Though *Sunny River* was lauded for its seriousness, critical judgment agreed that it needed a lot more of Edith Day's vivacity.

In 1956 Day married Henry Horne; they had no children. She appeared in nostalgic radio and television programs and returned to the London stage for Noël Coward's *Waiting in the Wings*, a 1960 play about aging actresses. In 1962, the year of her last radio appearance, she sang two songs in Coward's London production of *Sail Away*. Day died in London.

• Reviews, programs, and other material relating to Day's life and theatrical productions are on file in the Billy Rose Theatre Collection of the New York Public Library for the Performing Arts at Lincoln Center and at the Theatre Museum of the Victoria and Albert Museum, London. Her British radio and television career is documented in the archives of the British Broadcasting System, London. Day's London recordings are available on World Records SH 138. Gerald Bordman, *Days to Be Happy, Years to Be Sad* (1982), relates Day's career to Vincent Youmans's. Ethan Mordden, *Broadway Babies* (1983), places shows like *Irene* in their transitional context. A helpful obituary is in the *Times* (London), 3 May 1971.

JAMES ROSS MOORE

DAY, F. Holland (23 July 1864–6 Nov. 1933), publisher, photographer, and bibliophile, was born Fred Holland Day in Norwood, Massachusetts, the son of Lewis Day, an industrialist, and Anna Smith. The only child of wealthy parents, young Day was educated largely by private tutors. The family split their time between their Norwood house and an apartment in Boston, at that time considered the Athens of America. At fifteen Day accompanied his mother to Denver, where she recuperated from a lung disease. It was in Denver that he made his first sustained contact with a large colony of Chinese, and their art and material culture made a lasting impact on him. He began to draw with Chinese inks and brushes and purchased many Chinese artifacts; he remained fascinated by Oriental culture to his dying day. This fascination was abetted by the world-class Oriental collections at the Boston Museum of Fine Arts.

On returning from Denver at the age of sixteen, he entered Chauncy High School in Boston. Through friends there, he met many Harvard University students, including men like the art critic Bernard Berenson. In 1884 he graduated from Chauncy Hall, receiving a special gold medal for "the best scholarship in English literature." He had become an enthusiastic bibliophile, with early interests in Honoré de Balzac and John Keats. In 1885 Day went to work for about a year at A. S. Barnes & Company, a Boston bookselling firm.

Day's obsession with books led him to a practice known by Victorian bibliophiles as "extra-illustrating," "extending," or "grangerizing" a book. This consisted of collecting images in any graphic medium of people and places mentioned either as characters or as locations in both fiction and nonfiction. Since books were then often published in unbound signatures, the aim was to bind up signatures and the extra illustrations in a bibliophile's favorite morocco. Books thus bound vastly increased in value.

Day eventually established a magnificent personal library, featuring a rare edition of Keats printed on vellum. He was highly respected among Boston bibliophiles, with whom he helped to found the Club of Odd Volumes, the Boston equivalent of New York's Grolier Club. Having determined in 1887 to extra-illustrate an edition of Balzac, Day decided to take up photography preparatory to a trip to Europe, where he would serve as foreign correspondent for the *Norwood Review* and take as many pictures relating to Balzac's life and novels as he could find. Thus his literary interests led directly to his pursuit of photography, with an eventual membership in the Boston Camera Club in 1889.

When Day was twenty-two he met the woman who—besides his domineering mother—would have the strongest and most lasting influence on him. Louise Imogen Guiney was a published poet who was the darling of the Boston literati, including such formidable figures as Oliver Wendell Holmes. Day and Guiney shared an obsession with John Keats. Through Guiney, Day entered into the circle of her godmother, Louise Chandler Moulton, who had established literary salons in Boston and London.

Guiney was a devout Catholic, but, ignorant of what was appropriate in photography, she pressured Day to photograph saints and all things holy. He did take several fine portraits of her posing as Saint Barbara. This pursuit was interrupted by a trip to Europe in 1890 to see the passion play at Oberammergau, an event that stirred his imagination so profoundly that in the next decade he would photograph himself as Christ on the cross. Many of these pictures were unfortunately of negligible aesthetic interest, but his series called "The Seven Last Words of Christ," using close-ups of his bearded face topped with a crown of thorns, created a furor. The series was shown in England and France and was greeted with both admiration and shrill outcries of blasphemy.

Day brought home from Europe something else that would create much controversy: the hitherto unpublished letters of Fanny Brawne, John Keats's sweetheart, to his sister, Fanny Keats. He never succeeded in having these published, as the estate refused permission. Even Guiney, who had been instrumental in locating the letters, never saw them, and Amy Lowell, intent on writing a biography of Keats, could not persuade Day to let her see these crucial manuscripts, which were expected to alter important details of Keats's life. Despite frustration about the letters, Guiney joined Day in 1894 in establishing a memorial to Keats in a Hampstead church.

Day's visits to Europe transformed him from a bibliophile into a passionate aesthete. Simultaneously, he became deeply interested in psychic phenomena, often visiting the Society for Psychical Research in London. In 1889 he had met a like-minded Harvard student, Herbert Copeland, who became his partner in the publishing firm of Copeland and Day. Copeland brought Day into an exclusive Boston group called the Visionists, aesthetes and spiritualists all, including the poet Bliss Carman, the architect Ralph Adams Cram, the typographic genius Bruce Rogers, the printer Daniel Berkeley Updike, and only two female members, Guiney and her writer friend Alice Brown.

The Visionists decorated the walls of their hideaway with Egyptian symbols and played at being high priests of Isis, obviously under the influence of Helena Blavatsky's enormously popular book, *Isis Unveiled*, first published in English in 1877. Blavatsky's Theosophy was only one of many mystical systems that purveyed symbolism attractive to the fin-de-siècle "decadents," as they called themselves. (The term then referred to the *decade* of the 1890s.) Day joined several mystical societies and photographed the rituals involved.

The Visionists published two avant-garde magazines, *The Knight Errant* and *The Mahogany Tree* (1892–1894), in which the socialist and aesthetic ideologies of William Morris were promulgated, along with reverence for Japanese art and culture. The journals lasted only a few issues, but they remain important and rare. Day contributed reviews and notes of his personal acquaintance with Morris. In 1890, when Morris's influential Kelmscott Press was established, Day and Copeland decided to compete with him, and by 1893, the firm of Copeland and Day was in full operation. Day had agreements with John Lane, publisher of Oscar Wilde, and when Wilde's play *Salomé* was brought over, Boston was outraged, especially by Aubrey Beardsley's drawings.

One of Day's major accomplishments was to revive the publication of poetry, including Stephen Crane's *The Black Riders and Other Lines*, William Butler Yeats's *Poems*, Francis Thompson's *Sister Songs*, and Morris Rosenfeld's *Songs from the Ghetto*, translated from the Yiddish. The format of Copeland and Day's books followed the prescriptions of the Arts and Crafts movement, and all their books manifested an integrity of design and utilitarianism seldom matched.

Day did not neglect his photography during his publishing years. In fact, photography began to dominate his interests. Boston celebrities came to his Pinckney Street studio to have their portraits taken. High praise came from the critic Sadakichi Hartmann: "There is no photographer who can pose the human body better than he . . . He has pushed lyricism in portraiture as far as it can be . . . Day is indisputably the most ambitious and accomplished of our American portrait photographers." It was a portrait that won him election in 1895 to the prestigious London-based Linked Ring Brotherhood, a group that rejected the sharp-focus bias of British photography and lauded all attempts to make photography the equal of the fine arts.

Day joined the Links one year after Alfred Stieglitz had been elected to its membership. Stieglitz was then New York's most important editor, critic, and photographer. As editor of *Camera Notes*, Stieglitz gave Day's "Nubians" (some of the first sympathetic portraits of black Americans) the best reproductions in the very first issue. Stieglitz also collected Day's prints, including "The Seven Last Words of Christ," and was outspoken in his admiration. Day was perceived as a genius in the new art of photography, with the well-established society photographer Rudolf Eickemeyer

writing Stieglitz that Day stood alone and unique among contemporary photographers. Day's most sensational picture, "Ebony and Ivory," of a nude black man holding a white miniature statue, inspired other photographers, like his friend Clarence White, to emulate the extraordinary range of tones Day had accomplished.

In his search for models, Day occasionally found one among the poor immigrant children in the settlement houses of Boston. One of these was Kahlil Gibran, who, thanks to Day's support and goodwill, became his protégé; among other kind deeds, Day arranged an exhibition of Gibran's drawings at Wellesley College. There seems to have been no homosexual attachment between Day and Gibran, but Day was homosexual, as was his publishing partner, Copeland. Day was discreet, but he managed to shock Boston once again with the first frontal male nude photograph ever displayed in that city.

By 1899 Day had become one of America's most famous photographers, and, as one of the two acknowledged leaders of the pictorialist movement, he was able to collect outstanding prints from White, Gertrude Käsebier, and other art photographers. The idea of the pictorialists was that one did not merely *take* a picture; rather, one *made* a picture. Day urged Stieglitz to join him in establishing an "American Association of Artistic Photography." Unfortunately, Stieglitz had no intention of sharing the reputation of a leader with Day. His refusal forced Day to create his own entity, "The New School of American Photography." He took approximately 300 pictorialist prints to London for exhibition at the Royal Photographic Society in 1899–1900. Stieglitz was furious that Day had thus established himself as the leader of the new movement, and he wrote scurrilous letters to the English groups denouncing Day's selections as inferior, poor, secondrate prints. The rising young photographer Edward Steichen, who felt honored to be included in Day's exhibition, defended Day and denounced Stieglitz's misrepresentations.

One of the unfortunate outcomes of this quarrel was the refusal of Day to permit Stieglitz to reproduce his works in his new journal, *Camera Work*, begun in 1903. Day therefore was absent from what turned out to be the most important photographic journal of the pictorialist movement, and his absence denied him the later recognition his friends received. Although Day continued to exhibit in Europe, his American influence was diminished. The crowning blow was the 1904 fire that destroyed his Boston studio and many original works as well as his collection of Japanese prints and artifacts.

In 1904 or 1905, Day decided to buy Guiney's property in Maine, at Little Good Harbor on the then relatively underdeveloped Georgetown Island. He built a mansion there for summer living and frequently entertained Clarence White's family until White purchased his own property at Seguinland, a few miles away, where he founded an influential art school. Day was exceptionally generous to the White family, even supporting White's son, Maynard, through Brown University.

Day's publishing ventures petered out in the first decade of the twentieth century. In 1917, with his father dead and an ailing mother requiring his help, he returned to Norwood and literally took to his bed. He kept up with his friends with copious letter writing, but he had no lovers, and Copeland, a victim of alcoholism, died in 1923. Devoting himself to the study of horticulture and genealogy, Day passed his last years without the solace of his art of photography. His favorite medium had been gum bichromate over platinum, and with the First World War, platinum became unavailable. The loss was irremediable. By the time of his death, his love of classical themes and symbolism was also out of fashion. Day faded into an undeserved obscurity. Following the lead of his friends White and Käsebier, Day left his photographs to the Library of Congress.

• Manuscript sources include the archives of F. Holland Day at the Norwood Historical Society, Norwood, Mass.; the Library of Congress, which holds letters from Guiney to Day; and the Beinecke Rare Book and Manuscript Library, Yale University, which owns the archives of Alfred Stieglitz, with letters from Day. Joe Walker Kraus wrote "A History of Copeland & Day (1893–1899) with a Bibliographical Checklist of Their Publications" (master's thesis, Univ. of Illinois-Urbana, 1941). See also Hyder Edward Rollins and Stephen Maxfield Parrish, *Keats and the Bostonians: Amy Lowell, Louise Imogen Guiney, Louis Arthur Holman, Fred Holland Day* (1951). Interest in Day was revived in 1975 by Ellen Fritz Clattenburg in her catalog for the Day exhibition at the Wellesley College Museum. There followed Estelle Jussim's definitive biography, *Slave to Beauty: The Eccentric Life and Controversial Career of F. Holland Day, Photographer, Publisher, Aesthete* (1981). The London scholarly journal *History of Photography* published a special issue devoted entirely to F. Holland Day, edited by Verna Curtis of the Library of Congress (1994). Day wrote several articles for *Camera Notes*, the *British Journal of Photography*, and the *American Annual of Photography*.

ESTELLE JUSSIM

DAY, Frank Miles (5 Apr. 1861–15 June 1918), architect, was born in Philadelphia, Pennsylvania, the son of Charles Miles Day, an immigrant English tailor, and Anna Rebecca, a Philadelphia native. As a child Day traveled in America and Europe with his family before entering the architecture program of the Towne Scientific School of the University of Pennsylvania in 1879. He graduated in 1883, having been president and valedictorian of his class, and left for England. While there he attended the South Kensington School of Art (1884), the Royal Academy (1885), and the Architectural Association (1885). He also joined the atelier of Walter Millard and apprenticed under Basil Champneys; both architects were participants in the Gothic revival who drew Day's attention to craftsmanship and materials. Day also traveled through continental Europe, where he was particularly attracted to the ornament and work of the early Renaissance.

Returning to Philadelphia in 1886, Day worked as a draftsman for George T. Pearson and Addison Hutton. In late 1887 he opened his own firm and maintained an active practice that included residential, commercial, ecclesiastical, and collegiate work. Day's brother joined him as a financial manager in 1892, and in 1893 they adopted the name Frank Miles Day & Brother; in 1911 Day made his assistant Charles Klauder a partner, and in 1912 the firm went by Day & Klauder. Described as a "creative eclectic," Day produced designs that relied on a free interpretation of historical styles. He drew on medieval and early Renaissance styles, but he was also drawn to American colonial and Georgian architecture. For Day, however, ". . . style . . . [was] not an affair of archeology but an abstract quality, a subtle excellence very hard to define" ("Choosing a Style for the House," *Inexpensive Homes of Individuality*, 1912). He emphatically stated that the plan, material, site, and function of a building should determine the design. His own work subtly fused refined ornament with picturesque massing.

Day's notable early commissions include the Philadelphia Art Club (1888), Horticultural Hall (1894), and the Charles Bergner (1892) and Clement Newbold (1897) residences (both illustrated in *Stately Homes in America*, 1903); and he collaborated on the Free Museum of Science and Art (1893). After 1900 Day gained a reputation for campus planning and design. With the completion of athletic facilities for the University of Pennsylvania (1902), Day went on to design buildings for Princeton (1908), Cornell (1913), Pennsylvania State (1914), and the University of Colorado (1917); he also provided plans for Wellesley College (1916) and the University of Delaware (1915–1916). While the work for Penn State used classical sources and Colorado used Italianate, Day's work at the other schools made him a leader in collegiate Gothic. The Princeton buildings received praise from Ralph Adams Cram and the American Institute of Architecture Gold Medal (1918). Day's respect for historical styles made him an early contributor to historic preservation—perhaps most notably, he chaired the committee on the restoration of the Octagon, the AIA's headquarters in Washington, D.C.

Day's commitment to the professionalization of architecture went beyond his own practice to his involvement with a number of organizations: he became an active member of the T-Square Club in 1886 (serving as vice president in 1889 and 1890) and he taught courses at the Pennsylvania Academy of the Fine Arts, the University of Pennsylvania, and in 1906 at Harvard. His belief in the value of foreign study for architects resulted in becoming a trustee (from 1905) and director (1909) of the American Academy in Rome. His election to the Philadelphia Chapter of the AIA in 1887 began an association that included becoming a fellow and member of the board of directors (1895) and culminated in his presidency of the national AIA in 1906–1907. Under Day the AIA established committees on the regulation of competitions and licensing of architects and brought in a legal adviser.

Day received numerous awards throughout his lifetime and was elected a member of the Academy of Natural Sciences and the American Philosophical Society (1899), the National Fine Arts Council (1909), an honorary member of the Royal Institute of British Architects (1907), the National Academy of Design (1910), and the National Institute of Arts and Letters (1908). As a result of his work on competition regulations, Day sat on many design juries for important commissions throughout the country. Day had married Anna Blakiston in 1896; they had two children.

Frank Miles Day died in Philadelphia. His contributions to architecture came at a pivotal point in the professionalization of the discipline. One of the best-educated architects at the turn of the twentieth century, Day hoped to use his knowledge of architectural history and design to establish a modern American architecture. Unfortunately, recognition of his design accomplishments suffers from the demolition of many of his best buildings. Through his administrative and leadership skills, which included talents for diplomacy and oratory, he achieved significant results in the organization of architectural education and the administration of the profession. Day earned a high level of respect from his peers. According to Warren P. Laird, "Mr. Day combined to a rare degree the qualities of artist and executive, and his influence was potent in the advancement of both the quality of American architecture and the standards of professional practice under which it is wrought into being. To few men is it given thus to aid in moulding both the methods and ideals of a great profession" (*American Architect* 114 (3 July 1918): 15).

• Day's archives and papers are held in a number of repositories. A collection of family papers is located at The Architectural Archives of the University of Pennsylvania. The AIA Library and Archives also contains some papers. Day's own publications include the preface to *American Country Homes of Today* (1912), and *Suggestions in Brickwork* (1895). See the bibliography to the only full-length treatment of Day, Patricia Heintzelman Keebler, "The Life and Work of Frank Miles Day" (Ph.D. diss., Univ. of Delaware, 1980). For a list of Day's projects, see S. Tatman and R. Moss, *Biographical Dictionary of Philadelphia Architects* (1985), p. 192ff. See also Ralph Adams Cram, "The Work of Messrs. Frank Miles Day and Brother," *Architectural Record* 15, no. 5 (May 1904): 397–421. An obituary is in the *New York Times*, 18 June 1918.

MARIE FRANK

DAY, Jeremiah (3 Aug. 1773–22 Aug. 1867), professor and college president, was born in New Preston, Connecticut, the son of the Reverend Jeremiah Day, a Congregational minister, and Abigail Osborn. He was prepared for college by private tutors and entered Yale in 1789. Pulmonary problems interrupted his college years and delayed his graduation until 1795. After graduation he served as principal of the academy founded by Timothy Dwight (1752–1817) at Greenfield Hill, Connecticut, and then as a tutor at Williams College. He returned to Yale as a tutor in 1798, was licensed to preach by the New Haven West Association of Ministers in 1800, and became professor of mathematics and moral philosophy at Yale in 1801. His early professional years were marked by continued poor health; tuberculosis complicated by a hemorrhage interrupted his Yale career for two years until 1803. Soon thereafter he married; first in 1805 to Martha Sherman, who died the next year, and then in 1811 to Olivia Jones. No children resulted from either marriage. Between 1814 and 1817 he published three textbooks, respectively, on algebra, trigonometry, and surveying. Day had long been considered Timothy Dwight's handpicked successor as president of Yale. When Dwight died in 1817, Day was offered the position and after some hesitation accepted. He was inaugurated in July of that year, concurrent with his full ordination in the Congregational ministry.

Day served as president of Yale for twenty-nine years, longer than any other person who had held that office. Though often overshadowed by the more commanding personalities of his two predecessors, Ezra Stiles and Timothy Dwight, Day shaped Yale College in ways that continue to influence American higher education. Day inherited from Dwight the largest college in the country with a national student body and a plan to add professional schools to the collegiate base. Day enhanced this plan by creating a theological department, later the Divinity School, in 1822, which complemented the Medical School opened under Dwight in 1813. Yale affiliated with a proprietary law school in New Haven and listed the students in its catalog in 1824; in 1843 Yale took over the school and awarded the LL.B. degree for the first time. Day invigorated the role of faculty governance, which had languished under Dwight, and in 1823 eliminated the requirement that faculty take a religious oath.

The finances of the college were not adequate to sustain future growth upon Day's inauguration. He thus sought to increase aid from private donors as state support dwindled. Day encouraged the organization of the Society of the Alumni in 1827. In 1831–1832 Yale launched and successfully completed the Centum Milia Fund, which raised more than its $100,000 goal. With increased financial resources, Day was able to construct a new chapel, a new library with expanded holdings, new dormitories, and a new commons. In 1832, with the help of Benjamin Silliman (1779–1864), Day obtained Colonel John Trumbull's (1756–1843) paintings of the American Revolution and a building to house them. The Trumbull Gallery became the first art museum attached to an American college. Many aspects of student life, including Greek letter fraternities, secret societies, and publications such as the *Yale Literary Magazine*, began their existence under Day. The student body increased from 275 in 1817 to 349 undergraduates and 110 professional students in 1824. In the course of Day's presidency, over 2,500 young men gained their degrees from Yale.

Day's most lasting achievement was his influence on the liberal arts curriculum, which he expounded in the Yale Report of 1828. In response to a request from trustee Noyes Darling to drop the ancient languages and establish a more practical curriculum, Day, with the help of Professors James Luce Kingsley and Benjamin Silliman, prepared a report to the Yale Corporation that advocated the retention of the classical languages. More important, it stated that the purpose of a collegiate education was "to lay the foundation of a superior education." Day emphasized that a collegiate education was meant to prepare students for further education, not complete their education. By firmly delineating undergraduate or collegiate education from professional training, Day arrested any trend at Yale that might have led to early specialized education, as Thomas Jefferson proposed for the University of Virginia. Day's influence on the development of the American college extended far beyond New Haven as numerous Yale graduates went west before the Civil War to found new colleges based on the principles of the Yale Report.

Day's poor health dogged him continually, complicated by a heart attack in 1836 followed by angina. He made his first attempt to resign from the presidency in 1841 but was persuaded to stay on until 1846. Upon retirement he accepted a seat on the Yale Corporation, which he held for the next two decades. In these later years he gained a reputation for extreme conservatism, which some biographers incorrectly believed reflected on his earlier achievements. Always considered to be a quiet, unassuming man who was seen by students as interesting but not brilliant, Jeremiah Day died in New Haven a few weeks after his ninety-fourth birthday.

• The Day family papers, including materials on Day's presidency, are in Sterling Library at Yale University. Day's principal scholarly works are *An Introduction to Algebra* (1814), *A Treatise of Plane Geometry* (1815), *The Mathematical Principles of Navigation and Surveying* (1817), *An Inquiry Respecting the Self-Determining Power of the Will on Contingent Volition* (1838), *An Examination of President Edwards' Inquiry on the Freedom of the Will* (1841), *A Course of Mathematics* (1848), and *A Key to Day's Algebra* (1853). There is no major biography of Day, but various biographical sketches have been published. The best contemporary sketch is the funeral oration of Theodore Dwight Woolsey, *An Address Commemorative of the Life and Services of Jeremiah Day, Late President of Yale College, Delivered in the Center Church, New Haven, August 26, 1867* (1867). For early twentieth-century sketches see Timothy Dwight, *Memories of Yale Life and Men* (1903), and Franklin B. Dexter, *Biographical Sketches of the Graduates of Yale College with Annals of the College History*, vol. 5 (1911). For the most recent sketches of Day, see Reuben Holden, *Profiles and Portraits of Yale University Presidents* (1968), and Brooks M. Kelley, *Yale: A History* (1974).

JOHN S. WHITEHEAD

DAY, Leon (30 Oct. 1916–13 Mar. 1995), Negro League baseball player, was born in Alexandria, Virginia, the son of Ellis Day, a glass factory worker, and Hattie Leet. Day grew up in the Mount Winans district of Baltimore, Maryland, and finished the tenth grade before dropping out of school. As a youth, he was a fan of the Baltimore Black Sox of the Eastern Colored League, where he met his idol and future teacher, pitcher Lamon Yokeley. His career began in 1934 with the local semipro Silver Moons. As a right-handed pitcher, he used a deceptive no-windup delivery to deliver sneaky fastballs and roundhouse curves. He became known as an excellent fielding pitcher and an above-average hitter, and he sometimes played the field so that his bat would remain in the lineup. He quickly caught the attention of the Baltimore Black Sox player-manager Herbert "Rap" Dixon and finished the season with the team, earning $60 a month.

The following season Dixon jumped to the Brooklyn Eagles of the Negro National League and took Day with him. Named by Eagles manager Ben Taylor as his top pitcher, Day led the Eagles' staff in wins with a 9–2 record, which included a one-hitter, earning him his first selection to the prestigious East-West all-star game in Chicago, Illinois. In 1936 the Eagles were sold to Abe Manley and relocated to Newark, New Jersey. The next season Day enjoyed one of his finest campaigns, compiling a perfect 13–0 record and batting .320 with eight home runs. On 17 July 1939 Day married Helene Johnson; they had no children.

Except for missing most of the 1938 season due to a sore arm, from 1936 to 1943 Day was the undisputed staff ace. In 1942 he established a league record with 18 strikeouts in a game against the Baltimore Elite Giants, including future Hall of Fame catcher Roy Campanella three times. In the East-West all-star game that year in Chicago, Day struck out five of the first seven batters he faced, en route to a win. Overall, in his nine all-star pitching appearances, Day recorded 16 strikeouts in 21⅓ innings. That year, he was named by the *Pittsburgh Courier* newspaper as the "Best Pitcher" in the Negro Leagues.

In 1944 and 1945 Day fulfilled his military commitment as a corporal in the 818th Amphibian Battalion that landed in Normandy on Utah Beach during the Allied invasion on D-Day. After the victory celebration, Day pitched his service team to a win over a major league all-star team led by Cincinnati Reds pitcher Ewell Blackwell. In Munich, Germany, he pitched a one-hitter in the "GI World Series" before a reported crowd of 100,000 fans. Returning from the service in 1946, Day pitched the only Opening Day no-hitter in Negro League history, against the Philadelphia Stars. He finished the season with a 13–4 record and led the league in strikeouts, innings pitched, and shutouts, while batting a lofty .353. The Eagles, managed by Biz Mackey and paced by the power hitting of youngsters Larry Doby and Monte Irvin, defeated the powerful Kansas City Monarchs in the Negro League World Series, four games to three, with Day pitching in two games. That season Day was paid a reported $450 dollars a month, his Negro League career high. Contracts available from earlier years show that he had received $210 per month in 1941 and was given a raise of $15 per month the following year.

The 5'9", 170-pound Day played many winters in the Cuban (1937–1938, 1947–1948), Puerto Rican (1939–1942, 1949–1950), Mexican, and Venezuela leagues. During the 1941–1942 winter season, with the Aquadilla Sharks in the Puerto Rican League, he struck out a record 19 batters in an 18-inning marathon game. In three seasons with the Aquadilla team he hit .307, .330, and .351, while compiling a pitching record of 34–26. The three Puerto Rican campaigns saw 186, 149, and 168 batters strike out on Day deliveries. Day played in the Mexican Leagues for the Mexico City Reds in 1947 and 1948, before returning to the Negro National League in 1949 to help the Baltimore Elite Giants win the pennant. The following year Day joined manager Willie Wells's Winnipeg Buffaloes in the independent semipro Manitoba-Dakota (Man-Dak) League, where he hit .324 and compiled a 4–2 pitching record. In 1951, at the age of 34, he entered organized baseball, joining the Toronto Maple Leafs (AAA) of the International League. The following season he played with the Scranton Miners of the Eastern League, compiling a 13–9 record and batting .314. He finished his brilliant career with the Edmonton Eskimos of the Western International League (1953) and the Brandon Greys of the Man-Dak League (1954).

Upon retiring from baseball, he was employed by Tragfer Bakery, Revere Bass and Cooper, and the Liberty Security Companies as a security guard in Newark, New Jersey. He later worked as a substitute mail carrier for the Conmar Zipper Company and served as a part-time bartender for former Eagle teammate Leonard Pearson's sports bar Lennie's Lounge. He eventually returned to Baltimore's Harlem Avenue. After the death of his first wife, he married Geraldine "Jerry" Ingram from Wallace, North Carolina, in November 1980.

Former teammate Larry Doby remembers, "I don't see anybody in the major leagues that was better than Leon Day. If you want to compare him with Bob Gibson, stuff wise, Day had just as good of stuff. Tremendous curve ball, and a fast ball at least 90–95 miles an hour. You talk about Satchel [Paige]—I didn't see any [pitcher] better than Day." Another teammate, Monte Irvin confirmed this view, "People don't know what a great pitcher Leon Day was. He was as good or better than Bob Gibson. He was a better fielder, a better hitter, could run like a deer. When he pitched against Satchel, Satchel didn't have an edge. You thought Don Newcombe could pitch. You should have seen Day! One of the best complete athletes I've ever seen."

On 31 January 1992 Day was honored by Baltimore mayor Kurt L. Schmoke with a proclamation by the city for Leon Day Day. He was also honored for his baseball contributions by President George Bush in the White House on 19 February 1992 and by Maryland governor William Donald Schaefer on 18 May 1992. In 1993 he was elected to the Puerto Rican Hall of Fame. Day's final tribute came on 7 March 1995, when he received news of his election to the National Baseball Hall of Fame. Day died six days later in Baltimore.

On 30 July 1995 Day's wife Geraldine revealed something of Day's quiet, unassuming character by speaking at his induction in Cooperstown, New York.

She noted that Day was "a kind, gentle and humble man, and a wonderful athlete. He never bragged about his many accomplishments. He was always quick to praise others, and deserving of this great honor."

• A clipping file on Day is at the National Baseball Library in Cooperstown. For further information, see John B. Holway, *Black Ball Stars: Negro League Pioneers* (1988); James Riley, *Dandy, Day and the Devil* (1987); Dick Clark and Larry Lester, *The Negro Leagues Book* (1994); and Robert Peterson, *Only the Ball Was White* (1970). All-star statistics are compiled from actual box scores of the games. An obituary is in the *Baltimore Sun*, 14 Mar. 1995.

LARRY LESTER

DAY, Stephen (1594?–22 Dec. 1668), locksmith and printer, was born in England. Very little is known for certain about Stephen Day (also spelled Stephen Daye and Steven Day). He arrived from Cambridge, England, in New England in 1638 on board the *John of London* with his wife, Rebecca (widow of Andrew Bordman, a Cambridge baker), his two sons, and a stepson. He had made bond for two years' service to the Reverend Jose (also spelled Josse and Joos) Glover for his passage to New England. Glover, bringing a printing press to Cambridge, had probably engaged Day, listed in legal documents as "locksmith," to assemble the press, although nothing about the press or using Day as a printer appears in the bond.

Glover did not survive the journey. His widow, Elizabeth, was therefore responsible for settling the Day family and the press in a house in Cambridge, Massachusetts. In 1641 she married Henry Dunster, president of Harvard College, and moved the press to Dunster's house, thus making Harvard the proprietor of the first printing press in colonial America. The Day family was forced to leave the residence (now Holyoke Street) provided by the widow Glover and find other living quarters. The General Court records for 1641 state that Day, "being the first that set upon printing," was granted 300 acres of land as a reward for his services.

No real evidence exists that Day knew anything about the craft of printing; his handwriting shows that he was barely literate. Yet, as a locksmith, he apparently understood the workings of the press. The first issue from the Cambridge press was the "Freeman's Oath," a broadside (1639); the second, an almanac by William Peirce, mariner (1639); and the third, the *Bay Psalm Book*. Of these three, only the *Bay Psalm Book* is extant. In addition, Day is generally given credit for having printed nineteen other works: nine other almanacs (1640–1645 conjectural); five announcements of Harvard graduates' theses; the *Capital Laws* (1642); a spelling book (1643); Winthrop's *Declaration of the Narrowgansets* (1645); Norris's *Cathechism* (1648); and the *Book of General Laws and Liberties* (1649; in press 1648). Of a total of twenty-two attributed works, only nine are extant.

Since Stephen Day's name appeared on only one of these publications, he may not have printed all of them; an almanac for 1647 bears the imprint of Day's son, Matthew, also listed as "locksmith" in a legal document. Both George Parker Winship and George Emery Littlefield speculated that Matthew Day could have been taught printing before arriving in New England. Moreover, evidence exists in a letter from Samuel Green, Day's successor, to John Winthrop, Jr., that Green succeeded Matthew Day, not Stephen, as printer. Lucius Paige, a meticulous historian, also referred to Matthew as a printer.

In 1642 or 1643 Day became part of a group sponsored by John Winthrop, Jr., that attempted to start an iron factory and a new town known as "Plantation of Nashaway" (now Lancaster). Day, to purchase some cattle in 1642, mortgaged part of his property. In 1643 he was arrested for defraudment but was released two days later. While prospecting for iron ore, Day maintained his legal residence in Cambridge. Until his death he lived in a house bought by Matthew Day for the Day family. After about ten years and futile efforts to find ore, Stephen Day, who never actually resided in "Nashaway," abandoned the project and returned to Cambridge to work as a locksmith. General Court records also show that not until 1657 did Day receive the 300 acres promised in 1641 "for recompense of his care and charge of furthering the work of printing."

A lawsuit in 1656 (*Glover v. Dunster*) indicates that the widow's descendants believed they still had a claim to the press that had been sold to Harvard College after Dunster resigned as president in 1654. Detailed examinations of all records caused the court to charge Dunster with a little over £117, the press and paper accounting for almost 50 percent of this amount. The Glovers had originally brought from England the press, worth £20; one type font; and £60 worth of paper. Day was instrumental in helping to settle the suit with his depositions concerning the value of the press and equipment. In the same year he sued Dunster for £100 in recompense for services he claimed were unpaid during the time he had managed the press.

Day's wife died in 1658, and in 1664 he married Mary Fitch, a widow, who outlived him. A bronze tablet attached in 1907 to a building on the Day lot in Cambridge bears this inscription: "Here lived Stephen Daye / First Printer in / British America / 1638–68." Although the building was Day's legal residence from 1646, and although he lived there from about 1655 until his death, neither he nor it was connected during this time with printing. Regardless of which Day did the actual printing, Stephen Day is credited with being the first printer in colonial America. Samuel Green, not Matthew Day, is cited as the second.

• Much that has been written about Day is imaginative conjecture. What is certain is based on legal documents involving land grants, deeds, court cases, church records, correspondence, and the following entry for March 1640 in Winthrop's *Journal*: "A printing press was begun at Cambridge by one Daye, at the charge of Mr. Glover, who died on sea hitherward." Original source material exists at the Harvard University Archives, the Massachusetts Historical Society, and the American Antiquarian Society. Facsimiles of original publications for this period are found on microprint in *Early Amer-*ican Imprints (American Antiquarian Society), which is keyed by entry number to Charles Evans, *American Bibliography*, ed. Clifford K. Shipton (14 vols., 1941–1959). George Emery Littlefield, *The Early Massachusetts Press, 1638–1711* (1907; repr. 1969), should, in Samuel Eliot Morison's words, "be used with caution." Some of Isaiah Thomas's information in *The History of Printing in America* (1810; repr. and ed. by Marcus A. McCorison, 1970) has been proven false; McCorison's notes are helpful. A particularly detailed account of the *Glover v. Dunster* court case can be found in George Parker Winship, *The Cambridge Press, 1638–1692* (1945; repr. 1968). See also Lucius R. Paige, *History of Cambridge, Massachusetts* (1877); Andrew McF. Davis, "The Cambridge Press," *Proceedings of the American Antiquarian Society*, n.s., 5 (Apr. 1888): 295–302; and *Proceedings of the Massachusetts Historical Society* 5 (Feb. 1861): 154–56. Both Paige and Davis had access to original records.

MARION BARBER STOWELL

DAY, William Howard (16 Oct. 1825–2 Dec. 1900), educator and editor, was born in New York City, the son of John Day, a sailmaker, and Eliza Dixon, a seamstress. J. P. Williston, an inkmaker from Northampton, Massachusetts, first met Day during a visit to a school for black children in New York City. Williston was so impressed with the young student that he persuaded Day's mother to allow him, a white man, to adopt her son. Day spent five years in Northampton, where he attended school and was apprenticed as a printer at the *Hampshire Herald*. Refused admission to Williams College because of his race, Day enrolled at Oberlin College in Ohio (1843–1847). Soon after graduating, he was hired by the *Cleveland True Democrat* as a reporter, compositor, and local editor. He later published and edited the *Aliened American* (1853–1854), which aimed to promote education and defend the rights of African Americans. It was also the mouthpiece of the state's Negro Convention Movement, in which Day was a leading figure. Day married fellow student Lucy Stanton in 1852; one child was born to the marriage.

Five years out of college, Day organized a meeting in Cleveland to honor surviving black veterans of the revolutionary war and the War of 1812. It was in part a memorial to his father, a sailor in the War of 1812 who had died tragically in 1829, and also partly an expression of Day's conviction that such valor in the defense of the nation was grounds enough to be recognized as citizens. "We ask for liberty; liberty here—liberty on Chalmette Plains—liberty wherever floats the American flag," Day wrote. "We demand for the sons of the men who fought for you, equal privileges" (*Cleveland True Democrat*, 9 Sept. 1852). The struggle for equal rights dominated Day's life.

The failure of his newspaper and increasing discrimination prompted Day and his family to join the growing number of African Americans emigrating to Canada. There he became involved in John Brown's preparations for the 1859 attack on Harpers Ferry, printing Brown's constitution in an isolated shack outside Saint Catharines. Day was in Britain raising money for the fugitive slave settlement at Buxton, Ontario, when the attack occurred. He spent the next four years in Britain lecturing against slavery and working with the African Aid Society, an organization formed to support the efforts of Martin R. Delany, Henry Highland Garnet, Robert Campbell, and other advocates of African-American emigration to the west coast of Africa. By the time of his return to the United States in 1863, Day's marriage had fallen apart because of what he considered to be irreconcilable differences. It is difficult to determine what these differences were, but it is clear that Day's long absences from home must have been a contributing factor. William and Lucy Day were finally divorced in 1872, after years of wrangling. A few months later Day married Georgie Bell of Washington, D.C.; he had no children with his second wife.

After returning to the United States, Day settled in New York City, devoting most of his time to working with the American Freedmen's Friend Society, a black-led freedmen's aid organization, and as lay editor of the *Zion Herald*, the organ of the African Methodist Episcopal Zion church. In 1867 he was named by the Freedmen's Bureau as superintendent of schools for the freedmen of Maryland and Delaware. Day used this office to promote education, to support the construction of schools, and to work with local associations to increase educational opportunities for the freedmen. In spite of local and state opposition, Day reported significant growth in schools built and in attendance. Day lost his job in 1869 when the Freedmen's Bureau reorganized its local offices.

In 1872 Day moved to Harrisburg, Pennsylvania, after purchasing a local newspaper, *Progress of Liberty*, and changing its name to *Our National Progress*. Published simultaneously in Harrisburg and Philadelphia; Wilmington, Delaware; Camden, New Jersey; and New York City, Day saw the paper as both a regional and a national mouthpiece of African Americans. Despite its wide circulation, the paper ceased publication in 1875 largely on account of difficulties brought on by the economic depression of 1873. Day ran unsuccessfully for the Harrisburg School Board in 1873; five years later he became the first African American to be elected to the board. He remained a member for the rest of the century with the exception of brief periods in the 1880s when he refused renomination. In 1891 the board unanimously elected Day its president, a position he held until 1895. He finally retired from the board in 1899, ending an involvement in education lasting more than fifty years.

Day was a prominent force in central Pennsylvania Republican circles. His active involvement in the 1872 campaign led to his appointment to a clerkship in the state auditor general's office. But frustration with token appointments and the continued corruption of the state Republican machine under Simon Cameron led Day to break with the party in 1878. He temporarily threw his support to the Democrats but was back in the Republican fold in 1881. Although he remained an active supporter of the party, Day never again regained his place of prominence, nor was he, or any other black Pennsylvanian during Day's lifetime, ever nominated to significant office.

After his return from Britain in 1863, Day had become actively involved in the AME Zion church. His parents' home had served as a meeting place for the fledgling denomination in the 1820s, and Day had been baptized by James Varick, the first bishop of the church. By 1870 Day was unquestionably the most prominent member of the denomination in Pennsylvania. He was named secretary-general of the national body in 1876 and presiding elder of the Philadelphia and Baltimore Conference in 1885. As elder he supervised a district that included Washington, D.C., and parts of Pennsylvania, Maryland, and Delaware. He was later appointed secretary of the board of bishops.

Day, a contemporary observed, was "one of the grandest and most refined men of this country regardless of race" (*Harrisburg Telegraph*, 14 Apr. 1898). It was a fitting tribute to a man who had spent all of his adult life promoting the cause of freedom and equality in the United States. Day died in Harrisburg as a result of a series of strokes.

• A few letters from or about Day are in the American Missionary Association Papers, Amistad Research Center, New Orleans; the Anti-Slavery Collection, Cornell University Library; Bureau of Refugees, Freedmen and Abandoned Lands, National Archives; the Leon Gardiner Collection, Pennsylvania Historical Society; and the Gerrit Smith Papers, Syracuse University Library. Additional letters are in the microfilm edition of the *Black Abolitionists Papers, 1830–1865*, reel 11. See also William J. Simmons, *Men of Mark: Eminent, Progressive and Rising* (1887); Boyd B. Stutler, "John Brown's Constitution," *Lincoln Herald* 50–51 (1948): 20–24; B. F. Wheeler, *Cullings from Zion's Poets* (1907); and R. J. M. Blackett, *Beating against the Barriers: Biographical Essays in Nineteenth-Century Afro-American History* (1986). An obituary is in the *Harrisburg Telegraph*, 3 Dec. 1900.

R. J. M. BLACKETT

DAY, William Rufus (17 Apr. 1849–9 July 1923), associate justice of the U.S. Supreme Court, was born in Ravenna, Ohio, the son of Luther Day and Emily Spalding. Both his father and his maternal grandfather were lawyers and judges on the Ohio Supreme Court. He graduated from the University of Michigan in 1870 and spent the following year in its Department of Law. After settling in Canton, Ohio, in 1872, he began his law practice and married Mary Elizabeth Schaefer in August 1875. He practiced criminal and corporate law in the growing industrial town for twenty-five years while participating in Republican politics and becoming a close friend of William McKinley. Day was a legal and political adviser to McKinley as the latter won elections to the U.S. Congress, the governorship of Ohio, and the presidency.

Day, reluctant to accept political offices, did accede to McKinley's wishes and became first assistant secretary of state on 23 April 1897. As a part of several political moves, McKinley appointed John Sherman (1823–1900) secretary of state to open an Ohio seat in the U.S. Senate, but because of his increasing loss of memory, irascibility, and differences with administration policies, Sherman was ineffective in that position. Thus, with no diplomatic experience, Day was the de facto secretary and the secretary of state for twenty months during the Spanish-American War. The president and others went to Day for advice and direction at the State Department as the United States moved closer to war with Spain. The French ambassador to the United States, Jules Cambon, met frequently with McKinley and Day in an attempt to mediate between Spain and the United States on the issues related to Cuban independence. The various Spanish concessions were not acceptable to the Americans, however, and McKinley and Day agreed to the proposal to send the *Maine* to Havana. After war was declared, Day argued that the Spanish colonies other than Cuba should be returned to Spain, but he accepted McKinley's harsher terms for peace. His final diplomatic effort was to lead the U.S. peace commission in Paris and sign the Peace Protocol and Treaty of Paris.

Soon after Day's return from Europe, and despite his hope to return to private life, in February 1899 McKinley appointed Day to the U.S. Court of Appeals for the Sixth Circuit. Both future chief justice William Howard Taft and associate justice Horace H. Lurton were then already sitting on the sixth circuit court of appeals. The assassination of President McKinley in the summer of 1901 was a shock and tragedy for Day.

In 1902 President Theodore Roosevelt (1858–1919) twice offered the seat on the U.S. Supreme Court vacated by George Shiras, Jr., to William Howard Taft, but the then governor of the Philippines felt he could not leave his position there. Roosevelt then nominated Day in January 1903 to fill the vacancy. Day sat on the Supreme Court for almost twenty years during an era when the Court made numerous decisions that increased the involvement and police powers of both the federal and state governments in the economy.

Day wrote 439 opinions during his tenure on the Court, and only eighteen were dissents. Characterized as rigid and formalistic, and best known for his *Hammer v. Dagenhart* (1917) ruling, Day did advance state regulatory powers and the enforcement of antitrust laws, but the latter was the only federal economic police power that Day consistently supported. He argued that the Tenth Amendment did limit federal intervention and used that amendment to give assent to state regulations while denying regulatory power in most cases to the national government.

One of the first Roosevelt antitrust prosecutions, *Northern Securities Co. v. U.S.*, was decided by the Supreme Court in 1904 on a five-to-four vote with Day concurring with the majority. Day distrusted very large corporations and voted with antitrust majorities throughout his time on the Court. He sided with the government in the *Standard Oil, American Tobacco,* and *Union Pacific* cases in 1911–1912 and again in the *Southern Pacific* case in 1922. Day believed that Congress could regulate commerce but that constitutional power did not extend to the supervision of production.

Day accepted the logic of the *U.S. v. E. C. Knight* decision of 1895 that developed the distinction between commerce and production in the enforcement of the Sherman Antitrust Act. Chief Justice Melville Fuller in *Knight* wrote that regulation of interstate commerce did not include regulation of the manufacture or production of goods. Day used the same logic in his opinion in *Hammer v. Dagenhart*. That case grew out of the Federal Child Labor Act of 1916, which prohibited interstate transportation of products manufactured in factories that employed children under the age of fourteen, or children between fourteen and sixteen working more than eight hours a day or six days a week. Day was consistent in his belief that the commerce clause could not include regulation of production, even though the products would be transported over state borders. The decision frustrated the efforts of President Woodrow Wilson and the Progressives to control child labor, and it drew a harsh dissenting opinion from Justice Oliver Wendell Holmes (1841–1935).

Day was more comfortable with state regulation of social ills. His rulings in cases of state government intervention affirmed his belief that states could regulate economic power and social problems within individual state boundaries. In *Lochner v. New York*, Day voted with the minority in 1905 to limit work in bakeries to ten hours a day. Day wrote the dissent in *Coppage v. Kansas* in 1915, in which he upheld the constitutionality of the state law to outlaw yellow-dog contracts. Later, in 1921, he asserted the right of a state to regulate drug use in *Minnesota ex rel. Whipple v. Martinson*. For Day there was a constitutional limit on federal police powers that did not exist for state governments.

Day retired from the Supreme Court in October 1922 and died on Mackinac Island, Michigan.

• The William Rufus Day Papers are in the Manuscript Division of the Library of Congress. The standard biography is Joseph E. McLean, *William Rufus Day: Supreme Court Justice from Ohio* (1946). Also see Fenton S. Martin and Robert U. Goehlert, *The United States Supreme Court: A Bibliography* (1990); George W. Duncan, "The Diplomatic Career of William Rufus Day, 1897–1898" (Ph.D. diss., Case Western Reserve Univ., 1976); Vernon R. Roelofs, "William R. Day: A Study in Constitutional History" (Ph.D. diss., Univ. of Michigan, 1942) and "William R. Day and Federal Regulation," *Mississippi Valley Historical Review* 37 (June 1950): 39–60.

R. MICHAEL MCREYNOLDS

DAYHOFF, Margaret Oakley (11 Mar. 1925–5 Feb. 1983), research biochemist, was born in Philadelphia, Pennsylvania, the daughter of Kenneth W. Oakley, an industrialist, and Ruth P. Clark. When Margaret was about the age of ten, the Oakleys moved to New York City. There she attended Public School Number 32 and went on to become the valedictorian of the Bayside High School class of 1942. She was awarded a scholarship to Washington Square College of New York University, from which she graduated in 1945 magna cum laude, with honors in mathematics. In

1948 she married Edward S. Dayhoff; they would have two children. In that same year, Margaret Dayhoff received a Ph.D. from Columbia University in quantum chemistry.

Dayhoff received a research fellowship at the Rockefeller Institute in New York in 1948 and another at the University of Maryland in 1957. Joining the National Biomedical Foundation in 1959, she served as its associate director, a position she would hold for twenty-one years. During this time she was also professor of physiology and biophysics at Georgetown University Medical Center. Dayhoff had the distinction of being the first person to serve both as secretary and president of the Biophysical Society, an international organization of research scientists. She served on the editorial boards of three journals—*DNA, Journal of Molecular Evolution*, and *Computers in Biology and Medicine*—and was a fellow of the American Association for the Advancement of Science.

Dayhoff was a pioneer in the study of biological macromolecules (very large molecules, such as a polymer or protein). Early collaborative research on primordial planetary atmospheres (she developed a computer program for modeling these) led to her interest in the origin of life, particularly in deducing evolutionary relationships of early organisms from the information in protein sequences.

To provide a dataset for the support of her research on interrelationships and evolution of proteins, Dayhoff initiated the Protein Sequence Database (PSDB) with a collection of sixty-five sequences. Using this information, Dayhoff authored in 1965 a reference work that would prove invaluable to scientists, the first book in a series, *Atlas of Protein Sequence and Structure*. The series continued through 1981 with seven atlases of protein sequences and one of the nucleic acid sequences; through 1994 these volumes continued to be cited the world over more than 250 times per year. She developed the concept of a macromolecular sequence database as an evaluated, reviewed data compilation in which all data for each protein were merged into a single entry, with annotations reflecting current biological knowledge. The result was a new kind of research tool for scientists in many fields. She also developed the protein superfamily concept to organize distantly related protein families. This concept, now modified by more recent data on gene structures, continues to be widely used.

Dayhoff developed much of the early methodology in computational biology, including, in 1967, the first amino acid similarity scoring matrix (Mutation Data Matrix), one of the first methods for database search, sequence comparison, evolutionary tree building, and local similarity comparison. Some of the first protein evolutionary trees, derived with these methods, were published in 1966 in the second *Atlas of Protein Sequences and Structure*. A number of important new sequence homologies were discovered using these methods.

Dayhoff directed the development of the first document-based information retrieval system for the PSDB, as well as the on-line versions of both sequence databases (in 1980 and 1981). She helped direct the attention of the Committee on Data for Science and Technology to the importance of sequence databases, leading to the formation of a task group for biological macromolecules and to international cooperation for these databases. Her last major effort was to obtain funding for a Protein Identification Resource; this was established in 1984 and grew into the Protein Information Resource International, with collaborating databases in Europe and Japan.

Dayhoff and her colleagues contributed a number of papers supporting the hypothesis of the symbiotic origins of eukaryote cells and organelles from prokaryotes. Much of this work she summed up in her last paper, "Evolutionary Connections of Biological Kingdoms Based on Protein and Nucleic Acid Sequence Evidence." She used all applicable sequence data then available to derive a composite phylogenetic tree describing "early evolution starting with the anaerobic heterotrophic bacteria at the base." "A gene duplication of ferredoxin, probably predating all of the species divergences, permitted us to infer an ancestral molecule that can be placed on the tree to give the base." Dayhoff concluded that "this tree clearly supports the symbiotic origin of the eukaryote organelles" and suggests "that the earliest eukaryotes were unicellular and that the multicellular forms of plants, animals, fungi and slime molds arose independently."

In the foreword to a special commemorative issue of the *Bulletin of Mathematical Biology*, H. M. Martinez writes that Dayhoff will be remembered for "her outstanding pioneering work in collecting and comparing molecular sequences. . . . All of us working in molecular biology . . . have felt the impact of her work."

• Of Dayhoff's more than 150 publications, many early papers are included in two compendia: *National Biomedical Research Foundation Research Accomplishments* (1960–1970) and *National Biomedical Research Foundation Research Accomplishments* (1970–1975).

ROBERT S. LEDLEY

DAYTON, Jonathan (16 Oct. 1760–9 Oct. 1824), revolutionary war officer and congressman, was born in Elizabethtown (now Elizabeth), New Jersey, the son of Elias Dayton, a wealthy merchant and revolutionary war general, and Hannah Rolfe. Dayton probably attended Elizabethtown Academy (a grammar school). He entered the College of New Jersey (Princeton) about 1774 and graduated in 1776, although he missed the commencement because he had joined the Continental army.

Not yet sixteen years old, Dayton received a commission as ensign on 7 February 1776. Throughout the war he served first in the Second New Jersey Regiment and then in the Third New Jersey Regiment, each commanded by his father. Dayton was appointed lieutenant on 1 January 1777, captain-lieutenant on 7 April 1779, and captain (a rank he held for the remainder of the war) on 30 March 1780; he also served intermittently as regimental paymaster.

During the spring and fall of 1776 Dayton saw duty with his regiment along the Mohawk Valley, principally in the rebuilding of Fort Stanwix (Rome, N.Y.) and the construction of Fort Dayton (Herkimer, N.J.). He saw action at the battles of Brandywine, Germantown, and Monmouth. Much of his service in the New Jersey brigade occurred in the vicinity of his home at Elizabethtown, contending with British and Tory raiding parties. Dayton served as captain and aide-de-camp to General John Sullivan in the expedition against the Iroquois Indians in New York during the summer and fall of 1779. He participated in action versus British troops during the Springfield, New Jersey, raid of 7–23 June 1780. Dayton was captured on 5 October 1780 by a Tory band at Herd's Tavern in Connecticut Farms (now Union, N.J.), detained as a prisoner of war on Staten Island, and then quickly exchanged. He served with his regiment at the siege of Yorktown, assigned to the second brigade in General Benjamin Lincoln's division. After duty in New York state during late 1782, Dayton spent the remainder of the war at the Continental army encampment in the vicinity of New Windsor, New York. He left the army on 3 November 1783.

About the time of the war's end (the exact date is unknown), Dayton married Susannah Williamson of Elizabethtown, the daughter of militia general Matthias Williamson; they had one child. Dayton studied law and was admitted to the New Jersey bar by 1786. He helped to establish the New Jersey chapter of the Society of the Cincinnati (11 June 1783) and was a freemason. He served on the board of trustees for the First Presbyterian Church in Elizabethtown. With his father, he operated "E. Dayton and Son," a retail and wholesale mercantile firm. Dayton served in the New Jersey Assembly 1786–1787 and 1790.

When his father declined to be a delegate to the federal Constitutional Convention in 1787, Dayton took his place. At age twenty-six, he was the youngest delegate. William L. Pierce of Georgia, who made character sketches of the members of the convention, said that Dayton was talented, ambitious, well-educated, and a good orator; he had "an impetuosity in his temper that is injurious to him" but "an honest rectitude about him that makes him a valuable Member of Society" (Farrand, vol. 3, p. 90). Aligned with the so-called small state men, Dayton favored equal representation for all states in both houses of Congress. He also favored election of the president by state delegations in Congress voting as units. He supported a federal military establishment in peacetime but held that it should have jurisdiction over state militia only when in actual service of the United States. He opposed enumeration of slaves for the purpose of proportioning representation. He approved the final Constitution.

By legislative appointment, Dayton was a delegate to the Congress from November 1788 until the demise of the Confederation, 3 March 1789. He failed in seeking election to the First Congress under the Constitution in 1789. As one of the "East Jersey Junto" Dayton was opposed by the "West Jersey Junto" and Quakers, who pictured Dayton as one of those who wanted another war so "that they may make their fortunes."

During the 1780s Dayton bought up depreciated government securities, soldiers' certificates, and land warrants for a fraction of their original value, in expectation of making a huge profit when a new government (under the Constitution) should go into effect. He also invested in John Cleves Symmes's land deal. In 1788 Congress conferred on Symmes and his associates one million acres, at the cost of one dollar an acre in depreciated government paper. The land grant was located along the Ohio River, between the Great Miami and Little Miami rivers. The venture brought some settlement to the area. But owing largely to Symmes's mismanagement, failure to collect payments for land purchases, and allowing settlement outside the boundaries of the grant, the investors realized little profit, and Congress eventually reduced substantially the size of the land grant. Dayton, Ohio, settled in 1796, was named for Jonathan Dayton.

Dayton served in the House of Representatives from 1791 to 1799 and from 7 December 1795 to 3 March 1799 as Speaker. Although a Federalist, he had a reputation as a moderate and at times could be nonpartisan. Thus he achieved the Speakership when the Republicans had a bare majority in the House. As Speaker, Dayton acted mainly as a moderator, lacking powers later afforded the office, such as appointment of committees. As a holder of many military certificates, Dayton opposed James Madison's plan to discriminate in favor of the original owners. He proposed sequestration of British debts in the United States in reprisal for violations of the Treaty of Paris and reluctantly supported Jay's Treaty, casting a tie-breaking vote for appropriations to implement it. He favored enforcement of the Sedition Act and a war with France in 1798. Dayton accepted an appointment as brigadier general for the duration of the war scare, while being permitted to retain his congressional seat. Believing that John Adams had little voter appeal, Dayton wanted the Federalists to run Aaron Burr for the presidency in 1796 and in 1800 wanted Charles Cotesworth Pinckney to be the Federalist candidate.

Elected as a Federalist to the Senate in 1798, Dayton served from 4 March 1799 to 3 March 1805. He voted for the Louisiana Purchase and for the acquittal of Justice Samuel Chase at his impeachment trial. He was opposed to the repeal of the Federalist-passed Judiciary Act of 1801 and also opposed the Twelfth Amendment.

Dayton's public reputation greatly suffered beginning in 1800. In that year Francis Childs and William Denning, resentful of Dayton's suit against them for debt, published *Public Speculation Unfolded*, which showed Dayton's conflict of interest while working in Congress for land and public credit legislation that would have personally benefited him. In 1800 it was revealed that he had failed to settle congressional accounts and had kept $18,000 for personal use. Dayton repaid the money to the Treasury but without interest.

Dayton was linked to Burr's alleged western conspiracy. He supplied Burr with funds (originally intended for land speculation) and secretly attempted to secure Spanish aid for a western independence movement through that country's minister plenipotentiary to the United States, Don Carlos Martinez de Yrujo y Tacón. Dayton advised General James Wilkinson, governor of the Louisiana Territory, that President Thomas Jefferson was about to replace him as military commander for the western frontier. In a cipher letter to Wilkinson, Dayton declared: "You are not a man to despair, or even despond, especially when such prospects offer in another quarter. Are you ready? Are your numerous associates ready? Wealth and glory, Louisiana and Mexico" (Kline, vol. 2, p. 988). Fearing that his own complicity might soon be revealed, Wilkinson turned on Burr, who was charged with treason. Dayton and five others were also indicted on the same charge. At Burr's trial in the federal circuit court in Richmond, Virginia, a copy of the cipher letter was introduced but with changes and erasures made by Wilkinson to protect himself. After Burr's acquittal on grounds that there was no proof of an overt act of treason, Dayton's case was immediately dismissed for the same reason.

After his Senate term, Dayton retired to his home in Elizabethtown and gave some attention to farming. Losing the backing of Federalists because of his support for the War of 1812, Dayton was elected on the Republican ticket to the New Jersey Assembly; he served two terms (1814–1815).

Dayton lived quietly during his later years. In 1824 he helped raise funds for the Greek Independence movement. In the same year he had charge of troops assembled to honor the visit of the marquis de Lafayette to Elizabethtown; the French hero stayed at Dayton's home. One week after Lafayette left, Dayton died. Dayton had made and lost several fortunes during his lifetime. When he died he left an estate worth only about $3,000. Because he had been perceived as placing his own personal interests above that of the country while in high office and having flirted with treason, Dayton during his last years forfeited much of the esteem that he had once had from the public.

• Dayton papers are located at the New Jersey Historical Society, New-York Historical Society, Princeton University Library, and Rutgers University Library. For Dayton at the Constitutional Convention, see Max Farrand, ed., *The Records of the Federal Convention of 1787* (4 vols., 1937). Letters from Dayton are in Beverley W. Bond, Jr., ed., *The Correspondence of John Cleves Symmes* (1926), pp. 197–277. On the Burr conspiracy see Mary Jo Kline, ed., *Political Correspondence and Public Papers of Aaron Burr* (2 vols., 1983); Walter F. McCaleb, *The Aaron Burr Conspiracy* (1903); and Milton Lomask, *Aaron Burr*, vol. 2 (1982). Carl E. Prince et al., eds., *The Papers of William Livingston*, vols. 4–5 (1987–1988), has mention of Dayton. The only scholarly account of Dayton's life is in Richard A. Harrison, *Princetonians, 1776 to 1783: A Biographical Dictionary* (1981), pp. 31–42; this article has an extensive bibliography. For Dayton's long association with Elizabeth, New Jersey, see Theodore Thayer, *As We Were: The Story of Old Elizabethtown* (1964). A profile of Dayton's political career may be gleaned from Rudolph J. Pasler and Margaret C. Pasler, *The New Jersey Federalists* (1975); Ruth Bogin, *Abraham Clark and the Quest for Equality in the Revolutionary Era, 1774–1794* (1982); Richard P. McCormick, *Experiment in Independence: New Jersey in the Critical Period, 1781–1789* (1950); Carl E. Prince, *New Jersey's Jeffersonian Republicans: The Genesis of an Early Party Machine, 1789–1817* (1964); Donald H. Stewart, *The Opposition Press of the Federalist Period* (1969); James R. Sharp, *American Politics in the Early Republic: The New Nation in Crisis* (1993); and Bruce F. Fuller, *The Speakers of the House* (1909). An obituary is in the *New Jersey Journal & Elizabeth-Town Gazette*, 26 Oct. 1824.

HARRY M. WARD

DAYTON, William Lewis (17 Feb. 1807–1 Dec. 1864), politician and diplomat, was born at Baskingridge, New Jersey, the son of Joel Dayton, a shoemaker, and Nancy Lewis. After attending a local academy, he matriculated at Princeton College, graduating in 1825 as an "ordinary member" of his class. While teaching school he studied law in Somerville and was admitted to the New Jersey bar in 1830. In 1833 he married Margaret Elmendorf Van Der Veer; they had seven children.

Benefiting politically from the nationwide economic collapse in 1837, Dayton was elected to the New Jersey legislature as a Whig. He held his seat for only a few weeks before accepting an appointment at age thirty-one as an associate justice of the state supreme court. After occupying a seat on New Jersey's highest tribunal for less than four years, Dayton, lamenting that his judicial salary was too meager to support his growing family, resigned his judgeship in 1841 to reenter private law practice in Trenton. He had scarcely opened an office and begun to accumulate clients when in 1842 Governor William Pennington (1796–1862) appointed him—on the death of Dayton's distinguished cousin Samuel Lewis Southard—to fill the latter's unexpired term as a U.S. senator. Dayton was only thirty-five years old.

Reelected by the New Jersey legislature in 1845 for a full six-year term, Dayton was a senator until March 1851. His contributions to the legislation of this era were few, partly because his party was out of power much of the time and partly because of his cautious, self-effacing nature and his insistence on remaining politically independent, refusing to act against his personal convictions under pressure from leaders of the legislature, to which he was beholden for his Senate seat. Eschewing notoriety, he was esteemed more for his quiet common sense than for oratorical eloquence or vision.

On one issue Dayton stood out among his fellow senators. At a time when it would have been politically expedient in New Jersey, the northern state most sympathetic to the South's "peculiar institution," to refrain from antislavery pronouncements, Dayton voted against making war on Mexico as a way of expanding slave territory, supported the Wilmont Proviso excluding slavery from the lands acquired from Mexico, opposed the admission of Texas as a slave state, and spoke vehemently against the Compromise of 1850 as enhancing the power of slavery.

With the return of the Democrats to power in the New Jersey legislature, Dayton lost his Senate seat. In March 1851 he resumed the practice of law. He continued to be politically active, however, and in 1856 he joined the newly formed Republican party. Within a few weeks he became its first vice presidential nominee on the national ticket with John Charles Frémont, having outpolled Abraham Lincoln of Illinois in the scramble for delegate votes at the first Republican National Nominating Convention at Philadelphia.

Following the defeat of the Republican ticket in November, Dayton had hardly returned once more to his private law practice when he was appointed attorney general of New Jersey. He held that position from 1857 until early 1861, when he resigned to accept a diplomatic appointment from the first Republican president.

Lincoln, who as a young congressman had admired Dayton's independent antislavery stand in the U.S. Senate, wanted to make the New Jersey lawyer his minister to Great Britain. Only the determination of Secretary of State William Seward to have the London mission occupied by his friend Charles Francis Adams (1807–1886) persuaded Lincoln reluctantly to send Dayton to Paris instead.

At the court of the Emperor Louis Napoleon, Dayton served creditably as the American envoy, despite his inability to speak or to understand French. Ably supported by the American consul, John Bigelow, and wisely guided by Seward, Dayton helped to fend off European intervention on the side of the Confederate States of America that might have permanently divided the American Union. In scores of interviews with French officials, he vigorously argued against assistance to the Confederate cause, making good use of French suspicions of the British to undermine the "understanding" that the two European powers had developed with regard to the United States. Among the problems with which Dayton successfully grappled during the Civil War were Napoleon's sponsorship of Maximilian's puppet government in Mexico, southern efforts to construct warships in French shipyards, and the cotton shortage in Europe, which provided a pretext for Anglo-French intervention in the American conflict.

Inexperienced in international relations and therefore feeling his way at the outset of his mission, Dayton eventually became an able diplomatist. Dignified and diligent, he won the respect of two notable French foreign ministers, Antoine Edouard Thouvenel and Edouard Drouyn de Lhuys. Americans living in or traveling through Paris found him honorable, generous, affable, and urbane, and his colleagues in the corps diplomatique remarked upon his discretion and prudence as he labored to preserve amicable relations between the United States and France in the face of great danger of a Franco-American clash of arms.

An increasing addiction to the pleasures of the table exacerbated Dayton's chronic ill health by 1864. His sudden death late that year in the apartment of a well-known courtesan created a delicate situation when friends delivered his body unexpectedly to his wife at their Paris residence. He was eventually buried in Riverview Cemetery at Trenton.

Despite being in poor health much of his life, Dayton played a significant role in the political history of New Jersey. As the U.S. minister in France during the Civil War, he labored successfully to maintain good relations between his government and that of Napoleon III in circumstances where a more impulsive or less judicious diplomat might well have helped to trigger a transatlantic war.

• The only substantial collection of Dayton's papers is at the Princeton University Library. Scattered correspondence is in the collected papers of many contemporaries. All of Dayton's official correspondence during his ministerial service at Paris is in the State Department records, RG 59, National Archives. Nothing approaching a full-scale biography of Dayton has yet been published. Two sketches are Walter L. Whittlesey, "William Lewis Dayton, 1825: Senator—Presidential Candidate—Civil War Minister to France—A Forgotten Princetonian Who Served His Country Well," *Princeton Alumni Weekly* 30 (9 May 1930): 797–802, and J. P. Bradley, "A Memoir of the Life and Character of Hon. Wm. L. Dayton," *Proceedings of the New Jersey Historical Society*, 2d ser., 4 (1875): 69–118. Dayton's early career is discussed in Lucius Q. C. Elmer, *The Constitution and Government of the Province and State of New Jersey, with Biographical Sketches of the Governors from 1776 to 1845. And Reminiscences of the Bench and Bar, during More Than Half a Century* (1872). Dayton's diplomatic service during the Civil War is treated in John Bigelow, *Retrospections of an Active Life* (3 vols., 1909), and Lynn M. Case and Warren F. Spencer, *The United States and France: Civil War Diplomacy* (1970).

NORMAN B. FERRIS

DAZEY, Charles T. (12 Aug. 1855–9 Feb. 1938), playwright, was born in Lima, Illinois, the son of Mitchell Dazey and Albina Conover, farmers. Because his mother died two years after he was born, Dazey, who had no siblings, was raised by his father. He grew up in the countryside near Lima Lake, a hamlet that eventually disappeared when that shallow lake in the Mississippi River floodplain was drained.

After attending Adams County schools, Dazey studied at Methodist Episcopal College in nearby Quincy. At age fourteen he saw his first play—*Davy Crockett*, with Frank Mayo in the title role—at the Opera House in Quincy. From then on Dazey wanted to be a playwright, although his father urged him to study law. Mitchell Dazey had been born near Lexington, Kentucky, where he sent his son in 1872 to live with relatives and attend college. After one year in the Agricultural and Mechanical College of Kentucky University, Dazey transferred to the College of Arts where he studied off and on until 1877.

Dazey later attended Harvard University, where he was editor of the *Harvard Advocate* and was elected class poet. During his sophomore year his first play, a comedy entitled *Rustication*, was produced at the Boston Museum. After receiving his B.A. in 1881, Dazey read law for one year and then entered Columbia Law College in New York. Illness, however, forced him to quit school. During the early 1880s he wrote poetry for popular magazines and completed two plays, *An American King* (1884) and *For a Brother's Life* (1885), a Civil War drama that was his first full-length published work.

In 1887 Dazey married Lucy Harding and moved to North Dakota, where he tried ranching. About two years later they moved to Kansas, where he invested in real estate and wrote *The Little Maverick*.

After losing money in his real estate ventures, Dazey returned to Quincy, where he wrote his most famous play, *In Old Kentucky* (1893), during the winter of 1891–1892. A contrived but suspenseful four-act melodrama that centers around a horse race, *In Old Kentucky* employs character types that Dazey had recognized in Lexington. In a 1920 essay he described the writing of that play and his efforts to get it produced: "I had a commission from Katie Putnam, a well-known actress in 1892, to write a play for her. During the winter I completed the script and forwarded it to her. She read it and passed against it. The horse, she declared, was the star of the plot. . . . I took the script and went to Chicago. Jacob Litt at that time had his theaters in Milwaukee, St. Paul, and Minneapolis, and someone suggested that I send the play to him. I did so" (*Quincy Whig-Journal*, 22 Aug. 1920; repr. 25 Mar. 1979). After initially rejecting it, Litt produced *In Old Kentucky* in St. Paul on 4–6 August 1892. Although the play was moderately successful, Dazey quickly revised it before it was performed in Pittsburgh, New York, and other cities, where it attracted large audiences. During the next twenty-six years *In Old Kentucky* was performed thousands of times in the United States and was a huge success in England as well. Only *Uncle Tom's Cabin* was more frequently produced. In the twentieth century, such famous actors as Lionel Barrymore, Lynn Fontanne, Gary Cooper, and Katharine Hepburn appeared in the play.

In 1910 Dazey coauthored (with Edward Marshall) a novel based closely on the play, and the first of four film versions of *In Old Kentucky* was made in 1909 by the Vitagraph Company. The later movies were released in 1919, 1927, and 1935. Will Rogers starred in the last film, which varied considerably from the play text. Before his death in Quincy, Dazey wrote more than twenty other plays, including *The War of Wealth* (1895)—which was also a commercial success—*The Suburban* (1902), and *Home Folks* (1904). His last play, *Modern Madness*, was produced in Quincy in 1937.

None of Dazey's melodramas and comedies has significant literary value; his characters are types, and his plots are contrived. Even *In Old Kentucky*, which has such conventional characters as a humorously inept black servant and a wealthy Kentucky colonel, is notable chiefly for its enormous box office success. But through its reflection of a distinctive region, by means of characterization and setting, the play also antici-

pates more thoroughly realistic drama of the twentieth century.

• The best edition of *In Old Kentucky* was published in 1937. It includes Dazey's 1920 essay "How I Wrote 'In Old Kentucky.'" For a list of his plays, see *Who Was Who in the Theatre, 1912–1976*, vol. 2 (1978), pp. 618–19. A helpful sketch of his early life appears in *Portrait and Biographical Record of Adams County, Illinois* (1892), pp. 395–96. See also the brief article on Dazey (unsigned) in *Illinois Quest*, May 1937, p. 21, and his "Memories of Adams County" in that same issue, pp. 3–4. The most thorough obituary is in the *Quincy Herald-Whig*, 10 Feb. 1938.

JOHN E. HALLWAS

DEADY, Matthew Paul (12 May 1824–24 Mar. 1893), U.S. district judge for the District of Oregon, was born in Talbot County, Maryland, the son of Daniel Deady, a schoolteacher, and Mary Ann McSweeney. Following his mother's death in 1834, Deady lived in Baltimore for two years with his maternal grandparents, then returned to live with his father and four siblings on a southern Ohio farm.

In early 1841 Deady moved to nearby Barnesville, Ohio, where he spent four years as a blacksmith apprentice and earned a teaching certificate at the Barnesville Academy. He then taught school for a year in St. Clairsville, Ohio, before beginning law study with William Kennon, presiding judge of the local common pleas court. He joined the Ohio bar two years later, in 1847, and began a small practice with Judge Kennon's brother.

In 1849 Deady moved west, seeking greater opportunity. Convinced that gold mines disadvantaged a region by encouraging speculation and lawlessness, he chose as his destination Oregon rather than California. He settled in Lafayette, where he taught school and tended a store while establishing his law practice.

Deady quickly became a force in local Democratic politics. Elected to the territorial assembly in 1850, he won election to the council (upper house) in 1851 and became council president in 1852. He was a prominent member of the "Salem Clique" that, in an uneasy alliance with congressional delegate Joe Lane, controlled Oregon politics for nearly a decade.

In 1853 President Franklin Pierce appointed Deady to the territorial supreme court; he held that position until statehood in 1859. At that time Oregon voters elected him to the new state supreme court, but he chose instead to accept President James Buchanan's appointment as Oregon's first federal district judge, serving thirty-four years until his death.

Deady revered the law, especially the common law, as the foundation and guardian of a rational, orderly world. A devoted Anglophile, he read widely in English history and literature, and for him Westminster Hall was the supreme "bulwark of liberty and buttress of order." As he explained in "Law and Lawyers," an 1866 speech, "The common law is the source and panoply of all those features of our system which distinguish us from the subjects of absolute governments, ancient or modern—either by monarchs or majorities."

It was made by freemen for freemen." For Deady, as for others of his generation both within and outside the legal profession, constitutional and common law administered by wise and courageous judges represented the last best hope for control of political demagoguery and social disintegration.

Historians sometimes refer to Deady as Oregon's "Justinian" for his important role in drafting many of the state's early laws. He was president of the 1857 state constitutional convention and took an active part in many of its deliberations. He wrote the state's first codes of civil and criminal procedure, its first penal code, a landmark corporations statute, and many other miscellaneous laws. His thorough, annotated compilation of Oregon laws, completed in 1864, became known throughout the state for many years simply as the "Deady Code."

During his thirty-four years on the federal bench, Deady wrote hundreds of opinions, principally in admiralty, bankruptcy, public land law, constitutional law, criminal law, and immigration law. In general, he was deeply committed to the rule of law as a foundational norm of judicial decision making. Yet in areas lending themselves to more individualized, fact-based rulings, he also exhibited occasionally an activist willingness to reach results he believed were just as well as legal.

In admiralty, for example, Deady was part of a mid-century trend to extend greater federal protection to passengers, merchants, and sailors victimized in some way on the high seas. He interpreted federal admiralty jurisdiction expansively, ruled repeatedly for passenger and sailor victims of personal injury, extended wrongful-death protection to the high seas, and sought to balance the commercial needs of merchant shippers with those of merchant carriers. See, for example, *The Pacific* (1861), *Bernhard v. Creene* (1874), *Holmes v. Oregon & Calif. Ry. Co.* (1880), and *Olsen v. Flavel* (1888).

One important series of Deady opinions, extending over nearly two decades, were those interpreting the cornerstone of federal public land law in his region, the Oregon Donation Act of 1850. Those opinions helped resolve ownership of the valuable Portland and Salem land claims as well as title to millions of acres the federal government had granted for construction of five military wagon roads across the state.

Contrary to his general "fairness" orientation in admiralty disputes, Deady tilted toward "formalism" in litigation affecting land titles. He emphasized the importance to "civilized society" of secure land titles, common-law conveyancing rules undiluted by doctrines like estoppel, and literal interpretations of deed language. Although occasionally also invoking "equity" or "justice," his rulings in this area tended repeatedly to favor those who held formal legal title over those to whom the land arguably had been sold or given years earlier. See, for example, *Lownsdale v. City of Portland* (1861), *Fields v. Squires* (1868), *Stark v. Starr* (1870), and *Lamb v. Davenport* (1871).

Perhaps most notable among Judge Deady's many opinions were a remarkable series he wrote between 1876 and 1892 defending in outspoken terms the rights and sensibilities of immigrant Chinese. He repeatedly struck down discriminatory state and local laws, either as contrary to federal law or as beyond the state-delegated power of a municipality. He also construed sensibly and compassionately the federal Chinese Exclusion Acts of the 1880s, refusing to bar entry to the many Chinese immigrants manifestly not within the terms of the acts. And finally, in a dramatic, well-publicized 1886 charge to Portland's federal grand jury, he sought to protect the Chinese victims of white racism from mob violence by declaring such violence contrary to federal criminal statutes. For examples, see *Baker v. City of Portland* (1879), *In re George Moncan* (1882), *In re Wan Yin* (1885), and *In re Impaneling and Instructing the Grand Jury* (1886).

Deady married Lucy Ann Henderson in 1852. The couple had three children, all sons, two of whom became attorneys and one, a physician. In addition to his lengthy tenure as federal judge, Deady also served as first president of the University of Oregon Board of Regents and as longtime president of the Portland Public Library Association. He attended Trinity Episcopal Church regularly and died in Portland.

Matthew Deady dominated the Oregon legal landscape for forty years. A commanding presence both on and off the bench, he contributed a great deal to the orderly development of law and society in the early Far West. His service as Oregon's Justinian and his thirty-four years as its only federal district judge are his most notable and lasting achievements. He himself referred to them late in life as his "monument." In addition, however, the rectitude and dignity with which he always conducted both himself and his court contributed an important measure of moral leadership to his profession and to his community.

• Deady's papers, including an extensive collection of letters, are at the Oregon Historical Society in Portland. An early biographical source, written largely by Deady himself, is Hubert Howe Bancroft, *Chronicles of the Builders of the Commonwealth* (1890). Deady's diary, *Pharisee among Philistines: The Diary of Judge Matthew P. Deady 1871–1892*, ed. Malcolm Clark, Jr. (1975), is an important source of early Oregon legal, political, and social history. Two articles examining portions of Deady's life and career are Ralph James Mooney, "Matthew Deady and the Federal Judicial Response to Racism in the Early West," *Oregon Law Review* 63 (1984): 561–637, and "Formalism and Fairness: Matthew Deady and Federal Public Land Law in the Early West," *Washington Law Review* 63 (1988): 317–70.

RALPH JAMES MOONEY

DEALEY, George Bannerman (18 Sept. 1859–26 Feb. 1946), Dallas civic planning pioneer and newspaper publisher, was born in Manchester, England, the son of George Dealey, Sr., a shoeshop manager, and Mary Ann Nellins, the daughter of Dublin's William Nellins, one of Wellington's officers at Waterloo. Dealey's family moved to Liverpool, where he attended primary school and worked in a grocery, but after the family's bankruptcy in 1870, they sailed on a cotton windjammer freighter, the *Herbert*, for Galveston, Texas, where they had relatives and where his father began work as a tea and coffee merchant. During the next four years, young George worked as a Western Union telegraph messenger, as an errand runner for a cotton broker, for a saddle and harness manufacturer, at a leather and shoe firm, as a candymaker, in a hotel and a fruit store, and as a bell ringer and organ pumper for the Galveston Trinity Episcopal Church, although he was later active as a Presbyterian.

With little formal education, apart from some schooling in the first free public schools in Galveston and some night classes in the Island City Business College, young Dealey got his start in journalism in 1874, when he was hired as an office boy by the *Galveston News* for three dollars a week. By 1878 he was mail room clerk and later foreman, and by 1883 he had become the traveling agent and staff correspondent for the *News* in Waco, Austin, and Houston, where he was named head of the branch office. In April 1884, he married Olivia Allen, daughter of the copublisher of the Lexington, Mo., *Intelligencer*. They had five children.

Dealey was named business manager of the new *Dallas Morning News* when it was started by the *Galveston News* on 1 October 1885. His title was changed to manager in 1895 as the circulation of the Dallas paper exceeded that of the Galveston paper. Following the 1901 death of Colonel A. H. Belo, chief proprietor of the *News* operations since 1875, and the deaths of two other *News* senior executives shortly thereafter, Dealey became vice president and general manager of both papers in 1906. He declined to become president until 1920, after the deaths of Belo's widow in 1913 and her brother-in-law in 1919.

In 1923, as the Dallas paper suffered an advertising and circulation slump from the approaching depression, and since the Galveston paper had shown no profit since 1910, the *Dallas Morning News* sold the Galveston paper to a Galveston financier. In 1926 Dealey and associates bought the *Dallas Morning News* from the heirs of Colonel Belo. In 1928 Dealey's brother, James Quayle Dealey, a retired political science professor at Brown University and author of books on social and civic progress that influenced George, became editor in chief of the *Dallas News*. George was chairman of the board from 1940 until his death, but his ideas and ideals had guided the news and public service campaigns of the Dallas paper since before 1900.

Dealey was an activist publisher, practicing social responsibility, as he believed newspaper management should help shape news policies and take strong editorial positions even if they cost profits from advertising or circulation. Considered an independent Democrat, he generally supported Progressive and New Deal programs and campaigned to abolish the political corruption of the mayor-alderman type of government in favor of the more efficient and professional expertise of

the city commission and city manager forms, which he recommended for Dallas and other cities in the early 1920s.

Called "The Champion of Clean News," Dealey forbade sensational, inane, and vulgar news; he removed ads from page one and lost revenue when he refused ads for beer and liquor, dog and horse racing, and speculative oil drilling and production. When Adolph Ochs bought the *New York Times* in 1896 to remold it, he said (in 1928) that he got his "ideas and ideals for a clean, honest, high class newspaper" from the *Dallas Morning News* and the *Galveston News*.

Dealey's Christian charity and tolerance made him a philanthropic humanitarian. He raised money for victims of the 1900 Galveston hurricane. For needy and sick children and families unserved by scarce public agencies, he led efforts to establish the Texas Children's Hospital and the Dallas Family Welfare Bureau; to aid the rural poor in Texas, he sought to create programs for flood control and soil conservation. In the early 1920s, as a member of the National Commission on Interracial Cooperation, he forbade anti-Semitic references in the news and instructed editors to publish photos of distinguished African-American artists and scientists. Dealey and his *News* helped organize against the Ku Klux Klan. Staff writers prepared pamphlets and negative publicity which helped defeat the Klan candidate for Texas governor in 1924, although the *News* suffered heavy losses in ads and circulation.

Dealey's city planning zeal brought him national acclaim by planners and the press. The Cleaner Dallas League, which he organized in 1899, brought paved streets, garbage collection and sewer extensions, and sanitary inspectors for dumps, crematories, and sidewalk cuspidors. His own Dallas chapter of the American League for Civic Improvement in 1902 generated parks and flood control. Dealey brought the first city planner, George Kessler, to Dallas in 1910; helped secure Dallas as the site of the eleventh Federal Reserve Bank in 1913; campaigned for money and a site for Southern Methodist University in 1915; negotiated the removal of unsafe, ugly, downtown rail tracks and the construction of a unified rail terminal in 1916; and chaired a 1927 national conference on city planning in Dallas.

Although he declined public office, Dealey was an influential and active member of the National Municipal League and the American Planning and Civic Association. He was honored by Sigma Delta Chi, a professional journalism fraternity, as the "dean of American journalism" and in the *Southwestern Historical Quarterly* (17 Mar. 1947) as the "father of city planning in the Southwest." Journalists and planners admired him as an enlightened publisher whose business interests were combined with public service and defined ultimately by editors and writers enthusiastic about the Progressive and "City Beautiful" movements in the United States at the time. Dealey's Dallas experience was publicized in other cities and newspaper offices, where his emerging contemporaries faced similar urban challenges. These included not only Ochs, but Charles A. Dana of the *New York Sun*; James Gordon Bennett (1841–1918) of the *New York Herald*; Joseph Pulitzer of the New York *World*; and the publisher-planner of Kansas City, William Rockhill Nelson of the *Star*.

Dealey's death in Dallas brought telegrams from the White House and flags to half-staff in Texas in honor of its "first citizen," the English-Irish immigrant who realized the Horatio Alger dream. On 14 November 1949 a twelve-foot statue of Dealey was erected at the edge of the Dallas central business district in Dealey Plaza, near the Union Rail Terminal and *News* offices, and within a few yards of the spot where President John F. Kennedy was assassinated in 1963.

• Letters, correspondence, papers, documents, and photographs are catalogued and contained in the G. B. Dealey Library in the Hall of State in Dallas, operated by the Dallas Historical Society. Additional materials on Dealey are in the G. B. Dealey Collection at the *Dallas Morning News* and in the Fikes Hall of Special Collections and the DeGolyer Library Collection, both at Southern Methodist University. The two major biographical works are Ernest Sharpe, *G. B. Dealey of the Dallas News* (1955), and Sam Acheson, *Thirty-five Thousand Days in Texas: A History of the Dallas News and Its Forebears* (1938). See also Sam Acheson, "George Bannerman Dealey," *Southwestern Historical Quarterly*, 17 Mar. 1947, pp. 329–34; J. P. Dewey, "Romances of American Journalism," *Editor and Publisher*, 28 July 1928, p. 14; John E. Rosser, "G. B. Dealey of the News," *Southwest Review* 31 (Autumn 1946): 327–32; Dianne Hays Pingree, "George B. Dealey: The Mind, Heart and Conscience of the Dallas *News*," *Dallas Magazine*, Aug. 1977, pp. 33, 54–57. Biographical information can also be found in files at the Barker Texas History Center, University of Texas at Austin. Obituaries are in the *Dallas Morning News*, 27 Feb. 1946; the *New York Times*, 27 Feb. 1946; *Editor and Publisher*, 2 Mar. 1946, pp. 8, 70; *Proceedings, Philosophical Society of Texas* (1946), pp. 30–33; and *Texas House Journal*, reg. sess., 50th Legislature, 14 Jan.–21 Apr. 1947, p. 937.

GENE A. BURD

DEAN, Arthur Hobson (16 Oct. 1898–30 Nov. 1987), lawyer, government adviser, and diplomat, was born in Ithaca, New York, the son of William Cameron Dean, an engineering laboratory assistant, and Maud Campbell Egan. In 1915 Dean enrolled at Cornell University, where he earned money for expenses working as a night clerk at a hotel and as a bookkeeper at a bank. He interrupted his studies to serve in the navy during World War I. Returning to Cornell following peace, Dean received his A.B. in 1921. He then studied law at Cornell, where he was managing editor of the *Cornell Law Quarterly*. In 1923 he earned his LL.B. and gained admission to the New York bar. Dean then joined the prestigious New York City firm of Sullivan and Cromwell, which specialized in international law and where John Foster Dulles was senior partner. In 1924, following approval of the Dawes Plan for loans to promote Germany's economic recovery, Dulles chose Dean to help him negotiate financial and business transactions in Paris, Berlin, Rome, Milan, and London.

Dean traveled to Japan in 1927 to assist in arranging a bond issue of the Nippon Power Company worth $9 billion, which was opened to the American public the next year under terms unprecedented in the history of Japanese finance and investment. His reward for this stunning success was full partnership in 1929. For two decades thereafter, while providing advice to private businesses on assorted issues, Dean frequently served as legal counsel for English and American banks in corporate reorganizations and recapitalization of industrial firms, public utilities, and railroads in Asia and Europe. He also acted for many years as representative for Standard Oil of New Jersey. In 1932 Dean married Mary Talbott Clark Marden; they had two children. He began what would become regular service for the U.S. government a year later, when President Franklin D. Roosevelt named him to the Dickinson committee under the Department of Commerce, which prepared materials for drafting the Securities and Exchange Act of 1934. Thereafter, he helped write the Bankruptcy Act of 1938, the Trust Indenture Act of 1939, and the Investment Company Act of 1940. Dean served as well on several advisory committees to the Securities and Exchange Commission.

During World War II Dean instructed and supervised classes in piloting and navigation as an officer in the Coast Guard Reserve. Simultaneously, he served as counsel for the Investment Bankers Association and the Baltimore and Ohio Railroad. "The terrible destruction of World War II culminating in the dropping of the two atomic bombs" on Japan, he later recalled, "convinced me that it was imperative to set up a new, workable, and effective machinery for peace." In 1945, the year Dean resumed his law career, New York governor Thomas E. Dewey appointed him a trustee of Cornell University. Dean later became chair of the executive committee of Cornell's board of trustees and vice chair of the board of trustees for the New York state university system. After Dulles won a U.S. Senate seat in 1949, Dean replaced him as senior partner at Sullivan and Cromwell.

In September 1953 Dulles, who had become President Dwight D. Eisenhower's secretary of state, persuaded the president to appoint Dean as special deputy secretary of state with the rank of ambassador to head the delegation representing the United States and the sixteen other nations that had fought on the United Nations (UN) side in the Korean War in post-armistice negotiations with North Korea and China. Prior to his appointment, Dean visited South Korea and also served as adviser to the U.S. delegation during the special UN General Assembly session on Korea.

During the talks at Panmunjom from 26 October to 12 December 1953, Dean attempted to fulfill the provision of the Korean armistice agreement of 27 July 1953 that called for the convening of a political conference to determine Korea's future. His approach to negotiations with the Communists was "to listen, to be precise, determined, and willing to spend a lot of time, without any sign of being impatient, angry or annoyed." In accordance with his instructions, Dean proposed that only the belligerents participate in a conference devoted solely to deciding Korea's future. He advanced a compromise, however, that provided for the seating of five nonbelligerents without voting power along with the belligerents at a conference to convene in Geneva within twenty-eight to forty-two days after the preliminary meeting adjourned. Moscow could attend and vote but on the condition that it would accept the outcome. Despite employing a variety of ingenious legal maneuvers, Dean could not persuade either the Communists or President Syngman Rhee of the Republic of Korea to accept his formula.

Exchanges at the Panmunjom talks became increasingly vituperative. Dean called his counterparts "Soviet agents" who did not want permanent peace. On 9 December 1953 future Chinese foreign minister Huang Hua claimed that the United States was guilty of "deliberate treachery" in conspiring with Rhee the previous June to release thousands of North Korean prisoners of war who refused repatriation. Dean adjourned the talks because the Communists refused to apologize, and he left for home on 16 December. He reported to the American people that the "Chinese Communists are determined to keep North Korea politically and economically integrated into their own economy. They believe that at a long drawn-out conference the American negotiators will be forced by public opinion to give in." This was not enough for Republican senator Herman Welker of Idaho, who accused him of "appeasement." At a press conference in January 1954, Dean defended his record. "Communism is repugnant to every idea for which I stand," he declared. "In my judgment it should be fought tooth and nail."

Eisenhower persuaded Dean to interrupt his law practice again in 1958 and 1960 to serve as chief of the U.S. delegation at the Geneva Conference on the Law of the Sea. During these negotiations, several nations joined the Soviet bloc to support increasing the limits of the international definition of the territorial sea. Dean built enough support to block this plan but failed to secure approval for his compromise recognizing a six-mile limit. His efforts resulted, however, in agreements on fisheries, the high seas, the continental shelf, and right of access to the sea for landlocked nations. His reputation as a skilled negotiator prompted President John F. Kennedy to appoint Dean as head of the U.S. delegation to the Conference on Discontinuance of Nuclear Weapons Tests, which lasted from February 1961 to January 1962, and the Geneva Disarmament Conference, which met from January 1962 until February 1963, as well as U.S. representative at the UN General Assembly. Dean wrote several important weapons limitations proposals in these capacities, and he helped Special Adviser on Disarmament John J. McCloy draft the statute creating the autonomous Arms Control and Disarmament Agency (ACDA) in September 1961 to coordinate government policy on nuclear testing and disarmament.

Negotiations to control testing of nuclear weapons were at a standstill when Dean became chief U.S. negotiator. At issue were inspections. The United States wanted multinational teams to conduct frequent, mandatory, and reciprocal onsite inspections, but the Soviet Union insisted on a veto and inspection teams composed of nationals from the nation investigated. Kennedy instructed Dean to reassess the U.S. government's entire arms control policy. Dean then drafted the first comprehensive U.S. test ban treaty proposal, incorporating major concessions. His plan deleted the reciprocity provision, provided for equal membership from the West and Communist bloc on teams, and reduced the required number of annual inspections. However, the Soviets rejected his plan at Geneva in April 1961. By then Dean had concluded that the behavior of Moscow's delegates in these negotiations demonstrated "the ultimately hostile and revolutionary nature of Soviet goals," which were aimed at "the ultimate political victory of the Soviet Union over the rest of the world." The Soviet style was, he reported, "a curious mixture of feelings of arrogance and fear."

During September 1961 Dean helped Kennedy draft a sweeping plan for not just nuclear disarmament but eventual reduction of conventional forces to levels needed for maintaining internal order alone. When Dean presented the proposal in April 1962 at Geneva, the Soviets denounced it as "utterly unacceptable." He then, in August 1962, drafted two options for a limited test ban treaty, each option based on the fundamental premise that "reliable verification is the *sine qua non* for any disarmament proposals which are seriously meant." One option called for a partial, unsupervised ban covering sea and atmospheric tests at high altitudes, while the other was a comprehensive treaty providing for onsite inspections. That fall the Soviets rejected both options. In July 1963 Soviet leader Nikita Khrushchev accepted Kennedy's proposal to appoint personal emissaries to complete the negotiations. W. Averell Harriman finished the work on the Limited Nuclear Test Ban Treaty that Dean had begun. Kennedy personally invited Dean to attend the signing ceremony in Moscow on 5 August 1963. "After all," the president told him over the telephone, "it is your treaty." For Dean, his efforts had brought "the first breakthrough in all the years of effort since 1946 to reach some mutually satisfactory agreement with the Soviet Union on the control of nuclear weapons."

In July 1964 President Lyndon B. Johnson named Dean chair of the National Citizens Committee for Community Relations, an advisory body formed to assist in monitoring compliance with the Civil Rights Act of 1964. During 1965 he was cochair of the Lawyers Committee for Civil Rights under the Law and a member of a nonpartisan citizens group advising Johnson on foreign affairs. That same year Dean served on a panel studying ways to halt proliferation of nuclear weapons, which he saw as "the overriding arms problem of our time." In March 1968 he became a member of the Senior Advisory Group on Vietnam—the "Wise Men"—that considered the military's proposal to send 206,000 more troops. His advice helped to persuade Johnson to stop the bombing of

North Vietnam and propose peace negotiations. Meanwhile, Dean served as a trustee of the Bank of New York and general counsel of the American Metal Company, and he held directorships of several corporations. He also acted as rapporteur for the International Chamber of Commerce Association and worked on committees for bar associations both in New York City and the state of New York.

Dean provides valuable information and insights about his experiences as a disarmament negotiator in his book *Test Ban and Disarmament: The Path of Negotiation* (1966), which the author described as "too brief to be a history, too dry to be a memoir." He operated on the assumption that

disarmament and related problems are peculiarly big-power problems, [and] they are essentially political. . . . Just as Cain slew Abel, as long as there is greed and ambition, so long will men and nations be tempted to take what is not theirs. . . . Patience, persistence, calm toughness of mind, a nature impervious to insults, a constantly creative and resourceful mind, and unwillingness to be discouraged are all essential characteristics for the Western negotiator. (pp. 10, 47, 69)

Dean also authored *Business Income under Present Price Levels* (1949), and his articles appeared in *Fortune*, *Foreign Affairs*, the New York *Herald Tribune*, and several law journals. Dean retired in 1976, but he remained active in numerous philanthropic and civic organizations and was a trustee of North Country Hospital. He also served on committees studying state and federal legislation. He was a devoted collector of Americana and rare books, making it possible for Cornell to obtain a vast archive of manuscripts and printed materials on the public career of the marquis de Lafayette. An avid gardener and horticulturist, he turned his Oyster Bay estate into a floral showplace and created a wildlife sanctuary at his Nantucket summer home. Dean died in Glen Cove, Long Island.

• Most of Dean's papers are located at Sullivan and Cromwell, awaiting litigation to determine their disposition. His papers relating to negotiations on the Law of the Sea and a smaller amount of documents on disarmament are at Cornell University Library. Useful background on Dean's role in negotiations for the Limited Nuclear Test Ban Treaty appears in Harold K. Jacobson, *Diplomats, Scientists and Politicians* (1966), and Mary Milling Leeper, *Foreign Policy Formulation* (1971). Several sources provide details about his efforts to arrange a political conference to reunify Korea, including Rosemary Foot, *Substitute for Victory: The Politics of Peacemaking at the Korean Armistice Talks* (1990), Burton I. Kaufman, *The Korean War: Challenges in Crisis, Credibility, and Command* (1986), and David Rees, *Korea: The Limited War* (1964). See also *Current Biography* (1954); the *New York Times*, 22 Dec. 1953 and 15 Jan. 1954; and Nelson Lichtenstein, ed., *Political Profiles: The Kennedy Years* (1976). Dean's obituary is in the *New York Times*, 1 Dec. 1987.

JAMES I. MATRAY

DEAN, Bashford (28 Oct. 1867–6 Dec. 1928), zoologist and expert on ancient armor, was born in New York City, the son of William Dean, a lawyer, and Emma Frances Bashford. At the age of six Dean was fascinated by a helmet and other pieces of medieval armor at the house of a friend of his father. His interest in fishes began in childhood as well, during fishing trips with his father and then with an introduction to zoologist Edward Sylvester Morse.

He entered the College of the City of New York at the age of fourteen and graduated in 1886 with a degree in zoology. He began tutoring at that college and, at the same time, enrolled at Columbia University, where he received an A.M. in 1889 and a Ph.D. in zoology in 1890. His research there on American fossil fishes was directed by John Strong Newberry. Through Eugene Blackford, a friend of his father's, Dean began studying oyster beds in New York State. This work led to a position at the U.S. Fish Commission during summers from 1889 to 1901. In this capacity, he investigated oyster culture in several European countries and in Japan and visited many biological stations, which he described in a series of papers. On these trips he pursued his early interest in historic armor.

In 1890 Dean became the first director of the summer Biological Laboratory at Cold Spring Harbor, New York, for which he acquired a donation of land and a building. The next year he was appointed instructor at Columbia University and advanced to professor of zoology in 1904. Dean married Mary Alice Dyckman in 1893, who joined him on many travels; they had no children.

While teaching at Columbia University, Dean held other positions related to his dual interests. In 1903 he became curator of the department of fishes at the American Museum of Natural History in New York City and from 1926 was honorary (volunteer) curator there. He was also honorary curator of arms and armor at the Metropolitan Museum of Art in New York from 1906 to 1912, when he accepted a salary until 1927. During the First World War Dean advised the U.S. Army on protective armor and became a major in the ordnance branch, for which he designed a protective helmet for trench warfare.

In his studies of fishes Dean combined paleontology, embryology, and comparative anatomy. He published on fossil sharks and arthrodires, a group of armored fishes of the Devonian period. In his textbook *Fishes, Living and Fossil* (1895), he emphasized the older and more primitive forms, which are of special interest to students of evolution. In *Chimaeroid Fishes and Their Development* (1906), he presented observations on the embryology of this unusual group, from specimens that he had collected in the United States, Europe, and Japan, and he described fossil specimens and the anatomy of living forms. In several papers he described the embryology of the sturgeon, the garpike, the bowfin, and the hagfish. In the field he observed and later published on the nesting habits and spawning of these primitive fishes. Many of his publications are noted for his own carefully drawn illustrations, often as lithographic plates.

Dean's most significant publication was the three-volume *Bibliography of Fishes* (1916, 1917, and 1923), a monumental and carefully indexed listing of thousands of citations. The project began as his personal card file of references, to which he added constantly through the advice of colleagues and through visits to foreign countries. Dean's students also added entries to the file while they used it. In 1910, when the listing had become very large, Henry Fairfield Osborn of the American Museum of Natural History provided help in preparing it for publication. Several ichthyologists, including Louis Hussakof, Charles Rochester Eastman, Eugene Willis Gudger, and Arthur Wilbur Henn, participated in the editing and detailed indexing. Dean devoted considerable time to advising on the entire project, and he proofread the final text. On the publication of the third volume in 1923, the National Academy of Sciences awarded the Daniel Giraud Elliot Medal to Dean. Because of its completeness—its inclusion of materials on the pre-Linnaean period up until the ending date of 1914—this bibliography has continued to be useful to those who are tracing the taxonomy of fishes.

At the American Museum of Natural History, Dean had responsibility for the collection of fossil fishes, including Newberry's large collection and a great many specimens purchased for the museum from the estate of Edward Drinker Cope. Dean cataloged all of this material. He set up an exhibit of Devonian fishes and directed the installation of several mounted habitat groups of primitive fishes. He planned a full display on fishes, which, completed in 1928, was dedicated as the Hall of Fishes at the museum just before his death.

In 1906 Dean had first loaned many of his acquisitions of Japanese armor, which he had cataloged, to the Metropolitan Museum of Art. He later sold some pieces to the museum, and in 1914 he donated another 459 items. From 1910 he traveled to Europe almost yearly to acquire additional pieces of armor, and he was responsible for obtaining for the museum the large collection owned by William H. Riggs of Paris. In Syria he conducted archaeological investigations on the holy wars by the Knights Templar. The especial value of Dean's work was his knowledge and verification of the history and authenticity of each item. In his publications on armor he traced what he considered the evolution of its development. More than half of Dean's publications were on arms and armor, and he was recognized internationally as an expert.

At Columbia University Dean directed the research of graduate students, who enjoyed his two-handed use of the blackboard and what his biographer William K. Gregory called his "unassumed friendliness." Colleagues appreciated his thoroughness in detail and his enthusiasm. In his travels Dean enjoyed learning about foreign cultures, customs, and history. In 1910 France awarded him the Lamarck Medal and made him a chevalier of the Legion of Honor for his participation in advancing a memorial to the naturalist Jean Baptiste Lamarck. Dean died in Battle Creek, Michigan, where he had been seeking medical help.

• Dean's original card catalog on fishes has been incorporated into the ichthyological catalog at the American Museum of Natural History, which also has some of his letters related to the *Bibliography of Fishes* and some of his administrative letters in its Central Archives. Biographies are by William K. Gregory in *Science* 68, no. 1774 (28 Dec. 1928): 635–38; by "A. S. W." in *Nature* 123, no. 3090 (19 Jan. 1929): 99–100; by Henry Fairfield Osborn in *Natural History* 29, no. 1 (Jan.–Feb. 1929): 102–3; and in greatest detail by Gregory in *The Bashford Dean Memorial Volume*, published by the American Museum of Natural History (15 Dec. 1930), pp. 1–42, with bibliography. An obituary is in the *New York Times*, 8 Dec. 1928.

ELIZABETH NOBLE SHOR

DEAN, Dizzy (16 Jan. 1910–17 July 1974), baseball player, coach, and broadcaster, was born Jay Hanna Dean in Lucas, Arkansas, the son of Albert Dean and Alma Nelson, both migrant workers. "Dizzy," a nickname he acquired from his zany antics, had a younger brother, Paul, who also pitched in the major leagues. There has been some uncertainty about Dean's birthdate, birthplace, and baptismal name. According to Dean, the biographical confusion might stem from the fact that he liked to give every reporter a scoop. Dean said his other name, Jerome Herman, was adopted when he was seven years old. A playmate by that name died, and to console the boy's father, Dean said that he would take the youth's name as his own.

Dean attended school only until the fourth grade. While serving in the U.S. Army, Dean learned the basics of pitching. He later impressed St. Louis Cardinal scout Don Curtis at a tryout camp and was given a contract with St. Joseph, Missouri, of the Western League. Dean split the 1930 season between St. Joseph and Houston, of the Texas League, winning 25 decisions and losing 10 games. In September 1930 he tossed a three-hitter for the Cardinals against the Pittsburgh Pirates, gaining his first major league victory. The following year, Dean married Patricia Nash; they had no children. After hurling 304 innings and compiling 26 victories for Houston in the 1931 season, Dean joined the Cardinals permanently in 1932. The big right-hander won 18 contests and led the National League with 191 strikeouts and 4 shutouts his rookie season. For his efforts, the Cardinals paid him $3,000.

The following campaign, he became the workhorse of the Cardinal staff. He won 20 games and led the National League in games pitched (48), complete games (26), and strikeouts (199). The St. Louis team, which included Pepper Martin, Joe Medwick, Leo Durocher, Dean, and (beginning in 1934) Dean's brother Paul, was known as the Gas House Gang. This collection of diehard pranksters both on and off the field drove manager Frankie Frisch crazy with their usually good-natured antics. Dizzy, one of the era's most quotable players, proudly and regularly predicted tremendous successes for himself and his brother. These projected triumphs often were stated in unforgettable and grammatically aberrant English. Dean was saved, of course, because he almost always fulfilled the boast. He predicted that he and Paul collectively would win

45 games for the Cardinals in 1934, an incredible boast, since Paul had never pitched in the majors. Together they won 49 victories that year, with Dizzy becoming the only National League hurler since 1917 to post 30 victories. The Cardinals won the National League pennant that year and defeated Detroit in seven games to take the World Series.

The National League's most valuable player in 1934, in the balloting Dean outdistanced Paul Waner, who led the league with a .362 batting average. The following season, the Dean brothers teamed up to win 47 contests, 28 of which came in Dizzy's column. Over a four-year stretch beginning in 1933, Dean proved almost invincible on the mound. The 6'2" right-hander averaged better than 25 victories and 310 innings per season, led the National League in complete games each year, and paced the league in 1936 with 11 saves. Dean often aided his own cause with the bat. A .225 career hitter, he occasionally hit home runs.

On 21 September 1934, as the Cardinals battled the New York Giants for the National League pennant, Dean held the Brooklyn Dodgers hitless through seven innings. St. Louis won 13–0, on Dean's three-hitter. In the second game of the doubleheader, Paul Dean hurled a 3–0 no-hitter. Dizzy noted that he would have pitched a no-hitter against the Dodgers if he had known Paul was going to. The Cardinals won the 1934 World Series championship, as Dizzy and Paul each defeated the Detroit Tigers twice.

Dizzy pitched in the first All-Star game in 1933 and in each successive All-Star game through 1937. In the 1937 midseason classic, Dean started for the National League in Washington's Griffith Stadium. An Earl Averill line drive broke Dean's toe. Dean tried to return to the mound too soon and altered his stride to favor the injured foot, which strained his arm muscles, causing a very sore limb. Just before opening day of the 1938 season, the Redbirds traded Dean to the Chicago Cubs for pitchers Curt Davis and Clyde Shoun, outfielder Tuck Stainback, and $185,000. The Cardinals had informed Cubs owner Phil Wrigley of Dean's arm problems. Nothing remained but Dean's great control and baseball sense. Although he pitched only thirteen games for the Cubs in 1938, he won seven of eight decisions and recorded a 1.80 earned run average. Chicago edged the Pittsburgh Pirates for the National League pennant. Wrigley never believed that he had come up short in the deal, but Dean won only nine games over the next two campaigns for the Cubs. He was sent to Tulsa, Oklahoma, of the Texas League, during midseason in 1940.

Dean pitched one inning for the 1941 Cubs and served two months as a coach before becoming a St. Louis baseball broadcaster for Cardinals and Browns games on 12 July 1941. In 1947 Dean boasted that he could do as well as the Browns' pitchers. The Browns accordingly signed Dean to start the final game of the season. He hurled four scoreless innings and singled in his only at bat against the Chicago White Sox. Dean remained incredibly popular on the airwaves despite his frequent mangling of the English language. He started handling Game of the Week telecasts in 1950 and remained in sportscasting for twenty-five years. He was elected to the National Baseball Hall of Fame in 1953, his first year of eligibility. Dean's major league career included 150 victories, 83 defeats, 1,163 strikeouts, 26 shutouts, and a 3.02 earned run average in 317 games and 1,967.1 innings pitched. He died in Reno, Nevada.

• Biographical material is located in the Dizzy Dean File at the National Baseball Hall of Fame Library in Cooperstown, N.Y. For full-length biographies, see Vince Staten, *Ol' Diz: A Biography of Dizzy Dean* (1992), and Curt Smith, *Dean: America's Dizzy Dean* (1978). Complete statistical coverage of Dean's major-league career appears in *The Baseball Encyclopedia*, 8th ed. (1990), and in John Thorn and Pete Palmer, eds., *Total Baseball* (1989). Dean's life in broadcasting is recounted in Curt Smith, *Voices of the Game: The First Full-Scale Overview of Baseball Broadcasting, 1921 to the Present* (1987). Short biographies can be found in Martin Appel and Burt Goldblatt, *Baseball's Best: The Hall of Fame Gallery* (1977), Tom Meany, *Baseball's Greatest Players* (1953), David L. Porter, ed., *Biographical Dictionary of American Sports: Baseball* (1987), and Mike Shatzkin, ed., *The Ballplayers* (1990).

FRANK J. OLMSTED

DEAN, Gordon Evans (28 Dec. 1905–15 Aug. 1958), lawyer and public servant, was born in Seattle, Washington, the son of John Marvin Dean, a Baptist clergyman, and Beatrice Alice Fisken. A strong element of serendipity marked Dean's early career. As a student at the University of Redlands, he planned to be a teacher of English, but he changed his major to political science following his first traumatic encounter with students as an apprentice at a local junior high school. After graduating in 1927, he obtained a law degree at the University of Southern California (USC), where he came under the protective wing of the law school dean, Justin Miller. In 1930 Dean married Adelaide Williamson. They had two children before divorcing in 1953. Through the intercession of Miller, who in 1930 was appointed dean at Duke University, Dean that same year became assistant dean and instructor at Duke and acquired a master's degree in law from the university in 1932.

Dean's enthusiasm for teaching had not, however, notably increased from his undergraduate days, and in 1934 he accepted an offer from Joseph Keenan, special assistant to the U.S. attorney general, to join the Criminal Division of the Justice Department, headed by Brien McMahon. There Dean helped develop federal criminal law, the many loopholes of which were being profitably exploited by interstate felons, and he became chief of the Appellate Section in 1936. Between 1937 and May 1940 he served as special executive assistant, with responsibility for public relations, to two attorneys general, Homer Cummings and Robert Jackson. Resigning to join McMahon's Washington, D.C., law firm, Dean remained in private practice until 1943, when he joined Naval Intelligence with the rank of lieutenant, senior grade. In May 1945 Jackson, the newly appointed U.S. chief of counsel at the trial of the major war criminals at Nuremberg, Germany, assigned Dean to negotiate the tribunal's charter and rules of procedure with the other members and later to serve as head of press relations. Returning to the United States in the spring of 1946, Dean practiced law privately at Vista, California, and worked as a part-time professor of criminal law at USC.

In the second phase of his public career Dean assumed the leadership of the largest and most controversial governmental agency of the day during a period of intense domestic and international tension. Nominated by McMahon, now Democratic senator from Connecticut and chair of the Joint Committee on Atomic Energy, to fill the vacancy on the five-member U.S. Atomic Energy Commission (AEC) created by the resignation of William W. Waymack, Dean easily won Senate confirmation and took office on 24 May 1949. Although he possessed no scientific or technical expertise and was initially widely regarded as McMahon's proxy, Dean quickly established his independence. He immersed himself in the minutiae of atomic energy development and worked to clarify the tangle of jurisdictional conflicts that had sprung up among the commission, Congress, the military establishment, and private contractors. His collegial management style, civil service experience, and public relations skills were instrumental in the maintenance of harmonious relations both within the commission and among its various constituencies. In June 1950, following the retirement of the commission's first chair, David E. Lilienthal, Dean's reputation as a safe pair of hands combined with the energetic canvassing of McMahon secured him the position.

As chief commissioner, Dean presided over the first great postwar expansion of America's atomic energy capability, an initiative spurred by President Harry S. Truman's decision in January 1950 to proceed with the construction of thermonuclear weapons and by the deteriorating international situation created by the outbreak of the Korean War in June 1950. A vigorous Cold Warrior, Dean strongly supported both the thermonuclear bomb program and the development of tactical nuclear devices. Conscious of the strain imposed on the government's resources by the enormous growth of the atomic arsenal, however, he unsuccessfully opposed the building of a second national nuclear weapons laboratory at Livermore, California, as surplus to the nation's requirements. The Democratic defeat in the 1952 presidential election and the death of McMahon, his political patron, the same year ruled out the possibility of Dean remaining at the commission beyond his three-year term of office. On 30 June 1953 he resigned, yielding the chair to Lewis L. Strauss. That same year Dean married Mary Benton Gore; they had two children.

Dean's tenure as the head of the Atomic Energy Commission provided a much-needed period of stability after the organization's first turbulent years. While he was fortunate to escape the intense and often hostile scrutiny directed at his predecessor Lilienthal, who had accumulated many powerful political enemies in the course of a lengthy public career, Dean's congenial and unassuming personality, in addition to his relative anonymity, enabled him to reduce to a minimum the tensions inherent in the management of a vast, complex, and highly idiosyncratic organization whose activities were at once closely guarded secrets and the subject of intense public interest.

After his resignation, Dean, who moved to New York City, held directorships in several firms involved in banking and civil atomic energy production. He died when the commercial aircraft in which he was a passenger crashed at Nantucket, Massachusetts.

• Papers relating to Dean's tenure at the AEC are in the Atomic Energy Commission Files at the U.S. Energy Research and Development Administration in Washington, D.C. The most significant are collected in Roger M. Anders, ed., *Forging the Atomic Shield: Excerpts from the Office Diary of Gordon E. Dean* (1987). An unpublished, first-person manuscript, "The Reminiscences of Gordon Dean," is in the Columbia University Oral History Research Office. Covering the period from his birth until 1940, this manuscript provides much detail on his legal career. Dean's only significant publication, an explanatory text on atomic energy issues, is *Report on the Atom: What You Should Know about the Atomic Energy Program of the United States* (1953). Additional biographical information is in a publication of the Joint Committee on Atomic Energy, *Hearings before the Senate Section of the Joint Committee on Atomic Energy, Eighty-first Congress, First Session, on Confirmation of Gordon E. Dean and Henry DeWolf Smyth as Members of the Atomic Energy Commission, May 12 and 18, 1949* (1949). Dean's work at the AEC is also discussed extensively in Richard G. Hewlett and Francis Duncan, *A History of the United States Atomic Energy Commission*, vol. 2, *Atomic Shield, 1947–1952* (1969). An obituary is in the *New York Times*, 17 Aug. 1958.

R. M. DOUGLAS

DEAN, James (8 Feb. 1931–30 Sept. 1955), actor, was born James Byron Dean in Marion, Indiana, the son of Winton R. Dean, a dental technician with the Veterans Administration, and Mildred M. Wilson. While his mother encouraged his interest in music and drawing, relatives encouraged his interest in motorcycles and cars. They also remembered Dean's unusual kindness, cleverness, and stubborness.

In 1936 the VA transferred Dean's father to Santa Monica, California. Four years later Dean's mother died of breast cancer. His father sent Dean to his aunt, Ortense Winslow, and her husband, Marcus, in Fairmount, south of Marion. Dean lived on their farm until he graduated from high school in 1949.

His speech teacher, Adeline Nall, encouraged his talents as an actor. In his senior year she cast him as Kolenkov, the flamboyant Russian ballet-master, in *You Can't Take It with You*. That year Dean won a state forensic title and competed at the national championships with a dramatic monologue based on "The Madman's Manuscript," from *The Pickwick Papers*. He disobeyed Nall's instruction to shorten the piece and was disqualified for going overtime.

Following graduation, Dean returned to California to act professionally. Gene Nelson Owen at Santa

Monica Community College worked with him on *Hamlet*. Against her advice, he transferred to the University of California at Los Angeles and won the role of Malcolm in a mainstage production of *Macbeth* directed by Walden Boyle. Agent Isabelle Draesmer then signed him, and in early 1951 he appeared on television in a soft drink commercial and in a drama as John the Baptist. He also joined a class taught by actor James Whitmore, who told him about the Actors Studio in New York.

Dean moved to New York City in September 1951 and signed with agent Jane Deacy. Instead of auditioning for the Actors Studio, he worked in television. His reputation as a gifted actor and an unreliable co-worker grew. He was unable or unwilling to agree to one interpretation of a gesture, move, or speech and then repeat it. In a medium requiring precise coordination of cameras and actors, Dean's unpredictability exasperated nearly everybody. Nevertheless, the frequency and pattern of his work signifies that his talent outweighed fears about his lack of professionalism. Dean appeared in at least twenty-nine episodes of nineteen television shows between February 1952 and May 1955 and moved from supporting to featured roles.

His career onstage in New York did not fare so well. He was accepted at the Actors Studio in 1952 but clashed with its head, Lee Strasberg. He was cast in three plays, one of which never opened. The two that did, *See the Jaguar* and *The Immoralist*, impressed no critics, though Dean received good notices. For his role in the latter play, as a homosexual Morroccan houseboy, he won an award as the best newcomer of the 1953–1954 season and the attention of Elia Kazan. Kazan cast Dean as Cal, the rebellious son, in a movie of John Steinbeck's *East of Eden*.

Dean returned to California and completed Kazan's film by June 1955. Dean won two more parts: Jim Stark, a frustrated teenager, in *Rebel without a Cause* and Jett Rink, a violent ranch hand, in *Giant*, based on Edna Ferber's novel. None of the films was released before Dean's death in a high-speed automobile collision near Cholame, California. He received posthumous Academy Award nominations for best actor for his roles in *East of Eden* and *Giant*.

Dean's acting career does not account for the continuing interest in his life, although many think him to have been an actor as talented and exciting as Marlon Brando and Montgomery Clift, both of whom Dean admired. The most important feature of Dean's legend is the perception that his death represents the violent destruction of beauty. Further, it may be said that Dean died because of a character flaw, a reckless indulgence of personal whim; in the fatal instance, he simply wanted to drive his new sportscar as fast as possible. To this sorrow may be added the perception that the characters he played magnified conflicts in his private life with his father and with various friends, lovers, and co-workers, conflicts arising from his disdain for authority, his willingness to expose and exploit weaknesses in himself and others to achieve success, and his curiosity or confusion about his sexuality.

Homosexual men and heterosexual women found Dean's appearance and demeanor highly attractive. In the former group, James DeWeerd, a clergyman, and Rogers Brackett, an advertising executive and television producer, count most importantly. In Fairmount, DeWeerd introduced Dean to literature, the arts, and fine dining, as well as homosexual sex. In Los Angeles and New York, Brackett offered professional advice and social contacts. The roster of disciplined, successful women who nurtured and encouraged Dean is impressive. In addition to those already mentioned, Mildred Dunnock, Geraldine Page, Ruth Goetz, Julie Harris, Natalie Wood, and Elizabeth Taylor acted with him. Each found his talent breathtaking. Many others testify that his intelligence, sensitivity, and passion for life created intensely memorable relationships. Dean never married. Launched by three providentially posthumous films, the legend of James Dean is sustained by two dozen books, millions of photographs, and a festival in Fairmount that draws more than 50,000 persons on the anniversary of his death.

• The facts of Dean's life are not in dispute, but the types and intensities of the artistic and psychological influences in his life remain subjects of discussion, if not controversy. The following biographies adequately introduce the main questions: William Bast, *James Dean: A Biography* (1956), by a close friend; Venable Herndon, *James Dean: A Short Life* (1974), by a screenwriter and critic; Joe Hyams, with Jay Hyams, *James Dean: Little Boy Lost* (1992), by a veteran show business reporter; and Paul Alexander, *Boulevard of Broken Dreams: The Life, Times, and Legend of James Dean* (1994), by a former *Time* reporter and freelance journalist. All three of Dean's films and his television appearances on the television series "Tales of Tomorrow" are available on videotape, as are three other documentary retrospectives.

ARVID F. SPONBERG

DEAN, Julia (22 July 1830–6 Mar. 1868), actress, was born in Pleasant Valley, New York, the daughter of Edwin Dean, an actor, and Julia Drake, an actress. Dean's mother died after her birth, and her father soon remarried, leaving his daughter to be raised by his Quaker parents. When Dean was eleven, her father turned her over to his new wife to help at the boardinghouse they kept. Dean appeared in small parts with Noah Ludlow's company in the midwestern circuit of theaters established by Dean's grandfather, Samuel Drake. During the 1844–1845 season she performed in Mobile, Alabama, as a utility actress in a company with the young Joseph Jefferson (1829–1905).

In his autobiography Jefferson wrote of Dean with affection and recounted the circumstances that led to her rise from utility actress to leading lady. When the actress who was to play in *Wives as They Were and Maids as They Are* fainted and was unable to go on, the prompter suggested Julia Dean, who took the role despite the doubts of her manager. Dean made her New York debut as Julia in James Sheridan Knowles's *The Hunchback* on 18 May 1846 at the Bowery Theatre, where she became one of the most popular young actresses in America and made the role of Julia one of her most famous. Dean went on to become one of the leading juvenile actresses in America and several years later was engaged to perform at a theater managed by Jefferson in Charleston, South Carolina.

On 21 January 1855 Dean married Dr. Arthur P. Hayne, son of Robert Y. Hayne, a senator from South Carolina. The next year she accepted an offer to appear in starring roles from her repertoire in San Francisco, where she was an overnight success in performances of *The Hunchback, Romeo and Juliet*, and *Camille*, among other plays. She was adored on the West Coast and played a record thirty nights at the Metropolitan Theatre. She performed in many places in California, from Sacramento to the mining camps. She traveled as far north as Victoria, British Columbia, where she appeared on stage with the young David Belasco, who as a child had lived in Victoria before moving to San Francisco and later to New York as a producer, director, and playwright. DeWitt Bodeen wrote that "every man was at [Dean's] feet—from the coarse Sierra miner to the gilded youth of San Francisco. For almost ten years she was the star of the West" (p. 65). During this time Dean also had four children, two of whom survived infancy. However, the marriage was miserable and eventually led to a separation followed by public gossip and scandal.

In 1865 Dean finally obtained a divorce from Hayne, with whom she left her two living children, and decided to return to the East. She arrived in Salt Lake City by stagecoach from San Francisco with an entire company. She opened in *Camille* and was such a hit that she and her leading man, George B. Waldron, were hired to stay the season. In 1867, before she left Utah, she was married to James G. Cooper, a federal official.

Dean was never able to recapture her former renown, but she continued to do well outside of New York, appearing in Pittsburgh with Lawrence Barrett. However, her brilliance seemed to have been diminished by her unhappy marriage and perhaps by the less exacting audiences of the West. In *Annals of the New York Stage*, theater historian George C. D. Odell recorded that she was "no longer the radiant star of earlier years, but the saddened woman and rather coarsened artist, whose later work her former admirers deplored" (vol. 8, p. 162).

Critic Laurence Hutton described Dean's last appearance in the fall of 1867 at the Broadway Theatre: "Her support was indifferent, and her success not great. She occasionally delighted her audiences with bursts of her old force; but the performances as a rule still continued to offer sad contrasts to her early and perfect representations" (Hutton, p. 145). Dean died after childbirth in New York City and was buried with her baby daughter in Port Jervis, New York.

Julia Dean was the leading actress of youthful roles in America for ten years and was highly regarded for her natural style. Writing twenty years after her death, the theater critic William Winter remembered Dean with pleasure:

In person, Julia Dean was tall, stately, graceful, and interesting. Her voice was sweetly plaintive, the soft and gentle expression of her countenance harmonized with her voice and both fitly expressed a delicate, sensitive, refined, affectionate nature. As an actress, while she always manifested a quick imagination and gave a sense of power, she was most successful in delineating gentle phases of character and emotion and the milder aspects of human experience. (Winter, pp. 75–76)

• Clipping files on Dean are in the theater collections at the Harvard University Library, the Boston Public Library, and the New York Public Library for the Performing Arts, but many of the sources are unreliable, and many dates and details are contradictory. The major source of biographical material is DeWitt Bodeen's chapter on Dean in *Ladies of the Footlights* (1937). George C. D. Odell, *Annals of the New York Stage*, vols. 5–8 (1931–1936), documents her New York appearances, especially her performances in the role of Julia. Commentary on her acting is in Laurence Hutton, *Plays and Players* (1875), and William Winter, *Brief Chronicles* (1889). *The Autobiography of Joseph Jefferson* (1890) recounts the working relationship between Dean and Jefferson. Other references to her work and to her time in San Francisco are in Edmond M. Gagey, *The San Francisco Stage: A History* (1950).

SUSAN S. COLE

DEAN, Julia (13 May 1878?–18 Oct. 1952), actress, was born in St. Paul, Minnesota, the daughter of Albert Clay Dean and Susan Martin. She was named after her aunt, Julia Dean, a noted actress of the mid-nineteenth century. After the family moved to Salt Lake City, Utah, young Julia followed in her aunt's footsteps, making her first stage appearances in a local stock company.

Her first professional appearance was on 7 October 1897 in Joseph Jefferson's company in Portland, Maine. She was with the Jefferson company for one season, playing two small roles in *Rip Van Winkle* (Jefferson's signature piece) and the role of May Fielding in *The Cricket on the Hearth*. The next year found her at the Pike Theatre Stock in Cincinnati, Ohio, before she joined James F. Neill's company for three seasons playing lengthy engagements in leading western cities. The praise of two San Francisco critics won Dean her New York debut in *The Altar of Friendship* (1902) with Nat Goodwin and Maxine Elliott. This was followed with featured roles in *Merely Mary Ann* (1903) and *The Serio-Comic Governess* (1904). Although she was applauded for her sympathetic portrayal of Anna Gray, the title character in *The Little Gray Lady* (1906), the play was a failure, and she was once again relegated to a supporting role in her next play, *A Marriage of Reason* (1907). Dean played the saucy soubrette role in *The Round-Up* (1907) and appeared as Emma Brooks in *Paid in Full* (1908), which she also toured.

Critic Johnson Briscoe, writing in 1910, claimed that Dean had an "odd stage career. . . . While there has always been a ready demand for her services, she has played such a wide variety of parts, leads, soubrettes, ingenues, emotional and comedy parts that she has scarcely reached a position of real, established standing." However, Dean was on the verge of finding her métier in emotional roles. Portraying Christiane de Maigny in Belasco's *The Lily* (1909), she was praised for her "beautifully expressed emotionalism and fervor." She scored another success in the role of Virginia Blaine in *Bought and Paid For* (1911), in which she "assuredly makes the suffering seem real." Dean toured *Bought and Paid For* during the 1912–1913 season and followed that with *Her Own Money* (1913), in which she played the role of Mary Alden "with much charm and variety and a complete and very compelling suggestion of trying emotional experience." It was these roles that won Dean the admiration of legions of young "matinee girls" who ardently followed the actress's career. Although most of Dean's remaining stage roles followed in this vein of strong and vivid emotionalism, winning the actress high praise, the plays were critical failures. Her last major New York appearance was opposite George Arliss in *Poldekin* (1920).

During the advent of feature films, Dean had won minor notice in such movies as *Judge Not; or, The Woman of Mona Diggs* (1915), *How Molly Made Good* (1915), and *The Ransom* (1916). She did not actively pursue a full-time film career, however, until after a hiatus from the stage of over ten years and after she had moved to Hollywood. In 1944 she appeared as Julia Farren, a half-crazed character actress, in *The Curse of the Cat People* and in the role of Deria in *Experiment Perilous*. What followed was a series of films, both straight and musical, in which Dean played older women roles: Mrs. Allen in the musical *Do You Love Me?* (1946), Mrs. Wilton in *Magic Town* (1947), the Archduchess Stephanie in *The Emperor Waltz* (1948), the Old Lady in the star-studded (Cary Grant and Jeanne Crain) cast of *People Will Talk* (1951), and Aunt Clara in her final film, *You For Me*, in 1952. Dean was married to Orme Caldara. She died in Hollywood.

Never a star of note, Dean's sustained theatrical career, however, is typical of most actors and actresses through the ages. During the late nineteenth century she had played bit parts with old troupers and worked her way through the ranks of minor stock companies until she landed featured roles on Broadway. This hands-on training had provided her with a "thoroughly complete knowledge of her craft." Although applauded for her "wealth of versatility" as well as her "unlimited ambition and enthusiasm," Dean was unable to parlay that skill and ambition into a stellar career. Hampered by looks that she herself admitted were not beautiful (she often quoted one western critic who had written, "She's ugly, but she *can act*"), she remained primarily a supporting player, first on stage and later in film, to the end of her long career.

• Dean's career can be gleaned from occasional articles featuring the actress as well as reviews of her stage and screen performances. Scrapbooks of the actress's stage career are available in the Billy Rose Theatre Collection at the New York Public Library for the Performing Arts, Lincoln Center. Detailed accounts of Dean's early stage career are found in Johnson Briscoe, "The Younger Generation," *Green Book Album* 4 (Aug. 1910): 371–73, and in Burns Mantle, "Dry-Cleaning the Drama," *Munsey's Magazine*, Feb. 1914. An illuminating personal profile is found in David H. Wallace, "An Actress for Life," *New York Dramatic Mirror*, 1 Oct. 1913. An obituary is in the *New York Times*, 19 Oct. 1952, and *Variety*, 22 Oct. 1952.

JANE T. PETERSON

DEAN, Vera Micheles (29 Mar. 1903–10 Oct. 1972), international affairs specialist and teacher, was born in St. Petersburg, Russia, the daughter of Alexander Micheles, a Russian of German-Jewish background who immigrated to the United States in 1888 and later returned to Russia as a sales representative for the U.S.-based Gillette Company, and Nadine Kadisch, a translator of English novels into Russian. Growing up in Russia, the Micheles children received private tutoring and became fluent in seven languages. After the 1917 revolution, the family had to move to London for political reasons, and Vera was sent to Boston. There she attended business school, worked briefly as a stenographer, and then enrolled at Radcliffe College. After graduating with distinction in 1925, she earned an M.A. from Yale University. In 1928 she received her Ph.D. from Radcliffe in international law and international relations and became a U.S. citizen.

After graduation Micheles began working for the Foreign Policy Association (FPA), an organization with which she would be associated for thirty years. She also married William Johnson Dean, an attorney, in August 1929. After the death of her husband in 1936, she continued to support her two young children by lecturing and writing.

During her long career in international affairs, Dean served as director of research for the FPA (1938–1961) and edited the organization's bimonthly *Foreign Policy Bulletin*, designed to educate public opinion on matters of foreign affairs. She also taught international relations at many institutions: Barnard College (1946), Harvard University (1947–1948), Smith College (1952–1954), the University of Rochester (1954–1962), and New York University (1962–1971). In addition, she wrote articles on international relations for many scholarly and popular magazines and appeared frequently on radio and television. She traveled widely throughout the world, gathering firsthand material for her writings and lectures. She belonged to the Episcopalian church, the Cosmopolitan Club, and the American Women's Association.

Throughout her life Dean was an eloquent advocate for internationalism and collective security. She spoke out against isolationism before World War II. Her book *Europe in Retreat* (1939) was acclaimed as a masterful analysis of factors leading to the Munich settlement. Throughout the war she wrote on issues related to postwar reconstruction and stressed the need for structures of international cooperation. In 1945 she advised the U.S. delegation that founded the United Nations and, through her work with the FPA, energetically endorsed U.S. membership in the UN and other international organizations. For years, she served as the UN correspondent for India News and Feature Alliance, an Indian news service.

During and after the war Dean also stressed the need to build a cooperative relationship with the Soviet Union. Although she acknowledged the profound differences between Russia and the West, in books such as *Russia: Menace or Promise* (1947) she expressed the belief that existing divisions would soften as the systems of the two countries somewhat converged. She applauded the Soviet Union's dissolution of the Comintern in 1943 and argued that Russia was showing itself to be more interested in its own security than in expanding communism outside of its borders. Holding out the hope of future collaboration between the United States and the Soviet Union, she emphasized that the most important struggles of the postwar era ought to be against those forces that she believed caused warfare: poverty, disease, and illiteracy.

Greed and fear, she wrote, were among the most destructive forces of the time. She thus denounced the excesses of anticommunist crusaders, even as they denounced her views for being dangerous and "soft" on communism. In *Foreign Policy without Fear* (1953) she decried the narrowness of McCarthyite anticommunism and argued that greater tolerance for diverse views would enhance the credibility, and thus the security, of the United States in the world. By the late 1950s much of her writing was devoted to the growing importance of the non-Western world. For her contributions, Dean was awarded the French Legion of Honor in 1947 and the Jane Addams Medal in 1954.

After a series of strokes, Dean died in New York City. Her many books, articles, and pamphlets make up an impressive compendium of twentieth-century internationalist thought. By articulating an alternative to Cold War orthodoxies of a militant containment policy, she helped keep alive the traditions of progressive internationalism that focused on international cooperation and economic development.

• Some of Dean's correspondence, a clippings file, an outline for an autobiography (with her son's introduction), and her mother's autobiography are in the Vera Micheles Dean Papers in the Schlesinger Library, Radcliffe College. The Foreign Policy Association's publications, *Foreign Policy Bulletin, Foreign Policy Reports*, generally reflect her views. Her many books include *The Four Cornerstones of Peace* (1946), *The United States and Russia* (1947), *Europe and the United States* (1950), *The Nature of the Non-Western World* (1957; rev. ed., 1966), *New Patterns of Democracy in India* (1959), and *Builders of Emerging Nations* (1961). A sketch of her life appears in Judy Barrett Litoff and Judith McDonnell, eds., *European Immigrant Women in the United States: A Biographical Dictionary* (1994). A brief obituary is in the *New York Times*, 12 Oct. 1972.

EMILY S. ROSENBERG

DEANE, Charles (10 Nov. 1813–13 Nov. 1886), antiquarian and historian, was born in Biddeford, Maine (then part of Mass.), the son of Ezra Deane, a physician. Charles Deane's mother (given name unknown) was the daughter of Reverend Silas Moody of Kennebunkport. His father had practiced medicine in several different towns in Maine before settling in Biddeford. There Deane attended the public school and a classical school led by Phineas Pratt. The family intended for him to attend Bowdoin College, but this was prevented by the death of his older brother. He worked in two stores, one in Kennebunkport and one in Saco, before he went to Boston at the age of nineteen.

Deane found a salesman position with the dry goods house of Waterston, Pray & Company in Boston. He became a partner in the enterprise in 1840 and in the following year married Helen Waterston, the oldest daughter of the owner.

While continuing to work as a salesman, Deane became increasingly interested in the history of Massachusetts. By 1843 he had become aware of the distinct difference between the Plymouth Colony (1620–1692) and the Massachusetts Bay Colony (1629–1774). He did a great deal of reading on his own and by the late 1840s had become something of an expert on the early history of colonial New England. He continued working for the family company until his retirement in 1864. Made wealthy by his many years in industry, Deane was then able to devote himself entirely to what had become the passion of his life: the collection, dissection, editing, and writing of historical materials.

Deane was interested in a great variety of historical questions and researches. No piece of knowledge was too small or too unimportant to warrant his attention. He began his work by editing the first patent that had been given to the Plymouth Company in 1621. Continuing his interest in the pilgrims, he learned that the long-lost manuscript of Governor William Bradford had been located in the library of the bishop of London. Deane paid Joseph Hunter, the president of the Society of Antiquaries in London, forty pounds sterling to make an accurate transcript of the document. Deane added many scholarly footnotes to the work and published it in the *Collections* of the Massachusetts Historical Society in 1856. Little, Brown and Company published an edition the same year. On account of the initiative of Deane and the careful transcription of Hunter, Bradford's famous *Of Plymouth Plantation* became a standard source of knowledge and inspiration for Americans. The original manuscript was returned to Massachusetts in 1897 by Ambassador Thomas Bayard.

The securing of the Bradford manuscript was the greatest coup in Deane's scholarly career, but he went on to edit the first publication of the Prince Society, William Wood's *New England Prospect* (1865), and to research matters as obscure as the identity of the belfry in which the lantern was hung that signaled Paul Revere to begin his famous ride and the ancient rules of Harvard College. Nor was Deane's interest limited to New England. He took a great interest in early Virginia and researched the matter of John Smith and Pocahontas. He published the collected edition of John

Smith's writings as *True Relation of Virginia* (1860). The advent of the Civil War in 1861 was a painful matter for Deane, who loved both Massachusetts and Virginia, but during the war he remained a staunch Republican, loyal to the notion of an American nation that was indivisible.

In 1866 Deane went to Antwerp Belgium, to represent the American Antiquarian Society at the archaeological congress held there. He then visited London and parts of the English countryside, seeking out source materials for his work. In 1872 he made a trip through the southern states and maintained his strong interest in the history of the colonial origins of the American South. Numerous honors came to Deane throughout the last decades of his life. He was made a member of the Massachusetts Historical Society (1849), the American Antiquarian Society (1851), and the London Society of Antiquaries (1878). He received an honorary A.M. from Harvard in 1856 and an honorary LL.D. from Bowdoin in 1871. He died in Cambridge, Massachusetts.

Deane was one of a number of nineteenth-century Americans who combined a skill in business with a great interest in history. Both a man of affairs and a man with a passion for the past, he set an example that many historians would seek to emulate. His work was concluded prior to the formation of the American Historical Association (1884), but his tireless researches had already made their mark by that time.

Although some twentieth-century historians have tended to dismiss Deane as an antiquarian rather than a critical historian, his work was crucial in the development of an American historical tradition. Lacking the many centuries of history of European nations, the young United States greatly needed to embrace, enhance, and even mythologize its beginnings (the Mayflower, Bradford, John Smith, and Jamestown) simply in order to develop a national consciousness. Although this form of historical "nationmaking" has largely been rejected by post-1960 historians, the United States owes a large debt of gratitude to men such as Deane who created a sturdy edifice that can indeed be contested and shaken by his collegial descendants. Less known than Francis Parkman or George Bancroft, Deane was as important as those men in the building of a national consciousness.

• Many of Deane's voluminous writings are cataloged in Massachusetts Historical Society, *Proceedings*, 2d ser., 6 (1891): 224–28. The best single source for a study of Deane's life remains the memorial written by Justin Winsor, "Memoir of Charles Deane, LL.D.," *Proceedings*, 2d ser., 7 (1892): 45–89. Expressions of appreciation of him by many prominent Bostonians are in *Proceedings*, 2d ser., 5 (1890): 116–41. See also the entry on Deane in William Russell Foster's *Mount Auburn Biographies* (1953).

SAMUEL WILLARD CROMPTON

DEANE, Samuel (10 July 1733–12 Nov. 1814), writer and Congregational minister, was born in Dedham, Massachusetts, son of Samuel Deane, a deacon, and Rachel Dwight. His father was a blacksmith and tavern keeper, who in 1745 moved the family to Norton, where he opened a public house. Samuel graduated from Harvard College in 1760 at the advanced age of twenty-seven. Although an excellent scholar, a lover of the classics, and a poet of some ability, he was temporarily expelled in his junior year for "prevaricating with his tutor." This misfortune did not prevent him from serving as college librarian for a year and tutor for three years after he graduated. He contributed substantially from his small salary to replace books and instruments lost in the college fire of 1764.

Deane was ordained in October 1764 as pastor of the First Church of Falmouth (now Portland), Maine. His conciliatory personality attracted young people to a parish riven with dissension between New Lights and Old Lights. An Arminian (a believer in salvation through good works) who stressed ethics rather than theology, he was a tall, portly, dignified presence in the pulpit. His sermon style did not impress John Quincy Adams, who complained of "a whining sort of tone . . . which would have injured the sermons if they had been good."

Deane preached to the American army outside Boston in 1775 and fervently supported the Revolution. He complained of the burning of Falmouth by British naval captain Henry Mowat, "that execrable scoundrel and monster of ingratitude," who bombarded a community that refused to provide him with cannon, arms, and hostages to ensure its good behavior. In 1776 Deane married Eunice Pearson. The couple had no children.

After the war, Deane ran into trouble from Quakers, who sat in on his sermons and spontaneously disparaged them, because they were critical of the Quakers' lack of patriotism, as Maine's Quaker community was pacifist and opposed to Deane's support of a military war. His congregation reduced his salary from £100 to £75 per year. He declined election to the Massachusetts U.S. Constitutional Convention in 1788. Deane was becoming more interested in scientific agriculture than in religion and politics. A charter member of the American Academy of Arts and Sciences, in 1790 he published his magnum opus, *The New England Farmer or Georgical Dictionary, Containing a Compendious Account of the Ways and Methods in Which the Most Important Art of Husbandry in All Its Various Branches Is or May Be Practiced to the Greatest Advantage in This Country*. A review in *Massachusetts Magazine* (3 [1791]: 107) expressed hope that it would fulfill its purpose of ensuring that "the employ of farmers shall no more be treated with contempt; when the rich, the polite, and the ambitious shall glory in paying a close attention to their farms" as did the newly elected president, George Washington.

Deane himself conducted scientific and agricultural experiments at "Pitchwood Hill," his farm in Gorham, Maine, where he continued to write verse. He hoped to establish the first college in Maine in Portland but nevertheless worked hard on behalf of Bowdoin, located in Brunswick, and served as its vice president and a trustee from 1794 until his death. Brown University awarded him a D.D. in 1790 to honor his treatise on agriculture, the first such encyclopedia written and published in the United States.

A staunch Federalist and friend of Timothy Pickering, Deane opposed the Embargo of 1807 and regarded the Jeffersonian Republicans as "a few designing men, who are under a dreadful influence." He also advocated the separation of Maine from Massachusetts given its inadequate representation in the state legislature combined with heavy taxes on the frontier towns; one separatist convention met in his house. Deane died suddenly in Portland after announcing "Death has lost all his terrors—I am going to my friend Jesus, for I have seen him this night."

Deane symbolized the union of Christianity with enlightenment ideas that characterized many members of the seaboard elite in late eighteenth-century America. His interest in science and agriculture not only as scholarly pursuits, but as vehicles for national greatness, also typified men such as Franklin, Washington, and Jefferson.

• Deane's journals from 1761 to 1801, located at the Portland Public Library, have been partially published in *Journals of the Rev. Thomas Smith and the Rev. Samuel Deane, Pastors of the First Church in Portland*, 2d ed. (1849). Clifford K. Shipton, *Biographical Sketches of Those Who Attended Harvard College*, vol. 14 (1968), pp. 591–98, is a good short sketch.

WILLIAM PENCAK

DEANE, Silas (24 Dec. 1737–23 Sept. 1789), diplomat and politician, was born in Groton, Connecticut, the son of Silas Dean, a second-generation blacksmith, and Sarah Barker. He was the eldest surviving child in a family deeply rooted in the agricultural and artisanal endeavors of the stable community on the banks of the Thames. His father served one term in the colonial assembly and saw his son through Yale by 1758. Soon thereafter the younger Silas moved to Wethersfield, a more vibrant community on the Connecticut River. There he taught school by day and studied law by night. He also added the final *e* to his surname, and after the death of both parents in 1760 and 1761 brought his six siblings to live with him. By 1763 he had passed the bar and solidified his position by marrying a widow, Mehitable Nott Webb, who brought her five children to the marriage; the couple had one of their own. The ambitious Deane also gained capital from the Webbs' mercantile business as well as their contacts beyond the community.

Within two years of Mehitable's death in 1767 of tuberculosis, Deane made his second brilliant match by marrying Elizabeth Saltonstall Ebbets, granddaughter of Gurdon Saltonstall, a former governor of Connecticut. Through this match Deane gained entry into wider political circles. He was elected one of Wethersfield's two deputies to the General Assembly in 1768 and again from 1772 to 1775. The Deane-Webb-Saltonstall network, however, was fractured when the Webbs sued Deane over estate problems. The series of acrimonious intrafamilial suits concerning his handling of Webb funds and real estate hindered Deane's

rise in affluence, power, and trust. Settlement did not come until the 1790s. Here, as in later controversies, he appeared opportunistic, clever, and amoral.

Deane also rose in colonial politics with support from the Saltonstalls. His connections to the Susquehannah Company were equally important. This group of merchants was formed to use the sea-to-sea clause in Connecticut's royal charter of 1662 as a pretext to claim land in western Pennsylvania's Wyoming Valley. By 1774, with the support of the powerful Trumbull faction, Deane aided the company's cause by becoming the leading expansionist in the colony. He also ensured that Wethersfield stood at the forefront of efforts to aid Boston after its port was closed in 1774. As a result of these efforts he was named secretary of the Connecticut Committee of Correspondence. As representative of the upriver and eastern interests as well as a businessman, he joined Roger Sherman of New Haven and Eliphalet Dyer of Fairfield in 1774 as Connecticut's delegates appointed to the First Continental Congress.

With his attendance at the congress in the summer of 1774 a new stage of Deane's career opened. In the first congress as well as its successor in 1775, he quickly affiliated himself with like-minded men of commerce, most especially those from the middle colonies. No one doubted his patriotism or his keen eye for mercantile connections as he served on committees concerned with arming the Continental army and provisioning a nascent navy. He added to his reputation and gained the nickname "Ticonderoga" when in 1775 he authorized £300 to fund Benedict Arnold and Ethan Allen's expedition to capture Fort Ticonderoga. Deane basked in the resulting stunning success. The Connecticut Assembly, however, did not nominate him for a third term in October 1775. Apparently Sherman and Deane did not get along, and Sherman had more clout in the assembly. Deane's patron, Governor Jonathan Trumbull (1710–1785), told the irritated Deane that the Connecticut Assembly viewed him as "unteachable and incorrigible."

Rather than return home, Deane filled out his term. Scheming with internationally connected Robert Morris (1734–1806), netted him some assignments early in 1776. He became, in his own words, "involved in one scheme and adventure after another, so as to keep my mind in constant agitation." The Secret Committee (formed in 1775 to seek munitions and other supplies from abroad) contracted with him at 5 percent commission to go to France to purchase goods for trade with the Indians. Deane also entered into partnership with a number of delegates who sought to profit from international trade. Moreover, the Committee of Secret Correspondence (named to coordinate communications with American agents and informants overseas) dispatched him to France as their agent "to transact such Business, commercial and political . . . in Behalf and by Authority of the Congress of the Thirteen United Colonies." Primarily he was to ascertain French reaction to the move toward American independence and to seek arms. Deane and his partners passed on their losses to the government in order to maximize profits. (They put private shipments on board vessels chartered to Congress. If the vessel sunk or was captured by the British, they sought restitution from Congress.)

Deane's mission to France, in its initial stage, lasted from July to December 1776; he remained there as joint commissioner until the spring of 1778. The first official representative of the new nation abroad, he knew no French, was soon surrounded by British spies and French intriguers, and received few instructions from Congress. When the word spread of the Declaration of Independence, Deane was perplexed for he did not know if Congress wished to pursue connections with the court of Louis XVI. He was unable to secure credit to purchase goods for Indian trade but in July was received by the foreign minister, Charles Gravier Vergennes. This seasoned and industrious diplomat pushed a policy of rearmament and revenge.

Vergennes chose Pierre Augustin Caron de Beaumarchais, playwright and courtier, as agent to funnel aid to the American rebellion. The conduit was Rodrigue Hortalez and Company, which was loaned royal funds to purchase obsolete arms from government arsenals. These were to be sold on credit to Deane and Congress. By March 1777 the Frenchman and Deane had chartered merchantmen to convoy war material from royal arsenals to America. The weapons were rushed to New York to aid in defeating the British at Saratoga in the fall of 1777. Less successful were Deane's efforts to repay Hortalez. Sufficient American tobacco, as remittance, did not come to Beaumarchais. Arthur Lee of Virginia, Congress's agent in London, accused Deane of placing personal profit before public service. He visited Deane in August and claimed that the Hortalez shipments were in fact gifts from Louis XVI. Deane wrote Morris, "[I]t seems to me the present opportunity of improving our fortunes ought not to be lost, especially as the very means of doing it will contribute to the arms shipments." Vergennes, hiding behind the guise of neutrality, was in no position to acknowledge any form of governmental assistance and so could not clarify the matter. Congress later found Lee's interpretation convenient and withheld payments to Hortalez.

In the long run the Hortalez shipments proved to be Deane's most controversial accomplishment. Yet in the short run he exceeded his instructions and thus reaped mounting criticism from Congress that ended in his recall, voted by Congress on 21 November 1777. In the last five months of 1776 Deane had persistently badgered the cautious Vergennes to recognize the independent United States. Worse, he had contracted with myriad French army officers for the Continental army. These uneven appointments were vigorously resisted by American generals and politicians. For every Baron de Kalb or Marquis de Lafayette he helped to recruit, there were more numerous obnoxious line officers, such as Major Philippe C. Du Coudray. Also vexing in America were reports of Deane's complicity in a scheme to replace army commander George Washington with Charles-François, duc de Broglie, head of the king's own secret diplomatic service. From his Paris base Deane also recruited a pyromaniac to set fire to the British naval stores in Portsmouth, England, in the winter of 1776–1777. This mission misfired, and Vergennes was chagrined by the American's efforts to jeopardize France's neutrality.

In addition to congressional responsibilities, Deane entered into personal schemes with both French and American speculators. Although some revolutionaries such as Samuel Adams and Richard Henry Lee praised virtue and damned profit, Deane blurred the line between public and private interests by using his knowledge of the international scene to manipulate the London stock and insurance markets. To do this he employed in July 1776 Edward Bancroft, who, unbeknownst to Deane, was a double agent. In his role as Deane's secretary, Bancroft used government intelligence to play the market odds on when war might break out between Britain and France. He also compromised the secrecy of French-American negotiations. Arthur Lee and his brothers suspected Bancroft but could never prove that he was a spy. They also claimed that Deane cleared a profit of £60,000 from stock jobbing, although Deane maintained that his adventures had balanced profits against losses. A true accounting has never been made because of insufficient records.

In late December 1776 Deane progressed to another stage in his diplomatic career. He was yoked with Benjamin Franklin (1706–1790), who arrived from Philadelphia, and with Arthur Lee, who came over from London. Franklin, engaged in wide-ranging efforts to cultivate French opinion, genially left the details and commercial affairs of the Paris commission in the hands of Deane and his European cronies. Lee, when he was not dispatched in quests of militia diplomacy to Spain or Prussia, grew increasingly alienated, believing his compatriots less zealous and competent than himself. Despite growing dissension between Lee and his two colleagues, they managed to hold together through 1777.

At the end of the year Vergennes instructed his representative, Conrad Alexandre Gérard, to negotiate with the trio on their long-sought objective: a French-American alliance. By 6 February 1778 they had negotiated two alliances, one commercial and one military and political. The first pact was founded on the concept of commercial reciprocity. The second agreed that neither the United States nor France would quit the war until America had achieved independence and that neither ally would negotiate separately with the British. Within a month Deane, receiving news of his recall by Congress, joined Gérard in crossing the Atlantic. Gérard had been named France's first minister plenipotentiary to the United States. The American must have felt he had gained his diplomatic goal.

In fact Deane's life now entered its most controversy-filled stage. While Gérard was feted upon his arrival, Deane faced repeated frustrations at the hands of Congress. In September 1777 it had repudiated

Deane's contracts with French officers and two months later voted for his recall but failed to tell him why. In retrospect Deane could be seen as the victim of both factionalism within Congress and of the lack of clear communications between Congress and its envoys. In Congress Deane was criticized by his colleagues from Connecticut, by James Lovell and Samuel Adams of Massachusetts, and by Richard Henry Lee. Deane's champions came from the more commercial middle states; they rallied behind James Duane of New York. Ultimately, however, the vote for Deane's recall passed without dissent. Between 14 July and 5 December 1778 he waited in Philadelphia for a congressional audience. This was soon after R. H. Lee received first word from his brothers in Europe of possible wrongdoing by Deane. It was September before Congress openly considered substantive charges of misapplication of funds and dissension among the American trio in France.

Finally, in total frustration, Deane published a combative address in the *Pennsylvania Gazette* on 5 December 1778. This open public assault on the Lees opened a breach among the patriotic forces and precipitated a major war in the local press and a like cleavage in Congress. On Deane's side stood the more moderate, commercial-minded, and middle-states politicians. Deane's enemies rallied around the so-called Old Radicals of the Adams-Lee axis, those who had been in the forefront of early agitation and who emphasized a moral dimension in the Revolution. Gérard helped to widen the fissure, for he believed the Adams-Lee forces were anti-French. As the animosities played out, Congress refused to accept Deane's accounts, but they neither charged nor released him. Ultimately, after thirteen months, he was merely discharged. In 1779 Deane had the satisfaction of knowing that the Deanites gained revenge by unseating Arthur Lee and two cronies from their diplomatic posts.

Deane never went to Connecticut in the period from 1778 to 1780. He had arranged a network of kin from Connecticut to Virginia to the Caribbean to handle trade. He was determined to return to Europe in 1780 so as to avoid political infighting, to vindicate himself by settling his accounts, and most importantly to recoup his fortune. He failed in all three efforts. Without credit or capital he could make no headway in a scheme to supply masts to the allied navies. His connections with Robert Morris and other Pennsylvania notables led to ill-fated land speculations in the Illinois and Wabash companies. His unsettled accounts proved as vexing. In fact, it was not until 1841 that Congress guaranteed to Deane's heirs $37,000. Disillusionment led Deane to infamy. In the spring of 1781 a series of ill-timed "intercepted letters" were published by the Loyalist press in New York City. Some American patriots believed Deane had sold out to the British; most historians concur. These published missives voiced Deane's views that Americans should forsake alliances with France and seek reconciliation with Britain. At best he was labeled a defeatist; more often he was linked with Benedict Arnold as a traitor.

In 1781 Deane moved to Ghent, where he could live more cheaply than in Paris. By March 1783 he was living in London. His enemies joyfully reported his apostasy: he lived with a prostitute, and thieves stole his papers and in Paris offered them for sale to Thomas Jefferson. Edward Bancroft appeared to offer financial and medical assistance. Ever the grand schemer, Deane in 1785 began plans for a canal from Lake Champlain to the St. Lawrence River. In 1789 he boarded ship to return to America to pursue this and other adventures. Within four hours his illness forced the ship back to port in Deal, where he soon died. Contemporaries, and later detectives, have variously attributed Deane's death to stroke, tuberculosis, suicide, or murder. Bancroft, a known handler of drugs, has often been implicated because Deane's revelation of earlier espionage might have jeopardized the double agent's comfortable career in Britain.

While many of his peers in the American Revolution found their careers enhanced by the experience, Deane did not. His star seemed on the ascendancy in the early stages as he parlayed firm provincial political connections and entry through Robert Morris to the world of Atlantic merchants. Despite ambition and savvy his diplomatic assignments in France netted him frustrations, which he traced to his rivals, the Lees. Congressional debates and votes in 1778–1779 over the Deane-Lee imbroglio as well as his appeal for popular support broke the harmony of the original patriot leadership. They also hastened Deane's personal and financial depressions.

• Published sets of pertinent sources include Charles Isham, ed., *The Deane Papers* (5 vols., 1887–1891) (*Collections of the New-York Historical Society*, vols. 19–25), and *The Deane Papers: Correspondence between Silas Deane, His Brothers and Their Business and Political Associates, 1771–1795* (1930) (Connecticut Historical Society *Collections*, vol. 23). Official communiqués are found in Francis Wharton, ed., *The Revolutionary Diplomatic Correspondence of the United States* (6 vols., 1882–1889). A recent brief biography is Coy Hilton James, *Silas Deane—Patriot or Traitor?* (1975). Insight into his behavior is gained from Kalman Goldstein, "Silas Deane's Preparation for Rascality," *The Historian* 43 (1980–1981): 75–97. The intrigue surrounding Deane's death is charted in James West Davidson and Mark H. Lytle, *After the Fact*, vol. 1, 3d ed. (1992), pp. xiii–xxxiv.

LOUIS W. POTTS

DE ANGELIS, Thomas Jefferson (30 Nov. 1859–20 Mar. 1933), actor and musical performer, was born in San Francisco, California, the son of John "Johnny" De Angelis and Susan Loudenschlager, stage performers. He was thus born to a theatrical heritage. His uncle, Thomas Rosa, taught him dancing and gymnastics, and his father gave him voice lessons. De Angelis also attended a few classes in public schools in both Philadelphia and New York, but his formal schooling was sparse.

Although he had appeared often as a child, De Angelis considered a performance at the Odeon Theatre in Baltimore, Maryland, when he was about thirteen, his professional debut. During his youth he toured with various members of his family throughout the West, dancing, singing, clowning, tumbling, and acting in melodramatic theater productions. The family group, according to De Angelis, lacked funds to travel from St. Louis to San Francisco by rail, so they purchased wagons, hoping to play engagements in small towns along the way. The Midwest, however, had been impoverished by a grasshopper plague, destroying any hope for a profitable tour; the company arrived in San Francisco destitute.

De Angelis formed his own company after his father died and began a world tour in 1880, a venture lasting four years. His repertoire included *Uncle Tom's Cabin*, several farces, and operettas by Gilbert and Sullivan. A benefit performance in San Francisco raised $600 for the group, which was later to appear in South Africa, India, China, and other exotic places. Their first success came in Hong Kong, where they brought in between $6,000 and $7,000 a week for over three months, allowing them to pay off the company debts. In 1882 De Angelis's sister Sarah (La Petite Sally) died from an accidental pistol shot during this tour. The same year De Angelis married an actress, Florence Conliffe, a member of the company.

The company disbanded in Africa in 1884, whereupon De Angelis returned to India and leased several theaters. He eventually returned to San Francisco in 1887, where he appeared in Colonel McCaull's Opera Company, singing in more than 100 light operas. In 1890 he went to New York, where he worked regularly as the premier comedian at the Casino, taking such roles as Ali Baba in *Indigo*, Adrastis in *Apollo*, Baron Puck in *The Grand Duchess*, Tipple in *The Tyrolean*, and Punto in *The Vice Admiral*.

In 1895 De Angelis appeared as Vassili in *The Tzigane* and at Palmer's Theatre as Count de Vacarbilles in *Fleur-de-Lis*. The same year he played Pat O'Hara in *Brian Boru*. In 1897 he began a two-year run in *The Wedding Day*.

Critic Lewis Strang (in *Celebrated Comedians of Light Opera and Musical Comedy in America*) suggests that De Angelis's career up to 1898 was one of playing second fiddle to others of greater theatrical fame, only occasionally himself essaying stardom, never with success. Then in a commonplace comic opera, *The Jolly Musketeers*, he struck pay dirt at last, although Strang felt that De Angelis pushed the indifferent material through two seasons by his own talents. De Angelis later toured in *The Jolly Musketeers*, and in 1903 took *The Emerald Isle* on the road.

De Angelis returned to the Casino in 1907 in *The Great White Way* and two years later played General Samovar in *The Beauty Spot* at the Herald Square Theatre. In 1910 he played Ko-Ko in Gilbert and Sullivan's *The Mikado*, a role he was to play in eleven other productions. In 1911 De Angelis appeared in St. Louis in *The Royal Rogue* and in Chicago in *The Ladies' Lion*. He later appeared in *The Pearl Maiden* in Rochester, New York, and later in New York City. He appeared

as Dugald MacWheeble in *Rob Roy* in 1913 and Gabriel Smudge in *Mme Moselle* in 1914.

De Angelis continued his busy career in 1915, touring in *Some Baby*, followed by *Husbands Guaranteed* at the Winter Garden the next year. He appeared at the Winter Garden in *The Passing Show of 1917* and during the same season played Foxy Quiller in *The Highwayman*. The next season he starred in *The Passing Show of 1917* and *A Trip to Chinatown*.

After touring in 1921 in *Rockabye Baby* and as Bumerlil in a revival of *The Chocolate Soldier*, De Angelis made his last appearance in a musical show, playing Nish in a revival of *The Merry Widow*. The next year he acted in *Some Party* at the Fifty-ninth Street Theatre, and in 1927 he managed *The Royal Family*. He appeared in *Diana* in 1929 and finally, for the last time on any stage, in a New York comedy, *Apron Strings*.

De Angelis actively supported the formation of Actors Equity and served on its board of directors. He was also a major force in the Actors Fund, a benevolent society for elderly performers. His later years were spent in Yonkers, New York, and in East Orange, New Jersey. De Angelis died at the Orange Memorial Hospital. His first wife had died in 1926; he had married another actress, Charlotte Elliott, in 1931.

De Angelis rose to become one of the most noted figures in light opera in America. Strang commented favorably on his subtle and artistic clowning, considering him a character actor of no mean ability. Similarly, critic Philip Hale wrote of him "He is a character actor of genuine humour and uncommon skill. . . . His rakes, his old noblemen, his eccentrics, all differ in the expression of their amorous follies, or whims and caprices. . . . I know of no comedian . . . who is so legitimately amusing, intellectually and physically, as Mr. Jefferson De Angelis." Although De Angelis never achieved true stardom, he remained a great favorite for almost two generations, known for his comedic and acrobatic skills, a craftsman rather than a great artist, making a positive and substantial contribution to his profession.

• De Angelis published three articles: "How I Returned to the Stage," *Theatre* 48 (Sept. 1928): 17, 62; "My Beginnings," *Theatre* 5 (Aug. 1905): 205–6; and "Science and the Stage," *Green Book Album* 2 (Nov. 1909): 1084–88. De Angelis also wrote the play, *The Jolly Tar*, which was staged in Pittsburgh in 1910. His autobiography, *A Vagabond Trouper* (1931), describes his early life in some detail, skimming over the more successful portions of his career. A substantial interview appeared in the *New York Dramatic Mirror*, 23 Nov. 1895. Lewis Strang included an essay about De Angelis in *Celebrated Comedians of Light Opera and Musical Comedy in America* (1901). Obituaries appeared in the *New York Times* and the *New York Herald-Tribune*, both 21 Mar. 1933.

STEPHEN M. ARCHER

DEARBORN, Henry (23 Feb. 1751–6 June 1829), politician and soldier, was born in Hampton, New Hampshire, the son of Simon Dearborn and Sarah Marston, farmers. When Henry was seven years old the family moved to Epping, New Hampshire, where he attended local schools. The father died when Henry was fifteen, leaving the mother with a large family and scant resources. Unable to attend college, Henry studied medicine first under local doctors and then under Hall Jackson, a prominent physician in Portsmouth. In 1771 Dearborn married Mary Bartlett, with whom he had two daughters. The following year he began the independent practice of medicine in Nottingham, where as town moderator he soon became interested in politics, a profession he pursued for the remainder of his life.

Dearborn's other profession, that of soldier, began when as captain of the First New Hampshire Regiment he marched to the assistance of the patriots at Lexington and Concord. Dearborn took an active role in some of the major engagements of the American Revolution, including Bunker Hill, the march across Maine to Canada in 1775, and the battles of Saratoga, Monmouth, and Yorktown. Rising in rank to lieutenant colonel, he also served for a brief period toward the end of the war as deputy quartermaster general. Although his military experience was extensive, Dearborn at no time commanded more than 300 men in action; he obtained no experience in strategical or tactical planning; and his knowledge of logistics was limited.

After the death of his first wife, Dearborn married Dorcas Osgood Marble in 1780, with whom he had two children. Discharged from the army on 18 June 1783, he settled in Kennebec, Maine, at that time still a part of Massachusetts. In 1787 he was appointed major general of militia and in 1792 was elected to Congress, where he served until 1797. Like many other politicians of his day, Dearborn at first declared that he intended to remain aloof from party and base his decisions entirely on the merits of issues as they arose. As a congressman he soon changed his views. Opposed to most of the Federalist program advocated by Alexander Hamilton (1755–1804), he allied himself with James Madison (1751–1836) and Thomas Jefferson. From this time on he remained a consistent and faithful Republican.

Because of Dearborn's party loyalty, military experience, and northern constituency, Jefferson appointed him secretary of war in 1801, a position he held throughout Jefferson's presidency. During most of Jefferson's first term the United States had no serious enemies, foreign or domestic. Hence Jefferson and his secretary of war could safely carry out their plan to reduce the size of the armed forces built up by the Federalists. Dearborn faithfully executed Jefferson's policy of retrenchment and tried to convert an army dominated by Federalist officers into a truly republican army, in which the officers were drawn from all classes and the command structure was less rigidly hierarchical. At the same time, he tried to improve the training and discipline, the weapons, and the leadership of the force that remained. He supported the establishment of an officer training school at West Point

and responded to its needs, although the initiative here, as elsewhere, came from the president.

With regard to the American Indians, the administration's policy is often described as one of "civilization and assimilation." This meant trying to convert the American Indians to agricultural pursuits and to individual landownership. In order to make way for white settlement to counteract foreign influences in the vast Louisiana Purchase, thousands of acres east of the Mississippi River were acquired by the federal government. The details of dealing with the American Indians were left to Dearborn and his agents, who used manipulation and force when persuasion failed.

It is doubtful the policy of assimilation would have succeeded in any circumstances, but certainly it did not work after the threat of war with one or more foreign powers broke out, causing military alliances with the Indians to supersede peacetime plans. The general war between the nations allied to France and those allied to England was resumed in 1803, and especially after the Chesapeake affair of 1807, when a British warship bombarded the American frigate Chesapeake off Hampton Roads, Virginia, Jefferson felt the policy of reducing the armed forces should be revised. Efforts to reform the militia and make it a trained and disciplined force came to nothing because Congress failed to act. Shortly before he left office Dearborn presented a plan for enlarging the regular army, but Congress responded only partially, and little was accomplished.

Partly as a reward for his loyal service, Dearborn was appointed collector of customs at the Port of Boston in 1809. This office was lucrative and not greatly demanding, and after the death of his second wife, Dearborn in 1813 added substantially to the ease of his circumstances by marrying Sarah Bowdoin, widow of James Bowdoin (1752–1811). Meanwhile President Madison in January 1812 had appointed Dearborn senior major general of the U.S. Army, a position he accepted with reluctance. His diffidence was quite justified since he was then nearly sixty-two years old and his self-education, though extensive, was largely irrelevant to the military problems at hand. Dearborn was in charge of the northeastern sector from the Niagara River to the New England coast, where the main effort—an invasion of Canada via the Lake Champlain route—was to be directed. After establishing his headquarters at Greenbush, near Albany, Dearborn spent several weeks at Boston strengthening defenses along the East Coast and trying to deal with the New England governors, who refused to allow their militia, the best in the land, to be used in furtherance of offensive operations against Canada. The result was no major offensive in the East. Inaction in Dearborn's theater contributed to the loss of Detroit and general failure all along the border in 1812.

Dearborn's leadership in 1813 showed only slight improvement. All strategists of the time and later agree that the main effort should have been along the Lake Champlain route toward Montreal or Quebec since possession of these posts would have assured the fall of all that lay above. Instead of concentrating on the crucial line of attack, forces were scattered to the west, and although the army succeeded in taking York (now Toronto) and Fort George in April-May 1813, these operations produced no decisive results. Ill and unable to take the field, Dearborn was relieved of his command in July 1813. Later he had command of Military District Three at New York and served on the court-martial of General William Hull, an improper assignment since Hull could and did maintain that Dearborn had contributed to the disaster at Detroit for which Hull was held responsible.

Honorably discharged from the army in 1815, Dearborn spent the next few years active in Massachusetts politics. In 1822 President James Monroe appointed him minister to Portugal. From his diplomatic post Dearborn witnessed the repressive measures carried out by reactionary regimes in both Spain and Portugal. His dispatches reveal the loathing and disgust of an American thoroughly dedicated to republican principles. At his own request he was recalled in 1824.

Dearborn's greatest contribution was as a loyal and discriminating follower rather than as an effective and courageous leader. Neither a scholar nor a philosopher, he was perhaps typical of the average American of his day: a jack-of-all-trades. At one time or another, besides his main professions, he was a physician, pioneer, farmer, speculator, and government contractor. He met the various challenges of his long life with inveterate optimism, an amiable disposition, and in most cases, moderate success, the near total failure of his military command in the War of 1812 being the notable exception. He died in Roxbury, Massachusetts.

• Dearborn's public career is amply documented, his private life much less so. There is no extensive collection of his personal papers, but scattered letters are to be found in numerous collections listed in the works by Erney and Crackel mentioned below. Useful information may be found in a collection compiled by Dearborn's son, Henry Alexander Scammel, 7 manuscript vols., in the Maine Historical Society, Portland, Maine. Official letters, sent and received, are in the pertinent record groups of the Departments of War, Treasury, and State files in the National Archives, Washington, D.C. Official reports and other materials relating to the various offices he held are printed in Thomas C. Cochran, ed., *The New American State Papers* (13 vols., 1972). Other published collections include Lloyd A. Brown and Howard H. Peckham, eds., *Revolutionary War Journals of Henry Dearborn, 1775–1783: With a Biographical Essay by Herman Dunlap Smith* (1939). The only full-length biography is Richard A. Erney, *The Public Life of Henry Dearborn* (1979). Background material on Dearborn as secretary of war and as general may be found in Irving Brant, *James Madison: Commander-in-Chief, 1812–1836* (1961); Harry L. Coles, "From Peaceable Coercion to Balanced Forces, 1807–1815," in *Against All Enemies*, ed. Kenneth J. Hagan and William R. Roberts (1986); Theodore J. Crackel, *Mr. Jefferson's Army* (1987); and J. C. A. Stagg, *Mr. Madison's War: Politics, Diplomacy, and Warfare in the Early American Republic, 1783–1830* (1983).

HARRY L. COLES

DEARBORN, Walter Fenno (19 July 1878–21 June 1955), educational psychologist, was born in Marblehead, Massachusetts, the son of Josiah Weare Dearborn and Martha Mehitabel Dinsmore. In 1896 he entered his father's alma mater, Wesleyan University, from which he received a B.A. in 1900. For the next three years, Dearborn was engaged in graduate work at Wesleyan, funded during the latter two years by an appointment as vice principal of the local high school. Dearborn's interest in psychology was fired by one of his teachers at Wesleyan, Andrew C. Armstrong, who had steered earlier students, including Charles H. Judd and Edward L. Thorndike, in a similar direction. Perhaps the most directly influential of the Wesleyan faculty, however, was the experimental psychologist Raymond Dodge, for whom Dearborn had acted as a laboratory assistant. Dodge's important work on eye movement recording, some of which was carried out with Dearborn's help, earned Dodge a place in J. McKeen Cattell's list of the top thirty American psychologists in *American Men of Science* (1903).

Having obtained his M.A. from Wesleyan in 1903, Dearborn moved to New York to study for a Ph.D. under the direction of Cattell and Thorndike at Columbia University. Dearborn's doctoral thesis was an experimental study of eye movements in reading, for which he developed a modified version of Dodge's original photographic recording apparatus. (The importance of this early research can be gauged by its inclusion in Robert S. Woodworth's influential text *Experimental Psychology*, even as late as 1954.) After a period of study at the University of Göttingen during 1904, Dearborn completed his Ph.D. in 1905. He then took a post as instructor in educational psychology at the University of Wisconsin, in experimental psychologist Joseph Jastrow's department, where he became assistant professor of education two years later. During this period, Dearborn's interests gradually broadened to encompass other areas of educational psychology, such as intelligence testing.

Dearborn moved in 1909 to the University of Chicago as associate professor of education under Judd, the newly appointed head of the Department of Education. Dearborn remained there for the next three years, except for a period during 1911 spent at the University of Heidelberg. In 1912 he accepted an offer of an assistant professorship in educational psychology (with prospects of early promotion) at Harvard University. A further period of study in Germany during 1913 earned Dearborn an M.D. from the University of Munich. Dearborn advanced to full professor in 1917; that same year he married Ellen Kedean, with whom he had two daughters. With this promotion came Dearborn's appointment as director of the Harvard Psycho-Educational Clinic, which moved three years later into the newly founded Graduate School of Education.

Although his reading work continued, in the early 1920s Dearborn branched out into new areas. He designed several intelligence tests and, more important, embarked on the work for which he is perhaps best remembered: the Harvard Growth Study, which gathered data on the same group of schoolchildren during the period from 1922 to 1934. Although, as Dearborn himself noted, this was not the first such longitudinal survey carried out at Harvard, it was by far the most ambitious. Its aim was to chart, year by year over this twelve-year period, the intellectual and physical development of all children (some 3,500) entering the first grade of schools in three Boston suburbs in 1922. The data collection and management demands of the study were equally massive; for instance, the 1,553 children for whom there were complete records yielded about 190,000 physical measurements and 30,000 mental test scores. Unlike comparable longitudinal studies, such as that of gifted children begun at Stanford University in 1921 by Lewis M. Terman, the work was only modestly funded, with a start-up grant from the Commonwealth Fund. Consequently, Dearborn had to rely on several generations of graduate students for the detailed analysis and checking of the results. In the end, about 200 workers participated in the project, the successful completion of which attests to Dearborn's considerable organizational and administrative skills.

Research stemming from the Harvard Growth Study began to emerge from 1938 and included a monograph on the backgrounds of the young unemployed, written with John W. M. Rothney and titled *Scholastic, Economic and Social Backgrounds of Unemployed Youth* (1938). Dearborn and Rothney were also responsible for the study's most detailed summary, *Predicting the Child's Development* (1941). Indeed, the growth record data had become a major resource for other interested workers, particularly Frank K. Shuttleworth from the Institute of Human Relations at Yale University. Somewhat ironically, however, the most important overall finding was that little or no correlation existed between the physical and mental development of the children studied.

By the early 1940s, Dearborn, who was now effectively released from the administrative demands of the growth study, pursued even more vigorously his first experimental love, that of reading and eye movements. The culmination was a significant joint publication with Leonard Carmichael, *Reading and Visual Fatigue* (1947), which mixed an informal history of research on eye movement measurements and fatigue with an account of experiments jointly run or supervised by the authors. Dearborn also undertook some wartime research for the National Defense Research Committee into visual tests for selecting range finders.

Dearborn retired from Harvard in 1947 with the title of emeritus professor but immediately took up the reins again as professor of psychology and director of the psycho-educational clinic (which specialized in reading difficulties) at Lesley College in Cambridge, Massachusetts. He held this position until a severe cerebral hemorrhage in November 1953 left him incapacitated. He died in St. Petersburg, Florida.

Over his long academic career, Dearborn published numerous academic papers, books, and monographs on the subjects of reading, mental measurement, and the relationship between physical and mental growth; many were written in collaboration with current and former students. He was editor of *Harvard Monographs in Education* between 1923 and 1929. Dearborn belonged to several learned societies, most notably the American Academy of Arts and Sciences and the American Psychological Association, of which he was a fellow.

Dearborn was undoubtedly a beneficiary of the small and richly interconnected network that characterized American psychology in the early decades of this century. It is therefore not too surprising to see the same names and institutions emerging again and again during his climb up the academic ladder. However, the enormous amount of personal effort that Dearborn put into ensuring the successful completion of the Harvard Growth Study demonstrates his aptitude for moving easily and effectively between areas in psychology and education, a freedom not granted to the field's future specialists.

• The Walter Fenno Dearborn Papers, which chiefly relate to the work of the Harvard Psycho-Educational Clinic, are in the Harvard University Archives. Among Dearborn's works not already mentioned in the text are "The Psychology of Reading," *Archives of Philosophical Psychology and Scientific Methods* 4 (1906): 1–134; *The Psychology of Teaching Reading*, with I. H. Anderson (1951); *The Dearborn Group Tests of Intelligence* (1920); *Intelligence Tests: Their Significance for School and Society* (1928), based on his Lowell Institute lectures of 1925; and, with J. W. M. Rothney and F. K. Shuttleworth, *Data on the Growth of Public School Children (Harvard Growth Study)*, Monographs of the Society for Research in Child Development 3, no. 14 (1938). Obituaries by two former Harvard colleagues, Herbert S. Langfeld, in *American Journal of Psychology* 68 (1955): 679–81, and Gordon W. Allport, prepared specially for the Harvard Archives, provide useful biographical material, despite some inconsistencies.

A. D. LOVIE
PATRICIA LOVIE

DEARDEN, John F. (15 Oct. 1907–1 Aug. 1988), bishop, archbishop, and first president of the National Conference of Catholic Bishops, was born in Valley Falls, Rhode Island, the son of John Dearden, a manufacturing plant superintendent, and Agnes (maiden name unknown). He grew up first in Rhode Island and then in Cleveland, Ohio, attending parochial schools up to high school, when he attended Cathedral Latin School in Cleveland. In 1925 he went directly to seminary study at St. Mary Seminary in Cleveland and in 1929 to the Gregorian University through the North American College in Rome. Dearden was ordained in 1932 and shortly thereafter earned his doctorate in theology.

He began his priestly career in Painesville, Ohio, where he served as an assistant in St. Mary Parish. He soon moved over to teach in St. Mary Seminary and then to be its rector. While serving as rector of the seminary, Dearden coordinated many diocesan projects so calmly that others referred to him as "Iron John," a nickname that stuck with him through his years as bishop of Pittsburgh, Pennsylvania. In 1948

Pope Pius XII appointed Dearden as coadjutor bishop to Pittsburgh bishop Hugh C. Boyle, and Dearden succeeded Boyle as bishop of Pittsburgh when Boyle died two years later.

Dearden served as Pittsburgh's bishop until 1958, when he moved to Detroit, Michigan. While bishop of Pittsburgh he served as a conservative, rule-oriented leader who revitalized many lagging diocesan organizations and eliminated others. He championed Catholic Action within the diocese, as he encouraged the lay organizations for men (the Holy Name Society) and women (the Diocesan Council of Catholic Women) to reform society along Christian ideals. Dearden also purchased the lay-owned *Pittsburgh Catholic*, putting the oldest Catholic weekly paper in America under episcopal control. His firm manner and support for conservative Catholic doctrine confirmed his nickname as "Iron John."

Dearden's successful organizational and revitalization efforts in Pittsburgh earned him a promotion to Detroit, where he became archbishop of one of the nation's largest dioceses. While serving as archbishop of Detroit, he also served as treasurer for the National Catholic Welfare Conference, an organization of the American Catholic bishops established in the wake of the first world war to help coordinate and implement Catholic charitable work.

He attended the Second Vatican Council in Rome during the years 1962–1965 and became one of the world's leading advocates of liberal reform within the Catholic church. He played a central role in writing and revising the council's documents *Dogmatic Constitution on the Church* and *Pastoral Constitution on the Church in the Modern World* (both 1965).

Following Vatican II, the American Catholic bishops met as a body in Washington, D.C., and formed the National Conference of Catholic Bishops (NCCB) as their national episcopal organization. The bishops elected Dearden as the first president of the NCCB. As the first president, Dearden played a crucial role in shaping the NCCB and the United States Catholic Conference (USCC). In this role he was perhaps the person most responsible for implementing the sweeping reforms of the Second Vatican Council in the United States.

Dearden led the NCCB to implement the liturgical changes that derived from the Second Vatican Council. These reforms altered dramatically the way American Catholics worshiped on Sundays and understood their religion. The language used in the central liturgical experience for Catholics changed from Latin to the vernacular (English for most American Catholics). The laity played more visible and significant roles in the Mass, especially as lectors and Eucharistic ministers. The church dropped meatless Fridays, implemented Saturday Masses, and allowed the laity to receive Communion from the cup.

Dearden also played a crucial role in bringing the American Catholic church to address the major social concerns that Americans faced. If before the Second Vatican Council and the formation of the NCCB/USCC, American church leaders focused primarily upon nurturing and defending the institutional church itself, Dearden steered them afterward toward a more frank and sustained engagement with America's social, economic, and political problems. Under Dearden's leadership, the Bishops issued statements on the Vietnam War, conscientious objection, race relations, farm labor, Biafra, birth control and abortion, welfare reform, the environment, and the United Nations.

Many church leaders who worked with Dearden attributed his great success in large part to his persistence and low-key style. Dearden moved the church through extraordinary changes in areas long thought to be permanent. These changes clearly had potential for great euphoria or distress for Catholics, but Dearden's calm demeanor and persistent manner eased the transition for the institutional church. Archbishop Quinn reflected that Dearden would "point the direction toward a resolution that would be generally accepted and everybody would get along, and most people would be reasonably happy with it in the end."

Still, some conservative Catholics saw in the changes that Dearden helped to implement an unacceptable transformation of the church they had long viewed as unchanging. One well-known New York priest identified Dearden as one of four people responsible for the initiation of an "ecclesial war" within the American Catholic church, and in this characterization captured the tension that even the skillful Dearden could not completely allay. Pope Paul VI signaled his approval of Dearden's efforts in 1969 by making him a cardinal.

Dearden continued his service as NCCB president until 1971 and thereafter maintained a high profile among the American Catholic bishops. He served as the chair of the NCCB Ad Hoc Committee for Observance of the Bicentennial, and in this role he was instrumental in initiating the first Call to Action Conference in 1976. The following year he suffered a heart attack, however, and never completely regained his health. By 1980 he retired as archbishop of Detroit, and then lived for another eight years before dying in Detroit.

• Brief biographies of Dearden are in various places, such as the extended obituaries published at the time of his death, particularly that put out by the Catholic News Service and published in Catholic papers throughout America and in Francis A. Glenn, *Shepherds of the Faith: 1843–1993: A Brief History of the Bishops of the Catholic Diocese of Pittsburgh* (1993). Dearden's greatest work as president of the NCCB is highlighted in Hugh J. Nolan, ed., *Pastoral Letters of the United States Catholic Bishops*, vol. 3: *1962–1974* (1983), and Thomas J. Reese, *A Flock of Shepherds: The National Conference of Catholic Bishops* (1992). For a critical review of Dearden's influence on the American Catholic church, see George A. Kelly, *The Battle for the American Church Revisited* (1995). An obituary other than that distributed by the Catholic News Service is in the *New York Times*, 2 Aug. 1988.

TIMOTHY I. KELLY

DEARING, John Lincoln (10 Dec. 1858–20 Dec. 1916), missionary and theologian, was born in Webster, Maine, the son of Joseph Henry Dearing and Susan

Vinton Adams, farmers. Dearing earned his bachelor's and master's degrees at Colby College in Maine and graduated from the ministerial course at Newton Theological Institution in Massachusetts in 1889. For two years he was superintendent of schools in Deep River, Connecticut (1884–1886), and he served briefly as pastor of the Baptist church in Cambridge, Massachusetts (1889–1890).

Dearing became involved in the Student Volunteer Movement (SVM), an international organization of students on university campuses. At a meeting of the SVM in Cambridge, Massachusetts, in 1889, he was recruited for overseas work by William Ashmore, the famed Baptist missionary to China. Dearing was ordained to the Baptist ministry and was appointed as a student missionary of the American Baptist Missionary Union (ABMU) to Japan in 1889. After serving two years in Japan, he returned to Massachusetts and in 1891 married Mary L. Hinckley of Lynn, Massachusetts. They had two children. The Dearings returned to Yokohama in 1891 under full appointment of the ABMU and remained in that city for more than twenty years.

As a missionary, Dearing excelled in scholarship and human relations. He became the chief instructor at the Baptist Theological Seminary in Yokohama, teaching theology and ethics, and also served as its president from 1894 to 1908. He made many significant friends in the Japanese government, notably Marquis Okuma, the prime minister of Japan. On several occasions, Dearing carried diplomatic messages between the governments of Japan and the United States.

Dearing devoted his career as a scholar to the study of theology. He wrote the Baptist theological work in Japanese, *An Outline of Theology*, which the American Baptist mission board published in 1896. University of Chicago theologian and former roommate from Colby College days Shailer Mathews visited Dearing in Japan and assessed the book as a highly valuable contribution to Christian theology. Dearing was intellectually indebted to two of his former professors, George Dana Boardman Pepper at Colby and Alvah Hovey at Newton Theological Institution.

As a missionary, Dearing was well known in Japan, the United States, and other areas of the world. Highly committed to and involved in ecumenical work, he edited the *Christian Movement in Japan*, a periodical. He was also secretary of the Federated Mission Movement, an ecumenical association of mainline Protestant missionary organizations primarily located in Great Britain and North America, and at the conclusion of the Edinburgh Missionary Conference of 1910 he served as chair of the Continuation Committee for China.

Dearing wrote warmly of Japan and its people, hoping to raise awareness in the United States of the missionary opportunity there. He also became a significant apologist for missions to the Orient in general. Having surveyed the missions situation in both China and Japan, Dearing believed that Japan was a needier field that China and that better opportunities for Christian witness prevailed there.

In 1908 Dearing was appointed a general missionary (a supervisory field staff position) by the American Baptists, and he did much to focus attention on the Far East. He urged northern Baptists in the United States to enter West China, where he perceived both openness and a need for mission work. He wrote of the isolation and hardships to be faced by missionaries in western China, but he felt there would be ample spiritual rewards for teachers and evangelists willing to face the difficult conditions. A rising tide of localism among churches affiliated with the Northern Baptist Convention, however, led the American Baptist Foreign Mission Board (successor to the American Baptist Missionary Union) to eliminate the general missionary position in 1911, to Dearing's great regret.

For several years thereafter Dearing was a foreign minister in Japan for the First Baptist Church of Philadelphia, where he was a member and whose congregation actually underwrote the cost of his salary. His published reports to the church often focused on important emerging trends in Japan and China. For example, in 1912 he correctly identified Yuan Shihk'ai, a revolutionary leader who became president of China later that year, as a critical political bridge between the Chinese revolutionaries and the failing Manchu family. Dearing hoped that this statesman could achieve peace and stability for China.

In 1914 Dearing was chosen to coordinate the three-year evangelistic campaign for the Orient authorized by the Edinburgh Conference Continuation Committee. The result of this effort was an unprecedented cooperation among both older and younger churches in evangelism, education, literature, and reciprocal recognition of church discipline.

Dearing returned to the United States on furlough in 1916 and began a lecture tour. During a visit to Colgate Theological Seminary in Hamilton, New York, he contracted spinal meningitis and died at Clifton Springs, New York, a month later.

• Dearing's personal papers are in the denominational collections at the American Baptist Historical Society in Valley Forge, Pa. Dearing's own publications include an essay, "Is He the Chinese Washington? Yuan Shi Kai," in the *Standard*, 16 Mar. 1912, p. 655, and "Public Opinion in Japan," *Baptist Commonwealth*, 5 Mar. 1914, p. 2. He also wrote a useful tract for the American Baptist Foreign Mission Society, *The Golden Hour in West China: Where East Is West and West Is East* (1912). Informative obituary sketches are "Doctor John Lincoln Dearing, World Citizen," *Baptist Commonwealth*, 18 Jan. 1917, and in the *Pennsylvania Baptist Annual* (1917). Also see Shailer Mathews, "John Lincoln Dearing: An Appreciation," in the *Standard*, 1917, p. 581.

WILLIAM H. BRACKNEY

DEATH VALLEY SCOTTY. *See* Scott, Walter Edward.

DEAVER, John Blair (25 July 1855–25 Sept. 1931), surgeon, was born near Lancaster, Pennsylvania, the son of Joshua Montgomery Deaver, a physician, and Elizabeth Moore. His premedical education was limited to the public schools, and in 1878 he obtained an M.D. from the University of Pennsylvania. He served from 1880 to 1899 in the applied anatomy department of his alma mater, where he also conducted popular quiz classes for students in anatomy and surgery. In 1886 he became a surgeon in the German Hospital of Philadelphia and was made chief of the surgery department in 1896. (In World War I the unpopular name of the German Hospital was changed to Lankenau after its main benefactor.) In 1889 he married Caroline Randall; they had four children.

Like other nineteenth-century surgeons, Deaver engaged in "kitchen table surgery" in the home, performing such procedures as appendectomy, hysterectomy, Caesarean section, and drainage of abscesses. In such cases he operated with an assistant and an anesthetist. His surgery was swift, rough, and radical. He was regarded as a "slasher" who lacked the patience for fastidious techniques. As a staunch advocate of operating at once for acute appendicitis, his statement "an inch and a half, a minute and a half, a week and a half"—to designate the length of the incision, the duration of the operation, and the length of the patient's stay in the hospital—was often quoted. He dramatized his operations before admirers in his clinic with bravado demonstrations and catchy phrases. A favorite was "cut well, get well, stay well," in which he compared the results of operative versus nonoperative treatment.

Deaver's private practice was huge, unrivaled by any other Philadelphia surgeon. He saw patients in his office until 11 A.M. and then went to the hospital where he began operating shortly after noon, commanding three or four operating tables at one time. He performed a dozen or more procedures almost every afternoon. In his prime he did most of the surgery himself, but in later years he allowed more participation by his assistants.

In 1911 Deaver lectured on practical surgery at the University of Pennsylvania and in 1918 was appointed the John Rhea Barton Professor and Surgeon-in-Chief in the university hospital, where he served until 1922. He delivered many addresses at meetings of local, state, and national surgical societies and served as president of the American College of Surgeons (1921–1922). His scientific articles covered a wide spectrum of abdominal conditions, and most of his books went through multiple editions. He invented the "Deaver retractor," a version of the instrument used to hold back the edges of a wound that had a wider and more lengthy curve, which allowed better exposure of deeper regions of the abdomen.

Deaver, a robust, dynamic man, remained well until a few weeks before his death in Philadelphia. He developed an obscure anemia that failed to respond to transfusions and for which autopsy revealed no cause.

• Deaver manuscripts, reprints, and correspondence include over 300 items in the library and historical collections of the College of Physicians of Philadelphia. His important books are *Appendicitis* (1895); *Surgical Anatomy* (3 vols., 1899–1903); *Enlargement of the Prostate*, written with A. P. C. Ashurst (1905); *Surgery of the Upper Abdomen*, with A. P. C. Ashurst (2 vols., 1909–1913); *The Breast* (1917); and *Excursions into Surgical Subjects* (1923). Personal recollections by Deaver's colleague R. H. Ivy are in *Transactions and Studies of the College of Physicians of Philadelphia* 42 (1975): 249–51. An account of his surgical professorship is sketched by D. Y. Cooper III and M. A. Ledger in *Innovation and Tradition at the University of Pennsylvania School of Medicine—An Anecdotal Journey* (1990). His memoir as a member of the American Surgical Association appears in *Annals of Surgery* 95 (1932): 637–40.

FREDERICK B. WAGNER, JR.

DEBAPTISTE, George (1814?–22 Feb. 1875), abolitionist and businessman, was born in Fredericksburg, Virginia, the son of John DeBaptiste, a businessman, and Frances "Franky" (maiden name unknown). Although the details of DeBaptiste's early life are uncertain, he appears to have traveled to Richmond, Virginia, as a youth, where he learned to barber and where, perhaps in 1829, as a free black, he first helped a slave escape. While still in Virginia, he married his first wife, Maria Lucinda Lee, a slave, and bought her freedom. DeBaptiste subsequently remarried and had two children; his second wife's name is unknown. As a young man he demonstrated strong loyalty to his family, who remained in Fredericksburg. On two separate occasions in the 1820s he financially secured the property of two sisters when they faced significant debt (Fitzgerald, p. 53).

Between 1836 and 1838 DeBaptiste moved to Madison, Indiana, where he barbered, engaged in a number of other business enterprises, and served as a conductor for the underground railroad. Although the number of slaves he directly assisted is unknown, DeBaptiste gained a reputation as an abolitionist and conductor by crossing the Ohio River into Kentucky and escorting fugitive slaves into Indiana and Ohio. From there, they would go to Michigan and eventually Canada. His reputation as a conductor drew the ire of local whites. Probably as a result of his notoriety, the state of Indiana prosecuted George for residing in the state without paying the bond required of free blacks. He was saved from expulsion and possible sale into slavery by Stephen C. Stevens, a former member of the Indiana Supreme Court and prominent white attorney who opposed slavery. Stevens argued against the order expelling DeBaptiste, claiming that it was unconstitutional and did not specify his state of origin (where he was to be returned) as the law required. The court agreed only that the order was defective and allowed DeBaptiste to remain a resident.

While trading goods between Madison and Cincinnati, DeBaptiste met General William Henry Harrison and became Harrison's personal servant during the 1840 presidential campaign. After the inauguration DeBaptiste was a White House steward, attending the president until his death in 1841. He then returned to Madison and worked as a barber for seven years until he found the atmosphere too hostile and moved further north to Detroit, Michigan.

In Detroit DeBaptiste quickly became a leader in the black community. He bought an interest in a local barber shop and accepted a position as the chief clerk and salesman for a wholesale clothier. While living in Detroit he belonged to a secret society against slavery variously called the Order of the Men of Oppression, African-American Mysteries, and the Order of Emancipation. He also served as president of the black Union League and continued to participate in underground railroad operations. A letter to Frederick Douglass, dated 4 November 1854, demonstrates his commitment: "all the good news I have, is that the Underground Railroad Company is doing a very large business at this time. . . . We have had, within the last ten or fifteen days, fifty-three first class passengers landed at this point, by the Express train from the South" (Black Abolitionist Papers, frame 0230).

DeBaptiste also tried many different business pursuits while living in Detroit. After Robert Banks closed his clothing store in 1850, DeBaptiste purchased William Lee's bakery and ran it for a number of years. His next venture after selling the bakery was buying a steamboat, the *T. Whitney*. DeBaptiste employed a white captain because Michigan law did not allow a black man to hold a steamboat license. After selling the steamer, he went into the catering business. During the Civil War he and John D. Richards helped raise a black regiment for Michigan. DeBaptiste and Richards served in the regiment as sutlers, spending six months of 1864 in South Carolina. DeBaptiste returned to Detroit and to catering, later opening a restaurant, an ice-cream parlor, and finally, in 1874, a country house restaurant in Hamtramck. In 1867 his realty holdings in Detroit were valued at $10,000 (Katzman, p. 15).

In addition to his business ventures, DeBaptiste stayed active in community affairs, using his business success to help those less fortunate. He served as a temporary agent for the Freedmen's Association after the war, gathering supplies for freedmen's schools in Louisiana. His obituary in the *Detroit Advertiser and Tribune* credits him with working to have black children receive the same education as whites and to have them admitted to the public schools. He also helped organize a large celebration of the passage of the Fifteenth Amendment in Detroit's black community. DeBaptiste died in Detroit. A prominent member of the black community in Detroit, DeBaptiste was counted among its most wealthy figures. Throughout a variety of jobs and business ventures including being a hack, barbering, working as a personal servant, catering, and clerking, DeBaptiste remained an active abolitionist and assisted fugitive slaves in their flight northward.

• Despite his exceptional life, there is very little written directly about DeBaptiste. The most complete information can be found in the Burton Historical Collection, Detroit Public Library. David M. Katzman, *Before the Ghetto* (1973), is a study of the black Detroit community in the nineteenth century and provides a brief sketch of DeBaptiste. Ruth Coder Fitzgerald, *A Different Story* (1979), examines the black community in nineteenth-century Fredericksburg and raises interesting questions about DeBaptiste's early life among his siblings. Fitzgerald also finds that the Fredericksburg DeBaptistes enjoyed wealth and prominence during the early and mid-1800s, although their presence ends after 1850, at least partially owing to the refusal of the white community to allow them to educate their children. Emma Lou Thornbrough, *The Negro in Indiana* (1957), recounts DeBaptiste's Indiana prosecution. Robert Hayden, *History of the Negro in Michigan* (1957), describes some of DeBaptiste's life and cites a 1939 interview with his son Robert. *The Black Abolitionist Papers* (1981), microfilm version, contains a few documents connected to DeBaptiste. An obituary is in the *Detroit Advertiser and Tribune*, 23 Feb. 1875.

DAVID F. HERR

DE BAPTISTE, Richard (11 Nov. 1831–21 Apr. 1901), Baptist leader and race advocate, was born in Fredericksburg, Virginia, to free parents, Eliza (maiden name unknown) and William De Baptiste. Born in a slave state when individuals were fined and incarcerated for teaching blacks, enslaved or free, De Baptiste was fortunate to have parents who earnestly sought to educate their children and some relatives in their home, despite the law and heavy surveillance. In 1846 the De Baptistes moved to Detroit, Michigan. De Baptiste then received additional education and for some time attended classes at the University of Chicago. Having been the leading building and manufacturing contractor in Fredericksburg, the elder De Baptiste, after an unsuccessful partnership in a grocery enterprise, returned to his earlier work. Richard De Baptiste became a partner in the business before his twenty-first birthday and served for some years as its manager. From 1858 to about 1861 he also taught black youth in the public schools of Mount Pleasant, Hamilton County, Ohio.

De Baptiste was married three times. In 1855 he married Georgiana Brischo of Cincinnati, Ohio; by her death in 1872 they had at least three children. The death of his second wife, Mary, ended a marriage of only eight months. Finally, in 1890 he married Nellie Williams of Galesburg, Illinois.

Conversion at a revival meeting in 1852 in the Second Baptist Church of Detroit and affiliation with that church impressed De Baptiste with a call to the ministry, though he did not make this known until he had served for some time in a number of church positions. Licensed to preach by the church on his departure to Ohio in 1858, De Baptiste continued his preaching in Mount Pleasant and organized a Sunday school. In 1860 he was ordained as an elder, and three years later he assumed the pastorate of Olivet Baptist Church in Chicago, a post he held until 1882. His work there was very effective in terms of church construction and reconstruction after the 1874 Chicago fire, providing refuge and educational opportunities for African Americans as well as evangelistic outreach. Olivet became the city's largest assembly of African Americans. Despite the desire of the congregation that he remain, De Baptiste resigned in 1881 because of his children's poor health and reductions in church membership. He continued pastoral work in smaller Illinois congregations.

While De Baptiste maintained a fervent commitment to the ministry, he made great contributions in the organization and consolidation of Baptist groups among African Americans, especially in the Midwest and South. He was a popular official in various Baptist groups, winning frequent reelection. He played a major role in establishing and maintaining black denominations independent of white churches, though he himself had interracial church involvements. He served Baptist conventions as statistician, corresponding secretary, and president. De Baptiste was involved in the Wood River Baptist Association; the Northwestern and Southern Baptist Convention from its inception in 1865; the Consolidated American Baptist Missionary Convention, where he held the office of president from its organization in 1867 to 1871 and from 1872 to 1877; the American Baptist Free Mission Society, a biracial organization fiercely opposed to slavery, of which he was elected president in 1870; the Baptist General Association of Western Sates and Territories, of which he served as corresponding secretary; and the American National Baptist Convention from its organization in 1886, when he was elected corresponding secretary. De Baptiste also served as statistician of the American National Baptist Convention, demonstrating that black Baptist membership numbered more than a million, contrary to earlier counts by white Baptists who placed the number at 800,000. Finally, De Baptiste's strong emphasis on racial independence led him to support vigorously the founding of the National Baptist Convention (NBC) in 1895, the first permanent national organization of African-American Baptists. He also worked for the establishment of the NBC's publishing board and the active support of African missions work through the NBC and earlier black Baptist conventions.

De Baptiste, a prolific writer for both religious and secular news organs, edited a number of newspapers: the *Conservator*, the first black newspaper in Chicago, which he coedited with another minister; the *Western Herald*, during the period 1884 to 1885 the sole black Baptist news organ in the midwestern states and territories; the *St. Louis Monitor* and *Baptist Herald* (Keokuk, Iowa), for which he served as corresponding secretary; and the *National Monitor*, sponsored by the Consolidated American Baptist Missionary Convention and based in New York, for which he served on the editorial staff. As a pastor and denominational leader, race spokesperson and advocate, and journalist, De Baptiste was an outstanding religious leader of the nineteenth century.

• The impact of De Baptiste in both the nation and his denomination is captured by the contemporary writers William J. Simmons, *Men of Mark: Eminent, Progressive and Rising* (1887; repr., 1968), and Albert W. Pegues, *Our Baptist Ministers and Schools* (1892). Recent works on Baptist history illustrating the significance of this Baptist leader include James M. Washington, *Frustrated Fellowship: The Black Baptist Quest for Social Power* (1986), and Leroy Fitts, *A History of Black Baptists* (1985). Sandy D. Martin, *Black Baptists and African Missions* (1989), illustrates De Baptiste's involvement with African missions.

SANDY DWAYNE MARTIN

DE BAR, Benedict (5 Nov. 1814–28 Aug. 1877), actor and theater manager, was born in Chancery Lane, London, England, the son of a bank bookkeeper. His parents' names are unknown. The family moved to Ireland when Ben's father took a position as the steward of a nobleman's estate. In 1826 his father died, leaving the family to suffer financial hardships. The twelve-year-old Ben left school and entered the working world as a grocery clerk, a job he reportedly hated. He soon got his first taste of the theatrical life by running away and joining a strolling company. After returning home and working for a lawyer (his father had desired that he have a career in business or law), Ben finally persuaded his mother to accept his desire to perform. He moved to London and joined the ballet company of a minor theater. In 1832, at the Theatre Royal in Margate, Kent, he made his first full-scale acting appearance as the Page (a small role) in the farce *The Page and the Purse*. From there, he swiftly worked his way up on the English stages from "general utility" to "walking gentleman" to "leading man." (Actors in the nineteenth century, in both England and the United States, were employed by stock companies in specific "lines of business," meaning the categories of role in which they would be cast. A utility player might only have one line to deliver in an entire play; a walking gentleman or lady had slightly more substantial time on stage. The hierarchy of lines of business was quite elaborate and continued to prevail throughout much of the century.)

Many nineteenth-century American theatrical managers and agents recruited talent in England. In 1835 the 22-year-old De Bar came to the attention of James H. Caldwell, who had just finished building the St. Charles Theatre in New Orleans. De Bar crossed the Atlantic with his mother and sister and played for an attractive $15 a week at this theater (which he would later purchase), opening as Sir Benjamin Backbite in *School for Scandal*. After building a reputation in the South, he arrived in New York City in 1837. For about a decade, De Bar made the rounds of the city's several stock companies, performing sizable (though often not leading) roles in Shakespeare plays. He did a season at the Bowery Theatre, a well-known attraction for the legendary "b'hoys" (the flamboyant rowdies of the city's working class), and he took a hand at comanaging the Chatham Theatre with W. S. Deverna.

De Bar married Maria Conduit, a widowed English opera singer, circa 1837; they had one daughter. Sadly, Maria died within two or three years of their nuptials. In 1843 he married Henrietta "Hattie" Valle, a dancer and actress with whom he would make frequent appearances.

There was prestige, though not necessarily any increased security, in theater management and stardom—both of which De Bar attained in his career. After a brief return visit to England, he bought the St. Charles Theatre in New Orleans in 1853 and the Bates Theatre in St. Louis (which he promptly rechristened the St. Louis Theatre) in 1855. For more than twenty years he succeeded in keeping a vibrant legitimate theater in St. Louis, combining Shakespeare with the more modern forms of farce and melodrama at a time when other companies were increasingly turning toward burlesque and variety shows to stay solvent. Part of his success stemmed from his ability to attract a broad-based respectable audience. Aware that St. Louis had seen one company fail by attracting only the rowdy lower classes and another by bringing in only the wealthy elites, De Bar wisely aimed between the two extremes, charging prices and choosing plays that would appeal to the middle class. His theatrical house was nationally renowned for having some of the most up-to-date innovations in scenic design, stage illumination, and fire safety. He was also praised for his generosity in making his theater available for charity benefits including those for performing artists who had fallen upon misfortune. In the 1870s, as De Bar assumed control of yet another theater space in St. Louis and sought to expand his management into cities as far away as Montreal, the institution of the stable stock company was declining in favor of traveling combination companies. In these, De Bar was less interested.

In addition to managing, De Bar continued to perform star engagements, especially in the South. Having concentrated on dramatic roles in his earlier years, he now carved out a new niche as a comic actor, and during the last five years of his life he became one of the two most celebrated Falstaffs in America, playing the role in both *Henry IV* and *The Merry Wives of Windsor*. He did not, unfortunately, live to play that character on the English stage as he had hoped to do.

During his years in St. Louis, De Bar belonged to a professional and businessmen's lodge of Freemasons as well as to the Episcopal church. Because he was vociferously on the side of the Confederacy and had enjoyed a friendship with John Wilkes Booth, whose brother Junius was married to De Bar's sister, De Bar was briefly investigated, along with his niece Blanche De Bar, for possible complicity in the assassination of President Abraham Lincoln. They were both cleared. De Bar spent the last year of his life fighting off illness and trying to stave off financial setbacks. Although he had been quite well-to-do at one time, two financial panics plus the economic turmoil of the Civil War and its aftermath took a toll on his assets as he strove to meet the increasingly high cost of keeping star-quality talent on his stage.

To the last, though, De Bar worked hard at his craft and sustained public admiration for his acting talent and his managerial prowess. He is remembered as having strenghthened the legitimate theater in the South and West and holding forth with one of the last successful models of that dying theatrical institution,

the stock company. The *St. Louis Times*, in a 100-year retrospective of local theater, called De Bar "the most famous of all St. Louis producers and theatrical characters, without whose name no history of drama in this country would be complete" (10 Feb. 1871).

• The only book-length work on De Bar is Grant M. Herbstruth, "Benedict DeBar [*sic*] and the Grand Opera House in St. Louis, Missouri, from 1855 to 1879" (Ph.D. diss., Univ. of Iowa, 1954). A sketch of his life can be found in John Thomas Scharf, *History of St. Louis City and County* (1883), and portions of his career tangentially appear in George C. D. Odell, *Annals of the New York Stage* (1927–1949); Joseph N. Ireland, *Records of the New York Stage*, vol. 2 (1866); and John S. Kendall, *The Golden Age of the New Orleans Theater* (1952). An obituary is in the *New York Times*, 29 Aug. 1877.

BEN ALEXANDER

DEBARDELEBEN, Henry Fairchild (22 July 1840–6 Dec. 1910), industrial entrepreneur, was born in Autauga County, Alabama, the son of Henry DeBardeleben, a South Carolinian who moved to Alabama in the 1830s to become a cotton planter, and Mary Fairchild of New York. Upon the death of her husband in the early 1850s, Mary and her three children moved to Montgomery. In time, the family joined the household of a friend, Daniel Pratt, a former New Englander who had accumulated one of the largest fortunes in antebellum Alabama through cotton gin manufacturing. A free spirit who loved the outdoors and was never fond of formal schooling, the young DeBardeleben gladly left school as soon as his guardian would allow and became superintendent of Pratt's gin factory.

Although DeBardeleben, like Pratt, opposed secession, he enlisted as a private in the Confederate army but was soon drafted to supervise a Confederate factory. In 1863 DeBardeleben married Pratt's only surviving child, eighteen-year-old Ellen, with whom he had eight children. Increasingly, Pratt depended on his son-in-law to assist him in his business ventures.

After the war, Pratt, then ill but with some remaining capital, ventured into the mineral district of Alabama with DeBardeleben at his side. Although Alabama's antebellum economy was predominantly agricultural, limited industrial development had taken place by the time of the Civil War. In the postwar period, speculators, promoters, prospectors, and railroad men—attracted by iron ore, coal, and limestone—purchased land in Jefferson County and in 1871 laid out a new town named Birmingham after the English industrial city. In the spring of 1872 Pratt acquired a controlling interest in the Red Mountain Iron and Coal Company and placed DeBardeleben in charge of the enterprise, now renamed the Eureka Mining Company.

Although he succeeded in placing the war-damaged furnaces at Oxmoor back into operation, DeBardeleben's ignorance of the coal and iron industry, combined with the limited market for iron in Alabama, inexperienced labor, and the panic of 1873, spelled doom for the venture. DeBardeleben later declared, "And I came in and took charge of what I knew nothing about!" (Armes, p. 239). By the end of 1873 DeBardeleben submitted his resignation and the Oxmoor furnaces closed. With a cholera epidemic adding to the woes of Birmingham, activity in the district was at a standstill by the beginning of 1874.

But DeBardeleben had caught the speculative fever; with the death of Pratt in May 1873 and Pratt's wife less than two years later, he had access to an estate estimated at $250,000 with which he could begin to build his own fortune. Turning his back on the cotton gins of the Old South, the young man staked his future on the industry of the New South.

DeBardeleben's demeanor and speculative ventures mirrored the raucous, frontier atmosphere of early Birmingham. Described as a "dashingly good looking" man with a "hawk-like look," DeBardeleben had a "savagely energetic, restless, impatient" manner and appeared to always have one foot "in the stirrup, and to be itching to mount and be off and away" (Armes, p. 239). Exulting in the opportunities of the New South, he declared, "There's nothing like taking a wild piece of land, all rock and woods . . . and turning it into a settlement of men and women, making pay rolls, bringing the railroads in, and starting things going. There's nothing like boring a hillside through and turning over a mountain. That's what money does, and that's what money's for. I like to use money as I use a horse—to ride!" (Armes, p. 343).

Even in the depression years DeBardeleben was busy. When the ownership of the Oxmoor furnaces reverted back to him, he helped to sponsor an experiment in February 1876 that resulted in the first iron made in the district with coke rather than charcoal. But his main passion was to ride the hills and valleys searching for land to buy. Utilizing the expertise of one of the few mining engineers in Alabama, Joseph Squire of the Lancashire coal pits of England, DeBardeleben bought extensive coal lands. In 1878 he joined with Truman H. Aldrich, a mining engineer, and James W. Sloss, a developer of railroads, to organize the first big coal concern in Alabama, the Pratt Coal and Coke Company.

The three men placed all their assets in the project. DeBardeleben, as president, had the responsibility of obtaining money and land and promoting the endeavor; Aldrich took charge of the technical aspects. Opening the first mine in October 1878, the company also built coke ovens and constructed a rail line from the mines into Birmingham. In 1879 shipments of high-grade coking coal from the Pratt field brought life to the district's economy, but in a pattern that would be repeated, the headstrong DeBardeleben did not work well with his partners, who withdrew by 1881.

With Pratt coal fueling the great iron boom, Birmingham flourished in the 1880s. Known as Birmingham's biggest booster, DeBardeleben invested in a number of other ventures, including the Henry Ellen coal mines in the Cahaba River basin and the Alice Furnace Company, which erected the first blast furnace inside the city limits of Birmingham. By late 1881

DeBardeleben, exhausted and fearing that he had tuberculosis, decided to move to the drier climate of northern Mexico. In the first million-dollar deal of the district, on 29 December 1881 he sold the Pratt company to Enoch Ensley, a "moneyed man" from Memphis who headed a group of Tennessee investors. Subsequently, the Tennessee Coal, Iron and Railroad Company (TCI) absorbed Pratt Coal in 1886 in a $2.25 million stock deal and became the giant of the district.

Sheep ranching in Mexico, DeBardeleben not only recovered his health but also made contacts in Texas that would bring new capital to Birmingham. With a Kentucky lawyer, William Thompson Underwood, DeBardeleben constructed the Mary Pratt furnace (named after his daughter), which went into blast in 1883, but his largest new venture involved founding a city that he intended to rival Birmingham. Together with David Roberts, a young Welshman who secured additional investors from Charleston, Baltimore, and London, DeBardeleben incorporated DeBardeleben Coal and Iron Company in 1886 in Jefferson County, Alabama. Although he named their new town Bessemer after the English steel maker, DeBardeleben never realized his dream of establishing a steel plant; however, he fostered industrial development in western Jefferson County, continued to raise capital, and developed more companies.

By 1891 TCI officials feared DeBardeleben Coal and Iron Company as a rival. On 18 March 1892 an agreement was reached that merged the two companies, kept the TCI name, placed DeBardeleben and his associates on the board of directors, and made TCI the largest iron and coal company in the South. Content to serve as the first vice president for only a year before attempting to gain control through stock manipulation, DeBardeleben found himself defeated by the "Wall Street wilderness," lost most of his fortune, and was forced to sell his shares to his chief rival, New York speculator John Inman. He remained vice president until compelled to resign on 22 October 1894.

Although DeBardeleben continued to promote new industries and founded the Alabama Fuel and Iron Company, he never regained his fortune or a position of prominence in the district; the time of the freewheeling, laissez faire entrepreneur had passed. He suffered a heart attack while visiting his Acmar Mines and died three days later at his Birmingham home.

Once proclaiming that life was "one big game of poker" (Armes, p. 343), DeBardeleben was one of the first "big moneyed" men of Birmingham. Later judgments have held him at least partly responsible for the unstable boom or bust nature of Birmingham's early growth. Not an iron man, he was a speculator, promoter, and booster, responsible for bringing capital into the district. An investor remarked, "It's many a man has been lured upon the rocks of Alabama by that siren tongue of DeBardeleben!" (Armes, p. 331). Milton H. Smith, president of the Louisville & Nashville Railroad, declared that DeBardeleben was "the darndest man I ever knew in my life! Why, I've spent thirty millions following that man!" (Armes, p. 343). But he was a builder, and ultimately his properties became the center of the Birmingham holdings of the U.S. Steel Corporation, which took over TCI in 1907. By then, the times had passed DeBardeleben by, but the city he helped develop became the industrial capital of the New South.

• Business records of the DeBardeleben Coal Company (Collection No. 914) are in the Birmingham Public Library. The records of the Tennessee Coal, Iron and Railroad Company, U.S. Steel Corporation Records, Fairfield, Ala., contain information on some of the DeBardeleben companies that were absorbed by TCI. An early typescript history of TCI is W. B. Allen, "History of TCI," in U.S. Steel Corp. records. For vividly descriptive, contemporary accounts of DeBardeleben and other early entrepreneurs of the Birmingham district, see Ethel Armes, *The Story of Coal and Iron in Alabama* (1910), and Armes, "The Spirit of the Founders," *Survey* 27 (6 Jan. 1912): 1453–63. Candid comments on DeBardeleben and other Birmingham industrialists are in the diary of James Bowron, Jr. (a TCI official) in the James Bowron Papers, the University of Alabama Library, Tuscaloosa. Uncritical but interesting information is in George M. Cruikshank, *A History of Birmingham and Its Environs*, vols. 1 and 2 (1920). A comprehensive survey of DeBardeleben is Justin Fuller, "Henry F. DeBardeleben, Industrialist of the New South," *The Alabama Review* 39 (Jan. 1986): 3–18. DeBardeleben's efforts to enter the steel business are described in Fuller, "From Iron to Steel: Alabama's Industrial Evolution," *The Alabama Review* 17 (Apr. 1964): 137–48. Fuller, "History of the Tennessee Coal, Iron, and Railroad Company, 1852–1907" (Ph.D. diss., Univ. of North Carolina at Chapel Hill, 1966), contains information on the various mergers. Furnaces built by DeBardeleben are discussed in Joseph H. Woodward II, *Alabama Blast Furnaces* (1940). General overviews of DeBardeleben's role in the industrial development of the Birmingham district can be found in Leah Rawls Atkins, *The Valley and the Hills: An Illustrated History of Birmingham and Jefferson County* (1981), and Wayne Flynt, *Mine, Mill and Microchip: A Chronicle of Alabama Enterprise* (1987). An obituary is in the *Birmingham News*, 7 Dec. 1910.

MARLENE HUNT RIKARD

DE BERDT, Dennys (c. 1694–11 Apr. 1770), merchant and colonial agent, was born in London, England, the son of John De Berdt, a trader. Particulars regarding his mother have not survived. Following in his father's footsteps, De Berdt became a merchant in London, quickly establishing an interest in foreign trade. By 1748 he was deeply involved in the North American trade, and two decades later he admitted still having £50,000 "locked up in America" (Reed Collection). He was long associated with the firm of Wright, Burkitt & Sayre.

Doubtless it was his financial interests in North America that led De Berdt to assume a larger political interest in the area. In October 1750 he became part of a committee of six named by the Protestant Dissenting Deputies to carefully monitor any efforts to introduce bishops into America and to help protect Anglo-Americans against English attempts to diminish the strength or numbers of colonial churches. As a leading London Dissenter, De Berdt also gave generously to funds for the College of New Jersey and helped to collect money for the Reverend Eleazar Wheelock's Indian School, which later became Dartmouth College. In 1758 De Berdt persuaded a London publisher to print copies of a popular sermon by Virginia's Reverend Samuel Davies titled "The Curse of Cowardice" (1759), a passionate statement of the colonies' need for, and devotion to, England. De Berdt attached a preface to Davies's work dedicating it to the Earl of Halifax and noting the "ardent Zeal" of colonial Americans for English rights and privileges in general and for Halifax's policies and programs in particular. By 1763 he was offering advice to the Pitt administration on military operations in North America and was representing clients seeking land grants in Canada before the Board of Trade.

In 1765, on the recommendation of Dr. Samuel Avery, formerly chairman of the Protestant Dissenting Deputies, De Berdt was named special agent for Massachusetts to orchestrate that government's opposition to the Stamp Act. His habit of drafting his constituents' grievances into memorials that he then presented to various English officials and his ability to work closely with Lords Halifax and Dartmouth served Massachusetts well. In reward for his effective service in bringing about the repeal of the hated measure, the Massachusetts House of Representatives in 1766 designated him as the permanent agent for that colony, a post he held until his death. However, Massachusetts Governor Francis Bernard refused to accept De Berdt's selection and his council chose William Bollan as its spokesman in London. Though the Board of Trade quickly accepted De Berdt's credentials, Wills Hill, the Earl of Hillsborough later sought in 1768 to discredit his position on the basis that he represented only a single house of the Massachusetts legislature. De Berdt also represented Delaware as colonial agent in England until 1770, having replaced David Barclay, Jr., in 1765. As agent of both colonies he worked assiduously in 1766 for the repeal of the Currency Act, which forbade making colonial bills of credit legal tender and prohibited the publication of legal tender paper money. He preferred, as he said, "a good & solid Coin to a precarious & pernicious currency" (Matthews, p. 453).

De Berdt's opposition to British measures against the American colonies after 1763 was based both on constitutional and practical considerations. He maintained that originally American colonists had been driven from Great Britain by oppression and that they had then contracted with the crown through their colonial charters for certain liberties, among them the right to tax themselves. Thus, colonists had historically been permitted important constitutional safeguards, including the right to vote their own taxes and to regulate their internal affairs. Nonetheless, De Berdt preferred to emphasize practical arguments, insisting that British policies after 1763 ought to be discontinued because they disrupted transatlantic trade and diminished imperial commerce. He accepted the fact that Parliament could legislate for the colonies, but he denied that it could legally tax them.

In the late 1760s De Berdt's "Artillery Court" home became a favorite haunt for Americans in London. Several regular visitors, such as Arthur Lee and Stephen Sayre (who later became a partner in De Berdt's mercantile firm), came to act as his assistants. De Berdt had been an effective and efficient agent during the Stamp Act crisis, but following 1768 his effectiveness declined and his reputation suffered both in London and Boston. Increasingly he was characterized by friends and foes alike as naive in his political assessments. His unpopularity with Hillsborough, newly appointed secretary of state for the American colonies, personal feuds with Richard Jackson and Benjamin Franklin, and his unwillingness to work in concert with Bollan all contributed to this decline, as did his failing health.

Matters escalated in 1768 when Governor Bernard's criticism of Boston and its town meetings led to a decision to remove him from office. The Massachusetts House directed De Berdt to expedite Bernard's dismissal. However, because he was granted no power of attorney to prosecute the case, and because he was provided no compelling evidence against Bernard, De Berdt underwent a humiliating inquisition at the hands of the Privy Council and was forced to watch impotently as Bernard was acquitted of all charges. To blunt criticism in 1769 that he was too old (he was then seventy-five) and too ill to be an effective voice for Massachusetts in London, De Berdt arranged to have Joseph Reed act as his assistant, promising him half of his yearly Massachusetts salary of £300. Earlier De Berdt had helped Reed, son of one of De Berdt's American business associates, to obtain important administrative offices in New Jersey, including deputy secretary and clerk of the council.

De Berdt and his wife Martha had two children. The date of their marriage is unknown. De Berdt died in London, leaving an extensive but debt-ridden estate incapable of supporting his wife and children. He proved to be a valuable and conscientious friend to America, especially before 1768 when his sound advice, his enthusiasm in collecting information about the colonies, and his willingness to spend liberally in seeing that news of America reached important English officials, unquestionably benefited his Delaware and Massachusetts constituencies.

• No formal biography of De Berdt exists. Scattered De Berdt letters are found in the Reed Manuscripts Collection, New-York Historical Society; the Public Record Office, London; the papers of the Protestant Dissenting Deputies, Guildhall Library, London; the Massachusetts Archives, Boston; the Dartmouth College Library; and in the Dartmouth Manuscripts Collection in the William Salt Library, Stafford, England. Papers in the Stafford collection have been published by the Royal Historical Manuscripts Commission, *14th Report, Appendix, Pt. X, The Manuscripts of the Earl of Dartmouth, Vol. II (American Papers)* (1895) and *15th Report, Appendix, Pt. I, Vol. III* (1896). Biographical information can be gleaned from Albert Matthews, ed., "Letters of Dennys De Berdt, 1757–1770," in Colonial Massachusetts Society, *Publications* 13 (1912): 293–461. Biographical and genealogical materials also are found in William B. Reed, *Life and Correspondence of Joseph Reed* (2 vols., 1847); Reed, *The Life of Esther De Berdt* (1853); and John F. Roche, *Joseph Reed: A Moderate in the American Revolution* (1957). Extremely valuable is Michael G. Kammen, *A Rope of Sand: The Colonial Agents, British Politics, and the American Revolution* (1968), which assesses De Berdt's career as a colonial agent.

G. S. ROWE

DEBERRY, William Nelson (29 Aug. 1870–20 Jan. 1948), Congregational clergyman and social service worker, was born in Nashville, Tennessee, the son of Caswell DeBerry and Charlotte Mayfield, former slaves. His father was a railroad shop worker and a lay preacher in a local Baptist church; his mother's occupation is unknown. DeBerry was educated in Nashville schools and entered Fisk University in 1886, graduating ten years later with a B.S. degree. DeBerry then went to Oberlin College in Ohio where he received a Bachelor of Divinity degree in 1899. In that same year, he was ordained in the Congregational ministry, became the pastor of St. John's Congregational Church in Springfield, Massachusetts, and married Amanda McKissack of Pulaski, Tennessee; they had two children. After the death of his first wife (date unknown), DeBerry married Louise Scott in 1943.

DeBerry served as pastor of St. John's Congregational Church until 31 December 1930, during which time the church grew from approximately 100 members to about 500 members. In 1911 DeBerry launched St. John's Institutional Activities as the church's social outreach to the city's black population. Eventually, it offered boys' and girls' clubs, classes in cooking and sewing, an employment bureau, a music program, a playground, and a summer camp. In 1917 it became affiliated with the National Urban League. DeBerry was widely recognized for the work of St. John's Institutional Activities, the first systematic effort in Springfield to meet the social needs of its growing African-American community. In 1913 he was appointed to the Governor's Committee on Religious and Interracial Understanding, and a year later Lincoln University awarded him an honorary doctor of divinity degree. In 1915 he became the first alumnus to serve as a trustee of Fisk University. DeBerry was elected Second Assistant Moderator of the National Council of Congregational Churches in 1919, and in 1925 he was elected Recording Secretary of the American Missionary Association. In 1927 DeBerry received the Harmon Foundation's first award "for distinguished service in religion among Negroes of the United States," and the following year he was given the William Pynchon medal from the city of Springfield for "distinguished public service."

DeBerry directed a sociological survey of black Springfield in 1921, published in 1922, that studied the population growth and industrial opportunity for Springfield's black community during World War I. In a follow-up study two decades later, DeBerry edited and published *Sociological Survey of the Negro Popula-*

tion of Springfield, Mass. (1940), which discovered that the depression decade had caused a slight population decline and diminished black employment opportunities. DeBerry resigned from his pastorate in 1930 to devote his full attention to social work among blacks in Springfield. He became the executive director of the Dunbar Community League, an agency that absorbed St. John's Institutional Activities, and in 1935 DeBerry was appointed to the Springfield Board of Public Welfare. Although he retired from the league in 1947, he continued to direct Camp Atwater, a summer camp for black children that he had founded in East Brookfield, Massachusetts. He died in a Springfield hospital after a long illness.

William Nelson DeBerry was among a small group of African-American clergymen who, early in the twentieth century, saw the necessity of specialized attention to the secular needs of an urban African-American community. Through St. John's Institutional Activities, his ministry enriched and gave texture to the cultural, recreational, and social lives of Springfield's African-American community and pioneered the way for the social activism of black churches in the civil rights era and beyond. When he died, the *Journal of Negro History* remembered him as "one of the greatest churchmen of his time."

• There is neither a known collection of the manuscripts nor a biography of William Nelson DeBerry. Biographical information on his career can be found in Frank Lincoln Mather, ed., *Who's Who of the Colored Race* (1915); Lily Hardy Hammond, *In the Vanguard of a Race* (1922); "William Nelson DeBerry," *Journal of Negro History* 33 (July 1948): 384–85; *The History of St. John's Congregational Church, Springfield, Massachusetts, 1844–1962* (1962); and Nancy Weiss, "William Nelson DeBerry," in *Dictionary of American Negro Biography*, ed. Rayford W. Logan and Michael R. Winston (1982). Obituaries are in the *New York Times* and the *Springfield Union*, both 21 Jan. 1948.

RALPH E. LUKER

DE BOW, James Dunwoody Brownson (10 July 1820– 27 Feb. 1867), writer and publisher, was born in Charleston, South Carolina, the son of Garrett De Bow, a grocer, and Mary Bridget Norton. The family of five children enjoyed modest prosperity until De Bow's father failed in business. He died in 1826. De Bow's mother and older brother died of cholera in 1836, at which time he went to live with his older sister. De Bow was a studious youth, read widely, and graduated at the top of his class from the College of Charleston in 1843. He was admitted to the South Carolina bar on 15 May 1844.

De Bow began his literary career in July 1844 with the *Southern Quarterly Review*, edited by Daniel K. Whitaker, contributing the essay "The Characteristics of the Statesman." Attendance at a southern commercial convention in Memphis in 1845 fired his zeal for the economic improvement of the South. He moved to New Orleans that year. In 1846, recognizing that the South valued "ploughshares more than philosophy," he launched his famous *De Bow's Review*, originally titled *The Commercial Review of the South and West*, a monthly magazine devoted primarily to commerce, agriculture, trade, and finance. The magazine presented its readers with page after page of statistical data on the southern economy, as well as signed articles. De Bow kept his eyes on economic trends and patterns throughout the South and became a strenuous voice for modernization. However fact-laden his publication seemed, it also reflected its editor's idealistic and enthusiastic feelings about commerce and industry. He had a poetic sensibility about economic improvement and its place in advancing civilization. A champion of railroads in the South, De Bow called this industry "one of the great miracles of modern art and civilization" that promised great moral, social, and political gain.

In the late 1840s De Bow was made superintendent of the Louisiana Bureau of Statistics. At the national level, he was appointed by President Franklin Pierce to head the seventh U.S. Census (1850). In 1849 he enthusiastically took up a professorship of commerce at the newly established University of Louisiana in New Orleans. De Bow had championed reform in American higher education, impatient with the dominance of the classical curriculum and urging a more practical direction. In his romantic way, too, De Bow hoped to elevate the commercial classes to a social rank and prestige equal to those of the learned professions. Throughout its career, the *Review* always featured a literary section, and its editor urged the South on to advancement in the arts as well as in commerce.

De Bow's southern nationalism derived from his painful awareness of the region's economic backwardness and its dependency on the North. In 1850 De Bow used the editor's pages of the *Review* to decry this situation: "Who conducts our commerce, builds for us ships, and navigates them on the high seas? *The North!* Who spins and weaves, for our domestic use (and grows rich in doing it), the fabric which overruns our fields and not seldom fails to remunerate the labor that is bestowed upon it here? *The North.* Who supplies the material and the engineers for our railroads where we have any, gives to us books and periodicals, newspapers and authors, without any limit or end? *The North.*"

De Bow saw no connection between the South's economic plight and the primacy of slavery in the regional economy. From early on the *Review* defended the institution, through De Bow's own writings and essays he solicited from prominent slavery advocates. De Bow insisted that the well-being of merchants, traders, and all ranks of white labor were inseparable from the interests of the great planters and the slave system that sustained them. Nor did he have any doubt that American slavery fostered the moral, religious, and economic well-being of African Americans, which race, when left on its own, he averred, fell readily into barbarism. The South, he urged, had a God-given responsibility to nurture a backward race and ensure its benevolent protection by the prevailing arrangements.

De Bow fortified his views of racial hierarchy by adhering to a theory of multigenesis of human types. He accepted the opinion of those scientists and theologians who believed that separate creations of humans had occurred in different parts of the earth, each creation having its own distinct physical characteristics and different "habits and constitution" as well. He urged this view against orthodox Christian teaching, adding that the biblical account describes only one of the several origins of human life on earth.

Increasingly, De Bow became a party to the more extreme southern position in the politics of the 1850s. On one of the major issues, the "popular sovereignty" policy sponsored by the Illinois senator Stephen Douglas, De Bow broke with the Democratic party. He mistrusted popular sovereignty for being a device by which slavery could be voted out of the territories. De Bow, in fact, called for the expansion of slavery into the West, with which region he looked for an economic alliance, and he called for the reopening of the African slave trade, which had been terminated by Congress in 1808. By the middle 1850s De Bow sensed and welcomed the likelihood that the South, in order to protect its rights and interests, would have to go its own way. It should begin to train its own leaders for the future, a role he gave to southern colleges especially. The South must recall its youth from the North, he said, "subject them no more to the poison of Yale and Amherst, and even Harvard."

A bachelor until the age of thirty-four, De Bow married Caroline Poe, a cousin once removed of the great poet, in 1854. A daughter and son were born of the marriage, but the son died in 1857 and Caroline in 1858. A second marriage followed in 1860, to Martha Johns, of a prominent Nashville family. The couple had four children. De Bow presented a gaunt and lean figure and a head of thick, dark, disheveled hair and a black and shaggy beard. He had big ears, a wide mouth, and a long nose, though his dark, piercing eyes made him an arresting figure. Nonetheless, one description labeled him "ugly," and his marriage to the attractive woman from Tennessee inspired comments about "the beauty and the beast." By 1860 De Bow enjoyed considerable economic success from the *Review* and from investments in property he bought with his earnings. Although he fretted constantly about delinquent payments from his subscribers, De Bow had made the *Review* the most successful journal in the South, attaining a list of some 4,600 in 1855. Louisiana, Alabama, and Mississippi supplied the most readers.

De Bow considered the Civil War the product of northern fanaticism and misguided moral fervor represented by a small group of abolitionists and unreasoning Republicans. He believed that against this array all the South would rally together, including slaves and the free black population. He himself went to Richmond to volunteer his service to the Confederate government. The war fascinated De Bow, and he kept an extensive chronicle of events and personalities and offered commentary and judgment on political and military leaders. The war, however, cut deeply into the *Review*'s circulation, forcing suspension of publication in 1862 and then again for two years into 1864. Another suspension followed, and it did not renew publication until January 1866.

After the war De Bow received a presidential pardon, but his national reputation did him in. A Washington newspaper remembered that De Bow had been "active in inciting the secession of the states," and it echoed the sentiments of a Boston paper that "he be given into the hands of the negroes so that when they hang up 'de fiddle' they [might] at the same time 'hang up De Bow.'" De Bow did appear before the Joint Committee on Reconstruction and urged against any "vindictive" policies toward the defeated southern states. He assured that whites would willingly grant the new freedmen all civil rights, but he urged against their acquiring the right to vote.

De Bow toured the southern states in 1866 to survey the economic conditions and to find material to reestablish the *Review* and restore it to its earlier condition. He opened offices for the magazine in several cities and solicited some 2,500 subscribers. His death of peritonitis while visiting an ill brother in Elizabeth, New Jersey, the next year, however, virtually assured the end of the publication. Despite intermittent revivals, it made its last appearance in June 1880.

De Bow deserves his reputation as a major defender of southern interests and of the South's social and racial system. His nationalism, though, had a narrow focus. It centered almost entirely on the cause of economic improvement. De Bow seldom took note of the South's human problems, its poverty and disease, the cruelty and violence of slavery, the ignorance and moral improvidence—gambling and drinking—among the white classes. De Bow called himself a Jeffersonian, but a philosophy of human rights and freedom figured little in his thinking. Certainly, though, De Bow played a useful role in the Commercial Convention Movement in the South and awakened the region to the need for modernization. Forty years before Henry Grady championed the cause of a "New South," De Bow provided its essential outline.

• The J. D. B. De Bow Papers are at Duke University and contain business and personal correspondence, his diary, and his unpublished chronicle of the Civil War. A detailed biography of De Bow, somewhat sympathetic and offering much information about the progress of the *Review*, is Ottis Clark Skipper, *J. D. B. De Bow: Magazinist of the Old South* (1958). See also Diffee W. Standard, "*De Bow's Review*, 1846–1880: A Magazine of Southern Opinion" (Ph.D. diss., Univ. of North Carolina, 1970). For a history of *De Bow's Review*, see Frank Luther Mott, *A History of American Magazines*, vols. 1 and 2 (1938–1968). For some important selections from the *Review*, see Paul F. Paskoff and Daniel J. Wilson, eds., *The Cause of the South: Selections from De Bow's Review, 1846–1867* (1982). For the larger context of De Bow's ideas about slavery, see Larry E. Tise, *Proslavery: A History of the Defense of Slavery in America, 1701–1840* (1987).

J. DAVID HOEVELER, JR.

DE BRAHM, William Gerard (20 Aug. 1718–3 July 1799?), surveyor-cartographer and military engineer, was born in Koblenz, Germany, the son of Johann Phillip von Brahm, court musician to the elector of Triers, and Johannetta Simonet. A member of the lesser nobility, De Brahm secured a broad education that included exposure to the burgeoning experimental sciences of his day. After attaining the rank of captain engineer in Charles VII's imperial army, De Brahm married and renounced the Roman Catholic faith. Forced to resign his army commission because of his renunciation, he and his bride, Wilhelmina de Ger, found themselves nearly destitute.

Opportunity came when Samuel Urlsperger, a senior of the Evangelical Ministry of Augsburg who was recruiting Germans to settle in Georgia, put De Brahm in charge of a contingent bound for the colony. De Brahm was granted 500 acres of land for his services. Writing some weeks after De Brahm's arrival in 1751, James Habersham, a member of Georgia's board of assistants and royal council termed him "one of the most intelligent men I ever met with . . . will, I doubt not, make a very usefull colonist."

De Brahm was immediately put to work seeking out suitable land for the new immigrants, who soon were settled west of Savannah. In the spring of 1752 he was summoned to Charleston to undertake the design and construction of a comprehensive system of fortifications for the city. It was at this point that he exchanged von for De as his surname prefix. In 1754 De Brahm's fortunes rose sharply when he was appointed as one of the two first surveyors general in Georgia's newly instituted royal administration. Shortly thereafter he received an interim appointment as South Carolina's surveyor general and inspector of quitrents. Carolina's governor again sought him out in 1756 to survey the site and design and oversee the construction of ill-fated Fort Loudoun on the Little Tennessee River.

Georgia's colonial governor, like his fellow in neighboring South Carolina, "consulted with Mr. De Brahm . . . about what will be necessary to be done to put this Colony into a proper State of Defence." For Savannah De Brahm proposed a "well pallisadoed Intrenchment to envelop the city" and to provide a refuge for outlying planters, their slaves and stock, which was carried out according to his instructions. At the Savannah's mouth he constructed Fort George on Cockspur Island.

Realizing their almost total ignorance of the geography and resources of the newly enlarged American empire, in early 1764 George III's chief advisers recommended the establishment of two new imperial offices, the northern and southern surveyor generalships. They were charged with undertaking comprehensive and detailed surveys in their respective districts, which were separated by the Potomac River. In November 1764 De Brahm, an accomplished cartographer whose maps of Georgia and South Carolina had been published and well received in London, was selected for the Southern District. In addition, De Brahm was named surveyor general of lands in the newly organized British colony of East Florida. In the early months of 1765 De Brahm, with his wife and daughter (a son had died in childhood), left Georgia for St. Augustine. De Brahm's wife died that September. With a daughter to rear, De Brahm lost no time in remarrying, to the sister of a local planter and land surveyor named Row.

For six arduous years De Brahm explored, surveyed, and mapped the eastern coast of Florida and prepared detailed descriptions of the flora and fauna as well as other potential resources found there. Hurricanes, shipwrecks, attacks of fever, Indian threats, and bureaucratic opposition tested his endurance, but De Brahm managed to produce a large number of detailed and accurate maps and reports describing and analyzing a region that had been almost totally unknown to the British.

De Brahm's East Florida surveys were prematurely terminated in 1771 as a result of his feud with the colony's governor. In response to the governor's charges of malfeasance in the conduct of his provincial office, De Brahm was ordered to London for an official hearing. De Brahm took the opportunity to extend his observations of the Gulf Stream current. Upon his arrival in London, he addressed a lengthy letter to the editor of *Gentleman's Magazine* (41: 436) in which he informed the public that the Gulf Stream formed a safe seaway that could greatly accelerate voyages from the American colonies to Europe.

De Brahm lost little time in following up this notice with a book of sailing directions and original maps published in 1772 under the title *The Atlantic Pilot*. In it he included his "Hydrographical Map of the Atlantic Ocean Extending from the Southernmost Part of North America to Europe," the first published map to show the Gulf Stream as a continuous current through the North Atlantic.

While awaiting the convening of the Treasury Board that finally exonerated him on 28 July 1774, De Brahm enjoyed the patronage of the influential Lord Dartmouth, secretary of state for the Southern Department. He also personally presented his elegant multivolume manuscript "Report of the General Survey in the Southern District of North America" to King George III. During this London sojourn De Brahm became interested in the potential of the mercury barometer as a height-determining instrument. His second and third published works grew out of his barometric calculations and appeared in 1774.

Thanks to the support of Lord Dartmouth, De Brahm was provided with the armed ship *Cherokee* for his return to Florida and the continuation of the general survey of the Southern District. On the slow voyage, which lasted from mid-June until the first week in September, De Brahm conducted a pioneering oceanographic survey, the results of which remain unpublished. During the voyage the *Cherokee* went through a violent hurricane, and Mrs. De Brahm died. The surveyor general landed in Charleston on 9 September 1775 to attend her funeral, she having died the day before land was sighted.

Charleston was then immersed in political ferment, and the tide of rebellion was at flood stage. The *Cherokee* was removed from De Brahm's service for military use. De Brahm became persona non grata in the eyes of the Carolinians when he refused to abjure his allegiance to the king. Adding insult to injury, his nephew, Ferdinand De Brahm, joined the Americans as a military engineer. This situation led some contemporaries and several later historians to confuse the two and wrongly accuse De Brahm of duplicity if not treason in the revolutionary war.

In 1776 De Brahm entered into his third marriage, this time to the well-connected Charleston widow Mary Fenwick née Drayton, the widow of Edward Fenwick, a member of South Carolina's royal council. In the autumn of 1777 the Loyalist De Brahms left Charleston aboard a ship bound for France. In London De Brahm collected back salary due him as East Florida's surveyor of lands and received his last compensation for service as surveyor general of the Southern District. Now sixty years of age and in poor health, he appears to have suffered some sort of general breakdown; as he later explained, De Brahm spent the period from 1778 to 1784 "for the most part an invalid" in Topsham, Devon. In 1783 East Florida had been retroceded to Spain, and all hope of a return to his position and property there was dashed.

After his recovery in 1784, De Brahm returned to Charleston where, after long legal wrangling, he succeeded in having his name removed from the state's confiscation list and recouped a small part of the Fenwick estate. De Brahm's allegiance had not changed, however. In a letter to King George III sent from Charleston, De Brahm stressed his unbroken loyalty and dedication. In signing the letter, De Brahm styled himself "John De Brahm," as he would frequently henceforth. In the 1780s De Brahm embraced Quakerism and was guided by the tenets of the Friends as he pursued a path toward spiritual enlightenment no less energetically than he had pursued the muses of science and geography earlier in his life. All of his future publications would be devoted to biblical themes and revelations.

De Brahm returned to London in July 1788; there he continued to try bettering his fortunes through petitions for reimbursement of losses due to the war and a pension for his services to the Crown.

By 1791 the De Brahms had made their way via Charleston to Philadelphia, where the former surveyor general would publish three religiophilosophical books in the next three years. In 1796 De Brahm purchased an estate in Bristol Township, Philadelphia County. It was here, at the home called variously "Bellair," "Clearfield," or "Fairfield," that De Brahm spent his last three years in a style that contemporaries found both colorful and genteel. He died at his estate.

De Brahm is less well known than he deserves to be because his major contributions were devoted to East Florida, a colony that was part of the British Empire for two brief decades. Although his maps played an important role in the revolutionary war, the conflict brought an enforced halt to his official duties and may have contributed to his physical and emotional breakdown and consequent abandonment of scientific pursuits. De Brahm was largely forgotten in England, but early nineteenth-century Americans found his report and maps useful following the acquisition of Florida from Spain in 1821. More recently, researchers concerned with environmental changes in the Florida Keys and the Miami area have found his maps and reports to be both accurate and valuable. In at least two actions brought before the U.S. Supreme Court dealing with offshore and riverine boundaries in Florida, Georgia, and South Carolina, De Brahm's maps and reports were submitted as evidence by the litigants (*United States v. Florida*, 1972; *Georgia v. South Carolina*, 1981).

• In addition to *The Atlantic Pilot* (1772), De Brahm published two other scientific works in London, *De Brahm's Zonical Tables for the Twenty-five Northern and Southern Climates* (1774) and *The Levelling Balance and Counter-Balance; or, The Method of Observing by the Weight and Height of Mercury, on Any Place of Terra-Firma on the Terrestrial Globe, the Exact Weight and Altitude of the Atmosphere below and above the Place of Observation; Thereby to Ascertain How Much the Horizon of the Sea Is Lower than the Place Whereon the Observation Is Made* (1774). Four of his religiomystical books were published in Philadelphia, and one was issued from the press of Salomon Mayer in Ephrata, Pa. The Philadelphia volumes were *Time: An Apparition of Eternity* (1791), *Voice of the Everlasting Gospel* (1792), *Apocalyptic Gnomon* . . . (1795), and *Sum of Testimonies of Truth* (1795?). The Ephrata book is in German and is titled *Zeite Rechenschaft* (1794). Chapters from De Brahm's "General Report" were included in Plowden C. J. Weston, *Documents Connected with the History of South Carolina* (1856), and George Wimberley Jones De-Renne, *History of the Province of Georgia, with Maps of Original Surveys* (1849). It was not until 1971 that the full text of King George III's copy of De Brahm's "General Report" was published as *De Brahm's Report of the General Survey in the Southern District of North America*, ed. Louis De Vorsey, Jr. The 59-page introduction and numerous scholarly notes included in this volume constitute the fullest biographical profile on De Brahm available. A facsimile edition of *The Atlantic Pilot*, ed. De Vorsey, was published in 1974. De Brahm's personal copy of the "General Report"—similar but not identical to the King George III copy published by South Carolina in 1971—is at Harvard.

LOUIS DE VORSEY, JR.

DEBS, Eugene Victor (5 Nov. 1855–20 Oct. 1926), labor organizer and presidential candidate for the Socialist Party of America, was born in Terre Haute, Indiana, the son of Marguerite Bettrich and Daniel Debs, Alsatian immigrants and retail grocers. Following the completion of ninth grade, Debs left school to work as a paint scraper on the Terre Haute and Vandalia Railroad. Within a year he rose to locomotive fireman but was laid off in the sustained economic depression of the mid-1870s. Searching for work in St. Louis in 1874, he encountered extensive urban poverty for the first time.

When Debs returned to Terre Haute, he took a position as a clerk in Herman Hulman's wholesale grocery, but he retained an intense attachment to railroad work and railroad workers. When the Brotherhood of Locomotive Firemen (BLF) organized a local lodge in 1875, Debs became a charter member and was elected recording secretary. The BLF was less a trade union than a benevolent society that provided accident and death benefits. The organization accepted management's right to determine the nature of the workday and sought to encourage among its members responsible conduct and a harmonious feeling toward employers. This perspective, with its belief in individual effort, potential social mobility, and the absence of permanent class divisions, proved attractive to the young Debs.

At first glance, the outbreak of a nationwide railroad strike in the summer of 1877—the first national strike in American history—threatened those expectations. Although state and federal troops were called out in numerous cities, the strike in Terre Haute proved anything but violent, and Debs's role in it was anything but incendiary. In contrast with workers in some of the larger railroad centers, railroad workers in Terre Haute largely exempted their employer, William Riley McKeen, from attack. These workers did occupy the local rail depot, but they explicitly focused their anger at the corporate owners of the larger railroads, such as Thomas Scott, president of the Pennsylvania line. Scott's concentrated economic power, the strikers argued, forced their employer to follow his lead in instituting the wage cuts. Terre Haute's workers asserted a communality of interest between themselves and their employer and categorically rejected the advice of coal miners from a neighboring county to call a general strike.

Yet for the 22-year-old Debs, even a strike proclaimed for these ends proved too threatening to support. Although a leader of the local BLF lodge, Debs took no known position on the strike during July 1877, even as his fellow lodge officers were actively involved. The following September, however, at the brotherhood's annual convention, Debs clearly articulated his position in a long and well-received speech to the delegates who had just witnessed the strike's near total failure. "Does the Brotherhood encourage strikes?" he asked. "To this question we most emphatically answer, No, Brothers. To disregard the laws which govern the land? To destroy the last vestige of order? We again say No, a thousand times No."

In an important fashion, then, the 1877 strike did not immediately threaten Debs's expectations for social harmony and its attendant promise of social mobility. Indeed, following his speech at the convention, Debs was the only officer of the Terre Haute lodge returned to office, and he achieved even greater prominence within the national organization as well. By 1880 this young man who had only worked for the railroad a brief time had become the grand secretary treasurer of the brotherhood and the editor of its monthly, the *Locomotive Firemen's Magazine*. As the holder of the two most important positions within the brotherhood, he became a figure of some note nationally, as

what many called "the labor question" demanded more and more public attention.

In other ways as well Debs found that his response to the 1877 strike increased rather than diminished his standing. In 1879 he ran for city clerk as a Democrat, and the nature of the electoral coalition that led to his decisive victory over both Republican and Labor party candidates indicated the depth of his appeal. He received public support from former employers, including McKeen, a lifelong Republican, and won a clear plurality in the traditionally Republican Second Ward, the abode of many of the city's wealthier citizens. He also carried the wards with heavy concentrations of railroad and other working people by more than a 3 to 1 margin over his opponents' combined total.

Little occurred to threaten this experience of social harmony over the next five years. Debs became firmly entrenched as the national leader of the brotherhood, and he greatly expanded the group's organizing efforts with his incessant travels, crisscrossing the country time and again to attend local lodge meetings and to build the organization. Simultaneously, he easily won reelection as city clerk in 1881, and the same multiclass electoral coalition brought Debs the Democratic nomination and election to the Indiana Assembly in 1884. In 1885 he married Katherine Metzel. They would have no children. From a middle-class German immigrant family that owned a local drugstore, Katherine shared many of her husband's expectations of continued mobility and social prominence.

Debs's emphasis on harmony and cooperation as the key to industrial peace continued into 1886. He joined other brotherhood officials in urging members not to honor the strike of the Knights of Labor against Jay Gould's railways, and he remained publicly silent when the American Federation of Labor organized that December. Debs remained wary of strikes and confrontations with employers. Precisely because he came to these ideas honestly, as a reflection of his personal and social experience over the decade and a half since he entered the workforce, he could change his ideas in response to new circumstances. Indeed, by 1886 Debs had already begun to question his positions in private, even as he maintained, for the moment, a consistent public pattern. At the core of his thought was a commitment to the idea of an independent citizen living within a community of relative equals where acknowledged economic differences never weakened the common bond of citizenship nor allowed the emergence of permanent divisions within society. Increasingly, the actions of the nation's corporate employers and of the smaller businessmen who followed their lead caused Debs to question whether many of them retained their commitment to that reciprocal expectation of both worker and owner as expressed in the phrase "a fair day's work demands a fair day's pay."

The year-long strike against the Chicago, Burlington, and Quincy Railroad that began early in 1888 deepened Debs's concerns. The company's refusal to negotiate with the railroad brotherhoods influenced him to write in his editorials in *Locomotive Firemen's Magazine* a critique of Burlington officials and of others like them throughout American industry. Their actions, Debs stated repeatedly, threatened to destroy the proclaimed equality of all citizens and thus undermine the very foundation of American life. He also argued that the failure of the strike was in part the fault of the brotherhoods themselves. Their organizational structures emphasized craft distinctions, encouraged internecine warfare among the different brotherhoods, and made difficult a common purpose among working people.

The fact that Debs now accepted as social fact the distinction between employers and working people suggests something of the political distance he had traveled since 1886. His actions soon followed. Although he remained editor of the BLF magazine until 1894, he resigned his position as secretary treasurer in 1893 in order to devote more time to a new organization he helped establish, the American Railway Union (ARU). An industrial union, the ARU sought to enlist all railroad workers, regardless of the craft or level of skill, into one organization to more effectively confront employers. "The spirit of fraternity [is] abroad in the land," Debs exulted, and he worked feverishly to build the new organization.

The major test of the ARU came in 1894, when workers struck George Pullman's railroad car shops just outside of Chicago. As Pullman officials refused to negotiate, Debs and other strike leaders called for a national boycott of all Pullman cars, demanding that other railroads separate the famous Pullman sleeper car from their trains or face an immediate walkout by workers. The Pullman Company resisted the ARU as a member of the General Managers Association, an organization of executives from the twenty-four railroads with terminals in Chicago. The association orchestrated the employer response to the boycott, including arranging for the U.S. Department of Justice to appoint one of their own lawyers, Edwin Walker, as the government attorney with jurisdiction over the strike. By 4 July, using the interruption of the mail as justification, the leaders of the association succeeded in convincing President Grover Cleveland to send in federal troops to break the strike.

Faced with the direct power of the government, both in the form of troops and in a series of injunctions against strike activity by federal judges, the strike quickly collapsed. Debs and other ARU leaders were arrested on conspiracy charges and for contempt of court for disregarding the injunctions. Debs was sentenced to a six-month jail sentence in the Woodstock (Ill.) jail.

This prison experience established the central mythic image of Debs's public self. As he told it some years later, before Pullman "I had heard but little of Socialism," but during the strike, "in the gleam of every bayonet and in the flash of every rifle *the class struggle was revealed*." In this mood, Debs continued, he received a visit at Woodstock from Victor Berger, the Milwaukee Socialist leader, who bore as gifts the three

volumes of Karl Marx's *Das Kapital* (1867). That set "the wires humming in my system," Debs averred. Drawing on the archetype of Saul on the road to Damascus, Debs offered himself as one who, in a moment of blinding insight, had understood the systematic problems with capitalism and the promise of socialism. He emerged from jail a changed and charged man.

To accept this account at face value, however, strains credulity. The Pullman experience certainly affected Debs, but he did not jettison the democratic political ideology that had so informed his earlier career. Upon his release from jail, he delivered a speech to a crowd of over 100,000 in Chicago in November 1895 that was a paean to traditional concepts of American liberty. As he would for much of his future career, Debs portrayed himself as one seeking both to conserve the best of the American experience and to reinterpret it for his generation, and he pointed to the nation's industrialists as the real revolutionaries, whose actions would debase the meaning and the power of the idea of citizenship. He supported the People's Party ticket in 1896. The slow, circuitous path he traveled from the 1877 strike to public identification as a Socialist in 1897—a path he traveled by touch and feel rather than through theoretical discussions—explains Debs's particular merging of class realities with democratic belief. It also explains much about the appeal of this native son to Americans of his generation.

As a Socialist, Debs's continued emphasis on industrial unionism led him to fiercely critique the established craft unions; their national organization, the American Federation of Labor (AFL); and the AFL founding president, Samuel Gompers. Not surprisingly, in 1905 Debs welcomed the formation of the Industrial Workers of the World (IWW), a syndicalist industrial union dedicated to the workers' control of government and industry. However, by 1908 he had quietly allowed his membership to lapse, as he reacted to the IWW's rhetorical excesses and limited practicality. By 1913 he had publicly labeled IWW leader William "Big Bill" Haywood's call for sabotage and direct action "reactionary, not revolutionary," and he warned workers of the danger of being "most basely betrayed . . . and treacherously delivered to their enemies by the IWW Judases."

Although Debs remained an advocate of industrial unionism, his major effort in his speeches as he incessantly toured the country was to urge working people to vote for a democratic economic system by supporting the Socialist Party of America (SPA). In 1900 he represented the young and inexperienced SPA in the presidential campaign, receiving just under 100,000 votes. Four years later Debs's national total was more than four times that figure, and a growing number of Socialist candidates won election in local and state races. Expectations ran quite high in 1908, and the SPA leased a special railroad train, immediately dubbed "the Red Special," to carry presidential candidate Debs and his entourage into thirty-three states. The returns, however, barely matched the 1904 results.

Debs and his supporters thought the various reform efforts had detracted from their tally but took comfort from the belief, a maxim of Socialist faith, that when reform ultimately proved inadequate in alleviating capitalism's exploitation, socialism would attract the voters. In 1910 Victor Berger's election to the U.S. Congress, as nearly 100 Socialists also won election to local and state offices, buoyed these hopes as well. Debs was nominated for the fourth consecutive time in 1912, and in a four-way race that included incumbent Republican William Howard Taft, Democratic challenger and eventual winner Woodrow Wilson, and independent candidate and former president Theodore Roosevelt, his results seemed to confirm Socialist belief. With nearly one million votes, representing some 6 percent of the total, and with impressive local gains as well, Socialists looked forward to the coming electoral revolution.

Yet the 1912 results proved to be the high-water mark of SPA strength. Despite the attraction of many working people to Debs as a speaker and public figure, the overwhelming majority of workers simply would not vote for him. Contrary to Socialist belief, reform proved rather appealing as a practical solution to their needs, and the pull of the traditional parties, often grounded in ethnic and religious networks, remained dominant. Also, Socialist agitation addressed working Americans primarily as workers, an economic identity the majority simply did not accord a singular primacy in their lives. Debs suffered two collapses after 1912, and in 1916 he was too physically weakened to mount a national campaign. SPA loyalist Allan Benson ran a lackluster race instead. Debs did run that year as a candidate for Congress from Indiana's Fifth District. The campaign possessed an odd personal note for the 61-year-old Socialist leader, as he sought votes in the same district that, some thirty years earlier, had so applauded him for his more conventional Democratic politics. He finished a distant second to the Republican candidate.

Debs was confined to his sickbed, recuperating from severe physical exhaustion and psychological stress, during the tumultuous months of the American entry into World War One; a government-directed repression of Socialists, IWW members, unionists, and other dissidents; and the Bolshevik Revolution in November 1917. Dismayed by his inactivity in the face of his comrades' suffering, Debs rose from his bed in June 1918 to deliver a series of antiwar speeches. Following a speech at Canton, Ohio, federal agents arrested him under the Espionage Act of 1917, charging him with impeding the war effort. Sentenced to ten years, Debs reported for jail in April 1919, traveling from Cleveland to Moundsville, West Virginia, on a train staffed by union men in the various railroad brotherhoods he had organized almost forty years earlier. Shortly transferred to Atlanta Federal Penitentiary, Debs conducted his fifth and final presidential campaign from his jail cell in 1920. Federal prisoner 9653 received nearly a million votes, approximately 3 percent of the total.

In a surprise move, President Warren G. Harding released Debs and twenty-three other political prisoners on Christmas Day 1921, and the Socialist leader returned to Terre Haute. His remaining years were framed by a personal and political despondency. The Socialist movement he had led for so long had largely disintegrated, and he found his own prescriptions increasingly ignored in postwar American cultural and political life. Following a trip to Bermuda with his wife in 1926, he grew progressively weaker. Debs died at the Lindlahr Sanitarium just outside Chicago.

Although he never led a successful Socialist movement, Debs's public life was nonetheless significant and important. More forcefully than most in his era, he pressed Americans to recognize that their valued political traditions were themselves threatened, in a time of industrial expansion and concentration, unless the nation could expand its democratic sentiments into the economic realm. In this fashion Debs's career influenced progressives in his generation and in succeeding ones who raised, within a liberal political tradition, quite similar issues.

• The major Debs archive is in the Cunningham Library, Indiana State University, Terre Haute, and it is now available on microfilm. Other significant collections are in the Tamiment Institute, Bobst Library, New York University; the Perkins Library, Duke University, Durham, N.C.; and the Lilly Library, Indiana University, Bloomington. A useful three-volume edition of Debs's correspondence is *Letters of Eugene V. Debs*, ed. J. Robert Constantine (1990). The most comprehensive biography is Nick Salvatore, *Eugene V. Debs: Citizen and Socialist* (1982). Older works still of interest are McAlister Coleman, *Eugene V. Debs, A Man Unafraid* (1930), and Ray Ginger, *The Bending Cross: A Biography of Eugene Victor Debs* (1949). An obituary is in the *New York Times*, 21 Oct. 1926.

NICK SALVATORE

DEBUTTS, John Dulany (10 Apr. 1915–17 Dec. 1986), corporation executive, was born in Greensboro, North Carolina, the son of Sydnor deButts, a manager for the Atlantic & Yadkin railroad line, and Mary Ellen Cutchin. DeButts worked on a railroad during his youth and after finishing high school entered the Virginia Military Institute in Lexington. In 1936 he graduated as a captain with a B.S. in electrical engineering and served as valedictorian of his class.

Unable to serve a commission in the marines because of poor eyesight, deButts instead embarked on his long career with American Telephone and Telegraph (AT&T or the Bell System) as a trainee in the Richmond office of the Chesapeake and Potomac Telephone Company. He remained in the Richmond office until 1949, when he was transferred to AT&T headquarters in New York, serving there for two years before returning to Richmond. After working in Richmond from 1951 to 1955 as general traffic manager, whose territory included the entire state of Virginia, deButts served for two years in New York as an assistant vice president. In 1957–1958, deButts was in Washington, D.C., serving as assistant vice president of government relations, where he helped to direct AT&T's powerful political lobby. In 1958–1959, deButts was the general manager of New York Telephone's Westchester County office. He then got a considerable promotion when he returned to Richmond for three years as vice president of operations and engineering for the entire Chesapeake and Potomac group. In 1962 deButts became president of the Illinois Bell Telephone Company, his first assignment as a chief executive; at forty-six years of age, he was the youngest president in the Bell System. DeButts stayed at Illinois Bell until 1966, when he became executive vice president and later vice chairman of AT&T in New York, settling in that city for the rest of his AT&T career. Before nestling in the top echelons of the corporation, deButts experienced varied and extensive service in its ranks, allowing him to observe many facets of AT&T's vast operations. He displayed an extraordinary grasp of detail as well as an intense curiosity about the telephone business, and even as a corporate executive deButts joined work crews and personally installed telephone cables and repaired broken telephone lines to gain a complete understanding of all telephone operations.

On 1 April 1972 deButts became board chairman and chief operating officer of AT&T, succeeding Haakon Ingolf Romnes. AT&T was the world's largest corporation, employing more than 1 million workers, but it was beset by problems. Romnes, while a brilliant engineer, had been largely feckless as chief operating officer. Demand for new telephone service was outpacing AT&T's ability to accommodate new customers and systems. Operating costs were increasing while profits were shrinking, and morale among workers was low. Basic telephone service in major cities like New York, Boston, Houston, and New Orleans was horrendous. Frequent delays and breakdowns in Manhattan, where the financial district had experienced difficulties in getting dial tones, were as irritating to stockbrokers as they were damaging to the company's reputation. Perhaps most significantly, the federal government and new competitors were beginning to challenge AT&T's deeply entrenched monopoly.

DeButts, considered a strong leader and a manager par excellence, focused on AT&T's traditional strengths rather than enunciating a new vision for the corporation. Emphasizing the corporation's long heritage of service to the public, deButts coined the phrase "POTS"—plain old telephone service—as the standard to which AT&T employees should strive, and he stressed the mutually dependent relationship between good service and profits. "Service . . . is our only product, our only reason for being. If we don't meet the public's expectations, the public will make other arrangements," he warned, adding that such arrangements "will have to be made in any event if we don't remain a viable business—that is, a profitable one." DeButts took to the road, barnstorming the country to give pep talks to lower-level employees, toward whom he had always shown great concern, as one who himself had risen from an entry-level position in the AT&T system. He encouraged better communication between Bell headquarters in New York and the presidents of operating companies (the local phone companies throughout the country such as New York Telephone, Illinois Bell, and Pacific Bell). In May 1972, one month after becoming chairman, deButts invited the presidents of all Bell operating companies to Key Largo, Florida, for a corporate retreat during which he could elicit their comments and concerns. In October 1974 deButts launched an ambitious improvement program at AT&T, challenging the corporation to eliminate all "weak spots" in service by March 1976, the one hundredth anniversary of Alexander Graham Bell's first telephone transmission. (A "weak spot" in AT&T's performance was a failure to meet minimum monthly service standards.) DeButts's challenge startled his colleagues, who warned that his goal was unattainable. But by January 1976—two months ahead of schedule—all weak spots in Bell System service had disappeared.

An unabashed monopolist, deButts rejected the procompetition orientation of Romnes and instead defended AT&T's role as king of the American telephone system. DeButts subscribed to an idea that Theodore Vail, the first president of AT&T, developed, which argued that the telephone was a "natural monopoly" and therefore a multiplicity of telephone companies would impede market efficiency. DeButts warned that interference with AT&T's monopoly would force the company to change its pricing policies, which held down household phone bills by using long-distance profits to subsidize the cost of local calls; he predicted that the result of such interference would be at least a 70 percent increase in monthly home phone bills. (In 1977 he became one of the first corporation executives to appear in his own television commercials when he was featured in AT&T spots that ended with the line "The system is the solution.") In September 1973, appearing in Seattle before the National Association of Regulatory Utility Commissioners, deButts delivered an address legendary in the annals of corporate speeches. Reaffirming the words of former AT&T president Walter Gifford, deButts declared that the corporation had "an unusual obligation" to oppose competition in the telephone industry as a potential impediment to reliable, low-cost service. Such a business posture had served both the industry and the public well, he maintained. DeButts lashed out against government regulatory agencies as well as upstart companies who sought to enter the telecommunications field, the latter he charged with being motivated not by a sense of public obligation but rather by profit. (Although he did not mention adversaries by name in the speech, deButts objected to the Federal Communications Commission's allowing newcomers like Microwave Communications, Incorporated, or MCI—who were not responsible for local service—to compete with AT&T in long-distance service.) In unequivocal terms the speech established deButts's intention to protect AT&T's monopoly, throwing down the gauntlet to the government and to competitors who wished to challenge the corporation's preeminence.

In 1976 deButts lobbied heavily for congressional passage of the Consumer Communications Reform Act, the so-called Bell Bill that would have made AT&T the country's official monopoly, throwing all long-distance competitors off the playing field. De-Butts dispatched scores of lobbyists to Washington and spent more than $1 million to press for the bill's approval. But the bill was defeated, marking a fatal blow to deButts's hopes for AT&T's unchallenged supremacy in the telecommunications field. In 1979, when it became inevitable that AT&T would be dismantled, deButts stepped down as chairman, two years before the end of his term, to make room for a new team of executives who would preside over AT&T's breakup. The team was headed by the new chairman and deButts's hand-picked successor, Charlie Brown. DeButts never publicly criticized Brown's subsequent actions to dismantle the Bell System and felt that Brown ultimately had no choice. But by all accounts deButts was devastated by the breakup of his cherished monopoly.

DeButts retired to his farm in Upperville, Virginia, where he built a mansion from Virginia field stone. On land that sprawled over eighty-seven acres, he ranched, raised cows, and engaged in his favorite pastime of duck hunting. In 1983 circulation problems forced doctors to amputate his right leg, after which he spent much of his time in a wheelchair on his home's glass-enclosed back porch.

In 1939 deButts had married Gertrude Willoughby Walke; they had two children. A strapping figure who stood well over six feet tall and weighed more than 200 pounds, deButts's carriage and demeanor reflected his military training. He gave a firm handshake, and his large frame exuded leadership; gregarious and courtly, he had a gentle southern drawl but spoke with authority. One business associate commented that an exchange of views with deButts meant walking into the AT&T chairman's office with your own ideas and walking out with his.

By reaffirming AT&T's traditional goals of basic, efficient service, deButts redeemed the corporation's reputation, which by the early 1970s was tarnished. His leadership rectified the company's most urgent problems at the time—deteriorating service and flattening profits. At the time he retired, AT&T proclaimed that profits were up nearly 65 percent, and service was at peak efficiency. DeButts firmly believed that as a monopoly AT&T offered the best possible phone service to the American public, and he thought the federal government would accept his view. Thus, he thought that he could not only preserve but strengthen the monopoly. To detractors, deButts smacked of corporate arrogance and his intransigence only crystallized the resolve of the government and competitors to break the Bell System. Critics claimed that he underestimated the power of the deregulation movement of the 1970s. In the end, it was a movement too strong for deButts to resist. DeButts died in Winchester Medical Center near Upperville.

• Two books on the breakup of AT&T offer information on deButts: Steve Coll, *The Deal of the Century: The Breakup of AT&T* (1986), and Peter Temin with Louis Galambos, *The Fall of the Bell System: A Study in Prices and Politics* (1987). Profiles of deButts are: "Financial Wizards at AT&T," *Dun's* (Dec. 1974): 44–46, and A. M. Louis, "John deButts's Long March from Trainee to Chairman," *Fortune*, Dec. 1976, pp. 122–25ff. Interviews with deButts are in *U.S. News and World Report*: "Tomorrow's Phone Service," 9 Apr. 1973; "Tomorrow's Telephone Service—What It Will Be Like," 5 July 1976; and "Telephone Monopoly: Good or Bad?" 22 Nov. 1976. "Management Style of John deButts," *Harvard Business Review* (Jan. 1974), is also an interview. Obituaries are in the *New York Times* and the *Washington Post*, both 18 Dec. 1986.

YANEK MIECZKOWSKI

DEBYE, Peter Joseph William (24 Mar. 1884–2 Nov. 1966), physicist and physical chemist, was born Petrus Josephus Wilhelmus Debije in Maastricht, the Netherlands, the son of Wilhelmus Johannes Debije, a supervisor in a manufacturing firm, and Maria Reumkens. Debye attended Maastricht schools but did not intend to continue his education and never took the courses required for entrance to Dutch universities. In 1901 he changed his plans and enrolled in the Aachen Technical University in Germany, the academic center nearest Maastricht, where he received a degree in electrical engineering in 1905. In Aachen he transliterated his Dutch name into Peter Debye and studied with physics professor Arnold Sommerfeld, a future leader in the development of the quantum theory. Sommerfeld turned Debye's interest toward theoretical physics and took Debye with him in 1906 when he became a professor at the University of Munich. There Debye received a Ph.D. in physics in 1908.

Debye was a lecturer at Munich until 1911, when he succeeded Albert Einstein as professor of theoretical physics at the University of Zurich. Within one year he made two major contributions to physics. Max Planck had introduced the quantum concept in 1900, but its acceptance came slowly. Einstein in 1907 applied it to the specific heats of solids by attributing the ability of solids to absorb heat to the quantized vibrations of their atoms, but this theory proved inadequate. Debye in 1912 transformed the theory by arguing for a whole range of frequencies in atomic solids, instead of Einstein's assumption of only a single frequency, and provided a much better representation of their specific heats. Debye also proposed in 1912 that many molecules had permanent electric dipoles. The concept of the polar molecule was a striking innovation and of great importance for chemistry and physics, because the degree of polarity or dipole moment of a molecule made possible the determination of molecular structure.

Debye returned to the Netherlands in 1912 as professor of physics at the University of Utrecht. In 1913 he married Matilde Alberer, whom he had met at his

Munich boardinghouse; they had two children. His appearance at a 1913 quantum theory conference at the University of Göttingen in Germany so impressed the conferees that the university created for him a new professorship in experimental and theoretical physics. He moved to Göttingen and quickly entered the new field opened by Max von Laue's 1913 discovery of X-ray diffraction by crystals. Within one year, Debye developed a quantitative treatment of the subject, and in 1916, with his assistant Paul Scherrer, he introduced a new method to obtain X-ray scattering with powders. Physicists did not expect powders, fibers, or any amorphous material to be crystalline enough to act as a diffraction grating, but Debye argued that there was never a completely random arrangement of atoms in matter and that perfect crystallability was unnecessary for diffraction. The Debye-Scherrer powder method expanded X-ray diffraction to organic substances and giant molecules such as proteins and nucleic acids, providing another way to determine molecular structure.

The ailing postwar economic situation in Germany made an offer in 1920 from the Swiss Federal Technical Institute in Zurich attractive to Debye. In Zurich he demonstrated the wave-particle duality of light by offering in 1923 a convincing explanation of the Compton effect—the change in wavelength of X-rays diffracted by small particles—in terms of the radiation having both a particulate and a wave nature.

Debye's most important contribution to chemistry was a 1923 theory of solutions. The 1887 solution theory of Swedish physicist and chemist Svante Arrhenius posited the dissociation of electrolytes into separate ions to account for the conductivity of solutions. Solutions of strong electrolytes, however, did not exhibit the properties expected with complete ionization. Debye and Erich Hückel proposed a new theory of solutions, which adopted the total ionization of strong electrolytes but asserted that an ionic cloud created by oppositely charged ions shielded every ion, thereby retarding the mobility of the ions. This quantitative theory provided mathematical expressions to account for the behavior of solutions and quickly became the basis for teaching solution chemistry.

From 1927 to 1940 Debye was in Germany as professor of physics, first at the University of Leipzig, then, after 1934, at the University of Berlin. In 1936 he received the Nobel Prize for chemistry. With the advent of World War II, Nazi officials told him to become a German citizen or he would not be allowed to enter his laboratory. He felt strong ties to Germany but disliked National Socialism, his outlook having been formed in the fiercely independent Limburg province of the Netherlands and by his strong Roman Catholic faith. He had visited the United States several times and had received offers from American universities. In 1940 he went to Zurich for a lecture and then immigrated to the United States. From 1940 to 1952 he was professor of chemistry and head of the chemistry department at Cornell University. He became professor emeritus in 1952 but continued his investigations. His American period was a prolific one; one-third of his research articles were published during these years. He became an American citizen in 1946.

During World War II, Debye, as a Dutch citizen, was excluded for security reasons from full participation in the mobilization of scientists. He nevertheless contributed to the wartime synthetic rubber program. His interest in polymers aroused by this experience, he devoted the rest of his career to the study of macromolecules. In 1944 he proposed a light-scattering method by polymers in solution based on the idea that the wavelengths of visible light were comparable to the dimensions of polymer molecules. This method yielded information on the molecular size, shape, and weight of giant molecules, transformed the study of polymers into a more exact science, and led to a rapid development of high-polymer chemistry.

In retirement, Debye was a popular lecturer all over the United States. He attracted large audiences with his facility of expression and sensitivity to the level of understanding of such diverse audiences as schoolchildren, businessmen, and research experts. His American honors included election to the National Academy of Sciences in 1947 and the presentation of the National Medal of Science by President Lyndon Johnson in 1965. He was an active member until his death in the Pontifical Academy of Science at the Vatican. Friendly, generous, and accessible, he took a well-rounded approach to life, with a deep love of family and home, and an appreciation for the beauties of nature. His favorite recreations were gardening and trout fishing. He retained his love of opera from his childhood, when his mother had taken him to performances in Maastricht, and maintained his physical vigor and mental acuity throughout his life. Friends said that he did not seem to age and that his appearance went unchanged for many years up to his death in Ithaca, New York.

Debye introduced several major innovations in physics, especially in the area of the interaction of radiation and matter. In transferring his interests to chemistry, he revolutionized the way chemists approached solution chemistry and also provided organic, polymer, and biochemists with ways to determine the structure of molecules through his conception of the polar molecule and his diffraction methods. Indicative of his pervasive influence in twentieth-century physical science are the large number of concepts, units, equations, and methods that bear his name.

• Debye's papers that date from his American period are in the Cornell University Archives. His books available in English include *Quantum Theory and Chemistry* (1928), *Polar Molecules* (1929), *Dipole Moments and Electromagnetic Radiation* (1929), *Electron Diffraction* (1930), *The Dipole Moment and Chemical Structure* (1931), *The Structure of Molecules* (1932), *The Structure of Matter* (1934), *Topics in Chemical Physics* (1962), and *Molecular Forces* (1967). His most important articles are in *The Collected Papers of Peter Debye* (1954). Important biographical essays, each with a bibliography of his publications, are by Mansel Davies, *Biographical Memoirs* of the Fellows of the Royal Society 16 (1970): 175–232, and by J. W. Williams, National Academy of Sciences, *Biographical Memoirs* 46 (1975): 23–68. Eightieth birthday celebrations are in the *Journal of the American Chemical Society*, 5 Sept. 1964 issue, and in *Science* 145 (1964): 554–59, which includes an interview by several Cornell scientists with Debye that reveals his thoughts about quantum physics, chemistry, and science education. The *Journal of Physical Chemistry*, 20 Dec. 1984 issue, is a centennial tribute. Karl Darrow provides an excellent critical study of Debye in the *American Philosophical Society Yearbook* (1968): 123–30. A useful overview by W. O. Baker of Debye's accomplishments is in the *Proceedings of the Robert A. Welch Foundation Conferences on Chemical Research* 20 (1977): 154–99. An obituary is in the *New York Times*, 3 Nov. 1966.

ALBERT B. COSTA

DECAMP, Joseph Rodefer (5 Nov. 1858–11 Feb. 1923), painter, was born in Cincinnati, Ohio, the son of Lambert DeCamp, a brick layer and carpenter, and Lydia Garwood, a school teacher. His childhood was spent in the fashionable West End of Cincinnati, but it was nothing out of the ordinary. He began to sketch crayon copies of published lithographics at the age of twelve; this enabled him to draw living models easily years later. In 1873 DeCamp began a six-year study at the McMicken School of Design at the University of Cincinnati with academic painter Thomas S. Noble. At the age of nineteen he taught private drawing classes for women in Chillicothe, Ohio. During this experience DeCamp realized that teaching helped any instructor develop and better understand art and the techniques of painting.

Wishing to learn from fellow Cincinnati painter Frank Duveneck, DeCamp enrolled at Munich's Royal Academy in 1878 and trained for fourteen months with Duveneck, who taught students to render form with a brush using the somber, subtle color combinations used by the Dutch and Barbizon masters. With fellow classmates William Merritt Chase, John Henry Twachtman, Theodore Wendel, and others, DeCamp was known as a "Duveneck Boy" because he practiced Duveneck's painting method of using heavy strokes and dark colors. It was not until 1881 that Chase and Dennis Bunker influenced DeCamp to lighten his palette and to brush on paint more loosely.

Sacrificing to buy canvases, paint, and brushes with vision, determination, and little money, DeCamp, Twachtman and Duveneck painted living models in genres and landscapes in Munich and Polling-bei-Weilheim, Bavaria, and they enthusiastically exhibited in Munich the artistic results of these trips. With expatriate painter James McNeill Whistler and Duveneck, DeCamp painted in Venice and Florence while studying the painting techniques of the Dutch and Italian old masters.

On returning to the United States in 1881 DeCamp took a few lessons from the painters Edmund C. Tarbell and Frank W. Benson at the School of the Museum of Fine Arts in Boston and eventually taught with them. In 1884 he helped organize the School of Design at Cleveland's Western Reserve University, and the following year he taught at Wellesley College in Massachusetts.

DeCamp was as profoundly influenced by Tarbell as he had been by Duveneck. Tarbell inspired him to paint Jan Vermeer-like genre interiors of the genteel upper class and to create portraits in the grand manner of John Singer Sargent. After 1886 DeCamp earned the nickname "Tarbellite" because he copied many of Tarbell's subjects and mastered Tarbell's technique of painting color, light, and shadow with a soft-edged brush. Like Tarbell, Whistler, and Chase, DeCamp collected and incorporated into his art Japanese antiques and kimonos and utilized oriental philosophy by rendering on canvas portraits of people and places in a tonally harmonious and refined painterly manner.

In 1891 DeCamp married his student Edith Franklin Baker; they had four children. The family lived in West Medford, Massachusetts. DeCamp was an 1898 founding member of a group of artists known as "The Ten" with friends Chase, Twachtman, Edward Simmons, Tarbell, Robert Reid, and others. He exhibited with the group and gained awards and recognition as an eminent portrait and genre painter. Donelson Hoopes referred to DeCamp as "the pragmatist" of the Ten, citing his ability to carefully execute some of the finest turn-of-the-century portraits.

Accepting a position at Massachusetts Normal Art School in 1903, DeCamp taught students to work in the style of Tarbell and the Boston school of painting. He toiled painstakingly, but without hesitation, at perfecting each canvas or drawing. As a painter he depicted genteel female figures doing everyday chores (see *The Blue Cup*, Museum of Fine Arts, Boston). As a teacher he molded character with a clear, sensitive understanding.

In 1904 a fire at DeCamp's Harcourt Street studio in Boston destroyed most of his Munich oils and early impressionistic paintings. Although he helped to design and build the now-famous Fenway Studios in Boston, the Harcourt fire left DeCamp in financial ruin. He announced he would paint anyone's portrait for $50, and because he accepted too many portrait commissions, he anguished over the fact that he had too little time in which to paint the genre interiors and impressionistic landscapes he preferred.

In 1906 DeCamp was appointed instructor of painting at the Pennsylvania Academy of the Fine Arts, where he again worked with Chase. In 1908 he was commissioned by the White House to paint a portrait of President Theodore Roosevelt, and in that year he also completed *Guitar Player* (Museum of Fine Arts, Boston). After *The Seamstress* won the $1,500 Clark prize and silver medal at the Corcoran Gallery in 1909, DeCamp and his wife toured North Africa, Spain, France, and England. When he returned to Boston he was given his first one-man show of seventeen portraits at the St. Botolph Club.

For decades DeCamp, Tarbell, Benson, and Boston portrait painters William Paxton and Philip Leslie Hale taught in Boston and worked to teach the highest technical standards to their students. In 1914 they helped build the Riverway Studios and were founding members of the Guild of Boston Artists. Eventually moving to Boston's Beacon Hill in 1922, DeCamp painted portraits of famous artists, socialites, presidents, the premier of Canada, politicians, writers, and poets. Following Tarbell's example in painting realistic impressionism with soft-edged brush work, DeCamp came closer to emulating Tarbell than any other painter. His work was truthful to nature, and he painted life as he saw it, reckoning with and balancing two pronounced portraiture problems: the personality of the sitter and the art of the painter.

DeCamp moved to Philadelphia in 1915 to seek portrait commissions because Sargent, Tarbell, Benson, and Paxton were more sought after by Boston patrons. He taught students to think of themselves, not to be bound by artistic formulas, and to allow their spirits to live within their work.

DeCamp suffered with little complaint for sixteen years from a painful ulcer ailment. He painted his last canvas, *Blue Kimono*, in 1923, and he died later that year in Bocagrande, Florida. The Cincinnati Art Museum hung seventeen of his canvases in October 1924, and a memorial exhibition of forty-five canvases and three groups of drawings hung at Boston's St. Botolph Club commemorating DeCamp's refined, eloquent contribution to American portraiture and genre painting (7–26 Jan. 1924). Rose V. S. Berry stated that De-Camp was "one of the rare ones—a great American painter" (p. 182).

• For family papers see Donald Moffat's unpublished papers (1955–1957) on DeCamp held at the Frick Art Reference Library, New York City. For a comparison of DeCamp and Tarbell, see Edmund Von Mach, *The Art of Painting in the Nineteenth Century* (1908); Patricia Jobe Pierce, *The Ten* (1976) and *Edmund C. Tarbell and the Boston School of Painting* (1980); and Sadakichi Hartmann, "The Tarbellities," *Art News* 1 (Mar. 1897): 3–4. See also "Joseph DeCamp: An Appreciation" in the Student Association of the Massachusetts Normal Art School *Catalogue*, ed. Lee W. Court (1924); William Howe Downes, "Joseph DeCamp and His Work," *Art and Progress* (Apr. 1913): 918–25; "Fine Exhibits Mark Opening of Art Museum, Joseph DeCamp, Student of Duveneck, Noted for Sincerity," *Daily Times-Star* (Cincinnati, Ohio), 1 Oct. 1924. For newspaper clippings and exhibition records see the Cincinnati Art Museum artists' files, vol. 10. For history and exhibition records see Laurene Buckley, *Joseph DeCamp* (1995). An obituary is Rose V. S. Berry, "Joseph DeCamp: Painter and Man," *American Magazine of Art* 14, no. 4 (Apr. 1923): 182–89.

PATRICIA JOBE PIERCE

DE CASSERES, Benjamin (1873–6 Dec. 1945), author and journalist, was born in Philadelphia, Pennsylvania, the son of David De Casseres, a printer, and Charlotte Davis. On his father's side he was a collateral descendant of Spinoza. De Casseres left high school at thirteen and went to work as a four-dollar-a-week office boy for Charles Emory Smith, editor in chief of the *Philadelphia Press*. He was soon writing editorials

and reviewing plays, and would later describe himself as the youngest editorial writer in America on a first-class newspaper. He was with the *Press* until 1899.

In a varied and eclectic journalistic career that in the beginning included such duties as proofreader, book reviewer, editorial writer, and drama critic, De Casseres served with the *New York Sun* from 1899 to 1903, the *New York Herald* from 1903 to 1919 (interrupted by a 1906–1907 interlude as cofounder of *El Diario* in Mexico City), and as a special Sunday writer for the *New York Times* from 1919 to 1924.

In 1919 De Casseres married Bio Terrill, a woman chiefly known for her skill at palmistry. (Among admirers of her divinatory powers was Eugene O'Neill. On one occasion Mrs. De Casseres correctly predicted a favorable turn in the playwright's chaotic love life.) From 1922 to 1933 De Casseres was a regular critic for the magazine *Arts and Decorations*. During this period he also contributed to many well-known publications, such as *American Mercury, Smart Set*, and *Vanity Fair*. De Casseres's career with William Randolph Hearst's organization began in 1933 and ended with his death. His column, "March of Events," ran in the *New York Journal* (after 1937, the *Journal-American*) until 1943 and in the *New York Daily Mirror* from 1943 to 1945. De Casseres also wrote editorials and drama criticism for the Hearst papers.

As an author, De Casseres specialized in poetry, essays, and biography. His first book, a collection of poems called *The Shadow Eater*, was published in 1915. This was followed by *Chameleon* (1922), *Mirrors of New York* (1925), *James Gibbons Huneker* (1925), *Forty Immortals* (1925), *Anathema!* (1928), *The Superman in America* (1929), *Mencken and Shaw* (1930), *The Love Letters of a Living Poet* (1931), *Spinoza* (1932), *The Muse of Lies* (1936), *Don Marquis* (1938), and *The Works of Benjamin De Casseres* (3 vols., 1939). In 1935 De Casseres wrote a foreword to Nietzsche's *Germans, Jews, and France*. Though some critics dismissed De Casseres as a facile popularizer, no less a figure than Remy de Gourmont was sufficiently impressed by his work to translate much of it into French.

De Casseres described himself as being influenced by Heine, Ralph Waldo Emerson, Nietzsche, Schopenhauer, La Rochefoucauld, Victor Hugo, Spinoza, Walt Whitman, Montaigne, and Goethe. "My core passion is liberty," he declared. "I am a militant radical individualist. I hate Communism, Fascism, Socialism, and any system that suppresses the individual and enlarges the powers of the state." Nowhere was De Casseres's dislike of collectivism more apparent than in his World War II commentaries, as expressed in the "March of Events" column. During this honeymoon period of the Soviet-American alliance, when many conservatives joined liberals and leftists in praising the Russian war effort and "Uncle Joe" Stalin, De Casseres boldly bucked the tide. His predictions that Stalin and Hitler might make a separate peace and his speculations about the possibility of a Russo-American third world war outraged many people, including a New York publisher who reportedly urged a wartime ban on all works critical of the Soviet Union. Wryly amused by the opinion that his writings bordered on sedition, De Casseres wrote in his 16 July 1943 column that some of his critics probably thought he was "in the pay of Hitler or the Jap sun goddess."

De Casseres took an equally poor view of domestic communism and the New Deal, discerning a link between the two and urging that "the House of America be cleaned of bureaucratic parasites . . . Reds, fellow travelers—all 5th columnists of varying degrees." Fanatically hostile toward those he perceived as homegrown subversives, De Casseres declared in one column that "the Bill of Rights should apply to LOYAL AMERICANS ONLY." With this mind-set—ferocious Russophobia combined with contempt for the civil liberties of Americans whose loyalty he suspected— De Casseres was an ideological pioneer of the Parnell Thomas–Joseph McCarthy witch-hunts of the late 1940s and early 1950s.

De Casseres had a disturbing propensity to launch, with little or no apparent provocation, vituperative diatribes against individuals. It was one such attack that ended his long, close friendship with Eugene O'Neill. In 1934 O'Neill brought out *Days without End*, a play whose theme was reconciliation with the Catholic church. De Casseres, a freethinker, was so infuriated that he composed a venomous parody on O'Neill's work that he titled *Drivel without End*. The two men never spoke again, and De Casseres only relented two weeks before his death. "I'm sorry I wrote that about O'Neill," he told his wife. The final irony is that O'Neill never did return to Catholicism.

Another of his targets was Marcel Proust. The British poet Alfred Noyes had identified the underlying cause of France's 1940 defeat as moral decay exemplified by writers like Proust. Denying Noyes's charges, De Casseres exempted the French from any stigma of moral decay. The exemption did not extend to Proust. In a "March of Events" column De Casseres denounced the chronicler of things past as a "nut," a "queer," the author of "long-winded and boresome books," and a "nuisance who rang people up at 4 A.M."

De Casseres, whose health had been failing, was forced to suspend his column between March and August of 1945. His last entry appeared on 2 November. He died a month later in New York City.

The best insight into the psyche of this complex man was probably furnished by De Casseres himself. "I never think logically," he wrote. "I believe logic to be one of the lowest forms of mental activity and imagination the highest, although imagination has an invisible logic of its own. I think in images, flashes, and epigrams. Creators should spurn Reason as an eagle would spurn a ladder" (quoted in *Twentieth Century Authors* [1942], p. 360).

• A separate De Casseres file for 1944 is among the William Randolph Hearst Papers in the Bancroft Library at the University of California-Berkeley. Material on De Casseres can also be found in the H. L. Mencken and Robert H. Davis papers in the New York Public Library, in the Theodore Dreiser Papers in Special Collections at the University of Pennsylvania, in the Ezra Pound and Don Marquis papers in the Rare Books and Manuscripts Division of the Columbia University Library, in the James Gibbons Huneker Papers at Dartmouth College, and in the Cassius Cook Papers in the Rare Books and Manuscripts Division of the University of Michigan Library. References to the palmreading skills of Bio Terrill (Mrs. Benjamin De Casseres) as well as an account of the 1934 rupture between De Casseres and Eugene O'Neill are in Arthur and Barbara Gelb, *O'Neill* (1973). The De Casseres–O'Neill controversy is covered also in Frederic I. Carpenter, *Eugene O'Neill* (1979). An obituary is in the *New York Times*, 7 Dec. 1945.

JIM TUCK

DECATUR, Stephen (1752–14 Nov. 1808), merchant ship captain, privateersman, and naval officer was born in Newport, Rhode Island, the son of Etienne Decatur, a French seafarer of Dutch descent, and Priscilla Hill, of Newport, where Etienne had settled about 1750. Stephen was baptized on 7 June 1752, and the family moved shortly thereafter to Philadelphia. Etienne died when Stephen was a youth, leaving the family with little money. Stephen also went to sea and was master of a sloop by 1774. On 20 December of that year he married Ann Pine, a Philadelphian of Irish and Scottish descent. Four of their five children lived to adulthood; one daughter married an officer of the Marine Corps, and three sons, the most famous of whom was Stephen Decatur (1779–1820), became naval officers.

In March 1776 the Continental Congress approved Decatur's request for permission to sail the schooner *L'Esperance* to Hispaniola, from whence he proposed to import powder and arms for use in the rebellion. When the British captured Philadelphia in 1777, Decatur moved his family to the Sinepuxent Peninsula, on Maryland's eastern shore. After a brief return to Philadelphia in 1779 he settled in Cape May, New Jersey. Beginning in 1779 Decatur commanded successively larger privateers, all owned by Philadelphians. Whether the first, the galley *Retaliation*, commissioned on 11 June 1779, had any success is not known. The sloop *Comet*, commissioned on 9 September 1779, made prizes of four British merchantmen. While in command of the brig *Fair American*, of fifteen guns and a crew of 135, commissioned on 20 April 1780, Decatur frequently cruised in company with the brig *Holker*, captained by Roger Keane. The pair of brigs, owned by the same firm, made a number of valuable captures together, including a British packet and the armed ship *Richmond*, which submitted after stiff resistance. On 23 July 1781 Decatur took command of the *Royal Louis*, carrying twenty-two guns and a crew of 200, and shortly thereafter captured the Royal Navy brig *Active*. Decatur fell prisoner to the British on 8 October when HMS *Amphion* captured the *Royal Louis*. Released following a brief imprisonment at New York, Decatur commanded the thirteen-gun privateer ship *Rising Sun*, in which he made a cruise in European waters. After the war, Decatur was master and owner of merchant vessels in partnership with the Philadelphia firm Gurney & Smith. Francis Gurney had been an investor in Decatur's last two privateer commands.

In 1794 when Congress authorized the construction of six ships of war in response to depredations on American commerce by cruisers of the Barbary powers, Decatur unsuccessfully solicited one of the commands. Later, at the outset of the Quasi-War with France, he accepted a commission as captain in the U.S. Navy, dated 11 May 1798. On 7 July in command of the frigate *Delaware* Decatur made the first U.S. prize of the war. The French privateer schooner *La Croyable* had been plundering American merchant vessels along the New Jersey coast. When Decatur sighted *La Croyable*, he had the *Delaware*, a former merchant ship, maneuver as if it were a wary merchantman. *La Croyable* approached the intended victim, discovered the ruse, and, believing the vessel a British ship of war, headed for the neutral waters of Egg Harbor. Firing several cannon shots, Decatur forced the French captain to submit. Scorning the protests of his astonished prisoner that their two countries were not at war, Decatur took his prize into New Castle.

From July through September, *Delaware* joined the frigate *United States*, under Commodore John Barry, in a cruise against French armed vessels and merchantmen in the West Indies. In December Decatur, still in *Delaware*, was given command of a small squadron stationed off Cuba, where he remained until May 1799, earning the thanks of the merchants at Havana for the protection he gave their commerce. He was then promoted to command of a new and larger frigate, *Philadelphia*, at the request of the merchants of Philadelphia, who had advanced moneys to pay for the ship's construction. In May 1800 *Philadelphia* arrived in the West Indies, where Decatur took over the Guadaloupe squadron, stationed at St. Christopher. Before returning to Philadelphia the following March, *Philadelphia* captured five French armed vessels and recaptured six American ships taken by the enemy. At the end of hostilities, with the reduction of the navy under the Peace Establishment Act, Decatur was honorably discharged on 22 October 1801.

Before leaving the navy, Decatur had entered into the manufacture of gunpowder near Frankford, Pennsylvania, five miles from Philadelphia, and had begun supplying the navy. Decatur established his home, "Millsdale," at the site of the gunpowder manufactory. He passed his final years and died there.

As a privateersman and as a regular naval officer, Decatur proved himself aggressive, quick-thinking, spirited, and full of enterprise. In later life, he enjoyed hunting and fishing with friends on Cape Island, off Cape May, where he kept a record of the beach erosion and was noted among his companions for his excellent chowder, in which he took ostentatious pride.

• Decatur's participation in the American Revolution is documented in William Bell Clark et al., eds., *Naval Documents* of the American Revolution (9 vols., 1964–1986). Additional information on his privateering commands during the Revolution is in Charles H. Lincoln, comp., *Naval Records of the American Revolution 1775–1788* (1906). His service in the Quasi-War is recorded in U.S. Office of Naval Records and Library, *Naval Documents Related to the Quasi-War between the United States and France: Naval Operations from February 1797 to December 1801*, comp. Dudley W. Knox (7 vols., 1935–1938), and is discussed in Gardner W. Allen, *Our Naval War with France* (1909), and Michael A. Palmer, *Stoddert's War: Naval Operations during the Quasi-War with France, 1798–1801* (1987). The principal biographies of his son, Alexander S. Mackenzie, *Life of Stephen Decatur* (1846), and Charles L. Lewis, *The Romantic Decatur* (1937), contain some biographical information.

MICHAEL J. CRAWFORD

DECATUR, Stephen (5 Jan. 1779–22 Mar. 1820), naval officer, was born in a log cabin in Sinepuxent, Maryland, the son of Stephen Decatur, a merchant and privateer, and Ann Pine. Growing up in the maritime town of Philadelphia, Decatur was influenced to pursue a life at sea both by his father's profession and by the success that American merchant vessels had overseas in the wake of the Revolution. From an early age he displayed a tendency toward argument and physical violence—traits that would become important themes in his naval career.

Before Decatur signed on board the USS *United States* as a midshipman in May 1798, he had been accused of and tried for the murder of a Philadelphia prostitute. Acquitted of the charge, he joined the fledgling U.S. Navy and served in the limited naval war with France during 1798–1800. His courage and recklessness surfaced quickly in his relations with fellow officers. Decatur fought his first known duel in 1799, wounding his opponent in the hip, and served as a second in the notorious and bizarre Richard Somers duel. (Lieutenant Somers exchanged fire with three fellow officers in succession and was wounded twice.) In his lifetime, Decatur fought as a principal in at least two duels and participated as a second in three others.

Promoted to lieutenant in 1799, Decatur received his first command, of the USS *Argus*, in November 1803 and proceeded to the Mediterranean to serve in the Tripolitan War, which had been declared in 1801. He was reassigned to command the USS *Enterprise*, and he captured a Tripolitan ketch, the *Mastico*, which he renamed the *Intrepid*. The Tripolitans ran aground the USS *Philadelphia* and captured it. Decatur then embarked on the mission that would ensure his lasting fame, as Americans would long remember the image of his leading his men in the burning of the captured American frigate in the harbor of Tripoli on 16 February 1804. To American naval leaders the action was imperative, since the captured ship could serve as a model for the creation of a fleet of Tripolitan warships. Six months later Decatur led a gunboat division in hand-to-hand fighting in the same harbor; these two actions combined to make Decatur the most prominent and celebrated hero of the young U.S. Navy. Promoted to captain, Decatur returned to the United

States, where he soon met and married Susan Wheeler, the daughter of the mayor of Norfolk, Virginia; the couple had no children.

From 1804 to 1812 Decatur commanded in succession the USS *Constitution*, USS *Congress*, USS *Chesapeake*, and USS *United States*. He served as one of the judges in the court-martial of Captain James Barron, who had commanded the USS *Chesapeake* in its defensive action against HMS *Leopard* on 22 June 1807. When the court-martial barred Barron from service for five years, Barron blamed Decatur, and misunderstandings between the two men grew to bitterness as the years passed.

Decatur won fresh laurels early in the War of 1812. Commanding the USS *United States*, he met and defeated the British frigate HMS *Macedonian* on 25 October 1812. Decatur returned to New London, Connecticut, and the damaged prize was brought to Newport, Rhode Island, the first British warship ever displayed as a prize in an American port. Decatur basked in the glow of celebrations held in his honor, but he was soon blockaded in Long Island Sound by British ships. He made one effort to run the blockade but turned back on 1 June 1813, the same day that the USS *Chesapeake* was overpowered by HMS *Shannon*, making that day in American naval history "the Inglorious First of June."

Decatur transferred his command to the USS *President* in New York harbor and ran the blockade on 15 January 1815. He lost time as a result of running aground on a sandbar and, overtaken by several British ships, surrendered after a short fight in which he was wounded. Taken as a prisoner to Bermuda, Decatur was soon paroled—the war had ended three weeks prior to his capture—and he was absolved by a naval court of inquiry.

In May 1815 Decatur sailed to the Mediterranean as the commodore of a nine-ship squadron. Making record time on the voyage, he threatened and successfully intimidated the leaders of Algiers, Tunis, and Tripoli into signing treaties with the United States, ending the long American conflict with the North African powers. The North African leaders did not wish to enter into combat with Decatur, as they remembered his exploits from a decade earlier. Coming home to a hero's welcome, Decatur became a member of the Board of Navy Commissioners and in April 1816 delivered the toast that would outlast him by many generations: "Our Country! In her intercourse with foreign nations may she always be in the right; but our country, right or wrong."

Decatur purchased a mansion in Washington, D.C., and became prominent in the social life of the capital. Given his popularity, Decatur might have run for high political office; some historians conjecture that he would have run against Andrew Jackson in 1828. However, Barron's enmity toward Decatur grew over the years, and on 22 March 1820 the two men faced one another in a duel at Bladensburg, Maryland. Barron was wounded but survived; Decatur was wounded fatally and died twelve hours later. His funeral was attended by most of official Washington, and the newspapers responded with great sadness to the passing of one of the icons of the early U.S. Navy.

Decatur's spectacular naval career stood as a symbol for several generations of the vigor, dash, and aptitude of the early U.S. Navy. The burning of the *Philadelphia*, the hand-to-hand fighting with pirates, and the capture of the HMS *Macedonian* remained prominent in American military imagery for long after Decatur's death. In all of this, however, Decatur was more truly representative than he was exceptional; he was only the most heralded of a generation of American naval officers who led their flag to victory in the Mediterranean, on the Atlantic Ocean, and on the Great Lakes. Lesser-known naval leaders such as Thomas MacDonough did just as much as Decatur to develop a winning tradition in the navy. The darker aspects of Decatur's character—his touchiness, competitiveness with fellow officers, and his tendency toward dueling—have been largely overlooked in favor of his hero status. Examined under the lens of two centuries, Decatur's life and career more closely resemble the ideals of European Romanticism in all its glory and storminess than they do the aspirations of a young republic. His approach to naval warfare and his constant search for glory embodied many of the principles most admired by British sea captains during the era of the Napoleonic wars. The era of the sailing U.S. Navy was to some extent defined by Decatur; it was also in some respects limited by his emphasis on personal heroics and his insistence on protecting his reputation and honor.

• Decatur has been studied by many historians. The most accurate and valuable of the nineteenth-century writings is Alexander Slidell MacKenzie, *Life of Stephen Decatur, a Commodore in the Navy of the United States* (1846). Typical of the hagiographic approach is Charles Lee Lewis, *The Romantic Decatur* (1937). The works of Alfred T. Mahan, *Sea Power in Its Relations to the War of 1812* (1905), and Theodore Roosevelt, *The Naval War of 1812* (1898), remain valuable for their comprehensive and incisive portrayal of the war at sea. Recent studies have taken a closer and more critical look at Decatur; these include Leonard F. Guttridge and Jay D. Smith, *The Commodores: The U.S. Navy in the Age of Sail* (1969), and the articles of William M. P. Dunne, "'The Inglorious First of June': Commodore Stephen Decatur on Long Island Sound, 1813," *Long Island Historical Journal* 2, no. 2 (1990): 201–20, and "Pistols and Honor: The James Barron–Stephen Decatur Conflict, 1798–1807," *American Neptune* 50, no. 4 (1990): 245–59.

SAMUEL WILLARD CROMPTON

DE CISNEROS, Eleanora (31 Oct. 1878–3 Feb. 1934), opera singer and concert artist, was born Eleanor Broadfoot in Gramercy Park, New York City, the daughter of John C. Broadfoot, a Scotch-American writer, and Ellen Small. Schooled at a private Roman Catholic academy in Brooklyn, where her promising alto voice was discovered, Eleanor studied initially with Francesco Fanciulli, the academy's choirmaster, and subsequently with Mme. Murio-Celli in Manhattan.

Prompted by the legendary tenor Jean de Reszke, with whom Broadfoot began studying voice in 1899, the Metropolitan Opera Company's general manager, Maurice Grau, offered her a contract for the 1899–1900 season. Although no special mention of it was made by the critics when she made her debut as Rossweise in *Die Walküre*, the 21-year-old Eleanor Broadfoot became the first American-born singer to have made a Metropolitan Opera debut with no prior experience, here or abroad. (Two decades later, the critics and press would bestow that distinction upon another American, Connecticut-born Rosa Ponselle.)

Despite an impressive debut, Broadfoot was only given small parts to sing at the Metropolitan, and after that first season she decided that European experience would be a prerequisite to the major roles. In the meantime, in 1900 she married a Cuban journalist, Count François De Cisneros, with whom she relocated to France. She resumed her studies with de Reszke late in 1900, and in Turin in 1902 she made her second debut, as Countess Eleanora De Cisneros. In 1904–1906 critically acclaimed performances followed at Covent Garden, where she appeared in the first London performances of Francesco Cilea's *Adriana Lecouvreur* and Giordano's *Andrea Chénier*.

Although in demand throughout Europe, De Cisneros's growing reputation rekindled her interest in singing again in the United States, and in the 1906–1907 season she was Amneris in Verdi's *Aida*, quickly establishing herself as the leading contralto of Oscar Hammerstein's Manhattan Opera Company. In 1909 she returned to Europe to create the role of Clytemnestra in Strauss's *Elektra* at La Scala, where she had also created the part of the Italian countess in Tchaikovsky's *The Queen of Spades*. She also spent a season in Australia in 1911, touring in an opera company under Nellie Melba's direction.

De Cisneros returned to the United States in 1912 at the invitation of Cleofonte Campanini, for whom she sang leading roles in the Italian and German repertories at the Chicago Opera for four seasons. After another sojourn in Europe and Australia during World War I, she returned to America in 1917 but exchanged her operatic roles for the concert platform and vaudeville stage. In both settings De Cisneros was an ardent fundraiser for the Liberty Loan drives, reportedly selling more war bonds than any other opera singer except Enrico Caruso.

In 1919, a year after the armistice, De Cisneros and her journalist husband declared bankruptcy. Thereafter, she continued to concertize sporadically, but her career was essentially over. Her legacy was left to her meager phonograph recordings (made principally for the Edison and Columbia labels) to perpetuate her voice and artistic reputation. Her last appearance on an operatic stage took place in Italy, at La Scala in 1925, in a production of Strauss's *Salome*. Ten years later, never having fully recovered from the effects of bankruptcy, Eleanora De Cisneros died in Manhattan at the American Women's Association apartment building, her final residence.

• De Cisneros is referred to passingly in Robert Grau, *Forty Years Observation of Music and the Drama* (1909); in Henry Charles Lahee, *The Grand Opera Singers of To-day* (1912); and in Oscar Thompson, *The American Singer* (1937; repr. 1969). A more recent summary of De Cisneros's career is Robert Tuggle, *The Golden Age of Opera* (1983). An obituary is in the *New York Times*, 4 Feb. 1934.

JAMES A. DRAKE

DECKER, Sarah Sophia Chase Platt (1 Oct. 1855–7 Jul. 1912), clubwoman, suffragist, and community activist, was born in McIndoe Falls, Vermont, the daughter of Edwin Chase, a lumber dealer, paper manufacturer, and Baptist abolitionist known as the "Fighting Deacon," and Lydia Maria Adams. The family moved to Holyoke, Massachusetts, when Sarah was quite young. She graduated from high school in Holyoke and while still in her teens became active in community work as a trustee of a fund to aid the poor. In 1875 she married a Holyoke merchant, Charles B. Harris.

Sarah's interest in women's rights developed upon her husband's death in 1878, when she received only her "widow's third" dower rights to the wedding gifts of linen and silver she had received from her mother. In 1884 she married Colonel James H. Platt and moved with him to Queens, Long Island, New York. While living there, she served as a director of the Mineola Children's Home. The Platts moved in 1887 to Denver, where he opened a paper mill. They had one daughter before James Platt's death in 1894. Sarah Platt remained in Denver and in 1899 married Judge Westbrook S. Decker; he died in 1903.

Best known nationally for her work with the General Federation of Women's Clubs, it was in Denver that Sarah S. Platt Decker began building her reputation in voluntarism, reform, and politics. Throughout her career, she expressed her opposition to party machines and the spoils system. At the same time, she believed political progress for women could best be attained by organizing a woman's party. She worked for civil service reform, woman suffrage, free coinage of silver (after the 1893 mine closings in Colorado), conservation of natural resources, an end to child labor, and municipal improvements. She took a leading role in many Progressive Era organizations in Colorado, including the State Board of Charities and Corrections, the State Civil Service Commission, the Advisory Board of the Denver County Hospital, the American Institute of Civics and Child Labor League, the Women's Public Service League (a political action group), and the Denver Civic Federation. In addition, she worked as vice chair of the Colorado Woman's Bryan Club in 1900 and as vice president of the Denver Woodrow Wilson for President Club in 1912.

Notwithstanding Decker's many civic and political endeavors, she concentrated her activities in the woman's club movement. In 1894 she helped form the Woman's Club of Denver. Elected its first president, she served in that capacity for five years. Organized as a large, departmental club, the Woman's Club of Denver's interests reflected the activist concerns of its president: the reform department contained standing committees on public service, city improvement, temperance, public health, civil service, and legislation. Decker was soon recognized as a dynamic, capable leader at the national level. In 1898 at the Biennial in Denver, the General Federation of Women's Clubs (GFWC) elected her its vice president, although a large contingent wanted her to run for president. In 1904 she finally consented to run for president of the GFWC and won handily.

Decker served as president of the GFWC for two terms (1904–1908) and is generally credited with turning federated clubs toward a civic reform agenda. Rheta Childe Dorr, fellow clubwoman and author, recalled in *What Eight Million Women Want* (1910) that in her 1904 biennial address, Decker "simply laughed the musty study clubs out of existence" (p. 42). Dorr also cites one of Decker's often-quoted remarks: "Ladies, Dante is dead. He died several centuries ago, and a great many things have happened since his time. Let us drop the study of his *Inferno* and proceed in earnest to contemplate our own social order" (p. 42).

Decker also sought to make the Federation more responsive to the needs of individual clubs. She centralized and systematized its dealings with state federations and formed a Bureau of Information, which responded to requests for assistance on all aspects of club work. She promoted participation in Federation activities and strove to develop clubwomen's leadership qualities. She traveled extensively during her tenure as president, visiting forty state federations, encouraging cohesiveness within the growing Federation and promoting reform and philanthropic programs.

Decker made hundreds of speeches. An inspiring orator, she received accolades for her wit, wisdom, and common sense. In discussing the women's club movement before a California audience during her presidency of the GFWC, Decker commented: "We are sometimes told that the women's club makes women stay away from home; but it doesn't. There have always been things to keep a woman away from home—she has allowed matinees to keep her from home, and picnics and bridge whist. But the women's club teaches her to stay away from home properly."

Decker's charm and verbal skills enabled her to address controversial issues with aplomb and daring. For example, woman suffrage proved to be so divisive among women's clubs at the time she ran for president that the Federation declined to discuss it in a biennial forum. Decker's friends urged her to avoid the issue. However, she believed that candidates for Federation office should publicly state their views. She had actively participated in the successful 1893 Colorado campaign for equal suffrage, and she advocated national woman suffrage, although the Federation did not formally endorse it until 1914, two years after her death.

Conservation, too, occupied a central position in Decker's political agenda. As president of the GFWC, Decker received an invitation from President Theodore Roosevelt to a 1908 White House Governors'

Conference on the Conservation of Natural Resources. The only female delegate, her presence reflected the influence Roosevelt deemed clubwomen to wield during the Progressive Era.

In 1908, when Decker stepped down from the presidency of the GFWC, she continued to chair its Civil Service Reform Committee and to engage in public speaking. She urged that clubwork be regarded as a "real profession which has come to the women of this generation," not "a passing pleasure to be put on and off like a garment." She envisioned "a mighty company of earnest women" engaged in an "occupation for service of the world" (*Colorado Federation of Women's Clubs Yearbook* [1907–1908]).

At the 1912 San Francisco Biennial of the GFWC, Decker fell ill and died following emergency abdominal surgery. Flags flew at half-mast, and government offices closed for her funeral. Articles appeared in newspapers across the country to honor Decker's contributions to her community, state, and country. In his tribute to her in 1912, Colorado governor Alva Adams said: "In the days just preceding her tragic end it needed but her consent to have become a formidable aspirant for high place in the Colorado state house, or the capitol at Washington . . . She was the most popular and perhaps the greatest citizen of the state." At the time of her death in 1912, she had been suggested as a possible candidate for the U.S. Senate. The motto by which Decker lived spoke for a generation of women: "Never frown, never sigh, and keep step."

Certainly Sarah Platt Decker more than "kept step" with the events of the day. Her analysis of conditions and the programs she espoused promoting social change most definitely put her a step ahead.

• The principal sources of primary documents are extensive personal scrapbooks from the years 1894–1912, containing newspaper clippings, correspondence (including the letter to her from President T. Roosevelt), club paraphernalia, photographs, and other items. These scrapbooks are the property of the Denver Public Library. Records of the Woman's Club of Denver are in the possession of the Colorado Historical Society. Texts of Decker's prepared speeches before the General Federation of Women's Clubs appear in Biennial Convention Official Reports, GFWC, Washington, D.C. Biographical material and Governor Alva Adams's 1912 tribute to Decker are in the Archives of the General Federation of Women's Clubs. Brief biographies appear in Mildred White Wells, *Unity in Diversity: The History of the General Federation of Women's Clubs* (1953), and Ellis Meredith, *Favorite Poems of Sarah Platt Decker* (1912), a memorial booklet. See also Susan B. Anthony and Ida Husted Harper, eds., *The History of Woman Suffrage*, vol. 4: *1883–1900* (1902; repr. 1969); Mary I. Wood, *The History of the General Federation of Women's Clubs: For the First Twenty–Two Years of Its Organization* (1912); and Jennie June Croly, *The History of the Women's Club Movement in America* (1898). Additional biographical material and obituaries are in *Rocky Mountain News*, 8, 9, and 22 July 1912, and the *Denver Post* and the *Denver Republican*, both 8 and 9 July 1912.

DIANE HARRISON WERNE

DE CLEYRE, Voltairine (17 Nov. 1866–20 June 1912), teacher and anarchist lecturer and writer, was born in Leslie, Michigan, the daughter of Hector De Claire, a tailor, and Harriet Elizabeth Billings, a seamstress. Despite being raised in poverty, de Cleyre received formal schooling in a Catholic convent until age seventeen. Her experience in the convent influenced her turn to free thought and anarchism. In her speech "The Making of an Anarchist" she noted that "there are white scars on my soul yet" as a result of the convent life (*Selected Works*, p. 156).

In 1886 de Cleyre left her family and moved to Grand Rapids, where she began her association with the Free Thought movement, a group that challenged the power of religious authority over human reason on matters of religious belief. While in Grand Rapids, she published her first essays and stories under the pseudonym Fanny Fern in the *Progressive Age*, a small Free Thought weekly. She soon became its editor, a position she filled until she moved to Philadelphia in 1889. Her association with Free Thought eventually led her to anarchism in 1888. As her ideology evolved during this time, so, too, did her name, which she changed from Voltairine De Claire to Voltairine de Claire before settling on Voltairine de Cleyre in 1888.

During her time in Philadelphia, from 1889 to 1910, de Cleyre increased her activism with the Anarchist movement, began teaching English to Jewish immigrants (1891), and met Emma Goldman (1893). Also during this time, de Cleyre made her first suicide attempt, because of a particularly vicious fight with one of her lovers.

With Philadelphia as a home base, in 1897 de Cleyre traveled to Britain and France, where she met philosopher Pyotr Kropotkin, French anarchist Louise Michel, and Austrian historian of anarchism Max Nettlau, among others. In 1903 she journeyed to Norway and Britain. This travel and work took its toll on both her mental and physical health, resulting in extensive stays in the hospital during 1904, culminating in a second suicide attempt in 1905. The year 1906 provided improved health; the founding of Emma Goldman's *Mother Earth*, to which de Cleyre was a frequent contributor; and a chance to meet anarchist Alexander Berkman, with whom she had been corresponding since 1893. In 1910 de Cleyre lectured in New York, Ohio, and Michigan and resettled in Chicago, where she later died of a brain infection.

Although originally driven to the Free Thought movement by her convent experience, she eventually embraced anarchism, motivated by four interlocking factors: her rejection of women's traditional roles, her recognition of the plight of workers, her resistance to state interference in private affairs, and the injustice of the Haymarket trial. The Haymarket trial, which de Cleyre referred to as "the specific occasion which ripened tendencies to definition" (*Selected Works*, p. 156), convicted eight anarchist leaders for throwing a bomb that killed eleven people during a 4 May 1886 rally for an eight-hour working day. No evidence was ever produced that any of the eight were involved in making or throwing the bomb, yet all were convicted. Four were hanged, one committed suicide, and three eventually were pardoned in 1893.

However, the Haymarket injustice alone did not transform de Cleyre into an anarchist. In "Why I Am an Anarchist," first delivered in 1897, de Cleyre described her conversion as growing from

disgust with the subordinated cramped circle prescribed for women in daily life. . . . A sense of burning disgust that a mere legal form should be considered as the sanction for all manner of bestialities. . . . That in spite of all the hardship and torture of existence men and women should go on obeying the old Israelitish command, "Increase and multiply," merely because they have society's permission to do so, without regard to the slaveries to be inflicted upon the unfortunate creatures of their passions. (*Mother Earth*, Mar. 1908, pp. 20–21)

De Cleyre's anarchism led her to spend her life "making rebels wherever we can. By ourselves *living our beliefs* . . . we are revolutionists. And we shall use propaganda by speech, deed, and most of all, life—*being* what we teach" (*Lucifer*, 29 May 1891). She lived among and taught immigrant laborers in Philadelphia and Chicago, lectured for anarchism and Free Thought, and never became dependent (emotionally or financially) on another, although her teaching fees were low. She never lived with any of her male companions, who included James B. Elliot, Dyer D. Lum, T. Hamilton Garside, and Samuel Gordon. While waiting for a streetcar on 19 December 1902 she was shot by a former student, Herman Helcher. She did not press charges, arguing that the legal system would inappropriately treat her attacker, whom she believed was mentally ill. Instead she initiated a fundraising campaign to defray his legal costs. When she bore a child (named Vermorel Elliot by de Cleyre, who later changed his name to Harry de Cleyre), she refused to care for him and instead left him with his father, James B. Elliot, and paternal grandmother.

Chronic sinus infections that progressed to her middle ear and brain, coupled with psychological depression and the assassin's bullets that were never removed from her body, always made work, writing, and lecturing difficult and sometimes impossible. Yet, despite her physical and financial restraints, de Cleyre was an active lecturer. Her speeches demonstrate a keen understanding of the range of oppressions faced by U.S. industrial workers and women. Given the obstacles she faced, de Cleyre's extraordinary impact on her contemporaries was astounding. George Brown, the most popular anarchist orator in Philadelphia, wrote, "To me, she was the most intellectual woman I ever met. . . . She spent her tortured life in the service of an obscure cause. Had she done the same work in some popular cause, she would have been famous and the world would have acclaimed her . . . the greatest woman America ever produced" (quoted in Avrich, p. 101). Emma Goldman proclaimed her "one of America's great anarchists" (*Red Emma Speaks* [1972], p. 391).

Not content with her own speaking, de Cleyre created spaces in which others could lecture, helping form the Ladies' Liberal League in 1892, a forum for debating issues such as Prohibition, sex, crime, anarchism, and socialism. While the league primarily served its home audience of Philadelphia, it drew nationally recognized speakers. Ultimately the league merged with the Radical Library in 1895 and then disbanded a few years later. In 1901 de Cleyre was influential in the creation of the Social Science Club, an anarchist reading group that was soon the leading anarchist organization in Philadelphia.

In addition to leaving an eloquent legacy of speeches, de Cleyre was a voluminous writer, analyzing women's roles, anarchism, social oppression, literature, and education. Her prose was translated into numerous languages, including French, Italian, Spanish, Russian, Chinese, German, and Yiddish. She also translated others' works from Yiddish and French.

Unfortunately, de Cleyre's contributions long have been overlooked. First, her anarchist feminism is an early precursor to the radical critiques of women's status generated by the second wave of feminism. In particular, de Cleyre argued for sexuality separate from reproduction, critiqued the puritanism of the period, recognized rape in marriage, rejected motherhood as definitive of womanhood, and not only rejected marriage as an institution but rejected any "permanent relation of a man and a woman, sexual and economical, whereby the present home and family life is maintained" (*Mother Earth*, Jan. 1908, p. 502).

Second, de Cleyre's appeals to, and explanation of, emotion as a persuasive device are illuminating. Although involved with a movement that celebrated logic and rationality, she was able to make explicit and implicit appeals to emotion without being censured by other anarchists. For de Cleyre, feelings were more accurate barometers of social ills than was reason. De Cleyre equated sentiments, feelings, and instincts, and while reason might lead one to accept prevailing conditions, "the instinct of liberty naturally revolted not only at economic servitude, but at the outcome of it, class lines" (*Mother Earth*, Mar. 1908, p. 18).

Third, de Cleyre was a powerful eulogist, primarily because she was able to create eulogies in which the dead lived on. Her eulogies, particularly one written for Katherine Karg Harker, present a theory of being in which the individual, at death, transcends the bounds of the physical to combine with a universal "all." In her annual Haymarket memorials, such as "Our Martyred Comrades," delivered in 1900, she develops a framework to understand how martyrdom may support and energize a movement even though the movement rejects the religious underpinnings of martyrdom. In her eulogies de Cleyre created a secular afterlife for the Haymarket martyrs, repeating their words, keeping alive their memory, and incorporating their ideas into the present. For de Cleyre, eulogies were not occasions to consign the dead to the past but to reintegrate them into the present. All her extant Haymarket speeches are published in *The First Mayday: The Haymarket Speeches, 1895–1910* (1980).

Finally, de Cleyre functioned as "the leading apostle of tolerance within the anarchist movement, pleading for cooperation among all who sought the removal of authority, regardless of their economic preferences" (Avrich, p. 153). Hers was an anarchism without adjectives, rooted in the individual potential of each human being. This philosophy was best laid out in "Anarchism and American Traditions," which she delivered throughout 1909 and 1910.

De Cleyre's primary lesson of social action is contained in her call to action: "The first act of our life was to kick against an unjust decree of our parents, and we have unflinchingly stood for the kicking principle ever since. Now, if the word kicking is in bad repute with you, substitute non-submission, insubordination, rebellion, revolution, whatever name you please which expresses non-acquiescence to injustice" (*The Rebel*, 20 Oct. 1895, p. 18).

• The largest collections of de Cleyre's writings are in the Labadie collection (University of Michigan) and the Joseph Ishill Collection (Houghton Library, Harvard University). De Cleyre's pamphlets include *McKinley's Assassination from the Anarchist Standpoint* (1907), *Anarchism and American Traditions* (1909), *The Dominant Idea* (1910), and *The Mexican Revolt* (1911). A selection of her short stories is in *Selected Stories* (1916). While many of her essays and poems were printed in anarchist periodicals, such as *Mother Earth*, reprints of many of them are in *Selected Works of Voltairine de Cleyre* (1914) and *Written in Red: Selected Poems* (1990). Particularly intriguing are her speeches and writings on women, which include "The Gates of Freedom" (serialized in *Lucifer*, 10 Apr.–29 May 1891); "The Past and Future of the Ladies' Liberal League" (serialized in *The Rebel*, 20 Oct. 1895–Jan. 1896); "The Case of Woman vs. Orthodoxy" (*Boston Investigator*, 18 Sept. 1896); "Sex Slavery" (*Selected Works*); "Why I Am an Anarchist" (*Mother Earth*, Mar. 1908); and "They Who Marry Do Ill" (*Mother Earth*, Jan. 1908). The primary biographical source is Paul Avrich, *An American Anarchist: The Life of Voltairine de Cleyre* (1978). This book also details all the locations with materials by and about de Cleyre. For an analysis of de Cleyre's feminism, see Margaret Marsh's chapter on de Cleyre in *Anarchist Women: 1870–1920* (1981). For an analysis of de Cleyre's discourse on sexuality, see Catherine Helen Palczewski, "Voltairine de Cleyre: Sexual Pleasure and Sexual Slavery in the 19th Century," *NWSA Journal* 7, no. 3 (Fall 1995): 54–68. For a comprehensive rhetorical biography of de Cleyre and an annotated listing of all her speeches, see Palczewski, "Voltairine de Cleyre: Feminist Anarchist," in *Women Public Speakers in the United States, 1800–1925: A Bio-Critical Sourcebook* (1993).

CATHERINE HELEN PALCZEWSKI

DE CREEFT, José (27 Nov. 1884–11 Sept. 1982), sculptor and teacher, was born in Guadalajara, Spain, the son of Catalans Mariano de Creeft y Masdeu, a military officer, and Rosa Champane y Ortiz. When he was four the family moved to Barcelona, where in 1890 his father died. As a youth de Creeft helped support his family by modeling figurines for sale at the annual festival of Santa Lucia in 1895, and in 1898 he was an apprentice at the bronze foundry of Masriera and

Campins. Two years later he entered the Madrid workshop of Augustin Querol, the official government sculptor, and studied drawing and sculpture, the latter with Ignacio Zuloaga. In 1903 he first exhibited portrait sculptures at El Círculo de Bellas Artes.

De Creeft moved to Paris in 1905 and rented a studio in the Bateau Lavoir, a building in Montmartre that was also the home of Pablo Picasso, Georges Braque, and Juan Gris. On the advice of Zuloaga and Auguste Rodin, de Creeft improved his drawing and modeling by attending the Académie Julian. In 1911, desirous of learning how to cut stone, he began working at the Maison Greber, a firm that transferred and enlarged wax and clay models into permanent materials by the *mise aux point* technique. In 1915 de Creeft destroyed his clay and plaster portraits and allegorical figures as an act of rejecting traditional modeling and the use of pointing machines. From then on he preferred to carve directly his sculptures without preparatory drawings or models. By adopting what was then considered a progressive technique, de Creeft became one of the most avant-garde sculptors working in Europe.

The late 1910s and 1920s continued to be a period of great experimentation for de Creeft as he explored the soft material of lead, beating, flattening, and chasing its surface to create figures and heads that often incorporated negative space as well as positive, solid form. In 1925 he made *Picador* (Fundació Joan Miró, Barcelona) for a decoration of the Gran Bal Espagnol. This would be the first of several assemblages he constructed from scraps of found metal objects. Dadaist in spirit, these radical sculptures reflected the artist's sense of humor. Despite these creative excursions, direct carving remained de Creeft's primary technical process throughout his life. He exhibited frequently in Paris: at the Salon d'Automne (1920–1927), at the Société des Artistes Indépendants (1922–1925, 1927, and 1928), and at the Salon des Tuileries (1925–1927).

Although a friend of Picasso, de Creeft experimented with cubism only briefly. He was most inspired by primitive art: in 1902 he had been impressed by Eskimo art, and his first direct carved sculptures reflect African art in their themes, style, and material. After his initial foray with wood and African imagery in the late teens, de Creeft switched to stone, and this harder substance remained his preferred material. De Creeft and other modern primitivists extolled art created by non-Western craftsmen, for they believed that these native artists were more naive in their expressions, not hindered by generations of outworn traditions. Throughout his mature career de Creeft insisted that his personal response to the texture, grain, and color of wood and stone enabled him to understand his materials and thereby release from within them their innate beauty and spirit.

In 1927 de Creeft left Paris to execute a huge commission in Puerto Pollensa on the island of Mallorca. There, he devoted two years to decorating the terraced gardens of a fourteenth-century fortress owned by Argentine painter Roberto Ramonge. Assisted by the American sculptor Alice Robertson Carr, de Creeft created more than 200 gargoyle-like figures, fountain sculptures, and other decorative stone carvings.

The year 1929 was a pivotal one for de Creeft. He completed his large Mallorca commission, married Alice Carr in London (they eventually had two children), moved to the United States, and was given his first solo exhibitions. Before leaving Mallorca, de Creeft held an exhibition of his drawings and sculptures at the Galería Costa in Palma; and on visiting Seattle, his wife's hometown, he was invited to hold an exhibition of his recent sculpture at the Seattle Art Institute. Later that year, after settling in New York City, he held his first New York exhibition at Ferargil Galleries. De Creeft was well received and hailed as an important progressive artist. Numerous other exhibitions in a variety of cities were quickly forthcoming: 56th Street Galleries in New York (1930), Arts Club of Chicago (1930), Philadelphia Art Alliance (1933), and the Faulkner Memorial Art Gallery in Santa Barbara (1937). He was also accorded his first retrospective at the New School for Social Research in New York (1933). Three years later the dealer Georgette Passedoit in New York began holding exhibitions devoted to de Creeft's recent work almost annually until 1949.

Although he continued to exhibit in Paris and Mallorca for a few years after his arrival in New York City and almost annually visited the island until the Spanish Civil War in 1937, de Creeft became a significant figure in New York art circles. Not only did he exhibit widely, but he was an active promoter of modern art. In 1934 he became a board member of the Society of Independent Artists, in 1936 a founding member of the American Artists Congress, in 1938 a founding member of the Sculptors Guild, and in 1940 he formed the Federation of Modern Painters and Sculptors. By the end of the decade his art received official recognition as his work entered museum collections: the Brooklyn Museum purchased his stone *Semitic Head* (1936) in 1938, and two years later the Museum of Modern Art acquired the lead *Saturnia* (1939).

The stone carvings de Creeft created in the United States changed little after he developed his mature aesthetic. Relishing the hard substance, de Creeft cut glyptic forms that evince a powerful solidity and monumentality, no matter their size. He used a variety of stones of many colors and textures, often combining roughly chiseled passages with highly polished, mirrorlike surfaces. Usually depicting single figures or heads, de Creeft's work reflects his fascination with the physiognomy of exotic women. He was one of several American sculptors who created a new standard of beauty during the 1930s by transforming women from different races and lands into universal, timeless beings.

In 1932 de Creeft began a long teaching career. It was through his teachings as well as his art that he encouraged the next generation of American sculptors in the art of direct carving. For sixteen years until 1948 and again from 1957 to 1960 he was an instructor at the New School for Social Research. His other teaching stints included the Art Students League (1944–1948; 1957–1979), Black Mountain College, North Carolina (1944), Skowhegan School of Painting and Sculpture, Maine (1948–1949), and Norton Gallery and School of Art, West Palm Beach (1948–1951).

In 1940 de Creeft became an American citizen, and in 1944, five years after his divorce from Alice Carr, he married one of his students, Lorrie Goulet; they had one child. In 1946 he was elected to the National Sculpture Society (he became a fellow in 1958) and in 1948 an associate member of the National Academy of Design (he became an academician in 1963 and vice president in 1972). During the early 1950s he designed *Poet* for the Ellen Phillips Samuel Memorial in Fairmont Park, Philadelphia, and at the end of the decade his bronze *Alice in Wonderland* was dedicated in Central Park, New York City. In 1960 the American Federation of Arts organized and circulated his first retrospective exhibition, which opened at the Whitney Museum of Art. In 1974 the New School for Social Research accorded him another retrospective, and in 1980 the Fundació Juan Miró in Barcelona circulated his first major survey in Spain. The Smithsonian Institution organized a memorial exhibition a year after his death in New York City.

• De Creeft's papers (manuscripts, clippings of reviews, published material, etc.) are in the Archives of American Art, Smithsonian Institution. An unfinished manuscript for a book on the artist by Charlotte Devree is in the collection of Lorrie Goulet. Statements by de Creeft are in "Symposium: The Creative Process," *Art Digest* 28 (15 Jan. 1954): 14, 30, 32; and "Statement on Sculpture," *Seven Arts* 2 (1954): 63–68. The first monograph on the artist by Jules Campos, *José de Creeft* (1945), was followed in 1950 by the picture book *José de Creeft*, part of the American Sculptor's Series. The most inclusive chronology is in Carles Fontseré's exhibition catalog *L'Aventura Humana de José de Creeft* (1980). Information presented in the exhibition catalog by Charlotte Devree, *José de Creeft* (1960), was updated and corrected in the more scholarly catalog by Adelyn D. Breeskin and Virginia M. Mecklenburg, *José de Creeft: Sculpture and Drawings* (1983).

ILENE SUSAN FORT

DE CROIX, Teodoro (30 June 1730–8 Apr. 1791), Spanish colonial administrator, was born at the castle of Prevote, near Lille, France, which was his ancestral home. The names of his parents and the circumstances of his youth are unknown. He enlisted in the Spanish army at the age of seventeen and served in Italy as an ensign of grenadiers. He transferred to the Walloon guard in 1750. He was decorated in Flanders in 1756; in the same year he was promoted to lieutenant. In 1760 he became a colonel in the Walloon guard, and by 1765 he had become a captain of the Viceregal guard. His rise in the ranks was slow but sure, and his career began to accelerate once he went to the New World in 1765.

De Croix accompanied his uncle, the Marques de Croix, who went to Mexico in 1765 to assume his position as viceroy of New Spain. He was soon named collector of the port of Acapulco, which was the point of entry and departure for the galleons that made their way from Manila to the west coast of New Spain. During his tenure in this post, the revenues of the port increased greatly in size. In 1767 he collaborated with his uncle the viceroy and with José de Galvez, the visitador general of the king, in executing the instructions of King Charles III to suppress the Jesuit order in the Spanish dominions. De Croix was promoted to brigadier general in 1769. He returned to Spain with his uncle in 1771.

After several years of active duty with the army in Spain, de Croix returned to Mexico City in February 1777. At the recommendation of Galvez and others, de Croix had been named by King Charles III as the first commandant general of what were called the Interior Provinces of New Spain (Sinaloa y Sonora, Upper and Lower California, Nuevo Mexico, Nueva Vizcaya, Coahuila, and Texas). This administrative change was undertaken in order to strengthen the northern regions of New Spain in anticipation of attacks on those areas by Indians, Anglo-Americans, or Russians coming from Alaska.

De Croix remained in Mexico City until August 1777. He then departed and made a long journey through a large section of the provinces he was to govern. His journey was chronicled by the Franciscan friar Juan Agustín Morfi, who later wrote *Diario y derrotero, 1777–1781* (ed. Eugenio del Hoyo and Malcolm D. McLean [1967]). After returning to Chihuahua, de Croix undertook to strengthen the frontiers of his vast territory. He had at that time approximately 2,000 soldiers with which to defend an area as large as the thirteen English colonies that were at that time in rebellion against King George III.

De Croix created a special body of light infantry troops in 1778. These men were trained and equipped to travel lightly and to fight on foot. He also sought to establish a more rational system of presidios (forts and towns) along the frontier, but he was frustrated in this by the advent of Spain's participation in the war of the American Revolution. Starting in 1779, this participation made it difficult for Spain to send supplies and reinforcements to de Croix. He made the best of a bad situation for the most part, but he was completely prevented from carrying out a project that was close to his heart: an offensive war against the Apache Indians.

In June 1783 Yuma Indians destroyed a Spanish settlement on the California side of the Colorado River, killing 104 Spaniards. This war (or revolt) was the most serious reversal that occurred during de Croix's administration, and the Spanish never succeeded in regaining possession of the Yuma crossing. De Croix continued in his post until July 1783, when he was relieved by Don Felipe de Neve.

De Croix then received the greatest honor that his monarch could bestow upon him, the post of lieutenant general and viceroy of Peru. He left from Acapulco and arrived in Peru on 4 April 1784 and remained there until 25 March 1790. He distinguished himself in Peru and soon after his return to Spain he received the Grand Cross of the Order of Charles III. He became a colonel in the king's bodyguard in 1791, shortly before he died in Madrid.

De Croix was one of the capable administrators whom Spain sent to the New World in the late eighteenth century. The Spanish Bourbon monarchy had to a certain extent revived the fortunes of Spain and its colonies and men such as Bernardo de Galvez, José de Galvez, and Teodoro de Croix had a good deal to do with that revival. His diligence in office is shown by the extent of his correspondence, and his successor testified to an excellent state of affairs in the interior provinces of New Spain. De Croix's work was, however, incomplete. He never managed to pacify or subdue the Apache Indians, and events within a few years' time (the Nootka Sound controversy and the start of the French Revolution) undid much of the foundation he had labored to construct.

• A biography is Alfred Barnaby Thomas, ed. and trans., *Teodoro de Croix and the Northern Frontier of New Spain, 1776–1783* (1941), which reproduces many of de Croix's letters. There are two articles, Theodore E. Treutlein, "Los Angeles, California: The Question of the City's Original Spanish Name," *Southern California Quarterly* 55, no. 1 (1973): 1–7, and William A. Depalo, Jr., "The Establishment of the Nueva Vizcaya Militia during the Administration of Teodoro de Croix," *New Mexico Historical Review* 58, no. 3 (1973): 223–49. De Croix is mentioned as well in David J. Weber, *The Spanish Frontier in North America* (1992); Alfred Barnaby Thomas, *Forgotten Frontiers: A Study of the Spanish Indian Policy of Don Juan Bautista de Anza, Governor of New Mexico 1777–1787* (1932); and Peter Gerhard, *The North Frontier of New Spain* (1982).

SAMUEL WILLARD CROMPTON

DEERE, John (7 Feb. 1804–17 May 1886), manufacturer, was born in Rutland, Vermont, the son of William Rinhold Deere, a tailor, and Sarah Yates, a seamstress. His formal schooling was limited, and he became an apprentice blacksmith at age seventeen. He worked for several blacksmiths in Vermont before opening his own shop while in his mid-twenties. Deere's craftsmanship was highly regarded, but his luck was bad and his businesses failed. So in 1836 he left behind his pregnant wife, Demarius Lamb (whom he had married in 1827), and four young children (they eventually had nine) and joined the westward movement, heading for Grand Detour, Illinois. His family followed him the next year.

Deere found plenty of blacksmith work in that small town on the Rock River, and he became determined to solve a problem faced by the pioneer farmers in the area. The rich soil of much of the Midwest was so thick and sticky that plows were unable to turn it without considerable extra effort. Farmers had to stop frequently to scrape the dirt from the moldboards (the large, curved parts that actually turn the soil) of their walk-behind horse-drawn plows.

Deere recognized a need and through trial and error designed and built, in 1837, a plow with a uniquely designed polished steel moldboard that successfully "scoured" itself clean as it moved through the soil. He did not abandon his regular blacksmith work at first but built plows as a sideline. In 1839 he built and, importantly, sold ten of them, and this separated him from many other plow inventors of his time. As demand for his plows increased he gradually devoted all of his effort to their design, manufacture, and sale, forming a succession of partnerships. His solution eventually made him famous and wealthy and helped open vast areas to production agriculture.

In 1848 Deere moved to Moline, Illinois, and expanded his operations. This town was on the Mississippi River, which provided excellent waterpower and improved transportation, which was especially important because he imported steel from England and Pittsburgh. Again he formed a succession of partnerships and built a factory. By 1856 he was producing more than 13,000 plows per year in the largest plow factory in the western states. He modernized manufacturing processes and expanded the product line to include walking plows built in variations of five sizes and three popular sizes of breaking plows. In addition, he manufactured double plows, shovel plows, cultivators, and harrows.

Selling the ever-expanding line of plows was difficult. Although demand for his products was tremendous, "hard currency" was scarce due to the undeveloped and unregulated banking system, and most sales were on credit. Barter and sales on commission were common. Undeveloped methods of communication and distribution added to the difficulty. River transportation was hazardous, and the rivers froze in the winter. It was not until 1854 that the railroad (and the telegraph) reached the Moline area, and it was 1856 before the first rail bridge crossed the Mississippi, at nearby Rock Island. Despite these marketing obstacles Deere's field representatives, called "travelers," developed wholesalers and retailers in every state, plus Canada. In 1857 he even exported three plows to England.

Deere's increasing success allowed him to leave the actual operation of his factory to his assistants, and he was able to "fine tune" his products and improve their quality. He continually sought to improve and change his products, testing his new creations on local farms and often incorporating suggestions made by farmers. The concept of the interchangeability of parts was a relatively new one, and Deere had adopted it by the mid-1860s.

Deere also had time to concentrate on sales and marketing. He worked especially hard to get his travelers to require sales agents to pay cash for products consigned to them within specified time periods. He was an early user of illustrations in print advertising and was an early advertiser in *Prairie Farmer*. One of the best forms of advertising he used was to display his products at state and local fairs; in 1856 he even won a "first premium" at the Vermont State Fair, more than a thousand miles away. Plowing contests also provided valuable advertising.

The early 1850s were halcyon years for Deere, but the last part of the decade almost saw his undoing. The panic of 1857 ruined many businessmen, and Deere almost was among them because his company was suffering from its usual cash-flow problems and had substantial bills for raw materials. So he reorganized his company to protect his personal assets as well as those of the company. Some shrewd decisions were made, largely by his son Charles (who had joined his father as a bookkeeper in 1854), and the company survived. Although John remained as president of the reorganized company (it was formally incorporated as Deere & Company in 1868), day-to-day management fell to Charles, who was twenty-one years old in 1858.

While his son led the company to new heights, Deere pursued his personal interests. He always was experimenting with new ideas and products and farmed on a large scale. Retirement from active management of the implement business also provided him the opportunity to begin patenting some of his ideas: he secured his first patent (molds for casting steel plows) in 1864. His wife had died in 1865, and in 1866 he married her sister, Lusena Lamb. (This marriage was childless.) He was a local philanthropist and in 1873 was elected mayor of Moline, where he died.

John Deere possessed the necessary qualities to succeed as a manufacturer in what still was considered the West. He was energetic, able to select associates with skills that complemented his own, and had great leadership abilities. He had an unending commitment to producing quality products that met his customers' needs; he recognized that continual improvements, regardless of expense, needed to be made to gain and retain customers. Deere was reported to have said: "They haven't got to take what we make and somebody else will beat us, and we will lose our trade." A Deere & Company slogan proclaimed, "He gave to the world the steel plow." Because of the innovations he brought to the design, manufacture, and marketing of agricultural equipment, that was exactly what Deere did.

• Deere's personal and business papers are in the Deere & Company Archives in Moline. A company biography is Neil M. Clark, *John Deere: He Gave to the World the Steel Plow* (1937). The definitive work on Deere is Wayne G. Broehl, Jr., *John Deere's Company* (1984), which also includes an excellent bibliography. An interesting and fairly accurate article, titled "The John Deere Centennial," is in *Farm Implement News*, 14 Jan. 1937. Reasonably complete and accurate obituaries are in the *Chicago Tribune*, the *Moline Daily Republican*, and the *Davenport Daily Democrat*, all 18 May 1886.

LESLIE J. STEGH

DEERFOOT. *See* Bennett, Lewis.

DEERING, William (25 Apr. 1826–9 Dec. 1913), manufacturer, was born in South Paris, Maine, the son of James Deering and Eliza Moore. He attended first public schools, then Maine Wesleyan Seminary, in Readfield. He graduated in 1844 and began studying medicine, but his father, a successful woolen manufacturer, wanted him to help with the business; until about 1849, he managed his father's mill. He then turned his attention to the increasing opportunities in the West, where he invested in land, especially in Illinois and Iowa. When his wife, Abby Reed Barbour, whom he had married in 1849 and with whom he had one child, died in 1856, he decided to return to South Paris, opening there a dry-goods store. A year later he married Clara Hamilton; they had two children.

In 1861 he moved to Portland, Maine, to manufacture uniforms for the Union army. With the end of the war, he formed a partnership with Seth Milliken to sell woolens. Deering & Milliken was quite successful, adding offices in Boston and New York and growing to be one of the country's leading woolen goods merchants. In 1869 Deering withdrew from the partnership, possibly for reasons of health.

Years earlier, an old friend of Deering's from Maine, Methodist preacher Elijah Gammon, had moved to Illinois. There Gammon had invested in the Plano, Illinois, firm at which the Marsh brothers manufactured their harvester, a novel design on which men rode, binding by hand sheaves of grain as they were cut. It was an important improvement over self-rake reapers of the day that left the gavels (bundles of grain ready to be bound into sheaves) on the ground, requiring a team of binders to follow the machine tying sheaves. In 1870 Deering came west with $40,000 for land investments; instead he loaned the money to Gammon. In 1873 Gammon fell ill and asked Deering to superintend the company for three months. Deering agreed—and quickly recognized the commercial potential of grain-harvesting machinery. He moved to Illinois permanently, settling in Evanston in 1874. In 1875 Deering and Gammon bought out the other partners; in 1878 Deering bought out Gammon and moved the firm to Chicago. He incorporated the company in 1883 as William Deering & Company, changing the name to Deering Manufacturing Company in 1894.

In 1874 Deering began a pattern of pushing development of innovations, a pattern that defined his career as a manufacturer and constitutes his distinctive contribution. Over Gammon's objections, he bought the rights to manufacture a new self-binding mechanism using wire. Though reasonably successful, the McCormick Company came to market with a more successful design. But wire had serious drawbacks; pieces sometimes damaged threshing or milling machinery, and when left in hay they injured cows. Deering recognized the need to replace wire and quickly focused on developing a binding mechanism that would use twine instead. In 1878 he bought the rights to a twine binder that John Appleby had developed. Machines produced for the 1879 harvest were only marginally successful because Deering had been unable to find a twine that worked consistently well. Even so, he gambled his future, building 3,000 twine binders for the 1880 harvest. But cordage manufacturers were unresponsive to his entreaties. Then he turned to Edwin Fitler of Philadelphia. Initially uninterested, Fitler changed his mind when Deering said he would order ten carloads of a successful twine. Personally taking charge of the work, in just a few days Fitler developed a high-twist manila twine. Sent to Texas for immediate trial, the telegram came back, "Manila splendid."

Deering's success with the twine binder redefined the industry; demand for the wire binder collapsed; it was out of production by 1885. The Deering firm probably, briefly, surpassed McCormick. Deering continued to rely heavily on innovation to compete. He sought to develop (unsuccessfully) alternative, cheaper fibers—e.g., cotton, hemp, saw grass, flax— for use in binder twine. In the early 1890s Deering was the first to offer an all-steel binder, to use roller and ball bearings, and to offer farmers a "light" binder. Deering was the first to recognize the opportunity of line extension, that is, making and selling other harvesting equipment under the Deering name; it began with corn binders (harvesters) and hayrakes. Deering also led the industry in vertical integration, first with its own twine mill in 1886 to assure availability of the high-quality twines critical to the smooth operation of its machines, then with acquisition of its own steel mill and iron ore lands in the Masabi range, and by coking coal in Harlan County, Kentucky, by 1901. Deering was also the first to establish its own Canadian factory from which to supply the important and growing Canadian market. Symbolic of Deering's interest in innovation was his development, in 1894, of an automower; that is, a mower driven by an internal combustion engine. He later exhibited it with great fanfare at the great Paris Exposition of 1900.

As persistent and successful as Deering was with design innovation and vertical integration, he was less interested in production process and marketing. Deering never matched McCormick's low production costs and lagged behind McCormick by nearly a decade in establishing a credible European marketing organization (from 1892). Domestically, he sold farmers' notes to bankers for collection (unlike McCormick), thereby putting his goodwill at risk when those bankers pressed collections. As a result, by 1902 Deering, though holding perhaps 30 percent of the total market, had only three-quarters the sales of McCormick.

Deering had taken his two sons, James E. Deering and Charles W. Deering, into the business in 1880 and later brought in his son-in-law Richard F. Howe. But none were strong managers, and in 1898 he offered to sell his company to the McCormicks. They declined, because of the price asked and because they did not believe that they could alone manage effectively so large a company. In 1900 further negotiations came to nothing. In early 1902 Judge Elbert Gary, who had been the Deerings' chief legal counsel in the 1890s and was now chairman of the newly created United States Steel Corporation, urged renewed negotiations. Gary believed his company was threatened by the Deering expansion into iron, coal, and steel and feared McCormick would follow their lead, eroding U.S. Steel's dominance. Initially they made little progress; but at the urging of John D. Rockefeller, both sides turned to J. P. Morgan partner George W. Perkins. Perkins quickly succeeded; in August 1902 the five leading harvester manufacturers (McCormick, Deering, Plano, Champion, and Milwaukee) merged to create International Harvester. With the merger, Deering, who had been seriously ill in 1901, withdrew from management. (Enmity between the McCormicks and the younger Deerings continued for years, with the Deerings even apparently attempting to instigate a government antitrust suit in 1908 to break up the company and thus regain their firm.)

Deering performed limited public service, serving on the councils of two Maine governors in 1870–1873, as a director of the Metropolitan Bank of Chicago, as president of the Garrett Biblical Institute Trustees from 1887 to 1899, and as president of Board of Trustees of Northwestern University. He made large gifts to Northwestern, Garrett, and Wesley Hospital; he built and endowed the Deering School in Lake Bluff, Illinois. He died at his winter home in Coconut Grove, Florida.

• Some papers relating to the Deering Company are in the McCormick Collections at State Historical Society of Wisconsin, and a small collection of Deering correspondence is at the Garrett Theological Seminary. The following have a limited amount of material on Deering: Fred V. Carstensen, "' . . . A Dishonest Man Is at Least Prudent.' George W. Perkins and the International Harvester Steel Properties," *Business and Economic History* 2d ser., 9 (1980): 87–102; *William Deering* (1914); Deering Harvester Company, *Official Retrospective Exhibition of the Development of Harvesting Machinery* (1900), Esko Heikkonen, *Reaping the Bounty: McCormick Harvesting Machine Company Turns Abroad, 1878–1902* (1995); William T. Hutchinson, *Cyrus Hall McCormick: Harvest, 1856–1884* (1935); and John F. Steward, *The Reaper* (1931). Obituaries are in the *Chicago Evening Post* and the *Chicago American*, both 10 Dec. 1913, and the *Chicago Daily Tribune*, 11 Dec. 1913.

FRED CARSTENSEN

DEETER, Jasper (31 July 1893–31 May 1972), theater actor, director, producer, and teacher, was born in Mechanicsburg, Pennsylvania, the son of Jasper Newton Deeter, a successful businessman, and Sarah Mather, a singer and voice teacher. As a boy Deeter participated in amateur dramatics at the local Episcopal church. At Conway Hall prep school in Carlisle (Penn.), he performed in two school productions before graduating in 1911. Deeter withdrew from Lafayette College during his first term upon discovering that freshmen were denied participation in dramatics. In 1913, while working as a reporter and copyreader for the Harrisburg *Patriot*, he enrolled in Dickinson College, which he attended until 1915, never completing a degree. From 1910 to 1920 Deeter spent his summers at Lake Chautauqua in New York, studying interpretation and expression of, in his words, the "masterpieces of the drama" with his "great teacher" Silas Clark, the father of drama scholar Barrett Clark. Before moving to New York in 1918 to pursue an acting career, Deeter played in vaudeville in Chicago and worked in restaurants and for the Chicago news bureau.

Deeter's initial New York engagement was for actor/managers Charles and Ivah Coburn at the Greenwich Village Theatre in 1918, acting in a mob scene in *The Better 'Ole*. According to Sherwood Anderson in an article for *Esquire* (Oct. 1936), when the production "went up town and began to make money, Jap [nickname for Jasper] . . . began to ad lib. He made cracks about underpaid actors" and was fired from the play.

Deeter auditioned for the Provincetown Players on Macdougal Street in New York City and, accepted for their fifth season in 1919, was cast in every bill. In 1920 he played the lead in Eugene O'Neill's suicide drama *Exorcism* (later destroyed by the author). For the 1920–1921 season Deeter debuted the role of the Cockney trader Smithers (a part he played more than 200 times) in O'Neill's *The Emperor Jones*, with Charles Gilpin, on Deeter's solicitation, in the title role.

The Provincetown Players assigned Deeter to codirect *The Spring* in 1920 with the play's author, George Cram Cook. Deeter's recognized skill as a director then prompted the Provincetown to offer him the premiere of Susan Glaspell's *Inheritors* in 1921, in which he gave Ann Harding her first role, the play's leading part. The production was well received. On tour with *The Emperor Jones*, Deeter was soon dismissed from the Provincetown, stemming from his previous opposition to extending the production for a run on Broadway and then on tour. He subsequently joined a group in Chicago that was touring two plays by Henrik Ibsen, *The Master Builder* and *Ghosts*. In 1922 Deeter returned to the Provincetown at O'Neill's request to create sound effects for O'Neill's *The Hairy Ape*. Deeter's final Provincetown assignment was to direct in 1926 Paul Green's *In Abraham's Bosom*, which won a Pulitzer Prize.

As evidenced by the controversy surrounding Deeter's dismissal from the Provincetown, he considered the New York system of long-run productions detrimental to an actor's development. He envisioned a repertory company that would perform a different play every night, where "artists might work together to produce fine plays, where their freedom to create would be restricted only by the limitations of their own skills and imaginations" (quoted in Tanner). In the spring of 1923, amidst stressful negotiations for a directing contract with the Swarthmore Chautauqua in Pennsylvania, Deeter passed through Moylan-Rose Valley, fourteen miles from Philadelphia. In the town's Guild Hall, an old mill being used for community theater, he discovered his professional home.

On 21 April 1923 Deeter presented Shaw's *Candida* at the Guild Hall and thus founded Jasper Deeter's Theatre (later Hedgerow Theatre), a 165-seat suburban playhouse destined to become cosmopolitan in artistic scope and significance. In June of that year he invited Harding to recreate her role in a revival of *Inheritors*, the themes of which, namely the struggle for quality and the search for truth, came to constitute the "Hedgerow Bible." Through 1954, except during the war years, *Inheritors* was produced annually at the Hedgerow. Deeter's theater emerged not only as the inspiration for Eva LeGallienne's Civic Repertory Company in New York but also as the longest-running true repertory theater in the United States. By the time accumulated debts caused the Hedgerow to suspend operations in 1956, after thirty-three years under the artistic guidance of Deeter, the theater had produced 210 plays, 55 of which were either world or American premieres. The repertoire included scripts from more than a dozen countries, including five by Chekhov; seven each by Ibsen and Shakespeare; nine by O'Neill, who excused Deeter from paying royalties; and nineteen by Shaw. In 1939 Deeter produced the entirety of Shaw's *Man and Superman*, the first American production of the complete play.

Throughout Hedgerow's history, Deeter directed most of the productions and performed in nearly half of them. He maintained a company of about twenty actors, none treated as stars; they all lived in a nearby farm house, sharing the tasks of communal and theatrical life. During World War II Deeter drew national attention by petitioning the government (unsuccessfully) to exempt the Hedgerow actors from military service. Well-known actors who appeared at the Hedgerow include Richard Basehart, John Beal, Morris Carnovsky, Helen Craig, Van Heflin, Libby Holman, LeGallienne, and Sydney Machat.

As a director, Deeter was forever teaching acting to his actors. Sherwood Anderson dubbed him "a born teacher," and in 1946 Deeter officially opened a theater school to develop talent for Hedgerow and beyond. Henry Miller, who had visited Deeter at work and leisure, described Deeter as "a man who lives from the heart out" in an essay anthologized in *Remember to Remember* (1947). Moreover, Miller noted the "quiet way in which his authority communicated itself" and that "his great gift is the ability to inspire others." Even after the Hedgerow had ceased production, the Hedgerow School of Acting continued, with Deeter as head until his death in Media, Pennsylvania. In total he trained more than 700 students.

Deeter's pioneering spirit was tirelessly expansive. He enabled the Hedgerow to evolve administratively from his own operation, to a venture sharing policy decisions with the company of actors, to a cooperative run by committees, and finally in 1942 to a partnership with a board. Fiscally, his motto was "you can't budget nothing." Deeter's artistic achievement and interpersonal skills earned him contact and correspondence with notable playwrights, actors, and theatrical organizations. He also received commendation, as illustrated in a wartime letter from Irish playwright Sean O'Casey: "Long live the Abbey Theatre in Dublin! Long live the Art Theatre of Moscow! And long live the Hedgerow Theatre in the State of Pennsylvania!" Deeter was survived by his life companion Richard Brewer, whom he had met in the spring of 1953.

• The Hedgerow Theatre Collection, on permanent loan at Boston University's Twentieth Century Archives and partially on microfilm at the Historical Society of Pennsylvania, contains photographs, woodcuts, drawings, and directorial notes of various Hedgerow productions, speeches and unpublished articles written by Deeter, and transcripts of his acting and directing classes. The collection also includes a correspondence file, scrapbooks, newsclips, and actors' biographies. A special section covers the World War II years. Notated master scripts of 120 productions remain at the Hedgerow Theatre. For a writing by Deeter see "An Interpretation," *Theatre Arts Monthly* 20, no. 7 (July 1936): 541–42. Two essays illuminating Deeter's personality are Sherwood Anderson, "Jasper Deeter: A Dedication," in his *Plays: Winesburg and Others* (1937), first published as "The Good Life at Hedgerow," *Esquire*, Oct. 1936, pp. 51, 198A–99; and Henry Miller, "Jasper Deeter and the Hedgerow Theatre," in *Remember to Remember* (1947). See also John Calely Wentz, "The Hedgerow Theatre: An Historical Study" (Ph.D. diss., Univ. of Pennsylvania, 1954), which contains a thorough bibliography; and Dolores Tanner, "Jasper Deeter" (M.F.A. thesis, Univ. of Texas, 1957). An obituary is in the *New York Times*, 1 June 1972.

JOANNA ROTTÉ

DE FONTAINE, Felix Gregory (1834–11 Dec. 1896), journalist and author, was born in Boston, Massachusetts, the son of Louis Antoine de Fontaine, a French nobleman. His mother, whose given name is unknown, had the surname Allen and was said to have been from the family of the revolutionary war patriot Ethan Allen. Young de Fontaine received his education from private tutors and later studied phonography (shorthand). At age twenty-five he became a congressional reporter in Washington and reported the trial of a congressman charged with killing another man. In 1863 he married Georgia Vigneron Moore of Charleston, South Carolina.

On the eve of the Civil War, de Fontaine moved to Charleston. Before the outbreak of fighting, the *New York Herald* published a series of his articles on the antislavery controversy in the South. In 1861 the series was published in a booklet, *A History of American Abolitionism Together with a History of the Southern Confederacy*. During the bombardment of Fort Sumter on 12 April 1861, de Fontaine used his friendship with Confederate general Pierre G. T. Beauregard to provide the *Herald* with one of the first accounts of the fighting to appear in the northern press. However, de Fontaine's sympathies apparently were with the South, and he signed on as correspondent with the *Charleston Courier*. He accompanied the First South Carolina regiment to Virginia in May 1861. For the next three years de Fontaine covered the war, writing under the pseudonym "Personne."

De Fontaine became one of the best-known and most widely respected Confederate correspondents of the war. His stories for the *Courier* were widely reprinted by many newspapers in the South. De Fontaine reported on many of the war's major land battles and campaigns, including First and Second Manassas, Shiloh, Seven Days, Antietam, Charleston, Chattanooga, and Atlanta. Probably his greatest reporting work was done in September 1862 during the battle of Antietam, one of the bloodiest battles of the war. In his account, he described the scene in front of the Confederate center along a sunken road, later to become known as the "Bloody Lane." De Fontaine wrote

The air was filled with the white fantastic shapes that floated away from bursted shells. Men were leaping to and fro, loading, firing and handling the artillery, and now and then a hearty yell would reach the ear, amid the tumult, that spoke of death or disaster from some well aimed ball. . . . It is a hot place for us, but is hotter still for the enemy. They are directly under our guns, and we mow them down like grass.

De Fontaine also regularly reported on the privations of the ordinary Confederate soldier, who frequently suffered from insufficient food, clothing, and supplies. In December 1863 he described the distressing plight of troops in General James Longstreet's army, thousands of whom wintered in the rugged mountains of Tennessee with insufficient shoes: "The surface of the ground is as hard as a rock, and at every step the frozen edges of earth cut into naked feet, until the path of the army may be almost said to have been tracked in blood. To remedy the evil, I have seen these men, accustomed as they were at home to every luxury, strip their coats and blankets from their backs, and tie the rags around their feet."

In January 1864 de Fontaine became editor of the *Columbia Daily South Carolinian*, but he soon returned to the field as a correspondent for the newspaper. That year, he also published *Marginalia; or, Gleanings from an Army Note-book*, a collection of his news stories, praising the Confederate cause. In March 1865 General William T. Sherman's Union army captured Columbia and burned much of the city including the *South Carolinian*'s offices. De Fontaine and his staff fled the city before Union troops arrived.

After the war, de Fontaine remained in South Carolina for several years. In 1867 he was secretary of a convention held in Columbia to consider the abuses of carpetbag rule. Eventually de Fontaine moved to New York, and for much of the remainder of his professional life he was the financial editor and later the drama and music editor of the *New York Herald*. He wrote a series of articles, "Shoulder to Shoulder, Reminiscences of Confederate Camps and Fields," for the (Charleston) *XIX Century*. In 1873 he published *Cyclopedia of the Best Thoughts of Charles Dickens*, and in 1886 he published *De Fontaine's Condensed Long-Hand and Rapid-Writer's Companion*. At the time of his death in Columbia, he was writing a book on the missing records of the Confederate cabinet.

• Collections of Felix Gregory de Fontaine's Civil War correspondence are in *Marginalia; or, Gleanings from an Army Note-book* (1864) and *Army Letters of 1861–1865* (1896–1897). Biographical information on de Fontaine is in J. Cutler Andrews, *The South Reports the Civil War* (1970), and in an obituary, *Charleston News and Courier*, 12 Dec. 1896.

FORD RISLEY

DE FOREST, Erastus Lyman (27 June 1834–6 June 1888), mathematician, was born in Watertown, Connecticut; he was the only son of Dr. John De Forest and Lucy Starr Lyman. De Forest came from a family of better than comfortable means, a circumstance that created both opportunities and a lack of external challenges throughout his life. The De Forests, originally a Walloon family, dated their arrival in North America from 1623, and by the nineteenth century they had acquired considerable wealth and standing in the area of Watertown, Connecticut. At the age of sixteen he entered Yale College, his father's alma mater, from which he received a B.A. in 1854. De Forest's father celebrated his son's B.A. by endowing the De Forest Mathematical Prizes at Yale in 1855, and De Forest himself received a large bequest from his namesake and maternal grandfather, Erastus Lyman of Litchfield, Connecticut. De Forest remained at Yale for two years after his B.A., studying engineering at the Sheffield Scientific School, where he received his Ph.B. in 1856. Highly successful at Yale, he is said to have been regarded by a fellow student, the mathematical physicist J. Willard Gibbs, as one of the most brilliant and promising of Yale's students.

Shortly after receiving his Ph.B., De Forest's life took the one unusual turn of its otherwise unremarkable course. In February 1857 he traveled to New York, ostensibly with the aim of accompanying his aunt on a trip to Havana. Shortly before sailing he disappeared, leaving his luggage and no clue of where or why he had gone. The *New York Times* speculated that he had met with foul play, and an advertisement the family placed in the New York papers elicited an anonymous response stating that the body would be found in the East River. Despite their frantic inquiries, the family heard nothing about him until more than two years later, when a letter addressed to his father arrived from Australia. Depressed, De Forest had taken passage to California, where he had worked for a time in the mines and taught for a year in a public school before continuing on to Australia. There he had journeyed to Melbourne, where from 1858 to 1860 he had been engaged as an assistant master at the Melbourne Church of England Grammar School in South Yarra, teaching surveying and plan drawing as well as formal mathematics. In 1861 he returned to Connecticut by way of India and England, and aside from two extended trips to Europe (including the period 1863–1865) and a visit to Utah, he spent the remainder of his life close to home.

After 1865 De Forest devoted his life to the study of mathematics and to caring for his father. De Forest never married. From 1865 to 1867 he wrote three papers on interpolation, emphasizing applications to meteorology, and in 1867–1868 he undertook an assignment that would give a strong focus to the remainder of his work. At the invitation of his uncle Erastus Lyman, then president of Knickerbocker Life Insurance Company of New York, De Forest undertook the valuation of the policy liabilities of the company, and in the process he became attracted by problems in the graduation of mortality tables. These tables—essentially death rates classified by age, sex, and possibly other factors—tended to be rather rough when based

on only limited experience, as was generally the case. It was therefore thought desirable to graduate or smooth the tables in order to adjust the death rates so that those for nearby ages would be more nearly equal than were the raw figures. Between 1870 and 1885 De Forest wrote more than twenty papers on the graduation of series of numbers (smoothing by weighted averages), which were among the best and most perceptive on this topic to appear in the nineteenth century. In a tour de force that anticipated much of the work that would appear over the following half-century, he introduced formal optimality criteria for smoothness, and he borrowed statistical ideas from astronomy in developing and fully investigating the use of least squares methods in this area. Economist Irving Fisher later wrote of De Forest's work that "the idea of continuity of thinking could scarcely receive a better illustration." De Forest introduced a "runs test" (a way of testing for randomness by examining patterns in consecutive signs), and he used stochastic simulation in assessing the adequacy of fit of his methods in applications. In the 1880s he turned to questions involving symmetric and asymmetric error distributions in two and three dimensions and thereby partially anticipated some of the mathematics of correlation analysis, the methodology for the study of associations in multivariate data that was developed in England after De Forest's death by Francis Galton, Francis Edgeworth, and Karl Pearson.

Despite the excellence of De Forest's work, recognition came slowly or not at all. Publication of his first papers, which were submitted to the Smithsonian Institution, was delayed. The delay was principally due to a superficial lukewarm review that the secretary of the Smithsonian, Joseph Henry, obtained from the English mathematician James Joseph Sylvester; Sylvester was apparently sent only an incomplete version of the work. Most of De Forest's subsequent papers appeared in the *Analyst*, a little-known American mathematical journal published in Des Moines, Iowa. De Forest only became well known after his death, when later mathematicians came across his work and discovered that De Forest had anticipated them. In 1895 the English statistician Karl Pearson acknowledged De Forest's priority in the derivation of Pearson's Type III curve (the gamma distribution, an asymmetric curve best known through the particular case of the chi square distribution). Not until 1924, however, was De Forest's work accorded attention by insurance mathematicians, after the actuary Hugh H. Wolfenden rediscovered De Forest's work and, by championing it over his long career, introduced it widely to that public.

De Forest's father died in 1885, and his own health began to deteriorate not long thereafter. Shortly before his death in Watertown, he gave $10,000 to Yale College to found a chair, now known as the Erastus L. De Forest Professorship in Mathematics. De Forest was an able and original mathematician who worked at a level that was not yet expected in the United States. His only recognition was posthumous both because of the limitations he imposed on the scope of his analysis and because of his location, which was not only outside the active European mathematical community but outside any institutional framework.

• No archives of De Forest's papers are known. De Forest's life and work are discussed in S. M. Stigler, "Mathematical Statistics in the Early States," *Annals of Statistics* 6 (1978): 239–65. That paper, four of De Forest's papers, and an 1896 biographical article by J. Anderson, which includes a portrait, are reproduced in *American Contributions to Mathematical Statistics in the Nineteenth Century*, vol. 1, ed. Stigler (1980). One of De Forest's inventions is discussed in Stigler, "Stochastic Simulation in the Nineteenth Century," *Statistical Science* 6 (1991): 89–97. Some of the biographical detail presented here, including the identity of the referee responsible for De Forest's difficulty in publishing in the Smithsonian publications, comes from an unpublished account in this author's possession by H. H. Wolfenden, who devoted great energy to pursuing the meager facts of De Forest's life.

STEPHEN M. STIGLER

DE FOREST, John William (31 Mar. 1826–17 July 1906), writer, was born in Seymour, Connecticut, the son of John Hancock De Forest, a textile manufacturer, and Dotha Woodward. Little is known of De Forest's childhood, but it appears that frail health allowed him only intermittent school attendance, augmented by private tutoring. Although two of his older brothers graduated from Yale, De Forest did not attend college but, supported by a modest inheritance, devoted his twenties and early thirties to traveling in Europe and the Near East and to writing. Choosing literature as a career did not come quickly or easily to De Forest. He was unsure whether writing could be remunerative and whether, in Jacksonian America, a man of letters could be considered a man at all.

Between 1851 and 1859 De Forest published a work of history, two travel books, and two novels. Although De Forest often wrote of heroic deeds in the mysterious past, he acknowledged that "my forte is tittle-tattle concerning living men." At his best—and that was very good—he was an artist of the quotidian, illuminating contemporary manners and more.

In 1856 he married Harriet Silliman Shepard; they had one child. Family responsibilities intensified De Forest's need for income and his misgivings about writing as a vocation. In November 1859 he vowed to give up "book-making," and although there is no proof that he actually resorted to getting a job, he wrote little in the next two years.

The Civil War saved him. After raising a company of volunteer infantry for the Union, he was commissioned a captain in 1862. He served in the occupation of New Orleans, the siege of Port Hudson, Louisiana, and the battles of Winchester, Fisher's Hill, and Cedar Creek, Virginia. When the war ended, he transferred to the Freedmen's Bureau and was stationed in Greenville, South Carolina, at the rank of brevet major. Military service gave De Forest something to write about and reassurance that he was a worthy man despite being a writer. While in uniform or immediately thereafter, he published the works on which his reputation principally depends: magazine articles on the war, Reconstruction, literature, and society; and the novel *Miss Ravenel's Conversion from Secession to Loyalty* (1867).

De Forest's Civil War and Reconstruction articles portrayed historical events vividly and credibly enough to earn re-publication in *A Volunteer's Adventures* (1946) and *A Union Officer in the Reconstruction* (1948). Typical of his wryly unromantic reports of combat is this account of a retreat: "I did not properly creep, knowing that it would not do to raise my back; I rather swam upon the ground, catching hold of bunches of grass and dragging myself along. My ideas meanwhile were perfectly sane and calm, but very various in character, ranging from an expectation of a ball through the spine to a recollection of Cooper's most celebrated Indians." His essay calling for "The Great American Novel," published in *The Nation* in 1868, may have coined that phrase.

His masterpiece was *Miss Ravenel's Conversion*, wherein he successfully applied his gift for "tittle-tattle" to something as monstrous as war. The novel's namesake, Lillie Ravenel, is a Yankee woman with Confederate sympathies (like Harriet De Forest). In time she realizes the obsolescence and barbarity of the slaveholding southern way of life and "converts" to democracy and Unionism. The story's didactic allegory does not ruin the fiction. William Dean Howells later observed that the novel displays "an advanced realism before realism was known by that name." The book sold poorly, however, and was not reissued in its author's lifetime.

In 1868 De Forest took the risk of leaving the army to become a full-time, professional writer. He never again had a steady income. In order to increase sales of his novels (often serialized in magazines), he wrote what he thought people wanted to read: adventure, romance, political satire, even tales of religious inspiration. These were not his forte, and the eight novels he published between 1870 and 1881 never matched the quality of *Miss Ravenel's Conversion*. Reflecting his growing conservatism, these books scored politicians, immigrants, laborers, businessmen, nouveau riches, blacks, feminists, and the modern world in general with a vehemence that flattened fiction into polemic.

Harriet De Forest died in 1878. Thereafter, despite catering to what he considered the public taste, De Forest's books never gained much of a following or earned much in royalties. Consequently he railed against the philistinism of the reading public and, in weariness and despair, stopped writing novels. He did, however, compose a history of the De Forest family that asserted that they originated among the nobility in France. Although in his old age he published a novel and two volumes of poems that he had written much earlier, he had nothing new to say. His final years were spent in isolation in a hotel room near the railroad station in New Haven, where he died.

• Most of the novelist's few extant papers are in the John William De Forest Collection at the Beinecke Rare Book and Manuscript Library of Yale University. The De Forest Family Papers, also helpful, are in the Manuscripts and Archives Division at Yale. Manuscripts pertaining to Harriet Shepard De Forest and her family are in the Boltwood Family Papers, Burton Historical Collection, Detroit Public Library. Books published by De Forest but not already mentioned include *History of the Indians of Connecticut* (1851), *Witching Times* (serialized 1856–1857), *Kate Beaumont* (1872), *The Wetherel Affair* (1873), and *Playing the Mischief* (1875). His tales are collected in James B. Durham, "The Complete Short Stories of John William De Forest" (Ph.D. diss., Univ. of Arkansas, 1967). His important uncollected articles include "Charleston under Arms," *Atlantic Monthly*, Apr. 1861, pp. 488–505; "The 'High-Toned Gentleman'," *The Nation*, 12 Mar. 1868, pp. 206–8; and "Two Girls," *The Nation*, 6 Feb. 1868, pp. 107–9. For bibliographies, see E. R. Hagemann, "A Checklist of the Writings of John William De Forest (1826–1906)," *Studies in Bibliography* 8 (1956): 185–94; Clayton L. Eichelberger, et al., "John William De Forest (1826–1906): A Critical Bibliography of Secondary Comment," *American Literary Realism* 1, no. 4 (Fall 1968): 1–56; and Hagemann, "A John William De Forest Supplement, 1970," *American Literary Realism* 3, no. 2 (Spring 1970): 148–52. For biographies, see James F. Light, *John William De Forest* (1965), Frank Bergmann, *The Worthy Gentleman of Democracy: John William De Forest and the American Dream* (1971), and James A. Hijiya, *J. W. De Forest and the Rise of American Gentility* (1988). James W. Gargano, ed., *Critical Essays on John William De Forest* (1981), includes nineteenth- and twentieth-century criticism. Probably the single most important critique of De Forest is Edmund Wilson, *Patriotic Gore* (1962), chap. 15.

JAMES A. HIJIYA

DE FOREST, Lee (26 Aug. 1873–30 Jun. 1961), radio engineer and inventor, was born in Council Bluffs, Iowa, the son of Henry Swift de Forest, a Congregational minister, and Anna Margaret Robbins. He grew up in Iowa and (after 1879) Talladega, Alabama, where his father was president of the Talladega College for Negroes.

Demonstrating an interest in technical matters at an early age, de Forest followed his father to Yale, attending Sheffield Scientific School there and earning a general science bachelor's degree in 1896 and a Ph.D. in physics in 1899. His dissertation on "Reflections of Electric Waves of Very High Frequencies at the Ends of Parallel Wires" may have been the earliest American dissertation based on Hertzian waves—an experimental form of what became known as wireless. De Forest was interested in working further in wireless experimentation and by 1899 was reading widely in the scientific literature and so was aware of developments here and abroad. Specifically, he sought to perfect a detector of wireless signals to replace the then-standard crude magnetic "coherer" device. Nevertheless, de Forest was rejected for employment by Marconi, Nikola Tesla, and others.

De Forest began his career with American Telephone and Telegraph's (AT&T) manufacturing subsidiary, Western Electric, in Chicago and soon was working in the testing laboratory, again at wireless experimentation. He moved through several temporary or part-time jobs at Western and other firms while continuing his wireless development work, always seeking better detectors (reception) and transmitting devices. In 1901, in competition with Marconi, he used his wireless system to report on the America's Cup international yacht races off New York, but the inability to tune receivers selectively meant Marconi and de Forest were both drowned out in mutual interference.

De Forest's chief problem during the first two decades of the twentieth century was the conflict between his constant need for capital to support his inventive work and his desire to work without collaborators—what he called "independence of management." The tension between the two led to constant financial and legal problems between and among his various backers. He was involved in a bewildering number of companies during this period, several of which went bankrupt, and was defrauded by two of his backers. Many of the companies in which he played a central role were little more than stock speculation swindles that only increased public suspicion of wireless. Some of the companies built and operated shore stations to communicate with wireless units on board naval and mercantile vessels, using wireless devices of de Forest's design. To seek further financial support, he avidly pursued wireless publicity stunts, such as operating wireless apparatus at the St. Louis World's Fair in 1904 from a huge tower displaying his name in lights. He obtained thirty-four patents on various aspects of wireless telegraphy from 1902 to 1906.

De Forest's most important invention came in 1906, when he developed his "Audion," a three-element (triode) vacuum tube detector, on which later development of vacuum tube technology as well as long-distance telephone service were based. De Forest's innovation was to insert a grid between the anode and cathode inside a partial vacuum tube. The several patents he applied for would result in lengthy litigation with other inventors and firms—especially the expanding Marconi interests—which held rights to English electrical engineer John Ambrose Fleming's two-element or diode vacuum tube of 1904. De Forest's grid contributed a degree of control of electron flow absent in Fleming's device. The bankruptcy of one of de Forest's companies in 1911 and its subsequent takeover by American Marconi strengthened the Marconi firm's hand when it successfully contested de Forest's triode patents as infringing on the earlier diode device. But the 1916 verdict also held that Marconi had violated de Forest's patent rights, so the result was a draw: neither could manufacture tubes without agreement from the other. While a U.S. Navy–mandated patent pool existed during World War I, only RCA's creation of a postwar commercial radio patent pool resolved the standoff.

De Forest applied for several patents covering different aspects of the Audion tube, including one in October 1906 on a "device for amplifying feeble electrical currents"; this suggested he saw his device not merely as the improved signal detector he had sought since his Yale days, but as a possible amplifier as well. There is considerable scientific disagreement, however, on just how much of his device's potential was clear to de Forest at this point and even in later years. His laboratory notebooks and other records suggest some confusion over what the Audion could and might do—as does the fact that for some five years (until about 1912) he did little with his invention. This lapse resulted, in part, from a lack of research funds and the continued confusion over the rise and fall of de Forest-affiliated wireless firms. Furthermore, the Audion tube attracted little initial interest among other wireless experimenters of the time. There were several other, less expensive ways to detect wireless signals; the crystal detector, for example, was by then widely available.

De Forest's failure to develop the Audion also stemmed from his growing fascination with the potential of wireless telephony or broadcasting. De Forest began experiments with broadcasting music—using wireless to transmit recorded and live musical performances, first for four months in 1907 in New York, and then on his honeymoon in Paris with several broadcasts from the Eiffel Tower, one of which was picked up 500 miles away. In January 1910 he broadcast opera from the roof of the Metropolitan Opera, but reports on poor sound quality did not help promotion of broadcasting.

Only in 1912 did de Forest, then employed by Federal Telegraph, return to improving and expanding the applications of his device, this time with the help of several technical assistants. In August of that year the team discovered that under certain conditions the Audion could be an oscillator. Initially seen as a problem for Audion amplification, this tendency to oscillate hinted to de Forest (though only after others had discovered it) what became the Audion's crucial role: transmitting continuous radio waves required for effective broadcasting of voice and music.

De Forest's inventions were the subject of more than 120 patent suits, the longest-running of which was with Edwin H. Armstrong, who independently had come upon the regenerative or "feedback" role of multiple Audion tubes in the years just before World War I. Their nineteen-year fight ended only with a (second) Supreme Court decision (1934) awarding primacy to de Forest, though most engineers think that Armstrong better understood the device and its possibilities. The bitterness of this battle darkened the lives of both inventors for decades.

The first commercial application of the Audion came with the telephone. After lengthy evaluation, in July 1913 AT&T purchased for $50,000 (through an intermediary to keep the price down) all rights to the Audion except for wireless applications. AT&T began coast-to-coast long-distance service, using the Audion as a line amplifier, in early 1915. In 1914 and 1917, AT&T expanded its patent position by purchasing all remaining rights to use the Audion, save for de Forest's "personal rights," defined as the use of the device by amateurs to send music and news by radio. These, however, turned out to be essential to the Audion's later use in broadcasting, a field not contemplated in the AT&T agreements.

By 1920, with developing industry patent pools and plans for mass production of radio and wireless equipment, de Forest shifted his own work to broader applications of radio, turning first to developing a workable system of sound motion pictures. For several years he struggled to perfect an optical approach to recording sound directly on film. His "Phonofilm" system was widely demonstrated in the mid-1920s but did not attract sufficient film studio support, in part because of its poor quality tonal reproduction.

In 1930 de Forest moved permanently to Los Angeles. He often wrote or gave speeches critical of radio broadcasting and its excessive advertising and concentration on light entertainment. He also wrote about developments in television. His first book, *Television Today and Tomorrow* (1942), drew, in part, on his own work developing large-screen "theater" television systems, first based on mechanical approaches and later on electronic means. He predicted widespread use of such large-screen formats in the future.

In the mid-1930s de Forest briefly became involved in perfecting diathermy equipment. During the war he received patents on aviation, radar, and bomb projects, but without ties to manufacturing firms, and in his seventies he was primarily tinkering. Toward the end of the war he entered into an agreement under which Bell Labs (part of AT&T) obtained rights to develop his inventions, though little came of it. By the end of his productive life, de Forest had received 216 patents in radio, motion picture, television, and related fields.

De Forest's personality was often cited as a factor in both his successes and failures. Lloyd Espenschied, who was in the New York audience for de Forest's first public demonstration of the Audion (1907) and who later grew to know him well, said he was "good company, romantic, challenging and of an egotism so naive as to be enjoyable. He seemed to be a lone-wolf kind of Robin Hood, likeable, shrewd and knavish, intent on speculative patents and on stock certificates as a means of robbing the rich in the wondrous woods of wireless." A modern scholar, Hugh Aitken, summed up de Forest as "the egotistical romantic, rather sloppy in his research methods, but always ready to move ahead and try something new." He was not easy to work with, being described by many as dogmatic and single-minded to the point of frustrating others.

De Forest was married four times: first and only briefly to Lucille Sheardown (1906), who is not mentioned in his autobiography; second to Nora Blatch (1908–1911), a talented engineer and feminist who left when he would not allow her to continue her own work after their child was born; third, in 1912, to Mary Mayo, a Broadway chorus girl who bore him three more children before their divorce in 1930; and longest (from 1930 to his death) to Marie Mosquini, an aspiring Hollywood film actress when they met—she was twenty-four, and he was fifty-seven. De Forest died in Hollywood, California, leaving an estate of only about $1,200. There was so little money because he had little business sense with which to manage the income from several of his patents (he had even declared bankruptcy in 1936). His obituary in *Time* noted that he had burned through four fortunes.

De Forest's importance to the history of radio and broadcasting is threefold. First and most important was his development of the three-element vacuum tube (Audion). His work to promote public interest and investment in radio and broadcasting was significant as well. Finally, he was the quintessential tinkering seeker of fortune so prominent in the history of radio. Often blinded by his own ego, de Forest did not play the central role he and his backers perceived (they tried unsuccessfully to have him awarded a Nobel Prize in the 1950s), primarily because of his inability to combine science, technical tinkering, and clear business sense.

• De Forest's papers are in several locations. Some are at the Library of Congress; others are at Yale University. The largest collection of original materials was donated by his wife after his death to the Foothill College Electronics Museum, Los Altos Hills, Calif., though the material is only loosely arranged by decade. There are six major book-length sources: the authorized, laudatory biography by Georgette Carneal, *Conqueror of Space: The Life of Lee de Forest* (1930); the inventor's own romantically written *Father of Radio: The Autobiography of Lee de Forest* (1950); Israel R. Levine, *Electronics Pioneer: Lee de Forest* (1964), written for young adults; Hugh G. J. Aitken, *The Continuous Wave: Technology and American Radio, 1900–1932* (1985), the best modern technical treatment of de Forest's various radio roles up until 1920; Tom Lewis, *Empire of the Air: The Men Who Made Radio* (1991), which does a good investigative job of sorting out de Forest's role along with those of Armstrong and Sarnoff; and James A. Hijiya, *Lee de Forest and the Fatherhood of Radio* (1992), which is the most reasoned assessment of the key periods in the inventor's life. The first three sources must be used with care as they give inconsistent dates and company names. The last three are balanced, scholarly analyses placing de Forest in context. See also the three-part article by Samuel Lubell, "Magnificent Failure," *Saturday Evening Post*, 17, 24, 31 Jan. 1942, and Robert Chipman, "De Forest and the Triode Detector," *Scientific American* 212 (Mar. 1965): 92–100. For details on the patent battles, see W. Rupert Maclaurin, *Invention and Innovation in the Radio Industry* (1949). Susan Douglas, *Inventing American Broadcasting 1899–1922* (1987), offers excellent context for the crucial period of de Forest's life. De Forest's patents are listed with citations to full patent specifications in David W. Kraeuter, *Radio and Television Pioneers: A Patent Bibliography* (1992), which lists all 216 in chronological order (pp. 74–94). The confusing story of the many pre-1920 de Forest wireless companies is best clarified in both text and charts in Thorn L. Mayes, *Wireless Communication in the United States* (1989).

CHRISTOPHER H. STERLING

DEGAETANI, Jan (10 July 1933–15 Sept. 1989), mezzo-soprano and vocal teacher, was born in Massillon, Ohio, the daughter of Earl D. Ruetz, a lawyer, and Eleanor (maiden name unknown). She showed an early interest in music and as a teenager sang with the local church choir. Later she studied at the Juilliard School in New York with Henry Brant, Norman Lloyd, and Sergius Kagen. Kagen, an accomplished composer and pianist as well as a vocal coach, became an important influence on the development of her vocal style.

She remained affiliated with Juilliard following her graduation in 1955, initially as a teacher of sight singing. Her early career activities included a variety of musical forms, including small chamber choruses (the Riverside Singers and the Abbey Singers), opera (in workshops and as an apprentice with the NBC Opera), and early music (Noah Greenberg's New York Pro Musica Antiqua and the Waverly Consort). As a member of the Gramercy Chamber Ensemble she gave a 1959 performance of Arnold Schoenberg's *Pierrot Lunaire*, which established her as a formidable interpreter of contemporary music. In 1958 she had married Thomas DeGaetani, a stage manager; they had two children. The DeGaetanis divorced in the 1960s, but she retained the surname by which she was known professionally. She married Philip West, an oboist, in 1969. West served concurrently with DeGaetani on the Aspen and Eastman School faculties, and they performed together frequently.

DeGaetani was associated with the Contemporary Chamber Ensemble, founded by the conductor and bassoonist Arthur Weisberg in 1960, throughout the 1960s and 1970s. An important forum for twentieth-century music, the Contemporary Chamber Ensemble performed worldwide, presenting both modern repertory pieces and premiers of newly composed works. It also produced a series of recordings on the Nonesuch label, featuring works of Elliott Carter, George Crumb, Mario Davidovsky, Jacob Druckman, Peter Maxwell Davies, William Schuman, and Richard Wernick, among others. Another member of the ensemble, pianist Gilbert Kalish, had begun working with DeGaetani in the 1950s. Their partnership, including both recitals and recordings, spanned DeGaetani's entire career. She and Kalish recorded two volumes of Stephen Foster songs, shedding an entirely new interpretive light on material that was not previously well known.

Though she was an important figure in contemporary music, her performances and recordings with Kalish and with several orchestras and chamber groups include the work of Brahms, Berlioz, Schumann, Falla, Ravel, Rachmaninoff, Debussy, Tchaikovsky, and Mozart. The *New York Times* called her "that rare singer who has not only a rich, well-produced voice and warm feeling for singing, but also a precise intonation, an equally exact sense of rhythm and a handsome stage presence."

One common aspect of twentieth-century music is its often profound difficulty in terms of harmonic relations, melodic profile, rhythmic character, and mode of expression. DeGaetani was one of several performers who came of age after World War II with a natural talent for handling the complexities of contemporary music with complete, unassuming confidence. But she was more than just an "acrobat." The critic David Hamilton has observed that she "commanded her voice precisely as required by the old Italian tradition: on the one hand, she could move through her entire pitch range with a consistent dynamic and timbre (including degrees of vibrato) and any type of articulation; on the other, she could modulate any pitch seamlessly through the available dynamic and timbral range—plus any combination of the above" ("Jan DeGaetani: Her Art," in *A Tribute to Jan DeGaetani*, p. 7). Through her robust yet infinitely flexible vocal instrument DeGaetani was able to capture and express the nuances of both her contemporary and her traditional repertory.

In addition to her activities in performance and recording (her discography lists more than sixty recordings), she pursued a distinguished teaching career. She remained affiliated with her alma mater, Juilliard, throughout her lifetime and also taught at Bennington College and the State University of New York at Purchase. She began a long association with the Aspen Music Festival in 1971, and in 1973 she joined the faculty of the Eastman School of Music in Rochester, New York. Teaching was an important part of her musical personality, and the influence she shed on an entire generation of singers cannot be overestimated. In 1989 DeGaetani made her last recording: songs of Mahler and Berlioz's *Les Nuits d'été*, in chamber versions arranged by her husband. She died of leukemia later that year.

In January 1992, the Fritz Reiner Center for Contemporary Music at Columbia University paid "A Tribute to Jan DeGaetani" in three evenings of music dedicated to her, performed by singers who had studied with her and other musicians who were collaborators during her long career. The concert was broadcast nationwide.

• DeGaetani's personal library of scores is held by the Sibley Library at the Eastman School of Music in Rochester, N.Y., and her personal papers remain with Philip West. She coauthored *The Complete Sightsinger* (1980) with Norman Lloyd and Marsha Lloyd. *High Fidelity/Musical America* chronicles DeGaetani's career as its musician of the month in the April 1974 issue. *A Tribute to Jan DeGaetani at the Kathryn Bache Miller Theatre*, the extensive program booklet from the tribute at the Fritz Reiner Center for Contemporary Music in 1992, with contributions by Teresa Sterne and David Hamilton, provides the most complete overview of her life and her art and lists her numerous premieres and recordings.

CHRISTINE HOFFMAN

DEGANAWIDAH (fl. 1450), Huron spiritual leader and mystic and, according to Iroquois legends, principal founder of the League of the Hau-Dé-No-Sau-Nee, or People of the Longhouse. The oral traditions reveal little about his youth, personal life, or events after the formation of the league.

Sometime before A.D. 1450, Deganawidah, the great peacemaker between the Mohawk, Seneca, Cayuga, Onondaga, and Oneida, and his spokesman, Hiawatha, planted a Great Tree of Peace at the Onondaga village (Syracuse, N.Y.) to end a blood feud that threatened the very existence of Iroquoian identity.

Through this symbolic act, Deganawidah, who was a Huron from the Bay of Quinte region (in Ontario), hoped to institute three important principles—peace, unity, and clear thinking—among the Five Nations or People of the Longhouse.

Unlike later prophetic movements that would come as responses to European intrusion, this action was motivated by a need to end internal hostilities among the Iroquoian peoples. As it developed in succeeding centuries, the ultimate objective seems to have been the extension of this league for peace to all Iroquoian nations and their allies, an objective sometimes mistaken by historians for empire building. In the seventeenth and eighteenth centuries, by adopting members of other Iroquoian groups, such as the Huron and Tuscorora, the confederacy was able to maintain its demographic strength in the face of depopulation resulting from epidemics. In this way it could keep control of a large territory stretching from Lake Champlain to Lake Erie, to maintain its independence in the face of British and French imperial designs, and to profit from the fur trade with Europeans. Historians such as Daniel Richter, Georges Sioui, and Cornelius Jaenen now assert that so-called Iroquoian aggressiveness needs to be reviewed in terms of the need to establish internal order and to provide for self-defense.

Deganawidah was also said to have passed on Kaianerekowa, the Great Law of Peace, believed to have been the Creator's plan for the Iroquois confederacy. He claimed to have received a vision from the Great Spirit in which the principles of this law of brotherhood and peace were revealed. In accord with his vision, he crossed Lake Ontario to begin his mission among the Onondaga. Since he was not eloquent, an indispensable mark of leadership at the time, he did not attract a following. In fact, he suffered from a speech impediment. It was Hiawatha, his first convert and an eloquent and persuasive orator, who took up Deganawidah's crusade and rallied widespread support among the deeply divided Five Nations.

Deganawidah began his own mission among the Mohawk, who being more receptive than the Onondaga, became recognized as the founding nation of the confederacy. It took a miracle—a total eclipse of the sun (one of which is known to have taken place in the region in 1451)—to win over the Seneca. The Onondaga, particularly their chief Atotarho, were the principal resisters, but they were eventually won over when Deganawidah informed them that they would become the keepers of the central council fire and that the tree of peace would be planted in their central village (near present-day Syracuse, N.Y.). Each year, there would be a great confederacy council at Onondaga of the forty-nine chiefs, who were crowned with ceremonial antlers, to settle any disputes and to renew the peace.

To initiate this peaceful relationship between the Iroquoian peoples, Deganawidah insisted on a symbolic banishing of the Evil Mind, which was at the bottom of all dissension and hostility. The warriors were required to deposit their weapons at the roots of a large tree that grew over an underground cavern. Deganawidah then taught them the Good Mind philosophy consisting of three components: *Gaiwoh*, or righteous actions governing the relations between individuals and nations; *Skenon*, or healthy condition of body, mind, and interpersonal relations; and *Gashasdenshaa*, or power, especially spiritual power affecting customs and just behavior. This philosophy still guides Iroquoian elders.

Deganawidah then planted a large white pine to mark the compact among the Five Nations and to act as a reminder to future generations of the fundamental underpinnings of the Good Mind. This tree had four white roots going out to the cardinal points and so would reach out to other nations and offer them admission into the Great Peace. At the top of the tree, he placed an eagle symbolizing the need for vigilance and military preparedness on the part of the warriors. Figuratively, this tree needed to be watered frequently, and people needed to be reminded of the precepts for which it stood, especially not to take an unfair share of its fruits. Harmony, hospitality, and sharing, the great virtues of aboriginal peoples, were underscored in this way.

The Great Law was divided into paragraphs and was recited on certain occasions to remind the people of their pact and to educate the young. The law spelled out the duties of the tribal chiefs and the procedures for decision making. Elderly clan matrons nominated the chiefs of their own lineages. Council decisions were reached by unanimous consensus among all the nations. Deganawidah advised the chiefs that if a strong wind uprooted the Tree of Peace, they should find an elm in a great swamp and restore their confederacy. Following the American Revolution, the elm was planted on the banks of the Grand River in Upper Canada. Here the ancient forms of the league are still maintained.

• The first known reference to Deganawidah and the origins of the Great Peace was a manuscript by Christopher Pyrlaeus, a Moravian missionary among the Mohawk, which was cited by his successor John Heckwelder in *An Account of the History, Manners, and Customs of the Indian Nations, Who Once Inhabited Pennsylvania and the Neighboring States* (1819). This was followed by L. H. Morgan, *League of the Ho-Dé-No-Sau-Nee, or Iroquois* (1851); Horatio Hale, *The Iroquois Book of Rites* (1883); and Duncan C. Scott, "Traditional History of the Confederacy of the Six Nations," in *Transactions of the Royal Society of Canada*, 3d ser., vol. 5 (1912), sec. 2, pp. 195–246. More recent sources of information are Paul A. W. Wallace, *The White Roots of Peace* (1946); Anthony F. C. Wallace, "The Dekanawideh Myth Analyzed as the Record of a Revitalization Movement," *Ethnohistory* 5 (1958): 118–30, and William N. Fenton, "The Lore of the Longhouse: Myth, Ritual, and Red Power," *Anthropological Quarterly* 48 (1975): 131–47.

CORNELIUS J. JAENEN

DEGARMO, Charles (17 Jan. 1849–14 May 1934), college president and professor of education, was born in Muckwonago, Wisconsin, the son of Rufus DeGarmo and Laura Wilbur, farmers. His parents were members of the Society of Friends, as was DeGarmo throughout his life. In the Civil War, he served in the 149th Illinois Volunteers (1865–1866) but never saw battle. With the bounty that Illinois paid for his enlistment, he was able to buy prairie land, which he sowed to wheat. The yield brought him enough money to send him to Illinois State Normal University at Normal, Illinois, from which he graduated in 1873. After serving for a year as a school principal in Naples, Illinois (1873–1874), DeGarmo returned to the Illinois State Normal University, where from 1876 to 1883 he was head of the grammar department of the university's model school. In 1875 he married Ida Witbeck of Belvidere, Illinois; they had no children.

In the 1880s American education was developing rapidly at all levels, both quantitatively and qualitatively, and many American colleges were attempting to transform themselves into universities on the German model. In the last quarter of the nineteenth century, Germany was generally regarded as the leading source for pedagogical (educational) theory. Americans who wanted to establish education as a field of study sought their advanced education in German universities, in particular those at Jena and Halle. Jena, especially, was regarded as the mecca for those who wanted to be on the cutting edge of educational inquiry. By selling his Illinois farm, DeGarmo was able to finance three years of study at the Universities of Jena and Halle, receiving the Ph.D. from the University of Halle in 1886. While studying at Jena, DeGarmo became acquainted with the pedagogical doctrine of Johann Friedrich Herbart, who conceived of the mind's structure as built up from the "presentations" or ideas that develop in it. The structure of this "apperceptive mass" is modified to some extent by each new presentation, and the teacher's task is to base instruction on the structure of each individual child's mind. For Herbart, the aim of all instruction was moral development. The formation of the highest moral ideals and behavior depended on a unified curriculum and methods of teaching that provided social experience as well as knowledge. Herbart's followers at Jena had elaborated his ideas on education into five formal steps, based on comprehending one's new knowledge by relating it to one's previous knowledge. They advanced the theory of culture epochs (historical stages of culture) and concentration in studies (one subject such as history serves as the area of concentration) as a means of unifying the curriculum.

DeGarmo and two other educators who had already studied in Germany—Charles and Frank McMurry—brought these ideas to the United States and began to promote them. DeGarmo's two volumes, *Essentials of Method* (1889) and *Herbart and the Herbartians* (1895), did much to popularize Herbart's ideas on pedagogy in the United States, particularly the topics of apperception, concentration centers (curriculum synthesis), and the five formal steps. In reworking Herbart's ideas for American students, however, DeGarmo focused on the pedagogical ideas without relating them to Herbart's educational goal of developing morality. For

American Herbartians, education's purpose was basically cognitive. DeGarmo himself commented little on Herbart's individualized pedagogy. German Herbartianism had already ignored individualization as inapplicable if not impossible in the public schools with their classes of twenty-five or more pupils. DeGarmo's Americanized version of Herbart's ideas caught on like wildfire in normal schools and colleges, particularly the five formal steps of instruction. Sales figures indicate that *The Essentials of Method* was a bestseller among normal school textbooks.

In 1895 DeGarmo and the McMurrys organized the National Herbart Society, of which DeGarmo was president from 1895 to 1899. Nicholas Murray Butler, John Dewey, and Wilbur S. Jackman, educational leaders of the period, served on the society's executive council. The society included teachers and educators throughout the country, but its membership probably never exceeded 100 individuals. Despite its relatively small size, its influence was felt throughout the country. At meetings, members critically discussed each others' papers and educational issues of the day. Rather than promoting Herbartianism in America, the society's purpose, stated in its first *Yearbook*, was "to study and investigate and discuss important problems in education." The *Yearbook*'s papers concerned such problems as curriculum synthesis, character building, interest and effort in education, and, above all, the question What should the public schools teach? These problems have continued to be of vital concern to education. Out of the Herbart Society grew the present National Society for the Study of Education. Its *Yearbooks*, published without interruption since 1901, have continued to provide a forum for the discussion of questions about the purpose and means of education.

DeGarmo was professor of modern languages at Illinois State Normal University from 1886 to 1890, moved to the University of Illinois in 1890, and then became the fourth president of Swarthmore College in 1891. The founders of Swarthmore had originally shaped their vision for the college around teacher education; the institution would prepare Quaker teachers for children in the lower schools. This never became a major commitment, however, and, although DeGarmo thought that Swarthmore should invest in teacher education, he strongly favored maintaining good physical facilities and intellectual standards as high as those of important universities so that Swarthmore could better compete with other colleges and attract a full student body. (In the late 1880s Swarthmore had experienced a precipitous drop in enrollment.) DeGarmo was unable to obtain the financial support for these advances or to substantially increase enrollment. In 1898 he moved to Cornell University, where he was professor of the science and art of education. He retired in 1914, moving to Florida, where he resolved to limit his efforts in education to one field of thought. He chose esthetics in education because of his deep interest in that subject. He died in Miami, Florida.

By interpreting Herbart's ideas, DeGarmo influenced the course of American educational theory and practice. The curriculum of Dewey's Laboratory School at the University of Chicago was influenced by Herbart's culture-epochs theory and concentration centers, and the Herbart Society provided Dewey and other leaders with a forum for their theories. Variants of Herbart's steps of instruction have continued to be used in preparing and evaluating teachers. Perhaps most important of all are the questions that DeGarmo brought to the consciousness of educators, who continue to ask how teachers can be taught to teach and how the curriculum can be integrated so that it has greater meaning for the student.

• Letters from DeGarmo are in the James Morgan Hart Papers in the Cornell University Library. DeGarmo's presidential papers and biography files are in the Friends Historical Library, Swarthmore College. The Edmund Janes James Papers in the University of Illinois (Urbana) archives contain correspondence that includes letters from DeGarmo. Major works by DeGarmo include *Interest and Education* (1902), *Principles of Secondary Education* (1907–1910), *Aesthetic Education* (1913), *Essential of Design in Industrial Arts* (1924), in collaboration with Leon L. Winslow, and a translation of G. A. Lindner's *Manual of Empirical Psychology*, 2d ed. (1890). An obituary is in the *New York Times*, 15 May 1934.

LAUREL N. TANNER

DEGOLYER, Everette Lee (9 Oct. 1886–14 Dec. 1956), petroleum geologist, was born in Greensburg, Kansas, the son of John DeGolyer, an inveterate but unsuccessful minerals prospector and small businessman, and Narcissa Kagy Huddle. DeGolyer received his elementary education in public schools in and around Joplin, Missouri, and finished his secondary education at the University of Oklahoma's prep school in Norman, Oklahoma. In 1904 he enrolled in the mine engineering course at the university, where his contact with noted geologists Charles N. Gould and E. G. Woodruff helped him gain summer employment with the U.S. Geological Survey (USGS), first as a cook and later as a field assistant. His skill as a field assistant led USGS head C. Willard Hayes to hire DeGolyer away from the university just a few credits shy of completing his undergraduate degree. Hayes, then on leave from his USGS post, was employed as a private consultant exploring the Vera Cruz area in northern Mexico for the Mexican Eagle Oil Company, a subsidiary of the English firm of C. Pearson and Son. His early success in finding oil for Pearson allowed him to return to Norman in June 1910 and marry Nell Goodrich, whom he had met while in prep school. The couple had four children.

Though only twenty-four years old, DeGolyer led the exploring team that brought in the Potrero del Llano No. 4 well on 27 December 1910. Potrero del Llano was the largest, most spectacular oil strike to that time and for many years thereafter. It blew in with such force that it took DeGolyer and his crew almost ninety days to bring it under control while it spilled an estimated 90,000 barrels a day. This success secured

DeGolyer's reputation as a geologist and gave him the opportunity to keep a promise to his new bride by returning to the university to complete his B.A. in 1911. Later that same year, DeGolyer returned to Mexico in Pearson's employ. He left the company in 1914 to split his time between consulting for Pearson and doing his own private consulting.

Over the next few years, DeGolyer was not satisfied with just finding oil for others. He also led a geologic survey of Cuba for the U.S. Department of the Treasury and began publishing his research in scholarly journals. In 1918 he published two articles that emphasized the importance of studying the underground geologic structure and composition as a methodology of locating oil. In 1919, with the financial backing of Pearson, DeGolyer helped form the Amerada Petroleum Corporation, taking the posts of vice president and general manager.

In 1922 DeGolyer directed the world's first geophysical oil exploration, although it did not become successful until two years later at the Nash Dome. This venture was under the aegis of the Rycade Oil Company, one of the many companies DeGolyer would found in his lifetime. DeGolyer first advocated the torsion balance method and then the seismic refraction approach before focusing on the seismic reflection method of determining underground structure as the most useful research tool. In use since the eighteenth century, a torsion balance is an instrument that demonstrates gravitational, electrostatic, or magnetic forces by determining the amount of torsion exerted on a wire by those forces. DeGolyer had one built to his specifications to read different subsoil gravities. By the time the torsion balance method proved its worth by finding the Nash Dome, DeGolyer was experimenting with seismic refraction.

Rather than read the subsoil structure by gravitational attraction, seismic refraction measured the speed of sound waves, caused by an explosion at or near the surface, as the sound waves traveled through different types of rock. Since sound will, for example, travel through rock salt at twice the speed of either clay or shales, geologists could use the results of the test to identify where salt plugs and potential oil pools might be found. Seismic refraction was a huge success on the Gulf Coast because of the gulf's simple geologic conditions. It was less successful where various layers of rock were uniform, causing undifferentiated readings. By the time other oil seekers seized upon seismic refraction, DeGolyer was developing yet another method, seismic reflection. This process also used dynamite to make sound waves, but, by taking measurements of the time the sound bounced or reflected off subsurface structures, geologists could plot the results on a map to obtain a subsurface profile. Seismic reflection produced more detailed and deeper readings that greatly improved the chances of discovering potential oil bearing structures. As time and experimentation would show, each method had its application, but oil exploration would be changed forever. Seismic reflection remained the primary tool of petroleum geologists at the dawn of the twenty-first century. Science and not luck would be the path to petroleum riches for DeGolyer.

DeGolyer's belief in the use of geophysics led him in 1925 to found the Geophysical Research Corporation, as a subsidiary of the Amerada Corporation, to design and manufacture seismic equipment and to conduct explorations. By 1929 he was president of Amerada. In 1932, however, DeGolyer took another risk in the midst of the Great Depression by severing all ties with Amerada to establish two companies, Core Laboratories, to perform scientific examinations of drilling core samples, and Felmont Corporation, to conduct explorations. In 1933 he participated in developing the National Recovery Administration's Petroleum Code, which DeGolyer's biographer Lon Tinkle related as an unsatisfying experience for such an individualistic businessman. In 1935 he informally joined Lewis MacNaughton, a former employee, to provide consulting services for petroleum exploration; they formalized the partnership, which soon became the largest petroleum consulting firm in the world, as DeGolyer and MacNaughton.

With war in Europe, DeGolyer took a leave from the consulting firm in 1941 to join the Interior Department as director of conservation; conservation was an issue that he had long been pressing in industry circles. DeGolyer had been greatly bothered by the waste of flaming off natural gas at the wellhead and by the waste of both oil and gas when gushers blew in. As early as the 1920s he had predicted oil shortages. During the war he undertook secret missions to Mexico and Saudi Arabia for the U.S. government on petroleum-related issues. After the war DeGolyer was a founder and director in a company that acquired the Big Inch and Little Inch gasoline pipelines, which had been built during the war to eliminate oil losses from tanker sinkings. The partnership used the pipelines for transporting natural gas from Texas and Louisiana through the Ohio Valley to New Jersey to service the huge, and largely untapped, natural gas market in the Northeast. Previously, natural gas was flamed off at the wellhead, but transporting this so-called waste product made a fortune for members of the Texas Eastern Transmission Company and marked the beginning of the huge natural gas industry.

In 1950, with the onset of serious health problems, DeGolyer began to divest himself of many of his business interests. He suffered from aplastic anemia, a disease similar to leukemia that required blood transfusions, and from periodic bouts of depression in his last years. By 1956 he had also suffered two strokes and lost sight in one eye. Rather than continue the downward spiral of incapacitation, DeGolyer took his own life at his Dallas office.

Since his college days DeGolyer's quick mind and capacity for hard work won him the respect of his peers. For much of his life he was considered the nation's foremost petroleum authority. Among his many rewards were the 1941 Anthony F. Lucas Medal of the American Institute of Mining and Metallurgical Engineers, the 1942 John Fritz Medal of the Founder Societies (ASCE, AIME, ASME, and AIEE), the 1950 Sidney Powers Memorial Medal of the American Association of Petroleum Geologists, election to the National Academy of Sciences, and a 1956 appointment as a regent of the Smithsonian Institution. DeGolyer wrote hundreds of papers and reviews and actively encouraged his employees to publish their findings. He held prestigious university lectureships at the University of Colorado, Princeton University, and the University of Texas at Austin. His own writings ranged from editing a classic monograph, *Elements of the Petroleum Industry* (1941) to writing a biography of Santa Ana (published in the 1930 edition of the *Encyclopaedia Britannica*) and reviews of books on the history of the American Southwest. He served as a contributing editor of the *New Colophon* from 1948 to 1950 and of the *Southwest Review* from 1944 to 1956, and for more than fifteen years he owned the controlling interest in the famous literary periodical *Saturday Review*. He was an avid and increasingly sophisticated book collector from his late twenties on, and he developed three very notable collections in twentieth-century literature, history of science, and the American Southwest. In the depths of the depression of the 1930s, his book purchases often totaled in the thousands of dollars per month. He was considered one of the major American book collectors of the twentieth century. His government service included frequent appearances at congressional hearings as well as stints with the Treasury Department, National Recovery Administration, Atomic Energy Commission, Interior Department, and the Petroleum Administration for War. In 1943 he even declined an offer to become U.S. ambassador to Mexico.

DeGolyer was an inveterate risk-taker and left many sure and safe career tracks to move into new opportunities. Few businessmen ever had such successful melding of business, academic, and government service. Though estimated to be worth up to $100 million in 1950s dollars, he pursued knowledge as others pursued black gold. In 1961 *Fortune* magazine described DeGolyer as a "Renaissance Man," the most eminent of modern oil geologists, and a scholar. Throughout his life, DeGolyer professed luck as the most important ingredient in his success, yet his reputation was based on hard work and the application of science and scientific principles to petroleum exploration.

• DeGolyer's personal papers are at the DeGolyer Library of Special Collections at Southern Methodist University; see Linda Laury's guide to them, *Papers of Everette Lee DeGolyer, Sr.* (1988). A book-length biography is Lon Tinkle, *Mr. De: A Biography of Everette Lee DeGolyer* (1970). Lewis W. MacNaughton's memorial to his partner, in the *Bulletin of the American Association of Petroleum Geologists*, no. 41 (May 1957): 969–74, also includes a short bibliography of DeGolyer's writings. See also Carey Croneis, "E. DeGolyer, Sidney Powers Memorial Medalist," *Bulletin of the American Association of Petroleum Geologists*, no. 34 (May 1950): 971–74; Wallace E. Pratt, "Memorial to Everette Lee DeGolyer," *Proceedings of the Geological Society of America for 1957* (1958), pp.

95–103; MacNaughton, "E. L. DeGolyer, Father of Applied Geophysics," *Science* 125 (22 Feb. 1957): 338–39; Cleveland Amory, "Mr. De of Texas," *Saturday Review*, 26 Jan. 1957, pp. 35–37; and A. Rodger Denison, "Everette Lee DeGolyer," National Academy of Sciences, *Biographical Memoirs* 33 (1959): 65–86.

PATRICK J. BRUNET

DE GRAFF, Robert F. (9 June 1895–1 Nov. 1981), publisher, was born Robert Fair de Graff in Plainfield, New Jersey, the son of James W. de Graff, a notions salesman and distributor, and Carrie T. Milliken. He attended the Hotchkiss School, a private high school for boys in Lakeville, Connecticut, but left before graduating because of a nervous breakdown. He never attended college. At the age of eighteen he worked as an automobile mechanic in New Jersey. When the United States entered World War I in 1917, de Graff enlisted in the army, and his mechanical skills earned him a commission as a lieutenant in the Eighty-sixth Division's 311th Mobile Ordnance Repair Shop. He left the service in 1918 and two years later married Dorcas Marie Bomann. The couple had no children.

In 1920 de Graff joined his father as a notions salesman, dealing in household items such as combs, brushes, needles, and pins, and remained in that line of work until his father's business failed in 1922. That year de Graff's cousin, Frank Nelson Doubleday, offered him a job with his publishing house, Doubleday, Page & Co. After learning the book business as a salesman, de Graff became vice president of Doubleday and director of the company's reprint division, the Garden City Publishing Co., in 1925. Already recognizing the commercial potential of lower-priced editions, he concentrated on producing hardcover books that sold for as little as 39 cents. During his time with Doubleday he originated Star Dollar Books, a series of nonfiction reprints that sold more than 15 million volumes and increased the firm's yearly gross to almost $1.5 million.

De Graff left Garden City in 1936 intending to open a reprint company of his own but instead became president of Blue Ribbon Books, a successful publisher of clothbound reprints at prices from 39 cents to $1.98. With full executive authority for the first time, he made several bold moves. In 1937 he negotiated the purchase of the A. L. Burt Home Library, a long-established reprint house whose 2,000 titles, produced to sell at 50 to 75 cents, greatly enlarged Blue Ribbon's trade list. A pioneer in market research, de Graff began extensive testing and learned that books priced at 39 cents sold twelve times as fast as those offered at 75 cents. Acting on that knowledge in January 1938 he created Triangle Books, a series of clothbound reprints from Blue Ribbon's list selling for 39 cents. He also began exploring new locations for the sale of books and arranged wide distribution of Triangle Books to department stores, where they competed successfully with magazines.

A month after starting Triangle Books, de Graff left Blue Ribbon to undertake a market analysis for what has been described as "a revolutionary publishing plan to make bestselling books in unabridged form available for twenty-five cents a volume" (Tebbel, vol. 3, p. 508). He designed a compact book measuring about 4″ × 7″ with stiff, brightly illustrated cardboard covers and sent a sample printing of Pearl Buck's *The Good Earth* to 1,000 people asking if they would buy such a volume for 25 cents. He also mailed a questionnaire to 49,000 others asking their reading tastes and habits. The replies convinced him that there was a large market for inexpensive, easy-to-carry books. In partnership with three executives of the New York publishing house Simon & Schuster, Richard Simon, Max Lincoln Schuster, and Leon Shimkin, but keeping 51 percent of the stock for himself, de Graff launched Pocket Books, Inc., in June 1939. His carefully chosen initial list comprised ten titles, including four popular novels, three classics, one juvenile, one collection of light verse, and one mystery, in printings of about 10,000 each.

Contrary to the industry's expectations, the venture was an immediate success. In its first week, two of de Graff's titles sold out in New York City, where they were first offered for sale, and five sold more than one million copies within the year. When distribution was extended to the rest of the country in July, orders poured in from small towns that had never had a market for books before. By 1943 some 38 million Pocket Books had been purchased, and by 1969 the figure had topped a billion. Pocket Books was one of the greatest success stories in American publishing history. Begun with a capital investment of $30,000, the company was sold to Chicago department store and newspaper magnate Marshall Field in 1944 for $3 million and bought back in 1957 by a New York firm led by Shimkin and James M. Jacobson for $5 million. Four years later Pocket Books, Inc., became a public corporation, its stock valued at $72 million. The firm became a division of Simon & Schuster in 1966.

De Graff's success was due in part to the affordable price, shrewd selection of titles, and pleasing and portable format of his books, but his most important contribution to the industry was his innovative merchandising. In 1942 he explained it simply to Theodore English: "Pocket Books has wedded book and magazine distribution" (*Saturday Review of Literature*, p. 3). From the firm's first year bookstores accounted for only about 5 percent of Pocket Book sales, with department stores, newsstands, drug and cigar stores, five-and-dime stores, and bus and train stations responsible for most of the rest. Pocket Books and the many imitators that were to follow made a wide range of reading material conveniently available to a larger public than ever before. De Graff's imaginative methods of mass marketing paperbacks was to have a profound influence not only on the publishing industry but on American book-buying and reading habits as well.

De Graff remained president of Pocket Books until 1949, when he became chair of the board. A tall, energetic figure, he enjoyed sports and seldom read for pleasure. He continued working actively in his New York office until he retired in the early 1960s and devoted his last years to philanthropic and community work in Mill Neck, Long Island, New York, where he died in his home.

• References to the life and career of de Graff are in *Cue*, 25 Oct. 1941, p. 3; *Business Week*, 10 Jan. 1942, p. 28; the *Saturday Review of Literature*, 6 June 1942, pp. 3–4, 18; and Walter Clemons, "Ten Little Pocket Books and How They Grew," *New York Times Book Review*, 15 June 1969, pp. 8–11. The early history of Pocket Books, Inc., is given in John Tebbel, *A History of Book Publishing in the United States*, vols. 3 and 4 (1978, 1981), and in Piet Schrenders, *Paperbacks, U.S.A.* (1981). Obituaries are in the *New York Times*, 3 Nov. 1981, and the *Chicago Tribune*, 4 Nov. 1981.

DENNIS WEPMAN

DE GRAFFENRIED, Mary Clare (19 May 1849–26 Apr. 1921), labor investigator, was born in Macon, Georgia, the daughter of Colonel William Kirkland de Graffenried, a lawyer, and Mary Holt Marsh. Her father had opposed secession, but once the Civil War began, he supported the struggle and became a prominent member of Governor Joseph E. Brown's administration. De Graffenried, usually known as Clare, graduated from Wesleyan Female College in Macon in 1865, just as Federal troops, led by Colonel James Wilson, took control of the defeated city. Graduating at the top of her class, she abandoned her preapproved valedictorian speech and launched, instead, into a scathing attack on the behavior of the Federal troops encamped in the city. When Wilson heard of de Graffenried's actions, he threatened to close the college, but he changed his mind when he heard she had acted without the school's approval.

After such a controversial start to her adult life, de Graffenried appears to have lived quietly in Macon for the next decade or so, probably teaching school. In 1876 she moved to Washington, D.C., apparently for economic reasons, and taught literature and languages at Georgetown Female Seminary. Through her father's connections with L. Q. C. Lamar, secretary of the interior under Cleveland, de Graffenried secured a government position in the patent office in 1886. Within a few months she was working for the Bureau of Labor, and in 1888 she was one of the twenty labor investigators appointed by Commissioner Carroll Wright in the newly named Department of Labor.

As a labor investigator, de Graffenried visited factories and working-class homes throughout the United States, particularly in her native South and in the textile cities of the Northeast, collecting data and interviewing families. In 1892 de Graffenried traveled to Europe to gather statistics as part of a project headed by Wright to compare the lives of working-class families in Europe and the United States. She became particularly interested in two issues: the lives of working-class women and children and the importance of decent working-class housing. By the 1890s she was writing about these issues in many national journals and magazines, as well as lecturing around the country to religious and social organizations.

Her most famous article, "The Georgia Cracker in the Cotton Mill," published in the *Century Magazine* in February 1891, stirred great controversy. In the North, the article—based on de Graffenried's many interviews with poor white mill workers in Georgia—was praised for its combination of scientific research and evocative writing. In the South, however, and particularly in her native Georgia, de Graffenried angered all levels of society. Southerners were embarrassed by her depiction of millworkers as "an impressive example of race degeneration" who were "the butt of ridicule, shiftless and inconsequent, always poor though always working." Particularly offensive was her claim that women and children were "wrecked" because lazy husbands sat on porch steps "lounging, whittling sticks, and sunning their big lazy frames" while their wives and children, "baptized in suffering and sacrifice," went out to work. Such notions attacked both the dignity of southern womanhood and notions of male authority. Her calls for child labor reforms and safer working conditions upset southern manufacturers. Her claim that there was a "criminal indifference" to child labor laws offended politicians.

Her other writings were received more favorably. Her "Essay on Child Labor," published in the same year as "The Georgia Cracker," won the American Economic Association's prize for the best essay of the year on labor issues. Her articles were highly readable and yet carried a degree of statistical data unusual for the time. In "Need Of Better Homes for Wage-Earners," published in the *Forum* (May 1896), she opened her article by announcing that "the two civilizing agencies of highest values for laboring people, next to industrial training and baths, are bay windows and front door-bells." But her article continued in a less melodramatic, more scientific style, as she compared the average living space of workers in cities throughout the United States.

De Graffenried was a forerunner of later Progressive reformers, and, with Carrol Wright and others at the Department of Labor, she moved discussion of the working class from a purely impressionistic, subjective style to a more rational, statistical analysis. She was one of the earliest reformers to call for state intervention in working-class lives through child labor laws and better educational opportunities. Despite her own middle-class biases, sometimes evident in a rather condescending tone toward her working-class subjects, she was one of the earliest commentators to show a real concern for working-class women and children, and her work as an investigator for the Department of Labor gave her particular insight into working-class life.

Apart from extensive trips to Europe and Asia, de Graffenried lived in Washington, D.C., her whole adult life, socializing widely and turning her home into a "house museum" full of antiques and souvenirs. An acquaintance described her as a "highly-cultivated . . . original type" who "never gave a thought to her personal appearance." She was "courted in the highest social circles," including those of First Lady Ellen Wilson. Despite her criticisms of southern working conditions, the *Atlanta Journal*, in a series called "Georgia's Twenty-Five Greatest Women," characterized her as "intensely southern." After retiring in 1906, she ceased to write and died at home in Washington, D.C.

• The papers of the de Graffenried family are held in the Southern Historical Collection at the University of North Carolina at Chapel Hill. A useful family history, based upon the above papers is Thomas P. de Graffenried, *History of the de Graffenried Family* (1925). *The de Graffenried Family Scrapbook* (1958), by the same author, includes a listing of all of de Graffenried's publications. The fullest treatment of de Graffenried's life is Lala Carr Steelman, "Mary Clare de Graffenried: The Saga of a Crusader for Social Reform," in *Studies in the History of the South, 1875–1922*, ed. Joseph F. Steelman et al. (1966), pp. 53–83. For an interesting analysis of the controversy surrounding de Graffenried's article, "The Georgia Cracker in the Cotton Mills," see LeeAnn Whites, "The De Graffenried Controversy: Class, Race, and Gender in the New South," *Journal of Southern History*, 54, no. 3 (Aug. 1988): 449–78.

JULIA WALSH

DEGRASSE, John Van Surly (June 1825–1868), physician, was born in New York City, the son of George DeGrasse, a prosperous landowner, and Maria Van Surly. After obtaining his early education in both public and private schools in New York City, he entered Oneida Institute in Whitesboro (near Utica) New York in 1840. Oneida was one of the first colleges to admit African Americans, nurturing a strong antislavery stance. In addition to welcoming African Americans to its campus, the institute invited abolitionsts as lecturers and provided both a manual arts and academic program. In contrast to the graduates of all-black medical schools, African Americans like DeGrasse were seen as "manifestly more competent in their various callings for having graduated at institutions where they contended for mental superiority with the more favored class of white students."

In 1843 DeGrasse attended Aubuk College in Paris, France. Returning to New York City in 1845, he started medical training through an apprenticeship with Dr. Samuel R. Childs. After two years of clinical work and study under Childs, DeGrasse was admitted into the medical studies program at Bowdoin College in Brunswick, Maine, in 1847. Finishing his medical studies with honors in two years, he received an M.D. in May 1849. His admission to Bowdoin's medical course had been aided and sponsored by those Americans (organized as the American Colonization Society) who wanted to colonize free blacks and ex-slaves in Africa. The intent was to promote social equality by preparing black professionals who would then emigrate to Liberia in West Africa. For DeGrasse and other educated blacks, however, this plan to expatriate them did not materialize. Instead, with a medical degree in hand, DeGrasse returned to Europe and worked in various hospitals in Paris and London. He continued his professional development as an assistant surgeon to the French surgeon Velpeau.

In 1853 DeGrasse crossed the Atlantic again, this time working as a surgeon on the ship *Samuel Fox*, as he returned home to New York City. Prompted by the frequent capture of blacks under the Fugitive Slave Law of 1850, DeGrasse became a founding member of a Vigilante Committee of Thirteen, formed by free blacks to give protection to fugitive slaves.

After conducting a medical practice in his home city for about two years, DeGrasse moved to Boston, Massachusetts, where he continued his medical career. In Boston he was quickly recognized as a talented and skillful surgeon, and on 24 August 1854 he was admitted into membership in the Massachusetts Medical Society, in what is believed to be the first instance of the admission of an African American to a professional medical association in the United States. A Boston newspaper, the *Liberator* (24 Aug. 1854) reported of DeGrasse, "Earning a good reputation here by his diligence and skill, he was admitted a member," and observed that "others of his class may be stimulated to seek an elevation which has hitherto been supposed unattainable by men of color . . . Many of our most respectable physicians visit and advise with him whenever counsel is required. The Boston medical profession, it must be acknowledged has done itself honor in thus discarding the law of caste, and generously acknowledging real merit, without regard to the hue of the skin." DeGrasse was viewed as one of "the most accomplished" of the African-American medical pioneers in the pre–Civil War era.

An active abolitionist in Boston, DeGrasse helped to organize vigilante groups to intercept the movements of slave hunters on the streets of Boston during the enforcement of the 1850 Fugitive Slave Law in this city. In 1863 he volunteered to serve as a medical officer in the Union army in the Civil War. Being one of eight African-American physicians appointed to the Army Medical Corps, he served as an assistant surgeon in the U.S. Army. His meritorious service was celebrated when Governor John A. Andrews of Massachusetts presented him with a gold-hilted sword from the Commonwealth of Massachusetts.

One of the several free African Americans who were formally trained in and who practiced medicine in the North before the Civil War, DeGrasse continued as an active physician until his death and was a recognized leader in the African-American community in Massachusetts.

• Secondary sources include William C. Nell, *The Colored Patriots of the American Revolution* (1855), George Washington Williams, *History of the Negro Race in America* (1883; repr., 1968), and Leonard Johnson, Jr., "History of the Education of Negro Physicians," *Journal of Medical Education* 42 (1967): 439–46.

ROBERT C. HAYDEN

DEHNER, Dorothy (23 Dec. 1901–22 Sept. 1994), sculptor, was born in Cleveland, Ohio, the daughter of Edward Pius Dehner, a pharmacist, and Louisa A.

Uphof, a suffragist. Dehner spent her adolescence in Pasadena, California, and received instruction in painting and photography. At Pasadena High School she studied dance, music, and acting and performed in contemporary dramas with the Pasadena Playhouse. After one year at the University of California, Los Angeles, she moved to New York to pursue a career in theater. Dehner studied at the American Academy of Dramatic Arts and appeared in off-Broadway shows. She spent the bulk of 1925 traveling in Europe, predominantly in Italy but also in Switzerland and Paris, where she saw works by the cubists, the Fauves, and the German expressionists, among others.

On her return to New York in the fall of 1925, having been stimulated by her contact with European modernism, Dehner enrolled at the Art Students League. Initially she studied drawing because the sculpture produced there did not interest her. In 1927 Dehner married aspiring artist David Smith. Their union was childless. In this period, in a painting class with Jan Matulka (Smith's instructor as well), Dehner created her first cubist-related compositions.

In 1935 Dehner and Smith went to Paris, Brussels, Greece, and later the Soviet Union and Great Britain. She wandered through archaeological sites and visited museums where she saw examples of sculpture from the ancient world. Years later these cubic, hieratic, and simplified forms influenced her sculpture; titles chosen for her later work often refer to ancient sites or mythological personages. By the late 1930s Dehner had abandoned abstraction for a representational approach, a miniaturist style based on her interest in a book of medieval manuscripts. Many of her works from these years are lost; extant, however, is the Life on the Farm series, which depicts scenes from Dehner's daily life at Bolton Landing, New York, on the farm in the Adirondacks that she and Smith had purchased in 1929.

Dehner and Smith were inspired by the same images: the skeleton of a prehistoric bird they saw at the Museum of Natural History was the basis for Dehner's drawing *Bird of Peace* (1946) and for Smith's *Royal Bird* (1947). Both artists saw the prehistoric creature as a menacing predator—and likely as a reflection of their reaction to the destruction caused by World War II. But for Dehner, *Bird of Peace* held personal associations as well; the spectral presence of the skeletal creature and the barren, jagged peaks below it alluded to the anguish of her private life. Smith was actively competitive with her artistic achievements and had violent outbursts.

Only a few times in the 1940s did Dehner exhibit her work. In 1946 the Audubon Artists awarded her a first prize for drawing, and two years later Skidmore College organized a solo exhibition of her drawings and paintings. She found a copy of Ernst Haeckel's seminal study of natural forms, *Kunstformen der Natur* (1904), and embarked on a series of drawings of microscopic organisms, creating abstractions in gouache and ink. The repertory of biomorphic forms that Dehner introduced related to Paul Klee, Joan Miró, and Mark Rothko, among others. Unlike the surrealists, Dehner did not emphasize the disquieting aspects of her imagery but instead celebrated the animate energy of these unicellular life forms.

Dehner left Bolton Landing in 1950 and was divorced from Smith two years later. She took classes at Skidmore College and after obtaining a degree went to New York City, where she taught at various schools. In 1952 she had her first solo exhibition in the city, at the Rose Fried Gallery; she also studied engraving at Stanley William Hayter's Atelier 17 in New York and began to experiment with wax.

In 1955, the year Dehner began working at the Sculpture Center, she had a few pieces cast in bronze. For the rest of her life, Dehner would focus her energy on sculpture but would complement this work with drawings and prints. Also in 1955 she married Ferdinand Mann, and the calm that was brought to her life by this marriage is evident in her art of the 1960s and 1970s. The couple had no children together.

Dehner's sculpture emphasized contour rather than mass. She assembled her works out of disparate parts and used wax as an element in their construction. In the 1960s she braised and drew on wax slabs, then introduced other textures by adding small pieces of metal. To create a lively visual effect, she used faceted elements to form planes that shimmer when reflecting light. Though abstract, Dehner's sculptures derive from the natural world. Vertical compositions evoke a totemic presence, whereas the horizontal format can be viewed as a landscape. *Encounter* (1969), comprising six separate totem shaped sculptures, alludes, in composition as well as concept, to a chance meeting of individuals of varying sizes and shapes. Her abstract sculptures, abounding with circles, moons, ellipses, wedges, and arcs, constitute a personal iconography. Dehner's art, like that of her generation of artists of the New York School, asserts that abstract symbols, however personal, communicate universal meaning.

The Jewish Museum in New York City sponsored a major retrospective of Dehner's art in 1965. By the mid-1970s she had changed her medium from cast metal to wood and was constructing pieces out of small wooden elements. These ensembles feature thrusting verticals or stacked elements and suggest the architectural outline of a large city.

In the early 1980s Dehner began a new series of monumental sculptures constructed of fabricated steel and based on earlier works. *Demeter's Harrow* (1990), originally a small bronze cast from a wax model in 1970, reflects Dehner's lifelong penchant for imagery conveying personal associations. The composition, of polygonal and circular steel shapes extending outward, evokes the dynamic interplay between space and mass.

In 1993 major retrospectives of Dehner's sculpture and related drawings were held at the Katonah Museum of Art in Katonah, New York; and at the Corcoran Gallery in Washington, D.C. In 1995, the year following her death in New York City, a memorial exhibition was organized by the Cleveland Museum of Art.

Dehner had been awarded an honorary doctorate from Skidmore College (1982); the Women's Caucus for Art award for outstanding achievement in the visual arts (1983); and the Award of Distinction, National Sculpture Conference: Works by Women (Univ. of Cincinnati, 1987).

• The papers of Dorothy Dehner and David Smith are in the Archives of American Art, Smithsonian Institution, Washington, D.C. Exhibition catalogs include Joan Marter, *Dorothy Dehner and David Smith: Their Decades of Search and Fulfillment* (Zimmerli Art Museum, Rutgers Univ., 1984); Marter, *Dorothy Dehner, Sixty Years of Art* (Katonah Museum of Art [available through the University of Washington Press], 1994); and the essay by Jane Glaubinger in Cleveland Museum of Art, *Dorothy Dehner: Drawings, Prints, Sculpture* (1995). Also see Judd Tully, "Dorothy Dehner and Her Life on the Farm with David Smith," *American Artist* 47 (Oct. 1983): 58–61, 99–102. An obituary in the *New York Times*, 23 Sept. 1994, contains several inaccuracies corrected in the article above.

JOAN MARTER

DEHNERT, Dutch (5 Apr. 1898–20 Apr. 1979), professional basketball player and coach, was born Henry Dehnert in New York City. Dehnert grew up on the streets of Manhattan's West Side and attended public schools. He did not play high school basketball, however, and he never enrolled in college. Instead, around 1918 he began playing professional basketball with successful brief stints in the New York State League, Pennsylvania State League, and the New England League before joining the Original Celtics in 1919. The first Celtic team played from 1914 through 1917, but it did not emerge as the most celebrated of its time until the years from 1919 until 1922, when the team was joined by Dehnert, Johnny Beckman, Horse Haggarty, Joe Trippe, Pete Barry, Nat Holman (the only player with collegiate experience), Chris Leonard, Joe Lapchick, Oscar Grimstead, Davey Banks, and Nat Hickey. The team's nucleus, including Dehnert, came from the single New York City working-class neighborhood that ran from Twenty-third Street to Twenty-ninth Street between Eighth and Tenth avenues.

The Original Celtics profoundly transformed professional basketball. During the early 1920s there were hundreds of professional teams with revolving rosters. Players peddled their talent to the highest bidders, and they regularly played with "opponent" teams on any given night. In 1922 the Original Celtics' owner, James Furey, curtailed wildcat sports labor by signing his players to guaranteed annual contracts that averaged $7,500 a season, with the star players, like Dehnert, earning as much as $10,000.

The team popularized the young game (invented only thirty years earlier) by means of successful barnstorming tours throughout the East, Midwest, and South, playing professional, amateur, college, and local teams. Far more talented than most of their opponents, the Celtics experimented when comfortably ahead. Rather than running up the score, which doomed barnstorming popularity, they performed brilliant passing exhibitions. They often encountered the tough crowds of basketball's early years, fans who rooted against the country's dominant team. Local partisanship ran high, and occasionally the Celtics were despised in rural areas for their New York urban affiliation. Sometimes, when playing local opponents, they were harassed in their home city, too. The players, in fact, unanimously agreed that the South Brooklyn Prospect Hall (known as "The Bucket of Blood") was the toughest arena of all. Dehnert remembered dozens of men hanging from the rafters who "thought nothing of throwing a bottle at you when you were trying to shoot a foul" and the fans who tried to trip players if they ran too close to sidelines.

More than well-paid basketball missionaries, the Original Celtics were innovators. They revolutionized the game's offense. Dehnert's principal legacy was his perfection of the pivot play. During a 1926 game against a formidable industrial team, the Chattanooga Rail-Lites, he moved to the foul line where he received passes from the guards, and he returned them as his teammates moved toward the basket. The idea was hatched as a way to neutralize Chattanooga's defensive ploy of stationing a player in the free throw zone to restrict easy Celtic fast-break baskets and penetration down the lane. When the standing defensive guard challenged a cutting Celtic, Dehnert realized that "all I had to do was pivot to my left, take one step, and lay the ball up for a basket." The pivot quickly became central to the Celtics' offense over the next decade, and it remains a basketball staple. Dehnert became one of basketball's best-known and highest-paid players because of his speed, ball handling, adept passing from the pivot, and strong defense.

In 1925 the American Basketball League was formed, with franchises in Washington, D.C.; Boston; Rochester, New York; Brooklyn; Fort Wayne, Indiana; Detroit; Buffalo, New York; Chicago; and Cleveland. The new league standardized the game's rules and ended roster-jumping by signing players to exclusive annual contracts. The Original Celtics continued to play exhibition games, trouncing ABL teams and earning more money than any of their opponents. After the league's first season, opposing owners voted to blacklist them from playing their teams in exhibitions. Faced with the prospect of reduced revenue, the Celtics joined the ABL in 1926 and won successive league championships in 1926–1927 and 1927–1928.

The Celtics' domination so profoundly hurt fan interest and attendance around the young league that the ABL disbanded the team and distributed the players to other clubs. Dehnert, along with Lapchick, Beckman, and Barry, was acquired by the Cleveland Rosenblums in 1928. The "Rosenblum-Celtics" (by which name they were commonly called) ran away with the regular season championship and easily swept the playoffs against Fort Wayne. Max Rosenblum shocked the league by folding his franchise in December 1930, whereupon Dehnert, Barry, and Lapchick signed with the second-year Toledo club. Rosenblum's action presaged the collapse of other franchises

during the early depression years. The ABL itself folded in 1931. Dehnert, Lapchick, Banks, Hickey, and Carl Husta returned to the barnstorming life until 1936, but age and financial difficulties finally caught up with these once invincible veterans of the Original Celtics, and they formally retired. Dehnert and his colleagues made one final appearance at Madison Square Garden in a ten-minute preliminary game against the New York Giants' football team in 1941. In all, Dehnert played in more than 1,900 victories of the Celtics and Cleveland Rosenblums.

After 1936 Dehnert coached the Detroit Eagles to the World Professional Tournament championship in Chicago in 1941–1942. He then coached an ABL team from Harrisburg (1942–1943), the Sheboygan Redskins of the National Basketball League (winning the western division during the 1944–1945 and 1945–1946 seasons), and the Cleveland Rebels of the Basketball Association of America in 1946–1947, recording a 30–30 won-lost record for the season before being ousted two games to one by the New York Knicks in the playoffs. Dehnert compiled a 73–64 won-lost record over five seasons as a major league coach.

During his later years Dehnert worked as a mutual clerk at New York state racetracks. He was elected to Naismith Memorial Basketball Hall of Fame in 1968. He died in Far Rockaway, New York.

• Little is known about Dehnert's life apart from basketball. The best overview of the Original Celtics is in Zander Hollander, ed., *The Modern Encyclopedia of Basketball* (1973). Also useful are Ronald Mendell, *Who's Who in Basketball* (1973); Robert W. Peterson, *Cages to Jump Shots: Pro Basketball's Early Years* (1990); David S. Neft and Richard Cohen, *The Sports Encyclopedia: Professional Basketball*, 4th ed. (1990); Neil D. Issacs, *All the Moves* (1975); Glenn Dickey, *The History of Professional Basketball since 1896* (1982); and Joe Lapchick, *My Life in Basketball* (1965). An obituary is in the *New York Times*, 26 Apr. 1979.

STEVEN POPE

DEINARD, Ephraim (11 May 1846–24 June 1930), Hebrew author, bibliographer, and bookdealer, was born in Shossmaken, Courland, Russia, the son of Jekuthiel Gerson Deinard and Leah Cohen. In addition to attending traditional schools of Jewish learning, he also studied secular subjects with private tutors. By age eighteen he was contributing articles on current issues to the Hebrew weekly *Ha-Zefirah* and other East European periodicals. In 1866 he married Margolia Sara Jaffe of Shklov, and they had four children.

Deinard early established a reputation as a traveler, and in the course of his various journeys he pursued his interest in book collecting. While traveling in the Crimea he met the Karaite archaeologist Abraham Firkovich and served as his secretary. In Deinard's first book, *Toledot Even Reshef* (The Biography of Even Reshef, 1875), he attacked Firkovich and accused him of various forgeries. He also explored Europe and ventured into Asia and North Africa. Between 1899 and 1909 he made three trips to the Middle East, where he collected rare books and manuscripts. He also compiled ethnographic and demographic data regarding various Jewish communities. He wrote a number of books describing his extensive travels through the Crimean peninsula, Europe, and the Middle East.

After a visit to Palestine in 1881, Deinard settled in Odessa, where he was active as a bookdealer and participated in the Zionist movement. In 1888 he emigrated to the United States, where he would spend the rest of his life, except for the years 1913–1916, when he lived in Palestine.

In 1889 Deinard established the Hebrew weekly *Ha-Leumi* (The Nationalist), which appeared in New York City for twenty-three issues. He took its slogan from the book of Joshua: "You are indeed a numerous people possessed of great strength" (17:17), a verse that indicated his faith in the burgeoning American Jewish community. *Ha-Leumi* was dedicated to the Zionist program and to the encouragement of agricultural work among Jewish immigrants. It is noteworthy that later, in 1897, Deinard played a key role in an unsuccessful attempt to establish an agricultural colony in Nevada where land had become available for this purpose. His was but one of many such failed colonizing efforts by Eastern European Jewish immigrants at the end of the nineteenth century.

While in Europe Deinard had helped enrich the collections of various libraries and book lovers. Appalled by the paucity of the Hebrew holdings of American libraries, he continually stressed that they needed to be augmented so as not to be inferior to the depositories of the European libraries. Toward this end he performed an invaluable service by building up the Hebrew collections of leading libraries such as the libraries of the Jewish Theological Seminary of America, Columbia University, the Library of Congress, the University of California at Berkeley, Brown University, the Hebrew Union College, the New York Public Library, and Harvard University.

Deinard served as the principal agent of Philadelphia judge Mayer Sulzberger, who was an avid collector of Hebrew books. In 1896 Deinard issued a bibliography of Sulzberger's holdings entitled *Or Mayer* (The Light of Mayer), and these items were among those that the judge later presented to the library of the Jewish Theological Seminary of America. Deinard had the good fortune also of obtaining the support of prominent Jewish philanthropists in establishing depositories for his collections. In the case of Columbia University he benefited from the help of Oscar S. Straus. The Library of Congress was able to obtain its first two collections of Hebraica, totaling about 15,000 volumes, because of the support of Jacob H. Schiff, who later made possible the purchase of two additional collections of about 6,000 volumes. Deinard's last collection of some 12,000 printed volumes and twenty-nine manuscripts was acquired in 1930 by Harvard University with the help of Lucius N. Littauer. The collection contained sixteen incunabula, eleven in Hebrew and five in Latin, as well as many bibliographical rarities.

Throughout his life Deinard was a stormy petrel who engaged in sharp polemics. A prolific writer, he authored more than fifty books and pamphlets on history, Zionism, Jewish problems, and literature—his intemperate style often bringing him into conflict with his contemporaries. He opposed Hasidism, which he considered to be a sectarian and divisive movement and a departure from Orthodox Judaism. He also had little use for kabbalah and Reform Judaism. He delighted in republishing anti-Hasidic tracts to which he added his own vitriolic introductions.

Deinard's *Koheleth America* (1926), which contains a comprehensive listing of the Hebrew books printed in the United States from 1735 to 1926, focused attention on the body of American Hebrew literature that had been created and published here. In a preface he indicated that his book was being published on his eightieth birthday and that because of failing eyesight he had to take leave from his readers. Despite his handicap, however, Deinard was still able to produce several works up to his death four years later in New York City. He was convinced that the United States was destined to become a center of Jewish scholarship, and it was largely through his pioneering efforts that American libraries were better able to contribute to the fostering of Hebrew learning and the achievement of this goal.

• Deinard's papers, including correspondence from leading Hebrew writers, are in the library of the Jewish Theological Seminary of America in New York City. On these papers see Jacob Kabakoff, "Documents from the Deinard Collection" (in Hebrew), *Shoharim ve-Ne'emanim* (1978). Israel Schapiro, who served as head of the Hebrew section of the Library of Congress, evaluated Deinard's contributions and presented a bibliography of his books in "Ephraim Deinard," *Proceedings of the American Jewish Historical Society* 34 (1937): 149–63. See also Simcha B. Berkowitz, "Ephraim Deinard: Bibliophile and Bookman," *Studies in Bibliography and Booklore* 9 (1971): 137–52; this article is part of Deinard's biography submitted by Berkowitz toward the M.A. at Columbia University (1964). An obituary is in *Hadoar*, 11 July 1930.

JACOB KABAKOFF

DEITZ, John F. (3 Apr. 1861–8 May 1924), farmer and outlaw, was born in Winneconne, Wisconsin, the son of John Deitz (also spelled Dietz), Sr., a New York farmer who moved to Wisconsin before the Civil War. His mother's name and occupation are unknown. A few years after the war, the Deitz family moved north and west, seeking cheap farmland in the logged-over region of Wisconsin known as the Cutover. John, Jr., grew up in a log cabin, attended common school, and as a young man dabbled in real estate, ran for minor local offices, and eked out a marginal existence from a small farm. Like many another backwoods farmer, he also hunted, trapped, did odd jobs, and seasonally worked for the logging companies. In 1882 he married Hattie Young, a part-time schoolteacher, with whom he had six children.

In 1900 Deitz and his wife purchased a 160-acre farmstead abutting the Thornapple River in southeastern Sawyer County, in the heart of the Wisconsin pinery. On a corner of their property stood part of the Cameron Dam, one of many small wooden dams erected by logging companies on this important tributary of the Chippewa River. The dam itself was the property of the Chippewa Lumber & Boom Co., an affiliate of the vast Weyerhaeuser syndicate for whom Deitz had previously worked as a dam tender.

Throughout his life Deitz was a prickly and contentious man with a flair for promoting himself and for publicizing the wrongs he had suffered at the hands of "the corporations." He now claimed that the lumber company owed him back wages, and, in recompense, he demanded a toll on all logs sluiced downriver through the dam. Rifle in hand, he drove off representatives of the company and a series of sheriffs' deputies sent to serve warrants on him. For almost ten years he refused to permit any logs to be driven through "his" dam, defending it at gunpoint and foiling all attempts by local authorities to arrest him.

In 1904 a deputy sheriff and one of Deitz's sons were wounded in a gun battle on the farmstead, and the "Defender of Cameron Dam" attained national prominence as an outlaw-hero who stood up to the "lumber trust." Although his claims had no legal merit, Deitz was widely supported and admired by reformers, socialists, and ordinary people throughout the Midwest—somewhat to the embarrassment of Governor Robert M. La Follette and other Progressives whose rhetoric posed "the people" versus "the interests." Because Deitz was lionized by the press, La Follette was reluctant to marshal the full powers of the state against this outspoken backcountry anarchist.

In 1910, on one of Deitz's rare trips to the nearby town of Winter, he shot and wounded a local man in a street fracas. Shortly thereafter, two of Deitz's children were wounded by sheriff's deputies in an ambush gone badly awry. State authorities attempted unsuccessfully to negotiate a settlement, but Deitz refused all entreaties. Thereupon a large posse of deputies surrounded his farm. In the ensuing battle, a deputy died and Deitz was wounded and captured. In the trial at the county seat of Hayward, he defended himself against a charge of murder, contending that the state could not prove whose gun had fired the fatal bullet. But he was found guilty and received a life sentence. During and after his trial, a stage play and a movie portraying Deitz as a hero played to packed houses in Wisconsin and Minnesota.

Deitz served ten years in the state penitentiary, but continuing public pressure eventually persuaded Governor John J. Blaine to grant him a pardon in 1921. A cranky but charismatic figure of the Progressive Era, Deitz died in Milwaukee, estranged from family and friends but still protesting the righteousness of his cause.

• Information on Deitz can be found in two rich collections in the Wisconsin State Archives, State Historical Society of Wisconsin: the Executive Department Pardon Papers, ser. 1/1/10–7, and the Deitz Family Scrapbook (microfilm). The best sources for Deitz's colorful career are Paul H. Hass, "The Suppression of John F. Deitz: An Episode of the Progressive Era in Wisconsin," *Wisconsin Magazine of History*, 57 (Summer 1974): 255–309; Malcolm Rosholt, *The Battle of Cameron Dam* (1974); and *Dictionary of Wisconsin Biography* (1960).

PAUL H. HASS

DEJONG, David Cornel (9 June 1905–5 Sept. 1967), writer, was born Tjalmar Breola (or Breda) in Blija, Friesland, in the Netherlands. The uncertainty about his surname at birth is compounded by the confusion concerning his parents' names. Some sources identify his father, a carpenter, as Remmeren R. (or Raymond) DeJong; the maiden name of his mother, Jantje, is variously given as Cornel and DeJong. It is known, however, that David DeJong grew up in Wierum, where his family moved so that his father could take over his grandfather's building business. He attended school there until the age of eleven, but his education was frequently interrupted by illness stemming from acute allergies and was terminated because of financial reasons. When DeJong and his parents came to Grand Rapids, Michigan, in 1918, he found work digging up dandelions in a park while also taking care of his siblings because his ill mother was unable to. After high school, he continued his education at Calvin College in Grand Rapids. He studied at the University of Chicago and the University of Wisconsin and received his B.A. in 1929 from Calvin College. After teaching high school in Edmore, Michigan, DeJong returned to school on a fellowship at Duke University in Durham, North Carolina, where he completed his M.A. degree in English in 1932. Although he entered Brown University to work on a Ph.D. in English in 1933, he left school the next year, after his first novel was published, to devote his time to writing.

Over the next several decades he published short stories, juvenile stories, novels, articles, poetry, and his autobiography. Critics often found his work not to their liking; some described it as labored and dull, while others condemned it as distasteful and unpalatable. Negative reviews did not stop DeJong from writing, although this may reveal why he turned to children's books later in his life. However, not all of his books were poorly received; in fact, many were praised for their ability to help Americans see themselves in a different light, since the stories depicted a foreigner's experience in the United States. For example, *Belly Fulla Straw* (1934), his first published novel, tells the story of a Dutch immigrant family, a subject DeJong returned to in other works. He also worked with his native language, translating two books from the Dutch—*Old Man Daantje's Beard* (1935), by Leonard Roggeveen, and *Express to the East* (1937), by C. Spoelstra. DeJong received a Houghton Mifflin fellowship for *Old Haven* (1938). A few years later he published his first book of poems, *Across the Board* (1943), but it was not as well received as his fiction had been. His autobiography, *With a Dutch Ac-*

cent (1945), has been compared to those of Ole Edvart Rolvaag, Ludwig Lewisohn, Louis Adamic, and William McFee, in that the fresh perspective and objectivity of these books fostered a pride in America, both for the subjects of the autobiographies and for their readers. In addition, DeJong contributed to magazines and newspapers and was the editor of a poetry journal, *Smoke,* for five years (c. 1931–1937).

In 1945 DeJong married Helen Elizabeth Moffit; they had no children. During the 1950s DeJong taught creative writing at various workshop conferences and institutions, including the University of North Carolina and the University of Rhode Island; he also gave lectures and radio and television talks. Later, DeJong suffered a spinal injury that temporarily halted his writing and eventually limited his writing to shorter works. He began writing juvenile stories, beginning with *The Seven Sayings of Mr. Jefferson* (1959), and wrote six more over the next decade. Reviews of many of these books called them "delightful." Even those with less favorable reviews were not wholly dismissed: the reviewer of *Looking for Alexander* (1963), after describing the book as repetitious, admitted it "invited rereading." At the time of his death in Providence, Rhode Island, DeJong was working on two juvenile stories and two other works; he had four works in press.

While DeJong's works do not emanate from a consistent location or theme, he used his own experiences as the basis of many of his novels, which often deal with the lives and trials of Dutch families, either in their native country or as immigrants in the United States. No matter what his subject, he depicted the situations, at times quite dramatic or catastrophic, with poise and control, which were praised by reviewers. His best-known work is probably his autobiography, in which he displays his pride in being American, which explains why it was distributed to the American armed forces during World War II. Although he came to the United States a foreigner, his writings—whether depicting immigrant characters or telling a children's story—reveal he did not remain foreign to American culture for long.

• There is no complete collection of DeJong's papers, although some of his letters are in the University of Nevada Library at Reno; the Richard Johns Papers, University of Delaware Library; and the Willard Maas Papers, Brown University Library. Additional works by DeJong include *Light Sons and Dark* (1940), *Day of the Trumpet* (1941), *Benefit Street* (1942), *Domination in June* (1946), *Somewhat Angels* (1947), *Snow on the Mountain* (1949), *Two Sofas in the Parlor* (1951), *The Desperate Children* (1952), *The Unfairness of Easter* (1959), *The Happy Birthday Umbrella* (1960), *The Birthday Egg* (1962), *Outside the Four Walls of Everything* (1962), *Around the Dom* (1964), *Alexander, the Monkey Sitter* (1965), and *The Squirrel and the Harp* (1966).

Several of DeJong's novels include experiences of his life both in the Netherlands and in the United States; his autobiography, *With a Dutch Accent,* gives the story of his early boyhood. The 1944 edition of *Current Biography* gives an idea of what the longer work offers. An obituary is in the *New York Times,* 5 Sept. 1967.

MICHELLE M. PAGNI

DE KAY, George Colman (5 Mar. 1802–31 Jan. 1849), naval officer, was born in New York City, the son of George De Kay, a sea captain, and Catherine Colman. While he was very young, both of his parents died, and his family guardians enrolled him in a private school in Connecticut. Their plan was to prepare young George for college then send him to Yale for a degree, but he refused to follow the scenario. Lured by the mystique of the sea, he ran away from his protectors, enrolled as a common seaman on a merchant vessel, and began literally to learn the ropes. By the time he reached his majority, he was a skillful navigator, thoroughly versed in the workings of ships and their crews, and was captain of his own vessel. While sailing ships built by Henry Eckford under contract to clients in South American ports, De Kay became familiar with disputes between fledgling Hispanic republics. In 1826 he sailed to Buenos Aires, capital of the Argentine Republic, and discovered that the Río de la Plata was blockaded by a Brazilian squadron in a war with the Argentine Republic over the Banda Oriental, which later became Uruguay. Casting his lot with the *porteños* of Buenos Aires, he volunteered for service in the Argentine navy, commanded by Admiral William (Guillermo) Brown, a Scotch-Irishman. In June 1827 De Kay was given command of the eight-gun brig *Brandzen,* manned by a mixed crew of Argentinians and foreigners. Offered the rank of captain, he refused to accept it until he had proven himself as a naval officer.

Immediately after taking command of his ship, De Kay sailed the *Brandzen* in harm's way by breaking through the Brazilian blockade of the Río de la Plata. Encountering two Brazilian warships on 26 June, he engaged them in battle and captured one. Returning to port, he accepted a captain's commission then boldly set sail again. On this voyage, he captured three Brazilian ships before making contact with the brig *Cacique,* which was twice the size of the *Brandzen,* was armed with eighteen guns, and was carrying three times as many crew members. Undaunted, De Kay engaged the *Cacique* and, by using superior sea-fighting tactics, forced its surrender. He returned to Buenos Aires in triumph, was promoted to lieutenant colonel, a rank comparable to commodore in the U.S. Navy, and was given command of the *Cacique.* Accompanied by the *Brandzen,* he immediately sailed northward with his little squadron through the Caribbean to New York, where he put in for provisions and water. He was feted by the citizens, celebrated as "the Young Commodore of the Spanish Main." On his return voyage to Buenos Aires in June 1828 on board the *Brandzen,* his luck in running the Brazilian blockade finally ran out. Under imminent peril of being forced to surrender to a squadron of enemy warships driving his vessel inshore, he scuttled the *Brandzen* rather than allow it to be seized. He then swam safely ashore with his crewmen and traveled overland to Buenos Aires. Given command of three vessels of the defending squadron, he helped Admiral Brown fend off one final attack by the Brazilian fleet before peace was declared. He was furloughed home, and even though he pointedly invited his Argentinian hosts to recall him to active duty if the need should ever arise, his naval exploits were at an end.

In New York City, De Kay renewed his association with the shipbuilder Eckford, shortly thereafter delivering a newly constructed corvette to his naval friends in Buenos Aires. In 1831 he sailed another of Eckford's corvettes to Constantinople for delivery to the sultan of Turkey. He was accompanied on this voyage by his brother, James Ellsworth De Kay, a naturalist and writer, and by Eckford, who was appointed superintendent of Ottoman shipyards. When Eckford died the following year, De Kay returned Eckford's body to New York. In 1833 De Kay married Janet Halleck Drake, the only child of poet Joseph Rodman Drake and granddaughter of Eckford, thus cementing long-standing ties with a circle of literary people, including Fitz-Greene Halleck, William Cullen Bryant, and De Kay's brother. He and his wife had seven children, four of whom achieved fame as soldiers and writers.

In 1847 De Kay was called from his quiet family life in New Jersey to work for the relief of Irish famine victims. With Robert B. Forbes, another sea captain, he urged Congress to allow them use of the naval vessels *Macedonian* and *Jamestown* to carry cargoes of food to Cork. Although their request was unusual and although the United States was at war with Mexico at the time and needed all its warships, Congress passed a resolution allowing De Kay and Forbes to proceed with their plans. Public subscriptions were secured to pay for the project, and the two captains sailed with huge amounts of relief supplies to Ireland. However, De Kay had trouble collecting the money pledged for his part of the expedition and was compelled to pay some $30,000 in expenses from his own pocket. Unable to afford this loss, he proceeded to Washington to petition Congress for relief. While pursuing this frustrating employment, his health failed, and he died in Washington, D.C., leaving his family in arrears. Finally, Congress reimbursed his wife and children for the entire amount, but as Forbes observed, "Commodore De Kay may be said to have sacrificed his life to the voyage of the *Macedonian*."

• De Kay's life is surveyed in a manuscript by his brother, James Ellsworth De Kay, "The Book of the Children of De Kay," in the Library of Congress. See also an article by his youngest son, Charles De Kay, "Sea Fights on the Spanish Main," *National Marine* 2 (1918): 21–28, 72; and Fitz-Greene Halleck's *Outline of the Life of Commodore George C. De Kay* (1847). John Edwin Fagg, *Latin America: A General History*, 3d ed. (1977), provides background on his Argentinian adventures; and Robert B. Forbes, *Personal Reminiscences* (1878), describes his role in the *Macedonian* affair. An obituary is in the *National Intelligencer*, 3 Feb. 1849.

PAUL DAVID NELSON

DE KAY, James Ellsworth (12 Oct. 1792–21 Nov. 1851), zoologist, was born in Lisbon, Portugal, the son of George De Kay, an American sea-captain, and Catherine Colman, a young woman of Irish descent. His father returned to New York when his son was two and died when James was ten years of age; his mother died four years later. De Kay received his secondary education in Connecticut. He developed an early interest in natural history and in 1807, when not quite fifteen years of age, entered Yale College, from which he graduated in 1812.

In the summer of 1811 De Kay began the study of medicine with a physician in Guilford, Connecticut, or possibly in New York City, and from 1818 to 1819 he was enrolled at the University of Edinburgh, which granted him an M.D. in 1819. Returning to New York, De Kay spent little time with his medical practice but for several years gave serious consideration to a literary career; he was in fact much closer in outlook to writers and authors than he was to the scientific community for much of his life. In 1821 he married Janet Eckford, with whom he had at least three children.

De Kay was active as editor (1819–1830) and librarian (1826–1827) for the Lyceum of Natural History. He also served as recording secretary (1834–1836), corresponding secretary (1824–1836) and first vice president (1840–1846). He did much to develop that institution's collections and edited the first several volumes of its *Annals* (1825, 1828), to which he also contributed a number of papers on a wide range of zoological and geological subjects, giving particular attention to fossil animals. In addition, De Kay served as a curator of the Literary and Philosophical Society of New York in the mid-1820s. At various times, he contributed papers to the *American Journal of Science and Arts*, the *Transactions of the Albany Institute*, and the *Monthly American Journal of Geology and Natural Science* of Philadelphia.

In 1826 De Kay published his *Anniversary Address on the Progress of the Natural Sciences in the United States, Delivered before the Lyceum of Natural History of New York*, a useful summary of what had been accomplished by American natural historians to that time. This included some discussion of several of the federal exploring expeditions to the western United States.

In 1831 De Kay traveled to Turkey with his father-in-law, Henry Eckford, a marine architect and shipbuilder who had been invited to take charge of the sultan's navy yard at Constantinople. They traveled on a vessel that Eckford had built for the sultan, which was temporarily under the command of De Kay's younger brother, Commodore George De Kay of the U.S. Navy. Eckford died in Turkey the following year (1832), but prior to his return to New York, De Kay undertook a thorough study of Asiatic cholera.

De Kay responded quickly when asked to help treat patients during several outbreaks of cholera in the United States. Save for this emergency, however, De Kay continued to give most of his time to his natural history interests, rather than to medicine. He anonymously recorded his impressions of the Turkish nation and its people in *Sketches of Turkey by an American* (1833), which in its views concerning that country generally followed those held by several other knowledgeable Americans, including Commodore David D. Porter, the American minister, whom De Kay had met in Turkey.

In 1836 the New York Geological and Natural History Survey, "the oldest continuously functioning geological survey in the New World," was established by the state legislature. The legislature was responding in part to strong representations by the Lyceum of Natural History and several other organizations, which sought a statewide assessment of natural resources. There was a growing public interest in this subject, having particularly to do with coal. Offices for the survey were established in Albany, and De Kay was asked to take over as the agency's zoologist following the very brief tenure of another man who resigned to enter private business. De Kay's *Zoology of New York; or, The New York Fauna* (5 vols., 1842–1844) was a pioneering study that addressed both recent and fossil mammals, birds, reptiles, amphibians, fish, mollusks, and crustaceans. This was the second such set of state faunal accounts to appear, following a less elaborate set of volumes published by the state of Massachusetts. De Kay's work, which entailed a considerable amount of travel and research, was the most comprehensive put out by any state for some years and was a model effort for its time. Some 1,600 species of animals were identified and described, and common names were used as much as possible to facilitate use of the volumes by the general public.

Sections on mammals, birds, reptiles, and amphibia drafted by De Kay prior to his death were published in the *Catalogue of the Cabinet of Natural History of the State of New York and of the Historical and Antiquarian Collection Annexed Thereto* (1853). He died in Oyster Bay, Long Island, New York.

• There are no known manuscript collections attributable to De Kay. Lists of his papers on natural history are in Max Meisel, *A Bibliography of American Natural History: The Pioneer Century, 1769–1865*, vol. 2 (1926). Biographical information is in Clark A. Elliott, ed., *Biographical Dictionary of American Science: The Seventeenth through the Nineteenth Centuries* (1979). See also *American Journal of Science*, 2d ser., 13 (1852); and Arthur A. Socolow, ed., *The State Geological Surveys: A History* (1988). An obituary is in the *New York Herald*, 23 Nov. 1851.

KEIR B. STERLING

DE KOONING, Elaine (12 Mar. 1918–1 Feb. 1989), artist and critic, was born Elaine Marie Catherine Fried in Brooklyn, New York, the daughter of Charles Frank Fried, an accountant, and Mary Ellen O'Brien. She grew up in Brooklyn, and, encouraged by her mother, began to show a strong interest in art by the age of five. She attended Erasmus Hall High School, where she began her formal training in art. After a brief enrollment at Hunter College, Elaine Fried began to study at the Leonardo da Vinci Art School in Manhattan in 1937. A year later she switched to the American Artists School and, influenced by the political environment of the school, began to work in a social realist vein. Her artistic direction changed quickly, however, after she began private study with the Dutch-born painter Willem de Kooning, fourteen years her senior. He encouraged her to paint still lifes and to concentrate on formal problems such as the spatial relationships between objects. By 1939 Elaine Fried had begun to share Willem de Kooning's studio on West 22nd Street, and the two artists were married on 9 December 1943. During this period the couple participated in the vibrant life of the Chelsea artists' community.

Beginning in the mid-1940s, Elaine de Kooning began to concentrate on figure painting. In 1947–1948, under the influence of Willem, she turned briefly to abstract painting, producing some seventeen untitled abstractions in the summer of 1948 at Black Mountain College in North Carolina. She did not pursue this purely abstract direction, however, but returned to painting figures, embarking in the fall of 1948 on a series of energetically brushed paintings of baseball and basketball players in action, inspired by newspaper photographs. Although she again worked in a gestural abstract style in the mid-1950s, her primary commitment would be to figural painting for the rest of her career.

Despite her preference for figurative painting, de Kooning was an active participant in the social and intellectual activities of the abstract expressionists, frequenting the Cedar Street Tavern and the Eighth Street "Artists Club," where she regularly participated in panel discussions. She spent her summers with Willem in East Hampton, Long Island, a rural outpost of abstract expressionism. She also painted portraits of members of the abstract expressionist circle, including her husband, the critic Harold Rosenberg, critic and editor Thomas Hess, and poet and critic Frank O'Hara.

Perhaps de Kooning's most enduring contribution to the abstract expressionist movement was her art criticism, published in *Art News* from the late 1940s through the 1950s. Articles such as "Hans Hofmann Paints a Picture" (Feb. 1950), "David Smith Makes a Sculpture" (Sept. 1951), and "Vincente Paints a Collage" (Sept. 1953) remain important primary sources of information about the working methods of these abstractionists. But de Kooning also wrote on the work of figurative artists such as Edwin Dickinson (Sept. 1949) and Andrew Wyeth (Mar. 1950). Her widely read essay, "Subject: What, How, or Who?" (Apr. 1955) challenged the belief of writers like critic Clement Greenberg and painter Ad Reinhardt that abstract painting, in its "purity," was inherently superior to representational painting. She also published "Pure Paints a Picture" (Summer 1957), a brilliant satire of the popular *Art News* genre and a further attack, through subversive humor, on the Greenberg-Reinhardt position.

In 1956 de Kooning amicably separated from her husband. Her career followed its own path for the next two decades, before she reconciled with Willem in 1975, buying a house near his in East Hampton and building a new studio. In 1957–1958 de Kooning accepted a teaching position at the University of New Mexico, the first of seventeen visiting professorships she would hold over the next twenty-five years. She later recalled the impact of the experience of the southwestern scenery on her art: "The ruddy earth, the naked musculature of the Rockies, the brilliant colors of the sky behind them at twilight, the massive horizontality of the environment—it was all overpowering, and my painting responded" (Munro, p. 255). A trip to see the bullfights in Juárez, Mexico, inspired a series of dramatic bullfighting pictures, some of them wall-scale, that continued to occupy the artist after her return to New York.

In late 1962 de Kooning was commissioned to paint a portrait of President John F. Kennedy for the Truman Library in Independence, Missouri. She made studies of the president while he was vacationing in Palm Beach, Florida, in December 1962, and continued to work on images of Kennedy until, in her words, "the assassin dropped my brush" (Munro, p. 257). Traumatized by Kennedy's death, de Kooning stopped painting for about a year. During this time she turned instead to sculpture, executing fourteen bronzes while teaching at the University of California, Davis, in 1964. In the same year she was awarded an honorary doctor of fine arts degree by Western College in Oxford, Ohio, the first of five honorary doctorates she would receive over the next twenty-four years. On her return to New York, de Kooning resumed portrait work, painting her subjects in oil directly from life without the use of preliminary sketches, seeking, as she put it, "a spontaneous image that looked unstructured" (Munro, p. 260). Working in a loose, painterly style, she continued to paint both friends and strangers over the next decade.

In 1976 de Kooning began her series of vertical *Bacchus* paintings, drawings, and prints, based on a sculptural group of Dionysian revelers she had discovered in the Luxembourg Gardens in Paris. The *Bacchus* images, exuberant and sensuous evocations of flowing bodies ascending into the surrounding sky and treetops, are among the artist's most appealing. Another trip to France in 1983 to view the Paleolithic cave paintings at Lascaux, followed in 1984 by a trip to see more Paleolithic art in Altamira, Spain, inspired de Kooning's last major series, the *Cave Paintings*. In executing these works, she strongly identified with the prehistoric cave painters, whose immediate and powerful renditions of horses, deer, and bison showed, as she put it, an approach "much closer in spirit, in its directness to today's art than periods much closer to us" (Bledsoe, p. 41). De Kooning entered the hospital the day after the opening of her *Cave Paintings* show and died of lung cancer in Southampton, New York, three months later.

Although she participated energetically in the life of the New York avant-garde as a critic, and influenced students and artists around the country as a teacher and lecturer, Elaine de Kooning's first and last professional commitment was to her own art. Her paintings of athletes, her portraits, her *Bacchus* pictures, and her *Cave Paintings* represent a highly personal contribution to American art of the period 1948–1989, a contribution likely to receive increasing recognition as the status of figurative painting in postwar American art is reevaluated.

• Many of Elaine de Kooning's letters and other papers are in the Archives of American Art, Smithsonian Institution. Her memoirs, unpublished at her death, are under the editorship of her sister, Marjorie Luyckx. The major source on de Kooning's life and art is Jane K. Bledsoe, *Elaine de Kooning* (1992), an exhibition catalog that includes numerous reproductions of her works, an exhibition history, and a bibliography of her writings. Of interest is Lee Hall, *Elaine and Bill, Portrait of a Marriage: The Lives of Willem and Elaine de Kooning* (1993), though the book has been justly criticized for its numerous factual errors and questionable biographical interpretations. There is a detailed biography in *Current Biography Yearbook* (1982) and an autobiographical sketch in Eleanor Munro, *Originals: American Women Artists* (1979). An obituary is in the *New York Times*, 2 Feb. 1989.

DAVID CATEFORIS

DE KOVEN, James (19 Sept. 1831–19 Mar. 1879), Episcopal priest and educator, was born in Middletown, Connecticut, the son of Henry Louis De Koven, a banker, and Margaret Sebor. He grew up in a large and affluent family in Brooklyn Heights, New York, and at an early age showed exceptional intellectual ability. De Koven graduated from Columbia College in 1851 and the General Theological Seminary in 1854. While in seminary he helped form a "ragged school" for poor boys that met on Sundays.

De Koven emerged from seminary an advanced High Churchman, or ritualist, one of a small but growing group of Episcopalians who emphasized, in worship and doctrine, Anglicanism's Catholic as well as Protestant roots. This approach was based on High-Church principles, which—unlike the Low-Church faction, which focused on Scripture, and the Broad-Church party, which emphasized reason—stressed the importance of the sacraments and the episcopacy. The ritualists were inspired by the Oxford movement, which had begun in England in 1833 and which stressed Anglicanism's Catholic antecedents.

On being ordained deacon in 1854, De Koven traveled to Nashotah House, a twelve-year-old seminary in the wilderness twenty-eight miles west of Milwaukee, Wisconsin. There he taught church history and served as rector of the Church of St. John Chrysostom in nearby Delafield. The following year he was ordained priest, and in 1858 he founded St. John's Hall as a preparatory school for Nashotah. In 1859, its finances shaky in the aftermath of the panic of 1857, St. John's Hall united with Racine College. At twenty-eight De Koven became warden of the college, a post he held for the next two decades.

Under De Koven, Racine College, on Lake Michigan south of Milwaukee, became widely known for its high academic quality and ritualism. Chapel was held twice a day, evensong featured a vested choir, confession was available, and the daily Eucharist was celebrated for a time. De Koven was greatly beloved by students, providing for them a model of great learning, gracious manners, personal holiness, and extraordinary compassion. Racine College thrived under De Koven's leadership. At the time of the merger in 1859, there were 25 students; at the height of the college's success, there were 70 college students and 150 grammar students. He also helped establish several church institutions and parishes in the Racine area, including St. Luke's Hospital and Holy Innocents' Church.

A gifted orator, De Koven became known nationally for his eloquent efforts at three General Conventions of the Episcopal Church to defend ritualistic practices and teachings against critics who thought them dangerously close to the Roman Catholic faith. In 1871 he helped defeat an effort to prohibit such reverential acts in the celebration of Holy Communion as incense, crucifixes, processional crosses, altar candles, and eucharistic vestments. He also defended the teaching of the "Real Presence" of Christ in the Eucharist, showing it to be in harmony with thinking in the early Christian church and in the Church of England. De Koven became the acknowledged leader of what was now called the Anglo-Catholic movement in the Episcopal church.

At the general convention of 1874, despite a powerful effort by De Koven, a modest canon passed prohibiting several acts of adoration such as elevation of the elements in the Eucharist, the displaying of a crucifix in the church, and the use of incense. It was passed out of fear of schism and the desire to prevent actions implying belief in the "Real Presence" of Christ in the Eucharist. Anglo-Catholics dismissed its importance, and the measure was largely ignored until later repealed. In fact, by that time many measures designed by Anglo-Catholics to bring more beauty and reverence into Episcopal worship services were being accepted by the denomination at large. In 1877 De Koven stood virtually alone, however, in wishing to drop the word "Protestant" from the formal name of the church. A little more than a century later, that battle too would be won.

De Koven's "advanced" ideas and eloquent oratory prevented him from becoming a bishop. He was nominated five times and once elected, but he was refused confirmation by the Church Standing Committees. One of these defeats, which greatly saddened De Koven, was in his own diocese of Wisconsin. Opponents throughout the nation reviled him for condoning "papal abominations," although in fact he was openly critical of Roman Catholicism and was loyal to his church.

De Koven declined calls from two wealthy and prestigious eastern parishes in the late 1870s, choosing to remain at Racine College. He never married and devoted most of his prodigious energy to his institution and his church. Several of his sermons and speeches were published during his lifetime, and a book of sermons and a novel appeared posthumously.

While working to advance the "cathedral system" in his diocese to show the Catholic nature of Anglicanism by building cathedrals, De Koven died suddenly of a heart attack or stroke in Racine, Wisconsin. He left his fortune to Racine College. Episcopalians of all parties mourned the passing of a brilliant, holy, and courageous priest who had enriched the church with his pleas for more spiritual and reverent worship. In 1963 the Standing Liturgical Commission placed his name in the church calendar, noting that he "has left a permanent stamp upon the learning and piety of the Episcopal Church, through his reasoned and compelling defense of its Catholic heritage." That heritage is widely appreciated throughout the church and the entire Anglican Communion.

• De Koven's writings include *Sermons Preached on Various Occasions* (1880) and *Dorchester Polytechnic Academy: Dr. Neverasole, Principal* (1879). Thomas C. Reeves, ed., *James De Koven, Anglican Saint* (1978), includes excerpts from De Koven's writings. See also William C. Pope, *Life of the Reverend James De Koven, D.D., Sometime Warden of Racine College* (1899), and Frederick Cook Morehouse, *Some American Churchmen* (1892).

THOMAS C. REEVES

DE KOVEN, Reginald (3 Apr. 1859–16 Jan. 1920), composer and music critic, was born Henry Louis Reginald De Koven in Middletown, Connecticut, the son of Henry De Koven, a physician, and Charlotte LeRoy. At the age of eleven he went to Europe with his parents and, beginning in 1872, studied piano with Wilhelm Speidel at Stuttgart. His later studies included music theory with Dionys Pruckner (Stuttgart), light opera with Richard Genée and Franz von Suppé (Vienna) and Léo Delibes (Paris), and singing with Luigi Vannucci (Florence). In 1879, at the age of twenty, he earned a degree from Oxford University.

De Koven returned to the United States in 1882, and over the next three decades he was music critic for *Harper's Weekly*, the *New York World*, *Herald and Journal*, and the *Chicago Evening Post*. He wrote with authority on opera and operetta productions, concerts, and solo recitals; his critiques and opinions were generally highly regarded. In 1902 he established the Washington (D.C.) Philharmonic Orchestra, which he conducted during its first three seasons.

De Koven's output as a composer includes various short works for solo piano and a piano sonata, a suite for orchestra, ballet music, and two grand operas, *The Canterbury Pilgrims* (1917) and *Rip Van Winkle* (1920), which was completed just months before his death. He composed more than 200 songs, one of which, "Oh, Promise Me" (1890), became enormously successful as a song sung at weddings. Its popularity in this role lasted until well into the twentieth century and continues to be heard more than 100 years after its composition. The harmonic language of the song is richly chromatic in the manner of the late nineteenth-century German romantics, and the sturdy melodic line reaches a dramatic climax in the last phrase.

But it was as a composer of operettas that De Koven realized his greatest success. From 1887 to 1913 he produced a staggering twenty-six operettas, an average of one per year. Harry Smith was the librettist for most of these works. Many are set in exotic lands (exotic settings were especially popular with American theater audiences in the years around the turn of the century), and some took historical figures as their subject matter. His string of successes began with *The Begum* (1887) and *Don Quixote* (1889). These were followed by *Robin Hood* (1890), which featured "Oh Promise Me" and ran for 3,000 successive performances in Chicago. It was also popular in London, where it was retitled *Maid Marian*. There were other triumphs, but none matched the success of *Robin Hood*.

In the years after *Robin Hood*, De Koven produced *The Fencing Master* (1892), *The Algerian* and *The Knickerbockers* (both from 1893), *Rob Roy* (1894), *The Tzigane* (1895), *The Mandarin* (1896), *The Paris Doll* and *The Highwayman* (both from 1897), *The Three Dragoons*, *Papa's Wife*, and *The Man in the Moon* (all from 1899; the last in collaboration with Ludwig Englander), *Foxy Quiller* (1900), *Broadway to Tokyo* (1900, in collaboration with A. B. Sloane), *The Little Duchess* (1901), *The Red Feather* (1903), *The Jersey Lilly* (1903, in collaboration with W. Jerome and J. Schwartz), *Happy Land* (1905), *The Student King* (1906), *The Golden Butterfly* and *The Girls of Holland* (both from 1907), *The Beauty Spot* (1909), *The Wedding Trip* (1911), and *Her Little Highness* (1913). Broadly speaking, these works reveal a musical style that occupies a sort of middle ground between the elevated style, for example, of Verdi and Bellini, and the more colloquial musical language of songs from vaudeville and related genres.

In 1884 De Koven married Anna Farwell, an author and translator. Her book, *A Musician and His Wife* (1926), contains a good biographical profile of De Koven. De Koven was elected to the National Institute of Arts and Letters in 1898. He died in Chicago.

• For more information on De Koven, see J. W. Stedman, "Then Hey! For the Greenwood: Smith, DeKoven and Robin Hood," *Journal of Popular Culture* 12 (1978–1979): 432, and the entry by Ronald L. Byrnside in *Groves Dictionary of Music and Musicians*, 6th ed. (1980). An obituary is in the *New York Times*, 17 Jan. 1920.

RONALD BYRNSIDE

DE KRUIF, Paul Henry (2 Mar. 1890–28 Feb. 1971), bacteriologist and writer, was born in Zeeland, Michigan, the son of Hendrik de Kruif, a farm-equipment dealer, and Hendrika Kremer. As an undergraduate at the University of Michigan, he read an article about Paul Ehrlich, the German bacteriologist and Nobel laureate, which he credited with inspiring him to become a "microbe hunter." He received his B.S. degree in 1912 and remained at Michigan as a Rockefeller research fellow, working with Frederick G. Novy; after earning his doctorate, de Kruif was appointed assistant professor of bacteriology in 1916. He had married, and he and his wife, Mary, had two sons.

De Kruif's promising academic career was redirected by two events in 1917–1918. World War I sent the young researcher to France with the U.S. Sanitary Corps, to work on the analysis of the gas gangrene bacillus and develop a prophylactic serum. Returning to Michigan, he fell in love with a young laboratory assistant, Rhea Elizabeth Barbarin, and decided to divorce his first wife and marry Barbarin. De Kruif's need of additional income, to support two households, and his war experiences drove him to seek an audience for his belief in the pure rationality of science and the need to support scientific research and to ensure its freedom from materialism and commercialism.

De Kruif's work on hemolytic streptococcus attracted the attention of Donald D. VanSlyke, who encouraged him to apply for a research position at the Rockefeller Institute in New York. There from 1920 to 1922 de Kruif studied pulmonary infections; he was one of the first to differentiate between the "rough" and "smooth" colonies of Salmonella bacteria. He was also attracted to New York's literary scene, meeting authors and critics and falling under the influence of men such as H. L. Mencken. Encouraged by these new friends to express his personal views, and anxious to earn more money, de Kruif began writing.

One of de Kruif's first endeavors was a series of articles on modern medicine that appeared in the *Century* magazine in 1922 and were later published as *Our Medicine Men* (1922). These essays, signed "M.D.," described a profession corrupted by commercialism and easily swayed by fads and irrational cults; they included colorful and easily recognizable descriptions of several Rockefeller scientists. The identity of the author was an open secret, and on 1 September 1922 de Kruif was asked to resign by Simon Flexner, director of the Rockefeller. Although many, including de Kruif himself, believed that he had been fired for his outspoken criticisms, Flexner told colleagues that the young author's true error was that he had not signed his own name to the articles, attacking the Rockefeller and the medical profession anonymously.

De Kruif was now on his own. Having borrowed the money to secure a divorce, he married Rhea in December 1922 (they would have no children) and embarked on a literary collaboration. Just after leaving the Rockefeller, he had met Sinclair Lewis, who was looking for a modern hero for his next novel. Lewis was inspired by his talks with de Kruif to choose a medical researcher seeking truth in a world of materialism and personal ambition. The product of their turbulent two-year association, which included trips to Europe and the Caribbean, was *Arrowsmith* (1925). De Kruif's personal philosophy and devastating caricatures of former colleagues at the Rockefeller are prominent features of the novel; several of his targets believed the book to be his personal revenge on the institute. Although Lewis acknowledged de Kruif's assistance in the novel's preface, the scientist never felt his contribution had been sufficiently recognized.

De Kruif achieved international fame, however, with *The Microbe Hunters* (1926), a colorful, dramatic, and well-researched account of the lives and work of fourteen pioneers in the field of bacteriology, including Louis Pasteur, Robert Koch, and Paul Ehrlich. A generation of scientists attributed their first interest in the field to reading *Microbe Hunters*. Many of de Kruif's subsequent books continued his theme of the heroic, honest scientist struggling against ignorance, hypocrisy, and greed, as well as against pathogens and poor hygiene, to improve human welfare; these included *The Hunger Fighters* (1928), *Men against Death* (1932), *The Fight for Life* (1938), *The Male Hormone* (1945), *Life among the Doctors* (1949), *Man against Insanity* (1957), and the play *Yellow Jack* (written with Sidney Howard, 1934). In other works, less well received, he criticized the failures of American government and the medical and public health professions to provide adequate nutrition and health care for all citizens; *Why Keep Them Alive?* (1936), *Health Is Wealth* (1940), and *Kaiser Wakes the Doctors* (1943), embody aspects of these themes. In addition, de Kruif wrote many articles for *Reader's Digest* and other magazines on current research and new treatments.

De Kruif's work is characterized by an engaging, informal style, strong opinions and biases, and an ability to turn medical history into melodrama. Many scientists and physicians praised him for popularizing medical research and framing it as a moral endeavor; others criticized his sensationalism and his enthusiasm for some unproven therapies, such as lobotomy in mental illness and testosterone treatment.

In the 1930s de Kruif served as a consultant to state and city public health programs in the Midwest. He assisted in introducing an early treatment program for syphilis in Chicago and led a drive for increased funding for tuberculosis prevention in Detroit. In 1935 he was asked to join the research advisory committee of the President's Birthday Ball Commission, later (1938) incorporated as the National Foundation for Infantile Paralysis. De Kruif significantly influenced this body's early research initiatives and staff appointments; in 1941, however, a disagreement with other committee members over the funding of a program in nutrition research led to de Kruif's angry resignation. During World War II he was a congressional consultant on war-related medical issues.

De Kruif's last book was his dramatic and opinionated autobiography, *The Sweeping Wind* (1962), a tribute to his wife Rhea. As frankly critical of himself as he had often been of others, de Kruif begins the book by describing his first meeting with Rhea and ends with her death from cancer in 1957. He married again in 1959 to Eleanor Lappage. He was physically active for most of his life, enjoying walking, running, and swimming. Music, particularly Beethoven, was another of his passions. He died in Holland, Michigan, of a heart attack following a series of minor strokes.

• The main source for de Kruif's life is *The Sweeping Wind*. De Kruif papers are held by the Holland Historical Trust in the Netherlands Museum in Holland, Mich. Some material on de Kruif is at the Rockefeller Archive Center, Pocantico Hills, New York, and at the Rockefeller University Archives in New York City; in several collections at the Bentley Historical Library at the University of Michigan, Ann Arbor; and in the Simon Flexner Papers at the American Philosophical Society, Philadelphia. Saul Benison's oral history, *Tom Rivers: A Life in Medicine and Science* (1967), contains interesting information about de Kruif's work with the National Foundation for Infantile Paralysis. Charles Rosenberg's "Martin Arrowsmith: The Scientist as Hero," *American Quarterly* 15 (1963): 447–58 (repr. in Rosenberg, *No Other Gods: On Science and American Social Thought* [1976]), is a solid account of the de Kruif–Lewis collaboration. Albert Q. Maisel's "Fighter for the Right to Live," *Reader's Digest* 49 (Dec. 1946): 91–96 and 50 (Jan. 1947): 43–49, is a laudatory article published at the height of de Kruif's career. An obituary is in the *New York Times*, 2 Mar. 1971.

DANIEL M. FOX
MARCIA L. MELDRUM

DELAFIELD, Edward (7 May 1794–13 Feb. 1875), physician, was born in New York City, the son of John Delafield, a merchant, and Ann Hallett. He earned a bachelor's degree from Yale College in 1812. Delafield chose medicine as a profession and was apprenticed to Samuel Barrowe of Philadelphia while he took the course of instruction at the College of Physicians and Surgeons. After Delafield received his medical degree in 1816, he returned to New York to serve at New York Hospital. He traveled to Europe and spent much of 1817 studying with Astley Cooper and John Abernethy in London. In 1821 Delafield married Elina E. Langdon Elwin (some sources say Eliva Elwyn); they had six children.

On his return to the United States in 1820, Delafield joined John Kearney Rodgers in founding the New York Eye and Ear Infirmary. Both Delafield and Rodgers had studied at the London Eye Infirmary and modeled their institution after it. This was the second eye hospital in the United States, preceded only by Elisha North's infirmary in New London, Connecticut, founded three years earlier. The New York Eye and Ear Infirmary had its first home in two rooms on the second floor of a building on Chatham Street. Delafield served as attending surgeon there for thirty years and was subsequently elected consulting surgeon and vice president. His efforts in treating eye diseases brought him wide recognition as a pioneer American ophthalmologist, although he did not limit himself to that specialty.

In 1825 Delafield was made professor of obstetrics and diseases of women and children at the College of Physicians and Surgeons, a position he kept until 1838, when his extensive private practice required his resignation. In 1834 he was appointed one of the attending physicians of the New York Hospital. His wife having died, in 1839 he married Julia Floyd. Delafield was elected president of the College of Physicians of Surgeons in 1858, and he also became a member of the board of governors of Roosevelt Hospital.

By 1864 the handful of ophthalmologists practicing in America felt the need for a more direct exchange of ideas and experiences. Delafield, with Henry Drury

Noyes, a Dr. Bumstead of New York, and Haskett Derby of Boston, founded the American Ophthalmological Society in that year. Delafield was unanimously elected the first president of this organization, serving from 1864 to 1868.

Delafield was highly regarded as a teacher, described as "quiet, clear, methodical in his views; terse, elegant, and distinct in his mode of expressing them. No man more completely held the attention of his class, as in his earnest, dignified, and effective manner he laid before them the truths of medicine, and the great responsibilities involved in the practice of their noble calling" (Williams and Dix, p. 340).

Delafield edited the American edition of Benjamin Travers's *A Synopsis of Diseases of the Eye* (1825), the second book on the subject published in America. It contained numerous additions drawn from Delafield's own practice. In addition, he wrote numerous articles on ophthalmic surgery over a thirty-year period. Samuel W. Francis noted that if these were "collected in one volume [they] would bring before the community a work eminently calculated to ameliorate the condition of the blind and unfold suggestions of permanent utility to the oculist" (pp. 510–11).

Delafield also gained an outstanding reputation in pediatrics and obstetrics and was noted for his philanthropic efforts. The New York Eye and Ear Infirmary was a charitable institution where physicians donated their time. By 1866 7,000 patients a year were treated without charge. The institution served as a model for the founding of the Massachusetts Charitable Eye and Ear Infirmary in Boston and the Wills Eye Hospital in Philadelphia.

Delafield also established the Society for the Relief of Widows and Orphans of Medical Men, modeled after a London society; the charter was accepted in 1842. Delafield served as its president from 1842 until 1850. Through donations from benefactors, annual subscribers, and members for life, laymen as well as physicians, a fund was established to provide annuities for the widows and children of physicians. Delafield died in New York City.

• A biographical sketch of Delafield is Samuel W. Francis, "Biographical Sketches of Distinguished Living New York Physicians: XI, Edward Delafield," *Medical and Surgical Reporter* 15 (1866): 509. His obituary, written by Henry Willard Williams and John Dix, appeared in *Transactions of the American Ophthalmological Society* 2 (1873–1878): 339–41; a report of a tribute paid to Delafield in recognition of his philanthropic activities appeared in the *Medical Record* (1875): 215.

DANIEL MYRON ALBERT

DELAFIELD, Francis (3 Aug. 1841–17 July 1915), physician, was born in New York City, the son of Edward Delafield, a physician, and Julia Floyd. After graduating from Yale University (A.B., 1860), he entered the College of Physicians and Surgeons in New York and was awarded the M.D. in 1863. He then went to Europe to continue his studies and was strongly influenced by the theories of Rudolf Virchow, author of *Cellularpathologie* (1858), who showed that disease was understandable through cell theory. Virchow, at the pathological institute in Berlin, emphasized the postmortem examination as a procedure for obtaining new findings on the nature of disease and its effects on human organs.

Delafield studied in Paris, London, and Berlin and returned to the United States in 1865, having decided to devote his career to the practice of internal medicine, teaching, and research in pathology. In 1866 he was appointed curator at Bellevue Hospital with responsibilities for pathology and museum work. Delafield married Katherine Van Rensselaer in 1870; the couple had three children. In 1871 he was named first attending pathologist at Roosevelt Hospital. At the College of Physicians and Surgeons, Delafield was adjunct lecturer in pathology and the practice of medicine in 1875 and adjunct professor in 1876; from 1882 to 1891 he was professor of pathology at the college. He became a visiting physician at Bellevue Hospital in 1875 and was also on the staff of the New York Eye and Ear Infirmary and a consulting physician at St. Luke's Hospital.

From the beginning of his career Delafield gave many hours to work in hospital morgues, and he soon became recognized as an authority in pathology and clinical diagnosis. Esmond R. Long, in his *History of American Pathology*, writes that he "was New York's first laboratory clinician, distinguished for his combination of the old time clinical diagnosis, made by the five senses, with the inductive processes of the laboratory" (p. 137). Through his painstaking examinations of pathological tissues, which he compared with the clinical reports on the patient, he was able to study and classify a number of diseases that had not previously been precisely identified. For example, he was one of the first physicians to distinguish between acute lobar pneumonia and bronchopneumonia; he is also noted for clinical and pathological studies of nephritis, tuberculosis, pyemia, and diseases of the colon.

When Delafield joined the staff at the College of Physicians and Surgeons, pathology was not a separate department of medicine, but some physicians believed that it should be separate because of its importance in diagnosis and precise "cause of death" information. In 1877, when some of the alumni of the school raised $10,000 "for advancing the standard of medicine," Delafield successfully urged its use for the establishment of a histological and pathological laboratory at the college. He was its director from 1877 to 1882.

From his laboratory work and his years of postmortem examinations, Delafield wrote nearly a hundred scientific papers and books that were authoritative sources in pathology. His *Handbook of Post-Mortem Examinations and Morbid Anatomy* (1872) has been described as "the first significant book of its kind in America since Gross's [1839] *Elements of Pathological Anatomy*." It was later revised and enlarged with T. Mitchell Prudden in 1885; retitled *Text Book of Pathology*, it went through twelve editions and was the standard textbook for the great majority of American medical schools. Other major Delafield works were

Studies in Pathological Anatomy, published from 1878 to 1891, and *Manual of Physical Diagnosis* (1878), with Charles F. Stillman. Delafield also contributed important parts to other books, such as "Diseases of the Kidneys" in *Twentieth Century Practice* (1895) and "Pyaemia and Allied Conditions" in *The International Encyclopedia of Surgery* (1881).

The broad influence of Delafield as a writer was matched by his effectiveness as a teacher. In this vocation his subject matter came from his own research and not from other accounts. Students, including William H. Welch, who went on to organize the Department of Pathology at Johns Hopkins University, and Charles Norris, and associates alike knew that Delafield's conclusions were the result of "unwavering intellectual honesty" and that "he always taught the medicine of Delafield and not the medicine of the library." When he retired from professional duties in 1901 because of a decision he had made early in his life, it was against the wishes of all of his fellow teachers.

Along with such noted American physicians as William Osler, James Tyson, and William Pepper, in 1886 Delafield participated in the founding of the Association of American Physicians and became its first president. He was also a member of various local, state, and national medical societies and a member of the Century and Yale clubs. He died in Noroton, Connecticut.

Francis Delafield's contributions to American medicine were extraordinary; in his lifetime he was the leading authority in pathology and clinical diagnosis, and his writings were of enormous importance in disseminating his discoveries in a new medical specialization. His biographer Walter B. James wrote, "there can be no doubt that the clinical and pathological labors of Delafield constitute one of the important foundation stones upon which modern medicine rests."

• Numerous references to Delafield and his work are in Esmond R. Long, *A History of American Pathology* (1962). Other biographical accounts include those of Walter B. James in *Dictionary of American Medical Biography*, ed. Howard A. Kelly and Walter L. Burrage (1928), and Theodore C. Janeway, "Dr. Francis Delafield. In Memoriam," *Medical Record*, Nov. 1915, p. 929. An obituary is in the *New York Medical Journal*, 24 July 1915, pp. 202–3.

ROBERT F. ERICKSON

DELAFIELD, John (16 Mar. 1748–3 July 1824), merchant and underwriter, was born in Aylesbury, Bucks, England, the son of John Delafield, a cheese merchant, and Martha Dell. Most historians claim John Delafield accumulated considerable property in England as a young brewer from an ancient, distinguished family. Though obviously a man of means by American standards, Delafield may not have been as well off as supposed and could have moved to the newly independent United States at age thirty-five to better his business prospects. Delafield arrived in British-occupied New York City on 4 April 1783, bearing the first copy of the provisional treaty of peace to reach the new

republic. He immediately joined the Chamber of Commerce and started a mercantile, insurance, financial brokerage, and real estate business. He was so successful that he was soon one of the richest men in New York and was able to retire from active mercantile pursuits in 1798, though he continued in marine insurance.

The immigrant struggled somewhat during his first few years in New York, however, partly because revolution had devastated the economy of his adopted land. Delafield bought and sold jarred goods, butter, soap, wine, tea, and imported dry goods on his own account and sold others' wares on consignment. His frantic searching for good bills of exchange drawn on London to pay for these imports suggests that he did not have money or other liquid forms of wealth in England on which to draw. His early letters also mention some small debts he still owed in London.

The Englishman did all he could to invigorate New York's nascent money market. Despite his somewhat strapped circumstances, Delafield speculated in many of the paper securities of the American Revolution, including Morris's, Hillegas's, Pierce's, Barber's, and Pickering's notes, Virginia land warrants, and New Jersey certificates. Unlike many of his competitors, the newcomer was not shy about accepting the many types of paper securities in payment for goods and advertised this fact widely. It seems he used his regular mercantile trade to keep the brokerage side of his business well supplied with securities. He resold some of these securities to speculators, hypothecated others for loans, and used others to purchase confiscated estates and other lands. Delafield came to own large tracts in northern New York and elsewhere. He owned some $321,620 worth of securities, most of which he had obtained at a fraction of their face value, when they were finally funded during George Washington's first administration. Early on Delafield also acted as a banker-broker for those seeking specie in New York's ravaged money market. He used the Bank of New York (est. 1784), in which he owned two shares, to maintain his own liquidity while engaging in these extensive and risky operations. He also had an account with New York state's loan office. Delafield's correspondents included important capitalists Daniel Ludlow, William Constable, John Holker, and Daniel Parker.

The transplanted Englishman also delved into marine insurance. After some underwriting on his own account, he became an original director of the Mutual Assurance Company of New York in 1787 and was later president of the United Insurance Company. He also continued to underwrite on his own account and allegedly assumed some personal responsibility for his company's losses. In any event, foreign depredations on U.S. commerce during the Napoleonic Wars greatly depleted his resources. Though he did not fail, he was forced to press mortgage holders in Steuben County and elsewhere. The losses also forced him to assert claims on $12,128.12 of disputed loan office certificates he owned. Delafield's petition to Congress for funding of these securities led to several House reports and at least two abortive bills.

In 1789 Delafield was a steward in the fraternal organization St. George's Society. In 1792 he was involved in the Tontine association, a special survivorship insurance scheme. That same year he became a director in the New York branch of the Bank of the United States but served only one year. In 1821 Delafield may have served as treasurer of the New York Eye Infirmary under president William Few. In the early 1820s Delafield, along with bankers Charles Wilkes and Oliver Kane, may have owned an interest in the Ohio Land Company. These later activities are uncertain because by this time John, Jr., one of Delafield's sons, was quite active but rarely was clearly distinguished from his father. Part of the confusion may have been caused by the fact that Delafield's father was also named John, making it unclear why his son was sometimes referred to as a junior and not as the third.

In any event, Delafield raised a large and prominent family. He and his wife Ann Hallet, daughter of revolutionary officer Joseph Hallet and Elizabeth Hazard, had eleven children. The large brood resided in "Sunswick," a mansion on Long Island directly across the river from Manhattan, the site of many a genteel gathering. John Delafield, Jr., was his most famous offspring. After a stint of private banking in England during the War of 1812, John, Jr., returned to New York where he later became president of the Phoenix Bank (chartered 1817). Delafield died in New York City. Besides his large and successful family, Delafield was important because he brought much financial expertise and business leadership to the new republic at a time when it was desperately needed.

• The John Delafield Letterbook, 1783–1785, at the New York Public Library contains a wealth of information on Delafield's early business practices in this country, along with a few tantalizing tidbits concerning his personal and family relations. Some of Delafield's dealings with the Bank of New York and the New York branch of the Bank of the United States can be followed in the James O. Wettereau Papers at Columbia University. Record of his loan office account is in the Gerrit Lansing Papers at the New York State Library in Albany. His early advertisements are in the *New York Independent Journal*. For general treatments see Lyman Horace Weeks, ed., *Prominent Families of New York* (1897), and Margherita Hamm, *Famous Families of New York* (1902). Alfred Young, *The Democratic Republicans of New York: The Origins, 1763–1797* (1967), is the source claiming Delafield owned more than $300,000 of securities. Dixon Ryan Fox, *The Decline of Aristocracy in the Politics of New York* (1919), mentions Delafield's upstate land holdings, as do advertisements. For Delafield's Steuben County mortgages, see the *New York Herald*, 17 Apr. 1811. For Delafield's loan office certificate claims, see House Committee on Pensions and Revolutionary Claims, *Report on the Petition of John Delafield*, 15th Cong., 20 Mar. 1818. Delafield's activities in the 1820s can be followed in the *New York Spectator*, 24 Apr. 1821 and 25 Feb. 1823. Edward Pessen, *Riches, Class, and Power before the Civil War* (1973), may conflate this essay's

subject with his son of the same name, which is easy to do after 1815, because primary sources rarely clearly differentiate between the two.

ROBERT E. WRIGHT

DELAFIELD, John (22 Jan. 1786–22 Oct. 1853), merchant, banker, and farmer, was born in New York City, the son of John Delafield, a merchant, and Ann Hallett. The younger Delafield grew up in the city and on his father's summer residence, "Sunwick," on the East River, opposite Blackwell's Island. Because of his father's success in the merchant trade, Delafield enjoyed every privilege in his youth and attended Columbia College. Upon his graduation in 1802, he set out at once in his father's footsteps by becoming a confidential agent and supercargo aboard a merchant vessel.

Delafield's early employment appears to have been appropriate to his nature and his aptitudes; he soon came to own a ship of his own and to conduct merchant voyages on his own account. In the course of one of these voyages, he was forced by bad weather into the harbor of Corunna, Spain, a town that was under siege by Napoleonic armies during the Peninsular War. Coming under fire from French artillery on the night of 17 January 1808, Delafield had the ship's cable cut, and he left the harbor with both his crew and a number of Spanish notables. Delafield brought his ship, crew, and cargo safely to London, where he decided to remain for a time. He set himself up as a merchant banker in London and appears to have enjoyed commercial success during the years 1808–1810.

The onset of the War of 1812 brought peril to Delafield's situation. Bad feelings against Americans ran high in England, and, as a prosperous merchant Yankee, he was doubly suspect. He was nominally designated as a prisoner, but the influence of his English relatives (his father had emigrated from England in 1783) prevailed upon the government to treat him well. Delafield was allowed liberty of movement in a fifteen-mile radius of his country estate at Uxbridge, and he was granted the freedom of the city of London as well. In all, it was a genteel captivity, one that may have tried Delafield's patience but that did not hinder his business or personal affairs.

Delafield endured the lean business years of the War of 1812 and then prospered for several years afterward. In 1818 or 1819 he suffered financial reverses that were common in those years; in the United States the phenomenon was referred to as the panic of 1819. Sometime before 1819 Delafield had met and married an Englishwoman, Mary Roberts of Whitechurch, Buckshire. She was the first cousin of the American writer Washington Irving, who in 1819–1820 published his first bestselling book, *The Sketch Book of Geoffrey Crayon, Gent.* The fourth tale in the anthology, called "The Wife," may have related directly to Delafield. The protagonist of the sketch, Leslie, had lost his fortune and was extremely concerned that his wife would not be able to bear the news. Convinced by the narrator of the story that he should take the risk,

Leslie did so and was rewarded by a fuller, more complete harmony and understanding between him and his wife. Although the *Sketch Book* does not refer to Delafield by name, it is known that he and Irving were at least acquainted, and some scholars have suggested that Delafield either was the model for the protagonist or that Irving was inspired by Delafield's circumstances to write the story.

In 1820 Delafield returned to New York City. He became the cashier and the president of the Phoenix Bank, serving in that capacity from 1820 to 1838. In the latter year he became president of the New York Banking Company; again, his timing was unfortunate. The panic of 1837 hit hard soon after he took office, and for the second time in his life Delafield lost most of his fortune. He left New York City and purchased a farm he called "Oaklands" near Geneva in upstate New York. Within a few years he had turned his farm into a model, paying close attention to crop rotation, soil analysis, and other aspects of the science of agriculture. He became president of the New York State Agricultural Society.

Before he retired from banking, Delafield had been an active sponsor of New York City's cultural life. He raised funds for the University of the City of New York and played a role in the revival of the city's historical society. He was also a prominent member of the New York Philharmonic Society. Delafield had married a second time, to Harriet Wadsworth Tallmadge. He died at Geneva, New York.

Delafield's career was noteworthy but not spectacular. In some respects, he resembled the model farmer and citizen that Thomas Jefferson admired, a man who could be equally at home in the affairs of business, the world of letters, and the bucolic pursuits of plow and harvest. There was nothing rash or precipitate in his makeup; he appears to have been a man of science and system. Raised in comfortable economic circumstances, he endured the trials of losing two fortunes in his lifetime with a certain equanimity. In spite of his forward-looking and progressive spirit in business, banking, and farming, he appears to have belonged to the era of early American enterprise, in particular to the exciting years at the start of the nineteenth century when American ships were plying the Atlantic Ocean during the Napoleonic wars. His generous spirit and eclectic interests belong more closely to the age of Jefferson than to that of either Andrew Jackson or James K. Polk.

• Very little information has been found on Delafield's life and career. A sketch is in *Appleton's Cyclopedia of American Biography*, and his agricultural activities are described in *Transactions of the New York State Agricultural Society* (1847), p. 200. Further information can be found in Margherita Arlina Hamm, *Famous Families of N.Y.* (1902), and John Matthews, ed., *Matthews Am. Armory and Blue Book* (1901). Delafield's connection with Washington Irving is more fully explored in Ralph M. Alderman et al., eds., *Washington Irving, Letters*, vol. 1: *1802–1823*. An obituary is in the *New York Times*, 25 Oct. 1853.

SAMUEL WILLARD CROMPTON

DELAFIELD, Richard (1 Sept. 1798–5 Nov. 1873), army officer, was born in New York City, the son of John Delafield, a prominent merchant, and Ann Hallett. Delafield entered the U.S. Military Academy in 1814 and graduated at the head of the class of 1818. Commissioned a second lieutenant in the army Corps of Engineers, he served first as astronomical and topographical draftsman on the government commission established under the Treaty of Ghent for surveying the United States–Canada border. From 1819 to 1824 he worked as assistant engineer on fortification projects for the defense of Hampton Roads, Virginia, a key part of the army's system of seacoast defense launched in the aftermath of the War of 1812. For the next eight years, Delafield was stationed in the Mississippi Valley, where he supervised fortifications at Plaquemine Bend below New Orleans, oversaw navigational improvements on the Mississippi and Ohio rivers, and briefly served on loan as engineer of the New Orleans Canal and Banking Company. From 1832 to 1838 he directed construction of the eastern portion of the Cumberland Road as well as fortification and harbor projects on Delaware Bay. In July 1824 he married Helen Summers, who died four months later. In 1833 he married Harriet B. Covington, with whom he had eight children.

Delafield moved gradually up the promotion ladder, reaching the rank of major of engineers in July 1838. Later that year he replaced Major René E. De Russy as superintendent of the U.S. Military Academy. Believing DeRussy to have been lax in his administration, the new superintendent strove vigorously to tighten discipline among the cadets and required the senior faculty to devote more time to classroom teaching—moves that did not make him a popular leader. He also pushed architectural and programmatic improvements, including construction of a new library building and the introduction of riding instruction. Delafield left West Point in 1845, and for the next ten years he was primarily engaged in fortification duty in New York Harbor. As a member of the army's Board of Engineers for Fortification, he staunchly supported the engineers' increasingly controversial program, disparaging the argument that technological innovations, such as steam-powered naval vessels armed with rifled shell guns, rendered large masonry fortresses obsolete. Delafield also worked on civilian harbor and river improvements, and in 1853–1854 he served as chief engineer of the Department of Texas.

Early in 1855 Secretary of War Jefferson Davis selected Delafield to head a board of officers, including Major Alfred Mordecai of the Ordnance Department and Captain George B. McClellan of the cavalry, to observe the conduct of the Crimean War and report generally on the military art in Europe. French and Russian security restrictions prevented the group from reaching the Crimea before active operations had ended. Nevertheless, the officers carefully examined the battlefields with the aid of British officers, and they toured a wide variety of military installations in Russia, Germany, the Austrian Empire, France, Belgium, and Great Britain. On their return in April 1856, the members set about compiling reports on their specialties, which were eventually published by order of Congress. Delafield's large and elegantly illustrated volume appeared in 1860 and emphasized fortification and the conduct of the siege of Sevastopol, but it also included information on a range of other topics related to the "art of war," including small arms, gun carriages, the design of barracks and hospitals, and military schools. The Delafield board was the most ambitious American military mission to Europe during the antebellum era. Early in the Civil War, the Union government tried to suppress circulation of Delafield's report, lest the Confederates use its detailed drawings and data to design their own fortifications.

In September 1856 Delafield began a second tour of duty as superintendent of West Point. The dominant issue of his administration was a debate over the five-year program, introduced in 1854 to expand the coverage of liberal arts and military subjects in the traditionally technical curriculum. Cadets complained about the extra year of schooling, and the faculty gradually became disillusioned; in 1861, after the outbreak of the Civil War, the government ordered a return to the four-year program. As superintendent, Delafield also contended with the impact of the deepening sectional crisis on the corps of cadets. In January 1861 Captain Pierre G. T. Beauregard replaced him as head of the academy. However, the War Department, concerned about the secession of Beauregard's home state of Louisiana, reversed the appointment five days later, and Delafield continued to administer the school until early March.

Too old for vigorous field duty, Delafield served early in the Civil War on the staff of Governor Edwin D. Morgan of New York, advising the state government on the mobilization of its volunteers. From 1861 to 1864 his primary assignment was the supervision of coast defenses in New York Harbor. Delafield reached the rank of colonel in 1863 and, on the death of Chief Engineer Joseph G. Totten in April 1864, was promoted to brigadier general and chief engineer. He administered the central office of the Corps of Engineers until his mandatory retirement, at the rank of brevet major general, in August 1866. In his later years, Delafield served as a regent of the Smithsonian Institution, and he died in Washington, D.C. A consummate military professional, Delafield supported the development of formal military education during his nearly twelve years as superintendent of West Point, and his fortification work and European mission contributed to the army's increasingly scientific approach to the problem of national defense.

• A collection of Delafield's personal papers, the superintendent's letterbooks, and other records relating to his superintendency of West Point are preserved at the U.S. Military Academy Library, West Point, N.Y. A small collection of his papers, consisting mainly of accounts, is at the New-York Historical Society (New York City). Delafield's Crimean War report is *Report on the Art of War in Europe in 1854, 1855, & 1856*, 36th Cong., 1st sess., 1860, S. Exec. Doc. 60. His re-

ports on other subjects are also printed in the congressional serial set. For his views on fortification, see "Letter from the Secretary of War in Reference to Fortifications," 32d Cong., 1st sess., 1851, H. Exec. Doc. 5, pp. 234–49. For his annual reports as chief engineer, see *Annual Report of the Secretary of War*, 38th Cong., 2d sess., 1864, H. Exec. Doc. 1, pp. 29–43; and *Report of the Secretary of War*, 39th Cong., 1st sess., 1865, H. Exec. Doc. 1, pp. 913–27. Delafield's career is summarized in George W. Cullum, *Biographical Register of the Officers and Graduates of the U.S. Military Academy at West Point, N.Y., from Its Establishment in 1802, to 1890* (1891). For a biographical sketch and information on his family background, see John R. Delafield, *Delafield: The Family History* (1945). See also James L. Morrison, Jr., *"The Best School in the World": West Point, the Pre–Civil War Years* (1986); and George S. Pappas, *To the Point: The United States Military Academy, 1802–1902* (1993).

WILLIAM B. SKELTON

DE LAGUNA, Grace Mead (28 Sept. 1878–17 Feb. 1978), philosopher, was born Grace Mead Andrus in East Berlin, Connecticut, the daughter of Wallace R. Andrus, a soldier and accountant, and Annis Mead, a schoolteacher. De Laguna received a pioneer upbringing. In 1883, when she was about four years old, the family moved to Cheney in what is now eastern Washington State (then part of the Oregon Territory), where she attended a small school. They later moved to Tacoma, where de Laguna went to high school.

Determined to study philosophy in the East, de Laguna spent four years at the Tacoma Normal School and taught in the high school in order to save money for college. When she obtained a scholarship to study at Cornell University, she was on her way to receiving the excellent higher education she wanted. At Cornell she earned a bachelor of arts in 1903 and a doctorate in philosophy in 1906 with the thesis, "The Relation of the Mechanical Theory to Rationalism, with Special Reference to the Systems of Descartes, Spinoza, and Leibniz."

In 1905 Grace married Theodore de Leo de Laguna, also a Cornell Ph.D. and philosopher, and she accompanied him to Bryn Mawr College in Bryn Mawr, Pennsylvania, in 1907. They had two children.

De Laguna received her own appointments in the Bryn Mawr College Department of Philosophy as successively associate (1911) and full professor (1929). In 1944 she became professor emerita until her death. She had succeeded her husband as departmental chairperson when he unexpectedly died in 1930. The entire academic career that made her a well-known American philosopher developed at Bryn Mawr. De Laguna died at a nursing home in Devon, Pennsylvania.

De Laguna published a large collection of monographs, essays, articles, and discussions that earned her a wide reputation in philosophical circles, and she kept up a lively correspondence with a large number of philosophers and other academic professionals in various countries for many years. She wrote three books during her lifetime. With her husband she wrote *Dogmatism and Evolution: Studies in Modern Philosophy*

(1910; repr. 1977). Alone she wrote *Speech: Its Function and Development* (1927; repr. 1963, 1970) and *On Existence and the Human World* (1966).

Honors and achievements punctuated de Laguna's career. She was a cofounder in 1925 of the Fullerton Club for Philadelphia-area philosophers. She became president of the American Philosophical Association, Eastern Division (that year representing the whole association) in 1941; she delivered her presidential address to a standing ovation. Also, Adele A. Abrahamsen dedicated her book *Child Language: An Interdisciplinary Guide to Theory and Research* (1977) to de Laguna "in honor of the 50th anniversary of her pioneering book, *Speech.*"

De Laguna's philosophy was called by the Yale University philosopher Brand Blanshard "an evolutionary naturalism." Her philosophy of science showed deep influences from the naturalism, behaviorism, and evolutionism of her time, while her metaphysics was that of a process thinker, and these two trends in her thought were compatible with each other and also with a third continuous interest in value questions (moral, political, etc.). She wrote early in an 1899 paper that "The ultimate end of philosophy is the complete unification of all knowledge. All progress in science is towards this end."

De Laguna proceeded to follow such a program during a whole life of thinking, while studying a remarkably wide literature in the sciences and the branches of philosophy with an objectivity that became famous to her colleagues. In a posthumous paper she said, "I have argued for a similarity between the ontological understanding of Being and of the individual. But Being is not to be understood as an individual, nor is an understanding of the individual an understanding of Being. The understanding of one complements that of the other." The fact that such ideas are available to interested scholars but have not yet been appreciated widely enough makes up a challenging project in the real history of American philosophy.

• The Archives of Bryn Mawr College hold a sizable collection of valuable unpublished writings that form part of a proposed four-volume set of the author's complete writings. The single most important item is an unfinished book on epistemology, *Thought, Perception and a Common World*, that constitutes a bridge between her second and third published books and has remained unknown except to a very few faithful friends. Three remarkable notices about her books are Arthur O. Lovejoy, "Review of *Dogmatism and Evolution*," *Philosophical Review* 20 (1911): 535–45; L. Deme, "Review of *Speech*," *Acta Linguistica Academiae Scientiarum Hungaricae* 16 (1966): 387–93; and Maurice Natanson, "Nature, Value, and Action," *Man and World* 1 (1968): 293–302. A more recent comparative discussion of *Speech* can be found in C. Thomas Mason, "The Study of Language in Its Social Context: Dewey, Mead, de Laguna, Bentley," in *1980 Mid-America Linguistics Conference Papers*, ed. Michael M. T. Henderson. (1981). A serious discussion of her late thought was included in Brand Blanshard, "Memories and Reflections in Honor of Grace de Laguna" (typescript, 1979, Bryn Mawr College Archives). The complete bibliography of her published and unpublished writings and a discussion of her philosophy are included in Leopoldo M. Montoya, "On the Extant Writings of Theodore and Grace de Laguna" (typescript, 1982, Bryn Mawr College Archives).

LEOPOLDO M. MONTOYA

DE LAGUNA, Theodore de Leo (22 July 1876–22 Sept. 1930), philosopher, was born in Oakland, California, the son of Alexander Francisco López de Leo de Laguna, a private educator and businessman, and Frederica Henrietta Bergner. De Laguna was raised in the Californian home of his pietistic parents, two of the famous "pilgrims of 1848," one French and one German, as a frail and precocious child. His mother died while he was small. He studied first at home with his older sister Frederica and later attended the Oakland public schools and the University of California at Berkeley. At the university he earned a bachelor of arts in 1896 and a master of arts in philosophy and English literature in 1899. He then moved to Cornell University, and in 1901 he obtained his doctorate in philosophy with the thesis, "The Relation of Ethics to Evolution."

De Laguna then traveled to the Orient as a member of the first group of American teachers sent to the Philippines after the Insurrection. Specifically, he lived in a remote district on the island of Mindanao from 1901 to 1903 and taught English there. A bout of cholera put an end to that adventure, but he managed to visit Japan before his return to San Francisco. In retrospect, he commented that his foreign experience represented "a long and painful endeavour to escape from the trammels of the Lutheran pietism" in which he had been brought up. In perhaps his best-known essay, "The Way of Opinion" (1930), he stated:

I found it exceedingly hard to win freedom of thought, and probably should never have succeeded if I had not, in my middle twenties, been plucked away from home influences and set down for a time in the midst of a people of alien race to think my way to a clear self-consciousness.

De Laguna was back at Cornell University between 1903 and 1905 as an assistant in philosophy. In 1905 he married Grace Mead Andrus, then a graduate student in philosophy at Cornell. They had two children.

A quick appointment as assistant professor of education at the University of Michigan between 1905 and 1907 was followed by an offer from Bryn Mawr College in Bryn Mawr, Pennsylvania, to teach philosophy. There developed the entire professional career in philosophy and its teaching that would make him nationally famous. He was successively associate (1907) and full professor (1910) and became chairman of the college's department until his death. He unexpectedly passed away at Hardwick, Vermont, during a summer trip, from a massive stroke.

De Laguna wrote a large collection of monographs, articles, and reviews that made his name one of the staples in the field of American philosophy. He published three books during his lifetime. With his wife he wrote *Dogmatism and Evolution: Studies in Modern*

Philosophy (1910; repr. 1977). Alone he wrote *Introduction to the Science of Ethics* (1914, repr. 1972) and *The Factors of Social Evolution* (1926). Three of de Laguna's articles dealing with Plato were published in professional journals a few years after his death.

The English philosopher Alfred North Whitehead, who once credited de Laguna in print with a discovery in logic, wrote to de Laguna's widow after his death,

In thinking of him I realize his combination of keenness of mind with loveableness of character. In conversation he probed and analyzed, but his analysis was always directed to bring out the best points in the thoughts of others. This characteristic was so natural and intuitive for him that at first one hardly noticed it.

The American philosopher William Montague added, "This zestful and passionate concern for the life of reason which seems to me to have been uniquely characteristic of de Laguna stands out in bold relief if we view it in relation to his general philosophy. For he was both a sceptic and a pragmatist."

In spite of the fact that he was a noted scholar in the field of ancient Greek philosophy, de Laguna was truly a modern philosopher. This started in his student days, when he was taught mainly by a neo-Kantian (Professor G. H. Howison) and a left Hegelian (Professor Evander McGilvary), and it was followed by his encounter with the pragmatism of William James. Slowly and surely, he developed a radically skeptical way of thinking that included such tenets as there is no inductive reasoning, there cannot be a general theory of truth, there will never be a scientific philosophy systematically organized, there is no way to establish a hard distinction between knowledge and belief, and all ultimate questions are useless.

Confronted with such radical conclusions, de Laguna seemed to be moving toward a hermeneutic and linguistic-analytical way of philosophizing that would have been quite in tune with what was becoming predominant in English-speaking professional philosophy, if death had not taken him early. (He wrote one of the very first reviews of Wittgenstein's *Tractatus*, which much later was anthologized.)

De Laguna was a staunch feminist, believing in the intellectual equality of men and women and devoted to educating the latter to achieve their full potential. About his ability as teacher, we have the following testimonial of one of his many devoted students, Helen Parkhurst: "Unexampled patience, unfailing kindness and sympathy, lucidity, rare intellectual fervour, an inexhaustible enthusiasm for ideas—those were the invariable traits of his teaching."

• The archives of Bryn Mawr College hold a sizable collection of unpublished de Laguna writings in music, history, literature, science, and several branches of philosophy that form part of a proposed four-volume set of the author's complete writings. Two remarkable notices about de Laguna's books are Arthur O. Lovejoy, "Review of *Dogmatism and Evolution*," *Philosophical Review* 20 (1911): 535–45, and Frank Thilly, "Review of *The Factors of Social Evolution*," *Philosophical Review* 37 (1928): 607–11. An important celebration was that of Marion Edwards Park et al., "In Memory of Theodore de Leo de Laguna" (typescript, 1930, Bryn Mawr College Archives). The complete bibliography of his published and unpublished writings and a discussion of his philosophy are in Leopoldo M. Montoya, "On the Extant Writings of Theodore and Grace de Laguna" (typescript, 1982, Bryn Mawr College Archives).

LEOPOLDO M. MONTOYA

DELAHANTY, Edward James (30 Oct. 1867–2 July 1903), baseball player, was born in Cleveland, Ohio, the son of James Delahanty, a laborer and teamster, and Bridget Croke. Postfamine immigrants from Ireland, the Delahantys had eight children, five of whom played major league baseball. The oldest and most accomplished of the brothers, Ed was described by Connie Mack as an "Atlas, who carried the baseball world on his shoulders" (Mack, *My Sixty-six Years in Baseball*, p. 84).

The young and talented Delahanty rose rapidly to the competitive and highly visible semipro leagues of Cleveland. These successes clashed with his mother's middle-class values, which he tried to appease by enrolling in a local business college. Delahanty resolved this clash in 1887 when without his parents' consent he signed as a catcher with Mansfield in the Ohio League.

The next year Delahanty advanced to Wheeling, West Virginia, in the Tri-State League. Word of his batting exploits and his play at second base quickly spread among National League teams. By the end of May 1888 he was sold to the Philadelphia Phillies for a then-record price of $1,900. At twenty years old, Delahanty was earning $300 a month as "everybody's hero" (Ritter, *The Glory of Their Times*, p. 30). But Delahanty was an overmatched rookie, and he played in only seventy-four games. His manager attributed Delahanty's disappointing start to impatience and obstinance.

Delahanty's initial progress was also affected by a players strike in 1890 union strife that moved him to join the Cleveland Infants of the Players League. His return to Philadelphia the following season was forestalled by immaturity, nagging injuries, and the pressures of proving himself to his former team. It was not until 1892 that Delahanty gave notice that expectations of his ability were justified. For the next decade, he set standards that dominated his era. During these seasons he averaged a .375 batting mark with 197 hits, 122 runs and 62 extra base hits. In his career, Delahanty twice had six-hit games (1890 and 1894), once stroked nine hits in a doubleheader, and eleven times had games of five or more hits.

"Big Ed" also made ten consecutive base hits, and in 1896 he was the second person in history to swat four home runs (three out of the park) in a nine-inning contest. He hit .400 three times and was the first batter in modern times to win batting titles in both major leagues (.410 in 1899 with Philadelphia and .376 in 1902 with Washington). At five feet ten inches and 190 pounds, Delahanty had deadball hitting strength, skill, and renown that would later be compared with

Babe Ruth's. His .346 lifetime batting average ranked fourth among all batters, and second among all right-handed batters behind Rogers Hornsby, at the end of the twentieth century. Delahanty also was an excellent base runner and thrower, and he played every field position during his professional career.

Delahanty's career was a time of great management and player strife. Collusion among the owners after the 1890 strike cost players of Delahanty's caliber tens of thousands of dollars. These constraints did not deter the idolized Delahanty, who behaved as if baseball would always be an inexhaustible source of money and favors.

During the strike, Delahanty had signed contracts with three different clubs. Although he rejoined the Phillies, salaries were cut and a $2,400 salary cap was later enforced. In 1900, with the anticipation of a rival league, "Del" and teammate Napoleon Lajoie used their stature to demand $3,000 for a season. Delahanty's demands were met, but Lajoie took less, and went over to the new American League in 1901.

With his best years behind him, Delahanty jumped leagues in 1902 and signed a $4,000 contract with the Washington Senators of the new American League. The new contract was important to Delahanty, who had not saved his money. Living the life of an adored athlete, he had never even held a regular job. Instead, he pursued the limelight and craved the excitement of the racetrack. But after winning the American League batting title, Delahanty wanted one last chance to land a lucrative multiyear contract and to play with a contending team in a high-profile city. Lured by his old friend John McGraw, Delahanty signed a three-year deal for $4,000 a season with the National League New York Giants. After losing his signing bonus and advance money at the track, however, he was compelled by his new league to remain with the Senators. In debt and despondent by this denied opportunity, an out-of-shape Delahanty began the 1903 season. He played only forty-three games for the Senators and was batting .333 when the team suspended him for heavy drinking. On the trip from Detroit to Washington, with a stop to see McGraw in New York, Delahanty was put off the train for being intoxicated and disturbing passengers. Left late at night on the Canadian side of the Niagara River, Delahanty attempted to walk across a train bridge to Buffalo. A week later his bloated and mangled body surfaced below Niagara Falls.

Accident, suicide, and foul play were taken into account. Evidence indicates he stumbled off the bridge during an altercation with an elderly night watchman. Delahanty was survived by his wife, Norine Thompson, whom he married in 1894, and a young daughter. Left without insurance or money, his wife sued the Michigan Central Railroad for negligence. She lost the appeal and was dependent on friends and family for sustenance. In 1945, when Delahanty was elected to the National Baseball Hall of Fame, his plaque recited his achievements and omitted that his life was wrecked by self-indulgent fame. Sam Crane, a sportswriter who knew Delahanty well, lamented, "he never grasped the idea that the game afforded a field for improvement and betterment of habits and character that could firmly establish him . . . as a prosperous and successful man" (*New York Journal*, 10 Feb. 1912).

As a result, Delahanty's life and career are tainted by the circumstances surrounding his death. A product of a masculine urban subculture that revolved around the neighborhood firehouse, saloon, and ball fields, he celebrated his athletic feats through fraternal camaraderie. For second-generation Americans like Delahanty, sports represented totems to assimilation and vehicles for socioeconomic mobility. But professional sports could also evoke a self-indulgent lifestyle that devoured the weak-willed.

• The National Baseball Library in Cooperstown, N.Y., contains a clipping file on Delahanty. Other materials are owned by the estate of Norine Randall, Delahanty's granddaughter, in Mobile, Ala. Delahanty's career statistics are in *The Baseball Encyclopedia*, 9th ed. (1993). Contemporary descriptions of Delahanty's colorful career and tragic death are in the *Buffalo Evening News*, *Cleveland Plain Dealer*, *Cleveland Press*, *Detroit Times*, *Philadelphia Bulletin*, *Philadelphia Inquirer*, *Washington Post*, and other leading newspapers. Other sources of information include Frank Fitzpatrick, "A Baseball Mystery Is 85 Years Old," *Philadelphia Inquirer*, 3 July 1988; Frank Bilovsky and Rich Westcott, "Delahanty's Hitting Records Remain after Eight Decades," *Philadelphia Inquirer*, 19 Aug. 1984; and Robert J. Summers, "His Ticket Said New York City but Fate Said Niagara Falls," *Buffalo Courier Express Magazine*, 8 Sept. 1974, pp. 22–24. See also Frederick Lieb and Stan Baumgartner, *The Philadelphia Phillies* (1953); Lawrence Ritter, *The Glory of Their Times* (1966), Mike Sowell, *July 2, 1903* (1992); and Rich Westcott and Frank Bilovsky, *The New Phillies Encyclopedia* (1993). Obituaries are in the *Buffalo Evening News*, 8 July 1903, and the *Washington Post*, 12 July 1903.

JERROLD CASWAY

DE LANCEY, James (27 Nov. 1703–30 July 1760), jurist and politician, was born in New York City, the son of Stephen De Lancey, a Huguenot refugee who had established a leading mercantile house in New York, and Anne Van Cortlandt, heiress to a portion of one of the great New York manorial landholdings. James, at twenty, was sent to London for advanced education at Corpus Christi College, Cambridge and Lincoln's Inn.

De Lancey returned to New York in 1725 and, though he had declared that he would remain a bachelor, he was married in 1728 to Anne Heathcote, daughter of New York's receiver general and possessor of Scarsdale Manor. The couple had six children. Through subsequent marriages entered into by his brothers, De Lancey soon was allied to the Colden and Franks families of New York and Philadelphia. His sister, Susannah, married Sir Peter Warren, the hero at Louisbourg, who subsequently played an important role for De Lancey in the highest chambers of the English government. His wife's uncle, also in England, was Sir Gilbert Heathcote, director of the Bank of England, and his former tutor at Corpus Christi,

Thomas Herring, emerged as archbishop of Canterbury in 1747.

While such connections were important in De Lancey's business and political careers, his talents played a major role in his rapid rise to eminence. Being one of the best-trained legal minds in the colonies, he was named to the provincial council in 1729, soon after his admission to the bar. At the age of twenty-seven, he presided over the commission that drafted the famous Montgomerie Charter for the city of New York. By 1731 he was serving as second justice of the New York Supreme Court; he was promoted to chief justice in August 1733.

De Lancey's rapid rise in judicial status came at a time of political turmoil in New York politics with the arrival of William Cosby as governor in 1732. Cosby immediately embarked on a campaign to recover what he believed to be just compensation due him from the time he received his commission to the point of his arrival in New York. Cosby sought compensation through court action against Rip Van Dam, who had served as acting governor. When a question arose as to which court could exercise jurisdiction, Cosby determined it should be the supreme court in its capacity as a court of equity, with judges who were, not incidentally, gubernatorial appointees serving at his discretion. Lewis Morris, sitting as chief justice, publicly declared that his court lacked proper jurisdiction. At that point Cosby removed Morris and appointed De Lancey chief justice, which for all intents and purposes ended the suit. Cosby eventually dropped his complaint against Van Dam. The supporters of Van Dam's cause regarded this as a victory against the disliked governor.

Morris and his associates turned their fury to the creation in November 1733 of the *New York Weekly Journal*, printed by John Peter Zenger. They so successfully used the newspaper for their political attacks against Cosby that it was characterized as a weapon which hurled "invective and satire against the Governor." Cosby moved to silence the newspaper when, in January 1734, his newly appointed chief justice, De Lancey, acted on Cosby's request and charged the grand jury on the laws of libel and asked them to return an indictment against Zenger. Not receiving the desired response, De Lancey went before the next grand jury in October to seek an indictment against broadsides that had been published celebrating Morrisite victories in the general assembly elections of 1734. Again the grand jury refused to do his bidding.

Cosby then turned to the council for appropriate action against Zenger. The council agreed to order that four issues of the *Journal* be publicly burned and that Zenger be "taken into custody by the Sheriff and committed to prison." When Zenger's attorneys sought his release, De Lancey set bail at £400. Unable to raise such a sum, Zenger remained imprisoned for eight months during the lengthy trial. The Cosby opponents then painted Zenger as a martyr while continuing to publish the *Journal*.

Unable to obtain cooperation from a grand jury, Attorney General Richard Bradley in January 1735 used a legal device to start a prosecution against Zenger without grand jury action. James Alexander and William Smith, Zenger's attorneys, then challenged the commissions for De Lancey and Frederick Philipse as judges of the supreme court and claimed that Cosby had violated the laws of England and of New York by making them judges without obtaining prior consent of the New York council. De Lancey responded in April by disbarring Smith and Alexander. The Morris group then turned to Andrew Hamilton of Philadelphia, regarded by many as the best lawyer in America. The trial occurred on 4 August 1735 with De Lancey presiding. Hamilton delivered a carefully prepared brief to establish Zenger's innocence. The jury deliberated for only a few minutes before returning a verdict of not guilty.

Cosby's death in 1735 created a vacuum in local political leadership. George Clarke, who had served as Cosby's chief adviser, was commissioned as lieutenant governor. Clarke, however, had kept aloof from the leading merchants and active politicians in New York City while retaining strong friendships in the rural areas. De Lancey, on the other hand, cultivated the urban commercial and political elite. As a result, De Lancey soon had solid support in the general assembly, especially from those members who came from New York City. By 1737 De Lancey not only sat in the governor's council and served as chief justice but also controlled a bloc of votes in the assembly.

George Clinton served as New York's next governor, 1743–1753. De Lancey ingratiated himself to Clinton, who recognized De Lancey's power in the province. In September 1744 De Lancey received what he had long sought, a commission as chief justice during "good behavior," rather than during the governor's "pleasure," the equivalent of a lifetime interest in that position. Clinton, in return for De Lancey's support in obtaining a reasonable annual salary, placed De Lancey's friends in key provincial positions. Cadwallader Colden deplored De Lancey's control in these years when he later wrote that "all the officers of the Government became entirely dependent on the Chief Justice and his Faction in the Assembly both for the nomination to their offices and for their salaries or rewards for their services" (Colden to John Mitchell, 6 July 1749, *Letters*, pp. 20–21).

Clinton and De Lancey politically parted in 1746 when the two fought over a measure introduced by Clinton concerning the prevention of desertions from the New York regiments. Local New York merchants were using the deserters to man privateering vessels. Clinton succeeded in winning support for his measure over the objections of De Lancey's main supporters, the mercantile coalition. After the two openly quarreled at a public affair following the passage of the measure, De Lancey moved to increase his influence in the legislative bodies. Recognizing that if this should occur his own influence would be over, Clinton sought to introduce non–De Lancey supporters to the council while attempting to work with the assembly. A substantial part of the Clinton–De Lancey political warfare was carried out through the English patronage system, and both men turned to influential figures in England to bolster their positions in New York.

As early as 1747, De Lancey, through the influential participation of his brother-in-law Sir Peter Warren, was commissioned as lieutenant governor, over strenuous objections from Governor Clinton. The governor, however, successfully suppressed the actual delivery of the commission until shortly before he left New York for England in 1753. All was set for the arrival of Sir Danvers Osborne as the next governor and for De Lancey to serve only for a brief interim. The fates intervened, however; the newly arrived governor committed suicide. This left the provincial administration to De Lancey, who then continued to serve as acting governor until his death.

In this ultimate position, De Lancey sought to balance provincial and imperial needs on the eve of conflict between England and France. The issues of defense, logistics, troop supplies, and obtaining adequate revenues occupied his thoughts as the Great War for Empire began in 1754. De Lancey hosted the Albany Congress in June–July 1754 to which seven colonies sent delegates. At the congress De Lancey urged the colonists to unite in concerted actions in constructing fortifications and in seeking Iroquois support in the conflict. Even though New York was directly affected by military movements on its borders, De Lancey found great difficulty in obtaining adequate revenues and supplies.

At the same time, De Lancey became embroiled in the chartering of King's College in 1754. Through his connection with the archbishop of Canterbury and his own membership in the Anglican church, he felt obliged to support the move to place the college under Episcopal control in the face of Presbyterian opposition led by William Livingston, who sought no denominational control. A compromise arrangement was obtained whereby a college was chartered under Anglican supervision but without the support of public funds. Neither party was particularly pleased with the arrangement.

De Lancey was stricken by a fatal heart attack at his residence in New York City. He had built the first political faction in New York that would remain a major player in provincial affairs until the American Revolution. By a combination of his political astuteness, intelligence, extended family relations both in New York and England, sagacious use of the patronage system, and by being a driving force at a critical juncture in New York politics, De Lancey created a political force that challenged the authority of various governors as well as the ambitions of influential New Yorkers.

• For a descendant's observations about an illustrious ancestor see Edward F. De Lancey, "Memoir of the Honorable James De Lancey, Lieutenant-Governor of the Province of New York," in *The Documentary History of the State of New York*, vol. 4, ed. Edmund O'Callaghan (1851), pp. 1035–59. His own contemporaries left interesting accounts of De Lancey's political career. Two major sources are *The Letters and Papers of Cadwallader Colden*, Collections of the New-York Historical Society, 1917–1923, 1934–1935 (2 vols., 1918–1937); and William Smith, Jr., *The History of the Province of New-York*, Michael Kammen (2 vols., 1972). Stanley N. Katz has covered various aspects of De Lancey's career in a number of publications such as *A Brief Narrative of the Case and Trial of John Peter Zenger by James Alexander*, ed. Katz (1963), and *Newcastle's New York: Anglo-American Political Relations, 1675–1775* (1970). Summaries of De Lancey's career may be found in Patricia U. Bonomi, *A Factious People: Politics and Society in Colonial New York* (1971); and Leopold S. Launitz-Schurer, Jr., "Whig-Loyalists: The De Lanceys of New York," *New-York Historical Society Quarterly*, July 1972, pp. 178–98.

JACOB JUDD

DE LANCEY, James (6 Sept. 1747–2 May 1804), New York Loyalist, was born in West Farms, Westchester County, New York, the son of Peter De Lancey and Elizabeth Colden, colonial aristocrats. James De Lancey was a nephew of Chief Justice James De Lancey (1703–1760) and a grandson of Cadwallader Colden. Because of such family connections, James De Lancey rose quickly. On 5 October 1770 he was appointed sheriff of Westchester, a position that had been in his family for some time. He held the post until the American Revolution.

De Lancey's infamy started when he refused to join with the patriots. In 1776, after the British had invaded New York, patriot officer Thomas Mifflin ordered him to stay at his house unless granted permission to leave. As De Lancey never signed a parole or agreed to that demand, he felt free to flee and joined the British on Long Island. These circumstances led to the charge that De Lancey had violated parole, which he strongly denied.

After British forces seized New York City in September 1776, De Lancey had a dispute with a German officer, Colonel Andreas Emmerich. The cause of the argument is unknown, but angry comments quickly degenerated into a fist fight. Although De Lancey was incarcerated in the provost jail, it is unlikely that he was confined for long, for his prominent name and his important connections surely worked to secure his early release.

During March 1777 royal governor William Tryon placed De Lancey in charge of the remnants of the militia of his home county. De Lancey also began to recruit men for what became the Westchester Refugees, better known as De Lancey's Cowboys, though he did not become the unit's commander until 1780. The Refugees were an irregular body not connected with the regular Loyalist forces, which fought more traditional warfare. The Westchester Refugees were based at King's Bridge on the mainland and so guarded the approach to British-occupied Manhattan. Originally the Refugees were charged with apprehending deserters, but they were soon ordered to forage in Westchester for food supplies. Their seizures of cattle earned them the name of cowboys, which then had a criminal connotation. De Lancey later insisted that one-third of the foodstuffs that came within the British lines got there because of the Refugees' efforts, both by their raids and by their keeping the route to the Manhattan marketplace open for Westchester inhabitants.

Still another function of the Westchester Refugees was to kidnap patriots who could be exchanged for captured Loyalists. De Lancey claimed that the Cowboys captured more than 500 men who were used for that purpose. But during December 1777 De Lancey himself was caught by the rebels. Sent to Hartford, Connecticut, he defended himself against the accusation that he had violated parole in 1776. When given a parole in Connecticut, he carefully obeyed its provisions. He was exchanged in 1778, and during January 1780 the British promoted him to colonel.

De Lancey and the Refugees became objects of hatred, partly because of his famous surname and also because they operated in southern Westchester, most of which is the present borough of the Bronx. Lying between the lines of the competing armies, this section became a no-man's-land in which atrocities were committed by both sides. This "neutral ground" inspired James Fenimore Cooper to write his classic novel *The Spy* (1821). The most notorious military action involving De Lancey's Cowboys occurred on 14 May 1781, when patriot colonel Christopher Greene was killed by the Loyalists after a surrender had supposedly been negotiated. Despite the talk of surrender, two patriots suddenly shot at the Tories, who then turned vicious. Greene died after the fighting resumed. There is no proof that De Lancey ever tolerated outrages upon decency, for he demanded discipline from his soldiers and usually received it. In 1783 the colonel complained that everything disreputable that happened in Westchester was blamed on the Westchester Refugees. Most recent historians agree that the great majority of crimes were committed not by De Lancey's Cowboys but by a lawless element that took advantage of the anarchic conditions in the county.

Colonel De Lancey, who received no salary for his military service, was attainted by the rebels on 22 October 1779 and so lost his property. Hated in his homeland, he had no choice but to leave New York. On 3 April 1783 De Lancey resigned his command because the war was all but over. In his resignation, directed to Sir Guy Carleton, De Lancey complained about those who, envious of his zealous loyalty, had tried to smear him and his soldiers. General Carleton strongly recommended him to the British government. Apparently, De Lancey left America soon after his resignation.

During the war years, De Lancey had married Martha Tippett (d. 1827), also of Westchester. They had ten children. Taking some slaves with them, the De Lanceys settled in Annapolis County, Nova Scotia, after the war. He obtained an estate of 640 acres there. Soon after arriving, he became a justice of the peace. In February 1790 he was elected to the Nova Scotia Assembly. During 1794 De Lancey became a member of the colonial council and continued in that office until 1801. He died at his home near Annapolis, Nova Scotia.

• Few of James De Lancey's papers survive. A letter to John Jay of 14 Jan. 1778 is in the Jay papers, Columbia University. De Lancey's memorial to Carleton is in the British Headquarters Papers, New York Public Library. This institution also has De Lancey's claim for compensation in the Loyalist Transcripts. The only biography is Ronald S. Longley, "The Delancey Brothers, Loyalists of Annapolis County," *Nova Scotia Historical Society Collections* 32 (1959): 55–77. Genealogical information is in D. A. Story, *The deLanceys* (1931). There are references to him in Thomas Jones, *History of New York during the Revolutionary War* (2 vols., 1879), and Hugh Hastings, ed., *Public Papers of George Clinton* (10 vols., 1899–1914). Older works such as Otto Hufeland, *Westchester County during the American Revolution* (1926), are bitterly hostile to him. Far kinder are more recent accounts such as Philip Ranlet, *The New York Loyalists* (1986), and Catherine S. Crary, "Guerrilla Activities of James DeLancey's Cowboys in Westchester County: Conventional Warfare or Self-Interested Freebooting?" in *The Loyalist Americans*, ed. Robert A. East and Jacob Judd (1975), pp. 14–24, 153–55.

PHILIP RANLET

DE LANCEY, Oliver (16 Sept. 1718–27 Oct. 1785), colonial politician and Loyalist, was born in the province of New York, the youngest son of Etienne (Stephen) De Lancey and Anne van Cortlandt, who established the De Lanceys as a prominent New York mercantile family. The eldest son, James, the political head of the family in the 1740s, served as chief justice and lieutenant governor of the colony. Oliver De Lancey was educated in his father's business establishment. In 1742, in the Anglican church ritual, he secretly married a New York Jew, Phila Franks, who was from a wealthy merchant family with relatives in Philadelphia. The De Lanceys had seven children.

In 1746 De Lancey sent two sloops of provisions to supply British military forces at Louisbourg after its capture. In addition to being a merchant and an army supplier, De Lancey was a land speculator, with property throughout the city and province of New York and in New Jersey. Royal governor George Clinton disliked and distrusted both James and Oliver De Lancey. Seven years after Oliver De Lancey's marriage, Clinton condemned him for leading a mob attack on the home of an immigrant Dutch Jew, Judah Mears. De Lancey's attack on the Mears family may have been because of anti-Semitism, a projection of resentment against the Franks family, who were unreconciled to their daughter's marriage out of their faith, or may have resulted from business conflict. De Lancey was accused by authorities of participating in at least two other brawls, but no lawyer would prosecute the government's cases because of the power of James De Lancey. Finally in 1749 the governor issued a complaint denouncing him for contempt of God and king and the peace of the province.

A member of the aristocracy, De Lancey campaigned politically among farmers and artisans. His popularity among the city's tavern patrons may have been in part related to his well-known horsemanship and physical prowess. He could jump a horse from a standing position over five barrels. De Lancey appealed to voters in a tavern as early as 1749 with songs and "faction papers." He was perceived as riotous and tumultuous by enemies, who emphasized his belligerent and tough nature. Perhaps because James De Lancey was reserved and sedate as chief justice and lieutenant governor, Oliver De Lancey was free to mobilize the voting populace by developing new popular political techniques in the last decades of the empire.

During the French and Indian War, De Lancey was a city alderman from the Out Ward (1754–1757) and represented the county in the assembly from 1756 to 1760. In 1756 he was one of three paymasters of the New York troops and raised troops for the war effort. In 1758 he led his men at Fort Ticonderoga, for which service he was thanked by the assembly. Two years later his brother James, who was his benefactor and protector, died. In that year Oliver De Lancey was given a seat on the colonial council. For the next fifteen years he was the head of the De Lancey party, controlling it from the council. However, he was not as politically powerful as his eldest brother lacking his urbanity, humor, polish, and political sense. Nevertheless, De Lancey did continue his faction's involvement with mechanics and shopkeepers, maintaining an alliance with the Sons of Liberty longer than many mercantile friends thought desirable.

De Lancey moved in the political worlds of both the drawing room and the tavern. The 1768 assembly election, the first that he led as faction leader, was held in the traditional gentlemanly manner of eighteenth-century politics. However, the dissolution of the house, because of the Massachusetts Circular letter crisis, caused an election the following year. This time he led his party with new tactics in one of New York's roughest and most violent elections. The De Lancey–led aristocratic merchants won a majority of the seats by blatantly appealing to the Sons of Liberty, artisans, and shopkeepers as ardent defenders of rights against British policies. Gouverneur Morris, a critic of popular participation in politics, seems to have had De Lancey in mind when he recalled, "The troubles in America during Grenville's administration put our gentry upon this finesse. They stimulated some daring coxcombs to rouse the mob into an attack upon the bounds of order and decency. These fellows, became the Jack Cades of the day, the leaders in all the riots, the bell-wethers of the flock."

Street demonstrations, flagrant intimidation, slander, and other techniques developed during the Grenville and Townshend programs' crises were applied to the election. However, by the mid-1770s the demands of the Sons of Liberty were becoming too militant for the De Lanceys. Gouverneur Morris's wariness was appropriately applied to many De Lancey politicians, "The mob begin to think and to reason. Poor reptiles! . . . they bask in the sunshine and ere noon they will bite, depend on it. The gentry begin to fear this."

The alliance dissolved by 1775. The De Lanceys, fearful of the militant Sons of Liberty, were sliding toward support of royal governor William Tryon, while opposing the moderate Livingstons, who uneasily moved into an alliance with the Liberty Boys. The De Lanceys were similar to Rockingham Whigs, who also considered parliamentary authority supreme within the empire, but would not have this power applied to all political issues. Parliament should leave matters such as colonial taxation to be decided by the colonies. De Lancey and his followers applauded repeal of the Stamp Act and the Townshend Acts and overlooked the Declaratory Act as a political expediency. In 1775, as the Americans were seeking to create self-governing dominions in the British Commonwealth, De Lancey, the popular politician, was becoming increasingly anachronistic and irrelevant, a Loyalist in a war for independence.

De Lancey claimed that in June 1776 he was called before the New York rebel leaders and the Provincial Congress to explain his Loyalism and that on 20 June he fled to the British. When General William Howe's forces took Long Island in August 1776, De Lancey was appointed a brigadier general (the highest ranking colonial in the British forces) and was authorized to raise a brigade of three battalions with five hundred men each. During that winter he was one of a group of Loyalist leaders who unsuccessfully petitioned General Howe to restore civilian government in British-occupied areas of New York province in an effort to negate rebel propaganda that the British established martial law to destroy rights and privileges.

In retribution for British destruction of rebel property, on 26 November 1777 a rebel party slipped onto Manhattan Island and destroyed De Lancey's mansion at Greenwich Village along the Hudson River. Two years later, on 22 October 1779, De Lancey was one of fifty-nine outlawed by New York state in an act of attainder, and his property was forfeited. The statewide properties of nine such Loyalists, including James and Oliver De Lancey, were retained by New York because their high market value was used to back state paper money.

In the fall of 1778 General Sir Henry Clinton sent two battalions of De Lancey's brigade to Georgia and South Carolina, where they served well with Lord Cornwallis's campaign. The remaining battalion, under De Lancey's immediate command, stayed on Long Island to protect the Loyalists there and help gather wood for the port. At the end of the war, Oliver and Phila De Lancey moved to England; the three battalions evacuated to Nova Scotia.

On retirement the brigadier general was given the half-pay of a colonel. The Loyalist Commission of Parliament awarded De Lancey a stipend of £200 per year for his wife and £100 per year for his daughter. He estimated that the prewar value of his American property was £100,000 and that he lost £78,016. He was awarded £23,446. De Lancey died in Beverly, north of Hull (then Yorkshire, currently Humberside), England, where he was buried in a choir aisle of the Beverly cathedral; a memorial plaque marks the site. A major force in the development of colonial New York politics, De Lancey has been forgotten in the United States because he could not cross the barrier from being a liberal reformer within the British Empire to becoming a citizen of the new state.

• De Lancey's description of experiences during the revolutionary period and his appeal for property lost to the rebels appears in Public Records Office (London), Audit Office, Commission of Enquiry into the Losses and Services of the American Loyalists, "Transcripts of the Manuscript Book and Papers of the Commission . . . ," vol. 41 (1900), pp. 101–216. Significant data are in Gregory Palmer, ed., *A Bibliography of Loyalist Source Material in the United States, Canada, and Great Britain* (1982).

See the work of his son-in-law, the ardent Loyalist judge Thomas Jones, *History of New York during the Revolutionary War . . .* , ed. Edward Floyd De Lancey (2 vols., 1879), for a biographical sketch and scattered information on De Lancey. See also New-York Historical Society, *Orderly Book of the Three Battalions of Loyalists, Commanded by Brigadier-General Oliver De Lancey . . .* (1917); and I. N. Phelps Stokes, *The Iconography of Manhattan Island* (6 vols., 1915–1928). De Lancey's relation to the Franks family and Judah Mears is in Leo Hershkowitz and Isidore S. Meyer, eds., *Letters of the Franks Family (1733–1748)* (1968); Leo Hershkowitz, *Wills of Early New York Jews (1704–1799)* (1967); and Paul A. Gilje, *The Road to Mobocracy: Popular Disorder in New York City, 1763–1834* (1987).

De Lancey's political career is considered in Leopold S. Launitz-Schürer, Jr., "Whig-Loyalists: The De Lanceys of New York," *New-York Historical Society Quarterly* 56 (1972): 179–98. References to De Lancey are found in Cadwallader Colden, *The Letters and Papers of Cadwallader Colden*, New-York Historical Society, *Collections* (9 vols., 1917–1923, 1934–1935); William Smith, *Historical Memoirs . . .* , ed. William H. W. Sabine (2 vols., 1956); and Hugh Hastings and James Austin Holden, eds., *Public Papers of George Clinton, First Governor of New York* (10 vols., 1899–1914).

EUGENE R. FINGERHUT

DELAND, Margaret (23 Feb. 1857–13 Jan. 1945), novelist and short story writer, was born Margaretta Wade Campbell in Allegheny, Pennsylvania, the daughter of Sample Campbell, a clothing merchant, and Margaretta Wade. Her mother died in childbirth, and her elderly father died shortly thereafter. At two weeks old, she was sent to Maple Grove, Pennsylvania, to live with her mother's sister, Lois Wade, and Benjamin Bakewell Campbell (coincidentally of the same last name), whom Margaret regarded as parents. Family life, although strict Presbyterian, was lively and affluent, and "Maggie," as Deland recalls in her memoir, *If This Be I, As I Suppose It Be* (1935), was an imaginative and independent child who read widely and made up stories. At sixteen, when she became engaged to an older man, a friend of her uncle's, she was sent to Pelham Priory, a strict boarding school near New Rochelle, New York. In 1876, estranged from her family, she attended Cooper Union College in New York, where she studied design and drawing and became an assistant instructor in drawing and design at the Girls' Normal School (now Hunter College). In

May 1880 she married Lorin Deland, who worked in his father's printing and publishing company and later started an advertising business. The couple lived in Boston, Deland's primary residence for the rest of her life. Although not as well-off as the Campbell family, the couple appeared well matched, and, as she described in her memoir *Golden Yesterdays* (1941), they were very happy. They were active in community life and opened their home to unwed mothers, the beginning of Deland's lifelong concern with social and cultural issues affecting women, especially birth control and sex education. Later the Delands became leaders in Boston society, entertaining important literary and political figures of the day.

In 1886 Deland published her first book, *The Old Garden and Other Verses* (1886), a collection of conventional, sentimental poetry, very different from the work for which she would be best known. As a novelist and short story writer, she wrote about controversial issues, social and moral questions that challenged conventional responses. Her first novel, *John Ward, Preacher* (1888), depicting the breakup of a marriage over a conflict in religious ideals, shocked her family and others and gave evidence of her own questioning of her early faith. Such controversy was good for sales, and the Delands bought a summer home in Kennebunkport, Maine, with the profits. She began to write reviews, travel essays, advice, and realistic stories for *Harper's Bazaar*, *Atlantic Monthly*, and popular women's magazines. Her next novels, *Sidney* (1890) and *Phillip and His Wife* (1894), which dealt seriously with the question of marriage, were not as successful as her shorter works, the novelette *The Story of a Child* (1892) and a story collection, *Mr. Tommy Dove and Other Stories* (1893). She also began lecturing and in 1893 headed the Library Committee for Massachusetts that collected an exhibition of 100 books by Massachusetts women for the World's Columbian Exposition in Chicago.

Old Chester Tales (1898), a collection of realistic stories based loosely on Deland's childhood home, was a critical and popular success. Still exploring the value of the examined life and considered decisions, these stories ended happily more often than her earlier works. Deland's success continued with more Chester stories, *Dr. Lavendar's People* (1903), held together by her strongest male character, a man who combined the qualities of her friend and mentor, Boston minister Phillips Brooks, her uncle Dr. William Campbell, and her husband. She returned to this setting in *Around Old Chester* (1915), *An Old Chester Secret* (1920), *New Friends in Old Chester* (1924), and in several other novels.

Deland's most prolific period and her most acclaimed novels began with *The Awakening of Helena Richie* (1906). The main character defies society's rules by leaving her husband, a drunkard, to live with her lover. When her husband does not die as expected, she tries to live quietly with a seven-year-old orphan she has befriended. She is visited occasionally by a man she calls her "brother" but eventually must choose between her lover and her adopted son. Her awakening comes when she recognizes that she has a responsibility to the order of society, not only to her own happiness, and admits that with her background she cannot be a good parent. In the end, only when she is willing to give up her son for his own good does she become worthy of keeping him, and the two move west to start a new life. In the sequel, *The Iron Woman* (1911), Helena's son becomes involved in a similar situation, and to prevent the young woman who is trapped in a mismatched marriage from making the same mistake she did, Helena tells her story. The couple resolves to sacrifice their happiness to do what is right by society's standards; the realistic ending leaves unresolved the outcome of their decision. *The Rising Tide* (1916), one of Deland's few contemporary stories, attacks the extremists of the suffrage movement by demonstrating the shortcomings of the aggressive independence displayed by the protagonist, Frederica, and the senseless devotion to duty of her old-fashioned mother. A new ideal of womanhood, a person of intelligence, strength, and independent judgment, emerges as the balance between these extremes. Throughout her most powerful work, Deland shows women dealing with and coming to terms with the issues of their lives—sexual freedom, economic opportunity, and independent but responsible moral judgment.

Her husband's death in 1917 led to Deland's growing interest in spiritualism. Because of her serious research on the subject and reports of her successful communication with the dead, she was considered an expert and was asked to speak and write on the spiritual survival of individual identity. During World War I she traveled to France and became involved in war relief and writing essays supporting the war. She continued lecturing and writing. In 1926 she was elected to the National Institute of Arts and Letters. She died in Boston.

Throughout her career, Deland's work reflected the dilemmas facing women at the turn of the century and advocated moderation, balance, and individual responsibility as the best responses to the changing social order. Critic Diana Reep sums up Deland's strength as a storyteller and social commentator: "Her work is a mirror of the relationships, the problems, the moral crises of an age" (p. 116).

• After her death, Deland's reputation declined, and her nineteen novels and many story collections went out of print. *John Ward, Preacher* (1889; repr. 1967) and *The Awakening of Helena Richie* (1906; repr. 1969) are available in modern reprints. Her letters are available at Colby College Library, in the Barrett Collection of the University of Virginia, at the Western Pennsylvania Historical Society, and in the Library of Congress. Full-length studies of Deland's work with related criticism and bibliographies include Diana Reep, *Margaret Deland* (1985), and Phyllis Betz, "Balancing the Centuries: The Literary Career of Margaret Deland" (Ph.D. diss., Univ. of Maryland, 1989). Deland's works are treated in Grant Overton, *The Women Who Make Our Novels*, rev. ed. (1928); Loring H. Dodd, *Celebrities at Our Hearthside* (1959);

Barbara Welter, *Dimity Convictions: The American Woman in the Nineteenth Century* (1976); Herbert Smith, *The Popular American Novel, 1865–1920* (1980); and Nina Baym, *Novels, Readers, and Reviewers: Responses to Fiction in Antebellum America* (1984). An obituary is in the *New York Times*, 14 Jan. 1945.

CAROL BAKER SAPORA

DELANO, Alonzo (2 July 1806 or 1802–8 Sept. 1874), humorist, was born in Aurora, New York, the son of Frederick Delano, a doctor, and Joanna Doty. Delano, popularly known as Old Block, was educated at the Aurora Academy. In 1830 he married Mary Burt, also of Aurora, with whom he had two children. They migrated gradually westward, living several years in Ohio, followed by six years in South Bend, Indiana, until they finally settled in Ottawa, Illinois. Along the way, Delano earned his living as a self-described "counter jumper," selling produce, whiskey, and dry goods. Failing health led his physician to advise a change in environment. On 5 April 1849 Delano, then in his forties, left his wife and children in Illinois for an overland journey with a large company of others seeking health and fortune in the gold mines of California. They averaged fifteen miles a day and suffered serious deprivations before finally arriving at Sutter's Fort and the fledgling city of Sacramento at the end of September. Several days later, he and a companion departed for the Yuba River to mine for gold. Within two weeks they amassed approximately $600. Delano invested his share in general supplies and, for the next year, provided such mining camps as Independence, Nelson's Creek, and Rough-and-Ready with produce and other goods.

Delano's writing career appears to have coincided with the journal he kept of his travels to California. This account was later published as *Life on the Plains and among the Diggings; Being Scenes and Adventures of an Overland Journey to California: With Particular Incidents of the Route, Mistakes and Sufferings of the Emigrants, the Indian Tribes, the Present and the Future of the Great West* (1854). In it, Delano records his short career as a miner, his first three years in California, and an assessment of the state. He documents the rise in crime, precipitated by the mining out of gold and the influx of criminals from such British penal colonies as Sydney.

While running a produce business on Long Wharf in San Francisco, Delano began to contribute sketches about the mines and miners to local newspapers: the *Pacific News*, the *Sacramento Union*, the *California Farmer*, and the *Grass Valley Telegraph*. After the 4 May 1851 fire that destroyed Long Wharf and, with it, his business, he visited his wife and family in New York. He returned by ship to California in August 1852. As with many of his experiences and travels, his overland journey across the isthmus of Panama became the subject of a humorous sketch written for the *Pacific News*.

He became a Wells Fargo agent and settled in the growing town of Grass Valley, which had been founded on the discovery of gold-bearing quartz on nearby Gold Hill. Although Delano no longer mined, he continued to write throughout the 1850s and 1860s about mining, the miners, and the California experience, often with a bit of self-effacing humor. His sketches were published in such eastern newspapers as the *New York Times* and the *New Orleans True Delta*. In 1853 he published *Pen-Knife Sketches; or, Chips of the Old Block*, a collection of his contributions to the *Pacific News*. That year also saw the publication of his poem, *The Miner's Progress; or, Scenes in the Life of a California Miner*. The poem invokes John Bunyan's *Pilgrim's Progress* and features a "pilgrim from the Eastern shore" who suffers "his lust of gold." After a dream sequence, the miner strikes it rich, to the joy and benefit of his entire family. Both *Pen-Knife Sketches* and *The Miner's Progress* were illustrated by Charles Nahl, the German lithographer, whom Delano met while mining at the Rough-and-Ready camp.

Although he leveled many pointed and humorous barbs at his fellow Californians, Delano remained committed to its people, both indigenous and newly arrived. He befriended and traded with American Indians. He blamed the immigrants for most of the troubles between themselves and the Indians. When the bank ordered Delano to close his doors during the 1855 recession, he ignored the instructions, thereby preventing a crisis. When fire destroyed Grass Valley later that year, Delano further demonstrated his commitment to the town and its people by leading its rebuilding, and, through the years, serving as a treasurer and alderman. In 1856 he left Wells Fargo to open his own bank.

Delano continued to write and published his work in the region's more literary magazines: *Hutching's Illustrated California Magazine*, the *Hesperians*, and the *Golden Era*. In 1856 a second collection of his sketches appeared under the title *Old Block's Sketch Book; or, Tales of California Life*. The following year he wrote a two-act play, *A Live Woman in the Mines; or, Pike County Ahead*, which concerned the desperate plight of a young mining couple and featured such notable types as Old Swamp ("the Sermonizer"), High Betty Martin, Pike County Jess ("the Poet and Philanthropist"), Sluice ("the Plucked Pigeon"), and the gamblers Cash and Dice, characters already developed in his sketches.

In 1856 Delano's daughter joined him in Grass Valley, followed several years later by his wife, who had remained in the East to care for their invalid son. Unfortunately, his daughter suffered a mental breakdown and, by 1866, was committed to an asylum in New York. He was deeply affected by her departure, and, under the pretext of failing health, took a short trip to Nicaragua. His wife died in 1871 and was buried in Grass Valley. In August 1872 Delano married Marie Harmon of Warren, Ohio, "a handsome woman in her early forties," who was then visiting California. Delano died in Grass Valley. His passing was deeply mourned by the town.

Northern Californians resurrected Delano's writings by reprinting *Pen-Knife Sketches* (1934) and *The Miner's Progress* (1943) and by assembling another collection of his newspaper sketches under the title *A Sojourn with Royalty* (1936). This was followed by *Alonzo Delano's California Correspondence* (1952), a collection of his letters to newspapers. Critics have been quick to place Delano and his humor in the company of Bret Harte, John Phoenix, Mark Twain, and other noted humorists of the second half of the nineteenth century.

• In addition to his journal, sketches, and correspondence, the most extensive biographical work can be found in Edmund G. Kinyon's forward to *A Sojourn with Royalty*. G. Ezra Dane offers a biographical essay in his introduction to the 1934 reprint of *Pen-Knife Sketches; or, Chips of the Old Block*. An overview of his literary career can be found in Franklin Walker's *San Francisco's Literary Frontier* (1939). Glenn Loney includes Delano's *A Live Woman in the Mines* in *California Gold Rush Plays* (1983) and offers a brief assessment of Delano's life and writings.

RICHARD HENRY

DELANO, Amasa (21 Feb. 1763–21 Apr. 1823), New England mariner and author, was born in Duxbury, Massachusetts, the son of Samuel Delano and Abigail Drew. His father, a well-to-do shipbuilder, joined the American army when the Revolution broke out and was almost immediately taken prisoner. "Treated with great harshness and severity," he was released before the war ended and resumed his trade. Meanwhile, over his father's objections, Delano had entered the army at the age of fourteen and shipped out on the privateer *Mars* at sixteen. In 1782 he sailed on the *Peacock*, a new ship he built with his father, for the West Indies; he alternately sailed there and built ships until 1787, when he undertook a voyage to Ireland, which he described in his famous *Narrative* as "a beautiful country, which afforded every kind of provision in great abundance. The inhabitants are the most noble-minded, and possess the highest sense of honour of any that I ever was acquainted with." In 1787 he commanded a ship trading with Portugal, but on the return voyage it was wrecked off Cape Cod, and he was left deeply in debt and unemployed.

Delano's opportunity for fame and fortune came in 1790. A new ship, the *Massachusetts*, weighing 900 tons and 116 feet long, had been built at Quincy to engage in the recently opened and much-talked-about China trade. Delano booked on as second officer and began keeping the journal that would form the basis of his *Narrative of Voyages and Travels in the Northern and Southern Hemispheres, Comprising Three Voyages Round the World* (1817). He published this lengthy—about 600 pages—yet readable and frequently exciting story in Boston, and it was reprinted several times in the nineteenth century. The *Massachusetts*, "as noble a ship as ever swam the seas," was sold to a Danish company in the Dutch East Indies in December 1790, but Delano quickly booked passage on a British ship, the *Panther*. Despite the animosity between the two countries, the crew and officers treated him kindly. Delano remarks they were also "honest, generous, and friendly" to the natives they encountered in the South Seas: "Most of that of which we complain, of the character of the natives . . . is owing to ourselves, to our avarice and cupidity, to our selfishness and the disregard of our own principles."

If there is a theme to Delano's tales, which range over India, China, Polynesia, Africa, and South America, it is his open-minded curiosity and healthy respect for the diversity of cultures he encountered: "Virtue and vice, happiness and misery, are much more equally distributed to nations than those are permitted to suppose who have never been from home, and who believe, like the Chinese, that their residence is the center of the world, of light, of privilege, and of enjoyment." His impressions of China suggest this balanced viewpoint: the people "seem born for the active bustle of commerce. They are indefatigable, industrious, and will submit to any drudgery, however laborious, that is attended with a certainty of gain. Cunning, however, and deceitful to the last degree, they take a pride in imposing on Europeans." Observing the Malays' religious ceremony, which consisted almost entirely of music, he at first thought it "ridiculous and absurd, but it appears rational upon examination. . . . It is seldom just or useful for travellers to censure the forms of religion and devotion, which they find abroad, different from their own country."

Although he had no children with his wife, Hannah Appleton (date of marriage unknown), Delano was obliged to support two brothers and an invalid nephew. The exciting voyages he made on several ships were undertaken by a man who called himself "a child of misfortune." He takes pains in his *Narrative* to remind his readers that "in preparing for a long voyage, a man should take great care that his business should be settled, and agreements made so binding, that on his return home, he could keep clear of being dragged into the law, harassed, and poxed out of all his hard earnings." The *Narrative* enjoyed a modest success, and its sales helped Delano and his family over the last few years of his life.

Delano is most noted as the source of Herman Melville's short story "Benito Cereno." Apparently those who read Melville did not read Delano, for the connection was only discovered in 1928 by Harold H. Scudder. Delano told of how he rescued a Spanish ship that had been seized by the slaves it was transporting, its crew being forced by the slaves to pretend all was well until Delano was out of the way. But Delano spotted the ruse and brought the Spanish vessel into port despite his ambivalence about the slave trade. Melville adapted just one adventure in Delano's exciting and fascinating travelogue, which gives a real taste of what it was like to be a seaman in the early republic.

• Delano's own *Narrative of Voyages and Travels in the Northern and Southern Hemispheres, Comprising Three Voyages Round the World* (1817), with a biographical appendix, is the source on which all later authors have relied. Harold H. Scudder, "Melville's Benito Cereno and Capt. Delano's Voyages," *PMLA* 43 (1928): 502–32, links Delano and Melville. See also J. A. Delano, *Genealogical History and Alliances of the American House of Delano, 1621–1899* (1899).

WILLIAM PENCAK

DELANO, Columbus (5 June 1809–23 Oct. 1896), congressman and secretary of the interior, was born in Shoreham, Vermont, the son of James Delano and Lucinda Bateman. James died when Columbus was six, and Columbus came under the care of his uncle Luther Bateman, a farmer, with whose family he moved to Mount Vernon, Ohio, in 1817. Although obliged to work at an early age, he obtained sufficient schooling to study law in the office of Hosmer Curtis and was admitted to the bar in 1831. To supplement his practice he sought appointment as county prosecutor and, when that office became elective in 1832, won a three-year term, running as a National Republican. He resigned in his second term when his law practice had become larger. In 1834 he married Elizabeth Leavenworth, with whom he had two children.

In 1844 the local Whig congressional nominee died, and Whig leaders asked Delano, an excellent stump speaker, to take his place on the ticket. Delano prevailed in the election by just twelve votes. Antislavery was a burning issue in Delano's Western Reserve district, and he quickly identified with radical antislavery Whigs in Congress. He was one of only fourteen House Whigs who voted against the Mexican War, and he vigorously endorsed the Wilmot Proviso, which would have excluded slavery from territory acquired from Mexico. Although antislavery supporters backed him for governor, his controversial opinions prevented his nomination by the Whigs. Similarly disappointed by the Whigs' nomination of southern slaveowner Zachary Taylor for president in 1848, Delano angrily predicted the demise of the Whig party.

In 1850 Delano moved to New York City, where he was a banker for five years with Delano, Dunlevy & Company. Returning to Mount Vernon with capital to invest in sheep raising and farming, Delano again became interested in politics with the rise of the Republican party. When his ambitions were continually blocked by Radical leaders Salmon P. Chase and Benjamin F. Wade, Delano sided with more moderate antislavery elements in his party. He seconded Abraham Lincoln's nomination at the 1860 Chicago convention, and in 1864 he was Lincoln's chief Ohio supporter for renomination. Although frequently a contender for senatorial and gubernatorial nominations in the 1860s because of his support from party moderates, he always lost out to candidates with broader appeal.

Delano served briefly as commissary general for Ohio's troops at the beginning of the Civil War until responsibility for their subsistence was taken over by the U.S. government. In 1863 he was elected to the Ohio General Assembly for a two-year term and chaired the Judicial Committee, which endorsed voting by Ohio soldiers in the field. The following year Delano was elected to the Thirty-ninth Congress (1865–1867), where he chaired the Committee on

Claims. After Lincoln's assassination, he supported Andrew Johnson's efforts simply to restore, rather than reconstruct, the southern states but ultimately came to support federal guarantees of the civil rights of freedpeople in opposition to the president. He is classified, however, among the more moderate members of the party on constitutional and race issues. About this time Delano gave up the practice of law and, outside of politics, devoted himself entirely to sheep raising and banking in Mount Vernon. Delano was a strong advocate of tariff protection on wool, speaking vigorously in favor of the Wool and Woolens Act of 1867. Radicals distrusted Delano, who was apparently defeated for reelection by 271 votes in 1866, but he contested the count in several locations and resumed his seat on 3 June 1868.

Seeking to end factionalism and appreciating Delano's background in finance, President Ulysses S. Grant appointed him commissioner of internal revenue in 1869. Delano reorganized the department and increased revenue. He did not, however, personally address the problem of tax avoidance by whiskey distillers, which would soon result in scandal for the Grant administration. Grant appointed Delano to his cabinet as secretary of the interior in 1870. During his five years of service Delano implemented Grant's "peace policy" toward the Indians, which encouraged the extermination of the buffalo to force tribes onto reservations, used Christian organizations to teach agricultural life styles, and withheld annuities to punish Indians for noncooperation with governmental policies. The plan was disastrous for Native Americans, depriving them of economic and cultural resources and encouraging resistance rather than peace, and it anticipated the provision of individual homesteads for Indian families with the remainder of native lands opened to non-Indians. Democrats in Congress investigated allegations that inferior goods were supplied to some reservations during his tenure, but in this Delano was clearly not involved. His son, however, with Delano's apparent knowledge, did demand to be paid for participating in government surveys for which he did no work. Delano worked eagerly to promote the interests of western railroads. As a result, Democrats routinely portrayed him as a corruptionist, and he resigned his post in 1875 under a cloud. In retrospect Delano appears primarily to have tolerated rather than participated in corrupt activities.

Returning to Ohio, Delano served as president of the National Wool Growers' Association and advised Congress on tariff duties on wool as late as 1890. He endowed a grammar school at Kenyon College and served on the college's board of trustees for many years. He was a warden of the Episcopal church when he died at his estate outside Mount Vernon. Through much of his career, Delano promoted free labor, business growth, and economic development, important components of an expanding American capitalism, whose triumph justified, to his mind, almost any means.

• Delano's papers are at the Library of Congress and the University of North Carolina at Chapel Hill. See also the Records of the Office of the Secretary of the Interior (RG 48) in the National Archives. For biographical sketches see Joseph A. Smith, *History of the Republican Party in Ohio* (1898) and *Biographical Record of Knox County, Ohio* (1902). On Ohio politics see Stephen Maizlish, *The Triumph of Sectionalism* (1983), and Felice Bonadio, *North of Reconstruction: Ohio Politics, 1865–1870* (1970). On Indian affairs see Francis Paul Prucha, *The Great Father: The United States Government and the American Indians* (1984). An obituary is in the *New York Times*, 24 Oct. 1896.

PHYLLIS F. FIELD

DELANO, Jane Arminda (12 Mar. 1858–15 Apr. 1919), nurse and administrator, was born in Townsend, New York, the daughter of George Delano, a Union soldier who died of yellow fever in 1864, and Mary Ann Wright. Some sources list the year of her birth as 1862. Her mother later married Samuel Thomson, and Delano grew up in their home in Montour Falls, New York, where she attended a country school and Cook Academy. Delano taught in a country school for two terms; then, influenced by a friend preparing for missionary nursing in India, she enrolled in 1884 in the Bellevue Hospital Training School for Nurses in New York City, graduating in 1886.

After graduation Delano became a head nurse at Bellevue until a yellow fever epidemic in 1888 drew her to serve as superintendent of nurses at Sand Hills Hospital in Jacksonville, Florida. Her insistence on mosquito netting around each patient's bed ensured that her nurses avoided contracting the disease—even though mosquitoes had not yet been identified as the carriers. In 1889 Delano provided nursing care in Bisbee, Arizona, to the families of a copper-mining company's employees during a typhoid fever epidemic. She helped to establish a hospital for the company and served as superintendent of nurses. She then engaged in private-duty nursing for the next two years.

From 1891 to 1896 Delano served as assistant superintendent of nurses and instructor at the School of Nursing, University of Pennsylvania Hospital. She left nursing to attend courses at the University of Buffalo Medical School until she decided that becoming a doctor was not her calling. When the New York School of Civics and Philanthropy opened, Delano was one of its first students. From 1900 to 1902 she engaged in social work as the superintendent of the Girls' Department of the House of Refuge, Randall's Island, in New York City. Off duty, she entertained, guided, and educated young girls in her home. A trustee of the House of Refuge, impressed with Delano's selfless efforts, made her a beneficiary of his will, providing her with lifelong financial independence.

From 1902 to 1906 Delano was superintendent of Bellevue Hospital's Training School for Nurses, resigning to care for her mother in Charlottesville, Virginia, until the latter's death in 1908. Delano then traveled in Europe until returning home to become superintendent of the Army Nurse Corps (ANC) in 1909. As ANC superintendent she traveled to Hawaii, the Philippines, China, and Japan to obtain firsthand information on Army nurses' working and living conditions.

From 1900 to 1912 Delano served three terms as president of the Nurses' Associated Alumnae (later called the American Nurses' Association or ANA), which required extensive traveling, speaking, and writing. Throughout her career she wrote numerous articles, which were published in nursing journals. For ten years she wrote a monthly column, "Red Cross Nursing," for the *American Journal of Nursing*. She also served as president of its board of directors from 1908 to 1911. In 1913 she wrote, with Isabel McIsaac, *American Red Cross Textbook on Elementary Hygiene and Home Care of the Sick*, for the Red Cross's volunteer nurses' aides auxiliary corps she had helped to establish.

The American Red Cross had been reorganized in 1905 and had been working toward a solution whereby the nursing profession could provide the right numbers and types of nurses in times of war or national disaster. In 1909, in addition to becoming ANC superintendent and serving as president of the ANA, Delano was appointed chairman of the new National Committee on Red Cross Nursing Services. She now filled three key positions that could bring this dilemma to a resolution. She devoted her efforts to establishing a Red Cross nursing reserve, as well as to improving nurses' pay and working conditions and establishing nursing as a respected profession. To assist nurses in time of need, Delano established the Nurses' Relief Fund. In 1912 she resigned as ANC superintendent to concentrate on the Red Cross nursing reserve issue.

Delano, at her own request, was appointed first director of the Red Cross Nursing Service. In 1913 the War Department formally accepted Red Cross enrollment as the ANC reserve. When World War I began, Delano offered the services of Red Cross nurses, through the State Department, to each of the warring nations. Weeks later nurses departed for France, Germany, Belgium, Austria, Serbia, and England aboard the USS *Red Cross*, "the Mercy Ship." When the United States entered the war in April 1917, the Red Cross Nursing Service, owing to Delano's enormous recruiting efforts, could immediately supply 8,000 nurses. In 1918 Delano became director of the Red Cross Department of Nursing. By war's end she had supervised the mobilization of more than 20,000 nurses for overseas duty to the army, navy, and Red Cross, as well as recruiting nurses needed for the influenza epidemic that swept the nation in 1918.

Delano sailed for Europe in January 1919 to assess how the Red Cross could best help the devastated countries and to plan for future emergencies. Exposed to severe winter cold, she contracted a sore throat and ear infection, which developed into mastoiditis. After several unsuccessful operations, she died in Savenay, France.

Having no living relatives, Delano left her $500,000 fortune to nurses and nursing organizations, including the Bellevue Alumnae. Her will also established the Delano Red Cross Nursing Service, providing $25,000 to send nurses to locations unable to afford public health nurses. Her name now graces the nursing residence at Walter Reed Army General Hospital and numerous American Legion posts. She is honored further with memorials in Washington, D.C., and Bordeaux, France. Delano's vision, organizational skills, leadership, and tenacity were critical and instrumental in ensuring that the United States had a trained, competent, and ready reserve of nurses in sufficient numbers to care for its soldiers when it entered World War I.

• Delano's primary paper collection is located at Montour Falls Memorial Library in New York. In Washington, D.C., Delano papers are in the National Archives, American Red Cross collection; the U.S. Army Center of Military History, Nursing Archives; the U.S. Army Surgeon General's Office; and the National Library of Medicine, World War I Records and Archives. Delano papers are also at Mugar Memorial Library, Boston University; the Army War College, Records and Archives, in Carlisle, Pa.; and Bellevue Hospital Archives, Records and Newsletter Collection, in New York City. Mary E. Gladwin, *The Red Cross and Jane Arminda Delano* (1931), is the most comprehensive biography of Delano. The American Red Cross published a brochure, *Jane A. Delano: A Biography* (1952). Lyndia Flanagan, *One Strong Voice: The Story of the American Nurses' Association* (1976), includes two of Delano's speeches as president.

CONNIE L. REEVES

DELANO, William Adams (21 Jan. 1874–12 Jan. 1960), architect, was born at Madison Square, New York City, the son of Eugene Delano, a banker, and Susan Magoun Adams. His maternal grandfather, Dr. William Adams, was the parson of Madison Square Presbyterian Church, later the director of the Union Theological Seminary, and a descendant of two U.S. presidents, John Adams and John Quincy Adams. Delano's father began what was to be a successful banking career in New York City with Brown Brothers Harriman and Company, but the family was sent to Philadelphia in 1880 so that his father could run the Brown Brothers office there. It was here that young Delano first learned of his love for architecture during the building of the family country house in Bryn Mawr. After attending the Lawrenceville School (1887–1891) he went on to Yale College, graduating in 1895. As a member of the senior society, Scroll & Key, he became friends with Cornelius "Neily" Vanderbilt III, who later introduced him to some of his most important clients. After Yale Delano enrolled in Columbia's recently founded architectural school but soon withdrew to become an apprentice in the offices of Carrère & Hastings. Thomas Hastings, one of the partners, encouraged the younger man and sent him around 1897–1898 to study at the École des Beaux Arts in Paris, where he won a number of medals while at the *atelier* of Victor Laloux. He gained his diploma in 1902.

Upon his return from France in 1903, Delano joined his Carrère & Hastings colleague and École schoolmate Chester Holmes Aldrich in a small architectural office in New York. Almost immediately the pair garnered large and prestigious commissions. Through family connections, Aldrich was commissioned to design a house for John D. Rockefeller called "Kykuit," at the family compound in Pocantico, New York; meanwhile, Delano's chance European encounter with industrialist Henry Walters led to work in Baltimore—the Walters Art Gallery (1905–1910). The partnership generally functioned so that each man directed the design of his own jobs and acted as a critic for the other's projects. By 1910 the firm had built and published a dozen or more major residential, commercial, and institutional buildings, gaining national prominence. Delano also served on the Columbia architecture faculty from 1903 to 1910. He married Louisa Potter Sheffield in 1907 and in 1910 built the family a country house in Muttontown, Long Island, a place that became his spiritual home. They had one child.

Under Delano's leadership, the firm distinguished itself initially in the design of houses in the fashionable upper-class enclaves in and around New York City. A circa-1940s office register lists some 175 residential commissions, including city houses, country houses, and remodelings. Beginning with a series of handsome Georgian-classical townhouses in New York, such as those for Robert Brewster (1907), Willard Straight (1913–1915), and Harold I. Pratt (1919), Delano established a network of wealthy and socially prominent clients, many of whom he counted as close friends; these included Gertrude Vanderbilt Whitney, her cousin Mrs. James (Adele Sloane) Burden, Jr., the attorneys Bronson Winthrop and Egerton Winthrop, Vincent Astor, Mr. and Mrs. Paul Mellon, Victor Morawetz, and Mr. and Mrs. Benjamin Moore. His largest estate, "Oheka," was built at Huntington, Long Island, for the banker Otto H. Kahn (c. 1915–1930), while over a dozen more were constructed along the North Shore "Gold Coast." These restrained, bucolic country houses ranged in style from red-brick Georgian and French chateau-esque to English stuccoed cottages, each updated and adapted to client, site, and budget.

As he moved between the boardrooms of New York City and the country clubs of Long Island, Delano inevitably received commissions for institutions that were part of the exclusive universe of high society: clubs, schools, churches, and businesses. New York was graced by several of his elegant club buildings, including the Knickerbocker Club (1913) and Brook Association (c. 1915). The firm's only large New York commercial building, for Brown Brothers & Co. at 59 Wall Street, is no longer standing. Delano & Aldrich designed numerous buildings for the Lawrenceville School, Wright Hall, Sterling Chemistry Laboratory, and William L. Harkness Hall at Yale, the entire campus of the Yale Divinity School, and a significant master plan, including buildings, for the U.S. Military Academy at West Point in 1948. Of two dozen churches, the Third Church of Christ Scientist (1922–1924) at 583 Park Avenue in New York is the firm's best known.

Delano was proud of his record of public service, which began with a stint on the National Commission of Fine Arts under Calvin Coolidge in 1924. From this came his first renovation work on the White House; a continuing consulting role (from 1924) resulted in the celebrated second-story porch designed for President Harry S. Truman during 1949–1950. Delano noted in 1958 that he personally knew "every president of the United States from Teddy Roosevelt to the present day, except Harding" (New Yorker, 5 Apr. 1958). In 1927 Delano was appointed to the prestigious committee of architects who planned the massive Federal Triangle in Washington, designing the circular plaza on 12th Street and a new Post Office Department complex, though his design was left incomplete when preservationists managed to block his plan to demolish the old Post Office. But Delano's most cherished government commission was the U.S. Chancellery on the Place de la Concorde in Paris, completed in the early 1930s. A devoted Francophile, the architect took particular pleasure in seeing this classical project through construction while living in his favorite European capital.

During the latter years of his career, and after Aldrich had left the firm in 1935 to pursue other interests, Delano and his associates designed fourteen original buildings (1937–1940) for the so-called North Beach Airport in Queens, which eventually would become La Guardia Airport. Fiorello La Guardia himself appointed the architects for this WPA project, perhaps on the strength of their previous work for Pan American Airways. Never attracted to the modernist idiom, Delano acquitted himself well in the functionalist hangar buildings but was less successful with the small administration buildings, which eventually were replaced by terminals that were in use at the end of the century. In another confrontation with the machine aesthetic, in 1936 he was appointed to the seven-member Board of Design that oversaw plans for the New York World's Fair. There he watched the architectural world shift before him, away from the restrained traditional forms that he employed so persuasively over fifty years. Of the experience, he could only remark that "the Fair's many ultra-modernistic buildings . . . perhaps foreshadowed some of the confused thinking that exists today" (Nevins and Albertson, p. 82). Delano was "of counsel" to his firm through the 1950s. He died in New York.

William A. Delano was the epitome of a "gentleman architect"—one of the most successful and socially prominent of a large group of early twentieth-century designers who were graced with the patronage of the country's wealthiest families and most powerful business leaders. With his equally well-connected partner, Chester Holmes Aldrich, he produced a large and distinguished body of work during a career spanning a half-century. Their buildings were socially correct and traditional, but they were also highly rational in concept, refined in proportion, and built with up-to-date technologies. As a measure of the respect accorded him by his colleagues, Delano was honored in 1953 with the Gold Medal of the American Institute of Architects (AIA), the profession's highest accolade.

Delano's many other honors included fellowship, AIA (1912); honorary M.A., Yale University (1939); member, National Academy of Design (1938); member, National Academy of Arts and Letters (1937) and Gold Medalist in Architecture (1940); president, New York Chapter of the AIA (1928–1930); and president of the Society of Beaux Arts Architects (1927–1929). As a fully rounded man of his times, Delano manifested qualities that now belong to a bygone era. An artist, professional, philanthropist, civic leader, and confidant of politicians, business leaders, and the social elite, he gave to the term *architect* a rich, truly expansive significance, analogous to its Renaissance appellation: *uomo universale*.

• The most comprehensive collections of papers and drawings from the Delano & Aldrich firm are housed in the Architectural Archives of the Avery Architectural and Fine Arts Library, Columbia University, listed under the Delano Collection (1950) and the McIlvaine Collection (1986). Minor archives exist in the Museum of the City of New York and the New-York Historical Society. Delano's personal letters were given to the Yale University Libraries; firm documents to the American Academy of Arts and Letters. Although there is no published biography, the Columbia Oral History Project, under Allan Nevins and Dean Albertson, completed in 1950 a substantial autobiographical interview, "Reminiscences of William Adams Delano" (1972). Other reliable sources include Steven M. Bedford, "Delano & Aldrich," in *The Macmillan Encyclopedia of Architects*, vol. 1 (1982); and Mark A. Hewitt, "William Adams Delano and the Muttontown Enclave," *Antiques*, Aug. 1987, pp. 316–27, and "Domestic Portraits: The Early Long Island Country Houses of Delano & Aldrich," in *Long Island Architecture*, ed. Joann P. Krieg (1991). Only one book of the firm's work was published, *Portraits of Ten Country Houses Designed by Delano and Aldrich*, with drawings by Chester B. Price and an introduction by Royal Cortissoz (1924). Obituaries are in the *New York Times*, 13 Jan. 1960, and the *Journal of the AIA*, Mar. 1960.

MARK ALAN HEWITT

DELANY, Annie Elizabeth (3 Sept. 1891–25 Sept. 1995), dentist and author, was born in Raleigh, North Carolina, the daughter of Henry Beard Delany, an educator and Episcopal bishop, and Nanny James Logan. She grew up with her parents and nine siblings in Raleigh on the campus of St. Augustine's School, where her father, a former slave, served as priest and vice principal. After completing her studies at St. Augustine's in 1911, she taught school in Boardman, North Carolina, and then Brunswick, Georgia, before returning to school to take science courses at Shaw University in Raleigh.

In 1918 Delany moved, as did most of her brothers and sisters at about that time, to New York City, where she enrolled in 1919 in the dentistry program at Columbia University. She completed the D.D.S. in 1923, became only the second black female dentist licensed in the state of New York, and practiced her new profession in Harlem from 1923 until her retirement in 1950. She was well known in Harlem as "Dr.

Bessie," the "colored woman dentist," and her office was a meeting place for black leaders, including James Weldon Johnson and Franklin Frazier. During the depression of the 1930s she found herself twice evicted from her office, but she persisted in her work until her retirement.

During her childhood Delany had encountered the segregation and the discrimination of the Jim Crow South and the threat of violence that underlay the system. She remembered the first time she ran into Jim Crow when, as a child in the mid-1890s, she found she could no longer go to the park that she had previously played in, and she also recalled experimenting with the water from a "whites-only" fountain and discerning no difference in its taste. Yet she found that in the North, too, restrictions and dangers hemmed her in. Her closest brush with the Ku Klux Klan came on Long Island, and she attended Columbia instead of New York University, where her brother had studied dentistry, because NYU admitted only male students. Her mother had urged her as a young woman to decide whether she was going to marry and raise a family or be a doctor or dentist. As Delany said years later, it never occurred to anyone that a woman could have both a family and a profession, and she decided on a career. So did her older sister Sarah (known as Sadie), who taught in the New York City public schools from 1920 to 1960, and with whom Bessie lived for nearly eight decades either in New York City or nearby Mount Vernon.

Delany might have escaped notice by the wider world had she not in 1993 coauthored a bestselling memoir with her sister Sarah and with the assistance of Amy Hill Hearth. *Having Our Say: The Delany Sisters' First 100 Years* had its origins in an essay that Hearth had written for the *New York Times* at the time of Elizabeth's one-hundredth birthday. So enthusiastic were readers' responses to the article that Hearth continued her interviews and produced the book. Published when Bessie was 102 and Sadie was 104, *Having Our Say* offered a perceptive, witty review of the sisters' lives through the previous century. As Hearth observed in her introduction to the book, it was meant less as a study of black history or of women's history than of American history, but the sisters' age, race, and gender combined to provide a tart perspective on the past. These two black women spoke of their strong family, the racism and sexism that could have thwarted them, and their triumphs. They spoke of their experiences as teachers in the segregated South, their participation in the mass migration of African Americans from the South to the urban North, and their recollections of the Harlem Renaissance in the 1920s and the Great Depression of the 1930s.

Bessie Delany was a feisty woman who spoke her mind. "We loved our country," she observed, "even though it didn't love us back" (*Having Our Say*, p. 60). Asked her impression of the Statue of Liberty when she first entered New York harbor, she replied that it was important as a symbol to white immigrants but meant nothing to her. Regarding her experience at

Columbia she noted: "I suppose I should be grateful to Columbia, that at that time they let in colored people. Well, I'm not. They let me in but they beat me down for being there! I don't know how I got through that place, except when I was young nothing could hold me back" (p. 115). Delany twice saw Halley's comet. She died at her home in Mount Vernon.

• By the time Elizabeth Delany died, *Having Our Say* had sold nearly a million copies in hardback or paper; it had been translated into four foreign languages; and it was the basis for a Broadway play of the same name, reviewed by Vincent Canby in the *New York Times*, 7 Apr. 1995. A follow-up book, *The Delany Sisters' Book of Everyday Wisdom*, was published in 1994. Obituaries are in the *New York Times* and the *Washington Post*, both 26 Sept. 1995.

PETER WALLENSTEIN

DELANY, Martin Robinson (6 May 1812–24 Jan. 1885), black nationalist, was born in Charles Town, Virginia (now West Virginia), the son of Samuel Delany, a slave, and Pati Peace, a free black seamstress. In 1822 his mother moved the family to Chambersburg, Pennsylvania, to avoid punishment for violating state law after whites discovered that she had taught her five children to read and write. In 1823 Samuel joined the family after he had, with his wife's assistance, purchased his freedom. In 1832 Martin Delany moved to Pittsburgh, Pennsylvania, and the next year began an apprenticeship with Andrew N. McDowell, a local white doctor. In 1843 he married Catherine Richards. The couple had seven children, whom Delany proudly named after famous blacks. After being rejected by a number of medical schools, he entered Harvard Medical School in 1850 but was dismissed under the pressure of student protests.

While he practiced medicine at various points in his life, Delany, whose grandmother had taught him about his noble African heritage, nurtured a political and social activism that consumed most of his extraordinary talents. In Pittsburgh he became involved in black self-help organizations, a vigilance committee for the protection of fugitive slaves, and efforts to restore suffrage to black Pennsylvanians.

In 1843 Delany founded the *Mystery*, a short-lived abolitionist newspaper in which he attacked northern racial prejudice. During the late 1840s he was co-editor of Frederick Douglass's *North Star* and traveled as an abolitionist lecturer. His call for black economic self-determination and his critique of the black community's religiosity as an obstacle to achieving that end placed him among the most radical of abolitionists. In 1852 he published his argument for emigration as a means by which black Americans could break free of the psychological and physical domination of whites in *The Condition, Elevation, Emigration and Destiny of the Colored People of the United States*, which was well received by prominent black leaders but attacked by the white abolitionist press.

In 1856 Delany moved to Chatham, Ontario, where a significant number of blacks had settled and where he expected to find more support for his emigrationist

views. There he espoused a Pan-African philosophy that joined the destiny of American blacks with those of Africans and West Indians. In 1859 he explored the Niger Valley in West Africa, where he hoped to establish a settlement to grow cotton with free labor in direct competition with the slave South. He described the region and its prospects in his *Official Report of the Niger Valley Exploring Party* (1861). Although he was warmly received in Great Britain, where he lectured to publicize his venture, his African settlement failed to materialize. The African king with whom he had made a treaty by which to secure land for his settlement revoked the agreement. More importantly, the Civil War drew the attention of Delany and other African Americans back to the problem of slavery and emancipation in the United States.

Delany returned to the United States in 1861, became a recruiter of black troops, and in 1865 was commissioned a major in the 104th United States Colored Troops. After the war he served with the Freedmen's Bureau as a subassistant commissioner on the South Carolina coast at Hilton Head. There his message of black self-sufficiency merged with the Republican free-labor ideology of hard work and just treatment for the ex-slaves.

After receiving his military discharge in 1868, Delany became involved in South Carolina Republican party politics. In 1871 he continued his efforts to assist freedmen by attempting to persuade northern philanthropists to buy land and resell it to freedmen. The venture, he said, would be profitable for investors while it helped the ex-slaves to become good citizens. Delany, however, soon became disillusioned with his white Republican allies, who he believed were using the ex-slaves for their own political advancement. He therefore urged blacks to vote for whomever would serve their interests and threw his own support to the Democrats. Delany believed that such an alliance would be mutually beneficial because the interests of the state's white and black residents—capital and labor—were intertwined. This political shift did not, however, signal Delany's abandonment of his principles. In 1879 he published *Principia of Ethnology* in which he praised the accomplishments of African civilization.

In the late 1870s Delany edited the Charleston *Independent* for a brief period, served as a minor court official in Charleston for three years, and became involved in a short-lived Liberian emigration scheme. In 1880, after trying unsuccessfully to win a diplomatic appointment that would take him back to Africa, he returned to his family, which had resided since 1864 in the black community of Wilberforce, Ohio, where he died.

• Delany's personal papers were destroyed in a fire at Wilberforce University in April 1865. However, along with his published works, some insight into his thinking may be gained by examining original material in the seventeen-reel microfilm collection, *The Black Abolitionist Papers, 1830–1865*, ed. George E. Carter and C. Peter Ripley (1981). The bibliography of Cyril E. Griffith, *The African Dream: Martin R. Delany and the Emergence of Pan-African Thought* (1975), notes other collections that hold materials for Delany's postwar years. Griffith's work is essential for understanding Delany's intellectual development and may be supplemented with Robert M. Kahn, "The Political Ideology of Martin Delany," *Journal of Black Studies* 4 (June 1984): 415–40. Two biographies of Delany are Dorothy Sterling, *The Making of an Afro-American: Martin R. Delany* (1971), and Victor Ullman, *Martin Delany: The Beginnings of Black Nationalism* (1971). Also see Floyd J. Miller, *The Search for Black Nationality: Black Colonization and Emigration, 1787–1863* (1975). An obituary is in the Charleston *News and Courier*, 8 Feb. 1885.

PAUL A. CIMBALA

DELARGE, Robert Carlos (15 Mar. 1842–14 Feb. 1874), politician, was born in Aiken, South Carolina. His father was a free black tailor, and his mother was a cloak maker of Haitian descent; their names are unknown. Though several records claim that DeLarge was born into slavery, it is more likely that his parents were free blacks who owned slaves. This peculiar and paradoxical designation surely inspired the dual sensibilities that later characterized his political and social life as both an advocate for universal black enfranchisement and a member of South Carolina's propertied, often exclusionist, mulatto elite. Fortunate to receive the benefits of the prewar education available to free black children, DeLarge attended primary school in North Carolina and Wood High School in Charleston. For a short time he was employed as a tailor and farmer, and some sources indicate that he was also a part-time barber. During the Civil War, he amassed some money as an employee of the Confederate navy, a curious affiliation in light of his Republican activities during Reconstruction. He later donated most of his Civil War earnings to the state Republican party. By the time he became active in Reconstruction politics, DeLarge was a citizen of considerable standing in Charleston, as indicated both by his net worth of $6,650 in the 1870 census and his membership in the Brown Fellowship Society, a fraternal and charitable association founded in 1870 that admitted only mulattoes.

DeLarge's active political career began in 1865. Widely considered a "politician by inclination," he attended every political gathering he could get to and "talked continually at all of them" (Lamson, p. 37). An agent for the Freedmen's Bureau, he was named chairman of the Credentials Committee of the September 1865 Colored People's Convention in Charleston, where he mesmerized evening crowds with passionate speeches. Prompted by the lack of civil and educational rights for blacks in South Carolina following the Civil War, DeLarge and 102 colleagues drafted a petition to the state legislature calling for stronger civil rights provisions. The 1865 convention adopted DeLarge's resolution demanding the establishment of a universal public school system. Though he openly concurred with barring "ignorant" whites and blacks from voting, he also signed a petition asking for impartial male suffrage regardless of "race, color or previous condition." In November 1865 DeLarge attended the state black convention, and he chaired the Platform Committee of the 1867 South Carolina Republican Convention, where he was instrumental in advocating for public schools, the abolition of capital punishment, universal male suffrage with literacy restrictions, tax reform, welfare assistance to the poor of both races, funds for internal improvements like canals and railroads, and land distribution efforts.

Despite DeLarge's earlier activities, at the 1868 constitutional convention he emerged as an effective, though at times overly loquacious, leader. Described unimpressively as "a short man with brush sideburns and a receding hairline," he had a tendency to be stubborn and overbearing. His colleague Robert Brown Elliott referred to him as "a pigmy who is trying to play the part of a giant, elocutionizing himself into a perspiration which stood out upon his skin like warts." Nonetheless, DeLarge had considerable influence as a member of three standing committees. He supported the cessation of "further confiscation of lands and disfranchisement for political offenses" of ex-Confederates and former planters, which measure was ultimately defeated. Though he opposed laws to make school attendance compulsory, he argued successfully for a state-funded public school system. He advocated radical land redistribution initiatives, and the convention passed his resolution to ask Congress for a $1 million grant to purchase lands that would then be sold to the state's white and black poor. The petition was later denied at the federal level.

Elected to the state house of representatives following the convention, DeLarge served from 1868 to 1870 as chairman of the Ways and Means Committee and sponsored important railroad legislation. Also active as a civic leader, he cofounded the Enterprise Railroad Company, was a member of the Sinking Fund Commission and the board of regents of the state lunatic asylum, and served as a delegate to the 1869 state labor convention.

In April 1870, while still a member of the state legislature, DeLarge was appointed as C. P. Leslie's successor to head the troubled South Carolina Land Commission. According to DeLarge, the land monopolies that still existed in the postbellum South made "the rich richer and the poor poorer," and as head of the land commission he promised to heed "the voice of the impoverished people of the state." In March 1871 he reported that nearly 2,000 small tracts had been sold or would soon be taken over by homeowners who would have eight years to pay for them. Shortly thereafter, however, it became clear that DeLarge's public promises to facilitate the state's radical land experiment belied a series of unscrupulous private transactions at the expense of the commission. His tenure at the land commission was marked by fraud and mismanagement. The widespread opinion was that Governor Robert Scott, a Republican, had manufactured the appointment so that DeLarge could steal enough money from the coffers of the land commission to unseat Christopher C. Bowen, a white scalawag congressman. DeLarge subsequently defeated Bowen by fewer than 1,000 votes in the election of 1870. DeLarge was involved in some unauthorized and highly questionable exchanges of money, and when he resigned from the commission in March 1871, his successor, Secretary of State Francis L. Cardozo, discovered that DeLarge had kept no written records of the commission's operations or financial transactions.

DeLarge seized his victory over Bowen in the hotly contested congressional election as an opportunity to "demand for my race an equal share everywhere." While a member of Congress, he criticized the lawlessness of blacks and whites in both political parties and supported the Fourteenth Amendment and the quick readmission of ex-Confederates to political life. Despite his moderate successes as a statesman, he spent most of his short congressional career mired in controversy. In a speech during the 1870 campaign he said, "I hold that my race has always been Republican for necessity only." Consequently he was accused of advocating the creation of a "black man's party" as a challenge to the Republican party. Though he denied harboring such sentiments, DeLarge's occasional tendency to ally himself publicly with black nationalists like Martin R. Delany did not help bolster his cause with white Republicans and more integrationist black leaders. Furthermore, during the second half of his term in Congress DeLarge was largely preoccupied with trying to prove his right to keep his seat. On 24 January 1873, before his term expired, the House accepted a Committee on Election report that concluded that fraud and "other irregularities" were so common during the 1870 campaign between Bowen and DeLarge that neither candidate deserved a congressional seat. Shortly thereafter DeLarge was unseated and returned to Charleston, where he was quickly appointed a city magistrate by Governor Scott. DeLarge enjoyed considerable influence until his death of consumption in Charleston. The date of his marriage and the name of his wife are not known. He had one daughter.

DeLarge's life and career constitute something of a tragedy. A political figure committed at once to self-promotion and social justice, he was revered by the people of Charleston and yet unsuccessful in the halls of legislative power. DeLarge's social conservatism was often challenged during Reconstruction by his associations with more radical black peers. Nonetheless, on the day of his funeral city magistrates closed their offices to observe a day of mourning for the loss of their popular young colleague.

• No collection of DeLarge's papers exists. *Proceedings of the 1868 Constitutional Convention of South Carolina* help to locate DeLarge's ideas within the context of Reconstruction debates. For useful biographical sketches of DeLarge's activities, see William C. Hine, "Black Politicians in Reconstruction Charleston, South Carolina," *Journal of Southern History* 49 (1983); and Herbert Aptheker, "South Carolina Negro Conventions, 1865," *Journal of Negro History* 31 (1946). Good secondary works include Francis Simkins and Robert H. Woody, *South Carolina during Reconstruction* (1932); W. E. B. Du Bois, *Black Reconstruction in America, 1860–* *1880* (1935); Samuel Denny Smith, *The Negro in Congress, 1870–1901* (1940); Joel Williamson, *After Slavery: The Negro in South Carolina during Reconstruction, 1861–1877* (1965); Carol K. Rothrock Bleser, *The Promised Land: The History of the South Carolina Land Commission, 1869–1890* (1969); Peggy Lamson, *The Glorious Failure: Black Congressman Robert Brown Elliott and the Reconstruction of South Carolina* (1973); Thomas Holt, *Black Over White: The Negro in South Carolina during Reconstruction* (1979); and Eric Foner, *Reconstruction: America's Unfinished Revolution, 1863–1877* (1988).

TIMOTHY P. MCCARTHY

DELAVAN, Edward Cornelius (6 Jan. 1793–15 Jan. 1871), antiliquor leader, was born in Franklin, Westchester County, New York, the son of Stephen Delavan (occupation unknown) and Hannah Wallace. After his father died, the family moved to Albany, where the boy became an apprentice printer at Whiting, Backus & Whiting, from 1802 to 1806. He then attended the Reverend Samuel Blatchford's school in Lansingburgh for two years.

Young Delavan next clerked in his brother Henry's wholesale hardware business in Albany, became a partner at age twenty-one, and in 1815 moved to Birmingham, England, as the firm's import agent. In 1820 he returned to the United States and married Abigail Marvin Smith of Lyme, Connecticut. They had five children. Soon after his marriage, Delavan became a wholesale wine merchant in New York City. Amid the economic boom set off by the opening of the Erie Canal, he successfully speculated in real estate and around 1827 retired wealthy to the Albany area. He settled permanently in Ballston, Saratoga County, in 1833. His first wife died in 1848, and by 1850 he married Harriet Ann Schuyler, with whom he had one child. Continuing to invest in real estate, he had by 1860 accumulated $625,000, which made him one of the two dozen wealthiest New Yorkers.

Delavan devoted much of his fortune and most of his later life to the temperance movement. Shortly after Delavan's youthful retirement, the Reverend Nathaniel Hewitt recruited Delavan to the cause through a chance meeting on the street in Albany, and in 1829 Delavan played a key role in founding the New York State Temperance Society. Until the early 1830s temperance leaders tried to persuade Americans to stop or reduce the use of hard liquor, such as whiskey or rum. In 1831 Delavan became among the first to argue that the wealthy must give up wine, which was expensive, before ordinary Americans would quit drinking cheap hard liquor. At the suggestion of his coachman, he urged everyone to take the teetotal pledge, that is, to renounce all alcoholic beverages voluntarily. Delavan failed to get the state society to adopt his radical view, and in 1836 he quit. At a convention in Saratoga, New York, that same year he gave $10,000 to help launch the American Temperance Union on teetotal principles.

Delavan's attack on Christian communion wine produced controversy among temperance leaders in 1835. Delavan insisted that the "wine" mentioned in the Bible was unfermented grape juice. This dispute grew so bitter that Delavan left the Presbyterian church to become an Episcopalian. Delavan's religious argument did not appeal to his friends, abolitionist Gerrit Smith and Eliphalet Nott, president of Union College. They were willing to give up wine for ceremonial purposes but only on grounds of consistency and expediency. Smith and others scorned Delavan's approach, but, after a gentlemanly public disagreement, Nott yielded to Delavan, who became one of Union College's trustees from 1837 to 1870 and a major donor. He gave the college a substantial collection of minerals and shells in 1858.

Delavan frequently attacked commercial alcoholic beverages as impure. In 1835 he accused Albany's brewers of drawing water from a pond where a slaughterhouse and a glue factory dumped carcasses. He was sued for $300,000. In a celebrated case finally tried in 1840, he defended the truth of his charges and won an acquittal. In 1850 Delavan tried but failed to organize a life insurance company for abstainers. He believed, based on his knowledge of the wine trade, that adulterated beverages caused drinkers to die young.

In 1838 Delavan traveled to Europe to promote temperance. On the voyage over, he persuaded fifty-seven passengers to sign a petition urging the *Great Western* to withdraw liquor from its dining tables. He carried hundreds of antiliquor tracts with him and had them distributed and reprinted in England. Visits to France and Italy confirmed his disapproval of wine drinking countries, about which he later wrote a pamphlet, *Temperance of Wine Countries* (1860). In 1845 he established one of the first temperance hotels, Delavan House in Albany, which became a favorite resort for abstinent legislators. The hotel, however, lost money, and, much to Delavan's annoyance, the manager used a loophole in the lease to introduce liquor.

Delavan's greatest contribution to his cause was as a propagandist. According to his own count, he financed the publication and distribution of more than 36 million antiliquor tracts and periodicals. In 1837 he mailed an issue of the *Journal of the American Temperance Union* (1837–1865) to every member of Congress, minister, and postmaster in the United States. New, cheap printing technology made such action possible. Delavan employed one of the country's first steam-powered presses. In 1842 he commissioned a colored lithograph of Dr. Thomas Sewall's eight drawings of alcohol-diseased stomachs and furnished 150,000 reproductions to poorhouses, prisons, hospitals, and schools. In 1846 he sent a copy of one antiliquor leaflet to every household in New York State. No one had ever used direct mail advertising in that way before. In addition to the *Journal of the American Temperance Union*, he sponsored a series of periodicals, the *Temperance Recorder* (1832–1843), *American Temperance Intelligencer* (1834–1836), the *Enquirer* (1841–1847), and the *Prohibitionist* (1854–1856).

In politics Delavan followed William Henry Seward's reform faction in New York's Whig party. In 1845 he persuaded the New York legislature to enact local option prohibition, which voters throughout the state considered in 1846. More than 80 percent of the state's towns rejected liquor, but in 1847 many towns reversed themselves and voted to resume sales. In the 1850s Delavan advocated statewide prohibition, which New York adopted in 1855. The courts quickly overturned the law. Delavan then shifted to a program of voluntary abstinence. Embracing the American (Know Nothing) party, he publicly endorsed Millard Fillmore for president in 1856. By that time, Delavan's fanaticism against alcohol and disinterest in slavery placed him outside the mainstream of northern reformers.

During the Civil War, Delavan sent a million copies of a temperance tract to soldiers in the Union army. In 1868 he retired to Schenectady, New York, where he died. To the surprise of many, he left nothing to the antiliquor movement and gave his property, valued at $800,000 to $1 million, to his family. Liquorless towns in Wisconsin and Illinois were named in his honor.

• Some Delavan letters and an autobiographical fact sheet are at Union College. Other letters are in the Gerrit Smith Miller Collection at Syracuse University, in the John H. Cocke Papers at the University of Virginia, and in Miscellaneous Manuscripts at the Library of Congress. Important printed primary materials include *A Report of the Trial of the Cause of John Taylor vs. Edward C. Delavan* (1840) and Delavan's *Temperance Essays* (1865). A biographical sketch is in *American Temperance Magazine and Sons of Temperance Offering* 1 (1851): 30–41. Additional material may be found in Elmer M. Bennett, *The Delavan Family* (1940); Codman Hislop, *Eliphalet Nott* (1971); and John Marsh, *Temperance Recollections* (1866). Obituaries are in the *National Temperance Advocate*, Feb. 1871, and the *Schenectady Weekly Union*, 19 Jan. 1871. An article on the will is in the *New York Times*, 20 Jan. 1871.

W. J. RORABAUGH

DE LA WARR, Baron (9 July 1577–7 June 1618), governor of Virginia, was baptized Thomas West at Wherwell, Hampshire, England (probably also his place of birth), the son of Thomas West, the second baron De La Warr, and Anne Knollys. De La Warr began study at Queens College, Oxford, in 1592 but did not obtain a degree. He traveled in Italy during 1595. In 1596 he married Cecilia Shirley, the daughter of Sir Thomas Shirley; they eventually had seven children.

De La Warr was elected to and served in Parliament (1597–1599) for Lymington. He then served with the English army in the Netherlands and in Ireland, where he was knighted by the earl of Essex on 12 July 1599. De La Warr was later charged with complicity in the Essex Rebellion against Queen Elizabeth; briefly imprisoned in London, he was released after Essex testified that De La Warr was not involved in the rebellion. De La Warr succeeded to the peerage upon his father's death in 1602, becoming the third baron De La Warr. Considering the recent rebellion, it is remarkable that he became a member of Queen Elizabeth's privy council. Following the queen's death, he also sat on the privy council of King James I.

The second charter of the Virginia Company of London named De La Warr as a grantee, and he became a member of the council of that company in 1609. On 28 February 1610 the council named him governor and captain general of Virginia, with a lifetime appointment. He sailed for Virginia on 1 April 1610, and his expedition of 150 colonists, in three ships, arrived in early June. De La Warr had arrived just in time to prevent the abandonment of the colony as the settlers who had survived the notorious "starving time" were about to sail home. De La Warr came ashore at Jamestown on 10 June. He publicly gave thanks that the colony had been saved and had his commission read aloud. He sanctioned a new law code, titled the "Articles, Lawes, and Orders, Divine, Politique, and Martiall for the Virginia Colony." This code was severe, even considering English law of the period. Capital punishment was ordained for speaking against the governor, refusing to attend church, and committing any type of theft. Clearly, the company in London and De La Warr intended to set a new, more vigilant tone for the colony.

Like many English settlers, De La Warr was severely affected by the Virginia climate. He later wrote that he had been "welcommed by a hote and violent Ague," which was treated by bloodletting, and he also suffered from flux, cramps, gout, and scurvy. Nevertheless, he took charge of the colony. He had three forts built to protect against threats from the shore by Indians and from the sea by pirates or Spaniards. He set French workers he had brought with him to planting the first vines in Virginia. On a less positive note, he aggravated relations between the colonists and the Indians. He and Captain Christopher Newport coerced an Indian chieftain into agreeing to bring corn to Jamestown. When the Indian leader failed to deliver the corn, De La Warr sent men who burned two Indian villages and killed fourteen Indians—a melancholy foreshadowing of what English-Indian relations were to become.

Due to his illnesses, De La Warr sailed from Jamestown on 28 March 1611, seeking to reach the island of "Mevis" (probably Nevis). Blown off course, he eventually landed in the Azores where his scurvy was cured by fruit, especially lemons. He proceeded to England and after his arrival published *A Short Relation . . . Touching His Unexpected Returne Home . . .* (1611). In this report, De La Warr described his illnesses and mentioned that he had built "three severall Forts." He described Virginia as "wonderfull fertile and very rich," especially in its hemp, vines, cod fishing, and trees for masts. He urged the company to "further so worthy a worke, as will redound both to the Glory of God, to the Credit of our Nation, and to the comfort of all those that have beene Instruments in the furthering of it." What De La Warr did not mention was that he had incurred the hostility of many of the Indians and that 150 men had died of disease in the ten months he had spent in Virginia.

De La Warr remained in England for several years; in his absence deputy governors ran the colony. He sailed from England in 1618 with 200 more settlers. He and his company stopped at St. Michael's Island in the Azores, where they were feted. Soon after he reembarked, De La Warr fell ill. He died on 7 June, and twenty-nine of his men also died during the voyage (there was some suspicion that their hosts had poisoned them). His widow petitioned for and received a pension of £500 per annum.

It is difficult to evaluate De La Warr as governor since he was only in Virginia for ten months. He had the confidence of the Virginia Company of London, and his military background qualified him to lead men in dangerous situations. He clearly understood the significance of the Virginia colony, both in terms of its commercial and its imperial potential. On the negative side, he proclaimed a harsh law code and was swift to act against the Indians in Virginia. De La Warr typified both the strengths and the failings of the Elizabethan adventures: bold and clever, they were also shortsighted and class-minded. Had he remained in Virginia after 1611, De La Warr would have been hard pressed to develop workable solutions to the problems that his deputy governors faced: Indian conflicts, land squabbles, food shortages, and continuing resentments between the "gentlemen" and the common folk of the Virginia colony.

• The papers of the West family (which became the Sackville-West family in 1843) are at Buckhurst and Knole in England, but they apparently contain little information about Thomas West. There also appears to be no book-length biography as yet. Some sources exist in the writings of Alexander Brown, notably, "Sir Thomas West, Third Lord de la Warr," *Magazine of American History* 9 (Jan. 1883): 1–30. See also Brown, *The Genesis of the United States* (1890), which contains numerous primary sources relating to De La Warr, especially "A True and Sincere Declaration of the Purpose and Ends of the Plantation Begun in Virginia." De La Warr's statement to the Virginia Company is in L. G. Tyler, *Narratives of Early Virginia* (1907). Virginia's first law code is in Peter Force, *Tracts and Other Papers Relating Principally to the Origin, Settlement and Progress of the Colonies in North America* (4 vols., 1836–1846). Lacking a personal diary or record book, it is difficult to ascertain the personality and the inner motivations of Lord De La Warr.

SAMUEL WILLARD CROMPTON

DELBRÜCK, Max (4 Sept. 1906–10 Mar. 1981), physicist-turned–molecular biologist, was born in Berlin, Germany, the son of Hans Delbrück, a historian, and Lina Thiersch. Born into the Prussian intellectual and political elite, Delbrück's identity was shaped by the legacies of both his maternal and paternal families. His father, noted for his prolific scholarship in military world history, came from a family of political leaders; Delbrück's uncle (also called Max Delbrück) was a famous industrial chemist in Berlin. The world-famous chemist Justus von Liebig was Max Delbrück's maternal great-grandfather, and his maternal uncle (by marriage), Adolf von Harnack, was Germany's foremost modern theologian and founder and first president of the Kaiser Wilhelm Gesellschaft. Nurtured within that distinguished family and steeped in the ideals of

Wissenschaft and *Bildung*, the young Delbrück possessed solid foundations for scholarship and leadership.

Although his elementary education suffered, as did his childhood, from the devastation of World War I, his Gymnasium years were enriching. He received little exposure to natural science, but by the time he graduated in 1924, Delbrück had developed an intense interest in astronomy. That summer he began his university career as an astronomy student in Tubingen and soon after in Göttingen. While German astronomy was on the decline in the mid-1920s, Germany, and especially Göttingen, was spearheading the revolution in physics. A combination of disappointments in astronomy and excitement with quantum mechanics drove Delbrück toward physics, and he completed his rather unexceptional doctorate in 1930. After a postdoctoral year at Bristol University, England, Delbrück received a Rockefeller Fellowship in 1931 to study with Niels Bohr in Copenhagen and Wolfgang Pauli in Zürich. This was a turning point in his career.

It was the Copenhagen experience that forged Delbrück's lifelong commitment to biology and friendship with Bohr. Inspired by Bohr's philosophical musings about the relevance of the complementarity principle in physics to biological phenomena, Delbrück decided to pursue what he termed "the riddle of life." Complementarity, evolved by Bohr in the 1920s to reconcile quantum physics with scientific rationality, asserted that no complete description of a quantal system was possible and that no single set of physical measurements could fix simultaneously all the parameters needed to specify fully the state of an atomic or subatomic system. Bohr suggested that in biology, by analogy, experiments aimed at measuring molecular properties of a living organism were fundamentally incompatible with those aimed at studying the organism's life functions. While working on nuclear fission with Lise Meitner at the Kaiser Wilhelm Institute for Chemistry in Berlin, Delbrück collaborated with geneticists at the neighboring Kaiser Wilhelm Institute for Biology. Motivated by the goal of establishing complementarity as a guiding principle in biology, Delbrück hoped to show that fundamental knowledge of animate nature emerged out of uncertainty: just as in quantum physics, complete atomic accounts of organisms interfered with the essential properties of life. He began by studying the effects of X rays on mutations in Drosophila, providing explanations of genetic stability and change in terms of a quantum mechanical model. His approach, coupled with his talent for group organizing, gained him in 1937 a Rockefeller Fellowship in biology, which brought him to the California Institute of Technology.

Despite the recognition, Delbrück was not satisfied with his biological work and with the complex Drosophila as a mathematical genetic model. At Caltech's biology division (headed by Thomas H. Morgan) Delbrück stumbled upon bacterial viruses (phage), the simplest system of replication, which he envisioned as "atoms in biology." In the next couple of years Delbrück characterized phage replication rigorously and established it as a powerful conceptual model and experimental system of genetics. By then World War II had broken out. Being strongly opposed to the Nazis and having decided to remain in the United States, he accepted in 1940 a position in the physics department at Vanderbilt University in Nashville, with provisions to also continue his phage research. From 1940 to 1943, with Cold Spring Harbor on Long Island as a meeting ground for summer research, Delbrück was joined by microbiologists Salvador Luria and Alfred Hershey. Focusing on mechanisms of bacterial and phage replication and mutation and on genetic recombination in phage, they laid the foundation of what became known as the "phage school," one of the most important research schools in molecular biology.

In 1941 Delbrück married Mary Adeline Bruce Manny, a graduate of Scripps College in California. She became closely involved in his scientific and social life. She also made his life harmonious, grounding him in America and bearing him a large, strong-knit family. Their first two children were born in the 1940s; the second two in the 1960s.

Delbrück's remarkable effectiveness in science lay not only in his powers of theorizing but in his ability to inspire and lead. He became appreciated for his wit and critical inquiry: "I don't believe a word of it" became a hallmark of his perennial skepticism. In the summer of 1944, due to Delbrück's influence, phage workers decided to define and standardize the phage system and the experimental conditions. This accelerated the research, the coordination of results, and teaching. Anticipating and promoting the expansion of the new field, Delbrück in 1945 organized the annual phage course at Cold Spring Harbor, thereby setting off a rapid growth of phage research that continued into the 1960s—phage workers by then numbering in the hundreds. The technically minimalist, nonchemical approach, which coupled mathematics with mapping the genetic loci of viral recombinations, attracted many researchers to genetics. His program was instrumental in luring physicists to biology, thus altering its disciplinary nature. In 1947 the internationally acclaimed Delbrück returned to Caltech as professor of biology.

Due to Delbrück's intellectual leadership and charisma, Caltech became a world center of virus research. In addition to phage work, animal virology and its extension to tumor virology, cancer, and polio research were studied. By the late 1950s the collective works guided by Delbrück explained salient features of viral infection, organization of viral and bacterial genomes, their modes of replication, recombination, and mutation. By then, however, the elucidation of the double-helix structure of DNA by James D. Watson (member of the phage group) and Francis Crick (1953) underscored the explanatory power of biochemistry. This result effectively terminated Delbrück's personal quest to explain gene replication in terms of the complementarity principle. While continuing the management of phage genetics, his own intellectual efforts focused on neurophysiology. In search of the complementarity principle, he turned to phycomyces as the simplest model system for studying sensory transduction of signals. He pursued this project until his death, but he neither built a major research school nor attained his own epistemic goal.

Delbrück contributed also to the efforts to rebuild German science in the postwar years. Several areas in life science, especially genetics and molecular biology, languished in Germany during the decade after the war. After a 1956 visit to the University of Cologne, where he introduced phage genetics, it was agreed that an institute of genetics be founded in Cologne, with Delbrück as its first director. He directed the Institut für Genetik from 1961 to 1963. He was a member of the National Academy of Science, the Royal Danish Academy, the Deutsche Akademie der Naturforscher Leopoldina, the Royal Society of London, and the American Academy of Arts and Sciences. In 1969 he was awarded the Nobel Prize in Physiology and Medicine, shared with Luria and Hershey, for their contributions to molecular genetics.

Delbrück's remarkable influence in science stemmed only partly from his intellect and gift for teaching. Phage work in Pasadena, like physics in Copenhagen, was an enculturation. Colleagues and disciples participated in an unusual group experience—cohesiveness, collective intellectual criticism, jocular behavior, and camping trips. The Delbrücks' garden became an international meeting ground for colleagues, students, and visitors; their house, an intellectual and cultural sanctuary. Beyond his broad scientific and philosophical vision, Delbrück had a deep interest in music, a firm command of several languages, and a wide-ranging knowledge of classical and modern literature. These attributes added to his stature as an intellectual and eloquent spokesman on issues in both science and the humanities. Delbrück enjoyed life immensely, yet he knew how to confront death. After a multiple myeloma was discovered in 1978, Delbrück extracted as much enjoyment as possible from his remaining time. He died in Pasadena. At his request, the memorial service held at Caltech celebrated the joy he gave and received in life.

Because of his immense popularity and international following, Delbrück's program has been portrayed as "the origins of molecular biology" and his trajectory from physics to biology as unique. However, perspectives from more recent historical studies of molecular biology have revised some of these interpretations. Scholars have shown how the Rockefeller Foundation—the principal sponsor of the molecular biology program—has shaped the careers of hundreds of life and physical scientists by investing vast institutional resources in physicochemical biology. As a long-term recipient of Rockefeller support, Delbrück's scientific trajectory appears as an element within a larger movement in American and European science. This explains why, despite his relatively low personal output, his collaborative and group projects carried so much weight within the foundation's molecular biology program. The enormous prestige of phage genetics has contributed also to the exclusion of biochemistry from historical reconstructions of molecular biology. Recent correctives have challenged the historiographic hegemony of the phage school, pointing to the pivotal role that biochemistry played in and outside phage research. The reinterpretation of Delbrück's contributions has become an element in the reassessment of the history of molecular biology.

• The Delbrück papers, documenting his professional life, are housed at the California Institute of Technology; the Bohr-Delbrück Correspondence, spanning a period of thirty years, is at the American Institute of Physics. An oral history based on interviews with Carolyn Kopp, "Max Delbrück: How It Was," was published in *Engineering and Science*, Mar.–Apr. 1980, pp. 21–26, and May–June 1980, pp. 21–27. A festschrift for Max Delbrück, J. Cairns et al., eds., *Phage and the Origins of Molecular Biology* (1966; rev. ed., 1993), captures the cognitive and social aspects of the phage school. An official biography, co-written by one of his disciples, supplies vivid insiders' perspectives, Ernst Peter Fischer and Carol Lipson, *Thinking about Science: Max Delbrück and the Origins of Molecular Biology* (1988). Specific aspects of Delbrück's career are treated by Lily E. Kay in "Conceptual Models and Analytical Tools: The Biology of Physicist Max Delbrück," *Journal of the History of Biology* 18 (1985): 207–46, and "The Secret of Life: Niels Bohr's Influence on the Biology Program of Max Delbrück," *Rivista di Storia della Scienza* 2 (1985): 485–510. Several works contain significant discussions of Delbrück: Robert C. Olby, *The Path to the Double Helix* (1974); Horace F. Judson, *The Eighth Day of Creation: The Makers of the Revolution in Biology* (1979); and Kay, *The Molecular Vision of Life: Caltech, the Rockefeller Foundation, and the Rise of the New Biology* (1993). Two studies help contextualize Delbrück's career in biology: Robert E. Kohler, "The Management of Science: The Experience of Warren Weaver and the Rockefeller Program in Molecular Biology," *Minerva* 14 (1976): 249–93, and Pnina Abir-Am, "The Discourse of Physical Power and Biological Knowledge in the 1930s: A Reappraisal of the Rockefeller Foundation 'Policy' in Molecular Biology," *Social Studies of Science* 12 (1982): 123–43. Seymour Cohen, "The Biochemical Origins of Molecular Biology: Introduction," *Trends in Biochemical Sciences* 9 (1984):334–36, and Joseph Fruton, *A Skeptical Biochemist* (1992), offer alternative perspectives on the role of the phage group in the history of molecular biology.

LILY E. KAY

DELEE, Joseph Bolivar (28 Oct. 1869–2 Apr. 1942), obstetrician, was born in Cold Spring, New York, the son of Morris DeLee, a dry goods merchant, and Dora Tobias. He was the son of Jewish immigrants, and his father desired him to become a rabbi, but his mother encouraged him to become a doctor. DeLee attended the City College of New York. He received an M.D. from the Chicago Medical College (later Northwestern University Medical School) in 1891, and then completed an eighteen-month internship at the Cook County Hospital.

Following a tour of several European centers, DeLee returned to Chicago in 1894. Impressed with the work of New York's Lying-in Hospital and Broome Street Dispensary, he devoted his efforts to creating a similar institution in Chicago. In 1895 he opened the Chicago Lying-in (Maxwell Street) Dispensary to serve the poor in Chicago's slums. In 1902 this became the Chicago Maternity Center, of which he remained director until 1912. In 1896, upon the death of William Wright Jaggard, chairman of the Department of Obstetrics and Gynecology at Northwestern University Medical School, DeLee succeeded him. He served on the faculty of the department until 1929. In 1899 he founded the fourteen-bed Chicago Lying-in Hospital, which expanded to over 100 beds in 1917 and in 1931 opened at its present site on the campus of the University of Chicago. In 1929, when the Lying-in became officially affiliated with the University of Chicago, DeLee became the first chairman of the Department of Obstetrics and Gynecology of that institution's medical school. He served on the faculty of the University of Chicago until his death.

DeLee devoted his life to making childbirth safe for mothers and babies, and his crusade for improved maternity care for poor expectant mothers did much to reduce maternal and infant mortality in the United States. His medical and professional contributions included helping to establish the scientific basis of obstetrics. He had as a major aim the teaching of clinical obstetrics, and he was an influential writer both for the medical profession and for the lay press. Beginning in 1904, DeLee edited the annual *Year Book of Obstetrics*, including insightful editorial remarks on almost every subject. In 1913 he published *The Principles and Practice of Obstetrics*, a monumental text that was to go through seven editions under his hand (7th ed., 1938). A major contribution of DeLee was that of stressing "preventive" obstetrics and the "intelligent expectancy" of nonintervention, with minimal use of drugs and instruments during labor and delivery. He popularized low-segment cesarean section (involving a transverse incision in the lower portion of the uterus) in the United States, the use of prophylactic forceps for delivery, and episiotomy when indicated to minimize trauma to pelvic tissues from prolonged labor. Overall, Delee strove to raise the standards of obstetrical care in the United States. He did this by providing optimal care for home deliveries of the poor and deliveries at the Lying-in Dispensary/Maternity Center, by training competent specialists, and by writing extensively.

Beginning in the late 1920s, DeLee pioneered in making and using sound motion pictures for obstetric education. His films included instruction on proper use of the forceps, management of face presentation, cesarean section, and related subjects. He also devised many instruments, designing the obstetric stethoscope to fit on the clinician's head (1898–1915), modifying the obstetrical forceps, and devising a special bed for obstetrical delivery and an incubator for premature infants (1900–1902). DeLee's sister, Ida DeLee Neuman, founded the Mother's Aid Sewing Club in Chicago (1904, renamed the Mother's Aid Group in 1905), which supported the Lying-in Hospital (now the Joseph B. DeLee Building) and helped to promulgate DeLee's ideals of care for mothers and infants.

DeLee's life was devoted to improving obstetrical care. He not only provided his personal funds (estimated at over $300,000) for maternal and infant care and improvement but also lived in an apartment on the top floor of the Lying-in Hospital and seldom took vacations. Regarding his philosophy, DeLee noted that the first principle to teach medical students and nurses is that obstetrics is a "great science, complicated . . . and . . . far from complete," yet with "grand possibilities." Thus, he believed that one who practices obstetrics must be well grounded in the basic sciences and know everything possible about reproductive physiology, surgical principles, and the other specialties of medicine. In short, one must be an expert family practitioner as well as an obstetric specialist.

DeLee received numerous honors and awards. He served as president of the Chicago Gynecological Society (1908), vice president of the American Gynecological Society (1929), and chairman of the Section of Obstetrics, Gynecology and Abdominal Surgery of the American Medical Association (1933–1934). DeLee, who never married, died at his home in Chicago.

• DeLee's papers from the Chicago Lying-in Hospital are at the Joseph Regenstein Library of the University of Chicago. Among DeLee's works not already mentioned in the text are *Obstetrics for Nurses* (1941); "The Newer Methods of Caesarean Section, Report of Forty Cases," *Journal of the American Medical Association* 73 (1919): 91–95; "An Illustrated History of the Low or Cervical Caesarean Sections," *American Journal of Obstetrics and Gynecology* 10 (1925): 503–20; and "Low, or Cervical, Caesarean Section (Laparotrachelotomy), Three Hundred and Thirty Operations, with Two Deaths," *Journal of the American Medical Association* 84 (1925): 792–98. A biography is M. Fishbein and S. T. DeLee, *Joseph Bolivar DeLee—Crusading Obstetrician* (1949). See also F. L. Adair, "Joseph Bolivar DeLee, 1869–1942," *Transactions of the American Gynecological Society* 67 (1942): 367–68; D. N. Danforth, "Contemporary Titans: Joseph Bolivar DeLee and John Whitridge Williams," *American Journal of Obstetrics and Gynecology* 120 (1974): 577–88 (followed by a letter by A. J. J. Nuyens, 122 [1975]: 540); M. E. Davis, "Joseph Bolivar DeLee, 1869–1942: As I Remember Him," *Journal of Reproductive Medicine* 1 (1968): 33–44; and C. Moir, "Joseph B. DeLee," *Journal of Obstetrics and Gynaecology of the British Empire* 49 (1942): 444–46.

LAWRENCE D. LONGO

DE LEON, Daniel (14 Dec. 1852–11 May 1914), socialist, journalist, and polemicist, was born in Curaçao, Dutch West Indies, the son of Salomon De Leon, a surgeon and official in the Dutch colonial army, and Sarah Jesurun, who came from a wealthy family of Sephardic Jews. In the year that his father died (1864), Daniel's mother took her sickly twelve-year-old son to Europe for its more salubrious climate and educational opportunities. Although no evidence exists to prove that De Leon attended a Gymnasium in Germany or the University of Leiden in Belgium, as he later claimed, he did acquire some secondary education and knowledge of classical and modern languages.

De Leon immigrated to the United States in 1874. He settled in a Hispanic community in New York

City, supporting himself by teaching foreign languages in a private school in Westchester County and editing a newspaper for émigré Cuban revolutionaries. He also attended Columbia University Law School. After graduating with an LL.B. in 1878, he moved to Brownsville, Texas, where he practiced law. In 1882 De Leon married Sara Lobo, the daughter of a wealthy Venezuelan Sephardic Jewish family. They had four children, only one of whom, a son, survived. Sara died during childbirth in 1887.

De Leon returned to New York in 1883 to accept a prize lectureship in Latin-American diplomacy at Columbia. He held that position for only two three-year terms, sacrificing the prospect of reappointment and possible tenure to involve himself in radical politics. In 1886 De Leon joined the United Labor third-party mayoral campaign of Henry George, the noted land reformer and exponent of the single tax. After George's defeat and United Labor's split with the socialists, in 1889 De Leon joined the Nationalist movement founded by Edward Bellamy, the author of the best-selling utopian fantasy *Looking Backward*. An active participant in Nationalism, De Leon began to study Marxian political economy, a process that moved him away from the genteel middle-class utopianism of Bellamy and toward an emphasis on workers, the labor movement, and socialism. He had first revealed his interest in the labor movement in 1888, when he joined a local assembly of the Knights of Labor, the era's most notable mass labor organization. In 1890 De Leon affiliated with the Socialist Labor Party (SLP), the political arm of Marxism in the United States and an organization dominated by German-American and German-speaking members. As one of the few party members who could communicate effectively in English, De Leon rose rapidly within the SLP. By 1891 he served as the party's national lecturer and as an editor of its new English-language newspaper, the *People*, a weekly that became a daily in 1900. He was to remain its editor until his death. De Leon used his multiple roles as lecturer, editor, and party leader to Americanize the SLP and carry its message to English-speaking workers. In his role as national lecturer, De Leon met his second wife, Bertha Canary, whom he married in 1892 and with whom he had five children.

As party leader, De Leon proved himself to be adept at polemics, talented in sectarian conflict, but less successful in cultivating mass support. Committed to the belief that revolutionary socialism required the amalgamation of the political party and the labor movement, De Leon sought unsuccessfully to win control first of the Knights of Labor and later of the American Federation of Labor (AFL). Repulsed by the leaders of the two labor federations, De Leon condemned union leaders such as Terence Powderly of the Knights and Samuel Gompers of the AFL as "labor lieutenants of capitalism" and "labor fakirs." To build his own revolutionary labor organization, De Leon in 1895 created the Socialist Trade and Labor Alliance (STLA), which brought him into open conflict with Gompers and the trade unions in the AFL. His vituperative conflict with the AFL trade unionists caused dissension within the SLP, as other party members preferred compromise rather than warfare with the trade unionists. These "softer" or reform socialists also wanted the SLP to endorse immediate reforms rather than, as De Leon urged, to seek total revolution. The internal struggle in the SLP between factions loosely identified as "reformist" and "revolutionary" resulted in the secession of a majority of members who, after losing legally their claim to the Socialist Labor Party name, united with other socialists to form the Socialist Party of America (1901). Thereafter, the SLP and the STLA existed as tiny tributaries to the mainstream of socialism in the United States, which flowed in the direction of the SPA. From 1901 until 1914 De Leon and the SLP proved indistinguishable entities, attracting a minuscule number of followers, all of whom pledged absolute fealty to their leader's vision of a revolutionary socialism that disdained palliative reforms. Ever eager to win new allies and create a presence in the labor movement, De Leon joined with other labor radicals in 1905 to found the Industrial Workers of the World (IWW), an organization that condemned the AFL as a tool of capitalism. Within the IWW, De Leon again precipitated sectarian splits as he sought to turn its members into disciples and sycophants, not allies and comrades. In 1908 a majority in the IWW expelled De Leon from the organization, prompting him to create yet another schismatic body, the Workers' International Industrial Union, which proved as impotent as the deceased STLA. One IWW member who broke with De Leon in 1908 later characterized the SLP leader as "like a legendary South American who started a 'revolution' with twenty men, cut off the heads of nineteen and continued the revolution all by himself." Until his death in New York, De Leon led a revolutionary movement with a few loyal adherents, more enemies than friends among trade unionists, and the bleakest prospects for transforming society.

It is hard to evaluate De Leon's impact in the United States. He succeeded in Americanizing the SLP but only at the cost of splitting it. Like V. I. Lenin, whom De Leon's acolytes claimed borrowed ideas about revolution from the SLP leader, he wanted to make history. Unlike the Russian revolutionary, however, De Leon existed in a nonrevolutionary society. That was perhaps why his theories concerning socialism, revolution, and trade unionism had greater resonance overseas, especially in Great Britain, than at home.

• The De Leon papers and also those of the SLP are at the State Historical Society of Wisconsin, Madison, and are available in microfilm editions. For De Leon's own views, see *The Burning Question of Trade Unionism* (1957), *Two Pages from Roman History* (1959), and *What Means This Strike?* (1947). Two biographies provide the fullest accounts of his life and career, L. Glen Seretan, *Daniel De Leon: The Odyssey of an American Marxist* (1979), is critical, and Stephen Coleman, *Daniel De Leon* (1990), presents a more favorable portrait.

MELVYN DUBOFSKY

DE LEON, Thomas Cooper (21 May 1839–19 Mar. 1914), Alabama's first professional man of letters, was born in Columbia, South Carolina, the son of Mardici Heinrich De Leon and Rebecca Lopez-y-Nunez. His ancestors emigrated from Spain to the Spanish West Indies and then settled in the colonies before the American Revolution. De Leon's father was a distinguished physician and an ardent admirer of the former president of South Carolina College, Thomas Cooper, for whom young De Leon was named. He began his formal education at Fort Prevel, Maine, and then attended Rugby Academy in Washington, D.C. He graduated from Georgetown College in 1858 with a degree in engineering. His first inclination, however, was toward the world of letters. In college he formed a lifelong friendship with James Ryder Randall, the Maryland poet, and began to write essays, poems, and stories for various magazines, including the *Southern Literary Messenger*. From 1858 to 1861 he was an audit clerk in the Bureau of Topographical Engineering, Washington, D.C.

De Leon and his two brothers held important positions in the newly formed Confederate States of America. David Camden De Leon was appointed surgeon general by President Jefferson Davis. Edwin De Leon, upon resigning his consulate in Egypt, was sent to Europe to direct the Confederate propaganda campaign in foreign publications. In 1862 Thomas Cooper De Leon was commissioned a captain in the Confederate army and served throughout the conflict as private secretary to Jefferson Davis, who had been his friend and mentor before the war. This experience gave De Leon intimate knowledge of Confederate life and its leaders, and it became the source of his most important work, *Four Years in Rebel Capitals* (1890), reminiscences of political and social activities from the spring of 1861 in Washington to the fall of Richmond in 1865.

After the war De Leon turned to literature as a profession. In Baltimore he published his first book, *South Songs* (1866), one of the first collections of Confederate poems and songs. In that city he launched *The Cosmopolite* (1866), a pioneer among post–Civil War magazines devoted to preserving memories of the "Lost Cause." In New York City, from 1866 to 1867, De Leon wrote a series of widely circulated newspaper articles on politics under the pseudonym Dunne Browne, translated two French novels—Octave Feuillet's *Camors* (1866) and Ernest Feydeau's *Chalis* (1867)—and published segments of *Four Years in Rebel Capitals* in the *Mobile Sunday Times* and the *Philadelphia Times*.

In Mobile, where he lived the last forty-seven years of his life, De Leon found outlets for his boundless energies as author, editor, publisher, and entrepreneur. He always seemed happiest when engaged in several projects at the same time. In 1867 he became managing editor of the *Mobile Register*. When the theater claimed his attention, he wrote a burlesque, *Hamlet, Ye Dismal Prince: Ye Bigamist and Ye Ghoste.* Produced in 1870 at the Olympia Theater in New York, it

had a phenomenal run of 100 nights. Less successful were three other plays produced in New York between 1870 and 1874, including *Jasper*, based upon Dickens's *The Mystery of Edwin Drood*. From 1873 to 1884 he managed the Mobile Theatre. In 1873 he organized the Mobile Mardi Gras as a public celebration and directed the carnival for twenty-five years. His talents earned him a national reputation that kept him in demand for staging similar pageants in the South and in Washington, D.C. *Our Creole Carnivals* (1890) is a sprightly written history of these carnivals. Shortly after the death in 1877 of John Forsyth, editor of the *Mobile Register*, De Leon left the newspaper. In 1878 he edited a short-lived periodical, *The Gulf Citizen*. He established his own press, the Gossip Printing Company of Mobile, and reprinted a number of his books, wrote promotional reviews, and issued at irregular intervals a spicy little journal, *The Gossip*, later titled *Old Vets' Gossip*.

In the 1880s De Leon attempted a new genre, the travesty, which satirized the techniques of the popular domestic novel, such as the chaste heroine and the admirable hero. His first, *Coqsureus: A Lay of a Very Late Encampment* (1887), mildly ridiculed the soldier and war veteran. More successful was *The Rock or the Rye: An Understudy, after "The Quick or the Dead?"* (1888), a recognizable parody of Amélie Rives's best-selling novelette. Much in the same humorous vein is *Schooners That Bump on the Bar; or, An Automatic Tow from "Ships That Pass in the Night"* (1894), a satire on a popular novel by Beatrice Harraden. For effect, these novels depended upon exaggeration in plot and unrealistic dialogue. Their heroines are the antithesis of those in the works they were intended to satirize. A number of De Leon's novels focused upon the Civil War and featured intersectional love plots, though De Leon himself always remained a bachelor. The reconciliation motif of *Creole and Puritan* (1889) appealed to both northern and southern readers and was continued in a sequel, *The Puritan's Daughter* (1892). *John Holden, Unionist* (1893) was written in collaboration with Erwin Ledyard. Set in northern Alabama during the Civil War, it depicts the reluctant Confederate soldier. Benjamin Williams judged it De Leon's "most interesting and perhaps his most important work of fiction." In *A Fair Blockade Breaker* (1891), *Crag-Nest* (1897), *An Innocent Cheat* (1898), and *The Pride of the Mercers* (1898), De Leon also wrote in the Romantic manner of the local-colorists, in which setting was central and character portrayals were unrealistic. In these he continued the formula of modest praise for northerners while emphasizing genteel manners, family pride, and social standing of southerners.

De Leon's poems, though not wrought with craftsmanship, seem to have captured the emotions of the people on the occasions for which they were written. In his best known verse—such as "Asleep with Jackson" and "The Living Lee"—he paid tribute to Confederate leaders. After going totally blind in 1903, De Leon was called "The Blind Laureate of the Lost Cause." Despite his blindness, he learned to type and continued to write and publish novels, short stories, and miscellaneous pieces until his death. His last two important works were *Joseph Wheeler* (1899), a biography of a famous Alabama general who had served in both the Confederate army and the United States Army in the Spanish-American War, and *Belles, Beaux, and Brains of the Sixties* (1909), which is similar in content to *Four Years in Rebel Capitals* but deals solely with biographical reminiscences.

De Leon shunned active participation in politics, although he wrote on political topics in the *Mobile Register*; and two of his books—*The Rending of the Solid South* (1895) and *East, West and South* (1896)—were defenses of the Democratic party. He died in Mobile.

De Leon's fame faded after his death, and today he is known only to an occasional researcher or literary or social historian who discovers the value of his biographical sketches and Civil War reminiscences. Most of his works were written to appeal to the shifting tastes of the reading public of his day and thus have faded into obscurity.

• Apparently De Leon's manuscripts and papers have not been preserved. However, some of his pamphlets and his books are available in the Mobile Public Library and in the *Mobile Register* (on microfilm). Miscellaneous clippings are in the Museum of the History of Mobile and the Alabama Department of Archives and History, Montgomery.

Other major works by De Leon not listed above include *Cross Purposes* (1871), *The Soldiers' Souvenir* (1887), *Juny* (1890), *Society as I Have Foundered It* (1890), *Sybilla* (1891), *Out of the Sulphur* (1895), *A Novelette Trilogy* (1897), *War Rhymes, Grave and Gay* (1898), and *Inauguration of President Watterson* (1902).

The best assessment of De Leon's career is in Benjamin Williams, *A Literary History of Alabama: The Nineteenth Century* (1979). See also Louis de V. Chaudron's sketch of De Leon in *Four Years in Rebel Capitals*, 2d ed. (1892); T. M. Owen, *History of Alabama and Dictionary of Alabama Biography*, vol. 3 (1921); Erwin Craighead, *From Mobile's Past* (1925); Eleanor Fallin McKeller, "Life and Works of Thomas Cooper De Leon" (M.A. thesis, Alabama Polytechnic Inst., 1952); and Ray M. Atchison, "Southern Literary Magazines, 1865–1887" (Ph.D. diss., Duke Univ., 1956).

RAY M. ATCHISON

DE LIAGRE, Alfred (6 Oct. 1904–5 Mar. 1987), theatrical producer and director, was born Alfred Gustav Etienne de Liagre, Jr., in Passaic, New Jersey, the son of Alfred de Liagre, Sr., a textile manufacturer, and Frida Unger. De Liagre was born to wealth. After education at a private school and graduation from Yale University in 1926, he worked briefly on Wall Street. Then he traveled around the world as an aspiring journalist. It was travel in the grand style: he dined with eminences from former Kaiser Wilhelm II in Doorn to Mahatma Gandhi in India.

De Liagre, who had studied drama with Monty Woolley at Yale, next began to think of a career in the theater. "Dapper, red-haired . . . Mr. deLiagre is one of the numerous Yale contingent which descended on Longacre Square in the late '20s," wrote his Yale classmate Lucius Beebe (*New York Herald-Tribune*, 18 July

1937). Unlike other actors and actresses, de Liagre had come to stay. He began as an assistant stage manager at the Woodstock Playhouse in 1930. He was next employed by the producing firm of Macgowan and Reed in 1931 to be assistant stage manager for a repertory season; he liked to recount that his office was a dressing room also used on some nights by Katharine Hepburn in her first stage appearance.

Other summer stock work at Cape May, New Jersey, followed in 1932. There de Liagre had the opportunity to direct comedies. "I really tried my directing wings that summer," he told an interviewer (*New York Herald-Tribune*, 12 Nov. 1939). "I tried them and they didn't seem to let me down. So, when the season was over, I boldly decided that I was ready for Broadway." At Macgowan and Reed he had met a fellow employee, Richard Aldrich, who was another wealthy young theater lover. In 1933 the two, both still in their twenties, started their own producing firm. Their first presentation was a comedy, *Three-Cornered Moon* (1933), with de Liagre directing. Its success started the new producers on their way.

De Liagre's duties for the partnership allowed him time for the high life of a wealthy young bachelor playboy, "renting palazzos in Venice, throwing grand parties in Cannes, [and] piloting vintage motor cars around New Haven," always dressed in high style (*New York Times*, 26 Feb. 1978). A fedora worn rakishly on the side of his head became a sartorial fixture. In the next years after *Three-Cornered Moon*, he consistently produced and directed comedies for Aldrich and de Liagre, the most successful of which was *Petticoat Fever* (1935). "I have no illusions or pretensions," he said in one interview (*New York Times*, 28 Feb. 1937). "I know quite well that my bent is for comedy—and I am going to stick to it. Anything between farce and high comedy—that's my line."

His preference was also for the stage over films. Besides appearing as a dress extra in the Marx Brothers' film *The Cocoanuts* (1929), his only studio experience was in directing the movie version of *Springtime for Henry* (1934) in Hollywood, after directing its West Coast stage production. He came back resentful of the studios for turning out a "synthetic product" aimed at "the lowest possible common denominator of intelligence" (*New York Herald-Tribune*, 18 July 1937) and for luring good actors away from Broadway with long contracts (*New York Times*, 28 Feb. 1937).

In 1936 Hollywood lured away his partner Aldrich, and de Liagre became a producer on his own. His first presentation, which he also directed, was the comedy *Yes, My Darling Daughter* (1937). It succeeded on Broadway and a London production followed. His next few plays did less well, until in 1941 he produced and directed a very successful comedy-thriller, *Mr. and Mrs. North*. During the years of World War II, he produced, but did not direct, a romantic comedy that became one of the decade's smash hits: *The Voice of the Turtle* (1943), which ran for years in New York and London. In 1945 de Liagre married actress Mary Howard; they had two children.

One of the shining successes of de Liagre's career came in 1948, when he produced and directed the fantastic comedy *The Madwoman of Chaillot*. A success both in New York and London, his direction of the play won the New York Drama Critics Circle Award in 1949, and the same year brought de Liagre a decoration as chevalier of the French Legion of Honor. Other successes for him as producer, no longer director, followed in the 1950s: *The Deep Blue Sea* (1952), coproduced with John C. Wilson; *The Golden Apple* (1954), winner of the New York Drama Critics Circle Award for best musical; *Janus* (1955); and *J. B.* (1958), which won the Antoinette Perry Award as best play.

No such successes followed in the 1960s, and after *Love in E Flat* (1967), de Liagre was inactive on Broadway for years. Changes in public tastes were not to his liking. "It's distressed me enormously, the direction in which the theater has been going," he was quoted as saying. "I have been very upset over the preoccupation with obscenity and sexual deviation. I've grown weary of seeing actors trail their genitals across the footlights" (*New York Times*, 26 Feb. 1978). Also, he declared, "Playwrights today don't care very much about telling a story that has a beginning, a middle and an end. It's become a mood thing . . . [like] abstract impressionism . . . in painting and sculpture" (*New York Times*, 6 Mar. 1987). He turned instead to presenting productions by regional companies for the American National Theatre Academy and to productions at various theater companies and off-Broadway locations.

The play that brought him back to Broadway in 1978 was a comedy-thriller, *Deathtrap*, which de Liagre produced with Roger L. Stevens. He returned because "I thought it was a remarkably ingenious play, very well contrived, organized and brilliantly written. And also I think [playwright] Ira Levin succeeded in treading the very thin line between suspense and comedy" (*New York Times*, 26 Feb. 1978). Audiences agreed: the play ran four years. De Liagre now found himself an "elder statesman" of the theater, as he said in the *Times* article. His final production was a revival of the musical *On Your Toes* (1983), again in partnership with Roger L. Stevens. For de Liagre, it rounded out fifty years as a Broadway producer. Four years later, he died in New York City.

In de Liagre's *New York Times* obituary Katharine Hepburn called him "the last of the great gentleman producers." He was known for his courtliness of manner: "where some in his profession are like so much kindling wood when tempers flare on a set, Mr. de Liagre prevails serenely with expressions like 'Dear boy, would you mind trying it this way just once' or 'It would make me so very happy if you would change that to read like this'" (*New York Times*, 26 Feb. 1978). He was also known for uprightness in his dealings: "He was a traditional, old-fashioned gentleman," said the president of the Shubert Organization in the *Times* obituary. "Once he gave his word, you never had to look for him a second time."

The producer's career was a measure of how Broadway had changed in fifty years. When he began in the 1930s, producing was mainly a matter of finding a play (de Liagre estimated he read 500 to 1,000 a year) and backing with cash one's judgment that the public would like it. By the 1980s, producing was a matter of finding investors to take part in multimillion dollar risks. Even *Deathtrap*, a fairly modest production, required the money of six investors. Surviving into the 1980s, de Liagre, the grand old gentleman of Broadway, was a last reminder of an earlier era of American theater, when wealthy young men produced plays as much for love of the theater as for money—and could themselves afford the sums to do so.

• Materials on the life and career of de Liagre are in the Billy Rose Theatre Collection at the New York Public Library for the Performing Arts, Lincoln Center. A list of his productions and other activities and positions in the theater is in *Contemporary Theatre, Film, and Television*, vol. 5. An especially helpful article is by Warren Hoge, "The Last of the 'Gentleman' Producers?" *New York Times*, 26 Feb. 1978. Other information and reminiscence is found in Howard Kissel, "DeLiagre: Brahmin of the Caste on Broadway," *Women's Wear Daily*, 17 Feb. 1978. Three articles on de Liagre's early Broadway days are Lucius Beebe, "A Producer Talks Shop," *New York Herald-Tribune*, 18 July 1937; Bosley Crowther, "Turning the Spotlight on a Local Boy," *New York Times*, 28 Feb. 1937; and Jean Dalrymple, "Yes, the Stage Has Something Films Just Don't," *New York Herald-Tribune*, 12 Nov. 1939. An obituary is in the *New York Times*, 6 Mar. 1987.

WILLIAM STEPHENSON

DE LIMA, Agnes Abinun (5 Aug. 1887–27 Nov. 1974), progressive journalist, publicist, and educator, was born in Holywood, New Jersey, the daughter of Elias S. Abinun de Lima, a partner in D. A. de Lima and Sons, a banking firm, and Esther Abinun de Lima. Her parents were from Curacao. De Lima was raised in an upper-class home in New York City and Larchmont Manor, New York, and was taught by tutors and music teachers.

De Lima entered Vassar College in 1904. She took classes in English, charities and corrections, labor problems and socialism, social psychology, history, philosophy, economics, and education and studied the history of municipal government with progressive feminist Lucy Salmon. Her courses and her work in the College Settlement Association initiated her transition from the conservative values of her upper-class family to her adult commitments to feminism, reform, socialism, and support for organized labor.

Upon graduation in 1908 she moved to New York City, where she worked for three and a half years for the Bureau of Municipal Research and the Russell Sage Foundation as a researcher and writer on subjects such as municipal reform, education, and child nutrition. She studied at the New York School for Social Work, from which she received a master of arts degree in 1912.

De Lima lived briefly in San Francisco, where she researched and wrote for the Association of Collegiate

Alumnae a report titled *Some Conditions in the Schools of San Francisco* (1914). The report proposed a range of progressive policies, including increased taxation for schools, smaller class sizes, additional manual training classes, efficiency practices, and better newspaper coverage of education.

De Lima returned to New York City, where from 1916 to 1918 she conducted research and wrote publicity for the Women's Municipal League. The league's purposes were "to promote among women an intelligent interest in municipal affairs, and to aid in securing permanent good government for the city of New York without regard to party or sectional lines" (*Women and the City's Work*, 2 Jan. 1917, p. 2). The league studied city budgets and lobbied for better support of schools and for health and recreation programs for children and women. De Lima worked with Randolph Bourne in the effort, which quickly failed, to establish Platoon Schools in New York. These schools were a progressive innovation intended to promote student achievement and the efficient use of space by having one "platoon" of students studying in classrooms while another was learning in assembly halls, shops, libraries, and gymnasiums. In October 1918 de Lima began work for the Public Education Association, a citizens' organization that promoted adequate school funding, educational efficiency, and progressive school reforms.

From 1914 to 1918 Randolph Bourne had been the *New Republic*'s regular writer on education; after his death de Lima became one of the journal's most frequent writers on educational topics. During 1924 and 1925 she wrote for the *New Republic* and for the *Nation* a series of articles that she revised for publication as *Our Enemy the Child* (1925). This was one of the few books on education from this period that provided detailed descriptions of real life in progressive classrooms; partly for this reason it became one of the most widely quoted books on the history of progressive education. (It has been cited in at least twelve such histories; see representative titles below.) De Lima may have been the first writer to identify the three strands of progressive educators later described by historian Lawrence Cremin as "scientists, sentimentalists, and radicals." De Lima wrote: "Educational reformers are of three kinds: those who accept the established body of knowledge as necessary for the child to learn, but who admit that the methods of presenting it are at fault and must be changed; those who advocate changes in the curriculum so as to prepare children more adequately for a modern world; and those who view education as an organic process which changes and develops as the child himself changes and grows" (*Our Enemy the Child*, p. 125). De Lima was most supportive of the third group, often called organic or child-centered educators, and most critical of the first, whom she called "technicians" and who focused on "the measurement of intelligence, of classroom achievement, and improvement in method."

From about 1925 to 1928 de Lima ran a small progressive school in her home in Valley Cottage, New York. In 1929 she moved to Palo Alto, California, where she taught English for a year at the progressive Peninsula School.

De Lima returned to New York in 1937 and wrote historical and publicity materials for several progressive schools, including the Bank Street Schools and the Lincoln School. In 1939, with faculty members from the Lincoln School, she wrote about its elementary division in *A School for the World of Tomorrow*. In 1941, in conjunction with the high school staff, she wrote *Democracy's High School*, about the secondary division. In 1942, again with Lincoln School faculty, she wrote *South of the Rio Grande: An Experiment in International Understanding*.

Working with the staff of yet another progressive school, de Lima wrote *The Little Red Schoolhouse* (1942), for which John Dewey wrote an admiring introduction. The school had begun as Public School 41, and Dewey asserted that progressive education was effective in public as well as private settings. He wrote that the book provided "an immense public service. It supplies the much needed proof that nothing stands in the way of adoption of the new purposes and methods by schools operating under the conditions which affect public school work, even in a great city. This trait alone gives the book a deeply serious claim upon the attention of all who are concerned in making our public school system the power for good it is capable of becoming."

De Lima's books gave unusually detailed descriptions and interpretations of how progressive schools actually functioned, and expressed de Lima's conviction, which she shared with Dewey, that good teachers should begin instruction with the interests and needs of children, engage students actively in inquiry and discovery, and continuously guide them to serious and mature academic and intellectual achievement.

Over the years de Lima wrote articles and reviews for many magazines and newspapers, including the *New Republic*, the *Nation*, *Progressive Education*, the *Survey*, the *New York Herald Tribune*, and the *New York Times*.

In 1940 De Lima became director of public relations for the New School for Social Research, the leading progressive experiment in higher education. She held this position until 1960, when she retired. She spent much of her retirement in Greenwich Village doing volunteer work for the New School. She organized Randolph Bourne's papers and contributed them to the Columbia University Library and gave a substantial collection of letters from Alvin Johnson to the Yale University Library.

De Lima had a brief marriage during the 1920s with writer Arthur MacFarlane; it ended in divorce. She died in Woodcliff Lake, New Jersey. She had one daughter.

De Lima is remembered chiefly as the author of books, articles, and reviews about progressive education. Like her friend Randolph Bourne, she was instrumental in informing political progressives about developments in progressive schools. De Lima's work has received somewhat different interpretations by educational historians. Some, such as Patricia Albjerg Graham in *Progressive Education: From Arcady to Academe* (1967) and Larry Cuban in *How Teachers Taught: Constancy and Change in American Classrooms, 1890–1990* (1993), consider her an uncritical advocate of child-centered progressivism; others, such as Chester Bowers in *The Progressive Educator and the Depression: The Radical Years* (1969) and James M. Wallace, view her as selectively critical, especially of so-called scientific and radical progressivism. Lawrence Cremin, America's leading educational historian, considered *Our Enemy the Child* of sufficient historical significance to be included in a series of scholarly reprints in 1969. His editorial note said that these books "retain their place in the literature, having influenced educational thought and practice in their own time and having provided the basis for subsequent scholarship."

• Some of de Lima's letters and papers are in the Special Collections, Vassar College; the Alvin Saunders Johnson Collection, Sterling Memorial Library, Yale University; the Special Collections, Milbank Memorial Library, Teachers College, Columbia University; the Fogelman Library, New School for Social Research; and the Randolph Bourne Papers, Special Manuscript Collections, Butler Library, Columbia University. Other papers are in the possession of de Lima's daughter and of James M. Wallace, who is writing de Lima's biography. "Agnes de Lima and Progressive Education," chap. 8 of *Liberal Journalism and American Education, 1914–1941,* by Wallace (1991), discusses de Lima in the context of political and educational progressivism. The notes to that chapter identify other relevant sources. An obituary is in the *New York Times,* 28 Nov. 1974.

JAMES M. WALLACE

DELL, Floyd James (28 June 1887–23 July 1969), novelist and critic, was born in Barry, Illinois, the son of Anthony Dell, a butcher and laborer, and Kate Crone, a teacher. The experience of childhood poverty greatly influenced Dell's political views and writings. As an adolescent in Quincy, Illinois, and Davenport, Iowa, he despaired of his family's poverty and joined the Socialist party. Leaving high school after his junior year, Dell helped support his family by working as a reporter for Davenport newspapers from 1905 to 1908. In 1905 and 1906 he also wrote for and edited the *Tri-City Workers Magazine,* the main Socialist publication in the Davenport area.

Dell moved to Chicago in November 1908. The following spring he became associate editor of the *Chicago Evening Post*'s weekly supplement, the "Friday Literary Review." During the next two years Dell helped editor Francis Hackett turn the "Review" into one of the most influential literary publications in the United States. Hackett and Dell championed new European writers and such controversial American novelists as Theodore Dreiser and Upton Sinclair. In 1911 Dell became editor of the "Review," contributing many articles on literature and seven admiring essays on feminist leaders that were later collected in his first book, *Women as World Builders* (1913).

Dell married his first wife, Margery Currey, in August 1909; they had no children. By 1913 a community of innovative writers, artists, and theater people had coalesced around the Dells' apartments on Chicago's south side. Among their frequent guests were Dreiser, Sherwood Anderson, Maurice Browne (founder of Chicago's influential Little Theater), Margaret Anderson (founder of the *Little Review*), and Harriet Monroe (founder of *Poetry*). Within this remarkable community, which was largely responsible for the outpouring of cultural enterprises now known as the Chicago Renaissance, Dell was a tireless advocate of its disparate literary productions and a model of outlandish bohemian behavior.

In the fall of 1913 the Dells decided to divorce, and Dell departed for New York. He immediately became a prominent figure in Greenwich Village, where he worked as associate editor of the *Masses,* a magazine that mixed radical politics with art and literature. Dell summarized the irrepressible, eclectic spirit of the *Masses* when he wrote that "it stood for truth, beauty, realism, freedom, peace, feminism, revolution." Max Eastman, chief editor at the *Masses,* later remembered Dell as a brilliant editor who "brought to the *Masses* a gift of literary criticism as fine as we had in the country." From 1916 to 1918 Dell also worked as a playwright, actor, and director for the Provincetown Players. In 1918 Dell, Eastman, and several other editors at the *Masses* were tried twice for conspiracy to obstruct the draft. Both trials ended in hung juries, and in the fall of 1918 all charges were dropped.

In February 1919 Dell married Berta Marie Gage, a socialist and pacifist from Pasadena, California, settling soon afterward in Croton-on-Hudson, New York. They had two children. His second book, a defense of progressive education called *Were You Ever a Child?,* appeared in September 1919. A year later Dell published his first novel, *Moon-Calf,* a work that drew heavily on the experiences of his first twenty-one years. The book received wide critical acclaim and became a best seller in cities around the United States. His second novel, *The Briary Bush* (1921), also a largely autobiographical work, was inspired by Dell's years in Chicago.

In the course of the next fourteen years Dell published nine more novels, a collection of stories and poems (*Love in Greenwich Village*), a critique of modern trends in literary rebellion (*Intellectual Vagabondage*), a biography of Upton Sinclair, and a study on how modern economic conditions have transformed marriage and family (*Love in the Machine Age*). He also helped edit the *Liberator* (the successor to the *Masses*) and contributed articles to numerous other journals. In 1928 he coauthored with Thomas G. Mitchell *Little Accident,* a play based on one of Dell's novels, *An Unmarried Father.* The play became a Broadway hit and was later adapted for two Hollywood movies. In 1932 Dell published what was perhaps his finest work of fiction, *Diana Stair,* a historical novel set in the antebellum United States and concerned in part with abolitionism, early trade union struggles, and utopian communal experiments. His autobiography, *Home-coming*, followed in 1933.

Although a number of Dell's books met with critical and commercial success during the 1920s and 1930s, several factors combined to undermine his reputation. His third novel, *Janet March* (1923), was withdrawn by its publisher three months after publication because of its frank treatment of sex and abortion. During the 1920s Dell's novels were also attacked by younger writers who regarded his frequent focus on marriage and family as a sign of underlying conservatism. In addition, Dell's liberal socialism—inspired by writers like George Bernard Shaw and H. G. Wells—brought him into conflict during the late 1920s and early 1930s with growing numbers of Marxist writers. Partly as a result of these controversies, Dell's books generally sold poorly during the late 1920s and early 1930s. He found it especially hard to support his family by the pen after the stock market crash of 1929.

A solution to his economic problems came in 1935 when Dell was offered an editorial position in the Works Progress Administration (WPA) in Washington, D.C. He worked for the government until 1947, writing numerous reports on New Deal projects and speeches for government officials. A lifelong advocate of political reform, Dell derived considerable satisfaction from his work for the WPA. "I am still as proud of my governmental reports," he later wrote, "as of anything I have ever written."

After 1947 Dell continued to reside in the Washington area, where he worked on novels, poems, and essays, few of which he ever published. Although historians have frequently described him as an excellent example of the writers who came of age during the 1910s, Dell noted in his later years that he had often differed from many of his contemporaries, particularly in his rejection of experimental literature during the 1920s and of Marxism in the 1930s. He died in Bethesda, Maryland.

• Dell's papers are collected in the Newberry Library in Chicago. Dell's autobiography, *Homecoming* (1933), is an indispensable source of information on his life and era. The two novels that he based on his early life, *Moon-Calf* (1920) and *The Briary Bush* (1921), are also valuable, although they should be read as fictionalized, not purely factual, accounts. John E. Hart, *Floyd Dell* (1971), and George Thomas Tanselle, "Faun at the Barricades: The Life and Work of Floyd Dell" (Ph.D. diss., Northwestern Univ., 1959), are important sources. For other books and articles on Dell, see Judith Nierman, *Floyd Dell: An Annotated Bibliography of Secondary Sources, 1910–1981* (1984).

Important accounts of Dell's early years in Chicago are found in Bernard Duffey, *The Chicago Renaissance in American Letters* (1954), and Dale Kramer, *Chicago Renaissance: The Literary Life in the Midwest, 1900–1930* (1966). Daniel Aaron, *Writers on the Left* (1961), and James Burkhart Gilbert, *Writers and Partisans* (1968), provide valuable insights into Dell's career in New York. Robert Humphrey, *Children of Fantasy: The First Rebels of Greenwich Village* (1978), offers a critical view of Dell and his generation of literary radicals. Steven Watson, *Strange Bedfellows: The First American*

Avant-Garde (1991), places Dell among the founders of America's diverse avant-garde community of the 1910s. An obituary is in the *New York Times*, 30 July 1969.

DOUGLAS CLAYTON

DELMONICO, Lorenzo (13 Mar. 1813–3 Sept. 1881), restaurateur, was born in Marengo, Ticino Canton, Switzerland, the son of Francesco Delmonico and Rosa Longhi, farmers. He attended a parochial school for a short time but was largely self-educated. A bright, hardworking, ambitious person, Delmonico emigrated in 1831 to New York City, where his two uncles, Pietro and Giovanni, ran a small wine, confectionary, and catering concern. Delmonico was a quick learner with keen business instincts; his uncles eventually made him a junior partner.

The Delmonicos specialized in serving fine coffee, cakes, and chocolates in a little café, mainly to upper-class European immigrants and curious New Yorkers. From this beginning, they expanded into a larger combination restaurant and hotel. The business was destroyed in the great fire of 1835, but two years later they established a larger one.

The Delmonicos, particularly Lorenzo, sensed an opportunity in the food business that others had overlooked. The few American restaurants in the 1830s usually served meals at set times, the food overcooked and unimaginative, with limited choices. American culinary tastes favored simple, heavy meals, eaten quickly, washed down by quantities of water or various intoxicating beverages. The Delmonicos revolutionized such eating habits by turning the preparation and serving of food into a gastronomic art. Starting slowly, they at first specialized in introducing fine European foods, sauces, and wines. Their restaurant was open all day. The food was cooked to perfection, and prices were reasonable. A typical menu included a wide choice of items, with the names of dishes translated into English. The cuisine incorporated native ingredients, including game, vegetables, and salads.

Convinced that they could not rely on local marketers, they became their own chief suppliers of fresh items. They bought 200 acres of farm land in Brooklyn and used scientific methods of farming that they had learned in Switzerland. In 1848 Lorenzo assumed total management of the business. In 1856 he married Clemence Chanon Miege, a French widow who had two children by her first husband. The marriage was childless.

By the 1850s, Delmonico, now called "Lorenzo the Great" by admirers, established himself as the leading American epicure. As the fame of his operations increased, he further diversified by establishing a successful hotel and additional restaurants to keep pace with the city's expanding middle and upper classes. The principal Delmonico's restaurant was the famous site at Fifth Avenue and Twenty-sixth Street, facing Madison Square. Without a peer by the 1870s, Delmonico employed the best European chefs. His restaurants were the equal of the best in the civilized world and, more than anyone else, he had changed the traditional American diet and had turned eating into a form of entertainment.

Delmonico's services became indispensable as a caterer at fashionable New York weddings, parties, and receptions. He entertained visiting dignitaries, such as Charles Dickens, and boasted that he had served every president from Andrew Jackson to James A. Garfield. He maintained the daily operations of his businesses until late in life, supervising every aspect of his chain. He personally bought supplies, administered the preparation of foods, selected wines, and directed service to customers. Not everything turned out as well as his restaurant business. In 1861 he lost nearly $500,000 in a petroleum company and was almost forced into bankruptcy. Fortunately, his creditors were willing to wait, and Delmonico repaid his debts in a few years from the profits of his restaurants.

A man of few personal vices, beyond chain-smoking cigars, Delmonico was a noted philanthropist. He established a school in his native town and supported a variety of charitable institutions, chiefly those associated with the Catholic church. He died in Sharon Springs, New York.

• Delmonico left no personal letters. Relevant material appears in either contemporary newspapers or reminiscences. The best study of the Delmonicos, Lorenzo in particular, is Lately Thomas, *Delmonico's: A Century of Splendor* (1967). See also Esther B. Aresty, *The Delectable Past* (1964); W. Harrison Bayles, *Old Taverns of New York* (1915); Henry Collins Brown, *Delmonico's: A Story of Old New York* (1928); George S. Chappell, *Restaurants of New York* (1925); Maude Howe Elliott, *Uncle Sam Ward and His Circle* (1938); Meryl R. Evans, "Knickerbocker Hotel and Restaurants, 1800–1850," *New-York Historical Society Quarterly* 36 (Oct. 1952): 377–409; Lately Thomas, *Sam Ward: "King of the Lobby"* (1965); Leopold Rimmer, *History of Old New York Life and the House of Delmonico* (1898); and William G. Wilkins, *Charles Dickens in America* (1911). An obituary is in the *New York Times*, 4 Sept. 1881.

JEROME MUSHKAT

DELMORE BROTHERS, country singers, guitarists, and songwriters, were born Alton Delmore (25 Dec. 1908–8 June 1964) and Rabon Delmore (3 Dec. 1916–4 Dec. 1952) in Elkmont, Alabama, the sons of Charlie Delmore and Mary (called "Aunt Mollie," maiden name unknown). The parents were subsistence farmers. The brothers' uncle W. A. Williams was a prominent gospel singer and songwriter, and the family encouraged the two youngsters from a young age to attend a local singing school. Mollie, who played the fiddle, also taught her sons to play country fiddle tunes, and as early as 1925 she was writing gospel songs with Alton that were published locally. Alton and Rabon were heavily influenced by the bluesy recordings of white country star Jimmie Rodgers.

By 1926 the brothers were performing together, with Alton singing lead vocals and playing a standard guitar, and Rabon singing harmony and playing lead on a four-string, "tenor" guitar (tuned like a tenor banjo and not usually heard in country music). They began to build a local following and in 1931 made a single recording for Columbia Records. Though the record failed to sell, the brothers made a concerted effort to land a job on the prestigious Grand Ole Opry, originating out of Nashville, Tennessee. They finally succeeded in 1933.

In December 1933 the Delmores traveled to RCA's Chicago studios to record for the label's budget Bluebird division. They recorded several original songs with a blues flavor, including their signature song, the up-tempo "Brown's Ferry Blues," as well as "Big River Blues" (popularized in the 1960s by Doc Watson under the name "Deep River Blues") and the more sentimental "Gonna Lay down My Old Guitar." The success of these recordings and their popularity on the Opry led to several tours with other Opry performers, including old-time banjoist Uncle Dave Macon and the jazz-influenced fiddler and vocalist Arthur Smith. The Delmores also appeared as backup musicians on Smith's hit 1936 recording "There's More Pretty Girls Than One." But when the Opry adopted a more modern sound in the late 1930s, the duo pulled out of the show.

After working on several small radio stations, the brothers were hired in the late 1940s by Cincinnati's WLW, where they continued to perform as a duo. Later, with local guitarist Merle Travis and banjoist Grandpa Jones, who also worked at the station, they formed a gospel quartet, the Brown's Ferry Four. The quartet recorded on several occasions through the early 1950s, with the Delmores bringing in new members as necessary. The brothers also began recording again, this time for the local King label. They briefly separated when Rabon was drafted, but by the end of the war they were back together, working out of Memphis, and recording in a new style. Accompanied by blues harmonica player Wayne Ramey, along with electric guitar and piano, the duo recorded in a style that forecast the popular "rockabilly" sound of the mid-1950s that influenced the birth of rock and roll. They had their biggest hit in 1949 with the ever-popular "Blues Stay Away from Me," which reached number one on the country charts and remained on the charts for twenty-three weeks.

After brief stays at radio stations in Memphis, Chattanooga, and other smaller towns, by 1950 the Delmores made their way to XREF in Del Rio, Texas, where Alton suffered a heart attack. Tragedy struck again a year later with the deaths of their father and Alton's three-year-old daughter. Alton began drinking heavily, and Rabon relocated to Detroit to pursue a solo career. Rabon died of lung cancer in Athens, Alabama.

After his brother's death, Alton worked as a radio announcer and even recorded on his own. His son Lionel would sometimes perform with him, taking his deceased uncle's place. Alton also began to write semifictional stories and produced an autobiography, *Truth Is Stranger Than Publicity* (1977), which was published after his death.

• Alton's autobiography, edited by country scholar Charles T. Wolfe, was published by the Country Music Foundation in 1977. Wolfe also wrote an article on the duo in *Pickin'* 2, no. 8 (Sept. 1975). Bill C. Malone, *Country Music U.S.A.*, 2d ed. (1985), offers information on the Delmores and other brother groups of the period. Their original mid-1930s recordings were reissued on *Brown's Ferry Blues* (Country 402), while their later country-boogie flavored material is available on *Sand Mountain Blues* (County 110).

RICHARD CARLIN

DE LONG, George Washington (22 Aug. 1844–30 Oct. 1881), naval officer and explorer, was born in New York City, the son of Levi De Long and Catherine Greames (occupations unknown). He grew up in Brooklyn and was fascinated with stories of American naval heroes during the War of 1812. His protective parents tried vigorously to dissuade him—their only child—from going to sea, but he gained entrance on his own to the U.S. Naval Academy, which at the time was located at Newport, Rhode Island. He graduated with distinction in 1865, too late to participate in the Civil War. He was assigned as a midshipman aboard the U.S.S. *Canandaigua* and rose to ensign (1866), master (1868), and lieutenant (1869). He met Emma Wotton in Le Havre, France; they married in March 1871 and had one child. The couple moved to New York City and he continued on active duty. In 1873 he accompanied Captain Daniel L. Braine aboard the U.S.S. *Juniata* in its search for the men of the U.S.S. *Polaris* in the waters off Greenland. De Long became enamored of Arctic exploration during this duty and, soon afterward, he approached James Gordon Bennett, the proprietor of the *New York Herald*, to ask for assistance in developing an expedition to reach the North Pole. Bennett was interested, but their joint plans were put off until 1879; during the interim, De Long was the executive officer of the school ship *St. Mary's* in the Nautical School of the Port of New York.

In 1878 Bennett purchased the British steam yacht *Pandora*, which was rechristened the *Jeannette*. Bennett presented the ship to the U.S. Navy for the purpose of an expedition to reach the North Pole. Named to command the expedition, De Long brought the *Jeannette* from Europe to San Francisco. He applied idiosyncratic criteria to recruit a crew; he preferred Scandinavians to southern Europeans, and he wanted merry fellows, particularly musicians. De Long and his crew of thirty-two men left San Francisco on 8 July 1879 to a tremendous sendoff by the townspeople. Mrs. De Long accompanied the ship to the Golden Gate before being taken off by a boat.

De Long led the *Jeannette* northward, through the Bering Strait, hoping that Wrangel Land would serve as a guide to the pole. Instead, the *Jeannette* became caught in the ice pack near Herald Island on 6 September 1879 and remained so for nearly two years, drifting in a northwesterly direction. Using what he called "Edison's electric light" and a Baxter steam engine to generate electric power, De Long made the first, unsuccessful, attempt to use electric lights aboard a steamboat (14–30 Oct. 1879). He maintained an active

ship's regimen and worked to keep the men's spirits up. However, he had conflicts with Jerome Collins, the meteorologist, whom he considered incompetent and suspended from duty in December 1880. Later, he ordered Lieutenant Danehower off the work force (June 1881) and arrested Raymond Newcomb, the naturalist (July 1881), for insubordination to Danehower and William Ninedemann, a seaman (October 1881), for insubordination to De Long himself.

De Long and his men discovered two islands, Jeannette Island (sighted on 17 May 1881, but not landed upon) and Henrietta Island (landed on and claimed on 2 June 1881). The *Jeannette* broke up and sank on 13 June 1881 at 77° 15′ north latitude, 155° 50′ east longitude. De Long evacuated his men without any loss, and the company pushed on by foot, dragging three boats and their supplies, traveling about 600 nautical miles southward to Siberia. De Long discovered and claimed Bennett Island on 29 July 1881. The company stayed there nine days and then set out in two cutters and a whaleboat for the Lena Delta in Siberia. The boats were separated in a storm on 12 September. De Long's boat reached the shore on 17 September, Chief Engineer George Melville's whaleboat reached shore at another location, and the third boat was never heard from again. Melville's group met Tungus natives and settled down to recuperate. De Long and his men moved southward, lost in the many branches of the Lena Delta. Failing to meet any natives, De Long's men suffered from intense cold and hunger. On 3 October, De Long recorded that "Nearly everybody seemed dazed and stupefied, and I feared that some of us would perish during the night . . . such a dreary, wretched night I hope I shall never see again."

The suffering explorers began to die in the last week of the month. The final entry in De Long's journal read, "Sunday Oct 30—140th day—Boyd + Gortz died during night—Mr Collins dying." Presumably, De Long succumbed on 30 October 1881.

George Melville's rescue party found the bodies of the dead men on 23 March 1882. Melville buried the men in a cairn and rescued their journals and notes. The bodies were later taken from the burial place and brought—by deer train, horse sledge, train, and ship—to New York City, where they were interred on 22 February 1884. There was both a naval court of inquiry and a congressional hearing regarding the loss of the *Jeannette* and allegations that De Long was a martinet. The naval court of inquiry concluded that "special commendation is due to Lieutenant Commander De Long for the high qualities displayed by him in the conduct of the expedition." Testimony at the congressional inquiry made it clear that tempers were short and the patience of many members of the expedition was tried during two years of drifting in the ice pack. The voyage furthered Arctic exploration. De Long established that Wrangel Land was an island, not a continent, and he discovered Jeannette, Henrietta, and Bennett islands, which are collectively known as Ostrava de Longa (De Long Islands). A statue of De

Long was unveiled in Woodlawn Cemetery in New York City on 4 July 1928.

• De Long's journals are in the Naval Academy Museum, Annapolis, Md. True copies are in the National Archives. His wife edited his journals and published them as *The Voyage of the Jeannette: The Ship and Ice Journals of George W. De Long* (1884). The naval investigation and congressional inquiry into the Jeannette affair are published as U.S. Congress, House, *Proceedings of a Court of Inquiry into the Loss of the Exploring Steamer Jeannette*, 47th Cong., 2d sess., H. Ex. Doc. 108; and U.S. Congress, House, *Proceedings of an Investigation into the Jeannette by the Naval Affairs Subcommittee*, 47th Cong., 1st sess., H. Misc. Doc. 66. Accounts by members of the Jeannette expedition include Raymond Lee Newcomb, ed., *Our Lost Explorers* (1882), and George Wallace Melville, *In the Lena Delta* (1892). Edward Ellsberg told the story using Melville's voice in *Hell on Ice: The Saga of the Jeannette* (1938). Leonard F. Guttridge's *Icebound: The Jeannette Expedition's Quest for the North Pole* (1986) reveals conflicts between De Long and members of the expedition and the subsequent coverup of those conflicts by the naval inquiry.

SAMUEL WILLARD CROMPTON

DELORIA, Ella Cara (31 Jan. 1889–12 Feb. 1971), linguist and ethnologist, was born on the Yankton Sioux (Dakota) Reservation at Lake Andes, South Dakota, the daughter of Native Americans Philip Joseph Deloria, an Episcopalian minister, and Mary Sully Bordeaux. She and her siblings received their earliest education at St. Elizabeth's Mission, an institution associated with their father's parish on the Standing Rock Reservation at Wakpala, South Dakota. The Deloria household, where Dakota was spoken as the primary language, provided an environment that was supportive of both Christian values and traditional Dakota language and culture. Deloria continued to intertwine elements of both cultures throughout her personal and professional life.

After her schooling at St. Elizabeth's, Deloria continued her education at All Saints School, a boarding school, in Sioux Falls, South Dakota, where she excelled in her studies in the college preparatory course. She was awarded a college scholarship for high academic achievement and enrolled at Oberlin College in 1911. After two years at Oberlin she transferred to Columbia University and graduated from its teachers college in 1915. While at Columbia, she became acquainted with the anthropologist Franz Boas and assisted him and his students with translation and grammar of Dakota linguistic materials. At this time she also began to give talks and demonstrations on Dakota culture to various church groups and other organizations.

After graduation Deloria taught at both All Saints and St. Elizabeth's until 1919, when she was appointed health education secretary of Indian schools and reservations for the YWCA, a position that required much travel and brought her in contact with Native American groups throughout the United States. In 1923 she accepted a position to teach physical education, dancing, and other subjects at Haskell Institute,

a Bureau of Indian Affairs school in Lawrence, Kansas. While she was at Haskell, Boas contacted her and offered her financial support to do further work on the Dakota language. Deloria was also not entirely happy with her position at Haskell, and she remembered how much she had enjoyed her Dakota work for Boas twelve years earlier. She therefore resigned her teaching post in 1928 and was appointed research specialist in ethnology and linguistics for the Department of Anthropology at Columbia University the following year. Her collaboration with Boas continued until his death in 1942.

During her long association with Columbia, which also included work with Ruth Benedict until her death in 1948, Deloria recorded, translated, and annotated linguistic materials in all three Siouan dialects—Lakota, Dakota, and Nakota—collected in the field not only by herself but others as well. She did extensive field research, focusing both on linguistic texts and ethnographic material. In addition to becoming the foremost authority on language and culture of the Dakota, she was also keenly interested in Native American education and social issues. One of her goals was to disseminate knowledge about the Dakota, past and present, to the non-Native American community.

Deloria's earliest publication was an article titled "The Sun Dance of the Oglala Sioux," which appeared in the *Journal of American Linguistics* in 1929. Based on a field assignment she did for Boas shortly after leaving her job at Haskell, it was followed in 1932 by *Dakota Texts*, a selection of tales and their translations in all three Dakota dialects. These stories, collected in the field by Deloria and others, include extensive linguistic and anthropological notes as well as different examples of the same stories. Unlike Boas and other scholars who collected oral literature from informants, Deloria did not take notes or use a tape recorder. Instead she wrote the stories down later as she remembered them, imbuing them with her own creativity and imagination.

Although Boas did not often publish as a collaborating author, he made an exception in the case of Deloria, and the two coauthored "Notes on the Dakota, Teton Dialect," an article that appeared in 1933 in the *International Journal of American Linguistics* and *Dakota Grammar* (1941). What distinguished these two publications on the Dakota language from previous ones was an attempt to describe the language in terms of its own structure rather than relating it to English or Latin grammar and usage. During her years at Columbia Deloria also compiled a large amount of data for a Lakota dictionary, but she was never able to complete it.

Speaking of Indians, published in 1944, is a popular treatment of Native American culture in which Deloria describes the customs and ceremonies of traditional life as well as the many difficulties Native Americans encountered in facing rapid change and adjusting to reservation life. She pays particular attention to the importance of kinship in Dakota life. In fact, her own loyalty and sense of responsibility toward her family, especially her sister Susan and her father, during times of illness and need created occasional conflict between her personal and professional life.

Among the large amount of manuscript material that remained unpublished in Deloria's lifetime was *Waterlily*, completed sometime in the early 1940s. This fictional account of traditional Dakota culture and values as seen from a woman's perspective was turned down by publishers who believed it wouldn't have wide appeal; it was finally published posthumously in 1988.

Deloria continued to do research, writing, and lecturing throughout the 1940s, 1950s, and 1960s. Although she came to be considered the foremost authority on Dakota language and culture, she was never able to secure a permanent academic post, and she relied mainly on lecturing and consulting fees and small research grants to support herself and her artist sister Susan, who was her lifelong companion. In 1955 she assumed the directorship of her old school, St. Elizabeth's, but she left three years later to devote more time to writing and research.

In 1961 Deloria began her association with the University of South Dakota in Vermillion with a brief appointment as the Assistant Director of the W. H. Over Museum. She continued to compile Lakota language materials under a National Science Foundation grant awarded to the university's Institute of Indian Studies in 1962. Several of her articles on Dakota culture appeared in the university's publication *Museum News*. She continued working on Dakota materials, giving lectures, and attending conferences until becoming ill a year before her death in Tripp, South Dakota.

Deloria was a meticulous scholar who recorded, translated, and interpreted a voluminous amount of material on Dakota language and culture. But beyond that she was a person who cared deeply about Dakota traditions and wanted to make sure that their legacy was preserved for Natives and non-Natives alike. She has left behind a wealth of cultural and linguistic material from this distinctive period of American history.

• The majority of Deloria's unpublished manuscripts are housed in the Boas Collection of the American Philosophical Society in Philadelphia and the Dakota Indian Foundation in Chamberlain, S.D. The most complete biographical treatment is Janette K. Murray, "Ella C. Deloria: A Biographical Sketch and Literary Analysis" (Ph.D. diss., Univ. of North Dakota, 1974). Brief but valuable sketches of Deloria's life and scholarly contributions include introductory notes to 1992 editions of Deloria's *Speaking of Indians* and *Dakota Texts* by Agnes Picotte and Paul N. Pavich. See also the biographical sketch of Deloria by Picotte in *Waterlily*. Raymond J. DeMallie, in the afterword to *Waterlily*, offers valuable insights about the circumstances surrounding the writing of *Waterlily* and also offers a sensitive personal portrait of Deloria. As editor, Julian Rice approaches Deloria's collections of Dakota narratives from the point of view of literary criticism in *Deer Women and Elk Men* (1992), *Ella Deloria's Iron Hawk* (1993), and *Ella Deloria's the Buffalo People* (1994). A discussion of Deloria's writing from a feminist perspective is

Janet L. Finn, "Ella Cara Deloria and Mourning Dove: Writing for Cultures, Writing Against the Grain," *Critique of Anthropology* 13 (1993): 335–49.

MAIJA M. LUTZ

DE LUE, Donald Harcourt (5 Oct. 1897–26 Aug. 1988), sculptor, was born Donald H. Quigley in Boston, Massachusetts, the son of Harry T. Quigley, an iron and steel dealer, and Ida M. De Lue. De Lue grew up in Boston as the son of working-class parents of Irish and French descent. His home life during his childhood was troubled, but his mother encouraged his interest in art. By the age of twelve, after showing his drawings to the sculptor Bela Pratt, De Lue was allowed to enter the studio of Pratt's assistant, Richard Recchia, as an apprentice. In the next few years, in the studios of Pratt, Recchia, and the British-born sculptors Robert and Bryant Baker and at the School of the Museum of Fine Arts, Boston, De Lue learned the fundamentals of his craft.

Immediately following the armistice in 1918, De Lue signed on as a merchant seaman to work his passage to France. For the next four years he worked in various studios in Paris, Lyons, and London, including that of the Italian protégé of Rodin, Alfredo Pina, where he was influenced by Pina and by Pina's neighbor and rival, Antoine Bourdelle. After his return to the United States in 1922, De Lue entered the New York studio of Bryant Baker, where he became the chief modeler. De Lue's success in helping Baker gain commissions led him in 1937 to enter the APEX competition, the most important competition of the Section of Painting and Sculpture of the U.S. Treasury under the new Franklin D. Roosevelt administration. As one of four runners-up, De Lue was awarded the commission for the sculpture for the new federal courthouse in Philadelphia. This project was to be the first of a long series of major commissions for architectural sculpture, most of them working with the architect Paul Phillipe Cret or his students, Harry Sternfeld, John Harbeson, and Roy Larson.

In 1933, on his thirty-sixth birthday, De Lue married Martha Naomi Cross. Before his marriage, De Lue had been known as a hard-drinking, free-spending man-about-town. His wife, who was known by her middle name, encouraged him to settle down, taught him to save money, and began acting as his business agent. The couple remained childless by choice to enable them to turn all of their energies to his career. The beginning of De Lue's successful independent career dates from the time of his marriage, a marriage that lasted until Naomi De Lue's death in September 1982.

During the postwar years De Lue won almost all of the awards that were available to a young sculptor: not only a Guggenheim Fellowship but also gold medals from the Allied Artists of America, the American Artist Professional League, the American Numismatic Association, the American Numismatic Society, the Architectural League of New York, the National Academy of Design, and the National Sculpture Society. He was president of the National Sculpture Society from 1945 to 1948, succeeding Paul Manship. During this period his reputation as a sculptor of monumental figurative work increased. De Lue sculpted seven works for the Omaha Beach Memorial at St. Laurent, Normandy, France (1951–1958); the Virginia Polytechnic Institute chapel in Blacksburg, Virginia (1948–1960); work for the Harvey Firestone Memorial, Akron, Ohio (1950); the Crump Memorial, Memphis, Tennessee (1955–1956); *Stations of the Cross* and *Corpus* for the Sisters of St. Joseph Chapel, Willowdale, Toronto, Ontario (1959–1963); *Hercules as Athlete* for the U.S. Naval Academy, Annapolis, Maryland (1957); the controversial *Rocket Thrower*, for the 1964 World's Fair, Flushing Meadow, New York (1962–1963); *Quest Eternal*, Boston, Massachusetts (1967); *George Washington as Master Mason*, New Orleans, Louisiana (1959); Commemorative Tribute to the Boy Scouts of America, Washington, D.C. (1962–1964); three of the Gettysburg Battlefield monuments, *The Soldiers and Sailors of the Confederacy* (1964–1965), *The State of Louisiana Monument* (1967–1969), *The State of Mississippi Monument* (1970–1973); *The Mountaineer*, Morgantown, West Virginia (1967–1968); *The Green Beret*, Fort Bragg, North Carolina (1968–1969); *Thomas Jefferson*, Jefferson Parish, Louisiana (1975); *Leander Perez*, Plaquemines Parish, Louisiana (1976); *Washington at Prayer*, Valley Forge, Pennsylvania (1965–1967); *The Portal of Life Eternal*, Woodmont, Gladwyne, Pennsylvania (1967–1970); and a large number of smaller commissions and editioned bronzes. De Lue was also one of the finest medalists of his generation: he designed and executed twenty-six different commemorative medals for such organizations as the National Sculpture Society, the Society of Medalists, the Hall of Fame for Great Americans, the National Medal of Science, the Grand Lodge of Pennsylvania, the Daughters of the American Revolution, the National Academy of Design, and Brookgreen Gardens, South Carolina.

Donald De Lue has been called the most important American figurative sculptor of the third quarter of the twentieth century; he was also a passionate advocate for the figurative tradition in art during an age of ascendancy of abstract art in America. In his style, De Lue was firmly in the classical tradition of the ancient Greeks and Romans as transformed by the Italian Renaissance and the French and American Beaux-Arts tradition. His use of contra posto, figura serpentina, and Mannerist distortions of anatomy created heroic figures that made him perhaps the most Michelangelesque of all twentieth-century sculptors. De Lue greatly admired the Serbian sculptor Ivan Meštrović and might have been writing of himself in 1962 when he wrote an appreciation for Meštrović that began: "[The] master sculptor of our time has joined the great masters of the past. To those who worked in the tradition of Western Humanism starting with the Great Greeks, followed by the Renaissance and the massive genius of that time, Michelangelo, and more recently Rodin and Bourdelle, can now be added the name of Ivan Meštrović."

Throughout his career, in the tradition of those sculptors that he admired, De Lue chose to give his work a depth of meaning beyond the literal through the use of patriotic symbols, classical mythology, and the personification of spiritual emotions. His deeply held belief in both Western spiritual ideals and the classical tradition led him to be one of the most articulate and outspoken spokesmen in the New York art world of the 1950s and 1960s against what he viewed as the depredations of abstract and modern art. De Lue was quoted by the *New York Times* (15 Nov. 1951) on the subject of abstract and modern sculptors: "We don't like each other. They think we're old hat and we think they're incompetent." He was savagely attacked by the New York press, most notably by John Canaday in the *New York Times* (25 Apr. 1964), who characterized De Lue's *Rocket Thrower* as, among other things, "the most lamentable monster," and who viewed De Lue, his contemporaries in the figurative tradition, and his teachers as the discredited leftovers of a previous generation. De Lue, therefore, found that his later commissions were from more conservative organizations, such as the American Battle Monuments Commission, the Roman Catholic church, the Boy Scouts of America, Freedoms Foundation, and the Daughters of the Confederacy, among others. Nevertheless, De Lue lived to see his ideals confirmed by a younger generation of critics, scholars, curators and sculptors. In 1989 Joseph Veach Noble wrote: "[De Lue] stayed true to his vision of what sculpture should be. Some critics thought him to be old-fashioned and outdated. He fooled them all, and had the last laugh, by living long enough to see abstract, minimal, found objects and conceptual styles run their course. . . . the art world came full circle, and Donald's style is 'in' again." De Lue died in a hospital near Leonardo, New Jersey.

• The De Lue archives remain the property of the De Lue estate. The most complete and accurate study of De Lue is D. Roger Howlett, *The Sculpture of Donald De Lue: Gods, Prophets and Heroes* (1990), which also contains the fullest bibliography. Edward S. Cooke, Jr., in Katherine Greenthal et al., *American Figurative Sculpture in the Museum of Fine Arts, Boston* (1986), gives a good overview of De Lue's career but contains some errors in dating as well as an error in De Lue's mother's maiden name. A. Hyatt Mayor, *A Century of Sculpture: Treasures from Brookgreen Gardens* (1988), is useful for setting De Lue's work visually alongside that of his peers and colleagues. Joseph F. Morris, "Donald De Lue," *American Sculptors Series* (n.d. [c.1955]), which is primarily illustrations and captions, is the earliest monograph on De Lue and helps to establish the dating and titles of many works. Glenn B. Opitz, *Dictionary of American Sculptors: 18th Century to the Present* (1984), has good dictionary entries on De Lue and the other American sculptors of his generation. Beatrice Gilman Proske, *Brookgreen Gardens Sculpture* (1968), is an accurate text with interesting analyses of importance, style, and influences. Howlett, "Thirties Sculpture in the Manship Tradition Reborn in the Eighties," *Journal of Decorative and Propaganda Arts* 16 (1990): 22–39, analyzes the conditions that caused De Lue and four other sculptors to delay bronze editions of their smaller 1930s works until the 1980s. Howlett, "Donald De Lue and the Federal Government as Patron of the Arts," *American Art Review* 5, no. 1 (1992): 114–19, 146–51, gives an overview of shifting conditions, methods, and priorities in U.S. government commissions from the early 1930s to the 1980s through De Lue's experiences. *Uncommon Clay*, a film produced and directed by Thomas Craven (1951), shows De Lue at work on the Omaha Beach Memorial commissions. Obituaries are in the *Boston Herald*, 28 Aug. 1988; *National Sculpture Review*, Nov. 1988; the *Boston Globe* and the *New York Times*, both 27 Aug. 1988.

D. ROGER HOWLETT

DEMAR, Clarence Harrison (7 June 1888–11 June 1958), marathon runner, was born in Maderia, Ohio, the son of George DeMar, a farmer, and Carol Abbott. DeMar attended elementary school in Madisonville, Ohio, before the death of his father required him to help support the family by selling goods made by his mother. At eight years of age he pushed a cart filled with the items, which included soap, thread, and sewing implements, walking 10 to 20 miles a day. When DeMar was 10 years old, his family moved to Warwick, Massachusetts, to live in a house owned by his mother's relatives. Because his mother was unable to support him and his five younger siblings, the family split up; DeMar was sent to the Farm and Trades School on Thompsons Island in Boston Harbor. At age 16 DeMar left the school and went to South Hero, Vermont, where he worked for a fruit farmer and attended the Maple Lawn Academy. After graduating from the academy in 1908, he entered the University of Vermont. There he worked in the university print shop and as a delivery boy for the university experimental station. In the fall of 1909 DeMar quit school and returned to Melrose, Massachusetts, where he secured a job in a print shop to support his family.

Before leaving Vermont, DeMar had begun to race competitively, joining the cross-country team and finishing fourth in a four-mile race. In late 1909 he decided to compete in the Boston Athletic Association Marathon held annually on Patriot's Day, the third Monday in April. DeMar prepared for the race by running to and from work each day, a distance of about 14 miles. Representing the North Dorchester Athletic Association, he finished second in the 1910 Boston Marathon. The following year saw DeMar win the Marathon, running the 24.7-mile course in 2 hours, 21 minutes, and 39 seconds. In 1912 he was one of twelve runners who represented the United States in the Olympic Games marathon in Stockholm, Sweden; DeMar finished 12th in the race.

After the Olympic Games DeMar entered the Harvard University Extension School, and in 1915 he earned an associate of arts degree that qualified him to work as a print compositor. Although DeMar maintained a daily running schedule to and from work, he did not compete in the Boston Marathon again until 1917, when he finished third. Later that year DeMar joined the U.S. Army; following basic training at Camp Upton, Long Island, he was stationed first in Romsey, England, and later in St. Amand, France. Although he spent much time hospitalized with the flu

in 1918, he represented the army in track meets throughout France. As part of the Allied Occupational Forces in Coblenz, Germany, DeMar was an alternate on the U.S. team in the Inter-Allied Games in Paris in 1919.

In late 1919 DeMar returned to the United States and resumed working as a compositor in Boston area print shops. In 1922 he competed in the Boston Marathon for the first time in five years and won the race in a course record of 2 hours, 18 minutes, and 10 seconds. He won the race again in 1923 and 1924 for an unprecedented three consecutive titles. In 1924 DeMar finished third in the Olympic Games marathon at Paris, France, winning the bronze medal. He then finished second in the 1925 and third in the 1926 Boston Marathons. DeMar won two consecutive Amateur Athletic Union (AAU) marathon championships in Baltimore, Maryland, before returning to the victory stand in the 1927 and 1928 Boston Marathons. In 1928 he won a 44-mile race from Providence, Rhode Island, to Boston and finished 27th in the Olympic Games marathon in Amsterdam, Holland.

In 1929 DeMar married Margaret Ilsley and began working as teacher and printer at the Keene (N.H.) Normal School in 1929. The following year, at age 41, he won the Boston Marathon for the last time, becoming the oldest competitor to win the race. His time of 2 hours, 34 minutes, and 48 seconds was his personal record for 26.2 miles, the official Olympic marathon distance. DeMar competed in the Boston Marathon until 1954, when at age 66, he placed 78th out of 133 finishers. His last race, the 1957 New England AAU 15-Kilometer Championship, came a year after he was diagnosed with colon cancer, from which he died in Reading, Massachusetts. An autopsy of DeMar showed the benefits of a lifetime of running, as the coronary arteries of his heart were nearly free of sclerosis and three times normal size.

With seven Boston Marathon titles, DeMar remained the most successful performer in the history of America's prestigious long-distance running event at the end of the twentieth century. Only Bill Rogers of the United States and Cosmas Noleti of Kenya equalled DeMar's feat of three consecutive wins during the twentieth century. More important, DeMar was one of the first athletes to demonstrate that marathon running success could be achieved during middle age, and that the sport could be pursued into old age without any adverse effect upon the heart and vascular system.

• DeMar wrote an autobiography, *Marathon: The Clarence DeMar Story* (1937). A good account of DeMar's record as a marathon runner is in David E. Martin and Roger W. H. Gynn, *The Marathon Footrace: Performers and Performances* (1978), and John A. Lucas, "A History of the Marathon Race—490 B.C. to 1975," *Journal of Sport History* 3 (1976): 128–38. For the report of the DeMar autopsy, see James H. Currens and Paul D. White, "Half a Century of Running: Clinical, Physiologic and Autopsy Findings in the Case of Clarence DeMar ("Mr. Marathon")," *New England Journal of*

Medicine 265 (16 Nov. 1961): 988–93. Principal obituaries include the *Boston Globe* and the *New York Times*, both 12 June 1958.

ADAM R. HORNBUCKLE

DEMAREST, William Carl (27 Feb. 1892–28 Dec. 1983), actor, was born in St. Paul, Minnesota, the son of Samuel Demarest and Minnie Lingren, farmers. One of three sons, Demarest and his family moved to New Jersey when he was an infant. With his brothers, Ruben and George, "Willie" formed a trio, and their mother trained them for entering the entertainment business. Around 1906 they began performing in hotels in New Jersey as well as on Times Square street corners, with William playing the cello. Later, he and George worked up a vaudeville act in which they appeared in blackface and kilts and billed themselves as "The Demarestio Brothers, European Comedy Stars."

After the brothers broke up, Demarest did solo acts on the Pantages and Considine-Sullivan circuits. Later he teamed up with a violinist, Estelle Collette, who became his first wife. They did not have children, and the marriage ended in divorce. He served in the U.S. Army in 1917–1918 and subsequently toured for several years on the Keith-Orpheum circuit. A specialist in pratfalls and trick acrobatics, Demarest reached Broadway in 1925 in Ole Olsen and Chic Johnson's vaudeville revue *Monkey Business*. In 1926 he appeared in Earl Carroll's *Sketch Book* and performed in Carroll shows for two more years.

Demarest first appeared in films in 1926 with a role in *When the Wife's Away* for Columbia Pictures. He also appeared in the first all-talking featurette filmed in California, *A Night at Coffee Dan's*. In 1927 he began working for Warner Bros. and appeared in more than a dozen films that year, including *Finger Prints* and the first all-talking feature-length film, *The Jazz Singer*. Although Demarest was a national headliner in Carroll's *Vanities* by this time, he began to concentrate his efforts on films and moved to Hollywood permanently in 1933. He went on to appear in more than 130 films, his last in 1976.

During the 1930s Demarest worked at several studios, including Columbia, Fox, Paramount, and MGM. Among his films during this period were *Diamond Jim* (1935), *Murder Man* (1935), *Charlie Chan at the Opera* (1937), *The Hit Parade* (1937), *Rebecca of Sunnybrook Farm* (1938), *The Great Man Votes* (1939), and *Mr. Smith Goes to Washington* (1940). At one point during the decade, Demarest quit acting for a year to become a talent agent, discovering both Ellen Drew and Jane Wyman.

Demarest's most memorable film roles undoubtedly came in the 1940s in films by writer-producer Preston Sturges. Sturges's very popular Paramount films were invariably enhanced by his informal stock company of colorful and fast-talking character actors, including Demarest. He appeared in all eight of Sturges's films for the studio: *The Great McGinty* (1940), *Christmas in July* (1940), *The Lady Eve* (1941), *Sullivan's Travels* (1941), *The Palm Beach Story* (1942), *The Great Mo-*

ment (1944), *Hail the Conquering Hero* (1944), in which he played the tough marine sergeant, and *The Miracle of Morgan's Creek* (1944).

In the early 1940s Paramount signed Demarest to a long-term contract. According to film historian James Robert Parish, he had perfected the portrayal of characters who "excelled at the deadpan look of suspicion and exasperation." Other observers described him as "one of the master exponents of the characterization that includes the fish-eyed stare, crusty voice, and baleful countenance." Demarest's studio biography claimed that "when a director is casting about for an actor to play a loud-mouthed, not-too-bright character his mind automatically turns to William Demarest. . . . He is in a class by himself in such roles as prohibition bootleggers, marine sergeants, dumb cops and racetrack touts."

Demarest married Lucille Thayer, a nonprofessional actress, in 1938; they did not have children. During World War II he made many war bond tours and often volunteered his services as master of ceremonies at benefits and live shows to support the war effort. In 1946 he was nominated for an Academy Award for best supporting actor for his performance in *The Jolson Story*. During the 1950s, Demarest appeared in more than twenty films, including *When Willie Comes Marching Home* (1950), *Never a Dull Moment* (1950), *What Price Glory?* (1952), *Escape from Fort Bravo* (1953), and *Jupiter's Darling* (1955).

In 1959–1960 Demarest starred in the NBC television comedy series, *Love and Marriage*, and in 1961–1962 he joined the cast of NBC's *Tales of Welles Fargo* as the ranch foreman, Jeb Gaine. His late career fame, however, stemmed from his portrayal of Uncle Charley O'Casey in the CBS series *My Three Sons*. Demarest joined the series in 1965 after the death of actor William Frawley, stepping in as Frawley's brother, a crusty former sailor who helped the father, played by Fred MacMurray, run the household and advise the "sons." He continued to play the part until the series ended in 1972 and received an Emmy nomination for it. During those years he also appeared in the films *Pepe* (1960), *It's a Mad, Mad, Mad, Mad World* (1963), *Viva Las Vegas* (1964), and *That Darn Cat!* (1965).

In 1968 Demarest moved to Palm Springs and went into semiretirement, except for his involvement in *My Three Sons* and for appearances in his last two films, *The Wild McCullochs* (1975) and *Won Ton Ton, the Dog Who Saved Hollywood* (1976). He was also active in various charity groups, including the William Demarest Foundation, and he sponsored the Bill Demarest Golf Tournament, which raised more than $1 million for charitable causes. He received a star in the Hollywood Walk of Fame in 1979. He died at his home in Palm Springs.

After Demarest's death, film director Frank Capra described him as "one of the finest comedians this country ever saw. He had made people laugh more than anyone else because he was at it so long. He acted sour, but he wasn't, of course. He was a man without enemies. That's something, when you can say that." Demarest's seventy-year career spanned vaudeville, theater, film, and television.

• Biographical and career information on William Demarest can be found in James Robert Parish, *Hollywood Character Actors* (1978); Arthur F. McClure, Alfred E. Twomey, and Ken Jones, *More Character People* (1984); and "Little Willie Demarest—65 Years Later," *TV Guide*, 16 July 1966. Obituaries are in *Variety*, 4 Jan. 1984, and *Newsweek*, 9 Jan. 1984.

ARTHUR F. McCLURE

DEMARET, Jimmy (24 May 1910–28 Dec. 1983), professional golfer, was born James Newton Demaret in Houston, Texas, the son of John O'Brien Demaret, a carpenter; his mother's name is unknown. He grew up in Houston, began caddying at the age of eight, and won his first competitive tournament three years later in 1923. Demaret completed two years of high school before starting his professional golf career. He married a redhead named Idella Adams, and the couple had a daughter.

After brief stints in the pro shops of several clubs in the Houston area, as well as a number of singing gigs in nightclubs, Demaret achieved his first professional golf success in 1934 when he won the Texas PGA Championship in Dallas. Demaret spent the rest of the Great Depression touring and playing in minor tournaments in Texas and California. In 1938, after he won his fifth consecutive Texas PGA title, Demaret joined the regular tour and captured his first victory of national significance in the San Francisco Match Play tournament by beating Sam Snead. He soon developed a reputation as an extroverted, flashily dressed player with a solid game.

One of Demaret's finest seasons on the professional circuit was in 1940 when he won seven events, including the U.S. Masters and the Western Open. His Masters victory was record-setting in that he shot 67 in the first round. His score of 30 over the last nine holes, comprised of six birdies and three pars, was the lowest to that date and has been matched only a few times by the likes of Ben Hogan and Gary Player. In 1941 Demaret won three tournaments, among them the Argentine Open, and in 1943 he added two more minor events.

Demaret served in the U.S. Navy during World War II; his career was interrupted at the most unfortunate time because he was at his competitive peak in the early 1940s. After winning several minor tournaments in 1945–1946, Demaret came back in 1947 with another impressive season. That year he won six titles, including his second Masters, edging Byron Nelson by two strokes. He also collected the Vardon Trophy, given to the PGA tour player with the season's lowest stroke average, and he was the tour's leading money winner, collecting $27,936. In 1948 he broke the U.S. Open scoring record with a 278 at the Riviera Country Club, but finished two strokes behind Ben Hogan.

Demaret was one of Hogan's few close friends, and in 1954 he published *My Partner, Ben Hogan*, a book that chronicled the life and career of Hogan in the aftermath of his life-threatening auto accident. Demaret and Hogan were a feared match-play team in four-ball tournaments and in Ryder Cup matches. Demaret's Ryder Cup record from 1947 to 1951 was a perfect six wins and no losses. He won his third Masters, and his last major title, in 1950 when he shot 69 in the last round to overtake Jim Ferrier, former Australian Amateur and Open champion.

Over the next seven seasons, Demaret collected a handful of minor tournaments. In 1957, at age 47, he failed by one stroke to get into a playoff for the U.S. Open held at the Inverness Club in Toledo, Ohio. Though he never won the U.S. Open, the British Open, or the PGA Championship, he did win 44 professional events (31 sanctioned by the PGA), became the first man to win three Masters titles, and was elected to the PGA Golf Hall of Fame in 1960. Demaret retired from competitive golf in 1963.

Demaret spent the last twenty years of his life working as a television commentator, as host of the "Wonderful World of Golf" series during the 1960s, and as a consultant to a golf club manufacturer. The majority of his retirement, however, was spent managing the Champions Golf Club in Houston, which he co-owned with his lifelong friend Jack Burke. The course is one of Demaret's legacies to the game and was the site of the 1967 Ryder Cup matches and the 1968 U.S. Open. Demaret died of heart failure while working on the course he designed and built.

Demaret's professional record, while quite respectable, was overshadowed by his extremely popular personality and style. He was golf's most colorful figure in his era and, thus, a true gate attraction in the manner of Walter Hagen of the Golden Twenties. His trademark was not so much his solid and steady game as his sense of humor and outlandish wardrobe—particularly his collection of hats, or "lids," which ranged from a Scotch-plaid fedora to a Swiss yodeler's cap to the "wildest tam you ever did see." In an era when most golfers wore gray or white, Demaret adorned himself in electric blue, bright apricot, or canary yellow. Behind the smile was a respected and loved player who made a significant contribution as one of the game's finest ambassadors. Sam Snead observed, "Of all the guys on the tour, I think [Demaret] was more well-liked than anybody, by the pros and the fans both. He was a wonderful guy."

• Demaret's *My Partner, Ben Hogan* (1954) focuses primarily on Hogan but does include some information on Demaret's career, especially in the early years. Obituaries are in the *Houston Chronicle* and the *New York Times*, both 29 Dec. 1983.

STEPHEN R. LOWE

DEMBITZ, Lewis Naphtali (3 Feb. 1833–11 Mar. 1907), attorney and activist in public affairs, was born in Zirke, Prussia. His father, Sigmund Dembitz, was a surgeon whose degree from a Prussian university precluded his practicing in Austria, which required an Austrian degree. He, his wife Fanny Wehle, and their three children therefore led a wandering existence throughout other parts of the Austro-Hungarian Empire, particularly Poland, while Sigmund unsuccessfully sought a profitable practice in various small towns. The young Dembitz attended schools in Munchenberg, Brandenburg, Frangbord, and Sagan and graduated at age fifteen from the Gymnasium of Glogau University in Frankfort-on-the-Oder. Dembitz's family did not observe religious rituals. A schoolmate at Glogau introduced him to Orthodox Judaism when Dembitz was thirteen, however, and as an adult he adhered strictly to its tenets and rituals. His one semester of legal studies in Prague was interrupted by the unsuccessful political uprising of 1848. Although neither he nor his family were active participants, they found that the combination of their sympathy for the uprising's libertarian goals and their Jewishness, assimilated though it was, made life in the Empire uncomfortable. Thirty-five members of the interrelated Wehle, Dembitz, and Brandeis families therefore immigrated to the United States in 1849.

Dembitz read law in the offices of Walker and Kibler (Cincinnati, Ohio) and Dunn and Hendricks (Madison, Ind.). He also edited the newspaper *Der Beobachter am Ohio* from late December 1852 until early June 1853. The edition of 14 February 1853 contains part of a chapter of *Uncle Tom's Cabin* translated into German as *Onkel Tom's Hutte, oder: Das Leben unter den Niedrigen* "by the editor," an apparent reference to Dembitz, who became a strong abolitionist shortly after his arrival in the United States.

In 1853 he opened a law office in Louisville, Kentucky, where his sister Frederika had settled with her husband Adolph Brandeis. Dembitz and his cousin Wilhelmina Wehle, whom he married in 1857, had six children, one named after Henry Clay and a second after Abraham Lincoln. Dembitz not only served as a member of the Kentucky delegation to the abolitionist Republican party convention of 1860, becoming one of the convention's only two Jewish delegates, but was chosen to give one of the three nominating speeches for Lincoln.

Dembitz became a major figure in Louisville legal and public life in the late 1850s, working with such figures as future Supreme Court Justice John Marshall Harlan (1833–1911) and James Speed, Lincoln's attorney general. The Kentucky legislature designated him to write Louisville's tax law in 1884, the same year he was appointed assistant city attorney for Louisville in charge of tax matters. Four years later he drew up the first American voting law utilizing the Australian system of secret ballots for Louisville's municipal elections. In 1901 he was named commissioner from Kentucky to the Conference for the Uniformity of State Laws.

Dembitz read a dozen languages and was sufficiently versed in astronomy and mathematics to calculate the 1869 eclipse of the sun to the minute. He led the group of intellectuals known as the "Louisville Library," which met regularly to discuss books and ideas. His *Kentucky Jurisprudence*, published in 1890, be-

came the leading work on the subject. His two-volume *A Treatise on Land Titles in the United States* followed in 1895. He wrote numerous magazine articles and book reviews, many of them published in the *Nation* and the *American Hebrew*, as well as most of the articles on legal subjects in the *Jewish Encyclopedia* (1902–1905). The eclectic nature of his interests is reflected in his authorship of such diverse essays as "The Lost Tribes" in the 1889 *Andover Review* and "The Question of Silver Coinage" in the *Present Problem Series* (1896). The combination of his brilliance and his public activism led his teenage nephew, the future Supreme Court justice Louis D. Brandeis, to change his middle name from David to Dembitz.

Brandeis later recalled that Dembitz was not satisfied with "merely observing" orthodox law but sought to understand it by studying the history of the Jewish people. Dembitz insisted on defining orthodoxy for himself and refused to follow the example of many Orthodox Jews in considering other forms of Judaism to be heresy. He was one of the first American Zionists, expressing support at least as early as 1902 for Theodor Herzl's vision of a Jewish homeland in Palestine. Most Orthodox Jews abhorred Zionism, claiming that only the Messiah could create a Jewish homeland. In 1878, as a member of the executive board of the Union of American Hebrew Congregations, Dembitz was appointed to the commission on the plan of study for the Hebrew Union College, a Reform Jewish institution. Two decades later he chaired the organizing meeting of the Orthodox Jewish Congregational Union of America and was elected vice president of that body. He advised the founders of the Jewish Theological Seminary of America, the center of Conservative Judaism and a bastion of Zionism. In 1904 the seminary took the highly unusual step of awarding Dembitz an honorary degree of doctor of Hebrew literature, largely in recognition of his *Jewish Services in Synagogue and Home* (1898), which became the standard volume in the field. His acceptance by the varying strands of American Judaism, usually so mutually hostile that they avoided giving any institutional credibility to each other's members, was the greatest possible testament to his widely acknowledged scholarship and piety. It was also tacit recognition of a group of American Jews that became prominent in the late nineteenth and twentieth centuries and for many of whom Dembitz served as an exemplar. A literate member of the professional class, he was involved in American public life and active in causes such as abolition that emphasized the dignity of all human beings. And even though he supported the creation of a Jewish homeland abroad, he was secure in the belief that Jews were equally at home in the United States. Dembitz died in Louisville.

• In addition to the works mentioned above, Dembitz published *Law Language for Short Hand Writers* (1892). He also translated the books of Exodus and Leviticus for the Jewish Publication Society of America's edition of the Bible (1892–1901). Articles about him include Clarence E. Walker,

"Memoirs of Court Reporter," (Louisville) *Courier-Journal*, 11 Aug. 1918; an entry under his name in volume 44 of the *American Jewish Year Book* of 1942–1943; and John J. Weisert, "Lewis N. Dembitz and Onkel Tom's Hutte," *American-German Review* 19 (Feb. 1953): 7–8. He figures prominently in Allon Gal's *Brandeis of Boston* (1980). There is a eulogy in the *Maccabean*, Aug. 1907 (under "Report of Proceedings").

PHILIPPA STRUM

DEMBITZ, Nanette (22 Nov. 1912–4 Apr. 1989), lawyer and judge, was born in Washington, D.C., to Abraham Lincoln Dembitz, a lawyer, and Sarah Westheimer, a teacher. After graduating from the University of Michigan cum laude and Phi Beta Kappa in 1932, Dembitz went to work as a social worker in Baltimore. She found this unsatisfying and decided to follow the footsteps of her father, her grandfather, Lewis Naphtali Dembitz, and her second cousin, U.S. Supreme Court Associate Justice Louis Dembitz Brandeis, into law. She entered Columbia Law School as a James Kent Scholar in 1934, became an editor of the law review, and received an LL.B. in 1937. After graduation, however, she was unable to find a job in any New York City law office; at one firm, she was asked if she could type. The only way to avoid the pervasive sex discrimination of her day was to turn to public law: Dembitz became a legal research assistant to the New York State Constitutional Convention Committee preparing the constitutional amendments that were ratified in 1938. In 1939 she married attorney Alfred Berman and returned to Washington with him.

In 1942 Dembitz was hired as an assistant by Edward J. Ennis, special assistant to the attorney general and director of the Alien Enemy Control Unit. After President Franklin Delano Roosevelt issued the executive order under which Japanese Americans living on the West Coast were first placed under curfew and then removed to relocation camps, Ennis was given the job of overseeing the Justice Department's briefs in *Hirabayashi v. United States* and *Korematsu v. United States*, and assigned Dembitz to do the legal research for them. Ironically, both Ennis and Dembitz privately opposed the order but the Court upheld it. Dembitz resigned from the Justice Department in 1945 and published a lengthy law review article attacking the Court's decisions as well as the order itself, calling it "the first Federal measure of racial discrimination applicable to citizens."

Dembitz and Berman returned to New York City, he to go into private practice and she to study for an LL.M. degree in international law at Columbia (1946) and to raise their only child. She gradually developed a full-time career as a volunteer attorney for a number of social justice organizations. As a general counsel (1955–1967) for the New York Civil Liberties Union she helped decide which cases the organization would take, wrote briefs, and sat on the NYCLU's board of directors. During the same years she was a special counsel for the Legal Aid Society, in charge of appeals from the family court, and a volunteer lawyer for the American Ethical Society. She also sat on the Commission on Law and Social Action of the American Jewish Congress (1968–1980), again providing advice and guidance on the cases and approaches to take in areas such as religion and state, civil rights, and civil liberties.

New York mayor John Lindsay appointed her to the city's family court in 1967, after an article she wrote about that court led to the suggestion of her name by a number of city lawyers' organizations. She became well known for her dedication to children's rights, which occasionally led her to embrace positions that were at odds with her civil libertarian colleagues. She deplored what she saw as its advocacy of parental rights, for example, at the expense of the well-being of children. She approved of a Supreme Court decision upholding visits of social workers to the homes of those who received welfare payments for children, arguing that such visits were necessary to uncover neglect or unsanitary or other undesirable living conditions (*Wyman v. James*, 1971). Convinced that children should be adopted early rather than put in foster care, she applauded the Supreme Court's decision that unmarried fathers need not be sought out for their consent before the adoption of their children with whom they had established no relationship (*Lehr v. Robertson*, 1983). Similarly, she proposed ensuring children's welfare through the state by requiring, for example, that mental hospitals and hospital detoxification units report the release of any parent of a child under age sixteen.

Dembitz argued that children should be kept with their families whenever possible rather than institutionalized and that "the entire emphasis of the family court" should be on "decarceration." At the same time, she recognized that on occasion removal from the family environment might be in the child's best interest, and she articulated guidelines for the state's treatment of children under such circumstances. Dembitz maintained, for example, that urban children who did have to be institutionalized might have to be kept out of their community for two years or more rather than the usual period of less than one year. Although she later commented that it made her "a very hated judge," she disagreed "with those who say that the mother should always keep the child and that the child will always do better at home. My answer is that society and government have a duty to that child." She added, however, that a judge had an obligation to satisfy herself that committing a child to a particular institution "can reasonably be considered the best treatment for this type of child"; to judge the facts for herself, she visited upstate New York training schools for juveniles. She ordered counseling about contraceptives for teenage girls brought before her court and, insisting on responsibilities as well as rights, declared that a teenager's access to contraception implied a concomitant responsibility to use it. She also opposed attempts to require minors to get parental consent before they could obtain an abortion. She publicized many of these ideas in articles published in bar association journals and law reviews during the 1960s and 1970s.

In 1972 Dembitz ran for the New York State Court of Appeals, historically an all-male bench, saying that her candidacy was "a result of a movement by Independent Democrats to end the exclusion of qualified women from appellate judgeships in New York." A minor scandal erupted when the New York State Bar Association's Judiciary Committee found her the only candidate unqualified for the position. The *New York Times* wrote that she should be given a rehearing. Fourteen prominent lawyers sued unsuccessfully in the state supreme court to nullify the committee's finding, arguing that its secret deliberations and refusal to consider the endorsements of Dembitz by the Association of the Bar of the City of New York, the New York State Trial Lawyers Association, and the New York Women's Bar Association violated its own rules. While President Richard M. Nixon swept New York state in 1972 and only Republicans were elected to statewide office, Dembitz received the highest number of votes of any Democratic candidate running statewide.

Remaining on the family court, Dembitz was elected to the executive committee of Columbia Law School's board of visitors (1973–1981) and became active in the law school alumni association as well as a frequent moderator of discussions sponsored by the Committee on Lectures and Continuing Education of the New York City Bar Association. She was a member of an advisory committee to the U.S. attorney general (1971–7?), participating in a one-year study of juvenile justice coordinated by the Institute of Judicial Administration.

In 1982, one month before she reached the mandatory retirement age of seventy, Dembitz left the family court. She returned to Columbia Law School as a scholar in residence for 1983–84 and, from 1983 until her death, volunteered as a member of the Family Court Advisory and Rules Committee and the Advisory Committee to the Family Court, chair of the New York City Child Fatality Review Committee, a referee for the New York State Commission on Judicial Conduct, an appellate consultant to the City Corporation Counsel, and a director of the American Civil Liberties Union (1983–1986) and a member of its National Advisory Council (1988–89). Dembitz died in New York City.

• There is no known collection of Dembitz papers or letters, although a folder in the Columbia University Law School Alumni Office contains newspaper clippings and letters to the editor (primarily the *New York Times*) and to the law school by and about her. Among her articles are "Racial Discrimination and Military Judgment: The Supreme Court's Korematsu and Endo Decisions," *Columbia Law Review* 45 (1945): 175–234, "Congressional Investigation of Newspapermen, Authors, and Others in the Opinion Field—Its Legality under the First Amendment," *Minnesota Law Review* 40 (1956): 517–60, "Ferment and Experimentation in New York—Juvenile Cases in the New Family Court," *Cornell Law Quarterly* (1963): 499–523, "Law and Family Planning," *Family Law Quarterly* 1 (Dec. 1967): 103–13, "Should Public Policy Give Incentives to Welfare Mothers to Limit the Number of Their Children?" *Family Law Quarterly* 4 (1970): 130, "Justice for Children—for Now and for the Future," *American Bar Association Journal* 60 (1974): 588–91, and "Supreme Court and a Minor's Abortion Decision," *Columbia Law Review* 80 (1980): 1251–62.

"Relationship Between Promise and Performance in State Intervention in Family Life: A Panel," in *Columbia Journal of Law & Social Problems* 9 (1972): 28–62, includes comments by and about Dembitz, and "Judge Dembitz: A Life in Family Court" is in the *New York Times*, 31 Oct. 1982. An obituary appears in the *New York Times*, 5 Apr. 1989.

PHILIPPA STRUM

DEMEREC, Milislav (11 Jan. 1895–12 Apr. 1966), biologist, was born in Kostajnica, Austria-Hungary, the son of Ljudevit Demerec, a schoolteacher and school inspector, and Ljubica Dumbovic. After graduating from the College of Agriculture in Krizevci, Austria-Hungary, in 1916, Demerec worked as an adjunct at the Krizevci Experiment Station for three years before coming to the United States for graduate work. While attending Cornell University, he married Mary Alexander Ziegler in 1921; they had two daughters. Demerec received his Ph.D. in genetics in 1923. His dissertation, on the genetics of maize, was directed by leading maize geneticist Rollins A. Emerson. Immediately on finishing his degree, Demerec became a resident investigator at the Carnegie Institution of Washington's Department of Genetics at Cold Spring Harbor, on Long Island, New York. He became a naturalized U.S. citizen in 1931. Demerec remained at Cold Spring Harbor until 1960, when he joined the staff of Brookhaven National Laboratory, where he remained through 1965. In 1966 he served briefly as research professor of biology at the C. W. Post campus of Long Island University.

Upon arriving at Cold Spring Harbor, Demerec continued work on maize genetics. Wrapping up his collaboration with Emerson, Demerec showed that albinism, or lack of pigment, was determined by at least ten distinct genetic factors. Under the influence of Carnegie geneticist Charles Metz, Demerec soon switched his investigations to the genetics of *Delphinium*, or larkspur, and the fruitfly *Drosophila virilis*, a close relative of the more commonly studied *D. melanogaster*, which he later used. Demerec's interest focused on the genetics of mosaicism, also known as variegation or mottling. Patchy or speckled coloration, whether in fly eyes or corn kernels, results from spontaneous mutations in genes controlling pigmentation. Demerec and others used studies in mosaicism as an experimental lever to pry open the mechanisms of genetic mutation.

By the early 1930s Demerec became a leading figure in the community of scientists working on *Drosophila* and in genetics in general. Much of the power of *Drosophila* genetics comes from strains, or stocks, with particular gene combinations useful for designing experiments. Demerec made Cold Spring Harbor a clearinghouse for specialized *Drosophila* stocks that were cataloged and distributed to drosophilists throughout the eastern United States and internationally. Based on his experience with an informal newsletter that had for years circulated among maize geneticists, Demerec also established the *Drosophila Information Service* in 1934. With Caltech's gene-mapping genius Calvin Bridges providing tips and techniques and Demerec adding, editing, compiling, and distributing, the *DIS* newsletter soon became a staple of any fruitfly laboratory. The *DIS* is still in publication in the 1990s.

In the later 1930s and early 1940s Demerec also became an administrator. In 1936 he was appointed assistant director of the Carnegie Institution's Department of Genetics by the director, Albert Blakeslee. Blakeslee retired at the end of 1941, and Demerec was named acting director and the following year director. In 1941 the Carnegie's sister institution, the Biological Laboratory of the Long Island Biological Association, appointed Demerec director. As the head of both Cold Spring Harbor laboratories, Demerec's goal was to combine the Bio Lab's summer teaching and research program and fine land with the strong year-round research of the Carnegie Department of Genetics into a single world-class genetics institute. Though the two laboratories were not formally merged until 1963, three years after his departure, they functioned in increasing synchrony through the 1940s and 1950s.

In the 1940s Demerec once again switched organisms and took up the genetics of bacteria and bacterial viruses (bacteriophage). This move also marked a shift in his studies, from spontaneous mutations to mutations induced by X-rays, ultraviolet radiation, and chemicals. A major contribution was his 1945 description, with Ugo Fano, of the "T" system of phages, the set of viruses that predominated during this classic phase of bacteriophage research.

Demerec's move to bacterial and phage genetics was influenced by two major events of the 1940s, one scientific and one political. The summer of 1941 brought Max Delbrück on his first of many summer pilgrimages to Cold Spring Harbor, to attend the first Cold Spring Harbor Symposium that Demerec organized. The summertime research of Delbrück and his "phage group" fit with Demerec's overarching research program on the nature of the gene. At the annual CSH Symposium, organized by Demerec throughout the 1940s and 1950s, future Nobel laureates and other pioneers of molecular biology debated and probed the composition, structure, and behavior of the gene. Under Demerec, the Cold Spring Harbor Symposium and laboratories became a world center for this new science. The other event was World War II. As part of Cold Spring Harbor's contribution to the war effort, Demerec applied some of the new techniques of bacterial genetics to the practical problem of increasing the yield of the powerful new antibiotic, penicillin. His efforts more than doubled the yield from *Penicillium* bacteria. He also used techniques of induced mutations and genetic screening to address problems of bacterial resistance to penicillin and other drugs. After the war, Demerec continued investigations of *Salmonella*, *Staphylococcus*, and *E. coli*.

Through the 1950s Demerec continued to make substantial contributions to bacterial genetics. In 1956 work with Philip Hartman, Demerec mapped the fine structure of the *Salmonella* chromosome by using viruses to transfer genes between bacteria, a technique known as transduction. He showed that the bacterial chromosome is a complex structure, with genes organized in functional units, and that genes themselves could be subdivided into many mutational sites. He also edited the now-classic *Biology of Drosophila* (1950; repr. 1993).

Demerec was highly respected by his colleagues. He was elected to the National Academy of Sciences in 1946 and to the American Philosophical Society in 1952. He was also a fellow of the American Academy of Arts and Sciences, the New York Academy of Sciences, and the American Association for the Advancement of Science, as well as a member of many professional associations for general, bacterial, and botanical genetics as well as evolution and zoology. He served as president of the Genetics Society of America (1939) and the American Society of Naturalists (1954). In the 1950s he served on the genetics panel of the National Academy of Sciences' Committee on the Biological Effects of Atomic Radiation. International organizations honored him with memberships in the Academy of Sciences of Yugoslavia, the Royal Danish Academy of Sciences and Letters, the British Genetical Society, the Genetics Society of Japan, and others. He died in Huntington, New York.

• Demerec's papers are collected at the American Philosophical Society Library in Philadelphia. Cold Spring Harbor Laboratory also maintains a small collection of his correspondence and administrative paperwork. Demerec's significant publications include Demerec and Ugo Fano, "Bacteriophage-resistant Mutants in *Escherichia coli*," *Genetics* 30 (1945): 119–36; Demerec and P. E. Hartman, "Complex Loci in Microorganisms," *Annual Review of Microbiology* 13 (1959): 377–406; Demerec and Z. Hartman, "Tryptophan Mutants in *Salmonella typhinurium*," in *Genetic Studies with Bacteria*, Carnegie Institution of Washington Publication 612 (1956); and Demerec et al., "A Proposal for a Uniform Nomenclature in Bacterial Genetics," *Genetics* 54 (1966): 61–76. He is given extensive treatment in Bentley Glass and Nathaniel Comfort, *A History of Biology at Cold Spring Harbor* (1998). Glass, National Academy of Sciences, *Biographical Memoirs* 42 (1971): 1–27, offers biographical information and contains a complete Demerec bibliography. Other biographical notices include Glass, "Milislav Demerec, 1895–1966," Cold Spring Harbor Symposium on Quantitative Biology 31 (1966): xxi–xxii; A. D. Hershey, "Milislav Demerec," *Carnegie Institution of Washington Year Book* 65 (1966): 558; Robert P. Wagner, "Milislav Demerec: Jan. 11, 1895–April 12, 1966," *Genetics* 56 (1967): 21; and Philip Hartman, "Between Novembers: Demerec, Cold Spring Harbor, and the Gene," *Genetics* 120 (1988): 615–19. Detailed accounts of Demerec's research and administrative activities may be found in the annual reports of the Biological Laboratory at Cold Spring Harbor and the year books of the Carnegie Institution of Washington.

NATHANIEL C. COMFORT

DE MILLE, Agnes (18 Sept. 1905–6 Oct. 1993), dancer, choreographer, and writer, was born Agnes George de Mille in New York City, the daughter of William Churchill de Mille, a playwright, and Anna George, the daughter of American single-tax economist Henry George. De Mille was born into one of the entertainment world's most powerful families and was determined to make her own career independent of her father and her uncle, the movie director Cecil B. De Mille. Her family moved west in 1914, settling in Los Angeles in order that her father could work in the newly emerging film industry with his brother. De Mille spent much of her early life at the studio, watching films being made and occasionally appearing as an extra. She dreamed of a career as an actress. At the age of thirteen she was allowed to begin ballet lessons with the expatriate Russian dancer and teacher Theodore Kosloff. Despite her late start, a difficult body with short legs, and the constant discouragement of her father, de Mille persisted. From 1921 to 1925 she ceased her lessons to attend the University of California at Los Angeles, and after she graduated with an honors degree in English she moved to New York to seek her fortune in the theater. She was accompanied by her newly divorced mother and her sister.

Initially de Mille had little success at auditions; she did not qualify as a leggy chorus girl for the spectacular musical revues that dominated Broadway, and her ballet technique was not strong. After a brief stint as an actress in the spring of 1927 with the Fata Morgana Company, a second-rate outfit in Baltimore, she decided to try her hand at giving dance concerts. Between 1928 and 1939 de Mille worked as a recitalist, performing solo dances collected into a full evening's concert. She created a repertory of fifty-one theater pieces, combinations of dance and gesture that critics described as "character sketches in movement." She devised these works as showcases for her own unusual abilities as an actor-comedian-dancer and scaled them for intimate audiences in small theaters. Most of the characters in the narratives of her later dances can be traced to the heroines of these early solos. Particularly important was the frontier woman in her *Forty-Niner* (1928), the forerunner of the Cowgirl in her *Rodeo* (1942). The women in de Mille's concert dances possessed one common trait: they were ordinary rather than extraordinary. She shunned the larger-than-life women of Cecil B. De Mille's film spectacles and the archetypal austerity of her colleague Martha Graham to embrace that which she portrayed best, the ordinary, the awkward, and the hopeful.

De Mille performed her solos in a number of venues. She toured with Adolph Bolm's ballet company in 1928 and appeared in concert with other recitalists in New York. In 1929 she was hired to create the dances and to perform in a revival of the nineteenth-century spectacular melodrama *The Black Crook* at the Lyric Theatre in Hoboken, New Jersey. De Mille and her new partner, Warren Leonard, performed in incidental ballets, which she patterned after illustrations of the original 1866 production. *The Black Crook* provid-

ed de Mille with her first opportunity to choreograph for a large ensemble and with the experience of performing for an extended engagement.

In 1930–1931 de Mille joined forces with the newly emerging modern dancers in New York City's Greenwich Village. She performed solos in Dance Repertory Theatre concerts with Martha Graham, Doris Humphrey, and Charles Weidman. In 1931 she was elected president of the Concert Dancers' League, a cooperative organization designed to allow dancers to produce their own concerts. Unlike many of her colleagues in the league, de Mille was also interested in working in the popular theater on Broadway. The headstrong young choreographer who saw her dances as central to the production rather than as decoration gained a reputation with Broadway producers as uncompromising and difficult. In 1932, for example, she was hired by the Shubert Brothers to choreograph their revue, *Flying Colors*. While the production was still in out-of-town tryouts, de Mille was fired; however, her work, an African-American "Reefer Dance," remained in the show.

In the fall of 1932, discouraged by her lack of success in the United States, de Mille traveled to London. She sought independence from her mother and an environment in which she could improve her technique and her choreographic abilities. During the next six years she crossed the Atlantic frequently, returning to the United States to teach, choreograph, and perform. When in London she studied ballet with Marie Rambert and Antony Tudor, and she gradually enlarged her solos to fit a small group of English dancers. "Americana," which had been one of several themes in her early work, became increasingly important during her London years. It was her very Americanness, her outspoken frankness and quick humor, that separated her from her contemporary English choreographers. She also had firsthand knowledge of American modern dance and of Graham's technical innovations. In fact, her English colleagues referred to her as a "modern dancer" despite the fact that she had never formally studied modern dance. She experimented choreographically, incorporating her observations of modern dance and of American folk dance. In England in 1938 she presented the first all-female version of *Rodeo*, the foundation work at the core of her later ballet by the same name.

In the fall of 1938, when England began preparing for World War II by sending aliens home, de Mille was deported. She had just finished creating a suite of American dances, including *Rodeo*, with which she had hoped to tour the United States, but she was unable to bring any of her dancers with her. Back in New York she organized her own small company with dancers Katherine Litz, Sybil Shearer, and Joseph Antony to perform the works she had created in London. In 1939 she became a choreographer with a new ballet company, the Ballet Theatre (now the American Ballet Theatre). The company's founder, Richard Pleasant, stipulated that de Mille was not to perform in her own works. For the company's first season she presented an African-American work, *Obeah* or *Black Ritual*. The dance, based on voodoo rituals, was not a success, and de Mille returned to her work with her own company. On tour she performed the leading roles in the all-female version of *Rodeo* and in a comic ballet she had created in London, *Three Virgins and a Devil*, as well as her usual repertory of solos.

In 1941 Serge Denham, director of the Ballet Russe de Monte Carlo, hired de Mille to create an all-American ballet. She devised a scenario centered on an out-of-step rider, her character in *Rodeo*. The story, autobiographical as is much of de Mille's work, concerns the Cowgirl finding a man. De Mille chose as her collaborators composer Aaron Copland and designer Oliver Smith. Their resulting work, which premiered on 16 October 1942 at the Metropolitan Opera House with de Mille dancing the leading role, was a tremendous success. Unlike earlier largely Russian-style American projects by the Ballet Russe, the new *Rodeo* featured dancers as cowboys performing de Mille's unique blend of American modern dance, ballet, and mime. The dancers fought to control their imaginary horses and used dramatic gesture to tell a story.

De Mille's success with *Rodeo* attracted the attention of Richard Rodgers and Oscar Hammerstein II, who hired her to choreograph *Oklahoma!*, which opened at the St. James Theatre on 31 March 1943. Perhaps the most important aspect of that production was the "Dream Ballet" that closed Act 1, in which the dancers, juxtaposed as the principal characters, enacted the subconscious fears of the heroine, Laurey. *Oklahoma!*—particularly the dream sequence—is often cited as the beginning of a new direction in musical comedy choreography. The decorative lines of high-kicking-look-alike chorines gave way to serious artists who danced emotions and fears too ephemeral for words. For years after *Oklahoma!* dream ballets were popular devices.

On 14 June 1943, three months after *Oklahoma!* opened, de Mille married Walter Foy Prude, a soldier about to be sent overseas, who after the war entered the theatrical world as assistant to the impresario Sol Hurok. The couple had one son. De Mille followed *Oklahoma!* with a string of successful Broadway shows: *One Touch of Venus* (1943), *Bloomer Girl* (1944), *Carousel* (1945), and *Brigadoon* (1947). In 1947 she both directed and choreographed Rodgers and Hammerstein's musical play about Everyman, *Allegro*, which was not a successful production, and de Mille and Rodgers and Hammerstein parted ways. Although de Mille choreographed the film version of *Oklahoma!* in 1955, she never again worked with Rodgers and Hammerstein on Broadway. She choreographed several more Broadway shows, including *Gentlemen Prefer Blondes* (1949), *Paint Your Wagon* (1951), *The Girl in Pink Tights* (1954), *Goldilocks* (1958), *Juno*, based on Sean O'Casey's *Juno and the Paycock* (1959), *Kwamina* (1961), *110 in the Shade* (1963), and *Come Summer* (1970).

During the 1940s de Mille created two works for the Ballet Theatre, *Tally-Ho* (1944), in which she also performed the leading role of a young, tempted wife, and *Fall River Legend* (1948), a ballet about Lizzie Borden. In 1953 she organized her own company, the Agnes de Mille Dance Theatre, hiring the dancers with whom she had frequently worked on Broadway and featuring Gemze de Lappe and James Mitchell. She adapted dances from her Broadway shows for the concert stage. The dances from *Paint Your Wagon*, for example, became the ballet *Gold Rush* (1958). She also included selections from her early concert dances and at times performed them herself.

In the 1950s de Mille published the first of her autobiographies, *Dance to the Piper* (1952) and *And Promenade Home* (1958), and she created two television programs in the *Omnibus* series, "The Art of Ballet" (26 Feb. 1956) and "The Art of Choreography" (30 Dec. 1956), for which she won the *Dance Magazine* award. She continued an active work schedule in the 1960s, choreographing two musicals and several ballets, including *The Golden Age*, *Rib of Eve*, *Sebastian*, and *Wind in the Mountains*. She published three more books: *To a Young Dancer* (1962), *The Book of the Dance* (1963), and *Lizzie Borden: A Dance of Death* (1968). She became a frequent speaker on the lecture circuit, discussing the importance of federal support for the arts and the importance of the arts in our lives. In 1969 she was invited by the Soviet government to represent the United States as a judge for the International Ballet Competition in Moscow.

In 1975, hours before a fundraising concert by de Mille's newly founded company, the Heritage Dance Theatre, the choreographer suffered a massive stroke that paralyzed the right side of her body. Taking only a few months to relearn walking, and writing with her left hand, de Mille continued to work. In the year of the American bicentennial, she choreographed her ballet, *Texas Fourth* (1976), for the American Ballet Theatre; published *Reprieve* (1976), a book about her recovery from the stroke; and produced a lecture-demonstration with the Joffrey Ballet entitled *Conversations about the Dance*. Throughout the 1980s and until her death in 1993, de Mille continued to lecture, write, and choreograph. She reworked the dances from *Juno* into a ballet, *The Informer* (1988), about the Irish "troubles." Her last work, *The Other*, choreographed less than a year before she died, concerned death. She died in Manhattan, New York.

In the last years of her life, de Mille was awarded more than fourteen honorary doctorates and many national honors, including the Kennedy Center Award (1980) and the National Medal of the Arts (1986). Her contribution to American theater dance is her unique blend of folk dance, ballet, acting gesture, and modern dance and her ability to popularize the elitist art of classical ballet for the musical theater. Her gifted writing brought to life nearly a century of history in the world of American entertainment from the beginnings of Hollywood and of talking films to the stage spectacles of the 1990s. An articulate spokesperson for the arts, she persevered in the man's world of New York theater and achieved success as the first woman to both choreograph and direct on Broadway.

• De Mille's papers, including choreographic notebooks, book manuscripts, films and videos, correspondence, music scores, and scrapbooks are in the Dance Collection at the New York Public Library for the Performing Arts, Lincoln Center. The manuscript of *Dance to the Piper* and letters to her mother and husband documenting her stay in London in the 1930s are in the Sophia Smith Collection at Smith College. In addition to her books mentioned above she published *Speak to Me, Dance with Me* (1973); *Where the Wings Grow* (1978); *Martha, the Life and Work of Martha Graham, a Biography* (1991); a collection of biographical sketches, *Portrait Gallery* (1990); and *America Dances* (1980). For a complete biography see Carol Easton, *No Intermissions: The Life of Agnes de Mille* (1996), and for a book on her family see Anne Edwards, *The DeMilles, an American Family* (1988). For a critical look at de Mille's early work see Barbara Barker's "Agnes de Mille, Liberated Expatriate, and the American Suite, 1938," *Dance Chronicle* 19, no. 2 (1996): 113–51. See also Jack Anderson, *The One and Only: The Ballet Russe de Monte Carlo* (1981); Selma Jeanne Cohen and A. J. Pischl, "The American Ballet Theatre: 1940–1960," *Dance Perspectives* 6 (1960); Gerald Bordman, *American Musical Theatre* (1978); and John Martin, *America Dancing* (1936) and *John Martin's Book of the Dance* (1963). An obituary is in the *New York Times*, 8 Oct. 1993.

BARBARA BARKER

DE MILLE, Cecil B. (12 Aug. 1881–21 Jan. 1959), pioneer motion picture producer-director, was born Cecil Blount de Mille in Ashfield, Massachusetts, the son of Henry Churchill de Mille, a playwright and Episcopal lay minister, and Matilde Beatrice Samuel, a teacher and play broker. (Sources vary regarding the spelling of De Mille; even family members were not consistent in its use.) De Mille's father was a major influence on his son in childhood, both in his religious teachings and nightly Bible readings and in his work on plays at home with his co-writer, David Belasco. His father's early death from typhoid fever when De Mille was twelve left the family impoverished. His mother, through struggling to support the family as a teacher, managed to enroll him at Pennsylvania Military College in 1896. There the headmaster, "like Henry De Mille, was an unswerving fundamentalist," according to biographer Charles Higham, and the adolescent "learned and re-learned the truths of the Old and New Testament." In 1900 De Mille completed his education at the American Academy of Dramatic Art in New York in order to become an actor.

In his autobiography De Mille describes the experience he gained as a touring actor as "the best school a future director could attend," adding that the influences of actor-manager E. H. Sothern and, later, actor-manager Belasco are reflected in every one of his motion pictures. In particular he emulated Sothern's perfectionism and his skill at directing crowds. Seasons of touring allowed De Mille to become expert, he believed, in what audiences wanted to see. He also met his wife, actress Constance Adams, while on tour; they were married in 1902.

Between 1900 and 1912 De Mille tried his hand at many theatrical ventures without much success. In addition to acting, he was at times a singer, a stage manager, and business manager of the play agency his mother opened. Alone and in collaboration with his brother William he wrote several plays, all of which failed. He also collaborated with ex-vaudevillian Jesse Lasky on three marginally successful musical comedies. His life in these years was characterized by near poverty and failure, an unstable existence that was further exacerbated by the difficult birth of a daughter in 1908.

Ready to take any wild gamble, in 1913 De Mille entered into a partnership with Lasky and Lasky's brother-in-law, Samuel Goldfish (later Goldwyn), to produce on a low budget a "feature" film (one running about an hour). American film companies had been producing much shorter films that lacked the dramatic impact of a stage play, and the three believed that the growing movie audience would support American-made "features" like those recently imported from Europe. De Mille pawned his possessions and borrowed money to become a partner with a quarter interest in the Jesse L. Lasky Feature Play Company.

Having raised roughly $20,000, the partners decided to produce a movie version of a successful stage play about the Wild West, *The Squaw Man*, which premiered in 1901 and had recently been revived with Dustin Farnum in the lead role. Farnum, well known to theater audiences, was at liberty and willing to spend a few weeks "in the underworld of motion pictures," as De Mille's autobiography recalls Farnum's view of the fledgling industry. It was a good story, very exciting, but a primary reason for choosing a western was the necessity of shooting the film outdoors rather than in a studio, which the partners did not have. Scenery, story, and stars were the basics upon which De Mille built four decades of successful movie making.

De Mille was appointed director-general of the company, despite the fact that he had little or no experience with a camera. He and his partners were pioneers. They learned by doing. As De Mille later explained in an interview, "When I came to Los Angeles I knew nothing of the making of films, but I had the big idea. I had seen picture plays that were almost dramas." Trained in the theater, De Mille was certain he could make film dramas that were as compelling as those on stage. As for his lack of technical expertise, "When anyone told me that such and such a thing could not be done, I got someone who could do it" (*Photoplay*, Oct. 1915).

After some production tribulations, *The Squaw Man* was finally released in 1914. Fortunately for the partners it was a great success, earning $250,000. Other productions at the soon-erected Lasky studio quickly followed, and De Mille plunged into a frenzy of work, both as the director of his own films and as the supervisor of other productions. He introduced numerous innovations that later became standard in films: the listing of actors' names in cast credits on screen, the use of substantial sets rather than painted scenery for indoor scenes, and the use of additional lighting beyond sunlight in order to emphasize certain aspects of the screen image (he termed this "Rembrandt" lighting). Seemingly inexhaustible, he once directed two films at the same time, one by day and one by night. His twelve-hour days on the set constituted an athletic workout as he dashed from one point to another, and his tall, burly body stayed in prime physical condition for the rest of his life.

Ambitious and highly competitive, De Mille understood the value of self promotion. He was always available for interviews and made his director's garb a lifelong trademark: riding boots and breeches, open-necked shirt, a broad-brimmed hat covering his balding head, a whistle hanging around his neck, and a megaphone in his hand became the accepted image of what a movie director wore. Once his fame was established, he even "starred" in the "trailers," short promotional films shown in movie houses to promote his forthcoming feature films.

Within a few years, the impoverished New York actor was internationally known, a leading film director ranked with D. W. Griffith, and a millionaire several times over. De Mille invested his new wealth carefully—eventually having interests in land, oil, banking, racetracks, even an early airline—and he proved to be a shrewd, hard-bargaining businessman, but he also began to live in the style of a magnate, with a chauffeured limousine, a mansion home, a ranch, and a sailing yacht, and to indulge his desire to dominate. His niece, choreographer Agnes de Mille, was a keen lifelong observer of her uncle. She compared him in these years to "a young bull: dynamic, male, determined." Not one for subtlety he openly went after whatever he wanted, fiercely emboldened by his increasing power. The one moderating aspect of his personality was his great charm, something that the women on his studio staff greatly appreciated; some made serving him the central focus of their lives.

De Mille's early films were based on stage hits, fast-paced melodramas with clear-cut conflicts between good and evil that were prevalent on the stage at the beginning of the twentieth century. In 1915 he began to make movies based on original scenarios written by a young woman employee, Jeanie Macpherson. *The Cheat* (1915), made from one of her scenarios, tells the story of a foolish socialite who, after gambling away charity money, asks a wealthy man of her acquaintance for a loan, promising him sexual favors in return. After she reneges, the man physically brands her as his "possession," and she shoots and wounds him in retaliation. Her husband stands trial for the shooting and is found guilty, whereupon she confesses to save him and thereby bares the shameful brand. Her sacrificial honesty reconciles her husband to her. The possibility of teaching moral lessons by putting moral ambiguity on the screen fueled the deeply religious De Mille's films for years to come. He did not forget, either, that audiences liked dramas involving sex, sin, and high society.

In *The Whispering Chorus* (1918) De Mille explored moral ambiguity in a contemporary setting. Well ahead of its time, the film portrays a man's inner conflicts and weaknesses as faces that surround him and whisper contradictory commands, prompting him into reprehensible acts. At last, seeing what he has done, the man goes to a redemptive death. De Mille later called it the first psychological drama. The critics were not impressed. "The final scenes are unnecessarily terrible," the reviewer for *Photoplay* (June 1918) wrote, " with awful, subtle suggestions that will drive sensitive spectators almost into hysterics." The film was also a failure at the box office, and De Mille's faith that audiences wanted more sophisticated presentations of moral quandaries was deeply shaken.

Unwilling to lose his prominence as a money-maker for the studio, from 1918 until he left the studio late in 1924, De Mille made largely commercial films on the topics of sex, sin, and high society but with less ambiguity of character and a clearer moral message. His greatest successes were comedies that explored the causes of infidelity and/or questioned the necessity of strict class boundaries between lovers. In these films, erotic titillation meets modern luxury, especially in scenes where the heroine, usually played by Gloria Swanson, slowly discards her silken lingerie and steps, barely hidden from the camera, into an ornate bathtub. Bathtub scenes became a De Mille trademark. Some critics saw this change of direction as a calculation on his part, a violation of his personal Victorian morality in exchange for commercial success. Others said he was corrupting the public. One reviewer called *Why Change Your Wife?* (1920) "the most gorgeously sensual film of the month; in decoration the most costly; in physical allure the most fascinating; in effect the most immoral" (*Photoplay*, May 1920). De Mille protested that he was teaching a moral message about keeping married love alive.

Biographies of De Mille suggest a personal reason for his championing of infidelity in his comedies. The birth of his daughter had so physically harmed Constance De Mille that she could not risk another pregnancy. (The couple's three other children were adopted.) Although she was otherwise a loving wife, she ceased to be his partner in bed. De Mille eventually turned to other women he met at the studio but otherwise remained devoted to his wife. Thus there were personal reasons for his claim in one interview that, as in his comedies, a husband will come "galloping back" to his wife if she just has "the moral poise to weather his yieldings to the beast within" (*Photoplay*, Dec. 1920). Constance De Mille apparently had that moral poise. They remained married for fifty-six years.

In other films made between 1918 and 1924, De Mille portrayed the high living of high society in extreme melodramatic terms. It was his natural storytelling style, absorbed from the stage melodramas of his youth. As director Mitchell Leisen, who worked with De Mille from 1919 to 1932, recalled, his style was devoid of nuance. "Everything was in neon lights six feet tall: LUST, REVENGE, SEX." In the morality of these melodramas, the careless actions of wealthy people bring retribution, suffering, sacrifice, and, finally, redemption.

De Mille had long desired to film heroic tales of the past that would teach a moral, even religious, lesson. His first opportunity was *Joan the Woman* (1917), the story of Joan of Arc, through which he learned that he could direct thrilling battle scenes and handle thousands of extras on a set. Studio executives opposed "costume pictures," however, believing that the public would not pay to see them. Thus restricted from filming an entire story from the past, De Mille used "dream visions" and long flashbacks to past eras to illuminate moral points and to provide grand spectacle in many of his modern-day comedies and dramas.

Then, in 1923, De Mille claimed that moviegoers had selected, through a contest, the subject of the Ten Commandments, as the story they would most like to see told on the screen. In his *The Ten Commandments* (1923), De Mille used the biblical story of the Exodus and the giving of the Commandments to Moses on Mount Sinai as the prologue to a modern melodrama about how the Commandments applied in everyday life. The enormous cost of location filming of the biblical sequences appalled the financial backers, but the film's vast panorama and early use of Technicolor greatly contributed to its box office success. The *New York Times* reviewer called the first part "sublime" and "utterly impressive" but found the modern section "melodramatic" (22 Dec. 1923).

Executive complaints about De Mille's tendency to run over budget and behind schedule escalated, and at the beginning of 1925 De Mille parted company with the studio he had helped found. Financed in part by a wealthy and religious banker who wanted him to film the life of Jesus, he founded his own studio, called the Cecil B. De Mille Corporation. There his lordly ways continued. He appeared on the set with a personal retinue of assistants and poured sarcasm on any worker who displeased or disturbed him. One profile writer called him a "Hollywood Zeus" and described him as "a fearsome figure who may be loved or hated, but who must always be obeyed" (*New Yorker*, 28 Nov. 1925). At the same time, he was a loving family man and strongly loyal to long-time employees.

After he branched out on his own, De Mille's movie empire went into decline. His epic story of Jesus, *King of Kings* (1927), was a mammoth success worldwide, though some critics and religious leaders were outraged by De Mille's additions, such as an orgy scene at courtesan Mary Magdalene's luxurious palace. The studio's other productions lost money, however, and De Mille failed to adapt to audience demands for the new talking pictures. Finally forced out by other partners, he went to Metro-Goldwyn-Mayer (MGM), but his years there, 1928 to 1931, brought even more ignominy. *Dynamite* (1929), his first sound film, showed that he could adapt to the new technology. Indeed, to regain the camera mobility of silent films he created two devices that became standard in making talkies: a soundproof "blimp" camera covering so that the cam-

era could be moved without picking up extraneous sounds, and a microphone boom that enabled actors to move about the set and still be recorded. The film itself, though, was undistinguished 1920s' melodrama. *Madam Satan* (1930), a melodramatic musical, was a wild farrago that failed utterly at the box office. The bottom of De Mille's decline came with a wretched remake of *The Squaw Man* (1931) as a talkie. By then, both he and MGM wanted out of the contract.

In 1931, at age fifty, De Mille found himself a has-been without employment offers and in tax trouble with the U.S. government. He went back to his old studio, now called Paramount. He believed he could succeed with another historical drama, based on an 1896 stage drama he had liked in his youth, about oppressed Christians in pagan Rome. De Mille obtained a one-picture deal but was "on trial"; he had to accept a greatly reduced salary and remain strictly within budget. This he did, even shutting down production abruptly when an aide announced the budget was used up. His film version of *The Sign of the Cross* (1932) was a gamble that succeeded. Its message of faith and courage under oppression was what depression-era audiences wanted. The fast-paced narrative carried them along in rising excitement. Audiences also enjoyed the displayed decadence of Nero's Rome, the spectacle of the burning city, Empress Poppaea's milk bath, the orgy featuring an erotic dance, the sadistic torture scene, and the gladiatorial brutalities of the arena before lions are loosed on the Christians. The film reestablished De Mille as a "money" director. De Mille's next two films, both modern-day stories, lost money, and thereafter he played it safe with heroic tales of the past, beginning with *Cleopatra* (1934). De Mille, an independent by nature, was determined to withstand the dominant Hollywood studio system in which directors had to work like assembly line employees. Within a few years, as a result of his commercial successes, he had gained an independent unit for himself within Paramount, with its own "De Mille Gate."

De Mille's next historical saga, *The Crusades* (1935), did poorly despite the inclusion of some of his finest battle scenes. (There were complaints about its lack of a bathtub scene.) To publicize himself further, beginning in 1936 De Mille hosted the top-rated "Lux Radio Theatre." His trained actor's voice and genial manner made him a welcome visitor in millions of households. (He left the show in January 1945 after a union dispute.) Meanwhile, he produced several epic stories of the conquest of the North American continent: *The Plainsman* (1937), *The Buccaneer* (1938), *Union Pacific* (1939), *Northwest Mounted Police* (1940), and *Reap the Wild Wind* (1942). In the last two De Mille used Technicolor for additional visual splendor. The films were not so overtly moral as they were inspirational, showing the indomitable spirit of individual Americans against all odds.

De Mille's method now was to begin production of each film with a swift-moving story line, meticulously plotted out ahead of time, and never deviated from on the set. One-time associate Art Arthur described De

Mille as an excellent judge of a story's cinematic value, and he knew the best way to tell it on screen, demanding continuity, construction, and clarity. In his historical films De Mille had an "obsessive mania for authenticity in trivial details," according to film scholar Philip Kent, except when authenticity got in the way of thrills; then it was jettisoned. De Mille preferred florid, overripe dialogue, in the style of nineteenth-century drama, but his rich pictorial imagery overrode the prosiness.

During World War II De Mille produced and directed *The Story of Dr. Wassell* (1944), based on the real-life heroism of Dr. Corydon Wassell, who shepherded some wounded servicemen past Japanese lines. In the postwar years he returned to telling stories about the past, first making a frontier battle epic, *Unconquered* (1947), followed by a biblical film of sin and suffering and redemption by disaster, *Samson and Delilah* (1949). In 1949 he received the Irving G. Thalberg Award, his first Oscar in thirty-six years of work. Yet by then the general feeling was that he was an outdated vestige of the early days of Hollywood. In Paramount's *Sunset Boulevard* (1950), in which he plays himself, De Mille appears as much a relic of Hollywood's silent era as do Norma Desmond and the other silent-screen "waxworks" the movie puts on display. The difference is that De Mille was still active and successful, a lone survivor tenaciously hanging onto his film work and fame.

De Mille's last two films were major successes. *The Greatest Show on Earth* (1952) was set in modern times but in the rarefied world of circuses and their performers. The story moves thrillingly toward the climactic disaster in which the circus train wrecks, thereby resolving plot complications for the characters and resulting in an act of redemptive self-sacrifice. It won De Mille an Oscar for best picture of the year. De Mille's remake of *The Ten Commandments* (1956) was based as much on a popular historical novel, Dorothy Clarke Wilson's *Prince of Egypt*, as on the Old Testament. It was an immense, costly spectacle in which Moses and Pharaoh were portrayed as human beings, though heroically enlarged. Filming it caused the 75-year-old De Mille to suffer a serious heart attack, but he insisted on finishing despite his doctor's warnings. The public made the film a box office smash, and the Producers Guild gave De Mille its Milestone Award. De Mille never intended to retire, and he was planning a new film about the Boy Scouts at the time of his death in Hollywood.

It is hard to assess De Mille, a complex, sometimes baffling, set of contradictions. His films could be lurid and sensational, yet he was a master of rich visual storytelling. He could be demanding and imperious as a director, yet many people were devoted to him. He brought his values and outlook almost intact from the nineteenth century yet never lost his hold on the twentieth-century American public. He made seventy films in forty-three years; some of them set all-time box office records and continue to circulate on video. Criticizing him, as Philip Kemp has written, is "like throw-ing darts at Mount Rushmore." He is a giant figure in American film history.

• The papers of Cecil B. De Mille are at Brigham Young University. Materials on his life are in the Billy Rose Theatre Collection at the New York Public Library for the Performing Arts, Lincoln Center. The bibliography and factual guide by Sumiko Higashi, *Cecil B. DeMille: A Guide to References and Resources* (1985), is very helpful. A major source of facts and views is *The Autobiography of Cecil B. De Mille*, ed. Donald Hayne (1959). Useful biographical works, among the many published, are: Anne Edwards, *The DeMilles: An American Family* (1988); Charles Higham, *Cecil B. DeMille* (1973); and Philip French, *The Movie Moguls* (1969). Personal recollections are in Art Arthur, "C. B. DeMille's Human Side," *Films in Review*, Apr. 1967, pp. 221–25; Agnes de Mille, "The de Milles," in her *Portrait Gallery* (1990); and David Chierichetti, *Mitchell Leisen* (1995). Among the many critical appraisals, especially helpful are: Philip Kemp's entry on De Mille in *World Film Directors*, vol. 1, ed. John Wakeman (1987); Charles Wolfe's entry on De Mille in *American Directors*, vol. 1, ed. Jean Pierre Coursodon (1983); and the memo dated 16 Sept. 1953 in David O. Selznick, *Memo from David O. Selznick*, ed. Rudy Behlmer (1972). Other critical views can be found in Richard Griffith and Arthur Mayer, *The Movies* (1957). A collection of excerpted criticism and reviews is in Stanley Hochman, *A Library of American Film Criticism: American Film Directors* (1974). Also see K. Owen, "The Kick-In Prophets," *Photoplay*, Oct. 1915, pp. 82–85; Cecil B. De Mille as told to Adela Rogers St. John, "What Does Marriage Mean?" *Photoplay*, Dec. 1920, pp. 28–31; R. E. Sherwood, "The Hollywood Zeus," *New Yorker*, 28 Nov. 1925, pp. 11–12; and Vincent Canby, "For DeMille, Moses' Egypt Was Really America," *New York Times*, 25 Mar. 1984. Obituaries are in the *New York Times* and *New York Herald Tribune*, both 22 Jan. 1959, and *Variety*, 28 Jan. 1959.

WILLIAM STEPHENSON

DE MILLE, Henry Churchill (17 Sept. 1853–10 Feb. 1893), playwright, was born in Washington, North Carolina, the son of William E. de Mille, a merchant, and Margaret Blount Hoyt. After attaining A.B. and A.M. degrees from Columbia University in 1875, he taught school in Brooklyn and New York academies. In 1876 he married Mathilde Beatrice Samuel; they had three children.

De Mille had been fascinated by the theater since childhood, but family opposition led him initially to choose a career in education. He was active in amateur theater groups, both as an actor and as a budding playwright. Deeply devout, he was drawn to Episcopal church work and studied for ordination for some years. A particular influence on his thought came from the Christian Socialist writings of English clergyman and novelist Charles Kingsley.

De Mille's breakthrough into professional theater came in 1882, when he submitted his play *Robert Aclen* to the Madison Square Theatre. The play was rejected, but de Mille was hired as the theater's play reader. Here he became friends with two men soon to become eminent: Daniel Frohman, the theater's business manager, and David Belasco, its stage manager. Another play, *John Delmer's Daughters; or, Duty* was produced at the theater but failed after six performances. A change in the theater's top management led to de Mille completing his contract in 1885 as an actor. In 1886 he and his wife acted in a touring company.

By 1886 Daniel Frohman had established a stock company at the Lyceum Theatre. His play *The Main Line; or, Rawson's Y* (1886), written in collaboration with Charles Barnard and directed by Belasco, achieved solid success. The play made dramatic use of two important elements in the transcontinental growth of the United States: the railroad and the telegraph. Effects created by the theater's new electric lights made the simulation of a train wreck offstage gripping, and the "click" of the telegraph key and the "singing" of the wires became sound motifs.

From 1887 to 1889, de Mille was co-writer with David Belasco of a series of plays for the Lyceum company, all of which were enduring successes in New York City and on tour. The first was *The Wife* (1887), in which a woman confesses to her husband that she married him without love, but also without guilt from a previous attachment, and is forgiven by him. Next came *Lord Chumley* (1888), crafted largely as a starring vehicle for the company's E. H. Sothern, where a foppish aristocrat gradually reveals the strength of character that underlies his apparent superficiality. In 1889 de Mille and Belasco came forth with *The Charity Ball*, in which a minister forces his caddish brother to marry the woman he has wronged, although the minister loves her himself. The two collaborators worked out the development of each scene broadly, then created its speeches together as Belasco acted out the scene while de Mille wrote down the words. Beginning in 1888, de Mille became associate director of the American Academy of Dramatic Art, which had grown out of the Lyceum's acting school. As devoted an educator as ever, he told the *New York Times* (24 June 1888) that he saw a need for such a school because of the decline of the local resident stock companies where actors once received their training.

In 1890 de Mille and Belasco wrote their last play together (*Men and Women*) for the company Daniel Frohman's brother Charles had assembled at the Twenty-third Street Theatre. It was cut to the pattern of the previous plays and achieved a similar success. All contained the same effective theatricality of broad characters and "big" speeches in strong scenes, mixed with serious, even moralistic, themes. All showed in some way the struggle of moral values against the ruthlessness and greed present in contemporary American politics, banking, or stock speculation, along with the hypocrisy and destructive gossip of fashionable society. That same year, the pair came to an amiable end of their writing partnership, in order to follow different aspirations.

De Mille began 1891 by revising *The Main Line* as *The Danger Signal*, after which it continued its success on the road. He then undertook his first solo writing task in some years, a free adaptation for Charles Frohman of a German play, *Das Verlorene Paradies*. De Mille's adaptation, *The Lost Paradise*, another success

for him, followed along the lines of his work with Belasco, combining the theme of the rights of labor with a society situation. He next began work on an entirely original play, to be called *The Promised Land*, dealing with the social problem of poverty in America. It was never completed, as he contracted typhoid fever and died suddenly in Pompton, New Jersey.

Although the plays of de Mille fell from public favor after his death, he remains a significant figure as a playwright who successfully brought serious themes of American life to the theater. In doing so he raised the status of American dramatic works as compared to imports from England and France and made it easier for other American writers to gain a hearing. With his wife, he also founded a theatrical dynasty. As Beatrice de Mille, his wife became a prominent playwrights' agent. His sons were William C. de Mille, playwright and film scenarist, and Cecil B. De Mille, film director and producer. His daughter Agnes died in childhood. William C. de Mille's daughter was the choreographer Agnes de Mille.

• Original materials relating to de Mille are in the papers of William C. de Mille at the University of Southern California and also in the Billy Rose Theatre Collection at the New York Public Library for the Performing Arts, Lincoln Center. A collected edition of his plays, with critical introduction by Robert Hamilton Ball, is *The Plays of Henry C. DeMille* (1941). Gerald Bordman's *The American Theatre . . . 1869–1914* (1994), gives an account of each play's critical and popular reception. A detailed recollection of his life and work is given in Cecil B. De Mille's *My Autobiography* (1959), and further details of his personal life can be found in Anne Edwards's *The DeMilles, an American Family* (1988).

WILLIAM STEPHENSON

DE MILLE, William Churchill (25 July 1878–5 Mar. 1955), playwright and screenwriter, was born in Washington, North Carolina, the son of Henry C. de Mille, a playwright, and Matilda Beatrice Samuel. Not only was he destined to follow in his father's footsteps as a playwright, but he also ventured as a pioneer into the new medium of motion pictures, following his more famous younger brother, Cecil B. De Mille. Educated at the Horace Mann School and later at Columbia College, immediately following graduation in 1900 he enrolled at the American Academy of Dramatic Arts in New York, with which his father had been associated from its founding. He remained for one year of training and earned a diploma. He returned to Columbia for postgraduate work in 1901–1902. Between 1902 and 1910 de Mille supported himself and his family by teaching English literature at the Pamlico School for Girls in Pompton Lakes, New Jersey, and at the American Academy of Dramatic Arts. During this period he also wrote plays and vaudeville skits.

In 1903 de Mille married Anna Angela George, the daughter of Henry George, the chief advocate of the Single Tax movement. They had two children. By this time he was also achieving a modicum of success as a playwright. With the production of his *Strongheart* in 1905, a play about an American Indian's struggle to play football in the face of intolerance on a college campus, his career appeared to be off to a propitious start. He wrote more than two dozen plays, a few with his brother Cecil as collaborator. They include comedies, farces, and plays with serious themes, but with the exception of *The Warrens of Virginia*, a Civil War saga that was produced by David Belasco in 1907 and that enjoyed a lengthy run on Broadway and on the road in a touring production, most of de Mille's other plays are simply well-crafted plays of ephemeral interest.

In 1914, at the urging of his brother, de Mille set out for Hollywood to oversee the scripts that Cecil was transforming into movies. (He had previously declined his brother's offer to join in the formation of the movie company that later developed into the Paramount studio.) Once in Hollywood, he also worked for the Jesse L. Lasky Feature Play Company, the forerunner of Paramount, as head of the scenario department. Within a year de Mille began directing pictures, with *Anton, the Terrible* as his first venture. In all, he wrote seven scripts and directed more than fifty pictures, both silent and talking, and he saw the most successful of his plays, *The Warrens of Virginia*, turned into an equally successful movie directed by his brother in 1915. Like his plays, most of his early films have disappeared, but one of his directorial achievements, *Miss Lulu Bett* (1921), appears to have been a triumph of the silent era.

De Mille's work as a writer and director ran somewhat counter to the styles of the time in Hollywood's fast-growing movie industry, which had progressed from purveyor of short, pithy but relatively primitive films to sophisticated, often overproduced extravaganzas. Trying to remain honest and intelligent amid the new trends in movie making, de Mille favored restraint and reliance on good dialogue and plot. In 1931 he was elected president of the Academy of Motion Picture Arts and Sciences, but his own career in films was nearing its end. Although he continued writing and directing scripts for Paramount, Pathé, and Metro-Goldwyn-Mayer, he found himself increasingly out of step with the industry, and he returned to New York in the late 1930s to rekindle his career as a playwright. When nothing that he wrote was produced in New York, he returned to California, where he wrote his memoir, *Hollywood Saga* (1939). In 1941 de Mille was offered the job of developing a new drama department at the University of Southern California, at which he had given lectures over the years. He accepted the challenge with great enthusiasm and spent the rest of his career as a professor, retiring in 1953.

His marriage ended in 1928, and in the same year he married scriptwriter Clara Béranger, with whom he had no children. (An earlier affair with writer Lorna Moon produced a child who was adopted by Cecil in infancy.) De Mille died at his home in Playa del Rey, California.

• Most of de Mille's unpublished plays, scripts, and essays are in the New York Public Library for the Performing Arts, Lincoln Center. His daughter Agnes de Mille wrote about her father in her books of memoirs: *Dance to the Piper* (1952), *And Promenade Home* (1958), *Speak to Me, Dance with Me* (1973), and *Where the Wings Grow* (1978). See also *The Autobiography of Cecil B. DeMille* (1959) and Anne Edwards, *The DeMilles: An American Family* (1988). Obituaries are in the *New York Times* and *Variety*, 3 Mar. 1955.

MARY C. HENDERSON

DEMING, Barbara (23 July 1917–2 Aug. 1984), writer and activist, was born in New York City, the daughter of Katherine Burritt, who gave up her career as a singer to marry, and Harold Deming, a lawyer. Deming was born into a family that was influenced by her mother's association with an artistic group of friends in Greenwich Village and her father's association with Republican politics. She was educated at the Friends School of the Fifteenth Street Meeting in New York until she left for Bennington College in 1934.

During Deming's teens, her family owned a home across the river from New York in New City in a country neighborhood where friends included Norma Millay and her sister, poet Edna St. Vincent Millay, poet E. E. Cummings, photographer Consuelo Kanaga, sculptor Henry Varnum Poor, and writer Bessie Breuer and her daughter, the painter Annie Poor, who became Deming's lifelong friend. In this free and somewhat bohemian setting, Deming began to write poetry and, at the age of seventeen, had a passionate and formative love affair with her neighbor, Norma Millay. In 1974 she wrote retrospectively to her mother about this experience, "I have always been grateful to you for the fact that when you first told me about homosexuality you spoke of it very simply and did not condemn it to me as anything ugly. Because of this, when I fell in love with Norma I felt no hatred of myself."

At Bennington, Deming majored first in literature and then in drama. She received her B.A. in 1938 and a master's degree in drama from Western Reserve University in Cleveland in 1940. During her time at Bennington College, Deming met Vida Ginsberg, with whom she began a seven-year love affair, the first of three significant partner relationships during her lifetime.

Deming's first publication was a poem ("Listen/ cats love eyes") in *New Directions* in 1936. For ten years, her interest in theater and film overshadowed her poetry, but she began occasionally publishing poetry again in small magazines in the 1940s and the 1950s. She was discouraged by many rejections of her poetry but felt "rescued" when she began publishing her political writing and poetry in the *Nation* and *Liberation* in the 1960s.

During World War II, Deming worked for the Library of Congress national film library project based at New York's Museum of Modern Art. Her analyses of films during this period led to the writing of her first book, *Running Away from Myself—a Dream Portrait of America Drawn from the Films of the Forties* (1969). A bequest from an aunt in the early 1950s allowed Deming to travel in Europe, where she began writing the stories collected in *Wash Us and Comb Us* (1974) and also began a novel, *A Humming under My Feet: A Book of Travail* (1985).

In 1954 Barbara Deming met artist Mary Meigs at the Poors' family home in New City. The two became companions almost immediately, settling in a house in Wellfleet, Massachusetts, where Meigs painted and Deming wrote poems, stories, and essays that she published occasionally in the *New Yorker* and in *Partisan Review*. In 1959 Meigs and Deming traveled to India where Deming became interested in the work of Gandhi on nonviolence. She realized that she was "in the deepest part of myself a pacifist," and her life began to move from a personal search for truth to a political commitment to activism. A spontaneous interview with Fidel Castro during a trip to Cuba in March 1960 put her in touch with the Committee for Nonviolent Action and The Peacemakers. "Meeting them," she said, "felt like finding a long-lost family." She joined some of the first protests against nuclear-weapons testing and for unilateral disarmament. She was arrested on several occasions and jailed for protesting against the arms race and against racism.

In 1962 she corresponded with Martin Luther King, Jr., at the Southern Christian Leadership Conference, urging that the struggle for racial equality and the peace movement be joined, a plea that he answered by insisting that the registration of "nearly five million prospective Negro voters" would be more useful in removing the "conservative-militarist coalition which dominates our government" from power. Deming was jailed for civil rights protests in Birmingham, Alabama, and Macon and Albany, Georgia, during 1963–1964. Her book *Prison Notes* (1966) is an account of her imprisonment and her connections with her fellow prisoners who taught Deming about a life she had never lived. Her book *Revolution and Equilibrium* (1971) was an account of her participation in the anti–Vietnam War movement, particularly her travels to South Vietnam and to North Vietnam, where she witnessed and experienced the U.S. bombing of Hanoi.

Deming's commitment to human freedom and individual dignity brought her to the earliest stages of the peace movement and the civil rights movement and eventually to struggles that touched her own life most directly—feminism and gay and lesbian rights. After years of suppressing her "secret" life, in a 1971 letter to her comrade in the civil rights movement, Ray Robinson, Deming admits she has hit her own kind of bottom, "the bottom of being a homosexual. Facing always the threat of being despised for that." Since 1969, Barbara Deming had been living with her third lover and companion, Jane Gapen, whose former husband had threatened to never let her see her two children again. Deming's letter continues, "Our paying what amounted to ransom for the children quieted him. . . . But . . . the fear of what he might do is still in me."

Deming continued her struggle against violence, for several years focusing her political energy and her writing on issues of violence against women and the

historical roots of misogyny. Her books from this period include *We Cannot Live without Our Lives* (1974) and *Remembering Who We Are* (1981). In 1983 Deming was part of a Women's Encampment for a Future of Peace and Justice demonstration near the Seneca Army Depot in Romulus, New York, during which she and fifty-three other women were arrested. Her essay about this protest—which was her last—is included in the reprinted *Prison Notes* under the title *Prisons That Could Not Hold* (1985).

In February 1984 Deming was diagnosed with ovarian cancer. After painful surgery and chemotherapy, when Deming was quite certain she was dying, she left the hospital, summoned friends and family to come and visit her, and conducted nightly gatherings of women who sang, talked, and chanted as Deming, in her own words, "danced toward death." She died in her home at Sugarloaf Key, Florida.

In the introduction to an anthology of Barbara Deming's writings, activist and writer Barbara Smith assesses Deming's lifetime commitment to nonviolence. Deming, she wrote, is one of those who understood "the basic truth that activism often requires putting your body on the line," and that "nonviolence, militantly practiced," can make freedom possible. Deming's example to those who follow her, concludes Smith, is that she continued to grow and was willing to confront each issue her age presented to her.

• Deming's papers are housed primarily at the Schlesinger Library, Radcliffe College. A few early papers are at Boston University's Mugar Library. Permission to publish material from the papers can be obtained from Deming's literary executor, Judith McDaniel, Tucson, Ariz. Important publications not mentioned above include her interview with Castro prior to the Bay of Pigs, "Dialogues in Cuba," *Nation*, 28 May 1960, and "New Mission to Moscow: The Long Walk for Peace," *Nation*, 23 Dec. 1961. *We Are All Part of One Another: A Barbara Deming Reader*, ed. Jane Meyerding, was published in 1984. Meyerding's introduction and chronology of Deming's life were compiled with Deming's assistance shortly before her death. Deming's life was also featured in the film *Silent Pioneers*, interviews with gay and lesbian elders, produced by Pat Snyder, Harvey Marks, and Lucy Winer, and shown on the Public Broadcasting System in fall 1984.

JUDITH MCDANIEL

DEMING, Philander (6 Feb. 1829–9 Feb. 1915), author and pioneer in court stenography, was born in Carlisle, New York, the son of Julia Ann Porter and Rufus Romeo Deming, a minister in the Champlain Presbytery. As his father moved from one pulpit to another, Deming spent his childhood in various small towns in the Adirondack Mountain and Champlain Valley regions of New York State. In such circumstances his father's library provided much of his education, and he was steeped in writers of the New England tradition such as Emerson and Longfellow. After living for a time in Huntingdon, Quebec, the family returned to upstate New York and settled in the village of Burke in Franklin County. As a young man, Deming savored solitude, and could often be found walking about the countryside, fishing, hunting, and rambling. Among the inhabitants of Burke, he was considered "odd" and uncommunicative, yet he still managed to secure a teaching post there from 1852 to 1854. During that time Deming and his two brothers also built themselves a sawmill, which Deming helped operate as he prepared for college. After studying at Whitestown Seminary in Whitesboro, New York, he matriculated at the University of Vermont from which he graduated in 1861, having been elected Phi Beta Kappa. Three years later he received an advanced degree from the university, remaining active in its alumni programs throughout most of his life.

After graduation Deming settled in Albany, New York's capital, taking up work as a journalist. For two months he practiced the shorthand that he had learned as a child, and using the Albany newspapers as sources, he became adept at legislative reporting. By 1862 he was the legislative reporter for an Albany newspaper. The following year he served as assistant editor of the *Burlington Free Press* while simultaneously continuing his coverage of government activities. Then, in 1864 he became the *New York Times* reporter on the state legislature.

In 1865 Deming gave a courtroom demonstration that dramatically illustrated the importance of verbatim recording in legal proceedings and court testimony. He immediately became so engaged in court stenographic work and so busy traveling as an expert court reporter that he gave up journalism as a career. Immersed in the dramas of law, Deming took up the profession, graduating from Albany Law School in 1872; he was admitted to the bar that same year. He became the official stenographer for the Albany District Supreme Court, a position he maintained until his retirement around 1882. His pioneering work in court reporting continued with the publication of his handbook, *The Court Stenographer: Hints and Practical Suggestions in Regard to Court Reporting* (1879).

While working as a journalist and stenographer, Deming aspired to create "original literature," as he called it, writing essays that he submitted to the *Atlantic Monthly*, the publication he considered the "greatest magazine of the day." Unfortunately all of his efforts were rejected until he turned to fiction. By his own account, in 1871 he had a "vision" in which he saw his literary vocation as a short story writer. In a two-day burst of creative energy, he produced his first short fiction titled "Lost." Like all his best work, it is based on his experiences with the people and landscape of his youth in the mountains of New York. Blending his sense of courtroom drama with his sensitivity to the nuances of language that made him an adept reporter and recorder, Deming quarried a literary gem that William Dean Howells, editor of the *Atlantic Monthly*, recognized as a fresh impulse to realism and simplicity, just the sort of fiction Americans needed. In February 1873 "Lost" appeared in the magazine, and Howells began publishing Deming's short stories, placing him among the local color writers of American literature. These early stories and sketches were later collected in *Adirondack Stories* (1880) and *Tompkins and Other Folks* (1885).

Deming's sixteen published stories and the brief autobiographical sketches that accompanied them, most of the latter appearing as *The Story of a Pathfinder* in 1907, constitute his contribution to realism in American fiction. His stories engage themes that resonated from his observations in small mountain communities and Albany's courtrooms: self-reliance and personal justice, suspicion and silenced truth, the failure of romantic ideals. In "Lost" a small boy wanders away from the clearing around his Adirondack homestead. Without waiting for lawmen or local officials, folk from the area gather to mount a search for the child. As days pass without result, there are ugly rumors muttered about the father and the possibility that he has killed his little son. Just as the people are about to pass vigilante judgment on the man without due process, evidence, or a hearing, the body is found in the woods and the father is exonerated. Another story from the first collection, "Willie," opens with a young boy's voice: "It frightened us a good deal when we found the little dead boy" (p. 106). The startling discovery of a child's mangled and bloody corpse at a pasture's edge gives rise to speculation and dispute about the probable cause of death and then swift retribution on the animal presumed responsible. The old ram is killed in a passage typical of Deming's use of understatement and unsentimental realism: "In a moment a glittering keen knife flashed from somebody's keeping into the bright sunshine, and in a moment more a purple stream dyed the white wool around Buck's throat, and there was a red pool upon the grass, and a little later . . . 'some tough mutton'" (p. 117).

Deming's fiction reflects his years as a court reporter, during which time he witnessed stories of intense experience and suffering while not actually participating in them. Deming was profoundly, perhaps even obsessively, shy. Known to his college fellows as "the philosopher," he was a loner who preferred solitude to society, living in boarding houses where he could be an observer of some semblance of domestic life but not a part of it. He never married, and though he was much esteemed, he apparently had no intimate relationships. He died in Albany but was buried in the Adirondack village of Burke among the people who inspired and inhabited his stories.

• Philip G. Terrie, "Philander Deming," in *Writers Before 1880*, ed. Bobby Ellen Kimbel (1988), is most useful in putting Deming's work into the context of his life and literary times. Thomas F. O'Donnell, "Regional Fiction of Upstate New York" (Ph.D. diss., Syracuse Univ., 1957), and Kate H. Winter, "North Country Voices," in *Upstate Literature*, ed. Frank Bergman (1985), both provide biographical details and literary analysis. See also William Dean Howells, "Recollections of an Atlantic Editorship," *Atlantic Monthly*, Nov. 1907, p. 600.

KATE H. WINTER

DEMOREST, Ellen Curtis (15 Nov. 1824–10 Aug. 1898), publisher and businesswoman, was born Ellen Louise Curtis in Schuylerville, New York, the daughter of Henry Curtis, a farmer and manufacturer, and Electa Abel. She attended local schools and graduated from Schuylerville Academy at age eighteen. Exposed to the fashion industry from an early age—her father's factory made hats, and the nearby resort at Saratoga Springs regularly featured dapper visitors from across the nation—she established a prosperous local millinery business immediately after graduating. Within a year she had moved on to larger markets in Troy and finally—by the early 1850s—to New York City. Settling in Brooklyn, she met merchant William Jennings Demorest during a business transaction. They were married in 1858. In addition to raising two children from her husband's first marriage—he was a widower—Demorest would have two of her own. Unlike most couples of their era, the Demorests became equal partners in professional as well as domestic life.

The newlyweds lived in Philadelphia briefly—William had moved there to begin a business—but a chance discovery soon brought them back to New York and on their way to success. Ellen Demorest had given up her millinery business but retained an interest in fashion and had for years been especially interested, along with her sister Kate, in developing a new way to cut dresses. One day she watched her African-American maid cut out a dress using pieces of wrapping paper as a guide, and she was struck with an inspiration: provided with a proper pattern, which could easily be made from thin paper, any interested woman could become a competent home dressmaker. The newly popular domestic sewing machine, she knew, would only serve to augment the appeal of such a product. After she designed a few patterns and exhibited them to enthusiastic neighbors in her home, her husband was convinced that her idea would appeal to a mass market. The couple moved back to New York and set out to bring Demorest's idea to the women of America.

William Demorest, a marketing genius, supervised the initial manufacture of patterns and delivered them through *Mme. Demorest's Mirror of Fashions*. This magazine, founded in 1860 by both spouses, playfully invoked in its title the Paris vogue of the time and featured European fashions that Demorest and her sister fitted to more modest American sensibilities. Like other women's magazines of the time, it resembled a catalog, with color illustrations of dresses that women could make using Demorest's designs. The *Mirror* was unique, however, in also including in each issue an original dressmaking pattern. Ideally suited for home sewing, this pattern was the feature that distinguished the magazine and made it immediately popular. Despite the nation's absorption in the coming Civil War, the young publication flourished, partly as a result of its intimate connection with two other successful business ventures: Madame Demorest's Emporium of Fashions—an exclusive Broadway shop that attracted huge crowds to its semiannual shows—and a national network of local distribution agencies, organized by William, for the Demorest patterns. Capitalizing on her newfound appeal, Demorest soon also developed and successfully marketed a new hoop skirt, corsets, and a cosmetic line.

In January 1864 the Demorests purchased the *New York Illustrated News* and combined it with their already established fashion magazine to form *Demorest's Illustrated Monthly and Mme. Demorest's Mirror of Fashions*. The new forum featured not only the usual fashion pieces but also poetry (usually by Americans such as Edgar Allan Poe and William Cullen Bryant), musical scores, articles on topics ranging from health to architecture, and book reviews. Under the editorship of the Demorests, the magazine soon achieved a circulation of 60,000 despite the reading public's absorption in the ongoing war. The couple was aided by the able pen of chief staff writer Jenny June (Jane C. Croly), who in a regular section—"What Women Are Doing"—"took note of every woman rancher, banker, dentist or businesswoman of any sort who came to light in a distinctive way in any part of the country" (Ross, p. 228).

Jenny June's focus in this section was representative of the larger interests of the Demorests themselves. Not merely content to be successful entrepreneurs, they ultimately attached a moral purpose to their enterprise, both in their business practices—they made a point of hiring women in all their ventures and employed African Americans on the same terms as whites—and in the content of their magazine. Although the fashion section may have seemed only to appeal to feminine vanity, *Demorest's Monthly* on the whole "was urging women to live more sensibly—to cultivate their minds as well as their bodies, to educate their daughters, to make them read, to stop being slothful, to depend less on their servants and more on their own efforts, to discipline their children, to refrain from marrying young or for money" (Ross, p. 51).

The couple's interest in reform became more marked by the end of the decade. Demorest in 1868 helped to found the Sorosis Club, a trailblazing group of women who promised in their constitution to promote discussion of women's roles in society. In addition to serving as vice president and treasurer of the club, Demorest was treasurer of the New York Medical College for Women and chair of the board of the Welcome Lodging House for Women and Children, a shelter for the neglected or abused dependents of alcoholic men. Similarly, her husband became increasingly involved in temperance issues; he would eventually run unsuccessfully for lieutenant governor on the Prohibition ticket in 1885.

Meanwhile, business boomed. In 1876 the Demorests sold three million patterns through 1,500 distribution agencies, both in the United States and in Europe. Their son Henry opened a Paris office where patterns were printed in French; at the height of her popularity, Ellen Demorest accomplished the almost unthinkable—she brought American fashion to France.

In the next decade, however, business became more difficult. The Demorests had never patented their pattern idea, and they began to face increasing competition from rivals such as Ebenezer Butterick. William retired in 1885 to pursue his political interests, and two years later Demorest retired from the pattern business altogether, leaving her sons to run what in November 1889 became *Demorest's Family Magazine.* Alone after her husband's death in 1895, she died in New York City in 1898. That year the family's magazine was sold to Arkell Publishing Company, and it folded the next year.

Ellen Demorest created fashions that captured the attention of late nineteenth-century New York and took advantage of print and industry to carry those fashions directly to the women of America. She was a model of success for aspiring businesswomen and a crusader for the advancement of women in all fields. Perhaps her greatest accomplishment lay in her use of her fashion magazine—a publication that apparently catered to traditional notions of femininity—to create more opportunities and confidence for all women.

• Ishbel Ross, *Crusades and Crinolines: The Life and Times of Ellen Curtis Demorest and William Jennings Demorest* (1963), a full-length study of the couple and their industry, includes a complete bibliography. Margaret La Forge, "Fashions for Everyone: Ellen Demorest," in *Enterprising Women*, ed. Caroline Bird (1976), is also useful, as is information on the Demorests in Frank L. Mott, *A History of American Magazines*, vols. 3 and 4 (1957). An obituary is in the *New York Times*, 11 Aug. 1898.

W. FARRELL O'GORMAN

DE MOSS, Elwood (5 Sept. 1889–26 Jan. 1965), African-American baseball player and manager, was born in Topeka, Kansas. Little is known about his parents and early childhood, though according to a 1910 census De Moss was living at home with his mother Eley, a widow. In 1905 he began his baseball career as a shortstop with the Topeka Giants. Although his speed allowed him to cover extensive ground, an injured arm that year from a brief outing as a pitcher caused him to switch to second base. He is generally recognized as the best second baseman in black baseball prior to the formation of the Negro National League in 1920.

De Moss made appearances with strong independent teams such as the Kansas City (Kans.) Giants (1910–1912), the French Lick (Ind.) Plutos (1913–1914), the St. Louis Giants (1913), the West Baden (Ind.) Sprudels (1912–1914), and the Chicago Giants (1913). In 1915 he joined the Indianapolis ABCs, owned by Tom Bowser and managed by the legendary C. I. Taylor. He excelled at every phase of the game, exhibiting quickness and agility in the field and proving to be an offensive threat with the bat. Considered by baseball historians a "scientific" hitter, the right-handed De Moss hit the ball to all fields, depending on the pitcher's delivery. The players called him "Bingo,"

because, it was said, wherever he wanted to hit the ball, bingo, it would go there. An excellent bunter, master of the hit-and-run, and seldom a strikeout victim, he proved to be a valuable weapon in a team's batting order.

In his first year at Indianapolis, De Moss batted .316 and stole 34 bases in 50 games. In 1915 the ABCs lost to Rube Foster's Chicago American Giants in the playoffs. The American Giants won the first and third games, with the ABCs winning the second. A rematch occurred in September of the following year; the American Giants won three out of four games with scores of 3–1, 4–2, and 5–2, with their only loss by a 7–4 score. The ABCs, with De Moss, future Hall of Famer Oscar Charleston, and submarine pitcher William "Dizzy" Dismukes, then met the American Giants in October for a twelve-game series. Foster's Giants went down to defeat five games to four, with three games unplayed, and De Moss and his teammates claimed unofficial title to the world's black baseball championship.

In 1917 De Moss joined Foster's American Giants, who exhibited a more up-tempo, aggressive, and daring style of play that was better suited for De Moss's offensive skills. After World War I De Moss replaced Pete Hill, an outstanding hitter and outfielder, as captain of the team and held the position for the next six years. During this period the American Giants won the Negro National League (organized in 1920) pennants in 1920, 1921, and 1922, before relinquishing the title to the Kansas City Monarchs in 1923. During the 1923 and 1924 seasons the league was raided by the newly formed Eastern Colored League, weakening some of its original teams. League commissioner Rube Foster sent De Moss and George Dixon to the Indianapolis ABCs, after the 1925 season, in an attempt to balance power within the league.

De Moss was called by Homestead Grays owner Cumberland Posey "the king-pin of keystoners." Chicago American Giants manager Dave Malarcher said that De Moss "had the courage, confidence and ability written all over his face and posture. He was the smartest, the coolest, the most errorless ball player I've ever seen."

De Moss spent one season with the Indianapolis ABCs before the team folded. He joined the Detroit Stars in 1927 and was manger for the next four seasons. Although the Stars never captured first place, they compiled an impressive 195–158 won-lost record, a .545 percentage during De Moss's tenure. De Moss retired after the 1930 season, only to reemerge in 1942 as manager of a semiprofessional team called the Chicago Brown Bombers, capitalizing on boxer Joe Louis's moniker. The next year the Brown Bombers folded and De Moss went back into retirement.

In 1945 Branch Rickey started an experimental league, the United States Baseball League, to develop black ballplayers for possible integration into the major leagues. Rickey said he hoped the league would become a model for all leagues to follow and would eventually make the black players eligible to be drafted by major league clubs. One of six teams formed was the Chicago Brown Bombers, with De Moss named as manager. As manager he won 57 percent of his games. The new team with an old name played their games at Wrigley Field when the Chicago Cubs were out of town. De Moss won 57 percent of his games as manager of the Brown Bombers, who later became associated members in 1946, the last year of Rickey's provisional league.

After 1946 De Moss vanished from the baseball scene and lived a quiet life in Chicago until his death there. There is no record of him after 1946. League standings and game results were never published, and little information was available on the United States League. Little is known of his personal life, although he was survived by his wife Maranda (maiden name unknown) and two daughters. A brilliant manager and an excellent ballplayer, De Moss's contribution to baseball history has remained virtually unknown.

• Biographies of De Moss can be found in John Holway, *Voices from the Great Black Baseball Leagues* (1975); Robert Peterson, *Only the Ball was White* (1970); and James Riley, *All-Time All-Stars of Black Baseball* (1983). Game scores are from the weekly *Indianapolis Freeman* newspaper, 26 June 1915, 2 Sept. 1916, and 4 and 11 Nov. 1916.

LARRY LESTER

DEMPSEY, Jack (24 June 1895–31 May 1983), world heavyweight boxing champion, was born William Harrison Dempsey in Manassa, Colorado, the son of Hyrum Dempsey, a rancher and sharecropper, and Mary Celia Smoot. His parents had come to Colorado from West Virginia. The family was poor, and Hyrum Dempsey and his sons worked at a variety of jobs, none of long duration. Jack (who was actually called "Harry" by his family; his working name was derived from the nineteenth-century boxer Nonpareil Jack Dempsey) completed the eighth grade at Lakeview, Utah, one of a succession of western towns in which the family lived. He then became a miner and saloon fighter in Utah and Colorado, sometimes trained by his oldest brother, Bernie. Although still a slender boy, his practice was to enter a saloon and issue a general challenge to beat anyone available. Usually he won these fights, passing the hat afterward for his pay, but he would flee if the challenge was accepted by a rival who appeared too dangerous.

From 1911 to 1916 Dempsey lived as a hobo, working when he could and riding beneath railroad cars to travel from town to town. By late 1914 he was fighting professionally, in advertised boxing programs, beginning with a series of minor bouts in Salt Lake City. He used the name "Kid Blackie," won most of his fights by knockout, and gradually achieved a reputation in the mountain states. This encouraged him to travel to New York City in June 1916. There he attracted the attention of John "the Barber" Reisler, an unscrupulous manager of boxers, who took over Dempsey's affairs. After three fights, Dempsey decided to leave New York to escape from Reisler and returned to Utah. In later years, Reisler brought many unsuccessful lawsuits against Dempsey, claiming to be Dempsey's manager and thus entitled to a part of his earnings.

In 1916, back in Utah, Dempsey married Maxine Cates, a piano player in saloons and a prostitute who was fifteen years older. They lived together only a few months and were divorced in 1919. Early in 1917 Dempsey suffered his only knockout loss, to Jim Flynn in Murray, Utah. He then went to California and won a series of victories in four-round fights, defeating such well-known heavyweights as Gunboat Smith, Carl Morris, and Charlie Miller. While there he met Jack Kearns, an ex-fighter who became his manager and took him east in 1918. There Dempsey had a series of quick knockout victories, numbering among his victims Flynn, Bill Brennan, Arthur Pelkey, Battling Levinsky, and Fred Fulton, until then the highest ranked contender for the heavyweight title held by Jess Willard.

Dempsey's success attracted the attention of the boxing promoter Tex Rickard, who decided to hold a heavyweight championship fight between Dempsey and Willard. The two fighters met in Toledo, Ohio, on 4 July 1919. Perhaps this fight better than any other typifies Dempsey's impetuously aggressive, hard-hitting style. Willard was knocked down seven times and had his jaw broken, six teeth knocked out, and his face cut and badly swollen. He failed to answer the bell for the fourth round, and Dempsey's reign as heavyweight champion had begun.

During World War I Dempsey had seen no military service. On 23 January 1920 a letter was published in the *San Francisco Chronicle*, written by his ex-wife, accusing Dempsey of being a draft dodger. Following an inquiry both Dempsey and Kearns were indicted on charges of draft evasion. At a June 1920 trial held in San Francisco, Dempsey proved that he had been deferred as the sole support of his wife, mother, and younger siblings. Acquittal came after only ten minutes of jury deliberation, yet afterward Dempsey was regarded by many as a "slacker."

After his exoneration, Dempsey twice defended his title in 1920, knocking out Billy Miske in three rounds at Benton Harbor, Michigan, and Brennan in twelve rounds at Madison Square Garden in New York City. Miske, who suffered from Bright's disease but was still a highly capable fighter, gave Dempsey little trouble. Brennan fought Dempsey on even terms until knocked out by a sudden combination of terrific punches in the twelfth round. In 1921 Rickard brought the French war hero Georges Carpentier to the United States to challenge Dempsey in the much-heralded "Battle of the Century." The promotion for the fight skillfully contrasted Dempsey's rough appearance and manners with Carpentier's European urbanity. A giant wooden stadium was constructed for the event in Jersey City, New Jersey, and at least 80,000 fans packed it on fight day to produce the first million-dollar gate in boxing history. Although he fought valiantly, Carpentier lacked the necessary size and power needed, and Dempsey knocked him out in the fourth round.

Dempsey did not defend his title in 1922 but made two successful defenses in 1923. The first, on 4 July 1923 against Tommy Gibbons in remote Shelby, Montana, was an attempt to promote the town into national prominence and resulted in the failure of several Montana banks. Dempsey found Gibbons too shifty and clever to knock out, but he won decisively on points in fifteen rounds. The second, against Luis Angel Firpo of Argentina and promoted by Tex Rickard, was held in New York City and produced another million-dollar gate. It was arguably the most dramatic fight in heavyweight title history. In the first round Dempsey knocked Firpo down seven times, while Firpo dropped Dempsey to his knees once and to his hands once. Near the end of the round Firpo knocked Dempsey out of the ring, and Dempsey barely returned in time to beat the count. In the second round Dempsey quickly ended the fight with a terrific left hook.

In 1924 and 1925 Dempsey did not defend his title, but during these years he became tremendously popular. In 1920 he had appeared in the movie serial *Daredevil Jack*, and now he returned to the screen in the series *Fight and Win*, made at Universal Studios. He moved to Los Angeles, where he continued to make movies and where he met Estelle Taylor, an actress, whom he married in 1925. Their stormy relationship was complicated by bitter animosity between Taylor and Kearns and, together with Dempsey's growing independence, led to his separation from Kearns in 1926. Afterward Kearns became a bitter enemy, plaguing Dempsey with three unsuccessful lawsuits and other legal actions.

Dempsey's friendly, unaffected ways, plus his success in defeating two foreign challengers, contributed to his popularity. He was constantly in the news, through making movies, attempting an unsuccessful Broadway play with his wife, fighting exhibitions, and traveling. In England one of the many titled persons he met described him as "master of himself, easy, natural and unaffected, and free from any pose." He was champion of all the people, never placing himself above anyone. Yet in the ring his violence was barely controlled. Always on the attack and never fancy, he attempted to take the most direct way to victory, smashing his opponents with vicious left hooks and straight rights and fighting hardest when he was hurt. Smaller than many heavyweight champions at 6'1" and 185–190 pounds, he was one of the hardest hitters, quick of hand, fleet of foot, rugged, and utterly ruthless in the ring.

During much of the 1920s the African-American fighter Harry Wills was rated as the most logical contender for Dempsey's title. Dempsey claimed he would have fought him at any time, but politics kept them apart. In 1926 a match between them was actually made, but scheming behind the scenes prevented it from being held. Jack Johnson, another black boxer, who held the heavyweight title from 1908 to 1915 and

from whom Willard had won the championship, had been tremendously unpopular with whites and had been forced to flee the United States. Wills's personality was entirely different, but he was the victim of the lingering resentment toward Johnson. As a result Dempsey and Wills never fought each other. In October 1926, after Dempsey lost his title, Wills was badly beaten by Jack Sharkey and eliminated from contention.

After three years of inactivity, Dempsey defended his title against Gene Tunney on 23 September 1926 in Philadelphia. His long absence from competition had cost him much of his effectiveness, and Tunney outpointed him with clever boxing and hard hitting. Their fight drew the third million-dollar gate in boxing history. Dempsey regained sufficient form to knock out Jack Sharkey on 21 July 1927 in New York. On 22 September in Chicago, before the largest crowd ever to see a major fight and with a $2.5 million gate, Dempsey attempted to regain the heavyweight title from Tunney. For six rounds, Tunney outboxed Dempsey; in the seventh round Dempsey scored a knockdown but stood over the fallen Tunney instead of going to a neutral corner. This delayed the referee's count, allowing Tunney precious time to recover. After this controversial "long count," Tunney took command again in the next round and won decisively. This was Dempsey's last fight.

Dempsey lost most of the fortune he had amassed from his boxing career in the 1929 stock market crash. For the next twelve years he boxed in exhibitions and refereed boxing and wrestling matches, traveling constantly. He divorced his wife in 1930; in 1933 he married Hannah Williams, and they had two daughters. Theirs was a stormy marriage that ended in 1940 with a bitter divorce. During World War II Dempsey joined the Coast Guard; holding the rank of commander, he directed the Coast Guard's physical fitness program and later served as a morale officer in the South Pacific. Until 1974 he was co-owner of a restaurant on Broadway in New York City. He married Deanna Piattelli in 1959 and lived happily with her in New York City until his death there.

Dempsey's name is inseparably associated with the 1920s and the development of sports into a major financial industry. Known as the "Manassa Mauler," a name bestowed on him by sportswriter Damon Runyan, he is arguably the best-known fighter of all time. He was an inaugural inductee to the International Boxing Hall of Fame in 1990.

• The most authoritative source is the autobiography *Dempsey*, co-written with his stepdaughter Barbara Piattelli Dempsey (1977). Other autobiographies are *Round by Round: An Autobiography*, with Myron Stearns (1940) and *Jack Dempsey: Massacre in the Sun*, with Bill Considine and Bill Slocum (1960). The best biography is Randy Roberts, *Jack Dempsey: The Manassa Mauler* (1979), which also provides an extensive bibliography; another is Nat Fleischer, *Jack Dempsey: The Idol of Fistiana* (1929). Toby Smith, *Kid Blackie: Jack Dempsey's Colorado Days* (1987), is a description of Dempsey's early career. Dempsey was commemorated in Bert R. Sugar, "Jack Dempsey: A Legend for All Times," *Ring*, July 1983, pp. 24–33.

LUCKETT V. DAVIS

DEMPSEY, Nonpareil Jack (15 Dec. 1862–2 Nov. 1895), boxer, was born John Edward Kelly in Curran, County Kildare, Ireland, the son of Martin Kelly and Alicia Lennon. He came to the United States with his parents at the age of four. His family settled in Brooklyn, where he attended public schools. His father died during his childhood, and his mother later married Patrick Dempsey, whose name he assumed. Young Dempsey became a cooper and made his living by pounding hoops onto barrels. He also became a professional wrestler and won many matches in New York City, Boston, and other eastern cities.

Dempsey accepted his first boxing match in 1883 when he weighed only 128 pounds, knocking out Edward McDonald in 27 rounds on Staten Island. As with all of the fights that Dempsey would have until near the end of his career, the match was conducted under London Prize Ring Rules, in which bare fists or skintight gloves were used and a round ended when either man was knocked down or wrestled off his feet. Because such fights were illegal, they had to be held before small gatherings and in comparative secrecy; yet they were often reported in detail by newspapers and by tabloids such as the *National Police Gazette* The fighters fought for stake money, which was raised by contributions from gamblers and other interested persons, and the division of the stakes between winner and loser was prearranged.

Following his match with McDonald, Dempsey defeated the Irish lightweight champion Jack Boylan at Flushing, New York. He then fought the more experienced Harry Force on the beach sands at Coney Island, then a hangout for criminals, ruffians, and derelicts. Dempsey had Force hopelessly beaten by the end of the 11th round, when police arrived to stop the fight. In 1884 Dempsey won a series of fights, culminating in a match with George Fulljames in Great Kill, New York, on 30 July. Fulljames had claimed the middleweight championship, but the two men fought far below what was then the 154-pound middleweight limit. Dempsey knocked out Fulljames in the 22d round.

From the later months of 1884 until 1886, Dempsey continued to win all of his fights, usually by knockout. At last, on 3 February 1886, he gained some recognition as American middleweight champion by knocking out Jack Fogarty in 27 rounds in New York City. On 4 March Dempsey fought George LaBlanche, a brawling ex-lumberjack who also claimed the American title, in Larchmont, New York. Dempsey, a much cleverer boxer than LaBlanche, handed his opponent a terrible beating and knocked him out after 13 rounds to become the undisputed champion.

Dempsey did not fit the mold for prizefighters. Handsome, quiet-spoken, and gentlemanly, he made friends wherever he went. In the ring he used his intel-

ligence and agility to defeat his opponents, making good use of feints and a quick left jab. He outclassed his rivals so decisively that he attained the sobriquet of "Nonpareil," meaning "unequaled." Although his hands were small, he had good muscular development in the shoulders and chest, and he could hit hard with his right hand. Like so many men of his time, Dempsey was inclined to drink too much. In late 1885 he visited the Pacific Northwest, defeating two opponents. During this tour, he met Margaret Brady in Portland, Oregon. The two married on 27 July 1886, and they later had two daughters.

In 1887 Dempsey continued to fight frequently, only one or two draws interrupting his series of victories. On 13 December 1887 he defended his middleweight title against Johnny Reagan in perhaps his most famous battle. The fight began during the early morning hours, in a ring that was pitched on marshy ground near Maspeth, Long Island. Reagan wore borrowed spiked shoes and accidentally gashed Dempsey's legs badly in the early rounds. The ocean tide soon began to rise, inundating the ground and causing the fight to be interrupted after eight rounds. The fighters and onlookers boarded a tug, and after a two-hour trip the fight was resumed near Manhasset, Long Island. Dempsey soon began to dominate the battle, Reagan saving himself by frequently going to the ground intentionally. The battle continued for 45 rounds before Reagan's corner surrendered.

Dempsey's successes continued until 27 August 1889, when he fought another famous battle against his old foe LaBlanche in San Francisco, California. In the 32d round LaBlanche was near defeat, having suffered a bad beating, when he won the fight by suddenly swinging his body around and catching Dempsey on the point of the jaw, either with an elbow or a right-hand punch. This was the famous "pivot blow," which was later outlawed and considered at that time by many to be a foul. Although Dempsey was completely knocked out, he did not lose the middleweight title because LaBlanche weighed 161 pounds, far above the division limit. This was Dempsey's first defeat.

On 18 February 1890 Dempsey established himself as world middleweight champion by stopping Australian Billy McCarthy in 28 rounds in San Francisco. The first modern title fight in the middleweight division, it was conducted under Marquis of Queensberry rules, with padded gloves and three-minute rounds. On 14 January 1891 Dempsey lost his title under Marquis of Queensberry rules to Bob Fitzsimmons in New Orleans, Louisiana. No longer the effective fighter he had been, Dempsey suffered a bad whipping, bravely standing up under terrific punishment until he was knocked out in the 13th round. After this defeat Dempsey had just three more fights, the last of which was a world welterweight title fight on 18 January 1895 with Tommy Ryan, who knocked out Dempsey in three rounds.

Dempsey was suffering from the early stages of tuberculosis at the end of his boxing career. In his final years he lived mainly in Portland with his family until he died there, less than a year after his last fight. A few years later his attorney, M. J. McMahon, wrote a famous poem entitled "The Nonpareil's Grave," after supposedly finding Dempsey's grave unmarked. Contrary to legend, however, the grave had been marked by the family and the poem was not engraved on Dempsey's tombstone.

Dempsey was the most famous athlete in the United States during the 1880s, next to John L. Sullivan. Unlike Sullivan, Dempsey always had good public deportment as well as a happy family life. In modern terms, he was an excellent boxer-puncher and ring general who lost only three of his 64 fights. He was inducted into the International Boxing Hall of Fame in 1992.

• Dempsey's complete record appeared in Herbert G. Goldman, ed., *The Ring Record Book and Boxing Encyclopedia*, 1986–1987 ed. (1987). Elliott J. Gorn, *The Manly Art: Bare-Knuckle Prize Fighting in America* (1986), details the manner in which fights were conducted in the era during which Dempsey fought. Useful articles pertaining to his boxing career in *The Ring* magazine include Johnny Reagan, "The Mill on the Sands," Nov. 1931, pp. 26–27; Finley Park, "The Sporting Gazette," May 1933, pp. 8–9; Biddy Bishop, "Immortal Jack Dempsey," Jan. 1935, pp. 22, 42; A. D. Phillips, "Middleweights on Parade," Apr. 1938, pp. 16–17, 44; and anon., "The Mill in the Water," Apr. 1943, pp. 6–7. His fight with Reagan is also described in Lester Bromberg, *Boxing's Unforgettable Fights* (1962). An obituary is in the (*Portland, Ore.*) *Morning Oregonian*, 2 Nov. 1895.

LUCKETT V. DAVIS

DEMPSTER, Arthur Jeffrey (14 Aug. 1886–11 Mar. 1950), physicist, was born in Toronto, Ontario, Canada, the son of James Dempster, the owner of a wholesale bakery firm, and Emily Melissa Cheney. He received an A.B. and an M.A. from the University of Toronto in 1909 and 1910, respectively. In 1911 he went to Germany to continue his graduate work and spent the first year at the Universities of Göttingen and Munich. In 1912 he enrolled at the University of Würzburg to study with the German physicist Wilhelm Wien, who had discovered in 1898 that a gaseous stream of positive ions could be deflected by electric and magnetic fields. While Dempster utilized this effect to study electrical discharges in gases, in 1913 the British physicists J. J. Thomson and Francis William Aston reduced a stream of positive ions of the same element into a narrow beam, known as a positive ray, and projected this ray through a perforated, negatively charged electrode in a vacuum chamber so that the original beam separated into several smaller beams. This result suggested that positive rays consisted of constituent particles of uneven weight, which further suggested that subtle variations exist between atoms of the same element. Thomson and Aston also showed that natural neon molecules consist of atoms that have virtually identical chemical properties but possess different atomic weights; these variations were named isotopes in 1913 by the British chemist Frederick Soddy. Dempster's search for isotopes in other elements

became his life's work and, when combined with the work of Aston, formed the basis for the emerging field of mass spectroscopy.

Dempster's work in Germany was cut short in 1914 by the outbreak of World War I. Later that year he enrolled at the University of Chicago and received his Ph.D. degree in physics in 1916. After graduation he enlisted in the U.S. Army as a private and was assigned to the infantry. He soon transferred to the Signal Corps as a master signal electrician and was sent in 1918 to France, where he helped to develop methods to detect submarines, to send underwater and secret signals, and to improve the wireless telephone. That same year he was promoted to second lieutenant and became a naturalized citizen of the United States.

While in France, Dempster used his spare time to build the first mass spectrometer as a tool for determining the relative abundance of an element's isotopes. The Thomson-Aston experiment with neon utilized a device that discharged a stream of gaseous ions across both an electric and a magnetic field into a vacuum chamber, where the ions separated into a parabolic distribution according to mass and energy level. Because of the complexities arising from the use of two fields and the way in which the ions were distributed, this device yielded results that were difficult to interpret. Consequently, Dempster modified its design in three ways. He used only one field, similar to those he had experimented with at Würzburg, to deflect ions; he produced ions by evaporating a solid deposit of a particular element; and he projected the ions into a straight-line distribution. As a result, Dempster's mass spectrometer gave results that could be interpreted easily with an oscilloscope, and because it could produce ions of those elements not easily rendered into a gaseous state such as most metals, it could analyze the relative abundance of isotopes of virtually any element.

In 1919 Dempster was discharged from the army and returned to the University of Chicago as an assistant professor of physics. He discovered the isotopes of magnesium and lithium in 1921 and of potassium, calcium, and zinc in 1922. In 1923 he became an associate professor, and in 1927, the year after he married Germaine Collette, with whom he had no children, he was promoted to full professor. From 1923 to 1934 he experimented with the passage of proton streams through clouds of hydrogen, helium, and neon and in the process demonstrated that protons possess wave characteristics. He also devoted much of his time during this period to the development of the double focusing spectrograph, which he completed in 1935. Adapting his earlier spectrometer by refining the technique used by Thomson, he utilized both an electrostatic and a magnetic field to develop clear, sharp images of the various mass lines. With the new device he investigated the heavier elements of the periodic table and discovered the isotopes of platinum, rhodium, palladium, gold, uranium, and iridium in 1935; thorium, barium, cerium, iron, nickel, strontium, and tellurium in 1936; neodymium and tungsten in 1937; gadolinium, dysprosium, erbium, and ytterbium in 1938; hafnium, yttrium, lutetium, and tantalum in 1939; and cadmium and samarium in 1947.

Of all the isotopes discovered by Dempster, the one that had the most profound implications for the development of science and technology was the uranium isotope U-235, which he discovered in 1935. Because of the discovery of the neutron three years earlier by the British physicist James Chadwick, it was now known that the difference in isotopes' atomic weights resulted from a difference in the number of neutrons in their nuclei. U-235, which has three fewer neutrons than U-238 and occurs naturally at a ratio of about 1:139 to its heavier cousin, proved to be of great value as a source of fissionable material. Nuclear fission takes place when a nucleus splits apart as the result of neutron bombardment and continues when neutrons from the split nucleus cause a chain reaction by bombarding adjacent nuclei. Within four years of his find, scientists had discovered that, of all the naturally occurring isotopes, U-235 undergoes fission more readily because relatively slow-moving neutrons can split it apart and that it emits more neutrons during fission, thereby prolonging the chain reaction. Dempster's research gave further impetus to the discovery of nuclear fission when in 1938 he showed that protons and neutrons in the nuclei of the heavier elements contain much more energy than those of the lighter elements and estimated that 196 million electron volts of energy would be given off if a uranium nucleus were split.

In 1941 Dempster took a leave of absence from his academic duties to join the U.S. government's Metallurgical Laboratory at the University of Chicago. This laboratory eventually became part of the Manhattan Project, and Dempster contributed substantially to the development of the first atomic bomb. From 1945 to 1950 he continued his research with nuclear fission by serving as director of the Division of Mass Spectroscopy and Crystallography at the U.S. Atomic Energy Commission's Argonne National Laboratory in Chicago. He died while vacationing in Stuart, Florida.

Dempster was awarded the annual prize of the American Association for the Advancement of Science in 1930. He also received the Lewis Award and the Glasham Gold Medal of the American Philosophical Society. He was elected to membership in the National Academy of Sciences in 1937 and served as president of the American Physical Society in 1944.

Dempster contributed to the development of science by discovering and analyzing the stable isotopes of thirty elements. His research involving the energy levels contained in the nuclei of the heavy elements was one of many factors that contributed to the discovery of nuclear fission. His work with isotopes led to the discovery of the material from which the first atomic bomb was made.

• Dempster's papers have not been located. A biography, which includes a complete bibliography, is Samuel King Allison, "Arthur Jeffrey Dempster," National Academy of Sciences, *Biographical Memoirs* 27 (1952): 319–33. Obituaries are in the *New York Times*, 12 Mar 1950, *Newsweek*, 20 Mar. 1950, *Science* 111 (31 Mar. 1950): 348, and *American Journal of Physics* 18 (Sept. 1950): 401–2.

CHARLES W. CAREY, JR.

DEMPSTER, John (2 Jan. 1794–28 Nov. 1863), Methodist educator and minister, was born in Florida, Montgomery (Fulton) County, New York, the son of the Reverend James Dempster, a Scotsman and graduate of Edinburgh University, and his second wife (name unknown). His father came to New York in 1774 as one of John Wesley's missionaries but chose to retain his Presbyterian convictions and became a minister in the settlement of Florida. As a child, Dempster was "eccentric and thoughtless." His father died in 1803, and he failed to secure a formal education. At first he helped keep a tin store with one of his three brothers, but at the age of eighteen, while at a Methodist camp meeting, he was dramatically affected by a sudden religious impulse, through which he made a commitment to the Methodist ministry. He began to preach but also proceeded to harness his innate intellectual and scholarly abilities, educating himself in the classics, mathematics, theology, philosophy, and Hebrew. His metamorphosis, both spiritually and academically, was striking. For the rest of his life he would retire at nine and rise again at four to work, applying himself entirely to the investigation of a given subject or discipline.

Dempster entered itinerant ministry in 1815 and after being admitted to the Genesee Conference in 1816, often preached twenty-one times a week. Because his health was frail, he was on probation for four years. His first circuit was in Lower Canada, where the punishing climate made his health worse. He then took successive appointments in New York State (Paris, 1817; Watertown, 1818 and 1821–1822; Scipio, 1819; Homer, 1823; Auburn, 1824; Rochester, 1825–1826; and Cazenovia, 1827–1828), after which he served as presiding elder for both the Cayuga District of the Oneida Conference and the Black River District of the Black River Conference. In 1832 he became president of the newly founded Genesee Wesleyan Seminary in Lima, New York.

Prompted by continued ill health, on 14 October 1836 Dempster departed for Buenos Aires, where a Methodist mission had opened. He was one of the first Methodist missionaries in South America, and his contact was mainly with the Protestant population. He established day and Sunday schools, securing a college graduate as teacher for the school, and built a Methodist church, the first in Argentina. He visited Uruguay in 1838 and, in 1840, Brazil, where he again established a school.

In 1842 Dempster returned to New York City and spent the next three years as minister for two leading churches, Vestry Street in 1842 and Mulberry Street in 1843–1844. During these years his strong personality, mental agility, and presence as a preacher were increasingly recognized. His preaching was described by Bishop Kingsley as "simple, stirring and profound," but he tended toward a metaphysical and logical dialectic when reasoning theologically and addressing questions of Christian doctrine.

Dempster's commitment to establishing theological seminaries, his greatest legacy, emerged early in his ministry. Prompted by the observation that converts to Methodism tended to seek out educated ministers as their pastors, he appealed to Bishop Elijah Hedding to send better-trained ministers to the Cayuga District. On finding that such men were not available, he determined to devote himself to the cause of ministerial theological education, and this he did for the rest of his life. The idea of any formal theological training was generally unpopular at that time, except in New England, where the New England Wesleyan Education Association had formed in 1837 to promote a more formalized theological training for ministerial candidates. Corresponding with Dempster they formed in 1840 the Wesley Theological Association, which was invited to locate at the Newbury Seminary in Vermont. This department became known as the Newbury Biblical Institute and was, in effect, the first theological school of the Methodist Episcopal church. In 1844, as the institute's financial agent, Dempster was appointed its second president and a professor of theology. He tried to raise funds for the institute during his visit to Scotland and England as a delegate for the Evangelical Alliance in 1846. In 1847 the institute transferred to Concord, New Hampshire, and became known as the Methodist General Biblical Institute. Dempster was appointed its first professor of theology. In 1848 he was conferred DD by Wesleyan University, Middleton, Connecticut. His fundraising efforts would save the institute from total collapse, as for many years there was little support within the denomination for institutionalized theological training. With a final move to Boston in 1867, the department was renamed the Boston Theological School, becoming in 1871 the Boston University School of Theology.

In 1854 Dempster left the institute and moved to Evanston, Illinois, to become the first president of a second theological school, Garrett Biblical Institute, which he had helped his Northwestern Methodist colleagues found the previous year. When in 1856 the permanent faculty was organized, he was elected senior professor of systematic theology, a position he held until his death. During these years he spoke out against slavery and in 1860 was elected with W. W. Paton by Chicago ministers to petition Abraham Lincoln to issue a proclamation of emancipation.

In his last years, Dempster focused his energies on establishing a theological seminary in the West. In the wake of the financial panic of 1857, his attempt to establish a school near Missouri failed. He then looked toward the Pacific. He had planned to travel to California in January 1864 to provide funds (some his own) for a third ministerial school, but he died in Chicago about a month before the trip was set to begin. He was survived by his wife Lydia Clancey, one son, and three daughters. Because of his lifelong commitment to the promotion of Methodist ministerial educa-

tion, which led directly to the foundation of the denomination's first theological schools, Dempster is now regarded as the father of American Methodist theological education.

• A collection of Dempster's writings is at Garrett-Evangelical Theological Seminary in Chicago. His only published work was *Lectures and Addresses . . . with an Appendix Containing the Funeral Sermon and the Memorial Services Occasioned by the Death of the Author*, ed. Davis W. Clark (1864), in which can be found his theological positions and his views on ministerial education. Biographical articles can be found in *Methodist Quarterly Review*, July 1864, pp. 357–79; the *Zion's Herald*, 26 Aug. 1896 (which contains a portrait); and Charles E. Cole, ed., *Something More than Human* (1986). For a discussion of Dempster's role in the development of ministerial education in the Methodist Episcopal church, see Gerald O. McCulloh, *Ministerial Education in the American Methodist Movement* (1980). Obituaries are in the *Minutes of the Annual Conferences of the Methodist Episcopal Church 1864* (Bishop Kingsley, Rock River Conference) and *Zion's Herald and Wesleyan Journal*, 9 Dec 1863.

JOANNA HAWKE

DEMUTH, Charles Henry Buckius (8 Nov. 1883–23 Oct. 1935), painter, was born in Lancaster, Pennsylvania, the son of Ferdinand Andrew Demuth, a tobacco-shop owner, and Augusta Wills Buckius. Demuth's earliest education took place in Lancaster, but for serious art study he went to Philadelphia, first enrolling at the Drexel Institute of Art, Science, and Industry (1903–1905) and at the Pennsylvania Academy of the Fine Arts (1905–1910). His teachers at the latter included Thomas Anshutz, Hugh Breckenridge, Henry McCarter, and William Merritt Chase. It was during this period that he became acquainted with the poet William Carlos Williams, then a medical student. The connections established during these years remained strong, reinforced by Pennsylvania collectors Albert Barnes and Carroll Tyson, the latter also a painter. Demuth, who became one of America's leading modernist painters, spent most of his life in the historic southeastern Pennsylvania city of his birth, where the majority of his works were painted. Lancaster remained a lifelong source of creative inspiration and personal stability. Most significant of his Lancaster intimates was Robert Evans Locher, a designer of Art Deco interiors, costumes, and theater. Their friendship dates from 1909. Demuth's regional orientation to the state of his birth was as significant to his art as were his connections to the New York avant-garde.

In 1907 Demuth made his first trip abroad, spending about five months in Paris. More significant was his second visit to the French capital, where he remained from December 1912 until the spring of 1914, pursuing classes at the Moderne, Colarossi, and Julian academies. This period marks his most extended contact with European modernism, including the adventurous coloration of postimpressionism. During this time he became acquainted with Gertrude Stein, Jo Davidson, Ezra Pound, Marsden Hartley, and Arnold Rönnebeck; he visited Berlin with Hartley and Rönnebeck in 1914. His first serious exploration of cubism came during the winter of 1916–1917, which he spent in Bermuda with Hartley and the French painter Albert Gleizes. Typical of the modernist architectonic works that resulted from this sojourn is *Red Chimneys* (1918, Phillips Collection). The late work of Paul Cézanne also emerges as a significant influence during this period. Demuth made a third trip—his last—to Paris between August and November 1921, a visit during which the artist experienced the first symptoms of diabetes. Throughout the 1920s his health deteriorated, and despite insulin treatment, he suffered periodic debilitating attacks from the disease for the rest of his life.

Demuth and John Marin established their reputations as America's leading watercolorists of their time. Demuth exhibited regularly throughout his career, and his work was purchased by such leading collectors as Ferdinand Howald, whose extensive collection is now at the Columbus Museum of Art in Ohio. Demuth exhibited publicly for the first time in 1907, at the Pennsylvania Academy of the Fine Arts. In 1914 he held his first one-person show at the avant-garde Daniel Gallery in New York, which represented him throughout the 1910s and early 1920s. Alfred Stieglitz first presented his work at the Anderson Gallery in 1925 and continued to show it throughout the late 1920s and early 1930s, first at the Intimate Gallery and later at An American Place.

New York City, easily accessible by train from Lancaster, was the center of the American avant-garde, and Demuth was connected with the most advanced circles, participating in a lively bohemian life centered in Greenwich Village. He made regular visits to the city, staying at either the Brevoort or Lafayette hotels, but during the winter of 1915–1916 he maintained an apartment at Washington Square. The cabarets and restaurants he frequented were those popular among artists and writers and included the Purple Pup, the Golden Swan, and Marshall's. The social freedom of the gay subculture in which he participated is seen in a series of works based on homosexual themes, including *Dancing Sailors* (1918, Museum of Modern Art) and a remarkable nude self-portrait, *Turkish Bath* (1918, private collection). In Lancaster, his life was necessarily sexually discreet, though he associated with other gay residents of the city.

Most closely associated with the coterie centered around Alfred Stieglitz, Demuth's friendships with Hartley and Georgia O'Keeffe remained lifelong alliances. Also important to him was the French artist Marcel Duchamp and the dadaist group gathered around Walter and Louise Arensberg. Summer visits to Provincetown (he made his first trip there in 1914) and Gloucester, Massachusetts, throughout the 1910s reinforced connections previously made in New York to the literary and artistic milieu of playwright Eugene O'Neill and other authors. Demuth himself also produced an occasional piece of creative writing.

His earliest independent works, such as *Self Portrait* (1907, private collection), reflect the strong impact of his teacher Chase in their realistic treatment, dark coloration, and visible brushwork. His palette gradually lightened, and visits to New Hope, Pennsylvania, and Lambertville, New Jersey (1908, 1911, and 1912), show the combined impact of a loosely brushed late impressionism. By 1912 the influence of French artist Auguste Rodin is evident in a series of figural works inspired by vaudeville (Lancaster was a significant stop on this entertainment circuit) and New York nightclub performances; typical is *The Green Dancer* (1916, Philadelphia Museum of Art). These watercolors, characterized by bright colors, fluid lines, and luminous washes, mark his mature style. They are related to a series of never-published illustrations inspired by the work of Henry James (Philadelphia Museum of Art), Frank Wedekind, Émile Zola (Barnes Foundation, Merion, Pa.), Walter Pater, and Edgar Allan Poe. The late 1910s were productive years for the artist, and he began to paint still lifes of fruits, vegetables, and flowers, subjects he would continue to explore for much of his career.

By 1919 Demuth had embarked on a series of cubist-realist architectural paintings of industrial subjects inspired by the buildings of Lancaster that established his reputation as a major precisionist. These works were not popular with critics, who did not respond positively to the unusual structures depicted and their ironic titles. They also signal a shift in medium, as the artist increasingly employed oil and tempera. His most famous work in this series is *My Egypt* (1927, Whitney Museum of American Art). Between 1923 and 1929 he painted a series of poster portraits, creating emblematic visual homages to O'Keeffe, Williams, Marin, Arthur Dove, and others. Most are in the Collection of American Literature at the Beinecke Rare Book and Manuscript Library at Yale University, though several are elsewhere, including *I Saw the Figure 5 in Gold* (1928, Metropolitan Museum of Art) and *Calla Lilies (Bert Savoy)* (1926, Fisk University, Nashville, Tenn.). He returned to the figure in the early 1930s in a series of overtly homoerotic works, including *Three Sailors on the Beach* (1930, private collection). His last works were a series of figural watercolors inspired by Provincetown, where he spent the late summer and early fall of 1934. He died of diabetes in Lancaster.

• Demuth's correspondence with Alfred Stieglitz is part of the Collection of American Literature in the Beinecke Rare Book and Manuscript Library at Yale University. Additional correspondence from a Lancaster private collection has been microfilmed by the Archives of American Art (Smithsonian Institution, Washington, D.C.). In Lancaster, the Demuth Foundation has established a museum in the artist's house on East King Street and maintains a collection of artwork and memorabilia. The first scholarly monograph on the artist's work was Emily Farnham, *Charles Demuth: Behind a Laughing Mask* (1971), a study based on her doctoral dissertation (Ohio State Univ., 1959). A series of publications focused on the artist's Lancaster milieu have been authored by Betsy Fahlman: *Pennsylvania Modern: Charles Demuth of Lancaster* (1983); "Modern as Metal and Mirror: The Work of Robert Evans Locher," *Arts Magazine* 59 (Apr. 1985): 108–13; "Charles Demuth's Paintings of Lancaster Architecture: New Discoveries and Observations," *Arts Magazine* 61 (Mar.

1987): 24–29; and "The Charles Demuth Retrospective at the Whitney Museum," *Arts Magazine* 62 (Mar. 1988): 52–54. For a comprehensive treatment, see Barbara Haskell, *Charles Demuth* (1987). Of recent publications, most significant are Wanda M. Corn, *In the American Grain: The Billboard Poetics of Charles Demuth* (1991); Johnathan Weinberg, *Speaking for Vice: Homosexuality in the Art of Charles Demuth, Marsden Hartley, and the First American Avant-Garde* (1993); Robin Jaffee Frank, *Charles Demuth Poster Portraits, 1923–1929* (1994); and Gail Stavitsky et al., *Precisionism in America, 1915–1941: Reordering Reality* (1994).

BETSY FAHLMAN

DENBY, Charles (16 June 1830–13 Jan. 1904), lawyer and diplomat, was born at "Mount Joy," the home of his mother's family in Botetourt County, Virginia, and was the son of Nathaniel Denby, a Richmond merchant, and Jane Harvey. After attending Georgetown College in Washington, D.C., and the Collège Royal in Marseilles, France, he graduated with honors from Virginia Military Institute in 1850. He taught at the Masonic University in Selma, Alabama, before moving to Evansville, Indiana, in 1853. He read law while employed as political editor of the city's Democratic newspaper, the *Daily Enquirer*. Admitted to the bar in 1855, he served a term in the Indiana legislature in 1856–1857. In 1858 he married Martha Fitch, daughter of U.S. senator Graham N. Fitch. The couple had eight children.

Despite his southern origins, Denby volunteered for Federal service after the fall of Fort Sumter in 1861. Appointed lieutenant colonel, he helped organize the Forty-second Indiana Regiment. After being seriously wounded at the battle of Perryville in 1862, he was promoted to colonel of the Eightieth Indiana Regiment. In early 1863 he received a medical discharge.

Denby resumed his Evansville law practice and over the next twenty years became one of the most distinguished members of the state bar and a prominent figure in Democratic party politics. Although he resisted moves to nominate him for Congress, he served as a delegate to two Democratic national conventions and was a supporter of Thomas A. Hendricks of Indiana, Grover Cleveland's first vice president. In 1885 Cleveland rewarded Denby's party service by appointing him minister to China. After defeating Cleveland in 1888, Republican Benjamin Harrison retained his fellow Hoosier in Beijing, and with Cleveland's return to the White House in 1893 Denby remained at his post. All told he served thirteen years (1885–1898) as the chief U.S. diplomat in China, the longest tenure of anyone to hold that office.

Denby's service in China coincided with a pivotal era in the history of Sino-Western relations. As U.S. and European economic and military power grew dramatically in the nineteenth century, the Western nations increasingly pressured the weak Chinese monarchy for commercial and territorial concessions. Denby shared the capitalist, Christian, and social Darwinist faith in Western superiority over China that was common in his era. However, perhaps because of his experience as a trial lawyer, he advocated orderly diplomatic and legal processes in Western dealings with the Chinese. He was particularly concerned that, without strict adherence to treaties, Britain and Russia would move to divide China between them. In 1895 he capped his diplomatic career with an effort to mediate a peaceful settlement of the Sino-Japanese War.

The return of a Republican administration and declining health prompted Denby to relinquish his Beijing post in 1898. In 1899 President William McKinley appointed him to a federal commission to investigate allegations of mismanagement of military logistics during the Spanish-American War. Denby was also one of three commissioners whom McKinley sent to Manila in 1899 after the United States acquired the Philippines from Spain. The commission outlined a plan for Philippine government, under a U.S. governor-general, designed to protect both U.S. interests and the Filipinos' civil rights. An active writer and lecturer, Denby died in Jamestown, New York, after giving a speech.

• A collection of biographical information on Denby is in the Willard Library, Evansville, Ind. His extensive diplomatic correspondence is in the General Records of the Department of State in the National Archives, Washington, D.C. His diplomatic memoir, *China and Her People*, was published posthumously in 1906. See also David L. Anderson, *Imperialism and Idealism: American Diplomats in China, 1861–1898* (1985), and John William Cassey, "The Mission of Charles Denby and International Rivalries in the Far East, 1885–1898" (Ph.D. diss., Univ. of Southern California, 1959). Obituaries are in the *Evansville Journal-News*, 13 Jan. 1904, and the *New York Times* and the *Evansville Courier*, both 14 Jan. 1904.

DAVID L. ANDERSON

DENBY, Charles, II (14 Nov. 1861–14 Feb. 1938), diplomat, was born in Evansville, Indiana, the son of Charles Denby, a diplomat in China, and Martha Fitch. Charles was educated at home by private tutors for his primary and secondary schooling. He attended Princeton University, from which he earned a B.A. in 1882. After Princeton Denby intended to, like his father, pursue a career in law, and for three years he clerked in the offices of Garvin & Kumler in Evansville. In 1885, however, Grover Cleveland appointed his father minister to China, and the younger Denby followed him there as second secretary.

Denby had a facility for languages and readily learned Chinese during the course of his duties. He was soon able to conduct official business with his Chinese counterparts and thus greatly assisted his father in his diplomatic activities. Both father and son were committed to increasing American business opportunities in China and wherever possible assisted fledgling American efforts toward that end. In 1894 Charles Denby II was promoted to first secretary of the legation, and during his father's absences in 1894 and in 1896, he was in charge of the American diplomatic offices in Beijing (Peking). During the Sino-Japanese War of 1894–1895, Denby worked with the Japanese residents in China and represented them during the early stages of the war. He played a role as mediator in some of the early negotiations between China and Japan that led to an eventual treaty between the belligerents. In 1895 he married Martha Dalzell; they had three sons.

In 1897 Denby took advantage of the business relationships he had developed during his years in the consular service and left his government position, which had not been highly remunerative, to enter into business with Arnhold, Karberg & Co., a New York–based import/export firm, in Tientsin. Three years later, after the outbreak of the Boxer Rebellion in 1900, the occupying Allied powers appointed him as secretary general of the new provisional government in Tientsin. He held this post for two years, using his knowledge of the Chinese people and culture to improve the strained relations between foreigners and local Chinese that had developed as a result of the rebellion. Following this he spent three years from 1902 to 1905, as foreign adviser to the viceroy of the Chihli Province in northern China.

In 1905 Denby returned to the United States and settled in Washington, D.C., where he began an appointment as chief clerk of the State Department. Elihu Root succeeded John Hay, who had died suddenly in July 1905, as secretary of state and immediately launched a vigorous reorganization of the department's consular service. While Root struggled to expand the staffing of the department, Denby, who had nearly twenty years of experience in China, served informally as a one man Far Eastern division. In 1907 Denby's extensive knowledge of China resulted in his posting to Shanghai as consul general. Two years later he was transferred to Vienna in the same capacity. Although it was an unusual venue for someone whose experience had been largely limited to the Far East, Denby adapted to his new surroundings. He remained there until the end of 1914, when he resigned to return to the United States as a vice president of the Hupp Motor Car Company in Detroit.

When the United States entered World War I, Denby moved back to Washington in November 1917 to join the War Trade Board as director of the Bureau of Foreign Agents. In March 1918 he traveled to China as a special assistant to the State Department and spent the last months of the war reporting on local conditions for the War Trade Board. In December 1918 Denby returned to Washington and in March 1919 resigned his government position. He intended to retire to private life, but when his brother Edwin Denby became secretary of the navy during the administration of Warren Harding, Charles Denby entered public service for one last time. From October 1922 to October 1923 he served as a special representative on the U.S. Shipping Board in China. Upon completion of this assignment, he retired to Washington, D.C., where he died.

Denby devoted his career to promoting the expansion of American business in China. He believed that China represented a nearly unlimited opportunity for American business investment, which would improve the overall economy of the United States and at the same time help the Chinese become significant in the global economy at the end of the nineteenth century. More than a business entrepreneur in the guise of a government official, Denby brought to his government service and his business affairs a deep affection for the Chinese people, a clear understanding of Chinese society and culture, and a sincere belief that both the East and the West could benefit from increased trade.

• No collection of Denby's papers exists. He wrote several essays during his career, which can be useful summaries of his thought. Three representative samples include "America's Opportunity in Asia," *North American Review* 166 (Jan. 1898): 32–39; "The National Debt of China—Its Origin and Its Security," *Annals of the American Academy of Social and Political Science* 67 (Nov. 1916): 55–70; and "The Crisis of the Chinese Government," *North American Review* 209 (Mar. 1924): 301–10. Denby's obituary is in the *Washington Post*, 15 Feb. 1938.

EDWARD A. GOEDEKEN

DENBY, Edwin (18 Feb. 1870–8 Feb. 1929), U.S. congressman and secretary of the navy, was born in Evansville, Indiana, the son of Charles Denby, a lawyer and U.S. minister to China, and Martha Fitch. Charles Denby was minister during the administrations of Presidents Grover Cleveland and Benjamin Harrison. Educated in China, Edwin Denby gained valuable experience as his father's private secretary. He served in the Chinese Maritime Customs Service from 1887 until his return to the United States in 1894. He was recognized as an authority on Asian affairs because of his service.

Upon his return to the United States, Denby studied law at the University of Michigan, where he earned his LL.B. in 1896 and gained fame as a football player. After passing the bar, he practiced in Detroit as a partner in the firm of Chamberlin, Denby, Webster and Kennedy. In 1898, during the Spanish-American War, he enlisted in the U.S. Navy and achieved the rank of gunner's mate second class aboard the *Yosemite*.

Denby returned to practicing law after the war. Elected to the Michigan House of Representatives in 1903, he became the Republican congressman of the Michigan First District to the U.S. House of Representatives in 1905. Denby served from 4 March 1905 until 3 March 1911 in the Fifty-ninth, Sixtieth, and Sixty-first Congresses. Afterward, he married Marion Bartlett Thurber in 1911; they had two children.

Following his defeat in the election of 1910, Denby was active in business and banking. He founded the Hupp Motor Company and was an incorporator of the Federal Motor Truck Company and the Detroit Motor Bus Company. From 1913 to 1914 he was president of the Detroit Charter Commission. He also presided over the Detroit Board of Commerce from 1916 through 1917.

In 1917 Denby again left his practice and business interests to reenlist in the U.S. military. Beginning as a 47-year-old marine private, he advanced in six months to the rank of second lieutenant. He ended World War One as a major and remained in the Marine Corps Reserve, eventually achieving the rank of lieutenant colonel. Denby returned to Detroit after the war and was appointed chief probation officer in the recorder's court. He also functioned as chief probation officer in Wayne County Circuit Court until 1921.

On 4 March 1921 Denby became President Warren G. Harding's secretary of the navy. Denby was Harding's third choice, and his selection surprised the media. *Current Opinion* (Apr. 1921) described him as the "Dark Horse of the Harding Cabinet." A stunned Denby said he "was overwhelmed with surprise."

Not known for his intellectual prowess, Denby was respected for his dedication and commitment to the president and the Republican party. He supported a navy "equal to any other" in the world and promoted naval air power. A frugal administrator, Denby encouraged pay cuts to skilled laborers in shipyards to reduce costs while maintaining production of warships.

Denby's political career ended as a result of the Teapot Dome affair. He unwisely transferred the naval oil reserves to the Department of the Interior. Interior Secretary Albert Fall then leased the federal oil lands in Teapot Dome, Wyoming, and Elk Hills, California, to petroleum magnates Harry F. Sinclair and Edward Doheny for a personal consideration of nearly $400,000. A Senate investigating committee accused Denby of conspiring with Fall, Sinclair, and Doheny in the affair. Denby testified that his actions were taken in good faith with no improprieties on his part, because the transfers saved money by turning development over to the Department of the Interior. Denby believed that Fall's department was more experienced and better equipped to exploit the oil reserves. Furthermore, President Harding had approved the transfer on 26 May 1921.

Mounting hostility from Congress toward President Calvin Coolidge and investigations of the leasing eventually led to a Senate resolution requesting the resignation of the secretary of the navy. On 17 February 1924 Denby preempted the request in a letter to his commander in chief. His abdication, effective on 10 March 1924, saved the president any further embarrassment. Coolidge accepted his resignation "with the knowledge that your honesty and integrity have not been impugned."

On 28 February 1927 the Supreme Court held that Denby "took no active part in the negotiations and that Fall, acting collusively with Doheny, dominated the making of the contracts and leases." Furthermore, Senator Thomas James Walsh of Montana, head of the Senate investigation committee, acquitted Denby of any wrongdoing in the Teapot Dome affair. Denby left office to make his fortune in auto manufacturing, the banking business, and the law firm of Denby, Kennedy & O'Brien in Detroit, where he died of heart disease.

Denby was an indirect victim of partisan attacks against President Coolidge and Fall's rapacity. No evidence exists to suggest his complicity in the Teapot Dome affair. Denby had mediocre leadership abilities and never introduced farsighted naval policy as secretary. He was dedicated to his duties, however, and had unflagging commitment to the Republican party and the presidents he served.

• Denby's papers are located in the Burton Historical Collection in the Detroit Public Library. Secondary sources include Burl Noggle, *Teapot Dome: Oil and Politics in the 1920's* (1962); Robert K. Murray, *The Harding Era* (1969); William Allen White, *A Puritan in Babylon* (1938); Francis Russell, *The Shadow of Blooming Grove: Warren G. Harding in His Times* (1968); Donald R. McCoy, *Calvin Coolidge: The Quiet President* (1967); and Robert I. Vexler, *The Vice Presidents and Cabinet Members*, vol. 2 (1975), for prevalent information. Commentary on Denby's appointment and resignation is in "Denby, the Dark Horse of the Harding Cabinet," *Current Opinion*, Apr. 1921, pp. 471–73, and "Denby Out but Not Down," *Literary Digest*, Mar. 1924. An obituary is in the *New York Times*, 9 Feb. 1929.

JOHN KENT WIGGS

DENBY, Edwin Orr (4 Feb. 1903–12 July 1983), poet, dance critic, and actor, was born in Tientsin, China, the son of Charles Denby, Jr., an American diplomat, and Martha Orr. Denby lived in Austria and Detroit, Michigan, with his parents before attending Hotchkiss School in Connecticut, where he earned distinction as class poet. In 1919 he enrolled at Harvard University but left as a sophomore and went to England for a year. When he returned to the United States, he lived and worked on a farm in New Hampshire for five months, then tried Harvard once more before moving to Greenwich Village. He received no college degree. In 1923 Denby returned to Austria, where he underwent psychoanalysis for depression with Dr. Paul Federn, a colleague of Sigmund Freud's. With Federn's encouragement, Denby enrolled in 1925 at the Hellerau-Laxenburg School, where he earned a three-year degree in gymnastics and specialized in *Grotesktanz* (eccentric dancing). In 1929 he joined a German company known for its modern dance, the Hessisches Landestheater in Darmstadt, where he excelled as a comic dancer. There Denby performed satirical dances with the principal dancer, Cläre Eckstein, until 1934, when he felt the threat of Hitler's government. He taught dance and gymnastics in Switzerland before returning to the United States. In 1935, at the request of Orson Welles and John Housman, he adapted Eugène Labiche's farce, *Un Chapeau de Paille d'Italie*, for the stage. Titled *Horse Eats Hat*, the play was scored by Paul Bowles and performed in 1936 as a Works Progress Administration Federal Theater production. Afterward Denby embarked on a successful career as a dance critic.

As a critic Denby could draw on his own experience as a choreographer and dancer and, like poet-critics

Théophile Gautier and Stéphane Mallarmé, use his poetic faculties to describe in words what a dancer expresses in body movement. Denby's knowledge of the history of classical ballet, music, and theater also contributed to his understanding of a dancer's means of communication. Denby wrote about dance with a journalist's clarity and accuracy and a poet's subtlety and eye for detail. According to his friend, poet Frank O'Hara, for Denby, "attention equals life." In 1949 Denby outlined his standard for criticism in "The Critic." A critic, he wrote, should "appreciate in dancing the magic communal beat of rhythm and the civilized tradition of a personal and measured communication. I expect him to sharpen my perception sometimes to an overall effect, sometimes to a specific detail. I should not be surprised to find in some of his descriptions general ideas stimulating in themselves, even apart from his immediate subject, nor to find in other descriptions technical terms of dancing, of music, of painting or theater craft" (p. 416). Denby himself accomplished all these things.

He interpreted and evaluated in such meticulous detail the performances of famous dancers like Alicia Markova in *Giselle* that he gave readers of his reviews a system of criteria by which to judge and appreciate ballet. His descriptions of George Balanchine's choreographies made readers more sensitive viewers of dance performance. In his article "The Power of Poetry," published in *Looking at the Dance* (1968), Denby wrote about Balanchine's *Apollo*, "What you see on stage is strangely simple and clear. It begins modestly with effects derived from pantomime, a hint of birth pangs, a crying baby, a man dancing with a lute, and it becomes progressively a more and more directly classic dance ballet, the melodious lines and lyric or forceful climaxes of which are effects of dance continuity, dance rhythm and dance architecture" (p. 133).

Lincoln Kirstein, cofounder with Balanchine of the School for American Ballet, bestowed the highest praise on Denby when he equated the art of Denby's dance criticism with the art of the dance to which he was responding. Yet part of that art was Denby's focus on describing the visual performance at hand rather than on his own writing as an object of art. In "On Edwin Denby," Kirstein cited Denby's essay on Stravinsky and Balanchine's *Agon* (1957) as the best piece of dance criticism ever written. Denby's criticism enhanced the viewer's appreciation of a particular performance and the American public's appreciation of ballet in general. He wrote most of his dance criticism in a nine-year period, a time when both modern dance and ballet gained prominence and needed a proponent with Denby's talent for eloquent analysis. Denby wrote for *Modern Music* from 1936 to 1943 and, at the urging of his friend the composer Virgil Thomson, became dance critic for the New York *Herald Tribune* from 1942 to 1945. In 1945 Denby supplied the text to Alexey Brodovitch's 104 photographs collected in *Ballet*. Denby also freelanced for the *Nation, Hudson Review, Dance Magazine*, and other periodicals and newspapers. In 1948 he won a Guggenheim fellowship for dance criticism and in 1966 the Dance Magazine Award. His two books of criticism, *Looking at the Dance* (1949) and *Dancers, Buildings and People in the Streets* (1965), are considered primary sources for the history of ballet in the United States.

Though largely recognized for his dance criticism, Denby considered himself a poet first. When *Contemporary Poetry* asked him to describe his poetry, he said, "Theme: city. Form: sonnet." He used his keen visual memory to create portraits of New York City in poems appearing in *In Public, in Private* (1948) and later in *Snoring in New York* (1974). Denby's Proustian sonnets in *Mediterranean Cities* (1956), according to O'Hara, are deeper and stronger than the "Fulbright poems" of a typical American's experience in Europe. Denby expressed a Romantic sensibility in which sensitivity to environment leads to a blurring in the distinction between environment and writer. He won the Poets' Foundation Award in 1965.

In 1936 Denby began appearing in underground films, most of which were directed by his lifelong friend the photographer and filmmaker Rudolph Burckhardt. Their first film, *145 West 21* (1936), is also the address of the first apartment the two shared in New York. Denby appeared in ten other films, notably *Lurk* (codirected with Red Grooms in 1964) and *Money* (1967). Denby also wrote three opera librettos, one a collaboration with Aaron Copland, *The Second Hurricane* (1937).

Denby could withstand the deterioration of his body due to aging but not his mind. He committed suicide in New York City by taking an overdose of sleeping pills. His contribution to dance received further recognition with the publication in 1986 of *Dance Writings*. This collection includes more than 200 reviews and ten essays taken from the two earlier collections as well as previously unpublished work.

• The papers of Edwin Denby are held at the Detroit Public Library, Mich., in the Burton Historical Collection. For information on his life and career, see Denby's *Two Conversations with Edwin Denby* (1974); David Kaufman, "Denby on Dance: Angst and Beauty: The Life and Career of Dance Critic and Poet Edwin Denby," *Horizon*, July–Aug. 1987, pp. 38–40; Frank O'Hara's introduction to *Dancers, Buildings and People in the Streets* (1965); B. H. Haggin's introduction to the 1968 edition of *Looking at the Dance* (1949; repr., 1968); Lincoln Kirstein's "On Edwin Denby" and Ron Padgett's introduction, both published as part of Denby's *The Complete Poems* (1986); and William MacKay's "Edwin Denby, 1903–1983," in *Dance Writings*, pp. 11–34. Frank O'Hara discusses Denby's poetry in "The Poetry of Edwin Denby," first published in *Poetry* (Feb. 1957) and reprinted in *The Complete Poems*. Denby describes the role of the dance critic in "The Critic," an addendum to *Looking at the Dance*, pp. 410–18. For reminiscences of Denby by friends and colleagues, see the spring, summer, and fall 1984 issues of *Ballet Review* and the special Denby issue of *Mag City* 14 (1983), which includes an interview by Mark Hillringhouse. For additional poetry see *"C" Magazine* 1, no. 4 (Sept. 1963). An obituary is in *Ballet News* 5 (Oct. 1983): 30–31.

BARBARA L. CICCARELLI

DENEEN, Charles Samuel (4 May 1863–5 Feb. 1940), lawyer, governor of Illinois, and U.S. senator, was born in Edwardsville, Illinois, the son of Samuel H. Deneen, a professor of Latin and ancient history at McKendree College in Lebanon, Illinois, and Mary F. Ashley. Educated in local public schools during his formative years, Charles graduated from McKendree College in 1882. He taught in downstate schools and in Chicago prior to attending the Union College of Law (later Northwestern University School of Law) in Chicago, from which he graduated in 1888. He was admitted to the bar that same year but returned to teaching before entering the practice of law in 1890. In 1891 he married Bina Day Maloney; they had four children.

In 1892, with the support of William Lorimer, the "Blond Boss" of Chicago's westside Republicans, Deneen won election to the Illinois House of Representatives. After serving one term, he was named attorney for Chicago's sanitary district and in 1896 won election as state's attorney for Cook County. Reelected in 1900, Deneen gained wide notoriety for his vigorous prosecution. He won convictions against a state treasurer, prominent bankers, and several other well-known individuals. Meanwhile, he built a powerful political base and distanced himself from Lorimer and his machine. In Deneen's time, the office of state's attorney was funded by fees collected for the prosecution of cases, and he was accused by political opponents of overcharging. An Illinois Supreme Court investigation found no irregularities, and Deneen's political star continued to rise.

In 1904, after the Republican State Convention deadlocked for twenty-one days, Deneen emerged with the party's gubernatorial nomination on the fifty-eighth ballot. The stalemate ended after Republican governor Richard Yates threw his support to Deneen to keep an even more progressive candidate, U.S. representative Frank Lowden, from securing the nomination. During the campaign, Deneen allied himself with the progressive forces of President Theodore Roosevelt within the state and frequently found himself in conflict with archconservatives within his own party. After winning the general election by a wide margin, he brought about major reforms in Illinois state government. The management of the state's welfare institutions was consolidated and the employees placed under civil service. A State Highway Commission, with a salaried engineer, was created along with a state geological survey. A child labor law and improved provisions for workmen's compensation won approval in the legislature, and Deneen secured large increases in funding for education. He narrowly won reelection in 1908, defeating former U.S. vice president and postmaster general Adlai E. Stevenson. A tough, hard-nosed administrator, Deneen called out the National Guard to restore order following a race riot in Springfield in 1909. Working with the Illinois legislature, he secured the passage of Illinois's first statewide primary and the Presidential Preference Primary Law (1912), among the first such legislation enacted anywhere in the country. In 1912 he supported Roosevelt for the Republican presidential nomination, but he refused to abandon the Republican party and follow Roosevelt's Progressive "Bull Moose" party. The split among progressive Republicans and party loyalists cost Deneen a third term, and he was defeated by Edward F. Dunne, a progressive Democrat from Chicago.

A short, stocky, determined individual, Deneen set high ethical standards in a state where political chicanery was common. Although a progressive on many issues, he was not an idealist; he understood political realities and the need to compromise with party regulars. He was cautious and pragmatic, and in public he appeared cold and aloof. A straight-laced Methodist, he served nothing stronger than lemonade in Springfield's executive mansion, where he invited evangelist Billy Sunday to hold prayer meetings.

After losing his bid for a third term, Deneen returned to Chicago and his law practice. However, he remained active in state politics, and in 1924 he entered the Illinois senatorial primary against Republican senator Medill McCormick. Deneen's challenge to McCormick was supported by Chicago's powerful mayor, William Hale "Big Bill" Thompson, who hated McCormick for his excessively progressive policies. Deneen won the primary and the general election, and when McCormick died before the end of his term, Deneen was appointed to fill the vacancy in February 1925. In the Senate he supported the policies of President Calvin Coolidge and won respect for his integrity and knowledge of legal issues. In 1928 he returned to Illinois to lead a group of moderately progressive Republicans opposed to the reelection of Republican governor Len Small. Deneen's faction supported Louis L. Emmerson for governor and Judge John A. Swanson for Cook County state's attorney. During the bitter primary contest, known as the "pineapple primary," the homes of Deneen and Swanson were bombed. Deneen maintained that the bombings were the work of "organized and criminal classes of Chicago in their desperate efforts to retain control of the city and the county" (*Chicago Tribune*, 6 Feb. 1940). His faction was successful in both the primary and general elections. In 1930 Ruth Hanna McCormick, the widow of the former senator, defeated Deneen in the Republican primary, thereby denying him a second term in the U.S. Senate. He remained an energetic and vigorous backer of moderate, reform-minded Republicans, although his party had difficulty winning statewide races during the Great Depression of the 1930s. Nevertheless, speaking to fellow Republicans in Springfield in January 1940, the optimistic Deneen, now in his seventy-seventh year, stated, "We can win if we can get a good ticket that inspires confidence" (*Chicago Tribune*, 6 Feb. 1940). He died at his home in Chicago.

• The Illinois State Historical Library in Springfield holds the Charles Deneen Papers, including numerous printed speeches. For more information, see Robert P. Howard, "Charles Samuel Deneen," in *Mostly Good and Competent*

Men: Illinois Governors, 1818–1988 (1988), pp. 211–17; Robert P. Howard, *Illinois: A History of the Prairie State* (1972); Beth Blenz, ed., *Encyclopedia of Illinois* (1980); and *Blue Book of the State of Illinois* (1905–1932). An obituary is in the *Chicago Tribune*, 6 Feb. 1940.

MICHAEL J. DEVINE

DENHAM, Reginald (10 Jan. 1894–4 Feb. 1983), director, playwright, and actor, was born in London, England, the son of Harry Barton Denham, a government civil servant, and Emily Constance Chapman, a music teacher. He attended the City of London School from 1904 until 1911 and then studied music and singing with Cairns James at the Guildhall School of Music in 1913. He made his stage debut in 1913 as a walk-on in *Joseph and His Brethren* at His Majesty's Theatre. He then joined the Benson Shakespearean Repertory Company in 1914, with which he toured England until 1916. After leaving the company, Denham joined the Royal Irish Rifles, serving as a second lieutenant stationed at Clandeboye, Northern Ireland, until in May 1917 he was sent overseas and landed in the trenches just in time for Plumer's surprise attack on the Messines Ridge. He was then made a staff officer in the Tank Corps Cadet Battalion stationed near Winchester, where he trained cadets. He returned to the stage in 1919, appearing in relatively minor roles, such as Paris in *Romeo and Juliet*, Salanio in *The Merchant of Venice*, and Mishka in *The Government Inspector*. In 1922 *If Four Walls Told* appeared at the Comedy Theatre, the first play Denham directed in London. In 1920 he married Moyna MacGill, an actress; they divorced in 1925. The following year he married Lilian Oldland, an actress and playwright. Each marriage produced one child.

Between the end of World War I and 1940, Denham is said to have directed more than 200 plays in England, though his autobiography provides information on less than half that number. Among the plays were eleven classic dramas produced by the Oxford University Dramatic Society, of which he was made an honorary life member. They included *Heartbreak House, The Rivals, The Master Builder, She Stoops to Conquer* (all 1923–1924), *Peer Gynt,* (1925), and *The Tempest* (1927). At the end of the 1920s Denham solidified his reputation as a director of mystery and thriller plays and gained attention in the United States by directing *Rope* (1929), *Joseph Suss* (1930), and *Suspense* (1930) before their openings in New York.

In 1937 Denham began a long and fruitful relationship playwrighting with Edward Percy, and the two men coauthored many plays that Denham then directed. The first of these was *The Last Straw* (1937), followed by *Green Holly* (1938), *The Distant Hand* (1939), and *Ladies in Retirement* (1939). In 1940 Denham directed a play he wrote himself, *First Night*. He also directed two dozen films between 1933 and 1939, among them *The Village Squire* (Columbia, 1934) and *The Crimson Circle* (Du World, 1936).

In 1940 Denham shifted his home and his major activities to New York, though he continued to direct in England from time to time. He launched the new phase of his career with a New York revival of his most popular collaboration with Percy, *Ladies in Retirement*. During the 1940s Denham and Percy collaborated on several other plays, most of them directed by Denham in England, but in 1944 Denham began collaborating more frequently with actress and playwright Mary Orr, whom he married in 1947 (they had no children); he had divorced Oldland in 1946. During the next decade Denham and Orr wrote at least one production in New York or London every season, among them *Wallflower* (1944), *Dark Hammock* (1944), *Round Trip* (1945), *The Coral Snake* (1947), *The Platinum Set* (1950), and *Be Your Age* (1953). Denham and Orr also created more than 100 television scripts, including sixteen scripts for "Suspense" (CBS), and others for "The Schlitz Playhouse of the Air (CBS), "The Colgate Playhouse" (NBC), "The Boris Karloff Theatre," "Ellery Queen," and "Mr. and Mrs. North." Denham collaborated with Conrad Sutton Smith on *A Dash of Bitters*, presented in 1955 in Stockbridge, Massachusetts, and at the Margo Jones Theatre in Dallas. In 1951 Denham published his adaptations of three plays by the Spanish dramatist Alfonso Paso: *Recipe for a Crime, Blue Heaven,* and *Oh, Mama! No Papa!*, the last of which he directed at the Pasadena Playhouse in 1963.

Denham was particularly associated, as both a director and a playwright, with mystery and thriller drama, and he directed some of the best-known examples of this genre, among them Frederick Knott's *Dial "M" for Murder* (1952), Maxwell Anderson's *The Bad Seed* (1954), and Jack Roffey's *Hostile Witness* (1966). Other important productions that Denham directed during his later years include *Gramercy Ghost* (1951), *Sherlock Holmes* (1953), *Janus* (1955), *Hide and Seek* (1957), *A Mighty Man Is He* (1960), and *Once for the Asking* (1963). His last professional directing assignment was a 1969 production of George Bernard Shaw's *You Never Can Tell* at Washington University in St. Louis. He died in Englewood, New Jersey.

• Denham's published volume of his autobiography, *Stars in My Hair* (1958), covers most of his career. See also Mary Orr and Reginald Denham, *Footlights and Feathers* (1967), an account of their Australian and New Zealand theatrical tour in 1964. Obituaries are in the *New York Times*, 7 Feb. 1983, and *Variety*, 9 Feb. 1983.

MARVIN CARLSON

DENISON, Charles (1 Nov. 1845–10 Jan. 1909), physician, was born in Royalton, Vermont, the son of Joseph A. Denison and Eliza Skinner. Both his father and his grandfather were well-known physicians. He received his early education at the Academy in Royalton and the Kimball Union Academy in Meriden, New Hampshire, going on to Williams College, where he received a bachelor's degree in 1867. In 1869 he graduated as valedictorian from the Medical Department of the University of Vermont. He completed his studies in his initial specialties, diseases of the eye and surgery, in New York City.

In 1871 Denison settled in Hartford, Connecticut, where he served as the house surgeon of the Hartford City Hospital. A year later he realized that he had tuberculosis, the most dreaded disease and leading cause of death in nineteenth-century America.

In 1873 Denison moved to Denver, where in the restorative climate he quickly recovered his health. This led him to refocus his career on the study and treatment of tuberculosis. Enthusiastic about Colorado's climate, he became one of the state's most effective boosters; his book *Rocky Mountain Health Resorts* (1879) did much to attract tuberculosis sufferers to the state. Denison frequently extolled the healthful virtues of climate and altitude in works such as *Annual and Seasonal Climatic Maps* (1885), *Moisture and Dryness; or, The Analysis of Atmospheric Humidities in the United States* (1885), *The Climate of Colorado for Respiratory Diseases* (1898), and "How Does Colorado Climate Influence Tuberculosis?" in the October 1908 issue of the *Denver Medical Times*. He believed the beneficial effects he found in the mountains of Colorado were due to low humidity, "diathermacy" of the air, atmospheric electricity, increased ozone, and lessened atmospheric pressure; he claimed that the "altitude of approximate immunity from phthisis" was 6,000 feet. Denison was also fascinated by the therapeutic property of sunlight. In his will he established a prize of $10,000 every two years for an essay on "The Influence of the Sun's Rays on Health and Vital Functions."

Beyond his enthusiasm for the healing power of climate, Denison's research led him to believe as early as 1880—when most physicians still thought that tuberculosis was a hereditary disease—that the disease was communicable. After Robert Koch's 1882 discovery of the tubercle bacillus and 1890 discovery of tuberculin, which derived from cultures of tubercle bacilli and was used in the diagnosis and treatment of tuberculosis, Denison began treating patients with the new substance. In June 1891 he read his paper "Tuberculin: The Value and Limitation of Its Uses in Consumption" to the Colorado Medical Society, the first comprehensive report on tuberculin by an American physician.

Denison had a knack for inventing improvements on existing technology. His Denison stethoscope is described in a medical instrument catalog as having a hard rubber trumpet-shaped bell "inserted into fork and held by the patient about one inch in front of the open mouth, while the examiner makes forcible percussion." He also developed a spirometer, an emphysema jacket, an air inhaler and exhaler, a sleeping canopy to expose consumptives to fresh air, a rib cutter, a valvular empyema drainage tube, and a tuberculin syringe. His "sanitary cement-block house," designed for optimal ventilation, was exhibited as a model at the International Congress on Tuberculosis in Washington, D.C., in 1908. Denison also performed the first intubations of the larynx in diphtheria in 1887, and he devised new methods of withdrawing fluids from the middle ear and of immobilizing the hemithorax with adhesive plaster.

From 1873 to 1884 Denison treated 700 cases of tuberculosis. In 1883 he accepted the chair of diseases of the chest and of climatology at the University of Denver, retiring in 1895. He served as president of the Denver Medical Society in 1879 and as president of the American Climatological Association in 1890.

In 1877 Denison married Ella Strong; they had three children. After Denison's death in Denver, Ella Denison used her large inheritance to fund the building of the Henry S. Denison Research Laboratory (named for the Denisons' son and now known as the Denison Arts and Sciences Building) of the School of Medicine at the University of Colorado in Boulder. When the medical school moved to Denver, she donated a building for the Charles Denison, M.D., Memorial Library, along with a $50,000 trust fund.

• The Denison Memorial Library of the University of Colorado Health Sciences Center has a small collection of Denison's letters and personal effects, including a Denison stethoscope. Sally Davis and Betty Baldwin briefly discuss Denison's home and family life in *Denver Dwellings and Descendants* (1963). Florence Sabin provides an affectionate look at Denison in "The Contributions of Charles Denison and Henry Sewall to Medicine," *Science* 56 (1937): 357–64, originally an address she gave at the dedication of the Denison Library.

CARON SCHWARTZ ELLIS

DENISON, Mary Andrews (26 May 1826?–15 Oct. 1911), writer, was born in Cambridge, Massachusetts, the daughter of Thomas Franklin Andrews and Jerusha Robbins. There is little biographical information on Denison, and what exists is vague and sometimes contradictory. Sources do agree that she was educated in Boston schools. It appears that like many women writers of her period she first turned to writing to supplement a family income reduced by the death of her father. She married Charles Wheeler Denison in 1846, and his editorial connections to several periodicals were useful to her career. Shortly after their marriage, Charles Denison became assistant editor at the *Olive Branch*, a journal to which Mary Denison began to contribute and where she too worked as an editor.

In the 1840s Mary Denison contributed many short pieces to newspapers and magazines as well as writing longer works that were published separately, including *Edna Etheril* (a novel about a poor seamstress that includes a portrait of a noble and self-sacrificing doctor [1847]) and *Raphael Inglesse* (1848). *Home Pictures*, a collection of her journal pieces, was published by Harper's in 1853. In 1855 *What Not*, a second collection of her newspaper and magazine sketches, was published by Lippincott. It was reprinted in 1856 under the title *Orange Leaves* (perhaps the publisher's attempt to capitalize on the popularity of Fanny Fern's *Fern Leaves from Fanny's Portfolio*, the second series of which had been published in 1854). The publisher's preface to *Orange Leaves* boasted, "None excel her in throwing around everyday life a charm which elevates the seemingly commonplace." The collection includes a short essay titled "The Sacrifices and Recompense of Literary Life," in which Denison claims that writers persist because "the recompense of literary life is truly four-fold. It is to be remembered and cherished by thousands, whose mortal eyes you have never met. It is to be loved for sweet virtue's sake. It is to have your name spoken with tears by many, when the dust falls on your shroud. It is to build living monuments in grateful hearts that shall not crumble to decay but stand through eternity."

In 1853 Charles Denison was appointed U.S. consul to British Guiana, and for a few years the Denisons lived there. On their return in 1856 they moved to Buffalo, New York. Mary Denison continued to write both fiction and nonfiction, temperance tales and boys' adventures, books and short pieces aimed at juvenile and adult audiences, publishing in outlets as prestigious as the *Atlantic Monthly* and Harper's as well as with cheap book publishers like Ballou and Burdick. Most of her work was published under the name "Mrs. Mary A. Denison," but she also used "Clara Vance," "MAD," "N. I. Edson," and other variations of her name and initials. Although she wrote to appeal to public tastes, there were some issues explored in her work that seem to reflect strong beliefs. She consistently promoted the temperance cause (her husband worked for the National Prohibition party), wrote many "Sunday School" texts, and at least once wrote a strong condemnation of slavery, despite the risk of losing southern sales.

The *Boston Transcript* (17 Oct. 1911) obituary for Denison recalled, "Her fame was at its height at the time of the Civil War." One source of this fame may well have been her sensationalistic antislavery novel, *Old Hepsy* (1858). This tangled tale of incest, illegitimacy, miscegenation, and murder focuses on the responses of several women (including Hepsy, a manumitted slave who is 110 years of age as the novel opens, and Mabel Van Broek, a Quaker abolitionist) to slavery and its effect on the institution of the family, and especially on women's lives. The novel's incidents and characters stretch believability past the breaking point, but perhaps because it expressed some emotional truths about slavery or perhaps because of its sensational sex and violence, it was popular. The publisher claimed that in only two months 5,000 copies were sold.

The Denisons moved often in the 1850s and 1860s, spending time in Philadelphia and Washington, D.C., as well as some time in England, but eventually settled near Washington, D.C. Regardless of where she lived, Denison continued to write and publish. In 1877 she wrote what was perhaps her bestselling novel, *That Husband of Mine*. Said the *New-York Daily Times* reviewer (11 Aug. 1877), the novel's combination of "a worn out plot, bad grammar, slang expressions, and that disagreeable and too favorite American topic, the teeth, are not weighty enough to suppress the liveliness of this book, so strong are the animal spirits that bubble up through its pages." The book was a great success for Denison and the publishing firm of Lea

and Shephard. Sales of at least 300,000 copies are cited in discussions of her career. The plot concerns how one happily married couple manages (despite the husband's toothache) to eventually facilitate the marriage of some friends. Like a large number of her novels and stories, this one takes place in a safe and prosperous middle-class world. A sequel of sorts, *That Wife of Mine*, was published later in the year. It appears to have been based on a chapbook Denison published with a Toronto firm in 1872.

Although her publishing rate slowed, Denison continued to write and be published in the 1880s, and as late as 1895 a profile in the *Magazine of Poetry and Literary Review* reported her at work on a new book. She wrote poetry and plays in addition to prose works and words to accompany her husband's piano piece, "The Statesman's Dirge" (1852), dedicated to the family and friends of Daniel Webster. Although she did some nursing of the wounded during the Civil War and served as corresponding secretary for the League of American Penwomen, for the most part she is described as a woman who did not venture much into society. Nevertheless, her extremely varied output points to a lively imagination and a keen sense of the public's interests. Following the death of her husband in 1881, the childless Denison lived alone, primarily in Baltimore, Maryland. Her health declined in 1910, and she went to live with her brother, Dr. R. R. Andrews, in Cambridge, Massachusetts, where she died.

• A small number of items relating to Denison are in the Mary Edwards Walker Collection at Syracuse University. The entry on Denison in John S. Hart's *Manual of American Literature* (1873) summarizes her career to that date; additional information is available in brief entries on Denison in several nineteenth- and early twentieth-century biographical compilations, including the *National Cyclopedia of American Biography* (1893–), *Appletons' Cyclopedia of American Biography* (1888), and Allibone's *Critical Dictionary of English Literature* (1858). Her obituary in the *Boston Evening Transcript* is also helpful. Madeleine B. Stern discusses the confusion around her birth date in her bibliographic note at the end of the entry on Denison in *Notable American Women*, which also lists a number of short magazine profiles that appeared during Denison's lifetime. Denison's fiction is briefly discussed by Nina Baym in *Woman's Fiction*, 2d ed. (1993), and in several unpublished dissertations.

JoANN E. CASTAGNA

DENNETT, Mary Coffin Ware (4 Apr. 1872–25 July 1947), birth control and sex education reformer and pacifist, was born in Worcester, Massachusetts, the daughter of George Whitefield, a wool merchant, and Livonia Coffin Ware. When Dennett was ten her father died and the family moved to Boston, where she attended public schools and went on to Miss Capen's School for Girls in Northampton, Massachusetts. Dennett then studied at the school of the Boston Museum of Fine Arts, where she displayed a great talent for tapestry and leather design. From 1894 to 1897 she headed the Department of Design and Decoration at the Drexel Institute in Philadelphia. After a trip to Europe with her sister, during which they collected gilded Cordovan leather wall hangings, the sisters opened a handicraft shop in Boston. Dennett helped organize the Boston Society of Arts and Crafts in 1897. She served on the council of the society until 1905, when her interest in politics and social welfare began to supersede her interest in the arts. In 1900 she married William Hartley Dennett, a Boston architect with whom she had two sons. The marriage ended in divorce in 1913 with Dennett receiving custody of their children.

Dennett's political activism began in the suffrage movement in 1908. After serving two years as field secretary of the Massachusetts Women's Suffrage association, Dennett was elected corresponding secretary of the National American Women's Suffrage Association (NAWSA) in 1910. In 1915 Dennett resigned from NAWSA after becoming frustrated with the organization's political timidity, as her notions regarding social reform broadened. Her political courage can be measured by her pacifist activities once World War I began. Dennett was also active in the single tax movement and acted as chair of the Committee on New Voters of the Women's Henry George League. With the outbreak of World War I, Dennett became involved in the pacifist movement. To protest the entry of the United States into the war in 1917, she resigned as executive secretary of the Women's Section of the Democratic National Committee. She then became an organizer for the radical antiwar group, the People's Council, a board member of the Women's Peace Party, and a member of the Women's Peace Union and National Council of the International Free Trade League. She also served as the field secretary of the American Union Against Militarism. During the war, Dennett's commitment to civil liberties surfaced in the face of the government's harsh treatment of pacifists. This experience would shape her birth control work, encouraging her staunch dedication to individual rights.

Dennett's birth control work had begun when she helped to establish the National Birth Control League (NBCL) in March 1915. Dennett repudiated the militant tactics of birth control activist Margaret Sanger, who called for civil disobedience and class warfare, and instead focused on legislative reform to amend censorship laws. From 1917 to 1919 the NBCL lobbied the New York state legislature to remove birth control from the state censorship laws. Two frustrating years in Albany convinced Dennett that the federal obscenity law—the Comstock law of 1873—must be reformed to precipitate real social change, and she formed the Voluntary Parenthood League (VPL) in 1919 to work in the federal arena. Dennett served as director of the VPL and editor of its journal, the *Birth Control Herald*, from 1922 to 1925.

The VPL lobbied until 1926 for a bill that would exempt birth control information and materials from federal censorship laws. Dennett championed reforms on the grounds that "ignorance of scientific facts can never contribute to human progress, but knowledge and experience can. Liberty is dangerous, but anything less than liberty is even more dangerous" ("Liberty and Birth Control," n.d., box 36, MWD Papers). Dennett's appeal to scientific freedom and civil liberties was unique among birth control reformers. She spoke less about healthy mothers and babies than about the rights of citizens in a democratic republic.

As in New York, Dennett's efforts met with little success. In addition to a perceived lack of public demand, another reason for the VPL's failure was its rivalry with Sanger. In 1921 Sanger formed the American Birth Control League and in 1924 began working on her own federal reform campaign. Unlike Dennett's call for complete deregulation of birth control, Sanger's group attempted to pass a "doctors only" bill that would exempt physicians from birth control prohibitions. Dennett lost the support of many politicians and reformers and found it difficult to compete with her more popular and well-financed rival, who enjoyed the support of a powerful coalition of physicians.

By 1926 Dennett had abandoned lobbying, resigned as director of the VPL, and returned to her leather work. The "doctors only" position was popular in the birth control community and Dennett refused to compromise her principles, nor would she submit to Sanger's authority. She reappeared in the public eye in 1929, when she was indicted under the Comstock law for disseminating her pamphlet, "The Sex Side of Life." Written for her adolescent sons to explain human reproduction in plain terms, the pamphlet was published in 1918 and was widely distributed throughout the 1920s. In 1922 the Post Office declared it obscene and therefore unmailable, but Dennett continued her distribution. With the American Civil Liberties Union defending her, Dennett stood trial in 1928 and was convicted by the Federal District Court of Brooklyn. She refused to pay the $300 fine and appealed the conviction.

Dennett used the publicity from her trial to reintroduce her birth control work. She claimed she was being persecuted by the Post Office precisely because she had worked for so long to strip this body of its censorship power, not because of her sex education pamphlet. In 1930 Judge Augustus Hand of the U.S. Circuit Court of Appeals overturned her conviction and set an important legal precedent that took intent into account when evaluating obscenity. Dennett's trial was part of a series of decisions that eventually culminated in the 1936 ruling in *U.S. v. One Package*, which exempted birth control information and materials from obscenity laws when utilized by physicians. Dennett's trial reinforced her commitment to civil liberties and the connection between birth control and sex education. She was active for many years on the National Council on Freedom from Censorship and with the ACLU.

Dennett's emphasis on individual rights also shaped her reaction to the movement's tendency toward eugenic and racist rhetoric in the 1920s and 1930s. She expressed alarm at resolutions passed by various birth control groups to call upon countries to "limit their populations to their own resources." Dennett argued that any type of coercive policies represented "appalling paternalism as well as a shockingly unthinkable intrusion upon private life" ("Birth Control, War and Population," n.d., box 36, MWD Papers). Dennett supported birth control education but drew a distinction between spreading knowledge and dictating family size. She warned against eugenists who appealed to fears, "that the more prolific, undeveloped, unfit and dark-skinned peoples are sure to overwhelm the less prolific, highly civilized, more fit white skinned peoples" ("Birth Control, War, and Population"). Only international social and economic reform, not population control, Dennett contended, would solve the problems of less developed countries.

Dennett's political work revealed a sensitivity to personal freedom that was all but lost in the birth control movement as it developed an orientation toward population control. Her unique background in the peace movement and her personal experience with censorship made her wary of government power and protective of civil liberties. Dennett returned to leather work and peace activities in the 1930s and 1940s. She died in a nursing home in Valatie, New York.

• The Mary Ware Dennett Papers are collected at the Schlesinger Library, Radcliffe College, Cambridge, Mass. There is no full-length biography of Dennett, but biographies of Margaret Sanger and Sanger's autobiography include significant information on the years of rivalry between the two women. Dennett's three major works—Birth Control Laws (1926); her account of her trial, Who's Obscene? (1930); and The Sex Education of Children (1931)—provide insight into her reform strategies and evolving philosophy regarding obscenity and sex education. For more information on her obscenity trial, see the American Civil Liberties Union Archives at Princeton University. An obituary is in the New York Times 26 July 1947.

ROBYN L. ROSEN

DENNETT, Tyler Wilbur (13 June 1883–29 Dec. 1949), historian, government official, and college president, was born in Spencer, Wisconsin, the son of William Eugene Dennett, a Baptist preacher, and Roxena Tyler. He attended a small school in Pascaog, Rhode Island, where his parents moved shortly after he was born, and then the Friends School in Providence. His higher education included one year at Bates College in Maine and three years at Williams College in Massachusetts, where he was a scholarship student, edited the school paper, and played football.

After graduating with an A.B. in 1904, Dennett spent a year as secretary to the Reverend John H. Dennison, under whose influence he decided to enter Union Theological Seminary, graduating in 1908 with a B.D. After serving as a pastoral assistant in Washington, D.C., he worked in a Congregational mission in Seattle from 1909 to 1910 and for the Congregational church of Los Angeles from 1910 to 1914. In March 1911 he married Maybelle Raymond; they had four children.

In 1914 Dennett gave up his religious vocation to become a writer, although much of his writing and editing continued to be of a theological nature. Between 1915 and 1917 he edited the journal World Outlook. Following this, he was hired as publicity director for the Methodist Episcopal Missionary Centenary. Work for these two jobs took him to Asia twice, as a result of which he wrote a series of articles for the magazine Asia on the development of the region and its relationship to the United States. He argued that the United States was already heavily involved in Asia and that it was in the national interest to become more so. Many articles discuss the role and presence of missionaries in the region, publicizing their unglamorous but important work. These articles appear in collected form as The Democratic Movement in Asia (1918). For two years beginning in 1918, Dennett served as editorial secretary of the Inter-Church World Movement, during which time his second work, A Better World (1919), appeared.

In 1920 Dennett began work in the archives of the State Department, compiling reports on U.S. involvement in East Asia for the Washington Conference on the Limitations of Armaments in 1921–1922. Out of this work came Dennett's highly acclaimed third book, Americans in Eastern Asia (1922), a definitive study of nineteenth-century American policy in China, Japan, and Korea. It revealed for the first time the "Agreed Memorandum" between William Howard Taft and the then prime minister of Japan in which Theodore Roosevelt agreed to take responsibility for the maintenance of peace in the Far East, with the assistance of Japan and Great Britain. The books brought Dennett a reputation as a leading expert in U.S.–East Asian relations and earned him a lectureship in American history at Johns Hopkins University for the academic year 1922–1923. Johns Hopkins awarded him a Ph.D. in 1924. In the same year, he was appointed head of the division of publications and editor for the State Department. In this capacity he supervised the publication of American diplomatic correspondence during World War I, imparting to it a logic that earlier was often missing in government publications. Roosevelt and the Russo-Japanese War (1925) continued his narration of America's historical involvement in the Far East. Returning briefly to academia in 1927–1928, Dennett accepted a teaching post at Columbia University. The following year he gave up his position as editor for the State Department to become its historical adviser. In 1931 he was hired by Princeton University as professor of international relations in the School of Public and International Affairs.

After three years at Princeton, Dennett accepted the presidency of Williams College. In the first year of his tenure he radically revamped the college, which was then an expensive but academically weak school, catering more to the young aristocrat than the scholar. Dennett balanced the school's budget, raised the salaries of some teachers while weeding out others, reorganized both student government and the administrative system, and ended the daily chapel. His reforms and his stubborn personality evoked intense loyalty and affection in some but anger and alienation in others. One student described him: "He is human and sincere. He is caustic and inconsiderate. He is a real man." His biography of the former secretary of state John Hay, titled *John Hay: From Poetry to Politics*, was published in 1934 and won the Pulitzer prize for biography that same year.

Two separate incidents became focuses of dispute over Dennett's leadership. One was his refusal of federal funds for student scholarships made possible under the 1935 Federal Emergency Relief Administration because he believed that accepting the money would weaken the self-reliance of the student body. The second controversy erupted over his choice of words during a 1937 speech to alumni in Boston. By complaining that there were too many "nice boys" at Williams, Dennett intended to critique both the aristocratic air of culture that substituted for intellectual enthusiasm and the homogeneity of the student body. However, many interpreted the phrase as an unreasonable attack on well-bred young men who were being faulted for their upbringing and wealth. Conflict also developed between Dennett and the Williams board of trustees over the balance of power between president and board. Dennett resigned over these issues in July 1937.

After leaving Williams, Dennett returned to his earlier interest in the Far East, publishing articles on the region in leading periodicals, including the *American Historical Review* and the *American Journal of International Law*. He also taught in Australia and New Zealand as a Carnegie visiting lecturer in 1938–1939. He edited a volume of Hay's selected letters and journal entries, *Lincoln and the Civil War in the Diaries and Letters of John Hay* (1939), which covered the Civil War period when Hay served as Lincoln's private secretary. He died in Geneva, New York.

Dennett made significant contributions in all three major areas in which he worked. He was one of the first major scholars on U.S. policy in East Asia, and both of his books on the subject, but especially *Americans in East Asia*, became important texts in the field. Under his leadership, the publication division of the State Department was well run and produced unusually clear and well-organized publications. Finally, his leadership at Williams imparted to the college a new rigor in academic teaching, reorganized the administrative structure, and improved the faculty to an extent that prompted Howard Mumford Jones to comment in the *Atlantic Monthly* that teachers at Williams constituted the "liveliest college faculty" in New England.

• Dennett's papers are at Williams College. A biographical sketch is Richard M. Lovell, "Tyler Dennett—New England Frontiersman," *Sketch* (May 1939). For information on his influence at Williams, see Frederick Rudolph, *Perspectives: A Williams Anthology* (1983). For commentary on his work on East Asia, see Dorothy Borg, ed., *Historians and American*

Far Eastern Policy (1966), and Ernest R. May and James C. Thomson, Jr., eds., *American East Asian Relations: A Survey* (1972). An obituary is in the *New York Times*, 30 Dec. 1949.

ELIZABETH ZOE VICARY

DENNIE, Joseph (30 Aug. 1768–7 Jan. 1812), essayist, critic, and editor, was born in Boston, Massachusetts, the son of Joseph Dennie, a merchant, and Mary Green. To avoid the hostilities that threatened Boston, the family moved in 1775 to Lexington, Massachusetts, where they remained. In 1783 Dennie was sent back to Boston to prepare for a commercial career. After working for James Swan, Dennie went to live and study with the Reverend Samuel West of Needham, who prepared him for college. Dennie entered Harvard in 1787 as a sophomore; although suspended for the spring term in 1790 for insubordination to the tutors, he managed to graduate on time by continuing his studies with another minister in Groton. Soured by his collegiate experience, Dennie frequently denounced Harvard in both public and private writings.

With little aptitude or desire to follow his father into commerce, Dennie studied for the law with Benjamin West of Charlestown, New Hampshire. He did not pursue law, however, beyond one case in court and some small business in documents. In 1792 he turned his interests to literature and began to write a series of essays called "The Farrago," first in the *Morning Ray; or, Impartial Oracle*, a Windsor, Vermont, newspaper, then in 1793 in the *Eagle; or, Dartmouth Centinel*, located in Hanover, New Hampshire. With additional pieces appearing later in Dennie's own *Port Folio*, the series ended in 1802 with number twenty-nine. Typical is number eleven with its advice to the disappointed and defeated to drink and be merry.

In 1794 Dennie met Royall Tyler, who was practicing law across the Connecticut River from Charlestown in Guilford, Vermont. Both Federalists in politics and wits in literature, the two formed a partnership to contribute prose and poetry to newspapers under the rubric "From the Shop of Colon and Spondee." Dennie largely wrote prose (under the pen name Colon) and Tyler wrote poetry, although the attribution of individual pieces is sometimes difficult to make. This column and other writings secured Dennie's reputation as a stylist. After writing theatrical criticism for a Boston paper, the *Federal Orrery*, in early 1795, Dennie started his own magazine in Boston, the *Tablet*, in May of that year. The journal lasted thirteen weekly numbers and folded in August.

Moving his law practice and residence to Walpole, New Hampshire, Dennie began writing for a town newspaper, the *New Hampshire Journal; or, Farmer's Weekly Museum*. Drawing on service in 1792 as a lay reader for two churches, Dennie started a new essay series, "The Lay Preacher," in October 1795. Using a Bible passage as a beginning to each essay, Dennie's persona pursued political and cultural topics. His fervent opposition to democracy and its champions, such as Thomas Paine, led him in number five to denounce "he who jeers received truths, or who tells you that there is no distinction among men" as one whose "Favor is deceitful."

Dennie also acted as a paid editor of the *Museum* from 1796 until 1799. Through his selection of material and editorial comments, he established a reputation that spread throughout New England and beyond as an arbiter of taste. Citing Joseph Addison and Oliver Goldsmith as models, Dennie sought to reform American writing by a backward glance at eighteenth-century English prose. During his lifetime he earned the nickname of "the American Addison." Surrounding himself with other writers (many of whom were lawyers), including Tyler, his classmate Roger Vose, and Thomas G. Fessenden, Dennie became the center of a literary club that met at Crafts Tavern in Walpole.

After an unsuccessful run for Congress in 1798 and financial trouble at the *Farmer's Museum*, Dennie, a lifelong bachelor, moved to Philadelphia in 1799 to serve as private secretary to Timothy Pickering, the secretary of state, but lost his job when Pickering left the cabinet in May 1800. Dennie also became involved as writer and editor for the *Gazette of the United States*, a Federalist paper in Philadelphia. A staunch partisan, he deplored in print the growing popularity of Thomas Jefferson, whose election, he feared, would bring in French revolutionary principles and lead to the end of the class of "gentlemen" to which Dennie belonged.

Despite his serious doubts about the fate of the country, Dennie began in 1801 the work that would make him famous in his time. In January of that year he published the inaugural issue of *Port Folio*, which became under his guidance the most influential and longest-lasting literary journal of its time. Styling himself Oliver Oldschool, Esq., Dennie used the magazine to praise Goldsmith-like "simplicity" in style and to express contempt for the language of common people and their leader Jefferson. In 1803 he found himself named in a suit for sedition (he was eventually acquitted) when he printed an antidemocratic prediction of civil war. Although deliberately out of step with his times, Dennie nonetheless stayed in print by cultivating a theory of taste that appealed to a continuing Anglophilia among the literary elite.

Despite his constant criticism of American writers for their bad verse and prose, Dennie still encouraged or championed a number of writers who did not share his politics, including Joel Barlow, Charles Brockden Brown, and Philip Freneau. He seems to have exerted a strong influence on Washington Irving, whose attempt to be an English man of letters in America proved more successful than Dennie's. His friends and contributors during the *Port Folio* period included men who would have distinguished careers: John Quincy Adams, Nicholas Biddle, and British poet Thomas Moore. A stickler for style, he set a pattern for literary influence as editor and critic that would be followed by Edgar Allan Poe. Though combative, even ruthless in print, Dennie belonged to a circle of people

(Philadelphia's Tuesday Club) who valued his friendship and taste and who mourned his loss.

Dennie's career throughout his adult life was compromised by ill health. While remaining the nominal editor of *Port Folio* until 1812, he did little actual work during 1811. He appears to have suffered from tuberculosis; testimony from playwright William Dunlap and from Biddle suggests also that he became a heavy drinker during his last year. However, he was apparently lucid into his last hours and died in Philadelphia. His critical influence would last for another generation, but his writings have not earned for Dennie the fame he once openly courted.

• The largest collection of Dennie manuscripts and letters is at Houghton Library, Harvard; the Massachusetts Historical Society also has letters. Selections from his correspondence are in *The Letters of Joseph Dennie, 1768–1812,* ed. Laura Green Pedder (1936). Some of his essays were printed in book form as *The Lay Preacher; or, Short Sermons for Idle Readers* (1796); a modern collection of this series is available in Harold Milton Ellis, ed., *The Lay Preacher* (1943). The "Farrago" series was not printed as a book in Dennie's lifetime, but extant pieces have been collected as *The Farrago,* ed. Bruce Granger (1985). A parody of literary criticism from *Port Folio* is attributed to Dennie and reprinted by Harrison T. Meserole in "'A Kind of Burr': Colonial New England's Heritage of Wit," in *American Literature: The New England Heritage,* ed. James Nagel and Richard Astro (1981). The best biographical source is Harold Milton Ellis, *Joseph Dennie and His Circle: A Study in American Literature from 1792 to 1812* (1915). The best of the specialized articles on him include Randolph C. Randall, "Authors of the *Port Folio* as Revealed by the Hall Files," *American Literature* 11 (1940): 379–416; Randall, "Joseph Dennie's Literary Attitudes in the *Port Folio,*" in *Essays Mostly on Periodical Publishing in America,* ed. James Woodress (1973); Lewis Leary, "Joseph Dennie on Benjamin Franklin: A Note on Early American Literary Criticism," *Pennsylvania Magazine of History and Biography* 72 (1948): 240–46; Leary, "The Literary Opinions of Joseph Dennie," in *Soundings: Some Early American Writers* (1975); and Granger's "Joseph Dennie," in his *American Essay Serials from Franklin to Irving* (1978).

Obituaries are in the Philadelphia *American Daily Advertiser,* 9 Jan. 1812, and *Port Folio,* Feb. 1812. Biddle left a manuscript description of Dennie's last year and death that was published by Thomas P. Govan as "The Death of Joseph Dennie: A Memoir by Nicholas Biddle," *Pennsylvania Magazine of History and Biography* 75 (1951): 36–46.

JEFFREY H. RICHARDS

DENNIS, Alfred Lewis Pinneo (21 May 1874–14 Nov. 1930), historian, was born in Beirut, Syria (now in Lebanon), the son of James Shepard Dennis and Mary Elizabeth Pinneo, missionaries. Alfred spent most of his youth in Beirut, where his father was president of the Presbyterian Theological Seminary. He acquired an active interest in international affairs even before he attended college. After graduating from Princeton in 1896 he continued his study of modern history and diplomacy at Heidelberg College and Harvard and Columbia universities. In 1899 he married Mary Boardman Cable; they had two daughters. In 1901 Dennis earned his Ph.D. from Columbia and published his dissertation *Eastern Problems at the Close of the Eighteenth Century*; that year he also became an instructor in history at Bowdoin College. Dennis's rapid advancement at Bowdoin from instructor to full professor of history and political science by 1904 presaged a successful career as an academic. He became associate professor of history at the University of Chicago in 1904 and took a lectureship in history at Harvard for one semester the next year, temporarily replacing his friend and mentor Archibald Cary Coolidge, who was on leave. He spent his longest period in academia at the University of Wisconsin, where he became professor of history in 1906; for a time he served as chair of his department (exact dates unknown).

During his tenure at the University of Wisconsin, Dennis found himself, along with many of his fellow academics, drawn to Washington, D.C., and into the American effort in World War I. The declaration of war brought out both his patriotism and his interests in international relations and contemporary affairs. Fearing for American national security, he lobbied for acts that would establish national and state councils of defense even before U.S. entry into the war. Dennis hoped these councils would enhance U.S. preparedness for war. After congressional approval of these acts, Dennis served in 1917 as temporary secretary of the Wisconsin State Council of Defense. A year later he worked for the Military Intelligence Division of the U.S. Army general staff, holding the rank of captain. By the end of the war Dennis was assistant military attaché with the American embassy in London, reporting often to the Paris Peace Conference of 1919. His work throughout this period earned him the British Military Cross.

In 1920 Dennis left the University of Wisconsin in order to devote himself more fully to research and writing. As the titles of his works demonstrate, he retained his keen interest in contemporary affairs through the end of his life. In 1923 he published *The Anglo-Japanese Alliance*, written originally for use by the diplomats at the Washington Conference; that same year he became professor of modern history at Clark University in Worcester, Massachusetts. At Clark Dennis taught alternate semesters in order to preserve time for his research. Aside from occasional public lectures on current international affairs, including one given in 1925 to the Foreign Policy Association on developments in the Soviet Union, he worked single-mindedly on his scholarship. He contributed frequently to the *American Historical Review* and other journals, and during this period he published *The Foreign Policies of Soviet Russia* (1924), *Adventures in American Diplomacy, 1896–1906* (1928), and "John Hay," a biography in the series edited by Samuel F. Bemis, *The American Secretaries of State and Their Diplomacy* (1929). His success in finding unused historical sources made *Adventures in American Diplomacy* his most important work; it relied partly on previously unpublished documents from the State Department.

In all of his published works, Dennis drew not only on his abilities as a historian but on his international experience and his many acquaintances in the diplomatic world, particularly in Britain. In *Adventures in American Diplomacy*, dedicated to Harold W. V. Temperley of Cambridge University, he specifically acknowledged his many British friends. Yet his many connections never tempted Dennis away from his overriding purpose: scholarly and historical research in international relations and diplomacy. During his last years he began work on a study of British history from 1880 to the 1920s, which he hoped would become his magnum opus. By the time he died the first volume was almost complete, and the second was well under way. It was Dennis's driving insistence on completing this work that ultimately led to his illness in London during the last year of his life. He was forced to return to Worcester, where he died.

Dennis was one of the leading American historians of modern history and international relations. In the 1920s he was prescient about America's inability to continue its policy of isolationism from European affairs. Several years before he died he wrote that America "was apt to thank God for the Atlantic Ocean, which she imagined was a barrier against the old world and its troubles. Yet that ocean was not a barrier but a highway" (*Adventures in American Diplomacy*, p. 4).

• The Alfred Lewis Pinneo Dennis Papers are in the Clark University Archives in Worcester, Mass. The papers include Dennis's correspondence and typescripts of documents (1896–1906) relating to *Adventures in American Diplomacy*, his biography of John Hay, and his unfinished work on British politics. The papers also include transcripts of the sessions on Soviet foreign policy chaired by Dennis at the Williamstown (Mass.) Institute of Politics (1922), among other material. See also Mary Cable Dennis, *The Tail of the Comet* (1937). Obituaries are in the *New York Times*, 15 Nov. 1930; the *American Historical Review* 36 (Jan. 1931); the *Journal of Modern History* 3 (Mar. 1931); and the *Slavonic and Eastern European Review* (June 1931).

EMILY B. HILL

DENNIS, Eugene (10 Aug. 1905–31 Jan. 1961), American Communist party leader, was born in Seattle, Washington, as Francis X. Waldron, Jr.; he was to adopt the name he came to be known by in 1935. His father, the son of Irish immigrants, gave his son his own name but little else. The senior Waldron was a railroad worker and ne'er-do-well investor who drank heavily. Dennis's mother, Nora Veigs, of Norwegian immigrant stock, died when he was eleven. Dennis attended the University of Washington for a single semester, dropping out to support himself.

Seattle in the years of Dennis's childhood and adolescence had a rich working-class radical subculture, centered in the city's port and along its skid row. Dennis was fascinated by the labor organizers he met from the Industrial Workers of the World (IWW). The IWW had been weakened by wartime and postwar repression. A new organization created in 1919, the Communist party, laid claim to the spirit of the revolutionary militance of the IWW and attracted some of its former members. In 1926, at age twenty-one, Dennis joined the party. In 1927 Dennis moved to Los Angeles, where he became the party's educational director for southern California. In 1928, at a "Marxist summer school" he was directing for the party, he met his wife Peggy Carson. Although Peggy and Eugene Dennis were never legally married, they remained together for more than thirty years and had two sons.

As an organizer for the Trade Union Unity League (the party's vehicle for establishing a new revolutionary labor federation in the late 1920s and early 1930s), Dennis engineered a strike of 10,000 Mexican and Filipino lettuce pickers in the Imperial Valley of California in January 1930. The strike was broken, and Dennis was arrested and then beaten in his jail cell. He was arrested and beaten again that March after an unemployment demonstration in Los Angeles. In April a grand jury in the Imperial Valley indicted Dennis, along with sixteen others, for "criminal syndicalism" for their role in January's strike. To avoid imprisonment, Dennis fled to the Soviet Union.

For the next five years Dennis worked for the Communist International, serving as an underground courier in the Philippines, South Africa, and China. Peggy Dennis joined her husband in Moscow in 1931, with their young son. In 1935 the Dennises returned to the United States, but without their son; that he only spoke Russian was deemed a potential political embarrassment, since it raised questions about Dennis's political background at a time when the American Communist movement was stressing its indigenous roots.

It was on his return to the United States in 1935 that Francis Waldron used the pseudonym Eugene Dennis. (It was common in the Communist party for members to adopt a party name.) Dennis became state secretary of the Wisconsin Communist party. Later, after six months in Moscow in 1937 as the American representative to the Communist International, Dennis returned to the United States again, this time as a member of the party's ruling political committee in New York City. Dennis became a close ally of party general secretary Earl Browder, supporting his Popular Front policies against the criticisms of Browder's rival, party chairman William Z. Foster. Under the Popular Front, the Communists downplayed their revolutionary ideology and worked instead to create coalitions among all groups willing to oppose the spread of fascism.

The signing of the Nazi-Soviet pact in 1939 signaled a change in American Communist policies. The Communists became bitter critics of Franklin D. Roosevelt's efforts to aid Great Britain's fight against the Nazis. Dennis went underground once again, as part of an attempt to safeguard the party leadership. In June 1941 Eugene and Peggy Dennis were back in Moscow, but within weeks of their arrival the Nazis invaded the Soviet Union. They immediately returned to the United States, and Dennis resumed his post as a national leader.

In 1945 Earl Browder was denounced by the Communists on orders from Moscow for his wartime "revisionism" (including his decision to replace the party with a more loosely structured "political association"). Foster, Browder's longtime critic, was vindicated. Despite his close association with Browder, Dennis was appointed to the post of general secretary. Though his own political inclinations lay with the Popular Front politics of the 1930s, in the end he went along with Foster's more militant political stance. The Communists once again decided to go it alone, breaking with temporary allies. The new policies culminated in the decision to launch the ill-fated Progressive party campaign in 1948.

The Cold War brought a series of legal attacks on the Communist party. Dennis was a prime target. In 1947 he was convicted for contempt of Congress for refusing to answer questions before the House Un-American Activities Committee. In 1948 he was one of twelve top party leaders indicted for violation of the Smith Act, which made it a crime to conspire to teach or advocate the overthrow of the government. After a stormy trial, Dennis and the others were convicted in 1949. The case, known as *Dennis et al. v. U.S.*, was appealed to the Supreme Court, but in 1951 the Court upheld the verdict. Dennis was sent to the Atlanta penitentiary, where he served a five-year sentence.

After his release from prison, Dennis resumed party leadership. He called for a "new look" at the party's past failures. The revelation that Soviet premier Nikita Khrushchev made a "secret speech" in February 1956 denouncing his predecessor Joseph Stalin as a bloody tyrant seemed at first to strengthen the hand of would-be party reformers, like Dennis, against die-hard supporters of orthodoxy, like Foster. But the Soviet suppression of the Hungarian revolution in November 1956 swung the balance against the reformers. Once more the issue within the party became "defense of the Soviet Union." Dennis endorsed the invasion and made his peace with Foster. The party itself was decimated by the "de-Stalinization crisis," retaining only a few thousand members by 1958. Dennis was replaced as general secretary in 1959 by Gus Hall but held onto the largely honorary post of party chairman until his death in New York City.

• The papers of Eugene and Peggy Dennis are deposited at the State Historical Society of Wisconsin in Madison. Except for articles in the party press, Dennis left behind no written works. Peggy Dennis wrote *The Autobiography of an American Communist* (1977), an essential source on Dennis's life. Other books that deal with aspects of Dennis's life include Harvey Klehr, *The Heyday of American Communism: The Depression Decade* (1984), Joseph Starobin, *American Communism in Crisis, 1943–1957* (1972), and Maurice Isserman, *Which Side Were You On? The American Communist Party during the Second World War* (1982). A documentary film by Eric Stange, *Love in the Cold War* (1992), chronicles the marriage of Eugene and Peggy Dennis.

MAURICE ISSERMAN

DENNIS, Frederic Shepard (17 Apr. 1850–8 Mar. 1934), physician and surgeon, was born in Newark, New Jersey, the son of Alfred Lewis Dennis, president of the New Jersey Railroad and Transportation Company, and Eliza Shepard. After attending the Winchester Institute in Winchester, Connecticut, and Phillips Academy in Andover, Massachusetts, Dennis took his A.B. degree from Yale College in 1872. He next attended the Bellevue Hospital Medical College, from which he received his M.D. in 1874. In contrast to his lackluster academic record at Yale, Dennis was valedictorian at Bellevue. During 1876 and 1877 he completed work for a second medical degree, this time granted by the Royal College of Surgeons in London. Before returning to New York City he toured several European clinics and laboratories, including visits to Joseph Lister, who taught him the theory and techniques of antiseptic surgery, and to Louis Pasteur, who introduced him to the nascent germ theory of disease. Dennis married Fannie Rockwell on 5 February 1880; they had no children.

After returning to the United States Dennis established a private practice and also served as a surgeon at Bellevue Hospital and an instructor at the Bellevue Hospital Medical College. Listerian antisepsis had been introduced into the United States in 1867, but even a decade later its acceptance was incomplete; this was especially so at the Bellevue Hospital. "Its wards were redolent of the atmosphere of sepsis," wrote David Bryson Delavan, who was with Dennis at Bellevue, "the neighborhood reeked with an ill savor wafted far around" (p. xix). Dennis's training with Lister and Pasteur had convinced him not only of the efficacy of antisepsis but also of the truth of the germ theory. He pioneered (but did not—as later biographers would claim—introduce) antisepsis in the United States. His sound surgical results slowly convinced his surgical elders at Bellevue, such as James R. Wood and Austin Flint, Sr.; through years of lecturing and writing he also indoctrinated the next generation of surgeons. As professor of the principles and practice of surgery at Bellevue, he lectured often and well. William J. Mayo, one of his pupils, later observed that Dennis's clear distinction in both classroom and article "between the surgeon and the operator" contributed greatly to the progress of surgery. "Surgery is more a matter of mental grasp," Mayo continued, "than it is of handicraftmanship. I think all of us who have worked years in the profession understand that many very skillful operators are not good surgeons" (p. xvi). Some of Dennis's lectures were reprinted in the *Medical Record* (New York) and the *Journal of the American Medical Association*. Besides his work on antiseptic surgery, he advanced surgical technique for procedures such as the suprapubic lithotomy, amputation, and hernia; this work too was published in numerous articles. Contemporaries such as Samuel D. Gross praised the originality of his work, and other readers noted his use of statistics, then fairly uncommon. He contributed to *An American Text-book of Surgery* (ed. W. W. Keen and J. W. White, 1892, 1895). His own *System of Surgery* appeared in four volumes in 1895 and 1896, and *Selected Surgical Papers* (1934) was published posthumously in two volumes. He also wrote *The History and Development of Surgery during the Past Century* (1928).

Several notable physicians were associated with Dennis. He promoted William Henry Welch, whom he had known since preparatory school in Connecticut, for an instructorship at the Bellevue Hospital Medical College. An offer of the professorship of pathology at the newly founded Johns Hopkins University tempted Welch, who always preferred pathological research over clinical practice; to entice him to remain in New York, Dennis obtained a $50,000 donation from Andrew Carnegie to endow a physiological laboratory at Bellevue. Welch directed it for a year but left anyway in 1885 for Baltimore, and thereby ended their friendship. Dennis and Edward G. Janeway then assumed the directorship of the laboratory, which was among the first in the United States devoted to physiological research. Hermann Biggs, later known for his public health work in New York City, was another of Dennis's students. In the fall of 1885 four children in New Jersey were bitten by a presumably rabid dog. Dennis, knowing about Pasteur's newly developed rabies vaccine and using funds he obtained from Carnegie, had Biggs accompany the children to France for successful treatment overseen by Pasteur himself.

Dennis was additionally a surgeon at St. Vincent's Hospital and on the house staff of several other New York City area and Connecticut hospitals. He was professor of surgery at Bellevue Hospital Medical College from 1883 to 1898, and chair of clinical surgery at Cornell Medical College from 1898 until his retirement in 1910. He was also one of the founders of the Harlem Hospital.

Dennis played an active role in medical and surgical professional societies. He was a member of the New York Academy of Medicine, and a fellow of the American College of Surgeons and of the American Surgical Association, whose president he was in 1894. Foreign medical societies also honored him: he was elected to the Clinical Society of London, the German Congress of Surgeons, and in 1889 he became one of the first Americans to be made a fellow of the Royal College of Surgeons in London.

In addition to his New York City residence, Dennis had a house in Norfolk, Connecticut, and was active in that town's affairs. He and his wife organized the Norfolk Agricultural Society and in 1917 he published *The Norfolk Village Green*, which described the older houses of the town. He was proud of his achievements as a gardener, landscaper, and fancier and breeder of fine horses. He died in New York City.

David Bryson Delavan, a lifelong colleague and friend, summed up Dennis's character: "Possessed of excellent taste, a deeply affectionate nature, and a rarely beautiful character, his influence was uplifting and eminently helpful. . . . He was at once the accomplished man of society, the old-time gentleman and, before all, the true physician" (pp. xxiii–xxiv).

• Dennis's papers are at the New York Academy of Medicine. An excellent example of Dennis's advocacy of Listerism and his teaching style is "Some Practical Hints Upon the Technique of an Aseptic Surgical Technique," *Journal of the American Medical Association* (1886): 187–203; see also his *System of Surgery* (4 vols., 1895–1896) and *Selected Surgical Papers* (2 vols., 1934). William J. Mayo wrote the foreword to the latter, and David Bryson Delavan contributed "Frederic Shepard Dennis: An Appreciation" (vol. 1, pp. xvii–xxiv).

Dennis's friendship with Welch is described in Simon Flexner and James Thomas Flexner, *William Henry Welch and the Heroic Age of American Medicine* (1941, repr. 1993); on Biggs see C.-E. A. Winslow, "The Contribution of Hermann Biggs to Public Health," *American Review of Tuberculosis* 20 (1929): 1–28. The role of physiological laboratories in the development of medical science in America is narrated in W. Bruce Fye, *The Development of American Physiology: Scientific Medicine in the Nineteenth Century* (1987). The impact of antiseptic surgery and the germ theory is examined in Charles E. Rosenberg, *The Care of Strangers: The Rise of America's Hospital System* (1987). An obituary by William Mayo appeared in *Collected Papers of the Mayo Clinic* 26 (1935): 26; other obituaries are in *Proceedings of the Connecticut Medical Society* 142 (1934): 26, and *Transactions of the American Surgical Association* 52 (1934): 559.

THOMAS P. GARIEPY

DENNIS, Lawrence (25 Dec. 1893?–20 Aug. 1977), diplomat and far-right author, was born in Atlanta, Georgia, the son of Sallie Montgomery. Nothing is known of his biological father. His mother, however, was an African American, and Dennis was of mixed race parentage. In 1897 he was adopted by Green Dennis, a contractor, and Cornelia Walker. During his youth Dennis was known as the "mulatto child evangelist," and he preached to church congregations in the African-American community of Atlanta before he was five years old. By the age of fifteen he had toured churches throughout the United States and England and addressed hundreds of thousands of people.

Despite his success as an evangelist Dennis had ambitions to move beyond this evangelical milieu. In 1913, unschooled but unquestionably bright, he applied to Phillips Exeter Academy and gained admission. He graduated within two years and in 1915 entered Harvard University.

Dennis's decisions to attend these schools were more than steps away from his evangelical career. Born into the African-American world of the South, he now "passed" into white America and constructed a new racial identity for himself. By becoming "white" he opened up opportunities previously beyond his reach.

Dennis availed himself of these opportunities almost immediately. As a student he received military training and during World War One served as a first lieutenant in France. After the war he graduated from Harvard and in 1921 entered the U.S. Foreign Service. He served in Haiti, Romania, Honduras, and Nicaragua. His most notable assignment was in 1926 as chargé d'affaires in Nicaragua, where he presided over a peace conference between warring liberals and conservatives. Dennis resigned his position in 1927 and joined J. W. Seligman and Company, a banking firm, to be its representative in Peru.

In 1930, as the depression deepened, Dennis left the world of international finance and was soon writing articles and commenting in public forums on American foreign and economic policy. His earliest articles criticized American interventionism in Latin America. In his first book, *Is Capitalism Doomed?* (1932), he broadened his scope to analyze the sustainability of the American economy. He criticized businesspeople as incapable of providing the spiritual leadership needed to reinvigorate a now moribund capitalism, and he called on the state to find a solution to unemployment.

While the election of Franklin Roosevelt in 1932 mollified many Americans, Dennis condemned what he called the "planless Roosevelt revolution." In 1933 he became associate editor of the *Awakener*, a right-wing semimonthly publication, and entered the camp of far-right critics of the New Deal. By 1936, with the publication of his book *The Coming American Fascism*, Dennis made his reputation as a theorist of "fascism," or what he called an "authoritarian executive state." He believed that Americans would either descend into chaos with the depression or select some form of "totalitarian" system, such as communism or fascism. Liberalism had failed and fascism was the only likely and desirable choice for Americans. In 1933 Dennis married Eleanor Simson; they had two daughters before divorcing in 1957.

Dennis left the *Awakener* in 1935 and joined E. A. Pierce and Company, a New York brokerage firm, as an economist. Along with a partner in the firm, he traveled to Europe, where he met Adolf Hitler and Benito Mussolini. He then traveled around the United States for the company, speaking on political and financial issues to groups of businesspeople, where he established a reputation as an expert on these matters. He left his position in 1938 to publish his own subscription newsletter, the *Weekly Foreign Letter*.

In his newsletter Dennis gave investment advice and analyzed world political developments and American policy options. Dennis never sympathized with the ideology of nazism nor with anti-Semitism in his writings. He did, however, fight against American involvement in Europe. He denounced intervention as part of a "religious" war waged for an ideology of "internationalism." An outspoken isolationist, he found himself censured in 1941 by Secretary of the Interior Harold Ickes as an appeaser and "the brains of American fascism."

Dennis published his most ambitious book, *The Dynamics of War and Revolution*, in 1940. No longer using the controversial term "Fascist," he now argued that a "Socialist" world revolution was occurring and that democracies suffering from historical stagnation would "go Socialist." This would happen in the United States, he suggested, in the process of fighting a futile war against Germany, Italy, and Japan.

Dennis achieved a new level of intellectual respectability with this book, which was widely reviewed in political and academic journals. Yet with the outbreak of war, Dennis found that his reputation as an advocate for fascism and isolationism created serious legal problems. The army denied him a commission and considered removing him from the East Coast for security reasons. The postmaster general banned *The Dynamics of War and Revolution* from the mail, and in early 1944 the Justice Department charged Dennis and twenty-nine codefendants with sedition.

The charge against Dennis, conspiring with the Nazis to cause insubordination in the military, could not be sustained by the prosecution. The so-called Mass Sedition Trial ended after seven months, when the presiding judge died of a heart attack, and by 1947 the indictments were dismissed. In 1946 Dennis coauthored a scathing account of the episode, *A Trial on Trial: The Great Sedition Trial of 1944.*

The trial and Dennis's identification as "America's Number One Fascist" made him a political pariah. After World War II he retired to his Becket, Massachusetts, farm, where he resumed publication of his newsletter, renamed the *Appeal to Reason.* Though he was outspokenly hostile to communism, Dennis continued to endorse isolationism. He opposed Cold War confrontations in Korea and Vietnam and condemned political persecution in the guise of McCarthyism. In 1959 or 1960 he married Dora Shuser Burton; they had no children. Dennis published one last book, *Operational Thinking for Survival*, in 1968 and continued to publish the *Appeal* until 1972.

Though Dennis died in obscurity in Spring Valley, New York, he made his mark in the interwar years as a critic of liberalism and an outspoken isolationist. His criticism of liberal capitalism was often incisive. His advocacy of authoritarianism, however, made him an object of political derision and repression. He ended his life a political outcast.

• Dennis's papers are held by the Hoover Institution. His oral history, "The Reminiscences of Lawrence Dennis" (1967), is available on microfiche in the Oral History Research Office, Columbia University. Dennis's autobiography, written at age ten, *Life-Story of the Child Evangelist Lonnie Lawrence Dennis* (n.d.), is essential for information on his youth. For a list of Dennis's articles see Dennis, *A Trial on Trial*, pp. 447–48. An unpublished paper, Steven Leikin, "The Strange Career of Lawrence Dennis: Race and Far-Right Politics during the Great Depression," delivered at the Dec. 1995 meeting of the American Historical Association, has important information on his background, childhood, and thought during the 1930s. A number of sources deal with specific aspects of his life and thought during the 1930s, the 1940s, and the Cold War, including Leo Ribuffo, *The Old Christian Right: The Protestant Far Right from the Great Depression to the Cold War* (1983); Ronald Radosh, *Prophets on the Right* (1975); Justus Doenecke, "Lawrence Dennis: Revisionist of the Cold War," *Wisconsin Magazine of History*, Summer 1972, pp. 275–86; and Arthur M. Schlesinger, Jr., *The Politics of Upheaval* (1960). An obituary is in the *New York Times*, 21 Aug. 1977.

STEVEN LEIKIN

DENNISON, David Mathias (26 Apr. 1900–3 Apr. 1976), physicist, was born in Oberlin, Ohio, the son of Walter Dennison, a professor of classics at Oberlin College, and Anna L. Green. From 1902 to 1910 the family lived in Ann Arbor, Michigan, where David's father taught Latin at the University of Michigan. The Dennisons then moved to Swarthmore, Pennsylvania. His father died in 1917, the year in which David entered Swarthmore College. He had been introduced to experimental science by an Episcopal minister who often invited high school students to join him in dabbling after school hours. At Swarthmore, David strengthened the mathematical background he would need, receiving an A.B. in 1921. Meanwhile, a 1920 summer job at General Electric Research Laboratories with Irving Langmuir and Albert Hull provided additional experience; he entered graduate studies in physics at the University of Michigan in 1921. He did his doctoral research, on the structure of the methane molecule, under visiting theorist Oskar Klein; Dennison's dissertation was the first in theoretical physics at Michigan.

Following the receipt of his Ph.D. in 1924 and his marriage to Helen Lenette Johnson in August of that year, he departed for two years of postdoctoral research at Neil Bohr's Institute for Theoretical Physics in Copenhagen. He was in Copenhagen at the time of the birth of the new quantum mechanics, and he quickly adapted the new techniques to molecular structure problems. His 1926 paper on the rotational states of a symmetrical molecule was one of the earliest applications of the new matrix formulation of quantum theory.

The University of Michigan sponsored a third year of postdoctoral study in Europe for Dennison, which he split among Copenhagen, Zurich, and Cambridge. While at Cambridge in 1927, he undertook a theoretical calculation of the specific heat of hydrogen gas as a function of temperature. The existence of an intrinsic spin for the electron had been demonstrated by George E. Uhlenbeck and Samuel A. Goudsmit in 1925. Calculations of the specific heat of hydrogen, based on the assumption that the proton also has a spin, disagreed with the experimental measurements. Dennison added a new assumption, namely that the two known states of hydrogen gas (ortho- and para-hydrogen) are long-lived and would not transform from one form into the other over the period of the experimental measurements. Hydrogen gas is then a mixture of the two forms, each with its own specific heat dependency. Dennison found that an ortho- to para-hydrogen ratio of 3 to 1, the value expected if the proton has an intrinsic spin equal to that of the electron, gave the best fit to the experimental data. This work constituted the first quantitative evidence for nuclear spin, and, coming at a time when the concept of intrinsic spin was still very young, it is probably Dennison's most noteworthy contribution.

In 1927 Dennison and his wife returned to Ann Arbor, Michigan, where he took a position as instructor in physics. The University of Michigan was expanding its efforts in theoretical physics during this period and hired Uhlenbeck, Goudsmit, and Otto Laporte in addition to Dennison. The four young theorists, with the strong support of Harrison M. Randall, chairman of the physics department, organized a series of international summer symposia that brought outstanding theoretical physicists to Ann Arbor for a month or two each summer between 1929 and 1940. These seminars represented a new technique for conducting and communicating research in physics. The Dennisons also had two sons during this period, both of whom followed scientific careers.

In 1932 Dennison and Uhlenbeck collaborated on a quantum-mechanical calculation of the structure and transitions of the ammonia molecule (NH_3), which is pyramidal in shape, predicting that the nitrogen atom, at the apex of the pyramid, could "tunnel" through the plane formed by the three hydrogen atoms, and that this transition could be observed as an absorption of electromagnetic radiation of long wavelength. They enlisted a colleague who was working on the development of magnetron tubes, and the 1933 observation of this transition constituted the birth of microwave spectroscopy.

Dennison received a citation for exceptional service from the U.S. Navy for his work evaluating (VT) proximity fuses during World War II. The changes he recommended were based on both scale-model measurements, involving the towing of model airplanes past radio transmitters, and results from battlefield testing in the Pacific. A byproduct of this work was the postwar development, by Dennison and Lawrence N. Hadley, of evaporated reflection and transmission interference filters, now commonplace in the coating of camera lenses.

His interests also included nuclear physics. He investigated the stability of particle orbits in the racetrack synchrotron, and he and T. H. Berlin published a paper on orbit stability in 1946 that had important implications for subsequent generations of particle accelerators. In 1954 he applied techniques perfected in molecular spectroscopy to the interpretation of the nuclear energy levels of ^{16}O.

Dennison advanced rapidly through the academic ranks at the University of Michigan, becoming associate professor in 1930 and professor in 1935. He served as chairman of the Department of Physics from 1955 to 1965. From 1966 until his retirement in 1970 he held the position of Harrison M. Randall University Professor. He died in Ann Arbor. Honors accorded him include the University of Michigan Henry Russel Lecturer (1952); election to the National Academy of Sciences (1953); Distinguished Faculty Achievement Award (1963); and the naming of the new physics building in Ann Arbor in his honor in 1976.

Although best known for his application of quantum mechanics to molecules, Dennison, along with a handful of other young American physicists, also played an instrumental role in shifting leadership in physics from Europe toward the United States in the 1930s. An inspiring lecturer and mentor, Dennison felt that teaching was as important as his research. Indeed, his greatest legacy may well be found in the careers of several generations of graduate students and young faculty members who benefited from his kind and firm guidance.

• Dennison's papers are deposited in the Bentley Library, University of Michigan. For historical context, see Stanley Coben, "The Scientific Establishment and the Transmission of Quantum Mechanics to America, 1919–1932," *American Historical Review* 76 (1971): 442–66. A list of his publications is included in the obituary by H. Richard Crane in National Academy of Sciences, *Biographical Memoirs* 52 (1980): 139–59.

ROBERT G. ARNS

DENNISON, Henry Sturgis (4 Mar. 1877–29 Feb. 1952), manufacturer and social reformer, was born in Boston, Massachusetts, the son of Henry B. Dennison, a manufacturer, and Emma J. Stanley. Educated at Roxbury Latin School and Harvard University, Dennison joined his family's paper products company after his graduation from Harvard in 1899 and quickly demonstrated the combination of business ability and social activism that would make him one of the best-known executives of the twentieth century. As works manager after 1906 and as president after 1917, Dennison contributed substantially to the growth of Dennison Manufacturing. Under his stewardship the company embraced systematic organization and modern management and became a leading manufacturer of jewelers' boxes, crepe paper, tags, and labels. Most of all, it became a private social laboratory where Dennison applied his theories of industrial and social reform.

An impatient, almost frenetically active man who would "dart" rather than walk and "begin all sentences in the middle," Dennison was interested in music and science but above all in management, industrial relations, and the role of government in the economy (Galbraith, 1981, p. 61). He believed that reform required curbs on the powers of absentee owners, passive investors, and financiers; increased authority for operating managers; and a more secure and positive environment for workers. The key to these changes was a more rational, scientific approach to business. This conviction led Dennison to become involved in the scientific management movement and its many offshoots of the 1920s and 1930s. By the 1920s he was devoting as much time and energy to these causes as to his own firm.

Dennison began to introduce factory reforms in 1901. Over the next decade he installed many features of contemporary welfare capitalism: a clinic, library, cafeteria, and savings bank, for example. In 1913 he created a personnel department, and in 1916 he took a bolder step and introduced the innovation that made him famous, an unemployment insurance plan for Dennison employees. The Dennison plan was founded on the premise that most unemployment was preventable through careful operations and systematic planning. Benefit payments were a penalty the company paid for its failure to prevent unemployment. As a result, most Dennison employees of the 1910s and 1920s enjoyed steady year-round work and Dennison became the nation's leading authority on unemployment insurance.

In 1911 Dennison had inaugurated a complementary initiative: a plan to transfer control of the company from outside stockholders to the active managers. Under the Dennison plan, the stockholders would exchange their common stock for nonvoting, preferred shares and higher dividends. Current executives would receive annual bonuses in the form of common stock but could not sell the stock until they retired. Internal control was to continue as long as the company paid dividends. Support from Mrs. James Peter Warbasse, the largest stockholder, enabled Dennison to win approval for the reorganization. The Dennison ownership plan attracted wide interest but, unlike the unemployment plan, had little influence on other businesses.

Dennison added innovative industrial relations policies in the years during and after World War I, when industrial unrest became a popular concern. He became an outspoken champion of collective bargaining, introduced a company union for employees who were not members of other unions, and in 1920 expanded the executive stock dividend program to include veteran production employees. (The Dennison Company had negotiated with several skilled employee unions for years.)

From the mid-1910s, Dennison devoted more and more of his time to industrial reform causes. He became a convenient and accommodating figure for groups that sought business support for causes that most businessmen opposed. No one, however, questioned Dennison's sincerity or devotion. As an officer of the Boston Chamber of Commerce he developed close ties to Edward Filene and Lincoln Filene, prominent merchants and reformers. As a member of the Massachusetts State Pension Commission, he became an ally of Magnus W. Alexander, a General Electric executive and expert on employment issues. During World War I he served as assistant to Edwin Gay in the Planning and Statistics section of the War Industries Board, another organization that brought together activist managers. As president of the Taylor Society in the late 1910s, he helped make the society a magnet for innovative executives and a forum for industrial reform causes. In the 1920s he was a supporter of the International Management Institute, the National Bureau of Economic Research, and the Social Science Research Council. He wrote the essay on management for the landmark *Recent Economic Trends* (1929).

Dennison also served on numerous government committees and boards. He was a delegate to the Industrial Conference of 1919 and the Unemployment Conference of 1921 and was a director of the Federal Reserve Bank of Boston from 1937 to 1945. He was a management adviser to the U.S. Post Office in the 1920s and a member of many New Deal advisory committees.

In the 1930s Dennison increasingly devoted his attention to government policy. Impressed with the limits on private enterprise during the depression years, he advocated an expanded government role in economic life. Service on the Commerce Department's business advisory council in 1933 marked the beginning of a close association with the Roosevelt administration. In the mid-1930s, Dennison employed John Kenneth Galbraith to publicize his ideas on government planning and social policy. Two collaborative works, *Towards Full Employment* (1938) and *Modern Competition and Business Policy* (1938), reflected these concerns.

At a time when his ideas seemed to be winning acceptance, Dennison faced growing personal problems. The depression undermined the financial affairs of the Dennison company and its unique ownership arrangements; by 1939 it had to turn to outside financial markets for funds. Thereafter it gradually evolved into a conventional firm. Dennison's health also declined in the 1930s. Heart attacks suffered in 1937 and 1941 forced him to curtail his business and reform activities. Dennison's wife, the former Mary Tyler Thurber, whom he had married in 1901, and with whom he had had four children, died in 1936. In 1944 he married Gertrude B. Petri, who survived him. Dennison remained prominent in business and governmental affairs until his death in Framingham, Massachusetts.

• Dennison's private papers are available at the Baker Library of the Harvard Business School. Dennison also wrote extensively for publication. His essays appeared in the *Bulletin of the Taylor Society* and other business journals; he was the author of *Organizational Engineering* (1931); and he was coauthor of, with James Garrow, *Profit Sharing and Stock Ownership for Employees* (1926) as well as the books with John Kenneth Galbraith. The best single biographical account is Kim McQuaid, "Henry S. Dennison and the 'Science' of Industrial Reform, 1900–1950," *American Journal of Economics and Sociology* 36 (Jan. 1976): 79–97. Edward D. Berkowitz and McQuaid, *Creating the Welfare State: The Political Economy of 20th Century Reform* (1992), places Dennison in the reform movements of his time. Daniel Nelson, *Unemployment Insurance: The American Experience, 1915–1935* (1969), discusses Dennison's work on unemployment. Galbraith, *A Life in Our Times* (1981), includes a humorous account of his relationship with Dennison. An obituary is in the *New York Times*, 1 Mar. 1952.

DANIEL NELSON

DENNISON, William (23 Nov. 1815–15 June 1882), Ohio governor, was born in Cincinnati, Ohio, the son of William Dennison and Mary Carter, the proprietors of the Dennison House, a popular hotel. Dennison received a liberal arts education at Miami University, graduating in 1835. He studied law with Cincinnati attorneys Nathaniel G. Pendleton and Stephen Fales and was admitted to the bar in 1840. Moving to the state capital in Columbus to begin his practice, in 1840 he married Anne Eliza Neil, the daughter of the owner of an important stage line. They had seven children. Readily accepted among the elite, Dennison soon acquired important business interests and amassed a fortune. Appreciating the value of railroads for Columbus's growth, he served as president of the Columbus and Xenia Railroad and later promoted the Hocking Valley Railroad. He was president of the Exchange Bank, a member of the city council in the 1850s, and active in many civic organizations.

Dennison was a Whig in politics, and his first public speech in 1844 denounced the spread of slavery threatened by the acquisition of Texas. Despite his opposition to slavery extension, Dennison did not join the Free Soil party, and after he ran successfully for the state senate in 1848, Free Soilers joined with Democrats to deny him the senate presidency in a contest lasting two weeks. This legislature enacted the repeal, strongly supported by Dennison, of Ohio's discriminatory Black Laws. Dennison disliked the Compromise of 1850 on slavery but was an elector for Whig candidate Winfield Scott on a platform that endorsed it in 1852. With the Whigs' decline, however, he was among the first to join the new Republican party. He was an active leader in the first national Republican organizational meeting in Pittsburgh in 1856 and a prominent member of the convention that nominated John C. Frémont for president later that year. A frequent adviser on financial matters for Ohio's first Republican governor, Salmon P. Chase, Dennison was chosen in 1859 to run as his successor. Although the cool and aloof Dennison had never cultivated the common touch, he conducted a vigorous campaign, debating his opponent, Rufus Ranney, and calling in Abraham Lincoln, among others, to stump for him. He won with 51.9 percent of the popular vote.

The outbreak of the Civil War dominated Dennison's governorship. Like most northern governors, he found the task of organizing and equipping tens of thousands of volunteers an administrative nightmare. Unable to anticipate everything that might go wrong, he often had to react after disaster struck. Troops were ordered to assemble before they could be adequately quartered or fed. They suffered from disease in ill-chosen campsites. Weapons and supplies could only be found by paying exorbitant prices. Delays were inevitable but seemed intolerable to those who did not understand the difficulties. Dennison belatedly reorganized his staff, appointed George B. McClellan, who had extensive military and management experience, as major general over Ohio's volunteers, and systematized recruiting by mobilizing local elites into committees charged with organizing rallies and speakers. When he left office Ohio had met its recruitment goals and had a manpower surplus.

Dennison was well aware of the strategic importance of Ohio, which bordered on the slave states of Virginia and Kentucky. He halted arms shipments across the Ohio River, even though Kentucky had not seceded, and ordered telegraph companies not to accept civilian messages regarding troop movements, which angered journalists. He sought support from other Midwest governors for aggressive actions in the Border South and assured the Unionists in Virginia's western counties that Ohio would protect them. Dennison supplied Ohio volunteers not yet sworn into Federal service for McClellan's campaign into western Virginia to seize the terminals of the Baltimore and Ohio Railroad. When the men returned, they found they could not be paid for service outside the state. To some, Dennison's actions seemed arbitrary and his administration inefficient. He dodged criticism in the state legislature by taking money refunded to Ohio by the federal government and reapplying it toward new military expenditures, thus avoiding discussion of military appropriations by the legislators. He kept careful records with no hint of corruption, but his own attorney general had advised against it. Intent on forming a Union movement with loyal Democrats, Republicans dropped their controversial governor at the end of his term in 1861 and nominated an ex-Democrat, David Tod, to succeed him.

Dennison continued to serve his party during the war, organizing support against allegedly traitorous Ohio Democrats and chairing the Republican National Convention in 1864. To restore a seat for Ohio in the cabinet lost when Chase resigned, Lincoln appointed Dennison postmaster general in October 1864. Dennison had many Radical friends but was alarmed by the inflationary potential of greenbacks and preferred colonization as a solution to race problems. He tried to heal the growing breach between Radical and moderate Republicans, however, he only succeeded in making both factions distrust him. Following Lincoln's assassination, he supported Andrew Johnson, including Johnson's veto of the Freedmen's Bureau Bill, until required to endorse Johnson's call for a national Union movement with Democrats in 1866. He then resigned from the cabinet.

Although Dennison was considered for nominations to the Senate (1880) and the vice presidency (1872), the only post he held thereafter was the appointive one of commissioner for the government of the District of Columbia in 1874. He remained active in business and died in Columbus. Although unappreciated at the time, Dennison served his nation well in the crucial first months of the Civil War; his greatest problem was communicating to the public the necessity for his actions.

• No collection of Dennison manuscripts exists, although letters from him appear in the papers of prominent Republicans of the era. An important study is Thomas C. Mulligan, "Lest the Rebels Come to Power" (Ph.D. diss., Ohio State Univ., 1994). See also Richard H. Abbott, *Ohio's War Governors* (1962); George H. Porter, *Ohio Politics during the Civil War*

Period (1911); and William Alexander Taylor, *Centennial History of Columbus and Franklin County, Ohio* (1909). An obituary is in the *New York Times*, 16 June 1882.

PHYLLIS F. FIELD

DENNY-BROWN, Derek Ernest (1 June 1901–20 Apr. 1981), neurologist, was born in Christchurch, New Zealand, the son of Charles Brown, who was in the insurance business, and Marian Denny. The couple hyphenated their names at the time of their marriage. Denny-Brown was raised and educated in New Zealand and attended medical school at Otago University in Dunedin from 1919 until 1924. After graduation he was appointed lecturer and demonstrator in anatomy at the school. Subsequently he traveled to England and received an appointment as Beit Memorial Fellow for Medical Research, permitting him to work for three years in the laboratory of Sir Charles S. Sherrington at Oxford. Denny-Brown's work was seminal, demonstrating the slow motoneuron discharge of the stretch reflex, differences in the properties of red and white muscles, and the principle of the subliminal fringe. He received the degree of doctor of philosophy from Oxford in 1928. Denny-Brown then became a resident medical officer at the National Hospital, Queen Square, London, England, and subsequently was appointed as lecturer at the National Hospital from 1931 to 1939 and as registrar in neurology at Guy's Hospital from 1931 to 1935. From 1935 until 1941 he was assistant physician, National Hospital, and Neurologist, St. Bartholomew's Hospital, London. As a clinical neurologist, he studied the effects of removing small portions of brain tissue in monkeys and demonstrated that he could replicate disorders seen in humans with injury to these areas of the brain.

In 1936 Denny-Brown received a Rockefeller Traveling Fellowship to spend six months at Yale University in physiologist John Fulton's laboratory. There he learned the techniques of performing ablation procedures in primates. Denny-Brown met Sylvia Summerhays at the home of James Collier, a well-known neurologist who was married to Summerhays's aunt. In 1937 he and Sylvia were married and lived together happily until his death. The couple had four sons.

In 1939 Harvard University and the Trustees of the Boston City Hospital invited Denny-Brown to accept the position of professor of neurology at Harvard Medical School and director of the neurological unit of the Boston City Hospital. He accepted the position, but war broke out between Germany and England, and he was required to enter active status in the British army medical corps. While in the service he assisted in the care of patients with head injury at Oxford, England, serving in this post for two years and receiving the military decoration Order of the British Empire for his work.

The president of Harvard, James Conant, requested of British prime minister Winston Churchill that Denny-Brown be released from active duty to assume his position at Harvard. The request was granted, and in 1941 Denny-Brown was transferred to the army reserve and sent to Boston to take up his position as professor of neurology at Harvard Medical School and director of the neurological unit of the Boston City Hospital. There he initiated a series of basic laboratory investigations concerned with problems encountered in the war, including cerebral concussion, peripheral nerve injury, and motion sickness.

In 1944 the British army recalled Denny-Brown to active duty and sent him to India and Burma to care for patients with neurologic problems, including outbreaks of poliomyelitis and meningitis. He cared for prisoners of war rescued from Burma and Malaya, dealing with infections and malnutrition. He wrote a series of papers concerning his experience dealing with neurologic disorders resulting from dietary restriction, the care of patients with traumatic paraplegia, and the treatment of neurosyphilis. In these papers he was the first to differentiate nutritional ataxia and retrobulbar neuritis from beriberi.

Denny-Brown returned to Boston City Hospital in 1947 and worked there continuously for the next two decades. He made a series of remarkable discoveries in both basic and clinical neurology. He observed the importance of fibroblasts in the regeneration of nerve after experimental lesions, work that he used as a thesis for his M.D. degree. He was among the first to describe a sensory neuropathy associated with carcinoma in a paper published in 1948. He described the effectiveness of vitamin B_{12} in the therapy of combined system disease. In 1951 he described a hereditary form of sensory radicular neuropathy that is now often termed "Denny-Brown disease." He published a classic monograph with Raymond Adams and Carl Pearson describing the clinical and pathological features of diseases of muscle. Denny-Brown, together with L. L. Uzman, described the occurrence of aminoaciduria in Wilson's disease. Subsequently he demonstrated that the chelating agent BAL can improve the neurologic disorders of patients with severe Wilson's disease. In both humans and animals, he described the development of grasp reflexes after frontal lesions and of avoiding responses from parietal lesions. He was responsible for the concept of "amorphosynthesis" after parietal lesions, an important insight concerning the importance of the parietal lobe for the awareness and integration of both personal and extrapersonal space. He studied the effects of basal ganglia lesions on posture and movement, summarizing his findings in 1960 in the Croonian Lectures on diseases of the basal ganglia and their relation to disorders of movement. The work that constituted his most mature statement on the organization of the cerebrum was published in connection with his Sherrington Memorial Lectures, which were delivered in Liverpool and in which he defined the regions of the cerebral cortex that are important in the development of dystonia.

In 1967 Denny-Brown retired from his position as director of the neurological unit in Boston City Hospital and became chief of the section of neurophysiology and associate director of the New England Regional Primate Center. He worked there until 1972, working on sensory innervation and basal ganglia function in the developing primate. He proved that the area of loss of sensation from cutting a sensory nerve could be changed by medication, demonstrating the complex effects of recovery of nerve function after injury. In 1972 he became a Fogarty Scholar in Residence at the National Institutes of Health for one year and then entered a phase of semiretirement.

During his productive scientific career, Denny-Brown served as director of a residency program that usually accepted four trainees per year for a three-year program, and he was in charge of an active neurologic service with both inpatient beds and an outpatient clinic at Boston City Hospital. He also worked personally with a succession of postdoctoral fellows in his laboratory. He died in Cambridge, Massachusetts.

Denny-Brown's scientific achievements were outstanding. In addition to his research of "Denny-Brown disease," he demonstrated the pathophysiology of Wilson's disease and demonstrated a treatment for it that proved effective. He determined the principal cause of brain injury after head injury, the manner in which strokes affect the brain, and the neurological disorders resulting from various parts of the brain. In addition to his scientific contributions, he taught generations of physicians in neurology, and he provided training for many future professors and chairs of departments of neurology in the United States.

• Many of Denny-Brown's unique ideas are contained in three monographs that he published: *Diseases of the Basal Ganglia and Subthalamic Nuclei* (1946), *The Basal Ganglia and Their Relation to Disorders of Movement* (1962), and *The Cerebral Control of Movement* (1966). He also co-authored *Reflex Activity of the Spinal Cord* (1932) and *Diseases of Muscle* (1962). Additional information on Denny-Brown is available in *Centennial Anniversary Volume of the American Neurological Association, 1875–1975* (1975), which he edited. Obituaries are in *Neurology* 32 (1982): 1–6; *Annals of Neurology* 11 (1982): 413–19; *Archives of Neurology* 38 (1981): 603–04; *Canadian Journal of Neurological Sciences* 8 (1981): 271–73; and *Journal of the Neurological Sciences* 53 (1982) 137–39.

SID GILMAN

DENSMORE, Frances Theresa (21 May 1867–5 June 1957), ethnomusicologist, was born in Red Wing, Minnesota, the daughter of Benjamin Densmore, a civil engineer and cofounder of Red Wing Iron Works, and Sarah Adalaide Greenland. Her advanced musical studies in piano, organ, and harmony were at the Oberlin Conservatory in Ohio (1884–1887). She returned to Red Wing to be a piano teacher and church organist. Further training in piano was with Carl Baermann and Leopold Godowsky (1870–1938) and counterpoint with John Knowles Paine at Harvard.

Her lifelong interest in studying the music and cultures of Native American groups throughout southern North America had issued from hearing the drums and songs of a camp of Sioux across the Mississippi River from her home in Red Wing. In 1893 Densmore purchased Alice Cunningham Fletcher's *A Study of Omaha Music* and visited the Chicago World's Fair to see and hear the Native American presentations. She wrote later, "My interests were entirely musical, as I was teaching piano and lecturing on the Wagnerian operas, Indian music attracted me only as a novelty, but in 1895 I added it to my lecture subjects, presenting Miss Fletcher's material with her permission" (Hofmann, p. 102).

After several years of reading all the material on Amerindians that she could find, Densmore made her first personal contacts with Native Americans in 1901. She and her sister, Margaret, journeyed to Port Arthur (now Thunder Bay, Ontario) and around Lake Superior, where they encountered Chippewas. Back in Red Wing, she transcribed into conventional western musical notation several songs of a Sioux woman.

In 1903 she began her career as a writer on Amerindian culture with an article, "The Song and the Silence of the Red Man," in the *Minneapolis Journal*. At the St. Louis Exposition in 1904 she gave a lecture using a tom-tom, medicine rattles, and percussive sticks and sang her own collected examples plus some from Fletcher's publication. While in St. Louis, Densmore wrote down the song of an Apache, Geronimo, and studied the music of several Filipino groups. From a Moro woman she learned to play the gong-chime (*kulintang*) and subsequently claimed to be the first musician to seriously study their music.

In 1906 she began studying Sioux music and attended Chippewa events. The following year Densmore recorded twelve cylinders of Big Bear's Chippewa songs with borrowed equipment and witnessed sacred rituals involving the Midéwiwin. In a letter to the Bureau of American Ethnology at the Smithsonian Institution she reported these events. In response, the chief of the bureau sent her a small grant with which she purchased an Edison Home Phonograph. From this first scholarly study of Amerindian music the bureau supported her efforts until 1933 and reinstated her as a collaborator from 1939 to her death.

With a Columbia Graphophone purchased in 1908, Densmore recorded over 3,500 musical entities of the Northeastern Woodlands, Southeast, Northern Plains, High Plateau, Southern Plains, Southwest Pueblo, Southwest Nomad, British Columbia Plateau, Northwest Coast, Northern California, and Tule Indians of Panama. Her first two major monographs, *Chippewa Music* (2 vols., 1910, 1913), contained the largest collection (380 songs) from one cultural group to be collected by a single person. She transcribed each song into conventional staff notation with some modified signs to indicate pitch levels and minute rhythmic fluctuations. The ceremony, context, or use of each song, and its text and translation, accompanied each transcription along with a prose commentary. Extensive comparative tables supported her statements about the characteristics of Chippewa music, such as the importance of the rhythmic unit, the frequent independence of voice and drum, and the prominence of the descending minor third interval.

Similar transcriptions and comparative tables appeared in all of her subsequent music monographs and until *Choctaw Music* (1943) were cumulative to include the cultural group under study as well as comparisons with previously studied cultures in Densmore's purview. She concentrated on traditional material but distinguished songs according to age wherever possible. Unlike many ethnomusicologists, she did not neglect women's music and included lullabies and children's songs. Beginning in 1918, Densmore devised "a form of graphic representation . . . for the purpose of making the trend of . . . melodies more apparent to the eye than in musical transcription" (*Teton Sioux Music,* p. 51), a practice that she continued in *Northern Ute Music* (1922) and *Mandan and Hidatsa Music* (1923). Her graphs distinguished more clearly the melodic shapes of specific groups of songs and indicated how a certain profile distinguished for the Amerindian a specific genre.

Notational additions of a sign for glissando and humming occur in *Nootka and Quileute Music* (1939). Along with the recorded songs she obtained many artifacts and much contextual information, including numerous photographs, on her field trips, which were minimally supported by the Bureau of American Ethnology and in the late 1930s by the Southwest Museum of Los Angeles. She published twenty-one books and over 200 articles, almost all on Amerindian cultures.

To obtain the data for this amazing productivity, she traveled by various conveyances to remote areas and managed with makeshift quarters to record and interview her informants after obtaining their confidence. She was very meticulous to obtain the best possible recording. After discovering that the drums and rattles did not record well, she would have the informant use a cardboard box instead. Then Densmore would make several recordings of the same song, moving the horn in order to make sure that she had versions emphasizing either the voice or the percussive beat. Making use of developments in phonophotography, she checked her transcriptions and the relationship of voice and percussion.

In 1912 the Sioux chief Red Fox adopted Densmore as his daughter, and she subsequently used this relationship to facilitate her negotiations with other groups. At age seventy-eight, after studying Michigan Indians for the University of Michigan, she wrote: "I am now able to plan and carry through a 'stiff' field trip with its many decisions and its use of the old technique in getting information out of Indians" (Hofmann, p. 64). Nine years later she gave seminars at the University of Florida and did more fieldwork among the Seminole. Densmore continued writing until her death in Red Wing.

Although Densmore was the first to demonstrate that the creation and performance of music in Native-American cultures had to fulfill standards of excellence as vigorous as those of white culture, she supported the policy of "civilizing" these peoples through the learning of English and acculturating them into the dominant culture. At the same time, in studying their music she managed to avoid certain Eurocentric views in her analysis. However, she did not manage to view her informants as important sources of information beyond the songs they sang for her or for the context of the articles they displayed. In many cases her informants are not even named, and when a person is named, no historical or recent heritage of that person is provided.

• Densmore's papers are at the Smithsonian Institution and the Music Division of the Library of Congress. In her eighties she chose selections and prepared the booklets for seven recordings issued by the Library of Congress, the repository for the majority of her cylinders. Charles Hofmann edited *Frances Densmore and American Indian Music* (1968) with a complete bibliography, excerpts from her letters and articles, and a chronology of her life. Assessments of Densmore include Nina M. Archabal, "Frances Densmore, Pioneer in the Study of American Indian Music," in *Women of Minnesota,* ed. B. Stuhler and G. Kreuter (1977), and Gail Guthrie Valaskakis, "The Chippewa and the Other: Living the Heritage of Lac du Flambeau," *Cultural Studies* 2, no. 3 (1988): 267–93.

ELAINE KEILLOR

DENTON, Daniel (c. 1626–1703), author and local government official, was born in Yorkshire, England, the son of the Reverend Richard Denton, a Presbyterian minister, and Helen Windlbank. During the early 1640s Daniel accompanied his father to America. In 1644 Richard Denton became pastor at Hempstead, Long Island, where Daniel was made town clerk in 1650. Daniel relocated to Jamaica, New York, where he was one of the town's original grantees and where, in 1656, he became town clerk. Near the end of the decade he married Abigail Stevenson; they had three children. On 4 March 1662 he was appointed a magistrate of Jamaica, and the following year he became overseer of the poor. In 1664 he represented Jamaica in its boundary dispute with Flushing. Also, Governor Richard Nicolls commissioned him a justice of the peace for North Riding of Yorkshire, Long Island.

Business took Denton to London, and there he wrote and published *A Brief Description of New-York* (1670). Upon returning to New York, he found that his wife had committed adultery in his absence. Before the court, she was "accused for her Incontinency, & committing Adultery in the absence of her Husband, then about his Occasions in Europe." Faced with undeniable evidence, Abigail Denton confessed. The lower court sent the case to the provincial council, from which Denton obtained a bill of absolute divorce on 16 June 1672. After the divorce scandal, Denton left New York for Piscataway, New Jersey, where he became a magistrate in 1673. In 1676 he married Hannah Leonard, with whom he had six children. Denton returned to Jamaica, New York, in 1684. The following year he was chosen a commissioner of Jamaica, and, the year after, he once again became town clerk. In 1689 he became clerk of Queens County.

Though Denton maintained a busy and active presence in local government through much of his life, his lasting reputation rests on *A Brief Description of New-York*, the promotional tract he wrote in London. It was the first separately published work in English concerning the New York province and remains a minor classic of early American literature. The pamphlet reveals Denton's fondness for his home and his enthusiastic desire to improve New York. His description of Hell-Gate, a narrow passage leading into New York City, evidences his literary skill. The noisy and daunting channel, he explained, was "enough to affright any stranger from passing further, and to wait for some *Charon* to conduct him through; yet to those that are well acquainted little or no danger; yet a place of great defence against any enemy coming in that way, which a small Fortification would absolutely prevent" (p. 2). In this brief passage, Denton embodies the best of early American promotional literature. While discouraging the fainthearted, Denton encouraged those willing to risk the danger. With self-confidence and hard work, he suggested, a person could make New York a safe and profitable home.

Denton appealed to potential immigrants on multiple levels. Describing New York City as mostly "Brick and Stone, and covered with red and black Tile," he countered the traditional stereotype by letting his English readers know that they would not be immigrating to a howling wilderness. He also emphasized the colony's plentiful natural resources: timber, fruit, fish, and game. Furthermore, Denton appealed to the reader's aesthetic sensibilities. The city, he stated, "gives at a distance a pleasing Aspect to the spectators" (p. 3). Within the nearby woods, brightly colored songbirds "salute the ears of Travellers with an harmonious discord, and in every pond and brook green silken Frogs, who warbling forth their untun'd tunes strive to bear a part in this musick" (p. 6). He appealed to people with widely varying skills and interests—entrepreneurs, farmers, and tradesmen. He also emphasized the opportunities in New York that were unavailable in the Old World. Those denied a family inheritance in England could come to New York and procure "inheritances of land, and possessions, stock themselves with all sorts of cattel, enjoy the benefit of them whilst they live, and leave them to the benefit of their children when they die" (p. 18). Near the end of the work, Denton promoted New York through the use of another literary device commonly found within the promotional literature, the negative catalog: "Here you need not trouble the Shambles for meat, nor Bakers and Brewers for Beer and Bread, nor run to a Linnen-Draper for a supply, every one making their own Linnen, and a great part of their woollen-cloth for their ordinary wearing" (p. 18). There is no telling what effect Denton's work had on immigration to New York, but contemporary English readers would have recognized Denton's enthusiasm and fondness for the place. John Ogilby borrowed heavily from the pamphlet for the New York section of *America* (1671). After the works of Captain John Smith, Denton's *Brief Description of New-York* is the finest American promotional tract of the seventeenth century.

• *A Brief Description of New York* has been reprinted many times. It appeared as the first item in Gowans's "Bibliotheca Americana" series, edited and with notes by Gabriel Furman (1845). It was edited by John Pennington as a supplement to the Bulletin of the Historical Society of Pennsylvania (1845). Felix Neumann, "Denton's 'Brief Description of New York,'" *Publishers' Weekly* 61 (1902): 1173–75, 1354–57, contains much bibliographical information. Neumann's two-part article was incorporated into a new edition of the work (1902). A facsimile reprint by Columbia University Press (1937) includes an introduction by Victor Hugo Paltsits that contains much important biographical information. Additional biographical information can be found in George D. A. Combes, *Genealogy of the Descendant of Reverend Richard Denton* (1980).

KEVIN J. HAYES

DENVER, James William (23 Oct. 1817–9 Aug. 1892), soldier, governor of Kansas Territory, and lawyer, was born near Winchester, Virginia, the son of Patrick Denver and Jane Campbell, farmers of Irish extraction. In 1831 his family migrated to a farm near Wilmington, Ohio. After a grade school education, James taught briefly at Platte City, Missouri, graduated from Cincinnati College (now the University of Cincinnati) in 1844, and was admitted to the bar. He opened a newspaper and law office in Xenia, Ohio, but after less than a year, in 1845, returned to Platte City, where he continued to practice both professions. After the outbreak of the Mexican War on 4 March 1847, Denver was appointed captain in the Twelfth Regiment, U.S. Volunteers, commanding a company he had raised, and was ordered to Mexico. Sick much of the time, he was ordered home on 26 October 1847.

Denver resumed his two professions until the lure of gold discoveries in California prompted him to lead a party overland to Trinity County, California. In 1852–1853 he served in the state senate, and in 1853 he was appointed secretary of state. In 1852 Denver killed in a duel the editor of the *Alta California* after he took issue with the editor's verbal attacks on the governor. In 1854, running as a Democrat against the free-soil David Broderick faction, Denver was elected to the U.S. House of Representatives. He sat on the Military Affairs Committee and became chairman of the Select Committee on the Pacific Railroad. He strove unsuccessfully to push through a bill to aid in constructing a railroad and telegraph communication by a central route to California.

At maturity Denver was an impressive figure, standing six feet seven inches and weighing 260 pounds. In 1856 he married Louise Catherine Rombach; they had four children, one of whom, Matthew Denver, served in Congress for three terms.

After failing to be renominated for Congress, Denver was appointed by President James Buchanan on 17 April 1857 to be commissioner of Indian affairs—the first of two brief tenures. Denver's American Indian policy looked to reduce the size of reservations, thereby discouraging nomadism and encouraging agricultural and mechanical labor. His policies were not implemented. At this time he was making investments in western lands, which he continued to do until his death. Whether he exploited his privileged position is hard to determine.

When the two territorial posts in Kansas fell vacant and disorder persisted, Denver became acting governor and secretary; he was later confirmed as governor. A convention at Lecompton had written a proslavery constitution and scheduled a vote on it for 21 December. The free-soil legislature called for another referendum on 4 January. Widespread lawlessness prevailed, causing Denver to acknowledge that all his powers would be required to "prevent them [the settlers] from cutting each other's throats." The December vote strongly favored the proslavery constitution, but there were many abstentions; the January vote, with an additional 4,000 participants, overwhelmingly rejected it.

Denver urged Buchanan to reject the constitution or "risk a bloody civil war." He recommended a new constitutional convention, which he believed would lead to a free-state party fairly chosen. Denver's sage advice came too late: Buchanan had already pledged to southern leaders that he would support the Lecompton constitution.

While Congress was contriving a compromise and Buchanan was splitting his party, Denver was wielding a firm hand with the legislature and trying to maintain order in the territory. On 1 September 1858, after Kansans had voted on and rejected the compromise, which involved a popular vote and a land grant, Denver resigned (effective 10 Oct.), claiming that "peace now reigns where lately all was confusion." Meanwhile, early in 1858 gold had been discovered in a section of Kansas that is now Colorado, and a party sent out by Denver named a townsite for him; years later it became the capital of Colorado.

After briefly resuming his position as commissioner of Indian affairs, Denver returned to California in 1859, where he twice sought election unsuccessfully to the U.S. Senate. With the coming of the Civil War, he was appointed brigadier general of volunteers on 4 August 1861 and was assigned to duty in Kansas. On 14 May 1862 he was reassigned to the Fifth Division, Army of the Tennessee, where he commanded the Third Brigade in the march on Corinth. By early 1863, with his financial affairs in need of attention, assigned to noncombat duty, and weary of what he felt was public ingratitude for his public services, he resigned his commission.

Returning to law practice, Denver formed a partnership in Washington, doing much of his work in the court of claims. He maintained residence in Wilmington, Ohio, where he held farming and banking interests. Still interested in politics, however, he unsuccessfully sought the Democratic nomination for Congress in 1870 and 1886. In 1873 he helped organize the National Association of Mexican War Veterans, becoming lifelong president of the organization. He continued to practice law until he died in Washington.

• The Denver papers are mainly in the University of Oklahoma library, the University of Kansas library, and the Library of Congress. *The War of the Rebellion: A Compilation of the Official Records of the Union and Confederate Armies* (128 vols., 1880–1901) has numerous references, including Denver's report on the march on Corinth. Though inadequate, George C. Barns, *Denver the Man* (1949), publishes much valuable material and is the fullest biography. Edward Magruder Cook, *Justified by Honor* (1988), also contains helpful material. Edward T. Taylor, "General James W. Denver—An Appreciation," *Colorado Magazine* 17 (1940): 41–51, is useful. On the Kansas imbroglio, see James A. Rawley, *Race and Politics* (1969). Donald Chaput has a good short account of Denver as commissioner in *The Commissioners of Indian Affairs—1824 to 1977*, ed. Robert M. Kvasnicka and Herman J. Viola (1979).

JAMES A. RAWLEY

DENYS DE LA RONDE, Louis (2 Aug. 1675–25 Mar. 1741), French military officer, explorer, and spy, was born in Quebec City, Canada, the son of Pierre Denys de la Ronde, a landowner and merchant (the Crown had given the aristocracy in Canada permission to engage in trade), and Catherine Leneuf de la Potherie. He entered naval service in 1687 as a midshipman in France. During the war of 1689–1697 he served in exiled British king James II's expedition to Ireland, then off the coast of England, and finally on several voyages to New France and along the coast of New England. Captured at sea in 1695, he was soon released in an exchange of prisoners of war. He served in Pierre Le Moyne d'Iberville's final campaign in Hudson Bay in 1697. D'Iberville then selected him to join the two Mississippi expeditions (1699–1701) that established the colony of Louisiana.

The War of the Spanish Succession (1701–1713) took La Ronde back to combat. In 1702, while sailing to Quebec, he was severely wounded in the shoulder during the capture of a British ship. He resumed his naval career the following year; in 1704 he was taken prisoner again but soon returned in another exchange. In 1705 he went privateering off New England. By then he knew the coastline well, and in 1706 he boldly sailed right into Boston Harbor on the pretext of making inquiries about an exchange of prisoners. With his good command of English, La Ronde was well suited for spying. In the spring of 1707 he took part in the successful defense of Port Royal (Annapolis Royal, Nova Scotia) against a force from New England, then sailed with the news to the French court. He spent part of 1708 strengthening Port Royal's defenses in anticipation of a return attack before resuming privateering. Ending up in Plaisance (Placentia, Newfoundland), he joined Governor Philippe de Pastour de Costebelle's expedition against the English forts at St. John's, which fell New Year's day, 1709. La Ronde transported the prisoners to Quebec and there joined the forces massed in anticipation of an Anglo-American invasion. In the midst of this, he married Marie-Louise Chartier de Lotbinière, whose father was a prominent judge and member of the colony's Superior Council. The couple had six children.

In 1711 La Ronde resumed his career as a spy. Costebelle ordered him to sail into Boston under a flag of truce. There, while negotiating an exchange of prisoners, he was to learn everything he could about English plans and resources and attempt to sow doubt in the minds of the colonists about supporting the war effort, perhaps even to arrange a neutrality between New England and New France—precisely when the English were preparing to invade Canada. All went well until someone came upon a copy of La Ronde's instructions. He tried to make a run for it but was captured and thrown into prison. The General Court of Massachusetts condemned him to death but Governor Joseph Dudley intervened; this time La Ronde made good his escape. By then, however, his intelligence was of much less value; in August 1711 Sir Hovenden Walker's fleet had entered the St. Lawrence and met with disaster.

La Ronde then resumed his career as a colonizer. Newfoundland was surrendered to England by the Treaty of Utrecht in 1713, and he was ordered to help establish the new colony of Isle Royale (Cape Breton Island) north of Acadia (Nova Scotia), which had also been left to the English. He reconnoitered the island and later tried, unsuccessfully, to get the Acadians to move there. In 1719 Governor General Philippe de Rigaud de Vaudreuil had him transferred to the colonial regulars in Canada. Apparently unenthusiastic about this command, La Ronde avoided going to Quebec. The next year he was sent to assist in founding settlements on Ile St. Jean (Prince Edward Island). He was not prepared to do this for long and finally sailed for Canada.

Vaudreuil immediately used La Ronde as a plenipotentiary in New England. In 1723 he showed up once again in Boston. The nature of his mission is not exactly clear, though one task was to intervene in the colonists' war with the Abenaki, who were allies of the French. Back home, his foes accused him of pursuing his own interests. Like many Canadians, he was not averse to a bit of cross-border trading, however much the metropolitan governments of both colonies forbade it.

By the 1720s La Ronde was indeed interested in the fur trade—still the leading way to amass a fortune in Canada. In 1727 Governor General Charles Beauharnois de la Boische made him commander of Fort Chagouamigon (near present-day Ashland, Wisc.), a key post in the western fur trade. La Ronde got tangled up in the fight between Beauharnois and the colony's intendant Claude-Thomas Dupuy, who charged La Ronde with illegal trading. Beauharnois had to concede that this was true and cancelled his appointment. The minister of the Marine Jean-Frederic Phelypeaux, comte de Maurepas, announced that he no longer had confidence in La Ronde but stopped short of dismissing him. Resourceful as ever, La Ronde made friends with Gilles Hocquart, the intendant's successor, and resumed the command at Chagouamigon in 1731.

La Ronde learned that there were rich deposits of copper not far from the post at the western end of Lake Superior. He gathered samples of ore (which the Paris mint later established were over 90 percent pure copper) and then proposed to set up a mine and build two ships to transport the product eastward. Initially the French government took a keen interest, for copper was a strategic metal. Combined with the iron at Trois Rivières, it would produce bronze from which the best types of cannon could be cast, and Canada, indeed the French navy as a whole, was short of cannon. Canada, regarded as the white elephant among the French colonies, now looked as though it could become the western armory for the empire.

The proposal was approved in 1733 and La Ronde set up a partnership with several merchants. The costs were to be offset by a monopoly of trade at Chagouamigon, but progress was slow. Canada did not have the skilled artisans necessary to set up the mine and smelting furnace, and so La Ronde petitioned the king for assistance. In 1737 Maurepas instructed two Germans, Johan and Christoph Forster, to assess the feasibility of the whole operation. After an arduous voyage the Forsters finally reached their destination the next year. They spent a summer and winter in the west, returning to France in 1739. The miners reported that there were at least three rich copper deposits but concluded that exploiting them would be prohibitively expensive due to the great distance, harsh weather, and lack of manpower and material. Maurepas took the Forsters' report as decisive; he ordered an end to the enterprise, and wondered aloud whether the venture was just a scheme for La Ronde to tap into the fur trade. The evidence is hardly decisive but it is quite possible that the bold warrior who helped to establish two colonies seriously thought he could launch a great mine by force of will. He certainly paid for the failure. Despite the assistance of his fur trade income, La Ronde had not recovered from debt by the time of his death.

La Ronde was a man of enormous energy and determination, like his early protector d'Iberville. He was also headstrong and self-interested, which got him into trouble with several of his commanding officers. La Ronde repeatedly crossed the line between taking the initiative and following his own agenda. This conduct cost him: having reached the rank of infantry captain in 1707 he received no further promotion either in the navy or the colonial regulars. He did, after a long interval, receive the coveted Cross of St. Louis in 1721. La Ronde served himself as well as his king; he had no notion of separate "public" and "private" spheres. In this he was very much a man of his times, for blending personal and national interests was a hallmark of the ancien régime—in business as in war.

• Many letters, reports, and dossiers concerning La Ronde are preserved in the Archives Nationales, Paris, colonial series B and C ll. Most older accounts, for example, the one by Francis Parkman, are seriously out of date. The most detailed biography is still Bernard Pothier and Donald Horton, *Dic-*

tionary of Canadian Biography, vol. 3 (1974). See also Dale Miquelon, *New France 1701–1744, "A Supplement to Empire"* (1987).

JAY CASSEL

DE PALMA, Ralph (1883–31 Mar. 1956), race car driver, was born in Italy and raised in New York City. Little is known about his parents and early years. A high school graduate who also attended Stevens Institute in Hoboken, New Jersey, De Palma turned from racing bicycles to automobiles in 1908. Driving an Italian-built Fiat Cyclone, he immediately challenged the best American drivers of his era, including the flamboyant Barney Oldfield, who became a bitter rival. On a number of occasions Oldfield would leave the track rather than compete against De Palma. Conversely, Oldfield's association with Firestone prompted De Palma to boycott the company's high-quality racing tires. (Oldfield's car was emblazoned with the slogan "My Life Insurance—Firestone Tires.") In 1909, his first full year of racing, De Palma won 34 of 47 races and had eight second-place finishes.

De Palma soon gained an international reputation. In 1912 and 1914 he won both the prestigious Vanderbilt Cup race, in a Mercedes, and the national driving championship sponsored by the American Automobile Association (AAA). During a two-day period in May 1912 he set world speed records, in a Mercer, over eight different distances. De Palma finished sixth at the inaugural running of the Indianapolis 500 in 1911, and he led the 1912 race with fewer than two laps to go when a faulty connecting rod caused his Mercedes to stall. De Palma and his riding mechanic vainly tried to push the bulky car over the finish line before the other racers could roar by. This famous incident earned De Palma the nickname of "Hard Luck Ralph," and sportswriters repeatedly wrote of "the De Palma jinx."

In 1915 De Palma finally triumphed at Indianapolis. Enjoying the sponsorship of millionaire publisher E. C. Patterson, De Palma coaxed his sputtering Mercedes (again crippled by a bad connecting rod) across the finish line in a record speed of just under 90 miles per hour. To cap his day, the first ten finishers ran on Goodrich rather than Firestone tires.

After a brief yet distinguished career in the U.S. Air Service during World War I, De Palma secured a sponsorship from the Packard Motor Car Company and drove Packards to a world's land-speed record, on the sands at Daytona Beach, Florida, and to a sixth-place finish at the 1919 Indianapolis 500. The American press enthusiastically celebrated De Palma's record-breaking run at Daytona, which occurred on Abraham Lincoln's birthday, as a patriotic triumph since he had used an American-built car to wrest the land-speed record away from Germany's Mercedes Benz. The handsome Italian-American was heralded as the Enrico Caruso of auto racing.

De Palma was less fortunate at the Indianapolis 500 and other major races. Driving a French-built Ballot under his own sponsorship, he won the pole position at Indianapolis in 1920, but tire problems forced him to settle for fifth place. The following year his Ballot again captured the pole, only to fall out of the race after 112 laps with yet another faulty connecting rod. In 1922 De Palma returned to Indianapolis with a Dusenberg, which he qualified third and drove to a fourth-place finish. These failures to win at Indianapolis embellished the saga of "Hard Luck Ralph." But, in truth, De Palma was as stubborn as he was unlucky. Famous for demanding long hours and painstaking preparations from his crew, all of whom were required to don clean white uniforms whenever his car was on the track, De Palma nonetheless clung to his old bias against Firestone racing tires. The continued refusal to use Firestones necessitated frequent pit stops and severely handicapped De Palma in longer races, especially those run on board tracks. For a brief time he even campaigned in "outlaw" races, dirt-track contests that were not sanctioned by the AAA; but eventually he rejoined the regular racing circuit, on which he often competed against his nephew and former riding mechanic, Peter De Paolo.

The intrafamily rivalry came to a head at the 1925 Indianapolis 500 when De Paolo finished first and his uncle came in a credible (though to him disappointing) seventh. The traditional victory banquet, at which the winner and top finishers received both formal recognition and their share of the purse, became a family reunion as De Paolo publicly praised De Palma for providing both familial inspiration and expert technical training.

The 1925 race marked De Palma's last appearance in the Indianapolis 500, although he continued to thrive on the dirt tracks and capped his last full decade in competitive racing by winning the Canadian championship in 1929. In his later years De Palma became famous for a seemingly effortless style of driving, especially on dirt. To the casual fan, De Paolo later recalled, it might seem that his uncle was "driving as though he were out for an afternoon spin on the highway" instead of competing in one of the most dangerous of all spectator sports.

In 1934 De Palma retired from racing and, in a career move favored by many former drivers, worked for various motor companies as a test driver, spokesperson, and consultant. He once joked that he had donated at least seven teeth to the cause of developing a new braking system for Chrysler automobiles. De Palma continued to be an honored guest at the Memorial Day race at Indianapolis, until his death at his home in South Pasadena, California. In 1973 De Palma and De Paolo were both selected to membership in the Indianapolis 500 Hall of Fame.

Although precise records were not compiled during racing's earliest days, one estimate credits De Palma with competing in nearly 3,000 races and winning more than 2,500 of them. Certainly, he was one of the most successful drivers during the earliest years of the Indianapolis 500, a race for which accurate statistics are available. De Palma, who ran in ten Indianapolis races, completed nearly 1,600 laps and was the leader on 610 (nearly 40 percent) of them.

• Information on De Palma is in John Bentley, *Great American Automobiles* (1957); Peter De Paolo, *Wall Smacker* (1935); and Lyle Kenyon Engel, *The Indianapolis "500": The World's Most Exciting Auto Race*, rev. ed. (1972). See also two articles in *Indianapolis 500 Year Book* (1975): Bob Russo, "De Paolo Wins 1925 Race," pp. 124, 135–39; and Jack Fox, "Sixty Years Ago," pp. 150–51. An obituary is in the *New York Times*, 1 Apr. 1956.

NORMAN L. ROSENBERG

DE PAOLO, Peter (15 Apr. 1898–27 Nov. 1980), race car driver, was born in Roseland, New Jersey, the son of Tomasso De Paolo, a builder, and Giovinni De Palma, sister of the celebrated race car driver Ralph De Palma. De Palma's fame encouraged De Paolo to pursue a career of his own in automobile racing, and the training he received as an airplane mechanic during World War I convinced his uncle to let him join the fabled De Palma racing team. De Paolo traveled to tracks all over the world as De Palma's riding mechanic but became increasingly frustrated by his uncle's refusal to run on Firestone tires because of an ongoing feud with another racer, Barney Oldfield, who officially endorsed the Firestone brand. De Palma's continual problems with tires finally convinced De Paolo, reluctantly, to strike out on his own in 1922.

De Paolo's first year in racing proved a hectic one. Although he was a raw novice, he led the 1922 Indianapolis 500 when, on the 110th lap, a stupid, "rookie" mistake sent his car careening into the wall. Unhurt, De Paolo reentered the race as a relief driver and drove a Dusenberg to a tenth-place finish. He quickly became tagged as "Pile-up Pete" and "Wall Smacker." After De Paolo crashed again during a tragedy-filled race in Kansas City, he decided to settle down in California with his wife, Sally Lewis, whom he had married in June and with whom he would have two children, and abandon a driving career. De Paolo operated a service station in Los Angeles with his brother-in-law, and he briefly rejoined De Palma as a mechanic for the 1923 Indianapolis 500.

In 1924, however, De Paolo returned to racing. He convinced Fred "Daddy" Dusenberg to let him drive the Dusenberg racing team's slowest car, a vehicle that De Palma had driven during the 1922 Indianapolis 500. Serving as both chief mechanic and driver—a cost-saving move favored by Dusenberg—De Paolo piloted his aging car to a surprising sixth-place finish at the 1924 Indianapolis 500 and ran well enough during the entire season to finish in twelfth place in the American Automobile Association (AAA) championship standings.

De Paolo's best season occurred in 1925. Early successes at smaller tracks made him a top contender for that year's Indianapolis 500, a race that featured redesigned superchargers on most car engines, balloon-style tires, and the Brickyard's first front-wheel racer. After beating back the challenge of the numerous Miller racing cars that had been entered, De Paolo won the 500-mile race in a record speed of 101.13 miles per hour, a mark that stood until 1932. Perhaps the biggest winner in 1925, however, was his young son Tommy. De Paolo had used Tommy's baby shoes as good luck charms and had vowed that if he won the 1925 race he would buy his son's shoes for the rest of his life. On the occasion of the fiftieth anniversary of De Paolo's victory, *The Indianapolis 500 Yearbook* for 1975 claimed that Tommy had never yet had to pay for a pair of shoes.

The 1925 season began an exciting three-year run for De Paolo. That year he amassed more points than any previous AAA champion. The next season, despite a disappointing fifth-place finish at Indianapolis, De Paolo finished a strong third in the AAA standings. For 1927 De Paolo switched from a Dusenberg to a new, front-wheel drive Miller. Although De Paolo's car broke down at Indianapolis after only thirty-one laps, it ran so well during the season that De Paolo gained his second AAA national championship.

Having become financially secure, De Paolo decided to make the 1928 Indianapolis contest his last race, but a crash in practice prevented him from even qualifying for the race. Later, financial setbacks prompted De Paolo to change his plans and enter the 1929 Indianapolis 500, but steering problems with his Miller ended this third comeback after only twenty-five laps. De Paolo then worked in the promotional departments of car manufacturers until an abortive, fourth comeback in Europe during the 1934 season. A near-fatal accident during a race in Barcelona finally ended his career later in 1934—ironically, the same year that Ralph De Palma retired.

Although De Paolo never drove competitively again, he spent the remainder of his life around automobile racing—particularly the Indianapolis 500—primarily as a representative for various automotive-related companies. In 1973 he was voted to the Indianapolis 500 Hall of Fame (along with Ralph De Palma) and given the honor of singing the traditional pre-race song, "Back Home Again in Indiana." At the 1975 Indianapolis 500, which marked the fiftieth anniversary of his own victory, De Paolo and his wife were honored guests throughout the entire month of pre-race events at the speedway. De Paolo died in Costa Mesa, California.

De Paolo had a distinguished, if meteoric, career as a driver, but his place in the history of automobile racing also rests on his relationship with Ralph De Palma, his own postracing promotional work, and the staying power of his self-published memoir, *Wall Smacker* (1935). Indeed, since many of De Paolo's contemporaries did not live long enough or possess the literary skills to write autobiographies, *Wall Smacker* has remained a unique, and exceedingly accurate, account of automobile racing during its boom period of the 1920s.

• De Paolo's career is discussed in Lyle Kenyon Engel, *The Indianapolis "500": The World's Most Exciting Auto Race*, rev.

ed. (1972); Bob Russo, "De Paolo Wins 1925 Race," in *Indianapolis 500 Year Book* (1975), pp. 124, 135–39; and Brock W. Yates, *The Indianapolis 500* (1956).

NORMAN L. ROSENBERG

DE PARIS, Sidney (30 May 1905–13 Sept. 1967), jazz trumpeter, was born in Crawfordsville, Indiana, the son of Sidney De Paris, a trombonist, music teacher, and leader of the De Paris Family Band. De Paris's mother (name unknown) played alto horn, and his older brother, Wilbur, played trombone and later led a successful jazz band. De Paris received cornet lessons from his father, and starting in 1916 he toured the South with the band, playing at carnivals, tent shows, and vaudeville theaters. In 1924 he left the group to work in Washington, D.C., with pianist Sam Taylor, and the following year, moving to Harlem, he joined Andy Preer's Cotton Club Orchestra, making his first recordings with that band in November 1925. Starting in 1926 he worked on and off with Charlie Johnson's jazz orchestra at Small's Paradise, chiefly as a substitute for Jabbo Smith. In early 1927 he left New York to join his brother's band at the Pearl Theater in Philadelphia, but after about a year he rejoined Johnson as Smith's permanent replacement.

De Paris's blues-based growl style was first showcased on Johnson's Victor recordings of September 1928, "The Boy in the Boat" and "Walk That Thing," and on "Harlem Drag" and "Hot Bones and Rice" from May 1929. Throughout the late 1920s he was considered one of the best hot trumpeters on the Harlem scene, his facility with mutes and his mastery of the growl technique popularized by Bubber Miley being especially influential on such other young trumpeters as Rex Stewart, Bobby Stark, and Cootie Williams. The superior quality of his heated, heartfelt blues playing at the time, on both muted and open horn, can best be heard on the Johnson records and the November 1929 recordings of "Miss Hannah," "Peggy," and "Wherever There's a Will There's a Way" by McKinney's Cotton Pickers, a highly rated midwestern band then led by Don Redman. After leaving Johnson in 1931, De Paris briefly led his own group and played for a time in Benny Carter's orchestra, but in early 1932 he joined Redman's new big band, with which he remained through mid-1936.

After a short trip to Cleveland with Noble Sissle, whose orchestra was then sparked by soprano saxophonist Sidney Bechet, De Paris spent 1937 and 1938 in Willie Bryant's and Charlie Johnson's bands as well as participating in Mezz Mezzrow's inspired but ill-fated attempt to launch a racially mixed big band. During its brief existence late in 1937, Mezzrow's fourteen Disciples of Swing played at the Harlem Uproar House and the Savoy Ballroom, but racial pressures and lack of public support worked against the group's success. Beginning in October 1938 De Paris spent several months in Allie Ross's theater pit band for the *Blackbirds* show; he then returned to Redman briefly before forming his own eight-piece band for a job in Baltimore.

In September 1939 De Paris played alongside Bechet, Albert Nicholas, and Zutty Singleton on two Jelly Roll Morton recording dates for Bluebird, and from December through June 1940 he frequently augmented Singleton's trio at Nick's in Greenwich Village. At times during this residency, Singleton enlarged his trio, with Nicholas on clarinet, to a sextet, adding De Paris and others to fill out the ensemble sound of a traditional New Orleans jazz band. Bechet used him on a June 1940 record date with his own New Orleans Feetwarmers as well as engaging him for later jobs. After some occasional work, he again joined Carter's big band for a ten-month stay ending in September 1941, when he rejoined Singleton and spent a few weeks in the trumpet section of Charlie Barnet's popular swing band. In 1942, while working in pianist Art Hodes's combo, De Paris and Singleton appeared on a widely praised recording session for Decca. With solid connections such as Bechet, Singleton, Eddie Condon, and Hodes, De Paris became part of the New York small band jazz scene, while remaining active in big bands.

In the spring of 1943 the De Paris brothers, with Wilbur as leader, took their own sextet into Jimmy Ryan's on Fifty-second Street, and in February 1944 they received their first joint billing as leaders on the Commodore label. De Paris also had his own first date in June for Blue Note with an exceptional seven-piece group featuring clarinetist Edmond Hall, trombonist Vic Dickenson, and pianist James P. Johnson; one of the four numbers recorded, "The Call of the Blues," became his most memorable achievement. De Paris worked the summer months touring with Roy Eldridge's orchestra. From late 1943 until 1945 De Paris recorded as a sideman on dates led by Hall, Johnson, Eldridge, Bechet, Cliff Jackson, and J. C. Higginbotham; however, he did not record again as a leader until June 1951, when he assembled a New Orleans–styled sextet including clarinetist Omer Simeon, trombonist Jimmy Archey, and bassist Pops Foster for another Blue Note session. His most prolific period began in 1952, when as a featured member of his brother's Rampart Street Paraders he appeared on thirteen albums before the end of 1961.

In 1946 De Paris made several USO tours with Claude Hopkins's band, and in 1947 he rejoined his brother for engagements at Jimmy Ryan's, Child's Paramount, and the Palladium Ballroom. In the winter of 1950 the De Paris brothers were hired by Bechet's young disciple, Bob Wilber, for a stay at Storyville in Boston, during which time Wilbur decided to form another band—this one modeled on the style and organizational structure of Morton's late 1920s' Red Hot Peppers. In September 1951 the De Paris brothers opened at Ryan's for what would prove to be the longest-lasting run of any jazz band on Fifty-second Street. Not wishing to travel, De Paris led his own group at Ryan's when Wilbur took the band on a State Department–sponsored tour of Africa during the spring of 1957. However, De Paris resumed his role as sideman on his brother's return. De Paris's health had been failing for some time before the early 1960s, and increasingly trumpeter Doc Cheatham was called on to provide relief. But even at these times, De Paris doubled on cornet, flugelhorn, and tuba. He played infrequently in his last years and came to depend on his brother's daily care. He died in New York City.

• There is no biography of Sidney De Paris, and since he was extremely reticent no interviews exist. A big band section player for most of his career before 1952, his earlier activities can be gleaned only from accounts of the orchestras with which he worked. Albert McCarthy, *Big Band Jazz* (1974), is invaluable, as is Gunther Schuller, *Early Jazz* (1968) and *The Swing Era: The Development of Jazz, 1930–1945* (1989). Short biographical pieces are found in Dan Morgenstern, "Sidney De Paris", in the booklet accompanying *The Complete Edmond Hall/James P. Johnson/Sidney De Paris/Vic Dickenson Blue Note Sessions* (Mosaic MD4-109), and in John Chilton, *Who's Who of Jazz* (1985). Discographical information is in Brian Rust, *Jazz Records, 1897–1942* (1982), and Walter Bruyninckx, *Traditional Jazz Discography, 1897–1988* (6 vols.) and *Swing Discography, 1920–1988* (12 vols.).

JACK SOHMER

DE PARIS, Wilbur (11 Jan. 1900–3 Jan. 1973), jazz trombonist, was born in Crawfordsville, Indiana, the son of Sidney De Paris, a trombonist, music teacher, and bandleader. Nothing is known of his mother except that she played alto horn. In 1907 Wilbur also started playing the alto horn, and by 1916 he was playing baritone horn in his father's band. His younger brother Sidney, Jr., also had been added to the band on cornet. Throughout the 1910s the De Paris Family Band toured in carnivals and tent shows and played on the Theater Owners' Booking Association (TOBA) vaudeville circuit. After Wilbur had switched to trombone, sometime between 1919 and 1922, he joined Billy and Mary Mack's Merrymakers and traveled with them to New Orleans, where he sat in with trumpeter Louis Armstrong at Tom Anderson's Cabaret and worked with Armand Piron's orchestra. In 1925 he led a band in Philadelphia and later played in Harlem at Connie's Inn with LeRoy Smith and in Atlantic City with Bobby Lee's Cotton Pickers. In 1927 he led a big band at the Pearl Theater in Philadelphia, and from early 1928 through late 1937 he worked and/or recorded with Smith, Clarence Williams, Edith Wilson, Jelly Roll Morton, Bubber Miley, Dave Nelson, Benny Carter, Spike Hughes, Noble Sissle, the Mills Blue Rhythm Band, Edgar Hayes, and Teddy Hill, almost always as a utilitarian sectionman (he could play any part, whether lead, solo, or harmony). Still in the same capacity, between November 1937 and September 1940 he worked with the Louis Armstrong Orchestra and, following a brief stay with Ella Fitzgerald, toured with Roy Eldridge's big band.

In the spring of 1943 De Paris and his brother Sidney took a jazz sextet into Jimmy Ryan's on Fifty-second Street in New York City, and in 1944 he appeared on record dates led by Eldridge, Cliff Jackson, Eddie Condon, and George Wettling and recorded under the name of the De Paris Brothers for the first time. Re-

solved to become part of the burgeoning small-band jazz scene in New York, on 26 December 1944 De Paris organized a jam session concert at Greenwich Village's Pied Piper that featured Sidney Bechet, Bill Coleman, Hank Duncan, Mary Lou Williams, and others. In late 1945 he hired on with Duke Ellington, in whose orchestra he remained until the spring of 1947, when he reformed his sextet and played engagements at Jimmy Ryan's, Child's Paramount, and the Palladium Ballroom. Featuring his brother Sidney (who also doubled on trumpet and sometimes played tuba), clarinetist Edmond Hall, and drummer Cozy Cole, this was essentially a swing-styled unit that, like the similarly manned group he had led in 1944, also played traditional jazz numbers. In early March 1949, along with Bechet and Buster Bailey, De Paris played opposite saxophonist Charlie Parker's all-star bebop group in a "Battle of the Bands" concert at the Waldorf-Astoria, and in April 1950 he participated in Bechet's recording date for Commodore. The next winter he and his brother joined the band of Bechet's disciple, Bob Wilber, at the Storyville Club in Boston, a job that was to lead directly to the most fruitful engagement of his career.

Convinced that the time was ripe for a band dedicated to the principles of organized New Orleans–styled jazz as exemplified by Jelly Roll Morton's Red Hot Peppers, De Paris formed the Rampart Street Paraders. In September 1951, with a personnel including his brother, famed New Orleans clarinetist Omer Simeon, pianist Don Kirkpatrick, New Orleans banjoist and guitarist Danny Barker, and drummer Freddie Moore, the De Paris band opened at Ryan's for a residency that would last until early 1962, when the club was razed to make room for the new block-long CBS building. During this period De Paris was absent only twice, first in 1957 when he embarked on a fifteen-week State Department tour of Africa, during which time Sidney took over at Ryan's, and then in 1960 when the band appeared at the Cannes Jazz Festival in Antibes, France. In addition to being a major tourist attraction, the band also recorded thirteen successful albums and was showcased on radio and television. His film credits include *The Pirate*, a 1948 musical with Judy Garland and Gene Kelly, and *Windjammer*, a 1958 travelogue.

Considering its lengthy run the De Paris band maintained fairly constant personnel over the years, the major flux being in the rhythm section. When Simeon died in September 1959, his place was taken permanently by the versatile Garvin Bushell, who was not only a skilled clarinetist but also an expert jazz bassoonist. An earlier but less noticeable change took place in December 1954 when Sonny White replaced Kirkpatrick. Barker left in early 1952 and was replaced first by Eddie Gibbs and then by Lee Blair and John Smith. The succession of bass players went from Harold Jackson through Nat Woodley, Wendell Marshall, and Bennie Moten before De Paris finally settled on Hayes Alvis in early 1958. Moore was succeeded by Zutty Singleton in 1953, by George Foster in 1955, and from 1956 on by Wilbert Kirk, who also doubled on harmonica. On occasion trumpeter Doc Cheatham was added to the group, and as Sidney's health worsened in the early 1960s he was relied on even more frequently.

Compared to the best jazz trombonists of his time—Jack Teagarden, Jimmy Harrison, Tricky Sam Nanton, Benny Morton, J. C. Higginbotham, Dicky Wills, and Vic Dickenson—Wilbur De Paris was a dependable but bland player. Indeed, for the major part of his career he was employed as a sectionman in big bands, and it was not until the mid-1940s, with the renewed popularity of older styles of jazz, that he even considered forming a small band of his own. In March 1930 he had participated as a minor functionary on three successive recordings with Jelly Roll Morton, and these experiences with the dynamic leader so impressed him that when the opportunity came to him twenty years later he adopted the Morton format rather than return to the swing combo approach of his 1944 sextet. Accordingly, he enlisted the aid of Simeon, a ten-year veteran of the Earl Hines Orchestra and the clarinetist on most of Morton's best recordings. A devoted scholar of jazz history, De Paris developed a wide repertoire of compositions that went back to early ragtime cakewalks and previously overlooked songs of the 1920s, including a considerable number of Morton tunes and other jazz classics. To these he added several stylistically related, exotic compositions of his own. An astute bandleader, De Paris realized his own limitations as an improviser and gave most of the solos to others in the group, but his hand in the structure of his band's performances is always recognizable. A sincere lover of historic jazz and one of the rare analysts and intellectuals in the field of traditional jazz, De Paris was always ready to discuss the interweaving connections among the many ingredients that went into the making of jazz, from its seminal roots in African rhythms and polyphonic singing through its Creole and Caribbean influences to its flowering in late nineteenth-century New Orleans.

After the demise of Ryan's the band worked at the Broken Drum and the Room at the Bottom in Greenwich Village and in the summer of 1965 in a Mardi Gras Show at Jones Beach. De Paris never married. Relatively inactive after his brother's death in 1967, Wilbur De Paris opened a rehearsal studio in 1971, led another short-lived band, and then died at home in New York City.

• Because of his relative anonymity during the first three decades of his career, what is known about De Paris's prewar activities has been gleaned from cursory interviews with the subject and documentation of his work on recordings. The most useful sources in this regard are John Chilton, *Who's Who of Jazz* (1985); Brian Rust, *Jazz Records, 1897–1942* (1982); and Walter Bruyninckx, *Traditional Jazz Discography, 1897–1988* (6 vols., 1985–1989) and *Swing Discography, 1920–1988* (12 vols., 1985–1989). Although De Paris's most illustrious orchestral associations were with Louis Armstrong and Duke Ellington, none of the many books on these figures provides more than a passing mention of his name, if that.

Chilton, *Sidney Bechet: The Wizard of Jazz* (1987), acknowledges De Paris's working relationship with Bechet several times, but Arnold Shaw, *52nd St.: The Street of Jazz* (1971), refers to him only once, although it does offer much information on Jimmy Ryan's, the scene of De Paris's greatest triumph. An obituary is in the *New York Times*, 6 Jan. 1973.

JACK SOHMER

DEPAUW, Washington Charles (4 Jan. 1822–5 May 1887), businessman and philanthropist, was born in Salem, Indiana, the son of John DePauw, a merchant and lawyer, and Betsy Batiste. John DePauw was a prosperous landowner and a successful politician. Young "Wash," as he was called, was educated at the county seminary and assisted his father in various business enterprises. His father died when he was sixteen, leaving "Wash" $700 in cash and a small piece of property. Elijah Malott, a merchant, and Elijah Newland, a physician, acted as the boy's guardians. Malott appointed DePauw as his deputy in the county clerk's office before he was of legal age, and he won the position on his own in 1844. DePauw married his patron's daughter, Sarah Ellen Malott, in 1846; they had two children. He was an early success in business and freely admitted his determination to earn a fortune. He soon owned a flour mill, a saw mill, and a wool-carding mill and in 1850 erected both a brick commercial building and a railroad depot in Salem. He was active in Democratic politics and won reelection as county clerk by a large majority in 1851.

By the early 1850s DePauw's business interests were increasingly in the nearby Ohio River town of New Albany. He erected the DePauw House, New Albany's leading hotel, and was the largest investor and first president of the Merchants' and Mechanics' Bank. He also established a bank in Salem and played an active role in banking matters statewide. He declined election as county clerk in 1855 and withdrew from active politics by the end of the decade. In 1872 he received an unsolicited Democratic nomination for lieutenant governor but declined. Sarah Ellen DePauw died in 1851, and in 1855 he married Catherine Newland, the nineteen-year-old daughter of his former guardian; the couple had three children. DePauw was already a Methodist, but his new wife drew him more deeply into church affairs, and he soon became a generous supporter of Methodist institutions.

During the Civil War, DePauw's business interests flourished, particularly contracts to supply wheat and corn to the Union army. Soon after Kate DePauw's death in 1864 he moved his family permanently to New Albany. In 1867 he married Frances Marian Leyden; they had four children. Federal income tax records for 1864 show him as the richest man in Indiana, with an income of $307,450.

By the late 1860s DePauw was a leading businessman in a bustling industrial city. He erected the DePauw Block for stores and offices and the DePauw Hall for concerts and meetings. He owned majority interests in three of New Albany's six banks and a large minority interest in a fourth. The local agent of R. G.

Dun's credit-rating service noted in 1867 that "Mr. DePauw commands unlimited means for any business he may engage in." He invested in a variety of struggling industrial enterprises, providing capital for the expansion of existing firms rather than establishing new businesses of his own: the New Albany Woolen Mill, the Ohio Falls Iron Works, the New Albany Rolling Mill, and the Western Axe and Edge Tool Works, as well as two glass manufacturers. He eventually became sole owner of the American Plate Glass Works (formerly the Star Glass Works), the nation's foremost plate glass maker, but the firm did not earn a profit until 1879, after Congress enacted a protective tariff for which DePauw had successfully lobbied.

DePauw was the largest employer in New Albany after 1873. When he complained of high property taxes, the city council voted overwhelmingly to disannex thirty acres of his factory sites. A four-month strike for higher wages by plate glass workers in 1880 brought widespread public criticism, but DePauw took a high-toned, paternalistic position and outwaited the strikers. Well-paid and highly skilled glassblowers stood by "Uncle Wash." DePauw was clearly the dominant industrial and political figure in New Albany, although he wished to be regarded as pious and benevolent rather than simply as rich.

DePauw served as a trustee of Indiana Asbury University from 1856 until 1862, when he resigned in disgust at its chronic financial troubles. Urged by Methodist leaders to return to the board, he agreed in 1869 and played an active role in shaping educational policy as well as providing financial support.

Before leaving for an extended foreign tour in 1881, DePauw made a will providing for establishment of a university bearing his name. Methodist leaders offered to rename the struggling Indiana Asbury for DePauw in return for a substantial contribution, but he resisted their pleas for many months. Although he wished to create a university to perpetuate his memory, he feared public criticism if he did so during his lifetime. He also wished his university to be located in a major city, and Indiana Asbury refused to move from Greencastle, a small town west of Indianapolis.

DePauw eventually yielded to the desperate pleas of his fellow trustees and the leaders of Indiana Methodism. His gift was conditional upon additional contributions of $150,000 from church members and other friends of the university. They were unable to raise the full amount, and DePauw accordingly reduced his gift. Indiana Asbury changed its name to DePauw University in 1884, and DePauw donated $240,000, hinting that additional gifts might follow. As he had feared, critics were quick to say that he should provide all of the money now that the university carried his name. DePauw played an active role as trustee and provided generously for the university in his will.

DePauw died in Chicago, Illinois, and received a splendid public funeral in New Albany. Twice a widower, he was survived by his third wife and four of his children. His flourishing iron and glass enterprises were mismanaged by his two sons and devastated by the panic of 1893. Instead of the $1,300,000 it had been led to expect, DePauw University eventually received $210,000, but Washington C. DePauw is remembered for his philanthropy, just as he intended. The DePauw legend was elaborated by a respectful university, and his business success was ignored except as a source of donations for worthy causes. The DePauw family was Flemish and Catholic in origin, but the legend made it French and Calvinist.

DePauw was an investor and capitalist rather than an industrialist, a demanding employer at the same time that he was a generous supporter of Methodist charities. As a delegate to the Methodist Ecumenical Conference in London (1881) he spoke of consecrating "everything we have to Christ . . . our homes, our lives, our pocket books." So he wished to be remembered.

• Few DePauw business or personal papers survive, except for a small collection in the DePauw University archives. For personal and family matters the best source is a senior honors thesis at DePauw, Michael F. O'Brien, "A Nineteenth Century Hoosier Businessman: Washington Charles DePauw" (1966). Lawrence M. Lipin, *Producers, Proletarians, and Politicians: Workers and Party Politics in Evansville and New Albany, Indiana, 1850–87* (1994), offers a scholarly account of his business and political activities. Victor M. Bogle, "Nineteenth Century River Town: A Social-Economic Study of New Albany, Indiana" (Ph.D. diss., Boston Univ., 1951), provides a full local context. For his relations with DePauw University, see George B. Manhart, *DePauw through the Years* (1962), and Clifton J. Phillips and John J. Baughman, *DePauw: A Pictorial History* (1987).

PATRICK J. FURLONG

DEPEW, Chauncey Mitchell (23 Apr. 1834–5 Apr. 1928), public speaker, railroad president, and U.S. senator, was born in Peekskill, New York, the son of Isaac Depew, a shipowner, merchant, and farmer, and Martha Mitchell. After graduating from Peekskill Academy in 1852, Chauncey entered Yale where he forsook the Democratic faith of his father and sided with the antislavery forces of the newly created Republican party. After receiving his diploma in 1856, young Depew began the study of law in the office of a Peekskill attorney and was admitted to the bar in 1858. That same year he was a delegate to the Republican State Convention, and in 1862 and 1863 he served in the New York state legislature, becoming a leader of the GOP caucus during his second session. In 1863 he was elected New York's secretary of state, a post he held for two years. Throughout this period he developed a reputation as a campaign speaker who could sway a crowd in support of the Republican cause. In an age when oratorical skill was a prerequisite to political success, his gift for speaking proved an invaluable asset.

In 1866 Depew decided to leave public service, refusing an appointment as U.S. minister to Japan. Commodore Cornelius Vanderbilt (1794–1877) told him, "Railroads are the career for a young man; there is nothing in politics. Don't be a damned fool." Depew accepted the advice and signed on as an attorney for Vanderbilt's railroads. For the remainder of his long life he was associated with the Vanderbilt interests, specifically the New York Central Railroad. By 1874 he was a director of the Vanderbilt system and the next year became its general counsel. In 1882 he was named second vice president of the New York Central, advancing to the presidency of the railroad three years later. Meanwhile, in 1871 Depew married Elsie A. Hegeman, with whom he had one son. Elsie died in 1893, and eight years later Depew married May Palmer; they had no children.

During the 1870s and 1880s Depew not only developed into a leading business figure, but also enhanced his reputation as a public speaker. The nineteenth century was an era of great orator-politicians, and in the minds of his contemporaries Depew ranked among the most distinguished. In 1886 he delivered the principal address at the dedication of the Statue of Liberty; six years later he was chosen to speak at the laying of the cornerstone of Grant's Tomb; and also in 1892 he presented the dedicatory oration at the Chicago World's Fair. He was in constant demand as an after-dinner speaker, and his wit earned him fame as the most entertaining orator of his day. Depew once observed, "With an American audience no speech sticks unless there is some humor in it." During his lifetime, Depew's speeches were published in a series of volumes, winning him a following among many who had never heard him speak. One observer said of Depew in 1894, "He is probably the best-known American living today, with the sole exception of the President of the United States."

Speaking, however, was a hobby rather than a vocation for Depew. In fact, he regarded it as a form of recreation, a means of relieving the tension and anxiety arising from his duties as chief of the New York Central Railroad. "Speech-making is a tonic to me," Depew once remarked, and it was an elixir he indulged in for the rest of his life. At the age of eighty-six he won the rapt attention and roaring applause of delegates to the Republican National Convention, and when he was past ninety he continued to speak at the annual birthday dinners given in his honor by the Montauk Club of Brooklyn. At ninety-one he participated in the new age of communications when his birthday speech was broadcast over the radio.

During the late nineteenth century many Republicans sought to draw Depew back into public service. A contender for the U.S. Senate in 1881, Depew withdrew from the contest when the New York legislature became deadlocked in balloting for the position. Four years later he rejected entreaties to vie again for the Senate. In 1888 he was New York's favorite son candidate for president, but again he withdrew from contention, throwing his support to Benjamin Harrison (1833–1901). Depew repeatedly refused to accept appointments to Harrison's cabinet. In 1899, at an age when most men would be contemplating retirement, he stepped down as president of the New York Central

(though he remained chairman of the board) and embarked on a twelve-year tenure in the U.S. Senate.

In the Senate, Depew used his powers of debate and oratory to good effect. However, in 1905 his popularity suffered a setback when an investigation of the insurance industry, led by future New York governor and U.S. Supreme Court justice Charles Evans Hughes, revealed that the Equitable Life Assurance Company had been paying Depew an annual retainer of $20,000. Many observers concluded that the Equitable was purchasing political influence and that the venerable senator was a paid servant of the company's interests. Moreover, the fact that throughout his senatorial career, and until the end of his life, Depew remained chairman of the New York Central board caused some critics to claim that he was a hired lobbyist-legislator not only for the insurance giants but for the big railroad interests as well. Those suspicious of the power of big business called for Depew's resignation from the Senate, but he filled out his term, finally retiring in 1911.

For the remaining seventeen years of his life, Depew continued to act as the Prince Charming of capitalism, enlivening banquets with his witty, well-honed speeches and steadfastly supporting those twin pillars of his life, the New York Central Railroad and the Republican party. In an age when many Americans viewed railroad giants as ugly tyrants and rebelled at the Vanderbilts' public-be-damned attitude, the highly personable Depew was able to apply a genial face to corporate America and soften the harsh image of the business tycoon. In his written and oral reminiscences of seven decades in politics and business, he proclaimed his delight with living, and for his listeners and readers he momentarily masked the bitter struggles of industrial society with the attractive cosmetic of urbane rhetoric. He died in New York City.

• One collection of Depew's papers is at Yale University Library; another is at George Washington University Library. His reminiscences were published in *My Memories of Eighty Years* (1922). A discussion of Depew as a public speaker is Willard Hayes Yeager, *Chauncey Mitchell Depew, the Orator* (1934). A biographical sketch is in Joseph B. Gilder, ed., *Life and Later Speeches of Chauncey M. Depew* (1894).

JON C. TEAFORD

DE PEYSTER, Abraham (8 July 1657–2 Aug. 1728), colonial government official and merchant, was born in New Amsterdam, the son of Johannes De Peyster and Cornelia Lubbertse. His father, having settled in New Amsterdam in the early 1650s, created a thriving mercantile business that his son further developed by the early 1680s. While De Peyster began to rise in rank in the militia, he was also called upon in 1684 to become the city assessor and the following year became an alderman. While on a visit to Holland in 1684, De Peyster met and married a cousin, Catherine De Peyster. They had five children that survived to maturity. The province came to depend on De Peyster to supply local officials with monetary loans or food supplies for the militia. His continued inability to speak English did not deter local government agencies from calling on him for assistance whenever necessary.

New York was thrown into chaos when news reached the community in May 1689 of the accession of William and Mary to the English throne. Lieutenant Governor Francis Nicholson was a loyal supporter of James II, and when he found himself caught in the midst of rising local support for William and Mary, he threatened to "fire the town." At that point militia captain Jacob Leisler and a company of soldiers seized control of the fort. German-born Leisler, a wealthy international merchant, soon became the dominant authority in both the city and province of New York.

De Peyster was regarded, at first, as a Leisler supporter because the populace had split on ethnic and religious lines with Dutch inhabitants to a great extent supporting Leisler against the Anglican English. Leisler's arbitrary administrative methods alienated some of his earlier supporters, including De Peyster, who added his signature to a petition seeking redress from "the burthen of Slavery and arbitrary Power executed over us by the inraged fury of some ill men among us."

Once the so-called Leisler Rebellion had been crushed and Leisler executed in 1693 by Governor Henry Sloughter's order, a purge began in the provincial administration to remove Leislerian advocates. While many were ousted from provincial positions by Governor Sloughter, De Peyster actually gained influence by becoming mayor of New York in 1691. Perhaps because of De Peyster's continued prominence in commercial affairs, the governor found it expedient not to antagonize a leading member of the Dutch citizenry. Political divisions continued in New York, and the Crown named Richard Coote, the earl of Bellomont, as successor to Sloughter in 1698, with the hope that a new face would help ease tensions. Openly sympathetic to the Leislerians, Bellomont encouraged further local governmental involvement by the Dutch element. De Peyster soon became a member of the council, justice of the Supreme Court of Judicature, and commanding colonel of the militia of the city and county of New York. Upon the earl's death in March 1701, and with Lieutenant Governor John Nanfan away, De Peyster asserted that a majority of the governor's councillors should hold the reins of government until the return of the lieutenant governor or the appointment of a new governor. With anti-Leislerian councillors refusing to participate in such a move, De Peyster assumed control until Nanfan's return.

Continuing to sit as a supreme court justice, De Peyster became embroiled in the treason trial of Nicholas Bayard in 1702. Bayard, a leading anglicized Dutchman, had opposed Leisler and actively sought Leisler's execution. As of 1702 Bayard was accused of signing a petition attacking the recent Bellomont and Nanfan administrations. Found guilty of committing an act of treason, Bayard was sentenced to execution but was subsequently reprieved by the next governor, Edward Hyde, Viscount Cornbury, later that year. De Peyster's role in this dramatic trial remains enigmatic.

It appears that he worked behind the scenes to obtain a reprieve for Bayard. Bloodletting was not part of De Peyster's makeup; accommodation seemed to be his guiding principle. This made him appear as a political trimmer to his anti-Leislerian critics.

In 1721 Abraham De Peyster, Jr., succeeded his father as treasurer, at which time his father was described as being "closely confined by his family on that account without any hopes of his Recovery." De Peyster remained closely confined until he died in New York, after being "deprived of his senses and reason." Although not particularly active in religious affairs, he left bequests in equal amounts to the Dutch, French, and English churches.

• Papers relating to the activities of Abraham De Peyster and his brothers Johannes, Isaac, and Cornelius are in the De Peyster papers at the New-York Historical Society. William Smith, Jr., *The History of the Province of New-York*, vol. 1, ed. Michael Kammen (1972), makes note of De Peyster's career. Scattered references appear in Edmund B. O'Callaghan, ed., *Documents Relative to the Colonial History of the State of New York*, vols. 3–5 (1853–1855). An excellent biographical account may be found in Paul M. Hamlin and Charles E. Baker, *Supreme Court of Judicature of the Province of New York 1691–1704*, vol. 3 (1959). De Peyster's activities at the time of the Bayard trial are discussed by Adrian Howe, "The Treason Trial: Dramatizing Anglo-Dutch Politics in Early Eighteenth-Century New York," *William and Mary Quarterly* (Jan. 1990): 56–89.

JACOB JUDD

DE PRIEST, Oscar Stanton (9 Mar. 1871–12 May 1951), politician, was born in Florence, Alabama, the son of Martha Karsner, a part-time laundress, and Neander R. De Priest, a teamster and farmer. His father, a former slave, joined the Republican party. After a neighbor's lynching, the family moved to Salina, Kansas, in 1878. Young Oscar had sandy hair, blue eyes, and a light complexion and often fought over racial slurs made in his presence. After two years at Salina Normal School, he left home at seventeen, settling in Chicago. He apprenticed as a house painter and by 1905 had a successful contracting and real estate business. In 1898 he married Jessie L. Williams; they had one child.

De Priest was elected Cook County commissioner in 1904 and 1906 because he delivered a bloc of African-American voters from the city's Second and Third wards for the Republican party. He educated his constituency about city and county relief resources but lost the 1908 nomination over a dispute with First District congressman Martin B. Madden. For the next few years he maneuvered among various factions, sometimes supporting Democrats over Republicans. He reconciled with Madden and backed white Republican candidates for alderman against African Americans running as independents in 1912 and 1914.

In 1915 the growing African-American community united to elect De Priest to the city council. Significant support came from women, who had won the municipal ballot in 1913. As alderman, he introduced a civil rights ordinance and fought against job discrimination. Indicted in 1917 on charges of taking a bribe from a gambling establishment, De Priest claimed the money as a campaign contribution. He was successfully defended by Clarence Darrow but was persuaded not to run again. He campaigned as an independent in 1918 and 1919 but lost to black Republican nominees. In the 1919 race riots, his reputation was revived when, armed with pistols, he drove twice a day to the stockyards to supply his community with meat.

The riots helped De Priest renew ties to the Republican mayor, William Hale Thompson, and he was a delegate to the 1920 Republican National Convention. In 1924 he was elected Third Ward committeeman. His help in Thompson's 1927 election won De Priest an appointment as assistant Illinois commerce commissioner. In the 1928 election he again ran successfully for Republican delegate and Third Ward committeeman. That same year he supported the renomination of Congressman Madden, who died shortly after the primary, and used his influence with the Thompson faction of the Republican party to win the nomination for Madden's seat. After he was nominated, he was indicted for alleged gambling connections and vote fraud, charges that his supporters maintained were politically motivated. De Priest refused to withdraw and won the election to represent the predominantly black First District. The case against him was subsequently dismissed for insufficient evidence.

De Priest became the first African American to serve in the U.S. Congress in twenty-eight years and the first from a northern state. He considered himself "congressman-at-large" for the nation's twelve million black Americans and promised to place a black cadet in West Point, fight for enforcement of the Fourteenth and Fifteenth amendments, and secure work relief for the unemployed. But he vowed to "represent all people, both black and white."

While denying that he sought "social equality," De Priest used his position to secure the rights of citizenship for African Americans. When his wife's attendance at First Lady Lou Hoover's traditional tea for congressional wives in 1929 created controversy, De Priest used the publicity to promote a fundraiser for the National Association for the Advancement of Colored People (NAACP). He was much in demand as a speaker, urging audiences to organize and to vote, even in the South, where threats were made against his life. Although the Great Depression, which began shortly after his arrival in Congress, lured his constituents toward the Democrats, he won reelection in 1930 and 1932. He opposed federal relief, preferring state and local measures.

De Priest sponsored a number of bills to benefit his constituents, including pensions for surviving former slaves and appropriations for African-American schools in the District of Columbia. His most important legislative victory was an amendment to the 1933 bill creating the Civilian Conservation Corps barring discrimination based on race, color, or creed. After the infamous 1931 Scottsboro case in which nine Afri-can-American boys were sentenced to death after being convicted on questionable evidence by an all-white jury of raping two white women, De Priest called for a law to enable a trial to be transferred to another jurisdiction if the defendant was deemed not likely to get a fair trial. Warning that the country would suffer if one-tenth of its population were denied justice, he said, "If we had a right to exercise our franchise . . . as the constitution provides, I would not be the only Negro on this floor." The bill died in the Judiciary Committee, as did his proposal for an antilynching bill. He also fought unsuccessfully to integrate the House of Representatives restaurant, where he was served, but his staff was not.

By 1934 De Priest faced charges that his party was doing little to help African Americans hard hit by the depression, and he lost to Arthur W. Mitchell, the first African-American Democrat elected to Congress. De Priest was vice chairman of the Cook County Republican Central Committee from 1932 to 1934, a delegate to the Republican National Convention in 1936, and alderman from the Third Ward in 1943–1947. He lost the 1947 election for alderman, partly because of charges of cooperating with the Democratic mayor. He continued in the real estate business with his son Oscar De Priest, Jr., and died at his home in Chicago.

Skillful at organizing a coalition of black voters and using this bloc to pressure the dominant white political machine, De Priest was the forerunner of many local African-American politicians in the latter part of the twentieth century. His six years in Congress enabled him to raise black political consciousness. Kenneth Eugene Mann, writing in the *Negro History Bulletin* in October 1972, noted that De Priest "took advantage of his opportunities and frequently created them."

• The Arthur W. Mitchell Papers at the Chicago Historical Society have material on De Priest. For De Priest's speeches and resolutions in Congress, see the *Congressional Record*, 71st to 73d Congresses. De Priest's congressional career is summarized in Bruce A. Ragsdale and Joel D. Treese, *Black Americans in Congress 1870–1989* (1990), and Maurine Christopher, *Black Americans in Congress* (1971; repr. 1976). For aspects of his congressional career see Kenneth Eugene Mann, "Oscar Stanton De Priest: Persuasive Agent for the Black Masses," *Negro History Bulletin* 35 (Oct. 1972): 134–37; David S. Day, "Herbert Hoover and Racial Politics: The De Priest Incident," *Journal of Negro History* 65 (Winter 1980): 6–17; and Elliott M. Rudwick, "Oscar De Priest and the Jim Crow Restaurant in the U.S. House of Representatives," *Journal of Negro Education* 35 (Winter 1966): 77–82. For a contemporary account see Lester A. Walton, "The Negro Comes Back to the United States Congress," *Current History*, June 1929, pp. 461–63. Harold F. Gosnell, *Negro Politicians* (1935), gives an overview of his political life. Ralph Bunche, "The Thompson-Negro Alliance," *Opportunity*, Mar. 1929, covers his early years in politics. See Wanda A. Hendricks, "'Vote for the Advantage of Ourselves and Our Race': The Election of the First Black Alderman in Chicago," *Illinois Historical Journal* 87 (Autumn 1994): 171–84, on women in the 1915 election. For the depression period, see Rita Werner Gordon, "The Change in the Political Alignment of Chicago's Negroes during the New Deal," *Journal of American History* 56, no. 3 (Dec. 1969): 584ff.; and St. Clair

Drake and Horace Clayton, *Black Metropolis* (1945). Obituaries are in the *New York Times* and the *Chicago Tribune*, 13 May 1951, and the *Chicago Defender*, 19 May 1951.

KRISTIE MILLER

DE QUILLE, Dan (9 May 1829–16 Mar. 1898), humorist and journalist, was born William Wright near Fredericktown, Ohio, to Paxson Wright and Lucinda Markley, farmers. Wright was the oldest of nine children. In 1847 his father moved the family to a farm near West Liberty, Iowa, but died soon afterward, leaving Wright with the responsibility for the farm and the rest of the family. In 1853 Wright married Caroline Coleman and started his own family. Five children were born in quick succession to the couple, two of whom died in infancy.

Wright's family life is somewhat of a mystery. In 1857, attracted by the excitement of goldmining in California, Wright left his family and, except for one six-month period in 1863 and several months at the end of his life, did not return to Iowa. Nevertheless, he supported his family for most of his life, and both his wife and individual children came out west to live with him for periods of time.

Wright reached California by sail. Once there, he found that most of the goldfields on the coast had already been worked out, so he began prospecting on the eastern slope of the Sierra Nevada, between Death Valley and Lake Tahoe. Hearing of the newly opened silver mines in the Comstock Lode in the Nevada Territory, he moved there in 1860 and spent essentially the rest of his life in Virginia City.

Almost from the beginning of his western life, Wright composed travel letters and humorous squibs for newspapers and magazines in California and Iowa. The pen name he chose for himself was Dan De Quille, and that name soon became more widely known than his own and all but replaced it. He was known as an author by the time he moved to Nevada and contributed many items of literary and historical merit to such periodicals as San Francisco's *Golden Era* and the Cedar Falls (Iowa) *Gazette*. By 1861 De Quille gave up prospecting and joined the *Territorial Enterprise* of Virginia City, newly established by Joseph Goodman and Denis McCarthy; it soon became one of the most important papers of the West. He remained associated with the *Enterprise* for over thirty years. De Quille was universally respected as its mining editor, and as its local editor he occasionally contributed humorous items and short stories that earned him separate fame as a literary figure.

One of the most fateful events in his life occurred in 1862, when a young man named Samuel Clemens (soon to call himself Mark Twain) joined the *Enterprise*. The two men immediately became close friends and, sharing the same sense of humor and many of the same values, began to influence each other. Being slightly older than Twain and more experienced both in mining and in writing, De Quille taught Twain many tricks of the trade. In addition, Twain appropriated ideas and texts from De Quille that subsequently appeared in such later works as *Roughing It*, *Life on the Mississippi*, and *Huckleberry Finn*.

The two men lived and worked together in Virginia City until 1864, when Twain left for California and went on to fame. De Quille remained in Nevada, riding the boom of the silver mines of the Comstock Lode until they peaked in the late 1870s, and then riding the bust until 1898, when Virginia City was almost a ghost town. De Quille often capitalized on his association with Twain by writing reminiscences of him, and he secretly envied Twain's success and tried to imitate him, almost always less successfully. Inadvertently and unintentionally, Twain thus became a bad influence on De Quille.

De Quille became an alcoholic by the early 1870s and was laid off, sometimes for years, from the *Enterprise*. Instead of succumbing to his condition, De Quille controlled it and became more resourceful. He increased his freelance activity by sending short stories and essays to newspapers and magazines from San Francisco to New York and became a weekly correspondent for C. C. Goodwin's *Salt Lake City Daily Tribune* in 1885. Usually a gentle and witty writer, De Quille was outraged by America's abandonment of silver and bimetallism, and for years fulminated in the *Tribune* with uncharacteristic acrimony against the gold standard.

By the time the *Enterprise* ceased publication in 1893, De Quille had worked his way out from under Twain's shadow and entered upon his last period of original productivity. Ideas for plots came rapidly to him and he wrote furiously, sometimes completing but not placing, or even trying to place, his work. Perhaps the most important of his later writings is *Dives and Lazarus*, a Comstock novella modeled after Dante's *Divine Comedy*. By 1897, bent from arthritis and all worn out, De Quille was destitute. When John W. Mackay, the Comstock millionaire and a friend of De Quille, learned of his condition, he bestowed a monthly pension on De Quille and sent an agent to Virginia City to buy him a suit of clothes and accompany him back to West Liberty and the home of his daughter. De Quille left Virginia City for the last time on 14 July 1897. By January 1898 he was too weak to hold a pencil. He passed away in West Liberty two months later.

De Quille was the favorite and most beloved writer of the Comstock, where he was more highly thought of than Twain. In his day, De Quille had a national reputation as an author and journalist. His works were published and copied in scores of newspapers and magazines all across the country. At his best he was both a brilliant humorist and a writer of excellent fiction that was subtle and psychologically astute and that also reflected a surprising range of learning. But he was inexplicably diffident about collecting his work and promoting himself. Only *The Big Bonanza* (1876), the classic contemporary account of the Comstock Lode, was published in his lifetime as a book. It and a few choice works of humor and biography kept his name alive, as did his association with Twain. When scholars began to collect, study, and republish his short pieces in the 1980s, he was finally recognized as one of the most important, accomplished, and knowledgeable writers of the Old West, having lived in it and written about it for more than forty years.

Although Twain and De Quille are often lumped together as western writers, De Quille was unique. Whereas Twain's humor was often edged and aimed at some target, De Quille's typically was good-natured. Where Twain became angry and bitter in his old age, De Quille became more spiritual and affirmed his faith in God and an afterlife. For Twain, the West was a six-year episode—although a very important one—in his life. For De Quille, the West was everything. He loved it for itself, for the way of life it made possible, and for the high-spirited, independent, and colorful individuals who flourished in it.

De Quille is especially unusual among Old West authors in that he believed that money should not be an end in itself but rather a means to a moral life. As a consequence, even in relatively early works he often treated the attraction of wealth that drew so many to it as a danger and sometimes a curse. Although he served the silver kings of the Comstock for most of his life, toward its end he came to understand that the West had been exploited and despoiled, and in the works of the 1890s he empathized with those whose ways of life had been destroyed: the Indians, the prospectors, and the frontiersmen.

No other author of the Old West recorded as much of it as he, or wrote about it for a longer span of time. The corpus of his work is a loving but perceptive chronicle of his time and place. His literary skill ensures him the status of a minor classic.

• The largest and most important archive of De Quille manuscripts and papers is at the Bancroft Library of the University of California at Berkeley. The State Historical Society of Iowa, at Iowa City, also has a substantial archival collection. The Nevada Historical Society at Reno has important De Quille files and holdings of microfilms of newspapers for which De Quille wrote. No full biography of De Quille exists, but Lawrence I. Berkove's extensive introduction to De Quille's novella, *Dives and Lazarus* (1988) is largely biographical. Oscar Lewis's introduction to *The Big Bonanza* (1947) contains considerable biographical information relating to the publication of the book, and his *The Life and Times of the* Virginia City Territorial Enterprise (1971) is an important collection of memoirs by De Quille and some of his former colleagues. A discussion of how and why De Quille at the end of a life of tolerance developed bigoted attitudes toward Jews and Chinese, groups he had formerly befriended, is presented in Lawrence I. Berkove, "Free Silver and Jews: The Change in Dan De Quille," *American Jewish Archives* 41, no. 1 (Spring/Summer 1989): 43–51. Collections of De Quille's writings are Lawrence I. Berkove, ed., *The Fighting Horse of the Stanislaus: Stories and Essays by Dan De Quille* (1990); Berkove, ed., *The Gnomes of the Dead Rivers* (1990); James J. Rawls, ed., *Dan De Quille of the Big Bonanza* (1980); Richard A. Dwyer and Richard E. Lingenfelter, eds., *Dan De Quille, the Washoe Giant* (1990); Lingenfelter, ed., *Washoe Rambles* (1963); and C. Grant Loomis, "The Tall Tales of Dan De Quille," *California Folklore Quarterly* 5 (Jan. 1946): 26–71. Special editions of major but hitherto unpublished De Quille stories include Berkove, ed., "Pahnenit, Prince of the Land

of Lakes," *Nevada Historical Society Quarterly* 31, no. 2 (Summer 1988): 79–118, and Berkove, ed., *The Sorceress of Attu* (1994). Some of De Quille's correspondence is available in Berkove, "'Nobody Writes to Anybody Except to Ask a Favor': New Correspondence between Mark Twain and Dan De Quille," *Mark Twain Journal* 26, no. 1 (Spring 1988): 2–21. Substantial discussions about the relationship of De Quille and Twain can be found in Edgar M. Branch, *The Literary Apprenticeship of Mark Twain* (1966), and Henry Nash Smith, *Mark Twain of the Enterprise* (1957). New information that extends De Quille's influence on Twain is presented by Berkove in "Dan De Quille and 'Old Times on the Mississippi,'" *Mark Twain Journal* 24, no. 2 (Fall 1986): 28–35; "New Information on Dan De Quille and 'Old Times on the Mississippi,'" *Mark Twain Journal* 26, no. 2 (Fall 1988): 15–20; and "Dan De Quille and *Roughing It*: Borrowings and Influence," *Nevada Historical Society Quarterly* 37, no. 1 (Spring 1994): 52–57.

LAWRENCE I. BERKOVE

DERBIGNY, Pierre Auguste Charles Bourguignon (1767–6 Oct. 1829), governor and jurist, was born in Laon, France, the son of Auguste Bourguignon d'Herbigny and Louise Angeline Blondel. As members of the French nobility, the Derbigny family escaped the revolution by fleeing to the French West Indian colony on Santo Domingo. Subsequently, Derbigny moved to the mainland, probably because of the political unrest on the island. He lived in Pittsburgh, where he married Félicité Odile Dehault de Lassus. He moved to Missouri and then to Florida before settling permanently in New Orleans around 1800.

In New Orleans, Derbigny served in a succession of offices. He was the mayor's secretary during the brief period of French rule in 1803. His linguistic talents brought him to the attention of the new American regime. William C. C. Claiborne, the territorial governor of Lower Louisiana (Territory of Orleans), appointed him as official interpreter for the American government. During the territorial period (1803–1812), Derbigny also served as clerk of the court of common pleas and secretary of the legislative council.

Derbigny was very active in the volatile politics of the territory. Tensions between Louisiana's French inhabitants and the new American settlers surfaced soon after the French delivery of Louisiana to the United States (1803). Derbigny was sent to Washington as one of three commissioners, bearing a memorial to Congress (*Louisiana Remonstrance*), which detailed the many grievances of the French inhabitants, particularly the failure of the U.S. government to grant them immediate statehood. At the time, Derbigny wrote the *Esquisse de la Situation Politique et Civile de la Louisiane* (1804), a highly charged political attack on the territorial governor. The *Esquisse* focused attention on the transition in the civil courts from Spanish judicial forms to American procedures, which the local population resisted. The pamphlet also highlighted the growth in New Orleans of the "prodigious number of lawyers," who profited at the expense of impoverished litigants "by digging among the ashes of faded causes or by creating litigation where there was nothing but a shadow." Apparently, the *Esquisse* did not affect Derbigny's career as an appointed official, even though his authorship of the pamphlet was widely known. While in Washington, Derbigny wrote other tracts in support of the *Louisiana Remonstrance*, but the mission proved to be unsuccessful. Back in New Orleans, Derbigny played a key role in resisting the introduction of Anglo-American common law into the Territory of Orleans. He drafted the legislative resolution declaring that the existing Spanish and French laws must remain in force, a direct challenge to American policy in Lower Louisiana.

Derbigny also authored one of the principal legal briefs in another great issue of the territorial period, the fight between President Thomas Jefferson and Edward Livingston over a piece of Mississippi alluvial land known as the New Orleans Batture. Derbigny was the principal advocate for the public's right to the batture against claims of private ownership made by Livingston. When Livingston attempted to block members of the public from digging in the rich alluvial soil of the batture, Jefferson ordered the eviction of Livingston and his workers. Derbigny's published tract on the subject (1807) was the first entry in a lively pamphlet war over this hot legal dispute.

Derbigny was a regent of the University of Orleans, and when Louisiana became a state (1812), he was elected to the lower house of the first legislature. Subsequently, he was appointed as an associate justice of the Louisiana Supreme Court. In that capacity, he wrote the opinion for the court in the case of *Cottin v. Cottin* (1817), which declared that Spanish laws were still in force in Louisiana to the extent that the laws of Spain had not been specifically repealed. He also served as Louisiana's secretary of state (1820–1827).

Along with Livingston and Louis Moreau-Lislet, Derbigny was appointed as a redactor to prepare a revision of the Louisiana Civil Code, which had been adopted in 1808 as a digest of the laws then in force. Completed as a project in 1823, the work was the basis for the Civil Code of 1825, which served as the foundation of private law until another revision was adopted after the Civil War.

Derbigny was elected governor of Louisiana in 1828. During his brief tenure, he tried to ease the political tensions between French and American settlers. Before his first year in office was completed, Derbigny suffered a fatal injury as a result of a carriage accident. He died in Gretna, Louisiana.

• For more information on Derbigny see *Official Letter Books of W. C. C. Claiborne, 1801–1816* (6 vols., 1917); C. E. Carter, ed., *The Territorial Papers of the United States*, vol. 9 (26 vols., 1934–1962); George Dargo, *Jefferson's Louisiana: Politics and the Clash of Legal Traditions* (1975); Tulane Law School, *The Louisiana Civil Code: A Humanistic Appraisal* (1981); H. P. Dart, "History of the Supreme Court of Louisiana," *Louisiana Historical Quarterly* 4 (1921): 14–81; and W. K. Dart, "Justices of the Supreme Court of Louisiana," *Louisiana Historical Quarterly* 4 (1921): 113–24. An obituary is in the *Louisiana Courier* (New Orleans), 7 Oct. 1829.

GEORGE DARGO

DERBY, Elias Hasket (16 Aug. 1739–8 Sept. 1799), merchant, was born in Salem, Massachusetts, the son of Captain Richard Derby, an established ship master and merchant, and Mary Hodges, a merchant's daughter. His father's rise as a prominent general merchant was instrumental in lofting Derby to the position of one of the wealthiest and most successful merchants of his age. As an apprentice in his father's counting-house, young Derby assisted in the management of a burgeoning shipping business through the 1750s and 1760s. He became adept at keeping the firm's books and coordinating the flow of New England fish, lumber, and produce, West Indies sugar and molasses, and Southern tobacco and naval stores. As his aging father gradually withdrew from the business, the younger Derby assumed full control of counting-house operations, introducing new practices to adapt to the increasing complexity of the Atlantic trade. In 1761 he married Elizabeth Crowninshield; they had seven children.

At the close of the French and Indian War in 1763, during which the Derby family increased its fortune, Derby discerned fresh opportunities to expand the business and expedite his vessels' "ventures," or voyages. He cultivated a network of international agents to glean information about prices and demand throughout markets served by the Atlantic shipping lanes. This tactic also enabled him to consign cargoes directly to trusted intermediaries, thereby freeing his vessels from extended port calls. His captains assiduously scouted markets opened by British victory. Canada, Havana, Bermuda, and even the Barbary Coast hosted Derby vessels. Through the 1770s his vessels carried sugar and wine regularly to London, a market that his father had ignored. By the beginning of the Revolution, Derby's firm had become a major colonial business.

Derby's rise to business leadership was not an easy one. He entered the Atlantic trade during its "most dire trial," with "the old practices no longer fully suitable" (McKey, Ph.D diss., p. 65). After 1763 British imperial policy grew increasingly restrictive, closing lucrative markets and increasing the colonial merchant's costs of doing business. Melding idealism and self-interest, the Derby family, with a sole exception, opposed imperial regulations. "Piratical" seizures of Derby ships, targeted as smugglers by the British navy, especially outraged Elias Hasket. Furthermore, the family faulted British policy for a nasty postwar depression.

The flash of guns in April 1775 brought formal war with Great Britain and uncertain conditions for colonial commerce. With seven vessels plying the seas and "things . . . in such a confused state I know not what to write" (quoted in McKey, Ph.D. diss., p. 100), Derby had to trust to his captains' instincts. British reaction cleared the picture. By the winter of 1775 four of his vessels had fallen to enemy commerce raiders. He addressed British naval might directly. Along with the coastal trading vessels, armed privateers flying Derby colors sailed 110 cruises between 1775 and 1783, capturing 144 prizes, against nineteen losses. It was perhaps during this period that the fabled "Derby luck" became a topic of conversation—not all of it admiring—throughout Salem. While most colonial merchants suffered significant losses, Derby's investment, 5 percent of the colonies' entire privateering effort, made him one of the wealthiest merchants in the colonies. As his contribution to the colonists' victory was considerable, it also made him something of a local hero.

The Derby vessel *Astrea* brought home the first word of war's end in 1783; peace, however, did not improve economic conditions. Even relatively prosperous merchants like Derby found readjustment difficult, as they were forced to operate under stricter mercantilist regulations imposed by both Britain and their own former wartime allies. New England slumped into a calamitous depression; as late as 1786 the region's exports were still only one-fourth those of 1774. Derby responded to tighter postwar conditions by first employing a conventional strategy. Attempting to resume the traditional triangular coastal and West Indies trade routes, he quickly dispatched his fleet, but these twenty-five voyages between 1783 and December 1784 proved unfruitful. Trade in the Atlantic in the 1780s returned sharply reduced profits. Derby found it necessary to keep costs down, facilitate cargo collection, and avoid the prospect of flooding markets. In addition, he had to replace his wartime fleet of large, heavily-armed privateers with smaller schooners and sloops.

Derby adapted to the demands of the postwar era, establishing an economic basis for American resurgence. Scanning his maps for markets beyond the Atlantic, he targeted Mauritius, the Indian Ocean way station for France's Eastern trade, as a base for American commercial exploration. After an exchange of letters in 1785, in which his agents in Lorient identified articles best suited for the Eastern trade, Derby dispatched the *Grand Turk* to the Indian Ocean; she anchored at Port Louis in April 1786, the first American vessel to dock there. Remarkably, Derby gave responsibility for developing America's entry into the Eastern trade to his inexperienced 21-year-old son, Hasket. The adventurous Derby then organized three more voyages to the Cape of Good Hope in late 1786, even before French contacts informed him of a boom at Mauritius. Hasket immediately elected to sell Derby's pride, the *Grand Turk*, and in October 1788 sailed a newly acquired vessel to Bombay. His father's faith paid off. Through the next years, India emerged for Derby as an enormously profitable trade center.

During the next phase of commercial exploration, from 1791 to 1797, the Derby strategy focused on the search for new markets throughout the East. His captains made the first American calls at Bombay, Calcutta, Mocha, Rangoon, Manila, and assorted other ports in India, Ceylon, Sumatra, Siam, and Burma. Derby meanwhile developed a management strategy, striking a balance between writing minutely detailed instructions, based on his impressive knowledge of world

markets, and permitting his captains wide latitude. The formula was successful.

Derby's entry into the China trade was more coincidental and briefer. In 1786, before Hasket sold the *Grand Turk*, a French trader at Port Louis had chartered the ship to sail to Canton, making it the first New England vessel to reach China. The opportunity led Derby to project his Indian Ocean strategy farther afield, and by 1789 he had dispatched four more ships to Canton. However, Derby found the costs of operations in this arena prohibitive, and the difficulty of managing the demand for exotic goods in world markets made the Chinese leg of the Eastern trade less attractive. Relative profitability decided the issue; the Indian Ocean trade "compared too favorably" for Derby (McKey, Ph.D. diss., p. 262). Even before the last China ship returned at the close of 1790, Derby's strategy targeted the Indian Ocean and South Seas as his preferred theaters of commercial operations, using Salem and Mauritius as command centers.

Although Derby had shifted his attention to the East, he did not abandon the Atlantic trade. Rather, his strategic vision linked the two as essential complements of an interrelated world system of trade. He also redefined the scope of Atlantic commerce within this system. By the mid-1790s Derby realized that large imports of Eastern goods would not sell profitably in Salem, that he could avoid the time-consuming practice of collecting outgoing cargoes from disparate American, West Indian, and European marts, and that he could circumvent the expense of warehousing imports under the new Hamiltonian impost. Instead, he developed a strategy involving more triangular routes with briefer voyages, often using others' ships: from Salem they carried Indian goods to Europe and then brought European goods and currency to the East, returning to Salem, where eastern goods were broken into cargoes for the Atlantic and European trades or diverted directly to Europe.

Derby's career is a story of American business success. Although competitors such as John Jacob Astor soon adopted the role of commercial specialists, Derby succeeded as an incremental innovator, operating within a traditional commercial framework. The essential business of the House of Derby continued as it was when Derby took over the highly centralized family business was organized as a general merchant firm, dispatching cargoes of mixed goods across the globe. With the establishment of the eastern trade, he earned the popular sobriquet, "King Derby," and an encomium from the diarist William Bentley: "Wealth with full tide flows in on that successful man" (quoted in McKey, Ph.D. diss., pp. 293–94). When Derby died in Salem—by 1799 the sixth largest American city—he left a legacy of an estimated $1,000,000 in vessels, cargoes, warehouses, and other property.

Of greater historical significance, Derby was one of a handful of merchants who developed new business methods, pioneered new routes, and opened new markets to American commerce during a critical period of economic uncertainty. His entreaties to the federal government, for example, inspired the establishment of the bonded warehouse system. He was among the first American merchants to commission fast, copper-bottomed ships. Known for an almost reckless devotion to daring young mariners, he dispatched the famous "boys' voyage," sending the *Benjamin* on a three-year cruise with a nineteen-year-old captain and only one crewman over the age of twenty-one. Derby vessels brought home the first Indian native, the first zebra, and the first elephant to the United States. The products he off-loaded in Salem—coffee, tea, indigo, sugar, silks, pepper—expanded Americans' horizons and improved the quality of their lives.

• The Peabody-Essex Museum in Salem, Mass., houses the Derby Papers, along with a full range of secondary and related materials. A full-length treatment is Richard H. McKey, "Elias Hasket Derby, Merchant of Salem, Massachusetts, 1739–1799" (Ph.D. diss., Clark Univ., 1961), which provides an excellent synopsis of Derby's career. One might also consult McKey's published articles, "Elias Hasket Derby and the American Revolution," *Essex Institute Historical Collections* 97, no. 3 (July 1961): 166–96; and "Elias Hasket Derby and the Founding of the Eastern Trade," *Essex Institute Historical Collections* 98, no. 1 (Jan. 1962): 1–25 and 98, no. 2 (Apr. 1962): 65–83, both based on his dissertation. K. David Goss, "Pathway to Revolution: Salem, Massachusetts, 1763–1775" (master's thesis, Tufts Univ., 1977), analyzes the Derby family's role in the factional infighting that transformed Salem into a hotbed of revolutionary activity. See also the survey, "Elias Hasket Derby," *Essex Institute Historical Collections* 15 (1878): 306–7, Freeman Hunt's idiosyncratic sketch, "Life of Elias Hasket Derby," in *Lives of American Merchants* (1856), James Duncan Phillips's solid study of Richard Derby, *The Life and Times of Richard Derby, Merchant of Salem, 1712–1783* (1912), and Samuel Eliot Morison's excellent general study, *The Maritime History of Massachusetts, 1783–1860* (1961).

DANE A. MORRISON

DERBY, George Horatio (3 Apr. 1823–15 May 1861), soldier and literary humorist, was born in Dedham, Massachusetts, the son of John Barton Derby and Mary Townsend. Derby's father, a sometime lawyer and eccentric poet, abandoned his family in 1824, not long after George's birth. Derby entered West Point in 1842. There his practical jokes and comic drawings earned him both a number of demerits and the nickname "Squibob," one of the two chief pseudonyms with which he later signed his humorous writings. Derby graduated in 1846, seventh in a class of fifty-nine that included Stonewall Jackson and George B. McClellan (1826–1885). Initially commissioned a second lieutenant in ordnance, he was almost immediately transferred to the topographical engineers, the corps in which he served throughout the rest of his life. In April 1847 he was wounded at Cerro Gordo during the Mexican-American War and was subsequently assigned to the topographical bureau in Washington, D.C.

In Derby's day the topographical engineers were responsible for exploration and mapping and the construction of harbors, lighthouses, and military roads.

Derby spent most of his army career on the Pacific Coast, headquartered in California, also the site of his rise to fame as a humorist. He arrived in California in June of 1849, at the height of the gold rush. During the next two years he undertook four field expeditions, including mapping the mining country and the lower Colorado River.

Derby launched his literary career with the October 1850 publication of four humorous pieces in the *Alta California*, a San Francisco newspaper. By this time he had already established his reputation in the West as a practical joker and punster. So popular were his Squibob sketches over the next few years that by the spring of 1853 another California writer had begun signing his own work with Derby's pseudonym—whereupon Derby silenced his rival by publishing a piece that gave the particulars of Squibob's untimely death. Thereafter, Derby employed the new pseudonym John Phoenix.

Squibob's fame had not, however, extended outside California. Greater renown came only after Derby's guest editorship of the *San Diego Herald* later in 1853. Derby had first been stationed in San Diego in January of that year. In August the *Herald*'s editor, John Judson Ames, asked Derby to serve as temporary editor while Ames attended a Democratic party meeting in San Francisco. Derby's first act was to switch the newspaper's political allegiance to the Whig party. The six issues of the *Herald* edited by Derby were filled with comic writing and drawings, including a spoof of the era's illustrated newspapers and a vivid account of his mock-heroic combat with the returned "Judge" Ames (published *before* Ames's arrival). The San Francisco papers eagerly reprinted Derby's work for the *Herald*, and eastern editors thus discovered Derby.

In January 1854 Derby married Mary Angeline Coons; they had three children. In June of that year he began writing for the *Pioneer*, a San Francisco literary journal, while continuing to fulfill his military duties. Derby's literary reputation reached its zenith with the publication in December 1855 of *Phoenixiana; or, Sketches and Burlesques*, a volume consisting of thirty-four pieces edited by Ames of the *Herald*. As the book's subtitle indicates, burlesque was one of Derby's principal techniques, whether he was dealing with the effusions of Romantic poetry, the language of book reviews and music criticism, political oratory, or the rhetoric of the frontier boast. In "Pistol Shooting—A Counter Challenge," for instance, he debunks the frontier boast by claiming to have seen the following pronouncement by a St. Louis resident in the *Spirit of the Times*:

I will fit a dollar to the end of a twig two inches long, and while a second person will hold the other end in his mouth, so as to bring the coin within an inch and a half of his face, I engage to strike the dollar, three times out of five, at the distance of ten paces, or thirty feet. I will add in explanation that there are several persons willing and ready to hold the twig or stick described above, when required.

In response to this challenge Derby writes, with characteristic hyperbole:

I will suspend *two* dollars by a ring from a second person's nose, so as to bring the coins within three-fourths of an inch from his face, and with a double barrelled shotgun, at a distance of thirty feet, will blow dollars, nose, and man at least thirty feet further, four times out of five. I will add, in explanation, that, San Diego containing a rather intelligent community, I can find, at present, no one here willing or ready to have his nose blown in this manner; but I have no manner of doubt I could obtain such a person from St. Louis, by Adams & Co.'s Express, in due season.

Phoenixiana proved enormously popular. By the end of 1856 it had been reprinted eleven times; by 1890, over two dozen times. Early reviewers praised the vigor and originality of its humor, and Mark Twain was later to call Derby "the first great modern humorist."

Derby left California with his family in late October 1856, having been reassigned to the East. His military accomplishments on the Pacific Coast had included the construction of a dam in San Diego (1854) and road-building expeditions to Fort Vancouver and the Oregon Territory (1855–1856). The West had nurtured Derby's comic spirit, but the rigors of life on the frontier had also undermined his health. During the final years of his brief life, he was increasingly troubled by unexplained eye problems, rheumatism, and other illnesses. It was these physical disorders, not his transfer to the East, that prematurely ended his literary career.

Throughout 1857 Derby continued to publish humorous sketches in the East, principally in the *Knickerbocker* magazine and the *Boston Post*. His vision deteriorated further, however, after his assignment to Mobile, Alabama, in November of that year. The following month he published his last comic piece, a burlesque explication of Ralph Waldo Emerson's poem "Brahma." Yet Derby remained active as a military engineer for two more years, building lighthouses in Alabama and Florida. By late 1859, however, failing health had almost totally debilitated him, forcing him to take an extended leave. He died eighteen months later of what was diagnosed as "softening of the brain"—probably an undetected brain tumor.

Derby's death at age thirty-eight—just as the Civil War began and less than a year after his routine promotion to captain—brought to an end his military career but not his literary reputation. In 1865 Derby's widow and his friend Charles Poole edited a second collection of his writings, *The Squibob Papers*. But it was *Phoenixiana* that continued to win its author new readers throughout the nineteenth century.

Derby's readership has dwindled with the passage of time, even though much of his writing is still remarkably entertaining. While several critics have attempted to revive Derby's reputation, most notably

his biographer George R. Stewart, even Stewart concedes that "Derby is one of those who is more interesting when viewed as a character than when read as an author" (p. 177). Yet despite the brevity of his career and his rather small output, Derby remains of interest both to literary historians and to scholars of the western frontier. He was, after all, the first major humorist to emerge in that region. Moreover, Derby's zany comedy not only reflects the tall tale tradition of the West; it also anticipates the work of Robert Benchley, James Thurber, S. J. Perelman, and other *New Yorker* humorists in the twentieth century. Unlike these authors, however, Derby was essentially an amateur writer whose obligations to the army took precedence over his literary endeavors.

• Derby's papers are in the Bancroft Library at the University of California, Berkeley. Richard Derby Reynolds, a distant relative, has reprinted and annotated many of Derby's best sketches, together with pertinent letters, under the title *Squibob: An Early California Humorist* (1990). See also *The Topographical Reports of Lieutenant George H. Derby*, ed. Francis P. Farquhar (1933). George R. Stewart, *John Phoenix, Esq., the Veritable Squibob: A Life of Captain George H. Derby, U.S.A.* (1937), is the major biographical and critical source on Derby's life and reputation. Canice G. Ciruzzi, "'Phoenix' Revisited: Another Look at George Horatio Derby," *Journal of San Diego History* 26 (1980): 76–89, provides additional information on Derby's military career. Derby's literary influence, reputation, and achievement are also examined in Gladys Carmen Bellamy, "Mark Twain's Indebtedness to John Phoenix," *American Literature* 13 (1941): 29–43; Franklin Walker, *A Literary History of Southern California* (1950); Walter Blair and Hamlin Hill, *America's Humor: From "Poor Richard" to "Doonesbury"* (1978); and John Lang, "George Derby and the Language of Reasoned Absurdity," *Publications of the Missouri Philological Association* 3 (1978): 61–70.

JOHN LANG

DERBY, Richard (16 Sept. 1712–9 Nov. 1783), New England ship captain and merchant, was born in Salem, Massachusetts, the son of Richard Derby, a ship captain, and Martha Hasket. Richard's father died at the age of thirty-six in 1715, leaving four children to be raised by their mother and maternal grandmother. Little is known of Richard's early life, and he had no advanced education, but by the time he was twenty-four he had sailed to Cádiz in Spain as the captain of the sloop *Ranger*. He sailed on several voyages to Europe and the West Indies and began buying ships of his own. In 1735 he married Mary Hodges of Salem. The couple had three sons, all of whom entered the family business and joined their father in leading the town of Salem during the American Revolution, and three daughters. In 1770 Mary Derby died, and the next year Derby married a widow, Sarah Langley Hersey.

At the age of forty-five Derby retired from the sea to manage his burgeoning business. In 1755 he built Derby Wharf and a warehouse in Salem. Two years later he headed a subscription list to pay the town's soldiers arrears of wages from the Fort William Henry expedition. Specializing in supplying the Sugar Islands in the West Indies with New England timber and foodstuffs, Derby lost at least four ships to the French and British for trading illegally with French and Spanish islands during the French and Indian War. He protested the British seizures vigorously but in vain. Despite this, he seems to have done well privateering. In 1759 he bought a farm and in 1761 built a mansion on what is now Derby Street in Salem. He was then Salem's leading merchant.

Derby continued to lose vessels to British customs officials because of his trade with the French and Spanish West Indies in the 1760s. He did not accept this treatment gracefully. On 2 August 1768 the *Essex Gazette*, the first newspaper published in Massachusetts outside of Boston, appeared in Salem. It was printed by Benjamin Hall, formerly of Medford, who started the paper at Derby's invitation and with his capital. The paper attacked the five representatives to the General Court from Essex County who voted to rescind the circular letter in which the Massachusetts General Court invited the other colonies to cease importing goods from Britain to protest the Townshend Acts. The following May, four of the five were defeated, and Richard Derby, Jr., was chosen to represent Salem in the General Court for six of the next seven years, until he was elevated to the Massachusetts council.

Derby and his family spearheaded the resistance to British policy in Salem, although Derby himself held no political office commensurate with his great local prestige. A son-in-law, Dr. John Prince, made an appearance at the Boston Tea Party in December 1773. When the British troops came to Salem in February 1775 to seize artillery and ammunition held by the town, Derby led the local citizenry out to confront the soldiers. When ordered to surrender the guns, Derby replied: "Find them if you can, take them if you can, they will never be surrendered." Had not the commander withdrawn, the American Revolution might have begun in Salem two months before it did.

When hostilities broke out at Lexington and Concord that April, Derby offered his fastest ship, the *Quero*, commanded by his son John Derby, to take the news to England so the rebels could tell their story before General Thomas Gage's dispatches arrived home. Sailing on 27 April, John Derby ignored his orders to land in Ireland, made for the Isle of Wight and Southampton, and had his information in the hands of Massachusetts acting provincial agent Arthur Lee by the first of June. When the *Quero* returned on 19 July Congress asked for Derby's bill. He asked about £150 for expenses but as "to my time in executing the voyage from hence to London and back. . . . Nothing."

Derby left most of the business of supplying privateers for the Revolution to his son Elias Hasket Derby, but his approval and financial support were of course required to equip and send out eighty ships that over the course of the war employed 8,000 men, captured 144 British vessels, and constituted half of Salem's privateers. A Derby ship, the *Astraea*, brought back

word to America that peace had been concluded and independence recognized in 1783. Derby barely survived the news. He died that November in Salem, leaving an estate of over £20,000 in cash in addition to ships and real estate.

By interfering with Derby's trade, Britain turned this wealthy and influential merchant into Salem's leading revolutionary. The profits he won from attacking British commerce in turn laid the groundwork for his son Elias Hasket Derby's worldwide commercial empire and even greater fortune, which contributed significantly to America's rise as a maritime power.

• Miscellaneous manuscripts at the Essex Institute and in the Massachusetts Archives, Boston, mention Derby. James Duncan Phillips, "The Life and Times of Richard Derby, Merchant of Salem," Essex Institute, *Historical Collections* 65 (1929): 243–89, is the most complete treatment. See also Ronald N. Tagney, *The World Turned Upside Down: Essex County during America's Turbulent Years, 1763–1790* (1989).

WILLIAM PENCAK

DERCUM, Francis Xavier (10 Aug. 1856–23 Apr. 1931), neurologist, was born in Philadelphia, Pennsylvania, the son of Susanna Erhart and Ernest Albert Dercum, a German liberal émigré. After graduating in 1873 from Philadelphia Central High School (which later awarded him an M.A.), he attended medical school at the University of Pennsylvania, receiving an M.D. in 1877.

After graduation Dercum entered into practice and served for a time as consultant pathologist to the State Hospital for the Insane at Norristown, Pennsylvania, where he was the first to publish the institution's pathological reports. In 1879 he became assistant demonstrator in histology; in 1881, demonstrator in the physiology laboratory; and in 1882, instructor in nervous diseases at the University of Pennsylvania. From 1883 to 1892 he was chief of the nervous disease clinic at the Hospital of the University of Pennsylvania and joined the neurological staff at Philadelphia General Hospital in 1887, remaining in that position until 1911, when he became consulting neurologist to the hospital.

Dercum's early research included work on the sensory organs, the lateral line organs, and the semicircular canals (1878–1879). As a morphologist, he directed his attention toward anatomical issues of clear physiological significance, including mentation. "There is only one psychology," he insisted, "and that is the physiology of the brain." He also conducted anatomical studies of the nervous system in fish because, as he later explained, "In my early days the nervous system of man seemed to me to be hopelessly complicated, and I turned to the fishes, in which the fundamental problems of vertebrate structures are presented in a much simpler form."

At the same time, Dercum made important contributions to clinical neurology. With Eadweard Muybridge, Dercum was among the first to use, in 1884, a form of motion pictures to study patients with disorders of the nervous system. Photographs were taken with a series of aligned cameras and then arranged on a revolving wheel to produce moving images of male and female patients, stripped naked. They applied the technique most notably to convulsions; some of these, however, were artificially induced in the patients through hypnosis, a technique for which Dercum and Muybridge took some credit. In 1892 he published a lucid clinical description of adiposis dolorosa, which became known as "Dercum's disease." While president of the American Neurological Association, he edited *Textbook on Nervous Diseases by American Authors* (1895).

In 1892 Dercum became the first occupant of a new chair as clinical professor of nervous and mental diseases at Jefferson Medical College, a position he resigned in 1925 in order to devote more time to his private practice and literary endeavors. He served as consulting neurologist to the Jewish Hospital and St. Agnes Hospital in Philadelphia, the Asylum for the Chronic Insane at Wernersville, and the Pennsylvania Training School for Children. Beginning in 1915 he was on the consulting staff of the State Hospital for the Criminally Insane at Fairview.

Dercum was one of the founders of the Philadelphia Neurological Society in 1884 and remained one of its most active members. He was a founding member and served as president of the American Neurological Association and of the Philadelphia Psychiatric Society; he later belonged to the Association for Research in Nervous and Mental Diseases. Dercum was elected to the College of Physicians of Philadelphia in 1885 and became an active member. He also was a member of the American Medical Association and of state and local medical societies. In 1892 he married Elizabeth De Haven Comly; the couple had three children. He belonged to a number of social clubs and to virtually every important Philadelphia cultural institution, most notably the American Philosophical Society, of which he was president from 1927 to 1931.

Like most neurologists of his time, Dercum's interests included psychological as well as neurological problems, anatomy and physiology as well as pathology and therapeutics. In a talk before the Philadelphia Neurological Society in 1914, he rejected the traditional distinction between "functional" and "organic" neurological disturbances. He argued that all cases involved "changes of structure and function," as did the problems that arose in internal medicine and that "disturbances in metabolism" underlay all mental disease. He hoped that some nervous disorders (due to infection or exogenous poisoning) might be prevented through immunization; others (due to endogenous poisoning) he thought to be "hereditary and innate" and could only be dealt with through eugenics. On occasion, these views brought him into conflict with other neuropsychiatrists.

During World War I Dercum served on the Medical Advisory Board and the Medical Reserve Board and gave lectures to the Army and Navy Medical Corps. He was called in as a consultant during President Woodrow Wilson's long illness. Dercum's reputation was international. He was the second American to be elected a corresponding member of the Société de Neurologie of Paris and was later chosen for honorary membership in other medical and neurological societies of Vienna, Budapest, and London. Dercum was also honored by the French government in 1923 as chevalier of the Legion of Honor.

Dercum remained professionally active until the moment of his death, which occurred as he presided over a meeting of the American Philosophical Society in Philadelphia. Some found it appropriately symbolic that he died in Benjamin Franklin's chair, for Dercum was widely regarded not only as a neurologist but as one of the scientific leaders of his city.

• Dercum's books include *Rest, Suggestion and Other Therapeutic Measures in Nervous and Mental Diseases*, 2d ed. (1917), *Clinical Manual of Mental Diseases* (1913; 2d ed., 1917), *Hysteria and Accident Compensation* (1916), *Biology of the Internal Secretions* (1924), and *Physiology of Mind* (1925). See also his "Nervous and Mental Diseases and the Newer Pathology," *Journal of Nervous and Mental Diseases* 42 (1915), 358–69. For the outlines of Dercum's career, see "Francis Xavier Dercum, M.D.," *Pennsylvania Medical Journal* 34 (1931): 639–40; and *Annals of Internal Medicine* 5, no. 1 (July 1931): 92–94. More personal memoirs were written by C. W. Burr in the *Transactions of the College of Physicians of Philadelphia*, 3d ser., 54 (1932): ixv–ixxi; A. P. Brubaker in the *Proceedings of the American Philosophical Society* 71, no. 1 (1932): 39–48; and James H. Lloyd in *Archives of Neurology and Psychiatry* 25, no. 6 (June 1931): 1333–35. On his collaboration with Muybridge, see M. R. McVaugh, "Francis X. Dercum and Animal Locomotion," *Cadeuceus* 3 (1987): 1–33. An obituary is in the *New York Times*, 24 Apr. 1931.

BONNIE ELLEN BLUSTEIN

DEREN, Maya (29 Apr. 1917–13 Oct. 1961), avant-garde filmmaker, was born Eleanora Derenowsky in Kiev, Russia, the daughter of Solomon David Derenowsky, a psychiatrist, and Marie Fiedler, a teacher. The family immigrated to the United States in 1922. Shortly after their arrival they moved to Syracuse, New York, where Deren's father later became the director of the State Institute for the Feeble-Minded. The family name was changed to Deren in 1928. Eleanora, who took pleasure in cultivating an exotic public image, took the name Maya in 1943. A bright and articulate child, Deren shared a stormy relationship with her intellectual father, who taught her the importance of contemporary scientific theories and mathematics as complex systems by which one could understand the world. Her parents' rocky marriage led her mother to accompany Deren, an exceptional student, to Geneva, Switzerland, in 1930 to attend the League of Nations School.

Deren returned to New York in 1933, at the age of sixteen, to study journalism at Syracuse University. That same year she became active in the Youth party of the Socialists League. She married fellow member Gregory Bardacke in 1935 and followed him to New York City, where he became a union organizer; they had no children. The couple became more involved in the Trotskyist movement, and she completed her bachelor's degree at New York University.

In 1937 Deren entered the master's program in literature at the New School for Social Research in New York City. After her divorce from Bardacke in 1938 she left for Smith College in Massachusetts, from which she received her master's degree in 1939. Deren then spent three years in Greenwich Village, where she freelanced as a secretary, engaged in a series of short love affairs, and wrote poetry and short stories.

In 1940 Deren offered her secretarial services to the modern dance choreographer Katherine Dunham, who was also a trained anthropologist famous for her studies of the origins of black dance. From 1941 to 1942 Deren, Dunham, and Dunham's dance company toured the country with a production of the musical fable *Cabin in the Sky*, which starred Ethel Waters. It was this tour that prompted Deren's first article, "Religious Possession in Dancing" (*Educational Dance* [Spring 1942]), the first of her studies of Haitian culture. When the tour stopped in Los Angeles for several months, Deren met the Czechoslovakian experimental filmmaker Alexander "Sasha" Hackenschmied (he changed his name to Hammid in 1947), who had recently fled wartorn Europe. They were married in Los Angeles in 1942 and began a successful collaboration in which Hammid taught her the basics of filmmaking. They had no children.

The couple's first collaborative effort resulted in *Meshes of the Afternoon* (1943), a fourteen-minute film that is today probably the most well known avant-garde film in the country. Though the film reflects some of Hammid's stylistic and conceptual tendencies, Deren lent to it the intense emotions and striking mood for which it is so remarkable. The film, in which Deren plays a female subject who must contend with her own subjectification, exhibits the complex ideas about time, space, form, consciousness, identity, and sexuality that characterize Deren's later work. Her next work, *At Land* (1944), also focuses on a female protagonist (again played by Deren), whose physical movements are edited so as to appear continuous across changing backgrounds. In 1945 she directed *A Study in Choreography for the Camera*, a 2½-minute film of a Dunham company dancer performing one dance in several locations. Deren's *Ritual in Transfigured Time* (1946) concerns the rituals of courtship and marriage. That same year she became the first filmmaker ever to receive a Guggenheim award, although she never completed the proposed film. Rather, she used the award to make the first of three trips to Haiti to study Voudun rituals, the subject of her later full-length anthropological study.

Deren's films were often discussed by her critics and colleagues in terms of surrealism and the European avant-garde rather than as feminine discourse. Deren denied her films' identity with surrealism, however, suggesting instead their importance as rigorous intellectual systems. She began to take an active role in the exhibition and critical reception of her films, touring the country and screening her work, preparing program notes that guided audiences' and critics' interpretation of her films. She was the first filmmaker

to bring the ideas of New York's art culture to the Midwest and West.

In 1946 she published *An Anagram of Ideas on Art, Form and Film*, a collection of theories. From 1946 to the time of her death Deren devoted much of her time to traveling, writing, theorizing, lecturing, and encouraging community among independent film artists. Following her divorce from Hammid in 1947, Deren made a transition from producing art to participating in and organizing the critical discourse surrounding her films and independent filmmaking in general. According to filmmaker Joyce Wieland she became something of a "Pied Piper" to younger filmmakers. Deren's followers included filmmakers Stan Brakhage, Willard Maas, and Kenneth Anger. In 1953, the year she published *The Divine Horsemen: The Living Gods of Haiti*, Deren also organized the Film Artists Society, which gathered independent filmmakers from all over New York to discuss filmmaking and their own works, as well as to sponsor programs in local film festivals. By the mid-1950s Deren was but one voice in this dynamic and productive group of artists.

In 1955 Deren established the nonprofit Creative Film Foundation (CFF), the first foundation to award grants to independent filmmakers. Although the foundation maintained a distinguished board of directors whose names and affiliations lent prestige, the CFF was a one-woman show, run entirely from the apartment Deren shared with her third husband, the composer Teiji Ito, whom she married in 1960 (they had no children). Like all of Deren's efforts throughout the 1940s and 1950s, the foundation served to legitimize independent film's relationship to the other fine arts and to encourage the creativity of independent artists. Deren died in Queens, New York, after a series of brain hemorrhages. Film theorist Rudolf Arnheim eulogized her as one of cinema's "most delicate magicians."

• Deren's films and related materials are at the Anthology Film Archives in New York City. A collection of her writings and photographs is in Special Collections, Mugar Library, Boston University. Material on her family history is at the Syracuse University Archives. See also Lauren Rabinovitz, *Points of Resistance: Women, Power and Politics in the New York Avant-Garde Cinema, 1943–1971* (1991), and VèVè A. Clark, Millicent Hodson, and Catrina Neiman, eds., *The Legend of Maya Deren*, vol. 1, pt. 1 (1984), and pt. 2 (1988). Obituaries are in the *New York Times*, 14 Oct. 1961, and the *Village Voice*, 19 Oct. 1961.

JENNIFER M. BARKER

DE RIVERA, José (18 Sept. 1904–19 Mar. 1985), sculptor, was born José A. Ruiz in West Baton Rouge, Louisiana, the son of Joseph V. Ruiz, a sugar mill engineer, and Honorine Montamat. De Rivera apparently chose his last name to honor his grandmother. While growing up on the sugar plantation where his father worked, de Rivera practiced blacksmithing and maintained machinery, mastering materials necessary for constructing sculpture in metal. De Rivera graduated from high school in 1922 and after working on a sugar plantation, moved to Chicago in 1924. During the day he worked in various tool and die shops and at night took classes at the Studio School. John Norton, his instructor in life classes, appreciated the three-dimensional aspects of de Rivera's drawings and suggested that he try his hand at sculpture. In 1926 de Rivera married Rose Covelli, and they had one son.

By 1930 de Rivera had produced his first sculptures. These figurative pieces, including a bust of a female figure carved from a single brass rod, are related to the streamlined, elegant, Art Deco designs of the period. De Rivera's work of the early 1930s was indebted also to the cubist-inspired polished torsos of Alexander Archipenko, whose work was exhibited in Chicago during the 1920s, and to Constantin Brancusi's *Golden Bird*, a piece already in the collection of the Arts Club of Chicago.

De Rivera spent most of 1932 abroad, traveling in Spain, Egypt, North Africa, Greece, Italy, and France. He briefly resided in Paris, but he did not recall meeting avant-garde artists there. Returning to the United States, de Rivera moved to New York and soon met young American artists who were exploring vanguard concepts. For the rest of the decade de Rivera worked with a variety of materials, including stone and plaster, and experimented with different sculptural approaches, creating, for example, biomorphic pieces carved from stone and constructions made out of sheet metal and wire.

By 1938 de Rivera worked in the Sculpture Division of the Federal Arts Project, part of the Works Progress Administration (WPA), and during that period he produced one of his finest early works, *Flight* (1938, Newark Museum). Commissioned for the airport at Newark, New Jersey, this was the first of many commissions that the artist would receive for large-scale works in public places. Carved from solid aluminum rods, the sculpture was mounted on a high base, which further enhanced the suggestion of dynamic forms soaring upward in space. *Flight* is an abstracted image of a bird in flight, while the sleek surfaces of metal also allude to an aircraft. De Rivera often expressed his admiration for Brancusi's *Bird in Space*, made of polished bronze, and the indebtedness is noted in *Flight*, which fuses modern technology and abstracted natural forms in the creation of a new formal dialectic.

De Rivera's sculptural activity from the 1930s on was characterized primarily by exploratory studies with constructivist concepts. Through them he discovered that sculpture need not be approached simply in terms of bulk and stasis but rather as the interaction between the material and the space around it. Using hammered sheet metal and curved wire, he created openwork constructions that reveal his fascination with the concepts of space and time, especially as formulated by the Russian mathematician Herman Minkowski, whose scientific language he used to analyze and unite the static and dynamic properties of space and materials, as in *Black and Red (Double Element)* (1938, Solomon R. Guggenheim Museum, N.Y.). Cut from flat sheets of aluminum and hammered into curved shapes, the two elements of the piece were smoothly finished, and the surfaces were painted in primary colors. The elements were then positioned on a flat wooden base such that the curves partially enclose spatial volumes. Many of de Rivera's constructions were variations on this initial "shell" form and were made of copper, stainless steel, and other metals painted in primary colors. Some he built with a motor buried within the attached pedestal so that the construction would rotate.

After military service from 1942 to 1946, de Rivera developed what became known as his signature works: linear, tubular pieces that bend through and bring form to space. *Construction #1: Homage to the World of Minkowski* (1955, Metropolitan Museum of Art, N.Y.) is an example of his mature work. The reflection of light on the revolving surface serves to expose a myriad of forms, the movement of which illustrates the ongoing interaction between interior and exterior space. De Rivera and his wife divorced in 1955, and that same year he married Lita J. Jeronimo; they had no children.

Prodigious in his artistic output, de Rivera created all of his metal constructions in his studio. He was among the first American artists to put kineticism to effective use as a component of his sculptures, thereby merging his fascination with mathematical forms and the technology and materials of the twentieth century. He died in New York City.

• De Rivera's papers, including catalogs and newspaper clippings, are in the Archives of American Art, Smithsonian Institution, Washington, D.C. For a fuller discussion of his work and influences see Joan M. Marter, *José de Rivera* (1979). Exhibition catalogs include John Gordon, *José de Rivera* (American Federation of the Arts, 1961), and Thomas Tibbs, *José de Rivera: Retrospective Exhibition, 1930–1971* (La Jolla Museum of Contemporary Art, 1972). An obituary is in the *New York Times*, 21 Mar. 1985.

JOAN M. MARTER

DERLETH, August William (24 Feb. 1909–4 July 1971), author and editor, was born in Sauk City, Wisconsin, the son of William Julius Derleth, a worker in a wagon and blacksmith shop, and Rose Louise Volk. Derleth began his education in Catholic schools but finished in the local public system. He started writing short fiction at age thirteen, sold his first story at sixteen, and created his fictional detective Solar Pons while a student at the University of Wisconsin, from which he graduated with a B.A. in 1930.

Derleth moved to Minneapolis, Minnesota, in 1930 to edit the *Mystic Magazine*, for Fawcett Publications. Returning to Sauk City permanently in 1931, he collaborated with his friend Mark Schorer on ghost and horror tales and edited the *Midwesterner*. In 1933 he contracted with Loring & Mussey, New York publishers, to write six mystery novels featuring his genial detective Judge Peck. He wrote the first one, *Murder Stalks the Wakely Family* (1934), in ten days. In 1937 he published *Still Is the Summer Night*, which he called his first serious novel. Its triangular plot involves adultery and guilt in "Sac Prairie," his fictive equivalent of Sauk City, in the 1880s. In 1938, with recommendations from Sinclair Lewis and Edgar Lee Masters, he was awarded a Guggenheim Fellowship and was also sent by Wisconsin governor Philip LaFollette to represent the state at the Poet's Congress in New York City. Derleth corresponded for years with Howard Phillips Lovecraft, the reclusive science-fiction and mystery writer. In 1939 Derleth and Donald Wandrei established a publishing firm they named Arkham House, to reprint Lovecraft's works and other volumes of supernatural literature. "Arkham" derives from the mythic New England locale of many Lovecraft stories, fragments of some of which Derleth completed and published under the names Lovecraft and Derleth. Derleth was literary editor of the *Capital-Times* of Madison (1941–1971) and edited and published the *Arkham Sampler* (1948–1949) and the *Arkham Collector* (1967–1971).

Derleth taught courses at the University of Wisconsin on regional literature (1939–1943), bought property outside Sauk City, and built an ornate, financially-draining home called "Place of Hawks" (1939–1940). He was active—and abrasively opinionated—in civic affairs in Sauk City. In 1943 he and Master's daughter Maria Lee Masters Jennings announced their engagement, which, however, was broken a few months later.

In 1953 Derleth married Sandra Evelyn Winters. While honeymooning in Hollywood with his teenage bride, he wrote a few television scripts. He criticized California for attracting "crackpots," and the couple quickly returned to Sauk City. When they were divorced in 1959, Derleth was awarded custody of their two children. He edited a poetry magazine titled *Hawk and Whippoorwill* (1960–1963) and wrote "Wisconsin Diary," a column for the *Capital-Times*, begun in 1960 but discontinued in 1965 when his editor cut his comments favoring capital punishment.

Derleth wrote novels, stories of mystery and terror, nature books, poetry, books on Wisconsin history, biographies, and fiction for children. He wrote so rapidly that he sometimes had recourse to the following pen names: Romily Devon, Will Garth, Eldon Heath, Kenyon Holmes, Tally Mason, Michael West, and Simon West. He once estimated that he produced between 750,000 and 1 million words a year. He planned a *Sac Prairie Saga* in fifty volumes, of which he lived to write thirty-eight in several genres. He boasted that the venture was the most ambitious since the work of Honoré de Balzac. A fine Sac Prairie novel is *Evening in Spring* (1941), which features the idyllic young love of Steve Grendon, a Catholic, and non-Catholic Margery Estabrook and the prejudices they encounter in their families and among the townspeople. Derleth's best mysteries are his numerous pastiches, beginning with *In Re: Sherlock Holmes—The Adventures of Solar Pons* (1945). Derleth followed with more than sixty Solar Pons pieces, collected in a dozen books ending with the posthumous *Chronicles of Solar Pons* (1973).

Reviewers, including Ellery Queen, found these items to be neither imitations nor parodies but often worthy of Conan Doyle himself. Derleth's best nature book is *Walden West* (1961), in which he counterpoints nostalgic reminiscence and vignettes of small-town life and reveals his adoration of his region. Reviewers admired the work, some noting resemblances to efforts by Sherwood Anderson and Masters. *Return to Walden West* was Derleth's award-winning 1970 reprise. His poems are regularly simple and evocative. In "Walker-Errant," from *And You, Thoreau* (1944), Derleth characteristically wishes to speak for "nature, for freedom absolute / and wildness." His history books include *The Wisconsin: River of a Thousand Isles* (1942), nicely descriptive but borrowing excessively from his own previous works, and *Vincennes: Portal to the West* (1968), a moderate bestseller praised for its thorough research. His *Saint Ignatius and the Company of Jesus* (1956) earned him an apostolic blessing from Pope John XXIII in 1959. Derleth also wrote biographies of Zona Gale (1940), Lovecraft (1959), Thoreau (1962), and Emerson (1970)—the last two for young readers. Among ten "Steve-Sim" juvenile novels, often autobiographical, *The Pinkertons Ride Again* (1960) is representative; in it Steve Grendon, the adult hero from *Evening in Spring* (1941), is a boy and with his chum Sim Jones solves a crime adults are too busy to take seriously.

Derleth wrote too much, too fast. He published in more than 500 magazines and newspapers. He had unprofessional impatience when it came to revising. If he had taken Sinclair Lewis's advice to slow down and compose with greater care, he might have produced a dozen or so more enduring books. As it was, he is remembered mainly for the sincerity of his devotion—expressed in fiction, poetry, and nonfictional prose—to Sac Prairie, his Sauk City postage stamp on the big American literary map, for the popularizing of Lovecraft and his brand of terror fiction, and for continuing it. There is an August Derleth Society in Sauk City, which has published a newsletter since 1960. Derleth died in Sauk City.

• The bulk of Derleth's papers, which are deposited in more than three dozen locations, are in libraries at Brown University, New York University, Northwestern University, Princeton University, and the State Historical Society of Wisconsin at Madison. Allison M. Wilson, *August Derleth: A Bibliography* (1983), is exceptionally thorough, listing 736 items and including a chronology of Derleth's life. Edward Wagenknecht, *Cavalcade of the American Novel . . .* (1952), discusses Derleth's early works, especially the Sac Prairie novel *Wind over Wisconsin* (1938), briefly but well. Frederick S. Frank, *Through the Pale Door: A Guide to and through the American Gothic* (1990), includes pieces by Derleth, with a few critical synopses. L. Sprague de Camp, *Lovecraft: A Biography* (1975); Philip A. Shreffler, *The H. P. Lovecraft Companion* (1977); and John Clute and Peter Nicolls, eds., *The Encyclopedia of Science Fiction* (1993), reveal Derleth's considerable part in enhancing Lovecraft's popularity and completing some of his fragments. Critical commentary is in Harry Thornton Moore, "Derleth of Sac Prairie," *Amateur Writer* 1 (Nov. 1939): 3–6; Zealia Bishop, "A Wisconsin Balzac: A

Profile of August Derleth," *The Curse of Yig* (1953), pp. 153–75; Norbert Blei, "August Derleth: Storyteller of Sac Prairie," *Chicago Tribune*, 15 Aug. 1971; and Mark Schorer, *Pieces of Life* (1977). Obituaries are in the *New York Times*, 6 July 1971, and the *Washington Post*, 8 July 1971.

ROBERT L. GALE

DERN, George Henry (8 Sept. 1872–27 Aug. 1936), secretary of war, was born in Dodge County, Nebraska, the son of John Dern, a pioneer Nebraska farmer, mine operator, and industrialist, and Elizabeth, whose maiden name was the same as her married name, Dern. Both parents were German immigrants. Dern graduated from Nebraska's Fremont Normal College in 1888 and from 1893 to 1894 attended the University of Nebraska, where he was captain of the football team. In 1894 he accompanied his family to Salt Lake City, joining the Mercur Gold Mining and Milling Company, which his father served as president. Rising rapidly from bookkeeper to company treasurer, he was promoted in 1901 to general manager of the company, which had been reorganized as the Consolidated Mercur Gold Mines Company. Dern was coinventor of the Holt-Dern roaster, a furnace for carrying out the Holt-Christenson roasting process, a technique for recovering silver from low-grade ores. In 1899 he married Charlotte "Lottie" Brown; they had seven children.

Dern entered politics in 1914, running on a Democratic and Progressive fusion ticket in a Utah state senate district encompassing Salt Lake County. He was elected in 1914, serving until 1923 in the state senate, where he was twice selected as Democratic floor leader. His tenure there was marked by his strong advocacy of progressive legislation, including a landmark mineral leasing act that leased, rather than sold, Utah's mineral rights to private concerns.

Dern gained the Democratic nomination for governor in 1924, and during the campaign he received backing from the Utah Progressive party and an endorsement from Progressive presidential candidate Robert La Follette. Challenging incumbent Republican governor Charles R. Mabey, Dern ran on the catchy slogan "We want a Dern good governor, and we don't mean Mabey." Dern won by a plurality of 10,000 votes, 81,308 to 72,127, while the Republicans carried all the other statewide offices by a margin of 30,000 votes.

As governor, Dern focused on using Utah's rich natural resources to develop the state economy and devoted himself to education, social welfare, and tax reform, thus further embroidering his reputation as a progressive. Arguing that the general property tax was unfair as the sole source of state revenue, Dern secured the adoption of a state income tax and a corporate franchise tax against strong opposition. He also took a leading role in resolving important interstate problems related to the building of the Boulder Dam on the Colorado River. Dern, whose state had the disadvantage of being upstream from the dam, staunchly defended the theory that, with the exception of navigation, the waters of western streams were state rather than federal resources. This controversy brought Dern into direct conflict with U.S. secretary of commerce Herbert Hoover, who was attempting to mediate the dispute for the Calvin Coolidge administration.

Dern was reelected governor in 1928 by a margin of 31,000 votes, even though the Republican national ticket won in Utah by 14,000. He subsequently served from 1929 to 1930 as chair of the National Governors' Conference, where he worked with New York governor Franklin D. Roosevelt. Dern's record as a progressive western governor also commended him to Roosevelt, who after his November 1932 election to the presidency considered Dern for a cabinet position.

Roosevelt initially wanted Dern for the post of secretary of the interior but settled on appointing him to the War Department. Although he had no military experience and was reputed to have pacifist leanings, Dern won the support of military circles by promoting greater efficiency and readiness, calling for a military structure that could be expanded quickly and easily in a crisis. He also initiated a five-year plan to equip the army with newer airplanes, more tanks, semiautomatic rifles, and modernized artillery. He advocated increased strength for the army Air Corps and investigated charges of lobbying in the War Department, resulting in the court-martial and dismissal of two high-ranking army officers.

During Dern's tenure the War Department oversaw the administration of the Civilian Conservation Corps. Dern's department provided the CCC with food, clothing, transportation, and medical care for the 300,000 unemployed who joined its ranks for work in the preservation and conservation of America's public lands. The army's Corps of Engineers also began several important public works projects during Dern's tenure, including the dredging of the Mississippi and Missouri rivers, the construction of the Florida ship canal, and the building of the Bonneville, Passamaquoddy, and Peck dams. Dern worked closely with army chief of staff Douglas MacArthur on such projects. Dern was often at odds with President Roosevelt over plans to coordinate water resource development, and in 1935 and 1936 he opposed legislation to establish a permanent National Resources Board, even though it was strongly supported by Roosevelt. While still serving as secretary of war, Dern died in Washington, D.C., from heart and kidney complications following a bout with influenza.

Dern was fond of outdoor sports such as fishing and hiking and is remembered as a hard-working member of the Roosevelt cabinet, one who could also be an entertaining public speaker. After years of tight military budgets and an isolationist foreign policy, the War Department was a relatively inconsequential post during Dern's tenure. While he was generally well liked by other members of the cabinet, he never played a decisive role in the determination of administration policies.

• Dern's papers are at the Utah State Archives, but materials on Dern are also in the National Archives, the Franklin D. Roosevelt Library, the Library of Congress, and the Utah State Historical Society. A useful description of Dern's appointment to the War Department is in Frank Freidel, *Franklin D. Roosevelt: Launching the New Deal* (1973), while water policy differences between Dern and Roosevelt are discussed in Arthur Maass, *Muddy Waters: The Army Engineers and the Nation's Rivers* (1951). See also James Olson, ed., *Historical Dictionary of the New Deal* (1985); and Otis Graham, Jr., and Meghan Robinson Wander, eds., *Franklin D. Roosevelt: His Life and Times, An Encyclopedic View* (1985). An obituary is in the *New York Times*, 28 Aug. 1936.

CHRISTOPHER D. O'SULLIVAN

DE ROCHEMONT, Louis (13 Jan. 1899–23 Dec. 1978), film producer, was born Louis Clark de Rochemont in Chelsea, Massachusetts, the son of Louis L. G. de Rochemont, an attorney, and Sarah Wilson Miller. As a boy of twelve, de Rochemont made his own film camera with the help of a local machine shop and used it to film "newsreels" in neighboring towns, which he then sold to local movie houses to show. De Rochemont attended the Naval Aviation School of the Massachusetts Institute of Technology and the Naval Cadet School of Harvard University. He served for a year with British Military Intelligence through a program of the U.S. Naval Reserve Officers 'Training Corps. He then enlisted in the U.S. Navy in 1917, reaching the rank of lieutenant by the time he resigned in 1923. He remained in the naval reserve for another ten years. While he served in the navy, de Rochemont's interest in film continued. During his tour of duty abroad, he independently filmed the 1922 opening of King Tutankamen's tomb and, in the same year, Kemal Ataturk's capture of Smyrna, which led to the foundation of the Turkish Republic.

On returning to civilian life, de Rochemont went to work for International Newsreel and later for Pathé News as assistant editor. He married Virginia Conway in 1929; they had two children. During that time he began directing shorts for 20th Century–Fox, making two series, *Adventures of a Newsreel Cameraman* and *Magic Carpets of Fox Movie-tone News*. His first full-length documentary, *The Cry of the World*, a foreboding look at contemporary world events, was independently produced in 1933.

In 1934, in association with Roy E. Larsen of *Time* magazine, de Rochemont began production of his best-known work, the news documentary and editorial series called *The March of Time*. The first segment, *Metropolitan Opera*, was released in 1935, and another, *Inside Nazi Germany*, appeared in 1938. His first full-length documentary in the series, *The Ramparts We Watch* (1940), was a condemnation of American isolationism. *We Are the Marines* (1942) was produced with the support and cooperation of the U.S. Marine Corps. De Rochemont later fought censors to have the words "damn" and "hell" restored to the edited version of this movie. Acclaimed for its innovative combination of straight news and editorial viewpoint, the se-ries was awarded an Oscar in 1936 for "revolutionizing the newsreel."

De Rochemont left *The March of Time* project in 1943 to become a producer for 20th Century–Fox, though the series continued under the direction of his brother, Richard de Rochemont. His first assignment was the editing of sixty thousand feet of film taken over a fourteen-month period by navy photographers for an action film, *The Fighting Lady* (1944), which documented the adventures of an aircraft carrier. The final product received rave reviews and won de Rochemont the *New York Times* Film Critics Award and an Academy Award in 1944. *The House on 92nd Street* (1945) was a fictionalized account of an operation by the Federal Bureau of Investigation (FBI) against German spies, the basic plot of which was taken from J. Edgar Hoover's private files. It used authentic FBI footage and some actors who had undergone FBI training. The realism of this method combined with the excitement of Hollywood drama was enormously popular and set a new standard in film. Whereas earlier cinema had attempted to convey realism, de Rochemont's films, by using real-life settings and actors, achieved a palpably new level of authenticity. De Rochemont's next film, *13 Rue Madeleine* (1946), was about the operation of the Office of Strategic Services; although it was not as commercially successful as his earlier films, its powerful realism enhanced de Rochemont's reputation as a filmmaker. *Boomerang* (1946) again blended real-life events and cinematic realism to tell the story of an actual murder in Bridgeport, Connecticut; shot in a small Connecticut town with local extras, it was developed from an article in the *Reader's Digest*. De Rochemont later joined with the magazine in the formation of the RD-DR (*Reader's Digest*–De Rochemont) Corporation, created to facilitate the exchange of ideas and stories.

De Rochemont left 20th Century–Fox in 1946, frustrated by the sense of having to be "at the beck and call" of the studio. His contract was ended with the proviso that de Rochemont make no commercial features for eighteen months. He therefore created his own studio, Louis de Rochemont Associates, and, with Wallace Atwood, geologist and geographer, completed thirty-six twenty-minute instructional geographic films called *The Earth and Its Peoples*. Designed for children aged nine to eleven, the segments attempt to foster acquaintance with and acceptance of foreign cultures.

Lost Boundaries (1949), also developed from a *Reader's Digest* article, concerns a light-skinned African-American couple, Scott and Marsha Carter. Scott, a doctor, is first repeatedly denied jobs intended for African Americans because he looked too white and finally obtains a job by passing as a Caucasian. Scott's success in his profession leads to the couple's establishment as a socially prominent family in the small community of Keenham, New Hampshire, still passing as white. It is not until Scott and his son Howard attempt to enlist in the army during World War II that the family's African heritage is revealed, prompting both difficult questions of personal identity for parents and children (the couple also had a daughter, Shelley) and questions of racial acceptance for the entire community. The film's treatment of racial and social issues caused many distribution companies to decline it, and, when it was finally released, prompted great controversy, especially in the South. Like de Rochemont's earlier films, this was also shot at low budget using nonprofessional extras and genuine settings. Despite the low budget and surrounding controversy, the film was both a popular success and critically acclaimed. The *New York Times* said of it, "Viewed as emotional entertainment, as social enlightenment, or both, it is one of the most effective pictures that we are likely to have this year" (16 Jan. 1949).

His next film, *Windjammer* (1958), returned to de Rochemont's interest in the sea. It depicts a Norwegian trainee sailor aboard the ship *Christian Raditch*, and the cinematography, some of it produced underwater, is spectacular. To accommodate the showing of the film, New York's Roxy Theater had to remodel its auditorium and install a special, extra-large screen.

De Rochemont's later films included *Martin Luther* (1953), an acclaimed biographical portrait of the religious reformer; an animated version of George Orwell's *Animal Farm* (1954), which loses none of the novel's satirical edge; and a screen version of Tennessee Williams's *The Roman Spring of Mrs. Stone* (1961), starring Vivien Leigh, the story of an actress who decides to settle in Italy after her husband dies on vacation in Rome. De Rochemont died in a nursing home in York Harbor, Maine.

One of the most innovative documentary producers of his time, Louis de Rochemont changed the character of newsreels from their earlier bland incarnations to dynamic presentations of current events, often featuring dramatic reenactments. His fictional films, of which *Lost Boundaries* remains the best known, retain the authentic, real-life feeling of his nonfiction work. De Rochemont's influence on later filmmakers can be seen in the surge of police dramas in the late 1940s and in the work of directors like Henry Hathaway. *The March of Time* was influential enough to be satirized in the opening scenes of Orson Welles's *Citizen Kane* (1941). His films, while rarely screened today, remain generally available on videotape.

• Discussions of de Rochemont's work are in the *Christian Science Monitor*, 15 July 1949, the *New York Times*, 26 June 1949, and the *New York Herald Tribune*, 10 July 1949. See also Raymond Fielding, *The March of Time, 1935–1951* (1978), an excellent analysis of the newsreels, and Thomas Cripps, *Making Movies Black* (1993), an account of the production of and reactions to *Lost Boundaries*. Ephraim Katz, *The Film Encyclopedia* (1979), and Samantha Cook, ed., *The International Dictionary of Films and Filmmakers* (1993), include entries concerning his career. Brief summaries of some of his films are in Leslie Halliwell, ed., *Halliwell's Filmgoer's Companion* (1988). An obituary is in the *New York Times*, 25 Dec. 1978.

ELIZABETH ZOE VICARY

DERWENT, Clarence (23 Mar. 1884–6 Aug. 1959), actor, was born in London, England, the son of Charles Derwent, a diamond merchant, and Alice Falk. He was a desultory student at St. Paul's School, preferring theatergoing to homework. He idolized Sir Henry Irving and began slipping through the stage door and hiding behind a curtain to watch Irving rehearse. In 1902, after two years in the family business, he forged letters from a German shipping firm to convince his father that he had been offered a position in Berlin. He used money for the trip to join a provincial touring company. Shortly thereafter, he became a member of Frank Benson's Shakespearean touring company, where he developed into a versatile player of second leads. He appeared in ninety roles, including Iago in *Othello*, Cassius in *Julius Caesar*, Edmund in *King Lear*, and Claudius in *Hamlet*.

In November 1907 he joined the company of Annie E. Horniman at the Gaiety Theatre in Manchester. In his memoir he recalled that on his first day he was admonished by the director, B. Iden Payne: "We believe in natural acting here." Working in a repertory that included plays by George Bernard Shaw and John Galsworthy, Derwent received the same basic training in modern acting that he had acquired for the classics with Benson.

In the company with him was Lewis Casson, who was on the governing council of the Actors' Association. With Casson's encouragement, Derwent was elected to the council, beginning a lifelong affiliation with organizations that sought to improve conditions for actors and to develop theater as a cultural institution.

In 1910 Derwent began appearing in London, as well as touring the provinces and Europe. He alternated among light entertainments, classical roles, and modern or experimental plays. His sister Elfrida made her debut as an actress in a verse drama on the life of Buddha in which he played Prince Sidhartha. During this period Derwent received his first directing assignment, a production of *The Merchant of Venice*, in which he played Shylock, for a tour of the Netherlands.

World War I diminished opportunities for employment on the Continent, so Derwent and Elfrida moved to New York City in 1915. They spent the rest of their lives in the United States, living together and often traveling and working together.

Derwent's first American engagement was as Stephen Undershaft in the American premiere of *Major Barbara* with Grace George. He quickly established the pattern of his career: important secondary roles in productions in New York City or other major cities, varied with summer stock and directing. In 1923 Derwent directed his first American production, *Two by Two*, in which he cast Howard Lindsay as the lead and gave Una Merkle her first role. He made his musical theater debut in 1928 as King Louis XIII in *The Three Musketeers*, lavishly produced by Florenz Ziegfeld.

In 1932 Derwent played the art dealer in *The Late Christopher Bean* by Sydney Howard. During rehearsals, the playwright had difficulty finding an effective ending for the second act. Derwent suggested dialogue that brought the curtain down on a big laugh. Howard sent a telegram on opening night: "I don't know which to thank you for most—your performance or your second act curtain." The following year, Derwent repeated his role in a London production with Edith Evans and Cedric Hardwicke, the first of several appearances in his native city.

In 1935 Derwent went to Hollywood, California, but was unsuccessful in launching a movie career. He returned to New York City in 1937 for stage work. He was cast in the RKO film *The Story of Vernon and Irene Castle* (1939), with Fred Astaire and Ginger Rogers. After two more minor movies, Derwent left Hollywood, preferring to "earn a fifth of the money in the theatre to which I belong than here where I feel like a fish out of water." His earnings as a stage actor were enhanced by shrewd investments in the plays in which he appeared.

During the 1940s Derwent appeared in his usual mix of entertainments and more adventurous productions. These included S. N. Behrman's *The Pirate*, with Alfred Lunt and Lynn Fontanne; *The Innocent Voyage*, directed by Erwin Piscator; Brecht's *The Private Life of the Master Race; Lute Song*, with Mary Martin and Yul Brynner and directed by John Houseman; *Gypsy Lady*, a Victor Herbert operetta; and Jean Cocteau's *The Eagle Has Two Heads*, with Tallulah Bankhead and Marlon Brando.

In 1946 Derwent was elected president of Actors' Equity Association, serving two three-year terms. He was an articulate, if cautious, leader during times of controversy. When allegations of Communist party ties in the union became disruptive, he shepherded through a resolution directing the organization to concentrate on members' welfare instead of political diversions. "I never inquired into the political opinions of any member," he wrote in his memoir. "It was sufficient for me that each one, like myself, had taken an oath testifying to his freedom from any communist, fascist, or subversive alliance."

He strongly defended Equity's 1948 boycott of the National Theatre in Washington, D.C., for refusing to allow African Americans in the audience. "The time is approaching," he said, "when the actors and actresses of America must make up their minds as to whether they will continue to perform in the theater of the nation's capital so long as a large percentage of the population, asking nothing more than their rights as American citizens, are barred from admittance."

In 1945 he established the annual Clarence Derwent Awards in London and New York for best performers in supporting roles. "The struggle of the newcomer has always interested me," he said, "and this was an attempt to secure for the supporting player not only a badge of distinction supplemented by a little cash but a hallmark which might render a trifle easier the ascent to the coveted position of stardom."

Derwent made a notable appearance in 1948 as the president in *The Madwoman of Chaillot*. He left the cast to play Polonius in a production of *Hamlet* sponsored by the U.S. State Department at Elsinore Castle in Denmark in June 1949, followed by a tour of air force bases in Europe.

After leaving the presidency of Equity in 1952, Derwent became president of the American National Theatre and Academy, a position that capitalized on his talent as a speaker. He carried the message of American theater to communities throughout the country and at meetings of the International Theatre Institute in Europe. He continued to be active as an actor, appearing in *Uncle Vanya* in 1956 and a revival of *Lute Song* in 1959. He also returned to classical roles in guest appearances with college theaters. He played Creon in *Medea* at Rollins College and Shylock at the University of Kansas City and Stanford University. He died in New York City.

• Sound recordings of dramatic readings by Derwent and a film of a television production in which he appeared are at the Library of Congress. *The Derwent Story* (1953) is his memoir. *Current Biography* for 1947 gives a long summary of his career and roles. An obituary is in the *New York Times*, 7 Aug. 1959.

ARNOLD WENGROW

DE SCHWEINITZ, Edmund Alexander (20 Mar. 1825–18 Dec. 1887), leader of the Moravian church in America and first president of Moravian College and Theological Seminary, was born in Bethlehem, Pennsylvania, the son of Lewis de Schweinitz, a pastor and amateur botanist, and Louise Amalie Le Doux. De Schweinitz grew up in the Moravian village of Bethlehem during the period when its character as a closed religious community was crumbling. He studied classics and theology at Moravian schools in Nazareth and Bethlehem until 1844, when he spent several months at the University of Berlin. There he attended lectures in church history, a subject that would be the core of his academic writing. He taught briefly in Zeyst, Holland, before returning to the United States in 1847. From 1847 to 1850 he taught classics at his old school, Nazareth Hall. In 1850 he married Lydia de Tschirschky in Herrnhut, Germany; they had two sons and two daughters. Also in 1850 he was ordained and served in a number of short pastorates, including Dover, Ohio, and Lebanon, Philadelphia, and Lititz, Pennsylvania, before settling in Bethlehem. He was regarded as a good preacher with a scholarly and "ornate" style. He was also known to be formal and at times imperious as a pastor. These traits are evident in his published works.

De Schweinitz held a number of important ecclesiastical and academic positions while serving parishes. In 1855 he was made the editor of the new church weekly, the *Moravian*, a position he held off and on until 1867. He established the *Moravian* on a sound financial basis and used it as a forum to agitate for the independence of the American Moravians from German control. De Schweinitz worked successfully to move the Moravians away from the "heart religion" of Zinzendorf, with its mystical devotion to the crucified

Christ, and toward American evangelicalism. He also helped dismantle the communal and ecumenical structure of the church, remaking it into an independent American denomination.

De Schweinitz also taught theology at the theological seminary and in 1867 was made president of the newly combined Moravian College and Theological Seminary. He again demonstrated financial acumen in building up the new school in Bethlehem, and he lectured regularly on church history. During this period he published numerous articles in the new historical journal, *Transactions of the Moravian Historical Society*, as well as in several reference works. His most important works are *The Life and Times of David Zeisberger* (1870) and *The History of the Unitas Fratrum, or the Unity of the Brethren* (1885), volume one of a never-completed two-volume work. These were groundbreaking studies that were standards in their field for decades. His first wife having died in 1866, he married Isabel Allison Briggs in 1868; they had one daughter.

De Schweinitz was also active in denominational administration and finance, even writing a short work, *The Financial History of the American Province of the Unitas Fratrum and of Its Sustentation Fund* (1877). In 1857 he was the American representative to the General Synod in Germany and argued successfully for full independence for the church in America. Until that time many of the major decisions were controlled by the boards in Herrnhut. With the changes in the constitution, the two American provinces had full authority to supervise congregations, ordain pastors, create new congregations, control finances, and produce worship materials. Doctrinal matters needed to be approved by the Unity Board, but Americans had representatives in that body. This led to a period of growth for the church in America, and de Schweinitz was a major figure in organizing and enlarging it, serving as a member and, at times, president of the Northern Provincial Board from 1878 until his death in Bethlehem. During his administration the church began mission activities among the Inuit in Alaska and German immigrants in the Midwest. In 1870 he was elected a bishop.

De Schweinitz's writings, most notably *The Moravian Manual* (1859) and his *History*, did much to give the Moravian church in America a place among American denominations. He stressed the putative historic connections of the Moravian church with the old Czech Unitas Fratrum, defining that church in terms acceptable to American evangelicalism. As such, de Schweinitz was a crucial figure in the nineteenth-century redefinition of the Moravians as a mainline American denomination. Doctrinally, they were now similar to the Methodists; structurally, they were now like the Presbyterians.

• The bulk of de Schweinitz's papers, particularly relating to his governance of the church, are available in the Moravian Archives in Bethlehem, Pa. His published works are available in many libraries, but the entire corpus, including collections of his sermons, is housed in Reeves Library, Moravian College, Bethlehem. Two lengthy memoirs were published soon after his death: Charles Nagel, "A Sermon Preached in the First Church, Philadelphia, January 15, 1888 in Memoriam of Bishop de Schweinitz," *Moravian*, 8 Feb. 1888, pp. 83–84; and Edward Rondthaler, *Memoir of Edmund Alexander de Schweinitz* (1888). Both are available in the Moravian Archives in Winston-Salem, N.C.

CRAIG D. ATWOOD

DE SCHWEINITZ, George Edmund (26 Oct. 1858–22 Aug. 1938), ophthalmologist, was born in Philadelphia, Pennsylvania, the son of Edmund Alexander de Schweinitz, a bishop of the Moravian church, and Lydia Joanna de Tschirschky. De Schweinitz took his bachelor's degree in 1876 from the Moravian College in Bethlehem, Pennsylvania, where his father was president. He taught for the next two years at Nazareth Hall, a military academy in Nazareth, Pennsylvania, in order to finance his medical education and further prepared himself by reading medicine with a local physician. In 1878 de Schweinitz entered the University of Pennsylvania School of Medicine, from which he graduated with first honors in 1881.

Following internships at the Children's Hospital and University of Pennsylvania Hospital, de Schweinitz opened a general practice in Philadelphia in 1883. Over the next three years he also served as prosector for Joseph Leidy, the esteemed professor of anatomy at the University of Pennsylvania, and from 1882 to 1887 he taught therapeutics at the Medical Institute of Philadelphia.

Although he began his career in general medicine, de Schweinitz changed his emphasis to ophthalmology, largely through the influence of William F. Norris, professor of ophthalmology at the University of Pennsylvania. De Schweinitz rose quickly in his newly chosen field. In 1885 he was appointed ophthalmic surgeon to the Children's Hospital. In 1886 he was made ophthalmologist to the Orthopedic Hospital and Infirmary for Nervous Diseases, where he associated with neurologist S. Weir Mitchell and William Osler and developed his interest in the "sister specialties" of neurology and ophthalmology. In 1887 he was appointed ophthalmic surgeon to the Philadelphia General Hospital. In 1891–1892 de Schweinitz lectured on medical ophthalmoscopy at the University of Pennsylvania and assisted Norris in the outpatient department of the University Hospital. De Schweinitz was professor of ophthalmology at the Philadelphia Polyclinic and College for Graduates in Medicine from 1891 to 1893 and in 1892 was appointed clinical professor of ophthalmology at Jefferson Medical College, where he became professor of ophthalmology in 1896.

In 1902 de Schweinitz succeeded Norris as professor of ophthalmology at the University of Pennsylvania. One of de Schweinitz's students from this period later wrote of him that "I was most impressed by his untiring devotion to duty, the sterling uprightness of his character, the depth of his knowledge, his accuracy of diagnosis, his complete mastery of details, and his astounding memory, revealed in all discussions of

DE SCHWEINITZ • 479

ophthalmic subjects" (Carpenter, p. 347). In 1924 de Schweinitz became professor emeritus and a trustee of the University of Pennsylvania.

In his combined roles as investigator, clinician, surgeon, educator, and author, de Schweinitz was the leading figure in American ophthalmology by the mid-1890s. Of his several hundred articles and three books, his best-known contribution to ophthalmic literature is *Diseases of the Eye*, which appeared in ten carefully revised editions between 1892 and 1924. His most important published work, *The Toxic Amblyopias*, won the Alvarenga Prize of the College of Physicians of Philadelphia in 1894 and was published in 1896. His final monograph was *Pulsating Exophthalmos* (1908). De Schweinitz edited the *American Textbook of Diseases of the Eye, Ear, Nose and Throat* (1899), one in a series of authoritative texts on the various medical specialties issued by the W. B. Saunders publishing firm in the late 1890s, and was editor of the American editions (1899, 1901, 1903, 1905, 1909, 1910) of the atlases on eye diseases compiled by the Swiss ophthalmologist Otto Haab.

De Schweinitz was involved in many medical societies. He was elected a fellow of the College of Physicians of Philadelphia in 1887 and its president from 1910 to 1913. He was secretary of the Section on Ophthalmology of the American Medical Association in 1891–1892 and its chair in 1896–1897. In 1922 he was elected president of the AMA. In 1916 he became president of the American Ophthalmological Society and in 1922 president of the International Congress of Ophthalmology. The first American invited to deliver the Bowman Lecture to the Ophthalmological Society of the United Kingdom (1923), de Schweinitz was elected an honorary member of that society.

In 1908 de Schweinitz joined the Army Medical Reserve Corps as a lieutenant. During the First World War he was made a member of the Council of National Defense and was called up to active service. Promoted to major in April 1917, he was attached to the U.S. Army Surgeon General's Office and in October of that year was sent overseas. Upon his return to the United States in March 1918, he rejoined the surgeon general's office and established the School of Ophthalmology at Camp Greenleaf, Fort Oglethorpe, Georgia. By war's end de Schweinitz had risen to the rank of lieutenant colonel and was made a member of the editorial board of *The Medical Department of the United States Army in the World War*, published at Washington in fifteen volumes between 1923 and 1929. In 1922 he was promoted to brigadier general in the Medical Reserve Corps. De Schweinitz never married. He died at his home in Philadelphia.

De Schweinitz's contemporaries were effusive in their praise of both his professional and personal qualities. The Chicago-based ophthalmologist Casey Wood described him as "the most widely known and the most erudite of American ophthalmologists" and "a Gamaliel at whose feet I sat in wonder and admiration." De Schweinitz is still recognized for his research on toxic amblyopia, pulsating exophthalmos, iridocyclitis, papilledema, and eye manifestations generally.

• A small collection of de Schweinitz's papers in the archives of the College of Physicians of Philadelphia spans the period from 1901 to 1933 and consists largely of correspondence. One of the best evaluations of his character and work is J. T. Carpenter, "Memoir of G. E. de Schweinitz, M.D.," *Transactions and Studies of the College of Physicians of Philadelphia* 4th ser., 6 (1938–1939): 344–51. Obituaries are in the *Archives of Ophthalmology* 20 (1938): 1074–80; *Journal of the American Medical Association* 111 (1938): 957; and *Transactions of the American Ophthalmological Society* 37 (1939): 15–21.

CHRISTOPHER HOOLIHAN

DE SCHWEINITZ, Karl (26 Nov. 1887–20 Apr. 1975), social worker and educator, was born in Northfield, Minnesota, the son of Paul Robert de Schweinitz, a clergyman, and Mary Catherine Daniel. After attending Nazareth Hall and the Moravian Parochial School in Bethlehem, Pennsylvania, de Schweinitz received bachelor's degrees from Moravian College in 1906 and from the University of Pennsylvania in 1907. He spent two years as a reporter, first for the *Philadelphia Public Ledger* and next for the *Philadelphia Press*. He subsequently worked for a year in the circulation department of the Curtis Publishing Company; then in 1910–1911 he served as press representative for the University of Pennsylvania. The next two years he spent as executive secretary of the Pennsylvania Tuberculosis Society. He married Jessie Logan Dixon in 1911; they had two children.

De Schweinitz embarked on his social work career when he joined the staff of the Charity Organization Society (COS) in New York City in 1913. World War I broke out not long after, and once America entered the war, de Schweinitz wrote several Red Cross pamphlets. One of them, *This Side of the Trenches with the American Red Cross*, achieved a distribution of one million copies when it appeared in 1918. That same year De Schweinitz was appointed general secretary of the Philadelphia Society for Organizing Charity (later the Family Service of Philadelphia). While in Philadelphia he published a widely read book on social work, *The Art of Helping People Out of Trouble* (1924). Even more successful was *Growing Up: The Story of How We Become Alive, Are Born, and Grow Up* (1928, reissued 1974), which is generally considered the first American sex-education book for children. It was also published in Great Britain and Australia and was translated into nine languages.

As the Great Depression took hold during the winter of 1929–1930, de Schweinitz and a colleague established what they called the Committee of 100 on Unemployment (though they were the only members). For several months they held luncheon meetings with business and civic leaders to keep them abreast of the crisis the city was facing. When the Philadelphia Committee on Unemployment Relief was formed with private funds in 1930, de Schweinitz became secretary. Two years later, when the committee was forced to stop operating for financial reasons, the members helped persuade the state to establish the Pennsylvania State Emergency Relief Board. De Schweinitz served on the county branch of the board until 1935. He was named director of emergency relief for Pennsylvania in 1936; then a few months later he became deputy director of the Pennsylvania Welfare Department with the responsibility of administering programs under the new Social Security Act. He was appointed the state's first Secretary of Public Assistance in 1937 but resigned the following year in a protest over patronage. De Schweinitz and his wife were divorced in 1936. The following year he married Elizabeth McCord; they had no children.

Unlike many in his profession, de Schweinitz concluded as early as the 1920s that the government must take a major role in caring for the poor and the handicapped. Nevertheless, he believed that the private sector also had an important part to play, and he continued his work with private agencies through most of the depression, serving full time as executive director of the Community Council of Philadelphia from 1930 to 1933 and then part time until 1936. He also helped organize the Philadelphia Child Guidance Clinic, the Philadelphia Marriage Council, and the American Association of Social Workers (later the National Association of Social Workers).

De Schweinitz taught social administration at the University of Pennsylvania (1933–1936), headed the university's School of Social Work (1938–1942), and served as a training consultant for the federal Social Security Board (1942–1944). During the latter period he wrote *England's Road to Social Security* (1943), which received wide praise and reappeared in paperback in 1961. It traced the development of English social policy from Elizabethan Poor Law to the just-released Beveridge Report, which provided the design for England's postwar welfare state. From 1944 to 1950 de Schweinitz headed the committee for education and social security of the American Council on Education, designing and providing training programs for public welfare employees. As an outgrowth of this work he wrote *People and Process in Social Security* (1946).

De Schweinitz joined the social welfare faculty at the University of California at Los Angeles in 1950, while also remaining active in public life. In 1951 he headed the Social Security Mission to Egypt under the Point Four Program, which was initiated by President Harry S. Truman in 1949 to provide technical assistance to less developed nations. This mission was the first Point Four project in Egypt and the program's first social welfare endeavor anywhere. His book on the subject, *Social Security for Egypt* (1952), was published in both English and Arabic. He consulted for the United Nations (1952) and the Venezuelan government (1958), lectured at the University of Puerto Rico (1934), and studied as a Fulbright scholar at the London School of Economics (1956–1967).

After his retirement in 1958, de Schweinitz and his wife moved to Washington and later to Hightstown,

New Jersey. He gave a number of graduate seminars at Brandeis University, published many articles (some with his wife), presented lectures, and wrote a booklet with his wife, *Interviewing in Social Security* (1961), which was published in a number of countries as well as being translated into Braille. In 1962 the couple jointly received the Florina Lasker Award of the Columbia University School of Social Work. De Schweinitz died in Hightstown, New Jersey.

De Schweinitz's career spanned an historic transition in American social work, from the era when individualized private charity dominated the field to the vast expansion of public welfare programs under the New Deal. In 1931 he wrote: "Social work is on the brink of one of the greatest adventures it has ever known. Overnight we are becoming public social workers with our psychology changed from the idea of individual special treatment to the idea of equalization" (quoted in Wenocur and Reisch, p. 166). De Schweinitz devoted much of his career to exploring and discussing this new kind of social work—which, as he wrote, "while reaching the many must have meaning for the one." Many colleagues found the changes distressing, but de Schweinitz embraced the new challenge, and in so doing, he encouraged a generation of colleagues and students to do the same. "The great adventure, whether we will or no, is on us," he wrote. "Any social worker who is worth his salt will get into it" (quoted in Wenocur and Reisch, p. 166).

• There is no collection of de Schweinitz's papers, but correspondence with him appears in the papers of Survey Associates, Mattie Cal Maxted, the National Association of Social Workers, and the Community Service Society of New York, all in the Social Welfare History Archives, University of Minnesota Library. Other writings by de Schweinitz include *Home Service* (with Porter R. Lee) and *First Manual of Home Service* (with Mary Richmond), both published by the Red Cross in 1917. Articles written with his second wife, Elizabeth de Schweinitz, include "The Place of Authority in the Protective Function of the Public Welfare Agency," *Child Welfare League Bulletin* 25 (Sept. 1946): 1–6; and "The Contribution of Social Work to the Administration of Public Assistance," *Social Work Journal* 29 (July 1948): 108–13, and (Oct. 1948): 153–62. See also Frank J. Bruno, *Trends in Social Work, 1874–1956* (1957); Clarke A. Chambers, *Seedtime of Reform: American Social Service and Social Action, 1918–1933* (1963); Arthur E. Fink et al., eds., *The Field of Social Work* (1955); Louise Odencrantz, *The Social Worker in Family, Medical, and Psychiatric Social Work* (1929); Alan Keith-Lucas, *Decisions About People in Need: A Study of Administrative Responsiveness in Public Assistance* (1957); and Stanley Wenocur and Michael Reisch, *From Charity to Enterprise: The Development of American Social Work in a Market Economy* (1989). An obituary appears in the *New York Times*, 21 Apr. 1975.

SANDRA OPDYCKE

DE SEVERSKY, Alexander Procofieff (7 June 1894–24 Aug. 1974), aircraft designer and influential air-power advocate, was born in Tbilisi, Republic of Georgia (then part of imperial Russia), the son of Nicholas Procofieff-Seversky, a pioneer Russian sportsman-pilot, and Vera Vasilieff. A 1914 graduate of the Imperial Naval Academy of Russia, he attended the Military School of Aeronautics. In July 1915 on his first combat mission in World War I, de Seversky was shot down over the Gulf of Riga on a bombing mission, losing his right leg.

After convalescing, de Seversky served as an officer in charge of naval aircraft production. Later, with the special permission of Czar Nicholas II, he returned to flying and was named chief of Russian naval fighter aviation of the Baltic Sea. De Seversky became the best-known Russian navy pilot, getting credit for thirteen downed German planes in fifty-seven missions.

When his country's participation in the war ended with the Russian Revolution, the new provisional government sent de Seversky to Washington, D.C., early in 1918 as an assistant naval attaché for air. After the Bolsheviks seized power, de Seversky offered to don a pilot's uniform for the U.S. military. The Department of War, taking note of his production and engineering background, made de Seversky a consulting engineer and test pilot.

De Seversky made his mark quickly. In 1921 he developed inflight refueling techniques and worked closely with General Billy Mitchell on tests aimed at proving the superiority of the airplane over the battleship.

De Seversky developed the first fully automatic synchronous bombsight, which was completed in 1923 and bought by the U.S. and British governments. That device, along with technology fashioned by Elmer Sperry, Sr., laid the foundation for all gyroscopically stabilized flight instruments, leading in turn to the ubiquitous automatic pilot. With $50,000 from the army for the patent on the improved bombsight, in 1922 he formed the Seversky Aero Corporation, which he used as a base for further inventing, designing, and consulting work. In 1925 he married Evelyn Olliphant; they had no children.

De Seversky became a U.S. citizen in 1927 and was commissioned a major in the Air Corps Specialists Reserve. For the rest of his life, he was usually referred to as Major de Seversky.

In 1931, widening his development scope to include whole airplanes, not just systems, de Seversky organized Seversky Aircraft Corporation. He was elected president and served as general manager and chief designer. One of his projects evolved into the world's fastest amphibious airplane, the *Idofloat*, a powerful, low-wing monoplane, which had retractable wheels and floats with adjustable angles for water landings. The plane was never mass produced, but de Seversky did apply the technology to landing gear for aircraft that had to use plowed fields or rough terrain.

De Seversky's firm's most noteworthy accomplishments of the 1930s were tied to the fast-growing Army Air Corps. Seversky Aircraft designed and built the first all-metal basic training monoplane and the first all-metal skin-stressed single-seat fighter. The latter's design called for stresses to be carried by the metal wing covering rather than by conventional wing struts. That engineering approach, which allowed the wings to be used as fuel tanks, became a standard of airplane design.

Of more immediate importance, it linked the Seversky name with raw speed. The compact Sev-S2, the first aircraft in the world to exceed 300 miles per hour, won the prestigious Bendix Trophy three years in a row, beginning in 1937. Rewarding endurance and reliability as well as speed over a traditional closed circuit, the trophy went to the winner on a 2,050-mile course from Burbank, California, to Cleveland, Ohio.

The Sev-S2 was virtually identical to the P-35, the so-called *Sascha*, that, along with the Curtiss P-36, brought Army Air Corps fighter squadrons in the late 1930s to the brink of the rapid expansion in size and performance that would be a key to victory in World War II. With its Pratt & Whitney 1,000-horsepower, air-cooled, fourteen-cylinder, Twin Wasp engine, the P-35 led directly to the hefty P-47 *Thunderbolt*, which was modified with a turbo supercharger for high-altitude flying.

Despite sitting at the top of this successful corporation, Major de Seversky never really left the cockpit. He personally flight-tested all aircraft of his own design. And, demonstrating a flair for public relations, he broke numerous records in his combat planes. In the late 1930s de Seversky's new marks included New York to Havana, Havana to New York, New York to Washington, New York to Los Angeles, London to Paris, and Paris to Copenhagen.

But de Seversky didn't fare so well inside the company he started. Some of Seversky Aircraft's directors disagreed about the type of planes to be built. So while he was on company business in Paris in 1939, they refused to reelect him president and changed the name of the firm to Republic Aviation Corporation.

De Seversky had little trouble looking beyond that reversal, particularly with the approach of World War II. The global conflict gave him a chance to challenge long-held assumptions about warfare. Lobbying Congress and writing in mostly Hearst-owned newspapers and magazines, de Seversky made his greatest impact in 1942 with *Victory through Air Power*. The book sold more than 500,000 copies and was animated by Walt Disney in a film of the same name. At the 1943 Quebec Conference, British Prime Minister Winston Churchill asked that the film be shown to President Franklin D. Roosevelt. The president later said de Seversky "foresaw the technical necessity for the long-range escort fighter and devoted himself singlemindedly to its development."

De Seversky opened *Victory through Air Power* with these words: "The most significant single fact about the war now in progress is the emergence of aviation as the paramount and decisive factor in warmaking. . . . A realistic understanding of the new weapon [the airplane], of its implications in terms of national security, of its challenge to America, is not a matter of choice. It is the very condition of national survival."

Historian Charles A. Beard said of the book, "In my opinion, this book is more important to America than all the other war books put together." Added Walter Lippmann, "No one can afford henceforth to believe he is thinking about the war if he has not read carefully and opened his mind fully to what Major Seversky has to say."

At the end of World War II, during which control of the air had nearly always preceded a major ground action such as the invasion of Fortress Europe, de Seversky was appointed special consultant to Secretary of War Robert Patterson. Reporting back on the use of air power and the effects of bombing, he went to Europe and the Pacific theater and included a visit to the atomic bomb tests on Bikini Atoll.

The potential use of nuclear weapons was not lost on de Seversky, who became a leading voice for strategic deterrence via the specter of massive retaliation. He claimed that the threat of globe-girdling missiles and flexible tactical forces could help the United States and other nuclear superpowers such as the Soviet Union preserve the global status quo by inhibiting limited, conventional wars.

De Seversky pursued that theme in two more books, *Air Power: Key to Survival* (1950) and *America: Too Young to Die!* (1961). The latter book, published the year before the Cuban Missile Crisis, called for an unblinking U.S. strategic stance. "By the end of 1962," he said of his homeland, "the USSR will have enough ICBMs, IRBMs [intermediate-range ballistic missiles], and jet-bomber aircraft to blow us—together with our allies—off the face of the earth, unless we rise to the challenge, exert maximum effort, and match the Soviet threat. Otherwise, we will either be enslaved by a hostile ideology, or our nation will lie in ruins."

Taking that pessimistic note to a logical conclusion, de Seversky turned to work on defense against nuclear attack by the regime that had taken over his native land. His interest in fallout shelters and the problem of electrostatically removing radioactive particles during air intake led him to the discovery that heavier-than-air aircraft can get their lift as well as propulsion from ionic emission. So de Seversky patented a new lifting device called the Ionocraft. The same investigations resulted in a new development for air pollution control, a wet electrostatic precipitator for extracting impurities from industrial emissions developed at Seversky Electronatom Corporation.

De Seversky died in New York City. A member of the Aviation Hall of Fame and a recipient of the Medal of Merit from the U.S. government as well as awards from Russia, France, and Brazil, he had few equals in his contributions to military and commercial flying. De Seversky was a rare combination of tinkerer and thinker—pilot, engineer, and strategic theorist.

• Many of de Seversky's technical achievements are spelled out in Enzo Angelucci, *World Encyclopedia of Civil Aircraft from Leonardo da Vinci to the Present* (1982), the National Aeronautics and Space Administration's *Aeronautics and Astronautics, An American Chronology of Science and Technology in the Exploration of Space* (1961), and William M. Leary, ed., *Aviation's Golden Age* (1989). In its issue of 12 Jan. 1942, *Time* magazine briefly discusses de Seversky's problems with Seversky Aircraft's directors. He is mentioned frequently in a 9 Feb. 1942 *Time* article on bombers. Obituaries appear in the *Times* of London, 27 Aug. 1974, and the *New York Times*, 26 Aug. 1974.

DAVID R. GRIFFITHS

DESHA, Joseph (9 Dec. 1768–11 Oct. 1842), U.S. congressman and governor of Kentucky, was born in Monroe County, Pennsylvania, the son of Robert Desha and Eleanor Wheeler, farmers. Participating in the westward movement that took place during the Confederation period, the family moved to Kentucky in 1781 and to the Cumberland region of Tennessee one year later. Desha does not seem to have received any formal education beyond the common school. As a young man he fought Indians on the Tennessee frontier and lost two brothers in those conflicts. Another brother, Robert, born in 1791, would go on to serve in Congress from 1827 to 1831. In 1789 Joseph married Peggy Bledsoe; they would have thirteen children. Three years later the couple moved to Mason County, Kentucky. In 1794 Desha fought with General Anthony Wayne in the Indian campaign that culminated at the Battle of Fallen Timbers in August. In 1797, and again from 1799 to 1802, he served in the Kentucky house of representatives. In 1802 he was elected to the state senate, where he served until 1807.

Desha was elected to the U.S. House of Representatives in 1806 and reelected five times, serving from March 1807 to March 1819. He was an ardent Republican and a militant defender of American rights. While he supported the Embargo and other forms of commercial opposition to both Great Britain and France, Desha was an early advocate of stronger measures. In a lengthy speech delivered on 24 January 1810, he called for the conquest of Canada and made clear his hostility toward Great Britain: Is there, Desha asked, "a crime which can be perpetrated for which ready precedents cannot be found in the conduct of that perfidious Government towards America?" He also warned house members that if "you won't defend your rights, . . . your independence is not worth a straw." House Speaker Henry Clay placed his fellow Kentuckian and war hawk on the influential Foreign Affairs Committee. In 1813 Desha left Congress temporarily in order to serve as a major general with Kentucky volunteers. During this time he commanded a portion of William Henry Harrison's army at the Battle of the Thames in October 1813.

In his last years in Congress Desha opposed the rechartering of the Bank of the United States. In a sense this position foreshadowed his later career in Kentucky, where he became deeply embroiled in a struggle over the relief of debtors. Hoping to stimulate economic activity, Kentucky had chartered a host of new banks in 1818 and encouraged them to make loans in paper money. With the panic of 1819, both farmers and merchants found themselves in debt. The election of 1820 was a contest between Relief advocates who thought the government should aid debtors and Anti-Relief forces who opposed such measures. Relief leader John Adair was elected governor, and the legislature soon created the Bank of the Commonwealth, whose major function was to loan money to Kentuckians in debt. In December 1820 Kentucky also passed a replevin law that allowed debtors to postpone paying their creditors for up to two years. In May 1822, however, a county judge found the law unconstitutional, and in October 1823 the state appeals court took the same position.

In 1820 Desha ran for governor as a supporter of debtor relief but lost to the similarly minded Adair. In 1824 Desha ran alone on the Relief ticket and won 60 percent of the vote after a very bitter campaign. Although he has been criticized by some historians for tailoring his speeches to his audiences, Desha seems to have been a genuine partisan of the relief issue. His slogan, "Liberty or Slavery," was histrionic but not ambiguous. Moreover, he was flailed in the newspapers, which were controlled by the Anti-Relief party and which attacked all aspects of both his military and political careers. He did not put forward a detailed platform, but there is little doubt that the voters understood his sentiments.

Despite Desha's electoral success, the Relief party did not have a strong mandate. In order to get rulings more favorable to pro-debtor legislation, Desha supported the creation of a new court of appeals that was to be the creature of the legislature. When the old court refused to turn over its records, arguing that the new court was unconstitutional, state officials took the documents by force. As a result two courts were in existence until the legislative election of 1826 brought to power a substantial majority of Anti-Relief lawmakers, who quickly restored the power of the old court despite Desha's attempt to stop them. Desha did not achieve what he would have liked with respect to debtor relief, but he did play an important role in a critical moment in Kentucky history. The election of 1824 brought about a restructuring of state politics, and the factions that emerged were long-lasting: the Reliefers soon joined the Jacksonian Democratic party, and the Anti-Reliefers eventually merged with Henry Clay's Whig party.

Among Desha's other actions as governor, he attacked the University of Translvania as an aristocratic institution and advocated that the state support a system of common schools rather than giving money to higher education. Later, however, he suggested that school funds be invested in turnpike companies with only the dividends going to education. Desha was also criticized after he issued a pardon to his son, Isaac B. Desha, who had been found guilty of murder. When his term ended in 1828, Joseph retired to his farm in Harrison County. He died in Georgetown, Kentucky.

Desha grew up on the western frontier of the early Republic and qualified himself for political office by fighting Indians rather than attending college. He manifested an intense patriotism that grew out of his understanding of the events and principles of the American Revolution. He seems to have been consistent in support of liberty as he understood it, and that included the right of debtors to be assisted by the state. Desha was overshadowed by other Kentuckians such as Henry Clay, Richard Mentor Johnson, and Isaac Shelby, but he claimed to speak for the people of his state, and in a large sense he probably did.

• James A. Padgett, ed., "Joseph Desha, Letters and Papers," *Register of the Kentucky Historical Society* 51 (1953): 286–304, contains documents drawn from the Desha Papers in the Library of Congress. Little has been written about Desha's career in Washington. See his speeches in *Annals of Congress* and small references in many secondary works, especially Roger H. Brown, *The Republic in Peril: 1812* (1964). Desha's career as governor of Kentucky is better documented. See Thomas D. Clark, *A History of Kentucky*, rev. ed. (1960); Frank F. Mathias, "The Relief and Court Struggle: Half-Way House to Populism," *Register of the Kentucky Historical Society* 71 (1973): 154–76; and Paul E. Doutrich III, "A Pivotal Decision: The 1824 Gubernatorial Election in Kentucky," *Filson Club History Quarterly* 56 (1982): 14–29.

S. CHARLES BOLTON

DESILVER, Albert (3 Aug. 1988–7 Dec. 1924), civil liberties leader and lawyer, was born in Brooklyn, New York, the son of Carll Harrison DeSilver, a stockbroker and art patron, and Mary Henrietta Block. He attended private schools in Brooklyn and Connecticut and was graduated in 1910 from Yale University, where he was a member of Skull and Bones and the editorial board of the *Yale Daily News*. He was graduated from Columbia Law School in 1913, the year he also married Margaret Burnham. They had three children.

DeSilver was active in politics during his law school years. He was briefly a registered Republican, but in 1912 he joined the Progressive party and supported the election of Theodore Roosevelt. He soon drifted from electoral politics and became independent. During the labor unrest of the early 1900s, he wrote that most people "instinctively align themselves, either because of their economic position or because of their sympathies, with one or the other of the two great classes . . . They emotionally jump to the side to which they belong, and . . . endeavor, after the fact, to work out an intellectual justification for their position." DeSilver wanted "to belong to neither class, but to try to form part of the intellectual pivot upon which the balance of our civilization must be gained—to reason my way to a position *before* the fact and not after it."

DeSilver entered the general practice of law in 1913 with the New York City firm of Reynolds, Richards & McCutcheon and became a partner in 1916. When the United States entered World War I in 1917, he believed that participation would cause more harm than good, but he did not oppose the war. He subscribed heavily for Liberty Bonds and registered for the draft without mentioning his children, who would have entitled him to an exemption. According to his biographer, DeSilver saw no justification for regimenting thoughts and feelings about the war, and he felt strongly that "when utterance is not free, thought stagnates or goes rotten." He was among the first New York lawyers to volunteer to defend citizens and aliens against wartime espionage laws that penalized speech.

When the postmaster general suppressed the radical magazine *Masses*, DeSilver contributed substantially to its defense fund. At about the same time, he became a member of the direction committee of the National Civil Liberties Bureau, initially a unit of the American Union Against Militarism, an antiwar group, but later an independent body that evolved in 1920 into the American Civil Liberties Union (ACLU). Toward the end of the war he became associate director under Roger N. Baldwin; when Baldwin was sentenced to prison for opposing the draft act by refusing to serve, DeSilver became the sole executive of the bureau, serving without salary. One of his coworkers in the bureau, Lucille Milner, wrote in her autobiography that "Albert was one of those rare persons who found life exciting and adventurous; his gaiety was infectious and his good cheer permeated the atmosphere in which he worked."

In 1918 DeSilver resigned from his traditional law firm to avoid embarrassing his partners and to devote himself full time to civil liberties work. He continued in this vein for the ACLU, serving as its associate director. He wrote many briefs in a variety of legal proceedings, worked on bail cases, and engaged in publicity. DeSilver was often in charge of negotiations with lawyers and officials, and he directed legislative campaigns in Washington, D.C. Among other initiatives, in 1921 he drafted a memorandum on behalf of the ACLU for President Warren G. Harding supporting amnesty for 114 political prisoners in detention after the war. He was one of the founders, in 1922, of the National Bail Fund and served as its managing trustee from its inception until his death.

During the war and afterward, DeSilver thought of himself as a conservative and worked to preserve the American tradition of freedom of thought and expression. This dedication to free speech led him to support radicals of varied shades, but he agreed with them about little else. A half-century later he would have been regarded as a liberal or libertarian, who, in Baldwin's words, had "little or no sympathy with most of the wide variety of heresies whose right to expression he defended." DeSilver was consistent in his defense of civil liberties, serving as treasurer for a committee assisting the legal defense members of the Industrial Workers of the World and later opposing legislation aimed at suppressing the Ku Klux Klan. He was the largest financial contributor to the ACLU in its early years.

In 1923 DeSilver began taking a chemistry course at Columbia University, and the subject soon became his dominant interest, apparently giving him a sense of craft and of personal exploration that was lacking in his public work. He resigned from the ACLU's executive committee in 1924 to devote himself fulltime to studies in chemistry. When the chairman of the ACLU, Dr. Harry Ward, urged him to reconsider, he confessed that he lacked sufficient certainty "in this curious world" to continue with progressive movements. He wrote Ward that "on the one hand it seems to me to be quite fatuous to try to characterize human activity as right or wrong—good or bad. On the other, the outcome of human activity seems so unlikely even to approximate the expected desirability or undesirability." DeSilver recognized that "that sort of a feeling [cramps] the style of anyone engaged in social activity." As Walter Nelles wrote, his "eminently judicial mind could not fit in with indefinite satisfaction into the quick decisions, the assured championships that work in the civil liberties constantly demanded."

After attending the 1924 Harvard-Yale football game, DeSilver left his car in New Haven. Returning the next weekend by train to get it, he was thrown through an open door at a curve in Rye, New York, and was killed instantly. Baldwin wrote that "civil liberties in the United States sustained an irreplaceable loss."

• DeSilver did not leave papers to a library, but he is referred to in the archives of the American Civil Liberties Union, which are at the Mudd Library at Princeton University, and in the papers of Eugene V. Debs in the Library of Congress and Harry Weinberger at Yale University. Walter Nelles, DeSilver's colleague at the ACLU, wrote his biography, *A Liberal in Wartime: The Education of Albert DeSilver* (1940), with an introduction by Roger N. Baldwin. Nelles died before it was completed, so the work was edited by Lewis Gannett. DeSilver carried on an extensive correspondence, some of which is quoted in the Nelles biography. DeSilver's role in the ACLU is discussed in Samuel Walker, *In Defense of American Liberties: A History of the ACLU* (1990) and in books cited in Walker's extensive bibliography. An obituary is in the *New York Times*, 11 Dec. 1924.

NORMAN DORSEN

DESKEY, Donald (23 Nov. 1894–29 Apr. 1989), industrial and interior designer, was born in Blue Earth, Minnesota, the son of Robert Deskey, a German immigrant and proprietor of a dry goods and clothing store, and Fannie Katsky. In 1912, after graduating from high school, he left rural Minnesota and moved to California. During the following three years he worked at a variety of jobs, including bartending, drafting, and surveying. Beginning in 1915 he also attended the University of California, Berkeley, where he studied architecture and painting. He left college in 1917 to enlist in the army, but at the end of the war he resumed his peregrinations in the West. In 1920 he began a career in advertising and publicity in Chicago, and the following year he moved to New York, where despite meager resources he opened a successful advertising agency.

Within months, though, Deskey abandoned his business. Lured again by travel and notions of becoming a painter, he went to France. There he met his first wife, Mary Campbell Douthett, an American pianist whom he married in 1923; they had two children before divorcing in 1946. He returned in 1925 to visit the Paris Exposition of Modern Decorative and Industrial

Arts and to study at the École de la Grande Chaumière and in Parisian ateliers. In France and elsewhere in Europe he also saw the work of Bauhaus and De Stijl designers. Infused with the "hysteria" and the "glamour and excitement" of the art moderne movement surging through Europe, he returned in 1926 to New York committed with the "passion of a revolutionary" to introducing new decorative ideas and new utilitarian products to the United States.

Deskey debuted as a designer by creating decorative screens and window displays for two leading department stores in Manhattan, Franklin Simon and Saks–Fifth Avenue, and in the art gallery of the influential designer Paul Frankl. Employing industrial materials and boldly geometricized forms and metallic finishes, his designs brought him instant recognition in merchandising and artistic circles in New York. Numerous commissions followed, including an apartment (1927) for Adam Gimbel, then president of Saks–Fifth Avenue, that featured cork walls, copper ceilings, and Bakelite and metal wall trim. His first major interior composition, the Gimbel apartment distinguished Deskey as an innovative and skillful interpreter of European modernism.

In 1927, collaborating with business partner Philip Vollmer, Deskey received commissions to design furniture, consumer appliances, and stage sets for theaters. Their partnership lasted until 1931. In 1927 he also joined Frederick J. Kiesler, Paul Frankl, Lucian Bernhard, and others in founding the American Union of Decorative Artists and Craftsmen to promote modernism among artists and artisans in the United States. The following year he and the Swiss émigré architect William Lescaze introduced chromium-plated tubular steel chairs to Abraham and Straus, a Brooklyn department store. Adapted from prototypes designed by Ludwig Mies van der Rohe and Marcel Breuer, the tubular steel chairs became synonymous with "modern" home furnishings. Deskey's design, mass produced by the Ypsilanti Reed Furniture Company in 1928, found its way into households and offices throughout North America.

In 1928 Deskey also participated in the first of several "High Art Modern" exhibitions in the American Designers' Gallery in New York. His contributions to these exhibitions enhanced his reputation as an influential designer of zig-zag lighting fixtures, textured glass, streamlined furniture, rounded mirrors, geometric-patterned textiles, and Bauhaus-inspired wall and floor coverings.

In 1929 Edith Gregor Halpert, the Russian-born gallery impresario of Greenwich Village, arranged for Deskey to receive the first of three major commissions from the Rockefeller family, a gallery with lustrous Bakelite walls for Abby Aldrich Rockefeller (a work designed with Duncan Chandler). Subsequently, in 1932 the architects working on Rockefeller Center invited him to enter the competition for the International Music Hall (later renamed Radio City Music Hall). Staging a dramatic presentation before the jury, he won the competition; in only his sixth year as a prac-

ticing designer he emerged on the international stage at the summit of his profession, supervising the interior designs and furnishings of the world's largest theater. For this monumental endeavor, the most notable of his career, he assembled a team of twenty-one artists and artisans from the American Union of Decorative Artists and Craftsmen. Deskey personally designed the overall decorative motif, the lighting, the furniture, and the interiors of the auditorium and thirty lobby areas, foyers, and lounges including the men's smoking room, an imaginative composition in "visual jazz," featuring aluminum foil wallpaper. In collaboration with Wallace K. Harrison, he also designed the luxurious apartment for Samuel L. "Roxy" Rothafel atop the International Music Hall. His third and final work for the Rockefeller family was the apartment of Abby Rockefeller Milton (1933), an essay in white and silver praised for its "crystalline beauty" and "modern spirit."

Acclaim for Deskey's work at Rockefeller Center led to numerous commissions in the 1930s, including the interiors for the Richard M. Mandel house (1933–1935, Mt. Kisco, N.Y.), one of the first International Style houses in the United States (and designed in collaboration with Edward Durell Stone); exhibitions for the 1933 Century of Progress Fair in Chicago and the 1939 World's Fair in New York; the International Casino night club (1937, New York); and the Hollywood Turf Club (1937, Inglewood, Calif.). One of the most prolific designers in New York City during the 1930s, Deskey repeatedly experimented with new materials—cork, glass block, plastic laminate, wood veneers, plywoods, transite (asbestos), and aluminum—to sustain his reputation as an innovative designer. Drawing from his experiences in advertising and publicity, he also promoted his practice by publishing articles in art journals. In one article published in 1931, he predicted a future in which "the modern" would revolutionize architecture and decorative arts and bring about a "complete emancipation from tradition."

During the late 1930s and early 1940s Deskey shared with Louis Kahn and other influential architects an interest in designs for prefabricated housing. For eight years he experimented with development of a plywood-clad modular house. During 1946–1948 he marketed several hundred of these houses to veterans returning from the Second World War, but his business failed. He successfully returned, however, to his moorings in designing interiors for wealthy corporate clients. In 1947, working with Charles Eames, José de Rivera, Isamu Noguchi, and others, he was the lead designer for the rehabilitation of a luxury liner, the SS *Argentina*.

Through the 1950s and 1960s his New York–based firm, Donald Deskey Associates, grew into one of the largest interior design houses in the United States, with satellite offices in Denmark and England. His work during this period settled into a more conservative mode. The bulk of his commissions were packaging and showroom designs for large corporations such as Procter & Gamble, Sinclair Refining Company,

Union Carbide, and Westinghouse. Dozens of his packaging designs and product logos were recognizable to generations of consumers; some of these designs remained in use for more than forty years. He also designed bowling alleys, restaurant interiors, and in 1958 a spun aluminum "cobra-head" street light for the city of New York. Thousands of these street lights were installed in New York and imitated throughout the country. Notable among his works of the 1960s were exhibitions for the Seattle Century 21 Exposition and the New York World's Fair (1964).

Described as a "study in sophistication," Deskey habitually sported a mustache and wore English-tailored clothes. In the years following his retirement in 1975 he became a dean among American modernists. He was among the last survivors from the ranks of architects, artists, and designers who transformed New York during the late 1920s and 1930s into an international center of "High Art Modern." After living in Scotland, he moved to Vero Beach, Florida, where he died. Surviving him were two sons from his first marriage and his second wife, Katharine Godfrey Brennan, whom he had married in 1952.

A proselytizer for modernism, Deskey was instrumental in widening popular acceptance of modern home furnishings and interiors. During the late 1920s he was at the forefront of a small corps of designers who transmitted European models to the United States, and who simultaneously merged graphic and industrial design into the decorative arts.

• The primary source of information is the Donald Deskey Collection at the Cooper-Hewitt Museum of the Smithsonian Insitutution, to which Deskey donated his drawings and other archival materials. Two published works by Deskey illustrating his ardent commitment to modernism are "The Rise of American Architecture and Design," *London Studio* 5 (Apr. 1933): 266–73; and "Modern Wall Coverings," *Creative Art* 9 (Oct. 1931): 321–24. David A. Hanks and Jennifer Toher, *Donald Deskey: Decorative Designs and Interiors* (1987), is a definitive study that includes a scholarly essay by Jeffrey L. Meikle and a detailed bibliography. An admiring portrait by one of his early clients is Gilbert Vivian Seldes, "The Long Road to Roxy," *New Yorker*, Apr. 1933, pp. 22–26. See also Arthur J. Pulos, *American Design Ethic: A History of Industrial Design to 1940* (1983); Robert A. M. Stern, Gregory Gilmartin, and Thomas Mellins, *New York 1930* (1987); and Stern et al., *New York 1960: Architecture and Urbanism between the Second World War and the Bicentennial* (1995). For his work on Radio City Music Hall, see Alan Balfour, *Rockefeller Center: Architecture as Theater* (1978), and the *New York Times*, 27 June 1932. See also "Pretty Props for Furniture," *Life*, 8 Dec. 1958, pp. 107–8, 110. An obituary is in the *New York Times*, 30 Apr. 1989.

JEFFREY CRONIN

DE SMET, Pierre-Jean (30 Jan. 1801–23 May 1873), founder of missions among Native Americans, was born in Termonde (Dendermonde), Belgium, the son of Josse-Arnaud (Judocus) De Smet, a shipping merchant, and his second wife, Joanna Maria Buydens. At age twenty-one he was recruited by Charles Nerinckx, a Belgian parish priest who had served as a missionary in Kentucky and returned to his homeland to solicit people and money for North American missions. De Smet was one of several volunteers who left Belgium in 1821 and entered the Jesuit novitiate at Whitemarsh, near Baltimore, Maryland. In 1823 he was selected for a new novitiate to be founded at Florissant, near St. Louis, an establishment that eventually led to St. Louis University. He was ordained in 1827. Because of health problems he returned to Europe for a few years (1833–1837), where he in turn recruited more persons for work in North America. Shortly before his departure for Belgium he became a naturalized U.S. citizen, indicating his intention to return.

De Smet's first direct work with Native Americans came in 1838, when he was sent with a team to found a mission among the recently relocated Potawatomis, in the region of what is now Council Bluffs, Iowa. Despite some positive reports from De Smet, the Jesuit efforts there were not well received, and after less than eighteen months among the Potawatomis De Smet returned to St. Louis and requested reassignment; the mission continued to struggle and closed by 1841. De Smet's next assignment was among the Flathead or Salish people, who with the Nez Percé had sent four well-publicized delegations to St. Louis to request a Jesuit mission. He made a preliminary visit to the Pacific Northwest in 1840 and, after a fundraising period, returned with five others in 1841 to found St. Mary's Mission among the Salish, near Missoula, Montana. About a year later he returned again to St. Louis and was soon seeking mission funds in New Orleans, Boston, and Europe. Thereafter he spent some additional time in the Pacific Northwest but never as a resident missionary. Thus it is more accurate to refer to De Smet as a founder or promoter of missions rather than as a missionary who lived very long among Native Americans. His total residency with the Potawatomis and the Salish was less than two and a half years, and he never learned either language. When De Smet returned to the Northwest in 1844–1846, he spent most of his time traveling, visiting mission stations in the Columbia and Willamette river valleys, some of which he helped found, and generally serving as an administrator, promoter, and explorer. Some Jesuits complained that he was overly optimistic about mission prospects and made promises to Native Americans that were impossible to fulfill, and by 1847 he was relieved of his responsibilities as superior of Jesuit missions in the Oregon area. Recalled to St. Louis, De Smet was made provincial treasurer and secretary, marking the end of his formal missionary career. St. Louis became his home for the second half of his life, until his death there, but journeys frequently took him away. Biographers emphasize his indefatigable travels of over 180,000 miles in his lifetime, including eight trips to Europe.

De Smet's missionary travels in the upper Missouri River region and the Northwest during the 1840s had made him well known among many tribes, and the federal government began to turn to him as an intermediary. In 1851 he was asked to attend the first Fort

Laramie Peace Council as a "pacificator." In 1858 General William S. Harney requested De Smet as chaplain for military expeditions to Utah, in response to the Mormon rebellion and then to the "Yakima War" in Oregon. In 1864, 1867, and 1868 he was recruited to help with government peace missions on the northern plains. He generally declined to travel with the army, believing it would compromise his credibility, and instead traveled ahead, engaging in more private conversations and trying to bring delegations of Native American leaders to talks with government and military agents. Government leaders believed he had greater influence with Native Americans than "any other living white man," even in hostile settings. He gained great fame when he entered the camp of Sitting Bull in the face of threats to kill the first white man who appeared. General David S. Stanley reported that De Smet was told, "If it had been any other man than you, Blackrobe, this day would have been his last."

Among Native Americans, De Smet was a trusted friend and in some cases an adopted relative. He saw himself as an advocate for Indians and was critical of their treatment by the government, pointing out white American "provocations and injustice." De Smet wrote, "If our Indians become enraged against the whites, it is because the whites have made them suffer for a long time." In the face of advancing white settlement, he shifted from an earlier support of somewhat independent Indian nations to become an advocate of assimilation. Believing that he was supporting peace through tragic compromises, he generally encouraged Native Americans to accept government peace treaties and reservations. Thus he has been evaluated both as a heartfelt ally of Native Americans and as an agent of U.S. expansion.

• Manuscript materials relating to De Smet's life are found especially in the Jesuit Missouri Province Archives, St. Louis, and at Washington State University and Gonzaga University. Within De Smet's lifetime he published *Letters and Sketches: With a Narrative of a Year's Residence among the Indian Tribes of the Rocky Mountains* (1843), *Origins, Progress, and Prospects of the Catholic Mission to the Rocky Mountains* (1843), *Oregon Missions and Travels Over the Rocky Mountains in 1845–46* (1847), *Voyage au Grand Desert en 1851* (1853), *New Indian Sketches* (1863), and *Western Missions and Missionaries: A Series of Letters* (1863). These books mainly consist of letters and reports by De Smet, written and published to elicit support for mission efforts. Many of these letters were reorganized and republished, with additional materials, in the four-volume *Life, Letters and Travels of Father Pierre-Jean De Smet, S.J., 1801–1873*, ed. Hiram M. Chittenden and Alfred T. Richardson (1905), the most substantial published version of primary documents pertaining to De Smet. Biographies, often admiring, include Robert C. Carriker, *Father Peter John de Smet: Jesuit in the West* (1995); John J. Killoren, *"Come Blackrobe": De Smet and the Indian Tragedy* (1994); Eugen Laveille, *The Life of Father De Smet, S.J., 1801–1873*, trans. Marian Lindsay (1915); Helene Margaret, *Father De Smet: Pioneer Priest of the Rockies* (1940); and John Upton Terrell, *Black Robe: The Life of Pierre-Jean De Smet, Missionary, Explorer, and Pioneer* (1964). Surveys of Catholic missions give attention to De Smet; a significant example is Gilbert J. Garraghan, *The Jesuits of the Middle United States* (3 vols., 1938). George E. Tinker, *Missionary Conquest: The Gospel and Native American Genocide* (1993), is a Native-American critique focused on four revered mission figures, one of whom is De Smet.

BRUCE DAVID FORBES

DESMOND, Humphrey Joseph (14 Sept. 1858–16 Feb. 1932), editor and civic leader, was born near Cedarburg, Wisconsin, the son of Thomas Desmond, an educator and businessman, and Johanna Bowe. Desmond was a graduate of the University of Wisconsin, achieving his degree in three years (1877–1880). At the university, Desmond was a coeditor of the student newspaper with Robert M. La Follette, the future senator from Wisconsin. In 1881 Desmond was admitted to the Wisconsin bar and shortly thereafter began the practice of law. Desmond served as a member of the Milwaukee School Board from 1883 to 1890 and helped to initiate the industrial training system in the Milwaukee public schools.

At the same time, Desmond became the chief editorial writer for the *Catholic Citizen*, an independently owned Roman Catholic newspaper that originated in Milwaukee but had subscribers throughout the Midwest. By 1891, after nine years of association with the newspaper, Desmond became the president and general manager of the Citizen Company and thereby the publisher of the *Catholic Citizen*. Under Desmond's aegis, the *Catholic Citizen* acquired control over many other Catholic newspapers in the United States. Eventually, the *Citizen* would claim that it enjoyed the largest circulation of any Catholic newspaper in America. Under Desmond's editorship, the *Catholic Citizen* gradually shed its dominant Irish Catholic tone and began to appeal to a wider Catholic audience.

Desmond's talents as both editor and lawyer were reflected in the church-state issues involving the Wisconsin Bennett Law and the Edgerton Bible case. A compulsory education measure, the 1889 Bennett Law required that academic courses be taught in English. Desmond's editorial approach joined with both Catholic and Lutheran leaders in condemning the Bennett Law as an infringement of parental rights and as state interference in private parochial schools. Eventually, following the 1890 state elections, the Bennett Law was repealed. Elected to the Wisconsin State Legislature in 1890, Desmond was appointed chair of the Committee on Education. In that position he drafted a new compulsory education law to replace the Bennett Law; it became known as the Desmond Law and required school attendance for children under the age of thirteen.

On the issue of Bible reading in the public schools, in 1888 Desmond editorially supported a Catholic legal petition from the Wisconsin town of Edgerton that argued against the practice of reading from the King James version of the Bible in the local public schools. Eventually Desmond joined the legal team to argue against sectarianism before the Wisconsin Supreme Court. The legal decision of March 1890 vindicated Desmond's argument that the use of the King James version of the Bible constituted sectarianism in the public schools.

A consistent foe of nativism and bigotry, Desmond fought vigorously against the American Protective Association and its strident anti-Catholicism. Opposing the APA, he successfully argued for the placement of a statue honoring the Reverend Jacques Marquette in Statuary Hall in Washington, D.C.

Desmond's personal involvement in legal and social issues exemplified his commitment to activism that he believed all Roman Catholics should follow in American society. Desmond asserted that the Catholic church should identify itself with the needs and goals of the labor class in the United States. Supportive of labor unions and the justified use of strikes, Desmond employed the *Catholic Citizen* as a forum for prominent Catholic writers on economic and social justice issues to argue that American labor issues were truly moral and religious issues necessitating a Catholic response.

Desmond's support for Catholic activism in society was also reflected in his backing of lay Catholic congresses, of aid to immigrants, and of African-American Catholic meetings as well. Desmond continually defined social responsibility as part of religious responsibility. Eschewing a Catholic ghettolike mentality, Desmond urged Catholic activism in a world that was not to be avoided but rather grappled with.

Desmond's belief in an articulate Catholic populace led to his association with the founding of the Colombian Catholic Summer School in 1895. Its purpose was to acquaint Catholics with lecturers in subjects such as religion and science, literature, history, and the Bible. In addition, Desmond supported the establishment of Catholic reading circles for the purpose of stimulating intellectual curiosity among the Catholic public. In 1898 Desmond married Susan Ryan of Oshkosh, Wisconsin, with whom he had six children.

In a time of intense debate within the American Catholic hierarchy during the last decades of the nineteenth century, Desmond generally sided with those Catholic church leaders who advocated the church's becoming open to change and willing to work with non-Catholics, especially on issues of social reform.

In his editorial career with the *Catholic Citizen*, Desmond composed over 15,000 editorial columns and increased the circulation of his newspaper fourfold to more than 16,000 subscribers. As an author, Desmond published more than twenty-five books, including a legal text, *The Church and the Law*; the history of American nativism with *The Know-Nothing Party* and *The A.P.A. Movement: A Sketch*; collections of his editorials; and works of moral advice. He died in Milwaukee.

Desmond's career flourished during a period when the independent Catholic press came of age. He is credited with being one of the initiators of the Catholic Press Association. Founded in 1911, the CPA proposed to represent the interests of Catholic newspaper editors and to support the growth of Catholic publications in the United States. Desmond's significance is in establishing a network of newspapers with the *Catholic Citizen* as its mainstay; using that network he attempted to initiate dialogue within the Catholic community on a host of issues concerning that religious body. Desmond was a Wisconsin Progressive who communicated his faith and his social concerns through his newspaper. Secure in his belief in his religion and his country, Desmond strove to influence an activism within the Catholic community that would address both social concerns and religious issues. Journalism was his vehicle to educate the Catholic audience, fashioning it into an articulate body motivated by faith to contribute to the American environment.

• No known collection of Desmond's papers exists in a single depository, but primary resources are in the State Historical Society of Wisconsin, Madison; the Archives of the Archdiocese of Milwaukee; and the University of Notre Dame Archives. The best resource for Desmond's opinions is the pages of the *Catholic Citizen*, available on microfilm. Additional works of Desmond not mentioned in the text include collections of his editorials, *Outlooks and Insights* (1899), *Chats within the Fold* (1901), *Marked Copy: Being Paragraphs and Editorials Which in Their Time Attracted Attention Here Saved from Oblivion* (n.d.), and *The New Laity and the Old Standards* (1914). His works of moral suasion include *Your Better Self* (1918) and *The Ways of Courage* (1927). *Mooted Questions of History* (1895) and *Curious Chapters in American History* (1925) are both historical works. He also wrote *A Reading Circle Manual* (1901), a directory for education. Background information on the Desmond family is supplied in Humphrey J. Desmond, *A Memoir of Thomas Desmond* (1905). Academic treatises on Desmond include Richard J. Orsi, "Humphrey Joseph Desmond: A Case Study in American Catholic Liberalism," (M.A. thesis, Univ. of Wisconsin, 1965), and Richard Scheiber, "Humphrey J. Desmond, The *Catholic Citizen* and Catholic Liberalism," (Ph.D. diss., Marquette Univ., 1990). Background to the history of the Catholic church during the era of Desmond is in Aaron Abell, *American Catholicism and Social Action: A Search for Social Justice, 1865–1950* (1960); Robert D. Cross, *The Emergence of Liberal Catholicism in America* (1958); and David O'Brien, *Public Catholicism* (1989). An obituary is in the *Catholic Citizen*, 20 Feb. 1932.

RICHARD SCHEIBER

DESMOND, Johnny (14 Nov. 1920–6 Sept. 1985), singer and actor, was born Giovanni Alfredo de Simone in Detroit, the son of Anthony de Simone, a grocery store owner, and Lillian Buccellato. Johnny sang at age nine on a local radio show, "Uncle Nick's Children's Hour." He later attended the Detroit Conservatory of Music, then formed his own vocal group, the Downbeats. In the summer of 1940 the Downbeats were hired by the Bob Crosby band and performed as the Bob-o-Links. Ruth Keddington, who joined the Bob-o-Links that fall, became Desmond's wife (date unknown); they had two children. The date of his name change is unknown.

The Bob-o-Links met with mixed success. Desmond left in 1941 and joined Gene Krupa's band as a vocalist. After a year, Desmond entered the army where he was assigned to be a drummer. Feeling his talents were being wasted, he wrote Glenn Miller, asking to join his army band as a singer. He joined Miller's American Band of the Allied Expeditionary Forces in October 1943. It was his big break.

Desmond recalled that Miller told him to stop using vocal tricks, to lose that "look of a fish gasping for air." Whether it was owing to this advice, or simply through hard work and experience with highly professional musicians, Desmond became a huge success. His smooth baritone voice and good looks earned him nicknames such as the "G. I. Sinatra" and "Le Cremier." While stationed with the Miller orchestra overseas, he was given his own weekly radio show. He also sang in German on a few propaganda programs. By the time he returned to the United States in August 1945, he had fan clubs all over Europe.

A barrage of publicity greeted Desmond, who had secured a new radio show, a fat record contract with RCA Victor, and a movie contract. Two recorded songs, "Don't You Remember Me?" and "Guilty," hit the *Billboard* charts in 1946 and 1947. Surprisingly, all his enterprises failed, and Desmond's career stalled. "I just tried to do everything too fast," he recalled.

In 1949 an invitation to sing on the popular morning radio show "The Breakfast Club" turned into a six-year stay. Working on the program gave him "an understanding of what the public is like and what it wants," Desmond said. "In the final analysis, if you haven't got something the public accepts, you haven't got anything."

Desmond slowly resumed his recording career, first on the MGM label, then switching to Coral in the early 1950s. Several of his recordings reached the top twenties on the charts, including "C'est Si Bon," "Heart of My Heart," "Yellow Rose of Texas," and "Sixteen Tons." One hit, "Play Me Hearts and Flowers," was the title song from a 1955 "Philco Television Playhouse" episode, among Desmond's first TV appearances.

By the mid-1950s Desmond's career was again in full swing with many television, film, and nightclub appearances. Television shows (1953–1962) included episodes of "Danger," "Robert Montgomery Presents," the "Alcoa Hour," "Climax," "Sally," and the "U.S. Steel Hour." He was a regular on the short-lived situation comedy "Blansky's Beauties" (1957). His film debut was as a singer in *Calypso Heat Wave* (1957). Other films were *Escape from San Quentin* (1957), in which he sang his composition "Lonely Lament," *China Doll* (1958), *Desert Hell* (1958), and the 3-D science-fiction picture *The Bubble* (1967).

Amazing Adele (1956) marked Desmond's musical comedy debut. Intended for Broadway, the show closed out of town. His next show was the musical *Say, Darling* (1958). With music by Jule Styne, *Say, Darling* garnered favorable reviews and ran a respectable 338 performances on Broadway. Desmond later starred as Nicky Arnstein, replacing Sydney Chaplin, in Styne's hit show *Funny Girl* (1964) with Barbra Streisand. The few songs Desmond recorded after 1960 were mainly show tunes and popular ballads

from the 1940s and 1950s and an album of sacred songs.

Desmond's nightclub career lasted until a few months before his death. Over the years his performances elicited comments such as "crowd pleaser," "works hard and comes through to a big hand and encores," and has "surefire communication with audiences." Singer Mel Tormé noted that Desmond has "a tender brand of emoting, combined with a deep appreciation of what the lyricist tries to convey." A year before his death, *Variety* commented that "Desmond is in excellent voice. His notes are true, he projects feeling . . . a knowledgeable, competent and still handsome singer." At his death in Los Angeles, Desmond had nearly completed his autobiography and was working on a six-part television series on the big bands. The pilot for the series aired on PBS as "An Evening of Musical Memories of the '40s."

• Concise biographical and career entries on Desmond can be found in various standard reference works on popular music and jazz. Articles dealing with events in his career are in *Down Beat*, 31 Dec. 1952, p. 2, 2 Dec. 1953, p. 17, and 6 Oct. 1954, p. 3; *Variety*, 11 May 1955, p. 62, 28 Aug. 1968, p. 55, and 13 June 1984, p. 80. Obituaries are in the *Los Angeles Times*, 8 Sept. 1985, and the *New York Times*, 9 Sept. 1985.

JEANETTE L. CASEY

DE SOTO, Hernando. *See* Soto, Hernando de.

DESYLVA, B. G. (27 Jan. 1895–11 July 1950), lyricist and film and theatrical producer, was born George Gard DeSylva in New York City, the son of Aloysius Joseph DeSylva, a vaudeville performer turned attorney, and Georgetta Gard, daughter of a U.S. marshal. When he was two, his family moved to Los Angeles, where his father—who had played in vaudeville as Hal de Forest—tried to make a child star of DeSylva. His debut came at age four in a song-and-dance routine at the Grand Opera House, and for a time he toured on the Keith vaudeville circuit. But DeSylva's youthful show business career was terminated by his maternal grandfather, who insisted the boy receive a stable and normal education (Georgetta's father had earlier prompted the elder DeSylva to quit show business and seek a "respectable" profession as a condition for marrying his daughter).

After graduating from elementary school in Los Angeles and high school in Azuza, DeSylva, who was known popularly as "Buddy," enrolled at the University of Southern California, supporting himself as a shipping clerk and playing ukulele in a "Hawaiian" band that performed at country clubs. While at the university DeSylva began writing song lyrics. He sent one of those, "N Everything," to Al Jolson, who set it to music, performed it, and requested more. DeSylva responded with "Avalon," "Chloe," and "By the Honeysuckle Vine," among others, all of which Jolson set and performed in *Sinbad* at New York's Winter Garden in 1918. Still in Los Angeles, DeSylva received a royalty check for $16,000, giving him the means and impetus to move to New York, leaving college in his sophomore year, to make lyric writing his career.

Between 1919 and 1924 DeSylva's songwriting collaborations read like a who's who of the then-eminent or about-to-be-eminent lyricists and composers for the Broadway musical stage. In 1919, teamed with Arthur Jackson, he wrote the lyrics for *La, La, Lucille,* George Gershwin's first full score for a musical comedy. In 1920 DeSylva provided the words for "Look for the Silver Lining" and "Whip-poor-will" to Jerome Kern's music in *Sally,* and the following year, with music by Louis Silver, he wrote one of Jolson's biggest hits, "April Showers," first performed in *Bombo.* Two years later, during the tour of that show, Jolson introduced "California, Here I Come," with words by DeSylva and himself and music by Joseph Meyer. Meanwhile, DeSylva had been the lyricist for Victor Herbert's *Orange Blossoms* (1922), and that same year he teamed with Ira Gershwin on the words for George Gershwin's "I'll Build a Stairway to Paradise," performed in *George White's Scandals of 1922.* For the 1924 edition of the *Scandals,* DeSylva collaborated with Ballard MacDonald on the lyrics for one of Gershwin's most enduring ballads, "Somebody Loves Me."

The year 1925 was auspicious for DeSylva personally and professionally. On 15 April he married Marie Wallace, a Ziegfeld girl (they had no children), and that year he teamed up with co-lyricist Lew Brown and composer Ray Henderson to write the complete score for that year's *Scandals.* This began a partnership that lasted until the early 1930s, one whose song styles virtually defined the mood of the "Roaring Twenties" and whose string of hit shows marks DeSylva, Brown, and Henderson as the only successful long-term three-person collaboration in American musical theater history.

Not only were the shows successful in their own time, but numerous songs of DeSylva, Brown, and Henderson went on to become standards in the repertoire of American popular song. After the *Scandals* of 1925, they again wrote the full scores for the editions of 1926 and 1928, the 1926 show yielding two major hits, "Black Bottom" and "Birth of the Blues." Moving from revue to musical comedy, the trio in 1927 produced their biggest theatrical triumph, *Good News* (557 performances), whose most enduring songs were "Varsity Drag" and "The Best Things in Life Are Free." DeSylva cowrote the lyrics with Brown and also, with Lawrence Schwab, the libretto as well. This would become the pattern for their succeeding major musicals.

Manhattan Mary, which opened only three weeks after *Good News,* was not a success, but *Hold Everything!,* with a book by DeSylva and John McGowan, ran 413 performances and included two songs with some of the most charming lyrics in the DeSylva canon, "To Know You Is to Love You" and "You're the Cream in My Coffee." *Follow Thru* (1929), again with a libretto by DeSylva and Schwab, ran only ten fewer performances than their previous show and intro-

duced "Button up Your Overcoat" and "You Are My Lucky Star." The final DeSylva, Brown, and Henderson collaboration, *Flying High* (1930), closed after 347 performances and contained no songs that outlived the show's limited popularity. Perhaps the Great Depression accounts for the shorter run, or perhaps the combined powers of DeSylva and his cohorts were waning, for it was after this show that the trio broke up, each to follow his own pursuits.

Before the breakup, however, in 1929 DeSylva and his partners wrote scores for two film musicals, *The Singing Fool,* in which Jolson first sang their "Sonny Boy," and *Sunny Side Up,* which DeSylva also produced for Fox Studios. That producing assignment signaled a major career change for him. From that time forward he was to be a major producer of Hollywood films and, later, of such Broadway musicals as Cole Porter's *Dubarry Was a Lady* (1939) and *Panama Hattie* (1940) and Irving Berlin's *Louisiana Purchase* (1940). And while he collaborated on the librettos of the two Porter musicals, DeSylva would never again write lyrics of note.

With the breakup of the trio, DeSylva moved to Hollywood and became a producer for Fox, 20th Century–Fox, Universal, RKO, and Paramount. Among his films were five of Shirley Temple's most popular: *The Little Colonel, The Littlest Rebel* (both 1935), *Captain January, Poor Little Rich Girl,* and *Stowaway* (all 1936). In 1941 DeSylva became executive producer at Paramount, only stepping down from that post in 1944 because of poor health. Although he had ceased writing songs, DeSylva maintained an interest in the music industry, in 1942 helping to found Capitol Records in association with Johnny Mercer and Glenn Wallichs, and becoming Capitol's first chairman of the board.

After years of suffering from coronary disease, DeSylva succumbed to a heart attack in Hollywood. His career was singular in that he was enormously successful in both the creative and the managerial side of American popular entertainment, but in two entirely separate, sequentially distinct phases of his life.

• The fullest account of DeSylva's career as a songwriter is in the chapter "DeSylva, Brown, and Henderson" in David Ewen, *Great Men of American Popular Song* (1970), pp. 161–68, though Ewen glosses over DeSylva's second career as a motion picture producer. One of the most comprehensive listings of the shows he worked on, the songs he wrote, and the films he produced is included in the entry for DeSylva in *The ASCAP Biographical Dictionary of Composers, Authors, and Publishers* (1966). The best sources of information on the Hollywood phase of DeSylva's life are the obituaries in *Variety* and the *New York Times,* 12 July 1950.

JOHN BUSH JONES

DETT, R. Nathaniel (11 Oct. 1882–2 Oct. 1943), composer and educator, was born Robert Nathaniel Dett in Drummondsville (now Niagara Falls), Ontario, Canada, the son of Robert Tue Dett, a musician and music teacher, and Charlotte Johnson, a musician. The Detts were a highly literate and musically active family, especially interested in European concert traditions. For young Dett, the classical traditions formed his musical roots, and he would never lose touch with them.

Dett pursued formal musical study initially at Oberlin College, where he graduated in 1908. Thereafter Dett intermittently studied on the graduate level at Columbia University, the University of Pennsylvania, the American Conservatory of Music in Chicago, and at Harvard, where he won both literary and music prizes. He also studied advanced composition in Paris in 1929 with the renowned teacher Nadia Boulanger. For much of his professional life from 1913 to 1931 Dett served as director of music at the Hampton Institute in Virginia. Throughout these years he also devoted himself to musical composition. In 1916 he married Helen Elise Smith, with whom he had two children.

Both in his compositions and in his teaching at Hampton, Dett displayed ambivalence toward the issue of racial identification in art. During the early and mid-twentieth century, artists and critics discussed at length the roles and obligations of African-American artists. As with writers and painters, a key issue for composers concerned whether one should strive to be a consciously African-American composer or a composer who happened to be African American. Historians, journalists, and other commentators have tended to sympathize with the former position and, if only by implication, have criticized those who have chosen the latter course as having somehow sidestepped the center of cultural ferment. While the strengths and weaknesses of this perspective continue to be debated, Dett's career gives texture to this question.

Dett definitely saw himself as a composer who happened to be African American. At Hampton he insisted that his music students engross themselves in the classical traditions of Europe. When he took the Hampton Choir on tour he rarely performed spirituals or gospel music, though audiences in America and Europe eagerly hoped he would. Instead Dett preferred the mainstream choral literature. To Dett the question of a recognizable racial identity was best regarded as a kind of final layer, a cultural epidermis, which if given excessive attention could easily become distracting, obscuring the rest of the cultural body. In this regard he felt that many of the popular music forms such as ragtime, blues, and jazz had lost their artistic integrity, falling into titillation and pandering. In a letter Dett wrote:

We have this wonderful folk music, . . . but this store will be of no value unless we treat it in such a manner that it can be presented in choral form, in lyric and operatic works, in concertos and suites and salon music, unless our musical architects take the loose timbre of Negro themes and fashion from it music which will prove that we too have national feelings and characteristics.

As with the contemporary novelist William Faulkner, the ideal for Dett was to create art that was rooted in history and geography but that was also able to resonate among those unacquainted with that history and locale. The quotable hymn or folk fragment was not nearly enough; artful interpretations and settings were critical.

In 1926 Carl Engel, chief of the music division of the Library of Congress, asked Dett to write a quartet for piano, violin, saxophone, and banjo. Engel was seeking a piece that would merge African-American traditions with those of Western Europe. Dett politely declined the offer. In his refusal he stated, "Any effort from the outside to lay down rather strict lines along which art should develop can only result in self-consciousness and consequently in unartistic and insincere results."

In his compositions, Dett's work generally employed the harmonies and forms of traditional nineteenth-century symphonic and choral writing. But unlike many of the Romantics, Dett rarely sought to incorporate identifiable idioms into his music. Like the writers of his day who led the Harlem Renaissance, Dett chose to define himself in relation to established classical traditions; but, unlike them, he preferred no identification with any cultural movement. He wrote some well-regarded grand oratorios and several suites for solo piano. His most famous work is one of his piano pieces, *In the Bottoms Suite* (1913); it contains thematic, geographic, and dance references. Here Dett revealed his convictions about how the soul can be properly displayed. The work shows his brilliant command of setting and form, with head and heart in gentle harmony.

Dett's compositions remain known in the world of American concert music, particularly among lovers of choral and piano music, but his refinement may have limited his music's gaining broader appeal. Artists like Dett, who considered their race to be incidental, seem destined to be ignored as long as most enthusiasts of African-American arts seek racial consciousness from the artists they wish to promote. Ironically, this political priority limits the visibility of many great African Americans of the past. R. Nathaniel Dett warrants the attention he sought—as a mainstream American composer. Dett died in Battle Creek, Michigan.

• Much of Dett's musical manuscripts, as well as his correspondence and other papers, can be found at the library of Hampton University in Virginia. There are two good biographies of Dett. One is by Arlene Gray, *Listen to the Lambs* (1984); the other is by Vivian Flagg McBrier, *R. Nathaniel Dett, His Life and Works* (1977). Most anthologies on American music give at most a paragraph to Dett. One anthology that gives the composer greater depth of coverage is Eileen Southern, *The Music of Black Americans* (1971).

ALAN LEVY

DETWILER, Samuel Randall (17 Feb. 1890–2 May 1957), anatomist, was born in Ironbridge, Pennsylvania, the son of Isaiah H. Detwiler and Mary Hallman, farmers. After completing his secondary education he taught in the local public school for a year. From 1910 to 1912 he attended Ursinus College in nearby Collegeville as a day student; he then transferred to Yale University, where he planned to study medicine. However, he soon became more interested in anatomy and biology and devoted his academic career to these two subjects. After receiving his Ph.B. in 1914, he began teaching biology as an assistant instructor in the Department of Zoology while completing his graduate work. While working toward his A.M. degree, which he received in 1916, he became fascinated with the embryonic development of the nervous system and the function and structure of the optic organ, interests that he pursued simultaneously for the duration of his professional career. In 1917 he served briefly as a civilian physiologist for the U.S. Chemical Warfare Service and was also promoted to instructor of anatomy in the Yale Medical School. In 1918 he received his Ph.D. in zoology and anatomy.

In 1919 Detwiler married Susan Talmage; they had two children and were later divorced. In 1920 he accepted a position to teach anatomy at the Union Medical College in Peking (Beijing), China. He also enrolled in the school as a medical student and completed two years of coursework before returning to the United States in 1923 to become an assistant professor of zoology at Harvard University. In 1926 he was promoted to associate professor, and the next year he accepted a position with Columbia University as a professor and executive officer of the Department of Anatomy in the College of Physicians and Surgeons, a position he held for the rest of his career.

Detwiler's most important discoveries came in the field of experimental embryology, a field introduced in the 1880s by the German zoologist Wilhelm Roux. Prior to Roux, embryologists were largely content to observe and describe embryonic development, but following his lead, they began experimenting with embryos in an effort to determine why and how they developed as they did. Detwiler was one of the first Americans to recognize that many interesting and significant facts could be discovered through a carefully planned course of experimentation with embryos in various stages of development. His own research efforts focused on the development of the nervous system; specifically, he sought to understand how and why peripheral nerves grow and how the embryonic nervous system adjusts functionally and structurally to abnormal conditions.

Almost all of Detwiler's work in this regard involved experimenting with salamander embryos. In his earliest investigations he transplanted one or both of the anterior limbs to the head and other locations in order to observe the effect on the development of the embryo's neurological system. He was able to demonstrate that in almost every case the embryo adjusted to the relocation of the limb by growing the appropriate nerves, nerve networks, and peripheral nerve centers in positions appropriate to the relocated limb. Later he studied the effect of alterations to the spinal cord on the proliferation and differentiation of nerve cells. These experiments included replacing the cephalic end of the spinal cord with an extraneous medulla; transplanting the spinal cord so that the hindmost part of the brain was connected to the anterior limb region and vice versa; segmenting and transplanting the various pieces of the spinal cord in a number of rearrangements; and removing various parts of the forebrain and midbrain. The results of these experiments, many of which were brought together in his book *Neuroembryology* (1936), demonstrated that in almost every case the embryonic salamander is capable of adapting to the extirpation or rearrangement of the various major components of its central nervous system by modifying its development in order to compensate adequately for the changes. Moreover, Detwiler's findings were shown to have universal application when other scientists performed similar experiments on the embryos of birds and mammals and arrived at the same conclusions.

Detwiler's work with the eye was published in a number of scientific journals and synthesized in *Vertebrate Photoreceptors* (1943). The year before its publication he had married Gladys I. Hood, with whom he had no children. He studied the structural and functional features of the retinas of alligators, chinchillas, geckos, horned toads, lizards, rats, salamanders, and turtles, and he conducted experiments concerning their photomechanical responses and retinal pigment reactions. His most important finding was that visual acuity in vertebrates is a function of the size and number of visual cells per unit area in the retina.

Detwiler served as president of the American Association of Anatomists from 1954 to 1955 and was a member of the National Academy of Sciences. He served on the editorial boards of *Experimental Biology* (Monograph Series), the *Journal of Experimental Zoology*, and the Columbia Biology Series and was a member of the advisory board of *Human Biology*. He died in New York City.

Detwiler was a pioneer in the field of experimental embryology in the United States. His influence as a teacher, author, researcher, and editor did much to stimulate its acceptance and development in this country. As a researcher, he demonstrated the remarkable adaptability of the embryonic nervous system when forced to respond to disruptions in its normal growth pattern.

• Detwiler's papers are in the Osborn Zoological Laboratory at Yale. Biographies that include bibliography are John Spangler Nicholas, "Samuel Randall Detwiler," National Academy of Sciences, *Biographical Memoirs* 35 (1961): 85–111; and Russell L. Carpenter, "Samuel Randall Detwiler," *Anatomical Record* 131 (May 1958): 5–18. Obituaries are in the *New York Times*, 4 May 1957, and *Science*, 31 January 1958, pp. 227–28.

CHARLES W. CAREY, JR.

DETZER, Dorothy (1 Dec. 1893–7 Jan. 1981), peace lobbyist, was raised in Fort Wayne, Indiana, the daughter of August Jacob Detzer and Laura Goshorn. She attended the Chicago School of Civics and Philanthropy for two years but did not complete a college degree. Her family was Episcopalian and patriotic: her mother was in the Red Cross and an officer in the State Council of Defense; her younger brother attended Annapolis and embarked on a naval career; her older brother served with the army in France in World War I as did her twin brother, who was exposed to mustard gas at the battlefront and died a painful death from its effects a few years later. Detzer spent 1914–1918 working in Hull-House, Chicago, where she was inspired by the example of pacifist Jane Addams.

In 1920 Detzer traveled to Vienna to work for the American Friends Service's relief committee, moving to war-torn Russia in 1922 to serve with the Quakers once again at the "Volga famine front." In 1924 she returned to the United States and became the national executive secretary of the U.S. section of the Women's International League for Peace and Freedom (WILPF), an organization that had its origins in the opposition to World War I mounted by Addams and like-minded women. She lived in Washington, D.C., and devoted herself to building up the WILPF, which had nine branches with 2,000 members in 1921, and 120 branches with 13,000 members by 1937.

Detzer's main successes were as a congressional lobbyist. She believed in the effectiveness of public opinion and was contemptuous of Capitol Hill's special-interest lobbyists, such as the Firestone rubber corporation and the arms manufacturers. She brought pressure to bear on legislators through her charm and force of personality and by organizing, with the help of the "women's network" of reform activists and party and public officials that had sprung up in Washington by the 1930s, mass support among the nation's women—expressed through public meetings, petitions, letter-writing campaigns, and radio broadcasts and, Detzer could argue, at the polls. She and the WILPF set out to achieve a more equitable distribution of American freedoms: for example, she cooperated with the National Association for the Advancement of Colored People in demanding the desegregation of restaurants on the Hill and was arrested for attempting to have lunch in the Senate cafeteria with an African-American graduate of Bryn Mawr. Detzer also worked with the American Civil Liberties Union, the Southern Tenant Farmers Union, and the Women's Trade Union League. But she was at odds with the National Woman's Party, which had in 1923 initiated the campaign for an equal rights amendment that could have undermined women's protective labor legislation.

Detzer concentrated especially on foreign policy issues. She was an opponent of Adolf Hitler from as early as 1926. She insisted that the citizens of developing countries should be free from imperialist economic exploitation, criticizing U.S. invasions of Nicaragua and the Anglo-American manipulation of Liberia's rubber industry and labor force. Detzer and the WILPF vigorously pursued the cause of disarmament. Not satisfied by the efforts of successive Republican administrations to restrain naval expansion through multilateral agreements with other countries, she continued to press her antimilitarist arguments, subscribing to the view that the arms manufacturers, the "merchants of death," had been instrumental in causing World War I and America's entry into that conflict.

Many Americans agreed with this viewpoint, and, under the chairmanship of Gerald P. Nye of North Dakota, a major Senate investigation into the causes of World War I took place in 1934–1935. Against this background, Congress passed the neutrality laws of the mid-1930s. These were designed to eliminate U.S. participation in the arms trade and U.S. loans to belligerents in order to keep America out of any forthcoming European war. Detzer's lobbying skills and her knowledge of the workings of the Senate helped to bring about Nye's inquiry and to enable it to have a major impact on U.S. foreign policy. Senator Nye and journalist Drew Pearson were among those who observed that Detzer was the main driving force behind the munitions investigation, and the *New York Times* later concluded that she was "the most famous woman lobbyist" of the 1920s and 1930s.

But Detzer remained an ardent opponent of fascism, and when Nazi Germany helped General Francisco Franco's forces to defeat the weapons-starved Loyalists in the Spanish Civil War she began to have second thoughts on the desirability of the arms embargo. The outbreak of World War II only compounded the dilemma for Detzer; as pacifism could not be effectively pursued, she lobbied for the United States to fight the war as humanely as possible, for example by allowing Red Cross supplies to be delivered to war-affected countries.

In 1946 she resigned her job with the WILPF, and in 1954 she married Ludwell Denny, a journalist. In that year, she started a career as a freelance foreign correspondent. She continued to support the WILPF at home and never lost her enthusiasm for international correspondence. In the late 1970s, for example, she exchanged views on aging with British pacifist and socialist A. Fenner Brockway, who had been president of the British Council for Peace in Vietnam. In 1970 she had moved with her dying husband to Monterey, California, where she too died eleven years later.

Detzer's activities contributed to American isolation from world politics in the 1930s and slowed U.S. preparations for the forthcoming war against fascism. Yet her critique of militarism may also be viewed as part of a long tradition, beginning with George Washington's farewell address, of antipathy to foreign wars and other entanglements. In the context of American feminism, Detzer epitomized and helped to seal the link between women and the peace movement, and her lobbying successes, however controversial, helped to make her one of the more credible role models for other women who wanted to enter the political arena.

• Detzer's tenure as national secretary of the WILPF is documented in that organization's records in the Swarthmore College Peace Collection, Swarthmore, Pa., which is also the location of the Dorothy Detzer Papers, a source of information on her personal life. Detzer wrote an illuminating political autobiography, *Appointment on the Hill* (1948). Rosemary Rainbolt, "Women and War in the United States: The Case of Dorothy Detzer, National Secretary WILPF," *Peace and Change* 4 (Fall 1977): 18–27, is an overview of Detzer's career in the 1920s and 1930s. Rhodri Jeffreys-Jones, "Dorothy

Detzer and the Merchants of Death," in Jeffreys-Jones, *Changing Differences: Women and the Shaping of American Foreign Policy, 1917–1994* (1995), assesses her work in relation to the Nye inquiry.

RHODRI JEFFREYS-JONES

DEUTSCH, Albert (23 Oct. 1905–21 June 1961), historian and journalist, was born in New York City, the son of Barnett Deutsch and Kate Knopke. Raised on the Lower East Side, Deutsch was the fourth of nine children in a poor Jewish family that had recently emigrated from Latvia. At the age of five, following an accident, his right eye had to be enucleated. He was largely self-educated. Before finishing high school, he left home and traveled around the United States, working as a longshoreman, a field hand, and a shipyard worker. While on the road, he continued his education in public libraries around the country.

By the early thirties he had returned to New York City, where he found work doing archival research. In 1934, while surveying documents for a proposed history of the New York State Department of Welfare, he found records on the public care of the mentally ill. Recognizing the social as well as historical value of these records, he submitted a written proposal for a history of the subject to Clifford Beers, the founder of the National Committee for Mental Hygiene. He worked under contract with the committee for two years to complete *The Mentally Ill in America* (1937), a 530-page scholarly history of the care of the mentally ill from colonial times to the present. Remarkable because it was written by someone without a college education or any direct training or experience in psychiatry, this book immediately established Deutsch's reputation as the most important historian of American psychiatry up to that time.

Between 1936 and 1940 while employed at the New York Department of Welfare as a research associate, he wrote, with David Schneider, *The History of Public Welfare in New York State, 1867–1940* (1941). In 1938 he was elected to the newly formed Innominate Club, which later became the New York Society for the History of Medicine, where he presented many scholarly papers on the social history of psychiatry and medicine. He also published papers in learned journals including "Historical Inter-Relationships between Medicine and Social Welfare" in the *Bulletin of the History of Medicine* (1942). In 1944 he contributed scholarly essays on the history of the mental hygiene movement and military psychiatry during the American Civil War to *One Hundred Years of American Psychiatry*, a volume commemorating the centennial of the American Psychiatric Association.

In 1941 Deutsch began to write a daily column for the newspaper *PM*. Deutsch used this column to speak out on a wide range of contemporary social issues related to health care. In 1945 his columns criticizing the maltreatment of psychiatric patients in veterans hospitals led the House Committee on Veterans Affairs to demand that he name his sources. He refused and was voted in contempt of Congress. Later the committee rescinded its action, and many of Deutsch's suggestions for improved treatment were adopted by the Veterans Administration. In 1945 and 1946 the American Newspaper Guild gave him its Heywood Broun citation for this series of articles. In 1947 the New York Newspaper Guild honored him as "the most distinguished and effective humanitarian crusading in American journalism."

In 1948 he gathered together a series of articles on mental hospitals written for *PM* and published them, as well as numerous photographs, as *The Shame of the States*, a powerful indictment of state hospital care in the United States. The following year he won the Lasker Award "for his outstanding contribution to the advancement of mental health through his journalistic efforts." In 1958 he was made an honorary fellow of the American Psychiatric Association.

In addition to *PM*, Deutsch published articles on social issues in various popular magazines, including the *New York Times Magazine*, *Colliers*, *Woman's Home Companion*, *Saturday Evening Post*, and *Reader's Digest*. When *PM* closed he wrote briefly for other New York newspapers. In 1949 he gave up daily newspaper work in order to explore social problems more deeply. In 1950 he published *Our Rejected Children*, a book on juvenile delinquency. In 1955 he brought out another crusading book on the need for police reform, *The Trouble With Cops*. Neither of these works had as great an impact as Deutsch's earlier work on mental illness.

In his last years he was frequently invited to give lectures and participate in seminars on mental health problems. Although he devoted less time to medical history, he did present a paper on the "Deserving and Undeserving Poor," at the 1958 meeting of the American Historical Association. In 1956, under a grant from the National Association for Mental Health, he started a survey of mental health research in the United States—a project he did not live to complete.

Deutsch was married at age twenty-seven. His wife's name is not known; they had no children and were later divorced. He died in Roffey Park, England, while attending an international research conference convened by the World Federation for Mental Health.

• Some of Deutsch's correspondence is included in the records of Big Brothers of America at the University of Minnesota Library of Social Welfare History. Deutsch's scholarly articles include "Dorothea Lynde Dix: Apostle of the Insane," *American Journal of Nursing*, 36 (1936): 987–97; and "The Cult of Curability, Its Rise and Decline," *American Journal of Psychiatry*, 92 (1936): 1261–80. Works about Deutsch include: M. E. Kenworthy, "Albert Deutsch," *American Journal of Psychiatry*, 118 (1962): 1064–68; Jeanne L. Brand, "Albert Deutsch: The Historian as Social Reformer," *Journal of the History of Medicine and Allied Sciences*, 18 (1963): 149–57; George Mora, "Three American Historians of Psychiatry: Albert Deutsch, Gregory Zilboorg, George Rosen," in *Essays in the History of Psychiatry*, ed. Edwin R. Wallace IV and Lucius C. Pressley (1980); Mora, "Early American Historians of

Psychiatry," in *Discovering the History of Psychiatry*, ed. Mark S. Micale and Roy Porter (1994). An obituary is in the *New York Times*, 20 June 1961.

EDWARD M. BROWN

DEUTSCH, Babette (22 Sept. 1895–13 Nov. 1982), writer, editor, and translator, was born in New York City, the daughter of Michael Deutsch and Melanie Fisher. She grew up in New York, was a student at the Ethical Culture school, and attended Barnard College, graduating in 1917. She worked briefly for Thorstein Veblen. In 1921 she married Avraham Yarmolinsky, with whom she had two children.

Deutsch began publishing poems at Barnard, and in 1919 she published her first book of poetry, *Banners*. It was followed by six other volumes, the best selections of which are reprinted in her *Coming of Age: New and Selected Poems* (1959) and in *Collected Poems, 1919–1962* (1963). *The Collected Poems of Babette Deutsch* was published in 1969; subsequent poems appearing in journals have not been collected. Several poems are anthologized in collections such as *The New Yorker Book of Poems* (1969) and the *Treasury of Jewish Poetry* (1957).

Deutsch was also an active novelist, with *A Brittle Heaven* (1926), *In Such a Night* (1927), *Mask of Silenus* (1933), and *Rogue's Legacy* (1942) to her credit; a writer of critical studies, such as *This Modern Poetry* (1935), *Poetry in Our Time* (1952), and *Poetry Handbook* (1957); and, often in collaboration with her husband, a translator and editor of various works. Her writings for children and young people include fiction, nonfiction, and poetry; her biography of Walt Whitman won the Julia Ellsworth Ford Foundation Award for children's literature in 1941. Other of her notable juvenile works are *Heroes of the Kalevala* (1940), *The Reader's Shakespeare* (1946), *Tales of Faraway Folk* (1952), and the translation of *There Comes a Time* (1969).

Deutsch lectured at the New School for Social Research (1933–1935) and at Columbia University (1944–1971); she also lectured at the Poetry Center of the Young Men's Hebrew Association in New York. She was elected to the American Academy of Arts and Letters in 1958 and became its secretary in 1969. She was a member of P.E.N. and a chancellor of the Academy of American Poets. She was awarded the *Nation* Poetry Prize in 1926, won a William Rose Benét Memorial Award in 1957, and was an honorary consultant to the Library of Congress from 1960 to 1966.

Although some critics maintained that Deutsch's work, especially her poetry, lacked an emotional dimension and was overly "intellectual," others found great merit in her approach. A critic reviewing *Banners* for the *Dial* complained that Deutsch "embroiders too heavily upon her pattern" and declared that she needed to learn the virtues of dramatic economy. Another critic, writing for the *New Republic*, suggested that Deutsch, in her second book of poetry, *Honey Out of the Rock* (1925), was "far too self-conscious," which rendered her poetry "cold" and "imitative." On the

other hand, a *New Yorker* review called a later volume of poetry, *Animal, Vegetable, Mineral* (1954), "a mature and balanced performance." Among the many persons who praised her work were Marianne Moore, Louise Bogan, William Carlos Williams, Karl Shapiro, Hayden Carruth, George Garrett, and John Wain. In a review of her *Collected Poems, 1919–1962* in 1964, Lawrence Perrine spoke highly of Deutsch's "observant eye and . . . [her] way with metaphor."

Deutsch will probably be remembered primarily as a poet. Her sureness at depicting a scene and presenting an image may be seen in "Feeding the Chickens." "Yellow yellow yellow: you are the child's / First richness," it begins, evoking the cornbin's "hillocks." Two more lines tell of the farmer giving the girl a fistful of kernels that are "hard to hold," and thus "a few spill." Even so, the corn is "Hard to lose: the dribble of orange bright / Sunny white-tipped seeds." The rather unobtrusive language used in the poem and the easy repetition and parallelism lull the reader into a sense of serenity that is at odds with the striking picture. To the innocent delight of a child, the corn kernels are golden riches—an abundance, a spilling of a handful of suns. The technique at work here, typical of Deutsch's most successful poems, is also evident in poems such as "Lizard at Pompeii," in which the comparisons are always just but never strident. In five lines of progressively diminished length, the lizard quickly appears and is as quickly gone: the creature "flickers over stone," waits a moment in the shadow of vegetation, and then "Flashes emerald" before vanishing. Even in dealing with more abstract subjects, Deutsch's figures of speech fit the subject perfectly. In "History," for example, the "horrors" of history are shown in quiet comparisons that make a profound impact on a reader, the most startling being that of history closing in on the observer, who feels it to be "monstrous," likened to a doll "That is alive and bigger than the child / Who tries to hold it."

Deutsch's novels are certainly less successful than her poetry. One reviewer, Louis Kronenberger, spoke of Deutsch's second novel, *In Such a Night*, as a work "that deserves to be judged by high standards" but added that he was only willing to "applaud" Deutsch's "intention." Although all these novels display the craft of a skillful writer, Deutsch seemed to lack the narrative power necessary for a full-length work. Her other works are also in many respects praiseworthy, including her literary commentary, but they too may lack the quality found in her best poems. Nancy K. Mackenzie wrote of Deutsch's *Poetry in Our Time* in a review for the *New York Times* that the work was "more chronology than criticism," even though she generally praised Deutsch's efforts. Her *Poetry Handbook*, however, was useful to many teachers for several decades. It is probably fair to suggest that, recognizing the merits of her other works, Deutsch's poems will probably continue to be read long after her other books are forgotten.

Deutsch did not publish a book-length work after her husband's death in 1975. She died in New York City.

• Major collections of Deutsch's papers are at the American Academy of Arts and Letters Library, New York City, and at the Special Collections Department of Washington University Libraries, St. Louis, Mo. A listing of Deutsch's works, along with a brief commentary by Mark Van Doren, is in *Contemporary Poets* (1980). Reviews of her various works are in the *Dial*, Aug. 1919, p. 120; *New Republic*, Dec. 1925, p. 170; *Saturday Review of Literature*, 2 July 1927, p. 947; *New Yorker*, 12 June 1954, p. 120; *Poetry* 95 (1959): 116–21; *New York Times*, 8 Mar. 1964, p. 4; *Virginia Quarterly Review* 40 (1964): 326–29; *Sewanee Review* 73 (1965): 138–50; *Prairie Schooner* 39 (1965): 273–76; *New York Times*, 9 July 1966, p. 25; and *Poetry* 115 (1970): 277–80. Obituaries appear in the *New York Times*, 16 Nov. 1982, and *Time*, 29 Nov. 1982.

RICHARD E. MEZO

DEUTSCH, Gotthard (31 Jan. 1859–14 Oct. 1921), Jewish scholar and college professor, was born Eliezer Deutsch in Kanitz (Province of Moravia), Austria, the son of Bernhard L. Deutsch, a merchant, and Elise Wiener. He always called himself Gotthard, an attempted translation into German of his Jewish given name. Deutsch entered Breslau Jewish Theological Seminary in October 1876. While attending seminary classes, he also enrolled in afternoon classes at the University of Breslau. At the seminary, he was influenced by the noted Jewish historian Heinrich Graetz. Matriculating in 1879 at the University of Vienna, two years later he received his Ph.D. in history. While attending the university, he enrolled in a Talmudic course taught by Isaac Hirsch Weiss at Beth Hammidrash. During his studies in Vienna, Deutsch drew inspiration and guidance from both Weiss and Adolf Jellinek, an authority in midrashic research. Shortly after his graduation, Deutsch received Semichah (ordination) from Rabbi Weiss.

In 1881 Deutsch accepted a probational position as Sabbath schoolteacher for a Jewish congregation in Brünn. The following year he was appointed to teach religion at the city's German high school. After teaching for six years (1881–1887) at Brünn, he entered the rabbinate. His first and only charge came in 1887, in the town of Brüx. Deutsch was far from content at his new vocation. Soon, he yearned for an academic milieu and the opportunity of satisfying his craving for knowledge. While at Brüx he married in May 1888 Hermine Bacher; the couple had three sons and two daughters.

In 1891, at the invitation of Isaac Mayer Wise, Deutsch came to the United States to accept the chair of Jewish history and philosophy at Union Hebrew College in Cincinnati. After eleven years of teaching there, he was appointed dean. In February 1903, after the death of Moses Mielziner, he was designated acting president of the college, a position he held until October of the same year.

In 1912 Deutsch delivered lectures on Jewish history at the University of Chicago. While speaking at schools throughout the United States, Deutsch was also a guiding force at the local level. This included his association with the Cincinnati German Club and in 1909 his election to the Cincinnati Board of Education, a position he held for four years. Much of Deutsch's time was also spent as an editor and chief contributor to the *Jewish Encyclopedia*, as corresponding secretary for the Central Conference of American Rabbis, and as chairman of the conference's Committee on Contemporaneous History.

One of the turning points in Deutsch's life came with the United States's entry into World War I. His lifelong love for Germany had led Deutsch to support President Woodrow Wilson's neutrality while aligning himself with the People's Council of America for Democracy and Peace. In the tide of anti-German hysteria Deutsch found himself alone and ostracized. He spoke out singularly, sometimes bitterly, against his adopted country's wartime role. On 5 October 1917 federal agents and local detectives raided the council's headquarters. Shortly thereafter, at a friend's naturalization hearing, Deutsch refused to answer the question, "Who do you want to win in this war?" These activities and subsequent newspaper headlines led many colleagues and the public to demand his immediate removal from the college's faculty. Only the staunch support of his students, friends, and leading Reform rabbis enabled Deutsch to continue teaching.

Although a biblical scholar, Deutsch is also known for his two novels and works on history and language. One of the world's greatest Jewish scholars, Deutsch possessed a knack for memorizing facts, biblical scriptures, secular literature, and world history. He also wrote in several languages, including Hebrew, Yiddish, German, French, and English. Above all, however, Deutsch's gentlemanly traits separated and lifted him above the mundane. Kindness, enthusiasm, wit, humor, and a true concern for all mankind endeared him to friend and stranger alike. Children loved him for his friendly smile and for the sweets and gifts he always had available for them.

A prolific writer, Deutsch produced hundreds of newspaper and journal articles with commentary; these appeared mainly in the *Jewish Chronicle*, *American Hebrew*, *Central Conference of American Rabbis Yearbook*, *Hebrew Union College Journal*, *American Israelite*, and *American Journal of Theology*. Besides contributing to *Der Deborah*, he succeeded Isaac Wise in 1901 as its editor. His list of scholarly works is equally impressive: *Paradigmen-Tafeln zur hebräischen Grammatik* (1886), *Die Symbolik in Cultus und Dichtung bei den Hebräern* (1886), *Philosophy of Jewish History* (1897), *Andere Zeiten, eine Erzählung aus dem jüdischen Leben der jüngsten Vergangenheit* (1898), *Unlösbare Fesseln, eine Erzählung aus dem jüdischen Leben der Gegenwart* (1903), *Memorable Dates of Jewish History* (1904), *Four Epochs of Jewish History* (1905), *Israel Bruna, an Historical Tragedy in Five Acts* (1908), *The History of the Jews* (1910), *Der Glaube an Hobelspäne* (1914), *Scrolls* (2 vols., 1917; 3rd vol., 1919), and other pamphlets and reprints. His works are considered by many to be the authoritative word on questions relating to the Jewish faith.

Deutsch died at his home in Cincinnati. He was mourned by Jew and non-Jew, progressive and conservative; thousands filled the Cincinnati Crematory to pay their last respects. At the grave site of their friend and colleague, Rabban Gamaliel and Rabbi Eliezer illustrated best the void left by Deutsch: "Let us mourn the loss of this man and weep for him. When kings die, they leave their crowns to their heirs. When rich men die, they leave their wealth to their children. This great teacher took with him the most precious treasures in the world when he passed away."

• The Bernhard Felsenthal Papers, in the Hebrew Jewish Archives, contain an extensive record of correspondences between Deutsch and Felsenthal. Adolph S. Oko, *Selected List of the Writings of Gotthard Deutsch* (1916), presents an extensive bibliography of Deutsch's major publications. Biographical sketches of Deutsch are in Max Raisin, *Great Jews I Have Known* (1952), pp. 143–52, and an excellent unpublished sketch by Raisin in the Hebrew Jewish Archives. Celebrating Deutsch's semi-jubilee, the *Hebrew Union College Monthly* (2, no. 8 [May 1916]) published a series of tributes and editorials by E. L. Heinsheimer, Henry Englander, Abraham Jehiel Feldman, S. Felix Mendelsohn, H. B. Cantor, and Jacob I. Meyer, among others. These papers treat Deutsch's religious concerns, contribution to literature, and his role in Jewish history. A useful history of Hebrew Union College is Samuel E. Karff, ed., *Hebrew Union College–Jewish Institute of Religion at One Hundred Years* (1976). A comprehensive memorial by Henry Englander is in "Memorial Addresses and Resolutions: Gotthard Deutsch," *Central Conference of American Rabbis* 32 (1922): 145–49. Obituaries are in the *New York Times*, 15 Oct. 1921; *American Hebrew*, 21 Oct. 1921; *B'nai B'rith News*, Oct. 1921; *Hebrew Union College Monthly* 8, no. 5 (Mar. 1922); and *Jewish Advocate*, 20 Oct. 1921.

C. E. LINDGREN

DEUTSCH, Helene Rosenbach (9 Oct. 1884–29 Mar. 1982), psychoanalyst and psychiatrist, was born in Przemyśl, Poland, the daughter of Wilhelm Rosenbach, a lawyer, and Regina Fass. Her parents were Jewish, but she grew up a Polish nationalist. As early as 1898 she became romantically involved with a much older man, Herman Lieberman, who was a Social Democratic leader. Lieberman was married, however, and a divorce in those days was politically out of the question; nonetheless, their affair lasted for years. Although formal schooling was impossible in Poland for a woman, tutoring enabled her to enroll at the University of Vienna in 1907. From the outset she was interested in a psychiatric career.

While spending a year in Munich in 1910–1911 she finally broke off with Lieberman, who since 1907 had been a deputy from Poland in the Parliament in Vienna. In Munich she had met her future husband, Felix Deutsch, in medical school, and they were married in 1912. She received her medical degree from the University of Vienna in 1913.

Women could not then hold clinical psychiatric appointments at the University of Vienna, but the professor there, Julius Wagner von Jauregg, who won a Nobel Prize for psychiatry in 1927, had made a great impression on her. Once World War I broke out, physicians were needed by the Austrian military, and Deutsch was given tasks to perform at Wagner's clinic. She functioned as one of his assistants, a high post to which as a woman she could not formally be entitled.

In the fall of 1918 Deutsch left Wagner's clinic in order to undertake a personal analysis with Sigmund Freud, which lasted about a year. She had given birth to a son in 1917 and was uncertain about herself as both a mother and a wife. While for some in the history of psychoanalysis, particularly Freud's exceptionally talented male pupils, he could be a burden to their independent development, Deutsch found that Freud released her most creative talents. She could write as Freud's adherent and at the same time fulfill her own needs for self-expression. Her professional audience responded to her work as that of one of the most prominent leaders in psychoanalysis. She was no mere imitator of Freud, but within his system of thought she was able to express her own individual outlook.

The 1920s were Deutsch's most creative period; she emerged as one of the most successful teachers in the history of psychoanalysis. In 1924 she became the first to head the new Vienna Psychoanalytic Society's Training Institute, which meant that between 1924 and 1935 (when she left for Boston, Mass.) she had to evaluate those who came for instruction in analysis. She was much sought after for both as a training analyst and as a supervisor; her seminars were remarkable experiences for students, and her classes were remembered as vibrant and rich in clinical details. Her students included the next generation of the most prominent analysts who remained organizationally loyal to Freud.

Deutsch was the first psychoanalyst to explore feminine psychology. Her publications on the subject, beginning in 1924, along with those of Karen Horney, stimulated Freud himself to write about women. Deutsch was pioneering in her emphasis on the role of motherhood (Freud took mothers for granted) and was the one analyst to insist on its special significance for female psychology; in her private letters Deutsch went so far as to talk about the existence of a "female libido," a contradiction in terms according to Freud's thinking. Although she always expressed herself within Freud's conceptual framework, her writings were simultaneously the authentic outgrowth of her own most intense personal experiences. In 1930 she also published a textbook, *Psychoanalysis of the Neuroses*.

In Vienna Deutsch's caseload was, in large part, American, and in 1930 she visited the United States to attend the First International Congress of Mental Hygiene. She was already looking for a new position but was concerned about future possibilities for her husband, an internist who had also been Freud's personal physician when he first contracted cancer in 1923. Boston became the best choice for the Deutsches; a new psychoanalytic training institute was being founded there, and at the same time Stanley Cobb was creating a psychiatry department at the Massachusetts General Hospital. Cobb was interested in psychosomatic medicine, Felix's special field, so Cobb was eager to attract both of them. Helene came over in the fall of 1935 with their son, and Felix arrived in Boston in 1936.

Deutsch's mental stylishness, combined with the force of her personality, helped her attain a unique position in Boston. The analysts involved in setting up the Boston institute had mainly been students abroad when she was already established as one of Freud's favorites. Although she was not eager to be once again a participant in the politics of training candidates, which necessarily involves forwarding some students while discouraging others, she served as president of the Boston Psychoanalytic Society from 1939 until 1941.

During World War II Deutsch published her two-volume *The Psychology of Women* (1944, 1945). She wrote notably about the conflict in women between motherliness and eroticism, although she felt that she had missed out on both sides. In her mind, her preoccupation with work had cost her a heavy human price. Deutsch emphasized the realistic conflicts of young women. Her books were filled with case histories that an analyst would not have been expected to encounter because these patients came from such a variety of social classes. She was not afraid to sound old-fashioned about how sexual experience could take the place of love. She thought that in order correctly to understand pathologic behavior, we must understand normal human development. Deutsch argued that a woman's "intensified" inner life becomes a unique source of human superiority; women became, she thought, better psychologists thanks to their special conflicts.

Perhaps Deutsch's most famous clinical concept was that of the "as if" personality, which highlighted the sources of a woman's capacity to identify with others. At the same time her theories helped to account for her own tie to Freud. To Deutsch, victimization was a central danger of feminine masochism, while intensified self-love could be a self-preservative counterweight, protecting a woman from her masochistic tendencies. Although it has mistakenly appeared to many contemporaries that Deutsch was merely echoing Freud's own views, in fact she succeeded in using her own autobiography to revise Freudian thinking. He had, for example, objected to her label of "as if personality," but she went ahead anyway.

Deutsch's old age was as remarkable as the rest of her life. After her husband died in 1964, her publications accelerated. She kept on sustaining friends and acquaintances almost right up to her death in Cambridge. Although she was deeply influenced by Freud throughout her professional life, Deutsch was able to emancipate herself from theoretical dogmatism and develop her own original theories, which have continued to be appreciated.

• Helene Deutsch's papers are at Radcliffe College. Her first book, *Psychoanalysis of the Sexual Functions of Women*, was published in German in 1925; it was edited by Paul Roazen and published in English in 1991 (Eric Mosbacher, trans.). Her textbook and a selection of clinical papers were published as *Neuroses and Character Types* (1965). *Selected Problems of Adolescence* (1967), *A Psychoanalytic Study of the Myth of Dionysus and Apollo* (1969), and her autobiography, *Confrontations with Myself* (1973), were written in her extreme old age. A posthumous collection of her psychoanalytic papers, *The Therapeutic Process, the Self, and Female Psychology* (1992), was edited by Paul Roazen, who also wrote her authorized biography, *Helene Deutsch, a Psychoanalyst's Life* (1985; repr., with a new introduction, 1992). See also Marie Briehl, "Helene Deutsch: The Maturation of Women," in *Psychoanalytic Pioneers*, ed. Franz Alexander et al. (1966), pp. 282–98; Janet Sayers, *Mothers of Psychoanalysis: Helene Deutsch, Karen Horney, Anna Freud, Melanie Klein* (1991); and Brenda Webster, "Helene Deutsch: A New Look," *Signs* 10, no. 3 (1985): 553–71. An obituary is in the *New York Times*, 1 Apr. 1982.

PAUL ROAZEN

DEVENS, Charles, Jr. (4 Apr. 1820–7 Jan. 1891), soldier, jurist, and politician, was born in Charlestown, Massachusetts, the son of Charles Devens, Sr., a hardware merchant and town clerk, and Mary Lithgow. Charles Devens attended the Boston Latin School before being admitted to Harvard University. He graduated in 1838 and went on to Harvard Law School. He was admitted to the Massachusetts bar in 1840 and practiced from 1841 to 1849 in Franklin County, Massachusetts. From 1848 to 1849 he served in the state senate, and from 1849 to 1853 he held the post of U.S. marshal for the District of Massachusetts. While serving as marshal he became involved in a runaway slave dispute. After a U.S. Commissioner ruled that the slave was to be returned to his owner, Devens, as U.S. marshal, was required to carry out the order. This duty was most repugnant to him, and for several years he worked unsuccessfully for the release of the slave by offering to pay for his freedom. Eventually the slave gained his freedom during the Civil War, and Devens was able to find him a position in the federal government during the Rutherford B. Hayes administration.

In 1854 Devens returned to private law and also served as a city solicitor for Worcester from 1856 to 1858. During this time he gained a reputation as a public advocate and an outstanding speaker. He also developed a strong interest in military matters and rose to the rank of brigadier general in the state militia.

At the beginning of the Civil War, Devens was one of the first to answer President Abraham Lincoln's call for 75,000 volunteers. He was appointed a major in the Third Battalion of Massachusetts Rifles, and he and his battalion rushed to defend Washington, D.C. He was ordered from Washington to serve at Fort McHenry, Baltimore, Maryland. In July 1861 he was promoted to colonel and given command of a full regiment, the Fifteenth Massachusetts Infantry. At the battle of Ball's Bluff on 21 October 1861, Colonel Devens faced combat for the first time. This was a small battle, but it occurred shortly after the humiliating Union defeat at the first battle of Manassas in July. The battle took on severe political implications, not only because of the Union defeat but also owing to the death in the battle of a powerful U.S. senator, Edward Baker. Devens handled his troops well, receiving a minor wound when he was struck by a bullet right over his heart. His life was saved when the bullet's impact was absorbed by his uniform button.

On 15 April 1862 Devens was made a brigadier general of volunteers and assigned to a division in the Fourth Army Corps. He was involved in General George B. McClellan's Peninsular campaign in the spring of 1862 and was again wounded at the battle of Fair Oaks on 31 May 1862. While recovering from his wound, Devens was nominated for governor of Massachusetts by the "Peoples party." He was unable, because of his injury, to do any serious campaigning and was defeated by Republican candidate John A. Andrew. Devens's next major encounter was at the battle of Fredericksburg in December 1862. He again performed well despite another Union defeat, and his command covered the army's retreat across the Rappahannock River.

In May 1863, at the battle of Chancellorsville, Devens received a slight wound in his foot while leading a division of the Eleventh Army Corps. At the battle of Cold Harbor in June 1864, Devens was so crippled with rheumatism that he was forced to command his men from a stretcher. After the fall of Petersburg and Richmond in April 1865, Devens was awarded the honorary rank of brevet major general. Although the war ended in April 1865, Devens remained in service for another year and served as second in command in the Southeastern Military District in Charleston, South Carolina. He officially mustered out in June 1866 after more than five years of military service.

Returning to civilian life, Devens again took up the practice of law and politics in Worcester. In April 1867 he was appointed a justice of the Superior Court of Massachusetts, and in 1873 he was named to the Massachusetts State Supreme Court. When Hayes was elected president of the United States, he offered Devens the cabinet position of secretary of war. Devens refused that post but did accept the position of attorney general. At the end of this term he returned to his seat on the Massachusetts Supreme Court. Devens was also very involved in veterans' affairs, serving as the national commander of the Military Order of the Loyal Legion of the United States and the Grand Army of the Republic. Devens died in Boston. He never married.

Devens was one of Massachusetts's most well-known and distinguished citizens. He was said to be a handsome man with a commanding appearance. A thorough attorney who gave his clients his all, he was also known as a great orator and was in demand at many public functions. In 1894 the Massachusetts legislature commissioned a bronze statue of Devens in military uniform, which was erected on the state house grounds. A military training camp at Ayer, Massachusetts, was named for him during World War I.

• Devens's papers are at the Massachusetts State Library in Boston and the Massachusetts Historical Society, which holds his legal notebooks in seventy-one volumes. Devens's college and law school records are at the Harvard University Archives, and his Civil War military records and U.S. attorney general records are at the National Archives. Papers and newspaper items relating to Devens's law career are found at the Worcester Historical Museum and Worcester Public Library. Devens's orations were published by his nephew, Arthur Lithgow Devens, ed., *Charles Devens' Orations and Addresses in Various Occasions Civil and Military* (1881), which includes a memoir by John Codman Ropes. Short biographies are in Mark M. Boatner III, *The Civil War Dictionary* (1959); Ezra J. Warner, *Generals in Blue* (1964); and James L. Bowen, *Massachusetts in the War 1861–1865* (1889). For his term as attorney general see Kenneth E. Davison, *The Presidency of Rutherford B. Hayes* (1972). Thomas B. Wyman, *The Genealogies and Estates of Charlestown in the County of Middlesex in the Commonwealth of Massachusetts 1629–1818* (1879), provide family information. His activities in the Civil War are covered in detail in Bryon Farwell, *Ball's Bluff: A Small Battle and Its Long Shadow* (1990); Ernest B. Furgurson, *Chancellorsville 1863: The Souls of the Brave* (1992); *The War of the Rebellion: A Compilation of the Official Records of the Union and Confederate Armies* (128 vols., 1880–1901); and Andrew Elmer Ford, *The Story of the Fifteenth Regiment Massachusetts Volunteer Infantry in the Civil War 1861–1864* (1898). Extensive obituaries are in the *Boston Globe* and the *Boston Herald*, 8, 9 Jan. 1891, with funeral coverage on 12 Jan. 1891.

MICHAEL A. CAVANAUGH

DEVERS, Jacob Loucks (8 Sept. 1887–15 Oct. 1979), army officer, was born in York, Pennsylvania, the son of Philip Knoderer Jacobs, a jeweler, and Ella Kate Loucks. He attended the U.S. Military Academy at West Point and in 1909 was commissioned a second lieutenant of artillery. Devers completed a three-year assignment with the Fourth Field Artillery in Wyoming and subsequently returned to West Point as a mathematics instructor. He rose to captain in May 1917 while on the faculty and the next year performed temporary duty with the Ninth Field Artillery in Hawaii. Throughout the First World War, Devers functioned as a staff officer at the School of Fire (later Field Artillery School) at Fort Sill, Oklahoma. In 1919 he completed a brief tour of occupation duty in Germany and attended the French artillery school at Treves before returning to West Point as a field artillery instructor.

Devers remained at the military academy for five years before being nominated to attend the Command and General Staff School, Fort Leavenworth, in 1924. A major since 1920, he returned to Fort Sill in 1925 as director of the Department of Gunnery and there pioneered improved firing techniques. Devers next completed a period of staff duty with the War Department, attended the War College with distinction in 1932 and was promoted to lieutenant colonel in 1934. Between 1936 and 1939 he completed a third tour at West Point, where the rank of colonel was conferred. Devers then proceeded to the Panama Canal Department as chief of staff, and in May 1940 President Franklin D. Roosevelt appointed him to a board selecting army and navy bases on British possessions as part of the lend-lease agreement.

Devers rose to major general in October 1940 and assumed command of the Ninth Infantry Division at Fort Bragg, North Carolina. He handled his charge adroitly and caught the attention of Chief of Staff George C. Marshall, who in July 1941 directed him to lead the armored forces training school at Fort Knox, Kentucky. This proved Devers's most significant prewar assignment and he was instrumental in accelerating the design, development, and integration of military hardware such as the Sherman tank, the self-propelled 105mm howitzer, and numerous amphibious vehicles.

Devers remained at Fort Knox during the initial phases of American entry into World War II, and in September 1942 he was promoted to lieutenant general. In May 1943 his training endeavors culminated in a Distinguished Service Medal and transfer to England as commanding general of the European Theater of Operations (ETO) following the untimely death of Lieutenant General Frank Maxwell Andrews. In this capacity Devers was responsible for training and organizing U.S. forces for their eventual cross-channel invasion of Europe. His accomplishments culminated in a second Distinguished Service Medal, but General Dwight D. Eisenhower thought Devers lacked adequate combat experience and declined to include him in Operation Overlord, the invasion of Normandy. In January 1944 he became a deputy to General Sir Maitland Wilson, supreme Allied commander in the Mediterranean, and also functioned as the senior U.S. commander in that theater. For several months thereafter, Devers applied his instructional expertise in preparing Allied forces for the invasion of southern France.

Despite his lack of experience, Devers chafed in his role as a staff officer and sought a combat assignment. In July 1944 he was appointed commander of the Sixth Army Group, consisting of General Alexander M. Patch's Seventh Army and the First French Army under General Jean de Lattre de Tassigny. With this force Devers commenced Operation Dragoon, the invasion of southern France, on 15 August 1944. This move intended to relieve German pressure on Allied forces at Normandy and was entirely successful. Franco-American forces landed against scattered opposition and swept north through the Rhone Valley and Vosges Mountains until contact was established with General Eisenhower's army. Turning east, Devers's men conducted final mopping up operations in the Ardennes sector before turning on trapped German forces in the Colmar Pocket, near Strasbourg. Throughout January 1945 reduction of this strongpoint yielded more than 22,000 prisoners, eighty guns, and seventy tanks to the Allies. Devers then stormed and penetrated the formidable Siegfried Line east of the Rhine River and relentlessly pursued enemy forces into southern Germany and Austria. By April 1945 the cities of Nuremberg, Salzburg, and Munich had been captured along with Adolph Hitler's personal retreat at Berchtesgaden. On 6 May Devers received the unconditional surrender of German forces in western Austria and counted among his prisoners Marshal Hermann Goering, Generals Albrecht Von Kesselring and Gerd Von Runestedt, as well as the head of the former Vichy regime, Marshal Henry Philippe Pétain. In consequence of his services, Devers's final wartime rank was four-star general.

After the war Devers succeeded General Omar N. Bradley as commander of the Twelfth Army Group in September 1945. He subsequently served as chief of army ground forces until his retirement in September 1949. Devers then commenced a working relationship with the American Automobile Association, serving as president and chairman. He interrupted civilian pursuits in 1951 to function as United Nations military adviser during the Kashmir dispute between India and Pakistan. He also accepted civilian advisory positions with the Fairchild Corporation (1951–1959) and the Battlefield Monuments Commission (1960–1970). In 1911 Devers had married Georgia Hayes Lyon, with whom he had one child. After the death of his wife, he married his longtime friend Dorothy Caldwell Ham in 1975. Devers died in Washington, D.C.

Devers was one of the foremost administrators in American military history. A superb organizer, he was cognizant of the mounting complexities of modern warfare and tirelessly sought to integrate the latest tactics and technology. His training procedures were thorough, innovative, and designed to place American citizen-soldiery on par with their more professional adversaries. Devers was also a polished negotiator whose tact in dealing with foreign dignitaries was a prerequisite for successful coalition warfare. With four decades of military service behind him, Devers was one of the most competent professional officers of his generation and one of only three U.S. general officers (with Bradley and Mark Clark) to command an army group. Combat operations also revealed him to be a capable field commander and a solid contributor to the cause of victory in Europe.

• Much of Devers's official correspondence is in the War Department records at the National Archives, Washington, D.C. His personal papers are at the York County Historical Society, Pa., with scattered materials at the Center of Military History, Washington, D.C., and the U.S. Army Military History Institute, Carlisle Barracks, Pa. Biographical sketches are in Robert H. Shoemaker and Leonard A. Paris, *Famous American Generals* (1941); David G. Wittels et al., *These Are the Generals* (1943); and Martin Blumenson and James L. Stokesbury, "Masters of the Art: Jake Devers," *Army* (Feb. 1973): 26–31. For Devers's campaign in southern Europe consult Charles B. MacDonald, *The Last Offensive* (1973), and Seventh U.S. Army, *Report of Operations in France and Germany* (3 vols., 1946). An account in Devers's own words is "Operation Dragoon," *Military Affairs* (Summer 1946): 3–41. An obituary is in the *New York Times*, 17 Oct. 1979.

JOHN C. FREDRIKSEN

DEVIN, Thomas Casimir (10 Dec. 1822–4 Apr. 1878), soldier, was born in New York City, the son of Michael Devin, whose wife and occupation are unknown. Thomas Devin appears as a head of household for the first time in the 1850 census, having married Elizabeth Campbell in 1846. His occupation was listed as "painter," and he, his wife, a daughter, and an Irish-born servant lived in rented quarters in New York City's Seventeenth Ward. In 1860 Devin was still listed as a "painter" in the census, but he had by that time become a partner in a paint, varnish, and oil firm and had moved his family to newer rented quarters in the Nineteenth Ward. He had also become active in Irish-American fraternal activities and had risen to the rank of lieutenant colonel of the First New York State Militia.

At the outbreak of the Civil War in 1861, Devin recruited the first company of cavalry (known as the Jackson Horse Guards) to be dispatched from New York City to the defense of Washington, D.C. This company was soon absorbed into the First New York Cavalry, a three-month regiment that was mustered into U.S. service on 14 July 1861. When the First New York was mustered out on 23 October 1861, Devin reenlisted three weeks later for three years' volunteer service and was commissioned colonel of the Sixth New York Cavalry on 30 December 1861 (postdated to 18 Nov., three days after his reenlistment). Devin's regiment saw only limited action in northern Virginia and in the Shenandoah Valley during the first year of the war, but later in 1862 Devin and the Sixth New York participated with the Army of the Potomac in the critical battles of the Maryland campaign at South Mountain (14 Sept. 1862) and Antietam (17 Sept. 1862). When Major General A. E. Burnside took command of the Army of the Potomac in November 1862, a major reorganization of the command structure of the army's cavalry placed Devin and the Sixth New York in Colonel D. M. Gregg's Second Cavalry Brigade as part of the Left Grand Division of the Army of the Potomac. At Fredericksburg (13 Dec. 1862), Gregg was transferred to another division to replace a slain officer, and Devin inherited command of the Second Brigade (which included his own Sixth New York, the Fourth New York Cavalry, the Ninth New York Cavalry, two companies of the Third West Virginia Cavalry, and later on the Seventeenth Pennsylvania Cavalry). When the Army of the Potomac's cavalry was again reorganized under Major General Joseph Hooker in early 1863, Devin remained commander of the Second Brigade and now found himself part of the First Division of the new Cavalry Corps under the command of Brigadier General Alfred Pleasonton. Pleasonton was promoted to command of the entire Cavalry Corps in May 1863, and Devin's brigade received a new division commander, Major General John Buford.

It was under Buford that Devin's star shone brightest. Devin had already acquired a well-earned reputation as a disciplinarian and field tactician as colonel of the Sixth New York, which was commended by observers as "the best-drilled Regiment in the service." As one of Buford's two brigade commanders, Devin now became known as "Buford's Hard Hitter" and Buford's "Old War Horse." He took his brigade into action under Buford in major cavalry engagements at Brandy Station (9 June 1863) and Upperville (21 June 1863). It was at Gettysburg (1–3 July 1863) that Devin performed his best-known service for Buford. On the first day, as Buford's cavalry division attempted to delay the advance of the Confederate Army of Northern Virginia into Gettysburg so that the infantry of the Army of the Potomac would have the time to deploy and defend the town, Devin dismounted his Second Brigade and spread them out on the north side of Cashtown Road (on the northwest side of Gettysburg). Together with the dismounted troopers of the First Brigade, this thin screen of dismounted cavalry slowed the advance of superior numbers of Confederate infantry just long enough to permit the Army of the Potomac to occupy the high ground south and west of Gettysburg and thus ensure a Union victory over the next two days of the battle.

Devin continued to serve with the Army of the Potomac throughout its engagements in Virginia in 1863, most notably at Wapping Heights (23 July 1863), Bristoe Station (14 Oct. 1863), and Mine Run (26 Nov.–2 Dec. 1863). After Buford's untimely death in December 1863, Devin and his brigade performed scouting and outpost duties for Lieutenant General U. S. Grant's Overland campaign of 1864, including the battles of the Wilderness (5–7 May 1864), Spotsylvania Courthouse (8–21 May 1864), Totopotomy Creek (27–31 May 1864), and Cold Harbor (31 May–12 June 1864). Units from Devin's brigade also participated in the Kilpatrick-Dahlgren raid on Richmond (28 Feb.–4 Mar. 1864), although Devin himself had no role in the raid, in Major General P. H. Sheridan's Richmond raid (9–24 May 1864), and in the cavalry battles at Yellow Tavern (11 May 1864) and Trevilian Station (11–12 June 1864). In the summer of 1864 Devin and his brigade were attached to Sheridan's Army of the Shenandoah to subjugate the Shenandoah Valley. For his outstanding handling of his brigade at Front Royal (16 Aug. 1864), Devin was promoted to brigadier general, dating from 19 October 1864. He led his brigade in the important Shenandoah campaign battles at Opequon Creek (19 Sept. 1864) and Cedar Creek (19 Oct. 1864).

Devin and his brigade returned to the Army of the Potomac in March 1865, just in time to participate in the final battles at Five Forks (1 Apr. 1865), Sayler's Creek (6 Apr. 1865), and the surrender of the Army of Northern Virginia at Appomattox Courthouse (9 Apr. 1865). Devin was brevetted major general of volunteers on 13 March 1865 for his war services and was mustered out of U.S. service on 15 January 1866. However, unlike most volunteer officers in the Civil War, Devin chose to remain in the U.S. Army afterward. On 25 September 1866 he was offered the regular army rank of lieutenant colonel for the Eighth U.S. Cavalry and served at a series of military posts, beginning with the Carlisle Barracks (Nov.–Dec. 1866), Churchill Barracks, Nevada (July–Sept. 1867), Camp McDermitt, California, and Fort Whipple, Arizona Territory (Dec. 1867–Mar. 1870), and Fort Union and

Fort Bayard, New Mexico Territory (Nov. 1870–June 1873).

By this time, the injuries he had sustained during the Civil War and the hardships of army service in the West were taking a severe toll on Devin's health. In June 1873 he took the first of a series of medical leaves to deal with "chronic inflammation of the Eustachean tubes, Partial deafness of the left ear," gastroenteritis, hepatitis, and "general debility." He returned to his regiment in May 1874 and served with them at Fort Bayard and Santa Fe, New Mexico Territory, until November 1875 and at Fort Brown, Texas, until July 1877, when he took another medical leave (Aug.–Nov. 1877) at the White Sulphur Springs in West Virginia to deal with a "Malarial Rheumatic Affection of [the] Back and lower limbs." He had only just been promoted to colonel in June 1877 and given command of the Third U.S. Cavalry before taking his leave. So, in December Devin headed West for one final term of service with his new regiment at Fort Laramie, Wyoming Territory (Dec. 1877–Feb. 1878). From there he took his last leave of absence and returned to New York City, where he died two months later of cancer of the stomach (according to his widow's pension application in 1879).

• No significant collection of letters or manuscripts by Devin has survived, although a lengthy letter from Devin to his brother (or perhaps brother-in-law) dated 22 Apr. 1865 and describing the Confederate surrender at Appomattox was published as "Didn't We Fight Splendid," *Civil War Times Illustrated* 17 (Dec. 1978): 38–40. Devin's pension file at the National Archives (File WC 184-875) contains extensive documentation of his post–Civil War service and illnesses. A number of Devin's after-action reports and other notices are contained in *The War of the Rebellion: A Compilation of the Official Records of the Union and Confederate Armies*, 1st. ser. (128 vols., 1880–1901), especially in vol. 27, pt. 2, for his Gettysburg report and in vol. 29, pt. 1, for his brigade's action at Bristoe Station. Secondary sources touching on Devin include a biographical sketch in *The Union Army*, vol. 8 (1908), and Edward G. Longacre, *The Cavalry at Gettysburg* (1986).

ALLEN C. GUELZO

DEVINE, Andy (7 Oct. 1905–18 Feb. 1977), movie and television actor, was born Andrew Devine in Flagstaff, Arizona, the son of Tom Devine and Amy Ward, the owners of a local hotel. His mother was the daughter of Admiral James Harmon Ward, a founder of the U.S. Naval Academy at Annapolis. Devine began his film career in 1926 after coming to Hollywood to attend his father's funeral. While walking down Hollywood Boulevard he was stopped by a casting agent from Universal who, noticing the young man's athletic build (as well, no doubt, as his Santa Clara University football sweater, as Devine had excelled in both football and baseball there), hired him on the spot as an extra in the silent serial *The Collegians* (1926), which starred George Lewis and Dorothy Gulliver. Devine played minor parts in numerous silent films. But the development of sound pictures, Devine believed, would make an acting career impossible for him, with

his unusual, high-pitched, continually cracking voice (the result of a childhood accident). He joined the crew of a supply ship to the Bering Sea. On his return to California, he worked for a time as a lifeguard in Venice. In 1931 he returned to films in *The Spirit of Notre Dame* as Truck McCall, a somewhat befuddled football player. He drew critical acclaim for the role and in 1931 won a long-term contract at Universal Studios, where he invariably played the star's big, slow-witted but genial sidekick.

By 1933 Devine's film career was more established, and in October he married Dorothy Irene House. The couple had met on the set of a movie. They had two sons.

The family moved to Van Nuys, California, where Devine began investing in real estate. They avoided the fast-paced Hollywood life and dedicated themselves instead to raising their children. Devine was devoted to his family and in a 1957 interview said, "I made a deal with my boys years ago. If they'd do nothing to embarrass me, I'd do nothing to embarrass them. It's worked out fine." He preferred to stay near his home; when he had to be away, it was almost always for only a brief time.

During the 1930s and 1940s Devine was in constant demand by movie directors. He appeared in as many as six to nine films per year and estimated that by 1950 he had made more than three hundred movies in twenty-five years. *A Star Is Born* (1937) and *Stagecoach* (1939) were two of his outstanding films.

From 1935 to 1940 Devine regularly appeared on Jack Benny's enormously popular radio show. He often would appear in place of Eddie Anderson, who played Benny's valet, Rochester. Devine's role was that of a country bumpkin who would visit Benny. He later appeared on Benny's television shows.

In spite of all his movie work, Devine believed that his broadest exposure and greatest popularity came from playing Jingles, the happy buddy of Wild Bill Hickok, played by actor Guy Madison; the "Wild Bill Hickok" western television series ran for 113 episodes between 1951 and 1958. There was a concurrent radio version of the show on Mutual from 1951 to 1956, which also starred Madison and Devine. Devine later accumulated considerable income from the residuals of the series. When Smilin' Ed McConnell died in 1954, Devine replaced him on a Saturday morning television show retitled "Andy's Gang." It was primarily a local show from 1955 to 1960, with the exception of the 1957–1958 season, when it ran in the fall on the NBC television network.

Devine's roles were limited in range, but this never seemed to bother him; he said of his career that he "loved every minute" of it. He had no formal training whatsoever as an actor and claimed that much of his ability was due to a "lot of Arizona hayseed." When he was seventy, he stated, "It's been a helluva life. I can't think of anything I would want to change. Well, maybe I should have passed up *Yellowstone*," referring to a 1936 western for Universal that he always considered the worst clinker of his career. He once said, "I never won an Oscar but I've lent money to a lot of guys who did. . . . I never starred in pictures. I was always the second man through the door. I never got the credit when a picture was a hit, but I never got blamed for all the crap that I was in either."

Throughout his lifetime Devine was active in community affairs. He served as honorary mayor of Van Nuys for nearly twenty years, and after 1957, when the Devine family moved to Newport Beach, he served there on many local committees. He was proudest of his membership on the board of directors of the Orange County Boy Scouts. He was active politically and was a staunch supporter of Ronald Reagan, actively campaigning for him in the 1976 primaries.

Devine died at the University of California–Irvine Medical Center. At his funeral, cowboy singers serenaded outside the chapel where Devine's fellow actors eulogized him. Madison said that "Andy was an original." Lew Ayres reminded the mourners that Devine "left us a legend of happiness and laughter." Other actors in attendance at the service included John Wayne and James Stewart. The poem "A Cowboy's Prayer" was handed out at the service, and mourners filed out of the chapel to the strains of "Tumbling Tumbleweed."

• Biographical and career information on Andy Devine's motion picture, radio, television, and stage career can be found in James Robert Parish, *Hollywood Character Actors* (1978); Arthur F. McClure and Ken D. Jones, *Heroes, Heavies and Sagebrush* (1972); David Rothel, *Those Great Cowboy Sidekicks* (1984); and Arthur F. McClure et al., *More Character People* (1984). Obituaries are in the *New York Times*, 20 Feb. 1977, and *Variety*, 23 Feb. 1977.

ARTHUR F. MCCLURE

DEVINE, Edward Thomas (6 May 1867–27 Feb. 1948), social worker, writer, and lecturer, was born near Union, Iowa, the son of John Devine and Laura Hall, farmers. He attended Cornell College in Iowa where in 1887 he obtained his A.M.

After graduation and until 1890, Devine was a teacher and the principal of public schools in three Iowa towns, and in 1889 he married Harriet Scovel; they had two children. During these years, he met Simon Patten, an original economic theorist, who emphasized that the United States should focus on wealth distribution to alleviate social problems. In 1890 Devine traveled to the University of Pennsylvania to study under Patten, who soon became his mentor and friend. That same year, he journeyed to Halle, Germany, to study economics, as had Patten. By 1893 Devine had earned his Ph.D. and had begun lecturing on economics for the American Society for the Extension of University Teaching. For this organization, which he later served as executive secretary, he taught courses in Oxford, England, Edinburgh, Scotland, and in several American cities.

In 1896 Patten urged Devine to become general secretary of the Charity Organization Society of New York. This job, which he held until 1912, became the vehicle for Devine's career as a social worker and reformer.

Charity Organization Societies (COS) developed in the 1870s in response to problems created by urbanization and industrialization. These two factors, combined with high immigration rates, resulted in rising poverty and its associated consequences (slums, chronic diseases, and hunger). These organizations pioneered new empirical and cooperative methods to combat these social problems, breaking new ground by emphasizing science and efficiency. These individual societies did not, however, provide monetary relief. They functioned solely as administrative organizations to coordinate the delivery of services to the poor. Devine expanded his organization's scope by initiating public housing reforms. He also organized the Pittsburgh Survey, the first major attempt to survey one community's social conditions and the campaign to eradicate tuberculosis. In 1904 Devine established the New York School of Philanthropy, the first school of this type in America.

While initiating these programs, Devine (or as his colleagues called him, "Doctor") edited the new COS of New York publication, *Charities and the Commons*. He expanded this journal into a comprehensive social work periodical that in 1912, under new editor Paul Kellogg, became the *Survey*, the preeminent social work periodical for the next forty years.

Devine's prolific writing on social welfare began with his first major work, *Principles of Relief* (1904), which became a textbook for social work schools and agencies. In 1909 he published *Misery and Its Causes*, in which he expanded Patten's thesis that poverty had economic not moral causes and that the state needed to ensure a proper standard of living.

In 1906 President Theodore Roosevelt chose Devine to head American Red Cross Relief efforts in the aftermath of the San Francisco earthquake. His COS experience proved especially valuable as it prepared him to coordinate effectively a large bureaucracy. As manager of this emergency enterprise, he won praise for his sound judgment and clearly expressed views.

Devine worked actively with the Red Cross through World War I. In 1913 he supervised flood relief efforts in Dayton, Ohio. From 1917 to 1918, he led the Bureau of Relief and Refugees in France. "He organized the emergency activities of the American Red Cross," Paul Kellogg later wrote, "and set the pattern for their disaster relief in all the years since."

After the war, Devine lectured widely in the United States, hoping to increase the number of trained social workers and schools. He wrote that "social work had become so vital a factor in the nation that professional training had become imperative" (*When Social Work Was Young* [1939]). Between 1919 and 1926, while he visited over 344 cities and towns teaching social work classes, social work schools grew in number from fifteen to over forty.

From 1926 to 1928, he was dean of American University's Graduate School. In 1929 he directed the Bellevue-Yorkville Health Administration and in 1930 headed the Housing Association of New York. Simultaneously, Devine, who frequently worked with the Federal Council of Churches, chaired their committee on revision of social ideals, which advocated sexual and racial equality, and the elimination of poverty.

From 1933 to 1935 Devine directed relief efforts for Nassau County, New York. Still, he remained largely quiet during the New Deal era. In 1933 he wrote *Progressive Social Action*, in which he advocated New Deal style reforms. His institutional innovations at the COS of New York greatly influenced Frances Perkins, Harry Hopkins, and W. Frank Parsons, who led national changes in welfare policies for President Franklin Roosevelt (Trattner, p. 230).

In 1937 Devine retired from active social work and moved to Chicago. In 1939 he published *When Social Work Was Young*, his autobiography, which detailed his COS and Red Cross work and social work's transformation. "The social worker at his best," Devine wrote, "is an indefatigable crusader for specific reform or reforms, one who combines a knowledge of acts with a need for action." (*When Social Work Was Young*). He died in Oak Park, Illinois.

"The Dean of Social Welfare," according to the *New York Times*, Devine helped to advance the country's thinking on social work and reform in the early twentieth century. By running the nation's largest charity organization, and by publishing numerous articles and books "hasten[ing] the development of modern conceptions of science and professionalism in social work" (Trattner, p. 228), Devine took a leading role in advancing the federal government's social welfare policies. "It was he who threw the emphasis of what was to become social work over onto prevention," Paul Kellogg said, "bringing scientific method to bear on the causes that brought men and women and children to the concern of philanthropy."

• Devine left no personal collection of papers. The *Survey Associates Records Papers* contain useful editorial correspondence between Devine and staff members such as Paul and Arthur Kellogg. The Columbia University School of Social Work and the University of Wyoming hold some of his papers, yet neither provides a complete listing. He wrote sixteen books, including *Social Forces* (1910) and *Social Work* (1922), and his writings appear in *Charity and the Commons* and the *Survey*. Sandra Cornelius, "Edward Thomas Devine, 1867–1948: A Pivotal Figure in the Transition from Practical Philanthropy to Social Work" (Ph.D. diss., Bryn Mawr College, 1976), details his life until 1920. Because of Devine's extensive work in New York City, he is frequently cited in the *New York Times*. Walter Trattner, *Biographical Dictionary of Social Welfare in America* (1986), also contains good biographical material. Other books that provide valuable insights into social welfare during Devine's life include Stanley Wenocur and Michael Reisch, *From Charity to Enterprise* (1989), Clarke Chambers's biography of Paul Kellogg, *Paul U. Kellogg and "The Survey"* (1971), and Frank Bruno, *Trends in Social Work 1874–1956* (1957). Daniel Fox's biography of Simon Patten, *The Discovery of Abundance* (1967), provides excellent analysis of Patten's theories and his relationship with Devine. An obituary is in the *New York Times*, 28 Feb. 1948.

NICHOLAS SAMUEL PULLEN

DEVOTO, Bernard Augustine (11 Jan. 1897–13 Nov. 1955), journalist and historian, was born in Ogden, Utah, the son of Florian DeVoto, a teacher and freight agent, and Rhoda Dye. Educated well beyond the demands of the jobs he held, DeVoto's father could provide only a meager income and a very modest home for his small family. As the offspring of religious dissenters (his father was a lapsed Roman Catholic; his mother, a nonpracticing Mormon), DeVoto blamed his family's economic circumstances and religious nonconformity for alienating him from his birthplace. He grew up openly critical of the townspeoples' provincial ways and censorious attitudes.

After one year at the University of Utah, DeVoto enrolled at Harvard University, convinced that the intellectual stimulation he craved was to be found only in Cambridge. Harvard did in fact provide him with stimulation as well as a chance to flex his literary muscles and to engage in lively debate with a small but admiring group of students. In the spring of 1917, on the eve of his senior year, DeVoto trained with the Harvard ROTC Regiment and enlisted the following August; he was commissioned a second lieutenant in the infantry but saw only domestic service during World War I. Returning to Harvard after the war, he earned a bachelor's degree in 1920 (as of 1918), and in 1922, after a brief stint in Ogden as a high school teacher and an eighteen-month bout with depression (he would be forever plagued by fits of sheer, numbing panic), DeVoto left for Evanston, Illinois, and a teaching position at Northwestern University. There he developed his natural gifts as a teacher of composition and met a freshman, Helen Avis MacVicar, whom he married in 1923 and with whom he had two sons.

Despite his early success in the college classroom, DeVoto's goal was to succeed as a novelist, a dream he never realized, though he did publish some five novels under his own name between 1924 and 1947, and four works of popular fiction under the pseudonym John August. DeVoto repeatedly revised early drafts and made changes suggested by his publishers, but his novels were never more than mildly successful, and almost all reviews were only guardedly favorable. In fact, DeVoto never published a novel that met with unqualified praise or that sold over time. His earliest novels—*The Crooked Mile* (1924), *The Chariot of Fire* (1926), and *The House-of-Sun-Goes-Down* (1928)—reflect the author's preoccupation with the West, but the dialogue is often stilted and the outcome of emotional situations frequently predictable. Later novels, *We Accept with Pleasure* (1934) and *Mountain Time* (1947), offer more modern themes and settings as well as thinly disguised characterizations of DeVoto's friends and enemies, none very compelling—perhaps the essential weakness in all of his novels. *We Accept with Pleasure* focuses on the impact of World War I on a closely knit group of Cambridge intellectuals and features a subplot involving a young married couple from the Midwest who attempt an uneasy truce with the members of this entrenched social circle. Sales of *Mountain Time* were better than those of his earlier titles, but reviewers generally assigned it a failing grade.

DeVoto left Northwestern in 1927 and settled in Cambridge, willing to teach any course offered him in the English department at Harvard, yet his youthful goal—to be part of the East Coast literary circle (preferably at Cambridge but perhaps in New York City)—continued to elude him. As it turned out, beginning in the early 1930s, other creative outlets opened up for him, and DeVoto began to play the multiple roles that sustained him intellectually and financially for the rest of his life. To augment his income as well as satisfy the academic in him, DeVoto became part of the regular fiction teaching staff at the Bread Loaf Writers' Conference in Middlebury, Vermont. This two-week summer program was an exhilarating literary workout for DeVoto, who by then, though not a successful novelist, was nonetheless a professional writer who could talk persuasively about his craft and be rejuvenated by contact with other equally energetic and talented writers. And from the beginning, the message was clear: good writing was hard work.

Bread Loaf was not a full-time job, however, so DeVoto continued to teach part time at Harvard. In 1932 he published *Mark Twain's America*, which, with its concentration on detail and "ascertainable facts," established the writing stance that characterized much of his later nonfiction work. *Mark Twain's America* was DeVoto's first extended foray into nineteenth-century frontier life and its impact on Twain. In his view, Twain had benefited from his early exposure to the frontier. The book was a direct challenge to Van Wyck Brooks's psychoanalytical study, *The Ordeal of Mark Twain*. In his renunciation of Brooks's primary thesis—that the frontier, his mother, and his wife had smothered the artist in Twain—DeVoto argued that critics such as Brooks ignored the facts, relying instead on mere theories of art. Calling his own book "an essay in the correction of ideas," DeVoto set about rebutting Brooks's theory and arguing, instead, for the formative and positive influence the frontier had had upon Twain's work. Critics split fairly evenly between those who sided with Brooks and those who cheered for DeVoto.

In the latter half of the 1930s, DeVoto accepted a full-time (but temporary) teaching position at Harvard. To make ends meet, he also assumed the editorship of a column, "The Easy Chair," for *Harper's* and, shortly thereafter, editorship of the *Saturday Review*. DeVoto's tenure at the *Saturday Review* lasted only sixteen months, through which he maintained the posture struck in his first essay for the magazine: defender of observation and fact and avowed opponent of those critics and authors who, in his judgment, were all too ready in their analyses of American experience to indulge literary pretensions and ignore the facts and who, he believed, leaned precariously to the Left in their appraisals of American life. Rather typically, DeVoto announced his arrival with a certain bluster calculated to ruffle a few feathers. If he veered toward overstatement, so be it. He had been hired to rescue the *Saturday Review* by improving circulation, increasing subscriptions, and stimulating discussion. His efforts, though somewhat successful, were not enough. By January 1938 he had enlivened the magazine with reviews by talented writers but had not salvaged it financially. Given three-months' notice, and the freedom to seek another job, DeVoto tried one last time to acquire a full-time, permanent teaching position at Harvard. When that failed, he turned his attention to a new project, editing the Mark Twain Papers, while also concentrating on his column.

Throughout his life DeVoto was a skeptic, an individualist, and a believer in freedom of conscience and expression, and in his essays for "The Easy Chair," he countered the opinions or assertions of those who he believed had sacrificed fact to imagination or pandered to the least common denominator or replaced freedom of expression with mere yea-saying. Ideally suited by temperament and talent to be what his biographer, Wallace Stegner, called a speaker for the public conscience, DeVoto poured his energies into provocative, timely, and thoughtful responses to major issues in American culture in his role as editor of "The Easy Chair." The range of topics he covered over the course of two decades suggests the myriad interests he indulged: the dangers of isolationism as World War II approached; the Civil War and revisionist theories about its causes; book censorship; communism, ex-Communists, and Senator Joseph McCarthy, to name only a few examples. If his faith in facts often led him to become indignant and to be combative, that same strength of conviction made him the ideal "gadfly of the public conscience." In November 1955, as the twentieth anniversary of his editorship approached, DeVoto surveyed his efforts:

I hope that what I have said has been said gracefully and that sometimes it has been amusing, or informative, or useful. . . . The Easy Chair has given me a place in the journalism of my time. No one knows better than a journalist that his work is ephemeral. . . . [i]t is not important, it is only indispensable. The life or the half life of an issue of "Harper's" has never been calculated; the magazine has durable covers but even the copies kept in doctors' waiting rooms wear out and are dumped in the bay or ground up for pulp. But a historian knows that a lot of writing which has no caste mark on its forehead gets dumped in the bay too, and that he can count on finding bound files of "Harper's" in library stacks. He has to use them; he cannot write history without them.

As feverishly as DeVoto worked on his serious fiction, his journalism, and even, in the early years, on his hack work, he received substantial critical acclaim only for the three volumes of American history he published between 1943 and 1952: *The Year of Decision: 1846* (1943), *Across the Wide Missouri* (1947), and *The Course of Empire* (1952); these remain, along with his interpretive edition of *The Journals of Lewis and Clark* (1953), his lasting contribution to American letters. They earned him recognition and awards and were acknowledged by traditional historians as genuine achievements in a field where DeVoto had been viewed by some as a maverick.

In *The Year of Decision: 1846* DeVoto re-created that fateful year when the Mormons, the Donner Party, and soldiers serving in the Mexican War converged as they moved westward. For DeVoto, these events both argued for the theory of Manifest Destiny and pointed to the inevitability of the Civil War. DeVoto followed this first volume with another vivid historical account, *Across the Wide Missouri*; like *The Year of Decision*, it is crammed with facts and depictions of congruent events and encounters. Delving deeply into the 1830s, he traced the fur trade and, more important, the lives of the mountain men themselves. Side by side with these trappers he placed the Indians—all viewed up close. It is notable that whereas DeVoto the erstwhile novelist was unable to create convincing fictional characters, DeVoto the historian had no trouble bringing past figures to life. *Across the Wide Missouri* received both the Bancroft Prize and the Pulitzer Prize.

The Course of Empire was the final volume in DeVoto's panoramic exploration of American history. In it, his narrative field comprised the entire North American continent; the cast of characters, the Spanish, French, and British; the emphasis, the noble and not-so-noble motives that drove men across uncharted land in search of the "Western Sea." *The Course of Empire* received the National Book Award for history in 1953. Unfortunately for DeVoto, he was able to enjoy a sense of satisfaction and achievement for only a relatively short time before his death from a heart attack in New York City. It was fitting that the major work of his last years were the histories, as these books finally accomplished what his fiction had not.

• The most extensive collection of DeVoto's papers is in the Stanford University Library. The bibliography prepared by Julius P. Barclay and included in *Four Portraits and One Subject: Bernard DeVoto* (1963) is the most useful guide to the range of his writings; each essay in the collection focuses on a different aspect of DeVoto's life: Catherine Drinker Bowen, historical biographer, speaks of him as historian; Edith Mirrielees, creative writing teacher, recalls his essays, novels, histories, and personal correspondence; Arthur M. Schlesinger, Jr., historian, describes him as public citizen; and Wallace Stegner, novelist, concludes with his portrait of DeVoto's personality. Stegner's *The Uneasy Chair: A Biography of Bernard DeVoto* (1974) is a balanced interpretation by a friend and fellow writer. Stegner also edited *The Letters of Bernard DeVoto* (1975). Obituaries are in the *New York Times*, 14 Nov. 1955, the *Saturday Review*, 26 Nov. 1955, and the *New Republic*, 28 Nov. 1955.

MARY ELLEN BOYLING

DE VRIES, David Pietersen (1593–1655?), merchant adventurer and colonizer, was born in La Rochelle, France, the son of Pieter Jakobszoon de Vries, a ship captain, and a Dutch mother (name unknown). His father was from Hoorn, a northern Dutch province, and his mother from Amsterdam. They moved to La Rochelle in 1584 and back to Hoorn when David was four. He attended Latin school, obtained a knowledge of geography and astronomy, and learned French, Dutch, and English as a result of his family's contact with the international Calvinist community.

In 1608 de Vries accompanied his father to rescue the English Separatists of Scrooby, who settled in Leiden. (Some were later part of the group that founded the Plymouth colony.) In Leiden he worked for a printer of English religious books. He served as first mate and supercargo on his father's Baltic voyages. In 1615 he married Seitgen Huygh of Hoorn. Shortly after the birth of their only child, a daughter, in 1616, de Vries sailed on an Arctic trading venture for the Noordsche Compagnie. On this trip he killed a polar bear, contracted scurvy, and traded with Dutch whalers and Russian fur trappers before returning with a valuable cargo in a badly damaged ship.

De Vries is principally known for six eventful voyages from 1618 to 1644 to the Mediterranean, Asia, and America. During the first, to Genoa in 1618, Turkish galleys attacked his ship but were successfully repulsed. In 1620 he sailed for Newfoundland. On his return he carried a cargo of fish to Spain, where eight Berber pirate ships attacked. De Vries won the battle and built his reputation as a brave fighter. When the Strait of Gibraltar closed to Dutch ships in 1621, de Vries offered to help the duc de Guise fight the pirates. When Guise planned an attack against La Rochelle, however, de Vries resigned, sold his ship, and returned home in 1623.

De Vries entered a partnership in 1624 to sail to Canada for furs, but the newly chartered Dutch West India Company stopped the venture. In 1625 the king of France seized his ship in La Rochelle for military use. His American voyage temporarily frustrated, he sailed in 1627 as fleet captain to the Dutch East Indies, where he was appointed chief merchant and a councillor. By 1628 he managed the posts along the Coromandel Coast and on Ceylon. He began his return voyage to Holland in December 1629, arriving six months later. In terms of official duties and power, his three years of service in the East Indies marked the high point of his career.

In 1630 de Vries and eight directors of the Dutch West India Company associated to plant a colony named Swanendael on the South (Delaware) River of New Netherland. These patroons sent thirty-two men in 1631 to the outpost near present-day Lewes, Delaware, to hunt and process whales. In May 1632 de Vries sailed for America, just after hearing of the Indians' destruction of Swanendael. He arrived at the ruins in December. Delaware Indians explained the events leading to the massacre, and de Vries exchanged presents and made peace with Indian leaders.

Nevertheless, he was deeply suspicious of the Delawares as he explored the area in early 1633. He sailed to Virginia for corn, returned to Swanendael for whale oil, and then stopped at New Amsterdam, where he quarreled with the director general, Wouter van Twiller, who tried to search his ship. By the time he returned home, he was keenly aware of English competition in North America and disgusted with the West India Company's leadership in New Netherland.

De Vries sailed in 1634 to establish a patroonship in Suriname, carrying colonists there and establishing a governmental structure for them. After satisfying himself that the colonists could carry on without him, he delivered English refugees from Tortuga to Virginia in May 1635 while on the way to New Amsterdam. In September he returned to Virginia, where he wintered. After learning of the Suriname colony's demise, he decided to give New Netherland another chance and sailed there from Virginia in 1636. He registered a claim to Staten Island before returning in August to Holland, where he sought unsuccessfully the directorship of New Netherland. He returned in 1638 and soon settled "his people" (the colonists under his authority) on a Staten Island patroonship in partnership with Frederick de Vries of Amsterdam. Meanwhile, Director General Willem Kieft sent him on a diplomatic mission to the English in the Connecticut River valley, territory claimed by both nations, to assess the situation. His partner failed to supply more people for Staten Island, so in 1640 de Vries founded a third patroonship, Vriessendael, near present-day Edgewater, New Jersey.

For the remainder of his years in New Netherland, de Vries lived at Vriessendael as a prominent citizen, consistent critic of the colony's leadership, and sympathetic observer of Delaware Indian culture. He claimed to know their language well, and he gained a reputation among them as a trustworthy "good chief." In 1643 de Vries mediated between the Dutch and natives fighting Kieft's War. His small patroonships on Staten Island and at Vriessendael were destroyed nonetheless. He left New Netherland for the last time in October 1643 on a Rotterdam ship. With de Vries assisting as pilot, it stopped at the New Sweden colony and continued to Virginia, where he remained through the winter, spending some of his time there as a guest of Governor William Berkeley. In 1644 he returned safely to Hoorn, an event he said later in concluding his memoir "for which our God must be eternally praised, that he should have brought me again to my Fatherland, after such long and tedious voyages, and through so many perils of savage heathens."

Little is known of de Vries after his return to Hoorn. A portrait dated 1653 identifies him as an artillery master. He published his memoirs in 1655 as *Short Historical and Journal Notes of Various Voyages Performed in the Four Quarters of the Globe*. The date and circumstances of his death are unknown. De Vries exemplifies the entrepreneurial spirit and Calvinist zeal of Holland's "golden age." His unusually wide-ranging experiences and his position among the merchant elite brought him into contact with people and events of great historical interest. He described his book as "not embellished with ornaments of words—as is not to be expected of a person who has passed the most of his life upon the wild ocean waste." Yet there is much of value in his writing, especially his ethnographic descriptions of Native Americans and his firsthand accounts of the Dutch, English, and Indian competition for America.

• The principal source of information about de Vries is his memoir, *Korte Historiael, ende Journaels aenteyckeninge Van verscheyden Voyagiens in de vier deelen des Wereldts-Ronde, als Europa, Africa, Asia, ende Amerika gedaen* (1655), published in Alckmaer. The only reprint in Dutch, edited by H. T. Colenbrander (1911), includes the portrait of de Vries, two maps, and eighteen plates from the original. An English translation of the sections dealing with America was published as Henry C. Murphy, trans., *Voyages from Holland to America, A.D. 1632 to 1644* (1853), and then under the same title in the New-York Historical Society, *Collections*, 2d ser., 3, pt. 1 (1857): 3–136. A. J. F. van Laer revised parts of Murphy's translation in *Narratives of New Netherland, 1609 1664*, ed. J. Franklin Jameson (1909), and in *Narratives of Early Pennsylvania, West New Jersey, and Delaware, 1630–1707*, ed. Albert Cook Myers (1912). Charles McKew Parr, *The Voyages of David de Vries, Navigator and Adventurer* (1969), puts his life in context but reveals little new information outside of de Vries's own account. The location of Vriessendael is placed at Edgewater, rather than Tappan, New Jersey, in Reginald McMahon, "Vriessendael: A Note," *New Jersey History* 87 (1969): 173–00.

JAMES HOMER WILLIAMS

DEW, Thomas Roderick (5 Dec. 1802–6 Aug. 1846), economist and educator, was born in King and Queen County, Virginia, the son of Thomas Dew, a plantation owner, and Lucy E. Gatewood. He matriculated at the College of William and Mary and received an A.B. in 1820. In October 1826 he was appointed professor of political law at William and Mary, which required him to deliver lectures on political economy, government, and history. A decade later he became president of the college. Dew was reputed to have been an inspiring teacher and an effective academic administrator. Enrollments at William and Mary were strengthened under his leadership.

In 1829 Dew came to public prominence with the appearance of *Lectures on the Restrictive System*, a by-product of his professorial duties, which drew heavily on the free-trade doctrines of classical economists. Having studied for two years in England, France, and Italy after graduation from college, he had acquired a learned command of this literature. But his denunciation of tariff protection in the United States was more than a replay of the theoretical arguments that supported commercial freedom. In America, he maintained, tariff protection meant in practice that the manufacturing North "oppressed" the South, whose crops were traded in international markets. This policy was thus doubly objectionable: not only did it compromise economic efficiency, it offended against the constitutional protections assigned to states' rights. In 1831 Dew set out this case in a memorial to Congress.

Dew gained still more notoriety in 1832 with the publication of his *Review of the Debate in the Virginia Legislature, 1831–1832* (which became even more widely circulated when it was reprinted in 1852 in a collection of essays by southern writers entitled *The Pro-Slavery Argument*). This work was prompted by the turmoil following the Nat Turner revolt, during which some members of the Virginia legislature championed state support for gradual emancipation and deportation of slaves. Dew was harsh in his criticisms of legislators who expressed such views and defended the "peculiar institution" vigorously. In his judgment, "slavery has been, perhaps, the principal means for impelling forward the civilization of mankind." Those who sought to eliminate it might be well intentioned, but they were naive. Proposals to remove the black population through colonization in Africa and elsewhere were too expensive to be contemplated, but neither was emancipation without deportation a feasible option. Dew insisted "*that the slaves, in both an economical and moral point of view, are entirely unfit for a state of freedom among whites.*" Not only would emancipation disrupt the social fabric, it would impose irreversible economic damage. Dew was convinced that labor productivity in the South would decline if slaves were freed. Given the region's climate, the discipline of the slave system was essential: in its absence, workers in the "very warm or tropical latitudes" would succumb to indolence.

Dew drew a sharp distinction, however, between the circumstances of his native state and those of the rest of the South. Virginia, in his view, was better suited to free labor than to slave labor. He urged an ambitious program of state-financed internal improvements that would integrate Virginia's more isolated districts into a widened network of markets. Grazing land could then be brought under tillage by freeholders, thus expanding production, swelling commercial activities, and spurring employment opportunities through the growth of urban areas. Ultimately, economic forces might expunge slavery from Virginia's soil altogether. But, if this vision were to become the reality, the institution of slavery would have to continue to flourish elsewhere. Virginia's black population, Dew felt, should be shrunk by the sale of slaves to the parts of the South where their labor was required.

Dew approached the issue of slavery from a sweeping historical perspective. In his analysis, the emergence of the institution in the ancient world marked a crucial step in human progress. After all, it was far more humane when prisoners of war were no longer slaughtered, but treated as productive assets. In this manner, the conception of private property—a precondition for significant economic advance—also was solidified. This style of argument was further in evidence in his *Digest of the Laws, Customs, Manners, and Institutions of the Ancient and Modern Nations* (1853), a posthumous publication of lectures that he had delivered to history students. This work focused on the evolution of legal, social, and religious institutions—rather than on chronology, which was then common in the teaching of history—and was repeatedly republished for the rest of the century.

For Dew, the study of history—particularly as it informed an understanding of slavery—was more than an intellectual inquiry worth pursuing for its own sake. It also had lessons to teach about the rightness of southern institutions, and, as an educator, he felt obligated to convey them. He charged his students at William and Mary to "rally under our principles undivided and undismayed . . . and such a spirit, guided by that intelligence which should be possessed by slaveholders, will ever insure the triumph of our cause" (*An Address, Delivered before the Students of William and Mary, at the Opening of the College, on Monday, October 19, 1836*).

A pioneer among economists in the antebellum South, Dew argued that slavery was a "positive good" rather than a "necessary evil." His attempts to provide the proslavery position with intellectual underpinnings were received appreciatively in his native region. Ironically, his efforts may have heightened militancy among abolitionists. His message, as interpreted by some of his northern readers, suggested that there was no prospect that the South could reform itself from within and that peaceful resolution of the vexed question of slavery was increasingly unlikely.

Dew's writings on controversial issues of his day—particularly on the protective tariff and on slavery—brought him to the attention of a national audience. Although supporters urged him to run for a seat in Congress, he chose not to enter elective politics. He was nevertheless politically active as an informal adviser to state and federal officials. In the early days of the administration of his friend John Tyler (1790–1862), he was a member of the president's "kitchen cabinet."

Dew married Natilia Hay in 1845. He died unexpectedly—presumably from pleurisy or pneumonia—while on his wedding trip in Paris, France.

• Primary material on Dew's writings and activities at William and Mary is housed in the college's archives at Williamsburg, Va. For background on his career and his economic thinking, see Joseph Dorfman, *The Economic Mind in American Civilization*, vol. 2 (1946), and John K. Whitaker, "Early Flowering in the Old Dominion: Political Economy at the College of William and Mary and the University of Virginia" in *Breaking the Academic Mould: Economists and American Higher Learning in the Nineteenth Century*, ed. William J. Barber (1988), pp. 15–41. For additional details, see Stephen Mansfield, "Thomas Roderick Dew at William and Mary: 'A Main Prop of That Venerable Institution,'" *Virginia Magazine of History and Biography* 75 (Oct. 1967): 429–42, and Lowell Harrison, "Thomas Roderick Dew: Philosopher of the Old South," *Virginia Magazine of History and Biography* 57 (Oct. 1949): 390–404. Eugene D. Genovese's *Western Civilization through Slaveholding Eyes: The Social and Historical Thought of Thomas Roderick Dew* (1986) is also useful. Dew's membership in Tyler's "kitchen cabinet" is treated briefly in Norma Lois Peterson, *The Presidencies of William Henry Harrison and John Tyler* (1989).

WILLIAM J. BARBER

DEWEES, William Potts (5 May 1768–20 May 1841), obstetrician, was born in Pottsgrove (now Pottstown), Pennsylvania; his parents' names and occupations are unknown. After working for several years as an apothecary's apprentice, in 1787 he began studying medicine with William Smith, a Philadelphia physician, while attending the University of Pennsylvania. Upon receiving his M.B. in 1789, he opened a general medical practice in Abington, Pennsylvania. In 1791 he married Martha Rogers, who died shortly thereafter. He relocated his practice to Philadelphia in 1793, mostly because the epidemics of yellow fever that had swept that city for a number of years had greatly increased the demand for physicians. The next year he was one of only three medical practitioners to realize that yet another epidemic had broken out, and for the remainder of the decade he frequently attended victims of yellow fever at no charge.

Although he began as a general practitioner, Dewees evolved into a specialist in the treatment of women and children. At the time most women in labor were attended by midwives, primarily because the social conventions of the day prohibited a man from viewing, much less touching, the private parts of any woman other than his own wife. At the close of the eighteenth century most American medical schools taught their students very little about "midwifery," as obstetrics was then called, and most physicians had no idea how to assist during difficult deliveries. Dewees believed, however, that a woman's need for expert medical care overrode the need to avoid social impropriety, and this led him to become the first physician in Philadelphia to deliver babies routinely. By 1797 his obstetrical skill and experience were so great that he offered a full lecture course on obstetrics in his office. The course was canceled, however, because of low attendance.

In 1802 Dewees married Mary Lorrain, with whom he had eight children. He returned to the University of Pennsylvania in 1805 and received his M.D. the next year. His thesis, which identified ways to ease pain during labor and to facilitate difficult deliveries, was favorably received by the medical community.

In 1812 Dewees contracted a tubercular infection and was forced to give up his practice. He moved to Phillipsburgh, Pennsylvania, where over the next five years he lost money as a farmer but regained his health. In 1817 he returned to Philadelphia and the practice of medicine.

Dewees's major contribution to the development of obstetrics was *A Compendious Study of Midwifery* (1824), which went through twelve editions and was the first systematic textbook on obstetrics written by an American. This work popularized in the United States the classification and nomenclature of fetal presentations and positions developed by the French obstetrician Jean Louis Baudelocque. It also provided the reader with the full benefit of the author's practical experience as a deliverer of thousands of babies. Dewees insisted that physicians attending women in labor be well versed in the anatomy of the female pelvis, recommended prenatal examinations, and presented a convincing argument that delivery is most easily performed while the patient lies on her back instead of on her side, the preferred position of the day.

Dewees also authored a number of important medical works pertaining to fields other than obstetrics, two of which went through ten editions. *A Treatise on the Physical and Medical Treatment of Children* (1825) was the first work by an American to discuss pediatrics on a scientific basis. *A Treatise on the Diseases of Females* (1826) offered a complete discussion of the medical conditions peculiar to women that are not related to pregnancy.

In 1825 Dewees was appointed adjunct professor of midwifery at the University of Pennsylvania. Because of the extended illness of his superior, Thomas C. James, he provided most of the instruction in obstetrics until 1834, when James retired and Dewees was appointed to replace him. In 1835 his health deteriorated again, either as a result of a cerebral hemorrhage or a recurrence of tuberculosis, and he was forced to retire. After trying unsuccessfully to regain his health in the West Indies and Mobile, Alabama, he returned to his home in Philadelphia, where he died.

Dewees helped to develop obstetrics as a separate field of medicine in the United States. He played an instrumental role in breaking down the social and educational barriers that prevented physicians from delivering babies, thus greatly enhancing the probability that both mother and infant would survive childbirth.

• Dewees's papers are in the University of Pennsylvania's Van Pelt Library. A biography is Herbert Thoms, "William Potts Dewees and the First System of Obstetrics," in his *Chapters in American Obstetrics*, 2d ed. (1961), pp. 53–58. Dewees's contributions are discussed in Francis R. Packard, *History of Medicine in the United States* (repr. 1963).

CHARLES W. CAREY, JR.

DEWEY, Alice Chipman (7 Sept. 1858–14 July 1927), educator and feminist, was born in Fenton, Michigan, the daughter of Gordon Orlen Chipman, a cabinetmaker, and Lucy Riggs. Orphaned at an early age, Alice and her younger sister were raised by their maternal grandparents Fred and Evalina Riggs. The Riggses were freethinkers who raised the sisters to be socially responsible and self-reliant. After finishing high school in Fenton, Alice attended for a year the Fenton Baptist Seminary, where she studied music. She taught school for several years in Flushing, Michigan, before a desire for further education and a growing interest in women's rights spurred her to leave Fenton and enroll at the University of Michigan in 1882.

Alice Chipman was a junior at the University of Michigan when she met a young philosophy instructor named John Dewey, who had moved into the same boardinghouse on his arrival in 1884. Alice, who had a deep interest in philosophy coupled with a keen intellect, had taken a number of courses in the department before Dewey arrived. She completed most of the courses offered by the department, including three advanced courses taught by Dewey. By 1885 their friendship had deepened, and in the summer of 1886, after Alice's graduation and John's promotion to assistant professor, they were married. They made their home in Ann Arbor for the next eight years, with one year at the University of Minnesota. While John advanced to professor and head of the philosophy department, Alice managed the household, had three children, and actively encouraged her husband's growing interest in education. Often both Deweys practiced their theories of child development and education on their own children.

In 1894 John Dewey was invited to head a department combining philosophy, psychology, and education at the University of Chicago. The prospect of such a position, along with a sizable increase in salary, proved an irresistible lure. While Alice took the children to Europe for the summer, John taught summer school in Chicago. During this trip, two-year-old Morris died of diphtheria. The Deweys never fully recovered from this loss.

The Chicago years, from 1894 to 1904, were years of remarkable growth for both Deweys. They were socially and intellectually stimulated by the academic community as well as their association with Ella Flagg Young, then a district superintendent of Chicago schools, and Jane Addams, of Hull House. But it was the Deweys' involvement in educational experimentation through the establishment of the University of Chicago Laboratory School that offered the opportunity for Alice's direct influence on her husband's work. By all accounts, Alice was the primary impetus behind her husband's attempts to establish his educational ideas on a practical basis, and she was informally involved with every aspect of the school's operation. Both wanted to test their theories of how children learned and wanted their own children, including the three born in Chicago, to learn in a progressive, educationally innovative environment.

In 1901, due largely to her husband's efforts, Alice Dewey was appointed principal of the laboratory school in addition to directing its Department of English and Literature. She developed curriculum, taught classes, and solved problems involved in the daily operations of the school. Her decisiveness and down-to-earth realism, along with her intelligence and zeal in enacting Dewey's ideas, were important forces behind her husband's work and her own achievements at the laboratory school. However, her personality did not endear her to her colleagues. There was friction over her quick dismissal of allegedly incompetent teachers and fear that the school had become too much a Dewey family affair. When arrangements were made to merge the Parker Chicago Institute with the laboratory school, the opportunity arose to remove Alice Dewey as principal. In March 1904 President William Rainey Harper of the University of Chicago informed her that she was expected to resign. Ten days later both John and Alice Dewey submitted their resignations, and John went on to resign all of his positions at Chicago.

Columbia University was quick to offer John Dewey a position as a professor of philosophy, a post he held until his retirement in 1930. Before moving to New York, the Deweys, with all five children, sailed for a summer in Europe, after which Alice planned to remain with the children for a year of language study. Tragically, their son Gordon died of typhoid early in the trip, a death that their daughter Jane felt brought a lasting diminishment of her mother's energy and enthusiasm. When John Dewey rejoined the family in Italy after his first year of teaching at Columbia, they adopted an Italian boy about the same age as their dead son.

In New York both Deweys were involved in numerous political and social causes. Alice devoted her efforts most often to the woman suffrage movement. She supported her husband in his defense of the Russian writer Maxim Gorky, joining John in offering their home and the Deweys' prestige during Gorky's visit. Despite the negative media coverage—Gorky was controversial not only because of his support for the Russian revolution but also because he was accompanied by his common-law wife—Alice vowed that she and her children would starve before they would see John compromise his principles. She also continued her work on education, giving talks to teachers and teaching a course in elementary education at the New York School of Liberal Arts and Sciences.

Alice Dewey's health steadily declined after her move to New York. Max Eastman, a family friend, attributed her ill health primarily to the death of Gordon and the loss of her pivotal position with the laboratory school. He described her as increasingly querulous, resentful, and bitter, a depiction verified by other accounts. Although the Dewey children disputed Eastman's unflattering portrayal of their mother, John Dewey himself seems to have found his marriage more difficult during this period.

Between 1919 and 1921 the Deweys took an extended trip to Japan and China, where Alice spoke on behalf of women's rights. She lectured at Nanking University and was made an honorary dean of women, encouraging the feminist movement and women's education. In the summer of 1926 she traveled with her husband to Mexico but developed a heart ailment that forced her return home. Her condition deteriorated throughout 1926, and in the spring semester of 1927 John Dewey took a leave from teaching to tend to his sick wife. She died at their home in New York City.

Alice Dewey's commitment to her roles as an educator and as an outspoken advocate of women's rights matched her commitment to her roles as a mother and as the wife of an eminent public figure.

• A few of Alice Dewey's letters are in the Special Dewey Collection, Southern Illinois University, Carbondale. A full treatment of her life is Rose Spicola, "Alice Chipman Dewey" (1982), in the library of the Texas Woman's University, Denton. Other information on her life is in Jane M. Dewey's biography of her father, *The Philosophy of John Dewey*, ed. Paul Arthur Schilpp and Lewis Edwin Hahn (1951), and in Max Eastman's description of both John and Alice Dewey in *Great*

Companions (1959). An extensive account of the University of Chicago Laboratory School is by Katherine Camp Mayhew and Anna Camp Edwards in *The Dewey School* (1936). An obituary is in the *New York Times*, 15 July 1927.

JOANN WOOD

DEWEY, Chester (25 Oct. 1784–15 Dec. 1867), clergyman, educator, and scientist, was born in Sheffield, Massachusetts, the son of Stephen Dewey and Elizabeth Owen, farmers. After receiving a common-school education, he entered Williams College in 1802. While at Williams, Dewey excelled in mathematics and classical studies. Although he maintained the interest in the natural sciences he had developed in childhood, he felt compelled to enter the ministry after becoming a Christian in his senior year. Following his graduation in 1806, he studied theology in Stockbridge, Massachusetts, with Stephen West, D.D., and was licensed to preach by the Berkshire Congregational Association in 1807. He then briefly held a pastorate at Tyringham, Massachusetts, from July until November 1808, after which he returned to the Williams College campus as a tutor.

Dewey was appointed professor of mathematics and natural philosophy at Williams in 1810. In the same year he married Sarah Dewey, with whom he had five children; she died in 1823. Along with Amos Eaton, Dewey largely created the course of instruction in the natural sciences at Williams. Primarily responsible for providing instruction in botany and chemistry, in which he benefited from a brief period of study with Benjamin Silliman at Yale in 1812, he also taught mathematics, geology, astronomy, and mineralogy. Not content with classroom instruction alone, Dewey worked tirelessly to build up a museum of natural history at the college. He personally obtained numerous geological and botanical specimens, corresponding and exchanging materials with numerous professional colleagues across the United States and Europe.

Only recently founded, Williams College struggled for both students and funds and for a time seriously considered relocation from its relatively isolated situation to a more accessible site. Despite the demands of upgrading scientific instruction at the fledgling school, Dewey found time to conduct outside lectures on chemistry and botany, first at the Berkshire Medical Institution in Pittsfield, Massachusetts (beginning in 1822), and at the Woodstock, Vermont, Medical School (beginning in 1842). A popular teacher, Dewey provided inspiration to his students that did not end in the classroom. He also founded the first antislavery society in Massachusetts with members of the student body in 1823.

Pittsfield assumed an increasingly important role in Dewey's life when he met his second wife, Olivia Hart Pomeroy, there. They married in 1825 and had ten children. Relocating to Pittsfield in 1827, Dewey served as principal of the Berkshire Gymnasium, a secondary school for boys, for the next nine years.

In 1836 Dewey relocated to Rochester, New York, where he became principal at the high school (later the collegiate institute) of that city. When the University of Rochester was founded in 1850, he was appointed professor of chemistry and natural science. In addition to his efforts on behalf of the new university, Dewey expanded his own scientific research. Beginning in 1837 and continuing almost up to his death, Dewey recorded daily weather observations in Rochester. He conducted botanical research in his specialty, a class of the grass family (or Sedges) known as Carices. After publishing the first of a series of monographs ("Caricography") on the subject in 1824, he continued to work in the area throughout his long career, with the last of the monographs appearing in 1866.

A prolific writer, Dewey contributed "Sketch of the Mineralogy and Geology of the Vicinity of Williams College" to the first volume of the *American Journal of Science* in 1819; fifty-three subsequent volumes also contained articles under his authorship. He wrote *Report on the Herbaceous Plants and on the Quadrupeds of Massachusetts* (1840) and contributed the section on Carices to Alphonso Wood's *Class-Book of Botany* (1845).

Following his retirement from the university in 1861, Dewey, as professor emeritus, lived quietly and continued to write, publishing two reviews of Louis Agassiz's *Essay on Classification* (1859) in the *Princeton Review* (1863) as well as the essay "Examination of Some Reasonings against the Unity of Mankind" (also in the *Princeton Review*, 1862). He died in Rochester.

One of the first American naturalists, Dewey expanded the scope and content of instruction in the natural sciences at two major institutions of higher learning. He is best remembered today for this work as well as for his pioneering work in botany. The genus *Deweya* (umbelliferous plants in Calif.) bears his name in tribute to his efforts.

• The papers of Dewey are divided between the archives of Williams College, Williamstown, Mass., and the University of Rochester, Rochester, N.Y. His career receives attention in Frederick Rudolph, *Mark Hopkins and the Log: Williams College, 1836–1872* (1956). Older sources include L. W. Spring, *History of Williams College* (1917), and W. F. Peck, *History of Rochester, Monroe County, N.Y.* (1908). Obituaries are in the *Rochester Express* and the *Rochester Daily Democrat*, 16 Dec. 1867.

EDWARD L. LACH, JR.

DEWEY, George (26 Dec. 1837–16 Jan. 1917), naval officer, was born in Montpelier, Vermont, the son of Julius Yemans Dewey, a prominent physician and insurance company president, and Mary Perrin. His mother died when Dewey was just five years old. After study at Norwich University, Dewey entered the U.S. Naval Academy in 1854. The rambunctious plebe accumulated 113 demerits during his first year at the academy, but he graduated in 1858, fifth in his class of fifteen. After a cruise in the Mediterranean on the new frigate *Wabash*, he was commissioned a lieutenant and third in his class in April 1861.

Through the Civil War, Dewey served as executive officer on six major ships in eight campaigns as well as on patrol and blockade duty. While Dewey was executive officer on the old side-wheeler *Mississippi* during David G. Farragut's assault on New Orleans, his skipper entrusted him with navigating the ship on its dangerous movement through the barrier between Forts Jackson and St. Philip below the city. A year later, when the *Mississippi*'s pilot ran it at full speed on a mud bank before Confederate batteries at Port Hudson, Dewey supervised evacuation of the crew under heavy enemy fire. After a stint on Farragut's flagship, the screw sloop *Monongahela*, on the lower Mississippi, Dewey served in 1864 on the third-rate, double-ended gunboat *Agawan* on the James River. He finished the war as executive officer on the regunned frigate *Colorado* during the attacks on Fort Fisher in December 1864 and January 1865. He then held the rank of lieutenant commander.

The twenty-five years following the Civil War were for Dewey years of honorable service, slow promotions, and little opportunity to demonstrate distinction. In 1866 he sailed for Europe on the screw sloop *Kearsarge*, famed victor over the Confederate raider *Alabama*. This was followed by brief spells as executive officer on the sloop *Canandaigua*, as flag lieutenant for the commander of the European Squadron, and as executive officer of the *Colorado*. In 1867 he joined the faculty at the Naval Academy, and that year he married Susan Boardman Goodwin, the daughter of a former governor of New Hampshire. She died in 1872, five days after giving birth to their only child, George Goodwin Dewey. Dewey's first command (1870–1871), the third-class sloop *Narragansett*, was cut short when he was ordered in January 1871 to the *Supply*, one of three vessels designated to carry relief to French victims of the siege of Paris during the Franco-Prussian War. After an assignment at the Torpedo Station in Newport, Rhode Island, Dewey immediately secured command once more of the *Narragansett* in 1873 and spent two years surveying the Gulf of California and the west coast of Mexico. For the next six years he was ashore with the Lighthouse Service at Boston (1875–1878) and as secretary of the Lighthouse Board in Washington (1878–1882).

By 1882 Dewey was bound for the Asiatic Station in command of the old sloop *Juniata*. At Malta, however, he was stricken with typhoid and an abscess on the liver and was put ashore in a British hospital. After an extended sick leave and promotion to captain, in 1884 he briefly commanded the cruiser *Dolphin*, the smallest of the first four ships of the steam and steel navy. When the *Dolphin* failed its initial trials, Dewey was given command of the steam sloop *Pensacola*, flagship of the European Station, from 1885 to 1888.

Dewey in 1889 began a four-year term as chief of the Bureau of Equipment at the Navy Department. He continued his comfortable Washington career with appointments on the Lighthouse Board, eventually holding the presidency (1893–1895). In October 1895 he was named president of the Board of Inspection and Survey. While with the latter board, he presided over inspections of five of the navy's first six battleships and

in the spring of 1896 received his commission as a one-star commodore. Thanks in part to backing from the young assistant secretary of the navy, Theodore Roosevelt, Dewey commanded the Asiatic Squadron and broke his commodore's penant on his flagship, the *Olympia*, in Nagasaki Harbor on 3 January 1898.

Naval plans were already prepared for an attack on Manila should war break out between the United States and Spain. On 5 February 1898, just ten days after the sinking of the battleship *Maine* at Havana, Roosevelt alerted Dewey by a telegram marked "secret and confidential" that he should concentrate six ships of his command, all except the antiquated gunboat *Monocacy*, at Hong Kong and keep them coaled. Roosevelt further directed that, should war break out, Dewey was to prevent the Spanish squadron from leaving the Asiatic coast to attack the Philippines. At Hong Kong Dewey prepared his ships for action, impressed the new revenue cutter *McCulloch* into his service, and purchased the collier *Nanshan* and the British steamer *Zafiro* to transport supplies. Upon arrival of the cruiser *Baltimore* with much needed ammunition on 22 April, Dewey's squadron clearly outclassed the ships of the opposing Spanish in tonnage, speed, and gun power. He had assembled his ships at Mirs Bay, thirty miles up the China coast from neutral British Hong Kong, when on 24 April the Navy Department directed him to push ahead with "utmost endeavors" against the Spanish fleet and the Philippines.

After determining that the Spanish admiral, Patricio Montojo, was not waiting for him at Subic Bay, thirty miles to the north of Manila Bay, Dewey at midnight on 30 April led his five cruisers and single gunboat with attending train through Boca Grande into Manila Bay, without heed to possible mines or enemy shore batteries. At 5:00 A.M. the commodore sighted Montojo's ships drawn up before the naval station at Cavite to the southwest of Manila, and at 5:35 A.M., on the bridge of the *Olympia*, he calmly advised the flagship's skipper, Captain Charles V. Gridley, "You may fire when you are ready Gridley." The Americans passed three times to the west and twice to the east, firing into the Spanish ships. When at about 7:35 A.M. the Americans withdrew into the bay to count their ammunition, the Spanish ships were in flames and sinking. Dewey returned to battle at 10:50 A.M. Within two hours every Spanish ship was out of action, and the guns ashore at neighboring Sangley Point were silenced. After Dewey threatened to bombard the city, the Spanish halted their futile fire from Manila and surrendered the guns and magazines at the entrances to the bay on 2–3 May. Dewey cut Manila's cable link with the outside world when the Spanish governor general refused to extend its use to the Americans. In due course, the commodore dispatched the *McCulloch* to Hong Kong with a message for transmission to Washington announcing his destruction of the Spanish squadron. He also reported that, while he could take Manila at will, he could not hold the city.

Even before receiving Dewey's victory messages, President William McKinley had decided to dispatch an army expeditionary force to Manila along with the cruiser *Charleston* and the monitors *Monadnock* and *Monterey*. Spain, however, also responded by ordering east an outwardly impressive force under Admiral Manuel de la Camara. Madrid recalled the Camara expedition after the American victory at Santiago de Cuba released powerful American ships for possible operations against Spain. Britain, Japan, France, and Germany all sent ships to observe developments at Manila. Especially disturbing to Dewey were the Germans, who by late June had assembled a force under Vice Admiral Otto von Diederichs that surpassed Dewey's squadron in gun power and tonnage and engaged in various mysterious activities.

Ultimately of more serious consequence to Dewey than either the Spanish or the Germans were the Philippine insurgents, who like the Cubans wanted to break away from Spain. Initially, he found it convenient to encourage insurgent operations against the Spanish without, it seems, seriously considering Filipino moves to form a government or their declaration of independence. As American forces increased in Manila Bay, relations between Americans and Filipinos became difficult. The Filipinos had laid siege to Manila, but with the arrival of Major General Wesley Merritt and the Third Army contingent, the American army force of 10,000 men was quite sufficient to occupy and hold Manila without any assistance from the insurgents.

The Spanish proved willing to surrender the city to the Americans if the insurgents were kept out. Through the mediation of the Belgian consul, a charade was worked out whereby on 13 August, after some token firing by the Americans on Fort San Antonio to the south of the city, the Spanish surrendered, and the Americans occupied the city without a fight. Unknown to Dewey, the Spanish government had already accepted an armistice providing that the United States would "occupy and hold the city, bay, and harbor of Manila."

Dewey avoided taking a clear position on the future of the islands. He did advise the president that Luzon was the most important island in the group since, in addition to Manila, it embraced Subic Bay, which he judged the finest location for a naval base. Aware of the disintegration of relations between Americans and Filipinos, especially after Spain ceded the Philippines to the United States by the Treaty of Paris in December 1898, Dewey recommended that a civilian commission be sent to the Philippines on a mission of conciliation. Unfortunately, the first Philippine Commission only began its work in the islands months after the outbreak of hostilities that committed the United States to a long war of conquest. Dewey escaped from this unpleasant small war by securing orders to return to the United States on grounds of ill health.

Dewey's victory of 1 May had projected him to a position of immense public adulation. Two weeks after the battle Congress increased the number of rear admirals so Dewey could be given two-star rank. In March 1899 Congress created for him the rank of admiral of the navy with provision that he might remain on active service for life. His triumphal return to the United States was climaxed by a parade down Fifth Avenue in New York, President McKinley's presentation on the steps of the Capitol of a jeweled sword, and the gift from the nation of a mansion in Washington, D.C. In 1899 he married a prominent Washington matron, Mildred McLean Hazen; they had no children. His marriage was not popular, and the public was outraged when Dewey gave his mansion to his new wife. His announcement in March 1900 of his willingness to run for president failed to generate any significant support. A prestigious position was found for the distinguished officer in 1900 when Secretary of the Navy John D. Long appointed him president of the General Board of the Navy, which Long created to serve as the secretary's highest advisory body on naval policy. Dewey's rank as senior officer in either army or navy also brought him the position of senior and presiding officer of the Joint Army and Navy Board, established in 1903, which was in some respects the predecessor of the Joint Chiefs of Staff.

During his years as president of the General Board, Dewey and other American naval men were ever alert to the supposed menace of Germany in the Atlantic. In a naval spectacle during the winter of 1902–1903, Dewey assumed command of forces drawn from the North Atlantic, Europe, and South Atlantic to participate in combined maneuvers to test the navy's capacity to meet foreign (German) naval aggression in the Western Hemisphere. With Dewey presiding and Germany in mind, the General Board in 1903 recommended a building program designed to provide the United States by 1920 with forty-eight battleships and an appropriate number of armored cruisers, cruisers, and destroyers. Dewey also strongly supported, over vigorous opposition from conservatives within the service, the shift to construction of the all big gun dreadnought type of battleship.

The advent of Japan as a possible antagonist after 1906 was attended by the most serious challenge to Dewey's views during his seventeen years with the General Board. Since 1898 Dewey had championed Subic Bay as the finest site for an American naval base in the Philippines. In 1906, however, the navy's battleships were concentrated in the Atlantic Fleet, ready to meet an assault from Germany. At the height of the immigration crisis with Japan in June 1907, the Joint Board, with Dewey as senior officer present, resolved that, should war with Japan become imminent, the larger American ships in Asia should withdraw to the eastern Pacific, where they would join the battleships moving from the Atlantic and then proceed to the Philippines. The light naval forces remaining in Asia together with available army forces would join in defense of the still undeveloped base at Subic Bay. The following month President Theodore Roosevelt ordered the Atlantic Fleet to move from the Atlantic to the Pacific in a test of the strategy for war against Japan. The strategy, however, was immediately challenged by Major General Leonard Wood, commanding general in the Philippines, who insisted that Subic Bay could not possibly be held against Japanese attack until the arrival of the fleet from the Atlantic. The Joint Board proposed that the navy continue to use Subic Bay until a base could be constructed on Manila Bay. Dewey and the navy, however, never accepted Manila Bay as the site for the main naval base in the western Pacific. Given the impasse between the army and the navy, the United States built no naval base west of Pearl Harbor before Japan struck on 7 December 1941, perhaps as significant a legacy from Dewey as his victory at Manila Bay.

Except for Subic Bay, Dewey as General Board president avoided identification with rival groups and controversial positions during the Roosevelt and William Howard Taft administrations. A true test of his tact came with the arrival of Woodrow Wilson in the White House and the populist secretary Josephus Daniels in the Navy Department. Somehow Dewey commanded the devotion of both Daniels and Daniels's vigorous critic, Rear Admiral Bradley Fiske, the aide for operations. Dewey apparently escaped unscathed when, at the outset of the new administration, Wilson threatened to abolish both the General Board and the Joint Board if they persisted with recommendations that, he feared, might disrupt his efforts to conciliate Japan. Dewey's skills were again tested after the outbreak of World War I, when Fiske and the advocates of preparedness agitated for measures that seemed to contradict Wilson's determination to avoid any action likely to disturb public opinion. Dewey managed to prevent open collision when he advised that the General Board's recommendations for the fiscal year 1915 be submitted in two letters, an open letter proposing to continue the program of the previous year and an unpublished letter calling for increased personnel. Perhaps because he suspected the new office might render superfluous the General Board and his leadership in the navy, Dewey accepted with some reluctance the new position of chief of naval operations created in 1915.

Infirmities of age notwithstanding, Dewey in October 1915 signed the General Board's recommendation that became the basis for the 1916 program to build a navy second to none. Only days before the passage of this 1916 bill, Dewey gave a final, much-headlined interview to the distinguished newsman George Creel, in which he vigorously defended both the navy and Secretary Daniels. Dewey died in Washington, D.C.

• Collections containing Dewey's papers include the George Dewey Papers in the Manuscripts Division of the Library of Congress; the Records of the Office of Naval Records and Library, RG 45, National Archives; and the General Board Records, National Archives. Dewey wrote *The Autobiography of George Dewey* (1916). See also Ronald Spector, *Admiral of the New Navy, the Life and Career of George Dewey* (1974); William R. Braisted, *The United States Navy in the Pacific, 1897–1909* (1958); and Braisted, *The United States Navy in the Pacific, 1909–1922* (1972).

WILLIAM R. BRAISTED

DEWEY, John (20 Oct. 1859–1 June 1952), philosopher and educator, was born in Burlington, Vermont, the son of Archibald Sprague Dewey, a shopkeeper, and Lucina Artemisia Rich. Dewey's childhood and adolescence were influenced by his mother's strict Calvinism, his father's taste for British literature, and his contact with family friends on the faculty at the University of Vermont. His enrollment at the university in 1875 exposed him to Darwinian evolutionary theory and the speculative and social philosophy taught by Henry A. P. Torrey. Outside the classroom Dewey became an avid reader of progressive periodicals whose contributors espoused versions of evolution, positivism, and agnosticism. Undecided about a profession after his graduation in 1879, he taught high school on an interim basis and with the help of a relative secured a position in Oil City, Pennsylvania. In 1881 he left Oil City to teach in a small school near Burlington so that he could continue to study philosophy with Torrey.

Encouraged by the publication of his essay in the *Journal of Speculative Philosophy* in April 1882 and by support from Torrey, Dewey enrolled in his graduate school at the Johns Hopkins University in 1882. He studied logic with Charles S. Peirce and experimental psychology with G. Stanley Hall, but it was George Sylvester Morris who had the most immediate influence upon his development. Dewey later claimed that Morris's neo-Hegelian idealism helped him to resolve the "dualisms" of New England culture. Dewey was awarded his doctorate in 1884 and was soon hired as an instructor at the University of Michigan by Morris, who had become a full-time member of the Michigan faculty the previous year.

While at the University of Michigan Dewey published two essays in the British journal *Mind* in 1886 and his first major book, *Psychology* (1887), establishing his international reputation. These works attempt to unite into a single system the neo-Hegelianism of Morris and the experimental psychology of Hall, or, as Dewey put it, to identify psychology with "philosophic method." During these years he moved toward a more liberal religious stance as well as toward what he would later term "instrumentalism," the view that ideas are tools for resolving and reconstructing problematic situations. Dewey's second major book, a critique of Leibniz's *New Essays Concerning the Human Understanding*, followed in 1888.

Among Dewey's students during his first years at Michigan was Harriet Alice Chipman, a sensitive and energetic young woman whose interest in public affairs greatly influenced his own. Married on 28 July 1886, they had seven children.

In 1888 Dewey left Michigan to accept the chair of philosophy at the University of Minnesota. After just a few months, however, Morris died suddenly, and Dewey was recalled to Michigan as department head. There he wrote *Outlines of a Critical Theory of Ethics* (1891) and *The Study of Ethics: A Syllabus* (1894), works that reveal several important transformations in Dewey's thought. He abandoned the Hegelian notion of a super-conscious absolute spirit and accepted William James's characterization of the human being as a biological organism in a concrete environment, a responsible self that observes, judges, and makes. Consequently, he became convinced that the split in ethical theory posited by David Hume and others between the "is" and the "ought" was unwarranted and that ethics could be based on the scientific method. The "ought," he wrote in his essay "Moral Theory and Practice" (1891), is itself an "is"—the "is" of action. He also began to argue that metaphysics had "had its day"; that is, that a science of "direct, practical truths" was possible without metaphysics.

In 1894 Dewey accepted a position at the University of Chicago as head of the department of philosophy, which included psychology and pedagogy. At his urging, pedagogy was incorporated as a separate department of education, and he was appointed its head as well. One of Dewey's most important publications during his decade at Chicago was "The Reflex Arc Concept in Psychology" (1896), in which he attacked the basis of stimulus-response psychology and offered a more complex model of an organism interacting with its environment by means of selecting and conditioning its own stimuli. In 1942 this essay was voted the most important contribution to *Psychological Review* during the journal's first fifty years of publication. Dewey served as president of the American Psychological Association in 1899–1900.

The social ferment in Chicago during Dewey's years there profoundly altered his political views. Even though he thought the university's atmosphere unduly repressive, he avoided confrontation with the administration and urged his colleagues to do likewise. Nevertheless, Dewey's private correspondence during this period reveals a growing social progressivism, and he participated in the activities of Jane Addams's Hull House.

Dewey's social concern was also expressed in his growing commitment to pedagogical reform. His *School and Society* (1899) and the University Elementary School (also called the Dewey School and the Laboratory School), which he founded in 1896, sought a middle ground between two conflicting schools of pedagogy. At one extreme, the "curriculum-centered" view advanced by U.S. Commissioner of Education William Torrey Harris held that children should be drilled on the accumulated wisdom of civilization. At the other extreme, the "child-centered" view advanced by G. Stanley Hall argued that subject matter was secondary to the natural expression of the child's impulses. Dewey maintained that these conflicting views presented an artificial and unnecessary dichotomy: the aim of pedagogy should be to correlate impulse and subject matter and to find ways of subjecting ideas to the test of concrete experience. Dewey sought to develop a pedagogy that would take into account America's growing industrialization and urbanization and that would place educational practice in the context of a wider understanding of democracy. His *Experience and Education* (1938), for example, argued that education should conform both to the child's developmental stages and to the child's environment outside the classroom. His method of abstracting the best elements of opposing viewpoints and reconstructing them into novel alternatives became a hallmark of his life's work.

Dewey's Chicago years are also notable for his work in logic, which culminated in the publication with several colleagues of *Studies in Logical Theory* (1903). In this work Dewey articulated for logic a functional instrumentalism similar to the one William James had developed for psychology.

Growing differences between Dewey and University of Chicago president William Rainey Harper culminated in 1904 in the termination of Alice Dewey's appointment as principal of the Laboratory School. Both Deweys resigned, and John Dewey's friend James M. Cattell of Columbia University moved quickly to secure his services. In February 1905 Dewey assumed his duties as professor of philosophy with a joint appointment at Teachers College, Columbia's college of education. Dewey held these positions until 1930 when he was appointed Professor Emeritus of Philosophy in Residence at full salary.

Professional philosophy during Dewey's first decade at Columbia was embroiled in debates between realists, who generally held that things are as they are apart from knowing minds, and idealists, who believed that mind constitutes reality. Characteristically, Dewey's instrumentalism found a middle way. He argued that human organisms interact with the real facilities and constraints of lived environments and that they construct tools and artifacts of many types, including conceptual ones, in a continual modification and reconstitution of "reality." "Facts," Dewey argued, are neither the unconditioned entities of the realists nor the totally constituted ones of the idealists. They are instead always "the facts of a case"—the facts of and for an organism situated within an environment and continually adjusting to it by means of the production of new results. In these matters Dewey anticipated by some forty years the work of Ludwig Wittgenstein. Dewey's instrumentalism was further developed in *Ethics* (1908), written with James H. Tufts, the first text on the subject to include discussions of current social problems, and *How We Think* (1910), an instant classic in educational literature. Dewey's concern for the transaction of an organism with its environment figured prominently throughout his life's work, forming a central theme even in his last major work, *Knowing and the Known* (1949), a collaboration with Arthur F. Bentley.

Dewey's ground breaking work and increasing influence resulted in his election to the presidency of the American Philosophical Association for 1905–1906 and the vice presidency of the American Association for the Advancement of Science in 1909. His political activities during this period included participation in the formation of teachers unions, in the Henry Street Settlement on the Lower East Side of Manhattan, and in the woman suffrage movement.

Dewey reacted to the professional, national, and international stresses of the World War I years by intensifying his political activities. His support for U.S. intervention in the war as a means to the construction of a lasting peace precipitated a break with some of his most devoted disciples, including Randolph S. Bourne. But his support for the war was coupled with a staunch defense of peaceful dissent and academic freedom. He was among the founders of the Teachers League of New York (1913), the American Association of University Professors (1915), and the American Civil Liberties Union (1920) and was a regular contributor to the *New Republic*.

During the war years Dewey developed his instrumentalism still further. In his *Essays in Experimental Logic* (1916), he characterized the acquisition of knowledge as a kind of technological activity analogous to production in more patently industrial spheres. In *Democracy and Education* (1916), he identified education with growth and the development of habits that allow the control of the environment for human purposes. As such, he argued, education has "no end beyond itself." While on leave from Columbia from 1918 to 1921, Dewey lectured first at the University of California and Stanford University, and then at the Imperial University in Tokyo and the national universities of Peking and Nanking. Back at Columbia he published *Human Nature and Conduct* (1922), in which he rejected the view of human nature as the expression of instinct and offered instead an analysis of human impulse, habit, and intelligence with a view to establishing the empirical and naturalistic basis for moral behavior. This work was well received, and in 1944 was reprinted in a paperback edition for use by military personnel.

Dewey delivered the first series of the Paul Carus Lectures in 1922. These became the basis for *Experience and Nature* (1925), widely regarded as his most important work. Although it extended and refined his instrumentalism, it revealed that Dewey's emphasis had shifted from the biological and psychological factors of human life to the anthropological and historical. He also entered for the first time into a detailed treatment of aesthetic theory. Finally, in a move that puzzled many critics, he sought a reconstruction of metaphysics, which he treated as "a statement of the generic traits manifested by existences of all kinds, without regard to their differentiation into physical and mental," and as a "ground-map of the province of criticism."

Dewey's attention again turned to social and political matters during the next decade. He published essays in support of the socialist reforms he had witnessed in Mexico during the summer of 1926 when he had lectured at its national university. In *The Public and Its Problems* (1927), he deplored the disappearance of the "public" as a locus of discourse and the testing of ideas and argued that social inquiry must be reestablished on a scientific basis. His tireless professional activities continued despite Alice Dewey's death in 1927. In the summer of 1928 he visited schools in the Soviet Union as a part of an unofficial delegation of American educators. His generally favorable reports, published in the *New Republic*, included a call for his government's recognition of the Soviet Union; conservative factions responded by branding him a "communist."

In 1929 Dewey published *The Quest for Certainty*, in which he recast his instrumentalism in terms developed by physicist Percy W. Bridgman and others and known as "operationalism." Dewey argued that, whereas philosophy had traditionally aimed at attaining certainty, the real value of ideas is determined by their outcome, which is in turn based on continuing experimental tests. Some of the critics of this book accused Dewey of "scientism" or the view that science is the test of all experience. Despite such criticism, Dewey maintained a faith in the possibility that science and technology could ameliorate society. In *Individualism, Old and New* (1930), he argued that while rapid industrialization had alienated many men and women, technology properly embodied in social institutions could liberate personal energies and inspire jointly beneficial activities.

His attacks on dualistic thinking also continued, though in a different vein. During 1930 Dewey wrote that he was anxious to "get into a field I haven't treated systematically, and art & aesthetics has come to me." In *Art as Experience* (1934), an outgrowth of the William James Lectures he had given at Harvard University, he argued that in experience that is truly aesthetic means and ends cooperate. Where inquiry in the arts is successful, distinctions between "fine" arts and "useful" arts are obviated. The "work" of art involves not only the art object, but also its production and appreciation. Likewise, he maintained, the development of aesthetic appreciation is a kind of productive skill. Neo-Hegelian idealists applauded *Art as Experience*, and pragmatists professed shock at what both regarded as Dewey's return to idealism. Dewey, however, saw his work as a further development of his instrumentalism.

Dewey returned to his familiar theme in *A Common Faith* (1934), this time addressing the philosophy of religion. He argued that although the term "religion" refers at best to mutually contradictory cultural practices, the "religious" qualities of experience can nevertheless serve as a basis for a "common" faith that is able to cut across divisions of class, race, and sect and to take into account the demands of life in scientific-technological societies.

Liberalism and Social Action (1935) was in part a reply to Reinhold Niebuhr, whose *Moral Man and Immoral Society* (1932) had attacked Dewey for placing too much faith in scientific technology to reform society. Niebuhr had argued that reform would take place only through social conflict based on the "absolutizing moral principle" he termed Christian love, whose primary tools would be potent dogmas and popular oversimplifications. In his response, Dewey traced the history of liberalism from the seventeenth century and issued a call for its radical reform. The requisite liberalism, he argued, would overhaul outmoded institutions, reorganize common action, and apply the methods of science within the political sphere.

Although he demonstrated his deep concern for the plight of scholars who were fleeing fascism by participating in the formation of a "University-in-Exile" under the sponsorship of the New School for Social Research, Dewey nevertheless opposed U.S. intervention in the worsening problems in Europe and Asia. In 1937 Dewey served as chair of a commission to examine the charges brought against Leon Trotsky during the "Moscow Trials" of 1936–1937. Despite his advanced age he traveled to Mexico City, where Trotsky was living in exile, to chair a series of hearings. After numerous interviews with Trotsky and a lengthy examination of the evidence, the commission declared Trotsky not guilty of the charges brought against him in Moscow. Dewey's role in the work of the commission led U.S. communists to denounce him as a "fascist." Despite his opposition to U.S. intervention in Europe in the 1930s, on the home front Dewey actively opposed attempts by conservative organizations to limit academic freedom and to require teachers to take loyalty oaths. He also disapproved of religious instruction in the public schools.

Dewey continued to refine his version of the pragmatic theory of truth and the logical basis of his instrumentalism. In 1938 he published one of his least understood works, *Logic: The Theory of Inquiry*. Despite the increasing popularity of a formal approach to the subject, with its reliance on atomistic propositions with definable truth values, Dewey argued that such an approach to inquiry fails to reflect the richness of experience. Truth, he argued, is much more complex than a matter of the correspondence between statement and fact; it is "warranted assertibility."

Among Dewey's publications during 1939, *Theory of Valuation* and *Freedom and Culture* reflect his continuing interest in social criticism. The events following Hitler's invasion of Poland in 1939 caused Dewey to abandon his earlier advocacy of neutrality, in which he had warned of the growing influence of a "semi-military, semi-financial autocracy." He supported the Lend-Lease Bill in 1940 and America's entry into the war in December 1941. With Sidney Hook and others, Dewey formed in 1939 the Committee for Cultural Freedom, whose purpose was to "expose the repression of intellectual freedom." Because the committee condemned practices in the Soviet Union, as well as in Germany, Italy, Japan and Spain, Dewey once again became the target of communists. As the chair of the committee, Dewey supported Bertrand Russell when his appointment at the College of the City of New York was rescinded in 1940 on the grounds that Russell was an atheist and immoral.

In 1939 Dewey retired from Columbia, but his social activism did not diminish. He responded with vigor to the attacks on his educational theory advanced by advocates of a traditionalist "great books" approach led by Robert M. Hutchins and Mortimer Adler. He also opposed what he regarded as attempts by President Nicholas Murray Butler of Columbia to curb academic freedom during the war. Concerned about America's official praise of the Soviet Union, Dewey warned against the dangers of an uncritical acceptance of Joseph Stalin's repression. After the war, however, he opposed barring members of the Communist party from teaching in universities, and he deplored the "hysterical" activities of the House Committee on Un-American Activities.

In 1946 Dewey married Roberta Lowitz Grant, forty-two, the widow of Robert Grant, an engineer. Dewey had known her parents since the early years of the century when her father was a teacher. The couple adopted two young children. The occasion of Dewey's ninetieth birthday in 1949 was widely celebrated in the press, by numerous academic conferences that took his work as their theme, and by formal celebrations in New York City and Burlington, Vermont. During the last years of his life Dewey continued his long practice of regular correspondence, especially with his collaborator, Arthur Bentley. He also began work on a new edition of *Experience and Nature*.

Dewey died at his home in New York City. An urn containing his ashes was interred in a memorial monument at the University of Vermont. The event was commemorated on 26 October 1972. In 1968 the U.S. Post Office issued a thirty-cent stamp bearing Dewey's likeness, and in 1971 Grenada honored him with a five-cent stamp. In November 1991 astronaut Story Musgrave honored Dewey by taking a copy of *Experience and Education* with him into space.

Dewey's influence on American life can scarcely be underestimated. During his lifetime he was America's leading educational theorist, and his work continues to be a source of insight for reformers in that field. His social and political ideas, especially his radical conception of democracy, continue to be assaulted from both the right and the left. Together with Ludwig Wittgenstein and Martin Heidegger, Dewey is widely regarded as one of the three most innovative philosophers of the twentieth century. He was loved, honored, vilified, and attacked as perhaps no other major philosopher in American history. Although he was the recipient of scores of honors and awards, perhaps the most appropriate one was bestowed on him during the 1930s, when he became widely known as "America's Philosopher."

• Dewey's letters, papers, and memorabilia are at the Center for Dewey Studies and the Morris Library at Southern Illinois University at Carbondale. The critical edition of his works has been published by Southern Illinois University Press in three parts: *The Early Works: 1882–1898* (5 vols., 1969–1972); *The Middle Works: 1899–1924* (15 vols., 1976–1983); and *The Later Works: 1925–1953* (17 vols., 1981–1991). Dewey's correspondence with Arthur F. Bentley has been published by Sidney Ratner and Jules Altman with James E. Wheeler as *John Dewey and Arthur F. Bentley: A Philosophical Correspondence 1932–1951* (1964). Guides to Dewey's work include Jo Ann Boydston, ed., *Guide to the Works of John Dewey* (1970); Boydston and Kathleen Poulos, *Checklist of Writings about John Dewey 1887–1977* (2d ed., 1978); and Boydston with Robert L. Andresen, *John Dewey: A Checklist of Translations 1900–1967* (1969). The standard biography of Dewey is George Dykhuizen, *The Life and Mind of John Dewey* (1973).

Anthologies of Dewey's works include Richard J. Bernstein, ed., *On Experience, Nature, and Freedom* (1960); John J. McDermott, ed., *The Philosophy of John Dewey* (1973); and James Gouinlock, ed., *The Moral Writings of John Dewey* (1976).

Collections of essays evaluating Dewey's work include Paul Arthur Schilpp and Lewis Edwin Hahn, eds., *The Philosophy of John Dewey* (2d ed., 1989); Steven M. Cahn, ed., *New Studies in the Philosophy of John Dewey* (1977); and Sidney Morgenbesser, ed., *Dewey and His Critics: Selections from the Journal of Philosophy* (1977).

Modern interpretive works include Thomas M. Alexander, *John Dewey's Theory of Art, Experience, and Nature: The Horizons of Feeling* (1987); Richard J. Bernstein, *John Dewey* (1966); Raymond D. Boisvert, *Dewey's Metaphysics* (1988); Neil Coughlan, *Young John Dewey: An Essay in American Intellectual History* (1975); James Gouinlock *John Dewey's Philosophy of Value* (1972); Larry Hickman, *John Dewey's Pragmatic Technology* (1900); Steven C. Rockefeller, *John Dewey: Religious Faith and Democratic Humanism* (1991); Ralph Sleeper, *The Necessity of Pragmatism: John Dewey's Conception of Philosophy* (1986); J. E. Tiles, *Dewey* (1988); Robert B. Westbrook, *John Dewey and American Democracy* (1991); and Tom Burke, *Dewey's New Logic: A Reply to Russell* (1994).

LARRY A. HICKMAN

DEWEY, Melvil (10 Dec. 1851–26 Dec. 1931), educational reformer and librarian, was born in Adams Center, New York, the son of Joel Dewey, a general store owner, and Eliza Greene. As a child, Dewey adopted his parents' strict Republican and Baptist values and by the age of fifteen had defined his larger "destiny" as a "reformer" for the masses. In 1869 his family moved to Oneida, New York, where Dewey attended a local Baptist seminary. The following year he enrolled at Amherst College, where he began working in the college library in 1872. Perceiving a potential for libraries to educate the masses, he thereafter committed his life to improving librarianship. To that interest he added others like spelling and metric reform, all of which were aimed at saving time and eliminating waste. He once calculated that if children learned a simplified phonetic form of spelling and the metric system of weights and measures used by most of the rest of the world, educators could save students at least two years' time that could be better spent reading good books.

After Dewey graduated in 1874, Amherst hired him to manage its library and reclassify its collections. He worked there for two years, and in 1876 he published *A Classification and Subject Index for Cataloging and Arranging Books and Pamphlets in a Library*, better known as the "Dewey Decimal Classification," an innovative scheme that superimposed a system of decimals on a structure of knowledge first outlined by English philosopher Francis Bacon and later modified by American educator William Torrey Harris.

In the summer of 1876 Dewey moved to Boston, where he helped found the Spelling Reform Association, the Metric Bureau, and the American Library Association and served each as secretary and author of its constitution; he also served as editor of ALA's new *Library Journal* for four years. Lacking the capital to accelerate the reforms that he hoped these organizations would bring about, Dewey decided to merge treasuries into a single account to increase the collateral against which he could borrow. He failed, however, to inform the organizations of these unorthodox business practices. When several investors in the private Readers and Writers Economy Company, which Dewey had started in 1879, discovered that he had rolled these funds into company accounts, they obtained a court injunction in 1880 that denied him access to the RWEC treasury until the accounting mess he had created could be cleared up. Forced by the injunction to admit to the organizations what he had done, Dewey lost his credibility with them but not his office as secretary. In 1881 Dewey reached a settlement with RWEC in which he split company assets with investors, and two months later he established the Library Bureau, a library and office supplies company. As the bureau's president he resumed efforts to increase efficiency in library services and to advance spelling and metric reform, and slowly he reworked his way into the good graces of the organizations that he had helped start.

In the meantime (in 1878), Dewey had married Annie Godfrey. They were to have one child.

In May 1883 Dewey became librarian in chief at Columbia College, where he implemented many of the ideas he had been marketing through the Library Bureau. In five years he turned a collection of 50,000 poorly cataloged, indifferently classified, and infrequently used volumes scattered over nine departments into 100,000 uniformly cataloged and classified volumes located in a central library; at the same time he increased circulation 500 percent. Much of this was accomplished in the face of opposition from faculty and trustees who were angered when, without full authorization, Dewey opened the world's first library school in 1887 and admitted seventeen women to its first, twenty-member class. The consternation that his changes caused at Columbia led him to accept an offer by the regents of the University of the State of New York (USNY) in 1888 to become their secretary and the state librarian. The regents also agreed to let him move his library school to Albany.

As secretary, Dewey became instrumental in augmenting the power of the USNY regents in the period between 1889 and 1899, when New York's high school enrollment increased by 250 percent, higher education student enrollment by 182 percent, and higher education faculty by 223 percent. By carefully, often quietly, guiding bills favorable to the regents through the legislature, by using his office to create a statewide lobby for higher education, and by harnessing regent powers to examine and license professionals, Dewey established minimum standards for high school and college curricula, teachers, and libraries, and eliminated scores of bogus diploma mills. In the process, however, he made many enemies. By the time a movement toward the unification of New York's separately run common school and higher education systems gathered momentum in late 1899, Dewey was accurately perceived as an obstacle and was encouraged to resign as the regents' secretary. His situation was not helped that December, when he was caught using his office to protect the interests of a nephew who ran a New York City proprietary school in violation of its own university charter.

While the regents' secretary, Dewey pushed USNY into supporting an education extension system that he would be able to control through New York's public libraries. He hoped to make coursework prepared by USNY instructors available at public libraries so that the state's citizens could accumulate enough credits to qualify for a USNY degree. As state librarian, Dewey attempted to create an environment favorable to this system by organizing the New York Library Association; setting up extension sites in public libraries around the state; creating departments within the state library for facilitating interlibrary loans; publishing bibliographies of "best" books; and establishing a traveling library system that became a model for the rest of the country. In addition, he convinced the legislature in 1892 to create a book fund to which public libraries could apply for matching grants if their collections passed inspection by a state library employee.

During Dewey's tenure in Albany, the state library's collections had grown by 1905 to 500,000 volumes, making it the fifth largest library in the country. In addition, his library school had become a model for others opening across the country. Although his metric and spelling reform efforts languished in the 1890s, he did become ALA president in 1892–1893, during which time he organized a highly successful conference for the Chicago World's Fair at which ALA exhibited a "model library" whose contents were later published as a bibliographic guide for all American small public libraries. Dewey's Library Bureau weathered financial difficulties in the 1880s but by 1900 had tapped into lucrative markets with a card-index system that greatly reduced record-keeping costs, especially for banks and insurance companies. While Dewey wanted to subordinate the activities of the bureau to his own less profitable reform interests, his business partners were ultimately able to wrest control from him in 1901 when he sought capital for a new venture, the Lake Placid Club in upstate New York.

In 1894 Dewey and his wife had established the Lake Placid Club, an exclusive rest and recreation facility in the Adirondacks. Its clientele typically included social workers, librarians, and teachers at all levels of education. In 1896 the Deweys formed a company that owned and improved the land; members of the club were permitted to use its facilities for a fee. From the beginning, however, the club admitted no one against whom any member objected, and, as a result, all Jews, ethnic minorities, and consumptives were barred. In January 1905 several prominent New York Jews publicly called for Dewey's dismissal as state librarian because of the club's exclusionary practices. Under pressure, Dewey resigned later that year. The incident also served as a catalyst for several library school alumnae who were angered by Dewey's earlier unsuccessful efforts to move the library school from Albany and by reports that Dewey had sexually harassed several ALA women in public over the years. In 1906 they forced him out of active participation in ALA.

After Dewey moved permanently to Lake Placid, he continued the club's restrictive membership practices and worked hard to improve the club's resources and its parent company. What started as a five-acre endeavor with a few out-buildings surrounding a central clubhouse in 1894 had grown by 1925 into a 10,000-acre complex with scores of buildings, several large clubhouses, a concert hall, five golf courses, and twenty-one tennis courts. Over the years Dewey also cultivated winter sports at the club; by 1930 they had become so popular that the village of Lake Placid was chosen to host the 1932 Winter Olympics.

In 1922 Dewey turned over all his assets to a Lake Placid Club Education Foundation he had set up to carry on such reform causes as metric conversion and simplified spelling after his death. That same year his wife died, and in 1924 he married Emily Beal; they had no children. In 1926 he began to spend winters in Florida, and by the summer of 1927 opened a second club there that was characterized by the same exclusionary rules as its northern sister. His efforts to make the Florida Club a success were ultimately defeated by the onset of the Great Depression.

Dewey left a substantial legacy, for good and for ill. His decimal system evolved into a familiar organizing system for controlling library collections across the world, and his efforts to identify the best books evolved into a system of published bibliographic guides, like *Booklist*, *Public Library Catalog*, and *Fiction Catalog*, all serials that grew out of Dewey's 1893 ALA "model library." At the same time, however, his system imposed his perspective of the structure of knowledge on these collections, the arrangement of which mirrored the narrow priorities of the communities from which he and other librarians came. While his efforts as regents' secretary transformed USNY into a powerful organization that substantially improved the quality of New York's educational system, his successes in centralizing and standardizing controls had a homogenizing influence on curricula that undervalued and often ignored the needs of diverse cultures. Finally, his efforts at Lake Placid accelerated the development of the Adirondack resort and tourist industry, but his exclusionary practices perpetuated and amplified the region's reputation for racism. Dewey died at his Florida Club in Lake Placid, Florida.

• Dewey's diaries and papers are in the Rare Books and Manuscripts Reading Room at Columbia University's Butler Library. See also George Grosvenor Dawe, *Melvil Dewey: Seer, Inspirer, Doer, 1851–1931* (1932), Fremont Rider, *Melvil Dewey* (1944), and Sarah Vann, ed., *Melvil Dewey: His Enduring Presence in Librarianship* (1978).

WAYNE A. WIEGAND

DEWEY, Orville (28 Mar. 1794–21 Mar. 1882), Unitarian minister, was born in Sheffield, Massachusetts, the son of Silas Dewey and Polly Root, farmers. Dewey graduated from Williams College in 1814 as the class valedictorian, despite having contracted a case of measles that severely injured his vision during college. For some five years he was able to read only for limited periods, although he eventually regained full use of his vision. Dewey had a religious awakening in college that eventuated in his desire to enter the ministry, but he did not begin divinity studies immediately after his graduation, spending a year in Sheffield as a teacher and another year working in New York. He entered Andover Theological Seminary in 1817, hoping, as he explained, "to pursue my studies as well as I could without my eyes, expecting afterwards to preach without notes" (*Autobiography*, p. 40).

Dewey had been raised as a Calvinist, although many in Sheffield, including his father, had openly expressed dissent from the orthodox Calvinist position. He entered his studies at Andover "desirous of finding the Orthodox system true. But the more I studied it," he recalled, "the more I doubted" (*Autobiography*, p. 44). His doubts centered on the doctrine of the Trinity and were increased, ironically, by the teaching of Moses Stuart, Andover's leading biblical scholar and a defender of the orthodox position. Stuart, influenced by the German Higher Criticism, approached biblical interpretation from a modern and critical perspective, and as the young Dewey experienced Stuart's teaching, "many a solid text evaporated, and left no residuum of truth." Dewey also began to question what he termed "the living sense" of Calvinism, perceiving a troubling gap between its abstract logic and the consequences of those doctrines in life. The doctrine of eternal punishment, for example, "pressed more and more upon my mind, [until] it became too awful to be endured" (*Autobiography*, pp. 44–45).

Dewey graduated from Andover in 1819 feeling too insecure in his theological opinions to be a candidate for permanent settlement in a church, but he accepted an appointment to preach at various churches for the American Education Society. In the spring of 1820 he accepted an invitation to preach at the Congregational church in Gloucester, Massachusetts, after securing an agreement with the church that he would not discuss the question of his permanent position as minister there for a year because of his unsettled theological position. In 1820, during his year of preaching in Gloucester, he married Louisa Farnham; they had three children.

Dewey's continuing studies during his year at Gloucester confirmed his doubts about the doctrine of the Trinity, and he became a Unitarian, heavily influenced in his decision by the preaching of William Ellery Channing. Dewey entered the Unitarian ministry as Channing's assistant at the Federal Street Church in Boston from 1821 to 1823, and in 1823 he became minister of the First Church, Unitarian, of New Bedford, Massachusetts, remaining there until 1833. Dewey was successful as a preacher, but the stress of his pastoral work and the lack of pulpit exchanges because of New Bedford's geographical isolation left him exhausted. He suffered what he called "a certain nervous disorder of the brain" that incapacitated him for intellectual work completely for extended periods. He

achieved only temporary recovery through a European trip of 1833, and after another relapse, he resigned his New Bedford pastorate and moved in 1834 to his family home in Sheffield.

Dewey's move was a temporary retreat rather than a permanent retirement, for in the same year he received an invitation to preach from the Second Congregational (Unitarian) Church in New York. "I could preach, though I could not write," he explained. "My sermons . . . [delivered] in New Bedford, would be new in another pulpit, and I consented" (*Autobiography*, p. 75). Dewey was soon preaching to full congregations in New York, and in an era of great preachers, he was among the best. Although his church burned down in November 1837, many new people were attracted to his preaching in the temporary quarters of the Stuyvesant Institute. In 1839 his congregation built a new church on Broadway, naming it the Church of the Messiah.

Dewey's popular preaching was one of the most important reasons for the strengthening of the Unitarian presence in New York in the 1830s and 1840s, a period in which the Unitarian movement was establishing its identity as a denomination and moving outside Boston and eastern Massachusetts. When Henry Whitney Bellows became minister of New York's First Unitarian Church (later All Souls Church) in 1838, Dewey developed a close and mutually sustaining friendship with him, one of the most important friendships and professional relationships in the lives of both men.

From the 1830s on, Dewey published numerous articles, theological works, volumes of sermons, and travel writings. His extensive publications, combined with the popularity of his preaching, increased his influence during his New York pastorate, and he was given the important recognition of serving as president of the American Unitarian Association from 1845 to 1847. Despite his success in New York, Dewey continued to find his ministerial duties stressful and, after another crisis of health, went for an extended trip to Europe from 1841 to 1843. When he returned he remained minister of the Church of the Messiah until he moved back to Sheffield in the spring of 1848. After more occasional preaching at the church he resigned permanently in 1849. Retiring to Sheffield, he devoted more of his energies to lecturing and also served as minister of the New South Church in Boston from 1857 to 1861.

Influenced in his theology by Channing, Dewey rejected the Calvinist doctrine of depravity and stressed the potential, though not the assured fact, of human achievement. "There is a treasure in human nature of which most men are not conscious, and with which none are yet fully acquainted," he argued in 1835, taking a position that was central to the Unitarian attack on the Calvinist doctrine of innate depravity. Dewey remained theologically moderate within the Unitarian movement. While firmly opposed to slavery, he was also more cautious than many others in his support of the antislavery movement, remaining fervently committed to the preservation of the Union. His support of Daniel Webster's position in the Compromise of 1850 and in particular his view that the Fugitive Slave Law of 1851 was a disagreeable but necessary step to preserve the Union "laid him open to scornful and indeed vituperative attack" from more radical Unitarian abolitionists, as Conrad Wright has observed. When the war broke out, Dewey defended the Union cause as a "holy war" to preserve the Union. He spent his last years in retirement in Sheffield, where he died.

Dewey's most important work was his extension of the Unitarian presence in New York through his forceful pulpit oratory and his articulation of a liberal theological position in a time of religious change in the United States. Dewey "had every qualification for a great preacher," Bellows wrote, "in a time when the old foundations were broken up and men's minds were demanding guidance and support in the critical transition from the days of pure authority to the days of personal conviction by rational evidence" His great innovation, Bellows felt, was his capacity to bring his religious message to bear on "the whole sphere of human life," a dedication to a "practical preaching" that would "animate and elevate our daily life" (*Autobiography*, pp. 358–61).

• Among Dewey's many publications are *Discourses on Various Subjects* (1835); *The Old World and the New* (1836); *Moral Views of Commerce, Society, and Politics* (1838); *Discourses and Discussions in Explanation and Defence of Unitarianism* (1840); *Discourses on Human Life* (1841); *Discourses and Reviews upon Questions in Controversial Theology and Practical Religion* (1846); and *The Problem of Human Destiny* (1864). The best biographical source is *Autobiography and Letters of Orville Dewey, D.D.*, edited by his daughter Mary E. Dewey (1883), which contains Dewey's account of his life, a selection from his letters, and an 1879 tribute by Henry Whitney Bellows that assesses his accomplishments as a preacher. A sketch of Dewey that also concentrates on his preaching is contained in Henry Fowler, *The American Pulpit* (1856), pp. 267–88. On Dewey's important relationship with Bellows, see Walter Donald Kring, *Henry Whitney Bellows* (1979). Conrad Wright offers an important assessment in *The Liberal Christians: Essays on American Unitarian History* (1970), pp. 62–80. Further information on Dewey and the antislavery question is in Douglas C. Stange, *Patterns of Antislavery among American Unitarians, 1831–1860* (1977); and Donald Yacovone, *Samuel Joseph May and the Dilemmas of the Liberal Persuasion, 1797–1871* (1991).

DAVID M. ROBINSON

DEWEY, Thomas Edmund (24 Mar. 1902–16 Mar. 1971), prosecutor, governor of New York, and presidential candidate, was born in Owosso, Michigan, the son of George Martin Dewey, Jr., a newspaper editor, and Annie Louise Thomas. The Deweys were a Republican family of newspaper editors and publishers. During his youth in Owosso, Thomas showed promise as a baritone, and he studied both music and law at the University of Michigan from 1919 to 1923, graduating with an A.B. In 1923 Dewey moved to New York after winning a summer scholarship for further vocal training, but he also enrolled at Columbia Law School and ultimately decided to abandon music for the law. After graduating with an LL.B. in 1925, he worked at two Wall Street law firms and became active in Republican party politics in Manhattan in the late 1920s. During

this time he first encountered Herbert Brownell, a fellow New York lawyer and future U.S. attorney general under President Dwight D. Eisenhower, who would later become Dewey's campaign manager and closest political confidant. In 1928 Dewey married Frances Eileen Hutt, an Oklahoman he had first met at a singing competition in Chicago in 1923 who had also moved to New York City to pursue a singing career. The couple had two sons.

Dewey identified with the progressive, or "reform," element in the New York Republican party that battled the Tammany Hall Democratic machine for political control of New York City and New York State in the interwar years. In 1931 he abandoned Wall Street to take the position of chief assistant U.S. attorney for the Southern District of New York under U.S. attorney George Z. Medalie. When Medalie resigned in November 1933, Dewey succeeded him as interim U.S. attorney, a position he held for a few weeks until Democratic president Franklin Roosevelt appointed a replacement in December.

During his period at the U.S. attorney's office, Dewey played a major role in prosecuting organized crime figures and corrupt members of the Tammany machine. When the power of criminal rackets in the city appeared to be getting out of hand in 1935, Governor Herbert Lehman appointed Dewey (who had returned to private practice) as a special prosecutor to investigate and prosecute the racketeers. Dewey achieved the most spectacular success of his prosecutorial career when he obtained a conviction of New York's most notorious Mafia boss, Charles "Lucky" Luciano, on charges of running a prostitution racket in 1936.

Dewey's "racket-busting" activities made him a national hero and launched his career in city, state, and national politics. In 1937 he ran for district attorney in Manhattan on Fiorello La Guardia's Fusion ticket and overcame a 5 to 1 Democratic advantage in voter registration to become the first Republican to win that office in a quarter-century. Almost immediately Dewey came to the attention of national Republican leaders desperate for an attractive presidential candidate after the Republican electoral debacle in 1936. In 1938 he ran for New York governor against the popular Democratic incumbent Lehman and lost by just 1 percent of the vote. Despite this defeat, Dewey arrived at the June 1940 Republican convention in Philadelphia as one of the leading contenders for the presidential nomination. However, the international crisis created by the fall of France to Nazi Germany led the Republicans to choose the more interventionist contender, Wendell Willkie, over Dewey, who had little experience in foreign affairs, and the isolationist Ohio senator Robert Taft.

Dewey consolidated his position at the forefront of the GOP, however, by finally winning the New York governorship in 1942. Resoundingly reelected in 1946 and 1950, he served three terms as governor, creating a formidable record of accomplishments. While he was not a New Deal liberal, he did adhere to the tradition of Theodore Roosevelt and the turn-of-the-century Republican progressives. This was most evident in Dewey's strong conviction that government did occasionally have a legitimate role to play in promoting the public interest. In fact, as governor he often found that the strongest opposition to his new government programs came from conservative upstate Republicans, who dominated the malapportioned New York State legislature during his governorship. Overcoming this opposition, Dewey established New York's state university system in 1947, built the New York State Thruway, and introduced public health programs to deal with tuberculosis and other deadly diseases. A strong fiscal conservative who believed that new government programs had to be financed on a pay-as-you-go basis, he accomplished all of this while keeping the state budget in balance. When he left Albany in 1955, state taxes were also significantly lower than on his arrival twelve years earlier. Finally, Dewey, a strong proponent of civil rights for blacks, was the major proponent of New York's landmark civil rights law of 1945, which was the strongest antidiscrimination measure in the nation since the post–Civil War amendments to the Constitution and a model for the federal legislation that would later follow.

Outside New York, Dewey was the leading national figure in his party during the 1940s. With the help of Brownell and others, he constructed a formidable national organization that secured him the Republican presidential nominations in 1944 and 1948 and delivered the nomination to Eisenhower in 1952. Dewey's nominating coalition had as its geographic basis the internationally oriented states of the Northeast and the progressive states of the Pacific Coast. Together this alliance of the "two coasts" was able to outvote the conservative Republican heartland of the Midwest at Republican National Conventions between 1940 and 1952. Dewey's New York base and internationalist views on foreign policy also earned him strong support from Wall Street and the party's eastern establishment, still the major financial power centers within the national Republican party at that time. The New York governor's belief that the United States had to play an active role in world affairs, particularly participating in European collective security programs, was the main point of difference between Dewey and his midwestern, conservative archrival, Senator Taft. Dewey also claimed that his pragmatic, fiscally conservative but progressive approach to government provided a more electorally viable alternative to the New Deal Democrats than the harsh, antigovernment rhetoric of Senator Taft and Taft's allies in the congressional GOP.

In 1944 Dewey defeated Willkie in the Wisconsin primary, and at the Republican convention he easily won the presidential nomination over Taft's ally, Ohio senator John Bricker, who agreed to join the Republican ticket as the vice presidential candidate. Very much the underdog running against President Roosevelt while World War II was still raging, Dewey nevertheless fought a spirited campaign. While Dewey was easily defeated in the electoral college, his 46 per-

cent of the popular vote was the best Republican presidential performance since the 1920s.

Dewey's reputation was enhanced by his relatively strong showing in 1944, and despite some restiveness from GOP conservatives, he was once again the strong frontrunner for the Republican presidential nomination in 1948. In May of that year he defeated Harold Stassen in the Oregon presidential primary after demonstrating his strong civil libertarian convictions in a radio debate between the two candidates by attacking Stassen's proposal to outlaw the Communist party. At the Republican convention a month later, Dewey prevailed over the Taft and Stassen forces on the third ballot and chose California governor Earl Warren as his vice presidential running mate. Dewey and Warren embarked on a general election campaign that they appeared almost certain to win against an apparently unpopular incumbent, President Harry S. Truman, and a divided Democratic party. The Democrats had already produced two serious "splinter" presidential candidacies, former vice president Henry Wallace on the left and the southern segregationist governor J. Strom Thurmond of South Carolina on the right.

Always a rather stiff and severe personality, however, Dewey was not such a feisty and relentless campaigner as President Truman. Dewey also had the problem of running on the record of the Republican Eightieth Congress. Despite the pleas of Dewey and Brownell, Congress spurned the progressive Republican party platform when called into special session by the wily Truman, who then attacked Dewey and the Congress as "do-nothing" Republicans. While all the opinion polls predicted a Dewey triumph, Truman won with 49 percent of the popular vote to 45 percent for Dewey, and the Democrats swept back into control of Congress.

Despite a devastating second defeat, Dewey was by no means finished as a major force within the Republican party. When it became apparent that Senator Taft was the frontrunner for the Republican presidential nomination in 1952, Dewey felt obliged to prevent the unilateralist senator, who voted against the North Atlantic Treaty Organization (NATO) in 1949, from turning the Republican party in a direction that he believed would be disastrous for both it and the country. Dewey thus persuaded General Eisenhower to run against Taft and placed the still formidable Dewey-Brownell political organization at the general's disposal. After Eisenhower won a bitterly contested nomination over Taft at the 1952 Chicago convention, Dewey was instrumental in securing the vice presidential nomination for his protégé, California senator Richard Nixon, an ambitious politician from a lower-middle-class background in whom Dewey saw a mirror image of his younger self.

Dewey retired from the New York governorship at the end of his third term in 1955 and returned to New York City to practice law at the firm of Dewey, Ballantine, Bushby, Palmer and Wood. He remained active in the Republican party, however, and acted as an occasional adviser to Presidents Eisenhower and Nixon.

He was genuinely appalled by the fiscal profligacy of his Republican successor as New York governor, Nelson A. Rockefeller, and despite the latter's claim to the progressive Republican legacy, Dewey was much closer politically to Rockefeller's presidential rival Nixon. Preoccupied with his law firm and with caring for his ailing wife, who died in 1970, Dewey showed no interest in taking a federal government position in Washington, D.C. In 1968 he declined President-elect Nixon's offer of nomination as chief justice of the Supreme Court. Dewey died in Bal Harbor, Florida.

Dewey was a complex figure who aroused conflicting emotions of admiration and enmity. His most crucial role in twentieth-century American politics was to make the Republican party relevant and competitive once more after the electoral disasters of the 1930s. He did so by moving the GOP away from an isolationist position on foreign policy and toward acceptance of America's global role as the major world power during and after World War II. Dewey also helped revive the progressive Republican tradition, which became dormant following the departure of Theodore Roosevelt from the political scene but which became highly relevant once more in helping the Republican party reconcile itself to the more activist expectations of government after the New Deal. As governor, Dewey demonstrated the effectiveness of progressive Republicanism in action by blending innovative and active government with a traditional Republican emphasis on balanced budgets and fiscal rectitude.

Yet as a national party leader Dewey was a failure. A forceful administrator, he suffered from a somewhat rigid and aloof public persona on the presidential campaign trail. His prickly personality also perhaps explains why Dewey could never effectively communicate with or accommodate the conservative Republicans who dominated the congressional Republican party. The tragedy of Dewey's political career is that he will always be most remembered as the candidate who lost the 1948 presidential election to the underdog Harry Truman rather than as the successful prosecuting attorney who later became a major figure in both state and national politics.

• Dewey's private papers are in the Rush Rhees Library at the University of Rochester, Rochester, N.Y. His public papers have been published as *The Public Papers of Thomas E. Dewey* (12 vols., 1944–1957). Dewey's views on the major political questions of his time are set out in his own publications, *The Case against the New Deal* (1940), *Journey to the Far Pacific* (1952), and *Thomas E. Dewey on the Two-Party System*, ed. John A. Wells (1966). His uncompleted autobiography, *Twenty against the Underworld*, ed. Rodney Campbell (1974), deals with his career as a prosecutor. Richard Norton Smith, *Thomas E. Dewey and His Times* (1982), is a major biography, thorough and scholarly. His significance as a crime fighter is discussed in Mary M. Stolberg, *Fighting Organized Crime: Politics, Justice and the Legacy of Thomas E. Dewey* (1995). Barry K. Beyer, *Thomas E. Dewey 1937–1947: A Study in Political Leadership* (1979), is an analysis of Dewey's leadership skills in state and national politics. Dewey's presidential campaigns and his role in national Republican party politics are also discussed in Leonard Lurie, *The King Makers* (1971); James T. Patterson, *Mr. Republican: A Biography of Robert A. Taft* (1972); and Nicol C. Rae, *The Decline and Fall of the Liberal Republicans: From 1952 to the Present* (1989). An obituary is in the *New York Times*, 17 Mar. 1971.

NICOL C. RAE

DEWING, Arthur Stone (16 Apr. 1880–20 Jan. 1971), economics professor and author, was born in Boston, Massachusetts, the son of Charles Hamlet Dewing, a financial investor, and Eliza Dewing. From an early age he was burdened by eye troubles and was so afflicted with dyslexia that he did not learn to read until age twelve. A series of failed financial speculations by his father left the family all but destitute and forced his mother to take in boarders to maintain the family income. Dewing later attributed his mother's financial resourcefulness to his own interest in economics.

Dewing graduated from Cambridge (Mass.) English High School with an interest in the sciences, and in 1898 he enrolled in the Lawrence Scientific School, and later the engineering department, at Harvard. He then transferred to Harvard College and graduated magna cum laude in 1902 in philosophy. He entered the doctoral program in philosophy at Harvard, studying under William James, George Santayana, and Josiah Royce. As a graduate student Dewing studied at the University of Munich and taught science and philosophy courses at Harvard and local private schools. He was a master at undergraduate tutoring, helping struggling students, among them Franklin D. Roosevelt, prepare for their exams. He graduated with a Ph.D. in 1905 and within five years had published three volumes in philosophy and four highly profitable notebooks on scientific classroom instruction.

Between 1907 and 1913 Dewing taught philosophy at Simmons College in Boston, but he gradually transferred his scholarship to economics, reflecting his emerging belief that economics, not philosophy, would provide a more stable financial income. In 1910 he married Frances Hall Rousmaniere, whom he had met in a philosophy seminar at Harvard, and who was one of the first women to earn her Ph.D. in philosophy at Radcliffe. For a number of years the two taught in the same department at Simmons. They had three daughters. Dewing later taught economics in the School of Secretarial Studies at Simmons, and he also taught courses in political economy at Yale and the Boston School of Commerce and Finance. In 1919 Dewing accepted an invitation to join the faculty at the recently founded Harvard Business School; in 1927 he was promoted to professor of finance, a position he held until 1933.

While at Harvard Business School, Dewing developed an expertise as an international authority in the field of corporate law and finance, setting a standard for scholarly analysis of business enterprise. By 1920 Dewing had published three books on corporate finance, including his magnum opus *Financial Policy of Corporations*, first published in 1922 and revised five times over the next three decades for use in business school classes. In 1916 he published a widely circulated article that correctly predicted that the end of World War I would cause monetary instability. His later writings included textbooks on corporate finance and case studies of corporate mergers and reorganizations for use in universities and business schools.

As a teacher, Dewing combined his philosophical training in pragmatism and his expertise in finance to champion the case study method then gaining prominence at Harvard Business School. He asserted that business education should not teach truths, but rather should teach students to think in practical situations and to respond with intelligence and flexibility. In business education and practice alike, Dewing argued, "There should not be a single problem in use which is not capable of at least two intelligent solutions." He emphasized the role of the resourceful, competitive individual in business management and argued that the individual, not laws or bureaucracies, created economic value.

Dewing's faith in the paramount role of the individual in financial matters drove his decision to withdraw his entire bank holdings of about $30,000 of gold in 1933, blatantly challenging President Roosevelt's efforts to bolster the flailing bank system. In a dramatic public scene, the tall, bearded economics professor strode into his local bank in Harvard Square and lugged his bags of gold bars to his safe deposit box. Given Dewing's status as a leading authority on finance, the business school dean, Wallace B. Donham, considered that his action seriously threatened the reputation of the Harvard Business School. Already in conflict with the dean, who charged that Dewing's outside business commitments distracted him from his teaching, Dewing resigned.

Over the next forty years Dewing developed his investments, heading several water, gas, and real estate companies. He continued his collections of colonial houses and furniture and took on such eclectic investments as Florida alligators, rabbits, and a snake farm. An avid student of ancient history and philosophy, Dewing first visited Greece in 1901 and began collecting ancient Greek coins in 1929, eventually amassing more than 3,000 coins, which he donated to the Fogg Museum to become one of the most significant collections of Greek numismatic art.

A tall and distinctive figure with a short white beard, Dewing was a notorious character around the Boston area, who retained his great popularity with students at Harvard Business School years after his resignation. Dewing was one of the first to analyze in a scholarly fashion the rise and fall of giant financier-sponsored enterprises that grew and collapsed around the turn of the century. His emphasis on pragmatic knowledge of management and the definitive role of the individual was encapsulated in his writings and textbooks in American business schools through most of the twentieth century. He died in Boston.

• Records of Dewing's professional career can be found in the Archives of Harvard College, the Harvard Business School, and Simmons College. Dewing's career at the business school is recounted in Peter F. Rousmaniere, "Arthur Stone Dewing: Philosopher at the Business School," *Harvard Business School Bulletin*, May–June 1973, and in Jeffrey L. Cruikshank, *A Delicate Experiment: The Harvard Business School, 1908–1945* (1987). See also John Oleson, *Greek Numismatic Art: Coins of the Arthur Stone Dewing Collection* (1975). An obituary is in the *New York Times*, 21 Jan. 1971.

KATE ROUSMANIERE

DEWING, Maria Richards Oakey (27 Oct. 1845–13 Dec. 1927), painter, was born Maria Richards Oakey in New York City, the daughter of William Francis Oakey, an importer, and Sally Sullivan, a writer and socialite. The granddaughter of James Sullivan, second governor of Massachusetts, Maria Dewing was raised in a cultured familial atmosphere. Initially partial to a career as a writer, she became "swept with desire for art & achievement in it" (letter to Nelson C. White, 30 Aug. 1927) during the mid-1860s when she enrolled at the Cooper Union School of Design for Women in New York City. She studied at the National Academy of Design from 1871 to 1875 and in 1876 took private instruction in France with the academic painter Thomas Couture, after having previously studied informally with two of his American pupils, John La Farge and William Morris Hunt.

Artistically progressive from the outset of her career, Dewing joined forces with other European-trained painters in New York City who sought, throughout the late 1870s, to break the hegemony of the nativist National Academy of Design and to redefine America's artistic image in alignment with international art ideals. Consequently, she participated in the Cottier exhibition of 1875 and in the exhibitions of the Society of American Artists, an organization founded in 1877 to represent the aspirations of American artists seeking artistic interdependence with Europe. Her earliest artistic achievements, which consisted largely of now-unlocated figural pieces and portraits, anticipated the major thrust of her mature work: to infuse temporal subject matter with lyric and poetic significance. Concurrently, Dewing published several books and articles that reiterated her artistic aesthetic, including *Beauty in Dress* (1881) and *Beauty in the Household* (1882). She also dabbled in the decorative arts, creating needlework panels of embroidered appliqué that closely paralleled the overtly decorative still-life paintings of La Farge.

The thematic direction of Dewing's work changed following her marriage to Thomas Wilmer Dewing in 1881 and the birth of her only known surviving child in 1885. Familial responsibilities and her husband's status as one of America's leading figure painters may have prompted Dewing's growing devotion to still-life painting, either of tabletop bouquets or of outdoor garden scenes; contemporaneously, she became a self-trained botanist, developing her expertise in her garden at Cornish, New Hampshire, where she summered from 1886 to 1905. There, at the home she called "Doveridge," Dewing executed such original still-life conceptions as *Garden in May* (1895, National Museum of American Art, Washington, D.C.) and *Rose Garden* (1901, private collection). These depictions of isolated fragments of nature, inspired both by decorative and orientalist art, succeeded in probing beneath physical appearance to seize the "spiritual essence of each individual bloom" (Gerdts, p. 147).

The uniqueness of Dewing's outdoor garden pictures, specifically, brought her the patronage of the railroad magnate Charles Lang Freer and the newspaper editor Whitelaw Reid; she was asked to mount one-woman shows at the Pennsylvania Academy of the Fine Arts in 1907 and at Knoedler & Company, a gallery in New York City, in 1914. She was awarded bronze medals for such paintings at the World's Columbian Exhibition in Chicago in 1893 and for *Garden in May* and *Carnations* at the Pan American Exhibition of 1901. Her unusual talent for capturing the essence beneath the form was also acknowledged by her husband, with whom she probably collaborated on paintings such as *The Days* (1887, Wadsworth Atheneum), executing the floral elements.

After 1905 the Dewings summered in Green Hills, New Hampshire, and in Fryeburg, Maine, where her own gardens continued to inspire out-of-door still-life paintings such as *Bed of Poppies* (1909, Addison Gallery of American Art), purchased by the industrialist Edwin C. Shaw in 1923. Despite her recognition by contemporaries as the successor to La Farge and the American counterpart of the French still-life specialist Henri Fantin-Latour, Dewing bemoaned her commitment to flower painting; shortly before her death in New York City, she wrote, "This seems only a mockery I dreamed of groups & figures in big landscapes & still I *see* them" (letter to Nelson C. White, 30 Aug. 1927).

Notwithstanding her misgivings concerning her major professional achievement, Dewing produced some of the most unusual still-life pictures in late nineteenth-century American art. Royal Cortissoz, the art critic for the *New York Herald Tribune*, wrote, "The salient trait of Maria Oakey Dewing . . . was the strain of originality that characterized her deep feeling for beauty. . . . She knew how to interpret the soul of a flower. . . . We have had no one who could work with flowers the magic that was hers" (8 Dec. 1927). Although her reputation fell into obscurity in the years following her death, recent scholarly and popular interest has revived an appreciation of Dewing's career not only as a still-life painter but also as an active participant in progressive art circles in New York City during the 1870s.

• Dewing's papers are in the Archives of American Art, Washington, D.C.; see also Royal Cortissoz Papers, Collection of American Literature, The Beinecke Rare Book and Manuscript Library, Yale University, New Haven. A computerized inventory of Dewing's extant works is maintained by the National Museum of American Art in Washington, D.C. The most thorough considerations of Dewing's works and career are Jennifer A. Martin (Bienenstock), "Portraits of Flowers: The Out-of-Door Still-Life Paintings of Maria Oakey Dewing," *American Art Review* 4, no. 3 (1977): 48–55, 114–18; "Royal Cortissoz and Maria Oakey Dewing's 'Rose Garden,'" *Yale University Library Gazette* 52 (1977): 84–88; and "The Rediscovery of Maria Oakey Dewing," *Feminist Art Journal* 5, no. 2 (Summer 1976): 24–27, 44. Concerning Dewing's participation in progressive art activities, see Jennifer A. Martin Bienenstock, "The Formation and Early Years of the Society of American Artists: 1877–1884" (Ph.D. diss., Graduate Center of the City Univ. of New York, 1983). See also Doreen Bolger Burke et al., *In Pursuit of Beauty: Americans and the Aesthetic Movement* (1987), on Dewing's decorative art projects; Susan Faxon Olney et al., *A Circle of Friends: Art Colonies of Cornish and Dublin* (1985), on her years in Cornish; Ella M. Foshay, *Reflections of Nature: Flowers in American Art* (1984), and William H. Gerdts, *Painters of the Humble Truth: Masterpieces of American Still-Life 1801–1939* (1981), on Dewing's work discussed in the general context of late nineteenth-century American still-life painting.

JENNIFER A. MARTIN

DEWING, Thomas Wilmer (4 May 1851–5 Nov. 1938), artist, was born in Boston, Massachusetts, the son of Paul Dewing, a millwright, and Sophronia Durant, a former schoolteacher. Originally named Wilmer, during his teenage years the artist chose to adopt the more conventional "Thomas" as his first name. "Willie," as he was called by the family, took lessons at home from his sister Louise. He was twelve when his alcoholic father died, leaving the family of five children in difficult financial straits. Demonstrating his artistic talent at an early age, he apprenticed in a lithography shop, where he came to the attention of Belgian-born lithographer Dominique Fabronius, under whom he worked for a time in Boston.

During the early 1870s Dewing earned a reputation for meticulous black and white chalk portraits. In 1874–1875 he probably attended the anatomy lectures of sculptor-physician William Rimmer in Boston. Dewing also worked from live models in classes organized by students at the Lowell Institute. In the autumn of 1875 Dewing moved to Albany, where he drew portraits of Susan and Peter Gansevoort. He remained in Albany through the following spring doing further portrait commissions.

In July 1876 Dewing traveled to Paris, where he entered the Académie Julian; he was the first American student to enroll who would later achieve a reputation of note. There he studied under Gustave-Rudolphe Boulanger and Jules-Joseph LeFebvre. In October 1877 Dewing returned to Boston, where he taught at the newly opened school of the Museum of Fine Arts. He also exhibited small paintings of academic nudes. In 1878 he made his New York debut at the inaugural exhibition of the Society of American Artists, to which he was elected a member in May 1880.

Boston writers at this point were highly critical of Dewing, whose works they found eccentric and difficult to understand. His *Morning* (Delaware Art Museum, 1879), for example, contains no recognizable story line. Depicting two women in Renaissance gowns heralding the morning with long brass trumpets, the painting instead emphasizes angular patterns and mysterious color harmonies.

In October 1880, convinced that the larger metropolis would provide more sophisticated patronage, Dewing moved to New York City. That December he joined the staff of the Art Students' League, where he taught until 1888. At this time he met Maria Oakey, a portrait and still-life painter whom he married in April 1881; they had one child. During the 1880s the Dewings were part of a progressive circle of painters, writers, and musicians who met at the home of Richard Watson Gilder, editor of *Century Magazine*, and his wife, Helena deKay, a girlhood friend of Maria Dewing's. The artists around the Gilders included Augustus Saint-Gaudens, Albert Pinkham Ryder, Abbott Thayer, Waytt Eaton, Will H. Low, and J. Alden Weir. Literary figures that the group admired were British philosophers Matthew Arnold, John Ruskin, and Walter Pater. At this time Dewing painted society portraits and obtained mural commissions through his friend architect Stanford White. A typical example of the former is *Portrait of De Lancey Kane* (Museum of the City of New York, 1886), bearing the coat of arms of his wealthy client.

In June 1883 the Dewings went to Europe to purchase drawings and fine art reproductions for the Art Students' League. On their return, Dewing painted several works in the manner of British artists Sir Lawrence Alma-Tadema, Albert Moore, and Edward Coley Burne-Jones, whose studio he had visited in London. Among these paintings are *The Garden* (Museum of Fine Arts, Boston, 1883), *Hymen* (Cincinnati Museum of Art, 1884–1886), *Gloria* (Cleveland Museum of Art, 1884), and *Tobias and the Angel* (Metropolitan Museum of Art, 1887). The culmination of Dewing's work in the English Aesthetic tradition was *The Days* (Wadsworth Atheneum, 1886), a work inspired by a poem of the same name by Ralph Waldo Emerson. Suffused by delicate green tones, the canvas features a line of ethereal, classically gowned women, a composition that Dewing left vague intentionally, thereby leaving it open to interpretation. *The Days* won Dewing the Clark Prize for composition at the National Academy of Design, an honor that prompted his election as an associate in 1887 and to full membership in 1888.

Dewing's classically draped figures were succeeded by small paintings of contemporary women in studio settings. The artist's earliest work of this type is *Lady with a Lute* (National Gallery of Art, 1886). A similar figure entitled *Lady in Yellow* (Isabella Stewart Gardner Museum, 1888) established the artist's international reputation when it won a silver medal at the 1889 Paris International Exposition.

Dewing also became known for his elegantly dressed figures in softly lit landscapes, works inspired by Pre-Raphaelite and symbolist poetry as well as Japanese wood-block prints. The artist painted approximately a dozen of these outdoor themes that were prompted by his summers spent in Cornish, New Hampshire. During the late 1880s when Dewing went to Cornish, only a few artists lived there. A decade later the area had developed into a well-known art colony in which Dewing was the leading figure. Known for his gregarious personality, the artist was instrumental in organizing elegant dinner parties, dramatic masques, and tableaux vivants, some of which apparently provided motifs for his paintings.

Dewing's delicate color harmonies and exquisite themes won him the devotion of a select clientele, many of whom were railroad industrialists. Detroit railroad car manufacturer Charles Lang Freer, whom he met in 1890, became the artist's chief patron for nearly twenty-five years. Freer collected Asian art that he believed corresponded spiritually and aesthetically to works by his American protégés James McNeill Whistler, Abbott Thayer, Dwight Tryon, and Dewing. Freer eventually acquired twenty-six oils and fifteen works on paper by Dewing, all now in the collection of the Freer Gallery of Art, Smithsonian Institution, Washington, D.C.

The artist's other primary source of patronage was New Yorker John Gellatly. Aided by his wife Edith, heiress to a railroad car–building fortune, Gellatly began acquiring works by Dewing and other American artists during the late 1880s. Gellatly continued this patronage after his wife's death, assembling a large group of American paintings and European old masters that he gave to the National Museum of American Art, Smithsonian Institution, in 1929. His gift contained seventeen works by Dewing, whom he believed to be, along with Thayer and Ryder, a central figure in the "American Renaissance," that turn-of-the-century flowering of the arts considered at the time to be parallel in spirit and accomplishment to the Italian Renaissance. Dewing's diaphanous, three-figured *In the Garden* (National Museum of American Art, 1892–1894), for example, is reminiscent of the "three graces" in Sandro Botticelli's *Primavera*, one of Gellatly's favorite masterpieces.

Despite a reliable, albeit narrow, base of support at home, Dewing longed to try his fortunes abroad. In October 1894 he left for London, where he planned to stay for two years. Freer provided an introduction to Whistler, with whom Dewing worked periodically until March 1895. Dewing had hoped to exhibit his paintings at the Royal Academy but found that he was not welcomed by the British art establishment. He moved his family to Paris, from where he commuted weekly to the nearby village of Giverny. Although he exhibited three paintings at the Salon Champ de Mars in the spring of 1895 (*The Blue Dress, After Sunset*, and *The Carnation*, all Freer Gallery of Art, 1892, 1892, and 1893, respectively), Dewing became homesick for his native land. He returned to New York City, where he arrived on 13 July 1895. He never traveled abroad again.

Back in New York Dewing was heartened by a tribute to his work in *Harper's Magazine* written by critic Royal Cortissoz. Inspired by the lessons he had learned abroad, Dewing produced a series of Whistlerian canvases. One example is a fluidly painted, vaporous, green and gray interior with two women called *A Reading* (National Museum of American Art, 1897). Whistler probably also prompted Dewing's interest in screen painting as well. The greatest of his folding panels is the stunningly beautiful *Morning Glories* (Carnegie Institute, 1900), a composition framing three women in bowers of trumpet-shaped blossoms. Just as Whistler occasionally painted furniture, Dewing likewise decorated a gilded piano by Steinway and

Sons (National Museum of History and Technology, 1903). In celebration of their 100,000th keyboard instrument, the company presented it to the White House.

At the turn of the century Dewing turned almost entirely to painting female figures in sparsely furnished interiors. He believed that these works were more easily comprehended by the public than the landscape decorations of the previous decade—an important factor as he exhibited them on a regular basis. In December 1897 he had resigned from the Society of American Artists to join the progressive Ten American Painters, who staged annual spring exhibitions in New York City. The artist's first one-man exhibition occurred at the St. Botolph Club in Boston in 1898; a small retrospective followed at the Montross Gallery in New York in 1900. One of America's most respected and well-paid artists, Dewing was at the height of his powers occupying a niche just below that of Whistler and John Singer Sargent in the artistic hierarchy of the period.

At this time Dutch painting, particularly the works of Jan Vermeer and Gerard Ter Borch, provided him inspiration. The artist's well-known painting, and perhaps his masterpiece, *The Spinet* (National Museum of American Art, 1902), employs a back view of a woman at a keyboard. The pose and the rich surface treatment are particularly reminiscent of Vermeer. In 1901 Dewing contributed a number of interior subjects to the Pan-American Exposition in Buffalo, where he received a gold medal; he also won a gold medal at the 1904 Louisiana Purchase Exposition in St. Louis.

By depicting figures as they listen to music or hold musical instruments, Dewing established a mood of reverie similar to Vermeer's. He also seems to have been drawn to the enigmatic quality of the Dutch master's compositions. When Dewing placed a foreground figure with her back to a distant companion in his *Brocart de Venise* (Washington University, St. Louis, 1904), he employed a spatial disjunction typically used by Vermeer to suggest tension between figures.

Stimulated, perhaps, by the great Whistler memorial exhibitions of 1904–1905, Dewing next produced a series of single, profile figures that he painted periodically over the following decade. Early in 1907 critic Charles Caffin wrote that Dewing's works were becoming "less and less concerned with form as form, increasingly occupied with its suggestion of abstract expression." This interest in reduction and spareness is evident in *The Letter* (Toledo Museum of Art, 1906), in which broad foreground space contrasts significantly with tiny background figures. *The Necklace*, showing an isolated woman admiring herself in a looking glass, won first prize at the annual exhibition of the Carnegie Institute in 1908. It brings to a culmination various threads running through the artist's oeuvre: his veneration of Vermeer and Whistler, the abstraction he admired in Asian painting, and his devotion to the beauty of the painted surface.

In 1908 Dewing was elected to the National Institute of Arts and Letters, recognition that came just as a group of painters called The Eight burst upon the New York art scene. These artists propounded an urban realism at odds with the refined aestheticism cherished by Dewing. But it was the avant-garde European paintings showcased at New York's 1913 Armory Show that ultimately undermined his reputation as well as that of the other Ten American Painters. Nevertheless, Dewing continued to sell to a select clientele and to various museums.

After the mid-1920s Dewing painted little, content that he was well represented at the Smithsonian Institution, which eventually would contain sixty-five of his works, and in numerous museums across the country. In May 1923 the new Freer Gallery of Art devoted a large space to his paintings. In the spring of 1924 Dewing orchestrated his own exhibition at the Carnegie Institute in Pittsburgh, and in December the Corcoran Gallery of Art in Washington, D.C., staged an exhibition of his works on paper. Dewing died in New York City and was buried alongside his wife Maria at Mount Auburn Cemetery, Cambridge, Massachusetts.

From the first Dewing's experimental technique, subdued tonal range, and unsettling subjects separated his work from that of his peers. He created genteel realms of beauty and refinement that seem calculated to insulate viewers from an increasingly industrial landscape. The nuances and subtleties of his aestheticism fulfilled the ideals of his own time, one in which an attenuated delicacy signified the highest levels of cultural achievement. But with the advent of modernism, such benchmarks of quality and progress altered. From the 1930s through the 1960s Dewing was one of the most neglected figures in American art. This situation was remedied by the 1996 Dewing retrospective and its accompanying publication. Held at the Brooklyn Museum, the Smithsonian's Museum of American Art, and the Detroit Institute of Art, this traveling exhibition presents this surprisingly complex artist as a key figure for understanding turn-of-the century aesthetics, which Dewing himself defined as the need to "see beautifully."

• The papers of Thomas Dewing are in the Archives of American Art and the Freer Gallery of Art, Smithsonian Institution. The primary recent source on the artist is Susan A. Hobbs, with a contribution by Barbara Dayer Gallati, *Thomas Wilmer Dewing, Beauty Reconfigured* (Smithsonian Press in conjunction with the Brooklyn Museum, 1996). See also Susan Hobbs, "Thomas Wilmer Dewing: The Early Years, 1851–1885," *American Art Journal* 13 (Spring 1981): 4–35, and "Thomas Dewing in Cornish, 1885–1905," *American Art Journal* 17 (Spring 1985): 3–32. Charles de Kay wrote the first appreciation of Dewing in "The Ceiling of a Cafe," *Harper's Weekly*, 12 Mar. 1892, pp. 257–58. Royal Cortissoz followed with "Some Imaginative Types in American Art," *Harper's Magazine*, July 1895, pp. 164–79. Sadakichi Hartmann made key observations in *A History of American Art*, vol. 1 (1902), pp. 299–308, and "On the Elongation of Form," *Camera Work* 10 (Apr. 1905): 27–35. Charles H. Caffin linked Dewing to currents of modernism in "The Art of Thomas W. Dewing," *Harper's Magazine*, Apr. 1908, pp. 714–24, as did Catherine Beach Ely in "Thomas W. Dewing," *Art in America* 10 (1922): 225–29. Ezra Tharp, "T. W. Dewing," *Art and Progress* 5 (Mar. 1914): 155–61, is an incisive contemporary account based on the author's visit to

Dewing's studio. Dewing's art was evaluated by Royal Cortissoz in "An American Artist Canonized in the Freer Gallery: Thomas W. Dewing," *Scribner's Magazine*, Nov. 1923, pp. 539–46. More recently Kathleen Pyne wrote "Classical Figures: A Folding Screen by Thomas Dewing," *Bulletin of the Detroit Institute of Art* 59 (Spring 1981): 5–13, and "Evolutionary Typology and the American Woman in the Work of Thomas Dewing," *American Art*, Fall 1993, pp. 13–29. For Dewing's painting methods see Susan Hobbs et al., "Thomas Wilmer Dewing: A Look Beneath the Surface," *Smithsonian Studies in American Art* 4 (Summer/Fall 1990): 63–85.

SUSAN HOBBS

DE WITT, Lydia Maria (1 Feb. 1859–10 Mar. 1928), pathologist, was born in Flint, Michigan, the daughter of Oscar Adams, an attorney, and Elizabeth Walton. Her mother died when Lydia was five, and she was brought up by her father's second wife, the sister of his first wife.

After graduation from Flint High School, Lydia became a teacher. She married Alton D. De Witt, also a teacher, in 1878. The couple had two children. In 1884 Lydia De Witt enrolled in the Ypsilanti Normal College and obtained her certificate in 1886.

In 1893 De Witt changed careers and enrolled at both the Medical School and College of the University of Michigan, receiving her M.D. in 1898 and her B.S. in 1899. The De Witts separated in 1904.

Immediately after obtaining her M.D., De Witt became an assistant in histology at the University of Michigan. Her initial interest was microscopical anatomy, and she did research in neuroanatomy for G. Carl Huber, head of the school's department of histology and anatomy. During this time De Witt studied the structure of the pancreas and the nerves involved in the beating of the heart, making useful contributions. Her article, "Morphology and Physiology of the Areas of Langerhans in Some Vertebrates" (*Journal of Experimental Medicine* 8 [1906]: 193–239), reported pioneering results. "Observations in the Sino-Ventricular Connecting System of the Mammalian Heart" (*Anatomical Record* 3 [1909]: 475–97) was of value for both its techniques and its results. "Arrangement and Termination of Nerves in the Oesophagus of Mammals" (*Journal of Comparative Neurology* 10 [1900]: 382–98) became frequently cited. De Witt, however, gradually turned her attention to pathology, and George Dock, a well-known internist and pathologist at the university, invited her to join his staff. De Witt spent most of 1906 in Germany engaged in postgraduate studies; on her return to Michigan, she was promoted to instructor.

In 1910 De Witt moved to St. Louis, where for the next two years she was assistant city pathologist and bacteriologist and also served as an instructor in pathology at Washington University Medical School. Here she continued her efforts to improve histological techniques and procedures in bacteriology.

In 1912 H. Gideon Wells, professor of pathology at the University of Chicago and director of the recently founded Otho Sprague Memorial Institute, asked De Witt to join his staff as assistant professor of patholo-

gy. She was promoted to associate professor in 1918 and remained there until her retirement in 1926.

Around the turn of the century, the German biochemist and immunologist Paul Ehrlich (winner of the Nobel Prize for medicine in 1908) pioneered the use of dyes for staining tissues and the development of chemotherapy. De Witt became interested in these endeavors and devoted several years to related research with tuberculosis and other diseases. Between 1913 and 1925, pursuing the idea of combining dyes and toxic metals, she worked with chemists and wrote a long series of reports on the biochemistry and chemotherapy of tuberculosis. These articles, on dyes such as methylene blue, trypan red, and basic fuchsin and metals such as gold, copper, and mercury also served as models for later investigations. De Witt's research publications included about fifty articles. She also coauthored, with Wells and Esmond R. Long, the book *The Chemistry of Tuberculosis* (1923).

In addition to her scientific research and teaching, De Witt furthered the work of women in science and medicine. She was one of the first women given a regular faculty appointment at the University of Michigan Medical School and was a founder and first president of the Women's Research Club at that university. De Witt was also active in several professional organizations, serving as president of the Chicago Pathological Society (1924–1925). Suffering from Bright's Disease and arteriosclerosis, which damaged her health, De Witt retired in 1926 to Winter, Texas, to live with her daughter; she died there.

• There are no collections of De Witt's papers. A typescript memoir by the Women's Research Club (at the University of Michigan's Bentley Historical Library) is a good source of biographical information on De Witt and her children.

WILLIAM K. BEATTY

DE WITT, Simeon (25 Dec. 1756–3 Dec. 1834), cartographer, surveyor, and land developer, was born in Wawarsing, Ulster County, New York, the son of Andries De Witt, a physician, and Jannetje Vernooy. His early education was typical of what a scattered agricultural community could provide in that period. Later he received classical instruction from the local minister, and then, on the eve of the American Revolution, he enrolled at Queen's College (later Rutgers University) in New Brunswick, New Jersey. He was granted a B.A. degree in 1776 and an M.A. degree in 1788.

The British burned down the college at the end of his third year, and the students were dispersed. De Witt returned home, where he continued his studies. He spent much of his time with an uncle, James Clinton, then a colonel in the Continental army and brother of Governor George Clinton of New York State. De Witt marched as volunteer adjutant with a battalion formed in Ulster County, and when the battalion was formed into a regiment, De Witt continued to serve as a private, participating in the battles leading to John Burgoyne's surrender.

Some months later, when General George Washington was seeking a geographer (later designated as topographical engineer) for the Continental army, James Clinton recommended De Witt, who was given the position in 1778 as assistant to the Continental Army's geographer general, Colonel Robert Erskine. After Erskine's unexpected death two years later, De Witt became geographer of the United States in his place. Ordered to army headquarters in New Windsor, New York, De Witt immediately undertook the mapping of the roads to strategic military points, using all available scientific aids to improve the quality of military mapmaking. He remained attached to the army until the end of the campaign. On the march to Yorktown in October 1781, De Witt and his assistants, constantly engaged in surveying the land along the route, witnessed the surrender of General Charles Cornwallis. Although De Witt was anxious to be discharged, General Washington refused his application because his services continued to be needed.

Thereafter De Witt and his staff, working from a headquarters in Philadelphia, prepared final versions of the field maps to produce a cartographic history of the war to serve future peacetime needs. De Witt proposed to produce "A Map of the State of War in America" for publication, and although the project received a favorable reception from both the commander in chief and the Congress, the request for publication was rejected due to lack of funds. Nonetheless a subsequent congressional resolution recognized the value of the work and required that a copy of each of the maps be deposited in the office of the secretary of war in order to preserve a record of the war.

Having failed to obtain official support for his project, De Witt resigned his commission on 13 May 1784. He then sought to utilize his skills in public surveying. That same year, following the resignation of General Philip Schuyler as surveyor general of the State of New York, De Witt was appointed in his place. Although New York City remained the political capital, De Witt moved the office of the surveyor general to Albany (as established by law) as soon as it was feasible. His responsibilities were many and unremitting, for the western part of the state remained densely forested and had to be prepared for settlement. The boundaries with Pennsylvania remained generally obscure and productive of disputes over property ownership, making the permanent establishment of these boundaries a priority. Philip Schuyler, James Clinton, and De Witt were appointed commissioners for New York to undertake the survey, and David Rittenhouse and Andrew Ellicott were appointed for Pennsylvania; the work was completed during 1786 and 1787. Meanwhile in 1786, at the request of the New York legislature, De Witt began the preparation of a map of the state, which he successfully completed and published in 1802. In 1789 he married Elizabeth Lynott; the couple did not have children.

In 1796 President Washington nominated De Witt for the position of surveyor general of the United States and Congress approved it, but De Witt regretfully declined. Although fully occupied with his surveying activities, he had become deeply involved in education as well as other scientific activities. In 1798 he was elected a regent of the University of the State of New York, an office he retained until his death. In 1817 he was elected vice chancellor, and in 1829 he became chancellor of the university, remaining in that office also until his death.

When New York undertook development of canals in 1810, De Witt was named a member of the board of commissioners for "exploring the whole route, examining the present condition of . . . navigation, and considering what further improvement ought to be made therein." He made surveys of the streams and rivers between the Hudson River and Lake Erie.

Shortly after the death of his first wife in 1793, De Witt acquired from her relatives some 1,400 acres of lakeshore property at the head of Cayuga Lake, which he developed into a settlement that became the city of Ithaca. The community developed slowly at first, but after the War of 1812 had cut off the chief supply of gypsum from Nova Scotia, requiring thereafter that it be mined and processed chiefly near Union Springs on Lake Cayuga, Ithaca began to grow rapidly as a depot for barges whose cargoes were hauled overland on the Ithaca-Oswego turnpike. De Witt, based in Albany, employed a number of agents to handle his various properties in Ithaca, and it was not until 1831 that he moved his residence there.

De Witt was distinguished also in the field of science. Elected a member of the American Philosophical Society in 1790 on the recommendation of David Rittenhouse, his report of observations of a solar eclipse that occurred in 1806 was published in volume 6 of the Society's *Transactions*. He was a charter member of the Society for the Promotion of Agriculture, Arts and Manufactures, established in New York State in 1793, and served it in various offices, including president. The society published his papers on "A Plan of a Meteorological Chart, for Exhibiting a Comparative View of the Climates of North America, and the progress of Vegetations" and "Establishment of a Meridian Line in the City of Albany." In 1813 he published a volume on *The Elements of Perspective*. A founding member of the Albany Institute, he served as its vice president and published papers in the institute's *Transactions* on "A Table of Variations of the Compass Needle," "Observations on the Functions of the Moon, Deduced from the Eclipse of 1806," and "A Description of a New Form of Rain Gauge."

In 1799 De Witt married Jane Varick Hardenberg, with whom he had six children. In 1810, having been widowed a second time in 1808, he married Susan Linn. His third marriage was childless. An elder in the Dutch Reformed Church for twenty years, De Witt was an elder of the Second Dutch Church at the time of his death at Ithaca a few weeks short of his seventy-eighth birthday. De Witt's distinguished career as a military cartographer during the American Revolution and his subsequent work in the same field in New York State identify him as a major figure in the history of early American surveying and mapping.

• Some of De Witt's papers are in the Regional History and University Archives of Cornell University, in the De Witt Historical Society in Ithaca, N.Y., and in the Rutgers University Library in New Brunswick, N.J. The most comprehensive biographical account of De Witt is the *Eulogium on the Life and Services of Simeon De Witt, Surveyor-General of the State of New-York, Chancellor of the University, &c. &c. &c.* by T. Romeyn Beck, M.D., delivered before the Albany Institute on 23 Apr. 1835 and published in Albany in the same year. Other accounts of his life are to be found in Thomas G. Evans, *The DeWitt Family of Ulster County, N.Y.* (1886); Benson J. Lossing, *The Empire State* (1887); and William Heidt, Jr., *Simeon De Witt, Founder of Ithaca* (1968).

SILVIO A. BEDINI

DE WOLFE, Elsie (20 Dec. 1865–12 July 1950), actress and interior decorator, was born in New York City, the daughter of Stephen de Wolfe, a physician, and Georgina Copeland. She was baptized Ella Anderson de Wolfe. Her father had been raised in Nova Scotia and educated at the University of Pennsylvania; her mother, also reared in Canada, was born in Aberdeen, Scotland. Elsie attended private schools in New York until the age of fourteen and was then sent to Scotland to finish her education under the tutelage of her mother's cousin, Dr. Archibald Charteris. Owing to Charteris's connection to royal circles, she was presented to Queen Victoria and London society at age seventeen, an unusual honor then for an American girl. This experience focused her vision of life on elegance, refinement, fashion, and good taste.

When she returned to New York in 1884, she began to perform in amateur theatricals, becoming a professional actress in 1890, after her father's death left her with little money. She achieved a modest success during her fourteen-year acting career but was best known for her stylish couturier clothes on the stage. During this period she lived with Elisabeth Marbury (Bessie), who established herself as the leading theatrical and literary agent of her day.

It was at their house on Irving Place that de Wolfe began to experiment with her taste and ideas of interior decoration. She transformed the dark Victorian interior into a prototype of twentieth-century decoration by stripping away the clutter and replacing heavy furniture with eighteenth-century-style French pieces. From there she launched her career as America's first professional woman interior decorator. Backed by numerous wealthy, influential women, such as Anne Morgan, the daughter of the banker, J. P. Morgan, Anne Vanderbilt, and the Hewitt sisters, Sarah and Eleanor, her business was an immediate success.

In 1905 de Wolfe received her first major commission, to decorate the rooms of the Colony Club, an exclusive New York women's club whose architect, Stanford White, had been instrumental in obtaining the job for her. To impart an atmosphere of light and air, she introduced a number of decorative innovations that became her trademarks: flowered chintz or toile de Jouy fabrics in the bedrooms and sitting rooms, cream-colored furniture, the liberal use of mirrors, and the use of interior trellis work. De Wolfe's ideas of interior decoration were not original. By the turn of the century the resurgence of classical and colonial revival taste had led to the lightened appearance of rooms in general. Her taste and style were influenced by Ogden Codman, architect and decorator who advised her and collaborated with her on several houses. Codman's groundbreaking *The Decoration of Houses* (1897), written with Edith Wharton, called for the elimination of heavy draperies, knickknacks, and poorly designed furniture. Their credo—suitability, simplicity, and proportion—was popularized by de Wolfe in *The House in Good Taste* (1913). She directed her book at the emancipated American woman and imparted practical as well as artistic advice. Her emphatic claim that the decoration of the home belonged under the woman's domain did much to spawn the acceptability of decorating as a suitable occupation for women.

De Wolfe decorated residences and apartments throughout the country; some of her most notable commissions were for Henry Clay Frick of New York, Mrs. J. Ogden Armour of Chicago, Mrs. William Crocker of San Francisco, and Mrs. R. M. Weyerhaeuser of Minneapolis. Few, if any, of her interiors have survived.

As her career prospered, she spent increasingly more time at "Villa Trianon," the eighteenth-century house in Versailles that she and Elisabeth Marbury bought and restored, with the aid of Anne Morgan, in 1903. Drawn to novelty of all sorts, she was one of the first women to accompany Wilbur Wright on some of his test flights in 1908. She remained in France throughout the First World War and nursed the wounded, for which she was awarded the Legion of Honor. During the 1920s she maintained offices on both continents; her business acumen and flair for entertaining and self-promotion established her reputation as an international hostess. In 1926, at age sixty, she married Sir Charles Mendl, an attaché of the British embassy, and continued to stage extravaganzas at her residences in Paris and Versailles. When Villa Trianon was made a Nazi headquarters during the Second World War, Lady Mendl, as she was known after her marriage, and her husband fled to Hollywood, where she continued to be a trendsetter and hostess "extraordinaire." She is remembered for her individual sense of style as well as her contribution to fashion. She was never without white gloves and always maintained her fastidious appearance; she made it fashionable for older women to tint their hair blue. She returned to France after the war and died there at her home. Her success as a career woman led the way for the acceptance of American women in the professional world.

• Personal letters, scrapbooks, inventories of collections, and other memorabilia belong to the Elsie de Wolfe Foundation in Los Angeles. For her childhood, youth, and career on the stage, see clippings in the Players Collection and the Robinson Locke Scrapbooks in the Theatre Collection of the New York Public Library at Lincoln Center. Her autobiography is *After All* (1935); see also the autobiography of Elisabeth Marbury, *My Crystal Ball* (1923). The biography of Elsie de Wolfe, including extensive references, is by Jane S. Smith,

Elsie de Wolfe, a Life in the High Style (1982). For her decorating ideas, see her book, *The House in Good Taste* (1913). See also Ruby Ross Goodnow, "The Story of Elsie de Wolfe," *Good Housekeeping*, June 1913. For information on her later life, see Janet Flanner, *An American in Paris* (1940), and Ludwig Bemelmans, *To the One I Love the Best* (1955). Obituaries are in the *New York Herald Tribune* and the *New York Times*, 13 July 1950, and *Le Monde* (Paris), 14 July 1950.

PAULINE C. METCALF

DEWSON, Molly (18 Feb. 1874–21 Oct. 1962), politician and social reformer, was born Mary Williams Dewson in Quincy, Massachusetts, the daughter of Edward Henry Dewson, a Boston leather merchant, and Elizabeth Weld. Molly (as she was always known) attended Wellesley College, graduating in 1897. After college she joined the staff of the Women's Educational and Industrial Union in Boston, where she conducted research on domestic service and the professionalization of housework. In 1900 she became the superintendent of the parole department for the Massachusetts State Industrial School for Girls at Lancaster. In 1912 she resigned that post to join Boston reformer Elizabeth Glendower Evans and others in the successful fight to establish a minimum wage for women workers in Massachusetts, the first in the United States.

In 1911 Molly Dewson met Mary G. "Polly" Porter, with whom she shared her life for more than fifty years. The Porter-Dewsons (as they called themselves) operated a dairy farm in central Massachusetts from 1912 to 1917 and became active suffragists. In 1917 the partners (their word to describe their relationship) volunteered for duty in France with the American Red Cross. When they returned from the war in 1919, Dewson and Porter settled in New York City, alternating their time between Greenwich Village and Castine, Maine, where Porter had a spacious summer home.

Molly Dewson's subsequent career demonstrates the contributions that public-spirited women made to politics and social reform in the postsuffrage era. From 1919 to 1924, she was the research secretary of the National Consumers' League under Florence Kelley, where she concentrated on labor legislation and wrote the factual sections of Felix Frankfurter's unsuccessful brief in support of the minimum wage for women in *Adkins v. Children's Hospital* (1923). After a brief stint as the civic secretary of the Women's City Club in New York City, Dewson became president of the New York Consumers' League, a position she held until 1931. The professional and personal friendships forged in these groups greatly enhanced Dewson's political effectiveness.

Through her reform activity in New York in the 1920s, Dewson met Eleanor Roosevelt, an association that profoundly shaped the rest of her career. At Eleanor Roosevelt's request, she joined Al Smith's national Democratic campaign in 1928. By 1930 Dewson had transferred her loyalties to Franklin Roosevelt. In the 1932 campaign, the reformer-turned-politician organized women's activities for FDR's presidential bid. From 1933 to 1937 Dewson ran the Women's Division of the Democratic National Committee, where she worked for equal representation of women on party committees and initiated the Reporter Plan for Democratic women to study the impact of the New Deal on their communities. In the 1936 campaign the Women's Division counted 80,000 active supporters and supplied 90 percent of the literature for the general campaign in the form of brightly colored fact sheets called Rainbow Fliers.

Molly Dewson enjoyed a close personal and working relationship with both Franklin and Eleanor Roosevelt, and she used this friendship to lobby successfully for the appointments of unprecedented numbers of women to high-level positions in the New Deal administration. For example, she played a large role in the selection in 1933 of her longtime colleague and friend Frances Perkins as secretary of labor, the first woman to serve in the cabinet. In addition, as a member of the 1934 Committee on Economic Security, Dewson influenced the drafting of the Social Security Act, one of the Roosevelt administration's most significant legislative achievements. The New Deal represented the culmination of the reform agenda that many politically involved women had supported since the Progressive Era, and Dewson became one of Roosevelt's most loyal supporters. "I cannot believe I have lived to see this day," she told Arthur Altmeyer in a 1935 letter. "It's the culmination of what us girls and some of you boys have been working for so long it's just dazzling."

At the height of her political power in 1937, Molly Dewson returned to her old field of social welfare to become one of the three members of the recently created Social Security Board. She served for less than a year, however, and in 1938 left government service permanently, although she did return to Democratic women's politics to play a brief role in Roosevelt's 1940 campaign. Dewson spent the rest of her retirement with Polly Porter in New York and Maine, and, after 1952, exclusively in Castine, where she died. Polly Porter died in 1972.

• The Mary W. Dewson papers are divided between the Schlesinger Library of Radcliffe College, Cambridge, Mass., and the Franklin D. Roosevelt Library, Hyde Park, N.Y. Both collections include Dewson's unpublished autobiography, "An Aid to the End," which covers her political career. The papers of Eleanor Roosevelt and the Women's Division of the Democratic National Committee at the Roosevelt Library also have extensive documentation of Dewson's political activities in the 1930s. Susan Ware, *Partner and I: Molly Dewson, Feminism, and New Deal Politics* (1987), covers Dewson's entire career, whereas her earlier *Beyond Suffrage: Women in the New Deal* (1981) concentrates on the 1930s. An obituary appeared in the *New York Times*, 25 Oct. 1962.

SUSAN WARE

DEXTER, Aaron (11 Nov. 1750–28 Feb. 1829), physician and medical educator, was born in Malden, Massachusetts, the son of Richard Dexter and Rebecca Peabody, prosperous farmers. He received his A.B. degree from Harvard in 1776, when he was nearly twenty-six, six to eight years older than most Harvard graduates of the time. Following graduation, he studied medicine with Samuel Danforth, a member of a prominent Massachusetts family, influential Boston practitioner, and staunch Tory. Danforth was also known as the leading student of chemistry in the Boston area, but this subject was not well developed in Massachusetts, and Danforth's knowledge was only superficial, although he did possess some chemical apparatus.

After finishing his medical pupillage, Dexter struggled to establish himself as a physician and apothecary in Boston during the unsettled later years of the Revolution. He entered into a partnership with Thomas Welsh and two others to import drugs and in 1781 traveled to Europe to purchase a supply; he may have made one or two more trips. Dexter also served as a surgeon on board several privateers; he was captured and sent to Halifax, Nova Scotia, where he endured considerable suffering before he was exchanged.

On 22 May 1783 Dexter was elected professor of chemistry and materia medica in the newly founded Harvard Medical School. As the third and last member of the original medical faculty, he was the weakest, lacking either the outstanding academic credentials of Benjamin Waterhouse, professor of the theory and practice of medicine, or the teaching ability and enthusiasm of John Warren, professor of anatomy and surgery. Dexter served on the Harvard medical faculty from 1783 until his retirement in 1816 and was professor emeritus until his death. In 1793 he became the first Erving Professor of Chemistry and Materia Medica when his friend and patient, William Erving, a retired major in the British army and Harvard graduate (1753), bequeathed £1,000 to endow this chair, which Dexter held until his retirement.

Dexter's lectures were the first systematic teaching of chemistry at Harvard, addressed to undergraduates as well as to medical students. Although he was a poor and ill-prepared classroom teacher, his contacts with French officers in Boston during the War of Independence and his travel in Europe acquainted him with the revolutionary advances in chemistry being made, especially in France. During his visit to Boston in 1788, J. P. Brissot de Warville, a serious student of chemistry, was delighted to find Dexter using his mentor Foucroy's textbook, which incorporated many of these advances (*New Travels in the United States of America 1788* [1792; repr. 1964], p. 96). Dexter was perhaps the first teacher in an American college to teach the new French chemistry.

In 1787 Dexter enhanced his already strong social position in Boston by marrying Rebecca, the daughter of Thomas Amory. Energetic and personable, he enjoyed a large practice and was active, if not particularly influential, in professional affairs. He was an incorporator and first librarian (1782–1792) of the Massachusetts Medical Society, visiting physician at the Massachusetts General Hospital from its opening until 1829, and a member of the Board of Consulting Physicians in Boston from 1824 to 1828.

Dexter was also active in business, civic, and intellectual affairs. He was president of the Middlesex Canal Company and an early advocate of the Craigie Bridge connecting Boston with Lechmere's Point in Cambridge. He sold a portion of his farm in Chelsea to the national government for the building of the new United States Marine Hospital. Benjamin Waterhouse wrote that Dexter acquired a "fortune somewhat over one hundred thousand dollars" but "lost it all at one stroke by the villany [*sic*] of his own son" (*Memoirs, 1828–1836*, entry for Dec. 1833, Countway Library of Medicine, Harvard Medical School).

In 1787 Dexter, a strong Federalist, accompanied the expedition against Daniel Shays. From 1789 to 1796 he was on the Boston School Committee and from 1789 to 1826 was a member of the vestry of King's Chapel. He was president of the Agricultural Society and the Humane Society of the Commonwealth of Massachusetts. Dexter was also active in the founding of the Anthology Club, a precursor of the Boston Athenaeum, and of the *North American Review*. He was a member of the Wednesday Evening Club, the Massachusetts Historical Society, and the American Academy of Arts and Sciences.

Although he was active in many areas, Dexter's niche in American history rests solely on his having been a member of the original faculty of the Harvard Medical School and a pioneering teacher and student of chemistry in the infant United States.

• For the date and place of Dexter's birth, which is often incorrectly given, see Deloraine P. Corey, comp., *Births, Marriages and Deaths in the Town of Malden Massachusetts 1649–1852* (1903), p. 21. Primary material on Dexter is scarce and scattered; important brief biographies are found in Walter L. Burrage, *A History of the Massachusetts Medical Society with Brief Biographies of the Founders and Chief Officers 1781–1922* (1923); H. W. Foote, *Annals of King's Chapel from the Puritan Age to the Present Day*, vol. 2 (1882–1940), p. 480; and Charles C. Sweet, "Notice of Aaron Dexter," Massachusetts Historical Society, *Proceedings* 1 (1791–1835): 421–23. For Dexter's role as Harvard's first professor of chemistry and materia medica see Henry K. Beecher and Mark Altschule, *Medicine at Harvard: The First Three Hundred Years* (1977), and Thomas E. Moore, Jr., "Early Years of the Harvard Medical School, 1782–1810," *Bulletin of the History of Medicine* 27 (1953): 530–61. For a more complete account see Moore, "The Early Years of the Harvard Medical School: Its Founding and Curriculum, 1782–1810" (honors thesis, Harvard College, 1952). For Dexter's role in the early study and teaching of chemistry at Harvard see I. Bernard Cohen, *Some Early Tools of American Science: An Account of the Early Scientific Instruments and Mineralogical and Biological Collections in Harvard University* (1950).

PHILIP CASH

DEXTER, Al (4 May 1902–28 Jan. 1984), singer, was born Albert Poindexter in Jacksonville, Texas. The young Dexter showed a strong interest in music, learning to play French harp and banjo at fifteen and regularly playing organ in church services. Before long he could play just about any stringed instrument. He made his first guitar, he told a local newspaper, out of sweet-gum strips that he picked up around a box factory and a white pine drain board from a dismantled kitchen sink. Music became a hobby, and throughout the 1920s Dexter played informally with a variety of local groups in East Texas, performing at square dances and parties. He supported himself chiefly as a house painter, with his intermittent tips from performing as extra income, into the 1930s. Then the depression forced him to reexamine his career path. He decided to give music a full-time shot.

Dexter's family remembered that, at first, the young performer had wanted to write and sell religious songs—his first songwriting attempts were hymns—but when a friend asked him whether he would rather "write pretty songs or make money," Dexter began to concentrate on the upbeat bar ballads and swings that were gaining popularity in roadhouses throughout the area. Dexter formed or played with a variety of groups through the early 1930s before forming, in 1934, the Texas Troopers, the band that would help him to step into the national spotlight.

Dexter and his Texas Troopers began to perform throughout East Texas, gaining a popular following, before recording some original songs that gained the attention of larger recording labels. Dexter recorded for the OKeh and Vocalion labels in the late 1930s and for Columbia Records after the large label bought the two smaller recording companies in 1940. He also recorded for Decca, King, and Capital during his career. The uptempo style of playing that the band had learned and perfected in the many roadhouse bars that dotted the oil fields of Texas became known as "western swing" before becoming widely known by the description that Dexter himself introduced: "honky-tonk." Dexter's "Honky Tonk Blues," recorded in 1936, was the first song to use the term that became synonymous with this new, twangy, and upbeat form of country music.

Dexter—who owned and operated a roadhouse, the Round Up, in Turnertown, Texas—described the oil-boom taverns and roadhouses where honky-tonk was born as "beer joints up and down the road where girls jump in cars and so on." The mixture of a tightly packed, boisterous audience in close proximity to the performers, who more often than not did not even have a stage on which to perform, required an equally loud and boisterous, crowd-pleasing musical style. The popularity of the music quickly spread, carrying Dexter and his Troopers along.

Throughout the 1940s Dexter wrote and recorded fourteen songs that sold more than 1 million records each, including "Rosalita," "New Broom Boogie," "Guitar Polka," "Car Hoppin' Mama," and "Too Late to Worry, Too Blue to Cry." By far, though, his greatest success came in 1943 with "Pistol Packin' Mama," a song that sold more than 10 million records and remained in the number-one chart position for seventeen weeks. The song was a million seller as well for Bing Crosby and the Andrews Sisters, whose version was on the charts the same time as Dexter's original. The story behind the song varies. In a 1973 reminiscence, Dexter himself attributed the anecdote behind the song to a waitress who worked in his Turnertown tavern who had been chased and roughed up by the gun-toting wife of her boyfriend. More popularly, the story behind the song has been attributed to an event in the life of union organizer Aunt Molly Jackson, whose family ran an illicit whiskey still in Kentucky. Either way, the song became one of the top-selling novelty hits of the war years.

From the late 1940s and into the 1950s, as he concluded his recording career, Dexter remained a popular touring performer, appearing at nightclubs, county fairs, and rodeos throughout the country. He retired from touring in the 1970s to devote his attention to his Dallas nightclub, the Bridgeport Club, where he continued to perform, and to oversee his real estate investments.

Phil Hardy and Dave Laing have noted that the arrangement of steel guitar, accordion, and trumpet that Dexter and his Texas Troopers brought to country music influenced a great number of performers that followed, from Gene Autry to Johnny Bond (*The Faber Companion to 20th Century Popular Music* [1990]). Additionally, many well-known performers have had success covering Dexter's songs, including Frank Sinatra, Ronnie Milsap, and Bob Wills. Dexter estimated the total number of songs he had written to be around 300 and declared himself happy with his accomplishments, saying "I had my share of hits, I have had some dogs too." Dexter's nimble reach had extended from the dusty floorboards of countless Texas roadhouses to the gleaming walkways of the Songwriter's Hall of Fame in Nashville, Tennessee, into which he was inducted on 11 October 1971, by the time he died in Lake Lewisville, Texas. Dexter was survived by his wife, Frankie (maiden name unknown), a daughter, and two sons.

• All of Dexter's surviving papers and correspondence are in the possession of family members. While there is no definitive book-length biography of Dexter, no country music reference work fails to cite his accomplishments and influence. Dorothy Horstman's *Sing Your Heart Out, Country Boy* (1975) contains a complete transcript of "Pistol Packin' Mama" along with the 1973 letter in which Dexter recounts his version of the inspiration behind the song. The best sources of biographical materials are the local newspapers of East Texas. An obituary is in the *New York Times*, 1 Feb. 1984.

EDWARD WHITELOCK

DEXTER, Franklin Bowditch (11 Sept. 1842–13 Aug. 1920), educator, librarian, and historian, was born in Fairhaven, Massachusetts, the son of Rodolphus Williams Dexter, a businessman, and Mary Hathaway Taber. He attended the Williston Seminary in preparation for Yale College, in New Haven, Connecticut, from which he graduated with an A.B. in 1861. He received an A.M. in 1864 and a Litt.D. in 1902. He taught Greek at the Collegiate and Commercial Institute in New Haven from 1861 to 1863 before returning to work at Yale.

Dexter was professionally associated with his beloved alma mater for the rest of his long and active life. He was librarian of the Linonian Society in 1863. He tutored mathematics and Greek from 1864 to 1867. He was an assistant in the college library in 1867 and 1868, and in 1868 and 1869 he was an assistant in the office of the college treasurer. During these years he labored diligently on Yale's triennial catalog, which provided a directory of all living graduates and obituaries of all deceased ones. Finally Dexter was appointed to the position he liked best—assistant librarian of the college. He held that position from 1869 to 1912. During this span of forty-three years he was also registrar of the college faculty (1869–1892), secretary of the Yale Corporation (1869–1899), and Larned Professor of American History (1877–1888). In 1880 Dexter married Theodosia Mary Wheeler; the couple had one child. Dexter's research during his later years of teaching mainly concerned colonial and early regional history. He was named assistant librarian emeritus when he retired in 1912.

Any account of Dexter's outwardly uneventful life is largely a listing of his publications. Early in his career he prepared *A Catalogue of the Linonian and Brothers Library* (1873). Some years later he undertook his most formidable task—*Biographical Sketches of the Graduates of Yale College with Annals of the College History* (6 vols., 1885–1912). A related shorter and less onerous effort was his *Sketch of the History of Yale University* (1887). During most of his career he also did yeoman's work as an editor of *Acts of the General Assembly of the State of Connecticut with Other Permanent Documents Respecting Yale College* (3 vols., 1871–1889), *Historical Catalogue of the First Church, New Haven . . . 1639–1914* (1914), *The Documentary History of Yale University under the Original Charter of the Collegiate School of Connecticut, 1701–1745* (1916), *Extracts from the Itineraries and Other Miscellanies of Ezra Stiles, D.D., L.L.D., 1755–1794, with a Selection from His Correspondence* (1916), *Jared Ingersoll Papers* (1918), and *New Haven Town Records* (3 vols., 1917, 1919, 1962), completed by Zara J. Power.

More interesting to most modern readers are Dexter's edition of the *Diary of David McClure, Doctor of Divinity, 1748–1820* (1899) and especially his edition of *The Literary Diary of Ezra Stiles* (3 vols., 1901). McClure, a Yale graduate of the class of 1769, was a clergyman who preached briefly and unsuccessfully to Delaware Indians in the Ohio Valley in 1772 and 1773 and returned to New England to become a pastor and teacher in New Hampshire and then Connecticut. Dexter edited McClure's interesting diary with great care. Stiles was a clergyman, scholar, professor, and president of Yale from 1778 to 1795. In the preface to his edition of Stiles's diary, Dexter explained that he omitted repetitious passages, quotations readily accessible elsewhere, many meditative passages, and numerous comments on the Holy Scriptures and on current reading. Yet what follows totals 1,806 pages, meticulously prepared and exhaustively annotated. In addition, Dexter compiled an index of eighty double-columned pages—the work of weeks, if not months, of painstaking care.

Dexter also assembled *A Selection from the Miscellaneous Historical Papers of Fifty Years* (1918). In addition, he published several articles in periodicals, on antiquarian, demographic, historical, sociological, and pedagogical topics. In his *Selection of Historical Papers* he reprinted two of these essays, one on the influence of English universities on New England, and the other offering population estimates in the American colonies. Dexter's solid contributions to historical scholarship gained him membership in the Massachusetts Historical Society and in the American Antiquarian Society; he was elected vice president of the latter in 1893.

Dexter's biographical sketches of Yale graduates have been a mine of information used by later interpretive scholars. One might expect his short 1887 history of Yale—it is only 108 pages—to be pleasantly anecdotal; however, it is loaded with names and length of service of numerous faculty members, figures on gifts to the school, the cost of various buildings, numbers of graduates (even data on their longevity), and the like. Another proof of his willingness to perform burdensome tasks is the fact that he prepared handwritten library cards of thousands of books in the Yale Library, which under his unflagging supervision grew from 50,000 volumes in 1867 to almost eight times that number by 1907.

Dexter was singlemindedly assiduous in his documentary research and editorial work. Although he could never be praised for his analysis or for stylistic felicity in anything he produced, he was universally admired for his accuracy and thoroughness. Dexter died in New Haven.

• Dexter's papers are in the Manuscript Division of the Library of Congress and in the libraries of the Princeton Theological Seminary and Yale University. Richard Warch, *School of the Prophets: Yale College, 1701–1740* (1973), praises Dexter as "a thorough and resourceful historian" and includes a bibliography of his major works. Brooks Mather Kelley, *Yale: A History* (1974), mentions Dexter briefly. An obituary is in the *New York Times*, 14 Aug. 1920.

ROBERT L. GALE

DEXTER, Henry Martyn (13 Aug. 1821–13 Nov. 1890), editor and historian, was born in Plympton, Massachusetts, the son of Mary Morton and Elijah Dexter, a clergyman. At the age of fifteen Dexter attended his father's alma mater, Brown, but studied there for only a year. He transferred to Yale and, while acquiring enabling funds by teaching school every summer, graduated in 1840. For one full year he taught and served as principal of an academy in Rochester, Massachusetts, and in 1841 began theological studies at Andover Seminary. He graduated in 1844, received ordination shortly thereafter, and in the same year married Emeline Augusta Palmer. At the time of his marriage Dexter also took up his first ministerial responsibilities, serving as pastor of the newly organized Franklin Street Congregational Church in Manchester, New

Hampshire. Five years later he moved to Boston, ministering there at the Pine Street Congregational Church (later Berkeley Temple) from 1849 to 1867.

Upon arriving in Boston, Dexter contributed occasional pieces to a recently established denominational weekly named *The Congregationalist*. Within two years he was made a member of the editorial staff and in 1856 became editor in chief, retaining that office for the rest of his life except for a brief hiatus in 1866. Additional evidence of his concern for denominational affairs came in 1858, when Dexter was one of the handful who succeeded in founding the *Congregational Quarterly*. A ministerial invitation from California in 1867 proved to be a catalyst regarding career plans. Instead of remaining in the ministry, Dexter resigned all clerical office and assumed the position of editor, publisher, and co-owner of his first periodical together with an acquired pioneer of religious journalism, the merged efforts issued as the *Congregationalist and Boston Recorder*.

Through his writings Dexter helped define the image of Congregationalism in his day, and he influenced plans for its future development as well. A painstakingly accurate scholar, he manifested great interest in his denomination's origins in England and Holland. Some of his other studies provided data on William Bradford and William Brewster of Plymouth Colony, John Eliot and the Mather family of Massachusetts Bay Colony, and the question of how Roger Williams contributed to the practice of religious freedom. Dexter expended immense energy in tracking down documentary evidence, accumulating in the course of his scholarly forays an impressive personal library that he bequeathed to Yale. His editorial skills also benefited many readers through his work on King Philip's War, Benjamin Church's subsequent military campaigns, and Congregational church councils over the years. These and other publications in American colonial history remain valuable today for their factual information, shrewd analysis, and enormous bibliographical apparatus.

While open-hearted and genial, Dexter was a strong champion of democratic ways in denominational organization. He had a formidable bias in favor of the Puritans, and he was capable of producing one-sided narratives on their behalf. When discussing church policy he argued that Congregationalism was the closest version of the New Testament example to be found among contemporary churches. In 1877 he delivered the Southworth Lectures at Andover and two years later published them as *Congregationalism of the Last Three Hundred Years, as Seen in Its Literature . . . .* This volume appeared at an opportune time, adding its impetus to a burgeoning self-awareness as Congregational churches developed into a nation-wide denomination. He was recognized as one of the foremost expounders of his denomination's past and in 1880 served as moderator of the National Council of the Congregational Churches of the United States, where 276 delegates from twenty-five states and territories met to strengthen the church's prospects for growth.

Further notice of his eminence among ecclesiastical statesmen came in 1890, when Dexter was invited to preach the opening sermon at the first International Congregational Council to be held in London, England. He died at his home in New Bedford, Massachusetts, before the assembly convened.

• A large collection of Dexter's research notes is housed in the Congregational Library in Boston, Mass. In addition to printed sermons, tracts, and memorials, Dexter's most important books are *Congregationalism: What It Is; Whence It Is; How It Works . . .* (1865); *The Church Policy of the Pilgrims* (1870); and *A Handbook of Congregationalism* (1880). An unfinished work was edited and rewritten by his son Morton Dexter and published posthumously as *The England and Holland of the Pilgrims . . .* (1905).

HENRY WARNER BOWDEN

DEXTER, Samuel (16 Mar. 1726–10 June 1810), merchant and political leader, was born in Dedham, Massachusetts, the son of the Reverend Samuel Dexter, the minister of Dedham's first church, and Catherina Mears. Apprenticed to merchant Samuel Barrett in Boston, the younger Dexter made a sufficient fortune to enable him to retire at the age of thirty-six to his hometown. Meanwhile, in 1748 he married Hannah Sigourney, with whom he had five children, four of whom survived to adulthood.

Dexter switched from commerce to politics in the 1760s, representing Dedham in the Massachusetts House of Representatives from 1764 to 1768. He was elected to the Council, chosen by the incoming House of Representatives and outgoing Council, from 1766 to 1774, but his firm support of the revolutionary movement caused Governor Francis Bernard to veto his election in 1766 and 1767. He was allowed to sit then until 1774, when once again his political stance caused Governor Thomas Gage to veto him.

When Massachusetts revolted against Britain, Dexter was well positioned to take a place among the leaders. Chosen to the Supreme Executive Council of State, he was also elected receiver general, or treasurer, by the General Court but refused to serve in the latter position because he disagreed with other Massachusetts leaders over military strategy. Instead he suddenly retired from public life and moved from Dedham to Woodstock, Connecticut, in the spring of 1775. Dexter thought concentrating American militia near Boston to meet the trained British regulars in pitched battle sheer folly and simply abandoned the revolution when his plan to draw the redcoats into the countryside and overwhelm them was rejected. His abrupt move to Connecticut caused some to question his loyalty, which undoubtedly aggravated the second reason for his retirement. Dexter suffered from nervous disorders, perhaps psychosomatic, upset stomachs, and other ailments that by the fall of 1775 prevented him from going outdoors except in the best weather. He recovered sufficiently in Connecticut to resume his mercantile business. Dexter seemed content to stay out of the political world; he refused election to the Connecticut General Assembly in 1778.

Following a smallpox epidemic in Woodstock, Dexter returned to Dedham in 1784 and served in the Massachusetts General Court the following year. His wife died in 1785, and in 1786 he moved to Weston and in 1800 to Mendon, Massachusetts, where he died. Despite receiving a handful of votes for the Massachusetts legislature, he seems to have retired permanently from politics when he moved to Weston. Instead, he turned his attention to religion and wrote tracts, one of which survives: "Thoughts upon Several Passages of Scripture Both in the Old and New Testament, Relative to Jacob and Esau with Incidental Excursions" (1791). Here he defended Esau, who sold his inheritance for a mess of pottage when in dire straits and argued that the act was not sufficient to ensure Esau's eternal damnation. In an eccentric 37-page will Dexter left $5,000 to Harvard College for the study of divinity. The will also stipulated that he be buried in a 3.5-acre burying ground he left to the church of Woodstock, on the condition his grave have no marker. This final desire for obscurity symbolizes the life of a man who interested himself temporarily in the three great vocations of his time—politics, commerce, and religion—but who retired and moved on several occasions due to the strain he encountered dealing with a volatile and revolutionary world.

• Some of Dexter's letters are at the Massachusetts Historical Society. Clarence W. Bowen, *History of Woodstock, Connecticut* (1926), pp. 179–95, recounts nearly everything known about Dexter. See the obituary by Samuel Dexter, Jr., in the *Monthly Anthology* 9 (June 1810): 3–7, and C. A. Staples, *Samuel Dexter* (1892), for further information.

WILLIAM PENCAK

DEXTER, Timothy (22 Jan. 1747–22 Oct. 1806), merchant, was born in Malden, Massachusetts, the son of Nathan Dexter and Esther Brintnall, farmers. As a boy, after limited schooling, he was first indentured to a Malden farm. Later he apprenticed to a leather dresser in nearby Charlestown. In 1769 Dexter moved to Newburyport, a commercial entrepôt at the mouth of the Merrimack River, forty miles north of Boston. There he opened a leather shop called the Sign of the Glove. In 1770 Dexter married an older widow, Elizabeth (Lord) Frothingham, of moderate means and the mother of four children. They had two children of their own.

After the revolutionary war Dexter bought depreciated Continental notes well below face value. When the new federal government in 1791 resolved to redeem the currency at par, Dexter became wealthy. Soon he became famous for his bartering and speculative genius. Among his wilder reported ventures were shipments of warming pans and woolen mittens to the West Indies. The pans were sold to sugar plantations as ladles for molasses syrup, and the mittens were purchased by a Baltic-bound vessel. Dexter's trades became legendary and were embellished by him and by others.

Despite his affluence Dexter found that refined Federalist circles were beyond reach. In 1791 he ac-

quired the fine brick home of Nathaniel Tracy, a prominent merchant who had been ruined by wartime privateering losses. The gentry, although also mostly nouveau riche, were unimpressed. They viewed Dexter as crude, a vulgarian, and slighted him.

Dexter was a showman, known for histrionics and for letter writing, incessantly striving to increase his fame. An example was the 4 July 1793 wine studded opening soirée of the new Essex-Merrimack toll bridge, in which Dexter was a major investor. Standing atop a table, Dexter delivered an incoherent speech, reported later by his inebriated friends as "truly Ciceronian." He conveyed his good-natured views regularly to the Newburyport *Impartial Herald*. To the amusement of its readers, he wrote in chains of ungrammatical sentences lacking punctuation and riddled with misspellings. But with encouragement from flatterers, Dexter sustained an elevated opinion of his self-importance.

In 1795, responding to increasing congestion, Newburyport citizens clamored for an enclosed market house. Dexter offered to donate one provided it was called Dexter Hall, an offer rejected by town officials. Afterward he removed to Chester, New Hampshire, where people proclaimed him "Lord Timothy Dexter, King of Chester." He returned to Newburyport within two years, and the appellation stayed. Jonathan Plummer, Jr., a fish peddler, preacher, and longtime Dexter admirer, composed a welcoming ode signed "Poet Lauriet to his Lordship." Subsidized by Dexter, Plummer remained his laureate and boosted his patron with exalted praise.

The historian Mrs. E. Vale Smith wrote in 1854 that Dexter was viewed generally as "a fool, with a slight mixture of the knave," whose passion for vanity was so "inordinate as to lead him into all sorts of absurdities" (p. 175). He bought a three-story Georgian mansion crowned with an eagle-capped cupola, formerly owned by the distinguished merchant Jonathan Jackson. He made the residence and its grounds into a remarkable property. His biographer, Samuel L. Knapp, described the residence as "a princely chateau." Having achieved prominence by his magnificent home, a pleased Dexter welcomed a parade of visitors.

In 1801 Dexter announced plans to construct an outdoor museum on his grounds. It featured about forty life-sized statues representing world-renowned personalities, including Presidents Washington, Adams, and Jefferson, as well as Dexter himself, under which reportedly was written, "I am first in the East." Dexter's celebrity status rose; passers-by came to view this spectacle. He also built an elaborate tomb for himself on his property and arranged for a splendid mock funeral (conducted while he was still alive), in which his family participated. It was observed by a large invited crowd. He was also known for his public charity, like the church bell to the Presbyterian Society of Newburyport.

But Dexter's eccentric lifestyle also induced derision and an unwelcome notoriety. An 1805 full-length caricature shows Dexter strolling with a tall cane, wearing an oversized hat with tassels, a coat with tails, and pantaloons, tied at the ankles, followed by a pig-like dog. By his will, Dexter left $2,000, out of his total $35,000 estate, which had diminished, for the benefit of Newburyport's poor. His detractors, however, credited Dexter's conspicuous generosity to his publicity needs.

In later life, exacerbated by alcohol abuse, Dexter's actions became more bizarre. His family life in a shambles, the lonely and increasingly senile Dexter began to communicate his views publicly. In 1802 he produced a literary curiosity, a 24-page book entitled *A Pickle for the Knowing Ones; or, Plain Truths in a Homespun Dress*. This jumble of views on diverse, unrelated subjects during his life and time, written in his nonsensical style, was contemptuously critiqued. In it, Dexter wrote, "Ime the first Lord in the younited States of Amercary." An 1838 edition, which may have been a parody written by an editor, but reading like pure Dexter, included nearly a page of punctuation with an invitation that readers "may peper and solt it as they plese."

During his lifetime "Lord" Timothy Dexter, the individualist, had become romantic folklore. As the novelist John P. Marquand wrote in *Timothy Dexter Revisited*, parents began to point out Dexter "to their children as something rich and strange that should be remembered" (p. 292). He died in Newburyport and was buried not in the elaborate tomb of his museum but in a grave marked by a simple stone. Dexter continues to be a mysterious character: was he the deluded, vain, object of ridicule, or was he bantering with his amused public?

• The best books on Dexter are by John P. Marquand, *Lord Timothy Dexter of Newburyport, Mass.* (1925) and *Timothy Dexter Revisited* (1960), which are well researched and speak to Dexter the person. Early editions of Dexter's *A Pickle for the Knowing Ones* are in the James Duncan Phillips Library of the Peabody & Essex Museum, Salem, Mass. Samuel L. Knapp, of Newburyport, wrote an early biography, *Life of Timothy Dexter embracing Sketches of the Eccentric Characters That Composed His Associates* (1838), but it contains some errors. The following books have several pages on Dexter: John J. Currier, *The History of Newburyport, Massachusetts, 1764–1905* (2 vols., 1906–1909; repr. 1977–1978); Mrs. E. Vale Smith [E. Vale Blake], *History of Newburyport: From the Earliest Settlement of the Country to the Present Time* (1854); and William C. Todd, *Biographical and Other Articles* (1901).

RONALD N. TAGNEY

DE YOUNG, Michel Henry, Jr. (30 Sept. 1849–15 Feb. 1925), newspaper publisher, was born in St. Louis, Missouri, the son of Michel H. De Young, a banker, and Amelia Morange. De Young's father was a Dutch Jew who changed his name from Meichel De Jong when he immigrated to the United States and settled in St. Louis. His father's career proved unsuccessful, and he moved the family to California in 1854 but died en route. With his older brother Charles, De Young—who came to be called Harry—wrote for his high school paper. Since San Francisco had a large number of theaters, the two brothers decided in 1865 to publish a playbill titled *Dramatic Chronicle: A Daily Record of Affairs Local, Critical and Theatrical.*

The *Chronicle* was distributed free to readers and relied on advertising entirely at first to finance the operation. Circulation rose steadily from the initial 7,000 copies printed, and the De Youngs started charging for copies. In addition to notices about plays, the *Chronicle* soon used news items taken from the telegraph wires, editorials, and original contributions from rising local writers such as Mark Twain and Bret Harte. Gradually the De Young brothers developed their news-gathering skills and learned what type of items attracted readers. After the *Chronicle* scooped other San Francisco papers in publishing the news of President Abraham Lincoln's assassination, the De Young brothers considered transforming it into a regular newspaper. The shift was completed in September 1868 when the paper's name was changed to the *Daily Morning Chronicle* and sold for five cents per copy. The *Chronicle* appeared in a four-page, seven-column format. Like many dailies at this time, the paper also published a weekly edition for distant readers.

The *San Francisco Chronicle* expanded to eight pages in 1869 with its first Sunday edition. The paper remained on top of breaking news events, including an extra edition after an earthquake in 1868, but it was best known for sensational scandal-mongering. Charles's editorials gained notoriety for acid attacks on major public figures, yet the *Chronicle* maintained editorial independence. The paper added a sports editor in the 1870s, and single-tax advocate Henry George wrote several editorials for the *Chronicle* between 1870 and 1873. In 1875 De Young arranged for the *Chronicle* to launch its own wire service through an agreement with the Associated Press, where De Young was a director for twenty-four years. (De Young was also elected president of the Western Press Association in 1881.) When the *Chronicle* moved to a new building in 1879, it contained one of the first telephone switchboards in San Francisco and was the first West Coast daily to hire a correspondent to cover Pacific and Far East affairs. It also led West Coast papers in converting to Linotypes and the new stereotype presses in the 1880s. In 1885 the *Chronicle* started a weather warning service to aid fruit growers in protecting their orchards from freeze damage. By the mid-1880s the *Chronicle's* circulation ranged between 25,000 and 50,000, the largest of any San Francisco daily. De Young married a Gentile woman, Katherine Deane, in 1880 and he later converted to his wife's Roman Catholic faith. The couple had a son who died of typhus in 1913 and four daughters.

Both De Young and his brother Charles were noted for their fearless and reckless use of the *Chronicle* to attack individuals they disliked. As a result, San Franciscans showed little affection toward the family. After a particularly bitter mayoral campaign in 1879, the candidate opposed by the *Chronicle*, Isaac Kalloch of the Workingmen's party, won the election. Kalloch's administration was discredited in part by continued hostility from the *Chronicle*. Kalloch retaliated by verbally assailing De Young's brother from the pulpit of the church where Kalloch was the minister. Finally, in 1880, an angry Charles went to Kalloch's church and shot the mayor in the leg. Soon afterward, Kalloch's son entered Charles's *Chronicle* office and shot him to death. De Young took over complete operation of the *Chronicle* upon his brother's death and continued the sometimes vicious editorials made famous by his sibling. De Young also launched a gossip column in the *Chronicle*, but he usually offered to withhold printing salacious news if the target celebrity would pay a bribe. Once in the 1880s, the *Chronicle* attacked the integrity of the Spreckels family, who had built a major fortune from their Hawaiian sugar business and owned the *San Diego Union-Tribune*. In response, Adolph Spreckels entered De Young's office at the *Chronicle* and fired a shot at the editor, who ducked and was not wounded. The two families continued their bitter feud for decades thereafter.

Of course the *Chronicle* eagerly engaged major political issues, whether local, state, or national. A post–Civil War economic boom in California led major railroad and construction companies to engage in corrupt practices in their bitter competition for profits. The *Chronicle* was the only San Francisco newspaper to back a new constitution in 1878 supported by reformers as a means of eliminating corruption. The constitution recognized labor rights and established a state commission to regulate the railroads. When the railroads retaliated by sponsoring a press muzzling law in the legislature, the *Chronicle* fought fiercely for freedom of the press and the bill was defeated. Another constant issue in California after the Civil War was Asian immigration. Railroad and other large businesses recruited cheap Asian labor and wanted to keep the state open to immigrants. The *Chronicle* joined the Hearst-owned *San Francisco Examiner* in favoring various legislative proposals to limit or exclude Asian immigrants, primarily Chinese and Japanese, and frequently resorted to racist language in describing the Asian threat. The *Chronicle* exposed and opposed rampant local political corruption in San Francisco, especially during the era of Abraham "Boss" Ruef in the early years of the twentieth century.

From its founding in 1865, the *Chronicle* was staunchly Republican in politics, so that it usually opposed the Hearsts' Democrat-oriented *Examiner*. For example, it supported the Republican protective tariff policy. Yet it demonstrated that the party would not always determine its positions. While providing wide coverage to world news, the *Chronicle* supported an isolationist foreign policy that ran against the expansionist Republican foreign policy of the 1880s and 1890s. De Young was an active participant in state Republican party circles and served as delegate to three Republican national conventions. Most of the great newspaper families in California—De Young, Hearst, Spreckels—seemed to desire seats in the U.S. Senate, and De Young unsuccessfully sought the Republican nomination for the Senate in the 1892 election. The *Chronicle* opposed U.S. involvement in Cuba before the Spanish-American War as well as U.S. intervention in World War I before Congress declared war in 1917.

De Young's constant endeavors to promote San Francisco culture led to the establishment of an opera and a symphony orchestra. When De Young helped organize the San Francisco Mid-Winter Fair in 1885, the proceeds became the basis for founding a municipal museum later named in honor of the family. The permanent structure was situated in Golden Gate Park complete with a statue of De Young. The promotion of growth in San Francisco also revealed an ulterior motive for De Young, since he sold much of the real estate used in expansions. De Young's other civic contributions included service as chief executive officer for the 1894 San Francisco Exposition as well as participation in expositions held in Paris, Chicago, and Omaha. The *Chronicle*'s 1888 building, the city's first skyscraper, was severely damaged by the San Francisco earthquake of 1906. Nonetheless, De Young demonstrated his confidence in San Francisco's future by building a high-rise successor, the first new postquake downtown building. Although Sunday comic strips had existed for more than a decade, the *San Francisco Chronicle* became the first newspaper to print a daily cartoon in 1907 with the appearance of Bud Fisher's "Mutt and Jeff." De Young was able to acquire from longtime rival John Spreckels one of the *Chronicle*'s two morning competitors in 1913, the *San Francisco Call*, which suspended publication. Upon De Young's death in 1925, the *San Francisco Chronicle* continued to be operated by his four daughters.

De Young learned how to run a newspaper and print what the public expected at a very young age. He transformed his playbill into one of the nation's premier dailies. The *San Francisco Chronicle* demonstrated the importance of complete coverage of stories by reporters as well as unequivocal editorial positions. The *Chronicle* understood that its responsibility was more than just the local community, although promoting civic affairs remained a priority for De Young. Clearly, the De Youngs invited criticism by their use of gossip and scandal to promote sales of the paper. Finally, De Young was eager to embrace new technology and new formats to improve the communication with readers.

• The De Young papers are in the Bancroft Library at the University of California, Berkeley. De Young wrote an essay, "California Journalism," in *Making of a Newspaper*, ed. Melville Phillips (1913). The most authoritative biographical information about De Young is in Stephen D. Bray, "M. H. De Young," in *Dictionary of American Literary Biography: American Newspaper Journalists, 1901–1925*, ed. Perry J. Ashley (1984); and John Philip Young, *Journalism in California* (1915). An obituary is in the *San Francisco Chronicle*, 16 Feb. 1925.

DANIEL WEBSTER HOLLIS III

DE ZAVALA, Adina Emily (28 Nov. 1861–1 Mar. 1955), teacher and historic preservationist, was born at De Zavala Point, Harris County, Texas, the oldest of six children of Augustine De Zavala and Julia Tyrell. Her paternal grandfather was Lorenzo de Zavala, a native of Yucatan and first ad interim vice president of the Republic of Texas. In 1867 her father, a merchant and shipbuilder, moved his family to Galveston, Texas. Adina was enrolled as a student at the Ursuline Convent there from 1871 to 1878. In 1878 the family moved to Shavano, Bexar County, Texas, where Augustine De Zavala owned a ranch and general store. Adina De Zavala enrolled at Sam Houston Normal Institute in Huntsville, Texas, in 1879 and received a teacher's certificate in 1881. She taught elementary school in Terrell, Texas, from 1884 to 1886; in Austin in 1890; and in San Antonio from 1893 to 1907. Her father died in 1892, and in 1897 she and her mother and sisters moved from the ranch into a home in San Antonio, where she resided for most of the rest of her life. She resigned from the San Antonio school system in January 1907, after receiving a reprimand from the school board for "assuming an independent and insubordinate attitude toward her superior officers," and devoted the rest of her life to patriotic and historical organizations and to historical writing and journalism.

In 1889 De Zavala organized a group of largely middle-class Anglo-American San Antonio women to meet and discuss the teaching of Texas history and the preservation of sites connected with the Spanish and Mexican periods of Texas history. In 1892 this group began an effort to preserve the surviving grounds and mission buildings of the San Antonio de Valero Mission, better known as the Alamo, and in March 1893 the group was formally organized as the De Zavala Chapter of the Daughters of the Republic of Texas, a statewide patriotic group incorporated in 1891. The State of Texas had purchased the mission chapel from the Catholic church in 1883, but the adjacent convent, also known as the "long barracks," was owned by the Hugo-Schmelzer Grocery Company and had been remodeled into a retail store. Adina De Zavala obtained an option to purchase the Hugo-Schmelzer property in 1892 and then set about raising funds to do so. In 1904 she persuaded Clara Driscoll, a wealthy ranchwoman, to join the De Zavala chapter and purchase the property; in 1905 she drafted legislation that, when passed later that year by the Texas legislature, provided for the state to purchase the property from Driscoll and place control of it, and the Alamo chapel, with the Daughters of the Republic of Texas. However, De Zavala and Driscoll and their followers disagreed on restoration procedures. De Zavala and her followers wished to emphasize the site's history as a mission, while the Driscoll faction wished to focus on the 1836 battle, which they believed to have been fought primarily in the chapel. Despite De Zavala's opposition (at one point in 1908 she locked herself in the building for three days, receiving nationwide attention), most of the Hugo-Schmelzer property, which later proved to contain significant portions of the eighteenth-century mission convent, was destroyed and replaced with a landscaped wall that was felt to improve the setting of the chapel. The battle between the two factions for control of the state Daughters of the Republic of Texas organization went on in Texas courts until 1912, when a series of rulings settled it in favor of the Driscoll faction.

In 1912 De Zavala organized the Texas Historical and Landmarks Association, inspired, she said, by the success of Charles Lummis's California Landmarks Club in preserving the Spanish mission of California. The predominantly Anglo-American association eventually established chapters in New Braunfels, Goliad, Refugio, San Patricio, Harlingen, and Crockett and placed thirty-eight markers on significant sites. In 1915 De Zavala began efforts to preserve the eighteenth-century building on San Antonio's Military Plaza known as the Spanish Governor's Palace, which was finally purchased by the city in 1928 and restored in 1930. For many years, starting in 1902, she was active in the efforts to preserve the four Spanish missions in San Antonio, which now comprise San Antonio Missions National Historic Park. In the 1920s she led the opposition to replacing the Spanish street names of San Antonio with English ones. She collected historical documents for the Texas State Historical Association and the Texas State Archives, and in 1926–1928 her research was instrumental in locating and marking the sites of the Mision de San Francisco de los Tejas (1690–1693) and the Mision de Santisimo Nombre de Maria (1690–1692), the earliest Spanish missions in Texas.

In 1901 De Zavala edited Fr. Edmond J. P. Schmitt's *The "Antiquities of Mexico" by Lord Kingsborough: A Collation.* Her other publications include *The Story of the Siege and Fall of the Alamo: A Resume* (1911) and *History and Legends of the Alamo and Other Missions in and around San Antonio* (1917). From 1919 to 1923 she was editor of a San Antonio periodical variously titled the *Interstate Index*, the *Pioneer and Interstate Index*, the *Pioneer*, *Texasland*, and the *Texas Pioneer*. She was a charter member of the Texas State Historical Association and a member of the United Daughters of the Confederacy, the Texas Folk-lore Society, the Texas Philosophical Society, and the Texas Women's Press Association. She died in San Antonio.

De Zavala, who never married, was an early and lifelong advocate for the recognition of Texas's Hispanic heritage. She was inspired partially by her own Hispanic and Catholic heritage and partially by the romantic Hispanicism that characterized the attitude of many middle-class Anglo-Americans in the Southwest during the first two decades of the twentieth century. Although intensely proud of her grandfather's public record, her own associations in San Antonio were primarily with its Anglo-American rather than Hispanic population. She was active in women's patriotic and professional organizations but never became involved in party politics, in the suffrage movement, or in the many Mexican and Mexican-American organizations that existed in San Antonio during her lifetime. Although not a widely published scholar, she was an indefatigable researcher and publicist, and she made a significant contribution to the preservation of the major eighteenth-century structures remaining in Texas.

• De Zavala's papers are at the Center for American History at the University of Texas at Austin. The only biography is Luther Robert Ables, "The Work of Adina De Zavala" (master's thesis, Mexico City College, 1955). See also L. Robert Ables, "The Second Battle of the Alamo," *Southwestern Historical Quarterly* 70, no. 3 (1967): 372–413. An obituary is in the *New York Times*, 3 Mar. 1955.

LONN TAYLOR

D'HARNONCOURT, René (17 May 1901–13 Aug. 1968), museum director, was born in Vienna, Austria, the son of Hubert d'Harnoncourt, an amateur historian, and Julianna Mittrowsky. Both of his parents came from noble families with large landholdings in Austria and Czechoslovakia, and d'Harnoncourt was born with the title of count, which he later dropped. Having been tutored at home, he attended the University of Graz from 1918 to 1921, studying chemistry and pursuing his interest in art outside of school by painting, drawing, collecting prints, and mounting shows of contemporary art with a group of friends. In 1922 he went on to the Technische Hochschule in Vienna and wrote a thesis, "The Creosote Contents of Certain Coals in Southern Yugoslavia," which was published in the German technical journal *Brennstoff-Chemie*. D'Harnoncourt did not finish his degree, because in 1924 the breakup of the Austro-Hungarian Empire led to the loss of a family estate that was to have supported him.

Economic upheaval in Austria convinced René d'Harnoncourt to seek his fortune overseas; he first considered the United States, but, finding the immigration quota already full, he instead went to Mexico. Arriving in Veracruz in 1925, he quickly made his way to Mexico City, where he lived hand-to-mouth for a year, painting postcards, designing advertising posters, and arranging shop windows. In time he found work advising collectors of Mexican antiques and thus acquired his expertise in pre-Columbian and Mexican folk art. Hired to handle Mexican curios for the Sonora News Company, an antique store, d'Harnoncourt expanded his responsibilities to include contemporary folk art and painting and showed the work of Diego Rivera, Miguel Covarrubias, José Orozco, and Rufino Tamayo. His work at the store brought d'Harnoncourt to the attention of David Morrow, the American ambassador to Mexico, and his wife Elizabeth, whose Cuernavaca house he helped decorate with Mexican art and handicrafts and a mural he painted himself. In 1929 the Mexican Ministry of Education asked d'Harnoncourt to gather forty-eight collections of Mexican folk art to be sent to schools in each state then in the United States. In a bid to improve Americans' opinion of their southern neighbor, Ambassador Morrow convinced the Carnegie Corporation to finance a traveling show of Mexican art in 1930 and recommended d'Harnoncourt as the expert to oversee the project. Accompanying the show to eight American cities in fourteen months, d'Harnoncourt helped install it and gave more than 200 talks on Mexican art and handicrafts. During the Chicago leg of the exhibition, he met a fashion editor named Sarah Carr, to whom he became engaged; in 1932 he returned to Austria to obtain an emigration visa. He came back to the United States and married Carr in 1933; they had one child.

Moving to New York City in the mid-1930s, d'Harnoncourt produced a radio program called "Art in America" for NBC and taught art and art history at Sarah Lawrence College, but soon he began working with Native American art. In 1937 he accepted an appointment as assistant general manager of the newly formed Indian Arts and Crafts Board, an arm of the Department of the Interior. Working for the board through 1943, d'Harnoncourt helped Native Americans obtain some economic independence through native crafts. These efforts, combined with his earlier stint with the Mexican government, led to his involvement with the American Indian exhibition at San Francisco's Golden Gate International Exposition in 1939.

That show evolved into d'Harnoncourt's first project for the Museum of Modern Art (MoMA): as a guest curator and exhibit designer, he expanded the exhibition to more than 1,000 pieces to become Indian Art of the United States in 1941. Colored walls and dramatic lighting evoked the American landscape, Navajo sand painters were on hand to demonstrate their work in the galleries, and a totem pole outside the museum was visible from Fifth Avenue.

In 1943 Nelson Rockefeller, coordinator of the Office of Inter-American Affairs, brought d'Harnoncourt to work for him in the art section of that organization. But Rockefeller, who had long-standing ties to MoMA, thought d'Harnoncourt's tact, charm, and obvious ability might be of greater help at the museum. Moving to MoMA in 1944, d'Harnoncourt had a variety of titles until 1949, when he became director, although he had led the committee that directed the museum during much of his first five years there. One of his earliest and most important decisions was to retain the previous director (and MoMA founder) Alfred Barr, who had been removed from his post as a result of disagreements with the trustees. Barr and d'Harnoncourt worked together for the rest of their careers at MoMA, Barr providing the scholarly knowledge of art while d'Harnoncourt smoothed relations with the board and the staff.

Known throughout his career for his innovative and effective installation techniques, d'Harnoncourt was wary of its snares, commenting in 1960, "Installation is terribly dangerous. It's full of terribly seductive pitfalls. You mustn't just make things look desirable—dramatization for its own sake must be avoided. Your job is to help the visitor see for himself and judge for himself what the object has to offer." In shows like Timeless Aspects of Modern Art (1948), Ancient Art of the Andes (1954), Recent Sculpture USA (1958), and retrospectives of the work of Jean Arp and Pablo Picasso's sculpture, d'Harnoncourt was praised for achieving these goals. Remembered as a genial giant (he was more than 6'6" and weighed about 230 pounds) who had excellent diplomatic skills, he oversaw the physical expansion of the museum as well as its growing reputation in the art world. A fire in the building during a Georges Seurat show in 1958 demonstrated d'Harnoncourt's special dedication and skill with people: after accompanying firefighters in search of an employee believed to be trapped in the building, he helped hand paintings out to safety and then made sure each lender to the show received a telegram assuring them their artwork was safe. While d'Harnoncourt did not pretend to be an art connoisseur outside of his own field of expertise, in his role as museum director his charm and kindness may have been more important in establishing the museum on a sound footing.

D'Harnoncourt retired from MoMA in July 1968; a few weeks later, he was killed by a drunk driver while he was out for a morning walk near his cottage on Long Island.

• René d'Harnoncourt's papers are at the Museum of Modern Art. His years in Mexico are covered in Elizabeth Morrow, *Casa Mañana* (1932) and *The Mexican Years* (1953), as well as d'Harnoncourt's own *Mexicana* (1931). Robert Fay Schrader, *The Indian Arts and Crafts Board* (1983), discusses d'Harnoncourt's work there, while his years at MoMA are covered in Russell Lynes, *Good Old Modern* (1973), and in Sam Hunter's introduction to *The Museum of Modern Art, New York* (1984). "Imperturbable Noble," Geoffrey T. Hellman's profile of d'Harnoncourt in the *New Yorker*, 7 May 1960, pp. 49–112, is largely in the subject's own words. See also Museum of Modern Art, *Rene d'Harnoncourt: A Tribute* (1968), and Elizabeth Shaw, "Rene d'Harnoncourt," *Art News*, Oct. 1979, pp. 138–40. A 1968 interview with d'Harnoncourt is in the Oral History Collection of Columbia University. An obituary is in the *New York Times*, 14 Aug. 1968.

BETHANY NEUBAUER

DIAT, Louis Felix (5 May 1885–29 Aug. 1957), chef de cuisine, was born in Montmarault, France, the son of Louis Denis Diat, a shoemaker, and Anne Alajoinine. Trouble at school drove young Louis toward his life's work: left-handed, he was persecuted by a schoolmaster who rapped his offending hand with a heavy metal ruler. When he began to walk in his sleep, his parents made a plan; if he would try to write with his right hand, he would be allowed the honor of helping his mother in the kitchen. He proved so enthusiastic and adept that when he was fourteen his father purchased a two-year apprenticeship at Maison Calondre, a fine restaurant in nearby Moulins. Diat then moved to Paris to the kitchens of the Hôtel Bristol and then the Hôtel du Rhin.

In 1903 he became chef potager, making soups and stocks at the Hôtel Ritz in Paris. César Ritz was a connoisseur and inspirer of the refined, delicate cuisine that was evolving at the turn of the century, preferring nuances and flavor to the architectural pièces montées (often stale) and the parade of exotic dishes that had earlier characterized haute cuisine. Ritz sent Diat to his Ritz Hotel in London in 1906, where he served as assistant saucier under the celebrated chef de cuisine Émile Malley, son of his mother's best friend. So quickly did Diat rise that at the age of twenty-nine he was appointed chef de cuisine at the new Ritz-Carlton Hotel in New York City, built in 1910 by William Harris and Robert Goelet, who intended it to be the finest hotel in America. Arriving in New York in October 1910, Diat was naturalized in 1916. He married Suzanne Clemence Prudhon on 20 January 1913; they had one child.

Diat's intent was to create food at the Ritz-Carlton that would rival any served in the Old World. The kitchens occupied two basement floors of the hotel. This domain boasted a French bakery oven, an ice cream plant, huge water tanks for live trout and lobsters, and tremendous refrigerators and cold rooms. "We did everything for the kitchen right on the premises, everything. We roasted our own coffee, even made the chocolates and bonbons for the guests' gift boxes on such occasions as the openings of the opera and the horse show," Diat told his collaborator, the home economist and food writer Helen E. Ridley. Diat's staff of highly trained, well-paid workers numbered over 100. All the special chefs—potager, poissonier, entremetier, saucier, and pâtissier—had been recruited from Europe's finest restaurants.

Happily, there was always sufficient money to run the Ritz-Carlton's restaurants, including the Oval Room and the Oak Room, room service, and the many debutante parties, weddings, and society events. It took the new chef months, however, to find provisions that met his standards. The necessary fresh herbs, baby vegetables, shallots, leeks, and cress were unavailable at first. Soon, however, market gardeners began raising crops expressly for Diat. Cream that approximated the thick, prized cream of Normandy was shipped daily from a farm in Vermont. The kitchen staff worked from early morning to late at night, seven days a week. For forty-one years Diat worked fourteen-hour days, six days a week to obtain culinary perfection.

Diat created many dishes, but his most celebrated is vichyssoise, named for an important spa town in his native Burgundy. With vichyssoise the chef recalled his favorite breakfast, a hearty leek and potato soup that had warmed him on his long walk to school; Diat's genius was to turn a traditional hot soup into an elegant cold one. Before air conditioning, the Ritz added the Roof Garden restaurant, unimpeded by high-rise buildings, to catch the breezes from the Hudson and East rivers. Even so, cold food was welcome. Chilled, creamy vichyssoise, brightened by chopped chives, first appeared on the menu in July 1917. Diat asked Charles Schwab, chairman of U.S. Steel and a Ritz regular, to try the soup. "No one else has tasted it. If you like it, I'll put it on the menu. If you don't, I'll forget it," he said. Schwab later phoned to say that it was the best soup he had ever eaten. Vichyssoise remained, to delight diners from then on.

Diat gave many interviews and sought to improve the quality of America's food. In his publications, *Cooking à la Ritz* (1941), *Louis Diat's Home Cookbook: French Cooking for Americans* (1946), and *Sauces, French and Famous* (1951), he attempted to explain French cooking so that readers could duplicate it. In appreciation for "services in bringing to America the highest type of French culinary art," the French government made him *Chevalier du Mérite Agricole.*

A victim of ever-rising costs, an outmoded plant, and rising real estate values, the Ritz-Carlton closed in May 1951. Until the end Diat's standards remained unfailingly high and his staff of seventy-seven among the highest paid in the United States. With the assistance of Helen Ridley, who had helped with all his books, Diat regularly wrote a column in *Gourmet* magazine, beginning in 1946. He died in New York City, not living to see the publication of his last book, *Gourmet's Basic French Cooking* (1961).

• Diat's papers, including mementos and the indexed looseleaf notebooks in which his secretary had recorded his formulas for almost all of his dishes, were given to Helen E. Ridley by Diat's wife. Ridley and Diat wrote prefaces to *Gourmet's Basic French Cooking* (1961). An article on Diat by Helen E. Ridley appeared in *The Pleasures of Cooking* (Mar.-Apr. 1983). Portraits of Diat are in *Collier's*, 3 May 1945, and the *New Yorker*, 2 Dec. 1950. His long obituary in the *New York Times*, 30 Aug. 1957, contains the recipe for vichyssoise.

LYN STALLWORTH

DIAZ, Abby Morton (22 Nov. 1821–1 Apr. 1904), teacher, writer, and social reformer, was born Abigail Morton in Plymouth, Massachusetts, the daughter of Ichabod Morton, a shipbuilder, and Patty Weston. She descended from George Morton, author of "Mourt's Relation," the first printed record of the Plymouth settlement. After his wife's early death, Abby's father remarried and had five sons.

According to her own account, Abby grew up in a reform-conscious family, to which William Lloyd Garrison, Bronson Alcott, Lydia Maria Child, and Theodore Parker were heroes. Abby's father, a Unitarian, worked with Horace Mann to establish normal schools and engaged in the movements for temperance and the abolition of slavery. When Abby was four, he enrolled her in the "Fragment Society," founded and directed by his sister Sally Morton Stephens to distribute used clothing to the poor. At twelve she joined the Plymouth Juvenile Anti-slavery Society; she became its secretary and paid the twenty-five-cent weekly dues by knitting garters and going without butter.

After finishing at the Plymouth high school for girls (established by her father), Abby and two of her brothers pursued further study at Brook Farm, Sophia and George Ripley's transcendental community in Roxbury. In 1843 her father took the rest of the family to Brook Farm, but perceiving the association's instability, he soon moved the family back to Plymouth.

Abby, however, remained at Brook Farm, teaching with Georgiana Bruce Kirby in the Infant School. When Kirby departed in 1844, Abby replaced her as director. Ora Gannett Sedgwick, a Brook Farm contemporary recalled that Abby's "peculiar combination of liveliness and dignity, together with her beautiful singing, made her a favorite with all the members" (*Atlantic Monthly*, Mar. 1900, pp. 394–404).

In October 1845 Abby married Manuel A. Diaz, who had come from Havana to study at Brook Farm; he eventually became a Spanish instructor there. They remained at the farm until its demise in 1847. He and Abby had three children, one of whom died young. The couple apparently separated, and Abby supported the children thereafter, residing at her parents' home.

Putting into practice the Brook Farm ideal of combining thinker and doer in one person, Diaz pursued diverse careers. She taught in the public schools, held singing and dancing classes, regularly arranged social activities for both children and adults, did practical nursing, and one summer managed a residence in the then popular resort area of Clark's Island. During the Civil War Diaz worked for a Boston firm, passing out army clothing to be sewn by highly skilled women who she perceived were grossly underpaid. This observation motivated her later advocacy for working women.

In the early sixties Diaz began writing stories for both adult and juvenile magazines. Wit and inventiveness characterized her work. Her first story, "Pink and Blue," in which a droll male narrator details the process by which he won his wife, appeared in the *Atlantic Monthly* in May 1861. Diaz subsequently wrote stories and did editorial work for *Our Young Folks* and *Youth's Companion*. She also wrote for *Golden Rule*, *St. Nicholas*, and *Wide Awake*, and she produced more than a dozen juvenile books. She turned some of the early stories into her most famous books; *The William Henry Letters* (1870) and *William Henry and His Friends* (1872) remained popular into the twentieth century. Theodore Roosevelt referred to *The William Henry Letters* as "first-class, good healthy stories, interesting . . . and . . . teaching manliness, decency, and good conduct" (*An Autobiography*, 1913).

From the mid-seventies on, Diaz focused primarily on issues that continued to occupy feminists into the twentieth century—women's education and health, suffrage, sexual equality in the workplace and political arena, and shared parental responsibilities. Her epistolary *bildungsroman Lucy Maria* (1874), developed from earlier stories, features a 22-year-old protagonist who chooses education over marriage and advocates "*right*-forming" children so as to eliminate "*re-forming*" them. In "papers" first published in *Hearth and Home* and collected under the title *The Schoolmaster's Trunk* (1874), her male narrator illustrates how patriarchal attitudes turn women into "slaves of the rolling-pin," baking "Pies again! Always pies!" and deny them the educational and cultural opportunities that would make them better citizens, wives, and mothers. *A Domestic Problem: Women and Culture in the Household*

(1875) examines the issues of women's work, health, and education more extensively. Lamenting the scarcity of enlightened women and men, Diaz urges women to use women's clubs, the *Woman's Journal*, and the Women's Congress to effect change.

Diaz energetically followed her own advice. She gave her first public lecture in 1876 at the Woman's Congress in Philadelphia. Her *Neighborhood Talks*, essays on arbitration versus war, appeared in the same year, and in 1878, with N. A. Calkins, she contributed six booklets to a natural history series. Moving to the Boston area, and in about 1880 settling in Belmont, Massachusetts, where she maintained a household for three grandchildren, Diaz held leadership roles in organizations such as the Boston Woman's Christian Temperance Union and the Women's Exchange, the Massachusetts Women's Suffrage Association, the Belmont Suffrage League, and the Belmont Educational League. Politically, she identified with the Socialists and the Nationalists. Religiously flexible, she supported the Christian Socialist Society and wrote Christian Science pamphlets.

Diaz worked closely with Dr. Harriet Clisby to establish the Boston Women's Educational and Industrial Union in 1877 to educate women in marketable business skills such as stenography and bookkeeping, home management, languages, designing, health care, etc.; to provide a consignment outlet for women's products, including foods, clothing, and decorative objects; to provide legal assistance to women treated unfairly by unscrupulous employers; and generally to serve as a moral force in society. Diaz served as president from 1881 to 1892. She traveled widely, lecturing and establishing unions in cities such as Buffalo, Syracuse, St. Paul, Providence, and Washington, D.C. Two collections of her lectures—*Bybury to Beacon Street* and *The John Spicer Lectures*—appeared in 1887.

In her boldest work, *Only a Flock of Women* (1893), Diaz analyzed problems resulting from women's political inequality and universal exclusion from policymaking. She explained how the "degrading ideas of women" fostered by "the early Fathers of the Church" and their successors resulted in women's low self-esteem and public status. For Diaz, "a flock of women talking" was "a laying hold of the power that moves the world."

Through her writing and social action Diaz embodied the Transcendentalist principle she had imbibed at Brook Farm—uniting in one person the thinker and the doer. Her belief in equality of the sexes fired her writing, and her conviction that cooperation across class lines was mutually advantageous for women gave direction and strength to the Boston Women's Educational and Industrial Union, accounting, to a great extent, for the organization's national expansion and success. Diaz died in Belmont.

• A bibliography of Diaz's writings and talks is in the Diaz file, Sophia Smith Collection, Smith College. Diaz's correspondence is also at the Huntington Library, San Marino, Calif.; Smith College Library; and Cornell University Library. The most helpful accounts of her life are the obituary by Alice Stone Blackwell in *Woman's Journal*, 9 Apr. 1904, pp. 113, 116, 117; the obituary and editorial in *Boston Transcript*, 1 and 2 Apr. 1904; pieces in Frances E. Willard and Mary A. Livermore, ed., *A Woman of the Century* (1893); Karen J. Blair, *The Clubwoman as Feminist: True Womanhood Redefined, 1868–1914*, chpt. 5 (1980); and Lucy M. Freibert, "Creative Women of Brook Farm" in *Women in Spiritual and Communitarian Societies in the United States*, ed. Wendy E. Chmielewski, et al. (1993). Personal recollections by Diaz may be found in "Antislavery Times in Plymouth," *New England Magazine*, April 1899, pp. 216–24; in her "Personal Reminiscences of the Old Slavery Times," in *Woman's Journal*, 2 Aug. 1879, p. 246; and in Danvers [MA] Historical Society, *Old Anti-Slavery Days* (1893). Books on Brook Farm by John T. Codman, *Brook Farm: Historic and Personal Memoirs* (1894; repr. 1971), and Lindsay Swift, *Brook Farm, Its Members, Scholars, and Visitors* (1900), mention Diaz briefly but contain occasional inaccuracies. Records of Diaz's work with women's groups may be found in S. Agnes Donham's "History of the Women's Educational and Industrial Union" (1955), typescript at the Schlesinger Library, Radcliffe College, and in Jane C. Croly's *The History of the Woman's Club Movement in America* (1898).

LUCY M. FREIBERT

DIBBLE, Eugene Heriot, Jr. (14 Aug. 1893–1 June 1968), physician, was born in Camden, South Carolina, the son of Eugene Heriot Dibble and Sally Lee. He graduated from Atlanta University in 1915 and earned his medical degree at Howard University Medical College four years later. After a one-year internship at the Freedmen's Hospital in Washington, D.C., Dibble accepted a surgical residency at the John A. Andrew Memorial Hospital in Tuskegee, Alabama.

At that time, medical care for southern blacks was limited and often inferior. Dibble realized the urgent need for more black physicians to provide adequate health care. As assistant medical director of the John A. Andrew Memorial Hospital, he helped organize the first postgraduate course in surgery for southern black physicians.

By 1923 Dibble became the chief of the surgical section of the newly established Veterans' Administration hospital in Tuskegee. The large number of black World War I veterans created an acute medical demand and necessitated a solution to the problem of providing care and treatment for all who needed it. The Veterans' Bureau selected Tuskegee as the site for a hospital to rehabilitate disabled veterans. Community hostility toward black medical professionals resulted in violence, but eventually black physicians replaced white personnel.

The Tuskegee Veterans' Hospital supported six hundred patients, half suffering from neuropsychiatric disorders and half from tuberculosis. The latter patients were transferred to other facilities, and Dibble and his staff focused on veterans sick from manic depression, dementia, spinal cord injuries, and brain diseases. He modified traditional treatments for veterans, taking into account genetic, environmental, and socioeconomic factors; many veterans, white and black, lacked immunities to parasitic diseases such as syphilis, and physicians carefully evaluated viral vaccines to combat infections and prevent illnesses. Dibble also oversaw occupational therapy to assist veterans returning to their homes and employment.

In 1925 Dibble completed postgraduate work at Harvard University and returned as medical director of the John A. Andrew Memorial Hospital. In 1926 he married Helen A. Taylor; they had five children. During the early 1930s he became involved in a controversial public health experiment. Officials representing the Venereal Disease Program, Division of Special Health Services of the U.S. Public Health Service, wanted to study untreated syphilis. They approached Dibble in 1932, and he secured the approval of Dr. Robert R. Moton, the Tuskegee Institute's president.

Dibble emphasized that the research would be of "world wide significance" and give "added standing" to the hospital. He also stressed the "educational advantages," explaining that the work would provide training and employment for black nurses and interns. He had helped improve Tuskegee's nursing program and was discouraged that graduates were unable to secure work because of the depression and racism. Dibble also viewed the experiment as a way for black physicians, including himself, to acquire professional acceptance. He agreed to provide staff and facilities for examinations supervised by Dr. Raymond Vonderlehr, the Public Health Service officer in charge. Dibble also convinced county health officials and physicians to cooperate.

Local black men suffering from syphilis were promised hot meals and their burial costs paid in exchange for examinations, including lumbar punctures. Most residents were too impoverished to consult physicians and believed that they would receive treatment for syphilis and other health problems. One patient recalled that Dibble assured him that medicine was in his injection, which in fact was a spinal tap.

Appointed in 1933 as a special consultant in the U.S. Public Health Service, Dibble eagerly sought prestige and recognition for his "crucial role." He autopsied patients to determine the results of untreated syphilis, sending the brain tissues, spinal cord, and organs to the National Institutes of Health. Seeking the approval of his white colleagues, Dibble wrote Vonderlehr, "Please let me tell you how much both Doctor [Jerome J.] Peters and myself enjoyed the autopsy." In the 1970s details of the Tuskegee Syphilis Experiment were revealed, and medical ethics and individual morality were questioned. The public was outraged because only black patients were examined and were misled to think that they were being treated with potent medicine.

From 1936 to 1946 Dibble acted as manager and medical director of the Veterans' Administration hospital. During the next decade, the veterans' hospital reorganized and constructed more buildings, increasing bed space "to care for and to rehabilitate, where possible, the lame, halt and diseased defenders of our Country" (Morais, p. 239). Prominent visitors, including Franklin and Eleanor Roosevelt, military officers, and Hollywood stars, visited the hospital. In a 1943 speech, "Care and Treatment of Negro Veterans at Tuskegee," Dibble told how the hospital acquired modern equipment and his staff learned new scientific advancements and pharmaceutical treatments. During World War II, a cadet nurses program, which Dibble monitored, was established at Tuskegee. Owing to the shortage of army doctors, Dibble joined the military as colonel, the military position given to all veterans' hospital managers, and he was the first black medical officer to hold this rank. He was discharged from the U.S. Army Medical Corps in June 1946 and resigned from the veterans' hospital the following month.

After World War II Dibble assumed the medical directorship of the John A. Andrew Memorial Hospital. Throughout his career, Dibble sought to improve the professional status of black physicians and enhance medical care for the African-American community. He focused on eradicating diseases afflicting impoverished residents and was especially concerned with the high mortality rates of mothers and children. "Everything at the hospital is intended to impress unconsciously upon the student the fundamental laws of health," he stressed (Dibble, "Hospital Symposium," p. 138). He utilized the John A. Andrew Clinical Society, of which he was secretary, to achieve his goals.

From 1925 to 1965 Dibble developed this society as a means of postgraduate education of the "science and art" of medicine for black doctors. Although the profession was segregated, he arranged for talented white and black doctors, from rural and urban practices, to collaborate during seminars, lectures, and operations. Physicians were able to learn the most recent techniques and share ideas with distinguished colleagues with whom they would not have had contact otherwise. They focused on diseases prevalent in the South and concentrated on alleviating suffering.

Dibble hoped that participants, ranging from specialists to general practitioners, would learn skills so that they "may be better able to fulfill their life's work." Dibble "poured immeasurable creative energy" into the clinical society, serving as the "prime moving spirit" promoting "work, study, and service." The clinics "tremendously promoted professional interracial understanding and good will." Hoping to encourage racial harmony, Dibble invited Billy Graham and civil rights leaders to speak to clinic participants, city officials, and college students and faculty. He established clinic lectures named in honor of other black physicians to memorialize them. Dibble also used the clinics to mentor young minority doctors and then secured employment for them.

In 1958 Dibble joined a medical mission to the Far East and Africa sponsored by the Baptist World Alliance. He also served on the editorial board of the *Journal of the National Medical Association*, preparing special issues on the Tuskegee hospitals and revising papers presented at the clinical society. Dibble served on the board of trustees of Meharry Medical College. He was a member of the Medical Advisory Committee to the Children's Bureau, Department of Health, Education and Welfare; Dibble also helped establish the Macon County Medical Care Program, cooperating with the Alabama State Board of Health and Children's Bureau in counties surrounding Tuskegee.

The John A. Andrew Clinical Society presented Dibble the C. V. Roman Distinguished Service Medal in 1943. He received the National Medical Association's Distinguished Service Medal by unanimous vote in 1962, honoring his "career-long selfless dedication to the improvement of health care for the people he has served and the eminent success he has achieved as an organizer, administrator and promotor of activities for professional advancement." Howard University gave him an Alumni Distinguished Service Medal, and he was named an honorary member of Alpha Omega Alpha.

Dibble retired in 1965. His family worshiped at the St. Andrews Episcopal Church. Dibble was active in the U.S. Army Reserve, Alpha Phi Alpha, and the Masonic order. Diagnosed with bronchogenic carcinoma, he decided not to undergo therapy, which he feared would interfere with his medical duties. He worked until shortly before he died at home in Tuskegee and was buried in the Tuskegee Institute Cemetery on campus.

• Dibble's correspondence is held in the Tuskegee University Archives and in the Public Health Service records in the National Archives. Articles by Dibble include "Hospital Symposium: The John A. Andrew Memorial Hospital," *Journal of the National Medical Association* 22 (July–Sept. 1930): 137–39; with Louis A. Rabb and Ruth B. Ballard, "John A. Andrew Memorial Hospital," *Journal of the National Medical Association* 53 (Mar. 1961): 103–18; and, with C. O. Dummett, "Historical Notes on the Tuskegee Veterans Hospital," *Journal of the National Medical Association* 54 (Mar. 1962): 133–38. Information on Dibble and his work is in Herbert M. Morais, *The History of the Afro-American in Medicine* (1976); James H. Jones, *Bad Blood: The Tuskegee Syphilis Experiment*, rev. ed. (1993); Fred C. Collier, "Eugene Heriot Dibble, M.D., 1893–1968," *Journal of the National Medical Association* 60 (Sept. 1968): 446; "Dr. Eugene Heriot Dibble, Jr., Distinguished Service Medalist for 1962," *Journal of the National Medical Association* 54 (Nov. 1962): 711–12; "Eugene Heriot Dibble," *Journal of the National Medical Association* 35 (Sept. 1943): 175; and Asa G. Yancey, Sr., "Tuskegee Veterans Administration Medical Center: Genesis and Opportunities It Provided in Surgery," in *A Century of Black Surgeons: The U.S.A. Experience*, ed. Claude H. Organ and Margaret M. Kosiba (1987).

ELIZABETH D. SCHAFER

DIBBLE, Roy Floyd (12 Mar. 1887–3 Dec. 1929), author, was born in Portland, New York, the son of George E. Dibble and Miriam H. Quilliam, farmers. Little is known about Dibble's early life before he left home for college, but he appears to have developed strong ties to both his family and his native Chautauqua County. Rather than continue his education immediately after high school, Dibble divided the next two years between helping out on the family farm and caring for a sick brother. With a fondness for Shake-

speare and a desire to write, Dibble enrolled at Clark University, Worcester, Massachusetts, in 1908. He never married and had no children.

After graduating from Clark in 1912 with a B.A. in English, Dibble secured a teaching position in a small town in southern Connecticut. Two years later he moved to New York and entered the doctoral program in English at Columbia University. Aside from occasional visits home and summer trips to Europe, he remained in New York for the rest of his life.

At Columbia, Dibble found stimulating company in classmates Mark Van Doren, Joseph Wood Krutch, and Raymond Weaver. As a graduate student from 1914 to 1921, Dibble taught English and worked on a biography of Albion W. Tourgée, the outspoken Reconstruction advocate, carpetbagger, novelist, judge, and politician. It is unclear how Dibble developed an interest in Tourgée (they both grew up on farms on the shores of Lake Erie), yet the question is significant since Dibble's later writings continue his early interest in the type of subject Tourgée suggested: the exceptional yet "representative" American.

In 1921 Dibble's *Albion W. Tourgée* was published, the first biography of this difficult and unconventional subject. The book presents a somewhat critical evaluation of Tourgée, but it nevertheless remains an important reference. With his dissertation published, Dibble joined the faculty of Columbia as an instructor in English.

Dibble was exempted from military service during World War I because of poor health. Remaining in graduate school, he was asked to teach a prepackaged course on "war aims," with the effect that the obligation to teach against his beliefs seems to have helped to define them. In his autobiography, Van Doren recounts that Dibble was angered at this infringement and that, "fired by the example of Lytton Strachey's *Eminent Victorians*," he wrote a series of essays that are "strenuous and surprising, and successful enough to call for other work of their kind." The collection, titled *Strenuous Americans* (1923), contains biographical essays on seven of the most illustrious figures in nineteenth-century America: Jesse James, Admiral George Dewey, Brigham Young, Frances E. Willard, James J. Hill, P. T. Barnum, and Mark Hanna. Typical of Dibble's subjects, all of the people represented are historical figures important enough to influence public life, with personalities interesting enough to make the reading and writing entertaining.

Dibble found that each of these pop-culture heroes and villains manifested something "supreme in his particular field during his day; each represents, better perhaps than any of his contemporaries in the same field, some distinctive and significant trait of his time" (*Strenuous Americans*, p. 8). Complimentary reviews noted Dibble's ability to unite a "startling combination of Americans"; others noted his inclination to extend (or transcend) traditional boundaries of "academic" writing through the inclusion of colorful details from a subject's daily life, a tendency that placed him somewhere between a historian and a novelist. This approach (which he continued throughout his career) seemed to resonate with his creative side and appealed to popular and academic readers alike.

Over the next two years (1923–1925) Dibble continued to write and publish essays on similarly prominent figures of the nineteenth century, including John L. Sullivan, the famous boxer-turned-philanthropist; Robert G. Ingersoll, the vitriolic lawyer, Union officer, Illinois attorney general, and agnostic; James R. Day, the Methodist pastor-turned-autocratic chancellor of Syracuse University; and Anderson Hatfield, the patriarch of the feuding Hatfield clan. As figures of popular legend, those subjects challenged Dibble to explore the uncertain boundaries between myth, fiction, and history.

Encouraged by the success of his books and essays, Dibble expanded the short piece on Sullivan (which had first appeared in *American Mercury* as "Champion of Champions" in July 1924) into a full-length biography. *John L. Sullivan: An Intimate Narrative* (1925) delves into the personal life of the "hulking hero whose achievements elevated pugilism into the realm of epic poetry" ("Champion," p. 267). A "swarthy young Hercules," Sullivan is portrayed in his irresistible rise to fame as a likable bully, actor, ex-alcoholic, and good-hearted but abrasive temperance advocate.

Sullivan was so well received that later in 1925 Dibble left Columbia and abandoned teaching in order to devote himself full time to writing. In his next major work, *Mohammed* (1926), Dibble attempted to reconstruct a figure who "must forever remain largely ambiguous and enigmatical" (*Mohammed*, p. 26). Criticized for taking liberties inappropriate for a historical and religious subject (the book contains no references or notes), Dibble drew fire from the literary establishment and Muslim readers alike. With his history, called everything from a "heroic comedy" to "blasphemy," Dibble appears to have ignored his own earlier warning to historians: "It is perhaps too easy for the curious investigator of the past, who strives to keep scrupulously detached from all passionate interests and to hold aloof from every aim save a just and clearly limned portrayal of the manifold deeds of men, to regard history as a more dramatic spectacle than it really is" (*Strenuous Americans*, p. 70).

Nonetheless, as a "live, interesting human biography" and as an "informal," "entertaining," and "not too theological account" of its subject (to quote from contemporary reviews), *Mohammed* did find a receptive popular audience. And in Mohammed, Dibble found "a fusion of the furthest limits of charlatanism, demagoguery, bombastic egotism, and general intellectual incompetency, with the opposite extremes of willing martyrdom, unaffected simplicity and sincerity, and lightning flashes of divine poetry" (*Mohammed*, p. 44).

Dibble suffered increasingly from Addison's disease, but he continued to work. He returned to Hunter College to teach in 1927, and he finished a biography (unpublished) of Martin Luther. Dibble died in a New York hospital.

• Dibble's papers, including the Martin Luther biography, have not survived. In addition to his books, Dibble wrote essays for *The Nation, American Mercury, The Century, The Forum,* and the *New York Times Magazine.* An obituary is in the *New York Times,* 5 Dec. 1929.

SCOTT KELLEY

DICK, Elisha Cullen (15 Mar. 1762–22 Sept. 1825), physician, was born near Marcus Hook, Pennsylvania, the son of Archibald Dick, a wealthy farmer and horse-breeder, and Mary Barnard. Elisha received an excellent education in classics at the Pequea Academy in Lancaster County, Pennsylvania. After returning home at age sixteen, he studied under the Reverend Samuel Armor. In 1780 he began to study medicine, first under Benjamin Rush, and in 1781 under William Shippen. In March 1782 he graduated from the University of Pennsylvania with a bachelor of medicine degree. Dick began to practice medicine in Alexandria, Virginia, where he quickly became successful professionally and prominent socially. In October 1783 he married Hannah Harman; they had three sons.

A cultivated young man, Dick was accomplished in science, music, literature, painting, horsemanship, and fashion and even supported dueling. With maturity, he developed a more serious view of life and changed his church affiliation from Episcopalian to Presbyterian and then to Quaker. In keeping with his new beliefs, Dick threw his dueling pistols into a river and destroyed an organ he had built because he had come to believe it was a useless vanity.

Dick was one of the founders of the Masonic Lodge of Alexandria, serving as its worshipful master, a post also held at one point by George Washington. He conducted the masonic service at Washington's burial.

Dick was considered the outstanding physician in Alexandria during the period of his active practice there. He is said to have written extensively on medical subjects, but only two of his papers are extant, "Yellow Fever at Alexandria" ([N.Y.] *Medical Repository,* 2d Hexade, vol. 1 [1803]: 190) and "Facts and Observations Relative to the Disease Cynanche Trachealis, or Croup" (*Philadelphia Medical and Physical Journal* 3 [1806]: 242). He generally avoided performing surgery.

In 1793 Governor Henry Lee appointed Dick superintendent of quarantine at Alexandria during the yellow fever epidemic. Later he became health officer and a member of the local board of health, important and responsible positions in a busy seaport like Alexandria. Dick's career also included military and political experience. He commanded a cavalry troop during the suppression of the Whiskey Rebellion in Pennsylvania in 1794, and for several years following he was colonel of the cavalry regiment in Alexandria. In 1804 he was elected to the first of several terms as mayor of Alexandria.

Dick is chiefly remembered for his role in caring for George Washington during his terminal illness in December 1799. A neighbor and personal friend of

Washington, Dick was summoned to Mount Vernon by James Craik, the attending physician to Washington, and another physician, Gustavus Richard Brown of Port Tobacco, Maryland. Craik asked for this consultation when he realized that Washington's illness was quite serious. The patient developed difficulty breathing and swallowing on account of what he thought was an inflammatory condition. Apparently there was some disagreement between the consultants. Craik and Brown diagnosed Washington's condition as "quinsey." Today we define quinsy as a unilateral abscess of the peritonsillar tissue. However in the eighteenth century the term quinsey meant any condition of the throat that caused a feeling of strangulation. Usually when this term was used it implied generalized inflammation of the throat, for which the recognized treatment was bloodletting, counterirritation by blistering, and purges. This treatment was used on Washington. Therapeutic bloodletting, or more accurately "venesection," has recently been shown to temporarily inhibit the inflammatory response. However, Washington did not respond to the treatment. Dick initially recommended cessation of any more bloodletting based on his clinical observation. Current wisdom holds that Washington died from excessive blood loss by venesection. However, the amount of blood lost by Washington was not enough to cause shock or a compromised immune response. Rather Dick suggested that Washington was suffering from laryngeal edema and/or epiglottitis (cynanche trachealis) rather than quinsey (cynanche tonsillaris). In spite of the fact that there was no other treatment for cynanche trachealis recognized by authority other than bloodletting at that time, Dick recommended tracheotomy (cutting an opening through the skin into the windpipe below the larynx to bypass the obstruction caused by the swollen and inflamed tissues above) to prevent Washington from suffocating. Although tracheotomy was known from ancient times, it was seldom practiced. One year before Washington's fatal illness, tracheotomy was described authoritatively by two eminent surgeons in Paris, Desault and Bichat, who did not recommend the operation for any type of strangulation due to sore throat. After discussion among the three doctors, Dick was overruled, but he was later praised by Brown for his clear reasoning, accurate diagnosis, and use of common sense in his clinical judgment. Dick was ahead of his time in suggesting the tracheotomy, and, given our present knowledge, it probably would have been the correct thing to do. Dick and Craik wrote the official report of Washington's death that was published by newspapers. Dick is also remembered because he stopped the bedroom clock when Washington died.

From 1799 to 1825 Dick served several terms as mayor of Alexandria, was prominent in the Masonic Lodge, and became a devout Quaker. His major significance was his excellent clinical judgment and creative approach to the practice of medicine. Dick represented the type of physician who does not just confine his armamentarium to the security of known outcomes but who can be relied on to responsibly push the limits of the state of the art. Dick died at "Cottage Hill" in Fairfax County.

• Dick's letter, coauthored with James Craik, outlining the events of Washington's death was published in *The Times*, a newspaper printed in Alexandria, Va., in Dec. 1799. An important source is Wyndham B. Blanton, *Medicine in the Eighteenth Century* (1931), pp. 304–7. The best modern assessment is Walter A. Wells, "Last Illness and Death of Washington," *Virginia Medical Monthly* 53 (Jan. 1927): 629–42. An important biographical article is J. M. Toner, "A Sketch of the Life of Elisha Cullen Dick," *Transactions of the Medical Society of Virginia* 16 (1885): 267–79.

JOHN A. LANZALOTTI

DICK, George Frederick (21 July 1881–12 Oct. 1967), physician and bacteriologist, was born in Fort Wayne, Indiana, the son of Daniel Dick, a railroad engineer, and Elizabeth King. After two years of college at the Indiana University (1900–1901), Dick matriculated at the Rush Medical College of Chicago, where he received his M.D. in 1905. He then completed an eighteen-month internship at the Cook County Hospital, where he learned about the clinical practice of medicine as he rotated between different clinical services, including internal medicine, pediatrics, gynecology, pathology, and general surgery. Like many an ambitious, young physician of the early twentieth century who set his sights on an academic career, Dick traveled, in 1907, to Vienna and Munich, where he spent the year studying bacteriology. Although he maintained an active presence as a clinician throughout his career, it was his brilliant work in bacteriology that brought him international acclaim.

Dick returned to the United States at the end of 1908 and began his first academic appointment early the next year as an assistant professor in the pathology department at the University of Chicago. During his years at Chicago, he was associated most with the McCormick Institute for Infectious Diseases (1910–1924). He became a professor of pathology and medicine and remained on the University of Chicago faculty until 1933, when he was called to the professorship of medicine at his alma mater Rush Medical College. He retired from active teaching and research in 1946. During most of Dick's scientific career at both Chicago and Rush, he worked with his wife, Dr. Gladys Henry Dick, whom he had married in 1914. Trained as a physician at the Johns Hopkins Hospital and School of Medicine (M.D., 1908), Gladys Dick practiced as both an internist and a pathologist in the Chicago area as well as maintaining her laboratory career with George. Although she did not have an appointment at the University of Chicago, she was George's laboratory assistant and co-worker and was instrumental in their joint research on streptococcus. The Dicks had two children.

Dick's greatest contributions to the study of infectious diseases have to do with his researches on streptococcal infections and their relationship to the dreaded childhood disease: scarlet fever. Unlike other infectious diseases of childhood during the early twentieth century, such as tuberculosis, whooping cough, and diphtheria, the search for the causative organism for scarlet fever was long and elusive. Physicians of this era were puzzled by both the physical and bacteriological characteristics of the disease. For example, one debate during this period had to do with whether scarlet fever was infectious at all; other debates suggested different microbial agents, such as protozoa, as the etiologic cause of scarlet fever. Indeed, it was not until 1923 that physicians began to accept the concept that scarlet fever was, indeed, caused by a streptococcal organism; their acceptance was based largely on the experimental work of George and Gladys Dick identifying streptococcus as the cause. One of the major reasons research on the streptococcus was so difficult is that there are many nonpathogenic as well as pathogenic forms of this microbe. This work was greatly expanded on by Rebecca Lancefield, who developed the concept of type-specific immunity to different strains of the streptococcus organism in the 1930s.

Applying the strict principles of Robert Koch's germ theory, the Dicks injected streptococcus into the skin of volunteer patients (animal studies being eschewed because not all animals get scarlet fever) and created an experimental model for scarlet fever. Similar to the Schick skin test for diphtheria, the Dicks developed a process by which they neutralized the toxic filtrate, both *in vitro* and *in vivo*, using the blood of a patient ill with scarlet fever. This work also led to the development of a diagnostic test, called the "Dick Test," which took advantage of the erythrogenic toxin (a poison that yields a red skin rash) secreted by the type of streptococcus that causes scarlet fever.

Most importantly, the Dicks' discovery of the streptococcus (specifically group A beta-hemolytic streptococcus), allowed physicians to better manage and contain potential epidemics of scarlet fever. This extremely contagious disease had posed a dangerous public health risk: a small but significant percentage of those stricken with scarlet fever go on to develop the more serious rheumatic heart disease and, more rarely, kidney problems as a result of the toxins (poisons) secreted by the streptococcus organism. The Dick test also allowed the physician to check if the patient in question was susceptible to scarlet fever or immune to the disease because of a previous experience with the infectious organism. This test represented a notable achievement in an era when isolation, or quarantine, of the contagious was the only means physicians had for combating an epidemic. Prevention, rather than chemotherapeutic cure, was the major foci of physicians dealing with infectious diseases during this period. The development of the Dick test helped physicians to rein in potential scarlet fever epidemics before the advent of antibiotic chemoprophylaxix.

George and Gladys Dick retired to Palo Alto, California, where they lived for many years. George Dick died in Palo Alto.

• Among Dick's most important publications are, with Gladys Dick, *Scarlet Fever* (1938) and, all in the *Journal of the American Medical Association*, "Experimental Scarlet Fever," 81 (1923): 1166; "A Skin Test for Susceptibility to Scarlet Fever," 82 (1924): 265–66; "Prevention of Scarlet Fever," 83 (1924): 84–86; and "The Etiology of Scarlet Fever," 82 (1924): 301–2. See also George Rosen, "Acute Communicable Diseases," in *The History and Conquest of Common Diseases*, ed. W. R. Bett (1954), pp. 26–38, and Howard Markel and Frank A. Oski, "If Your Baby Had Scarlet Fever," in *The H. L. Mencken Baby Book* (1990), pp. 145–55.

HOWARD MARKEL

DICK, Robert Paine (5 Oct. 1823–12 Sept. 1898), jurist and politician, was born in Greensboro, North Carolina, the son of John McClintock Dick, a jurist, and Parthenia P. Wilson. Dick received his college preparatory training at the Caldwell Institute and entered the sophomore class at the University of North Carolina, graduating with distinction in 1843. He then studied law with his father, by then a state superior court justice, and George C. Mendenhall. He began his legal practice in 1845, working first in Wentworth and later in Greensboro. In 1848 Dick married Eloise Adams of Pittsylvania County, Virginia; the couple had five children.

Dick entered the political arena in 1852, supporting Franklin Pierce at the Democratic National Convention. The next year President Pierce appointed him U.S. district attorney, and he served in that post until 1861. During this period Dick accepted the existence of slavery though he disliked the institution and was devoted to the Union. At the party's national conventions in 1860 and through the subsequent campaign, Dick broke with other North Carolina Democrats to support the candidacy of Stephen A. Douglas as the best means of preserving the Union.

While strongly opposing the secession of southern states in early 1861, he and other North Carolina Unionist leaders voted for an ordinance of secession when Abraham Lincoln called for troops after the firing on Fort Sumter. Yet he never actively supported the Confederate cause, and by 1864, recognizing the futility of continued resistance, he joined the state "peace movement" led by William W. Holden. Dick was elected to the state senate on a platform that proposed calling a convention that, together with other southern states, might negotiate a separate peace with the Union since the Confederate government refused to come to terms.

In May 1865 Dick was one of twelve North Carolinians summoned to Washington, D.C., by President Andrew Johnson to devise the best method for restoring the state to the Union. Pressing Johnson to be forbearing, Dick remonstrated against the idea of confiscating the estates of large slaveholders and also called for a general amnesty for former Confederates. Feeling unable, subsequently, to subscribe to an "ironclad" oath attesting to his prior loyalty, Dick declined to serve as a federal district judge or a state judge under Holden, who had been appointed the provisional governor. He did serve in the 1865–1866 state constitutional convention, but Dick neither chaired major committees nor spoke out on important issues.

While he had advocated generous treatment of former Confederates in the immediate aftermath of the war, by 1866 Dick had become one of the leading advocates of the Fourteenth Amendment and endorsed Holden's efforts to have the state reenter the Union under its terms. After conservative white southerners spurned the amendment, Dick participated in the formation of the state's Republican party, and at an 1867 convention he offered the resolution that formally organized it. In the state elections held the next year, Dick was elected to the North Carolina Supreme Court at the same time that Holden won the governorship. He remained close to Holden, who counted on him to turn out the vote in Greensboro. Dick was criticized by members of the state bar for continuing to take an active role in Republican politics while on the bench. In 1872 he resigned to accept a presidential appointment to the federal judgeship for the Western District of North Carolina. He served until 1898 when health problems forced his retirement.

Dick served with great distinction throughout his judicial career. He was acclaimed for his role in molding North Carolina's system of jurisprudence in the wake of the precedent-breaking 1868 constitution. As a federal judge he was prominent in the enforcement of federal laws against illegal distilling. He fought corruption and the abuses of power of internal revenue officers and was also known for his leniency in sentencing petty offenders. Dick, in addition, conducted a private law school with John H. Dillard that was distinguished for the outstanding training given to its many young students.

In private life, Dick was a biblical scholar, an ardent advocate of temperance reform, and an elder in the First Presbyterian Church in Greensboro, where he died.

• There is no collection of Dick papers, but much of his correspondence has been preserved in the William W. Holden collections at the North Carolina Division of Archives and History, the Southern Historical Collection at the University of North Carolina, and Duke University. Biographical information is available in William S. Powell, ed., *Dictionary of North Carolina Biography*, vol. 2 (1986); B. D. Caldwell, *Founders and Builders of Greensboro* (1925); Jerome Dowd, *Sketches of Prominent and Living North Carolinians* (1888); and John H. Wheeler, *Reminiscences and Memoirs of North Carolina and Eminent North Carolinians* (1884). Dick's work as a federal judge is discussed in Wilbur Miller, *Revenuers & Moonshiners: Enforcing Federal Liquor Law in the Mountain South, 1865–1900* (1991).

HORACE W. RAPER

DICKENSON, Vic (6 Aug. 1906–16 Nov. 1984), jazz trombonist, was born Albert Victor Dickenson in Xenia, Ohio, the son of Robert Clarke Dickenson, a plastering contractor and amateur violinist. (His mother's name is unknown.) Using his brother Carlos's instrument he began to play trombone in high school. In 1921 he played with the Elite Serenaders while also

working days for his father as a plasterer, but after suffering a severe back injury as a result of a fall from a ladder, he decided to concentrate on music exclusively. Around 1922 his family moved to Columbus, where he and his brother, now a saxophonist, started working with local bands. In 1925 he played his first professional job with Don Phillips in Madison, Wisconsin, and after returning home he heard and was influenced by trombonists Claude Jones and Dicky Wells. He was particularly impressed by their smooth tones and facile techniques, virtues that he had already admired on records by Miff Mole, Charlie Green, Benny Morton, and Jimmy Harrison.

In May 1927 Dickenson joined Willie Jones's band in South Bend, Indiana, and in November made his first records with that group, later working with the bands of Bill Broadhus, Wesley Helvey, and Leonard Gay. Dickenson stayed with Gay through a summer 1929 residency in Madison and then joined the Toledo-based Speed Webb band for about a year. In December 1930 he went with Zack Whyte's Chocolate Beau Brummels to work at the Savoy Ballroom in New York City and on a five-band tour, but he left in early 1932 and moved to Kansas City, where he played in a Bennie Moten spin-off band, led by trombonist Thamon Hayes, that also included Count Basie, Hot Lips Page, and Buck Clayton. Also in 1932 Dickenson married Otealia Foye; the couple had no children. With the exception of a brief job in Ohio with Clarence Paige's Royal Syncopators, he remained with Hayes into 1933. From the summer of 1933 through early 1936 Dickenson toured the theater and ballroom circuit with singer Blanche Calloway's band, after which he spent three years in Claude Hopkins's orchestra, most often in residence at the Roseland Ballroom in New York City. In the spring of 1939 he joined Benny Carter for extended stays at the Savoy, where he met pianist Eddie Heywood, an important transitional figure in his career. In January 1940 Dickenson replaced one of his longtime friends, Benny Morton, in Count Basie's band, but because almost all of the trombone solos fell to another early mentor, Dicky Wells, he left in January 1941, rejoining Carter in February for a job at Nick's in Greenwich Village and a midwestern tour. That summer he played with Sidney Bechet at a summer resort in upstate New York and then returned to Manhattan to work with trumpeter Frankie Newton.

Later in 1941 Dickenson went to Chicago with Page and in 1942 resumed working with Newton, first in Boston and then at New York's Café Society Downtown. The Newton group played opposite the Eddie Heywood Trio, and when Newton left to take another job, Heywood enlarged his trio to a sextet, using Dickenson as his first choice for the three-horn front line. From September 1943 through October 1946, with the exception of a brief layoff because of illness in early 1946, Dickenson remained with the Heywood group, playing long residencies in both New York and Los Angeles and making himself known to the larger community through a remarkably diverse and prolific series of record dates with other jazzmen.

After a lengthy period of freelancing in Los Angeles between 1947 and 1948, during which time he led his own group at Billy Berg's, in the spring of 1949 Dickenson settled in Boston, where he worked primarily in Edmond Hall's band at George Wein's Savoy Café and Storyville Club. During this time he also appeared at various New York jazz concerts and worked with Bechet in New York and Philadelphia. During 1951 he played with Bobby Hackett and in October 1953 reunited once again with Bechet at Storyville, and in 1956 he played with Hackett in several venues. In early 1958 he moved to New York permanently and began working in Red Allen's band at the Metropole. That July he played with Bechet on a European tour, and in the summer of 1959 he led his own group at the Arpeggio in New York. Between 1961 and 1963 Dickenson worked with Wild Bill Davison and for five years starting in 1963 co-led the Saints and Sinners with pianist Red Richards.

Throughout the 1960s he toured with Wein's Newport Jazz Festival All-Stars and also worked occasionally at Eddie Condon's in New York City. In March 1964 he toured Australia, New Zealand, and Japan with a Condon band that included Buck Clayton, Pee Wee Russell, Bud Freeman, and Jimmy Rushing; the next year he embarked on a solo tour of England and Europe, while stateside he continued to work with his own Saints and Sinners. Dickenson co-led a popular quintet with Hackett between 1968 and the spring of 1970, when they enjoyed a successful residency at Manhattan's prestigious Roosevelt Grill. At this same time he also began a lengthy association with the World's Greatest Jazz Band, an all-star group that, during Dickenson's tenure from 1970 to 1974, included, among others, Yank Lawson, Billy Butterfield, Hackett, Lou McGarity, Morton, Bob Wilber, and Freeman. In 1973 he worked regularly with Hackett and also appeared with Jimmy McPartland. In March 1975 he worked at the new Eddie Condon's Club and spent the remainder of the decade freelancing and traveling, appearing at the Newport, Nice, and other jazz festivals. He died at his home in New York City.

During his career, Vic Dickenson participated in close to 300 recording sessions, from his first date with Willie Jones in 1927 through a blinding array of big-name associations that ended with Wilber in 1982. In the early period he played almost exclusively in larger bands, but a few recorded solos stand out, such as "Catch On" (1934) and "I Need Some Lovin'" (1935) with Blanche Calloway; "Twinkle Dinkle," "Ja Da," and "Walkin' the Dog" (1937) with Claude Hopkins; "My Favorite Blues" (1941) with Benny Carter; and "I Never Knew," "Louisiana," "Let Me See," "Blow Top," "The World Is Mad," and "Rockin' the Blues" (1940–1941) with Count Basie. Stand-outs from his first small band dates include "Blues in the Air" and "The Mooche" in 1940 and "After You've Gone," "Bugle Call Rag," and "St. Louis Blues" in 1943 with Sidney Bechet. From 1944 on, though, Dickenson recorded much and in many different settings, most frequently with Louis Armstrong (1946–1947), Count Basie (1956, 1977), Ruby Braff (1954–1981), Buck Clayton (1957–1976), Bobby Hackett (1969–1970), Ed Hall (1943–1958), Eddie Heywood (1944–1946), Art Hodes (1944, 1959), Jimmy McPartland (1950–1977), Pee Wee Russell (1946–1959), Saints and Sinners (1960–1968), George Wein (1954–1974), and the World's Greatest Jazz Band (1970–1974). He also recorded in groups such as Big Eighteen (1958), Dixieland All Stars (1959), Dixieland at Carnegie Hall (1958), Jazz at Storyville (1951), Jazz from a Swinging Era (1967), Jazz Giants (1956), Manassas Jazz Festival (1969), New York Jazz Repertory Company (1974), Tribute to Louis Armstrong (1974), and Tribute to Bobby Hackett (1980).

Though his style is not easily categorized, it is convenient to think of Dickenson as a Dicky Wells disciple who also had the flexibility to fit in with a variety of mainstream approaches, from so-called "dixieland" through modern swing. That he could improvise just as convincingly in relatively traditional settings with such diversely talented giants as Sidney Bechet, Edmond Hall, Pee Wee Russell, and Bobby Hackett as he could in more modern environs with Roy Eldridge, Coleman Hawkins, and Lester Young speaks eloquently enough for his adaptability. That does not, however, explain the essence of his style, a basic element of which lay in Dickenson's personality. Humor was never very far from the surface in his playing, and to this purpose he used his gruff, sly, insinuating tone, sardonic growls, patented single-note triplets, and invariably imaginative, well-structured lines to advance his agenda of "storytelling." Indeed, where the growl technique of Tricky Sam Nanton was used to marvelously somber and thrilling effect, in Dickenson's hands it took on a wholly different, irreverent, self-parodic character. When he growls, smears, or bends his already shaggy pitch, the listener is frequently compelled to smile, a reaction rarely prompted by other jazz trombonists.

• Valuable firsthand accounts of Dickenson's life and career as well as pertinent editorial comments on his style are in Whitney Balliett, *American Musicians: 56 Portraits in Jazz* (1986), and Stanley Dance, *The World of Swing* (1974). See also Dale Curran, "Vic Dickenson—Trombone," the *Jazz Record*, July 1944, pp. 4–6, and the short biographical entry in John Chilton, *Who's Who of Jazz* (1985). For information on his early orchestral associations, see Albert McCarthy, *Big Band Jazz* (1974), and Warren Vaché, Sr., *Crazy Fingers: Claude Hopkins' Life in Jazz* (1992), while critical comment on some of his recorded solos can be found in Chilton, *Sidney Bechet: The Wizard of Jazz* (1987) and *The Song of the Hawk: The Life and Recordings of Coleman Hawkins* (1990). Specialized discographical listings are in both Robert Hilbert, *Pee Wee Speaks: A Discography of Pee Wee Russell* (1992), and Manfred Selchow, *Profoundly Blue: A Bio-Discographical Scrapbook on Edmond Hall* (1988), but complete coverage is in Brian Rust, *Jazz Records, 1897–1942* (1982), and two works published serially between 1985 and 1989 by Walter Bruyninckx, *Traditional Jazz Discography, 1897–1988* (6 vols.) and *Swing Discography, 1920–1988* (12 vols.). An obituary is in the *New York Times*, 18 Nov. 1984.

JACK SOHMER

DICKERSON, Carroll (1895–Oct. 1957), was a jazz and popular bandleader and violinist. His birthplace, family, and upbringing are unknown. Through the 1920s Dickerson led jazz bands in Chicago, including residencies at the Entertainers' Café (1921) and Sunset Café (1922–1924), where cornetist George Mitchell and clarinetist Buster Bailey were among his sidemen, playing for a revue that featured singer Frankie "Half-Pint" Jaxon. Trombonist Honore Dutrey and pianist Earl Hines joined Dickerson's orchestra at the Entertainers' and remained with him when, after the club closed, Dickerson made a 42-week tour of the Pantages theater circuit, taking the band to the West Coast and Canada into 1926.

The success of the tour earned Dickerson an engagement in Chicago at the Sunset, where trumpeter Louis Armstrong joined the orchestra. Dickerson sidemen such as Hines and drummer Zutty Singleton later participated in Armstrong's Hot Five and Savoy Ballroom Five sessions, which are among the most important recordings in jazz history. Dickerson's excessive drinking led to his firing in February 1927; Armstrong was made nominal leader and Hines the music director. By February 1928 Dickerson had become violinist and conductor in pianist Clarence M. Jones's band at the Metropolitan Theater, playing alongside Armstrong and Singleton. Jones moved over to the Vendome Theater and then in April, under Dickerson's leadership, the bulk of the group began a residency at Chicago's new Savoy Ballroom. The following month Dickerson's group "tore the roof off the Congress Hotel" according to a review in the *Chicago Defender* (quoted in Collier, p. 165).

In the spring of 1929 the orchestra left Chicago for New York, with Armstrong as its leader and Dickerson as conductor. Initially it presented the musical revue *Hot Feet*, created by Fats Waller, Harvey Brooks, and Andy Razaf. From June, Armstrong sprinted nightly between these performances uptown with Dickerson to those at the downtown location for the show at the Hudson Theater, where it acquired its better-known title, *Hot Chocolates*. This show introduced the hit song "Ain't Misbehavin'." Dickerson's group also accompanied Armstrong for a week at the Lafayette Theater late in June and the following week recorded "Symphonic Raps" and "Savoyagers' Stomp" under Dickerson's name, with Armstrong and Hines as the featured soloists (replacing trumpeter Willie Hightower and pianist Gene Anderson). From the late summer of 1929 Dickerson's group supported Armstrong at Connie's Inn in Harlem for Waller and Razaf's show *Loads of Coal*, a spin-off of *Hot Chocolates* that introduced a new hit, "Honeysuckle Rose."

Armstrong broke away from Dickerson at the end of 1929, and the band quickly unraveled without its star. Dickerson played briefly with the Mills Blues Rhythm Band. Having recorded with King Oliver during the first part of 1930, he served as Oliver's manager, conductor, and violinist while they toured with little success through the midwestern and south-central states that spring and summer. He then returned to Chicago, where he led lesser-known bands. In 1934 and 1935 Dickerson's band filled in at the Grand Terrace while the resident group, Earl Hines's big band, was on tour. In this capacity they participated in the 1934 debut of *Rhythm for Sale*, a musical revue created by English composer Paul Denniker and lyricist Razaf. The number of well-respected jazzmen playing with Dickerson during this period—trumpeters Guy Kelly and Zilner T. Randolph, trombonists Preston Jackson and Al Wynn, reed player Franz Jackson, pianists Charlie Beal and Zinky Cohn, drummer Zutty Singleton—suggests that this was a fine band, but it never recorded. In 1937 Dickerson temporarily ceased full-time playing. He resumed early in 1939, and during the 1940s he held a long residency at Chicago's Rhumboogie Club. He died in Chicago.

Evidently Dickerson was comfortable in styles as different as hot jazz and light classics. According to Hines, Dickerson "was a very strict guy so far as playing instruments was concerned. He wanted everything to be just right." Audiences "had never seen tap dancing and comedy like we had" at the Sunset, Hines said. "For beautiful picture numbers, the producer would find very hard music, like *Black Forest Overture*, *Poet and Peasant Overture* and *Rhapsody in Blue*" (Dance, pp. 40–41, 46). Dickerson's orchestra was prominent in Chicago's night life of the 1920s, but it left scarcely any recorded legacy and few published accounts. Hence lasting memories of Dickerson are not for what he did in his own right but for his having nurtured Armstrong and those sidemen who made great music with Armstrong, independent of Dickerson.

• A few glimpses into Dickerson's personality and musical concerns are found in an interview with Hines in Stanley Dance, *The World of Earl Hines* (1977; repr. 1983), pp. 38–47. A brief essay on Dickerson's career is in Albert McCarthy, *Big Band Jazz* (1974), p. 26. Further bits and pieces may be extracted from Thomas J. Hennessey, "The Black Chicago Establishment, 1919–1930," *Journal of Jazz Studies* 2 (Dec. 1974): 15–45; Dempsey J. Travis, *An Autobiography of Black Jazz* (1983); James Lincoln Collier, *Louis Armstrong: An American Genius* (1983); John Chilton, *Who's Who of Jazz: Storyville to Swing Street*, 4th ed. (1985); and Barry Singer, *Black and Blue: The Life and Lyrics of Andy Razaf* (1992).

BARRY KERNFELD

DICKERSON, Mahlon (17 Apr. 1770–5 Oct. 1853), New Jersey political leader, secretary of the navy, and iron mine operator, was born in Hanover Neck, Morris County, New Jersey, the son of Jonathan Dickerson and Mary Coe. Dickerson's father owned substantial property in Morris County, including an iron mine that Dickerson later inherited. The younger Dickerson grew up privileged. He enjoyed preparatory school near home, and further education at the College of New Jersey (later Princeton University). Graduating from Princeton in 1789, Dickerson studied law in Morristown and in 1793 was admitted to the local bar. Although his political leanings were strongly favorable to the nascent Jeffersonian-Republican cause, Dickerson volunteered for duty in militias organized to suppress the Whiskey Rebellion of 1794 in western Pennsylvania. Although perhaps motivated by visions of military glory, Dickerson saw no direct action.

During the bitter political struggles of the 1790s Dickerson served the Jeffersonian cause in both New Jersey and in Philadelphia. Attracted to the cosmopolitanism of the nation's capital as well as to its political significance, in 1797 Dickerson moved, with two of his brothers, from Morris County to Philadelphia. He commenced a law practice but spent much of his time doing political chores and writing polemics for William Duane's ardently Jeffersonian paper, the *Aurora*. In 1799 Dickerson was chosen a member of Philadelphia's common council, the first of more than a dozen elected or appointed offices he would hold during a remarkably successful political career.

Dickerson allied himself with Philadelphia's Democratic Society and worked assiduously on behalf of Thomas Jefferson's election to the presidency in 1800. He was subsequently rewarded with appointments as commissioner of bankruptcy (1802), adjutant general of Philadelphia (1805), and recorder of the City of Philadelphia (1808). Always interested in politics in his native state, and increasingly uncomfortable with the bitter infighting among Philadelphia Jeffersonians after 1805, Dickerson recognized that his political prospects were better in New Jersey than in Pennsylvania. In 1810 he left Philadelphia forever and assumed responsibility for running the family mine at Succasunna in Morris County. It contained one of the richest iron ore deposits in the eastern United States and supported Dickerson comfortably for the rest of his life. Imitating his political idol Thomas Jefferson, Dickerson built a mansion on his property, "Ferromonte," that became his home base and the focus of his creative energies.

Within months of his move to Morris County, Dickerson was heavily engaged in state politics. Over the next thirty years he jostled with other formidable Jersey politicians, including Samuel L. Southard, Robert Stockton, Peter D. Vroom, Lewis Condict, William L. Dayton, and Garret D. Wall, coming away with an ample share of the best offices in the state. Between 1811, when he was elected to the state assembly from Morris County, and 1841, when he resigned an interim appointment as a federal district judge for New Jersey, Dickerson was rarely out of public office. He served on the state supreme court (1812–1815), as governor (1815–1817), in the U.S. Senate (1817–1833), and as secretary of the navy (1834–1838) under Presidents Andrew Jackson and Martin Van Buren.

In important respects Dickerson's career resembled that of his main rival, Samuel L. Southard, though Dickerson never achieved the mastery of Democratic party organization as Southard did for the New Jersey Whigs. As a politician Dickerson was best known for his tenacious advocacy of a protective tariff, particularly during his service as chairman of the committee of manufactures in the Senate during the great tariff debates of 1832–1833. In 1833, when John Randolph of Roanoke was visiting the U.S. Senate floor while Dickerson was declaiming on the merits of protection, Randolph turned to a friend and observed, "I heard that speech sixteen years ago." Dickerson's tariff advocacy required some tact and wishful thinking during election campaigns, since few Democratic nominees for the White House favored protection at levels Dickerson favored. Dickerson was tolerated for his unorthodox views on the tariff and banking policy because he was respected as a Democratic workhorse.

In 1834 Dickerson was invited to join Jackson's cabinet as secretary of the navy. He served for four years in the post but made little mark beyond his consistent advocacy of a better educated naval force. As navy secretary, Dickerson was often in the uncomfortable position of privately dissenting from administration policies. Publicly, he always played a loyalist's role. Dickerson was present at the attempted assassination of President Jackson at the U.S. Capitol in 1835.

Dickerson's tenure in the Navy Department was marred by a controversy over his leadership in organizing an exploration of Antarctica. Naval officers responsible for the expedition were frustrated by his apparent lack of energy and focus and expressed their dissatisfaction with Dickerson both privately and in the public prints, embarrassing both the secretary and President Van Buren. In 1838, as Dickerson grew more frustrated with his job and his health was affected, he sent Van Buren a resignation letter, which the president readily accepted.

Back in Morris County in semiretirement Dickerson successfully kept his mining operation afloat during the worst of the depression of 1838–1840. He also remained active in politics, speaking on behalf of Jacksonian candidates and assisting his brother Philemon Dickerson in particular. Between 1840 and 1841 Dickerson served as a federal district judge for New Jersey, in effect holding the position for his brother while the latter conducted an unsuccessful bid for reelection to the U.S. House of Representatives. Aside from his service at the state constitutional convention in 1844, the judgeship was his last public office. He did serve for two years in the mid-1840s as head of the protectionist American Institute of New York and might have accepted a diplomatic post had his friend Lewis Cass been elected to the presidency in either 1844 or 1848. Cass failed to win the Democratic nomination in 1844, however, and was narrowly defeated in the election of 1848.

Dickerson never married, and, despite the active interest he took in the affairs of his Canfield nieces and nephews, to whom he was related through his sister, his life was often lonely. His diary reveals that he spent Christmas Day each year alone at Ferromonte, working among his books, papers, and mementos of political life. Shortly before his death there he turned the daily operation of his mines over to the Canfields.

Dickerson's political career was remarkable only in his uncanny ability to achieve and hold significant offices in two states. His wealth and social standing launched him in politics, and his keen ear for what was popular helped sustain a career that was largely unmarked by substantive achievement. That his political success was achieved as a Jacksonian Democrat while his views on public issues were closer to those of mainstream Whigs suggests that ideology was but one element among many in the operation of the second American party system.

• Most of Dickerson's surviving personal papers are housed at the New Jersey Historical Society. They are organized discretely as the Mahlon Dickerson Letterbook, Mahlon Dickerson Mss., Mahlon Dickerson Diary, and as Dickerson papers within the Canfield Genealogical Collection. A small collection of Dickerson papers, including a portion of his diary, can be found in the Special Collections Department of the Rutgers University Library. Robert Russell Beckwith, "Mahlon Dickerson of New Jersey, 1770–1853" (Ph.D. diss., Columbia Univ., Teacher's College, 1964) is the only full-length biography. Significant secondary works on Dickerson include Josiah C. Pumpelly, "Mahlon Dickerson: Industrial Pioneer and Old Time Patriot," New Jersey Historical Society, *Proceedings*, 2d ser., vol. 11 (1891), pp. 133–56; William J. Dunham, "Mahlon Dickerson: A Great but Almost Forgotten Jerseyman," *New Jersey Historical Society, Proceedings*, vol. 68 (Oct. 1950), pp. 297–321; and Robert Russell Beckwith, "Mahlon Dickerson," in *The Governors of New Jersey*, ed. Paul A. Stellhorn and Michael J. Birkner (1982).

MICHAEL J. BIRKNER

DICKERSON, Philemon (26 June 1788–10 Dec. 1862), politician and jurist, was born in Succasunna, New Jersey, the son of Jonathan Dickerson, a landowner and owner of an iron mine, and Mary Coe. Philemon Dickerson graduated from the University of Pennsylvania in 1808 and immediately began studying law in Philadelphia at the instigation of his elder brother Mahlon, then a rising political figure in New Jersey. In 1813 Dickerson was licensed in Philadelphia to practice law. Three years later he moved from Philadelphia to Paterson, New Jersey, where he spent the rest of his life. In 1816 Dickerson married Sidney Stotesbury; they had one daughter and two sons (the second son, Edward Nicoll Dickerson, became a prominent New Jersey attorney, scientist, and inventor).

As a result of the War of 1812 and the new emphasis on American industrial self-sufficiency, Paterson enjoyed a surge of economic development and remained one of the fastest growing cities in the United States during Dickerson's lifetime. Dickerson's relocation to Paterson positioned him effectively in a power center of New Jersey politics, and like most lawyers in this era, Dickerson was active politically. His older brother Silas had been an important figure in the New Jersey Jeffersonian Republican party until his early death in a mill accident. His brother Mahlon became one of the most prominent New Jersey Jeffersonians, helping build the Jacksonian party in the state. Like Mahlon, whose lead in politics he consistently followed, Philemon Dickerson adhered to a heterodox Jacksonian creed. He believed in limited government, but at the same time he strongly supported protective tariffs and government-sponsored internal improvements. As a member of Congress from 1833 to 1836, Dickerson loyally supported the Jacksonian program, however, including the president's war against the Bank of the United States.

In 1836, when popular Democratic governor Peter D. Vroom declined another term, the Jacksonian legislative caucus turned to Dickerson, who resigned his congressional seat to accept the governorship. His single one-year term as governor was turbulent. With a majority in the Legislative Council, Whigs refused to cede patronage appointments to the Democrats. Because the council failed to compromise on this issue, the legislature adjourned without having a joint sitting, in which both houses met simultaneously to act on issues before them. Nor did matters go more smoothly in a special session Dickerson called in the summer of 1837 to deal with the deepening economic depression. As the party in power, Jacksonians took the brunt of voter discontent in the fall elections, and Dickerson lost his job.

A year later Dickerson won a narrow victory as part of a Democratic congressional slate in a hotly contested race. Whigs charged that the Democrats had prevailed only because of fraudulent voting. The new Whig governor, William Pennington, certified the Whig candidates as the true victors in the election by affixing the state seal to their certificates of election, assuring that Whigs would control the House. The ensuing "Broad Seal War" led to a long congressional investigation and, ultimately, the seating of Dickerson and his Democratic colleagues in time to vote for the independent Treasury program proposed by President Martin Van Buren. Like Van Buren, however, Dickerson went down to defeat in the Whig election landslide of 1840; he never again held elective office.

In June 1840, when New Jersey federal district judge William Rossell died, Dickerson indicated his desire for the position. His brother Mahlon interceded with President Van Buren on Philemon's behalf, but Van Buren feared that Philemon's absence from Congress would harm the Democrats' prospects in New Jersey. Consequently, Van Buren named Mahlon Dickerson to the post ad interim, with the understanding that whatever resulted from the election results in November, Philemon Dickerson would replace him. After a difficult confirmation proceeding in the U.S. Senate, with the Whigs doing their best to make the president's life difficult, Philemon indeed succeeded Mahlon.

Dickerson served on the federal bench for the rest of his life. He enjoyed the prestige of the position and the workload, which remained small and mundane until the Civil War. According to one contemporary, he was possessed of a "dry humor" and dignified demeanor. Though enjoined from a too open political activism, he worked with his brother Mahlon throughout the 1840s to promote the presidential prospects of Michigan Democrat Lewis Cass, and he served for many years as mentor to rising lawyers and politicians in Paterson.

As a gray eminence in Paterson, Dickerson helped procure the city's corporate charter in 1851. Five years later he published *The City of Paterson, Its Past, Present, and Future* (1856). He died in Paterson.

• A modest collection of Dickerson's correspondence and miscellaneous personal documents is at the New Jersey Historical Society. Many Philemon Dickerson letters can be found in the papers of his brother Mahlon, housed at the New Jersey Historical Society and Rutgers University Special Collections; and in the Canfield Genealogical Collection at the New Jersey Historical Society. For a brief contemporary memoir, see Lucius Q. C. Elmer, *The Constitution and Government of New Jersey* (1872). The best scholarly account of Dickerson is W. Robert Fallaw, "Philemon Dickerson," in *The Governors of New Jersey: Biographical Essays, 1664–1974*, ed. Paul A. Stellhorn and Michael J. Birkner (1982).

MICHAEL J. BIRKNER

DICKEY, Bill (6 June 1907–12 Nov. 1993), baseball player, was born William Malcom Dickey in Bastrop, Louisiana, the son of John Dickey, a railroad worker, and Laura (maiden name unknown). Bill spent his childhood in Kensett, Arkansas. His family moved to Little Rock, Arkansas, when he was sixteen, and he maintained a home there until his death. Dickey demonstrated his baseball potential while attending Little Rock Junior College. After playing one year of semiprofessional ball, the New York Yankees purchased his contract for $12,500 in 1928. Dickey married Violet Ann Arnold in 1932; they had one child.

Dickey joined the Yankees in 1928 and became the team's regular catcher the following year. He spent his entire major league career with the Yankees, the most dominant team of the period. He caught over 100 games a year for 13 straight seasons, establishing a major league record (later tied by Johnny Bench). During his career Dickey played with Babe Ruth, Lou Gehrig, and Joe DiMaggio. This was both a blessing and a curse for the catcher because he was often overshadowed by these legendary giants. But playing with some of the greatest teams in baseball history, most notably the 1936 Yankees, provided Dickey with visibility, particularly in the World Series. Dickey's brilliance from 1936 to 1939, along with the last great years of Gehrig and the emergence of a young DiMaggio, were instrumental in a Yankee resurgence. After winning just two pennants in Dickey's first seven years, the Yankees won four World Series championships in a row in 1936–1939.

Dickey was a close friend and roommate of Yankee immortal Lou Gehrig. In 1940 Dickey had his worst season as the Yankees foundered and fell to third place. Many attributed Dickey's bad season and the team's decline to the aftermath of Gehrig's disease and retirement. Dickey and the Yankees bounced back in 1941, winning the American League pennant and the World Series.

The left-hand-hitting Dickey appeared in 1,789 games over his seventeen-year career. At the end of the twentieth century his lifetime average of .313 was topped among catchers only by Mickey Cochrane of the Philadelphia Athletics and Detroit Tigers. He hit 202 home runs and had 1,209 runs batted in during his career. Over an eleven-year period (1929–1939), Dickey hit over .300 ten times. His greatest seasons were 1936, with 22 home runs, 107 runs batted in, and a .362 batting average, which set a record for the highest single season average for a catcher (tied by Mike Piazza in 1997); and 1937, with 29 home runs, 133 RBI, and a .332 batting average. In 1938 and 1939 he hit over 20 home runs, drove in over 100 runs, and hit over .300, the only catcher to do so over a four-year period until Piazza did so from 1993 to 1996. Dickey hit over one-half of his career home runs over those four seasons as he adapted his batting stroke to the short right field porch in Yankee Stadium. In addition to being a great clutch hitter, Dickey excelled on defense and had a strong throwing arm. He was considered a good handler of pitchers.

Dickey played in eight World Series and the Yankees won seven world championships during his career. Dickey hit five home runs and drove in 24 runs in 38 World Series games, hitting .225. Dickey was an All-Star every year from 1933 to 1943 except 1935. In the 1934 All-Star game he singled to break the legendary strikeout streak of Carl Hubbell, who had fanned future Hall of Famers Ruth, Gehrig, Jimmy Foxx, Al Simmons, and Joe Cronin consecutively.

Dickey was well respected by teammates and opponents. He was a quiet, unassuming star, but he is remembered for an incident that belied his typical demeanor. After a collision at home plate with Carl Reynolds of the Washington Senators on 4 July 1932, Reynolds headed back for the plate. Dickey apparently thought that Reynolds was ready to fight and leveled the Senators outfielder with one punch that broke his jaw. Dickey was fined $1,000 (a significant portion of his $14,000 salary) and suspended for thirty days.

Dickey was the only active Yankee to play himself in the movie *Pride of the Yankees* about Gehrig. He also played himself in *The Stratton Story*, a movie about Monty Stratton, a promising pitcher for the Chicago White Sox until a hunting accident cost him a leg.

Shortly after hitting the home run that clinched the 1943 World Series, Dickey enlisted in the U.S. Navy. He spent 1944 and 1945 in the service as an organizer of recreational activities in the Pacific theater. He returned to the Yankees as a part-time player in the 1946 season. He also managed the Yankees for part of the 1946 season, taking over from Joe McCarthy. Dickey had a managerial record of 57–48, but he claimed that he was temperamentally unsuited to managing and resigned when the Yankees were eliminated. Other accounts claim he was miffed because the Yankees failed to give him a long-term contract. He seemed to have trouble making the transition from being one of the players to managing his peers.

Dickey returned home and managed in the minor league Southern Association with the Little Rock Travelers, finishing in last place. He returned to the Yankees as a coach in 1949 and helped develop his successors behind the plate, Yogi Berra and the Yankees' first black player Elston Howard. Berra, the master of the malaprop, gave his mentor a great deal of credit, claiming that "Bill Dickey learned me all his experiences." Manager Casey Stengel doubted Berra could become a good major league catcher, but Dickey was convinced. As a Yankee coach, Dickey was part of seven more World Series winners.

After he retired from coaching in 1957, Dickey went home to Little Rock and scouted for the Yankees in the area for two seasons. He had success in Little Rock as a securities representative in the largest brokerage firm off Wall Street after retiring as a scout in 1959. He retired from the business in 1977.

Dickey is regarded as one of the best catchers in baseball history (along with Johnny Bench and Yogi Berra) and the best of his time (his contemporaries were Gabby Hartnett and Mickey Cochrane, also considered among the greatest catchers of all time). Dickey was elected to the National Baseball Hall of Fame in 1954. In 1972 the Yankees retired his uniform number eight (also worn by Berra). A plaque honoring him in Monument Park at Yankee Stadium recognized Dickey as "First in Line of Great Yankee Catchers. The Epitome of Yankee Pride."

• A clipping file on Dickey is at the National Baseball Library, Cooperstown, N.Y. Newspapers are the best primary source for information about Dickey and the Yankees, including the *New York Times*, the *New York Herald Tribune*, and the *New York Daily News*. Among the best books that include interviews with Dickey and his contemporaries are Mike Shatzkin, *The Ballplayers* (1990), and Anthony J. Connor, *Voices from Cooperstown: Baseball's Hall of Famers Tell It Like It Was* (1982). For a statistical analysis of Dickey's career, see Bill James, *The Bill James Historical Baseball Abstract* (1986). A number of books evaluate the all-time greats of baseball, including Larry Klein, "Bill Dickey: Baseball's Immortal Catcher," in *Sport Magazine's All-Time All Stars*, ed. Tom Murray (1977), which rates Dickey as its all-time greatest catcher; Lowell Reidenbaugh, *Cooperstown: Where Baseball's Legends Live Forever* (1983); Maury Allen, *Baseball's 100: A Personal Ranking of the Best Players in Baseball History* (1981); and Eugene McCaffrey, *Major League Baseball Players Vote on the All-Time Greats* (1987).

RICHARD L. PACELLE, JR.

DICKEY, Sarah Ann (25 Apr. 1838–23 Jan. 1904), teacher of freedwomen, was born near Dayton, Ohio, the daughter of Isaac Dickey and his wife, whose maiden name was Tryon. Following her mother's death in 1846, Sarah Dickey was placed with farming relatives who neglected their promise to educate her. At age sixteen, having averaged ten to fifteen days of schooling per year, she remained illiterate. It was with understandable shock and some amusement that her family received her announcement that she wanted to become a teacher.

Undeterred, Dickey struck a bargain with a neighboring family to work in exchange for board and the long-coveted opportunity to attend school. After three years, to her family's astonishment, she earned a teaching certificate, and over the next seven years she taught in country schools near Dayton.

Driven inward by her early deprivations, Dickey relied on promptings from visions, dreams, and a voice she viewed as God's. In 1858 she joined the Church of the United Brethren in Christ, later the Evangelical United Brethren. She applied for missionary work in Africa but was denied. In 1863 the Emancipation Proclamation prompted the American Missionary Association (AMA) to establish a freedmen's school in Vicksburg, Mississippi. They selected Dickey and two other teachers to open it. Conditions in the wartorn city were shocking; one of Dickey's fellow teachers died of typhoid fever. Following Appomattox, the AMA was forced to abandon the school, calling her north again.

Feeling the need for more education, Dickey set her sights on Mount Holyoke Seminary. Borrowing money from her church, she set out for Massachusetts, arriving in South Hadley with thirty-four cents in her pocket and conspicuously missing her trunk, which she had been forced to leave as collateral for the last leg of her trip. Dickey managed to secure a place and, through Mary Lyon's famous domestic work system, earned her way through the four year course, graduating in 1869. Deeply affected by her experience, and consulting as always her guiding voice, Dickey felt charged with a divine mission: to establish a Mount Holyoke for freedwomen.

Dickey began teaching in a freedman's school in Raymond, Mississippi, in January 1870. A year later she moved on to a newly opened school in nearby Clinton, which a local politician declared an unmitigated outrage against Clinton's white citizens. Harassed daily by whites and threatened by the Ku Klux Klan, Dickey was offered lodging by Senator Charles Caldwell, one of the most powerful black leaders in the state. Warning shots fired over her head during class and open threats in the street prompted her response that she had come south to do God's work and would be removed only by death.

While teaching at the free school, Dickey laid the foundation for her seminary, tirelessly soliciting funds and recruiting a biracial board of trustees headed by Caldwell. She secured a charter in 1873 and the following year procured a suitable building on 160 acres of land. Much of the money came from freedmen, despite their destitution. She was making final preparations when Clinton exploded in race riots on 4 September 1875, forcing a delay. For Dickey, the chaos only underscored the need for her school. On 4 October 1875 the Mount Hermon Female Seminary, a nonsectarian school for young black women, opened its doors. Two months later Caldwell was killed by a white mob.

Dickey modeled Mount Hermon as closely as possible after Mount Holyoke. She instituted a domestic work system, setting exacting standards for cleanliness, punctuality, and industriousness. In addition to the elementary course, Dickey offered a three-year, and later four-year, normal course, featuring yearly English and Bible courses, liberal science offerings, music, and education theory. The catalog promised that students completing the course would have no trouble obtaining teacher's certification, and this proved true. In fact, Mount Hermon students were so well prepared that many obtained certification without completing the course.

Dickey's dream for a Mount Holyoke for freedwomen, however, rested on the advanced course, which included Latin, philosophy, further science, English, and religious studies. Only one student graduated the course, yet Dickey continued to offer it until her death, believing that nothing less would do her students justice. Economic and social turmoil and the strong demand for Mount Hermon teachers drew most students away before entering this level.

Though it fell short in that aspect, Mount Hermon exerted tremendous influence in the community. When Clinton closed its free school, Dickey admitted the local children as day students. The Mount Hermon commencement was a source of pride and a big social event, the students acquitting themselves so well that it inspired the grudging respect of many in the white community. Many displaced children found a home at Mount Hermon, and Dickey helped families as she could, offering financial advice and accompanying workers to the cotton markets to ensure fair compensation. In the mid-1890s she bought 120 acres of land and offered tracts on credit to freedmen to build homes. They promptly built the Holy Ghost Baptist Church on the first lot of "Dickeyville," as the neighborhood was called. This was one of the thirty-eight churches burned in Mississippi in 1964. Over the decades the white community began to perceive the value of her work. By 1889 Dickey could write that all of the prejudice against her had been erased.

In 1896 Dickey was ordained a minister of the United Brethren in Christ. However, despite years of tireless solicitation and creative financial endeavors, she was unable to secure permanent funding for her school. Following her death in Clinton at age sixty-five, the school was entrusted to the AMA, whose interests lay in its nearby Tougaloo University. The school fell into neglect and was closed in 1924. Only the brass bell and the gravesite, dedicated and maintained by the Mississippi State Federation of Colored Women's Clubs, remain of Mount Hermon. A memorial building at Tougaloo and a laboratory at Mount Holyoke bear Sarah Dickey's name.

• A book-length biography is Helen Griffith, *Dauntless in Mississippi*, 2d ed. (1966), which is based on Dickey's letters, class newsletters, and other material from the Mount Holyoke College Archives; on legal documents (deeds, wills, etc.) in state offices at Jackson, Miss.; and on interviews with students and friends. See also the three-part article by Elizabeth F. Flagg, "The Mary Lyon of the South," *Woman's Voice* (Boston), 29 Aug. and 5 and 12 Sept. 1896; and F. G. Woodworth, "The Life and Work of Sarah A. Dickey," *Mount Holyoke* (Jan. 1905): 207–12.

ELIZABETH PALERMO GONZALEZ

DICKINS, John (24 Aug. 1747?–27 Sept. 1798), early American Methodist preacher and publisher, was born in London, England, of unknown parentage. He was educated, it is thought at Eton, in English, Latin,

Greek, the natural sciences, and mathematics. He emigrated to North Carolina sometime before the revolutionary war, possibly as an indentured tutor for a colonial planter's family.

In about 1774 Dickins experienced a religious conversion, and by 1776 he was serving as a Methodist local preacher in Sussex County, Virginia. In May 1777 he joined the Methodist connection of unordained itinerant preachers, the evangelical wing of the Anglican church. Between 1777 and 1779, when many Methodists in America threatened to separate from the Church of England because it would not ordain Methodist preachers to administer the sacraments, Dickins sided with the southern preachers, including the allies of the Irish lay preacher Robert Strawbridge, who encouraged the unordained preachers to provide the rites of baptism and communion for their followers.

In 1778 Dickins married Elizabeth "Betsy" Yancey, also a Methodist, of Halifax County, North Carolina. The couple named their first child, born in 1780, Asbury after the Methodist leader Francis Asbury, with whom Dickins was developing an enduring friendship. In 1781, possibly because of ill health or disruptions from the revolutionary war, Dickins briefly left the itinerancy and farmed a portion of his father-in-law's plantation in Halifax County, where he was listed in the tax records of 1782 as owning several slaves and assorted livestock.

In June 1783, at the conclusion of the war, Dickins was appointed by Asbury as the stationed preacher at Wesley Chapel in New York City, where he was expected to revive the flagging congregation. He also taught school, as he may have done in later years, in Philadelphia. In December 1784 he was among the preachers who attended the Christmas Conference in Baltimore that established the Methodist church. Dickins, who was ordained a deacon, is credited with moving the resolution whereby the new denomination was to be named the Methodist Episcopal church. The following spring or early summer Dickins and his family returned briefly to North Carolina. Here, the new deacon, one of the few educated men among the itinerants, traveled an assigned circuit and edited and revised the Methodist *Discipline* into its standard American form. In September 1786 he was ordained elder and was restationed in New York City.

In May 1789 Dickins received his appointment as the first book steward of the Methodist Episcopal church. The next month he moved his family to Philadelphia, the new nation's cultural capital. Here he opened shop (for what by 1792 was called the Methodist Book Concern) with the publication of two Methodist standards, *An Extract of the Christian's Pattern* (John Wesley's abridgment of Thomas à Kempis's devotional tract) and Wesley's *Primitive Physic* (already in its twenty-first edition), and the first of two volumes of the *Arminian Magazine* (1789–1790), modeled on Wesley's periodical of the same name. Although Methodist books had been issued previously in America or imported from Britain, Dickins published some of the earliest accounts of the American Methodist experience in the *Arminian Magazine* and later in the *Methodist Magazine* (1797–1798). By 1793 his book list comprised twenty-eight titles, mostly of English origin but including *The Experience and Travels of Mr. Freeborn Garrettson*, the autobiography of an American preacher; and the first volume of Asbury's *Journal*. Dickins's edition of the English bestseller *A Pocket Hymn Book* appeared in 1790; the first American edition of extracts from Wesley's *Journal* in 1795.

Under Dickins's stewardship the Methodist church produced approximately 114,000 copies of Methodist books and tracts. Because the book business was expected to subsist on the sale of these items, usually at low prices, on the preachers' circuits and on monies invested from the Chartered Fund for the support of retired preachers, Dickins was, in short, "editor, treasurer, and general flunky, as well as book steward for the whole church" (Pilkington, p. 96). Initial operating capital was provided by Dickins himself, and he continued to shore up the increasingly expensive operation thereafter. By the mid 1790s, to support his family, Dickins had begun a small business as a stationer, bookseller, and bookbinder, first at 44 North Second Street and then at 41 Market Street, where he tended numerous Methodist as well as non-Methodist customers. He also served as Asbury's accountant. By the time of his death, the Methodist book business had accumulated a substantial debt, much of it tied to Dickins's estate. Methodist publishing was placed on secure financial footing by the stringent fiscal policies of Dickins's successor, Ezekiel Cooper.

Dickins was admired by his less well-educated Methodist contemporaries for his intellect and at the same time for his lack of affectation. Early in their friendship, Asbury described Dickins as "a gloomy countryman of mine, and very diffident of himself" (*Journal and Letters*, vol. 1, p. 358). Reflecting on his long years of urban residence, Dickins wrote to fellow preacher Edward Dromgoole in November 1791: "As far as I know myself, I am the same plain man that I was ten years ago. Living in these polite cities has not polished off any of my roughness" (quoted in Sweet, p. 143). He declined to leave his post as stationed preacher in Philadelphia at the time of the 1798 yellow fever epidemic, during which he and his eldest daughter died. He was survived by his wife and five children.

• The John Dickins Account Books (1795–1798) are in the Loudoun Collection, Historical Society of Pennsylvania, Philadelphia. The Dickins family Bible is housed at the Library of the Methodist Publishing House in Nashville. Dickins's various imprints, 1789–1798, are in Charles Evans, *American Bibliography, 1639–1800*. The best treatment of Dickins's life and career is in James Penn Pilkington, *The Methodist Publishing House: A History* (1968). See also Ezekiel Cooper, *A Funeral Discourse, on the Death of That Eminent Man[,] the Late Reverend John Dickins* (1799). On early American Methodist imprints see Leland D. Case, "Origins of Methodist Publishing in America," Bibliographical Society of America *Papers* 59 (First quarter 1965): 12–27, and Frank Baker, *Union Catalog of the Publications of John and Charles Wesley*, rev. ed. (1991). Materials relating to Dickins and the Methodist book business appear throughout publications related to the Methodist Episcopal church: *Minutes* (1773–1798); John Wesley, *Letters*, vol. 8. (1931); Francis Asbury, *Journal and Letters* (3 vols., 1958); and William Warren Sweet, ed., *Religion on the American Frontier*, vol. 4, *The Methodists* (1946). The naming of the Methodist Episcopal church is attributed to Dickins in *Sketches of the Life and Travels of Thomas Ware* (1839).

DEE E. ANDREWS

DICKINSON, Anna Elizabeth (28 Oct. 1842–22 Oct. 1932), orator and lecturer, was born in Philadelphia, Pennsylvania, the youngest child of John Dickinson, a merchant who never recovered from the Panic of 1837, and Mary Edmondson. Devout Quakers, the Dickinsons were active members of the local antislavery society. Dickinson was two when her father died, and her mother kept the family together by teaching school and taking in boarders. Dickinson attended a series of Friends' educational institutions, but her formal training ended by the time she was fifteen.

Determined to help support her family, Dickinson worked as a copyist for publishing houses and law firms, a teacher, a milliner, a government clerk, a writer, and an actress both before and after she had gained and lost fame and fortune as a public lecturer. Although she flirted briefly with Methodism, she finally followed the Quaker tradition that encouraged a public role for women as preachers and provided her with a platform, an audience, and benefactors in the early stages of her career. At the height of her career (1863–1875) Dickinson could command a thousand dollars a lecture; by 1872, when she was known as the "Queen of the Lyceum," she was earning more than $20,000 per year and was more popular on the national lyceum circuit than any other speaker except Henry Ward Beecher.

Dickinson's remarkable public career began in 1856 when William Lloyd Garrison published in the *Liberator* a letter young Dickinson had written protesting the apparent indifference and political apathy of northerners to the tarring and feathering of a Kentucky schoolteacher who had criticized slavery. Four years later Dickinson delivered her first public address, "The Rights and Wrongs of Women," at Clarkson Hall in Philadelphia. Her extemporaneous, sarcastic response to a man's suggestion that women were suited only for the role of homemaker drew a favorable response from the crowd. That day she made the acquaintance of social reformers Ellwood Longshore and Dr. Hannah Longshore, who encouraged Dickinson to speak out on the subjects of woman's rights and antislavery before local audiences. When she spoke before the Philadelphia Anti-Slavery Society in 1860, she received favorable and widespread reviews by the press. Soon thereafter Lucretia Mott introduced her to an audience of 800 at Concert Hall in Philadelphia, where she spoke for two hours on woman's rights.

Working twelve-hour days at the office of the U.S. Mint in Philadelphia for $28 a month, Dickinson lectured as an avocation. Following the Union disaster at the Battle of Ball's Bluff, in late 1861, she delivered a scathing attack on General George McClellan (1826–1885). The northern press vilified General Charles P. Stone for the costly defeat, but Dickinson blamed fellow Philadelphian McClellan and accused him of treason. She was promptly fired for her political sentiments, and almost in desperation turned to lecturing as a source of financial support. Garrison arranged several engagements for her throughout New England, where she shared the stage with such notables as Wendell Phillips and Ralph Waldo Emerson.

Despite Dickinson's popularity, due in part to her youth, demure appearance and sharp wit, and her ability to speak for hours without resorting to notes, she found it difficult to earn a living as a lecturer before church groups and antislavery societies. Crowds were large, but the pay was a modest $20 a lecture. In her spare time, she volunteered at soldiers' hospitals, and on the lecture circuit she wove those experiences into her repertoire.

In New Hampshire in fall 1862 Benjamin Franklin Prescott, an influential man in the Republican party, heard Dickinson speak and was captivated by her youth, energy, and popular appeal. The party's popularity was declining, and the March 1863 gubernatorial race was considered too close to call. In a daring move, Prescott convinced the party to hire Dickinson to stump the state. Partly due to her exhortations the Republicans retained the state house. Fresh from this success she spoke to an enthusiastic New York crowd at Cooper Union Institute in May 1863 and earned $1,000. A triumphant Dickinson returned to Philadelphia where that summer she shared a platform with Frederick Douglass and her close friend William D. Kelley. The threesome delivered stirring speeches, which were reprinted frequently, promoting the enlistment of blacks, a favorite topic of Dickinson's.

The following year Dickinson was invited to speak before the U.S. House of Representatives. Her historic lecture on 16 January 1864 marked the first time a woman spoke before members of Congress. Her performance delighted the radical element of the party as she castigated Democrats, praised blacks' contributions to the war effort, and rebuked Lincoln's Proclamation of Amnesty and Reconstruction plan for its leniency.

When the Civil War ended Dickinson was almost twenty-three, the age at which many women of her generation retreated into domesticity. Although she did not lack for suitors, she never seriously considered marriage. Instead she turned her wartime experiences into a successful career as a public speaker in the national lyceum movement, which reached its zenith in the decade following the Civil War. Between 1865 and 1875 Dickinson followed the lecture circuit from October to May. While a good season might net her over $20,000, the pace—five to six lectures per week in a different city each night—taxed her health. Her stock of lectures included civil rights for the former slaves, women's rights, universal education, attacks on nativism and racism, the evils of prostitution and polyga-

my, the political corruption of Grant's administration, and the life of Joan of Arc.

When Republican party leaders supported Grant's bid for a second term, Dickinson broke with party regulars and endorsed Horace Greeley's candidacy. In 1861 Dickinson's political sentiments had resulted in the loss of her government job; now her support for Greeley cost her bookings on the national lecture tour. After 1872 her speaking career declined. Having saved no money, she attempted to revive her flagging career during the next few years, but to no avail.

In 1868 Dickinson tried her hand at novel writing. *What Answer?* was a polemical piece about a handsome, wealthy Union Army officer who weds, despite his family's objections, a beautiful, cultured, educated "quadroon" and perishes with her in the 1863 New York Draft Riot. Harriet Beecher Stowe lauded the book for its "powerful appeal to the heart and conscience of the American nation on the sin of caste," but otherwise it was not well received. *A Paying Investment* (1876) was an appeal for universal education and technical training as a cure for the social ills of crime and poverty. In 1879 she depicted her lyceum experiences in *A Ragged Register (of People, Places, and Opinions)*.

Dickinson also flirted with a career in the theater, writing plays and acting. Her first play, *A Crown of Thorns, or Anne Boleyn*, opened in 1876 at Boston's Globe Theatre with Dickinson playing the part of the doomed queen. She finished a second historical drama, *Aurelian*, in 1878 and achieved modest success with *An American Girl*, which opened in New York in 1880 and starred the popular actress Fanny Davenport. At forty Dickinson briefly returned to the stage as Hamlet, but ridicule by the press led her to quit the theater.

Defeated in spirit, and impoverished, Dickinson retired from public life. Moving to West Pittston, Pennsylvania, to live with her ailing mother and her sister, she succumbed to illness and bouts of depression. In 1888 she temporarily came out of retirement when the Republican party hired her to tout Benjamin Harrison's (1833–1901) candidacy. Summoning up her old attack style, she railed against Grover Cleveland and the Democratic party. However, her too frequent references to the Democrats' past misdeeds when the party stood for slavery led partisan papers to question her lucidity.

Thereafter Dickinson's physical and mental health deteriorated. In 1891 her sister had her committed to the State Hospital for the Insane in Danville, Pennsylvania. Dickinson eventually secured her own release and sued the doctors for signing the commitment order. Although she eventually won her suit, the monetary award was negligible. Befriended by Sally and George Ackley, Dickinson lived with them for almost forty years and died in Goshen, New York.

In an era when the prevailing wisdom frowned on female participation in the political process, Anna Dickinson's brief career as a celebrated, paid political speaker stands out. She successfully capitalized on her wartime experiences with a career in the lyceum movement where she gained a national following and out-earned all but two men. However, what catapulted Dickinson to fame was not what she said or how she said it but the novelty of her youth and striking appearance. Once those advantages naturally faded, her career was doomed. The public stage was less kind to middle-aged women than to middle-aged men in the political culture of nineteenth-century American life.

• Dickinson's papers are located in the Manuscript Division, Library of Congress. An excellent example of her rhetorical style is in "Addresses of the Honorable W. D. Kelley, Miss Anna E. Dickinson, and Mr. Frederick Douglass, at a Mass Meeting, Held at National Hall, Philadelphia, July 6, 1863, for the Promotion of Colored Enlistments," in the University of Texas Library. See also Elizabeth Cady Stanton, "Anna Elizabeth Dickinson," in *Eminent Women of the Age*, ed. James Parton (1868). More recent sources include James Harvey Young, "Anna Elizabeth Dickinson and the Civil War" (Ph.D. diss., Univ. of Illinois, 1941); Giraud Chester's biography *The Embattled Maiden* (1951), which makes excellent, although undocumented, use of primary sources but also takes literary license with invented dialogue; Joseph Duffy, "Anna Elizabeth Dickinson and the Election of 1863," *Connecticut History* 25 (1984): 22–38; and George Philip Prindle, "An Analysis of the Rhetoric in Selected Representative Speeches of Anna Elizabeth Dickinson" (Ph.D. diss., Stanford Univ., 1972).

KATHLEEN C. BERKELEY

DICKINSON, Anson (19 Apr. 1779–9 Mar. 1852), portrait miniaturist, was born in Milton, Connecticut, the son of Oliver Dickinson, Jr., a master carpenter who designed and built the town's Trinity Episcopal Church, and Anna Landon. Art historian Frederic Fairchild Sherman reported that Oliver Dickinson also painted portraits and was thought to have given his son his first lessons in painting. Recent research, however, has found no evidence that Oliver ever painted, and it appears that Sherman confused him with Obadiah Dickinson, Jr. (no relation), a Connecticut portrait painter. No information has come to light regarding Anson Dickinson's earliest instruction in art, and it is likely he was self-taught. He was apprenticed around 1796 to the Litchfield, Connecticut, silversmith Isaac Thompson (or Thomson), and a silver spoon in the collection of the Litchfield Historical Society marked "A. Dickinson" is either his work or that of his brother Ambrose.

An advertisement in the *Connecticut Journal* of 27 May 1802 is the earliest evidence of Dickinson's activity as an artist, though no works painted in response to the ad have been located. From the beginning he seems to have concentrated on painting miniatures. On 1 September 1803 he began to keep a record of his commissions and travels. This account indicates that in 1803 he charged $20 to $25 for a watercolor-on-ivory miniature and up to $7 for a profile portrait executed probably on paper or Bristol board. His earliest-known miniature is of his uncle Abel Dickinson, painted on New Year's Day 1803 (private collection). Confirmed in his choice of a career, in May 1804 he began a two-month visit to New York City, where he

painted nine miniatures and was himself painted by Edward Greene Malbone; the portrait of Dickinson (Stamford Historical Society, Stamford, Conn.) depicts a handsome young man with a serious, sensitive face. Malbone, two years older than Dickinson, was then the leading miniaturist in America. The younger artist must have hoped to learn what he could from talking with Malbone, watching him paint, and afterward having his miniature to study. Dickinson may also have taken lessons from his fellow Connecticut artist Elkanah Tisdale, whose miniatures bear a stylistic similarity to Dickinson's work.

Dickinson's friends and neighbors in the Milton-Litchfield area provided him with commissions over the years, but in order to earn a livelihood he had to travel to other cities and towns. New York City served as his base for much of his professional life. From there he traveled up and down the eastern seaboard as far north as Quebec and as far south as Charleston, South Carolina. In Albany, New York, in 1810 he met and was befriended by writer Washington Irving, who praised him in a letter to Mrs. Josiah Ogden Hoffman as "an artist of highly promising talents, and of most amiable demeanor and engaging manners . . . He is not a mere mechanic in his art, but paints from his imagination" (P. M. Irving, *The Life and Letters of Washington Irving*, vol. 1 [1863], pp. 243–45). Irving encouraged Dickinson to return to New York City, but he remained in Albany for another year before going to Montreal, where he worked from September to December 1811. He then journeyed south to Charleston, where he worked until May 1812. It was not, however, a successful stay; despite being then the only artist in town, he received only eleven commissions. Finally, following Irving's advice, Dickinson returned to New York City, where on 30 June 1912 he married Sarah Brown. The couple had no children but around 1824 adopted William Edmund and Mary Ann Walker, the two children of their friends William and Mary Ann (Wright) Walker, following the death of the elder Mary Ann Walker.

From 1812 to 1820 Dickinson worked almost exclusively in New York City and painted nearly three hundred miniatures. Among his subjects were the diarist and future mayor Philip Hone, the physician David Hosack, General Peter B. Porter, and Maria Gansevoort Melville, the mother of the writer Herman Melville. By 1820, however, Dickinson was receiving far fewer commissions, perhaps a result of the economic depression of the previous year, and therefore returned to the life of an itinerant artist. While maintaining his residence in New York City, he traveled to Canada, where he painted miniatures in Montreal and Quebec for several months in 1820, 1821, and 1822. For most of 1823 he remained in Boston, where he painted more than forty miniatures. Among his sitters were the prominent merchant Amos Lawrence (Massachusetts Historical Society) and the well-known artist Gilbert Stuart (New-York Historical Society); Stuart, who seldom sat for other artists, paid Dickinson the high compliment of commissioning miniatures of himself and his daughter Jane.

In late October 1823 Dickinson hit the road again. In Philadelphia, between November and January 1824, he painted eight miniatures; in Baltimore, from January to May, he painted a dozen miniatures. His most famous Baltimore sitter was Charles Carroll of Carrollton, a signer of the Declaration of Independence. Painted when Carroll was nearly eighty-seven, the miniature (Maryland Historical Society, Baltimore) depicts the statesman as quite elderly but still spry. Between January 1825 and November 1826 he worked in upstate New York, Canada, and Connecticut and painted more than eighty miniatures. In January 1827 he went to Washington, where he worked off and on for the next three years, usually when Congress was in session. During this period he painted such notables as General Jacob Brown, Sam Houston (then a Tennessee congressman), Stephen Van Rensselaer (whose portrait by Stuart Dickinson he had copied in miniature two decades earlier), the statesman Edward Livingston (Metropolitan Museum of Art, New York), the noted lawyer William Wirt and his wife (both private collection), and Charles Francis Adams, son of President John Quincy Adams and himself later American minister to Great Britain (National Museum of American Art, Washington). He also painted a copy in miniature of Charles Willson Peale's 1772 portrait of George Washington, the earliest-known likeness of the first president. Washington's adopted son, George Washington Parke Custis, commissioned the miniature; Dickinson was much pleased with his work and had it engraved by James W. Steel so impressions could be sold to the public.

The bulk of Dickinson's output was, naturally, portraiture, but he also executed the occasional genre or "fancy" piece. His best work in this line is *Cupid and the Graces* (1816, Stamford Historical Society), which he painted as an exhibition piece to display his virtuosity.

Around 1833 Dickinson and his family moved to New Haven. He continued to make frequent visits to Litchfield and traveled periodically back to New York City and to upstate New York. From 1842 to 1846 he spent much time in and around Buffalo. He ceased his professional travels after 1846 but continued to paint miniatures in Connecticut until four months before his death in Milton.

Dickinson hit his stride as a miniaturist early on, around 1804, and his style and ability remained constant thereafter. The widespread use of photography after 1839 dealt an ultimately fatal blow to the art of miniature painting, but Dickinson was apparently not seriously affected by this development, and unlike other miniaturists, his art was never influenced by photographic realism. His miniatures are attractive, well-executed, direct portrayals, many of well-known figures. His papers contain a passage in his handwriting copied from Jonathan Richardson's *An Essay on the Theory of Painting*: "A Painter's language is his Pencil, he should neither say too Little, nor too Much,

but go directly to his Point, and tell his Story with all possible Simplicity." Dickinson's miniatures demonstrate that this was his guiding principle. In 1834 William Dunlap called him "the best miniature painter in New York City." He certainly ranks among the best American miniaturists of the nineteenth century.

• Dickinson's papers are owned by the Connecticut Historical Society, Hartford; additional papers relating to his life and career are in the collection of the Litchfield Historical Society. The Stamford Historical Society owns several of his miniatures; other works by him can be found in collections of the National Museum of American Art in Washington, D.C., the Metropolitan Museum of Art in New York, the Philadelphia Museum of Art, and the Yale University Art Gallery. His work is recorded in the National Portrait Gallery's Catalog of American Portraits, the National Museum of American Art's Inventory of American Painting, and at the Frick Art Reference Library in New York. Dickinson's account book was edited by Mary Helen Kidder and published by the Connecticut Historical Society in 1937. The society mounted an exhibition of his work in 1983; the accompanying catalog by Mona L. Dearborn, *Anson Dickinson: The Celebrated Miniature Painter, 1779–1852*, contains a biographical sketch and a chronology of his career. Dickinson is mentioned also in William Dunlap, *A History of the Rise and Progress of the Arts of Design in the United States* (1834).

DAVID MESCHUTT

DICKINSON, Daniel Stevens (11 Sept. 1800–12 Apr. 1866), politician, was born in Goshen, Connecticut, the son of Daniel T. Dickinson and Mary Caulkins, farmers. In 1807 the family joined the westward migration from New England to New York, settling in Guilford in the Chenango valley. Dickinson aspired to be a lawyer, but his parents, who could only provide him with a common school education, insisted he learn the trade of clothier. When he reached legal age, however, he taught school and surveyed land while continuing a course of intensive self-study begun during his apprenticeship. In 1822 he married Lydia Knapp, with whom he had four children. Finally completing his legal education in the offices of Clark and Clapp in Norwich, New York, he was admitted to the bar in 1828. He set up practice in Guilford but moved to the larger Binghamton in 1831. Able to analyze the intricacies of cases and to speak persuasively before juries, he became a highly successful lawyer.

Dickinson became the first president of Binghamton after its incorporation in 1834, served as a delegate to the Democratic National Convention in 1835, and was elected to a four-year term in the state senate in 1836. His service coincided with the panic of 1837. Many Democrats blamed the depression on the banking system and state spending on internal improvements such as canals and railroads, but Dickinson considered government aid for economic development, especially the completion of the Erie Railroad through Binghamton, very important. Challenging deflationary and antidevelopment views in debate in the senate, Dickinson won recognition as a leader of the "Hunker" faction of the Democratic party. In 1840 the state convention, deciding to represent both factions on the ticket, nominated Dickinson for lieutenant governor. The Whigs won that election, but in 1842 Dickinson was renominated for the position and the ticket triumphed. During Dickinson's two-year term he presided over the state senate and the court of errors and served on the canal board.

An ardent nationalist, Dickinson vigorously supported James K. Polk and territorial expansion in 1844. Faced with two upcoming vacancies in the U.S. Senate in December 1844, Democratic leaders divided the seats between the party factions, with the governor appointing Dickinson for the remaining six weeks of N. P. Tallmadge's term and the legislature confirming the ensuing full term. Dickinson served on the Senate's Finance Committee, which he eventually chaired. On the floor he argued for the annexation of Texas, the acquisition of all the Oregon Territory occupied jointly with Great Britain, and the war with Mexico. He opposed the Clayton-Bulwer Treaty (1850) because it permitted Britain to join the United States in guaranteeing the neutrality of any future Isthmian canal.

As territorial expansion made the extension of slavery an issue, Dickinson responded by denying its relevance. Slavery, he insisted, would die out if left alone; agitating it could only lead to civil war. Those raising the issue did so only to further selfish ambitions, he averred. He thus opposed, despite instructions to the contrary from the state legislature, the Wilmot Proviso, which demanded that territory acquired from Mexico be free soil. In 1847 Dickinson introduced resolutions that called for territorial legislatures to control domestic policy, foreshadowing the doctrine of popular sovereignty on slavery. During the heated debates over the Compromise of 1850 he coolly disarmed Senator Henry Foote, who had drawn a pistol on Senator Thomas Hart Benton on the Senate floor. He served on the Committee of Thirteen, which hammered out the elements of the eventual compromise, and won the gratitude of Whig compromisers Henry Clay and Daniel Webster.

The slavery issue exacerbated Democratic factionalism in New York, with Free Soil Democrats refusing to support the national Democratic ticket in 1848. Dickinson blamed the Free Soil element, which had been welcomed back to the party in 1849, for the Whigs regaining control of the state legislature, which cost him reelection to the Senate in 1850. To Dickinson the only way to stop the sectionalism threatening the nation was to punish it severely; he bitterly impugned the motives of Democrats willing to forgive the Free Soil exodus and demanded that Free Soil advocates be prescribed from holding office.

This quarrel formed the basis of a new Democratic factionalism pitting hardliners ("Hards") like Dickinson against the more accommodating "Softs" like William Marcy and Horatio Seymour. In 1853 President Franklin Pierce offered Dickinson the position of collector of the New York port as an incentive for compromise, but Dickinson firmly declined. With Dickinson leading the upstate Hards and active at most

conventions, the party remained divided through the 1850s, causing endless grief to the Pierce and Buchanan administrations, facilitating the growth of Republicanism in the state, and preventing any New York Democrat from winning a presidential nomination.

Until the Confederate attack on Fort Sumter, Dickinson, who supported southern Democrat John Breckinridge in 1860 and blamed northern sectionalists for the secession crisis, was considered prosouthern. With war a reality, however, Dickinson concluded that only complete support for the Abraham Lincoln administration could save the nation. Advocating an end to politics as usual, he cooperated with the Republicans as a War Democrat. He addressed patriotic gatherings throughout the North and recruited troops for the army. Selected to run for state attorney general in 1861 on a People's (Union) ticket, he triumphed along with the entire ticket. In office he argued for the constitutionality of conscription and of soldiers voting in the field. He was mentioned as a candidate both for the U.S. Senate and for governor, but his enemies mobilized against him.

Rejecting Lincoln's offer of a place on the commission to study the northwest boundary, Dickinson schemed to replace the president with Salmon P. Chase on the 1864 ticket; Dickinson himself was an unsuccessful candidate for the vice presidential nomination. One of Lincoln's last appointments before his assassination was to name Dickinson district attorney for the Southern District of New York, a post he accepted. At the time of his own death in New York City, Dickinson was a supporter of Andrew Johnson's Reconstruction plans and anticipated party realignment. His firmness of conviction had proved valuable during the war, but it had also factionalized his party and cost him all opportunities for major offices after leaving the Senate.

• John R. Dickinson, ed., *Speeches and Correspondence, Etc., of the Late Daniel S. Dickinson* (2 vols., 1867), contains a biographical sketch, Dickinson's most important speeches, and many letters. A few other letters are in the William Corcoran Papers, Library of Congress. See also Christopher Dell, *Lincoln and the War Democrats* (1975), and De Alva S. Alexander, *A Political History of the State of New York*, vols. 2 and 3 (1906, 1909). An obituary is in the *New York Times*, 14 Apr. 1866.

PHYLLIS F. FIELD

DICKINSON, Donald McDonald (17 Jan. 1846–15 Oct. 1917), lawyer and postmaster general, was born in Port Ontario, New York, the son of Asa C. Dickinson, a voyager, and Minerva Holmes. In 1848 Donald moved with his family to Michigan's St. Clair County and then four years later to Detroit, where he attended the Detroit public schools. He graduated from the University of Michigan Law School in March 1867 and was admitted to the Michigan bar on 2 May 1867. A successful young attorney, Dickinson in 1869 married Frances Platt. The Dickinsons had seven children, five of whom died in one year, 1878, from spinal meningitis.

Dickinson first became actively involved in state politics in 1872 when he served as a delegate to the Democratic State Convention and then as secretary of the Democratic State Central Committee. It seemed his association with the Democratic party would be shortlived when he abruptly resigned from the committee after the election, charging that some fellow Michigan Democrats had contributed to the defeat of Horace Greeley, their party's presidential nominee.

By 1874 Dickinson had returned to the Democratic fold, and in that year his campaign speeches helped Democrats score substantial gains in the state legislature. Michigan also sent three Democrats to the U.S. House of Representatives, the first elected to the House from that state since the Civil War. Named chairman of the Democratic State Central Committee, Dickinson managed a brilliant political campaign in 1876. Although the Wolverine State still went Republican, Michigan recorded the nation's largest Democratic gain over 1872. The *Detroit Evening News* exulted, "Never was a political campaign in this state managed with more tact and energy than the recent one by Don M. Dickinson of this city, chairman of the Democratic State Central Committee."

By 1880 the Democrats named Dickinson chairman of their delegation to the national convention. By 1884 he was a member of the Democratic National Committee, only the second Michigan Democrat to become well known nationally, the first having been Lewis Cass, the 1848 Democratic presidential candidate. He supported Grover Cleveland's nomination and became one of his confidants after Cleveland won the election. In 1885 Cleveland offered him a seat on the Civil Service Commission, but Dickinson declined, saying that he had been "not merely a strong and devoted Democrat, but a hard and a contentious partisan." Dickinson did not want his own partisanship to discredit President Cleveland's reform program.

On 16 January 1888 the Senate confirmed Dickinson's nomination as postmaster general. In that position he was successful in defeating legislation that would have granted an $800,000 subsidy to steamship companies carrying mail to South and Central American ports. He issued an order placing employees of the Railway Mail Service under civil service. When certain employees of the Chicago, Burlington and Quincy Railroad went on strike, he refused to employ troops to break the strike as management desired and insisted that the federal government had no obligation to pay additional compensation to railroad companies because of inconveniences caused by a strike.

After Cleveland lost the 1888 election, Dickinson returned to Michigan where he again practiced law. It was during this time that he successfully prevented railroad interests from pushing a number of Michigan homesteaders off their farms. For this he took no compensation. One Jackson newspaper reported that "in the cabins of the homesteaders of the Upper Peninsula Mr. Dickinson's name is a household word, and he is revered by them as the one man who at all times and places has proved their true friend." As a tribute to

Dickinson, one Upper Peninsula county bears his name.

In 1892 Dickinson led the Michigan delegation at the Democratic National Convention. He proved to be a successful floor leader of the Cleveland forces as the Democratic party again nominated Cleveland for president. Later Dickinson headed the Democratic National Campaign Committee that engineered a Cleveland victory in November.

Although Cleveland offered Dickinson various posts in his second administration, Dickinson declined any official position. However, he continued advising Cleveland concerning the appointment of others. Cleveland felt indebted to Dickinson, exclaiming, "I am constantly wondering why there are not, within the circle of my life, more [Daniel] Lamonts and Dickinsons." On another occasion Cleveland expressed a wish for "about twenty Dickinsons in the country."

Dickinson, who opposed free silver, became disillusioned with the Democratic party when it nominated William Jennings Bryan in 1896 and again in 1900. In 1900 he backed the Republican ticket of William McKinley and Theodore Roosevelt (1858–1919). In 1912 he supported Theodore Roosevelt for president. By then Dickinson had become convinced that the federal government should be less laissez-faire and that it should play a more positive role in the life of the nation. Roosevelt had proposed a new nationalism that regarded "the executive power as the steward of the public welfare." Dickinson agreed with much of Roosevelt's program, for he stated that Roosevelt had "been the victim of the reactionary teachings of both old parties."

In 1896 Cleveland had named Dickinson chief counsel for the United States before the Joint High Commission on Bering Sea Claims. When Theodore Roosevelt became president, he named Dickinson in 1902 to an arbitration tribunal commissioned to settle a dispute between the United States and Salvador (present-day El Salvador). Later Dickinson wrote, "As to my positions under the National Government, I esteem my professional positions in international matters, both as counsel for the United States and as arbitrator, more highly than any mere political place."

Dickinson died at his home in Trenton, Michigan. President Woodrow Wilson saluted Dickinson upon his death as one "who leaves a memory that will be cherished and revered not only by the people of his state, but by the people of his nation."

• Six boxes of Dickinson papers are held by the Library of Congress. The Burton Historical Collection in the Detroit Public Library has a small collection of Dickinson material. The only major biography is Robert Bolt, *Donald Dickinson* (1970). A shorter biographical sketch by Arthur Pound is in *Michigan and the Cleveland Era* (1948), ed. Earl D. Babst and Lewis G. Vander Velde. See also the *Biographical Directory of the United States Executive Branch 1774–1971* (1971). An obituary is in the *Detroit News*, 17 Oct. 1917.

ROBERT BOLT

DICKINSON, Edwin De Witt (19 May 1887–26 Mar. 1961), legal educator, was born in Bradford, Iowa, the son of William Elihu Dickinson, a farmer, and Edna Jessie Hickock. After obtaining a B.A. from Carleton College in 1909, he taught history for two years at Dartmouth University and earned a master's degree from that institution in 1911. He studied political science at Harvard University from 1911 to 1913 and received a doctorate in government and international law on completing his dissertation in 1918. To these scholarly achievements he added a J.D. in 1919 from the University of Michigan Law School, where he had been a Carnegie Fellow in International Law (1917–1918). In 1913 he married May Luella Hall, a former Carleton classmate; they had no children.

Dickinson joined the law faculty at Michigan in 1919 and for the next fourteen years helped to develop a strong program in international law. He advocated the use of the case method in teaching international law but insisted that casebooks must incorporate a broad range of materials—treaty provisions, state papers, extracts from treatises and historical works—in addition to representative court decisions. His pragmatic and relativistic approach to international legal problems reflected the empirical temper of the social sciences in the 1920s and found expression in two widely used casebooks: *A Selection of Cases and Other Readings on the Law of Nations* (1929) and *Cases and Materials on International Law* (1950). Throughout a prolific publishing career Dickinson attacked legal fictions and called for a realistic assessment of the needs and values of individual states to be based upon such factors as geography, history, and politics. His first book, *The Equality of States in International Law* (1920), argued that an effective international organization could only be built upon a rule of law that acknowledged inequalities in national power and rights. In *Law and Peace* (1951), his last major work, he urged that the jurisdiction of international tribunals be expanded to resolve many disputes conventionally classified as matters of domestic policy.

Dickinson became professor of international law at the University of California Law School at Berkeley in 1933 and served as dean of California's School of Jurisprudence from 1936 to 1948. In 1938 President Franklin D. Roosevelt appointed him U.S. commissioner on the Inter-American Permanent Commission of Investigation and Conciliation, a hemispheric peacekeeping agency established under the Montevideo Protocol of 1933. During World War II Dickinson briefly held several other government posts. He was a special assistant to the U.S. attorney general from 1941 to 1943 and worked on alien enemy registration problems. He then became general counsel for the American-Mexican Claims Commission (1943–1944), assistant diplomatic adviser to the United Nations Relief and Rehabilitation Administration (1944), secretary to the Committee on Legal Problems at the United Nations Conference on Legal Organization (1945), and chairman of the Alien Enemy Repatriation Hearing Board, which handled cases involving Japanese aliens (1945–1946). On his return to the University of California he supervised plans for a new law building but resigned his deanship in 1948 to resume full-time teaching and research at the University of Pennsylvania Law School.

Named to the Permanent Court of Arbitration at The Hague in 1951, Dickinson remained a member of that tribunal until 1960. The position was largely honorary, since few cases came to the court for determination. He also served as president of the Association of American Law Schools in 1949 and was president of the American Society of International Law in 1952–1953. His presidential address to the society, "Progress: The Middle Way" (1953), praised "the emerging adjustment techniques of modern world society," which "exist to ameliorate and reconcile in ways best calculated to conserve a decent minimum of order in harmony with such ideals of fairness as have come to have a wide or substantial acceptance." Summarizing a lifetime of scholarship, he defined international law as a comprehensive and uncertain process rather than a set of black-letter rules. But he tempered his functionalism, as he had always done, with appeals to the values of freedom and justice found in Western political philosophy. "Without ideals," he warned, "there can be no progress, only change."

A friendly and unassuming man, Dickinson inspired generations of students and contributed lucid and insightful articles to such general publications as the *New Republic* as well as to specialized legal journals. When he retired from the Pennsylvania Law School in 1956, he returned to California and taught for two years at Hastings College of Law in San Francisco. He died at his home in St. Helena, California. The University of Michigan named a professorship in his honor in 1965.

• William W. Bishop, Jr., provides a valuable assessment of Dickinson's career and discusses his major writings in "Edwin D. Dickinson," *American Journal of International Law* 55 (1961): 637–44. For a personal tribute from an old friend, see Herbert F. Goodrich, "Edwin DeWitt Dickinson," *University of Pennsylvania Law Review* 109 (May 1961): 919–21. An obituary is in the *New York Times*, 27 Mar. 1961.

MAXWELL BLOOMFIELD

DICKINSON, Emily (10 Dec. 1830–15 May 1886), poet, was born Emily Elizabeth Dickinson in Amherst, Massachusetts, the daughter of Edward Dickinson, an attorney, and Emily Norcross. The notation "At Home" that summed up her occupation on the certificate recording her death in that same town belies the drama of her inner, creative life even as it accurately reflects a reclusive existence spent almost entirely in the Dickinson Homestead. That home, built by her grandfather Samuel Fowler Dickinson, represented her family's ambition. Edward Dickinson's young family shared the Homestead first with his parents and (after Samuel Fowler Dickinson's financial collapse as a result of overextending his resources on behalf of Amherst College) with another family before moving in 1840 to the home on North Pleasant Street where

Emily spent her adolescence and young womanhood. In 1855 Edward Dickinson celebrated the family's renewed prosperity by repurchasing the Homestead, where Emily Dickinson remained until she died. Although her father and grandfather held prominent places in the town as lawyers and college officers, it is indicative of changing reputations that the Homestead is maintained today by Amherst College as a memorial to this woman, who has become an American legend for the poems she wrote in its kitchen pantry and in her second-story chamber. Like the "Circumference"-seeking songbird of one of her poems, Dickinson is now as much "At home—among the Billows—As / The Bough where she was born—" (*Poems* 798 [P798], p. 604).

Dickinson grew up in a Connecticut Valley environment that drew close linkages among religion, intellectual activity, and citizenship. She studied at Amherst Academy, then greatly influenced by the scientist-theologian Edward Hitchcock of Amherst College, and worshiped at the First Church (Congregational) during the period of revivalistic evangelical Protestantism known as the Second Awakening. Her father played an active role in the town's political and business affairs, served as treasurer of the college, and was a leading figure in the church community even though not actually converted and eligible for membership until the revival of 1850. Her mother had joined the church when pregnant with Emily, her second child. The poet had an older brother, William Austin, and a younger sister, Lavinia, as well as a close circle of girlhood friends.

Letters written during Dickinson's one year at Mount Holyoke Female Seminary (1847–1848) reflect tendencies evident even in her academy years: maintenance of close family ties and intense friendships with chosen intimates, preference for solitude over society, intellectual curiosity, pride in her ability to write wittily, and hesitation to commit herself to Christ in the manner expected by her friends and spiritual counselors, including Mount Holyoke's redoubtable foundress, Mary Lyon. Those tendencies grew more pronounced when she returned home to Amherst and its lively community of young people. Although aware of local developments such as the coming of the Amherst-Belchertown Railroad and involved to some extent in reading groups and the cultural offerings of a college town, she increasingly narrowed her circle to family and a few friends—notably Susan Gilbert. When Austin Dickinson married Sue in 1856, Edward Dickinson built a house next door to the Homestead for the young couple, thereby squelching any impulses to move west. With her closest friend only a short walk away, Emily visited frequently for the next several years but apparently avoided most of her sister-in-law's ambitious social entertainments. Gradually she discontinued even those visits but retained close ties to Sue as well as to some of Sue's and Austin's friends, notably Samuel Bowles of the *Springfield Republican*, his assistant Josiah Gilbert Holland, and Holland's wife, Elizabeth. Shrinking from public exposure,

Dickinson also ceased going to church by the early 1860s and never attempted to join it through profession of faith. Nonetheless she maintained friendships with successive ministers of the First Church while pursuing her independent spiritual journey.

Two events impelled Dickinson beyond her domestic sphere. Her father's election to the U.S. House of Representatives precipitated family visits. Although Emily remained at home with Sue and a cousin, John Graves, when her mother and Lavinia visited Washington, D.C., in 1854, she did accompany her sister to the capital the following year, staying at Willard's Hotel and visiting tourist attractions such as the U.S. Patent Office and Mount Vernon. On the return trip the sisters visited their Coleman cousins in Philadelphia, where they probably stopped at the Arch Street Presbyterian Church and met its minister, the Reverend Charles Wadsworth. In 1864 and 1865 Dickinson required treatment by a Boston specialist, Dr. Henry W. Williams, for an eye disorder. While under his care Dickinson stayed at Mrs. Bangs's Boardinghouse in Cambridge with cousins Lavinia and Frances Norcross. Upon her return to Amherst, Dickinson confined herself to the Homestead, declaring, "I do not cross my Father's ground to any House or town" (*Letters* 330 [L330], p. 460). Yet she kept up with current literature through extensive reading, chiefly in English and American Romantic writers, and maintained lively correspondences with many friends.

Unfortunately the record of that correspondence lapses from the mid-1850s to the early 1860s after Sue's return from teaching in Baltimore and Austin's from law school, even though that was when Dickinson wrote most of her poems. There had been some clever valentines and a few lyrics in the early 1850s as well as references in letters to Jane Humphrey and Abiah Root to some "strange things—bold things" that she had undertaken (L35, p. 95). Around 1858 she started copying poems and stitching them into little booklets now known as fascicles. These poems, remarkable for their distilled wit, ambiguous manner, and stylistic idiosyncrasies, were shared with friends but apparently not offered for publication. The ten that were printed in the *Springfield Republican*, in several New York and Boston journals, and in Helen Hunt Jackson's *A Masque of Poets* between 1852 and 1878 appeared anonymously and, it seems, without the poet's consent. Dickinson evidently valued her privacy too much to risk the fate of a nineteenth-century literary celebrity and protected herself by adhering to standards of genteel reserve imposed by society on ladies of her age and station. Nonetheless, she cultivated connections with literary figures in positions to promote her work, not only with Bowles and Holland but also with Thomas Wentworth Higginson, whom she appointed as her "preceptor" from 1862 until her death, and Helen Hunt Jackson, who had volunteered to serve as her reticent friend's literary executor because "you are a great poet—and it is a wrong to the day you live in, that you will not sing aloud" (L444a, p. 545).

Dickinson's poetry is remarkable for its emotional and intellectual energy as well as its extreme distillation. In form, everything about it is tightly condensed. Words and phrases are set off by dashes, stanzas are brief, and the longest poem occupies less than two printed pages. Yet in theme and tone her poems grasp for the sublime in their daring expression of the soul's extremities. Stylistic tendencies such as her inclination toward symbolically freighted words such as "Circumference," her ironic wit, her adoption of personae, her penchant for oxymoron ("sumptuous—Despair—" [P505, p. 387]; "Heavenly Hurt" [P258, p. 185]), her punctuation that withholds traditional syntactic markers, her omission of titles, her recording of poems in multiple versions with variant words and stanzas, her willingness to leave poems unfinished, and even the distinctive amount of white space she left on the page force readers to involve themselves directly in this poetry in a way that forecloses definitive readings even while encouraging an exceptional degree of intimacy between reader and poet. Dickinson's imagery ranged widely from domestic and garden metaphors, through geographic and scientific references drawn from her education, to literary allusions (especially to the Bible, Shakespeare, Dickens, and the Brontës). The poems express extremes of passion—love, despair, dread, and elation—and do so in many voices (that of the child, for instance, or the bride, the nobleman, the madwoman, or the corpse).

Although these lyrics characteristically withhold evidence of the occasions that precipitated them, they suggest various narratives of religious searching and of romantic love reciprocated but unfulfilled. Consequently there has been much speculation about whatever crises in Dickinson's life may have spurred her to poetic expression: literary ambition in conflict with both societal restrictions on women and her own reticent disposition, the eye problems that threatened her lifelines of reading and writing, or perhaps a religious conversion or even a psychological breakdown. Much of that speculation focuses on presumed romantic attachments to Charles Wadsworth and/or Samuel Bowles, both married men and therefore unattainable. Whether either of these men was the "Master" she addressed in three passionate letter drafts apparently written in 1858 and 1861 remains a question. The only romantic attachment that has been documented was with Judge Otis Phillips Lord, a widowed friend of her father, from the late 1870s to 1884, many years after most of her poems were written. Other candidates for the role of Dickinson's forbidden lover include Susan Gilbert Dickinson and Sue's friend Kate Scott Anthon Turner. Letters as well as poems demonstrate the intensity of the poet's engagement with her friends while leaving to the reader's imagination whatever private dramas she may have concealed when telling Higginson that "my life has been too simple and stern to embarrass any" (L330, p. 460).

We do know that Dickinson took profound pleasure in her reading, her gardening, her friendships, and her share in nurturing Austin's and Sue's three children. She also devoted herself, as did her sister, to long-term care of their invalid mother. Her life was marked increasingly by deaths within the family (her father in 1874, her mother in 1882, and her eight-year-old nephew in 1883) and in her circle of friends. Samuel Bowles died in 1878, Josiah Holland in 1881, Charles Wadsworth in 1882, Otis Phillips Lord in 1884, and Helen Hunt Jackson in 1885. She felt bereaved by deaths of favorite authors also, including Elizabeth Barrett Browning (1861), George Eliot (1880), and Ralph Waldo Emerson (1882). Grief confronted her repeatedly with religious doubts she had coped with earlier in poems exploring her "Flood subject" of immortality (L319, p. 454), though Dickinson's late writings, especially letters, suggest an increasingly hopeful sense of her relationship with God. She suffered from kidney disease, perhaps associated with hypertension, for several years before she died.

Were Emily Dickinson known only by public achievements, she would soon have been forgotten. While the poet died, however, her poems lived. Back in 1862, opening her correspondence with Higginson, she challenged that man of letters to tell whether her verse "breathed" (L260, p. 403). Lavinia Dickinson, who came upon a box with the stitched fascicles and other poetic manuscripts while settling her sister's affairs, resolved to display Emily's genius to the world and eventually enlisted Mabel Loomis Todd, a friend and their brother's mistress, to edit them. Higginson assisted with publication and promotion of *Poems by Emily Dickinson* (1890) and *Poems by Emily Dickinson* (1891). Todd alone then responded to public interest by publishing an 1894 edition of selected Dickinson letters and a third collection of *Poems* in 1896. Roberts Brothers of Boston brought out all four volumes, the first of which sold out rapidly with eleven editions printed within a year. A legal dispute between Lavinia Dickinson and Todd over Austin's estate then put an end to Todd's editing. No further Dickinson writings came to press until after Susan Dickinson's death in 1913, when her daughter, Martha Dickinson Bianchi, published a selection of poems her aunt had sent to her mother as *The Single Hound* (1914). Bianchi followed that with correspondence and biography reflecting her own sense of family tradition in *The Life and Letters of Emily Dickinson* (1924), personal reminiscences in *Emily Dickinson Face to Face* (1932), and successive volumes of poems. After Bianchi died, Todd and her daughter, Millicent Todd Bingham, brought out the remaining poems in their possession as *Bolts of Melody* (1945). Gradually, as public acceptance of Dickinson's writing grew, editors represented poems more in accordance with her wording, spelling, and punctuation. When Thomas H. Johnson presented *The Poems of Emily Dickinson* (1955) in a scholarly three-volume variorum edition, he was hailed for making her art available to readers in its full brilliance. Since then, however, Ralph W. Franklin's two-volume facsimile edition of the poet's fascicles in *The Manuscript Books of Emily Dickinson* (1981) has shown that Dickinson's lineation was often less conventionally hymnlike than it appears in Johnson's edition, that the poems occupy space in more revealing ways than can be reproduced in print, and that variants play a significantly complicating role in an inherently ambiguous, open-ended poetry that resists editorial closure while demanding reader engagement.

From the first appearance of *Poems* during the 1890 Christmas season, readers have responded variously to Emily Dickinson. Arlo Bates, a Boston critic, remarked ambivalently that Dickinson's poetry was "so wholly without the pale of conventional criticism, that it is necessary at the start to declare the grounds upon which it is to be judged as if it were a new species of art." Yet William Dean Howells declared that "if nothing else had come out of our life but this strange poetry we should feel that in the work of Emily Dickinson America, or New England rather, had made a distinctive addition to the literature of the world" (Buckingham, pp. 29, 78). Dispraise of her style (initially perceived as crude and unpolished) and admiration for her daring treatment of subject matter—both religious and erotic (often in one poem)—was matched by popular curiosity about the poet's life. Attention focused early on the mysteries of her seclusion, with speculation about the romantic disappointment readers typically detect in Dickinson's poetry when they construct narratives to link her lyrics (a tendency first encouraged by the Todd-Higginson editions with a section of each book devoted to "Love" poems and later by Johnson's attempt to group poems chronologically in a way that makes them look autobiographical).

Although interest in one or more lovers continues, as does attention to the poet's religious quest and to her quiet subversion of gender assumptions, Emily Dickinson's poems steadily gain recognition as works of art, both individually and collectively, especially when read in her original fascicle groupings, which establish not just her unquestionable brilliance but her frequently underestimated artistic control. The regard Dickinson has won in the little more than a century since her poems introduced her to the world has established her as the most widely recognized woman poet to write in the English language and as an inspiration, both personally and in terms of craft, to modern women writers. As a voice of New England's Protestant and Transcendental cultures in fruitful tension and of the spiritual anxieties unleashed by the Civil War (during which she wrote the great majority of her poems) and as an avatar of poetic modernism, Emily Dickinson now stands with Walt Whitman as one of America's two preeminent poets of the nineteenth century and perhaps of our whole literary tradition.

• The two major collections of Dickinson manuscripts and other research materials are held by Harvard University's Houghton Library and Amherst College's Special Collections. Joel Myerson, *Emily Dickinson: A Descriptive Bibliography* (1984), records the publication history of her poems and letters. Thomas Johnson's editions of *The Poems of Emily Dickinson* (1955) and *The Letters of Emily Dickinson* (1958) remain the preferred scholarly editions, supplemented by R. W. Franklin's facsimile edition of *The Manuscript Books of*

Emily Dickinson (1981). Critiques of Johnson's editing appear in Franklin, *The Editing of Emily Dickinson: A Reconsideration* (1967), and Martha Nell Smith, *Rowing in Eden: Rereading Emily Dickinson* (1992). Although Dickinson's poems and letters have been released gradually and in varying forms since 1852, the Johnson editions are generally preferred to earlier printings as representations of the poet's intent.

Documentary materials providing a context for Dickinson's life may be found in Jay Leyda, *The Years and Hours of Emily Dickinson* (1960), and Polly Longsworth, *The World of Emily Dickinson* (1990), which provides a pictorial record of the poet's environment. The most important biography remains Richard B. Sewall, *The Life of Emily Dickinson* (1974). Cynthia Griffin Wolff, *Emily Dickinson* (1986), combines biography with extensive critical analysis. Many critical studies of Dickinson attempt with varying degrees of plausibility to draw biographical insights from readings in poems, letters, and fascicle groupings. Among these are John Cody's psychobiography, *After Great Pain: The Inner Life of Emily Dickinson* (1971), William H. Shurr's *The Marriage of Emily Dickinson: A Study of the Fascicles* (1983), and Judith Farr's *The Passion of Emily Dickinson* (1992). Willis J. Buckingham has collected early responses to Dickinson's poetry in *Emily Dickinson's Reception in the 1890s: A Documentary History* (1989). Bibliographic reviews of subsequent Dickinson criticism include Buckingham, *Emily Dickinson: An Annotated Bibliography—Writings, Scholarship, Criticism, and Ana, 1850–1968* (1970), and Karen Dandurand, *Dickinson Scholarship: An Annotated Bibliography, 1969–1985* (1988). Joseph Duchac's two annotated guides to *The Poems of Emily Dickinson* trace commentary published on individual poems from 1890 to 1977 (1979) and from 1978 to 1989 (1993). Numerous articles appear in literary journals around the world, and the Emily Dickinson International Society sponsors two publications entirely focused on her work: the *Emily Dickinson Journal* and the *Emily Dickinson International Society Bulletin*.

JANE DONAHUE EBERWEIN

DICKINSON, John (8 Nov. 1732–14 Feb. 1808), statesman and political pamphleteer, was born in Talbot County, Maryland, the son of Samuel Dickinson, a plantation owner and merchant, and his second wife, Mary Cadwalader. Owners of extensive properties in Delaware as well as Maryland, the family moved in John's youth to Kent, near Dover, Delaware. He was tutored at home until the age of eighteen when he began the study of law in the office of John Moland. Three years later he left for London for further legal training at the Middle Temple, the Inns of Court, and Westminster. After completing his studies in 1757, he returned to Philadelphia to open a law office. His extensive knowledge of legal history and precedent as well as his skills in writing and presentation soon earned him an outstanding reputation.

The family property in Delaware kept Dickinson closely tied to that colony, and in 1759 he was elected to the Delaware assembly; the next year he was chosen Speaker. In 1762, having not been returned to his seat in the Delaware assembly, he was elected to the Pennsylvania assembly. Conservative by nature, Dickinson disagreed with Benjamin Franklin's opposition to the proprietary government, arguing that if the petition sponsored by Franklin and Joseph Galloway against the proprietors was successful, the colony might have imposed on it a royal government that was even more pernicious. A pamphlet war ensued. Dickinson was returned to the assembly while Franklin and Galloway lost their seats. Their supporters, however, still controlled the majority, and the petition was carried to Parliament by three agents of the colony, including Franklin.

The Sugar Act of 1764 and the Stamp Act of 1765 vindicated Dickinson's fears of arbitrary parliamentary action. He was selected as one of a four-member delegation from Pennsylvania to the Stamp Act Congress of 1765, where he drafted the Declaration of Rights and Grievances of that body. In a broadside addressed to "Friends and Countrymen" in November 1765 Dickinson advised ignoring the Stamp Act. "If you behave in this spirited manner," he wrote, "you may be assured, that every colony on the continent will follow the example of a Province so justly celebrated for its Liberty." In that same month he published a pamphlet, *The Late Regulations Respecting the British Colonies,* purported to be a "Letter from a Gentleman in Philadelphia to his Friend in London." Dickinson argued that Britain as well as the colonies would be adversely affected by the trade regulations. "We can never be made an independent people, except it be by Great Britain herself; and the only way for her to do it, is to make us frugal, ingenious, united and discontented." Determining that such acts of Parliament infringe on the "natural rights" of the colonists, including the right to levy taxes on themselves, Dickinson concluded that resistance to such acts was not rebellion. His *Address to the Committee of Correspondence in Barbados* (1766) accuses that group of ignorance of the source of human rights: "They are created in us by the decrees of Providence, which establish the laws of our nature. They are born with us; exist with us; and cannot be taken from us by any human power, without taking our lives."

Although the Stamp Act was repealed, subsequent acts of Parliament continued the perceived threat to the rights of the colonies. In response, Dickinson produced his *Letters from a Farmer in Pennsylvania.* Published in the *Pennsylvania Chronicle* beginning 2 December 1767 and reprinted in nineteen of the twenty-three newspapers then in existence in the colonies, they were subsequently gathered into pamphlet form and widely circulated in Paris and London as well as in America. The *Letters* address specifically the Quartering Act of 1765, the Restraining Act of 1766, and the Townshend Duties of 1767. The ideological bases of his arguments concern threats to liberty, the loss of colonial control over taxation, and the dangers of a standing army. Dickinson's purpose was unequivocally stated in the third letter: "The meaning of [these letters] is, to convince the people of these colonies that they are at this moment exposed to the most imminent dangers; and to persuade them immediately, vigorously, and unanimously, to exert themselves in the most firm, but most peaceable manner, for obtaining relief." Throughout he supported his arguments with appeals to Greek, Roman, and British history as well

as to legal theory. The strength of the *Letters,* however, lies in the power of Dickinson's rhetoric, not in the originality of his arguments.

Exploiting a pastoral tradition, the first letter introduces an idealized American, a gentleman farmer who possesses the qualities of industry and frugality but who is also a rational, educated man with the leisure for study and contemplation. Having established his credibility as knowledgeable but disinterested, the farmer proceeds to warn his countrymen of imminent danger. He then examines the relationship between the colonies and the mother country (*Letters* 2–4) and the grievances of the colonies (*Letters* 5–8). The following three *Letters* offer further reflections on the subjects discussed and the last urges the unity and vigilance of the colonies.

Although on the surface separate, the letters appear to have been conceived as a whole, with the overall pattern of a classical oration. Underlying Dickinson's arguments are the assumptions that the colonists have a right to be "happy"; they cannot be happy without being free; and they cannot be free without being secure in their property. A testimony to the persuasive power of the *Letters* is the accusation in the Tory *Critical Review* that the farmer was "inciting the colonies to independence."

Dickinson was married in 1770 to Mary Norris of Philadelphia; they had five children, three of whom died in infancy. Dickinson continued to speak and write against British taxes and tariffs. As a member of the Pennsylvania assembly in 1771 he assisted in drafting a petition asking the king to intercede with Parliament in obtaining a repeal of importation taxes on tea and other items. The Tea Act of 1773 prompted Dickinson to send an anonymous "Extract of a Letter" to the *Pennsylvania Journal* analyzing it. He followed this with a letter signed "Rusticus" warning against the threats to American freedom and liberty but urging moderation in response. Dickinson's stance in this period was firmly against any royal or parliamentary encroachments on the rights of the colonies, but he continued to be cautious about colonial use of force or violence. At a mass meeting called in May 1774 in response to the closing of the port of Boston, he urged that a special session of the Pennsylvania assembly be called and that a committee of correspondence be appointed. He then proceeded to address four anonymous letters to "The Inhabitants of the British Colonies"; among other suggestions, he urged a general congress of representatives of all colonies. Elected chair of a Philadelphia committee of forty-three to engage in correspondence with other colonies as well as other parts of Pennsylvania, Dickinson delivered the major address to a convention of provincial representatives, presenting arguments on Great Britain's powers and the constitutional rights of the colonists as Englishmen.

Initially excluded from the Pennsylvania delegation to the First Continental Congress by the maneuvering of Joseph Galloway, Dickinson joined that body in October 1774. However even before his selection he was at work on a draft of colonial rights and grievances. He contributed to the "Address to the People of Quebec" seeking their support and the "Address to the King." He also took an active role in the deliberations of the Second Continental Congress that convened in May 1775 in Philadelphia.

Dickinson was determined that readiness for war be accompanied by strenuous attempts to peacefully settle the disputes between the colonies and the mother country, a position described by John Adams as "having a sword in one hand and an olive branch in the other" (Flower, p. 129). Dickinson accepted a commission as colonel of the "First Battalion of Associators in the City and Liberties of Philadelphia." At the same time he chaired a committee of the Congress to prepare a second "olive branch" petition to the king. The following month, June 1775, he prepared the final draft of the Congress's "Declaration of the Causes and Necessity of Taking Up Arms."

Dickinson's moderate stance, although it made him unpopular with the more militant members of the Congress, evidently won the approval of his constituents for he was reelected to the Pennsylvania assembly in the fall. With public sentiment for independence growing throughout the winter and spring of 1776, however, Dickinson's position became increasingly difficult. He opposed the Declaration of Independence and voted against it in July, citing the lack of foreign allies, the colonies' poor state of military preparedness, and the lack of unity among the colonies. Yet he served on the congressional committee appointed to prepare the articles of confederation as well as the committee preparing a plan to seek foreign treaties. Then, as colonel of the First Philadelphia Battalion he led his troops north to face the British in northern New Jersey.

Dickinson's disaffection with the new leadership in Pennsylvania led to his resignation of his commission and his retirement from the Pennsylvania assembly. He moved his family to their estate in Delaware, eventually joining the Delaware militia as a private. In February 1779 he accepted selection to the Congress as representative from Delaware. Although not wishing to participate in Delaware politics, he reluctantly accepted election to the executive council and in November 1781 was named president of Delaware, the only dissenting vote being his own. His more natural political and personal ties were with Pennsylvania, however, and in October 1782 he was elected to the Supreme Executive Council of Pennsylvania and was named president of that state. Two months later he resigned his Delaware position, preferring to involve himself in the affairs of the state where he had been more politically and professionally active.

Attacks by radicals on the conservative Dickinson began in Pennsylvania even before his election. He was accused of opposing the Declaration of Independence, opposing the new state constitution, deserting his battalion, and advising his brother to refuse the new Continental currency. Of these, only the charge of desertion was false. One especially vicious critic, who

signed himself "Valerius," prompted Dickinson to respond in a series of letters that began appearing in the *Pennsylvania Gazette* in December and were reprinted by the three other Philadelphia newspapers. Financial and political affairs of the state occupied Dickinson for the next several years. In addition to serving as the chief executive officer of the state, the president of the executive council also served as head of the judiciary, and Dickinson's legal experience was valuable in establishing judicial precedents. In September 1783 the assembly established a college at Carlisle named after him. Dickinson's three-year term as president, plagued by economic problems and political disputes, ended in October 1785, and he and his family retired to Wilmington, Delaware.

Weaknesses in the Articles of Confederation began to surface shortly after the end of the war. When the Constitutional Convention convened in 1787, Dickinson was one of Delaware's five-man delegation. He favored the establishment of a legislature that would protect the representation of small states such as his own, but recognized the need for a strong central government. Delaware was the first state to ratify the new federal constitution. Dickinson's enthusiastic support of the constitution drafted by the convention is reflected in nine letters signed "Fabius" that appeared in 1788, first in the *Delaware Gazette* and later in pamphlet form. In the letters he analyzed the organization of the government as it was set forth in the new constitution and defended the theory underlying that organization. He especially defended the balance of powers in the new government, responding to critics concerned about the division of responsibilities. "The power of the people pervading the proposed system" he wrote, "together with the strong confederation of the states, forms an adequate security against every danger that has been apprehended."

For the next several years poor health caused Dickinson to decline all public offices; in 1791, however, he agreed to represent New Castle County at the Delaware Constitutional Convention and was elected president of that convention. He consented to serve again in the assembly but resigned in 1793, citing poor health.

For the next fifteen years Dickinson did not hold public office but remained involved in community, state, national, and international affairs, carrying on a voluminous correspondence with a number of public figures and writing letters and pamphlets on critical issues. He opposed the treaty negotiated by John Jay with Britain and in January 1797 published an ode sympathetic to France. Three months later, again writing as Fabius, he began the publication of a series of letters in Philadelphia's *New World*. The fifteen letters praised France for the establishment of a republic, decried the treatment of France by other European powers, and defended the pro-French position of the democrats. These were immediately collected and published with his earlier Fabius letters defending the Constitution. He followed this the next year with a small pamphlet titled *A Caution; or, Reflections on the Present Contest between France and Great Britain*

(1798). In 1803 he again addressed his writing talents to the subject of the United States' relationship with France, but this time he expressed alarm at recent developments, including Napoleon's conquest of Spain and France's control of Louisiana.

As a statesman and legal theorist, Dickinson employed his skills in political analysis and in writing through a long career that spanned a critical time in the history of this country, from the first protests against Great Britain's taxation of the colonies to the establishment of the United States as a maturing nation and an international power.

• Collections of Dickinson's papers are at the Library Company of Philadelphia, the Historical Society of Pennsylvania, the Public Archives of the State of Delaware, the Historical Society of Delaware, and the Massachusetts Historical Society. An early collection is *The Political Writings of John Dickinson* (2 vols., 1801). See also Paul Leicester Ford, ed., *The Writings of John Dickinson, 1764–1774* (1895). The first biography was by Charles J. Stille, *The Life and Times of John Dickinson* (1891); Milton E. Flower, *John Dickinson: Conservative Revolutionary* (1983), is a comprehensive biography that draws from letters, diaries, newspapers, and other contemporary accounts to detail Dickinson's political and personal life. David L. Jacobson, *John Dickinson and the Revolution in Pennsylvania, 1764–1776* (1965), deals with Dickinson's early career and writings.

Useful assessments of Dickinson's best-known writings include A. Owen Aldridge, "Paine and Dickinson," *Early American Literature* 11 (Fall 1976): 125–38; Bernard Bailyn, ed., *Pamphlets of the American Revolution* (1965); Stephen H. Browne, "The Pastoral Voice in John Dickinson's First *Letter from a Farmer in Pennsylvania*," *Quarterly Journal of Speech* 76 (1990): 46–57; Richard M. Gummere, "John Dickinson, the Classical Penman of the Revolution," *Classical Journal* 52, no. 2 (1956): 81–88; Carl F. Kaestle, "The Public Reaction to John Dickinson's *Farmer's Letters*," *Proceedings of the American Antiquarian Society* 78, no. 2 (1969): 323–53; and Pierre Marambaud, "Dickinson's *Letters from a Farmer in Pennsylvania* as Political Discourse," *Early American Literature* 12 (Spring 1977): 63–72.

ELAINE K. GINSBERG

DICKINSON, John (24 Feb. 1894–9 Apr. 1952), jurist, scholar, and public official, was born John Sharpe Dickinson in Greensboro, Maryland, the son of Willard Dickinson and Caroline Schnauffer. In 1903 the family moved to Baltimore, where John completed his secondary education at the Boy's Latin School. By all accounts, he was a brilliant student. After majoring in classics and graduating from Johns Hopkins University in 1913, at age nineteen, Dickinson proceeded to study history, politics, and jurisprudence at Princeton and attained his A.M. the following year. He then taught history at Amherst College and finished his Ph.D. at Princeton in 1919. He moved to Harvard Law School, where he completed his law degree in two years.

From 1917 to 1918 his Dickinson served as an economist on the War Trade Board and then as a first lieutenant with the Army General Staff in Washington. He thus exhibited an analytical mind of amazing breadth and energy. Schooled in classics, philosophy, literature, history, political science, economics, law, and jurisprudence, he was well prepared for a career as a teacher, scholar, administrator, and statesman.

In 1921 Dickinson joined the law firm of William G. McAdoo, and he supported McAdoo's unsuccessful bid for the Democratic presidential nomination in 1924. In 1925 Dickinson returned to Harvard as a lecturer in the Department of Government. During the two years he taught at Harvard, he completed his *Administrative Justice and the Supremacy of Law* (1927), considered the classic study of American administrative law.

In 1929 Dickinson took a position of professor of law at the University of Pennsylvania Law School. Described as a "highly successful teacher" and an "inspiring colleague," he had a profound and immediate impact on the jurisprudential debate of his age. Dickinson's legal scholarship was largely an exploration of the role of reason in judicial decision making. As a trenchant critic of legal realism, he attempted to demonstrate the role of determinate legal principles that underlie the law and inform judicial decision making. By focusing on how legal decision making requires the use of accepted legal principles, Dickinson tried to steer a middle course between traditional jurisprudence and the new school of legal realists. The latter argued that law was ultimately a matter of judges making political decisions and hence legislating public policy. Dickinson viewed judicial decision making as the balanced interaction between legal rules and judicial discretion. He allowed that judicial decision making was indeed political, which is not to say unprincipled. In the final analysis, judges must take on the role of judicial statesmen. In his later writings on legal education, Dickinson was highly critical of the narrow technical specialization that had come to characterize law schools. His understanding of the lawyer's need for a liberal education was clearly informed by his own experience. He retired from his law professorship in 1948.

Throughout his life, Dickinson maintained strong ties to the Democratic party and was a close associate of some of the party's most powerful figures. During his tenure as a law professor, he twice held appointed political office. In 1933 the newly elected president, Franklin D. Roosevelt, invited him to become assistant secretary of commerce. Dickinson played a leading role in drafting the administration's plan for industrial recovery. Drawing upon an article published a few years earlier, he advocated a relaxation of antitrust laws as one way of stimulating economic growth. While holding this position in the Department of Commerce, Dickinson also served as chairman of the General Statistical Board in 1934 and 1935. In 1935 he moved to the office of the assistant attorney general, in charge of the anti-trust division. Under his direction, the Department of Justice launched a major investigation into collusive bidding practices in a number of industries. His tenure in the Roosevelt administration can be characterized as his attempt to provide a pragmatic defense of the administration against its most conservative, free-enterprise critics in the business community.

Following Roosevelt's reelection in 1936, Dickinson left the administration to join the legal staff of the Pennsylvania Railroad, rising to the position of vice president by 1946. In litigation representing the railroad, he displayed his forensic skills, winning a number of landmark cases on the railroad's behalf.

In 1938 Dickinson married Lula Martin McIver Scott; they had one daughter. Following his retirement from the law school, he maintained an active legal practice until his death from an embolism in Baltimore. His range of scholarship and his ability to practice law, teach, write, and hold political and corporate office all at the same time were remarkable. His impact on American jurisprudence is likely to grow as the full extent of his legal philosophy comes under greater scholarly scrutiny.

• Among Dickinson's writings, those most important for understanding his philosophy of law and jurisprudence are "The Law behind Law," *Columbia Law Review* 29 (1929): 113–46, 285–319; "The Problem of the Unprovided Case," *University of Pennsylvania Law Review* 81 (1932); "Legal Rules," *University of Pennsylvania Law Review* 79 (1931); *My Philosophy of Law: Credos of Sixteen American Scholars* (1941); *Administrative Justice and the Supremacy of Law in the United States* (1927); *Death of a Republic* (1963); and his translation of selections from the medieval political philosopher John of Salisbury's book *Policraticus* (1159) under the title *The Statesman's Book* (1963). The best available scholarly article on Dickinson is George L. Hoskins, "John Dickinson 1894–1952," *University of Pennsylvania Law Review* 101 (Oct. 1952): 1–25. Neil Duxbury, *Patterns of American Jurisprudence* (1995), provides a succinct discussion of Dickinson's criticism of legal realism and his place in the tradition of American legal thought. Also see William C. Chase, *The American Law School and the Rise of Administrative Government* (1982), and John Henry Schlegel, *American Legal Realism and Empirical Social Science* (1995).

PATRICK MALCOLMSON

DICKINSON, John Woodbridge (12 Oct. 1825–16 Feb. 1901), educator, was born in Chester, Massachusetts, the son of William Dickinson and Elizabeth Worthington, farmers. His education was limited to occasional winter terms in district schools and a short period of preparatory work at Greylock Institute and Williston Seminary. He was twenty-three when he enrolled in Williams College, graduating in 1852. There he developed a lifelong friendship with Mark Hopkins.

From 1852 to 1856 Dickinson taught on the faculty of the Westfield normal school in Westfield, Massachusetts, serving as its president between 1857 and 1877. While there, he made Westfield a national center for object teaching, a Pestalozzian-based method of teaching that revolted against the older American education system of rote memory and oral recitation. The educator Edward A. Sheldon observed at Westfield before opening his normal school in Oswego, New York, and Lowell Mason, another lifelong friend of Dickinson who promoted musical education in Bos-

ton, was a continual visitor and supporter of the school.

Dickinson brought other innovations to teacher training, such as formal child study and courses in psychology. He believed in health and nutrition as a necessity for successful learning, so he required daily physical exercise for all his pupils. He regulated their hours of rest and gave lessons on healthful dress and living habits. He even introduced gymnastic exercises set to music as part of graduation exercises. In 1857 he married Arexine Parsons, an instructor of French and drawing in the school. They had two children.

During his tenure at Westfield, Dickinson lectured widely in the West, served as president of the Massachusetts Teachers Association, traveled to Europe for further study in 1869, and was offered the presidency of many of the new public colleges of the western states. In 1877 he was appointed to Horace Mann's old post as secretary of the Massachusetts Board of Education. There he remained until 1893.

As secretary Dickinson presided over significant changes in public education. He advocated expansion of high schools and kindergartens and successfully lobbied for the consolidation of rural school districts and for the hiring of professional superintendents to run them. His long association with normal schools committed him to the professionalization of the teaching cadre as well as to the improvement of employment conditions for teachers. His greatest misfortune was that he was employed during a period of economic hardship in Massachusetts, when increasing urbanization under the flood of immigrants frightened the Massachusetts establishment and caused it to withdraw its support for public education. The new business and education leadership in the state advocated vocational and manual training as the basis for public education, contradicting Dickinson's belief that the classical liberal arts could serve the children of the poor and the rich equally well.

During his later years Dickinson continued to lecture widely. He was elected to vice presidencies in the National Education Association in 1877, 1882, and 1887. Although he achieved national prominence, in Massachusetts, his views were considered as old-fashioned as his dress and manner. His wife died in 1892, just as the state legislature intervened to undo the normal school training program he had built. He resigned his position in 1893 and retired to the home in Newton, Massachusetts, that he shared with his daughter. He joined her on the faculty of the Emerson School of Oratory in Boston and continued to write and lecture on the training of teachers until his death in Newtonville, Massachusetts.

Dickinson represented the pre–Civil War reformist views of New England that believed in knowledge and hard work as the keys to social advancement. He was important in the transfer of the child-centered pedagogy of Europe into American classrooms and, at the same time, in the foundations of the professionalization of teacher preparation.

- Dickinson's educational theories can be found in his books, especially *The Limits of Oral Training* (1890) and *Principles and Methods of Teaching, Derived from a Knowledge of the Mind* (1899). Also of value are the "Reports of the Secretary" in *Annual Report of the Board of Education of Massachusetts*, particularly vols. 42–44 (1878–1880). Biographical materials appear in Robert Brown, *The Rise and Fall of the People's Colleges: The Westfield Normal School, 1839–1914*, and in the obituary by Hosea Ballou, "The Educational Services of the Late Hon. J. W. Dickinson," *Education* 22 (Oct. 1901): 65–77.

ROBERT T. BROWN

DICKINSON, Jonathan (22 Apr. 1688–7 Oct. 1747), Presbyterian minister, was born in Hatfield, Massachusetts, the son of Hezekiah Dickinson, a merchant, and Abigail Blakeman. Little is known about Dickinson's early life before he entered one of the earliest classes of Yale College, from which he graduated in 1706. The source of his theological training is not known, but by 1708 he was in Elizabeth Town, New Jersey, preaching to a group of New England Congregationalists who had recently migrated to northern New Jersey. About the same time that he began his work as a minister, Dickinson in 1709 married Joanna Melyen, the sister of his predecessor. They had nine children, including one son, also Jonathan Dickinson, whose dissolute life and rejection of religion was a sore trial for the family. After his first wife died, the elder Dickinson married a widow from nearby Newark, Mary Crane, in April 1747; that ceremony was performed by the young revivalist, David Brainerd, who had become Dickinson's close friend.

On 29 September 1709 Dickinson was ordained by the Fairfield County (Conn.) Consociation of Congregationalists for service in the Elizabeth Town parish, which then included Rahway, Springfield, Westfield, and other localities that soon became separate towns with their own churches. Along the way, Dickinson also began to practice medicine, at which he gained considerable reputation, especially after publishing a treatise on the "throat distemper" (diphtheria) in 1740. From 1715 Dickinson met regularly with Philadelphia Presbyterians; in 1717 he led his congregation into formal association with the Presbyterian church. Dickinson's effectiveness as a preacher, his gracious personality, his clear theological vision, and his skill with the pen made him one of the Presbyterians' most respected leaders.

Dickinson is remembered for his role in three important episodes. During his first decade as a Presbyterian, he was embroiled in a struggle over whether ministers and elders in the colonies' new Presbyterian church should be required to sign (or subscribe to) the Westminster Confession of Faith and Catechisms as the expression of their faith. Dickinson, whose loyalty to New England's congregational polity was strong, led the forces against subscription. In a memorable sermon preached at the opening of the Presbyterian annual synod in 1722, he set out a position he would argue through shifting circumstances over the next quarter century: "We may not so much shut out of Communion, any such Dissenters, as we can charitably hope Christ won't shut out of Heaven: But should open the *Doors of the Church* as wide, as Christ opens *the Gates of Heaven*; and *receive one another*, as Christ also received us, to the Glory of God" (*A Sermon* [1723], pp. 22–23).

Dickinson's view prevailed then, but in 1729 the Synod of Philadelphia passed an Adopting Act that required ministers to "declare their agreement in, and approbation of" the Westminster Confession (*Records*, p. 94). Conceded to Dickinson and like-minded ministers was the privilege for ministers to declare their "scruples" about any aspect of the Confession and still be ordained, if presbyteries felt the scruple did not touch a material aspect of the faith. In a debate that would be repeated time and again in the later history of American Presbyterianism, Dickinson upheld an English Puritan ideal of informal evangelical communion against a Scottish or Scotch-Irish ideal of orderly ecclesiastical consistency.

The revivals that broke out in the colonies during the late 1730s pushed Dickinson once again to the fore. Among Presbyterians, a party of Scotch-Irish evangelicals led by William Tennent and his four sons eagerly welcomed the British itinerant George Whitefield when he began his spectacular preaching tours in the late 1730s. An opposing party of Scotch-Irish conservatives came to the conclusion that Whitefield threatened everything sound in the church. Dickinson and the other former New England Presbyterians stood in between. Dickinson had welcomed Whitefield to his church in November 1739 and April 1740 and rejoiced when a quickening of religion began at Elizabeth Town in June 1740, but he also feared the excesses of revival—especially the tendency to antinomianism, or the belief that a person touched by God's grace no longer needed to pay attention to the requirements of God's law.

Dickinson was thus quick to play the mediator. One of his most effective works was a dialogue published in 1742, *A Display of God's Special Grace*, in which he attempted to defend revival while maintaining the church's need to promote order, discipline, and stable holiness. Soon, however, the obduracy of the Old Light conservatives proved too much. In 1745 Dickinson and his colleagues in northern New Jersey and New York joined the Tennent New Lights from western New Jersey and Pennsylvania in forming a Synod of New York as an alternative to the Synod of Philadelphia.

A sharp issue dividing the Old Lights from the New Lights was the question of ministerial training. In an attempt to curtail the influence of informal academies, especially the "Log College" conducted by William Tennent, the Old Light Philadelphia Synod had passed a regulation requiring elaborate ministerial examinations for any candidate who had not graduated from a European university, Harvard, or Yale. After the establishment of the New York Synod in 1745, Dickinson joined with three other ministers, including Aaron Burr, Sr., of Newark, and three wealthy laymen from New York, in advancing a scheme to found a full-fledged college. On 22 October 1746 interim New Jersey governor John Hamilton signed the charter for a new institution of higher learning.

The college was designed by New Light Presbyterians, but its charter was broad enough to provide for the education of young men from various denominations and for vocations other than the ministry. Dickinson, to no one's surprise, was selected the first president of the College of New Jersey (which later moved to Princeton and, still later, was renamed Princeton University). Classes began in the last week of May 1747 at Dickinson's house in Elizabeth Town with eight or ten undergraduates, several of whom had earlier been studying privately with Dickinson. Dickinson, however, died of a sudden attack of pleurisy in Elizabeth Town only five months after instruction began.

Throughout his career, Dickinson's theology blended the doctrines of Puritan Calvinism with the more contemporary experiences of evangelical revivalism. With contemporaries like Jonathan Edwards in Massachusetts and John Maclaurin in Scotland, Dickinson advocated a lively faith, yet one that took due account of the age's intellectual advances. The type of religion he desired informed his closing appeal from a sermon published in 1742: "Whatever Darkness, whatever Deadness, whatever Afflictions, or Temptations you may meet with, still repair to him [Christ], that you may *obtain Mercy, and find Grace to help in a Time of need*, that *of his Fulness you may receive even Grace for Grace*. You can't trust too little your selves; nor too much to him, in the Way of Duty" (*True Scripture-Doctrine* [1742], p. 217).

Not the least of Dickinson's memorable traits was a predilection for controversy. While he was intimately involved in the turmoils of the Presbyterians, his concerns also stretched further afield. Against Anglican Episcopalians he entered the lists on questions of church order, he attacked Nicholas von Zinzendorf and the Moravians for errors in theology, and, both early and late in his career, he defended the baptism of infants against Baptist contentions for adult immersion.

• A few of Dickinson's manuscript letters and unpublished sermons are in the archives of Firestone Library, Princeton University. Nearly thirty separate works of Dickinson were published in the eighteenth century. Among older biographical sketches, two are most reliable, William B. Sprague, *Annals of the American Pulpit*, vol. 3, *Presbyterians* (1868), pp. 14–18, and Franklin Bowditch Dexter, *Biographical Sketches of the Graduates of Yale College . . . October, 1701–May, 1745* (1885), pp. 45–52. There is no comprehensive modern biography, but two helpful dissertations are Keith Jordan Hardman, "Jonathan Dickinson and the Course of American Presbyterianism" (Ph.D. diss., Univ. of Pennsylvania, 1971), and Herbert L. Samworth, "Those Astonishing Wonders of His Grace: Jonathan Dickinson and the Great Awakening" (Th.D. diss., Westminster Theological Seminary, 1988). Bryan F. LeBeau, "The Subscription Controversy and Jonathan Dickinson," *Journal of Presbyterian History* 54 (1976): 317–35, covers its subject well. The two finest articles differ in their conclusions: Leigh Eric Schmidt argues for a consistent pattern in Dickinson's convictions compounded of Puritan traditions, the moderate Enlightenment, and a mediating revivalism, in "Jonathan Dickinson and the Making of the Moderate Awakening," *American Presbyterians* 63 (1985): 341–53; Schmidt is more persuasive than David C. Harland, who pictures Dickinson's course as zig-zagging from ardent revivalist to frightened conservative in "The Travail of Religious Moderation: Jonathan Dickinson and the Great Awakening," *Journal of Presbyterian History* 61 (1983): 411–26. Official documents are in *Records of the Presbyterian Church in the United States of America* (1904). For more general context, two works from the 1940s remain indispensable: Leonard J. Trinterud, *The Forming of an American Tradition: A Re-examination of Colonial Presbyterianism* (1949), and Thomas Jefferson Wertenbaker, *Princeton, 1746–1896* (1946).

MARK A. NOLL

DICKINSON, Philemon (5 Apr. 1739–4 Feb. 1809), revolutionary soldier and congressman, was born in Talbot County, Maryland, the son of Samuel Dickinson, a merchant, planter, and judge, and Mary Cadwalader. Shortly after Dickinson's birth his family moved to Jones Neck, Kent County, Delaware. His early education and that of his older brother, John Dickinson (1732–1808), was overseen by his mother and a succession of tutors. William Killen, later the first chancellor of Delaware, also lived with the Dickinsons and served as a sometime instructor.

In 1757 Dickinson moved to Philadelphia to live with his uncle, Dr. Thomas Cadwalader, and to attend the College of Philadelphia. Upon graduating in 1759 Dickinson studied law under the direction of his brother, who by then had established a law office in Philadelphia. Although Dickinson became a clerk in his brother's office, he soon discovered that the law was not for him and left to oversee his family's estates. Before leaving Philadelphia he joined his brother and other wealthy young Philadelphians as members of the Mount Regale Fishing Company, one of the city's elite social organizations. The Dickinson brothers also shared an interest in politics. Both signed the Nonimportation Agreement of November 1765. Upon his father's death in 1760 Dickinson became an executor of the vast Dickinson properties. He renounced his executorship in favor of John and sold most of his share of the Delaware estates to his sibling. On 14 July 1767 he married Mary Cadwalader, his first cousin, daughter of Thomas Cadwalader, and moved to a farm near Trenton.

In 1775 Dickinson was named colonel of the Hunterdon County, New Jersey, militia. In October of that same year he was commissioned brigadier general of the state's militia. He also served briefly in the Provincial Congress of New Jersey in 1776. December of that year found him in camp with his battalion, worried about his family, which had been forced to flee their home when it was occupied by British troops. He participated in the Trenton campaign, at one point ordering his artillery to shell his own residence, which was being employed as a British command post. In January 1777 he won acclaim from George Washington when he successfully deployed his militia against one of Lord Cornwallis's foraging parties near the Somerset County courthouse and recaptured more than three dozen wagons, one hundred horses, and a herd of cattle and sheep. In June 1777 he was commissioned major general and commander in chief of the New Jersey militia. Later that same year he pressed Washington to allow him to occupy Staten Island in support of assaults on Long Island. Although Washington rejected much of his proposal, he agreed with its general strategy and ordered Dickinson to attack Staten Island. His militia landed successfully, failing to destroy British troops there only because they rapidly evacuated the area.

On 9 May 1778 Dickinson's militia repulsed Major John Maitland's attack on Trenton. When Henry Clinton evacuated Philadelphia on 16 June with his army and 3,000 Loyalists and retreated across New Jersey, headed for New York, Dickinson with 800 militia impeded them by destroying bridges and obstructing roads. Dickinson remained on Clinton's flank and kept Washington apprised of British movements. Washington later attributed much of the American success at Monmouth to Dickinson and his men. In June 1780 Dickinson also won praise for his efforts in the battle of Springfield, New Jersey.

On two occasions Dickinson became embroiled in the partisan bickering that characterized the times. He briefly became the target of suspicion in December 1776 when a letter to him from his brother allegedly advocating that he refuse to recognize the legitimacy of continental money, that he resign his commissions, and that he go over to the enemy was intercepted by Pennsylvania Whigs. If the incident caused embarrassment for John Dickinson, Philemon's patriotism was never seriously questioned. In July 1778 he served as a second to his cousin, General John Cadwalader (1742–1786), when Cadwalader challenged (and wounded) General Thomas Conway for disparaging remarks concerning Washington.

For three consecutive years (1778, 1779, 1780) Dickinson was a New Jersey gubernatorial candidate, losing in each instance to William Livingston. He was named commissioner of the state's new loan office in 1781 and during his brother's tenure as president of Delaware was named one of Delaware's representatives to the Continental Congress (Feb. 1782). There he urged the cession of western lands to the national government. The following year he was elected to the New Jersey Council, where he served as vice president for two years. In 1785 he was named to a congressional committee to select a site for a national capital. He competed unsuccessfully for the U.S. Senate in 1789 against William Paterson. However, when Paterson later became governor, Dickinson completed his senatorial term (1790–1793) before retiring from public service.

A slaveholder, Dickinson resisted arguments for emancipation. In 1793 he also deflected criticism from his brother, who urged him to manumit his blacks. He claimed to favor gradual abolition but argued that he could not at present support any program that would deny him the slaves' labor. He did not have the resources of his brother and told him he could not "make so great a sacrifice as you request." Born a Quaker, Dickinson, like his brother and father, never accepted full association with that sect. Mary Cadwalader was an active Quaker, as was Dickinson's second wife, Mary's sister, Rebecca, whom he married shortly after Mary's death in 1791. Dickinson died at his home near Trenton.

Despite his willingness to take up the American cause and his impressive military contributions after 1776, Philemon Dickinson remained chary of many of the forces unleashed by the Revolution. He exhibited a greater conservatism than did most of his gentry counterparts in New Jersey, continuing to embrace slavery long after others encouraged its termination and adhering to conventional political forms while others profitably turned to more popular practices. Always conscious of his family's position and influence, and its tradition of public service, Dickinson held important public offices, but clearly he was viewed as less popular and less able than such men as William Livingston and William Paterson.

• There are Dickinson papers in the New Jersey Historical Society, Newark. Letters to, from, and about Philemon Dickinson can be found in various other collections, including the Dickinson papers in the Logan collection at the Library Company of Philadelphia and the Gratz, Dreer, and Loudoun collections at the Historical Society of Pennsylvania, Philadelphia. No biography of Philemon Dickinson exists, but a few letters to, and numerous references about, Dickinson can be found in George H. Ryden, ed., *Letters to and from Caesar Rodney, 1756–1784* (1933). Relevant materials also appear in the *Papers of the Continental Congress*, microfilm ed. (1971); Worthington C. Ford, ed., *Journals of the Continental Congress, 1774–1789* (34 vols., 1904–1937); John C. Fitzpatrick, ed., *The Writings of George Washington* (39 vols., 1931–1944); and *The Debates and Proceedings in the Congress of the United States . . . Second Congress* (1849). Much information on the Dickinson family can be found in Milton E. Flower, *John Dickinson: Conservative Revolutionary* (1983), though it is poorly indexed regarding coverage of Philemon. A brief biographical sketch of Dickinson is provided by Wharton Dickinson, "Philemon Dickinson: Major General, New Jersey Militia—Revolutionary Service," *Magazine of American History* 7 (1881): 420–27. Dickinson's congressional career is discussed in John A. Munroe, "Nonresident Representation in the Continental Congress: The Delaware Delegation of 1782," *William and Mary Quarterly* 9 (1952): 166–90. His military exploits can be followed in part in Christopher Ward, *The War of the Revolution* (2 vols., 1952). An obituary is in the *Trenton Federalist*, 6 Feb. 1809.

G. S. ROWE

DICKINSON, Robert Latou (21 Feb. 1861–29 Nov. 1950), gynecologist and sexologist, was born in Jersey City, New Jersey, the son of Horace Dickinson, a hat manufacturer, and Jeannette Latou. During Dickinson's childhood the family business was located in Brooklyn, New York, where the Dickinsons and Latous were civic and cultural leaders. Dickinson enjoyed a privileged childhood in Brooklyn Heights, with summers on an uncle's Connecticut farm. When he was twelve, his father took the family to Europe for four years, during which the children were privately tutored and attended schools in Switzerland and Germany. The Dickinsons returned to the United States in 1876. Robert entered Brooklyn Polytechnic Institute and completed the equivalent of the last years of high school in 1879.

Dickinson considered a career as a commercial artist, but an interest in medicine had been inspired by a childhood boating accident that left an eight-inch scar on his abdomen, and he entered the medical school of Long Island College Hospital in 1879. He completed course work in 1881, but receipt of the M.D., which then served as a license to practice, was delayed a year because candidates were required to be at least twenty-one years old. Dickinson spent his twenty-first year as an assistant to Alexander J. C. Skene, whose *Treatise on Disease of Women* (1888) dominated the textbook market in gynecology for a decade and featured 161 illustrations by Dickinson.

Dickinson began building a successful private practice in 1882, but his strong interest in the reform politics of Brooklyn mayor Seth Low drew him into service as a Republican ward captain, ambulance surgeon, examiner for the police and fire departments, and unsuccessful candidate for the office of coroner. In 1886 Long Island College Hospital hired him as a lecturer in obstetrics, and he remained an active teacher there and at other local hospitals until he retired from clinical practice. As Skene's protégé, Dickinson took great pride in developing new techniques for both surgery and teaching, which he described in more than one hundred publications. His writing competed with his busy schedule as a healer but provided an outlet for his talent as an illustrator and his desire to raise the standards of his profession. In 1890 he married Sarah Truslow, a banker's daughter and Packer Institute graduate with whom he shared an Episcopalian commitment to the social gospel. They had three children.

Early in his practice Dickinson began to make detailed records of female sexual anatomy and to interview his patients systematically about their sexual experience. Convinced that women were frequently the victims of sexual maladjustments deriving from ignorance or dysfunctional social values, he published a series of articles that described autoeroticism in women, urged his colleagues to counsel patients actively on the need for sexual fulfillment in marriage, advocated dress reform and physical education, and declared his conviction that birth control was essential to strong families. Dickinson became convinced that his ideal of the doctor as marriage counselor was just as important to the future of his specialty as were advances in basic scientific research. Known as a Christian gentleman and orthodox physician, Dickinson commanded a tolerant reception for his unorthodox work, but he chafed constantly over the reticence of his colleagues in matters of sexual reform. He successfully lobbied for election as president of the American Gynecological Society in 1920 in order to secure a platform from

which to make his case for sex research and counseling as an essential medical responsibility. The experience represented by his own database of more than 5,000 heavily illustrated patient records convinced him that he should turn from his lucrative ordinary practice to full-time sexology. Following service in World War I in the medical section of the National Council of Defense (1917) and as medical adviser to the Army General Staff (1918–1919), he closed his Brooklyn office-home and moved to Manhattan, where he lived on his investments and devoted all his time to sexual reform.

In 1923 Dickinson founded the Committee on Maternal Health (in 1930 "National" was added to the title) to provide an institutional sponsor for the campaign for medical sex research and marriage counseling. His first agenda item was to conduct a clinical study of contraceptive methods that would disprove irresponsible claims by medical leaders that safe and effective contraceptive practice was not possible. Even Dickinson's group of distinguished physicians could not obtain a license for a birth control clinic in New York State, but through cooperation with Margaret Sanger, the founder of the American Birth Control League (1921) and of the unlicensed Birth Control Clinical Research Bureau (1923), Dickinson played a key role in the publication of the first definitive studies on the effectiveness and safety of contraceptive practice. He waged a long lobbying campaign that led to a 1937 American Medical Association resolution that recognized contraception as a legitimate and essential part of medical practice.

During the 1930s the National Committee on Maternal Health emerged as a clearinghouse for information on human fertility. A series of definitive monographs, such as Dickinson's *Control of Conception* (1931), *One Thousand Marriages* (1931; with Lura Beam), *The Single Woman* (1934; with Beam), and *Atlas of Human Sex Anatomy* (1933), served as handbooks for doctors interested in sexual counseling and as justification for shifts in medical opinion. Committee publications on the physics and chemistry of contraception helped to define standards for commercial products, while studies on sterility and abortion brought new issues to the table for professional debate. Dickinson was also an active member of the Committee for the Study of Sex Variants, which conducted major studies of lesbianism, described in G. W. Henry's *Sex Variants* (1941). He wrote introductions and provided illustrations for works ranging from sex education pamphlets for adolescents to academic benchmarks such as Clellan Ford and Frank Beach's *Patterns of Sexual Behavior* (1951). As the most influential person in American sexology before Alfred Kinsey, Dickinson received and answered hundreds of letters from colleagues asking his opinion on sexual issues they encountered in their practices. In collaboration with sculptor Abram Belskie, he developed a series of sculptures depicting the cycle of conception, fetal growth, and birth that was viewed by more than 2 million people at the 1939 World's Fair, in one of the most successful efforts at sex education ever staged.

Dickinson was characterized by directed exuberance in both work and play. His artistic skills and love of nature—he was an avid walker, cyclist, and sailor—were reflected in hundreds of sensitive medical illustrations, as well as in *Palisades Interstate Park* (1921) and the *New York Walk Book* (1923; with Raymond Torrey and Frank Place). Dickinson blended the ethical idealism of his New England ancestors with great social skill in raising funds and mobilizing colleagues in support of his goal, the maintenance of stable families in a changing world. His career as a sexologist was inspired by an essentially religious vision of a richer existence if barriers to erotic fulfillment could be removed. He was a mediator of the transition from the Victorian code of "civilized sexual morality" to the embrace of personal erotic fulfillment characteristic of modern society, yet he maintained a strong, prescriptive commitment to his ideal of heterosexual, monogamous, married parents as the cornerstone of social order. He died in Amherst, Massachusetts.

• Dickinson's papers are in the Countway Library of Medicine, Boston, Mass. For his biography, see "Robert L. Dickinson and the Committee on Maternal Health," part 3 of James Reed's *From Private Vice to Public Virtue: The Birth Control Movement and American Society since 1830* (1978). On Dickinson's work with the Committee for the Study of Sex Variants, see Jennifer Terry, "Lesbians under the Medical Gaze: Scientists Search for Remarkable Differences," *Journal of Sex Research* 27, no. 3 (Aug. 1990): 317–39. Obituaries are in the *New York Herald Tribune* and *New York Times*, both 30 Nov. 1950.

JAMES W. REED

DICKINSON, William Preston (9 Sept. 1889–25 Nov. 1930), painter, was born in New York City, the son of Watson Dickinson, a sign painter and interior decorator, and Matilda Preston Jones. Dickinson was probably encouraged to choose art as a profession by his father. He was educated in New York City public schools and attended classes at the Art Students League from 1906 to 1910. Training at the league fostered a lifelong commitment to beautiful imagery, fine craftsmanship, and organization. Studying portraiture under the impressionist painter William Merritt Chase and outdoor landscape painting in summer classes at Woodstock, New York, under Birge Harrison and John Carlson, Dickinson developed an impressionist style. While he was working as an office boy for Suburban Engineering Company, Henry G. Barbey, the firm's founder, admired his art. Barbey helped pay for Dickinson's education at the league and, with future art dealer Charles Daniel, provided him with the funds to go to Europe.

Dickinson was abroad between 1910 and 1914, traveling in France, Belgium, Germany, and England but residing primarily in Paris. There he attended the École des Beaux-Arts and the Académie Julian. Unimpressed by his conservative teachers, he later stated that his own visits to the Louvre had a greater impact on his art. In Paris Dickinson exhibited in the Salon des Artistes Français and the Salon des Indépendants, and according to his sister Enid he wrote about art for French newspapers.

Although no artworks can be dated with certainty to his Parisian period, judging from what he exhibited after returning to New York, Dickinson clearly had been exposed to modern art, particularly cubism. Renewing his association with Daniel, he showed his earliest precisionist works in group shows at the Daniel Gallery in 1914 and 1915, abstractions inspired by Upper Manhattan locations such as *High Bridge*, a charcoal drawing on rice paper (c. 1915, Cleveland Museum of Art). (Precisionist artists worked in an impersonal, almost mechanical manner, emphasizing sharply focused details and geometric forms in response to the increasingly technological and urban American scene.) Thereafter Dickinson was a regular contributor to Daniel exhibitions, having solo shows in 1923, 1924, and 1927.

By 1916 Dickinson was experimenting in a variety of styles, creating more painterly, colorful work inspired by French fauve painting and Japanese art. By the late 1910s and early 1920s his paintings were similar to Paul Cézanne's landscapes and Pablo Picasso and Georges Braque's cubist art. Though he worked in a precisionist manner later on, most notably in the mid-1920s, Dickinson altered his style to fit his subject, sometimes traveling to distant locations to be inspired by their picturesque qualities.

While in Omaha, Nebraska, in 1924, Dickinson executed a major series of precisionist works of the granaries and industrial complex of Peters Mills, such as *Grain Elevators*, a graceful and majestic mixed-media drawing (Columbus Museum of Art), and *Power Station, Night*, a pastel and pencil drawing (Wadsworth Atheneum, Hartford, Conn.). Along with his still life drawings of the following year, which concentrated on wine bottles, decanters, and glasses, these works were instrumental in establishing sleek, industrial forms and machine-made artifacts as subjects of significance for the precisionists. In contrast are the works he made during sojourns in Quebec, Canada, in 1925–1926 and 1929: *Old Quarter, Quebec* (1927, Phillips Collection, Washington, D.C.), an oil painting, features a richly colored, energetically executed city view conveying quaint, old world charm. His late still lifes, such as the oil painting *Still Life with Yellow Green Chair* (c. 1928, Columbus Museum of Art), are complex, dynamic compositions of sharply angled forms seen from multiple viewpoints.

Dickinson's work also appeared in major exhibitions outside of the Daniel Gallery. He won a bronze medal for watercolor and drawing in 1926 in Philadelphia's Sesqui-Centennial International Exposition. His work was included in the influential survey of European and American modernism organized by the Société Anonyme held from November 1926 to January 1927 at the Brooklyn Museum, and in the exhibition Paintings by Nineteen Living Americans held at the

Museum of Modern Art from December 1929 to January 1930.

In a review of Dickinson's one-man show in 1924, critic Forbes Watson praised the consistent high quality of Dickinson's work, stating,

From the beginning his work gave evidence of clear-cut individuality, hard and positive, and of a lucid and inventive mind capable of great concentration, sure of itself and of its aims. . . . In his work there is no thoughtless painting, not an inch that is accidental. His designs are compact, intentional, and logical.

Although his works were well received critically and purchased by prominent collectors such as Duncan Phillips and Ferdinand Howald, Dickinson led a troubled life in the 1920s, the result of economic instability, family problems, and alcoholism. When he traveled to the Basque provinces in France and Spain in 1930 with painter Oronzo Gasparo, it was to escape the deprivation of the Great Depression, live cheaply, and have a new start. His last drawings, executed in and around San Sebastian, Spain, were emotionally charged and reminiscent of El Greco's art. Before he was able to explore this new emphasis in depth, however, his financial situation worsened along with his health. Stricken with influenza, Dickinson died from complications resulting from pneumonia in Irun, Spain.

Part of the modern art movement in the United States at a time when Americans had their first major exposure to avant-garde art, Dickinson is best remembered as a stylist. The Armory Show of 1913, which opened in New York City and traveled to Chicago and Boston, small exhibitions of contemporary work in Alfred Stieglitz's "291" Gallery in New York, and firsthand experience with modernism abroad made American artists of Dickinson's generation aware that they could choose from a broad spectrum of styles or invent their own. Along with Charles Sheeler and Charles Demuth, Dickinson was an originator of precisionism, an American movement that presented industrial and urban subjects in carefully composed, geometric arrangements. His stylistic exploration and his discovery of beauty in machine-made artifacts and industrial architecture encouraged other artists to break free from the restrictions of academic art to produce personal work focusing on the contemporary scene.

• The best early published sources on Dickinson are Forbes Watson, "Preston Dickinson," *Arts* 5 (May 1924): 284–88, and Louis Bouché, "Preston Dickinson," *Living American Art Bulletin* (Oct. 1939): 2–4. The most comprehensive studies of his life and art are Ruth Cloudman, *Preston Dickinson, 1889–1930*, an exhibition catalog for the Sheldon Memorial Art Gallery in Lincoln, Nebr. (1979), which is the best published source of illustrations of Dickinson's art, and Richard Rubenfeld, "Preston Dickinson: An American Modernist with a Catalogue of Selected Works" (Ph.D. diss, Ohio State Univ., 1985). A short, unpublished biographical sketch of the artist, written by his sister, Enid Dickinson Collins, in 1934, at Smith College Museum of Art, Northampton, Mass., corrects a number of errors in published accounts of the artist's life.

RICHARD RUBENFELD

DICKMAN, Joseph Theodore (6 Oct. 1857–23 Oct. 1927), army officer, was born in Dayton, Ohio, the son of Joseph Theodore Dickman, a soldier and politician, and Mary Weimer. Appointed to the U.S. Military Academy in 1876, Dickman graduated in 1881 after a one-year suspension "for interfering with and striking a new cadet." Commissioned a second lieutenant in the cavalry, he participated in campaigns against American Indians, bandits, and Mexican revolutionaries in the West and was both a student and an instructor at the Infantry and Cavalry School, Fort Leavenworth, Kansas. In 1882 Dickman married Mary Rector; they had four children.

During the Spanish-American War, Dickman was a staff officer in the Santiago campaign in Cuba, and in 1899–1900 he commanded an infantry regiment against insurgents on the island of Panay in the Philippines. In 1900 he was also chief of staff of the American relief forces in China during the Boxer Rebellion. From 1900 to 1917 Dickman rose steadily in rank from captain to brigadier general while holding a variety of staff and troop assignments in the United States and the Philippines, including command of the Second Cavalry Regiment. Well-read in military history and the writings of European strategists and tacticians, he gained a reputation as one of the army's outstanding tacticians. In 1905, while serving with the War Department General Staff, he prepared the first American edition of the *Field Service Regulations*. This "military bible," modeled after the German army regulations, guided the organization, administration, and tactics of the U.S. Army in the field.

Several months after the United States entered World War I in April 1917, Dickman was given command of the Eighty-fifth Division, then in training at Camp Custer, Michigan, with the temporary rank of major general. Later that year he was made commander of the Third Division at Camp Greene, North Carolina, and in May 1918 he took the division to France. Within a month Dickman and part of his division were rushed into the line at the Marne Crossings at Château-Thierry to assist the wavering French, and in their first action Dickman's eager but green troops made a good showing in stopping a German attack across the river. In July Dickman was charged with defending the Marne line directly east of Château-Thierry, as the Germans prepared to launch a new offensive to expand the Marne salient. Wisely ignoring French instructions to hold the river "with one foot in the water," he thinned his forces along the river to minimize the destructive effect of the German preparatory artillery bombardment, fashioned a defense in depth, and skillfully sited his artillery to cover the open ground on his front and right flank. When the Germans attacked on 15 July in what came to be known as the second battle of the Marne, Dickman's outnumbered men, often fighting German infantry in fierce melees, stood firm despite terrible losses. Dickman's division played a vital role in repulsing the last major German offensive and helped demonstrate that the American reinforcement made an Allied victory in the war certain.

Dickman's cool performance at the Marne led General John J. Pershing, commander of the American Expeditionary Forces (AEF), to make him commander of the IV Corps in August 1918. In September Dickman carried out a successful assault against the south side of the St.-Mihiel salient during the St.-Mihiel offensive. Some of the victory's luster was tarnished, however, by the Americans' failure to keep the Germans from evacuating large numbers of men before Dickman's corps linked up with the corps attacking from the salient's west side. As part of Pershing's shake-up of his top commanders after the American First Army's advance in the Meuse-Argonne offensive stalled, Dickman on 12 October became commander of the I Corps, which was situated on the extreme left of the First Army. After two weeks of preparation, he led the I Corps in the American army's breakthrough in the Meuse-Argonne sector following an attack on 1 November and the subsequent pursuit of the retreating Germans to the Sedan area on the Meuse River. For Dickman, however, the success was marred when a division in the V Corps misinterpreted its orders and marched across the front of his corps. He complained bitterly for years afterward that other American generals had embarrassed him and the American army in the eyes of the Allies through their tactical ineptitude.

Shortly after the armistice on 11 November 1918, Dickman was appointed commander of the American Third Army, the American force assigned to occupy Germany. In the spring of 1919, however, he was relieved from this post because of his strained relations with the French, who believed he was too lenient in his handling of the defeated Germans. For a brief time Dickman, then a permanent major general, headed a board of officers charged with developing and setting forth the lessons of the war and then served as commander of the Southern Department and the VIII Corps Area until his retirement in October 1921.

Burly and strong-willed with an annoying tendency to be pompous and take himself too seriously, Dickman was a competent, well-trained commander who knew how to run an efficient military machine. He possessed an outstanding soldier's eye for ground in analyzing a tactical situation and preparing his battle plans and was an aggressive troop leader. He was widely regarded as a skilled military technician, second to none among generals in the American army during World War I. Dickman died in Washington, D.C.

• Dickman's *The Great Crusade: A Narrative of the World War* (1927) is a straightforward narrative of his experiences during World War I. Robert L. Bullard, another major AEF general, includes a sympathetic biographical sketch of Dickman in *Fighting Generals* (1944). Astute comments on Dickman as a military commander are in Edward M. Coffman, *The War to End All Wars: The American Military Experience in World War I* (1968), and Frank E. Vandiver, *Black Jack: The Life and Times of John J. Pershing* (2 vols., 1977). For biographical information see *General Cullum's Biographical Register of the Officers and Graduates of the U.S. Military Academy*, vols. 4, 5, and 6 (1901, 1910, and 1921), and *Sixtieth Annual Report of the Association of Graduates of the United States Military Academy* (1929). An obituary is in the *New York Times*, 24 Oct. 1927.

JOHN KENNEDY OHL

DICKSON, David (6 July 1809–18 Feb. 1885), cotton planter and agricultural reformer, was born in Hancock County, Georgia, the son of Thomas Dickson and Elizabeth (maiden name unknown), farmers. Thomas Dickson was a Virginia revolutionary war veteran who migrated to southern Georgia. David spent his boyhood on his parents' farm, where he received only a common school education. At age twenty-two Dickson began a successful fourteen-year career as a merchant in Sparta, Georgia. Coveting the social status reserved for planters, Dickson in 1845 purchased a farm of 266 acres; stocked it with slaves, livestock, and farm implements; and for a time abandoned his career in merchandising to become a full-time agriculturist. Because his soil was infertile, in 1846 he applied Peruvian guano, a fertilizer that had first become available in the United States the previous year, on some of his crops. The resulting improvement in crop yields was so dramatic that Dickson soon developed a new system of culture based on heavy usage of guano, in conjunction with deep plowing and shallow cultivation. When chemical fertilizers came on the market during the 1850s, Dickson empirically experimented with various mixtures of guano and chemicals until he found a combination that was very effective on his land. Dickson capitalized on his success by manufacturing and marketing his fertilizer throughout the Southeast.

During his early years as a cotton grower, Dickson imported Petit Gulf cottonseed from New Orleans and adapted this prolific Mississippi cotton to Georgia soils by careful selective breeding, eventually becoming one of the few Georgians who made a financial success of selling name-brand cotton. Dickson also developed, manufactured, and marketed an improved sweep, a light plow for shallow working of cotton and corn. By 1860 he had amassed a fortune of $500,000, including 250 slaves and 15,000 acres of land in Hancock and Washington counties, Georgia, and 10,000 acres in Rush County, Texas. Nevertheless, his fortune was not the result of individual effort alone, for apparently he inherited many of these slaves and much of the land from his equally prosperous deceased older brother, Thomas Dickson.

Dickson's most significant achievement was to adjust his prewar farming methods to the utilization of free labor after Emancipation. He experimented with various forms of tenancy for several years and then adopted a system of sharecropping under which his workers received only one-third of the crops they produced. Dickson furnished his many tenants with food and supplies from his commissary, holding back one-third of their shares of the crops to cover future emergencies and to ensure that their debts to him would be paid. His tenants accepted this relatively unfavorable division of the crops because crops raised by Dickson's methods were unusually large, providing better living standards for his sharecroppers than was usual on Georgia farms.

Dickson's postwar financial success attracted the attention of agriculturists throughout the lower South, and his growing reputation expanded the market for his fertilizer, cotton seeds, and farm implements. In 1870 his voluminous writings that had appeared in such farm journals as the *Southern Cultivator* were edited and published as *A Practical Treatise on Agriculture*, which included a somewhat exaggerated autobiographical sketch. This work sold widely in several editions, contributing to Dickson's reputation throughout the South as an outstanding cotton grower and agricultural expert.

Dickson died on his Hancock County plantation, leaving most of his property in Georgia to his African-American mistress, Amanda A. Dickson, and their children.

• Dickson's papers were not preserved. His writings appeared as mentioned above and in G. E. Hunnicutt, ed., *David Dickson's and James M. Smith's Farming* (1910). The most thorough scholarly study of Dickson's career is Chester McArthur Destler, "David Dickson's 'System of Farming' and the Agricultural Revolution in the Deep South, 1850–1885," *Agricultural History* 31 (July 1957): 30–39. Willard Range, "The Prince of Southern Farmers," *Georgia Review* 2 (1948): 92–97, also includes useful information. An obituary is in the *Atlanta Constitution*, 19 Feb. 1885.

JOHN HEBRON MOORE

DICKSON, Leonard Eugene (22 Jan. 1874–17 Jan. 1954), mathematician, was born in Independence, Iowa, the son of Campbell Dickson, a merchant, banker, and real estate investor, and Lucy Tracy. Early in his childhood Dickson moved with his family to Texas, which he thereafter considered his home state. He attended the University of Texas, where he came under the influence of the outspoken mathematician, historian of mathematics, and promoter of non-Euclidean geometry, George Bruce Halsted, who taught an unusually strong undergraduate curriculum in mathematics for the day. Dickson received a B.S. in 1893 and an A.M. in mathematics in 1894 from Texas. He then undertook graduate work at the University of Chicago in the fall of 1894.

The University of Chicago, which had just opened in 1892, boasted the strongest mathematics faculty yet assembled on American shores. Under department head Eliakim Hastings Moore, Dickson earned his Ph.D. in 1896. His thesis, "The Analytic Representation of Substitutions on a Power of a Prime Number of Letters with a Discussion of the Linear Group" (*Annals of Mathematics* 11 [1897]: 65–143), represented an important extension and generalization of the work of French mathematician Camille Jordan and formed the basis of Dickson's first major book, *Linear Groups, with an Exposition of the Galois Field Theory* (1901).

After earning his doctorate, Dickson, like many American mathematical aspirants in the last decades of the nineteenth century, studied for a year in Europe. In 1896–1897 he journeyed to Leipzig to seek out the brilliant Norwegian mathematician, Sophus Lie, and to Paris to learn personally from Camille Jordan. On his return to the United States, he became an instructor of mathematics at the University of California. In 1899 he left the West Coast to assume an associate professorship at the University of Texas and in 1900 made his final academic move to the University of Chicago. There, he rose successively through the ranks from assistant professor in 1900 to Eliakim Hastings Moore Distinguished Service Professor of Mathematics in 1928. In 1902 he married Susan McLeod Davis; they had two children.

At Chicago, Dickson participated fully in all aspects of the mathematical mission as defined by Moore and his original colleagues, Oskar Bolza and Heinrich Maschke. Besides teaching and doing research, Dickson served the broader American mathematical community as editor of the *American Mathematical Monthly* from 1902 to 1908, joint editor of the *Transactions of the American Mathematical Society* from 1910 to 1916, and vice president and then president of the AMS in 1910 and 1917–1918, respectively. He also worked diligently as a mentor to future researchers.

During his lengthy career, Dickson produced a prodigious amount of seminal, original work, which established him as one of the world's foremost algebraists. In particular, his early work on linear groups codified important aspects of the theory of finite simple groups, an area that American mathematicians would soon come to dominate. His research beginning in 1903 on the theory of algebras also resulted in fundamental discoveries, most notably on division algebras and cyclic algebras. During the 1910s Dickson divided his research time between pure investigations on algebras and primarily historical work on number theory. As he stated in the preface to his massive, three-volume *History of the Theory of Numbers* (1919–1923), the result of a nine-year effort, his decision to embark on such a project "fitted in with his convictions that every person should aim to perform at some time in his life some serious, useful work for which it is highly improbable that there will be any reward whatever other than his satisfaction therefrom." In the case of Dickson's treatise, however, reward had come in the form of sustained reputation; the volumes have remained an authoritative encyclopedia of results in the theory of numbers.

Dickson successfully merged his interests in algebras and number theory in his extremely influential *Algebras and Their Arithmetics* (1923), which won the first prize of the American Association for the Advancement of Science for the most notable contribution to science in 1924. Expanded and translated into German as *Algebren und Ihre Zahlentheorie* (1927), the monograph played a key role in the evolving ideas of the German mathematicians Emmy Noether, Helmut Hasse, and Richard Brauer. In 1932 these three mathematicians, together with Dickson's student A. Adrian Albert, resolved one of the key problems in the area: the classification of all finite-dimensional division algebras over the field of rational numbers. Awarded the prestigious Cole Prize of the AMS in 1928 for the German edition of his book, Dickson then undertook extensive number-theoretic researches on the so-called Waring problem, which would define the focus of his mathematical activities for the rest of his career.

Although not especially gifted in the classroom, Dickson adeptly engaged the interests of the graduate students at the University of Chicago in his work as an adviser. With a keen sense of where interesting, original problems lurked, he directed some sixty-seven students in their doctoral researches. One such student, Albert, carried on his adviser's algebraic legacy in the department of mathematics at Chicago following Dickson's retirement in 1939.

A hard-bitten character, Dickson tended to speak his mind bluntly; he was always sparing in his praise for the work of others. At the University of Chicago, he was somewhat of a fixture in the faculty Quadrangle Club. There, along with colleagues such as physicist A. A. Michelson, he indulged his serious passions for bridge and billiards and reportedly did not like to lose at either game.

After his retirement, Dickson and his wife moved back to Texas, where he effectively gave up mathematical research and concentrated on more recreational activities, such as poker and his beloved bridge. He died in Waco, Texas. One of the first generation of American-trained mathematicians to achieve international prominence in research-level mathematics, Dickson established what has since become a strong American research tradition in the theory of algebras and in the closely related field of ring theory.

• Although isolated letters written by Dickson may be found in various archives, most notably in the papers of Eliakim Hastings Moore at the University of Chicago, Dickson destroyed his personal papers after his retirement from active teaching. Dickson's mathematical papers have been published as *The Collected Mathematical Papers of Leonard Eugene Dickson* (6 vols., 1975; repr. 1983). Among Dickson's books that have not already been mentioned are *Algebraic Invariants* (1914); *Linear Algebras* (1914); *Theory and Applications of Finite Groups*, with G. A. Miller and H. F. Blichfeldt (1916); and *Modern Algebraic Theories* (1926). Dickson also wrote several elementary course textbooks, including *College Algebra* (1902); *A First Course in the Theory of Equations* (1922); and *Plane Trigonometry with Practical Applications* (1922). On Dickson's life, consult Raymond C. Archibald, "Leonard Eugene Dickson," in *Semicentennial History of the American Mathematical Society* (1938), pp. 183–94; and A. Adrian Albert, "Leonard Eugene Dickson 1874–1954," *Bulletin of the American Mathematical Society* 61 (1955): 331–46, which both include bibliographies of Dickson's works; the former also contains a list of most of Dickson's doctoral students. For technical discussions of some of Dickson's early work, see Karen Hunger Parshall, "A Study in Group Theory: Leonard Eugene Dickson's *Linear Groups*," *Mathematical Intelligencer* 13 (1991): 7–11; and Parshall and David E. Rowe, *The Emergence of the American Mathematical Research Community 1876–1900: J. J. Sylvester, Felix Klein, and E. H. Moore* (1994).

KAREN HUNGER PARSHALL

DICKSON, Robert (c. 1765–20 June 1823), fur trader and British Indian Department officer, was born in Dumfries, Scotland, the son of John Dickson, a merchant. His mother's name is unknown. Robert Dickson emigrated to the United States in 1785–1786, soon after the American Revolution and was first employed at Oswego (N.Y.), where "he began his apprenticeship, which induced him to adopt the fur trade as a life-long occupation" (Cruikshank [1931], p. 88). Within a few months, Dickson was removed to the Niagara area, where his duties included selling and shipping goods to the fur-trade posts and managing accounts. As he was closely connected with some of the most respected and influential Loyalist families along the Niagara, Dickson enjoyed preferential treatment in both the choice and flexibility of his work. As a result of this good fortune, Dickson took the opportunity to leave the drab routine of his work at Niagara and in July 1786 was pleased to be transferred to the "Island of Michilimackinac" (MacKinac Island, Mich.) in order "to learn the art and mystery of commerce" (Cartwright papers, 10 July 1786).

Until the War of 1812 Dickson resided in the upper Mississippi region "in the character of a mercantile Trader" (Wood, vol. 1, p. 419) and acquired an extensive knowledge of the country and of the customs and distribution of the several Indian nations. In the spring of 1797 he married, probably in the custom of the country, To-to-win (Helen Dickson), a Dakota woman (Santee Sioux) and the daughter of an influential chief. The union strengthened Dickson's connections with the Sioux and surrounding Indian nations. For the next several years, the Dickson family (eventually including four children) were established at Lake Traverse (Upper St. Peter River, Minn.) and conducted a trade in furs.

By early 1812 war between Britain and the United States was imminent. Dickson and the other British and Canadian fur traders in the upper lakes south and west of Michilimackinac had economically suffered since the Jay Treaty (1794), through American encroachment and the imposition of heavy customs duties on British goods passing through border crossings such as Michilimackinac. The war offered them an opportunity to cooperate with the British military and hopefully gain a renewed paramountcy in the region. Thus, motivated by both economic self-interest and loyalty to the Crown, Dickson responded in June 1812 to a "Confidential Communication" from Major General Isaac Brock (commander of British forces in Upper Canada), which sought the cooperation of Dickson and his Indian "friends." In his reply, Dickson reported that he had collected about 250 to 300 friends and they were "ready to march." Indeed, Dickson was eminently successful in collecting, organizing, and dispatching Indian allies for the British war effort. These chiefs and warriors were instrumental in the resounding and critical victories of Crown forces over the Americans in the summer of 1812 at Michilimackinac and Detroit. As a result of this overwhelming success, Dickson was appointed on 1 January 1813 as agent and superintendent "for the Indians of the Nations to the Westward of Lake Huron." Until October 1813 Dickson solicited the military assistance of the upper lakes Indian nations for the defense of Upper Canada. But with the utter collapse of the British Right Division and the death of the inspirational Shawnee leader Tecumseh at the battle of Moraviantown on the Thames (5 Oct. 1813), Dickson was happily restricted to mustering His Majesty's Indian allies to the defense of the fur-trading region of the upper Mississippi. For the Indian nations, the military alliance with the British and Canadians was convenient and worthwhile, as both allies fought for protection and survival against the common enemy, the Americans. Among the Sioux, Dickson, "a large man, of full face, tall and commanding" and possessed of flaming red hair, was affectionately known as "the Redhead"—Mascotapah—in the Dakota language. Throughout the duration of the war, Dickson was tireless in recruiting Indian allies, and his set policy speech, delivered on numerous occasions and at several locations to Indians assembled, prompted the Dakota ever after to refer to the War of 1812 as "Pahinshashawacikiya," meaning "when the Redhead begged for our help" (Peter Douglas Elias, *The Dakota* [1988]).

Dickson spent the winter of 1814–1815 at Prairie du Chien (Fort Mckay), which had been captured by the British in July 1814, and continued his efforts in organizing the Indians in support of the king. During this time, he became snarled in a feud with the British commander over the distribution of food to the various Indian bands, with Dickson apparently showing favoritism to the Sioux families. This conflict resulted in Dickson being recalled to Michilimackinac. The case was referred to London, and in a hearing at Québec Dickson was exonerated and rewarded for his services to the Crown with the title of lieutenant colonel. With the war over, Dickson was retired from the British Indian Department with a pension.

The War of 1812 ruined Dickson's fur-trading career. While in Scotland for a brief visit after the war, he applied unsuccessfully for the vacant position of superintendent for the Indian Department at Amherstburg on the Detroit River. He subsequently drifted back to the upper Mississippi, where he remained popular with the Indian people. He tried various business endeavors, including the provisioning of beef to the Red River Colony (Selkirk's colony, Manitoba). All failed, and somewhat aimlessly, Dickson worked and traveled around the upper lakes region. He died near Michilimackinac at the British post of Drummond Island (Ontario).

Robert Dickson proved invaluable to the British in the successful defense of Canada during the War of 1812. His efforts in collecting and organizing the various Indian nations of the upper Mississippi also stalled the inexorable advance of the American frontier and allowed the indigenous people to preserve for a few more years their traditional lands and cultural values. In particular, the Dakota people retained a strong attachment to the British Crown, largely as a result of the efforts of the Redhead. This economic and military partnership was well remembered most poignantly in 1862 and again in 1876–1877 when Sioux refugees, fleeing the wrath of the revengeful Americans following the Minnesota Sioux War and the battle of the Little Big Horn, sought and were granted sanctuary in Canada as compensation for assisting the king during the War of 1812.

• Among the printed and unpublished primary material, the following sources are particularly useful: R. G. Thwaites, ed., "Dickson and Grignon Papers, 1812–1815," *Wisconsin State Historical Society Collections* 11 (1888): 271–315; Queen's University Archives, "Richard Cartwright, Letterbooks, 1785–1802"; and National Archives of Canada, MG19, E5 (Fur Trade and Indians), Bulger papers, which contain detailed correspondence relating to the Bulger-Dickson feud at Prairie du Chien during the winter of 1814–1815. For general reading on the life and times of Dickson, see Robert S. Allen, *His Majesty's Indian Allies: British Indian Policy in the Defence of Canada, 1774–1815* (1992), esp. pp. 123–66 and Appendix C, "Speech of Robert Dickson Esquire to Indian Tribes, 18 January 1813," pp. 223–24. Also recommended is E. A. Cruikshank, "Robert Dickson, the Indian Trader," *Wisconsin State Historical Society Collections* 12 (1892): 133–53; L. A. Tohill, "Robert Dickson, British Fur Trader on the Upper Mississippi," *North Dakota Historical Quarterly* 2 (1928): 5–49, 3 (1929): 83–128, 182–203; Cruikshank, "The King's Royal Regiment of New York," *Ontario Historical Society Papers and Records* 27 (1931): 1–131; William Wood, ed., *Selected British Documents of the Canadian War of 1812* (3 vols., 1920–1928); G. F. G. Stanley, "British Operations in the American North-west, 1812–15," *Society for Army Historical Research Journal* 22 (1943–1944): 91–106; Allen, "Canadians on the Upper Mississippi: The Capture and Occupation of Prairie du Chien during the War of 1812," *Military Collector and Historian* 31 (1979): 188–23; and A. R. Gilpin, *The War of 1812 in the Old Northwest* (1958).

ROBERT ALLEN

DICKSON, Samuel Henry (20 Sept. 1798–31 Mar. 1872), physician, was born in Charleston, South Carolina, the son of Samuel Dickson and Mary Neilson, Presbyterians of Scotch-Irish descent who had emigrated from Belfast, Ireland, before the American Revolution. Dickson received his early education from his father, a schoolteacher, and at private schools in Charleston. At the age of thirteen he entered Yale College as a sophomore and graduated with a B.A. in 1814 a few days before his sixteenth birthday.

Dickson returned to Charleston and began his medical training with Dr. Philip Grendron Prioleau in 1816. During the yellow fever epidemic of 1817 in Charleston, he devoted much of his time to the care of the sick patients at the Marine and the Yellow Fever Hospitals, and at twenty-one years of age, he was placed in charge of both institutions. For two years he practiced without a license, but, after attending two courses of lectures at the Medical School of the University of Pennsylvania, he received an M.D. in 1819; his thesis was a history of the Charleston yellow fever epidemic of 1817. He married Elizabeth Brownlee Robertson in 1821. In 1822 and 1823 he conducted free lectures in physiology for thirty-two students as a prelude to the establishment of a medical school in Charleston. With the aid of two colleagues and the support of the Charleston Medical Society, in 1824 the Charleston Medical College was established, and Dickson was appointed professor of the institutes and practice of medicine. The following year, suffering from hemorrhaging associated with tuberculosis and tormented by other debilitating illnesses, Dickson went to southern Europe, where he spent two years recuperating. Tuberculosis and his general poor health would plague him throughout his lifetime.

A controversy ensued between the medical faculty and the Charleston Medical Society over the appointment of a successor in the chair of surgery. The faculty choice was ignored, and Dickson, along with the entire faculty, resigned in 1832. The following year a charter for a new medical school, the Medical College of South Carolina, was granted to Dickson and his colleagues, and he was elected to the chair of the institute and practice of medicine. After the death of his wife in 1832, in 1834 he married his sister-in-law Irene Robertson, who died in December 1842; in 1845 he married Marie Seabrook Dupré. According to renowned surgeon Samuel D. Gross most of his children died from tuberculosis.

In the spring of 1847 Dickson accepted an appointment as professor of the theory and practice of medicine at the University of New York. He remained at that school for three years, but at the urgent request of the Medical College of South Carolina he returned as professor of the institute and the practice of medicine. During his tenure in Charleston as a medical practitioner and teacher Dickson enjoyed a thriving medical practice.

Dickson was an outstanding public speaker, having received training early in his career in Charleston. From the time of his graduation from medical school, as a resident of Charleston, Dickson lectured on the "Southern Circuit," on a broad range of medical and literary subjects. The "circuit" was equivalent to the Chautauqua, New York, meeting, which provided a wide range of cultural activities. He was one of the founders and a director of the first railroad built in South Carolina and an active participant in medical, scientific, civic, social, and benevolent organizations in Charleston.

In 1858 Dickson was invited to join the faculty of the Jefferson Medical College of Philadelphia as professor of the practice of medicine, replacing his good friend John Kearsley Mitchell, who had died earlier that year. He became the sixth chairman of the department and served in that capacity from 1858 to 1872. Dickson came to Jefferson an experienced, elegant, and articulate teacher. In addition to his regular teaching assignment, he taught a course on pathology at the "Summer Course," a program instituted in 1866 that

provided medical students with additional learning opportunities during the long summer recess. In 1868, at the age of seventy, Dickson served for one year as college dean. Although always in pain because of the debilitating and ravaging effects of tuberculosis and various intestinal ailments, Dickson did not subscribe to the common use of heroic medicine, which consisted of blood-letting (venesection, cupping, leeching) and purging, as a cure for his medical problems. Dickson relied on the use of stimulants and anodynes to alleviate the pain. In spite of a long history of illness and pain he continued to lecture at Jefferson Medical College until about a month before he died.

Dickson's many articles and monographs on medical subjects, philosophy, history, and current events appeared primarily in the *Southern Quarterly Review* and *Chapman's Philadelphia Journal*. His articles on the yellow fever epidemic of 1817 and 1829, dengue fever in 1828, and heat stroke in 1829 appeared in the *American Journal of the Medical Sciences*. His essay "Life, Sleep, Pain and Death" (1852) was an example of the eloquence of his writing.

Dickson was a slave owner, a southern sympathizer, and one of the early writers on racial anthropometry. Being dependent on student fees, when the Civil War appeared imminent and the southern students at Jefferson left Philadelphia for home, his income dropped precipitously and he was never able to recover financially. Because his private practice was small and Philadelphia physicians were reluctant to send their patients to consultants, his income was limited, and he died a poor man.

In 1860 Dickson said of himself

"I have passed my whole life in Minorities—political, religious, professional. I was one of the few Democrats in college in the War of 1812—I was a Clay Whig and Union Man in the Midst of Calhounism and Nullification. I am a Southern Slaveholder living among Abolitionists. I am a Unitarian-Rationalist-Free-thinking man. I have been always a Humoralist—almost alone for much of my life. I became an early convert a Contagionist and quaicurtinist [i.e., an advocate of quarantines]." (quoted in Radbill)

He died in Philadelphia.

• Among Dickson's most outstanding works were *A Manual of Pathology and Practice of Medicine* (1839), *Essays on Pathology and Therapeutics* (2 vols., 1845), and *Elements of Medicine* (1855). Biographical accounts of Dickson can be found in Edward Lewis Bauer, *Doctors Made in America* (1963), pp. 143–46, 174, and in Burton A. Konkle, *Standard History of the Medical Profession of Philadelphia*, ed. Frederick P. Henry (1977), pp. 257–58. Other sources include Samuel X. Radbill, "Samuel Henry Dickson: Pioneer Southern Medical Educator," *Annals of Medical History* 3d ser., 4 (1942): 382–89, and Frederick B. Wagner, *Thomas Jefferson University: Tradition and Heritage* (1987). Wagner's private papers include the unpublished manuscript "Samuel H. Dickson, M.D. (1798–1872): Confederate Sympathizer." Obituaries are in *Medical Times*, 15 Apr. and 1 May 1872, and the *Philadelphia Press*, 2 Apr. 1872.

SAM ALEWITZ

DIDDLE, Edgar Allen, Sr. (12 Mar. 1895–2 Jan. 1970), college basketball coach and administrator, was born in Gradyville, Kentucky, the son of John Haskins Diddle, a tobacco farmer, and Mary Elizabeth Hughes. Gradyville was little more than a general store, post office, a few houses, and a one-room schoolhouse for elementary grades. Between his chores and school Diddle played sandlot baseball and sharpened his basketball skills on outdoor, dirt courts. By the time he entered Columbia High School he excelled in both sports.

In 1915 Diddle entered Centre College in Danville, Kentucky, where the 5'10", 165-pound freshman quickly became a standout in baseball (center field), basketball (all positions), and football (halfback). In a slow drawl the ever-confident Diddle simply and exactingly highlighted his football skill, stating, "you know, the first football [game] I ever saw I played in. And I did pretty well, too." While Diddle had played basketball prior to his college days, the results were similar to those on the gridiron; he did pretty well at that sport too. Diddle worked to pay his way through college, and academics had a low priority after sports and work. Following the entry of the United States into World War I, he left school to join the navy in 1918. In the fall of 1919 Diddle returned to campus, where he played for noted football coach Madison A. "Matty" Bell. He was a stalwart on Centre's football team that went undefeated 9–0 and lost only one of 17 games during his last two seasons. Diddle also captained the basketball team to consecutive 11–0 finishes.

After his athletic eligibility expired, Diddle left Centre College in the spring of 1920 without completing his degree. In January 1921 he became head basketball coach at Monticello High School, Kentucky, where he guided the team to a 16–2 record and the semifinals in the state tournament. Diddle's strong year at Monticello gained him a position at Greenville High School, Muhlenburg County, Kentucky, coaching football and basketball. In his first season he guided his Cagers to a 26–2 record.

As a basketball coach Diddle was ahead of his time in strategy and techniques. He was one of the first coaches to implement the fast break and to bring all five players into the front court on offense. His innovative coaching style quickly attracted the attention of Western Kentucky Teachers College (later University) officials. In the fall of 1922, after some apprehension, Diddle accepted the university's offer of head coach in basketball, football, and baseball. The basketball position also included coaching the women's program. A star player on the women's basketball team that first year was Margaret Louise Monin. The two were married in 1923 and had two children.

Western Kentucky Teachers College had no basketball court, and the team played in tobacco warehouses against teams from small colleges in Kentucky and Tennessee and against the junior varsity squads from major colleges. Diddle stated, "I went to Western for $150 a month. That was $100 less than I was making in high school. But I knew I could build athletics at the school and I knew eventually the money would come." Success, recognition, and no doubt salary did come to Coach Diddle. In a short time a gymnasium was built on the campus. The team began to go up against varsity foes from the southern and southeastern conferences and played occasionally at Madison Square Garden in New York. In his first eight seasons, Diddle's teams won only 73 games and lost 57. But his recruiting skills and the availability of scholarships enabled him to attract highly talented players. With talent, motivation, and a strong belief in basic game fundamentals, his teams began to win consistently, recording 217 wins and 46 losses during the 1930s.

As his programs flourished, Diddle's coaching responsibilities became focused on the men's programs in basketball and baseball. But basketball gained Diddle national recognition and attracted considerable attention to Western. "Uncle Ed," as he was called, was homespun, easygoing, and preached a simple yet direct basketball philosophy. "If you play the game right you're gonna win. And if you don't win, you're in trouble. Real bad, awful trouble. If there's anything I can't stand, it's a happy loser." Spectators enjoyed Diddle's sideline manner—especially his habit of waving and chewing on a trademark red towel. His innovative coaching techniques quickly raised the Hilltoppers to become consistent winners and a national power.

Diddle spent forty-two years as coach at Western Kentucky, compiling 759 wins and 302 losses and only five losing seasons, two in his final seasons. Western Kentucky won or shared 32 championships in three different conferences and played in three National Collegiate Athletic Association and eight National Invitational Tournaments. At the time of his retirement in 1964, Diddle was the only coach to have directed more than 1,000 games at one college. Though not considered a master strategist, he inspired his players to perform at their best. Diddle, however, credited his friend and longtime assistant coach Ted Hornback for much of Western's basketball success. Aside from coaching, Diddle gave extensively of himself to the university as athletic director and to the community of Bowling Green, Kentucky. To his players, who until the 1950s lived in a campus home at the rear of his own house, Diddle was more than a coach. He and his wife were always there to provide a sympathetic ear to any of the youngsters' problems.

In 1952 Diddle suffered the first of thirteen heart attacks. But he continued to coach with the same vigor and success before turning the reins over to one of his former All-Americans, Johnny Oldham, in June 1964 on the advice of his physician. One of the greatest tributes to Diddle was the $3 million, 13,800-seat arena that the university built and named for him in 1963. A final heart attack took his life in Bowling Green, Kentucky. In 1971 Diddle was inducted into the Naismith Memorial Basketball Hall of Fame.

Diddle's colorful coaching style, which included pounding the floor and consulting with fans during a game, was popular with fans and media. He believed in winning with basic, fundamental basketball. But he occasionally tinkered with the basics, as in his early use of the fast break and the five-man offense. Generations of coaches have Diddle to thank for his pioneering efforts in college basketball's evolution. His spirit and dedication as a motivator of young athletes is worthy of emulation.

• The Edgar A. Diddle File, Naismith Memorial Basketball Hall of Fame, Springfield, Mass., contains numerous articles and newspaper accounts pertaining to his life and specific games. Significant print and film materials, and some memorabilia, can be found at Western Kentucky University, Bowling Green. A good general history of Diddle's life and career is Lowell H. Harrison, "Kentucky Biographical Notebook: Coach E. A. Diddle, Motivator of Men," *Filson Club History Quarterly* 67, no. 2 (Apr. 1993): 277–85. For statistics, his record, and a comparison with other college coaches see Neil D. Isaacs, *All the Moves: A History of College Basketball* (1984). William G. Mokray, ed., *Ronald Encyclopedia of Basketball* (1963), has accounts of games, records, and some of Diddle's colorful anecdotes; Alexander M. Weyand, *The Cavalcade of Basketball* (1960), includes game accounts and coaching records; and the *New York Times*, Mar. 1952, has National Invitational Tournament accounts. An obituary is in the *Bowling Green Daily Journal*, 3 Jan. 1970.

JERRY JAYE WRIGHT

DIDIER, Eugene Lemoine (22 Dec. 1838–8 Sept. 1913), author and editor, was born in Baltimore, Maryland, the son of Franklin James Didier, a physician, and Julia LeMoine. He studied English literature and composition for four years at St. Vincent's Academy in Baltimore and attended classes at Loyola College, also in Baltimore, for four more years but left without a degree. For three years he worked as an accountant in a commission firm, during which time he continued studying literature. He founded and edited *Southern Society* (1867–1868), a journal of southern writings. In 1869–1870 he worked as the private secretary of Salmon Portland Chase, who was then chief justice of the U.S. Supreme Court.

While employed by Chase, Didier had ample time to study and write. He contributed articles to *Appleton's Journal*, *Harper's Magazine*, *Lippincott's Magazine*, and the *National Quarterly Review*, using the pen names Lemoine and Timon. After resigning from Chase's office, on the ground of visual impairment, Didier, who always had plenty of money, began research on Edgar Allan Poe, whom he called "America's greatest genius." In 1873 he married Mary Louisa Innocentia Northrop. The couple had one child. Didier's father-in-law, Lucius Bellinger Northrop, had been Poe's fellow student at West Point and graduated from the academy in 1831.

Before publishing on Poe, Didier availed himself of Northrop's West Point recollections; discussed Poe with Maria Clemm, who was Poe's mother-in-law; and corresponded with Sarah Helen Whitman, who briefly been Poe's fiancée late in his life and had written *Edgar Poe and His Critics* (1860) and who shared letters from Poe with Didier. He published *The Life and Poems of Edgar Allan Poe; and Additional Poems* in 1877. This work was so popular that it went through nineteen editions. Its fourteen chapters are arranged in simple chronological order, with one chapter devoted to "The Raven," another to Poe's "Last Year," and a concluding, laudatory one on his appearance, manners, disposition, habits, industry, and well-deserved fame. In the last half of the book, Didier reprints forty-five of Poe's poems and two of his critical essays. Now labeled inept, sentimental, and even mawkish, Didier's book on Poe is discussed by scholars only in connection with Poe's friendship with Sarah Whitman and her cooperation with Poe's headstrong British biographer, John Henry Ingram. Ingram and Didier loathed each other. Ingram adversely reviewed Didier's book, and Didier in turn accused Ingram of stealing Poe manuscripts and letters loaned him.

Didier followed with *The Life and Letters of Madame Bonaparte* (1879). His subject, Elizabeth Patterson of Baltimore, was married there in 1803 to Jerome Bonaparte, the youngest brother of Napoleon, who promptly ordered him home—alone. The underage lad ranted and stalled but in 1805 abandoned his pregnant wife in Lisbon, later married Catharine of Württemberg, and became king of Westphalia. Elizabeth Bonaparte gave birth to his child in Camberwell, near London, and subsequently—never marrying again—made a dramatic career for herself as an international beauty combining vivacity, vanity, sharp wit, bitterness, and generosity. She died in Baltimore in 1879 at age ninety-four. Didier made great use of recently discovered Madame Bonaparte letters in presenting a thoroughly captivating, old-fashioned biography. It sold four editions in one month, was republished in England, and was translated into French.

The remainder of Didier's professional life was not very attractive. In 1879 Didier, always cocky and aggressive, published a sarcastic book called *American Publishers and English Authors*. As by Stylus, it advocates protecting foreign copyrights—but only so that Americans might become independent of England culturally and politically. In 1881 he founded the short-lived *Timon* magazine. In the early 1880s he edited several *Primers for the People*, designed to disseminate information on a variety of subjects, at ten cents a book. Topics included health, history, literature, marriage, money, and politics. One little book, his own 46-page *Primer for Criticism*, came out in 1883; in it, boldly reactionary, he rebukes "Henry James, jr." and "William D. Howells," among other exemplars of the new realism. Late in 1883 Didier went abroad, to England, France, Italy, Greece, and Turkey; while there, he sent dispatches back as special correspondent to Boston's *Literary World* and San Francisco's *Alta California*. In 1884 he published a harsh little pamphlet called *The Political Adventures of James G. Blaine*. He lived in New York from 1884 through 1887, offered for auction his library of 1,000 volumes and 800 engraved portraits in 1888, and reestablished himself permanently in Baltimore. He founded the monthly *No Name Magazine* (1889–1892), notable for some Poe material he published in it. In 1893 he founded another monthly, called *Success: An Illustrated Magazine for the People*, which soon failed. In his last book, *The Poe Cult, and Other Poe Papers* (1909), he assembles twenty or so of his earlier pieces, in some of which he violently criticizes Ingram. Didier died in Baltimore.

Didier should be remembered for helping to rescue Poe from temporary disfavor and for writing the definitive biography of Napoleon's unacknowledged American sister-in-law.

• Frank Luther Mott, in *A History of American Magazines, 1885–1905* (1957), mentions Didier's editorial work very briefly. David Saville Muzzey, in *James G. Blaine: A Political Idol of Other Days* (1934), does not cite Didier's publication on Blaine. Arthur Hobson Quinn, in *Edgar Allan Poe: A Critical Biography* (1941), mentions Didier but mainly to criticize him adversely. Problems involving Didier, Poe, Ingram, and Sarah Whitman are discussed in *Building Poe Biography* (1977) and *Poe's Helen Remembers* (1979), both by John Carl Miller. John Niven, in *Salmon P. Chase* (1995), mentions Didier only once, in passing. Obituaries are in the *Baltimore Evening Sun*, 9 Sept. 1913, and the *New York Times*, 10 Sept. 1913.

ROBERT L. GALE

DIDRIKSON, Babe (26 June 1914?–27 Sept. 1956), athlete, was born Mildred Ella Didriksen in Port Arthur, Texas, the daughter of Ole Nickolene Didriksen, a ship's carpenter and cabinetmaker, and Hannah Marie Olsen, an accomplished skater and skier. Didrikson herself was later to change the last syllable of the surname from *-sen* to *-son*. In 1915 her Norwegian immigrant parents moved to a working-class neighborhood in Beaumont, Texas. Her father, obsessed with physical fitness, required his children to exercise, and the husky young girl performed sports with her four brothers. As the sixth child in the family, she was given the nickname "Baby"; later, she was called "Babe" because she often, like Babe Ruth, hit tape-measure home runs.

Didrikson led the Beaumont Senior High girls' basketball team as a junior, sometimes outscoring the opposition's entire team. Melvin McCombs, who coached athletic programs for the Dallas Employees Casualty Company, recruited her in February 1930 to work as a clerk-typist for $75 a month and to play forward for his Golden Cyclones basketball team. In June 1930 she graduated from Beaumont High School. Didrikson earned All-America honors in 1930, 1931, and 1932, helping Dallas reach the Amateur Athletic Union tournament semifinals in 1930, capture the championship in 1931, and attain the finals in 1932. At the 1931 tournament, she tallied 106 points in five games and led scorers in a 28–26 title victory over the Wichita Thurstons.

Representing her company, Didrikson also excelled in track and field. The raw-boned, muscular 5'6", 130-pounder won the javelin throw at the 1930 AAU women's championships and the 80-meter hurdles and the long jump the following year. By 1932 the *Famous Athletes of Today* series listed Didrikson as "the world's greatest girl athlete." During July 1932 she dominated the Olympic trials at the AAU women's championships in Evanston, Illinois. Within 150 minutes she entered eight events, winning the shot put, javelin throw, 80-meter hurdles, and baseball throw, while sharing the high jump title with Jean Shiley. She tallied 30 points, eight better than the 22-member second-place Illinois Women's Athletic Club. Her 11.9-second 80-meter-hurdle heat, 139'3" javelin throw, and 5'3 3/16" high jump set world records.

American Olympic officials limited Didrikson to just three events at the Los Angeles Summer Olympic Games. On the opening day she threw the javelin 143'3 11/16" to earn the gold medal and shatter her world record. Three days later, she edged out a win in the 80-meter high hurdles after making two false starts; she was awarded a gold medal, being clocked in 11.7 seconds to top the world record by one-half second. Didrikson and Jean Shiley each broke the world high jump record, clearing the bar at 5'5 1/4". The bar was raised half an inch, but neither competitor cleared that height. Olympic officials then disqualified Didrikson for diving headfirst and awarded her second place, declaring Shiley the champion. Sportswriter Grantland Rice persuaded Didrikson to join his threesome for a round of golf the next day at the Brentwood Golf Club's difficult course in Santa Monica. Although she had golfed only ten other times, Didrikson drove the ball 260 yards from the first tee and scored a 43 on the back nine holes.

The AAU suspended Didrikson in December 1932 because she appeared in an automobile advertisement. She then turned professional, touring in 1933 and 1934 as one of three female members of the Babe Didrikson All-American basketball squad and the only female member of the bearded House of David baseball team. She also staged a billiards exhibition with Ruth McGinnis, a professional billiards player. In 1934 she pitched one shutout inning for the St. Louis Cardinals against the Philadelphia Athletics in a major league spring training baseball game. The *New York Tribune* in 1933 filmed Didrikson throwing a baseball 296 feet, an Olympic record, and a football fifty yards. She missed the women's 100-yard freestyle swimming record by one second, won a diving championship, and performed well at lacrosse, soccer, handball, fencing, cycling, and ice skating. Her annual earnings approached $50,000, enabling her to support her parents, put several relatives through school, buy an annuity, and invest. She resented press stereotypes degrading her athletic abilities. Sportswriters frequently had penned that female athletes should not be taken seriously. One sportswriter, Paul Gallico, had claimed that female athletes were "at best second-rate imitations of the gentlemen"; he would later change his assessment. Didrikson especially detested being called a "muscle moll." In "I Blow My Horn" (*American Magazine*, June 1936) she wrote, "They seem to think I'm a strange unnatural being. . . . The idea seems to be that Muscle Molls are not people."

Didrikson began taking golf lessons from Stan Kertes, a young golf professional, in 1933 and qualified for the Fort Worth Invitational tournament in November 1934. Her first golf victory came in April 1935 at Houston, where she won the Texas Amateur Championship. The U.S. Golf Association that summer, however, barred her from further amateur competition because of her professional involvement in other sports. In 1936 she captured the Eastern Open title, one of only two women's tournaments allowing professionals at the time, and she gave golf exhibitions for $150 a day with Gene Sarazen, Horton Smith, and Joyce Wethered in the United States and Australia.

In 1938 Didrikson was paired with George Zaharias, a prosperous, 285-pound professional wrestler and promoter, at a Los Angeles golf tournament. They were married in St. Louis, Missouri, in December 1938; they had no children. Zaharias managed Didrikson's career, having her sit out the required three years to regain amateur status, which she needed in order to play in the top tournaments. Eleanor Tennant, noted coach for Alice Marble, instructed Didrikson in tennis for three months in 1942 at the Los Angeles Tennis Club and predicted that Didrikson would win a championship within two years. The U.S. Lawn Tennis Association, however, banned her from amateur competition.

Didrikson participated in professional golf tournaments from 1940 to 1943, but she declined monetary prizes. In 1940 she began taking daily lessons from golfer Tommy Armour and captured the Western and Texas Open tournaments, her first victories in five years. During World War II she staged several golf exhibitions to boost War Bond sales. In January 1943 the U.S. Golf Association restored her amateur status, and Didrikson promptly won the Western Open that year. In the 1944 Los Angeles women's match play tournament she averaged four strokes per hole for 99 holes. Although she learned of her mother's death before finishing the semifinal round of the 1945 Western Open, the next day she became the event's first three-time titlist. She suffered her first golf setback in seven years at the Western Amateur tournament in August 1945, but she rebounded to win the Texas Open and the Broadmoor Invitational.

Didrikson won seventeen consecutive golf tournaments in 1946 and 1947. Her 1946 victories included the Trans-Mississippi, Broadmoor Invitational, and All-American Open events as well as her only U.S. National Amateur championship. During early 1947 she won six titles in six weeks and took the Titleholders Championship in a driving rainstorm. The same year she became the first American woman to win the British Amateur tournament.

Already the holder of every major amateur golf title, Didrikson turned professional in August 1947 and began an exhibition tour. In October 1947 she shot 293 in 72-hole medal play tournament golf, a women's record at the time.

In January 1948 Didrikson and five others organized the Ladies Professional Golf Association, setting up a seven-event tour. From 1948 to 1951 she led the tour in earnings with nearly $40,000. Patty Berg, Betty Jameson, Beverly Hanson, Betsy Rawls, and Louise Suggs furnished her principal competition. Didrikson won three tournaments, including the U.S. Open, in 1948, and she earned two titles the following year. The tour expanded to nine events in 1950, with Didrikson winning six. She became the first woman to sweep all three major tournaments in the same year, winning the Titleholders, U.S. Open, and Western Open. After winning half of the fourteen tour events in 1951, the next year she won her third Titleholders and three other tournaments.

Major colon cancer surgery sidelined Didrikson in April 1953, but she returned that summer to win one title. Her five 1954 victories included the Tam O'shanter All-American Open and her third U.S. Open. Between 1935 and 1955 she won thirty-one LPGA titles and fifty-two other golf crowns. She recorded her last two victories in 1955, the year the cancer recurred. Before her death in Galveston, Texas, she and her husband established a fund to support cancer clinics and treatment centers.

The Associated Press named Didrikson Woman Athlete of the Year in 1932, 1945, 1946, 1947, 1950, and 1954, making her the only six-time recipient. In 1950 the news service overwhelmingly acclaimed her "Woman Athlete of the Half Century." "The Babe," Grantland Rice wrote, "is without any question the athletic phenomenon of all time, man or woman." Sportswriter Paul Gallico called her "the most talented athlete, male or female, ever developed in our country." Didrikson made women's golf a colorful, entertaining, power game. During her lifetime she earned around $1 million in prize money, mostly for her golf activities. She attracted sizable galleries, outdrawing most male golfers. Natural sports talent, a dedicated work ethic, patience, concentration, character, a warm personality, self-confidence, a competitive, aggressive spirit, and an indomitable will combined to make her a superb and versatile champion. She symbolized through her talents and achievements what women could accomplish in sports, and she paved the way for big-time women's professional sports.

• Didrikson's letters to William and Ruth Scurlock are at the John Gray Library, Lamar University, Beaumont, Tex. Her autobiography, written with Harry Paxton, *This Life I've Led*, was published in 1956. The most comprehensive, objective biography is William Oscar Johnson and Nancy P. Williamson, *"Whatta-Gal": The Babe Didrikson Story* (1977), based on their *Sports Illustrated* articles of 6, 13, and 20 Oct. 1976. George Zaharias, "Babe and I," *Look*, 11 Dec. 1956, provides a personal perspective. See also Betty Hicks, "Babe Didrikson Zaharias," *Womensports*, Nov. and Dec. 1975, for reminiscences by a golf competitor. Assessments by sportswriters include Paul Gallico, *Farewell to Sport* (1938), and Grantland Rice, *The Tumult and the Shouting: My Life in Sport* (1954). Obituaries are in the *New York Times*, 28 Sept. 1956, and *Life*, *Newsweek*, and *Time*, all 8 Oct. 1956.

DAVID L. PORTER

DIEBENKORN, Richard (22 Apr. 1922–30 Mar. 1993), painter, was born Richard Clifford Diebenkorn, Jr., in Portland, Oregon, the son of Richard Clifford Diebenkorn, a hotel supplies sales executive, and Dorothy Stevens. In 1924 the family moved to San Francisco, where Diebenkorn attended local schools. At an early age he was interested in art, and he later noted, "I drew and painted all through grammar school. For me, the high point of the day was when the paints came out" (Gruen, p. 82). In 1940 Diebenkorn enrolled in Stanford University. After enlisting in the U.S. Marine Corps Officer Training Program in his junior year, he briefly studied physics at the University of California at Berkeley in 1943. Transferred to the marine base in Quantico, Virginia, later in 1943, Diebenkorn spent weekends visiting art collections in Washington, D.C., particularly the Phillips Collection, where he was fascinated by Henri Matisse's *The Studio, Quai St.-Michel* (1916). Returning on leave to California, Diebenkorn married Phyllis Gilman in 1943; the couple had two children. One of Diebenkorn's earliest works dates from this same period: *Palo Alto Circle* (1943, Santa Cruz Island Foundation Collection). The painting is a precise rendering of a hotel in a style clearly reminiscent of the work of Edward Hopper, another early influence on Diebenkorn.

Discharged from the marines in 1945, Diebenkorn returned to California and enrolled at the California School of Fine Arts (CSFA) in San Francisco. At the CSFA Diebenkorn studied with David Park, one of the first abstract painters to work in California; Park became a friend and mentor. With the aid of a special grant, the Albert Bender Award, Diebenkorn moved to Woodstock, New York. On periodic trips to New York City he studied the work of Joan Miró and Piet Mondrian at the Museum of Modern Art.

When Diebenkorn went back to California in 1947, he began teaching at the CSFA. Among the other instructors at CSFA at this time were Clyfford Still, a senior faculty member, and Mark Rothko, who taught summer sessions. Stirred by their work, with its large fields of color that dominated the canvas, Diebenkorn started to paint in a more abstract vein, which may be seen in such works as *Painting II* (1949, Oakland Museum). In 1948 he was given his first solo exhibition at the California Palace of the Legion of Honor in San Francisco. The following year Diebenkorn returned to Stanford to complete his degree.

Fascinated by photographs he had seen of the American Southwest, Diebenkorn moved to Albuquerque, New Mexico, in 1950. There, he enrolled in the masters degree program at the University of New Mexico and received his degree in 1952. Diebenkorn's works from his New Mexican period, such as *Untitled 'M'* (1951, San Francisco Museum of Modern Art), while remaining abstract, are more open and less dependent on the work of Still and Rothko. After receiving his degree, Diebenkorn spent a year teaching art at the University of Illinois, Urbana. Not liking the formalistic teaching style, he moved his family to New York City in June 1953. He became acquainted with the abstract painter Franz Kline, and through Kline he formed an association with the Poindexter Gallery. But, uncomfortable with the atmosphere of the New York art world, Diebenkorn quickly returned to California in late 1953 to settle in Berkeley.

In 1955 Diebenkorn became an assistant professor of drawing and painting at the California College of Arts and Crafts, where he remained until about 1960. The following year he had his first solo exhibition in New York City at the Poindexter Gallery. He was moving away from his abstract work to a more figurative style, and as Diebenkorn later commented, he "wasn't going to get stuck in any dumb rut" (Gruen, p. 84). When he joined drawing sessions with David Park and Elmer Bischoff, the three painters were dubbed the "Bay Area Figurative School." Drawing on many of the Abstract Expressionists' precepts concerning color and field/ground, the Bay Area figurative style retained at the same time traditional elements of the figure. Over the next few years Diebenkorn's work concentrated on landscape, the figure, and still lifes. Such works as *Girl on A Terrace* (1956, Neuberger Museum, SUNY-Purchase), *Girl with Three Coffee Cups* (1957, Yale University Art Gallery), and *Ingleside* (1963, Grand Rapids Art Museum) illustrate Diebenkorn's new fascination with figurative art while retaining the vibrant palette of his abstract years.

In 1964 Diebenkorn toured the Soviet Union on behalf of the U.S. State Department's cultural exchange program. Traveling to Leningrad (now St. Petersburg) and Moscow, he showed examples of his paintings and visited Russia's great collection of the works of Matisse.

Appointed professor of art at the University of California at Los Angeles in 1966, Diebenkorn moved into the Santa Monica studio belonging to the artist Sam Francis. While Francis was vacating the space, Diebenkorn worked in a small room in the same building. He later remarked: "What I was doing was things that were representational, but they were getting very, very flat. Very, very simplified. It represented a great change in my figurative painting" (Gruen, p. 86). After moving into the larger space Diebenkorn began working on large canvases and suddenly "abandoned the figure altogether" (Gruen, p. 86). These abstract works were the first in his Ocean Park series. Diebenkorn would be consumed with the theme for nearly the remainder of his life; over the next twenty years, he completed more than 140 works in the series. Commenting on this series, named after the Santa Monica neighborhood where his studio was located, Diebenkorn said, "I probably went to Santa Monica's Ocean Park district because of the light, but I didn't know it until I started realizing that I was very involved with this light" (Gruen, p. 86).

Composed of rectangular color areas divided and intersected by lines and smaller color patches, the Ocean Park series has a remarkable range of design that encompasses both abstraction and representation. Works in the series include *Ocean Park #16* (1968, Milwaukee Art Museum), *Ocean Park #27* (1970,

Brooklyn Museum), *Ocean Park 64* (1973, Carnegie Museum of Art, Pittsburgh), and *Ocean Park #107* (1978, Oakland Museum). The Ocean Park series received nearly unanimous critical praise. John Russell of the *New York Times* called it "One of the most majestic pictorial achievements of the second half of this century, in this country or anywhere else" (5 Dec. 1976).

Diebenkorn was the subject of a major retrospective exhibition organized by Buffalo's Albright-Knox Art Gallery in 1976. On the occasion of the exhibition's opening at the Whitney Museum of American Art in 1977, Diebenkorn noted that "New York has always been a nervous-making place for me" (*New York Times*, 10 June 1977). The New York art establishment had a tenuous relationship with him, identifying him "with New York's one-dimensional conception of California culture" (Gopnik, p. 97) and slightly jealous of his position as a key figure who oversaw "the rise of California from a provincial backwater to an artmaking capital equal to New York" (Gopnik, p. 97).

Though primarily known for his paintings, Diebenkorn was also an excellent draftsman. His drawings were praised in the *New York Times* (4 Jan. 1969) by critic Hilton Kramer, who noted that "The art of drawing is, in his hands, not only an accomplished and accurate technique of representation, but also a natural language of feeling." At the showing of Diebenkorn's drawings at the Museum of Modern Art (New York City) in 1988, Robert Hughes noted in *Time Magazine*, that "He is, quite simply, one of the best painters America has ever produced" (12 Dec. 1988).

Diebenkorn's health began to decline, and he underwent heart surgery twice in his last two years in addition to suffering from pneumonia. He left southern California to return to the Berkeley area in 1988. His health problems limited his ability to paint, though he continued to create drawings and other small-scale works until his death at his home in Berkeley, California.

Among Diebenkorn's lasting contributions are his introduction of the alternating cool and hot palettes that to some extent define the popular conception of California. His use of blue, green, and a harsh white embody the spirit of the West Coast. Achieving worldwide fame from his home there, Diebenkorn created a small crack in New York City's hegemony in the American art world.

• Although there are no public collections of Diebenkorn's papers, the Archives of American Art (Smithsonian Institution) has a number of taped interviews with him, and he figures in the papers of numerous others held by the archives. Works are in the collections of the Metropolitan Museum of Art, the Whitney Museum of American Art, and the Museum of Modern Art in New York City; the Corcoran Gallery of Art and the Phillips Collection in Washington, D.C.; the Oakland Museum (Calif.); the San Francisco Museum of Modern Art; and many others. John Gruen's interview with the artist, "Richard Diebenkorn: The Idea Is to Get Everything Right," *ARTnews*, Nov. 1986, pp. 80–87, provides a wealth of biographical detail. *Richard Diebenkorn* (1991), the catalog to the exhibition held at the Whitechapel Art Gallery, London, with an essay by John Elderfield, is also useful. See also Adam Gopnik, "Diebenkorn Redux," *New Yorker*, 24 May 1993, pp. 97–100; the Museum of Modern Art exhibition catalog, *Drawings of Richard Diebenkorn* (1988); Gerald Nordland, *Richard Diebenkorn* (1987); and Susan Landauer's catalog from the San Francisco Museum of Modern Art, *The San Francisco School of Abstract Expressionism* (1996). Obituaries are in the *New York Times*, 31 Mar. 1993, the *Washington Post*, 1 Apr. 1993, the *Washington Times*, 4 Apr. 1993, and the *Christian Science Monitor*, 5 Apr. 1993.

MARTIN R. KALFATOVIC

DIEGEL, Leo H. (27 Apr. 1899–8 May 1951), professional golfer, was born in Detroit, Michigan, the son of William G. Diegel, an industrial worker, and Elizabeth Kebbe. As a ten-year-old parochial school student he began caddying and became something of a teenage phenomenon. At age thirteen he won the city caddy championship, and four years later, as an assistant professional at the Country Club of Detroit, he won the Michigan Open title. He rose to national prominence in 1920 when he tied for second place, behind Englishman Ted Ray, in the U.S. Open at Inverness Country Club in Toledo, Ohio. This event proved to be a turning point in American golf. It marked the end of British dominance in major tournaments and the emergence of American professionals such as Diegel, Walter Hagen, Gene Sarazen, and the transplanted "Silver Scot," Tommy Armour, as well as amateur Bobby Jones. It was also the first national championship in which professionals, heretofore considered socially inferior employees, were extended full clubhouse privileges. The Open at Inverness also began a period that spawned the modern tournament circuit, or "tour," of the Professional Golfers Association (PGA), founded in 1916.

From his first official victory in 1920 to his thirty-first and last in 1934, Diegel was a tour pioneer. Having won one tournament each year from 1920 through 1923, he entered the prime of his career in 1924. That year he earned his first significant victory, the Canadian Open; he would also win this event in 1925, 1928, and 1929. Five titles in 1925 earned him the number one position that year among the top 25 competitors. He won four tournaments each in 1928 and 1929, including consecutive PGA championships, and in so doing he broke Hagen's string of four straight triumphs. Three victories in 1930 concluded this exceptional span. Thereafter, he won once in 1933 and twice in 1934. Because of his superb record he played on four Ryder Cup teams (1927, 1929, 1931, 1933) in the biennial matches against British professionals. For the period 1916 to 1929, he ranks third (behind Hagen and Johnny Farrell) in PGA winnings.

During a time when golf professionals rarely earned a living strictly from playing in tournaments, Diegel parlayed his growing reputation and engaging personality into a succession of prestigious club positions. In 1921 he became head professional at Lochmoor Country Club in Detroit. The next year he moved to the New Orleans Country Club, and in 1925 he became affiliated with the Fenimore Country Club in White Plains, New York. From 1929 to 1933 he was associated with the new Agua Caliente course in Tijuana, Mexico, as winter professional for the then princely salary of $15,000. During the late 1920s he was also a private teaching professional; his clients included motion picture mogul Adolph Zukor, film producer Joseph Schenck, and actor Douglas Fairbanks. The Hollywood connection resulted in Diegel and his friend Hagen costarring in a Mack Sennett golf comedy. In 1934, during the second of his 12 years with the Philmont Country Club in Philadelphia, he married Violet Bird. The couple was childless.

After 1934 Diegel's tournament presence and performance abruptly declined. He injured his right shoulder in 1935 while roughhousing with fellow tour player Harry Cooper and was forced to forgo much of the 1936 season. A second injury in 1938 to his right hand and thumb, the result of being struck by an automobile while crossing a street, was a further setback. His last noteworthy, top-25 finish in a PGA event occurred in 1939. During World War II he chaired the PGA Rehabilitation Committee, actively promoted golf in the convalescence of wounded service personnel, and raised some $600,000 for the construction of golf facilities at veterans' hospitals. In 1945 he became the professional at the El Rio Country Club in Tucson, Arizona; returned to the Detroit Country Club in 1949; and in 1950 relocated in southern California. A heavy smoker, Diegel was diagnosed in 1947 with throat and lung cancer, the cause of his death in North Hollywood, California. In 1955 he was posthumously elected to the PGA Hall of Fame.

Because he came close but never won either the U.S. Open or the British Open, Diegel is remembered as a near-great player who fell short of expectations. Writers have attributed this predicament to his temperament, variously described as high-strung, jittery, and fidgety; the golf historian Al Berkow referred to it as something akin to "exposed ganglion." His frenetic tournament behavior included sticking the lighted end of a cigarette in his mouth and ramming a two-foot putt into a sand trap. He was especially vulnerable to psychological manipulation during match, or head to head, play involving the irrepressible Hagen, his competitive nemesis but close personal friend. To combat his tendency to jerk critical short putts to the left, in 1924 he adopted a unique style in which he bent over from the waist, aligned his arms almost horizontally over the target line, and locked his hands so as to eliminate all wrist movement from the stroke. While "Diegeling," as it was called, was effective in lesser tournaments, it never produced the foremost national championships. This limitation was especially apparent in the U.S. Open; he told an interviewer in 1929 that he could never seem to develop "the proper frame of mind" for the event (Price, *American Golfer*, p. 122). Fellow professionals held his wood and iron play in high regard, and when his "arms-akimbo" or "flying elbows" putting technique was working "the Dieg" was considered unbeatable. Bernard Darwin, the Lon-

don *Times* golf writer, referred to him as "in a way the greatest golfing genius I have ever seen" (Wind, *American Golf*, p. 254). His grasp of the game matched his execution, as revealed in his respected instructional book, written with Jim Dante, *The Nine Bad Shots of Golf and What to Do about Them* (1947), which justified seven printings. His notion of an arms-and-hands putting stroke anticipated a more mechanical approach in the latter half of the twentieth century. Ironically, a few missed putts denied him the greatness equated with "major" tournament victories.

• During Diegel's prime in the late 1920s, W. D. Richardson, golf writer for the *New York Times*, contributed "Diegel the Dazzling" to the *American Golfer* magazine; it was reprinted in Charles Price, *The American Golfer* (1964), a collection of articles from that magazine. Herbert Warren Wind analyzes Diegel's brilliance and his failures in *The Story of American Golf: Its Champions and Its Championships* (1948; repr. 1986) and to a lesser extent in *Following Through* (1985). Robert Sommers, *The U.S. Open: Golf's Ultimate Challenge* (1987; 2d ed., 1996), is insightful regarding the elusive American championship. Al Barkow, *Golf's Golden Grind: The History of the Tour* (1974) and *The History of the PGA Tour* (1989), cover Diegel's role as a tour pioneer; the latter title, when used with John P. May, ed., *The Golf Digest Almanac, 1984* (1984), presents his career statistically. Additional insights are in Bernard Darwin, *Golf between Two Wars* (1944; repr. 1985); the editors of *Golf Digest*, *All about Putting* (1973); Will Grimsley, *Golf: Its History, People & Events* (1966); Walter Hagen, *The Walter Hagen Story* (1956); George Peper, ed., *Golf in America: The First One Hundred Years* (1988); and Charles Price, *The World of Golf: A Panorama of Six Centuries of the Game's History* (1962). Obituaries are in the *Detroit News* and the *Los Angeles Times*, 9 May 1951.

JAMES A. WILSON

DIES, Martin (6 Nov. 1901–14 Nov. 1972), U.S. congressman, was born in Colorado, Texas, the son of Martin Dies, Sr., himself a member of the U.S. House of Representatives for ten years, and Olive Cline. After graduating from National University in Washington, D.C., in 1920, Dies married Myrtle Adams that same year. They had three children. After moving back to Texas, Dies practiced law in the Orange, Texas, firm of Dies, Stephenson, and Dies. Not yet thirty when first elected to Congress in 1931 as a Democrat, he became the protégé of John Nance Garner, the powerful Speaker of the House, and received an appointment to the important Rules Committee after the Roosevelt-Garner ticket captured the White House in 1932. A tall man (6'3") with blond hair, Dies had an unaffected, folksy style and was the first president of the House's tongue-in-cheek Demagogues Club. Members pledged never to vote for a tax bill or against an appropriation bill.

Like many other southern Democrats, Dies at first supported the New Deal, but during Franklin D. Roosevelt's second term he objected to the president's increasing emphasis on urban constituencies. Dies was particularly troubled by the administration's apparent sympathy for sit-down strikers in the automobile factories of Flint and Detroit, Eleanor Roosevelt's persistent advocacy of antilynching legislation and other human-rights issues, the court-packing scheme of 1937 that would have added administration supporters to the U.S. Supreme Court, and FDR's attempt to purge the party of anti–New Deal southern Democrats during the 1938 primary elections. A coalition of Republicans and conservative southern Democrats managed to bring the New Deal to a halt and even to launch modest offensives. One such offensive came with the approval in 1938 of Dies's resolution to establish the Special Committee to Investigate Un-American Activities. The intent was to both discredit political radicalism and roll back what the Dies Committee later called, in its 1942 report, the "creeping totalitarianism" of the executive's "effort to obliterate the Congress of the United States as a coequal and independent branch of government."

The Dies Committee had a mandate to probe "the extent, character, and object of un-American propaganda activities in the United States." Since World War I, Congress had periodically investigated radical activities under the leadership first of Lee S. Overman (D.-N.C.) in the Senate in 1920 and then during the early 1930s of Hamilton Fish (D.-N.Y.) and Samuel Dickstein (D.-N.Y.) in the House. No congressional proponents ever precisely defined the term "un-American." J. Parnell Thomas (R.-N.J.), the Dies Committee's senior Republican member, may have come closest. Un-American activities, he later told the *New York Times*, encompassed "the four horsemen of autocracy . . . Fascism, Nazism, Bolshevism, and New Dealism."

Dies concentrated on the last two, recognizing no important distinction between the New Deal's social and economic reforms and the more radical plans of communist revolutionaries to overthrow the government and abolish capitalism. In a series of spectacular hearings and reports during the late 1930s, he charged the Roosevelt administration with incompetence and negligence in failing to confront the domestic communist threat. "Stalin," he wrote in *The Trojan Horse in America* (1940), "baited his hook with a 'progressive' worm, and [the] New Deal swallowed bait, hook, line, and sinker." To prove it, he released a barrage of official papers detailing alleged communist infiltration of the New Deal's alphabet agencies as well as liberal organizations (notably the Congress of Industrial Organizations [CIO]) that were part of the New Deal coalition.

An avalanche of newspaper publicity accompanied these charges, particularly during the committee's first two years. Indeed, in 1940 Dies received more than 3,000 invitations to speak before various patriotic societies and business associations. Un-American activities had become a thorn in the administration's side, in the process earning Dies a permanent place in the nation's political history.

Roosevelt responded to Dies on two fronts. Rejecting the advice of Interior secretary Harold Ickes, who favored a public confrontation, he at first ignored the Dies Committee investigations. After the German blitzkrieg of spring and summer 1940, however, he abandoned this tactic. Concluding that Dies's activities were interfering with the administration's preparedness campaign, he met with Dies at the White House, after which the committee was briefly more restrained. On the other front, Roosevelt had J. Edgar Hoover's FBI investigate Dies, personally passing on a spurious rumor reported by Supreme Court Justice Felix Frankfurter. The committee chairman's campaign manager, Frankfurter said, had received $20,000 from an agent of Hitler's Reich. For his part, Hoover pursued a love-hate relationship with the Dies Committee. Although sharing Dies's convictions about the nature of New Deal reform and the subversiveness of New Deal personnel, the FBI director saw the committee as a rival and never fully cooperated with it.

Dies was an unsuccessful candidate for the Senate in 1941, running fourth in a special election. After that, he largely lost interest in un-American activities and in 1945 retired from Congress. Reelected to the House in 1952, he returned to Washington in 1953 with McCarthyism in full bloom, and hoping to capitalize on the issue's notoriety he unsuccessfully sought a seat on his old committee (now a regular standing committee known by the acronym "HUAC"). Dies's contemporaries either hailed him as prophet and trailblazer or condemned him for sullying the good name of anticommunism. Following another failed Senate bid in 1956, Dies sat two more years in the House and then returned to his Texas law practice. His last words on the Red menace came in an autobiography written, he said, "lest I be asked on Judgment Day, 'Why did you sin by silence when you knew the truth?'"

Yet Dies never suffered silence, although his activities commanded differing popular attention. Thus, while during the Dies Committee's first month of existence the *New York Times* alone gave him more than 500 column inches, in 1963 no one paid much attention to his autobiography. By the time he died, in Lufkin, Texas, he had spent years in obscurity. Still, the *Times* ran his obituary on the front page.

• The Roosevelt Library in Hyde Park, N.Y., has a transcript of the FDR-Dies conversation and thousands of other documents and public correspondence. The autobiography, *Martin Dies' Story*, was published by an obscure house called Bookmailer and thus had little chance of gaining wide circulation. By contrast, Dies's *The Trojan Horse in America* had been published by Dodd, Mead and became a bestseller. Kenneth O'Reilly, ed., *The FBI File on the House Committee on Un-American Activities* (1986), a microfilm edition of the bureau's holdings, includes Hoover's "Official and Confidential File" on the chairman himself. Chapter 2 of O'Reilly's *Hoover and the Un-Americans* (1983) evaluates Dies based on this new FBI evidence. Although much has been written on Dies, the scholarship on his career and life is scant. William Gellerman, *Martin Dies* (1944), remains the only biography of note, and August Raymond Ogden, *The Dies Committee* (1945), is the only book with that narrow a focus.

KENNETH O'REILLY

DIETRICH, John Hassler (14 Jan. 1878–22 July 1957), Unitarian minister and a leader of the humanist movement in twentieth-century Unitarianism, was born in Chambersburg, Pennsylvania, the son of Jerome Dietrich and Sarah Sarbaugh, farmers. He graduated from Franklin and Marshall College in 1900 and studied at the Reformed Theological Seminary, Lancaster, Pennsylvania, from 1902 to 1905. He began his ministerial career in 1905 at the Reformed church at St. Mark's Memorial Church in Pittsburgh. His early career was marked by conflict with his denomination over a number of issues, some related to the parish politics at St. Mark's, others arising as a result of his growing liberalism in theology. In 1911 he was tried for heresy by the Allegheny Classis of the Reformed church, which cited his lack of belief in the infallible truth of the Bible and the supernatural nature of Jesus.

Dietrich chose not to defend himself against the charges and was expelled from his ministry, but with the assistance of Walter L. Mason, minister of the First Unitarian Church in Pittsburgh, Dietrich gained ministerial fellowship as a Unitarian, moving to Spokane in 1911 and then to the First Unitarian Society in Minneapolis in 1916. In 1912 he married Louise Erb, with whom he had two children before her death in 1931. In 1933 he married Margaret Winston.

Dietrich's preaching emphasized the aspiring spiritual capacity of humanity, not a God conceived in supernatural terms as a separate being. Denoting his position on humanism (he was one of the first Unitarians to embrace the term), Dietrich argued that this new conception of religion marked a major departure in human thinking. In his tract of 1934, *Humanism*, he argued that "for centuries, the idea of God has been the very heart of religion; it has been said 'No God, no religion.' But Humanism thinks of religion as something very different and far deeper than any belief in God."

While Dietrich's preaching struck a responsive chord in the liberal religious community, his conversion to Unitarianism did not shield him from controversy; the humanist movement became a subject of debate within Unitarian circles, dominating Unitarian theological discourse in the 1920s and early 1930s. One particularly important moment in this interchange came at the 1921 meeting of the Unitarian National Conference in Detroit, when Dietrich debated William L. Sullivan, a defender of the theist position.

With Curtis W. Reese and Charles F. Potter, Dietrich offered the humanist movement important intellectual leadership, and his preaching of humanism did much to make it an acceptable position within the Unitarian denomination. In *Humanism* Dietrich explained the rise of religious humanism as the result of two factors: the rise of modern science, which has taught human beings "to refer every event to natural causes," and a heightened interest in social reform, which reflected the increasingly held belief that human destiny was controlled by the social and political decisions of human society. The humanist philosophy, he wrote, must be constructed on the basis of "the self-existing continuousness and trustworthiness of the cosmic process," a process that "is not aware" of the individual "and surely is in no sense partial to him." This naturalistic, nontheistical view of the cosmos, with its refusal to posit any divine ordinance or sanction for historical events, "adds immeasurably to the significance of human conduct," which in Dietrich's view was the channel for "the best in individual and social life." As Dietrich's emphasis on "the significance of human conduct" suggests, he regarded humanism as a religious philosophy that placed primary emphasis on ethical choice and social responsibility, building on the long tradition of Unitarian emphasis on human spiritual potential and on a theology of character building. He recognized that modern skepticism about theistic religion might well imply a similar skepticism about moral responsibility, but the humanism he preached responded to such skepticism with a positive conception of human ethical potential.

Dietrich retired from his influential ministry in Minneapolis in 1938 and moved to Berkeley, California, in 1941, where he lived until his death. Along with Curtis W. Reese and Charles F. Potter, he was prominent in the struggle to legitimize humanism as a viable theological alternative within the Unitarian denomination, and he provided the movement with important intellectual leadership. The continuing presence and influence of nontheistic forms of theology within contemporary Unitarian Universalism is in part a testament to Dietrich's intellectual legacy.

• Selected sermons from Dietrich's Minneapolis ministry were published and distributed monthly and gathered into seven annual volumes as *Humanist Sermons* (1927–1934). These provide the most detailed exposition of his mature theological views. In addition to *Humanism*, he also authored for the American Unitarian Association a tract titled *The Significance of the Unitarian Movement* (1927). For biographical information, see Carleton Winston, *This Circle of Earth: The Story of John H. Dietrich* (1942). For a reading of Dietrich's career in the context of American Unitarianism, see Charles H. Lyttle, *Freedom Moves West: A History of the Western Unitarian Conference* (1952), and David Robinson, *The Unitarians and the Universalists* (1985). The most thorough and helpful analysis of Dietrich's ministerial career, his theological positions, and his leadership in the humanist movement, is Mason Olds, *Religious Humanism in America: Dietrich, Reese, and Potter* (1978).

DAVID M. ROBINSON

DIETRICH, Marlene (27 Dec. 1901–6 May 1992), actress and singer, was born Maria Magdalena Dietrich in Berlin, Germany, the daughter of Louis Erich Otto Dietrich, a policeman, and Wilhelmina Elisabeth Josephine Felsing. Dietrich trained as a concert violinist at the Hochschule für Musik in Berlin, but a hand injury at the age of twenty-one led her to shift her ambitions to acting. She adopted the surname Marlene for her stage name by combining syllables of her first two names.

In 1922 Dietrich auditioned for, but was denied entry to, Max Reinhardt's acting school in Berlin, so she joined a musical revue for several months until a later successful audition. During the rest of the 1920s she acted in Reinhardt's stage productions as well as performed occasionally in cabarets and on film. Her first film role was a bit part in *Der kleine Napoleon* (1923). In 1924 she auditioned for a movie role at Universum-Film Aktien-Gesellschaft (UFA Studios), Germany's largest film company, where she met Rudolf Emilian Sieber, a casting assistant, whom she married in May. They had one child, Maria, who also became an actress. The couple later separated but never divorced.

By 1926 Dietrich was starring in major stage roles in Berlin and Vienna, including the German production of the American play *Broadway*. During the remainder of the decade she starred in other plays and films and recorded songs for Telefunken Records. Movie director Josef von Sternberg (who later became her mentor as well as her lover) was so impressed by her stage performance in *Zwei Krawatten* that he immediately asked her to star opposite Emil Jannings in his movie production of Heinrich Mann's novel *Professor Unrat*. Dietrich played the amoral singer Lola Lola in two versions directed simultaneously by von Sternberg, one in German titled *Der blaue Engel* and the other in English titled *The Blue Angel* (1930). The German version had an extremely successful premiere in Berlin on 31 March 1930, and that evening Dietrich left Germany for Hollywood and Paramount Studios.

The English-language version of *The Blue Angel* was so popular in the United States that Paramount Studios signed Dietrich to a long-term contract. Paramount and von Sternberg unleashed a huge publicity drive that promoted Dietrich as the studio's answer to Greta Garbo, the popular foreign star under contract to Metro-Goldwyn-Mayer (MGM). By shedding thirty pounds and undergoing the then-novel process of plastic surgery to narrow her nose, Dietrich was transformed from a chubby cabaret showgirl into a svelte Venus. Paramount publicity photos displayed her wearing gorgeous costumes in exotic locales, as did her roles in a series of films directed by von Sternberg, *Morocco* (1930), *Dishonored* (1931), *Shanghai Express* (1932), *Scarlet Empress* (1934), and *The Devil Is a Woman* (1935).

The persona created by Dietrich and Paramount paralleled that erected by Garbo and MGM. Both played icy and aloof foreign exotics whose husky voices and occasional cross-dressing hinted at transsexuality. In public Dietrich professed nothing but gushing admiration for Garbo; in private, she was an intense rival and had affairs with several of Garbo's lovers, including actor John Gilbert and screenwriter Mercedes de Acosta. Dietrich and Garbo met only once, brought together by Orson Welles at a party, after which Dietrich commented to Welles: "Her feet aren't as big as they say."

After the success of *Shanghai Express*, Dietrich renegotiated her contract with Paramount. She received $125,000 per film, making her the studio's highest-paid star. When disputes over artistic control caused von Sternberg to leave Paramount, Dietrich stayed with the studio. She limited herself to a small number of roles in productions by major filmmakers: Ernst Lubitsch (*Desire* in 1936 and *Angel* in 1938), David Selznick (*Garden of Allah* in 1936), and Alexander Korda (*Knight without Armor* in 1937). In all of her films she actively perpetuated her film image and insisted on particular lighting and camera angles that would highlight her distinctive appearance.

Dietrich's movie career began to sag near the end of the thirties. Most of her films after von Sternberg left Paramount were undistinguished. Critics began to complain that her glamour had become stereotyped, and her movie audiences dropped off. In 1938 the Independent Theater Owners of America published announcements in *Variety* and other trade journals that Dietrich and several other actresses (including Garbo) were no longer popular with their movie audiences. Dietrich publicly assumed a dismissive attitude and told a reporter: "All I know is that whenever the guys in the front office want to pay their mortgage, they call me up with an idea for a picture."

Her next film, however, embodied a complete change of image in a comedy role in Joseph Pasternack's western *Destry Rides Again* (1939). Movie audiences loved her performance as the rowdy dancehall singer Frenchy—a return to her origins in Berlin cabarets—and her unforgettable rendition of "See What the Boys in the Back Room Will Have." She and Pasternack made several other popular films that bolstered her standing in Hollywood, but she temporarily abandoned her movie career in 1943 to join the United Service Organizations (USO) and entertain American troops overseas.

Dietrich was fervently anti-Nazi and had spurned an offer in 1937 from Adolf Hitler's propaganda minister, Joseph Goebbels, to return and star in any German film she wanted. Her films were subsequently banned in Germany. Dietrich filed naturalization papers in 1937 and became an American citizen in 1939. When the United States entered World War II, she participated in war bond drives and made anti-Nazi broadcasts in German for Allied radio services. After the Allies invaded Normandy, she paid her own expenses to travel with the USO to the European theater of war to entertain Allied troops, giving more than 500 performances in the years 1943–1946, many times performing near the line of battle. After the war, President Harry S. Truman awarded her the Medal of Freedom and the French government made her a Chevalier of the Legion of Honor.

Dietrich remained in Europe after the war to star opposite Jean Gabin in the French film *Martin Roumagnac* (1946), which opened in the United States as *The Room Upstairs* (1948). She then returned to Hollywood to appear in *Golden Earrings* (1947) and *A Foreign Affair* (1948). Her appearance in 1950 in Alfred Hitchcock's *Stage Fright* was followed in 1951 by *No Highway in the Sky*; both productions were British, but she returned to the United States for *Rancho Notorious* (1952).

During the mid-1950s Dietrich temporarily stopped appearing in movies. Although critics had praised her performances, her films were not box-office successes. The movie studios were hurting financially from television's competition, so they began cutting back on productions and laying off talent. A highly paid star like Dietrich found herself priced out of the movie industry. She began to explore other venues for her performances. In 1952 she hosted two radio series, "Cafe Istanbul" for ABC and then "Time for Love" for CBS, but neither was a success. Dietrich also made several recordings for Columbia Records in 1953 and then, after studying Judy Garland in rehearsals for her one-woman show, embarked on a solo nightclub act. Dietrich debuted at the Hotel Sahara in Las Vegas, Nevada, and went on to appear in New York, London, Jerusalem, and in various other cities around the world. She made only one postwar visit to Germany, where many conservatives considered her a traitor for her wartime work. Nevertheless, her Berlin show was unexpectedly successful and attracted only a few hecklers. She later developed her nightclub act into a full-scale musical revue, opening on Broadway at the Lunt-Fontanne Theatre on 9 October 1967 for a six-week run.

Dietrich still retained an interest in movies and resumed working with independent producers in the late 1950s. She alternated her theatrical tours with appearances in Billy Wilder's *Witness for the Prosecution* (1958), Orson Welles's *Touch of Evil* (1958), and Stanley Kramer's *Judgment at Nuremberg* (1961).

Dietrich moved her residence to Paris in 1972 and made her last stage appearance in a 1975 Australian tour, which ended when she collapsed onstage in Sydney on 29 September 1975 and broke her leg. Thereafter she lived a virtually reclusive life, except for an unusual appearance in a quirky and unsuccessful film directed by David Hemmings, *Just a Gigolo* (1978). She also provided voice-over narration, but did not appear in, Maximilian Schell's documentary *Marlene* (1978). She died in Paris.

• No Dietrich papers are available to the public, but portions of her correspondence and other relevant documents are located in the Kurt Weill Papers at the Kurt Weill Foundation for Music in New York City and in the USO Camp Show Publicity Records, Billy Rose Theatre Collection, New York Public Library. Dietrich published two revealing memoirs, *Marlene Dietrich's ABC* (1962; rev. ed., 1984) and *Marlene* (1989), but is the subject of numerous biographies, including one by her daughter, Maria Riva, *Marlene Dietrich* (1993). See also Donald Spoto, *Blue Angel: The Life of Marlene Dietrich* (1992); Steven Bach, *Marlene Dietrich: Life and Legend* (1992); and Homer Dickens, *The Complete Films of Marlene Dietrich* (1992). She is discussed in the autobiography of her early mentor Josef von Sternberg, *Fun in a Chinese Laundry* (1965), and in that of her lover Mercedes de Acosta, *Here Lies the Heart* (1960). Dietrich's role as a sexual icon and her place in popular culture are discussed in Gaylyn Studlar, *In the Realm of Pleasure: Von Sternberg, Dietrich and the Masochistic Aesthetic* (1988). Obituaries are in the *New York Times* and the *Washington Post*, both 7 May 1992, and in *Variety*, 11 May 1992.

STEPHEN G. MARSHALL

DIETRICHSON, Johannes Wilhelm Christian (4 Apr. 1815–14 Nov. 1883), Lutheran clergyman, was born in Fredrikstad, Norway, the son of Fredrik Dietrichson, a military officer, and Karen Sophie Henriette Radich. The Dietrichson family, originally from Denmark, was of the upper class, the so-called officialdom. In 1837 he completed studies for a theological degree at the Royal Frederick University in Christiania (later the University of Oslo) and the following year passed the "practical" examination that qualified him to serve as a pastor in the Church of Norway. During his academic years he was influenced by Grundtvigianism, a churchly movement of Danish origin, which, in addition to the more influential Haugean lay movement, was part of the religious ferment within the Church of Norway during the nineteenth century. During the years preceding his ordination he was engaged in teaching and studying and served as assistant to the prison chaplain in Christiania. In November 1839 Dietrichson married Jørgine Laurentze Broch, who died a year and a half later, a few weeks after giving birth to a son. In June 1846, while on his trip to Norway, he married Charlotte Josine Omsen Müller. They had two children.

Peter Sørensen, a mission enthusiast who was concerned about the growing number of emigrants to America, urged Dietrichson to travel to America to minister to their spiritual needs. He offered to provide financial support for the proposed mission effort. Regarding this request and offer of support as a divine call, Dietrichson accepted it. On 23 February 1844 he was ordained by Bishop Christian Sørenssen to serve as pastor to Norwegian emigrants in America.

Leaving Norway in May 1844 Dietrichson arrived at his destination in southern Wisconsin in August. During the 1840s Norwegian immigrants were coming in increasing numbers to northern Illinois and southern Wisconsin. It was his mission "to bring about orderly church life" among them by organizing congregations through which the spiritual heritage of the Church of Norway would be transplanted to America. He proceeded to carry out this mission systematically and vigorously. After visiting several Norwegian communities, he chose the Koshkonong Prairie settlement, located southeast of Madison, as his headquarters. There he organized two congregations, East and West Koshkonong, that comprised the parish that called him to be their pastor. They were the first of several congregations that he established in southern Wisconsin, all of which were committed to the doctrine and liturgy of the Church of Norway, with some permissible modifications required by the American situation. The congregational constitutions that he prepared served as models for Norwegian-American Lutheran congregations established in the future.

In May 1845 Dietrichson returned to Norway to recruit young pastors to serve as missionaries among their countrymen in America. His efforts did not bring immediate results, but while in Norway he published *The Travel Narrative*, an invaluable source of information about his year's experience as a pastor in America and about life and conditions among the Norwegian settlers. He returned to his Koshkonong parish in September 1846.

Dietrichson had a high view of the ordained ministry, insisting that pastors have requisite qualifications and be properly called. From the beginning he stressed his pastoral authority. For many of the immigrants he was an uncomfortable reminder of class distinctions they thought they had left behind in Norway, where the clergy were of the official class. In addition he was by nature rigid and authoritarian, which caused tensions between him and some parishioners as well as other members of the community. When Dietrichson arrived in southern Wisconsin, there were already two pastors on the scene who were ministering to Norwegian immigrants, Elling Eielsen and Claus L. Clausen. Each had been ordained in America in 1843 by a Lutheran pastor. Neither had been theologically trained for the ministry. Dietrichson and Clausen enjoyed a friendly, cooperative relationship in which Dietrichson was dominant, but he and Eielsen, the former Haugean lay preacher, disagreed sharply about many things. The validity of Eielsen's ordination was challenged by Dietrichson, and he regarded Eielsen's evangelistic activity in Norwegian communities to be disruptive and questionable.

Dietrichson proposed that the newly established congregations unite in a church body, for which he prepared a constitution. His efforts to achieve such an organization were unsuccessful because the congregations feared that their freedom would be jeopardized. But in 1853 his proposed constitution was utilized with some modifications as the basis for the formation of the Norwegian Evangelical Lutheran Church of America (popularly known as the Norwegian Synod).

In 1850 Dietrichson returned to Norway, having fulfilled the terms of his call, never again to set foot on American soil. Although he was in America for only a short period of time, he played a decisive leadership role in the formative period of Norwegian-American Lutheranism as an effective frontier missionary pastor and organizer of well-ordered congregations.

In Norway, Dietrichson served as pastor in three different parishes during the period 1850–1876. His career in the homeland was a stormy one, marked by conflicts and tensions in the congregations he served. He left the ministry and from 1876 until his retirement in 1882 he was postmaster in Porsgrund. He died on a visit to Copenhagen.

• Two historically valuable documents written by Dietrichson, *The Travel Narrative* and *The Koshkonong Parish Journal*, are in *A Pioneer Churchman: J. W. C. Dietrichson in Wisconsin, 1844–1850*, edited and with an introduction by E. Clifford Nelson (1973). Chapters devoted to his career in the United States are in *Norsemen Found a Church*, ed. J. C. K. Preus et al. (1953) and in E. Clifford Nelson and Eugene L. Fevold, *The Lutheran Church Among Norwegian-Americans*, vol. I (1960). See also J. Magnus Rohne, *Norwegian American Lutheranism up to 1872* (1926), and Rasmus Malmin et al., eds., *Who's Who among Pastors in All the Norwegian Lutheran Synods in America, 1843–1927* (1928).

EUGENE L. FEVOLD

DIETZ, Howard (8 Sept. 1896–30 July 1983), lyricist and publicity director, was born in New York City, the son of Herman Dietz, a jeweler, and Julia Blumberg. While a student at Townsend Harris Hall, a public high school for unusually able students, Dietz took a job as a copyboy on a newspaper, the *New York American*. Finding journalism much to his liking, he applied for admission to Columbia University, where he intended to study in the university's recently opened School of Journalism. While he was there, the *New York American* appointed him its Columbia correspondent. He also wrote for the Columbia *Jester*, a humor magazine, and for the university's newspaper, the *Spectator*. In addition, like many other ambitious young writers, he frequently submitted verses to the popular humor column of Franklin P. Adams, "The Conning Tower," in the *New York World*.

In 1917 Dietz came to the realization that much in the Columbia curriculum held no interest for him, and he left the university. Philip Goodman, the owner of a small advertising agency, offered him a job. One of Goodman's clients was the film producer Samuel Goldwyn, and Dietz designed the logo for Goldwyn's company, a growling lion wreathed in film emblazoned with the slogan "Ars Gratia Artis" (art for art's sake). Dietz chose the lion as the Goldwyn emblem because it was also the Columbia mascot. Years later, in 1924, when Goldwyn merged his company with Metro Pictures and the company of Louis B. Mayer to form Metro-Goldwyn-Mayer, the logo became known worldwide.

When the United States entered the First World War, Dietz gave up his position with Goodman, enlisted in the navy, and awaited a call for service. The year 1917 also marked his first effort at lyric writing, when a theater producer offered him the opportunity to supply words for a song in a vaudeville sketch. In 1918 he married Elizabeth Hall, whom he had met when she was a student at Barnard College. They had no children. Eventually Dietz was called up by the navy and put to work at the Hampton Roads naval base as the editor of *Navy Life*, a magazine published for seamen. He continued this assignment until the war ended.

Following his discharge Dietz sought a position with Goldwyn and was given a job in publicity and advertising. After the formation of Metro-Goldwyn-Mayer Dietz stayed on with the new organization in the same position, eventually becoming head of the department. In 1925 he joined the board of directors of Loew's, the parent company of MGM, and in 1942 he was made a vice president.

In 1923 Dietz embarked on a second career, one for which he would become better known to the general public than he ever could in his position at MGM. Jerome Kern, having heard of Dietz as a writer of light verse, invited him to write the lyrics for his songs for a new musical, *Dear Sir*. Although the show was unsuccessful, it produced happy results for Dietz. Arthur Schwartz, a young lawyer who wished to give up the law and become a musical comedy composer, wrote to Dietz, whom he had not yet met, to suggest that they collaborate on a revue. In his reply Dietz held out only faint hope to Schwartz, but eventually they formed a partnership that led to the creation of such highly acclaimed revues as *The Little Show* (1929), *Three's a Crowd* (1930), *The Band Wagon* (1931), *Flying Colors* (1932), and *Inside U.S.A.* (1948). Both men sometimes worked with other collaborators, however, and among Dietz's major successes was his translation of the lyrics of Johann Strauss's operetta *Die Fledermaus* for the Metropolitan Opera in 1950. A second operatic translation, the libretto of Puccini's *La Bohème* in 1952, which was also sung at the Metropolitan, met with critical disapproval and was soon discarded. In 1953, for a film titled *The Band Wagon* (but not based on the revue of the same name), the team wrote a new song, *That's Entertainment*, that soon became a show-business anthem.

Dietz and his wife were divorced after nineteen years of marriage, and in 1937 he married Tanis Guinness, an Englishwoman whom he had met in Hollywood. The couple had one child. Although this marriage ended in divorce in 1951, it did so without rancor, and the couple maintained friendly relations. In 1951 Dietz was married a third time, to Lucinda Ballard, a distinguished Broadway costume designer. No children were born of the marriage.

In 1954 Dietz became afflicted with the first stages of Parkinson's disease. Although he responded somewhat favorably to various forms of treatment, including brain surgery, his activities were sharply diminished for the remainder of his life. Eventually he found himself too incapacitated to remain in his position at Metro-Goldwyn-Mayer. He continued to write, however. With Schwartz he wrote the scores for what would prove to be his final musicals, *The Gay Life* (1961) and *Jennie* (1963). Despite the excellence of the songs, both shows were failures, the first because of miscasting in a leading role and the second because of problems created by the star of the show, Mary Martin. Having invested heavily in *Jennie*, Dietz suffered a severe financial loss. In 1974 he published his memoirs, *Dancing in the Dark*, the title of one of the most popular songs in the Dietz-Schwartz catalog.

Dietz, a gregarious, good-natured man blessed with a keen sense of humor and a talent for friendship, was much admired in Hollywood and Broadway circles. From 1959 to 1966 he served on the board of directors of the American Society of Composers, Authors, and Publishers (ASCAP). He was the first recipient, in 1983, of the ASCAP/Richard Rodgers award. Proud of his accomplishment as an amateur painter, he used some of his paintings as illustrations of his memoirs. He died in New York City.

• Autograph letters, manuscripts, and other documents by Dietz are held by the Library of Congress and the New York Public Library. The ASCAP headquarters in New York houses an oral history interview of Dietz by Mike Whorf, originally recorded for broadcast by radio station WJR in Detroit. The best source of facts about his life, although frequently lacking precise dates, is Dietz's own *Dancing in the Dark* (1974). See also David Ewen, *American Songwriters* (1987), and the ASCAP *Biographical Dictionary*. Some sketchy information about Dietz's career in the film industry may be found in Bosley Crowther, *The Lion's Share* (1957), a history of Metro-Goldwyn-Mayer. An obituary is in the *New York Times*, 31 July 1983.

MALCOLM GOLDSTEIN

DIETZ, Peter Ernest (10 July 1878–11 Oct. 1947), Roman Catholic priest and labor activist, was born in New York City, the son of Frederick Dietz, a varnisher, and Eva Kern. His parents had emigrated from Bavaria, and the family was large and poor. After attending parish schools and a series of Catholic colleges in Pennsylvania and New York, Dietz, in 1900, entered the novitiate of the missionary community of the Society of the Divine Word in Moedling, Germany. Two years later, however, hoping to found a new religious order, he withdrew from the community. His plans came to naught, and in 1903 he returned to the United States, subsequently studying at Catholic University and at St. Mary's Seminary in Baltimore. Dietz affiliated himself with the diocese of Cleveland, Ohio, and was ordained to the priesthood by Cardinal James Gibbons at the end of 1904.

Dietz's youth and early academic training coincided with the large-scale industrialization and urbanization of the late nineteenth century and the controversies it provoked between labor and capital. Catholic social teaching on these issues was also taking shape, Pope Leo XIII's encyclical *Rerum Novarum* (1891) offering a prescription for the ills of the age. Leo was deeply concerned about the abuses of laissez faire capitalism but equally fearful of the growing influence of socialism. The pontiff called for a return to a corporative social order, which would curtail the excesses generated by the rugged individualism of modern capitalism but resist the collectivist-statist solution. The papal letter strongly impressed Dietz who, despite the fact that his bishop had made him pastor of a parish in Elyria, Ohio, vigorously pursued these issues on the lecture circuit and through the written word. He called upon the church to work for social justice, believing it might thereby diminish the attractions of socialism to workers.

Dietz spent 1909–1910 as an editor of the English section of *Central Blatt and Social Justice*, a publication of the Central Verein, a German Catholic federation. He then joined the American Federation of Catholic Societies, which created, at his suggestion, a standing Committee on Social Reform. From 1911 to 1918 he edited the committee's bulletin and wrote a widely disseminated newsletter devoted to social issues, which was reprinted in many Catholic newspapers.

Though seeking to build a broad Catholic reform effort, Dietz—wanting a more active role in public affairs and the shaping of legislation—began to focus his energies on the trade union movement. His desire that American trade-unionism be free of socialist influence led him to establish the Militia of Christ for Social Service in 1910 for Catholic members of the American Federation of Labor (AFL). Though the group never acquired a large membership and did not survive past 1914, Dietz remained a fraternal delegate of the American Federation of Catholic Societies to the AFL through 1922 and regularly spoke at AFL conventions. His association with men like Samuel Gompers, John Mitchell, and Philip Murray was an important bridge between the Catholic church and the labor movement.

Dietz eventually lost favor with his bishop, John P. Farrelly of Cleveland, who insisted that he spend more time on parochial duties. As a result, Dietz was incardinated in 1912 into the archdiocese of Milwaukee, whose bishop, Sebastian G. Messmer, had come to know and appreciate Dietz through the American Federation of Catholic Societies. Dietz had permission to remain outside the diocese, and Messmer gave Dietz virtual carte blanche to pursue his social justice interests.

Dietz was highly instrumental in the establishment of schools to educate laborers in social work, the social sciences, parliamentary law, and Catholic social teachings. His first effort, the American Academy of Christian Democracy for Women, opened in Hot Springs, North Carolina, in 1915. However, difficulties financing such an operation in the largely non-Catholic South and the scarcity of large-scale industrial operations in the vicinity led him to move the school to Cincinnati in 1917. Despite recurrent financial woes and resistance from local ecclesiastical authorities, Dietz, largely with help from friends in the AFL, also established a pioneering National Labor College, offering programs for union members, in the Cincinnati suburb of Ault Park.

Eventually Dietz's work with labor unions led him to tangle with business leaders. He, furthermore, antagonized Archbishop Henry Moeller of Cincinnati, who, though generally sympathetic to Dietz's ideas, took exception to his uncompromising and rather intolerant manner. After general warnings to be more circumspect, Moeller lost his patience when the priest publicly supported the presidential candidacy of Ohioan Warren G. Harding in the election of 1920 and opposed American membership in the League of Nations. In December 1920 Dietz received a request from Moeller to leave the archdiocese of Cincinnati. After a series of stalling actions, including lobbying by officers of the AFL and other admirers, Dietz moved to Milwaukee in 1923.

Dietz thereafter faded from the scene, hampered by the weakness of the labor movement in the twenties and occupied by his work as pastor of St. Monica's Parish in Whitefish Bay, Wisconsin. He died in Milwaukee.

Dietz might be honored as a minor prophet of American Catholic social teaching. Murray wrote that he "strongly voiced the right of labor to organize and bargain collectively . . . at a time when few figures were willing to do so" (letter to Mary Harrita Fox, 28 Dec. 1949). His efforts to educate and mobilize Catholic workers would be imitated extensively by "labor priests" of the 1930s who encouraged the industrial unionism of the Congress of Industrial Organizations.

• Dietz's personal papers are in the hands of family members. Additional information can be gleaned from the archives of the Central Verein in St. Louis, the papers of the Social Action Department of the National Catholic Welfare Conference in the archives of the Catholic University of America, and the extant papers of the Federation of American Catholic Societies in the archives of the University of Notre Dame. The best secondary source is Mary Harrita Fox, *Peter E. Dietz: Labor Priest* (1953). John J. Mitchell, *Critical Voices in American Catholic Economic Thought* (1989), contains an essay on Dietz. An obituary is in the *Milwaukee Catholic Herald-Citizen*, 18 Oct. 1947.

STEVEN M. AVELLA

DIETZGEN, Peter Joseph (9 Dec. 1828–15 Apr. 1888), writer and socialist philosopher, was born in Blankenberg near Cologne, now part of Germany, the son of Gottfried Dietzgen, a master tanner, and Margaret Lückeroth. He had an elementary education and some high school in Cologne prior to learning his father's trade. In hours of recreation from the tannery he studied literature, economics, and philosophy and became fluent in French. His studies of French economists, the *Communist Manifesto*, and the conditions of the times "made a class-conscious socialist out of him in 1848," according to his son. The reaction following 1848 drove him to the United States, where he worked at various jobs, tramped over part of the country, and made some acquaintance with the land and its people.

In 1851 he returned to Germany to work in his father's tannery and two years later married Maria Cordula, a devout Catholic with whom he lived in close harmony despite his naturalistic views. The couple had four children. He opened a combined tannery and grocery store but planned his work to devote half a day to study. To achieve greater economic independence he moved to Montgomery, Alabama, in 1859 and there wrote his first essay, "Schwarz oder Weiss," arguing that truth is not passion or something a priori in the mind but rather generalization of manifold appearances of economic fact. He returned to Germany when he saw some friends lynched as Yankee sympathizers shortly before the outbreak of the Civil War.

Dietzgen operated his father's tannery in Uckerath until 1864 when the Russian government employed him to manage its tannery in St. Petersburg. He greatly increased its productivity in a few years, wrote articles on *Capital* that Marx found perceptive, and completed his first and major book, *The Nature of Human Brain Work: A Renewed Critique of Pure and Practical Reason by a Manual Worker* (1869), presenting his theory of knowledge and ethics.

Dietzgen strenuously opposed pure speculation or a priori thinking that seeks to arrive at truth independently of experience. The typical product of such speculation is metaphysics in the great historic systems such as Hegel's. The way to genuine knowledge, rather, lies in the inductive method, a posteriori thinking based on perceptible material. Even mind or thought is something we perceive (*wahrnehmen*) as sensibly as we perceive walking or pain. It is not tangible (*greifbar*) but perceptible and thus as actual as the scent of a rose or heat of a stove. All these things, while differing among themselves, have a common nature as being "perceptible, material, i.e., actual" (*sinnlich, materiell, das heisst wirklich*). Though some propositions appear to be true a priori, they turn out to be, Dietzgen held, tautologies. "Where only the wet is called water, we don't need any special transcendental faculty to know categorically that water must be wet."

In clarifying sensuous fact by finding the general in particulars, genuine or a posteriori thinking is dialectical. It sees how all things are alike as well as different, one as well as many. Consciousness "recognizes that all nature, all being, lives in contradictions, that everything is what it is only in cooperation with its opposite." For this view of knowledge Dietzgen acknowledged his debt to Bacon, Kant, and particularly Ludwig Feuerbach who showed him that true philosophy must identify itself with natural science. "My philosophy," Dietzgen repeated after Feuerbach, "is no philosophy." It is no speculative metaphysics.

On this basis Dietzgen developed an inductive or "materialistic" theory of morals based on perceived desire and need, not uninformative a priori principles. Moral reasoning is not a mere catalog of desires and needs but criticizes them by distinguishing the general from the particular. Action is most reasonable when found by induction to be the means of realizing its end "in the widest, broadest, most general way." "The end is the sum of all its means." But only those ends are truly good that are themselves means to the totality of ends defining human welfare in given circumstances. Murder achieves some ends but is bad in frustrating a wider totality of ends. Because ends are the sum of their means and themselves means to other ends, both ends and means may be judged scientifically, inductively.

After returning from St. Petersburg in 1869, Dietzgen operated a tannery in Siegburg and continued his writing and studies. Relatively detached from immediate political affairs he was, nevertheless, a delegate to the Hague International Congress in 1872 where Marx introduced him saying, "Here is our philosopher." He was arrested in Cologne for speaking on socialism and was held in custody for three months during the hysteria from an attempt to assassinate the emperor. Three years later he ran unsuccessfully for a seat in the Reichstag.

In the years around his third emigration to the United States in 1884, settling first in New York and then Chicago, Dietzgen wrote *Letters on Logic* (1890–1893) and *The Positive Outcome of Philosophy* (1887). In contrast to his first and major book, they defended a monistic view of the world, not merely in the sense of all things having a common nature in perceptible material but as being parts of one organic whole. Here he was especially attracted to the pantheism of Spinoza and Jakob Böhme. To establish the "absolute world-being" or "world god" he resorted to the ontological arguments of Anselm and Descartes, precisely the a priori reasoning he had attacked in *The Nature of Human Brain Work*. He also championed his erstwhile enemy, Hegel, as a "hero of thought" who rightly makes all things rise, pass, move, and necessarily belong together. Though Marx and Engels found repetitions and confusions in Dietzgen's first book, they commended its several insights, remarkable for having come from a self-educated workingman. Marx had Dietzgen's later reversal on Hegel in mind when he said, "I hold the case to be incurable."

In spite of confusions and self-contradictions in Dietzgen's thought, there were distinct achievements. His view of knowledge as based on perceptible material anticipated Ernst Mach's "empirical monism," used in William James's "radical empiricism." Dietzgen's moral theory strikingly anticipated John Dewey's as it rooted moral value in "concrete experiences of desire and satisfaction" and the interrelation of means and ends determined inductively. Dietzgen went beyond Marx to view nature as "absolute world-being"—a questionably consistent achievement.

After the Haymarket bomb exploded (1886) and the editors of the *Chicagoer Arbeiterzeitung* had been arrested, Dietzgen volunteered to edit three socialist papers and tried to lessen differences between anarchists and socialists as required by his dialectical principle. After his death in Chicago, he was buried beside the imposing Haymarket monument in the Waldheim Cemetery.

• Joseph Dietzgen's first and major book, *The Nature of Human Brain Work*, trans. W. W. Craik, appears with *Letters on Logic* and *The Positive Outcome of Philosophy* in a single volume titled *The Positive Outcome of Philosophy* (1906). One of Dietzgen's later books, *Excursions of a Socialist into the Domains of Epistemology* (1887), and several articles are in his *Philosophical Essays* (1906). Together, *The Positive Outcome of Philosophy* and *Philosophical Essays* contain most of the first and second volumes of *Joseph Dietzgens Sämtliche Schriften*, ed. Eugene Dietzgen (3 vols., 1910, 1920).

The main biographical source is Eugene Dietzgen's "Sketch" of his father's life, trans. E. Untermann, at the beginning of Dietzgen's *Philosophical Essays*. *Dietzgen Brevier Für Naturmonisten*, ed. E. Dietzgen (1915), contains topically grouped selections on theory of knowledge, nature-monism, and religion. Jonathan Rée, *Proletarian Philosophers* (1984), presents Dietzgen's main views in relation to their influence on British socialism. Viktor Thomas, *Das Erkenntnisproblem* (1921), provides details on Dietzgen's "empirical monism" in relation to positivism, including Mach's. V. I. Lenin, "Joseph Dietzgen," *Labour Monthly* 9 (1927): 117–19, or *Collected Works* 19 (1913): 79–82, gives a "hard line" estimate of Dietzgen's views.

Loyd D. Easton

DIGGES, Dudley (9 June 1880–24 Oct. 1947), actor and director, was born in Dublin, Ireland, the son of James Dudley Digges and Catherine Forsythe. He received his education at the Christian Brothers' School from 1886 to 1890 and at St. Mary's College, Dublin, from 1890 to 1893. Digges embarked on his career on stage as an actor with the Abbey Players in Dublin at the turn of the century. Describing Digges's performance in 1902 in *Deirdre*, by George Russell, one Dublin theatergoer stated that "Digges made an admirable 'Naisi,' realising the role with excellent dramatic impressiveness and telling declamatory effect as the text demanded" (Holloway, p. 16). Digges moved to the United States after the Abbey Theatre decided not to accept an invitation to the 1904 International Exposition in St. Louis, Missouri. Digges believed that it was important to have the Irish theater in attendance at the event—important enough to quit the theater and strike out for America. An actress from the Abbey named Maire Roden Quinn agreed and left with him. Digges and Quinn were married in 1907.

Digges made his American debut in New York City in 1904 with the celebrated actress Minnie Maddern Fiske. This performance was the advent of a New York career that spanned almost five decades. It was his work with the Theatre Guild that would give Digges his rise to prominence, though. On 28 April 1919 Digges appeared in multiple roles in Jacinto Benavente's *Bonds of Interest* with the Guild. His hit performance as James Caesar in *John Ferguson* (opened 12 May 1919) helped cement the reputation of the Guild and is, in large part, responsible for helping it become a permanent organization. The play and Digges received a bounty of positive reviews: "It is true, of course, that by far the best performance in the play was that of Dudley Digges who plays the part of Jimmy Caesar, a cowardly, braggart, oily tradesman. It would be difficult to imagine a more unsympathetic role, but Digges plays it so that the audience first laughs, then stops laughing, and then begins to consider whether it would not be in order to cry" (Heywood Broun, *New York Dramatic Mirror*, 10 June 1919).

The Guild would become Digges's artistic home for the rest of his professional career. He would appear on its stage more than 3,500 times after *John Ferguson* in a plethora of role types in plays such as *George Washington Slept Here*, *R.U.R.*, *Candida*, *Major Barbara*, *The Brothers Karamazov*, *On Borrowed Time*, and *Outward Bound*. One of his most startling portrayals was that of Mr. Zero in Elmer Rice's expressionistic *The Adding Machine* (1923). Digges is noted for giving the hero of the play a definitively human portrayal. Held up as the model example of American expressionist drama, *The Adding Machine* established Rice as a major playwright and won Digges numerous accolades.

He also eventually staged four plays for the Guild later in his career: *Heartbreak House*, *The Doctor's Dilemma*, *Pygmalion*, and *Man's Estate*. Drama critic Walter Pritchard described Digges's handling of Shaw's texts as "splendid," but *New York American*

critic Gilbert Gabriel wrote that *Man's Estate* was "unhappily ordinary, untidy and unhinged." Not only did Digges direct, but he also played one of the principal roles in Shaw's story of a young idealist trapped in a midwestern town.

Critics praised Digges's last role for the Guild, that of Harry Hope in Eugene O'Neill's *The Iceman Cometh* (1946). The play is set in the back of a saloon owned by Hope, who has not been outside in twenty years. Despite the play's objectionable four-hour length, it received commending reviews. Drama critic Brooks Atkinson said of Digges's portrayal of Hope, "To anyone who loves acting, Dudley Digges performance as the tottering and irascible saloon proprietor is worth particular cherishing. Although the old man is half dead, Mr. Digges' command of the actor's art of expressing character and theme is brilliantly alive; it overflows with comic and philosophical expression" (*New York Times*, 25 Oct. 1947).

Digges not only directed and acted, but he also worked behind the scenes at times. Early in his career, he worked as stage manager for George Arliss from 1911 to 1918, managing *Paganini*, *Hamilton*, and *Disraeli*. Digges acted only in small roles with Arliss, because Arliss was unsure of Digges's acting abilities but confident of his capabilities as a stage manager.

Digges is less well known for his forays into celluloid, though he acted in more than fifty films, most notably *The Maltese Falcon* (1931), *The Voice of Bugle Ann* (1936), *The General Died at Dawn* (1936), *Love Is News* (1937), and *The Light That Failed* (1939). But both the quantity and quality of his stage career have continued to overshadow his work in film.

During his career Digges was vice president for Actor's Equity and a member of the Lambs and Players clubs, and he received an award from the American Irish Historical Society for outstanding achievement as an American citizen of Irish descent. He died in New York City.

Digges is best known for his ability to give depth and insight into characters that may seem only two dimensional on the pages of the script. Throughout his career he continually received praise for his psychologically motivated and moving portrayals of generally stereotypical characters. In his obituary in the *New York Times* he was described as "one of the most beloved actors on the American stage" (25 Oct. 1947).

• Little biographical material on Digges exists. Some discussion of his work at the Abbey can be found in Peter Kavanagh, *The Story of the Abbey Theatre: From Its Origins in 1899 to the Present* (1950), *Joseph Holloway's Abbey Theatre: A Selection from His Unpublished Journal, Impressions of a Dublin Playgoer*, ed. Robert Hogan and Michael J. O'Neill (1967), and Lennox Robinson, *Ireland's Abbey Theatre: A History, 1899–1951* (1951). Many references to his Guild career can be found in Roy S. Waldau, *Vintage Years of the Theatre Guild: 1928–1939* (1972); Walter Prichard Eaton, *The Theatre Guild: The First Ten Years* (1929); and Norman Nadel, *A Pictorial History of the Theatre Guild* (1969). Though references abound in these books, little detailed information is given about Digges's personal history. Detailed comments on his acting style and ability from various critics can be found in Anthony Slide, ed., *Selected Theatre Criticism* (3 vols., 1982–). A filmography is in Leslie Halliwell, *The Filmgoer's Companion* (1977).

WOODROW HOOD

DIGGES, Thomas Attwood (4 July 1742–6 Dec. 1821), gentleman, confidential agent, ne'er-do-well, and novelist, was born in Warburton, Maryland, the son of William Digges and Ann Attwood, the owners of "Warburton Manor," Digges was sent abroad to be educated. Family tradition holds that he attended Oxford University, but his Catholic faith and the absence of his name in university records make this unlikely. In 1767, after being disowned by his family for reasons that are not known, Digges purportedly went to live in Portugal, where he stayed until 1773 or 1774. In a subsequent letter to Benjamin Franklin (1706–1790), Digges calls Lisbon a place where "I am well known & a little respected." Digges's novel, *Adventures of Alonso*, which was published anonymously in London in 1775, displays considerable familiarity with Portugal and Spain. It opens in Lisbon and contains lengthy discussions of Portuguese politics, especially Marquês de Pombal's government. Some critics speculate that it is in part autobiographical, but not enough information about Digges's life is available to verify this claim.

Sometimes described as the first novel by an American, *Alonso* combines elements from the picaresque, sentimental, and travel traditions of the novel. It recounts the adventures that follow when its protagonist, Alonso, elopes with Donna Eugenia, the bride of an elderly Portuguese gentleman. Alonso, a picaro, steals a diamond from an employer in Brazil, becomes a smuggler in the Spanish colonies, and is captured and sold into slavery in Algeria—all before repenting his misdeeds. But his repentance comes too late for him to reunite with Donna Eugenia, who has died while awaiting his return from the New World. In the manner of the sentimental novelist, Digges invites his readers' sympathies for his characters' illicit romantic love: "a silent tear would now and then steal down his cheeks, claiming the sympathy of Eugenia: she again catching the sorrowful state of his mind, would be so sunk in dejection and grief, as to require all his tenderness and love to alleviate." Digges shows little interest in exploring the moral ambiguity of this love affair or the questionable ethics of his protagonist.

During the revolutionary war, Digges resided in London but actively supported the American cause. As a confidential agent, he passed on political gossip from London coffee houses, lists of American prisoners of war, and reports on activities in Parliament to Arthur Lee and William Lee (1739–1795) of Virginia as well as to Benjamin Franklin and John Adams (1735–1826). He also smuggled war supplies to America via Spain and aided prisoners of war held in Forton and Old Mill prisons. In april 1778 Digges served as a liaison between British member of Parliament David Hartley and Franklin about the former's secret peace

plan. Although the plan failed, Digges's efforts gained Franklin's approval. But in 1781 he lost this respect when it was discovered that he had embezzled funds intended to aid prisoners of war. Franklin, outraged, called him "the greatest villain I have ever met with." There appear to have been some extenuating circumstances for Digges's misappropriation of funds, in that he had aided prisoners out of his own pocket, and although they promised to repay him when released, usually they did not. In 1782 Digges was again engaged as the intermediary for a secret peace plan, this time between Hartley and John Adams. However, Lord North's ministry, which had sanctioned the plan, fell while Digges was in Amsterdam meeting with Adams. For his efforts, Digges was thought by some to be a spy for Lord North.

After the war, Digges remained abroad in England and Ireland, continually troubled by debt. In 1785 Digges was imprisoned for debt in the Four Courts Marshalsea in Dublin. Of this imprisonment, Jonathan Williams, Jr., wrote Franklin, his uncle, that Digges "is now paying severely for his Folly & Wickedness." What Williams was referring to is not known. In the 1780s and early 1790s Digges encouraged emigration to the United States, smuggling artisans and shipping machinery from the British Isles to America. These were dangerous enterprises; as Digges told Alexander Hamilton (1755–1804) in 1792: "By the laws of England . . . the smallest particle of machinery, tools, etc. will stop the ship if informed against.—The person attempting to inveigle away an artist is subject not only to very rough treatment, but a fine of £500 and 12 months imprisonment." While the nature of the connection remains mysterious, Digges also worked with the Irish patriot Theobald Wolfe Tone on Irish nationalist activities. In 1791 Tone's diary records that Digges advised him to seek Irish independence; the diary also notes that Digges was arrested for shoplifting while on a trip to Scotland with Tone and his associates. From 1794 until 1797 Digges was back in England, where he unsuccessfully pursued his claim to Chilham Castle Manor, the family's ancestral English seat. The estate was inherited by members of a younger line despite being strictly entailed.

Digges returned to America in 1798 to assume proprietorship of Warburton Manor, which he inherited after his younger brother George's death in 1792. Upon his return he dined on a number of occasions with family friend George Washington at Mount Vernon, which was just across the Potomac River from Warburton. He had corresponded with Washington while abroad, sending him books that he had requested in 1777 and seed potatoes in 1798. Digges was one of the few people Martha Washington invited to her husband's funeral. In 1794, when an attempt was made to confiscate Warburton on the basis of Digges's alleged wartime misconduct, Washington had written warmly on his behalf: "I have no hesitation in declaring that the conduct of Mr. Thomas Digges toward the United States during the War . . . has not been only friendly, but I might add zealous." At Warburton,

Digges became involved in a series of disputes over the construction of Fort Washington on his estate. The fort was designed to prevent hostile naval traffic on the Potomac. After it was destroyed in 1814 when the British burned Washington, Pierre Charles L'Enfant, the designer of Washington, D.C., was in charge of its reconstruction, which resulted in Digges becoming his friend and patron. He was interested in politics, supporting Thomas Jefferson and James Madison (1751–1836); he also corresponded with Jefferson about agriculture and politics. He moved from Warburton to Washington, where he died at Strothers Hotel. Digges's obituary in the *National Intelligencer* described him as an "undeviating republican and patriot" and praised his hospitality at Warburton.

A minor historical figure and author, Thomas Digges played bit parts in the revolutionary war, the cause of Irish nationalism, the transport of technology to the newly formed United States, and the founding of the American novel. Although he corresponded and met with many of the most influential people of his age, he remains a shadowy figure, his ethics questionable and his motives uncertain. Neither his life nor his novel will ever elicit major interest, but his career will remain a colorful footnote to his age.

• Digges's novel, *The Adventures of Alonso*, was reprinted in a facsimile version in 1943, and his letters have been collected and published as *Letters of Thomas Attwood Digges* (1982). For useful biographical overviews of his career, see Robert H. Elias and Eugene D. Finch's introduction to Digges's letters and Katharine A. Kellock's, *Colonial Piscataway in Maryland* (1963), pp. 18–20. For historical assessments, see William Bell Clark, "In Defense of Thomas Digges," the *Pennsylvania Magazine of History and Biography* 77 (1953): 381–438, which examines Digges's activities during the revolutionary war; Carroll W. Pursell, Jr., "Thomas Digges and William Pearce: An Example of the Transit of Technology," *William and Mary Quarterly* 21 (1964): 551–60, which explores Digges's efforts to transport technology to the United States and the subsequent career of an inventor whom he persuaded to emigrate; and Lynn Hudson Parsons, "The Mysterious Mr. Digges," *William and Mary Quarterly* 22 (1965): 486–92, which recounts the relationship between Digges and Theobald Wolfe Tone. For critical overviews of *Alonso*, see Robert H. Elias, "The First American Novel," *American Literature* 12 (1940–1941): 419–34, and Henri Petter, *The Early American Novel* (1971), pp. 285–87.

DAVID M. CRAIG

DIGGS, Annie LePorte (22 Feb. 1848–7 Sept. 1916), Populist orator and journalist, was born in London, Ontario, Canada, the daughter of Cornelius LePorte, a French-Canadian lawyer, and Ann Maria Thomas. While Annie was still a small child, her father moved the family to New Jersey. She had a private governess then attended public schools and a convent school, but she always regretted her lack of a college education. Deciding on a career in journalism, she lived briefly in Washington, D.C., before moving west in 1873. She worked in a Lawrence, Kansas, music store demonstrating pianos until she married Alvin S. Diggs, a postal clerk, that September. The couple had three children.

Her career as a social reformer began in 1877. After serving as a poll watcher in a prohibitionist campaign in Lawrence, she joined the Woman's Christian Temperance Union. A liberal in religion, Diggs became a lay preacher in the Unitarian church. In 1881 she was a founder of the Kansas Liberal Union, a free religion society comprising such nontraditionalists as Spiritualists, materialists, Unitarians, Socialists, and agnostics. That winter a meeting of the Free Religious Association in Boston that she attended elected her a vice president to succeed Lucretia Mott, the pioneering feminist, whom she greatly admired. While in the East she investigated the social conditions of the poor. On her return to Kansas in February 1882, she and her husband began jointly publishing the *Kansas Liberal* from their home in Lawrence.

Active in the Kansas suffrage movement, Diggs began speaking at national woman suffrage conventions in 1885. She believed that a suffrage amendment was not necessary, as women's rights were implicitly protected by the Constitution; women should simply lobby to have those rights enforced. The Nationalist movement formed by admirers of Edward Bellamy's utopian socialist novel, *Looking Backward* (1888), also attracted her. In 1895 she wrote to Henry Demarest Lloyd, a crusading Chicago journalist and antimonopolist, proposing a "Colorado Co-operative Colony." She supported the somewhat novel idea of silkworm cultivation in the West as an economic base for social reformers.

In the late 1880s drought caused a series of crop failures in Kansas, exacerbating the long-term problems of falling agricultural prices, high transportation costs, and interest rates of up to 18 percent on mortgages. Thousands of Kansans lost their farms due to foreclosures. Seeking relief, the Farmers' Alliances turned to political action. Diggs took up the farmers' cause, volunteering to write a column in the *Lawrence Journal*, the leading Republican newspaper in town. The paper printed a statement disassociating itself from her views but allowed her to continue writing. In March 1890 she was appointed associate editor of the *Alliance Advocate*, which quickly became the leading reform weekly in the state.

As an experienced speaker and writer, Diggs was a natural choice as a spokeswoman for the Kansas Populist party formed in June 1890 to provide a platform for the farmers' grievances. Campaigning through Kansas that summer and fall, she tried to link the farmers' problems with those of the eastern working class. At Osborne on 25 October she asked her audience, "Why there are so many poor men out of employment . . . why women and children are forced into the workshop to earn their daily bread, so that even Sitting Bull says he 'Don't see how white men can treat their squaws so'" (Clanton, p. 266). Diggs also pointed out the effect of poverty on farm women in the reform journal *Arena* (July 1892), citing a "startling report of the physicians that American farms were recruiting stations from whence more women went to insane asylums than from any other walk in life." In December 1890 she spoke at a Southern Farmers' Alliance meeting in Ocala, Florida, where the Kansas delegation promoted the idea of a national third party.

Kansas Populists were divided over the issues of prohibition and woman suffrage. At a Cincinnati reform convention she attended in 1891 to urge formation of a national third party, Diggs defended the omission of a prohibition plank on the grounds that it would be divisive. A woman suffrage bill was passed by the Kansas House in 1891 but was defeated in the Kansas Senate. The Populist Speaker of the state house opposed it; Diggs and the *Advocate* defended it. The Kansas amendment passed both houses in 1893 and was submitted to a referendum. Elected vice president of the Kansas Equal Suffrage Association in 1894, Diggs argued for passage of the amendment at both the Republican and Populist state conventions. The Republicans refused to endorse it but allegedly promised the women "on the sly" that they would vote for it. After a heated floor fight, Diggs secured an official endorsement from the Populists. Still, the proposed amendment was rejected in the referendum. Women achieved full suffrage in Kansas in 1912. They had received the Municipal suffrage in 1887, after a campaign in which Diggs had been active.

Diggs was a delegate to the Omaha convention of the People's party in 1892, which officially launched the Populists as a national third-party movement. She toured California and the West that fall with General James B. Weaver, the party's presidential candidate, and Mary Elizabeth Lease, its best-known woman orator, famous for the admonition to "raise less corn and more hell." Lease and Diggs were rivals, both politically and personally. Lease got more acclaim, but many Populists considered Diggs more intelligent and a better organizer. She tried to build bridges to the labor movement, advocating raising a strike fund for Eugene Debs's American Railway Union in the Pullman strike of 1894 and urging a Populist congressman to introduce a bill that foreshadowed the New Deal's Civilian Conservation Corp by calling on the federal government to employ a half-million men on conservation projects and other public works.

In the presidential election year of 1896, William Jennings Bryan, "the boy orator of the plains," was nominated for president on both the Democratic and Populist tickets. A member of the Populist National Committee that year, Diggs accepted the principle of "fusion"—subordinating the separate identity of the Populists to support Bryan, who endorsed free coinage of silver, an important Populist issue, and who had a real chance of being elected. Bryan's defeat splintered the Populist party, but Diggs continued to advocate the fusion principle. At a Kansas state convention of Populists, Bryan Democrats, and Silver Republicans in 1900, she was acknowledged as the leader of the fusion forces and succeeded in having the convention endorse the tactic. By this time, however, she described herself as a Debs socialist.

In spite of the failure of the Populist party, Diggs continued her political and reform activities. An original member of the Organization Committee of the National American Woman Suffrage Association, in 1899 she was elected president of the Kansas Equal Suffrage Association. In 1898 a fusion administration named her Kansas state librarian. Skeptical of U.S. involvement in the Spanish-American War, in 1899 Diggs wrote a poem, "Little Brown Brother," condemning American imperialism in the Philippines. She joined the Western Co-operative Association of Kansas City, which sent her to England in 1902 to an International Co-operative Congress at Manchester. She remained in England for two years, writing and traveling. She returned home in 1904 and the next year became president of the Kansas Woman's Press Association.

In 1906 she moved to New York City to live with her son and to work for civic reform. She subsequently wrote two books: *The Story of Jerry Simpson* (1908), a biography of a leading Populist, and *Bedrock* (1912), which lobbied for the creation of employment agencies. In 1912 the family moved to Detroit, and Diggs died there. She was buried in Lawrence, Kansas.

Diggs was a major figure in the Populist insurgency and important to the western suffrage movement as well. Perhaps her most striking accomplishment was to become an effective politician without the benefit of suffrage. She did not mourn the passing of the People's party; it had raised the issues important to the farmers and forced both the Democrats and the Republicans to deal with them. "It wasn't the name particularly that I cared about," she told the press in 1907. "It was the principles . . . 'Clodhoppers' or anything would have served the purpose just as well" (Clanton, p. 234).

• The Kansas State Historical Society contains some original material on Diggs in its Kansas Scrapbooks and an unsigned manuscript, "Annie Diggs." A copy of "Little Brown Brother," issued in 1899 as a pamphlet, is also there. She published articles in leading reform journals, including "The Farmers' Alliance and Some of Its Leaders," *Arena* 5 (Apr. 1892): 601–3; "The Women in the Alliance Movement," *Arena* 6 (July 1892): 161–79; "A Captain of Industry," *Arena* 10 (June 1894): 112–16; "The Garden City Movement," *Arena* 28 (Dec. 1902): 626–33; "An English Garden City," *Cosmopolitan* 35 (June 1903): 190–95; "Republics Versus Woman: A Review and a Rejoinder," *Westminster Review* 160 (July 1903): pp. 190–95; and "Co-education in the United States," *Westminster Review* 160 (Dec. 1903): 665–72. There is no biography, and detailed information on her life is rare and scattered. The best source is O. Gene Clanton, *Kansas Populism: Ideas and Men* (1969). There are brief references to her in Florence Finch Kelly, *Flowing Stream* (1939); Elizabeth C. Stanton et al., *History of Woman Suffrage*, vol. 4 (1902); and the *New York Daily Tribune*, 22 July 1896. An obituary is in the *Detroit Free Press*, 9 Sept. 1916.

HELEN C. CAMP

DIHIGO, Martin (25 May 1905–22 May 1971), Negro League baseball player, was born in Matanzas, Cuba. Little is known about his parents or his early life. Dihigo played more than three decades of professional baseball. He began his professional baseball career in 1922 at the age of seventeen with the Havana Reds. The following year he made his first trip to the United States to play in the inaugural season of the Eastern Colored League. He was signed by Alejandro Pompez, owner of the Cuban Stars, one of six teams in the new league. Initially he was a middle infielder, playing second base and shortstop. He was immediately recognized by his peers for his skill, ability, and grace on the field. As a hitter, he developed quickly. Dihigo continued to return to the United States each summer to play Negro League baseball. He remained with the Cuban Stars through the 1927 season. In 1926 he led the Eastern Colored League in home runs while posting a .421 average. Dihigo opened the 1927 season in a spectacular fashion. On opening day against the Hilldales, he drove in nine runs with two grand slams and one solo home run. He finished the season hitting .370 and tied for the league home run title.

During this period Dihigo was returning home to Cuba each winter. Playing in Havana, he hit .413 during the winter of 1926–1927 and .415 the following winter. Dihigo left the Eastern Colored League in 1928 to play with the independent Homestead Grays. In 1929 he was traded to the Philadelphia Hilldales of the American Negro League. By this time Dihigo was one of the biggest names in black baseball and was being paid a team high salary of $400 per month; this put him in the top 10 percent of player salaries in the Negro Leagues during this period. He finished the 1928 season second in the league in home runs with a .386 batting average. In 1930 Dihigo returned to the Cuban Stars and hit .393 for the season.

It was during the 1930s that Dihigo began making more appearances as a pitcher. In 1931 with the Hilldales his pitching record was 6–1. After leaving the Hilldales, Dihigo appeared briefly with the Baltimore Black Sox in 1931, after which he spent three seasons in the Venezuelan League. Salaries in Latin America were generally higher than in the United States for black players during this period. While playing in Venezuela, his pitching was outstanding. In 1932 he pitched a no-hitter, and in 1933 he compiled a record of 6–0 with a 0.15 ERA.

Dihigo returned to the United States in 1935 as player-manager for the Negro National League's New York Cubans. That season he received the most votes of any outfielder in the balloting for the annual East-West All-Star game. Illustrating his versatility, he both played center field and pitched during the contest. That season, with a .372 average and a 7–3 pitching record, he led his team to the second-half title in the Negro National League. Dihigo was the winning pitcher in game one and game four of the championship series, but the Cubans lost the series to the Pittsburgh Crawfords four games to three.

That winter Dihigo returned to Cuba as player-manager of the Santa Clara team. At age thirty he posted an 11–2 pitching record and won the batting title with a .358 average, and his team won the Cuban League championship. The potent talent in Cuba and other Latin American countries made his numbers all the more impressive. Dihigo returned to the United States with the New York Cubans for the 1936 season. In 1937 he played in the Dominican Republic with Aquilas Cibaenas, recording a 6–4 pitching record and a team-leading .351 batting average.

In 1938 Dihigo went to Mexico to play, and he made his presence felt immediately in the Mexican League. In September 1938 Dihigo pitched the first no-hitter in Mexican League history. He ended the 1938 season leading the league in hitting (.387) and in pitching (18–2, 0.90 ERA). Dihigo played in Mexico through the 1944 season. Well into his thirties, he continued to be a dominant player. In 1942 he led the league with 211 strikeouts and a 2.53 ERA. In 1943 he again led the league in strikeouts (134). He finished his Mexican League career with a lifetime pitching record of 119–57. In Cuba, he finished with a lifetime record of 115–60. In 1945 Dihigo returned to the United States for his final season of professional baseball. Although he only hit .204 for the season with a 1–2 pitching record, he was selected to pitch in the 1945 Negro League East-West All-Star game.

Dihigo was a national hero in Cuba. After retiring from baseball he was involved in radio play-by-play broadcasting. After Fidel Castro came to power he appointed Dihigo minister of sports in Cuba, a position Dihigo held until his death in Cienfuegos, Cuba.

During the course of his career Dihigo played every position on the field and played it well. His command and proficiency at each position has earned him the ranking by many historians as being the best all-around baseball player in the early twentieth century. Dihigo is also remembered fondly in every country where he played. He has been called the most versatile man ever to play baseball. In his homeland of Cuba he was known as "El Maestro," while in Mexico he was called "El Immortal." His career accomplishments earned his election to three halls of fame: the Cuban Baseball Hall of Fame in 1951, the Mexican Sports Hall of Fame in 1964, and the National Baseball Hall of Fame in Cooperstown, New York, in 1977.

• Many articles and career highlights information are available at the National Baseball Library in Cooperstown, N.Y. Other notable sources are John Holway, *Blackball Stars* (1988), and Jim Riley, *The Biographical Encyclopedia of the Negro Baseball Leagues* (1994).

TODD BOLTON

DILL, James Brooks (25 July 1854–2 Dec. 1910), corporate lawyer and judge, was born in Spencerport, New York, the son of the Reverend James Horton Dill and Catherine D. Brooks. When Dill was four years old the family moved to Chicago, where his father became pastor of the South Congregational Church. After Dill's father died in battle in 1862 while serving as a Civil War chaplain, the family moved to New Haven, Connecticut.

Dill attended Oberlin Academy (1868–1871), Oberlin College (1872), and Yale College (1872–1876). After graduation, Dill taught for a year in a private school in Philadelphia and studied law with equity lawyer E. Copes Mitchell. He then taught Latin and mathematics at Stevens Institute in Hoboken, New Jersey, while studying law at night at New York University Law School, from which he graduated in 1878 as class salutatorian. Dill was admitted to the New York bar in 1878 and was to become an attorney and counselor in New Jersey as well in 1894.

Dill worked for two newspapers, the *Jersey City Evening Journal* and later the *New York Tribune*, while establishing a law practice. His reputation as a corporate lawyer grew after he won a case in 1879 for John G. Tappan, a director of an insolvent corporation, McKillop, Sprague & Co. The corporation had failed and had liabilities in the millions. Dill obtained the dismissal of the suit against Tappan on an argument of statutory interpretation, although the other directors had been found individually liable for the debts of the corporation. This victory helped Dill build his practice around the new field of corporate law.

In 1880 Dill married Mary W. Hansell; they had three daughters. In 1881 he formed the law firm of Dill, Chandler, & Seymour. He advocated the new corporate form of business organization, including the large firms and trusts that developed in the 1880s.

In response to the early antitrust movement that threatened clients such as Standard Oil, Dill convinced New Jersey governor Leon Abbett to call for the amendment of the state's laws to allow corporations greater freedom. Between 1888 and 1896, the New Jersey State legislature did liberalize the state's corporate laws. Following what was called a "charter-mongering" strategy, these laws were designed to entice big business to incorporate in New Jersey by legalizing trusts and allowing corporations to own stock in other corporations, as well as allowing other privileges that had been denied by previous state laws. In response, many major corporations flocked to New Jersey to incorporate under the favorable laws. These corporations, such as Standard Oil, flourished, as evidenced by the merger wave of 1896–1904. New Jersey benefited from the incorporation fees and corporate franchise taxes that poured into the state's coffers and helped the state eliminate its Civil War debt and its property tax.

Dill and Abbett also had a financial interest in the new policies. In 1892 Dill founded the Corporation Trust Company of New Jersey to satisfy the legal requirements of out-of-state businesses that sought the benefits of New Jersey's corporate laws. The firm handled the necessary paperwork for a fee, and Abbett and New Jersey Secretary of State Henry Kelsey served as directors.

During his career in private practice, Dill served as legal counsel and director of many banks and corporations and also aided in establishing others. He was a director and general counsel for National Steel Company; American Tin Plate Company; Seventh National Bank of New York; Westinghouse Company of Pittsburgh; New England Street Railway Company of Boston; Savings, Investment and Trust Company and the People's Bank of East Orange; and the North American Trust Company of New York, as well as fifty smaller companies.

Dill also is credited with settling a celebrated falling out between Andrew Carnegie and Henry C. Frick that threatened the steel industry in 1900. The settlement led to the formation of United States Steel Corporation. Dill's fee of $1 million was reputed to be the highest fee ever paid to an American lawyer.

Dill was recognized as an authority in the field of corporate and business law. Among his extensive writings on corporate law were *The Statutory and Case Law Applicable to Private Companies under the General Corporation Act of New Jersey* (1898), *The Laws of New Jersey Relating to Banks and Banking, Trust Companies and Safe Deposit Corporations* (1899), and *Business Corporations* (1910). He also delivered addresses on business or corporate law topics. An address he made to the Seminary in Economics of Harvard University was published as "National Incorporation Laws for Trusts" in the *Yale Law Journal* (11 [1902]: 273–95). In 1898 Dill served as chairman of the committee that revised New Jersey's financial laws, and he compiled New Jersey's corporate laws. He also served on law revision committees in New York (1899) and in Canada (1904–1905).

Dill was appointed in 1905 as a lay member of New Jersey's then-highest court, the Court of Errors and Appeals. In contrast to his career as a corporate lawyer, Dill's five-year tenure on the court was less distinguished. Dill resigned from the court just before his death.

According to the *New Jersey Law Journal*, Dill was known as being a person who was "[a]ffable to an unusual degree," but who nevertheless was "one of the most able and painstaking lawyers practicing at the New York bar." Although Dill's practice was centered in New York, he made his home in East Orange, New Jersey, where he maintained his private library of 10,000 books. He also had a farm in Connecticut and was a devotee of horseback riding and outdoor activities. Dill belonged to numerous social organizations. He was a member of the Brick Presbyterian Church in East Orange and served as its chairman of the Board of Trustees. Dill was also a Thirty-third Degree Mason and was a commander of the Knights Templar. He served two terms as president of the New York University Law School Alumni Association. He died at his home in East Orange.

• Dill's role in corporate law is discussed in Christopher Grandy, *New Jersey and the Fiscal Origins of Modern American Corporation Law* (1993), and Henry N. Butler, "Nineteenth-

Century Jurisdictional Competition in the Granting of Corporate Privileges," *Journal of Legal Studies* 14 (Jan. 1985): 129, 161–62. A biographical sketch with a photograph of Dill is in *Banking Law Journal* 10 (1894): 375–76. Obituaries are in the *New York Times*, 3 Dec. 1910, and the *New Jersey Law Journal* 33 (10 Dec. 1910).

ANDREW T. FEDE

DILLARD, James Hardy (24 Oct. 1856–2 Aug. 1940), educator and promoter of racial harmony, was born in Nansemond County, Virginia, the son of James Dillard and Sarah Brownrigg Cross, planters. Dillard spent most of his early years on the family's plantation with its over three hundred slaves. At the age of twelve he was sent to school in Norfolk. He enrolled in Washington and Lee University in 1873 where he excelled in history and received a master's degree in 1876 and a bachelor of laws in 1877. Although Dillard considered building a legal practice, his parents' poverty in the aftermath of the Civil War forced him to accept the principalship of the Rodman School in Norfolk, Virginia, in 1877 in order to immediately assist his family. Five years later he married Mary Harmanson and accepted an administrative position at Norfolk Academy.

Dillard supplemented his income in 1885 by teaching Latin for the Sauveur Summer School of Languages. Thereafter, he spent the next fifteen summers with the school, which offered courses at various collegiate institutions. In 1887 Dillard accepted the principalship of Mary Institute at Washington University in St. Louis, where he earned a reputation as an able administrator. He left St. Louis for New Orleans in 1891, however, to accept a professorship in Latin at Tulane University. His administrative ability led to his eventual appointment as dean of the College of Arts and Sciences in 1894. Two years later he suffered a personal tragedy when his wife died, leaving him with six children to raise alone. In 1899 he married Avarene Lippincott Budd, with whom he had four children.

Dillard's reputation in New Orleans extended beyond Tulane. He developed an interest in progressive causes, which he translated into an active civic life. In addition to serving as president of the city's public library and Child Welfare Association, Dillard received the most renown for his antilynching activities. Shortly after his arrival in New Orleans, the lynching of an African American occurred near Dillard's home. The failure of New Orleans's civic leaders to condemn the act angered the professor; subsequently, he delivered addresses and wrote articles publicly condemning lynching. He also served as a trustee for four African-American colleges and universities in Louisiana. Two of these schools eventually merged in 1930, and the founders of the new institution honored the former principal by naming it Dillard University.

Dillard frequently recounted a youthful incident that he recognized as the source of his sensitivity to injustices committed against African Americans. He had coaxed an African-American boy on his family's plantation away from watching cattle, and the overseer caught and whipped the African-American youth. But Dillard, who believed himself responsible, went unpunished.

Dillard's work attracted the attention of proponents of African-American education, including Booker T. Washington, who urged him to become president of the newly endowed Anna T. Jeanes Negro Rural School Fund in 1907. Dillard eventually accepted the appointment after some initial hesitation. Overcome by the offer of an annual $6,000 salary—or a thousand dollars more than his income at Tulane—he resigned from the university to assume the new post.

Under Dillard, the Jeanes Fund provided African-American teachers for black schools throughout the South. These teachers worked in concert with local primary public schools, providing instruction in "industrial education," which included such crafts as carpentry for boys and sewing for girls. Dillard also assumed the directorship of the John F. Slater Fund in 1910, which provided aid for training black teachers in manual arts. Additionally, Dillard used the fund to subsidize the development of industrial "county training schools" to provide African Americans opportunities for secondary education. Gradually, many such schools evolved into high schools, offering academic as well as manual training. Dillard also required school systems that accepted aid from either endowment to provide matching funds, thereby increasing the commitment of white-controlled school boards to black education.

In addition to his labors on behalf of African-American education, Dillard worked to promote racial harmony. Although not a founding member of the Southern Sociological Congress, he encouraged its efforts to improve race relations. Dillard was instrumental in convincing that body to conduct integrated meetings on issues that concerned race. He also organized the University Commission on Southern Race Questions in 1912, which consisted of delegates from the South's white state universities. Dillard encouraged the commission to publicly identify areas of unnecessary racial conflict and to try to convince whites to accept the idea of black economic, educational, and social progress through its annual conferences. Likewise, Dillard helped organize the Commission on Interracial Cooperation in 1919, which conducted biracial meetings throughout the South. That particular commission sought to alleviate tensions created by the return of black servicemen from the First World War, who after fighting for democracy abroad demanded equal rights upon coming home. In all of these efforts, Dillard believed education, whether delivered in a conference hall or in a classroom, to be the best means to remove prejudices that led to racial conflict.

Dillard's desire to turn his work over to younger administrators led him to retire from the Jeanes and Slater Funds in 1931. Nevertheless, he continued to concern himself with racial issues, serving from 1935 to 1936 as chairman of the American Scottsboro Committee, which worked on behalf of nine African Americans convicted of raping two white women on slight evidence in Alabama. He also continued to serve as rector of the Board of Visitors for the College of William and Mary, where he fought for academic freedom and against lowered scholastic requirements for athletes. His work on racial and educational matters ended only with his death in Charlottesville, Virginia.

Dillard's contemporaries almost unanimously described him as a congenial open-minded man with the capacity to charm either poor, rural black teachers or wealthy, urban white philanthropists. Admirers praised him as a humanitarian who worked for black education and better race relations, while his critics viewed him as a paternalist whose support of industrial education for African Americans actually hindered their educational progress by limiting their training to menial skills. Likewise, civil rights activists deplored Dillard's emphasis on educational answers to racial problems at the expense of political solutions.

Dillard, however, was aware of the weaknesses of industrial education and wanted black and white children to be given a combination of both academic and manual instruction. Extremely cautious, he feared that moving too quickly toward equalizing black educational opportunities would alienate whites and provoke a reaction to his efforts. Dillard, nevertheless, abhorred paternalism, and, unlike most white educators, he wanted African Americans to operate their own schools and escape the patronizing influences that prevented black institutions from achieving their full potential. Dillard defined himself as a liberal, characterizing his beliefs in the *South Atlantic Quarterly* (Jan. 1917) as favoring "the constant improvement of the masses of people through self-development and the fair opportunity." Although a prolific writer who advocated equal educational and other public services for African Americans, Dillard still tolerated segregation. Ultimately, his gradualist approach to social change did little to help white southerners accept the civil rights movement that followed World War II.

• An extensive collection of Dillard's papers, including his diary, were donated in 1971 to the Alderman Library, University of Virginia. Only one of five books by Dillard gives insight into his philosophy: *From News Stand to Cyrano* (1935). Dillard also wrote articles on race and education for numerous journals and newspapers, some of which are included in James Hardy Dillard, "Selected Writings of James Hardy Dillard," *Occasional Papers of the Trustees of the John F. Slater Fund*, vol. 27 (1932). For biographical information see Benjamin Brawley, *Doctor Dillard of the Jeanes Fund* (1930), a celebratory account of Dillard's accomplishments. More scholarly, but nevertheless complimentary, is John Edward McNeal, "James Hardy Dillard: Southern Humanitarian" (Ph.D. diss., Univ. of Virginia, 1971), which focuses on Dillard's liberalism. McNeal's footnotes are an excellent source for locating Dillard's published articles. Neither biography, however, reveals much about Dillard's personal life. D. Ralph Davison, Jr., "James Hardy Dillard: A Christian Educator in the Segregated South," *Historical Magazine of the Protestant Episcopal Church* 55 (Dec. 1986): 113–26, argues that Dillard's humanitarian impulses stemmed not from liberalism but from deeply held religious convictions. Unlike McNeal, Davison had access to Dillard's papers at the University of Virginia. An account of Dillard's time at Tulane is found in John P. Dyer, *Tulane: The Biography of a University 1834–1965* (1966). Obituaries are in the *New York Times* and the *New York Herald Tribune*, both 3 Aug. 1940.

DAN R. FROST

DILLER, Angela (1 Aug. 1877–30 Apr. 1968), pianist and music educator, was born in Brooklyn, New York, the daughter of William A. M. Diller, a church organist and choirmaster, and Mary Abigail Welles. As a child, she played piano by ear; when she was twelve she began studying with Alice Fowler, whom she described as "an inspiring teacher" and with whom she studied until she was seventeen. Soon after that she took her first teaching position at St. John the Baptist School for Girls, a New York boarding school, where some of her pupils were her own age. Diller took students to New York Philharmonic concerts, first educating herself about the works to be played by studying scores borrowed from the public library so that she could discuss the music with her students.

In 1896 Diller concurrently enrolled at Barnard College and attended Columbia University, where she studied harmony, counterpoint, orchestration, and composition for seven years with Edward MacDowell, then head of the music department. In 1899 she became the first person to receive the Mosenthal Fellowship for music composition at Columbia. She also studied for a time with Johannes Schreyer in Dresden, Germany.

Diller joined the faculty of the Music School Settlement in New York City in 1899; she later became head of the theory department there. The settlement had been founded in 1894 by Emilie Wagner, a venturesome educator deeply interested in social issues, in order to provide underprivileged children with opportunities for music study. The school was the first of its kind in New York. In a 1958 interview for *Music Journal* Diller recalled that "the children of the neighborhood clamored for lessons. On Saturday mornings the house was so crowded that one child, I remember, was taking a violin lesson at the turn of the stairs, because there was no studio available. The children tumbled over themselves to come and learn about music."

In the settlement, Diller learned much about teaching music. There, too, she made many friends among both teachers and students, one of the most important of whom was her teaching colleague Elizabeth Quaile. After leaving the Music School Settlement in 1916, Diller and Quaile taught together at the Mannes School of Music for five years. In 1921 they founded the Diller-Quaile School of Music in New York City, a progressive school for the instruction of children and young people, with a training school for teachers. In partnership with Quaile, Diller developed a curriculum of musicianship for graded classes that was closely coordinated with each student's individual instrumental lesson. As Diller explained: "what was learned in class about chords, structure, style, etc., was used at once in the piano lessons" (*New York Times*, 2 May 1968, p. 46). Although Diller once stated, "I don't teach a method; I try to open people to music," the close correlation between the students' theoretical work and the music being studied for performance was the characteristic of the Diller-Quaile approach to music study distinguishing it from the conventional approach at the time, that of studying theory apart from music studied for performance. Diller administered the school until 1941, after which she taught part time until the last years of her life.

With Quaile, Diller coauthored over forty instructional books, which averaged sales of twelve thousand copies a year. The success of the books, along with the proven effectiveness of Diller and Quaile's techniques, contributed greatly to the rapid dispersion of their teaching approaches. She also collaborated in publications with Kate Stearns Page, a teaching colleague, musical collaborator, and long-time friend with whom she shared a home for over twenty-five years. In addition, Diller and Quaile collaborated with pianist Harold Bauer in the publication of *A Piano Method for Class and Individual Instruction* (1931).

Diller taught and lectured extensively in the United States and Europe. She taught at the University of Southern California, Mills College, the University of Louisville, Brown University, Baylor University, and Ohio State University, as well as at conservatories in Boston, Toronto, and Ottawa, and at the Worcester Art Museum in Worcester, Massachusetts. In addition, she lectured in Philadelphia and many other cities in the United States and abroad. Although widely acclaimed as a pedagogue, Diller insisted that she didn't teach any one method, but that she simply tried to open her students to the beauty of all music. Once, after playing MacDowell's "To a Water Lily" to an interviewer, she paused and remarked: "That's what I mean about music's being indestructible. Monet's 'Water Lilies' at the Museum of Modern Art went up in smoke, but nothing, by George, can happen to *this* water lily" (*New Yorker*, 20 Sept. 1958).

In 1953 Diller received a Guggenheim Foundation Award to write *The Splendor of Music* (1957), a book about her life in teaching. She collaborated with Margarethe Dessoff in founding the Adesdi Chorus of women's voices in 1924 and the A Cappella Singers of New York in 1929; the two ensembles later combined to form the Dessoff Choirs.

Through her teaching, writing, and lecturing, and through her novel approach to music instruction—one that integrated theory studies with applied instrumental study—Diller achieved fame in musical circles and was an important influence in the development of music education both at home and abroad. She died in Stamford, Connecticut, never having married.

• Diller's writings not mentioned in the text include *First Theory Book* (1921), *Keyboard Harmony Books* (4 vols., 1936–1949), and *Keyboard Music Study Books* (2 vols., 1936–1937). Two of the most important biographical pieces are "Personal Recollections of a Music Teacher" *Music Journal* 16 (Apr.–May 1958): 36–37, 64; and "Teachers' Teacher," *New Yorker*, 20 Sept. 1958, pp. 33–34. An obituary is in the *New York Times*, 2 May 1968.

S. MARGARET WILLIAM MCCARTHY

DILLER, Burgoyne (13 Jan. 1906–30 Jan. 1965), painter and arts administrator, was born in the Bronx, New York, the son of Andrew Diller, a violinist and conductor, and Mary Burgoyne. Diller's father died in 1908. In 1919 his mother married Adrian Adney, an engineer, and the family moved to Battle Creek, Michigan. Diller attended Battle Creek High School and, subsequently, Michigan State College in East Lansing. A marginal student, Diller was successful only in his art classes and on the track team. Leaving Michigan State before graduating, he moved in 1928 to Buffalo, where he lived with his maternal grandfather.

In Buffalo, Diller worked briefly at a number of jobs before landing a steady position as a janitor. At this time he began to sell a few artworks. This income, combined with his savings, allowed him to move to New York City, where he enrolled in the Art Students League in 1929. Diller was an immediate success at the League and was soon awarded a scholarship job in the League bookstore.

Diller continued to take classes and work at the League bookstore until 1933. Among his instructors were Boardman Robinson, William von Schlegell, and, most significantly, Jan Matulka. Matulka was a proponent of abstract art, particularly cubism, and taught not only Diller but other abstract artists, including David Smith and Irene Rice Pereira.

In his early work Diller had been influenced by Paul Cézanne and Georges Seurat. Under the tutelage of Matulka and exiled German Hans Hofmann (with whom Diller studied at the League during 1932–1933), his work began to reflect cubism, with flat planes of color enlivened by biomorphic shapes.

In 1930 Diller married Sarah "Sally" Bernadette Conboy; they did not have children. Conboy worked in the classified department of the *New York Times*, and her steady income helped the couple maintain a modest lifestyle throughout the depression. Their friends felt the couple were a "prince and princess in fairy land" (Haskell, p. 36).

After his first solo exhibition at the Contemporary Arts Gallery (New York City) in 1933, Diller's work made a dramatic change. Abandoning cubism, he began to work in the abstract modes of constructivism, de Stijl, and neoplasticism. His paintings became more austere, composed of geometric shapes in primary colors floating on a flat, often white, picture plane.

In late 1933 Diller's position at the League bookstore was eliminated for financial reasons. Almost immediately, however, he was selected for the Public Works of Art Project (PWAP), a New Deal relief effort for artists that terminated in 1934. At first appointed to the easel division of the PWAP, Diller worked on mural projects in 1934–1935 for the Temporary Emergency Relief Administration (TERA), completing mural projects started by the PWAP.

When the Federal Art Project (FAP) was established as part of the Works Progress Administration in 1935, Diller was hired as an artist and quickly promoted to assistant project supervisor of the mural division in New York City. By 1937 he was the sole supervisor of the mural division. In this influential position, Diller oversaw the creation of hundreds of murals and the employment of numerous artists. Though the majority of murals created reflected the social realism that predominated in the work of the FAP, Diller employed a number of abstract artists, including Stuart Davis and Arshile Gorky. Major abstract murals supervised by Diller include those at the Newark Airport by Gorky and the Williamsburg Housing Project by Ilya Bolotowsky, Byron Browne, and Paul Kelpe, among others.

Additional work that Diller completed for the FAP included designing and installing the Federal Art Gallery, teaching at the Design Laboratory, and serving as the WPA's liaison to the 1939 New York World's Fair, for which he oversaw the Contemporary Arts Pavilion and designed benches for the gallery.

Diller's support and encouragement of abstract artists during the depression is significant in that it gave work to a group of artists who would form the core of the New York art scene in the postwar years. Among the most promising artists supported by Diller through the FAP, in addition to Gorky, Davis, and Bolotowsky, were Jackson Pollock and Willem de Kooning.

In 1937 Diller was a key figure in the formation of the American Abstract Artists, a group devoted to the support and propagation of abstract art. However, his administrative duties for the FAP and his own work kept him from actively participating in their activities, and he dropped out in 1940, only to rejoin in 1947.

Alleged Communist infiltration of the WPA led to Diller's temporary suspension (along with other WPA supervisors) in 1941. No evidence was found to incriminate Diller, and he was soon reinstated. With the entry of the United States into World War II, the arts projects were reformed into the Graphic Section of the War Services Division. In 1943, at age thirty-seven, Diller enlisted in the U.S. Navy. Assigned to the U.S. Navy Training Aids Development Center in New York City, he invented a hand-held Morse code training device. More than three million of the devices were made, and Diller was awarded a patent in 1945. After being released from active duty in November 1945 as a lieutenant junior grade, he remained in the naval reserve, retiring in 1954 with the rank of full lieutenant.

In 1946 Diller was hired as an assistant professor at Brooklyn College and soon promoted to full professor. In 1948 he designed a studio for himself in Atlantic Highlands, New Jersey, where he spent summers painting. He was granted tenure in 1949.

During the late 1930s and early 1940s Diller's work moved closer to the neoplasticism of Piet Mondrian and Theo Van Doesburg. His more notable paintings from this period include *Construction* (1940, Yale University Art Gallery), *First Theme* (1942, Museum of Modern Art, New York), and *Third Theme* (1946–1948, Whitney Museum of American Art). In 1951 Diller described his work as falling into three themes, which delineate the ways that geometric forms and complex line patterns interact on the plane of the canvas.

With the rise of abstract expressionism in the early 1950s, Diller, with his cool, analytical abstractions, found himself isolated from the art scene. Though always a heavy drinker, he turned more frequently to alcohol during this time. Sally Diller's own alcoholism contributed to her death in 1954 of cirrhosis of the liver, just months after she retired from the *New York Times*. That summer, while visiting his mother and stepfather in Michigan, Diller met Grace Kelso LaCrone, just separated from her husband. After her divorce was finalized, Diller and LaCrone married in 1955; no children resulted from this union. Leaving New York City, the Dillers moved to a house near his studio in New Jersey.

By 1956 Diller's health had seriously declined after years of smoking and alcohol abuse. Exhibiting only occasionally since the 1940s, in 1958 he participated in a group show at Galerie Chalette in New York City. The gallery began to handle his work and gave Diller a number of solo exhibitions over the next six years. In the 1960s Diller transferred his geometric themes to the three-dimensional medium of sculpture. Diller died of complications of heart disease and pulmonary edema at French Hospital in New York City.

• Diller's works are at the Art Students League, New York City; the Albright-Knox Art Gallery, Buffalo, N.Y.; the Hirshhorn Museum and Sculpture Garden at the Smithsonian Institution; the Metropolitan Museum of Art, New York City; the Whitney Museum of American Art, New York City; the Yale University Art Gallery; and the Baltimore Museum of Art. A large collection of papers, including records of Diller's work on the Federal Art Project, is located in the Archives of American Art at the Smithsonian. Also held by the Archives of American Art are taped interviews with Diller. Barbara Haskell's catalog for the Whitney Museum's exhibition of the same name, *Burgoyne Diller* (1990), provides comprehensive biographical information on the artist. See also Anita J. Ellis, "Burgoyne Diller: A Neo-Plasticist" (master's thesis, Univ. of Cincinnati, 1975), and David Hoyt Johnson, "The Early Career of Burgoyne Diller: 1925–45" (master's thesis, Univ. of Arizona, Tucson, 1978). An obituary is in the *New York Times*, 31 Jan. 1965.

MARTIN R. KALFATOVIC

DILLINGER, John (22 June 1903–22 July 1934), criminal, was born John Herbert Dillinger in Indianapolis, Indiana, the son of John Wilson Dillinger, a grocer, and Mary Ellen Lancaster. When he was three, his mother died, and his seventeen-year-old sister took over his care. He attended public schools in Indianapolis, disliked arithmetic, enjoyed reading, and excelled in schoolyard fights. In 1920 his father, by then remarried, moved to nearby Mooresville with his family, including two stepsons, and Dillinger quit school and began to work in a machine shop and furniture factory. In 1923 he joined the navy, was punished for being absent without leave, deserted, and was dishonorably discharged. He married Beryl Hovious in 1924; they had no children. Dillinger worked as an upholsterer in Mooresville, but he got drunk with a friend and was caught trying to rob a grocer. He served time in the Indiana reformatory at Pendleton and then the state prison at Michigan City. He attempted to escape, was ordered to serve more time, and was punished for gambling and disorderly conduct. His wife divorced him in 1929 and remarried. Though sentenced to ten to twenty years, he was paroled in May 1933 and promptly went on a crime spree, usually with accomplices who were often less lucky than he.

In a botched robbery in Monticello, Indiana, Dillinger shot and wounded a mill manager. He was involved in at least five bank robberies, in Indiana (Daleville, Indianapolis, and Montpelier) and Ohio (Bluffton and New Carlisle), netting more than $50,000, and in one tavern robbery. He was also suspected in three other bank robberies before being arrested in September in Dayton, Ohio. He was charged with multiple bank robberies and jailed in Lima, Ohio. Four days later ten of Dillinger's friends broke out of the Indiana State Prison with guns he had smuggled to them earlier. On 12 October four of these men—Russell Clark, John Hamilton, Charles Makley, and Harry Pierpont—and a friend named Harry Copeland killed the Lima sheriff and freed Dillinger. Between capers that summer, Dillinger and a pair of girlfriends attended the World's Fair in Chicago, and he amused himself by photographing a policeman. Later in October Dillinger, Pierpont, and a friend raided two police stations in Indiana (Auburn and Peru) for guns and bulletproof vests; then Dillinger, Clark, Copeland, Makley, and Pierpont took $75,000 from a bank in Greencastle, Indiana, after which Dillinger returned to Chicago.

November was crime filled. Authorities set a trap for Dillinger outside a Chicago dermatologist's office, but he and Evelyn Frechette, a new girlfriend, shot their way out. Copeland was arrested in Chicago and later sentenced to twenty-five years for the Greencastle robbery. Dillinger, with Clark, Hamilton, Makley, Pierpont, and a friend named Leslie Homer, robbed a bank in Racine, Wisconsin, wounded two men, kidnapped two others and one woman, and escaped; Homer was arrested in Chicago and later sentenced to twenty-eight years for the Racine robbery. In December Chicago authorities placed Dillinger and eight cohorts, including two women—Pearl Elliott and Mary Kinder—on their list of public enemies and organized a forty-man "Dillinger Squad." Dillinger was a suspect in several other robberies. While he and his gang were spending the Christmas season in Florida, police raided an apartment in Chicago and killed three criminals mistakenly thought to be members of his gang.

In January 1934 Dillinger, Hamilton, and others never identified robbed an East Chicago, Indiana, bank of $20,000, during which a policeman named William Patrick O'Malley was killed, and Hamilton was wounded. Ten days later Dillinger, Clark, Frechette, Kinder, Makley, and Pierpont were captured in a hotel in Tucson, Arizona. Extradited to Indiana for the O'Malley murder, Dillinger, while in jail in Crown Point, whittled a toy gun out of wood and blackened it with shoe polish. In March he threatened guards with the toy and escaped, with an inmate named Herbert Youngblood and two hostages, in the sheriff's car. For crossing state lines in a stolen vehicle, he was placed on a federal complaint. J. Edgar Hoover, director of the Federal Bureau of Investigation, named agent Melvin Purvis to head a team to capture Dillinger. Forming a new gang including Eddie Green and Lester "Baby Face Nelson" Gillis, Dillinger robbed a bank in Sioux Falls, South Dakota, of $49,500. While robbing a bank in Mason City, Iowa, of $52,000, Dillinger and Hamilton were wounded. Youngblood was killed by police in Port Huron, Michigan. Pierpont and Makley were sentenced to death in Lima, Ohio; Clark was given a life sentence. Dillinger, Frechette, and longtime friend Homer Van Meter shot their way out of an FBI trap in St. Paul, Minnesota. While dying of wounds and delirious in St. Paul in April, Green revealed information of much value to the FBI. Frechette was captured by Purvis in a Chicago tavern, but Dillinger escaped unseen. He and Van Meter stole guns and vests in Warsaw, Indiana. Dillinger, Hamilton, and Nelson shot their way out of a botched FBI trap at the Little Bohemia Lodge near Rhinelander, Wisconsin; Nelson killed one agent, and agents killed one civilian and mortally wounded Hamilton, whom Dillinger helped bury outside Oswego, Illinois.

In May, in the wake of new federal anticrime laws, Dillinger, Nelson, and Van Meter were indicted in Madison, Wisconsin, for conspiracy. Substantial rewards were posted for Dillinger's capture. Plastic surgeons in Chicago altered his face and that of Van Meter. In June grand juries indicted Dillinger on sundry charges. In Chicago he met Polly Hamilton, celebrated his thirty-first birthday with her in a nightclub, and through her met Anna Sage, a prostitute and madam from Romania. Dillinger, Nelson, Van Meter, and others robbed a bank in South Bend, Indiana, of $30,000, killing a policeman in the process. Dillinger returned to Chicago. Sage, seeking to avoid being deported, informed Purvis that on 22 July Dillinger would take her, along with Polly, to a movie at the Biograph Theater on Lincoln Avenue. Purvis assembled a large team of federal agents and Chicago policemen, including Martin Zarkovich, to surround the place. When Dillinger emerged, he was shot in the head and left side and died within five minutes.

Questions immediately arose. Who actually shot Dillinger? Did he ever draw a weapon, or was he simply executed? What was the background of Sage, the "Woman in Red"? Did Zarkovich, who was her lover, take money from the dead man's pockets? Why did Purvis resign from the FBI in 1935? Why was Sage deported in 1936? Was Dillinger ever killed, or was a petty criminal set up by the authorities in his place? The metamorphosis of the Dillinger legend follows a classic pattern. The hero, who had a deprived childhood, never robbed from the poor; he managed fabulous escapes and acclaimed reappearances; his associates gained fame; he was betrayed by a woman; his fall paradoxically proved that crime does not pay; the victors argued over who deserved the most credit; memorabilia, including his alleged weapons and even traces of his blood, were treasured; rumors of his grand sexuality circulated; and he may have survived after all.

• The John Dillinger Historical Museum in Nashville, Ind., has Dillinger memorabilia. Alanna Nash, "Maybe I'll Learn Someday, Dad, You Can't Win in This Game," *New York Times*, 7 Mar. 1976, describes the museum. G. Russell Girardin, with William J. Hemler, *Dillinger: The Untold Story* (1994), is the definitive biography. Athan G. Theodoris and John Stuart Cox, *The Boss: J. Edgar Hoover and the Great American Inquisition* (1988); Anthony Summers, *Official and Confidential: The Secret Life of J. Edgar Hoover* (1993); and William W. Turner, *Hoover's F.B.I.* (1993), detail activities, carelessness, blunders, and coverups of the FBI under Hoover in connection with Dillinger. Richard Gid Powers, *G-Men: Hoover's FBI in American Popular Culture* (1983), traces permutations in the Dillinger legend. Jay Robert Nash, *Dillinger: Dead or Alive?* (1970), presents evidence that Dillinger was not killed in Chicago in 1934. A long obituary, with portrait, is in the *New York Times*, 23 July 1934.

ROBERT L. GALE

DILLINGHAM, Benjamin Franklin (4 Sept. 1844–20 Aug. 1918), businessman, was born in West Brewster, Cape Cod, Massachusetts, the son of Benjamin Clark Dillingham, a shipmaster, and Lydia Sears Howes. Dillingham was educated in the public schools of Southboro and Worcester, Massachusetts. He left school at age fourteen to become a seaman on the merchant ship *Southern Cross*, captained by his uncle Benjamin Perkins Howes. On his third voyage, the *Southern Cross* was captured and destroyed in June 1863 by a Confederate raider, the *Florida*. Part of the crew, including Dillingham, was transferred to a French merchant ship that put them ashore in Brazil. Dillingham repatriated himself to New York.

Dillingham returned to sea in 1864 as first mate of the bark *Whistler*. On his third voyage, while ashore in Honolulu in July 1865, Dillingham fractured his leg in a riding accident. During a lengthy convalescence in the U.S. Marine Hospital in Honolulu, he was befriended by a missionary, Rev. Lowell Smith. In 1869 Dillingham married Smith's daughter Emma Louise Smith. They had four children.

In 1865 Dillingham was employed as a clerk by Henry Dimond, a Honolulu hardware merchant. In 1869 Dimond sold his store to a partnership between Dillingham and Alfred Castle, the son of S. N. Castle, one of Hawaii's business leaders. The partnership lasted until Alfred Castle's death five years later. Dillingham continued as sole manager and agreed to share the profits with Castle's widow and family. The store was incorporated as the Pacific Hardware Company in 1885. In 1879 Dillingham founded a small farm called "Woodlawn." He established a dairy business there that was incorporated as the Woodlawn Dairy and Stock Company in early 1884. Neither of his businesses proved to be particularly successful.

During the first half of the 1880s Dillingham discovered that real estate speculation was a more profitable business. In 1885 James Campbell, one of Oahu's biggest landowners, offered Dillingham a one-year option to acquire 60,000 acres of poor quality grazing land. Dillingham believed that the land had potential for redevelopment through subdivision and irrigation. However, he failed to raise the capital to purchase the land—despite two extensions to his option.

In 1888 Dillingham decided that he might have more success in raising funds for his real estate project if he combined it with a railroad project. He obtained a railroad concession from the Hawaiian legislature and quickly succeeded in raising capital to build the railroad. The Oahu Railway and Land Company (OR&L) was incorporated in February 1889. Dillingham became the railroad project's contractor and ceased to be actively involved in the Pacific Hardware Company. The first section from Honolulu to Halawa was completed within a year, and the line was officially opened in November 1889. It was fully completed in July 1890.

Dillingham's success in raising capital for the railroad led him to revive his attempt to purchase the Campbell properties in June 1889. In November 1889, having failed once again to raise the necessary capital, Dillingham persuaded Campbell to grant him a fifty-year lease instead. Dillingham sold this lease to the OR&L. In 1889 he commissioned a survey of the Campbell properties by two Californian hydrographic engineers; they suggested that sufficient water existed for the development of sugar plantations. Dillingham was able to sublease part of the Campbell properties to the founders of the Ewa and Kahuku sugar plantations.

In the early 1890s Dillingham's railroad company and real estate developments experienced severe financial difficulties. The McKinley Tariff Act of 1890 had offset the benefit to Hawaii of the 1875 Reciprocity Treaty, which allowed the duty-free entry of its principal export staple, sugar cane, into the United States.

The Wilson-Gorman Tariff of 1894 restored the benefits of the Reciprocity Treaty to Hawaii's sugar industry. This enabled Dillingham to embark upon the development of the Oahu Sugar Company plantation at Waipahu in 1894. The German-owned H. Hackfeld and Company provided the capital that enabled the plantation to be developed successfully and subsequently incorporated in 1896. Dillingham's development project at Waialua was not such a quick success. Together with other investors, he acquired during 1897 and 1898 7,000 acres of potential sugar cane land at Waialua that the OR&L had connected to its railroad system. Dillingham persuaded Castle & Cooke to underwrite the foundation of the Waialua Agricultural Company. However, it was ten years before the plantation succeeded because irrigation proved to be unexpectedly difficult.

In 1899 he founded the B. F. Dillingham Company, Ltd., into which he placed a major share of his financial assets and liabilities. In the same year Dillingham began a number of projects that nearly bankrupted him because he mistakenly predicted a rise in the price of sugar. Two of the projects were based in the outer islands of Maui and Kauai. In both of these undercapitalized projects, Dillingham acted as a promoter and invested only a small amount of his own money.

In 1899 Dillingham had also become involved in the establishment of two plantations on the island of Hawaii, the Puna and Olaa Sugar Companies, in the latter of which he was the principal investor. As on Oahu, he also founded a railroad to provide his real estate development with access to markets. However, unlike the OR&L, the Hilo Railroad was not a financial success because Hawaii (unlike Oahu) was too sparsely populated to generate sufficient traffic. The plantations remained unprofitable even after the merger of the Puna plantation with the Olaa Sugar Company in 1902.

In 1903 Dillingham had a nervous breakdown, and his son Walter became increasingly involved in his business empire. However, Dillingham continued as general manager of his most successful business, the OR&L, until 1916; he retained the presidency of the railroad until his death.

Dillingham's disastrous investments of 1899 resulted in a financial crisis in his principal company, the B. F. Dillingham Co., in 1904. It was estimated that Dillingham and the company together owed $3 million and held assets slightly in excess of this amount. However, both the Californian and Hawaiian creditors allowed Dillingham and his son Walter to reorganize their debts. Nevertheless, Dillingham's business interests remained on the edge of bankruptcy until 1907. Olaa Sugar remained a sizable loss-maker. However, the OR&L was rather more successful. The completion of a branch line to Wahiawa in 1906 allowed the railroad to benefit from the success of the new pineapple industry in this area. That same year Dillingham sold the Pacific Hardware Company. In 1907 he had a stroke.

As Dillingham recovered, sugar prices began to rise; most of his business interests also experienced a recovery. However, in 1908 his Maui plantation was sold to raise cash to support the B. F. Dillingham Co. Two years later the Woodlawn Dairy and Stock Company sold the last of its animals and divided its Manoa property for sale as house lots. Dillingham also tried to make the Hilo Railroad profitable by extending it. However, by the time the extension was completed in April 1913, it had overrun its initial estimated cost of $1 million by nearly $2.7 million. This folly forced Dillingham and his son to reorganize the railroad in 1916. A new company was formed to take it over, the Hawaii Consolidated Railway. Dillingham died in Honolulu.

Dillingham played an important role in the economic development of Oahu and Honolulu, particularly during the latter half of his life. However, during his lifetime his business ventures were normally so heavily indebted that he himself was not the principal beneficiary of them; it was the foresight of Dillingham, combined with the fortuitous gullibility of a series of backers who were apparently as naive as he in matters financial, that enabled his son Walter to lead a prosperous life.

• The Bernice Pauahi Bishop Museum in Honolulu, Hawaii, holds Dillingham's business records, letters, and miscellaneous papers and photographs. Further information about Dillingham can be found in a biography commissioned by the B. F. Dillingham Company, Ltd., Paul T. Yardley, *Millstones and Milestones: The Career of B. F. Dillingham* (1981). A short biography can be found in George F. Nellist, ed., *The Story of Hawaii and Its Builders* (1925). An obituary is in the *Pacific Commercial Advertiser* and the *Honolulu Star-Bulletin*, both 8 Apr. 1918.

RICHARD A. HAWKINS

DILLINGHAM, Charles Bancroft (30 May 1868–30 Aug. 1934), theatrical producer, was born in Hartford, Connecticut, the son of Edmund B. Dillingham, an Episcopal minister, and Josephine Potter. From Hartford public schools Dillingham launched himself into journalism. In Chicago he wrote alongside George Ade and Finley Peter Dunne. In 1896, the year of his marriage to actress Jennie Yeamans, he was doubling as the *New York Sun*'s drama critic and as an aspiring playwright. His failed play, *Ten P.M.* (1896), caught the eye of producer Charles Frohman, who hired him to adapt a French farce. He became Frohman's press agent, his general righthand man on Frohman's play-gathering expeditions to England. In 1898 Dillingham became Julia Marlowe's production manager, and in 1903 he began a producing career that ended more than two hundred shows later.

Dillingham's fame dawned with *Mademoiselle Modiste* (1905), the first of nine Victor Herbert operettas. Its "Kiss Me Again" became the signature of Fritzi Scheff, from then on a Dillingham star. Herbert's *The Red Mill* (1906) featured another star who stayed with Dillingham for decades, the nonchalant acrobatic clown Fred Stone, as well as Broadway's first illuminated sign, a windmill in front of the theater with electric lights hanging from its blades.

The genial, expansive Dillingham inspired strong personal loyalties. Richard Rodgers wrote, "He was a tall, courtly, neatly mustached gentleman who treated me as if I were doing him the greatest honor merely by visiting him." Ethan Mordden, historian of the musical theater, called Dillingham's productions for Stone "clean shows, friendly shows, with a few thrills, some hurdy-gurdy slapstick and sweethearts to toodle."

Dillingham's musicals were always large. In 1910 he helped build the Globe, which became the flagship of his increasingly far-flung theatrical holdings. The Globe's roof could open on warm summer evenings. Its first show, *The Old Town* (1910), had Stone jumping in and out of a spinning lariat and a beautiful, kilted chorus playing bagpipes against a glowing California backdrop.

In 1911 Dillingham began a long association with Jerome Kern, although Kern's best work was usually done for others. Dillingham had better luck with Irving Berlin. In 1913, the year of Dillingham's second marriage, to actress Eileen Kearney (he had no children in either marriage), Dillingham hired the current "ragtime" king to write the first Broadway ragtime musical, *Watch Your Step* (1914) for the creators of the Dancing Craze, Vernon and Irene Castle. Berlin's biographer says *Watch Your Step*'s orchestrator taught Berlin to write for the theater.

Berlin wrote *Stop, Look, Listen!* (1915) for Dillingham, but the show foundered because of the antics of its star, the notorious Gaby Deslys, Europe's hottest ticket. Dillingham is said to have finally told an aide, "Take her around and show her the town, take her over to the Statue of Liberty; take her for a nice long ride up and down Manhattan." When Deslys asked why, he said, "I just wanted you to get a good look at the city, my dear, because you're never going to see it again—that is, at my expense."

In 1914 Dillingham acquired the Hippodrome Theater, temporarily Broadway's largest, and there he presented vaudevillean musicals such as *Hip Hip Hooray* (1915) with John Philip Sousa and a company of skiers. Soon to the huge stage came swimmer Annette Kellerman and two hundred mermaids. *The Big Show* (1916) introduced ballerina Anna Pavlova to the United States along with ballplaying elephants and the song "Poor Butterfly."

Dillingham's collaborations with Florenz Ziegfeld had begun in 1912. In 1916 they acquired the large but out-of-the-way Century Theater, and there they scored a hit with *The Century Girl*, with music by both Herbert and Kern, heavenly sets by Joseph Urban, and a finale in which "the Laces of the World" promenaded. Its successor, *Miss 1917*, was a legendary flop. Urban's groves of trees losing their leaves as the seasons changed were ironically symbolic. Kern and Herbert fought over whose songs Vivienne Segal should sing. After a five-hour dress rehearsal, the two producers spent the night "reshuffling, chopping and tearing their hair." The show still ran until half-past midnight and bankrupted their Century Amusement Corporation.

The year 1917 was a turning point for Dillingham's brand of musical theater. He still had Stone, diving horses, and a locomotive full of hoboes, but in that year Kern, P. G. Wodehouse, and Guy Bolton created *Leave It to Jane*, an intimate musical comedy that subordinated spectacle and star turns to witty, contemporary lyrics and storytelling. Dillingham now starred the Castles' young successors, Fred and Adele Astaire. In their 1919 *Apple Blossoms*, Dillingham's English director invented the Astaires' signature dance, the Oompah Trot.

Dillingham passed the Hippodrome to B. F. Keith in 1922. As the twenties boomed, he completed his string of homes and apartments with a large house in Palm Beach, Florida. His clothes were always hand-tailored; he pampered his stars with chauffeured Rolls-Royces. He had boasted that his *Man and Superman* (1905) was the first production to make George Bernard Shaw any money, and for several years in the 1920s he focused on nonmusical productions. These

included *Bulldog Drummond* (1921) and, in 1924, Frederick Lonsdale's *Aren't We All?* In 1925 Lonsdale's *The Last of Mrs. Cheyney* cemented Ina Claire's claim as the leading American comedienne of manners.

In that same year Kern's *Sunny* (introducing the classic "Who?") began a run of 517 performances. It was Dillingham's last success. Perhaps what the *New York Times* called his "1890s convictions"—the theater as a place of beauty and a forum for the exchange of ideas—had suddenly been overtaken by the times. Perhaps his attention to production detail—or his luck—simply flagged. His two musical comedies with Beatrice Lillie—her first in the United States—failed. Goaded by Ziegfeld's new theater, Dillingham splurged. His 1927 *Lucky*, Broadway's first $6.60 ticket, lost $250,000.

By 1930 Dillingham was producing on a shoestring in smaller theaters. He appeared briefly in a Ziegfeld-produced talking motion picture, *Glorifying the American Girl* (1929). The stock market collapse that soon bankrupted Ziegfeld claimed Arthur Hammerstein and Dillingham as its first victims. He remortgaged the Globe, his last asset.

During Kern's *The Cat and the Fiddle* (1931) Dillingham apparently absconded with one week's receipts and retired in disgrace. A friend collected donations so he could live on $100 weekly. His 1933 bankruptcy petition listed liabilities of $7 million and assets of $100,000. The estates of his longtime partners, Abe Erlanger and Ziegfeld, were the largest creditors. In 1934 he accepted a salary for lending his name to Leonard Sillman's revue *New Faces*. He died at the Hotel Astor in New York City.

During the first third of the twentieth century Dillingham partially succeeded in combating theatrical triviality and vulgarity, especially by encouraging serious playwrights. However, the lavish, decorous musicals especially associated with his name were swept away by livelier, more original musical comedies. Like many a producer, Dillingham is remembered for his kingly manners and his complete downfall.

• No full-length biography of Dillingham has been published, although he is mentioned at significant length in the biographies of his contemporaries. These include Lawrence Bergreen, *As Thousands Cheer: The Life of Irving Berlin* (1990); Billie Burke, *With a Feather on My Nose* (1949); Gerald Bordman, *Jerome Kern: His Life and Music* (1980) and *Days to Be Happy, Years to Be Sad: The Life and Music of Vincent Youmans* (1982); Randolph Carter, *The World of Flo Ziegfeld* (1974); Daniel Frohman and Isaac Marcosson, *Charles Frohman* (1916); James Gardiner, *Gaby Deslys: A Fatal Attraction* (1986); Richard Rodgers, *Musical Stages: An Autobiography* (1975); Tim Satchell, *Astaire* (1987); and Ian Whitcomb, *Irving Berlin and Ragtime America* (1987). Ethan Mordden, *Broadway Babies: The People Who Made the American Musical* (1983), and Bordman, *Chronicle of the American Musical* (1992), are invaluable general sources. An obituary is in the *New York Times*, 31 Aug. 1934.

JAMES ROSS MOORE

DILLON, Clarence (27 Sept. 1882–14 Apr. 1979), investment banker, was born in San Antonio, Texas, the son of Samuel Lapowski, a merchant, and Bertha Steenback, the daughter of Swedish Lutheran immigrant mine and land owners. Samuel, a Polish Jewish immigrant, took his mother's maiden name around 1900. Clarence showed mathematical ability at Harvard, and after an undistinguished career he graduated in 1905. He became associated with Newport Mining Company and Milwaukee Coke & Coal Company, firms headed by the father of Armin A. Schlesinger, a close friend from his college days.

In 1907 Dillon fractured his skull in a freak accident. Ordered to rest, he left with his bride, Ann McEldin Douglass, for Europe, where he studied painting and architecture for pleasure. Their son, Clarence Douglas Dillon, born in Geneva on 21 August 1909, later became President John F. Kennedy's secretary of the treasury. The couple also had a daughter, Dorothy Anne. The Dillons returned to Milwaukee early in 1910. Clarence bought a half interest in the Milwaukee Machine Tool Company from his brother-in-law and became president. The partners sold the moderately prosperous firm at a good price in 1913.

William A. Phillips, a Harvard classmate, introduced Dillon to his employer, William A. Read, a leading bond underwriter. Dillon accepted a position in Read's Chicago office. At first, he later acknowledged, "Banking meant less to me than most things," but he soon found himself "interested, then enthusiastic." At Read's insistence, in March 1914 Dillon moved to the Wall Street headquarters where he became Read's protégé. He was made a partner on 1 April 1916. Six days later, Read died, and the other partners asked Dillon to "take the helm." From 1920 on, he headed William A. Read Company.

Bernard Baruch, whom President Woodrow Wilson had appointed chairman of the War Industries Board in 1918, recruited Dillon to serve as one of his three executive assistants. Dillon "had already made a mark as one of the keenest minds in Wall Street, and was to make a much more impressive one after the war . . . ," Baruch noted in his memoirs. He took Dillon to Versailles as an assistant on the German Reparations Committee.

Dillon returned to Wall Street after the peace conference. On 1 January 1921, he changed the firm's name to Dillon, Read & Company. The firm's first major underwriting success was a project to save Goodyear Tire & Rubber Company from bankruptcy. The syndicate formed by Dillon, Read provided the distressed manufacturer with working capital and funds to repay its bank loans. Dillon represented bond holders on the three-person voting trust, which took over control from Frank A. Seiberling, Goodyear's founder. Dillon, Read's constructive role in the May 1921 reorganization was recognized in an out-of-court settlement with dissident shareholders in May 1927, terminating the voting trust; the firm acted as bankers when twenty-one issues were refinanced to reduce fixed charges.

In the spring of 1921 Dillon, Read outbid the London Rothschilds for a $50 million Brazilian government issue, and for the remainder of the decade it was the leading lender to Brazil. One of the first American investment banks to get German business after World War I, Dillon, Read ranked third among American firms in volume of foreign flotations. By 1929 it was also the most prominent firm dealing in Canadian issues.

Investment trusts, familiar to British investors since the late 1800s, enabled small shareholders to diversify risk. Dillon perceived an untapped American market for them. United States & Foreign Securities Corporation, organized in October 1924, was the first such trust in the United States formed by an investment bank. In 1928 the $10 million surplus accumulated by the trust was used to form United States & International Securities. In 1958 Dillon, Read launched the first sizable closed-end investment company to appear after the 1929 crash, the $33-million American–South African Investment Company, which held diversified shares of South Africa's firms, especially gold mines.

The heirs of the Dodge Brothers Manufacturing Company sold the third largest automaker to Dillon, Read in 1925 for a net cash price of $146 million, $14 million above what General Motors, through J. P. Morgan & Company, had bid. Dillon reincorporated the firm, sold to the public $159 million in Dodge bonds, preferred stock, and 56.7 percent of the non-voting common (Class A), while retaining the remaining 43.3 percent as well as all of Class B (voting) common. Walter P. Chrysler acquired Dodge from Dillon, Read for common stock with a market value of $160 million in the summer of 1928 in the largest consolidation in the history of the auto industry up to that time. In January 1926 Dillon had sold 1.1 million shares of National Cash Register Company stock for $55 million, the largest common stock offering until then.

Dillon had quickly convinced the financial community "of his inherent honesty, his unfailing dependability and his dauntless courage," B. C. Forbes stated in his magazine on 15 May 1925. The eminent business editor and publisher called Dillon "the brightest rising star in the financial firmament." By the mid-1920s some were hailing Dillon as "The Wizard of Wall Street," second only to J. P. Morgan (1837–1913). The *American Review of Reviews* described Dillon as a new leader who had "joined the long procession of men who have made Wall Street famous."

By 1927 Dillon, Read ranked third among investment banks. Over the next four years, as many issues of inferior quality flooded the market, its share fell to 4.75 percent. Dillon, Read issued almost $4 billion from the beginning of 1919 to mid-1933. On 30 June 1933 only 7.7 percent of the total were in default. A buyer of all securities sponsored by the firm over those fifteen years who sold the defaulted ones on 30 June

1933 would have earned over 4.5 percent a year over the entire period and would have had enough cash income to make up the capital loss on the defaulted obligations.

Dillon pointed this out to the Senate Banking Committee investigating stock exchange practices as the first witness when the series of famous hearings resumed after a three-month hiatus. However, the next morning the front page of the *New York Times* of 4 October 1933 headlined the Senate Banking Committee's finding that Dillon, Read came to rule $90 million in its investment trusts' assets, with a $5.1 million initial investment. The firm insisted on the "splendid showing" of its trusts. Between the end of 1927 and mid-1933, as the Dow Jones Index fell 51 percent, shares of United States & Foreign declined only 28 percent. United States & International lost only 14 percent of its end-1930 value by mid-1933, while the Dow Jones dropped 41 percent. Dillon urged the committee "to find the way to reopen the markets for long-term capital so that the requirements of industry may be met and so that labor may be reemployed." He wanted the 1933 Securities Act amended to provide continuing current information on corporations for the investing public. According to his son, "The hearings turned him off investment banking. . . . the new securities laws made it harder to try new financings. He got bored."

In 1934 Dillon bought a leading Bordeaux wine estate, Château Haut-Brion, to which he devoted a great deal of attention. He subsequently expanded his French holdings, acquiring several Paris hotels and shares of Baccarat Glass. He was made an officer of the Legion of Honor in 1935 and a commander in 1938. In 1938 James V. Forrestal, a partner since 1923, became president of Dillon, Read. Dillon remained chairman, though no longer actively managing the firm, and, by virtue of his holdings and knowledge, remained the ultimate source of power. Dillon continued to influence strategy, his son, who had joined the firm in 1931, serving as his liaison. The two were the stockholders when Dillon, Read became a corporation on 12 March 1945. C. Douglas Dillon was chairman of the board from 1946 until he entered government service in 1953. Clarence Dillon retired from active business practice in the 1950s but continued to exercise ownership control and to oppose undue risk taking by the firm. He agreed to retire completely in September 1971. His son became chairman of the executive committee, a position he held for the next decade. Dillon, Read was manager or agent for 6.5 percent of all negotiated issues from 1934 to 1949. It was in first place in private placement of securities and seventh in dollar volume of sealed-bid issues managed. In 1960, as in 1950, it ranked twelfth in underwriting dollar volume. By 1965 Dillon, Read dropped to eighteenth place, rising to sixteenth in 1970 and fifteenth in 1980. Clarence Dillon died in Far Hills, New Jersey, where he had owned an estate since 1928.

• See Robert Sobel, *The Life and Times of Dillon Read* (1991); U.S. Congress, Senate Committee on Banking and Currency, *Stock Exchange Practices*, 73d Cong., 2d sess., Pt. 4 Dillon, Read & Co., 3–13 Oct. 1933 (1933); U.S. District Court New York (Southern District), Corrected Opinion of Harold R. Medina . . . in *United States of America v. Henry S. Morgan* . . . (1954), a comprehensive review of the investment banking industry and Dillon's role in it; Robert C. Perez and Edward F. Willett, *Clarence Dillon: A Wall Street Enigma* (1995); Frank J. Williams, "A New Leader in Finance: Clarence Dillon," *American Review of Reviews* 73 (1926): 146–48; and Vincent Carosso, *Investment Banking in America* (1970). An obituary is in the *New York Times*, 15 Apr. 1979.

BENJAMIN J. KLEBANER

DILLON, John Forrest (25 Dec. 1831–6 May 1914), lawyer, was born in Montgomery County, New York, the son of Thomas Dillon, a hotel owner, and Rosannah Forrest. In 1838 Thomas Dillon brought his family to Davenport, Iowa, a frontier town on the west bank of the Mississippi River, to open a hotel. As one of the first settlers, Thomas Dillon quickly became a trustee and councilman and a member of a group of boosters who worked with the town proprietor to promote development. John F. Dillon was a product of this male, urban, booster ethos. After attending the town's first school, Dillon acquired the rest of his education in the hotel lobbies, newspaper offices, professional offices, semiannual circuit courts, and streets of Davenport, where he learned what he needed to know while making friends and acquiring mentors who would facilitate his professional advancement.

In 1850 Dillon received an M.D. at the Davenport College of Physicians and Surgeons associated with the University of Iowa. Dillon's nascent career as a doctor was cut short, however, by an injury that resulted in a hernia, which made it impossible for him to ride the long distances required by frontier practice. When a lawyer friend in Farmington, Iowa, suggested he become a lawyer and advised him on what books to read, Dillon undertook the study of law by himself; when he had questions or needed guidance in legal practice and procedures, he consulted local lawyers or officials. In 1852 a friend moved his admission to the bar, and Dillon was welcomed into the local legal fraternity. Attorney John D. Cook, a prominent Whig and family friend, took him in as a partner. No doubt because of his disability, which precluded riding the circuit, the members of the local bar nominated Dillon for the position of prosecuting attorney of Scott County; he was elected that year. The next year Dillon married Anna Price, the daughter of Hiram Price, future congressman and commissioner of Indian affairs. The couple became prominent members of Davenport's local elite.

In 1858 Dillon was elected judge of the district court of the Seventh Judicial Circuit of Iowa. In 1862 he was reelected by the unanimous acclaim of the members of the local and circuit bar. In 1863 Dillon, a Republican, was "promoted" to a six-year term on the Supreme Court of Iowa. He performed with such brilliance that he was easily reelected in 1869. However, before his second term commenced, President Ulysses S. Grant appointed him to the U.S. Circuit Court for the Eighth Judicial District, which included the states of Iowa, Minnesota, Missouri, Kansas, Arkansas, Nebraska, and later Colorado. During his tenure he traveled thousands of miles by rail and acquired countless friends and associates in the regional bar.

During Dillon's tenure as judge, in both the Supreme Court of Iowa and the federal circuit court, he codified laws and introduced innovations into the legal process. His *Digest of the Decisions of the Supreme Court of Iowa, 1839–1860* (1860) became a standard work. Dillon encouraged lawyers to seek relief for their clients in federal courts in his *Removal of Causes from State Courts to Federal Courts* (1875), and, as a result, case loads in the Eighth Circuit increased tenfold during his tenure. His most important contribution as a legal thinker was his *Treatise on the Laws of Municipal Corporations* (1872), which, with Thomas M. Cooley's *Constitutional Limitations* (1868), established the theoretical foundations of the so-called laissez-faire constitutionalism, a doctrine that protected individuals and corporations from government regulation and taxation.

Dillon's philosophy of legal formalism suited the need for law to adjust to turbulent times. His ideas were rooted in his reading of Blackstone and Edmund Burke, as well as his approbation of John Marshall, who, Dillon believed, had assured that the constitution would become the "ultimate national protection" of the "rights of life, liberty, property, freedom of commerce, sanctity of contracts, and equality before law" (Dillon, ed., *John Marshall*, vol. 1, p. 385). But Dillon's ideas were equally rooted in his personal and professional experience as an urban booster, a railroad lawyer, and a jurist.

As one of the best known judicial thinkers in the nation in the 1870s, Dillon accepted a position as professor of law at Columbia College in New York and opened a law office on Wall Street. While teaching property and equity, an activity he apparently did not particularly enjoy, he dramatically expanded his practice, becoming the general counsel for the Union Pacific Railroad (of which his uncle Sidney was president), the Western Union Telegraph Company, and the Manhattan Elevated Company, as well as the attorney for Jay Gould and his estate. Within three years Dillon chose to concentrate on his practice and resigned his position at Columbia. In ensuing years he became a regular speaker at bar association meetings. He also added a useful compendium of railroad laws, *Pacific Railroad Laws* (1890), and his derivative treatise, *The Laws and Jurisprudence of England and America* (1894), to his published works. During 1891–1892 Dillon served as president of the American Bar Association. By the time of his death in New York City from the flu, Dillon had appeared as counsel before the U.S. Supreme Court more times than any other lawyer in the country.

In both Davenport and New York, Dillon and his wife lived the genteel lifestyle of the provincial professional upper-middle class drawn to the metropolis. Anna Price Dillon had to accept the fragmented character of the life of a "circuit court widow," spending much of her time moving from city to city and living in rented quarters with her husband, who was on the circuit six to eight months a year for over twenty years. The couple had four children; a fifth died in infancy. Over the years, in addition to traveling for Dillon's work, they visited family and friends across the West and journeyed to Europe several times. Increasingly the Dillons traveled for the benefit of the health of their divorced daughter, Annie Dillon Oliver, who suffered from lameness in her foot and chronic "neuralgia." It was on such a trip that Mrs. Dillon and Annie perished on 4 July 1898 when the French liner *La Bourgogne* collided with a freighter off Halifax and quickly sunk. True to his character, John Dillon hired a ship to try to recover the bodies of his wife and daughter; however, this effort failed. Dillon never really recovered from the loss but assuaged his grief by having privately published *Anna Price Dillon, Memoir and Memorials* (1900), an intriguing portrait of his wife and family.

• The John F. Dillon Papers in the Iowa State Historical Society in Iowa City are fragmentary. The standard work on Dillon's ideas is Clyde E. Jacobs, *Law Writers and the Courts, the Influence of Thomas M. Cooley, Christopher G. Tiedeman, and John F. Dillon upon American Constitutional Law* (1954). See also Thomas G. Barnes, "Introduction," in the Legal Classics Library's reprint of John F. Dillon, *The Laws and Jurisprudence of England and America* (1995). Still useful is Edward H. Stiles, "John F. Dillon," in *Recollections and Sketches of Notable Lawyers and Public Men of Early Iowa* (1916), and Stiles, "Judge John F. Dillon," *Annals of Iowa* (1909). Both note many of his numerous published addresses and court decisions, as well as court and bar association proceedings concerning Dillon. An obituary is in the *New York Times*, 6 May 1914.

TIMOTHY R. MAHONEY

DILLON, Sidney (7 May 1812–9 June 1892), railroad constructor and financier, was born in Northampton, Montgomery County, New York, the son of Timothy Dillon, a farmer who had fought in the revolutionary war. His mother's name is unknown. He grew up in humble circumstances and at the age of seven accepted work as a water boy on the Mohawk & Hudson Railroad from Albany to Schenectady, New York. He carried water to the laborers who were employed on the grating and received one dollar per week for his efforts.

When Dillon's first assignment was completed, he went on to perform similar humble tasks on the Rensselaer and Saratoga line. He found an opportunity to expand his horizons through accepting work in Sharon, Massachusetts, on the Boston and Providence Road, where he rose slowly to the position of overseer and then foreman on the line. He worked for the Stonington Railroad and the Western Railroad of Massachusetts before gaining his first contract for railroad building, which he completed successfully in 1840. In

1841 he married Hannah Smith of Amherst, Massachusetts; the couple had two children.

Whether intentionally or by default, Dillon had acquired the skills of contracting for railroad work. During the 1840s and 1850s he worked on the Troy and Schenectady Road, built twenty-nine miles of the Central Railroad of New Jersey, and constructed a tunnel from Grand Central Station in New York City to the Harlem River (this work was done for Cornelius Vanderbilt). In all of these tasks Dillon appears to have succeeded through a rare combination of technical skill, bulldog tenacity, and a rugged physique that allowed him to continue working when others were exhausted. He had made his fortune by 1860, but he continued to ply new opportunities and in the mid-1860s came upon the enterprise that would mark the acme of his career: the building of the first transcontinental railroad.

The desire for a railroad to connect the East and West coasts was accelerated by the events of the Civil War, and in July 1862 President Abraham Lincoln signed the bill that initiated the process. Dillon entered the picture in 1865 when he purchased a large amount of stock in the Crédit Mobilier, which became involved in the affairs of the Union Pacific Company that was building from east to west, where it would meet with the Central Pacific. Dillon directed the overall course of construction for the Union Pacific for three crucial years (1866–1869), and he figured prominently in the ceremony at which the last spike was driven at Promontory Point, Utah. He kept one of the spikes in his possession for the rest of his life. Again it appeared that he had reached a summit in his career and that no additional efforts would be necessary.

Early in his construction career Dillon had made a practice of accepting shares of stock as payment for his work in lieu of cash. By 1870 he had accumulated a substantial fortune and lived comfortably in New York City and in a country home in Connecticut. However, he remained active in the affairs of the Union Pacific Railroad and was simultaneously occupied with managing his fortune in stocks. Dillon first met the financier Jay Gould in the early 1870s. Although the two men appeared to have little in common, their relationship blossomed into one of mutual admiration, and they became firm and lasting business associates. Dillon assisted Gould in many of his financial endeavors during the heyday of railroad construction during the 1870s and 1880s; in return Dillon was rewarded with a place on the boards of directors of numerous companies.

Dillon served twice as president of the Union Pacific Railroad Company (11 Mar. 1874–10 June 1884; 26 Nov. 1890–27 Apr. 1892). In the first instance he became active in a side business of raising cattle. One byproduct was that the town of Dillon, Montana, was named for him. However, Dillon found he was unequal to the task of meeting the financial crisis that developed in 1883, and he resigned his post while remaining on the board of directors of the Union Pacific. For a time he enjoyed himself fishing and sailing off the coast of Long Island while his replacement in the presidency, Charles F. Adams, who represented Boston interests, struggled with the exigencies created by the financial crisis. In 1890 Dillon was again persuaded to take the reins of leadership in the company. At age seventy-eight he struggled manfully but could not cope with the enormous demands of the position. He resigned from the presidency in April 1892 and was immediately voted into the post of chair of the board of directors (a spot that was created specifically for him). Dillon died soon afterward in New York City.

Dillon exhibited great energy, verve, intelligence, and skill during his long career in railroad construction. More truly a Horatio Alger success story than most railroad magnates, Dillon rose to the top of his profession through a combination of skill, luck, and endurance. What seems most consistent and remarkable about the man was the extent to which he was absorbed in his work; he could easily have retired in 1860, in 1869, or in 1884, but he chose instead to carry forth the business of the "iron rail" into the American West. There is little doubt as to the importance of his career; he helped to bring the construction methods he had learned in upstate New York during the early nineteenth century to the Rocky Mountains and beyond in the latter part of the century.

Although Dillon is recognizable first and foremost as a railroad man, he belongs most truly to the larger spirit of business enterprise that was active in the mid- to late nineteenth century; a spirit that relished the prospect of large challenges in the areas of transportation, communication, and finance. Dillon was a true representative of the heroic age of enterprise in the realm of American transportation.

• Dillon's business papers are in the Union Pacific Archives held in Omaha, Nebr., and Portland, Oreg. Dillon himself described the importance of the transcontinental railroad in "Historic Moments: Driving the Last Spike of the Union Pacific," *Scribner's Magazine*, Aug. 1892, pp. 253–59. The best way to find information about Dillon is to examine the books relative to the Union Pacific Railroad, including Maury Klein, *Union Pacific: The Birth of a Railroad 1862–1893* (1987); Robert G. Athearn, *Union Pacific Country* (1971); and Klein, *The Life and Legend of Jay Gould* (1986). A substantial obituary is in the *New York Times*, 10 June 1892.

SAMUEL WILLARD CROMPTON

DIMOCK, Susan (24 Apr. 1847–7 May 1875), physician and surgeon, was born in Washington, North Carolina, the daughter of Henry Dimock and Mary Malvina Owens. Her father, the son of a physician, was the editor of a small newspaper, while her mother, a strong influence in Dimock's life, taught her at home and in a private school that she had organized. At age thirteen Dimock entered the Washington Academy, where she studied Latin and became interested in medicine. A family physician loaned her books and took her on house calls. The Civil War interrupted her studies when Washington became occupied by Union troops, forcing townspeople to evacuate. Her father died during the occupation, and with her mother, she traveled north to live with relatives in Sterling, Massachusetts. There she befriended Elizabeth Greene, the daughter of Colonel W. B. Greene, a wealthy Boston reformer. While teaching in a local school, Dimock became acquainted through Greene with Dr. Marie Zakrzewska, a pioneer woman doctor in Boston and founder of the New England Hospital for Women and Children. Zakrzewska gave her medical books and encouraged her to begin clinical study at her hospital. In 1867, she was rejected, together with the English pioneer woman doctor, Sophia Jex-Blake, for admission to Harvard Medical School.

On the suggestion of Dr. Zakrzewska and with the financial support of the Greene family, she applied in 1868 to the University of Zurich, which had just become the first university in Europe to admit a woman student. She sailed for Europe in September 1868 and began her studies at Zurich in the fall term. Dimock found the professors friendly and the students supportive. "Oh, it is so nice to get here," she wrote her mother, "at a word, what I have been begging for in Boston for three years." She became a leader among the small number of women studying medicine in Zurich. Completing the normally five-year course in three years, she wrote a dissertation on "The Different Forms of Puerperal Fever" and became the fourth woman to graduate in medicine on 26 October 1871. At her dissertation defense, her professor of anatomy, Hermann von Meyer, announced that "You have shown by your example that it is possible for women to devote themselves to the medical profession without denying your female nature." On leaving Zurich, she did further clinical study in Vienna and Paris, returning to the United States in July 1872 as one of the two or three best-prepared women physicians in America.

Dimock then began a three-year appointment as resident physician at the New England Hospital for Women and Children. She was a pioneer among women physicians in performing a number of important surgical operations, including a case of vesico-vaginal fistula. Dr. Samuel Cabot, a Boston friend and mentor, predicted that had she lived she would have become a great surgeon. She acquired a reputation as a shrewd diagnostician and a capable manager. She ran the hospital, one observer reported, "like a little Napoleon." The hospital's school of nursing owed much to her energy and organizing skill. Hospital record-keeping was improved, and the fever chart was introduced. After her three-year term was completed, she was offered a renewal and accepted it on the condition that she be given a five-month leave of absence to revisit Europe.

In April 1875 she set sail with Elizabeth Greene and another friend on the *Schiller* for England, but the ship foundered on a reef off the Scilly Islands and went down on 7 May. Her remains were returned to Boston for burial. The funeral was attended by many of the most influential physicians of the city. Mary Putnam Jacobi, America's best-known woman physician, described Dimock as having been "as fresh and girlish as if such qualities had never been pronounced by com-

petent authorities to be incompatible with medical attainments. She had . . . a certain flower-like beauty, a softness and elegance of appearance." The memory of Dimock was important to many women, said Jacobi, "in the difficult enterprise of hewing out for women an equal place in the medical profession."

• A few unpublished manuscript letters from Dimock, along with other materials, are in the Sophia Smith Collection at Smith College. Many of her other letters, especially those from Zurich, were published in *Memoir of Susan Dimock* (1875), edited anonymously by Ednah Dow Cheney. Her Zurich experience is covered in Hanny Rohner, *Die ersten 30 Jahre des medizinischen Frauenstudiums an der Universität Zürich 1867–1897* (1972), and in Victor Böhmert, *Das Studieren der Frauen mit besonderer Rücksicht auf das Studium der Medicin* (1872). Two useful, brief accounts of her life are Irma Henderson-Smathers, "Medical Women of North Carolina," *Medical Woman's Journal*, 56 (Nov. 1949): 38–40, and "Nineteenth Annual Banquet of Women's Medical Society of New York State in Honor of Dr. Eliza M. Mosher's Fifty Years in Medicine," *Medical Woman's Journal*, 32 (1925): 221–22. Obituaries appeared in *Medical Record*, 15 May 1875, *Boston Medical and Surgical Journal*, 10 June 1875; and *Boston Daily Transcript*, 2 June 1875.

THOMAS NEVILLE BONNER

DINGLEY, Nelson, Jr. (15 Feb. 1832–14 Jan. 1899), politician and congressman, was born in Durham, Maine, the son of Nelson Dingley, a farmer, owner of a general store, and tavern keeper, and Jane Lambert. Dingley went to schools in Parkman and Unity, Maine, read avidly, and took an intense interest in politics. He started a diary when he was in his early teens and added regular entries until he became fatally ill. He spent several years at Waterville Academy and continued on at Waterville College (now Colby) until 1853, when he left in a dispute with the faculty. He finished his undergraduate work at Dartmouth College, graduating with the class of 1855. He studied law and was admitted to the bar. Dingley married Salome McKenney in 1857; they had five children.

Dingley's life changed in 1856, when he became part owner and editor of the *Lewiston Journal*. He promised readers that the paper would "give our hearty support to the Republican party" as long as it remained true to its principles (Edward Nelson Dingley, pp. 46–47). Dingley was outspoken against slavery, and his newspaper work during the late 1850s drew him into the politics of the Maine Republicans as the Civil War approached. He became a close associate of James G. Blaine at this time. By 1861 Dingley was selected to run for the state legislature from his county. He won with a small majority and was reelected three succeeding times. He twice served as Speaker of the Maine House of Representatives. The voters returned him to the legislature in 1868 and again in 1873. In state politics Dingley was identified with the temperance wing of the Republican party.

In 1873 Dingley's party nominated him as its candidate for governor. He defeated the Democratic choice, Joseph Titcomb, by more than 12,000 votes. In his 1874 inaugural address, Dingley said that railroads were "public works" and that it was "the right and duty of the state to see to it that they are so managed as to serve the public" (Edward Nelson Dingley, p. 109). During his administration, railroads found their taxes to the state increased. He was reelected in 1875 for a second one-year term.

For the next five years, Dingley participated actively in state politics. He led the Republican opposition to the inflationary Greenback movement. In 1881 Blaine's nomination as secretary of state in President James A. Garfield's cabinet brought Congressman William P. Frye to the U.S. Senate as Blaine's successor. In turn, Dingley was chosen as the Republican nominee for Frye's seat from the Second Congressional District in Maine. His Democratic opponent withdrew before the election on 12 September 1881, and Dingley won easily. He was reelected in 1882 and served in the House of Representatives until his death.

Dingley devoted himself to the protective tariff as a House member, immersing himself in the minutiae of that subject. As Thomas B. Reed, a House colleague from Maine, put it, "He'd rather have a pad and pencil on his knee than a pretty girl" (Bolles, p. 20). A small, bald man with a full mustache and beard, Dingley became an advocate of the gold standard and the encouragement of the American merchant marine. He assisted the chairman of the Ways and Means Committee, William McKinley, in the preparation of what became known as the McKinley Tariff of 1890. Dingley opposed the Democratic tariff policy in the second Cleveland administration that resulted in the Wilson-Gorman Tariff of 1894. When the Republicans recaptured the House of Representatives after the 1894 elections, the new Speaker, Reed, named Dingley as chairman of the Ways and Means Committee.

When McKinley won the 1896 presidential election, he offered Dingley the position of secretary of the Treasury. The congressman declined on account of his uncertain health, saying, "I can do more for the success of your administration where I am than in the Treasury" (Edward Nelson Dingley, p. 413). As Dingley guided a tariff bill through the House during the spring of 1897, the wife of a Democratic congressman watched his performance and reported in her diary, "Dingley of Maine is ill, querulous, and resentful of any criticism of the bill bearing his name" (Webb and Webb, pp. 6–7). The measure raised duties on wool, silk, cattle hides, industrial goods, and luxury products. With a heavy Republican majority in the House, the bill passed easily on 31 March 1897. In the Senate version and the conference committee that followed, the Dingley Tariff grew even more protectionist before it became law in late July 1897. As prosperity returned during the late 1890s, high-tariff Republicans gave the credit to the Dingley law. When attitudes toward protectionism cooled after 1900, the Dingley Tariff was seen as the embodiment of business lobbyists and special interest groups shaping tariff policy for their own purposes.

Dingley was an important figure during the second year of the McKinley administration. He spoke out for the gold standard and had a significant role in shaping revenue policy during the war with Spain. The president appointed him to the Joint High Commission to resolve disputes over Canada with British and Canadian delegates. Dingley participated in the deliberations of that body during the autumn of 1898. In December he fell ill with pneumonia, and his weak heart gave out. He died in Washington, D.C.

Dingley's historical fame rests on the tariff law that bears his name. Praised by Republicans when it was passed, it has receded in historical importance except as it seems to represent a failed economic policy of protectionism. Dingley's legislative career has not been explored, and he has faded in comparison to Reed and McKinley, his House colleagues. He was one of those lawmakers who were important in their own time but whose effect on history was transitory.

• A small collection of Dingley Family Papers is at the Fogler Library, University of Maine, Orono. It includes an autobiography that Dingley wrote during the early 1870s, some of his diaries, a few of his own letters, and a small number of documents from Dingley's gubernatorial terms. The William McKinley Papers, Library of Congress, have several Dingley letters. Some of Dingley's speeches were published. The only biography was written by his son, Edward Nelson Dingley, *The Life and Times of Nelson Dingley, Jr.* (1902). Dingley's service on the Ways and Means Committee is covered in Donald R. Kennon and Rebecca M. Rogers, *The Committee on Ways and Means: A Bicentennial History, 1789–1989* (1989). For the tariff measure that bears his name, see U.S. Congress, House, Committee on Ways and Means, *Tariff Hearings before the Committee on Ways and Means*, 54th Cong., 2d sess., 1897, H. Doc. 338, and Lewis L. Gould, "Diplomats in the Lobby: Franco-American Relations and the Dingley Tariff of 1897," *The Historian* 39 (Aug. 1977): 659–80. Comments about Dingley are in Walter Webb and Terrell Webb, eds., *Washington Wife: Journal of Ellen Maury Slayden from 1897–1919* (1963), and Blair Bolles, *Tyrant from Illinois: Uncle Joe Cannon's Experiment with Personal Power* (1951). See also U.S. Congress, *Memorial Addresses on the Life and Character of Nelson Dingley* (1899). Obituaries are in the *New York Times*, 14 Jan. 1899, and the *Lewiston Weekly Journal*, 14 Jan. and 19 Jan. 1899.

LEWIS L. GOULD

DINKELOO, John Gerard (28 Feb. 1918–15 June 1981), architect, was born in Holland, Michigan, the son of William Dinkeloo, a painter and contractor, and Bessie Brouwer. He attended Hope College from 1936 to 1939 and received a bachelor's degree in architectural engineering from the University of Michigan in 1942. In that same year he began work as a designer with the six-year-old firm of Skidmore, Owings and Merrill (SOM) in Chicago. Shortly thereafter, he put his career on hold to join the war effort. From 1943 to 1946 he served as a lieutenant in the U.S. Navy in the South and Central Pacific. Before departing for duty, he married Thelma Ann Van Dyke in 1943; they had seven children.

Following the war Dinkeloo returned to SOM's Chicago office to become chief of production in charge of working drawings. He functioned primarily as a production man, leaving the designing to colleagues such as Gordon Bunshaft and Harry Weese, who later became famous for their work. Taking advantage of the postwar construction boom and government contacts resulting from wartime commissions such as Oak Ridge, Tennessee (1942), SOM increasingly obtained large government commissions—military installations, public housing projects, and veterans hospitals. Legions of young architects like Dinkeloo provided the firm with a surplus of talent in exchange for experience.

In 1950 Dinkeloo left SOM to become the chief of production for Eero Saarinen and Associates in Bloomfield Hills, Michigan. In charge of technical development, working drawings, specifications, and construction supervision, Dinkeloo advanced to full partner in 1956. At this time Saarinen's firm was involved with the construction of the General Motors Technical Center in Warren, Michigan (1956), one of the largest and most technically sophisticated postwar projects. For his part, Dinkeloo pioneered the usage of structural Neoprene gaskets for the sealing of exterior walls. Adapted from a technique used to seal automobile windshields, the gasket was remarkably easy and economical to produce, install, and maintain. Over the next decade Dinkeloo refined this and other glazing techniques until it was said that his glass facades stood technologically in a class by themselves.

In the fall of 1961 Saarinen died. Dinkeloo and fellow partners Kevin Roche and Joseph N. Lacy endeavored to complete his many unfinished works, while simultaneously relocating the office to Hamden, Connecticut, following a decision made by Saarinen the previous spring. Ultimately, the office constructed ten major Saarinen projects, including the Trans World Airlines Terminal at Kennedy International Airport (1961), the Deere & Company headquarters in Moline, Illinois (1964), the CBS Building in New York (1965), and the Gateway Arch of the Jefferson National Expansion Memorial in St. Louis, Missouri (1965).

Colleagues credited the successful transition of the office to the courage and strength of Dinkeloo who, according to Roche, was also instrumental in pushing the office toward new goals. Dinkeloo understood that in order to complete Saarinen's work, the office had to be healthy and vital, which meant that a new practice had to be established with new commissions. The first such project was the Oakland Museum (1968). Removed from consideration after Saarinen's death, the reorganized firm had to request an interview with the museum's selection committee. After their entry was chosen and built, the final design was widely acclaimed. The unique urbanistic approach provides for terraced public spaces on top of the museum complex.

No longer executing Saarinen's designs, the firm changed its name in 1966 to Kevin Roche John Din-keloo and Associates. The change was in accordance with Saarinen's wishes that the title be changed within a five-year period following his death, when the new leaders of the firm would have emerged. By many counts, Dinkeloo had the right qualities for such leadership. Fellow architect Walter McQuade later wrote of Dinkeloo in the *Journal of the AIA* (Aug. 1981): "He was affable, unflappable, handsomely saturnine but never sarcastic, one who bore no grudges. . . . His laconic, low-key approach defused contractors and clients alike. He was also practical; he knew how to invest a firm's cash on hand for the best available return."

Dinkeloo frequently presented technical papers before professional societies and is credited with major technical innovations. First, to reduce heat load and energy costs in buildings with substantial glazing, he placed a metallized mirrorlike glass on exterior walls. Because this glass deflects heat, air conditioning requirements could be substantially reduced. Second, he was the first to use Cor-Ten steel, a low-alloy weathering steel that oxidizes to acquire a dark reddish, protective patina, in building construction. Its great strength makes possible the reduction of support columns and thus provides for more spacious interiors and larger windows. Along with his pioneering usage of Neoprene gaskets, these innovations allowed building construction to keep pace with modern design, particularly the usage of glass curtain walls.

Despite his accomplishments, Dinkeloo maintained a low profile throughout his career. Both he and his partner Roche were known for their reticence—as well as pragmatism. To Dinkeloo the process of building, and the omnipresent search for solutions, defined the nature of architecture. When discussing design in *Architectural Forum* (Mar. 1974), Dinkeloo stated, "You have to understand how we do things. And if you understand that, you can almost forget about design—because design is the way something is carried out."

The success of numerous high-profile commissions gained Roche Dinkeloo much acclaim. In 1974 the company was awarded the Architectural Firm Award, the highest honor that the American Institute of Architecture confers on a firm. Many of their well-known works, such as the Ford Foundation Building (1967) and the plan for the Metropolitan Museum of Art (1969–1989), incorporate vast expanses of glass wrapped around indoor gardens or courtyards.

Dinkeloo continued to work out of the firm's Connecticut office until his death while on vacation in Fredericksburg, Virginia. A talented engineer with an innate sense of the proper use of materials, Dinkeloo was instrumental in the advancement of modern architecture. As a key figure in three of America's most influential architectural firms in the second half of the twentieth century, Dinkeloo helped facilitate an era of distinctive design.

• A comprehensive look at the firm's development and work is Yukio Futagawa, ed., *Kevin Roche, John Dinkeloo & Asso-*

ciates, 1962–1975 (1977), with an introduction by Henry-Russell Hitchcock, which includes a bibliography. More commentary on the firm's early work is in the entire issue of *Architectural Forum* 140 (Mar. 1974). Analysis of the firm's later work is in the entire issue of *Architecture and Urbanism* (Aug. 1987). Obituaries are in the *Journal of the AIA* 70 (Aug. 1981) and the *New York Times*, 16 June 1981.

LISA A. TORRANCE

DINSMOOR, Robert (7 Oct. 1757–16 Mar. 1836), poet, was born in Windham, New Hampshire, the son of William Dinsmoor and Elizabeth Cochran, farmers. The second of ten children, Robert was educated at home until the age of nine. When a local school was established, he attended regularly for four years and then intermittently for several more, during which time he taught his younger brothers and sisters. A robust young man, he enlisted in 1775 in the New Hampshire troops commanded by General John Sullivan and at age twenty took part in the battle of Saratoga. On returning to the farm, he taught school for five winters to subsidize his farm income and in 1782 married Mary "Polly" Park, who died sixteen years later, leaving Dinsmoor with eleven children (two others had died in infancy). In 1801 he married Mary Davidson Anderson; they had no children.

Long interested in writing, Dinsmoor's poems occasionally appeared in local newspapers such as the *Haverhill Gazette*. These poems were published along with others in a subscription volume of his works, *Incidental Poems . . . with a Preface and Sketch of the Author's Life* (1828). According to the preface, Dinsmoor "wrote from the untutored impulses of his own mind," an assumption apparently acceptable to the poet, who sometimes used "Rustic Bard" as his signature. Several of his poems, written in the Lowland Scottish dialect common around Londonderry, New Hampshire, employed traditional Scottish line and stanza forms that were later made widely familiar by Scottish poet Robert Burns in his Kilmarnock volume (1786).

Most of the pieces in Dinsmoor's collection are not spontaneous effusions but studied verse epistles to particular individuals—whose verse replies are sometimes included—on subjects ranging from personal affection to partisan politics to his orthodox Presbyterianism (Dinsmoor was deacon at Windham Church and clerk of session at the age of thirty). Once aware of Burns, however, he sometimes wrote in conscious imitation, as when he used Burns's "To a Mountain Daisy" as a model for "The Sparrow." Dinsmoor died in Windham.

Among several tributes to Dinsmoor in *Incidental Poems* is the first John Greenleaf Whittier poem to appear in a book, "J. G. Whittier to the 'Rustic Bard,'" itself written in the Lowland Scottish dialect. Whittier, who knew Dinsmoor, wrote in 1850 an appreciative essay on aspects of the man and his work, from his genial personality and complete integrity to his use of elements of common life and New England legend in his poetry, an example that directly influenced Whittier's own. In part through this essay, Dinsmoor is remembered as one who realized that "the Yankee, after all, is a man, and as such his history could it be got at, must have more or less of poetic material in it" (Whittier, p. 247). Dinsmoor's works were published again as *Poems of Robert Dinsmoor: "The Rustic Bard,"* edited by Leonard Allison Morrison (1898). The compilation opens with an additional long narrative poem, "Jamie Cochran, the Indian Captive," an example of Dinsmoor's use of his own family history in writing about the New England experience.

• Several Dinsmoor letters are in collections at the Boston Public Library, Middlebury College, and Yale University. The Boston Public Library has two manuscripts; Brown University Library has a manuscript volume of letters and poems. Biographical information supplied by Dinsmoor in his *Incidental Poems* is added to by the poet's nephew James Dinsmoor in the Morrison compilation of 1898. "Robert Dinsmore" (a variant spelling) is included in "Old Portraits and Modern Sketches," *The Writings of John Greenleaf Whittier*, vol. 6: *Prose Works* (1889; repr. 1892). Interesting information about both poets is presented by Theodore Garrison in "The Influence of Robert Dinsmore upon Whittier," *Emerson Society Quarterly* 50 (1968): 55–60.

VINCENT FREIMARCK

DINWIDDIE, Emily Wayland (14 Aug. 1879–11 Mar. 1949), social worker and housing reformer, was born in Greenwood, Virginia, the daughter of William Dinwiddie, a Presbyterian evangelical minister, and Emily Albertine Bledsoe. Emily grew up on a farm where she developed a love for the outdoors, participated in climbing, hiking, and swimming, and studied plant life. She graduated with a B.A. from Peace Institute in Raleigh, North Carolina, in 1898 and remained at the school for two years as a Latin teacher. She never married.

Encouraged by an aunt, in 1900 Dinwiddie joined the staff of the New Jersey State Board of Children's Guardians as an investigator, which launched her into a career in the social services. In 1901 Dinwiddie signed up for a course in social work at the Summer School for Philanthropic Workers. Following its completion she was hired by the New York Charity Organization Society (COS) and worked from 1901 to 1902 as an investigation bureau visitor, assistant district agent, and acting agent. She then became the editor of the *Charities Directory*.

In 1903 Dinwiddie became an investigator and assistant in the First Deputy Commissioner's office of the Tenement House Department. She also served as a special investigator for Octavia Hill Association in Philadelphia from 1903 to 1904. In this capacity she examined the problems of newly arriving immigrants housed in the tiny apartments of tenement buildings. Owing to landlord neglect these tenements had become dirty and dilapidated. As a result of her experiences Dinwiddie wrote *The Tenants' Manual*, designed to educate and provide information on housing to both tenement dwellers and settlement workers on how to achieve better living conditions. While on these various assignments, she took graduate courses in economics and sociology at the University of Pennsylvania from 1903 to 1904. In 1904 she accepted the position of assistant secretary of the Tenement House Committee for COS and returned to New York. She served in this capacity until 1905 when she became the secretary. Her work on the committee lasted until 1909.

On assignment in Pittsburgh in connection with housing problems there between 1907 and 1908, Dinwiddie worked under Lawrence Veiller, a noted housing reformer. The committee's recommendations were formulated into laws that made old buildings habitable and set guidelines for the construction of new buildings.

With added experience and knowledge Dinwiddie was prepared to move ahead in her field. The opportunity presented itself when muckrakers denounced church tenement properties, claiming that they were plagued by structural defects, poor sanitary conditions, and housed saloons and gambling parlors, thus encouraging prostitution. The vestry property committee of one such church, Trinity, requested that Dinwiddie evaluate their holdings. Trinity was one of the largest owners of tenement properties on the Lower West Side of New York City. Dinwiddie found that muckraking claims against Trinity were untrue and showed that in most of their 334 properties, the church had not raised rents and maintained home environments equal to or above average of those in most tenements. After her investigative work and the publication of a series of articles, Trinity's Board of Directors hired Dinwiddie as supervisor of dwellings. She served in this capacity from 1910 to 1918.

Responsible for implementing housing reforms and instituting policies that would lead to improvement on the properties and for the tenants, Dinwiddie worked with efficiency and tact to correct any existing abuses. Said to have drawn "her salary for bringing soap and sunshine into Trinity's tenements," Dinwiddie's work resulted in establishing Trinity Church as an example of a model landlord. She provided for a policy of affordable rents and ensured that large families had priority in obtaining an apartment. During her tenure, 180 buildings were razed to make way for low-rise buildings with yards for children's play. Other buildings had repair work begun and any crime and illicit activities were stopped as were home manufacturing and use of the apartments for rag or junk shops. Dinwiddie encouraged tenants to make improvements on their properties through sanitary living conditions, and by planting gardens in unused yard spaces.

In 1918 Dinwiddie left Trinity to take an assignment in France with the American Red Cross. For a year she served as director of a social service exchange giving aid to war refugees. She then returned in 1919 to Washington, D.C., where she became the associate director of the Red Cross Information Service, advancing to director in 1921, and to assistant executive secretary of the Red Cross in 1922. After leaving the Red Cross a year later, Dinwiddie became a social work consultant to St. Elizabeths Hospital in Washington D.C., and over the next four years she took courses in psychiatry while also lecturing in social casework at George Washington University. In 1927 she left Washington and took a position as director of the Children's Bureau of the Virginia Department of Public Welfare, coordinating the bureau's work with that of the state's public and private welfare agencies. Her comprehensive report on Virginia's mental hospitals detailed the services provided for the mentally ill in that state.

Her next job sent her to Kansas in 1934 where, in the middle of the Great Depression, she became a state case supervisor of the Kansas Emergency Relief Committee and then assistant state superintendent of relief and state superintendent of the child welfare program from 1936. She headed the committee's children's program, overseeing the allocation of federal funding to provide training for local workers and coordinating local welfare activities to improve services for children. In 1938 she retired, returning to Virginia where she remained until her death in Waynesboro.

A leader in the era of Progressive reform, Dinwiddie persistently attacked the problems plaguing overcrowded cities through her evaluations of poor housing and worked toward rectifying the abuses that she found. Expanding her social service duties, she found solutions to improve the quality of life for city dwellers crowded into tenements, alleviated housing problems faced by Trinity Church, and provided cooperation and funding between agencies and recipients. Maintaining her perspective, humor, and wit, Dinwiddie remained an effective investigator, researcher, and administrator, implementing the techniques for improvement that she had learned through charity and investigative work.

• Biographical information can be obtained from Lillian Brandt, *The Charity Organization Society of the City of New York, 1882–1907* (1907), pp. 236–37; and through the Presbyterian Historical Society and the Historical Foundation of Presbyterian and Reformed Churches. Dinwiddie's writings include *Housing Conditions in Philadelphia* (1904); "The Work of New York's Tenement House Department," *Charities and the Commons*, 6 Oct. 1906, pp. 11–12; "The Truth about Trinity's Tenements," *Survey*, 26 Feb. 1910, pp. 797–809; and "The Tenant's Responsibility," National Housing Association, *Process* 1 (1911): 52–60. Some mention of her publications is in Robert A. Woods and Albert J. Kennedy, *Handbook of Settlement* (1911): 200–201. Dinwiddie's reports on Trinity's properties can be found in the *Trinity Church Year Book and Register* (1911–1916). Her scholarly research on Virginia's state mental institutions appears in *Virginia State Hospitals for Mental Patients—Report on Receiving System and Hospitalization Needs* (1934). Other information on Dinwiddie and tenement house reform can be found in Roy Lubove, *The Progressive and the Slums* (1962). COS can be further examined in Frank Dekker Watson, *The Charity Organization Movement in the United States* (1971). Her obituary is in the *New York Times*, 13 Mar. 1949.

MARILYN ELIZABETH PERRY

DINWIDDIE, Robert (3 Oct. 1692–27 July 1770), royal customs official and lieutenant governor of Virginia, was born in Glasgow, Scotland, the son of Robert Dinwiddie, a merchant, and Elizabeth (or Sarah) Cumming. He attended the University of Glasgow and probably served in his father's mercantile house. He may have visited North America before settling in Bermuda some time late in the 1710s. As a merchant and ship owner Dinwiddie made a considerable amount of money, and about the mid-1730s he married Rebecca Auchinleck (in some early accounts the surname appears as Affleck), daughter of an Anglican clergyman of Bermuda. They had two children.

Dinwiddie's personal involvement in commerce and his close association with public officials in Bermuda gave him an opportunity to view close up the operations of the British commercial system, and from time to time he submitted informal reports on some of its features to his friends in London. Probably as a result, his friends arranged in 1738 for him to be appointed surveyor general of the royal customs for the southern district of North America, consisting of the Bahamas, Jamaica, and the mainland colonies from Pennsylvania southward. Dinwiddie made inspection tours of his district and energetically proceeded against officials suspected of impropriety. He tangled with Charles Dunbar, the surveyor general for the southern Caribbean, and he was both praised and criticized for proceeding against Edward Lascelles and others in Barbados with what the commissioners of the customs politely characterized as "more zeal than prudence."

Dinwiddie's commission as surveyor general allowed him to become a member of the council of one of the colonies, and he chose Virginia, settling there, probably in Norfolk, early in 1741. Disagreements about whether he should serve as a full member of the council or as a member ex officio with a limited role delayed his actually taking his seat, and although he lived in Virginia off and on for about five years, he sat in the council for only a few months in 1745. In 1741 he presented the borough of Norfolk with a silver seal, and in 1754, while lieutenant governor, he gave the borough a beautiful silver mace, both of which are extant.

In July 1751 Dinwiddie was appointed lieutenant governor of Virginia to succeed Sir William Gooch. He speedily concluded an agreement with the absentee royal governor, William Anne Keppel, second earl of Albemarle, concerning the division of the salary and fees of the office and moved to Virginia and took the oaths of office in Williamsburg on 21 November 1751. Until his retirement and departure in mid-January 1758, Dinwiddie labored diligently at his duties. He was a tireless dictator of letters and kept up an informative correspondence with a wide variety of people in Virginia and elsewhere. As a dedicated administrator

he appears to have been well above average, and as a persistent advocate of the wider British interest he appears to have been consistent and inflexible. Dinwiddie remained financially ambitious, and along with many native Virginians he cast covetous eyes on the unsettled western lands.

His public duties and his private proclivities soon led him into trouble, in the famous pistole fee controversy. In April 1752 Dinwiddie requested and received approval from his council to charge a fee of one pistole (the value of a Spanish coin worth approximately sixteen shillings) for every land patent he signed. Taking fees for services performed was routine in the colonies, and other governors charged and received similar fees for similar services. Dinwiddie's action appeared to some people to be a mere act of greed, but he also insisted that persons claiming western lands under warrants and surveys obtain patents for the lands and pay the required quitrents. Many prominent speculators had avoided the payment of quitrents by the simple expedient of postponing the application for the patent, so Dinwiddie's action was both personally rewarding and calculated to enrich the royal treasury. The imposition of the fee sparked a bitter and protracted dispute with the House of Burgesses, in which the speculators were influential. No Virginia governor had dared to impose a fee without the approval of the General Assembly for more than half a century; the burgesses declared the fee unlawful and sent Attorney General Peyton Randolph to London to lobby against the governor's assertion that he had the right to levy it. Ultimately the Board of Trade issued a split decision that upheld the governor's authority to charge the fee but limited its applicability. The long argument produced some of the first prerevolutionary public discussions in Virginia about the division of constitutional authority between the royal governor and the General Assembly and between the authorities in Great Britain and those in Virginia. Dinwiddie also took the losing side in a contest over the appointment of a new president for the College of William and Mary; the two incidents permanently strained his relationship with the powerful burgesses.

Dinwiddie's most important actions as governor involved the West. In 1753 he selected Major George Washington as his agent to deliver a message to the French commanders south of the Great Lakes, demanding that they leave the lands claimed by the British crown and the colony of Virginia. Dinwiddie's demand and the French rejection of it precipitated the French and Indian War. Dinwiddie gave Washington his first field commands, first as lieutenant colonel and later as colonel of the First Virginia Regiment. Dinwiddie and Washington clashed over military policies and the relationship between the British army and the Virginia militia. Both men were highly opinionated and determined to have things their own way, but Dinwiddie's patronage was of significant importance in advancing Washington's military career. Dinwiddie participated in important intercolonial conferences in Alexandria and Annapolis in the spring of 1755 and in

Philadelphia early in 1757. In spite of tireless efforts, he was often frustrated by the unwillingness of the Virginia General Assembly to respond with what he regarded as sufficient promptitude or adequate appropriations to the demands that he and the king's ministers made for more troops, money, and supplies. In part because of the legacy of the pistole fee controversy, the General Assembly forced Dinwiddie to accept appropriation bills that placed control over expenditures with a joint committee of burgesses and councilors. The need to obtain the committee's approval restricted his capacity to bring Virginia's resources fully into the field during the war.

Old, weary, and frustrated, Dinwiddie requested permission to retire, and he left Virginia on 12 January 1758 and never returned. Granted a pension of £400 per annum and holding his commission as surveyor general for several more years, he lived in quiet retirement in England, chiefly at Bath, although he made at least one tiring trip to Scotland. His health waxed and waned until his death in the city of Bristol.

• Dinwiddie's correspondence with the secretaries of state and the Board of Trade is in PRO, CO 5 and CO 324, and his letters to the bishop of London are in the Fulham Palace Papers, Lambeth Palace Library, all now accessible through the microfilm of the Virginia Colonial Records Project. Dinwiddie's letterbooks, together with a genealogy, have been published in Robert A. Brock, ed., *The Official Records of Robert Dinwiddie, Lieutenant-Governor of the Colony of Virginia, 1751–1758* (2 vols., 1883–1884), supplemented by Louis Knott Koontz, ed., *Robert Dinwiddie Correspondence Illustrative of His Career in American Colonial Government and Westward Expansion* (2 vols., 1951), microfilm. The most detailed biography is Louis Knott Koontz, *Robert Dinwiddie; His Career in American Colonial Government and Westward Expansion* (1941); the most judicious is John Richard Alden, *Robert Dinwiddie, Servant of the Crown* (1973); and the most recent informed assessment of his administration in Virginia is in Paul Randall Shrock, "Maintaining the Prerogative: Three Royal Governors in Virginia as a Case Study, 1710–1758" (Ph.D. diss., Univ. of North Carolina, 1980), pp. 187–286. A lucid account of the pistole fee controversy and some important documents are in Jack P. Greene, ed., "The Case of the Pistole Fee; The Report of a Hearing on the Pistole Fee Dispute before the Privy Council, June 18, 1754," *Virginia Magazine of History and Biography* 66 (1958): 399–422.

BRENT TARTER

DIRKSEN, Everett McKinley (4 Jan. 1896–7 Sept. 1969), U.S. senator, was born in Pekin, Illinois, the son of Antje Conrady and Johann Dirksen. The latter, a design painter, died when Everett was nine. Everett and his four brothers (one was his twin, Thomas Reed) were raised by their widowed mother under conditions bordering on poverty. Everett was the only one of the boys to finish high school and attend college. He did odd jobs to attain three years of higher education at the University of Minnesota (1913–1917). In 1917 Dirksen enlisted in the army, received a commission as a second lieutenant, and served in France as a balloon observer for the artillery.

After his World War I service, Dirksen returned to Pekin and for the next ten years became involved in small business enterprises. He helped found the local chapter of the American Legion. As a result of his leadership abilities and prowess as an orator, Dirksen soon found himself involved in politics. In 1926 he was elected to the Pekin City Council. One year later he married Louella Carver. They had one daughter, Joy, who later became the wife of Senator Howard Baker (R-Tenn.). In 1932 Dirksen ran for Congress as a Republican and was elected. He served in the U.S. House of Representatives from 1933 to 1949, leaving office because of an eye ailment (from which he recovered in 1950). Early in his House career Dirksen gave substantial support to New Deal measures while positioning himself as a staunch isolationist in foreign policy matters. He studied law privately and was admitted to the Illinois bar in 1936. In 1944 he made an unsuccessful bid for the GOP presidential nomination. By the end of his seven terms, Dirksen had become more critical of New Deal and Fair Deal programs while shifting to an internationalist outlook in foreign policy.

In 1950 Dirksen ran for the Senate against Democratic majority leader Scott Lucas and gained national attention by winning the election. At the 1952 Republican National Convention Dirksen supported Senator Robert A. Taft of Ohio while denouncing Governor Thomas E. Dewey of New York. He also joined the anti-Communist crusade led by Senator Joseph McCarthy of Wisconsin. But after Taft's death in 1953 and the Senate's condemnation of McCarthy in 1954, Dirksen became a leading spokesman for the administration of Dwight D. Eisenhower. In 1957 he was chosen Senate minority whip by his Republican colleagues, and in 1959 he became the minority leader—a post he held until his death.

Dirksen's brand of leadership in the Senate was marked by brilliant oratory, collegiality, and parliamentary skill. It was marked by partisan fervor, as well, but in the final analysis Dirksen displayed a willingness to compromise. Although he and Senate majority leader Lyndon B. Johnson of Texas were political adversaries, Dirksen developed a close personal relationship with his Democratic counterpart. Dirksen loved to entertain colleagues or members of the press with humorous stories and anecdotes. He enjoyed electrifying audiences with his magniloquent rhetoric, often creating colorful phrases dubbed "Dirksenisms" by the media. He once chided a colleague, "That idea has as much effect as a snowflake on the bosom of the Potomac." In a floor debate, when an opponent began to filibuster, Dirksen announced, "I shall invoke upon him every condign imprecation." Within Republican ranks Dirksen played the role of mediator between the western and midwestern ultraconservatives and the more liberal eastern wing of the party. He personally supported Eisenhower's brand of modern Republicanism on domestic issues and defended Ike's internationalist foreign policy.

After John F. Kennedy was elected president in 1960, Dirksen led the Republican opposition to much of the New Frontier program. Dirksen objected to deficit spending and to the enlargement of the federal bureaucracy. In matters of foreign policy, however, he tended toward bipartisanship. Dirksen refrained from criticizing JFK over the Bay of Pigs fiasco and strongly backed him during the Cuban Missile Crisis. He provided Republican votes for implementing the Peace Corps, ratification of the Nuclear Test Ban Treaty, and U.S. government purchases of bonds issued by the United Nations.

Although Dirksen realized that the right-wing stance of Arizona senator Barry Goldwater lacked national appeal, he nevertheless nominated him for president at the 1964 Republican National Convention and tried to promote party harmony. Following the landslide election of Lyndon B. Johnson over Goldwater, Dirksen had difficulty in leading the small number of Republicans in the Senate in effective opposition to the president's Great Society initiatives. He warned repeatedly that the many costly programs of the Johnson administration would increase the national debt drastically while creating welfare dependency among the poor it was supposed to help. Yet his opposition to Johnson's domestic agenda was neither reflexive nor absolute. Motivated by his own conscience, Dirksen acted in a statesmanlike manner in getting sufficient Republican votes for cloture to end the filibuster by southern Democrats that had blocked passage of the Civil Rights Act of 1964. He also delivered GOP votes to ensure passage of the Voting Rights Act of 1965.

Dirksen gave valuable support to President Johnson in the realm of international affairs. As minority leader, he defended LBJ's Vietnam War policy. Dirksen not only helped silence Republican criticism; he often chastised dovish Democrats for their attacks upon the president as well. In Dirksen's judgment the Vietnam War was a noble crusade to preserve the principle of self-determination in South Vietnam.

During the 1960s Dirksen voiced strong disapproval of many decisions handed down by the U.S. Supreme Court. He was particularly disturbed by Chief Justice Earl Warren's one man–one vote decree in the case of *Reynolds v. Sims* (1964). In an attempt to nullify this reapportionment decision, Dirksen sponsored an amendment to the U.S. Constitution to allow states to apportion one house of a bicameral legislature on a basis other than population alone. He was fearful that urban domination would bring the ultimate demise of congressional Republicans because of rampant gerrymandering of districts by Democratic-controlled state legislatures. This amendment failed, as did his other constitutional amendment, which would have overthrown the ban on prayer in public schools as decreed by the Warren Court in *Engel v. Vitale* (1962).

In 1968, running as a hawk who believed in the morality of U.S. actions in the Vietnam War, Dirksen won a fourth term in the Senate. By this time, he was a national celebrity. His weekly television appearances to present the Republican position on issues of the day along with GOP House minority leader Gerald R. Ford, which began in 1965 and was called the "Ev and Jerry Show" by the press, gave Dirksen nationwide coverage. He was extremely telegenic, and his curly silver locks, mellifluous voice, wit, and showmanship helped make Dirksen a popular television personality. He also gained some fame as a recording artist. Dirksen recorded four best-selling albums, one of which, "Gallant Men," sold over 500,000 copies and in 1967 was awarded a Grammy by the National Academy of Recording Arts and Sciences. Dirksen's sonorous bass voice and theatrical renditions of poetry and patriotic texts made him a septuagenarian symbol of America's traditions. Dirksen reveled in the accolade that he was the Senate's "Golden Voice." At the same time, his liberal critics labeled him the "Wizard of Ooze," claiming that his flamboyant oratory actually camouflaged a reactionary stance on the issues and a crass political expediency. And it is true that when he spoke on the Senate floor, Dirksen sought to ensnarl adversaries in a web of words or tried to weave a bridge of rhetoric that would permit opponents to cross over to his side. His motto was, "The oil can is mightier than the sword."

Dirksen's modus operandi as minority leader was to employ the amendatory process in order to fashion legislation acceptable to both conservatives and liberals. This was especially true in the case of his efforts to cut the cost of Great Society programs. His extemporaneous speeches were verbal weapons forged in the heat of political battle. Their purpose was to influence the course of vital legislation, not to be inscribed in stone. Dirksen was no arm twister, preferring to win opponents over by moral suasion, intellectual arguments, shrewd cajoling, or emotional appeals. When tempers flared, Dirksen would inject a little levity in the proceedings by advocating one of his pet notions, that the marigold be named the national flower. This usually initiated a mock debate to the enjoyment of all.

When Richard M. Nixon was elected president in 1968, Dirksen's leadership role was eclipsed. Nixon seldom sought Dirksen's counsel, relying instead on his White House staff. The Ev and Jerry Show was canceled as Nixon took the spotlight with his own presidential press conferences. Nixon even made high-level appointments over Dirksen's objections.

Dirksen suffered from many illnesses during his later years, but when he died following an operation for lung cancer at Walter Reed Hospital in Washington, D.C., both the Senate and the public were stunned. His body lay in state in the Capitol Rotunda for twenty-four hours. Only four other senators had ever been so honored. As minority leader, he left his imprint on many major laws. In practicing the art of minority statecraft, the venerable Dirksen achieved a level of power and influence denied to many leaders who found themselves perpetually playing the role of party spokesperson for the loyal opposition.

• The papers of Everett Dirksen are located at the Everett McKinley Dirksen Congressional Leadership Research Center in Pekin, Illinois. Other archival material relating to his political career can be found in the presidential libraries of Dwight D. Eisenhower, John F. Kennedy, and Lyndon B. Johnson. Dirksen's wife, Louella, wrote (with Norma Lee

Browning) a memoir titled *The Honorable Mr. Marigold: My Life with Everett Dirksen* (1972). There are two biographies of Dirksen: Edward L. and Frederick H. Schapsmeier, *Dirksen of Illinois: Senatorial Statesman* (1985), and Neil MacNeil, *Dirksen: Portrait of a Public Man* (1970). Excerpts from Dirksen's speeches are found in Annette C. Penny, *The Golden Voice of the Senate* (1968). Three articles by Edward L. and Frederick H. Schapsmeier dealing with varied aspects of his career are "Senator Everett M. Dirksen and American Foreign Policy," *Old Northwest, A Journal of Regional Life and Letters* 8 (1981–1982): 359–72; "Everett M. Dirksen of Pekin: Politician par Excellence," *Journal of the Illinois State Historical Society* 86 (1983): 2–16; and "Dirksen and Douglas of Illinois: The Pragmatist and the Professor as Contemporaries in the United States Senate," *Illinois Historical Journal* 83 (1990): 75–84.

EDWARD L. SCHAPSMEIER

DISALLE, Michael Vincent (6 Jan. 1908–15 Sept. 1981), attorney and politician, was born in New York City, the son of Anthony DiSalle, an entrepreneur, and Assunta D'Arcangelo. In 1911 his family moved to Toledo, Ohio, where DiSalle grew up. After graduating from Central Catholic High School, he attended Georgetown University to study law. In 1930 he married Myrtle Eugene England; they had five children. He graduated in 1931 and returned to Toledo to practice law.

DiSalle entered politics in 1937, winning a seat in the Ohio House of Representatives. After serving one term, he failed to win election to the Ohio Senate but remained active in Toledo politics. At the end of World War II, for example, he successfully navigated his municipality through the rash of labor strife that plagued the nation. While serving as vice mayor in 1945, he developed the Toledo Labor-Management Citizens Committee to lessen the likelihood of labor strikes in his city. This successful arbitration board earned DiSalle national notoriety and helped him win election as mayor in 1947, an office he held until 1950.

As mayor, DiSalle drew on his city's progressive past to solve many of its current problems. He saw the implementation of a 1 percent income and business tax, which gave the government adequate funds to retire its debt. His capacity for hard work and his pleasant manner endeared him to his constituents. Following his tour of Toledo with DiSalle, the former king of Romania commented favorably on the mayor's uncommon familiarity with the public, as most people called the Ohio politician by his first name. In a friendly retort, DiSalle replied, "You might still be King if your people had called you 'Mike'" (*New York Times*, 4 May 1950).

DiSalle's innovative successes in addressing the labor and financial burdens at the municipal level caught the attention of President Harry S. Truman. Having to deal with these same problems on a national scale, the president in December 1950 asked DiSalle to head the Office of Price Stabilization (OPS). Following the onset of hostilities in Korea in June 1950, the United States faced the problem of runaway inflation. To head off a dangerous increase in prices, Di-

Salle instituted a thirty-day freeze while his office explored possible solutions. Although he attempted to implement voluntary controls in cooperation with industry, his office recommended to the president the institution of numerous price regulations.

Following Republican success in the 1952 presidential election, DiSalle resumed his private law practice. In 1958 he won election as Ohio's governor on a prolabor platform. Beating his conservative opponent C. William O'Neill, whom the press called the new "Mr. Republican," DiSalle capitalized on a Democratic groundswell as voters overwhelmingly rejected Republican candidates. As governor, DiSalle faced two well-publicized problems, Ohio's budget deficit and capital punishment. To decrease the Buckeye State's debt, DiSalle successfully pushed the legislature into increasing taxes on consumer goods and corporate franchises. He was less successful at convincing lawmakers to abolish the state's death penalty. Taking his contention to Ohio's Judiciary Committee, he argued that the policy of using convicted murderers on the executive mansion's household staff illustrated the success of rehabilitation. His statement, however, failed to convince the legislature.

During his first year as governor, DiSalle agreed to endorse the presidential hopeful, Senator John F. Kennedy (D.-Mass.) at the 1960 Democratic National Convention. Kennedy had visited Ohio regularly since 1956 and had created a base of support around the state. Kennedy used his popularity to pressure DiSalle, threatening to run against the governor's favorite son campaign. The governor hesitated but, after a survey of the state, concluded that Kennedy would defeat him in the 1960 primary. Thus DiSalle became the first governor outside of New England to support Kennedy. His support helped Kennedy make headway months before the convention. California governor Edmund "Pat" Brown, for instance, started to lean toward Kennedy in January, in part because he was "most impressed" by DiSalle's early commitment.

DiSalle won the favorite son nomination from his state and at the 1960 Democratic National Convention delivered every Ohio delegate to Kennedy on the first ballot. This marked the height of DiSalle's political fortunes, however; in 1962 he lost his reelection bid. In 1966 he joined the Washington, D.C., law firm Chapman, Duff, & Paul. Although his political influence was limited, he remained active in the Democratic party for the remainder of his life. At the 1968 Democratic National Convention he headed a drive to nominate Senator Edward Kennedy (D.-Mass.) for the presidency. In his last national function as a politician, he was honorary chairman of Edward Kennedy's 1980 campaign for the Democratic presidential nomination. DiSalle died in Italy.

DiSalle's political career exemplifies important characteristics of the Democratic party during his lifetime. As the child of an immigrant and a Catholic living in an urban center, he naturally chose the Democratic party, which had come to represent the interest of urban ethnics. His relationship with John Kennedy's campaign for the presidential nomination in 1960 illustrates an important aspect of the presidential nominating process. Before the reform of the primary system in the 1970s, candidates relied on Democratic state leaders to deliver delegate votes at the national convention. Kennedy could count on Ohio's delegates because, although DiSalle had won the Buckeye State's primary as a favorite son, he had publicly promised these votes to Kennedy. DiSalle's political tenure, however, coincided with the decline in the power of local party leaders. By the time of Senator George McGovern's (D.-S.Dak.) nomination in 1972, reforms in the nominating process increased the power of the open presidential primary elections and thereby decreased the influence of the traditional party leaders, who had previously commanded their state's delegates.

• DiSalle's personal papers are at the Ohio Historical Society in Columbus, Ohio. The Harry S. Truman Presidential Library, Independence, Mo., has microfilm copies of files from his tenure as director of the OPS. The John F. Kennedy Presidential Library, Boston, Mass., has an oral history, in which DiSalle speaks of his relationship with the former president and his actions as Ohio's governor from 1959 to 1963. In an oral history for the Lyndon B. Johnson Presidential Library, Austin, Tex., DiSalle reflects about his associations with Johnson while head of the OPS and about his governorship. DiSalle wrote about his opposition to capital punishment in *The Power of Life or Death* (1965) and *Second Choice* (1966). An obituary is in the *New York Times*, 17 Sept. 1981.

R. SCOTT HARRIS

DISNEY, Walt (5 Dec. 1901–15 Dec. 1966), animator and motion picture producer, was born Walter Elias Disney in Chicago, Illinois, the son of Elias Disney, a building contractor, and Flora Call, a teacher. After a childhood near Marceline and in Kansas City, Missouri, Disney studied at the Chicago Institute of Art in the evening while attending McKinley High School during the day. In 1918 he enlisted in the American Ambulance Corps, serving in France and returning to employment as an artist at the Pesmen-Rubin Commercial Art Studio, where he befriended artist Ub Iwerks. After learning the rudiments of animation at a subsequent job at the Kansas City Film Ad Service, Disney began to produce his own animated films. In 1922 he formed Laugh-O-Gram Films. He was soon joined by Iwerks and a staff, including Hugh Harman and Rudolf Ising, to produce theatrical and sponsored films.

In 1923 Disney relocated to Los Angeles and incorporated the Disney Bros. Studio in partnership with his brother Roy. The signing of a contract with distributor Margaret Winkler to produce the "Alice Comedies," which combined live action and animation in emulation of the successful Fleischer "Out of the Inkwell" series, gave his product national distribution. Marriage in 1925 to Lillian Bounds of the studio's ink and paint department followed. The union would produce two daughters. Disney's distributor in 1927 arranged for the "Oswald the Lucky Rabbit" series of cartoons to be distributed through Universal, which gave Disney films regular access to theaters and introduced the filmmaker to the benefits of product licensing through the merchandising of "Oswald the Lucky Rabbit" chocolate bars. Disagreements with Charles Mintz (husband of Margaret Winkler) resulted in Mintz hiring away many of Disney's animators in order to force Disney to work directly for him, rather than as an independent contractor. Outraged, Disney broke with Mintz.

While the artists now under contract with Mintz completed the last of Disney's Oswald films, Ub Iwerks worked in seclusion animating *Plane Crazy*, the first of a projected series starring Disney's new character, Mickey Mouse. *Gallopin' Gaucho*, the second of the series, was begun, but no distributor could be found. Looking for some way to differentiate his new Mickey Mouse cartoons from the silent Oswald series, Disney made an agreement with former Universal executive Pat Powers to animate cartoons using the Powers' Cinephone sound process. The result was *Steamboat Willie* (1928). Earlier sound animated films made by competitors Max Fleischer and Paul Terry enjoyed limited success, but the coupling of synchronized sound with the engaging new character made *Steamboat Willie* a sensation.

At the suggestion of his musical director Carl Stalling, Disney inaugurated the "Silly Symphony" series with *Skeleton Dance* (1929). While the character-based "Mickey Mouse" films used music as an accompaniment to the action, the "Silly Symphonies" created stories through the use of music. *Skeleton Dance* was animated completely by Ub Iwerks. Since production costs were rising faster than returns, Disney pressured his distributor for more money and urged Iwerks to abandon the practice of animating straight through in favor of the more efficient technique of drawing key poses and letting lower-paid assistants sketch the in-between poses. In 1930 the disgruntled Iwerks accepted Powers's offer to set up a rival company, Celebrity Productions. Carl Stalling resigned shortly after.

In contrast with the previous debacle with Mintz, Disney now owned the copyright to his characters, and the popularity of Mickey Mouse ensured a quick transition of distribution to Columbia. Prior to Iwerks's and Stallings's departures, Disney had been hiring experienced animators from New York that were to include Bert Gillett, David Hand, Dick Huemer, Ben Sharpsteen, and Grim Natwick. He also began training local talent such as Eric Larson, Wolfgang Reitherman, Les Clark, Milt Kahl, Ward Kimball, Marc Davis, Ollie Johnston, Frank Thomas, and John Lounsbery (later known as the "Nine Old Men"). A more significant move was to expand his economic base, hiring Herman "Kay" Kamen in the United States and William Banks Levy in the United Kingdom to act as merchandising agents. Licensing fees added substantially to studio revenue, as did the introduction of Iwerks's Mickey Mouse comic strips, continued after Iwerks's departure by Win Smith and then Floyd Gottfredson. Mickey Mouse Clubs, which promoted Disney films and products, reached a peak membership by 1932 larger than the Boy Scouts of America and the Girl Scouts combined.

The decline in popularity of Mickey Mouse in the mid-1930s was compensated by the introduction of other characters such as Donald Duck, Pluto, and Goofy. With a stable financial base, Disney sought expensive refinements to animation technique, introducing the "pencil test" (in which the animator's original pencil drawings are photographed sequentially on motion picture film and projected in order to test the action) to check work in progress. Story development became an elaborate process, closely monitored by Disney himself. Through the establishment of links to the Chouinard School of Art and in-house training sessions led by Don Graham, the studio developed an unrivaled degree of expressive virtuosity. Disney was hailed by critics as creating an American art form exhibiting "that same delicate balance between fantasy and fact, poetry and comic reality, which is the nature of all folklore. In Disney's studio . . . by a system as truly of the machine age as Henry Ford's plant at Dearborn, true art is produced" ("The Big Bad Wolf," *Fortune*, 5 Nov. 1934, p. 88). Disney's moral homilies set in rural or small-town surroundings, like *The Three Little Pigs* (1933), *The Wise Little Hen* (1934), and *The Band Concert* (1935), were seen as embodying peculiarly American values by contemporary critics. In contrast to the earlier "cartoony," gag-oriented, and often risqué films made by his New York competitors, Disney's films were patterned after Hollywood live-action films, with linear narratives, mimetic design, and, as Disney put it, "not an obvious moral, but a worthwhile theme" (quoted in Douglas W. Churchill, "Disney's 'Philosophy,'" *New York Times Magazine*, 6 Mar. 1938, p. 9).

A believer in technological progress, Disney was quick to embrace innovations, producing the first cartoon using the three-color Technicolor process (*Flowers and Trees*, 1932) and assigning camera department head William Garity to develop the multiplane camera, which allowed the use of three-dimensional effects beginning with *The Old Mill* (1937). Increasing costs of the films were met by more lucrative distribution contracts with United Artists and then Radio Keith–Orpheum. Disney's banker, Joseph Rosenberg, authorized loans from the Bank of America that underwrote the application of new skills and technology to *Snow White and the Seven Dwarfs* (1937), which was the first animated feature film with sound and color.

Income resulting from *Snow White and the Seven Dwarfs* ($4.2 million from the initial release in the United States and Canada alone) allowed Disney to build a state-of-the-art studio in Burbank, California, as he proceeded with the even more elaborate *Pinocchio* (1940); *Fantasia* (1940), which had the first stereophonic sound track; and *Bambi* (1942). The wartime loss of foreign markets and the declining critical reaction to his increasingly ambitious projects led to the company's first public stock offering in 1940 and to retrenchment during the war period with modest productions like *The Reluctant Dragon* (1941) and *Dumbo* (1941). To ensure the success of his films, Disney became an early user of George Gallup's audience research from the pre- to postproduction stages of his films' development.

In the aftermath of a 1941 strike, talents such as Art Babbitt, Vladimir Tytla, David Hilberman, Zachary Schwartz, and John Hubley defected to other studios, while Virgil Partch and Walt Kelly left animation altogether. After the war, Disney appeared as a friendly witness before the House Committee on Un-American Activities to name strike leaders as communists. During the strike, following a request by John Hay "Jock" Whitney, director of the Motion Picture Section of Nelson Rockefeller's Office of the Coordinator of Inter-American Affairs, Disney went on a goodwill tour of South America to develop markets to replace those lost in Europe and Asia during wartime hostilities. This led to projects aimed at the Latin American markets, such as *Saludos Amigos!* (1943) and *Three Caballeros* (1945). Production of government propaganda and training films contributed to the war effort and kept the studio afloat financially. Disney self-financed *Victory through Air Power* (1943), based on the book by aviation advocate Alexander de Seversky. Winston Churchill arranged for Franklin Roosevelt to see the film at the Quebec Conference in 1943. Roosevelt's subsequent order that *Victory through Air Power* be shown to the Joint Chiefs of Staff may have influenced air strategy.

The war's end saw a declining market for short films with greater competition from animation units at Warner Bros. and M-G-M. As animation became increasingly expensive in relation to live action, Disney scaled down production of unprofitable shorts. At Roy Disney's urging, the company increased live-action production in films like *Make Mine Music* (1946), *Song of the South* (1946), *Melody Time* (1948), and *So Dear to My Heart* (1949). The release of the all-animated feature *Cinderella* (1950) was followed by the studio's first entirely live-action feature, *Treasure Island* (1950), which began a string of live-action adventures, including *The Sword and the Rose* (1953) and *Twenty-thousand Leagues under the Sea* (1954). A documentary series of "True-Life Adventure" films began with *Seal Island* (1949). Other forms of product diversification included film projects for Firestone and General Motors.

On Christmas Day 1950 NBC broadcast Disney's foray into television—a special on the making of *Alice in Wonderland* (1951) called *One Hour in Wonderland*, which Roy Disney credited with adding millions to the box office for the film, stating his belief that "television can be a most powerful selling aid for us, as well as a source of revenue. It will probably be on this premise that we enter television when we do" ("Interim Letter to Shareholders," 31 Mar. 1951).

Disney's entry into television synchronized his activities with those of his business allies. Disney's company acquired a 34 percent interest in Disneyland, Inc., which was to develop an amusement park in Anaheim, California. Plans for the park were commissioned in 1952, and it opened in 1955. The other principal stockholders (later bought out) were American Broadcasting–Paramount Theatres, Inc.; Western Printing and Lithographing Company; and Walt Disney himself. ABC's financing of Disneyland was contingent upon the Disney production of a weekly "Disneyland" series for the network, which marked an unprecedented commitment by a major Hollywood movie studio to television production. It became ABC's first hit series. Western Printing had held exclusive rights to reproduce Walt Disney's characters for juvenile books, coloring books, and comics since 1932. Disneyland, Walt Disney Productions, the "Disneyland" show on television, and publications based on the films, shows, and theme park would all promote one another. Interlocking business relationships among these leisure industries created interlocking systems of promotion. The Disneyland park and television series became the linchpin of these systems.

Disney developed similar relationships among his ventures and those of the U.S. government and major corporations. Monsanto, Atlantic Richfield, TWA, Douglas Aircraft, American Motors, Pepsi-Cola, and other companies became sponsors of rides or exhibits at Disneyland. As part of the "Atoms for Peace" program, the U.S. Navy and General Dynamics participated in the construction of an "atomic submarine" ride at Disneyland, as well as in the production of the "Disneyland" telefilm *Our Friend the Atom* (1957), which promoted the use of atomic energy. Government scientists such as Willy Ley and Wernher von Braun cooperated in telefilms publicizing government rocketry programs, such as *Man in Space* (1956) and *Mars and Beyond* (1957), as well as with the design of the "Trip to the Moon" ride at Disneyland.

For the State Department during the Cold War, Disneyland became a convenient simulacrum of America. One official observed that there really was no reason for showing foreign dignitaries anything but Disneyland—everything was right there. Disney was also a consultant to the American Exhibition in Moscow and the Brussels World's Fair, where the American pavilion featured Disney's 360-degree film in its Circarama theater. For the New York World's Fair, Disney technicians designed the Ford, General Electric, and Pepsi-Cola/UNICEF "It's a Small World" exhibits, as well as developing the mechanized "Audio-Animatronics" system of presidential effigies used in the Hall of Presidents. Disney was also active in the field of education, being instrumental in the establishment in 1961 of the California Institute of the Arts, to which he was to leave almost half his estate.

Disney's other ventures for ABC included "The Mickey Mouse Club" (1955–1959) and "Zorro" (1957–1959). These and such "Disneyland" broadcasts as the Davy Crockett series led to a bonanza from the licensing of such products as Mickey Mouse Club hats, Zorro swords and capes, and Davy Crockett coonskin caps. Through careful market positioning of his product amid those of major film corporations, Disney fo-

cused on family entertainment. Live-action films took historical and often patriotic subjects in *Johnny Tremain* (1957), *Old Yeller* (1957), *Tonka* (1958), *The Swiss Family Robinson* (1960), and *Polyanna* (1960). *The Shaggy Dog* (1959) began a series of low-budget comedies such as *The Absent Minded Professor* (1961) and *Son of Flubber* (1963) that became mainstays of the company's production. Popular fantasies like *Darby O'Gill and the Little People* (1959) and *Babes in Toyland* (1961) led to the blockbuster *Mary Poppins* (1964). Animation continued in *Peter Pan* (1953), *Lady and the Tramp* (1955), *Sleeping Beauty* (1959), *One Hundred and One Dalmatians* (1961), *The Sword in the Stone* (1963), *Winnie the Pooh and the Honey Tree* (1966), and *The Jungle Book* (1967).

In 1961 Disney changed his broadcasting alliance from ABC to NBC with "Walt Disney's Wonderful World of Color" and the less successful "Disneyland after Dark" series. With more than one-third of corporate income coming from the leisure park, Disney began development of the Mineral King resort. Stalled by ecological concerns, Disney initiated a new theme park near Orlando, Florida, in 1964. The project was awarded municipality rights by the Florida legislature, giving it unprecedented powers for a corporation. This Disney World park was to be built in conjunction with the Experimental Prototype Community of Tomorrow (EPCOT). In Disney's words, EPCOT was to be "a controlled community, a showcase for American industry and research, schools, cultural and educational opportunities" (quoted in Holliss and Sibley, p. 87). While Roy Disney was to supervise the completion of Walt Disney World, which opened in 1971, final realization of the EPCOT project after Walt Disney's death in Burbank, California, of acute circulatory collapse following lung cancer bore little resemblance to the original vision.

Years after his death, Walt Disney retains a centrality in American culture granted to few twentieth-century figures, "because of the manner in which his work in film and television is connected to other projects in urban planning, ecological politics, product merchandising, United States domestic and global policy formation, technological innovation, and constructions of national character" (Eric Smoodin, ed., "Introduction: How to Read Walt Disney," *Disney Discourse: Producing the Magic Kingdom* [1994], pp. 4–5). Assessments are deeply divided. Earlier evaluations of Disney hailed him as a patriot, folk artist, and popularizer of culture. More recently, Disney has been regarded as a paradigm of American imperialism and intolerance, as well as a debaser of culture. Publications on Disney, ranging from company-sponsored hagiographies to fanciful exposés, are numerous enough to be categorized as an industry of their own. Disney remains the central figure in the history of animation. Through technological innovations and alliances with governments and corporations, he transformed a minor studio in a marginal form of communication into a multinational leisure industry giant. Despite his critics, his vision of a modern, corporate utopia as an extension of traditional American values has possibly gained greater currency in the years after his death.

• Correspondence and company records are at the Walt Disney Archive in Burbank, Calif. A biography is Bob Thomas, *Walt Disney: An American Original* (1976). Considerations of Walt Disney's work can be found in Robert D. Feild, *The Art of Walt Disney* (1942); Christopher Finch, *The Art of Walt Disney* (1973); Richard Holliss and Brian Sibley, *The Disney Studio Story* (1988); Mark Langer, "Why the Atom Is Our Friend: Disney, General Dynamics and the USS *Nautilus*," *Art History* 18, no. 1 (Mar. 1995): 63–96; Russell Merritt and J. B. Kaufman, *Walt in Wonderland: The Silent Films of Walt Disney* (1993); Richard Shale, *Donald Duck Joins Up: The Walt Disney Studio during World War II* (1987); and Frank Thomas and Ollie Johnston, *Disney Animation: The Illusion of Life* (1981). Obituaries are in the *New York Times*, 16 Dec. 1966, and *Variety*, 21 Dec. 1966.

MARK LANGER

DISSTON, Hamilton (23 Aug. 1844–30 Apr. 1896), land developer, was born in Philadelphia, Pennsylvania, the son of Henry Disston, an industrialist, and Mary Steelman. At the age of fifteen Disston started as an apprentice in one of the divisions of his father's factory, Keystone Saw, Tool, Steel and File Works, setting a precedent for other family members. The firm, later renamed Henry Disston and Sons, eventually became the world's largest saw manufacturing company. A few years later, much to the dismay of his father, Hamilton and other young men from the Disston factory volunteered for Union army service during the U.S. Civil War. Returning to the firm at the end of the war in 1865, Hamilton continued an active role in the company, becoming its president in 1878 upon the death of his father.

The year before Disston assumed the reins of Henry Disston and Sons, he traveled to Florida for a fishing excursion with a friend, Henry S. Sanford. Sanford, who had pursued a U.S. diplomatic career, was a scion of a wealthy Connecticut family and had real estate investments along Florida's St. Johns River. It is very possible that Disston's interest in a Florida land project began at this time. Whatever the turn of events, Disston eventually met with Florida governor William D. Bloxham and signed a land deal considered by many historians as essential to the future development of the state.

Back in 1850 the federal government had transferred ownership of several million acres of federal lands in Florida to the state. Within five years the Florida legislature had established a board of internal improvements to administer the disposition of these lands for railroad, canal, and other construction projects. By the 1870s the Internal Improvement Fund was mired in debt from the default of antebellum railroad companies, and land sales could not even meet interest obligations. A bondholder of the fund sued in federal court to stop the board from selling additional tracts. The court responded in 1877 by placing the Internal Improvement Fund in receivership, thus making it very likely that the state would lose title to the properties. Then in 1881 Disston and his associates signed a drainage contract with the trustees of the Internal Improvement Fund "to drain and reclaim by draining all overflowed lands in the State of Florida practicable and lying south of Township 23 and east of Peace Creek." This included a large portion of south and central Florida below present-day Orlando. Disston and his associates were to receive one-half of the lands recovered. Because legal proceedings had state lands tied up in receivership, tracts reclaimed by Disston could not be transferred to him. This legal obstacle led to another agreement between Disston and Governor Bloxham, which is known as the Disston land purchase. Under this deal, which was quite controversial within the state, Disston purchased 4 million acres of land for $1 million. This discharged the debt incurred by the Internal Improvement Fund and cleared the way for land transfers.

The first drainage project joined the Caloosahatchee River to Lake Okeechobee, thus permitting Florida's largest lake to drain into the Gulf of Mexico. The second project connected by canal a series of lakes around the upper Kissimmee valley. As the development of the upper Kissimmee River proceeded, several thousand acres of the drained lands were converted to agricultural production. Around 1887 at St. Cloud, Disston was cultivating sugar and rice. Later in 1891 he persuaded the federal government to establish an agricultural experiment station near St. Cloud. Not only did the station conduct research with sugar cane varieties but also with many types of fruits and vegetables.

Eventually Disston was deeded 1,652,711 additional acres of land by the state of Florida for his drainage efforts. Canal construction and river improvements made water transportation possible from Kissimmee through Lake Okeechobee and the Caloosahatchee River to the Gulf of Mexico. Although his drainage projects were probably too ambitious for private capital and did not accomplish all that was planned, central and south Florida were opened to development and settlement years earlier than would have been the case without Disston's activities. Several scholars of the Disston land deal maintain that had the Board of Internal Improvements been forced to sell all lands in 1881, the consequences would have been disastrous. For example, the state would not have kept ownership of any of the lands as it had under the Disston contract and it could not have offered lands as an incentive to railroad, canal, and other development companies. Thus developers such as Henry B. Plant and Henry M. Flagler—who played a key role in the development of the state—might never have invested in the state or might have waited until a later period.

Unfortunately, Hamilton Disston's reinvestment of profits in additional projects coupled with the economic depression of 1893 produced a financial strain on his personal finances. Furthermore, Florida railroad expansion had diminished the profitability of his steamboat companies. Apparently believing he had brought financial ruin to the family business, Henry Disston and Sons, Disston committed suicide at his Philadelphia residence as creditors were preparing to foreclose on a $1 million loan. As others in his family had little or no interest in the Florida properties, and funds were required to secure the firm's indebtedness, the land was sold for a fraction of its value.

• Business records of Disston and Sons are at the factory site in Tacony, Pa. An excellent study of Hamilton Disston's Florida land development projects is an unpublished undergraduate paper written at the University of North Florida by Jack W. McClellan, "Hamilton Disston in Florida" (1987). Two other helpful articles, which appear in the *Florida Historical Quarterly* are J. E. Dovell, "The Railroads and the Public Lands of Florida, 1879–1905," 34 (1955): 236–58, and T. Frederick Davis, "The Disston Land Purchase," 17 (1939): 200–210. See also R. E. Rose, *The Swamp and Overflow Lands of Florida* (1916), and Charlton W. Tebeau, *A History of Florida* (1971). A well-written general account of the Disston family business is Harry C. Silcox, *A Place to Live and Work: The Henry Disston Saw Works and the Tacony Community of Philadelphia* (1994). An obituary is in the *Philadelphia Record*, 1 May 1896.

MARY ELLEN WILSON

DISSTON, Henry (24 May 1819–16 Mar. 1878), manufacturer, was born in Tewkesbury, England, the son of Thomas Disston, a machinist, and Ann Harrod. His grandfather owned a textile mill, and his father invented a lace machine. An ambitious group of English businessmen arranged for Thomas Disston to set up his lace-making device in the United States. Taking his eldest daughter and fourteen-year-old son, Henry, with him, Thomas Disston reached Philadelphia in early 1833. When his father died three days after their arrival, young Henry apprenticed himself to a company of sawmakers in Philadelphia, where he learned all aspects of the manufacture of saws. Seven years later he started his own business with his savings. Also in 1840 Henry married Amanda Mulvina Bickley. After only one year of marriage Amanda died while giving birth to twins, who survived only a few hours. By 1843 Henry had married Mary Steelman; they had nine children, eight of whom survived infancy. The five sons would eventually join their father's business.

Disston's company, the Keystone Saw, Tool, Steel and File Works, later renamed Henry Disston & Sons, established a fine reputation for the manufacture of various types of saws, but he encountered several financial setbacks between 1840 and 1850. To protect himself from capricious landlords, Disston purchased land in Philadelphia in 1850 to construct his own shop. By 1855 he decided to make his own steel as a cost-saving measure, something that the other Philadelphia sawmakers did not do. Realizing that higher quality steel would result in a better quality saw, Disston secured steelworkers from Sheffield, England, where Americans obtained most of their saw steel. Simultaneously he diversified his line of manufacturing by adding various types of saws, knives, trowels, squares, and other items. These kinds of innovations allowed Disston to outdistance his local business rivals and to compete effectively with English-made saws, which dominated the market in the United States.

During the Civil War the demand for war materials and the imposition of a tariff on foreign saws doubled the business of the plant. As the company's prosperity continued into the postwar years, fed by the brisk growth of the American lumber industry, Disston decided in 1871 to relocate several miles northeast of Philadelphia to accommodate expansion of the enterprise. "Tacony" was the name of the site selected. During the next few years, as the transfer occurred, many new machines were procured to perform tasks that had been handled manually, thus making the plant one of the most efficient in the world. By increasing productive capacity, the Disston company was positioned to emerge as the premier saw company in the United States and the world.

In association with the manufacturing establishment at Tacony, Disston constructed housing for his workers, a dispensary, a soup kitchen during economic downturns, a public park, and a music hall. Disston firmly believed that providing for the necessities of his employees was crucial to the success of the firm. He arranged a building and loan association, so workers could become homeowners. He provided company sports teams with the necessary recreational facilities. Furthermore, Disston developed a program to provide employee sickness insurance. His Tacony community became a classic example of nineteenth-century industrial paternalism through which he hoped to maintain good owner-employee relations, forestall strikes, and encourage loyalty to the firm.

Largely responsible for Disston's success was his continuous search for better processes to improve quality and increase production. On a visit to Paris, for example, he discovered the bandsaw, a continuous blade of steel with teeth; a bandsaw could be up to ten feet in height. It was a considerable improvement over the older circular saw. After purchasing two of the bandsaws, Disston utilized them in the construction of saw handles, thereby increasing production. Another secret to the prosperity of the firm was the participation of Disston family members. Disston brothers became involved in the supervision of the business. As the Disston sons and nephews joined the business, they started as shop apprentices and worked their way up to management positions, learning all facets of the operation. Furthermore, Disston encouraged his factory hands to participate in quality improvement.

Other factors also contributed to the company's emergence as the number-one saw company in the world. Disston was very knowledgeable about lumbermill operations. Realizing that different types of wood required different saw teeth, Disston tailored saws for the specific purposes of his customers in lumber companies and other industries. This knowledge and the resulting product development gave the Disston company a competitive advantage. He also purchased saw patents and experimented to learn what types of saws would best cut various types of wood. Throughout his active years Disston was responsible for more than twenty improvements in the manufacture of saws, including the development of inserted-tooth circular saws. With inserted-tooth saws, lumber companies could cut operating expenses by purchasing the saw teeth separately from the saw body. Another development was crosscut saws with raked teeth, which became a first choice for timber cutters.

When he died in Philadelphia, the Philadelphia *Public Ledger* commented, "Henry Disston created a new American industry. He gave to the United States the greatest saw works in the world." With perseverance, ingenuity, skillful management, and good labor relations, Disston transformed a two-man operation into the leading saw-manufacturing firm in the world.

• Henry Disston & Sons published two important publications that provide technical information on saws, *The Disston Lumberman's Handbook* (c. 1921) and *The Disston Saw, Tool, and File Book* (1940). Biographical information about Disston is contained in a pamphlet written by his grandson Jacob S. Disston, *Henry Disston (1819–1878): Pioneer Industrialist, Inventor and Good Citizen* (1950). By far the best source of information on Disston and his company is Harry C. Silcox, *A Place to Live and Work: The Henry Disston Saw Works and the Tacony Community of Philadelphia* (1994).

MARY ELLEN WILSON

DITHMAR, Edward Augustus (22 May 1854–16 Oct. 1917), journalist, was born in New York City, the son of Henry Dithmar and Anna (maiden name unknown). His father was foreman of the composing room at the New York *Evening Post*. Dithmar's public school education ended at seventeen when he joined his father at the *Evening Post*. He remained there until moving to the *New York Times* in 1877, serving successively as night editor (1882–1884), drama critic (1884–1901), London correspondent (1901–1902), book review editor (1902–1907), and editorial writer (1907–1917). Upon his appointment as night editor in 1882, he married Ella B. Knapp.

It was Dithmar's eighteen-year service as drama critic that brought him public recognition, but his colleagues at the *New York Times* knew him as a trusted adviser in the shaping of the newspaper's policy and as a constant contributor of book reviews and editorials, no matter what position he held on the staff. His colleague Francis W. Halsey wrote at length of "the sincere and cordial interest he had in the paper from the beginning." Dithmar's interests ranged from literary subjects to American and British politics to civic affairs. Noteworthy among his public-spirited crusades were his successful effort to prevent commercial encroachment upon city park spaces and his call for American military preparedness in the early days of World War I. He was deeply respected for his soundness of judgment. According to one posthumous tribute, Dithmar "could ever be depended upon to exhibit that poise of thought and utterance which made his words always sane and his thought not trivial, but fundamental. In his estimate of persons he was ever generous."

Dithmar's public-spiritedness comes across even in a piece of dramatic criticism, as in his review of Bronson Howard's *Shenandoah* (*New York Times*, 10 Sept.

1889) in which he relates the material of the play to larger issues in American history and life:

The author has spared no effort to emphasize the sentimental idea of the brotherhood of the contesting parties in our terrible war, and the recognition by individuals on either side of the natural ties which bound them to their foes. . . . Of course the true drama of the Civil War will not be written in our time. Mr. Howard has made a popular play, which, happily, is good enough to deserve popularity, but he touches very lightly on the causes of the rebellion and the feelings that prevailed during that dreadful period, in spite of his background of carnage, his signal lights and bugle calls, and the fleeting vision of glorious Phil Sheridan on horseback.

As a drama critic, Dithmar was especially admired for his fairness. He had a remarkable long-term memory for details of staging or performance in productions he had seen. His ability to analyze and evaluate the art of the actor was "unfailingly just and true," and yet he was "singularly little disturbed by mere badness in play or players. He simply passed the matter by as not worth getting wrought up about, so escaping the common fault of wasting denunciation on ignoble subjects." As another tribute expressed it, "what he said was quoted and respected, because there were many things he did not choose to say." A friend of his, the great actor John Drew, recalled that "he told me when he thought I was right and told the public too, and told me also when he thought I was wrong."

Dithmar was also credited with encouraging the unknown Clyde Fitch, who was to become the leading playwright of his day. Dithmar persuaded actor Richard Mansfield to commission Fitch's first play, *Beau Brummel* (1890), in which Mansfield triumphed, launching Fitch's prolific career. John Drew recalled that Dithmar was "the guide, philosopher, and friend to Clyde. We may judge, of course, from Mr. Fitch's growth how valuable that close friendship was, what worth Dithmar contributed to the art of the American playwright." Dithmar also published two books: *Memories of Daly's Theatres* (1897) and *John Drew* (1900). Dithmar died at Roosevelt Hospital in New York City.

• Dithmar's scrapbooks are in the Billy Rose Theatre Collection of the New York Public Library. Two samples of his reviewing are included in Montrose J. Moses, ed., *The American Theatre as Seen by Its Critics 1752–1934*. He is also listed in *Who's Who in Music and Drama* (1914) and *Who Was Who in America*, vol. 1: *1897–1942*. The *New York Times* published a number of tributes at the time of Dithmar's death; these include an editorial, 17 Oct. 1917; his obituary and a special tribute by John Drew, 18 Oct. 1917; the *Brooklyn Daily Eagle* obituary and a letter to the editor from Jerome H. Eddy, 19 Oct. 1917; a letter to the editor from Rush C. Hawkins and Dithmar's funeral eulogy by Rev. Charles J. Smith, 20 Oct. 1917; and a tribute by Francis W. Halsey, 21 Oct. 1917.

FELICIA HARDISON LONDRÉ

DITMARS, Raymond Lee (22 June 1876–12 May 1942), zoo curator and popular writer on reptiles, was born in Newark, New Jersey, son of John Van Harlingen Ditmars, a furniture dealer and Confederate veteran, and Mary Knaus. When Raymond was six the family moved to New York City. His interest in nature began with visits to Central Park, which had a small menagerie and natural areas teeming with snakes and other creatures, and to the salt marshes on the outskirts of Brooklyn, where his family spent the summer. These experiences captivated his interest, and, although his family intended for him to attend the U.S. Military Academy at West Point, his mind was on snakes.

When he was fifteen Ditmars and some like-minded boys founded a nature club, the Harlem Zoological Society, and through it he was introduced to the American Museum of Natural History where, in 1893, he became an assistant in its entomology department. He maintained collections of live snakes at the museum and at his parents' apartment, but by 1897 the meager salary at the museum forced him to take a stenographer's job at an optical instruments company. In July 1898 he became a reporter for the *New York Times*. One of his assignments was to interview William T. Hornaday, first director of the newly formed New York Zoological Society, which was soon to open its zoo in the Bronx. The interview led to an offer to become assistant curator (in charge) of reptiles.

Ditmars began his career at the New York Zoological Park in July of 1899; he remained there until his death. He later took on the posts of curator of mammals (1926) and curator of insects (1940), but reptiles remained his chief interest. His private hoard of snakes became the nucleus of the zoo's collection, which he quickly built into the country's largest. He fully recognized the public's fascination with snakes and, because of his theatrical flair, rarely missed an opportunity to stage some event—such as the feeding of a large python or milking the venom from a rattlesnake—to obtain maximum publicity for the zoo and himself. Soon, through his zoo work, public lectures, and publications, he became America's leading popular authority on snakes and other reptiles.

In 1903 Ditmars married Clara Elizabeth Hurd. They had two daughters. Since 1900 he had been working on his first book, *The Reptile Book* (1907), and it promptly became a standard. This was the first book to review the reptiles of North America, in text and illustrations, in a comprehensive yet nonscientific manner. It was reissued in an expanded edition in 1930, and together with his four other books on reptiles—*Reptiles of the World* (1910), *Snakes of the World* (1931), *Reptiles of North America* (1936), and *Field Book of North American Snakes* (1939)—it established his reputation. These books had a widespread influence and stimulated a large number of students to study reptiles professionally.

Ditmars also wrote highly popular books for the general public. The first, *Strange Animals I Have Known* (1931), was followed by several autobiographical books. Despite his claim to being a scientist, however, Ditmars published very few scientific papers based on his own research, and he was dismissed by many in the scientific community as merely a showman. His reptile books were not considered to be sufficiently complete or accurate, and many scientists objected to his exaggeration of information for effect. For many years Ditmars had used the title "doctor," even though he never attended college, but in 1930 Lincoln Memorial College in Tennessee awarded him an honorary Litt.D. degree.

Despite little credit from scientists, Ditmars was a pioneer in the production of nature films. He had a small studio in his home in which he produced short films to use in his numerous public lectures, and he eventually produced his first feature-length film, *The Jungle Circus* (1910), one of a series of popular nature movies.

Ditmars was also instrumental in the establishment in the United States of an institute for the manufacture of antivenins. Shocked by the death of a close friend from a snakebite, Ditmars began by developing techniques for the long-term storage of snake venoms. For several years he was the American distributor of antivenins manufactured in Brazil. U.S. law at that time did not permit importation for sale, so Ditmars gave supplies away. In 1926 Ditmars joined with several others to establish the Antivenin Institute of America, in Glenolden, Pennsylvania, to produce antivenins for treatment of victims of snakebite in North America.

Ditmars died in New York City.

• Ditmars's correspondence and office records are in the New York Zoological Society Archives, Bronx, N.Y. He wrote several autobiographical books, including *Thrills of a Naturalist's Quest* (1932), *Confessions of a Scientist* (1934), and *The Making of a Scientist* (1937), as well as books on insects, pets, prehistoric animals, and life in zoos. His biography was written by Laura N. Wood, *Raymond L. Ditmars, His Exciting Career with Reptiles, Animals and Insects* (1944). A biography from a scientific point of view is in Kraig Adler, ed., *Contributions to the History of Herpetology* (1989). An obituary and editorial is in the *New York Times*, 13 May 1942.

KRAIG ADLER

DITRICHSTEIN, Leo (6 Jan. 1865–28 June 1928), actor and playwright, was born Leo James Ditrichstein in Tamesvar, Hungary, the son of Count Sigismond Ladislav Ditrichstein and Bertha von Etvoes, daughter of the renowned Austrian novelist Joseph von Etvoes. Ditrichstein apprenticed in Berlin and performed at the Royal Theater in Hamburg, where, because of his acting skills, he became the company's leading actor. In 1890, at the request of Gustav Amberg, who hired German-speaking actors, Ditrichstein immigrated to the United States. He first appeared in German plays at the Amberg Theatre in New York while he studied English. After three years he had acquired fluency in English (although he spoke with a noticeable accent throughout his acting career), and he signed with Charles Frohman for John Drew's company. Ditrichstein's first English-speaking role was in

William Gillette's farce *Mr. Wilkinson's Widows* (1890); the play lasted for 140 performances at Proctor's Twenty-third Street Theatre. He made his New York debut under Frohman in *The Other Man* in 1893 and two years later came to the public's attention as Zou Zou in Paul M. Potter's *Trilby*, which lasted for 208 performances. Ditrichstein excelled in comic roles, such as Otto Whisky in *A Stag Party* (1895) and Achille Rabon, a mad scientist, in *Under the Polar Star* (1896). Also in 1896 he married Josephine Wehrle.

Early in his career Ditrichstein began to adapt plays as well as act in them. His earliest adaptation, along with renowned playwright Clyde Fitch, was *The Superfluous Husband* (1897), from a German source. Although one review chastised Ditrichstein and Fitch for not giving meaty roles to star actors Joseph and E. M. Holland, the critic described the adaptation as "a comedy with many merits, including those of ingenuity, originality, and fidelity to nature, and to human nature at that."

In 1898 Ditrichstein played George Tesman in the first New York performance of *Hedda Gabler*, earning rave reviews for his portrayal of the naive, diligent, and devoted husband of an aristocratic woman who fears scandal yet desires to manipulate the lives of others and to die beautifully. One critic wrote of Ditrichstein's performance that it was "beautiful in its illuminative power, and remarkable for its fidelity to Ibsen and to nature, and also for the quality of personal charm." Another critic applauded his interpretation of the "scholarly Tesman" as "beautiful in its perfection. I have seen no better piece of acting, comparatively speaking, all this season." Other notable Ditrichstein roles were Colonel Larivette in *Before and After* (1905), which Ditrichstein adapted from the French; the cynical Bernard in *The Lily* (1906); the philandering pianist whose long-suffering wife finally takes steps to stop him from cheating on her in *The Concert* (1910); Jacques Dupont in *The Temperamental Journey* (1913); and Sascha Tàticheff, whose wife sees him as her imagined lover in his adaptation of Hungarian playwright Ferenc Molnár's *The Phantom Rival* (1914).

Ditrichstein's portrayals were almost always praised by the critics. The headline of one theater review of *The Concert* gushed: BRILLIANT COMEDY BEAUTIFULLY ACTED. This was followed by a review that lauded Ditrichstein's adaptation of Herman Bahr's work but acclaimed his portrayal of Gabor Arany even more, calling it "the sort of achievement which comes along only once in so often to show how piffling and unimportant much of that which passes for acting on the stage is." Ditrichstein gave "a complete and wholly gratifying impersonation, and by long odds the finest example of genuine comedy acting to be seen on our stage at present." Likewise, the headlines of one review of *The Temperamental Journey* asserted that "BELASCO PROVIDES EXQUISITE COMEDY: With Leo Ditrichstein's Splendid Artistry to Charm." The critic continued that the play, another adaptation from a French source, "provides one of those exquisitely delightful evenings in the theatre when to the charm of an exhileratingly [sic] humorous tale is added the grace of a bit of tender sentiment genuinely expressed." The play concerns a failed artist who cannot sell his paintings. His unsuccessful career, exacerbated by his overbearing wife, renders life intolerable, so he decides to commit suicide. After writing a suicide note, he attempts to drown himself but fails at that too. Word of his supposed death resuscitates his reputation as an artist, and comedy ensues as he reveals himself as being still among the living.

Ditrichstein often worked with other playwrights, producers, and directors. He collaborated with Frederic and Fanny Hatton on *The Great Lover* (1915), a three-act drama that ran for 245 performances (three years). Ditrichstein played the title role. His character, Jean Paurel, is an actor who is notorious for playing the role of Don Giovanni off stage as well as on. After he loses his voice, Paurel's many female admirers quickly desert him. As he laments the loss of his voice and women, an admirer he has previously ignored telephones him and expresses interest in him. The drama created a stir because the set clearly resembled the Metropolitan Opera House and because the name of Ditrichstein's character resembled that of Metropolitan opera star Victor Maurel. The title of the drama also suited Ditrichstein, who became famous for his romantic leads. As one critic noted in a review of *The King* (1917), a comedy in which Ditrichstein played a monarch whose love life intersects with his political career, "Ditrichstein himself has been a main factor in making us accept a certain kind of lover as great, and now it is he who has produced 'The King,' which is quite the limit of his achievement in amorous and theatrical adventure."

Ditrichstein later co-produced (with Lee Shubert) and directed *The Americans in France* (1920), a comedy about the conflict between American and French ways of life, in particular, American preoccupation with modernization and change as opposed to French notions of convention and custom. Ditrichstein gave his last performance, as a businessman whose wife interferes with his work, in *The Business Widow* (1923), a comedy that he co-directed with Edward Elsner. Because it lacked realism, the play was unsuccessful at the box office.

While he was still a popular and successful actor, Ditrichstein retired from the New York stage, partly because he was concerned that the American motion picture industry was beginning to overshadow the theater. He spent much of his retirement in Florence before traveling to Auersperg, Yugoslavia, where he died. Although Ditrichstein began with small parts, partly because he was not an English native speaker, he gradually assumed larger ones—not only because he performed in his own adaptations but also because he was extraordinarily skilled as an actor. He was especially good in comic roles and considered by some critics to be one of the finest comic actors of his day. Several of his adaptations, such as *The Concert* (1910) and *The Temperamental Journey* (1913), also were quite successful. Ditrichstein's skills as an actor and playwright rendered him a prominent force on the New York stage during the early part of the twentieth century.

• Some of Ditrichstein's correspondence and photographs are in the S. C. Woodward Manuscripts in the Lilly Library, Indiana University, Bloomington. For more information on Ditrichstein's career see, in addition to entries on him in the standard biographical reference works, the *New York Times Theater Reviews* from 1890 to 1923; Samuel L. Leiter, *Encyclopedia of the New York Stage: 1920–1930* (1985); and Gerald Bordman, *American Theatre: A Chronicle of Comedy and Drama: 1869–1914* (1994). Obituaries are in the *New York Times*, 30 June 1928, and *Variety*, 4 July 1928.

ERIC STERLING

DITSON, Oliver (20 Oct. 1811–21 Dec. 1888), music publisher, was born in Boston, Massachusetts, the son of Joseph Ditson, a merchant, and Lucy Pierce. In 1823, having graduated from the Eliot School, Ditson began to work for Colonel Samuel H. Parker, a local bookseller and publisher who over the next three years introduced him to sheet music engraving. Through this association, Ditson was later able to trace a tortuous if unconvincing pedigree for his firm, from Parker back to 1783 and Ebenezer Battelle's book shop, which Ditson then argued to be America's first music publisher.

Next working for Isaac R. Butts and Alfred Mudge, Ditson at last set up his own shop in 1835 and rejoined forces with Parker the next year. The Parker & Ditson imprint appeared on dozens of song sheets over the next seven years and established the conservative character of Ditson's catalog, with its polite and sentimental songs rather than black minstrelsy and tastefully drab caption headings rather than stunning chromolithograph covers. In this period, sometime around 1840, he married Catherine Delano; they would have five children. In 1857 Ditson's imprint became Oliver Ditson & Co., now reflecting a partnership with John C. Haynes, who had worked for the firm since 1845.

Although Ditson flourished during the Civil War, his catalog of hundreds of new editions each year never achieved the distinction of that of Root & Cady in Chicago, which could call on the good name of the composer George F. Root; or those of Firth, Hall, & Pond in New York or Lee & Walker in Philadelphia, which were located in musical centers of greater breadth; or those of the Peters family, whose members in Baltimore, Pittsburgh, Cincinnati, and Louisville were in better touch with southern and frontier tastes. Ditson's imprint appeared on several Stephen Foster first editions, but nothing is known of any personal dealings between the two men. Ditson also published the nation's leading music periodical, *Dwight's Journal of Music*, from its fifth year until two years before its demise (1858–1879). However appropriate the journal's viewpoints were to Boston's musical tastes, little is known of Ditson's dealings with John Sullivan Dwight, editor of the journal and a former Brook Farm denizen. Throughout Ditson's career, his name was known, but he was not.

In 1856 Ditson became the first president of the Board of Music Trade, a music publishers' association formed to combat piracy—music copyright was just beginning to be appreciated—and to establish pricing practices both among members and between them and others in the emerging regional markets. Through Ditson's efforts, the board's massive *Complete Catalogue* appeared in 1870; its short, classified entries for roughly 100,000 titles was the first national bibliography of music in print.

The *Complete Catalogue* was clearly a boon to Ditson, who in the depressed years after the Civil War had been buying up other firms with less capital. Minor ones were acquired first; then, in 1867, Firth, Son & Co. of New York and in 1875, Lee & Walker of Philadelphia (these became branches of Oliver Ditson & Co. and were managed by his sons Charles H. Ditson and James Edward Ditson, respectively). In 1873 Miller & Beecham of Baltimore was acquired; in 1875, Wm. Hall & Son of New York; in 1877, G. D. Russell & Co. of Boston and J. L. Peters of New York; in 1879, G. André and in 1890, F. A. North & Co., both of Philadelphia. In addition, Ditson's capital was used to create new firms in other cities, the most famous of them being John Church in Cincinnati in 1860 and Lyon & Healy of Chicago in 1864. Ditson was also a president of the Continental Bank of Boston for twenty years as well as a supporter of local musical institutions, including the New England Conservatory.

At his death in Boston, Ditson, the preeminent music publisher of the nineteenth century, was eulogized as one who "made the business of publishing music a great industry, and if he did not confine himself to symphonies and oratorios . . . he did send sweet song into many a humble home, and helped make 'music' part of the daily life of the American citizen." An apologetic tone is discernible in these words, but as the speaker noted, if Ditson's firm had "issued so much poor music, where does one go for all the good music if not there. This influential firm . . . but responded to the demands of the times. It is a tradesman's right to do so."

Ditson's musical tastes and impact are apparent also in the subsequent history of his firm. International copyright, which Ditson had successfully opposed, was enacted in the copyright law of 1891. Following an unfavorable court decision on 6 February 1894, other firms slowly withdrew from the Board of Music Trade, often also in deference to the growing musical instrument market. By 1900, however, Oliver Ditson & Co. was still the country's largest music publisher, with nearly 100,000 titles in its catalog. The firm moved to successively larger quarters in 1891, 1904, and 1917. Responding to the critics who decried Ditson's modest tastes in marketing sentimental songs, his successors established the ambitious Musician's Library series (1903–1928), consisting of sixty-eight anthologies of songs and piano solos edited by various musical luminaries (among them, William Foster Apthorp, Vincent d'Indy, Henry T. Finck, Philip Hale, W. J. Henderson, Rupert Hughes, James Gibbons Huneker, Henry Edward Krehbiel, Ernest Newman, and Cecil Sharp) and printed at the Merrymount Press by Daniel Berkeley Updike. Ditson's firm was absorbed by the Theodore Presser Co. of Philadelphia in 1931, not so much because of any inflexibility in the face of changing musical tastes but rather as a result of the Great Depression.

• The Ditson archives were destroyed, and extant letters from Ditson himself are scarce and scattered. His publications are widely represented in the sheet-music collections of American libraries. The Ditson firm's history is William Arms Fisher, *Notes on Music in Old Boston* (1918), revised as *One Hundred and Fifty Years of Music Publishing in the United States* (1933). Dena J. Epstein's introduction to the reprint of the Board of Music Trade's *Complete Catalogue of Sheet Music and Musical Works* (1973), revised as "Music Publishing in the Age of Piracy," *Notes* 31 (1974): 7–29, describes the music publishing milieu in which Ditson worked.

D. W. KRUMMEL

DIVINE, Father (1877?–10 Sept. 1965), religious cult leader, was born George Baker, apparently on Hutchinson Island, Georgia, in obscure and indeterminate circumstances. It is difficult to recover specifics about Divine, a black sharecropper's son who spent his youth in the rural, post-Reconstruction South. This difficulty has been compounded by his own efforts to hide his prosaic origins because he eventually claimed to be God on earth. Most inquirers agree, however, that until the early 1900s the subsequently acclaimed deity was probably George Baker, who in his early life experienced racial prejudice, inadequate education, and poverty. By 1899 he resided in Baltimore, Maryland, where he taught Sunday school and preached occasionally at a Baptist church. Around 1906 he came under the influence of Samuel Morris, who took the biblical passage about the spirit of God dwelling within and arrogated it to himself alone. Baker served as "the Messenger" for Morris, but by 1912 he began claiming his own divinity. Such preaching in Valdosta, Georgia, two years later resulted in a lawsuit that listed Baker's identity as "John Doe, alias God." Jurors found the defendant (who was charged with disrupting congregations and general troublemaking) of unsound mind but recommended leniency if he left the state.

The arrival of this ardent visionary in New York City around 1915 coincided with the major northward push of Negro population. He soon moved to Brooklyn where a small band of disciples lived together, avoiding liquor and tobacco and sharing the warmth of religious communion. As spiritual leader of this commune he skillfully directed its economic organization and in 1919 moved the enlarged family to Sayville, Long Island. Known by then as "Major J. Devine," he was by 1919 formally recognized as husband to a woman named Pinninnah. He also adopted the title of reverend, while followers called him "Father," and consequently "Father Divine." Externally he projected the image of a modest suburbanite, though to his inner circle of believers he embodied the divine spirit. Divine often obtained jobs for his followers, who in turn surrendered their wages to the communal revenues. This allowed him to expand housing and provide free weekly banquets. By 1926 his personal magnetism attracted the first white converts, who mingled easily with black believers; together they lived chaste lives dedicated to harmony among all humankind.

As the Great Depression deepened, larger crowds attended Divine's apparently inexhaustible banquets. Though most followers came from Harlem and other urban ghettos, whites as well as blacks consumed opulent meals. The Reverend M. J. Divine welcomed all, charged nothing, and promised hospitality regardless of race, color, or creed. Increased crowds led to local resentment and charges of disturbing the peace. In 1932 at a trial presided over by Judge Lewis J. Smith, who conducted more of an inquisition than an inquest, Divine assumed the image of a martyr. When Smith fell dead three days after imposing the maximum sentence, adherents' belief in Divine's control over events rose to unprecedented heights. "I hated to do it," he said upon release, and soon moved his headquarters to Harlem.

In 1933 Divine's following received its permanent name of the Peace Mission Movement. Its divine leader spoke to the poor and powerless to assure them that they were still close to God. The Peace Mission gave him the moral sanction and institutional base for urging programs of social and economic change. By 1936 he developed a platform with fourteen planks dedicated to achieving human rights and racial equality. The platform sought to repress base passions such as prejudice, lust, and selfishness in addition to lesser evils like cosmetics and movies. But the most significant efforts centered on abolishing color barriers among believers. Even words like "white" or "Negro" were forbidden, and followers were enjoined to live together in harmony under a leader who refused to acknowledge distinctions of race.

In 1942 Divine acquired a large estate outside Philadelphia and established it as the center for branches formed in most northern cities. He was not known for compelling pulpit oratory, though a weekly paper recorded his every word for those who acclaimed his deity. His movement had no clergy, creed, or scripture. Its meetings featured no formal worship but rather were occasions for impromptu speeches, jubilant songs, and banquets as a form of communion. Divine had urged chastity among his people, and so his second marriage in 1946 to Edna Rose Ritchings raised questions. The fact that his new bride, called "Sweet Angel," was white and fifty years his junior presented even more difficulties. But Divine explained that this was a spiritual union and the occasion for his first wife, who had simply disappeared in 1937, to inhabit a new body. In the later years of his life he continued to exemplify the ideals of social and racial harmony, which his cult represented and which he wished the whole of American society could achieve. Ill with diabetes, he died in Woodmont, Pennsylvania, but even that event did not endanger the belief that Divine remained spiritually present in the movement, directing its details as before.

• Indispensable sources for sermons, letters, interviews, and office talks relating to Father Divine are the weekly journals *Spoken Word* (1934–1937) and *New Day* (1936–). The better secondary sources for biographical material are Robert A. Parker, *The Incredible Messiah: The Deification of Father Divine* (1937), and Sara Harris with Harriet Crittenden, *Father Divine* (1953; repr. 1971). These are now superseded by Robert Weisbrot, *Father Divine and the Struggle for Racial Equality* (1983). An obituary is in the *New York Times,* 11 Sept. 1965.

HENRY WARNER BOWDEN

DIX, Beulah Marie (25 Dec. 1876–25 Sept. 1970), playwright and screenwriter, was born in Kingston, Massachusetts, the daughter of Henry Dix, a factory foreman, and Maria (maiden name unknown). The family moved to Plymouth, Massachusetts, an important revolutionary war site that Dix used later as a backdrop for her early plays and novels. The Dix family eventually moved to Chelsea, where sixteen-year-old Beulah was valedictorian at Chelsea High School.

"From the very beginning I meant to be a writer," Dix declares in the *Junior Book of Authors*. Write she did; her writing career spanned sixty years and included historical romances, plays, novels, and silent-movie scripts. In 1893 Henry Dix sent Beulah Marie to Radcliffe College in spite of the high cost of education. At Radcliffe she studied history and English, combining the two subjects in plays and essays for her classes and the Idler, the drama club. The research she did for her history courses served as good preparation for establishing the settings she later used as backdrops to her plays: the Thirty Years' War, the Boston Tea Party, and seventeenth-century England. One of her sophomore essays, which dealt with the Thirty Years' War, was later sold to *Lippincott's Magazine*. At age twenty Dix received her A.B. summa cum laude. She was also the first woman to win the George B. Sohier Prize, given to a Harvard or Radcliffe student who presents the best thesis. In the year that Dix returned to college to get her A.M., she sold her first book, *Hugh Gwyeth: A Roundhead Cavalier* (1896), to the Macmillan Company. A second commission from Macmillan convinced Dix that she could support herself by becoming a writer rather than a teacher; the latter was what her family encouraged her to be.

Even though Dix relied on military events to frame her early plays and fiction, she was a pacifist, and the themes of peace and forgiveness dominate her novels, plays, and children's books. As she matured as a writer, Dix weaned herself from the trappings of historical romances and clarified her arguments for peace. In contrast to the detailed settings of her early plays, the stage directions in *Across the Border* (1915) are rather vague, citing neither war, time, nor place: "The people in the play speak English, but they are no more meant to be English than they are meant to be Austri-

an, French, German, or Russian." Dix risked her career by publishing *Across the Border* and another antiwar play, *Moloch* (1915), when the United States was on the brink of entering World War I. Nevertheless, she insisted on asking her audience the same crucial question that the hero in *Across the Border* confronts: "Did you do anything yourself to stop it?"

A self-confirmed tomboy from childhood, Dix did not seek feminine companionship during her lifetime. In fact, little boys are the main characters in Dix's plays written when she was a child because she "found them more exciting than little girls." However, she did acknowledge two very important women in her life, one of whom was Evelyn Sutherland. In contrast to Dix and her bluestocking lifestyle, Sutherland was married, twenty years Dix's senior, and well established in Boston society. Yet, together, Dix and Sutherland collaborated on *The Breed of the Treshams* (1903) and *The Substitute* (1908). Another collaborative play, *The Road to Yesterday* (1906), was a standard of Sir John Martin Harvey's repertory, which Dix later rewrote as a script when she went to Hollywood. As was the custom of the day, Sutherland and Dix wrote their plays using the male pseudonym "John Rutherford" in order to make the play more acceptable to English audiences.

Dix's personal life was influenced by Sutherland as well. Sutherland's adopted son Alan Rowe had numerous college friends, including George Flebbe, a German immigrant who came to the United States to be a junior partner in a book firm. Flebbe admired Dix's writing very much, and they married soon after they met in 1911. As a successful book importer in Boston, Flebbe provided Dix with a comfortable writing atmosphere. They had one child, named after Sutherland. When searching for words to describe her mother's marriage, Evelyn Flebbe Scott conceded that "*contented* may not be the right word for Mother's marriage; *satisfied* might do." Mother and daughter remained close throughout Dix's life.

The other important woman in Dix's life was her New York agent, Beatrice de Mille. By 1916 de Mille was living in Hollywood, California, near her movie director sons, William de Mille and Cecil de Mille. Beatrice de Mille invited Dix and her daughter to join her in California for a brief vacation in 1916. Dix never left. Polio was raging on the East Coast, and the world war had crippled Flebbe's book-importing business. After a year settling his accounts in Boston, Flebbe joined his family and went to work for the oil industry in California. Meanwhile, Dix's standards and experience as a playwright easily transferred to the demands of both the silver screen and screen director William de Mille.

During the depression, Dix continued to be the main provider for her family by working for Bertram Millhauser at RKO studios. She was in great demand as a writer because she could create strong, historically accurate characters. She also had a talent for writing about violence, which directors liked. Aside from her career as a silent-movie scriptwriter, Dix continued to experiment with other forms of writing. By 1927 she had abandoned the historical romance format. *The Turned About Girls*, a children's book of rhymes, was published in 1927. Almost in direct contrast to the children's book, her novel *Their Own Desire* is loosely based on the life of William de Mille and his divorce, a risqué subject for that time. Ironically, Dix's career as a silent-film scriptwriter ended because directors assumed that scriptwriters were not versatile enough to write dialogue for the new "talkies."

Dix is remembered primarily as a playwright of historical romances. Not much is known about her scripts because scriptwriters did not begin to receive credit for their work until the Screen Writer's Guild was formed in 1936 (twenty years after Dix began working as a screenwriter). By then most of her scripts were assumed to be company property by MGM and RKO, as was the accepted policy of the time. Dix's solitary nature also contributed to her anonymity as a silent-screen scriptwriter. Even though she was in the midst of Hollywood's heyday, she was selective about the company she kept. She died at her home in Hollywood.

• Dix's children's novels include *Soldier Rigdale* (1899), *The Fair Maid of Graystones* (1905), *Merrylips* (1906), *The Lilac Room* (1906), and *Blithe McBride* (1916). Her plays include *The Road to Yesterday* (1906), *Allison's Lad* (1910), *Fighting Blade* (1912), *Hands Off!* (1920), and *Pity of God* (1932). *The Wedding Eve Murder* (1941) is her last novel. See also Evelyn Flebbe Scott, *Hollywood: When Silents Were Golden* (1972), a biographical account of Dix's career as a screenwriter and mother. For Dix's contribution to the movie industry and literature, see M. S. Logan, *The Part Taken by Women in American History* (1972).

TAMARA HORN

DIX, Dorothea Lynde (4 Apr. 1802–17 July 1887), social reformer, was born in Hampden, Maine (on the Penobscot River), the daughter of Joseph Dix, a minister, and Mary Bigelow. During her early years Dorothea shared a small cottage with her parents and two younger brothers. Because her family was quite poor, she often traveled to Boston to live with her grandparents. In 1816 she began a career as a teacher. Five years later Dix opened her own school for young women in Boston. During this early period of her life, Dix worked diligently, teaching during the day while reading and writing late into the evening. Included among her students were the daughters of influential Bostonian William Ellery Channing, who became one of her early supporters.

In 1827 Dix became severely ill with tuberculosis. In an effort to regain her health, she spent the spring and summer that year at Channing's country retreat in Portsmouth, Rhode Island. Following this, Dix dedicated herself to writing while also working to regain her health. Having already published a science textbook for young students titled *Conversations on Common Things* (1824), Dix subsequently produced other books, including *Ten Short Stories for Children* (1827), *Meditations for Private Hours* (1828), *The Garland of Flora* (1829), and *The Pearl or Affection's Gift: A Christmas and New Year's Present* (1829).

With her health still not fully restored, Dix again joined the Channing family for a vacation in the fall of 1830. This time they traveled to St. Croix. After an extended retreat, Dix returned to teaching in Boston in 1831. For the next five years she followed an exhaustive schedule, which now included caring for her aging grandmother. During this time she complained to her friend Anne Heath in Brookline, Massachusetts, "There is so much to do, I am broken on a wheel." In the spring of 1836 she collapsed. Suffering frequent pain and hemorrhaging, she soon lost the use of a lung. In an effort to recover her strength once again, Dix sailed to Liverpool, England, where she stayed in the home of William Rathbone, a wealthy merchant and friend of Channing. Often bedridden and extremely weak, Dix stayed in Liverpool for a total of eighteen months.

In England Dix learned of the work of Philippe Pinel, a French doctor who had campaigned for prison reform during the late eighteenth century. She also became familiar with the efforts of William Tuke, Rathbone's grandfather, who founded a sanctuary for the mentally ill in England called the Retreat at York. The careers of these two men soon would inspire her to investigate the plight of the insane in the United States.

After hearing of the death of her grandmother, Dix returned to Boston in 1837. Shortly thereafter, she received an inheritance that freed her from the need to work as a teacher. During the next few years Dix remained preoccupied with her health. Advised to avoid the New England winter, she spent time in Washington, D.C., and in Oakland, Virginia.

By 1841 Dix had regained her strength. That winter she visited a jail in East Cambridge, Massachusetts, after being invited to teach a Sunday school class. Having heard rumors of the horrible conditions that existed in the jail, she took the opportunity to inspect the facility herself. After listening to the concerns of a group of women prisoners, she asked to see where the "insane" were kept. Taken to a dark, underground cavern, Dix discovered a number of mentally ill women in cold, filthy cells.

Shocked by this experience, Dix consulted with her friend Channing. He advised her to talk with influential men in the community in order to arouse public opinion regarding the plight of the mentally ill. She visited with educator Horace Mann, abolitionist Charles Sumner, and the head of the Perkins Institute for the Blind, Samuel Gridley Howe. Gaining the support of these men, known at the time as "the three horsemen of reform" in Massachusetts, Dix began an eighteen-month tour of poorhouses and prisons in the state. During this time, she visited approximately 500 towns in search of the mentally ill. In many cases she found individuals kept in cages, chained to walls, or otherwise mistreated.

In support of Dix's efforts, Howe published an article in the *Boston Daily Advisor* on 8 September 1841 that criticized the treatment of the mentally ill throughout Massachusetts. Along with other letters published around the same time, Howe's description sparked significant public response. Encouraged, Dix decided to take up the cause of the mentally ill full-time. Two years later she composed the first of what would become several "memorials" to state legislatures throughout the country. In *A Memorial to the Massachusetts Legislature* (1843) she described what she had seen during her tour and called for immediate reforms. "Men of Massachusetts," she wrote, "I implore. I demand pity and protection for these of my suffering, outraged sex." With the support of Howe, Mann, and others, Dix's petition was approved and a bill was passed that soon provided needed funds for the mentally ill at the Worcester State Hospital. After this first victory, she expanded her campaign to the states of New York, New Jersey, Pennsylvania, Maryland, Ohio, Kentucky, and Tennessee.

On 10 April 1844 the *Providence Journal* printed an article by Dix describing the living conditions of Abram Simmons, an insane man held in a jail near Providence, Rhode Island. Titled "Astonishing Tenacity of Life," Dorothea wrote describing Simmons's cell:

Six to eight feet square, built entirely of stone and entered through two iron doors, excluding both light and fresh air, and entirely without accommodation of any description for warming and ventilating. The internal surface of the walls was covered with a thick frost . . . the only bed was a small sacking stuffed with straw. The bed itself was wet, and the outside covering was completely saturated with drippings from the walls and stiffly frozen.

She then offered a portrait of Simmons himself. "In utter darkness, encased on every side by walls of frost, his garments [were] constantly more or less wet, with only wet straw to lie upon, and a sheet of ice for his covering, has this most dreadfully abused man existed through the past inclement winter." She suggested that "his teeth must have been worn out by constant and violent chattering for such of length of time, night and day." With this vivid account, Dix created new opportunities for mental health reform.

While in Providence, Dix visited the home of wealthy businessman Cyrus Butler to ask for money to help improve treatment of the mentally ill. To her surprise, Butler agreed to donate $40,000 to her cause. This allowed several hundred of the city's "mentally incompetent" to be transferred to a new hospital. Following this success, Dix turned her attention to New Jersey, where she presented a memorial to the state legislature. The New Jersey lawmakers approved her proposal to establish a new state hospital in February 1845. A similar decree also gained the necessary votes in the Pennsylvania legislature the same year.

By the end of 1845, Dix had traveled approximately 10,000 miles, visiting eighteen state penitentiaries, 300 county jails, and more than 500 poorhouses in much of the U.S. Midwest and South, as well as in portions of eastern Canada. At this point, she had helped to establish six new hospitals for the mentally ill and had influenced the improvement of numerous other facilities. During the following three years she continued to lobby state legislatures on behalf of the mentally ill.

Beginning in 1848 Dix increasingly devoted her energy to reforms at the federal level. She began a new project that proposed that revenue collected from the sale of public land be used to establish a federal fund for the mentally ill, blind, deaf, and mute across the nation. Despite significant support for the measure, Congress turned down her request. Quickly, she appealed again. This time Dix more than doubled the amount of public domain requested. In her memorial to Congress, she described the conditions she had observed in jails, poorhouses, and other facilities, where inmates were "bound with galling chains, . . . lacerated with ropes, scourged with rods, and terrified beneath storms of profane execrations and cruel blows; now subject to gibes and scorn and torturing tricks, now abandoned to the most loathsome necessities, or subject to the vilest and most outrageous violations." Recognizing her determination, Congress designated a special alcove in the Capitol library for Dix. Despite her persistence, however, approval of her proposal continued to be frustrated by political delays in Washington. With the opening of the 1850 Congress, Dix again increased the amount of land requested and worked to gain additional support. Further action was unsuccessful, however, until early 1854. At that time the Senate voted to approve Dix's bill by a two-thirds majority. In August the House also passed the measure. When the bill reached the desk of President Franklin Pierce, he vetoed it. Asked why he disapproved of the legislation, Pierce said that he feared it would make the federal government responsible not only for the "indigent insane" but also "all the poor of the United States." Although Pierce's veto had killed Dix's bill, it did not end her determination to champion the cause of the mentally ill.

Dix left for Liverpool in September 1854. In February of the following year she traveled to Scotland, where she resumed her reform campaign. Working constantly, Dix conferred with notable London doctors and visited several institutions in both Scotland and England. By April she had generated sufficient interest to persuade Queen Victoria to appoint a Royal Commission to investigate the condition of the mentally ill. Two years later, Parliament approved a law that allocated funds for the improvement of asylums in Scotland.

After her success in the United Kingdom, Dix then set her sights on the European continent. Beginning in June 1855, she traveled for approximately one year, visiting institutions in France, Switzerland, Italy, Greece, Turkey, Russia, Sweden, Norway, Denmark, Holland, and Germany. In Rome she appealed to Pope Pius IX, who later facilitated the creation of a new asylum. Cyrus Hamlin, a Turkish doctor who had hosted Dix in Constantinople, later conveyed his impression of her to biographer Francis Tiffany: "She had two objects in view, the hospitals and prisons. To these she seemed wholly devoted, although her conversation and her interest, embraced a vast variety of subjects . . . Miss Dix made the impression [of being] a person of culture, judgement, self-possession, absolute fearlessness in the path of duty, and yet a woman of refinement and true Christian philanthropy." As with her experiences in Italy and Turkey, Dix's talent as well as her tireless dedication brought about important changes in the treatment of the mentally ill in many of the countries she visited.

In the fall of 1856 Dix returned to New York. For the next five years she continued to work for mental health reform in the United States and Canada. In 1860 her earlier efforts in Washington finally bore fruit. Her bill, allocating funds for the New Jersey State Hospital in Trenton, passed both the House and Senate and was signed by President James Buchanan. That same year Dix's lobbying prompted the Tennessee legislature as well as private donors in the state of Pennsylvania to provide significant sums dedicated to the treatment of the mentally ill.

In 1861 the outbreak of the Civil War temporarily suspended Dix's advocacy for the mentally ill. On 10 June 1861 she was appointed superintendent of U.S. Army nurses. For the next few years Dix trained approximately 180 young women, including Louisa May Alcott, for medical duty during the war. One doctor testified to Dix's dedication during this period by writing that she "was a very retiring, sensitive woman, yet brave and bold as a lion to do battle for the right and for justice. . . . She was very unpopular in the war with surgeons, nurses, and any others, who failed to do their whole duty." As with her deep commitment to the cause of mental health reform, Dix's service during the war won the respect of many. She received special recognition for her service during the war in December 1866 when Secretary of War Edwin M. Stanton awarded her two national flags for "the Care, Succor, and Relief of the Sick and wounded Soldiers of the United States on the Battle-Field, in Camps and Hospitals during the recent War."

Following the war, Dix resumed her career as an advocate for the mentally ill. Traveling the country as before, she continued to visit institutions and lobby state legislators. In Washington, Dix persuaded the visiting Japanese chargé d'affairs to help establish facilities for the mentally ill in his country. In late 1875 she was pleased to learn that an asylum had been built in Kyoto.

At the age of seventy-nine, Dix, who never married, took her final tour to parts of New England and New York. After this, she retired in Trenton, New Jersey, where, after a convalescence of five years, she died.

In her lifetime, Dorothea Dix brought about significant changes in the care of the mentally ill in North America and Europe. Her work influenced conceptions about those held in prisons and asylums by identifying mental illness as a medical rather than moral issue. Her efforts helped pave the way for improved treatment of the mentally ill as well as the creation of more than 120 new mental health facilities. As biographers Charles Schlaifer and Lucy Freeman wrote, "It was Dorothea Lynde Dix who lifted the status [of the insane] from that of wounded beasts who were brutalized, chained, thrown food as though they were vicious dogs, and left to freeze in the cold, to that of troubled mortals who could be helped to regain their senses as they received understanding care that helped them reach the roots of their inner disturbances" (p. 161). Dix's compassionate work and dedicated effort for over forty years helped open the eyes of many to the plight of the mentally ill. Her distinguished career as an advocate for reform has earned her an important place in history as well as the respect of people around the world.

• Dix's papers are at Houghton Library, Harvard University. Francis Tiffany's *Life of Dorothea Lynde Dix* (1891) offers the first and most detailed biography of Dix, including a number of letters exchanged with her friends William Ellery Channing, Samuel Gridley Howe, Horace Mann, Anne Heath, Mrs. Hare, Daniel Tuke, Mr. and Mrs. William Rathbone, Mrs. Samuel Torrey, and others, as well as interviews with various people who knew her. Other biographies include Helen E. Marshall, *Dorothea Lynde Dix: Forgotten Samaritan* (1937); Rachael Baker, *Angel of Mercy* (1955); Dorothy Clark Wilson, *Stranger and Traveler: The Story of Dorothea Lynde Dix, American Reformer* (1975); and Charles Schlaifer and Lucy Freeman, *Heart's Work: Civil War Heroine and Champion of the Mentally Ill, Dorothea Lynde Dix* (1991).

ANDREW G. WOOD

DIX, Dorothy (18 Nov. 1861–16 Dec. 1951), journalist and personal advice columnist, was born Elizabeth Meriwether on her family's plantation in Montgomery County, Tennessee, the daughter of Will Douglas Meriwether, a horse breeder, and Maria Winston. Her mother died when Elizabeth was a child; her father was the benefactor of inherited wealth and a descendant of the explorer Meriwether Lewis. The Civil War changed the family fortunes, and the remarriage of her father to a cousin, Martha Gilmer Chase, changed the family structure to one of strict discipline.

Taught by a family member how to read, Elizabeth read voraciously from her great-grandfather's library. Eventually the family moved to Clarksville, Tennessee, and she attended the female academy and later completed one semester at Hollins Institute in Virginia. Attracted to the debonair George O. Gilmer, her stepmother's brother and ten years her senior, Elizabeth married him in 1882. They had no children.

George Gilmer had a small amount of success as an inventor of methods for distilling turpentine, but the family struggled with its finances. During this period, while living in Clarksville, Elizabeth submitted short stories and sketches to newspapers. Although her husband became irrational and his erratic moods were diagnosed as a mental illness, Elizabeth refused to leave him throughout their marriage, which lasted for forty-seven years. In the early 1890s Elizabeth herself had a nervous breakdown and left for a rest on the Mississippi Gulf Coast, where she met Eliza Nicholson, publisher and owner of the *New Orleans Picayune*.

Nicholson bought one of Elizabeth's stories for three dollars and in 1894 hired her to work on the paper writing obituaries and recipes. The editor, Major Nathaniel Burbank, at first did not approve of her but soon realized that she was a "first rate newspaperwoman." Shortly after, the newspaper employed her to write an advice column for women titled "Sunday Salad." Choosing the pseudonym of Dorothy Dix, by which she became well known, she gained popularity with a casual writing style and simple language. Her writing encompassed many feminist subjects such as dress reform, health care, and education. After the turn of the century she petitioned for women's right to the franchise and campaigned with many suffrage activists. A number of her early columns related to her own life and spoke to women concerned with the financial difficulties that they encountered when faced with supporting themselves. Dix wrote in her column of 5 September 1897, "Nothing could be more meaningless than a discussion of a woman's right to earn money. It would be . . . just as profitable to debate her right to breathe."

As her column became more popular it was renamed "Dorothy Dix Talks," and Dix received fan mail and letters from women who trusted her advice. In 1900 she was asked by William Randolph Hearst to join the *New York Journal* but turned him down at the time. Eliza Nicholson had died, and Dix remained loyal to Burbank at the *Picayune* until his death in 1901. She then took the job with Hearst.

At the *Journal* Dix's trial period was spent covering the headline story of temperance leader Carry Nation. As she followed the story of Nation, who went into saloons smashing bottles of liquor, Dix wrote a dramatic and lively account of the event and quipped that it was "a waste of good liquor." Concluding the story, she headed for New York, where she went to work covering courtroom scenes at murder trials and became famous as one of the nation's "sob sisters," a woman writer who could recognize a personal story—reminiscent of a soap opera—and relate it to the public.

After fifteen years of sitting in courtrooms and feeling that advice was more valuable than reporting crime, Dix signed on with the Wheeler Syndicate in 1917 to write her column, "Dorothy Dix Talks." The column appeared six days a week; she devoted three days to actual advice and three days to previously published letters and answers. In the same year, she returned to New Orleans, where she bought a home, and in 1928 Dorothy Dix Day was held in a New Orleans park. Her husband, who had alternately lived with her and in hospitals, died in a mental institution in 1929. Dix continued to write her column without the use of ghost writers until 1949 and died two years later in New Orleans.

At the height of her career Dix received as many as four hundred to five hundred letters a day, had nearly sixty million readers, and earned an annual income in excess of $90,000 a year. As one of the first personal advice columnists in America, she was popularized as the "mother confessor to millions." She believed that people should practice what they preach, and for her entire career she stayed in a marriage of hardship and advocated that women work things out rather than divorce. Her common-sense advice kept up with the changing times. She called women the "architects" of their own fate, always stressing their need to receive an education in order to support themselves. Dix felt that her purpose in life was helping others work out their problems. The hundreds of letters she received each day told her she had accomplished that goal.

• Some of Dix's letters are in the archives at Tulane University. The Meriwether Family Papers, which include some of her letters, are at Western Kentucky University. Dix's work appeared Sundays in the *New Orleans Picayune*, 1895–1901, and in the *New York Journal*, 1901–1917; after 1917 her column was widely syndicated. She also contributed regular features to *Good Housekeeping* and other women's magazines. Her books, some of which consist of her columns, include *Fables of the Elite* (1902); *Dorothy Dix on Woman's Ballot* (1908); *Woman's Lack of Pride* (1912); *Mirandy* (1914); *Hearts à la Mode* (1915); *Mirandy Exhorts* (1922); *My Trip Around the World* (1924); *Dorothy Dix—Her Book: Every-day Help for Every-day People* (1926); *Mexico* (1934); and *How to Win and Hold a Husband* (1939). Biographical information about Dix is often inaccurate, and a full-length biography, Harnett T. Kane, *Dear Dorothy Dix: The Story of a Compassionate Woman* (1952), written in collaboration with Ella Bentley Arthur, is anecdotal and sometimes cites sources imprecisely. See also Herman Deutsch, "Dorothy Dix Talks," in *Post Biographies of Famous Journalists* (1942). For a discussion of Dix's early work see Madelon Golden Schilpp and Sharon M. Murphy, *Great Women of the Press* (1983); Dorothy M. Brown, *Setting a Course: American Women in the 1920s* (1987); and Margaret Culley, "Sob-Sisterhood: Dorothy Dix and the Feminist Origins of the Advice Column," *Southern Studies* 16 (Summer 1977): 201–10. An obituary appears in the *New York Times*, 17 Dec. 1951.

MARILYN ELIZABETH PERRY

DIX, John Adams (24 July 1798–21 Apr. 1879), politician and general, was born in Boscawen, New Hampshire, the son of Timothy Dix, a merchant, and Abigail Wilkins. He received a varied liberal education, including a year at Phillips Exeter Academy and fifteen months at the College of Montreal. At age fourteen, while being tutored in Boston, Dix pleaded to join the army to defend the nation in the War of 1812. His father, a major, helped him to obtain a commission, and he served in battles at Chrysler's Field (1813) and Lundy's Lane (1814). His father's death during the war caused Dix to stay in the army to help support his stepmother and siblings. Serving as an aide to Major General Jacob Brown, the handsome, well-spoken young man made the most of duties in New York and Washington to meet prominent men such as James Madison (1751–1836) and John C. Calhoun and to begin writing for party newspapers such as the *National Intelligencer* and the *New York Statesman*. While rising to the rank of major, Dix still managed to read law and was admitted to the District of Columbia bar in 1824.

In 1826 Dix married Catharine Morgan, the adopted daughter of a New York congressman with sizable upstate landholdings. The couple eventually had seven children. Dix resigned from the army in 1828 to become his father-in-law's managing agent in Cooperstown, New York. Dix, long active in factional politics, united with the Jacksonians in 1828 out of a strong dislike for their Anti-Masonic opponents, whom he considered irrational for their attacks on Free Masons. Within three years the young lawyer was appointed adjutant general, a position that enabled him to exert party leadership in the "Albany Regency," an informal group who made patronage decisions. As New York secretary of state (1833–1839), he initiated improvements in teacher training and organized a state geological survey. When the Whigs regained the statehouse, Dix edited the *Northern Light*, a literary and scientific journal (1841–1843), and traveled to southern Europe, later publishing *A Winter in Madeira, and a Summer in Spain and Florence* (1850). Dix was chosen by the legislature in 1845 to fill the remaining five-year Senate term of Silas Wright, recently elected governor. Like his mentor Martin Van Buren, Dix was distressed by President James K. Polk's unfriendly policies toward northern Democrats, and he supported the Wilmot Proviso restricting the expansion of slavery into territory acquired from Mexico, although he never attacked slavery as morally wrong. Dix reluctantly followed Van Buren into the Free Soil party in 1848, running as its gubernatorial candidate. The Whig triumph over the divided Democrats cost Dix reelection to the Senate in 1849. The New York Democrats reunited following the Compromise of 1850, and Dix spoke extensively for Franklin Pierce in the 1852 election. Southern Democrats, however, remembered Dix's former apostasy and kept him from any major patronage appointments in the 1850s.

Dix moved to New York City in 1849 and became a highly respected railroad attorney and financier. In 1860 President James Buchanan, embarrassed by corruption in the New York post office, named Dix postmaster. Dix made overtures to southern Democrats by running as the Breckenridge (southern Democratic) gubernatorial candidate in 1860, arguing to northerners that southerners were not secessionists. When southern states seceded after the election, Dix felt betrayed. As Buchanan's secretary of the treasury in early 1861, Dix not only helped calm financial markets and obtained needed loans, but he galvanized northern opinion by ordering New Orleans officials to instantly shoot anyone lowering the American flag. When war erupted in 1861, he was made president of New York City's Union Defense Committee, which was responsible for raising money, supplies, and volunteers for the war.

Dix's nationalism was attractive to President Abraham Lincoln, who needed to demonstrate bipartisan support for the Union effort. Dix was named a major general in the army and served in administrative posts in politically sensitive areas. As head of the Department of Maryland, he arrested secessionists but also returned fugitive slaves. Named commander of the Department of the East following the July 1863 New York City draft riots, Dix asserted national authority by peacefully carrying out the draft in August. In 1864 he shut down the *World* and *Journal of Commerce*, Democratic newspapers that had printed a false draft call, but refused to let General Benjamin F. Butler's (1818–1893) troops occupy the city in force during the fall elections, as the general urged.

As a War Democrat Dix stood between traditional Democrats and Republicans, a valuable symbol for those on either side trying to broaden their parties' support at election time. But in an era of extreme partisanship, Dix had also alienated the hardliners in both parties, subtly eroding his ability to lead. After the war he supported President Andrew Johnson's unsuccessful National Union Movement and was appointed minister to France (1866–1869). In 1872 the Republicans, concerned about Democratic overtures to the Liberal Republicans, nominated Dix for governor. Although elected easily, neither traditional Republicans nor Democrats gave him consistent support as governor. Despite a competent administration, Dix's political woes were compounded by the panic of 1873, and he was defeated by Samuel J. Tilden in 1874. He died in New York.

• Dix's papers are at the Columbia University library. The basic biographical source is *Memoirs of John Adams Dix* (1883), compiled by his son, Morgan Dix. The only modern book-length study is Martin Lichterman, "John Adams Dix, 1798–1879" (Ph.D. diss., Columbia Univ., 1952). See also Jerome Mushkat, *The Reconstruction of the New York Democracy, 1861–1874* (1981), Ernest A. McKay, *The Civil War and New York City* (1990); and Christopher Dell, *Lincoln and the War Democrats* (1975). Obituaries are in the *New York Times*, 21–23 Apr. 1879.

PHYLLIS F. FIELD

DIX, Morgan (1 Nov. 1827–29 Apr. 1908), Episcopal clergyman, was born in New York City, the son of John Adams Dix, a politician and military officer, and Catharine Morgan. He spent his youth in Albany while his father was New York's secretary of state. The family moved to New York City in 1842 but went to Europe soon afterward, spending time on the Island of Madeira and in Florence and Rome because of Catharine Dix's poor health. After a year of studies in a private school in New York, Dix entered Columbia University in 1845 and graduated in 1848. Beginning but then abandoning the study of law, in 1849 he entered the General Theological Seminary, from which he graduated in 1852. Ordained a deacon in 1852 and a priest in 1853, he served from 1852 through 1855 as the assistant rector of St. Mark's in Philadelphia.

Dix's maternal grandfather and father were vestry members of Trinity Parish, the oldest and most important of the Episcopal churches in New York City, and his father played an important role in the financial planning for Trinity Chapel, a satellite congregation created in response to urban growth and changing residential patterns. When the chapel was completed in 1855, Trinity's rector, William Berrian, added Morgan Dix and two other clergy to the Trinity Parish staff to deal with the increased responsibilities.

Berrian assigned Dix as an assistant minister at St. Paul's Chapel, another of Trinity's satellite congregations. Dix devoted much of his attention there to a new parish school for girls, but his pastoral responsibilities also included visits to a mission house in the Bowery. He found time for writing as well, publishing the *Manual for the Young Children of the Church* (1857). St. Paul's flourished under the ministry of Dix and his colleague Francis Vinton.

To the chagrin of some of his senior colleagues, Dix was chosen as Berrian's assistant in 1859. When an illness prevented Berrian from exercising active leadership, Dix spoke for the parish during the first years of the Civil War. That was a difficult and complex job; from the time of the rectorship (1816–1830) of John Henry Hobart, clergy at Trinity had avoided any reference to political matters from the pulpit. Dix, whose father served as a major general in the New York State Volunteers, broke the tradition of silence, but he did it in a way that satisfied the vestry. When Berrian died in 1862 Dix was chosen as the successor.

Dix soon rose to the level of national prominence enjoyed by rectors of Trinity Parish. He served from 1868 to 1908 as the chairman of the Diocese of New York's Standing Committee, the body that functions as a council of advice for the bishop and, in the absence of a bishop, as the highest authority in the diocese. Dix also represented his diocese at the General Convention (1877–1898) and served as the president of the General Convention's House of Deputies (1886–1898). He was an unsuccessful candidate for bishop coadjutor of the Diocese of New York in 1883.

Dix's work at Trinity Parish was characterized by an emphasis on orthodoxy in what he perceived as a climate of increasing unbelief. "This is an irreverent age," he declared in *Sermons: Doctrinal and Practical* (1878), "and that irreverence appears even in good and religious people." He described those who discarded belief in hell or final judgment as subject to a "delusion, run riot through the land," and he warned against a belief that "becomes intellectualized and refined" to the degree that "it lose[s] its power."

Dix advocated a moderate ritualism. He had entered the General Seminary in the decade during which students were first exposed to the theological ideas of the Oxford Movement and the liturgical innovations of the Cambridge Camden Society. Edward Pusey, John Henry Newman, and other theologians at Oxford University had accentuated the authority of the church and the power of its sacraments; John Mason Neale and other members of the Cambridge Camden Society had recovered forms of worship from the pre-Reformation era. Dix's interest in ritualism had already been evident during his tenure in Philadelphia, a post he had left when his rector refused to allow the use of a covering on the holy table. The series *A History of the Parish of Trinity Church in the City of New York*, begun in 1898 (Dix edited the first four volumes in 1898, 1901, 1905, and 1906), describes Dix's litur-

gical innovations at Trinity: "Here the choir was vested in cottas, the altar was decorated with flowers and candles, the priests were again clad in their traditional robes, churchly music was revived, and the Order of the Eucharist was reverently observed. Daily celebrations of the Holy Communion were held . . . Other parishes followed this lead, and some went much further . . . But Trinity has never espoused extremes, nor would her great rector have tolerated them" (vol. 5 [1950], pp. 43–44).

Dix wrote extensively on the liturgy, producing devotional manuals, liturgical offices not provided in the Book of Common Prayer, and lectures on liturgical theology. He served on the General Convention's Joint Committee on the Book of Common Prayer (1883–1886), and after becoming the president of the House of Deputies, he guided the committee's proposals through several conventions, producing in 1892 a new edition of the Book of Common Prayer.

Dix encouraged the revival of Gothic church architecture. His interest in the setting of worship was already evident in his *Plea for the Use of Fine Arts in the Decoration of Churches* (1856). Trinity Parish had turned to Gothic revivalist Richard Upjohn to design its new building, completed in 1846, and its Trinity Chapel. As rector, Dix turned to Upjohn again for St. Chrysostom's Chapel, completed in 1879. Dix also served as a trustee for what would become the centerpiece of Gothic architecture for Episcopalians in New York City: the Cathedral of St. John the Divine. He encouraged Trinity's vestry to donate $100,000 toward the project.

Dix worked hard to help the poor, the weak, and the recent immigrant. During his years at Trinity the parish initiated regular services for German-speaking immigrants, started a program to improve the conditions of tenement dwellers, and established a number of mission houses and infirmaries. Recognizing the effectiveness of female church workers, he strongly supported women's ministries. In 1866 he became the chaplain to the newly formed Community of St. Mary, the Episcopal church's first traditional religious order. In 1873 he invited three sisters from the order to work at Trinity Infirmary, a medical clinic designed to meet the needs of the poor. Three years later he welcomed women from an English order, the Community of St. John the Baptist, to engage in settlement house work. Dix was president of the House of Deputies when in 1889 that body adopted a canon standardizing the office of deaconess, which previously had been established only by parish and diocesan initiatives.

In June 1874 Dix married Emily Woolsey Soutter. They had two children. Dix died in the parish rectory. He was a representative of what was best in the late nineteenth-century Episcopal church in New York. Although a member of the upper class, he was tireless in his efforts on behalf of the poor and the recent immigrant. Literate and possessing a refined sense of aesthetics, he was nonetheless genuinely concerned with the piety of everyday men, women, and children. He was deeply involved with the national leadership of his denomination and yet closely involved with day-to-day projects in his city.

• Dix's personal papers are preserved in the archives of Trinity Church but are currently not open to the public. His liturgical works include *A Guide for the Instruction of Adult Candidates for Holy Baptism* (1862), *The Book of Hours* (1866), *A Manual of Instruction for Confirmation Classes* (c. 1867), *The Churchman's Altar Manual, and Guide to Holy Communion* (c. 1880), *Lectures on the First Prayer Book of King Edward VI* (1881), and *The Sacramental System Considered as the Extension of the Incarnation* (Paddock Lectures at the General Seminary, delivered in 1892 and published in 1893). Dix wrote two biographies: *Harriet Starr Cannon, First Mother Superior of the Sisterhood of St. Mary* (1896) and *Memoirs of John Adams Dix* (1883). The latter work, about his father, contains some information about Dix's early years. His later years were so deeply connected with Trinity that histories of the parish are the best source of information about him. Clifford P. Morehouse, *Trinity: Mother of Churches* (1973), devotes a considerable amount of space to Dix.

ROBERT W. PRICHARD

DIXON, Amzi Clarence (6 July 1854–14 June 1925), minister and evangelist, was born in Shelby, North Carolina, the son of Thomas Dixon, a Baptist minister, and Amanda Elvira McAfee. Converted at one of his father's revival meetings, Dixon determined as a youth to enter the ministry. After earning an A.B. at Wake Forest College in 1873, Dixon began his peripatetic pastoral career by serving two Baptist churches in Mount Olive and Bear Marsh, North Carolina, from 1874 to 1875; he was ordained in the latter church in 1875. Dixon studied for six months with John A. Broadus, the prominent professor of New Testament and homiletics, at the Southern Baptist Theological Seminary in Greenville, South Carolina, before returning to North Carolina to serve the Baptist church in Chapel Hill in 1876. In 1880 he became pastor of First Baptist Church in Asheville, North Carolina. That same year he married Susan Mary Faison, with whom he had five children. After turning down the presidency of Wake Forest, Dixon accepted a call to Immanuel Baptist Church in Baltimore in 1882. Intent on attracting members from the poor and working classes, he persuaded the church to construct a larger and less pretentious building and to abolish the practice of pew-rents.

A traditional Southern Baptist, Dixon adopted the new premillennial dispensational theology and Keswick holiness teaching that had gained popularity among some mainline Protestants in the late nineteenth century. In contrast to postmillennial eschatology, which taught that Christ would return to this world to establish a millennial kingdom *after* a 1,000-year period of peace, dispensational premillennialists held that Christ would return *before* the millennium and that the modern era, the sixth dispensation, was about to come to an end and the final dispensation, the millennium, was about to dawn. During his Baltimore pastorate, Dixon was drawn into the premillenarian movement through his friendship with the great revivalist Dwight L. Moody. After hearing another revivalist, A. J. Gordon, speak at a Bible conference in Chicago in 1889, Dixon became a zealous proponent of the doctrine of the premillennial return of Jesus Christ. That same year he attended the second World's Sunday School Convention in London, where he met Charles H. Spurgeon, his boyhood idol, and spoke at his church, the Metropolitan Tabernacle.

Dixon became the pastor of Hanson Place Baptist Church in Brooklyn in 1890, and, like other premillennialists, he established a Bible training school and periodical, the *Living World*. He joined Moody's evangelistic campaign at the World's Columbian Exposition in Chicago in 1893 and was a regular speaker at a variety of Bible conferences organized by prominent premillennialists. In 1901 he became pastor of Ruggles Street Baptist Church in Roxbury, Massachusetts, where he also served as president of the Evangelical Alliance of Boston and A. J. Gordon's Bible and Missionary Training School.

During a visit to England, Dixon attended a Keswick conference and, like other revivalists, added the personal holiness teaching to his theology. The Keswick holiness doctrine taught that Christians could receive a "second blessing" of the Holy Spirit, which would repress their inclination to sin, produce a purity of heart, and furnish a new desire to serve God through ministry. Although Dixon was a member of both the northern and southern Baptist conventions, for whom he served as a delegate to the Baptist World Alliance Convention in London in 1905 and in Stockholm in 1923, he became pastor of Moody's nondenominational Chicago Avenue Church in 1906. A lifelong temperance advocate, he used a series of evangelistic services in 1908 in North Carolina to campaign for the Prohibitionist party's candidate for governor, who won the election that year.

In the first decade of the twentieth century Dixon and other conservative Protestant theologians grew more hostile toward the spread of theological modernism, the higher criticism of the Bible, and Darwinism. Although he considered these developments to be signs of the "end-times," Dixon aggressively opposed their spread. "Above all things I love peace," he told an ecumenical missions conference in 1900, "but next to peace I love a fight, and I believe the next best thing to peace is a theological fight." Through Reuben A. Torrey, dean of the Bible Institute of Los Angeles, Dixon was introduced to two wealthy laymen, Milton and Lyman Stewart of the Union Oil Company. The latter offered to fund the publication of a collection of essays that would address the foundational beliefs of the conservative Protestant faith, and he asked Dixon to supervise the project. Dixon edited the first five of the twelve volumes of *The Fundamentals*, which were distributed at no charge to some three million ministers, missionaries, and laypeople throughout the English-speaking world between 1910 and 1915.

The Fundamentals marked the emergence of a fundamentalist coalition through which different types of conservative Protestants began to actively cooperate in opposition to modernism in the early twentieth century. As the work's first editor, Dixon was largely responsible for forging this coalition. The articles articulated the core of non-negotiable, or fundamental, Christian beliefs, among them the virgin birth and supernatural resurrection, that the conservatives believed most Protestants shared, and they helped to foster a greater sense of mutual identity among the conservatives, or fundamentalists, all of which helps to account for the popularity of the volumes. The terms "fundamentalist" and "fundamentalism" were later coined by Curtis Lee Laws, editor of the *Baptist Watchman-Examiner*, in 1920 to describe those conservatives who deemed a short list of doctrines as essential Christian beliefs. Many of the articles in *The Fundamentals* also offered criticisms of Roman Catholicism, Mormonism, and, more important, liberal Protestant theology, German higher criticism, Darwinism, and the naturalistic presuppositions upon which they were built. Yet at this point the movement had not become belligerent, as evidenced by the scholarly, carefully reasoned, and moderate tone of the majority of articles.

Although Dixon remained a committed Baptist throughout his life, he helped to foster the growth of various parachurch institutions that came to serve as surrogate ecclesiastical institutions for the premillennialist faction of the fundamentalist coalition after the defeat of the fundamentalist movement in mainline Protestant churches in the 1920s and 1930s. In 1911 he became the pastor of Spurgeon's Metropolitan Tabernacle in London, where he remained until 1919, when he returned to the United States to lecture at the Bible Institute of Los Angeles and at various Bible conferences.

Dixon's career reflects not only the nineteenth-century roots of one major party in the twentieth-century fundamentalist movement but also the changing nature and role of conservative Protestantism in the United States during the late nineteenth and early twentieth centuries. His opposition to modernism grew more strident after the First World War when he helped organize the Baptist Bible Union, which sought to halt the spread of liberalism in Baptist institutions. He denounced the teaching of evolution at Wake Forest and in 1922 went to China and Japan where, under the auspices of the Baptist Bible Union, he tried to prevent the spread of modernism among Baptist missionaries. In 1921 he returned to Baltimore to pastor the University Baptist Church. After his first wife died in 1922, he married Helen Cadbury Alexander in 1924. Dixon died the following year in Baltimore.

• Dixon's papers are in the library of the Southern Baptist Historical Library and Archives, Nashville, Tenn. In addition to numerous pamphlets and articles, Dixon published more than a dozen books, including *Milk and Meat* (1893), *Heaven on Earth* (1897), *Light and Shadows of American Life* (1898), *Back to the Bible* (1912), and *The Birth of Christ* (1919). Helen C. A. Dixon, *A. C. Dixon: A Romance of Preaching* (1931), is a friendly biography. Dixon's roles in both the premillennialist movement and the larger funda-

mentalist movement are discussed in George M. Marsden, *Fundamentalism and American Culture: The Shaping of Twentieth-Century Evangelicalism: 1870–1925* (1980); Ernest R. Sandeen, *The Roots of Fundamentalism: British and American Millenarianism, 1800–1930* (1970); and Timothy P. Weber, *Living in the Shadow of the Second Coming: American Premillennialism, 1875–1982*, rev. ed. (1983).

P. C. KEMENY

DIXON, Dean (10 Jan. 1915–4 Nov. 1976), orchestra conductor, was born Charles Dean Dixon in New York City, the son of Henry Charles Dixon, a lawyer and hotel porter, and McClara Dean Ralston. Both of Dixon's parents were West Indian—his mother was born in Barbados and his father in Jamaica. Because more than two decades elapsed before his parents secured their U.S. passports, according to Dixon, "[T]here is a lot of legal questioning as to whether I am an American or whether I only have an American passport. Both [of] my parents were Commonwealth citizens when I was born" (Dunbar, pp. 189–90).

Before reaching the age of four, Dixon was studying the violin, using one purchased at a local pawn shop for $15. Though his mother had no musical training, she was able to recognize talent. Such was evidenced for her when she saw young Dean holding two sticks in violin position. An avid concertgoer, particularly to New York City's Carnegie Hall, she generally carried her son along. She taught him to read music almost before he learned his ABCs.

Dixon began taking three lessons per week, with monitored daily practice of four to five hours, and before long he was performing at church and lodge concerts. When he was thirteen, his instructor suggested that his lessons be discontinued, believing that a career in classical music was unrealistic for an African American. Both Dixon and his mother ignored the advice, although Mrs. Dixon began to consider a medical career for her son, planning for Dixon to offer private lessons on the piano and violin to defray the cost of his medical study.

As Dixon approached his graduation from DeWitt Clinton High School in 1932, the head of the music department convinced Mrs. Dixon that her son should pursue a career in music and exerted his influence to secure Dixon's acceptance into the Institute of Musical Art (the Juilliard School). Dixon was admitted on the basis of a violin audition and pursued a violin degree for the first half year; he then began following the music pedagogy course of study. In 1932 Dixon organized the Dean Dixon Symphony Orchestra, with one violin and one piano, using a pencil for a baton. They rehearsed at the Harlem Young Men's Christian Association, and within a short period of time the number of musicians reached seventy. Dixon received a B.S. degree from Juilliard in 1936 and an M.A. degree from Columbia University Teachers College in 1939, while concurrently studying conducting on a graduate fellowship at Juilliard under Albert Stoessel.

Dixon conducted his first professional orchestra concert in 1938 at Town Hall with the League of Music Lovers Chamber Orchestra. In 1939 he and several of the city's finest instrumentalists formed the New York Chamber Orchestra.

Struggling financially, but prospering artistically, good fortune struck for Dixon and the Dean Dixon Symphony Orchestra in the late 1930s, when a women's group began offering them a subsidy. Having reached the attention of First Lady Eleanor Roosevelt, the orchestra presented a concert at Heckscher Theater in May 1941. In attendance was NBC music director Samuel Chotzinoff, who was so impressed that he contracted Dixon to lead the famed Arturo Toscanini's NBC Symphony Orchestra for two concerts. Other important engagements followed: performances with the New York Philharmonic Orchestra (1942), the Philadelphia Orchestra (1943), and the Boston Symphony (1944, "Coloured American Night"). In 1944 Dixon also organized the American Youth Orchestra.

Dixon merited a chapter in David Ewen's book *Dictators of the Baton* when it was reissued and enlarged in 1948. The same year Dixon received Columbia University's Alice M. Ditson Award of $1,000 "for outstanding contributions to American Music" and was designated "Outstanding Conductor of the Year," by Columbia. Yet, between 1944, when he last conducted the Boston Symphony, and 1949, no invitations came from any established organization. When in 1949 he received an invitation from the Radio Symphony of the French National Radio, he accepted, beginning a "self-imposed" exile from the United States. At a later date, Dixon remarked, "I felt like I was on a sinking ship and if I'd stayed here, I'd drown."

Before leaving the country, Dixon distinguished himself with several orchestral innovations. In his programs for children four years old and older, in which he sat the children among the instrumentalists to be fascinated by both sight and sound, created quite a bit of excitement. His "Symphony at Midnight" concerts given at a reduced price for those who could not attend at the regularly scheduled hour, were also quite popular. Most innovative for the late 1930s and early 1940s was the "blindfold test" technique in which musicians auditioning for Dixon's orchestra displayed their skills for the maestro while his back was turned. When he worked with various training ensembles, including the Works Progress Administration and the National Youth Administration Orchestra in the late 1930s, Dixon consistently changed the seating arrangements, often placing string players among woodwinds and brasses among strings, a method that helped his players listen better and learn the complete score.

By 1952 Dixon had become America's most active musical ambassador abroad. The American press reported that during the 1951–1952 season, Dixon led thirty-two concerts in nine different European countries. It was also announced that in 1953 he would become resident conductor of the Göteburg (Sweden) Symphony, where he remained until 1960. His next major appointment was with the Hesse Radio Symphony Orchestra in Frankfurt, Germany (1961–1974). During this tenure he was also principal conductor of the Sydney Symphony Orchestra in Australia (1964–1967). He frequently received guest conducting invitations from other organizations, including symphony and radio orchestras in Amsterdam, Athens, Barcelona, Belgrade, Berlin, Budapest, Copenhagen, Florence, Leipzig, London, Mexico City, Rome, Salzburg, Stockholm, Tokyo, Vienna, and Zurich.

Dixon's first substantial American conducting invitation came in 1970. After twenty-one years abroad, he returned to conduct the New York Philharmonic in three park concerts and enjoyed guest stints with the Pittsburgh Symphony at Temple University's Ambler Festival and with the Saint Louis Symphony at the Mississippi River Festival. A 1971 conducting tour, sponsored by the Schlitz Brewing Company, included the Kansas City, Minnesota, Milwaukee, and Detroit symphony orchestras, while a 1972 tour included appearances with the National, Chicago, and San Francisco symphony orchestras.

Having recently retired as musical director of the Frankfurt Radio Orchestra, Dixon was called back to the Sydney Symphony Orchestra in 1975, first for a two-week season, then for a twenty-four concert tour of Australia, conducting also the Melbourne Symphony Orchestra. After only nine concerts, however, it was necessary for Dixon to return to his home in Switzerland and undergo open-heart surgery. He continued his guest conducting activities in early 1976, but he died later in the year in Zug, Switzerland.

News of Dixon's death appeared in the press worldwide. Ronald Smothers captioned his entry for the *New York Times* (5 Nov. 1976), "Dean Dixon, 61, Dies, Conductor in Exile/First Black to Lead Philharmonic/Left the U.S. in 1949 to Build His Reputation in Europe." During the course of his life, Dixon had three wives: Vivian Rivkin, an American Caucasian whom he married in 1947; Mary Mandelin, a Finnish woman reared in France whom he married in 1954; and Roswitha "Ritha" Blume, a German whom he married in 1973. He had two daughters.

• Coverage of Dean Dixon's early career in America appears in David Ewen, *Dictators of the Baton* (1948). Full coverage of his life and career appear in D. Antoinette Handy, *Black Conductors* (1995). Two very detailed articles concerning his return to America after twenty-one years are Beatrice Berg, "Dixon: Maestro Abroad, Stranger at Home," *New York Times* 19 July 1970, and Gail Stockholm, "Dean Dixon: A Return with Laurels," *Music and Artists* (June–July 1970): 7, 10–14. For an informative interview conducted with Dixon in Frankfurt, Germany, see Ernest Dunbar, ed., *The Black Expatriates: A Study of American Negroes in Exile* (1968). Noah Andre Trudeau reflects very positively on Dixon the man, Dixon's career, the state of affairs in America during the 1940s, and Dixon's recordings in "When the Door Didn't Open: A Cool Classicist and a Soldier for Social Equality," *High Fidelity* 35 (May 1985): 57–58.

D. ANTOINETTE HANDY

DIXON, Dorsey Murdock. *See* Dixon Brothers.

DIXON, George (29 July 1870–5 Jan. 1908), boxer, was born in Halifax, Nova Scotia, Canada, but was brought by his parents to Boston when he was eight years old. There he attended school and, in 1884, began working for Elmer Chickering, a photographer who specialized in making portraits of boxers. While working on a job assignment Dixon saw boxing matches at the Boston Music Hall and decided to pursue a boxing career. After a few amateur bouts he attracted the attention of Tom O'Rourke, a former boxer himself, who taught Dixon and managed him throughout most of his career.

Dixon became a serious professional boxer in 1888, and by the end of the year he was well known in the Boston area through a thrilling series of fights with a local hero, Hank Brennan. Weighing less than 100 pounds, Dixon proved to be an extremely clever boxer, good at defense and capable of landing hard punches frequently with both fists. In 1889 he grew into the featherweight division, the weight limit at that time being 116 pounds. He made rapid progress and ended the year by making his first New York City ring appearance, in which he scored a two-round knockout of the highly regarded Eugene Hornbacker.

On 7 February 1890 Dixon boxed Cal McCarthy in Boston for the American featherweight title. The fight, which started after midnight and ended nearly five hours and 78 rounds later, was called a draw because both men had fought themselves to exhaustion. O'Rourke then launched his man on a campaign to become world featherweight champion, taking him to England, where he knocked out a British contender, Nunc Wallace. After returning to the United States, Dixon scored a 40-round knockout of contender Johnny Murphy. On 31 March 1891 in New York, he knocked out McCarthy in 22 rounds; in July in San Francisco he won a five-round knockout over contender Abe Willis, the Australian champion; and finally on 27 June 1892 in Brooklyn, he knocked out British champion Fred Johnson in 14 rounds. These victories gained worldwide featherweight championship recognition for Dixon.

During this era of boxing it was the right of the champion to set the weight limit at which his title would be defended. Because Dixon's fighting weight was only between 114 and 116 pounds at this time, he initially set the limit below 120 pounds, but the limit was increased as he added weight. His first defense, in New Orleans on 6 September 1892, was against noted amateur Jack Skelly, at 116 pounds, with Dixon winning by a knockout in eight rounds. This bout was significant in two respects: it was the first boxing match held in New Orleans before a racially mixed audience, and it was part of a series of championship fights leading to the world heavyweight title match between John L. Sullivan and James John Corbett. In 1893 in Brooklyn, New York, Dixon made two successful defenses at 120 pounds, against Eddie Pierce and Solly Smith, knocking out his opponents in three and seven rounds, respectively.

Dixon had reached the zenith of his career; he had lost only twice, once by a disqualification early in his career, and on a four-round decision to Englishman Billy Plimmer in 1893 in a nontitle fight. He seemed almost unbeatable in the ring, but his personal affairs were less satisfactory. He often drank heavily, gambled his money away on horseracing, and even bought race horses that were mortgaged and then lost when he could not make payments. In addition to his genuine ring battles he made theatrical tours, taking on all comers.

First married at age fifteen, Dixon later married O'Rourke's sister. Dixon was brown-skinned, hence his popular name of "Little Chocolate," and claimed to be one-fourth black and three-fourths white. During his theatrical tours he was forced to take lodgings at "colored" boarding houses apart from his wife, who stayed in "white" hotels along with his manager.

In 1894 and 1895 Dixon fought two epic nontitle battles with the famous Australian fighter Young Griffo, who outweighed him by many pounds. Both fights were called draws, the first in 20 rounds in Boston, 29 June 1894, and the second in Brooklyn in 25 rounds, 19 January 1895. On 27 August 1895 he again successfully defended the featherweight title, at 128 pounds, against Johnny Griffin in Boston over 25 rounds. In the next two years he fought several important nontitle fights, including another with Young Griffo, three with Frank Erne, and another with Griffin.

Dixon lost the featherweight title by decision to Solly Smith, at San Francisco on 4 October 1897, in 25 rounds. Smith soon lost the title to Dave Sullivan, and Dixon defeated Sullivan by disqualification in 10 rounds on 11 November 1898, to regain it. In 1899 he won nine of 10 fights against dangerous opponents, including seven title defenses. On 9 January 1900 he made his last title defense and was knocked out in eight rounds by Terry McGovern in New York.

Dixon continued to fight until 1906, but he lost most of his remaining battles. At times he showed traces of his former boxing brilliance, but he was no longer a title contender. He went to Great Britain and boxed there for more than two years to stay active. O'Rourke refused to continue handling his affairs, and his second wife left him. After returning to the United States, he suffered a crushing two-round knockout in Philadelphia by Tommy Murphy and finally retired after a few more inconsequential fights. Dixon was then penniless and had no means of supporting himself. He lived on the charity of others, drank heavily, and eventually died in New York City of acute alcoholism.

Almost all of Dixon's fights were pleasing, action-filled affairs, and he never took part in a fake fight. For many years he was the standard against which featherweight champions were measured, and he was long considered to be the greatest fighter of all time at that weight. He was elected to the International Boxing Hall of Fame in 1990.

• Dixon's complete record is available in Herbert G. Goldman, ed., *The 1986–87 Ring Record Book and Boxing Encyclo-*

pedia (1987). The main source of information on his career is Nathaniel S. Fleischer, *Black Dynamite*, vol. 3, *The Three Colored Aces, George Dixon, Joe Gans, and Joe Walcott* (1938). Detailed accounts of his fights may be found in contemporary newspapers such as the *Philadelphia Item*. His obituary, "George Dixon, Greatest Fighter of His Age, Is Dead," is in the *Philadelphia Item*, 7 Jan. 1908.

LUCKETT V. DAVIS

DIXON, George Washington (1801?–2 Mar. 1861), blackface minstrel and newspaper editor, was born probably in Richmond, Virginia. Little is known about his parents other than that his father might have been a barber and his mother a domestic. One account claims that Dixon was educated in a charity school. Around age fifteen he became an apprentice in a traveling circus and subsequently performed with several such troupes throughout the 1820s. By 1827 Dixon was enjoying renown as a singer of popular stage songs, especially those of a comic nature, which allowed him to advertise himself as "The American Buffo Singer." His leap to fame came in New York City in 1829, when he put on blackface makeup and sang "Coal Black Rose," impersonating an African American. He was, thus, one of the very first to practice a genre of stagecraft that came to be called blackface minstrelsy.

In 1830 Dixon published *Dixon's Oddities*, a small collection of texts to some of his songs, which was reprinted throughout the decade. His star as a performer rose during the early 1830s and probably reached its apex in 1834, when he sang what became his signature song, "Zip Coon," in blackface. The song became one of the most popular in all minstrelsy, and its tune survives yet as "Turkey in the Straw."

Even before this success, Dixon was embarking on another career, one that he claimed on his deathbed to have been his calling—that of a newspaper editor. In 1833 he was living in Connecticut, where he opened the *Stonington Cannon*, but the publication quickly folded. In 1835 he relocated to Lowell, Massachusetts, where he edited *Dixon's Daily Review*, which reflected Dixon's Whig party principles. Dixon also claimed a central role for the press in maintaining community mores, especially those condemning the seduction of working-class females by upper-class males. Dixon lived in New England until 1838 and published several other short-lived newspapers, some of which suggest that he was sympathetic to antislavery causes. It was also during this period that he spent time in jail awaiting trials on charges brought against him for (on separate occasions) fraud, theft, and forgery, against all of which he successfully defended himself.

By June 1838 Dixon had moved to New York City, where he continued to perform for several more years. But more important, he established the *Polyanthos and Fire Department Album*, by far the most influential and successful of his newspapers. He immediately attacked the immoral behavior of some prominent citizens, on occasion with tragic consequences. By year's end at least two of his subjects were dead, one a sui-

cide. The next year Dixon faced a libel suit for his published exposés. In one of the period's most widely followed trials, he established the veracity of his sources and was exonerated. But another libel suit followed, this one brought by the Reverend F. L. Hawks. Although Dixon initially pleaded not guilty, he uncharacteristically changed his plea at the last moment, was silent during his mitigation, and served a six-month sentence in the state penitentiary. He claimed later to have received substantial payment from Hawks in return for the plea change, ostensibly preserving the reverend's reputation. (Although ironically, or perhaps tellingly, Hawks was soon relieved of his pulpit by his congregation and moved to Mississippi.) Back from incarceration, Dixon reestablished the *Polyanthos* as a moral reform press. He enjoyed particular success in his attack on Madame Restell, an abortionist, and managed to have her arrested, brought to trial, and convicted. Dixon later published an anonymous account of the circumstances surrounding Restell's arrest and conviction.

Dixon became the leader of a group of young editors who were then attempting to turn the power of the press against what they saw as rampant moral turpitude. Their efforts at moral reform were modeled on rituals long in use among the common classes, such as the charivari, in which seemingly contradictory modes of understanding and expression coexist. According to these rituals, only by turning an unjust world topsy-turvy, usually through manipulation of symbols of power, does a better reordering become possible. For example, the moral-reform press sometimes ranked brothels for cleanliness, hospitality, and the beauty of the inhabitants, thus endorsing what it considered appropriate expressions of sexuality; this enabled it then to rail all the stronger against "inappropriate" cross-class sexual philandering.

Dixon's personal life often seemed to be lived at similar cross-purposes; he never thought that being a crusader for the reform of sexual behavior was in any way compromised by his frequent association with some of New York's most famous madams. Despite such an apparent contradiction, he was deadly serious in the moral changes he was trying to bring about, acting out of a sense of community (and, in truth too, a hope for profit). Dixon never flinched in his commitment; in addition to serving time in prison, he endured several street floggings, including one in which he was wounded in the head by an ax.

In the early 1840s Dixon continued to sing and edit and tried out several other occupations as well, including hypnotist and professional athlete (he was a marathon pedestrian, one who walked for extraordinary spans of time or distance for prizes or ticket receipts). In spite of these efforts, Dixon never rose substantially above a state of impecuniosity. Less is known about his life after he left New York during the mid-1840s. It appears that he was a filibuster in the Yucatán in 1847, which would be in keeping with his lifelong commitment to American republicanism and manifest destiny. After the Mexican expedition, he moved to New

Orleans, where he lived the rest of his life, apparently in penury. One city directory listed his address as "Literary Tent." He died in the New Orleans Charity Hospital.

Dixon, who never married, was surely one of the most complex, controversial, eccentric, and enigmatic men ever to have flourished in the American public eye. A singer of undeniable gifts and arguably the father of blackface minstrelsy, the most popular form of musical theater in the nineteenth century, he chose to pursue an undistinguished literary career that nevertheless succeeded in blazing the way for others. Although he was deeply committed to moral reform, he was also something of a rogue. To his adoring audiences and many admirers (generally, the weak, vulnerable, or powerless), he was a man of estimable stature, one not to be dismissed. An obituary in the *Baton Rouge Daily Gazette and Comet* observed that "his errors were those of the head, rather than of the heart."

• A few of Dixon's letters are at the Massachusetts Historical Society. The most extensive treatment of Dixon's life is to be found in Dale Cockrell, *Demons of Disorder: Early Blackface Minstrels and Their World* (1997). His antiabortion crusade against Madame Restell is covered in Clifford Browder, *The Wickedest Woman in New York: Madame Restell, the Abortionist* (1988). A two-part biography by one of Dixon's colleagues in the moral-reform press is "Some Passages in the Life of G. W. Dixon: The American Coco la Cour," *New York Flash*, 11 Dec. 1841 and 18 Dec. 1841. Because the piece is a vendetta of sorts, it must be consulted with great care. An obituary is in the *Baton Rouge Daily Gazette and Comet*, 23 Mar. 1861.

DALE COCKRELL

DIXON, Howard Briten. *See* Dixon Brothers.

DIXON, James (5 Aug. 1814–27 Mar. 1873), congressman, was born in Enfield, Connecticut, the son of William Dixon, a lawyer, and Mary Field. The Dixons were well-known residents of Enfield, which William served as town clerk, probate judge, and state representative. At age sixteen James entered Williams College. After graduating in 1834, he returned to Enfield, where he studied law at his father's office and where he resided when he was admitted to the bar and began his legal and political career.

In 1837 and 1838 he won election as a Whig to represent Enfield in the Connecticut House of Representatives. In 1839 he moved to Hartford, continuing his Whig political activity and becoming a law partner of Connecticut's governor, William W. Ellsworth. A year later he married Elizabeth Lord Cogswell. They had four children.

Dixon was a conservative Whig who disliked slavery. In 1844 he served a third term as a Connecticut representative, but the next year he won a congressional seat, which he held until 1849. An advocate of the protective tariff, he contended that it created jobs and produced prosperity. Opposed to the Mexican War as an attempt by the "slavocracy" to extend slavery, he strongly favored the Wilmot Proviso to exclude

that institution from any territory acquired from Mexico.

As the leader of a political faction, Dixon had enemies among Connecticut's Whigs, many of whom also objected to his antislavery stand. Consequently, in 1849 the party denied him a third congressional term, but he remained in public office by winning a seat in the state senate. In 1854 he was reelected but lost a bitter contest for a U.S. Senate nomination. The same year, the Whig party died, and Dixon affiliated with the nativist Know-Nothing or American party. An outspoken critic of nativism in 1846, a decade later Dixon embraced it as politically expedient and ran as the Know-Nothing nominee for a U.S. Senate seat, which he wrested from Democrat Isaac Toucey. Connecticut's Republicans had attempted to prevent Dixon's election, but failing to elect their own candidate, some Republicans voted for Dixon to defeat the Democrat. Dixon's nativist affiliation disturbed many Republicans, who backed him reluctantly. Their suspicion did not, however, preclude his joining the Republican party when the Know-Nothings declined soon after his election.

As a senator, Dixon remained successful at factional politics, gaining reelection in 1862. Opposed to the spread of slavery in the 1850s, he voted against the admission of Kansas to the Union as a slave state and denounced the annexation of Cuba. Hoping to prevent the disintegration of the Union and the onset of civil war following Abraham Lincoln's election as president in 1860, he favored compromise with the South. Dixon said his constituents were prepared to make sacrifices on the slavery issue, and he supported congressional proposals to guarantee slavery's permanence, thus incurring the wrath of advanced antislavery forces in Connecticut's Republican party.

During the Civil War, Dixon backed Lincoln and the war effort but battled the radical Republicans in Connecticut for control of the state party organization. Exercising influence with Lincoln, he manipulated federal patronage and attempted to turn the president against his enemies. In 1864 he sought to draw the radicals into openly endorsing Treasury Secretary Salmon P. Chase for the presidency. Warned of Dixon's machinations in advance of the Republican state convention, the radicals abandoned Chase and joined in choosing Lincoln. By orchestrating this selection, Dixon demonstrated his loyalty to the president, but when Democrat George B. McClellan (1826–1885) seemed the likely victor in the presidential contest, Dixon wavered in his support for Lincoln. With the reelection of Lincoln, Dixon's political influence plummeted.

After Lincoln's assassination in 1865, Dixon turned even further from the Republican party. Unlike most Republicans, he firmly supported the lenient southern reconstruction policy of Lincoln's successor, Andrew Johnson. In 1868, after Dixon voted to acquit Johnson of impeachment charges, he was denied renomination for a third Senate term. The next year he declined an offer by Johnson to become minister to Russia and ran unsuccessfully for Congress as a Democrat. He died of heart disease in Hartford, Connecticut, two years after his wife's death in 1871, and was survived by his four children. An intriguer rather than a statesman, the conservative Dixon was increasingly alienated from the Republican party. He left a modest legacy based on his opposition to the extension of slavery.

• Letters from Dixon are in the Dixon Correspondence, Hoadly Collection, Holley Family Papers, and Mark Howard Papers in the Connecticut Historical Society, Hartford; the Beekman Family Papers in the New-York Historical Society, New York City; and the Joseph R. Hawley Papers and Gideon Welles Papers in the Library of Congress, Washington, D.C. The Connecticut Historical Society also has copies of Dixon letters, the originals of which can be found in the Connecticut State Library, Hartford, and the Library of Congress, and speeches delivered by Dixon in Congress. Especially informative are the biographical sketches in *Commemorative Biographical Record of Hartford County, Connecticut* (1901) and Oscar Jewell Harvey, *The Harvey Book* (1899); and the obituary in the *Hartford Courant* (28 Mar. 1873). The most complete biography is Nelson R. Burr, "United States Senator James Dixon: 1814–1873, Episcopalian Anti-Slavery Statesman," *Historical Magazine of the Protestant Episcopal Church*, 50 (Mar. 1981): 29–72. Significant references to Dixon can be found in J. Robert Lane, *A Political History of Connecticut during the Civil War* (1941); Harry J. Carman and Reinhard H. Luthin, *Lincoln and the Patronage* (1943); John Niven, *Connecticut for the Union: The Role of the State in the Civil War* (1965); and Niven, *Gideon Welles: Lincoln's Secretary of the Navy* (1973).

ROBERT D. PARMET

DIXON, Joseph Moore (31 July 1867–22 May 1934), politician, was born in Snow Camp, North Carolina, the son of Hugh Woody Dixon, a farmer and small-scale manufacturer, and Flora Adaline Murchison. Snow Camp was a small Quaker, Republican enclave, dominated by Dixon's intensely religious father and uncle. Dixon was educated in neighboring Quaker schools and at Earlham and Guilford colleges (A.B., 1889). His education provided him with a lifelong enthusiasm for history and biography and skill in debate and oratory.

In 1891 Dixon arrived in Missoula, Montana, to study law in the office of a kinsman. Apparently he had left Snow Camp on account of his religious apostasy and his political aspirations. He capitalized on the fluid social, economic, and political structure of the West. Quickly admitted to the practice of law, he soon became county attorney and a state legislator. He invested in real estate, and in 1900 he bought a Missoula newspaper, the *Missoulian*, which was a necessity for an aspiring politician in a state where "the newspapers spouted mud in a manner to cause the Yellowstone geysers to look like toy fountains" (29 Aug. 1924). In 1896 he married Caroline M. Worden, whose family was prominent in western Montana; the couple had seven children, six of whom survived to adulthood.

Dixon exploited the internal dissension afflicting the Democrats to rise rapidly in politics. In 1902 and 1904 he won congressional races, and in 1907 the Montana legislature chose him for a U.S. Senate seat. His early years in Washington, D.C., were marked by his adroitness in producing a disproportionate share of federal benefits for Montana. Yet Dixon was cognizant that he was politically vulnerable to future internecine political warfare involving Senator Thomas H. Carter and "The Company" (the Amalgamated Copper Company), which was a vital force in both parties.

On his first trip to Washington, after the 1902 election, Dixon met President Theodore Roosevelt, who exerted an almost hypnotic effect on him. Like so many other ardent Rooseveltians, Dixon never recovered from this spell. Moreover, as he attained more insight into the complexities of the U.S. government and the economy, he adopted Roosevelt's mildly reformist outlook and philosophy. Thus he became an associate of the senatorial insurgents soon after President William Howard Taft's inauguration. He strayed from Republican doctrine on tax questions and railroad legislation. Since the Carter wing of the Montana Republicans remained orthodox, Dixon's position at home became increasingly tenuous.

After Roosevelt finally decided in 1912 to try to wrest the Republican nomination from Taft, he persuaded Dixon to be his campaign manager. It was a shrewd appointment. Dixon was a southerner by birth and a westerner by choice. He had spent a decade in Washington and was a graduate of what the *Butte Miner* characterized as the "Montana school of politics, which means that there is nothing concerning the game that any eastern leaders can teach him." But Roosevelt's campaign for the Republican nomination and his third-party candidacy, both directed by Dixon, were unsuccessful. Running on the Progressive ticket, Dixon also lost his Senate seat.

Dixon, who had not left Washington to campaign for himself, returned to Missoula in the spring of 1913. He found his business affairs chaotic and his newspaper threatened by a competing daily financed by the Amalgamated Copper Company. Within a few months Dixon prevailed against Amalgamated Copper and acquired its Missoula newspaper. He actively controlled both the editorial and business sides of both papers. He vigorously championed a variety of reforms and continued to denounce the Company. Though his foreign policy was characterized by anti-Wilsonism, between 1915 and 1917 he shifted from unreserved neutrality to advocating strong measures against Germany and ultimately war.

The decay of the Bull Moose party impelled Dixon to return to the GOP in 1916, not as a penitent, but as a former leader intent on regaining his influence. Carter's political heirs, backed by major economic interests, continued to fight Dixon and his associates.

Dixon's desire to terminate his career as a publisher and editor continued to grow apace. While there were certain phases he relished, he grumbled that publishing kept him "tied down, day and night, Sundays and holidays" (letter to Miles Taylor, 24 Nov. 1915). Missoula was not large enough to make "the newspaper game an easy one financially" (letter to Tom Stout, 15

Mar. 1917). Ever uneasy about Amalgamated Copper's economic power, he feared that the Company could endanger the solvency of his newspapers. Finally, convinced that he would never again seek an elective office, he did not require the newspapers for political advantage. Hence he sold them in 1917, and ultimately they came under the ownership of Amalgamated Copper.

Dixon then retired with his family to his new ranch at Flathead Lake. As a typical gentleman farmer, he was prepared to support his establishment with his investments in real estate.

Politics in Montana were confused in 1920. Amalgamated Copper had become the Anaconda Copper Mining Company (ACM) in 1915, and its allies were confronted by the Nonpartisan League (NPL), which had moved into the state from North Dakota determined to take over the Democratic party. Dixon, a political animal, announced his candidacy for the governorship, positioning himself between the extremes. Primary day was a disaster for ACM. Burton K. Wheeler, a Butte lawyer, led an NPL sweep. Dixon, running against five opponents, qualified for the November ballot by capturing 35 percent of the GOP vote. Without a candidate, and anxious to regain control of the Democratic party, ACM was compelled to treat Dixon with benevolent neutrality. He rode the national Republican tide to victory.

Dixon's administration was ill-fated. Montana suffered from a severe agricultural depression, worsened by drought in some sections. Consequently there were widespread bank failures. The finances of the state government were chaotic. Party affiliations were irrelevant since the legislature continued to prove susceptible to ACM's blandishments. Hence the legislature killed Dixon's recommendations for a broad spectrum of reforms, including a strong tax commission (approved by referendum in 1922) and increased taxes on mining.

Both ACM and the Dixonites girded for 1924. The Company struck first by establishing a well-financed front, a new Farmer-Labor party, to attack Dixon from the left. The Dixonites replied with an initiative providing for a 1 percent tax on the gross production of metal mines. Needing a plausible gubernatorial candidate, ACM tapped Judge John E. "Honest John" Erickson of Kalispell. Here was a classic example of the molding of an impressive candidate out of appealing external characteristics and an inner void. Although Dixon barnstormed for seven weeks, his defeat was almost preordained. He was not only saddled with the continuing agricultural depression, but he had meager campaign funds, a makeshift organization, and the undeviating support of only two dailies and a scattering of weeklies. In contrast, the Company and its allies waged their campaign against Dixon with remarkable skill and almost unlimited funds. As regular Democrat J. T. Carroll later wrote Senator Thomas J. Walsh, "I recognize the mighty influence a large number of papers will have if they turn loose on a man.

Witness Dixon for example" (Walsh manuscripts, Library of Congress, 1926).

Ironically, although Erickson won by 14,675 votes, the tax initiative carried even more decisively. Apparently Montanans supported it with the cynical intention of shifting part of the tax burden from themselves.

Although Dixon is now generally conceded to have been Montana's most imaginative and most competent governor, the results of his four years in office were relatively meager. He had attempted to awaken the political consciousness and arouse the conscience of Montanans, to modernize the archaic financial and political structure of their government, and to end the almost complete domination by ACM and its allies over the internal political life of the state. Nevertheless, his attempts at a Rooseveltian revolution failed.

The last decade of Dixon's life was anticlimactic. On his return to Missoula he engaged in frenetic real estate activity. In 1928, however, the lure of politics seduced him into running for Wheeler's Senate seat. (In 1922 T. J. Walsh had presided over a rapprochement between Wheeler and ACM.) Dixon campaigned on orthodox Republican principles and tied himself closely to Herbert Hoover. But after Dixon lost by 12,000 votes, he explained that Wheeler had effectively "sold himself to the labor groups and the farmers, as the only honest-to-God crusading Sir Galahad that ever went to Washington. They were not so much anti-Dixon as pro-Wheeler" (letter to John Wilson, 9 Dec. 1928). The following spring Dixon returned to Washington for a four-year stint as assistant secretary of the Interior.

Before Dixon returned to Missoula, where he died the following year, he vented his disillusionment to trusted friends. In 1932 he wrote to one: "I have lost much of my former faith in the intelligent action of the 'dear people.'" He told another: "I know how fickle the dear people are and how ignorant the mass may be of actual conditions." He warned a young Montanan, who proposed tax reforms in 1932: "You must realize in advance that when you have taken a bloody head in making the fight for the dear people they will not appreciate your efforts." He replied to a cynical friend: "Like you, when I get older and have seen more of life, I have largely backed away from my enthusiastic dreams of the years that are past." Dixon's loss of faith in the electorate's wisdom was paralleled by his philosophic skepticism. In December 1932 he confided to an old friend: "I have seen much of life in my 65 years and still I wonder what it is all about. I have no religion or hope of another existence."

Imbued with Quaker ethics and a desire to improve the quality of secular life through political action, Dixon had moved to a Montana tainted by widespread corporate corruption and despotism. The reversal of Dixon's political fortunes and his subsequent disillusionment stemmed from his inability to persuade Montanans to end Amalgamated Copper's fiefdom. Eventually, only corporate financial reverses could chasten the Company, leading to its departure from the state.

• Dixon's voluminous correspondence is in the University of Montana library. Other repositories have copious quantities of material on the Progressive party and the Republican fissures. The following also have illuminating material on Dixon's roles in the Senate and in Montana. Particularly useful are the Thomas J. Walsh, Thomas H. Carter, and William Allen White manuscripts in the Library of Congress. See also the Charles D. Hilles manuscripts at Yale University. Also relevant are the reminiscences of William L. Hunt, Chester C. Davis, Ormsby McHarg, and M. L. Wilson, which can be found in the Oral History Collection at Columbia University. Documents relating to Dixon are scattered among the papers of Warren G. Harding and E. Mont Reily at the Ohio Historical Society. The Montana Historical Society has a wide-ranging collection of state newspapers, daily and weekly, as well as state government files and bank records. It also has the manuscripts of trusted Dixon lieutenant O. A. Bergeson and a memoir prepared by Charles D. Greenfield, a reporter for the Helena *Daily Record*, a Carter mouthpiece. The illuminating memoirs of ardent Dixonite Peter Rorvik are in the possession of the Rorvik family, Moses Lake, Wash. The only biography of Dixon is Jules A. Karlin, *Joseph M. Dixon of Montana* (2 vols., 1974). For additional details about the political battles in which Dixon was engaged, see Burton K. Wheeler's lively memoir, *Yankee from the West* (1962); J. Leonard Bates, "Senator Walsh of Montana, 1918–1924: A Liberal under Pressure" (Ph.D. diss., Univ. of North Carolina at Chapel Hill, 1952); and Shirley DeForth, "The Montana Press and Joseph M. Dixon, 1920–1922" (M.A. thesis, Univ. of Montana, 1959). Obituaries are in the *Billings (Mont.) Gazette*, the *Great Falls Tribune*, and the *Missoula Sentinel*, all 23 May 1934.

JULES A. KARLIN

DIXON, Luther Swift (17 June 1825–6 Dec. 1891), judge, was born in Underhill, Vermont, the son of Luther Dixon, a prosperous farmer. (His mother's name is unknown.) During the War of 1812 Dixon's father headed a regiment that he placed under federal command over the objections of a temporizing governor. He sent his son Luther to the Norwich Military Academy, where he learned republican virtue by reading classical authors and undergoing strenuous military exercises. Dixon read law with Luke P. Poland, one of the state's most eminent lawyers, and was admitted to the Vermont bar in 1850. The next year he moved to the bustling lumber town of Portage, Wisconsin, where he quickly built a large practice by exhibiting good judgment, sound grasp of the law, and independence of mind. Refraining from party politics, he nevertheless was elected district attorney in 1851 and held the office until 1856.

In the last year of his term, Dixon tried a notable murder case in Madison, the state capital. His performance against two of the state's best lawyers was so impressive that in August 1858 Republican governor Alexander W. Randall appointed him as a circuit judge to preside over trials in Madison and surrounding towns. Although he was only thirty-three, Dixon won the admiration and devotion of the local bar. "Unostentatious, simple and direct in manner as a child, cordial and generous," his brother lawyers recalled, Dixon presided "with a befitting dignity so blended with kindness, patience and consideration for every

advocate who appeared before him as to make him loved and honored by the whole brotherhood of the bar" (*Wisconsin Reports* 81, pp. xxxv, xxxi).

At the time of Dixon's appointment, Wisconsin was consumed by a great legal controversy. In 1854 the abolitionist editor Sherman Booth was arrested by order of the federal district court for his part in the rescue of escaped slave Joshua Glover, who was being held for his Missouri master under the Fugitive Slave Act of 1850. The Wisconsin Supreme Court granted Booth's application for a writ of habeas corpus on the ground that the act unconstitutionally abridged the rights of northern states. The federal court rearrested, tried, and convicted Booth, only to see the editor freed yet again by the state judges, who, for good measure, refused to make the official record of their proceedings available for an appeal to the U.S. Supreme Court. The high court heard the appeal nonetheless, and in *Ableman v. Booth* (1859), Chief Justice Roger B. Taney upheld the act and federal judicial supremacy.

In April 1859 Governor Randall appointed Dixon chief justice of the state supreme court, upon the death of the incumbent. The month before, the Wisconsin legislature had condemned Taney's decision in the Booth case. Dixon was soon called on to enter Taney's order in his court's record. His vote, however, could make no difference to the outcome because Justice Byron Paine, having been Booth's lawyer, could take no part in the decision, and Justice Orsamus Cole was sure to vote against the federal court, so the three-justice court would lack a majority to enter the order. Further, by acknowledging the order Dixon would jeopardize his chances for reelection the following year. He nevertheless voted to recognize the authority of the federal courts and issued a remarkable opinion, which, while acknowledging the passion on both sides, followed "the plain letter and spirit of the constitution, leaving the adjustment of such matters to the people who made, and who can unmake and amend it" (*Wisconsin Reports* 11, p. 523).

Renounced by the Republicans, Dixon narrowly won reelection in 1860 as an independent. The bar labored hard in his cause, thrilled by his "manly" devotion to duty. "I had voted for BYRON PAINE," a lawyer recalled, "but I gloried in Judge DIXON" (*Wisconsin Reports* 81, p. xlv). Dixon presided over the court for another fourteen years. He faced another strong challenge in 1863 from farmers who were angered by his decisions to enforce mortgages that had been obtained by unscrupulous railroad agents. But Dixon was no minion of capital. He struck down laws that gave railroads too free a use of the eminent-domain power, he forbade publicly funded donations to railroads, and he held railroads liable for the negligent conduct of their employees, notwithstanding the contrary precedents of eastern states.

Finding that his judge's salary failed to keep pace with his family's growing financial needs, Dixon resigned in 1874 and commenced private practice in Milwaukee. He helped defend Wisconsin's "Potter Law," which set railroad rates, and in the appeal of these "Granger cases" to the U.S. Supreme Court he prevailed over former attorney general William Evarts, a pillar of the Wall Street bar. Another railroad case took him to Colorado, where he discovered that the climate relieved a respiratory condition that had dogged him in Milwaukee. In 1880 he moved to Denver and built a substantial appellate practice. One mining case came before the U.S. Supreme Court three times between 1888 and 1891. Returning from arguing the case in Washington in late November 1891, Dixon stopped over in Milwaukee, where a cold that he had acquired in transit suddenly worsened, and he died of pneumonia "with his professional harness upon him" (*Colorado Reports* 17, p. xxvi).

Regional pride accounts for much of Dixon's lasting fame. To the former midwesterner Gilbert Roe, Dixon and his successor Edward Ryan showed that the eastern bench had no monopoly on judicial talent. Still more important was what Dixon, by his action in the Booth case, came to symbolize for elite lawyers who had been made anxious by the innovative social legislation of turn-of-the-century America. Successfully withstanding the "wild torrent of politics," he represented "one great idea above all others"—the supremacy of the law as administered by fearless and incorruptible judges (*Colorado Reports* 17, p. xxiv; Winslow, p. 393). In life Dixon mixed rectitude with "an earnest, honest soul" (*Wisconsin Reports* 81, p. xxxiii). After his apotheosis, the human traits that made him an exemplary judge too often fell from view.

• Dixon's opinions appear in vols. 9–35 of *Wisconsin Reports* and in Gilbert E. Roe, *Selected Opinions of Luther S. Dixon and Edward G. Ryan, Late Chief Justices of the Supreme Court of Wisconsin* (1907). Wisconsin chief justice John Bradley Winslow celebrates Dixon for lifting "the Supreme Bench above the plane of party politics" in *The Story of a Great Court* (1912). Robert S. Hunt discusses Dixon's role in the "farmer mortgage controversy" and the Potter Law in *Law and Locomotives: The Impact of the Railroad on Wisconsin Law in the Nineteenth Century* (1958). Lawyerly assessments include Parker McCobb Reed, *The Bench and Bar of Wisconsin* (1882); Edwin E. Bryant, "The Supreme Court of Wisconsin," *Green Bag* 9 (1897): 116–21; and John R. Berryman, *History of the Bench and Bar of Wisconsin* (1898), as well as the eulogies collected in *Colorado Reports* 17 (1893): xix–xxv and *Wisconsin Reports* 81 (1892): xxxi–lv. Obituaries are in the (Denver) *Rocky Mountain News* and the *Milwaukee Sentinel*, 7 Dec. 1891.

DANIEL R. ERNST

DIXON, Roland Burrage (6 Nov. 1875–19 Dec. 1934), anthropologist and natural historian, was born in Worcester, Massachusetts, the son of Louis Seaver Dixon, a physician, and Ellen R. Burrage. Appointed an assistant at the Peabody Museum after graduating from Harvard in 1897, he engaged in the archaeological excavation of burial mounds in Madisonville, Ohio. After earning his M.A. in 1898, he joined the Jesup North Pacific Expedition, doing fieldwork in British Columbia and Alaska. He was also a member of the Huntington Expedition in California in 1899. His 1900 Harvard doctoral dissertation dealt with the language of the Maidu Indians of California. It was included by its de facto supervisor, Columbia anthropologist Franz Boas (who had been a member of the Jesup Expedition and was the most influential teacher of cultural anthropology in the United States), in the first volume of the *Handbook of American Indian Languages*. In 1905 Dixon published a monograph on the Maidu and another on the Shasta. Later he collaborated with anthropologist Alfred L. Kroeber in proposing various historical connections among California indigenous languages. Dixon also organized the statistical presentation of results on the American Indian population from the 1910 U.S. Census.

While advancing through the ranks of the Harvard faculty and the Peabody Museum (to the positions of professor and curator of ethnology, respectively), Dixon traveled extensively in Asia and the Pacific. From 1918 to 1919 he participated in a U.S. congressional inquiry on political conditions in Central Asia and was a member of the U.S. delegation to the Paris Peace Conference, which produced the Treaty of Versailles ending World War I and redrawing political boundaries in Europe and European colonies.

Following his California fieldwork (the last of which he undertook in 1907), Dixon's scope expanded: first to the indigenous languages of the entire North American continent, then to a survey of Oceanic mythology, and on to the geographical distributions of cultural traits around the world. For *The Racial History of Man* (1923) he cross-classified three physical measurements for all the peoples of the world for whom there were data, computed the proportions of each of the eight resulting combinations in various populations, and tried to fit the results to facts of history and geography. As Kroeber put it, "Dixon's reliance on the objectivity of his method induced him to follow it even when it led to fantastic results, evidently due to factors which he had omitted from consideration; and the use of his wide range of knowledge in attempts to prop some of his less probable findings, only made matters worse."

In opposition to Robert Lowie and others of Boas's later students, Dixon, along with John Swanton, Edward Sapir, and Clark Wissler, maintained what Kroeber characterized as "a sane and constructive interest in tribal and ethnic migrations" and cultural distributions. Lowie, in particular, maintained that no history could be extracted from myths. Dixon et al. looked at tribal myths as containing historical nuggets, especially about the direction of prehistorical migrations.

In his magnum opus, *The Building of Cultures* (1928), Dixon refined the age and area method (in which the center of geographical distributions of a trait was assumed to be the place of origin) by distinguishing components of culture traits more finely than was usual in such work and exhaustively analyzing similarities in material objects in order to understand the early movements of peoples over the world and to propound a theory of the diffusion of cultural traits. Environment (especially geographic location), diffusion from contact with other cultures, population density, and the giftedness of particular peoples were the factors Dixon saw as shaping the growth of human cultures in their physical, social, and religious aspects as well as the degeneration of some.

Dixon was regarded by fellow anthropologists as exceptionally erudite and icily impersonal. Harvard colleague Alfred Tozzer spoke of Dixon's "almost inhuman objectivity" and added that, besides being "unbending and rigid in his ideas," Dixon "shrank from personal contacts" (pp. 292–93). Dixon did not have disciples, and his theory of diffusion (of peoples and of tools, including languages) was neither used nor refined by later anthropologists. A major turn away from treating cultures as collections of unrelated parts (traits) and toward regarding them as tightly integrated wholes was already under way during the last decade of Dixon's life. Anthropologists began to stress the complexity in the cosmology and knowledge of the environment that were common in hunting and gathering groups and to eschew taking societies with "primitive" technologies and without nonlocal (state) organizations as a window to prehistory. Not only Dixon's models but what he modeled ceased to be of interest to anthropologists.

Dixon did not marry but was "cared for by his chauffeur and the latter's wife" (Coon, p. 135). Dixon died at his home (set on a large wooded grounds) in Harvard, Massachusetts, having lectured earlier that day.

• Dixon's other important publications include "Maidu Myths and the Northern Maidu," *Bulletin of the American Museum of Natural History* 17 (1905): 33–346; "The Shasta," *Bulletin of the American Museum of Natural History* 17 (1905): 381–498; "Maidu," *Handbook of American Indian Languages* 1 (1911): 679–734; with John Swanton, "Primitive American History," *American Anthropologist* 16 (1914): 376–412; *Oceanic Mythology* (1916); and with A. L. Kroeber, "Linguistic Families in California," *University of California Publications in American Archaeology and Ethnology* 16 (1919): 47–118. For assessments of his work and place in American anthropology, see Alfred M. Tozzer and Alfred L. Kroeber, "Roland Burrage Dixon," *American Anthropologist* 38 (1936): 291–301; and Stephen O. Murray, "Historical Inferences from Ethnohistorical Data," *Journal of the History of the Behavioral Sciences* 19 (1983): 335–40. Glimpses of the person are provided by Carleton S. Coon in his autobiography, *Adventures and Discoveries* (1981).

STEPHEN O. MURRAY

DIXON BROTHERS, country music songwriting and performing duet, comprised Dorsey Murdock Dixon (14 Oct. 1897–17 Apr. 1968) and Howard Briten Dixon (19 June 1903–24 Mar. 1961). Dorsey and Howard were born in Darlington, South Carolina, the sons of William McQuillan Dixon and Mary M. Braddock, textile mill workers in the newly industrialized South. Their father worked as a steam engine operator for the Darlington Cotton Manufacturing Company, and an older sister began working as a spinner in the mill when she was eight years old, earning pennies a day. Howard began mill work when he was ten, and Dorsey started at age twelve. These experiences

formed the basis of several of the topical songs for which the brothers would later become famous, but they also formed the impetus for them to try to escape from the cotton mills as quickly as possible. One way was through music.

Both Dorsey and Howard learned old American and British ballads from their mother when they were very young, as well as gospel songs and spirituals. Dorsey got his first guitar when he was fourteen and soon taught himself to play; a local teacher also taught him to play the fiddle, and soon he was performing in local Sunday school classes. Howard was even more intrigued with the guitar, and a chance meeting with a professional entertainer named Jimmie Tarlton (who later became famous through his recording of "Birmingham Jail") inspired him to adapt the slide technique in which he "noted" the instrument with a heavy piece of steel. (This was a forerunner of the bluegrass dobro, as well as the electric steel in later country music.)

By the time they were teenagers, the Dixons were performing at a movie theater in nearby Rockingham, North Carolina. During this time both were still working for the mills, except for a stint at working on the railroad during World War I. (In later years, even after their success as performers and recording artists, both would continue to work in the mills.) Dorsey's jobs took him to Greeneville and Lancaster, South Carolina, and to East Rockingham, North Carolina, as well as a short time in a rayon plant in New Jersey.

As teenagers, the brothers honed their skills singing at local dances and church events, and by 1934 they were playing over WBT, a major clear-channel radio station in Charlotte, North Carolina, that could be heard across the South at night. Now billed as the Dixon Brothers, they were sponsored by the patent medicine company Crazy Water Crystals. By now Dorsey was starting to create his own songs, including a local ballad called "The Cleveland Schoolhouse Fire."

These songs, as well as the brothers' versatile musicianship, attracted the attention of Eli Oberstein, an executive with RCA's Bluebird record company. He invited them to a recording session on 12 February 1936 at a temporary studio in Charlotte, where he recorded six selections by them. These included two that would become among their best-known songs, "Weave Room Blues" (a bitter protest song about mill work) and a tale of comic surrealism called "The Intoxicated Rat." The records were widely distributed and sold through Montgomery Ward's famed mail order catalog. A second Bluebird session soon followed, in which the brothers were joined by guitarist/vocalist Mutt Carey.

The Dixon Brothers went on to record forty-nine selections between 1936 and 1938. Other popular sides featured more of Dorsey's original songs: comic pieces like "Fisherman's Luck" and "Sales Tax on the Women"; labor protest songs like "Spinning Room Blues"; and songs about tragedies, such as "Down with the Old Canoe" (about the *Titanic*) and "I Didn't Hear Nobody Pray" (about a local automobile wreck). The latter was made into a hit in the 1940s by Grand Ole Opry star Roy Acuff, who had recorded it not knowing it was Dixon's composition and who called it "The Wreck on the Highway." (Acuff later acknowledged Dorsey's authorship and paid royalties.) Unlike other popular duet acts of the day, such as the Blue Sky Boys or Karl and Harty, who sang in clean, precise, close harmony, the Dixons preferred a looser, bluesy, more soulful style and featured Howard's steel guitar.

In 1927 Dorsey had married Beatrice Moody, who also was a singer; they had four children. Howard also married young, in 1920, to Mellie Barfield of Darlington, North Carolina, and they had eight children. In September 1938 the Dixon Brothers recorded their last sides as a formal duo. Howard joined forces with Frank Gerald, and, under the name the Rambling Duet, they recorded twenty-two more sides for Bluebird in 1937 and 1938. While they had no especially noteworthy hits, they did have successful songs with "Hobo Jack, the Rambler" and "The Bootlegger's Story." Dorsey recorded additional sides with his wife. Later, in about 1940–1941, Howard also worked in Wade Mainer's popular radio band over WWNC radio in Asheville, North Carolina, and during the 1950s and 1960s he sang in a local gospel quartet called the Reaping Harvesters. During much of this time, he also continued to work in the East Rockingham mills.

By the 1940s Dorsey was relatively inactive as a musician, but in 1962 he was visited by folklorists like Archie Green who encouraged him to begin performing again. He did so, appearing as a solo act at the Newport Folk Festival and recording a pair of LPs that appeared in the mid-1960s. During the 1980s many of the Dixon Brothers records from the 1930s were issued on LPs by the Old Homestead company, recycling their distinctive style and songs for newer generations. Dorsey died in Plant City, Florida, and Howard died in East Rockingham, North Carolina.

• The most readily available accounts of the Dixon Brothers are the entries by Ivan M. Tribe in *Definitive Country*, ed. Barry McCloud (1995).

CHARLES K. WOLFE

DIXWELL, John (c. 1607–18 Mar. 1689), regicide, was born at Cotton Hall in Warwickshire, England, the son of William Dixwell and Elizabeth Brent. Little is known of his early years. In 1643, after the death of his brother, Mark Dixwell, John Dixwell received large estates in Kent to hold in trust for his brother's children. Dixwell sided with the parliamentary cause during the English Civil War, and in 1646 he was elected to Parliament from Dover. His great claim to fame or to notoriety in English history comes from the events of early 1649; Dixwell was one of the fifty-nine men who signed the death warrant of King Charles I. Dixwell's signature was the thirty-eighth in line on the document, and it is interesting to note that his handwriting was much more legible than that of most of his fellow judges.

Dixwell became a colonel in Cromwell's forces in 1650, was a member of the Council of State (1651–1652), and served in the Protectorate Parliaments (1654, 1656). Therefore, Dixwell was a marked man when King Charles II was restored to the throne in 1660. Dixwell and all the other regicides were excepted from the Act of Pardon and Oblivion; the regicides who were still alive fled from England to continental countries (except for Edward Whalley and William Goffe, who went to America). Dixwell fled to Hanau, Germany, and probably stayed there for several years.

Dixwell made his appearance in colonial America in February 1665, when he visited Whalley and Goffe at their secret hiding place—the home of John Russell, the pastor of the frontier town of Hadley, Massachusetts. Whalley and Goffe had stayed at Boston, New Haven, and Milford, Connecticut, before settling at Hadley. Dixwell's historical trail vanished for several years until 1670 when he appeared at New Haven, where he soon became a regular member of that community. Dixwell called himself "James Davids," an alias that he kept for the rest of his life. Known in New Haven as a quiet, pious, and somewhat mysterious person, Dixwell married a widow, Joanna Ling, who died shortly after their wedding in 1673. Dixwell married again in 1677, to Bathshaba Howe, with whom he had three children. There is no record of Dixwell having married during his years in England.

Like his two fellow regicides eighty miles to the north in Hadley, Dixwell kept a strong belief in the Puritan cause. Although the year 1666 did not bring the apocalyptical changes he desired, Dixwell remained confident that the Puritan cause would eventually prevail and that the Stuart royal family would again be humbled. Save for the adoption of his alias, Dixwell lived openly in New Haven, a far cry from Whalley's and Goffe's lives in Hadley. One compliment later paid to Dixwell came from the pen of a British subject of Queen Victoria, totally loyal to the memory of the house of Stuart: "Time went by and the Hadley regicides wasted away in their cellar, while Dixwell thus flourished like a bay-tree in green old age" (*Blackwood's Edinburgh Magazine*, p. 346).

In March 1689 Dixwell transferred his claim to the estates in Kent to his wife and son, and later that month Dixwell died in New Haven. Only five weeks later, the news reached Boston that King James II had been deposed and that William and Mary had taken the throne at the request of Parliament. Dixwell had died just too soon to witness the end of the Stuart family's attempt to re-create absolute government. Edmund Ludlow in Switzerland was the only regicide who survived Dixwell. Dixwell's widow and son later tried to regain the estates in Kent, but their attempts proved to be in vain. In 1849 one of Dixwell's descendants erected a memorial to the regicide behind Center Church in New Haven, where Dixwell had been buried.

The lore, legend, and fascination with the three English regicides who came to America is considerable. Nourished by the literary efforts of Thomas

Hutchinson, Ezra Stiles, Sir Walter Scott, Nathaniel Hawthorne, and others, all three regicides became enshrined in the nineteenth-century American canon; indeed, it has been said that Ezra Stiles's admiration of the three judges "amounts almost to idolatry." The image of the three men making their way through a bleak and unfamiliar American landscape has excited poets, historians, and novelists. Dixwell is probably the least well known of the three men, which is ironic since he was the most visible of the three in America. Just as King Arthur is expected to rise and defeat Britain's enemies, so do the judges loom as protectors and guardians of liberty in the American mind.

Dixwell's life and career form an illuminating vignette of early American history. His presence in New Haven seemed to indicate to the Puritan faithful of his generation that the Puritan struggle was not in vain— that popery and absolutism would eventually be vanquished. His years in America provide the basis for some understanding of the Puritan mentality between the Restoration of King Charles II and the Glorious Revolution. Certainly Dixwell was aware that the Puritan commonwealth existed on both sides of the Atlantic. The people who sheltered him at New Haven, and those who had sheltered Whalley and Goffe, were all liable for the punishment of execution, which was meted out to Lady Lisle after she sheltered two fugitives during Monmouth's Rebellion in 1685. It was no small matter to harbor a regicide; the fact that it was done indicates the strong faith of the Puritans in both old England and New England—their community of saints would eventually rise and triumph, no matter how long the battle lasted.

• Dixwell's papers are at the New Haven Colony Historical Society. There is as yet no biography of Dixwell. However, because of his years in New Haven, there is a fair amount of tangible evidence about Dixwell's life and hence, perhaps, less possibility of the development of legends. Some of the standard accounts are Ezra Stiles, *A History of the Judges of King Charles I* (1794), Lemuel A. Welles, *History of the Regicides in New England* (1927), and Israel P. Warren, *The Three Judges* (1873). In addition, there are several important journal articles, including F. B. Dexter, ed., "Dixwell Papers," *New Haven Colony Historical Society Papers* 6 (1900): 337–74; Mark L. Sargent, "Thomas Hutchinson, Ezra Stiles, and the Legend of the Regicides," *William and Mary Quarterly* 49, no. 3 (1992): 431–48; Douglas C. Wilson, "Webb of Secrecy: Goffe, Whalley, and the Legend of Hadley," *New England Quarterly* 60 (1987): 515–48; Cora E. Lutz, "Ezra Stiles and the Monument for Colonel John Dixwell," *Yale University Library Gazette* 55, no. 3 (1981): 116–20. The British travel writer's essay is "The Cave of the Regicides," *Blackwood's Edinburgh Magazine* 61, no. 377 (Mar. 1847): 333–49. There is an intriguing hypothesis about Ezra Stiles and his connections with the regicides proposed in James W. Mavor, Jr., and Byron E. Dix, *Manitou: The Sacred Landscape of New England's Native Civilization* (1989).

SAMUEL WILLARD CROMPTON

DOAK, Samuel (1 Aug. 1749–12 Dec. 1830), Presbyterian minister and educator, was born in Augusta County, Virginia, the son of Samuel Doak and Jane

Elizabeth Mitchell, farmers who had emigrated from northern Ireland. Doak began his classical studies at age sixteen under Robert Alexander, founder of Augusta Academy (now Washington and Lee University), and later attended West Nottingham Academy in Colora, Maryland, where he paid some of his expenses by working as an assistant teacher. In 1773 he entered the College of New Jersey (now Princeton), where he studied with John Witherspoon; he received a B.A. two years later. After graduation he studied theology and served as an assistant teacher in the school of Robert Smith in Pequea, Pennsylvania.

In 1775 Doak married Esther Houston Montgomery; they had seven children. In 1776 the Hanover Presbytery appointed Doak second assistant to Samuel Stanhope Smith, the rector of the newly founded Prince Edward Academy (now Hampden-Sydney College) in Virginia. He likely continued theological studies there under Smith and later under William Graham, the rector of Liberty Hall in Timber Ridge, Rockbridge County, Virginia. On 31 October 1777 Doak was licensed to preach by the Hanover Presbytery; the following year, he served as itinerant supply minister for congregations without ministers in southwestern Virginia.

In 1778 Doak accepted a call to the Holston River settlements in North Carolina, becoming the first minister to settle in present-day Tennessee. Because the appointment was temporary and there was the threat of Indian attacks, Doak moved to the Nollichucky River settlements in October 1781. There, on Little Limestone Creek in Washington County, Tennessee, he organized Salem Church. He also built a log schoolhouse on his farm, the "first educational institution in the Mississippi Valley" (Thompson, p. 114). Doak assisted in organizing a number of other churches in Washington and Greene counties. With Scotch-Irish pouring into the back country after the Revolution and with the number of clergymen limited, Doak and other Presbyterian ministers and licentiates were often asked by the Hanover Presbytery to act as supply pastors or missionaries for congregations in Presbyterian communities. Doak's preaching was apparently "original, bold, pungent, and sometimes pathetic" with a delivery that was "natural and impressive" (Sprague, p. 396).

Doak labored to prevent the spread of the "new divinity," or Hopkinsianism, in eastern Tennessee. In 1796 he and four other ministers accused Hezekiah Balch, the minister of Mount Bethel Church, of abandoning the covenant theology of Calvinism by modifying the doctrines of predestination, atonement, and original sin. The Hopkinsians did not accept the doctrine of limited atonement, that Christ died only for the elect. Though supporting general atonement, they believed that only those granted God's sovereign grace would acquire salvation. The doctrine of original sin was unacceptable; sinners were responsible for their own sinfulness. Despite the efforts of Doak and others, "Tennessee was the only southern state in which the 'new divinity' secured a firm footing" (Thompson, p. 355).

Doak supported the revolutionary cause. On 26 September 1780, when hundreds of riflemen from Sullivan and Washington counties gathered at Sycamore Shoals on their way to King's Mountain, Doak apparently delivered a stirring prayer and invocation. Active in the affairs of Washington County, Doak served as delegate to the first general convention of transmontane counties, held in Jonesborough in August 1784. That convention charged North Carolina's government with neglecting western interests; petitioned Congress to accept the Cession Act of April 1784, by which North Carolina had agreed to cede its western lands to the United States; and formed an association of counties that evolved into the independent but short-lived state of Franklin.

Though a slaveowner himself, Doak favored emancipation of slaves but ultimately joined with other Presbyterian clergymen who believed that there was no practical solution for freeing them. Nonetheless, a number of Doak's students, including David Nelson and John Rankin left the South and became active figures in the abolition movement that emerged in the region north of the Ohio River and west of the Alleghenies in the 1830s.

Doak's small school was incorporated by the General Assembly of North Carolina as Martin Academy in 1783, reincorporated by the state of Franklin two years later, and finally chartered as Washington College by the Assembly of the Southwest Territory in 1795 with Doak continuing as president and teacher. Two students received bachelor's degrees in the first graduating class of 1796. Doak obtained the nucleus of a college library in 1798 while attending a meeting of the General Assembly of the Presbyterian church in Philadelphia. The donated books were transported by packhorse across the mountains to become one of the first school libraries in Tennessee.

James G. M. Ramsey, a historian and student of Doak, recalled Doak's "stentorian voice" and countenance that "expressed strong intellect, manly good sense, calm dignity, and indomitable firmness." Each student was allowed to move as rapidly as his "industry and his abilities enabled him to do." The primary objective of Doak's instruction was mental discipline training the student "to think accurately and profoundly, to think for himself, and to beget a spirit of manly reliance upon his own powers of independent investigation and vigorous thought" (Sprague, p. 395). Doak's teaching reflected his experience as a student of John Witherspoon at the College of New Jersey, particularly the Scottish philosophy of common sense expounded by Witherspoon. According to this philosophy, as noted by Doak in his lectures on human nature, there are certain principles that comprise the "foundation of all reasoning, and without them there can be no reasoning. To become acquainted with human nature we must ourselves examine it, not depending on the hypotheses of metaphysicians on the subject, but, directed by certain axioms of self-evident truths established by consciousness and common sense" (Doak, pp. 7–8). Doak had a passion for philology and taught languages until his death. Ever a student, after age sixty he mastered and taught both Hebrew and chemistry.

Doak married Margaretta Houston McEwen of Nashville, Tennessee, in 1818, his first wife having died in 1807. They had no children of their own. Also in 1818, after years of financial struggle at Washington College, Doak resigned as president and moved to Bethel in Greene County, Tennessee, where he and his son Samuel Witherspoon Doak opened a classical school, Tusculum Academy (later Tusculum College). During its early years the academy operated with no formal charter, president, or board of trustees. The school was incorporated by the Tennessee legislature on 1 February 1842. His older son, John W. Doak, served as president of Washington College until his death in 1820. At that time Doak was asked to return to Washington College, but he declined and remained at Tusculum until his death there.

Doak was one of many Presbyterian ministers who were graduates of the College of New Jersey and were committed to the Revolution and to an expansive vision of their role in creating a moral society. Such ministers built churches and spurred much of the educational advance in the Old Southwest, while engaging in important political and social issues of the frontier.

• The Doak Family Papers and Samuel Witherspoon Doak Papers, including Samuel Doak's diary (1768–1775) and his transcriptions of John Witherspoon's lectures on moral philosophy, are in the Tennessee State Library, Nashville. An important source, including twenty-two of Doak's lectures as transcribed by his students, is *Lectures on Human Nature Adapted to the Use of Students at Colleges, Academies, or in Other Schools, or in Private. To Which Is Added an Essay on Life by Rev. John W. Doak* (1845). The minutes of the Hanover Presbytery (1769–1785) and the minutes of the Synod of the Carolinas (1788–1826), found in the Union Theological Seminary in Richmond, Va., and the minutes of the Abingdon Presbytery (1805–1834), located in the Historical Foundation of the Presbyterian and Reformed churches in Montreat, N.C., all chronicle Doak's work in the church and his involvement in the new divinity controversy. The *Journal of the Proceedings of the Board of Trustees of Washington College* (1795–1818), provides information on Doak's presidency. For a sketch of Doak, see William B. Sprague, *Annals of the American Pulpit*, vol. 3 (1969). Howard Ernest Carr, *Washington College: A Study of an Attempt to Provide Higher Education in Eastern Tennessee* (1935), is the most complete history of its subject yet published; also see Joseph T. Fuhrmann, *The Life and Times of Tusculum College* (1986). For genealogy, see William Gunn Calhoun, *Samuel Doak, 1749–1830: His Life, His Children, Washington College* (1966), and Harry E. Mitchell, *The Mitchell-Doak Group: History, Biography, Genealogy* (1966). Samuel Cole Williams, *History of the Lost State of Franklin* (1924), presents Doak as one of the Franklinites. Useful for placing Doak in the broader context of Presbyterian history in the Old Southwest are William Henry Foote, *Sketches of North Carolina, Historical and Biographical, Illustrative of the Principles of a Portion of Her Early Settlers* (1846); Walter Brownlow Posey, *The Presbyterian Church in the Old Southwest, 1778–1838* (1952); and Ernest Trice Thompson, *Presbyterians in the South, 1607–1861*, vol. 1 (1963).

RUBY J. LANIER

DOANE, George Washington (27 May 1799–27 Apr. 1859), Episcopal bishop, was born in Trenton, New Jersey, the son of Jonathan Doane, a builder and contractor, and Mary Higgins. He graduated from Union College, Schenectady, New York, in 1818 and there came under the influence of Thomas Church Brownell, later the third bishop of Connecticut, who directed him toward the ministry. He entered the General Theological Seminary, New York City, which had been established in 1817. "I was one of three, who studied and recited, when the whole Seminary was accommodated in a second story room over a saddler's shop, downtown" (Doane, vol. 1, p. 27). At General he began his friendship with Bishop John Henry Hobart, leader of the High Church party in the Episcopal church. While in New York, Doane established a school for boys, which began his later career as an educator. He also assisted George Upfold, later the second bishop of Indiana, in establishing St. Luke's Church, New York City.

Bishop Hobart ordained Doane priest on 19 April 1821, and he became Hobart's assistant at Trinity Church, New York City. On 6 August 1823 Hobart ordained him to the priesthood. Soon after Brownell became bishop of Connecticut he took steps to establish Trinity College, which opened on 23 September 1824 under the name Washington College. (It changed its name to Trinity College on 24 May 1845.) Doane became professor of belles-lettres and oratory. After the *Churchman's Magazine*, which had been founded in 1808 by Bishop Hobart to propagate High Church ideals, suspended publication in 1827, Doane began publishing and editing the *Episcopal Watchman* on 26 March 1827 to defend High Church principles. "The *Episcopal Watchman* stood in a unique position in that it was at once the successor of the first periodical of the Episcopal Church, the *Churchman's Magazine*, and the forerunner of the first enduring weekly periodical, the *Churchman*" (C. Morehouse, p. 245). In the first editorial, Doane and his colleague William Croswell pledged themselves to "the elucidation and defense . . . of the doctrines, discipline and worship of the Protestant Episcopal Church, its divinely instituted ministry, existing from the Apostles' time in three orders, with the power of ordination exclusively in the first; its blessed sacraments opening the kingdom of heaven, and conveying the means of grace, to the devout and faithful recipient; its primitive and apostolical rites and usages; its liturgy, simple, comprehensive, fervent, and almost inspired; and its government . . . judicious, wholesome, and equitable" (Doane, vol. 1, p. 101).

The motto of the *Episcopal Watchman* was "the Gospel of Christ in the Church of Christ." This editorial and this motto describe Doane's Pre-Tractarian High Church position, a position developed and propagated by Bishop Hobart. It was a High Churchmanship that preceded the impact of the *Tracts for the Times* of the Oxford Movement, which were first published in the United States in 1839. This High Church position emphasized the threefold order of ministry—bishops, priests, and deacons—and insisted on ordination only by bishops in apostolic succession. This ministry was instituted by Christ and has existed since the time of the apostolic church. It also taught that there are two sacraments—baptism and the eucharist—instituted by Jesus Christ and that those two sacraments are not just pledges of grace but are the means of grace. Sacraments administered by persons not ordained by a bishop in apostolic succession were invalid. These High Churchmen stressed the faithful and consistent use of the *Book of Common Prayer* and considered it as second only to the Bible as a doctrinal guide. They had a high view of the church as a divine society and as the Body of Christ. The Evangelical party stressed the centrality of the Bible, preaching as the primary means of grace, the church as a gathered group of believers, and a personal conversion experience.

In 1828 Doane became the assistant minister at Trinity Church, Boston, and in 1830 he became the rector. While in Boston he and Croswell edited the *Banner of the Cross*, which used as its motto Bishop Hobart's watchword, "Evangelical Truth and Apostolic Order." It also defended High Church principles but lasted only from 3 September 1831 to 24 November 1832. During its brief existence, it published some poems of the English poet-priest, John Keble. In 1829 Doane married Eliza Greene Callahan Perkins, the widow of James Perkins; they had one child, a son.

On 3 October 1832 Doane was elected the second bishop of New Jersey, a position he held until his death. He was consecrated on 31 October 1832 at St. Paul's Chapel, New York. On 3 August 1833 the vestry of St. Mary's Church, Burlington, elected him rector, and he accepted the position on 1 October 1833.

As bishop of New Jersey, Doane founded the *Missionary*, which was in existence from September 1834 to December 1837. The stated objective of the *Missionary* articulated Bishop Doane's theology and also carried the Hobartian watchword: "Evangelical Truth: Apostolic Order." The evangelical truth was "The Cross of the Lord Jesus Christ—the Lamb of God who taketh away the sins of the world, lifted up from the earth that he might draw all men unto him. Man lost—God incarnate for his recovery—'Christ crucified' the price of his restoration—justification by faith,—faith working by love,—love purifying the heart,—salvation wholly by grace." The apostolic order was the church, "the body of the Lord Jesus . . . which he hath purchased with his own blood. Its ministers, its sacraments, its worship—the appointment of the Lord, the means of Grace" (C. Morehouse, p. 268).

Doane also founded two schools; St. Mary's Hall for girls opened on 1 May 1837 in Burlington, and in 1846 Burlington College for boys opened. After both schools fell deeply in debt, several persons in the diocese accused Doane of financial irregularities. These persons, especially William Halsted, convinced three evangelical bishops, William Meade of Virginia, Charles P. McIlvaine of Ohio, and George Burgess of Maine, to make a presentment against Doane in the House of Bishops. Eventually the House of Bishops dismissed the case. Doane was not guilty of any crime but was a poor manager of money. On 25 September 1835 Doane preached the sermon at the consecration of Jackson Kemper as the first missionary bishop of the Episcopal church, a sermon that elevated the missionary task of a bishop.

Although Doane was a leader of the High Church party and sympathetic to the Oxford Movement, he was critical of any Roman Catholic intrusions into the Episcopal church. As a High Churchman, he edited the first American edition of John Keble's *Christian Year* (1834). When one of Doane's sons, George Hobart, joined the Roman Catholic church, Bishop Doane had to depose him from the ministry of the Episcopal church. Not only a leader of the High Church party, Doane was also its poet. Three of his hymns, *Softly Now the Light of Day*, *Thou Art the Way*, and *Fling out the Banner*, have been particularly popular. He was an educator, editor, missionary, and significant advocate for High Church principles. He died in Burlington, New Jersey.

• Doane's papers and sermons are in the Archives of the Diocese of New Jersey, Trenton; the Archives of the Episcopal Church, Austin, Tex.; and the Archives of the General Theological Seminary, New York City. The major study of him and the fullest collection of his published materials was done by his son William Croswell Doane, *The Life and Writings of George Washington Doane, D.D., LL.D., for Twenty-Seven Years Bishop of New Jersey, Containing His Poetical Works, Sermons, and Miscellaneous Writings: With a Memoir by His Son* (4 vols., 1860–1861). Some of his poetry was published as *Songs by the Way* (1824). Material related to Doane's trial was published in pamphlet form, *The Protest and Appeal of George Washington Doane, Bishop of New Jersey; as Aggrieved, by the Right Reverend William Meade, D.D.; the Right Reverend George Burgess, D.D.; and the Right Reverend Charles Pettit McIlvaine, D.D.: And His Reply to the False, Calumnious, and Malignant Representations of William Halsted, Caleb Perkins, Peter V. Coppuck, and Bennington Gill; on Which They Ground Their Uncanonical, Unchristian and Inhuman Procedure, in Regard to Him* (1852), *The Record of the Proceedings of the Court of Bishops Assembled for the Trial of the Rt. Rev. George Washington Doane* (1852), *The Record of the Proceedings of the Court of Bishops Assembled at Camden, New Jersey, Sept. 1st, 1853, for the Trial of the Rt. Rev. George Washington, Doane* (1853), and George Weller, *An Historical Review of the Proceedings in the Case of Bishop Doane* (1853). Doane is treated rather fully in George M. Hills, *History of the Church in Burlington, New Jersey* (1885), and in Frederick C. Morehouse, *Some American Churchmen* (1892), and briefly in Nelson R. Burr, *The Anglican Church in New Jersey* (1954), and George E. DeMille, *The Catholic Movement in the American Episcopal Church* (1941). His work as an editor is discussed in Clifford P. Morehouse, "Origins of the Episcopal Press from Colonial Days to 1840," *Historical Magazine of the Protestant Episcopal Church* 11 (Sept. 1942): 199–318.

DONALD S. ARMENTROUT

DOANE, William Croswell (2 Mar. 1832–17 May 1913), Episcopal bishop, was born in Boston, Massachusetts, the son of George Washington Doane, the second Episcopal bishop of New Jersey, and Eliza Greene Callahan Perkins, the widow of a James Perkins. Doane's father was consecrated bishop of New Jersey in 1832, and the family moved to Burlington, New Jersey, where William grew up. Bishop Doane founded Burlington College, and William graduated from it in 1850.

Doane studied for the ministry under his father and was ordained deacon in 1853. Shortly after his ordination, Doane married Sarah Katharine Condit of Newark; they had two children.

His first ministry was as assistant to his father at St. Mary's Church, Burlington. Doane was ordained priest in 1856 and then founded St. Barnabas Free Church in northern Burlington, where he served as rector from 1856 until 1860. During the six years from 1854 until 1860, in addition to his parochial responsibilities, he taught English literature at Burlington College. When his father died, young Doane succeeded him as rector of St. Mary's Church and served there from 1860 until 1863.

Doane's reputation as a preacher and pastor grew rapidly, and he was called to be the third rector of St. John's Church, Hartford, Connecticut. He was instituted in 1863 and served until 1867. While at Hartford he taught English literature at Trinity College, where his father had taught before him. At St. John's he was active as a social reformer and was a great supporter of missions. During Doane's tenure as rector, St. John's Church established two daughter missions—St. John's in East Hartford and the Church of the Good Shepherd in Hartford. Following in the tradition of his predecessor, Arthur Cleveland Coxe (later bishop of western New York), Doane was intensely devoted to the church's liturgy and insisted on daily morning and evening prayers. He also was an opponent of the practice of auctioning off pews, which he considered an indecent and unchurchly transaction.

In 1867 Doane became the rector of St. Peter's Church in Albany, New York, and remained there until he resigned in 1869. While at St. Peter's he had a weekly celebration of the Eucharist and daily morning and evening prayer.

At this time the Episcopal church was rapidly expanding in New York state, and many people realized that it needed additional episcopal supervision. The General Convention of 1868 voted to divide the Diocese of New York and create two new ones: Albany and Long Island. The Primary Convention of the Diocese of Albany met at St. Peter's Church in December 1868 and elected Doane bishop on the ninth ballot. There was strong opposition to Doane as a High Church ritualist by part of the Evangelical party, and some of them circulated a pamphlet in which his ritualistic practices were vehemently denounced. Among these practices were colored eucharistic vestments, altar lights, processions, lay servers, and incense. Shortly after Doane's election, a determined but unsuccessful effort was made to block the confirmation of the election by a majority of the standing committees. Doane was consecrated the first bishop of Albany in February 1869 and served in that position until his death.

In his address to the Diocese of Albany convention in 1869, Bishop Doane said, "God helping me, if I live long enough, the Diocese of Albany will have the reality of a cathedral with all that involves of work and worship, in frequent services, in schools and houses of mercy of every kind" (DeMille, *Pioneer Cathedral*, p. 7). He began his cathedral system by opening St. Agnes' School for Girls in 1870. A new congregation was organized in conjunction with the school by members of two other parishes, and property was donated for a cathedral building. In 1872 the congregation of All Saints began to meet for worship in an unused machine shop. By 1875 a cathedral chapter was in existence, and a hospital had begun. To staff the hospital, Bishop Doane formed a new order of nuns, the Sisterhood of the Holy Child Jesus. In 1873 Doane set apart Helen Dunham as the first sister. In 1883 St. Margaret's House for Babies opened. The cornerstone for the cathedral building was laid in 1884, and the Cathedral of All Saints was dedicated in November 1888.

Doane published a number of significant books and articles. His most important publication was the four-volume *Life and Writings of George Washington Doane, with a Memoir* (1860–1861). In 1882 he published *Mosaics; or, The Harmony of Collect, Epistle and Gospel for the Sundays of the Church Year*. He was an accomplished poet and in 1901 published *Rhymes from Time to Time*. His most successful hymn was "Ancient of Days," written in 1886 for the bicentennial celebration of Albany.

Doane was a leading High Church bishop committed to a weekly Eucharist, daily morning and evening prayers, and the sacrament of penance. He was a champion of the cause of the American family and a great opponent of divorce. Doane also opposed the remarriage of divorced persons. He was unalterably opposed to woman suffrage and called the suffragists "silly women." Doane always insisted on the outward show of episcopal dignity and following the English custom wore the episcopal costume of apron, pectoral cross, knee breeches, gaiters, and a shovel hat. He referred to himself as "William of Albany." He died in New York City.

• Doane's papers are in the Archives of the Episcopal Church, Austin, Tex. George Lynde Richardson, *William Croswell Doane, First Bishop of Albany* (1933), is a major study of Doane. His ministry at Hartford is discussed in Nelson R. Burr, *A History of Saint John's Church, Hartford, Connecticut, 1841–1941*, and his ministry at St. Peter's is treated in Joseph Hooper, *A History of Saint Peter's Church in the City of Albany* (1900). Doane's work in establishing the Cathedral of All Saints is discussed in George E. DeMille, *Pioneer Cathedral* (1972). Other helpful studies are Daniel Sylvester Tuttle, "Bishop Doane as a Member of the House of Bishops," *Spirit of Missions* 78 (1913): 446–47; Reese F. Alsop, "Bishop Doane as a Member of the Board of Missions," *Spirit of Missions* 78 (1913): 447–48; and DeMille, "The Doane Consecration: A Skirmish in the Second Ritualistic War," *Historical Magazine of the Protestant Episcopal Church* 17 (1948): 287–96. Obituaries are in the *Living Church* 49 (24 and 31 May 1913), the *Week* 104 (31 May 1913), the *Churchman* 107 (24 May 1913), and the *New York Times*, 18 May 1913.

DON S. ARMENTROUT

DOBBS, Arthur (2 Apr. 1689–28 Mar. 1765), colonial governor of North Carolina, was born in Givran, in Ayrshire, Scotland, the son of Richard Dobbs, a landed gentleman and British army officer, and Mary Stewart. His mother had been sent to Givran to escape the turmoil in Ireland following the Glorious Revolution. His father owned an estate at Castle Dobbs near Carrickfergus in County Antrim, Ireland. As a member of northern Ireland's small Anglican elite, Dobbs easily achieved local prominence. After serving two years in the British army in Scotland, Dobbs returned to manage the family estate at the age of twenty-four. His marriage to Anne Osburn Norbury in 1719 increased his wealth; the couple had three children. In 1720 he was appointed high sheriff of Antrim and elected mayor of Carrickfergus.

Dobbs soon took a leading role in Irish affairs. A reflective man, he believed that Ireland's stability and prosperity depended on its ties to other parts of the British empire. As a member of the Irish Parliament beginning in 1727, he supported the ruling Whig administration. Through Sir Robert Walpole's favor, he was appointed engineer and surveyor general of Ireland in 1733. Dobbs even advocated Irish parliamentary union with Britain, but he took a reformist approach to Anglo-Irish relations. Ireland would most enhance British and imperial strength, Dobbs argued, if Britain served Irish interests by lifting restrictive navigation acts and by allowing Irish Catholics to hold longterm leases on their lands. Under such favorable circumstances, he hoped, the Catholic majority might even convert to Protestantism.

In his efforts to realize his ambitions for himself and the empire, Dobbs looked beyond Ireland to North America. In his memorandum, "Scheme to Enlarge the Colonies and Increase Commerce and Trade," which had brought Dobbs to Walpole's attention in 1730, Dobbs argued that a more aggressive colonial administration might enable Britain to win its ongoing struggle against France. He even suggested in a later treatise that this conflict would lead to a "millennium following the world-wide supremacy of Protestantism and English arms" (Clarke, p. 133). Dobbs's recommendations for achieving this lofty end paralleled his hopes for imperial reform in Ireland. British power in America could only be secured, he argued, if the mother country promoted colonial growth and development. This entailed fostering new settlements and allowing free trade. He also proposed that Britain could eliminate French influence and promote true religion only by treating the Indians fairly. Indeed, he suggested that colonial women might be offered premiums to marry Indian men, thus promoting harmony and unity.

During the 1730s and 1740s Dobbs not only continued to write about America; he also became personally involved in American enterprises. Patriotic, religious, and financial goals, combined with a genuine interest in exploration and scientific investigation, led him to promote the discovery of a northwest passage. He and a group of London merchants petitioned the British government, insisting that the Hudson's Bay Company had irresponsibly neglected such an opportunity to check French Canada and enhance British wealth. Despite financing two independently organized expeditions, Dobbs and his associates failed to discover a viable northwest passage. Nevertheless, Dobbs continued to insist on its existence.

Somewhat more fruitful were his investments in North American land further south. In 1745 Dobbs's London mercantile associates, led by Henry McCulloh, sold North Carolina lands totaling 400,000 acres (in what are now Mecklenburg and Cabarrus counties) to Dobbs and a partner, Colonel John Selwyn. By the mid-1750s Dobbs had convinced some 500 Protestant Irish to emigrate and settle on these lands. He was also a founding member of the Ohio Company, a transatlantic group of speculators who in 1749 received a land grant of 200,000 acres in the Ohio Valley. In this, as in his other American ventures, Dobbs served his personal interests while promoting his vision of a strong empire of interdependent parts.

The same combination of motives induced him to use his connections at court to obtain the governorship of North Carolina in 1753. After he reached the province in October of the following year, Dobbs sought to rationalize the administration and to harmonize the interests of this contentious, rapidly growing colony.

He enjoyed partial success during his early years as governor because he refused to favor either the northern or southern regional faction, whose struggles had crippled his predecessor's administration. By calling the assembly to meet at the central town of New Bern and by emphasizing a common cause in the current struggle with France and its Indian allies, Dobbs achieved an unprecedented degree of unity. Throughout his administration, he also attempted to bring North Carolina more into the imperial mainstream by strengthening the Anglican church in the province.

By 1760 the assembly united against Dobbs, despite his attempts to act even-handedly. His efforts to resolve disputes over land titles and to make the treasurer and other public officials more accountable alienated many who had profited from disorganization and corruption. Dobbs undoubtedly believed that his appointment of several Irish friends and relations to public office would check the influence of corrupt factions, but his opponents regarded this as an abuse of executive power. The governor especially alienated Francis Corbin and Thomas Child, successive agents of the proprietary interest of the earl of Granville (John Carteret) in the northern part of the colony. They enjoyed considerable support in the assembly, and both

profited from their positions at the expense of the settlers and Lord Granville. The governor removed Corbin from the council because he viewed Corbin as inimical both to the province's interest and to that of his partner in land speculation, Henry McCulloh, whose claims in the Granville district Corbin had fought. The assembly, nevertheless, defended Corbin. When Child succeeded Corbin as Granville's agent, he hoped not only to line his own pockets but also to obtain the governorship for himself. He therefore helped instigate the assembly's petition in 1760 to have Dobbs removed from office.

Dobbs survived politically, however. While opposition to the governor continued, the provincial elite after 1760 evinced an unprecedented awareness of their stake in compromise and political stability. As had occurred in more developed colonies earlier, legislative opposition led by unscrupulous individuals evolved into a more principled ideal of institutional privilege against executive encroachment. As Dobbs complained in 1760, the assembly "think themselves entitled to all Privileges of a British House of Commons." Ironically, Dobbs maintained some political standing by cultivating the regional factionalism that he had earlier tried to eliminate. He appointed southern leaders to provincial office and, his first wife having died, cemented the alliance by marrying the fifteen-year-old daughter of one of them, Justina Davis, in 1762. When the governor added insult to injury by calling the assembly to meet at Wilmington in the far south, he so alienated northern politicians that they boycotted legislative sessions. With his southern allies, even after a debilitating stroke in 1762, Dobbs obtained passage of bills that he believed would benefit both the province and the empire, including legislation to facilitate navigation of the Cape Fear River and to provide funding for the building of churches and schools.

In 1764 Dobbs requested leave to return to the British isles for health and personal reasons, and the home government appointed William Tryon as lieutenant governor. While packing for his journey, perhaps believing that he would never return to America, Dobbs died at his home in Brunswick. Dobbs had begun to promote a more vigorous imperial role in America, but North Carolina still deviated significantly from British standards. His successor, Tryon, realized this keenly when he learned that there was no Anglican clergyman available to read the burial service for Governor Dobbs. Nevertheless, Dobbs had articulated an ideal of empire that imperial officials might have heeded in the crisis of the ensuing decade—an ideal of a diverse empire united for mutual benefit and common purpose.

• Dobbs's papers are located at the Public Record Office of Northern Ireland, Belfast. They are also available on microfilm at the Southern Historical Collection of the University of North Carolina at Chapel Hill. Dobbs's writings include *Essay on the Trade and Improvement of Ireland*, published in two parts in 1729 and 1731. He also published scientific essays in *Transactions of the Royal Society* 32 (1722–1723), 34 (1726–1727), 36 (1729–1730), 44 (1746–1747), and 46 (1749–1750), and published several essays in the debate over a northwest passage. A list of Dobbs's writings, published and in manuscript, is included as an appendix of Desmond Clarke's thorough biography, *Arthur Dobbs, Esquire, 1689–1765 . . .* (1957). Much of Dobbs's public correspondence as governor of North Carolina is in William L. Saunders, ed., *The Colonial Records of North Carolina*, vol. 5 (1887), and vol. 6 (1888). While Dobbs has often been portrayed as a stubborn proponent of the royal prerogative against a rising assembly, Roger A. Ekirch presents a more complex view in *"Poor Carolina": Politics and Society in Colonial North Carolina, 1729–1776* (1981), placing Dobbs's political struggles in their proper socioeconomic context.

J. RUSSELL SNAPP

DOBBS, Ella Victoria (11 June 1866–13 Apr. 1952), leader in elementary education and founder of the Department of Applied Arts at the University of Missouri, Columbia, was born in Cedar Rapids, Iowa, the daughter of Edward O'Hail Dobbs, a railroad employee, and Jane Jackson Forsythe. Ella's mother, an invalid, died after a long illness when her daughter was only eight years old. Ella did not know her father well but developed a deep affection for her stepsister, who became a mother to her. A delicate child, Ella early had a desire to be a first-grade teacher. Ill health interrupted her schooling, but she supplemented her education with independent reading and extension courses.

At the age of nineteen, Dobbs began teaching with a second-grade certificate granted upon "a satisfactory examination in all the branches required by law and the regulations of the State Superintendent." It allowed her to teach for one year in a one-room rural school in Silver Ridge, Nebraska. In 1886, while teaching in Illinois, she developed tuberculosis and moved to a drier climate in Utah. She continued teaching in rural schools at Salina and Hyrum, Utah.

While teaching in Logan, Utah, Dobbs first encountered manual training, which had been introduced in the Logan Agriculture College by a teacher from St. Louis. The new study was derived from Swedish *sloyd*, a system of teaching techniques of trade for broader education. It instilled a love for work and developed habits of order, attention, and self-reliance as well as a sense of form and a high degree of manual dexterity.

By 1895, with good health restored, Dobbs left Logan to teach in Pasadena, California. There she also enrolled in Throop Polytechnic Institute to study Swedish *sloyd*. She received a diploma from the institute in 1900 and became a supervisor of handwork for grades 3 and 4 in the Los Angeles public schools. In 1902, in addition to her work in the public school system, she became a member of the faculty at Throop, where she had charge of the manual arts courses in the absence of the regular instructor, Arthur H. Chamberlain. A year later she moved to Helena, Montana, where she became supervisor of all the manual work in the public schools. Her students prepared samples of their work for an exhibit at the St. Louis World's Fair in 1904, and during the fair Dobbs spoke to the Na-

tional Education Association about her work. She became one of the first educators in the nation to correlate handwork with the conventional subjects taught in primary and elementary schools.

Always searching for ways to make education enjoyable and meaningful for boys and girls, Dobbs decided she needed more formal education, so in 1907 she enrolled in Teachers College at Columbia University in New York City. After receiving her bachelor of science degree in 1909, she became an instructor in the manual arts department at the School of Education, University of Missouri, Columbia. There she developed design courses and taught applied design and art metal work. In 1913, after further study, she received her M.A. degree from the University of Missouri.

Dobbs organized the applied arts department at the University of Missouri in 1924 and served as its first chairwoman. Six years later she became associate professor of applied arts and full professor the following year. During her years at the university she published four books on handwork for children, the first works to be published on this subject. These included *Primary Handwork* (1914), *Illustrative Handwork for Elementary School Subjects* (1917), *First Steps in Art and Handwork* (1932), and *First Steps in Weaving* (1938). She dedicated her 1932 book to "little children everywhere with the hope that each day they may find beauty and happiness more closely linked together in the common affairs of life." She believed handwork could be used to illustrate various topics of interest to children.

Dobbs helped found the National Council for Primary Education and served as its first chairwoman from 1915 to 1925. She also edited the council's bulletin during most of those years. Later the council was renamed the Association of Childhood Education International.

A leader in many educational and civic organizations, she helped found the Pi Lambda Theta honorary society of education in 1910, served as its national president from 1921 to 1925, and edited the *Pi Lambda Theta Journal* from 1921 to 1933. Pi Lambda Theta established a scholarship in her honor in 1923. Dobbs was elected president of the Missouri State Teachers Association in 1924, the second woman to hold that office.

An active member of the Equal Suffrage Association of Missouri, Dobbs often spoke on the subject of woman suffrage. When the League of Women Voters organized a Columbia branch in 1920, she served as one of the first local presidents (1923–1924) and as state education chairman of the Columbia branch (1920–1931). She also held offices in the state and national organizations. Her name appears with the names of fifty-five other women on a plaque in the state capitol commemorating pioneer efforts in the Equal Suffrage Movement.

Dobbs also held offices in the American Association of University Women, the Missouri Federation of Women's Clubs, the Columbia Tuesday Club, and Delta Kappa Gamma, an honorary educational organization in which she served as parliamentarian for the national, state, and local groups from 1933 to 1936.

In her spare time, Dobbs worked with various materials, including wood, metal, clay, textiles, leather, paper, reed, cardboard, and raffia. Ceramics became a favorite medium during the later part of her teaching career.

In 1936 Dobbs was named professor emeritus of applied arts. She died in Macon, Missouri.

• Dobbs's papers are located in the Western Historical Manuscripts Collection, University of Missouri-Columbia. The major biography of Dobbs is Verna M. Wulfekammer, *Ella Victoria Dobbs: A Portrait Biography* (1961). Short biographies are Dorothy J. Caldwell, "Ella Victoria Dobbs," in *Show Me Missouri Women: Selected Biographies*, ed. Mary K. Dains (1989), and Caldwell, "Missouri Women in History: Ella Victoria Dobbs," *Missouri Historical Review* 67 (Apr. 1973): inside back cover. An obituary is in the *Columbia Missourian*, 14 Apr. 1952.

MARY K. DAINS

DOBIE, Gilmour (21 Jan. 1879–23 Dec. 1948), college football player and coach, was born in Hastings, Minnesota, the son of Robert Dobie, a well driller, and Ellen Black. Dobie first played football in high school at Hastings as a 150-pound end and halfback. He graduated from Hastings High School and entered the University of Minnesota at Minneapolis in 1899. After joining the Minnesota Golden Gophers football team as an end in 1899, Dobie became quarterback and led the Gophers to the Western (later Big Ten) Conference Championship in 1900. He remained at quarterback until graduating from the University of Minnesota in 1902, after which he entered the University of Minnesota Law School and began a three-year tenure as a Minnesota assistant football coach. In 1902 he also coached the South Side Minneapolis High School football team to an undefeated season and the state championship. As an assistant coach, Dobie directed the Minnesota junior varsity football team to three consecutive undefeated seasons. Dobie graduated from law school in 1904 but never worked as an attorney.

In 1906 Dobie joined North Dakota Agricultural College (now North Dakota State University) as its football coach, basketball coach, and athletic director. In his first season he directed the football team to four wins and no losses, and the subsequent season witnessed three wins and no losses. As North Dakota's first basketball coach, Dobie directed the team to eleven wins and one loss from 1906 to 1907 and six wins and four losses from 1907 to 1908. His undefeated coaching record in football at North Dakota marked the beginning of one of college football's greatest winning streaks. In 1908 Dobie became the football coach at the University of Washington in Seattle, where he maintained an undefeated record for nine consecutive seasons. From 1908 to 1916 the Huskies compiled a record of 58 wins, no losses, and three ties and outscored their opponents 1,930 to 118 points. Although many of Washington's victories came at the expense of high schools, service teams, and athletic clubs that

could not match Washington's strength and talent, it should be noted that Washington State, Oregon, and Oregon State, the Huskies' toughest rivals, altogether managed only to tie Washington once in twenty-one games. In 1917 Dobie resigned from the University of Washington following a disagreement with President Henry Suzzalo over the role of athletics in the university.

In 1917 Dobie became the football coach at the U.S. Naval Academy in Annapolis, Maryland. He coached the Midshipmen for three years and lost only one game each season, for a record of 18 wins and three losses. Navy's defeat of West Point by the score of 6–0 in 1919—the Midshipmen's first triumph over Army since 1912—marked Dobie's greatest moment as Navy's coach. Despite his fortune, Dobie decided against renewing his contract, citing that there were "too many admirals trying to run football at Navy, who should be at sea." While at the Naval Academy, Dobie married Eva M. Butler in 1918.

After coaching football at the Naval Academy, Dobie joined Cornell University in Ithaca, New York. From 1920 to 1923 he led Cornell to a 26-game winning streak. In 1922 Cornell captured the national championship, led by the outstanding offensive backfield performances of George Pfann, Eddie Kaw, Floyd Ramsey, and Charles Cassidy. Dobie's football fortunes declined after 1924, and he resigned from Cornell in 1936. The death of his wife in an automobile accident in 1927 further marred this bleak period in his life. Dobie, an original member of the American Football Coaches Association, served as the organization's president in 1928. In sixteen years at Cornell, Dobie won 82, lost 36, and tied seven games.

In 1936 Dobie became the head football coach at Boston College and built the Eagles into a national football power. In his brief two-year tenure at Boston College, Dobie recorded 16 wins, six losses, and five ties. His most memorable moments at Boston College came with a 13–12 upset of Holy Cross in 1936 and a 26–26 tie with Temple in 1938. Dobie's influence on Boston College persisted beyond his retirement in 1938, as many of his former players comprised the Eagles squad that enjoyed an undefeated season in 1940, capped by a 19–13 triumph over the University of Tennessee in the Sugar Bowl. Dobie died from injuries sustained in an automobile accident in Hartford, Connecticut.

Dobie, who compiled a career record of 180 wins, 45 losses, and 15 ties, for a .781 winning percentage, ranks as one of the most successful football coaches of the twentieth century. While at the University of Washington, sportswriters nicknamed him "Gloomy Gil" because he always predicted that his teams were unconditioned and ill prepared, and that they would lose. He was elected posthumously to the College Football Hall of Fame in 1951.

• Information on Dobie is in biographical files located at the Boston College Sports Information Office, the Cornell University Sports Publicity Office, the North Dakota State University Sports Information Office, the U.S. Naval Academy Athletic Association, the University of Minnesota Archives, and the University of Washington Sports Information Office. See also Edwin Pope, *Football's Greatest Coaches* (1956), and John D. McCallum and Charles H. Pearson, *College Football U.S.A. 1869–1973* (1973). An obituary is in the *Ithaca (N.Y.) Journal*, 24 Dec. 1948.

ADAM R. HORNBUCKLE

DOBIE, James Frank (26 Sept. 1888–18 Sept. 1964), writer, folklorist, and educator, was born on his family's 7,000-acre ranch in Live Oak County, Texas, the son of Jonathan Richard "R. J." Dobie and Ella Byler. He preferred his mother's infectious love of standard eighteenth- and nineteenth-century books to his father's habit of reading the Bible and singing Methodist hymns. He grew up rigidly moral, attended ranch schools, and lived with his grandparents in Alice, Texas, to go to high school there (1904–1906). After earning a B.A. in 1910 at Southwestern University in Georgetown, Texas, he worked briefly for the *San Antonio Express*, then taught high-school classes at Alpine, Texas (1910–1911), was a reporter for the *Galveston Tribune* (1911), and taught and was the president's secretary at Southwestern (1911–1913). He obtained an M.A. at Columbia University (1913–1914), livening his routine there by frequenting bookstores and attending plays, and returned to his home state to resume his teaching career at the University of Texas at Austin.

In 1916 Dobie married Bertha McKee, whom he had known at Southwestern. They had no children. He also became a member of the Texas Folklore Society. He joined a U.S. Army artillery unit (1917), went overseas but saw no action, and was mustered out as a first lieutenant in 1919. He taught again at the university but resigned to help an uncle manage his Texas ranch (1920–1921). While there, he listened to campfire and bunkhouse yarns, often related by a vaquero named Santos Cortez, and decided to transmute them—and allied folktales and historical data—into what became his unique brand of writing. He returned to teaching in 1921 and became secretary-editor of the Folklore Society (1922–1943). He felt held back by his lack of a Ph.D., writing a dissertation for which he called "transferring bones from one graveyard to another." After chairing the English department at Oklahoma Agriculture and Mining College (1923–1925, now Oklahoma State University), he returned to Austin with a promotion, published voluminously in journals, and was appointed full professor (1928). Dobie collaborated with a cowboy named John Young to tell his story, in *A Vaquero of the Brush Country* (1929). Also in 1929 he initiated "Life and Literature of the Southwest," one of the most influential courses in American academic history. Out of it came his *Guide to Life and Literature of the Southwest* (1943; rev. ed., 1952).

For the rest of his life Dobie combined teaching, collecting written and oral material, writing, public appearances, and convivially hunting. He was aided at every turn by his feisty wife. Monetary success came with his *Coronado's Children* (1930), which won the Literary Guild Award a year later. Expanding on earlier essays—always his habit—it fictionalizes legends concerning the cities of Cíbola, the San Saba and Padre mines, Guadalupe and the Wichitas, and much else. Four books followed, all in his characteristically tangy prose: *On the Open Range* (1931), *Tongues of the Monte* (1935, New Mexican legends in picaresque form; reissued as *The Mexico I Like* in 1942), *Tales of the Mustang* (1936), and *The Flavor of Texas* (1936). Then came his masterpiece, *Apache Gold and Yaqui Silver* (1939), stories about gold and silver mines in the Southwest left hidden from record when natives drove out the greedy Spaniards. Beginning in 1939 and continuing until the year he died, he wrote Sunday columns for ten or so Texas newspapers, ultimately totaling more than 1,200 items. He was also prolific in writing for regional and national magazines, ultimately amassing a total of more than 500 such publications. He also contributed pieces to well over a hundred books by others.

Dobie wrote four books on aspects of Texas natural history. The first was *The Longhorns* (1941), a superb record in many genres of the descendants of the noble cattle that Spanish explorers brought to the Southwest. The other three are *The Voice of the Coyote* (1949), combining folklore, history, and science; *The Mustangs* (1952), describing how those tameless, fleet horses spread over a vast region, influenced human life, had their heyday, and declined to a marginal existence; and *Rattlesnakes* (posthumously published in 1965), blending observation, speculation, legends, and fanciful gossip relating to one of nature's most feared creatures.

Two years after *The Longhorns* was published, Dobie enjoyed a momentous adventure. He was invited to lecture on American history at Cambridge University in England (1943–1944), where his professional modesty and articulate charm made him an enormous success. He wrote about his varied experiences in *A Texan in England* (1944). Trouble began soon after his return to Texas. Always abrasively liberal, Dobie disturbed conservative Texans by being prolabor and pro–African American, labeling two governors incompetent and Davy Crockett ignorant, and saying that a revered Alamo monument resembled a grain elevator. The university administrators and regents objected to his public statements as well as to his four-year leave of absence—extended so he could lecture in England and on the Continent under U.S. Army auspices (1945–1946) and then return to do research back home. He was dismissed in a much-publicized case in 1947. At this time he was called a communist for supporting Henry Wallace's candidacy for president. Later in the 1940s and in the early 1950s Dobie lashed out against administrators, regents, and rich alumni of the University of Texas for supporting Senator Joseph McCarthy, whom he regarded as a pseudo-patriotic scoundrel.

The Ben Lilly Legend (1950) weaves together facts and fables about a professional southwestern bear-and-lion hunter of legendary prowess; through it all runs a thread of nostalgia because this footloose folk hero represents a way of life long gone. Then came lesser collections—some for juvenile readers—of more narratives, reports, and legends about Texas, its cowboys, and their cattle, culminating in *Cow People* (1964). Work on these books was less efficient because Dobie developed a heart condition in 1957 and had a serious automobile accident five years later. Though ill, he visited his old friend President Lyndon B. Johnson in the White House in April 1964 but had to let his wife accept the Presidential Medal of Freedom from the president that September. He happily fondled an advance copy of *Cow People* on the day he died at "Paisano," his home near Austin.

J. Frank Dobie regarded as peers his friends folklorist Stith Thompson; writer-artist Tom Lea; historian Walter Prescott Webb; literary critics Joe B. Frantz, Jay Hubbell, and Henry Nash Smith; naturalist Roy Bedichek; and many other distinguished persons. They in turn regarded Dobie as a folklorist and historian of aspects of Texas and the Southwest without equal. His nicknames included "Professor Pancho" and "Mr. Texas." The symbol he chose for himself was the roadrunner.

• The main collection of Dobie's papers, library, and western art objects is in the Harry Huntt Ransom Humanities Research Center at the University of Texas. Lesser collections of Dobie material and Dobieana are at Texas A&M University, in the Cody Memorial Library at Southwestern University, and at Baylor University. Bibliographies are Mary Louise McVicker, *The Writings of J. Frank Dobie: A Bibliography* (1968); Spruill Cook, *J. Frank Dobie: Bibliography* (1968); and Jeff Dykes, *My Dobie Collection* (1971). Bertha Dobie, "Dobie's Sunday Pieces," *Southwest Review* 50 (Spring 1965): 114–19, concerns the bulk of her husband's weekly newspaper columns. A partial autobiography is *Some Part of Myself*, ed. Bertha McKee Dobie (1967). John Graves, "The Old Guard: Dobie, Webb, and Bedichek," in *The Texas Literary Tradition*, ed. Don Graham et al. (1983), pp. 16–25, places Dobie in context. Biographical studies include Ronnie Dugger, ed., *Three Men in Texas* (1967), reprinting the Dobie memorial issue of the 24 July 1964 *Texas Observer*; Winston Bode, *A Portrait of Pancho; the Life of a Great Texan: J. Frank Dobie* (1965, largely illustrations; repr. 1968, as *J. Frank Dobie: A Portrait of Pancho*); Francis Edward Abernethy, *J. Frank Dobie* (1967); Ralph W. Yarborough, *J. Frank Dobie: Man and Friend* (1967); and Lon Tinkle's thorough *An American Original: The Life of J. Frank Dobie* (1978). The *New York Times* published an extended obituary, 19 Sept. 1964.

ROBERT L. GALE

DOBSON, Thomas (1751–9 Mar. 1823), bookseller, printer, and publisher of the first comprehensive encyclopedia produced in the United States, was born probably near Edinburgh, Scotland. His family and early professional backgrounds are unknown, but by 1777, when he married Jean Paton of New North Parish, he could claim to be a member of the Edinburgh bookselling fraternity. Three daughters were born in

Scotland, and a son, Judah, who later became a full partner in the firm of Thomas Dobson and Son, was born in Philadelphia around 1792.

Dobson emigrated to America in the spring of 1784, settling permanently in Philadelphia. In February 1785 he opened a bookstore in Front Street and soon became one of the leading dealers of medical, professional, and scientific books in the United States. By early January 1788 he had relocated to "No. 41, south Second street, at the Stone House," an address he was to make famous with his American editions of recent British publications, including the first American edition of Adam Smith's *Wealth of Nations* (1789). Following the model of booksellers in Edinburgh, he cultivated close relationships with local learned societies and the faculty of the University of Pennsylvania, thereby establishing the clientele, capital, and credit he would require to see him through his most ambitious publishing venture.

Dobson began to gather subscribers for his American edition of the third edition of the *Encyclopaedia Britannica*, which had recently commenced publication in Edinburgh, on 31 March 1789. No book approaching the magnitude of this one, which was originally advertised as fifteen quarto volumes, had previously been published in the United States, and many potential patrons were at first skeptical of its chances of success. By December 1789, however, Dobson had collected enough signatures to begin printing and soon found himself able to double the number of impressions from 1,000 to 2,000. The first volume was ready for distribution on 18 June 1790, and the entire work, now numbering eighteen volumes, was finished almost eight years later, on 19 May 1798. A *Supplement* extending the work to twenty-one volumes, one more than the British original, was advertised as completed on 2 June 1803. Each volume contained between 700 and 800 pages, and the full set was illustrated by 595 copperplates. All the paper was manufactured in Pennsylvania, and all the engravings were executed by American artists; the type was cast in Philadelphia, although a fire on 8 September 1793 nearly destroyed Dobson's printing office and forced him to use imported fonts for some of the middle volumes. His commitment to American manufacturing was a critical ingredient in his campaign for subscribers, for it provided reluctant Americans, long accustomed to identifying quality workmanship with Europe, with a patriotic rationale for investing in his rather than in the British publication.

Though dependent on the text of the Edinburgh edition, Dobson's *Encyclopaedia*, as it was popularly known, was not merely a reprint like the British books republished in Dublin at the end of the eighteenth century. Important articles on America and New England were revised or newly written by Jedidiah Morse, who in addition provided new biographies for the *Supplement*. Addenda by John Ewing, Jasper Yeates, Samuel Miller, David Hosack, and David Rittenhouse, among other American notables, also helped to make the book an important if underrated contribution to

American intellectual and cultural history. Although new material accounted for a relatively small percentage of the text, enough was added to stamp the work unmistakably with the Federalist ideology of the period, a political philosophy that Dobson seems to have embraced.

Besides being a publisher and printer, Dobson was the author of several books for children and a number of works on religion that argued for the universal salvation of humankind and the necessity of free inquiry into religious matters. The most important of these is probably *Letters on the Existence and Character of the Deity, and on the Moral State of Man* (1799), to which Dobson added a second part (1802) and then a second volume (1804) in an attempt to explain views that may best be described as broadly Unitarian and Universalist in outlook, though idiosyncratic on certain points. His role as a publisher of Unitarian texts, including works by the English refugee Joseph Priestley, is on the whole of more significance to the history of that religion in the United States than are his own compositions.

Dobson's prominence as a publisher had already begun to fade before the final volume of the *Supplement* was published, in part because the *Encyclopaedia* seriously drained his resources. As many as 896 sets of the *Supplement*, for example, or almost half the total number, remained unsold when he went out of business in 1821, and a substantial number of subscribers who had received their volumes probably also remained permanently delinquent. In addition, Dobson speculated in copper during the War of 1812 and shortly afterward, again most likely with large losses. Yet he continued to publish, achieving in 1814 another landmark with the first Hebrew Bible published in the United States. It was to be his last work of national importance.

On 1 February 1817 Dobson took his son Judah into a short-lived partnership in the bookselling business. Early in 1818 his wife of more than forty years died, and Dobson himself soon suffered the first of several apparent strokes that eventually left him without the power of speech. Deteriorating economic conditions in the United States between 1817 and 1821 accelerated his financial decline, and finally, on 14 May 1821, the firm of Thomas Dobson and Son was forced to declare insolvency, assigning all its assets for the benefit of creditors. Dobson died in Philadelphia. Although he had by that time almost totally forgotten, he merits recognition for his early leadership in transforming American publishing from a provincial cottage industry into a self-consciously nationalistic and commercially competitive enterprise that in turn prepared the way for still more revolutionary transformations in printing, publishing, and book distribution in the nineteenth century.

• The few surviving papers of Thomas Dobson, consisting mostly of receipts and correspondence, are located at the Historical Society of Pennsylvania, with additional letters at the Boston Public Library, Massachusetts Historical Society,

and Yale University (Morse Family Papers). In addition to works mentioned in the entry, books written by Dobson include *First Lessons for Children, The Holiday, or Children's Social Amusement,* and *Pleasing Instructions for Young Minds* (all 1797); *Index to the Bible* (1804); *Thoughts on the Scripture Account of Faith in Jesus, and Life through His Name* (1807); and *Thoughts on Mankind, Considered as Individuals, Originally Created Upright; Their State under Discipline, Rendered Needful by Their Disobedience; and Their Recovery by Jesus Christ* (1811). For a comprehensive discussion of Dobson's career, including volume-by-volume details of the publication of the *Encyclopaedia,* see Robert D. Arner, *'Dobson's Encyclopaedia': The Publisher, Text, and Publication of America's First 'Britannica,' 1789–1803* (1991). The same author also discusses another of Dobson's major business investments in "Thomas Dobson's Rolling Mill for Copper: A Note on the Publisher of the *Encyclopaedia,*" *Pennsylvania Magazine of History and Biography* (Jan.–Apr. 1994): 117–36. Additional details about Dobson not included in either of the above studies is in Arner, "Thomas Dobson's American Edition of the *Encyclopaedia Britannica,*" in *Notable Encyclopedias of the Late Eighteenth Century: Eleven Successors of the "Encyclopédie",* ed. Frank A. Kafker (1994), pp. 201–54. A contemporary eulogy of Dobson, one that, somewhat oddly, scarcely mentions his publishing or printing, is "The Death of Thomas Dobson," *New England Galaxy and Masonic Magazine,* 28 Mar. 1823, p. 4.

ROBERT D. ARNER

DOBZHANSKY, Theodosius (25 Jan. 1900–18 Dec. 1975), biologist, was born in Nemirov, Russia, the son of Grigory Dobzhansky, a mathematics teacher, and Sophia Voinarsky. On completing secondary school in 1917, he entered the University of Kiev in the fall, just as the Bolshevik revolution was beginning. Despite the political turmoil, he graduated from the university in 1921 with a degree in biology. He remained to teach at Kiev until 1924, when he took a position as lecturer in genetics at the University of Leningrad under the new department head, Yuri Filipchenko. In Leningrad, Filipchenko introduced Dobzhansky to the new and exciting work on genetics in the fruit fly *Drosophila melanogaster,* which was centered in the laboratory of Thomas Hunt Morgan and his group at Columbia University in New York. Filipchenko set up his own genetics laboratory, where Dobzhansky carried out his first genetic studies on what was known as the pleiotropic, or multiple, effects of individual genes. In 1924 he married Natalia "Natasha" Sivertzeva, an accomplished biologist who was then working with the renowned evolutionary biologist Ivan I. Schmalhausen. The Dobzhanskys had one daughter, Sophie Dobzhansky Coe, who became an anthropologist at Yale University.

In 1927 Dobzhansky applied for and was awarded a fellowship from the International Education Board of the Rockefeller Foundation, allowing him to spend two years in Morgan's laboratory. Although he found the physical conditions of the small "fly room" cramped and dirty, the dedication to research and the enthusiasm of the group was stimulating. When Morgan moved his laboratory to the California Institute of Technology in 1928, Dobzhansky followed and a year later was appointed assistant professor of genetics at Caltech; he was promoted to professor in 1936. In 1940 Dobzhansky returned to Columbia University as professor of zoology, a position he held until he moved to the Rockefeller Institute (now Rockefeller University) in New York in 1962. After reaching emeritus status at Rockefeller in 1970, he accepted an appointment as adjunct professor of biology at the University of California, Davis, where he remained until his death (in Davis) from the long-term effects of lymphatic leukemia.

Dobzhansky was an energetic researcher and a lucid and prolific writer, authoring over a dozen books and hundreds of journal articles. The subjects ranged from technical papers on field and laboratory studies in genetics and evolutionary theory to broadly philosophical monographs dealing with science and religion, eugenics, and human perfectibility. Though primarily a laboratory geneticist, Dobzhansky brought from Russia to the United States a background and experience in field natural history that was rare among American geneticists. His major accomplishment over the years was to apply the methods of the Morgan laboratory, namely cytogenetics (the detailed microscopic study of chromosome structure) to the study of evolution in natural populations. Much of this work was contained in a series of thirty-nine articles published between 1938 and 1968, all having the primary title, "The Genetics of Natural Populations." These articles, along with Dobzhansky's 1937 book, *Genetics and the Origin of Species*, became major cornerstones in the synthesis of genetics and evolutionary theory in the 1940s and 1950s (the so-called "evolutionary synthesis").

One of the unresolved issues raised by Darwinian theory during the first decades of the twentieth century was the origin and extent of the variations on which natural selection could act. Although Mendelian genetics had made major gains in the period between 1910 and 1930, both geneticists and evolutionary biologists were skeptical about how much light laboratory genetics could throw on the mechanism of evolution in nature. Many evolutionists did not believe that the types of mutations geneticists studied, such as a change from red to white eye color in *Drosophila*, were the sort of "slight individual differences" on which Darwin's theory was based. In *Genetics and the Origin of Species*, Dobzhansky surveyed the research literature and used his own studies to show clearly that mutations of the sort encountered in *Drosophila* and other laboratory species were exactly the sorts of variations in which selection could and did act, thus demonstrating that Mendelian genetics provided the missing evidence regarding variation needed to complete the Darwinian theory.

At the same time, both geneticists and evolutionists maintained that mutations occurred only rarely and would generally be deleterious because they upset the delicate and finely tuned genic balance that natural selection had produced in the species over thousands of generations. This view led to the conclusion that natural populations would be expected to contain very little variation, thus making the evolutionary process so slow that it could not be studied experimentally or quantitatively in an individual's lifetime.

In the early 1930s the work of R. A. Fisher and J. B. S. Haldane in England and Sewall Wright in the United States had taken the first steps toward uniting Mendelian and Darwinian theory by applying the principles of genetics not to individual organisms but to whole populations. Fisher, Wright, and Haldane showed independently that it was possible to treat evolution quantitatively as a change in gene frequencies within a population over time. With mathematical models, they were able to test theories about how various factors such as intensity of selection, population size, or breeding patterns could affect the frequency of given genes in successive generations. While mathematical modeling opened up a whole new approach to the study of evolution and was a major stepping stone to the synthesis of evolution and genetics, it was largely theoretical. The extent to which the modeling applied to populations in the wild depended in part on how much variation actually existed in natural populations. Dobzhansky set out to investigate this question in the mid-1930s.

One of the problems with studying variability in a natural population is that most variation is "cryptic"— that is, it is present in the form of recessive genes, which do not show their effects if their dominant counterparts are present. Because it would take hundreds of random breeding experiments to begin to uncover such variations at the genetic level, Dobzhansky sought another method. Using cytogenetics, Dobzhansky began a long-term collaboration with Alfred H. Sturtevant in Morgan's laboratory to record inversions of chromosome segments (segments that have become detached from the chromosomes and reinserted upside down) in natural populations of the fruit fly *Drosophila pseudoobscura* collected from different geographic locations throughout the West and Southwest. Dobzhansky's work showed that a large variety of chromosomal inversions existed in nature and that each population had its own frequency of each inversion type. Moreover, these frequencies often varied seasonally within any given population, suggesting that selection could act rapidly in response to changing environmental conditions. Although he did not know at the time in what ways the chromosome inversions might be affecting various traits in the fly populations, he assumed their effects were heritable and that different arrangement types were adaptive under different conditions. In the early 1940s Dobzhansky began another fruitful collaboration, this time with Wright, who used his mathematical skills to devise models of selection that Dobzhansky could then test in the field. What the work of Fisher, Wright, and Haldane had originally lacked, Dobzhansky could now provide: strong empirical field work as support for the union of genetic and evolutionary theory. Dobzhansky's work contributed significantly to the view that populations were not composed of largely uniform "types" but could be understood best as groups showing definable ranges of variation at the genetic level. These conclusions greatly stimulated other architects of the evolutionary synthesis, including Ernst Mayr (systematics), George Gaylord Simpson (paleontology), and G. Ledyard Stebbins (botany), each of whom applied Dobzhansky's approach to their own fields.

Dobzhansky was also interested in problems at the interface between biology and the social sciences and humanities. Provoked by the bigotry surrounding issues of race in the early decades of the century, he authored a number of papers on the biological basis of race and one book on the subject, *Heredity, Race and Society* (1946), with his close friend and Columbia colleague for many years, L. C. Dunn. Dunn and Dobzhansky argued that, contrary to eugenical claims, there was no evidence that social or personality traits are genetic in origin or that any racial group displays more of such traits than any other. On these grounds they strongly criticized interwar American and British eugenics and, after 1933, Nazi race hygiene. In the 1940s and 1950s Dobzhansky also vigorously opposed the theories of Russian agronomist T. D. Lysenko, who revived earlier theories of the inheritance of acquired characteristics as the basis for Soviet agricultural breeding. Also concerned with the role of religion in human life, Dobzhansky authored several papers on the evolutionary foundation of religious belief. Because he thought that evolutionary theory addressed both old philosophical and moral issues as well as raised new ones of its own, in his book *The Biology of Ultimate Concern* (1967), he particularly criticized the antievolutionary views of Pope Pius XII along with those of Protestant fundamentalists.

During his lifetime Dobzhansky received many honors and awards, including the presidencies of the Genetics Society of America (1941), the American Society of Naturalists (1950), the Society for the Study of Evolution (1951), and the American Society of Zoologists (1953). He was also a member of the National Academy of Sciences (U.S.), the American Philosophical Society, the American Academy of Arts and Sciences, and the Academia Nazionale die Lincei (Italy). Dobzhansky received honorary degrees from some twenty universities in Europe and the United States. He received both the Daniel Giraud Elliot Medal (1940) and the Kimber Genetics Award (1958) from the U.S. National Academy of Sciences, the Darwin Medal from the Academia Leopoldina (1959), the A. E. Verrill Medal from Yale University (1966), and the Gold Medal Award for Distinguished Achievement in Science from the American Museum of Natural History (1969). He also received the National Medal of Science from President Lyndon B. Johnson in 1964.

• Dobzhansky's personal papers, including copies of many letters and manuscripts from his Russian days, are in the library of the American Philosophical Society, Philadelphia. An extensive interview, both on tape and in transcript form, is contained in the archives of the Columbia University Oral History Project, New York. Dobzhansky's most important published scientific papers, the Genetics of Natural Populations series, was reprinted by Columbia University Press in 1981 with extensive introductions by population geneticists Richard Lewontin and Bruce Wallace and historian William Provine. Among his most important books that have not already been mentioned are *The Biological Basis of Human Freedom* (1956), *Mankind Evolving* (1962), and *Genetics of the Evolutionary Process* (1970). Dobzhansky's work with Sewall Wright is discussed at length in Provine, *Sewall Wright and Evolutionary Biology* (1986). Mark B. Adams, ed., *The Evolution of Theodosius Dobzhansky: Essays on His Life and Thought in Russia and America* (1964), contains discussions about many aspects of Dobzhansky's career, especially his early field and genetic studies in the USSR. Particularly appreciative and extensive biographical memoirs are by Francisco Ayala in *Journal of Heredity* 68 (1977): 3–10, and by Howard Levene et al., in *Essays in Evolution and Genetics in Honor of Theodosius Dobzhansky*, ed. William Steere (1970). An obituary, by Ayala, is in National Academy of Sciences, *Biographical Memoirs* 55 (1985): 163–213.

GARLAND ALLEN

DOCHEZ, Alphonse Raymond (21 Apr. 1882–30 June 1964), bacteriologist and internist, was born in San Francisco, California, the son of Louis Dochez and Josephine Dietrich. No record of Dochez's early life exists until his mother moved to Indianapolis, Indiana, where he received his early education. Subsequently the family moved again to Harford County, Maryland, where they lived with Dochez's mother's family on their farm. Dochez continued his education by commuting to Baltimore and attending Johns Hopkins University, receiving his bachelor's degree in 1903. Following the recommendation of his uncle, Dochez went on to study medicine and earned his M.D. from Johns Hopkins Medical School in 1907. The year after graduation, he worked in the pathology laboratory at Johns Hopkins Hospital, studying the effect of an iodine-free diet on animals.

When Dochez heard of the new Rockefeller Institute, he traveled to New York City and applied to director Simon Flexner for a position. Flexner hired him; his first position at the Rockefeller Institute was working with Eugene L. Opie. Their two-year collaboration resulted in the publication of four papers on the activation of trypsin and other enzymes.

The Rockefeller Hospital, officially opened on 10 October 1910, was a novel institution—a research hospital organized for the clinical study of diseases. It was to be staffed by young physicians who were given time and materials for intensive clinical research. When the hospital opened, Rufus Cole, its first director, gave Dochez a position as a bacteriologist. Having little training in bacteriology, Dochez asked Hideyo Noguchi whether he could learn to be a bacteriologist in three weeks. Despite Noguchi's doubts, Dochez assumed this clinical position and remained at the hospital for five years as an intern and then as resident.

Rufus Cole had chosen lobar pneumonia for his field of investigation, and Dochez became a major contributor to the progress of this work. In 1913 he published on the classification of the types of pneumococci that caused lobar pneumonia. Later in 1917, with Ostwald T. Avery, Dochez discovered the substance that conferred specificity to type-specific pneumococci. This finding led to an explanation of why earlier serums used to treat pneumonia had failed.

With specific serums, Dochez and Avery were able to precipitate a specific soluble substance; they found that it originated from the capsule of the pneumococcus. In further studies they demonstrated that this substance was frequently detectable in the blood and urine of patients in the acute stages of pneumonia. Dochez and Cole also demonstrated the importance of type-specific serum in the treatment of pneumonia, work that eventually resulted in the development of a type-specific anti-pneumococcus horse serum useful in the treatment of type I pneumonia. Later, the horse serum and a type-specific serum produced in rabbits—especially the purified globulins from rabbit antisera—were the only effective treatments of lobar pneumonia until the introduction of the sulfa drugs and penicillin.

Dochez's work was of great importance in understanding infectious diseases and their treatment. Not only were his specific discoveries important; his careful and systematic use of the bacteriological and chemical laboratories served as an example for future investigators.

During World War I Dochez served as a major in the Army Medical Corps in 1918–1919 and continued his studies on respiratory diseases. On discharge from the service, he returned in 1919 to Johns Hopkins Medical School as associate professor of medicine. At this time he began studies on the relationship of streptococcus to scarlet fever. In 1921 he was appointed professor of medicine at the College of Physicians and Surgeons of Columbia University, where he continued his work on streptococcal infections. The important result of this work was Dochez's demonstration of the direct relationship of scarlet fever to streptococcal pharyngitis ("strep throat"). Dochez also demonstrated that the streptococci isolated from cases of scarlet fever all belonged to a single strain. His work on streptococcal diseases was terminated when the patent rights for the streptococcal serum were awarded to Gladys H. Dick and George F. Dick of Evanston, Illinois. Although Dochez had obtained a British patent for the serum before the Dicks, his American patent for the type-specific anti-pneumococcus serum was of a later date. This was the basis for the decision that Dochez had infringed on the Dicks' patent. Dochez then shifted his interest to studies of upper respiratory infections, centering mainly on the cause of the common cold. This work led to the demonstration that the common cold could be caused by a filterable virus.

After 1930 Dochez's time became increasingly taken up with administration. He became a member of the National Academy of Sciences in 1933. In 1940 he was appointed chair of bacteriology at the College of Physicians and Surgeons of Columbia University; he remained in that post for nine years. Dochez, who never married, retired in 1949 with the title of John E. Borne Emeritus Professor of Medical and Surgical Research

and continued studying medical problems until his death in New York City. In his last years, he was interested in studies of the etiology of cancer.

During World War II Dochez was an active member of the Office of Scientific Research and Development and a member of the Board for Coordination of Malarial Studies, the Board for the Control of Influenza and Epidemic Diseases, and the Hoover Commission on the reorganization of the executive branch of the government. For these services to his country from 1942 to 1945 he was awarded the Medal of Merit. For his contribution to medicine and science he was awarded the Kober Medal of the New York Academy of Medicine.

• A detailed biography of Dochez is Michael Heidelberger et al., National Academy of Sciences, *Biographical Memoirs* 42 (1971): 30–46. On Dochez's work with Avery at the Rockefeller Institute see Rene J. Dubos, *The Professor, the Institute, and DNA* (1976), and George Washington Corner, *A History of the Rockefeller Institute, 1901–1953* (1964). An obituary is in the *New York Times*, 1 July 1964.

DAVID Y. COOPER

DOCK, George (1 Apr. 1860–30 May 1951), physician and educator, was born in Hopewell, Pennsylvania, the son of Gilliard Dock, the owner of a machine shop and then a superintendent of a coal mine, and Lavinia Lloyd Bombaugh. Dock was classically educated in preparatory school, and later he often corrected his students' Latin as well as their English. He graduated in 1884 from the University of Pennsylvania's three-year medical course at the time when "men got the title of doctor of medicine with many elaborations in Latin, without having to handle a sick man" (Davenport, 1987).

Dock taught himself physical diagnosis and interned (1884–1885) in a Philadelphia Catholic hospital whose German nuns taught him conversational German in preparation for an eighteen-month trip to Austria and Germany. Dock studied under Ehrlich, Virchow, Waldeyer, and Weigert, and he learned German medical methods including conduct of a pathological examination, care of tuberculous patients, and veterinarians' methods of detecting worms. William Osler, who had become professor of clinical medicine at the University of Pennsylvania in 1884, joined John Herr Musser in establishing a clinical pathology laboratory in the university's hospital, and he summoned Dock back from Europe to run it. Later Osler said that Dock knew more about clinical laboratory procedures than anyone in the United States.

In 1888–1891 Dock was professor of pathology at the Texas Medical School in Galveston, where he attempted to prove that mosquitoes are the vector of malaria. He failed because the island swarmed with *culex*, which do not carry the malaria plasmodium, rather than with *anopheles*, which do. In 1891 Dock was recruited to be the University of Michigan's professor of internal medicine by Dean Victor Vaughan, who was assembling a notable preclinical faculty that included John Jacob Abel, Arthur R. Cushny, and J. Playfair

McMurrich, among others distinguished for research. Dock was ruefully aware that the clinical faculty had no research reputation. He began with almost nothing, but by the time he left Michigan in 1908 he had a hospital-based medical service of about 120 beds whose adult and pediatric patients were referred from all over Michigan and the surrounding states. All patients were used for teaching, and Dock's students had responsibility for them on the wards. He had a small staff that ultimately went on to responsible positions elsewhere, competent dieticians, disciplined nurses, and a good clinical pathology laboratory.

Dock left Michigan for Tulane University, ostensibly because he expected to find what he did not have at Michigan, an adequate teaching laboratory. He had alienated his Michigan colleagues and the university administration by his sharp tongue and outspoken scorn of religion. Dock left Tulane in 1910 to become dean and professor of internal medicine at Washington University in St. Louis, Missouri, a school undergoing reorganization with Abraham Flexner's advice and Carnegie Foundation money. Dock's deanship was soon terminated by quarrels with his colleagues, but he ran a large and tightly organized internal medical service. Reforms at Washington University included institution of the full-time plan in which a faculty physician abjures private practice. Although Dock's own private practice was small, he thought the full-time plan fatally limited a physician's range of experience. He resigned in 1922 to enter private practice in Pasadena, California, and he continued to practice until well past age eighty.

Dock married Laura McLemore of Galveston, Texas, in 1882 and with her had two children. The marriage ended with her death. Dock's second marriage, in 1927 to Miriam Gould, was childless.

Dock, like Osler, collected rare medical books, and he left more than 1,500 volumes to the Los Angeles County Medical Society's library. Also like Osler, he was an acute diagnostician: his identification of coronary occlusion in four living patients, confirmed at autopsy, was made in 1896, sixteen years before James B. Herrick, who gets the credit, made the same observation. Dock taught his students that a thorough physical examination will resolve most diagnostic problems, that they must make complete blood counts and examine urinary sediments in office practice, that they must diagnose tuberculosis early when it is still curable, that they must keep up with the French and German as well as with the English medical literature, and that patient care comes before fee collection. Dock carried the same message to a profession still laden with many "so-called physicians" by lecturing to many county and state medical societies. He had an encyclopedic knowledge of the manifestations of disease but, like Osler, did not do research to find their causes. He rejected Cushny's identification of atrial fibrillation as the cause of absolute irregularity of ventricular beat because Cushny had studied animals, not patients. Dock was a nineteenth-century physician and teacher at the bedside, not a twentieth-century clinical scientist in the laboratory.

• A complete list of publications by and about George Dock is available from the Los Angeles County Medical Society. A typescript of Dock's tedious and uninformative autobiography written when he was seventy-five is in the society's library. The typescript of "George Dock, Clinical Notes," 16 vols. (1899–1908), in the University of Michigan's Bentley Historical Library is a superlative source of information about Dock as a physician and teacher of medicine as well as about medicine in the period. Horace W. Davenport, *Dr. Dock: Teaching and Learning Medicine at the Turn of the Century* (1987), is a distillation of the "Clinical Notes." See also Dock's *Outlines for Case Taking as Used in the Medical Clinic of the University of Michigan* (1902). Davenport, "George Dock at Michigan, 1891–1908," in *Medical Lives and Scientific Medicine at Michigan, 1891–1969*, ed. Joel D. Howell (1993), offers biographical data. Davenport, *Fifty Years of Medicine at the University of Michigan, 1891–1941* (1986), describes the Michigan medical background in Dock's time in Ann Arbor. James R. Arneill, *Clinical Diagnosis and Urinalysis* (1905), by Dock's Michigan assistant, describes Dock's laboratory methods. The typescript of Nathan D. Munro, "George Dock, M.D.," in the *Proceedings of the Victor Vaughan Society* in the University of Michigan's Taubman Medical Library reproduces a letter to Munro from Dock's son William evaluating his father. George R. Herrmann, *Methods in Medicine: The Manual of the Medical Service of George Dock, M.D., D.Sc.* (1924), is a good account of the way Dock worked at Washington University.

HORACE W. DAVENPORT

DOCK, Lavinia Lloyd (26 Feb. 1858–17 Apr. 1956), nurse, suffragist, and social reformer, was born in Harrisburg, Pennsylvania, the daughter of Gilliard Dock and Lavinia Lloyd Bombaugh, landlords. Dock, who later came to think of herself as a feminist, received what she called an "oldfashioned and conventional" education at a local female academy. Her life was basically carefree until her mother died when Dock was eighteen, leaving her and her older sister with the responsibility of raising their four siblings.

Financially independent—she and her siblings each derived an income from land their parents had inherited—Dock was inspired by an article in *Century* magazine about the Training School for Nurses at Bellevue Hospital in New York, enrolling there in 1884 and graduating in 1886. In the spring of 1889 she helped Clara Barton aid the victims of the Johnstown, Pennsylvania, flood. She established herself as a leader in the nursing field with the publication of *Textbook for Materia Medica for Nurses* (1890); the first manual of drugs for nurses, it served as the standard nursing textbook for a generation. In 1890 Isabel Hampton, who advocated improvements in the education of nurses and standardization in nursing practices, appointed Dock assistant superintendent of nurses at the new Johns Hopkins Hospital. At the 1893 international conference on hospitals held during the World's Columbian Exposition in Chicago, Dock argued that nurses needed their own profession in order to buttress their authority within the practice of medicine. Toward that end Dock organized and became secretary of the American Society of Superintendents of Training Schools in 1893 and that same year also formed the Nurses Associated Alumnae (later the American Nurses Association), which was modeled after the American Medical Association.

In 1896 Dock joined the community of women living at Lillian Wald's Nurses Settlement on Henry Street in New York City's Lower East Side. "I never began to *think* until I went to Henry Street and lived with Miss Wald," Dock later said. There she formed what she later called "a strong sympathy with oppressed classes, a lively sense of justice and a keen love of . . . 'freedom' and 'liberty.'" For twenty years Dock worked with other public health nurses to provide preventive care and health education to poor immigrants. Their activities made these nurses the chief authorities on immigrant health and public health reform in New York City.

At the International Council of Women held in London in 1899, Dock and Ethel Gordon Fenwick, leader of British nurses, founded the International Council of Nurses, of which Dock became secretary. This organization linked nurses from around the world toward the goal of improving public health. Among nurses she was known as the editor of the "Foreign Department" of the *American Journal of Nursing*, a column through which she dispensed information on the practice and status of nursing and of public health worldwide. With Adelaide Nutting, her former student at Hopkins, Dock wrote the two-volume *History of Nursing* (1907; revised and two volumes added, 1912). She also helped to organize the National Association of Colored Graduate Nurses in 1908.

The innovative atmosphere at Henry Street led Dock to battle the sexual double standard for men and women. In *Hygiene and Morality* (1911) she opposed state regulation of prostitution and was among the first publicly to advocate the treatment of venereal disease. In 1907, however, her political allegiance began to shift from nursing to suffrage as the basis of her reform activism. That year she joined the Equality League of Self-Supporting Women (later the Women's Political Union), recently founded by American activist Harriet Stanton Blatch who based the league on the activities of British suffragists. By 1915 this shift had introduced strains in her relationship with Henry Street reformers, who, being leaders in the mainstream suffrage movement, distanced themselves from Stanton's aggressive style. The rift between Dock and her Henry Street friends never healed. In 1917 Dock moved to Washington, D.C., and became a member of Alice Paul's advisory council for the National Woman's Party. She picketed the White House and was jailed (briefly) three times that year for militant suffrage activities. Dock advocated the passage of the Equal Rights Amendment in 1921.

Dock, who became increasingly deaf in her later years, retired to her home in Fayetteville, Pennsylvania, in 1922 and was joined by her four sisters, all of whom were single. In 1947 she was honored for her achievements at the International Council of Nurses

convention. She died in a hospital in Chambersburg, Pennsylvania, after having broken a hip in a fall.

• Dock's papers can be found at the Library of Congress, the Pennsylvania State Archives at Harrisburg, the Lillian Wald Papers at Columbia University, and (available on microfilm) the New York Public Library. See also the Adelaide Nutting Papers, Teachers College, Columbia University; the Nursing History Archives, Boston University (which include valuable clippings by and about Dock from the *British Journal of Nursing*); the Leonora O'Reilly Papers at the Schlesinger Library, Radcliffe College; and oral history interviews with Isabel M. Stewart in the Oral History Collection, Columbia University, and with Alice Paul in the Bancroft Library, University of California at Berkeley. Dock's other publications include *Short Papers on Nursing Subjects* (1900) and *The History of American Red Cross Nursing* (1922). For biographical information, see her "Self-Portrait" of 1932, published in *Nursing Outlook*, Jan. 1977; Mary M. Roberts, *American Nursing: History and Interpretation* (1954); and obituaries in the *American Journal of Nursing* 57 (May 1956), and the *New York Times*, 18 Apr. 1956.

KATHRYN KISH SKLAR

DOCKSTADER, Lew (7 Aug. 1856–26 Oct. 1924), minstrel-vaudevillian, was born George Alfred Clapp in Hartford, Connecticut, the son of Chester Clapp, a bartender, and Harriet Gouge. Dockstader's aptitude for the life of a minstrel appeared during his childhood years. He could play any musical instrument he picked up, yet until he was seventeen he confined his talents to an amateur minstrel band that brought him only local fame. He made his professional debut in 1873, joining the Earl, Emmet and Wilde Minstrels; at the same time he took the professional name of Lew Dockstader. A year later he toured the country with the Whitmore and Clark Minstrels, achieving great popularity with his song "Peter, You're in Luck This Morning." (Every minstrel show was a virtual potpourri consisting of softshoe dancing, comedy routines, brisk songs, and sentimental ballads. All of them were performed by white artists made up in blackface, who played on African-American stereotypes purportedly originating in the South.)

The next several years saw Dockstader gaining both experience and popularity with several traveling companies. He formed a partnership with Charles Dockstader, who, despite his name, was not related. On his partner's death, Dockstader became the sole owner of the troupe, but the venture was not successful, and four years later he had to disband it for lack of funds. In 1885 he married Lucene Brown; they had one child.

Early in the 1890s Dockstader entered vaudeville, and in 1898 he teamed with George Primrose to form the "Primrose and Dockstader Minstrel Men," which soon became America's most famous blackface group. When the team split up in 1904, Dockstader formed "Lew Dockstader's Minstrels" with a company of forty people. Success was immediate, and Dockstader became the foremost minstrel man of his day.

The major part of Dockstader's vaudeville act was composed of blackface characterizations of major figures of the times. One of the most successful was his "singles act" in which he appeared immaculately dressed and fitted out in every detail, even to the prominent teeth, as Colonel Theodore Roosevelt in his Rough Rider uniform. His mere entrance always brought a roar of laughter and applause. But, as Dockstader grew older and heavier, he was forced to abandon blackface, and in its stead he became a monologist. He was still able to poke fun at the political favorites of the day, and he even made friends of a few of them, especially Governor Alfred E. Smith of New York. As late as 1920 the *New York Dramatic Mirror* observed: "He is the only monologist today who can skillfully touch upon the campaign candidates and do it in just the humorous satirical manner that an audience will take kindly to."

Dockstader almost single-handedly kept the spirit of the minstrel show alive in the early years of the twentieth century. His greatest coup probably came in 1908 when he discovered a young man then singing blackface on one of the minor vaudeville circuits. The singer was Al Jolson, and Dockstader was quick to recognize his talent. He hired him immediately for "Lew Dockstader's Minstrels," thus guaranteeing Jolson exposure as well as an education from the greatest of minstrel men. Individual earnings in minstrel shows were much lower than in vaudeville, but Dockstader signed Jolson for weekly salaries of $75 for the first season, $100 for the second, and $125 for the next three. The $125 figure was the same as his own. Jolson soon won a featured spot in the show, and he remained with Dockstader until 1911 when the Shubert Brothers offered him a small role in a musical to be staged in their handsome new theater, the Winter Garden. Jolson's success was immediate, and he soon rose to stardom as one of the great entertainers of his time.

Dockstader, meanwhile, continued to tour at the head of his own company, to which he had acquired sole rights some years earlier. But the minstrel show was beginning to die, as vaudeville and, later, motion pictures became more popular, and in 1913 he decided to return to vaudeville. He immediately became a headliner on the Keith-Orpheum vaudeville circuit, a role he held for another decade, and he continued to perform as he had for many years—in shoes that were two feet long and a coat with a thirty-inch tail. His best song had now become "Everybody Works But Father." In January 1923 he suffered a severe fall in New Brunswick, New Jersey, as he was returning to his hotel from a performance at Keith's Star Theater. While recuperating, he received a letter of sympathy from Governor Smith of New York, to which he replied: "If I had to fall, I wish it had been on the sidewalks of New York and not on the sidewalks of New Brunswick, New Jersey." Dockstader never fully recovered his health, and in December 1923 he was forced to give up performing. He soon became completely incapacitated. He died in New York City.

• Information on Dockstader's career, on minstrel shows, and on vaudeville in the later nineteenth and early twentieth centuries can be found in Gerald Boardman, *The Oxford Companion to the American Theatre* (1984); Herbert G. Goldman, *Jolson: The Legend Comes to Life* (1988); Dailey Paskman, *Gentlemen Be Seated: A Parade of the American Minstrels* (1976); Anthony Slide, *The Vaudevillians* (1981); Robert C. Toll, *On with the Show: The First Century of Show Business in America* (1976); and Don B. Wilmeth and Tice L. Miller, eds., *The Cambridge Guide to American Theatre* (1993). Obituaries appeared in the *New York Times*, the *Hartford Courant*, and the *New York Herald Tribune*, 27 Oct. 1924.

CHARLES W. STEIN

DODD, Bella Visono (Oct. 1904–29 Apr. 1969), teachers' union lobbyist and lawyer, was born Maria Assunta Isabella Visono in Picerno, Italy, southeast of Naples, the daughter of Rocco Visono, a grocer, and Teresa Marsica. She was raised in the nearby village of Avialano by foster parents until she was old enough to join her family in New York City at the age of five. Her family moved several times and finally out of the tenements into a large house in Westchester left to her mother by two elderly women for whom she had worked. Determined to become "an American," Bella excelled in school, rejected Catholicism, and, after World War I, avidly began reading newspapers.

Her studies were interrupted when, in 1916, a trolley car accident necessitated the amputation of her left foot. She began high school the following year and earned a state scholarship based on achievement in English, history, and science. She wrote later that her mother "made me feel I could accomplish anything I set my heart on, despite my physical limitation" (*School of Darkness*, p. 21). At Hunter College she became president of her junior class and was president of the student council during her senior year. She graduated in June 1925 with honors and became a substitute teacher of history at Seward Park High School. In 1926 she accepted an offer to teach political science at Hunter and attended the Teachers College of Columbia University, realizing the "powerful effect Teachers College could have on American education with thousands of teachers to influence national policy and social thinking" (*School of Darkness*, pp. 42–43). She received her master's degree in 1927 and enrolled in the New York University Law School. After graduating in 1930 and passing the bar exam, she took a leave of absence from Hunter and traveled through Italy and Germany, where she saw the devastating effects of fascism. She left teaching on her return to serve a clerkship with corporate lawyer Howard Hilton Spellman and in September 1931 married John Dodd, whom she had met abroad. Financial difficulties the following year forced her to resume her post at Hunter.

When the depression jeopardized the jobs of untenured teachers, Bella Dodd began her long and somewhat troubled career in activism and politics. To support New York teachers, she joined the Instructors Association and helped establish the short-lived American Association of University Teachers. In addition, she joined the Communist Anti-Fascist Literature Committee. At the time, Dodd's interests and those of the American Communist party appeared mutual: antifascist, antiwar, and a commitment to working-class rights. After helping pass a bill on college teachers' tenure, Dodd became legislative representative of the Teachers Union Local 5 in 1936 and, thus, an officer of the American Federation of Labor (AFL). As such, she joined an already active communist faction within the AFL. With the help of this faction she was chosen as delegate to the AFL Central Trades and Labor Council of New York, helping to pass two union bills, and was elected delegate to the State Federation of Labor convention. At the 1936 May Day parade, Dodd led more than 500 teachers in a march with communists. Though she lost a bid for a position in the State Federation of Labor, Dodd gained popularity. She eventually resigned from Hunter in 1938 to devote herself to the Teachers Union at a reduced salary. When in 1939 the Teachers Union was investigated by the anticommunist Rapp-Coudert Committee, Dodd organized "Friends of the Free Public Schools" to fight for communist teachers. She continued her affiliation with the Communist party, even after the Soviet-Nazi pact in 1939, believing in its support of the Teachers Union and its antiwar stance. In 1940 she led the Women's Trade Union Committee for Peace, which picketed the White House and went on the air with pro-German speakers. The same year she and her husband separated, divorcing two years later.

In March 1943 Dodd accepted an invitation from Gil Green, the New York State chairman of the Communist party to become an official member and open party leader. She withdrew from the Teachers Union a year later. By January 1944 she was legislative representative for the party's New York district, organizing legislative programs for women and youth organizations and for government workers' unions on local, state, and national levels. When the American Communist party changed its name to the less imposing Communist Political Association, Dodd was elected a member of the national committee.

With increased involvement, Dodd realized that the party's goal was not social reform for the disadvantaged but, rather, building party membership. By 1945 she expressed her disenchantment and tried to leave but was told "no one gets out; you either die or are thrown out." The party nominated her for attorney general in the 1946 state elections but later withdrew her name. False charges brought against Dodd in 1949 resulted in her expulsion from the party.

In her autobiography, *School of Darkness* (1954), Dodd wrote that her "memory of God" and habit of living by "eternal standards of truth and justice" facilitated a belief in communism, run as it was by "men who masquerade as saviors." According to reviewer R. L. Duffus in the 12 December 1954 issue of the *New York Times*, what attracted her to the movement was "sympathy for the common man and a belief that the Communists, including the small governing clique in Moscow where men dealt out life and death, really wanted to help the common man."

After renouncing communism, Dodd remained in New York City, continued to practice law and in 1952 was welcomed back into the Roman Catholic church. Between 1952 and 1957 she was subpoenaed and testified several times before the Internal Security Subcommittee of the U.S. Senate, which investigated communist activities of teachers. In 1955 she formed the law firm Dodd, Cardiello, and Blair, which represented the interests of the disadvantaged. Twice—in 1965 and 1966—she failed in attempts to be elected to the New York State Supreme Court as a conservative. In 1968, again as a conservative, she made an unsuccessful bid for a New York State congressional seat. She died in New York City.

• Dodd's papers are in the records of the New York City Teachers Union at the Kheel Center for Labor-Management Documentation and Archives at Cornell University. For correspondence see the papers of Oakley C. Johnson at the State University of New York at Stony Brook. For more information on the Teachers Union, see Celia Lewis Zitron, *The New York City Teachers Union 1916–1964: A Story of Educational and Social Commitment* (1968). Dodd's autobiography is the most detailed source for an account of her life up to 1954. For information beyond that date see obituaries in the *New York Times*, 30 Apr. 1969, and the *National Review*, 20 May 1969.

BARBARA L. CICCARELLI

DODD, Bobby (11 Nov. 1908–21 June 1988), college football coach, was born Robert Lee Dodd in Galax, Virginia, the son of Edwin Dodd, a businessman, and Susan Nuckolls. The family also lived in Bluefield, Virginia, where they owned a small furniture factory. Because the nearest high school was located in Kingsport, Tennessee, Dodd attended school there. Academics were not as important to him as were sports, and his high school football accomplishments won him a scholarship to the University of Tennessee. There his athletic ability brought Dodd his first national fame. As quarterback he led Tennessee to a 27–1–2 record between 1928 and 1930. In 1930 Dodd was named to what was then the only All-American team, a unit selected for *Collier's* magazine by the noted sportswriter Grantland Rice.

Dodd was still in his junior year at Tennessee when his football eligibility ran out. Consequently, in 1931 he accepted the post of assistant coach at Georgia Tech under Bill Alexander, and he remained in this capacity until 1944. Shortly after assuming this position, Dodd married Alice Davis; the couple would have two children. In 1945 Dodd was promoted to head coach at Georgia Tech, becoming only the third person to hold that post. Over the next twenty-two years he would create a football legend.

At Georgia Tech Dodd utilized the "T-formation" offense, which allowed for a faster, more wide-open game. He developed players who specialized in various aspects of the game, and he emphasized that playing the game should be fun. Recognizing the problems he encountered because of his own failure to finish college, Dodd strongly urged his players to complete their college degrees, despite the fact that all students at Georgia Tech were then required to take calculus. Dodd was among the first head coaches to allow assistant coaches to teach their specialties while he supervised. He also believed that practices should bring his squad up to the edge of competition while leaving them hungry for contact with the opposition. Possessing a genuine concern for his players as persons, Dodd allowed them to live personal lives as did other students; girlfriends were given a bench on the sidelines so that they could leave the field with the players after a game, and players were allowed to marry.

While the academic and humanitarian aspects of his coaching technique caused some to scorn him as "soft," Dodd's record left no room for criticism. His peers included such great football coaches as Bear Bryant of Alabama, Shug Jordan of Auburn, and Robert Neyland of Tennessee; yet Dodd was recognized by all of them as "the best on Saturday." Dodd's career record was 165–64–8, including victories in 9 of 13 postseason bowl games and a perfect 12–0 season in 1952. After the 1952 season the International News Service named Georgia Tech the national champion, while the *New York Daily News* named Dodd the "Coach of the Year." The college football coach of the year award was later named for Dodd. During his career Dodd coached 21 first team All-Americans.

Dodd's character won him admiration as much as did his skill as a coach. Called the "Gentleman Coach of College Football" and the "Gray Fox," Dodd was scrupulous in following the rules. None of his coaching or recruiting practices was ever questioned or investigated by the National Collegiate Athletic Association. Dodd said, many years after his retirement, "I stood for honesty." This character perhaps shone brightest in the 1956 Sugar Bowl in New Orleans, Louisiana. At that time many southern colleges refused to play against teams that included African-American players. Dodd and Blake Van Leer, the Georgia Tech president, were under pressure from Georgia governor Marvin Griffin and members of the university's board of regents to conform to this policy. But when offered the chance to play in the Sugar Bowl against the University of Pittsburgh and its African-American fullback Bobby Grier, Dodd firmly accepted the invitation. There was much speculation in the press as to how the Tech team would play against an African-American, but after the game ended in a 7–0 victory for Georgia Tech, Grier congratulated the Tech players, saying, "They are all fine sportsmen." Football experts noted that the Tech players had several opportunities to "gang up" on Grier but declined to do so. Dodd's coaching and attitude were evident in the behavior of his team.

Dodd had become athletic director as well as head coach in 1950. After the 1966 season he gave up his coaching duties and remained as athletic director until 1976. From 1976 until his death in Atlanta Dodd served as a consultant with the Georgia Tech National Alumni Association. In 1993 he was inducted into the National Football Foundation College Football Hall of Fame in recognition of his coaching career. A member of the Hall of Fame as a player since 1959, he became one of three people to be inducted as both player and coach.

• There is no known collection of Dodd's papers. The sports information office at Georgia Tech maintains a collection of notebooks with clippings from Dodd's years as coach. Additional materials are at the National Football Foundation Hall of Fame, South Bend, Ind. Dodd wrote an autobiography, *Dodd's Luck* (1977). See also Al Thomy, *The Ramblin' Wreck: A Story of Georgia Tech Football* (1973); and Robert B. Wallace, *Dress Her in White and Gold* (1963).

MICHAEL R. BRADLEY

DODD, Frank Howard (12 Apr. 1844–10 Jan. 1916), publisher, was born in Bloomfield, New Jersey, the son of Moses W. Dodd, a publisher, and Rachel Hoe, whose brothers manufactured high-speed newspaper presses. Dodd finished his preparatory training at Bloomfield Academy in 1859 and took a temporary position in his father's firm, M. W. Dodd Publishers, at the age of fifteen. He was to have attended Yale, but because of the Civil War he stayed on in the business instead. Dodd soon proved to have quite an aptitude for the publishing trade. He never did attend college but spent the next ten years apprenticing in every department of the firm. Moses Dodd gradually relinquished control of the business to his son, whose early successes included publishing a series of twelve classics in fine bindings when he was only nineteen and accepting Martha Finley's highly popular *Elsie Dinsmore* juvenile series, launched in 1867. In 1868 Dodd married Martha Bliss Parker, daughter of former Union Theological Seminary president Joel Parker; the couple had four children.

On Moses Dodd's retirement in 1870, Frank Dodd became head of the firm. He had been planning a reorganization, and he immediately brought in his cousin Edward S. Mead to form Dodd & Mead. (Edward S. Mead himself was a prodigious writer, turning out fiction—often under the name of Richard Markham—until his death in 1894.) Struggling at first during a period of economic depression, the reorganized publishing house had its first great success in 1872 with E. P. Roe's *Barriers Burned Away*, a historical novel based on the great Chicago fire of 1871. Roe, a minister, went on to write some twenty more fiction titles, and Dodd & Mead used *Barriers Burned Away* to launch an innovative series of cheap reprints of works still under copyright. Bleecker Van Wagenen was brought in as partner in 1876, when the company changed its name to Dodd, Mead & Co. The firm's retail activities increased dramatically when Dodd's brother Robert H. Dodd brought his expertise in rare books to the firm in 1873.

Frank Dodd expanded the house's list to include many titles of general interest. In 1899 he suggested that Paul Leicester Ford write a novel of the American Revolution, and the successful *Janice Meredith* series was born. In the late 1890s Dodd introduced the works of a number of new poets, including Robert W. Service and Paul Laurence Dunbar. The house's fiction and nonfiction list grew during Dodd's lifetime to include writers such as G. K. Chesterton, Joseph Conrad, Jerome K. Jerome, George Barr McCutcheon, Hamilton Wright Mabie, and H. G. Wells.

To publish several of these writers Dodd shared rights with British publishers. Until passage of the International Copyright Act in 1891, Dodd had arranged to publish British works through informal agreements, but in the mid-1890s he energetically began to cultivate working relationships with authors and publishers on the other side of the Atlantic.

Trips to the British Isles yielded many cooperative publishing ventures. Dodd's editor James MacArthur persuaded him to pursue American publication of Ian Maclaren's *Beside the Bonnie Briar Bush* (1894), which proved a strong seller in the United States. Maclaren (Dr. John Watson) introduced Dodd to William Robertson Nicoll, editor of the London literary journal *Bookman* and the *British Weekly*, a religious newspaper. Dodd arranged with Nicoll to bring out an American version of the *Bookman* beginning in February 1895. By design the two monthlies published a great deal of material in common, but the focus of the American version gradually shifted to American contributions, one sign of a growing national literature.

In his later years Dodd devoted much of his attention to the publication of a new American encyclopedia. In 1884 Dodd, Mead had purchased the rights to *Alden's Library of Universal Knowledge*, itself based on *Chambers' Encyclopedia*. Under the editorship of scholars Daniel Coit Gilman, Harry Thurston Peck, and Frank Moore Colby, Dodd revised the work extensively as the *International Cyclopedia*. As the new century approached, he further revised and expanded the encyclopedia—modeling it on the principles of the German Brockhaus & Meyer encyclopedia—and issued it from 1902 to 1904 as *The New International Encyclopedia* in seventeen volumes. Three supplementary volumes were brought out in 1906. A second edition appeared in twenty-three volumes between 1914 and 1917; the *New International Yearbook* was added beginning in 1907.

In 1910 the firm moved to newer quarters at Fourth Avenue and Thirtieth Street—the first enterprise to establish itself in the vicinity—but in so doing relinquished its retail operations. Dodd was a proponent of commercial development in the area.

Dodd's lifelong promotion of the publishing industry was acknowledged in his election as president of the American Publishers' Association; during his years in the position, he strongly supported net pricing. In addition, Dodd was active in civic and financial affairs: he served as president of the Riverside Association and the Fourth Avenue Associations and was a trustee of the New York Kindergarten Association and the Greenwich Savings Bank. He also was a member of the Century and City clubs (New York) and the National Club (London).

Dodd died in New York City. Over the course of his fifty-seven years in the book business, he had transformed his father's publishing house from a small firm with a list of mostly religious titles into a respected leader of American book publishing.

• Significant collections of Dodd, Mead papers (including some of Frank H. Dodd's) are in the Hugh Morris Library at the University of Delaware, and two boxes of records dated 1839–1900 are at the American Antiquarian Society. The standard source of information on the Dodd dynasty is Edward H. Dodd, Jr., *The First Hundred Years: A History of the House of Dodd, Mead, 1839–1939* (1939). Frank E. Comparato, *Chronicles of Genius and Folly: R. Hoe & Company and the Printing Press as a Service to Democracy* (1979), contains a lengthy biographical section. A thorough entry on Dodd appeared in the *New International Yearbook, 1916* (1917), pp. 187–88. Obituaries include Claudius Clear [William Robertson Nicoll], "The Late Mr. Frank Dodd of New York: Some Memories," *British Weekly* 20 (20 Jan. 1916): 3331, and the *New York Times*, 11 Jan. 1916.

BARBARA A. BRANNON

DODD, Thomas Joseph (15 May 1907–24 May 1971), U.S. senator, was born in Norwich, Connecticut, the son of Thomas Joseph Dodd, a building contractor, and Abigail Margaret O'Sullivan. After graduating from Providence College (1930) with a degree in philosophy, he received his law degree from Yale University (1933). In 1934 he married Mary Grace Murphy; they had six children. A son, Christopher Dodd, also became a senator.

Dodd had a varied and interesting career, beginning as an agent with the Federal Bureau of Investigation in 1933. The highlight of his two years with the agency was his participation in an unsuccessful trap set for famed gangster John Dillinger. In 1935 he returned to Connecticut to direct the state's National Youth Administration (NYA). In this post he developed excellent connections with state Democratic leaders, which helped him secure the post of special assistant in the U.S. Department of Justice, a position he held from 1938 to 1945, successfully prosecuting a number of industrial sabotage and espionage cases on the East Coast during World War II. In 1945–1946 he served as executive trial counsel at the Nuremberg war crimes trials at the special request of Justice Robert H. Jackson, chief prosecutor at the trials.

In 1946 Dodd returned to Connecticut with a presidential citation and the Medal of Freedom and became a partner in the Hartford law firm of Pelgrift, Dodd, Blumenfeld, and Nair. Attempting to capitalize on his well-publicized and colorful background, he tried unsuccessfully for the Democratic gubernatorial nomination in both 1946 and 1948. In 1952 he captured the nomination for the House of Representatives from the First Congressional District (Hartford). He won the general election handily despite the landslide victory of President Dwight D. Eisenhower and was reelected in 1954, leading the state Democratic ticket. In 1956, however, the Eisenhower tide proved too much, and Dodd failed in his attempt to unseat Republican senator Prescott Bush. In 1958 he tried again and won election to the Senate, where he would serve two terms.

Dodd enjoyed prestigious assignments in the Senate, including seats on the Foreign Relations, Judiciary, Space, and Appropriations committees. Although not an active or influential committee member, he excelled at gaining publicity for frequent hard-line anticommunist pronouncements—such as on Berlin—which placed him at odds with Democratic leaders in the Senate. On domestic issues, he consistently supported New Frontier–Great Society policies, voting for civil rights and welfare measures, Medicare, and immigration reform. Dodd was best known during his Senate years as a proponent of gun control and a crusader against television violence and drug abuse, but no important piece of legislation ever bore his name.

From the beginning, rumors of financial misdeeds surrounded Dodd. His critics raised questions about his connections with foreign lobbyists (he had earned over $60,000 per year as a registered agent for Guatemala between his stints in the House and Senate), and it was later revealed that some on his staff were concerned about a discrepancy between campaign contributions and actual campaign expenditures during his successful 1964 bid for reelection. In January 1966 Washington columnist Drew Pearson began a series of reports alleging serious ethical violations on Dodd's part; Pearson's sources were four disaffected members of Dodd's Senate staff. These allegations included claims that Dodd had intervened in government matters on behalf of clients of his law firm, had falsely labeled vacations as government trips in order to be reimbursed, had used campaign contributions to pay for personal expenses, had "double-billed" the government for trips that were already paid for, and had carried persons on his payroll who performed no duties.

The Senate was slow to respond, but in self-defense Dodd himself called for an investigation. The recently constituted Senate Committee on Standards and Conduct undertook a yearlong inquiry, and on 23 June 1967 the Senate considered two counts of censure recommended by the committee. Dodd's colleagues voted overwhelmingly to censure him on the first count, diversion of over $100,000 in campaign contributions for his own use; by a narrow vote they exonerated him on the second charge, "double-billing" expenses to the government. Dodd remained in the Senate, though with little influence. In 1968 the Senate amended its rules to provide for more stringent standards of ethical conduct for both senators and employees.

Only the seventh U.S. senator to be censured, Dodd maintained his innocence of wrongdoing and, despite being denied nomination by his party, in 1970 ran for a third Senate term as an Independent. He received slightly less than 25 percent of the vote in the general election, contributing to the defeat of the regular Democratic nominee and the election of Republican Lowell Weicker. Six months after his defeat, Dodd died at his home in Old Lyme, Connecticut.

• Dodd's papers have been deposited at the Connecticut State Library in Hartford but as of 1991 were unavailable to researchers. No scholarly study of Dodd's career has been published, but the story of his censure is recounted at length in two works: Drew Pearson and Jack Anderson, *The Case against Congress: A Compelling Indictment of Corruption on Capitol Hill* (1968), and James Boyd, *Above the Law* (1968). An extensive obituary is in the *New York Times*, 25 May 1971.

GARY W. REICHARD

DODDRIDGE, Philip (17 May 1773–19 Nov. 1832), attorney and congressman, was born in Bedford County, Pennsylvania, the son of John Doddridge and Mary Wells, farmers. Growing up on his family's farm, young Philip experienced little if any formal education before being sent to Johnson's School in Charlestown, Virginia (now Wellsburg, West Virginia). Without benefit of a college education, he studied law on his own, was admitted to the Virginia bar in 1797, and began a lucrative but physically grueling practice consisting mostly of land title litigation. Routine cases required trips on horseback over perilous roads into Ohio and western Pennsylvania. As his reputation grew, he was called more often to cross the Alleghenies and the Blue Ridge to the Virginia Court of Appeals in Richmond, a punishing journey of 300 miles. Later, Doddridge appeared from time to time before the U.S. Supreme Court. In 1800 he married Julia Parr Musser of Lancaster, Pennsylvania. They raised their six children on a comfortable 56-acre estate overlooking the Ohio River.

Doddridge's oratorical skill and phenomenal command of detail enabled his rapid ascent in the legal community. In 1808 he became the state's attorney for Ohio County, and from that position he advanced predictably into legislative politics, serving three stints in the Virginia House of Delegates (1815–1816, 1822–1823, and 1828–1829). A western-style Jeffersonian, he was both more democratic in principle and more nationalist in outlook than his eastern Virginia counterparts. Representing the remote Brooke County, which bordered the Ohio River between Wheeling and Pittsburgh, Doddridge maintained a following of nonslaveholding grain farmers who needed banks and internal improvements—state or federal—to bolster their unstable frontier economy. Government in Virginia, however, remained based on the constitution of 1776, an undemocratic instrument by early nineteenth-century standards. Under its provisions, scarcely half of the adult white males in the state held enough property to qualify as voters. In legislative representation, the constitution favored the eastern parts of Virginia and denied power to the western districts, which were rapidly being settled by a hardworking population who, in Doddridge's eyes, constituted the incorruptible "marrow and backbone of the nation." As for the monied eastern elite, he judged that "its fruits are pride and arrogance, with sloth and idle habits" (quoted in Willey). Doddridge served on an unusual number of committees, ranging from banking, finance, and taxation concerns to roads and navigation, schools, and courts of justice. These assignments exposed him to a full range of state issues, including many that directly pitted frontier interests against the oligarchical Tidewater. Without success, for example, he pushed for a connected public school system from primary grades up, similar to Thomas Jefferson's vision of a network of academies and colleges not just for the rich but also for the middle classes.

In 1829 western pressure finally resulted in the calling of a state constitutional convention in Richmond. There, representing several frontier counties, Doddridge championed a reform agenda that included proposals for universal white male suffrage, the election of governors by the voters instead of the legislature, and the democratizing of local government. The reformers' most important goal was changing the legislative apportionment system to allow more western influence in the Virginia General Assembly. Tidewater slaveholders, however, won the day by defeating a western scheme that counted only whites and not slaves when calculating the population basis for representation. Western delegates went home with no important gains in the new constitution of 1830 and only a slightly more suitable ratio of legislative seats. In frustration Doddridge left early and was absent for the final vote. The "equal and just claims" of the western districts, he announced to his constituents, "were betrayed and lost." Real democratic reform would have to wait until the convention of 1850, after the population west of the Blue Ridge had overtaken that of the east.

The Virginia convention overlapped part of Doddridge's first term in the U.S. House of Representatives. After fruitless bids in 1822 and 1824, he defeated Joseph Johnson for the coveted seat in 1828 and, despite uncertain health, held it until his death four years later. The congressional interests of his western Virginia district translated into support for Henry Clay's Maysville Road Bill, which in 1830 proposed a federally-subsidized turnpike to link central Kentucky to the Ohio River trade. Doddridge regularly backed legislation to improve transportation improvements in western regions of the country. He voted for recharter of the ill-fated Bank of the United States in 1832 and vowed allegiance to protective tariffs as long as the British excluded American beef, pork, and breadstuffs from their West Indian markets. Along with Chief Justice John Marshall, he thought federal authority usually superceded states' rights. When South Carolina radicals in 1830 advanced a bill to end the Supreme Court's power to review state decisions, Doddridge sputtered that it was like "a proposition to repeal the Union" (*Register of Debates*, 25 Jan. 1830). In late 1831 he advocated federal sponsorship for a bridge over the Ohio River at Wheeling, never doubting the power of Congress to authorize such a project. As the chairman of the committee for the District of Columbia, he received a flood of petitions from abolitionists urging an end to slavery and the slave trade in the national capital. But to these pleas he turned a deaf ear, believing that Congress should not violate the good faith of Virginia and Maryland, the states that had ceded the district originally, until those state governments eradicated the evil institution within their own boundaries. As of 1830 Doddridge himself owned just one slave, a female house servant.

While at work on a legal code for the District of Columbia, a job that fitted his turn of mind, Doddridge fell ill suddenly and died at Gadsby's Hotel in Washington, D.C. Paying final tribute, the *National Intelligencer* declared that "in intellectual power, and useful qualities, he has left hardly an equal in the body of which he was a member."

• Doddridge's personal and legal papers are widely scattered. A few pieces may be found at the Virginia Historical Society, Richmond, and the University of Virginia Library, Charlottesville. Some valuable biographical information appears in W. T. Willey, *A Sketch of the Life of Philip Doddridge* (1875). On his role in the Virginia Constitutional Convention of 1829–1830, see *Proceedings and Debates of the Virginia State Convention of 1829–1830* (1830); Merrill D. Peterson, ed., *Democracy, Liberty, and Property: The State Constitutional Conventions of the 1820s* (1966); and Robert P. Sutton, *Revolution to Secession: Constitution Making in the Old Dominion* (1989). For Doddridge's record in the Twenty-first and Twenty-second Congresses, see Joseph Gales and William W. Seaton, comps., *Register of Debates in Congress, 1825–1837* (29 vols., 1829–1837). An obituary is in the *National Intelligencer*, 21 Nov. 1832.

JOHN R. VAN ATTA

DODDS, Baby (24 Dec. 1898–14 Feb. 1959), jazz drummer, was born Warren Dodds in New Orleans, Louisiana, the son of Warren Dodds. His father played quills (a type of musical pipe made from reeds), his mother (name unknown) played the melodeon, his sisters were accomplished on both organ and harmonica, and his older brother Johnny Dodds became an outstanding jazz clarinetist. Named for his father, Warren Dodds at an early age became "Baby," an appellation he carried for life. As a child he was given a tin flute, but he never mastered it and eventually gave it to Johnny. His father thought drums were too noisy, but Dodds nevertheless constructed a primitive set out of tin cans in which he punched holes; he used discarded chair rungs as his sticks. Finally, at age seventeen, he obtained a rope bass drum and a snare drum. He rounded out his first set of real drums with others he picked up at pawnshops. Lacking formal lessons, he was basically self-taught.

To trace Dodds's subsequent career is to mention virtually every major personality in the rise of New Orleans jazz. His first paying jobs came in 1912 at small New Orleans clubs. Dodds also played street parades with Frankie Dusen's and Bunk Johnson's bands and occasionally sat in with Armand Piron's group. For several years he periodically performed with childhood friend Willie Hightower's American Stars, playing at times for ice cream. His initial inspiration on drums was Mack Murray, who also performed in both the popular street parades and the John Robichaux band. But influences were everywhere: an early teacher was "Rabbit" from Ma Rainey's band, and drummer Walter Grundy taught him to read music. He admired drummers Henry Zeno, Henry Martin, Tubby Hall, Louis Cottrell, Roy Palmer, and Dave Perkins.

Oscar "Papa" Celestin hired Dodds briefly in 1917 for roadhouse work, including the 101 Ranch in New Orleans, a popular venue for aspiring musicians. As jazz spread in popularity, bassist George "Pops" Foster got him jobs on riverboats plying the Mississippi. There he played with Louis Armstrong in a group led by Fate Marable called the Jaz-E-Saz Band. Photographs dated 1918 or so show Dodds on board the SS *Capitol* and the SS *Sydney*, both of which were run by the St. Louis–based Streckfus family, pioneers of the floating dance hall. At this time Dodds was already noted for having a great smile and an utterly reliable beat, two of his most memorable traits.

Although classified as a drummer, Dodds was also accomplished on washboard, a novelty instrument popular in the 1920s. He mastered the use of cowbells, wood blocks, tom-toms, and other crowd pleasers, sometimes being accused of overexuberance. Additionally, for some listeners, he tended to overuse the bass drum. Yet others credit him as the first to extract the full potential of this percussion instrument.

In 1921, while playing on the riverboat *St. Paul*, King Oliver asked Dodds to accompany him to San Francisco as drummer with Oliver's famous Creole Jazz Band. While there, he also played with Kid Ory. During this period Dodds made yearly visits to Chicago either with Oliver and Armstrong or on his own. In 1924 he returned to Chicago with Lil Hardin Armstrong. Once there, he also played with Freddy Keppard, Willie Hightower, and his brother Johnny. He in fact stayed with his brother off and on until 1940, when Johnny died. The two did not always get on smoothly because Baby drank and Johnny did not.

As his reputation spread, Dodds in 1926 played in the Hugh Swift Band at the Evergreen Golf Club, which included doing some radio broadcasts and playing concert and semiclassical pieces, not jazz. The year 1927 found him with the Charlie Elgar band in Chicago. Popular white bandleaders such as Paul Whiteman and Guy Lombardo were impressed with Dodds, both for his skills and the sheer number of songs he knew. A high point in Dodds's career occurred in 1927, when Louis Armstrong formed his Hot Seven Band, with Armstrong on trumpet, Lil Hardin on piano, Johnny Dodds on clarinet, Kid Ory on trombone, and Johnny St. Cyr on banjo (these first-named also constituted the equally famous Hot Five), along with Pete Briggs on tuba and Baby Dodds on drums. This association burnished his reputation.

During the depression years Dodds played a variety of Chicago clubs. By the early 1940s, his fame well established, Dodds recorded and played with many different groups. He performed with Bunk Johnson, Jelly Roll Morton, Jimmie Noone, Sidney Bechet, Mezz Mezzrow (including a trip to France in 1948), Art Hodes, Miff Mole, Bob Wilber, and Lee Collins. Dodds also led several groups of his own during this period.

Dodds was the first of the influential drum stylists, and he revolutionized the drumming of his time. In contrast to many of his contemporaries, he was light-handed, yet he seldom used brushes. Actually, Dodds was more of a percussionist than a drummer. He thought in terms of tonal colors and how to mix them. He correctly realized that drums and cymbals were pitched and needed tuning and that they had a wide range of tonal variations. They could fit harmonic as well as rhythmic patterns. Unfortunately, there exists little recorded evidence of Dodds's genius. On most of his early recordings he is virtually inaudible; but he may not have been playing anything other than wood blocks, since early audio technology could not accommodate the sound of actual drums.

Louis Armstrong encouraged Dodds to play an even four beats instead of emphasizing the second and fourth, which was more characteristic of the time. The result lightened the pounding drum sound immeasurably. Dodds also developed breaks, brief drum solos that fill the gap at the end of another instrument's solo. This eventually led to the drum solo, which has become so much a part of jazz since then. He attempted to play behind soloists—to whom he was always attentive—not overpower them. His playing has been recognized for its subtle nuances. As his later recordings attest, his drumming provided the pulsating rhythmic undercurrent that exemplified jazz.

Dodds was married at least twice (his second wife's name was Ruth). He died in Chicago after a series of strokes, starting in 1949, that gradually incapacitated him.

• Interviews Dodds gave for the *Jazz Record* in 1946 have been preserved in Art Hodes and Chadwick Hansen, eds., *Selections from the Gutter* (1977). In 1955 he gave extensive interviews to the *Jazz Journal*, much of which has been reprinted in Nat Shapiro and Nat Hentoff, eds., *The Jazz Makers* (1957). The best recordings that display Dodds's drum techniques are on the Folkways label, *Baby Dodds: Talking* and *Drum Solos*. In addition, he did a number of sides for the American Music label in the 1940s and early 1950s. He can also be heard (although the audio quality often obscures his playing) on the Armstrong Hot Seven tracks collected on Columbia.

WILLIAM H. YOUNG

DODDS, Harold Willis (28 June 1889–25 Oct. 1980), college president and professor, was born in Utica, Pennsylvania, the son of Samuel Dodds, a Presbyterian minister and professor of chemistry, physics, and Bible at Grove City College, and Alice Dunn. In 1909 Dodds graduated Phi Beta Kappa from Grove City College, then taught high school Latin and English for two years before taking graduate courses in politics at Princeton University and in social ethics and theology at Princeton Theological Seminary. After receiving an A.M. from Princeton University in 1914, he taught economics for two years at Purdue University; he earned his Ph.D. at the University of Pennsylvania in 1917. That year he married Margaret Murray; they had no children.

During World War I, Dodds was executive secretary of the United States Food Administration in Pennsylvania. Between 1919 and 1925, he lectured in political science or municipal government at Western Reserve University, the University of Pennsylvania, Swarthmore College, and New York University. His service with the National Municipal League (secretary, 1920–1928; editor of the *National Municipal Review*, 1920–1933; and president, 1934–1937) gained him the recommendation of Secretary of State Charles Evans Hughes. Dodds drafted the Nicaraguan electoral law (the so-called "Dodds Law") in 1923 that ensured relatively peaceful presidential elections in 1924, but he was asked to return to oversee registration for the 1928 election; to prevent "repeaters," a voter's finger was stained with Mercurochrome. Dodds was also technical adviser (1925–1926) to the Tacna-Arica Plebiscitary Commission, chaired by General John J. Pershing, on the dispute between Chile and Peru; and he was consulted by Cuba in 1935 on election law procedures.

Joining the Princeton University faculty in 1925, he was promoted to associate professor (1926) and full professor (1927) of politics. He taught municipal problems and public administration and chaired the administrative committee of the School of Public Affairs (renamed in 1948 the Woodrow Wilson School of Public and International Affairs); he also supervised a faculty study of New Jersey's finances and administration.

Elected Princeton's fifteenth president by the trustees in 1933, Dodds was its third youngest president and second layman after Woodrow Wilson. Proposing "no stirring platform of educational policy or radical reform," Dodds demonstrated superior administrative ability as he successfully led Princeton through the depression, World War II, and into the Cold War era. Between 1933 and 1956 the faculty increased from 327 to 582, as Princeton hired promising young scholars and endowed thirty new professorships. Undergraduate enrollment climbed from 2,309 to 2,948, while its graduate enrollment rose from 293 to 636. A liberal arts education was achieved, Dodds believed, by balancing programs among the humanities, natural sciences, and social sciences. Princeton established seven of nine research units in the social sciences, created new departments of music and religion, opened a school of architecture, and developed new programs in the creative arts, the humanities, Near Eastern studies, American civilization, and European civilization. The physical plant expanded with the construction of the Herbert Lowell Dillon Gymnasium and the Harvey S. Firestone Library and the 1951 purchase from the Rockefeller Center for Medical Research of what became the James Forrestal Research Center (Project Matterhorn's thermonuclear research facility, the Jet Propulsion Center, and the Department of Aeronautical Engineering). From 1933 to 1957 Princeton received over $60 million in gifts, legacies, and funds; the market value of its endowment, construction, and expendable funds reached about $123 million. Impor-

tant sources of support were alumni annual giving, initiated in 1940, and government- and industry-financed scientific and engineering research.

During his administration, Princeton celebrated two important anniversaries: in 1946–1947 the bicentennial of its founding as the College of New Jersey and in 1956 the centennial of Woodrow Wilson's birth. Princeton's bicentennial, which launched the $57 million Third Century Fund, featured sixteen conferences and three major convocations, attended by hundreds of academic and political dignitaries, including President Harry S. Truman, who received an honorary LL.D., Herbert Hoover, and General Dwight Eisenhower. In his addresses during both occasions, Dodds expanded on Wilson's vision of a liberal education in a residential university.

In the 1950s Dodds had to respond to attacks on academic freedom. On the one hand, he was president of the Association of American Universities when it released, in 1953, its statement, "The Rights and Responsibilities of Universities and Their Faculties," specifying that Communist party membership disqualified a person from a faculty position and that universities had the obligation to cooperate with governmental inquiries into subversion. On the other hand, he refused the House Un-American Activities Committee's request for a political science professor's list of books and would not block, in April 1956, a student debating society's invitation to Alger Hiss.

He gave athletics their due, but in 1951 Princeton, Harvard, and Yale issued a joint admission policy on athletes and outlawed athletic scholarships. In 1956 the Ivy League for intercollegiate athletic competition was formalized with the scheduling of round-robin competition in football among all eight of the so-called "Ivy League" colleges.

Because of limited scholarship funds, Dodds only partially realized his "ideal for Princeton," a student body that would "always represent a cross-section, geographically and economically, of the best elements in American life." Princeton's reputation for exclusiveness persisted because of its required chapel attendance and its annual "bicker" system that left 15 to 20 percent of the sophomores outside the prestigious dining and social clubs for juniors and seniors. Dodds, who was liked by the students, supported their efforts to achieve "100 per cent Bickers" from 1941 to 1943 and again from 1950 to 1956; in 1956 he announced preliminary plans for dormitories with dining and social facilities, similar in concept to the Harvard house plan and the Yale college system. But campus anti-Semitism persisted, gaining national attention in 1958, when twelve of the twenty-three men who did not receive bids were Jews. Not until 1963 would the university begin actively to recruit African Americans, although it had received its first four black students in 1945 through the navy's V-12 program.

Believing that "an academic social scientist is improved by some contact with practice," Dodds continued throughout his career to serve on many boards, committees, and foundations: the General Education

Board, Rockefeller Foundation, and Carnegie Foundation for the Advancement of Teaching. His federal government service included the following chairmanships: American delegation to the Anglo-American Conference on the Refugee Problem, held in Bermuda (1943); the President's Committee on Integration of Medical Services of the Government (1946); a task force studying personnel and civil service for the Second Hoover Commission on Organization of the Executive Branch (1954); and the James Madison Memorial Commission (1960). As a member of President Truman's Advisory Commission on Universal Military Training (1947), Dodds opposed "blanket deferment of college students." He was designated a commander of the Belgian Order of King Leopold (1937). In 1956 Dodds received the Stockberger Award of the Society of Personnel Administration. By 1957, Dodds had been awarded thirty-eight honorary degrees from colleges and universities in the United States, Canada, and Europe.

After retirement in 1954 Dodds published *The Academic President—Educator or Caretaker?* (1962), supported by a Carnegie grant. "Presidents especially have an obligation to draw likely junior faculty into the administration to try them out and to give them experience," said Dodds, who recommended that current "academic chief executives" study the careers of such past presidents as Andrew D. White of Cornell, Charles W. Eliot of Harvard, Daniel Coit Gilman of Johns Hopkins, and Woodrow Wilson of Princeton.

Dodds continued to live in Princeton in later years. In 1965 he chaired the Citizens for a Mercer County Community College and was chosen as one of eight trustees for the new two-year institution. The Greater Princeton Chamber of Commerce and Civic Council voted to honor him as its "Man of the Year" in 1971. Four years later the National Academy of Public Administration voted to make him an honorary member. Dodds died at the Meadow Lakes retirement village in Hightstown, New Jersey.

"A college president," said Dodds, "has two choices. One is to lean toward being a public figure. I decided to throw my weight toward Princeton." During his administration, observed Joseph R. Strayer, "Princeton became a real university, a major contributor to knowledge and understanding throughout the world," while maintaining excellent undergraduate teaching (quoted in Leitch, p. 140). Dodds understood, wrote Charles G. Osgood, "that the Liberal Arts, combining Science and the Humanities in just proportion, constitute the indispensable discipline for a free and enduring democracy" (p. 46).

• The papers of Harold Willis Dodds, which are unprocessed and closed for fifty years from the date of their origin, are in the Seeley G. Mudd Manuscript Library, Princeton University Archives. A box of chronologically arranged biographical files, university press releases, and clippings and several scrapbooks are open for examination. Dodds was interviewed for the Columbia University Oral History Project both on his administration (9 Feb. 1962) and on his committee service for the Carnegie Foundation for the Advancement of Teaching

(17 June 1968). Significant publications not mentioned in the text include: *Procedure in State Legislatures* (1918); "United States and Nicaragua," *Annals of the American Academy of Arts and Sciences* 132 (July 1927): 134–41; "American Supervision of the Nicaraguan election," *Foreign Affairs* 7 (Apr. 1929): 488–96; *Out of This Nettle, Danger . . .* (1943), a collection of addresses in which Dodds defended "old-fashioned liberalism" and advocated a liberal arts education; "Memorandum on Government Grants-in-Aid to Universities in Great Britain," in *Government Assistance to Universities in Great Britain, Memoranda Submitted to the Commission on Financing Higher Education*, by Harold W. Dodds et al. (1952), pp. 91–133. Many of his Princeton addresses were reprinted in *Vital Speeches of the Day*. The *Princeton Alumni Weekly*, *Time*, *Newsweek*, and the student *Daily Princetonian* contain articles documenting Dodds's career. For a discussion of Dodds's administration and his addresses during the bicentennial, see Charles G. Osgood, *Lights in Nassau Hall: A Book of the Bicentennial, Princeton 1746–1946* (1951). Joseph R. Strayer's concise sketch of Dodds's career appears in Alexander Leitch, *A Princeton Companion* (1978). An obituary is in the *New York Times*, 26 Oct. 1980.

MARCIA G. SYNNOTT

DODDS, Johnny (12 Apr. 1892–8 Aug. 1940), jazz clarinetist, was born John M. Dodds in Waverly, Louisiana, the son of Warren Dodds, a farm worker, warehouse employee, and handyman, and Josephene (maiden name unknown). Raised in New Orleans from 1901, at age seventeen Dodds was given a clarinet by his father, an amateur musician who sang religious songs with the family and played a variety of instruments. A high school graduate, Dodds studied clarinet with legendary Creole master Lorenzo Tio, Jr., and bandsman Charlie McCurdy. He also began paying serious attention to Sidney Bechet, who, though five years his junior, was already a skilled jazz improviser. In 1911 bassist Pops Foster heard Dodds practicing clarinet while on a lunch break from his job at a rice mill; impressed with his abilities, Foster brought him to the attention of Kid Ory. Dodds sat in with the trombonist's band at the Globe Hall and was hired immediately for his first professional job in neighboring Gretna. During this time Dodds also took jobs with Jack Carey's and other marching bands.

In 1917 Dodds traveled to Chicago with Billy and Mary Mack's Merrymakers. He then played from May to September 1918 on the Streckfus line riverboat SS *Sidney* with Fate Marable's twelve-piece band, whose personnel included Louis Armstrong, banjoist Johnny St. Cyr, Foster, and Dodds's younger brother, drummer Warren "Baby" Dodds. On his return to New Orleans, Dodds rejoined Ory in 1919, and in January 1920 he returned to Chicago to join King Oliver's new band. In June 1921 Oliver began an extended engagement at the Pergola Dance Pavilion in San Francisco, leaving in September for a series of ballroom and theater engagements in Los Angeles and other West Coast cities. Back in Chicago in the spring, Oliver's Creole Jazz Band began its historic residency at the Lincoln Gardens in mid-June, and in late August its ranks were strengthened by the addition of Armstrong, completing the personnel of the first truly great jazz band in history. However, after recording thirty-seven performances from April until December 1923 (most of them featuring Dodds), in early 1924 dissensions resulted in the band's partial breakup. The Dodds brothers, trombonist Honoré Dutrey, and bassist Bill Johnson, along with cornetist Freddie Keppard and pianist Charlie Alexander, left the Gardens to work at Bert Kelly's Stables, a regular club job for Dodds through New Year's Day 1930.

From 1925 until 1929 Dodds enjoyed his most prolific period of recording, appearing not only on the classic Armstrong Hot Five and Hot Seven series, with Ory, Lil Hardin Armstrong, St. Cyr, and Baby Dodds, but on dates with Jelly Roll Morton and others, including many recorded under his own leadership. Throughout the 1930s Dodds continued to lead small groups, usually with Dominique, Baby Dodds, and pianist Leo Montgomery, at such clubs as the Three Deuces, the New Stables, and the Hotel Hayes. On 18 May 1937 the Dodds quartet appeared in concert at the Congress Hotel opposite Roy Eldridge's swing band, Zutty Singleton's sextet, and the Bob Crosby orchestra at a benefit for pneumonia-stricken pianist Joe Sullivan. In January 1938, eight and a half years after his last recording session, Dodds made his first and only visit to New York to record with Lil Armstrong and members of John Kirby's sextet, but in May 1939, while leading a sextet at the Hotel Hayes, he suffered a stroke, his second in a year and one that left him unable to play for many months. Despite dental problems, as well, he then worked occasionally with his quartet, now under Baby Dodds's contractual leadership, at the 9750 Club (Jan.–Mar. 1940). In June, equipped with full dentures, he recorded two titles for Decca's *New Orleans Jazz* album, and from mid-July he played at 5400 Broadway. After suffering a third stroke, he died in Chicago.

In direct contrast to his highly emotional, expressive musical persona, Dodds was a serious and sober man who disapproved of his younger brother's wild and carefree lifestyle. On stage he always conducted himself in a professional manner, and he expected the same of his bandsmen. Similarly, as a family man, while earning top salaries in the 1920s, he started investing in real estate, ultimately acquiring clear title to a three-story apartment building, as well as maintaining a financial interest in his older brother's taxicab company and garage. Even after the onset of his physical problems, he supported his wife and three children on the income from his investments.

Although his playing was integral to the artistic success of the records he made with Oliver, Armstrong, and Morton, most of Dodds's own more fully realized performances are on the 1926–1929 dates issued under his own name or such sobriquets as the New Orleans Wanderers, New Orleans Bootblacks, Chicago Footwarmers, and the Beale Street Washboard Band. He worked exceedingly well with Armstrong, yet he usually played at his best in the company of less commanding cornetists such as George Mitchell, Natty Dominique, and Herb Morand. As Bechet had done

earlier, Dodds developed a strong lead style by the mid-1920s, and although he never lost his skill at ensemble counterpoint, by the late twenties he was clearly the major force in the front line.

Dodds's reputation as the best blues and stomp clarinetist in jazz history is not unfounded. Throughout his career he played with an inventiveness, rhythmic drive, technical assurance, and variety of timbral expression that many critics feel was surpassed only by Bechet on soprano sax. Frequently he would play with a warm intimacy in the broad, dark, lower recesses of his range and then, with bold, darting lines, either leap or gradually ascend to a raw, almost savage, visceral intensity in his searing upper register. By no means, though, was this a formulaic pattern; his performances are valued for their unpredictability as much as for their consistency. Like Bechet, he favored a hot, throbbing vibrato and a free-flowing, almost rubato phrasing, but because his sound was personal and part of an age forgotten by the later 1930s, his later years were spent in comparative obscurity. Dodds's greatest period of influence occurred following the New Orleans Revival of the mid-1940s, when hundreds of young white clarinetists attempted to duplicate his tone and feeling.

Johnny Dodds was perhaps the most uncommercial, aesthetically pure jazz clarinetist of all time. Well into the swing era, when big bands prevailed, Dodds still played the same informal, heartfelt small-band jazz that he had played in the 1920s, his slashing, blues-drenched sound soaring above his surroundings, untouched by the changes in the world around him.

• The most comprehensive treatment of Johnny Dodds's life is Baby Dodds, *The Baby Dodds Story*, as told to Larry Gara (1959), while important details of his early career are discussed in Pops Foster, *The Autobiography of Pops Foster*, as told to Tom Stoddard (1971); John Chilton, *Sidney Bechet: The Wizard of Jazz* (1987); Max Jones and John Chilton, *Louis: The Louis Armstrong Story, 1900–1971* (1971); James Lincoln Collier, *Louis Armstrong: An American Genius* (1983); and Walter C. Allen and Brian Rust, *King Oliver*, rev. ed., by Laurie Wright (1987). William Howland Kenney, *Chicago Jazz: A Cultural History (1904–1930)* (1993), offers information on the sociological background of Dodds's milieu, while his musical contributions receive intelligent analyses in Bob Wilber, notes to *Johnny Dodds* (Time-Life *Giants Of Jazz*, 1982), Joe Muranyi, notes to *Johnny Dodds: Blue Clarinet Stomp* (RCA, 1990), and Richard Hadlock, notes to *Johnny Dodds: South Side Chicago Jazz* (MCA, 1990). Further biographical treatment is found in Frank K. Kappler, notes to *Johnny Dodds* (Time-Life *Giants Of Jazz*, 1982), Brian Peerless, notes to *Johnny Dodds: 1926–1928* (JSP, 1990), and, in abbreviated form, John Chilton, *Who's Who of Jazz* (1985). The most accurate listing of Dodds's recorded works is Brian Rust, *Jazz Records, 1897–1942*, 5th ed. (1982).

JACK SOHMER

DODGE, Augustus Caesar (2 Jan. 1812–20 Nov. 1883), politician and diplomat, was born in Ste. Genevieve, Missouri, son of Henry Dodge and Christina McDonald. His father was a soldier and politician, who served the territory and state of Wisconsin as governor, congressional delegate, and U.S. senator. At age fifteen, after minimal formal schooling, young Dodge moved with his family to Galena, Illinois, to take advantage of the prosperity being generated by the lead mining industry in the area. Here he worked at numerous and varied jobs. He was with his father during the Winnebago War and later served him as aide-de-camp during the Black Hawk War. In 1837 he married Clara Ann Hertich, daughter of a teacher in Ste. Genevieve. They had three children.

Through the influence of his father and an uncle, who was a Missouri senator, in 1838 Dodge secured an appointment by President Martin Van Buren as Registrar of the Land Office in Burlington, Iowa, which he made his permanent place of residence. A lifelong Democrat, as was his father, Dodge was elected a delegate to Congress from the Iowa Territory in 1840 and served in this capacity until 1846. In Congress he unsuccessfully sought to resolve a boundary dispute between Iowa and Missouri, later adjudicated by the U.S. Supreme Court. He was more successful in persuading Congress to approve various appropriations for Iowa, largely to pay for internal improvements and help defray expenses of the territorial government.

When Iowa became a state in 1846, Dodge and George W. Jones were selected as the new state's first U.S. senators. Dodge initially held the short term but was elected to a full term in 1849. In the Senate he fully supported all components of the Compromise of 1850. A member of the Committee on Public Lands, he endorsed legislation for free homesteads and sought, unsuccessfully, to secure a grant of land for Iowa in 1852 to aid railroad construction. A supporter of the construction of a transcontinental railroad, in 1853 he introduced in the Senate a bill to organize the Nebraska Territory that in 1854 became the Kansas-Nebraska Act, which he heartily endorsed.

The political turmoil unleashed by passage of the Kansas-Nebraska Act cost Dodge his Senate seat in 1855, when Republican James Harlan was selected in his stead. President Franklin Pierce named Dodge minister to Spain in 1855. Though not really qualified for this post, Dodge served his country to the best of his abilities. He helped ease strained relations growing out of the *Black Warrior* incident, in which Spanish authorities had seized an American merchant ship in Havana in 1854. He could not, however, secure a treaty of friendship and commerce or acquire Cuba from Spain. For reasons of national security as well as domestic politics, the United States wished to acquire Cuba. Spain rejected all American overtures for the island, including President Polk's offer in 1848 of one hundred million dollars for its purchase. He reluctantly continued in his post until early 1859. He learned sufficient Spanish to be able to make his departing remarks in that language.

Dodge returned to Iowa in time to be nominated by the Democrats as their candidate to oppose Republican Samuel J. Kirkwood in the gubernatorial election of 1859. Joined in a series of debates with his opponent, Dodge proved to be a political anachronism no longer in tune with Iowa's voters. His endorsement of slavery as a civilizing, Christianizing, and, beneficial institution fell upon a largely unhearing audience. His role in helping to secure passage of the Kansas-Nebraska legislation also harmed his campaign. He was hurt further by Republican characterizations of him as a person of superior airs and pomposity. Democrats were unable effectively to refute such characterizations, which probably stemmed from the formal manners and style of dress that his diplomatic assignment required. Following his loss in the election Dodge returned to Burlington, where he lived in semiretirement but remained politically active, even making one last unsuccessful bid for the U.S. Senate in 1860. He was a delegate to the Democratic National Convention in 1864 and eight years later endorsed Horace Greeley for the presidency. In 1874 he was elected mayor of Burlington for a two-year term. In 1879 he was made chairman of the state Democratic convention. He also served as a member of an investigative committee to examine the state reform school. He died in Burlington.

Dodge's politically productive period lasted from 1840 to 1855 and coincided with Iowa's early formative years. Changes in the political climate of the state—generated partially by increasing numbers of antislavery newcomers from the northeastern states and abroad—combined with Dodge's inability to shed his long-held antiblack, proslavery proclivities to terminate his successful political career. By the midpoint of the final antebellum decade, Dodge and the Democratic party of Iowa had been relegated to minority status.

• Many of Dodge's private papers have been lost or destroyed. The State Historical Society of Iowa at Iowa City contains some documents, however. An old essay by William Salter, "Augustus C. Dodge," appeared in Jan. 1887 in the *Iowa Historical Record*, and a lone biography, *Augustus Caesar Dodge* by Louis Pelzer, was published in 1908. A useful account of the election of 1859 may be found in Morton Rosenberg, *Iowa on the Eve of the Civil War: A Decade of Frontier Politics* (1972).

MORTON M. ROSENBERG

DODGE, Bernard Ogilvie (18 Apr. 1872–9 Aug. 1960), plant pathologist, mycologist, and educator, was born in Mauston, Wisconsin, the son of Eldridge Gerry Dodge, and Mary Ann Nourse, farmers. Dodge credited his parents with the early education of their children and for instilling in them a passion for knowledge and music. Because his help was needed to run the family farm, Dodge attended high school on an infrequent basis and graduated in 1892, at the age of twenty. Over the next fourteen years he would alternate between teaching high school and attending the University of Wisconsin, from which he received a bachelor of philosophy degree with the class of 1909.

While at the University of Wisconsin, Dodge was influenced by R. A. Harper, one of the United States' leading botanists. Harper helped cultivate Dodge's passion for learning and provided him with an opportunity to study more fully a class of plants called fungi. Upon graduating, at Harper's suggestion Dodge decided to pursue graduate studies. He followed his mentor to Columbia University, where he accepted a position as a research assistant in the department of botany and in 1912, at the age of forty, received a doctor of philosophy degree. He had married Jennie S. Perry in 1906; they had no children.

Dodge remained at Columbia University from 1912 to 1920 as an instructor in the botany department. There he began to study plant pathogens, publishing his first paper on the subject, "Fungi Producing Heart-Rot of Apple Trees," in 1916 (*Mycologia* 8: 5–15). During this time he described a number of plant pathogenic fungi, one of the most notable being *Polyporus admirailis*, which at the time was attacking apple trees in Connecticut and southeastern New York. He also began to study the life cycle, morphology, and cytology of the rusts, particularly *Gymnosporangium*. The quality of this early work led to his being offered a position as a plant pathologist with the U.S. Department of Agriculture's Bureau of Plant Industry in Washington, D.C., in 1920.

At the Bureau of Plant Industry, Dodge was charged with the study of fruit diseases. He also continued his investigations on rust fungi. During this period he coauthored publications with famous plant pathologists and mycologists such as C. L. Shear, N. E. Stevens, F. A. Wolf, and R. B. Wilcox. In 1926 Dodge and Shear were assigned to study a newly isolated fungus they would later name *Neurospora*. In 1928, two years after beginning this assignment, Dodge left the USDA and accepted a position as senior plant pathologist at the New York Botanical Garden, where he was assigned to the study and control of diseases of ornamental plants and continued his studies on the fungus *Neurospora*.

Remaining at the NYBG until his retirement in 1957, Dodge published extensively on diseases of a number of ornamentals, including iris, marigold, and, his favorite, roses. According to Pascal Pompey Pirone, Dodge's greatest contribution to plant pathology was the book he coauthored, at the age of seventy-one, with H. W. Rickett, *Diseases and Pests of Ornamental Plants*. The first in its field to be published in the United States, the book became the standard text on ornamental diseases and insect problems at universities offering courses in plant pathology.

In his spare time Dodge continued his studies on the *Neurospora*. He characterized the life cycles of three *Neurospora* species: *N. erythraea*, *N. sitophila*, and *N. tetrasperma*. He was the first to demonstrate that *N. erythraea* and *N. sitophila* were haploid organisms and that phenotypic markers would segregate according to Mendelian rules similar to those known to exist in plants and animals, making these species useful for studying the mechanism regulating inheritance. Dodge also demonstrated the difference between a fungus in the diploid state and one that is heterothalic using *Neurospora*. G. W. Beadle and E. L. Tatum received the Nobel Prize for their 1941 paper in biochemical genetics titled "Genetic Control of Biochemical Reactions in *Neurospora*." In their acceptance speeches both researchers credited the work of Dodge and thanked him for laying the foundation on which future generations of scientists could build.

Dodge's work on the genetics of *Neurospora* would become his legacy. In his 48-year career he published a total of 162 papers (more than half after the age of fifty), forty-six of which were on *Neurospora*. A strong proponent of the study of the fungus, he took it upon himself to enlighten the scientific world about it. Dodge's work showed that the fungus used a mechanism similar to plants and animals to control the inheritance of traits. It had, however, several advantages as a research organism: *Neurospora* could be grown under defined conditions, reached sexual maturity in a matter of days, and thousands of generations could be studied in just a few months. Whenever he had occasion to speak to other professors or graduate students, whether at a formal meeting or a relaxed social gathering, inevitably the conversation would turn to the wonders of *Neurospora*.

Outside of science, Dodge's interests included a love of classical music and baseball. In his retirement he would go to his laboratory in the morning and then leave to attend an afternoon baseball game at Yankee Stadium before returning home for the evening. He died in New York City.

• It is not known if a comprehensive collection of Dodge's writings exists. Some primary sources are at Columbia University and the New York Botanical Garden. In-depth biographical and bibliographic information is in William J. Robbins, "Bernard Ogilvie Dodge, April 18, 1872–August 9, 1960," National Academy of Sciences, *Biographical Memoirs* 36 (1962): 84–124. See also Robbins et al., "Torreya: Bernard Ogilvie Dodge," *Bulletin of the Torrey Botanical Club* 88 (1961): 111–21; Carl T. Nelson, "Bernard Ogilvie Dodge," *Bulletin of the New York Academy of Medicine* 38 (1962): 117–19; Donald P. Rogers, "Dr. Dodge's *Neurospora*," *Garden Journal of the New York Botanical Garden* 3 (1953): 140–42, 158; Fred J. Seaver, "Bernard Ogilvie Dodge," *Bulletin of the Torrey Botanical Club* 74 (1947): 197–98; and Harold W. Rickett, "Bernard Ogilvie Dodge (1872–1960)," *Taxon* 10 (Mar.–Apr. 1961): 65. An obituary is in the *New York Times*, 11 Aug. 1960.

TERRENCE M. CALLAHAN

DODGE, Grace Hoadley (21 May 1856–27 Dec. 1914), social welfare worker and philanthropist, was born in New York City, the daughter of William Earl Dodge, Jr., a wealthy businessman and active supporter of evangelical causes, and Sarah Hoadley. She was educated at home, except for an unhappy year spent at Miss Porter's School. Perhaps because she was unusually tall and heavy-set, she suffered throughout her life from feelings of awkwardness. She shied away from intimacy; some friends thought that she was the loneliest person they had ever known. For many years she fulfilled what she termed her "sacred" duties of nurse-companion for her chronically ill mother, and of hostess for her father. She never married. To be an "old maid," she wrote, was to have the opportunity to "bring cheer or gladness into many a home instead of only one."

Rather than enter upper-class society, she chose to serve the less fortunate. In 1874 she began to teach Sunday school at the Madison Square Presbyterian Church and to teach basic household skills in the "industrial" schools established by the Children's Aid Society. She was recruited by Louisa Lee Schuyler, a family friend, to help work for efficient administration of public welfare. But Dodge craved more personal, more sisterly, relations with the poor than were contemplated by spokeswomen for the New Charity. Instead, like the settlement-house workers of the next generation, whom she would admire, Dodge identified emotionally with those she wished to help—especially the growing number of young, single women in the urban work force. In 1881 she brought together a group of working girls for weekly fellowship and discussion of such "practical" matters as health, purity, clothes, men, and family. Dodge was painfully anxious not to patronize. Her sisterly affection and utter lack of officiousness muted resentment of her privileged position. She frequently insisted that she, too, was a working girl, whose wages had been paid "in advance." Dodge also had great talent as an organizer and manager. By the 1890s, though treasuring the group for the sorority she found there, Dodge was increasingly preoccupied with creating a national organization of Working Girls Societies.

Dodge worked steadily to improve "industrial education," and to offer it to more young people. Admiring the theories of Friedrich Froebel and the classes Emily Huntington had organized for young girls, she helped found the Kitchen Garden Association in 1880. Four years later this organization became the Industrial Education Association, with the aim of spreading the gospel and providing the specialized teacher training that industrial education required. In 1886, as one of the two first women appointed to the New York City Board of Education, Dodge tried to promote industrial education. Regarding herself as the "especial representative" of New York's thirty-five hundred women teachers, she invited them to visit her at her Madison Avenue home. The president of the IEA in 1887, Nicholas Murray Butler, was less committed to philanthropy than to professionalism and in 1892 succeeded in transforming the association into Teachers College of Columbia University. Dodge worried that the college might lack "spirituality" but ruefully recognized that she lacked the education to shape college policy. As its treasurer, she loyally raised large amounts of money from her friends, contributed much herself, and closely monitored expenditures.

Dodge devoted much of the last decade of her life to strengthening the Young Women's Christian Association. As late as 1905 the movement was split between an American board, which was centered in midwestern colleges, evangelical in commitment, and tightly organized; and an international board, which was largely eastern, loosely administered, but dominated by upper-class women. Empathizing with both groups, Dodge succeeded between 1905 and 1906 in creating a single national organization with headquarters in New York City. As its elected president, she raised money, kept in daily touch with headquarters, and wrote thousands of letters of advice and encouragement to the young women organizing or managing YWCAs in other parts of the country. For these young women, she helped create a National Training School in New York, whose program stressed biblical studies and Christian character.

Dodge personified, and helped define, a transition in the way women served women. She wholeheartedly agreed with charity-organizers like Louisa Schuyler that upper-class women had a special obligation to organize and to manage welfare work. She also deeply admired settlement-house workers like Jane Addams, and she reveled in establishing close personal relations with working girls, with New York City school teachers, and with YWCA secretaries. At the same time, she was neither a feminist nor a suffragist. Vida Scudder, the radical social gospeler, would protest that Dodge failed to realize that capitalist, urban America ineluctably denied many young women the ability to "improve themselves." But Dodge's compassion touched thousands of women, and she helped to create enduring institutions, such as Teachers College and the modern YWCA, which would continue to empower young women in ways that Dodge had not dreamed of. She died of apoplexy in New York City and bequeathed about $1.5 million to the causes she had served.

• Some of Dodge's papers are held by Mrs. Cleveland E. Dodge, Jr., of Pownal, Vt.; others are in the archives of the National Board of the YWCA and in the archives of Teachers College, Columbia University—both in New York City. Scrapbooks in the YWCA archives preserve a good selection of the many newspaper and magazine articles Dodge wrote. See also her *A Bundle of Letters to Busy Girls on Practical Matters* (1887) and her introduction to Annie MacLean, *Wage-Earning Women* (1910). An enthusiastically admiring biography is Abbie Graham, *Grace H. Dodge: Merchant of Dreams* (1926). A much fuller and more judicious account is Esther Katz's "Grace Hoadley Dodge: Women and the Emerging Metropolis, 1856–1914" (Ph.D. diss., New York Univ., 1980).

On the Working Girls Societies, see Joanne Reitano, "Working Girls Unite," *American Quarterly* 36 (Spring 1984): 112–34. Dodge's work in education is discussed in Ellen C. Lagemann, *A Generation of Women: Education in the Lives of Progressive Reformers* (1979), and in Richard Whittemore, *Nicholas Murray Butler and Public Education, 1862–1911* (1970). Some of Dodge's other reform commitments are discussed in David Pivar, *Purity Crusade* (1973). The memories of family members are nicely represented in Phyllis B. Dodge, *Tales of the Phelps-Dodge Family: A Chronicle of Five Generations* (1987).

ROBERT D. CROSS

DODGE, Grenville Mellen (12 Apr. 1831–3 Jan. 1916), civil engineer and army officer, was born in Danvers, Massachusetts, the son of Sylvanus Dodge, a peddler, and Julia Theresa Phillips. Despite a nearly impoverished childhood and the need to find employment at an early age, Dodge demonstrated a strong desire for a formal education. Following one semester of preparatory study at New Hampshire's Durham Academy, he entered in 1848 Norwich University in Vermont, where he learned the scientific and engineering skills that would serve him well in life. After his graduation in 1851, he lived briefly at nearby Captain Alden Partridge's Military Academy and then headed west to market his talents.

Joining two school friends in Peru, Illinois, in 1851 Dodge surveyed town lots for a brief time, but this proved tedious and financially unrewarding. Amid the Illinois railroad building mania of the pre–Civil War decade, he found new opportunity among a group of engineers who worked for the Illinois Central Railroad. Under the guidance of Peter A. Dey, chief engineer for the Mississippi and Missouri Railroad, Dodge became chief assistant engineer for the railroad, and in 1852 he headed the survey from Davenport to Council Bluffs, Iowa, for the Mississippi and Missouri. The latter frontier community became his permanent home. In 1854 he married Ruth Anne Brown; they had three children.

Beginning in 1856 Dodge wisely invested his money in diverse businesses such as banking, real estate, mercantilism, and railroad construction, all of which greatly benefited his adopted community of Council Bluffs. He pursued an interest in the newly opened lands of Nebraska just across the Missouri River from his home and made several forays onto the Great Plains to trade with Indians, freight supplies to military posts, and assess the topography for future railroad routes. On the heels of the 1859 Colorado gold rush, he expanded freighting operations into the fledgling community of Denver and established a mercantile house under the name of Baldwin, Pegram and Company. Financial reverses during the panic of 1857 and scandals caused by some of his business associates harmed Dodge but did not destroy his reputation for honesty. In addition to retaining his position as a civic and business leader, he organized and commanded the Council Bluffs Guards in 1856 and conducted financially lucrative surveys for the St. Louis, Chillicothe, and Council Bluffs Railroad. When Illinois attorney Abraham Lincoln visited Council Bluffs in August 1859, Dodge gave him a tour and tried to interest his guest in investing in a railroad to run from the banks of the Missouri River to the Pacific Ocean.

The Civil War brought Dodge to even greater prominence. Rather than accept a federal army commission as a captain, he received appointment as a colonel in the Fourth Iowa Volunteer Regiment and eventually rose to the rank of major general. Serving initially under General John C. Frémont in Missouri, he distinguished himself as a brigade commander at the 7 and 8 March 1862 battle of Pea Ridge, Arkansas, where he was wounded. Dodge achieved additional successes in the battles for western Kentucky and Tennessee and commanded the Second Division of the Army of Tennessee as it advanced through northern Mississippi and Alabama during early 1863. Throughout the Vicksburg campaign of mid-1863 he not only commanded fighting troops but also utilized his engineering skills to reconstruct numerous bridges and railroads essential to the Union victory. Severely wounded on 19 August 1864 during the Atlanta campaign, he was temporarily furloughed from duty, only to return in December 1864 as commander of the Department of Missouri and subsequently to serve against Sioux and Cheyenne warriors who were disrupting overland trails through the central plains.

Honored by General Ulysses S. Grant for his wartime engineering feats, Dodge was in a good position to win the coveted role of chief engineer for the Union Pacific Railroad, whose eastern terminus was in Omaha, Nebraska, just a few miles from his Council Bluffs doorstep. Although some track had already been laid prior to his appointment in January 1866, the Union Pacific was almost totally his project, and when linked with the Central Pacific Railroad at Promontory Point, Utah, in May 1869 it represented the nation's first transcontinental railroad. The railroad's success assured Dodge's financial independence, made his name a household word, and earned him the nickname of "Long Eye," a moniker given by plains Indians, who observed his habit of carrying a telescope during the construction activities.

Dodge never tired of new railroad-building ventures, and in 1871 he accepted the position of chief engineer for construction of the Texas and Pacific Railway, which stretched from Shreveport, Louisiana, to San Diego, California. He became the railroad's president in 1880. By the end of the 1880s, he had participated in the construction of nearly 9,000 miles of track across the Southwest, forming associations with numerous railroads, including the Denver, Texas, and Forth Worth; Denver, Texas, and Gulf; New Orleans–Pacific; Missouri, Kansas, and Texas; International; Fort Worth and Denver; and the Mexican Railroad from Laredo, Texas, to Mexico City. Dodge not only designed many of these roads, he also served as president of most of them as well as of several other midwestern lines. His last such venture occurred in Cuba, where he helped to organize the Cuba Railroad Company, which, by 1903 linked Santa Clara to Santiago.

Despite the great demands on his time by business concerns, Dodge actively participated in Republican party politics. He had served as a popular Iowa representative to Congress in 1867–1868, only to decline renomination so that he could accept the chief engineer's position with the Union Pacific Railroad. He assumed a visible role in all elections from 1861 to 1912 and served as a delegate to the national Republican conventions of 1868, 1872, and 1876. He utilized these numerous political contacts as a masterful lobbyist and strongly influenced legislation that affected railroads. In 1898 President William McKinley appointed him chairman of the Dodge Commission to investigate the military supply scandal that had erupted during the

Spanish-American War, especially within the Commissary Department.

Shortly after this last public act, Dodge retired to a comfortable life in Council Bluffs with his wife. Although stricken with cancer in 1914, he recovered enough to resume correspondence with important national dignitaries and to oppose U.S. entry into World War I. After his death in Council Bluffs, nine companies of the Iowa and Nebraska National Guard escorted his body at his funeral to the local cemetery, and the entire town closed down in honor of its most distinguished citizen. Dodge's ultimate legacy was measured by the numerous miles of track that he had helped design across the West and the incalculable numbers of towns that grew up alongside those rails.

• Dodge's private papers and an incomplete autobiography are available at the Iowa State Department of History and Archives in Des Moines and the Council Bluffs Public Library. His own account of the most fascinating part of his life appears in *How We Built the Union Pacific Railway* (1910). He also published *The Battle of Atlanta* (1911); *Romantic Realities: The Story of the Building of the Pacific Roads* (1889); and *Personal Recollections of President Abraham Lincoln, General Ulysses S. Grant, and General William T. Sherman* (1914). A comprehensive and well-documented study appears in Stanley P. Hirshson, *Grenville M. Dodge: Soldier, Politician, Railroad Pioneer* (1967). Also see J. R. Perkins, *Trails, Rails and War: The Life of General G. M. Dodge* (1929).

MICHAEL L. TATE

DODGE, Henry (12 Oct. 1782–19 June 1867), soldier, governor of Wisconsin Territory, and U.S. senator, was born at Post Vincennes (now Vincennes), Indiana, the son of Israel Dodge, a farmer and businessman, and Nancy Ann Hunter. His father moved the family to Kentucky and then to Ste. Genevieve on the Missouri frontier in 1796. By the time Henry was born his father had become a wealthy landowner. Henry had little formal education, but worked on his father's farms and in his mills, distilleries, and mines. In 1800 Henry Dodge married Christina McDonald; they had thirteen children, but only nine survived infancy. He succeeded his father as sheriff of the Ste. Genevieve district in 1805.

A year later, Dodge made an effort to join Aaron Burr's (1756–1836) band of adventurers in a mysterious expedition down the Mississippi River. Burr's objectives remain unclear, but Dodge seems to have believed that he was off to conquer Mexico. President Thomas Jefferson thought otherwise, and Burr was arrested and tried for treason. Dodge returned to Ste. Genevieve to find that he was under threat of indictment by a grand jury. It has been alleged that Dodge soundly whipped nine of the jurors and that after this confrontation, the jury was "persuaded" that no further action was necessary.

Apparently Dodge's association with Burr did not adversely affect his reputation. He continued to serve as sheriff for sixteen years and then was appointed U.S. marshal for the territory of Missouri by President James Madison (1751–1836). During the War of 1812, Dodge enlisted in the Missouri militia and rose quickly to the rank of brigadier general. The only action he saw was defending the settlers of Boone's Lick in northwestern Missouri, who were suffering from attacks by Indians. Dodge's militia unit routed the Indians and restored order.

After the war Dodge returned to Ste. Genevieve and his flourishing lead-mining business. By the 1820s, however, the miners around Ste. Genevieve found themselves in serious competition with the newly opened Fever River mines in northwestern Illinois. Hearing of the rich mining fields around Dodgeville, Wisconsin, then part of the Michigan Territory, Dodge moved his family to that region in 1827. Shortly after he settled in the area, a series of conflicts between the Indians and whites erupted into war, and Dodge became the commander of a mounted volunteer force that fought in both the Winnebago War of 1827 and the Black Hawk War of 1832.

In the Black Hawk War, Dodge fought a number of skirmishes, rescued captives from the Indians, and participated in the final destruction of the Black Hawk warriors at Bad Ax Creek, above Prairie du Chien. His role in these Indian wars brought him recognition as a local hero and an appointment by President Andrew Jackson as major of a battalion of mounted rangers recruited to patrol the frontier of the Upper Mississippi River Valley. In the following year (1833), Dodge became colonel of a regiment of dragoons that patrolled the Indian frontier from the upper waters of the Red River to the Rocky Mountains.

In 1836 Dodge was made governor of the newly formed territory of Wisconsin, which had been carved out of the old Michigan Territory and included what are now the states of Wisconsin, Minnesota, Iowa, and parts of the Dakotas. He was a straightforward frontiersman who wore pistols and a Bowie knife in his belt, even on civic occasions. When the land west of the Mississippi was separated from the Wisconsin Territory and organized as the territory of Iowa in 1838, Dodge continued as governor of Wisconsin. But in 1841, when the Democratic party lost the presidency, Dodge was removed from office. He was elected, however, as a delegate from the territory of Wisconsin to the U.S. Congress, serving until 1845. As a delegate he worked to maintain the tariff on the production of lead and voted in favor of bills designed to improve the harbors along the shores of Lake Michigan. In April 1845 Dodge was reappointed as territorial governor. When the Democratic party regained the presidency in 1846, he labored constantly during the next two years for statehood.

In 1848 Wisconsin became a state, and the legislature elected Dodge as one of its first senators. In the sectional Compromise of 1850, he supported the admission of California to the Union and the abolition of the slave trade in the District of Columbia, but voted against the Fugitive Slave Bill. Because he was instructed to do so by the Wisconsin legislature, he voted against the Kansas-Nebraska Act in 1854.

Although he consistently voted against slavery, Dodge did not participate in drafting any major pieces of legislation. The longest speech he gave in Congress would not fill a newspaper column. His biographer, Louis Pelzer writes, "He belongs . . . to that class of Senators who are industrious and capable, and who have regard for their oath of office in which they promise to perform their duties to the best of their abilities." Dodge retired from the U.S. Senate in 1857 and spent the last ten years of his life in his home in Wisconsin and in Burlington, Iowa, where he died.

• Most of the original material on Dodge consists of commissions, military order books, and letters in the History Department of the University of Iowa at Des Moines. There is one book-length biography of Dodge: Louis Pelzer, *Henry Dodge* (1911). In addition, there are two biographical sketches: James I. Clark, *Henry Dodge: Frontiersman* (1957); William Salter, "Henry Dodge," *Iowa Historical Record*, vols. 5 and 6 (Oct. 1889–Apr. 1890). For general histories of Wisconsin that also discuss Henry Dodge, see Robert Nesbit, *Wisconsin: A History*, 2d ed., updated by William F. Thompson (1973), and Richard N. Currant, *The Civil War Era, 1848–1873*, vol. 2 of *The History of Wisconsin* (1976).

MARGARET HORSNELL

DODGE, Henry Chee (1857?–7 Jan. 1947), Navajo political leader, was born in Fort Defiance, Arizona, the son of a Navajo woman of the Coyote Pass (Ma'iideshgizhnii) clan and, in all likelihood, Henry L. Dodge, an agent for the federal government. Although it has often been suggested that Dodge's father may have been a Hispanic man named Juan Cocinas, the conclusion by government agent William F. M. Arny, stationed at Fort Defiance, that Henry L. Dodge was indeed the parent of the young Navajo boy altered the course of Dodge's life. Dodge was orphaned at an early age. Although one of his mother's sisters looked after him for a time, agent Arny believed Dodge would be an ideal candidate for schooling. Here, he probably concluded, was a survivor—a boy of mixed descent who had made it through the trauma of the enforced incarceration of the Navajo people at Fort Sumner, New Mexico, as well as the difficulties of the Long Walk, as the forced march to Fort Sumner would become known. Unlike most Navajo children, Dodge would have access to education, and unique among his peers, he would develop fluency in English. Dodge took full advantage of his months of formal instruction at the Fort Defiance Indian School.

By the early 1880s Dodge's career as a translator, cultural broker, and leader was already under way. He worked for the federal government as an interpreter and assisted agency personnel in some challenging tasks, including the interrogation of Navajos suspected of crimes. His employment also gave him the chance to earn and to save money. In 1890 Dodge became a partner in the Round Rock (Ariz.) trading post; he also married his first wife, Asdzaa Tsi'naajinii, and started to own livestock and farm near Crystal, New Mexico. But he could not remain removed from Navajo political affairs. In 1892 Dodge,

as an agency employee, became involved in the celebrated Black Horse incident, which symbolized Navajo resistance to the compelled school attendance of their children. Black Horse and his followers had captured agent Dana L. Shipley, beaten him, and imprisoned him. Dodge's talents in both the Diné language and the English language and his familiarity with the cultural values of Navajo and American societies enabled him to defuse an explosive situation. Without Dodge's intervention, Shipley might have been killed. Dodge was able, however, to extricate Shipley without further harm being done to the agent.

Even though Dodge was willing to support federal personnel, he did not always do so. Although he recognized the need for his people to adapt and adjust to changing circumstances, he did not want the Navajos to do so at any price. He believed that the people should continue to speak Navajo language, even though English would also be a useful additional language. He also believed that attendance at a Christian church should not mean antagonistic relationships with traditional Navajo religious healers and that customary marital patterns could be continued. For example, after he divorced his first wife, Dodge remarried. As a number of prominent Navajo men did at this time, he now had not one wife but two, for his wife's sister also joined his household. When the well-known agent from Shiprock, New Mexico, William T. Shelton, tried to arrest a man from the tribe for having more than one wife, Dodge naturally objected. It is by no means clear how many women Dodge married or how many children these marriages produced. In the context of Navajo culture, such statistics were of secondary importance. Dodge was a wealthy man, capable of supporting a large family; he may have been the father of six children.

During the last decades of the nineteenth century and the first two decades of the twentieth century, in contrast to the experiences of most other Native American communities, the Navajo reservation expanded in size and enjoyed a period of economic growth. Urged on by government agents as well as traders whose posts now dotted the land, the Navajos substantially increased their livestock holdings, especially their flocks of sheep. Sheep had become central to the workings not only of the economy but of the culture itself, for the animals were used to feed people at religious or social gatherings, for wool to teach young girls how to weave, and for payment to religious leaders who presided over ceremonies. Dodge was one of many Diné who profited personally from this period of economic expansion. His lands and livestock holdings increased. One who appreciated symbolism as much as utility, Dodge was among the first Navajos to purchase an automobile. He liked his Buick not only for the impression it gave but also for its assistance in getting him over the rugged Colorado Plateau terrain.

By the beginning of the 1920s Dodge had become the most prominent Navajo man of his time; yet political leadership remained largely local rather than tribal. Particularly in the northeastern portion of the reservation, around greater Shiprock, New Mexico, people were more concerned about their immediate area than the development of the entire Navajo reservation. The discovery of oil deposits in this area fueled the need for a Navajo political entity that could authorize exploration and drilling. No such body existed. Dodge and two other men, Charley Mitchell and Dugal Chee Bekiss, gained authority in 1922 to serve as this initial council. Jacob C. Morgan soon challenged the leadership that Dodge attempted to assert. The product of Hampton Institute in Virginia and a conservative Christian in his religious beliefs, Morgan represented not only northern New Mexico but a different attitude about social and cultural change. Dodge's association with another part of the reservation and his friendship with the Franciscan fathers at St. Michael's mission in Arizona did not endear him to Morgan or his followers.

Dodge did not embrace assimilation as did Morgan, and he was far more willing to serve as a cultural broker. Older than Morgan, he saw the need for a slower transition to the demands of the outside Anglo-American culture; he also felt more at home in the most rural reaches of Navajo country. Dodge had the generosity of spirit that at times accompanies a person of wealth; he expected the best of white ministers, traders, and government officials and was not always disappointed by their behavior. Morgan was more suspicious of outsiders and less at home in the workings of internal Navajo society. Although he would champion the rights of the average rural Navajo and take advantage politically of Navajo resentment over any federal interference in their lives, Morgan felt more at home with others of his tribe who had been away to school and who had adopted some of the trappings of contemporary American society.

The 1920s brought not only oil but an escalating concern over the condition of the Navajo range. Even before the selection of John Collier as commissioner of Indian affairs in 1933, Navajos had been told that they held too many sheep and that their sheep and other livestock were responsible for overgrazing the land. During the era of the Dust Bowl, Navajo soil erosion was cause for concern. Although Collier was more sympathetic to many elements of Navajo culture than past commissioners had been, he and his associates sought to reduce rapidly and significantly the numbers of sheep, goats, horses, and cattle owned by the people. This effort at livestock reduction turned Navajo political life into a maelstrom.

Dodge was in his seventies during the New Deal era, but his status had not diminished. If anything, age brought him increased respect within a society that associated increased years with accumulated wisdom. Thus, although he had stepped somewhat aside from a position of leadership in the late 1920s, in part to allow for the growth of his son Thomas's career, the events of the following decade did not allow him the luxury of distance from the Navajo political scene. Dodge was centrally involved in the heated debates over livestock reduction and the Indian Reorganization Act of 1934.

As an owner of large numbers of stock, Dodge represented the views of wealthy Navajos who understood the need to cull their herds and had the number of livestock that made such a process less financially damaging. Morgan sided with the more sizable ranks for Navajos who owned smaller numbers of stock and for whom the prospect of livestock reduction proved more problematic. Although Morgan remained unsympathetic to traditional Navajo culture, he recognized the issue for its political worth and exploited it at every turn. Both men had their doubts about the Indian Reorganization Act, which among other features attempted to create tribal constitutions and more formal tribal governments. Morgan opposed it without hesitation. Dodge recognized the need for a stronger and more cohesive reservationwide approach to Navajo issues. At the same time, as the difficulties with livestock reduction became more apparent, he became more uncertain about supporting something Collier backed. In the end, Navajo voters gave the act a narrow defeat at the polls. Morgan became chairman of the tribal council in 1937, but he was more effective as a critic of Dodge than as a political leader. Dodge succeeded him as chairman in 1941, a position he would hold until his death.

Before his death Dodge witnessed the gradual ending of the livestock reduction program and the gradual rise of tribal rather than exclusively local allegiances. Even though the Navajos had rejected the act, they had tried to move forward in efforts to create a government of their own that would be more responsive to their needs. The Second World War no doubt hastened the popular understanding for more access to formal schooling for Navajo children and for a stronger tribal government to defend Diné interest, a feeling that had been awakened by the excruciating years of livestock reduction. Returning veterans and others who had worked in war-related industries had come to appreciate what Dodge had preached all along: the need for more education, for more effective political representation of Navajo interests, and for a flexible approach to the demands of the present. In his long life and career, Dodge had symbolized both the need for constructive, incorporative change and the ability of the Navajos to make such changes. With the war over and livestock reduction coming to an end, at the time of Dodge's death the Navajos looked once again to the future with a greater degree of optimism. Many have acknowledged the central role that Dodge played in helping the people survive as Navajos, with a distinct identity and the largest population and land base of any Indian community in the United States.

• There is no collection of Dodge's papers. The best single source on Dodge is the essay by David M. Brugge, "Henry Chee Dodge: From the Long Walk to Self-Determination," in *Indian Lives: Essays on Nineteenth- and Twentieth-Century Native American Leaders*, ed. L. G. Moses and Raymond Wilson (1985). For a discussion of Dodge in the larger context of Navajo politics and society, see Robert W. Young, *A Political History of the Navajo Tribe* (1978), and Peter Iverson, *The Navajo Nation* (1981). Donald L. Parman, *The Navajos and the New Deal* (1976), offers information about Dodge during the turbulent years of the 1930s and 1940s.

PETER IVERSON

DODGE, Horace Elgin. *See* Dodge, John Francis, and Horace Elgin Dodge.

DODGE, John Francis (25 Oct. 1864–14 Jan. 1920), and **Horace Elgin Dodge** (17 May 1868–10 Dec. 1920), automobile manufacturers, were born in Niles, Michigan, the sons of Daniel Rugg Dodge and Maria Casto. Daniel Dodge operated a foundry and machine shop near the St. Joseph River, and as children John and Horace worked there, becoming familiar with marine engines and learning mechanical skills that later built their reputation and fortune in the automobile business. From early childhood the two brothers forged a close relationship that endured throughout their lives. John was very outgoing, while Horace was a more private individual.

The family subsequently moved to Port Huron, Michigan. Horace, who never finished high school but was the more mechanically gifted of the two brothers (as well as an accomplished, self-taught musician), worked with John and their father for the Upton Manufacturing Company, makers of farm machinery. In 1886 the family moved to Detroit, and John and Horace found work at Tom Murphy's Boiler Shop, building boilers and repairing boats. The brothers worked there for six years and then moved to Windsor, Ontario, Canada, where they made bicycles for the Dominion Topography Company. There John and Horace gained proficiency at working with precision tools such as micrometers and calipers; they also developed their first mechanical invention, a dirt-proof, easily adjustable ball bearing for bicycles.

In 1892 John married Ivy Hawkins, a Canadian-born dressmaker. They had one son and two daughters. Ivy died of tuberculosis in 1902. In 1896 Horace married Christina Anna Thompson, a Scottish-born piano teacher. They also had one son and two daughters.

The Dodge brothers briefly took over the Dominion Topography Company in 1897, but it soon went bankrupt. They moved to Detroit and, using machinery from the Dominion operation, set up their own shop. Their business received a tremendous boost when carmaker Ransom Olds, who had formed the first automobile company in Michigan, asked them to make 3,000 transmissions for him, an unusually large order for that day. The Dodge Brothers' business expanded, and in 1902 they moved into a new, three-story plant and hired more workers. John and Horace were fiercely industrious machinists, often laboring up to twenty hours a day, working well into the night and sleeping on benches at their factory so as to begin work at 6 A.M. They showed an unflinching determination to succeed in a blue-collar city crowded with competing machine shops.

Automaker Henry Ford gave the Dodge Brothers a big business opportunity when he approached them with plans for a new car. Horace redesigned the car, and by late 1902 the brothers had produced a working prototype for Ford. The following year the Dodge Brothers took a business gamble by abandoning their lucrative work for Ransom Olds and signing a contract with Henry Ford to produce 650 chassis that included engines, transmissions, frames, and axles. These chassis formed the basis for the two-cylinder, eight-horsepower Ford Model A, the enormous success of which helped the Dodge Brothers to recover the costs they had incurred in retooling and hiring new employees to produce the Ford chassis. By 1903 they had 150 employees and had enlarged their assembly building. But later that year, when Ford failed to pay John and Horace, the brothers instead each received fifty shares of the newly formed Ford Motor Company (FMC), pursuant to a contract clause that stipulated that Ford's assets would be surrendered to the Dodge Brothers if Ford failed to make payments. As the value of the FMC stock appreciated, John and Horace received thousands of dollars in dividends. John became vice president of FMC in 1907.

In 1903 John married his housekeeper, Isabelle Smith, who had been caring for John's three children after the death of his first wife. This unhappy union was largely a marriage of convenience, since Isabelle was living in John's home and effectively ran the house, and John wanted the marriage kept sub rosa. The wedding ceremony was small, and even after their marriage he referred to Isabelle only as "my housekeeper." In reality, John was deeply in love with his secretary, Canadian-born Matilda Rausch, who was eighteen years his junior. Isabelle moved out of John's house after they had been married just over one year, but she refused to divorce him, believing that his feelings for Matilda would attenuate. They did not, and in 1907 John finally convinced Isabelle to agree to a divorce, which was kept a secret. Later that same year John and Matilda were married. They had one son and two daughters.

The Dodge Brothers manufactured parts for new Ford models, and FMC was enjoying prosperous business, especially after the introduction of the revolutionary Model T in 1908. The Dodge Brothers continued to receive enormous payments in dividends, which by 1910 grew to $200,000, and by 1913 to over $1 million. Still, the brothers were dissatisfied. They felt that Ford owed them more in dividends and underpaid them for the parts that they were supplying to him. They were also troubled by Ford's lack of loyalty to his business associates; moreover, as Ford was their sole customer, the Dodge Brothers worried that FMC might someday face a business decline or develop on its own the parts that the Dodge Brothers supplied.

These concerns led John and Horace to lay plans to manufacture their own car. They already owned the best-equipped machine plant in Detroit, and in 1910 they began construction of a new, 5.1 million-square-foot plant in Hamtramck, Michigan. In 1913 the brothers gave their required one-year notice to Ford that they would terminate their contract with him and subsequently announced plans to begin production of their own car the next year. They incorporated their new firm in 1914. John was the president of the new company, largely in charge of business affairs, and Horace, the vice president, supervising mechanical operations. The two brothers formed an indivisible team and even refused to answer mail if the "B" in Dodge Brothers was not capitalized; they saw the capital "B" as emphasizing the closeness and permanence of their relationship. To accommodate their new production plans, the Dodge Brothers added new buildings to their factory and increased their workforce from 2,000 in 1913 to 7,000 by 1915.

The Dodge Brothers built a four-cylinder touring car. Horace, having decades of experience with mechanical work, designed a highly efficient engine. The car had several distinctive features, including an all-steel body, appearing at a time when wooden coachwork was the industry standard; a dynastarter unit that restarted the car automatically in case it stalled with the ignition on; and an advanced air-pump system to bring gasoline forward to the carburetor that enabled the car to climb steep hills at a time when many Model T Fords had to use the reverse gear and back up hills. The Dodge Brothers also adopted the innovative policy of adding improvements to their car at any time, rather than waiting for a new model year. Dependability and durability were key selling points for their vehicles, and John and Horace conducted crash tests, extensive track tests, and special tire tests that involved rolling tires from the roof of their factory. The Dodge Brothers, who enjoyed a reputation as the best mechanics in Michigan and as the men responsible for Henry Ford's success, had no trouble in generating interest in their cars and in attracting dealerships. Before the first Dodge car was even produced, 22,000 firms applied for Dodge dealerships.

The rise of the new Dodge Company was meteoric. In November 1914 the first Dodge car rolled out of their factory. The Dodge Brothers produced 45,000 cars in 1915; 124,000 in 1917. At just $785, the car was an immediate consumer hit, and the Dodge factory could not keep pace with demand. In 1915 the Dodge Brothers introduced a two-passenger roadster. The following year the company secured a contract with the government, and General George Patton used Dodge cars in his raids in Mexico against Pancho Villa, who also adopted a Dodge car for his use; the vehicles handled admirably in the difficult Mexican terrain. By 1916 the Dodge factory had expanded to encompass seventy-two acres of factory floor space, and the assembly lines there included many of Horace's inventions that streamlined production to the point that it took only two hours and thirty-five minutes to assemble a Dodge car. They were the fourth-largest automaker in the United States and, having produced 100,000 cars by the end of 1916, had set a record for the volume of cars manufactured in a two-year period.

But the Dodge Brothers' success bred resentment from Henry Ford. Believing that his new competition had used profits from his company to underwrite their success, Ford stopped paying dividends to the Dodge Brothers and also cut his own car prices by $80 to make them more competitive. The Dodge Brothers were furious, because they had indeed been counting on continued dividend payments to help underwrite their business expansion. They also believed that Ford's plans for plant expansions would drain FMC dividends. They decided to sue Ford to force him to distribute three-quarters of his company's retained earnings as dividends. In 1916 they received a court order demanding distribution of Ford's retained earnings and preventing him from proceeding with his River Rouge plant expansion. The celebrated 1917 trial eventually produced a verdict favorable to the Dodge Brothers that ordered Ford to distribute $19 million to stockholders immediately (of which the Dodge Brothers received $2 million), forced him to continue to make annual disbursements of retained earnings, and additionally barred him from some planned expansions. In 1919 John and Horace sold their remaining FMC shares back to Ford for $25 million.

During World War I the Dodge Brothers conducted considerable business with the U.S. government. Fiercely patriotic, in March 1918 they completed a $10 million munitions plant built to manufacture a recoil mechanism for howitzers designed to prevent the gun from ripping apart when fired. The government also used the Dodge touring car as a standard army vehicle in Europe and adopted a new Dodge truck for military service. Additionally, the government ordered Dodge trucks for use as ambulances. In 1919 the Dodge company began producing its first all-steel, four-door sedan, which came with velvet upholstery. By 1920 the Dodge company hit its meridian, becoming the second-largest automaker in America; it employed 18,000 workers and produced 625 cars daily.

The spectacular success that the Dodge Brothers achieved in their automotive work—even before they launched their own company—allowed them to enjoy lives of opulence. In 1910 Horace moved into a mansion in the affluent Detroit suburb of Grosse Pointe; his home had a dock that overlooked Lake St. Clair, and Horace enjoyed watching the boats sailing the lake. He designed a 100-foot diesel steam yacht, the *Hornet II*, which he acquired in 1910. He donated another yacht, the 180-foot *Nokomis I*, to the government during World War I for use as a submarine chaser and had naval architects build a new 243-foot yacht, the *Nokomis II*, in 1917.

John owned a home on East Boston Boulevard in Detroit as well as a country estate, "Meadow Brook Farm," that sat on more than 300 acres near Rochester, Michigan. In 1919 he began planning a palatial mansion in Grosse Pointe that was to have 110 rooms, twenty-four baths, a ballroom, and an indoor swimming pool. But in January 1920, while in New York City for the National Automobile Show, both Horace and John contracted influenza. While Horace recovered, John developed pneumonia and died at his hotel. (John's unfinished Grosse Pointe mansion was eventually demolished in the 1940s.)

Horace was devastated by the death of his brother and lifelong business partner. His strength sapped by this loss and by his illness, he spent the balance of the winter of 1920 in Palm Beach, Florida, with his wife Anna. Later in the year she persuaded him to buy a Spanish villa in Palm Beach. In the months after the double blows of influenza and the death of his brother, Horace—who was now president and treasurer of the Dodge company—occasionally visited the plant. But John's death had left Horace's interest in the business bloodless, and he left the bulk of his work to his assistants. In November 1920 Horace died of cirrhosis of the liver in Palm Beach. The brothers who had forged an inseparable bond in life died just eleven months apart.

Apart from their fame as machinists and later as automobile manufacturers, the Dodge Brothers were known for their volatile tempers and sometimes fractious behavior. Respiratory problems that included a bout with tuberculosis had led John to drink whiskey as a remedy, and Horace obligingly followed. Both men possessed powerful, husky frames and surly, blunt-spoken personalities that made them well-suited not only for manufacturing work but also for barroom brawls. Raucous incidents during their long weekend evenings in saloons grew notorious. Horace once punched a man who snickered as he labored to crank-start his car. John forced a bar owner at gunpoint to dance on a table, then threw glasses at the bar mirror in applause. In a particularly appalling display of brutality, John and another man beat a handicapped attorney during a bar fight. Both John and the other man were arrested and released on bail, and John settled the lawsuit that followed by paying a substantial sum.

While these incidents earned the Dodge Brothers some opprobrium in the Detroit community, John and Horace also were noted philanthropists and popular company leaders among their workers. The two men showed concern for their employees by, for example, installing a medical clinic in their Hamtramck factory and supplying sandwiches and free beer during morning and afternoon work breaks. The brothers, especially Horace, were also generous supporters of the Detroit Symphony Orchestra, which attended Horace's funeral in toto and later gave a concert in his memory. Horace also donated $50,000 to the Good Samaritan Hospital in Palm Beach to establish an isolation building for patients with contagious diseases. The Dodge Brothers also returned to their hometown of Niles every year and gave private financial help to needy residents.

After the death of the Dodge Brothers in 1920, ownership of the company passed to their widows. In 1925 the New York banking firm of Dillon, Read and Company bought the business, but badly mismanaged it. In 1928 the Chrysler Corporation bought the concern, and it enabled Chrysler to become one of the "Big Three" automobile manufacturers. Walter P. Chrysler later said that the greatest thing he ever did was to buy the Dodge company.

• The National Automotive History Collection of the Detroit Public Library maintains files on both John and Horace Dodge. Two biographies are by Jean Maddern Pitrone, *Tangled Web: Legacy of Auto Pioneer John F. Dodge* (1989) and *The John Dodge Story* (1978). Another biography is Pitrone and Joan Potter Elwart, *The Dodges: The Auto Family Fortune and Misfortune* (1981). An essay on the Dodge Brothers by Pitrone is in *Dodge Brothers/Budd Country Historical Photo Album*, ed. John Velliky (1992). Information on the Dodge Brothers' business relationship with Henry Ford is in Allan Nevins and Frank Ernest Hill, *Ford: Expansion and Challenge, 1915–1933* (1957). Obituaries for John and Horace are in the *New York Times*, 15 Jan. and 11 Dec. 1920, respectively.

YANEK MIECZKOWSKI

DODGE, John Wood (4 Nov. 1807–15 Dec. 1893), portrait miniature painter, was born in New York City, the son of John Dodge, a goldsmith and watchmaker, and his Canadian-born wife, Margaret Wood. He was apprenticed to a sign and overmantel painter. He "conceived a desire to pursue some higher branch of art" and found that he had an aptitude for copying portrait miniatures. After his apprenticeship he rented a studio and began work as a miniature painter. He had no formal training but in 1826–1827 practiced drawing from casts at the National Academy of Design. He first exhibited there in 1830 and thereafter annually through 1838. On 10 May 1832 he was notified of his election as an associate member. His exhibition piece was of his wife, Mary Louise Dodge, a cousin whom he had married in 1831 and with whom he had eight children.

In 1828, the first year of his surviving account book, he earned $393 painting forty-five miniatures. He was paid, sometimes, in kind: a pair of boots and once (in 1831) "By Pugilism." By 1835 his income had grown to $1,875 for just forty-two miniatures.

In 1838 Dodge went south for the winter because of his health. He was admired by contemporaries, including William Dunlap, who in the *History of the Rise and Progress of the Arts of Design in the United States* praised Dodge as "among the prominent professors of the art [of miniature painting] in New York" (vol. 3, p. 254). The portraitist Charles Ingham said only one or two miniaturists could compare with Dodge.

Dodge rented a studio in Huntsville, Alabama, and advertised "A Rare Opportunity," in the *Huntsville Democrat* in February and March 1839, stating "that all pictures coming from his hands shall be equal to any painted in the U.S." The Posey family drummed up business for him. That year he earned $2,529 for forty-two miniatures, and his cough improved greatly. He spent the spring and summer of 1839 in Marietta, Ohio, where a brother lived, and where his wife joined him. He returned to Huntsville during the winter of 1839–1840 but determined it was too small to be his permanent residence. Dodge arrived in Nashville,

Tennessee, in May 1840 and was welcomed effusively in the newspapers. He did a specimen piece for the Reverend Robert Boyt C. Howell, pastor of Nashville Baptist Church, who praised it in the *Baptist Banner*, a denominational paper published in Louisville, Kentucky.

Dodge's studio was on Union Street. He again accepted diverse methods of payment, including "By violin and cash" from William Edward West, another artist, and by dental work for his wife, from another subject. In 1841 he also made trips to St. Louis and Harrodsburg Springs, Kentucky, a resort. In Nashville he painted in the 1840s Governor James C. Jones and Governor Aaron V. Brown; Dr. Philip Lindsley, president of the University of Nashville; and various relations of Andrew Jackson. In 1842 he painted Jackson himself. The sitting began on 15 March 1842, Jackson's seventy-fifth birthday. It was completed three weeks later. The six-inch-square miniature on ivory is unlocated, but a reduced version is at the Tennessee State Museum. On 28 April 1842 Jackson wrote to Dodge, "I have heard many of those long and best acquainted with me observe that this is the best and most perfect [likeness] of any they have seen of me" (Dodge's manuscript autobiography, Archives of American Art).

Backed by Jackson's testimonial, Dodge exhibited the portrait at the Library of Congress, then in the Capitol. Dodge paid New York engraver Mosley I. Danforth $570 to engrave a plate from the miniature. By March 1843 the plate was ready, and impressions sold briskly at $2 each. The New York *Plebian* said, "No Democrat should be without this portrait in his house."

Dodge was a Whig, however, and appealed to Tennessee party leaders to persuade Whig presidential candidate Henry Clay of Kentucky to sit for a portrait. Dodge wrote, "Your politics are undoubtedly a recommendation to me," but Clay was reluctant, believing his head and face hard to depict sympathetically. But in June 1843 he sat for Dodge at Brennan's Hotel in Lexington. Clay was quite pleased with the result (National Museum of American History, Smithsonian Institution). He also did a cabinet-size oil of Clay that was engraved by Francis D'Avignon.

Dodge stayed in New York City during much of 1843 and 1844. Then, to improve his health, he and his wife visited Mexico before returning to Nashville.

In 1846 Dodge purchased 5,000 acres, which he named "Pomona Fruit Ranch," in Cumberland Mountain, approximately 150 miles east of Nashville. To pay for his estate he collaborated with Thomas Jefferson Odell on four dioramas (such as "Interior of St. Peter's Church, Rome") that he exhibited in Nashville, Memphis, Louisville, New York, and Hartford.

In December 1848 he visited Natchez, painting Varina Howell, later the wife of Jefferson Davis (National Portrait Gallery, Smithsonian Institution). He sold his dioramas in New Orleans, returned to Nashville, and again was in Natchez from December 1849 to April 1850. Most of the rest of 1850 Dodge spent at Pomona; he painted miniatures in Nashville during the winter only. By this time the realistic depictions offered by photography were reducing the demand for miniatures, and in the 1850s Dodge began coloring photographs taken by a hired assistant.

Dodge lived in St. Louis for two years and spent much of 1854 in Huntsville, Alabama. During most of the 1850s, however, he was occupied developing his orchards at Pomona. In 1857 his name appeared in the Nashville city directory as "horticulturalist." Three times his apples won prizes at the state fair.

In June 1861 Tennessee voted to secede. The Dodges were outspoken Unionists, and Dodge was threatened if he did not leave Tennessee. The family made their way to Ohio, where they sold their wagons for passage to New York City. There Dodge opened a studio in November 1861, mostly taking photographs. President Andrew Johnson sat for Dodge in May 1865, and Dodge produced and sold a photographic portrait of him. In the late 1860s Dodge moved to Chicago. He became a member of the Chicago Academy of Design after 1871 and served as vice president in 1874–1875. He showed miniatures at the academy, but mostly he painted large oils and colored photographs. In 1873 his watercolor of *Washington after Houdon's Cast* was displayed at the Chicago Interstate Industrial Exposition. In 1878 he painted ASPCA founder Henry Berge.

Dodge returned to his orchards in Pomona in 1889. There he retouched and made a copy of his 1849 miniature of Varina Davis at her request. By this time Dodge was nearly deaf, but his eyesight was unimpaired. He painted miniatures, portraits, landscapes, and still lifes almost until the time of his death in Pomona. His career after the Civil War was unremarkable, but during the 1840s and 1850s he was one of America's premier miniaturists.

• Film 960 at the Archives of American Art, Smithsonian Institution, contains Dodge's account book, book of recommendations, manuscript autobiography, business letters, and a manuscript biography by the Reverend James McNeilly (1908). Dodge's family papers have been made available to the author by Leonard Mee, Santa Rosa, Calif. Other sources are James C. Kelly, "John Wood Dodge, Miniature Painter," *American Art Review* 6, no. 4 (1994): 98–103, 160; Anne Elliott, "A Master of Miniatures," *Southern Woman's Magazine*, Jan. 1917; Frances R. Summers, "John Wood Dodge, Miniaturist" (unpublished typescript, Alabama Department of Archives and History); and Edgar B. Chesnutt, "Miniature beyond the Grave," *Chattanooga Sunday Times*, 8 Apr. 1934. An obituary is in the *New York Times*, 31 Dec. 1893.

JAMES C. KELLY

DODGE, Josephine Marshall Jewell (11 Feb. 1855–6 Mar. 1928), leader in the day-nursery movement and antisuffragist, was born in Hartford, Connecticut, the daughter of Marshall Jewell, a successful businessman, and Esther Dickinson, an early suffragist. Her father was elected governor of Connecticut three times and was appointed by President Grant to be ambassador to Russia and then U.S. postmaster general. Josephine attended Vassar College from 1870 to 1873. In 1875 she married Arthur Murray Dodge, a New York businessman from a family known for its wealth and Christian philanthropies. They had six children. Whereas Arthur's niece, Grace Hoadley Dodge, committed herself to the well-being of "working girls," Josephine Dodge joined the "day-nursery" movement, which, following the lead of the Parisian crèches, sought to provide daycare for the children of women who were obliged to work outside the home. By 1888, when she founded the Jewell Day Nursery, Dodge had come to believe that the day nursery might provide children with the "mothering" they would otherwise miss, at the same time that it instilled in the children patience, ambition, industry, and religious devotion. With an abiding faith in organization, Dodge in 1895 formed and presided over the Association of Day Nurseries of New York City; in 1898 she helped form—and for many years actively supported—the National Federation of Day Nurseries. At her death, a writer on the *New York World* asserted that "to mention day nurseries is to invoke the memory of Mrs. Dodge."

Dodge did not consider that her strenuous advocacy of the right sort of day nurseries involved women in "politics," which, in her view, dealt with political and economic advantage. Men were suited for politics; women had higher "civic responsibilities." Dodge saw no reason to doubt that the male political powers-that-be would listen dutifully to the admonitions of the right sort of women. As evidence pointed to the enlightened social laws passed by states like Massachusetts, where women could not vote but seemed to exercise a decisive influence for the good in public affairs. Through the last years of the nineteenth century, Dodge remained largely uninterested in the campaign for woman suffrage, satisfied that there had never been a time of greater opportunity for "women of judgment and energy" to help promote the public welfare.

In the early twentieth century, as both the proponents and opponents of woman suffrage intensified their efforts, heightened their rhetoric, and radicalized their tactics, Dodge came to believe that the suffrage movement was not only unnecessary but that it was dangerous. With its reckless disregard for conventions, it played, she argued, into the hands of socialists and populists intent on social revolution, encouraging women to forget their primary obligations to home and family; it demeaned the whole sex. In the face of such dangers Dodge felt obliged, despite her aversion to public controversy, to engage—only "temporarily," she profoundly hoped—in the politics true women instinctively eschewed.

In 1911 the National Association Opposed to Woman Suffrage (NAOWS) was organized in her home. As president, she edited the *Woman's Protest*, a journal designed to rebut every destructive proposal and ridicule every inanity perpetrated by the suffragists. She campaigned in many states that were considering woman suffrage. She testified before congressional committees, and she wrote articles. At every opportu-

nity she insisted on two intrinsically political points: first, that the NAOWS was *not* a small coterie of specially favored, upper-class women, but it included many working-class and professional women; second, that most women, though they naturally chose not to join publicly the battle over suffrage, much preferred not to have the suffrage thrust on them. The NAOWS, Dodge protested, spoke for a sex, not for a class.

By 1917 a great many states had committed themselves to woman suffrage. With the only remaining question being whether Congress would endorse a constitutional amendment, Dodge turned over the leadership of NAOWS to women in Washington, D.C. She resumed her work with the day-nursery movement, supported the Welfare Council of New York, the Public Education Association, and the National Civic Federation.

Her husband had died in 1896, and she spent an increasing amount of time with her sons. She died in Cannes, France.

Throughout her life Dodge tried to fulfill the public obligations incumbent on a woman of education and social standing. Though her antisuffragism proved to be an anachronistic battle to protect women from the corruption of "politics," her sense of the need to provide city children with daycare that was nurturing, not just custodial, anticipated a central concern of future generations of working women.

• Dodge's papers have not been collected. The fullest bibliography of her writings is given by Jane Jerome Camhi, "Women against Women: American Antisuffragism, 1800–1920" (Ph.D. diss., Tufts Univ., 1973). Dodge contributed regularly to the *Woman's Protest* from 1911 to 1917. Her visceral distaste for suffragists is revealed in a letter to the *New York Times*, 12 Mar. 1913. Her "Woman Suffrage Opposed to Woman's Rights" appeared in the *Annals of the American Academy of Political and Social Science* 56 (Nov. 1914): 99–104. Dodge's early "child-saving" work is placed in context in Margaret O'Brien Steinfels, *Who's Minding the Children? The History and Politics of Day Care in America* (1973), and Susan Tiffin, *In Whose Best Interest? Child Welfare Reform in the Progressive Era* (1982). The rationale of antisuffragism is nicely developed in Aileen S. Kraditor, *The Ideas of the Woman Suffrage Movement, 1890–1920* (1965). Anne M. Benjamin, *A History of the Anti-Suffrage Movement in the United States from 1895 to 1920* (1991), is exhaustive but too easily scornful of antisuffragists like Dodge. An obituary is in the *New York Times*, 7 Mar. 1928.

ROBERT D. CROSS

DODGE, Joseph Morrell (18 Nov. 1890–2 Dec. 1964), banker and government financial official, was born in Detroit, Michigan, the son of Joseph Cheeseman Dodge, an artist, and Gertrude Hester Crow. After graduating from Central High School in Detroit in 1908, Dodge became a clerk for the Standard Accident Insurance Company. In 1909 he joined the Central Savings Bank, where he advanced from messenger to general bookkeeper. After brief employment as an accountant, Dodge spent five years beginning in 1911 as a bank and securities examiner for the state of Michigan. He then went to work for the Bank of Detroit as an operating officer in 1916. In that same year he married Julia Jane Jeffers, and they had one son.

Dodge moved into sales in 1917, when he became vice president and general manager of the Thomas J. Doyle Company, which marketed automobiles. Dodge resigned in 1932 because of the company's financial difficulties arising from the Great Depression. He then joined the First National Bank, which failed during the national banking crisis in early 1933. As vice president, Dodge helped organize the National Bank of Detroit, which incorporated assets from the First National. He then became president of the Detroit Bank in December 1933, a position he held until January 1953.

During World War II, Dodge served as a price adjuster, monitoring defense contractors for price gouging and profiteering. He worked in that capacity first for the Army Air Forces (1942–1943) and then briefly for the War Department (1943) before chairing the War Contracts Price Adjustment Board (1943–1944), which regulated the costs of defense procurement for six federal agencies, including the armed services.

Dodge made his first trip outside the United States in August 1945, when he went to Berlin as financial adviser to the U.S. military government in Germany. His first important achievement in Germany was a reorganization of the banking system, which went into effect in the U.S. occupation zone in 1947. His other noteworthy accomplishment was a plan for the stabilization of the German currency. Delayed for two years by disagreements among the occupying powers, the currency reform was only partially implemented in the British, French, and U.S. zones in June 1948. The immediate effect of the new currency was to stimulate consumption by discouraging hoarding and bartering. This reform also precipitated the Berlin Blockade, since the Soviets considered it another step toward the consolidation of the western occupation zones into a state closely aligned with the West.

Dodge, however, had turned from German to Austrian affairs before the implementation of either the banking or currency reforms. In 1947 he became the U.S. representative to the Austrian Treaty Commission and also served as an adviser on Austrian matters at the London meeting of the Council of Foreign Ministers.

Dodge rendered his most significant government service by leading a U.S. mission in 1949 to revitalize the Japanese economy. The Dodge mission was a product of the "reverse course," a shift in U.S. occupation policy in Japan away from liberal reform (which included recognition of the equality of women, new laws supporting labor unions and the right to strike, and educational reform, among other changes) and the dismantling of big business and toward the reconstruction of industrial strength. Dodge recommended balancing Japan's national budget, establishing a single exchange rate for the yen, and expanding exports by shifting control of foreign trade from the government to private enterprise. This was harsh medicine, since it required the elimination of subsidies and preferences that cost both profits and jobs. Dodge insisted that such austerity was necessary to raise productivity so that Japanese industry could compete in foreign markets. The "Dodge Line" had mixed effects—the first postwar balanced budget and lower inflation but at the cost of increased unemployment, sluggish industrial growth, and widespread popular discontent. The Korean War, however, created an economic boom in Japan, the effects of which Dodge helped to channel. The results were higher exports, greater self-sufficiency, and closer alignment with the United States.

In January 1953 Dodge became President Dwight D. Eisenhower's director of the Bureau of the Budget. Like Eisenhower, Dodge gave high priority to curbing inflation by restraining government spending. He helped formulate a revised budget for fiscal year 1954 that reduced former president Harry S. Truman's projected deficit of $10 billion by almost half. Dodge achieved such results by requiring all government agencies to rank their proposed programs and then cutting low-priority spending. As Dodge explained, "This is something you do all the time in business. But the subtractive process had all but disappeared in the government until we restored it" (Sloan, p. 72). As the first budget director who was a member of the cabinet and the National Security Council, Dodge supported the New Look, the administration's effort to balance defense needs against the requirements of a healthy economy. Yet despite a $5 billion reduction in defense spending under the New Look, Dodge was unable to balance the fiscal 1955 federal budget, the last he prepared before resigning in March 1954.

After returning to the Detroit Bank as chairman, Dodge accepted several presidential appointments to government committees and advisory boards. He counseled Eisenhower on foreign economic policy during 1954–1956. After becoming chairman of the reorganized Detroit Bank and Trust Company in 1956, he served Eisenhower again as a member of the Special Committee to Study the Military Assistance Program (1958–1959) and as a consultant to the National Security Council (1959). His last public service was as treasurer of the Tractors for Freedom Committee (1961), which unsuccessfully tried to ransom the prisoners from the Bay of Pigs invasion in return for farm equipment. He died in Detroit.

Contemporaries admired Dodge for his organization, meticulousness, and fiscal orthodoxy. He adhered to a banker's conservative philosophy—a sound currency, balanced budget, and financial stability. He was a technical expert rather than a policy maker. While he was not an architect of the reverse course or the New Look, he designed economic and financial programs that made them a reality.

• Dodge's papers are in the Dwight D. Eisenhower Library, Abilene, Kans. His published works include *An Introduction to the Business of Management* (1939) and *Editorials on Our Changing Banking* (1941). There is no full biography, but a brief account of his life is in Duncan Norton-Taylor, "The Banker in the Budget Bureau," *Fortune*, Mar. 1953, pp. 136–44. For Dodge's contributions to German banking and currency reform, see Lucius D. Clay, *Decision in Germany* (1950), and John H. Backer, *Winds of History: The German Years of Lucius DuBignon Clay* (1983). The best discussion of Dodge's role in stabilizing the Japanese economy is in Howard B. Schonberger, *Aftermath of War: Americans and the Remaking of Japan, 1945–1952* (1989). Also valuable are Michael Schaller, *The American Occupation of Japan: The Origins of the Cold War in Asia* (1985), and Theodore Cohen, *Remaking Japan: The American Occupation as New Deal* (1987). For Dodge's service as budget director, see John W. Sloan, *Eisenhower and the Management of Prosperity* (1991); Iwan W. Morgan, *Eisenhower Versus "the Spenders": The Eisenhower Administration, the Democrats and the Budget, 1953–60* (1990); Larry Berman, *The Office of Management and Budget and the Presidency, 1921–1979* (1979); and Chester J. Pach, Jr., and Elmo Richardson, *The Presidency of Dwight D. Eisenhower*, rev. ed. (1991). An obituary is in the *New York Times*, 3 Dec. 1964.

CHESTER J. PACH, JR.

DODGE, Mary Abigail (31 Mar. 1833–17 Aug. 1896), best known as an author and journalist under the pseudonym Gail Hamilton, was born in Hamilton, Massachusetts, the daughter of James Brown Dodge, a farmer, and Hannah Stanwood. Abby Dodge, as she preferred friends to call her, entered the Congregational church in her early years and enjoyed a country childhood marred only by an accident that permanently injured one eye. As a daughter of a family belonging to the landed gentry, Dodge received one of the best educations possible for a girl of her day. She benefited from her mother's having been a schoolteacher before her marriage, and she attended the village school. At twelve she went to Cambridge for one year to attend a boarding school. The following year she moved to the Ipswich Female Seminary and graduated in 1850.

During her early working years, Dodge pursued the employment common to many unmarried New England women. She taught at the Ipswich school until 1854 before moving to the Hartford Female Seminary in Connecticut for one year. She ended her career in Hartford at the high school. Her notebooks and writings show that she was discouraged by the long hours of teaching and its low pay. She tried writing and sent some of her early essays to Gamaliel Bailey, editor of the antislavery *National Era*. In 1858 she went to Washington, D.C., as governess to Bailey's children but returned to Hamilton in 1860 to care for her mother. In the early 1870s, after her mother's death in 1868, Dodge began to winter in Washington with the family of her cousin Mrs. James G. Blaine.

Dodge's periods in Washington with the Bailey and Blaine families introduced her to various networks essential to her development as a writer and journalist. Bailey's *National Era* published many of the leading antislavery polemicists including Harriet Beecher Stowe. As Gail Hamilton, Dodge became a regular columnist for the *Independent*, and she contributed essays to the *Atlantic Monthly*. She used the pseudonym Cunctare for reports on the doings of Congress for the

Congregationalist. In the 1860s James T. Fields, whose firm Ticknor and Fields published well-known Boston and Cambridge authors including William Cullen Bryant, Oliver Wendell Holmes, Nathaniel Hawthorne, and Henry Wadsworth Longfellow, issued a collection of her essays. The success of *Country Living and Country Thinking* (1862) led to the publication of four more volumes in the 1860s. Soon Gail Hamilton could command a good price for her essays.

Dodge's concerns fall into that broad category known as New England reform. Hoping to free individuals from arbitrarily imposed restrictions that limited self-development, she opposed slavery, favored the Civil War, and hoped to improve the conditions under which working men and women labored. Besides these concerns, her predominant subject was women and reform of the domestic lives of wives and daughters in middle-class homes. Never an ardent proponent of woman suffrage, Dodge proposed that reform of women's domestic situation should precede that political innovation. Woman suffrage, she believed, could never break the barriers to self-development in most women's home lives.

In the home, Dodge wrote, women suffered under the yoke of too much housework, which often was more difficult than some men's work. She found all the detail of "ordinary woman-life" "wearisome and intolerable." A housewife, she observed, becomes a worn-out woman "shattered in nerves, health and temper." She wrote to her friend Henry James (1811–1882) that if she had married she "should be digging in the dark, down in a cellar where all the dead-alive women are." She saw that "bright and intellectual women" were buried "under the household ruins." A young woman with a husband intent on improving himself would find herself tied down "by the endless details of housekeeping and the nursery." Meanwhile he "reads and reasons" and "attends to business, by intercourse with intelligent people, by journeys, growth, and contact." She argued that wives needed similar opportunities for intellectual development and stimulation.

As a resident of the Blaine household, Dodge came into contact with important Republicans and Washington figures. She is reputed to have helped Blaine write his speeches and did assist with his memoirs *Twenty Years of Congress* (1884–1886). Like Blaine, Dodge opposed civil service reform. As Gail Hamilton, she contributed a major series of fifty articles on the subject to the *New York Tribune* in 1877 and 1878 in which she stated that reform would transform the civil service from the ideal form of public service that educated citizens (which she imagined had existed in the Hamilton of her childhood) to a preserve for career officeholders.

Dodge never acquired the fame of some of her writer friends such as John Greenleaf Whittier, Sara Parton (Fanny Fern), and Harriet Beecher Stowe. Her sentimental novel, *First Love Is Best: A Sentimental Sketch* (1877), was no blockbuster; her editing jobs and essay writing offered her a sure, steady income that she said kept her well stocked "in bread and but-ter and calicoes" but not in "furs and diamonds and laces." According to her obituary in the *New York Times*, Dodge gained a national audience "by reason of her witty and aggressive style." The development of her ideas remind us that not every nineteenth-century liberal made the transition from support of antislavery in the 1850s and 1860s to support of civil service re-form in the 1870s. As a reformer, Dodge remained true to the New England romanticism of her youth. She belongs to the first phase of nineteenth-century liberalism when reformers sought to break down the structures barring self-development. Dodge died at her family homestead in Hamilton.

• The most substantial manuscript collection for Mary Abi-gail Dodge is in the Essex Institute, Salem, Mass. Other col-lections are in the Clarke Historical Library, Central Mich-igan University, Mt. Pleasant, Mich.; the Library of Congress; the Sophia Smith Collection at Smith College, Northampton, Mass.; and the University of Virginia Library. Also see *Gail Hamilton's Life in Letters*, 2 vols., ed. H. Augus-ta Dodge (1901). There is no full-length biography. Informa-tive articles are Maurine Beasley, "Mary Abigail Dodge: 'Gail Hamilton' and the Process of Social Change," *Essex In-stitute Historical Collections* 116 (1980): 82–100, and Susan Coultrap-McQuin, "Gail Hamilton," *Legacy* 4 (1987): 53–58. Obituaries are in the *New York Times*, 18 Aug. 1896, and *Woman's Journal*, 22 Aug. 1896.

LOUISE L. STEVENSON

DODGE, Mary Elizabeth Mapes (26 Jan. 1831?–21 Aug. 1905), editor and author, was born in New York City, the daughter of James Jay Mapes, an agricultural reformer, and Sophia Furman. She and her siblings were educated at home, mainly by their father, a bril-liant but impecunious self-taught chemist, inventor, and publisher. In a home where intellectual endeavors were valued as highly as material goods, the Mapes children frequently encountered scientists, poets, mu-sicians, journalists, and statesmen, giving them access to a truly liberal education. Lizzie, as the young Mary Elizabeth was known, was an avid reader of English literature, and by her teens she was assisting her father in editorial duties.

In 1848 the family moved to a rundown farm on the outskirts of Newark, New Jersey. The farm purchase was financed with the help of a friend, a New York lawyer named William Dodge, whom Lizzie's father knew through a social club. In 1851 Lizzie Mapes married William Dodge and moved to New York City; they had two children. In 1858 William Dodge, with his finances in disarray and the health of his older son in question, disappeared from their home and was found several weeks later, drowned. His widow moved with her sons back to the family home in New Jersey.

Over the next decade Lizzie Dodge developed a suc-cessful writing career, contributing essays and stories to leading magazines and editing her father's publica-tion, the *United States Journal*. Her first full-length book, *The Irvington Stories*, was published in 1864,

followed by *Hans Brinker; or, The Silver Skates* at the end of 1865. *Hans Brinker*, one of the most successful children's books ever published, was printed in five languages and 100 editions during its first thirty years. It remains a popular classic of children's literature.

During this period Dodge developed many useful friendships in the literary community, from estab-lished figures like John Greenleaf Whittier and Horace Greeley, personal friends of her father, and Alice and Phoebe Cary, who held an influential New York liter-ary salon, to newcomers such as Horace Scudder and Richard Watson Gilder, who became important pub-lishers. These contacts became crucial to Dodge when her father died in 1866, leaving debts that she spent fifteen years paying off. She was the sole support not only of her two sons, who were approaching college age, but also of her mother and her two unmarried sis-ters. Despite the success of her freelance writing ca-reer, she needed a dependable income, so she turned to editing.

After a brief stint as associate editor of a short-lived magazine, *Hearth and Home*, in 1873 Dodge was asked by publisher Roswell Smith to found a new juvenile publication to be a companion to his firm's *Scribner's Monthly*. Dodge was a conscientious parent and had conducted voluminous correspondence with Horace Scudder on the need for a children's magazine that would not be simplistic, didactic, or bland, so she agreed to the project. Smith gave her complete control over the new journal, even to choosing its name, *St. Nicholas* (*SN*). Smith also gave her the full backing of the prosperous publishing house of Scribner's, includ-ing the services of its excellent art director, printer, and editorial staff, including J. T. Trowbridge and Tudor Jenks. Dodge was allowed to choose her own assistant editor; with an unerring eye for talent, she hired Frank Stockton, later one of the most popular novelists of the late nineteenth century. After his de-parture in 1878, she hired William Fayal Clarke, an equally talented young man, to replace him.

From its beginning *SN* was an unqualified success. It was created at a moment when the middle class was making itself felt as a cultural influence, and *SN* was middle class to its bones. Moreover, Dodge had a fine instinct for giving America's children what they want-ed—"a shade of grandiloquence—a little introducing of the heroic"—and never preaching or talking down to them, never "pouring the lees of our experience upon them in a stream of twaddle" (letters to Scudder, 23 July 1866 and 9 May 1867, Huntington Library). At the same time Dodge subtly inculcated the virtues of American Victorian morality—patriotism, dili-gence, thrift, prudence, neatness, honesty, and cour-age. Lawrence B. Fuller wrote that *St. Nicholas* taught "historical awareness, the importance of money and success for a happy life, the primacy of science and technology in modern Western civilization, and the cultural superiority of the Caucasian race, primarily of its northern European and North American branches. That *St. Nicholas* [presented] these themes in the guise of richly illustrated fiction, poetry and information suggests the likelihood that young readers assimilated the messages eagerly and unwittingly" ("Mary Mapes Dodge and *St. Nicholas*: The Magazine as Educator," M.A. thesis, Pennsylvania State Univ., 1983).

The magazine became a desirable market for writers and illustrators throughout the country. Dodge aggressively sought out the finest, while at the same time searching for undiscovered talent. Contributors included Joel Chandler Harris, Bret Harte, Robert Louis Stevenson, Rudyard Kipling, Jack London, Henry Wadsworth Longfellow, John Greenleaf Whittier, and Alfred Tennyson. Dodge wooed Louisa May Alcott away from *Youth's Companion*, *SN*'s biggest competitor, and serialized her *Eight Cousins* in *SN*. Mark Twain was persuaded to write a sequel to *Tom Sawyer* for its pages, and Frances Hodgson Burnett, at one time reduced to borrowing $30 from Dodge, made her first big triumph in the pages of *SN*, serializing her novel *Little Lord Fauntleroy*. Selma Lanes, in *Down the Rabbit Hole* (1971), says that *SN* "did as much to open up the unexplored hinterland of literature [for children] as the railroads did to open up the vast expanses of the West to their parents and grandparents."

Dodge was equally insistent on high standards of layout and illustration. "Pictures," she wrote in "Children's Magazines," "should be heartily conceived and well-executed. . . . If it be only the picture of a cat, it must be so like a cat that it will do its own purring and not sit a dead, stuffed thing, requiring the editor to purr for it." Contributing illustrators were the best to be found, including Howard Pyle, Frederic Remington, and Kate Greenaway. Almost more impressive is the list of children who contributed their juvenilia to the magazine's "St. Nicholas League" and who went on to become noted writers: Bennett Cerf, Edna St. Vincent Millay, Robert Benchley, Eudora Welty, Ring Lardner, Henry Steele Commager, Stephen Vincent Benet, and E. B. White.

Dodge directed *SN* for thirty-two years, leaving an indelible imprint on American juvenile publishing. She was still titular editor at the time of her death at Onteora, a literary community near Tannersville, New York, in the Catskills. Her policies were continued by William Fayal Clarke for another twenty-three years, and her legacy of excellence endured even beyond *SN*'s demise in the 1940s. The ephemeral nature of *SN* was mitigated by the fact that families could send in a year's run of issues and have them bound. These "red volumes" were placed on many household shelves and in many community libraries, where favorite stories, poems, and historical sketches could be reread by their original owners and enjoyed by future generations of readers. They remain on many shelves to this day, as a testimony to Dodge's editorial genius and as a lode of material to be mined by scholars of the history of American Victorian childhood.

• The main body of Dodge's papers is in the Princeton Library in four collections. A smaller collection is in the Alderman Library at the University of Virginia, and Dodge's voluminous correspondence with Horace Scudder is in the collection of his papers at the Huntington Library, San Marino, Calif. See Mary Mapes Dodge, "Children's Magazines," *Scribner's Monthly* 6 (July 1873): 352–54, for her philosophy of children's literature. Catherine Morris Wright, *Lady of the Silver Skates: The Life and Correspondence of Mary Mapes Dodge* (1979), is a comprehensive biography and is an important source of family memories, letters, and documents not found elsewhere. Susan R. Gannon and Ruth Anne Thompson, *Mary Mapes Dodge* (1992), provides a critical reading of Dodge's published works. See also Lucia Gilbert Runkle, "Mary Mapes Dodge," *Our Famous Women* (1884), for a personal memoir by a close friend. For information on Dodge's editorial abilities see Fred Raymond Erisman, "The Utopia of *St. Nicholas*: The Present as Prologue," *Children's Literature* 5 (1976): 66–73; Mary June Roggenbuck, "*St. Nicholas* Magazine: A Study of the Impact and Historical Influence of the Editorship of Mary Mapes Dodge" (Ph.D. diss., Univ. of Michigan, 1976); and Wright, "How *St. Nicholas* Got Rudyard Kipling and What Happened Then," *Princeton University Library Chronicle* 35 (Spring 1974): 254–89. Dodge's obituaries are in the *New York Times* and the *New York Tribune*, both 22 Aug. 1905.

MARY JANE HORSTMAN

DODGE, Raymond (20 Feb. 1871–8 Apr. 1942), psychologist, was born in Woburn, Massachusetts, the son of George Smith Dodge, an apothecary and Congregational minister, and Anna Pickering. Interested from an early age in mechanics, Dodge often experimented in the tool shed at the back of his father's yard, a hobby that later developed into the invention of scientific instruments. He attended Williams College, graduating in 1893 with an A.B. in philosophy. After graduating, Dodge worked briefly as an assistant librarian at Williams while saving money to fund his graduate work. In 1894 he traveled to the University of Halle in Germany to pursue a doctorate in philosophy, but while working with Benno Erdmann, a scholar whose interests included both philosophy and psychology, his focus shifted to psychology.

At the time, experimental psychology was just emerging as a field of study, growing out of practical investigations of traditional philosophic questions. Two events precipitated Dodge's change of focus. Erdmann told his student that he would probably not go far as a philosopher, and at the same time he expressed a pressing need for a new device that could control the length of time a stimulus was presented to a viewer. This need led to Dodge's first invention, the Erdmann-Dodge tachistoscope, a device that could expose an object to a subject for a very brief and precisely determined period of time. Dodge's student years in Germany were ones of tight financial constraint, and he often barely had enough money to eat. His dissertation, *Die Motorischen Wortvorstellungen* (The kinesthetic imagination) (1896), discussed the close relationship between verbal imagery and kinesthesia, the sensation of muscular movement. Experimentation into motor perception was a popular topic of psychological investigation at the time. Dodge was awarded a Ph.D. in 1896.

Dodge's monograph *Psychologische Untersuchungen uber das Lesen* (Psychological investigations of reading)

(1899), co-written with Erdmann and drawing on experimentation made possible by the new tachistoscope, cast doubt on an older theory of reading that argued that humans progress letter by letter through a word in order to recognize it. Instead, building on the work of American psychologist James McKeen Cattell, the experimenters argued that words, rather than letters, are the fundamental units of recognition in reading. Their work also showed that effective visual stimulation occurred only during periods of eye fixation, not during eye movement. Using mirrors, they discovered a new type of eye movement called the saccadic movement, which shifts the eyes as quickly as possible from one fixation point to another.

Dodge returned to the United States in 1896 and began teaching at Ursinus College in Pennsylvania. In addition to psychology, his heavy teaching load required him to lead classes in logic, the history of philosophy, ethics, aesthetics, pedagogy, and the history of English literature. In August 1897 he married Henrietta C. Cutler; they had no children. The following year Dodge was hired by Wesleyan University in Middletown, Connecticut, where he taught for the next twenty-six years. In 1902 Dodge was promoted to a full professor at Wesleyan. His article, "An Experimental Study of Visual Fixation," published in the *Psychological Review Monograph*, supplement, in 1907, was the first to argue that the function of peripheral vision in reading is to aid in making predictions about upcoming text. For one year (1913–1914) he worked with physiologist Francis G. Benedict at the Nutrition Laboratory in Boston, testing the psychological effects of moderate doses of alcohol. He presided over the American Psychological Association in 1916–1917 and chaired the Division of Anthropology and Psychology of the National Research Council in 1922–1923.

During World War I, Dodge served in the navy, where he advanced to the rank of lieutenant commander. He served as a consultant psychologist to the chemical warfare service and as a member of the committee on fatigue of the Council of National Defense. He developed a highly successful method of selecting and training naval gun pointers. His other war-related service included an extensive study of the effects of frequent gas mask wearing, including a comparative analysis of different designs.

In 1924 Dodge left Wesleyan to accept a position at Yale as a professor of psychology. There he helped found Yale's Institute of Psychology. With Robert M. Yerkes and Clark Wissler, Dodge supervised the school's growth; in 1929 it expanded to include psychiatry and other social sciences and was renamed the Institute of Human Relations. Dodge retired in 1936, when Parkinson's disease had begun to erode his mental facilities. He lived the remainder of his life in Tryon, North Carolina, where he died.

Although not well known for his work in theoretical or clinical psychology, Dodge is remembered for his contributions to the development of techniques for the study of human behavior and instruments for its measurement. He developed three instruments for the study of reading methods that allow precise manipulation of light and readability. He discovered two methods of recording eye movements, the first of which tracked the eye while a subject read and the second recorded ocular movements behind closed eyes. He also refined the techniques used to measure involuntary reflexes of the eyelid, increasing instrumental sensitivity and reducing distortion. His other significant inventions include a pendulum photochronograph, which measures small intervals of time by photographic traces from a beam of light, and a precision oil resistance myograph, which records ocular muscle contractions. Eye movements had always played an important role in older theories of both space perception and reading, and theorists had assumed whatever eye movements supported their hypothesis. Dodge's new instruments allowed for more precise observation of eye movements, which enabled the refutation of incorrect theories and the support of correct ones.

More thoroughly than his predecessors, Dodge studied the phenomena of visual perception, and the conclusions he reached had a major impact. His most important experimental contributions were in the discovery and articulation of the processes of visual perception, especially regarding eye movements in reading and in the differentiation between a subject and its background. His work has had implications for the study of animal conditioning and nystagmus, a condition in which the eye darts involuntarily from side to side.

• Dodge's other important publications include *Visual Fixation* (1908); *Elementary Condition of Human Variability* (1927); *Experimental Analysis of the Sensori-Motor in Consequences of Passive Oscillation, Rotary and Rectilinear* (1928), with Roland C. Travis; and *The Craving for Superiority* (1931), with Eugene Kahn. An autobiographical article by Dodge is in Carl Murchison, ed., *A History of Psychology in Autobiography*, vol. 1 (1930). For contextual background, see Eleanor J. Gibson and Harry Levin, *The Psychology of Reading* (1975), and E. B. Huey, *The Psychology and Pedagogy of Reading* (1908). Obituaries are in the *American Journal of Psychology* 55 (Oct. 1942); the *Psychological Review* 49 (Sept. 1942); *Science*, 8 May 1942; and the *New York Times*, 9 Apr. 1942.

ELIZABETH ZOE VICARY

DODGE, Theodore Ayrault (28 May 1842–25 Oct. 1909), soldier, businessman, and military historian, was born in Pittsfield, Massachusetts, the son of Nathaniel Shattswell Dodge, a wealthy writer and a U.S. War Department official, and Emily Pomeroy. His great-grandfather fought at Bunker Hill. When Theodore was eight years old, his father was appointed American commissioner to the London Exhibition, and the family moved to Europe. Theodore was sent to school at the College des Josephites in Tirelmont, Belgium, and was tutored in Berlin. There he lived with the family of retired Prussian general Gebhardt von Froerich, attended the Friedrich Werderschen Gymnasium, and absorbed the Prussian work ethos, including dedication to the profession of arms and commitment to the importance of ideas in war. He graduated from the University of London in 1861.

Enrolling in the 101st New York Volunteers in August 1861, Dodge participated as a first lieutenant in the Peninsula and Manassas campaigns of 1862. At Second Manassas his regiment lost half of its members. Dodge was wounded at Chantilly; he returned to duty in November 1862 with the newly organized 119th New York Regiment, which was a part of General Carl Schurz's Third Division, Eleventh Army Corps. He fought at Chancellorsville, and at Gettysburg his regiment was virtually wiped out as it withdrew to Cemetery Hill on the afternoon of 1 July 1863. At age twenty-one, Dodge endured amputation of his right leg below the knee.

After the war Dodge lived in Washington, D.C., working for the War Department until he was mustered out of the army as disabled in April 1870. In 1865 he married Jane Marshall Neil; they had three sons and two daughters. In 1866 he obtained an LL.B. from Columbian College (now George Washington University) Law School, was admitted to the bar, and became interested in patent law.

After his forced retirement from the army, Dodge moved to Cambridge, Massachusetts, where his father was a literary figure and the president of the Papyrus Club of Boston and the Loyal Legion of Massachusetts. Settling down to make his fortune, Dodge worked for the McKay Sewing Machine Company from 1870 to 1880. Meanwhile he purchased patents for the Tapley burnishing machine, which was widely used in cotton textile manufacture, and worked with Robert Cowen, who was experimenting with cotton woven hose—the forerunner of rubber tires. In the 1880s the bicycle craze emerged, and in the 1890s the automobile became popular. The Boston Woven Hose Company, of which Dodge was president, became one of the largest producers of single-tube tires in the country.

Through it all Dodge remained fascinated by the military. During the 1880s he began to join active veterans' groups in presenting military history lectures, which were part of the post–Civil War "lecture craze" of Victorian America. In 1880 he gave three papers to the Military History Society of Lennox, Massachusetts. Out of these came his first two books, *The Campaign of Chancellorsville* (1881) and *A Bird's Eye View of Our Civil War* (1882). An 1888 lecture to the Lowell Historical Society on "great captains" outlined his publishing ventures for the next twenty-one years. He produced *Alexander: A History of the Origins and Growth of the Art of War, from the Earliest Times to the Battle of Ipsus* (2 vols., 1890); *Hannibal: A History of the Art of War among the Carthaginians and Romans Down to the Battle of Pydna* (2 vols., 1891); *Caesar: A History of the Art of War among the Romans, from the Second Punic War Down to the Fall of the Roman Empire* (2 vols., 1892); *Gustavus Adolphus: A History of the Art of War from Its Revival after the Middle Ages to the End of the Spanish Succession War* (2 vols., 1895); *Na-*

poleon: A History of the Art of War from the Beginning of the French Revolution to Waterloo (4 vols., 1904–1907); and two unpublished volumes on Frederick the Great. More than 40,000 of Dodge's volumes were in print by 1910.

After Dodge's first wife died, he married Clara Isabel Bowden in 1892; they had no children. Her wealth and social position complemented his own, and thereafter Dodge was financially independent. He gave up active business management and moved to Europe, living first in Paris and then, beginning in 1908, in a château on the Oise River. Having secured a good contract with a major American publisher, Houghton-Mifflin, he applied his passionate interest to his work and developed a readable style for the military history to which he devoted himself.

As historian, Dodge had begun lecturing and writing a "veteran's history"—expanded personal memoirs that included accounts of battles and wars in which he had participated. But gradually he entered into scholarly historical debate and was forced to defend his conclusions. In developing his vision of modern American military history he departed from traditional approaches in which military history was written by professional officers who described war in what came to be known as the "battles and leaders" school or by popular writers who focused on diplomacy and heroic, romantic images of war. Dodge chose to pattern his work after two European writers who by the 1880s had begun to influence the study of war: Leo Tolstoy, the author of *War and Peace* (1869), and Hans Delbrück, the first modern military historian and author of *The Art of War in the Framework of Political History* (4 vols., 1900–1920). Both writers began with primary sources but added exact technical details, including topography, weapons, supplies, and casualties—the material circumstances of military life.

Dodge employed these innovations and wrote history that was both comparative and quantitative. For example, he compared Caesar, Alexander, and Frederick the Great using specific data concerning the size of their armies and campaigns. He was writing for an educated American audience that valued entertainment but also wanted a certain realism and authenticity. Like Tolstoy and Delbrück, Dodge's work reached both the professional military officer and the educated layman. He read primary sources with a critical eye and traveled frequently, making eighty trips to Europe during the 1880s and 1890s by some accounts. He walked over the battlefields to determine whether details in ancient accounts of war were possible. Although he wrote as a soldier, he applied the dispassionate skills of a scholar to his work.

Dodge's image of military history was limited. Despite the controversies in which he engaged, it was impossible for others to verify his arguments because he gave few clues regarding where his descriptions had originated. Nevertheless, his understanding of past wars was good, based as it was on his own war experiences and his immersion in valid primary and secondary sources. His life was full. As a soldier he was wounded and decorated. As a businessman he gained financial independence. As a historian he was read by both fans of military history and professional historians, securing him a distinguished place among late nineteenth-century American military writers. Dodge died near Nanteuil-le-Haudouin, France, and is buried in Arlington National Cemetery.

• Dodge's papers are privately held. The Massachusetts Historical Society in Boston and the Houghton Library at Harvard have some of Dodge's materials. See Thomas L. Livermore, "Memoir of Theodore Ayrault Dodge," *Proceedings of the Massachusetts Historical Society* 43 (1909–1910); and A. H. Pomeroy, *History and Genealogy of the Pomeroy Family* (1912). Dodge's work is compared to modern military history in Arden Bucholz, *Hans Delbrück and the German Military Establishment* (1985), and in Bucholz, *Delbrück's Modern Military History* (1997). An obituary is in the *New York Times*, 27 Oct. 1909.

ARDEN BUCHOLZ

DODS, John Bovee (26 Sept. 1795–21 Mar. 1872), amateur physician and popular author and lecturer on mesmerism and Spiritualism, was born Johannes Dods Bovee in the town of Florida in Montgomery County, New York, the son of Jacob Mathias Bovee, a farmer and merchant, and Jane Dods. After serving in the War of 1812, he took as his surname Dods, probably out of respect for the maternal uncle who cared for him after his father's untimely death. Little is known about his early education, but his father's will stipulated that he "be educated in wreading [sic] writing arithmetic and English Gramer [sic]."

Dods served for many years as a Protestant minister, first in Levant, Maine, and then, from 1836 to 1842, at the Universalist Society Church in Provincetown, Massachusetts. In his sermons, some of which were published in 1842 as *Thirty Short Sermons on Various Important Subjects, Both Doctrinal and Practical*, he joined a rising challenge to orthodox Calvinism and generated some sectarian tension in Provincetown by outspokenly defending the liberal theology of universalism. He preached gradual spiritual growth and universal salvation, rejecting older notions of sudden conversion, eternal punishment, and the divinity of Christ. He also harbored a growing interest in the phenomena and philosophy of animal magnetism, or mesmerism, which became an American fad during the 1830s and 1840s. His Provincetown activities also included the establishment of a school called the Academy, where he taught, and the publication of an English grammar that went through several editions.

Dods left the ministry in 1842. His investigation of human spirituality and regeneration led him deeper into mesmerism, according to which an invisible but universally pervasive and empirically demonstrable magnetic fluid operates on the body, mind, and soul, linking them to the higher spiritual powers of the universe and providing a mechanism for physical and emotional healing. He devoted the remainder of his life to studying and publicizing what he called "electrical psychology," believing that the mind and soul

could be understood and analyzed in terms of the action of the mesmeric fluid upon them. He was convinced that he had found a scientific approach to human psychology and religiosity at a time when many religious groups and medical reform movements sought to tap the growing cultural authority of science and the unknown potential of magnetism and electricity.

Dods lectured on mesmerism and "electrical psychology" to large audiences throughout New England and the Northeast during the late 1830s and early 1840s, publishing his teachings in *Six Lectures on the Philosophy of Mesmerism* (1843) and *The Philosophy of Electrical Psychology* (1850). He proposed that spiritual forces operated on the individual by means of the absorption of the magnetic fluid in the process of breathing and the consequent transformation of it into a nervo-vital fluid that energized the physiological and mental systems. Usually called "Dr. Dods" despite his amateur status, he applied this idea by entrancing physically and spiritually ailing family and congregation members in an effort to harmonize them with the universe and induce spiritual and physical healing and by becoming one of the first to experiment with the therapeutic use of electricity. More broadly, he concluded that God was an impersonal mind that generally operated automatically or "involuntarily" on nature through the universal mesmeric fluid, adhering to natural law and only rarely exercising the "voluntary" power of miraculous intervention. Still, he presented his ideas as a supplement to rather than a replacement for Christian doctrine. His lectures and writings were very popular and won him a following. His books passed through several editions and a group of U.S. senators wrote to him requesting that he speak in Washington, D.C.

Like many other Americans who had been involved with Universalism and mesmerism, Dods took a lively interest in Spiritualism when it began to attract widespread attention in the 1850s. He admitted the authenticity of the phenomena produced in the presence of entranced mediums and attempted to explain them in terms of his theories of mind. Joining contemporaries such as Edward Coit Rogers and Karl von Reichenbach, who offered neurological and electrical explanations of mediumship, he suggested in *Spirit Manifestations Examined and Explained* (1854) that the phenomena resulted from the involuntary release of an "electro-nervous force" that accumulated in the medium's cerebellum when the voluntary powers of the cerebrum were rendered passive. Within a few years, however, he rejected this theory in favor of the Spiritualist explanation, which postulated the existence of spirits that mediated between humanity and an impersonal deity by using the magnetic fluid to operate on mediums and, more subtly, on all individuals. Grafting Spiritualism onto his previous theories of mind and spirit, he worked with his daughter Jennie (Amelia Jane), a medium, to spread his new belief system and investigate its applications to spiritual and mental healing.

In using mesmerism and then Spiritualism to suggest that the divine acts within the individual, Dods expressed an important theme in nineteenth-century American religious life that became for many Americans an article of faith: that the person should look within for spiritual guidance. He also articulated an American religious theme repeated with greater impact later in the nineteenth century by Mary Baker Eddy, on whom he had a documented influence, and in the twentieth century by Norman Vincent Peale, Scientology, and Transcendental Meditation: that spiritual and physical healing and well-being can result when the individual achieves a positive orientation toward the workings of the universe.

Dods was married three times. He had four children, including Jennie, with his first wife, Mercy A. Hodgdon, whom he married in 1820 and who died in 1831. In 1834 he married Julia A. Holden, who died in 1844; they had one child. In 1861 he married Phebe C. Reybert; they had no children. He died in Brooklyn, New York.

• In addition to the works mentioned above, Dods published *The Second Death Illustrated* (1832), a Universalist sermon; and *Immortality Triumphant* (1852). Genealogical information about Dods may be found in Everett Filgate's privately published *Bovee and Bovie Families in America* (1996). Information about his career and his ideas is available in Emma Hardinge Britten, *Modern American Spiritualism* (1870); Frank Podmore, *Modern Spiritualism*, vol. 1 (1902); Simeon G. Smith, *Leaves from an Old Church Record Book* (1922); R. Laurence Moore, *In Search of White Crows: Spiritualism, Parapsychology, and American Culture* (1977); and Robert C. Fuller, *Mesmerism and the American Cure of Souls* (1982).

BRET E. CARROLL

DOE, Charles Cogswell (11 Apr. 1830–9 Mar. 1896), associate justice and chief justice of the state of New Hampshire, was born in Derry, New Hampshire, the son of Joseph Doe, Jr., a storekeeper and landowner, and Mary Bodwell Ricker. Doe's paternal ancestors had lived in New Hampshire since at least 1663, and by the time of his birth the family was prosperous enough to ensure him a good education. After attending the academies of South Berwick, Maine, Exeter, New Hampshire, and Andover, Massachusetts, and spending a year at Harvard College, Doe was graduated from Dartmouth College in 1849. He then studied law for about three years in Dover, New Hampshire, and in 1853 enrolled at Harvard Law School. Completing only the first of two terms, he returned to Dover without a law degree and in January 1854 was admitted to the state bar.

Doe's father, a supporter of banks and of industrial development at a time when the Jacksonian majority opposed most acts of incorporation, had also been a leading spokesman for the Whigs in the New Hampshire legislature. Doe, by contrast, came to age in a New England torn by abolitionism. Committed to the rule of law, he became a pro-Union Democrat. A frequent speaker at party rallies throughout the state, Doe was rewarded by an appointment as county solici-

tor, or prosecutor, of Strafford County. In 1856 he was "addressed" out of that office by the Republican-controlled legislature. Despite some lingering bitterness he became a Republican three years later, explaining that "adoption" of the *Dred Scott* decision "in 1857 by the Democratic party drove me out of that party." He not only believed that the ruling violated the U.S. Constitution, but he was also troubled by its implication; he concluded that it meant the South would never compromise. Though he put the cause of national unity first, Doe was antislavery. He then became the foremost Republican stump speaker in southern New Hampshire until 1859, when he was appointed to the state supreme court. At age twenty-nine Doe became an associate justice on the state's only court of record, which meant that he presided at jury trials as well as serving as an appellate judge deciding appeals from the trial term. He remained an associate justice until 1874, and from 1876 until his death he served as chief justice.

As an appellate judge Doe achieved such renown that he has been universally ranked among the nation's ten greatest common-law jurists. In an age of judicial formalism he stood out as an original genius with an open disdain for precedent that would have marked him as unique even in the most instrumentalist of times. "The maxim which . . . requires courts to follow decided cases is shown by thousands of overruled decisions, to be a figurative expression requiring only a reasonable respect for decided cases," Doe wrote in *Lisbon v. Lyman* in 1870. Without legislative aid he reformed civil procedure in New Hampshire in a series of brilliantly crafted decisions from a practice "almost proverbial for its severity" to a process so informal that during his final decade on the bench no lower-court rulings were appealed, a record probably then unmatched by any other American jurisdiction. His main instrument was amendment. By permitting parties to amend pleadings, Doe transformed them from substance law in control of the proceedings to mostly formalities, no longer capable of determining the outcome of litigation. Rather than dismiss a case for inadequacy of procedure, Doe not only allowed a defendant to amend from an incorrect writ to the proper one, but also to amend from law to equity.

Less well known, however, was Doe's development of an American theory of torts, perhaps because credit usually is given to Oliver Wendell Holmes, Jr. Working from both treatises and English legal history, Doe formulated the theory that a person is liable for damage resulting from an accident for which he or she is legally at fault; for damage resulting from an intention to inflict an injury not justified or privileged at common law; for damage resulting from unlawful actions; and for damage resulting from the assumption of an unreasonable risk. Before this time recovery for injury at common law depended on linking a cause of action to a proper writ, such as trespass, which required a direct blow, or case, which turned on consequential damages. As a result of the work of Doe and Holmes, lawyers no longer concentrated on the physical act that had caused an injury, but now could argue in court why a person should be liable for damage that he or she inflicted on another.

Doe made his most original contribution to common-law jurisprudence in the law of evidence. Nineteenth-century judges, he thought, deluded themselves into believing that there can be unmixed legal presumptions, that is presumptions that are entirely "of law," for the court's determination, and not "of fact," properly the jury's province. No matter how much judges change fact into law, factual issues remain to be resolved. To say, for example, that recent and exclusive possession of stolen property creates an unmixed legal presumption of guilt suggests that issues of recentness and exclusiveness are determined by legal formulas. Yet, the question of recentness has to be one of fact under the circumstances. Better to admit that any such presumption properly belongs to the triers of fact. By recognizing that most issues arising in the course of a trial are questions of fact for the jury and are not reviewable by the court, Doe's fact-law distinction reshaped New Hampshire legal theory and in time was recognized as the hallmark of the state's jurisprudence. Outside of New Hampshire it made less headway and was frequently misunderstood, most notably Doe's striking contributions to the law of criminal insanity. The general rule is that the definition of an exculpatory mental illness is one of law. It is also the rule that to return a verdict of not guilty by reason of insanity the jury must find that the disease caused the accused to commit the act. In a startling original ruling, Doe formulated what is known as the New Hampshire Doctrine, holding not only that the definition of criminal insanity is a question of fact for the jury, thus opening trials to unrestricted psychiatric evidence, but also that it was for the jury to determine whether it is necessary to establish that the disease had *caused* the defendant to commit the crime of which he is accused. Doe's work in the law of criminal insanity did not gain wide recognition until the 1950s when the U.S. Court of Appeals for the District of Columbia promulgated the *Durham* Rule, a test that although based more on medical than on legal principles reflected much of the theory of the New Hampshire Doctrine.

Remembered today as one of the country's greatest common-law judges and as America's premier adjudicatory reformer, Doe is less renowned for constitutional law. The reason is that during his tenure constitutional law was less tolerant of the unorthodox and less receptive to eccentric genius than was common law. Doe's bold originality is demonstrated by the use he made of the theory that New Hampshire's constitution is a social compact. By the conventional rules of constitutional construction, under which a constitution is organic law, not a contract, the government is held to have inherent powers limited by certain enumerated provisions (as, for example, the federal Bill of Rights). In a situation in which the liberty of a citizen is pitted against the authority of the state, the citizen must cite specific wording in the organic law to prove

the government is restrained from exercising power. A constitution that is a compact, by contrast, has no doctrine of inherent power. Whatever authority the state enjoys is "manufactured"—created by the people through the compact.

By starting with the theory that the government under the "contract" is an agent while also holding that the privileges of the citizen are absolute except where specifically surrendered by that contract, Doe relieved the citizen of the burden of proving that the government's power is limited. Instead, the burden falls on the state to prove that it has been delegated the authority that it seeks to exercise. Thus, Doe held, civil rights are not immunities but "privileges which society has engaged to provide in lieu of the natural liberties given up by individuals" under the contract (*Wooster v. Plymouth*, 1882). To say that the compact made government an agent and rights absolute unless specifically surrendered meant that the citizen did not have to argue for constitutional limits on state authority. The constitutional benefit conferred on individuals by Doe's contractarian constitutionalism was the principle of equality. "The bill of rights," he ruled, "is a bill of [the people's] equal, private rights, reserved by the grantors of public power." Equality, he concluded, is "practically the source and sum of all rights, and the substance of the constitution," the most fundamental of the civil rights protecting nineteenth-century Americans (*State v. Express Co.*, 1880).

While an associate justice Doe married Edith Haven of Portsmouth, New Hampshire, in 1865. They had nine children. A plain, unassuming man, his costume never varied: a brown frock coat, coarse trousers, and heavy boots that were never polished. Famous throughout New England for his eccentricities, Doe even wore woolen mittens when serving as a pall bearer. He insisted at all times on fresh air, not only removing all the windows on the second floor of his house, but also on occasion from his courtroom even in the dead of winter. He died at the railroad station in Rollinsford, New Hampshire, on his way to the state capital.

Charles Doe's immense reputation rests on remarkably few judicial opinions. As a judge on the court of a very small state, he did not have many opportunities to write great law. In several instances—as, for example, the leading nineteenth-century tort decision *Brown v. Collins*—he asked the parties to stipulate the facts he needed to expound the law and the reasoning that he wished to promulgate. Despite this handicap, Doe is remembered as the leading judicial lawmaker of the second half of the nineteenth century, as the nation's most successful reformer of procedure, and as one of the most original thinkers ever to sit on an American court.

• Doe's extant letters and papers, including recently discovered trial notes, are in the New Hampshire Historical Society. The most extensive discussion of Doe's life and work, with documentation of primary and secondary sources, is John Phillip Reid, *Chief Justice: The Judicial World of Charles*

Doe (1967). For reaction to Doe's New Hampshire Doctrine of criminal insanity see Reid, "Understanding the New Hampshire Doctrine of Criminal Insanity," *Yale Law Journal* 69 (1960): 367, and Louis E. Reik, "The Doe-Ray Correspondence: A Pioneer Collaboration in the Jurisprudence of Mental Disease," *Yale Law Journal* 63 (1953): 183.

JOHN PHILLIP REID

DOHENY, Edward Laurence (10 Aug. 1856–8 Sept. 1935), oil developer, was born in Fond du Lac, Wisconsin, the son of Patrick Doheny, a laborer, and Ellen (in some sources Eleanor Elizabeth) Quigley, a schoolteacher. Doheny received his education in the Fond du Lac public schools and graduated from high school in 1872 at the age of fifteen. He left home soon after his graduation hoping to join a surveying party leaving from Atchison, Kansas. He arrived too late for that adventure but stayed in Kansas working odd jobs. Sometime around 1876 he headed west as a prospector, which led him to New Mexico in 1880. He settled in the mining camp of Kingston in 1883 and married Carrie Lou Ella Wilkins. They had two children, one of whom lived to adulthood. While in Kingston Doheny worked as a prospector, mine owner, and company superintendent but struggled to make ends meet. He also operated a lead mine in Silver City, New Mexico, for a short time before he moved to California in 1891.

Doheny began mining for gold near San Bernardino but in 1892 ended up in Los Angeles. There he and Charles Canfield, another former New Mexican, successfully dug an oil well that inaugurated the Los Angeles City oil field. No market for fuel oil existed in the city at the time, but he eventually secured a contract to supply fuel oil for the Southern California Railway, the local subsidiary of the Santa Fe Railroad. By 1896 Doheny was the largest producer in the field, but his aggressive overexpansion of the business sent his company into receivership. In 1897 he went to work developing oil lands exclusively for the Santa Fe and opened up the Fullerton and Brea Canon oil fields to commercial development. Two years later he set up a new operation, the Petroleum Development Company, as one of the pioneer companies in the Kern River oil district near Bakersfield. By the time he sold that company to the Santa Fe in 1902 he was perhaps the most well known and successful oil promoter in the state. After divorcing his first wife, Doheny married Carrie Estelle Betzold in 1900. They had no children.

Doheny's reputation achieved legendary status when he began prospecting for oil in Mexico in 1900. His Mexican Petroleum Company, established west of Tampico, was the first company to obtain large quantities of oil in Mexico and the first to secure sales contracts for Mexican fuel oil. Doheny began by supplying his own asphalt-refining company, which was paving streets in Mexico's major cities, and progressed to providing fuel for more than three-quarters of the rail lines in the country. He also supplied manufactured gas to Mexico City and other urban areas beginning in 1910. From this period through the mid-1920s Doheny's Huasteca Petroleum Company struck several huge Mexican gushers, making him the largest crude oil producer in the world. He also reentered the California oil business in 1908 and set up a number of independent companies that kept him active in the West Coast petroleum industry. His influence grew primarily with the rising importance of Mexican fuel oil to American and European markets, and shares of "Mexican Pete" led the oil stocks on the New York Stock Exchange. In 1916 Doheny set up the Pan American Petroleum and Transport Company as the holding company for his entire operation.

Politically, Doheny was a lifelong Democrat. His Irish-Catholic roots made him a member by tradition, and his years as a miner made him an ardent supporter of William Jennings Bryan's free silver campaign in 1896. In 1912 Doheny was a large contributor to Woodrow Wilson's successful election, and four years later he served as a presidential elector at the Democratic convention. As a fixture among California Democrats, Doheny was largely credited behind the scenes for helping Wilson win that state and the national election in 1916. Doheny was briefly considered as a vice-presidential nominee in 1920 and received a favorite son nomination from the California delegation.

During the First World War Doheny was conspicuous among the offices of the State Department in Washington, D.C., lobbying on behalf of his Mexican oil companies. He also served as a member of the National Petroleum War Services Committee, which coordinated the nation's oil resources during the war. Because the Mexican Revolution threatened foreign-owned property, Doheny tried to promote a forceful Mexican policy by the Wilson administration. Although his efforts failed to move the president's focus away from Europe, he came closest to success in 1919, when the oil lobby sponsored Senator Albert B. Fall's official Investigation of Mexican Affairs. But this too fell short of pushing the U.S. government into action against Mexico.

Although Doheny was one of the richest men in the United States by the early 1920s, he had not been one to publicize his exploits and was not yet a national figure. That changed as a result of the Teapot Dome oil scandal in 1924. At that time the public learned that Doheny had made a personal loan to Secretary of the Interior Fall while he was negotiating for valuable leases on Naval Petroleum Reserve lands at Elk Hills, California. The federal investigation into these dealings began with a review of Fall's arrangements with another oilman, Harry Sinclair, for government oil land at Teapot Dome, Wyoming, but it was the $100,000 loan Doheny made to Fall that garnered the most attention. Initially, Fall lied about who had given him the money, and it was left to Doheny to appear before the investigating committee several months later and admit the truth about the loan. Doheny also revealed that he had given large sums of money to both political parties and that he had employed a number of former cabinet officers from the Wilson administration as legal advisers for his oil business, including Wilson's son-in-law and former secretary of the Treasury, William Gibbs

McAdoo. In early 1924 McAdoo was the leading Democratic candidate for the presidency, but Doheny's statement that McAdoo had been on retainer for a number of years linked him to the oil scandal and caused irreparable damage to his campaign.

In the end, despite having constructed vital oil storage and dock facilities at Pearl Harbor, Hawaii, in exchange for royalty oil from Elk Hills, Doheny's government leases were cancelled by a federal judge in 1925 after a review of his relationship with Fall. In a criminal trial the following year, however, Doheny and Fall were acquitted of having conspired to defraud the government. As his legal problems continued, Doheny sold his Mexican oil lands to Standard Oil of Indiana in 1925 and most of his California holdings to the Richfield Oil Company in 1927. Then, in the final court battle over the $100,000 loan, Fall was convicted in October 1929 of having accepted a bribe from Doheny while he was a government official. In a separate trial a few months later, Doheny was acquitted of having offered a bribe to Fall in return for the leases at Elk Hills. In both cases, substantial evidence pointed to the personal nature of the loan. The difference in the outcomes turned on the intent of each defendant and the fact that the jury in Fall's trial perceived a clear conflict of interest in his acceptance of any money while he was administering public lands. Doheny was the more appealing character and at his trial documented a lifelong habit of giving money to friends whenever they asked for it. Despite this legal vindication, Doheny's reputation was left in tatters, and Fall became the first cabinet officer to go to jail for crimes while in office.

Doheny had retired from the oil business by this time, and his health declined rapidly. He lived his last years largely in seclusion. His son was murdered in 1929 in a notorious Beverly Hills crime, driving him further from public view. Doheny died at his home in Los Angeles.

• Doheny's personal and business papers were destroyed soon after his death. A small collection of letters written to and from his second wife in the early 1900s and a few pieces of business correspondence are in the Estelle and Edward L. Doheny Collection at the Archival Center of the Archdiocese of Los Angeles, San Fernando, Calif. Public sources on Doheny are scattered throughout government archives dealing with the Mexican oil situation during World War I. In particular, the records of the Department of State concerning the foreign affairs of Mexico and the military intelligence files for the same period are significant. Some correspondence between Doheny and Fall dealing with Mexico and the oil trials is in the Albert B. Fall Papers at the Huntington Library, San Marino, Calif., and in the collection of Fall material at New Mexico State University in Las Cruces. Most of the work on Doheny has been done by partisans for or against his role in Mexico and his complicity in the oil scandal. The laudatory works include Fritz Hoffman, "Edward L. Doheny and the Beginnings of Petroleum Development in Mexico," *Mid-America* 24 (Apr. 1942): 94–108; Lucille V. Miller, "Edward and Estelle Doheny," *Ventura County Historical Society* 6 (Nov. 1960): 3–20; and Ward Ritchie, *The Dohenys of Los Angeles* (1974). For a negative interpretation see Dan La Botz, *Edward L. Doheny: Petroleum, Power and Politics in the United States and Mexico* (1991), which relies on unsubstantiated attacks against Doheny in a savage review. A full-scale interpretation of Doheny's importance is Martin R. Ansell, *Oil Baron of the Southwest: Edward L. Doheny and the Development of the Petroleum Industry in California and Mexico* (1998). Two basic overviews are in the front-page obituaries in the *Los Angeles Times* and the *New York Times*, both 9 Sept. 1935.

MARTIN R. ANSELL

DOHERTY, Catherine de Hueck (15 Aug. 1896–14 Dec. 1985), Catholic social activist and author, was born Catherine Federovna Kolyschkine in Nizhni Novgorod (now Gorki), Russia, the daughter of Theodore Kolyschkine, a businessman and diplomat, and Emma Thomson. Catherine's mother, immersed in the Russian Orthodox faith, taught her to "see the faith of Christ in the poor" while warning her that she was "born under the shadow on the Cross." Born into Russian nobility, she was educated in a Catholic school in Alexandria, Egypt, from 1903 until 1906, when her father's career in international business necessitated the relocation of his family. This early sojourn was a portent of things to come, for her wanderings around the world and her interest in Roman Catholicism led to a fervent desire to bridge the gap separating the Eastern and Western branches of Christianity.

When the family returned to St. Petersburg in 1910, their aristocratic life began to unravel, owing to the forces set in motion by the Russian Revolution. In 1912 Doherty married a cousin, Boris de Hueck, and embarked on a tortuous personal journey. The marriage was a troubled one, and Boris's emotional cruelties brought her much pain and suffering. Their immediate crisis, however, was shaped by the larger historical context.

Doherty accompanied her husband when he fought during World War I, serving from 1915 to 1918 as a Red Cross nurse in the 130th Division of the Russian army on the western front. The chaos of the Bolshevik revolution and the ensuing civil war exposed them to a death sentence at the hands of the Red forces. In 1918 they escaped to Finland, where Doherty resolved to dedicate her life to Christ in thanksgiving for surviving the ordeal.

Life as refugees took them to Scotland, then to England, where in 1919 Doherty converted to Roman Catholicism, convinced that God had a special mission for her. In 1921 the couple set sail for Canada, hoping for a new life. As immigrants, they adopted the titles of baron and baroness. They had one son, whom Doherty consecrated to the Blessed Virgin Mary. Simultaneously, she became the "mother" to the Russian immigrant community in Canada.

Driven from Canada by her husband's scandalous infidelities and financial failures, Doherty moved to New York in 1924, searching for a way to support the family. She found employment as a public speaker, traveling first with the Chatauqua Lecture Bureau (1924–1925), telling the adventuresome tale of her harrowing escape from the Communists. Later she spoke on behalf of the Catholic Union (1925–1926), focusing on the reunification of the Orthodox and Catholic churches. The family migrated to Montreal in 1929, but the marriage continued to deteriorate.

Searching for a greater purpose in her life and a way to follow her mandate to do God's work, Doherty in 1930 founded the first Friendship House in Toronto on the advice of Archbishop Neil McNeil. This ministry, a form of Catholic settlement house, was designed to assist refugees and to provide for the physical and spiritual needs of the poor, offering meals, clothing, Catholic literature, and fundamental social education. The "Baroness," influenced by the papal encyclicals and the example of Dorothy Day's Catholic Workers, was determined to fight communism in the slums. Doherty's vocation as a Catholic social worker was linked with her intense personal holiness in the formation of a unique lay apostolate based upon the simple premise of a loving God. Preaching the Gospel message, she believed, would promote harmony and understanding and allow the apostles of Friendship House to counter communism, which she saw as fueled by hate, with Christian love.

Harmony, however, gave way to conflict, and the controversies that swirled around Friendship House—personality conflicts, disagreement about the proper direction of the ministry, and troubles with ecclesiastical authorities—drove Doherty back to New York in 1937. In 1938 she founded another Friendship House in Harlem with an agenda of confronting racial injustice in addition to comforting the poor and saving souls. This Friendship House served as a magnet for many prominent Catholics, such as Thomas Merton and John LaFarge, drawn by the opportunity to volunteer and support its mission. Archbishop Francis Spellman gave his blessing to the endeavor, and Paul Hanley Furfey became Doherty's personal spiritual adviser. Furfey saw her as a woman destined for great things but not without great sacrifice and more suffering along the road to her greatest achievement.

Irretrievably broken by 1931, Doherty's marriage was legally dissolved, and it was eventually annulled by her church in 1942. A reporter, Eddie Doherty, visited her in 1940 to write a story about the work of Friendship House. Married in 1942, they had no children. Together the Dohertys carried on the work of Friendship House in Chicago, to which they had moved in 1946, but tensions with the staff over their life style and her leadership developed once again. Feeling betrayed by her spiritual children and concerned that her spiritual vision and work were being compromised by the exclusive focus on racial issues, Doherty moved back to Canada in 1947.

From the ashes of this defeat rose the vision of Madonna House, founded in 1947 in Combermere, Ontario, the culmination of Doherty's long pilgrimage and the fulfillment of her dreams. At once a rural house of hospitality reaching out to the poor and a consecrated spiritual community of priests and laypersons, Madonna House was dedicated to preaching the Gospel and living a life of Christian witness in keeping with the traditional vows of poverty, chastity, and obedience. Doherty's unique contribution is in the distinctive blend of Eastern and Western spirituality, symbolic of her goal of Christian unity and the restoration of all things in Christ. She wrote several books on Eastern Orthodox spirituality. After a restless and difficult journey, Doherty finally found peace and success under her new patroness, "Our Lady of Combermere." Before her death in Combermere, Ontario, the seeds she had planted at Madonna House in Canada had taken firm root and borne much fruit, encompassing branches in the United States, the West Indies, France, and Africa.

In her final talk with her staff at Madonna House, Doherty offered these words of advice and wisdom, "Be willing to move with the needs of the time." They were equally evocative of her personal dynamic faith and testimony to the effectiveness of the ever-widening mission of a woman sometimes referred to as "the Dorothy Day of Canada." She was a woman of destiny, courage, and uncompromising principle. Having experienced the collapse of worldly ideologies in her native Russia, she became a "revolutionary for Christ," never losing faith (despite some dark moments) in the conviction that God's love could change the world.

The thriving community Doherty established at Madonna House, infused with a spirituality characterized by simplicity, duty, and a passionate love of God, was a living testament to the significance of her contribution to the Catholic church. As the simple words on the wooden cross that marks her final resting place attest, "She loved the poor." Doherty was a pioneer in seeking to implement the social encyclicals, in the campaign for racial justice and equality, and in establishing a vibrant and effective apostolate for laypersons seeking to live the faith.

• Doherty was the author of over twenty books. The most representative and useful for understanding her life are *Poustinia: Christian Spirituality of the East for Western Men* (1975), which best summarizes her spiritual vision and view of prayer in the silence of the heart; *Friendship House* (1947); *The Gospel without Compromise* (1976); and the autobiographical *Fragments of My Life* (1981). The most comprehensive biography of Doherty is Lorene Hanley Duquin, *They Called Her the Baroness: The Life of Catherine De Hueck Doherty* (1995), which is based on the papers in the Madonna House Archives, numerous secondary sources, Doherty's books, and oral interviews with clergy and other members of the Madonna House community. Other good sources include Robert Wild, *Journey to the Lonely Christ: The Little Mandate of Catherine de Hueck Doherty* (1987); Emile Briere, *Katia: A Personal Vision of Catherine de Hueck Doherty* (1988); and Eddie Doherty's memories, *Tumbleweed* (1948).

KATHLEEN L. RILEY

DOISY, Edward Adelbert (13 Nov. 1893–23 Oct. 1986), biochemist and Nobel Prize winner, was born in rural Hume, Illinois, the son of Edward Perez Doisy, a traveling salesman, and Ada Alley. Though neither parent had a high school education, Doisy's mother insisted that he attend college; when he graduated from the local high school at the age of sixteen he received a scholarship to the University of Illinois and began a two-year premedical course there. Wishing to earn a degree, he took extra courses in bacteriology and physiological and organic chemistry, as well as a special study on the chemistry of nervous tissue that resulted in two publications with the instructor, C. G. MacArthur. He received the B.A. in 1914, and MacArthur persuaded him to stay on for graduate work, resulting in an M.S. in 1916. The year before he had received a scholarship for graduate study at Harvard University, and he began work with chemistry professor Otto Folin. World War I intervened, and Doisy spent 1917–1919 first as a lieutenant in the Army Sanitary Corps and then at Walter Reed Hospital and the Rockefeller Institute, where he learned blood-gas determination with the chemist Donald Van Slyke and protein nitrogen analysis with medical researcher Simon Flexner. In 1918 he married Alice Ackert; they had four children. After discharge from the army he finished his Ph.D. at Harvard in 1920 with a dissertation on microdetermination of sodium, potassium, and chlorine in brain tissue.

In 1919, after a summer spent investigating nitrogen metabolism and its uric acid end products, Doisy accepted a position as instructor in biochemistry at Washington University in St. Louis, Missouri, becoming associate professor three years later. In 1923 he moved to the School of Medicine of the University of St. Louis as a professor and was named head of the Department of Biochemistry that year. He spent the remainder of his professional career there. During the Washington years Doisy, with a colleague, Edgar Allen, began his first major research study, which focused on female sex hormones. These were initially isolated from the follicles surrounding the ova of mice in estrus, but in work that continued at St. Louis University the major hormone was isolated as well from the follicular liquid of sows, cattle, sheep, and humans; from the urine of pregnant women; from human and sheep ovaries; and from human placentae and corpora lutea. The first such estrogen was obtained in pure form and reported in 1929 under the name "theelin"; it is now called "estrone." It was quickly followed by estradiol and estratriol. Doisy took out a number of patents on these and other compounds, which proved to have widespread application in human and animal medicine. He assigned the patents to the university; they earned more than a million dollars over the years and funded construction of Doisy Hall, a research wing at the School of Medicine. The work on sex hormones resulted in Doisy's only book-length publications, *Sex Hormones* (1936) and *Sex and Internal Secretions* (1939, with Allen and Charles H. Danforth).

In the late 1930s Doisy took up the study of vitamin K, which is implicated in blood clotting. He was inspired by the interest of one of his graduate students, Ralph W. McKee, in the work of the Danish chemist Henrik Dam, with whom Doisy would share the 1943 Nobel Prize in Physiology or Medicine. Dam had found that chicks living on an artificial diet developed subcutaneous hemorrhages that showed no clotting tendency. The hemorrhaging did not respond to treatment with vitamins, cholesterol, fats, or oils but only to a diet of grain or seeds. Having ruled out all other dietary factors, Dam concluded that the active material was a new, fat-soluble vitamin to which he gave the name K, as this was both the next available letter in the alphabet and the initial of the German word *Koagulation*. Dam prepared vitamin K in a form pure enough for medical applications, principally in the prevention of hemorrhage in neonates, but was not able to isolate it in pure crystalline form. Working with McKee, Doisy quickly found that vitamin K was two compounds, K_1 and K_2 and by 1938 McKee produced crystalline K_2, which could be chemically characterized and its structure determined. Vitamin K_1 followed within the year, and in September 1939 the *Journal of the American Chemical Society* reported the synthesis of K_1 by Doisy's group as well as two others, at Harvard and in Europe. This work was supported by grants from the university and from the drug firm Parke-Davis and Company, which also provided the help of company chemists Stephen Binkley, Lee Cheney, and Walter Holcomb. As he had done earlier, Doisy assigned his patent rights to the university.

Doisy continued his work on both the estrogens and vitamin K for the remainder of his career, retiring from the School of Medicine in 1965 but maintaining an office and an active emeritus status for many years thereafter. The importance of Doisy's work over his lifetime lay in isolation and characterization of active compounds found in biological extracts with specific physiological effects. When the pure compound was sorted out from the mixture it could be synthesized and used as a therapeutic agent in sex-hormone and blood disease treatment.

Many honors came to Doisy in addition to the Nobel Prize, including some eight honorary doctorates, the Gold Medal of the St. Louis Medical Society, the Conné Medal of the Chemists' Club, the St. Louis Award, the Gibbs Medal of the American Chemical Society's Chicago Section, the American Pharmaceutical Manufacturers Association Award, and the St. Louis University Fleur de Lis. Doisy's wife died in 1964, and the next year he married Margaret McCormick, his wife's good friend and his longtime secretary; they had no children. Doisy died at his home in St. Louis.

• Doisy's own "An Autobiography," *Annual Review of Biochemistry* 45 (1976): 1–9, gives reminiscences over a lifetime. Probably the most complete and knowledgeable article on Doisy's life and work is that by Jane A. Miller in *The Nobel Prize Winners, Physiology or Medicine*, vol. 1 (1991); it contains a partial bibliography of primary sources as well as numerous secondary articles. A brief but informative sketch may be found in Wyndham D. Miles and Robert F. Gould, eds., *American Chemists and Chemical Engineers*, vol. 2 (1994). Another treatment is Theodore Sourkes, *Nobel Prize*

Winners in Medicine and Physiology, 1901–1965 (1966). Obituaries are in the *New York Times*, 25 Oct. 1986, and the *St. Louis Post-Dispatch*, 24 Oct. 1986.

ROBERT M. HAWTHORNE JR.

DOLE, James Drummond (27 Sept. 1877–14 May 1958), businessman, was born in Jamaica Plain, Massachusetts, the son of Charles Dole, a Unitarian pastor, and Frances Drummond. Dole was educated at Roxbury Latin School in Boston, Massachusetts, and entered Harvard University in 1895. Part of his university studies included horticulture and agricultural science (for example, food processing technology). After he graduated in 1899 with an A.B. degree, Dole decided to move to Hawaii where his second cousin Sanford Ballard Dole was a leading politician. Dole's decision was also influenced by a Hawaiian government pamphlet promoting agricultural opportunities—in particular, coffee growing.

In July 1900 Dole acquired sixty-one acres of land at Wahiawa on the island of Oahu. He had concluded that coffee growing would be unprofitable and so decided to become a truck farmer specializing in the cultivation of pineapples. At that time it was impossible to export fresh pineapples to the North American West Coast without excessive spoilage, so Dole decided to can his pineapples. He raised capital in New England and founded the Hawaiian Pineapple Company in December 1901. In 1903 Dole succeeded in raising further capital from California food canner J. H. Hunt. The Hawaiian Pineapple Co. packed its first canned pineapple in 1903. Production grew rapidly between 1903 and 1906. In 1906 Dole married Belle Dickey of Honolulu. They had five children.

By 1908 Dole and other Hawaiian pineapple canners found that their principal market—the U.S. West Coast—was saturated. Dole concluded that decisive action was required. He initiated the first of three successive industry associations formed during his leadership of the Hawaiian Pineapple Co. As the first president of the Hawaiian Pineapple Growers' Association (HPGA), Dole argued that the solution to the industry's problem was price cutting, better marketing, and cooperative advertising. In 1908 the HPGA became the first American food industry to adopt nationwide cooperative advertising. The advertising helped expand the market for canned pineapple from the American and Canadian West Coast to the American Midwest and East Coast.

Another important part of the success of the Hawaiian Pineapple Co. was Dole's investment in research and development of pineapple processing technology. Dole felt that the existing machinery imported from the mainland was unsatisfactory. In 1911 he employed Henry Gabriel Ginaca, chief draftsman of the Honolulu Iron Works, to invent a more efficient machine. After several attempts, Ginaca succeeded in 1913. The "Ginaca Machine" resulted in a substantial increase in productivity, as it was the first device to allow the canner to peel and core pineapples in one operation with a single machine. Dole continued to invest in research and development, and, just before he lost control of his company in 1932, he discovered a way of processing canned pineapple juice. This new product was a great success during the 1930s.

During World War I Dole participated in the American war effort. He served as chairperson of the Honolulu Chamber of Commerce Committee on Agriculture and, subsequently, between 1917 and 1918 also served as chairperson of the Territorial Food Commission. The purpose of these two organizations was to promote diversification away from sugar cane production, which dominated Hawaiian agriculture. Dole was one of the few planters in Hawaii to succeed in producing a commercial crop other than sugar cane.

During the 1920s Dole found it increasingly difficult to acquire land to grow enough fruit to meet the growing demand for canned pineapple in the United States. As a result, he embarked upon an ambitious expansion project with the acquisition of most of the island of Lanai in 1922 for $1.1 million, where he redeveloped a former ranch into a 13,000-acre pineapple plantation. Dole financed this project with several million dollars borrowed from a syndicate of Hawaiian banks and finance houses and by selling a share in his company to a sugar plantation company affiliated with the sugar agency Castle & Cooke.

In 1931 the Hawaiian Pineapple Co. lost over half of its market in the United States as a result of the Great Depression and had heavy losses. Dole's company was unable to service the debt incurred largely as a result of the Lanai project. However, Dole's creditors were unwilling to reorganize his debt partly because he had lost the support of Castle & Cooke by switching his company's shipping contract in 1931 to the Isthmian Steamship Co. from the Matson Navigation Co., which was affiliated with Castle & Cooke. Dole's creditors forced him to reorganize the Hawaiian Pineapple Co. and to resign as president of the company. He was appointed chairman but without any management role and sent on a long vacation. Castle & Cooke and its affiliate, the Waialua Agricultural Co., gained majority control of the company in December 1932.

Dole returned to the mainland where, on 5 August 1933, he was appointed chief of the Food Products Section, Processing and Marketing Division, Agricultural Adjustment Administration (AAA), by the Roosevelt administration. Dole was responsible for formulating codes for food products. Cynical about the benefits of his work to the consumer, he resigned from the AAA in January 1934.

After leaving Washington, D.C., Dole moved to San Francisco, where he became interested in gold mining and invested in the Arroyo Seco Gold Dredging Company. Although the mine produced gold for several years, Dole's other gold mining investments were less successful. He also organized the Chemical Process Company in 1936 to manufacture exchange materials for improved sugar purification. It became the leading company in its field and later became part of the Diamond Shamrock Company after a merger.

In December 1937 Dole formed a venture capital general partnership, James D. Dole & Associates, with three partners and turned over all of his gold projects to the partnership, which continued until his retirement in 1954. In 1938 the partnership and a group of associates, including the food processing company S & W Fine Foods, invested in the Schwarz Engineering Co., Inc., of Redwood City, California (later renamed the James Dole Engineering Co.). At the time of the acquisition, this company had just developed a process for packing natural carrot juice after four years of research and experimentation. Dole had financed the development of this process by Henry Schwarz in 1937. In 1940 the company also developed a process for canning and bottling natural apple juice. In 1941 S & W formed a joint venture with Dole Engineering to produce canned apple juice in the S & W plant in Redwood City. Later, the company perfected a canned milk process. Dole resigned as chairman of the board of the Hawaiian Pineapple Co. in 1948. However, the company continued to pay him royalties for the use of his name. He died in Honolulu, Hawaii.

Dole was not the first entrepreneur to see the commercial possibilities of canning Hawaiian pineapple. However, he can be regarded as the founding father of a commercially successful Hawaiian canned pineapple industry. He was responsible for some of the most important technological developments in the industry and also led the development of its successful cooperative advertising strategy. After Dole lost control of the Hawaiian Pineapple Co. he developed a new career in food technology based in California.

• The archives of the Hawaiian Pineapple Company, which include scrapbooks from 1907 and board minutes, are held by the University of Hawaii at Manoa Library. Dole was the author of a number of articles, including "The Pineapple Industry," *Report of the Governor of Hawaii to the Secretary of the Interior* (1904), and "The History of the Pineapple Industry from the Early Days," *Pacific Commercial Advertiser*, 9 Feb. 1921. Interviews with Dole can be found in the *Pacific Commercial Advertiser*, 11 Sept. 1913, and in "The Hawaiian Pineapple Industry," *Canning Trade* 45, no. 7 (10 Oct. 1921): 12–18. "Impressions of Five Months in Washington August, 1933, to January, 1934" (1934) is a collection of interviews on his experience as a New Deal administrator originally published in the *New York Herald Tribune*. Further information about Dole can be found in a biography coauthored by his grandson and daughter, Richard Dole and Elizabeth Dole Porteus, *The Story of James Dole* (1990). Short biographies can be found in George Ferguson Mitchell Nellist, ed., *The Story of Hawaii and Its Builders* (1925), and in Nellist, ed., *Men of Hawaii: A Biographical Record of Men of Substantial Achievement in the Hawaiian Islands* (1935). An account of Dole's years at Harvard can be found in Harvard University, *Class of 1899: Fiftieth Anniversary Report* (1949). A short article about Dole's business venture in Calif. can be found in the *Honolulu Star-Bulletin*, 19 Aug. 1941. Obituaries are in the *Honolulu Advertiser*, 15 May 1958, and the *New York Times*, 16 May 1958.

RICHARD A. HAWKINS

DOLE, Sanford Ballard (23 Apr. 1844–9 June 1926), president of the Republic of Hawaii and governor of the territory of Hawaii, was born in Honolulu, Hawaii, the son of Daniel Dole and Emily Hoyt Ballard, Congregational missionaries to the islands who superintended Punahou School. His father also served as pastor at the Seamen's Bethel in Honolulu. His mother died when Dole was four days old, and he was cared for by other missionary families, first the Chamberlains and then the Bishops, until 1846, when his father married Charlotte Knapp, who raised him as her own son. Dole attended Punahou School, then spent his senior year (1866–1867) at Williams College in Williamstown, Massachusetts. Upon graduation he studied law for a year in Boston. On 10 September 1868 he passed the bar examination and was admitted to practice law in Suffolk County. "I look upon law," Dole wrote to his parents, "as a possible stepping stone to influence and power in Government, where they need good men, and where a good man could, I think, do more for the nation, for morality and justice, than preaching to the natives." He returned to Hawaii to open his law practice. In 1873 he married Anna Prentice Cate. They built a home on Emma Street in Honolulu and attended the Fort Street Church. Along with law, Dole continued numerous hobbies, from bird watching to yacht racing.

In January 1880 Dole began to involve himself in politics by organizing mass meetings against King Kalakaua and his cabinet. Dole opposed the king's appointment of Celso Caesar Moreno, thought to be dubiously credentialed, as premier and minister of foreign affairs, calling the action a scheme toward absolute monarchy and inconsistent with the principles of constitutional government. The king withdrew the appointment of Moreno, and Dole congratulated the king in a speech applauded by masses of Hawaiians at Kaumakapili Church. Dole continued to organize mass public meetings to hold the king and his cabinet accountable for arbitrary actions, such as granting Claus Spreckles, a sugar magnate from California who played cards with the king, the privilege of importing Chinese immigrants after the license had already been granted to the Pacific Mail and the Occidental and Oriental Steamship companies. Dole also objected to the king's support for a lottery bill and the licensing of opium, which were in Dole's mind immoral. Elected to the Hawaiian legislature in 1884 and 1886, he was associated with the Opposition party, a reform group opposed to the king's royalists or Palace party, and was dedicated to ending political abuses within the Hawaiian monarchy. The reformers cut across ethnic boundaries and enjoyed wide support. W. D. Alexander wrote of the crisis, "A considerable reaction had taken place among the natives, who resented the cession of the Wailuku Crown lands to Spreckles, and felt a profound distrust of Walter Murray Gibson [the king's chief minister]." The legislatures of 1884 and 1886 attempted to vote money in reason and proportion, but Kalakaua continued his extravagance and offered no plan to reduce debt. Dole wrote: "Dissatisfaction grew. With no legal way of overriding the king's veto, there seemed no hope of desirable reforms by legislative methods. Late in 1886, the feeling became so intense that a proposal to organize developed." In January 1887 the reformers formed the Hawaiian League, a voluntary organization to secure "efficient, decent, and honest government in Hawaii." Membership in the league was kept secret, but by the following year it had over four hundred members. The league openly discussed its options, including forming a republic. In 1886 King Kalakaua, over the protests of the reformers, had signed an act licensing the sale of opium, and a scandal developed over the king's taking bribes from more than one bidder for the opium license. During this "intolerable" crisis, the Honolulu Rifles, a local militia organized by the Hawaiian League, and the league's executive Committee of Thirteen forced the king on 6 July 1887 to sign a new constitution, known as the Bayonet Constitution, which limited the king's power.

In December 1887 the king appointed Dole an associate justice of the Supreme Court of Hawaii, a position he held until the monarchy was overthrown in 1893. King Kalakaua died in 1891, and the two years of Queen Liliuokalani's reign echoed much of the political turmoil that had characterized her brother's seventeen-year rule. In 1886 Liliuokalani, fearing domination by foreigners, had opposed the second reciprocity treaty with the United States because it involved the lease of Pearl Harbor. The early moments of her rule suffered the effects on Hawaii of the McKinley Tariff, which destroyed the advantage Hawaiian sugar had enjoyed since reciprocity was signed. Now annexation by the United States for economic gain was openly talked about in reforming circles. Liliuokalani wanted "Hawaii for the Hawaiians," the royalists' motto, and immediately attempted to promulgate a new constitution to replace the one forced upon her brother. At the same time, she planned to initiate a lottery. Dole recalled that the lottery "promoters promised the government a princely annual tax for the license; she wanted to have personal control of the government; and the loss of the royal prerogative resulting from the constitution of 1887, was a grief to her."

The reformers saw the queen's actions as revolutionary or unconstitutional. As the queen attempted to issue a constitution on 14 January 1893, the Hawaiian League was organized to act in the emergency, and the Annexation Club authorized a Committee of Safety "to take whatever measures it might consider necessary to protect the public interests." On 16 January at a mass meeting held at the armory, the Committee of Safety was given power "to further devise such ways and means as might be necessary to secure the permanent maintenance of law and order and the protection of life, liberty, and property in Hawaii." Dole instructed the Committee of Safety, and he asked the U.S. minister to Hawaii, John L. Stevens, to land troops from an American warship, the USS *Boston*, for protection

against the queen's guard. Dole resigned from the Hawaiian Supreme Court to accept the presidency of the evolving provisional government. On the evening of 16 January Liliuokalani promised not to make changes to the constitution except through channels allowed in the constitution of 1887, but her offer was too late and was not accepted. The reformers were supported by the Honolulu Rifles, who took control of the government buildings and proclaimed a new regime. Minister Stevens recognized the Dole government, which looked now toward annexation by the United States. The 270 Hawaiian soldiers at the royal barracks stacked their arms, refusing to fight to defend the monarchy. Liliuokalani surrendered the government buildings, including the police station, to the Committee of Safety, vacated the palace, and retired to her private home, "Washington Place." However, she protested the presence of American forces ashore and professed to yield her authority to these forces pending an investigation by the U.S. government, after which she hoped to be reinstated as monarch. Princess Kaiulani, heir to the throne, traveled to Washington, D.C., where she implored President Grover Cleveland to restore the monarchy. The Dole government suspended the writ of habeus corpus on Oahu and proclaimed martial law. The provisional government organized military forces, created a national guard, established the powers of government, passed laws against sedition and treason, and repealed the lottery and opium licenses. Troops from the USS *Boston* remained in the streets to preserve order.

Representatives Lorrin Thurston, William R. Castle, Joseph Marsden, C. L. Carter, and William Wilder were sent to Washington to secure a treaty of annexation, but the recent election of President Cleveland temporarily impeded their cause. President Cleveland wished to restore the queen, and he assigned James H. Blount, the new minister to Hawaii, to lead an investigation of the circumstances surrounding the overthrow of the monarchy. Blount withdrew the protectorate that former minister Stevens had placed over Hawaii, lowered the U.S. flag over the islands, and evacuated the troops back to the *Boston*. Mainland newspapers from California to Maine discussed the Hawaii question, with Republican tracts usually in favor of and Democrats usually against annexation. Stevens had supported annexation "as a Maine Republican, journalist, and diplomat of long experience," wrote Dole's biographer Ethel Damon, adding, "Stevens in his reports to Washington, had repeatedly urged the value to the United States of annexing Hawaii." An article in the *Boston Transcript* on 16 June 1893 noted: "Sanford Dole's unusual ability . . . anticipated for him a useful career. . . . In the community Mr. Dole is esteemed for clear sense, moderation, and rectitude." During a September–October 1893 visit to Honolulu, Robert Louis Stevenson expressed his support for the royalist cause and his British conviction that Princess Kaiulani should sit upon the throne. The London government hinted that England,

France, and Germany might not acquiese to U.S. annexation of Hawaii.

After Blount's return to Washington, Cleveland named Albert S. Willis as minister to Hawaii with instructions to reinstate the queen. Throughout the United States, Republicans, such as Senator Joseph R. Hawley of Connecticut, condemned Cleveland's "secret, underhand instructions to Willis" (Damon, p. 269). Dole and the provisional government determined "to resist to the last" and to continue the move for annexation "as a conspicuous feature of our foreign policy." On 23 December 1893, in a reply to Cleveland's request that the provisional government reinstate the queen, Dole wrote that he did not recognize the president's right to interfere in Hawaii's domestic affairs. Cleveland stipulated that, if reinstated, the queen must pardon those who had overthrown her government. However, she would not promise amnesty, saying that "she would abide by the law of her country, which carried for traitors the death penalty with confiscation of property" (Damon, p. 292). President Cleveland, upon hearing of the queen's response through Willis, allowed the decision on restoration to be placed before Congress.

With annexation not yet forthcoming, the government in Hawaii proclaimed the Republic of Hawaii on 4 July 1894, and Dole was elected president. He drafted a tentative constitution for the republic, which was the basis for discussion in the constitutional convention that ratified the new instruments of government. In 1895 the royalists staged an unsuccessful counterrevolution, during which a cache of weapons was found in the queen's garden, and she was imprisoned in Iolani Palace. The queen sent Dole her formal abdication and pledged allegiance to the republic. At the trials of the royalist insurrectionists, Dole modified the three death sentences to imprisonment. Many American newspapers, such as *Kate Field's Washington*, continued to support Dole and the move for annexation. From 7 January to 4 March 1898 Dole visited Washington, D.C., to speak with President William McKinley on behalf of the annexationists. His case had gained strength as U.S. ships stopping in Hawaii on their way to the Philippines during the Spanish-American War emphasized the stategic importance of the islands. In June and July Congress passed a joint resolution for political union. At the formal ceremonies of annexation on 12 August 1898, the sovereignty of the Hawaiian Islands was passed to the United States, and Hawaii became a territory. The Organic Act (14 June 1900) became the basic law of Hawaii after acceptance in Congress, and in June 1900 Dole was appointed as the first governor of the territory of Hawaii. After McKinley's assassination, Theodore Roosevelt continued Dole's appointment, and Dole often talked about statehood for Hawaii in the future. Republican delegate to Congress Jonah Kuhio Kalanianaole spoke for the Dole government and Hawaii, and Dole encouraged Kuhio's Hawaiian homesteading laws. During Dole's governorship, the Chinatown fire was set in 1900 by the board of health to combat the plague, the

trolley and the transpacific cable were developed, and pineapple production became a major industry through the pioneering efforts of his cousin James D. Dole, who founded the Hawaiian Pineapple Company.

Dole did not seek another term as governor. In 1903 he was appointed a U.S. district judge, and he was reappointed in 1909. In 1907 he served as Hawaiian branch president for the American Red Cross and in 1908 supported the founding of the Children's Hospital and the Outrigger Canoe Club. He toured Europe in 1911, and in December of that year he was an honored guest, along with former queen Liliuokalani, at the opening ceremonies celebrating the newly widened channel into Pearl Harbor. In 1916, at the end of his second term as judge, he retired to private life. During World War I, Dole was head of a group supporting war orphans and widows. In 1918 his wife died. From 1922 to 1926 he served as a commissioner of the Hawaii Territorial Archives, which he had helped organize during his governorship. After his death in Honolulu, a new addition to the Hawaii State Archives was named Sanford Ballard Dole Hall.

• Dole's private papers are in the possession of his heirs. His public papers are in the Hawaii State Archives, which also has invaluable photographs of the republic and territorial periods. The archives of the Hawaiian Mission Children's Society, Honolulu, and the archives of the Hawaiian Historical Society, Honolulu, have personal information relating to Dole's missionary family background. Ethel M. Damon, *Sanford Ballard Dole and His Hawaii* (1957), is the best source available, for Damon was selected as Dole's personal biographer and was given access to his personal papers by his heirs. Damon's book includes Dole's "Thirty Days of Hawaiian History," which describes in journalistic fashion the revolution against the Hawaiian monarchy. Lorrin A. Thurston, *Memoirs of the Hawaiian Revolution*, ed. Andrew Farrell (1936), is also an excellent contemporary account by a friend and colleague of Dole. Gavan Daws, *The Shoal of Time: A History of the Hawaiian Islands* (1968) and Ralph Kuykendall, *Hawaiian Kingdom* (3 vols., 1938–1967), offer excellent interpretive accounts. See also W. D. Alexander, *History of Later Years of the Hawaiian Monarchy and the Revolution of 1893* (1896).

BARBARA BENNETT PETERSON

DOLLAR, William (20 Apr. 1907–28 Feb. 1986), dancer, choreographer, and teacher, was born in East St. Louis, Illinois, the son of Edward Dollar, a Hungarian grocer, and Catherine Hoffman. Because his mother was opposed to dance he did not inform her when, in his senior year of high school, he began taking classes in "acrobatic adages" with a local teacher, a Miss Clark, who did not charge him. There he was seen by Bob Alton, who immediately billed him and his partner into the vaudeville shows that were given between films at the Missouri Theatre. Alton's wife then sent Dollar to New York to see Mikhail Mordkin, the Russian dancer and teacher, who got him a scholarship at the Murray Anderson school, where Mordkin taught. In 1930 Dollar went with the Mordkin company to Philadelphia, where that same year Catherine Littlefield invited him to join her company. With her he danced in movie houses in Philadelphia and went with the company to Paris, where he studied briefly with Alexandre Volonine.

Back in the United States, Dollar went to New York, where he performed at the Capitol Theatre and at Radio City Music Hall. He also studied dance with Michel Fokine, danced with Fokine's group at Lewisohn Stadium, and performed with the Metropolitan Opera Ballet. In Hollywood, he danced in the *Goldwyn Follies* (1938).

Dollar was first really noticed as a dancer, an excellent technician who could jump and turn, when he first performed with George Balanchine's American Ballet in 1936, dancing Amor in the opera-ballet *Orpheus and Eurydice*, the Joker in *Card Party*, and Melancholic in *The Four Temperaments*, as well as roles in *Ballet Imperial*, *Concerto Barocco*, and *Serenade*. He was also in Lincoln Kirstein's Ballet Caravan, in the Marquis de Cuevas Ballet International, and was a principal with Ballet Theatre, where he danced in the Fokine ballets *Les Sylphides* and, as Harlequin, *Carnaval*. All of these companies also included Dollar's ballets in their repertory.

As a choreographer, Dollar created the first of eighteen works, *Concerto* (to Chopin's Piano Concerto no. 2), in 1937. It was really a music visualization, expressing in movement what he heard in the music, the creation of which was encouraged by Balanchine, who choreographed the second of the three movements (Dollar choreographed the outer movements). Revised by Dollar and renamed *Constantia*, it was performed in New York in 1944 and later revived by the Original Ballet Russe, Ballet International, the Grand Ballet de Monte Carlo, Ballet Theatre, and American Ballet Theatre. In 1988 it was staged by Yvonne Patterson, Dollar's common-law wife, for the Ballet du Nord. John Martin in the *New York Times* called this an "intelligent job of composition by a choreographer of unmistakable talent," if derivative in style. Another work, *A Thousand Times Neigh*, was performed by American Ballet Caravan at the New York World's Fair in 1940—ten times a day for six months.

The best known of Dollar's works is *The Duel* (music by Rafaella de Banfield), created for and first performed by Roland Petit's Ballets de Paris in 1949 under the title *Le Combat*. An effective dramatic showpiece, the initial version was a duet between the Christian knight Tancred and his critically wounded opponent, who turns out to be his love, the Saracen maiden Clorinda. As staged for the New York City Ballet in 1950, it was a fuller work with warriors and a prologue. Although some critics found it slight in form, it was praised in content, invention, and expression, particularly the use of movements that give the impression the characters are mounted on horseback. Ballet Theatre presented still another version in 1953 called *The Combat*. This work has been widely staged and is an audience favorite.

Dollar served as ballet master for the American Concert Ballet in 1943 and the Ballet Society in 1946.

After he stopped performing in 1956, owing to arthritis, he helped found the Ballet Academy in Iran, taught at the Ballet Theatre School, and worked in Japan and in Rio de Janeiro on several occasions, one under the auspices of the U.S. State Department. He died in Flourtown, Pennsylvania.

Dollar was highly regarded as a teacher. In his choreography he was a classicist who showed the influence of both Balanchine and Fokine. He possessed an innate sense of craftsmanship, and he preferred flowing movements. William Dollar's role as a substantial figure in American ballet during its most critical stages has yet to be fully explored.

• The Dance Collection of the New York Public Library for the Performing Arts has clippings and program files for Dollar as well as files on *Constantia* (*Concerto*) and *The Duel* (*The Combat*). There are also numerous articles in *Dance Magazine* (see, especially, Apr. 1950, p. 9, and Sept. 1980, pp. 44–46); *Dance and Dancers* (London), Nov.–Dec. 1988; *Ballet Today*, Dec. 1955; and *Dance News*, Nov. 1946. Lynn Asinof's article "When It All Began," *Ballet News*, Nov. 1980, pp. 14–16, talks about some of Dollar's lesser-known works for Ballet Caravan. At the New York Public Library for the Performing Arts is a tape of an oral interview with Paul Sutherland by Marilyn Hunt that discusses Dollar as a teacher. Obituaries are in *Dancing Times* (London), Apr. 1986, and *Dance Magazine*, May 1986.

DAWN LILLE HORWITZ

DOLLARD, John (29 Aug. 1900–8 Oct. 1980), psychologist and sociologist, was born in Menasha, Wisconsin, the son of James Dollard, a railroad engineer, and Ellen Brady, a former schoolteacher. Following his service as a private in the U.S. Army during the First World War, Dollard attended the University of Wisconsin at Madison, where he studied commerce and English and earned his B.A. in 1922. At Wisconsin, Dollard met the physicist Max Mason, who became, in Neal Miller's words, Dollard's "model and second father"; following several years as a fundraiser for the Wisconsin Memorial Union, Dollard went on to work as Mason's assistant at the University of Chicago when Mason was its president. With Mason's encouragement, Dollard entered graduate school at Chicago and received his M.A. (1930) and his Ph.D. (1931) in sociology. His doctoral dissertation, published in 1931 as *The Changing Functions of the American Family*, was supervised by the prominent Chicago sociologist William Fielding Ogburn. The dissertation used statistical methods to analyze how the American family had changed over a thirty-year period, from 1900 to 1930, particularly with regard to its roles as provider of education, promulgator of religious values, and protector of health.

At the conclusion of his graduate studies, Dollard accepted a year-long Social Science Research Council Fellowship in social psychology to study psychoanalysis at the Berlin Psychoanalytic Institute, under the supervision of Hanns Sachs and Karen Horney, among others. There, Dollard later wrote, "the writings and views of Freud [became] so thoroughly worked into my thinking that I ascribe to him a major orientation of my thought" (*Caste and Class*, p. 38n). Upon his return in 1932, Dollard worked with Edward Sapir, the linguist and anthropologist, on a year-long seminar on the impact of culture on personality that was held at Yale University. Dollard was subsequently appointed research associate in psychology at Yale's Institute of Human Relations. Max Mason, as president of the Rockefeller Foundation and as a believer in an integrated "science of man," supported Dollard's work at Yale, continuing his early interest in and influence on the social scientist. Dollard remained at Yale for the rest of his career, becoming professor of psychology there in 1952 and professor emeritus in 1969. In 1930 he was married to Victorine Day Dollard and divorced in 1959; the couple had four children. In 1961 he married Joan Ganis Palance; that marriage lasted until his death.

In all of his work, Dollard attempted to integrate the psychoanalytic insights of Freud, the learning theory of the Yale behaviorist psychologist Clark Hull, and social scientific descriptions of the social and cultural contexts in which personality is formed. The Institute of Human Relations, of which Dollard became a leading member, nurtured this integrative enterprise. Because its directors encouraged cooperation across disciplinary lines, Dollard was able to meet and to collaborate with psychoanalysts, psychologists, sociologists, and anthropologists.

Dollard's first work at the institute was a monograph, *Criteria for the Life History* (1935), on his method of taking "life histories" of individuals to understand their personality development. He subsequently used this method to study the personality development of "Negroes" in a small town in the Deep South. He soon discovered that he could not understand individual personalities apart from the social structure of the community and so turned to describing that structure rather than the trajectories of individual lives.

The book that resulted, *Caste and Class in a Southern Town* (1937), was Dollard's best-known, most influential, and most controversial work. Using Freudian terminology and social scientific methods, he sought "to grasp and describe the emotional structure which runs parallel to the formal social structure in the community" (*Caste and Class*, p. 17). Southern society depended on a caste system, Dollard argued, that afforded whites economic, social, and sexual privileges while keeping blacks subservient. Unlike class, which was relatively fluid, caste was a fixed and rigid system that "replaced slavery as a means of maintaining the essence of the old status order in the south" (*Caste and Class*, p. 62).

Dollard described various forms of white aggression against blacks, ranging from lynching to moral intimidation, that he believed arose from white fear of the lower caste, especially from the mixture of fear and repressed desire that whites felt for interracial sexual relations. He delineated the frustrations that the caste system imposed on blacks and their accommodation to and repression of aggressive tendencies toward whites.

For Dollard, the caste system was deeply antidemocratic and required a complex of defensive rationalizations "to conceal the disparity between social justice according to our constitutional ideal and the actual caste treatment of the Negro" (*Caste and Class*, p. 365).

Despite his criticisms, Dollard stressed his objectivity as an observer of southern society and made no explicit recommendations for changes in policy. He concluded that race prejudice was always "irrational," yet he believed that no changes to the caste system in the South were imminent. Regarded by sociologists as a model approach to the study of race relations, *Caste and Class* was widely praised as revealing "the forces retarding the solution of the race problem and social progress" in the South, at the same time that it was banned in Georgia and South Africa (the *New York Times*, 11 Oct. 1980, p. 20).

Dollard's findings in *Caste and Class* formed the basis for his next book, a theoretical work he published with several colleagues. In *Frustration and Aggression* (1939), Dollard and his collaborators again employed a combination of Freudian ideas and behaviorist methods to advance the hypothesis that aggression is always a consequence of frustration and to use the hypothesis to explain a wide range of human behavior. In 1940 Dollard returned to the study of race relations by collaborating with the anthropologist Allison Davis on *Children of Bondage*, a book based on Davis's research on the personality development of Negro youth in the urban South. In 1941 Dollard collaborated with the Yale psychologist Neal E. Miller on *Social Learning and Imitation*, which used the behavioristic laws of learning to explain crowd behavior and the diffusion of culture.

From 1942 to 1945, Dollard served as a consultant to the Department of War. He and Miller studied the reactions of infantry to fear in battle, using veterans of the Spanish Civil War as interview subjects, to gather data useful for training servicemen in World War II. In this period, Dollard wrote *Victory over Fear* (1942), a popular self-help book designed to encourage people to overcome their fears of everything from sex and intimacy to war and social change. He also wrote a self-help manual specifically for soldiers called *Fear in Battle* (1943), in which he advises soldiers that fear is a normal response to danger and that a calm, rational understanding of this response would help them deal with it. Dollard also served as president of the Commission on Mental Health of the U.S. Public Health Service from 1949 to 1952.

In the last few publications of his career, Dollard continued to pursue the synthesis of the social sciences that he had envisioned years earlier. *Personality and Psychotherapy* (1950), written with Neal Miller, attempted to integrate Hull's behavioristic studies of learning with anthropological reports of the social and cultural conditions under which learning takes place and to apply this knowledge to explain Freudian psychoanalytic observations of human behavior. Dollard and Miller argued that neurosis is a learned behavior, that new ways of coping can be taught, and that the psychotherapist was therefore a special kind of teacher. *Step in Psychotherapy* (1953), written with Frank Auld, and *Scoring Human Motives* (1959), with Auld and Alice M. White, were both attempts to codify and systematize the results of psychoanalysis.

At a time when few American social scientists were followers of Freud, Dollard attempted to give Freudian psychoanalytic theory a firm basis in objective observation and experiment. He envisioned a synthesis of diverse sciences—psychoanalysis, behaviorism, anthropology—sciences often considered incompatible. The unified social science that resulted fulfilled the social engineer's dream: in Dollard's hands, it became a tool for the rational management of the nation's most pressing social and political problems.

Dollard died in New Haven, Connecticut.

• Dollard's papers are in the archives of Yale University. His coauthors on *Frustration and Aggression* were Neal E. Miller, Leonard W. Doob, O. H. Mowrer, and Robert R. Sears, in collaboration with Clellan S. Ford, Carl Iver Hovland, and Richard T. Sollenberger. Substantive assessments of Dollard's life and thought can be found in two obituaries, one in the *New York Times*, 11 Oct. 1980, and the other by Neal Miller in *American Psychologist* 37 (1982): 587–88; and in Daniel Patrick Moynihan, "Remembering John Dollard," *New York Times Book Review*, 9 Nov. 1980.

NADINE WEIDMAN

DOLLIVER, Jonathan Prentiss (6 Feb. 1858–15 Oct. 1910), U.S. senator, was born near Kingwood, Virginia (now W.Va.), the son of James Jones Dolliver, a Methodist circuit rider, and Eliza Jane Brown. In 1868 the Dolliver family moved to the outskirts of Morgantown, West Virginia, where Jonathan entered the preparatory department of West Virginia University. At age thirteen Jonathan began his collegiate studies at the university and graduated four years later. He spent the years 1875 to 1878 teaching school and studying law in Illinois and Iowa. Then in the spring of 1878 Dolliver moved to Fort Dodge, Iowa, where he began the practice of law.

At first the earnings from his legal business were meager, but in 1880 Dolliver was elected city solicitor, a post that ensured him a steady supplemental income. Though his legal fortunes did not soar, his reputation as a public speaker won Dolliver the attention of many in northwestern Iowa, including former governor Cyrus C. Carpenter. In part through Carpenter's influence, Dolliver was chosen the keynote speaker for the 1884 Iowa Republican Convention, where he delivered a rousing political address. Because of this oratorical success, he was chosen to stump the eastern United States for the Republican candidate for president, James G. Blaine. Blaine lost the White House, but Dolliver won recognition as a coming leader whose speaking skills could prove invaluable for the GOP.

After failing to secure the Republican nomination for the U.S. House of Representatives in 1886, Dolliver returned to the fray and won the GOP endorsement in 1888. Defeating his Democratic opponent, Dolliver

entered the House in 1889 and remained there for the next eleven years. In the House he earned a reputation as an orthodox Republican who favored high protective tariffs, the gold standard, and President William McKinley's policy of colonial expansion. Dolliver became unusually close to Iowa's preeminent legislator, Senator William Boyd Allison, who nurtured the younger man's political career. Dolliver, however, maintained harmonious relations with all factions of Iowa Republicans. He was a good friend of sometime Allison critic Governor William Larrabee, a leading proponent of railroad regulation, and Dolliver's younger brother married Larrabee's daughter. In 1895 Congressman Dolliver married Louise Pearsons. They had three children.

In 1900 Dolliver was seriously considered as a vice presidential running mate for McKinley. Dolliver, however, was not interested in the position, which instead went to Theodore Roosevelt. That same year Dolliver's career benefited from the death of Iowa senator John Henry Gear. Iowa's governor appointed Dolliver to succeed Gear in the Senate, and in the 1902 session the Iowa legislature seconded the governor's choice, electing Dolliver to fill out the remainder of the term. In January 1907 the legislature chose to continue him in office, electing him to a full six-year term.

As senator, Dolliver remained unswerving in his loyalty to the conservative Allison, but he also became a staunch supporter of the reform agenda of Roosevelt. In fact, Dolliver was the principal figure in guiding the Roosevelt-endorsed Hepburn Act of 1906 through the Senate. This act empowered the Interstate Commerce Commission to fix maximum rail rates and was especially popular among Dolliver's midwestern constituents, who had long chafed under the discriminatory rates of the railroads. Yet as late as 1908 Dolliver fought a bitter battle against Iowa's leading progressive reformer, Albert Cummins, when the latter sought unsuccessfully to defeat the dying Senator Allison in the state's first senatorial primary election.

In 1908 Republican William Howard Taft won the presidency after a campaign in which he promised a lowering of the tariff rates. During the first decade of the twentieth century, many of Dolliver's constituents, who had previously accepted Republican protectionism, grew increasingly critical of high duties, believing that the tariff protected monopolistic eastern manufacturers while raising the cost of living for heartland consumers. Likewise, Dolliver's faith in the necessity of a high tariff waned as he became increasingly concerned about the privileged status of big business. Consequently, in 1909, when Nelson Aldrich, the Republican leader of the U.S. Senate, proposed a tariff measure that did not sufficiently decrease the rates, a number of midwestern lawmakers, including Dolliver, were outraged. Even more infuriating was the apparent complicity of President Taft in this plot to maintain high duties. Together with Wisconsin's senator Robert La Follette and Indiana's senator Albert Beveridge, Dolliver led the fight against Aldrich on the tariff issue, earning a reputation as an "insurgent." Unleashing his ample speaking skills, he lambasted Aldrich and his supporters, presenting a series of widely acclaimed speeches against the Payne-Aldrich Tariff. "I do not propose now to become a party to a petty swindle of the American people," Dolliver told his fellow senators. He also spoke of his "indignation" at being "duped with humbug and misrepresentation" by the Aldrich forces. Despite Dolliver's dramatic attack, the tariff measure passed both houses of Congress and was signed by the pliant President Taft. "President Taft," Dolliver observed in response, "is an amiable man, completely surrounded by men who know exactly what they want."

The Payne-Aldrich clash was not the only battle in the war between Dolliver and Taft. The Iowa senator sided with Gifford Pinchot, chief of the federal forestry bureau, who charged that Taft's secretary of the interior, Richard Ballinger, allowed private exploitation of government-owned natural resources. Moreover, Dolliver opposed the Mann-Elkins Bill as originally proposed by the Taft administration, claiming that it would weaken the Interstate Commerce Commission.

Exhausted by his battles against Aldrich and Taft, Dolliver sought rest in Fort Dodge, where he died of a heart attack. By the time of his death, he had won a reputation as a courageous crusader for progressive reform. Like his circuit-riding father, Dolliver was a man with a strong sense of morality and an even stronger voice, which during his final years he used to support insurgency in the Senate. Though for decades he had been a true believer in the GOP party line, at the close of his career he was one of the heroes of progressivism, a figure whose integrity equaled his oratory.

• Dolliver's papers are in the State Historical Society of Iowa. The definitive biography of Dolliver is Thomas Richard Ross, *Jonathan Prentiss Dolliver: A Study in Political Integrity and Independence* (1958). For the early development of Dolliver's speaking skills, see Gordon F. Hostettler, "Jonathan Prentiss Dolliver: The Formative Years," *Iowa Journal of History* 49 (1951): 23–50. The whole issue of *The Palimpsest* 5 (Feb. 1924) is devoted to Dolliver. Another useful source is a series of sketches devoted to Dolliver in *Annals of Iowa* 29 (July 1948): 335–65. For memorial addresses on Dolliver, see the *Congressional Record* 46 (1911): 2832–43. An obituary is in the *New York Times*, 16 Oct. 1910.

JON C. TEAFORD

DOLLY SISTERS, identical-twin celebrities, were born Janszieka Deutsch and Roszika Deutsch (25 Oct. 1892–1 June 1941) in Budapest, Hungary, to Julius Deutsch, a tailor, and Margaret Weiss, a painter. Janszieka became known as Jenny Dolly; her sister as Rosa Dolly. Raised and educated in Queens, at age eight the Dollys were performing with an acrobatic troupe; by 1909 they were dancing at B. F. Keith's Union Square Theatre. Later, their four-week engagement at the Palace set a vaudeville record for a sister act. After their 1910 appearance in the musical comedy *The Echo*, Florenz Ziegfeld signed them for his 1911 *Follies*. After two 1912 musical comedies, *A Winsome Widow*

and *The Merry Countess*, the Dollys, so apparently temperamentally akin that one might finish the other's sentence and so physically alike that news stories often confused them, were famous, largely because of their glittering off-stage lives. Legend holds that the *bon vivant* "Diamond Jim" Brady gave Rosy a Rolls-Royce automobile wrapped in ribbons.

Onstage, the Dollys, who never successfully portrayed anyone else, wore stylish clothes and specialized in graceful synchronized dancing. A co-star in *The Honeymoon Express* (1913), matinee idol Harry Fox, divorced his wife to marry Jenny in that year. They formed their own vaudeville act. They had no children and divorced in 1921. Theater historian Gerald Bordman claimed the ensuing publicity helped prolong Fox's career, but marriage separated the Dollys. In the same year Rosy married composer Jean Schwartz. They had no children and also divorced in 1921.

During the sisters' separation Rosy appeared in the musical comedies *The Beggar Student* (1913) and *The Whirl of the World* and *Hello, Broadway* (both 1914) as well as the D. W. Griffith film *The Lily and the Rose* (1915), supporting Lilian Gish as a predatory exotic dancer. In 1916 the Dollys reunited on Broadway for *Her Bridal Night*. They appeared as themselves in the 1918 Metro film *The Million Dollar Dollies*, wherein they had to earn enough money to match their prospective suitors' fortunes by convincing a rich but hypnotized maharajah to love his beautiful bride. They never returned to films. After an undistinguished tour of *Oh, Look!* (1919), the Dollys went to London for revue producer Albert deCourville's lavish *Jig Saw* (1920).

The Dollys' international career truly began in London with Charles Blake Cochran's revue *The League of Notions* (1921). Cochran's biographer said Rosy and Jenny "electrified the audience with their looks and their dash." They appeared in a pageant of brides down through the ages; garbed as statues they clog-danced; in The Dollies and Their Collies, an act borrowed from their American shows, they performed with dogs who "danced wonderfully for dogs"; in pearly costumes they did a "witty pastiche of old time music hall"; in black top hats and coachmen's silken cloaks they urged the audience to join them in beating tambourines. This "inconsequential process of music, dance and dramatic interlude" delighted many viewers, as did the production's sheer gaudy expense.

In the absence of its ill impresario, Cochran's next show, *Fun of the Fayre* (1921), was foundering when the Dollys, who were still appearing in *The League of Notions*, rushed over after its curtain to dance a pony trot with the Indianan from Piccadilly, Clifton Webb. The patrons returned. In Cochran's Christmas pantomime *Babes in the Wood* (1922) the playful Jenny was Douglas Fairbanks while the more reflective Rosy was Mary Pickford.

Performing in such cabarets as the Kit Kat Club, Jenny and Rosy became glamorous London fixtures, their stylish Borzoi hounds always in tow. They collected such rich admirers as yachtsman-teagrower Thomas Lipton and American department-store tycoon Gordon Selfridge. Selfridge set aside a vast room in his London mansion for the sisters. French soubrette Gaby Deslys's biographer noted that Jenny's "passion for emeralds was eventually instrumental in Selfridge's losing control of the store he had founded." Between 1922 and 1924 the Dollys also lived the high life in France, where the exchange rate neared 50 francs to $1.

Returning to the States in 1924, the Dollys, eventually called by the *New York Times* "a mirror of an era's taste," were newsworthy for their cloche hats, black shirtwaists, brown tailormade skirts, lizard skin shoes, and bare tanned legs. In *The Greenwich Village Follies of 1924* their "French vividness" was acclaimed in a show mainly noted for its looks. They left (replaced by Toto the Clown) after a contract dispute but not before receiving the accolade of parody when Gertrude Lawrence and Beatrice Lillie spoofed them abroad in *Charlot's Revue* as the Apple Sisters, Cora and Seedy. The Dollys helped a road company of the Guy Bolton–P. G. Wodehouse–Jerome Kern musical *Sitting Pretty* (1924) outrun its Broadway version.

Later in 1924 the Dollys made their Parisian music hall debut at Les Ambassadeurs. They subsequently appeared at the Casino de Paris, the Moulin Rouge, and the Palace, where in *Oh! Les Belles Filles!* they demonstrated "Le Dancing Crazy" and parodied themselves in a stock exchange skit, "The Dollar Sisters." By 1925 the Dollys had remodeled the new dance craze, the Charleston, into the Dirty Dig, "less acrobatic than the Black Bottom." They specialized in surprising entrances—perhaps from a huge straw hat. If Jenny left a robe provocatively askew, Rosy would shoot her a reproving glance. One critic praised their version of the Can-Can as "extra dry." In 1926 the Dollys successfully sued the Moulin Rouge for billing the soubrette Mistinguette higher than themselves. The 550,000 francs ($18,500) they were awarded went to Parisian charities. Their eyelids shaded, their cheeks round and pink, their lips cupid's bows, and their black hair in bangs, they were the very image of the 'twenties.

Back in America, in 1927 Rosy married Mortimer Davis, Jr., heir to a Canadian brewing fortune, in a ceremony kept secret from Davis's father, who threatened disinheritance. They divorced in 1931; she received a settlement rumored to be worth $2 million. They had no children. In 1927 the sisters announced their retirement from show business. In 1928 Jenny won a reported $625,000 at Cannes, converting most of it into jewelry. She acquired the chateau at Fontainebleu. Rosy reportedly won $400,000 at Cannes. Soon Davis was back in Canada and Rosy was living in St. Moritz.

In 1929 Rosy had to give back a $280,000 pearl necklace because Davis had not paid its Parisian vendors. In 1929 Jenny adopted two Hungarian girls, Klari and Manzi, five and six years old, from a Budapest orphanage. In 1930 she won $280,000 at Le Tou-

quet. In 1932 Rosy married Irving Netcher in New York's Waldorf Hotel, where Mayor Jimmy Walker performed the ceremony. They had no children. In 1933 Jenny was injured in an automobile accident near Bordeaux. For nearly three years, she avoided public view, enduring a series of surgeries. Her jewels were auctioned off, and in 1934 she was fined for evading French luxury tax on a diamond ring bought with her 1928 Cannes winnings.

In 1935, after the sisters' rumored return to show business did not materialize, Jenny married Bernard Vissinsky, who also adopted Klari and Manzi. In 1937 at their Chicago apartment a man threw white pepper into Jenny's eyes, blinding her for ten days. Jenny committed suicide in Hollywood, fashioning a noose from heavy draperies and hanging herself from a curtainrod. Four years later, *The Dolly Sisters*, an engaging Hollywood motion picture musical, was made with Betty Grable as Jenny and June Haver as Rosy.

In a 1952 interview Rosy attributed the sisters' success entirely to luck. When Netcher died in 1953, she was on the Isle of Capri. She became a regular at the Hamptons in Long Island and in 1958 enlivened American documentary television, recalling for Edward R. Murrow's "Person to Person" her friends Rudolph Valentino, Maurice Chevalier, and Marlene Dietrich. In *Variety*'s words, she portrayed "a silken dowager dame in tufted surroundings . . . weighted down with a heavy, glittering three-strand necklace and long drop two-strand earrings." In 1962 she was found unconscious in her New York apartment from a drug overdose. Having never completely recovered from a broken hip, Rosy died in New York.

• Programs and news clippings regarding the Dolly Sisters are found in archives such as the Billy Rose Theatre Collection of New York Public Library for the Performing Arts and the Theatre Museum, London, which also includes such Parisian publications as Louis Roubaud, *Music Hall* (1929), P. Bost, *Le Cirque et Le Music Hall* (1931), and C. Georges-Michel, *Nuits d'Actrices* (1933). The Dollys are mentioned in Charles B. Cochran's many volumes of memoirs, as well as biographies such as James Harding, *Cochran* (1988), and James Gardiner, *Gaby Deslys* (1986). The liveliest obituary and accompanying memoir is Rosy's in *Variety*, 4 Feb. 1970.

JAMES ROSS MOORE

DOLPH, Joseph Norton (19 Oct. 1835–10 Mar. 1897), U.S. senator, was born in Dolphsburg, New York, the son of Chester V. Dolph and Eliza Vanderbilt, farmers. Dolph attended public schools in New York until the age of sixteen, when he took a job on the Chemung Canal. Two years later he began attending classes at Genesee Wesleyan Seminary, teaching in local schools, and studying law under Jeremiah McGuire of Havana, New York. Dolph was admitted to the New York bar in 1861 and began a practice in Binghamton. In the spring of 1862, Dolph enlisted in an expedition known as the "Oregon Escort," a military force charged with protecting migrants from

American Indian attacks, and headed west. He settled in Portland, Oregon, and, in 1864, married Augusta E. Mulkey. They had six children.

Shortly after arriving in Portland, Dolph formed a legal partnership with John H. Mitchell, and it quickly became one of the most influential legal firms in the state. They specialized in land litigation and railroad right of way cases, establishing themselves as experts in railroad issues. Among their clients were Ben Holladay and Henry Villard, two of the most prominent business tycoons in the West. Dolph served as counsel for the Oregon Steamship Company, the Oregon Transcontinental Company, and other big corporations. He eventually became vice president of Villard's Northern Pacific Railroad. Both Dolph and Mitchell would parlay the wealth and power deriving from these contacts into political careers.

Similar to so many other lawyers, Dolph entered politics in a legal position, as attorney for the city of Portland in 1864. One year later President Abraham Lincoln appointed him U.S. district attorney for Oregon. Dolph served in the state senate from 1866 to 1872 and again in 1874, and for two years he chaired the state's Republican central committee. When Oregon's electoral votes in the presidential election of 1876 were disputed because of voting irregularities, Dolph prepared the brief that contested the decision of the governor to certify a Democrat as one of the state's electors. Congress approved Dolph's position and awarded all three of Oregon's votes to Republican candidate Rutherford B. Hayes, helping Hayes defeat Samuel J. Tilden.

In 1882 Dolph was elected to the U.S. Senate, following his former partner Mitchell, who had been elected in 1872. Dolph served two terms in the Senate and was chosen as chairman for the Committee on Coast Defenses. He also served on the Commerce Committee and the Committee on Foreign Relations. As a Republican senator, Dolph supported the party's insistence on high tariffs but also championed the creation of the Interstate Commerce Commission and advocated woman suffrage. He quietly provided financial support for Oregon suffrage leader Abigail Scott Duniway, not least because she used her writings to associate Democrats with liquor and prostitution. Like many other legislators from the West Coast, Dolph also vigorously opposed the immigration of Chinese workers.

As with many western Republicans, Dolph found it difficult to deal with the issue of silver coinage. He voted for the Sherman Silver Purchase Act in 1890 and opposed its repeal three years later. However, while Dolph was willing to consider the partial use of silver as a monetary standard, he remained firmly opposed to the unlimited coinage of silver. This partial concession on silver coinage was not enough to satisfy the generally prosilver position of Oregon's GOP. Amid widespread allegations charging Dolph with fraud and vote buying in the state legislature and at the behest of Mitchell, Dolph was replaced by a prosilver Republican, George McBride.

Dolph retired from public life after his defeat. When Mitchell resigned from their law firm to become a senator, Dolph had expanded the firm by bringing in new partners, including his brother Cyrus A. Dolph. The firm's continued success and Dolph's own business contacts allowed him to maintain a considerable fortune and his prominent position in the community. He served as state grandmaster for both the Masons and Odd-Fellows. Dolph died in Portland soon after his retirement from politics, when attempts to trim a corn and ingrown toenail resulted in gangrene in his leg.

As it did for many others, a successful career as a corporate lawyer turned into a political career for Dolph. His political service was unspectacular but not without merit. He generally served as a loyal Republican legislator while trying to find some middle ground on free silver. If Dolph did not stand out from the crowd, it was because his career path was one so commonly traveled by Gilded Age politicians.

• Dolph's papers are at the University of Oregon. The best source for Dolph's attitudes on public questions is the *Congressional Record* (1883–1895). Also helpful are E. Kimbark MacColl, *Merchants, Money, and Power: The Portland Establishment, 1843–1913* (1988), and T. T. Geer, *Fifty Years in Oregon* (1912). Dolph's obituary is in the *New York Times*, 11 Mar. 1897.

WILLIAM T. HULL

DOLPHY, Eric (20 June 1928–29 June 1964), jazz musician, was born Eric Allan Dolphy, Jr., in Los Angeles, California, the son of Eric Dolphy, Sr., and Sadie Gillings. He showed a strong interest in music during his preschool years and began playing clarinet in the first grade. He participated in musical activities throughout his grade school years, and he studied privately with Lloyd Reese, a well-known Los Angeles music teacher who also taught jazz musicians Buddy Collette, Dexter Gordon, and Charles Mingus. After graduating from high school, Dolphy enrolled in music classes at Los Angeles City College. By this time he also was playing alto saxophone with local bands, and he made his first recordings with a big band led by drummer Roy Porter. After serving in the army during the early 1950s, he returned to Los Angeles and reentered the music profession. Early in 1958, his friend Buddy Collette recommended him to drummer Chico Hamilton, who needed a woodwind player. Dolphy moved from local to national prominence in jazz, playing flute, clarinet, bass clarinet, and alto sax in Hamilton's quintet. (He is heard on Hamilton's album *Gongs East*, Dec. 1958.) The group at the time was well known for playing a type of gentle bebop popularly known as "cool" jazz, although Dolphy's style leaned toward the more exuberant in that idiom.

At the end of 1959 Hamilton's quintet broke up, and Dolphy soon began working and recording with Mingus in New York City, appearing with him prominently on the album *Charles Mingus Presents Charles Mingus* (20 Oct. 1960). Mingus's groups played an energetic, almost chaotic brand of jazz, combining elements of bop, Duke Ellington's music, and basic classical techniques in a style much better suited to Dolphy's taste than that of Hamilton's quintet. During his tenure with Mingus, Dolphy recorded with other players and made his first recordings as a leader, most notably on the album *Out There* (15 Aug. 1960). After a year he left Mingus's group and recorded some highly regarded and historically important albums with other leaders, including Ornette Coleman's *Free Jazz* (21 Dec. 1960), Oliver Nelson's *Blues and the Abstract Truth* (23 Feb. 1961), and George Russell's *Ezz-Thetic* (8 May 1961). He also participated in some of composer Gunther Schuller's concerts and recordings of third-stream music, which attempted, sometimes successfully, to blend jazz and European-style classical music.

Intermittently from 1961 until 1963 Dolphy wrote arrangements for and played with saxophonist John Coltrane appearing on *Spiritual* (1 Nov. 1961) and on concert recordings made in Europe (Nov. and Dec. 1961). Coltrane at the time was the most prominent avant-garde player in jazz, so Dolphy's association with him was professionally as well as musically important. During the same period he also rejoined Mingus's group for short stays and led groups of his own. He took part in a short European tour with Mingus in April 1964 and remained on the Continent to perform on his own. On June 27 he began a night club engagement in Berlin, but he was too sick to complete the first night's performance. Two days later he died of a heart attack, possibly triggered by a diabetic condition. His body was flown to Los Angeles for burial.

Dolphy had a solid musical background in bebop, the jazz style that Dizzy Gillespie, Charlie Parker, and others had developed in the 1940s. Indeed, Dolphy's style of improvisation held many similarities to Parker's. But he went beyond the bebop idiom's norms of harmony, melody, and tone quality and became a leading figure in the "free jazz" or "action jazz" idiom. This stylistic evolution was aesthetically rewarding but economically costly. Free jazz, then as now, was the least understood and least liked of jazz styles, and he often went without playing jobs. For a time, he supported himself mainly by private teaching. He found steadier work and more sympathetic audiences in Europe than in the United States.

Like Coltrane, Dolphy had a thorough command of his instruments and of both the bebop and the post-bebop jazz styles. In the early 1960s the music that Dolphy and Coltrane created was often attacked by the jazz audience and press. When a widely read critic labeled their music "nonsense," "nihilistic exercises," "anti-jazz," and "gobbledegook," the two men felt compelled to defend their music in print. In their published interview, Dolphy explained that some of what he played on flute imitated bird calls, including the nonstandard pitches that bird calls contain. He believed his music to be inspiring and moving, and he wished that critics would ask the performers about the music before writing uninformed reviews that could hurt the musicians economically.

Dolphy dedicated himself untiringly to developing his forceful personal style and to mastering several instruments, principally alto saxophone, flute, and bass clarinet. He remains the principal bass clarinetist in jazz history. His unaccompanied bass clarinet solo, "God Bless the Child" (8 Sept. 1961), recorded in Copenhagen, is a landmark. His album *Iron Man* (July 1963), on which he mainly plays alto saxophone, is a prime example of his mature playing. In some of the album's pieces he creates melodies with wide leaps, sudden changes of direction, and rapid flurries of notes; these freely ranging, angular melodies have little obvious connection with the harmonies of the themes. Yet on the ballads his command of the traditional harmonic vocabulary of jazz is clear and idiomatically consistent.

• The famous negative review by John Tynan of Dolphy's and Coltrane's music appeared in *Down Beat*, 23 Nov. 1961, as did the Coltrane/Dolphy interview in response to it, 12 Apr. 1962. Two of the best articles on Dolphy are by Jack Cooke, *Jazz Monthly*, Jan. 1966, and David Keller, *Jazz Times*, Nov. 1981. A useful chapter appears in John Litweiler's *The Freedom Principle: Jazz after 1958* (1984), an informative section in Robert Gordon's *Jazz West Coast: The Los Angeles Jazz Scene of the 1950s* (1986), and a good article by Barry Kernfeld in *The New Grove Dictionary of Jazz* (1988). Works devoted to Dolphy are Vladimir Simosko and Barry Tepperman, *Eric Dolphy, a Musical Biography and Discography* (1974); Uwe Reichardt, *Like a Human Voice: The Eric Dolphy Discography* (1986); and Raymond Horricks, *The Importance of Being Eric Dolphy* (1988). An obituary is in *Down Beat*, 13 Aug. 1964.

THE EDITORS

DONAHOE, Patrick (17 Mar. 1811–18 Mar. 1901), editor and publisher, was born in County Caven, Ireland, the son of Terrence Donahoe and Jane Christy. The father's occupation is unknown, but the family was clearly poor. In 1821 Patrick and his father immigrated to Boston, Massachusetts, where the boy received a basic education and entered the printing trades in 1825. Patrick worked as a printer for several Boston newspapers and became co-owner of *The Jesuit*, a local Catholic paper, in 1831. He soon changed the name of the paper to *The Literary and Catholic Sentinel* and in 1835 changed the name again, this time to the *Boston Pilot*, in an effort to link it to Daniel O'Connell's *Dublin Pilot*. The following year he married Kate Griffin. During the late 1830s, Donahoe suffered a series of economic setbacks, and publication of the *Pilot* was suspended in 1837.

Donahoe revived the *Pilot* in 1838 and took over sole ownership in 1839. During these years, he was reporter, editor, printer, and circulation manager, all in one. In an effort to increase circulation, Donahoe revamped the *Pilot* in the 1840s by targeting more specifically the growing number of Irish immigrants in the city. The paper published news of Ireland and championed O'Connell's movement for greater Irish independence. The Boston Irish responded to the change in the paper, and by the mid 1840s the circulation had grown from 600 to 7,000 subscribers. The success of the *Pilot* during these years was further fueled by Donahoe's charismatic editor, Thomas D'Arcy McGee, who joined the paper in 1844.

As a prominent Irish-American citizen of Boston, Donahoe contributed to a number of social causes, including the Young Catholic Friends Society, an organization founded to care for dependent children; the temperance crusade led by Irish priest Theobald Mathew; and the New England Land Company, an organization established to help Irish immigrants move west and colonize undeveloped land. An ardent Democrat and loyal Catholic, Donahoe favored the gradual emancipation of the slaves, but he opposed abolitionism, a movement he believed to be made up of "bigoted and persecuting religionists."

In 1849 Donahoe hired Father John T. Roddan as editor. Roddan found a national audience for the *Pilot* by shifting the paper's focus from Irish nationalism to a mixture of Irish news and Catholic piety. "It was during Roddan's editorship from late 1849 to 1858," noted historian William L. Joyce, "that the *Pilot* started the growth that was to give it the highest circulation and the great national influence it enjoyed as the foremost Irish-American journal of the 1870s."

With his paper in capable hands, Donahoe turned his attention to other business enterprises. He found great success in book publishing. As early as the 1830s, Donahoe had published popular fiction in the pages of the *Pilot*, and the appeal of these stories added to the success of the paper in the 1840s. The popularity of serialized stories by Mary Anne Sadlier and other writers led Donahoe to publish their work in book form. Among the most popular titles were Sadlier's *Willie Burke; or, The Irish Orphan in America* (1850); Hugh Quigley's *The Cross and the Shamrock; or, How to Defend the Faith* (1853); and Peter McCorry's *The Lost Rosary; or, Our Irish Girls, Their Trials, Temptations and Triumphs* (1870).

The onset of war in 1861 turned Donahoe's attention and the focus of the *Pilot* to the preservation of the Union. After the secession of the southern states, Donahoe took an active part in organizing volunteers into the Ninth Regiment of Massachusetts. The Twentieth Regiment also received Donahoe's support. In the years following the war, the circulation of the *Pilot* rose steadily. Among the most popular features of the paper during these years was "Records of Irish American Patriotism," stories of the Civil War exploits of the Irish-American soldiers who fought to preserve the Union.

By 1870 Donahoe was a wealthy man, publisher of a paper with a national circulation of over 100,000 subscribers. Donahoe also operated the largest Catholic publishing house in the nation, a book store, a bank, and a travel agency, all located in the "Donahoe Buildings" in downtown Boston.

But Donahoe suffered an "avalanche of misfortune" in November 1872 when fire swept the Boston business district, destroying the Donahoe buildings, and a second fire ten days later destroyed what little he had left. His losses from the two fires were reported to be

$350,000. Although Donahoe struggled to pay his debts for the next four years, he was forced into bankruptcy in 1876. As one part of the settlement, Donahoe sold his beloved *Pilot* to his editor, John Boyle O'Reilly, and Archbishop John Williams.

Donahoe began to rebuild his business enterprises in 1878 with the establishment of *Donahoe's Magazine*, a publication that grew in popularity during the 1880s. The magazine reflected Donahoe's own liberal views—a friend of liberal bishops such as John Williams and James Gibbons, he favored more lay involvement in church affairs, opposed parochial schools, and generally promoted efforts that would assimilate Catholics into the mainstream of American life. The success of the magazine marked Donahoe's return to prominence in the Boston business community. He found great satisfaction in repurchasing the *Pilot* in 1890 and in receiving the Laetare Medal from the University of Notre Dame in 1893 as the "Catholic who had done the most in defense of the Faith in America."

A year after his first wife's death in 1852, Donahoe had married Anne E. Davis. Donahoe died in Boston the day after his ninetieth birthday. His funeral was something of a civic affair, with thousands of Irish Americans attending his funeral. Even Pope Leo XIII sent an apostolic blessing for this loyal servant of the Catholic Church.

• There is no significant body of Donahoe papers. An excellent and very thorough biography is Mary A. Frawley, *Patrick Donahoe* (1946). Donahoe's contributions to the development of Boston Catholicism are discussed in Robert H. Lord et al., *History of the Archdiocese in Boston*, vol. 2 (1944). Three more recent studies that touch on Donahoe's editorial and publishing career are Donna Merwick, *Boston's Priests, 1848–1910* (1973); William L. Joyce, *Editors and Ethnicity* (1976); and Charles Fanning, *The Irish Voice in America* (1990). Obituaries are in the *Boston Pilot*, 23 and 30 March 1901.

TIMOTHY WALCH

DONAHUE, Sam (8 Mar. 1918–22 Mar. 1974), jazz and popular tenor saxophonist and bandleader, was born Samuel Koontz Donahue in Detroit, Michigan. His parents' names and occupations are unknown. Donahue began clarinet at age nine and saxophone in high school. He played in the Redford High School band while also working locally as a sideman and with his own band from 1933 until 1938. In the latter year he gave his Detroit band over to arranger Sonny Burke and became a soloist in Gene Krupa's big band. Donahue's tenor saxophone playing may be heard on such recordings as "Apurksody" (1938), "The Madam Swings It" (1939), and "Who" (1940). Donahue was a capable but not significant jazz soloist. Like a number of leading white tenor saxophonists of the day, he focused on the more aggressive aspects of solo styles pioneered by Coleman Hawkins, Chu Berry, and other African-American tenor players. After brief stands with the big bands of Harry James (summer 1940) and Benny Goodman (October 1940), Donahue was reunited with Burke in autumn 1940 and took back the leadership of his band, which recorded "It Counts a Lot" in December of that year. The band's final recording session was in July 1942.

Drafted into the navy, Donahue was assigned to Artie Shaw's big band in November 1942. In this capacity he toured the South Pacific. After Shaw's discharge in December 1943, Donahue took over leadership of this navy band and in April 1944 embarked for Europe. Donahue spent considerable time in London, where the band regularly made radio broadcasts. Evidently he married there. Details of the marriage are unknown, but Donahue's children lived in London. In 1945 his navy band recorded for the V-Disc label in New York and the Armed Forces Radio Service in Hollywood.

Donahue occasionally led another band after the war, and he taught music lessons at the Hartnett Studios in New York City. During the Korean War he was recalled into the navy for six months in 1951. He played with Tommy Dorsey's orchestra from late 1951 to early 1953 and directed the Billy May Orchestra on tour from January 1954 through 1956. From 1957 to 1959 he led his own band again, performing at Birdland and the Blue Note in New York. Toward the end of a stay with Stan Kenton from September 1960 to September 1961, Donahue taught in Kenton's summer jazz workshop; listeners especially remembered his wrenchingly beautiful ballad playing as a featured soloist with the student band from North Texas State College.

In October 1961 he took over the memorial Tommy Dorsey Orchestra, which visited Japan, South America, and Europe in 1964 and 1965. During his British tour in 1964, Donahue expressed disappointment that his beloved big-band music had fallen completely out of fashion, to be replaced by a new popular music (heralded by the Beatles) that he intensely disliked and severely underestimated. In 1965 the band worked with singer Frank Sinatra, Jr., rather than being billed as the Dorsey Orchestra. By the following year Donahue was no longer able to finance a big band, and the group was reduced to an octet before he disbanded it. After another involvement with Kenton's jazz education efforts in 1967, Donahue became a music director, first at the Playboy Club in New York City, from 1969 at the Nugget Casino in Sparks, Nevada, and finally at casinos in Reno, where he died of cancer.

Donahue was a moderately well-known bandleader in the last years of the swing era and a musically conservative keeper-of-the-flame in the decades that followed. Ironically, in the mid-1970s his son Jerry became lead guitarist with the English rock group Fairport Convention.

• Interviews of Donahue are Max Barker, "The Ghost Band," *Crescendo* 2 (Jan. 1964): 20, and Garry Brown and Jack Dorsey, "They Only Buy the Name," *Crescendo* 2 (Mar. 1964): 11. William F. Lee, *Stan Kenton: Artistry in Rhythm*, ed. Audree Coke (1980), details his affiliation with Kenton. See also Albert McCarthy, *Big Band Jazz* (1974), and George T. Simon, *The Big Bands*, 4th ed. (1981). A catalog of his recordings as a leader is by Charles Garrod and Bill Korst, *Sam Donahue and His Orchestra* (1992). An obituary is in *Melody Maker*, 20 Apr. 1974.

BARRY KERNFELD

DONALDSON, Henry Herbert (12 May 1857–23 Jan. 1938), neurobiologist, was born in Yonkers, New York, the son of John Joseph Donaldson, a banker, and Louisa Goddard McGowan. Donaldson was a friendly, levelheaded young man, always characterized as honest and straightforward. His fascination with science and nature began at an early age, when he entered Phillips Academy in Andover, Massachusetts. As a Phillips student, he undertook the academic challenges that lay before him with eagerness, fervor, perseverance, and the same dedication that would mark his future work.

Donaldson earned his B.A. in 1879 from Yale University, where he forged strong and lasting relationships with many professors. Still unsure about his future career, he chose to remain an extra year to study the effects of arsenic poisoning under the guidance of Professor Russell Chittenden. This work resulted in Donaldson's first publication in a scientific field, an article written with Chittenden that appeared in the *American Chemical Journal* in 1881.

In 1880 Donaldson began medical studies at the College of Physicians and Surgeons in New York. After one year, however, he realized that medicine was not to be his calling and instead accepted a fellowship in physiology at Johns Hopkins University. There he worked with H. Newell Martin on the effect of digitalis on the heart and with G. Stanley Hall, a pioneer in American psychology, on the detection of stimuli moving across the skin.

In 1884, while working on tactile motion perception, Donaldson noticed that his metal probe elicited sensations of cold only at certain spots on the skin. Intrigued by this incidental finding, he began to map the cold-sensitive spots on different parts of the body. After he found out that Magnus Blix, a Swede, and Alfred Goldscheider, a German, had just published papers on the punctate sensitivity of the skin, Donaldson improved his methodology and began to conduct additional experiments on both cold and warm spots. This research formed the basis of the doctoral dissertation that Donaldson submitted for his degree in 1885.

Donaldson evaluated changes in temperature sensitivity over time by marking the spots with ink. He even tried to identify the specific receptors for cold and warm by excising a cold sensitive spot from his leg and a heat-sensitive spot from his forearm. His stained samples revealed many nerves beneath the two kinds of spots, but he could not detect any significant morphological differences between the two samples.

Donaldson's most unique contribution to somesthesis came when he elicited the help of a few Baltimore eye surgeons who were using cocaine as an anesthetic. He examined some of their patients and found that, when cocaine was administered locally to block pain and pressure sensations, cold and heat could still be detected by the eye. To convince himself that the modality dissociation was really occurring, he even had the procedure conducted on one of his own eyes.

In 1886, a year after publishing two papers on temperature sensitivity, Donaldson coauthored a paper with G. Stanley Hall on the perception of movement on the skin. He then left for Europe for more extensive training in neuroanatomy. His year and a half abroad brought him in contact with the leading European neuroanatomists of the day, including August Forel in Zurich, Bernhard von Gudden in Munich, Theodor Meynert in Vienna, and Camillo Golgi at Pavia.

In 1889 Donaldson left Johns Hopkins to become an assistant professor of neurology at Clark University in Worcester, Massachusetts. Josiah Clark had recently recruited G. Stanley Hall to head the new research university, and it was Hall, with whom he had worked on the skin senses, who enticed him to move. While at Clark, Donaldson was entrusted with the brain of a blind and deaf mute, Laura Bridgman, who had been taught to communicate. In order to understand the aberrant features of her brain, which seemed to be due to arrested growth caused by the loss of sensory organs, Donaldson tried to learn all he could about normal brain development from birth to maturity. His celebrated papers on the case of Laura Bridgman appeared a few years later, in 1891 and 1892.

Donaldson moved in 1892 to the University of Chicago, where he served as professor of neurology and as dean of the Ogden School of Science. In 1895 he published *The Growth of the Brain: A Study of the Nervous System in Relation to Education* and, in 1898, a chapter of well over one hundred pages on the central nervous system in the *American Text Book of Physiology*. Although he then suffered a crippling tubercular infection of the knee that left him permanently lame, Donaldson continued to write about the anatomy of the human and infrahuman (usually frog) nervous systems. As time passed, however, and as the result of the work of one of his assistants, Dr. S. Hatai, Donaldson came to the conclusion that the best available mammal for controlled developmental studies was the white rat.

In 1906 the board of directors of Philadelphia's recently reorganized Wistar Institute invited Donaldson to become the institute's professor of neurology and director of research. The board informed him that the institute must be devoted to research, especially in the neural sciences. Donaldson accepted the challenge and, joined by Hatai, moved from Chicago to Philadelphia.

Once at the Wistar Institute, Donaldson began to write papers on the growth of the brain and spinal cord in the rat. He and his associates also set to work producing a purebred strain of white rats for researchers. These endeavors eventually led Donaldson to undertake a source book for investigators planning to work with rats. In 1915 he published *The Rat*, a long-awaited work that he felt compelled to expand just nine years later.

Donaldson remained active in research and writing up to the time of his death in Philadelphia. In accordance with his will, his brain was removed and donated to the Wistar Institute, and the rest of his body was cremated. Donaldson had been married twice. His first marriage, in 1884, was to Julia Desboro Vaux, who died in 1904, leaving him with their two children. In 1907 he married Emma Brace; they had no children.

During Donaldson's distinguished career he was a member of the National Academy of Sciences (1914) and also served as president of several elite societies, including the Association of American Anatomists (1916–1918), the American Society of Naturalists (1927), and the American Neurological Association (1937). To the scientists who knew him, he had been a man of exemplary integrity and foresight and an American pioneer in developmental neurobiology and neuroanatomy.

• Donaldson's thesis research on the punctate sensitivity of the skin appeared as "On the Temperature Sense" in *Mind* 10 (1885): 399–416. His related papers from this period are "Action of Muriate of Cocaine on the Temperature Nerves," *Maryland Medical Journal* 12 (1885): 475, and "Motor Sensations on the Skin," with G. Stanley Hall as first author, in *Mind* 11 (1886): 557–72. The Laura Bridgman papers appeared as "Anatomical Observations on the Brain and Several Sense Organs of the Blind Deaf Mute, Laura Dewey Bridgman," *American Journal of Psychology* 3 (1891): 293–342 and 4 (1891): 248–94, and as "The Extent of the Visual Cortex in Man as Deduced from the Study of Laura Bridgman's Brain," *American Journal of Psychology* 4 (1892): 503–13. One of Donaldson's first papers on the rat was "A Comparison of the Albino Rat with Man in Respect to the Growth of the Brain and of the Spinal Cord," *Journal of Comparative Neurology* 18 (1908): 345–92. A biography of Donaldson, which includes a list of approximately one hundred of his publications and a photograph, was written by E. G. Conklin for the National Academy of Sciences, *Biographical Memoirs* (1939): 229–43. For obituaries of Donaldson, see *Science* 88 (1938): 72–74, *Archives of Neurology and Psychiatry* 39 (1938): 1313–14, and *Journal of Comparative Neurology* 69 (1938): 173–79.

CLARA LAJONCHERE
STANLEY FINGER

DONALDSON, Mary Elizabeth (12 Jan. 1851–1930), physician and social activist, was born Mary Elizabeth Cracker in Reedsburg, Wisconsin, the daughter of Zachariah Cracker and Elizabeth Delia Brown, farmers. Donaldson grew up in a family strongly dedicated to the Baptist religion and intellectual pursuits. She completed her education through high school, then taught for four years in Reedsburg schools until her 1871 marriage to a man named Hesford. In 1873 Donaldson bore a daughter, who died at age four; soon after the child's death she and her husband divorced. Following the divorce Donaldson escorted her ailing brother James to Idaho to recuperate. In Idaho she obtained work as a teacher while nursing James to full recovery.

During this period Donaldson met and married her second husband, Thomas L. Johnston. While married to him she pursued her lifelong desire to enter the medical profession. In 1889 she began her studies at the medical department of the University of Wooster (later the College of Wooster), where she was the only woman to graduate with an M.D. in 1892.

Donaldson returned to Idaho after completing her medical education and established a private practice in Boise, where she also opened a sanitarium with a staff of two nurses. The sanitarium was successful, and Donaldson then moved on to Milton, Oregon, where she established a second lucrative practice as well as the first sanitarium in Oregon. She next went to Portland, Oregon. She directed the Portland sanitarium for four years and then returned to Boise, where, with the help of her husband, she built the Idaho Sanitarium Institute in the spring of 1898. After its opening Donaldson provided services to patients free of charge. Her husband died later that year.

In Boise Donaldson demonstrated her philanthropic character further; she adopted five orphaned children, rearing them in her comfortable home and inspiring them to follow fulfilling careers. Not only was she a pioneer in the medical field; she also took initiative in social and political issues. She was a charter member of the American Woman's League, frequently contributing to its publications. She was a cofounder of the *Idaho Magazine* in 1903, the first of its kind in Idaho, and she organized and directed the Prohibition Alliance. The active doctor was also an editor and publisher of the *Reform Appeal*, a journal addressing public issues. The election of a Democratic mayor in Republican-dominated Boise was credited to the journal. Donaldson became friends with Captain Gilbert Donaldson, a businessman who shared her philanthropic ideals and social activism, and they married on 9 January 1912.

A later medical establishment of Donaldson's was the Donaldson Home for the Aged, which was inspired by her visit to a similar institution in Philadelphia in 1881. Since then the desire had remained with her to establish such a home. After campaigning for funds from friends, businessmen, and many other charitable citizens, her vision became a reality in 1920 at Donaldson Heights in Boise. There, too, Donaldson provided free care for the patients. Nothing is known about the last ten years of her life; even the date of her death seems not to be recorded, although she is believed to have died in 1930.

• Hiram T. French, *History of Idaho* (1914), is an excellent source on Donaldson's accomplishments and character until 1914. J. Hawley, *History of Idaho*, vol. 2 (1920), also traces her medical and social activism with frequent reference to her humanitarian traits. Louise Shadduck, *Doctors with Buggies, Snowshoes, and Planes* (1993), provides a synopsis of information in these sources.

KIMBERLY HALL

DONALDSON, Walter (15 Feb. 1893–15 July 1947), popular-song composer, lyricist, and publisher, was born in Brooklyn, New York. The names of his parents are not known. Although his mother was a music teacher, Donaldson seems never to have taken music lessons; instead, he learned to play the piano by ear. While still in high school, he began writing songs, and after graduation he found employment on Wall Street, but he soon gave that up in favor of popular music. For a time he worked as a Tin Pan Alley song plugger at $15 a week; however, his addiction to writing his own songs during working hours cost him his job. His first song to make a public impression was "Just Try to Picture Me Down Home in Tennessee" (1915; lyrics by William Jerome), about a state he had never seen. World War I found him in the Entertainment Division of the U.S. Army, where he met Irving Berlin. After returning to civilian life, Donaldson joined the firm of Irving Berlin, Inc., and remained there as an administrator and songwriter for about a decade. A tireless worker, he wrote piece after piece for individual publication and for a variety of Broadway musical productions.

His "How Ya Gonna Keep 'Em Down on the Farm?" (1919; lyrics by Sam Lewis and Joe Young) increased his fame after it was taken up by Sophie Tucker and Eddie Cantor. Then came an extraordinary hit, "My Mammy" (1920; lyrics by Lewis and Young), made famous by Al Jolson, who performed it in blackface, wearing white gloves, on bended knee, with arms flung out to embrace the audience. It was the progenitor of numerous "mammy" songs by other songwriters, which singers presented in the Jolson fashion. Collaborating with the lyricist Gus Kahn, Donaldson composed several more striking successes: "My Buddy" (1922), "Carolina in the Morning" (1922), "Yes, Sir, That's My Baby" (1925), "Love Me or Leave Me" (1928), "Makin' Whoopee" (1928), and "My Baby Just Cares for Me" (1930). The tune for "My Buddy" came to Donaldson as Kahn's child played with a music box that Donaldson had brought him. "Carolina in the Morning" was first sung by Bill Frawley in vaudeville, but its huge success did not come until Willie Howard and Eugene Howard used it in *The Passing Show of 1922*. This song also figured in the Eva Gauthier–George Gershwin recital given in Aeolian Hall on 1 November 1923, famous for introducing American popular songs into a concert of art music.

Donaldson was noted for conceiving his melodies while playing billiards, or golf, or while watching football games, prize fights, and racing events. One example is his immensely successful "My Blue Heaven" (1927; lyrics by George Whiting). The melody is said to have occurred to Donaldson while he was waiting his turn at billiards at New York's Friars' Club. Whiting, a vaudeville headliner, failed in his attempt to popularize the song on stage, but three years later Tommy Lyman won it a wide following by singing it repeatedly on radio and, still later, Gene Austin's recording of the piece sold millions of copies.

In 1928 Donaldson left the Irving Berlin music establishment to cofound the music publishing firm of Donaldson, Douglas, and Gumble, which quickly became highly successful. The firm published, among other songs, at least three hits for which Donaldson wrote both the words and music: "Just Like a Melody Out of the Sky" (1928), "You're Driving Me Crazy" (1930), and "Little White Lies" (1930). In 1929 he went to Hollywood to compose music for movie musicals. Three well-received songs from 1930s films were "When My Ship Comes In" (1934; lyrics by Kahn), "Did I Remember?" (1936; lyrics by Harold Adamson), and "You" (1936; lyrics by Adamson). Former actress Walda Mansfield became Donaldson's wife in 1935. They had two children and were divorced after ten years. He died of a liver ailment at his home in Santa Monica, California.

Donaldson's approach to composition was to conceive a tune and mentally work on it (sometimes for many weeks) before putting it down on paper. He supported his catchy melodies with resourceful harmonies and attractive rhythms. Donaldson labored to put together songs that would reach a wide public rather than please a sophisticated elite. His tunes won the affection of millions.

• Details on Donaldson's life and work are scarce and can be found mainly in his obituary in the *New York Times*, 16 July 1947; David Ewen's *All the Years of American Popular Music* (1977); and Mark White's *"You Must Remember This . . . "* (1985). Information on individual songs is supplied in David Ewen's *American Popular Songs: From the Revolutionary War to the Present* (1966) and David A. Jasen's *Tin Pan Alley* (1988).

NICHOLAS E. TAWA

DONELSON, Andrew Jackson (25 Aug. 1799–26 June 1871), presidential aide, diplomat, and politician, was born near Nashville, Tennessee, the son of Samuel Donelson, who kept a store in partnership with his brother-in-law Andrew Jackson, and Mary Smith. In 1805 Jackson became his namesake's guardian, Donelson's father having died and his mother having remarried. Raised at the "Hermitage," Donelson studied at Cumberland College in Nashville and later at the U.S. Military Academy. In 1820, after only three years, he graduated from West Point, second in his class. He subsequently served Jackson, by then territorial governor of Florida, as aide-de-camp. Donelson left the army in 1822 to study law at Transylvania University in Kentucky. Admitted to the bar the following year, he established a practice in Nashville. In 1824 he married a cousin, Emily Tennessee Donelson, whose dowry included both land and slaves. Establishing their home adjacent to the Hermitage, the couple eventually had four children.

The same year as his marriage Donelson became Jackson's political helpmate, managing the general's correspondence and helping plot his effort to be elected president. After Jackson lost the presidency through what both men regarded as "corrupt bargain" in the House of Representatives, Donelson tried to keep "Old Hickory's" name before the public by cultivating friendly newspaper editors. When Jackson finally reached the White House in 1829, Donelson came with him. Jackson's wife (Donelson's aunt Ra-

chel) having died shortly after the election, the Donelson family took up residence in the executive mansion; Emily Donelson became the White House's official hostess and Donelson served as private secretary. Because this position was not publicly funded, Donelson also performed routine duties at the General Land Office. However, he devoted the bulk of his energies to overseeing Jackson's correspondence, serving as a liaison with Congress, and helping craft official messages. Jackson had a habit of recording his thoughts on bits of paper, often carrying them about in his hat for some time before delivering them to Donelson, who would synthesize them into formal statements.

Donelson and Jackson's professional relationship and their close personal ties came close to collapsing in the course of the famed Peggy Eaton affair. The Donelsons were among the official families of Washington that shunned Mrs. Eaton, the wife of the secretary of war and object of various rumors alleging marital indiscretions. Jackson, on the other hand, proved an ardent defender of Mrs. Eaton and was particularly galled by the Donelsons' power to make the Eatons feel unwelcome in his own home. Donelson's position was further complicated by the fact that, in the factionalism that divided the administration, he was less friendly toward Secretary of State Martin Van Buren than he was to Vice President John C. Calhoun, whom Jackson increasingly saw as the power behind the Eatons' discomfiture. With the Donelsons refusing to accede to Jackson's demand that they make amends to the Eatons, matters reached such a pass that Emily exiled herself to Tennessee in 1830. For a brief time, Donelson and Jackson were reduced to communicating by letter even though they resided in the same household. Tensions eased after John Eaton resigned his position in the cabinet shuffles of 1831 and Emily resumed her place at the White House in the autumn of that year. Interestingly, Donelson—the only prominent tormentor of the Eatons to remain in Jackson's inner circle—seems thereafter to have played a more significant role in administration affairs, having a hand in shaping the noted message accompanying Jackson's veto of the recharter of the Bank of the United States, Jackson's proclamation on nullification, and the Specie Circular. Donelson left his post late in Jackson's second term to tend to his ailing wife, who died of tuberculosis in December 1836. In 1841 he married Emily's niece, Elizabeth Martin Randolph. They had a child the following year.

Donelson, dwelling in "Tulip Grove," the home he had constructed near the Hermitage, remained closely tied to Jackson during the latter's retirement. He continued to compose letters for Jackson and, their families' finances having become entwined, both men found themselves plagued by debt. In September 1844, after a treaty annexing Texas had failed in the Senate, President John Tyler appointed Donelson chargé d'affaires to the Lone Star Republic, hoping he might exercise some influence over Texan leader Sam Houston, a Jackson protégé. Donelson's mission was to facilitate annexation by a second means—the passage and acceptance by Texas of a joint resolution of Congress. Donelson pressed Congress to pass such a resolution before Great Britain and France could broker a deal that would perpetuate Texas's independence by gaining Mexico's official acquiescence in it. Congress having acted in February 1845, Donelson persuasively lobbied Texans to accept annexation, assuring the publicly noncommittal president, Anson Jones, that American forces would guarantee the republic's security until statehood could be accomplished. Donelson's success in Texas was followed the next year by his appointment as minister to Prussia. There he observed the nationalist and liberal upheavals of 1848, and that year he was named by President James Polk the American envoy to the German Confederation. Donelson returned to the U.S. in 1849, subsequently assuming the editorship of the *Washington Union*, a Democratic paper. Finding his pay insufficient to support his family, Donelson resigned in 1853 and returned to Tennessee.

Considering who his mentor was, it is not surprising that Donelson treasured the preservation of the Union over the militant assertion of states' rights—although he was reported to have termed his 100 slaves "proof and guarantee of his fidelity to the institutions of the South" (Gohmann, p. 132). At both sessions of the Nashville Convention of 1850 he supported compromise of sectional issues and opposed southern radicalism. It was surely his unionism that by 1855 had drawn him out of the Democratic party and into affiliation with the Know Nothings, but he gave voice as well to the group's nativism and anti-Catholicism. The American party nominated Donelson, a Southerner and Jacksonian Democrat, for vice president in 1856, running on a ticket headed by former Whig president Millard Fillmore of New York. The pair fared poorly, winning only a single state (Maryland) and earning 21.6 percent of the popular vote. Finding that his political course had soured relations with certain family members and friends, Donelson sold Tulip Grove in 1858 and moved to Memphis, Tennessee. There he practiced law while also superintending his cotton plantation in Bolivar County, Mississippi. Though the wartime action of federal troops and the consequent collapse of slavery disrupted his planting, Donelson never embraced the Confederate cause. He died in Memphis.

Though never a leading man in American politics, Donelson played important supporting roles across three decades—from serving as a vital member of Jackson's inner circle to helping secure the annexation of Texas and later running for the vice presidency in one of the more significant elections in American history.

• Donelson's papers are at the Library of Congress, Manuscripts Division, Washington D.C. His correspondence as chargé d'affaires to Texas is published in William Manning, ed., *Diplomatic Correspondence of the United States: Inter-American Affairs, 1831–1860*, vol. 12: *Texas and Venezuela* (1939); see also John Spencer Bassett, ed., *Correspondence of Andrew Jackson* (7 vols., 1926–1935). Various aspects of Donelson's life and career are covered in Robert Satterfield, "Andrew Jackson Donelson: A Moderate Nationalist Jacksonian" (Ph.D. diss., Johns Hopkins Univ., 1962); Harriet C. Owsley, "Andrew Jackson and his Ward, Andrew Jackson Donelson," *Tennessee Historical Quarterly* 41 (1982): 124–39; Charles F. Bryan, Jr., "The Prodigal Nephew: Andrew Jackson Donelson and the Eaton Affair," *East Tennessee Historical Society's Publications* 50 (1978): 92–112; Annie Middleton, "Donelson's Mission to Texas in Behalf of Annexation," *Southwestern Historical Quarterly* 24 (1920–1921): 247–91; Stephen Lawrence, "Tulip Grove: Neighbor to the Hermitage," *Tennessee Historical Quarterly* 26 (1967): 3–22; Sister Mary de Lourdes Gohmann, *Political Nativism in Tennessee* (1938); Pauline Burke, *Emily Donelson of Tennessee* (1941); and Jonathan M. Atkins, *Parties, Politics, and the Sectional Conflict in Tennessee, 1832–1861* (1997). Considerable information on Donelson is also in Robert Remini's three-volume biography of Andrew Jackson: *Andrew Jackson and the Course of American Empire, 1767–1821* (1977), *Andrew Jackson and the Course of American Freedom, 1822–1832* (1981), and *Andrew Jackson and the Course of American Democracy, 1833–1845* (1984).

PATRICK G. WILLIAMS

DONELSON, John (c. 1718–1725–11 Apr. 1786), land speculator and explorer, was born in Somerset County, Maryland, the son of John Donelson, a merchant and seaman, and Catherine Davis. Following his father's death in 1736, Donelson entered the shipbuilding business. He then migrated to Virginia in 1743, settling near the town of Pastoria in what was Accomack County. About that time he married Rachael Stokely, daughter of prominent landowner and member of the House of Burgesses Alexander Stokely. They had eleven children; the tenth, Rachel, later became the wife of President Andrew Jackson.

Donelson prospered in Virginia, aided by his family connections. He removed to what became Pittsylvania County, Virginia, in 1744. There he was appointed to the county court by Lieutenant Governor Francis Fauquier, became an elder in the Presbyterian church, and acquired a plantation called "Markham." Donelson became county surveyor in 1767 and in 1769 was elected to the Virginia House of Burgesses.

As county surveyor, Donelson became involved on behalf of the colony in a joint enterprise with North Carolina to establish a mutual border. This effort was made necessary by the Treaty of Locabar (1770) with the Cherokees that eliminated American Indian control of land separating the two colonies. Donelson was also selected as a militia lieutenant for his county and participated in the Cherokee War of 1776 that culminated in the Treaty of Long Island (1777). Donelson's surveying and military activity caused his private affairs to suffer and left him near financial ruin. He decided to leave Virginia for what appeared to him to be a "land of promise, that Terrestrial Paradice and garden of Eden" in the area of present-day Tennessee (Spence, p. 163).

Donelson had discovered the area of extreme western Carolina or southern Virginia while on his military and surveying expeditions. He had also become acquainted with Judge Richard Henderson of North Carolina and James Robertson (1742–1814), a leader of the outlawed Watauga Association in present-day Tennessee. Henderson, who had established claims to Cherokee lands in the Cumberland River valley, convinced Donelson to head the colonization of the lower part of that area along with Robertson.

In late 1779 Donelson moved his family to a site near present-day Kingsport, Tennessee. He had agreed to lead a river flotilla that would travel the Tennessee River and the Cumberland River and meet an overland party led by Robertson that would precede him to the French Lick (now Nashville, Tenn.). Donelson was to bring family members and supplies via the water route, while Robertson led the bulk of the males and livestock overland to the settlement already established in the previous year at the French Lick.

The choice of Donelson for the 985-mile river expedition was logical based on his previous nautical experience. The flotilla consisted of some thirty to forty flatboats, dugouts, keelboats, and canoes. The party left Fort Patrick Henry; proceeded down the Holston River about 142 miles to Knoxville; continued via the Tennessee River to the Ohio River, a distance of some 635 miles; then moved up the Ohio River to the Cumberland, about fifteen miles. The final stage was up the Cumberland to the French Lick, a distance of 193 miles. On board those "vessels" were men, women, and children, including thirty blacks; in all, between 160 and 300 persons began the trip. Donelson's flagship was the *Adventure*, which housed about thirty persons.

The journal kept by Donelson constitutes a marvelous account of the harrying journey to join Robertson at Nashville. The trip took from 22 December 1779 to 24 April 1780. The flotilla was attacked by American Indians, experienced capsized vessels in strong currents, and suffered an outbreak of smallpox. During the voyage, some thirty-one persons died, including an infant born during the trip.

It was an extraordinary voyage, one that prompted author Donald Davidson in his work *The Tennessee* (1946) to term it "the most famous voyage in the annals of the pioneer" (vol. 1, p. 150). It was a trip that contributed as much to the history of the old Southwest, in Davidson's estimation, as did the *Mayflower* to that of New England. That view may be excessive, but without a doubt the successful voyage can be marked as one of the great achievements of the settlement of the old Southwest.

After arrival in Middle Tennessee, Donelson settled his large family along the Stones River where it joined the Cumberland River at a place called the Clover Bottom. He participated in writing one of the premier frontier governmental documents, the Cumberland Compact, a written constitution designed primarily by Henderson, Robertson, and Donelson to establish government in the far western region of North Carolina. This mutual compact, signed by the male inhabitants in and around Nashville, went into effect on 1 May 1780.

Life in the Cumberland region, despite formal government and well-established stations and forts, proved too dangerous for Donelson. Frequent American Indian attacks convinced him to move his family to the safer area of Kentucky in 1781. They settled near Harrodsburg at the juncture of the Kentucky and Dix rivers.

Despite living in Kentucky, an area belonging to Virginia, Donelson became involved in a number of activities that involved Tennessee. He was appointed in 1783 by Virginia's governor as a commissioner to negotiate with the Chickasaw Indians in the Cumberland area. While so involved, Donelson went to North Carolina to contact a prominent official there, former governor Richard Caswell, who put Donelson into contact with William Blount, a Carolina politician, businessman, and speculator in western lands. Donelson became an agent of Blount and was soon involved in schemes to develop a new state in and around the Muscle Shoals of the Tennessee River. He also became active in land development in the Cumberland region, which now was included in the Blount-inspired military reservation established there to compensate North Carolina soldiers for revolutionary war service with land in the state's western area.

Donelson became official surveyor for both the Muscle Shoals and the military reservation. In November 1783 Donelson and the other commissioners concluded a peace treaty with the Chickasaws, a move calculated to improve the safety of the western areas, particularly the Cumberland River area.

Throughout 1784 and into 1785, Donelson was engaged in surveying activities in the Big Bend of Muscle Shoals area of the Tennessee River. In March 1785 he sent his family back to the Cumberland area, and on 11 April 1786 Donelson, along with two companions, set out for Nashville to join the family. He was believed to be carrying a large amount of money with him. When the trio stopped for water, Donelson, allegedly in a hurry, went ahead. His two traveling companions stated that they heard shots in the distance, and when they found Donelson he was severely wounded in the stomach and leg. According to the two men, Donelson refused rest until they camped later in the evening. He died during the night. His two companions buried him there but lost his belongings while crossing a river en route to Nashville.

Donelson's death, despite intriguing questions about his traveling companions, was finally attributed to American Indians but at best remains a mystery. He helped open a wilderness to settlement and conducted one of the most breathtaking and significant river voyages in the history of western exploration.

• Primary source material on Donelson is somewhat fragmented due to his mobility. For his early career in Virginia, the *Journals of the House of Burgesses, 1766–1769*, ed. J. P. Kennedy and H. R. McIlwaine (1905–1915), and *The Executive Journals of the Council of Colonial Virginia*, ed. H. R. McIlwaine et al. (1925–1966), vol. 6 (20 June 1754–3 May 1775), are useful. The *Official Letters of the Governor of Virginia*, ed. R. A. Brock (1882–1885), n.s. 3, is also significant concerning the negotiations with the American Indians. Donelson's post-Virginia activities are found in the Draper collections at the Wisconsin Historical Society, of particular value being the Tennessee Papers, the William Preston Papers, and the Kings Mountain Papers. Microfilm copies are available at the University of Tennessee McClung Library. The *John Gray Blount Papers*, ed. Alice Barnwell Keith (1952–1982), particularly vol. 1 (1764–1789), are helpful concerning Donelson's Tennessee career, as is Donelson's journal of his river voyage, found in the collections of the Tennessee Historical Society at the Tennessee State Library and Archives and published in *Three Pioneer Tennessee Documents*, ed. Robert T. Quarles and Robert H. White (1964). The *Papers of Andrew Jackson*, ed. Smith and Owlsly, vol. 1, contains significant genealogical data on Donelson and his family, as does the often overlooked work by Pauline Wilcox Burke, *Emily Donelson of Tennessee* (2 vols., 1941). The best secondary material on Donelson is Charles M. Pope, "John Donelson: Pioneer" (M.A. thesis, Univ. of Tenn., 1969). See also Richard D. Spence, "John Donelson and the Opening of the Old Southwest," *Tennessee Historical Quarterly* 50 (Fall 1991): 157–72, to which the present writer is much obligated.

THOMAS H. WINN

DONGAN, Thomas (1634–14 Dec. 1715), colonial governor, was born in Castletown, Kildare, Ireland, the son of Sir John Dongan, a baronet, and Mary Talbot. After the execution of King Charles I, Dongan left for France where he served in a regiment of Irishmen in King Louis XIV's army and eventually became a colonel there. Dongan attached his fortunes to those of Charles Stuart, who became King Charles II at the Restoration in 1660. Called to England in 1677 and named the lieutenant governor of Tangier, Africa, Dongan served in that capacity from 1678 to 1680. Returning again to England, Dongan was named lieutenant governor of the colony of New York and its dependencies—Pemaquid, Martha's Vineyard, Nantucket and others—by James, the duke of York. The appointment made Dongan essentially the acting, or de facto, governor, and the duke's instructions (issued 27 Jan. 1683) stipulated that he should call a council, issue writs, and summon a general assembly of the freeholders, something that had not happened in the nineteen years since England had taken New Netherland from the Dutch and renamed it New York.

Dongan arrived in New York City on 25 August 1683. What he found was an underdeveloped colony, smaller in population than its New England neighbors. In many letters to London, Dongan stressed the weakness of the colony and urged that Connecticut and New Jersey be annexed to New York. Dongan appointed a council and summoned New York's first general assembly, the representatives of which presented a "Charter of Libertyes and Priviledges," that asserted their rights to enjoy traditional English liberties. These included the right of the freemen to vote for representatives, the right to a trial by jury, and the specification that "Noe aid, Tax, Tallage, Assessment, Custome, Loane, Benevolence or Imposicon whatsoever" would be made without the consent of all three governing bodies: governor, council, and assembly. Dongan gave his assent to the document and forwarded it to England. The duke of York signed the bill but did not return it, and when he became King James II, the new monarch declared that the charter was "repealed and disallowed." The charter assembly had three sessions between 1683 and 1685, but it did not meet again, and the first attempt at a partially representative government in New York came to an end.

Dongan confronted the danger of possible incursions from French Canada. Although he was a Catholic and had served in King Louis XIV's army, Dongan was assertive in his letters to his opposite number in Canada, the marquis de Denonville. Both Dongan and Denonville lacked the soldiers and money to carry out a truly aggressive policy, and the balance of power lay in the hands of the five Iroquois tribes. Dongan's diplomacy paid off in 1684 when the Onondagas and Cayugas agreed that "Wee have putt ourselves under the Great Sachim Charles that lives over the great lake." Dongan persuaded the Iroquois to display the duke of York's arms in their villages as a symbol of English sovereignty.

Dongan conducted this diplomacy at his own initiative and expense and therefore was greatly relieved when James II wrote to him in November 1687 that "we have thought fitt to own the five nations or Cantons of Indians" as subjects. By contrast the Iroquois perceived themselves as free allies. Dongan also clashed with the marquis de Denonville on the subject of the French Jesuits who went among the Iroquois. Dongan and Denonville chastised each other for transgressions; when the French governor accused the English of trying to subvert the Iroquois with liquor, Dongan retorted that "our rum doth as little hurt as your Brandy and in the opinion of Christians is much more wholesome."

Despite his vigorous leadership, Dongan was replaced by Sir Edmund Andros in August 1688. King James II declared that he was well pleased with Dongan's performance, but a decision had been made to merge all colonies north of Pennsylvania into the Dominion of New England, headed by Andros. Dongan chose to remain in New York seeking to recoup his fortune, which had been depleted in both Tangier and New York. Therefore, Dongan was present during the uprising against Andros that followed the news of the Glorious Revolution in England. In the interim period of 1689–1691 (known in N.Y. as Leisler's Rebellion) Dongan was accused of having been a player in a suspected conspiracy to hand New York over to Catholic New France. Harassed and threatened, Dongan fled to Long Island, then to Connecticut, and finally to Boston, where he took a ship for England in 1691.

With the Stuarts in exile Dongan's political capital was gone. His brother had fought for James II at the battle of the Boyne (1690) and therefore was attainted—he lost all his honors and estates. It is therefore surprising that Dongan appears to have succeeded to the earldom of Limerick after his brother's death in 1698, although he never recovered the bulk of his family's estates. Nearly all sources maintain that Dongan never married, but *The Complete Peerage of England,*

Scotland, Ireland, Great Britain, and the United Kingdom (1910) lists a wife, Mary, who died in 1720. He clearly had no male heirs, and after his death at St. Pancras, Middlesex, the earldom became extinct.

Dongan was a great advocate for the English cause in New York. Ambitious for himself and his patron James II, he sought to upgrade New York from a small colony to a powerful one. His negotiations with the Iroquois gave New York a vital edge in its competition with New France for the fur trade and the loyalty of the Five Nations, although that alliance was not firmly established until 1713 at the Peace of Utrecht. It is ironic that Dongan, an Irish Catholic gentleman, who had served in the French army, was so vigorous in his advocacy of the English cause in North America. It is equally ironic that his record was misunderstood to the extent that many people in New York perceived him to be preferential to New France. This misperception was eventually corrected, and Dongan was afterward regarded as one of the most effective and prescient of the colonial governors of English North America.

• Dongan's official correspondence is contained in *Documents Relative to the Colonial History of the State of New York*, vol. 3 (1853). Dongan's disputes with the marquis de Denonville and his negotiations with the Iroquois are well covered in both Francis Parkman, *Half Century of Conflict* (1897), and Herbert Osgood, *The American Colonies in the Seventeenth Century* (1907). David Lovejoy, *The Glorious Revolution in America* (1972), covers Dongan's governorship in some detail, emphasizing the importance of the Charter of Liberties and New York's first assembly. See also John H. Kennedy, *Thomas Dongan, Governor of New York, 1682–1688* (1930), and Thomas P. Phelan, *Thomas Dongan, Colonial Governor of New York, 1683–1688* (1933). Francis Jennings, *The Ambiguous Iroquois Empire* (1984), describes Dongan and other colonial governors as less than successful in their attempts to manage the Iroquois nations.

SAMUEL WILLARD CROMPTON

DONIPHAN, Alexander William (9 July 1808–8 Aug. 1887), soldier and lawyer, was born near Maysville, Mason County, Kentucky, the son of Joseph Doniphan and Anne Smith, farmers. His father died when Doniphan was not quite five years old. He attended a private school at Augusta, Kentucky, graduating from Augusta College at the age of nineteen. After two years of studying law in the office of Martin Marshall, Doniphan was admitted to the bar in Kentucky and Ohio. He moved to Missouri in 1830, settling initially at Lexington. Three years later, he reestablished his law practice at Liberty in Clay County, where he shared a law office with David Rice Atchison, another young lawyer recently arrived from Kentucky. Doniphan quickly gained a reputation as a defense lawyer in murder trials, handling some 180 over the next thirty years. In 1837 he married Elizabeth Jane Thornton. They had two children.

Shortly after moving to Liberty in 1833, Doniphan began a complicated legal involvement with members of the Mormon church, who had recently been driven from their homes in Jackson County, Missouri, by hostile neighbors. He and Atchison were hired by Mormon leaders to help them regain their lost property in Jackson County or secure compensation for it. Elected to the state legislature as a Whig in 1836, Doniphan secured the creation of Caldwell and Daviess counties in western Missouri with the tacit understanding that the former would be the Mormons' exclusively. Within two years after settling there, their numbers proved too many for one county alone; they began to spread into surrounding areas. When difficulties broke out between the Mormons and their neighbors in Daviess County during an election for sheriff in August 1838, Doniphan found himself caught between divided loyalties. He had risen to the rank of brigadier general in the local militia, which was now called out by Governor Lilburn W. Boggs, an anti-Mormon from Jackson County, to quell the disturbances. Doniphan and Atchison sought in vain to mediate between the state authorities and the Mormon leaders. Convinced that the Mormons were the root cause of the disturbances, Boggs now issued his famous "Exterminating Order," calling on the militia to either "exterminate" the Mormons or drive them from the state. Several Mormon leaders, including Joseph Smith (1805–1844), surrendered, while the remainder of the Mormons fled to Nauvoo, Illinois. In the ensuing trials Doniphan again served as one of the Mormon attorneys and won acquittal for those who had not escaped. He was reelected to the legislature in 1840 and 1854.

At the outbreak of the war with Mexico in May 1846, Doniphan organized the First Regiment of Missouri Mounted Volunteers at the request of Governor John C. Edwards and was elected its colonel. The following month Doniphan and his men joined the Army of the West under General Stephen W. Kearny at Fort Leavenworth for the march overland to New Mexico. After taking Santa Fe, Kearny moved on to California, leaving Doniphan in command at the New Mexican capital. Doniphan was not only given military control of the territory but was also instructed to draft a constitution and code of laws for the conquered region. He accomplished the latter with the assistance of Frank Blair, Jr. (1821–1875), and Charles Bent. During this time Doniphan secured peace with the Navajo, who had been harassing white settlers.

Leaving Santa Fe in the command of Colonel Sterling Price, who had arrived with a fresh body of men, Doniphan took his command of 800 men south on 14 December 1846 to join forces with General John E. Wool at Chihuahua. En route south, they encountered a superior force of some 1,200 Mexicans at the Bracito River on Christmas Day and routed them after a fierce fight with the loss of only seven Americans. They entered El Paso without resistance two days later. Continuing south, at the pass of the Sacramento they encountered in late February 1847 an even larger force of Mexicans, which they routed, capturing large amounts of supplies. Doniphan lost only one man while the Mexicans counted 304 dead. Doniphan entered Chihuahua unopposed on 1 March. With the term of enlistment of his men nearly expired, Doniphan and his men went first to Saltillo and then to Brazos Santiago, from where they embarked for New Orleans and were mustered out. After being feted at several celebrations, Doniphan returned to Liberty and resumed the practice of law. He accepted appointment as commissioner of public schools for Clay County in 1854 and inaugurated an aggressive program of building new schoolhouses and opening new schools where they were needed. He was the Whig candidate for the U.S. Senate in 1855 to succeed Atchison, but the legislature deadlocked and failed to elect. Personal tragedy struck Doniphan during the 1850s with the accidental deaths of his two sons, one by poisoning and the other by drowning. His wife's health failed in 1853, and she remained a semi-invalid thereafter.

During the secession crisis of 1860–1861, Doniphan, although a slaveowner, urged that Missouri maintain a strict neutrality. Chosen by the legislature as a delegate, he participated in the Peace Conference held at Washington in February. While there he learned of his election as a member of the state convention to decide the issue of secession. Although opposed to secession, he also expressed his fear of excessive federal power. He served briefly as major general of the Missouri State Guard in the crisis following the capture of Camp Jackson in May 1861 but relinquished the command a few weeks later. He was appointed a commissioner of claims by President Abraham Lincoln in 1863 and moved to St. Louis, where he also established a legal practice. In 1868 he moved to Richmond in Ray County, where he practiced law until his retirement in 1875 and served as president of the Ray County Savings Bank. He died in Richmond.

• Doniphan's papers, including a manuscript autobiography, are in the Missouri Historical Society, St. Louis. The best biographical sketches may be found in Howard L. Conard, *Encyclopedia of the History of Missouri*, vol. 2 (1901), and W. L. Webb, *Battles and Biographies of Missourians* (1900). Doniphan's legal career is well analyzed in Hugh P. Williamson, "Colonel Alexander W. Doniphan: Soldier, Lawyer, Statesman," *Journal of the Missouri Bar* (Oct. 1952): 180–85. Doniphan's role in the Missouri Mormon controversies is detailed in Stephen C. LeSueur, *The 1838 Mormon War in Missouri* (1987). The best contemporary account of Doniphan's role in the Mexican War is Frank S. Edwards, *A Campaign in New Mexico with Colonel Doniphan* (1847; repr. 1966). John T. Hughes, *Doniphan's Expedition and the Conquest of New Mexico and California* (1907), George R. Gibson, *Journal of a Soldier under Kearny and Doniphan* (1935), and Jacob S. Robinson, *A Journal of the Santa Fe Expedition under Colonel Doniphan* (1932), are also useful.

WILLIAM E. PARRISH

DONN-BYRNE, Brian Oswald Patrick (20 Nov. 1889–18 June 1928), Irish-American writer, was born in New York City, the son of Thomas Fearghail Donn-Byrne and Jane D'Arcy McParlane. His parents, natives of South Armagh, Ireland, were on a business trip to the United States. The family returned to Ireland soon after Donn-Byrne's birth.

In a letter, Donn-Byrne said of his family: "We were about the only one of the four big Irish families of the gap in the North to still keep our mouths, if not our heads, above water." At age fourteen, he met Bulmer Hobson, founder of the Irish volunteer movement. Hobson took him to an early meeting of the volunteers (1906), where Hobson was accompanied by Robert Lynd of the *Daily News* (London). Lynd wrote about that meeting, mentioning the singing of a little fair-haired boy (Donn-Byrne). Through his association with Hobson, Donn-Byrne acquired a taste for Irish history and nationalism that pervaded Irish culture at the turn of the century. He entered local Irish festivals (Feiseanna) using the name Brian O'Beirne, and he frequently won. He was equally fluent in Irish and English, having grown up in an area were Gaelic was still spoken.

In 1907 Donn-Byrne went to the University of Dublin to study Romance languages. While at the school he published poetry and stories in the student magazine, the *National Student*. At this time he also met Dorothea "Dolly" Cadogan. After graduation he moved to Paris and Leipzig to continue his studies at the Sorbonne and Leipzig University, with the hope of joining the British Foreign Office as a diplomat. He turned down his Ph.D. when he learned that he would have to wear evening clothes to his early morning examinations, which no true Irish gentleman would ever do.

He gave up his hope of being a diplomat in 1911 and moved to New York. There he began working first for the *Catholic Encyclopedia*, then the *New Standard Dictionary*, and finally the *Century Dictionary*. In December 1911 he married Dolly in Brooklyn, New York. They had four children. Soon after, in February 1912, his poem "The Piper" appeared in *Harper's* magazine. His first short story, "Battle," was sold to *Smart Set* magazine for $50 and appeared in the February 1914 issue. During this time he also explored the field of journalism but decided to become a freelance writer instead, writing under the pseudonym of Donn Byrne.

Throughout the following year Donn-Byrne sold more of his stories to various magazines such as *Scribner's* and *Ladies Home Journal*. Some of these were anthologized in his first book, *Stories without Women* (1915). He soon earned the financial security he needed to begin working on his first novel, *The Stranger's Banquet* (1919). This was followed by *The Foolish Matrons* (1920), *Messr Marco Polo* (1921), *The Wind Bloweth* (1922), *Changeling, and Other Stories* (1923), *Blind Raftery* (1924), *O'Malley of Shanganagh* (1925), *Hangman's House* (1926), *Brother Saul* (1927), *Crusade* (1928), *Destiny Bay* (1928), and *Ireland, the Rock Whence I Was Hewn* (1929).

His novel *Field of Honor* was published posthumously in 1929. It was followed by *A Party of Baccarat* (1930) and the short story anthologies *Rivers of Damascus* (1931), *A Woman of the Shee* (1932), *The Island of Youth* (1933), *An Alley of Flashing Spears* (1934), *The Hound of Ireland* (1935), and *A Daughter of the Me-*

dici (1935). His poems were collected into an anthology and published as *Poems* (1934).

Donn-Byrne's early novels can be said to be quite mediocre, noted as "potboilers" by Thurston Macauley, his earliest biographer. *Polo* tells the story of the Italian adventurer, and *Wind* is a romantic novel of the sea. Both contain some highly lyrical passages intermixed with the plain language of real life. With *Raftery*, however, the author seems to reinvent the saga style, the prose breaking off into musical verse now and then as it tells the story of a blind poet wandering Ireland and avenging his wife's dishonor.

His later novels invited comparison with Irish novelist George Moore, especially in their romantic and historical themes. In *Hangman's*, Donn-Byrne began to identify himself with the traditional Irish storytellers, noting in his preface ("A Foreword to Foreigners") that: "I have written a book of Ireland for Irishmen. Some phrase, some name in it may conjure up the world they knew as children." It is also in this novel that Donn-Byrne returns to his Irish nationalist ide as by alluding to the ongoing strife of the Irish Civil War and fight for independence. *Destiny Bay* is a collection of stories tied together by recurring characters and their narrator, Kerry MacFarlane, perhaps a self-portrait. The tales evoke a landscape of nostalgia and idealistic beauty that seems almost real (there is no actual Destiny Bay). A recurring Byrne image of horse racing here produces one of his best (and most anthologized) short stories, "Tale of the Gypsy Horse." *Field of Honor*, Byrne's last and most accomplished novel, presents an excellent portrait of Napoleon, the true hero of the story. Unusually, Napoleon's character is treated kindly throughout.

Despite both his wife's success as a playwright and his own increasing popularity as an author, the family's financial straits forced them to sell their house in Riverside, Connecticut, and return to Ireland. Eventually the family bought Coolmain Castle near Bandon in County Cork, where Donn-Byrne lived until his death in a car accident.

Donn-Byrne seems to have been caught up in the neo-Romantic view of the mythical and pastoral beauty of Irish history. His writing hauntingly evokes these images, sometimes seeming to want to preserve them. "It seemed to me," he said in *Wind*, "that I was capturing for an instant a beauty that was dying slowly, imperceptibly, but would soon be gone." Donn-Byrne is buried in Rathclarin churchyard, near Coolmain Castle. His headstone reads, in Irish and English: "I am in my sleeping and don't waken me."

• The majority of Donn-Byrne's papers are held by the New York Public Library, including the author's scrapbooks. Winthrop Wetherbee, Jr., *Donn Byrne: A Bibliography* (1949), is "practically a catalogue" of this collection. John J. Doherty, "Donn Byrne: An Annotated Bibliography," *Bulletin of Bibliography* (June 1997), is an extensive work detailing and evaluating Byrne's novels and stories. The most complete biography of Donn-Byrne is still the rather uncritical *Donn Byrne: Bard or Armagh* (1929), by Thurston Macauley. This is notable, however, for the access Macauley had to the family and papers of Donn-Byrne. The most notable obituary, with an examination of the author's life and work, is on the front page of the *New York Times*, 20 June 1928.

JOHN J. DOHERTY

DONNELL, Clyde Henry (4 Aug. 1890–10 Oct. 1971), physician, was born in Greensboro, North Carolina, the son of Smith Donnell, a real estate developer, and Lula Ingold. Donnell was raised in Greensboro, where he attended the public schools for African Americans and the high school operated by North Carolina Agricultural and Technical University. He received an A.B. in 1911 from Howard University and an M.D. in 1915 from Harvard University. While at Harvard he studied under Milton J. Rosenau, world-renowned scientist in preventive medicine and founder of the world's first school of public health, at Harvard in 1909. Since few hospitals would accept African Americans as interns at the time of Donnell's medical school graduation, he rotated as a fellow and observer at Boston City Hospital, Massachusetts General Hospital, and the Children's Hospital from 1915 to 1916. Donnell's subsequent career was devoted to African-American health education, insurance, and banking.

African-American insurance companies, intended to provide financial protection against sickness and aid at the time of death, were organized in the American South in the mid-nineteenth century. White insurance companies actively competed for African-American business during the mid- to late nineteenth century. In 1881, however, Frederick L. Hoffman, statistician for the Prudential Insurance Company, published a study arguing that "excessive mortality among this element [African-American] of the population [is such] that unless the company adopted a restrictive course, it would soon find itself in difficulty because of inordinate losses experienced on this class of policy-holders" (Hoffman, p. 137). Fearing greater exposure to risk, as a result white insurance companies reduced the size of policies they were willing to write for African Americans and significantly increased the premiums. One of the effects of the new policy was to promote the growth of black-owned insurance companies. In October 1898 the North Carolina Mutual Life Insurance Company was formed in Durham—later to become the largest African-American-owned financial institution in the United States. By 1920 the company had approximately $33 million of insurance in force.

During its formative years the company noted an exceptionally poor mortality experience. Throughout the 1920s N.C. Mutual paid more in death benefits than anticipated. In 1920 whites died at the rate of 12.4 per 1,000 population; African Americans at 18.7 per 1,000. In some urban areas the African-American death rate was close to twice that for whites. Tuberculosis was the principal cause of this excess mortality, a fact generally attributed to differences in socioeconomic and sanitary conditions. Tuberculosis accounted for 11 percent of all African-American deaths in the United States in 1930 (Weare, p. 125). N.C. Mutual ascertained that to sustain itself it needed not only to select healthier customers but also to improve African-American health in general.

Donnell received a North Carolina medical license in 1916, moving from Boston to Greensboro in 1917. He met in Durham and married in 1919 Martha Merrick, youngest daughter of John Merrick, one of the founders of N.C. Mutual. They had no children. Another founder was Dr. Aaron M. Moore, Durham's first African-American physician. Donnell became associated in a general medical practice with Moore. Their office shared a building with N.C. Mutual. To help address the problem of death and disability among the company's customers, Donnell was hired by N.C. Mutual in 1917; Moore and Donnell created the company's Life Extension Department.

Donnell became the company's medical director following Moore's death in 1923. He hired black physicians to replace white physicians to conduct field examinations of prospective policyholders. This represented a conscious effort to build the clinical practices of black physicians. Complex cases or prospective purchasers of large policies were referred to Donnell for a definitive examination. Donnell hired another African-American physician, Roscoe Brown, a former employee of the U.S. Public Health Service, as his assistant. Donnell used the second floor of the Durham company's home office both for his private practice and for company work, and every day he saw a large number of patients, including company employees. Donnell had a special interest in tuberculosis as well as in the therapeutic use of ultraviolet light. His Life Extension Department conducted lecture tours, showed films, and distributed health promotion bulletins from state and federal health departments along with a variety of its own pamphlets. Sales agents also distributed health education materials. Health hints were provided to policyholders, medical information was given to field agents, and continuing education was provided to field physicians.

There was, however, no clear decline in mortality among the company's policyholders following the establishment of the Life Extension Department. The company's financial status did not significantly improve until it hired Asa Spaulding, the United States' first African-American actuary. Combining Donnell's medical knowledge with Spaulding's actuarial training, the company instituted significant underwriting reforms and insurance practices particularly suited to the health status of southern African Americans. These significantly contributed to the company's profitability. Changes in the economic and social status of African Americans in this period make it difficult to identify a particular benefit from the Life Extension Department, although it clearly served the company as a valuable marketing tool.

Donnell was deeply committed to continuing medical education for African-American physicians, who maintained their own structure of local, state, and national medical associations—similar to the better-known all-white societies. Donnell was founder in 1918 and primary mover in Durham's Academy of Medicine, Pharmacy and Dentistry. He was secretary-treasurer of the Old North State Medical Society for thirty-two years. He was also active in the National Medical Association, serving as journal business manager and secretary-treasurer from 1924 to 1928. Donnell was also chairman of the board of trustees of Durham's Lincoln Hospital, a 150-bed African-American facility.

Donnell is remembered as an ebullient, gregarious, generous, outgoing "people person." Acquaintances recall him as being "full of fun," always ready with a joke, and fond of socializing. He enjoyed walking in Durham's African-American neighborhoods and chatting with tradesmen. Donnell rose in N.C. Mutual to become vice president and a member of the board of directors. N.C. Mutual was closely tied to Durham's African-American-owned Mechanics and Farmers Bank. At the time of his death in Durham, Donnell was chairman of the bank's board of directors.

His life's work illustrates the efforts of African Americans to improve their health status through public health education and the continuing medical education of physicians. In Donnell's case these efforts were undertaken for altruistic reasons as well as for the economic benefits to the insurance company and his fellow African-American physicians.

• The definitive scholarly history of the N.C. Mutual Life Insurance Company, and Donnell's association with it, is W. B. Weare, *Black Business in the New South: A Social History of the North Carolina Mutual Life Insurance Company* (1973). The Duke University Library Archives contains E. E. Waite, Jr., "Social Factors in Negro Business Enterprise" (master's thesis, Duke Univ., 1940), an excellent review of the early history of African-American insurance enterprises in the United States and the early history of N.C. Mutual. Documentary material of the early history of the company is in the Charles Clinton Spaulding Papers and the William Jesse Kennedy, Jr., Papers in the possession of the company. The company monthly magazine, the *Whetstone*, which began publication in the 1920s, frequently cites Donnell's work. The magazine is available on microfilm at the Duke University Library. The nineteenth-century study that changed the attitude of white insurance companies toward African Americans is recounted in Frederick L. Hoffman, *History of the Prudential Insurance Company of America* (1900). Valuable supplementary information was gleaned from interviews with Drs. Charles Johnson and Charles Watts and with Albert Starr. Donnell is briefly cited in the *AMA Directory, 25th Edition*, pt. 3 (1969), p. 2937 and his career is reviewed in the *Journal of the National Medical Association* 52 (Sept. 1960): 382. An obituary is in the *New York Times*, 11 Oct 1971.

EDWARD C. HALPERIN

DONNELL, Robert (4 Apr. 1784–24 May 1855), minister, was born in Guilford County, North Carolina, the son of William Donnell and Mary Bell, farmers. Donnell's parents were Scotch-Irish Presbyterians, and his father was an elder in a congregation served by the Reverend David Caldwell. Donnell was a self-educated man, who by age seven was said to have memorized the Westminster Shorter Catechism and read the Bible through three times. In 1793 his family moved to

Sumner County, Tennessee. Five years later Robert's father died, leaving the fourteen-year-old Donnell to operate the family farm. Influenced by the evangelical fervor of the Second Great Awakening, he became a professed Christian during a camp meeting in 1800 and joined the Spring Hill Presbyterian Church in Wilson County. Some of the ministers in this revival movement had studied under David Caldwell in a tutorial program he conducted in his home.

In 1806 Donnell became a candidate for the ministry in Cumberland Presbytery of the Presbyterian church. At that time the presbytery was involved in a theological controversy that had led to the suspension of a number of ministers and would lead that year to the dissolution of the presbytery by Kentucky Synod. The suspended ministers had expressed doubts concerning the doctrine of predestination and had supported revivalism; They also had argued, given the circumstances on the frontier, that a tutorial program for candidates for the ministry might be substituted for study in a regular college. In 1810 three of the suspended ministers reorganized Cumberland Presbytery. Donnell, who had been sympathetic to the views of the suspended ministers, was listed as a candidate for the ministry. The presbytery enrolled him in a tutorial program, in which he read from a list of books that included "Stewart's *Philosophy*, Paley's *Natural Theology*, Watts's *Logic*, and Ferguson's *Astronomy*." He was licensed to preach in 1811 and on 20 February 1813 was ordained by Cumberland Presbytery.

Repeated overtures by Cumberland Presbytery to be received back into Kentucky Synod were unsuccessful. At a meeting in April 1813 the presbytery appointed Donnell and Finis Ewing to prepare a statement describing "the rise, doctrines, etc., of the Cumberland Presbytery" to be published in the third edition of *Buck's Theological Dictionary*. Later that year Cumberland Presbytery was divided into three presbyteries, and Cumberland Synod was formed. These developments signaled the beginning of the Cumberland Presbyterian church. In its first meeting on 5 October 1813, the synod appointed Donnell and three other ministers as a committee to revise the Westminster Confession, which had been adopted by the American Presbyterian church in 1729. The proposed revision, consisting largely of the deletion of the doctrines of predestination and limited atonement from the section on Divine Decrees, was adopted in 1814.

As a member of Elk Presbytery, Donnell threw himself immediately into the task of conducting camp meetings and forming new congregations in Tennessee and Alabama. Records indicate that he organized as many as ten congregations, including those in Huntsville, Alabama, and in Memphis and Nashville, Tennessee. In 1817 he was elected moderator of Cumberland Synod.

In 1818 Donnell married Anne Smith, daughter of Col. James W. Smith, a wealthy planter in Jackson County, Alabama. They had five children, only one of whom survived infancy. With the considerable dowry his wife had received from her father, Donnell bought a farm at Mooresville in Limestone County, Alabama. Because of his ownership of slaves, Donnell was able to maintain a farming operation in conjunction with his ministry.

In 1828 Anne Donnell died. Three years later Donnell left on an extensive missionary itinerary to introduce the Cumberland Presbyterian church to communities in east Tennessee, Kentucky, Virginia, and Pennsylvania. While in Pennsylvania he met and later married Clara W. Lindley, daughter of the Reverend Jacob Lindley, one of the founders and first president of Ohio University. On returning with his new bride, Donnell purchased land and built a home at Athens, Alabama. No children were born to this marriage.

In 1837 Donnell was elected to the highest office in the denomination, moderator of the General Assembly. In 1842 he served as a member of a commission of the General Assembly that recommended the establishment of a college in Lebanon, Tennessee, which later became Cumberland University. From 1846 to 1848 he was pastor of the Cumberland Presbyterian Church in Lebanon and also served as lecturer in theology at the college. In 1849 Donnell returned to Athens, where he died six years later. He was buried in the family cemetery on the grounds of "Pleasant Hill," the antebellum home he had built in Athens.

Robert Donnell was a leader in developing and shaping the Cumberland Presbyterian church during the first four and one-half decades of its existence. Through his preaching and writing, and through an educational institution that he helped to establish and in which he taught, he influenced the shape of the theology of the church. His book, *Miscellaneous Thoughts on Several Subjects of Divinity* (1832), was widely circulated. It is one of two books published between 1810 and 1840 that gives insight into the theology of the founders of the church.

Born soon after the United States of America had been formed, Robert Donnell is an example of the creative, pioneering spirit that opened up the West to the growing nation. It is not surprising that he regarded the denomination he helped to establish as one that was in tune with the mind and spirit of the new nation. He wrote of the Cumberland Presbyterian church: "She was born in this land of liberty, and is properly called an American church, if not the only one."

• Donnell's papers are in the Historical Archives of the Cumberland Presbyterian Church, Memphis, Tenn. Relevant historical records on deposit in the library of Memphis Theological Seminary include Minutes of Cumberland Presbytery 1803–1807, 1810–1813; and Minutes of Cumberland Synod 1813–1828. A revised edition of Donnell's *Miscellaneous Thoughts on Several Subjects of Divinity* was published posthumously as *Thoughts on Various Subjects* (1856), which included articles appearing earlier in the *Theological Medium*, a Cumberland Presbyterian journal. Published biographical materials include David Lowry, *Life and Labors of the Late Robert Donnell of Alabama, Minister of the Gospel in the Cumberland Presbyterian Church* (1867); Richard Beard, *Brief Biographical Sketches of Some of the Early Ministers of the Cumberland Presbyterian Church*, vol. 1 (1867); and Winstead P.

Bone, *A History of Cumberland University* (1935). For an analysis of the theology of Robert Donnell see Hubert W. Morrow, "The Background and Development of Cumberland Presbyterian Theology" (Ph.D. diss., Vanderbilt Univ., 1965).

HUBERT W. MORROW

DONNELLY, Charles Francis (14 Oct. 1836–31 Jan. 1909), lawyer, was born in Athlone, County Roscommen, Ireland, the son of Hugh Donnelly, a woolen draper, and Margaret Conway, a teacher. While Donnelly was a child, his family moved to New Brunswick, subsequently to Nova Scotia, and then to Providence, Rhode Island. He was educated in private schools. He read widely throughout his life, although with an abiding sense of how "absurd as well as sinful" it was to read "what is not good or useful." In his youth he wrote poetry and stories for magazines in New York and Boston. Deciding against entering the priesthood, he read law, studied for a year at Harvard Law School, was admitted to the Suffolk County (Mass.) bar in 1859, and began a legal career in New York City.

In 1861, after the Civil War had broken out, Donnelly returned to Boston, where for nine months he was a lieutenant who succeeded in recruiting many Irish Americans for the Fifty-fifth Massachusetts Regiment. He resumed the practice of law, and in 1867 he was appointed legal counsel by John Joseph Williams, a Roman Catholic bishop (subsequently the first archbishop) of Boston—a position he held for forty years. Donnelly shared Williams's conviction that it would be possible to win a respected place for the Catholic church, in Massachusetts life, and to do so without antagonizing non-Catholic America, which, in all but its religion, he admired. Donnelly was proud of his Irish heritage and was a member of the Charitable Irish Society, but he publicly insisted that he was "absolutely and unreservedly" American—not Irish. Donnelly was confident that appeals to the legal and constitutional order would secure to Catholics the fundamental rights they as Americans were entitled to.

Donnelly played an important part in creating a network of Catholic charitable institutions. In 1864, alarmed by the number of children whose families had not recovered from the shock of immigration, or whose fathers had been killed in the Civil War, and fearing that aggressively Protestant "child-saving" agencies might subvert the children's faith, Donnelly helped found the Home for Destitute Catholic Children. He drafted the articles of incorporation, as he did for virtually every Catholic institution founded in Massachusetts while he was Williams's counsel, and he remained a director most of his life. He later persuaded the legislature to guarantee that every ward of the state would be raised in the faith of his or her parents.

Donnelly strongly supported efforts to secure for Catholics in prisons, reformatories, and state asylums freedom from the obligation to attend Protestant religious services, as well as access to Catholic chaplains. In 1875 he was appointed to the State Board of Health, Lunacy, and Charity (subsequently the State Board of Charity) on which he served continuously until 1907—with the exception of a period from 1883 to 1884, when Governor Benjamin Butler, angered at Donnelly's refusal to countenance Butler's free-swinging attacks on the state almshouse, did not reappoint him. Butler's successor did reappoint him—as did every governor thereafter. And Donnelly was enormously gratified that although none of his colleagues on the board were Catholic, they elected him chairman for several years.

One of his accomplishments on the board was to persuade the legislature to provide special treatment for dipsomaniacs. Effective as he was in shaping the charitable efforts of the state, Donnelly always believed, as he insisted in a paper prepared for the World's Parliament of Religions in Chicago in 1893, that religiously motivated, church-sponsored efforts would always be "in advance of the state in all examples of beneficence."

In Massachusetts during Donnelly's lifetime the most intractable conflicts between secular and religious authority centered around the schools. Having adopted compulsory school laws, the towns and the state were forced to agonize over what should be taught to a religiously diverse student population. As early as 1866 Donnelly had been appointed by the state to help prosecute a public school teacher in Shirley, Massachusetts, who had beaten two of his students for refusing to recite a Protestant version of the Lord's Prayer. Although most public schools managed to eliminate such egregious sectarianism, an increasing number of Catholic clergy and laymen, regarding even religiously neutral schools as unsatisfactory, began to build their own, mostly parochial, schools. The anti-Catholicism of the 1880s found its most virulent expression in fears that these schools not only failed to provide the basic education all American children needed but also inculcated un-American ideals.

In 1888 the Massachusetts legislature's Committee on Education held five hearings on a bill that mandated regular "inspections," by local school boards to determine if the curriculum and the teachers in private schools measured up to those of the public schools. The next year the committee held fifteen hearings on a bill that stipulated the use of English and imposed penalties on the use of "threats" to coerce parents into sending their children to parochial schools. At the request of Archbishop Williams, Donnelly served as counsel for the opposition to these bills. He vigorously contested every slur, however preposterous, made against Catholicism and the Catholic schools. He celebrated the opposition to the bill voiced by non-Catholics like President Charles Eliot of Harvard and the venerated Unitarian author Edward Everett Hale.

His argument for the near-complete autonomy of the parochial schools was founded on American constitutionalism rather than on theological or ecclesiastical precept. Stresing that parents had the moral responsibility to get their children educated, Donnelly disparaged as "socialism" the claim that the legislature had the right to decide what schools parents might employ. Should a parent not meet his responsibility to his children, Donnelly was confident that a court would take appropriate action.

The legislature passed neither bill, specifying instead that students should receive twenty weeks of education "in the branches of learning taught in the public school." Donnelly was no doubt gratified that until the legislature helped finance the parochial schools, and so gained a property right in them, it was not likely to cripple them with gratuitous regulations.

In 1893 he married Amy Frances Collins of Providence, Rhode Island; they had no children.

Donnelly's confidence in the American political process was shaken by the willingness of many women suffragists in Massachusetts to make common cause with critics of the parochial schools. In 1895 he joined other prominent Catholics in founding the Man Suffrage Association. Donnelly died in Boston.

• Donnelly's papers have not been collected. Extensive quotes from his speeches and memoranda in the school hearings are given in Katherine E. Conway and Mabel W. Cameron, *Charles Francis Donnelly* (1909), and in "The Relations of the Roman Catholic Church to the Poor and Destitute" in *The World's Parliament of Religions*, vol. 2, ed. J. H. Barrows (1893), pp. 1032–36. A selection of his verse, *Roma, and Other Poems*, was published posthumously by his wife in 1909. See also Donnelly's introduction to a translation of *Eliza Despres*, a French tract cautioning against enjoying novels 1861. A brief biography is provided in Robert H. Lord et al., *History of the Archdiocese of Boston*, vol. 3 (1945), pp. 401–2. See also James J. Kenneally, "Catholicism and Women Suffrage in Massachusetts," *Catholic Historical Review* 53 (1967): 43–57. An obituary is in the *Boston Globe*, 1 Feb. 1909.
ROBERT D. CROSS

DONNELLY, Dorothy Agnes (28 Jan. 1880–3 Jan. 1928), actress, playwright, and librettist, was born in New York City, the daughter of Thomas L. Donnelly, a theatrical manager, and Sarah Williams, an actress. After the early death of her father, Donnelly was raised in the home of her uncle Fred Williams, stage director for Daniel Frohman. Other family members were successful actors. She completed her education at the Convent of the Sacred Heart in New York City and also received dramatic training from her uncle. Her family encouraged her early interest in writing and music, but she decided to enter the family profession of acting.

In three seasons with the Murray Hill Stock Company, run by her brother Henry, she proved herself a professional as she advanced from small parts to leads. Public acclaim came to her when she joined Arnold Daly's company and played the title role in the first American production of Shaw's *Candida* (1903). Though only a few matinee performances were anticipated, the play caught on and ran for a season.

The height of Donnelly's acting career came with *Madame X* (1910). Its first night brought "a conscientious actress still struggling for stellar recognition . . . the cheers of an audience gone mad . . ." (*New York*

Telegraph, 12 June 1910). The drama told a grim story of a Parisian woman who strayed from virtue, became a degraded addict of ether drinking, ended in the gutter, and died after a murder trial in which her defense attorney proved to be her long-lost son. The *New York Times* reviewer exclaimed over the "innumerable little ways she conveys the impression of mental and physical fatigue and worse, the loss of the natural faculties, the slow, certain hideous undermining of the woman's constitution . . . bringing at the end, as well, a touch of beautiful tenderness and mother's pride to complete the complex picture" (3 Feb. 1910). After other actresses had turned down the sordid role, audiences found Donnelly's Madame X a compelling portrait. The play ran on Broadway and on tour for more than a year.

It proved to be a problem for Donnelly that she did not fit neatly into the typecasting of the period. An interview in 1904 describes the "startling variety" of her personal appearance: "Instead of the cream and roses of the famed Irish complexion . . . hers by Hibernian descent, her olive skin is rather suggestive of lace mantillas, castanets and the sunny skies of Spain. Yet again, her swinging, self-reliant walk is entirely American." In demeanor quiet and intelligent, she has "earnest gray eyes, round almost to childishness, [yet] with occasional, unexpected gleams of roguishness" (*Theatre Magazine*, July 1904). Her versatile ability to play comedy and character parts also made her difficult to pigeonhole as a "type," reviews show. Her abilities brought her work but, apart from Madame X, no public recognition as a star attraction.

That play's emotional demands were great and brought Donnelly "not 'blues' but 'blacks'" (*Theatre Magazine* Aug. 1918). As her next play, she went into a comedy about a carnival snake charmer, *Princess Zim Zim* (1911). It was a failure and closed during out-of-town tryouts, yet it had a lasting effect on Donnelly's life. Its author was the young, handsome, successful playwright Edward Sheldon, in whom the progressive illness that would leave him paralyzed and blind was not yet evident. His biographer, Eric W. Barnes, says Donnelly "lost her heart forever to Ned Sheldon." Meanwhile, her acting career stagnated. She had only one more successful play, *Maria Rosa* (1914), playing a Spanish woman who unknowingly marries the murderer of her husband. From 1914 to 1916 she appeared in three silent films, the last one a screen version of *Madame X* (1916).

A new career as a playwright began in 1916, when Donnelly grew tired of waiting to be offered suitable roles and decided to write something for herself. Collaborating with Charlotte E. Wells, she wrote an adaptation of a Danish play with a good female lead part, under the English title *The Riddle: Woman*. Donnelly seems to have had a modest view of her talents, for she usually collaborated with others in her writing and mainly made adaptations of works written by others. But as a complete theatrical professional, she was gifted with a keen sense of what would "play" with American audiences and was soon offered further writing assignments, even while *The Riddle: Woman* went unproduced.

Donnelly's real success as a writer came from her work on musicals. Her light, entertaining humor brought her success in 1916 with revisions to the book for *Flora Bella*, a musical comedy from England. Further success came in 1917 with her revision of the farce *Johnny Get Your Gun*, and in 1918 with her collaboration with Edgar Smith on the musical comedy *Fancy Free*. By 1918, Donnelly no longer desired to find acting roles. Citing the hardships and dislocation of going on tour, she told an interviewer "Life is more livable for the playwright" (*Theatre Magazine*, Aug. 1918). When *The Riddle: Woman* was produced in 1918, Donnelly was not in the cast.

Another factor in the turn from stage roles was Donnelly's war work after the entry of the United States into World War I. She put together Sunday evening programs for military men for the Stage Women's War Relief, then went to France to stage entertainments for the troops. After the Armistice and a last acting appearance in a benefit for the Actors Fund in 1919, she went to Germany to stage shows for the Army of the Occupation. A play based on her experiences of the interaction of German civilians and American soldiers, titled *Forbidden*, was produced in 1919.

In the 1920s Donnelly began a professional association with composer Sigmund Romberg that resulted in several of the era's most successful and enduring operettas. The first was *Blossom Time* (1921), a romanticized version of the life of Franz Schubert. Donnelly adapted the libretto from a German original and wrote lyrics for Romberg's popularization of Schubert melodies. The pair's greatest success came in 1924 with *The Student Prince*. Again, Donnelly adapted an old play and wrote words to Romberg's melodies. As with *Blossom Time*, the new operetta was romantic in tone and again told a story of undying devotion to an unfulfilled love. Book and lyrics are often overlooked in assessments of operettas, but her contribution to *The Student Prince* was noted in the *New York Times* review: "Dorothy Donnelly . . . has done a first-rate job for the purpose in hand." The reviewer found that "[n]ot even the comparative absence of the comic element is of importance . . . the piece concentrates so successfully on its prime ingredients [romance and presentation of songs] that nothing more is needed" (3 Dec. 1924).

In private life Donnelly remained close to Sheldon, by now bedfast. Over the months from 1923 to 1924 she worked with Sheldon on a play, "The Proud Princess," which was tried out but never produced. In other work she collaborated with composer Stephen Jones on a successful musical comedy for W. C. Fields, *Poppy* (1923). She was further "prominent in the affairs of [Actors] Equity and . . . served on its Executive Committee" (*New York Times*, 4 Jan. 1928). She had by now developed serious kidney trouble. In 1925 the *New York Times* (10 Aug.) noted her return from four months seeking recuperation in Europe; she also brought back an adaptation of a Schnitzler play, titled *The Call of Life* (1925), and the script for a musical version of *Seventeen* (produced in 1926 as *Hello, Lola*). The year 1927 brought two more operettas with Romberg. The first, *My Maryland*, a musical version of *Barbara Frietchie*, was successful; the second, *My Princess*, based on her play written with Sheldon, was not.

By late 1927 Donnelly's health was failing. Sheldon's biographer says that "when she could no longer visit him they still talked together daily by telephone. In the hospital when her strength was almost gone she begged that Ned might be brought to her so that she could see him once more." She died of nephritis-pneumonia in New York City. She never married.

Her place in theatrical history is not so much as an actress, talented though she was, but as a theater professional who merged various gifts to succeed as a writer for the musical stage. In the 1920s she helped to create some of the landmarks of American operetta. Her name as lyricist is on half a dozen of the period's great standard songs: "Song of Love" (*Blossom Time*); "Deep in My Heart, Dear," "Golden Days," "The Drinking Song," and "Serenade" (*The Student Prince*); and "Your Land And My Land" (*My Maryland*).

• Materials on the life and career of Dorothy Donnelly are in the Billy Rose Theatre Collection at the New York Public Library for the Performing Arts, Lincoln Center. Informative articles on her professional life are Ada Patterson, "A Morning's Chat with Candida," *Theatre Magazine*, July 1904, pp. 171—72; "Creating the Role of Madame X," *Theatre Magazine*, Mar. 1910, p. 71; Eileen O'Connor, "From Mme. X to Musical Comedy," *Theatre Magazine*, Aug. 1918, p. 84; and "Dorothy Donnelly Wrote 'Forbidden' as a Tribute to Occupation Army," *New York Tribune*, 28 Dec. 1919. Information on her association with Edward Sheldon is in Eric W. Barnes's biography of Sheldon, *The Man Who Lived Twice* (1956). Obituaries are in the *New York Times*, 4 Jan. 1928, and *Variety*, 11 Jan. 1928.

WILLIAM STEPHENSON

DONNELLY, Ignatius Loyola (3 Nov. 1831–1 Jan. 1901), politician and author, was born in Philadelphia, Pennsylvania, the son of Philip Donnelly, an Irish-born physician, and Catherine Gavin, a pawnbroker. He attended Central High School, a premier academy, where he was drilled in English literature. He read law with Benjamin H. Brewster, who served as U.S. attorney general during President Chester Arthur's administration. Active in politics, Donnelly was a passionate (James) Buchanan Democrat in 1856, denouncing Republicans as nativists.

Donnelly, who had few political and fewer economic advantages, felt his opportunities were limited in Philadelphia. He decided to settle in Minnesota, where, with his wife Katherine McCaffrey, whom he had married in 1855, he tried to establish a city, Nininger (named for his silent partner, John Nininger), on the Mississippi River. The panic of 1857 ended the venture and left him debt-ridden and land poor.

Donnelly turned to politics but, influenced by his business connections and dislike of slavery, became a

Republican. He was placed on the 1858 Republican state ticket to secure ethnic and religious balance and was elected lieutenant governor. Denied a military commission at the outset of the Civil War (Minnesota's governor and later senator Alexander Ramsey doubted his ability to lead troops), Donnelly served in Congress from 1863 to 1869. He sought land grants for western railroads, strongly advocated Radical Republican positions, and invariably raised a storm of controversy whenever he ran for office, usually turning each campaign into a personal contest rather than one of issues. His congressional career was tainted by charges that he was using his office to solicit funds from railroads. A contretemps with Illinois congressman Elihu Washburne, whose brother was Donnelly's rival in Minnesota, resulted in his censorship by the House. Recognized as a threat to Senator Ramsey's Republican political organization, Donnelly was denied reelection. He worked briefly as a Washington lobbyist on behalf of John C. Frémont's ill-fated Atlantic and Pacific Railroad scheme and for Jay Cooke.

In 1872 Donnelly returned to Minnesota and to politics as a spokesman for the disadvantaged, beginning a new career that would see him espouse issues and principles rather than party loyalty. He became in time a Liberal Republican, a Greenbacker, a Granger, a Democrat, and a Populist. He boasted, "No party owns me." He was the beneficiary of the era's political structure that allowed party coalitions. He established and edited a newspaper, the *Anti-Monopolist*, and ran successfully for the state senate on an Anti-Monopolist ticket, which was a Granger-Democratic fusion, and served from 1874 to 1878. Donnelly was almost unbeatable in his home district, both because of his record and the fact that it embraced heavily Irish-Catholic and working-class West St. Paul. But running statewide for Congress on a fusion Greenback-Democratic ticket, Donnelly lost a bitterly fought election to William D. Washburn (Elihu's brother had dropped the *e*). It was an election marked by Republican voter fraud; lumber companies marched their workers to polls to vote for Washburn.

Disgusted with the election's outcome, Donnelly turned from politics to literature. A speculative and imaginative turn of mind, a remarkable capacity to juxtapose disparate facts, a vigorous prose style, and a lawyer's gift for advocacy led him to write a variety of books, including fiction, during the final decades of his life. In *Atlantis; the Antediluvian World* (1882) Donnelly sought to validate Plato's narrative by studying myths. The following year he wrote *Ragnarok: The Age of Fire and Gravel*, arguing in part from geological evidence that the earth had encountered a comet. Although ridiculed in the scientific community, the theory continues to win converts. In *The Great Cryptogram* (1887) Donnelly claimed to have found a mathematical cipher in Shakespeare's plays proving that they were authored by Francis Bacon. Donnelly wrote scores of articles for newspapers and magazines, including the *North American Review*, defending his assertions. His publications, his oratorical skill, and

his natural wit also led him to the lecture circuit, where he earned a living and enhanced his reputation.

Politics, however, remained his first love, and he was easily lured back to run (unsuccessfully) for Congress as a Democrat in 1884 and for the state legislature (successfully) on an Independent ticket in 1887. His primary constituencies were farmers and laborers. An organizer of the Minnesota Farmers' Alliance, he turned it into a political force and, over the protests of its more partisan members, into the agrarian wing of the Populist party. His disillusionment with political corruption and his profound concern about the direction of American society prompted him to write a series of highly successful social novels. *Caesar's Column: A Story of the Twentieth Century* (1890) rejected Edward Bellamy's utopian view of the nation's future, *Looking Backward*, and depicted a bleak country of economically and politically oppressed, half-brutalized, and mongrelized people controlled by a dictatorial Jewish elite. (The novel raised questions about the anti-Semitic nature of Populism.) *Doctor Huguet* (1891) reaffirmed Donnelly's opposition to racism by pointing out that the most virtuous and talented white man, if placed in black skin, would be denied success. A third novel, *The Golden Bottle* (1892), was a free-silver political tract.

Donnelly played a leading role in the Populist party. He drafted its famous 1892 platform preamble that embodied Populist social criticism: "From the same prolific womb of governmental injustice we breed to great classes—paupers and millionaires." He also ran for governor in 1892 but suffered a crushing defeat. Although he advocated bimetallism (using both gold and silver as legal tender), Donnelly was more interested in a monetary system where the government managed the economy by controlling the amount of money in circulation. He supported William Jennings Bryan and the Populist-Democratic fusion ticket in 1896. Rejecting Bryan's stand on the Spanish-American War and his retreat from bimetallism, Donnelly became a middle-of-the-road Populist, favoring an independent course for the party and advocating that position in his newspaper, *The Representative*. In 1900 Donnelly was the vice presidential candidate of the virtually defunct Populist party.

Like many nineteenth-century reformers, Donnelly was often praised as a sage or denounced as a crank. He retained the image of a rebel against formal religion (he left Catholicism), urbanization, political parties, and the scientific and cultural establishment. But he never lost faith in the open marketplace of ideas or in the democratic system and reform through the political process. He never became a socialist. Many of the reforms that he advocated, such as woman suffrage, direct election of senators, and government regulation of the economy, later became commonplace. Donnelly's family life, unlike that of some radical reformers, was traditional. He reared three children and enjoyed a close relationship with his wife, who died in 1894. In 1898 he married his young secretary, Marion Hanson, whom he called his typewriter. Donnelly died in St.

Paul. He was always a politician, living by the last election and for the next one.

• The Donnelly papers, including correspondence, book manuscripts, and scrapbooks, are in the Minnesota Historical Society (microfilm edition is available). For a campaign biography of sorts, see E. W. Fish, *Donnelliana: An Appendix to "Caesar's Column," Excerpts from the Wit, Wisdom, Poetry and Eloquence of Ignatius Donnelly* (1892). For a brief biography that emphasizes Donnelly's literary career, see David D. Anderson, *Ignatius Donnelly* (1980). For a detailed study, see Martin Ridge, *Ignatius Donnelly: Portrait of a Politician* (1962). For the general histories of Populism that refer to Donnelly, see John D. Hicks, *The Populist Revolt: A History of the Farmers' Alliance and the People's Party* (1931), and Lawrence Goodwyn, *Democratic Promise: The Populist Movement in America* (1976).

MARTIN RIDGE

DONNER, Frederic Garrett (4 Oct. 1902–28 Feb. 1987), automobile industry executive, was born in Three Oaks, Michigan, the son of Frank Donner, an accountant for the Warren Featherbone Company, which manufactured corset stays and buggy whips, and Cornelia Zimmerman. During high school Donner worked in a bank and a drug store. He enrolled at the University of Michigan and compiled a sterling academic record, benefiting from his contact with his economics professor, William Paton. In 1923 he graduated Phi Beta Kappa with a degree in economics. After graduating, Donner worked for three years for a Chicago accounting firm, Rackitt Benington Leclear.

Albert Bradley, a University of Michigan graduate and a General Motors (GM) executive, wrote to his former classmate Paton, asking him to recommend a bright, promising student with an analytical mind whom Bradley could recruit to GM. Paton suggested Donner. Bradley brought Donner to the company in 1926, beginning Donner's long career with GM with a position as an accountant for the company at its New York financial offices. In 1929 Donner married Eileen Isaacson; they had one son and one daughter.

Donner specialized in finance and worked at a number of jobs at GM, including cost studies; he became regarded as the company expert on cost controls and product pricing. Donner rose steadily through the corporate ranks, becoming an assistant treasurer in 1934, a general assistant treasurer in 1934, and a vice president in 1941 at age 39. One of the youngest men ever to attain such a high post at GM, he became known as "GM's boy wonder." In 1942 Donner was elected to GM's board of directors. In 1956 he became the executive vice president of finance. During his steady climb up GM's corporate ladder, Donner earned a reputation for having a formidable mind that could absorb an impressive array of facts, figures, and information.

During World War II, Donner established one of the first bank-credit deals, providing GM $1 billion in wartime financing—enough working capital to meet greater wartime production demands. In the postwar period he helped formulate a revised and expanded pension plan as well as benefits programs, wage scales, and stock purchase plans for GM's salaried employees. He was also prominent in renegotiating the company's defense contracts after the war.

Although Donner thought that his 1956 ascension to the post of executive vice president of finance would be the pinnacle of his career at GM, in 1958 he was elected to the highest position in the corporation: chairman and chief executive officer (CEO). His election to both positions represented a shift in the power structure at GM, because since 1946 the titles had been held by separate executives. Moreover, Donner worked at GM's financial offices in New York City rather than at its manufacturing headquarters in Detroit, and he enhanced the voice of GM's New York City operation in directing the corporation. The heads of GM's automotive divisions were piqued because Donner, a financial expert and the first nonengineer to hold the CEO post, was running GM. They complained that he knew little about factory operations and seemed more interested in numbers and stock, and they worried that the power of GM's financial men would eclipse that of its division heads and engineers. He held the positions of chairman and CEO for nine years, which at the time represented the second-longest tenure at the top in GM history (only Alfred Sloan had been chief executive officer longer: 1923–1956).

At the time Donner was named to head GM, the automobile giant was reeling from various blows. A national recession during the mid-1950s weakened the company, and its market share dropped. GM's automobiles gained a reputation as stodgy and devoid of innovation. Ford and foreign automobile manufacturers began to challenge GM's primacy in the domestic market, and GM seemed to falter against the new competition.

But Donner effected a remarkable turnaround and presided over a tremendous growth in the company. Although GM faced stiffer competition from modernized Ford and Chrysler corporations during Donner's last years at the helm, he presided over a tremendous growth in the company. GM almost doubled its sales during his nine-year tenure and expanded its worldwide production of cars and trucks to more than 7 million units, compared to under 4 million during his first full year as GM head. Although not normally given to hyperbole, Donner once observed, "We lead the industry in plant, in engineering organization and in dealer organization," and he attributed GM's success in large part to good management.

Donner's tenure witnessed the beginning of government regulation of the automobile industry, intervention that he deprecated. He felt that GM dutifully fulfilled its federal obligations by paying its taxes, and deemed unnecessary any government impingement on the company's operations. Donner bristled at suggestions that GM should deliberately limit its huge market share, and he defended the company's preeminence in the market, fighting calls for the Justice Department to take antitrust action against GM.

One expression of the federal government's growing supervision of the automobile industry was a Senate subcommittee investigation into automobile safety. For Donner, the Senate hearings had added significance because of the controversy surrounding the Corvair, a small, sporty, rear-end–engine vehicle that GM introduced in 1960 as an import fighter (designed especially to challenge the popular German import, the Volkswagen Beetle). In his celebrated 1965 book *Unsafe at Any Speed*, consumer advocate Ralph Nader launched a withering attack against the Corvair, charging that the car was unstable and beset with many other inherent defects that endangered its owners. Nader's charges threatened to damage GM's reputation. Yet when Donner testified before the Senate subcommittee in 1965, he displayed a singular reluctance to accept more rigorous federal safety standards, warning against government interference in the economic market place and stressing the consumer's right to accept or reject new safety devices.

But Donner was swimming against the tide. As the 1960s wore on, government pressure for increased automobile safety grew more intense, and plummeting Corvair sales reflected the public's concern with this issue. As a consequence, Donner and GM began to accept government demands for improvements in automobile safety, exhaust emissions, and working conditions at GM plants. After retiring in 1967 as GM's chairman and CEO, Donner served as chairman of the Alfred P. Sloan Foundation from 1968 to 1975.

Donner had a quick, often sarcastic wit that was known to liven up press conferences and tedious stockholder meetings. Colleagues praised him for his sharp mind and encyclopedic knowledge of myriad subjects—including the most complex knowledge of GM operations displayed by any GM executive. When one questioner asked about his facility in using numbers and statistics, Donner replied with characteristic modesty: "Some people can sketch, but to me it comes easily to use figures, almost like a language." Donner was an avid reader whose interests ranged far beyond business and finance: he was known to enthusiastically read economics, history (especially concerning the U.S. Civil War), foreign policy, Charles Dickens, and mystery stories. It was not uncommon to hear Donner, while discussing a matter such as GM's immense size, cite a parallel from Thucydides's *Peloponnesian Wars*.

Donner shunned publicity and seldom granted interviews. Although known as a laconic man, he once tried to clarify accounts that characterized him as diffident or as a walking calculator: "I am not taciturn, I am not shy. I am not afraid of people, and I don't even own a slide rule. People build up an image of a financial man that has no relation to reality" (*Time*, 22 Sept. 1958). Donner studiously guarded the privacy of his family, living in a modest, middle-class home in Port Washington, Long Island, and spending winter months in a Manhattan apartment on Fifth Avenue, close to GM headquarters. He died in Greenwich, Connecticut.

• The National Automotive History Collection at the Detroit Public Library maintains a file on Donner. His book *The World-Wide Industrial Enterprise: Its Challenge and Promise* (1967) represents an expansion of a series of lectures he delivered at Columbia University in the spring of 1966. An informative article on Donner is "Product of the System," *Time*, 18 May 1962. Other articles on Donner include "New Top-Riding Team at GM," *Life*, 13 Oct. 1958; R. Sheehan, "GM's Remodeled Management," *Fortune*, Nov. 1958; and "GM's Donner Looks down the Road," *Business Week*, 11 June 1966. A brief interview with Donner is in *Time*, 22 Sept. 1958, p. 79. An obituary is in the *New York Times*, 1 Mar. 1987.

YANEK MIECZKOWSKI

DONNER PARTY. *See* Breen, Patrick.

DONOGHUE, John Talbott (1853–1 July 1903), sculptor, was born in Chicago, Illinois, the son of immigrants from western Ireland whose names and occupations are unknown. Details of his early life are also unavailable. A change of city administration forced Donoghue out of his job as a clerk in the recorder's office and signaled the beginning of his career as an artist. In 1875 he enrolled in classes at the Academy of Design in Chicago and there was awarded a scholarship for his bust of a vestal virgin. In 1879 Donoghue applied to follow a course of study at the École des Beaux-Arts in Paris, though he may have been training in Paris as early as 1877. Donoghue contributed a plaster bust, *Phaedra* (present location unknown), to the Salon of 1880. He exhibited in the prestigious annual five times during his career.

Donoghue came back to the United States in 1881 and set up a studio in Chicago, where he completed commissions for bronze portrait reliefs. At that time, he met Oscar Wilde, then on an American lecture tour. After seeing the reduced model for *Young Sophocles Leading the Chorus of Victory after the Battle of Salamis*, Wilde called it a "piece of the highest artistic beauty and perfect workmanship" (Lloyd Lewis and Henry Justin Smith, *Oscar Wilde Discovers America* [1936], p. 180). He sang the sculptor's praises and garnered patronage for him. His influence on Donoghue was considerable, as evidenced by the latter's adoption of Wilde's eccentric dress and personality traits. The *Collector* mentions that Donoghue "took to wearing dark green Roman togas lined with shrimp pink. . . . And [his] hats were wonderful to behold" (1 Feb. 1894, p. 111). Wilde's support probably helped to attract a patron, enabling the sculptor's return to Paris in 1882 or 1883, where he studied with Alexandre Falguière. While there Donoghue completed a bronze bas-relief, *Seraphim* (1883), and sent it to the Salon of 1884.

By 1885 Donoghue had moved to Rome, and in that year he executed a heroic-sized plaster of *Young Sophocles*. The piece, which is unquestionably the triumph of his otherwise spotted career, is based on Edward Hayes Plumptre's translations of the Greek dramatist's writings. One writer for the *Studio* paid Donoghue a high compliment, writing in 1893 that he "has modelled his statue in a manner which sends the mind back to the statues of antiquity." The original plaster was shown in the Paris Salon of 1886, where it received an honorable mention. At the 1893 World's Columbian Exposition in Chicago, it was accorded a first-place prize. The Art Institute of Chicago, the St. Louis Art Museum, and the Metropolitan Museum of Art have full-size bronze casts. Around 1890 Donoghue commissioned the Barbedienne foundry of Paris to cast 44½-inch reductions (Isabella Stewart Gardner Museum, Boston).

Following several years in Rome, Donoghue's peregrinations found him completing portraits in Boston between 1887 and 1888. Bronze busts of Hugh O'Brien (1888) and John Boyle O'Reilly (1897) are in the collection of the Boston Public Library. Donoghue executed a statue, *The Boxer* (1887; present location unknown), based on the contemporary boxing legend John L. Sullivan. The sculptor conceived the piece as emblematic of perfect manhood. Early in 1888 he displayed three works—*Young Sophocles*, *The Boxer*, and *Hunting Nymph*—in Boston's Horticultural Hall. *Hunting Nymph* (present location unknown) had been previously exhibited in plaster at the Salon of 1887.

For two years around 1890 Donoghue was in London, where, in addition to submitting *Young Sophocles* to the Royal Academy exhibition, he included a bust of Mrs. Ronalds (present location unknown). He then moved to Rome in order to model a colossal figure for the World's Columbian Exposition. According to contemporary accounts, he even rented part of the Baths of Diocletian to complete his foremost intellectual effort, *The Spirit Brooding over the Abyss*. The seated winged figure, thirty feet high, was based on a line from Milton's *Paradise Lost*. Donoghue's efforts yielded only fierce disappointment, as the piece never reached its intended destination. Instead, when he was unable to pay for the cost of shipping, half the sculpture sat deteriorating on a Brooklyn dock; the rest remained in Rome. The entire piece was eventually destroyed. Three works—*Young Sophocles*, *Hunting Nymph*, and *Kypros*—were exhibited in Chicago in its stead.

Donoghue lived in New York during the 1890s, completing ornamental and architectural sculpture. Among his projects were statues for the decorative programs of two major monuments: *St. Paul* for the Library of Congress, Washington, D.C., and *St. Louis of France* for New York's Appellate Court House (1896–1900). On a smaller scale, he experimented with the production of tinted Tanagra-like statuettes, small figures in action, produced in ancient Greece and popularized in the mid- to late nineteenth century, with the hope that they would provide a steady income. He also took up painting, completing landscape and figure subjects. Toward the end of his life he became interested in psychic processes; the April 1897 issue of *Art News* announced that he had authored a book, *X Rays with Religions*. Donoghue's ultimate frustration was the rejection of his ambitious plan for the proposed McKinley Memorial in Philadelphia due to expense. Defeated and financially insolvent, the artist committed suicide on 1 July 1903 on the shores of Lake Whitney, near New Haven, Connecticut. He had never married or had children. Although Donoghue's limited oeuvre consists of only a few portraits and ideal subjects, his contribution to American sculpture is measured in his skilled appropriation of classical themes and contemporary French formal properties.

• S.[adakichi] H.[artmann], "John Donoghue," *Camera Work* 21 (Jan. 1908): 223–26, recounts his life, stressing its tragic aspects. J. C. McCord, "Pathos of the Career of John Donoghue, Sculptor," *Brush and Pencil* 12 (Aug. 1903): 364–68, provides a summary of the artist's career and details his most ambitious work, *The Spirit*; biographical details are occasionally inaccurate. "Romance of a Baffled Genius: Crosses and Losses Endured by the Sculptor John Donoghue, Which Ended in Suicide," *New York Herald*, 2 Aug. 1903, is one of several newspaper articles that assess the circumstances leading to Donoghue's demise. "Donoghue's Young Sophokles," *Art World* (Jan. 1917): 236–38, is an account of the artist's greatest sculpture. Obituaries are in the *New York Herald* and the *New Haven Evening Register*, both 6 July 1903.

THAYER TOLLES

DONOVAN, Hedley Williams (24 May 1914–13 Aug. 1990), magazine editor, was born in Brainerd, Minnesota, the son of Percy Williams Donovan, a mining engineer, and Alice Dougan, a former schoolteacher. Donovan grew up in Minneapolis. At the University of Minnesota, Donovan was editorial chairman of the *Minnesota Daily*; he earned his B.A. in 1934. A Rhodes scholar, Donovan took a second degree at Hertford College, Oxford. Donovan had hoped to do graduate work in history upon returning to the United States in 1937 but had to settle for a reporting job at the *Washington Post* to save enough money for his studies. While working he fell in love with journalism. He married Dorothy Hannon in 1941; they had three children. During World War II, he served in Naval Intelligence. In late 1945 Donovan joined the staff of *Fortune* magazine, a business monthly published by Time Inc. In 1953 he became editor. Six years later, Henry R. Luce, founder and editor in chief of Time Inc., named Donovan editorial director, his second in command.

Early in 1964, Donovan succeeded Luce as editor in chief. He was responsible for the content of the nation's most influential and popular periodicals, including *Time*, *Life*, and *Sports Illustrated*, and answerable only to the Time Inc. board of directors. Appointed by Luce himself, Donovan appeared a safe choice. He had no serious disagreements with Luce on politics and policy, only differences in temperament. Luce could be volatile and opinionated; Donovan, in contrast, was quiet and judicious. Yet he lacked Luce's creative genius. Donovan was a manager, not an entrepreneur.

Exasperated by the Republican party's turn rightward in 1964, Donovan had *Life* endorse Lyndon B. Johnson's election to a second term. Luce did not disagree. In other ways, Donovan followed the founder. He continued to support U.S. intervention in Vietnam, which he forcefully defended in *Life*. By late 1967, however, Donovan began to have misgivings, which could be seen in *Life* commentaries on the war. Early the next year, *Life* recommended a negotiated settlement, to the fury of President Johnson.

Donovan had already been urging *Time* editor Otto Fuerbringer to soften the magazine's coverage of Vietnam. "Occasionally a kind of cheerleader tone turns up in our treatment of the war and Washington decisions about the war," Donovan wrote in 1966. For many years, he realized, *Time*'s smug advocacy of the Cold War had been infuriating some readers, many of whom had been abandoning the magazine in favor of *Newsweek*. Donovan replaced Fuerbringer with Henry Grunwald in 1968. Although *Time* remained the more conservative of the two newsmagazines, under Grunwald's direction the periodical became less strident and more judicious in its analyses. "The portentous all-knowing tone could be slowly changed, and was," Donovan recalled. Donovan, *Newsweek* editor Osborn Elliott admitted, "did bring a balance and straightness and integrity to the operation that was needed."

The move of Time Inc. to the center could also be seen during the Nixon presidency. Although an independent, Donovan had voted for Nixon three times. *Life* had endorsed him in 1960, 1968, and 1972. But as the nation learned more and more about the administration's improprieties, Donovan abandoned the president, and *Time* in November 1973, in its first editorial, urged Nixon to resign.

Life posed the greatest challenge to Donovan. Although immensely popular, *Life* faced an uncertain future. The main problem, Donovan recognized, was *Life*'s audience. *Life*'s circulation, while impressive, paled when compared to the audiences for network television. Donovan had long recommended that *Life* seek a more select readership, akin to *Time*'s, which would appeal to advertisers coveting well-to-do customers neglected by mass advertising on television. *Life* did, in fact, begin playing to more affluent, better-educated readers in the late 1960s. "We had finally abandoned the idea that *Life* could be for everybody," Donovan wrote. In the process, *Life* assumed a less mainstream attitude toward cultural reporting. This shift, however, alienated some long-time middle-class readers, many of whom let their subscriptions lapse. At the same time, sharply increasing mailing costs portended only more red ink. Donovan ordered the suspension of *Life*'s publication on 7 December 1972, "the most painful day of my professional life," he later admitted. Although reborn as a monthly in 1978, *Life* never regained its once substantial hold on American culture.

Donovan oversaw other changes at Time Inc. *Money*, which offered tips on investing and spending, commenced publication in October 1972. *Fortune* became a fortnightly in January 1978. That year, Donovan encouraged the company to purchase the moribund *Washington Star*. Time Inc. could not, despite generous underwriting, make the *Star* profitable and closed the daily in 1981.

Donovan had little to do with the greatest editorial success of Time Inc. during his tenure. Early in 1974 the company launched *People*, a weekly focusing on personalities, mostly in show business. It had all the lightness and none of the aspiration of the old *Life*. Many colleagues found *People*'s self-conscious frivolity embarrassing. Still, Donovan welcomed the challenge: "Could I help create an important new national magazine of which I myself was not necessarily the first and most natural reader?" *People* was earning money eighteen months after its launch, well ahead of schedule.

The success of *People* notwithstanding, magazines became less important at Time Inc. in the 1970s. A Time Inc. pay cable system, Home Box Office (HBO), unexpectedly proved a major revenue source. Donovan insisted on magazines' primacy to the corporation and had fought attempts to invest in motion picture studios. But by the time he retired as editor in chief in 1979, periodical publication accounted for less than half the total revenues of Time Inc.

Soon after leaving Time Inc. in mid-1979, Donovan became a senior adviser to President Jimmy Carter. Carter had been urged, Donovan recalled, "to broaden the White House staff: to bring in one or more non-Georgians 'with gray hair' acquired in business or the professions." Donovan mainly counseled the president on foreign policy. Carter often ignored Donovan's suggestions and he quit after one year. In retirement, Donovan traveled and wrote two books. He died in New York City.

• Donovan's memoir, *Right Places, Right Times: Forty Years in Journalism Not Counting My Paper Route* (1989), is unusually detailed and often helpful, especially on his early years. See also an earlier memoir, *Roosevelt to Reagan: A Reporter's Encounters with Nine Presidents* (1985). The Oral History Project of Columbia University has a long oral history conducted in the late 1960s for which Donovan was interviewed. Donovan is among the protagonists in Joan Simpson Burns, *The Awkward Embrace: The Creative Artist and the Institution in America* (1975), and Curtis Prendergast and Geoffrey Colvin, *The World of Time Inc.: The Intimate History of a Changing Enterprise, 1960–1980* (1986). See also Robert T. Elson, *The World of Time Inc.: The Intimate History of a Publishing Enterprise, 1941–1960* (1973). His obituary is in the *New York Times*, 14 Aug. 1990.

JAMES L. BAUGHMAN

DONOVAN, James Britt (29 Feb. 1916–19 Jan. 1970), lawyer and educator, was born in the Bronx, New York, the son of John D. Donovan, a surgeon, and Hattie F. O'Connor, a piano teacher. Donovan received a B.A. in English from Fordham University in 1937. Throughout his schooling he pursued interests in journalism and writing, and upon graduation he persuaded his wealthy father to buy him a small newspaper, with the condition that he complete law school first. Donovan received an LL.B. from Harvard in

1940. He joined a law firm in New York City that represented several newspaper interests. Publishing and insurance law quickly became permanent interests. Donovan married Mary E. McKenna in 1941; the couple had four children.

When World War II broke out, Donovan became general counsel of the Office of Scientific Research and Development, which supervised the development of the atomic bomb, radar, and other scientific war projects. He entered the U.S. Navy in 1943 as an ensign but was assigned as general counsel to the Office of Strategic Services, which conducted secret intelligence operations, working under its commander, Major General William Donovan (no relation). In May 1945 Donovan was appointed to the staff of Justice Robert H. Jackson, the American chief counsel for the prosecution of major European war criminals. As an associate prosecutor at the principal Nuremberg trial in 1945 and 1946, Donovan was responsible for all visual evidence, including captured enemy photographs and motion pictures. He was discharged from the navy as a full commander in 1946.

Upon returning to the United States, Donovan became general counsel for the National Bureau of Casualty Underwriters, a position he continued to hold after he, Thomas Watters, Jr., and Myron Cowen formed the law firm of Watters, Cowen, and Donovan in 1951, which specialized in insurance law.

In 1957 the Brooklyn Bar Association recommended him to represent Rudolf Abel, the highest-ranking Soviet intelligence agent to be tried in the United States up to that time. Abel was charged with failure to register as a Soviet agent and with conspiracy to obtain and transmit defense secrets. Donovan accepted the assignment as a public duty, later stating, "The constitutional issues had nothing to do with whether Abel was a Soviet spy. At issue were the rights of us all." He donated his $10,000 fee to the law schools of Fordham, Harvard, and Columbia Universities.

Donovan structured Abel's defense on attacking the credibility of key prosecution witnesses, including an army master sergeant who confessed during the trial that he had sold the Russians information while serving at the American Embassy in Moscow. Abel was found guilty on 15 November 1957, fined $3,000, and sentenced to thirty years in prison. Donovan asked that Abel not be sentenced to death, so that possible future trades with the Soviets would not be jeopardized. In 1958 the Second U.S. Circuit Court of Appeals upheld the conviction unanimously. In March 1960 the U.S. Supreme Court rejected, 5 to 4, Donovan's argument that Abel's Fourth Amendment rights had been violated by use of a civil alien detention writ rather than a search warrant. Two months later the same body refused an appeal for re-argument.

In 1961 the U.S. government asked Donovan to begin secret negotiations with the Soviets to exchange Abel for captured American U-2 pilot Francis Gary Powers. The successful culmination of these efforts on 10 February 1962 was praised by President John F. Kennedy in a letter to Donovan. During the ensuing months, Donovan conducted negotiations with Cuban president Fidel Castro for the release of 1,163 survivors of the Bay of Pigs invasion as well as thousands of other political prisoners, including thirty-five American detainees and their families. These efforts continued even during the Cuban missile crisis and resulted in the release of more than 9,700 individuals from Castro's jails by the spring of 1963 in exchange for medicine, drugs, and baby food.

In part because of the fame resulting from these efforts, Donovan was chosen by New York State Democrats to oppose Senator Jacob Javits in his bid for reelection in 1962. Donovan accepted the nomination but campaigned in a distracted manner and lost by 975,000 votes.

During the later years of his life Donovan devoted increasing amounts of time to education. In 1961 he was appointed vice president, then president, of the Board of Education of New York City. As president he became embroiled in a controversy over an integration program for the city that seemingly satisfied no one. In 1964 critics engineered a boycott of the public schools in an attempt to force Donovan's resignation, but he stood firm and was reelected to the post.

In January 1968 Donovan became president of Pratt Institute in New York City, where he immediately faced campus disruption over black students' demands and antiwar protests. He attempted to deal with the unrest by threatening to expel students who committed vandalism, denied other students access to classes, or incited nonstudents to action. These measures were answered by a faculty strike that forced Donovan to tone down his policy.

In January 1970 Donovan was admitted to Methodist Hospital in Brooklyn suffering from influenza. He died there of a heart attack a few days later.

• Donovan published two books, *Strangers on a Bridge* (1964), about his experiences in Abel's trial and the negotiation of his exchange for Powers, and *Challenges* (1967), an outline of his public career. He also published numerous articles in law journals, including the *Duke Law Journal* and *Law and Contemporary Problems*. See also, Louise Bernikow, *Abel* (1970). The best obituary is in the *New York Times*, 20 Jan. 1970.

REBECCA S. SHOEMAKER

DONOVAN, William Joseph (1 Jan. 1883–8 Feb. 1959), lawyer, soldier, and intelligence official, was born in Buffalo, New York, the son of Timothy Patrick Donovan, a railroad yardmaster, and Anna Letitia Lennon. After starting college at Niagara University, Donovan transferred to Columbia University from which he received an A.B. in 1905 and an LL.B. in 1907. He joined the law firm of Love and Keating in Buffalo. In 1912 he and Bradley Goodyear formed a partnership that merged with Buffalo's leading firm, O'Brian and Hamlin, to become O'Brian Hamlin Donovan and Goodyear. Hamlin's withdrawal led to the firm's dissolution in 1920. Meanwhile, in 1914, Donovan married socially prominent Ruth Rumsey. They had two children.

In October 1911 Donovan had joined the New York National Guard as a private and rose to captain within a year. During World War I he traveled in several European countries with the Rockefeller Foundation's War Relief Commission. He left the commission in mid-1916 when his guard unit was called up for service on the Mexican border and was mustered out in March 1917. In July, after the United States entered the war, he joined the guard's "Fighting Irish" Sixty-ninth Regiment, which became the 165th Regiment in the Forty-second Division, the "Rainbow Division" of the American Expeditionary Force. While training new recruits in France, and pushing them hard, Donovan won the nickname "Wild Bill." It stuck to him for life, and he liked it, but it was the opposite of his personality and character.

Donovan commanded the 165th's First Battalion. He was wounded several times in combat and demonstrated such unusual leadership that he became a national hero. He won a Distinguished Service Cross, a Distinguished Service Medal, and the Medal of Honor. (Years later, in 1957, he was awarded the National Security Medal and thereby became the first person to receive the country's four highest decorations.)

After the Armistice and two months of service in Siberia in 1919, he returned to Buffalo and resumed his law practice. In 1922 he was appointed U.S. attorney for New York's Western District. He enforced the controversial prohibition law so strictly that, after issuing a warning, he raided the prestigious Saturn Club, of which he was a member. In 1922 he was also the Republican candidate for lieutenant governor of New York but lost out to the Democratic ticket headed by Alfred E. Smith. (He also met defeat in 1932 when he ran for governor.)

In 1924 he moved to Washington, D.C., when the new attorney general, Harlan Fiske Stone, his former law school teacher, brought him into the Department of Justice as an assistant attorney general. He ran the Criminal Division from August 1924 to March 1925 and then the Anti-Trust Division until 1929. He was the acting attorney general in mid-1928. Donovan's legal victories and speeches and articles on current policy issues buttressed general expectations of a still brighter future for him. At the time a former law partner said Donovan "won't be satisfied until he's the first Catholic President of the United States." He had hoped to be appointed attorney general when Herbert Hoover became president, but Hoover chose William D. Mitchell. Disappointed, Donovan in 1929 moved to New York City where he formed a law firm known most of his years as Donovan Leisure Newton Lumbard and Irvine.

In Manhattan he continued to make news with articles, speeches, various public service assignments, and, after 1933, with his spirited opposition to Franklin D. Roosevelt's New Deal. Still a soldier at heart, Donovan was drawn by the rise of Hitler and looming European war clouds to the issue of war and peace. At his own expense he made intelligence trips to Ethiopia, Spain, Germany, and other parts of Europe. In 1940, after World War II began, his friend Frank Knox, a Republican, became secretary of the navy and, with Roosevelt's approval, immediately sent Donovan to England to assess its survivability. Out of this and a later Mediterranean trip came Donovan's recommendation, worked out with William S. Stephenson, Britain's intelligence chief in New York, for a new American intelligence position, coordinator of information (COI). The post was established and given to Donovan on 11 July 1941. He quickly created an organization to carry out, as needed, research and analysis, propaganda broadcasts, economic warfare, espionage, sabotage, subversion, and commando operations.

However, on 13 June 1942, Roosevelt replaced the COI with the Office of Strategic Services (OSS), still under Donovan but subordinate to the Joint Chiefs of Staff. Donovan hoped to make OSS a permanent agency, but his 1944 proposal to that end was fatally leaked to the press in February 1945. President Harry S. Truman, unsympathetic to Donovan, abruptly abolished the agency in October. Even so, Donovan's plan, in modified form, was the blueprint for the Central Intelligence Agency, which Truman established in July 1947.

In the postwar world Donovan campaigned hard for the establishment of the CIA and for a vigorous anti-Communist policy. Hence in 1953 at age seventy he became ambassador to Thailand, whose pro Western position he strengthened, but policy differences, financial needs, and ill health brought on his resignation in 1954. He died, a hero of two world wars, at Walter Reed Army Hospital in Washington, D.C.

• Donovan's personal papers are at the U.S. Army Military History Institute in Carlisle Barracks, Pa. Nearly 4,000 cubic feet of OSS records have been deposited by the CIA in the National Archives in Washington, D.C. There is no good, much less definitive, biography of Donovan. Authors focus on his wartime years to the neglect of his 1920–1940 and post-1945 legal and political activity. A glimpse of Donovan in World War I is found in Francis P. Duffy, *Father Duffy's Story* (1918). More of Donovan's early life is found in Richard Dunlop, *Donovan: America's Master Spy* (1982). The OSS story will be found there and in Anthony Cave Brown, *The Last Hero: Wild Bill Donovan* (1982); Corey Ford, *Donovan of OSS* (1970); Bradley Smith, *The Shadow Warriors: O.S.S. and the Origins of the C.I.A.* (1983); and R. Harris Smith, *OSS: The Secret History of America's First Central Intelligence Agency* (1972). Thomas F. Troy, *Donovan and the CIA: A History of the Establishment of the Central Intelligence Agency* (1981), focuses on the conception and realization of the idea of central intelligence in COI, OSS, and CIA. Although there is considerable newspaper coverage of Donovan, other periodical literature is sparse and generally thin. Obituaries are in the *Washington Post* and the *New York Times*, 9 Feb. 1959.

THOMAS F. TROY

DOOLE, George Arntzen (12 Aug. 1909–8 Mar. 1985), airline executive, was born in Quincy, Illinois, the son of George Andrew Doole, a banker, and Naomi Arntzen. Educated in local schools, Doole graduated from the University of Illinois in 1931 with a B.S. in business administration. A member of the Army Reserve Officers' Training Corps, he rode with the elite cavalry unit while in college and won a jumping prize. Following graduation, Doole later recalled, he had two job choices, either work in his father's bank or join the military. He chose the military.

Doole had been interested in aviation ever since Charles A. Lindbergh's dramatic transatlantic solo flight in 1927. Although he had read widely on the subject, he had never flown. Realizing that there was no future in the cavalry, he applied for and was accepted in the highly competitive U.S. Army aviation cadet program. In 1932, following a year of training at Randolph Field, Texas, he received his wings and was commissioned a second lieutenant. Two years on active duty followed with assignments in Hawaii and Panama.

Released from the U.S. Army Air Corps in 1934, Doole secured a position with the Brownsville Division of Pan American World Airways (Pan Am), flying Douglas DC-2s between Brownsville, Texas, and Mexico City. In 1936 he flew Ford Trimotors on the Guatemala-Panama route and, for a brief time, managed Panama Airways, a Pan Am subsidiary that operated a 47-mile shuttle between Cristobal and Balboa.

In 1939, while flying DC-3s between Rio de Janeiro and Buenos Aires, Doole obtained a leave of absence and entered Harvard University's two-year M.B.A. program. He had completed only one year, however, when he was called back by Pan Am to take over as chief pilot of Sociedad Colombo–Alemana de Transportes Aéreos (SCADTA), a Colombian airline and subsidiary that was renamed Aerovías Nacionales de Colombia (Avianca). Doole remained in Bogota, Colombia, until September 1942, when he was reassigned to Pan Am's Atlantic division as assistant chief pilot.

By 1946, Doole had ended his active flying career to become Pan Am's regional director for the Middle East and Asia. He participated in negotiations for postwar bilateral air agreements, and in 1949 he was instrumental in the formation of Middle East Airlines.

While working for Pan Am, Doole had retained his commission in the Air Force Reserves, rising to the rank of colonel in 1948. Three years later, because of the war in Korea, he was recalled to active duty to become chief of estimates for the Middle East in the U.S. Air Force's Office of Intelligence, headed by Lieutenant General Charles P. Cabell. Doole and Cabell had a longstanding friendship that went back to their service together as junior officers in Panama.

On 6 July 1953, after President Dwight D. Eisenhower had appointed Cabell as deputy director of the Central Intelligence Agency (CIA) under Allen Dulles, Cabell brought Doole into the CIA as an appointed employee to "clean up the mess" with the agency's air proprietary in Asia. As Doole soon learned, the CIA in 1950 secretly had purchased Civil Air Transport, an airline that had been formed in China after World War II by Claire L. Chennault and Whiting Willauer. The Taiwan-based airline had provided air-

craft and personnel for CIA covert operations during the Korean War, all the while giving the appearance of a normal commercial operation. The CIA, however, had grown concerned about the amount of subsidy required by its airline and about control problems in the field.

Doole quickly established Washington's authority over Civil Air Transport's operations. As president of the Pacific Corporation, part of the corporate structure developed by the CIA, he exercised detailed supervision over the various components of a growing air complex. During the 1960s, the major subsidiaries of the Pacific Corporation included Air America, a contract airline that operated primarily in Southeast Asia; Civil Air Transport, a commercial airline with passenger routes from Korea to Thailand; and Air Asia, a large maintenance complex on Taiwan. At its height in 1968 the Pacific Corporation had assets of over $50 million, more than 8,000 employees, and a fleet of nearly 200 transports, small aircraft, and helicopters. While most of the air proprietary's business involved normal air transport operations, it also was used to support covert CIA operations in Indonesia, Tibet, China, Southeast Asia, and elsewhere. During this time the CIA's role in these operations was not common knowledge in the U.S. government.

Widely disliked by most employees because of his abrupt personality, Doole ruled over the air complex with an iron hand, exercising a strict managerial control of the business and of the aviation aspects of covert operations. It was a style of management that tolerated little discussion from subordinates. At the same time, he proved to be a skilled bureaucratic fighter, winning numerous battles inside the CIA in favor of the directorate of administration versus the directorate of operation over control of the air proprietary. Thanks largely to his reputation for turning a losing economic enterprise into a profitable one and to the support of Deputy Director Cabell, Doole withstood all challenges to his authority over the proprietary.

Doole retired from the CIA on 31 August 1971. Five years later the agency liquidated the air complex, returning $20 million to the U.S. Treasury. Doole, who never married, managed a family enterprise, Arntzen and Company, until his death in Washington, D.C.

• No collection of Doole's personal papers exists, and documentation of his career with the CIA remains unavailable for researchers. His battle to gain control over the air proprietary is detailed in William M. Leary, *Perilous Missions: Civil Air Transport and CIA Covert Operations in Asia* (1984). Information on his background was provided by Mr. Doole in a number of interviews with the author.

WILLIAM M. LEARY

DOOLEY, Ray (30 Oct. 1896–28 Jan. 1984), comedienne, was born Rachel Rice Dooley in Glasgow, Scotland, the daughter of Robert Rogers Dooley, a noted circus clown and theatrical manager, and Mary Dougherty. The family immigrated to the United States while Rachel was still an infant, eventually settling in Philadelphia. Dooley attended public schools and studied theater under her father's minstrel act, which also included her three older brothers.

Dooley continued to appear in the minstrel shows for the next few years, and in 1910, at the age of fifteen, she eloped with a fellow actor, Eddie Dowling, who later became an influential director and producer. The couple eventually had two children. By 1914 Dooley had left her father's company and formed her own group, the Ray Dooley Minstrels (also known as Ray Dooley and her Metropolitan Minstrels), which premiered at the Palace Theatre in New York. The following year Dooley made her debut in vaudeville as a producer of Tim McMahan's *Watermelon Girls* in New York, later touring with the group. In 1917 she appeared as Gazzoleen in *Words and Music* at the Fulton Theatre and subsequently played Kate in *Hitchy-Koo, 1918* at the Globe Theater in New York. Dooley gained the role of Kate almost by accident—the baby buggy used for the character was too small for another actor, and Dooley, petite, five feet tall, and weighing 100 pounds, stepped into the baby part. The role changed her career, and Dooley continued to do baby impersonations for the next three years in the Ziegfeld *Follies* of 1919, 1920, and 1921, originating the character of Baby Snooks (a brat character given to temper) to parents W. C. Fields, Will Rogers, Leon Carroll, and Fanny Brice. Regarding her performance in the *Follies* of 1920, a *New York Times* critic commented that "the talented Ray Dooley . . . is hilariously funny in a skit which depends entirely upon her own gifts as a comedienne" (23 June 1920). The same critic regarded the following year's edition, which featured a prize fight between Dooley and Brice, as the "best of them all" (22 June 1921). Despite her success, Dooley soon tired of the baby roles, but the *New York Times* reported that Florenz Ziegfeld convinced Dooley to sign contracts by promising a change in her act. Unfortunately the change was never worked into the show, and Dooley finally left the *Follies*.

After her departure Dooley appeared as Evie Dallas in *The Bunch and Judy* at the Globe Theater in November 1922 and in another review, *The Nifties of 1923*, at the Fulton Theatre in September 1923. In 1924 Ziegfeld convinced Dooley to return to the *Follies*, where she remained until 1926, when she finally left vaudeville for the musical stage. Dooley appeared first in *No Foolin'* at the Globe Theater in June 1926 and then scored a huge hit in October of the next year as Gertie in *The Sidewalks of New York*, a musical that featured her husband as both actor and director. The musical was successful and raised Dooley, according to the *New York Times*, to the "azure ranks of musical play stardom" (4 Oct. 1927). In 1928 she costarred in the seventh edition of *Earl Carroll's Vanities* with W. C. Fields and returned for the eighth edition the following year.

In 1931 Dooley returned to vaudeville with her husband but left to appear in his production of *Thumbs Up!*, which opened at the St. James Theatre in December 1934. The *New York Times* reported that Dooley had "returned with her bag of comic antics, her worried countenance, and her acrobatic nimbleness" (28 Dec. 1934). When the play closed, Dooley retired from acting to raise her newborn daughter and to devote more time to her family. In 1948 Dooley returned briefly to the stage in her husband's production of *Hope's the Thing*, a series of three one-act plays in which Dooley played Josey in *Home Life of a Buffalo*. After her husband's death in 1976, Dooley devoted her time to her daughter and three grandchildren. She died at home in East Hampton, New York.

Despite her objections, Dooley is remembered primarily for her baby impersonations. Her short stature and elfin-like face gave her an advantage in the roles, and her personality endeared her to audiences, despite the frequent tantrums in which her characters engaged. Dooley used her physical stature and dexterity as an integral part of comic routines. In her introduction of the baby character played by an adult, Dooley created what would become a staple in the vaudeville variety show, and she remained the definitive baby impersonator throughout her career.

• Clippings on Dooley's performances can be found in the Billy Rose Theatre Collection at the New York Public Library for the Performing Arts, Lincoln Center. Ray Dooley is included in the *Biographical Encyclopaedia and Who's Who of the American Theatre* (1981) and *Who Was Who in the Theatre* (1978). Her obituary is in the *New York Times*, 29 Jan. 1984.

MELISSA VICKERY BAREFORD

DOOLEY, Thomas Anthony, III (17 Jan. 1927–18 Jan. 1961), medical missionary, was born in St. Louis, Missouri, the son of Thomas A. Dooley, Jr., a railroad executive, and Agnes Wise. Dooley was raised in a devoutly Catholic, upper middle-class Irish-American family in St. Louis. After enrolling at the University of Notre Dame in 1944, Dooley enlisted in the navy's corpsman program and served at a naval hospital in New York. In 1946 he returned to Notre Dame and in 1948 entered St. Louis University Medical School, where he was known for impulsive acts of kindness to young hospital patients. A careless student, he was forced to repeat his final year of medical school before graduating near the bottom of his class in 1953. He reenlisted in the navy and served his residency at Camp Pendleton, California, prior to duty at the naval base in Yokusuka, Japan. In August 1954 Dooley was assigned to temporary duty on the USS *Montague*, which had been ordered to North Vietnam to aid in the evacuation of refugees who were fleeing the Communist Viet Minh for the South.

Lieutenant Dooley's medical work in the refugee camps of Haiphong provided the "cover" for an additional assignment in medical intelligence. An extraordinarily driven, charming, and charismatic individual, he soon came to the attention of Lieutenant Colonel Edward G. Lansdale, who led the CIA detail in Saigon that was dedicated to winning support, in both Vietnam and America, for the fledgling regime of the Catholic mandarin Ngo Dinh Diem. Lansdale, a former advertising executive, annointed Dooley the key symbol of Vietnamese-American cooperation and friendship. Dooley received the highest award of the Republic of South Vietnam and was encouraged to write an account of his heroic medical work among the refugees. *Deliver Us from Evil* was excerpted in *Reader's Digest* and published with great fanfare in April 1956. This bestselling book established Dooley's legend as a militant anti-Communist who was inspired by the Vietnamese refugees' struggle for religious freedom. The Catholicism he shared with those refugees only enhanced his stature because the mid-1950s saw the birth of an ecumenical movement within American religion and society. He was a hero to Catholics for his devotion to the Church and to people of all faiths for the fervent Americanism he unabashedly espoused to the Vietnamese.

Dooley had embarked on a whirlwind lecture tour on behalf of the book, the navy, and Diem's American supporters in January 1956 but was forced to resign from the service in late March following a lengthy investigation into his homosexual activities while on the lecture circuit. In a state of desperation he was approached by influential members of the loose coalition of intelligence agents, publicists, and international relief specialists later dubbed the "Vietnam Lobby" and offered an assignment in Laos as a "jungle doctor." Laos, which had only come into existence in 1954, was considered at the time even more vital than Vietnam to American interests in Southeast Asia. Under the sponsorship of the International Rescue Committee, Dooley—aided by three former navy corpsmen from his Vietnam days—established a clinic in Vang Vieng, Laos, in the fall of 1956. He would later build small hospitals at Nam Tha, Muong Sing, and Ban Houei Sai, all near "the rim of Red hell," as Dooley called the Lao-Chinese border. In Laos, where his patients were Buddhists or animists, he replaced proselytism with gentle sharing and even came to exalt certain aspects of Laotian life over the rugged materialism of America. By preaching love and service in his bestselling works *The Edge of Tomorrow* (1958) and *The Night They Burned the Mountain* (1960), Dooley became a hero of idealistic young Americans, while his grass-roots anticommunism anticipated the flexible counterinsurgency that the Kennedy administration's foreign policy would enshrine.

In 1959 Dooley contracted malignant melanoma and returned to New York in August for cancer surgery. The operation was filmed for a CBS documentary, "Biography of a Cancer," in which Dooley urged Americans to overcome their fear of the disease. He also used the opportunity to dramatically promote his work in Laos, now under the rubric of a voluntary agency called MEDICO (Medicine for International Cooperation). As the product of modern public relations strategies, Dooley was vulnerable to charges that his work was less genuine than that of his putative role model, Dr. Albert Schweitzer, and Schweitzer's hospital at Lambaréné in French Equatorial Africa. Dooley replied to his critics that "Madison Avenue" enabled him to treat many more patients than humble

physicians in underdeveloped nations could ever see. Dooley's illness greatly enhanced his fame, as he was now perceived as a martyr and perhaps even a saint in tireless pursuit of a noble calling. A lecture tour in 1959 raised over a million dollars for MEDICO, and the results of the annual Gallup Christmastime poll showed that Dooley was the seventh most admired man in the world among Americans.

During the final months of his life Dooley sought vainly to provide MEDICO with a solid foundation that might survive his own passing. Hospitals were established throughout Southeast Asia as well as in Kenya and Haiti. Yet Dooley's genius for personalizing the cause of the world's sick could not be simply conferred upon his successors. Shortly after his death in New York City, President John F. Kennedy cited Dooley's example in launching the Peace Corps, which attracted many young people who were initially inspired by Dooley's message of service. Dooley was a controversial figure in death as in life. While ardent supporters launched a campaign for his canonization as a Roman Catholic saint, others derided him as a dupe of American imperialism who bore at least some of the responsibility for America's entry into the Vietnam War. Many others continued to extol his memory as they sought ways to assist the less fortunate throughout the world.

• The official depository of Dooley's papers is the Western Historical Manuscripts Collection at the University of Missouri in St. Louis. There is also an outstanding collection of Dooley materials at the Pius XII Library of St. Louis University. A full-length biography is James T. Fisher, *Dr. America: The Lives of Thomas A. Dooley, 1927–1961* (1997). Dooley's mother and his devoted secretary authored hagiographical biographies in the 1960s: Agnes W. Dooley, *Promises to Keep: The Life of Dr. Thomas A. Dooley* (1962), and Teresa Gallagher, *Give Joy to My Youth* (1965). A more balanced early account is offered in an oral biography edited by James Monahan, *Before I Sleep: The Last Days of Dr. Tom Dooley* (1961). An effort to place Dooley in his historical context is Fisher, *The Catholic Counterculture in America, 1933–1962* (1989). The most substantial obituary is in the *St. Louis Post-Dispatch*, 19 Jan. 1961.

JAMES TERENCE FISHER

DOOLIN, William (1858–25 Aug. 1896), cowboy and bank and train robber, was born in Johnson County, Arkansas, the son of Michael Doolin and Artemina Beller, farmers. Bill Doolin had a normal childhood and remained on the family farm until 1881. He was a tall, slender man, lacking a formal education and barely literate but generally regarded as intelligent and personable. At twenty-three, Doolin left home to seek his fortune on the closing frontier. He quickly became a proficient cowboy for Oscar Halsell and other ranchers operating near the Cimarron and Arkansas rivers of the Oklahoma Territory. For several years Doolin worked his way across the western ranges of Wyoming, Montana, California, Arizona, and New Mexico, earning the reputation of a reliable, capable, and good-natured hand. He was considered to be a fine rider, an excellent shot, and a natural leader when he returned to the cattle ranches of Oklahoma.

Doolin and several other cowboys visited nearby Coffeyville, Kansas, for the Fourth of July celebration in 1891 and perhaps inadvertently launched a prominent career in crime. When local constables attempted to confiscate the visitors' illegal beer, a gunfight erupted, and the lawmen were shot. Probably already bored with ranch life, Doolin joined the notorious Dalton gang of train robbers. For thirty-three years the former cowboy had lived an ordinary life, giving no indication of a proclivity for criminal behavior, but within months Doolin would be widely known as a desperate, dangerous fugitive, and "King of the Oklahoma Outlaws."

Doolin soon participated in several Dalton depredations in the Indian Territory, but although he was credited with at least six killings, he remained only a peripheral member of the outlaw band. On 5 October 1892 the Daltons attempted to rob two banks simultaneously in Coffeyville, Kansas. The raid proved disastrous, with four members of the gang killed by townsmen. Doolin either escaped or was not involved in the fighting. Instead, he quickly emerged as the new leader of a reorganized and even more formidable outlaw organization. Doolin's gang struck repeatedly at trains and banks in Kansas, Missouri, and the Oklahoma Territory. About twenty individuals participated in these offenses, but typically only three to five members were involved in any specific act. The robberies were marked by careful planning, rapid execution, violence when necessary, and skillful escape.

The leader of these versatile and active criminals found time for a family. In 1893 Doolin married nineteen-year-old Edith Ellsworth, daughter of a Methodist minister. The couple had one son, Jay. Doolin and his criminal colleagues enjoyed good relations with many settlers, furnishing them with provisions and money in return for information and warnings of any efforts at apprehension. Helpful spies for the gang included two young women, Annie McDoulet and Jennie Stevens, popularly known as "Cattle Annie" and "Little Breeches."

Doolin's robbers usually operated from Ingalls, a small community in the Oklahoma Territory about ten miles east of Stillwater. Deputy federal marshals learned of this center for crime, realized the futility of direct attack, and decided to infiltrate the settlement by masquerading as homesteaders hiding in covered wagons. On 1 September 1893 the plan reached its climax with the "Battle of Ingalls," one of the bloodiest confrontations between outlaws and lawmen on the frontier. Doolin and most of the gang escaped, leaving four members of the posse and one innocent citizen killed or fatally wounded in the five-hour gunfight. The raid on Ingalls was a disastrous effort to apprehend the outlaws, but it led to the gradual disintegration of their organization.

A massive manhunt involving federal marshals, private detectives, and local peace officers began. The reward offered for Bill Doolin reached $5,000 "dead or alive," despite which he continued to direct robberies for two years. Public support for the outlaws eroded, however, and such members of the gang as "Arkansas Tom" (Ray Daugherty), Bill Dalton, "Tulsa Jack" Blake, Charley Pierce, and George "Bitter Creek" Newcomb were killed. By 1895 the surviving outlaws had scattered. Doolin sought refuge under an assumed name on the ranch of Eugene Manlove Rhodes in the mountains of eastern New Mexico. The fugitive also attempted, without success, to negotiate a surrender in return for a reduced charge and sentence.

Suffering from rheumatism, Doolin finally sought relief at the bathing resort of Eureka Springs, Arkansas. Deputy federal marshal Bill Tilghman diligently followed the trail and on 15 January 1896 arrested him in the Davey Hotel. News of the apprehension attracted a multitude of spectators to Guthrie, Oklahoma Territory, where Tilghman had taken his prisoner. Doolin was taken on a tour of the town, during which he shook hands with hundreds of fascinated citizens.

Confined for the first time in his life, the notorious outlaw declined the offer of a fifty-year sentence in return for a plea of guilty to the killings at Ingalls. On the night of 5 July 1896, still awaiting trial, he joined thirteen other prisoners and broke out of the federal jail at Guthrie. The escapees quickly scattered; most were never recaptured.

Doolin hid on the Cimarron River near his wife and son, who were then living in Lawson (later Quay), a small community some ten miles east of Ingalls. A local informant furnished information on the fugitive's movements, and Deputy Federal Marshal Heck Thomas planned an ambush. Just after sundown on 24 August 1896 Doolin said goodbye to his wife and walked down a road, where the posse was waiting. A fusillade of shots brought an immediate end to the outlaw's life. He had never been convicted of any crime.

Bill Doolin was quietly buried at Guthrie three days later. For decades only a rusting buggy axle marked the grave. Marshal Thomas eventually collected only $1,435 of the promised reward, a sum that did not cover his expenses.

• Leading sources include Bailey C. Hanes, *Bill Doolin: Outlaw O. T.* (1968); Glenn Shirley, *West of Hell's Fringe* (1978); and Paul Wellman, *A Dynasty of Western Outlaws* (1961).

FRANK R. PRASSEL

DOOLITTLE, Amos (18 May 1754–31 Jan. 1832), engraver, was born in Cheshire, Connecticut, the son of Ambrose Doolittle and Martha Munson (occupations unknown). Doolittle apprenticed under Eliakim Hitchcock, a silversmith, but he may have taught himself to engrave copper plates. By 1774, he was living in New Haven, where he remained until his death. He appears to have prospered, owning a house and shop on College Street in which he rented out a large room to individuals and organizations, including the Masons, who met there from 1801 to 1826. Doolittle was himself a dedicated Mason from 1792 until his death.

Like most eighteenth-century engravers, Doolittle was versatile by necessity. He engraved maps, political cartoons, invitations, bank notes, labels, music, bookplates, diplomas, certificates, tickets, Masonic aprons and ephemera, charts, book and magazine illustrations, religious and moralizing prints, portraits, and historic scenes. Connecticut newspaper accounts also advertised his work as a jeweler, a calico printer, and an engraver of clock faces.

Doolittle is known to have designed, printed, and published many of his own prints (*A Display of the United States* [1788] indicates that he owned a "rolling press"), but he was also associated with the publishers Shelton & Kensett, of Cheshire, Connecticut, from 1813 to 1817.

As a member of the Governor's Second Company of Guards (now known as the Governor's Foot Guards), Doolittle marched under Captain Benedict Arnold, to Cambridge, Massachusetts, in 1775 after news of the battles of Lexington and Concord. This trip led to his earliest and most famous works, a series of four handcolored copperplate engravings titled *The Battles of Lexington and Concord*, published in New Haven in December 1775. Based on sketches that Doolittle prepared in collaboration with Ralph Earl, the four engravings provide the only pictorial record by a contemporary American of these significant revolutionary battles. The identifiable buildings and the realistic details gleaned from eyewitness accounts add to their value as historical documents. The prints also show an emerging American artistic sensibility, one that emphasizes realistic description and literal narrative through minute detail, decorative pattern, and a primitive flattened space.

Doolittle executed other single prints that marked historic moments and the beginning of national pride. *Federal Hall the Seat of Congress* (1790) depicts George Washington's inauguration on 30 April 1789 and was engraved after a drawing by Peter Lacour. *A Display of the United States of America*, with its central portrait of George Washington, was so successful that similar prints were issued to mark the presidencies of John Adams and Thomas Jefferson. Splendid Victories Gained by the United States Frigates over the British (1813) celebrates three decisive American naval victories during the War of 1812.

Doolittle was an accomplished political cartoonist. One of the earliest American political prints, *The Looking Glass for 1787*, deals with Connecticut's adoption of the federal Constitution. While published anonymously, the print is almost certainly by Doolittle. In 1813, during the War of 1812, Doolittle issued two cartoons. One, *Brother Jonathan Administering a Salutary Cordial to John Bull*, was issued under the pseudonym "Yankee-Doodle." The other, *The Hornet and the Peacock, or, John Bull in Distress*, is signed. A fourth political cartoon, *Bonaparte in Trouble*, was published around 1814 and verifies the interest Americans had in contemporary European events.

Doolittle's other important works include four scenes from the biblical parable of the prodigal son (1814), executed in the tradition of eighteenth-century English morality prints. They transpose the story to New England by using American dress and home furnishings.

Doolittle also engraved maps throughout his life. The maps in Jedediah Morse's *Geography Made Easy* (1784) appear to be his earliest. Some of his most notable map engraving was done for William Blodget's *A Topographical Map of the State of Vermont* (1789), Seth Pease's *Map of the Connecticut Western Reserve* (1798), and Almon Ruggles's *Map of the Fire Land* (1808).

Doolittle was married three times. His first wife, Sally (maiden name unknown), died in 1797; they had two children, both of whom died in early adulthood. Later in 1797 he married Phebe Tuttle, with whom he had one child. He was widowed again in 1825, and that same year he married Esther Moss; they had no children together.

Amos Doolittle was one of America's earliest and most prolific copper-plate engravers. His engravings are often naive, but the vigor and directness of his best work complements the dramatic emotions and events depicted. Today, his prints of historic events, issues, and people are among the most rare and important early American graphics.

• The only biography of Amos Doolittle is William A. Bearsley, "An Old New Haven Engraver and His Work: Amos Doolittle," *Papers of the New Haven Colony Historical Society* 8 (1914): 132–51. The research notes of Thomson Harlow (Director Emeritus) at the Connecticut Historical Society contain further information about Doolittle, as does his article "Connecticut Engravers, 1774–1820," *Connecticut Historical Society Bulletin* 36, no. 4 (1971): 102–8. Other articles and books on specific prints of Doolittle's are Francis W. Allen, "Notes of the Bookplates of Amos Doolittle," *Old-Time New England* 39 (Oct. 1948): 38–44; John Warner Barber, *History and Antiquities of New Haven, Connecticut* (1836); Frank J. Metcalf, "Amos Doolittle, Engraver and Printer," *American Collector* 4 (May 1927): 53–56; William Murrell, *A History of American Graphic Humor* (1933–1938); Ian M. G. Quimby, "The Doolittle Engravings of the Battle of Lexington and Concord," *Winterthur Portfolio* 4 (1968): 83–108; William Sawitzky, "Ralph Earl's Historical Painting (A View of the Town of Concord)" *Antiques* 28 (Sept. 1935): 98–100; and Frederic Fairchild Sherman, "The So-Called Ralph Earl Originals of Doolittle's Concord and Lexington Engravings," *Art in America* 24 (Jan. 1936): 43–44. A genealogy of the Doolittle family is in William F. Doolittle, *The Doolittle Family in America* vol. 3 (1903). There is an obituary by Benjamin Silliman in the *American Journal of Science and Arts* (July 1832): 183–85.

KATE STEINWAY

DOOLITTLE, Hilda (10 Sept. 1886–27 Sept. 1961), poet and novelist, was born in Bethlehem, Pennsylvania, the daughter of Charles Leander Doolittle, a professor of astronomy, and Helen Eugenia Wolle. With two older stepbrothers and one older and two younger brothers, the writer who later established herself as "H.D." was early sensitive to the defining nature of her gender. She was also aware of her special upbringing within the Moravian traditions of her mother's religion in contrast to her father's scientific and mathematical aspirations for her. Later in memoirs, poetry, and fiction she would palimpsestically return to these tensions between mother and father, spirit and science, mythic understanding and measured reality.

H.D. was first educated at Moravian schools, then privately in Philadelphia, where her circle of friends widened. In 1901 she met Ezra Pound; in 1905, William Carlos Williams. She graduated from Friends' Central School in the same year, then for three semesters attended Bryn Mawr College, where Marianne Moore was a classmate. Between 1905 and 1908 she and Pound became intimate friends, and the more worldly writer influenced her reading and poetic aspirations. Later H.D. reflected on this early friendship as well as on her subsequent relations with Pound in her memoir *End to Torment* (1979).

In 1910 she met Frances Gregg, who soon became her lover. H.D.'s complex relationship with both Pound and Gregg, which encapsulated her struggles with her own bisexuality, later became the basis for her autobiographical novel *HER* (1981; retitled *HER-mione* by the publisher, New Directions). In the summer of 1911 H.D. sailed with Gregg and her mother to Europe. When the Greggs returned to America in the autumn, however, H.D. remained in London, where through Pound she met other writers and artists, among them Wyndham Lewis, Ford Madox Ford, John Cournos, and Richard Aldington, whom she married in 1913.

During the first years of their courtship and marriage, the Aldingtons established themselves as writers. In 1912 Pound labeled their early verse "Imagiste" and, slashing away with red pencil at what he felt were excessive phrases, signed her poems "H.D." before sending them off to Harriet Monroe at *Poetry*. This "naming" was to become symbolic of the struggle for her own identity that H.D. confronted as a woman and writer throughout her life. Her early poems were gathered with verse by others into the modernist anthology *Des Imagistes*, edited by Pound in 1914. Through work on this volume, H.D. began important friendships with D. H. Lawrence and Amy Lowell. H.D.'s poems appeared in subsequent imagist anthologies in 1915, 1916, and 1917, and her first volume of verse, *Sea Garden*, was published in 1916. This free verse seemed to her contemporaries "crystalline," "pure," "hard," and "Greek." Certainly it was new, experimental, and modernist—its stark power exemplified by H.D.'s most anthologized poem, "Oread." May Sinclair called H.D. "the best of the Imagists," yet "imagist" was a label H.D. struggled to escape throughout her life as she grew beyond the "doctrine of the image" toward the epic poetry and larger themes of her mature years.

The advent of war in 1914 distressed H.D. Her husband resisted his initial impulse to enlist, becoming increasingly hostile to the social and economic forces causing the war, but he enlisted just before conscription in 1916. H.D. had a stillborn daughter in 1915; she lived alone in Devon and London during Aldington's absence on the western front. When Aldington returned for officers' training in 1917, the couple enjoyed a brief period of renewed intimacy; but when they went back to London at the end of the year, the tensions between them intensified. Aldington took a lover, Dorothy Yorke, and soon after he returned to the front in 1918, H.D. left London for Cornwall with the musician Cecil Gray. In July she met Winifred Ellerman (known as Bryher). H.D. also became pregnant in Cornwall with her only child, Frances Perdita, born in 1919. The events of this period became the basis for H.D.'s autobiographical novel *Bid Me to Live* (1960) and for two novels she did not publish, *Asphodel* and *Paint It Today* (both published posthumously in 1992), as well as for her collection of interrelated stories, *Palimpsest* (1926).

In 1919, after efforts at reconciliation, H.D. left Aldington and began a lifelong relationship with Bryher. They visited Greece together in 1920 and America in 1920–1921. This pattern of frequent travel persisted until illness in the 1950s made it impossible. H.D. balanced periods of retreat in Switzerland with more social periods in Paris and especially in London. Her literary circle grew to include such figures as Sylvia Beach, Nancy Cunard, Norman Douglas, and Dorothy Richardson. After a period of estrangement in the 1920s, H.D. resumed an epistolary friendship with Aldington that continued, with an interruption in the late 1930s and early 1940s, until her death. She divorced Aldington in 1938.

Bryher's first marriage of convenience (1921–1927) to Robert McAlmon also shaped H.D.'s experience. He was an ally in her intense and often upsetting friendship with Bryher, whose early threats of suicide gave way in the 1920s to more complex manipulation of the woman she supported and loved. H.D. was alternately upset and affirmed by Bryher, whose second marriage of convenience, to Kenneth Macpherson in 1927, veiled an affair of H.D.'s. Her experiences with Macpherson are fictionalized in *Narthex* (1928), *Kora and Ka* (1934), *The Usual Star* (1934), and *Nights* (1935). Encouraged by Bryher's and Macpherson's interest in film, H.D. published reviews in *Close Up* in 1927–1929 and starred with Paul Robeson in *Borderline*, an avant-garde film produced and directed by Macpherson and edited by H.D. and Bryher.

H.D.'s interest in psychoanalysis began at least as early as her first sessions with Havelock Ellis in 1919. In 1931, at Bryher's urging, H.D. began analysis with Mary Chadwick in London. In 1931–1932 she had analytic sessions with Hanns Sachs, and in 1933 and 1934 she underwent periods of analysis with Sigmund Freud in Vienna. Her analysis and friendship with Freud later formed the basis of her memoir *Tribute to Freud* (1974).

In the late 1930s H.D. became increasingly interested in the hermetic tradition; in the 1940s, in spiritualism and astrology. Her interest in these dimensions of experience influenced such autobiographical novels as the unpublished "The Sword Went Out to Sea" and "White Rose and the Red." During the Second World War, H.D. left Switzerland for London, where she remained until 1946. This war, which seemed to her a recapitulation of 1914–1918, was fraught with psychological tension exacerbated by the real physical threats of living in England during the blitz. Her verse trilogy—*The Walls Do Not Fall* (1944), *Tribute to the Angels* (1945), and *The Flowering of the Rod* (1946)—gives evidence of her struggles and her spiritual reconciliation of them.

Artistic resolution did not resolve H.D.'s psychic distress, however, and in 1946 she suffered a serious emotional breakdown. She went to a clinic near Zurich, where she recovered, and settled in Switzerland, first in hotels, but after 1956 because of physical ill health in clinics, for the rest of her life. She continued to write throughout the 1950s, and numerous memoirs and reflective journals from this period are among her unpublished work.

H.D.'s relationship with Bryher endured as, ironically, did her relationship with Aldington. These friendships and H.D.'s important relationship with Norman Holmes Pearson, a professor of English at Yale whom she first met while on a visit to the United States in 1937, became especially significant to her in her years of increasing isolation before her death in Zurich. Pearson played a crucial role in arranging publication of H.D.'s work after the war and encouraged her to preserve letters and manuscripts. H.D.'s final years were productive despite incapacitating physical illness, and shortly before her death she finished the epic poem *Helen in Egypt*, the work many critics feel is her most successful voicing and resolution of the dualities she struggled with throughout her life and work.

During her formative years as a writer and in association with imagism, H.D. was highly regarded by her contemporaries. Aldington never ceased to champion her poetry, and she was praised in print by F. S. Flint and by later scholars of the period, including Glenn Hughes in his pioneering *Imagism and the Imagists* (1931). But the very movement that established H.D. as a serious artist also froze her reputation, and she strove to overcome the finally trivializing label that ceased to characterize her work at least by the publication of *Hymen* in 1921 and *Heliodora and Other Poems* in 1924. Later readers often regretted that she had moved beyond the short, comparatively lucid early poems to the more experimental, complex, and challenging prose and poetry of her maturity. As the work of Pound and T. S. Eliot came to define the era for many critics, H.D. was marginalized: as woman and artist, she was not taken seriously by mainstream scholars establishing the canon. In the late 1960s, with the advent of the women's movement and fresh attention to the nature of modernism, H.D. began to be read and reread. Many of her books were reissued, and previously unpublished work appeared in print for the first time. Critical and biographical attention from scholars and poets influenced by her writing (such as Robert Duncan and Adrienne Rich) called into question H.D.'s reputation as merely an imagist and established her for many readers as a writer worthy of the same attention

as that given to her more widely read male contemporaries. H.D. is now regarded as a major poet, a versatile writer whose exploration of her identity as both woman and artist is central to an understanding of literary modernism.

• H.D.'s papers, which include voluminous correspondence as well as unpublished work, are in the Collection of American Literature at the Beinecke Library at Yale University. Other important material by H.D. is in Bryher's papers, also at Yale. Additional letters are at several other libraries in the United States, including those at Southern Illinois University, the Harry Ransom Humanities Research Centre at the University of Texas, Temple University, and Indiana University.

Major works by H.D. not mentioned above include the translations *Choruses from Iphigeneia in Aulis and the Hippolytus of Euripides* (1919) and *Euripides' Ion* (1937); the volumes of poetry *Red Roses for Bronze* (1931), *What Do I Love?* (1944), *By Avon River* (1949), *Hermetic Definition* (1972), and *Collected Poems: 1912–1944*, ed. Louis Martz (1983); the novel *Hedylus* (1928); the essays included in *Notes on Thought and Vision and the Wise Sappho* (1982); and the memoir of her Moravian childhood, *The Gift* (1982).

Important biographical studies include Janice Robinson, *H.D.: The Life and Work of an American Poet* (1982); Barbara Guest, *Herself Defined: The Poet H.D. and Her World* (1984); and Caroline Zilboorg, ed., *Richard Aldington and H.D.: The Early Years in Letters* (1992). Important book-length critical studies include Susan Stanford Friedman, *Psyche Reborn: The Emergence of H.D.* (1981); Rachel Blau DuPlessis, *H.D.: The Career of that Struggle* (1986); Deborah Kelly Kloepfer, *The Unspeakable Mother: Forbidden Discourse in Jean Rhys and H.D.* (1989); Gary Burnett, *H.D. between Image and Epic: The Mysteries of Her Poetics* (1990); Susan Stanford Friedman, *Penelope's Web: Gender, Modernity, H.D.'s Fiction* (1990); and Donna Krolik Hollenberg, *H.D.: The Poetics of Childbirth and Creativity* (1991). Two significant collections of essays include biographical, critical, and bibliographical material: Michael King, ed., *H.D.: Woman and Poet* (1986), and Susan Stanford Friedman and Rachel Blau DuPlessis, eds., *Signets: Reading H.D.* (1990).

CAROLINE ZILBOORG

DOOLITTLE, James Harold (14 Dec. 1896–27 Sept. 1993), aviator and air force commander, was born in Alameda, California, the son of Frank Henry Doolittle, a carpenter and gold prospector, and Rosa Shepard. Doolittle grew up in California and Alaska, where his parents moved in the gold rush of the period. He was educated in Nome, Alaska; at Los Angeles Junior College; and, for three years, at the University of California. He left the university at the beginning of his senior year when the United States entered World War I.

Enlisting as a flying cadet in the Army Reserve Corps in 1917, Doolittle was assigned to the Signal Corps and trained at the School of Military Aeronautics at the University of California and at Rockwell Field, California. Also in 1917 he married Josephine Elsie Daniels; they had two children. On 11 March 1918 he was commissioned a second lieutenant in the Signal Corps's Aviation Section. He served in a number of assignments as a flight leader and gunnery instructor. In July 1920 he was promoted to first lieutenant, regular army, in the Army Air Service and attended the Air Service Mechanical School at Kelly Field, Texas, and the aeronautical engineering course at McCook Field, Ohio.

On 4 September 1922 Doolittle made the first transcontinental flight across North America within twenty-four hours (twenty-one hours, nineteen minutes) from Pablo Beach, Florida, to San Diego, with only one refueling stop at Kelly Field. For this feat, he received the Distinguished Flying Cross and gained international acclaim.

In 1922 he was granted a bachelor of arts degree from the University of California (as of 1918). He then went to the Massachusetts Institute of Technology for advanced aeronautical engineering training and received a master of science degree in 1924 and a doctor of science degree in aeronautics in 1925.

Between 1925 and 1930 Doolittle was assigned to a series of testing stations, where he raced and demonstrated aircraft and performed a wide range of other aviation activities. He won the prestigious Mackay Trophy for setting aviation speed records and a number of other awards. In 1928, while assigned to Mitchell Field on Long Island, he helped to develop the artificial horizontal and directional gyroscopes that paved the way for instrument flying. In September 1929 he made the first blind instrument-controlled landing, subsequently receiving the Harmon Trophy for his pioneering work in this area.

In February 1930 Doolittle resigned his active commission, retaining the reserve rank of major. He became the aviation manager for Shell Oil Company, where he helped to develop better aviation fuels. Continuing to race airplanes, he set a world speed record in 1932, winning both the Bendix and the Thompson trophies. He also served on various government and military consultative boards on aviation matters during this period.

In July 1940 Doolittle returned to active duty as a major in the Army Air Corps. His first assignment was as assistant district supervisor of the Central Air Corps Procurement District at Indianapolis, where he was involved in converting civilian industry to war production. He was promoted to lieutenant colonel in January 1942 and reassigned to Headquarters Army Air Force in Washington. His duty was to plan the first aerial raid on Japan. He volunteered to lead the attack and on 18 April 1942 led sixteen B-25 twin-engine bombers from the carrier USS *Hornet* on a daring raid 740 miles to the Japanese mainland to bomb Tokyo, Yokohama, Kobe, Osaka, and Nagoya. The first strike back at the Japanese after Pearl Harbor, it gave a huge boost to American morale at a time when the Japanese seemed invincible in the Pacific. Although he had to bail out over China, he was rescued and eventually made his way back to the United States, where he was promoted to brigadier general and awarded the Congressional Medal of Honor.

After the raid, Doolittle was sent to England, where he was assigned to the Eighth Air Force. In September 1942 he was named commander of the Twelfth Air Force, directing the air forces in support of Operation TORCH, the invasion of French North Africa. In 1943 he became the commanding general of the Allies' Northwest African Strategic Air Forces and then the Fifteenth Air Force, directing strategic air operations against German forces in the Mediterranean theater of operations. In 1944 he was promoted to lieutenant general and commanded the Eighth Air Force in strategic operations against German industry and V-weapons facilities from airbases in England and in the attacks that preceded the Normandy invasion. After Germany surrendered, Doolittle was transferred to the Pacific theater, but he saw little action, as the war ended shortly after his arrival. In January 1946 he returned to reserve status.

Doolittle rejoined Shell Oil in a senior executive position. From 1946 until 1959 he served first as a vice president and then as a director. He retired from Shell Oil and the Air Force Reserve in 1959. After the war and up until his death, he remained active in science, aviation, and national security matters, serving on a number of important advisory boards and commissions, including the National Advisory Committee for Aeronautics (1948–1958), the Air Force Science Advisory Board (1955), the President's Science Committee (1957), and the Board of Space Technology Laboratories. President Ronald Reagan promoted him to four-star general in 1985, and President George Bush awarded him the Presidential Medal of Freedom in 1989. He died at Pebble Beach, California.

Doolittle was one of the pioneers of aviation in the United States; the techniques and instruments that he developed became, according to *Aviation Week & Space Technology* (4 Oct. 1993), the "cornerstone of practical air commerce." During wartime, he played a pivotal role in establishing the role of aviation in modern warfare. His raid on Japan raised American morale when it was needed most. He helped lead the Allied air forces in the offensive campaign that ultimately made a signal contribution to the defeat of Nazi Germany. After the war, he continued to have an impact on science and aviation. William F. Rickenbacker, the son of World War I ace Eddie Rickenbacker, described Doolittle as proof that "heroes have lived among us" (*National Review*, 1 Nov. 1993).

• Doolittle tells his own story in *I Could Never Be So Lucky Again* (1991), providing new insight into his early years as an aviator and shedding light on his role as an operational air commander during World War II. The best overall narrative of the Tokyo raid can be found in Carroll V. Glines, *Doolittle's Tokyo Raiders* (1964). The most complete biography of Doolittle is Lowell Thomas and Edward Jablonski, *Doolittle: A Biography* (1976). Another important and very complete source that addresses Doolittle's wartime contributions in the greater context of the overall European air campaign is Wesley F. Craven and James L. Cate, eds., *The Army Air Forces in World War II* (6 vols., 1948–1955). An obituary is in the *New York Times*, 29 Sept. 1983.

JAMES H. WILLBANKS

DOOLITTLE, James Rood (3 Jan. 1815–27 July 1897), U.S. senator, was born in Washington County, New York, the son of Reuben Doolittle, a prosperous blacksmith and iron maker, and Sarah Rood. Doolittle grew up near the village of Hampton and in Genesee County in western New York. He attended a local district school, later praising his teacher for requiring that he properly enunciate his words. Doolittle then attended Middlebury Academy in Wyoming County, and in 1834 he graduated from Geneva (now Hobart-Smith) College, an institution to which his father had generously contributed. In 1836 Doolittle moved to Rochester, New York, where he read law and in 1837 was admitted to the bar. That same year he married Mary Lovina Cutting; they had six children.

In 1841 Doolittle moved to Wyoming County, New York, where he entered politics as a Democrat, first as an unsuccessful candidate for the state legislature and then as an active Martin Van Buren supporter of the "Barnburner" faction, whose enemies held them ready to destroy the country over the slavery issue. In 1847 Doolittle was elected district attorney, and the next year, as a delegate to the Democratic state convention, Doolittle introduced the cornerstone resolution opposing the extension of slavery to free soil territory, a pledge that became the distinguishing principle of the Free-Soil party, which he subsequently supported. In 1851 Doolittle and his family moved to Racine, Wisconsin, where he built the large residence he maintained for the rest of his life. A handsome six-footer with a strong voice and an active law practice, Doolittle was elected a judge of the first judicial circuit. He was active in the state of Wisconsin's campaign to nullify the controversial fugitive slave provision of the Compromise of 1850, which made it easier for slaveholders to return escaped slaves to the South. Doolittle resigned his judgeship in 1856 and joined the newly formed Republican party. During the political realignment that shuffled partisan attachments everywhere during the 1850s, he joined thousands of American men in changing his political allegiance to the Republicans, who were committed to no extension of slavery in the territories. In 1857 Doolittle was elected to the U.S. Senate as a Republican.

As a senator, Doolittle combined his opposition to slavery in the territories with a firm commitment to colonization for all African Americans, who, he believed, should be returned to Africa or sent to South America. He also developed what he called a "homestead policy" for free blacks to take up land in Haiti, Jamaica, and Honduras. His commitment to colonization was his solution to the growing tension over slavery, for he held that "the only question which can imperil the union is the negro question." Viewing national unity as more important than the eventual end of slavery, he opposed the abolitionists, who, he believed, jeopardized the nation's survival.

During the campaign of 1860 Doolittle campaigned for Abraham Lincoln, and during the ensuing secession crisis he was vigorously Unionist. In Congress Doolittle opposed the Crittenden Resolutions, which would have extended slavery across the southwestern United States, adding to them his own proposal for a constitutional amendment denying the right of any state to secede from the Union. Throughout the Civil War he continued to tie the emancipation of African-American slaves to their voluntary colonization as freedmen in Haiti or Liberia. In time he became a dependable supporter of Lincoln's policies, well known for his patriotic slogan "Fill up the ranks and press on the columns." Considered a moderate Republican by his senatorial colleagues, Doolittle in 1864, as a member of the Senate Committee on Indian Affairs, offered a resolution to investigate the actions of Colonel John Chivington of the Colorado militia in its attack on the Cheyenne, known as the Sand Creek Massacre. Reelected to the Senate in 1863 by the Wisconsin legislature, Doolittle remained a loyal supporter of the president's policies. At a campaign rally in Springfield, Illinois, during the election of 1864, he rallied the president's supporters with the words: "I believe in God. Under Him I believe in Abraham Lincoln."

After Lincoln's assassination Doolittle gave his support to the new president Andrew Johnson, and when Johnson tried to form a new political organization that would include conservative Republicans and Democrats, he became a prominent figure in the short-lived National Union party. Unlike other Republican senators, such as Charles Sumner of Massachusetts, Doolittle held to the doctrine that the Union was unbroken, a condition that limited congressional power over the defeated South. Hence, he opposed many of the Republican initiatives during Reconstruction, including the Freedman's Bureau and the Fifteenth Amendment. He continued to encourage colonization, at one point encouraging Texas to cede her unoccupied lands to African-American veterans of the Union army. During the impeachment trial of Andrew Johnson, Doolittle was one of only ten Republicans to vote against the conviction of the president. Ignoring the instructions of the Wisconsin legislature to vote impeachment, he insisted that the charges against Johnson were weak and partisan. In response, in 1868 the Wisconsin legislature passed a resolution calling for his resignation from the U.S. Senate, which he ignored. After his second term as a senator ended in 1871, he was not reelected. In later campaigns for the governorship in 1871 and for Congress in 1886, Doolittle ran as a Democrat and was defeated. Always interested in public life, he was disappointed in his hopes for an ambassadorial appointment. His last years were spent as a lawyer in his firm's Chicago office and in Racine. He died in Providence, Rhode Island.

• Doolittle's letters are scattered, but several are in the Robert Todd collection of Abraham Lincoln papers and in the Andrew Johnson papers at the Library of Congress; both sets of papers have been microfilmed. Miscellaneous documents relating to Doolittle are available in *Publications of the Southern Historical Association* (nos. 9–11) and at the Wisconsin Historical Society. See also Duane Mowry, "An Appreciation of James Doolittle," *Proceedings of the Historical Society of Wisconsin* (1909), p. 291; James Sellers, "James Rood Doolittle," *Wisconsin Magazine of History* 17 (1933–1934): 168–78, 277–306, 393–401; Biagino Marone, "Senator James Doolittle and the Struggle against Radicalism, 1857–1866" (Master's thesis, Marquette Univ., 1955); Claude Albright, "Dixon, Doolittle, and Norton: The Forgotten Republican Votes," *Wisconsin Magazine of History* (Winter 1975–1976): 91–101. An obituary is in the *Chicago Tribune*, 28 July 1897.

JEAN H. BAKER

DORAN, George Henry (19 Dec. 1869–7 Jan. 1956), book publisher, was born in Toronto, Canada, the son of Annie Oliver and James Doran. Little is known of Doran's parents; in his autobiography, Doran stressed principally their staunch Presbyterianism and described his father only as a "simple-minded inventive genius of few words." Doran left school at fourteen, attracted by a sign in the window of the Willard Tract Depository reading, "Smart Boy Wanted." After working for this religious publishing company for nearly ten years, in 1892 he moved to Chicago, where he became a traveling salesman for another religious publisher, Fleming H. Revell. He married Mary Noble McConnell in 1895; they had one child.

In 1896 Doran became a U.S. citizen and was also named vice president of Revell. Meanwhile, he encouraged the company's expansion into general publishing, soon growing impatient with his employer's cautious pace. Sent east to bolster the firm's New York City office, Doran spent a "hellish" year of divided responsibility and then resigned. He made some successful business investments in Canada, but the panic of 1907 plus, he said later, his "insatiable longing to be back among books" led him to return to publishing. With the help of several investors, he established the George H. Doran Company in Toronto in 1908 and shortly thereafter opened his main office in New York City.

Among Doran's backers was the British firm of Hodder & Stoughton, which granted him reprint rights to many of their books. In addition, several authors followed him from Revell, including Ralph Connor, whose novel *The Foreigner* helped launch the fledgling company by selling 125,000 copies. In his first year, Doran cleared a net profit of $40,000 on an initial investment of $10,000. "How many times later on I prayed for similar results!" he recalled. "It was the most thrilling adventure of my life." In 1909 he had another great success with a British novel, Arnold Bennett's *The Old Wives' Tale*. Doran's gamble—at his wife's urging—on the relatively unknown Bennett marked the beginning of a relationship that would last for years and enrich both author and publisher. Through Bennett, who became a good friend, Doran met other important young British writers, including Hugh Walpole and Frank Swinnerton. He began to spend several weeks each year at London's Savoy Hotel, enjoying the social pleasures of British literary life and signing up new authors. Meanwhile, the company's prosperity enabled Doran to buy out several of his smaller investors.

When World War I broke out in Europe in 1914, Doran was asked by the British Ministry of Information to help build U.S. sympathy for the Allied cause by publishing the ministry's books and pamphlets under his own imprint, without any indication as to their original source. Over the next four years, Doran became, in the words of one publishing historian, "virtually a one-man publishing factory for Prime Ministers and other government notables." Because some of the books were by eminent British authors, the arrangement gave Doran an opportunity to broaden his list. Even more important, he said later, was the "gratification of being in actual service in the cause of my race, the Anglo-Saxon hegemony." Doran also published works by leading Americans who supported the country's entry into the war, including Theodore Roosevelt and Mary Roberts Rinehart. His professional association with Rinehart lasted long after the war, adding an enormously popular novelist to his list. Their ties became even closer in 1919, when Rinehart's son Stanley married Doran's daughter and joined the firm; Stanley's younger brother soon signed up as well.

During the 1920s Doran grew troubled by the outspoken language and controversial themes of some of the best new writers. He had no use, he said, for the "vulgar nudity of intellectualism." He broke a contract rather than accept D. H. Lawrence's *The Rainbow*, ended his association with John Dos Passos after publishing *Three Soldiers*, and rejected books by Ernest Hemingway and "that ruffian" Theodore Dreiser. Nevertheless, with the encouragement of young staff members such as Rinehart and John Chipman Farrar, Doran did publish many talented new writers, including Stephen Vincent Benét, DuBose Heyward, Hervey Allen, Michael Arlen, Aldous Huxley, and W. Somerset Maugham. (Indeed, the "revolutionary" character of some of his books led to tension with his British partners.) Doran also made an important literary contribution with the *Bookman*, a monthly journal he bought in 1918 and published throughout the 1920s. The *Bookman* made little money, but the firm as a whole prospered. By 1925 Doran was able to buy out his British partners and take sole ownership of his company.

In 1927 Doran agreed to merge with Doubleday, Page and Company, creating a new firm, Doubleday, Doran and Company, the largest trade publisher in the United States. Doran and his editors hoped to retain their independence in the new organization, but it soon became clear that F. N. Doubleday had no intention of relinquishing control. Accordingly, Farrar and the Rineharts left to start their own firm in 1929, and Doran resigned a year later, complaining that "the auditor-in-chief and not the editor-in-chief was the final arbiter of publishing policy." He worked for a few years for the Cosmopolitan Book Corporation, which had been acquired by Farrar & Rinehart, but relations grew strained, and he retired in 1934. After publishing a lively account of his publishing career, *Chronicles of Barabbas* (1935), and traveling for several years, Doran settled on a ranch in Tucson, Arizona. Then in

1949 he returned to Toronto, where he took up residence in a grand hotel suite, much lionized by his local admirers. He died in Toronto.

A friend once described Doran as "a bit of an imperial," with his spats, neat mustache, walking stick, and gold-tipped cigarettes. Throughout his career, he inspirited the world of publishing with his colorful style, infectious geniality, and zest for his calling. He also treated his authors well; Bennett's literary agent said of him, "He is certainly most attentive, . . . and it is impossible altogether to resist the effect of his diplomacy." His author and fellow publisher, Frank Swinnerton, observed, "Other men in the book trade had judgment and more consistent success. Doran had genius." He combined a willingness to take professional risks with a flair for reading the public taste. All publishers, said Swinnerton, "owed much to this generous and flamboyant man."

• The Aldous Huxley Papers at Stanford University include some unpublished letters from Doran. The liveliest, though not entirely accurate, source on Doran's life is his own *Chronicles of Barabbas* (1935), whose title is taken from the legend that Lord Byron, sent a copy of a Bible by his publisher, returned it with the line "Now Barabbas was a liar" changed to "Now Barabbas was a publisher." Descriptions of Doran's publishing career appear in Charles A. Madison, *Book Publishing in America* (1966); Donald Sheehan, *This Was Publishing* (1952); and John Tebbel, *A History of Book Publishing in the United States*, vols. 2 and 3 (1975, 1978). Doran's dealings with particular authors are described in Ted Morgan, *Maugham* (1980); Reginald Pound, *Arnold Bennett: A Biography* (1952); and *Letters of Arnold Bennett*, vol. 3, ed. James Hepburn (1970). An obituary is in the *New York Times*, 8 Jan. 1956. See also "People Who Read and Write," *New York Times Book Review*, 8 Jan. 1956.

SANDRA OPDYCKE

DORÁTI, Antal (9 Apr. 1906–13 Nov. 1988), conductor and composer, was born in Budapest, Hungary, the son of Sándor Doráti, a violinist, and Margit Kunwald, a pianist, violinist, and violist. Doráti began his musical studies with his parents at an early age. Late in his life he remarked, "Since my earliest childhood the strongest impressions and influences which pointed my way, emanated from my father and mother. Both were musicians through and through" (*Notes of Seven Decades*).

In 1920 Doráti enrolled at the Liszt Academy in Budapest, where he studied with Zoltán Kodály and Leo Weiner. He graduated from the academy in 1924. Doráti also studied philosophy at Vienna University at this time. At the recommendation of the opera conductor Miklós Radnai, Doráti obtained his first professional position as *repetitor* at the Budapest Royal Opera, a post he held until 1928. In 1928 Fritz Busch, the general music director at the Dresden Opera, asked Doráti to be his special assistant with the company. Aided by an unusual "vacation" stipend from the Hungarian government, Doráti left for Dresden. The following year he was appointed conductor of the Münster Opera at the Municipal Theater, and he held the post until 1932. In the same year, encouraged by

his developing professional career, Doráti married Klári Kórody. They had one child.

Doráti was given frequent guest conducting opportunities outside of Münster, which led in part to his decision to move to Berlin in 1932. By 1933 Doráti had become disgusted with the growing racism and fascism in Germany and suddenly moved to Paris. As Doráti recalled, he was "starting over" in France. He found his first work in Paris as a vocal coach similar to his early work in Budapest. Doráti then organized and conducted the first opera broadcast on the Post, Telegraph, Telephone (PTT), the new state radio station.

After an engagement as guest conductor with the Ballet Russes de Monte Carlo, Doráti joined the company in December 1933 as associate conductor to Efrem Kurtz. The company, which toured throughout Europe, North America, and Australia, was under the direction of Colonel W. de Basil, Serge Diaghilev's successor. Doráti's inspired conducting and wide exposure led to many international opportunities.

Doráti made his first recordings in London in 1936. His debut concert in the United States was with the National Symphony Orchestra in 1937. This was one of the many important orchestras with which Doráti recorded. After the Ballets Russes de Monte Carlo had divided into two companies, Doráti toured Australia as musical director of the de Basil half in 1938. He moved to New York in 1939 and soon began conducting studio concerts for ABC Radio there. He then went on tour in Australia with the de Basil company.

From 1941 to 1944 Doráti was the music director of the newly formed American Ballet Theater. He established a high professional standard for this group from the outset. The number of Doráti's appointments and engagements dramatically increased from this time on. His reputation as an orchestral conductor, trainer, and organizer was secure.

Doráti served as the music director of the Dallas Symphony from 1945 to 1949. In 1947 he became an American citizen. Doráti succeeded Dimitri Mitropoulos as the director of the Minneapolis Symphony Orchestra (MSO) in 1949, and he remained at that post until 1960. Recording was a main focus of the orchestra under Doráti, and they made more than 100 recordings together.

In the 1950s Doráti returned to his youthful interest in composing. He premiered his symphony in Five Movements (1957) and his cantata, *The Way* (1956), with the MSO during this period. Composition remained central to him thereafter.

Doráti held the post of principal conductor with the BBC Symphony Orchestra from 1964 to 1966 and with the Stockholm Philharmonic from 1966 to 1970. Between 1970 and 1973 Doráti recorded the complete Haydn symphonies with the Philharmonia Hungarica. He was later appointed that orchestra's honorary president. In 1970 Doráti became the music director of the National Symphony Orchestra (NSO) in Washington, D.C., and conducted the inaugural concert of the Kennedy Center on 9 September 1971. Doráti remained with the NSO until 1977. He was then appointed music director of the Detroit Symphony, a post he held until 1981. Doráti was also principal conductor of the Royal Philharmonic in London from 1975 to 1979 and was named its conductor laureate in 1978.

In 1984 Doráti was given the distinction of honorary knight commander of the Most Excellent Order of the British Empire. He was also made a chevalier de L'Ordre des Arts et Lettres by the French government and a knight of the Swedish Order of Vasa. Doráti's conducting career was distinguished by an impressive list of recordings and by his expertise in many areas, including opera, ballet, and symphonic music. He ranks among the great conductors of the twentieth century.

Doráti's compositions were written with his audience in mind. His music is never experimental and generally reflects a respect for the traditions of the past. One unnamed critic commented that it is "much more contemporary than it sounds." Doráti's more than forty works include *Magdalena* (1961); *Night Music* (1968); *Die Stimmen* (1975); Cello Concerto (1977); String Quartet (1980); and *The Chosen* (1984).

• Works by Doráti include *Notes of Seven Decades* (1981) and "Bartokiana (Some Recollections)," *Tempo*, no. 136 (1981). See also G. Turner, "Antal Doráti Talks," *Record and Recordings* 18, no. 2 (1974), which includes a discography; J. Rockwell, "Orchestras Play Better for Me," *New York Times*; C. MacDonald, "Antal Doráti: Composer, a Catalogue of His Works," *Tempo*, no. 143 (1982); and K. S. Walker, *De Basil's Ballet Russes* (1983).

LEWIS ROSENGARTEN

DORCHESTER, Daniel (11 Mar. 1827–13 Mar. 1907), Methodist clergyman and statistician of American church history, was born in Duxbury, Massachusetts, the son of the Reverend Daniel Dorchester, a Methodist clergyman, and Mary Otis. He attended Wesleyan University in Middletown, Connecticut, for two years; in 1847 he entered the Methodist ministry. In April 1850 he married Mary Payson Davis; they had seven children. Mary died in 1874, and in 1875 Dorchester married Merial A. Whipple.

After serving as pastor of several churches in the Providence Conference, in 1858 Dorchester joined the New England Conference, where he served as pastor of ten churches and three times as presiding elder. In 1884 and 1888 he was a member of the General Conference of the Methodist Church. While still in his twenties, he was elected for a term in the Connecticut Senate; in his fifties he served briefly in the Massachusetts General Court. He considered the crusade against intemperance as compelling as the war against slavery and was for many years president of the National Temperance League; in 1884 he published *The Liquor Problem in All Ages*.

Sadly aware of the denominational splintering of Protestantism in America, Dorchester felt obliged both to celebrate what made Methodism distinctive and to show the way toward "greater unity of faith and fellowship among all Christian believers." He praised those aspects of Methodist polity that distinguished it from the polity of other evangelical denominations: "connectionalism" rather than autonomous congregations; "itinerancy" rather than a settled clergy; and the right and obligation of the bishop to provide a congregation with a pastor (*The Way of Methodism* [1888]). The Methodist polity, he argued, resembled the state and national polity: neither aristocratic nor democratic, but republican; while laymen had an important role, they did not rule.

In his *Concessions of "Liberalists" to Orthodoxy* (1878, repr. 1890) and *Christianity Vindicated by Its Enemies* (1896), Dorchester anthologized quotations from Unitarians and Universalists, from Voltaire, Charles Darwin, and John Fiske in an attempt to show that even such advanced thinkers assented, however inadvertently or reluctantly, to such central orthodox beliefs as the immortality of the soul, the divinity of Christ, and future retribution. It was obvious to Dorchester that because orthodoxy "wonderfully [and completely] satisfies the spiritual necessities of our being," right-thinking liberals would soon return to the fold.

Dorchester was much less sanguine about Roman Catholics. Their ecclesiastical machinery was detrimental to genuine piety. And Catholics exercised a malign influence on American public life, most especially in efforts to build an effective system of public schools. Dorchester was convinced that the Catholic hierarchy supported parochial schools only for the purpose of preventing Catholic children from adapting to American civilization. In the 1880s he joined other Massachusetts evangelical leaders in proposing that parochial schools be required by law to conform to demanding state regulations. Checkmated by the opposition not just of Catholics but of Protestants like President Charles W. Eliot of Harvard and the Reverend Phillips Brooks of Trinity Church, Dorchester published *Romanism versus the Public School System* (1888), in which he worried that there are "two peoples struggling in the womb of the nation" (p. 4). He was sure that all children would benefit from attending public schools. Although Dorchester acknowledged that even "irreconcilable minorities" had rights, the general welfare of the nation depended on the rapid Americanization of every individual.

In 1888, President-elect Benjamin Harrison nominated Thomas Jefferson Morgan, a Baptist minister and passionate exponent of public schools, to be commissioner of Indian affairs and Dorchester to serve as superintendent of Indian schools. Many of the schools were maintained under contract to the Catholic church, and many Catholics fought the nomination of both men as bigots determined to replace all church-sponsored schools with public schools. As superintendent, Dorchester worked strenuously to direct the Indian students "towards civilization and self-support." In 1893 he estimated that he had traveled more than 90,000 miles while inspecting schools in more than 100 reservations. But he was never optimistic about the redeemability of the Indians. "No class of people," he lamented, "more readily fall from stages of progress"; even the best students in the schools, he concluded, lacked "staying power." In 1892 some Catholics made the Morgan-Dorchester approach to Indian affairs an issue in the presidential campaign; and President-elect Cleveland declined to reappoint either man.

But the Indians' failure to progress did not weaken Dorchester's confidence in the inevitable triumph of Christianity. In *The Problem of Religious Progress* (1881) and subsequently in his most important and most massive book, *Christianity in the United States, from the First Settlement to the Present Day* (2 vols. 1888; rev. ed., 1895), Dorchester separated himself from the "carping and unjust depreciation of our times, a whining tone of distrust, and an exaggerated confession, often both unintelligent and unmanly" (*The Problem of Religious Progress*, p. 294). There had never been a golden age, but progress was unmistakable. Evolutionary science, biblical scholarship, new departures in philosophy—modernisms that seemed so threatening to some Christians—seemed no challenge at all to Dorchester. "Christianity," he declared, will lose "nothing of its inherent original self—only that which human imperfection, subtlety, and folly have attached to it, trammeling and falsifying it" (p. 118). Protestantism in America in the late nineteenth century, he triumphantly concluded, transcends "in magnitude and significance anything ever before seen in the history of Christianity" (p. 423).

To substantiate this triumphalism, Dorchester relied not on theological argument or the testimony of believers, but on "statistical science." Acknowledging the pioneering work of Auguste Comte and Henry Buckle, he studied the statistics reported by governmental censuses and denominational publications. "The realm of spiritual religion," he declared, is not "so hidden that it is impossible to measure." Tables and graphs of church membership, of denominational colleges, and of numbers of clergymen constituted for Dorchester irrefutable and "philosophical" proof of the growing power of American Protestantism. He retired from the ministry in 1899; he died in West Roxbury, Massachusetts.

• In *A Half-Century Discourse* (1897), Dorchester summarizes his career and his convictions. In addition to the books cited, see the collection of his sermons, *Giving and Worship: The Old Wedlock Restored* (1882). See also *Reports of the Superintendent of Indian Schools* (1890–1893) and Dorchester's many articles in the *Methodist Quarterly Review*, *Zion's Herald*, and *Christian Advocate*. Obituaries are in the *Boston Globe* and the *Boston Herald*, both 13 Mar. 1907.

ROBERT D. CROSS

DOREMUS, Robert Ogden (11 Jan. 1824–22 Mar. 1906), chemist, teacher, and inventor, was born in New York City, the son of Thomas Cornelius Doremus, a merchant who was one of the founders of New York University, and Sarah Platt Haines, a social worker and philanthropist. He began his undergraduate study in New York at Columbia College but moved

after a year to New York University, where he received his A.B. in 1842, his M.A. in 1845, and his M.D. in 1850. In 1847 he studied chemistry and metallurgy in Paris, and during all of his graduate school years, from 1843 to 1850, he was assistant to the English-born chemist at New York University, Dr. John W. Draper, with the chemical laboratory of the University's medical department in his sole charge. Nor were these his only activities while he finished his medical training. In 1848 he and Charles Townsend Harris established a laboratory for instruction in analytical chemistry and for commercial analysis, where he also lectured to students from the New York College of Pharmacy until 1861. He became a professor at that institution in 1849. In 1850 he married Estelle Emma Skidmore. They had eight children, of whom one, Dr. Charles A. Doremus, adopted his father's profession of chemistry teacher, serving for some years at City College. In 1850 Doremus was also active in founding the New York Medical College, and he equipped its analytical laboratory at his own expense.

Doremus was elected professor of natural history at the New York Free Academy (later the College of the City of New York) in 1852. Except for time in France in 1862–1863, he remained at City College until his emeritus retirement in 1903, becoming professor of chemistry and physics in 1863 and occasionally serving as vice president. His teaching and lecture demonstrations were memorable, causing Johns Hopkins's Ira Remsen to recall, many years later, that "my own interest in chemistry . . . was due to what I saw and heard in these lectures." Doremus interested himself in lighting, for example, producing for demonstration an arc light operated by an enormous battery of Bunsen electrochemical cells (the dynamo being an invention of the future). He also improved gas lighting by adding oxygen to the gas flame; he is said to have piped oxygen to the street lights in the Twenty-third Street area around City College.

Besides his work at City College Doremus pursued a further academic career as well as becoming an inventor and a public health and forensic investigator. In 1858–1859 he helped to found the Long Island Hospital Medical College in Brooklyn, setting up its student laboratory and acting as professor of chemistry and toxicology. In 1861 he did the same for the Bellevue Hospital Medical College, acting as treasurer and holding the chair of chemistry, toxicology, and medical jurisprudence from 1864 to 1897. Meanwhile, in 1858 he was called as an expert witness in the case of James Stephen, whose wife was killed with arsenic. This led to consultation and court appearances for many years thereafter as a forensic toxicologist.

Doremus's work in public health began in 1853 when he demonstrated that much commercially available soda water was poisonous because its carbonic acid dissolved copper and lead from the pipes and tanks employed in its preparation and use. The problem was solved with glass-lined apparatus. During the 1850s, as a member of a municipal medical advisory committee, Doremus fought to improve sanitary conditions in slaughterhouses and in the tenement housing of New York City. In 1865 he was the first to employ chlorine water to disinfect an incoming ship that carried passengers who had been diagnosed with cholera; use of this agent eventually eliminated the forty-day quarantine period for arriving vessels. Later the same disinfectant was employed in hospital wards, particularly those of Bellevue. Doremus crusaded against adulteration of milk supplies and worked for modern purification of drinking water.

Doremus's inventions include a number of chemical fire extinguishers, for which he took out patents; hydrogen peroxide bleaching methods for feathers and delicate fabrics; a system of railway signals worked out with Thomas Seavey Hall; improvements in the ballistic pendulum, a device for measuring the speed of a projectile; and treatment of building materials with paraffin to protect them against frost. This last development stopped the weathering of "Cleopatra's Needle," the sandstone obelisk with hieroglyphs in Central Park, when melted paraffin was forced into the soft stone. Perhaps the most curious outcome of his activity in invention resulted from his discovery that compressed, granulated gunpowder was more effective than loose powder, which led to adoption of the granular form by the U.S. government. A demonstration of granular powder before the French emperor Napoleon III resulted in its use by the French government and also led to a friendship between Doremus and his wife and Napoleon and the empress Eugenie. This continental visit (during which he also formed a friendship with the biologist Louis Pasteur, whom he later induced to form an institute in New York) accounts for the hiatus in his years at City College in 1862 and 1863.

Doremus's principal outside interest was music. A singer in his younger days, he was also a cornetist of solo quality who formed a brass band and composed music. He was the first amateur to be named president of the New York Philharmonic Society (1867–1870), and he brought many European vocal and instrumental soloists to perform in this country. The Doremus household was a gathering place for notable persons in both the sciences and the arts.

Doremus's most important and lasting contributions occurred during his teaching and in his founding of many laboratories and departments of chemistry. Honors came to Doremus throughout his life. He was president of the Medico-Legal Society of New York from 1885 to 1886 and was a fellow of the New York Academy of Sciences and the American Geographical Society. Doremus died in New York City.

• Some of Doremus's manuscripts are in the archives of the Massachusetts Institute of Technology as part of the papers of the law firm of Blatchford, Seward, and Griswold. Manuscript class notes, with plates, from Doremus's lectures on anatomy, physiology, and hygiene in 1861–1862, by student Edward Frankel, are held in the Columbia University libraries. An interesting article on the dedication of the City College chemistry building, 14 May 1908, with some information on Doremus, is found in *Science* 27 (1908): 969–83. Biographical information on Doremus appears in W. Miles, ed., *American Chemists and Chemical Engineers* (1976), *City College Quarterly*, Dec. 1906, and Charles F. Chandler, *Science* 33 (1906): 513–14, are less complete than this source. An obituary and follow-up are in the *New York Times*, 23 and 26 Mar. 1906.

ROBERT M. HAWTHORNE JR.

DORGAN, Tad (29 Apr. 1877–2 May 1929), cartoonist, was born Thomas Dorgan in San Francisco, California, the son of Thomas Dorgan, a laborer, and Anna Tobin. He grew up with four brothers and four sisters in the working-class Mission District south of Market Street known as "South of the Slot" and showed an early taste for sports, especially boxing. He set up a punching bag for himself when he was seven and often engaged in street fights. At an age variously reported as ten and thirteen, he lost the last three fingers of his right hand in an accident. This dashed his dreams of a career in the ring, but he set himself to learn to draw with his left hand. His father hoped he would become a bookkeeper, but he hated desk work and regular schedules, and at the age of fourteen he left school and found a job in the art department of the *San Francisco Bulletin*. For a year he did menial graphic tasks like lettering and shading for the regular artists at three dollars a week before he worked his way up to illustrating the news, caricaturing local celebrities, and drawing filler art for the classified ad pages. When he had a chance, he slipped his own political cartoons into the paper. In his spare time he studied in a local art school, where a teacher named Aloysius Donnegan so inspired him that he took Donnegan's first name as his own middle name. His new initials, T.A.D., provided him with the newspaper signature he was to use for the rest of his life. Dorgan married a woman named Izole (maiden name unknown); apparently the couple had no children.

Dorgan's inventive and often acerbic cartoons earned him a local reputation that prompted the city's leading paper, the *Chronicle*, to hire him to do sports illustrations and his first comic strip, *Johnny Wise*, in 1902. A weekly color feature about an Irish immigrant with a weakness for drink, the strip ran for less than a year. Dorgan had already become one of the most prominent sports cartoonists in San Francisco by that time, however, and a short time later William Randolph Hearst offered him a large increase in salary to come east and work on his *New York Journal*. As Dorgan later admitted, "'the call of the tame'—money—yelled so loud I had to listen to it."

In 1905 Hearst was running for mayor of New York as an independent against the Democratic party's candidate, and he wanted Dorgan to lampoon his opponent's Tammany Hall political machine as Thomas Nast had done forty years earlier. Dorgan had no taste for editorial cartooning, but his powerful images of Tammany boss Charles F. Murphy as a convict almost won Hearst the election. When the publisher gave up his political aspirations, Dorgan resumed his specialty, drawing ball games, horse races, and boxing matches. The highest-paid and most respected sports cartoonist in the country by then, he was known for both the fidelity and the fluid grace of his renderings. Realist painter George Bellows has been quoted as saying "In catching the complex beauty of prize-fighters in action, T. A. Dorgan is without a rival" (Henry Morton Robinson, p. 64).

It was as a sardonic humorist, however, that Dorgan had his widest appeal to the newspaper-reading public. In 1910 he launched a series variously called *Judge Rummy's Court*, *Old Judge Rumhauser*, and, finally, *Silk Hat Harry's Divorce Case*. An unsparing burlesque of bureaucracy and middle-class pretension as well as of the American courts, it featured a cast of stock comic types thinly disguised as dogs. Another Dorgan creation of the period was the single-panel series alternately labeled *Outdoor Sports* and *Indoor Sports*, which was as much about the "sports" of business, courtship, marital infidelity, and social climbing as about prize-fighting and pool. *Daffydills* were riddles, verses, and fanciful little stories leading up to outrageous plays on words, all illustrated with stick figures. Less original was his last creation, a bland domestic comic strip created in the 1920s. Variously called *Home—That's All* and *For Better or Worse*, it starred the dim-witted couple Webster and Lil Blink of Hopeville-by-the-Dump and burlesqued suburbia with heavy-handed humor.

One of the most noteworthy characteristics of Dorgan's many and diverse creations was the racy slang in which his characters expressed themselves, and the cartoonist has been credited with adding significantly to the vernacular speech of his times. Many of his colorful terms may be traced to the argot of the ring, the racetrack, the pool hall, and the saloon, but whether or not Dorgan actually coined such expressions as "lounge-lizard," "hot dog," "four-flusher," "drugstore cowboy," or "nickel-nurser," he certainly did much to put them in general circulation through his sports columns and cartoon features.

In much of Dorgan's comic art, a note of dark, even cruel, humor underlies the zany fun. The catchphrases for which he became known were usually cynical and bitter: "You'll find sympathy in the dictionary" was typical, as was "Half the world are squirrels and the other half are nuts." His objective was usually to deflate and expose, and he was not gentle or kindly in doing so. Historian Jerry Robinson has noted, "His forte was the put-down. . . . The caustic comments of the background players mocked the assorted pomposities of the others" (p. 226). Dorgan was often personally as acid-tongued as his characters, but while some of his colleagues found him forbidding, he was convivial with his friends and widely respected for his personal generosity. His deep disgust with what he called "two-dollar words" and "high-hat manners" may have derived from an insecurity and defensiveness born of his impoverished childhood, his lack of formal education, and his maimed right hand, but it also reflected a genuine contempt for hypocrisy and pretension.

In 1920 Dorgan suffered a massive heart attack while attending a prize fight, and for the rest of his short life he was virtually an invalid. Prevented from attending sports events or even going to his newspaper office, he stalwartly continued sending in work daily from his home in Great Neck, Long Island, where his neighbors included former heavyweight boxing champion James J. Corbett and the writer Ring Lardner, both close friends. He died in Great Neck.

• No extended study of the work of Tad Dorgan has been produced, but he was widely discussed by his colleagues in the press. Articles about his life and work include John B. Kennedy, "Tad—The Funniest Man in America," *New Age Illustrated*, Nov. 1927, pp. 44–45, 81–82; Henry Morton Robinson, "Tad for Short," *Century*, Autumn 1929, pp. 63–70; and Gilbert Seldes, "Tad," *New Republic*, 15 May 1929, pp. 358–60. More formal examinations of Dorgan's life and art are in Maurice Horn, ed., *World Encyclopedia of Comics* (1976), and Ron Goulart, ed., *The Encyclopedia of American Comics* (1990). For histories of the comics with material on Dorgan, see especially Coulton Waugh, ed., *The Comics* (1947); Stephen Becker, *Comic Art in America* (1959); Jerry Robinson, *The Comics* (1974); Robert C. Harvey, *The Art of the Funnies* (1994); and Ron Goulart, *The Funnies* (1995). Long obituaries and editorials on Dorgan appeared in many newspapers, including the *New York Times*, *New York Evening Journal*, *New York American*, *New York Herald-Tribune*, *New York Evening Post*, and *Chicago Tribune*, 3 May 1929.

DENNIS WEPMAN

DORHAM, Kenny (30 Aug. 1924–5 Dec. 1972), jazz trumpeter, was born McKinley Howard Dorham on a ranch near Fairfield, Texas. His nickname was originally "Kinney" (also spelled "Kinny"), from McKinley. His parents' names are unknown. His father, a sharecropper, played guitar; his mother and sister, piano. From age seven, Dorham learned piano by ear, and around that time he began to appreciate Louis Armstrong's records. In 1939 he played trumpet in the Anderson High School marching band in Austin, Texas, as well as with jazz-oriented spinoffs from that band.

Dorham attended Wiley College in Marshall, Texas, for two years, first to study chemistry, but then turning to music theory; in his second year he played in the college band. He also worked in Milt Larkin's big band, then playing in clubs throughout Texas. He was drafted into the army in 1942, and for about one year he served on a service boxing team while occasionally performing on trumpet. He considered a career in boxing, but on being discharged he returned to music. After trying but failing to secure steady work on the West Coast in late 1943, he went to Houston as a member of trumpeter Russell Jacquet's band. Dorham did not record during these years. Reportedly he played in a swing style, using vocalized growls and trumpet mutes for diverse timbral effects.

In July 1944 Dorham went to New York City and immediately became involved in playing at Minton's Playhouse, one of the centers of a new jazz style, bop. Any earlier stylistic inclinations he may have had gave way to a concentration on rapid, multinoted melodic lines. By this point he had married Rubina Corbin (date unknown), with whom he would have five children. He first worked in New York with trumpeter Frank "Fat Man" Humphries at the Savoy Ballroom, and in the spring of 1945 he joined Dizzy Gillespie's bop big band, playing trumpet and doubling as a blues singer. From December to early January 1946 he replaced Fats Navarro in Billy Eckstine's bop big band. He returned to Gillespie and also worked with the big bands of Mercer Ellington (1946–1947) and Lionel Hampton (1947).

During this period Dorham was a ghostwriter for the then overcommitted arranger Gil Fuller, and he contributed all or parts of arrangements to the bands of Harry James, Jimmy Dorsey, and Gene Krupa. In August 1946 he began recording with small bop groups, initially as leader of the Be Bop Boys. He revealed himself to be "l'eternal second," a fine soloist, but not on a par with Gillespie for improvisatory imagination, with Fats Navarro for tone and melodic architecture, or with the as yet undeveloped Miles Davis for nuance. These shortcomings are apparent on sessions from September 1946, in which Dorham improvises head-to-head with Navarro.

In December 1948 Dorham replaced Davis in Charlie Parker's quintet at the Royal Roost. With Parker in May 1949 he performed at the Paris Jazz Fair, and he broadcast regularly with the group until mid-1950. In 1949 he recorded with trombonist J. J. Johnson, including "Opus V." Dorham continued freelancing with Parker over the next few years, while he studied arranging and composition at the Gotham School of Music in New York. Outside of music, he worked in California for Republic Aviation, the U.S. medical depot in Oakland, and a sugar refinery in Salinas, to support his family.

In December 1953 he recorded his first album as a leader, *The Kenny Dorham Quintet*, including his blues "An Oscar for Oscar." That tune had been captured two months earlier in a performance at Birdland in New York, which included Horace Silver, with Art Blakey's quintet. From this association came the hard bop group the Jazz Messengers, which began as a cooperative, recording under Silver's name and transferred to Blakey's leadership by the time *The Jazz Messengers at the Cafe Bohemia* was recorded in November 1955, by which point Blakey had persuaded Dorham to return to music full time. On Silver's catchy tunes "Doodlin'" (Nov. 1954) and "The Preacher" (Feb. 1955), Dorham moved away from perpetual motion solos and instead invented relaxed, creative melodies. In 1956 his own quintet, modeled after the Jazz Messengers, recorded the album *Kenny Dorham and the Jazz Prophets*. The group came to an abrupt end when Clifford Brown was killed in an automobile accident, and Dorham took his place in Max Roach's hard bop quintet in mid-July. While playing with Roach until 1958, Dorham also recorded as a freelance. His album *Jazz Contrasts* from May 1957 demonstrates his continuing struggles with creativity at fast tempos, as in a rapid passage in the midst of his

solo on "Falling in Love with Love," but that same solo and others on the album find him improvising sophisticated melodies and playing with a beautiful, romantic timbre.

After leaving Roach, Dorham worked as a freelance and led his own groups. He taught trumpet at the School of Jazz in Lenox, Massachusetts, in the summer of 1958. After recording the album *Blue Spring* early in 1959, he visited Paris to collaborate with drummer Kenny Clarke, pianist Duke Jordan, and saxophonist Barney Wilen on two films, playing the soundrack for and acting in *Un témoin dans la ville* (also released as *Witness in the City*) and acting in director Roger Vadim's *Les Liaisons Dangereuses 1960* (1959). Back in the United States, he again taught at the School of Jazz and continued recording regularly, including *Quiet Kenny* (1959), *Jazz Contemporary* (1960), *Whistle Stop* (1961), and *Matador* (1962), all of which show off his strengths as an improviser.

He performed in Rio de Janeiro in July 1961. In 1962 tenor saxophonist Joe Henderson and Dorham formed a quintet. Since the mid-1950s Dorham had been composing themes, and the best known of these, *Blue Bossa*, appeared on Henderson's album *Page One* in 1963. Dorham performed in Scandinavia in December 1963–January 1964; he then participated in the Jazzmobile program, bringing jazz to young people in central Harlem. By the spring of 1964, Henderson had joined Horace Silver, but he and Dorham recorded with a sextet led by Andrew Hill and continued recording with their own quintet, including Dorham's album *Trumpet Toccata* from September 1964. Later, in 1967, Henderson and Dorham formed a rehearsal big band, from which Dorham would gain modest posthumous fame when Henderson reassembled the band for acclaimed performances in the 1980s and 1990s.

In the late 1960s, while Dorham was working on a master's degree at NYU, his health was failing as the result of high blood pressure and kidney disease. He worked occasionally with Hank Mobley and with reed player Bobby Jones, participated in concerts for Charlie Parker month in Chicago in August 1972, and worked on Monday nights at the Playhouse (formerly Minton's), even while spending fifteen hours per week on a kidney machine. He died in New York of kidney failure.

Dorham never entirely abandoned many-noted playing, but once he had found paths away from that style of improvising, he became one of the most creative and lyrical trumpeters in the bop and hard bop styles.

• Dorham gives a colorful summary of his life from childhood through the mid-1950s in "Fragments of an Autobiography," *Down Beat Music '70* (1971), pp. 30–34. Interviews include Leonard Feather, "Durable Dorham," *Down Beat*, 15 May 1958, pp. 33–34; "Kenny Dorham's 3 Careers," *Down Beat*, 19 Feb. 1959, pp. 20, 43; and Gene Feehan, "Durable Dorham," *Down Beat*, 27 Sept. 1962, pp. 16–17. These in turn form the basis for Jean-Pierre Binchet, "Kenny

Dorham: l'eternel second," *Jazz Magazine*, Oct. 1967, pp. 16–22, 50, including several excellent photographs.

Information on Wiley College and Milt Larkin appear in Stanley Dance, "Wild Bill Davis," *The World of Duke Ellington* (1970), pp. 238–39. Details of Dorham's brief affiliation with Eckstine are in Bernard Niquet and Kurt Mohr, "Mister B. Goes to Swing," *Le point du jazz*, June 1977, pp. 31–39. Dorham remembers his years with Parker in Robert Reisner, ed., *Bird: The Legend of Charlie Parker* (1975), pp. 79–81.

Surveys of Dorham's recordings are H. A. Woodfin, "Kenny Dorham," *Jazz Review*, Aug. 1960, pp. 6–9, and Michael James, "Kenny Dorham: Soloist Extraordinary," *Jazz and Blues*, Jan. 1972, pp. 4–9. Three comprehensive catalogs of his recordings are "Kenny Dorham Discography," *Swing Journal*, Mar. 1973, pp. 260–67; Bo Raftegard, *The Kenny Dorham Discography* (1982); and Claude Schlouch, *The Unforgettable Kenny Dorham* (1983). A concise but comprehensive obituary is "Kenny Dorham: 1924–1972," *Down Beat*, 1 Feb. 1973, p. 10; another appeared in the *New York Times*, 6 Dec. 1972.

BARRY KERNFELD

DORION, Marie (c. 1790–5 Sept. 1850), interpreter, was born into the Iowa tribe as Marie Aioe, or Marie L'Aguivoise; both versions of her maiden surname, variations on the word "Iowa," appear in early nineteenth-century records of Oregon and Washington territories. Nothing is known of her life until she became the common-law wife of a half Sioux, half French-Canadian fur trader, Pierre Dorion, Jr., around 1806 in the vicinity of what is now Yankton, South Dakota. Pierre Dorion, Sr., had been an interpreter and a guide with the Meriwether Lewis and William Clark expedition (1804–1806). By 1811 Marie had become the mother of two sons, who themselves became interpreters and guides in later life.

Early in 1811 Pierre Dorion was invited to become an interpreter with the overland division of the Wilson Price Hunt expedition on their journey to Fort Astoria, the Pacific Fur Company outpost being built at the mouth of the Columbia River. Despite the objections of Hunt, the expedition leader, Dorion insisted that Marie and their sons accompany him, and the party left St. Louis in March, traveling up the Missouri River by keelboat.

Disembarking at the present site of Pierre, South Dakota, the Hunt expedition continued westward by land. During the arduous journey, Marie Dorion gave birth to a third son, who lived eight days. On 15 February 1812 the travelers finally reached Fort Astoria, in what is now Oregon; since their departure from St. Louis, they had traveled 3,500 miles. Their arrival was due in large part to the interpreting skills of Marie Dorion. Later chroniclers, including Washington Irving, singled out Marie for her steadfastness and courage during the trek, which saw several members of the party drop out from exhaustion.

After spending more than a year at Fort Astoria, the Dorions joined a beaver-trapping expedition to eastern Oregon in July 1813. A campsite was established some 300 miles from Astoria at the confluence of the Boise and Snake rivers, on what is now the Idaho-Oregon border. Marie and her children remained behind while Pierre Dorion and a trapping party went off to catch beavers. Sometime early that winter, Marie set out to join her husband, perhaps to warn him of an impending Indian attack. In January 1814, however, she learned that Pierre Dorion, along with the rest of the trappers, had been massacred by Indians; when she returned to the campsite, she discovered that everyone who had remained behind had also been killed by Indians.

Marie Dorion fled on horseback with her two children and headed northwest to the Columbia River. Again she faced hardship as bad weather forced her to camp for nearly two months in the Blue Mountains before she and the children were given shelter by friendly Walla Walla Indians. In April, resuming her journey, she reached the Columbia and encountered the surviving members of the original Hunt expedition who were returning to St. Louis. The party took her and her sons to Fort Okanogan, a Canadian-owned fur-trading station nearly 200 miles to the north. Here she settled, apparently without incident, for a number of years. A liaison with a French-Canadian trapper named Venier resulted in the birth of a daughter in 1819.

Sometime in the early 1820s, Dorion began living with a French-Canadian interpreter named Jean Baptiste Toupin; a son was born to the couple in 1825, followed by a daughter two years later. In 1841 the family moved westward to a farm in the Willamette Valley, near the present site of Salem, Oregon. In July of that year Dorion and Toupin were formally married in a Roman Catholic ceremony. By this time the story of Marie Dorion was widely known throughout North America, the consequence of its appearance in Washington Irving's book *Astoria* (1836), an account of the expedition and settlement, and in published memoirs of early settlers.

Dorion died near Salem, apparently from natural causes. The priest who officiated at her burial service noted incorrectly that her age was "about 100," an indication that the harshness of her life had taken its toll on her appearance. Acclaimed during her lifetime as a heroine of the wilderness and the equal of Sacajawea, the renowned Indian guide and interpreter on the Lewis and Clark expedition, Dorion fell into obscurity after her death; her feats and contributions were rediscovered in the twentieth century.

• Early accounts of Marie Dorion's life appear in Gabriel Franchère, *Relation d'un Voyage à la Côte du Nord-Ouest de l'Amérique Septentrionale* (1820; English trans., 1854, 1967); Ross Cox, *Adventures on the Columbia River* (1831; repr. 1957); and Alexander Ross, *Adventures of the First Settlers on the Oregon or Columbia River* (1849). Part of Washington Irving's *Astoria* is based on Franchère's and Cox's accounts. Biographical information is also found in J. Neilson Barry, "Madame Dorion of the Astorians," *Oregon Historical Quarterly* 30, no. 3 (Sept. 1929): 272–78, and T. C. Elliott, "The Grave of Mme. Dorion," *Oregon Historical Quarterly* 36, no. 1 (Mar. 1935): 102–4.

ANN T. KEENE

DORMAN, Isaiah (?–26 June 1876), frontiersman and interpreter, was known as "Teat," or the Wasicun Sapa (Black White Man), among the Sioux of Dakota Territory. Nothing is known of his life before he entered the territory as a young man around 1850; he is thought to have been an escaped slave who fled to the wilderness to avoid capture. Sioux tribal history records his presence in their midst from that date; he became known to white settlers in 1865, by which time he had become fluent in the Sioux dialect. About this time he married a Sioux woman and built a log cabin near Fort Rice, in Dakota Territory, not far from present-day Bismarck, North Dakota. For a while he earned a living cutting wood for the fort and for a trading firm, Durfee and Peck.

In November 1865 Dorman was hired by the U.S. Army to carry the mail between Fort Rice and Fort Wadsworth, some 180 miles away. Dorman's hard work and reliability earned him respect from army officials, and he was often called upon to perform other jobs as well at Fort Rice, earning an average monthly salary of $60, a considerable sum at the time. In 1871 Dorman served for several months as guide and interpreter for the survey crew of the proposed Northern Pacific Railroad, and in October of that year he was appointed post interpreter at Fort Rice at a salary of $75 per month. According to official army records, Dorman was an asset to the post; his language skills, coupled with a natural ability to mediate differences, helped avoid potential conflict at the post between white settlers and Indians. Dorman's ease in handling the Sioux was also attributed to the large stores of smoking and chewing tobacco that he always kept on hand and willingly shared.

Although the situation at Fort Rice was relatively stable, conflict with Sioux elsewhere in the territory was escalating by the mid-1870s. This was largely a consequence of a dramatic increase in the white population, caused by both the building of the Northern Pacific Railroad and the discovery of gold in the Black Hills in August 1875, which quickly drew thousands of prospectors to the region. The man responsible for the Black Hills gold rush was U.S. Army general George A. Custer, who had made his discovery while leading a military expedition to the territory.

In May 1876 Custer was ordered to lead the Seventh Cavalry against hostile Sioux settled farther west, along the Little Bighorn River in what is now southern Montana. Dorman's reputation as an outstanding civilian employee of the army was widespread, and he was the natural choice of Custer as interpreter for the expedition. He assumed his new duties on 15 May, again at the salary of $75 a month.

On 25 June 1876 Custer's forces assembled some fifteen miles east of the Little Bighorn, at a landmark known to the Indians as the Crow's Nest. There Custer divided his command, and Dorman, along with most of the other civilian employees, was assigned to Major Marcus A. Reno's battalion of three companies. Reno's battalion crossed the Little Bighorn, and the next day they attempted an attack on the Sioux but were driven back to the west bank of the river. In the course of the fighting, Dorman was fatally shot in the chest with a rifle by an Indian marksman. An army burial detail that recovered his body a few days later reported that he had been stripped and mutilated.

No records show Dorman to have fathered any children, and he apparently left no survivors, including his wife, since his back pay of $102.50 was never claimed.

• Biographical information on Isaiah Dorman can be found in Roland C. McConnell, "Isaiah Dorman and the Custer Expedition," *Journal of Negro History* 33 (July 1948): 344–52, and Edward C. Campbell, "Saving the Custer Muster Rolls," *Military Affairs* 10, no. 2 (Summer 1946): 49–57. See also M. A. Reno, *Report of Battle of the Little Big Horn*, in the National Archives, Record Group 94.

ANN T. KEENE

DORO, Marie (25 May 1882–9 Oct. 1956), actress, was born Marie Kathryn Stuart in Duncannon, Pennsylvania, the daughter of Richard H. Stuart, an attorney, and Virginia Weaver. She was an accomplished pianist and singer from childhood. After finishing her education at Miss Brown's School in New York City, she took her delicate brunette beauty and winsome charm into the professional theater, adopting the stage name "Doro" from "Adorato," a youthful nickname.

Doro first appeared in *Aristocracy* with a St. Paul, Minnesota, stock company in 1901. Two years with touring companies followed. She first appeared on the New York stage in *The Billionaire* (1903) and went on to several appearances in musical comedies. A major producer, Charles Frohman, saw her star potential and featured her in productions with several of his established stars, mainly William Gillette. She appeared as leading lady to Gillette in *The Admirable Crichton* (1904), *Clarice* (1905), a revival of *Sherlock Holmes* (1905), *Electricity* (1910), and a revival of *Diplomacy* (1914). Her first appearance in a principal role for Frohman, in *Friquet* (1905), was not successful, but success and stardom came in *The Morals of Marcus* (1907).

In following years, Doro alternated between appearances in New York, London, and on the road. She knew she did best in "light" roles suited to her looks and personality. The titles of some of these vehicles, such as *The Richest Girl* (1909) and *The New Secretary* (1913), are indicative of their nature. Describing her, reviewers used such terms as "elfin" and "a Dresden china doll." She told an interviewer (*Cosmopolitan*, May 1913) that she felt unsuited to heavier roles, naming the one she undertook in *A Butterfly on the Wheel* (1911), where she played a woman "racked through the ordeal of divorce." Her petite figure allowed her to play the title role in an all-star revival of *Oliver Twist* (1912); the *New York Times* reviewer found her "a lovely and highly sympathetic little Oliver" (27 Feb. 1912). In other successful revivals of the period, she played Patience in Gilbert and Sullivan's *Patience* (1912) and Dora in *Diplomacy* (1914).

In the New York run of the latter play, she appeared with young actor Elliott Dexter, whom she married in 1915; they had no children. Both went into film appearances in 1915 and made several films together. In her first film, *The Morals of Marcus* (1915), she repeated her stage role. After making a dozen movies in 1916 and 1917, she returned to the stage in *Barbara* (1917). The reviewer for the *New York Times* (6 Nov. 1917) found her appeal to audiences stronger than ever: "By some magic, her girlish prettiness and charm have been touched with the flame of a real beauty—a beauty that is as compelling as it is exquisite and unaffected."

After her brief marriage ended in divorce at an unknown date, Doro pursued her long-time love of Europe and lived abroad repeatedly after World War I. In 1919 and 1920 she made films in England and Italy. Her final New York stage appearance came in *Lilies of the Field* (1921). Her last film appearance was in *Sally Bishop*, made in England in 1923. She might well have become an outstanding actress of the silent screen had she not decided to retire: the *New York Times* reviewer of her British film *12:10* (1919), called her "a pantomimist of unusual talent. Her actions, especially in emotional scenes, have plain meaning and subtle significance. She seems to realize that what she does before the camera must convey to spectators something definite about what she feels."

Doro withdrew from professional life after her last film, however, to explore other interests in life. Her public persona had become confining. As Constance Clark writes, "Interviewers expressed surprise at finding an erudite and witty woman behind her stage personality." In fact, she was considered "a brilliant conversationalist" and an authority on "the Shakespeare sonnets and Elizabethan poetry" (*New York Times*, 10 Oct. 1956). In retirement, she traveled abroad frequently except during World War II. She never remarried.

In later life, Doro lived quietly in New York City under her birth name of Marie Stuart. She studied religion at Union Theological Seminary and Princeton Theological Seminary. She wrote and published popular songs, as she had since the start of her career. The last one, "I See You Clearly," appeared in 1956. Doro died in New York City. In 1958 the Actors Fund of America announced her bequest of $90,000.

Marie Doro figures in theatrical history as a woman astutely able to parlay good looks and unique charm into years of stage and film stardom, along the way gaining recognition as an actress as well as a beauty. Then, financial independence achieved, she was able to retire at the crest of her career to escape its constraints and live a life of personal fulfillment.

• Materials on the life and career of Marie Doro are in the Billy Rose Theatre Collection at the New York Public Library for the Performing Arts, Lincoln Center. An extensive biographical sketch by Constance Clark is in *Notable Women in the American Theatre* (1989). A list of her stage appearances can be found in *Who Was Who in the Theatre 1912–1976* (1978). To assemble a complete roster of her film appearances, consult the *American Film Institute Catalog* for 1911–1920 (1988) and 1921–1930 (1993); *Enciclopedia dello Spettacolo*, vol. 4 (1957); *Filmarama*, vol. 1 (1975) and vol. 2 (1977); and *Who Was Who on Screen* (1974). Portraits and production photographs can be found in three books by Daniel C. Blum, *Great Stars of the American Stage* (1952), *A Pictorial History of the American Theatre* (1960), and *A Pictorial History of the Silent Screen* (1953). An obituary is in the *New York Times*, 10 Oct. 1956.

WILLIAM STEPHENSON

DORR, Julia Caroline Ripley (13 Feb. 1825–18 Jan. 1913), author, was born in Charleston, South Carolina, the daughter of William Young Ripley, a merchant, and Zulma DeLacy Thomas. Dorr's mother and her family, natives of France, had come to Charleston from the West Indies after a slave revolt dispossessed them in the late 1700s. Julia, an only child, moved with her family to Vermont because of her mother's ill health; the change of region failed to help, however, as Zulma Ripley died on the day following her arrival. Julia was reared in Vermont and, for a time, in New York City. Her education has been characterized as "irregular" and "haphazard," but she apparently had some talent in Latin and attended classes at the Middlebury seminary in Vermont. At the age of twenty-two, she married Seneca M. Dorr, a young businessman who apparently shared Julia's interests in literature and elite culture, and they made their home in Ghent, New York, for a decade before moving to Rutland, Vermont, to join Julia's father (who had established successful careers as the owner of marble quarries and as a bank president).

Dorr had from childhood written poems and stories for the amusement of her family, but she had never thought of herself as a writer until her husband, allegedly without her knowledge, submitted one of her poems to *Union Magazine*, a new "literary" journal originally edited by the novelist Caroline Kirkland. When Dorr's poem was published in 1848, she joined the ranks of other *Union* contributors like Henry Wadsworth Longfellow, James Russell Lowell, and Edgar Allan Poe (whose "To Helen" and "The Bells" first appeared there). She went on to win a $100 prize from *Union*'s successor, *Sartain's Union Magazine of Literature and Art*, for her first short story, "Isabel Leslie," in 1848.

It was as a novelist that Dorr first achieved recognition, even though she published her earliest work of fiction under the pen name "Caroline Thomas." *Farmingdale* (1854), set in small-town Vermont, recounts the story of Mary Lester, an orphan girl who endures a miserable life of family bitterness and unrelenting work under the lash of tyrannical Aunt Betsy. Mary redeems her brother from a similar exploitation and wins success as a teacher in a female seminary, at once a triumph of "womanly" sacrifice and "manly" achievement. A similar female despot terrorizes her plucky daughter, Bessie, in Dorr's second novel, *Lanmere* (1856). The young girl outwits her religiously obsessive mother and wins vindication when the local minister asks to marry her. Both of these novels have been praised for their realistic depiction of the rigors of domesticity in northern New England and for Dorr's devotion to "a reformation of the matriarchy" (Baym, p. 240). Another such novel was *Sybil Huntington* (1869).

Gothic horror looms over rural Vermont in *Expiation* (1873), which features hereditary insanity, hidden secrets, attempted matricide, premature burial, and other assorted shocks, no less dismaying because narrated by a sensible, middle-aged spinster. Dorr's last novel, *In Kings' Houses: A Romance of the Days of Queen Anne* (1898), incorporates her increased knowledge of English culture and history, but her reputation as a fiction writer rests chiefly on her earlier portrayals of regional American life.

Yet it was as a poet that Dorr's contemporaries knew her, and Dorr herself felt that her poetry was her finest literary achievement. Moreover, her more renowned contemporaries agreed with this judgment. In the 1850s her verse began to appear with regularity in important American magazines like *Scribner's*, *Harper's*, and *Atlantic Monthly*. Ralph Waldo Emerson included one of Dorr's poems in his anthology of poetry, *Parnassus*, in 1874, and the most popular American anthologist of the nineteenth century, Edmund Stedman, published her verse in *An American Anthology* (1900). Dorr corresponded with Oliver Wendell Holmes (1809–1894), was awarded a doctor of letters degree from Middlebury College, and wrote poetry consistently for over seventy years.

Her diligence was rewarded by the publication of nine collections of her poetry, beginning with *Poems* (1872). More exotic themes dominate in *Friar Anselmo and Other Poems* (1875). The poems in *Afternoon Songs* (1885) are wistful and death haunted. With Dorr's poetic reputation waxing, Scribner's published *Poems . . . Complete Edition* in 1892, followed by *The Fallow Field* in 1893. As she aged, Dorr's poetic productivity seemed to increase: four collections appeared after her seventy-fifth birthday—*Afterglow* (1900), *Poems, Complete* (1901), *Beyond the Sunset, Latest Poems* (1909), and *Last Poems* (1913).

Some of the dramatic monologues in Dorr's poetry have the bite of her iconoclastic fictional realism, but her lyrics tend to be somewhat more formal and stilted. Even so, domestic problems figure frequently in Dorr's narrative poetry, and her women are often torn by unresolved problems associated with gender in rural New England. Whatever the case, none of the vast body of Dorr's poetry is particularly revolutionary in theme or original in form. She was quoted as claiming that her work shunned all expressions that she could not with propriety read to children. Thus, Victorian caution marks the poetry in ways that it does not the more gritty and quotidian world of the Vermont fiction. Probably only in *Farmingdale* and *Lanmere* will analysts find enough verity and scope for any revivification of the literature of Julia Dorr.

In her later years, Dorr wrote several successful travel books. A winter trip with Seneca just before his death in 1884 was the inspiration for *Bermuda: An Idyl [sic] of the Summer Islands* (1884). In 1895, travels in Great Britain produced "*The Flower of England's Face*": *Sketches of English Travel* (1895), with a long section devoted to the Haworth of the Brontë sisters. *A Cathedral Pilgrimage* (1896) is a bit more pedestrian, but Dorr's imagination gives free rein to legends of martyrs and knights among crumbling and picturesque ruins.

A pillar of the Rutland community, Dorr was founder of the Free Library and its first president in 1885. Her book of advice, *Bride and Bridegroom* (1873), to some degree took the sting out of her realistic fictional portrayals of the torment of rural life by underscoring the sentimental potential of matrimony for the young. Dorr died in Rutland.

• Some of Dorr's manuscripts and papers are in the Rutland Free Library. Little has been written about Dorr. A feminist reading of her fiction is in Nina Baym, *Women's Fiction: A Guide to Novels by and about Women in America, 1820–1870* (1978). Edmund Stedman's estimates of her verse are in *Life and Letters of Edmund Clarence Stedman*, ed. Laura Stedman and George M. Gould (1910). Dorr's obituaries remain major sources of information: *Harper's Weekly*, 1 Feb. 1913; *Nation*, 23 Jan. 1912; *Rutland Herald*, 20 Jan. 1913; and *Burlington Free Press*, 20 Jan. 1913.

CHARLES BASSETT

DORR, Rheta Childe (2 Nov. 1866–8 Aug. 1948), journalist and feminist, was born in Omaha, Nebraska, the daughter of Edward Payson Child, a druggist, and Lucie Mitchell. Christened Reta Louise Child, Dorr later adopted the "Rheta Childe" spelling. In 1884 her father enrolled her at the University of Nebraska, where she took the "opportunity to loaf to my heart's content." Finding her "soul's reflection" in Henrik Ibsen's play *A Doll's House*, Dorr left college in 1885 against her family's wishes and found her first job as a post-office clerk.

At the age of twenty-four Dorr went to New York to attend the Art Students League and write poetry. In 1892 she married forty-year-old John Pixley Dorr, a Seattle businessman, and moved with him to Seattle. She gave birth to a son in 1896 but soon "began to break bounds" by seeking out "Baldy Rogers and Wah Chung and a number of other persons distinctly not in society" (*Woman of Fifty*, p. 66). She sent stories about people she met who came through Seattle during the Klondike gold rush to the *New York Sun* and wrote a book about Alaskan native people, *The Thinklets of Southeastern Alaska* (1896), with the missionary Frances Knapp. Dorr's husband could not accept her newspaper reporting, and in 1898 Dorr left him and returned to New York with her young son whom, with some help from her husband's New York relatives, she supported throughout his childhood and adolescence. She found a few freelance jobs, sold many of her possessions, and got noticed in 1901 by major newspapers when she was hired to supervise news photographers covering Theodore Roosevelt's acceptance of the vice-presidential nomination on the Republican ticket. She became a reporter in 1902 at the *New York Evening Post*.

Told to "write well enough to attract department store advertising," she focused on fashion, housekeeping, and women's club activities. With encouragement from *Post* editors, in a signed weekly column, "Woman and Work," she began to write "sob" stories about girls who "don't belong in jobs nohow," including the immigrant adolescents from New York's Lower East Side who worked in airless factories preparing gold leaf for books and picture frames and young women artists employed by Tiffany glass works who threatened male trade union jobs. Despite reader interest in her stories, Dorr was unable to persuade editors to promote her or to raise her weekly salary of $25.

Dorr became an activist, allying with women's groups that supported woman suffrage, union organization, minimum wage laws, an eight-hour work day, city playgrounds, and day nurseries. The General Federation of Women's Clubs appointed her to chair a committee on industrial conditions of women and children, and in association with the Women's Trade Union League (WTUL), her committee persuaded President Theodore Roosevelt and Congress to investigate the working conditions of women. The 1905 Bureau of Labor's report, "Statistics of Women at Work," was the first government study to document women's role in the work force. Widely reported in the press, it showed that the number of women wage earners was increasing faster than the number of men in industrial jobs.

Earning a "salary lower than that of any man on the paper" and with no hope of advancement at the *Post*, in 1906 Dorr took what would be the first of nine trips to Europe. Supported by freelance commissions that included *Harper's Weekly* and the *Boston Transcript*, her stories included coverage of Russian revolutionaries whom she met in St. Petersburg, the International Woman Suffrage Alliance quinquennial meeting in Copenhagen, and the beginning of the suffragist movement in England.

Returning to New York in November 1906 Dorr worked for more than a year in jobs in department stores, the garment industries, and a cotton mill in Fall River, Massachusetts. She argued in her autobiography, *A Woman of Fifty* (1924), that she was the first woman writer to "throw herself into the ranks of manual workers with a view of surveying their conditions in relation to the whole social fabric" (p. 163). "Christmas from behind the Counter" and other stories that provided insight into the world of women as workers and consumers appeared in popular magazines, including the *Independent* and *Harper's Weekly*. Dorr joined the Greenwich Village branch of the Socialist party, spoke at trade union meetings about "the race of dispossessed women" who "toiled for miserable wages" she met on the job, and agreed to write a series for *Everybody's Magazine*, owned by John Wanamaker, the department store magnate. When the series was published, as "The Woman's Invasion" in 1908–1909, Dorr believed that William Hard, hired as coauthor,

distorted her research and portrayed women workers as a "triumphant army of invasion" who "had broken all shackles [to] spend money on clothes and pleasures like men" (*Woman of Fifty*, p. 197).

Ben B. Hampton, the muckraking editor, hired Dorr in 1910 at *Hampton's Magazine*, where she researched new stories about working women and children, education, women's clubs, and woman suffrage. She later acknowledged that Hampton taught her to write "publishable stuff." This work became the basis for *What Eight Million Women Want* (1910), which centered on the idea that women were independent human beings and citizens who had become permanent producers in the workplace.

Beginning in 1912 Dorr spent the next several years traveling and meeting with suffragists and feminists in Europe, Washington, D.C., and New York. During this period she was a founding member of Heterodoxy, the feminist discussion group organized in New York in 1912 by Marie Jennie Howe. In England she worked with Emmeline Pankhurst on her 1914 autobiography, *My Own Story*, and published articles about the suffragist in *Good Housekeeping*. Having attended a lecture by Elizabeth Cady Stanton and Susan B. Anthony in Lincoln, Nebraska, Dorr had joined the National Woman Suffrage Movement at the age of twelve. Later, in 1914, she founded and became the first editor of the *Suffragist*, the official publication of the Congressional Union for Woman Suffrage, which publicized the fight for the Nineteenth Amendment, giving women the right to vote. A leading proponent and instigator of the new methods of "publicity, street meetings and parades," Dorr earned the description given to her by the *New York Times* as a "militant suffragist" and "one of the country's leading feminists."

Hired in 1915 by Edward E. Rumely at the *New York Evening Mail*, Dorr challenged the Tammany political machine in articles supporting the reelection of mayoral candidate John Purroy Mitchel because of his position on improved schools. In a signed and syndicated daily editorial, "As a Woman Sees It," she wrote about subjects of her choice, including support of the Allied effort in the war in Europe in which she praised men and women who worked together for the human race. Because he supported the Nineteenth Amendment, Dorr campaigned for the Republican presidential candidate, Charles Evans Hughes. In 1916 she joined the Republican party and later campaigned for Warren G. Harding and Calvin Coolidge.

Sent by the *New York Evening Mail*, Dorr went to Russia in early 1917 to write about the revolution. Printed after she returned to New York, her newspaper stories and book, *Inside the Russian Revolution* (1917), marked a final break with radical friends. Anti-Bolshevik, she described simple-minded Russian workers in need of practical democracy, education, and American business leaders. With her son serving in the American Expeditionary Force, Dorr spent three months in France as a war correspondent for the *Evening Mail*, although the French authorities would not recognize her credentials because she was a woman. Joining the YMCA and traveling freely under its auspices, she published articles for the *Evening Mail* about her experiences and a patriotic, sentimental book, *A Soldier's Mother in France* (1918), "written especially for soldiers' mothers to read." Dorr resigned from the *Evening Mail* after its editor was arrested for buying the *Evening Post* with German currency. She was seriously injured when struck in 1919 by a motorcycle on a Washington, D.C., street.

Despite suffering mental and physical impairment during much of the 1920s, Dorr continued to write and to be active in politics. She campaigned for Republicans Harding and Coolidge and spent three years in Europe, writing articles about the Dawes Committee, Communism in Bulgaria and Rumania, and Benito Mussolini's rise to power, which were published in the *New York Herald Tribune* and other newspapers. She assisted Anna Viroubova, an intimate of Czarina Alexandra, on her book, *Memories of the Russian Court* (1923). In 1928 she published *Susan B. Anthony: The Woman Who Changed the Mind of a Nation*, a feminist biography of the suffragist that was the first study to appear since the 1898 authorized biography. In *Drink: Coercion or Control?* (1929), Dorr encouraged compromise in the Prohibition controversy. Most important, *A Woman of Fifty*, published when Dorr was fifty-seven, chronicled her career and personal struggles as a divorced working mother. It was among the few firsthand accounts to document conditions of working women in department stores and industrial trades.

The death in 1936 of Dorr's son, the U.S. vice consul to Mexico, contributed to a further decline in her health. She lived in a sanatorium in Bucks County and later in New Britain, Pennsylvania, at her doctor's home, where she died.

Dorr sought but was never given equal status to men in her career as a journalist, yet as she concluded in her autobiography, "I think the greatest thing my generation of women accomplished was the freeing of younger women to go farther than ourselves" (*A Woman of Fifty*, p. 446).

• Dorr's correspondence and other papers are in the General Federation of Women's Clubs Archives, Washington, D.C.; the Library of Congress; and the Newberry Library, Chicago, Ill. Additional autobiographical information may be found in "A Convert from Socialism," *North American Review* (Nov. 1927): 498–504. Sources concerning specific periods of Dorr's life and work include William H. Chafe, *The Paradox of Change: American Women in the 20th Century* (1991); Susan Porter Benson, *Counter Cultures: Saleswomen, Managers, and Customers in American Department Stores, 1890–1940* (1986); Agnes Hooper Gottlieb, "Women Journalists and the Municipal Housekeeping Movement: Case Studies of Jane Cunningham Croly, Helen M. Winslow, and Rheta Childe Dorr" (Ph.D. diss., Univ. of Maryland, 1992); Ellen Carol Dubois, "Making Women's History: Activist Historians of Women's Rights, 1880–1940," *Radical History Review* 49 (1991): 61–84; Zena Beth McGlashan, "Club 'Ladies' and Working 'Girls': Rheta Childe Dorr and the New York Evening Post," *Journalism History* 8 (1981): 7–13; and McGlashan, "Women Witness the Russian Revolution: Analyzing Ways of Seeing," *Journalism History* 12 (1985): 54–61.

Also see Nancy F. Cott, *The Grounding of Modern Feminism* (1987); Madelon Golden Schlipp and Sharon M. Murphy, *Great Women of the Press* (1983); Maurine Beasley and Sheila J. Gibbons, *Taking Their Place: A Documentary History of Women and Journalism* (1993); Louis Filler, *Crusaders for American Liberalism* (1950); and Ishbel Ross, *Ladies of the Press* (1936). An obituary is in the *New York Times*, 9 Aug. 1948.

JENNIFER L. TEBBE

DORR, Thomas Wilson (5 Nov. 1805–27 Dec. 1854), political and social reformer, was born in Providence, Rhode Island, the son of Sullivan Dorr, a wealthy merchant and business leader, and Lydia Allen, a prominent socialite and sister of noted inventor Zechariah Allen and Rhode Island governor and U.S. senator Philip Allen. Dorr, studious and dutiful as a youth, graduated with honors in 1823 from Harvard, the second-ranking pupil in his class. He then studied law in New York City under Chancellor James Kent, passed the bar, toured the country, practiced law for a time in New York, and returned to Providence in 1833 to begin a life of public service.

As a Whig state legislator (1834–1837), a Democratic state chairman (1840–1841), a political insurrectionary (1842), and the leader of the Equal Rights wing of the Rhode Island Democratic party (1842–1854), Dorr was the catalyst that hastened the demise of the royal charter of 1663 and the adoption of a written state constitution. Ironically, neither document met with his approval, for his egalitarian philosophy was best expressed in the so-called People's Constitution, of which Dorr was the principal draftsman. It was Dorr's attempt to put this constitution into effect by invoking his version of the Lockean doctrine of popular constituent sovereignty that precipitated the Dorr War in 1842. Dorr's political goals—"free suffrage" with no discrimination against the foreign-born, "one-man, one-vote," an independent judiciary, a more powerful and dynamic executive, the secret ballot—though not permanently achieved in Rhode Island during his lifetime, placed him in the front rank of the political reformers of Jacksonian America.

Late in December 1841 the progressive People's Constitution was approved in a three-day referendum by a majority of Rhode Island's free white adult males acting in defiance of the existing state authorities. In April 1842 Dorr was elected the "people's governor" under this new regime, and the state was confronted with two rival governments. Generally, urban Whigs and rural Democrats opposed the Dorrites and united to form the Law and Order party. These conservatives prevailed, and Dorr, after surrendering to them, was tried, convicted, and imprisoned for treason against the state. The Whig-led Law and Order coalition dominated state politics for the remainder of the decade, despite a brief intraparty dispute in 1845 over whether or not to liberate Dorr. The vanquished reformer was actually confined to a state prison for a total of twenty months, counting the time he spent awaiting trial, an ordeal that shattered his fragile health and contributed to his political and physical demise. Dorr's liberation, finally achieved on 27 June 1845, stirred national interest and was a Democratic issue in the 1844 presidential campaign, as evidenced by the slogan "Polk, Dallas, and Dorr."

Dorr's rebellion was no tempest in a teapot; it had national repercussions and has enduring significance. The most important and controversial domestic occurrence of the John Tyler administration, it eventually involved the president, both houses of Congress, and the Supreme Court. Of even greater significance, the Rhode Island upheaval inspired the substantial contributions of John C. Calhoun, John L. O'Sullivan, Orestes Brownson, Joseph Story, Daniel Webster, Horace Greeley, Benjamin Hallett, and others of similar stature to the theories of suffrage, majority rule, minority rights, and constitutional government.

Much less known but no less significant were Dorr's economic and social concerns. Despite his patrician status, Dorr gradually evolved into a laissez-faire Democrat with a deep aversion toward economic privilege. As a young state legislator he sponsored the first comprehensive statute regulating state banks, a measure that led to his break with the local Whig party. The People's Constitution was permeated with equal rights (Locofoco) economic doctrine that sought to curb the abuses of special corporate "privilege" and monopoly grants from government.

Dorr was also a pioneer of free public education, and his People's Constitution made education a fundamental right. As a member then chairman of the Providence School Committee (1836–1842), Dorr established that city's secondary school system and made significant improvements in teacher education, recruitment and certification, administrative reorganization, and physical facilities. When the famed educational innovator Henry Barnard came to Rhode Island in 1843 and observed the workings of the Providence school system, he announced that his goal as state commissioner was to bring the schools in the other towns up to the standards established by Dorr in the city of Providence.

Dorr was intensely concerned with the status of minorities. His support of equal voting rights for Irish Catholic immigrants was exploited by his opponents and led to the breakup of his reform coalition. Though not an abolitionist, Dorr actively opposed slavery, urged civil rights for blacks, and worked with the leaders of the American Anti-Slavery Society as a delegate to that group's national convention. Dorr, a bachelor, worked well with local women's rights leaders, and they played a major role in the agitation leading to his liberation from prison.

Beginning in 1851, Dorr's uncle, Philip Allen, the new leader of Rhode Island's reform Democrats, captured the governorship for three successive one-year terms because of the defection of the rural Democrats from the Law and Order party. When the Allen faction (called "Dorr Democrats") pardoned Dorr, reversed his treason conviction, and attempted to reenact the People's Constitution, the agrarians again defected. At this juncture, Know-Nothingism and the rise of the Republican party produced a major political realignment in Rhode Island.

Dorr participated in the equal rights resurgence of the early 1850s as political strategist and adviser to his popular uncle. As the tide of reform began to ebb, he died in Providence from respiratory problems aggravated by his twenty-month imprisonment in a damp, poorly ventilated state prison. Dorr is best known as the determined leader of the Dorr rebellion, Rhode Island's crisis in constitutionalism, but he was much more than merely a "rebel" or a political reformer. He was a man of quality education, high social standing, and diverse intellectual and social interests.

Some American historians have suggested the name "Age of Egalitarianism" for the period from the mid-1820s to the mid-1850s, because a passion for equality of opportunity was the overriding theme of political, social, and economic activists. A more broadly-based democracy, an assault on neomercantilism and government-granted privilege, and a crusade for a more just, humane, and upwardly mobile social order were hallmarks of the era. This was the first great age of American reform, and Dorr was in the midst of it as an archetypical equal rights proponent. By the end of the turbulent 1850s, the Republicans, who revived the Law and Order coalition, dominated state politics and would continue to do so until the New Deal. The urban wing of the Democratic party, appealing mainly to equal rights advocates and Irish Catholics, was consigned to minority status until well into the twentieth century. They enshrined Dorr as their hero, and in 1935, when the state's Democrats finally gained control of the governorship and both houses of the general assembly via the "Bloodless Revolution" for the first time since 1854, Governor Theodore Francis Green justified the coup by telling a statewide radio audience that his party's success was inspired by "the spiritual presence of the patron saint of the Democratic Party in Rhode Island—Thomas Wilson Dorr!"

• The extensive Dorr papers and correspondence are at the John Hay Library of Brown University, and many of his letters survive in other depositories, especially the Rhode Island Historical Society Library. Dan King, *The Life and Times of Thomas Wilson Dorr* (1859), is a biography by Dorr's political ally. An excellent brief glimpse into Dorr's complex personality is C. Peter Magrath, "Optimistic Democrat: Thomas W. Dorr and the Case of *Luther vs. Borden*," *Rhode Island History* 29 (Aug. and Nov. 1970): 94–112. Also useful are Chilton Williamson, "The Disenchantment of Thomas W. Dorr," *Rhode Island History* 17 (Oct. 1956): 97–108; and Amasa M. Eaton, "Thomas Wilson Dorr and the Dorr War," in *Great American Lawyers*, ed. William Draper Lewis (1908). Patrick T. Conley, *Democracy in Decline: Rhode Island's Constitutional Development, 1776–1841* (1977), puts the Dorr rebellion in historical perspective and contains the most information in print about Dorr's political career. Arthur May Mowry, *The Dorr War* (1901), is an older, conservative view that upholds the position of the Law and Order party. Marvin E. Gettleman, *The Dorr Rebellion: A Study in American Radicalism*

(1973), views the Rhode Island reform movement from a New Left perspective. George M. Dennison, *The Dorr War: Republicanism on Trial, 1831–1861* (1976), analyzes the impact of Dorr's movement on the development of American republican theory.

PATRICK T. CONLEY

DORRANCE, John Thompson (11 Nov. 1873–21 Sept. 1930), business owner and inventor, was born in Bristol, Pennsylvania, the son of John Dorrance, a businessman, and Elizabeth Cottingham Thompson. After graduating from the Massachusetts Institute of Technology in 1895, he received a Ph.D. in chemistry from the University of Göttingen in 1897. He turned down teaching positions offered by several colleges and became a chemist at the Joseph Campbell Preserve Company, a Camden, New Jersey, food-processing firm controlled by his uncle Arthur Dorrance. The Campbell operation was producing nearly 200 products at the time, including several types of soup that did not sell particularly well. Inspired by the widespread consumption of soup he had witnessed in Europe and noting the inability of the three most prominent American soup manufacturers to attain profitable national distribution, Dorrance immediately began experimenting with condensed soups. The technology of condensing soups proved to be rather simple; the process involved little more than reducing the amount of water in conventional recipes. Condensed soup had significantly reduced packaging and distribution costs relative to the large, water-laden cans then on the market, and thus could be sold at about a third of the price.

The new product was introduced in 1899, with some resistance from Dorrance's uncle. Dorrance gained his uncle's confidence by quickly selling a carload of the new soup during a visit to Boston retailers. National success was soon realized, and Dorrance was rewarded by being named a director and vice president of Campbell's in 1900. He was named general manager of the company in 1910.

The popularity of Campbell's condensed soups was based in part on the cost to the consumer; whereas competitors' soups cost thirty cents or more per can in the early 1900s, a can of Campbell's sold for a dime. Extensive advertising assured consumers that the product, while inexpensive, was still wholesome and nutritious. Although Campbell's earned only a fraction of a cent per can, the product's superior value and the company's large-scale investment in advertising generated such widespread demand for the product that Campbell's enjoyed consistent profits and sales growth during Dorrance's tenure with the firm. The low profit margin also discouraged competitors from entering into the product market. The promotional efforts of the food-processing industry in general brought increased consumer demand for convenience foods that could be quickly prepared and served; Campbell's products required only heat and a little water.

Dorrance aggressively purchased stock in Campbell's and became the company's sole owner in 1915.

Soon after Dorrance's ascent to the presidency of the company, he discontinued the manufacture of the jams, jellies and other condiments that had been the original focus of the business. Dorrance then devoted the company's resources almost exclusively to the manufacture of soup and changed its name to the Campbell Soup Company in 1922. The only non-soup product that the company continued to manufacture was pork and beans, produced only on Mondays. This was a matter of efficiency; the Campbell's factory was idle on Sundays, and when production resumed the next day, broth needed to simmer for many hours before the canning of soup could begin. The company's reliance on a narrow product line allowed it to maintain a relatively small sales force, which kept distribution costs low. Volume discounts were rare, encouraging the placement of Campbell's products in small "mom and pop" retail stores. Campbell's dominated the nation's canned soup market, at times controlling nearly 90 percent of the field, during Dorrance's years as head of the firm.

In 1915 Campbell's purchased the Franco-American Food Company of Jersey City, New Jersey. Franco-American, founded in 1887, had been the first commercial manufacturer of canned soup in the United States. Dorrance's brother Arthur was named president of the Franco-American subsidiary. Campbell's management typically rose from within the organization. A long-standing ritual for top executives was participation in the daily soup tasting sessions.

Dorrance had married Ethel Mallinckrodt of Baltimore in 1906; the couple raised five children. The family settled in Cinnaminson, New Jersey, in 1911, a few miles from the Campbell's plant in Camden. Their house was owned by Campbell's and leased back to Dorrance. In 1925 the family moved to "Woodcrest," a Tudor-style mansion on a 118-acre estate in Radnor, Pennsylvania, a suburb of Philadelphia.

Although he was active outside of the soup company, serving as a director of several railroads and financial firms and holding positions in social clubs and the Episcopal church, Dorrance generally eschewed publicity. Possessing epicurean tastes, he traveled throughout the United States and Europe.

After his death in Cinnaminson from heart disease, Dorrance, who had started working at Campbell's at a weekly wage of $7.50, left an estate valued at $115 million, which at the time was thought to be the third largest estate ever probated in the United States. The bulk of the estate was Campbell's stock, of which Dorrance held all 120,000 preferred shares and all but nine of the one million common shares. Dorrance declared himself a New Jersey resident in his will, which was prepared in 1927. However, Pennsylvania authorities successfully argued in their state's courts that Dorrance was a resident of that state, a claim vigorously denied by the executors of Dorrance's estate. After losing their appeal to the Pennsylvania Supreme Court, the executors paid inheritance taxes of more than $14 million. Soon afterward, New Jersey officials contended that Dorrance's domicile was in New Jersey, as

Dorrance had himself claimed in his will. New Jersey authorities refused to deduct the amount of the inheritance taxes paid to Pennsylvania when calculating the taxable value of the estate, arguing that the Pennsylvania tax had been illegal. The matter was heard by the U.S. Supreme Court, which refused to intervene in what it labeled a matter to be determined solely by the two states involved, and Dorrance's executors were forced to pay more than $12 million in inheritance taxes to New Jersey. The Campbell Soup Company continued under private control of the Dorrance family until 1954.

• Perhaps because of his private nature, little has been written about Dorrance. Articles discussing both the history of the Campbell Soup Company and the extensive tax litigation following Dorrance's death appear in "Campbell's Soup," *Fortune*, Nov. 1935, pp. 69–139. Dorrance's business achievements are briefly discussed in Earl Chapin May, *The Canning Clan* (1937). An obituary is in the *New York Times*, 22 Sept. 1930.

PEYTON PAXSON

DORSETTE, Cornelius Nathaniel (c. 1852–7 Dec. 1897), pioneering black physician, was born into slavery at Eden in Davidson County, North Carolina, the son of David Dorsette and Lucinda (maiden name unknown). Two months after his birth, he was separated from his mother. When he was freed with the Emancipation Proclamation of 1863, he lived with his grandmother on a small farm and attended school in Thomasville, North Carolina.

Dorsette moved to Virginia, where he attended Hampton Institute. He thrived in the educational environment, and his classmates included Booker T. Washington. Dorsette graduated in 1878. A Hampton Institute trustee, Dr. Vosburgh, offered Dorsette employment in Syracuse, New York, where Vosburgh was a physician. Dorsette became Vosburgh's driver and handyman. Encouraged by his employer to become a doctor, Dorsette studied Latin to prepare for medical school and enrolled at Syracuse University College of Medicine but soon quit as a result of ill health, fatigue, and a lack of sufficient funds for tuition. After his health was restored and Vosburgh offered to pay his expenses, Dorsette applied to the Medical Department of the University of the City of New York. He was refused because he was black. The University of Buffalo Department of Medicine accepted him, and Dorsette received his M.D. in 1882.

Eager to establish himself professionally and reimburse Vosburgh (which he did in full by 1884), Dorsette practiced in a variety of positions during the next two years. He was assistant physician of the Wayne County, New York, almshouse and insane asylum and conducted a part-time general practice in Lyons, New York. He also worked in the mental ward at the Lyons hospital.

Desiring more opportunities than were available in New York, Dorsette contacted his college friend Booker T. Washington, who convinced Dorsette to move to Alabama. "In all the South, I know of no place that would afford a better opening for you than Montgomery," wrote Washington, assuring Dorsette that there were not yet any black doctors in the city, which was 59 percent African American in 1880. Observing that a black doctor in Atlanta then earned $2,000 annually, Washington stated, "Don't see why one can't do as well in Montgomery. There are some good progressive col. people in Montgomery whom I know you could depend on." Washington also emphasized that a white minister, Robert Charles Bedford, was "very anxious for you to locate here" and promised to introduce him to Montgomery's white and black ministers to establish a clientele. Noting that Tuskegee was only forty miles northeast of Montgomery, a two-hour train ride away, Washington promised, "I could give you an introduction that would go a good ways." Offering to assist Dorsette whenever needed, Washington invited him to Tuskegee Institute's commencement because "it would be a good opportunity to get advertised" (28 Feb. 1883).

Dorsette visited Montgomery and decided to stay. In 1884 he passed the six-day state medical examination and became Alabama's first licensed black physician. At the National Educational Association meeting that summer, Washington spoke of Dorsette's accomplishments, commenting that "when his white brother physicians found out . . . that he had brains enough to pass a better examination, as one of them said, than many of the whites had passed, they gave him a hearty welcome" (*Booker T. Washington Papers*, vol. 2, p. 257). Montgomery's white physicians offered Dorsette assistance in setting up his practice and also agreed to consult on cases.

Dorsette told Washington that although the white town leaders accepted him, Montgomery's blacks were hostile toward him. Suspicious and distrustful, the African-American community gradually approached Dorsette for health care. During his early days in Montgomery, Dorsette often drove into the surrounding countryside to deliver babies and treat patients. He claimed that he was an "idol" to the "country folk." He also traveled to Tuskegee as Washington's personal physician and to care for his family, faculty, and students. When a smallpox epidemic threatened central Alabama's public health, Dorsette was praised for using his knowledge of vaccines, previously unavailable in Alabama, to protect the populace.

Despite his successes, Dorsette encountered racial violence. White residents misinterpreted comments Dorsette made about the South; they also disliked his promotion of the black race. He was accused of having a "big head" and was threatened. He wrote Washington on 17 April 1888, "I have been on the go day & night and have not been molested though have met some of the bullies after mid night." The situation worsened, and three days later he commented, "I see signs of an undercurrent of sentiment that I dont [*sic*] like and while I hope for the best yet I dare not trust them. However I am here & here to stay unless removed by death. I trust the God that cares for a sparrow will care for me."

Feeling wronged, Dorsette longed for quiet, claiming he was tired of "this cussed nonsense." He vowed, "I have never flinched nor do I intend to even if death stars [*sic*] me in the face." Believing that opening a business would convince his harassers that he could not be intimidated to leave, he told Washington, "I am now determined to open a Drugstore if I only have one bottle on the shelves." Although he lacked money to finance a business, he asked Washington for assistance because "I am more and more convinced that my only safety & stability depends upon my owning something visible and that denotes permanency" (Dorsette to Washington, 19 Apr. 1888).

By May 1888, Dorsette had opened a drugstore underneath his office, proving that he intended to remain in the community. Located on a prominent corner of Dexter Avenue near the state capitol, the three-story brick Dorsette building contained professional offices and an auditorium. Harassers ceased their threats toward Dorsette, and he recruited professional blacks to work in Montgomery. Physicians, a dentist, a pharmacist, and a lawyer rented office space, and the *Montgomery Argus*, a black weekly newspaper, was edited in the building. He also helped physicians prepare for the state medical examination.

Establishing the Hale Infirmary, the state's first black hospital, was Dorsette's most significant accomplishment. In 1884 or 1885 he had married Sarah Hale, the daughter of James Hale, Montgomery's wealthiest and most influential black resident. Dorsette emphasized to James Hale the great need for an infirmary to treat black patients. He explained how most black Alabamians lacked access to quality health care professionals. Hale donated land for Dorsette's infirmary, which operated in Montgomery from 1890 to 1958.

Washington praised Dorsette for his "wonderful success" and often cited him as an example of what blacks could accomplish. Congratulating him for breaking racial barriers and for having the "largest practice of any colored physician in the country," Washington considered Dorsette a medical missionary to the African-American community. As Washington's "closest ally" in Montgomery, Dorsette supported Tuskegee Institute financially, offered to consult with the governor on the school's behalf, provided medical assistance, and served as a member of the school's board of trustees from 1883 to 1897. He gave the students oysters for Christmas dinner and a "large school bell." Dorsette introduced speakers at the annual Tuskegee Conference. He was pleased when Washington hired his sister, Cornelia, as a spelling teacher.

Dorsette helped organize the National Medical Association for black physicians and served as the group's first president. He was active in the state Republican party, acting as a delegate to the Republican National Convention, and especially studied legislation affecting education and health care. A member of "secret orders," he was captain of the Capital City Guards, the Colored Battalion of the National Guard.

Dorsette advised black residents how to handle racial threats and violence. In autumn 1895, he acted as assistant commissioner of the Negro Building at the Atlanta Cotton States and International Exposition, organizing the Alabama exhibits.

Dorsette and his first wife, Sarah Hale, had no children, and she died within a year of their marriage. He married Lula Harper in 1886; they had two daughters and lived near his professional building on Union Street. Dorsette suffered chronic illnesses. In 1892 he confided to Washington that he was "having trouble with my head" and worried about his health. Despite the damp, cold weather, Dorsette went hunting on Thanksgiving Day 1897 and developed pneumonia. He died shortly thereafter.

His funeral procession, consisting of fraternal orders and a fire company, paraded down crowded streets "while many windows were open and full of gazing people. Whites were nearly as prominent as the colored" (*Booker T. Washington Papers*, vol. 4, p. 348). An obituary in the *Montgomery Advertiser* stated that "Dr. Dorsette had so conducted himself as to win the respect of the white people of the city, and he was a good citizen, and has always struggled to better the condition of his race and his people." Tuskegee's trustees reflected in "Resolutions of Love and Respect" (25 May 1898), "His kind and genial ways endeared him to us all."

• Dorsette's letters to Booker T. Washington are in Washington's papers at the Library of Congress and Tuskegee University. See also *The Booker T. Washington Papers*, ed Louis R. Harlan (14 vols., 1972–1981). Biographical accounts are William Montague Cobb, "Cornelius Nathaniel Dorsette, M.D., 1852–1897," *Journal of the National Medical Association* 52 (Nov. 1960): 456–59, and in Herbert M. Morais, *The History of the Afro-American in Medicine* (1976).

ELIZABETH D. SCHAFER

DORSEY, Anna Hanson McKenney (12 Dec. 1815–25 Dec. 1896), author, was born in Georgetown, District of Columbia, the daughter of William McKenney, a chaplain in the navy, and Chloe Ann Lanigan. Anna was educated at home. As a girl she wrote poetry and published some of her verse in magazines. In 1837 she married Lorenzo Dorsey; they had five children. (Ella Loraine, the youngest, became a popular Catholic writer like her mother.) Both Dorsey and her husband converted to Catholicism in 1840, influenced by the English Oxford Movement in America. Lorenzo worked in the government post office in Washington, D.C., until his death in 1861.

Between 1847 and 1887 Dorsey published approximately thirty books, mostly prose but some poetry. Her works are religious in tone and are primarily concerned with the Catholic church. *The Student of Blenheim Forest* (1847), for example, is an account of the alienation of Louis, a Catholic, from his anti-Catholic father, Colonial Clavering, who is an important Virginian. Mrs. Clavering, Louis's mother, secretly baptizes Louis. The book has a pro-Catholic tone. In addition to presenting the history of Catholicism in

Maryland, the novel contains explanations of various Catholic traditions such as confession, the adoration of the Virgin Mary, High Mass, priestly vestments, the Benediction, and convents. In the preface to the second edition of *The Student of Blenheim Forest*, Dorsey explained that the work

does not pretend to be a complete system of instruction in Catholic dogmas, although several of the doctrines and practices of the Church are explained in a manner quite simple enough to be understood by all. [My] object has been to illustrate some of the difficulties which those who become converts to the True Faith are frequently destined to encounter from the persecutions of the world.

In *The House at Glenara* (1887), Dorsey describes the history of Christianity in Ireland. *Zoe's Daughter* (1888) is a historical novel set in Maryland during the days of Lord Baltimore. The first Lord Baltimore, George Calvert, wanted to establish a colony north of the Potomac for patriotic and commercial reasons as well as to create a safe place for oppressed Catholics. He died before the colony could be formed, but the land was issued to his son Cecil Calvert, the second Lord Baltimore, who founded the colony of Maryland in 1634.

Pope Leo XIII gave Dorsey special blessings twice, the University of Notre Dame awarded her the Laetare Medal, and her work was praised by Catholic ecclesiastics in America. Nevertheless, Dorsey was modest about her writing, noting in the preface to *Flowers of Love and Memory* (1849) that she did not have "the genius of a Longfellow or the highly attuned talent of a Hemans."

Dorsey died in Washington, D.C. A description of her funeral in the *Ave Maria* (16 Jan. 1897) attests to the influence of her work: the commentator noted that many people "who had learned to love her through her books" came to her home, "hoping that they might be permitted to gaze on her face." One gentleman had his request honored; he said that he had "found consolation and instruction and refreshment as of clear waters" in Dorsey's books, and he felt she had been "to him as a guiding light." Dorsey's work is a notable part of American literary history, and she made significant contributions to American Catholic literature.

• Other works by Dorsey include *Woodreve Manor* (1852), *Nora Brady's Vow* (1869), *Palms* (1887), *Adrift* (1887), and *Coaina: The Rose of the Algonquins* (1867). Colleen McDannell, *Catholic Women Fiction Writers, 1840–1920* (1991), includes Dorsey among the Catholic women in the study. An obituary is in the (Washington, D.C.) *Evening Star*, 26 Dec. 1896.

SANDRA M. GRAYSON

DORSEY, George Amos (6 Feb. 1868–29 Mar. 1931), anthropologist, was born in Hebron, Ohio, the son of Edwin Jackson Dorsey, a schoolmaster, farmer, and merchant, and Mary Elma Grove. He graduated with bachelor of arts degrees from Denison (1888) and Harvard (1890) Universities. In 1894 he received his Ph.D. from Harvard University with a thesis focusing on the necropolis of Ancón, Peru. His thesis topic stemmed from his graduate work of collecting anthropological materials in Peru, Ecuador, Chile, and Bolivia in 1891–1892 for an exhibition at the World's Columbian Exposition, presented in 1893 in Chicago. While still a graduate student he had been appointed honorary commissioner and superintendent of archaeology at the exposition, which was organized in recognition of the 400th anniversary of Columbus's discovery of the Americas. Dorsey married Ida Chadsey in 1892; they had two children. His second marriage, in 1924, was to Sue McLellan; they had no children.

After receiving his Ph.D. (the first granted by Harvard in anthropology), Dorsey was appointed an instructor at Harvard from 1895 to 1896. He then accepted a position as assistant curator of physical anthropology at the Field Columbian Museum in Chicago (now the Field Museum of Natural History). He held the rank of curator from 1898 to 1915, and he maintained joint appointments as a professor of comparative anatomy at the Northwestern University Dental School (1898–1913) and as an anthropologist at the University of Chicago (1908–1915). In 1909 he received an honorary LL.D. from Denison.

At Harvard Dorsey had acquired an interest in physical anthropology that led to his appointments in Chicago in that academic area. During his years in Chicago he contributed to the young field of forensic anthropology (physical anthropology applied to medico-legal problems). This interest might have been generated through his study of anatomy under Thomas Dwight, who is generally regarded as the "father" of forensic anthropology in the United States. In 1897 and 1898 Dorsey offered scientific testimony in the highly publicized Luetgert murder trials in Chicago. Adolph Luetgert, a local sausage maker, was accused of killing his wife and disposing of her remains in a vat at the sausage facility. Dorsey offered testimony regarding small bone fragments found within the vat. For this effort (or perhaps in spite of it, since the testimony was very controversial), and for his publications in this field, he is regarded as an early pioneer in forensic anthropology.

While at Harvard, Dorsey had also been influenced by Frederic Ward Putnam, the Peabody Professor of Anthropology at Harvard and the director and curator of the Peabody Museum of Archaeology and Ethnology. This led to a career-long interest in ethnology and material culture of New World aboriginal peoples. By 1900 his research interests had shifted away from physical anthropology toward ethnology, especially that of the Plains Indians. From 1900 to 1906 Dorsey conducted fieldwork among Caddoan-speaking Indians of the Plains that led to numerous ethnographic reports. His fieldwork included work for the anthropology section of the 1904 Louisiana Purchase exposition. His responsibility in this exposition included creating exhibits focusing on the Osage, Arapaho, Cheyenne, Pawnee, and Wichita tribes. Among anthropologists today he is best known for his ethnographic work, especially in documenting the mythology of the Pawnee, Wichita, Arikara, and Caddo tribes and for his study of ceremonial dance among the Hopi, Cheyenne, Ponca, and Arapaho. In 1908 Dorsey traveled for the Field Columbian Museum to the Pacific, Australia, Asia (including the Philippines and India), and Europe. He participated in the first exploring party to travel across Bougainville, the largest island in the Solomon group.

Dorsey was a correspondent from 1909 to 1912 for the *Chicago Tribune*, studying the issue of American immigration from Italy, Austria, and Eastern Europe. He also examined the political and social situations in South Africa, Australia, Japan, China, and India.

In 1915 Dorsey received a commission as lieutenant commander in the U.S. Navy, accepting an appointment as assistant naval attaché in Lisbon, Portugal, and Madrid, Spain. In 1919 he participated in the Paris Peace Conference. In 1921 Dorsey returned to civilian life, serving as a correspondent for the *London News* and writing a number of popular and successful books, including *Why We Behave like Human Beings* (1925) and *The Nature of Man* (1927), comparative treatments of human development and the human condition.

Dorsey was a member of the American Folklore Society and served as its president in 1903. He was also a member of the American Society of Naturalists, the American Association of Museums, the Anatomical Society of America, the Chicago Geographical Society (twice elected president, 1908 and 1909), Phi Beta Kappa, Sigma Xi, the Royal Anthropological Institute of Great Britain, the Société des Américanistes de Paris, the Anthropological Societies of Stockholm, Paris, and Berlin, the American Numismatic Antiquarian Society, and the Adventurer's Club (elected president).

Dorsey's principal academic impact was to advance the early development of forensic anthropology, to document aspects of aboriginal cultures of peoples around the world (especially in the Plains area of the United States), and to contribute to the understanding of human behavior through his numerous writings and lectures. He is remembered for his broad interests, extensive travel, and publications. He died in his home in New York City.

• Other significant publications by Dorsey include "Lumbar Curve in Some American Races," *Essex Institute Bulletin* 27 (1895): 57–73; "A Study of the Size of the Articular Surfaces of the Long Bones in Aboriginal American Indians," *Boston Medical and Surgical Journal* 137 (1897): 80–82; "The Skeleton in Medico-Legal Anatomy," *Chicago Medical Recorder* 16 (1899): 172–79; "The Mishongnovi Ceremonies of the Snake and Antelope Fraternities," *Field Columbian Museum Publication* 66 (1902): 159–261; "Arapaho Sun Dance: The Ceremony of the Offerings Lodge," *Field Columbian Museum Publication* 75 (1903); "Traditions of the Arapaho," *Field Columbian Museum Publication* 81 (1903); "Mythology of the Wichita," *Carnegie Institution of Washington Publication* 21 (1904); "Traditions of the Arikara," *Carnegie Institution of Washington Publication* 17 (1904): 1–102; "Traditions of the Osage," *Field Columbian Museum Publication* 88 (1904); "The

Cheyenne," *Field Columbian Museum Publication* 99 (1905); "The Ponca Sun Dance," *Field Columbian Museum Publication* 102 (1905): 61–88; "Traditions of the Caddo," *Carnegie Institution of Washington Publication* 41 (1905); "Pawnee Mythology (Part I)," *Carnegie Institution of Washington Publication* 59 (1906); and "Notes on Skidi Pawnee Society," *Field Museum of Natural History Publication* 479 (1940): 67–119.

A comprehensive summary of Dorsey's life and contributions can be found in Fay-Cooper Cole, "George A. Dorsey," *American Anthropologist* 33 (1931): 413–14. For perspectives on Dorsey's contributions to physical anthropology, especially forensic anthropology, see T. D. Stewart, "George A. Dorsey's Role in the Luetgert Case: A Significant Episode in the History of Forensic Anthropology," *Journal of Forensic Sciences* 23 (1978): 786–91, and Stewart, "History of Physical Anthropology," *Perspectives on Anthropology 1976*, ed. A. F. C. Wallace (1977). Clyde Collins Snow, "Forensic Anthropology," *Annual Review of Anthropology* 11 (1982): 97–131; and T. D. Stewart, "Forensic Anthropology," in *The Uses of Anthropology*, ed. W. Goldschmidt (1979). An obituary is in the *New York Times*, 30 Mar. 1931.

DOUGLAS UBELAKER

DORSEY, James Owen (31 Oct. 1848–4 Feb. 1895), ethnologist and missionary, was born in Baltimore, Maryland, the son of Thomas Anderson Dorsey and Mary Sweetser Hance. As a child, James showed an aptitude for languages, learning to read Hebrew by the age of ten. He entered Central High School in Baltimore in 1862 and in 1867 began studies at the Protestant Episcopal Theological Seminary in Alexandria, Virginia. Ordained as a deacon in 1871, Dorsey immediately left for the Dakota Territory, where he began missionary work among the Ponca Indians, a Siouan tribe. He quickly learned to speak the Ponca language well enough to communicate without an interpreter, and he was working on a Ponca grammar and dictionaries in 1873 when serious illness forced him to return east. Dorsey contacted the Smithsonian Institution, hoping to have his materials published, but his work was judged to be insufficiently professional.

Dorsey spent the next five years working in a parish in Maryland. In 1877, however, a family friend recommended him to accompany Major J. W. Powell's Rocky Mountain Survey as an ethnologist. In addition to studying the region's geology, Powell sought to examine American Indian peoples and the influence of the land on their culture. Dorsey was hired to develop a grammar and dictionary of Ponca, and in July 1878 Powell sent him to the Omaha reservation in eastern Nebraska for two years of fieldwork. When the Bureau of American Ethnology (BAE) was established under Powell in 1879, Dorsey was engaged as an expert on Siouan languages and tribes, particularly the Omaha, Ponca, Quapaw, and Kansa. While missionaries had collected much of the existing information on Native Americans available at that time, Dorsey was the only missionary on the staff of the BAE.

After 1880, with a few exceptions, Dorsey spent his life in Washington, D.C., drawing on his earlier experiences in the field to write about Native American linguistics and culture. In 1883 he traveled to Canada and the Indian Territory to study Tutelo and Quapaw, two Siouan languages. In 1885 he reluctantly agreed to study the linguistic groups of Oregon, in which he had no particular expertise. Dorsey's final fieldwork took place in 1892, when he spent two months in Louisiana with the last surviving Biloxi speakers. However, throughout this period Dorsey also worked in Washington, D.C., with individual native speakers who were hired by the BAE, and his years in the West had left him with ample material to collate and synthesize. In particular, his fieldwork contributed to Powell's 1891 classification system for Native American languages. While at the BAE, Dorsey contributed to the bureau's annual reports and bulletins and also wrote an 812-page treatise on the Omaha language for Powell's 1890 *Contributions to North American Ethnology*. In addition to languages, Dorsey wrote on dwellings, furniture, implements, kinship and marriage arrangements, and mythology.

Dorsey, like many of his contemporaries in the field, had no professional training in anthropology, but he was known to have an excellent ear and to be unusually quick and methodical in recording. He noted astutely the inconsistency of speakers of any language, remarking on the changes in linguistic habits that result from age and contact with outsiders. In his vocabularies and grammar analyses, he attempted to retain native categories in describing parts of speech, rather than imposing Western models on them. As an anthropologist and as a missionary, Dorsey wanted to understand the culture as well as the language; Powell thought that Dorsey was "actuated by an earnest desire to acquaint himself fully with primitive modes of thought." He remained an active supporter of the peoples of the northern Plains and helped the Ponca write letters requesting improvements in reservation conditions.

Dorsey's work was admired by his contemporaries, including Franz Boas, who recommended his work as a model of linguistically based ethnology and thought his writing showed "deep insight into the mode of thought of the Indian." Possessing a sympathetic patience and a desire to understand in order to save American Indian culture, Dorsey retained, even in his work for the bureau, some aspect of his evangelical mission. Dorsey, who never married, died in Washington, D.C.

• Among Dorsey's most important works are "Omaha Sociology," in the BAE *Annual Report* 1881–1882; "An Account of the War Customs of the Osage," *American Naturalist* 18 (1884); and, with J. R. Swanton, *A Dictionary of the Biloxi and Ofo Languages* (1912). For a short biography, see Curtis M. Hinsley, Jr., *Savages and Scientists: The Smithsonian Institution and the Development of American Anthropology, 1846–1910* (1981). On Dorsey's place in anthropology in the late nineteenth century, see Neil M. Judd, *The Bureau of American Ethnology: A Partial History* (1967).

BETHANY NEUBAUER

DORSEY, Jimmy (29 Feb. 1904–12 June 1957), clarinetist, alto saxophonist, and bandleader, and **Tommy Dorsey** (27 Nov. 1905–26 Nov. 1956), trombonist and

bandleader, were born James Francis Dorsey in Shenandoah, Pennsylvania, and Thomas Francis Dorsey, Jr., in Mahanoy Plane, Pennsylvania, respectively, the sons of Thomas Francis Dorsey, Sr., a miner, and Theresa "Tess" Langton.

Jimmy started on "slide trumpet" (a soprano trombone) from about age six. His father, a part-time music teacher and leader of brass bands, gave him rigorous instruction on cornet and clarinet. Around the age of twelve, Jimmy took up the alto saxophone as well. The family moved to Lansford, Pennsylvania, around 1920. Perhaps it was here that Jimmy spent his only year in high school; the chronology is unclear.

Receiving the same rigorous instruction from his father, Tommy started on alto horn, baritone horn, and cornet (he occasionally played cornet throughout his career) before settling on trombone about the age of twelve. He worked as a delivery boy for a meat market, and, although he did not attend high school, he proved to have a brilliant mind and multifaceted talent; later in life he deeply regretted not having had a college education.

Jimmy's brief tenure in the mines as a blacksmith's helper ended disastrously but without lasting harm when he accidentally hit the blacksmith with a sledgehammer. Probably in the summer of 1922 the brothers left home to play at Carlin's amusement park in Baltimore, using the band name Dorseys' Wild Canaries. Around 1923 Jimmy joined the Scranton Sirens, which he persuaded to hire his brother. In the summer of 1924 Jimmy became a member of the California Ramblers, including Adrian Rollini, at the California Ramblers Inn on Pelham Bay, New York; Tommy joined the band soon afterward. Jimmy joined Jean Goldkette's orchestra in 1925; Tommy followed in the spring of 1926. Later in 1926 Jimmy joined Paul Whiteman's orchestra, with which he was featured on alto sax on "Whiteman Stomp" (1927); Tommy, after playing with Roger Wolf Kahn's orchestra, followed in 1927.

From 1925 each brother also extensively freelanced in public performances, on radio, and on recordings. Jimmy independently recorded Dixieland in Red Nichols's groups (including "That's No Bargain" and "Hurricane," both from 1926) and alongside Bix Beiderbecke under Frankie Trumbauer's leadership. He toured Europe with Ted Lewis in 1930. Tommy independently participated in Beiderbecke's first recordings as a leader in 1925, including "Davenport Blues," and from that year he, even more than Jimmy, was involved in ever-changing freelance affiliations. At a fervent all-star jazz recording session including Henry "Red" Allen and Pee Wee Russell in 1932, he supplied a memorable and contrasting moment of calmness by playing a sustained lip trill to begin his solo on "Who Stole the Lock?" (released under banjoist Jack Bland's nominal leadership).

In 1928 a considerable portion of joint freelancing became formalized as the Dorsey Brothers Orchestra, which used a brass instrumentation distinctive for big bands: one trumpet and three trombones (together with the usual complement of reeds, piano, guitar, bass, and drums). Bouncy versions of Bing Crosby's "Stay on the Right Side of the Road" (1933) show its style, perched between Dixieland and swing. In 1931 the brothers also worked in the Broadway show *Everybody's Welcome*.

Jimmy married Jane Porter in November 1927; they had one child. In later years they often were separated. Tommy's first wife was Mildred "Toots" Kraft; they had two children. The date of the marriage is unknown. Tommy and his family lived in Freeport, New York, before moving to Bernardsville, New Jersey, around 1934.

In the spring of 1934, with Glenn Miller writing many of the arrangements, the Dorsey Brothers Orchestra began playing steadily in public in New England and then in the New York City area, culminating in an engagement at the Glen Island Casino from 15 May 1935. At month's end, in a celebrated incident, Tommy quit. Despite their years of working together, the brothers were fierce rivals who fought constantly in overt and subtle ways.

For the next eighteen years their careers merged only infrequently, and from that time the group was the Jimmy Dorsey Orchestra, with virtuoso trombonist Bobby Byrne replacing Tommy. According to Bing Crosby, Jimmy was "soft-spoken . . . an inveterate punster . . . shy and self-effacing." Jimmy shared his brother's exacting approach to music, but he was far less aggressive and far better at getting along with people. Hence, by comparison with Tommy, the personnel of his band was stable. Among his steady sidemen, singer Bob Eberly (originally Eberle), drummer Ray McKinley, and arranger Toots Camarata made significant contributions. In January 1936 the orchestra began an eighteen-month residency in Hollywood on Crosby's Kraft Music Hall radio series, and Crosby's fame brought the band popularity, even without its having a hit record. It performed on the soundtrack to the movie *Shall We Dance?* (1937), the Gershwins' musical starring Fred Astaire and Ginger Rogers. Rigorous tours and prestigious ballroom engagements followed into the 1940s.

In April 1940 the orchestra recorded its theme song "Contrasts," an updated excerpt from Jimmy's composition "Oodles of Noodles," which the brothers had recorded in 1932; it featured his sensuously romantic alto saxophone. On recordings made earlier that month, singer Helen O'Connell, whom Jimmy hired in 1939, showed a gift for light comedy in the mock-Latin song "Six Lessons from Madame La Zonga" (which was surpassed the next year by her rendition of "Arthur Murray Taught Me Dancing in a Hurry"), while on "The Breeze and I" a long passage based on a bolero-like rhythm introduces Eberly's ballad singing. Proceeding from "Breeze," a series of popular records followed in 1941 and 1942. Each of them featured Eberly, followed by the ensemble with Dorsey soloing on saxophone or clarinet, and finally O'Connell, and each used a formula unusual for a big band of the swing era; in spite of the threat to conventional dancing, each ar-

rangement changes mood, tempo, and rhythmic character, the idea having originated in Camarata's arrangements for the finale of a weekly radio show for which dancing was not an immediate consideration. Among these recordings, the tango-like introduction to "Amapola" (1941) and the rumba-like rhythms beneath O'Connell in the last parts of "Yours" (sung in Spanish) and "Brazil" (both 1942) continue the combination of Latin rhythm with swing. But the biggest hits in this series, "Green Eyes" and "Tangerine" (both 1941), use the formulas (Eberly—ensemble and Dorsey—O'Connell; shifting tempos) without the explicit Latin rhythm.

The Tommy Dorsey Orchestra experienced a heavy turnover in personnel from its inception in 1935. Tommy was a musical perfectionist, a severe disciplinarian, and "a fighter—often a very belligerent one—with a sharp mind, an acid tongue and intense pride," according to big band chronicler George T. Simon. Exceptionally, though, Tommy had a deep love of jazz and consequently an unusual tolerance for a looseness and an eccentricity that characterized some of the finest jazz musicians, including tenor saxophonist Bud Freeman (who was in and out of the band) and drummer Buddy Rich, who joined in 1939. This was never more true than for the spectacular trumpeter Bunny Berigan, whom Tommy hired as a sideman, encouraged as an independent bandleader, and rehired, until finally Berigan's alcoholism became so debilitating that he could no longer continue.

Initially the orchestra formed mainly from members of Joe Haymes's group. After a college tour, it made its debut at the Lincoln (later Edison) Hotel in New York, and in October 1935 it recorded what became Tommy's theme song, "I'm Gettin' Sentimental Over You." Tommy became justly famous for the smooth perfectionism of his trombone playing on this title, and by 1936 he had acquired his lasting motto: "the sentimental gentleman of swing." He was, though, far more versatile than the catchphrase implies, and indeed he was dedicated to playing in as many contemporary popular and jazz styles as possible. Through the late 1930s Dixieland-oriented jazz was heard for the most part from a band within the big band, his Clambake Seven (actually nine, including Dorsey and singers Edythe Wright or Jack Leonard), which late in 1935 recorded a hit record, "The Music Goes 'Round and Around." But the division of repertory was by no means strict, and often individual pieces were stylistic conglomerates. The principal example is the orchestra's rendering of "Marie" (recorded early in 1937), in an arrangement which by various accounts was either purchased from, traded for, or stolen from Doc Wheeler's Sunset Royal Serenaders. (In any event, it was Tommy who supplied the spark that made it a hit.) "Marie" begins with another example of his trombone control, in an unadorned rendering of the melody; then Leonard sings the melody in the same straightforward, clear-toned, and pretty manner, while the bandsmen interject rhythmically syncopated and swinging comments on the lyrics; then Berigan takes over, improvising one of his most acclaimed jazz solos. The tune was requested so often that, to avoid boredom, Dorsey commissioned a series of arrangements along the same lines, extending from "Who?" with Leonard (1937) to "Blue Skies" with Frank Sinatra (1941).

Eclecticism marked the band's recordings of the 1940s. A different series, "swinging the classics," stemmed from the popularity of an adaptation of Rimsky-Korsakov's "Song of India" (recorded at the same time as "Marie"), again featuring Dorsey and Berigan. From 1937 Deane Kincaide supplied Dixieland-oriented arrangements for the big band, including the recording of "Milenberg Joys" (1939), which featured trumpeter Yank Lawson. At decade's end, arranger Sy Oliver joined from Jimmie Lunceford's big band and thereby enabled Tommy to embrace a jazz style firmly oriented in swing, for which the finest example, "Opus No. 1," came later, in 1944. In the early 1940s Tommy began to feature dreamy, romantic performances by Sinatra and the Pied Pipers (eight vocalists, soon trimmed down to four, including Jo Stafford), whose biggest hit was "I'll Never Smile Again" (1940); this tendency was taken further with the addition of a string section in 1942. In that same year, by which time Stafford was also being featured in this romantic manner, Tommy recorded a version of "Blues in the Night," on which Stafford shows a command of idiomatic, blues-tinged singing.

The Tommy Dorsey Orchestra broadcast nationally in mid-1936 from Dallas and then from the Los Angeles area. Tommy joined comedian Jack Pearl's radio show, and in the summer of 1937 he took it over, while also playing at the Palomar Ballroom. In 1939 he started a newspaper, *The Bandstand*, which he was forced to abandon after it proved too expensive. When his radio sponsorship ended late in 1939, he temporarily cut back, but Sinatra's impact more than compensated for this loss, and the orchestra flourished through the war years. On Halloween 1940 it opened a new ballroom, the Hollywood Palladium.

For several years both orchestras played for soundtracks and appeared in movies, including Jimmy's appearance in *The Fleet's In* (1942) and Tommy's in *Du Barry Was a Lady* (released that same year but made earlier while Rich and trumpeter Ziggy Elman were still bandsmen). Tommy formed his own publishing companies, Sun Music Company and Embassy Music Company, to gain a greater share of royalties from his hit records. In the spring of 1941 he formed his own booking agency, Tommy Dorsey, Inc., after years of disputes with MCA. Then the brothers formed a joint publishing company. During these years of great affluence for the Dorseys, Jimmy lived at Toluka Lake, California. Tommy, having divorced his first wife around 1941, married movie actress Pat Dane in 1943. This marriage also ended in divorce. In a dispute over money with the Hollywood Palladium in the summer of 1944, he opened his own Casino Gardens in Ocean Park, California, in partnership with Harry James and

Jimmy, although Tommy took over as its sole proprietor after the war.

In 1946 the brothers contributed to the disappointing, fictionalized movie *The Fabulous Dorseys* (1947). They were among the prominent swing era leaders who disbanded at the end of 1947, but this proved to be only temporary, and both resumed leading independently. Tommy's last marriage was to Jane New, in 1948; they had two children. In 1953 the expense of maintaining a big band finally led Jimmy to be reunited with Tommy, ostensibly in a new Dorsey Brothers Orchestra, although in practice it was Tommy's group. The band was featured on Jackie Gleason's television series, where the Dorseys introduced a young star, Elvis Presley.

Tommy died at his home in Greenwich, Connecticut, from choking on food after taking an overdose of sleeping pills. A memorial Tommy Dorsey orchestra later toured under the leadership of trombonist Warren Covington (1958), saxophonist Sam Donahue (1961–1965), and trombonist Buddy Morrow (late 1970s into the 1980s). Shortly before Tommy's accidental death and without Tommy's presence, the Dorsey Brothers Orchestra recorded "So Rare" under Jimmy's leadership (1956). It proved to be a posthumous hit song; by the time of its release, Jimmy was dying of cancer in a New York hospital.

Jimmy Dorsey's virtuosic command of the clarinet and alto saxophone was admired by jazz musicians as important as Lester Young and Coleman Hawkins. Such was his stature as a swing era bandleader that the "third Dorsey," trumpeter Lee Castle, successfully toured as the leader of a memorial Jimmy Dorsey orchestra until his death in 1990.

Tommy Dorsey was unsurpassed in his ability to render strict, formal, pretty melodies on the trombone. Although as a player he stuck carefully to this approach, as a bandleader he had a wide-ranging interest in jazz and popular music and an extraordinary talent for making that music commercially successful.

• A bibliography of early periodical sources on the Dorseys appeared in *Current Biography 1942*; it supplies a great deal of unique material. A concise, friendly survey of their careers, including interviews, is Richard English, "The Battling Brothers Dorsey," *Saturday Evening Post*, 2 Feb. 1946, reprinted in *Eddie Condon's Treasury of Jazz*, ed. Eddie Condon and Richard Gehman (1957), pp. 303–18. An entertaining casual biography is Herb Sanford, *Tommy and Jimmy: The Dorsey Years* (1972). George T. Simon, *The Big Bands*, 4th ed. (1981), has chapters on the history and style of the brothers' band and their individual bands; additional comments on the Dorseys permeate the book. Surveys of jazz-oriented aspects of the Dorsey Brothers Orchestra and Tommy's big band can be found in Albert McCarthy, *Big Band Jazz* (1974), pp. 193–95, 219–22; this topic is pursued in greater detail, with a discussion of Jimmy's big band as well, in Gunther Schuller, *The Swing Era: The Development of Jazz, 1930–1945* (1989).

On Jimmy alone, see the obituary in the *New York Times*, 13 June 1957. Charles Garrod, *Jimmy Dorsey and His Orchestra* (1980), catalogs his recordings as a leader. Richard M.

Sudhalter vividly summarizes his career in liner notes to the boxed Time-Life LP set *Jimmy Dorsey* (1984).

On Tommy alone, see his obituary in the *New York Times*, 27 Nov. 1956. A catalog of his recordings as a leader is Charles Garrod et al., *Tommy Dorsey and His Orchestra*, vol. 1, *1928–1945*, and *Tommy Dorsey and His Orchestra*, vol. 2, *1946–1956* (n.d.). Robert L. Stockdale identifies Tommy's birthplace in his discography *Tommy Dorsey: On the Side* (1995). Reminiscences from former sidemen appear in Steve Voce, "Talking of Tommy," *Jazz Journal International*, Feb. 1985, pp. 20–22. Bruce Crowther surveys Tommy's career in "Tommy Dorsey: The Sentimental Gentleman," *Jazz Journal International*, Nov. 1989, pp. 10–11, 13.

BARRY KERNFELD

DORSEY, John Henry (28 Jan. 1874–30 June 1926), Roman Catholic priest, was born in Baltimore, Maryland, the son of Daniel Dorsey and Emmaline Snowden. He was baptized the same year at St. Francis Xavier Church in Baltimore, the oldest black Catholic parish in the United States. As a young boy Dorsey was encouraged to study for the priesthood by Father John Slattery, S.S.J., the superior of the Mill Hill Fathers (later the Josephites), who was very interested in encouraging religious vocations among African Americans. In 1888 Dorsey was sent to St. Thomas College, a minor seminary in St. Paul, Minnesota. In 1889 he entered the newly opened Mill Hill (later Josephite) Seminary, Epiphany Apostolic College, in Baltimore. Four years later in 1893 he entered St. Joseph Seminary, at that time residence for the Josephite seminarians taking courses at nearby St. Mary's Seminary.

On 21 June 1902 Dorsey was ordained a priest in the Baltimore cathedral by Cardinal Gibbons. He sang his first Mass the following day at St. Francis Xavier Church in Baltimore. He was the sixth African American to be ordained a Catholic priest following the ordination of James Augustine Healy in 1854. He was the second black priest to be educated and ordained in the United States. In many places black priests still faced either outright hostility or subtle resistance. Slattery, the preacher at Dorsey's first Mass, delivered a forthright and somewhat angry sermon calling for the ordination of more black priests and denouncing the racism within the American Catholic church. Within the year Slattery had resigned his position and a few years later left the priesthood and the Catholic church.

Dorsey was a powerful and impressive preacher. He became an immediate success with black Catholics in both the South and the North as he was sent on a preaching tour to black congregations immediately following his ordination. He was described as "projecting an air of authority." Dorsey's popularity among African Americans was seen as the proof that an increase in the number of black priests would greatly increase the number of black converts to Catholicism. Following his first tour of preaching missions, he was given a position in 1903 at the St. Joseph Catechetical College in Montgomery, Alabama. He stayed there a year and a half and was then assigned to the black parish in Pine Bluff, Arkansas. In the spring of 1905 he was made pastor.

Dorsey was the first black priest to become a pastor of a parish in the South. Almost immediately he met with hostility and suspicion from the local white pastor, a former Confederate army officer, and even from some of the black sisters in the school who would have preferred a white priest. Charges were leveled against him concerning the administration of the parish and misconduct with one of the women whom he had converted. None of these charges was proved. In fact, many in the parish signed a petition in support of their pastor. Notwithstanding, the bishop of Little Rock, John B. Morris, requested the superior of the Josephites to remove Father Dorsey. In 1907 the superior of the Josephites was forced to comply.

From 1909 to 1917 Dorsey was part of a team of three priests who traveled throughout the South preaching missions mainly to African-American Catholics. Here Father Dorsey was eminently successful. He was equally popular with many black Protestant listeners to whom he explained the teachings of Catholicism. He was also instrumental in the formation of the Knights of Peter Claver, an African-American Catholic fraternal organization. He along with three other Josephite priests and three black Catholic laymen established the organization in 1909 in Mobile, Alabama. He served as national chaplain for fourteen years.

Despite his success and achievements, Dorsey faced relentless criticism and hostility because of his race. He was caricatured in the anti-Catholic southern press as a black ape wearing a stole and listening to the confessions of a young white woman. Weariness, racial prejudice, and loneliness resulted in illness and overweight. He became an alcoholic. His ill health forced his retirement from the preaching circuit. In 1918 he was assigned to St. Monica's Church, a poor black parish in south Baltimore.

At this time the newly elected superior general of the Josephites, Louis B. Pastorelli, officially introduced a policy of no longer accepting black candidates for the priesthood into their seminary. The policy was adopted as a result of the many difficulties experienced by the black clergy up to this point and the many complaints against black priests by some southern bishops and whites. Aware of the new policy, Father Dorsey supported those black Catholics in Baltimore who publicly challenged the Josephites on their exclusion policies in the African-American press. These actions further alienated him from the leaders of the Josephite society. John Henry Dorsey died in Baltimore after a long illness resulting from blows to his head inflicted by an irate father—a former convict—angered by the disciplinary action taken by Dorsey against his daughter in the parish school.

John Henry Dorsey's experience as one of the first black Catholic priests in the United States is a witness to the hardships and misunderstanding faced by these priests in this country. Many bishops and priests had little sympathy for the idea of a black Catholic priesthood and gave no support to black priests. As a result of activity by the Holy See a seminary was eventually opened in Mississippi by members of the Society of the Divine Word for the training of African-American men for the priesthood in 1920.

• Information regarding John Henry Dorsey is in Stephen Ochs, "The Ordeal of the Black Priest," *U.S. Catholic Historian* 5 (1986): 45–66. The same author places Dorsey within the context of African-American priests in *Desegregating the Altar: The Josephites and the Struggle for Black Priests, 1871–1960* (1990). For an older look at Dorsey, see Albert Foley, S.J., *God's Men of Color: The Colored Catholic Priests of the United States, 1854–1954* (1955).

CYPRIAN DAVIS

DORSEY, Sarah Anne Ellis (16 Feb. 1829–4 July 1879), writer, was born in Natchez, Mississippi, the daughter of Thomas G. P. Ellis, a wealthy planter, and Mary Magdalen Routh. Although she was born just outside of Natchez on the family plantation, she was raised primarily in Natchez. Her family's wealth enabled her to receive a fine education, which she finished by traveling to England. In 1853 she married Samuel Worthington Dorsey and moved to Louisiana; the couple had no children.

As a devout Episcopalian, Dorsey believed it was her duty to establish a church and a school for the slaves on her plantation. James Davidson, author of *The Living Writers of the South* (1869), described Dorsey as "one of those practical Christian slave-owners, who illustrated the precepts of the creed in her relations to her slaves." He also remarked that after emancipation, Dorsey's former slaves stayed with her and Dorsey continued to teach them each Sunday. In fact, Dorsey's work with her slaves inadvertently led to her writing career. The *Churchman* published a question regarding music in church services, and Dorsey responded with a letter describing her services with her slaves. To a subsequent letter from her the editors affixed the name "Filia Ecclesiae" (daughter of the church); Dorsey liked the name and later used Filia as her pen name.

Dorsey wrote several serial stories that were published in such periodicals as the *Churchman, Church Intelligencer*, and the *Southern Literary Messenger*. She was also the author of four novels and a biography. *Lucia Dare* (1867), her first full-length novel and her least popular, was a war story based on the lives of Philip and Jane Noland of Natchez. Philip Noland, a lieutenant in the U.S. Navy, married Jane against her family's wishes. Shortly after their marriage, he went to sea and never returned. Jane mourned her husband, who was presumed dead, and died soon afterward. In her preface Dorsey explained that as a writer, "I write principally what I see and what I know. I may idealize, but I have little talent for invention." Although *Lucia Dare* was not as well received as her later novels, one reviewer noted, "It shows cleverness, it has vivacity, it contains incident, and is intelligent" (quoted in Davidson, p. 156). *Athalie; or, A Southern Villeggiatura* (1872) and *Panola: A Tale of Louisiana* (1877) were both more popular. In 1869 Dorsey published *Agnes Graham*, a revised version of *Agnes*, which had ap-

peared serially in the *Southern Literary Messenger* in 1863–1864. The New York *Roundtable* printed a favorable review of Dorsey's work:

[Agnes's] whole conduct and bearing through life, her struggles with sorrow which knows no healing and spreads like a pall over her whole existence, are depicted in a manner which shows that the author has an appreciation of genuine pathos which appeals at once to the heart of the readers. . . . "Filia" possesses many of the most important qualifications for a good novelist, and her faults are only those of immaturity. (quoted in Tardy, p. 80)

Although Dorsey's novels received favorable reviews, she is best known for her biography, *Recollections of Henry Watkins Allen* (1866). Allen was a brigadier general in the Confederate army and a former governor of Louisiana. His private secretary wrote of the biography, "It is the most faithful and thorough portrait of him that could be drawn, the best word-likeness that has been produced this century" (quoted in Tardy, p. 78). In *A History of Southern Literature*, Carl Holliday states, "Unlike many American biographies of ante-bellum type," Dorsey's text "is free from far-stretched, extravagant praise, free from all attempts to make a god of an erring human being" (p. 270). Nonetheless, Dorsey clearly wrote from a southern perspective. In the preface to *Recollections*, she argued, "It is very essential, for the sake of Southern honor, and the position which may be accorded us in the future pages of impartial history, that we, Southern people, should also put on record on the files of Time, so far as we can, our version of the terrific struggle" (p. 9).

This statement, as well as her actions before and after the war, appear to justify Hudson Strode's description of Dorsey as a "devout believer in the Confederate cause" (*Jefferson Davis: Private Letters*, p. 445). She spent two years in Texas working in a Confederate hospital. Although her family's wealth was greatly reduced during the war, she never lost faith in the southern cause nor in its leader, Jefferson Davis. In fact, Dorsey served as Davis's amanuensis while he wrote *The Rise and Fall of the Confederate Government* (1881). Davis worked on his manuscript at Dorsey's estate, "Beauvoir." Dorsey arranged in February 1879 to sell Beauvoir to Davis, but when she died of cancer in New Orleans, Davis had made only one payment; however, Dorsey left Beauvoir and most of her assets to Davis.

Dorsey will probably remain a minor figure in history owing to her connection to Jefferson Davis, but her novels have been forgotten, victims of changing tastes that no longer find idealized heroes and complex plots appealing. Nonetheless, Dorsey's work for a time influenced the ideas of southern readers and writers.

• Biographical information about Dorsey can be found in her biography of Henry Watkins Allen as well as in Mary T. Tardy, *The Living Female Writers of the South* (1872), and James W. Davidson, *The Living Writers of the South* (1869). For a critical assessment of her writing, see Charlotte E. Lewis,

"Sarah Anne Dorsey: A Critical Estimate" (M.A. thesis, Louisiana State Univ., 1940), and Van Akin Burd, "A Louisiana Estimate of an 'American Rousseau': Sarah Anne Dorsey on Henry David Thoreau," *Louisiana History* (Summer 1964): 296–309. Brief mentions of Dorsey appear in Hudson Strode, *Jefferson Davis: Tragic Hero* (1964) and *Jefferson Davis: Private Letters, 1823–1889* (1966), and in Ishbel Ross, *First Lady of the South: The Life of Mrs. Jefferson Davis* (1958).

VENETRIA K. PATTON

DORSEY, Stephen Wallace (28 Feb. 1842–20 Mar. 1916), entrepreneur and U.S. senator, was born in Benson, Vermont, the son of John W. Dorsey and Mary (maiden name unknown), farmers. Dorsey's parents, Irish-born Congregationalists, settled in the 1850s in Oberlin, Ohio, where Stephen attended Oberlin College. When the Civil War began in April 1861, he enlisted in an Ohio regiment. Attaining the rank of artillery captain, he saw combat in the western and eastern theaters from Perryville through the fall of Richmond. He served under Generals James A. Garfield and Ulysses S. Grant, with whom his later political career would intertwine. In 1865 he married Helen Mary Wack. They had three children and adopted another.

Attracted to the postwar South like many Union veterans, Dorsey in 1865 took a position as postmaster of Demopolis, Alabama, where he opened a dry goods store. In 1866 he returned to Ohio, where he helped establish the successful Sandusky Tool Company. He engaged in politics as chair of the Erie County Republican Central Committee and as a Sandusky city councilman. In 1871 Ohio and Arkansas investors persuaded him to give up his Sandusky ventures and return South as president of the Arkansas Central Railway, the projected central line in a regional network focused around Helena, Arkansas, and financed in part with public funds. Political favoritism and probably a measure of corruption were features of the Arkansas Central project, as was the case with many Southern railroads with public funding during Reconstruction. Political opponents, however, distorted and exaggerated charges against Dorsey and his partners as a way to discredit the Southern Republican party.

By fall 1872 Dorsey was active in Arkansas Republican politics. Although he had been in the state less than two years, the businessman had received favorable attention for his railroad venture. Republicans turned to Dorsey as an attractive U.S. Senate candidate tied to none of the party's feuding factions and capable of gaining votes from Democratic legislators. Soon after Dorsey's election in January 1873, however, the bipartisan coalition that chose him crumbled. Joseph Brooks, the Liberal Republican candidate for governor, disputed the apparent victory of Dorsey's ally, Republican Elisha Baxter. To secure Democratic support to stay in office, Baxter questioned the constitutionality of state funding for railroads. This compelled Dorsey to join with Republican senator Powell Clayton, who had opposed Dorsey's Senate candidacy, in an attempt to seat Brooks. When the Grant ad-

ministration and Congress refused to intervene, Democrats turned this so-called Brooks-Baxter war into a vehicle for ousting the Republicans altogether and "redeeming" the state in fall 1874.

A virtual lame duck two years into his term and his incomplete railroad in receivership, Dorsey was fated to make little impression on the Senate. He did win notice within his party for effective work with the Republican Congressional Committee during the 1876 campaign. Disaffected by the Rutherford B. Hayes administration's civil service and southern policies, which combined to preclude Dorsey from using patronage to rebuild an Arkansas political base, the senator associated himself with New York senator Roscoe Conkling's patronage-conscious Stalwart Republicans. Dorsey cut his ties to Arkansas when he left the Senate in March 1879. In 1880 Republican leaders attempted to ensure the cooperation of disgruntled Stalwarts in Garfield's presidential run by appointing Dorsey secretary of the National Committee. Praised for "executive qualities" (Marcus, p. 42) even by anti-Stalwart Republicans who suspected his integrity, Dorsey sought to provide Garfield's campaign with a degree of coordination unusual in the Gilded Age's decentralized politics, but historians doubt the efficacy of these efforts.

In February 1881 Vice President-elect Chester A. Arthur encountered much criticism when he appeared to praise questionable features of Dorsey's Indiana campaign during a testimonial dinner at Delmonico's in New York. On becoming president in September 1881, Arthur, determined to rise above his Stalwart background, ordered the vigorous prosecution of Dorsey and eight others in the alleged scheme to overcharge the post office on western mail contracts known as the Star Route affair. In part through a resourceful defense mounted by Dorsey's friend and counsel, the agnostic lecturer Robert G. Ingersoll, Dorsey secured a hung jury in a summer 1882 trial and then an acquittal in a melodramatic retrial that endured from December 1882 through June 1883. A careful study concludes that Dorsey was "certainly guilty" of taking advantage of political connections and legal loopholes to win mail contracts through rigged bids and then having the contracts revised so as to provide fraudulently high payments. But the government weakened its case by portraying the politician as the central mover behind what was really a broad pattern of abuse (Lowry, "Portrait of an Age," p. 417).

After his acquittal, Dorsey hoped to rebuild his personal and political fortunes at a large cattle ranch in Colfax County, New Mexico Territory, that he had acquired while in the Senate. By 1884 Dorsey's operation could ship more than 10,000 head of cattle in a year. The ex-senator constructed an unusual rambling mansion—half log house, half sandstone Gothic fantasy—in which he displayed a European art collection and entertained with an extravagance that must have seemed bizarre in the New Mexico hills. Yet Dorsey proved unsuccessful when he challenged Thomas B. Catron's leadership of the New Mexico Republicans.

Clouds hung over his land titles, which stemmed from a forged Mexican grant that Dorsey may have purchased in good faith. He could not shake off debts incurred in Arkansas and in his Star Route defense. At odds with former partners and dogged by lawsuits, Dorsey converted his mansion into a tuberculosis sanatorium and left New Mexico in the early 1890s. Through mining and other western ventures, Dorsey recouped his finances enough to spend his last years prosperous and respected in Los Angeles, where he died. After his first wife's death in 1897, he had married Laura Bigelow, who died in 1915.

Dorsey left few papers, and he alienated articulate friends such as Ingersoll, who in exasperation over their joint ranching ventures eventually proclaimed Dorsey a "great scoundrel" (Caperton, p. 37). It is difficult, therefore, to delve behind the bleak portrait of an opportunist left by enemies. In a measure of Dorsey's repudiation, Arkansas in 1885 tried to erase evidence of its prior embrace of this Reconstruction senator by changing the name of Dorsey County to Cleveland County.

• Thomas J. Caperton's brief biography, *Rogue* (1978), also serves as a guide to the Dorsey Mansion State Monument in Raton, N.Mex. Sharon K. Lowry's judicious "Portrait of an Age: The Political Career of Stephen W. Dorsey, 1868–1889" (Ph.D. diss., North Texas State Univ., 1980), includes a bibliography of legislative hearings and legal documents through which Dorsey's tribulations and trials may be traced. Dorsey's role in the Republican organization during the 1880 campaign is described in Robert D. Marcus, *Grand Old Party* (1971), and Thomas C. Reeves, *Gentleman Boss: The Life of Chester Alan Arthur* (1975), which also explains the Arthur administration's actions in the Star Route prosecutions. Mark W. Summers, *Railroads, Reconstruction, and the Gospel of Prosperity* (1984), places Dorsey's Arkansas Central project in context. Two articles that consider Dorsey's N.Mex. years are Morris F. Taylor, "Stephen W. Dorsey, Speculator-Cattleman," *New Mexico Historical Review* 49 (Jan. 1974): 27–48; and Lowry, "Mirrors and Blue Smoke: Stephen Dorsey and the Santa Fe Ring in the 1880s," *New Mexico Historical Review* 59 (Oct. 1984): 395–409. Obituaries are in the *Los Angeles Times* and the *Arkansas Gazette*, 21 Mar. 1916.

ALAN LESSOFF

DORSEY, Susan Almira Miller (16 Feb. 1857–5 Feb. 1946), educator, was born in the Finger Lakes region of New York, near Penn Yan, the daughter of James Miller and Hannah Benedict, dairy farmers of English and Huguenot descent. Her parents encouraged their daughter's intellectual curiosity beyond the education provided by Penn Yan's public elementary school. She attended Penn Yan Academy and Vassar College, where she earned a B.A. in classics in 1877. After graduation, she moved to Chambersburg, Pennsylvania, to teach Latin and Greek at Wilson College, a Presbyterian school for women, returning to Vassar the next year as an instructor of classics.

In 1881 she married Patrick William Dorsey, a Baptist minister, and moved to Los Angeles. Patrick, a graduate of the University of Rochester, became a pastor of the city's First Baptist Church, and Susan performed her duties as a minister's wife and also joined the newly formed Los Angeles chapter of the Women's Christian Temperance Union to work for social reform. She returned to teaching in 1893 at a short-lived Baptist institution in Los Angeles. The couple's only child was born in 1888. For reasons unknown, in 1894 Patrick left his wife, taking their son with him. Mother and son corresponded over the years but were not close. Little else is known of Dorsey's family life, although a niece lived in Los Angeles and was with her when she died.

In 1896 the 39-year-old Dorsey began her association with the Los Angeles public schools. Laws prohibited the board of education from hiring married women as teachers, although it made some exceptions, and the records fail to indicate whether the Dorseys divorced or not. Her first classroom assignment was teaching classics at Los Angeles High School. She rose quickly through the ranks, and in 1902 she became vice principal and in 1913 the district assistant superintendent. In 1914 the Southern Section of the California Teacher's Association elected her president, and in January 1920 she became superintendent of the Los Angeles city schools. Nationwide, over 90 percent of elementary teachers were female, yet few women had achieved such success in the male-dominated profession of school administration. Joining Ella Flagg Young of Chicago, Dorsey became the second woman to head a large urban district.

For the next decade Dorsey shaped the Los Angeles public schools. She believed that the role of educators was to train children to become useful citizens and to prepare them for their life's work. She focused her attention on three areas: Americanization of immigrants, vocational education, and moral training. The year before Dorsey took office, Los Angeles had a school population of 90,609; nine years later when she retired, it had risen to 222,670. Many of the arrivals were non–English-speaking immigrants, many from Mexico. To ease the problems of assimilating the growing number of the city's foreign-born, Dorsey expanded Americanization programs for children in neighborhood schools and for adults in evening schools, and she provided district support for the Home Teacher Act, a state law encouraging school districts to provide certified teachers for classes in English and American culture in the homes and workplaces of immigrant women. She fought off conservative attempts to dismantle Americanization programs by creating separate school departments, one for immigrant education—to continue and expand social services such as school lunches, after-school playgrounds, and home teachers—and another for naturalization—to provide citizenship training. Her tenure coincided with the end of the Progressive Era, when state and national conservatism was on the rise, and a reluctance to rely on government for social reforms was increasing. Dorsey argued that Los Angeles schools had more than their share of immigrants and that the responsibility of educating them should be shared by the state and federal governments.

Although Dorsey had not initiated vocational or industrial education, she wholeheartedly supported these programs. Under her stewardship, Los Angeles citizens passed multimillion-dollar school bond drives in 1920, 1922, and 1924, providing funding for new schools, including trade schools that emphasized vocational training. At the same time, she insisted that schooling offer all students the basic curriculum that included moral guidance to shape their characters and help them on their way to self-sufficient adulthood. To this end, she expanded student government, school assemblies, and school-related clubs and activities.

Dorsey had continued her predecessor's policy of intelligence testing, but she was highly critical of slavish reliance on test results as indicators of intelligence. In an address to the National Congress of Parents and Teachers in 1927, she noted that the tests did not measure intelligence but achievement, not mental ability but mental experience.

Although Dorsey hired some nonwhite teachers, including the second Chinese-American teacher in the system, and increased the numbers of African-American teachers, she accepted the prevailing ideology that sanctioned racial separation. She participated in the deliberate segregation of Mexican and African-American children and denied some qualified teachers positions because of their race.

Dorsey's superintendency was not without controversy. In 1923 she became embroiled in a bitter school-board election campaign pitting elementary teachers against principals. At stake were policy issues that included the continuance of social services, curriculum reconstruction that promised efficiency, and teachers' salaries. Many teachers felt Dorsey had allied too closely with the city's political and fiscal conservatives, yet her strong commitment to higher salaries, tenure, and sabbatical leaves helped overcome those reservations, and few teachers openly attacked her. Conservatives won the election, and Dorsey's position was not challenged again.

Dorsey retired in 1929 but continued her vigorous life. A lifelong Republican, she supported Alfred Landon's presidency in 1936 and was outspoken in her distrust for Democratic gubernatorial candidate Culbert L. Olson in 1938 for what she called his "lack of understanding" of educators and the children they teach. She criticized Eleanor Roosevelt's suggestion, made in the depths of the depression, that school districts hire male over female teachers to support beleaguered families. To Dorsey, and many female teachers, this course of action was anathema. She was an honorary member of the Los Angeles Women's Club and, like many of its members, supported universal peace organizations. She served as chair of the Southern California Committee on the Cause and Cure of War and was vice president of the Women's Law Observance Association. She never ceased her interest in educational policy and administration. She participated in the movement to consolidate smaller California school districts and served as a trustee to Scripps College and the University of Redlands. During her retirement years, she was an editorial consultant to the journal of the National Education Association. In 1934 the association named her its honorary life president, an honor it had bestowed only once before, on John Dewey. In 1937 a new high school in Los Angeles was named for her, and she was present at its dedication. She died in Los Angeles.

• Dorsey is profiled in Georgette F. McGregor, "The Educational Career of Susan M. Dorsey" (Ph.D. diss., Univ. of California, Los Angeles, 1949). Dorsey's educational views can be found in her many articles and addresses, including "The Place of the Junior College in Public Education," *Journal of the National Education Association* 12 (Sept. 1923): 265–66; "A Defense of Youth," *Journal of the National Education Association* 15 (June 1926): 177; "Mrs. Pierce and Mrs. Dorsey Discuss Matters before the Principals' Club, February 12, 1923," *Los Angeles Teachers' and Principals' School Journal* (Mar. 1923): 58–61; and *Los Angeles Examiner*, 27 May 1927. See also James M. Guinn, *A History of California*, vol. 3 (1915); John S. McGroaty, *Los Angeles*, vol. 3 (1921); and Judith R. Raftery, *Land of Fair Promise: Politics and Reform in Los Angeles Schools, 1885–1941* (1992). An obituary is in the *Los Angeles Times*, 6 Feb. 1946.

JUDITH R. RAFTERY

DORSEY, Thomas Andrew (1 July 1899–23 Jan. 1993), blues performer, gospel singer, and composer, was born in Villa Rica, Georgia, the son of Thomas Madison Dorsey, a preacher, and Etta Plant Spencer. Dorsey's mother, whose first husband had died, owned approximately fifty acres of farm land. Dorsey lived in somewhat trying circumstances as his parents moved first to Atlanta and Forsyth, Georgia, and then back to Villa Rica during the first four years of his life. In Villa Rica the Dorsey family settled into a rural lifestyle supported by marginal farming that was slightly mitigated by his father's pastoral duties.

Though economically pressed, Dorsey's parents found enough money to purchase an organ, and it was on this instrument that their young son began to play music at around six years of age. Dorsey was exposed not only to the religious music that pervaded his home but also to the secular music—especially the emerging blues tradition—that encompassed the music universe of a young black American growing up in rural Georgia in the early twentieth century. His experience with secular music came through his friends as well as his uncle Phil Plant, who picked the guitar and wandered across southern Georgia as a bard. His mother's brother-in-law Corrie M. Hindsman, a more respectable member of the local black establishment, gave Thomas a rudimentary formal music education, including singing out of the shape-note hymnals and learning some of the antebellum spirituals.

In 1908 the family moved to Atlanta after Dorsey's parents finally tired of the lack of opportunities available to black Americans living in rural Georgia. Both worked at a variety of menial jobs while the elder Dorsey occasionally also worked as a guest preacher. Atlanta's higher cost of living meant a decline in social and economic status, however, and young Thomas dropped out of school after the fourth grade. He slowly became part of the commercial music scene that revolved around Decatur Street and the Eighty-one Theater in particular. By his mid-teens Dorsey was regularly working as a pianist at the clubs and at local Saturday night stomps, house parties, and dances sponsored by organizations such as the Odd Fellows.

For three years, between the summers of 1916 and 1919, Dorsey shuttled between Atlanta and Chicago in search of more lucrative and steady musical employment. He was principally a blues pianist who occasionally performed with small combos that played jazz, and well into the early 1920s Dorsey was still struggling to survive on his meager earnings from music. Although he attended the 1921 National Baptist Convention in Chicago (his Uncle Joshua invited his nephew to accompany him) and after the convention became music director of Chicago's New Hope Baptist Church, Dorsey remained committed to the secular world. He was in a good position to cash in on this music when the blues records of Bessie Smith, Alberta Hunter, and Gertrude "Ma" Rainey gained popularity in the mid-1920s. For several years he served as Rainey's pianist and arranger, touring the country playing tent shows and vaudeville stages. In 1928 he teamed with Tampa Red, and they soon had a hit with "It's Tight Like That"; until 1932 the duo earned a steady living playing on stage and recording for the Vocalion label. Dorsey also worked as a music demonstrator in Chicago music stores from 1928 on and as an arranger and session organizer for Brunswick and Vocalion records.

Dorsey's personal life had changed in August 1925 when he married Nettie Harper, who had recently arrived in Chicago from Philadelphia. He was given to occasional bouts with depression, and his marriage helped to stabilize him. When these periods descended upon him he turned not only to Nettie but also to his own religious upbringing. As early as 1922 Dorsey began publishing sacred songs in addition to blues. His 1926 composition, "If You See My Savior, Tell Him That You Saw Me," came during one of his depressive periods and is perhaps the first "gospel blues" piece ever published. Dorsey pioneered this genre by combining sacred lyrics with the harmonic structure and form of the popular blues songs. In 1928 Dorsey met and mentored seventeen-year-old Mahalia Jackson, one of the first singers he knew who was able to combine the emotional feeling of blues with the sentiments of his new gospel songs.

Almost exactly seven years after their marriage, Nettie died in childbirth, followed within a day by their infant son, their only child. Dorsey fell into deep melancholy that lasted for months. He finally started to climb out of his depression by writing "Take My Hand, Precious Lord," and from that point until his own death Dorsey devoted his life to gospel performing, composing, and organizations. During the decade after his wife's death, Dorsey worked tirelessly to promote gospel music, first in Chicago and then across the United States.

As early as a year before Nettie's passing Dorsey had been turning more and more of his attention to the sacred music realm. He founded and helped to direct the first gospel choir at Chicago's Ebenezer Baptist Church in late 1931. One year later Dorsey, along with gospel singer Sallie Martin, was instrumental in establishing the National Convention of Gospel Choirs and Choruses, formed in response to the steadily growing number of gospel choruses. These proved to be popular, though controversial, innovations within the black-American church. The old-line, more conservative mainstream church members proved resistant to change; they protested the showmanship that accompanied these groups' programs and were appalled by the clapping, highly syncopated rhythms, choreographed movement, and overt emotionalism that Dorsey instilled into the gospel choruses with which he worked. Undeterred, though sometimes troubled by the criticism he received, Dorsey's final major contribution during this early period was to open the Thomas A. Dorsey Gospel Songs Music Publishing Company. This fledgling company sold thousands of copies of early gospel songs for ten cents apiece, disseminating them mainly at local churches and the early annual meetings of the National Convention of Gospel Choirs and Choruses.

Dorsey worked tirelessly over the next two decades in service to the growth of gospel blues and the organizations that he helped found. He traveled across the country teaching workshops, leading choruses, and occasionally singing, all the while retaining his Chicago base. He published scores of sacred songs during this period, including "There'll Be Peace in the Valley" (1938), "Hide Me in Thy Bosom" (1939), "Ev'ry Day Will Be Sunday By and By" (1946), and "I'm Climbing Up the Rough Side of the Mountain" (1951). In 1940 he married Kathryn Mosley, with whom he had two children, and in the 1960s and 1970s he served as an assistant pastor at the Pilgrim church.

Slowed by age and the desire to stay closer to his Chicago home, Dorsey became less prolific over the last four decades of his life, composing fewer than twenty songs. Throughout his life Dorsey remained proud of his work in blues and of his guidance of Mahalia Jackson early in a career that eventually touched millions of Americans, black and white. By the late 1950s pop singers Pat Boone and Elvis Presley had underscored Dorsey's impact on modern gospel music through their influential recordings of "Peace in the Valley" and other Dorsey-inspired compositions. The 1982 documentary film *Say Amen, Somebody* pays warm tribute to Dorsey and other gospel pioneers. During the final years of his life Dorsey became recognized as the patriarch of the gospel blues movement, which he lived to see from its inception to its widespread acceptance today. After several years of severely diminished health, he died in Chicago.

• For more information on the life and career of Thomas Dorsey, see Michael Harris, *The Rise of Gospel Blues—The Music of Thomas Andrew Dorsey in the Urban Church* (1992), and Robert M. W. Dixon and John Godrich, *Blues and Gospel Records, 1902–1943* (1982). An obituary is in the *New York Times*, 25 Jan. 1993.

KIP LORNELL

DORSEY, Tommy. *See* Dorsey, Jimmy, and Tommy Dorsey.

DOS PASSOS, John (14 Jan. 1896–28 Sept. 1970), writer, was born in Chicago, Illinois, the son of John Randolph Dos Passos, a lawyer, and Lucy Addison Sprigg Madison. His parents were married in 1910, when his father's first wife died, and in 1912 the boy took his father's name of Dos Passos; before that he was known as John Roderigo Madison. As an illegitimate child he had lived a rootless life, traveling much in Europe with his mother. She died in 1915. The necessary secrecy of his boyhood, the mixture of admiration and fear Dos Passos felt toward his powerful father—who was both an important corporate lawyer and the author of books on trusts and the stock market—and his dependence on his beautiful, often unhappy southern mother affected him deeply. A timid boy, Dos Passos found excitement in reading, studying languages, and observing the art of the time; he discovered his greatest joy in writing. His early poems, with those of E. E. Cummings and others, appeared in 1917, shortly after his graduation from Harvard, in the collection *Eight Harvard Poets*.

The grandson of a Portuguese immigrant, Dos Passos led a privileged life, graduating from Choate before entering Harvard. He nevertheless defined himself as an outsider, an "Ishmael" among his Harvard friends. Fascinated by the common American culture, he tried to become part of it rather than the elite society he was immersed in. In his writing he analyzed his love-hate relationship with the traditions of American life and consistently questioned the American dream, in novels ranging from *One Man's Initiation* (1917) and *Three Soldiers* (1921), with their bitter antiwar sentiment, to the portraits of bewildered college students in *Streets of Night* (1923) and the modern urban citizen in *Manhattan Transfer* (1925).

Serving with the Norton-Harjes Ambulance Service in Italy, Dos Passos knew firsthand the inhumane destruction of World War I. He also thought he understood the implicit inhumanity of capitalism and, during the 1920s, was much attracted by the Russian experiment. Like others of his generation, he protested the arrest of Nicola Sacco and Bartolomeo Vanzetti, two anarchists charged with murder and widely regarded as martyrs. Dos Passos himself was arrested during a protest march before their execution. In 1927 he published his defense of them, *Facing the Chair: Story of the Americanization of Two Foreignborn Workmen*. Partly because of his disappointment with the American system of justice and partly because of his aesthetic interest in Expressionist drama and the films of Sergei Eisenstein, he visited Russia in 1928 but returned to the United States feeling that he had escaped the totalitarian regime. He later referred to his enthusiasm for Communism as "illusion" and commented, "In the end we were to discover . . . that Marxism, hardened into a crusading quasi-religion, turned loose more brutal aggressions than the poor old capitalists ever dreamed of " (preface, *One Man's Initiation* [1917; repr. 1968]). Even in the midst of his interest in the Russian experiment, Dos Passos maintained his close friendships with the writers and artists from his Paris years during the 1920s—Ernest Hemingway, Gerald Murphy and Sarah Murphy, Blaise Cendrars, Zelda Fitzgerald and F. Scott Fitzgerald—and could frequently be found at the Murphys' home in the South of France.

During the 1920s and 1930s Dos Passos lived by his writing, publishing a collection of poems, travel essays collected into books, and the three plays that were important to the development of American theater: *The Garbage Man: A Parade with Shouting* (1926) (produced as *The Moon Is a Gong*), *Airways, Inc.* (1928), and *Fortune Heights* (1933). Strongly influenced by the work of John Howard Lawson and by E. E. Cummings's play *Him*, Dos Passos drew into his plays elements from the real world and created remarkable pastiches of popular culture. His most important work began shortly after his involvement in theater, however, when he used that dramatic montage technique of juxtaposing disparate elements in his fiction.

The first of his *U.S.A.* volumes, *The 42nd Parallel*, appeared in 1930 to enthusiastic comments about his innovative modernist techniques and his biting criticism of various American ways. The many characters that were to wind through the three volumes of *U.S.A.* represented all aspects of American attitude and life, from women who had become interior decorators to avoid the boredom of traditional women's roles, to public relations men, pilots, factory workers, secretaries, and the politically involved. Juxtaposed with these stories about fictional characters from modern life were three other kinds of narrative: (1) the prose poem "biographies," portraits of Thomas Edison, Henry Ford, Isadora Duncan, and other living people who Dos Passos felt represented American culture in important ways; (2) the "newsreels," Dos Passos's collages of news headlines, lines from popular songs, and catchphrases of the time combined with ironic commentaries on the United States in the twentieth century; and (3) the impressionistic "Camera Eye" sections, haunting prose poems that drew largely from Dos Passos's own life and created his consciousness as the narrative observer of the events in the trilogy. The blended and interrupted story lines created mock confusion similar to the narrative effect of his earlier *Manhattan Transfer*, but much more intense. By the time the other two volumes of the trilogy appeared (*1919* in 1932 and *The Big Money* in 1936), many readers had abandoned the fiction because of its sheer difficulty; the trilogy became a landmark of American modernism, however, and led Jean-Paul Sartre and other writers worldwide to consider Dos Passos as important a writer as Ernest Hemingway or William Faulkner.

Dos Passos's *U.S.A.* trilogy also appeared to place him firmly in the camp of Marxist and Communist critics and readers, and as a result his work was consistently praised by *New Masses* and other Marxist journals. Because he had criticized much about American capitalism, Dos Passos was seen as a Communist—which he never was. Dos Passos was intent on justice, not on political affiliation. He went to Harlan County to write about the plight of the Kentucky miners; he reported on strikes in Michigan; he wrote about the Scottsboro boys, nine young black men accused of raping two white women; he covered the veterans' marches in Washington and Chicago; he actively participated in protests to effect social change; but his involvement did not necessarily imply political allegiances. In his later writing he was as critical of the injustice of labor unions as he had been earlier of the abuses of capitalism. His empathy was with the individual person who was trying to live a respectable life and trying to make it in a competitive system, regardless of what skills or ambitions had been given to him or her. Unlike most other American modernist authors, Dos Passos created several convincing women characters and was interested throughout his career in the characterization of women.

For all the importance of his fiction, Dos Passos earned much of his living through travel writing and journalism. In 1922 he published *Rosinante to the Road Again*; in 1927, *Orient Express*; in 1934, *In All Countries*; in 1937, *The Villagers Are the Heart of Spain*; and in 1938, *Journeys between Wars*. As the world political situation intensified, he became more involved in its currents and spent time in Spain during the Spanish Civil War. His disillusion at the execution of the attaché José Robles, a good friend, led to his break with Ernest Hemingway, one of his best friends. The situation was complicated by the fact that in 1929 he had married Katharine ("Katy") Smith, one of Hemingway's boyhood friends from Michigan. (Dos Passos settled his score with Hemingway in his portrayal of George Elbert Warner in his 1951 novel, *Chosen Country*.) The primary motivation of Dos Passos's life was his art: most of his good friends were writers and painters, and most of the events of his life were grounded in his writing. His wife was also a writer, and his comparatively late marriage allowed him to continue the primacy of his identity as writer.

Political events as the world moved toward fascism disturbed Dos Passos, and he turned in his writing to somewhat utopian subjects. He began the series of writings on American political figures that would dominate his late years. Most notable are his many books on Thomas Jefferson, but he also wrote about Tom Paine in 1940 and, in 1941, various other American political philosophers. He also began what would become another trilogy of novels, publishing *Adventures of a Young Man* in 1939. In this novel of a disillusioned young American Communist in Spain, Dos Passos was able to vent his anger at the blindness of political enthusiasts. The two other volumes of this *District of Columbia* trilogy—*Number One* (1943) and *The Grand Design* (1949)—were poorly received, and from this time until his death Dos Passos's writing received only sporadic attention. The magical combination of technique and subject matter that had occurred in *Manhattan Transfer* and the *U.S.A.* trilogy was not repeated, and the great quantity of writing Dos Passos did in his last twenty years is now almost entirely out of print.

Dos Passos always called himself a "chronicler" of American life, and his turn to outright history late in his career legitimates that definition. In his probing studies of historical figures like *The Men Who Made the Nation* (1957), his biographies of Jefferson, and such historical studies as *Mr. Wilson's War* (1962) and *The Shackles of Power: Three Jeffersonian Decades* (1966), Dos Passos located and presented the qualities that he thought made America a viable and promising experiment. In fact, some of the power of his earlier fiction came back into his last writing. In 1961, *Midcentury* was a successful amalgam of events and trends in America as Dos Passos continued to observe his country; in 1964 he collected his essays in *Occasions and Protests*; and in 1966 he published his autobiography, *The Best Times: An Informal Memoir*. He continued to write about foreign cultures as a way of earning money and in 1963 published *Brazil on the Move*, followed by *The Portugal Story: Three Centuries of Exploration and Discovery* (1969) and *Easter Island: Island of Enigmas* (1971). Perhaps the best of his late work is the posthumously published *Century's Ebb: The Thirteenth Chronicle* (1975). Here Dos Passos uses the moon shot as the luminous image of American promise, the utopian glimpse of new worlds to explore and inhabit.

Dos Passos's writing career expressed the kind of spirit his life itself evinced: indefatigable promise. When his beloved wife Katy was killed in the same 1947 car accident in which he lost an eye, Dos Passos—in spite of intense depression—kept writing. In 1949 he married Elizabeth Holdridge, and the next year their child, Lucy, was born. For the next twenty years he lived a happy and stable family life in Virginia, enjoying his career as both writer and family man. His increasing turn to conservatism was mediated by his sense of humor as he watched the promise he had believed inexhaustible slowly grind America into the "two countries" the wandering "Vag" of *U.S.A.* had watched so sadly.

• Most of Dos Passos's manuscripts and letters are housed at the Alderman Library at the University of Virginia in Charlottesville. Other materials are at the Houghton Library, Harvard University, and the Beinecke Library Collection of American Literature, Yale University. David Sanders, *John Dos Passos, A Comprehensive Bibliography* (1987), is the authoritative bibliography; Townsend Ludington, *John Dos Passos: Twentieth Century Odyssey* (1980), is the authoritative biography. Other biographies include Melvin Landsberg, *Dos Passos's Path to U.S.A.: A Political Biography, 1912–1936* (1972), and Virginia Spencer Carr, *Dos Passos* (1984). Ludington has also edited Dos Passos's letters (*The Fourteenth Chronicle: Letters and Diaries of John Dos Passos* [1973]); Donald Pizer has edited *John Dos Passos: The Major*

Nonfictional Prose (1988), Dos Passos's largely uncollected pieces from 1914 to 1971; and Barry Maine has edited *Dos Passos: The Critical Heritage* (1988).

Critical studies include John H. Wrenn, *John Dos Passos* (1961); John D. Brantley, *The Fiction of John Dos Passos* (1968); George J. Becker, *John Dos Passos* (1974); Linda W. Wagner, *Dos Passos: Artist as American* (1979); Robert C. Rosen, *John Dos Passos: Politics and the Writer* (1981); Michael Clark, *Dos Passos's Early Fiction, 1912–1938* (1987); and Donald Pizer, *Dos Passos' U.S.A.: A Critical Study* (1988). See also Blanche H. Gelfant, *American City Novel* (1954); Stanley Cooperman, *World War I and the American Novel* (1967); and John Diggins, *Up from Communism: Conservative Odysseys in American Intellectual History* (1975).

LINDA WAGNER-MARTIN

DOSTER, Frank (19 Jan. 1847–25 Feb. 1933), jurist and reform advocate, was born in Morgan County, Virginia (now W.Va.), the son of Alfred Doster and Rachel Doyle, farmers. The family moved to Clinton County, Indiana, in 1848. In early 1864, while still a teenager, Doster joined the Eleventh Indiana Cavalry in the Civil War, seeing much action in Tennessee and Mississippi. After the war, his regiment patrolled the Santa Fe Trail in Kansas in 1865. Mustered out as a corporal in the fall of that year, he returned to Indiana, where he studied at Thornton Academy and attended, but did not graduate from, Benton Law Institute and the state university. In 1870 he moved to Monticello, Illinois, was admitted to the state bar, and married Caroline Riddle. They had seven children, five of whom survived to adulthood.

In the following year the young couple settled in Marion (then called Marion Centre), Kansas. There Doster built up a moderately prosperous practice. Later in 1871 he was elected as a Republican to a term in the state legislature. Thereafter Doster embraced a number of radical movements and in 1878 ran unsuccessfully for Kansas attorney general and the U.S. Congress on the Greenback ticket. He was also briefly affiliated with the Union Labor party in 1879. After publishing an article in *Woodhull and Claflin's Weekly* in 1874, "God and the Constitution," in which he denied that the United States was officially a Christian nation or that its laws were derived from the Christian religion, his opponents branded him, unfairly, as an atheist, and as an advocate of free love for publishing in a weekly run by Victoria Woodhull and her sister Tennessee Claflin, both open advocates of free love. While by no means an orthodox Christian, Doster kept an open mind on religious questions. In his private life he was devoted to his wife and family. He was a charter member of the Kansas Bar Association, was active in the Grand Army of the Republic, and continued to practice law.

Despite Doster's association with advanced reform measures and groups, Republican governor John A. Martin appointed him judge of the new twenty-fifth judicial district in 1887. With the support of most of the district's bar, he won a full term later that year. When he sought reelection in 1891, he was by then thoroughly identified with the People's (Populist) party and seen by many as a dangerous radical. A coalition of Republicans and Democrats succeeded in defeating him.

Emerging soon thereafter as one of the most articulate spokesmen of Kansas Populism, Doster gave his enemies further ammunition when in 1891 he delivered an address in which he asserted that "the rights of the user are paramount to the rights of the owner." He explained then and later that he meant that the owners of property dedicated to a public use, notably railroads, were subject to regulation—a principle that the U.S. Supreme Court had endorsed in *Munn v. Illinois* (1876). Over the years his expansive interpretation of the *Munn* decision's public interest doctrine became the cornerstone of his advocacy of a socialistic society.

Doster made an unsuccessful bid for election to the U.S. Senate in 1893. During the administration of Populist governor Lorenzo D. Lewelling (1893–1895) Doster argued the Populist side in litigation arising out of the "Legislative War" of 1893 and served as the state's judge advocate general. In 1896 he was elected chief justice of the state supreme court on the Populist-Democratic fusion ticket. During the campaign, *Emporia Gazette* editor William Allen White denounced him as a "shabby, wild-eyed rattle-brained fanatic."

On the bench Doster proved not to be the extremist the Republicans warned against, but he consistently voted to uphold reform legislation, such as antitrust laws, railroad regulation, and measures to protect labor. For two years of his six-year term (1897–1903) he and fellow Populist Stephen H. Allen formed a majority on the three-man court. But when Allen did not win reelection in 1898 and the court was enlarged to seven members, Doster became a one-man minority. With the collapse of the People's party he was defeated in a try for a second term, despite support from several Republicans who had come to respect his judicial abilities and fairness.

After leaving the court Doster took up private practice in Topeka, serving for a time as an attorney for the Missouri Pacific railroad. Although he found a new political home in the Democratic party (and made a halfhearted attempt to be the party's candidate in the 1914 race for the U.S. Senate), he called himself a socialist. By attendance of party gatherings and an occasional speech Doster championed most of the major reform causes of the early twentieth century, including regulation of business and woman suffrage. In the 1920s he espoused internationalism, strongly backing America's entry into the League of Nations, and spoke out against bigotry, religious intolerance, and prohibition. Like many other Civil War veterans, he enthusiastically supported the Spanish-American War and World War I. He did, however, condemn overseas imperialism, denouncing American acquisition of the Philippine Islands in a 1901 article in *The Arena*.

In common with many of his generation, Doster's political and economic views were eclectic; his thinking was a blend of the ideas of such eighteenth- and nineteenth-century thinkers as Jean-Jacques Rousseau, Louis Blanc, Elisha Mulford, and Karl Marx. In his later years he defended communism and said that he was a "communist in economic belief." Doster served the cause of American reform until the end: he suffered a fatal stroke in Topeka while helping the Kansas legislature draft a bill to protect tenant farmers from landlord abuses.

Shy and withdrawn in his social relations, Doster gave others an erroneous impression of coldness. Perhaps with the intention of shocking his audiences, he employed a rhetorical style that often made his views appear more radical than they were. Nevertheless, his commitment to reform was genuine and consistent.

• Michael J. Brodhead, *Persevering Populist: The Life of Frank Doster* (1969), is a full-length biography. For valuable interpretations and further information see also O. Gene Clanton, *Kansas Populism: Ideas and Men* (1969); Norman Pollack, *The Just Polity: Populism, Law, and Human Welfare* (1987); and R. Douglas Hurt, "Populist Judicial Response to Reform" (Ph.D. diss., Kansas State Univ., 1975). Obituaries are in the *Kansas City* (Mo.) *Star*, 27 Feb. 1933, and the *Topeka Capital*, 26 Feb. 1933.

MICHAEL J. BRODHEAD

DOTEN, Alfred (21 July 1829–12 Nov. 1903), journalist and diarist, was born in Plymouth, Massachusetts, the son of Samuel Doten, a ship captain, and Rebecca Bradford. The family was socially stable and financially comfortable, and the children were well educated. Alfred was briefly apprenticed to a carpenter when his schooling was completed and also spent a summer fishing for cod on the Grand Banks. In 1849, attracted by the news of gold, he took ship for California as a crew member.

Once in California, Doten prospected for gold as a placer miner, without much success, and worked at a variety of other jobs, including farming and ranching, and he became an occasional correspondent to a Plymouth newspaper. In 1863 Doten crossed the Sierra Nevada eastward to participate in the silver boom of Nevada's Comstock Lode, first in Como and then in Virginia City. Of all of his jobs, journalism was the one that he found most agreeable, and he served as correspondent for several California newspapers as well as some western Nevada papers in the Comstock mining region, particularly the *Como Sentinel*, the *Virginia Daily Union*, the *Territorial Enterprise*, and the *Gold Hill News*. The last paper increasingly occupied him, and in 1872 he bought it, becoming its owner and editor. Under Doten, the *News* became one of the leading Comstock newspapers.

Doten's journalistic involvement with the Comstock made him an intimate of its society. He was a close associate of such well-known Comstock journalists as Mark Twain, Dan De Quille, Joe Goodman, Denis McCarthy, Rollin Daggett, Sam Davis, and Jim Townsend. As his reputation and influence grew he also became friendly with the powerful political and financial figures of the area: William Sharon, Adolph Sutro, Senator John P. Jones, and the "silver king," John Mackay. An ardent Republican, Doten was active in the Nevada party and held a variety of positions in it, such as delegate to the state convention of 1876 and secretary to various county conventions. In 1873, at the peak of his success, he married Mary Stoddard, with whom he had four children.

By 1878 Doten's career began to decline. Like many Comstockers, Doten had invested heavily in mining stocks. As long as the region prospered, his stocks made him financially comfortable. But when the price of silver began to drop, the Comstock mines began to lose their value. Doten remained mistakenly optimistic and continued to buy stocks until he went so deeply into debt that he eventually lost the *Gold Hill News*. Hired as editor by the new owner, Doten resisted direction and was fired in 1881. He subsequently moved in 1882 to Austin, Nevada, where he briefly edited the *Reese River Reveille* until his unsuitability for that post became apparent. Always a hard drinker, Doten now became a drunkard. He served as occasional correspondent for the *Territorial Enterprise*, one of many part-time and sometimes menial jobs he took to raise cash. In 1885 friends arranged a political job for him in Carson City. It did not last long, nor did any of the other various jobs he subsequently obtained, only a few of which were in journalism. He returned to drinking, and his family paid him to stay in Carson City, away from them in Virginia City. Despite some flashes of his old spirit and demonstrations of his former journalistic ability, he steadily declined into a mockery of his former self and died alone in a rented room in Carson City.

Most of what Doten published was ephemeral journalism. At his best, he was a versatile and highly competent reporter and a respected editorial voice. He also wrote some short stories that showed ability. Of more lasting value are the memoirs and historical reports he composed at various times of his career. Because of his wide acquaintance with personalities and events, his accounts are unusually detailed and accurate.

The most important single work of Doten's career, however, was nothing that he wrote for publication but instead, unsuspectedly, his diary. He faithfully and frankly recorded in it the day-to-day events in his life and abodes from the time in 1849 when he boarded ship to leave Plymouth until the last night of his life. The entries reveal Doten as the diarist of the Comstock, perceptively and vividly reporting his own foibles and amours as well as somehow selecting and boiling down to their quintessence the mundane activities, successes, hopes, fears, and tragedies of the times and places his entries cover. The diary manuscripts traveled from one family attic to another for half a century, were then purchased by a dealer of western Americana, and were finally acquired by the University of Nevada in 1961, which had them edited and published in 1973. The diary is a unique, detailed, extensive, fascinating, well-written, and invaluable record of Old West life in California and western Nevada. Read in its entirety, it is a better portrait of Doten than any biography could possibly be. It is hardly possible that Doten had any notion that he was composing a classic document of American history. But now that we have it, this eminently personal and candid labor of daily routine is indispensable to an understanding of the Comstock and its age.

• The main archive of Doten papers is at the University of Nevada–Reno, which also has microfilms of some of the newspapers for which Doten worked. The nearby Nevada Historical Society also has microfilms of the *Gold Hill News* and other Comstock newspapers. A substantial treatment of Doten is *The Journals of Alfred Doten, 1849–1903*, ed. Walter Van Tilburg Clark (3 vols., 1973). Before the publication of this excellent edition, Doten was referred to only fleetingly, superficially, and anecdotally in such historical discussions of the Comstock as Samuel Post Davis, ed., *The History of Nevada* (2 vols., 1913), and Wells Drury's autobiographical memoir, *An Editor on the Comstock Lode* (1936). Information on Comstock personalities, including Doten, may also be found in the Bancroft Library of the University of California, Berkeley, and in the archives of the Mark Twain Project.

LAWRENCE I. BERKOVE

DOUBLEDAY, Abner (26 June 1819–26 Jan. 1893), soldier and reputed inventor of baseball, was born in Ballston Spa, New York, the son of Ulysses F. Doubleday, a newspaper editor and later a congressman, and Hester Donnelly. He apparently was educated at schools in Auburn, New York, and Cooperstown, New York. In 1838 he received an appointment to the U.S. Military Academy at West Point. Graduating in 1842, ranked twenty-fifth in a class of fifty-six, Doubleday was commissioned a lieutenant in the First Artillery Regiment. During the Mexican War he served at Monterrey and Buena Vista under General Zachary Taylor, and in 1847 he was promoted to first lieutenant.

After the war Doubleday served on inspection boards, including a commission in 1852–1853 that investigated what proved to be fraudulent claims pertaining to the wartime destruction of mines. In January 1853 he married Mary Hewitt; it is unknown if they had any children. He also participated in military campaigns against the Apaches in the Southwest (1854–1855) and the Seminoles in Florida (1856–1858). Promoted to captain in 1855, Doubleday spent the next few years at various posts along the Atlantic Coast. In December 1861, when South Carolina seceded from the Union, he was second in command of the U.S. garrison under Major Robert Anderson at Fort Moultrie, in Charleston Harbor. Because Fort Moultrie was considered vulnerable to attack, the garrison evacuated it in December 1860. Doubleday led the first company of soldiers who journeyed to Fort Sumter, a partially constructed installation on an artificial island in the harbor. On 12 April 1861 the first shots of the Civil War were fired in a Confederate bombardment on Fort Sumter. Doubleday later claimed that he aimed and ordered the fort's first retaliatory cannon shot, writing that in doing so "I had no feeling of self-reproach, for I fully believed that the contest was inevitable." After the ensuing skirmish, which lasted a day and a half, the Federals, their food and supplies exhausted, were allowed by the Confederates to leave the fort.

In May 1861, following a short tenure in the defenses of Washington, D.C., Doubleday was promoted to major and given command of the Seventeenth Infantry Brigade in the makeshift Union army that had been organized to check Confederate incursions into the Shenandoah Valley. In February 1862 he was appointed brigadier general of volunteers and assigned a brigade command in the First Division of General Irvin McDowell's First Corps. After engaging the Confederates in an August 1862 skirmish on the Rappahannock River, Doubleday's brigade fought in the second battle of Manassas at the end of that month. There it acquitted itself well in two engagements near Groveton, Virginia. The following month, during the battle of South Mountain, General John Porter Hatch was wounded, and Doubleday took his place as division commander. This move was made permanent when Union commander George B. McClellan reorganized the Army of the Potomac. Doubleday led the division in the battles of Antietam and Fredericksburg, after which he was promoted to major general of volunteers in November 1862. He commanded the Third Division, First Corps, during the battle of Chancellorsville, although the division did not see action in this battle, and remained in this position into the summer of 1863.

On 1 July 1863 Doubleday succeeded to command of the First Corps after the death of corps commander John F. Reynolds in the opening stages of the battle of Gettysburg. Doubleday's management of his position, just west of the town of Gettysburg, was steady but uninspired, and that afternoon he had to order his men to retreat through the town and take up a position along Cemetery Hill. That evening Union commander George G. Meade decided to name John Newton as Reynolds's permanent replacement and to return Doubleday to his division command. During the second and third days of the battle Doubleday's division engaged in heavy combat, and on the third day a Vermont brigade under his command played a key role in repelling the final Confederate assault. In September 1863 Doubleday was promoted to lieutenant colonel in the regular army.

Gettysburg proved to be Doubleday's last major battle, however. He left the Army of the Potomac afterward, believing that Meade was planning to reorganize the army along political lines, and held administrative duties in Washington for the remainder of the war. Humiliated by Meade's decision to replace him as corps commander, Doubleday resented Meade's treatment of him. Before long he began to circulate rumors that Meade had planned to retreat after the second day of the battle. He repeated these charges in an appearance before the Joint Committee on the Conduct of the War in March 1864.

Mustered out of the volunteer service in January 1866, Doubleday remained an officer in the regular army. Commissioned colonel of the Thirty-fifth Infantry in September 1867, he was later transferred to the Twenty-fourth Infantry. He served in Texas, first at Galveston and then at Fort McKavett. From 1869 to

1871, a period during which he was not assigned to active duty, Doubleday helped promote the first cable railroad in San Francisco, California.

Retiring from the military in 1873, Doubleday took a serious interest in establishing his claims to greatness at Fort Sumter and Gettysburg. In 1876 he published *Reminiscences of Fort Sumter and Moultrie in 1860–61*, and in 1882 he wrote *Chancellorsville and Gettysburg*. The core of the latter account was a reiteration of Doubleday's contention that Meade planned to retreat at Gettysburg. The book, which falls far short as an account of the events at Gettysburg, generated significant controversy. William Swinton, in *Campaigns of the Army of the Potomac* (1883), argued that Doubleday's contention was without "a scintilla of evidence" and that such a statement attacked Meade's reputation. In response, Doubleday wrote a letter to the editor of the *New York Times* (1 Apr. 1883) defending his assertion. Doubleday died in Mendham, New Jersey, and he was buried in Arlington National Cemetery.

Although during his lifetime Doubleday was noted for his military accomplishments, the historical significance attributed to him has been based primarily on his supposed invention of the game of baseball. In 1905 a commission was established to determine whether baseball had uniquely American origins or was descended from rounders, a game of English origin. Arranged at the behest of sporting goods manufacturer and baseball executive Albert Goodwill Spalding, who believed firmly in the indigenous nature of the game, the commission consisted of seven men with ties to the fledgling enterprise of organized baseball. The de facto leader of the commission was Abraham G. Mills, a former president of the National League, who in this capacity spent two years collecting written anecdotal recollections from interested persons nationwide on the matter, but he acquired little substantive evidence to support either claim. One such anecdote that piqued Mills's interest was provided by Cooperstown resident Abner Graves, who testified that he and Doubleday were schoolmates and that in 1839 Doubleday redesigned a game played by local residents known as "town ball." Doubleday, he said, instituted a smaller number of participants and a new set of rules and renamed the game "base ball." Doubleday may have played a game similar to that of baseball as a child or teenager in Cooperstown, but his status in 1839 as a second-year cadet at West Point makes a prolonged appearance in Cooperstown at that time unlikely. Moreover, no record has been found, even in Doubleday's many writings, that he ever played baseball.

Regardless, in December 1907, on the basis of Graves's testimony, Mills published the commission's report proclaiming that baseball originated in the United States and that, "according to the best evidence available to date, [baseball] was invented by Abner Doubleday at Cooperstown, N.Y., in 1839" (Alexander, pp. 94–95). In 1939, the presumed centennial of the game, major league baseball officials held a series of celebratory events, including the founding of the National Baseball Hall of Fame in Cooperstown. Although somewhat embarrassed by the claims of Bruce Cartwright that his distant relative Alexander Cartwright actually invented the game of baseball and that he could prove the claim, baseball officials proceeded with the planned celebration, having already made substantial public relations and financial commitments to perpetuating the role of Doubleday. As a result, according to baseball historian Harold Seymour, "the Doubleday myth was crystallized and given complete form by Organized Baseball" (Seymour, p. 14).

Baseball scholars have largely discredited the claim that Doubleday invented the game. Nevertheless, the Hall of Fame has continued to recognize Cooperstown as the "birthplace of baseball," and the ballpark adjacent to the Hall of Fame has continued to bear Doubleday's name.

• A small collection of Doubleday's papers is at the National Baseball Library, Cooperstown, N.Y. In addition to the works mentioned above, Doubleday wrote *Gettysburg Made Plain: A Succinct Account of the Campaign and Battles with the Aid of One Diagram and Twenty-nine Maps* (1888). The New York State Monuments Commission for the Battlefields of Gettysburg, Chattanooga, and Antietam prepared a biographical account, which includes tributes from Doubleday's friends and fellow officers, *In Memoriam, Abner Doubleday, 1819–1893, and John Cleveland Robinson, 1817–1897* (1918). A more recent biography is David M. Ramsey, "The 'Old Sumpter Hero': A Biography of Major-General Abner Doubleday" (M.A. thesis, Florida State Univ., 1980). Information regarding Doubleday and the origins of baseball is in Harold Seymour, *Baseball: The Early Years* (1960); Charles C. Alexander, *Our Game: An American Baseball History* (1991); and David Q. Voigt, "The History of Major League Baseball," in *Total Baseball*, 3d ed., ed. John Thorn and Pete Palmer (1993).

BROOKS D. SIMPSON
MATTHEW E. VAN ATTA

DOUBLEDAY, Frank Nelson (8 Jan. 1862–30 Jan. 1934), book publisher, was born in Brooklyn, New York, the son of William Edwards Doubleday, a hat manufacturer, and Ellen M. Dickinson. Doubleday's formal education was limited. After completing public primary school, he attended Brooklyn Polytechnic Institute for only "two or three years" (*Memoirs*, p. 3) because his father's hat business failed in 1876, when he was fourteen. As a result, Doubleday was forced to leave the institute and seek employment. Already interested in publishing, in 1877 Doubleday joined Charles Scribner's Sons. During his twenty years at Scribner's, he worked his way up to become editor of the *Book-Buyer*, a publication he resurrected in 1884, and subsequently to manage the newly launched *Scribner's Magazine* in 1887.

In 1886 Doubleday married Neltje De Graff, an author, under the name Neltje Blanchan, of several books on nature and gardening that Doubleday published in its Nature Library. They had one son and one daughter and adopted Doubleday's nephew.

In 1897 Doubleday decided to establish his own firm, and together with Samuel S. McClure of S. S. McClure and Company, publishers of the popular *Mc-*

Clure's Magazine, he formed the Doubleday and Mc-Clure Company. After dissolving the partnership with McClure in 1900 Doubleday joined Walter Hines Page, a former editor of *Atlantic Monthly* and *Mc-Clure's*, in founding Doubleday, Page and Company, which soon became one of the nation's major publishing houses. During 1908 Doubleday purchased the book publishing division of McClure, Phillips and Company from his former partner. Doubleday retained the name Doubleday, Page and Company when Page became ambassador to Great Britain and resigned his position with the firm in 1913. Finally, in 1928 Doubleday "absorbed" (*Memoirs*, p. 123) the George H. Doran Company and renamed the company Doubleday, Doran and Company. In addition, following the death of William Heinemann in 1920 Doubleday purchased half interest in W. Heinemann and Company, a British publishing house, which he owned outright by 1924.

Frank Doubleday contributed several innovations to the publishing business. According to Christopher Morley, Doubleday was the first in the industry to "visualize" book publishing as "a business, not merely as a dignified literary avocation" (*Effendi*, p. 6). In addition to more vigorous advertising and promotion of his publications, Doubleday was the first to employ independent auditors to calculate and verify royalties. Other innovations included magazine and book subscription plans, the publication of all the books of a major author in a collection, and direct ownership of a chain of bookstores, which comprised fifteen during Doubleday's lifetime.

Believing in "the money value of good surroundings" for his employees (*Memoirs*, p. 131), Doubleday was one of the first American businessmen to make his firm an attractive place in which to work. In 1910 he moved the printing and distribution center of his business to Garden City, Long Island, and there he established the Country Life Press in an attractive structure built on a fifty-acre tract landscaped to resemble a garden. Theodore Roosevelt laid the cornerstone of the building. This plant was reputed to be "one of the first daylight industrial plants in this country" (*Publishers Weekly*, 3 Feb. 1934, p. 584). In addition to pleasant surroundings, Doubleday employees at Garden City had a small hospital, a dental office, life and illness insurance benefits, a generous stock participation plan, and entertainments provided. "No other company could match Doubleday's munificence" (Tebbell, vol. 3, p. 50). Similarly, after he had purchased Heinemann, Doubleday also established Windmill Press in the English countryside near Kingwood in Surrey.

In addition to his business acumen—Doubleday was reputed to have "the best accounting system in the publishing business" (*Fortune*, p. 179)—his success was also the result of an extensive tradebook list that featured a large number of prominent authors. These included Booth Tarkington, O. Henry, Frank Norris, Edna Ferber, Sinclair Lewis, Ellen Glasgow, Jack London, Joseph Conrad, and Rudyard Kipling. In addition, he published several major periodicals, including the *World's Work*, *Country Life*, and *American Home*. Three literary personalities with whom he developed particularly close relationships were Conrad, Kipling, and T. E. Lawrence ("Lawrence of Arabia"). Kipling nicknamed Doubleday "Effendi," a word play on Doubleday's initials and also the Arabic and Turkish word that means "chief," or one who commands respect or attention. Indeed, Doubleday nursed Kipling back to health in 1899 when he was stricken with pneumonia while visiting New York City, and on one occasion he provided funds to enable the impoverished Conrad to continue writing.

Doubleday, who shared the public morality of his time, refused to publish the works of all the authors recommended by his editors and readers. Thus, Doubleday viewed Theodore Dreiser's *Sister Carrie* as "immoral," even though it was highly recommended by Frank Norris and approved for publication by Walter Page. Nevertheless, Doubleday fulfilled Dreiser's contract by publishing only 1,008 copies of the book, but he provided no publicity or advertising for the work.

In February 1918, while on a journey to the Far East as a commissioner for the Red Cross, Doubleday's wife Neltje died in Canton, China. Later the same year, Doubleday married Florence Van Wyck.

By the end of his life, Doubleday was one of America's most prominent citizens who included among his close friends a large number of influential Americans, including Andrew Carnegie, John D. Rockefeller, Sr., and Theodore Roosevelt. Following an illness of several years, Doubleday died of a heart attack in Coconut Grove, Florida, where he was spending the winter.

In spite of the fact that "he sold more books per title published than any American [publisher] of his time" (*Fortune*, p. 172), Doubleday did not succeed in his efforts to make his firm the largest publishing house in the United States; it was his son, Nelson, who accomplished this objective. But Doubleday's sound financial planning and his genuine interest in his authors and in good writing laid the foundation for the company's success in the twentieth century.

• Beginning in 1928 Doubleday began to privately publish recollections and reflections on his publishing career for the edification of his family. In 1972, in connection with Doubleday's seventy-fifth anniversary, Doubleday's grandson Nelson, Jr., published the recollections as *The Memoirs of a Publisher*. In 1910 Doubleday published *A Plain American in England* under the pseudonym Charles L. Whitefield. Other sources of information on Doubleday include Florence Doubleday, *Episodes in the Life of a Publisher's Wife* (1937); Charles A. Madison, *Irving to Irving: Author-Publisher Relations 1800–1974* (1974); John W. Tebbell, *A History of Book Publishing*, vols. 2–3 (1975–1978); Christopher Morley, *Effendi (Frank Nelson Doubleday, 1862–1934)* (1934); "Frank Nelson Doubleday (1862–1934)," *Publishers Weekly* (3 Feb. 1934), 583–86; and "Doubleday, Doran and Company," *Fortune* 13 (Feb. 1936): 73–181. A lengthy obituary on Doubleday with a photograph is in the *New York Times*, 31 Jan. 1934.

JOAN B. HUFFMAN

DOUBLEDAY, Nelson (16 June 1889–11 Jan. 1949), publisher, was born in Brooklyn, New York, the son of Frank Nelson Doubleday, the founder of the Doubleday publishing empire, and Neltje De Graff, a naturalist. Doubleday attended the Friends School in New York City and Holbrook Military Academy in Ossining, New York, from which he graduated in 1908. Numerous childhood illnesses, including typhoid fever, prevented his regular attendance at school. He was privately informed that the ensuing weakness of his heart would prevent labor-intensive work. Doubleday failed to reveal this dictum to his father, which led to a later breach between the two men, and they maintained a strained relationship throughout their lives. Doubleday also traveled extensively overseas with his family and spent two years at New York University before dropping out to pursue an independent career in publishing and merchandising.

Doubleday's penchant for publishing revealed itself early, and as a child Doubleday wrote to Rudyard Kipling urging him to publish a book of informative animal stories. Intrigued, Kipling wrote *Just So Stories*, published by Doubleday in 1902. The book sold a half-million copies by the mid-1930s and yielded to Nelson the royalty of one penny a book until his death, a deal he negotiated with his father for persuading the renowned author to write the book.

In 1912 Doubleday began a career independent of his father by founding Nelson Doubleday, Inc., a company geared toward half-priced, month-old magazines sold as deferred subscriptions. His profits exceeded $1,000 a month, but he abandoned the magazine sales when the post office increased its rates. With these profits he published several books under his own imprint, including an etiquette guide, and eventually exceeded a million reprints annually of nonfiction works.

In 1916 Doubleday married Martha J. Nicholson of Providence, Rhode Island, but the marriage ended in divorce in 1931. In 1932 he married Ellen McCarter Violett of Rumson, New Jersey. She had two daughters from a previous marriage, and they had two children together.

At the onset of the United States' involvement in World War I, Doubleday enlisted in the U.S. Navy and attained the rank of lieutenant, but he never served overseas. Following his discharge from the navy, Doubleday joined his father's firm in 1918. He began as a junior partner and became vice president by 1921. He became president in 1928, a year after the company's merger with George H. Doran, which changed the company name to Doubleday, Doran and Company. Frank Doubleday died in 1934, and Nelson assumed the position of chairman of the board in addition to his presidency.

The Great Depression affected the company financially, and Doubleday, moving quickly to save his legacy, sold the recently acquired Heinemann Publishing to its directors in England and disposed of all the magazines, including *Country Life* and *American Home*. Doubleday purchased 49 percent of a book club, the Literary Guild, in 1929 (becoming sole owner in 1934), and this proved to be the stimulus for further marketing innovation. Zealous in his desire to find a price at which every book would sell, Doubleday revived the Book League of America and created several new book clubs, targeting specific audiences.

Some of these imprints included the Young People's Division of the Literary Guild, the Junior Literary Guild, the Crime Club, the Doubleday One Dollar Book Club, the Family Reading Corporation, the Home Book Club, the Dollar Mystery Guild, and Book Club Associates in addition to Nelson Doubleday, Inc. By 1946 the Literary Guild and the Doubleday One Dollar Book Club had become the largest book clubs in the world. The combined Doubleday book clubs had a subscription list of 2.25 million customers. Doggedly, Doubleday watched his enterprises, and if anything proved unprofitable he was quick to terminate it. In 1937 he moved his offices from Garden Center to New York's Rockefeller Center.

During World War II Doubleday was able to increase his paper allotment and add medical books to his firm's offerings by purchasing the Blakiston Company of Philadelphia. In 1944 he also added to his company a second book manufacturing plant, in Hanover, Pennsylvania. Finally, he established editorial and business offices in Philadelphia, San Francisco, and Canada in addition to existing Doubleday offices in New York and London.

Although not a reader himself, Doubleday's biggest contribution was making books available to the masses. Edna Ferber once said of him, "He thought that books should not be treated as literature only. He thought they should be food. Not caviar, but bread. . . . He was a genius at devising ways to put books into the hands of the unbookish" (*Nelson Doubleday*, p. 28).

In 1946, ill with cancer, Doubleday retired as president of Doubleday and Company, Inc., but continued to serve as chairman of the board until his death. By 1948, the last year of Doubleday's tenure at the helm of Doubleday and Company, the firm, which boasted 4,765 employees, was publishing over 200 new titles per year and enjoyed sales of approximately 30 million books annually, making it the world's largest book publishing company. *Fortune* magazine declared, "If Nelson Doubleday ever decided that there is money to be made out of selling reprints of the *Congressional Record* for seventy-nine cents a year, he will probably turn out to be right" (Feb. 1936, p. 180). In addition, the company's Country Life Press also manufactured more than 120,000 books daily, some of which were produced for other publishers.

Doubleday's innovations in publishing and his book clubs allowed the American populace to enjoy books that may have been prohibitively costly otherwise. During the Great Depression, Doubleday's One Dollar Book Club and his Literary Guild brought books to the masses, enlisting a staggering number of members. Possessing a gift for marketing and managing,

Doubleday's innovative techniques positioned his publishing empire to enjoy continued success.

• Neither the Doubleday family papers nor the records of the Doubleday company, called the "Sphinx of Publishing," are available for consultation. Nelson Doubleday, Jr., supplied information for this sketch. The most significant source of information is a small memoir, *Nelson Doubleday 1889–1949*, privately printed. Nelson's uncle, Russell Doubleday, produced a biography of him titled "Nelson Doubleday: A Publisher in the Making," published in *Famous Leaders of Industry*, 5th ser., ed. Joseph A. Moore (1945). A good source on Doubleday and his company is John W. Tebbel, *A History of Book Publishing in the United States*, vols. 3 and 4 (1978 and 1981). Two informative articles are "Doubleday, Doran and Company," *Fortune*, 13 Feb. 1936, and "Doubleday Plans Fiftieth Anniversary Celebration in 1947," *Publishers Weekly*, 21 Dec. 1946. For additional information consult Charles A. Madison, *Book Publishing in America* (1966), and George H. Doran, *Chronicles of Barabbas* (1935). An informative obituary is in the *New York Times*, 12 Jan. 1949.

JOAN B. HUFFMAN

DOUBLEDAY, Neltje de Graff (23 Oct. 1865–21 Feb. 1918), natural history writer, was born in Chicago, Illinois, the daughter of Liverius de Graff, owner of a men's clothing store, and Alice Fair. She attended St. John's School in New York City and the Misses Masters' School in Dobbs Ferry, New York. In 1885 her family moved to Plainfield, New Jersey. On 9 June 1886 she married Frank Nelson Doubleday of New York; they had three children.

Frank Doubleday was editor of *Book Buyer* at the time of their marriage. He later became the manager of *Scribner's Magazine* and a founder of the Doubleday publishing company. Neltje Doubleday began writing for many of the magazines associated with the family publishing business, most notably *Country Life* and *Ladies' Home Journal*. She used the pen name Neltje Blanchan, so her ties with the publisher were not evident to readers. Her subjects varied greatly, including such topics as gardening, antique furniture, Indian basket weaving, biography, wildflowers, and birds.

Doubleday's first book, *The Piegan Indians* (1894), was an anthropological treatise that seems not to have been influential. Three years later she published the first of her six books on birds, riding and contributing to a rising tide of interest in birds and conservation in general. *Bird Neighbors* (1897) presented vignettes of many common birds. These were scientifically accurate for the time but included a few questionable anecdotal observations and occasional anthropomorphism. John Burroughs, a prominent naturalist of the day, wrote a flattering introduction for the book. *Bird Neighbors* went through numerous printings, the last of which (1937) added plates by the eminent bird artist Louis Agassiz Fuertes. All of Doubleday's books were lavishly produced and well illustrated for the period.

Birds That Hunt and Are Hunted (1898) focused on North American hawks, falcons, owls, and game birds in much the same way that *Bird Neighbors* presented songbirds. However, Doubleday often made strong moral judgments against the raptors' predatory behavior. She was particularly angry in her attack on the accipiters—birds that eat other birds—describing them as "vicious," "villains," and "murderers." She referred to the northern goshawk as the "most destructive creature on wings." Buried beneath her anthropomorphism and moral judgments, however, was good biology. Nonetheless Doubleday helped to perpetuate needless slaughter of birds of prey.

How to Attract the Birds (1902) and *Birds That Every Child Should Know* (1907) were ostensibly written for children, but the writing style and message seemed more aimed at teachers and members of the newly established National Association of Audubon Societies. A number of similar books were produced by competing publishers. *Birds Worth Knowing* (1917) included forty-eight color plates, many by Fuertes, and a well-written introduction assessing the bird conservation movement of the time. Doubleday's last book, *Birds* (1926), was a posthumously published anthology of material from earlier publications.

Doubleday also wrote two flower books, *Nature's Garden* (1900) and *The American Flower Garden* (1909). The first dealt with wildflowers and the second with cultivated flowers, in a format similar to that of her successful bird books but somewhat more encyclopedic. The flower books contain a good deal of anecdotal information and interesting folklore. *The American Flower Garden* is directed to the owners of spacious gardens with hired help, reflecting Doubleday's prosperous life, with homes in New York City and on Long Island.

Doubleday was a skilled and influential writer of popular natural history. She was not trained as a scientist and occasionally introduced emotion and anthropomorphism into her work, but her critics generally had neither the skill nor the inclination to interpret science for the general public as she did. Her influence on bird conservation at the turn of the century was in general quite positive.

Doubleday is perhaps best known for her bird books and her moralistic commentary on birds of prey, crows, and other birds she despised, but she figured in another episode of moral judgment, for which the primary evidence is the word of a disgruntled author. In 1900 the Doubleday firm published Theodore Dreiser's *Sister Carrie*, considered by many at the time to be a scandalous story glorifying a sinful life and replete with profanity. The book had been accepted by Frank Doubleday's partner while Frank and Neltje were in France. Upon their return and discovery that the book had been accepted, they were much disturbed. Doubleday honored the contract but printed only 1,008 copies, nearly half of which remained in storage, and did no advertising for the book. Dreiser blamed the book's failure squarely on Neltje Doubleday and took every opportunity to tell others so.

In addition to her writing career, Doubleday was quite active in charitable work, especially with the Red Cross Society of Nassau, Long Island. In December 1917 she and her husband traveled to China on a mission for the Red Cross. While in Canton she died suddenly. A memorial service was held on 18 March 1918 in the Mattinnecock Neighborhood House, one of her philanthropic projects at Locust Valley, Long Island.

• A brief biography is in Deborah Strom, *Birdwatching with American Women* (1986). The Dreiser incident is discussed in Robert H. Elias, *Theodore Dreiser: Apostle of Nature* (1970). An obituary is in the *New York Times*, 23 Feb. 1918.

JEROME A. JACKSON

DOUBLEHEAD (?–Aug. 1807), Cherokee leader whose Indian name was Tal-tsu-ska, was born probably on the Little Tennessee River. He has been described as the brother of the influential Cherokee chiefs Old Tassel and Tolluntuskee and rose to prominence in the wars that followed the murder of the former by North Carolinians in June 1788. Although he described himself as "but a boy" in 1793, he was of sufficient standing to put his name to the treaty of the Holston in 1791, which he signed against the name "Chuqualatague, Doublehead."

After the death of Old Tassel, Doublehead threw in his lot with the Lower Cherokees or Chickamaugas who waged a guerrilla war against the American settlements encroaching on Indian lands. A small man with a fine but solid build, a dark complexion, and piercing eyes, he had an explosive temper occasionally exacerbated by drunkenness and earned a reputation as an unusually ferocious warrior. He was party to the treaty of the Holston, in which William Blount, governor of the territory south of the Ohio, induced the Cherokees to surrender more land in Tennessee and to agree to free navigation on the Tennessee River, but disregarded his commitment to peace on 19 January 1792, killing two members of the Sevier family near what is now Clarksville.

A man of some oratorical ability, Doublehead accompanied John Watts to Pensacola to collect supplies from the Spaniards in 1792 and participated in the subsequent Chickamauga offensive against the Tennessee frontiers. On 25 September 1793 he was a leader of the Indians who captured Alexander Cavett's station below Knoxville. The occupants, three men and ten noncombatants, surrendered on terms offered by the Indians, but Doublehead, eager to avenge losses, massacred the prisoners with the exception of a child, rescued by Watts himself. In 1793 Doublehead also led a Cherokee delegation to the neighboring Chickasaw tribe, seeking to bring them into the war. June 1794 saw his diplomatic talents in use again, at the head of a Cherokee party sent to Philadelphia to negotiate with the U.S. government. He asserted that peace would be made and induced the Americans to increase Cherokee annuities due for the Holston treaty from $1,500 to $5,000. Entrusted with the annuity for the coming year, Doublehead infuriated his people by distributing it among his own followers.

Doublehead assured Blount in October that he was determined to remain peaceful, but on 11 November he led an attack on Valentine Sevier's station, near Clarksville, killing five or six women and children and throwing their mutilated bodies into the flames of burning buildings. "It was a horrid sight," recalled a witness, "some scalped and cut to pieces, some tomahawked very inhumanly, and poor helpless infants committed to the torturing flames." Doublehead was evidently incensed by the many punitive expeditions John Sevier, Valentine's brother, had led against the Cherokees.

Peace was eventually established in the Cherokee country in 1795, and Doublehead maintained a town of some 140 Indians at Muscle Shoals on the lower Tennessee (present-day Ala.). He became speaker or spokesman for the Cherokee National Council and, briefly, the most influential member of the tribe. From 1801 the character of Doublehead's career changed. Hitherto he had been the implacable enemy of the Euro-American, but now he eagerly embraced the "civilization" policy promoted by the United States. This encouraged the Indians to relinquish their extensive hunting grounds to white settlers and to invest the proceeds in the capital stock needed to "improve" the native economy. The Cherokees were urged to intensify their agriculture, raise stock, spin and weave cotton, and profit from the maintenance of inns and ferries along the roads through Indian lands. It was hoped they would abandon the common ownership of tribal land and become independent farmers, producing for the market. The "civilization" policy of the United States was partly philanthropic, intending to integrate the Indian into national life; but it was also motivated by a desire to secure aboriginal land, and it struck deeply at traditional Indian customs, values, and attitudes.

Influenced by John D. Chisholm, a white partner, as well as by U.S. Indian agent Return Jonathan Meigs, Doublehead became the most important Cherokee exponent of "civilization." He was remarkably entrepreneurial. In November 1802, for example, he was seeking the construction of a keelboat with which he intended to trade with New Orleans and the Arkansas tribes, as well as the erection of cotton gins and mills, with the employment of mechanics, in his part of the nation. He became wealthy, using black slaves to farm substantial land and raise cattle, and he levied tolls to pilot boats through the rapids at Muscle Shoals as well as exercising the right to salvage wrecks.

Doublehead's conversion proved useful to American agents eager to alienate Cherokee land. Meigs admitted the chief was "a vindictive, bloody-minded savage" but discovered in him "uncommon powers of mind." An acquisitive, ambitious man, Doublehead was easily bribed. In 1803 he helped Meigs gain Cherokee permission for a road from Nashville to Augusta, earning the right to maintain a ferry and public houses on the route and to have a track cut from it to his store at Muscle Shoals. The treaty of Tellico (25 Oct. 1805), by which the tribe released large tracts of land north of the Duck River and elsewhere, was to a great extent the work of Doublehead and Tolluntuskee, who received, in addition to shares in the sums granted the nation as a whole, reservations on the ceded areas, awarded in secret clauses. Doublehead and his brother then accompanied Meigs to Washington, D.C., with a Cherokee delegation. There the remaining hunting lands between the Duck and Tennessee rivers were ceded on 7 January 1806, and again Doublehead received special consideration, including a hundred-square-mile reservation north of the Tennessee at Muscle Shoals. Meigs expected the chief to establish a model Indian community on the reservation, exhibiting the advantages of "civilization," but Doublehead began leasing it out to white settlers.

By then Doublehead's activities had outraged many of his fellow tribesmen, especially those among the Upper Cherokees, who had derived little benefit therefrom. Critics pointed out that he had eschewed the traditional attempts to gain a political consensus and worked with a cabal of Lower Cherokee chiefs and American officials; that he had surrendered great tracts of territory for which many had affection, and which facilitated the hunting numerous Cherokees still found attractive; and that he was claiming as private reservations resources that properly belonged to the nation. Doublehead handled money tactlessly. Even before leaving Washington in 1806, he and his delegation had purloined $2,000 of the payment made for the cession and agreed with Meigs that the balance should be applied solely to liquidate debts the tribe owed to traders.

On 7 August 1807 Doublehead arrived at Hiwassee to watch a ball game. He had a stormy confrontation with an Indian named Bone Polisher and in a fracas shot his opponent dead. Doublehead then rode to a tavern at Walker's Ferry. As he sat drinking, the candle on his table was extinguished, and a bullet, fired by a party of Upper Cherokees, struck him in the face. Although the attack probably owed something to the death of Bone Polisher, it seems that a plot to assassinate Doublehead had already been in motion. The chief survived and was borne to a nearby house, but his presence was soon discovered by his enemies, who broke in and murdered Doublehead with guns, knives, and tomahawks.

A somewhat unpleasant, violent man, rumored to have beaten his pregnant wife to death, Doublehead has been reappraised. In his own day white observers lamented his activities as a warrior but commended his vision in modernizing the Cherokees. They regretted the passing of a valuable ally. More recently historians sensitive to the Indian perspective have reversed that judgment. Robert S. Cotterill, for example, remarked that he "formerly faithfully defended and lately faithlessly betrayed the interests of his countrymen." He consistently abrogated his responsibility for the welfare of the community as a whole to further his own interests, repudiating the ideals of the Cherokee civil leader. However, his career is not without interest, for it mirrored the turbulent history of his tribe at the beginning of the nineteenth century. Earlier he exemplified the old warrior-hunting society; later, in his efforts to develop the tribal economy, he presaged the immediate future of the Cherokee people.

• Valuable sources for Doublehead's career are contained in *American State Papers, Class II, Indian Affairs*, vol. 1 (1832–1834), and the files of the Cherokee Indian Agency, 1801–1835, RG 75, National Archives, microfilm no. M208. Relatively little secondary material is available, but valuable accounts are given by John P. Brown, *Old Frontiers* (1938); Robert S. Cotterill, *The Southern Indians* (1954); Thurman Wilkins, *Cherokee Tragedy* (1970); and William G. McLoughlin, *Cherokee Renascence in the New Republic* (1986).

JOHN SUGDEN

DOUGHERTY, Dennis Joseph (16 Aug. 1865–31 May 1951), Roman Catholic ecclesiastical leader and archbishop of Philadelphia, was born in Honesdale, Schuylkill County, Pennsylvania, the son of Patrick Dougherty and Bridget Henry, both refugees from the potato famine in County Mayo, Ireland. His parents' occupations are unknown. Educated in a public school in Girardville, Pennsylvania, Dougherty entered Saint Mary's College in Montreal, Canada, in 1879. Two years later, he transferred to Saint Charles Borromeo Seminary in Overbrook, Pennsylvania, to begin studies for the priesthood. Dougherty was then sent to the North American College in Rome, where he excelled academically and formed a lifelong attachment to orthodoxy and the papacy. He was ordained in Rome on 31 May 1890 and sent back to teach at his alma mater in the United States.

After thirteen happy years at Saint Charles, Dougherty was consecrated the first American bishop of the Philippines on 14 June 1903. During his service to the Dioceses of Nueva Segovia and Jaro, he concentrated on the rebuilding of churches, schools, convents, and seminaries destroyed during the Spanish-American War. In 1916 Dougherty was sent to the see of Buffalo, where he demonstrated the same administrative talents so evident in the Philippines.

On 30 April 1918 Dougherty succeeded his friend, Archbishop Edmond Prendergast, as archbishop of Philadelphia, the first native Pennsylvanian to do so. Three years later, on 7 March 1921, he became the fourth American-born prelate to be elected to the College of Cardinals. In 1937 Dougherty was again honored by being named the first American papal legate *a latere* to an international eucharistic congress in Manila.

During his thirty-three years as archbishop of Philadelphia, Dougherty acted on his belief that the Catholic church, and especially the papacy, was under attack from the forces of secularism and atheism throughout the world. He demanded of himself as well as of his clergy and laity a militant and unquestioning loyalty to the pope, especially since, after the devastation of World War I, only the United States had the wherewithal financially to support the universal Church.

In order to provide that support, however, Catholicism in the United States had to grow more rapidly than before. As Dougherty saw it, despite the massive influx of immigrants into the United States, Catholic growth had been hampered by a shortage of priests, the frequency of mixed marriages, and the enrollment of many Catholics in public schools. All three problems could be remedied only by encouraging vocations to the priesthood.

Accordingly, in 1926, Dougherty began construction of a vast new seminary building at Saint Charles Borromeo, where he insisted on academic excellence and strict discipline. As a result, 2,000 priests were ordained in Philadelphia during his episcopacy. Likewise, Dougherty was very strict with his ordained clergy. Priests were to observe a dress code and to perform liturgical celebrations with perfection. Priests were not permitted to own automobiles or to become involved in political or civic affairs. Priests were to attend only Roman universities or the Catholic University in Washington, D.C., for advanced studies, and they were permitted to study only theology or canon law.

Largely because of his priestly emphasis, Dougherty downplayed the role of the laity. In the parishes, the pastor was the master of spiritual and temporal affairs. Nevertheless, parish life, and especially parochial education, was a top priority for Dougherty. He created 112 new parishes, 145 parochial schools, fifty-three Catholic high schools, and four Catholic colleges. This school system was free to all Catholic children and financed entirely from the Sunday contributions of the parishioners. Only by maintaining such a separate educational system, Dougherty believed, could Catholic life and values be preserved from the corrupting influences found in public education.

One-quarter of the parishes founded between 1919 and 1927 were national ethnic parishes. Dougherty was afraid that aggressive Protestant proselytizing, especially among Italians and African Americans, would lead to further losses to Catholicism in the United States. He imported priests from Italy, placed young American priests who had studied in Rome in Italian missions, and collected money from the richer parishes for the construction of new settlement houses in Italian neighborhoods. Dougherty also promoted the foundation of new parishes for black Catholics and the education of blacks in Catholic high schools and colleges.

In various other ways, Dougherty attempted to insulate Catholics from "outside" influences. He promoted the placement of Catholic orphans in exclusively Catholic institutions. Because he insisted that every Catholic family should have a Catholic newspaper to read, he expanded the circulation of the *Catholic Standard and Times*, which he controlled with an iron hand. In 1927 he went to war against what he saw as the movie industry's preoccupation with sex and crime, even instituting in 1934 a diocesan-wide boycott of all movies, which was still in effect at his death in 1951.

Dougherty was always anxious to prove that Catholics were good, patriotic citizens and not the alien threat portrayed by nativist demagogues. He did this by throwing his support behind government efforts in World War I and World War II and by placing all available diocesan institutions and personnel at the disposal of the secular authorities to help deal with ca-

tastrophes such as the influenza epidemic of 1918. He was also one of the staunchest opponents of atheism and communism in the country. He organized two mass demonstrations during his episcopate: one in 1935 against the persecution of religion in Mexico and another in 1946 against the imprisonment of Archbishop Stepinac by the Communist Jugoslav government. The only press conference Dougherty ever summoned during his whole tenure as archbishop of Philadelphia was on 8 February 1949, when he denounced the imprisonment of Cardinal Mindszenty by the Communist Hungarian government.

In his relations with state and national secular authorities, Dougherty commanded respect. In 1927 he was instrumental in having a Pennsylvania pro–birth control law defeated. The same year, under pressure from Dougherty, a bill to tax church property was defeated. In 1939 he won his campaign against a sterilization bill and one giving boroughs the right to tax funerals. It was largely due to Dougherty's influence that in 1944 the Allies refrained from bombing the city of Rome. The following year he was influential in getting President Harry S. Truman to appoint prominent Catholic lawyer James McGranery as U.S. attorney general. In 1948 Dougherty gave the invocation at both the Republican and Democratic National Conventions, the first time in United States history that the same clergyman had done so, and quite in keeping with Dougherty's policy of not taking sides in political contests. He also studiously avoided involvement in labor-management affairs, although he was often courted by both sides.

Dougherty died in Philadelphia after celebrating Mass commemorating his sixty-one years as a priest.

• Dougherty's correspondence while archbishop of Philadelphia is in the Dennis Cardinal Dougherty Papers at the Philadelphia Archdiocesan Historical Research Center in Wynnewood, Pa. Secondary works include Hugh J. Nolan, "The Native Son," in *The History of the Archdiocese of Philadelphia*, ed. James F. Connelly (1976), pp. 339–418; Nolan, "Cardinal Dougherty's Services," *Ave Maria*, 8 Sept. 1951, pp. 295–96; Nolan, "Cardinal Dougherty: An Appreciation," *Records of the American Catholic Historical Society of Philadelphia* 62 (Sept. 1951): 135–41; *Official Jubilee Volume: Life and Work of His Eminence D. Cardinal Dougherty and History of St. Charles Seminary, June 10th 1928* (1928); and George E. O'Donnell, *St. Charles Seminary, Philadelphia* (1964). An obituary is in the *Catholic Standard and Times*, 1 June 1951.

JOSEPH J. CASINO

DOUGHTON, Robert Lee (7 Nov. 1863–2 Oct. 1954), politician, was born in Laurel Springs, North Carolina, the son of J. H. Doughton, a farmer and captain in the Confederate army, and Rebecca Jones. He grew up on the family farm and was educated in the public schools of Laurel Springs and Sparta, North Carolina. Little is known of Doughton's early life; even the dates of his first marriage and the death of his first wife, Boyd Greer, are unknown. In 1898 Doughton married Lillie Sticker Hix; they had four children.

Doughton was a farmer, banker, and small businessman before entering politics. After holding appointed positions, he won a seat in the state senate as a Democrat in 1908. Two years later he defeated the incumbent Republican in his area to become a member of Congress. He held that seat until his retirement in 1953. His lengthy service in Congress eventually earned him the chairmanship of the House Ways and Means Committee from 1933 to 1947 and from 1949 to 1953.

As Ways and Means chair, Doughton rose to national prominence. His elevation to that position coincided with the beginning of the New Deal, and as chairman of the congressional committee overseeing taxation, he was instrumental in steering many New Deal measures through Congress, including the National Recovery Administration (NRA), the Reciprocal Trade Act, the Social Security Act, and the tax bills used to fund the New Deal, World War II, and the first years of the Cold War.

Like much of the country, Doughton was unsure of the soundness of many of Franklin D. Roosevelt's proposals. He went along with them out of desperation, explaining to his supporters, "Old methods have failed. . . . To pursue the road we have been travelling means not only economic disaster but revolution." However, Doughton believed the New Deal was to be a temporary solution rather than a fundamental change in American government and society. To this end, he often modified New Deal legislation in the Ways and Means Committee. This becomes apparent in later New Deal measures that Doughton did not support, such as the Fair Labor Standards Act (1938).

However, Doughton thought three New Deal programs should be permanent—the Federal Deposit Insurance Corporation (FDIC), the Reciprocal Trade Act, and Social Security. Doughton, who was president of a small North Carolina bank, thought "some Federal guarantee of bank deposits is necessary if banks are to fully retain the confidence of the public." Throughout his career, he supported lower tariffs. He saw the Reciprocal Trade Act as a way to ensure that the country would pursue a liberal trade policy. Social Security was necessary, in Doughton's eyes, "to prevent the distress and suffering which so frequently arise from our industrial economy."

Although a loyal party man much of the time, Doughton maintained his independence from the national Democratic party on many key issues. In 1928 he opposed the nomination of Al Smith on the Prohibition issue and later referred to the repeal of Prohibition as a "colossal mistake." Despite his sponsorship of tax legislation to this effect, Doughton was skeptical of Harry Truman's conduct of the Cold War, noting that he did "not believe we can stop the march of communism by the expenditure of any amount of money."

Even when he acceded to his party's wishes, Doughton served his own interest. This is seen most clearly in his acquiescence to President Roosevelt's plea that he forgo a run for the governorship of North Carolina in 1936 and keep the Ways and Means Committee in hands Roosevelt considered friendly. Doughton was rewarded by having his candidate chosen by Roosevelt as state Works Progress Administration (WPA) director, ending a bitter patronage struggle among North Carolina Democrats in Doughton's favor.

Doughton's reputation for hard work and stubbornness earned him the nickname "Muley." Contemporary press accounts had him routinely working days well over twelve hours, often from around 6:00 A.M. until around 7:00 P.M. Both in committee and on the floor, he was a forceful proponent of measures he supported and an intractable foe of those he opposed. His favorite tactic was to point out fallacies in the positions of his opponents. Despite his advancing years, Doughton remained a vibrant and active legislator until his retirement. He died the next year at his home in Laurel Springs, North Carolina.

To his contemporaries and to later scholars, Doughton attracted most interest as the architect of the nation's tax policy during his reign over the Ways and Means Committee. His personal vision of what constituted a fair system of taxation helped to guide America's tax system during the expansion of the federal government from the nascent New Deal welfare state to the warfare state created by World War II and the Cold War. He supported a tax system based on ability to pay, calling the graduated income tax "the fairest, soundest, and most equitable form of taxation developed in the history of government." At the same time, one of the press's favorite Doughton quotations cautioned against excessive taxation, noting, "You can shear a sheep year after year, but you can only skin it once." He believed that government should extract enough revenue from those able to pay to operate without running a deficit, but it should not take so much that no incentive would be left for future private investment. The tax structure that he created for the country during the 1930s and 1940s reflects his best efforts to achieve that balance.

• Doughton's papers are in the Southern Historical Collection, University of North Carolina Library, Chapel Hill, N.C. Contemporary views of Doughton are in Gerald Movins, "He'll Take a Bite Out of You," *Saturday Evening Post*, 17 Jan. 1942, pp. 27, 53–56; "Exit Muley," *Time*, 25 Feb. 1952, p. 26; *U.S. News and World Report*, 9 June 1950, pp. 34–37; *Newsweek*, 12 Apr. 1943, p. 52; and J. T. Slater, ed., *Public Men in and out of Office* (1946). Doughton's congressional career is discussed in Douglas Abrams, *Conservative Constraints: North Carolina and the New Deal* (1992); Susan Hartmann, *Truman and the 80th Congress* (1971); Harold Ickes, *The Secret Diary of Harold Ickes: The Lowering Clouds, 1939–41* (1955); James T. Patterson, *Congressional Conservatism and the New Deal* (1967); Frances Perkins, *The Roosevelt I Knew* (1946); Jordan Schwarz, *The Interregnum of Despair: Hoover, Congress, and the Depression* (1970); and Schwarz, *The New Dealers* (1993). On Doughton's role in southern politics see Elmer Puryear, *Democratic Party Dissension in North Carolina, 1928–1936* (1962). Doughton and fiscal policy are covered in John Morton Blum, *From the Morgenthau Diaries: Years of Crisis, 1928–1938* (1959) and *From the Morgenthau Diaries: Years of Urgency, 1938–1941* (1967); A. E. Holmans, *United States Fiscal Policy 1945–1959* (1961); Walter Kraft Lambert, "New Deal Revenue Acts: The Politics of Taxation" (Ph.D. diss., Univ. of Texas, 1970); Mark Hugh Leff, *The Limits of Symbolic Reform: The New Deal and Taxation, 1933–1939* (1984); Randolph E. Paul, *Taxation in the United States* (1954); and Herbert Stein, *The Fiscal Revolution in America* (1969). The *New York Times*, 2 and 4 Oct. 1954, and the *Washington Post*, 3 Oct. 1954, contain obituaries discussing Doughton's national significance.

G. DAVID PRICE

DOUGHTY, Thomas (19 July 1793–22 July 1856), lithographer and landscape painter, was born in Philadelphia, Pennsylvania, the son of James Young Doughty, a ship carpenter, and Mary Young. He was apprenticed to a leather merchant when he was sixteen and continued in this occupation for approximately ten years. Doughty apparently taught himself how to paint, and around 1816 he painted his first landscapes. It was also at this time that he listed his occupation as "painter" in the Philadelphia register, among the first American artists to do so. He was an avid hunter and fisherman whose intense love of nature inspired him to capture the serenity and joy he experienced in the wooded hills and along the quiet streams of the Northeast.

Doughty began his career painting topographical views of gentlemen's estates as practiced by late eighteenth- and early nineteenth-century American landscape artists, such as William Guy Wall. Among these were at least six depictions of "Beech Hill," the estate of the Baltimore collector Robert Gilmor, Jr., who later became Doughty's patron, including *View of Baltimore from Beech Hill, the Seat of Robert Gilmor, Jr.* (1822, Baltimore Museum of Art). To compensate for his lack of formal training, Doughty studied the works of Dutch and English landscape artists whose works he found in his native Philadelphia and in Gilmor's personal collection. The influence of these artists upon Doughty's work can be seen in his painting *In the Catskills* (1836, Reynolda House, Museum of American Art, Winston-Salem, N.C.). He soon won attention for his tranquil views of the Pennsylvania and Hudson rivers as well as the Catskill and Adirondack mountain ranges that captured the recognizable American qualities of the native landscape. During this time he gained a reputation as one of the nation's foremost landscape painters, and in 1824 he was elected a member of the Pennsylvania Academy of the Fine Arts.

In the summer of 1828 Doughty left Philadelphia for Boston but, disliking the climate, returned to Philadelphia less than two years later. From 1830 to 1832 he produced lithographic plates for a monthly magazine called *The Cabinet of Natural History and American Rural Sports*, which he edited and published with his brother John. When the series failed, Doughty took his wife and five children and returned to Boston. Between the years 1832 and 1837 he achieved his greatest fame and found himself exhibiting and working in Boston, Philadelphia, and Baltimore. In order to support his large family he ran a painting school in Boston. Throughout the 1820s and 1830s Doughty exhibited regularly at the Pennsylvania Academy of the Fine Arts, the National Academy of Design in New York City, and the Boston Athenaeum, as well as abroad. He was not a prolific painter, but his paintings sold quickly. The majority of his works, such as *Delaware Water Gap* (1826) and *Hudson River Near West Point* (1827, Montclair Art Museum, Montclair, N.J.), were depictions of scenes along the banks of the Delaware, Pennsylvania, Hudson, and Susquehanna rivers. Doughty's painting *In Nature's Wonderland* (1832, Detroit Institute of Fine Arts) is considered by many to be his best work for anticipating the themes and style of the Hudson River School painters, such as Thomas Cole, Asher B. Durand, and Jasper Cropsey. Cole studied Doughty's work, which he saw while living in Philadelphia between 1823 and 1825. *In Nature's Wonderland* exemplifies Doughty's refined landscape style. The painting is small (24.5 × 30 ins.), and although the location depicted is unknown, it is a simple river scene with a wooded foreground. A solitary wandering figure, in this instance a hunter, symbolizes the artist's own direct relation to nature and reveals the central theme: the pastoral ideal of man's harmony with nature. The pigments are modified through the use of silvery gray tones, but it is Doughty's treatment of the sky that is the most innovative. Through the careful blending of paint infused with varying degrees of light applied in a painterly manner, he is able to capture subtle atmospheric effects. Each of these elements in Doughty's work foreshadowed the accomplishments of the painters connected with the Hudson River School.

During the 1820s and 1830s Doughty traveled in Europe and became widely known in part through numerous engravings of his work. Works like *Fanciful Landscape* (1834, National Gallery of Art, Washington, D.C.), with its inclusion of an ancient ruin set atop a promontory, reflect the influence of his experiences there. By May 1838 Doughty was back in New York. Influenced by his exposure to the English landscape artist John Constable, Doughty continued to develop an increasingly painterly approach to his style that included softening the features of the landscape, blurring outlines, and experimenting with the effects of atmospheric light. From 1839 to 1840 Doughty was in Newburgh, New York, located near the Hudson River, where he continued to paint light-filled landscapes.

In the 1830s Doughty's popularity slowly began to decline, and by the 1850s his work was no longer in favor. Contemporary critics, artists, and historians, such as William Dunlap, and even Doughty's own patron, Gilmor, expressed dissatisfaction with his work. These criticisms reflected the demands of critics and patrons alike for a definitively nationalistic art. While Doughty had achieved success for his ability to evoke the essential qualities of the American landscape in his paintings, his works were increasingly regarded as generalized distillations that were too rooted in eighteenth-century European conventions. Changing tastes were calling for images that were more precisely identifiable American scenes. The paintings done by Cole, for example, of American forests, mountains, and rivers were insistent exultations of national identity. While Doughty's influence on the younger artist has been recognized, Cole quickly surpassed him by setting a new standard for accuracy, atmospheric effects, and sublime color. By comparison, Doughty's landscapes appeared outdated. Works like *Gilpin's Mill on the Brandywine* (1827, Carolina Art Association, Gibbs Art Gallery, Charleston, S.C.) and *Early Winter* (1850) were small, unassuming, and subdued in color and did not reflect the emerging romantic sensibility that was brought forth in the majestic landscapes of Cole, Durand, and Cropsey. In the fall of 1852, perhaps to escape the harsh criticisms of his detractors, Doughty moved to Oswego, New York. While he had attempted to keep pace with the rapidly evolving monumental landscape mode, incorporating elements such as panoramic vistas and the meticulous observation of nature in his own work, Doughty's ambitions exceeded his abilities. He died a depressed and poor man.

Doughty was among the first American painters to replace the topographical approach in landscape painting with a more personal response to nature. His outstanding contribution to American painting was that he was one of the first to choose landscape exclusively for subject matter. Doughty's personal, more direct approach to landscape painting, which resulted in lyrical, pastoral depictions of the American wilderness, made him an innovator in this country, and his achievements prepared the way for the sublime celebrations of the Hudson River School painters.

• Sources of information on Doughty's life are few, and particulars are greatly lacking. Brief biographical essays appear in E. P. Richardson's *Painting in America* (1965) and in Oswaldo Rodriguez Roque's biography on Doughty in the catalog *American Painting in the Metropolitan Museum of Art*, vol. 1 (1994), coauthored by Roque and John Caldwell. The one indispensable work on Doughty is the exhibition catalog done for the Pennsylvania Academy of Fine Arts by Frank H. Goodyear, Jr., *Thomas Doughty, 1793–1856: An American Pioneer in Landscape Painting* (1973).

BRITT STEEN ZUÑIGA

DOUGLAS, Aaron (26 May 1899–2 Feb. 1979), artist and educator, was born in Topeka, Kansas, the son of Aaron Douglas, Sr., a baker, and Elizabeth (maiden name unknown), a domestic. Educated in segregated schools until high school, Douglas's early artistic influences included his mother's paintings and drawings and fellow African-American artist Henry Ossawa Tanner's *Christ and Nikodemus* (1899), which young Douglas saw reproduced in a magazine.

Torn between becoming a lawyer and an artist after graduating from Topeka High School, Douglas, like thousands of other black laborers, headed to the urban centers of the North in search of a factory job. Unlike most of them, however, Douglas was intent on saving enough money to attend college in the fall. Arriving in Detroit, Michigan, he worked as a plasterer, but finding this work too much for his slight frame, he worked for Cadillac, loosening molding sand from automobile radiators. In his spare time Douglas attended free evening art classes at the Detroit Museum of Art (now the Detroit Institute of Arts). In July 1917, after only two months, Douglas left Detroit for Dunkirk, New York, where a friend had arranged a job for him at Essex Glass factory. These experiences may have influenced Douglas's idealized portrayals of the African-American working class in his art work.

After a brief return home to Topeka, Douglas went to Lincoln, Nebraska, determined to enroll in the University of Nebraska, regardless of the fact that the term had already begun. He had none of the materials necessary for his college application, but he was conditionally accepted by the chairman of the Fine Arts Department. Douglas worked as a busboy to finance his education. When World War I broke out, Douglas joined the Student Army Training Corps (SATC), only to be summarily dismissed, probably on racial grounds. Determined to serve, Douglas transferred temporarily to the University of Minnesota, worked at the Minneapolis Steel Machinery Company, and volunteered for the Minnesota SATC, attaining the rank of corporal. While in Minneapolis, Douglas frequently visited the Walker Art Center, where he studied Leonardo Da Vinci's drawings. Returning to Lincoln with the armistice, Douglas received his B.F.A. from the University of Nebraska in 1922. After receiving his B.A. from the University of Kansas in 1923, he spent the summer of that year as a waiter with the Union Pacific Railroad's Short Line. In the fall he became an art teacher at Lincoln High School in Kansas City, Missouri, where he stayed until the spring of 1925, educating himself about modernism, cubism, and German expressionism and taking a correspondence course in art. Douglas quit his teaching job with the intention of going to Paris to become an artist, stopping in Harlem en route. This detour was decisive to his career.

While still in Kansas City, Douglas had made several contacts with high-ranking members of the National Urban League, including its director, Charles S. Johnson, through his friend Ethel Ray, the secretary of the local branch. On his arrival in New York, Douglas was quickly assigned illustrations for the Urban League's respected journal, *Opportunity*. Attracted by the nascent "New Negro" movement, Douglas decided to stay in New York rather than continue on to Paris. Also known as the Harlem Renaissance, the New Negro movement was characterized by an emphasis on the African aspects of black American culture, white patronage, racial pride, and a collaborative spirit. Dominated by literary figures such as Zora Neale Hurston, Langston Hughes, Claude McKay, Jean Toomer, and Countee Cullen, the movement was spearheaded by Dr. Alain Locke of Howard University. Aaron Douglas is widely acknowledged to be the most significant visual artist of the Harlem Renaissance.

Soon after arriving in New York, Douglas met German artist Winold Reiss, who became an important influence. Reiss offered Douglas a two-year scholarship to attend classes with him. It was as Reiss's protégé that Douglas was included in Locke's *The New Negro* (1925), the manifesto of the Harlem Renaissance. Douglas's woodcut-like, stylized black-and-white illustrations graced many important books of the period, including the 1927 reprint of James Weldon Johnson's *The Autobiography of an Ex-Colored Man* (1912) and his *God's Trombones* (1927), Wallace Thurman's *The Blacker the Berry* (1929), Langston Hughes's *Fine Clothes to the Jew* (1927), and Claude McKay's *Home to Harlem* (1928), *Banjo* (1929), *Banana Bottom* (1933), and *A Long Way from Home* (1937).

Throughout this period Douglas continued to contribute his modernist illustrations, which blended elements of art deco, art nouveau, cubism, Egyptian art, and West African sculpture, to *Opportunity*. He was also a regular contributor to *Crisis* (where he served briefly in 1927 as art editor), edited by the respected and influential African-American leader William Edgar Burghardt DuBois. His celebrated *Emperor Jones* series, inspired by the Eugene O'Neill play of the same name, then starring Paul Robeson, first appeared in the February 1926 issue of *Theatre Arts Monthly* magazine. Also in 1926, the year of his marriage to Alta Sawyer, Douglas helped to found the celebrated, if short-lived *Fire!!* In his memoir, *The Big Sea*, Langston Hughes recalls *Fire!!*'s editor Wallace Thurman insisting that the journal, the collaborative effort of the leading lights of the Harlem Renaissance, "had to be [printed] on good paper . . . worthy of the drawings of Aaron Douglas."

Douglas's contributions to magazines decreased after 1927, when he became involved in other projects. In 1928 he received a one-year Barnes Foundation fellowship, after millionaire art collector Albert C. Barnes saw Douglas at work on his first mural, commissioned in 1925 for the popular Harlem cabaret, Club Ebony. Commuting between New York and Merion, Pennsylvania, Douglas studied Barnes's extensive collections of modern and African art. In the summer of 1930, Douglas and his wife moved temporarily to Nashville, Tennessee, while he worked on his cycle of murals for the newly built Fisk University Library. Painted on canvases that were then attached to the walls, the murals tell "the story of the Negro's progress from central Africa to present day America," as Douglas once explained in a speech. While at Fisk, Douglas also accepted and worked on two other mural commissions: the unfinished College Inn Room mural for the Sherman Hotel in Chicago (destroyed), and a mural depicting slave leader Harriet Tubman for Bennett College for Women in Greensboro, North Carolina. In 1931 Douglas and his wife spent a year in Paris, where Douglas enrolled in L'Académie Scandinave, receiving training in sculpture and painting from Charles Despiau and Othon Friesz, respectively. While in Paris he met fellow African-American artist Hale Woodruff and his childhood role model, Henry O. Tanner.

Returning to the United States, Douglas entered the most political period of his career, joining the American Communist Party sometime in the early 1930s. Serving as president of the Harlem Artists Guild, Douglas challenged the racist practices of the Works Progress Administration, helping to gain recognition for black artists. His new political awareness informed *Aspects of Negro Life*, a mural cycle commissioned in 1934 by the Public Works Administration for the Countee Cullen Branch of the New York Public Library. Executed in Douglas's characteristic two-dimensional style but infused with his newly discovered passion for Marxism, the mural is widely accepted as the masterpiece of Douglas's oeuvre. His mural for New York's 135th Street YMCA, also completed in 1934, marks the end of the period of his greatest artistic activity.

Douglas received two travel fellowships from the Rosenwald Foundation, which enabled him to visit the American South in 1937 and Haiti and the Dominican Republic in 1938. In 1940 Douglas entered into an arrangement with Charles S. Johnson, now president of Fisk University, in which he developed Fisk's art department while attending Columbia University Teacher's College in New York City. He received his M.A. in 1944, eventually became chairman of the department at Fisk, and taught until his retirement in 1966. Douglas was invited by President John F. Kennedy to attend the centennial celebration of the Emancipation Proclamation. He exhibited regularly in both one-man and group exhibitions throughout the United States until his death in Nashville.

Douglas, "the father of African-American art," incorporated African themes, subjects, and techniques into American art for the first time. In the process, he encouraged African Americans to take pride in a heritage that previously had been a source of shame, mystery, and confusion for many. As the "dean" of the Harlem Renaissance, Douglas was also the first African-American artist to use a modernist visual vocabulary to depict the lives of people of African heritage, from cotton fields to cabarets, factories to palaces.

• Douglas's papers, including his eighteen-page manuscript autobiography, are in Fisk University Special Collections. Some of his papers are also held by the Schomburg Center for Research in Black Culture. Amy Helene Kirschke, *Aaron Douglas: Art, Race, and the Harlem Renaissance* (1995), provides a thorough treatment of Douglas's life and a detailed discussion of his art. Another important source is Romare Bearden and Harry Henderson, *A History of African-American Artists from 1792 to the Present* (1993). See Theresa Dickason Cedarholm, *Afro-American Artists: A Bio-bibliographical Directory* (1973), for an exhaustive listing of works, exhibitions, awards, and reference sources.

JEANNINE DELOMBARD

DOUGLAS, Adèle Cutts (27 Dec. 1835–26 Jan. 1899), Washington belle and hostess and wife of Stephen A. Douglas, was born in Washington, D.C., the daughter of James Madison Cutts, an official in the U.S. Treasury Department, and Ellen Elizabeth O'Neale (or Neale), the descendant of a prominent Roman Catholic family in Maryland. Adèle's grandfather,

Richard Cutts, in whose house on Lafayette Square she lived as a child, had also served in the Treasury Department, as well as serving twelve years in Congress. Her aunt was Rose O'Neale Greenhow, the celebrated Confederate spy. When Adèle was a young girl, her great-aunt, Dolley Madison, moved into the Cutts home following the death of her husband. Adèle and Dolley frequently spent summers together at White Sulphur Springs, and at Madison's public receptions in Washington young Adèle met presidents, congressmen, and other notables while developing the social graces for which she later became famous.

Adèle was brought up a Roman Catholic and educated at Madame Burr's school and the Academy of the Visitation in Georgetown, where she excelled in the study of French literature. On her eighteenth birthday she was presented to Washington society. Seen often at receptions and balls, she made an unforgettable impression, winning praise for her beauty and her distinguished bearing. Addie (as her friends called her) was described by one admiring reporter as "tall, elegantly formed, with a sweet oval face, large brown eyes, [and] small Grecian forehead" around which the "braids of her glossy and abundant chestnut hair" were intertwined (Chicago *Democratic Press*, 25 Nov. 1856).

It is uncertain whether Adèle first met Illinois senator Stephen A. Douglas at a public reception or in the home of a Senate colleague. In any event, when they met, Douglas, the national leader of the Democratic party, had just been passed over for the 1856 presidential nomination. He remained a powerful member of Congress, however, and, ever since his authorship of the Kansas-Nebraska Act in 1854, the center of political controversy. A brief courtship followed, interrupted by Douglas's trip to Illinois to campaign for James Buchanan. In November 1856, following Buchanan's election as president, Adèle and Douglas's marriage was solemnized by a Roman Catholic priest in what was widely reported as the social event of the season in the national capital. Their wedding trip to New York (to visit Douglas's mother) and Chicago was marked by public suppers and receptions, at which every detail of Adèle's dress and appearance was recorded in the press. "It is difficult to say," wrote one observer, "whether the genius of the husband or the beauty of the wife attracts the most homage" (*Harper's Weekly*, 26 Dec. 1857).

To many the couple appeared an unlikely match. A widower with two small sons, Douglas was twenty-two years older than Adèle and lacked the refinement for which she was known. Since his first wife's death in 1853, Douglas had shunned society, allowed his whiskers to grow, and assumed a decidedly shabby appearance. Marriage to Adèle worked a remarkable change. He shaved his whiskers and trimmed his hair, cut down on his drinking, and appeared in a new, neat-fitting suit. From a frequenter of "crossroads taverns and city oyster saloons" Douglas had been transformed "into quite a genial and courtly aristocrat" (*New York Herald*, 20 Dec. 1856).

Adèle's influence was noted in other ways as well. After his marriage, Douglas built a splendid mansion, complete with a ballroom, that quickly became a center of Washington's social activity. Presiding over dinner parties, afternoon receptions, and public receptions, Adèle became the most popular hostess in the capital, the envy of other Washington wives. She assumed responsibility for Douglas's two sons and placed them in a Roman Catholic school. She also took a strong interest in his political career, accompanied him on campaign trips, and sat regularly in the Senate gallery when he spoke. When Douglas returned to Illinois to stump the state against Abraham Lincoln in the 1858 senatorial campaign, Adèle was at his side, despite a recent miscarriage. She attracted attention wherever they went, winning compliments for her dignity and grace even from Douglas's Republican opponents. The following year, Adèle gave birth to a daughter, but the baby survived only a few months and Adèle herself lay desperately ill with puerperal fever. She recovered in time to travel with Douglas on his campaign tour of the Deep South in 1860, following his nomination for the presidency. She was at his side again in the spring of 1861 when he returned to Illinois following the firing on Fort Sumter to mobilize support for Lincoln's prosecution of the war against the seceded states. She kept vigil at his bedside during his final illness, until he died in Chicago on 3 June 1861.

Following Douglas's death, Adèle went into seclusion in Washington, refusing to take part in the capital's social events until after the Civil War. Early in 1866 she married Captain Robert Williams, a Virginian who had remained in the Union army. Ulysses S. Grant was one of the witnesses of their marriage ceremony. In the years that followed, Adèle accompanied her new husband to a number of western army posts. They had six children, the three elder ones born in Washington and the younger three in the West. She never resumed her earlier role as a society hostess. In 1892 Williams was promoted to brigadier general and appointed adjutant general of the U.S. Army; he retired the following year. Suffering from declining health, Adèle died in Washington, D.C., six years later.

• There is no known collection of Adèle Cutts Douglas's papers. Three letters (one written by her and two written to her by Douglas) are included in Robert W. Johannsen, ed., *The Letters of Stephen A. Douglas* (1961). For biographical information, see Virginia Tatnall Peacock, "Adèle Cutts," in her *Famous American Belles of the Nineteenth Century* (1901), and Sister Marie Perpetua Hayes, "Adèle Cutts, Second Wife of Stephen A. Douglas," *Catholic Historical Review* 31 (1945): 180–91. References to Adèle's life with Douglas are in Robert W. Johannsen, *Stephen A. Douglas* (1973).

ROBERT W. JOHANNSEN

DOUGLAS, David (25 June 1799–12 July 1834), botanist, was born in Scone, Perthshire, Scotland, the son of John Douglas, a stonemason, and Jean Drummond. He spent a few years in the parish schools and was then apprenticed, at the age of eleven, at the earl of Mansfield's gardens. Through reading, field studies, and practical gardening, Douglas developed an enthusiasm for natural history, especially botany, which would be the single passion of his life. In 1820 he obtained a post at the botanical garden in Glasgow, and there met the famous botanist William Jackson Hooker. Hooker became his mentor and then his close friend, and the two went on many botanizing expeditions in the Scottish Highlands and Islands.

In 1823 Douglas entered the employ of the Horticultural Society of London and was sent on a journey to eastern North America to investigate fruit culture and send back samples of new trees and other specimens. He returned in 1824, and the society's officers were so pleased with his work that they sent him off within six months on what would be the first of two journeys to the American Northwest. In July 1824 he sailed on a Hudson's Bay Company ship, *William and Ann*, for the voyage around Cape Horn and arrived at the mouth of the Columbia River in April 1825. The purpose of his trip was to explore the region, study its plant life, and send back seeds and specimens to the society. Hooker was very enthusiastic about the Northwest, saying it was "highly interesting country" about which there was little botanical knowledge.

Douglas, now twenty-five years old, was described as excessively modest and shy, but his contemporaries believed him to be a man of enthusiasm and intelligence. He also possessed a strong spirit of adventure and was well endowed with personal courage. The journey itself was a daunting prospect, and Douglas, at the time of departure, said he doubted he would ever see England again. However, his enthusiasm for botany was unbounded, and he combined this with a strong religious faith as his support in life.

Douglas spent two years in North America, years filled with difficult travel, interesting and sometimes dangerous encounters with Indians, and extraordinary successes in botanizing. He sent back to England collections of seeds and plants; included were many species new to English botanists—evening primrose, wild hyacinth, ocean spray, the Oregon grape, honeysuckle, and many others. He also described the giant fir, *Pinus taxifolia*, later given the name of Douglas fir (*Pinus Douglasii*), and further emended, in botanical nomenclature, to *Pseudotsuga menziesii*.

From Fort Vancouver on the Columbia, Douglas traveled across half the continent to York Factory on Hudson Bay; from there he sailed back to England, arriving in October 1827. He had traveled more than 10,000 miles in North America by canoe, on horseback, and on foot; had climbed peaks in the Rocky Mountains; and had fulfilled the mission of his journey beyond anyone's expectations.

Douglas spent the next two years as a public figure, the recipient of many honors, including membership in the Linnean Society and a fellowship in the Zoological Society of London. Douglas had introduced into England more plants than had ever been introduced into a single country by an individual hitherto. Much of the value of the Douglas contributions lay in the fact that they were readily adaptable to the English climate. Not only were society members relieved at his safe return, they were overwhelmed by the results of his expedition.

Toward the end of this period in his life, it became obvious that Douglas had no defined status in either the social or the scientific circles of his time. He was not well educated in a formal sense, and his humble origins gave him no social status at all. He did not qualify as a scientist, and there seemed to be no position that he could fill; in truth, many of his contemporaries regarded him as a successful plant collector, no more and no less. This situation caused him much distress, but he was rescued from it when his lifelong friend and patron William Hooker arranged for him to go on a second expedition to America. He sailed from England in October 1829 and, after a stop in the Sandwich (Hawaiian) Islands, he reached the Columbia River in June 1830. His new travels in the Northwest included what are now Washington and California. In the latter he spent nineteen months, visiting Franciscan missions, collecting new specimens, and sending many back to England. Included were mariposa lilies, fairy lanterns, the scarlet bugler, bush poppies, and the blazing star. His new contributions were enthusiastically received by the Horticultural Society. On 15 May 1883 Hooker wrote to his friend John Richardson, "What a glorious collection has Douglas sent me from California." Douglas himself wrote that he hoped the new species would give his "good friend, Dr. Hooker . . . material for two new volumes of the Flora" (letter to Joseph Sabine, 26 Oct. 1832).

Never to return to England, in the last two years of his life, Douglas made two more voyages to the Sandwich Islands, the second expedition sponsored by the Royal Horticultural Society with support from the Colonial Office and the Hudson's Bay Company. This was a land that held a great fascination for him; he thought it more interesting than California and suggested to Hooker that he might consider doing a "Flora of these Islands." Along with plant collecting on the island of Hawaii, he explored the island's mountains, including the active volcano Kilauea. He also made a trek to the summit of Mauna Loa, whose crater he measured. At this time, Douglas was ill, and his condition might have contributed to his death on Hawaii. His failing eyesight was his principal malady, and it is believed that, while on a trail, he missed his footing at a bullock pit (a large hole dug for the purpose of capturing wild cattle) and, falling into it, was gored to death by the captured beast.

News of Douglas's death produced an outpouring of praise and recognition of his special achievements. Not only had he introduced into Britain hundreds of new plants and an enormous fund of botanical information, he also was the first botanist to make a comprehensive study of the flora of the Pacific Northwest and made unique observations in the Hawaiian Islands. He was one of the preeminent natural history explorers of his generation of Europeans.

• The letters and journals of Douglas are at the Royal Horticultural Society, London, and other materials are in the letters and manuscripts of W. J. Hooker at the Royal Botanic Gardens, Kew. There are two important sources for the story of the life of David Douglas. The first is William Jackson Hooker, "Brief Memoir of the Life of Mr. David Douglas, with Extracts from His Letters," in his *Companion to the Botanical Magazine*, vol. 2 (1836) (repr. *Hawaiian Spectator* 2 [1839]; *Oregon Historical Quarterly* 5 and 6 [1904, 1905]). The second is the Royal Horticultural Society's book, *Journal Kept by David Douglas during His Travels in North America 1823–1827* (1914). There is a lengthy critical discussion of both these sources in Susan Delano McKelvey, *Botanical Exploration of the Trans-Mississippi West, 1790–1850* (1955; rev. ed. 1991), chap. 14; chap. 18 is a continuation of the Douglas story.

Of the numerous secondary sources, excellent biographies are A. G. Harvey, *Douglas of the Fir* (1947), and W. Morwood, *Traveler in a Vanished Landscape* (1974). Harvey's work is notable for its extensive bibliography, including depositories of manuscripts. For another list of books and articles about Douglas and his contemporaries, reference should be made to F. Stafleu, *Taxonomic Literature*, vol. 1 (1976), pp. 674–75.

ROBERT F. ERICKSON

DOUGLAS, Donald Wills (6 Apr. 1892–1 Feb. 1981), aeronautical engineer and airplane manufacturing executive, was born in Brooklyn, New York, the son of William Edward Douglas, a banker, and Dorothy Locker. He attended a Brooklyn elementary school and was later sent to the Trinity Chapel School in Manhattan, an Episcopal preparatory school. Douglas enjoyed a comfortable middle class upbringing, spending considerable time sailing at the New York Yacht Club, where his father was a member. As a boy he also became enthralled with the exploits of Orville Wright and his brother Wilbur, Samuel Langley, and other aviators. During the summer of 1908, Douglas visited Fort Myer, Virginia, and saw a demonstration of aeronautics by the Wright brothers. This experience confirmed his eagerness to make aviation his life's work.

In 1909 Douglas completed his schooling at Trinity and received an appointment to the U.S. Naval Academy. As a midshipman, he advocated in classes the development of aircraft as a naval weapon but found little sympathy for his belief. Since opportunities in aviation were limited in the navy, he eventually resigned his appointment to pursue aeronautical engineering at the Massachusetts Institute of Technology (MIT). After graduating with a B.S. in 1914, Douglas remained at MIT to work for Jerome C. Hunsaker, one of the foremost aeronautical engineers in the United States, helping to develop the first wind tunnel.

In August 1915, on a recommendation from Hunsaker, Glenn L. Martin, the aviation pioneer and head of Martin Aircraft Company based in Los Angeles, hired Douglas as his chief engineer. A year later Douglas left Martin briefly to serve a stint with the U.S. Army Signal Corps as its chief civilian aeronautical engineer. He married Charlotte Marguerite Ogg in 1916; they would have five children. He returned to Martin in 1917, this time working at the Cleveland factory. Though he rose to the vice presidency by 1920, Douglas wanted full control of the design effort and decided to form his own aircraft company.

In 1920 Douglas returned to southern California with $600 and the dream of building a streamlined monoplane. He chose this region because he believed it had ideal weather for flight testing over several terrains and because his wife thought the warm, arid climate would improve their children's health. He formed a partnership with David R. Davis, a millionaire sportsman and pilot, who wanted to be the first man to make a coast-to-coast nonstop flight and believed they could build an aircraft that would allow him to achieve that record. The Davis-Douglas Aircraft Company set up shop in the back room of a barbershop and began work on what became known as the "Cloudster." In June 1921 Davis took off for Long Island in Douglas's aircraft, but the flight ended over Texas when the engine failed. Losing his dream to two army pilots soon thereafter, Davis dissolved the partnership in 1921.

Douglas was not dissuaded from his own dream, however, and he persuaded fifteen local businesspeople to lend him $1,000 each to keep the company going. He also convinced the navy in 1921 to give his company a contract for $120,000 to build three Cloudsters that could be used for torpedo bombing and opened a plant at an old Santa Monica motion picture studio. The ensuing DT-1 was a successful design, incorporating innovative features such as folding wings for sea launch and options for either float or wheel undercarriages. The navy placed orders for ninety-three more DT-1's the next year, beginning a long partnership with Douglas Aircraft Company.

Douglas was able to secure additional government contracts during the 1920s. In 1923 the army approached Douglas with a request to build four variants on the DT-1, a plane that officials believed was rugged enough to fly around the world without major overhaul and enhance U.S. prestige abroad. Douglas responded, and in 1924 two of the four aircraft completed the circumnavigation of the globe, impressing foreign leaders, army officials, and Douglas. Also in 1924 Douglas entered an army competition for observation aircraft and out of the trials received a contract for fifty airplanes. By the late 1920s, Douglas's firm had grown to over 500 employees, most of whom were working on military contracts.

The most significant aircraft developed by Douglas before World War II, and perhaps ever, was started in 1932 as a contract for Transcontinental and Western Airlines (TWA), who wanted a new all-metal, monowinged airliner. As a result, the famous Douglas Commercial (DC) series emerged. The DC-1 prototype of 1932 became the DC-2 that filled the TWA order and then developed in 1936 into the revolutionary DC-3 commercial transport. It was an instant success. Between 1937 and 1941 Douglas delivered 360 DC-3's to the airlines. In all, Douglas built 803 commercial DC-3's; they were the mainstay of airlines around the world for a generation. This airplane, with its efficient engines, favorable lift/drag ratio, high payload capability, relative comfort, and ease of operation, helped make passenger aviation profitable without government airmail contracts.

World War II proved a great boon to Douglas's aircraft business. He made the decision in 1942 to expand his manufacturing greatly, operating plants in El Segundo, Santa Monica, and Long Beach, California; Tulsa and Oklahoma City, Oklahoma; and Chicago. By 1944, for example, Douglas employed a total of 160,000 personnel, compared to less than 2,000 when he started building the DC aircraft. By 1945 Douglas Aircraft Company had built 29,385 aircraft in four years and had become one of the largest aircraft firms in the nation due in large measure to Douglas's aggressive business leadership and engineering acumen.

Military purchases of the DC-3, designated C-47's, had much to do with Douglas's success during the war. The army and navy bought 10,123 aircraft and used them in every theater. Nevertheless, while Douglas concentrated on designing and producing transport aircraft, he remained involved in naval aviation and secured a contract in 1940 to develop the SBD "Dauntless" dive bomber. It became the premier carrier-based strike aircraft for the navy during the war. In all, Douglas manufactured nearly 6,000 SBD's, some of them an army version. Although a slow aircraft—a navy wit suggested that SBD stood for "slow but deadly"—the military prized the aircraft's ruggedness, heavy armor, size and variety of firepower it could carry, and its distinctive tail gunner position. Douglas's company also developed the A-26 "Invader" bomber for the army and entered into coproduction agreements with other companies to produce B-17's and B-24's.

In anticipation of postwar demand from commercial airlines for a new generation of transports, in 1942 Douglas began the development of another pathbreaking four-engine transport, the DC-4. He hoped it would protect his company from depending solely on military contracts to remain solvent. Initially successful, the DC-4 and its DC-6 and DC-7 variants, however, were the last of the great propeller-driven commercial airliners. His very success with these aircraft, indeed, led Douglas to a major error in not foreseeing the shift from prop to jet aircraft. He continued manufacturing these aircraft long after their technology had become obsolete and, therefore, lost much business to Boeing's 707 commercial jetliner during the early 1950s. In a frenzy to catch up, in 1956 Douglas built the DC-8 as a Boeing competitor. While the DC-8 was a moderately successful design, Douglas's company never really recovered from the earlier miscalculation. He also developed the DC-9, a short-range aircraft, in the early 1960s to secure a place in that market and competed with Boeing and McDonnell to develop the first wide-bodied jetliners in the mid-1960s. In the process of this competition, however, Douglas exhausted the resources of his company, and in 1967 he was forced to merge with McDonnell, a specialist in building military fighters, to survive. McDonnell, which had tied its business to military contracts, had prospered. In seeking independence from the military and in not anticipating the importance of jet airliners, Douglas lost control of his company.

McDonnell-Douglas Aircraft Company was a giant in the industry throughout the rest of Douglas's life, but he could not control it the way he had his own company. He chafed under the rules of the merger, in which he had only figurehead status, as he had while working for Martin. Douglas died in Palm Springs, California, still regretting the business decisions that had ruined his company. Without question his most significant legacy was the early DC series of commercial airliners his firm produced. They had revolutionized passenger transportation and helped to create the commercial aviation industry as it emerged in the post–World War II era.

• There is no formal collection of Douglas's papers. Material by and about him can be found at the Douglas Aircraft Company, Long Beach, but access is restricted. Some of his letters are available in the Henry H. Arnold Papers, Library of Congress. Additional information about Douglas can be found in Frank Cunningham, *Sky Master: The Story of Donald Douglas and the Douglas Aircraft Company* (1943); Jeffrey A. Fadiman, "Dreamer of the Drawing Board: Donald Wills Douglas (1892–1981)," in *Business Entrepreneurs in the West*, ed. Ted C. Hinckley (1986); Barrett Tillman, "Douglas Aircraft: Armorer of Naval Aviation," *Journal of the West* 30 (Jan. 1991): 58–68; Douglas J. Ingells, *The Plane That Changed the World: A Biography of the DC-3* (1966); Ingells, *The McDonnell-Douglas Story* (1979); and John B. Rae, *Climb to Greatness: The American Aircraft Industry, 1920–1960* (1968). An obituary is in the *New York Times*, 3 Feb. 1981.

ROGER D. LAUNIUS

DOUGLAS, Helen Gahagan (25 Nov. 1900–28 June 1980), actress and politician, was born in Boonton, New Jersey, the daughter of Walter Hamer Gahagan, a civil and contracting engineer, and Lillian Rose Mussen. In 1905 the family moved to an exclusive neighborhood in Brooklyn, New York. Helen's authoritarian father made all the family decisions; her mother stressed education and the religious values of the Episcopal church. She also had a penchant for the opera and took Helen to every performance of the Metropolitan Opera. As a child Helen often staged dramatic presentations atop her father's billiard table for siblings and friends. Although bright, she was a poor student and dreamed of being an actress, a career choice neither parent found acceptable.

After attending Berkeley Institute for Girls, Helen Gahagan enrolled in Capen's School, a college preparatory school in Northampton, Massachusetts, where she nearly failed academically. Seeing the benefits a fine college might offer, she finally pulled up her grades and in 1920 was accepted at Barnard College. For Gahagan the college had two advantages: it was close to New York and Broadway and had a drama department. She soon played the leads in school productions, participated in debates, took drama courses, and became a member of the drama society, Wigs and Cues.

Gahagan developed a friendship with another student, Alis de Sala, and together the two combined their talents to write a one-act play, *Shadows on the Moon*, for a term paper. A former Berkeley professor offered to have it staged at the Lenox Little Theatre and cast Gahagan in the lead. Her acting career escalated, resulting in two small parts in Off-Broadway productions and a three-year contract with Broadway producer William A. Brady. She signed the contract against her father's wishes and dropped out of college in 1922.

Although Gahagan's first Broadway role as the lead in *Dreams for Sale* (1922) was a dismal failure and the play closed after thirteen performances, she won recognition and was lauded as a sensational new talent. Gahagan played numerous roles as she fulfilled her contract obligations with Brady. She played Paula in *Fashions for Men* (1922), Jean Trowbridge in *Chains* (1923), and Leah in *Leah Kleschna* (1924). In 1925 she appeared in *Beyond* and *The Sapphire Ring*. She felt the latter was a disaster, but for the first time her father accepted her career in the theater, telling her, "You build character."

Gahagan's last performance under contract with Brady was also in 1925 in *Enchanted April*. Needing new challenges and direction, she signed a contract in November of that year with George Tyler and performed in *Young Woodley*. Critically hailed as one of the most promising actresses, she was compared to Ethel Barrymore and was called one of the twelve most beautiful women in the world. On tour Gahagan passed the offstage hours with lessons in French, German, and Italian. She read numerous biographies, works on art and philosophy, and literature, and she studied music and diction. After 260 performances the highly successful *Young Woodley*, which had launched Gahagan as a major stage actress, ended. She did two more plays with Tyler, *Trelawney of the Wells* (1927) and *Diplomacy* (1928).

Tyler had afforded her the chance to perform in wonderful productions with excellent casts but had not introduced her to the classics. For this she needed wider experiences of Off-Broadway training that she had not yet attempted. Despite this limitation, she loved her chosen career yet longed to be challenged by directing and playwriting.

On one of her tours Gahagan had met Madame Sophia Cehanovska, an opera coach, and had begun studying with her. Gahagan became intensely interested in singing and in 1928 pursued an operatic career, a dream that her mother had always wanted. She made two European tours in 1929 and 1930. After moderate success she returned to the United States but was not able to get work singing. Instead she accepted the part of a frustrated opera singer in David Belasco's production of *Tonight or Never* (1930). She played opposite Melvyn Douglas. The two fell in love and married in 1931 before the opening. The movie rights were purchased by Samuel Goldwyn in the same year, and the

entire cast, except Gahagan, was hired. Instead Gloria Swanson was signed to take her place. The Douglases moved to Hollywood. They had two children.

Until she witnessed the plight of California's migrant workers during the 1930s, Gahagan had only a vague sense of the world around her. Although she had read widely, she did not concern herself with international events or the social and economic problems of the nation. In the height of the Great Depression she became aware of the troubled lives of migrants who were out of work and living in boxcars. Although she did not become politically active at this time, the experience changed her outlook, and she thought that the Democrats and the New Deal had the right programs to handle the difficulties of hard times.

After her marriage Gahagan became more selective in her roles as her husband's career as a leading man grew. In 1932, after a benefit performance of *Aïda* in New York, Gahagan took the leading role in *The Cat and the Fiddle* in San Francisco. In 1934 she returned to Broadway as Emily Brontë in *Moor Born*, opposite her husband in *Mother Lode*, and as Queen Mary in *Mary of Scotland*. The following year she acted in her first and only film, *She*. Unsuccessful at the time, many years later it became an acclaimed classic horror film. Gahagan had a role on Broadway in *And Stars Remain* (1936).

Gahagan returned to Europe for a singing tour in 1937. In Europe she realized the effects of the Nazi regime on Germany and Austria. When she sang in German, she was appalled when she was approached by someone who, assuming she was a supporter of Hitler, wanted her to seek out American sympathizers for the Nazi cause. The incident moved her beyond her own self-contained world. Upon her return to California she joined the Anti-Nazi League and was initiated into activism. "The current of the times," she once explained, "carried me."

At a meeting of the John Steinbeck Committee to Aid Migratory Workers, Helen Gahagan Douglas suggested to the group that they ask merchants for toys for a Christmas party for 2,000 children of migrant workers. She was put in charge of the event and later became chairman of the Steinbeck Committee. She and her husband attracted many volunteers, but when she noted that many of those joining the organization were Communists, the couple quit.

After Helen Douglas entered the Women's Division of the Democratic party, she became acquainted with Eleanor and Franklin Roosevelt. The president appointed Douglas to the State Advisory Committee of the National Youth Authority and the National Advisory Committee of the Works Progress Administration in 1939. Douglas's political interest heightened, and in 1940 she was elected national committeewoman for California. In a few months she was also made vice chairman of the California State Committee. Her ability to speak effectively brought demands for appearances all over the country. In 1941, following the presidential election, she held a regional conference convention in which she engineered a meeting of labor leaders over continued jurisdictional strikes. The meeting helped to resolve the differences. As head of the Women's Division, she appointed capable women to important positions and elevated their status in the party.

Douglas became an active campaigner in the 1942 election. Financial troubles loomed when her husband entered the army. Without an income Douglas managed her household without help. When it came to her own campaign for Congress in 1944, female aides said she ran it on "pennies." No meeting place was too small for Douglas as she campaigned rigorously, speaking before the people of her Los Angeles district. She won the election, representing various ethnic and blue-collar neighborhoods. Shedding her star image, she took her political office seriously. She coauthored the McMahon-Douglas Bill, which placed atomic patents under civilian control. In 1946 and 1948 she won reelection.

Persuaded by women leaders and California liberal Democrats, Douglas ran for the U.S. Senate in 1950. Because she was a liberal who had supported many causes, including advocating blacks to serve as soldiers during World War II and introducing legislation to protect the rights of citizens who appeared before congressional committees, she became vulnerable to attacks. Richard Nixon, her Republican opponent, accused her of being "soft on communism," often quoting her out of context. His campaign workers made anonymous calls slandering Douglas and her supporters. These "red smear" measures helped Nixon win. (During the Watergate hearings of 1974, bumper stickers read, "Don't blame me. I voted for Helen Gahagan Douglas.")

Douglas quit politics after the defeat and moved to New York City. She appeared in a final Broadway production, *First Lady* (1952), and published *The Eleanor Roosevelt We Remember* (1963). Lectures topped her busy schedule as she spoke to audiences on concerns of nuclear disarmament. She often campaigned for Democratic candidates for national and state political posts. A delegate at the second Soviet-American Women's Conference, Douglas also represented President Lyndon B. Johnson at the inauguration of the president of Liberia in 1964. Her autobiography, *A Full Life*, was published two years after her death in New York City.

A woman who possessed natural charisma and talent for the stage, Helen Gahagan Douglas employed these assets to serve her country in the political arena. An idealist wishing to preserve the country and obtain peace for the average American, she showed her greatest influence when she engaged in public speaking. She became a role model for women in politics and as a candidate willing to stand forcefully against her opponent.

• Helen Gahagan Douglas's papers are in the Carl Albert Congressional Research Center, Western History Collection, University of Oklahoma. Other collections containing theatrical and political documents are in the New York Public Library Performing Arts Research Center at Lincoln Center; the Bancroft Library at the University of California, Berkeley; the Franklin Delano Roosevelt Library, Hyde Park, N.Y.; and the Library of Congress. Her oral history, *Helen Gahagan Douglas Project* (1981–1982), is in the collection of Women in Politics Oral History Project at the Bancroft Library. Her life is best depicted in her autobiography and in Ingrid Winther Scobie, *Center Stage: Helen Gahagan Douglas, a Life* (1992). Other sources on her life and career are Eleanor Roosevelt and Lorena A. Hickok, *Ladies of Courage* (1954); William Miller, *The Memoirs of a Congressional Doorkeeper* (1977); Scobie, "Helen Gahagan Douglas and the Roosevelt Connection," in *Without Precedent: The Life and Career of Eleanor Roosevelt* (1984); Ronald Brownstein, *The Power and the Glitter: The Hollywood-Washington Connection* (1990); Scobie, "Douglas v Nixon: A Campaign on the Conscience," *History Today* 42 (Nov. 1992): 16–24; Maria Braden, *Women Politicians and the Media* (1996); and Karen Foerstel and Herbert N. Foerstel, *Climbing the Hill: Gender Conflict in Congress* (1996). Her obituary is in the *New York Times*, 29 June 1980.

MARILYN ELIZABETH PERRY

DOUGLAS, H. Ford (1831–11 Nov. 1865), abolitionist and military officer, was born in Virginia, the son of a white man, William Douglas, and a slave, Mary (surname unknown). His first name was Hezekiah, which he chose to abbreviate. Sometime after his fifteenth birthday, he escaped from slavery and settled in Cleveland, Ohio, where he worked as a barber. Self-educated, he became an active member of the antislavery movement and the Ohio free black community in the 1850s. He served as Cleveland agent for the *Voice of the Fugitive*, a black newspaper published in Canada that was devoted to the "immediate and unconditional abolition" of slavery.

Douglas became a leader in the black state convention movement of Ohio. He supported William Lloyd Garrison's position that the U.S. Constitution was a proslavery document that recognized the slave trade, approved slavery, and provided for the recapture of fugitive slaves. Unlike those abolitionists who sought to uproot slavery through moral suasion or political activity, Douglas advocated African-American emigration. He soon gained a reputation as an eloquent orator and at age twenty-two was appointed one of the vice presidents of the 1853 Ohio State Convention of Colored Freemen in Columbus. Achieving prominence at the 1854 National Emigration Convention in Cleveland, Douglas delivered a brilliant defense of emigration. He argued that African Americans could not wait indefinitely for change in the United States after 200 years of oppression and little improvement in their status. While Douglas knew that African Americans would never achieve equality as long as slavery continued, he believed that this system was destined to last for a long time. Under these circumstances, he refused to proclaim allegiance and loyalty to the United States.

After the 1854 National Emigration Convention, Douglas moved to Chicago, where he became a proprietor of the *Provincial Freeman*, a black newspaper published in Canada. He also became active in the Illinois black state convention movement. At the 1856 meeting in Alton, he chaired the Committee on Declaration of Sentiment, which denounced the racial prejudice that African Americans encountered in their "native land." Remaining in Chicago for only a few years, Douglas soon moved to British-controlled Canada West (now Ontario), where he believed black people could give their allegiance to a government that protected them. He described the United States as a country that robbed, kidnapped, plundered, raped, and murdered black people "with the cant of liberty, democracy and Christianity upon her lips."

Douglas married Statira Steele in October 1857; they had one child. In 1858 Douglas returned to Chicago. The emigrationist movement, which had once considered Canada as the ideal destination, turned its attention to Africa and Haiti. Douglas, however, became interested in Central America and signed up as an agent for Francis P. Blair, Jr.'s Central American Land Company. Blair, a congressman from Missouri, advocated settling free blacks in Central or South America. With assistance from the U.S. government, Blair argued, African Americans could lead comfortable and prosperous lives in an area free of slavery. Blair proposed Honduras as a suitable location that could also assist the United States in its competition with Great Britain for control of trade in Central America. Because of the area's climate, Blair argued that whites could not settle the region but that blacks would thrive there. Blair's proposal made little progress, however, especially because the Guatemalan government, which controlled the territory of Honduras, opposed the scheme.

In May 1860 Douglas made his first visit to New England at the invitation of Parker Pillsbury, a Garrisonian whom Douglas had met during a lecture tour through the Midwest. Douglas was soon much in demand as an abolitionist speaker. Newspaper accounts of his 4 July 1860 address to an antislavery rally in Framingham, Massachusetts, describe him as having "a physique so noble and a presence so attractive as to charm and interest the listener at once." In that speech, Douglas criticized the United States for not measuring up to the standard of a great nation because it supported slavery. He argued that on the slavery question there was not much difference between Stephen A. Douglas and Abraham Lincoln.

Douglas lectured widely throughout New England during the latter part of 1860 as a traveling agent for the Massachusetts Antislavery Society. With growing praise for John Brown (1800–1859) and his raid on the federal arsenal at Harpers Ferry, Virginia, Douglas increasingly favored the use of violence to end slavery. He remained in New England through January 1861, when he returned to Chicago as an agent for James Redpath's Haitian Emigration Bureau. His duties involved recruiting prospective emigrants, informing them about Haiti, and describing the facilities offered by the Haitian government.

With the outbreak of the Civil War, Douglas traveled to Kansas, where he encouraged slaves from Missouri to escape to freedom. He later passed for white

and joined Company G of the 95th Regiment Illinois Infantry Volunteers in July 1862, in Belvidere, Illinois. Six months later, Douglas, who was overjoyed at Lincoln's freeing the slaves, wrote Frederick Douglass about the Emancipation Proclamation and his role in the war. He encouraged Douglass to support the war by recruiting and commanding a black regiment to prove that black men deserved equality. Once the Union army officially enlisted black troops, Douglas requested a transfer to a black unit. Brigadier General John P. Hawkins, Commander of the South, assigned him to the 10th Louisiana Regiment of African Descent (Corps d'Afrique) in June 1863. While stationed with the Corps d'Afrique in Mississippi, Douglas contracted malaria and returned home to Chicago to recover. He rejoined the military in July 1864 and recruited an independent battery of light artillery of which he became captain. Douglas was one of fewer than thirty black commissioned officers in the Union army and was probably the only black combat captain during the Civil War.

He left the service in July 1865, still suffering from malaria. He tried unsuccessfully to operate a restaurant in Atchison, Kansas, but died there four months after his discharge. Although not as well known as Frederick Douglass, H. Ford Douglas was a popular and effective antislavery speaker. As was true of Douglass, his complexion and physical features made clear to audiences the tragedy of slavery. Contrary to Douglass, however, he advocated emigration on the grounds that African Americans would never achieve their full potential in the United States until the nation abolished slavery.

• Douglas's surviving correspondence, speeches, editorials, and reports are reproduced in C. Peter Ripley, ed., *The Black Abolitionist Papers 1830–1865* (5 vols., 1985–1992). Robert L. Harris, Jr., "H. Ford Douglas: Afro-American Antislavery Emigrationist," *Journal of Negro History* 62, no. 3 (July 1977): 217–34, is the most complete essay on Douglas. Materials relating to his military career are in Records of the Adjutant General's Office, 1780s–1917, in the National Archives, Washington, D.C., Record Group 94 and Pension File Number 191423.

ROBERT L. HARRIS, JR.

DOUGLAS, Lewis William (2 July 1894–7 Mar. 1974), businessman and government official, was born in Bisbee, Arizona, the son of James Stuart Douglas, a mine owner and banker, and Josephine Leah Williams. In 1906 he was sent east to be educated and subsequently attended the Hackley School in Tarrytown, New York, the Montclair Military Academy in New Jersey, and Amherst College in Massachusetts, from which he graduated in 1916. In addition, he spent a year (1916–1917) at the Massachusetts Institute of Technology, studying geology and metallurgy. During World War I, he was commissioned a second lieutenant in the field artillery and was a participant in the Argonne offensive of 1918. After the war, he took temporary positions as a history instructor at Amherst and a teacher of chemistry at the Hackley School but in 1921 decided to return to Arizona, where he became engaged in copper mining and citrus fruit growing near the town of Jerome. In 1921 he married Margaret "Peggy" Zinsser; they had three children.

In 1922 Douglas was elected to the Arizona state legislature, where he served for two years (1923–1925) and involved himself particularly in fighting labor legislation, the Colorado River Compact, and the Ku Klux Klan. In 1926 he became the Democratic nominee for U.S. representative from Arizona, was victorious in the election, and retained his seat in the elections of 1928, 1930, and 1932. In Congress he served on the House Military Affairs, Appropriations, and Reclamation Committees, articulated a philosophy of small government and free markets in the Grover Cleveland tradition, and became known particularly for his opposition to the development projects for Boulder Canyon and the Tennessee River, his votes against veterans' pensions, and his advocacy of strict governmental economy and a balanced budget. In 1932 he sponsored the resolution creating a special economy committee for the House and subsequently became a member of it. In addition, he was a strong critic of the Smoot-Hawley Tariff of 1930, but as an Arizonan he favored tariff protection for copper and succeeded in making this a part of the Revenue Act of 1932.

During the presidential campaign in 1932, Douglas established close relations with Franklin D. Roosevelt and was convinced that Roosevelt's campaign promises to reduce the federal budget by 25 percent were sincere. In December 1932, after visiting Roosevelt at his Hyde Park estate, Douglas began work on an economy bill, and in early 1933 he resigned from Congress to accept an appointment as Roosevelt's director of the budget. In March he was able to secure the Economy Act, reducing federal salaries and veterans' benefits and empowering the president to implement other economy measures. He became a close presidential adviser, writing presidential messages, acting as a liaison to Congress, participating with the inner circle in policy conferences, and becoming a regular member of the "Bedside Cabinet" that met with the president each morning. He was unable, however, to prevent the passage of new public works, relief, and monetary expansion measures, and by early 1934 Douglas had become thoroughly disillusioned with the course the New Deal was taking. On 31 August 1934 he resigned, citing philosophical differences with the president's fiscal goals and program. In 1935, particularly in articles published in the *Atlantic Monthly* and in a book of lectures entitled *The Liberal Tradition*, Douglas became a sharp critic of New Deal economics, especially of Roosevelt's failure to balance the budget, the lack of actions to stimulate the capital goods industries, and the embrace of "collectivism" rather than "true liberalism." In 1936, after writing and publishing "A Declaration of Principles for Conservative Democrats" (*New York Times*, 3 June 1936), he became an adviser to Republican presidential candidate Alfred M. Lan-

don, and in 1940 he was an organizer of the Democrats for Willkie movement.

Following his departure from government in 1934, Douglas took a managerial position in New York with the American Cyanamid Company. He soon became bored, however, with his business duties and in January 1938 accepted a position as principal and vice chancellor of McGill University in Montreal, Canada. There he spent the next two years, seeking in particular to put the institution on a sound financial basis and to develop new programs that would help to counteract socialism. In 1940 he moved back to New York, where he became the head of the Mutual Insurance Company of New York and continued to be associated with the company until 1972. As its president (1940–1947), he was responsible for the company's reorganization and revival, and as chairman of the board (1947–1959) and chairman of the executive committee (1959–1972), he continued to play a significant role in its management. In the 1940s and 1950s he also accepted directorships in other major corporations, the most prominent of which were General Motors, the Union Corporation, and the International Nickel Company of Canada.

As World War II approached, Douglas became a strong interventionist, an important figure in the activities of the Committee to Defend America by Aiding the Allies, and a champion of lend-lease assistance. Following Pearl Harbor, he accepted a position as deputy lend-lease expediter in Britain, and in February 1942 he became the deputy administrator of the War Shipping Administration in charge of allocating all shipping resources available. In this position, he worked closely with the British and was soon involved in clashes with the American military, who tended to see him as too pro-British in the positions he took. In March 1944 Douglas resigned his position and returned to his duties at Mutual Insurance. In April 1945 he was again in the limelight with a controversial article in the *Atlantic Monthly* calling for government withdrawal from shipping once the war was over.

Following World War II, Douglas served briefly as a financial adviser to General Lucius Clay in Germany, turned down an offer to head the World Bank, and became a strong advocate of German economic reconstruction as the key to promoting European recovery and curbing communism. In 1947 President Harry Truman offered him the ambassadorship to Great Britain, and as ambassador from 1947 to 1950, he not only made his residence a center of London social life but was heavily involved in the British-American negotiations concerning the Marshall Plan, German currency reform, the North Atlantic Treaty Organization, and the fate of Palestine. While in Britain, he was involved in a fishing accident that cost him an eye and was troubled with sinus problems that finally led to his resignation and return to the United States in 1950.

On his return, Douglas moved to Tucson, Arizona, where he had earlier bought a ranch and a controlling interest in the Southern Arizona Bank and Trust Company (subsequently a subsidiary of Western Bancorporation). There he continued to manage his business interests and also to involve himself in such matters as national unity, foreign aid, weather modification, solar energy, juvenile delinquency, business education, and American Indian policy. In the early 1950s he chaired the American Assembly's National Policy Board, an agency seeking to build national cooperation between the leaders of business, government, labor, and education. In the years from 1953 to 1967 he served on a variety of presidential study groups and task forces and took a particular interest in the work of the Institute of Atmospheric Physics, which he had helped to establish at the University of Arizona. He continued to follow national politics, usually supporting the Republican candidates in presidential elections but expressing disgust with McCarthyism in the 1950s, refusing to support Barry Goldwater in 1964, and becoming an early critic of the Vietnam War.

Douglas liked to think of himself as the epitomy of "rugged independence" whose "whole educational foundation rested upon international liberalism," but the antistatism that led him to break with the New Deal and support its political foes also had room for a powerful warfare state, a strong national security apparatus, and a society ordered through corporate organization and intergroup cooperation as well as free markets. His ideological rigidity, moreover, was always tempered by his mastery of the political arts and the attractiveness and seemingly irresistible charm of his personality. Tall and strapping with a lean and lined face, a ready grin, a pleasing and forceful voice, and a cheerful, alert, and energetic manner, he was a person whom people liked, even when they disagreed with him. This helped to explain his successes both in the business world and in the governmental posts that he occupied. He died at his home in Tucson.

• Douglas's papers are at the University of Arizona in Tucson. His own writings include *The Liberal Tradition: A Free People and a Free Economy* (1935) and *There Is One Way Out* (1935; originally published in *Atlantic Monthly*). The only biography is Robert Paul Browder and Thomas G. Smith, *Independent: A Biography of Lewis W. Douglas* (1986), which is based in part on Smith, "From the Heart of the American Desert to the Court of St. James's: The Public Career of Lewis W. Douglas of Arizona, 1894–1974" (Ph.D. diss., Univ. of Connecticut, 1977). Useful articles include Smith, "Lewis Douglas Grows Up," *Journal of Arizona History* 20 (1979): 223–38; B. Cosulich, "Mr. Douglas of Arizona," *Arizona Highways* 29 (Sept. 1953): 2–11; and Smith, "Lewis Douglas, Arizona Politics, and the Colorado River Controversy," *Arizona and the West* 22 (Summer 1980): 125–62. An obituary is in the *New York Times*, 8 Mar. 1974.

ELLIS W. HAWLEY

DOUGLAS, Lloyd Cassel (27 Aug. 1877–13 Feb. 1951), minister and novelist, was born in Columbia City, Indiana, the son of Alexander Jackson Douglas, a minister and educator, and Sarah Jane Cassel, a teacher. His father had been a farmer, school superintendent, lawyer, and state senator before becoming pastor of a rural Lutheran church; his mother smothered young Lloyd with "maternal supervision," and he grew up a solemn and sheltered child. By working at various jobs, especially playing the organ, Douglas put himself through Wittenberg College in Springfield, Ohio, and the Hamma Divinity School, a Lutheran seminary connected with Wittenberg, receiving his B.A. in 1900 and his B.D. in 1903.

Ordained as a Lutheran minister, Douglas served his first parish in North Manchester, Indiana (1903–1905). While there he married Bessie Io Porch, a classmate at Wittenberg; they had two children. From 1905 to 1909 he served a Lutheran congregation in Lancaster, Ohio. In 1909 Douglas became minister of the Luther Place Memorial Church, a prominent congregation in Washington, D.C. While there he developed doubts about conservative Lutheran theology, but he did not discover any satisfactory alternative; he therefore decided to leave the pastoral ministry. In 1911 he accepted a position with the Young Men's Christian Association (YMCA) as director of religious work at the University of Illinois. Although effective in this capacity, he yearned to return to the pulpit.

Discussions with the pastor of the local Congregational church helped Douglas redefine his personal faith, and the reverent, adaptable, dignified style of this denomination led him into its ministry. From 1915 to 1921 he served the First Congregational Church of Ann Arbor, Michigan, and attracted many faculty and students to its services. During the last six months of World War I he chaired the YMCA War Fund and spent much of his time in New York City. His desire for a new challenge took him in 1921 to the First Congregational Church in Akron, Ohio. Although his ministry there was successful, he failed to fulfill his goal of making the church into a famous institutional center that provided a broad range of educational, social, and recreational services for the community, and in 1926 he accepted a call from the First Congregational Church of Los Angeles. When a group within this congregation sharply criticized his style of ministry, which focused more on sermon preparation and community involvement than on visiting parishioners and attending all the meetings of various church groups, he resigned in 1928.

While serving his church in Washington, Douglas began writing short stories and essays. During subsequent pastorates he published a few articles in the *Atlantic Monthly*, as well as several books, including *Wanted: A Congregation* (1920) and *The Minister's Everyday Life* (1924). In *These Sayings of Mine: An Interpretation of the Teachings of Jesus* (1926), Douglas expanded and interpreted some of Christ's parables through the use of novelistic scenes. A collection of his sermons was issued in 1927 as *Those Disturbing Miracles*. When Douglas resigned from his Los Angeles congregation, he was working on a novel, *Magnificent Obsession*. Published in 1929 by a small Chicago firm that specialized in religious books, it tells the story of a rich playboy whose life is saved by a saintly surgeon's sacrifice of his own life. Inspired by this act and the dead man's journal, the hero experiences a spiritual rebirth—a central theme in most of Douglas's books—

and continues the surgeon's work. Sales of the novel began very slowly, and Douglas accepted a pastorate at St. James United Church in Montreal, where he stayed until 1933. By 1932, however, *Magnificent Obsession* had become a bestseller, eventually selling almost three million copies. While in Canada, Douglas wrote two other popular books, *Forgive Us Our Trespasses* (1932) and *Precious Jeopardy* (1933), published by Houghton Mifflin, as were the rest of his novels. The first addresses the problem of how people could escape from the encumbrances that blocked the development of their personalities; the second tells the story of a businessman who through an accident learns to live more fully and happily.

Douglas's success led him to return to the United States, where he eventually settled in Los Angeles, and to begin writing full time. His fourth novel, *Green Light*, topped the charts in 1935. Originally published in installments in *Cosmopolitan*, the book urged readers to free themselves from the burdens of frustrations and old bitterness. By the mid-1930s Douglas was the nation's most popular novelist. He made numerous lecture tours to promote his books and received thousands of letters from admirers, often requesting advice. Many readers identified Douglas with the protagonist of *Green Light*, the Episcopal rector Dean Harcourt, who appears in several subsequent novels and dispenses wise guidance based on his convictions that God watches over all people and that the world is making progress.

In the second half of the 1930s Douglas published five successful novels: *White Banners* (1936), *Home for Christmas* (1937), *Doctor Hudson's Secret Journal* (1939), *Secret Passage* (1939), and *Invitation to Live* (1940). His most popular novel was *The Robe* (1942), which remained on the bestseller lists from 1942 to 1945, eventually selling more than three million copies. The book describes the impact of the robe Jesus wore to his crucifixion on those who possessed it after his death, especially a young Roman soldier who was forced to supervise Christ's execution.

Ill health, especially arthritis and fatigue, curbed Douglas's literary output after 1942, but the publication of *The Big Fisherman* (1948), which traces the slow progress of Peter from a simple, rugged, often hasty individual to the chief apostle, gave Douglas another bestseller, with total sales of 1.3 million. *Magnificent Obsession*, *The Robe*, and several other of Douglas's novels were made into movies.

Although immensely popular, Douglas's novels received mixed reviews from critics. While some praised their substance, coherence, inspirational themes, narrative techniques, convincing dialogue, and humor, others argued that his plots were contrived and confusing, his characters simple and plastic, and his prose sentimental, poorly written, and filled with clichés and "saccharine platitudes" (*New York Times*, 17 Mar. 1935). Although Douglas stressed the importance of the spiritual life, critics protested, characters who were faithful to God typically received material rewards. They noted that except in his more theologically complex novels—*The Robe* and *The Big Fisherman*—he solved the problem of evil in the world simply by ignoring it. Seeking to explain the popularity of Douglas's novels, Edmund Wilson concluded that he was "a genuine man of God of the type who used to do his best in the American small-town pulpit and that the community felt it could rely on" (pp. 207–8). Carl Bode insisted that Douglas was successful because his emphasis on moral purpose, doing good, and spiritual rewards was "more congenial to the American reader than the words of almost any other contemporary novelist" (p. 352).

Douglas underwent a spiritual pilgrimage in his own life that his writings reflect. In *These Sayings* and *Those Disturbing Miracles* he is uneasy with the basic doctrines of Christianity, including biblical miracles, which he attempts to explain in psychological terms, and the divine nature of Christ. Although his novels of the 1930s have a religious purpose, they minimize the supernatural. In *The Big Fisherman*, however, Christ is consistently depicted as divine, and miracles no longer require reasonable explanation. Chastened by the depression, war, and personal infirmity, Douglas seems to have reaffirmed the orthodox Christian beliefs he held as a young pastor.

A popular preacher, Douglas was described by Calvin Davis as "facile in speech, powerful in imagery, dramatic in delivery, . . . quick to utilize a pithy saying or humorous anecdote" (quoted in Dawson and Wilson, p. 6). He encouraged congregations to engage in philanthropy and social work but insisted that their highest calling was to provide inspirational worship services, the ministerial function he most enjoyed. A man with few hobbies other than reading and listening to classical music, Douglas devoted his time to his family, his pastoral work, and his writing. He died in Los Angeles.

• The principal sources of information on Douglas's life are his memoir, *A Time to Remember* (1951), which discusses his life through his years in college, and *The Shape of Sunday: An Intimate Biography of Lloyd C. Douglas* (1952), by his daughters, Virginia D. Dawson and Betty D. Wilson; the latter provides much information about Douglas's work as both a pastor and a novelist and includes many of his letters. *The Living Faith* (1955) contains a good sample of his sermons. The best critical analysis of his books is Carl Bode, "Lloyd Douglas: Loud Voice in the Wilderness," *American Quarterly* 2 (Winter 1950): 340–52. Several general works on American literature discuss his novels: Robert van Gelder, *Writers and Writing* (1946); Frank L. Mott, *Golden Multitudes* (1947); Edmund Wilson, *Classics and Commercials* (1950); and Alice P. Hackett, *Seventy Years of Best Sellers* (1967).

GARY SCOTT SMITH

DOUGLAS, Melvyn (5 Apr. 1901–4 Aug. 1981), actor, was born Melvyn Hesselberg in Macon, Georgia, the son of Edouard Hesselberg, a Russian-born concert pianist, and Lena Shakelford. Two major elements of his personality were established in early life. One was his strong social conscience as a defender of society's outsiders, with a special sensitivity to anti-Semitism.

During his family's recurrent moves, to Nashville, then Toronto, then Lincoln, Nebraska, he observed his highly cultured parents being treated as outsiders who "always seemed on the verge of belonging without ever quite arriving," says his autobiography (p. 7), and in his early teens he learned of his father's Jewish descent. The other element was a penchant for stage work, resulting from appearances in a high school play and with local amateur groups in Lincoln.

Douglas matured into a tall, blond, good-looking youth of athletic build, not easily confined to school routine. In 1916, in Toronto, he tried unsuccessfully to enlist in the Canadian army to fight in World War I. In Lincoln he was expelled from high school in his junior year for drinking, smoking, and belonging to a secret fraternity. At seventeen he enlisted in the U.S. Army and served ten months as a medical orderly at Fort Lewis, Washington.

Out of military service in 1919, Douglas came to Chicago in search of the city's exciting artistic and intellectual life. After a series of short-lived jobs, he decided to make the stage his profession. Coaching by actor William Owen led to a place in a Shakespearean repertory company organized by Owen: "I was fortunate to start my work in the theatre," Douglas said, "with an old man who had a tremendous and very real love of it, which adds up to what I suppose could be called idealism. Up to then, the theatre was just something I thought of as fun. It gave me a chance to sleep late and meet actresses. Owen struck something in me that responded" (Millstein, p. 32). His first stage appearance came in 1919, as Bassanio in *The Merchant of Venice*.

After two years with the repertory troupe, Douglas found work with stock companies in midwestern cities for two more years. A European interlude of five months let him experience the expatriate life of Paris, though he never attained the study with Max Reinhardt in Berlin that he had planned. He returned to Chicago for more work in stock and in 1925 was hired by actress Jessie Bonstelle for her repertory company. At her urging he took the stage name of Douglas from a forebear in his mother's old Kentucky family. In 1925 he married Rosalind Hightower; the birth of a son was followed by divorce in 1926.

Douglas's work with the Bonstelle company brought him a three-year contract with a New York producer, William Brady, in 1926. After some stage work in other cities, he made his New York debut in the featured role of a gangster in the Brady production *A Free Soul* (1928). Other Broadway plays followed. The most notable and successful of these was *Tonight or Never* (1930), which starred the singing actress Helen Gahagan. Her strongly liberal political and social concerns resonated with his, the play's torrid love scenes had their effect, and Douglas and Gahagan were married in 1931. Another result of the play was that Douglas was signed by Samuel Goldwyn to a motion picture contract and repeated his stage role in a film version of *Tonight or Never* (1931) opposite Gloria Swanson. At Goldwyn's instigation, he grew the pencil-line mustache that became an integral part of his 1930s screen image as a debonair sophisticate.

Douglas was never at ease with Hollywood life, and in 1932 he terminated his contract with Goldwyn so that he and his wife could take a trip around the world to observe conditions. They returned just in time for the birth of a son in 1933 (a daughter later completed their family). In 1934, after more film appearances, he went to Broadway as a star and director of various productions, none of which was more than a succès d'estime. Douglas resumed work in motion pictures in 1935 and became known as a reliable leading man for female stars from Claudette Colbert (*She Married Her Boss*, 1935) and Irene Dunne (*Theodora Goes Wild*, 1936) to Greta Garbo (*Ninotchka*, 1939) and Joan Crawford (*A Woman's Face*, 1941). Though he showed an acting range from screwball comedy to romantic drama, Douglas remained at costar level, never achieving stardom in his own right. Much energy went into his social and political activism. He raised contributions for the loyalists of the Spanish Civil War, was a stalwart of the Democratic party in California, was involved in union affairs with the Screen Actors Guild, and in 1940 became the first actor ever to be a delegate to the Democratic National Convention. To those who called him a "radical," as some in California did, he replied that "he was a radical only if you choose to call the New Deal radical."

When the United States entered the war in 1941, Douglas went to Washington, D.C., as director of the Arts Council of the Office of Civilian Defense. In 1942 he enlisted in the army as a private, then became a captain heading an Army Entertainment Production Unit in the China-Burma-India war zone. There he learned that Helen Gahagan Douglas had been elected to the U.S. House of Representatives. After his discharge from the army as a major in 1945, he was a co-producer of the hit Broadway revue *Call Me Mister* (1946), about soldiers returning to civilian life.

Douglas was not eager to resume his old screen roles as a suave playboy, nor in postwar America was there much demand for them. After a series of disappointing films, he determined to return to Broadway and did so in a successful comedy about government bureaucracy, *Two Blind Mice* (1949). His wife's defeat by Richard Nixon in a savage campaign for U.S. senator in 1950 left the couple ready to abandon California altogether for life in New York City.

In 1952 Douglas starred in a long-running comedy, *Time Out for Ginger*, as a father trying to deal with three rambunctious teenage daughters. He had first played a father in the film *Captains Courageous* (1937) and would have many more such roles. A series of stage appearances in succeeding years established him as an actor of stature, and two permitted him to affirm his social values as well: in *Inherit the Wind* (1955), replacing the ailing Paul Muni, he won artistic respect for his masterful portrayal of a character much like Clarence Darrow; and in *The Best Man* (1960), he played an idealistic aspirant to the presidency. For his performance in *The Best Man*, he won the Antoinette

Perry Award. In between he was the disillusioned father of two sluttish daughters in *Waltz of the Toreadors* (1957).

In the 1960s, when Hollywood's studio era was over and its ultraconservative political climate of the 1940s and 1950s was in the past, Douglas returned to films in character roles of substance. He remained active in films for the rest of his life. His performance as the hard-bitten, upright father of Paul Newman in *Hud* (1962) won him an Academy Award as best supporting actor. He was nominated again for his role as a tyrannical, selfish parent in *I Never Sang for My Father* (1970). He was Robert Redford's father, a shrewd and cynical politician, in *The Candidate* (1972), and he won a second Academy Award for his role as a political kingmaker near death in *Being There* (1979). In addition, for his performance as an aged man in the television drama *Do Not Go Gentle into that Good Night* (1968) he won the Emmy Award for outstanding performance. Only four actors before him had won all three awards—the Tony, the Oscar, and the Emmy—for performances in theater, film, and television.

In his later years Douglas suffered a heart attack and was beset by arthritis and other illness. He told one interviewer, "As [my life] is now, I'm either in pain or I'm medicated to the point of insensibility, which is not pleasant" (*New York Times*, 30 Mar. 1980). Yet he stayed alert and interested in current conditions; the interviewer described him as "a classy gent, proud and literate, inspired to fine-grained opinions on everything and driven to leavening serious statements with dry, jaunty little laughs." He kept up his acting to the end of his 62-year career. At the time of his death in New York City, three of his films were still awaiting release. Alan Alda, who worked with him in *The Seduction of Joe Tynan* (1979), summed up both his co-star's career and character thus: "Melvyn is a person who has survived—no small achievement for an artist. He has survived with his art intact, with dignity and integrity. If somebody says to you that actors are children or narcissists or not very bright, say the name Melvyn Douglas and let them be quiet" (*Women's Wear Daily*, 29 Feb.–7 Mar. 1980).

• Materials on Douglas's life and career are in the Billy Rose Theatre Collection at the New York Public Library for the Performing Arts, Lincoln Center. His autobiography, written with Tom Arthur, is *See You at the Movies* (1986). Two biographical sketches are Gilbert Millstein, "Melvyn Douglas," *Theatre Arts Monthly*, Jan. 1960, and "Melvyn Douglas" in James L. Parish and Ronald L. Bowers, *The MGM Stock Company* (1973). A roster of his major acting appearances and other creative work is in *Contemporary Theatre, Film and Television*, vol. 1 (1984). His film work, both as leading man and character actor, is considered in Kevin Lewis, "The Two Careers of Melvyn Douglas (1901–1981)," *Films in Review*, Oct. 1981 and Nov. 1981. Information on the actor's marriage to Helen Gahagan Douglas is in Ingrid Winther Scobie, *Center Stage: Helen Gahagan Douglas* (1992). Extensive television credits are in David Inman, *The TV Encyclopedia* (1991), and Tim Banks, *The Complete Directory to Prime Time TV Stars* (1987). Two articles focusing on his later years are John Byrne, "A View from a Co-Star," *Women's Wear Daily*, 29 Feb.–7 Mar. 1980, and Helen Dudar, "Melvyn Douglas: A Portrait of the Artist at 79," *New York Times*, 30 Mar. 1980. An obituary is in the *New York Times*, 5 Aug. 1981.

WILLIAM STEPHENSON

DOUGLAS, Paul Howard (26 Mar. 1892–24 Sept. 1976), economist, educator, and U.S. senator, was born in Salem, Massachusetts, the son of James Howard Douglas and Annie Smith. The latter, a laborer, died when Paul was four. His father remarried but soon became an alcoholic and abandoned his wife and son. Douglas worked his way through Bowdoin College, from which he received a B.A. in 1913, and won a scholarship to Columbia University, where he earned an M.A. in 1915 and a Ph.D. in economics in 1921.

Douglas identified closely with the working class. He advocated federal ownership of the means of production, particularly industry, even to the extent of emulating the socialist model of the Soviet Union. While never a Communist, he did favor close diplomatic ties and U.S. friendship with the USSR. After teaching economics at various colleges, Douglas became a professor at the University of Chicago and remained on the faculty from 1920 to 1948. He was a prolific researcher and writer and soon acquired a national reputation as an economist. Douglas published articles in leading economic journals and authored the following major works: *American Apprenticeship and Industrial Education* (1921), *The Worker in Modern Economic Society* (coauthored, 1923), *Wages and the Family* (coauthored, 1925), *Adam Smith* (1928), *Real Wages in the United States* (1930), *The Problem of Unemployment* (1931), *Standards of Unemployment Insurance* (1933), and *Social Security in the United States* (1936). His books dealing with politics include *The Coming of a New Party* (1932), in which he discussed the formation of a viable socialist party; *Economy in the National Government* (1952), dealing with the problem of sustaining a welfare state without resorting to deficit spending; and *Ethics in Government* (1952), which set forth guidelines for the ethical behavior of members of Congress. The code of conduct outlined in the last-named work is still cited by the Senate Ethics Committee in cases dealing with conflict of interest. In 1947 Douglas was elected president of the American Economic Association.

Because Douglas was a Quaker, he opposed military participation in World War I. He did, however, serve as an industrial relations consultant for the Emergency Fleet Corporation. In 1930, following the advent of the Great Depression, Douglas served as acting director of the Swarthmore Unemployment Study, secretary of the Pennsylvania Commission on Unemployment, and economic adviser to the New York Commission on Unemployment (appointed by Governor Franklin D. Roosevelt), and in 1931 was a member of the Illinois Housing Commission. When FDR became president, he appointed Douglas to the Consumer's Advisory Board of the National Recovery Administration in 1933 and to the Advisory Committee to the Social Security Administration in 1937. Douglas participated in formulating the original Social Security Act of 1935 and in its revision in 1939. In Illinois he played a key role in drafting the Utilities Act of 1933, Old Age Pension Act of 1935, and State Unemployment Act of 1937.

After visiting the Soviet Union in 1937 as an economic adviser to a trade union delegation and witnessing the totalitarian power wielded by Joseph Stalin, Douglas became much less enamored of communism in action there. He became totally disillusioned with Stalin in 1939 when the Communist leader signed the Nazi-Soviet Pact. Douglas resigned from the American Society for Cultural Relations with Russia and also denounced the Committee for Democracy and Intellectual Freedom as constituting a Communist front for propagating Stalinism. Likewise, after visiting Italy in 1938 and hearing one of Benito Mussolini's balcony performances, Douglas reexamined his Quaker pacifism. He came to the realization that Hitler, Stalin, and Mussolini were dire threats to world peace and that if decent people did not stand up to them, all humanity would suffer the tragic consequences. Following Germany's defeat of France and the British withdrawal from Dunkirk, Douglas renounced his pacifism and openly supported FDR's interventionist foreign policy. He became an active member of the Committee to Defend America by Aiding the Allies.

Douglas's first marriage to Dorothy Wolff in 1915 ended in a 1930 divorce. He then married Emily Taft, daughter of sculptor Lorado Taft, in 1931. Emily was an author and politician, who served in the U.S. House of Representatives from 1945 to 1947. Through her influence, Paul became interested in seeking elective office. He failed in his attempt to win the Chicago mayoral nomination in 1935, but he won election to the city council as an alderman from the Fifth Ward in 1939 and served until 1942. Douglas steadily gravitated toward the Democratic party, coming to believe the New Deal served the national welfare better than socialism. In 1942 he sought the Democratic nomination for the U.S. Senate but was defeated by the Cook County Democratic organization (the so-called Kelly-Nash machine).

After his defeat, at age fifty, Douglas enlisted in the U.S. Marines as a private. He was assigned to the First Marine Division and served in the Pacific theater. Douglas was wounded in combat at Peleliu and Okinawa and was awarded both the Purple Heart and the Bronze Star, the latter for "heroic achievement." His left arm was permanently disabled (he called it a "paper weight"). After fourteen months in a military hospital, he was discharged as a lieutenant colonel. Douglas returned to Illinois after the war and resumed his professorship, but in 1948 he won the Democratic nomination for the U.S. Senate. He campaigned vigorously against incumbent senator C. Wayland Brooks. He advocated civil rights, public housing, federal aid to education, rent and price controls, repeal of the Taft-Hartley Act, high price supports for farmers, antimonopoly measures, expansion of Social Security benefits, a strong national defense, and active support for the United Nations. Douglas defeated the GOP and Progressive party candidates, obtaining a plurality of 407,000 votes.

Douglas's three terms as a senator spanned the presidential administrations of Truman, Eisenhower, Kennedy, and Johnson. He set rigid ethical standards for himself, which gave him a reputation of being incorruptible, and he was respected as a man of principle; but Douglas championed causes with such inflexibility that he was often ineffective as a legislative leader. As a liberal idealist, he resisted compromise and did not fraternize with those with whom he disagreed politically. He was also less than charitable toward those who opposed the liberal welfare state. This dogmatic stance did little to endear him to his colleagues, especially conservative southern Democrats.

In foreign policy matters, Douglas was an avowed Cold Warrior. He voted for the Marshall Plan as well as military and economic aid to Greece and Turkey. He also supported the formation of the North Atlantic Treaty Organization and the Southeast Asia Treaty Organization, backed Harry Truman's Point Four foreign aid program for underdeveloped countries, favored the rearmament of West Germany, and endorsed the concept of reciprocal trade via the General Agreement on Tariffs and Trade. Douglas believed the United States should exert its influence as leader of the Free World by strengthening the peacekeeping role of the United Nations. He believed both the Korean and Vietnam wars to be morally justified and necessary to preserve the principle of self-determination and prevent the expansion of Communist imperialism. Douglas opposed diplomatic recognition of the People's Republic of China and denounced the Soviet Union for making Communist satellites out of the nations of Eastern Europe. He favored continued support to Israel.

Domestically Douglas supported the Fair Deal, New Frontier, and Great Society programs that became associated with the evolution of the welfare state. He advocated strict federal regulation of monopolies and active government involvement in providing all Americans with adequate housing, education, and health care, as well as assuring them of a standard of living above the poverty level. He voted for Medicare, federal assistance to depressed areas, food stamps for the poor, the Model Cities Act, federal aid to education, and the Civil Rights acts of 1964 and 1968. He was also a major force in gaining public support for enactment of the Truth-in-Lending Act of 1968.

In 1966 Douglas was defeated in his campaign for a fourth term by Republican Charles Percy. His pro–Vietnam War position and his strong civil rights record proved liabilities. After leaving the Senate, he taught at the New School for Social Research in New York City. He also served as chairman of a commission on urban problems appointed by President Lyndon Johnson and as organizing chairman of the Committee for Peace with Freedom in Vietnam. The latter included as members former president Dwight D.

Eisenhower and General Omar Bradley. In 1968 Douglas was a delegate-at-large at the Democratic National Convention in Chicago, which nominated his longtime friend Hubert Humphrey for president. He participated in Humphrey's campaign and also helped raise funds for Democratic senators up for reelection in 1970. Douglas ceased to be active in politics only after suffering a disabling stroke. He died in Washington, D.C.

• The papers of Paul H. Douglas are located in the archives of the Chicago Historical Society. His autobiography is *In the Fullness of Time* (1973). Two biographical articles coauthored by Edward L. and Frederick H. Schapsmeier are "Paul H. Douglas: From Pacifist to Soldier-Statesman," *Journal of the Illinois State Historical Society* 67 (June 1974): 307–23, and "Dirksen and Douglas of Illinois: The Pragmatist and the Professor as Contemporaries in the United States Senate," *Illinois Historical Journal* 83 (Summer 1990): 75–84. See also Irwin Ross, "The Independent Gentleman from Illinois," *Reader's Digest*, Dec. 1958, pp. 129–31; Richard T. Cooper, "The Hardest Campaign of Paul Douglas' Career," *New Republic*, 22 Oct. 1966, pp. 9–10; and Charles Manzel, "Paul Douglas: Man Ahead of His Time," *Look*, 13 June 1967, pp. 110–11. An obituary is in the *New York Times*, 25 Sept. 1976.

EDWARD L. SCHAPSMEIER

DOUGLAS, Robert L. (4 Nov. 1882–16 July 1979), professional basketball player and team owner, was born in St. Kitts, British West Indies. No information is available concerning Douglas's parents or his early education. He observed his first basketball game shortly after arriving in New York City in 1902. Approximately 1919 Douglas and some friends organized the Spartan Field Club, which provided black New York City youths with opportunities to participate in cricket, soccer, track, and basketball at the amateur level. Coach Douglas's basketball team, the Spartan Braves, were very successful, and at times he joined them on the court.

In 1922 Douglas ran into problems with the Metropolitan Basketball Association, an amateur organization, over the amateur status of a couple of his players. Because of this controversy Douglas organized the New York Renaissance, a professional basketball team. He approached the owner of the Renaissance Ballroom in Harlem, agreeing to use the name "Renaissance" in return for practice and playing space. The name was soon shortened to the Rens. Three of the members, Leon Monde, Hilton Slocum, and Frank Forbes, had played for Douglas as Spartan Braves. The Rens played the first game of their 26-year existence on 3 November 1923. In that game they defeated the Collegiate Five, a white team, 28 to 22. The Rens finished their first season with a record of 15–8.

The Renaissance team was the first full-salaried black professional basketball team. Before it was common practice, Douglas required contracts from his players. Steeped in a West Indian immigrant culture that emphasized economic self-sufficiency, Douglas displayed an astute business sense. Though he lacked a high school or college education, he worked hard and persevered to become a winning coach and top businessman in the 1920s and 1930s.

By the late 1920s the Rens were playing up to 150 games each year. They played any and all teams—both amateur and professional—including clubs, Young Men's Christian Associations, and colleges. Douglas booked his team for games as much as one year in advance, requiring a guarantee plus expenses for their appearance.

In the 1930s the Rens became a barnstorming team, traveling in the Midwest and the South to play opposing teams. While on the road the players faced constant racism and discrimination. They had difficulty finding hotels and restaurants that would house or serve them. Because of this the Rens traveled in a custom-designed team bus called the "Blue Goose," where they often slept and ate their meals out of brown bags. Douglas believed that touring enhanced the image of his team and also helped to improve the quality of the game itself among blacks. He provided encouragement to southern black teams by arranging games between them and his Rens. The Renaissance team traveled four months out of the year, playing usually seven or eight games per week.

Before many of the rule changes in the mid-1930s, players were required to face a jump ball after every basket. Games were low scoring and accompanied by poor officiating. Nonetheless, Douglas insisted that his players be disciplined and work as a team. Initially, due to slippery ballroom floors, the Rens developed a system of fast breaks made up of passing. Rather than dribbling the ball down the court, the ball passed from player to player and ended up in the basket. This style of play quickly became a Ren trait.

In the 1932–1933 season, the Rens won 88 consecutive games and had an overall 127–7 record. They were one of the few teams to consistently beat the Original Celtics, the top white team of the era, although it was the Original Celtics who ended the Rens' winning streak of 1932–1933. The Rens won 100 or more games over fourteen straight seasons. The popularity of Douglas's Rens was evident in that they drew up to 15,000 spectators, both black and white, per game during the mid-depression years.

In 1939 in Chicago the Rens won the first World Professional Championship Basketball title. After claiming victories against the New York Yankees and the Harlem Globetrotters, the Rens went on to defeat the Oshkosh All-Stars, a white team, by a score of 34 to 25. During World War II Douglas was forced to curtail the number of games his team played due to gas rationing. Many of his players traveled to Washington, D.C., on the weekends and played as the Washington Bears. After the war ended, Douglas gathered his team back together and resumed normal play.

The New York Rens moved to Ohio and became the Dayton Rens in 1948, the first black team to join the National Basketball League. They served as a replacement for the Detroit Vagabonds, an all-white team. The financially troubled Dayton Rens had a 16–43 season, playing their last game ever against the Denver Nuggets in Rockford, Illinois, on 21 March 1949.

Over twenty-six years, the Rens' record stood at 2,318 wins and 381 losses. According to Arthur Ashe, the Rens "were the first black team to win a world professional title in any sport and led the way for the post–World War II surge of blacks who eventually dominated the sport [basketball] at every level" (p. 50).

In 1963 the 1932–1933 Renaissance team was inducted into the Naismith Basketball Hall of Fame. Members of this team included Clarence "Fats" Jenkins, James "Pappy" Ricks, Eyre "Bruiser" Saitch, John Holt, Bill Yancey, Charles "Tarzan" Cooper, and "Wee" Willie Smith. Douglas, now referred to as the "father of black basketball," was elected to the Hall of Fame as a contributor in 1971, the first black individual to be so honored. In 1975 the Robert L. Douglas Basketball League, the summer professional league in New York, was named for him. Douglas served as the first president of the New York Pioneer Athletic Club and until 1973 managed the Renaissance Ballroom in Harlem. He was married twice, although little information is available. Sadie (maiden name unknown) died, and Douglas was married to Cora Dismond (date unknown). He never had any children. Douglas was the oldest living member of the basketball Hall of Fame when he died in New York City at the age of ninety-six.

• A file on Douglas is at the Naismith Memorial Basketball Hall of Fame, Springfield, Mass. Important primary sources on Douglas and the Renaissance team include the *New York Amsterdam News*, the *Pittsburgh Courier*, the *Chicago Defender*, and other black newspapers in the 1920s and 1930s. An excellent secondary source is Arthur Ashe, *Hard Road to Glory: A History of the African American Athlete, 1919–1945* (1988). See also Ocania Chalk, *Pioneers of Black Sport* (1975); Glenn Dickey, *The History of Professional Basketball since 1896* (1982); Art Rust and Edna Rust, *Art Rust's Illustrated History of the Black Athlete* (1985); and Nelson George, *Elevating the Game* (1992). Because so little is known about Douglas, reference works such as David L. Porter, ed., *Biographical Dictionary of American Sports: Basketball and Other Indoor Sports* (1989), and Ronald L. Mendell, *Who's Who in Basketball* (1973), are valuable. An obituary is in the *New York Times*, 17 July 1979.

SUSAN J. RAYL

DOUGLAS, Stephen Arnold (23 Apr. 1813–3 June 1861), U.S. senator and presidential candidate, was born in Brandon, Vermont, the son of Stephen Arnold Douglass, a college-educated physician, and Sarah Fisk (he dropped the final "s" in his name in 1846). Following his father's death, while Stephen was still an infant, he lived with his mother on the farm of a bachelor uncle, who with an outspoken and eccentric grandfather exerted an important influence on the boy. While serving as an apprentice to a Middlebury cabinetmaker, Douglas was captivated by the image of Andrew Jackson; during the presidential campaign of 1828, he supported Jackson's candidacy by pulling down opposition handbills from walls and fences. "From this moment," Douglas later recalled, "my pol-

itics became fixed, and all subsequent reading, reflection and observation have but confirmed my early attachment to the cause of Democracy" (by which he meant both the party and the principle).

The experience not only aroused his ambition for a career in politics but also stimulated his interest in an education. In 1830 he moved with his family to upstate New York where he entered Canandaigua Academy, studying the Latin and Greek classics, mathematics, and English literature. Canandaigua was a cultural center of swirling ferment and unrest. The recently completed Erie Canal had opened the region to economic development, and the area was alive with a spirit of reform and change that Douglas could neither ignore nor resist. The Anti-Masonic movement had sparked political protest a few years before, religious revivals drew people to nearby towns and villages, and only a few miles north of Canandaigua, Joseph Smith (1805–1844) was organizing the Mormon church. The excitement further stimulated Douglas's interest in politics. Early in 1833 he left the academy to study law in the office of a local attorney.

Douglas had already developed the driving energy that would later cause others to dub him a "steam engine in breeches." A young man in a hurry, he chafed at the long period of preparation required by New York law for admission to the bar. After six months of study, he headed for the "western country" where legal training and qualification were less formal. After brief stops in Cleveland, Cincinnati, Louisville, and St. Louis, he settled in Jacksonville, Illinois, in November 1833. Within months he was writing in glowing terms of the opportunities that awaited him. Illinois was "the Paradise of the world," he informed his family. "I have become a *Western* man, have imbibed Western feelings principles and interests and have selected Illinois as the favorite place of my adoption." Admitted to the bar in 1834 after a cursory examination before a judge (who cautioned him to learn more of the law), Douglas entered the rough-and-tumble arena of frontier politics as a zealous partisan of Andrew Jackson and Jacksonian democracy. The mix of New Englanders who had settled Jacksonville and the area's farmers who had migrated from Kentucky and Tennessee added to his enthusiasm. "The people of this country," he wrote of his future constituents, "are more thoroughly Democratic than any people I have ever known . . . democratic in principle and in Practice as well as in name."

Douglas brought with him from New York innovative techniques of party organization, which he unhesitatingly applied to Illinois politics. To him, the political party was a necessary instrument for accommodating diverse views and protecting democratic government. To be effective, he believed, it required a tight organization and strict discipline. A network of committees on the county, district and state levels was developed, nominating conventions were introduced, and a new sense of party loyalty was encouraged. Douglas was instrumental in bringing the Jacksonian party system to Illinois, to the discomfiture of the older politicos who had monopolized state politics. Illinois's Democratic party became an extension of Douglas's own ambitions and personality. Before his twenty-second birthday, he was elected state's attorney for an eight-county judicial district. In August 1836 he was elected to a seat in the lower house of the state legislature. Serving with Douglas were Abraham Lincoln, whom he had first met two years before, two future U.S. senators, one future governor, and five future congressmen—"more talent," commented one newspaper, "than any legislative body ever before assembled in Illinois."

But Douglas's ambition knew no rest. He could not remain in any political office for long. In March 1837 he moved to the new state capital when he was appointed register of the Springfield land office. In 1840 he assumed the post of secretary of state. Finally, in 1841, Douglas was elevated to the Illinois state supreme court, at the age of twenty-seven the youngest person ever to hold a seat on that high tribunal. From this time on, he was always addressed as Judge Douglas.

In 1838 Douglas ran for a seat in Congress, losing by a narrow margin to his Whig opponent; and in 1842 he was an unsuccessful candidate for the U.S. Senate. (Actually, he was not yet old enough to qualify for that body.) The following year, after the redistricting of the state, he won election to the House of Representatives. In December 1843 he took his seat in Congress, beginning a career as a national legislator that terminated only with his death. After serving two terms in the House, he was elected to the Senate in 1846, where he became one of the most powerful and controversial political figures in the country. Reelected in 1853 and in 1859, Douglas was involved in every major issue that came before Congress during one of the nation's most critical periods. In 1852 and 1856 he was a leading contender for the Democratic presidential nomination but was passed over each time because of his identification with controversial measures.

Douglas's physical appearance belied his power and influence. Standing only five feet four inches in height, yet brash, aggressive, and full of nervous energy, he reminded people of a scrappy bantam cock. Although a product of New England, he seemed more representative of the boisterous and turbulent spirit of frontier America. Early in his career he was dubbed "the Little Giant." He loved furor and never dodged conflict. As a debater he had "excellent prize fighting qualities." When John Quincy Adams observed Douglas in heated debate removing his cravat and unbuttoning his waistcoat, he saw only a "half-naked pugilist" who had lashed himself into "such a heat that if his body had been made of combustible matter it would have burnt out." Douglas's oratorical power became legendary; the galleries of the Senate were packed whenever he spoke, and even his opponents expressed admiration for his eloquence.

The political outlook that Douglas carried into national politics was rooted in the fierce independence and individualism of his native Vermont. There, he

recalled, he had "first learned to love liberty." In Illinois his vision expanded. "I came out here . . . ," he remarked, "and found my opinions enlarged when I got on these broad prairies, with only the Heavens to bound my vision." Although his arguments were well informed, he was a man of action rather than intellect; he was distrustful of doctrinaire thinkers. Beneath Douglas's pragmatism, however, was his faith in the will and wisdom of the people. His creed was Jacksonian: the sovereignty of the people, regard for the rights of the states, and the sanctity of the indestructible Union. To Douglas, the United States must remain true to its revolutionary origins, a "confederation of sovereign states" ever responsive through the exercise of local self-government to the wishes and aspirations of the people. That was what democracy was all about.

This abiding faith in democracy and the Union defined Douglas's belief in America's mission, and this sentimental attachment to his country tied him to the romantic spirit of the times. Douglas's vision of America's future was boundless. From his earliest years, he explained, he had "indulged an enthusiasm, which seemed to others wild and romantic, in regard to the growth, expansion, and destiny of this republic." For Douglas, America's destiny had always been manifest.

When Douglas entered Congress in 1843, he drew up a program that would develop the West and encourage settlement. His grand project was the construction of a Pacific railroad that would link the Mississippi Valley with the Pacific Coast. To attract farmers who wished to improve their condition and establish new homes, he urged the adoption of a free land policy, and in 1849 he introduced his first homestead legislation. Douglas gave little thought to the American Indians who stood in the path of western settlement, charging that they were simply a barrier to the "onward march of civilization" and should be brushed aside. Finally, he fought for the extension of American institutions to the western frontier by creating territorial governments and admitting new states. He was chairman of the Committee on Territories, first in the House of Representatives and then in the Senate. The citizens of the territories looked to Douglas as their special representative—the guardian of their interests and promoter of their self-government. He wrote, modified, and sponsored bills for the creation of seven territories: Oregon, Minnesota, Utah, New Mexico, Washington, Kansas, and Nebraska.

Douglas's goal, as he often said, was to make this "an ocean-bound republic," by making the area of liberty as broad as the continent itself. He was in the forefront of the effort to annex Texas, and he insisted that the United States acquire all of Oregon. Sharing the Anglophobia of his generation, he saw in Great Britain's North American presence a constant monarchical threat to American democracy. War with the British over Oregon held no terrors for Douglas; in fact, he denied Britain's right to a single foot of land in North America. He supported the war with Mexico, which he described as "a fervent, glorious, patriotic zeal to advance the great cause of freedom," and even contemplated volunteering for service in the conflict. The acquisition of New Mexico and California, he felt, was necessary, the latter to fulfill the nation's destiny "as the first maritime nation" in the world. But he opposed the Treaty of Guadalupe Hidalgo, which ended the Mexican War, because it seemed to foreclose the possibility of further expansion to the south. American expansion, for Douglas, was a law of nature, sanctioned by God and therefore inevitable. "You cannot fix bounds to the onward march of this great and growing country," he shouted from the floor of the Senate. "You cannot fetter the limbs of the young giant."

In 1847, following his election to the Senate, Douglas married Martha Martin, the daughter of a wealthy plantation and slave owner in North Carolina. Shortly afterward, he moved his residence from Quincy, Illinois, where he had resided (but seldom visited) since his term on the state supreme court, to the burgeoning lake city of Chicago, where he invested in real estate. Upon the death of her father in 1848, Martha inherited a 2,500-acre plantation with over 100 slaves on the Pearl River in Mississippi. Douglas was designated manager of the plantation, for which he received 20 percent of its income. After less than six years of marriage and the birth of two sons, Martha died in 1853, and the plantation passed to the children. In 1857 Douglas sold the plantation and, on behalf of his sons, established a new one near Greenville, Mississippi, in partnership with a Baton Rouge planter. His political opponents tried on a number of occasions to make a political issue of Douglas's involvement with slavery, but their efforts were to no avail.

Like many Americans, Douglas hailed the triumphant end of the Mexican War as the beginning of a new era. Events quickly dashed his expectation. The most important consequence of the war was the re-entry of the slavery issue into national politics, raising again the question of slavery's relation to territorial expansion. The introduction of the Wilmot Proviso in the summer of 1846, stipulating that slavery would be barred forever from all lands acquired from Mexico, initiated a bitter sectional debate that increased in intensity until 1850, when the Union itself appeared to be in danger. Douglas rejected both the northern antislavery position that the national government had the power to prohibit slavery in the territories and the southern proslavery argument that the Constitution sanctioned the existence of slavery in the territories. Instead he proposed, as the only fair and just course, to allow the people of the territories to decide the question for themselves without the intervention of the national government. This doctrine of popular sovereignty, Douglas believed, satisfied the yearnings of westerners for self-government and removed the divisive slavery question from national politics. The conflict finally culminated in the passage of the Compromise of 1850, in which Douglas played a leading role. The territories of Utah and New Mexico were organized on the basis of popular sovereignty, and California was admitted to the Union as a free state in accordance with the wishes of its inhabitants.

Douglas was not proslavery, as many of his opponents charged, but he was aware of the dangers involved in debating the right or wrong of slavery. He condemned the abolitionists as irresponsible agitators. Privately he deplored slavery's existence and hoped it would some day disappear, but he was unwilling to risk the destruction of the Union. To Douglas, there was no tribunal on earth that could decide the moral question of slavery to the satisfaction of each side. In the interest of maintaining the Union, slavery must be dealt with as a "political question involving questions of public policy." He was confident that it was poorly adapted to western conditions and that the people of the territories, if left to settle the question for themselves, would decide against it. The growing momentum of the antislavery movement and the rising strength of the proslave southern political leadership, however, made it increasingly difficult to adhere to this position without being misunderstood.

Douglas's dilemma became clear in 1854 when the issue of slavery in the territories was revived by the passage of the Kansas-Nebraska Act. Written and introduced by Douglas, the act organized two new territories out of the old Louisiana Purchase area. Although slavery had been barred from the region by the 1820 Missouri Compromise, Douglas nonetheless provided for popular sovereignty, intending neither to introduce nor to exclude slavery but to leave the people free to decide the question. Southerners, however, pressed him for an explicit repeal of the Missouri Compromise, and Douglas agreed in order to secure the bill's passage, although he predicted it would raise a "hell of a storm." Antislavery opponents denounced the repeal as a "gross violation of a sacred pledge" and a betrayal of freedom made to promote Douglas's ambitions.

The act was followed by a realignment of political parties, as the Whig party fell into ruins and the Republican party rose in its place. The sectional conflict entered a more violent and dangerous stage. The emergence of the Republican party marked the transition of the party system from a national to a sectional orientation. Meanwhile, Kansas was plunged into chaos, as proslave and free-state factions vied for control of the government.

In 1856 Douglas married 21-year-old Adèle Cutts (Adèle Cutts Douglas) a grandniece of Dolley Madison who was known and respected in Washington social circles for her grace and beauty. She accompanied him on his campaign trips and, being an accomplished hostess, made their home a center of social activity in the national capital.

Douglas persisted in his conviction that popular sovereignty offered the only national solution to the issue of slavery in the territories, against a growing opposition from the Republicans and the increasing disenchantment of southern Democratic leaders. He blamed the breakdown of order in Kansas on outside groups. He was undaunted when the U.S. Supreme

Court, in the 1857 *Dred Scott* decision, affirmed the southern position that slavery had a constitutional right to exist in all the territories, without interference from the federal government or from popular sovereignty. Arguing rather unconvincingly that popular sovereignty formed no part of the decision, he further argued that no matter what the court might decide in relation to the abstract question, the people in a territory might still exclude slavery if they wished by enacting unfriendly legislation that would effectively prevent its introduction into their midst. This philosophy was later known as the "Freeport Doctrine," after the Illinois town in which he best expressed it during his 1858 debates with Lincoln. When an effort was made in Congress during the winter of 1857–1858 to admit Kansas to the Union as a slave state under its Lecompton constitution, Douglas stood defiantly against the proslave southern political leadership and its northern allies, including President James Buchanan, denouncing the proslave constitution as a fraud and a travesty on the will of the people in Kansas. His courageous move attracted Republican support and strengthened his campaign for reelection to the Senate in 1858 against Abraham Lincoln. Both men traversed the state in an encounter that reflected the national debate over slavery in microcosm. Their seven joint debates have assumed an almost legendary importance in the story of the sectional conflict and the coming of the Civil War.

As he parried the thrusts against him from both northern Republicans and southern slavery expansionists, Douglas became more inflexible in his devotion to popular sovereignty. "I do not intend to make peace with my enemies," he shouted, "nor to make a concession of one iota of principle."

It was a losing battle. In the charged atmosphere of the late 1850s, as arguments became more extreme, emotional, and abstract, it became clear that there was little room for one who counseled a middle road. In April 1860 the Democratic presidential convention met in Charleston, South Carolina, to nominate a presidential candidate and to frame a platform. Douglas had the most support, but he was unacceptable to southerners and to those Democrats who sided with the Buchanan administration. Popular sovereignty was equally unacceptable, for the southern delegations insisted on a federal slave code that would guarantee slavery in the territories. Eight southern state delegations withdrew from the convention. The remaining delegates, unable to conduct their business, adjourned, planning to meet in Baltimore in June. There the fragmentation of the party was completed. Douglas was nominated for the presidency by his northern supporters, and Vice President John C. Breckinridge, of Kentucky, was nominated by the southern delegations.

Unlike his competitors—Breckinridge, the Republican nominee Abraham Lincoln, and John Bell (the candidate of the Constitutional Union party)—Douglas conducted an active campaign. He spoke in New England and the Deep South, sections in which opposition to his position was strongest. The real issue, he maintained, was not the slavery question but rather the Union. Following Lincoln's election he made one last effort, appealing to the southern people to accept the election results and arguing that, with Democratic majorities in Congress and a Supreme Court against him, Lincoln was to be more pitied than feared. His election, Douglas pleaded, was not sufficient cause to destroy the "best government of which the history of the world gives an example." Southerners were not convinced; secession soon became a reality.

Douglas fought hard during the last few months of the Buchanan administration to find a compromise that might yet save the Union and avert a civil war, but he failed. The firing on Fort Sumter signaled the beginning of the sectional war he had so dreaded. Pledging his support to President Lincoln, Douglas returned to Illinois. Speaking to the Illinois General Assembly on 25 April 1861, he recalled that almost daily for eighteen years he had stood on the portico of the Capitol and surveyed a "prosperous, happy, and united country on both sides of the Potomac." Now he contemplated the destruction of that happy country. "To discuss these topics," he lamented, "is the most painful duty of my life. It is with a sad heart—with a grief that I have never before experienced, that I have to contemplate this fearful struggle."

Less than two weeks later, worn out physically and broken in spirit, Stephen A. Douglas, who had suffered attacks of rheumatism before following periods of great stress, died in his room at the Tremont Hotel in Chicago. His last words were a message to his two young sons: "Tell them to obey the laws and support the Constitution of the United States."

• The largest collection of Douglas letters, mostly incoming, is in the University of Chicago Library. Collections of letters written by Douglas are in the Illinois State Historical Library, Springfield; the Chicago Historical Society; and in scattered collections in the Library of Congress. Most of the known Douglas letters have been published in Robert W. Johannsen, ed., *The Letters of Stephen A. Douglas* (1961). Douglas's speeches in his debates with Lincoln during the 1858 Illinois senatorial campaign may be found in Robert W. Johannsen, ed., *The Lincoln-Douglas Debates of 1858* (1965). For his speeches during the 1859 campaign in Ohio, see Harry V. Jaffa and Robert W. Johannsen, eds., *In the Name of the People: Speeches and Writings of Lincoln and Douglas in the Ohio Campaign of 1859* (1959). The definitive biography of Douglas is Robert W. Johannsen, *Stephen A. Douglas* (1973). Other less complete studies are George Fort Milton, *The Eve of Conflict: Stephen A. Douglas and the Needless War* (1934), and Damon Wells, *Stephen Douglas: The Last Years, 1857–1861* (1971). See also Robert W. Johannsen, *The Frontier, the Union, and Stephen A. Douglas* (1989).

ROBERT W. JOHANNSEN

DOUGLAS, William Lewis (22 Aug. 1845–17 Sept. 1924), shoe manufacturer and governor, was born in Plymouth, Massachusetts, the son of William Douglas, a sailor, and Mary C. Vaughan. Attending public schools sporadically throughout his boyhood, Douglas was sent to work for his uncle, a shoemaker, at age seven, two years after his father's death at sea. As a shoe pegger, he worked long hours and faced habitual mistreatment, but by age eleven he began to train formally as an apprentice under his uncle. Becoming a journeyman shoemaker at age fifteen, he was first employed at a cotton mill in Plymouth, where he earned thirty-three cents a day. He continued in the shoemaking trade in Hopkinton and later South Braintree under the well-known bootmaker Ansel Thayer until 26 February 1864, when he enlisted in the Fifty-eighth Massachusetts Regiment. Wounded at the battle of Cold Harbor in that same year, Douglas spent months in army hospitals and was discharged in 1865. In 1866 he headed west to Colorado, settling in Black Hawk and later Golden City. There he received training in designing, drafting, cutting, and fitting shoes—knowledge that allowed him to be classified as a professional shoemaker—and opened a retail boot and shoe store. He returned to Massachusetts in 1868 and that year married Naomi Augusta Terry. They had three children.

Applying his knowledge to the shoe manufacturing industry, from 1870 to 1875 Douglas was superintendent at the shoe factory of Porter & Southworth in North Bridgewater (now Brockton), Massachusetts. With a loan of $875, he started his own manufacturing company in 1876. In the early years the company claimed five employees and a daily output of forty-eight pairs of shoes. Douglas functioned as buyer, cutter, and salesman as well as director and frequently put in eighteen and twenty hours a day. By 1879 the size of the factory had doubled, and daily production rates reached 840 shoes. Douglas constructed a three-story factory in 1881. Embracing advertising in 1884, he communicated a "promise of integrity" through his portrait, which appeared both on the soles of his products and in the newspapers. His image and goods became famous throughout the country, and in 1892 he incorporated his business as W. L. Douglas Shoe Co., capitalized at $2.5 million. As president of the firm, Douglas erected a larger factory at Montello Station in Brockton, employing 4,000 workers and producing 20,000 pairs of shoes daily, and established a chain of retail stores.

Douglas entered political life as a member of the Brockton Common Council (1883–1884, 1891), and then served as a Democratic member of the Massachusetts House of Representatives (1884–1885), as a Massachusetts state senator (1886–1887), and as mayor of Brockton (1890). He also served as a delegate to the Democratic National Conventions of 1884, 1892, and 1896 and as a delegate at large in 1904. Ever sympathetic to the interests of the worker, he drafted the State Weekly Payment Law, which guaranteed that employees working in manual trades would receive their wages on a weekly basis. As senator, Douglas introduced a bill that resulted in the founding of the Massachusetts Board of Arbitration and Conciliation, the first body of its kind in the country.

Although Massachusetts had been the site of progressive reform during the later nineteenth century, political conservatism had been the rule since the Civil War. Nevertheless, on 8 November 1904 Douglas was elected governor, defeating the incumbent Republican, John Lewis Bates, by an overwhelming majority. Douglas's victory, however, had more to do with his popularity and Bates's failings as governor than a general embrace of political progressivism. Bates presented himself as an enemy of labor, unwilling to limit the working hours of women and children, and during his governorship he also alienated state farm groups by advocating the reorganization of the State Board of Agriculture. He annoyed Civil War veterans by vetoing a bill intended to grant a bounty of $125 to all veterans who had previously not received a state gratuity. Finally, a waning state economy and a textile workers strike in Fall River in the summer of 1904 sealed Bates's defeat.

Douglas held office from 1905 to 1906, and while he faced a Republican-dominated legislature that prevented him from having much influence on law making, his efforts were instrumental in settling the six-month-long textile strike on 19 January 1905. A champion of tariff revision for all industries in Massachusetts, he also pleaded for reciprocity with Canada, citing "free hides" and "free coal" as potential benefits, though he did not realize this goal. Highly esteemed by members of both parties, Douglas chose not to run for a second term, stating that he had "no taste for office-holding" and much preferred his "business and quiet home life to the constant strain incident to public responsibilities" (*Boston Herald*, 27 May 1905).

After his term as governor, Douglas returned to his business and engaged in philanthropic activities. He gave the Brockton Hospital a surgical building, organized the Brockton Day Nursery for working mothers, and established the Douglas Eye and Ear Fund. His first wife died in 1911, and in 1913 he married Alice Kenniston Moodie, his former housekeeper. They had no children.

Though a self-made millionaire, Douglas was a simple, moral man who preferred to express himself through actions rather than words. Never ashamed of his impoverished beginnings, his compassion lay with the worker, and as a result strike activity was rare at his Brockton plant. His diplomacy in labor negotiations also won him the respect of labor unions. Frequently forgoing public ceremonies and limiting himself to two short vacations a year, he regarded work as his primary recreation throughout his life. Douglas died in Boston.

• No manuscripts or personal papers of Douglas are known to exist. An informative history of Douglas's career is in *The Boy Who Pegged Shoes* (n.d.), a short pamphlet published by the W. L. Douglas Shoe Co. Also helpful is the *Boston Herald*, 6 Jan. 1905–30 Apr. 1907. A detailed history of Massachusetts politics during this period is Richard Martin Abrams, "Mass Politics, 1900–1912: Conservatism in a Progressive Era" (Ph.D. diss., Columbia Univ., 1962). Also see *The Biographical Directory of the Governors of the United States*

(1789–1978), vol. 2 (1978), and *A Legislative Souvenir of Massachusetts Legislature*, vol. 14 (1905). An obituary is in the *Boston Transcript*, 17 Sept. 1924.

JILL MASSINO

DOUGLAS, William O. (16 Oct. 1898–19 Jan. 1980), U.S. Supreme Court justice, New Deal administrator, and environmentalist, was born William Orville Douglas in Maine, Minnesota, near the North Dakota border, the son of Julia Fisk and William Douglas, a Presbyterian minister. The family moved to southern California in 1901 and then to eastern Washington, near Yakima, a year later.

When Orville, as the family called him before he became the adult Bill, was six, his father died. Thereafter the family lived in various stages of poverty with the children working as best they could to bring additional money home. His father's death was the second searing experience for the young Douglas. While still living in Minnesota he had contracted polio. Initially it was feared he would die; that was upgraded to losing the use of his legs. His mother spent hour after hour massaging his legs, saving their use. Always weaker than his childhood peers because of the effects of polio, Douglas turned to hiking to strengthen himself. "This period is when I became a loner. Throughout my life I have enjoyed company but seldom sought it out. I preferred to eat lunch alone. I preferred to walk or exercise alone. I became a very lonely, introspective person." Indeed, he would have few close friendships as an adult. Instead he indentified with society's outcasts and misfits: the Wobblies, hobos, and racial minorities he traveled with as a youth.

With hard work he conquered the aftereffects of polio. With hard work he would conquer any obstacle. One of his driving qualities was a belief in the Protestant ethic; before his father's death the latter had instilled in the youth the lasting lesson of the importance of "self-reliance and hard work." As an adult he would never ask another to do what he would not do, but neither would he tolerate those around him who did less than he did. In part this accounts for his biting assessment of so many of his contemporaries.

Because he brought extraordinary intelligence with his work ethic, he excelled at all academic endeavors, though the need for employment always meant that he never gave full attention to his studies. He was valedictorian of his Yakima High School class (with the yearbook predicting he would become president of the United States); at Whitman College in Walla Walla he held three jobs simultaneously so that he could send money back to his mother; despite a lucrative tutoring business, working on the prestigious law review, and serving as a research assistant to a professor, he graduated number two in his law school class at Columbia. The ability to do several different tasks simultaneously would assist his meteoric rise during the New Deal but plague him on the Supreme Court. Probably no justice since the legendary John Marshall so awed his brethren with his intellect; yet Douglas infuriated them by

his seemingly cavalier treatment of the Court's opinion writing function.

He went to Whitman College because it offered him a scholarship. After his sophomore year, in the summer of 1918 he attempted to enlist in the navy, but failed because of color blindness. He then tricked his way into an army ROTC program, but World War I ended before he left the West Coast. The patriotic fervor that impelled his enlistment never flagged; one side of his tombstone in Arlington Cemetery says simply: "William O. Douglas Private United States Army."

Doulgas graduated from Whitman in 1920 and returned to Yakima as a high school teacher. During that two-year period, he met Mildred Riddle, an Oregonion also teaching at Yakima High School, and he married her in 1924 while he was a student at Columbia Law School.

Following graduation from Columbia, he accepted a job with the prestigious Wall Street law firm of Cravath, deGersdorff, Swaine, and Wood. There he practiced corporate law, especially railroad reorganizations, for two years; he also taught part-time at Columbia Law School. An attempt to return to Yakima to practice small-town law lasted but a few months, ending in 1928 when Columbia offered him a full-time position as an assistant professor. This allowed him, in his words, "to reenter one of the mainstreams of American life."

Columbia was one of the nation's leading law schools, on the cutting edge of the development of legal realism, a profound jurisprudential movement that shook the underpinnings of American law as no other movement has. Legal realism severely questioned whether judicial opinions did anything beyond masking the real (presumably extralegal) reasons why judges decided cases as they did. Columbia's president, Nicholas Murray Butler, was sufficiently worried about legal realism—or "sociological jurisprudence" as it was often called during the 1920s—that he appointed a law school dean who opposed it. The appointment came without faculty consultation and resulted in an exodus of some of the major faculty members, including Douglas, who was recruited to the Yale Law School by its boy-wonder dean Robert Maynard Hutchins.

Douglas's academic status was quickly established. In 1930 Hutchins became the president of the University of Chicago and offered Douglas the astronomical salary of $20,000 per year to follow him. Douglas accepted, delayed his move, and then reversed himself by accepting Yale's promotion to the prestigious Sterling Professor of Law, leapfrogging his colleagues. Thus Douglas remained at Yale during the time it was the most exciting place in American legal education, indeed probably in the history of American legal education, and he contributed fully to its intellectual life. The early 1930s were productive years for Douglas. As a corporate law expert, he produced seven casebooks, all from the realist perspective, on various aspects of corporate and partnership law. It was this period when his only two children were born. Douglas, however, was largely an absentee father, preferring work and its resultant status to time with his children. "I doubt if I rated high as a father" may have been an understatement.

Douglas's reputation as a bankruptcy whiz brought him some consulting opportunities under the secretary of commerce at the end of the Hoover administration. But in 1934 Douglas took a one-semester leave of absence from Yale to work on a study for the newly created Securities and Exchange Commission dealing with bankruptcy reorganizations. The semester leave extended for a lifetime.

The chairman of the SEC was Joseph P. Kennedy. His no-nonsense attitude toward the agency's business found a match in Douglas, who became a lifelong family friend. Unlike later, Kennedy was then on excellent terms with the president, who bowed to Kennedy's entreaties first, in January 1936, to appoint Douglas to a seat on the SEC and then, in the summer of 1937, elevate him to the chairmanship. Douglas would now have his own entrée to Franklin D. Roosevelt.

The SEC was the New Deal's showcase agency. As the regulatory policeman of Wall Street, it was responsible for enforcing the Securities Acts of 1933 and 1934 and overseeing the "death sentence" provisions of the Public Utilities Holding Company Act of 1935. Douglas's two most public actions as chairman were refusing the demands of the New York Stock Exchange to close the exchange during a steep sell-off in early September 1937 and then taking over the exchange in the wake of disclosures that former exchange president Richard Whitney had misappropriated funds. In the former case he acidly noted his view that he always assumed markets could go down as well as up. In the latter he commented, "It's goddamned lonely in the front line trenches these days." But his most important contribution was his tireless energy and administrative ability, plus consistent sixteen-hour days, in organizing and structuring the SEC to be a viable regulatory agency despite an incomplete statutory scheme. In an era that produced excellent administrators, he was the best.

Douglas became an unofficial economic adviser to FDR in addition to his SEC duties. Business was often mixed with pleasure, and Douglas became a regular at the president's poker games and eventually "perfected" the dry martini, becoming FDR's favorite bartender.

Douglas expected to return to Yale and told the president so. In 1937 the chairmanship of the SEC forestalled his projected return, but in early 1939 Douglas was selected as the next dean of the Yale Law School, and he told the president of his intent to return. Douglas reports FDR as replying "we'll see." On 13 February 1939 Justice Louis Brandeis retired. Roosevelt, having already made three appointments to the Court, had previously publicly indicated that the next appointment would go to the West Coast, which had not had a Supreme Court justice since 1925. Douglas,

in the political campaign of his life, first had to reestablish his bona fides as a westerner, and second, become the westerner ahead of the likely nominee, Washington senator Lewis Schwellenbach. With the help of Washington's other democratic senator, Homer Bone, Douglas established his bona fides with support from the chief justice of the state supreme court, the Washington State Bar Association, and most important, Idaho senator William Borah. In the meantime Douglas worked to line up his support in the capital, from the ubiquitous "Tommy the Cork" Corcoran, to Attorney General Frank Murphy, to newspaperman Arthur Krock. Douglas also shored up his own liberal credentials with a well-timed speech condemning the financial community and supporting regulation. On 19 March FDR nominated him; on 4 April the Senate confirmed the nomination 62–4 (the dissenters arguing that Douglas was but a tool of Wall Street!); and on 17 April he took his seat, the second youngest Supreme Court justice in history, bested only by Joseph Story 128 years earlier.

The Supreme Court Douglas joined only two years after FDR's failed court-packing plan was firmly in the control of New Dealers and Douglas fit right in. Their first and foremost belief was that governments had to have the authority to regulate business as they saw fit. The use of the due process clause of the Fifth and Fourteenth Amendments to protect business from regulations, exemplified by *Lochner v. New York* (1905) and its invalidation of a sixty-hour work week meant for the welfare of bakery employees, had to be wholly repudiated. Douglas and Hugo Black favored denying that corporations were "persons" within the meaning of the Constitution, but no one else agreed. As an alternative, in *Olsen v. Nebraska* (1941), Douglas wrote for the Court in a way that reached a similar conclusion indirectly: issues of "wisdom, need, or appropriateness" of legislation were exclusively a legislative function. Notions of public policy about economic and social legislation were not found in the Constitution and therefore could not serve as a guide to interpreting the Constitution.

His two other major opinions of his early years also involved business regulation. *United States v. Socony Vacuum Oil Co.* (1941) held that a combination to fix prices was a per se violation of the Sherman Antitrust Act and therefore no further inquiry into the reasonableness of the behavior was appropriate. And in *Federal Power Commission v. Hope Natural Gas* (1944) he freed rate-setting agencies from any specific formula in determining a reasonable rate of return to a regulated corporation.

Although Douglas became known as a "liberal absolutist" in regard to the First Amendment and otherwise a staunch protector of civil liberties, that was not his view when he joined the Court. Like other New Dealers he was sympathetic to claims of racial or religious injustice, but he was also willing to support state regulation of expression when prejudice was not the animating reason for the state's policy. Thus in *Minersville School District v. Gobitis* (1940) he joined with the other New Dealers in an opinion by Felix Frank-furter ruling that school children could be expelled if they did not participate in a compulsory flag salute, even if nonparticipation was impelled by religious scruples. *Gobitis* set off a wave of liberal denunciation of the Court as well as a number of simultaneous at-tacks on the Jehovah's Witnesses. Two years later Douglas, along with Black and Frank Murphy, recant-ed in *Jones v. Opelika* (1942), and a year later in *West Virginia v. Barnette* (1943) the Court overruled *Gobitis.*

Barnette must be contrasted with the federal govern-ment's decision to remove all persons of Japanese dis-sent from the West Coast, a policy supported by then California attorney general Earl Warren as well as President Roosevelt and a majority of Supreme Court justices. Like those of the majority, Douglas's views of civil liberties stopped where the war powers began. He voted to sustain the Japanese Relocation program, with its forced internment of American citizens of Jap-anese descent in both *Hirabayashi* (curfew) (1943) and *Korematsu* (duty to report to relocation centers) (1944). He wrestled with his position and even drafted a dissent, but when the time to vote came he joined the majority in the single greatest blot on twentieth-cen-tury civil liberties. Additionally Douglas dissented in *Cramer v. United States* (1945), in which a majority, reversing a treason conviction of a naturalized Ger-man, interpreted the Treason Clause restrictively. He saw ample evidence to justify conviction in the case. His voting was hardly different from the record, sus-taining government when it was important, civil liber-ties when to do so was nearly cost free. As the Court's resident expert on corporate law, he believed that cor-porations had the power to submerge the individual. He did not yet believe that government, especially one headed by a man he respected, carried a like power.

Douglas's contacts with Roosevelt did not end with his appointment to the Court. FDR considered mov-ing Douglas from the Court to a position of domestic czar during the war, but ultimately did not. Then as the 1944 Democratic Convention was approaching and the decision to drop Vice President Henry Wal-lace from the ticket was finalized, FDR had to choose a running mate. Douglas and Harry Truman were his choices. The latter was the choice of the party bosses, the former of the remaining New Deal liberals. Emu-lating the 1916 example of Justice Charles Evans Hughes, whom he greatly admired, Douglas remained aloof—in the Wallowa Mountains of Oregon—and waited for a draft that never materialized. When asked later what would have been different if he had suc-ceeded FDR, he responded that he would not have dropped the atom bombs on Japan. In 1948 while Douglas was again in the Wallowas, Truman would offer him the vice presidency, but Douglas, believing Truman would be defeated, spurned the opportunity: "I won't be a number two man to a number two man." Never again would Douglas be considered for elective office.

Prior to 1949 Douglas had never left the country. But throughout the next decade he used the Court's summer recess to travel extensively in Asia. Douglas was a cold war liberal who believed that in the ideolog-ical fight with communism the best weapon of the United States was its commitment to individual free-dom. During this period he began writing a book a year. The books, which often chronicled his travels, carried three messages: innate human dignity, the degradation of the environment and the need to pro-tect it, and the supreme importance of liberty and freedom.

These ideas were also central to his voting on the Court. Travel, the passing of his presidential ambi-tions, and the new understanding, thrust to the fore by the federal government's domestic security program, that government could suppress individual liberty, changed Douglas's judicial philosophy. The main-stream New Dealer of the 1940s vanished and in its place emerged a "liberal absolutist" and the new phrase "Black and Douglas dissenting." Seemingly alone amid the hysteria of the early 1950s, Black and Douglas explained the hysteria, drew parallels with communist behavior, and documented the Court's abandonmment of the Bill of Rights. To the argument that judges should not presume to substitute their views for those of the other branches, Black and Doug-las responded that the Constitution controlled those views, and so long as judicial review existed it was the judicial duty to enforce the Constitution even when to do so was unpopular. Together they were laying the groundwork for the Warren Court revolution of the 1960s. In the 1960s, however, they split over issues in-volved in the mass demonstrations and sit-ins of the civil rights movement. Black ultimately prevailed in arguing that property, whether private or public, could be declared off limits to protest, while Douglas wrote possibly his most powerful dissent on behalf of free speech rights, *Adderly v. Florida* (1966).

Douglas's best-known religion opinion is *Zorach v. Clauson* (1952), in which he sustained a release-time program and wrote that "we are a religious people whose institutions presuppose a Supreme Court." Yet *Zorach* was an aberration, a throwback to his 1940s views. Subsequently his Establishment Clause views hardened to where he was the sole dissenter against tax exemptions for church property in *Walz v. Tax Com-mission* (1969). His free-exercise opinions, like his speech opinions, also moved to absolutism as his ca-reer continued.

During Douglas's tenure the Court dismantled the South's policy of segregation, and Douglas was always with or a step ahead of the Court in the process. He was one of the four justices ready to overrule the sepa-rate but equal principle after the first oral argument in *Brown v. Board of Education* (1954); his expansive views of state action in *Bell v. Maryland* (1964) would have prohibited racial discrimination by private busi-nesses without the need for the Civil Rights Act of 1964; he eventually rejected, in *Keyes v. Denver School District No. 1* (1973), the de facto–de jure distinction in public education and believed that all racially isolated schools, no matter what their cause, should be legally desegregated.

Douglas was also at the forefront of the Warren Court's criminal procedure changes. Not until Clarence Thomas would another twentieth-century justice have the direct experiences with poverty that Douglas had, and Douglas, especially from the 1950s on, was keenly aware of the willingness of governments to impose law on the less fortunate. He tried to equalize the law as best as possible. In the 1940s he supported Black's position that the Fourteenth Amendment "incorporated" the entire Bill of Rights; see *Adamson v. California* (1949). In the 1960s he saw that position become law with respect to all the significant guarantees. Unlike some of his brethren, he refused to water down provisions of the Bill of Rights, such as the requirement of unanimous juries, once they became applicable to the states, as in *Apodaca v. Oregon* (1972).

One could argue that Douglas's liberal absolutism was a matter of degree apart from the views of his Warren Court brethren. But his views of the relation of humans to the environment were of a whole different order. From his vision of Mount Adams at his father's funeral to hiking in the Cascades to conquer polio and fears, the mountains became a sacred place for him. He could take only so many months in urban America without needing to flee to the wilderness to replenish himself. It saved him; he would save it. In 1954 he organized a hike along the Chesapeake and Ohio Canal towpath to create publicity against a proposed parkway. He succeeded, and today the C&O, controlled by the National Park Service, is officially dedicated to William O. Douglas.

The C&O hike was the first of many to protect places of solitude, beaches, forests, white water rivers. Years before environmentalism became fashionable Douglas was developing strategies to protect the wilderness. In his books, passages describing nature have an unmistakable spiritual quality. Civilization is artificial; the wilderness is real. Civilization brings out the worst in humans; wilderness the best: equality, self-reliance, respect, community. In his attempts to protect nature as best he could, Douglas also tried to craft relevant legal doctrine. In *Sierra Club v. Morton* (1972), he argued that any natural site should have "standing" in its own right and that any person should be able to sue to protect such a site. In *Udall v. Federal Power Commission* (1967), he maintained that an expert agency like the FPC is not owed deference by the courts if it proceeds with an action based on an inadequate examination of the facts and a failure to consult significant interested parties (in this instance, the secretary of the interior, who sought to block a dam on the Snake River). And he drew upon the National Environmental Policy Act of 1970 to require additional studies before actions affecting natural sites could be pursued.

Douglas advocated a Wilderness Bill of Rights because he felt the existing protections were insufficient. He knew that clean water and clean air were not inexhaustible; he also understood that neither was liberty. As he entered his third decade of service, he began looking for ways to refocus the Constitution to better protect the needs of late twentieth-century Americans. From a man initially concerned with corporate power came the view that the function of the Bill of Rights was to take government off the backs of the people. Ironically, this required him to revisit and distinguish his participation in the Court's eradication of *Lochner* because what he believed must be done required substituting judicial views of wise policy for those of legislatures. In *Griswold v. Connecticut* (1965), which laid the foundations for *Roe v. Wade* (1973), he found a right of marital privacy in "penumbras, formed from emanations," of the specific guarantees of the Constitution. To many, including Black, the constitutional right to use contraceptives looked like the rejected natural law philosophy of *Lochner*. Similarly in *Harper v. Virginia Board of Elections* (1966) he found state poll taxes unconstitutional because, despite their long lineage, times change. Then in *Papachristou v. City of Jacksonville* (1972), concerning a challenge to a vagrancy law, Douglas enshrined a right to wander and loaf because such conduct can promote independence, creativity, and self-confidence.

Papachristou extolled the "honored right to be a nonconformist and the right to deny submissiveness." These were rights Douglas personally embodied. He stated that "the only soul I have to save is my own" and acted on that. He was never a good father or, until his fourth marriage, a good husband. In 1953 he was divorced from his first wife Mildred; a year later he was remarried, to Mercedes Davidson. They were divorced in 1963. Douglas had already lined up his third wife, Joan Martin, some forty years his junior, whom he married the same year. That marriage lasted but two years, and before its end Douglas was eying Cathleen Heffernan, also some forty years his junior, whom he wed in 1966.

His latter two marriages were public scandals in Washington, D.C., and the two young brides, especially Cathy, were socially ostracized. Douglas was becoming an icon; to a generation in college that believed that no one over thirty could be trusted, Douglas was a hero. An outspoken critic of Vietnam and other Johnson policies, his 1969 book, *Points of Rebellion*, was a direct and unsophisticated appeal to the nation's youth to seek new paths. Its reference to the "establishment" as the "new George III" and to the time-honored right of revolution were unjudicial and inflamatory in the opinion of the new Republican administration. In the spring of 1970, in the confluence of the demise of the Warren Court, the forced resignation of Justice Abe Fortas, and the failed nominations of Clement Haynsworth and G. Harold Carswell, President Richard Nixon had House Republican leader Gerald Ford spearhead an effort to impeach Douglas. The goal was to remove the premier liberal from the Court and add yet another vacancy for Nixon to fill, therby speeding its transformation into conservative dominance. Ironically, Douglas, bored with the Court and having the ability to seek other outlets, had been planning to retire. But it was never in his nature to succumb to pressure. Although Ford offered some specific charges against Douglas, the real reason for the impeachment effort was the belief that Douglas was radically out of step with the nation and therefore unfit for the Court. Like all previous attacks on the independence of the judiciary, this one ended in failure. In December 1970 a subcommittee of the House Judiciary Committee ruled there were no grounds for impeachment, and the matter died.

On 31 December 1974 Douglas suffered a stroke. Partially paralyzed, he never recovered his full faculties, though he lingered on the Court until November 1975, when he retired, having served thirty-six and a half years, the longest tenure in the Court's history. He died in Washington, D.C.

It is difficult to evaluate Douglas because the normal criteria do not measure the man. From the traditional doctrinal perspective, he left little legacy besides sloppiness. His commitment to legal realism and his disdain for Frankfurter and his academic disciples resulted in Douglas's belief that judicial opinions were little more than "Harvard fly paper." The legal community has cast a strong dissent to that position. Yet as a jurist, when everyone else was cowering from hysteria, he stood tall. This is an unappreciated trait despite a generally held professional belief in an independent judiciary. Furthermore, unlike most late-twentieth-century justices, Douglas had a life both before and during his tenure. Although he was appointed at an exceptionally early age, he was already an important figure and would have been so without judicial service. Again, unlike other justices, he managed a second career, environmentalism, for which he might be significant without judicial service. Yet traditional criteria see this as incompatible with judicial norms. Only time will give perspective on this extraordinary individual; he broke the mold.

• Douglas's voluminous papers are collected in the Library of Congress. Vern Countryman, *The Douglas Opinions* (1977), provides an edited selection of his judicial productivity, while Melvin Urofsky and Philip E. Urofsky do the same for his voluminous correspondence in *The Douglas Letters* (1987). Douglas wrote two volumes of autobiography, *Go, East Young Man* (1974) and *The Court Years* (1980). The latter volume is highly unreliable. The best single volume biography is James Simon, *Independent Journey* (1980), and the best analyses of his career are in Stephen Wasby, ed., "He Shall Not Pass This Way Again" (1990), which also contains a superb bibliography and a list of all of Douglas's opinions.

L. A. POWE, JR.

DOUGLASS, Andrew Ellicott (5 July 1867–20 Mar. 1962), astronomer and dendrochronologist, was born in Windsor, Vermont, the son of the Reverend Malcolm Douglass and Sarah Hale. Raised in Episcopalian rectories in Vermont and Massachusetts, Douglass early showed an interest in astronomy and performed well in high school science and mathematics classes. In the fall of 1885 he entered Trinity College in Hartford, Connecticut, where he served as an assistant at the campus observatory and graduated in 1889 with honors in astronomy, mathematics, and physics. Financially unable to continue his education because of his father's death two years earlier, Douglass accepted an assistant's position at Harvard College Observatory. He accompanied the Harvard expedition to establish a southern hemisphere observatory at Arequipa, Peru, in late 1890, remaining in South America for the next three years.

A few months after his return from Peru, Douglass met wealthy Boston financier and amateur astronomer Percival Lowell, who had decided to finance an observatory in the American Southwest to observe the planet Mars. Working closely with Harvard staff members, Lowell chose Douglass as his principal assistant and dispatched him to Arizona Territory to survey potential observatory sites during the spring of 1894. Douglass provided the data on atmospheric quality that convinced Lowell to locate his facility on a mesa west of Flagstaff. Although Lowell directed the work of the observatory after its founding in April, he rarely spent long periods of time in Arizona. Douglass served as acting director during his employer's absences and coordinated the facility's research activities. Lowell made extensive use of the Martian observations from Flagstaff to support his imaginative theories of an intelligent civilization on the planet, which he advocated in several popular books and various articles and addresses. Increasingly disturbed by the impact of these publications on the reputation of the observatory, Douglass attempted to convince Lowell to refrain from claiming scientific evidence for his theories. Such challenges to Lowell's ideas led to Douglass's dismissal in July 1901.

Douglass remained in Flagstaff for the next five years, serving variously as Coconino County probate judge, instructor at Northern Arizona Normal School, and mineral assayer. He married Ida Whittington, a local music teacher, in 1905. Although the couple would remain childless, Douglass continued to seek the more stable employment offered by an academic position, and in the fall of 1906 he joined the faculty of the University of Arizona in Tucson. Despite a heavy teaching load, Douglass spent much of the next decade attempting to establish an astronomy program at the small university. Efforts to secure funding for a suitable telescope proved fruitless until 1916, when Lavinia Steward gave the university $60,000 to endow an observatory in honor of her late husband. Delayed by World War I, the Steward Observatory was completed in the late summer of 1922. Its 36-inch reflecting telescope was one of the largest in the United States, although the observatory continued to suffer until budgetary constraints until the 1960s.

Douglass's most original contribution to science, however, was his intensive study of the annual growth rings of trees. Noticing that trees in the desert Southwest responded primarily to rainfall in their growth patterns and believing that sunspots played an important role in determining terrestrial weather, Douglass viewed tree rings as a potential indicator of solar phenomena. By 1909 he had found a clear relationship between rainfall and tree growth, which seemed to show the same eleven-year cycle as sunspots. Douglass spent much of the rest of his career attempting to determine the precise parameters of the relationship between sunspots and weather but remained unable to establish anything other than suggestive correlations.

Douglass made a far more specific contribution to science in another area of dendrochronological studies. Living trees that showed the required ring-width patterns indicating wet and dry years were rarely more than a few hundred years old. Older trees, such as sequoias and redwoods, grew in areas characterized by less dramatic responses to rainfall. In order to extend his tree-ring record, Douglass worked with archaeologists in the Southwest to obtain beams and other wood artifacts from the region's ancient ruins. Throughout the 1920s Douglass collected and examined various wood and charcoal samples, gradually building various chronologies by overlapping characteristic patterns from different specimens. By July 1929 he had constructed a tree-ring record that began in A.D. 700 and showed clear patterns of wide and narrow rings. These patterns could be compared with similar patterns in wood specimens from ruins to provide archaeologists with a usable calendar. By the mid-1930s Douglass had further extended his chronology, offering archaeologists a record from A.D. 11 to the present and allowing them to place ruins in precise historical perspective.

Douglass retired as director of the Steward Observatory in late 1937, a few months after his seventieth birthday. His activities continued, however, as he accepted the directorship of the newly established Laboratory of Tree-Ring Research at the University of Arizona. In addition to archaeological endeavors, Douglass coordinated the expansion of tree-ring dating into climatological research, laying the foundation for many of the laboratory's most dramatic contributions. He retired during the summer of 1958, after which his health declined steadily until his death in Tucson.

Douglass's contributions to science rest equally in the disciplines of astronomy and dendrochronology. The two major observatories he helped to establish led to the Southwest's later emergence as a center for optical astronomy. His development of tree-ring dating techniques, made possible by the unique environment of the arid Southwest, immediately revolutionized archaeology and soon provided a crucial data source for climatological research. Although Douglass performed his own work within the tradition of the individual researcher, his contributions have been integrated into the modern practice of team research and large-scale funding.

• The primary collection of Douglass's papers is in the Special Collections Department of the University of Arizona Library, Tucson. A more restricted collection is the Douglass papers of the Lowell Observatory Archives in Flagstaff.

Douglass's principal published work is the three-volume *Climatic Cycles and Tree Growth* (1919, 1928, 1936). Among the most significant of his published articles are those that appeared in *Popular Astronomy* (Feb. 1899), *Popular Science Monthly* (May 1907), *Monthly Weather Review* (June 1909), and *National Geographic* (Dec. 1929). The standard biographical study is George E. Webb, *Tree Rings and Telescopes: The Scientific Career of A. E. Douglass* (1983). Obituaries are in the *New York Times* and the (Tucson) *Arizona Daily Star*, both 21 Mar. 1962.

GEORGE E. WEBB

DOUGLASS, David (?–1786), actor and theatrical manager, was born in England. His parents' names and occupations are unknown. Little is known of his early life, but in 1754 the actor John Moody organized a company of British actors in London that he planned to take to Jamaica. However, when Moody was offered a job by England's leading actor David Garrick, he turned over the reins of the new troupe to Douglass. In Jamaica, Douglass's company and that of Lewis Hallam, Sr., merged. Shortly thereafter, Hallam died; Douglass married Hallam's widow in 1758, taking over the leadership of the company that same year.

Immediately following his marriage, Douglass went to New York City as the head of Hallam's Company of Comedians, which he had merged with a small company of his own. His wife and her son Lewis Hallam, Jr., were the leading actors. Local authorities were not pleased with the arrival of the players, but Douglass, a resourceful politician, indicated that he was interested in presenting "Dissertations on Subjects, Moral, Instructive, and Entertaining" and was permitted to open a series of thirteen performances with a production of Nicholas Rowe's 1713 play *Jane Shore* on 28 December 1758. At this performance, his wife spoke a prologue that expressed the values of the art of theater (a necessary argument given the local opposition):

> Much has been said at this unlucky time
> To prove the treading of the stage a crime.
> Mistaken zeal, in terms oft not so civil,
> Consigns both play and players to the devil.
> Yet wise men own, a play well chose may teach
> Such useful morals as the parsons preach;
> May teach the heart another's grief to know,
> And melt the soul in tears of generous woe.

Douglass's troupe played in a temporary theater that Douglass had constructed on Cruger's Wharf until 7 February 1759, when his permit to perform in New York expired and he took the troupe to Philadelphia. There, despite harangues from local Quakers and other religious groups, he was allowed to perform in a new theater on Society Hill. He opened with a production of *Tamerlane*, which was well received. After a time in Philadelphia, Douglass's troupe played in Maryland and Williamsburg, Virginia, before embarking on a tour of New England in the summer of 1761. As anti-British sentiment grew in the colonies, Douglass in 1763 wisely changed the name of his company to the American Company of Comedians. For nearly two decades, Douglass led the company in tours of the East Coast. Their procedure was generally to erect temporary theaters in the towns in which they played, but in 1766 Douglass built the first permanent theater in the United States in Philadelphia. Called the Southwark, this theater thrived despite intense opposition from Philadelphia's Puritan citizenry. The next year, Douglass built New York's John Street Theatre. Other permanent theaters credited to Douglass include the Chapel Street Theatre in New York and the New or Third Dock Street Theatre in Charleston, South Carolina.

Although Douglass was the first American to play Falstaff and King John, he was not highly regarded as an actor. His stepson Lewis Hallam, Jr., was generally considered the company's outstanding actor. Douglass's skills as a manager, however, were unparalleled in his time. He was well known for his tact and business acumen, and when the company encountered local opposition to its appearance, Douglass's skillful diplomacy usually eased the way. In April 1767 Douglass heralded the first professional production of a play by a United States–born writer, a comic opera by Thomas Forrest (writing under the pseudonym Andrew Barton) titled *The Disappointment; or, The Force of Credulity*. However, this production did not come together and was replaced by Thomas Godfrey's previously unproduced 1759 play *The Prince of Parthia*, a tragedy in five acts that had been published by Godfrey's friend Nathaniel Evans following Godfrey's death. Douglass's production opened on 24 April 1767 at the Southwark and is regarded as the first native tragedy to be presented professionally in the United States. In this era, John Henry joined Douglass's company and later succeeded Douglass as the head of the theater. Under Douglass's direction, the company's repertory featured the latest London hits along with a strong sampling of classics, all strongly influencing the taste of the early American theater audience.

Shortly before the start of the American Revolution in 1775, Douglass and his company returned to the West Indies, where Douglass became significantly involved in civic matters during the last decade of his life—first as a justice, then as a militia officer, and finally as a member of the Council. At his death in Jamaica, Douglass left an estate totaling £25,000.

• For information on Douglass see Jared Brown, *The Theatre in America during the Revolution* (1995); Barnard Hewitt, *Theatre U.S.A., 1668 to 1957* (1959); Glenn Hughes, *A History of the American Theatre, 1700–1950* (1951); Walter J. Meserve, *An Outline History of American Drama* (1965; rev. ed., 1970); Jordan Y. Miller, *American Dramatic Literature: Ten Modern Plays in Historical Perspective* (1961); Don B. Wilmeth and Tice L. Miller, eds., *Cambridge Guide to American Theatre* (1993); Garff B. Wilson, *Three Hundred Years of American Drama and Theatre from Ye Bare and Ye Cubb to Chorus Line* (1982); and Jürgen C. Wolter, ed., *The Dawning of American Drama: American Dramatic Criticism, 1746–1915* (1993).

JAMES FISHER

DOUGLASS, Frederick (Feb. 1818–20 Feb. 1895), abolitionist, civil rights activist, and reform journalist, was born Frederick Augustus Washington Bailey near Easton, Maryland, the son of Harriet Bailey, a slave, and an unidentified white man. Although a slave, he spent the first six years of his life in the cabin of his maternal grandparents, with only a few stolen nighttime visits by his mother. His real introduction to bondage came in 1824, when he was brought to the nearby wheat plantation of Colonel Edward Lloyd. Two years later he was sent to Baltimore to labor in the household of Hugh and Sophia Auld, where he remained for the next seven years. In spite of laws against slave literacy, Frederick secretly taught himself to read and write. He began studying discarded newspapers and learned of the growing national debate over slavery. And he attended local free black churches and found the sight of black men reading and speaking in public a moving experience. At about age thirteen he bought a popular rhetoric text and carefully worked through the exercises, mastering the preferred public speaking style of the time.

Literacy and a growing social consciousness made Frederick into an unruly bondsman. In 1833, after being taken by master Thomas Auld to a plantation near St. Michael's, Maryland, he organized a secret school for slaves, but it was discovered and broken up by a mob of local whites. To discipline Frederick, Auld hired him out to a local farmer who had a reputation as a "slave breaker." Instead he became increasingly defiant and refused to allow himself to be whipped. Hired out to another local farmer, he again organized a secret school for slaves. Before long, he and his pupils had plotted to escape to the free state of Pennsylvania, but this too was discovered. Expecting further trouble from Frederick, Auld returned him to Baltimore in 1836 and hired him out to a local shipyard to learn the caulking trade. Taking advantage of the relative liberty afforded by the city, Frederick joined a self-improvement society of free black caulkers that regularly debated the major social and intellectual questions of the day.

After an unsuccessful attempt to buy his freedom, Frederick escaped from slavery in September 1838. Dressed as a sailor and carrying the free papers of a black seaman he had met on the streets of Baltimore, he traveled by train and steamboat to New York. There he married Anna Murray, a free black domestic servant from Baltimore who had encouraged his escape. They soon settled in the seaport of New Bedford, Massachusetts, where Frederick found employment as a caulker and outfitter for whaling ships, and began a family; two daughters and three sons were born to the union in a little more than a decade. At the urging of a local black abolitionist, he adopted the surname Douglass to disguise his background and confuse slave catchers. He also joined the local African Methodist Episcopal Zion church and became an active lay leader and exhorter.

Soon after arriving in New Bedford, Frederick Douglass was drawn to the emerging antislavery movement. He began to read the *Liberator*, a leading abolitionist journal edited by William Lloyd Garrison, and to attend antislavery meetings in local black churches, occasionally speaking out about his slave experiences. His remarks at an August 1841 convention of the Massachusetts Anti-Slavery Society on Nantucket Island brought him to the attention of Garrison and other leading white abolitionists. Society officials, impressed by Douglass's eloquence and imposing presence, hired him as a lecturing agent. Over the next two years, during which time he moved his family to Lynn, Massachusetts, he made hundreds of speeches for the society before antislavery audiences throughout New England and New York State. In 1843 he joined other leading abolitionist speakers on the One Hundred Conventions tour, which sought to strengthen abolitionist sentiment in upstate New York, Ohio, Indiana, and western Pennsylvania. His oratorical skills brought him increasing recognition and respect within the movement. But antislavery lecturing was a hazardous business. Douglass and his colleagues were often subjected to verbal assaults, barrages of rotten eggs and vegetables, and mob violence. And, as a fugitive slave, his growing visibility placed him in constant danger of recapture. He had to conceal or gloss over certain details in his life story, including names, dates, and locations, to avoid jeopardizing his newfound freedom.

Douglass's growing sophistication as a speaker brought other difficulties in the mid-1840s. At first, his speeches were simple accounts of his life in bondage. But as he matured as an antislavery lecturer, he increasingly sought to provide a critical analysis of both slavery and northern racial prejudice. His eloquence and keen mind even led some to question whether he had ever been a slave. As Douglass's skills—combined with his circumspection—prompted critics to question his credibility, some white abolitionists feared that his effectiveness on the platform might be lost. They advised him to speak more haltingly and to hew to his earlier simple tale. One white colleague thought it "better to have a *little* of the plantation" in his speech (quoted in McFeely, p. 95).

Douglass bristled under such paternalistic tutelage. An answer was to publish an autobiography providing full details of his life that he had withheld. Although some friends argued against that course, fearing for his safety, Douglass sat down in the winter of 1844–1845 and wrote the story of his life. The result was the *Narrative of the Life of Frederick Douglass, Written by Himself* (1845). The brief autobiography, which ran only to 144 pages, put his platform tale into print and reached a broad American and European audience. It sold more than 30,000 copies in the United States and Britain within five years and was translated into French, German, and Dutch. Along with his public lectures, "the *Narrative* made Frederick Douglass the most famous black person in the world" (David W. Blight, ed., *Narrative of the Life of Frederick Douglass* [1993], p. 16).

Although the *Narrative* enhanced Douglass's popularity and credibility, it increased the threat to his liberty. He was still a fugitive slave—but now one with a bestselling autobiography. Antislavery colleagues advised Douglass to travel to Britain to elude slave catchers, also hoping that his celebrity would mobilize British abolitionists to bring international pressure against American slavery. He sailed in August 1845 and remained abroad twenty months, lecturing to wildly enthusiastic audiences in England, Scotland, and Ireland. Douglass broadened his reform perspective, grew in confidence, and became increasingly self-reliant during this time. English antislavery friends eventually raised the funds necessary to purchase his freedom from the Aulds and permit his return home. They also collected monies to allow him to begin his own antislavery newspaper in the United States. In December 1847 Douglass moved his family to Rochester in the "burned-over district," a center of reform activity in upstate New York. There he launched the weekly reform journal *North Star*, which promoted abolitionism, African-American rights, temperance, women's rights, and a host of related reforms. Like his later journalistic ventures, it was well written and carefully edited and carried Douglass's message to an international audience. While it served as a personal declaration of independence, it initiated an ever-widening rift between Douglass and his Garrisonian colleagues, who sensed that they were losing control of his immense talent.

Douglass's movement away from Garrisonian doctrine on antislavery strategy also signaled his growing independence. Unlike Garrison, who viewed moral suasionist appeals to individual conscience as the only appropriate tactic, Douglass was increasingly persuaded of the efficacy of politics and violence for ending bondage. He attended the Free Soil Convention in Buffalo in 1848 and endorsed its platform calling for a prohibition on the extension of slavery. In 1851 he merged the *North Star* with the *Liberty Party Paper* to form *Frederick Douglass' Paper*, which openly endorsed political abolitionism. This brought a final breech with the Garrisonians, who subjected him to a torrent of public attacks, including scandalous charges about his personal behavior. Nevertheless, Douglass endorsed the nascent Republican party and its moderate antislavery platform in the elections of 1856 and 1860. At the same time, he increasingly explored the possibilities of abolitionist violence. As early as 1849 Douglass endorsed slave violence, telling a Boston audience that he would welcome news that the slaves had revolted and "were engaged in spreading death and devastation" throughout the South (Benjamin Quarles, *Allies for Freedom* [1974], p. 67). After passage of the Fugitive Slave Act of 1850, which put the federal government in the business of capturing and returning runaway slaves, he publicly urged resistance to the law, with violence if necessary. And he became active in the Underground Railroad, hiding numerous fugitives in his Rochester home and helping them on the way to Canada West (now Ontario). Douglass's growing attraction to violence is evident in his 1852 novella, *The Heroic Slave*, generally considered to be the first piece of African-American fiction, which glorified the leader of a bloody slave revolt. Later in the decade Douglass became involved in the planning for John Brown's 1859 raid at Harpers Ferry, Virginia, and secretly helped raise funds for the venture, although he thought it ill conceived. When the raid failed, he fled to Canada East (now Quebec), then on to England, fearing arrest on the charge of being Brown's accomplice. He returned home in 1860, disillusioned about African-American prospects in the United States, and planning to visit Haiti in order to explore the feasibility of black settlement there.

The coming of the Civil War revived Douglass's hopes. From the beginning of the conflict, he pressed President Abraham Lincoln to make emancipation a war goal and to allow black enlistment in the Union army. After Lincoln issued his Emancipation Proclamation in January 1863, Douglass spoke widely in support of the measure. Believing that military service might allow black men to demonstrate their patriotism and manhood, winning greater equality as well as helping to end slavery, he recruited for the Massachusetts Fifty-fourth Colored Infantry, the first African-American regiment organized in the North. His stirring editorial, "Men of Color, to Arms," was often reprinted in northern newspapers and became a recruiting poster. Nevertheless, Douglass was disgusted by the government's failure to keep its recruiting promises and met with Lincoln to protest discrimination against black troops. Before long, the War Department offered him a commission to enlist and organize African-American regiments among the slaves fleeing to Union lines in the lower Mississippi Valley. He stopped publication of *Douglass' Monthly*, which he had begun in 1859, and waited. But the commission never came, and Douglass, refusing to go South without it, continued to lecture and recruit in the North. As the war wound toward a conclusion in 1864–1865, he worked to shape public memory of the war and the character of the peace. He reminded audiences that the conflict had been fought to abolish slavery; it would only be successful, he argued, if the former slaves were granted equal citizenship rights with other Americans.

The end of the war and the Thirteenth Amendment outlawing slavery posed a crisis for Douglass. After a quarter of a century as the preeminent black abolitionist, he wondered if his career was at an end. But he soon recognized that important work remained to be done. In an 1865 speech to the American Anti-Slavery Society, many of whose white members were calling to disband the society, he forcefully argued that "the work of Abolitionists is not done" and would not be until blacks had equal citizenship rights with other Americans. Although he vigorously supported the Fourteenth Amendment and other civil rights stat-

utes, he believed that a meaningful Reconstruction required two essential elements: keeping the old leadership elite from returning to power in the South, and giving the freedmen the vote. Putting the ballot in the hands of black men, he argued, would prove the key to uplifting and protecting African-American rights. When President Andrew Johnson refused to endorse these principles in an 1866 meeting with Douglass, the race leader became one of his most vocal critics. He lobbied hard for passage of the Fifteenth Amendment, even at the cost of a breach with many friends who opposed the measure unless it also granted women the vote.

The 1870s were a "time of troubles" in Douglass's life. An 1872 fire destroyed his Rochester home and the files of his lengthy journalistic endeavors. He moved his family to Washington, D.C., where two years earlier he had purchased the *New National Era*. Through careful editorial guidance, he attempted to shape the weekly into a mouthpiece for the race. But persistent financial troubles forced him to stop publication of the paper in 1874. That same year Douglass was named president of the Freedman's Savings Bank, a federally-chartered savings and lending institution created to assist the economic development of former slaves. He soon found that the bank was in severe financial distress; it was forced to declare bankruptcy in a matter of months. These two failed ventures cost Douglass thousands of dollars and some public respect. Other black leaders increasingly criticized his alleged moderation on key race questions, his devotion to American individualism (most clearly seen in his oft-repeated lecture, "Self-Made Men"), and his unswerving loyalty to the Republican party. They openly attacked his failure to criticize the party's abandonment of the Reconstruction experiment in 1877.

The end of Reconstruction dashed Douglass's hopes for a meaningful emancipation. Even so, he never abandoned the fight for African-American rights. And he still regarded the Republican party as the likeliest vehicle for black advancement. A skilled practitioner at "waving the bloody shirt"—linking Democrats with slavery and the Confederacy—he campaigned widely for Republican candidates during the 1870s and 1880s. Partisanship brought rewards. President Rutherford B. Hayes appointed Douglass as the U.S. marshal for the District of Columbia (1877–1881), and President James A. Garfield named him the district's recorder of deeds (1881–1886). These offices made him financially secure. But changing family circumstances unsettled his personal life. His wife Anna died in 1882. Two years later he married Helen Pitts, his white former secretary. This racially-mixed marriage stirred controversy among blacks and whites alike; nevertheless, it failed to limit Douglass's influence.

Douglass was not lulled into complacency by partisan politics. He pressed Republicans as forcefully as ever on issues of concern to the African-American community, while continuing to campaign for party candidates. President Benjamin Harrison rewarded him with an appointment as U.S. minister to Haiti

(1889–1891). In this capacity he became an unwitting agent of American expansionism in the Caribbean, unsuccessfully attempting to negotiate special shipping concessions for American business interests and the lease of land for a naval base at Môle St. Nicholas. He eventually resigned his post and returned home in disgust.

Douglass continued to claim the mantle of race leader in the 1890s. He denounced the wave of disfranchisement and segregation measures spreading across the South. He threw much of his energy into the emerging campaign against racial violence. Between 1892 and 1894 he delivered "Lessons of the Hour"—a speech attacking the dramatic increase in black lynchings—to dozens of audiences across the nation. He personally appealed to Harrison for an antilynching law and used his position as the only African-American official at the 1893 World's Columbian Exposition to bring the issue before an international audience. He had just returned from another lecture tour when he died at his Washington home.

The most influential African American of the nineteenth century, Douglass made a career of agitating the American conscience. He spoke and wrote on behalf of a variety of reform causes: women's rights, temperance, peace, land reform, free public education, and the abolition of capital punishment. But he devoted the bulk of his time, immense talent, and boundless energy to ending slavery and gaining equal rights for African Americans. These were the central concerns of his long reform career. Douglass understood that the struggle for emancipation and equality demanded forceful, persistent, and unyielding agitation. And he recognized that African Americans must play a conspicuous role in that struggle. Less than a month before his death, when a young black man solicited his advice to an African American just starting out in the world, Douglass replied without hesitation: "Agitate! Agitate! Agitate!" (Joseph W. Holley, *You Can't Build a Chimney from the Top* [1948], p. 23).

• A wealth of primary sources document Douglass's life. Personal papers, including letters, manuscript speeches, and the like, are in the Frederick Douglass Collection at the Library of Congress. Three autobiographies offer detailed accounts of his beginnings in slavery and his career, as well as his ongoing attempts to construct a public image. In addition to the *Narrative*, Douglass wrote *My Bondage and My Freedom* (1855) and *Life and Times of Frederick Douglass* (1881; rev. ed., 1892). Hundreds of editorials can be found in the four reform journals he edited: the *North Star* (Rochester, N.Y., 1847–1851), *Frederick Douglass' Paper* (Rochester, N.Y., 1851–1860), *Douglass' Monthly* (Rochester, N.Y., 1859–1863), and the *New National Era* (Washington, D.C., 1870–1874). Many of these documents are available in modern published editions, especially *Life and Writings of Frederick Douglass*, ed. Philip S. Foner (5 vols., 1950–1975); and *The Frederick Douglass Papers: Speeches, Debates, and Interviews*, ed. John W. Blassingame (5 vols., 1979–1992).

Secondary sources on Douglass's life and career are equally numerous. The best biographies are Benjamin Quarles, *Frederick Douglass* (1948), and William S. McFeely, *Frederick Douglass* (1991). Dickson J. Preston, *Young Frederick Douglass: The Maryland Years* (1980), offers insights into his family background and his life in slavery. Aspects of his developing thought are explored in Waldo E. Martin, Jr., *The Mind of Frederick Douglass* (1984); David W. Blight, *Frederick Douglass' Civil War: Keeping Faith in Jubilee* (1989); Leslie F. Goldstein, "Violence as an Instrument for Social Change: The Views of Frederick Douglass," *Journal of Negro History* 61 (1976): 61–72; and Peter F. Walker, *Moral Choices: Memory, Desire, and Imagination in Nineteenth-century American Abolition* (1978). Useful analyses of his autobiographies and short fiction include C. Peter Ripley, "The Autobiographical Writings of Frederick Douglass," *Southern Studies* 24 (1985): 5–29, and William L. Andrews, ed., *Critical Essays on Frederick Douglass* (1991). Frederick S. Voss, *Majestic in His Wrath: A Pictorial Life of Frederick Douglass* (1995), is an excellent photographic record of Douglass's career.

ROY E. FINKENBINE

DOUGLASS, Harlan Paul (4 Jan. 1871–14 Apr. 1953), Congregational clergyman and sociologist, was born in Osage, Iowa, the son of Truman Orville Douglass, a clergyman, and Maria Greene. He grew up in a Grinnell, Iowa, parsonage. In 1887 he entered Grinnell's Iowa College. There he was influenced by the belief of the college's new president, George Augustus Gates, that the ultimate reality of the universe was personal. After graduating in 1891, Douglass studied theology in seminaries at the University of Chicago and in Andover, Massachusetts, and took courses in philosophy and the psychology of education with William James and Josiah Royce at Harvard University. He returned to Iowa in 1894, was ordained in the Congregational ministry, and served churches at Manson and Ames. In 1895 he married Rena Sherman; they became the parents of one child. As a graduate student of the radical Christian socialist George D. Herron at Iowa College, Douglass became an able interpreter of Herron's controversial social Christianity and received an M.A. in 1896.

In 1900 Douglass became the pastor of the First Congregational Church at Springfield, Missouri. He also taught psychology and philosophy at nearby Drury College. He was disturbed by white exploitation of the African-American community in Springfield. On 14 April 1906 a white mob sought three black men, who had been jailed. Two of the men were accused of assaulting a white woman, and the third was charged with murder. The mob of several thousand people broke into the county jail, seized the suspects, and hung them from an electric light tower, which was surmounted by a replica of the Statue of Liberty. Their bodies were cut down and burned at the foot of the tower. State militia saved the black section of Springfield from the torch, but Douglass, whose ancestors had been Scotch-Irish opponents of slavery, charged that "we might as well have had a jelly fish for a sheriff and a set of rag dolls for police." A grand jury found that the white woman had not been assaulted, and the mob had released from jail the man who was probably guilty of the murder. But all charges against the mob leaders were eventually dropped.

In 1906, despairing of his ability to improve Springfield's race relations, Douglass moved to New York to become superintendent of education for the American Missionary Association's seventy-five schools in the South. Initially regarded as "a dangerous radical" by AMA conservatives, Douglass advocated new measures such as hiring married women and African-American faculty members, turning primary and secondary schools over to local authorities, and placing southern black and white men on black college boards of trustees. Asked for an analysis of the AMA's work, Douglass published *Christian Reconstruction in the South* (1909). It invoked memories of evangelical abolitionism's heritage and visions of the social gospel's hope for an age to come. It was both a thoughtful study of race relations in the South and a theological critique of racism. The segregation mandated by white racism, Douglass argued, violated the sacred worth of human personality and brotherhood. From 1910 to 1918 Douglass was corresponding secretary of the AMA.

When he left the AMA at the end of World War I, Douglass became a sociologist of religion and a leader in ecumenical affairs. After serving briefly with the Young Men's Christian Association and the Interchurch World Movement, he was director of research for the Institute of Social and Religious Research from 1921 to 1933. He directed the China Survey of the Laymen's Foreign Missions Inquiry from 1930 to 1934. During this period his published sociological surveys of rural and urban Protestant churches and missions put the findings of an empirical sociology at the service of the church. Douglass was secretary of the Federal Council of Churches' Commission to Study Christian Unity from 1937 to 1942, and he edited two ecumenical journals, *Christendom* (from 1938 to 1948) and the *Ecumenical Review* (from 1948 to 1950). In these capacities, he facilitated the dialogue that worked toward greater cooperation among Protestant denominations in the United States.

Douglass died in Montclair, New Jersey. His career of more than five decades focused on the relationship between Christianity and society. In its early years, his major contribution was to challenge white racism by insisting that black people were persons created in the image of God and that discrimination against them was an offense to God. Later, as a sociologist of religion, Douglass eschewed the theoretical approaches of European sociology in favor of empirical studies of the social contexts of American congregations. Finally, as an important ecumenist, Douglass contributed to the maturation of cooperative efforts among American Protestant denominations.

• The Harlan Paul Douglass Papers and the Douglass Family Papers are at the Amistad Research Center, Tulane University. Papers from Douglass's later career as a sociologist of religion are at the Drew University library. On his early career see Robert T. Handy, "George D. Herron and the Kingdom Movement," *Church History* 19 (June 1950): 91–115; Katherine Lederer, "And Then They Sang a Sabbath Song," *Springfield!* (Apr.–May and June 1981); Lura Beam, *He Called Them by the Lightning: A Teacher's Odyssey in the Negro South,* *1908–1919* (1967); James M. McPherson, *The Abolitionist Legacy* (1975); and Ralph E. Luker, *The Social Gospel in Black and White: American Racial Reform, 1885–1912* (1991). On his later career see Edmund deS. Brunner, "Harlan Paul Douglass: Pioneer Researcher in the Sociology of Religion," *Review of Religious Research* (Summer and Fall 1959), and Frederick A. Shippey, "The Concept of Church in H. Paul Douglass," *Review of Religious Research* (Spring 1963). An obituary is in the *New York Times*, 15 Apr. 1953.

RALPH E. LUKER

DOUGLASS, Mabel Smith (11 Feb. 1877–21 Sept. 1933), college dean, was born Anna Mabel Smith in Jersey City, New Jersey, the daughter of James Weaver Smith, a merchant, and Wihelmine Joanne Midlige. She attended public schools in Jersey City and graduated from Barnard College in 1899.

Following her graduation, Mabel Smith taught for three years in the New York City public schools. She left teaching in 1903 to marry William Shipman Douglass, a New York commission merchant, with whom she had two children. She was, in her own words, "just a well-to-do woman with two children and a lovely home" when, in 1911, she joined the campaign of the New Jersey Federation of Women's Clubs to secure "speedy admission" of women to all-male Rutgers College, the land-grant college of New Jersey. At that time there was one small private college for women in the state and no public institution so that most young women seeking a liberal arts education had to enroll in colleges outside of New Jersey. Since Rutgers was supported by federal and state funds, the federation argued, it should admit both women and men. Douglass agreed to chair the subcommittee formed to pursue that objective.

Early on Douglass discovered that the trustees of Rutgers College were opposed to coeducation but not totally averse to the idea of a coordinate women's college on the order of Barnard, particularly if the new students of such a college "should bring with them a sort of dowry, a building to serve for dormitory and classrooms." Shifting gears, she launched a campaign for the establishment of a women's college, conducting surveys, visiting dignitaries, speaking to interested groups, even organizing a $1 subscription campaign among federation members in the hope of raising a $150,000 dowry. This activity came at a cost. In a 1913 letter detailing her son's serious illness, she wrote, "I am going to peg and peg away—but sometimes the task seems very heavy." In 1915 she suffered a nervous breakdown and was forced to withdraw from leadership of the campaign. She recovered quickly, but family crises—the death of her beloved mother and the illness and death of her husband—followed. Though sidelined herself, she had earned for her cause the valuable support of influential groups, and the campaign had moved forward. A confluence of events and the acquisition of the requisite dowry brought the effort to a successful conclusion. In May 1918 the trustees of Rutgers College approved the establishment of a college for women as a department of the state university, to open in September with an anticipated enrollment of ten to fifteen students. Shortly thereafter, Douglass accepted the invitation of the trustees to become the first dean of the college. The trustees understood that Douglass's vitality, intelligence, and indisputable administrative skills were more important to the success of the new college than more traditional, scholarly credentials.

Douglass had just three months in which to transform an idea into a working institution. She saturated the state high schools with materials about the "adequate faculty and facilities" of the new college that would open in September. Just where they would come from she did not know, but she did know that she "had need of students." Having secured the publicity front, she set out, with the aid of Elizabeth N. Greene, the first registrar-bursar, to organize the college. During that summer she did everything from fundraising to supervising workers renovating the mansion in which the college was to be housed to organizing a curriculum that would provide a sound liberal arts education for women. Her energy was palpable. According to Greene, "She was always on top of the wave."

The New Jersey College for Women opened on schedule, with fifty-four students. The flu epidemic of 1918 and a defective heating system made the first year difficult for both staff and students, but the college survived. Dean Douglass was technically under the supervision of a board of managers appointed by the Rutgers trustees, but in effect she ran the college. Her ingenuity was legendary. To accommodate the expanding student body during the college's second year, she transformed a barn into a science building and created a gymnasium out of packing boxes that had been used to ship Liberty motors to France during World War I. In the following decade state funding provided three permanent classroom buildings. The federation, whose loyalty Douglass retained, funded a music building, and a private donor endowed a chapel. In the college's first year, instruction was provided by Rutgers faculty. By 1933 the college had its own faculty of more than one hundred, and departments of art, music, and library science, none of which existed elsewhere at Rutgers, had been established. Enrollment was more than 1,000.

When the New Jersey College for Women opened in 1918, it offered three courses of study: liberal arts and sciences, teacher training, and home economics. The college received state support, and the vocational courses were a practical response to the desire of New Jersey taxpayers that young women be trained as teachers and dieticians. But for Douglass, the goal had always been to establish what she called "a true *college* for women," at which they would be intellectually challenged by the liberal arts. "The duty of a college," she once said, "is primarily cultural."

Despite personal tragedy—the suicide of her son in 1923—and health problems, Douglass was unremitting in her quest to build a college of distinction with a sound fiscal base. In 1932, plagued by recurring depression, she took a leave of absence from which she never returned. She officially resigned the deanship on 1 July 1933. After a stay in an upstate New York sanatorium, she retired to her summer cottage on Lake Placid. On 21 September she went out for a row from which she did not return. Her body was recovered thirty years later with every indication that her death had been a suicide.

A colleague once described Mabel Smith Douglass as a woman for whom obstacles simply did not exist: "She managed at the same time to face them and not see them." This quality above all others enabled her to persist in the grueling campaign for the establishment of the New Jersey College for Women. In 1955 the college that she had created was renamed in her honor.

• Douglass's papers, including her account of the founding of the college, *The Early History of the New Jersey College for Women* (1929), are in the Douglass College Library, as are other materials related to the history of the college. The most complete history is George P. Schmidt, *Douglass College: A History* (1968). See also George C. Orloff, *A Lady in the Lake: The True Account of Death and Discovery in Lake Placid* (1985), for a full account of the somewhat bizarre circumstances surrounding the recovery of her body from Lake Placid. An obituary is in the *New York Times*, 22 Sept. 1933.

LOUISE DUUS

DOUGLASS, Mrs. Lewis Hallam. *See* Hallam, Lewis, and Mrs. Lewis Hallam Douglass.

DOUGLASS, Sarah Mapps (9 Sept. 1806–8 Sept. 1882), abolitionist and educator, was born in Philadelphia, Pennsylvania, the daughter of Robert Douglass, Sr., a prosperous hairdresser from the island of St. Kitts, and Grace Bustill, a milliner. Her mother was the daughter of Cyrus Bustill, a prominent member of Philadelphia's African-American community. Raised as a Quaker by her mother, Douglass was alienated by the blatant racial prejudice of many white Quakers. Although she adopted Quaker dress and enjoyed the friendship of Quaker antislavery advocates like Lucretia Mott, she was highly critical of the sect.

In 1819 Grace Douglass and philanthropist James Forten established a school for black children, where "their children might be better taught than . . . in any of the schools . . . open to [their] people." Sarah Douglass was educated there, taught for a while in New York City, and then returned to take over the school.

In 1833 Douglass joined an interracial group of women abolitionists in establishing the Philadelphia Female Anti-Slavery Society. For almost four decades, she served the organization in many capacities. Also active in the antislavery movement at the national level, she attended the 1837 Anti-Slavery Convention of American Women in New York City. The following year, when the convention met at Philadelphia's ill-fated Pennsylvania Hall, which in 1838 was burned by an antiabolitionist mob, she was elected treasurer. She was also a delegate at the third and final women's antislavery convention in 1839.

Douglass repeatedly stressed the need for African-American women to educate themselves. In 1831 she helped organize the Female Literary Association of Philadelphia, a society whose members met regularly for "mental feasts," and on the eve of the Civil War she founded the Sarah M. Douglass Literary Circle.

Throughout the 1830s Douglass wrote poetry and prose under the pseudonyms "Sophanisba" and "Ella." Her writings—on the blessings of religion, the prospect of divine retribution for the sin of slavery, the evils of prejudice, and the plight of the slave—were published in various antislavery journals, including the *Liberator*, the *Colored American*, the *Genius of Universal Emancipation*, and the *National Enquirer and Constitutional Advocate of Universal Liberty*.

During the 1830s and 1840s Douglass was beset by financial problems. Her school never operated at a profit, and in 1838, deciding she could no longer accept the financial backing of her parents, she asked the Female Anti-Slavery Society to take over the school. The experiment proved unsatisfactory, however, and in 1840 she resumed direct control of the school, giving up a guaranteed salary for assistance in paying the rent. In 1852, now reconciled with the Quakers, she closed her school and accepted an appointment to supervise the Girls' Preparatory Department of the Quaker-sponsored Institute for Colored Youth. From 1853 to 1877 she served as principal of the department.

For more than forty years Douglass enjoyed a close friendship with abolitionists Sarah and Angelina Grimké. After an uneasy start, the relationship between the daughters of a slaveholding family and the African-American teacher deepened into one of great mutual respect. Sarah Grimké, fourteen years Douglass's senior, eventually became her confidante. After her mother's death in 1842 left Douglass as unpaid housekeeper to her father and brothers, Grimké sympathized with her: "Worn in body & spirit with the duties of thy school, labor awaits thee at home & when it is done there is none to throw around thee the arms of love."

In 1854 Douglass received an offer of marriage from the Reverend William Douglass, a widower with nine children and the minister of Philadelphia's prestigious St. Thomas's African Episcopal Church. Grimké considered him eminently worthy of her friend. He was a man of education, and his remarks about her age and spinster status were only proof of his lively sense of humor. As for Douglass's apprehensions about the physical aspects of married life, the unmarried Grimké assured her, "Time will familiarize you with the idea." The couple were married in 1855. The marriage proved an unhappy one. On her husband's death in 1861, Douglass wrote of her years "in that School of bitter discipline, the old Parsonage of St. Thomas," but she acknowledged that William Douglass had not been without his merits.

In one respect, marriage gave Douglass a new freedom. A cause she had long championed was the education of women on health issues. Before her marriage,

she had taken courses at the Female Medical College of Pennsylvania. In 1855 she enrolled in the Pennsylvania Medical University and in 1858 embarked on a career as a lecturer, confronting topics that would have been considered unseemly for an unmarried woman to address. Her illustrated lectures to female audiences in New York City and Philadelphia drew praise for being both informative and "chaste."

Through the 1860s and 1870s Douglass continued her work of reform, lecturing, raising money for the southern freedmen and -women, helping to establish a home for elderly and indigent black Philadelphians, and teaching at the Institute for Colored Youth. She died in Philadelphia.

As a teacher, a lecturer, an abolitionist, a reformer, and a tireless advocate of women's education, Sarah Mapps Douglass made her influence felt in many ways. Her emphasis on education and self-improvement helped shape the lives of the many hundreds of black children she taught in a career in the classroom that lasted more than a half-century, while her pointed and persistent criticism of northern racism reminded her white colleagues in the abolitionist movement that their agenda must include more than the emancipation of the slaves.

• In her will, Douglass instructed her family to destroy all her private correspondence, as well as her "lectures on Anatomy and Natural History to Mothers." However, a number of letters to and from Douglass are in the Weld-Grimké Papers at the University of Michigan and the Antislavery Manuscripts at the Boston Public Library. Much of her correspondence with the Grimkés has been reprinted in Gilbert H. Barnes and Dwight L. Dumond, eds., *Letters of Theodore Dwight Weld, Angelina Grimké Weld, and Sarah Grimké, 1822–1844* (2 vols., 1934). Douglass's role in the antislavery movement is documented in the records of the Philadelphia Female Anti-Slavery Society at the Historical Society of Pennsylvania and in the published proceedings of the three national women's antislavery conventions held between 1837 and 1839. For other accounts of Douglass's career, see Anna Bustill Smith, "The Bustill Family," *Journal of Negro History* 10 (Oct. 1925): 638–44; Henry J. Cadbury, "Negro Membership in the Society of Friends," *Journal of Negro History* 21 (Apr. 1936): 153–99; Dorothy Sterling, ed., *We Are Your Sisters: Black Women in the Nineteenth Century* (1984); Kenneth Ives, *Black Quakers: Brief Biographies* (1986); and Julie Winch, *Philadelphia's Black Elite: Activism, Accommodation, and the Struggle for Autonomy, 1787–1848* (1988).

JULIE WINCH

DOUGLASS, William (Oct. 1681–21 Oct. 1752), doctor, historian, and pioneer in colonial philanthropy, was born in Gifford, Scotland, the son of George Douglass, chamberlain to the marquis of Tweeddale, and Katherine Inglis. His father, a man of distinction in local affairs, was able to afford a fine education for his son. William earned his master's degree in 1705 from Edinburgh University where, influenced by Dr. Archibald Pitcairne, he decided on a medical career. At the University of Leyden he studied under Dr. Herman Boerhaave and then earned his medical degree from the University of Utrecht in 1712. His medical dissertation, *Animalium Hydraulisin*, was on the circulation of the blood.

Douglass had a peripatetic early career as he worked in Paris and England before he decided to seek opportunities in the New World. He arrived in Boston in early 1716 but stayed less than a year and resumed his travels to the West Indies and to the mid-Atlantic colonies. In 1718 he settled permanently in Boston; as the only physician with a university medical degree, he enjoyed a successful practice.

For the European-trained Douglass, the medical techniques of local physicians were appalling: "bleeding, vomiting, blistering, [and] purging; if the Illness continued, there was *repetendi* and finally *murderandi*." For the rest of his life Douglass sought to advance colonial medicine and to reform it along the lines of European institutions. He imported medical books, introduced new medicines, instructed local physicians, and began research on epidemic diseases such as smallpox. When smallpox broke out in 1721, he used Thomas Sydenham's "cold regimen" but to little avail as the worst epidemic in Boston's annals swept through the town.

At this juncture Cotton Mather, the foremost minister in Boston and long interested in medical affairs, proposed the use of a new procedure, variolous inoculation. All of the town's physicians, except Zabdiel Boylston, rejected it as new and untested. In a bold experiment, Boylston inoculated his son, and it proved to be an effective treatment. Yet Boylston disregarded basic medical precautions when he failed to isolate the inoculees. Douglass opposed the unscientific way in which Boylston introduced inoculation and considered it a dangerous innovation that lacked medical controls. Despite orders from town authorities to desist and strong opposition from the populace, Boylston continued his inoculations.

The clash between Douglass and Boylston led to the famous "inoculation controversy" with scathing polemics from both sides. Douglass led the opposition with two anti-inoculation pamphlets and attacks in local newspapers, especially in James Franklin's *New England Courant*. As the controversy continued, the issues broadened to include the question of the clergy's involvement in medical affairs and the regulation of medical practitioners. By 1722 Douglass accepted inoculation, but he never forgave Boylston and believed that the careless introduction of inoculation added to the deaths in the epidemic.

After the epidemic Douglass focused his medical research exclusively on smallpox, determined to reduce the mortality rate of the disease in Boston. Before he could complete his work on a new method of treatment, another epidemic occurred in 1730. This time Douglass approved the use of inoculation but insisted upon strict medical controls. In 1730 he also published the preliminary results of his research, *A Practical Essay concerning the Small Pox*. A concise scientific treatise, this was the first colonial publication to utilize large-scale statistics for medical purposes.

Douglass acquired additional prominence during the "throat distemper" epidemic of the 1730s, which had a high mortality among New England's children. An acute observer, he studied the pathology of the disease, introduced mercurials as a new treatment, and in 1736 published a clinical description, *The Practical History of a New Eruptive Miliary Fever*. As the first modern analysis of scarlet fever, it was his most important medical publication and a notable contribution to epidemiology; it preceded European accounts by a dozen years.

In 1736 he founded the Boston Medical Society, the first organization of doctors in colonial America. In other ways Douglass tried to advance the medical profession with proposals for a chair of medicine at Harvard College and efforts to publish a medical journal. He also sought to regulate the medical profession with a board of doctors to examine and license practitioners. But his ideas for medical reform were too advanced for colonial physicians, and they came to naught.

Like many men of the Enlightenment, Douglass had broad scientific interests and owned an excellent library. He collected more than 1,000 plants for botanical study, compiled extensive weather data, prepared a map of New England from recent surveys, published the almanac *Mercurius Nov Anglicanus* (1743), and corresponded with the learned men of the Atlantic world. In 1740 he wrote *A Discourse concerning the Currencies*, an excellent analysis of paper money and the colonial monetary system.

His grand history, *A Summary, Historical and Political, of the . . . British Settlements in North America*, was first issued in serial form in 1747, then published in two volumes in 1749 and 1752. Opinionated and encyclopedic, it was an impressive achievement with an informative, if digressive, account of colonial life. Incomplete at his death, the *Summary* is an important source book, and it enjoyed a wide circulation among American and European intellectuals. Adam Smith used it in his research for *The Wealth of Nations* and had praise for the "honest and downright Dr. Douglass."

Douglass, known for his medical charity among Boston's poor, expanded his philanthropic endeavors late in life. He proposed a series of orphanages for Massachusetts, sought to reform the system of colonial poor relief, and was a generous benefactor to the town of New Sherburne, whose grateful inhabitants renamed it "Douglas" in his honor.

His most important humanitarian work was with the Scottish-American community, particularly with the Scots Charitable Society, the oldest benevolent organization in the colonies. He joined it in 1716, was elected vice president in 1721, and president in 1736 until his death. Under his leadership the society expanded its philanthropic work to include pensions for the elderly, benefits to widows, aid to war veterans, and extensive social services for Scottish immigrants. Douglass reformed the society's operations with sound management and a strong fiscal policy, making it the model for New England's benevolent organizations.

As a Scotsman in an English world, Douglass had strong opinions and enjoyed a contentious public life. He lampooned the Great Awakening and its leader George Whitefield, attacked the politics of Governor William Shirley, and criticized Admiral Charles Knowles for the impressment of Boston men. His worship at an Anglican church and his later deism rankled local Puritans, and he responded with a hearty anticlericalism. Douglass was an exceptionally well-educated man in a provincial world, versatile and with a trenchant pen for polemics. Abrasive and argumentative, he had his share of enemies, but historians have too readily accepted the opinions of his critics.

Douglass developed strong ties to Boston and affectionately considered it his "*Altera Patria*." Although he never married, he fathered a son, William, in 1745 and deeded his vast library to the boy. Prosperous and a large land owner, Douglass lived in the Green Dragon Tavern, where he continued extensive research on smallpox. He developed his "cool regimen" of treatment, and in the smallpox epidemic of 1752 it was applied by the town's physicians on a large scale. It helped reduce the mortality rate in Boston from 146 per 1,000 in 1721 to 97 per 1,000 in 1752, a significant triumph against the deadly disease. This was Douglass's most important medical achievement. Exhausted by his work in the epidemic and his efforts to complete the *Summary*, Douglass died of a stroke at his son's home.

• Most of the William Douglass Papers disappeared after his death; what survived were letters to Cadwallader Colden, which are at the New-York Historical Society in New York City. They were published in various volumes of *The Letters and Papers of Cadwallader Colden* from 1918 to 1937. Also important are the Scots Charitable Society Papers at the New England Historic Genealogical Society in Boston. The standard biographical sources are Charles J. Bullock, "The Life and Writings of William Douglass," *Economic Studies* 2 (1897): 265–90; George H. Weaver, "Life and Writings of William Douglass, M.D., 1691–1752," Society of Medical History of Chicago *Bulletin* 2 (1921): 229–59; and Raymond Muse, "William Douglass, Man of the American Enlightenment, 1691–1752" (Ph.D. diss., Stanford Univ., 1948). More recent is John M. Bumsted, "Doctor Douglass's *Summary*," *New England Quarterly* 37 (1964): 242–50; David F. Hawke, "William Douglass's *Summary*," in *The Colonial Legacy: Some Eighteenth-Century Commentators*, ed. Lawrence H. Leder, vol. 2 (1971), pp. 43–74; James W. Schmotter, "William Douglass and the Beginnings of American Medical Professionalism," *Historical Journal of Western Massachusetts* 6 (1977): 23–36; and Peter R. Virgadamo, "William Douglass," in *The Biographical Dictionary of Social Welfare in America*, ed. Walter I. Trattner (1986), pp. 247–50.

PETER R. VIRGADAMO

DOUVILLIER, Suzanne (c. 1778–30 Aug. 1826), ballerina and choreographer, also known as Mme Placide, was born Suzanne-Théodore Taillandet in Dole, France, the daughter of François Taillandet and Louise Jantie (or Jauntie). Douvillier danced in 1784 and 1785 at the renowned Comédie Française, said to have had the "prettiest" corps de ballet in Paris. She probably danced in the festive wedding scene for Beaumarchais's *Le Mariage de Figaro*, which had its premiere at this time. In 1786 she was honored to be accepted into the school of the Royal Academy of Music, where she studied with Deshayes. For two years the young girl danced at the Paris Opéra and was granted permission to appear daily at Nicolet's Théâtre des Grands Danseurs du Roi. By the time she was around twelve years old, Mlle Théodore, for such was her Parisian stage name, had already earned a reputation as one of the most beautiful and talented Columbines in all of Paris.

Lessons in stagecraft from these two institutions served her throughout her life. Her repertoire was unusually varied, particularly at a time when specialization was the rule: she could perform not only elegant dances from the *danse serieux* repertoire of the Paris Opéra but also, and equally well, comical or melodramatic roles from the popular theaters. In all, she danced almost 150 roles in her American career, more than 100 of them in full-length ballets, operas, or pantomimes.

At Nicolet's, too, she first encountered the celebrity Alexandre Placide, an acrobat and pantomimist. In 1788 Douvillier adopted the stage name of Mme Placide and left Paris with the thirty-year-old star. They toured Haiti from October 1788 until July 1791, shortly before the slave revolt broke out.

She debuted with the French Company from Paris, as Placide billed them, in Annapolis, Maryland, on 29 October 1791. In Baltimore they premiered six new ballets in six weeks, then joined the Old American Company for a tour that took them from New York to Philadelphia to Boston, where they opened the city's first theater in the fall. After the sheriff enforced legal prohibitions against dramatic entertainments, the company withdrew to Newport, Rhode Island, where they remained throughout the summer of 1793. Her daughter was probably born that spring.

At first, she often danced Columbine opposite Placide's Pierrot in commedia dell'arte pantomimes. Placide composed several comical "dancing ballettes," such as *The Bird Catcher*, which became her standard opening night vehicle. Mostly, however, she starred as the virtuous heroine in Jean-François Arnould-Mussot's melodramatic pantomime-ballets, including *The American Heroine*, *Le Maréchal aux Logis*, *Sophie of Brabant*, and *La Forêt Noire*. The historian Lillian Moore erroneously credited Haitian ballerina Mme Gardie with performing the first "serious" ballet-pantomime produced in the United States (*La Forêt Noire*, 1794), but the accolade belongs to Mme Placide for appearances in other Arnould-Mussot ballet-pantomimes, dating from 1791. In Charleston in 1794 they were joined by Jean Baptiste Francisqui, Douvillier's classmate at the Paris Opéra. Moving away from comedy and melodrama, the repertoire expanded in the direction of light-hearted ballets from the Opéra. Her most popular were title roles in Jean-Georges Noverre's *Les Caprices de Galathée* and Pierre Gardel's *Mirsa*.

Two years later the Charleston-based troupe disbanded owing to scandalous goings-on. Placide and a handsome young opera singer fought a duel on the public streets for Suzanne's hand. Louis Douvillier won her heart, and possibly the duel. They were said to have married in June 1796, whereupon the two headed north with her daughter but left her infant son behind. They joined Francisqui at Lailson's Circus in Philadelphia, appearing in French opera, ballets, and melodramas. Sometime prior to 1801 the Douvilliers moved to New Orleans, where they opened the Café de St. Dominigue and settled down. Her second son was born in 1802 but did not survive. Neither did her marriage, for her husband permanently abandoned her in favor of a soprano with whom he shared leading roles at the opera house on St. Pierre Street.

Theater records prior to 1805 have not survived, but a fragment of a playbill dated September 1799 lists Francisqui dancing with an unnamed ballerina, who was most likely Douvillier, since there was no other danseuse in New Orleans for years after that. In 1808 she evidently was the proprietor of a short-lived theater, named Le Théâtre de la Gaîté [*sic*] after Nicolet's theater in Paris. She choreographed several pastorale ballets that summer, most of them dealing with unrequited love or fantasies of revenge: *Echo and Narcissus; or, Love and Vengeance* and *Amour et les Nymphes ou Diane Vaincue par Cupidon*. Then she resumed her career at the opera house on St. Pierre. Not only was she the ballerina, but she also succeeded Francisqui as ballet master. She trained a corps de ballet that included her daughter, better known as an opera singer, and choreographed incidental dances for the operas. One of her ballets, *L'Indépendance Americaine ou l'Apothéose de Washington*, remained in the repertoire for many years and was trotted out regularly for patriotic occasions.

In 1814 the once-beautiful ballerina was afflicted with a disease that consumed the flesh on her nose and mouth. She was forced out of hiding by poverty in April 1818, even though she could no longer speak. Theater manager Noah Ludlow described her as "tall and commanding in her bearing, fine hair and eyes, splendid bust, and beautifully rounded figure." Despite her mask, he claimed that he had never observed "such truly *speaking* pantomime" performed with "exquisite grace and ease." Douvillier was cast as the abandoned Donna Anna in a ballet adaptation of Gluck's *Don Juan*. Ironically, it was her former husband, Louis Douvillier, who enacted Don Juan's descent into hell while she danced Vengeance in "The Ballet of the Furies." She returned to a hermit's life and died eight years later in New Orleans. Suzanne Douvillier was the first professional ballerina to tour the United States, as well as the first woman choreographer and ballet master of an American opera company.

• Douvillier's Haitian career is described in Maureen Needham Costonis, "French Ballet in 18th Century San Dominigue," Society of Dance History Scholars, *Proceedings of Sixth Annual Conference* (1983), pp. 214–29; and her American career is traced by the same author in "Ballet Comes to America, 1792–1842: French Contributions to the Establishment of Theatrical Dance in New Orleans and Philadelphia" (Ph.D. diss., New York Univ. 1989). Noah Ludlow's anecdotal account of his career in the theater is in his *Dramatic Life as I Found It* (1880). Since Douvillier's career interfaced with that of another French dancer who came to the United States at the same time, see Maureen Needham [Costonis], "The American Career of Jean Baptiste Francisqui," *Bulletin of Research in the Humanities* (Winter 1982): 430–42.

MAUREEN NEEDHAM

DOVE, Arthur Garfield (2 Aug. 1880–23 Nov. 1946), illustrator and modernist painter, was born in Canandaigua, New York, the son of William George Dove, an affluent brickmaker, building contractor, and civic activist, and Anna Elizabeth Chipps. In 1882 the family moved to Geneva, New York, where they eventually occupied a mansion in an upper-class neighborhood. Dove received many educational opportunities, including painting lessons. After Dove graduated from high school in 1899, he attended Hobart College, located in Geneva, and then Cornell University in Ithaca, New York, where he took art classes. Dove graduated from Cornell in 1903 and found work as an illustrator in New York City with magazines such as *Century*, *Collier's*, *Harper's*, *Life*, the *Saturday Evening Post*, *Scribner's*, the *Illustrated Sporting News*, *McClure's*, and *St. Nicholas*.

While in New York, Dove expanded his social circle to include some of the most forward-thinking artist-illustrators of his day, including John Sloan, Ernest Lawson, and other members of the avant-garde group known as The Eight. In addition to illustrating, these artists painted in a variety of progressive modes. They held a common desire to free art from the conservative establishment. Dove's association with the group was fitting because he had been a progressive thinker since childhood. He even resigned from his church at age twelve, as he remembered it, "owing to a difficulty over Robert Ingersoll," who was an atheist, "having the right to his opinions whether we agree with them or not."

In 1904 Dove married Florence Dorsey, whom he knew from Geneva. Shortly thereafter he decided to give up illustration. Following the lead of his liberal colleagues, he made plans to try his hand at painting. Although the decision brought him considerable financial difficulty in the coming years, Dove eventually attained renown for his abstract compositions.

Dove's opportunity to begin his career as a painter came during his year spent in France in 1908–1909. In Paris he met and befriended Alfred Maurer, who had connections in the Paris art world, and other modernist American artists. These figures introduced him to the latest trends in painting. Dove worked steadily throughout the year, producing brushy landscapes in the impressionist style, and then brighter fauve-inspired pieces. He exhibited one of these works in the avant-garde Salon d'automne of 1908, and another at the same salon in 1909. Always preferring the country to city living, Dove also spent time outside Paris in Moret, and in Cagnes, a town near Nice, France. He also took short trips to Spain and Italy. Dove sketched and painted in the rural locations he frequented, often in the company of Maurer.

Dove returned to New York in the summer of 1909 and arranged to show the fruits of his year abroad in a three-day exhibit at Hobart College. He also took a job as a newspaper illustrator but, dissatisfied with urban living, gave it up almost immediately. Instead he purchased a house in Westport, Connecticut, a town that became a haven for artists, writers, and other creative intellectuals within a few years of his move there. Dove hoped to earn a living as a farmer and fisher in order to make more time for his painting than illustration afforded. Just before the couple moved in 1910, Florence gave birth to their only child.

About the time that he returned from France, in 1909 or early 1910, Dove made the acquaintance of Alfred Stieglitz, the well-known photographer, gallery owner, and modern art patron. Stieglitz played a crucial role in the painter's development as an artist. He invited Dove to show at his gallery at 291 Fifth Avenue (called 291) in the ground-breaking Younger American Painters exhibit in 1910. Dove showed *The Lobster* (1908), one of the fauve-inspired still lifes that he created while in France. The piece portrays a lobster, a pitcher, fruit, and other items and, although executed primarily in neutral colors, reveals the influence of Henri Matisse in its flat, patterned background.

After the show Stieglitz encouraged Dove to work more abstractly. For the next several years Dove devoted his energies to developing a personal style wherein general forms derived from nature predominated. He reduced forms to their essences and exaggerated and simplified the results. Bodies of water, for instance, became rows of softly undulating lines. As Dove put it, "I gave up trying to express an idea by stating innumerable little facts, the statement of facts having no more to do with the art of painting than statistics with literature" (Wight, p. 37). Occasionally Dove's works bore only a slight resemblance to nature. Such is the case with a group of pastels known as the Ten Commandments (1912). These pieces caught the attention of the public. Like work by so many modern artists, however, much of the attention he received for them was negative. Critics reviewed the abstractions as incomprehensible, freakish, and even immoral. They failed to see the spiritual or poetic component Dove believed himself to have captured.

Dove continued to paint despite negative criticism. Soon he began to establish a reputation for works such as *Foghorns* (1929, Colorado Springs Fine Arts Center). In this oft-reproduced painting, four purple forms made up of concentric circles hover over gray horizontals. The forms, each made up of concentric circles radiating from a central round core, suggest sound waves. The sound waves in turn suggest the peal of foghorns at sea. The gray striations call up images of the ocean without portraying it realistically.

Dove's farming work, a new endeavor as a chicken grower, and then in 1918 full-time work again as an illustrator consumed much of his time. Nevertheless, he continued to exhibit. Dove showed sixteen works at the Anderson Galleries' Forum Exhibition in 1916, two at the Society of Independent Artists' first exhibition in 1917, and two more at the Philadelphia Academy of Fine Art's show Paintings and Drawings Showing the Later Tendencies in Art in 1921. In addition, Dove participated in several small shows, most at Stieglitz's galleries.

Dove experienced a notable period of creative growth beginning in 1921, possibly as a result of the fact that his father, who never supported his painting, died. Dove left his wife later the same year and moved in with Helen Torr, who was married to cartoonist Clive Weed. Dove married Torr, whose nickname was "Reds," in 1932. His first wife, who had refused to grant him a divorce, died that year. Dove's style changed to include mechanical as well as nature imagery, and he created his first "assemblages." Influenced by the cubist collage technique, these works utilized bits of everyday objects such as magnifying glasses, pages from hymnals, and pieces of cloth. Often serving as symbolic portraits of acquaintances, these witty pieces challenged common definitions of art making. Dove's most well-known assemblage is *Goin' Fishin'* (1926, Phillips Collection, Washington, D.C.), which utilizes bits of bamboo, bark, and the sleeves from a denim shirt to suggest fishing rods and attire.

Dove exhibited twenty-five of his new works, including several assemblages, at Stieglitz's Seven Americans show staged at Anderson Galleries in 1925. Stieglitz himself showed in this exhibit, along with Georgia O'Keeffe, John Marin, Marsden Hartley, Charles Demuth, and Paul Strand. The show met with success, and Dove received most of the critical attention. Thereafter Dove showed with Stieglitz once a year, except once, for the rest of his life. When 291 closed, Stieglitz exhibited Dove at his Intimate Gallery and then at An American Place.

Although by the mid-1920s Dove had received critical acclaim for his art, his works failed to sell well enough to provide him with enough money to cover his living expenses. He and Reds constantly experienced financial difficulty. They lived on a 42-foot sailboat moored off Manhattan and then off the town of Halesite, on Long Island, during 1922 to 1933. There was no real studio space on the boat. At several points the couple acted as caretakers for a house on Pratt's Island near Westport. Only when art collector Duncan Phillips, of the Phillips Memorial Gallery (now the Phillips Collection, Washington, D.C.), discovered Dove and began a regular patronage of his paintings did the artist experience financial security.

Although Phillips first saw Dove's works in the early 1920s, he did not purchase any until 1930, when Dove first showed at An American Place. At that time he purchased two works through Stieglitz, then three others by 1933. In May 1933 Phillips wrote Dove proposing that he acquire three more paintings shown at An American Place. Thereafter, Phillips chose works from Dove's annual show and paid for them on an installment plan. He gradually came to think of his patronage of Dove as a stipend or subsidy. Over the years Phillips's monthly payment to Dove increased, but it was never assured. As such, it offered Dove little peace of mind.

In 1934 Phillips attempted to enroll Dove in the federal Public Works of Art Project of the Works Projects Administration, but Dove declined, even though he needed the money. Although many artists found respite under the program, Dove felt, with reason, that the committee would disapprove of his abstract style and that he would have to change his work to satisfy them. He also felt that the salary offered him of $34 per week was insufficient even to cover the cost of materials, let alone the value of his paintings.

The death of Dove's mother in 1933 did little to increase his financial stability. Although the family had amassed great wealth, virtually all of it was in real estate, which was difficult to sell during the depression. Dove, who with his brother Paul inherited the family's holdings, sold the houseboat and moved with Reds to Geneva in order to live rent-free in the family's various dwellings. They lived in Geneva for five years while Dove and his brother divested themselves of the estate, and Dove continued to paint. Dove showed in several noteworthy exhibitions during these years, including the Whitney Museum of American Art's show Abstract Painting in America in 1935, the Museum of Modern Art's Fantastic Art, Dada, Surrealism in 1936–1937, and its Art in Our Time exhibit in 1939. In 1946 he showed at the Whitney's Pioneers of Modern Art in America exhibition.

Living in Geneva, Dove and Reds felt cut off from the intellectual set to which they were accustomed, and when their financial situation improved after the sale of some properties, Phillips's continued patronage, and the sale of a painting to the University of Minnesota for the then-large sum of $1,000, they determined to move closer to New York City. In 1938 the couple purchased a small house on Long Island Sound, where they lived for the remainder of their lives. The acquisition of the house, unfortunately, coincided with the deterioration of Dove's health. He contracted pneumonia the week after its purchase and never fully recovered. He suffered a relapse in 1939 and was bedridden for months. Over the next eight and a half years he experienced the effects of a weakening heart and the kidney malfunction known as Bright's disease.

Remarkably, Dove experienced a last creative period beginning around 1940, when he recovered sufficiently to paint but to do little else. No longer plagued by chores, business, or other interruptions, Dove painted steadily for long periods. The results were canvases that were more abstract than any before. Correspondingly, the 1940 show at Stieglitz's was a dramatic success, and Phillips's purchases totaled more than $2,000. A good example of Dove's late style is *That Red One* (1944, William H. Lane Foundation, Leominster, Mass.). Seemingly nonobjective, the piece depicts a black circle with a green center flanked by two vertical red rectangles. Blue, yellow, orange, and green angular shapes suggesting 1960s hard-edged paintings form a backdrop.

Though World War II raged during Dove's last years, it caused him only minor inconveniences. His main trial became getting into the city to see his shows at Stieglitz's, which he was unable to do because of travel restrictions. His son was drafted in 1942, along with his personal doctor, but was discharged unharmed in 1945. Dove staged his last exhibit at Stieglitz's in 1946. Because of his rapidly deteriorating health, he only submitted nine new paintings. Stieglitz, too, was ill, and he passed away suddenly just a month after the show closed. The death of his friend and dealer affected Dove greatly and probably contributed to his own expiration. In the months following Stieglitz's death, Dove suffered a stroke that left him unable to paint. He died in New York at Huntington Hospital.

Dove is remembered for his contribution to American modernist painting and for his relationships with patrons Alfred Stieglitz and Duncan Phillips. Interestingly, few studies of Dove treat him with scholarly acumen. Instead, most investigations recapitulate Dove's biography. This dearth of critical attention to the painter may be a result of several factors. First, Dove's reputation as a simple person at one with nature has impeded recognition of him as an intellectual. Second, an alternate view of the artist as breaking revolutionary ground in painting has made it difficult to realistically evaluate his achievements. Third, Dove's reluctance during his lifetime to share his views on art and life has left scholars little with which to construct discourse. Clearly, he produced a body of work that merits consideration on its own terms.

• Archival resources for Dove include papers at the Beinecke Rare Book and Manuscript Library, Yale University; the Archives of American Art, Smithsonian Institution; the University of Pennsylvania Library; the Phillips Collection, Washington, D.C.; the Newberry Library, Chicago; the Whitney Museum of American Art, New York; the Metropolitan Museum of Art, New York; and the New York Public Library. Bibliographic resources include Sherrye Cohn, *Arthur Dove: Nature as Symbol* (1985); Anne Cohen Depietro, *Arthur Dove and Helen Torr: The Huntington Years* (1989); Barbara Haskell, *Arthur Dove* (1974); Dorothy Rylander Johnson, *Arthur Dove: The Years of Collage* (1967); Ann Lee Morgan, *Arthur Dove: Life and Work, with a Catalogue Raisonné* (1984); Ann Lee Morgan, ed., *Dear Stieglitz, Dear Dove* (1988); Sasha Newman, *Arthur Dove and Duncan Phillips: Artist and Patron* (1981); Alan Solomon, *Arthur G. Dove* (1954); and Frederick S. Wight, *Arthur G. Dove* (1958).

CATHERINE MCNICKLE CHASTAIN

DOW, Alden Ball (10 Apr. 1904–20 Aug. 1983), architect, was born in Midland, Michigan, the son of Herbert Henry Dow, an industrial chemist and founder of the Dow Chemical Company, and Grace Ball. As the son of a very successful scientist-businessman, Dow enjoyed all the advantages of position in a small town whose chemical industry competed on an international scale. After dutifully trying to follow in his older brother's footsteps by attending the University of Michigan's chemical engineering department for two years, Dow convinced his father to send him to the school of architecture at Columbia University. He received his bachelor of architecture degree in 1931, the same year he married Vada Bennett; they had three children.

Dow designed for Midland a wide range of building types that interpreted a set of ideals associated with Frank Lloyd Wright, whose Imperial Hotel he had first seen on a trip to Tokyo in 1923. In the summer of 1933 Dow joined the new apprenticeship program Wright had set up at his Wisconsin country home, "Taliesin." The five months he spent with Wright completed Dow's architectural education and molded his style, which combines Wright's natural geometries and materials with the more refined style often called art deco, after the 1925 decorative arts exhibition in Paris. Dow's association with Wright placed him in a critical position in mid-twentieth-century American architecture, and he is one of a small number of former apprentices of Wright whose work extends Wright's example in a creditable way.

Before his direct contact with Wright, Dow was chiefly influenced by the modernism of the decorative arts exhibition in Paris, particularly evident in his first architectural commission, the Midland Country Club, completed before his graduation from Columbia. After working at Taliesin, Wright's plan forms, materials, and ground-hugging horizontals became more prominent in Dow's work. Upon his return to Midland in 1933 and throughout the 1930s, the ready clientele of managers at his father's chemical company commissioned Dow to build a number of houses. The effects of the depression did not stop construction in Midland, owing to the continued success of the Dow Chemical Company. With the contribution of constructional and ornamental details provided by his assistant Robert Goodall, who had also been at Taliesin, Dow designed outstanding, modern, yet relatively modest houses that were built on the quiet streets of Midland and that were featured in numerous architectural journals of the time.

The square grid of specially designed concrete blocks comprises the distinguishing visual element in Dow's early houses. Although he was intrigued by Wright's experiments with concrete blocks ten years earlier in California, Dow simplified both their surfaces and construction. Patented as "unit blocks" by Dow in 1936, their geometric discipline linked spatial volumes banded by windows and stucco. One of the most spatially intricate of these houses, the John S. Whitman house, won the grand prize for residential architecture at the Paris Exposition of Arts and Technology in 1937.

The most stunning use of unit blocks is in Dow's own studio in Midland, which he built in 1934, soon after returning from Taliesin. The building, a magical interweaving of nature and architecture along a stream at the edge of his father's landscape garden, shows Dow successfully translating various influences into a unique individual expression. The unification of architecture and nature is completely in the compositional control of the architect, with nature not so much found as arranged. Dow dammed the stream to create a reflecting pool, and he strategically planted willows, pines, and birches. The geometry of the blocks moves freely from building to terraces and stairs to stepping stones in the pond. The gently sloped green copper roofs, whose pattern of standing seams lines up with the grid of the concrete blocks, contrasts with the varied pattern of leaves, branches, and ripples. The studio and house, added later, were put on the National Register of Historic Places in 1989.

Dow spent the years during World War II on the gulf coast of Texas, where Dow Chemical was expanding its works; there he designed the buildings for the town of Lake Jackson and houses for the town of Freeport. In 1941 Dow completed his residence attached to the studio in Midland and began spending his summer months there. By the end of the war he was spending most of his time in Midland, where he eventually died. In the late forties and fifties, his business expanded in size and range. In addition to houses, the churches, libraries, fire stations, and facilities for the chemical company that Dow designed gave Midland a vernacular of its own. Of his many designs, the First Methodist Church (1950) was given an award of merit by the American Institute of Architects in 1956. The scope of Dow's institutional designs, which include the Phoenix Civic Center, various college and university facilities, and civic institutions, precluded the type of personal statements that Dow had made in earlier house designs. The enlarged scale and complexity of such institutional designs demanded an abstract, problem-solving method, as opposed to his more effective, if limited, approach to design using an image of formal and textural contrasts that produced his earlier unit block houses. This "picturesque" way of composing architecture came naturally to Dow, who used it most successfully for his own outstanding home and studio.

Dow's financial resources and his association with Wright make it easy to attribute his success to these factors and to underestimate his genuine contribution to mid-twentieth-century American architecture. National recognition, which he did not actively pursue from his peaceful world in Midland, diminished after World War II, as his practice moved beyond the residential scale of the thirties. Dow was fortunate enough to enjoy the financial freedom to develop his talent more or less unconstrained by external forces. Compared to Wright's architecture, Dow's is successful in the more restricted scale of residences where his delight in visual contrasts softens any intellectual toughness. The composure and delicacy of his life and work are remarkable for their internal consistency. Dow produced outstanding architecture and a gentle philosophy, which he initially called "composed order" and later expanded to "way of life." Ideally, according to Dow's philosophy, man, thought, and place are fused into one beautifully composed creation.

• Dow's papers and drawings are located at his office, 315 Post Street, and at Northwood University, both in Midland, Michigan. Publications by Dow are "An Architect's View of Creativity," *Journal of the American Institute of Architects*, Feb. 1959, pp. 19–26; "The Continuity of Idea and Form," in *Four Great Makers of Modern Architecture* (1963; rpt. 1970; the verbatim record of a symposium held at Columbia Univ., 1961); and *Reflections* (1983). The standard monograph on Dow's architectural career is Sidney K. Robinson, *The Architecture of Alden B. Dow* (1983). An obituary is in the *Midland Daily News*, 22 Aug. 1983.

SIDNEY K. ROBINSON

DOW, Blanche Hinman (9 Feb. 1893–24 May 1973), educator and college president, was born in Louisiana, Missouri, the daughter of Ernest Wentworth Dow, an educator and minister, and Carrie Ann Reneau, a teacher. At the time of Dow's birth, her father was president of McCune College, a small denominational school, and he alternated between college presidencies and pastorates in New York, Massachusetts, and Missouri throughout her childhood. Dow received an A.B. in French from Smith College in 1913; she received both an A.M. (1925) and a Ph.D. (1936) from Columbia University. Her dissertation, *The Varying Attitude toward Women in French Literature of the 15th Century: The Opening Years*, was published in 1936.

After attending Samuel S. Curry's School of Expression in Boston during the summer of 1913, Dow taught speech and dramatics at the Milwaukee-Downer College in Wisconsin during the 1913–1914 academic year. In 1914 she rejoined her family in Gallatin, Missouri, where her father had reopened and assumed the presidency of Grand River College. She taught in the college's Department of Expression until late 1917 when she became a clerk for the third assistant postmaster general in Washington, D.C. A member of various acting companies in the nation's capital, she briefly considered pursuing a career as an actress.

In 1919 Dow accepted a position as instructor in French language and literature and as dramatics coach at Northwest Missouri State Teachers College (now Northwest Missouri State University) in Maryville. She advanced steadily at the state institution, becoming a full professor and chair of the foreign languages department in 1935. In 1941 she was named chairman of the humanities division.

Much admired by her students, Dow gained a reputation as "a superb teacher, with a warmth and humanness of approach" (*Northwest Missourian*, 4 May 1949). In addition to teaching, she assumed a public relations role on behalf of the college, speaking at high schools throughout the region. Her personality and gifted public speaking abilities also made her a favorite

with area organizations, where she gave dramatic readings and talked about her travels.

In 1921 Dow was present at the formative meeting of the Missouri Division of the American Association of University Women (AAUW). She assumed an active role in the organization and in 1930 became president of the Maryville chapter. Throughout the 1930s and 1940s she served on numerous state and national committees, and in 1937 she began a two-year term as president of the Missouri Division. She helped establish a chapter of the American Association of University Professors at the Maryville school, serving as its first secretary in 1934. Her active participation earned her a membership on the national council from 1937 to 1940 and the presidency of the Missouri chapter in 1940–1941.

While at Northwest Missouri State, Dow became increasingly interested in international affairs and the role of women in promoting world peace. In 1928 she traveled to Europe for the first time and studied at the Sorbonne in Paris that summer. While studying at the Sorbonne again in 1931–1932 she attended the disarmament conference held in Geneva. Back in Missouri she wove her impressions of the conference and her views on the need for an international perspective into her public appearances. At the same time she began recruiting foreign students for the college. In 1933 she became chair of the state AAUW Committee on International Relations and two years later a member of the national-level committee.

By the mid-1940s Dow had become dissatisfied with her duties at Northwest Missouri State, and for unexplained reasons she decided she could not work with J. W. Jones, the newly appointed president. Consequently, she began to look elsewhere for a position. In 1949 she requested a six-month leave to tour Europe. Just before her departure from the United States, Cottey College, a small junior college for women in Nevada, Missouri, selected Dow as its sixth president. Founded in 1884, the college had been owned and operated by the PEO Sisterhood, a women's organization, since 1927. Dow assumed the presidency following her return from Europe in late summer and was inaugurated on 28 November 1949.

At Cottey, Dow turned her considerable public speaking skills and indefatigable personality toward enhancing the quality of education at the school. The *Kansas City Times* (12 Mar. 1965) paraphrased her views on the three-part goal of education: "self-discovery of one's real abilities, development during college and . . . a commitment to use those abilities for the good of society." She proved to be an excellent fundraiser and public spokesperson, popular with both local civic organizations and PEO groups around the nation. Reflective of her continuing interest in internationalism, she promoted the recruitment of foreign students; she also persuaded the governing board to admit African-American women.

Concurrent with her presidential duties, Dow maintained her active role in the AAUW. From 1949 to 1953 she served as vice president of the Southwest

Central Region, from 1953 to 1957 as first vice president of the national organization, and from 1963 to 1967 as national president. She also served as the assistant treasurer and later treasurer of the International Federation of University Women.

Dow retired as president of Cottey College in 1965, receiving the rank of president emerita. During her retirement she finished her national AAUW presidency and continued her contributions to other organizations and conferences related to women and internationalism. Never married, Dow helped support her mother and younger siblings. Throughout most of her Maryville years, she lived with a close friend, college art professor Olive DeLuce. Dow died in North Kansas City, Missouri.

As a college administrator, Dow enlarged the scope of a small women's junior college and promoted its ties to the larger world. Her activities in the AAUW focused on increasing "representation and status of women on college and university faculties," "fellowships for women students," and "continuing education of mature women, college-educated or not" (Harvey, p. 97). Dow's major significance was in her influence on the lives of her students. She was a compelling teacher for both sexes and a role model for young women at a time when few women held administrative positions in higher education.

• Small collections of Dow's papers are in the Northwest Missouri State University Archives, Maryville, and in the Cottey College Archives, Nevada, Mo. Included in the latter collection is a lengthy unpublished biography of Dow written by her nephew David Dow Harvey, "'A World of Love': The Life and Letters of Blanche Hinman Dow, 1893–1973" (n.d.). Information on her tenure as president of Cottey College is in Orpha Stockard, *The First 75 Years: Cottey College* (1961), and a biographical sketch appears in Mary K. Dains, ed., *Show Me Missouri Women: Selected Biographies* (1989). Obituaries are in the *Washington Post*, 25 May 1973, and in the *Kansas City Star* and the *Nevada (Mo.) Daily Mail*, both on 24 May 1973.

LYNN WOLF GENTZLER

DOW, Daniel (19 Feb. 1772–19 July 1849), Congregational clergyman, was born in Ashford, Connecticut, the son of Daniel Dow and Elizabeth Marsh, farmers. Dow's father died when Daniel was three months old, but financial support and encouragement from his mother enabled him to enter Yale College as a sophomore in 1790. There he fell under the influence of Yale's president, the moderate Calvinist Ezra Stiles, who nurtured Dow's piety. "Instead of merely speculating about the truth of the gospel," he recalled, "I became reconciled to it." He made a public profession of faith before graduating with high honors in 1793. Having spent his inheritance on his schooling, he then taught psalmody for two years while he studied theology under Elizur Goodrich (1734–1797) of Durham, Connecticut, and Enoch Pond of Ashford, Connecticut.

Pond taught him the doctrines of the New Divinity, a theological movement rooted in the sophisticated Calvinism of Jonathan Edwards (1703–1758) and refined by Edwards's students Joseph Bellamy and Samuel Hopkins (1721–1803). The New Divinity theologians emphasized the sovereignty of God, the "natural" liberty but "moral" bondage of the sinner's will, the incapacity of unregenerate sinners to improve their state merely by frequenting such means of grace as sermons and prayers, and the legal obligation of the regenerate to love God and neighbor with a selfless, disinterested benevolence. Dow accepted most of the New Divinity doctrines, though on a few points—such as the teaching that an original sin inherited from Adam preceded sinful choices—he stood with the so-called Old Calvinists, like Stiles, who criticized the Edwardseans for appearing to equate sinfulness with sinful choices.

In 1795 he married Hannah Bolles of Woodstock, Connecticut. The couple would have nine children, only four of whom survived him. In May 1795 the Congregational Association of Windham County, Connecticut, licensed him to preach. For several weeks he traveled as a visiting preacher to parishes in Douglas, Massachusetts, and Eastford and East Woodstock, Connecticut, but in August the Congregational church in Thompson, Connecticut, called him as its pastor, and on 20 April 1796 he was ordained there. He remained the pastor in Thompson throughout his ministry.

Dow preached regularly in ten remote neighborhoods in the parish. To supplement his salary of $300, he purchased a small farm and also prepared young men for the ministry. He proved to be an adept farmer; the year after he died, his wife valued the farm at $3,000. Students remembered him fondly. One recalled that he rose at four or five o'clock every morning, read the Greek New Testament, and sang a hymn before beginning the day's activities. After a brief flirtation with Arminian views of the freedom of the will—he later attributed the lapse to "erroneous books"—Dow preached Calvinist doctrine to his congregation and defended it in theological debates with other clergy.

His first effort at theological polemics came in a defense of trinitarian doctrine in *Familiar Letters to the Rev. John Sherman* (1806), which he supplemented the next year with an argument for infant baptism in *The Pedobaptist Catechism* (1807). His *Dissertation on the Sinaitic and Abrahamic Covenants* (1811) repeated the conventional formula that God's covenant with Moses on Sinai remained binding only in its moral commandments; the ceremonial features of the entire Sinai dispensation, such as the sacrificial altar and the Jewish priesthood, were types that merely foreshadowed Christ the true sacrifice and priest, so they no longer bound Christians. God's covenant with Abraham, on the other hand, was the same covenant of grace that received its fullest manifestation in Christ, and because God had sealed the Abrahamic covenant with circumcision—a typological prefiguring of baptism—Christians were obligated to baptize their children.

In 1824 Dow became a fellow of Yale College, but he soon felt deeply troubled by the theological doctrines taught by Nathaniel William Taylor in the Yale Divinity School. When Taylor began to teach that God could not, in a moral system, prevent sin by free agents, that infants bore no taint of sinfulness until they sinned, and that the preacher could appeal to a morally neutral self-love in the unregenerate sinner, Dow joined the alliance of conservatives who in 1833 tried to counter Taylor's influence at Yale by forming the Theological Institute of Connecticut in East Windsor (later moved to Hartford and renamed Hartford Theological Seminary). He became one of the first trustees of the new institution.

In 1834 Dow published his *New Haven Theology, Alias Taylorism, Alias Neology*, in which he collected quotations from Taylorite theologians and tried to refute them. For the most part, his refutation consisted of a restatement of the position of the Edwardsean New Divinity in opposition to Taylor's New Haven Theology. Dow thought that Taylor's doctrine compromised the Calvinist vision of God's sovereign grace, and he could not accept Taylor's theory of self-love, defending instead the New Divinity position that all self-regard in religion revealed that true conversion had not yet occurred.

Dow shared in the reformist and evangelical temper of antebellum New England Calvinism, serving as a member of the American Board of Foreign Missions from 1840 until his death and taking an active part in the temperance movement. In his theology and in his allegiance to the new seminary in East Windsor, he represented the effort to preserve older Calvinist doctrines in the face of challenges from both Unitarian critics and the innovators at New Haven.

Dow died in Thompson after a ministry of fifty-four years to the same congregation. His death occurred on the same day that he preached a funeral sermon titled "Be Ye Also Ready."

• For an autobiographical reminiscence, see Daniel Dow, *Reminiscences of Past Events: A Semi-Centennial Sermon Preached in Thompson, Conn., April 22, 1846* (1846). A former student, William A. Larned, wrote a memorial for the *Annals of the American Pulpit*, ed. William B. Sprague vol. 2 (1857).

E. BROOKS HOLIFIELD

DOW, George Francis (7 Jan. 1868–5 June 1936), antiquarian, editor, and museum curator, was born in Wakefield, New Hampshire, the son of George Prince and Ada Bingham Tappan. He grew up in Topsfield, Massachusetts, and lived there most of his life. After attending a commercial school in Boston, Dow entered the wholesale metal business, in which he was engaged from 1885 to 1898. During this time he became increasingly interested in local history and material culture. In 1893 Dow began to publish a local newspaper, the *Topsfield Townsman*. He organized the Topsfield Historical Society in 1894 and edited *The Historical Collections of the Topsfield Historical Society*. In 1898 Dow was offered the post of secretary of the Essex Institute in Salem, Massachusetts, a large and distinguished local historical organization. In this position, which he held for twenty years, Dow published the *Historical Collections* of the Essex Institute while managing the organization's museum and library.

Displaying energy and imagination as the Essex Institute secretary, Dow succeeded in raising both the attendance and the public profile of the Essex Institute by persuading the institute to open its museum on Sundays and holidays, as well as encouraging public schools' interest in the museum. Dow believed that in a period of rapid change and social dislocation, Americans could find both instruction and inspiration in an idealized reconstruction of colonial New England, and it was to this end that he devoted the rest of his life. When a new building was added to the Essex Institute in 1907, Dow rearranged the institute's exhibit hall. The exhibits now included clothes, utensils, and some fragments of old Salem buildings that had been demolished. Next he created "period rooms" by using old woodwork and furnishings to construct rooms that had the appearance of an earlier time. Finally, he acquired the John Ward house (c. 1684) in Salem and had it moved behind the Essex Institute to create one of the nation's first outdoor museums. When the house was opened to the public in 1912, it featured not only rooms with period furniture but also women who lived in the house and dressed in homespun fabrics to greet visitors.

Dow's Salem exhibits gained national attention. In 1910 officials from the Metropolitan Museum of Art visited the Essex Institute to view the period rooms. When the museum opened its "American Wing" in 1924, it featured period rooms based on those that Dow had constructed in Salem. Dow was consulted as the American Wing took shape and hailed it as the answer to the destruction of period architecture throughout the country. He built a national reputation restoring colonial houses beginning in 1913 with the Parson Capen House in Topsfield, then elsewhere in New England.

Dow's formal association with the Essex Institute ended in 1918. The following year he went to work in Boston for the Society for the Preservation of New England Antiquities (SPNEA) as curator of its museum and the editor of the SPNEA *Bulletin*, which Dow renamed *Old-Time New England*. He revamped the contents of the magazine as well, enlarging its scope to consider every aspect of New England history that could be demonstrated by documents or artifacts. Up until the time of his death he divided his time between the SPNEA and writing a series of illustrated books on New England history—collections of documents on a wide variety of subjects—at his home in Topsfield.

In partnership with a Topsfield neighbor, William A. Perkins, Dow formed the Marine Research Society of Salem. In 1922 Dow and John Robinson published the society's first book, *The Sailing Ships of New England, 1607–1907*. This was followed by *Whale Ships and Whaling* (1925) and *Slave Ships and Slaving* (1927). Dow understood the commercial implications of his subjects; he connected the contemporary interest in sailing ships with the increase in market value for pictorial representations and models. He underlined the cruelty of slavery but added to his book an eccentric introduction by a retired British naval officer who compared conditions on slave ships favorably with those for impressed seamen.

William Perkins also operated the Wayside Press in Topsfield, and he published several books by Dow, including *The Arts & Crafts in New England, 1704–1775* (1927), a collection of newspaper advertisements by painters and craftsmen; and *Domestic Life in New England in the Seventeenth Century* (1925), a lecture given in connection with the opening of the American Wing at the Metropolitan Museum of Art. Dow urged the SPNEA to publish books, and in 1935 the society produced his own *Every Day Life in the Massachusetts Bay Colony*, again a collection of source materials.

Admitting the imperfections of his New England predecessors, Dow nonetheless presented a romantic image of New England colonial life, perhaps most memorably when he was commissioned by the town of Salem to commemorate its tercentennial in 1930 by constructing an entire village. The opening of Pioneer Village was marked by a pageant of costumed townspeople, and the village became a permanent attraction intended to introduce schoolchildren and newcomers to a fictional past. Dow's "restorations" were historical fantasies, the rooms in his houses displaying a modern functionalism that had no counterpart in colonial times. For a nation increasingly attuned to consumerism, Dow presented history as a marketable commodity.

Dow had married Alice Goldsmith Waters in 1920. Apart from his publishing and preservationist activities, Dow had served as a Massachusetts state legislator in 1900 and as chairman of both the Topsfield Town Library and the Topsfield Park Commission. He died in Topsfield.

• There is a collection of Dow's correspondence at the Massachusetts Historical Society. Additional correspondence can be found in the records of the SPNEA. Other primary sources are the annual reports of the Essex Institute, 1898–1918, and issues of *Old-Time New England*, 1919–1936. See also his article on "Museums and the Preservation of Early Houses," *Bulletin of the Metropolitan Museum of Art* 17, pt. 2 (Nov. 1922): 16–20. For an extended discussion of Dow's life and career, see Charles B. Hosmer, Jr., "George Francis Dow," in *Keepers of the Past*, ed. Clifford L. Lord (1965), pp. 157–66; and James M. Lindgren, *Preserving Historic New England: Preservation, Progressivism, and the Remaking of Memory* (1995). Obituaries are in the *New York Times*, 6 June 1936; the *Boston Evening Transcript*, 6 June 1936; and *Old-Time New England* 27 (July 1936): 37.

MOREY ROTHBERG

DOW, Herbert Henry (26 Feb. 1866–15 Oct. 1930), chemist and industrialist, was born in Belleville, Ontario, the son of Joseph Dow, a master mechanic, and Sarah Bunnell. Dow's early life was spent in Connecticut, but in 1878 his family moved to Cleveland, Ohio,

where he graduated in 1888 from the Case School of Applied Science. While at Case he became fascinated with the possibility of extracting bromine, a substance used to produce drugs and photographic chemicals, from the salt-impregnated waters (brines) often associated with oil and gas wells. By 1889 he had developed a novel electrolytic process for doing this. After an initial attempt at commercialization failed, Dow secured new backing and in 1890 formed the Midland Chemical Company. He moved operations to Midland, Michigan, near rich, easy to tap brines, and by 1894 he had developed one of the earliest commercially successful electrochemical processes in the United States. In 1892 Dow married Grace Ball, a Midland schoolteacher; they had seven children. The oldest child, Willard Dow, eventually succeeded his father as head of the Dow Chemical Company.

In 1894, because the backers of Midland Chemical opposed his plans for diversification into chlorine and bleaching powder production, Dow resigned as general manager. With new investors he formed the Dow Process Company and eventually built an experimental plant to extract chlorine from Midland Chemical's waste brine. The Dow Chemical Company, incorporated in May 1897, absorbed the experimental plant and soon initiated commercial production of chlorine bleach. By 1900 Dow Chemical had absorbed Midland Chemical, and by 1910, after surviving extended price wars with foreign competitors, had become an established chemical producer. Continuing to promote diversification along lines related to established company products, in 1900 Dow began to produce sulfur chloride from surplus chlorine. A few years later, he began to manufacture chloroform from surplus sulfur chloride. By 1914 Dow Chemical's electrolytic cells had been improved to extract not only bromine and chlorine from brines, but also magnesium and calcium compounds.

The outbreak of World War I eliminated German imports and created a growing market for chemicals. Dow responded by renewing research on synthetic indigo, previously one of the most widely imported German dyes, and marketed the first American synthetic indigo in 1916. Simultaneously, Dow Chemical entered other chemical markets previously dominated by Germany, including phenol, magnesium, and aspirin. During the postwar adjustment, Dow poured resources into research and, between 1916 and 1927, quadrupled the number of chemists and engineers on staff. Stressing creativity, Dow asserted that if his company could not make a chemical cheaper and better than anyone else, he would not make it at all. With this philosophy, Dow Chemical flourished in the 1920s, improving its processes and steadily increasing product offerings. The exploding demand for leaded gasoline for automobiles in the late 1920s, however, put pressure on Dow's traditional resource base—the natural brines from which it extracted bromine for conversion to ethylene dibromide, a key ingredient of leaded gas. To meet this crisis Dow promoted research in several directions. One was the use of seawater as a source of bromine.

Although Herbert Dow initiated planning for an Atlantic Coast bromine extraction plant, he did not live to see the plant completed. Shortly after receiving the prestigious Perkin Medal of the Society for Chemical Industry in 1930, he died in Rochester, Minnesota. The company that he had created to manufacture one chemical in 1897 was, by then, manufacturing 150 chemicals and had contributed significantly to the emergence of an independent American chemical industry.

• Dow's surviving papers are in the Post Street Archives, Midland, Mich. The collection is described in E. N. Brandt and Barbara Schettig Brennan, *The Papers of Herbert H. Dow: A Guide for the Scholarly* (1990). The only book-length account of Dow's life is Murray Campbell and Harrison Hatton, *Herbert H. Dow: Pioneer in Creative Chemistry* (1951), but additional information can be found in Don Whitehead, *The Dow Story: The History of the Dow Chemical Company* (1968), and Robert S. Karpiuk, *Dow Research Pioneers: Recollections 1888–1949* (1984). Finally, Thomas Griswold, Jr., one of Dow's close associates, provides some revealing snippets on Dow's character in his autobiographical *The Time of My Life* (1973).

TERRY S. REYNOLDS

DOW, Lorenzo (16 Oct. 1777–2 Feb. 1834), itinerant Methodist evangelist, was born in Coventry, Connecticut, the son of Humphrey Dean Dow and Tabitha Parker, poor farmers. Dow was raised by his parents according to the Calvinism of the established Congregationalist church in New England with its emphases on predestination and original sin. Dow emphatically rejected this Calvinism as a teenager when he heard itinerant Methodist evangelists who came through town to speak. Dow became convinced that one becomes a Christian through one's own volition and by a conversion that results in a dramatic experience of salvation. Following a traumatic several years in which he received visions and dreams, experienced a severe bout with asthma, and contemplated committing suicide, Dow had his own conversion at the age of seventeen.

Following this conversion, Dow experienced another five months in sickbed during which he received more dreams and visions summoning him to preach the gospel. In November 1794 Dow had his first public speaking engagement and, to the relief of his parents, it was not a success. Eventually in the spring of 1796 Dow left home to become an itinerant evangelist.

In September 1796 Dow passed the exam necessary to become a licensed preacher in the Methodist church, but he was persuaded to forego the license. Shortly after, he was granted a license as reports of his conversions came in. This marked the first of many conflicts in which Dow's religious and political populism and egalitarianism regularly put him at odds with ecclesiastical authority. Although he was never ordained to the Methodist church, he always encouraged his converts to become Methodists.

In 1798, against the will of his Methodist superiors, Dow traveled to Ireland to preach and precipitated a crisis over the differences between American camp meeting revivalism and British Methodism. While in Ireland he contracted smallpox and was tended by Dr. Paul Johnson and his wife, Letitia, whom Dow called the only happily married couple he ever knew.

In 1801 Dow returned to the United States. He preached first in New York, and then in January 1802 he sailed to Georgia, where he conducted more camp meetings. In November 1802 Dow returned to the South where he preached in Alabama, North and South Carolina, Tennessee, and Virginia. While preaching in the Mohawk Valley of New York in 1802, Dow met Peggy Holcomb. They became engaged and in September 1804 were married; they had one daughter, who apparently died in infancy.

In 1804 Dow again traveled along the eastern seaboard preaching at between 500 and 800 camp meetings. In 1805 he traveled some 10,000 miles, including his second journey to Great Britain. In June 1807 he returned to the United States and began a preaching tour from New England to Florida, and from Mississippi back to New England. In 1808 Dow went through the West, in 1809 he traveled through Louisiana, and in 1810 he went through Georgia, North Carolina, and then back up to New England.

Dow's travels became less extensive after this, but he took one more trip to England in 1818. He returned in 1820 on hearing that Peggy, who had always been sickly, was ill with tuberculosis. Shortly after his return, she died on in January 1820. Three months later, however, Dow married Lucy Dolbeare, the daughter of a well-to-do farmer in Montville, Connecticut, in April 1820. Dow, who had become quite wealthy from the sales of his books and pamphlets, devoted most of his time and energy to land speculation and to "Lorenzo Dow's Family Medicine," which he patented in 1820. He died suddenly and unexpectedly in Georgetown, Maryland.

Dow's enormous reputation as "Crazy Dow" and his self-description as a "cosmopolite" during his life resulted from his appearance as well as from his preaching manner. A contemporary described him as a "forbidding" person with a forcible voice "adapted to the feminine key" who had a habit of "protracting some tones in his voice to a painful length, which was truly disgusting to a delicate ear: still it passed for perfection in him, because it was an attribute in his peculiar character" (Sellers, p. 95). Dow was tall, thin, and fragile looking. He had long, straggly hair that fell over his stooped shoulders, a long beard, and piercing blue eyes. His dark clothes were remarkably unkempt and dirty, which led to constant criticism from the more refined and stable clergy of the day.

In addition to his eccentric appearance, Dow was not above using tricks in his camp meetings to get conversions. On one occasion he had a young African-American boy named Gabriel hide in a tree and blow his trumpet during a sermon on the second coming as Dow uttered the words, "suppose that at this moment you should hear the sound of Gabriel's trumpet!" On other occasions he would discuss the future torments of hell for sinners, only to fake an epileptic fit and "die"—in order to induce people to repent from their sins and escape sudden damnation.

The most important reason for Dow's reputation, however, was the dramatic manner in which he combined Jeffersonian democracy and a message of spiritual conversion to fight against political and religious elitism and Calvinism. "If all men are 'BORN EQUAL,'" declared Dow, "and endowed with unalienable RIGHTS by their CREATOR, in the blessings of life, liberty, and the pursuit of happiness— then there can be no just reason, as a cause, why he may or should not think, and judge, and act for himself in matters of religion, opinion, and private judgment." By preaching against political and religious tyranny, Dow helped make American Christianity a religion of individual choice and conscience.

• Dow's own writings, consisting of over 700 pages, are contained in *All the Polemical Works of Lorenzo Dow* (1814); and *History of the Cosmopolite: or, the Four Volumes of Lorenzo's Journal* (1814), which recounts his itinerant travels. A biography of Dow is Charles Coleman Sellers, *Lorenzo Dow: The Bearer of the Word* (1928). Richard Carwardine, *Transatlantic Revivalism: Popular Evangelicalism in Britain and America, 1790–1865* (1978), and Nathan Hatch, *The Democratization of American Christianity* (1989), both have useful information on Dow.

WESLEY SMITH

DOW, Neal (20 Mar. 1804–2 Oct. 1897), politician and social reformer, was born in Portland, Maine, the son of Josiah Dow and Dorcas Allen, operators of a tanning business. He received a basic education at the Portland Academy and later at the Friends' Academy in New Bedford, Massachusetts. He also received an education in social involvement from his parents, who were ardent Quakers, committed to various types of social reform. As a child Neal witnessed escaped slaves moving through his home, which was a station on the Underground Railroad. His father traveled widely in New England in the interests of antislavery, with the support of the Society of Friends. Dow wanted to attend college and become a lawyer, but his parents objected, so he went into partnership with his father in the family business. In 1830 he married Maria Cornelia Durant Maynard; they had nine children, five of whom survived to adulthood.

Success in the tanning business placed Dow in the circle of important businesspeople in Portland, and he soon was recognized for his leadership capabilities. He was a bank director, the president of the Portland Gaslight Company, and the chief of the Portland Deluge Engine Company. By the late 1840s Dow reaped the benefits of wise investments and became one of Portland's most influential citizens.

Dow's family had a long history of involvement in American political life. His father had been an active Federalist and then joined the National Republican party in the elections of 1824 and 1828. When the Ad-

ams faction was transformed into the new Whig party, Dow and his father followed the affiliation, although they had difficulty with the nomination in 1836 of Henry Clay, who supported dueling, which the Dows abhorred, and who was perceived to be proslavery. In 1840 Dow campaigned for William Henry Harrison, and he became a charter member of the Republican party in 1856.

Dow's politics became focused on social reform as early as 1828, when he made a speech to his fire engine company denouncing the liquor traffic. He joined various organizations that supported prohibition, including the Maine Temperance Union. As one of the founding members of the union, he worked tirelessly to educate the public about the values of total abstinence from alcohol. His reforming conscience and his experiences supervising intoxicated workers at his firm led him into the Washingtonian movement in the early 1840s. Dow's social reform efforts did not follow the familiar antebellum path of religious enthusiasm. Early in life he jettisoned formal ties to the Friends and offered only indirect support to Unitarian and Congregational churches in his neighborhoods, while being critical of clergy and denominations that would not take a strong stand against the liquor traffic. However, his Quaker upbringing and family tradition informed his abolitionist stand from an early age.

Elected as mayor of the city of Portland in 1851, Dow was selected by the Portland City Council to chair a committee to petition the legislature for a bill to drive the illegal liquor trade from the city. His persuasive powers convinced many legislators, and the bill that he wrote passed with substantial majorities and was signed into law on 2 June 1851 by Governor John Hubbard. With the now-famous "Maine Law" in hand, Dow returned to Portland and strictly enforced its provisions. His campaign to clean up Portland proved so successful that he was reelected as mayor in 1855, serving until 1857. In June 1855, however, a riot broke out, prompted by opponents of the prohibition legislation. The reaction spread across the state, and the legislature repealed Dow's Maine Law. Following another wave of positive public opinion, however, the law was again restored in 1858.

Dow's reputation as the father of the Maine Law grew far beyond the state, and he became active in the international prohibition movement. In 1853 he served as the president of the World's Temperance Convention, and in 1857 he toured England on behalf of the United Kingdom Alliance, for which he gave lectures.

With the same fervor he showed in forwarding the temperance movement, Dow supported antislavery. When the Civil War broke out in 1861, Dow, who was fifty-seven, enlisted in the Maine State Volunteers and served as a colonel of the Thirteenth Regiment. In February 1862 he joined General Benjamin Butler's command and was commissioned as a brigadier general of volunteers in the Gulf Department. During the battle of Port Hudson, Louisiana, he was wounded; while recuperating behind Union lines, he was captured and incarcerated at the Libby Prison in Richmond, Virginia, and subsequently in Mobile, Alabama. On 14 March 1864 he was exchanged for Confederate general Fitzhugh Lee and released from military service. His eight-month and 24-day imprisonment was costly to his health, and he returned to Portland to recuperate.

At work again in 1865 in support of national prohibition, Dow began another lecture tour, which took him to Great Britain in 1866–1867 and 1873–1875. His reputation in the United States had grown considerably, and in 1880 he ran for president on the Prohibition party ticket, with H. Thompson of Ohio as the vice presidential candidate. Even though he did not campaign, Dow received 10,305 votes, losing to James A. Garfield. His critics pointed out that he had not been committed fully to the principles of the Prohibition party and remained a Republican in disguise. Back in Maine, at seventy-six years old, he campaigned for an amendment to the state constitution, which was his last successful crusade. In the Portland mayoralty campaign in 1888, he ran unsuccessfully against "rum democracy" to embarrass the Republicans, who he felt lacked the courage of their convictions by refusing to support prohibition.

Small in stature, feisty, and fanatical in his reforming temperament, Dow attracted a large following and as many detractors. Hailed as the "Apostle of Temperance" and the "Prophet of Prohibition," Dow died at his Congress Street mansion in Portland. He had a lifelong interest in book collecting and left one of the largest private libraries in Maine's cultural history.

• Archival resources relating to Dow and the Maine Law may be found in the Maine State Library and Archives in Augusta. The chief published source on Dow's career is his autobiography, *Reminiscences of Neal Dow: Recollections of Eighty Years* (1898). The best biography is Frank L. Byrne, *Prophet of Prohibition: Neal Dow and His Crusade* (1961). His role in the prohibition crusade is the subject of Henry S. Clubb, *The Maine Liquor Law: Its Origin, History, and Results* (1856). The early development of the temperance movement is analyzed in Ian R. Tyrell, *Sobering Up: From Temperance to Prohibition in Antebellum America, 1800–1860* (1979). Dow's role in the Prohibition party and the election of 1880 is covered in K. Austin Kerr, *Organized for Prohibition: A New History of the Anti-Saloon League* (1985). A personal appreciation is expressed in Frederick Neal Dow, *Presentation of a Portrait and Commemorative Tablet of General Neal Dow to the Young Men's Christian Association, Portland Maine* (1927).

WILLIAM H. BRACKNEY

DOWIE, John Alexander (25 May 1847–9 Mar. 1907), religious sectarian, was born in Edinburgh, Scotland, the son of John Murray Dowie, a tailor and lay preacher, and Ann Macfarlane-McHardie. Early years in the family were marked by poverty, piety, and illness. A move to Australia in 1860 alleviated conditions somewhat, and young Dowie became successful in the dry goods business. In 1868, however, he decided to enter the ministry and studied at the University of Edinburgh for two years. Upon returning to Australia he was ordained minister of the Congregational church in

Alma in May 1870. In 1876 he married Jane Dowie, a cousin whose family was initially quite opposed to the union; they had two children. Over the next few years Dowie held pastorates in Sydney and one of its suburbs, Newtown. However, in 1878 he decided that it was wrong for ministers to be salaried, and so he turned to independent evangelistic work. This proved to be so successful that he was soon able to build a large nondenominational tabernacle in Melbourne.

From the age of six onward Dowie had been strongly opposed to alcohol and tobacco. Many of his sermons were moralistic warnings against those and other pitfalls to upright living. But by the early 1880s he began to offer people a chance to be healed through prayer, and his audiences swelled immensely in response to this new emphasis. He organized the International Divine Healing Association to institutionalize his sincere, and ego-enhancing, efforts to combine physical health with spiritual rectitude. In 1888 Dowie expanded his evangelical empire to the United States, developing over the course of two years a string of modest congregations in cities along the Pacific coast. His most important career move came in 1890 when he established a following in Chicago. Attendance increased so much because of his emphasis on divine healing that in 1893 it was possible to build the first Zion Tabernacle. The following year saw the appearance of Zion Publishing House, which issued a weekly paper, *Leaves of Healing*, and a monthly, *A Voice from Zion*. Most of the material printed there were Dowie's sermons and other writings. At first these publications purported simply to interpret and implement God's word as found in Scripture; in time they implied that Dowie's words were congruent with and equal to divine truth. In 1895 Chicago's clergy and physicians took Dowie to court no fewer than one hundred times on charges of misrepresenting the possibilities of healing. He won every case, enhancing his claim to spiritual authority.

In 1896 Dowie judged his support to be strong enough for another step. He organized the Christian Catholic Apostolic church as an improvement over all extant denominations. He named himself general overseer, and as church membership grew, publications flowed unabated, and popular interest in healing remained strong, the leader's image of himself swelled to megalomania. In 1899 the general overseer announced that he was Messenger of the Covenant, as the prophet Malachi had foretold. Two years later he informed followers that he was a prophet himself, Elijah the Restorer. This psychological metastasis culminated in 1904 when Dowie, standing before a stunned audience dressed in a flowing robe of satin and gold, consecrated himself as the First Apostle of Jesus Christ. "Clothed by God with Apostolic and Prophetic authority," he asserted, "I now have the right to speak as the instructor of all nations" (Lindsay, p. 235). Most of Dowie's followers continued their allegiance to him despite, or perhaps because of, his pretentions to exalted spiritual status. His downfall was the result of more mundane developments.

In 1899 Dowie had created Zion City, a township some forty miles north of Chicago, to be occupied exclusively by members of his flock. Thousands of people settled there and submitted to rules that banned smoking, drinking, theaters, dance halls, pharmacies, and medical doctors. Dowie owned all local industries and the bank, plus a fledgling college and an ambitious printing facility. The apostle did not manage funds well, and there were murmurs about the new opulence that he did not try to hide. Further, he spent hundreds of thousands of dollars in 1903 during a dismal revival effort in New York. Refusing to accept public rejection, he spent lavishly on a trip around the world. Few realized how much his quixotic schemes had depleted Zion's resources until in 1905 he suffered a paralytic stroke and while recovering in Jamaica was forced to relinquish control of the town's corporations. Those who took up the task, including Wilbur Glenn Voliva, Dowie's closest friend and adviser who also had his power of attorney, were astonished at how investments had become imperiled and funds misappropriated. Within six months they deposed the apostle in order to rescue themselves from financial ruin. The surprised, ousted leader challenged his expulsion in civil court, but the dismissal was found to be legal. Dowie was allowed to stay in Zion while leadership was in dispute, and he died there, an embattled and embittered man.

• Edna M. Sheldrake compiled and edited a useful collection, *The Personal Letters of John Alexander Dowie* (1912). Biographical information can be found in Rolvix Harlan, *John Alexander Dowie and the Christian Catholic Apostolic Church in Zion* (1906), Arthur Newcomb, *Dowie: Anointed of the Lord* (1930), and Gordon Lindsay, *John Alexander Dowie, Whose Trials—Tragedies—and Triumphs Are to Most Fascinating Object Lesson of Christian History* (1951; repr. with shorter title, 1986). An obituary is in the *Chicago Tribune*, 10 Mar. 1907.

HENRY WARNER BOWDEN

DOWLING, Eddie (9 Dec. 1894–18 Feb. 1976), actor, director, and producer, was born Joseph Nelson Goucher in Woonsocket, Rhode Island, the son of Charles Goucher and Bridget Mary Dowling. The fourteenth of seventeen children, Dowling attended parochial schools, but by age ten he had run away to Boston and started his performing career by singing Irish ballads in music shops and outside barrooms. At eleven, having taken his mother's maiden name, Dowling became a cabin boy on the Fall River Line.

Dowling first appeared on stage in Providence as an extra in a 1909 production of *Quo Vadis?*, followed by further stints as a cabin boy on the ocean liners *Mauretania* and *Lusitania*. While in London in 1911, he joined the boys' choir of St. Paul's Cathedral and then toured with a boys' choral group. On returning to Providence he made his professional stage debut as part of a vaudeville troupe but also took dramatic roles with a New England stock company. By 1919 Dowling had established himself as a leading musical-comedy performer, making his Broadway debut that year in *The Velvet Lady* and landing a spot in Ziegfeld's *Follies* of 1919 with Will Rogers, Fannie Brice, and Ray Doo-

ley, the vaudeville headliner he had married in 1914. Their marriage produced two children and lasted until Dowling's death.

For many years Dowling's fame as a song-and-dance man kept him from pursuing his interest in serious drama. His well received but melancholy 1918 sketch *The Stowaway* depicted an immigrant facing deportation, but with critics comparing him to George M. Cohan, Dowling enjoyed much greater success in sprightly musical comedies such as *Sally, Irene, and Mary* (1922), *The Fall Guy* (1925), and *Honeymoon Lane* (1926). Having first shared star billing in *Sidewalks of New York* in 1927, Dowling and his wife performed together in vaudeville revues during the early 1930s, including *Thumbs Up!* in 1934. A friend and supporter of President Franklin D. Roosevelt, Dowling became head of the vaudeville project of the WPA (Works Progress Administration) Federal Theatre in 1935, but soon after his wife retired from performing, Dowling himself decided to abandon the vaudeville stage.

With his landmark 1937 production of Shakespeare's *Richard II*, featuring Maurice Evans in the title role, Dowling began the most important phase of his career. Early in 1938 he produced, to great acclaim, *Shadow and Substance*, by the Irish playwright Paul Vincent Carroll; late that year Dowling produced Philip Barry's cosmic morality play *Here Come the Clowns*, also playing the lead role of Dan Clancy, the spiritually troubled stagehand—a personal and critical triumph for Dowling though not a box-office hit. The following year Dowling produced Carroll's *The White Steed*, toured with Thornton Wilder's *Our Town*, and won both the Pulitzer Prize and the Drama Critics' Award for his work with the Theatre Guild as director, coproducer, and leading actor in William Saroyan's *The Time of Your Life*. In 1940 he produced another Saroyan play, *Love's Old Sweet Song*.

In 1942 Dowling defied the escapist tendencies of the wartime theater by trying to set up a repertory theater to showcase literate playwriting. He produced Saroyan's one-act *Hello Out There* on a bill with G. K. Chesterton's *Magic*, but despite praise for Dowling's acting the show closed quickly, forcing Dowling to disband his repertory group. In 1944, having suffered large financial losses, Dowling served as assistant director in Herbert Kubly's *Men to the Sea*, whose theme of infidelity among soldiers' wives boldly flouted patriotic wartime sentimentality. During the war Dowling also organized and served as the first president of USO–Camp Shows.

Also in 1944, though deeply in debt, Dowling decided to support a much-rejected script by an unknown playwright named Tennessee Williams. As coproducer, codirector, narrator, and actor, Dowling was a driving force behind the huge success of *The Glass Menagerie*, which ran on Broadway for almost seventeen months during 1945 and 1946, followed by two national tours. Besides launching a new playwright, Dowling's production of *The Glass Menagerie* eased his financial difficulties and affirmed his place among the country's top directors. It also led to his involvement with another major American play of this period, Eugene O'Neill's *The Iceman Cometh*. Dowling, offered the lead role of the salesman Hickey, declined it to direct the play. Though O'Neill became increasingly dissatisfied with his directing, Dowling's work was generally praised by critics.

Dowling continued working in theater until the early 1960s, but his best work was done between 1937 and 1946. Several of his later productions closed during pre-Broadway tryouts, but a 1948 bill of one-acters, featuring *Hope Is the Thing with Feathers*, enjoyed modest success. Meanwhile, Dowling continued acting; in 1952 he succeeded James Barton—the man who played Hickey in *Iceman*—in the part of Ben Rumson in the musical *Paint Your Wagon*. In 1961 he founded the Eddie Dowling University Theatre Foundation to support college and university productions. Dowling died in Smithfield, Rhode Island.

Dowling's career traces a shift in American theater from the prevalence of vaudeville and musical comedy to an increasing demand for more probing, realistic dramas. Besides launching, reviving, or solidifying the careers of major playwrights such as Williams, O'Neill, and Saroyan, Dowling's work in *The Iceman Cometh*, *The Glass Menagerie*, and other important plays of the 1930s and 1940s helped bring the American stage to a new level of aesthetic maturity and international renown.

• Autobiographical data on Dowling may be found in *The Reminiscences of Eddie Dowling* (1977). His work as a director is covered in Gary Vena, *O'Neill's "The Iceman Cometh": Reconstructing the Premiere* (1988); John Mason Brown, *Dramatis Personae* (1963); and George Jean Nathan, *The Theatre Book of the Year, 1944–1945* (1972). See also William Lindsay Gresham, "Eddie Dowling: Hoofer, Actor, Producer," *Theatre Arts* 30 (1946): 632–39; and Lawrence Langner, *The Magic Curtain* (1951). An obituary is in the *New York Times*, 19 Feb. 1976.

KURT EISEN

DOWNER, Silas (16 July 1729–15 Dec. 1785), scrivener and lawyer, was born in Norwich, Connecticut, the son of Samuel Downer and Phebe Bishop, farmers. The family soon moved to Sunderland, Massachusetts. Downer entered Harvard in 1747 and was ranked twenty-eighth in a class of thirty. Since Harvard students were then ranked according to their family's social standing, Downer's low ranking indicates his relatively humble origins. As an undergraduate, he won Brattle and Hollis scholarships. After receiving an M.A. in 1750, he moved to Rhode Island, settled in Providence, and became a scrivener. He married Sarah Kelton in 1758; within a decade the couple had five children.

Although it is not clear how he obtained his training, Downer became one of Rhode Island's leading lawyers and helped produce the 1767 revised digest of the colony's laws. During the 1760s, he was quite active in local affairs. In 1760, he joined others in petitioning for the enactment of a law that would legalize

smallpox inoculations. Four years later Downer subscribed £2 8s. toward the founding of Rhode Island College. He served as librarian of the Providence Library from early 1762 until early 1767. In 1767, inspired by seeing Philadelphia's public market, Downer called for the creation of a municipal market house in Providence; he continued to champion the plan until it produced results. The market opened in 1773.

Downer, whose income was small and who never held elected office, was one of Rhode Island's most ardent revolutionaries. But Downer, who said of himself in 1766 that "I am a very Small Man in Stature besides my diminutive Size in other Respects," did not seek nor gain the public spotlight. As a member of what John Adams (1735–1826) called "the Political Clubb" of Providence, Downer worked surreptitiously with others to oppose Britain's efforts to regulate colonial trade more effectively and to tax the colonists. A driving force in the local Sons of Liberty, he served as the group's clerk and also authored or helped author position statements. In 1767 he secretly journeyed to New York to cement contacts with other Sons of Liberty.

Downer's claim to fame rests on the fact that he was the first revolutionary who openly and unequivocally said that the British Parliament did not have the right to legislate for the colonies. By 1768 some radical colonists were beginning to formulate arguments that might, if carried to their logical extreme, deny parliament that right. In newspaper essays published in early 1768, William Hicks, writing under the pen name "A Citizen," maintained that the colonists could both remain loyal to and dependent on the British monarch and reject the claim that the British Parliament had unlimited sovereign power to legislate for the colonies. Although he employed some bold rhetoric, Hicks also seemed to concede that parliament had some right to legislate for the colonies. Downer would make no such concession. On 25 July 1768 he spoke to a large crowd gathered for the dedication of Providence's Liberty Tree. He opened his address by proclaiming that the colonists "chearfully recognize our allegiance to our sovereign Lord, *George* the third, King of *Great-Britain*, . . . but utterly deny any other dependence on the inhabitants of that island, than what is mutual and reciprocal between all mankind." Stressing the historic existence of legislatures in the colonies and a people's "natural right" to have a hand in the creation of the laws that governed them, he later boldly asserted: "I cannot be perswaded that the parliament of *Great-Britain* have any lawful right to make *any laws whatsoever* to bind us." In addition to advancing this stunningly radical theory, Downer reiterated standard arguments about British abuse of Americans amounting to "an unwarrantable combination against the liberties of his [the King's] subjects in *America*." In doing so, he articulated the democratically inclined view that the people had "natural liberty" and that a civil magistrate "is only the people[']s trustee." A Providence printer quickly published Downer's oration under the title "A Discourse, Delivered in Providence, . . . July, 1768, at the Dedication of the Tree of Liberty, from the Summer House in the Tree" (1768). The pamphlet was not, however, sufficiently popular to get reprinted elsewhere in the colonies.

Downer's argument that the colonists were linked to Britain only through the allegiance they owed the King, and therefore the British Parliament had no legislative authority over the colonies, anticipated the dominion system that the British developed in the nineteenth century. His forward looking analysis was not publicly embraced by more noted revolutionaries until James Wilson and Thomas Jefferson advocated that argument in separate publications which appeared almost simultaneously in 1774. Both John Adams and the Continental Congress espoused that stance in 1775.

In the 1770s, Downer at times held minor public posts as a secretary or clerk of various Rhode Island political bodies. Although he also developed a reputation as a cryptographer, no record exists of how often—if ever—he performed this work during the Revolution. Sometime after 1781, possibly because of debts, Downer left Rhode Island. He was visiting a cousin, Dr. Eliphalet Downer, when he died at Roxbury, Massachusetts.

• Documents relating to Downer, not just prepared by Downer as a public scrivener, exist in collections of the Rhode Island Historical Society and in the John Carter Brown Library, both located in Providence. Important biographical sketches of Downer appear in Clifford K. Shipton, *Sibley's Harvard Graduates . . . in the Classes 1746–1750* (1962), and in David R. Downer, *The Downers of America* (1900). The definitive analysis of Downer's public life, which rests on an extensive search of manuscript materials, is Carl Bridenbaugh, *Silas Downer: Forgotten Patriot—His Life and Writings* (1974). As the title indicates, this volume contains the works, including "A Discourse," that Downer authored or may have authored. When comparing Downer's arguments to those developed by William Hicks, one must be sure to consult the Philadelphia, not the less complete New York edition, of Hicks's *The Nature and Extent of Parliamentary Power Considered . . .* (1768).

JOHN K. ALEXANDER

DOWNES, John (23 Dec. 1784–11 Aug. 1854), naval officer, was born in Canton, Massachusetts, the son of Jesse Downes and Naomi Taunt. His father was purser aboard the frigate *Constitution*, forty-four, and in September 1800 Downes joined him on that vessel in the capacity of waiter. He subsequently accompanied Captain James Barron on the frigate *New York*, and there, on 1 June 1802, he received his midshipman's warrant. Downes fought in the Tripolitan conflict and in May 1803 distinguished himself in Lieutenant David Porter's attack on enemy feluccas. Downes advanced to lieutenant on 6 March 1807 and two years later rejoined Porter, now captain, on board the frigate *Essex*, thirty-eight.

On 28 October 1812 Downes sailed with the *Essex* on its epic voyage from the Delaware Capes to the Pacific. Between April and June 1813 his boat attacks captured five valuable British prizes, including the whaler *Georgiana* and the privateer *Hector*. Downes

took command of a large prize, renamed *Essex Junior*, and conducted several independent forays. While refitting at Nuku Hiva (Marquesas Islands) on 27 November 1813, he was attacked by a large body of natives. Downes skillfully drove off his assailants but sustained a broken leg in battle. He then accompanied Porter back to Valparaiso, Chile, where on 28 March 1814 the *Essex* succumbed to the British warships *Phoebe* and *Cherub* after a stiff engagement. *Essex Junior* was converted into a cartel (prisoner exchange) vessel, and both Downes and Porter sailed back to the United States. While at sea he had been promoted to commander on 24 June 1813.

After the war, Downes enjoyed a varied and far-ranging career. Beginning in May 1815 he commanded the brig *Epervier* as part of Commodore Stephen Decatur's squadron during the Algerian conflict. On 17 June Downes played a prominent role in capturing the frigate *Mashuda* and two days later the brig *Estido*. Decatur was impressed with Downes's sailing ability and appointed him to command his flagship *Guerriere* in consequence. He received promotion to captain on 5 March 1817 and subsequently commanded the frigate *Macedonian* during a Pacific cruise, 1819 to 1821. Downes later took charge of the frigate *Java* in the Mediterranean from 1828 to 1830. In 1821 he married Maria Hoffman. Their son, John Downes, Jr., was a noted naval commander of the Civil War.

On 9 February 1831 pirates from the Malaysian village of Quallah Battoo (Kuala Batu) seized and looted the Salem merchant vessel *Friendship*, killing three of its crew. Merchants trading to the East Indies thereafter petitioned President Andrew Jackson for assistance, pointing out that no U.S. warship had ever shown its flag in Sumatra. In response, Downes was directed to assume command of the Pacific Squadron. He arrived off Quallah Battoo on 6 February 1832 with the frigate *Potomac* and landed 282 sailors and marines ashore. Four forts were stormed in a battle lasting two and one-half hours, and the village was captured and burned. The Americans killed an estimated 150 inhabitants, including their leader, Rajah Po Mahomet, and suffered a loss of two dead and eleven wounded. Downes secured a pledge of good behavior from the Sumatran survivors, but he was criticized at home for employing excessive force. Nonetheless, Sumatrans continued molesting American shipping until a second attack by Commodore George C. Read on 1 July 1839.

Downes remained with the Pacific Squadron until May 1834, when he returned to the United States and formally concluded his sailing career. He functioned as commandant of the Charlestown Navy Yard, Boston, from 1835 to 1842 and again from 1849 to 1852. He also served as Boston port captain from 1843 to 1845 and lighthouse inspector from 1852 to 1853. Downes died at Charlestown.

Though somewhat obscure, Downes was part of a naval cadre that established naval professionalism in the Tripolitan conflict and the War of 1812 and nurtured its growth in the decades that followed. His punitive action at Quallah Battoo marked the first armed intervention in Asia and was a prelude to the aggressive maritime expansion that followed. Downes was an efficient officer whose thirty-four years at sea and fifteen years ashore constitute an impressive record of achievement.

• Downes's official correspondence is in Record Group 45, Captains' Letters, National Archives. Scattered materials also exist in the Clements Library, University of Michigan; the New-York Historical Society; and the Franklin D. Roosevelt Library, Hyde Park, N.Y. Printed references are in Herman F. Kraft, "Commodore John Downes from His Official Correspondence," *United States Naval Institute Proceedings* 54 (1928): 36–48; Dudley W. Knox, ed., *Naval Documents Related to the United States Wars with the Barbary Powers* (6 vols., 1939–1944); William S. Dudley, ed., *The Naval War of 1812* (3 vols., 1985); and Edwin S. Bearss, *Charlestown Navy Yard, 1800–1842* (1984). Details on his War of 1812 activities appear in Loyal Farragut, *Life and Letters of David Glasgow Farragut* (1879); and David Porter, *Record of a Cruise Made to the Pacific* (1822). For his subsequent Pacific operations consult David F. Long, "'Martial Thunder': The First Official American Armed Intervention in Asia," *Pacific Historical Review* 42 (1973): 143–62; Jeremiah N. Reynolds, *Voyage of the United States Frigate "Potomac"* (1835); and Celia Woodworth, "The USS *Potomac* and the Pepper Pirates," in *America Spreads Her Sails*, ed. Clayton R. Burrow (1973). Brief biographical sketches include "Sketch of the Life of John Downes," *American Monthly Magazine* 8 (1876): 71–78; and Henry Hill, *Recollections of an Octogenarian* (1884). Perspective on the navy in which Downes served is in Christopher McKee, *A Gentlemanly and Honorable Profession* (1991).

JOHN C. FREDRIKSEN

DOWNES, Olin (27 Jan. 1886–22 Aug. 1955), music critic, was born Edwin Olin Downes in Evanston, Illinois, the son of Edwin Quigley and Louise C. Downes. Downes's music education included study of harmony with Homer Norris in Boston and piano lessons with Louis Kelterborn and Carl Baermann. Downes had little academic training in music, but his passionate interest and wide reading made him one of the most influential music critics in the United States during the first half of the twentieth century. He married Marion Amanda Davenport in 1910; they had three children. Their son, Edward Olin Davenport Downes, also became prominent as a music critic and broadcaster.

Downes was the senior music critic for the *Boston Post* from 1906 to 1924, which during those years was the largest daily newspaper in America. In this position Downes was an early and ardent champion of the music of Jean Sibelius. He also established himself as an open-minded, if not entirely sympathetic, observer of new musical trends, recognizing the value in music by Claude Debussy and Richard Strauss, and later Sergei Prokofiev and Dimitri Shostakovich. Downes was among the first to appreciate the lively artistic qualities of ragtime and jazz (even before the style acquired the name).

In 1924 he replaced Richard Aldrich as music critic for the *New York Times*, where he remained until his death. The 1920s and 1930s were turbulent years in the New York musical scene, and Downes was among New York's most astute observers. While often denigrated as being too conservative by the more "ultramodern" of the young composers and musical activists, many of Downes's thoughts on their activities have often stood the test of time. One of the most significant of his reviews was that of the premiere of two movements from Charles Ives's 4th Symphony at a Pro Musica concert in January 1927. Downes wrote:

There are ineptitudes, incongruities. The thing is an extraordinary hodge-podge, but something that lives and that vibrates with conviction is there. It is not possible to laugh this piece out of countenance. . . . There is . . . real vitality, real naivete and a superb self-respect. . . . [and] the conviction of a composer who has not the slightest idea of self-ridicule and who dares to jump with feet and hands and a reckless somersault or two on his way to his destination. (*New York Times*, 30 Jan. 1927)

With respect to more mainstream repertoire, Downes was, like most of his contemporaries, particularly attuned to the late nineteenth-century music of Richard Strauss and Johannes Brahms and, perhaps paradoxically, was a fervent advocate of Arturo Toscanini's "objective" and anti-romantic approach to music. Downes wanted each member of the audience to be his or her own critic, and to some extent he took his cues from the audience of which he saw himself a part.

Awarded Finland's Order of the Commander of the White Rose in 1937 for his promotion of Sibelius in America, Downes was also invited to speak at the celebration of Sibelius's Seventy-fifth birthday in 1940. He received an honorary doctorate in music from the Cincinnati Conservatory in 1939. Throughout his career he gave occasional lectures around the country and for several years produced a radio program during intermissions of the Metropolitan Opera Saturday broadcasts. Downes served as chairman of music for the New York World's Fair of 1939 but resigned when the classical programs were canceled. In 1939 he divorced his first wife and soon after, in 1940, married Irene Lenore Miles. They had no children. During the later years of his tenure at the *Times*, Downes engaged in friendly competition with Virgil Thomson, the chief critic for the *New York Herald-Tribune*, whose criticism was thought by some to be a brilliant and less responsible counterweight to Downes's more mainstream opinions.

Downes wrote four books: *The Lure of Music* (1918), *Symphonic Broadcasts* (1931), revised as *Symphonic Masterpieces* (1935), and *Sibelius the Symphonist* (1956). In addition, he edited a volume of *Select Songs from Russian Composers* (1922) and compiled and annotated *Ten Operatic Masterpieces, from Mozart to Prokofiev* (1952). After his death in New York City, his wife published a selection of his criticism under the title *Olin Downes on Music* (1957).

Downes epitomized the musical culture of his times through his unflagging devotion, his openness to a certain degree of innovation, and his conviction that art music was something that the "average person" could come to understand. As a largely self-taught man, he had a not uncommon American suspicion of academic learning that made him feel a certain inferiority, but his private lifelong education provided a base for observations about music and musical culture that were above average for any period or place. Downes stated his position in a 1941 lecture titled "Be your own music critic": "What comes out of you [immediately after the concert] when the impression is white-hot is most spontaneous and intuitive. And it happens that vigor, directness and individual approach are characteristics of the best American musical criticism."

• Downes's papers are in the archives of the University of Georgia and are described by Jean Réti-Forbes in "The Olin Down Papers," *Georgia Review* 21 (1967): 165. Two Ph.D. dissertations that include studies of Downes's music criticism are: Lloyd Weldy, "Music Criticism of Olin Downes and Howard Taubman in the "New York Times," Sunday Edition, 1924–29 and 1955–60" (Univ. of Southern California, 1965), and Barbara Mueser, "The Criticism of New Music in New York: 1919–1929" (City Univ. of New York, 1975). Downes's criticism is sampled and interpreted in Joseph Horowitz, *Understanding Toscanini* (1987). Selections from Downes's correspondence appear in *Arnold Schoenberg Correspondence: A Collection of Translated and Annotated Letters Exchanged with Guido Adler, Pablo Casals, Emanuel Feuermann and Olin Downes*, ed. E. M. Ennulat (1991). An obituary is in the *New York Times*, 23 Aug. 1955.

RON WIECKI

DOWNEY, June Etta (13 Jul. 1875–11 Oct. 1932), psychologist, was born in Laramie, Wyoming, the daughter of Colonel Stephen Downey and Evangeline Owen. Both parents were strongly committed to public service. Colonel Downey, a trial lawyer, was one of the first territorial delegates from Wyoming to the United States House of Representatives, while Evangeline Downey was active and influential in church, educational, and political affairs in the town of Laramie. Although socially prominent in their community, the Downeys were not wealthy. June Downey recalled that as children she and her nine siblings lived in a small crowded house in somewhat narrow circumstances. And after her father died in 1902, when her youngest sibling was not yet seven, Downey's mother began handpainting china to help support her family. Downey herself never married and continued to reside throughout her life with her mother in the family home.

In the fall of 1890, the year that Wyoming became a state, June Downey was one of seven students in the freshman class at the University of Wyoming founded four years earlier. She received her B.A. from the university in 1895 and then taught for a year in the Laramie public schools. In 1896 she began graduate work in philosophy and psychology at the University of Chicago where she served as an assistant to the director of the psychological laboratory, James Rowland Angell. After earning her M.A. in 1898 with a thesis on Berkeley's theory of the will, she returned to the University of Wyoming as an instructor in English. Downey was

appointed instructor of English and philosophy in 1899 and, in the summer of 1901, studied at Cornell University, gaining exposure to the approach of the influential experimental psychologist Edward Bradford Titchener. After promotion to assistant professor of philosophy in 1902 and to professor of philosophy in 1905, Downey left Wyoming for a year to return to the University of Chicago where she completed work for a doctorate in psychology awarded in 1907. Her dissertation, directed by Angell, was an experimental study that used the method of introspection to investigate the variables controlling the act of handwriting. Back at the University of Wyoming after earning the Ph.D., Downey was made head of the department of philosophy, a post she held until 1915 when she was named professor of psychology and philosophy and head of the combined departments, a position she held until her death.

Downey's contributions to psychology were as an experimentalist, but she is not readily identified as an adherent of any particular school. Among her contemporaries she was probably best known for the personality test she devised, the Will-Temperament Test, first published in 1919. Her investigations encompassed a variety of other topics, including the creative process, color blindness, and handedness. Much of her early work was concerned with the subject of imagery, an interest that persisted throughout her life. However, the topic of handwriting, the subject of her dissertation, occupied Downey for most of her academic career. Exploring the links between handwriting and personality in the decade following the receipt of her Ph.D. led Downey to develop her personality scale, which purported to measure temperament. Her book *The Will-Temperament and Its Testing* (1923) presented her view of personality as an intra-individual relationship of parts. What mattered for Downey was the relative dominance of various traits within the individual, not how that individual ranked on a trait in comparison with other individuals. Further, Downey was not interested in the absolute scores obtained by individuals on her will-temperament test, insisting that personality is better expressed in terms of a pattern or profile of personality traits. Appearing at a time when mental testing—especially intelligence testing—was coming into its own in the United States, Downey's scale was the first devised to measure nonintellectual traits.

In the fourth edition of the directory *American Men of Science*, published in 1927, Downey's name was prefixed with a star indicating that she was recognized as one of the leading scientists in her field. In 1929 she was one of the first two women to be elected to the Society of Experimental Psychologists, an elite group founded by E. B. Titchener, who had enforced a ban on women as members until his death in 1927. A bibliography of Downey's work compiled after her death by a colleague credited her with 143 publications including eight books. In addition to her substantial contribution to the psychological literature, Downey also wrote a book of poetry, seven plays, and many stories, essays, and popular articles.

Downey was remembered by her colleagues and students as a modest and shy person but also someone with personal warmth, a whimsical sense of humor, and a talent for public speaking. This characterization accords with her self-perception revealed in an article published in the year of her death in which she described herself as very introverted by nature. She explained the extrovert aspects of her personality as having developed through the pressure of circumstances that accompanied her professional life. Admitting that habits or reactions acquired in this fashion could come to mask one's natural dispositions, she added wryly that she realized this belief was not in harmony with the prevailing view of personality as merely the sum total of more or less unrelated bits of behavior. In fact, her emphasis on the patterning of traits within an individual as the key to understanding personality could be regarded as her unique contribution to psychology. But, as she correctly recognized, it was a view that was at odds with the direction the field was taking, and would continue to take, for the next several decades.

Taken ill in August 1932 while attending the Third International Congress of Eugenics in New York City, Downey died in Trenton, New Jersey, in the home of one of her sisters following an operation for stomach cancer.

• Materials relating to the life and career of Downey are located in the American Heritage Center, University of Wyoming, Laramie. *In Memoriam* (1934), a volume published by the University of Wyoming, contains a bibliography of Downey's writings, some of her poems, and personal reminiscences of colleagues. An obituary by R. S. Uhrbrock is in the *Journal of General Psychology*, 9 (1933): 353–64.

LAUREL FURUMOTO

DOWNEY, Morton (14 Nov. 1901–25 Oct. 1985), singer, composer, and businessman, was born in Wallingford, Connecticut, the son of James Andrew Downey, the fire chief of Wallingford and a tavern keeper, and Elizabeth Cox. When Downey was eight, he received $5 for singing at a church social. Engagements at picnics, political rallies, and Elks Club meetings followed. He developed an act with Philip Boudini, both playing accordions. For Downey, the accordion was mostly a prop. By the time he was fourteen people were paying $15 to hear him sing.

When he was seventeen Downey left Lyman Hall, a private high school, and worked at a factory. His next job was as a newshawk and candy salesman on trains running between Wallingford and Hartford. He sang songs up and down the cars and finally earned enough money to leave for New York City to begin a career as a singer. Although he sometimes made ten to fifteen dollars a week in song publishing houses as a singer for artists looking for new songs, success eluded him. Fortunately, he was befriended by James J. Hagan, a Tammany Hall leader, who took the broke and homeless Downey to his home. Downey stayed with the Hagans for six years.

In 1919 Downey joined Max Spiegel at the Sheridan Square Theater in Greenwich Village, where Spiegel was running a western thriller. Downey, in cowboy pants, boots, and a sombrero, sang "Mother Machree." He was heard by a talent scout for orchestra leader Paul Whiteman, auditioned, and was offered a job singing with one of Whiteman's bands.

By 1922 Downey had been assigned to Whiteman's SS *Leviathan* orchestra. Before actually joining the ship, the band played at New York City's Palace Theater. Downey brought down the house with his singing of "Molly Malone"; he was such a hit that his salary was raised from $100 to $250 a week, and he was given equal billing with the band. After a national tour, the orchestra and Downey crossed the Atlantic twenty times.

In 1926 Downey left the band and appeared in Ziegfeld's *Palm Beach Nights* revue, in Florida. After this success, he went to Europe in 1927, singing in supper clubs in London, Paris, and Berlin, and on the French Riviera and gaining an international reputation. One evening, when Downey was working at the Cafe de Paris in London, he answered the request of the prince of Wales for "You Took Advantage of Me" by singing it eleven times. Downey first sang on the air over BBC from London in 1928 and became enthusiastic about singing on radio when he returned to the United States.

But first he went to Hollywood and in 1929 starred in the movie *Syncopation*, in which he sang the hit song "I'll Always Be in Love with You" to his costar Barbara Bennett (sister of Constance and Joan). When filming was complete, he married his costar in January 1929; they had five children. *Syncopation*, the first sound musical, was produced by Joseph P. Kennedy, who became a lifelong friend of Downey. Downey made another film in 1929, *Mother's Boy*, and his final film, *Lucky in Love*, in 1930.

Downey returned to New York City in 1930, opened his own nightclub, Delmonico's, and made his radio debut when WABC broadcast his show from there. As a vocalist on radio he achieved his greatest fame, and over the next two decades his voice was heard over the networks of the United States and Europe. His first show, "The Morton Downey Show," which was aired under several different names, ran in both fifteen-minute and thirty-minute versions from 1930 to 1951. In 1931 CBS signed him for "The Camel Quarter-Hour," and Downey began receiving 95,000 fan letters a week. By 1932 his annual earnings were estimated at $250,000, and in 1933 he was voted Best Male Singer of the Year in a *World-Telegram* poll.

In 1936 Downey sang at the coronation celebration for King George VI; he later entertained President Franklin D. Roosevelt at the White House. As a result of the Great Depression and a "messy divorce," finalized in 1941, Downey's popularity and income declined. However, he accepted a five-year contract with Coca-Cola in 1943 for a program called "The Coke Club," with Downey as the featured singer. It ran from 1943 to 1951, when his contract was extended two years. Downey did three fifteen-minute broadcasts over, initially, two hundred stations, and made it a point to be photographed as often as possible in the company of a Coca-Cola bottle. Downey became the company's greatest salesman and a stockholder.

Throughout the 1940s Downey sang on his own show, sang on "The Coke Club," and did guest appearances on radio shows such as "The Andrews Sisters," singing a song he made famous, "Carolina Moon." He also continued to perform in nightclubs all over the country. Downey once said the only state he had not sung in was Idaho.

In 1949 Downey had his first television show, sponsored by Mohawk Carpets and called the "Mohawk Showroom." He was with the show from May to December 1949. Although the show started off as "something of a sleeper," it soon became a hit. What the viewer saw was the same thing that nightclub audiences had been paying well to see: Downey at the piano, running through an apparently inexhaustible supply of songs, and making it all look like fun. Downey later hosted "Star in the Family" for one season (1955) and guest-starred in other television shows, including "Life Begins at Eighty."

In addition to his work in clubs and on radio and television, Downey wrote more than thirty songs, including "Now You're in My Arms" and "That's How I Spell Ireland." His biggest seller was "Wabash Moon," which sold a million copies in sheet music. He also made more than 1,500 recordings, dating back to 1916, when he was fifteen.

Downey was not only an entertainer but was also an investor, mostly in business properties in New York City and Chicago. As Downey noted, "I stuck pretty close to Joe [Joseph P.] Kennedy . . . I hoped some of his smartness would rub off on me" ("Downey in the Dough," p. 48). Downey's friendship with Kennedy extended over the years through correspondence, business involvement, and social engagements. He sang a traditional Communion song at Kennedy's funeral mass in 1969. Downey was on the boards of the Coca-Cola Bottling Company of Chicago and General Aniline & Film Corporation. He owned one-third of a perfume concern and one-half of a chemical-patent holding firm. Downey did so well with his investments and his singing that he was dubbed the "singing millionaire."

In 1951 Downey married Margaret Boyce Thompson Schulze; they had no children. She died in 1964. Downey retired to Florida in 1970 and married Ann Van Gerbig the same year. Once called by Bing Crosby "the oldest choirboy in the world," Downey, at age eighty-two, was still able to sing Rose Kennedy her favorite song, "My Wild Irish Rose." He died in Palm Beach, Florida.

A consummate showman, Downey entertained in night clubs, on radio during the 1930s and 1940s, and on television in the 1950s. He became one of America's most popular singers. Known, variously, as the "Irish Thrush," the "Irish Troubadour," and the "Irish Nightingale" for his melodious Irish tenor and repertoire of Irish songs, the Connecticut-born Downey made being Irish his signature. He once estimated that he had sung "When Irish Eyes Are Smiling" 10,000 times.

• Many collections of his songs were published, including *The Morton Downey Song Album,* comp. George McConnell (1933). Biographical information may be found in Richard Lamparski, *Whatever Became of . . . ?* (1968). See also Collie Small, "My Wild Irish Downey," *Collier's,* 19 Mar. 1949, pp. 19, 54; "'Oldest Choirboy,'" *Newsweek,* 23 May 1949, p. 55; "Downey in the Dough," *Newsweek,* 26 Dec. 1949, pp. 47–48; and Carol Hughes, "The Come-Back Triumph of Morton Downey," *Coronet,* May 1951, pp. 129–34. Obituaries are in the *Boston Globe,* the *Chicago Tribune,* and the *New York Times,* all 27 Oct. 1985.

MARCIA B. DINNEEN

DOWNEY, Sheridan (9 Mar. 1884–25 Oct. 1961), U.S. senator, was born in Laramie, Albany County, Wyoming Territory, the son of Stephen Wheeler Downey, an attorney and politician, and Evangeline Victoria Owen. Sheridan Downey grew up in Laramie, attended the University of Wyoming, and received an LL.B. from the University of Michigan Law School in 1907. He subsequently returned to Laramie to practice law, and in 1908 he was elected district attorney of Albany County as a Republican. In 1910 he married Helen Symons; they had five children. In 1912 Downey split Wyoming's Republican vote by heading the state's "Bull Moose" revolt in support of Theodore Roosevelt, thus leading to a Democratic victory statewide.

In 1913 Downey moved to Sacramento, California, and continued to practice law with his brother, Stephen Wheeler Downey, Jr. During his first few years in California, he devoted most of his time and energy to his law practice and various real estate interests. In 1924 he supported Robert La Follette's Progressive party campaign for the presidency, and in 1932 he became a Democrat and campaigned for the election of Franklin D. Roosevelt. In October 1933 Downey announced that he was running for governor of California, but after a series of meetings with the writer Upton Sinclair, who also had designs on the governorship, Downey agreed to run for lieutenant governor as Sinclair's running mate. With Sinclair, Downey campaigned on the End Poverty in California (EPIC) platform. EPIC began as a mass movement, calling for an economic revolution to lift California out of the depression. The EPIC platform called for state support for the creation of jobs, a massive program of public works, and an extensive system of state-sponsored pensions and radical changes in the tax structure. Before long, more than 2,000 grassroots EPIC clubs sprouted throughout the state, and the most popular EPIC anthem, "Campaign Chorus for Downey and Sinclair," was made into a phonograph record for mass distribution featuring Downey, among others, singing. While EPIC suffered a landslide defeat to Republican Frank Merriam in November 1934, Downey, who had been subjected to less vitriol than Sinclair during the campaign, remained a viable political force in the state. Downey actually garnered 123,000 votes more than his running mate, and he gained a statewide reputation as a champion of progressive politics.

After the election, Downey became an attorney for Dr. Francis Townsend, whose $200-a-month pension plan had won a large following in California, particularly among retirees. In 1936 Downey published the book *Why I Believe in the Townsend Plan.* Defeated as a Townsendite candidate for Congress that year, Downey ran in the Democratic primary for the U.S. Senate in 1938 against incumbent senator William Gibbs McAdoo. McAdoo was the leader of the more conservative or "regular" faction of the California Democratic party, while Downey had the support of more liberal and progressive Democrats and of many who had enthusiastically supported the EPIC campaign in 1934. Downey also had the backing of organized labor, which viewed McAdoo with hostility, and the highly mobilized retirement groups in California, who identified with Downey's support for old-age pensions. Despite the strong backing McAdoo received from the White House and a personal campaign appearance by President Franklin Roosevelt to endorse the incumbent, Downey won the primary and went on to victory in November.

In the Senate, Downey introduced a series of pension bills, and in 1941 he was named chairman of a special Senate committee on old-age insurance. He took an early stand supporting a military draft but opposed the Roosevelt administration's plans to requisition industries in time of war. During World War II he called for the creation of a committee to investigate the status of blacks and other minorities in the armed forces and advocated a postwar United Nations, international control of atomic energy, increased veterans' benefits, and federal pay raises. At the end of the war he opposed continuation of the military draft. During his years in the U.S. Senate Downey often represented the interests of California's powerful motion picture industry.

After his narrow reelection to the Senate in 1944, defeating Republican lieutenant governor Frederick F. Houser by 52 percent to 48 percent, Downey began a push for the California Central Valley project, which had been initiated during the 1930s as part of the New Deal's vast array of public works projects, such as power dams and irrigation canals. In a 1947 book titled *They Would Rule the Valley,* Downey argued that the federal Bureau of Reclamation sought "to rule" the rich Central Valley farmlands by limiting the size of irrigated holdings. Downey's critics began to charge that the senator had become conservative over the years owing to his support for large growers and the oil industry. This shift may also have reflected the tensions within the California Democratic party that distinguished between white pensioners and union members and the many African-American or Hispanic laborers of the state. These shifts in Downey's political views made him vulnerable to a challenge from the left of his party, and in 1950 he was challenged in the Democratic primary by Representative Helen Gaha-

gan Douglas, who characterized him as being in the pocket of the California oil industry and beholden to big business and large-scale agriculture concerns. In early 1950 Downey dropped out of the race, citing ill health, and threw his support in the Democratic primary behind Manchester Boddy, the conservative and wealthy publisher of the *Los Angeles Daily News.* After Republican representative Richard M. Nixon's election over Douglas in the November general election, Downey resigned his seat several weeks early to give the incoming freshman an advantage in Senate seniority. After his departure from the Senate, Downey became a lobbyist representing the city of Long Beach and the large petroleum concerns leasing its extensive waterfront. He died in San Francisco.

During his years in the Senate Downey was often described as slight, grayish, and strikingly handsome. His political career in many ways typified the transformation of millions of Republican progressives who supported Theodore Roosevelt and the "Bull Moose" movement of 1912 into Democratic supporters of Franklin Roosevelt and the New Deal in the 1930s. During the 1930s and early 1940s Downey was one of California's most significant progressive politicians. While he was often overshadowed in state politics by Republican progressives like Hiram Johnson and Earl Warren, Downey left a significant mark because of his tireless advocacy of old-age pensions, organized labor, and racial justice. His conservative turn after his reelection in 1944, when he increasingly represented the interests of big business, large agribusiness concerns, and the oil industry, has obscured his historical reputation as a onetime liberal and progressive force in California politics.

• Downey's papers are in the Bancroft Library at the University of California at Berkeley. His other books include *Onward America* (1933) and *Highways to Prosperity* (1940). A useful introduction to Calif. politics and the Progressive movement in particular is in Royce D. Delmatier et al., eds., *The Rumble of California Politics* (1970). More specific aspects of Downey's career are examined in Abraham Hotlzman, *The Townsend Movement* (1963), and Jackson K. Putnam, *Old-Age Politics in California* (1970). Downey's role in the 1934 EPIC campaign is discussed in Greg Mitchell, *The Campaign of the Century* (1992). His decision to drop out of the 1950 Senate race and his role in the subsequent Nixon-Douglas campaign is discussed in Roger Morris, *Richard Milhouse Nixon* (1990). An obituary is in the *New York Times,* 27 Oct. 1961.

CHRISTOPHER D. O'SULLIVAN

DOWNING, Andrew Jackson (31 Oct. 1815–28 July 1852), nurseryman and landscape gardener, was born in Newburgh, New York, the son of Samuel Downing, a wheelwright turned nurseryman, and Eunice Bridge. His youthful experiences in the Hudson Valley inspired his later interest in landscape and architectural design. As Newburgh grew from village into small industrial city, and as farmers increasingly raised fruits and vegetables for urban markets, Downing's career evolved from that of selling garden stock to the landscaping of grounds and the design of rural and suburban homes. And as the pace of urban growth accelerated, he became the most influential early advocate of spacious parks within cities and codified the suburban ideal for middle- and upper-class Americans.

Upon finishing schooling at the age of sixteen, Downing joined his brother Charles Downing in managing the family business, Botanic Garden and Nurseries, in Newburgh. During the next decade he wrote dozens of articles for horticultural magazines and read extensively in the history and theory of landscape design. Perhaps as early as 1836 he had begun writing a book on the use of trees in gardening and in late 1838 had employed Alexander Jackson Davis to prepare finished illustrations for the book. Much expanded in content, it was published in 1841 as *A Treatise on the Theory and Practice of Landscape Gardening*. Downing rejected the classical styles prevalent in landscape and architectural design and introduced readers to the Beautiful and the Picturesque, aesthetic categories that reflected the romantic movement evident in literature and art. The *Treatise* drew heavily upon previous English works, most notably those by Humphry Repton and John Claudius Loudon, but consciously "adapted" those ideas to the climate and social conditions of the United States. Although most of the book is devoted to descriptions of trees, advice on laying out grounds, and ornamental uses of water and statuary, Downing also included a brief summary of the historical evolution of styles in landscape design, an analysis of the "beauties and principles of the art," and a chapter devoted to rural architecture. Gracefully written and handsomely illustrated, the *Treatise* went through four editions during the next twelve years; it sold approximately 9,000 copies.

The following year Downing published *Cottage Residences*, a series of designs for houses of modest size. This was arguably the first of the new genre of house pattern books, which depicted the home in its landscaped setting, plans of the grounds, and ornamental details, along with an explanatory text to assist the reader in choosing a residence appropriate to his or her circumstances. Unlike the larger houses Downing used to illustrate in the *Treatise*, most of the designs in *Cottage Residences* were smaller and more appropriate to an emerging middle class. Downing later explained that he intended his cottage designs for "industrious and intelligent mechanics and workingmen, the bone and sinew of the land." *Cottage Residences* also reached a large audience: several of its designs were reprinted in agricultural or horticultural periodicals, and numerous extant houses still bear testament to the popularity of Downing's designs. So great was his influence that novelist Catharine Sedgwick reported that "nobody, whether he be rich or poor, builds a house or lays out a garden without consulting Downing's works."

Even as he was writing for a more general audience, Downing had begun compiling information for *The Fruits and Fruit Trees of America* (1845). This book included technical information on fruit nomenclature as well as advice on planting and the care of orchards. *Fruits and Fruit Trees* also proved enormously popular: it sold 15,000 copies prior to 1853 and earned its author membership in several European horticultural or scientific societies. Shortly thereafter Downing prepared an American edition of Mrs. Loudon's *Gardening For Ladies* (1846) and one of George Wightwick's *Hints to Young Architects* (1847), for which he added "Additional Notes and Hints to Persons About Building in This Country."

Downing's final book, *The Architecture of Country Houses* (1850), is both a culmination of his views on domestic architecture and a catalogue of the works of a rising generation of architects, including Alexander Jackson Davis, Gervase Wheeler, and Richard Upjohn. In the preface Downing attributed a moral and social influence to domestic architecture and asserted that a properly designed home was "a powerful means of civilization." The text presented the characteristics of such eclectic or historical styles as Gothic, Romanesque, Italianate, and Bracketed and explained how each style and building type—cottage, farmhouse, villa—was appropriate to different settings and economic situations. Downing included chapters on the treatment of interiors and furnishings as well.

Shortly after delivering *Country Houses* to its publisher in June 1850, Downing traveled to England. He recorded the impressions of his travels in a series of eight letters, published in the *Horticulturist*, that described various English estates, public buildings, and landscapes; visits to arboretums and botanical gardens; and the social influence of the public parks he visited there. He returned in the fall of 1850 accompanied by Calvert Vaux, a young English architect, and shortly thereafter established a "Bureau of Architecture" in a new wing he added to his home. Less than two years later Downing and Vaux were joined by Frederick C. Withers, another English architect, in what quickly became a flourishing business. The office, Downing informed John Jay Smith, was "full of commissions, and young architects, and planning for all parts of the country." Among the commissions Downing's firm enjoyed were the Matthew Vassar estate, "Springside," in Poughkeepsie, New York; the Daniel Parish house, Newport, Rhode Island; and the Dodge houses in Washington, D.C. These and other designs are illustrated in Vaux's *Villas and Cottages* (1857).

Equal in significance to Downing's books and his professional commissions was his monthly magazine, the *Horticulturist*, which began publication in July 1846. As its subtitle indicated, Downing devoted its pages to broader questions of "rural art and rural taste." He crusaded against free-roaming pigs that menaced the streets of countless towns, for the formation of village improvement societies, and for sensible yet tasteful designs in rural architecture. He provided plans for such commonplace structures as ice houses as well as residences, schools, and churches. Rural economy was as important as matters of taste. Because he realized that farmers were wastefully extracting nutrients from the soil and in older settled areas were experiencing declines in productivity, Downing became one of the earliest advocates of public agricultural education. In 1849 he was appointed one of eight commissioners to develop a plan for an agricultural college and experimental farm in New York, and the following year he and Alexander Jackson Davis prepared a design for such an institution. In the commission's report and in a leader in the *Horticulturist*, Downing advocated that the curriculum of the school teach both practical farming and its scientific underpinnings. Convinced that wisdom was "knowledge put into action," he hoped that graduates of the school would improve agricultural practices and reinvigorate the overall quality of rural life. Although nothing came of his proposal at this time, a decade later Congress enacted the Morrill (or Land Grant Colleges) Act to provide for agricultural and industrial education.

Downing supported agricultural education because he considered farmers the "great industrial class of America." At the same time, the urban population was increasing at the fastest rate in American history, and Downing recognized the need for open spaces within cities and promoted the establishment of public parks. In 1848 he described parks as the "pleasant drawing-rooms" of European cities, places that promoted a more democratic social life than was the case in American cities. In succeeding years Downing elaborated on the role of parks as part of a reformist program that also included publicly supported libraries, galleries of art, and opportunities for social interaction. "Popular refinement," as he termed this broad initiative in 1851, "takes up where the common school and the ballot-box leave it, and raises the working-man to the same level of enjoyment with the man of leisure."

In late 1850 Downing was commissioned to landscape the public grounds in Washington, D.C. This 150-acre tract extended west from the foot of Capitol Hill to the site of the Washington Monument and then north to the president's house. Downing saw this as an opportunity not simply to ornament the capital but also to create the first large public park in the United States. He believed that the Washington park would encourage cities across the nation to provide healthful recreational grounds for their citizens. Although only the initial stages of construction had been completed at the time of his death, Downing's commission, as well as the influence of his writings, merited the epithet "Father of American Parks."

Downing was also an early proponent of the suburb as a middle ground between city and county. He recognized that railroads and other transportation technologies had made possible the separation of workplace and domicile, and he urged the creation of suburban communities that combined a spacious setting for single-family homes and proximity to urban jobs and cultural institutions. In his essay "Our Country Villages," Downing rejected the rectangular plat so common to most suburban development and advocated instead the curving lines that characterized his principles of landscape design. He also proposed that each suburban community have a centrally located park, which would function as the "nucleus or *heart of the village*" and provide opportunities for communal activities.

In 1852 Downing was thirty-six years old. He had written four books and conducted a monthly journal; he had established impressive practices in landscape gardening and architecture; and he had outlined a series of initiatives that would improve the quality of rural and urban life. He must have anticipated greater successes in the years to come. On July 28, however, he died in the burning of the Hudson River steamboat *Henry Clay* near Yonkers, New York. His death, Harvard botanist Asa Gray noted, was "a truly national loss." Downing was survived by his widow, Caroline DeWint Downing, whom he had married in 1838.

Downing achieved fame during his brief life as a tastemaker for the nation. He guided the prevailing taste away from geometric patterns in the garden and classical styles in architecture to less formal, picturesque or romantic forms. In addition to his own commissions, buildings and grounds designed according to his principles were evident in every region of the United States. But perhaps his greatest legacy was the construction of large parks in most American cities. Calvert Vaux and Frederick Law Olmsted (1822–1903), co-designers of New York's Central Park, attributed the creation of the park to Downing's work and in 1889 honored their friend by designing Andrew Jackson Downing Memorial Park in Newburgh, New York.

What united Downing's various endeavors was an enduring concern for the future of the American republic. He believed strongly in the need to raise the level of "*social* civilization and social culture" in the United States. He considered his landscape and architectural commissions, as well as his books and the pages of the *Horticulturist*, vehicles for popularizing models of design appropriate to a middle-class society. Downing anointed his readers "Apostles of Taste" and charged them with the responsibility of providing examples of landscape and architectural design worthy of being imitated by other Americans.

• Most of Downing's surviving correspondence consists of letters to A. J. Davis, housed at the Metropolitan Museum of Art; the New-York Historical Society; the New York Public Library; and Avery Architectural and Fine Arts Library, Columbia University, all in New York City. Other important collections are the John Jay Smith Papers, Library Company of Philadelphia, now deposited in the Historical Society of Pennsylvania, Philadelphia, which also includes letters from Caroline Downing, Charles Downing, Calvert Vaux, and Asa Gray to Marshall P. Wilder written shortly after Downing's death; the Vassar College Archive, Poughkeepsie, N.Y., which documents Downing's designs for Matthew Vassar's estate; and the Records of the Commissioners of Public Buildings, National Archives and Records Service, Washington, D.C., which provides information on Downing's planning of the public grounds in that city. There is no full-length biography of Downing; the most comprehensive works are George Bishop Tatum, "Andrew Jackson Downing: Arbiter of American Taste, 1815–1852" (Ph.D. diss., Princeton Univ., 1950), and George B. Tatum and Elisabeth B. Mac-Dougall, eds., *Prophet with Honor: The Career of Andrew Jackson Downing, 1815–1852* (1989).

DAVID SCHUYLER

DOWNING, George Thomas (30 Dec. 1819–21 July 1903), abolitionist, businessman, and civil rights advocate, was born in New York City, the son of Thomas Downing, a restaurant owner, and Rebecca West. His father's Oyster House was a gathering place for New York's aristocracy and politicians. Young Downing attended Charles Smith's school on Orange Street and, with future black abolitionists J. McCune Smith, Henry Highland Garnet, Alexander Crummell, and Charles and Patrick Reason, the African School #2 on Mulberry Street. He completed his schooling privately and in his mid-teens was active in two literary societies.

Before he was twenty Downing participated in the Underground Railroad and worked with his father to lobby the New York legislature for equal suffrage. In 1841 both were delegates to the initial convention of the American Reform Board of Disenfranchised Commissioners, one of many organizations formed by African-American males to fight for the elective franchise in New York. That same year George Downing married Serena Leanora de Grasse, the daughter of a German mother and a father from India. She attended Clinton Seminary in Clinton, New York, and spent vacations at the home of a classmate, the daughter of political abolitionist Gerrit Smith; it was here Downing courted her.

Downing started his own restaurant in 1842 in New York. In the summer of 1846 he opened a branch of his father's restaurant in Newport, Rhode Island; four years later he began a catering business in Providence. He set roots down in Newport in 1855 when he built the Sea Girt House, a luxurious summer resort (for whites only). Although he traveled extensively, lived in Providence and Boston before the Civil War, and managed the House of Representatives dining room in Washington, D.C., during and after the Civil War, Newport was his home.

Outside of his real estate, catering, and restaurant interests, Downing devoted himself to fighting for his race. An early abolitionist, he participated in several rescues of fugitive slaves, including the famous cases of James Hamlet (1848) and Anthony Burns (1854). He zealously asserted the right of black children to equal education and was a member of the first board of trustees of the New York Society for the Promotion of Education among Colored Children (1847). In 1857 he began and financed a successful nine-year campaign to integrate the schools of the Rhode Island's three major cities, Providence, Newport, and Bristol. Downing questioned a manual labor school proposal by Frederick Douglass, in part because it was racially exclusive.

His opposition to the largely white American Colonization Society's efforts to persuade blacks to migrate to Liberia was both persistent and passionate. He believed blacks should stay and fight for their freedom. When Henry Highland Garnet formed a parallel black African Civilization Society to encourage emigration, Downing led a bitter fight to neutralize its efforts, using parliamentary maneuvers, personal attacks, and threats of violence in conventions of 1859, 1860, and 1864.

Downing's devotion to equal rights for African-Americans lasted a lifetime. When Louis Kossuth, the Hungarian rebel leader, arrived in New York in 1851, Downing and a reception committee welcomed him as a "living Apostle" of the precept that men have "a right to the full exercise of [their] faculties and powers" in their native land. In 1860, over the protests of Boston officials, he and a handful of black leaders held a large meeting honoring the first anniversary of John Brown's death. The Civil War raised the question of enlisting black troops; before recruiting, Downing secured from Massachusetts governor John A. Andrew a pledge that there would be equality of treatment "in every particular" for black soldiers. During and after the war, he supported Senator Charles Sumner's attempts to advance civil rights and was instrumental in removing the color ban from the U.S. Senate gallery.

In a well-publicized 1866 interview of a dozen black leaders with President Andrew Johnson, Downing told the president, they had come as "friends, meeting a friend. . . . We are in a passage to equality before the law." He asked for legislation to enforce the Thirteenth Amendment and for the right to vote. To do less, he said, "will be a disregard of our just rights." Johnson's reply was long, rambling, and negative, but over the next decade the Fourteenth and Fifteenth amendments and the 1875 Civil Rights Act gave the race a fleeting taste of victory.

While Downing never lost his fervor for equal rights, he maintained his interest in economic affairs. His real estate holdings in 1856–1857 were valued at $6,800. Shortly after the war, he tried without success to create "a great mercantile house" in New York and "establish business relations" with the South. He was a key figure in organizing the Colored National Labor Union in 1869 and served as the first convention's temporary chair and the union's initial vice president. Downing condemned the racial intransigence of the white National Labor Union and urged freedmen to seek loans, not donations, from northern capitalists to underwrite their business efforts.

His ties to the Republican party began to loosen as early as 1869, when he told the Colored National Labor Union convention that the party deserved "respect and support," but it "should have been more consistent, more positive" in confronting the race's "enemies." He predicted that after the ratification of the Fifteenth Amendment, the party's "adhesive element" would dissipate and new issues such as labor would emerge. His 1873 attack on Rhode Island Republicans for blocking the repeal of a law against racial intermarriage provoked charges of apostasy from regulars of both races.

Downing's support for the 1879 Exodusters challenged Frederick Douglass and chastised Republican president Rutherford B. Hayes for a failed southern policy. The Kansas migrants from Louisiana and Mississippi were victims of southern oppression, he affirmed, because the South "is not ready to accept . . . equality before the law for all men" (Foner and Lewis, *Black Worker*, p. 321). The next decade saw Downing firmly in the Democratic camp. He favored Grover Cleveland for president in 1884 and, with Democratic support, tried three times without success to win a Rhode Island legislative seat, an effort that nevertheless weakened "the blind adhesion of the colored people to one party" (*New York Freeman*, 16 Apr. 1887). When Senator William Sprague was elected governor in 1887, he recognized Downing's support by appointing him to the state Prison Commission and to an ad hoc committee of leading citizens.

George Downing was a light-complexioned, tall, "commanding" figure, whose vigorous commitment to equality often created friction within the race. He understood the vulnerability of the powerless, learning, wealth, moral character, and the ballot, he asserted in 1859, were the keys to power. In childhood he experienced racial taunts and abuse, and as an adult he was ejected from a railroad car. Yet he remained an optimist, believing that race blending would eradicate barriers. "The world has no such beauties as are the product of the Africo-American with other races in America," he wrote in 1884.

Downing retired from business in the early 1880s, financially secure and recognized as "one of the institutions of Newport" (*New York Freeman*, 3 July 1886). He devoted his time to his dogs and his collections of memorabilia. He told a friend in 1899 that his writing aimed "to force the inevitable on prejudiced Americans." Downing died at home in Newport, Rhode Island. The *Boston Globe* called him "the foremost colored man in the country" and praised his efforts in behalf of liberty, adding in an editorial: "Narrowness was never safe where George T. Downing was present" (22, 23 July 1903).

• Houghton Library, Harvard University, has a small collection of Downing correspondence. Individual letters may be found in the collections of Frederick Douglass (Anacostia), John Jay (Columbia University), Blanche K. Bruce (Howard University), and Alexander Crummell (Schomburg Division, New York Public Library). A number of early Downing letters to newspapers are cited in Lawrence Grossman, "George T. Downing and Desegregation in Rhode Island Public Schools, 1855–1866," *Rhode Island History* 36 (1977): 99–105. Downing published two essays in the *AME Church Review*, "The Africo-American Force in America," 1 (1884): 157–62, and "A Sketch of the Life and Times of Thomas Downing," 4 (1887): 402–10. Downing's oldest daughter, Serena, published a brief laudatory biography: S. A. M. Washington, *George Thomas Downing: Sketch of His Life and Times* (1910), much of which is drawn, sometimes verbatim, from a biographical sketch by T. McCants Stewart in the *New York Freeman*, repr. in the *Cleveland Gazette*, 2 May 1885. Several volumes of *The Frederick Douglass Papers*, ed. John W. Blassingame, Series One, vols. 2–4 (1982–1991), have substantive references to Downing, including the interview with President Andrew Johnson (vol. 4). Philip S. Foner and Ronald L. Lewis, eds., *The Black Worker*, vol. 2 (1978), covers Downing's participation in the nascent labor movement. Helpful secondary works include Irving Bartlett, *From Slave to Citizen: The Story of the Negro in Rhode Island* (1954); Rhoda G. Freeman, *The Free Negro in New York City in the Era before the Civil War* (1994); John H. Hewitt, "Mr. [Thomas] Downing and His Oyster House: The Life and Good Works of an African-American Entrepreneur," *New York History* 74 (1993): 229–52; and Benjamin Quarles, *Black Abolitionists* (1969). Obituaries are in the *New York Times*, 22 July 1903; the *Cleveland Gazette*, 1 Aug. 1903; and, with editorial comment, the *Boston Globe*, 22, 23 July 1903.

LESLIE H. FISHEL, JR.

DOWSE, Thomas (28 Dec. 1772–4 Nov. 1856), bibliophile, was born in Charlestown, Massachusetts, the son of Eleazer Dowse, a tanner and leather dresser, and Mehitable Brenthall. The family's home was destroyed by fire when the British burned Charlestown during the battle of Bunker Hill in June 1775. The Dowses took up temporary residence in Holliston, then resettled in Sherborn, Massachusetts, where Eleazar Dowse renewed his trade. At age six Thomas was injured in a fall from an apple tree; the injury, coupled with a later bout with rheumatic fever, left him lame for life. Unable to participate in vigorous physical activities, the sickly child turned to books for "occupation and amusement." He became an omnivorous reader, spending his every cent on books. He came to idolize Sir Walter Scott, the celebrated Scottish poet and novelist, because he also had suffered from lameness. Dowse later said that "lameness drove us both to books—him to making them, and me to reading them." Dowse's extensive reading compensated for a scant formal education. Like Benjamin Franklin (1706–1790), another of his heroes, Dowse was the quintessential autodidact.

Dowse followed in his father's footsteps and became a leather dresser after a ten-year apprenticeship in Roxbury, Massachusetts. In 1803 he opened his own shop in Cambridgeport, a Cambridge, Massachusetts, neighborhood. Because of his honesty, trustworthiness, industriousness, punctuality, and intelligence, he prospered in his trade and acquired sufficient capital to build a three-story wooden structure in Cambridgeport in 1814. His workshop was on the ground floor and his residence in the two upper stories. The most imposing room in his personal quarters was his library, where he spent most of his free time. He read before and after work and on Sundays, forgoing church. He displayed only two art objects in his library: a marble bust of Sir Walter Scott by Sir Francis Legatt Chantrey and an unfinished portrait by Gilbert Stuart of his friend and fellow bibliophile Edward Everett.

Dowse never married and was, possibly because of his lameness, a social recluse. Everett described him as "a taciturn, lonely, self-reliant man, drawing solitary enjoyment from the deep cold wells of reading and thought." Although he had acquired books since childhood, Dowse became a serious collector when he moved into his Cambridgeport home. He committed practically every cent not needed for his business and living expenses to his library. It is estimated that he spent over $40,000 on his collection. He bought from Boston book shops and, using catalogues, from London dealers. Lacking a reading knowledge of foreign languages, he collected mostly English literature, the best contemporary translations of Greek and Latin classics and German, French, Italian, and Portuguese literary works. He also purchased many standard American publications. By 1856, after more than fifty years of active collecting, his library numbered 4,665 volumes. In size and quality it was one of the premier private libraries in New England. A contemporary author described Dowse's English literature holdings as "the richest and fullest . . . of any owned by a private individual in New England."

While interested primarily in content, Dowse also sought books with beautiful bindings. Having tanned skins for Boston bookbinders, he had a keen knowledge and appreciation of fine bindings. The books in his library were "all decently, many elegantly, a few magnificently bound," many in calf and morocco. As his collection grew, Dowse's reputation as a connoisseur of books increased. He became known in Boston-Cambridge bookish circles as the "literary leather dresser."

In 1856, knowing that his life was nearing its end, Dowse became concerned about the disposition of his library and so arranged for a printed catalogue of the collection. Then, using as an intermediary George Livermore, his neighbor, trusted friend, and one of the two men he selected as executors of his estate, he offered his library to the Massachusetts Historical Society, which had been founded in 1791 and was the nation's first such organization. Livermore was a resident member of this exclusive society, which had a maximum elective membership of 100. Dowse was not a member and, because he lacked social position and status as a tradesman, was never considered for membership, notwithstanding his love of books and history. It is doubtful that he would have accepted membership, even if it had been offered, for he was not a sociable person. As Everett noted, "He kept no company, he joined no clubs, belonged to no mutual-admiration societies, talked little, wrote less, published nothing." In making his offer to the society, Dowse stipulated two conditions: that his books remain in one room "for ever" and that they be used only in that room. The society agreed to the conditions and accepted the gift in the summer of 1856. It set aside a special room, designated the Dowse Library, for his collection. It also commissioned Moses Wight to paint Dowse's portrait and placed it in the room. Since 1856 the society has been located in three different buildings in Boston, all of which have featured a Dowse Library in honor of the institution's "greatest benefactor" and one of New England's most notable bibliophiles. He died in Cambridgeport.

• There is no extant collection of Dowse papers. The most important sources on Dowse's life and library are Edward Everett, "Eulogy," *Massachusetts Historical Society Proceedings*, 1st ser., 3 (1855–1858): 361–98; Walter Muir Whitehill, "The Centenary of the Dowse Library," *Massachusetts Historical Society Proceedings*, 71 (1953–1957): 167–78; and *Catalogue of the Private Library of Thomas Dowse of Cambridge, Mass., Presented to the Massachusetts Historical Society, July 30, 1856* (1856). Genealogical information can be found in William B. H. Dowse, *Lawrence Dowse of Legbourne, England, His Ancestors, Descendants and Connections* (1926).

LOUIS LEONARD TUCKER

DOYLE, Alexander Patrick (28 Feb. 1857–9 Aug. 1912), Roman Catholic priest, was born in San Francisco, California, the son of Richard S. Doyle, a contractor, and Matilda Shea. The Doyle and Shea families were California pioneers who had migrated to San Francisco at the time of the gold rush and had prospered with the city's development. Alexander Patrick graduated from St. Mary's College, San Francisco, with an A.B. degree in 1875. In the same year he entered the Missionary Society of St. Paul the Apostle (Paulist Fathers), in New York, having heard the Paulists preach at his local church.

Ordained a priest on 22 May 1880, Doyle was assigned to the Paulist Mission Band in New York City. Parish missions were a program of sermons or instructions presented in local churches over a period of one to two weeks. The Paulists specialized in a form of mission that encouraged lapsed Catholics to return to the practice of their faith and invited non-Catholics to consider conversion. For the next twelve years Doyle traveled throughout the northeastern and midwestern United States, preaching missions to both Catholics and non-Catholics.

In September 1892 Doyle left mission preaching to become editor of the *Catholic World*. The popular Catholic monthly was begun in 1865 by Paulist founder Isaac Thomas Hecker. An advocate of low-cost, popular Catholic literature, Doyle altered the scholarly format of the journal in order to reach the largest audience possible, introducing photographic images, travelogues, and short stories. While older subscribers complained that the journal had lost its former depth, circulation increased during his editorship. As editor, Doyle supported rapid assimilation of Catholic immigrants into American society, temperance, and Catholic participation in the Spanish-American War. His successor and former assistant, John J. Burke, restored the journal's original format in 1905.

During his tenure as editor, Doyle resided at the Church of St. Paul the Apostle in New York City. From 1860 to 1890 the semirural area was transformed into a set of crowded neighborhoods filled with tenements, gas storage tanks, docks, and a railroad yard. Doyle began a campaign of neighborhood reform that led to the closing of brothels and saloons and the creation of a parish-sponsored settlement house in 1901. His reform efforts brought him into collaboration with

Police Commissioner Theodore Roosevelt (1858–1919), who became a lifetime friend.

Doyle promoted the cause of temperance among Catholics, and from 1894 to 1898 he became the national secretary and the guiding spirit of the Catholic Total Abstinence Union of America. Founded in 1872 as a national network of parish-based temperance societies, the union reached a membership of 100,000 Catholics in 1896. Membership growth was due in part to Doyle's efforts to increase union publications and circulate inexpensive temperance tracts. In 1894 he created the union's national monthly, *Temperance Truth*, and served as its editor until 1898.

In cooperation with fellow Paulist Walter Elliott, who sought to develop missionary programs directed to non-Catholics, Doyle both raised funds and developed large consignments of apologetic literature for free distribution. In 1896 the two priests founded the Catholic Missionary Union to encourage national support among the bishops for the work of conversion. In the same year, Doyle began publication of the *Missionary*, a monthly magazine that served as the official organ of the union.

In 1903 Doyle moved to Washington, D.C., to serve as first rector of the Apostolic Mission House on the campus of the Catholic University of America. The Mission House was an institute designed to train diocesan priests in the methods of missionary preaching and the work of non-Catholic conversion. With these new responsibilities, he resigned the editorship of the *Catholic World* in 1904. Under his direction the Mission House also served as a center for the printing and distribution of missionary literature.

In 1905 Cardinal James Gibbons (1834–1921) appointed Doyle to serve as liaison between the Catholic bishops and the White House for the recommendation of priests as military chaplains. Prior to Doyle's appointment, a committee of American bishops had met infrequently to nominate candidates. Doyle worked closely with Theodore Roosevelt and his successor, William Howard Taft. In addition to appointments, Doyle was given oversight of all Catholic chaplains in the army and navy. In 1908 he opened a central office in Washington where chaplains could meet and report on their activities. Doyle's office was to develop into the Military Ordinariate or Diocese of the United States following the First World War.

A chronic sufferer of diabetes, Doyle was diagnosed in 1912 with nephritis or Bright's disease. In late July, overworked and seriously ill, he traveled to his native San Francisco to visit his family. Upon his arrival he was immediately hospitalized, and he died two days later.

• The Doyle papers are housed at the Paulist Archives in Washington, D.C.; the archives also contain materials related to the *Catholic World* and the Apostolic Mission House. Files of the Catholic Total Abstinence Union and *Temperance Truth* are housed at the Archives of the Archdiocese of Philadelphia, St. Charles Borromeo Seminary. Files on Doyle's years as liaison for military chaplains are at the Military Archdiocese of the United States in Silver Spring, Md. Obituaries are in the *New York Times*, 10 Aug. 1912, and the *San Francisco Monitor* and the *Brooklyn Tablet*, both 17 Aug. 1912.

PAUL GERARD ROBICHAUD

DOYLE, James Henry (29 Aug. 1897–9 Feb. 1981), naval officer, was born in Astoria, New York, the son of John Joseph Doyle, the assistant chief clerk in the Department of Health in Jamaica, New York, and Elizabeth Acheson Johnson. Winning an appointment to the U.S. Naval Academy in 1916, James Doyle made wartime summer cruises in the battleships *Arkansas* and *Connecticut* and was commissioned as a member of the class of 1920 on 6 June 1919.

For the next seven years Doyle served aboard a variety of warships. In 1924 he married Eleanor Ruth Fields; they had two children. In 1926 he was detailed to the office of the judge advocate general. Attending George Washington University Law School from 1926 to 1929, he graduated with distinction and was admitted to practice in the District of Columbia and before the Supreme Court. Over the next decade Doyle's sea assignments were generally aboard destroyers, including duty as commanding officer of the *Sands* in 1937–1938. Following service in the Philippines, he in August 1940 advanced to command of Destroyer Division Sixty-seven and oversaw the transfer of his warships to the Royal Navy in Halifax, Nova Scotia, Canada, the following month as part of the Destroyers-Bases Agreement.

In September 1940 Doyle took the helm of the assault cargo ship *Regulus*, thereby beginning his long association with the navy's amphibious forces. He participated in the initial landings at Guadalcanal and Tulagi and in the operations that followed until the conclusion of the Solomon Islands campaigns in July 1943, earning the Legion of Merit for "outstanding ability . . . utmost courage, perseverance and heroic devotion to duty."

Doyle then returned to Washington, where he served in the Office of the Chief of Naval Operations from November 1943 to April 1945. Going to sea again as captain of the light cruiser *Pasadena*, he won the Bronze Star with Combat "V" for directing his vessel in three antishipping strikes and in shelling the Japanese home islands.

With peace came more shore duty. In 1946 Doyle was detailed to the United Nations (UN) Security Council as a member of its Military Staff Committee. Following his promotion to rear admiral on 7 August 1947, he took the post of inspector-instructor of naval reserves in the Thirteenth Naval District and then assumed the amphibious training command of the Pacific Fleet on 26 March 1948.

In January 1950 Doyle was transferred to head up Amphibious Group One, and he was overseeing a training exercise in Japanese waters when the Korean War broke out in June. While his ships prepared to rush troops of the U.S. First Cavalry Division from Japan to Korea, Doyle considered landing them at Inch'ŏn but ultimately chose P'ohang for their 18 July debarkation.

As the navy's amphibious expert, Doyle was then drawn by General of the Army Douglas MacArthur, commander of the United Nations Forces, into organizing the Inch'ŏn riposte. Doyle's earlier studies now laid the groundwork for the UN counteroffensive. Given the constricted approaches to the harbor, the swift currents in its channels, and its 33-foot tidal range, Doyle expressed his reservations to MacArthur on 23 August; "The best I can say is that Inch'ŏn is not impossible."

Following the general's decision for a landing on 15 September, Doyle directed the planning of the large and complex operation in only twenty-three days, "a record which seems likely to stand in military history" (Cagle and Manson, p. 84). Of necessity, telephone conversations took the place of written directives. Lacking time for any rehearsals, Doyle ordered that lower-ranking personnel be informed of the broad details of the assault so they could exercise initiative intelligently.

Doyle personally assumed command of the Attack Force, a job that included coordination of the naval gunfire and close air support for the troops. On 15 September he risked the capture of his valuable landing craft by ordering them stranded overnight on the tidal flats so they could serve as depot ships for the troops. Following the success of the invasion, Doyle received the army's Silver Star for "conspicuous gallantry." MacArthur named Doyle, along with Admiral Arthur D. Struble and General Oliver P. Smith, as having "delivered a performance in planning and execution which not only sustained our country's great naval tradition, but which in ultimate effect is probably unexcelled in the history of warfare."

After the United Nations offensive into North Korea, Doyle moved to the eastern side of the peninsula to command the Attack Force at the Wŏnsan landings on 19 October. Following Allied reverses in the late fall, he was placed in charge, as commander of Task Force 90, of the withdrawal of United Nations forces from Hungnam. In a two-week operation beginning on 10 December, Doyle skillfully oversaw, at small cost, the evacuation of 105,000 UN soldiers and 91,000 civilian refugees.

For his able conduct from the beginning of the war, Doyle won the Distinguished Service Medal and was elevated in September 1951 to president of the navy's Board of Inspection and Survey. In May 1952 he was appointed chair of the Joint Amphibious Board at Little Creek, Virginia. He retired on 1 November 1953 with the rank of vice admiral. After various consulting jobs, he made his home in Austin, Texas, and resumed his legal career, becoming a member of the Texas bar. Doyle died in Oakland, California. His older son, James H. Doyle, Jr., also enjoyed a distinguished naval career, becoming the third deputy chief of Naval Operations (Surface Warfare) and retiring, like his father, as a vice admiral.

During his 37-year career, Doyle gained a reputation as an officer with an unusual affinity for his sailors and their families. He ably filled a wide array of assignments, but he made his most lasting mark in the power projection role of amphibious warfare.

• A biographical sketch of Doyle is "Amphib Commander Honored," *Surface Warfare*, Aug. 1982, pp. 8–9. His Korean War service is detailed in Malcolm W. Cagle and Frank A. Manson, *The Sea War in Korea* (1957). An obituary is in the *New York Times*, 11 Feb. 1981.

MALCOLM MUIR, JR.

DOYLE, John Thomas (26 Nov. 1819–23 Dec. 1906), lawyer, was born in New York City, the son of John Doyle, a noted bookseller, and Frances Glinden. Doyle was raised in New York City and Ireland. He graduated as valedictorian in 1838 from Georgetown College in Washington, D.C., from which he obtained an additional A.M. degree in 1840. He studied law at Columbia Law School and was admitted to the New York bar in May 1842.

Doyle practiced law in New York until 1851. In that year, while on vacation in Nicaragua, he met industrialist and financier Cornelius Vanderbilt (1794–1877), who induced Doyle to accept a position as general agent of the American Atlantic & Pacific Canal Company. Through this company Vanderbilt hoped to build an interoceanic canal. Remaining in Nicaragua for a year, Doyle built a road from Lake Nicaragua to the Pacific and organized a transportation service across the country. While there, he became interested in the former Spanish colonial administration, particularly its relation to the Roman Catholic church.

When Vanderbilt failed to obtain the capital needed for his canal project, Doyle resigned and moved to San Francisco, where he resumed the practice of law in January 1853. Archbishop Joseph S. Alemany retained him to recover possession and title to the old Spanish missions of California through the land claim proceedings. (In the late years of Mexican California most of the mission buildings and gardens had been seized and sold by the government.) Doyle successfully established the illegality of these sales and reclaimed the church buildings and immediately surrounding lands for the Roman Catholic church. In 1863 he married Antonia Pons. Three years later they moved to Menlo Park, California, where they raised eight children.

As a distinguished trial lawyer, Doyle participated in many of the important legal controversies of late nineteenth-century California. His most famous legal cause was his representation of the California Roman Catholic church in the Pious Fund litigation. The case, which would occupy Doyle intermittently for more than four decades, traced its roots to the early eighteenth century, when several wealthy Spanish Creoles in Mexico founded a trust for the support of the California missions. Mexico seized the assets of the trust fund in 1842, while promising to pay 6 percent interest to support the missions. However, it soon defaulted. The California archbishop hired Doyle in 1857 to file a claim for this lost income stream should opportunity present itself. Doyle spent years diligently investigating the obscure origins of the claim. In 1870 a Mixed Claims Commission was appointed by Mexico and the United States for the investigation and confirmation of private claims accruing after 1848. After many hearings and much delay, Doyle secured a judgment that the interest on the misappropriated trust was $904,700.99 for the years 1848 to 1869. The commission ordered Mexico to pay the California Roman Catholic church one-half of that sum, that for Alta California, in annual installments of $43,080.99 over twenty-one years.

Mexico paid those installments but then disclaimed any further liability for additional interest. The United States and Mexico submitted the controversy to further arbitration at The Hague in 1902. Doyle continued as one of the attorneys representing the California Roman Catholic church. The Court of Arbitration ordered Mexico to pay $43,050 to the church as a permanent annual annuity. Mexico made payments, including the arrearage, until 1912, when it ceased payment altogether. The Pious Fund arrearage was finally settled and the perpetuity feature waived when Mexico made a lump sum payment in 1967.

Throughout his long career, Doyle actively undertook a wide variety of civic responsibilities. For thirty years he was a trustee of the San Francisco Law Library. He was a regent of the University of California (1868), a state commissioner of transportation (1877–1878), and, beginning in 1874, a trustee of the town of Menlo Park. He was a critic of the railroads, and his call for the abandonment of direct government regulation of freight rates and the substitution of rates based on a classification of goods and distance to be carried was an advancement in the eventual development of the modern tariff.

Doyle published numerous articles and pamphlets. Most were on topics arising out of the Pious Fund litigation, but other publications discussed such diverse topics as California railroad policy, the discovery of San Francisco Bay, the California missions, and the Electoral Commission of 1877. He was also proficient in French, Spanish, and Italian and maintained an extensive library. After noting the civil law court procedure in Nicaragua, he resolved certain questions regarding Shakespeare's legal accuracy in the *Merchant of Venice* in an article for the *Overland Monthly* (July 1886), which was favorably credited by Shakespearean scholars.

In an address at Santa Clara College in 1870, Doyle urged the formation of a California Historical Society. It was organized, and Doyle was one of its trustees. Although the society soon fell into desuetude, it was revived in the 1880s, and Doyle became its president in 1887. The 1880s incarnation of the California Historical Society likewise was abandoned, and the present society traces its continuous history only to 1922. During its 1870–1875 epoch, the society published a four-volume edition of Francisco Palóu's *Noticias* and

Felipe de Neve's *Reglamento*. Doyle edited all five volumes and contributed a foreword to the Palou series. Zephyrin Englehardt, the Franciscan historian, claimed that Doyle's edition of Palou's early history of California "abounds" in misprints.

Sometime before Doyle's retirement from active law practice in 1888, he became interested in wine production and established a vineyard in Cupertino, California. Combining that interest with his energetic civic activities for several terms he served as viticultural commissioner of California. He died in Menlo Park.

Oscar T. Shuck in his *History of the Bench and Bar of California* (1901 ed.) called Doyle "impatient and irascible" but also praised him as "good-natured at heart" and having "materially aided many younger members of the profession." The California historian Hubert Howe Bancroft, a keen appraiser of human talent and failings, wrote in 1890 (*History of California*, vol. 7) that Doyle was "a very conspicuous and reputable jurist . . . among the ablest lawyers on the coast . . . [and] a scholar of rare culture and refinement."

Doyle made his greatest mark as a lawyer. His acclaimed triumphs were the recovery of the California mission lands for the Roman Catholic church and the success of the Pious Fund claim against Mexico.

• Doyle's papers are located primarily in the California State Library and California Historical Society Library. Doyle was a friend of William T. Sherman, and the two maintained a correspondence. There are numerous writings about the Pious Fund litigation, all of which have information on Doyle, including Kenneth M. Johnson, *The Pious Fund* (1963); Francis J. Weber, "The United States Versus Mexico: The Final Settlement of the Pious Fund of the Californias," *Southern California Quarterly* 51 (1969): 97–152; and one of Doyle's many pieces, "Recovery of the Pious Fund," in *History of the Bench and Bar of California*, ed. Oscar T. Shuck (1901), pp. 81–91. Short biographical articles are in Francis J. Weber, "John Thomas Doyle: Pious Fund Historiographer," *Southern California Quarterly* 49 (1967): 297–304, and Oscar T. Shuck, ed., *History of the Bench and Bar of California* (1901), pp. 518–20. An obituary is in the *San Francisco Chronicle*, 24 Dec. 1906.

DAVID J. LANGUM

DOYLE, Sarah Elizabeth (23 Mar. 1830–21 Dec. 1922), educator and activist, was born in Providence, Rhode Island, the daughter of Thomas Doyle, a bookbinder, and Martha Dorrance Jones. Her father died when Sarah was eleven years old. Her brother, Thomas Arthur, was mayor of Providence between 1864 and 1886, possessing a strong commitment to public schools and urban planning. Sarah Doyle attended the local public grammar school, then entered Providence High School in 1843, its first year, graduating in 1846. She began nearly four decades of teaching immediately after high school, first teaching for ten years in private schools. In 1856 Doyle joined the girls department of Providence High, serving as department principal from 1878 until her retirement in 1892. Doyle was an active and influential teacher, responsible for supervising her colleagues. She was a vice president of the Rhode Island Institute of Instruction, a teachers' continuing-education organization, and she headed the literature section of its reading circle for several years. Doyle impressed many of her women students with her skill and dedication, and several who became teachers founded the Sarah E. Doyle Club in her honor. Organized in 1894 for the "mutual assistance and culture of members," for decades the club served hundreds of Providence teachers through lectures and classes. She became the first woman to preside over a meeting of the National Education Association when president Thomas Bicknell gave her the gavel for a single session in Madison, Wisconsin, in 1884.

Concomitant with her teaching career, Doyle pursued an active public life, especially in organizations dedicated to women. Suffrage was a hard fight in the state, and Doyle's long involvement in the Rhode Island Suffrage Association included lobbying unsuccessfully for a suffrage clause in the 1897 state constitution. In the 1870s she served on the board of Lady Visitors to Penal Institutions, a role that disappointed her because it lacked real power. Naturally, many of Doyle's public interests involved education. She joined the Providence Free Kindergarten Association to encourage this innovation in the public schools. In 1898 she was named by the mayor as the only woman in a group of five citizens to investigate the administration of Providence schools, which were in danger of shutting down because of fiscal difficulties. The investigative group lambasted the school committee's management and recommended changing the large ward-based committee to a small board of education. Doyle also joined with a group of prominent Rhode Islanders in founding the coeducational Rhode Island School of Design (RISD). Following two decades of advocacy, RISD was created in 1877, when members of the Women's Centennial Commission contributed their remaining exhibition funds. Doyle was one of four RISD officers, serving as secretary from 1877 to 1889. She served as a director of the Providence Athenaeum (1899–1903), and she supported the American Women's Table at the Zoological Station in Naples, Italy, a method for sustaining women's research opportunities.

Doyle's most prominent leadership developed through the women's club movement, which she viewed as an avenue for the advanced education that women of her generation rarely received in colleges or universities. With four other Providence women, she founded the Rhode Island Women's Club in 1876 and served as its first president until 1884. This club, and its subsequent involvement in the General Federation of Women's Clubs, absorbed Doyle's energies for a number of years, allowing her access to a national network. Doyle helped to create a constitution for the new national General Federation, and she pushed Rhode Island to create a state federation in 1895.

In Doyle's view, women's clubs combined literary education with utilitarian purpose: "the education of women for work they ought to do." She viewed the clubs as advancing both self-education and activism for women, urging members first to educate themselves and then to speak out for suffrage, education, women's self-support, and better urban conditions. She stressed women's need for training in public speaking and clear thinking, noting, "It is not enough to have right beliefs, it is necessary to know how to express them so as to move others in the right direction." Although acknowledging the prevailing Victorian notion of a "sphere" of proper activity for women, Doyle asserted that this "so-called sphere is one with an infinite and indeterminable radius."

In the 1890s, Doyle helped to invigorate an effort to admit women to Brown University, an activity that became the center of her most effective leadership and fundraising. The premier college in the state, Brown had resisted earlier appeals by women's advocates. However, the new university president, E. Benjamin Andrews, and his wife showed themselves to be supporters of women, and joined with women's groups to open university resources. In 1891 women were permitted to take examinations; the next year, to earn graduate and undergraduate degrees. But all teaching for women was strictly outside the university, by sympathetic male professors who offered parallel courses for women. Limited resources notwithstanding, the venture soon proved very popular, making obvious the need for a secure affiliation and a permanent structure.

With Andrews's encouragement, the women organized the Rhode Island Society for the Collegiate Education of Women (RISCEW) in 1896, with Doyle as president (a post she held until 1919). Like many men's institutions, Brown resisted incorporating its women's college until the venture could pay for itself, a fact accomplished in 1896 through the successful efforts of Doyle and RISCEW. The group raised $75,000 for a women's building on land the university provided; in only one year, they had raised sufficient funds to begin construction. The large, commodious Pembroke Hall was dedicated and turned over from RISCEW to Brown in 1897, with only $600 remaining on its debt.

RISCEW served as more than a fiscal patron of the new Women's College and Doyle as more than its chief fundraiser. With no women faculty or administrators on campus, RISCEW took responsibility for monitoring women's academic and social lives. The organization hosted teas, provided lectures, offered administrative support, and significantly, created a loan fund for female students. Even after a woman dean was hired in 1900, Doyle continued to chair the Women's College Advisory Committee and regularly offered chapel talks along with her administrative expertise. Over several decades, RISCEW raised money for a gymnasium and other buildings, as well as Women's College furnishings. Only when women's position on campus had solidified could the early advocates ease their daily involvement. Doyle was eighty-eight years old when she resigned the presidency of RISCEW; she died in Providence three years later. She never married.

Doyle's legacy to women has been honored by Brown University, which has acknowledged her leadership in sustaining the early women's college. Brown made her the first woman to receive an honorary degree (1894) and in 1975 created the Sarah Doyle Women's Center as the focus for women's campus organizations.

• There is no known collection of Doyle's papers; the papers of the Women's Club are housed at Rhode Island Historical Society. Her only publications are her *History of the Rhode Island Women's Club, 1876–1893*, printed as the club's 1893 annual report (Rider Collection, John Hay Library, Brown University) and her speech for the 1897 dedication of Pembroke Hall (Brown University Archives). Her leadership activities are best understood through the *Records of the Rhode Island Society for the Collegiate Education of Women* (manuscript volumes, John Hay Library, Brown University). Annual reports of the Rhode Island Women's Club and the Rhode Island Suffrage Association are less detailed. Contemporary accounts of women's club activities that cover Rhode Island include Jane Cunningham Croly's *The History of the Woman's Club Movement in America* (1898). More recent scholarship on women's clubs and on the early years of the Women's College at Brown University have clarified the contributions of both Doyle and women's organizations. See Grace Hawk, "Sarah E. Doyle: Gifted Organizer Of Pembroke's First Friends," *Pembroke Alumna* (Apr. 1967), and Hawk, *Pembroke College in Brown University, the First Seventy-Five Years, 1891–1966* (1967); Linda Eisenmann, "Women at Brown University, 1891–1930: Academically Identical, But Socially Quite Distinct" (Ed.D. diss., Harvard Univ., 1987); and Polly Welts Kaufman, *The Search for Equity: Women at Brown University, 1891–1991* (1991). An obituary is in the *Providence Journal*, 22 Dec. 1922.

LINDA EISENMANN

D'OYLEY, Edward (1617–1675), founder of English Jamaica, was born at Albourne, Wiltshire, England, the second son of John D'Oyley and Lucy Nicholas. D'Oyley's was "no inconsiderable family, but persecuted these many years for the cause of religion." Their puritanism was no bar to an advantageous marriage, however, and D'Oyley was to rely upon his namesake, Sir Edward Nicholas, secretary of state to both Charles I and Charles II, for protection and promotion. D'Oyley's puritanism took him from his legal education at the Inns of Court to join the parliamentary army in 1642. By 1650 Lieutenant Colonel D'Oyley stood at the head of the new English military profession. He was the dedicatee of Major Richard Elton's *The Compleat Body of the Art Military* (1650, 1659), which celebrated the rise of the meritorious gentleman volunteer to command of the army of the state.

In 1654 D'Oyley was commissioned in "the Western Design," the expedition Oliver Cromwell dispatched to conquer a base in the West Indies for the war against Spain. D'Oyley took command of a regiment recruited from Barbados laborers (by Colonel Lewis Morris, the founder of the New York family). Rebuffed from Hispaniola, the English army seized Jamaica in May 1655. D'Oyley, a veteran of Ireland, and his men, former servants in Barbados, began to implement Cromwell's policy of Irish-style military planta-tion. By October, D'Oyley was president of the army's council of war and one of the few officers prepared to cooperate with Major General Robert Sedgewick of Massachusetts, the conqueror of Nova Scotia and Newfoundland, whom Cromwell had ordered to fortify and to farm Jamaica and to recruit it from the other English colonies. From Nevis and Barbados, Sedgewick was successful, but his emissary Daniel Gookin could not persuade either Massachusetts men or Virginians to transplant and remained in New England to cultivate the Algonquians.

In September 1657 D'Oyley became "Commander in Chief of all his Highness Forces in America." His journal of proceedings "during the time he held the chief command in the Island of Jamaica (19 Nov. 1655–27 M[a]y 1662)" is for the second stage of English colonization what Smith's Winthrop's, and Bradford's journals had been for its first generation: the record of a society's founder. Unlike his predecessors, however, D'Oyley was a military conqueror and the agent of a modern state. So the Jamaican institutions that he created were the template of the military executive model afterward imposed on England's formerly autonomous American provinces.

D'Oyley adopted the new model of the garrisoned town, with its special-purpose government buildings, for his provincial headquarters at Villa La Vega (St. Iago). He constructed a modern port citadel at Cagway (Port Royal). Thence he led the forces that ended five years of guerilla war with the Spanish by two decisive victories, at the Ocho Rios in October 1657 and at the Rio Nuevo in June 1658. D'Oyley's infantry were drawn from soldier settlers, a militia. He had converted each of his six regiment's quarters into a plantation, endowing every officer and soldier with land. Some of D'Oyley's redcoats became cowboys. Cattle hides purchased provisions from New England until agrarian self-sufficiency was achieved with the help of civilian settlers from the Leeward Islands. D'Oyley promised them that, quitrents aside, they were "to have no other taxation laid upon them except what they shall consent to by their deputies for the defence of the Island."

Representative government was delayed until the collapse of the protectorate and the end of the war with Spain. Instead, Jamaican belligerency and lawlessness were enhanced when, in 1657, D'Oyley invited the English buccaneers to transfer their base from Tortuga to Jamaica. Jamaican raiders captured from Cuba the wherewithal of plantation development in Jamaica. Goods captured from the Spanish also underwrote trade with England. In July 1660 D'Oyley freighted the *Edward*, the first ship built in Jamaica, with a mixed cargo of Cuban captures and Jamaican produce. D'Oyley's initiatives had produced two, ultimately incompatible, Jamaican lifestyles: planting and civil government; privateering and martial law. The planter party would be led by one of D'Oyley's captains, Sir Thomas Lynch, and the privateering party by another, Sir Henry Morgan, and, such was the continuing conflict between England's own mercantile and imperial parties, they were successive island executives.

In August 1660 D'Oyley's militarism manifested itself once more when Jamaica's libertarians revolted. Civilian settlers and merchants, General D'Oyley complained, "not being under the Military Power have traitorously and seditiously dared to infuse into the soldiers principles of liberty and freedom from my authority" and had demanded "constables and civil officers" in place of provost martials and martial law. The dissident's quarters were surrounded and their surrendered leaders convicted and shot, but D'Oyley, hearing of the royal restoration in England and so the presumptive end of his command, feared that he might have murdered the mutineers. In January 1661, however, the royal authorities, including the Cromwellian general George Monck, the engineer of the restoration, and Sir Edward Nicholas, restored as secretary of state, decided to reappoint D'Oyley as governor, with full martial power.

On 8 February King Charles signed the commissions and instructions for Edward D'Oyley that carried the imperial policies of the Cromwellian protectorate into the Stuart restoration. The elements of royal authority in America were to be the king's commission and instructions to his viceroy, the customs and constitutions of other colonies, and executive discretion. Imperialism's instruments were to be both martial law and civil courts, headed by the governor and composed of his councilors. D'Oyley received the royal instructions on 2 June 1661. He constituted his field officers as his council. With them, he regulated labor, prices, and wages, defining the island's civil economy and shaping its society until he was replaced by one of the king's callow "young lords," Thomas, Lord Windsor, in August 1662.

In September 1662 D'Oyley set out on an epic voyage home. After receiving the royal pardon for his acts in the interregnum, D'Oyley recommended a militant imperial policy. So he was pensioned off by the pacific ministry of the earl of Clarendon. Living a retired life in St. Martin-in-the-fields, D'Oyley died just when his brand of Protestant imperialism was revived by the Danby regime. Edward D'Oyley left no heirs, but he did bequeath Jamaica to the empire, "the vastest expence and greatest design that was ever made by the English."

• D'Oyley's journal is Additional Manuscripts (Add. Mss.) 12423, British Library. The records of his administration are in Add. Ms. 12401–12440, 11410, 11411; and Egerton Ms. 2395. His commission and instructions are in Add. Mss. 12428, 6–13b, Colonial Office 138 (Jamaica Entry Books) / vol. 1, 3b–10, and are calendared in W. Noel Sainsbury et al., eds., *Calendar of State Papers, Colonial Series, America and West Indies, 1661–1668*, nos. 20 and 22. D'Oyley's pension is recorded in Add. Mss. 15897, 23. Other printed primary sources include Thomas Birch, ed., *A Collection of the State Papers of John Thurloe, Esq. . . .* (1742); C. H. Firth, ed., *The Clarke Papers*, vol. 3, Publications of the Camden Society, n.s., 61 (1899); and *The Narrative of General Venables*, Publications of the Camden Society, n.s., 59, 60 (1899, 1900). The histories of Jamaica all depend upon Edward Long, *The History of Jamaica* (1774). Modern specialist studies include Stanley Arthur Goodwin Taylor, *The Western Design: An Account of Cromwell's Expedition to the Caribbean* (1965); Agnes M. Whitson, *The Constitutional Development of Jamaica, 1660–1729* (1929); and Clarence Henry Haring, *The Buccaneers in the West Indies in the XVII Century* (1910). The fullest biography is Frank Cundall, *The Governors of Jamaica in the Seventeenth Century* (1936), pp. 1–9. Complete citations and an extended consideration of Edward D'Oyley's career is in Stephen Saunders Webb, *The Governors-General: The English Army and the Definition of the Empire, 1569–1681* (1979), especially chap. 4.

STEPHEN SAUNDERS WEBB

DOZIER, Edward Pasqual (23 Apr. 1916–2 May 1971), anthropologist, was born in Santa Clara Pueblo, New Mexico, the son of Thomas Sublette Dozier, a Euroamerican lawyer, teacher, and Indian arts and crafts dealer, and Leocadia Gutierrez, a member of Santa Clara (Tewa) Pueblo. In 1893 Thomas Dozier had left his law practice in Cameron, Missouri, to accept a civil service position as a day school teacher at Santa Clara Pueblo in New Mexico Territory. He quickly developed a keen interest in Tewa language and culture. In his writings and field collecting for museum anthropologists, Dozier aspired to be an ethnologist, but it was Edward, the youngest of the eleven children, who would realize his ambitions.

In Edward Dozier's life there were three recurring themes: language, education, and multiculturalism. In his youth, he was trilingual, learning his mother's native Tewa language, his father's English language, and the Spanish language from nearby New Mexican communities. His knowledge of languages and his writing abilities served him well in his assimilation to cultures outside of Santa Clara. When he attended Santa Clara Day School (1926–1928), the U.S. federal policy of Indian education required Indian students to learn English. At St. Michael's Catholic school in Santa Fe, which Dozier attended from seventh grade through high school, he was one of a small number of American Indians in a primarily Hispanic school where Spanish and English dominated the classrooms and schoolyards. In his senior year in high school, Dozier began to express an interest in ethnology and American Indian history and studied his father's manuscripts and family history. Taking advantage of the new college loan program offered under the Indian Reorganization Act, Dozier attended the University of New Mexico from 1935 to 1937. The transition to college life was difficult. Dozier's grades were not encouraging. Consequently, he left school temporarily from 1937 to 1939 and worked as a clerk at both the U.S. Indian School in Albuquerque and at the Indian Bureau in Washington, D.C.

Dozier enlisted in the U.S. Army Air Force in 1941. In the last summer of military duty, Dozier conducted a social study of the Chamarros in Charankanoa village on Saipan Island in the Marianas as a personal educational project. On 19 November 1945 he was honorably discharged.

The GI Bill made it financially possible for Dozier to return to the University of New Mexico to continue his anthropological studies. In 1947 he completed his undergraduate degree. Two years later he earned his master's degree with the thesis "Tewa Verb Structure II," a linguistic analysis of his native Santa Clara dialect. Dozier began his formal study of linguistics as an indigenous anthropologist by blending data from other native speakers with his personal knowledge of the Tewa language.

Transferring to the new Ph.D. program at UCLA, Dozier studied under linguist Harry Hoijer and ethnologists Ralph Beals and Walter Goldschmidt. In 1952 Dozier received the first doctoral degree in anthropology from UCLA and became the first American Indian academic anthropologist. His dissertation fieldwork was conducted at Tewa village (Hano) on First Mesa at the Hopi Reservation in Arizona. A major contribution to acculturation studies in anthropology was Dozier's framing of the complex relationships between two American Indian communities. Dozier subverted the typical approach of making hegemonic comparisons between a dominant Euroamerican community and a subordinate American Indian community and instead focused on the changing power relations (resistance and accommodation) in social and ceremonial organization between the Tewa and Hopi. In his lifetime, Dozier's creative approach to acculturation studies at Tewa village was never fully acknowledged as an innovation in ethnology made by an indigenous anthropologist. Later, Watson Smith acknowledged Dozier's contribution, but his innovation had no effect on the way future acculturation studies were conducted (Smith, *American Antiquity* 21:324–25).

During his twenty-year career as an anthropologist, Dozier held several teaching positions in ethnology and linguistics: instructor at the University of Oregon (1951–1952), instructor (1953–1954), assistant professor (1954–1957), and associate professor (1958–1959) at Northwestern University, and professor at the University of Arizona (1960–1971). At the University of Arizona, Dozier held positions as American Indian student adviser and chair of the Indian Advisory Committee and the American Indian Studies Program. He was a Fellow at the Center for Advanced Studies in the Behavioral Sciences at Stanford University (1958–1959) and served on the board of directors of the Association on American Indian Affairs in New York City (1955–1971). He was the recipient of numerous grants, including the John Hay Whitney Foundation Opportunity Fellowship, the Social Science Research Council, the Wenner-Gren Foundation, and the National Science Foundation.

As a nonindigenous anthropologist, Dozier wrote a Philippine ethnography on the peace pact system as practiced in 1959–1960 by the Kalingas in northern Luzon province in the Philippines. Some critics believe that Dozier did not receive full membership among his professional peers until he conducted the Kalinga research, as only then did Dozier fulfill a basic tenet of anthropological practice at that time by studying the "anthropological other."

Dozier married his first Anglo wife, Claire Elizabeth "Betty" Butler, in 1943. The marriage ended in divorce in 1948. Their only child, a daughter, was raised as a Tewa child by her grandmother, aunts, and uncles at Santa Clara Pueblo. Dozier's second marriage was to Marianne Fink in 1950. They had two children. At age fifty-five, Dozier died of a heart attack at his home in Tucson, Arizona.

Dozier's professional career marked a turning point in the social and political relationships between anthropologists and North American Indians. Earlier contributions were made by numerous American Indian individuals from diverse native cultures as "informants" and interpreters, by field-trained ethnographers, and by museum anthropologists. Dozier extended this intellectual tradition in a modest and innovative manner with his academic accomplishments as an indigenous anthropologist of his native Tewa culture and the interrelated pueblo cultures in the American Southwest.

• The Edward P. Dozier Papers, including his Hopi-Tewa and Kalinga field notes, are in the Arizona State Museum's Archives at the University of Arizona. His dissertation was published as "The Hopi-Tewa of Arizona" in the *University of California Publications in American Archaeology and Ethnology* (1954) and as *Hano: A Tewa Indian Community in Arizona* (1966). For a synthesis of Dozier's research on pueblo communities in the American Southwest, refer to *The Pueblo Indians of North America* (1970). His major Kalinga publications are *Mountain Arbiters: The Changing Life of a Philippine Hill People* (1966) and *The Kalinga of Northern Luzon, Philippines* (1967). For a biography of his early life based on archival materials in the Dozier papers, see Marilyn Norcini, "The Education of a Native American Anthropologist: Edward P. Dozier (1916–71)" (master's thesis, Univ. of Arizona, 1988). For an obituary and bibliography of Dozier's work, refer to the *American Anthropologist* 74 (1972): 740–46.

MARILYN NORCINI

DRAGGING CANOE (?–?1792), Cherokee war leader, was born probably near the Little Tennessee River (Tenn.), the son of White Owl. His Indian name was Chincanacina or Tsi-yu'gunsi'ni. By 1775, when he emerged as a leader of the Cherokees resisting European-American expansion, he had a fully grown son and was an important headman among the Overhill Cherokees of the Little Tennessee. In March of that year a group of speculators under Richard Henderson of North Carolina met Cherokee leaders at Sycamore Shoals on the Watauga River to purchase 27,000 square miles between the Cumberland, Ohio, and Kentucky Rivers, most of present-day Kentucky. Dragging Canoe was willing to cede land north of the Kentucky (already surrendered to Virginia) and a path from the Watauga to the Kentucky. He passionately protested the wider cession accepted by some of the older chiefs, however, and aborted one day of negotiations by storming from the conference. His celebrated warning that "a dark cloud" hung over Kentucky ("it was the bloody ground, and would be dark and difficult to settle") may have suggested that he intended resisting occupation. If so, he was challenging not only Henderson but also established Cherokee chiefs such as Attakullaculla, the Raven, and Oconostota.

In 1776, at the outbreak of the American Revolution, Dragging Canoe was more concerned with resisting encroachment on unceded Cherokee land on the Watauga, and in March he was at Mobile seeking supplies from the British. The British saw value in diversionary raids against the frontiers but wanted Dragging Canoe to wait until more support could be given him. In July, however, a party of Shawnee and other northern Indians visited Chote on the Little Tennessee and inflamed the younger Cherokees with the war spirit. Dragging Canoe wanted to attack the Wataugans before they could prepare proper defenses and used the visit of the northerners to muster enough support for a Cherokee offensive, contrary to the advice of both older chiefs and British officials.

Dragging Canoe led a party of Overhills against settlements on the upper Holston and Watauga but was defeated by American militia at Island Flats, near present-day Kingsport, Tennessee, in July 1776. Nevertheless, war parties scourged the frontiers of Virginia, the Carolinas, and Georgia. Retaliating armies destroyed Lower, Valley, Middle, and Overhill Cherokee towns, and in 1777 the Indians were compelled to cede more land in the Carolinas and Tennessee. Dragging Canoe was unimpressed, and with perhaps 500 warriors, mainly Overhills, and their families withdrew down the Tennessee, to Chickamauga Creek. Receiving British provisions from Florida, the "Chickamaugas" (as whites called the band) accompanied Loyalists on attacks in Georgia and Carolina and obstructed the revolutionaries' communications along the Tennessee to the Mississippi. Dragging Canoe's hostility was not moderated by American invasions of the Chickamauga settlements in 1779 and 1782. He simply transferred his people to the more inaccessible lower Tennessee, where the state lines of present-day Georgia, Alabama, and Tennessee meet. Thereabouts five new Chickamauga towns were established, Dragging Canoe's own being Running Water (Marion County, Tenn.).

After the Revolution Dragging Canoe refused to negotiate or recognize land treaties and waged a guerrilla war against white settlements throughout Kentucky and Tennessee. Traders from Spanish-held Florida resided at the Chickamauga towns, which also received assistance from the Upper Creeks after 1786 and Cheeseekau's party of Shawnees. Increased pressure on Indian land from settlers and speculators encouraged by North Carolina and Georgia and the failure of the U.S. government to protect the boundary established in the Hopewell treaty of 1785 also brought Dragging Canoe occasional support from the Upper Cherokees, particularly after borderers murdered the senior Cherokee chief, Old Tassel, in 1788.

The Chickamaugas directed their greatest efforts to isolating the settlements on the Cumberland, founded in 1780; resisting efforts of the Tennessee Company to colonize Muscle Shoals on the lower Tennessee, which

Dragging Canoe successfully cleared in 1786 and 1791; and opposing encroachments in eastern Tennessee, particularly those made by the splinter state of Franklin, formed in 1784. Dragging Canoe's followers levied a cumulatively formidable toll of lives and resources on the expansionists, but they won no major victories, incited retaliation against the more pacific but accessible Upper Cherokees, and failed to arrest the long-term reduction of Indian landholdings.

In July 1791 the Chickamaugas finally joined in discussions with William Blount, the governor of the territory south of the Ohio, at Knoxville. Once again the Cherokees were induced to surrender territory, this time between the French Broad and the Holston, as well as to permit the navigation of the Tennessee. Although some of his followers accepted the treaty, particularly after the annuities awarded the Cherokees were increased, Dragging Canoe himself regarded it as irrelevant and spent the last months of his life trying to build an anti-American confederacy among the southern Indians, inspired by the success of pan-Indianism north of the Ohio. In the spring of 1792 his brother, White Owl's Son, returned from a visit to the British on the Great Lakes with an invitation from the northern Indian confederacy, its confidence increased by its victory over Arthur St. Clair's army, to join a united effort against the Americans. Dragging Canoe traveled first to the Creek leader Alexander McGillivray and then to Piomingo's Chickasaws promoting a southern confederation, but he had little success. He died immediately on his return to the Chickamauga towns, in February or March. Under the military leadership of John Watts the Chickamauga maintained their resistance to the United States for another two years.

In standing against land cessions and breaking with the greater part of the Cherokee people, Dragging Canoe showed courage and resolution, qualities that seldom deserted him. A leader in the same mold as Cochise and Sitting Bull, he was able to maintain a considerable local influence, but his most notable trait was durability. His militance was proof against numerous adversities, including three major invasions of his towns. For almost twenty years his warriors were the most consistent defenders of the aboriginal Old Southwest.

• The most conscientious study of Dragging Canoe is in John P. Brown, *Old Frontiers* (1938), although some of the details are unreliable. Other useful accounts are Robert S. Cotterill, *The Southern Indians* (1954); James Paul Pate, "The Chickamauga" (Ph.D. diss., Michigan State Univ., 1969); and E. Raymond Evans, "Dragging Canoe," *Journal of Cherokee Studies* 2 (1977): 176–89. An older work, John Haywood, *Civil and Political History of the State of Tennessee* (1823), contains extensive details of Chickamauga hostilities but nothing on Dragging Canoe himself.

JOHN SUGDEN

DRAGON, Carmen Martin (28 July 1914–28 Mar. 1984), arranger, conductor, and composer, was born in Antioch, California, the son of Frank Dragon, a building contractor, and Rose Dedio. Both parents were born in Italy. His background in music came naturally: Sunday evenings and holidays were spent making music, with his parents on violin and guitar and Dragon and his brothers Peter and Roland alternating on accordion, clarinet, piano, saxophone, string bass, trombone, and trumpet. Dragon also had perfect pitch. He attended San Jose State College, where his major was music and his minor was psychology. In order to make money, Dragon often interrupted his college education to work, and he did not return to complete his senior year.

Dragon began his professional music career in 1936 by arranging music for a concert orchestra radio broadcast. He had been performing in his own dance band throughout college, but it was his skills as an arranger that drew the attention of composer Meredith Willson, the creator of the musical *The Music Man*, in 1936. Willson, who was the music director of the Western Division of the NBC Radio Network, encouraged Dragon to move to San Francisco. Soon Dragon would quit performing and devote all of his time to arranging. When Willson left NBC in 1937, he took Dragon with him to Hollywood to work as an arranger and conductor on the radio program "Show Boat." Dragon married soprano Eloise Rawitzer, a chorus member of "Showboat," in 1938; they had five children. Rawitzer, whose stage name was the "Voice of Eloise," sang in almost all of Dragon's radio shows, and all five of their children entered the music industry. (His older daughter Carmen became a concert harpist and conductor, and one of Dragon's three sons, Daryl, was a performer with the Beach Boys and was one-half of the music duo the Captain and Tenille, popular in the 1970s and early 1980s.)

Dragon began a career as an arranger for movie musicals, which starred performers such as Gene Kelly, James Cagney, and Spencer Tracy. His work on films began in 1941 with *Time Out for Rhythm*, starring Ann Miller. In 1945 Dragon shared an Academy Award with Morris Stoloff for their score of Jerome Kern's songs in the musical *Cover Girl*, beating thirteen other nominees in the field. In total, Dragon is credited with arranging or scoring thirty films, most of them musicals in the 1940s and 1950s; he also did the score for the horror classic *Invasion of the Body Snatchers* in 1956.

Unable to join active service in World War II because of a leg injury, Dragon instead kept busy in various media. In addition to working in the movies, he composed, arranged, and conducted music for phonograph recordings by entertainers such as Al Jolson, Jane Powell, and Gordon MacRae. Throughout the 1940s he also worked as a conductor for radio shows such as "Baby Snooks," starring comedienne Fanny Brice, and "The Railroad Hour," for which he was the musical director of material ranging from musical comedies to operas. Dragon's musical scope in radio was broad: in addition to comedies and musical programs, he also served as the music director on the "Don Ameche" variety program (1946–1948) and the

"Prudential Hour" drama series (1948–1950). Ultimately, he worked on more than 3,000 hours of radio broadcasts in his career.

In 1949 Dragon was appointed as the music director of the Standard School of Broadcasting, and that same year he began his symphonic career by conducting the Standard Symphony Orchestra of San Francisco. That year also marked the beginning of his work producing programs for the Chevron School Broadcasts, heard weekly in more than 60,000 classrooms across the United States. This he continued until 1975. Later Dragon became the music director/conductor of Chevron's Community Concert series.

When television began growing as a new medium, Dragon was there. In 1951 he was the musical director and conductor of "The Standard Hour," a TV series of musical, orchestral, and ballet performances. He continued his television work on shows such as "The Colgate Comedy Hour" (1954–1956) and an episode of "Dr. Kildare" (1961). He was a prolific recording artist, too, conducting on more than sixty diverse albums for Capitol Records. Among these are *The Music of Christmas*, *L'Italia*, *Echoes of Spain*, *An Evening with Cole Porter*, the seven-volume *Melodies of the Masters* series, and *Americana*, which includes his popular arrangement of "America the Beautiful."

Dragon's symphonic career in the "pops"—popular or light classical arrangements that were first enjoyed in the concert halls of London at the end of the nineteenth century—began when he conducted an annual concert of Gershwin songs at the Hollywood Bowl in the early 1950s. He continued to serve as a guest conductor of the Hollywood Bowl Orchestra summer concerts from 1950 to 1964. He also made guest appearances at the competition-festival "Music In May" in 1968 in Forest Grove, Oregon, and wielded the baton with the symphony orchestras of Chicago, Cincinnati, Cleveland, Los Angeles, Montreal, Portland, and San Francisco. He was referred to as a "virtuoso conductor" in a review of his July 1961 performance as the leader of England's Philharmonia Orchestra (*Musical Opinion*, Aug. 1961, p. 664).

Among Dragon's international appearances were those with the British Broadcasting Company Concert and Symphony Orchestras, the London Symphony, the Royal Philharmonic Orchestra, the Munich Symphony, and the Mozarteum Orchestra in Salzburg. He was also invited, while on a tour of Latin America in February 1962, to conduct Chile's Vina del Mar Sinfonica. When its regular director, Izidor Handler, visited the United States and attended a concert in Cincinnati that Dragon conducted, Dragon invited Handler to take over at the podium for the overture of *Marriage of Figaro*, a surprise delight for the audience.

As a composer, Dragon wrote the patriotic band song "I Am an American" and composed the *Santa Fe* Suite, a work for chorus and orchestra with sound effects. The suite premiered on 8 February 1958 as part of the pops concert of the National Symphony in Constitution Hall in Washington, D.C.

From the mid-1960s until his death, Dragon was the musical director and conductor of the Glendale Symphony Orchestra, founded in 1923 in Glendale, California. Although his association with the Glendale Symphony went back to the West Coast premiere of his *Santa Fe* Suite on 21 November 1958, it was not until the 1965–1966 season that Dragon was officially named its music director. In fact, Dragon had led the Glendale Symphony to a number of "firsts" even before he became its music director. He conducted the orchestra's first appearance on color television in January 1964 (the orchestra had been performing on television specials since 1962). Dragon won an Emmy Award in 1964 for his production of the orchestra's 18 December 1964 special television broadcast, "The Sounds of Christmas," on the NBC network, and he also took his spot on the podium for the orchestra's first concert in their new venue, the Dorothy Chandler Pavilion, on 30 January 1965. This program, played before a capacity audience, included Dvorak's *Carnival* Overture, Wagner's *Forest Murmurs*, and Brahms's Symphony No. 1 in C Minor—the latter described as "the pièce de résistance for Maestro Dragon" (Bobbitt, p. 45). An example of one of Dragon's "pops" programs with the Glendale Orchestra (given 20 August 1978 at the Starlight Bowl) included material as diverse as selections from the Alan Jay Lerner and Frederick Loewe musical *My Fair Lady* and Strauss waltzes. He also recorded *The Bee Gees Music*, an album with the Orchestra of his arrangements of songs of the rock group the Bee Gees.

On 6 November 1976 Dragon's tenth anniversary as the music director of the Glendale Symphony was celebrated. He was given a gold baton from the Glendale Chamber of Commerce and received citations from organizations including the state senate, the state assembly, and the American Symphony Orchestra League. Dragon was also honored in 1989 with a posthumous star on the Hollywood Boulevard Walk of Fame. He died in Santa Monica, California.

• The Glendale Public Library in Glendale, Calif., maintains an extensive clipping file on Dragon. A large collection of his manuscripts is housed at the University of Wyoming's American Heritage Center. Copies of Blanche G. Bobbitt, *The Glendale Symphony Orchestra, 1924–1980* (1980), and some personal papers, programs, and other materials relating to Dragon's career are maintained by the Glendale Symphony. Copies of Dragon's arrangements, recordings, a roster of his guest-conducting appearances, and his 1969 unpublished autobiography are held by Dragon Music Company in Malibu, Calif. For information on Dragon's Hollywood work, see Jay Robert Nash and Stanley Ralph Ross, *The Motion Picture Guide* (1987). Details about Dragon's work as a conductor are given in Henry Roth, "Glendale Symphony: A Musical Phenomenon," *Inter-American Music Bulletin* 48 (July 1965): 4–7. Dragon's name appeared in a number of music journals, whether to note the American and world premieres of his *Santa Fe* Suite or his appearances in London, England. Most of these articles appear between 1959 and 1961 in *American Music*. Obituaries are in the *New York Times*, 29 Mar. 1984; *Variety*, 4 Apr. 1984; and *International Musician* (June 1984).

MARIANNE FEDUNKIW STEVENS

DRAGONETTE, Jessica (14 Feb. 1905?–18 Mar. 1980), popular soprano of the radio, was born in Calcutta, India, the daughter of parents about whom little is known. Orphaned early in life, Dragonette was brought to the United States at the age of six; throughout her childhood she was placed in various institutions operated under the auspices of the Roman Catholic church. She completed her compulsory education at the Philadelphia (Pa.) Catholic High School and later matriculated at Georgian Court College in Lakewood, New Jersey, where she studied languages and religion. The cloistered environment of this school, part of which housed a convent, played a major role in shaping Dragonette's personality, which—even at the height of her celebrity—was one of introspection and humility. Her lifelong devotion to the Roman Catholic faith may be traced to these formative years spent among the sisters of the convent, many of whom provided Dragonette with the foundations that enabled her to realize her goal of becoming a concert singer.

Upon graduation from college, Dragonette went to New York and further studied singing with Estelle Liebling, a renowned teacher whose pupils later came to include Beverly Sills, America's great coloratura soprano of the midcentury. The stage and film director Max Reinhardt assigned Dragonette the offstage singing part of an angel in his production of *The Miracle*; and no less a luminary than the celebrated Russian basso profundo Feodor Chaliapin praised the stature of Dragonette's singing in this production as "beautiful, a superb voice," in a retrospective article on the soprano's rise to fame that was published in the *New York Times* (19 July 1931). The female lead of Kathie in Sigmund Romberg's operetta *The Student Prince* on Broadway quickly followed, as did an engagement for the *Grand Street Follies*. Radio executives also agreed with Chaliapin's glowing assessment of the young singer's vocal appeal, with the result that Dragonette began one of the longest, most successful tenures in radio broadcasting in 1926.

As a pioneer in the world of radio entertainment, Dragonette had few serious competitors within any of the several networks for which she broadcast over the span of a quarter-century. Her quicksilvery soprano voice, likened by many as combining the best attributes of such musical colleagues as Jeanette McDonald in popular and semiclassical music and Grace Moore in opera, was heard successively over the WJZ, WEAF, and WABC networks. Dragonette reached the zenith of her career in 1935 when she was voted "Queen of the Radio" by an overwhelming majority of listeners polled nationwide by *Radio Guide*. That she was versatile in her programming, as well as beguiling in the manner in which she performed, may be evidenced from a perusal of selections that constituted a typical Dragonette broadcast. She went easily from the Viennese-style operettas of Sigmund Romberg, Franz Lehar, Rudolf Friml, and Oscar Straus to popular American songs composed by Stephen Foster, Victor Herbert, and Jerome Kern, while demonstrating to her concert audiences that she also possessed the technique to do justice to composers in the standard classical canon. This last point was perhaps best displayed in Dragonette's 1938 appearance with the New York Philharmonic-Symphony Orchestra at Lewisohn Stadium, wherein she performed arias and songs by Jules Massenet, Franz Schubert, Nikolai Rimsky-Korsakov, Antonín Dvořák, and Leo Delibes for an in-house audience exceeding 15,000 listeners. These same programming ideas were also to be savored at the musicales held at Georgian Court College, where Dragonette returned to perform on an annual basis. She sang many times for various charities and performed for the benefit of American service personnel during the years of World War II.

Dragonette married Nicholas Meredith Turner, a New York contractor and builder, in June 1947 in a private Roman Catholic ceremony conducted by Francis Cardinal Spellman. After her marriage, she gradually withdrew from public performance, singing only on special occasions—usually for the benefit of Roman Catholic organizations. Dragonette was honored by the church numerous times: she received the Papal Medal, Pro Pontifice et Ecclesia Cross, from Pope Pius XII in April 1942 and the Lady Grand Cross of the Equestrian Order of the Holy Sepulcher from Cardinal Spellman (on behalf of Pope Pius XII) in September 1955. She also received the Ribbon of the Order of Isabella the Catholic from the Spanish government in 1948 for her advocacy of Spanish music, as well as an honorary commission as first colonel at Will Rogers Field from Colonel Earl H. DeFord of the U.S. Armed Forces in 1942.

Dragonette continued to take an interest in world and human affairs and performing arts as a private citizen until her death from a heart attack at her New York home. As America's "Queen of the Radio," she will always be remembered for her lilting performances on "The Philco Hour," the "Ford Summer Show," and as the star of the popular CBS vehicle, "Saturday Night Serenade."

• Dragonette's autobiography, *Faith Is a Song* (1952), offers the soprano's life story through her marriage and impending retirement from public performances. An obituary is in the *New York Times*, 20 Mar. 1980.

LEIGH DAVIS SOUFAS

DRAGSTEDT, Lester Reynold (2 Oct. 1893–16 July 1975), physiologist and surgeon, was born in Anaconda, Montana, the son of John Albert Dragstedt, the foreman of an industrial blacksmith shop, and Caroline Selene. Both parents were Swedish immigrants. After his primary and secondary education in Anaconda, Dragstedt attended the University of Chicago, where his lifelong interest in physiology was aroused by his association with the eminent physiologist Anton J. Carlson, a friend of the Dragstedt family. At Chicago he received the B.S. in 1915, the M.S. (physiology) in 1916, the Ph.D. (physiology) in 1920, and the M.D. (from Rush Medical College and the University of Chicago) in 1921. His pursuit of the last two degrees

was interrupted by appointments to the faculty in pharmacology and physiology at the University of Iowa (1916–1918 and 1919) and by enlistment in the U.S. Army, Sanitary Department (1918–1919, second lieutenant). He was married to Gladys Shoesmith, of Guthrie Center, Iowa, in 1922; they had four children.

Dragstedt's long teaching career at the University of Chicago began in 1920, while he was still a medical student, with his appointment as assistant professor of physiology. In 1923 he was named the Nathan Smith Davis Professor and chairman of the Division of Physiology and Pharmacology at Northwestern University, but he returned to the University of Chicago as associate professor of surgery in 1925. Dallas B. Phemister, first chairman of surgery at the University of Chicago's newly organized medical school, selected Dragstedt for his original surgical faculty because Phemister wanted a professorial staff that could apply physiological principles to clinical problems, could teach and apply the scientific method, and could conduct independent basic research in physiological problems related to the field of surgery. To overcome Dragstedt's inexperience in the field of surgery, Phemister sent him to Europe where, during a fifteen-month sojourn, he was able to observe and actively acquire surgical skills in the clinics of several eminent surgeons. Dragstedt became professor of surgery in 1930 and was appointed the Thomas D. Jones Professor of Surgery and chairman of the Department of Surgery in 1948 upon Phemister's retirement. In 1959, having reached mandatory retirement age at the University of Chicago, he left Chicago to become Research Professor of Surgery and Physiology at the University of Florida in Gainesville, where he remained actively engaged in research and teaching until his death at his summer home in Elk Lake, Michigan, at the age of eighty-one.

Dragstedt became widely known because of his many pioneering contributions to the advancement of basic science, chiefly in the field of gastrointestinal physiology, and because of his equally important innovations in clinical surgery. His work is documented in more than 360 articles published in various scientific journals. Principal among his achievements were the introduction of the operation of vagotomy (severing the vagus nerves to the stomach) for the treatment of peptic ulcers and the elucidation of the important role played by the distal part of the stomach (the antrum) in regulating the secretion of acid by the stomach.

Vagotomy had been tried by surgeons for a variety of intra-abdominal conditions, but without a rationale or clear indication for its use, it had been abandoned. Dragstedt's elucidation of the importance of acid in causing ulcers and the role of the vagus nerves in maintaining high levels of gastric acidity enabled him to formulate a sound physiological basis for the potential usefulness of vagotomy. He performed his first vagotomy for duodenal ulcer in 1943, and he subsequently proved that the operation was effective in lowering gastric acid secretion and curing peptic ulcers, particularly those in the duodenum. His clinical results demonstrated persuasively that there were far fewer complications, postoperative deaths, and adverse side effects after vagotomy than there were after the only other effective ulcer operation, subtotal gastrectomy (the removal of three-fourths or more of the stomach). During the 1940s and 1950s there was widespread resistance among surgeons to the adoption of this simpler operation, but the soundness of the rationale for vagotomy, the excellence of its clinical results, and the effectiveness of Dragstedt's advocacy eventually convinced surgeons throughout the world of its superiority. Although the introduction of effective medical methods for controlling the secretion of gastric acid during the last two decades of the twentieth century greatly diminished the need for surgery in duodenal ulcer disease, vagotomy remains the sine qua non of surgical therapy in those cases in which the complications of duodenal ulcer preclude successful medical management.

Dragstedt's investigations of the physiology of the gastric antrum resulted in a succession of landmark papers, published between 1948 and 1954. He and his colleagues proved conclusively that the antrum manufactures and releases a hormone, "gastrin," that stimulates gastric acid secretion; they showed, further, that food in the stomach or distention of the antrum stimulates release of gastrin and that this function is governed by an autoregulatory mechanism that inhibits release of the hormone when acid is present in the antrum. (J. S. Edkins, in 1905, had published experiments that suggested the existence of an antral hormone, which he named gastrin, but his work was not confirmed by others and was largely unaccepted by physiologists.) A thorough knowledge of these important attributes of antral function is of vital importance in understanding certain disease states and in planning all upper-abdominal operations that involve the stomach.

Of equal, or perhaps even greater, importance when compared to these and other of Dragstedt's specific accomplishments was his position of leadership in the vanguard of those surgeons who, in the middle third of the twentieth century, transformed surgery from a largely anatomic exercise into the scientific discipline, based on an understanding of physiology and pathophysiology, that it is today. Previous generations of surgeons had concentrated on the anatomic—one might almost say the mechanical—aspect, that is, removing part of all of a diseased organ, closing a perforation, and removing or bypassing an obstructing lesion, but the physiologist-surgeons effected a dramatic change in this simplistic approach. They recognized that only by understanding the cause of the pathological process and the factors that govern normal function of the diseased organ system could they devise procedures that would not only correct the anatomic abnormality but would also prevent recurrence of the disease process and restore function to as nearly normal a state as possible. Dragstedt was also among the first of the educator-surgeons of his era to incorporate research experience into the surgical training program.

He did this because he saw the merit of teaching surgeons to apply scientific method to the analysis of clinical problems and because he wanted to stimulate at least some of these young people to pursue the kind of academic career that he, himself, had found so rewarding. Today, virtually all academic surgical training programs offer or require such an experience.

Dragstedt's lectures, whether to scientific peers or to lay audiences, were brilliant examples of lucidity, organization, erudition, and convincing logic, presented with a unique blend of personal warmth, good humor, and humility. Widely sought as a lecturer, he could be found on podiums throughout North America and Europe even in his eighth decade. He was a capable and compassionate clinician and an artful master of surgical technique. These attributes, coupled with his interest in people from all walks of life and his generosity of spirit, endeared him to three generations of colleagues, students, and friends. In recognition of his many contributions to science, education, and the welfare of patients, he received many honorary degrees and awards, chief among which he valued his election to the National Academy of Sciences and his award by the king of Sweden of the Order of the North Star.

• Principal sources of biographical information are John H. Landor, "L. R. D.—Recollections and Reminiscences," *Surgery* 81 (1977): 442–45; Owen W. Wangensteen and Sarah D. Wangensteen, "Lester R. Dragstedt," National Academy of Sciences, *Biographical Memoirs* 51 (1980): 63–95; Landor, "Lester Reynold Dragstedt—Physiologist-Surgeon," *Gastroenterology* 80 (1981): 846–53; and Irvin M. Modlin and Marc Basson, "The Lester Dragstedt Centennial," *Journal of the American College of Surgeons* 179 (1994): 84–102. Obituaries were published in many medical journals, including one in *Gastroenterology*, 70 (1976): 2–4, and one in *Proceedings of the Institute of Medicine, Chicago*, 30 (1975): 289.

JOHN LANDOR

DRAKE, Benjamin (1795?–1 Apr. 1841), writer and lawyer, was born in Mays Lick, Kentucky, the son of Isaac Drake and Elizabeth Shotwell, poor homesteaders who had emigrated from Plainfield, New Jersey, in 1788. (Edward Mansfield, a close friend of the family, writes that Drake was born in 1795, but Drake's birthdate appears in some other sources as 22 November 1794). By the time Drake was born, his parents had managed to secure a freehold title of 200 acres, where they raised sheep, corn, and wheat. Like that of many farmer's children, Drake's early schooling was crude, and his father owned only a handful of books, including a Bible, Dilworth and Webster's spellers, Scott's *Lessons in Elocution, Aesop's Fables*, and *Franklin's Life*. Greatly influenced by his elder brother Daniel, who had left the farm to become a successful doctor and author, Drake followed him to Cincinnati in 1807. Working first as an errand boy for an apothecary and then as a partner in his brother's general store in 1814, he studied law on the side and by 1825–1826 was working with the firm of William R. Mones. By 1829 Drake had established his own office on Jones Row, where he practiced until shortly before his death.

Drake shared his brother's literary tendencies and developed his talents through diligent self-education. He also participated in his brother's literary salons, which evolved from playful readings and private theatricals to the more formally organized Semi-Colon Club, which included James Hall, Edward Mansfield, Calvin Stowe, Harriet and Catherine Beecher, and Caroline Lee Hentz. In this milieu he established in 1826 the *Cincinnati Chronicle and Literary Gazette*, a weekly eight-page newspaper, which he edited until 1834 and which published Harriet Beecher Stowe's first story, "Cousin William."

In 1826 Drake also spent two months gathering information with Edward Mansfield to publish *Cincinnati in 1826* (1827), a book similar to one published by his brother Daniel titled *Pictures of Cincinnati in 1815*. Although Drake and Mansfield's book was hastily put together, it is a cogent statistical and descriptive account of the young city, listing the number and variety of its churches, schools, and other associations while also discussing Cincinnati's fledgling cultural scene. Drawing attention to the prevalence of industrious mechanics in the city and the lack of rich or poor, *Cincinnati in 1826* was later published in London and Germany, where it served as a guide for prospective immigrants. Despite the outbreaks of cholera that ravaged Cincinnati between the 1830s and 1850s, Drake remained an enthusiastic civic booster, publishing a follow-up essay in *Western Monthly Magazine* in January 1836 that hailed Cincinnati's recent growth and the industrial potential of new railway and canal access.

Drake's most enduring achievement, however, was his work as a historian. His first history, *The Life and Adventures of Black Hawk* (1838), is an even-handed discussion of Black Hawk and the tribal history of the Sauk, the Fox, and the Sioux. Drawing on local interviews corroborated by materials provided by fellow historian James Hall, Drake generally defends Black Hawk's conduct but corrects inaccuracies published in Black Hawk's autobiography. Although Drake praises some individual federal agents, he characterizes Black Hawk's "war" as a three-month flight from federal misdeeds. Drake points out that the United States acted as the aggressor, breaking the terms of the 1804 treaty of St. Louis and firing twice on Black Hawk's attempts to surrender. The study also discusses how leadership rivalry with fellow chief Keokuk, who largely collaborated with U.S. forces, alienated Black Hawk from both his peers and the federal government. The book concludes with a very moving portrait of Black Hawk's waning influence among his tribesmen.

In 1838 Drake also published *Tales and Sketches from the Queen City*, a collection of many of the essays that he had published in newspapers since 1825. The stories are tinged with frontier nostalgia, describing the life of riverboat gamblers, Indian battles, natural scenery, and romances. This text was followed by a superficial campaign biography, co-written with Charles Todd, titled *Sketches of the Civil and Military Services of William Henry Harrison* (1840).

Drake's last work, the *Life of Tecumseh* (1841), continues to be one of the most succinct and reliable accounts of Tecumseh's life. Profiting by access to living witnesses, Drake's style as a historian is best characterized by his discussion of Tecumseh's death. Although unable to conclude who did kill Tecumseh, Drake provides varying accounts to suggest that he was not killed by Richard Johnson, as was widely thought at the time. Only days after correcting the final galleys of the book, Drake died in Cincinnati after enduring a long and painful pulmonary illness. In the obituaries published after his death, he was remembered by his friends for his plain and finished writing style, his well-mannered integrity, and his central, though unpretentious, role in Cincinnati society.

• Precise details of Drake's life are scarce. The best sources of information are Edward D. Mansfield, *Memoirs of the Life and Services of Daniel Drake* (1855), and Mansfield, *Personal Memories* (1879). See also the essay by another friend, James Hall, in the *Cincinnati Chronicle*, 7 Apr. 1841. For Drake's place in Cincinnati history, see William Venable, *Beginnings of Literary Culture in the Ohio Valley* (1891); Charles Greve, *Centennial History of Cincinnati* (1904); and Lewis A. Leonard, *Greater Cincinnati and Its People* (1927). For information on the Drakes and the Semi-Colon Club, see Louise Tucker, "The Semi-Colon Club of Cincinnati," *Ohio History* 73 (Winter 1964): 13–26, and Joan Hedrick, *Harriet Beecher Stowe* (1994). Drake's role as editor is thoroughly discussed in John Nerone, *The Culture of the Press in the Early Republic* (1989). An obituary by Mansfield is in the *Cincinnati Chronicle*, 2 Apr. 1841. Another obituary appears in the *Cincinnati Gazette*, 2 Apr. 1841.

GRANVILLE GANTER

DRAKE, Charles Daniel (11 Apr. 1811–1 Apr. 1892), U.S. senator and jurist, was born in Cincinnati, Ohio, the son of Daniel Drake, a physician, and Harriet Sisson. After attending several academies in Cincinnati and Kentucky, he entered the U.S. Naval Academy in 1827 but resigned three years later because of a sudden decision to study law, which he undertook with his uncle Benjamin Drake in Cincinnati. Admitted to the bar in 1833, he moved to St. Louis the following year. Drake married Martha Ellen Taylor Blow in 1835 and, following Blow's death, wed Margaret Austin Cross in 1843. He returned to Cincinnati to practice law in 1845, then in 1849 went to New York, where he served for a year as treasurer of the Presbyterian Board of Foreign Missions. Returning to St. Louis in 1850, he resumed the practice of law. Initially a Whig, Drake turned first to the Know Nothings and then joined the Democratic party following the breakup of the Whigs in the mid-1850s. He was elected to the legislature as a Democrat in 1859; there he antagonized many of the state's Germans and their political allies through his advocacy of strict blue laws.

Drake did not play an active role in the secession crisis and as late as July 1861 denounced agitation against slavery; but, as guerrilla warfare began to wrack Missouri, he underwent a metamorphosis. By early 1862 he began speaking out against slavery as the principal cause for the war and all the evils associated with it. A strident but effective orator, Drake was elected to fill a vacancy in the state convention, which had originally decided the secession issue and had been meeting periodically since then in conjunction with the provisional government that it had established. When it reconvened in July 1863, Drake led the "Charcoal" element, so named because of its extreme position of demanding uncompensated emancipation by January 1864. The convention instead opted for 4 July 1870.

Drake now played a major role in establishing the Radical Union party, which adopted a platform calling for immediate emancipation, a new constitution, and the disfranchisement of southern sympathizers. Gaining strength in the legislature in spring 1864, the Radicals pushed through a referendum for a constitutional convention with the simultaneous election of delegates in case it passed. In the fall 1864 elections, they triumphed overwhelmingly, carrying the convention referendum and electing a strong majority to that body while also sweeping all the state offices.

Drake became the dominant force in the constitutional convention that convened in January 1865. It quickly passed an ordinance providing for immediate emancipation. Then, rallying a hard core of St. Louis supporters with a majority of the Radicals from rural Missouri, who had suffered great hardships at the hands of Confederate guerrillas, Drake ramrodded a new constitution. This document provided for the stringent disfranchisement of southern sympathizers by requiring an ironclad oath, one that guaranteed past as well as future loyalty, for voting and holding public office. At the same time the constitution established a broad framework to encourage industrial and corporate growth and assist with the orderly development of Missouri's natural resources. It also provided strong state support for public education for both whites and blacks. Although Drake favored suffrage and office holding for the newly emancipated blacks, he did not push that issue for fear that it would lead to the constitution's defeat. As it was, the so-called "Drake Constitution" was passed by only 1,862 votes out of 85,478 cast in a referendum in early June 1865.

Drake was rewarded by the strongly Radical legislature with a seat in the U.S. Senate. There he followed the lead of the more extreme Radicals in calling for a harsher reconstruction policy. His control over Missouri's Radical party began to loosen in 1869 with the election of Carl Schurz to fill the state's other Senate seat. Led by Schurz and former senator B. Gratz Brown, the more moderate element in the Missouri party broke with Drake and the extreme Radicals at the 1870 state Republican convention over the Radicals' refusal to endorse the reenfranchisement of southern sympathizers. Establishing the Liberal Republican party, the moderates elected Brown as governor with Democratic support.

Drake promptly resigned his Senate seat to accept appointment from President Ulysses S. Grant as chief justice of the U.S. Court of Claims, where he served until his retirement in 1885. He died at his home in St. Louis.

• Drake left a manuscript "Autobiography," which is in his papers at the State Historical Society of Missouri, Columbia. It only goes up to his election to the Senate in 1867. His rhetoric in the early stages of the Radical movement may be sampled in Charles D. Drake, *Union and Anti-Slavery Speeches Delivered during the Rebellion* (1864). The only biography is David D. March, "The Life and Times of Charles Daniel Drake" (Ph.D. diss. Univ. of Missouri–Columbia, 1949). March condensed the dissertation in "Charles Daniel Drake of St. Louis," the *Bulletin of the Missouri Historical Society* 8 (Apr. 1953). Drake's wartime and Reconstruction careers are covered in William E. Parrish, *Turbulent Partnership: Missouri and the Union, 1861–1865* (1963) and *Missouri under Radical Rule, 1865–1870* (1965).

WILLIAM E. PARRISH

DRAKE, Daniel (20 Oct. 1785–5 Nov. 1852), physician, naturalist, and educator, was born near Bound Brook, New Jersey, the son of Isaac Drake and Elizabeth Shotwell, farmers. The family moved west in 1788 to Mays Lick, Kentucky. At the age of fifteen Drake was apprenticed to Dr. William Goforth of nearby Cincinnati for training in medicine and surgery, then attended medical lectures in Philadelphia during the winter of 1805–1806. Drake returned to Mays Lick but went to Cincinnati in 1807 to take over Goforth's practice and to marry Harriet Sisson. Five children were born to the couple, although only two survived childhood, and Harriet herself died in 1825 when their youngest was only six.

Drake's first scientific publication was "Some Account of the Epidemic Diseases Which Prevail at Mays-Lick, in Kentucky" (*Philadelphia Medical and Physical Journal* 3, pt. 1 [1808]: 85–90). It consisted of observations in the form of facts from which conclusions might be drawn: "In most cases [of fever], quotidian intermissions, or remissions, were observable." "There was, I think, more east-wind than usual." More polished pieces followed, including two substantial volumes, *Notices Concerning Cincinnati* (1810–1811) and *Natural and Statistical View; or, Picture of Cincinnati and the Miami Country* (1815). All retained the character of the first work, as collections of data—on botany, on the geology and climate of the Ohio Valley, and on the natural, civil, and medical history of Cincinnati.

Drake was also practicing medicine during these years and laying the basis for what would become an extensive consulting practice (by mail) with patients and other physicians; buying, leasing, and managing Cincinnati real estate, in partnership with his wife's uncle Jared Mansfield, surveyor general of the Northwest Territory and then of the United States; with his brother Benjamin and then also with their father, merchandising drugs and medicines, patent medicines, groceries, paints, dyes, surgical instruments, stationery, books, and "artificial [i.e., artificially carbonated] mineral waters." In 1813 he was elected a trustee of the Cincinnati City Corporation. In 1818 he was appointed a director of the Cincinnati branch of the Bank of the United States. In 1818 Drake also was made a corresponding member of the nation's two most prestigious learned societies, the American Philosophical Society (Philadelphia) and the American Antiquarian Society (Worcester, Mass.).

As early as 1812 Drake began preparing to make Cincinnati a center for medical education by creating the institutions necessary for "literary culture" to flourish—learned societies, libraries, museums, schools—and in 1815–1816 returned to Philadelphia to obtain an M.D., thus qualifying for the professorate. His appointment to the medical faculty at Transylvania University in Lexington in 1817–1818, announced by the Transylvania trustees shortly after his return to the West, may indeed have been intended to prevent Drake from establishing a competing medical college in Ohio. By May 1818, however, Drake was advertising the availability of medical lectures in Cincinnati and petitioning the Ohio legislature for charters of incorporation for a Cincinnati College, a Medical College of Ohio (both granted in 1819), and a Commercial Hospital and Lunatic Asylum (granted in 1821) for clinical instruction.

The motifs in these activities are multiple, as are our readings of them. Drake's publications contributed to scientific knowledge of the West but also sought to establish Cincinnati's habitability—its climate and geology supported *democracy* as well as agriculture, he said—and especially to assert its competitive advantage vis-à-vis its regional rivals, Lexington, Louisville, and St. Louis, slaveocrat cities where the spirit of enterprise could not be expected to flourish. The institutions Drake founded in Cincinnati were those normally founded in order to bring the advantages of "civilization" to the new cities of the American West, but when Drake wrote about them, as in *An Anniversary Discourse, on the State and Prospects of the Western Museum Society* (1820), he implied that their establishment would make Cincinnati into the Philadelphia of the West, perhaps even—because Cincinnati was a new chance for a new civilization—the Philadelphia of America. For science's sake he sought to encourage the cultivation of natural history as an amateur pursuit among Cincinnati's elite but thereby created a local constituency for higher education and a potential market for scientific courses taught at *his* medical school.

At least until the mid-nineteenth century, colleges and medical schools, like learned societies and museums, were local institutions, serving the needs of their constituencies rather than their own (institutional) need for permanence, or the needs of "science" for continuity in the collection, dissemination, and preservation of knowledge. Thus they closed their doors because of lack of funds or lack of interest and reopened—reappeared—when some new group obtained control of the charter and began doing new business under the old name, or the old trustees ended their squabbles and agreed to try again. The continuous life of colleges and medical schools in particular was rarely longer than a couple of years. So it was that

Drake's professorial career took him from city to city and from institution to institution. He kept teaching; the colleges came and went.

Drake taught again at Transylvania from 1823 until 1827. Then he became coowner and coeditor of the *Western Medical and Physical Journal* and, from 1828 until 1838, editor and sole proprietor of its successor, the *Western Journal of the Medical and Physical Sciences*. Commonly called "Drake's" journal as the contemporary *American Journal of Science and the Arts* was "Silliman's," and with a national circulation, it made Drake into the public representative of science (and medicine *as* science) in the West, and the West's representative in the halls of science. It also provided him with an alternative classroom in which to teach the profession about its obligations and a way to encourage the collection of data in botany and natural history, geology, and meteorology. He was also a regular contributor to the newspapers, opposing medical quackery; advocating temperance, antislavery, the preservation of the union, and the candidacy of his friend Henry Clay for the presidency; and debating the character and extent of municipal responsibility for public health, especially in response to the cholera epidemic.

During the 1830s Drake tried to revitalize medical education in Cincinnati, through a medical department of Miami University, a reorganized Medical College of Ohio, and finally through a medical department of the Cincinnati College. In 1839 he accepted an appointment at the Louisville Medical Institute and in 1840 agreed to serve also as senior editor of its publication, the *Western Journal of Medicine and Surgery*.

In 1822 Drake began preparing a comprehensive "Treatise on the Diseases of the Western Country." This became a life's work, and it was finally published in 1850 and 1854, in two parts comprising 1,863 pages, as *A Systematic Treatise, Historical, Etiological, and Practical, on the Principal Diseases of the Interior Valley of North America, As They Appear in the Caucasian, African, Indian, and Esquimaux Varieties of Its Population*. Like the contemporary "miscellany" (of which Thoreau's *Walden* is the best known), it was the great repository of all he knew and saw—and also what he taught, for he routinely used his lectures to develop text for publication, and drafts of chapters as the basis for his teaching. Today it is almost unreadable, but the *American Journal of Medical Sciences* (July 1850) called it "the most valuable and important original production . . . that has yet appeared from the pen of any of our physicians."

In 1849 Drake sent the first volume of the *Systematic Treatise* to the printer and resigned from all duties in Louisville, presumably to devote full time to finishing the project. Nonetheless, he accepted appointments at the Medical College of Ohio for 1849–1850, at the Louisville Medical Institute, 1850–1852, then at a revived Medical College of Ohio until his death in Cincinnati midway through the term, teaching, as usual, the subjects on which he was then writing, especially the causes of disease. In the end, the *Systematic Treatise* could not be completed, and his editors cobbled together a second volume out of Drake's 3,000-page manuscript. Neither the diligent collection of data nor its orderly presentation could explain what caused what. Drake's generation continually looked for additional facts, seeking the missing specimen for the set instead of the missing link in the sequence.

Drake was one of the last physician-naturalists for whom facts were *things* that might be collected and stored for future use, and whose descriptions of nature were intended to elucidate the meaning of America as new world and as environment. By the time of his death, the autonomy of facts had begun to be questioned. By then also, America was no longer new, and its meaning had been transformed into a series of specialists' questions on the impact of environment on the evolution and distribution of species and of human institutions. The result for Drake has been a minor reputation as civic booster and pioneer this or that, while the scientific work that brought him national prominence, and his activities as a medical educator, have come to be seen as *merely* the precursors of modern medicine, modern science, and modern education.

• Because Drake published almost everything he wrote, few manuscripts survive, but materials are at the Cincinnati Historical Society and the Medical Heritage Center Library of the University of Cincinnati and at the Ohio Historical Society (relating to real estate investments, in the Jared Mansfield Papers). Student notes on his classroom lectures are in the Transylvania College Library and the National Library of Medicine, which also has Drake's own student notes from his first visit to Philadelphia. Henry D. Shapiro, "Daniel Drake's 'Sensorium Commune' and the Organization of the Second American Enlightenment," *Cincinnati Historical Society Bulletin* 27 (1969): 43–52, and "Daniel Drake and the Crisis in American Medicine of the 19th Century," *Journal of the American Medical Association* 254 (1985): 2113–16, locate Drake in the intellectual context of his time, as do the introductory essays and headnotes in Shapiro and Zane L. Miller, eds., *Physician to the West: Selected Writings of Daniel Drake on Science and Society* (1970), which also contains a complete bibliography of Drake's writings. Biographies are Emmet Field Horine, *Daniel Drake (1785–1852): Pioneer Physician of the Midwest* (1961), which also contains traces of Drake's voluminous correspondence as a consulting physician; Otto Juettner, *Daniel Drake and His Followers: Historical and Biographical Sketches* (1909), even more laudatory but rich in information about the careers of Drake's physician contemporaries; and Edward D. Mansfield, *Memoirs of the Life and Services of Daniel Drake, M.D., Physician, Professor, and Author* (1855).

HENRY D. SHAPIRO

DRAKE, Frances Ann Denny (6 Nov. 1797–6 Sept. 1875), actress and theatrical manager, was born in Schenectady, New York, the daughter of John Denny, a sea captain; her mother's name is unknown. Her family moved to Albany when Captain Denny died at sea in 1800. Her mother was an independent and well-connected woman who ran an inn two blocks from the Green Street Theatre. Frances was well educated (for this time period) and had attended finishing school. Known for her skill in recitation, she was naturally drawn to the many actors who stayed at her mother's

establishment. She met Samuel Drake and his theatrical family while they were performing in Albany in 1813–1814. She became friendly with Drake's son Alexander and often attended rehearsals.

When Samuel Drake was invited to take a theater company to the Kentucky frontier, Frances begged her mother to be allowed to go. Eventually Mrs. Denny relented and Frances joined the company as a supporting juvenile actress, even though she had never been on stage before. In order to pay their way, the company acted in each town they encountered. Thus Frances Denny acted her first role, that of Julia in *The Midnight Hour*, at Cherry Valley, New York.

In one of the most intrepid adventures ever undertaken in the history of the American theater, the company traveled overland and downriver, arriving on the "wild frontier" of Kentucky in 1815. The Drake family and the five neophyte actors who traveled with them established the first significant professional theater company in the West.

During these early years in Kentucky Frances Denny served a remarkable apprenticeship because every actor in the company had to undertake a variety of jobs connected with the theater. She learned about theater management, stagecraft, sets, costumes, but above all she learned about acting. The company was forced to perform with a minimum of sets and costumes and had to rely almost entirely on its dramatic talents. Frances played every type of role from low comedy to high tragedy. In her first season in Kentucky the company performed almost one hundred different plays and she was in most of them. Fellow actor Noah Ludlow noted that she had a "firm and clear" speaking voice but that her singing was "inflexible and unmusical." Her first tragic role was the title role in Monk Lewis's *Adelgitha* (1815).

Frances Denny left Kentucky and the Drake Company in 1819 and enjoyed successful seasons in stock companies in several East Coast and Canadian cities including Boston, Montreal, and New York, where she became a regular member of the company at the Park Theater. Her first appearance in New York was at the Park in the leading role of Helen Worret in *Man and Wife* (1820). By that time the Park had abandoned the stock system in favor of visiting star players.

In 1822 Alexander Drake visited Frances in New York, and they were married later that year or early in 1823. She returned with Alexander to Kentucky, and together they took over the growing Drake theatrical empire. She performed regularly in the theaters owned by the Drakes in Kentucky and Ohio but took frequent trips east and south to play "star" roles. By 1830 she was the most prominent theatrical figure in the West and was known as the "tragic lioness of the Southwest." That year Frances Drake's husband died suddenly at the age of thirty-two, when her powers were at their height. The couple had four children, two of whom, Samuel and Julia (who subsequently married the "riverboat king" Harry Chapman), went into the theater.

In the mid-1830s Drake married a lawyer from Cincinnati, Captain George Washington Cutter, but the marriage was short and unsuccessful and they soon separated. Following their divorce she resumed her use of the Drake name and continued acting. She managed the theater in Louisville and frequently performed there. She also continued to make frequent trips to the East Coast and performed in some of the major theaters. Frances Trollope, an English traveler not given to praising what she found on her visits to America, met Drake during a stay in Cincinnati, pronounced that she had a "decidedly first rate" talent, and described her acting as having "deep and genuine feeling, correct judgement and the most perfect good taste" (p. 130).

Drake was an imposing woman, over six feet tall, and is described in Ford as a "handsome woman and plenty of her" (p. 179). Although she played a wide range of roles, she is best known for tragedy. The *New York Mirror* (15 Mar. 1834) called her "a fine actress and an ornament to the American stage." She is frequently referred to as "the Siddons of the West," although this accolade might have more to do with her being the first native-born actress of note than with her abilities as an actress. She did, however, challenge the domination of the early American stage by English-based actresses, in particular Fanny Kemble. In 1835 when the Kemble mania was at its height Drake opened as Julia in Sheridan Knowles's *The Hunchback* at the Park Theatre. This part had originally been written for Fanny Kemble and the Park took a big risk in mounting the play. There ensued much debate among the critics as to who was the superior actress. One critic said that Drake "has a noble commanding art . . . and acquitted herself with much ability." Her obituary notices claimed that when Kemble was playing in New Orleans, a rival theater brought in Drake "who proved the greater attraction."

Drake was said to be a woman of great taste and integrity who read a great deal. Although she owned a handsome residence in Covington, Kentucky, she retired to the old Drake farm, "Harmony Farm," in Oldham County, Kentucky, where she became the matriarch of an ever-expanding theatrical dynasty, which included several generations of Drake actors as well as Julia Dean and the Chapman sisters. Her strong abolitionist views caused her some distress during the Civil War. She was shunned by her neighbors, most of whom were slaveowners. Harmony Farm was overrun and looted by both sides during the war and for some years she was almost destitute. She died at Harmony Farm ten years after the war's end.

• The most complete recent account of Drake's life and the theater of early Kentucky is contained in West T. Hill, Jr., *The Theatre in Early Kentucky, 1790–1820* (1971). An anecdotal and entertaining history of the actors of this early period is given by Drake's great-grandson George D. Ford in his *These Were the Actors: A Story of the Chapmans and Drakes* (1955). The fullest, though not always accurate, contemporary account of Drake's life is Noah M. Ludlow's *Dramatic Life as I Found It* (1880). Other contemporary accounts include Frances Trollope, *Domestic Manners of the Americans* (1832); T. Allston Brown, *History of the American Stage* (1870); Bernhard, duke of Saxe-Weimar Eisenach, *Travels through North America* (1828); and Joseph L. Cowell, *Thirty Years Passed among the Players in England and America* (1844). A chronicle of Drake's appearances on the New York stage is in Joseph Ireland, *Record of the New York Stage* (1866), and George C. D. Odell, *Annals of the New York Stage*, vols. 2–8 (1927–1938). A not very accurate obituary appears in the *Louisville Courier-Journal*, 4 Sept. 1875.

ANTHONY R. HAIGH

DRAKE, Sir Francis (1542 or 1543–Jan. 1595), circumnavigator, was born in Crowndale, near Tavistock, Devonshire, England, the son of Edmund Drake, a sailor, farmer, and preacher, and (first name unknown) Mylwaye. When Francis was a boy the family moved to the north coast of Kent on the Thames estuary, near London, where he was apprenticed to the master of a coasting vessel. By his early twenties Drake had joined his influential relatives, the Hawkins family, in Plymouth. From this port the Hawkinses were making mercantile voyages via West Africa to the Caribbean, then controlled by Spain, and directly back to England. In 1569 Drake married Mary Newman and the next year began to make voyages on his own account. During a voyage in 1572–1573, like Vasco Núñez de Balboa sixty years earlier, Drake crossed the Isthmus of Darien and first saw the Pacific Ocean. He captured a Spanish mule train carrying silver across the isthmus and returned to England a rich man.

His ambition now was to sail in the Pacific, a voyage made possible by the patronage of a number of the most powerful people in England including, probably, Queen Elizabeth I. A small squadron of five ships was assembled at Plymouth for the expedition, the objectives of which are not entirely clear. Some have conjectured that it was to found an English settlement in southernmost South America, or to find a passage through North America from the Pacific—the legendary Strait of Anian. Whatever the purpose, the ships set sail late in 1577 and reached the Atlantic entrance to the Strait of Magellan in June the next year. Here the squadron was reduced to three ships, which passed through the strait in sixteen days, a record for the century.

As they entered the Pacific, the ships met a severe storm, which drove them southward and led to the discovery of Drake Passage, the body of water between Tierra del Fuego and Antarctica. One ship was lost, and another returned to England while Drake, in the *Golden Hind*, progressed northward along the Pacific coast of South America. With the help of pilots he picked up along the way and stores he took from ships and Spanish settlements that he raided, Drake reached the North Pacific. Taking a captured vessel in tow, the *Golden Hind* sailed to the midlatitudes in this ocean beyond any settlement in New Spain and farther north (48°?) than any previous expedition. Drake returned to 38° north latitude to an area in present-day California that he designated *Nova Albion* (the first New England) on 17 June 1579, to careen and refresh. Drake's precise location in California remains a subject of controversy.

Drake took possession of *Nova Albion* from the Miwok Indians, and after sojourning there for five weeks the *Golden Hind* set sail across the Pacific. Navigating by way of Palau and the Philippines, Drake reached the Moluccas in November; there he made a commercial treaty with the sultan of Ternate. Some have seen this as the forerunner of the English East India Company. After many adventures in the Indian Ocean, Drake returned via the Atlantic to Plymouth, arriving on 26 September 1580. His was the first expedition to circumnavigate the earth in which the commander himself returned to report his accomplishment (Magellan died on the way). The "Famous Voyage," as it became known, was the greatest of many achievements.

Back in England, Drake was received by Queen Elizabeth, who had him knighted aboard the *Golden Hind*. He became a national figure, especially popular with the ordinary people, and continued to make notable contributions to his country. In 1581 he became the mayor of Plymouth. His wife died shortly after this. He was elected a member of Parliament in 1584 and in the next year married Elizabeth Sydenham, a maid of honor at the court of Queen Elizabeth. In 1585–1586 Drake took a large fleet to the West Indies and in 1587 delayed the Spanish armada by raiding Cadiz. When the armada came into the Channel in July 1588, Drake, serving as vice admiral of the English fleet, greatly distinguished himself in defeating the invaders.

Drake sailed once more to the West Indies in 1595; he died of dysentery at sea and was buried off Portobelo a few miles from the eastern end of what is now the Panama Canal. He was an expert navigator, a charismatic leader, and the greatest English sailor up to his time. Britain's claim to the northwest coast of North America two hundred years later, when it was visited by James Cook (1798) and George Vancouver (1792), was based on Drake's prior exploration of the area.

• Much was written on Drake in his lifetime, and much more has been since. Contemporary accounts are detailed in Benjamin P. Draper, "A Collection of Bibliographical Items, 1569–1659," in *Sir Francis Drake and the Famous Voyage, 1577–1580*, ed. Norman J. W. Thrower (1984). Among the many modern books on the subject is John Sugden, *Sir Francis Drake* (1990), with an up-to-date bibliography especially good on modern works.

NORMAN J. W. THROWER

DRAKE, Francis Marion (30 Dec. 1830–20 Nov. 1903), army officer, railroad promoter and executive, and governor of Iowa, was born in the western Illinois hamlet of Rushville, the son of John Adams Drake, a merchant and small-time capitalist, and Harriet Jane O'Neal. Drake grew up in a family of modest means. In 1837 his father relocated the family to the raw frontier settlement of Fort Madison, Iowa, then part of Wisconsin Territory. The Drakes stayed in this Mississippi River community until March 1846, when they moved to inland Davis County. There Francis's father founded the town of Drakesville and pursued agricultural and banking interests. Like his thirteen brothers and sisters Francis received rudimentary formal education. He attended public schools in Fort Madison, although he never graduated from high school. But Drake expanded his knowledge through his own initiative; he read widely and enthusiastically and associated with "learned" people.

During the early 1850s Francis Drake revealed his love for adventure and risk-taking. In 1852 he organized a wagon train from southern Iowa to the gold fields of northern California. Once there, however, Drake turned to stock raising and remained in the Sacramento area for about a year. He returned to the Midwest in 1854 but soon set out again for the Golden State. This time he drove a herd of dairy cows. While Drake accomplished this perilous undertaking, he nearly lost his life on the trip home; he survived both a shipwreck and a shipboard fire. Once safely back in Iowa, Drake worked for his father and brothers in their Drakesville-based business enterprises. Then in 1859 he struck out on his own and settled in the nearby Appanoose County village of Unionville, where he operated a general store.

During the Civil War Francis Drake rallied to the Union colors. He raised a company of volunteers for an Iowa infantry unit, and he saw active combat service. Later the Iowa governor commissioned him as a lieutenant colonel and asked him to recruit more troops. Once again Drake endured hostile fire. He was wounded severely and captured by Confederate forces. Eventually Drake won parole and rejoined his regiment. When he left the military in 1865, he wore the uniform of a brigadier general.

After the war Drake abandoned his occupation as a minor merchant. He studied law and won admission to the local bar. And he left Unionville for neighboring Centerville, the bustling seat of Appanoose County. The quintessential community booster, Drake became keenly interested in improving his region's transportation. That, of course, meant railroads. In 1866 he launched the Iowa Southern Railroad, which soon joined the Keokuk & Western Railway (K&W), a road that by 1872 linked Keokuk, Iowa—via Alexandria, Missouri—with Centerville, a distance of ninety miles. Eight years later the K&W, which Drake headed, reached Van Wert, Iowa, fifty-eight miles west of his adopted hometown. Drake also saw need for better rail service to the north of Centerville. He subsequently spearheaded construction of the 24-mile Centerville, Moravia & Albia Railroad that tied Centerville with the strategically located Monroe County seat of Albia, situated on the Chicago, Burlington & Quincy (then the Burlington & Missouri River Railroad) and the Iowa Central.

And there were other railroad projects. Drake assisted in the development of two central Iowa branch lines for the Iowa Central (then the Central Iowa). Built under the corporate banner of the Iowa Central & Northwestern Railway in 1881 and 1882, these pikes connected Hampton with Belmond and Minerva Junction with Story City. A much larger undertaking involved constructing the 110-mile Indiana, Illinois & Iowa Railroad, commonly called the "Three I Road." Opened between Streator, Illinois, and North Judson, Indiana, in 1883, this surprisingly profitable bridge and terminal road within a decade reached South Bend, Indiana, forty miles east of its original terminus. Drake would serve as Three I president from its inception to his retirement in 1898.

In all likelihood Francis Drake represented various investors in his railroad schemes. Evidence suggests that he worked closely with Russell Sage, the shrewd Wall Street stock-trader. Yet Drake's business activities made him a millionaire, and thus he possessed the financial means to expand independently his railroad interests.

By the time of his death in 1903, due to the complications of diabetes, Francis Marion Drake had become a household name to Iowans. While fellow residents may not have immediately associated him with railroads, they knew that he had been the principal benefactor of Drake University in Des Moines, and that this Republican party wheel horse had served as the state's governor between 1896 and 1898. Just as important, though, was Drake's role in creating modest-size railroads during the Gilded Age. Indeed, such railroads became vital building blocks for subsequent railroad systems after the turn of the twentieth century. In Drake's case the Chicago, Burlington & Quincy acquired the K&W; the Iowa Central leased the Centerville, Moravia & Albia (which later became an independent electric road); and the New York Central absorbed the Three I.

• The Francis M. Drake Papers are held by the State Historical Society of Iowa, Iowa City. For further information on Drake, see Leland L. Sage, *A History of Iowa* (1974), and *Annals of Iowa* 6 (Jan. 1904): 307–9.

H. ROGER GRANT

DRAKE, Francis Samuel (22 Feb. 1828–22 Feb. 1885), historian, author, and antiquarian, was born in Northwood, New Hampshire, the son of Samuel Gardner Drake and Louisa M. Elmes. His family moved to Boston, Massachusetts, where his father became the proprietor of a popular antiquarian bookstore, wrote books concerning American history and Indians and edited other such books. Drake was educated in the Boston public schools, mainly at the Mayhew School, after which he worked in his father's store and then as an accountant for a Boston company.

In 1848 Drake, by then a lieutenant in the Boston Light Guard, participated in a ceremony for the placing of the cornerstone of the Washington Monument in Washington, D.C. By 1856 he was married to E. M. Valentine; they had one child. In 1862 he went with his younger brother Samuel Adams Drake (who later became a soldier, journalist, editor, and historian) to Leavenworth, Kansas, where Drake sold books. During the Civil War, Drake was a Union army adjutant. In 1867 he returned to Boston. Beginning in the 1850s he became interested in collecting biographical data. It is likely that he used and built on his father's extensive genealogical and biographical materials.

The long titles of the books written by Drake often describe their contents. In 1872 he published *Dictionary of American Biography, Including Men of the Time; Containing Nearly Ten Thousand Notices of Persons of Both Sexes, of Native and Foreign Birth, Who Have Been Remarkable, or Prominently Connected with the Arts, Sciences, Literature, Politics, or History of the American Continent, Giving Also the Pronunciation of Many of the Foreign and Peculiar American Names, a Key to the Assumed Names of Writers, and a Supplement.* Drake's stated aim was to present in one volume, at a moderate cost, a reference "manual" of important Americans, including many then still living. The abundance of New England and New York material, as well as data concerning clergymen, political figures, and writers, threatened, Drake believed, to make the work comparatively neglectful toward artists, engineers, industrialists, inventors, and practical scientists. He listed thirty-one authors of authoritative reference works he consulted. He identified authors who had used as many as 245 pen names. Each one-paragraph entry included places and dates of birth and death, titles and ranks, main activities, and citations of sources. This enormous work of 1,019 two-column pages proved sufficiently popular to justify at least four later editions.

In 1872 Drake also published *List of Members of the Massachusetts Society of the Cincinnati, Including a Complete Roll of the Original Members, with Brief Biographies Compiled from the Records of the Society, and Other Original Sources.* It was reissued in 1873, in which year he also prepared *Memorials of the Society of the Cincinnati of Massachusetts.* It is likely that Drake, who did not belong to the Society of the Cincinnati, was hired to assemble the contents of these works in a form specified by the membership. In 1873 Drake also compiled *The Life and Correspondence of Henry Knox, Major-General in the American Revolutionary Army,* a comparatively short work and in a limited edition for subscribers only. These books are all reliable but pedestrian.

Drake next turned to more challenging work. He published *The Town of Roxbury: Its Memorable Persons and Places, Its History and Antiquities, with Numerous Illustrations of Its Old Landmarks and Noted Personages* (1878). In 475 pages, this work amply fulfills Drake's purpose to present material of "historical interest"; to elucidate the manners, customs, and way of life of former inhabitants of Roxbury; and to describe such tangible "memorials" of their past "as have escaped the ravages of time." Drake had gained such respect as a researcher that Justin Winsor, while compiling his *Memorial History of Boston* (1880), asked him to contribute essays on Roxbury and Brighton. Drake edited *Indian Tribes of the United States* (1884), a shortened version of Henry Rowe Schoolcraft's influential *History and Statistical Information Respecting the History,*

Condition, and Prospects of the Indian Tribes of the United States (6 vols., 1851–1857). From his painstaking abridgment Drake prepared his own *Indian History for Young Folks* (1884), an exciting narrative well deserving of at least four subsequent editions.

Drake's final work was *Tea Leaves: Being a Collection of Letters and Documents Relating to the Shipment of Tea to the American Colonies in the Year 1773, by the East India Tea Company, Now First Printed from the Original Manuscripts* (1884). This source book includes Drake's own 184-page introduction. He explains that the letters and documents were taken in March 1776, when the British and certain Tories escaped from Boston, and were given to a man in Halifax, who sold them to Abel Brown, a Boston engraver and publisher who planned to publish them but died without doing so. Drake obtained the collection from Brown's two daughters, living in Chelsea, Massachusetts. The materials cover some of the troubles that led to the American Revolution. Drake provides biographical information (often minimal) on fifty-eight Boston Tea Party activists identified earlier and on forty-two others later identified mainly from family traditions. The book includes portraits, reproductions of autographs, other illustrations, and maps.

In his last years in Boston, Drake was the proprietor of a stationery shop, a circulating library, and a periodical store. He died unexpectedly of pulmonary apoplexy while in Washington, D.C., representing the Boston Light Guard, his old military unit, at the dedication of the Washington Monument. At the time of his death, he was working on a revision of his *Dictionary of American Biography*. Shortly after his death, his collection of autographs, broadsides, historical manuscripts, and portraits was sold at auction.

• Drake's correspondence and notes relating to the Massachusetts Society of the Cincinnati (1872–1873) and his manuscripts and notes relating to his *Tea Leaves* are in the New England Genealogical Society collections in Boston, Mass. Samuel Gardner Drake, *Genealogical and Biographical Account of the Family of Drake* (1845), provides personal background data. Obituaries are in the *Washington Post*, 23 Feb. 1885, and the *Boston Transcript*, 24 Feb. 1885.

ROBERT L. GALE

DRAKE, Joseph Rodman (7 Aug. 1795–21 Sept. 1820), writer of verse, was born in New York City, the son of Jonathan Drake and Hannah Lawrence, aristocrats. Drake's father died when he and his three sisters were quite young; his mother remarried and moved to New Orleans with her daughters. Drake stayed in New York and grew up with close relatives, the Hunts and the Rodmans. He studied medicine and in 1816 received his degree from Queen's College, a private school. Shortly thereafter, he married Sarah Eckford, the daughter of shipbuilder Henry Eckford; they had one child. After the wedding, he visited Europe with his wife. On their return to New York in March 1819 he sent the first of his "Croaker" verses to the New York *Evening Post*; for a time, his coauthorship of a series of sometimes witty and satiric verses that ap-

peared in the *Post* was kept secret. Nearly half of the forty verses were written by Drake; the remainder by Drake's friend Fitz-Greene Halleck. The verses were attributed to "Croaker," "Croaker, Jr.," or "Croaker & Co."

Drake's posthumous recognition as a writer has been based on this series of newspaper verses, later reissued as *The Croakers* (1860), and on a work published as the title piece of *The Culprit Fay and Other Poems* (1835). A number of Drake's verses were widely admired and anthologized, such as "The American Flag," which in addition to having a patriotic theme is typically sentimental. In the piece, Drake apostrophizes "Freedom['s] . . . symbol" in a series of flowing but easy clichés:

> Flag of the free heart's hope and home,
> By angel hands to valor given;
> Thy stars have lit the welkin dome
> And all thy hues were born in heaven!

The poem has been printed separately and set to music by several composers. Drake was also remembered for the lines written by Halleck in tribute: "None knew thee but to love thee, / Nor named thee but to praise." The extravagant praise given Drake's work by literary nationalists may have provoked the negative responses from critics such as Edgar Allan Poe and Edmund Gosse.

Drake, who was never a practicing physician, became a partner in a drugstore in 1819, but the state of his health was soon to be a serious problem. He visited New Orleans for his health during the fall of 1819, and when he returned to New York in the spring of 1820, the "consumption" (pulmonary tuberculosis) from which he suffered had rapidly progressed. On his deathbed, Drake reportedly called his verse "valueless" and asked that all his writings be destroyed. His work, however, was preserved, and his daughter later published a selection, *The Culprit Fay and Other Poems* (1835).

Critics of Drake have called him "a third-rate versifier widely acclaimed" and "a gentle imitative bard of the forth or fifth order." Nevertheless, despite his facile, redundant, and derivative style and his relative want of imagination, Drake's contribution to the development of an American literature should not be underestimated. The literary historian Barrett Wendell, for example, writes with regard to one of Drake's "pretty fancies" ("The Culprit Fay"): "This conventional tale of some tiny fairies, supposed to haunt the Hudson River, is so much better than American poetry had previously been that one is at first disposed to speak of it enthusiastically." The lengthy work (640 lines), reportedly written in three days, does illustrate Drake's strengths and weaknesses as a writer. Drake's strong points were his fine ear for a melodic line, his occasionally felicitous images, and his enthusiasm for a national literature. It is regrettable that Drake's work illustrates so well the adverse effects of a lack of artistic discipline.

• Drake and Halleck's collaboration first appeared in book form as *Poems, by Croaker, Croaker and Co., and Croaker Jun.* (1819); the 1860 edition is available on microfiche in the Library of American Civilization. Selections from Drake's work appear in Duyckinck and Duyckinck, *Cyclopaedia of American Literature* (1856; repr. 1965). A biography is in Frank L. Pleadwell, *The Life and Works of Joseph Rodman Drake (1795–1820): A Memoir and Complete Text of His Poems and Prose, including Much Never before Printed* (1935). Bibliography and commentary may be found in Jacob Blanck, *Bibliography of American Literature* (1955); Kendall B. Taft, ed., *Minor Knickerbockers* (1947); Robert E. Spiller et al., eds., *The Literary History of the United States* (1948; with *Supplements*, 1959, 1963); Barrett Wendell, *A Literary History of America* (1900; repr. 1968); Vincent Buranelli, *Edgar Allan Poe* (1961); and Edmund Gosse, *Has America Produced a Poet? Questions at Issue* (1889).

RICHARD E. MEZO

DRAKE, Pete (8 Oct. 1932–29 July 1988), steel guitarist, music producer, and music publisher, was born Roddis Franklin Drake in Atlanta, Georgia, the son of Rev. Johnny Drake, a Pentecostal minister, and Nora Blevins. Beginning his musical pursuits on the acoustic guitar, Drake was inspired at around the age of eighteen by hearing steel guitarist Jerry Byrd playing at the Grand Ole Opry. Drake purchased a lap steel at a local Atlanta pawnshop and began to teach himself to play it. Further inspiration came a few years later from hearing Webb Pierce's 1953 recording of "Slowly," on which steel guitarist Bud Isaacs achieved bending-note effects with a pedal-activated, pitch-altering mechanism on his guitar. Fashioning his own pedal guitar, Drake became one of Atlanta's first pedal steel guitarists. He soon formed his own band, the Sons of the South, which at one time included such notable country music figures as Jerry Reed, Joe South, Doug Kershaw, and Roger Miller. This group achieved significant notoriety in the Atlanta area, making regular appearances on radio and television as well as working many nightclub dates.

By 1959 Drake desired to be closer to the center of the country music scene and decided to move to Nashville with the duo with whom he had been currently performing, Wilma Lee and Stoney Cooper. He recalled that he "starved to death the first year and a half," but a turning point came when singer Roy Drusky heard him one night playing at the Opry, was impressed with his individuality of style, and asked Drake to record with him. The result was the 1960 hit "Anymore." An appearance on another chart hit, George Hamilton IV's "Before This Day Ends," soon followed, and Drake's career as a Nashville session player was in high gear. In the late 1960s, he described the pace as "fifteen sessions per week, usually three a day."

Over the course of his recording career, Drake played on 118 gold and platinum albums and recalled that at one point in the mid-1960s he appeared on fifty-nine of *Billboard* magazine's top seventy-five singles. Under his own name he produced five singles, including one that sold a million copies ("Forever"), and

roughly a dozen LPs for various record labels. Drake's playing style always tended toward tasteful understatement, and he was at his best when providing soulful instrumental commentary behind a singer. As country music producer Owen Bradley put it, "Some steel players might play more than you need. Sometimes you just need a little touch, and Pete was good at that" (quoted in Kienzle, p. 17).

Meanwhile, Drake had also been exploring other musical styles and directions. Sometime in the 1950s, he saw a Kay Kyser movie in which steel guitarist and big-band leader Alvino Rey was imitating human speech patterns on his guitar through sliding the steel bar and swelling the volume. Drake took this concept further and in 1961 completed the invention of his own "talking steel" device, in which a small speaker driver feeds the guitar's sound through a plastic tube, the other end of which is inserted into the player's mouth. The player then shapes the sounds with his mouth cavity as if forming vowels and uses a microphone to pick up the shaped sounds. Drake first used his talking steel commercially on the 1963 Roger Miller recording "Lock, Stock, and Teardrops," and in 1964 he created his own million-selling instrumental single, "Forever," with it. In historical retrospect, Drake's talking steel episode must be seen largely as the momentary popularization of a novelty effect. Nonetheless, it also bore witness to his inventiveness in searching for new and different musical sounds. It also had the influence of bringing the steel guitar, the role of which had been diminished around this time during the country music industry's "pop" phase, back to the public's attention.

In the later 1960s and early 1970s, Drake also made the steel guitar known to folk and rock audiences. While he had already played on a number of recordings by noncountry artists, his most influential appearances were on a series of albums by Bob Dylan: *John Wesley Harding* (1968), *Nashville Skyline* (1969), and *Self Portrait* (1970). Both *Nashville Skyline* and the Byrds' *Sweetheart of the Rodeo* (1968, featuring steel guitarist Lloyd Green) were particularly significant in establishing "country rock." Appearances by Drake on George Harrison's *All Things Must Pass* (1970) and Ringo Starr's *Beaucoups of Blues* (1970) furthered this market crossover influence.

Beginning in the 1960s, Drake pursued other musical enterprises in addition to playing. In 1962 he founded, with his older brother Jack, the Window Music publishing company, which by the early 1970s had assembled a catalog of some 3,000 songs. In the mid-1960s, Drake began working as a producer and also began his own record label, Stop Records. As in his playing, Drake the producer did not hesitate to cross market boundaries, producing recordings for rock and pop artists such as Bob Dylan, Leon Russell, and Ringo Starr as well as country performers. His favorite projects as producer were *Ernest Tubb: The Legend and the Legacy* (1979), produced in honor of Tubb's sixty-fifth birthday, and B. J. Thomas's *Amazing Grace* (1981), which won Grammy and Dove awards. In the mid-1970s, Drake opened his own recording studio, Pete's Place, and initiated another record label, First Generation Records, dedicated to recording traditional country artists.

While in high school in Atlanta, Drake had married Rebecca (maiden name unknown); they had six children and divorced in 1972. In 1982 he married Rose Trimble; they had no children together. Drake had two children out of wedlock.

For his tireless and innovative efforts as a player, producer, and publisher, Drake received many awards in the music industry. In 1964 he was voted as Instrumentalist of the Year by *Cash Box* magazine and as Fastest Climbing Instrumentalist by *Record World*. In 1970 he was inducted into the Country Music Hall of Fame's Walkway of Stars. In 1987 he was awarded the Nashville Entertainment Association's Master Award and inducted into the International Steel Guitar Hall of Fame. As *Billboard* writer Gerry Wood noted in his obituary tribute, "most important, he won the friendship and respect of those that worked with him" (20 Aug. 1988, p. 28). Drake died at his Brentwood, Tennessee, home of complications resulting from lung disease.

• A selected discography of Drake's recordings includes *The Amazing and Incredible Pete Drake* (1963), *Forever* (1964), *Talking Steel and Singing Strings* (1965), *Country Steel Guitar* (mid-1960s), *The Greatest Steel Guitarist in the World* (mid to late 1960s), *Steel Away* (late 1960s–early 1970s), *The Fabulous Steel Guitar Sounds of Pete Drake* (late 1960s–early 1970s), and the posthumous release *Pete Drake* (1996). For a complete discography of Drake's recordings, see Joe Goldmark, *The International Steel Guitar and Dobro Discography*, 8th ed. (1997). The most extensive biographical sources are Tom Bradshaw, "Steel Guitar," *Guitar Player* 3, no. 5 (Oct. 1969): 23–25, and Douglas Green, "Pete Drake: Everyone's Favorite," *Guitar Player* 7, no. 6 (Sept. 1973): 22ff. First-hand accounts of Drake's sessions with Beatles members George Harrison and Ringo Starr can be found in Patrick North, "Pete Drake and the Steel Beatle," *Rolling Stone*, 23 July 1970, p. 6, and North, "Ringo and Friends in Country Country," *Rolling Stone*, 6 Aug. 1970, pp. 6–7. An obituary is Rich Kienzle, "Pete Drake Remembered," *Guitar Player* 22, no. 11 (Nov. 1988): 17.

DANIEL JONES

DRAKE, Samuel (15 Nov. 1768–16 Oct. 1854), actor, theatrical manager, and pioneer of professional theater in the West, was born in England of unknown parentage. Very little is known of his early life. It is said that he was born Samuel Drake Bryant but later adopted Drake as a stage name. He was apprenticed as a printer but broke his apprenticeship and joined an acting troupe. He became a manager of a small provincial theater in the west of England and married Alexina Fisher (date unknown), sister of the manager of the theater in Exeter. They had five children and, in the tradition of great English stage families, founded a theatrical dynasty. Martha Drake, their eldest child, was an actress who married a Frankfort, Kentucky, businessman and returned to England. Samuel Drake, Jr., was a talented musician but an average actor. Alexan-

der Drake, who suffered from deafness but was an excellent singer and low-comedy actor, married the celebrated actress Frances Ann Denny, the "Siddons of the West." Julia Drake was known as a great beauty and natural actress who specialized in high comedy and whose daughter, Julia Dean, was one of the best known actresses of her generation. James Dean, Samuel's youngest son, was perhaps best known as a singer during his performing days.

Samuel Drake came to the United States with his talented family in 1809 and was engaged by the theater manager John Bernard to act and stage manage for the Federal Street Theatre in Boston. At that time, before the advent of directors, the stage manager was responsible for everything that happened on stage. Drake and his wife performed for three seasons in Boston before accompanying Bernard to Albany, New York, in 1813. There Drake again combined stage management with acting, playing roles such as Lear and Julius Caesar. In 1814 Drake's wife died, and Bernard announced his plans for retirement. Drake's future looked uncertain until, in the fall of that year, he met the actor Noble Luke Usher. Usher had come to Albany to find a stage manager for a proposed professional theater company in Kentucky, at that time the frontier of the "Western wilderness" (Ludlow, p. 5). For several years Usher's father, Luke Usher, a Kentucky merchant with interests in the umbrella business, innkeeping, and the theater, had been trying to persuade John Bernard to establish a company in Kentucky. Usher's son Noble was an actor who had worked for Bernard in 1806 and had toured the United States and Canada. The Ushers had established theaters in Lexington, Louisville, and Frankfort.

Drake promised the younger Usher that he would recruit a company and set off for Kentucky in the spring of 1815. When Usher died on the return journey, his father offered Drake the management of the company and encouraged him to stick to the original timetable. The Drake company arrived in Kentucky in December 1815.

The principal record of their trip westward is provided by Noah Ludlow, one of the actors in Drake's company. His account of their journey forms part of his invaluable but often inaccurate autobiography published in 1880. Along with Ludlow in this initial acting troupe were Mr. and Mrs. Lewis, Frances Ann Denny, and Joe Tracy, all of whom also took on some extra administrative or technical role: Ludlow acted as advance agent, Mr. Lewis was the general manager of the company, and Tracy was the stage carpenter. The rest of the company was made up of the Drake children, who ranged in ages from thirteen to twenty. Given the primitive state of transport and the wildness of the country, it is unlikely that any other theater company in the annals of the American stage can have undertaken so hazardous or intrepid a journey.

They left Albany in May 1815 on foot, with their scenery, costumes, and baggage loaded onto a cart. They carried six scenes: a wood, a street, a parlor, a kitchen, a palace, and a garden. They also hauled with them a stage floor, made up of green baize cloth, and a portable proscenium arch that could fit into almost any space. The whole thing, with scenery and painted backdrops, could be put up and taken down in two or three hours. Usher's job was to go ahead of this motley crew and arrange performances along the way. These performances paid for their trip. Their first such performance was in the courthouse of the small town of Cherry Valley, New York, where they presented two farces, *The Prize* and *The Purse*, followed the next night by the debut of eighteen-year-old Frances Ann Denny in the leading role of Julia in *The Midnight Hour*. Thus they continued from town to town, playing as they went. At Cooperstown, Ludlow notes that James Fenimore Cooper was in the audience to "encourage our pioneer efforts in the cause of Drama" (p. 9).

Drake's company had serious confrontations with Native Americans, wolves, and indignant locals on their journey. When they arrived at Olean, New York, Drake traded in his wagon for a flat-bottomed boat, and the group embarked on a hazardous 200-mile trip down the Allegheny River to Pittsburgh. They arrived in Pittsburgh in August and were joined by five other actors. They presented a season of plays there in an old converted building, inappropriately named the New Theatre. Their repertoire included *The Honeymoon*, *The Castle Specter*, *Speed the Plough*, *No Song, No Supper*, and *Pizarro*. Mr. Williams, one of the newcomers, was determined to do this latter piece so that he could play the part of Rolla. Drake had to paint new scenery, and Williams had to recruit a number of extras to play "temple virgins." The entrance of this group brought the play to a halt as the audience and actors, in fits of laughter, watched two beautiful young ladies followed by one elderly woman, one child, the theater's cleaning woman, and the prop man in drag, come on stage in long white dresses to the sound of slow, dramatic music.

In mid-November the group set off on the second leg of their adventure: a 400-mile journey down the Ohio River in a flat-bottomed boat. They landed in Kentucky at Limestone (now Maysville) some sixty miles upriver from Cincinnati. The rest of the trip, to the state's capital city of Frankfort, was made by wagon. Regular professional theater on the frontier could be said to have started on 4 December 1815, when Drake's company, augmented by several local actors, performed *The Mountaineers, or Love and Madness* in the Frankfort Theatre. The company's repertoire had been perfected "on the road," so that by the time they arrived in Kentucky they had an extensive list of plays from which to choose.

In February 1816 Drake moved on to Louisville, having hired John Vos to renovate the theater there. These frontier theaters were often little more than barns or warehouses, but Drake wanted to convert them into playhouses that "were little inferior to those in the eastern states" (*Western Courier*, 15 June 1815). Louisville was growing fast as the industrial center of the state, and Drake made it his theatrical home. From there he established the Louisville-Lexington-Frankfort theater circuit that was the basis of his success.

Once this circuit was established, Drake encouraged his younger actors to set off on their own to play in some of the smaller towns in Kentucky and beyond. Several of them consequently went on to become actor-managers in their own right. Drake also tried, somewhat unsuccessfully, to establish touring circuits in St. Louis, Vincennes, and Cincinnati. In 1823 he handed over management of his Kentucky theater empire to his son Alexander and daughter-in-law Frances Ann Denny Drake. Samuel Drake retired to his farm in rural Oldham County, where he died.

Drake's company was prolific and provided its audience with a constant diet of new productions. During one season in Louisville the company performed twenty-four different plays in twelve days. They generally performed two plays a night, often with musical entertainment between shows. Ludlow complained of the sheer volume of work required of actors in those days; he felt that actors who had to study new plays daily had little chance of understanding their roles (p. 73). Drake, himself an accomplished actor, musician, and fencer, had his company specialize in farce and sentimental comedy, where "moral tendency is emulated, and where instruction is blended with innocent amusement" (*Western Courier*, 28 Feb. 1816). In this way he established the theater as a respectable form of entertainment and frequently performed benefits for hospitals, churches, and charities.

Although it might be overstating the case (as Ludlow often did) to say that Drake was the first to bring professional theater to the West, Drake's vision of refurbished theaters that played an active role in the community, where one could see plays suitable for ladies and gentlemen of taste, with visually stimulating scenery and quality actors, formed the basis for the first really successful theatrical enterprise in the West.

• The most thorough and detailed account of Drake's life and work to date is West T. Hill, Jr., *The Theatre in Early Kentucky: 1790–1820* (1971). The most entertaining account is Noah M. Ludlow, *Dramatic Life as I Found It* (1880), which was reprinted in 1966 with an introduction by Francis Hodge. The reader must be careful with Ludlow's account; as he looks back on events that happened sixty-five years previously his memory is somewhat flawed and his own importance somewhat inflated. Other works of note are Mable Tyree Crum's two-volume dissertation for the University of Kentucky, *The History of the Lexington Theatre from the Beginning to 1860* (1956), George D. Ford, *These Were Actors: A Story of the Chapmans and Drakes* (1955), and Barnard Hewitt, *Theatre U.S.A.: 1665–1957* (1959).

ANTHONY R. HAIGH

DRAKE, Samuel Gardner (11 Oct. 1798–14 June 1875), bookseller and historian, was born in Pittsfield, New Hampshire, the son of Simeon Drake and Love Muchmore Tucke, farmers. Drake was a slender and delicate child who loved the woods near his home more than he did the local school. In 1816 he joined his older brother John Drake and worked as an underclerk for his uncle Samuel J. Tucke, an importer of paints and oils, in Boston. Following a six-month stay in Baltimore on business for his uncle, Drake returned to New Hampshire and taught in a school in Loudon, New Hampshire. This was followed by a schoolteaching stint in New Jersey (1819–1820), a study of medicine in Pittsfield, New Hampshire, and then a return to teaching (1820–1823). Although he did not "find himself" in these endeavors, Drake brought the purposefulness that he had developed to what would become the great passions of his life: collecting antiquarian materials and bookselling.

In 1825 Drake came across a 1772 edition of Benjamin Church's *Entertaining History of King Philip's War*. Drake resolved to bring out a new edition of Church's book and quickly located the requisite subscribers for his project. This project was the first of many that would follow; Drake's interest in the history of early New England (in particular the relations between the Puritans and the Native Americans) led him to publish *Indian Biography* (1832), *Old Indian Chronicle* (1836), *Indian Captivities* (1839), and *Book of the Indians* (1841). In the pursuit of these works, Drake developed a large collection of materials relative to early American history, and he soon became the authority on the subject. It is important to recall that Drake lived in an intensely "historical" age; the 1830s and 1840s witnessed the production of many books on early New England.

In 1828 Drake set himself up as a bookseller in Boston. He established his own "Antiquarian Book-Store" on Cornhill Street on 10 July 1830; this endeavor became the most productive and consuming of his life. He was awarded an honorary master's degree from Union College in 1843, and he was well on his way to becoming the most sought-after authority for an understanding of early American books.

Drake was one of five men who collaborated in the founding of the New England Historic Genealogical Society in 1845. He served as the first corresponding secretary of the organization for twelve years and was its president in 1858. Drake was also the true founding father of the periodical of the organization, the *New-England Historical and Genealogical Register*, which printed its first issue in January 1847. In both the organization and its periodical Drake was a guiding light at the time of the foundation and for many years afterward.

Wishing to find more books, and wanting to find out about the state of American books abroad, Drake went on a trip to England and France in November 1858. He enjoyed London but was even more impressed with Paris, which was undergoing an architectural renovation during the Second Empire of Louis Napoleon. Drake found that London, which had at least 1,500 bookselling establishments, contained very few books about America or by American authors. Determined to rectify this situation by encouraging younger American scholars to write for European audiences, Drake took a steamship for home in May 1860, bringing with him books that were estimated to be worth £400.

There is little record of Drake's sympathies or feelings regarding the American Civil War. It can only be assumed that he continued to focus on his antiquarian researches during that time period; indeed, he could present as the result of his work *Result of Some Researches among the British Archives* (1860) and a *Brief Memoir of Sir Walter Raleigh* (1862). Before his European trip, Drake had intended to write a general history of New England; despairing of the size of the subject, he contented himself with *History of Boston*, which came out over four years (1852–1856).

Drake made his last visit to his bookstore on 8 June 1875; he died six days later. At the time of his death, he left 15,000 volumes and 30,000 pamphlets on the subjects of American history, biography, genealogy, poetry, theology, and education. Some 10,417 items were cataloged and sold in May 1876.

Drake married twice, the first time in 1825 to Louisa Elmes, with whom he had five children, and the second time, after his first wife died, to a relative, Sarah Jane Drake. Drake and his second wife had no children. Two of his sons became historians.

Drake was one of the first great collectors and chroniclers of the American experience. He found his calling in the 1830s, when American historiography was undergoing a revival; before that time, the visions of American history had changed little since the time of Cotton Mather. Many legendary and semilegendary episodes were clarified by the more careful scholarship of Drake's time. Without being cognizant of the fact, Drake also stood at a critical intersection in American history and literature; although he identified himself much more strongly with the "serious" writers of history (such as George Bancroft and Jared Sparks), Drake's researches also allowed for a greater probing of the American past by the novelists of his era (Nathaniel Hawthorne among them). In the case of both the historians and the novelists, the scholars and the popularizers, the work of Samuel G. Drake was instrumental in bringing together a sizable body of knowledge that encouraged a greater understanding of the American past. Certainly not on a scholarly par with Bancroft or Sparks or on a literary footing with Hawthorne, Drake was nevertheless their true contemporary, and in some respects their equal in terms of his importance in bringing the American past to life.

• Drake's own works are the best method by which to study his scholarship. There is little in the way of personal information, other than a memoir in the *New-England Historical and Genealogical Resister* 17 (1863): 197–211. The catalog of his life's work and collections is in *Catalogue of the Private Library of Samuel Gardner Drake, A.M.* (1876).

SAMUEL WILLARD CROMPTON

DRAKE, St. Clair, Jr. (2 Jan. 1911–15 June 1990), anthropologist, was born John Gibbs St. Clair Drake, Jr., in Suffolk, Virginia, the son of John Gibbs St. Clair Drake, Sr., a Baptist pastor, and Bessie Lee

Bowles. By the time Drake was four years old his father had moved the family twice, once to Harrisonburg, Virginia, and then to Pittsburgh, Pennsylvania.

The family lived in a racially mixed neighborhood in Pittsburgh, where Drake grew to feel at ease with whites. His strict Baptist upbringing led him to understand religious organizations from the inside. His father also taught him to work with tools and to become an expert in woodworking, a skill Drake later employed in his field research.

A trip to the West Indies in 1922 with his father led to major changes in Drake's life. Rev. Drake had tried to instill in his son a deep respect for the British Empire, but the sight of the poverty in the Caribbean led him to abandon his support of racial integration and convert to Marcus Garvey's ideas in favor of racial separation and a return to an African homeland for the black diaspora. He quit his pastorship and went to work as an itinerant organizer for Garvey. Drake was to trace his interest in anthropology to this trip with his father.

While his father worked for Garvey as an organizer and was constantly away from home on trips, Drake and his mother moved to Staunton, Virginia. In contrast to his Pittsburgh experiences, Drake encountered the caste system in full force in Virginia. These experiences led him to an appreciation of the radical African-American poets of his day, particularly Langston Hughes, Countee Cullen, and Claude McKay. They also led him to combine action with study.

After graduating with honors from Hampton Institute in Hampton, Virginia, in 1931, Drake worked with the Society of Friends on their "Peace Caravans." These caravans worked for racial harmony and civil rights. Once again Drake met with whites in a common cause as an equal. He continued to work with the Quakers while teaching at one of their boarding schools. For a time he considered becoming a member of the Society of Friends; however, the realization that there was still prejudice in such a liberal group kept him from converting to the religion.

Drake decided to study anthropology in an effort to better understand the roots of human behavior. After teaching high school at the Christianburg Institute in Cambria, Virginia, from 1932 to 1935, he became a research assistant at Dillard University in New Orleans. There he combined his field research with action, joining the Tenant Farmers Union and the Farmers Union in Adams County, Mississippi. By his own accounts in "Reflections on Anthropology and the Black Experience," these periodic forays into activism nearly cost him his life on a number of occasions. A lynch mob once chased him and his fellow workers; they barely escaped. Drake recounts that on another occasion he was badly beaten and left unconscious.

After a year at Columbia University in 1936, Drake entered the University of Chicago in 1937 on a Rosenwald fellowship. There he met the sociologist Horace Cayton and joined his research under the auspices of the Public Works Progress Administration (WPA), specializing in the African-American church and the urban black population. This work became the basis for his contributions to *Black Metropolis* (1946), which he jointly authored with Horace B. Cayton. Drake married sociologist Elizabeth Dewy Johns in 1942; they had two children.

During the Second World War, Drake became actively involved in the struggle of African Americans for equality. He concentrated his efforts on the conflict in northern war industries and housing. He worked with various African-American organizations for which he gathered hard data, joined in work actions, and served on various war boards concerned with presenting African-American grievances to the federal government. While gathering data for *Black Metropolis*, Drake worked in a war plant and experienced inequality firsthand. Drake grew bitter at his fellow citizens who so enthusiastically fought fascism abroad but were unwilling to combat it in the United States. In response to these experiences Drake joined the merchant marine, in which he believed he would not encounter the same prejudice and segregation that he might have in the U.S. armed forces.

Following his discharge from the service, Drake completed his Ph.D. in anthropology at the University of Chicago in 1946 and accepted a position teaching at Roosevelt College that same year. Drake worked extensively in Africa, teaching in both Liberia and Ghana. In 1961 he developed a training program for Peace Corps volunteers in Africa. Over the years he was a personal adviser to many African leaders, including Kwame Nkrumah in Ghana and various high officials in Nigeria. However, as military rule steadily replaced civilian rule in the 1960s, Drake left Africa, refusing to work with dictators.

A prolific scholar, Drake focused his writing on racial concerns such as the problem of inequality, the plight of the urban poor, religion, race relations, and the relationship of African Americans to Africa. His major works include *Race Relations in a Time of Rapid Social Change* (1966), *Our Urban Poor: Promises to Keep and Miles to Go* (1967), and *The Redemption of Africa and Black Religion* (1970). He edited numerous journals and books and brought intellectuals together to discuss the issues of the day and propose actions to meet these problems.

In 1969 Drake moved to Stanford University, where he established the Center for Afro-American Studies, an Afro-American studies department that became a model for other universities. Drake refused to bow to the demand of radicals who wanted the department to be a center exclusively for black students, where others interested in African and Afro-American history would not be welcome. He refused to teach Afrocentric notions that saw Africans as the center of all civilizations and the inventors of all wisdom. He resisted the efforts of black militants outside and inside academia—Stokely Carmichael, James Turner at Cornell, Felix Okoye, and others—who believed that a person's skin color accredited or discredited him or her as an expert in African and Afro-American studies.

Drake insisted on establishing his center on solid academic grounds.

Throughout his life, Drake showed personal integrity in working to achieve his goals of equality and respect for African Americans and their accomplishments. He founded the American Society for African Culture and the American Negro Leadership Conference on Africa in the early 1960s. He was never afraid to risk his life in pursuit of his goals. Drake died at his home in Palo Alto, California.

• Some of Drake's manuscripts are in the collection of the Schomburg Library of the New York Public Library. Patrick W. Romero, *In Black America, 1968: The Year of Awakening* (1969), contains an article by Drake on the civil rights movement as well as bibliographic references of his work. Similarly, Joseph R. Washington, Jr., *Jews in Black Perspective* (1984), has an article by Drake on the African and Jewish diasporas as well as bibliographic notes on his work. See also Okon Edet Uya, *Black Brotherhood: Afro-Americans and Africa* (1971), which has an essay by Drake on the poets of the Harlem Renaissance, a major influence in his self-perception. Other noteworthy writings by Drake are "Black Studies and Global Perspectives: An Essay," *Journal of Negro Education* 53 (1984): 226–42; "Anthropology and the Black Experience," *Black Scholar* 2 (1980): 2–31; "What Happened to Black Studies?," *New York Educational Quarterly* 10, no. 2 (1979): 9–16; "Reflections on Anthropology and the Black Experience," *Anthropology and Education Quarterly* 9, no. 2 (1978): 85–109; and "The Black University in the American School Order," *Daedalus* 100 (1971): 833–97. Wyatt MacGaffey, "Who Owns Ancient Egypt," *Journal of African History* 23, no. 3 (1991): 515–19, includes a discussion of Drake's *Black Folk Here and There: An Essay in History and Anthropology* (1987). An obituary is in the *New York Times*, 21 June 1990.

FRANK A. SALAMONE

DRAPER, Charles Stark (2 Oct. 1901–25 July 1987), aeronautical engineer, was born in Windsor, Missouri, the son of Arthur Draper, a dentist, and Martha Washington Stark, a former schoolteacher. From the beginning, Draper was a free spirit whose intellectual drive could not be contained within any one discipline. He matriculated at the University of Missouri in 1917 but transferred to Stanford University in 1919 when his parents moved to California. After receiving his B.A. in psychology in 1922, he abandoned his plan to become a physician and instead embarked on a career as a ship's radio operator. He attended Herald's Radio College in 1922 and then went along for the ride with a friend who was traveling to Cambridge, Massachusetts, to attend Harvard University. Draper was so taken with Cambridge in general and the Massachusetts Institute of Technology (MIT) in particular that he immediately enrolled in MIT. In 1926 he received his B.S. in electrochemical engineering. His graduate coursework was such a free-form collage of mathematics, chemistry, physics, metallurgy, and aeronautical engineering that his M.S., which he received in 1928, was awarded from no particular department. In 1929 he began working as a research assistant in MIT's aeronautical engineering department while pursuing a

doctorate and was promoted to assistant professor in 1935. Again, his interests could not be confined to one narrow field of study. Not until 1938, after MIT demanded that he focus on *something* long enough to get a degree, did he satisfy the requirements for an Sc.D. in physics. Also in 1938 he married Ivy Hurd Willard. They had four children.

In 1939 Draper became a full professor of aeronautical engineering, and from 1951 until his retirement in 1966 he served as chairman of the department. He also found a field to which he could devote himself single-mindedly—automatic control and guidance. In 1939 he founded and became the first director of MIT's Confidential Instrument Development Laboratory, renamed the Instrumentation Laboratory in 1945. The laboratory's first major development was a single-degree-of-freedom gyroscope, which he adapted for use in the Mark 14 gunsight. Because it semiautomatically adjusted for range, wind, and the pitch and roll of a ship's deck, the Mark 14 proved to be an invaluable tool for directing naval antiaircraft weapons and was particularly effective in protecting American naval vessels against Japanese fighter and "kamikaze" attacks during World War II. After the war, Draper designed the A-1 and A-4 sight control systems for F-86 fighter planes. These sights, which relied on automatic radar ranging, gave the U.S. Air Force a decided advantage against Soviet-built fighters in "MIG Alley" during the Korean War.

In the late 1940s Draper began working on an inertial guidance system that would revolutionize navigation. As a reserve officer in the Army Air Corps in the 1920s, he had been greatly concerned about the unreliability of cockpit instrument panels. Moreover, because conventional navigational systems and devices required outside reference points, such as star sightings and radio signals, the usefulness of such systems and devices was greatly compromised by inclement weather and jamming. Draper's invention, known both as Spatial Inertial Reference Equipment (SPIRE) and "astronomy in a closet," eliminated the need for such reference points. Built around three reduced friction gyroscopes like the ones used in the Mark 14, SPIRE measured acceleration, velocity, and distance. Connected to an altimeter, compass, and computer, the device constituted a self-contained guidance system. In order to prove to the multitude of skeptics that SPIRE would work, in 1953 Draper took an Air Force crew and seven MIT engineers on a twelve-hour flight from Massachusetts to California in a B-29 bomber equipped with his 2,700-pound system. Except during takeoff and landing, no one touched the controls as the huge plane "flew" itself. In 1954 Draper and his colleagues at MIT developed a miniature version of SPIRE, called the Ships Inertial Navigation System (SINS), for use in nuclear submarines. In the late 1950s SINS was adapted for use on submarine-launched and intercontinental ballistic missiles such as Polaris, Atlas, and Titan I. The development of SINS was one of several major technological advances that allowed the United States to use the threat of nuclear deterrence as an instrument of foreign policy during the Cold War.

Draper's most impressive achievement was the development of the guidance system used by the National Aeronautics and Space Agency's (NASA) Project Apollo. In the early 1960s Draper began assigning lunar navigation problems as thesis work to his graduate students while the laboratory began designing a system to do the job automatically. Essentially an inertial guidance device connected to telescopes and a sextant, in 1969 Draper's system successfully piloted the Apollo 11 astronauts on their round trip to the Moon.

Draper received a great many honors for his achievements, including the Sylvanus Albert Reed Award for designing the Mark 14 (1945), the U.S. Air Force's Exceptional Service Award (1951), the U.S. Navy's Distinguished Public Service Award (1956), the Holley Medal of the American Society of Mechanical Engineers (ASME) (1957), the William Proctor Prize of the Scientific Research Society of America (1959), the Louis W. Hill Space Transportation Award of the Institute of the Aeronautical Sciences (1962), the National Medal of Science (1964), the Daniel Guggenheim Medal of the United Engineering Trusts (1967), the Founders Medal of the National Academy of Engineering (1970), and the ASME's Rufus Oldenburger Medal (1971). He was elected to the National Academy of Sciences (1957) and the National Academy of Engineering (1965). In 1973 the Instrumentation Laboratory was renamed the Charles Stark Draper Laboratory. He died in Cambridge, Massachusetts.

Draper was a feisty fellow, regarded by some of his colleagues as pugnacious, irritating, and fanatical. Others considered him brilliant, stimulating, and contagiously enthusiastic. All regarded him as one of the foremost engineers of his day. James Killian, Jr., a former president of MIT, stated that Draper's "technological achievements clearly placed him in the category of genius." He dominated the field of automatic control and guidance for more than thirty years, and his research led to the creation of the inertial instruments and systems industry. His greatest contributions were to space exploration and the defense of his country.

• Draper's papers are located in the Library of Congress. Sidney Lees, ed., *Air, Space, and Instruments* (1963), a festschrift celebrating Draper's sixtieth birthday, provides an excellent account of the importance of Draper's work up to that date as well as much useful biographical information. Don Murray, "'Doc' Draper's Wonderful Tops," *Reader's Digest*, Sept. 1957, pp. 63–67, offers a more personal glimpse of Draper and his work. An obituary is in the *New York Times*, 27 July 1987.

CHARLES W. CAREY, JR.

DRAPER, Dorothy (22 Nov. 1889–10 Mar. 1969), interior decorator and columnist, was born in Tuxedo Park, New York, the daughter of Paul Tuckerman and Susan Minturn. She grew up in the environs of New York in an exclusive resort community where her parents were among the founding members in 1886. Educated primarily at home with a governess and tutor, her formal schooling was minimal, including two years at the Brearley School, a private girls' school in New York City. Annual trips to Europe gave her a cosmopolitan exposure to the world, and she was presented at Sherry's in 1907. Although she did not have any academic design training, her background and upbringing among the elite families of the Northeast contributed to her subsequent success as a decorator. She had complete confidence in her taste, and her social connections proved to be important in acquiring future clientele.

In 1912 she married George Draper, with whom she had three children before their divorce in 1930. Her interest in interior decorating began when she successfully renovated several houses that she owned in Manhattan and Washington. Eager to apply her energies and natural flair beyond her own domestic environment, she started a small business in 1925 called the Architectural Clearing House in which she coordinated the renovations of friends' houses with the assistance of local architects. In the early 1930s, through Douglas Elliman, a real estate developer, she received the commission to decorate the lobby of the Carlyle Hotel in New York City, the first of many important hotel commissions. The lobby displayed many features that came to represent her trademarks, including large square black and white marble floor tiles, chintz fabric and wallpaper in oversize patterns, and the display of busts and other classical forms as decorative elements.

In 1929, as her business grew with the successful renovation of several apartment house lobbies in the classical–Art Deco idiom, the name of the firm was changed to Dorothy Draper and Company. Draper's natural talent for public relations as well as her reputation in the area of nonresidential design resulted in the 1937 commission for the entire thirty-seven story Hampshire House apartment hotel in Manhattan, the largest commercial decorating contract to be given to a woman at that time. She believed that the entire project should be conceived comprehensively and designed everything from the interior architecture to bellboy liveries and china. Combining furniture styles and design motifs of various historical periods, she tried to make the impersonal public spaces more homelike, creating the atmosphere of a London townhouse instead of the customary hotel look, which was monochromatic and undistinguished. While stark contrasts of black and white, fanciful plasterwork in the neo-baroque style, large expanses of mirror, and innovative uses of materials such as patent-leather and metal gave these spaces theatrical drama, the walls and furniture of bedrooms were decorated with a patterned fabric of huge cabbage roses in brilliant reds and emerald greens. This fabric became a well-known signature of the Dorothy Draper style, produced by the fabric house of F. Schumacher & Co., which sold more than a million yards of this bright-colored chintz throughout the 1930s and 1940s. Wallpaper with wide pink and white stripes, chenille bedspreads, and white organdy curtains completed the Draper scheme and became ubiquitous in tasteful American bedrooms. Another innovation at the Hampshire House was the use of sliding glass doors instead of shower curtains in the bathrooms.

Draper was known for her vivid use of colors. Large, strong, and bold were her catchwords. From the 1930s to the mid-1950s her innovative design statements could be seen in all kinds of environments. In the striking use of scale and light, her style reflected the influence of the surrealist movement. Besides hotel interiors, Draper's work included clubs, restaurants, retail stores, and some private homes. She became a national celebrity largely due to her newspaper columns and publications. From 1939 to 1946 she wrote for *Good Housekeeping* magazine, and later she wrote a syndicated column for Hearst newspapers, "Ask Dorothy Draper." The author of three books—*Decorating Is Fun* (1939), *Entertaining Is Fun* (1941), and *365 Shortcuts to Home Decoration* (1965)—she also had a radio show called "Lines about Living," and she appeared on the covers of *Time* and *Life* magazines.

Some of her best-known commissions include the Gideon Putnam Hotel in Saratoga Springs (1933), Arrowhead Springs resort in California (1939), the Drake Hotel (Camellia House Restaurant) in Chicago (1940), the Mayflower Hotel in Washington, D.C. (1944), the Quitandinha Hotel in Petropolis, Brazil, and the "Dorotheum" restaurant-cafeteria of the Metropolitan Museum of Art in New York City (1954). Most of her work for those buildings has been altered beyond recognition. Her surviving tour de force is the Greenbriar resort in White Sulphur Springs, West Virginia, which was totally redecorated in 1947 with all her trademark motifs. She was also the color coordinator for the 1952 Packard Automobile, parts of the International Hotel at Kennedy Airport (1958), and the interior of the Convair 880 airplane (1960).

One reason given for her particular fondness for large-scale patterns and grandiose architectural detailing was her statuesque height, which was close to six feet. Her commanding presence was frequently crowned by a stylish hat, and her influential design aesthetics earned her the title of the grande dame of American interior decorating. Like most of the first generation of women decorators in America, she lacked the credentials of a professional designer. But because of the enormous impact her firm had on the industry, she was eventually admitted to the American Institute of Decorators (AID) in the early 1950s. Despite the infamous slur leveled at Draper by Frank Lloyd Wright, who referred to her as an "inferior desecrator," her reputation remains unchallenged with respect to the influence of her style on commercial hotel design. In 1960 she sold her company to Leon Hegwood (who has since died) and the designer Carlton Varney; the latter continued to use her name in the design of commercial interiors. Draper died in Cleveland, Ohio, and is buried in Newport, Rhode Island.

• The firm of Dorothy Draper and Company, Inc., also known as Carlton Varney, New York City, has the records of the firm, scrapbooks containing articles about Dorothy Draper, and some renderings of her commissions. Two of her drawings for the Convair airplane interior are at the Cooper-Hewitt Museum in New York City. A biography is Carleton Varney, *The Draper Touch: The High Life and High Style of Dorothy Draper* (1988). See also Mark Hampton, *Legendary Decorators of the Twentieth Century* (1992), and Robert A. M. Stern et al., *New York 1960* (1995). Draper was interviewed by Edward R. Murrow on CBS's "Person to Person" on 17 May 1957. An obituary is in the *New York Times*, 12 Mar. 1969.

PAULINE C. METCALF

DRAPER, George (21 May 1880–1 July 1959), physician and pioneer of constitutional and psychosomatic medicine, was born in New York City, the son of William Henry Draper, a prominent clinician, and Ruth Dana, a musician and daughter of Charles Dana, editor of the *New York Sun*. Draper grew up in a family that was both culturally and economically privileged.

Draper completed his A.B. at Harvard in 1903. Three years later he received an M.D. from the Columbia College of Physicians and Surgeons and began a two-year internship at Presbyterian Hospital in New York. In 1908 the young physician took up residence at the University of Munich for further training at the clinic of Friedrich von Mueller, Germany's most renowned clinical researcher at the time, who trained hundreds of newly minted American physicians before World War I.

Returning to the United States in 1909, Draper held residencies at Pennsylvania Hospital in Philadelphia (1909–1910) and the hospital of the Rockefeller Institute for Medical Research (1910–1912). Collaborating with fellow Rockefeller physicians Raymond Dochez and Francis W. Peabody, he published *A Clinical Study of Acute Poliomyelitis* in 1912. Hailed as a model for clinical research, the monograph became a classic on its subject, establishing Draper among the rising stars of internal medicine. When Franklin D. Roosevelt was struck with an acute attack of polio, Draper served as his physician. In 1912 Draper left the Rockefeller Institute to join the staff of Presbyterian Hospital.

It was Draper's involvement with polio four years later that set the agenda for the remainder of his career. As a New York City medical officer during the polio epidemic of 1916, he observed that many polio victims possessed physical similarities. He speculated that there might be definite "types" of individuals, with particular physical and mental "constitutions," who were susceptible to specific diseases. Thus began Draper's career of exploring the relationship between human constitution—as seen in an individual's physique, physiology, and temperament—and disease. Months later, with private donations, he established the constitution clinic at the Columbia-affiliated Presbyterian Hospital.

Draper defined constitution broadly, as "that aggregate of hereditarial [*sic*] characters, influenced more or less by environment, which determines the individual's reaction, successful or unsuccessful, to the stress of the environment" (Draper et al., "Studies in Constitution I.: Clinical Anthropometry," *Journal of the American Medical Association* 82 [1924]: 431). He also emphasized the role of the psyche in the disease process. This holistic approach to disease ran against the current of scientific medicine in America, which had focused reductionistically on specific pathogens and their attendant lesions since the late nineteenth-century rise of the germ theory. Constitutionalism was just one of several alternative holistic approaches within American academic medicine during the early twentieth century; others included social medicine, psychosomatic medicine, and the integration of social services and the social sciences in medicine.

Between his founding of the constitution clinic in 1916 and his retirement in 1946, Draper focused most of his research on the development of a disease-based human taxonomy, a means of classifying humankind according to individuals' constitutional predisposition to specific diseases. His three monographs on human constitution—*Human Constitution* (1924), *Disease and the Man* (1930), and *Human Constitution in Clinical Medicine* (1944)—articulated his research program for the study of the individual's four "panels of personality": anatomy, physiology, psychology, and immunology. It was an ambitious program designed to restore a vision of the whole patient within medicine, to provide a scientific basis for the work of the general practitioner, and to reintegrate a medical profession Draper regarded as overspecialized and excessively reductionistic.

Draper's work found support from an eclectic range of individuals and institutions, including eugenicists Charles Davenport and Harry Laughlin, biologist and constitutional researcher Raymond Pearl, and psychosomaticist H. Flanders Dunbar. The Josiah Macy, Jr., Foundation, which promoted the integration of medicine with the social and biological sciences, funded much of Draper's work in the early 1930s, as did private individuals and friends. In 1942 the U.S. Navy enlisted Draper to screen candidates for its flight training school. His greatest patron, however, was Alan Gregg, director of the Rockefeller Foundation's Division of Medical Sciences. Gregg was particularly interested in integrating psychiatry and psychology with general medicine, and Draper's work on the psychological dimensions of human constitution and disease susceptibility fit nicely with his program. The constitution clinic received funding from the Rockefeller Foundation from 1936 to 1946, allowing Draper to expand his studies substantially and to garner the respect of many previously skeptical colleagues at Columbia.

Interestingly, at the twilight of his career, in 1945, Draper confessed to Gregg that he was now convinced that "morphology, gross physiology, and psychiatry" would not unlock the secrets of constitutional specificity but must step aside for "magnificent new chemical, physical, and biological techniques" whose "target . . . must be the intimacies of the individual cell." Having spent years fighting the reductionism inherent in laboratory investigation, Draper had now become its champion. It is important to realize, however, that constitutionalists like Draper had always employed a wide range of reductionistic analyses to investigate their patients before reconstituting them as wholes. Today, as the origins of disease are increasingly sought in the genetic and molecular fabric of life, and as researchers explore the relationship between psychic state and physical disease, Draper's words and work seem prescient: he was a pioneer in exploring the psychosomatic and hereditary nature of disease.

George Draper died at his home in New York City after a long illness. He was survived by his second wife, Elizabeth Carrington Low, whom he married in 1935, after divorcing Dorothy Tuckerman in 1930; he had three children from his first marriage.

• There is no official body of Draper's papers, but the papers of Raymond Pearl and Charles Davenport, both at the American Philosophical Society in Philadelphia, contain the correspondence of these men with Draper and their correspondence to others about Draper's work. Informative correspondence between Draper and Alan Gregg is held in the Rockefeller Archive Center, North Tarrytown, N.Y. Besides those cited in the text, Draper's monographs include *I. Human Constitution, Its Significance in Medicine and How It May Be Studied; II. The Influence of Sex in Determining Human Disease Potentiality; III. The Patient and His Physician*, Beaumont Foundation Lectures No. 7 (1928), and *Infantile Paralysis* (1935). For biographical information, see his obituary in the *New York Times*, 2 July 1959; and David Riesman, ed., *History of the Interurban Clinical Club, 1905–1937* (1938), pp. 113–14. For an exploration of Draper's relationship to American constitutional medicine, see Sarah W. Tracy, "George Draper and American Constitutional Medicine, 1916–1946: Reinventing the Sick Man," *Bulletin of the History of Medicine* 66 (1992): 53–89. See also Tracy, "An Evolving Science of Man: The Transformation and Demise of American Constitutional Medicine, 1920–1950," in *Greater Than the Parts: Holism in Biomedicine, 1920–1950*, ed. Christopher Lawrence and George Weisz (1998).

SARAH W. TRACY

DRAPER, Henry (7 Mar. 1837–20 Nov. 1882), astronomer, was born in Prince Edward County, Virginia, the son of John William Draper, a noted physician, chemist, and educator, and Antonia Gardner, a Portuguese woman of noble birth. Draper was two years old when his father accepted a position as professor of chemistry at the University of the City of New York and moved the family to New York City, where Draper lived for the rest of his life. Draper's father kindled in him an early interest in science, often permitting his precocious son to assist in his university lectures and scientific investigations. When Draper was thirteen, his father taught him the art of taking photographs through a microscope. From this period dates Draper's lifelong interest in photography, a field in which he later attained great eminence.

Draper enrolled in the collegiate department of the University of the City of New York at age fifteen but left it to enter the University's medical department at the end of his sophomore year, largely on the advice of his father (who was then president of the faculty of medicine). By 1857 Draper had completed a thesis and had successfully passed all of his examinations but was only twenty, one year shy of the minimum graduation age. He therefore decided to go abroad with his older brother for a year of study and recreation. On his return in 1858 he received his medical degree with distinction and joined the staff of Bellevue Hospital, where he remained for eighteen months. In the fall of 1860 he accepted a position as professor of natural science at his alma mater.

To this appointment Draper added the chair of analytical chemistry in 1862, and he retained both positions until 1882. In 1866 he was simultaneously appointed professor of physiology in the medical department and dean of the faculty but resigned from these last two positions in 1873. Finally, after the death of his father in 1882, Draper was chosen to succeed him as professor of chemistry. He held this position only until the end of that academic year, at which time he severed his connection with the university.

During his 1857–1858 European sojourn, Draper had attended the annual meeting of the British Association for the Advancement of Science in Dublin. Afterward, he had visited the famous six-foot reflecting telescope of the earl of Rosse at Birr Castle, Parsonstown. There, he had conceived of the possibility of combining photography and astronomy. Accordingly, as soon as he returned, he began construction of a telescope and observatory on land that belonged to his father's estate at Hastings-on-Hudson. His tedious grinding and polishing of a speculum metal mirror came to an abrupt end in February 1860 when the speculum split in half one night because of the expansive force of freezing moisture. On the advice of Sir John Herschel, he quickly began experimenting with silvered-glass mirrors, grinding and polishing more than one hundred of them over the next two years.

By the fall of 1862 Draper had completed a 15½-inch glass mirror, which he installed at the Hastings observatory. He spent the greater part of 1863 taking photographs of the planets, sun, and moon. Draper took some 1,500 lunar photographs; about 1¼ inches in diameter, they bore enlargement to three feet (and in one case to fifty inches) with excellent results. They were the best photographs of the moon taken up to that time. At the request of Joseph Henry, the secretary of the Smithsonian Institution, Draper wrote the monograph *On the Construction of a Silvered-glass Telescope 15½ Inches in Aperture, and Its Use in Celestial Photography* (1864), which quickly became the standard reference on telescope making.

He began construction of a 28-inch glass mirror in 1867. After its completion in May 1872 Draper immediately used it, at his father's urging, to see if it could photograph stellar spectra. His initial attempts on Vega were only partially successful, however; his photographs, ½-inch long by ¹⁄₃₂-inch wide, revealed a faint continuum but no spectrum lines.

Repeated experiments enabled Draper to improve his technique, and on 1 August 1872 he succeeded in obtaining the first photograph of a star (again Vega) that showed distinct Fraunhofer lines, a series of dark absorption lines in the stellar spectra whose pattern depends on (and therefore helps scientists identify) the chemical composition of the star's atmosphere. Draper's closest competitor, the British astrophysicist William Huggins, could not duplicate that feat for four years. Draper followed this pioneering work with further photographic studies of the spectra of Vega, Altair, the sun, Venus, and Jupiter. Within a short time, he succeeded in making photography—especially spectrum photography—the best means of studying the sky.

Draper also achieved spectacular results in the direct photography of the Orion nebula. His success here resulted from his use of the new dry photographic plates (suggested to him by Huggins), an excellent 11-inch Alvan Clark photographic refractor, and his technical skill in constructing an excellent driving clock for it. In March 1882 he took a superb 137-minute exposure of the nebula, which constituted by far the most brilliant success achieved by celestial photography up to that time.

In 1867 Draper married Mary Anna Palmer, the daughter of a prominent and wealthy New York businessman. Anna Draper took an intense interest in her husband's work and proved to be a valuable assistant, both in his laboratory attached to their New York residence and in the Hastings observatory. She was also a renowned hostess and frequently entertained celebrated politicians and scientists in their spacious Madison Avenue home. They had no children.

Draper regularly spent a few weeks every fall hunting on horseback in the Rocky Mountains. On one such trip in 1882, he was caught overnight in a blinding snowstorm without shelter and was unusually weary on his return to New York, where he died less than a month later of double pleurisy. After his death, his wife established the Henry Draper Fund at the Harvard College Observatory, which enabled the observatory to carry out fundamental research on the photography and classification of stellar spectra.

Despite the fact that Draper's medical training did not give him the mathematical background necessary for meaningful theoretical work in astronomy, his technical skills and innovative research placed him on the cutting edge of the astronomy of his day.

• Draper's papers, five boxes of correspondence, are in the New York Public Library. A small collection of his letters is reprinted in Nathan Reingold, ed., *Science in Nineteenth Century America: A Documentary History* (1964). A full-length modern assessment is Howard Plotkin, "Henry Draper: A Scientific Biography" (Ph.D. diss., Johns Hopkins Univ., 1972), which also contains a complete listing of his writings. See also Owen Gingerich, "Henry Draper's Scientific Legacy," and Howard Plotkin, "Henry Draper, Edward C. Pickering, and the Birth of American Astrophysics," both in *Symposium on the Orion Nebula to Honor Henry Draper, Annals of the New York Academy of Sciences* 395 (1982): 308–

20 and 321–30; Dorrit Hoffleit, "The Evolution of the Henry Draper Memorial," *Vistas in Astronomy* 34 (1991): 107–62; and Plotkin, "Henry Draper, the Discovery of Oxygen in the Sun, and the Dilemma of Interpreting the Solar Spectrum," *Journal for the History of Astronomy* 8 (1977): 44–51.

HOWARD PLOTKIN

DRAPER, John (29 Oct. 1702–29 Nov. 1762), journalist and publisher, was born in Roxbury, Massachusetts, the son of Richard Draper, a Boston shopkeeper, and Sarah Kilby. Draper grew up in a home stressing religious values; his father was a deacon at the Brattle Street church as well as a Boston selectman. Draper also was deeply religious and joined his father's church in 1727. He was apprenticed to Bartholomew Green, Sr., publisher of the *Boston News-Letter*, the oldest newspaper in America. The Green family virtually dominated printing in Connecticut, tracing their roots back six generations to Samuel Green, a printer in Cambridge, England. Draper worked hard and impressed the family so much that in 1726 he married his employer's daughter, Deborah Green; they had three children. After Deborah's death in 1736, he married Elizabeth Avery the following year; with his second wife, Draper had two children.

Draper had use of Green's press and in 1726 printed his first imprint, a 350-page book of sermons. In September 1731 Draper took another job, printing the first forty-seven issues of Jeremiah Gridley's *Boston Weekly Rehearsal*, a political paper of a Boston club. The 190 imprints of Draper's first decade as master printer, from 1733 to 1742, indicate the nature of his business. The majority (42 percent) were religious: primarily sermons, the Westminster Catechism, a biography of George Whitefield, and the Church of Scotland's translation of the Old Testament Book of Psalms. The main religious authors whom Draper published were Mather Byles, Charles Chauncy, Benjamin Colman, Samuel Cooper, Samuel Mather, Thomas Shepard, and Gilbert Tennent. Government documents (38 percent) were the next largest category, including laws, proclamations of the governor, speeches, and tax warrants. In 1733 he had become the official printer to the governor and Council of Massachusetts, a position he held for the next thirty years. The third most frequent titles (11 percent) were printing jobs for Harvard University. In 1733 he became the official printer of Harvard College, printing catalogs and undergraduate and graduate theses until his death. During his lifetime the prolific Draper and his apprentices printed 587 titles.

The vast majority of these titles were printed for booksellers, who in turn sold them from their stores. The booksellers who most often hired Draper were Daniel Henchman (Boston's most aggressive bookseller), Joseph Edwards and Hopestill Foster, and Charles Harrison, all of Cornhill Street, John Parker near the town dock, Nathaniel Procter of Fish Street, and Thomas Hancock in Ann Street. By 1742 Draper, while continuing as a printer, raised his occupational status by becoming a bookseller, hiring other printers to print titles for him. His printing house was on Newbury Street, and he opened his bookstore on Cornhill Street. One of his bestselling titles was Nathaniel Ames's almanac. The almanac was printed for the first few years by Green, but then from 1733 until 1762 Draper printed it annually. Ames's 24-page almanac was a printing job of up to 60,000 copies that Draper shared with three other houses.

After the death of Bartholomew Green on 28 December 1732, John Draper became the third publisher of the *Boston News-Letter*. Over the next thirty years, Draper changed the name of the paper twice, but always retained "News-Letter" as part of the title. In 1734 he suffered a temporary setback when his printing house on Newbury Street burned to the ground, and he lost the press. Fellow printers loaned him a press until he could purchase a new one from England. Under his editorship the paper added new features such as poetry, letters to the publisher, and an expanded section of advertisements. The most significant change was more extensive coverage of religious news. Most of Draper's business revolved around the printing of his weekly newspaper (printed every Thursday with a circulation of 1,500 and an annual charge of 6 shillings, 8 pence lawful money). Usually printed on durable rag paper, ten by fifteen inches, the paper lasted numerous readings. Coffeehouses and taverns carried his newspapers for their customers to read. The *News-Letter* circulated to the west along the road to Worcester, Springfield, Northampton, Hartford, and New Haven and was also carried south by riders to Providence and Newport. In order to sell his newspaper to an audience with a wide political and religious perspective, Draper kept the *News-Letter* nonpartisan. For example, he generally, but moderately, supported the Great Awakening of 1740–1745.

In addition to newspapers and imprints, probably half of Draper's annual business came from "job printing," such as labels, blank forms, handbills, ballads, posters, broadsides, petitions, and election notices. However, this business is difficult to substantiate since the materials were for quick reading and disposal and rarely carried the printer's name.

John Draper symbolized many New England printers for whom printing was a deeply ingrained family business. He married into a printing family and then trained as apprentices several of his relatives, including his son Richard, and three nephews, Edward Draper, Samuel Draper, and John Green, who married Draper's daughter Lydia. When Draper died in Boston, his son Richard wrote his obituary and praised him for his "industry, fidelity, and prudence in his business," his "charity and benevolence, his pleasant and sociable turn of mind," and especially for his "piety."

• For information on printing see Bernard Bailyn and John B. Hench, eds., *The Press & the American Revolution* (1981). James H. Stark, *The Loyalists of Massachusetts and the Other Side of the American Revolution* (1907); E. Alfred Jones, *The Loyalists of Massachusetts: Their Memorials, Petitions and*

Claims (1930); and Thomas Draper, *The Drapers in America* (1892), pp. 193–99, provide valuable family information. Although they technically begin coverage after Draper's death, additional helpful information may be found in Mary Ann Patricia Yodelis, "Boston's Second Major Paper War: Economics, Politics, and the Theory and Practice of Political Expression in the Press, 1763–1775" (Ph.D. diss., Univ. of Wisconsin, 1971); and Timothy Barnes, "The Loyalist Press in the American Revolution, 1765–1781" (Ph.D. diss., Univ. of New Mexico, 1970). For all imprints by John Draper and their full citations see *Eighteenth-Century Short Title Catalog* (1992), CD-ROM. Determining the actual number of imprints is tricky as you must subtract imprints that the CD-ROM incorrectly attributes to him (subtract imprints by his kinsman Samuel Draper who for 5 years printed in partnership with Zachariah Fowle; imprints by Somerset Draper, a proflic London printer; imprints by patriot John Draper; imprints printed by other printers but only for sale at his store; and forged copies of Ames's Almanac). First publication of the notice of John Draper's death was in the *Boston News-Letter*, 2 Dec. 1762.

DAVID E. MAAS

DRAPER, John William (5 May 1811–4 Jan. 1882), scientist, educator, and historian, was born near Liverpool, England, the son of John Christopher Draper, an itinerant Wesleyan minister, and Sarah Ripley. Draper attended a Methodist grammar school and completed his premedical studies at University College, London, immersing himself in the philosophies of Benthamism and positivism, to which he would return later in life.

Draper married Antonia Gardner in 1831. They had six children, including three sons who went on to become prominent scientists. Always maintaining a close relationship with his family, in 1832 Draper immigrated to the United States with his wife, mother, and sisters. Arriving too late to accept a promised teaching position in Virginia, the Drapers nevertheless settled in Mecklenburg County in that state. While the Draper women opened a school for girls that provided family income, John Draper constructed a laboratory and pursued his interest in science, publishing several papers on a variety of subjects. He then completed his medical studies at the University of Pennsylvania in 1836 and returned to Virginia as professor of chemistry and natural philosophy at Hampden-Sydney College in Prince Edward County. There he researched the chemical effects of light and the application of physics and chemistry to physiology. It was also at Hampden-Sydney that Draper began to consider pedagogical issues and the creation of a scientific-minded community in America. He recruited students to record the weather on a daily, systematic basis, and in 1838 he proposed that all colleges train students to do this work. When the graduates returned to their homes, Draper argued, they would be prepared to implement the establishment of a federal weather bureau.

In 1839 Draper accepted the chair of chemistry at the University of the City of New York (now New York University). Working primarily on experiments concerning light and heat, he published voluminous-

ly. He also became interested in daguerreotype photography and is credited with having taken the first portrait of an individual (although his primacy is sometimes contested), as well as the first photographs of the Moon and of an object under a microscope. Draper also developed spectrography and techniques for enlarging and reproducing photographs. As his principal biographer, Donald Fleming, wrote, "Probably no other man did as much to measure the furthest reach of photography as a means to knowledge."

In 1841 Draper became involved in the founding of the medical college at New York University. Moving on from his experimental photography, he continued to work in theoretical physics and chemistry, particularly in studies of radiant energy and its impact on light. In 1850 he added a chair of physiology and was appointed president of the medical college, serving himself in those capacities while also keeping his chair in chemistry until his retirement in 1873. Much of the funding for his laboratory, as well as for the entire chemistry department during this time, came from Draper's own personal resources, which included royalties from a number of textbooks he wrote on chemistry and physiology. Among the most prominent of these publications were *A Treatise on the Forces Which Produce the Organization of Plants* (1844), *Text-book on Chemistry* (1846), *A Text-Book on Natural Philosophy* (1847), and *Human Physiology, Statical and Dynamical; or, The Conditions and Course of the Life of Man* (1856). Draper was also actively involved in professional and graduate education at New York University outside of the medical college, proposing instruction in civil engineering and authorizing the granting of a degree of bachelor of science that deleted the requirement for knowledge of Greek and Latin, as well as granting of the degree of doctor of philosophy.

The 1856 publication of *Human Physiology* marked a significant shift in Draper's career. Thereafter he essentially concluded his strictly scientific work and began to concentrate on historical analysis and the social ramifications of science. In a speech given in 1859 to inaugurate the Cooper Union, Draper summarized the thoughts that would guide him for the remainder of his scholarly work, expressing the belief that nations, like organisms, inevitably pass through "an unavoidable career, and then die, some earlier, some more maturely, some at still a later date. In their infancy, some are cut off by mere feebleness, some are destroyed by civil diseases, some commit suicide, some perish of old age. But for every one there is an orderly way of progress—the same pursued by the individual and assigned to the Globe."

Draper's mission was to be the "universal man," a complete multidisciplinary theorist. He attempted to fit history into the framework of natural science. Benthamism and the positivism of Auguste Comte, which he had studied in London, came back to the forefront of his intellectual pursuits.

In 1862 Draper published *A History of the Intellectual Development of Europe*. Actually written prior to Darwin's *Origin of the Species* (1859), it was also preceded by a notorious speech given by Draper at the convocation of the British Association at Oxford University in 1860; he spoke for more than an hour and delayed the famous debate on Darwinism between Bishop Samuel Wilberforce and T. H. Huxley. *The Intellectual Development of Europe* was an attempt to write the history of Western thought from the beginning of civilization to the present day. Its main thesis was that Roman Catholicism had attempted to hold back the development and acceptance of science and the scientific spirit. Other books Draper published in this decade included *Thoughts on the Future Civil Policy of America* (1865) and the three-volume *History of the American Civil War* (1867–1870), the first serious study of the war.

The work for which Draper is probably best known is *History of the Conflict between Religion and Science* (1874), essentially a revised version of his *Intellectual Development of Europe*. Draper wrote, "The history of science is not a mere record of isolated discoveries; it is a narrative of the conflict of two contending powers, the expansive force of the human intellect on one side, and the compression arising from traditionary faith and human interests on the other." Once again, the target of his criticism was the Roman Catholic church. Fueled by encyclicals and actions of the church beginning in the 1860s that responded to perceived threats to Roman supremacy, Draper noted several factors that he argued had created a "great and rapidly-increasing departure" from religious faith in Europe and America: the declaration of war on modern civilization by the pope, the recently declared claim of papal infallibility, the political role of Roman Catholic churches in Germany and France, and the literal interpretation of *Genesis* creation stories. These circumstances, according to Draper, were holding back the universal dominion of the scientific spirit.

Going through fifty American and twenty-one British printings and translated into at least ten other languages, *History of the Conflict* was the bestselling of the hundred-odd volumes of the International Scientific Series edited by Edward Livingston Youmans. The Spanish edition, published in 1876, was placed on the church's index of prohibited books. Together with a later work by Andrew Dickson White in 1896, Draper and *History of the Conflict* reset the terms of the controversy, brought on with renewed force by the debates surrounding Darwinism, over the relationship between Christianity and science.

Draper remained prominent in American scientific circles throughout his career. In 1875 he was awarded the Rumford Medal by the American Academy of Arts and Sciences for his work on radiant energy, and in 1876 he was elected the first president of the American Chemical Society. He became a member of the National Academy of Sciences in 1877. But while the historical treatises he wrote do not merit serious consideration under the standards of contemporary historiography, and while the logic of his arguments concerning the conflict between religion and science often seem enigmatic, they are the matters for which he is chiefly remembered. After several years in retirement, Draper died at his home in Hastings-on-Hudson, New York.

Regardless of what can be said about his abilities as a historian or social critic, however, Draper was certainly committed to intellectual liberty and the progress of science. As Fleming concludes, "Draper deserves . . . to be remembered for his honorable record as a research scientist, for his pioneering in new kinds of history, and for his courage in popularizing unpopular ideas. But his chief merit, in spite of grave equivocations, was to bring his weight down hard on the side of free inquiry and the free play of the minds of men."

• According to his biographer Donald Fleming, Draper's correspondence was destroyed at his request at the time of his death, but many letters and other papers remained in the possession of his granddaughter, Dorothy Draper Nye, in the Mrs. Henry Draper Papers of the New York Public Library and in the archives of New York University. The most comprehensive biography of Draper is Fleming, *John William Draper and the Religion of Science* (1950), which includes a lengthy bibliographical essay. Good discussions of Draper's influence in the debate over the relationship between religion and science can be found in James R. Moore, *The Post-Darwinian Controversies: A Study of the Protestant Struggle to Come to Terms with Darwin in Great Britain and America, 1870–1900* (1979), and David C. Lindberg and Ronald L. Numbers, *God and Nature: Historical Essays on the Encounter between Christianity and Science* (1986).

GREGORY A. HILE

DRAPER, Lyman Copeland (4 Sept. 1815–26 Aug. 1891), historical collector and writer, was born in Erie County, New York, the son of Luke Draper, a grocer and farmer, and Harriet Hoisington. From 1834 to 1836 he studied at Granville College in Ohio (later Denison University), where he became an ardent Baptist and Democrat, and deepened his growing interest in western history. He completed his formal education at the Hudson River Seminary near Albany, New York, in 1836–1837.

Raised on the New York frontier and steeped in family tales of the War of 1812, Draper acquired an early interest in American history. At eighteen he began to publish historical articles in the *Rochester Gem* and other papers. After college he tried his hand at editing a newspaper and at farming in Mississippi, and worked for a time as a clerk on the Erie Canal. During most of his life, however, he found ways to support himself by doing what he most cared about, collecting the raw materials of western history. His interest grew out of a critical reading of earlier historical writings in which he found numerous errors. He found a patron in Peter Remsen, husband of his cousin Lydia Chadwick, who subsidized his efforts to find descendants of early western settlers and paid him to manage the household while Remsen himself was away on business.

Draper's stated objective was to record the true story of western expansion and to rescue from oblivion such heroes as Daniel Boone, George Rogers Clark, and John Sevier, pioneers whom he revered. In 1844 he traveled for five months through Tennessee, Kentucky, and Virginia, carefully recording interviews with aging pioneers. There were many other such trips. By 1868 he had logged 46,000 miles in the interest of research and had collected thousands of documents. His notebook was always within reach. He also carried on a massive correspondence with other historians, and his collection soon attracted national attention.

In 1852 Draper moved to Madison, Wisconsin, at the invitation of his college friend Charles Larrabee, who was interested in putting the new historical society on a firm basis. Draper helped to draft a charter that established the State Historical Society of Wisconsin and became its corresponding secretary; he served in that capacity until his retirement in 1887. Besides continuing to add material to his private collection, Draper used his connections to create a model institution. From fifty volumes in a church basement, the society's collection grew to 65,000 titles by 1876, when it was located on the second floor of the new state capitol building. In 1853 he married Remsen's widow, Lydia Chadwick Remsen; they had one child, an adopted daughter.

Draper's responsibilities at the historical society included extensive writing. Each year he produced an annual report, and he also edited and contributed to the ten volumes of Wisconsin Historical Collections that were published during his tenure. In addition he wrote a 48-page promotional pamphlet for Madison and coauthored *A Helping Hand for Town and Country* (1869), a book of useful household and farming information. But his major ambition was to tell the story of the western pioneers in a series of works that would secure their place in history. Although he clearly possessed both material and energy for such an undertaking, only one of his planned books—*King's Mountain and Its Heroes* (1881)—was ever published. Draper missed the battle's centennial by a year, and, although reviews were generally favorable, only 1,300 copies were sold.

Draper suffered from indecision about which of his major works to complete first and, because he continued to turn up new information, fear about premature publication. When the actual writing began, he developed writer's cramp and other physical ailments. Standing less than five feet tall and weighing only about a hundred pounds, he had a vulnerable constitution and sought a variety of cures for his many physical and psychological problems. In later life he even abandoned his Baptist faith for spiritualism.

Recognizing that he needed help with his writing, Draper tried to work with coauthors, but three literary partnerships proved fruitless. In 1846 he published a two-page circular that described his collection and announced plans for a series of "Sketches of the Lives of Pioneers." Several works, including "The Mecklenburg Declaration of Independence," and "Border Forays," which was written with Consul W. Butterfield, never found publishers. Others, such as his projected life of Daniel Boone, were never completed.

A Granville College professor called Draper the "Plutarch of Western History," and the title was often used to describe him. William A. Croffut, one of his coauthors, noted that Draper had published virtually nothing. He was "naturally a gleaner rather than a compiler," said Croffut. Moreover, he found ways to avoid reaching his own goals. Sometimes he courted distractions, as when he served a term as Wisconsin's superintendent of public instruction, a post he filled with distinction from 1858 to 1859. After the death of his first wife in 1888, he married Catherine T. Hoyt in 1889. He died in Madison, Wisconsin.

Although it was never Draper's intention to find fame as a collector, his work had a profound influence on historical scholarship. His emphasis on the West, and the 478-volume collection that he left to the State Historical Society of Wisconsin, helped to create the intellectual environment that would nurture historian Frederick Jackson Turner and the frontier thesis that Turner developed. Later scholars wrote biographies of Boone, George Rogers Clark, Simon Kenton, and others, books that Draper himself had planned. Historians have used the Draper manuscripts to revive the memory of many of his heroes, men whose lives and deeds would be largely unknown without his diligence as a collector and promoter of history.

• In addition to the Draper Manuscript Collection, the State Historical Society of Wisconsin holds fifty boxes of the Draper and Wisconsin Historical Society Correspondence, a rich source of information about Draper himself. William B. Hesseltine, *Pioneer's Mission: The Story of Lyman Copeland Draper* (1954), is the only full-length biography. Shorter accounts include Larry Gara, "Lyman Copeland Draper," in *Keepers of the Past*, ed. Clifford L. Lord (1965), pp. 40–52; Louise Phelps Kellogg, "The Services and Collections of Lyman Copeland Draper," *Wisconsin Magazine of History* 5 (Mar. 1922): 244–63; and Reuben Gold Thwaites, "Lyman C. Draper, the Western Plutarch," *Magazine of Western History* 5 (Jan. 1887): 335–50. Thomas Waln-Morgan Draper, *The Drapers in America, Being a History and Genealogy of Those of That Name and Connection* (1892), pp. 186–91, contains a summary of Draper's life.

LARRY GARA

DRAPER, Margaret Green (fl. 1750–1807), was a printer and a publisher. Nothing certain is known regarding her parentage or the place of her birth, although some sources suggest that she was a granddaughter of printer Bartholomew Green and the daughter of Thomas Green and Ann (maiden name unknown). What is known is that she married Richard Draper on 30 May 1750 in Boston. The son and grandson of Boston printers, Richard Draper took control of the *Boston Weekly News Letter and New England Chronicle* in 1762. He changed the name of the newspaper in the following year to the *Massachusetts Gazette and Boston News-Letter*. The Drapers lived in a brick house on Newbury street in Boston, and, though they had no children, they adopted Margaret's niece around 1766.

Nothing is known of the relationship between husband and wife, whether they were a true partnership couple or whether theirs was a traditional relationship of wife serving her husband. Following the death of Richard Draper on 5 June 1774, Margaret Draper took control of the newspaper. Along with the paper, she inherited a partnership that her husband had formed with John Boyle one month prior to his death. Boyle was apparently in favor of the new patriot movement in Boston, while Margaret Draper was a firm Loyalist; the two ended their business relationship in August 1774. She soon took another printer, John Howe, into partnership, although his name did not appear with hers on the masthead until May 1775.

Draper ran the newspaper from 9 June 1774 to its last issue on 29 February 1776. This was a heady time to be in charge of a newspaper, as the events of Lexington, Concord, Bunker Hill, and the siege of Boston all fell within this two-year period. At the outset of her printing and publishing career, Draper applied an even-handed approach to the news. Even when the battles of Lexington and Concord were fought, she appears to have approached the situation with some objectivity. But as the siege of Boston wore on, she became more strident in her opinions, showing conclusively her Loyalist sympathies. One example came on 28 September 1775, when she declared in the paper that "such is the abundance of fuel, and provision for man and beast, daily arriving here, that instead of being a starved, deserted town, Boston will be, this winter, the emporium of America for plenty and pleasure" (Frothingham, p. 239).

Draper's optimism was not entirely in error, of course. The British and Loyalists in Boston did enjoy an easier winter than the army of patriots that surrounded the city during 1775-1776. However, the appearance of the artillery pieces brought by Colonel Henry Knox from Ticonderoga to Dorchester Heights in March 1776 ended British control of the city. When British general Sir William Howe sailed from Boston on 17 March 1776, he took with him a great many Boston Loyalists, Margaret Draper among them.

Draper went with the British fleet to Halifax, Nova Scotia, and then on to England, where in 1784 she applied for restitution of losses caused by the revolutionary war. Her property and printing materials had indeed been confiscated, and the British committee that examined her claim awarded her a pension of £100 sterling per year, as well as a one-time payment of £940 (she had claimed £2,093 sterling in losses). Nothing is known of the rest of her years in London. She died in that city, and her will was proved on 12 February 1807.

Margaret Draper was a headstrong woman with firm convictions. Little different in character from her patriotic counterparts, such as Mercy Warren, she believed strongly in the right of King George III to govern the colonies. She had the distinction of publishing the only newspaper in Boston during 1775–1776 and of carrying on a printing tradition that certainly existed in her husband's family and that may have existed in her own.

• There is a frustrating paucity of material on Draper. Some of the best sources are Isaiah Thomas, *The History of Printing in America* (1810); Richard Frothingham, *History of the Siege of Boston* (1896); Gregory Palmer, *Biographical Sketches of Loyalists of the American Revolution* (1984); James H. Stark, *The Loyalists of Massachusetts* (1910); and Sally Smith Booth, *The Women of '76* (1973). See also Susan Henry, "Margaret Draper: Colonial Printer Who Challenged the Patriots," *Journalism History* 1, no. 4 (1974–1975): 141–44.

SAMUEL WILLARD CROMPTON

DRAPER, Mary Anna Palmer (11 Sept. 1839–8 Dec. 1914), philanthropist, was born in Stonington, Connecticut, the daughter of Courtlandt Palmer and Mary Ann Suydam. Her father had been a successful hardware merchant in New York City but lost most of his money in the panic of 1837. He invested what little capital he had left in real estate in New York City and became very wealthy, leaving a large fortune to his three sons and daughter when he died in 1874. Relatively little is known about Mary Anna Palmer's education and early life. It is evident that she and her brother Courtlandt, who was educated at Williams College and Columbia University Law School, shared an interest in liberal causes, salon discussions, and philanthropy toward technical activities, which may indicate the influence of their parents and teachers as well as the connections they had with other patrons of science, art, and education in New York City.

In 1867 Anna (as she was called by friends and family) Palmer married Henry Draper, a professor of physiology and chemistry at the University of the City of New York, later New York University, and a skilled astronomical observer with a special interest in stellar spectroscopy. She began to assist him in making observations and soon became an expert technician. They had no children, so much of their life together revolved around their shared interest in his astronomical work. He constructed a 28-inch reflector telescope in a private observatory at the home of his father, John William Draper, at Hastings-on-Hudson, New York, and each summer the young couple would reside at Dobbs Ferry and then drive together to the observatory to work in the evening. Together they began experimenting with photographs of stellar spectra and, using wet plates, she coated the glass with collodion in preparation for the photography. In May and August 1872 Henry Draper successfully photographed the spectrum of Vega and made the first observation of four dark lines on this star. In 1878 the two went to Rawlins, Wyoming, in order to observe the total solar eclipse. Draper sat patiently in the tent and called out seconds as the eclipse occurred while her husband observed the phenomenon and took photographs. During the winter they lived in a home built by her father on Madison Avenue that was well suited for entertaining. Henry Draper utilized a laboratory over the stables, attached to the house by an enclosed passageway, where the photographs could be studied and results calculated and analyzed for publication. Then, abruptly, Henry Draper died of pneumonia in the fall of 1882. His widow turned her attention to the work he had begun and devoted much of the rest of her life and wealth to advancing physical astronomy and contributing to cultural life in New York City.

Although Anna Draper initially thought of erecting an observatory in New York City in honor of her husband, she turned to Professor Edward C. Pickering of the Harvard College Observatory for advice. He had been a friend and colleague of her husband and was also interested in photographing stellar spectra. In 1886 she established a memorial to further such research at the Harvard College Observatory. Initial successes led her, in 1887, to extend the funding of the project to include all available facts about the stars and to establish a thorough classification of stars based on identified characteristics. She frequently visited the observatory in Cambridge and continued to provide the monthly financial support for ongoing observations, laboratory work, and tabulations by "computers," many of them women, including Pickering's exceptionally able administrator Williamina P. Fleming. The first *Draper Catalogue of Stellar Spectra* was published in 1890 and classified some 10,351 spectra. This was followed by publications that detailed about 5,000 spectra of the brighter and northern stars. Annie Jump Cannon joined the observatory in 1896 and during the course of her career there extended the total classification to nearly 400,000 stars, from the brightest to the barely visible on the Harvard plates, in *The Henry Draper Catalogue* (9 vols., 1918–1924) and *The Henry Draper Extension* (2 vols., 1925–1949), thanks to ongoing support and then an endowment bequest. Anna Draper thus made an unprecedented contribution to modern astronomy by funding these publications that provided new data for discussions of stellar evolution and the connection between variability and changes in spectra. The observations made with her patronage also resulted in discoveries of novae, variable stars, and gaseous nebulae. She always took a personal interest in the work, visiting regularly and giving advice on matters of policy.

The Drapers had frequently entertained literati and scientists in their home, including colleagues like Simon Newcomb and others, who admired Anna Draper's engaging personality and "intellectual sympathy" with her husband's work. After her husband's death, Anna Draper continued to organize scientific lectures and transformed their home laboratory into a lecture and exhibition room that could seat two hundred people. She hosted receptions and exhibitions for the meetings of the National Academy of Sciences and the American Astronomical Society, in whose work she took considerable interest. Her endowment of the Henry Draper Medal, a gold medallion, in 1883, allowed the NAS to honor outstanding and original work in astronomical physics. She was also influential in the establishment of the Mount Wilson Observatory in California under the supervision of the Carnegie Institute (1902).

Her own personal activities were multiple. She became particularly interested in archaeology and amassed an extensive collection of ancient Near Eastern, Greek, and Roman artifacts. She was also a supporter of the New York Public Library and aided its development under John S. Billings; in her will she included a memorial fund of $200,000 to the reference department that he had directed. Draper died at her home in New York City.

• Draper's correspondence relating to the Harvard College Observatory is in the Harvard University Archives, and other correspondence is in the New York Public Library. On the Draper family see Donald Fleming, *John William Draper and the Religion of Science* (1950; repr. 1980). On Draper's archaeological collection see Garrett Chatfield Pier and David Proskey, *Catalogues of Rare Gems, Ancient Greek, Roman and Other Coins, Amulets, Rosaries, and Other Objects of Archaeological Interest, Collected by the Late Mary Anna Palmer Draper* (1917). See also Lyle G. Boyd, "Mrs. Henry Draper and the Harvard College Observatory, 1883–1887," *Harvard Library Bulletin* 17 (Jan. 1969): 70–97, and Bessie Zaban Jones and Lyle G. Boyd, *Harvard College Observatory: The First Four Directorships, 1839–1919* (1971). Obituaries are in *Science*, 12 Mar. 1915; the *New York Times*, 9 Dec. 1914; and the Harvard College Observatory's *Annual Report for 1915*.

SALLY GREGORY KOHLSTEDT

DRAPER, Richard (24 Feb. 1727–5 June 1774), Massachusetts Loyalist, printer, and publisher was born in Boston, Massachusetts, the son of John Draper, the publisher of the *Boston News-Letter*, and Deborah Green. His mother came from a family of official printers in Connecticut going back six generations to Samuel Green, originally a printer in Cambridge, England. Richard Draper was educated at the Boston Public Latin School. He grew up in the family printing business, learning the trade from his father, and soon became a silent partner. In 1749 he married Margaret Green, a cousin and the granddaughter of the printer Bartholomew Green. Apparently childless, the couple adopted their niece, Margaret Collier.

Richard Draper's first imprint was a sermon by Jonathan Mayhew (1751). After his father's death in 1762, Draper inherited the printing and bookseller stores. In 1763, mainly because of a weak physical constitution, he took his cousin Samuel Draper (who died in 1767) into partnership. After petitioning Governor Francis Bernard, Draper became the official printer for the governor and council of Massachusetts.

Under Draper the newspaper went through six name changes, always retaining "News-Letter" as part of the title. He trained a number of apprentices including his cousin Edward Draper, who boarded in his home. In addition, Draper employed a staff of three. Most of Draper's business revolved around his weekly newspaper (printed every Thursday with a circulation of 1,500 at an annual charge of 6 shillings, 8 pence lawful money). Usually printed on 10-by-15-inch durable rag paper purchased from a mill in Milton, Massachusetts, the paper lasted through numerous readings. Draper claimed the *News-Letter* circulated to the west along the road to Worcester, Springfield, Northampton (to the north of Springfield), Hartford (southward again), and New Haven and was carried south by riders to Providence and Newport. He made money from subscriptions but more significantly from advertisers. From 1763 to 1775 advertising filled an average of 39 percent of his newspaper and nearly defrayed printing costs. A large number of the advertisements in Draper's paper came from either merchants (37 percent) or legal/government ads (20 percent).

Draper had such strong Tory feelings that in 1763, after his appointment as the official printer of the governor and council, he started decorating his newspaper with the royal coat of arms. That same year, however, he promised his readers that he would print only news of trade and commerce while avoiding "all Party disputes and personal Invectives." At first he kept his promise and maintained political neutrality. From 1763 to 1775, of the seven major Boston newspapers, Draper's contained the least amount of political columns (only 12 percent of the space, in contrast to 85 percent for Ezekiel Russell's *Censor*). During the same time, Draper printed twenty-three pro-British political sermons and seventeen anti-British tracts. During the Stamp Act crisis, Draper reflected the general consensus and opposed the tax, editorially calling it a "terrible String" of duties. He solicited from John Adams the Braintree town resolves against the Stamp Act and printed his paper without attaching the required stamps. Although most residents suspected that Jonathan Mayhew, the pastor of the West Church, had inflamed mobs during the Stamp Act, Draper for financial gain published Mayhew's sermons.

Opposition to the Stamp Act was a position espoused by most Americans, both patriots and Loyalists, but by 1770 Draper had resumed his normal pro-Tory stance and become the mouthpiece for royal governor Thomas Hutchinson and his supporters. An example was the exchange between Governor Hutchinson and the Massachusetts General Court, from 1770 to 1773, over Hutchinson's removal of the General Court from Boston to Cambridge. Draper printed both sides of the official correspondence between the governor and the House of the General Court.

During the controversy Isaiah Thomas's *Massachusetts Spy* became the favorite newspaper for patriot essays attacking Hutchinson. Draper's paper printed the Loyalists' responses under such pseudonyms as "Aquitas," "Constitutionalis," "Publius," "Verus," and "Chronus." Both printers became involved personally when Isaiah Thomas altered the release of his paper from Tuesdays to Thursdays. Since Draper printed the *Boston News-Letter* every Thursday, he claimed in an editorial that Thomas deliberately changed his usual day of publication to "injure" him and that Thomas published authors who "leap over every barrier of Truth and Decency to gratify malice and party rag." Thomas countered by charging that Draper was controlled by the Tory party. Draper denied this by an "appeal to the impartial public to decide, whether Mr. Thomas, or his Assistants had the least shadow of reason for their unfriendly censure— I disclaim all masters and all undue influence in my publications— and profess to be governed by reason, justice, decency and truth."

From 1770 to 1773, of sixteen Tory articles submitted to Boston papers, almost half were printed in the *Boston News-Letter*. From 1773 to 1776, of the twenty-three major Loyalist essays printed, nine were in the columns of the *Boston News-Letter*. In 1774 Draper published the famous Loyalist essays written by Daniel Leonard under the signature "Massachusettensis," which were rebutted by John Adams in the guise of "Novanglus." Patriots began referring to Draper's paper, with its royal arms masthead, as the "court gazette."

In addition to the newspaper, Draper took on outside printing contracts, such as sermons, religious hymn books, all of the Harvard theses from 1767 to 1770, and Ames's Almanac. Nathaniel Ames's 24-page almanac was a lucrative printing job of up to 60,000 copies that Draper shared with three other printing houses.

In 1771 Draper engaged in another controversy with his rival Isaiah Thomas because Thomas successfully convinced the Harvard undergraduates to let him print the single sheet listing commencement theses. Draper permanently lost the account, which would have been about fifty copies per student or a total of three thousand sheets. Draper and Thomas, along with their supporters, exchanged heated words in print over the issue. A Draper supporter characterized Thomas's newspaper as "the engine of all ill"; another described Thomas as a "dunghill-bred Journeyman Typographer." Among subsequent titudes, a defender of Thomas portrayed Draper as a "grand slavish Conformist to ministerial Instructions," a "ministerial hypocritical Slave," and a "haughty Advocate for Prerogative" who possessed a "haughty arbitrary Mind."

Draper's father had made the transition from printer to bookseller, and Draper continued this trend. Most of his imprints were produced not for others but for sale at his own store. However, in contrast to his rivals, Draper's non-newspaper printing was slight. Draper's imprints dropped from a total high of 966 pages in 1763 to a low of 54 pages in 1770. Furthermore, in his lifetime he and his apprentices only produced 249 imprints, less than half his father's production. It is unclear if Draper's business declined because of his poor health, his pro-British position, or the competition from newly established printing firms. Twenty-one towns in Massachusetts had printers from 1764 to 1783, more than any other colony. In 1775 readers could buy any of ten Massachusetts newspapers, seven of which were published in Boston.

Draper's newspaper and imprints were just part of his business. Probably half his annual business came from "job printing" including labels, blank forms, handbills, ballads, posters, broadsides, petitions, and election notices. However, this work is difficult to substantiate since such materials were for quick reading and disposal and rarely carried the printer's name.

Draper built a substantial brick house on Newbury Street in Boston. The family owned one slave, who worked in their home rather than at the printing shop. In 1765 both Richard and Margaret Draper were admitted to full communion in the West Church of Boston. Apparently Draper suffered from a lingering consumptive disorder; because of this illness, in May 1774 he went into partnership with the printer John Boyle.

Less than a month later, Draper died in Boston. The *News-Letter*'s black-bordered masthead told readers that it was now published by Margaret Draper and Boyle. However, Boyle became a patriot, so in August 1774, with British general Thomas Gage's encouragement, Margaret Draper assumed total control of the business. She ran the only pro-British newspaper during Boston's occupation, was official printer for the governor and council, and eventually went into partnership with John Howe. In January 1775 the Worcester Convention urged citizens no longer to subscribe to her paper since it "assist[ed] enemies by publishing their Scandalous performances." Margaret Draper printed at least eleven imprints. When she left Boston with the British army in March 1776, the *News-Letter* ceased publication, after 3,770 weekly issues spanning a 72-year history.

Richard Draper's prominent prewar position as the printer to the king and his wife's support of the British cause led to confiscation of their property, which was sold at public auction. Margaret Draper claimed £2,093 in losses before the Commissioners on American Loyalists, a board appointed by Parliament to recompense American Loyalists. It allowed her £929 and an annual pension of £100.

Richard Draper's career parallels that of many New England printers for whom it was an inbred family business. His life also reflects the anguish of a printer who desired to remain neutral, but increasingly found himself forced into the Tory camp.

• For all imprints by Richard Draper and their full citations see "Eighteenth-Century Short Title Catalog" (1992), CD-ROM. The CD-ROM incorrectly attributes to him imprints by his kinsman Samuel Draper who for five years printed in partnership with Zachariah Fowle; imprints by Somerset Draper, a prolific London printer; imprints by patriot John Draper; and imprints by other printers, but only for sale at his store; as well as forged copies of Ames's Almanac. For Margaret Draper's petitions see American Loyalists Claims, Public Record Office, Audit Office 12/105/62; AO 12/109/124; and AO 13/44, London. For information on printing see Bernard Bailyn and John B. Hench, eds., *The Press & the American Revolution* (1981). James H. Stark, *The Loyalists of Massachusetts and the Other Side of the American Revolution* (1907); E. Alfred Jones, *The Loyalists of Massachusetts: Their Memorials, Petitions and Claims* (1930); and Thomas Draper, *The Drapers in America* (1892), pp. 193–99, provide valuable family information. Additional helpful information can be found in Mary Ann Patricia Yodelis, "Boston's Second Major Paper War: Economics, Politics, and the Theory and Practice of Political Expression in the Press, 1763–1775" (Ph.D. diss., Univ. of Wisconsin, 1971), and Timothy Barnes, "The Loyalist Press in the American Revolution, 1765–1781" (Ph.D. diss., Univ. of New Mexico, 1970).

DAVID E. MAAS

DRAPER, Ruth (2 Dec. 1884–30 Dec. 1956), actor/monologist, was born and raised in New York City, the daughter of William H. Draper, a physician, and Ruth Dana, his second wife. Her maternal grandfather was Charles A. Dana, editor and part owner of the *New York Sun*, and her parents were affluent as well as educated. The seventh of William Draper's eight children (he had had two by a previous marriage), Draper was a shy, frail child, and school disagreed with her. Her parents hired a German governess, Hannah Henrietta Hefter, to school her at home, and it was thanks to Hefter that Draper carried a love of literature and languages throughout her life and work.

From an early age Draper showed a talent for impersonation, which eventually led her to develop character sketches that she performed in programs before wealthy New Yorkers beginning in 1902. In 1910 the pianist Ignace Jan Paderewski, a family friend, encouraged her to turn professional. Against her mother's wishes she decided to do so and began to develop a more extensive repertoire. By 1913 she was performing for the elite of London. After one of her performances, Queen Mary wrote in her diary that Draper recited "too delightfully."

Not a conventional actress, Draper rarely performed material that she did not write herself. Early on she played a lady's maid in *A Lady's Name*, starring Marie Tempest, in 1916, and in 1917 she appeared in August Strindberg's *The Stronger*, which ran on the same bill with her own sketch, *The Actress*, a piece that came to be viewed as one of her most brilliant character sketches. But reviews and her own strong feelings convinced Draper that she should confine herself to her own material. According to Neilla Warren, editor of Draper's letters, except for a couple of roles in a few all-star benefits in later years, after 1917 Draper never appeared in a program that she did not create for herself.

Draper's performances consisted of combinations of various five- to fifty-minute character sketches in which she often played multiple characters—and evoked many others—with the help of only a few props, hats, and shawls. Both dramatic and comic sketches found their way into her repertoire, which she continually expanded with new sketches until about 1940, after which she relied on older material. Draper was careful to acknowledge her debt to comedienne Beatrice Herford, whom she had seen in 1912 in a minimal production of *The Yellow Jacket*, staged with no scenery and few props. Draper appeared at the White House and began a series of foreign engagements; she was equally popular in the United States and Europe, owing in part to her ability to speak several languages, including French, in which she was fluent. Late in life, in 1955, she performed for three weeks with her nephew, dancer Paul Draper.

A few of Draper's popular character sketches included "The Actress," "Vive la France!," "A Scottish Immigrant at Ellis Island," "The Italian Lesson," and "The German Governess." As her obituary in the *New York Times* opined, Draper, "like most great artists,

. . . had imitators, but probably no equal in the art of creating taut one-woman shows. The emotional range of her thirty-seven sketches and fifty-eight characters was as extraordinary as her devotion to her work." Much of Draper's material was derived from personal experience, obtained through extensive travel and keen powers of observation. Many of her monologues were recorded on a five-volume disk collection entitled *The Art of Ruth Draper* (Decca, 1954–1955).

Draper never married, but she had a passionate—though short-lived—affair with Lauro deBosis, a brilliant poet, scientist, and antifascist Italian revolutionary. Seventeen years her junior, deBosis happened into Draper's life when she was forty-three, and the couple spent only three and a half years together. DeBosis was killed in 1931 after a flight over Rome, during which he dropped 400,000 antifascist pamphlets on the city. Draper never completely recovered from his death. She convinced Oxford University Press to publish *The Golden Book of Italian Poetry*, a collection of poems deBosis had edited, and she translated his play, *Icaro*, into English and later had it translated into French. In 1934 she also set up, at Harvard, the Lauro deBosis Lectureship in the History of Italian Civilization, which continues to fund important Italian scholars.

Although Draper looked upon New York and London as her theatrical homes, by the end of her life she had performed on all five continents, in most of the countries of the world, always with great success. A map of what Draper called her "strange wandering life"—in which each place in the world that she visited is marked with a gold star—is in a special reading room for children of members of the New York Society Library. Draper's friends, including notables in the arts and in society, were scattered across Europe, Great Britain, and North America.

Committed to helping those in need, Draper gave numerous benefit performances for various charities, including but not limited to churches, the Red Cross, and the Actors Benevolent Fund. In 1951 King George VI of England conferred upon her the Insignia of Honorary Commander of the Most Excellent Order of the British Empire in recognition of her generosity to British philanthropies, especially during and after World War II; he also awarded her the honorary title of C.B.E. Draper received several honorary degrees from U.S. and British universities, including Cambridge University.

Draper died in her sleep at her New York apartment following a performance at the Playhouse Theatre. Her influence continues to be felt. Illustrious one-woman shows, including those of Lily Tomlin and Anna Deveare Smith, can be compared to the versatile performances that Draper gave nearly half a century before. Sometimes lonely, always full of dignity, Draper committed herself to performing but also to good works. Her letters are the succinct yet compassionate expressions of a citizen of the world during the first half of the twentieth century. She so impressed her friend and contemporary Lugné-Poë that he wrote, "I have never met an actress so sincerely humble when she steps out of her profession, whose success however she perfectly admits. . . . In my eyes she is always a great woman" (quoted in Warren, p. 38).

• The most satisfying volume for studying Draper is *The Letters of Ruth Draper 1920–1956*, compiled and edited, with narrative notes, by Neilla Warren (1979). Also extremely helpful is *The Art of Ruth Draper*, both the book by Morton Zabel (1960), which includes a biography and many of Draper's monologues, and the five-volume set of disk recordings by Spoken Arts. Various references to Draper are included in Arthur Rubinstein, *My Young Years* (1973); Joyce Grenfell, *Joyce Grenfell Requests the Pleasure* (1976); Alexander Woollcott, *Going to Pieces* (1928); and Malvina Hoffman, *Heads and Tails* (1965). An obituary is in the *New York Times*, 31 Dec. 1956.

CYNTHIA M. GENDRICH

DRAPER, William Franklin (9 Apr. 1842–28 Jan. 1910), textile machinery manufacturer and inventor, congressman, and ambassador to Italy, was born in Lowell, Massachusetts, the son of George Draper and Hannah Thwing. His grandfather, Ira Draper, had patented the first self-acting rotary temple for cotton looms in 1816 and had established a plant to manufacture the new machine part in Weston, Massachusetts. By 1842 Ira's son Ebeneezer had taken control of the business and had moved the plant from Weston to Hopedale, Massachusetts, where he became a member of the Reverend Adin Ballou's Christian commune.

In 1853 William Draper's father moved to Hopedale, and with his brother Ebeneezer formed the E. D. and G. Draper Company. From the beginning the company was devoted to the technological improvement of weaving, and George Draper alone acquired patents to more than 100 improvements in weaving machinery, the most important of which was for the first high-speed spindle. The Drapers' manufacturing plant quickly became the main financial support of Ballou's commune, and eventually the brothers owned the majority of the commune's shares. George Draper had little sympathy for the economic aims of the commune and forced its dissolution in 1856. The Drapers bought out all the remaining shareholders, and Hopedale became a company-owned town. Hopedale still retained much of the communal atmosphere, though, and during the late nineteenth and early twentieth centuries it became famous as a model company town and the Draper Company as the epitome of the paternalistic company.

After his family moved to Hopedale, William Draper began school at the Hopedale Academy. He studied there until he was sixteen and then spent three years at various textile plants studying weaving machinery. In 1861 he passed the entrance examinations for Harvard College but never attended. Instead, with the advent of the Civil War he enlisted in the Twenty-fifth Massachusetts Regiment, receiving a commission as a lieutenant. He later served with the Thirty-sixth Massachusetts Regiment and advanced steadily in rank to become a colonel in 1863. He fought in many battles, including Fredericksburg and Antietam and was seriously wounded twice. After his second injury in October 1864, Draper was discharged from the army; he returned to work for E. D. and G. Draper Company. In 1865, though, he was promoted to brigadier general in recognition of his service.

In April 1868 William succeeded his uncle as a member of the firm, which was renamed George Draper and Son (George Draper and Sons after 1876, when his brother George A. Draper also joined). After his father's death in 1887, William Draper became president of the firm—renamed Draper Company in 1896—a position that he held until 1907. Like his father, Draper saw that the key to profitability in the textile machinery business lay in developing and patenting improved equipment. He sold his first invention in 1867 for $10,000 and went on to patent many more improvements to weaving machinery. Even before his father's death, Draper was responsible for the firm's patents and for patent litigation; under both father and son's leadership, Draper Company devoted much of its revenue to patent litigation. It also bought up competing spindle patents to create one of the first "patent pools," as the partnerships aimed at controlling vital patents in an industry were then known. At its height, Draper Company's pool owned more than 200 spindle patents, which gave it control of almost the entire spindle industry. Indeed, most of the company's revenue was derived from licensing fees paid on spindles manufactured by other companies. Once he became company president, Draper devoted these profits to research and development of new machinery. In 1892 this reinvestment paid off when Draper Company perfected the Northrop automatic loom. The Northrop loom cut the labor cost of weaving in half, and the Draper Company became the largest manufacturer of looms in the world.

It was, however, Draper's insistence on continued technical improvement that led to the end of his service as Draper Company president in 1907. His brothers (Eben had joined in 1880), who were more interested in steady profit than continued development, decided over his objections to reduce expenditures on research and development and to concentrate on the production of the current models of machinery. Foreseeing that this shortsighted decision would cause the gradual decline of Draper Company's dominant position in the textile machinery market, William Draper resigned from the company and sold all his shares.

Draper married twice. In 1862 he had wed Lydia Warren Joy, with whom he had five children. After his first wife died in 1884, he married Susan Christie Preston, the daughter of Confederate general William Preston, in 1890; they had one child.

While an astute businessman, Draper was also a successful politician. The Draper family members' political involvement grew out of their advocacy of a protective tariff, which they considered vital to their business. (George Draper was a founder of the Home Market Club, and William served twice as its president.) William Draper's formal political career, though, began when he served as a delegate to the Republican National Convention in 1876. In 1887 he was chair of the committee on resolutions at the Republican State Convention, and in 1888 he was a Republican presidential elector. He was elected to the U.S. House of Representatives in 1892 and served two terms (1893–1897). While in Congress he continued to pursue his interests in patent law and the tariff, and during his second term he successfully steered to passage a new U.S. patent code. In addition, he worked for a stronger tariff and against U.S. intervention in Cuba. In 1897 Draper was appointed by President William McKinley as ambassador to Italy, where he served until 1900. After his return to Massachusetts, he remained active in state Republican party politics as an unswerving advocate of a protective tariff. In 1904 he worked successfully to prevent the state's Republican convention from adopting a resolution in favor of free trade with Canada. He retired to Washington, D.C., where he died.

Draper's career provides an outstanding example of the combination of entrepreneurship, technical innovation, and political influence that contributed to the rise of American industry in the late nineteenth century.

• The main source on Draper is his own memoirs, *Recollections of a Varied Career* (1908). Short biographical profiles of him can also be found in William F. Moore, *Representative Men of Massachusetts, 1890–1900* (1898), and Ruth Lawrence, *Draper, Preston and Allied Family Histories* (1954). The Library of Congress, Manuscript Division, contains a collection of 120 of his letters, most of which date from 1862–1863. His views on industrial relations can be found in "Testimony of William F. Draper," in Albert Clarke, ed., *Report of the Industrial Commission on the Relations and Conditions of Capital and Labor*, vol. 14 (1901). John S. Garner, *The Model Company Town: Urban Design through Private Enterprise in Nineteenth Century New England* (1984), and Edward K. Spann, *Hopedale: From Commune to Company Town, 1840–1920* (1992), both discuss the development of Hopedale during Draper's years as company president. Irwin Feller, "The Draper Loom in New England," *Journal of Economic History* 26 (1966): 320–47, concentrates on the history of the Northrop loom. The best account of Draper's business methods, however, is in Thomas R. Navin, *The Whitin Machine Works since 1831* (1950), which also provides a detailed account of the close relationship and rivalry between Draper Company and the nearby Whitin Machine Works in Whitinsville, Mass.

JOHN POTTER

DRAYTON, John (22 June 1766–27 Nov. 1822), governor of South Carolina, was born in Drayton Hall on the Ashley River in South Carolina, the son of William Henry Drayton, a judge, and Dorothy Golightly. Members of this planter family were descended from Thomas Drayton, who came to South Carolina from Barbados in 1679, and who may have brought the first slaves to South Carolina; they were quite influential in colonial and state politics for several generations. Drayton was educated in Charleston until he was ten years old; then he accompanied his father, a delegate to the Continental Congress, to Little York, Pennsylvania, where he went to school. Later he entered the grammar school at Princeton, New Jersey. He was admitted to the College of New Jersey (now Princeton University) but attended only a short time, if at all, before his father's death in 1779 required his return to South Carolina. He continued his studies in Charleston, reading law with General Charles Cotesworthy Pinckney, a schoolmate and friend of this father, after his mother's death in 1780. In 1788 he began a legal practice in Charleston. In 1794 he married Hester Rose Tidyman; they had seven children before her death in 1816.

Soon after establishing his legal practice, Drayton became active in public life. He served as warden of Charleston in 1789, as a member of the South Carolina House of Representatives from 1792 to 1798, and as lieutenant governor from 1798 to 1800. When Governor Edward Rutledge died in office on 12 January 1800, Drayton took over the executive office on an interim basis; he was elected to a full two-year term on 4 December 1800.

Drayton had a keen interest in developing public education in South Carolina. His *Letters Written during a Tour through the Northern and Eastern States of America*, which he published in 1794, portrayed the shortcomings of the South Carolina educational system through a comparison with schools in Boston, Massachusetts. In 1801 he obtained a charter from the state general assembly for South Carolina College in Columbia. An act providing for its establishment was passed by the legislature and was approved by Drayton in December 1801; the school later became known as the University of South Carolina.

In 1802 Governor Drayton published another book on South Carolina, *A View of South Carolina, as Respects Her Natural and Civil Concerns*. Modeled after Thomas Jefferson's *Notes on Virginia*, the book includes a botanical catalog that reflected Drayton's interest in and knowledge of botany. The work was translated and favorably reviewed in England, Hanover, and Switzerland. Partly as a result of the favorable reviews of the book, the Royal Society of Sciences of Göttingen admitted him to membership in 1804.

Drayton served as president of the board of trustees of the South Carolina College until 1802. During 1807 he argued a case before the U.S. Supreme Court, *Rose v. Himely*. From 1805 to 1808 he served in the South Carolina Senate, after which he again won election as governor (1808–1810). After Drayton's last term as governor, President James Madison appointed him federal judge of the U.S. District Court in South Carolina; he remained in this position until his death.

In 1821 Drayton drew upon his father's papers to publish under his own name a two-volume book, *Memoirs of the American Revolution, from its Commencement to the Year 1776, Inclusive; as Relating to the State of South-Carolina and Occasionally Refering [sic] to the States of North-Carolina and Georgia*. The compilation contains a brief biographical sketch of his father and his father's memoirs from 1753 to 1776. A posthu-mously published book, *The Carolinian Florist of Governor John Drayton of South Carolina* (1943), draws upon unpublished manuscripts and marginalia of Drayton to give a complete accounting of his botanical knowledge, which was considerable. Drayton was also an amateur painter and, especially late in life, an amateur planter. He died in Charleston.

Drayton had a very high regard for the policies and values of his country and state; in his will, he gave instructions that his son Alfred Rose Drayton should be educated in this country, "that he may be informed of its Local politics and governmental interests, hence I am opposed to his going abroad for any Education until his manners and affections be first formed to Suit his native Country." Drayton's instructions were, however, not carried out; for health reasons, his only son was sent to Cuba when he was about seventeen years old, and later he entered a Charleston bank.

• Drayton's papers are in the possession of the University of South Carolina and the Charleston Library Society. Family members own copies of the autobiographical "Family History" and the family Bible containing ancestors' notes (see the Preface to *The Carolinian Florist of Governor John Drayton of South Carolina* for details). Some early publications, including the *Dictionary of American Biography*, vol. 3 (1930), portray Drayton as having had a postrevolutionary legal education in England, probably as a result of errors contained in J. B. O'Neall's *Biographical Sketches of the Bench and Bar of South Carolina*, vol. 1 (1859). Drayton himself contradicted the misinformation in an autobiography he prepared for his children; it is reflected in the *National Cyclopedia of American Biography*, vol. 12 (1904) and other works. The discrepancies are discussed in the Preface to *The Carolinian Florist of Governor John Drayton of South Carolina* (pp. xiii–xiv).

BETHANY K. DUMAS

DRAYTON, Percival (25 Aug. 1812–4 Aug. 1865), naval officer, was born in Charleston, South Carolina, the son of Ann Gadsden and William Drayton (1776–1846), a lawyer and, later, U.S. congressman and president of the Second Bank of the United States. Percival Drayton was heavily influenced by his father's nationalistic and antinullification views, and like his father, he would eventually call Philadelphia home.

On 1 December 1827, at the age of fifteen, Drayton was appointed a midshipman in the U.S. Navy. He attended naval schools at Norfolk and New York and served for two years with the navy's Brazilian Squadron on the USS *Hudson*. During this period Drayton advanced from appointed midshipman to warranted midshipman, and on 12 July 1833, after successfully passing his examination, he was warranted a passed midshipman.

In July 1835 Drayton was assigned to the USS *Constitution* and in 1838 was promoted to lieutenant. Throughout the 1830s and 1840s Drayton had a career typical of an American naval officer, serving in the Brazilian, Pacific, and Mediterranean squadrons. He also saw duty at the naval observatory in Washington, D.C., and at the New York Navy Yard, where he tested ordnance and became a close friend of David G.

Farragut. In October 1855 Drayton was commissioned commander and in 1858 was assigned to the staff of Commodore William B. Shubrick during the Paraguay expedition. Drayton was detached from active sea duty in May 1859. He became a member of the Board of Examiners for the Naval Academy.

Drayton was a well-known figure in the pre–Civil War navy. He was considered brilliant by his contemporaries in maritime and ordnance matters and was highly praised for his work with the manufacturing of the Dahlgren gun. He was also fluent in several foreign languages. He was never married but devoted himself to his career.

A strong backer of national government, Drayton was on duty at the naval yard in Philadelphia during the secession crisis. To show his loyalty, he requested in February 1861 that his nativity on the naval register be changed from South Carolina to Pennsylvania. His favoring of the national government was declared "infamous" by the South Carolina legislature. For the first months of the war Drayton supervised the outfitting of vessels at Philadelphia until September 1861, when he applied for sea duty with the squadron being organized by Captain Samuel Francis Du Pont. Assigned to the gunboat *Pocahontas*, Drayton commanded the vessel during Du Pont's attack on the Confederate fortifications at Port Royal, South Carolina, which were commanded by his older brother Thomas F. Drayton.

The day after the battle of Port Royal Percival Drayton was given command of the gunboat *Pawnee* and with that vessel carried out reconnaissance missions in the region's rivers and sounds, securing enemy forts and liberating slaves. Besides believing slaves could be seized as contraband, Drayton also considered slavery a disgrace to civilization. His experiences along the southeastern coast convinced him that freed slaves would become productive citizens. He participated in expeditions against Fernandina, Florida, and St. Marys, Georgia, and on 28 May 1862 Drayton commanded the naval squadron that entered the Stono River, and later he directed his vessels in support of the army in June and July during the Secessionville campaign.

Drayton's service with the South Atlantic Blockading Squadron earned him the rank of captain on 16 July 1862. Sent to New York in September, he took command of the unfinished ironclad *Passaic*, the first of a new class of monitors designed and constructed by John Ericsson. While in New York Drayton worked closely with Ericsson to improve the *Passaic* and its sisterships by giving the vessels a compass, towing apparatus, an improved anchor harness, and better ventilation. Though his alterations increased the fighting ability of the monitors, Drayton believed the vessels to be underpowered and undergunned for operations against Confederate fortifications. As commander of the *Passaic*, Drayton participated in the March 1863 attacks against Fort McAllister and was part of Du Pont's ironclad squadron that was turned back at Charleston on 7 April 1863.

In the aftermath of the Charleston attack, Drayton joined Du Pont in criticizing the offensive capabilities of the monitors. In May he was detached from the *Passaic* and became the superintendent of ordnance for the New York Navy Yard, a position he held until December, when he was ordered to the West Gulf Blockading Squadron as fleet captain. Serving with Rear Admiral Farragut, Drayton assumed the responsibilities as his chief of staff and captain of the steam sloop *Hartford*, Farragut's flagship.

As captain of the *Hartford* Drayton took part in the 5 August 1864 attack against Mobile Bay. When Farragut climbed into the rigging to view the battle, Drayton ordered the admiral lashed in place to keep him from falling overboard. Highly praised by Farragut for his actions both before and during the battle, Drayton continued to serve with the West Gulf Blockading Squadron until December 1864, when he and Farragut returned to New York on the *Hartford*. Farragut said of Drayton, "Drayton does not know fear, and he would fight the devil himself; but he believes in acting as if the enemy can never be caught unprepared." On 28 April 1865 Drayton was appointed chief of the Bureau of Navigation. He died after a brief illness in Washington, D.C.

• A large collection of Drayton papers can be found in the bound volume *Naval Letters from Captain Percival Drayton, 1861–1865* (New York Public Library, 1906). Drayton documents not reprinted in *The Official Records of the Union and Confederate Navies in the War of the Rebellion* (30 vols., 1894–1922) can be found in the National Archives, Record Group 45. Letters from Drayton to Rear Admiral Du Pont are located at the Eleutherian Mills Historical Library, and some are reproduced in John D. Hayes, ed., *Samuel Francis Du Pont: A Selection from His Civil War Letters* (3 vols., 1969).

STEPHEN R. WISE

DRAYTON, William (21 Mar. 1732–18 May 1790), jurist, was born at "Magnolia," the family plantation, near Charleston, South Carolina, the son of Thomas Drayton, a planter and colonial legislator, and Elizabeth Bull, the daughter of Lieutenant Governor William Bull. Admitted to the Middle Temple in London in 1750, William was called to the English bar in 1755. A year later he returned to South Carolina, where he began a law practice and in 1767 became Berkeley County justice of the peace in Charleston. He served six years in the assembly, beginning in 1756, and was briefly private secretary to Governor William H. Lyttelton. In 1759 Drayton married Mary Motte, daughter of Jacob Motte, royal treasurer of South Carolina. The Draytons had five children who survived infancy.

Drayton's acquaintance with Governor James Grant of East Florida led to his temporary appointment as chief justice and member of the council of that colony. In 1765, after the death of Drayton's intended replacement, Drayton's office became permanent. He accordingly moved his family to St. Augustine, where he became a considerable landowner. After his death, his heirs unsuccessfully claimed about 6,000 acres under some fifteen British grants.

Drayton apparently raised no major complaints to Grant's administration, but in June 1770 he denounced the lack of an assembly. When Lieutenant Governor John Moultrie, a fellow South Carolinian, became acting governor in 1771, Drayton became his most vocal critic. In an address to the governor, Drayton deplored the condition of East Florida and urged the convening of a representative assembly. Henceforth Moultrie had to deal with continued opposition from Drayton.

In August 1773 Drayton was censured by the council for his apparent dilatoriness in discharging his duties as chief justice. Drayton called his colleagues "a Damn'd Dirty Sett or House," for which he was suspended from the council. Because of differences over constitutional issues with both Moultrie and his successor Patrick Tonyn, who assumed the governorship in March 1774, Drayton was twice suspended from his chief justiceship. In his unpublished "An Inquiry into the Present State, and Administration of Affairs in the Province of East Florida with Some Observations on the Case of the Late Chief Justice There" (1770), Drayton maintained that Tonyn's military background led him to adopt arbitrary policies that in turn gave rise to an opposition. Drayton charged Tonyn with untruthfulness, waste of public funds, unpunctuality in making payments, and showing political favoritism.

Tonyn, for his part, considered Drayton and his ally and fellow councilor, Andrew Turnbull, as leaders of a dangerous faction that advocated political principles "of the leveling kind," similar to those in the rebellious colonies. The governor exaggerated, but Drayton did refer to the elected houses of assembly as "the great bulwark of American liberty." Drayton believed that the failure to allow East Floridians to have such a body violated their rights as Englishmen.

Drayton again became suspect in 1774, when he helped Jonathan Bryan, a Whig leader from Georgia and former acquaintance, to lease from the Creeks the Apalache Old Fields, an estimated five million acres of land in East Florida. Allowing Bryan to escape, Drayton refused to issue a writ to arrest Bryan on charges of violating the Proclamation of 1763, and Tonyn accused Drayton of Whig sympathies. Drayton was again reprimanded when he ordered that the presentments of a recent grand jury decrying the lack of an assembly be published in the Georgia and South Carolina gazettes. Although the council censured Drayton, the next grand jury praised him for his ability, integrity, and uprightness.

In February 1776 the council brought charges against Drayton for his involvement with Bryan, obstruction of justice, failure to divulge all of William H. Drayton's letters, and influencing the grand jury to criticize the governor and council. The council voted that month to suspend him without addressing the legal issues raised in his defense. Although the council was hardly impartial, a general suspicion against Drayton appeared to exist even among members who were less partisan. Tonyn was further insulted by an address written by Turnbull and Drayton's supporters, but before Turnbull could be summoned before the council, he and Drayton sailed for England. Drayton appeared before the Board of Trade prior to the arrival in London of Tonyn's countercharges and was restored to office with full pay from the date of suspension. To add insult to injury, Lord George Germain rebuked Tonyn for party prejudice and private animosities.

After Drayton's vindication, Tonyn continued to denounce him for criticizing the government and undermining the governor's credibility. Drayton openly spoke of the blunders of the government and declared he would be the first to sign a petition for Tonyn's removal. Tonyn brought charges of insubordination against Drayton before the council in December 1777. In spite of a long written defense, the council concluded that Drayton should be suspended. Drayton decided to return to England a second time to make his own case. While he was there, his wife died, and before any disposition of his case was made, he resigned as chief justice.

Drayton returned to his native Charleston after the city was captured by the British in May 1780 and soon recovered his status. In about 1780 he married Mary Gates; they had one child. He became chairman of the local committee of the South Carolina Society of Agriculture in 1785, and in 1789 he was appointed a judge of the Admiralty Court of South Carolina. From March until October 1789 he was appointed a judge of the Admiralty Court of South Carolina. From March until October 1789 he was an associate justice of the state supreme court. In November 1789 President George Washington named him the first judge of the U.S. Court for the District of South Carolina, a position he held for only six months prior to his death at Magnolia Plantation.

At the time of his death Drayton was grand master, Fraternity of South Carolina Ancient York Masons. In his rather pathetic will he lamented his poor financial standing, which he blamed on the length of the war and his failure to win compensation for his lands in East Florida. As a placeman, he owed his position and fortune to the British government. In spite of Tonyn's charges, little evidence supports accusations that Drayton was the leader of an American faction. Arrogant and contentious in his advocacy, he insisted that East Florida, like the other American colonies, should have an elected assembly. Apparently the loser in this contest, Drayton returned to Charleston, where he received prestigious appointments owing to family connections and his superior education. His contemporaries regarded him as a "gentleman of unusual talents and great professional knowledge."

• The William Drayton Papers are in the Library of Congress. Numerous Drayton family papers, including several genealogies, are in the South Carolina Historical Society, Charleston. Useful sources include Charles L. Mowat, *West Florida as a British Province, 1763–1784* (1943); Wilbur H. Siebert, *Loyalists in East Florida, 1774–1785* (2 vols., 1929);

and J. Leitch Wright, *Florida in the American Revolution* (1975). Also see Mowat, "The Enigma of William Drayton," *Florida Historical Quarterly* 22 (July 1943): 3–33; Emily H. Drayton Taylor, "The Draytons of South Carolina and Philadelphia," *Publications of the Genealogical Society of Pennsylvania* 8 (1923); and three later studies that amplify the East Florida context, Alan Gallay, *The Formation of a Planter Elite: Jonathan Bryan and the Southern Colonial Frontier* (1989), Paul David Nelson, *General James Grant, Scottish Soldier and Royal Governor of East Florida* (1993), and E. P. Panagopoulos, *New Smyrna: An Eighteenth Century Greek Odyssey* (1966). Also helpful is Keith Krawczynski, ed., "William Drayton's Travel through the South Carolina Backcountry in 1784," *South Carolina Historical Magazine* 97, no. 4 (Oct. 1996). An obituary is in the *City Gazette or the Daily Advertiser* (Charleston), 19 May 1790.

R. FRANK SAUNDERS, JR.

DRAYTON, William (30 Dec. 1776–24 May 1846), attorney and member of Congress, was born in St. Augustine, East Florida, the son of William Drayton, a chief justice of the province, and Mary Motte. In 1778 his parents went to England. His mother died there, and Drayton was left in the care of Dr. Andrew Turnbull, who raised him and whose son, Robert J. Turnbull, would later oppose Drayton in the nullification controversy. During the Revolution the Turnbull family moved to Charleston, South Carolina, where Drayton's father had settled in 1780. Drayton subsequently returned to England for schooling, but upon the death of his father in 1790 he was forced to return to South Carolina because of reduced finances. With his formal education ended at age fourteen, he became assistant to his brother Jacob Drayton in the clerk's office of the Court of General Sessions and Common Pleas for Charleston District. In 1797 he was admitted to the bar, and Langdon Cheves, Keating Lewis Simons, and Drayton soon became the leading attorneys in Charleston. By 1812 Drayton was quite wealthy, and he invested heavily in commercial enterprises.

Politically, Drayton was a Federalist and a protégé of Edward Rutledge. Like most members of his party, he opposed the War of 1812, yet he volunteered his services to President James Madison and was commissioned a lieutenant colonel in the army. He rose to the rank of colonel and on 1 August 1814 was appointed inspector general. Later in life he was commonly addressed as "Colonel Drayton." In 1815 he resigned his commission, returned to Charleston, and resumed his law practice. The following year Andrew Jackson proposed his name to President James Monroe as secretary of war.

Drayton served as recorder of the City Court of Charleston (1819–1823) and presided over the Inferior City Court. In 1824 he was elected to Congress as a Democrat to replace Joel R. Poinsett, who had become minister to Mexico. In Congress Drayton initially supported the ambitions of John C. Calhoun and opposed the protectionist tariff of 1828, but he believed that the disunion threatened by opposition to the tariff would be a calamity. As a leader of the Anti-Convention or Union party in South Carolina, he opposed the views of his foster brother, Robert Turnbull, one of the architects of nullification, the principal that states can nullify federal legislation if it is judged to infringe on states' rights. In the 1830 congressional election Drayton campaigned against nullification and was reelected without opposition even though he opposed the idea of a state veto. Willing to compromise, he urged lower tariffs and asked President Jackson not to use federal troops in South Carolina. In 1831, when Secretary of War John H. Eaton resigned, Jackson offered the position to Drayton, but he declined.

In 1828 Drayton supported slavery against abolitionist attacks in Congress as a necessary evil. "Slavery, in the abstract, I condemn and abhor," he said. Northern slave traders were the villains, and southern slaveholders were the victims, forced to maintain their inherited curse. In the debate over the petition of Marigny D'Auterive requesting compensation for war-damaged property, a slave, Drayton led the South Carolina delegation in opposition to the few northern congressmen who balked at classifying a human being as property. He threatened that southerners would walk out if Congress challenged slaveholders' constitutional rights to hold private property and to receive compensation for property lost under eminent domain. Such an action would force South Carolinians "to calculate the value of the Union." In the end, Congress granted the petition.

At the end of his term in 1833 Drayton declined to stand for reelection and moved to Philadelphia. He remained in private life except for a brief period in the early 1840s, when he became president of the Bank of the United States. After a last-ditch effort to revive the institution, he placed the bank's remaining assets in the hands of its receivers and supervised its closing.

Drayton was married twice, first to Ann (or Anna) Gadsden, with whom he had four children. His second wife was Maria Heyward; they had five children, only two of whom reached adulthood. Drayton died in Philadelphia.

Though he was born into a well-known South Carolina family, Drayton began his legal career in modest circumstances and rose quickly to wealth and prominence on his own. In both Congress and South Carolina he achieved notoriety for his opposition to nullification and his leadership of the Union party. While more open to compromise than some of his more radical contemporaries, he nevertheless shared their strong commitment to defending the institution of slavery against its detractors.

• Drayton's papers are in the Historical Society of Pennsylvania in Philadelphia. The most complete biographical sketch is in John Belton O'Neall, *Biographical Sketches of the Bench and Bar of South Carolina*, vol. 1 (1859; repr. 1975). His role in the defense of slavery and the nullification controversy is treated in William W. Freehling, *Prelude to Civil War: The Nullification Controversy in South Carolina, 1816–1836* (1965). Brief references are in Robert V. Remini, *Andrew Jackson and the Course of American Freedom, 1822–1832* (1983), and John Niven, *Martin Van Buren: The Romantic*

Age of American Politics (1983). Obituaries are in the (Philadelphia) *Pennsylvanian*, 26 May 1846, and the *Charleston Courier*, 28 May 1846.

A. V. HUFF, JR.

DRAYTON, William Henry (Sept. 1742–3 Sept. 1779), revolutionary leader, was born at Drayton Hall in St. Andrew Parish, South Carolina, the son of John Drayton, a wealthy planter and member of the provincial council, and Charlotta Bull, daughter of Lieutenant Governor William Bull. Like the sons of many wealthy South Carolinians, William Henry was sent to England in 1753 to complete his education. His father forced his return in late 1763 before he could finish his degree at Balliol College, Oxford.

In 1764 Drayton married seventeen-year-old Dorothy Golightly, one of the wealthiest heiresses in the colony. Their union produced four children, only two of whom reached adulthood. Financially secure and politically well connected, Drayton naturally sought public office. He won a seat in the South Carolina General Assembly in 1765 but lost it in the following election for supporting parliamentary authority during the Stamp Act controversy.

Drayton invited further public censure in July 1769 when he wrote a polemic in the South Carolina *Gazette* opposing the popular extralegal nonimportation association as "*a base, illegal decree*" designed "*to ruin and overthrow our happy constitution*" (28 July 1769). This letter started a five-month public debate with several other colony leaders in which Drayton managed to offend the lower classes and convey the impression that he was a pompous political upstart. Local merchants responded by refusing to buy his crops. Ostracized politically, socially, and economically, Drayton sailed for England where his views would find greater acceptance.

In England, Drayton was introduced at Court as a staunch supporter of the royal prerogative. To further display his loyalty, in 1771 he published *The Letters of Freeman*, a compilation of most of the newspaper articles on the nonimportation debate. Drayton's allegiance did not go unrecognized; in March he was rewarded with a position on the provincial council in Charleston, where he joined his father.

Drayton's aspiration for additional posts was frustrated, however, by an increasing number of Englishmen appointed to the most desirable offices in the colony. Although his uncle recommended Drayton for the vacant berths of assistant judge in 1770 and deputy postmaster general for the Southern Department in 1771, both offices went to Englishmen. Drayton's distaste for these "placemen" increased when John Stuart, a Scotsman serving as the Crown's superintendent of Indian affairs for the Southern Department, foiled his scheme to wrest 144,000 acres from the Catawba Indians. Finally, in January 1774 Drayton filled a vacancy as assistant judge, but a barrister from England soon superseded him.

In August 1774 Drayton vented his personal and intellectual frustration with the Crown and Parliament in *A Letter from Freeman*, a pamphlet addressed to the First Continental Congress in which he outlined American rights and encouraged the delegates to vigorously oppose the recently enacted Coercive Acts (dubbed in the colonies the Intolerable Acts). Reflecting on his own dashed aspirations, he had become convinced that the "liberty and property of the American [were] at the pleasure of a despotic power" (*A Letter from Freeman*, p. 5). But equally influential in his conversion to the patriot cause was Parliament's passage of the Intolerable Acts, which "increased my alarms in [such] a progressive degree," remarked Drayton, that "it prevented my saying one word in favor of administration" (*A Letter from Freeman*, pp. 7–8). He called for the establishment of an independent and permanent branch of legislature between the Crown and the American people, the selection of council members from residents of the colony, the creation of American courts of ordinary and chancery, and the abolition of writs of assistance. Realizing that others would question his sudden conversion to the revolutionary cause, Drayton explained that "the same spirit of indignation which animated me to condemn popular measures in the year 1769 . . . actuates me in like manner, *now to assert* my freedom *against the malignant* nature of the late five Acts of Parliament" (*A Letter from Freeman*, p. 5).

During his tour of the circuit courts in November 1774, Drayton, speaking as a "servant, not to the King, but to the Constitution," urged grand jurymen to select "freedom over slavery" and defy British authority; he argued that English people "cannot be bound by any law unless by their consent, expressed by themselves or their Representatives of their own election" (Peter Force, *American Archives*, 4th ser., vol. 1, p. 959). After he returned to Charleston, Drayton publicly defended the recently enacted nonimportation association adopted by Whig leaders. He was suspended from the provincial council in March 1775.

Drayton's outspoken views made him one of the leading Whigs in the colony. Even before his suspension from the council, Drayton was selected as a member of the Provincial Congress (an extralegal body serving as the colony's de facto government) and to all significant revolutionary committees. He also had the critical responsibility of planning the colony's defense. As the most radical member of the revolutionary faction in Charleston, Drayton led raids against the city's royal post office and armories, thereby obtaining both crucial information regarding the intentions of the British ministry and arms for the patriot forces.

In July 1775 the revolutionary Council of Safety (of which he was a member) sent Drayton on a six-week tour of the backcountry to attempt to convert the large number of Loyalists in the region. Although Drayton's efforts were largely unsuccessful, he managed to procure a treaty of neutrality from some of the Loyalist leaders at a conference in the town of Ninety Six on 16 September 1775.

After he returned to Charleston, Drayton was elected president of the Provincial Congress. In this capacity he struggled to develop a navy and directed attacks against British warships in Charleston harbor in hopes of hastening a war with England. Speaking to the Provincial Congress on 6 February 1776, Drayton openly called for establishment of a new government and separation from Great Britain. The next month that body drafted a constitution replacing the royal charter. For his important and persistent service, Drayton earned a position as chief justice in the new government as well as membership in the privy council and general assembly. As chief justice, Drayton continued to champion the idea of independence in fiery speeches to Charleston's grand juries; when Britain made an offer of peace (without American independence) in October 1776, Drayton blasted the proposal as an invitation for Americans "to exchange an independent Station for a servile and dangerous Dependence!" (*To Their Excellencies Richard Viscount Howe . . .* , p. 2).

In January 1777 Drayton went to Savannah, Georgia, to propose a union with its younger and weaker southern neighbor. The Georgians stoutly rejected Drayton's proposal. Near the end of that year, Drayton temporarily assumed the duties of president of the state and was, in the words of Henry Laurens, "Father & Mother" in creating the new state constitution adopted in 1778 (Smith, *Letters of Delegates*, vol. 9, p. 685).

Containing both conservative and liberal elements, the 1778 constitution raised property qualifications for the highest offices while reducing them for representatives, replaced the legislative council with a popularly elected senate, and disestablished the Anglican church. In January of that year Drayton also proposed numerous amendments to the recently published Articles of Confederation. Attached to his proposal was an alternative plan of confederation, augmenting the power of individual states and protecting southern interests. He included provisions preventing the abolition of slavery, and he increased the number of votes in Congress necessary to pass a law from nine to eleven in order to prevent the South's subjugation by northern states.

Early in 1778 Drayton was elected to the Second Continental Congress. An indefatigable worker, Drayton served on nearly ninety committees during his seventeen months in Congress—more than any other delegate except New York's Gouverneur Morris. Drayton focused his efforts on protecting southern interests and opposing British attempts at reconciliation. Drayton also assiduously compiled documents for a history of the Revolution, an undertaking left unfinished when he died of typhus in Philadelphia.

An "upright, candid gentleman" with polished manners (*Pennsylvania Packet*, 31 Sept. 1779), William Henry Drayton was a zealous, energetic, and articulate spokesman for independence and one of his state's foremost constitutional theorists. Some of his writings were widely read in America and Great Britain and translated into several languages. Drayton helped lead the colony toward independence; he aided in establishing a new, yet still conservative govern-

ment, and he consistently sought to protect the interests of the southern states.

• Drayton's surviving manuscripts are strewn throughout numerous repositories in the United States and Great Britain. For a listing of the most important ones, see the bibliography in William Dabney and Marion Dargan, *William Henry Drayton and the American Revolution* (1962). The two most comprehensive collections of Drayton's writings include Robert W. Gibbes, *Documentary History of the American Revolution . . . Chiefly in South Carolina*, vols. 1–2 (1855), and John Drayton, *Memoirs of the American Revolution . . . As Relating to South Carolina. . . .* (2 vols., 1821), the latter of which contains the surviving documents Drayton had planned for his history of the Revolution. For a modern edition of his letters in the nonimportation debate, see Drayton, *The Letters of Freeman*, ed. Robert M. Weir (1977). Drayton's speeches on British colonial policy include *A Letter from Freeman of South Carolina, to the Deputies of North America* (1774) and *A Charge on the Rise of the American Empire, Delivered . . . to the Grand Jury for the District of Charlestown* (1776). His opposition to British attempts at reconciliation can be found in *To Their Excellencies Richard Viscount Howe, Admiral; and William Howe, Esq.* (1776) and *The Genuine Spirit of Tyranny . . .* (1778). Drayton's constitutional philosophy appears in his *Speech to the Assembly, 20 January 1778* (1778). Much of Drayton's public correspondence can be found in the *Papers of Henry Laurens*, ed. Philip Hamer et al. (1961–), and Paul H. Smith, ed., *Letters of Delegates to Congress, 1774–1789* (1976–).

KEITH KRAWCZYNSKI

DREIER, Katherine Sophie (10 Sept. 1877–29 Mar. 1952), artist and art patron, was born in Brooklyn, New York, the daughter of Johann Caspar Theodor Dreier, an iron distributor, and Dorothea Adelheid Dreier, his cousin. The youngest of five children, she grew up in a family with strong Germanic ties and a long-standing commitment to social and humanitarian reforms. Until art took precedence in her life, Dreier involved herself in a number of Progressive Era reforms, beginning in 1898 with her service as treasurer of the German Home for Recreation of Women and Children in Brooklyn, an institution cofounded by her mother. In 1903 she helped launch both the Manhattan Trade School for Girls and the Little Italy Neighborhood House in South Brooklyn. Dreier was also active in woman suffrage, serving as a delegate to the Sixth Convention of the International Woman Suffrage Alliance held in Stockholm in 1911 and heading the German-American Committee of the Woman Suffrage party in New York in 1915. In 1918 she spent five months in Argentina surveying that country's fledgling social reforms.

Throughout her life, however, Dreier consistently directed her greatest energy toward making and promoting art. She commenced her studies of art at the Brooklyn Art Students League in 1895–1897. Following a year in Europe, she studied privately for five years with Walter Shirlaw, whose emphasis on individual expression helped prepare her for her later immersion in modernism. From 1909 to 1911 Dreier lived and painted in London, where her art displayed a strong affinity with the tonal nocturnes of James Abbott McNeill Whistler and she enjoyed her first solo exhibition at the Doré Galleries. In 1911 Dreier married the American painter Edward Trumbull, also known as Edward Trumbull-Smith, but the marriage was quickly annulled when it was learned that Trumbull was already married with children. Dreier made her decisive turn toward modernism in 1912 after viewing the massive Cologne Sunderbund Exhibition. She was particularly attracted by the many paintings of Vincent Van Gogh in the exhibition, and the following year, after meeting Elisabeth Huberta du Quesne-Van Gogh, the artist's sister, and purchasing one of his works, published her own English translation of the sister's *Personal Recollections of Vincent Van Gogh* (1913). In her introduction to the volume, Dreier attributed the strength and legitimacy of the modern movement to its probing explorations of the nonmaterial essence of the modern world, a viewpoint that revealed her already strong grounding in the theoretical writings of Wassily Kandinsky. That same year, Dreier exhibited two paintings in the Armory show and had her first American solo exhibition at New York's Macbeth Gallery. Despite her growing sympathy for modernism, she did not, however, immediately launch her campaign on its behalf. Instead, from 1914 to 1917 she oversaw operations of the Cooperative Mural Workshops in New York, an art school-workshop in the tradition of John Ruskin and William Morris.

In 1917 Dreier met the French dadaist and art iconoclast Marcel Duchamp while serving on the board of directors of the newly formed Society of Independent Artists. The two became lifelong friends, and over the years Dreier acquired some of Duchamp's most important works, including *Tu'M* (1918) and *The Bride Stripped Bare by Her Bachelors, Even* (1915–1923). In 1920, with the help of Man Ray, Dreier and Duchamp founded the Société Anonyme, Inc., to advance the cause of international modern art in the United States. The organization bore witness to the mocking spirit of dada both in its name, proposed by Man Ray, which meant literally "Incorporated, Incorporated," and in several of the programs and publications sponsored during its first year. In 1923, following an eighteen-month trip through China, Dreier assumed virtually sole responsibility for the organization and its programs. For the remainder of its twenty-year history, she served as the organization's president, exhibitions organizer, chief publicist, and principal financial backer. On repeated visits to Europe, Dreier established important contacts with the leading avant-garde artists active in Germany, France, and Italy between the two world wars. Her philosophy of art, set forth in her book *Western Art and the New Era* (1923), evinced a committed understanding of Theosophy and a continuing sympathy for the theosophical idealism of Wassily Kandinsky, whom she made honorary vice president of the Société Anonyme in 1923.

As the most consistently avant-garde and international organization active in the United States during the 1920s and early 1930s, the Société Anonyme staged exhibitions, presented lectures and symposia, issued pamphlets, and compiled a reference library in support of international modern art. In an effort to reach audiences outside the existing gallery network, Dreier arranged programs in community centers, private clubs, university halls, and trade schools as well as in commercial galleries. Important exhibitions were also held outside New York City. The Société Anonyme purchased and exhibited the works of cubists, constructivists, expressionists, futurists, and dadaists as well as artists associated with the Bauhaus and de Stijl. The organization introduced many Russian, German, and East European artists to American audiences and gave important solo exhibitions to Kandinsky, Fernand Léger, Paul Klee, Joseph Stella, and Heinrich Campendonk. In 1926–1927 the Société Anonyme organized its most ambitious undertaking, an impressive exhibition of more than 300 works of art at the Brooklyn Museum, with smaller displays in Buffalo and Toronto.

Throughout her years as president of the Société Anonyme, Dreier continued to paint, mostly symbolic abstractions, and in 1933 the Academy of Allied Arts mounted a retrospective of her work. The founding of the Museum of Modern Art in 1929, coupled with Dreier's own weakened financial situation, meant a significant slowing of the Société Anonyme's activities in the 1930s. In 1941 Dreier and Duchamp donated the organization's massive art collection to Yale University. Portions of Dreier's private collection followed, bringing the Yale holdings to more than 1,000 objects. Both the collection and the organization that sponsored it bear vivid testimony to Dreier's pioneering achievements as a perceptive and indefatigable promoter in the field of international modern art. Dreier died in Milford, Connecticut.

• Dreier's papers and documents relating to the Société Anonyme are in the Beinecke Rare Book and Manuscript Library at Yale University; the organization's art collection is at the Yale University Art Gallery. Most of the Société Anonyme's principal publications have been reprinted in *Selected Publications Société Anonyme: (The First Museum of Modern Art, 1920–1944)* (3 vols., 1972). See also *Collection of the Société Anonyme: Museum of Modern Art, 1920* (1950). For Dreier's experiences in Argentina, see her *Five Months in the Argentine: From a Woman's Point of View* (1920). The most complete assessments are Ruth L. Bohan, *The Société Anonyme's Brooklyn Exhibition: Katherine Dreier and Modernism in America* (1982), and Robert L. Herbert et al., eds., *The Société Anonyme and the Dreier Bequest at Yale University: A Catalogue Raisonné* (1984). Aline B. Saarinen, *The Proud Possessors* (1958), contains a brief biography. See also Bohan, "Katherine Sophie Dreier and New York Dada," *Arts Magazine*, May 1977, pp. 97–101. An obituary is in the *New York Times*, 30 Mar. 1952.

RUTH L. BOHAN

DREIER, Mary Elisabeth (26 Sept. 1875–15 Aug. 1963), labor reformer and suffragist, was born in Brooklyn, New York, the daughter of Theodor Dreier, a partner in an iron firm and elder in the German

Evangelical church, and Dorothea Adelheid. Mary Dreier attended George Brackett's School in Brooklyn and was tutored in music, art and language. Her parents raised Dreier and her siblings to be independent and morally responsible. After her father died in 1897, her mother founded a rest and recreation home for poor women in his memory before she died two years later. A large inheritance allowed her to live comfortably and dedicate her life to social reform.

In 1904 Dreier attended the New York School of Philanthropy, following in the footsteps of her bright, assertive older sister Margaret. Both served on the board of directors at Asacog House, a Brooklyn settlement house where they met garment worker Leonora O'Reilly. O'Reilly persuaded both sisters to join the Women's Trade Union League (WTUL), an alliance of middle-, upper-class, and working women who sought unionization and better labor conditions. Dreier recruited women through lectures at settlement houses and women's organizations. The friendship of Dreier and O'Reilly blossomed, and in 1907 Dreier bought her a house; she continued to financially support O'Reilly throughout her life.

Margaret Dreier became president of the WTUL, but when she married and moved to Chicago, Dreier took over her presidency in 1906 and remained until 1914. A quiet, reserved woman, she had trouble at first in her new leadership role, but before long Dreier became a confident spokeswoman. She believed that one had to endure "hardship and discomfort for a cause of someone else" to truly understand his or her plight. Her commitment convinced working women that their allies' motivation was sincere and helped to create a coalition between the two classes.

In November 1909 Dreier joined striking picketers in front of the Triangle Shirtwaist Company. Police arrested her along with other strikers but dismissed her when they realized she was a prominent citizen. But newspapers published details of her arrest and brought public notice to the issues of poor wages and working conditions. The publicity lured thousands of working women to join the strikers. Although most demands were not met, the women proved they were capable of organization.

In 1911 a fire erupted at the Triangle Shirtwaist Company killing 146 women. Almost immediately the New York State Factory Investigating Commission was established, and Dreier was appointed as the only woman. For four years she served on the commission, helping to develop a study of factory conditions, hours, wages, and fire prevention methods. Their efforts resulted in the introduction of sixty bills, fifty-six of which were made into law, including one for a 54-hour work week that became a state law in 1913. Dreier's service on the commission won her an appointment to the Board of Education by New York's mayor. She held that position from 1915 to 1917.

In 1916 Dreier redirected her efforts toward suffrage. She was particularly disturbed over the treatment of women by the American Federation of Labor and decided that the only way to get protective and minimum wage laws passed was if women voted for them. In a letter to O'Reilly she stated that "enfranchisement of all women is the paramount issue for me." Dreier retired from her WTUL position and from 1915 to 1917 she campaigned for suffrage as the chairwoman of the New York City Woman Suffrage party's industrial section. In 1917 women won the right to vote in New York State.

During World War I Dreier headed the New York State Women in Industry Committee for the Council of National Defense. Following the war she helped to establish the International Congress of Working Women. From 1921 to 1927 she was a member of the executive committee of the New York Council for the Limitation of Armaments. Her appeal for international cooperation extended into World War II, when she hoped for a continued alliance between the United States and the Soviet Union. She spoke out against Nazism and sponsored a number of Jewish families fleeing from Nazi Germany.

From 1918 to 1924, and again in 1926, Dreier chaired the Women's Joint Legislative conference to push for protective measures through legislation and compensate for the union's failure to do so. Her efforts succeeded in the passage of a state law limiting the work week to forty-eight hours. In the 1930s she again worked with the committee, resulting in the passage of a bill that extended compulsory education in New York State from fourteen to sixteen years of age. In 1924 she was elected to the WTUL's National Executive Board, and in 1935 she became vice president and stayed with national until its demise in 1950.

As an activist for unemployment relief during the depression, Dreier served on a committee working with President Herbert Hoover's Organization on Unemployment Relief in 1931. She also chaired a New York commission that designed relief proposals, especially those helping unemployed industrial women. Dreier was secretary of the joint New York Conference for Unemployment Insurance from 1933 to 1935.

Dreier corresponded with many trade union women and sometimes invited them to vacation at the Dreier farmhouse in Stonington, Connecticut. She enjoyed writing pageants for WTUL programs, and in 1950 she published a biography of her sister, *Margaret Dreier Robins: Her Life, Letters, and Work*. Although in poor health during her last years, she still wrote letters to congress supporting labor legislation that she felt should be passed.

Throughout her lifetime Dreier was infatuated with her brother-in-law, Raymond Robins, and corresponded with him frequently. Although Margaret Robins wished her husband to marry her sister should anything happen to her, Raymond persuaded Dreier to forget him and commit herself to reform work instead. Dreier never married. In 1905 she invited Frances Kellor, a fellow reformer, to live in her household and Kellor stayed until her death in 1952. Eleven years later Dreier died in Bar Harbor, Maine.

Congenial and warm, Dreier drew her inspiration for reform from a strong religious conviction, and in later years she joined the Presbyterian church. Until the 1920s when her inheritance began to dwindle, she generously supported the WTUL, taking pride in the training that the organization gave to women. The compassionate alliance that Dreier formed with working women empowered them to develop their talents to the fullest and assume leadership positions in labor organizations.

• Mary E. Dreier's papers are at the Schlesinger Library, Radcliffe College. Other important sources are Margaret Dreier Robins Papers, University of Florida; Raymond Robins Papers, State Historical Society of Wisconsin; New York WTUL Papers, New York State Labor Library, New York City; and National WTUL Papers, Library of Congress. Details of her work with the WTUL can be found in "Who's Who—National League Officers," *Life and Labor Bulletin* 9 Oct. 1926, p. 3. Additional information is in Gladys Boone, *The Women's Trade Union Leagues in Great Britain and the United States of America* (1942); Rose Schneiderman, *All for One* (1967); Cecyle S. Neidle, *America's Immigrant Women* (1975); George Martin, *Madam Secretary: Frances Perkins* (1976); Barbara Mayer Wertheimer, *We Were There: The Story of Working Women in America* (1977); James J. Kenneally, *Women and American Trade Unions* (1978); Nancy Schrom Dye, *As Equals and as Sisters* (1980); Philip S. Foner, *Women and the American Labor Movement* (1980); Meredith Tax, *The Rising of Women: Feminist Solidarity and Class Conflict, 1880–1917* (1980); Elizabeth Anne Payne, *Reform, Labor, and Feminism: Margaret Dreier Robins and the Women's Trade Union League* (1988); and Gus Tyler, *Look for the Union Label: A History of the International Ladies' Garment Workers' Union* (1995). Her obituary is in the *New York Times*, 19 Aug. 1963.

MARILYN ELIZABETH PERRY

DREISER, Theodore (27 Aug. 1871–28 Dec. 1945), author, was born Hermann Theodore Dreiser in Terre Haute, Indiana, the son of Johann Paul Dreiser and Sarah Schänäb. Dreiser's father had emigrated from Germany in 1844 and had been a moderately successful wool dealer until 1869, when a fire destroyed his factory in Sullivan, Indiana. The family never recovered either economically or psychologically from the disaster. Theodore, the twelfth of thirteen children, was born into poverty, and in his childhood his parents moved from town to town in search of employment. His family life was emotionally unstable, and he had few educational opportunities. These experiences colored his worldview and influenced the character of his writing. In addition, his youth was further darkened by the strict Roman Catholic training he received in German-American parochial schools, an experience that fed his later anti-Catholicism and deeply influenced his quest for alternative forms of religious experience.

In *Dawn* (1931), an autobiography of his youth, Dreiser gives a vivid picture of his German-speaking, Catholic, downwardly mobile family and offers a classic account of the financial, social, and emotional pressures facing nineteenth-century ethnic families. Dreiser describes the typical bilingual and bicultural experiences of first- and second-generation Americans. Some of his best fiction, as well as his autobiographical writing, draws from these experiences. Examples from the fiction are the novel *Jennie Gerhardt* (1911) and the Edward Butler/Aileen Butler sections of *The Financier* (1912). In such works, as in Dreiser's life story, one finds certain themes: the figure of the foreign-born father who fails to understand his children's American ways and loses authority over the family, the second generation's rebellion against Old World religious and moral values, the role of the public school system in the Americanization process, and the isolated, beleaguered mother who attempts to mediate between traditional customs and the emotional needs of her children.

Although a good student, Dreiser never finished high school. He felt shame over the conduct of his siblings, especially the sexual adventures of his sisters. He also became depressed over his family's poor economic standing in the community, and as a result he left Warsaw, Indiana, at age sixteen to find work in Chicago. There he held a few commonplace jobs, from which he was rescued by a former teacher, Mildred Fielding, who paid his way to Indiana University (Bloomington) for one year (1889–1890). But his real education began as a reporter in Chicago. In June 1892, two months before his twenty-first birthday, he wrote his first news story for the *Chicago Globe*. Three years later he abruptly abandoned journalism by walking out of Joseph Pulitzer's New York *World*, where as a space-rate reporter he was being paid, like a garment worker in the city's sweatshops, by the inch.

As a journalist, Dreiser never came close to realizing his dream of having his own byline, a column the public would read because his name appeared above it. But he showed enough talent to get decent assignments—as drama critic, special feature writer, and investigative reporter—for the *St. Louis Globe-Democrat*, the *St. Louis Republic*, and the *Pittsburg Dispatch*. Dreiser drew many of the images and stories for his later fiction from his observations as an urban reporter in the 1890s. He was especially adept at writing special feature stories for the newspapers, in which he was able to experiment with local-color settings, dialogue, and character sketches. In addition, he was encouraged by editors and fellow journalists to write fiction. He wrote poetry; worked on a script for a comic opera, called "Jeremiah I," of which only a fragment survives; and began to experiment with short stories.

After he left the *World*, Dreiser went to work in the office of Howley, Haviland, publisher of the songs of his brother, Paul Dresser, remembered today mainly as the author of the Indiana state song, "On the Banks of the Wabash." Theodore became "editor-arranger" for the firm's publication, *Ev'ry Month*, which billed itself as a "Woman's Magazine of Literature and Music." As editor, he wrote reviews, editorials, and a "Reflections" column, in which he formulated his ideas on the leading social and philosophical issues of the day.

In 1897 Dreiser left *Ev'ry Month* and spent the next three years as a freelance writer for the national magazines. For O. S. Marden's *Success* he interviewed the famous of the day, including Andrew Carnegie, Thomas Edison, Marshall Field, William Dean Howells, and Philip Armour. For other magazines he wrote articles on a wide range of subjects, such as America'a fruit-growing industry, the meatpacking business in Chicago, and the making of stained-glass windows. He continued to write poetry and fiction. The first four short stories he published were written in the late 1890s: "Nigger Jeff," "When the Old Century Was New," "Butcher Rogaum's Door," and "The Shining Slave Makers."

In 1898 Dreiser married Sara Osborne White, a schoolteacher from Missouri whom he had met when he covered the 1893 World's Columbian Exposition as a reporter for the *St. Louis Republic*. With her encouragement and that of his friend Arthur Henry, a novelist and former editor of the *Toledo Blade*, Dreiser began writing his historic first novel, *Sister Carrie* (1900). He began the book with a story based on his own sister Emma's affair with Harry Hopkins, a married man who had run off with funds embezzled from his employer. In the pages of what is now generally considered the first great urban novel in America, he also included philosophical speculations and much of what he had learned as a reporter and observer of city life, and he created one of the most memorable characters in American literature, George Hurstwood, a dramatic portrait of a well-to-do gentleman who degenerates into a derelict on the Bowery and then a suicide buried in a potter's field.

Even before *Sister Carrie* was published, Dreiser began *Jennie Gerhardt*, a novel that tells the story of a German-American girl compelled by economic forces to abandon her family life for the larger American world of her lover, Lester Kane, the son of a wealthy Irish immigrant. The character of Jennie was based in part on his sister Mame; Lester, on her future husband, Austin Brennen; and Jennie's father was modeled after Dreiser's own father, who like the fictional Old Gerhardt, disowned his daughter when she became pregnant outside the bonds of marriage.

Dreiser wrote forty chapters of the novel before it and his writing career were interrupted by an extended nervous breakdown, brought on, Dreiser claimed, by the suppression of *Sister Carrie*. The publisher, Doubleday, Page, did, in fact, try to renege on its contract. When Dreiser refused to give in to the firm's pressures, the company did nothing to promote a book that its president, Frank Doubleday, considered "immoral." Frank Doubleday was on vacation when his staff, which included novelist Frank Norris, read the manuscript of *Sister Carrie*. Norris enthusiastically recommended it as the best work of American realism he had ever read, and a contract was issued. When Doubleday returned and read the new work, he protested. It was said, but later denied by Doubleday, that Doubleday's wife was the person most adamant in her opposition to the novel. In later years Dreiser developed this episode into a story of censorship and "puritanical" repression that became legendary, and

the book became a symbol of literary freedom for an entire generation.

Dreiser's disability lasted nearly three years, after which he recovered enough to seek employment in editorial jobs with *Smith's* and *Broadway*. By 1907 he had worked his way up to become editor in chief of the prestigious Butterick Publications. In the meantime *Sister Carrie* continued to enjoy an underground reputation, and a new edition was issued in 1907. Dreiser continued at Butterick until 1910, when an infatuation with an employee's seventeen-year-old daughter cost him his job. With the encouragement of his friend, critic H. L. Mencken, Dreiser completed *Jennie Gerhardt*, and he once again became a full-time writer. With this, Dreiser's life changed dramatically. He separated from his wife, moved into the artistic community developing in Greenwich Village, and began the lifelong practice of what he called "varietism," a term he used to describe his practice of being sexually involved with more than one woman at the same time.

Dreiser had close relations with the liberal thinkers and artistic avant-garde of the 1910s. He associated with leading political radicals such as Max Eastman, Daniel DeLeon, and Floyd Dell; supported the birth-control movement of Margaret Sanger; befriended anarchist Emma Goldman; and wrote for left-wing journals such as *The Masses*, as well as magazines with more purely aesthetic goals, such as *Seven Arts*. Dreiser was nothing if not eclectic in his interests, and although generally progressive in his social thought, he was too eccentric and independent a thinker to fit into any one ideological camp.

For more than a decade after 1911, H. L. Mencken's reviews in the *Smart Set* promoted his friend's case as America's greatest living realist. Despite such support, the threat of censorship haunted everything Dreiser wrote between 1900 and 1925. Publishers often refused to issue manuscripts as Dreiser wrote them. Fiction such as *Jennie Gerhardt* and nonfiction such as *A Traveler at Forty* (1913) were drastically cut by editors before publication. Moreover, censorship was not always limited to publishers and editors. The New York Society for the Supression of Vice caused *The "Genius"* (1915), an autobiographical novel, to be removed from the bookshelves, precipitating a court battle that lasted for years before the book was finally reissued in 1923. Dreiser was further embattled during the period of the First World War, when some of his critics attacked his "barbaric naturalism" and unconventional writing style as representative of "a new note in American literature, coming from the 'ethnic' element of our mixed population."

Despite such problems, Dreiser continued to write, and he did so prolifically. Although Dreiser is remembered primarily for his novels, he wrote in many genres. In fact, of his twenty-seven published books only eight were novels, one of which was published posthumously. Besides journalism, which he wrote throughout his life, he published volumes of poetry, *Moods, Cadenced and Disclaimed* (1926; enlarged ed., 1928) and *Moods, Philosophical and Emotional* (1935); short stories, *Free and Other Stories* (1918) and *Chains, Lesser Novels and Stories* (1927); plays, *Plays of the Natural and Supernatural* (1916) and *The Hand of the Potter* (1918); travel books, *A Traveler at Forty*, *A Hoosier Holiday* (1916), and *Dreiser Looks at Russia* (1928); autobiographies, *Newspaper Days* (1922) and *Dawn*; philosophical essays, *Hey Rub-a-Dub-Dub* (1920); social criticism, *Tragic America* (1932) and *America Is Worth Saving* (1941); character sketches, *Twelve Men* (1919) and *A Gallery of Women* (2 vols., 1929); and *The Living Thoughts of Thoreau* (1939).

His novels, however, remain the center of critical attention and the main source of his reputation. After the publication of *Jennie Gerhardt*, Dreiser turned to a very different subject. At the center of his first two novels are women who battle poverty and the conventional prejudices of society; for this third novel he portrayed an American Nietzschean Superman, Frank Algernon Cowperwood, a character based on the Philadelphia and Chicago "traction king" Charles T. Yerkes. Dreiser decided that he needed a trilogy to explore this character, and he named it "The Trilogy of Desire." The first book, *The Financier*, was soon followed by *The Titan* (1914), but he did not return to the third volume, *The Stoic* (1947), until the last year of his life. Although the trilogy is based on the life of Yerkes, readers have often identified the drives and aspirations of Cowperwood with Dreiser himself—particularly in the financier's love of beauty, his sexual appetites, and his will to power. The censor again intervened when Dreiser's publisher, Harper and Brothers, decided that *The Titan* would be too risky to publish, due in large part to Cowperwood's promiscuous sexuality. Fearing a repeat of the *Sister Carrie* conflict, Dreiser signed with English publisher John Lane Company.

Despite all the controversies surrounding Dreiser's books, they enjoyed critical esteem rather than high sales. Dreiser's distrust of publishers kept him constantly embattled in contractual disputes. He often depended on minor work for the magazines to make ends meet, and he diverted other energies to projects for movie scripts, most of which were unsuccessful.

In 1919, when he was at a low point financially and mentally, he met Helen Patges Richardson, a distant cousin who had decided to pursue a career as an actress in Hollywood. They immediately began a stormy 25-year relationship that survived periods of separation and many other romantic affairs on Dreiser's part. He went to Hollywood with Richardson in 1919 and settled in a small bungalow to write as she worked in films that are now forgotten. Dreiser tried to write *The Bulwark* (1946), the story of a Quaker family whose children and traditional values are exposed to the corrupting forces of modern American life. He struggled with it but was distracted from his writing by attempts to cash in on the big money offered for Hollywood film scripts.

More significantly, he began to be obsessed by a story that was rooted in a youthful love affair he had had in Chicago. There in 1892 he had met Lois Zahn, a

friend of one of his sisters. They had dated and planned to be married. Zahn was from the same working-class background as the young Dreiser, and with her he found himself making invidious comparisons to the wealthy girls he saw in the city. He dreamed of marrying one of those girls and thereby escaping poverty and raising his social status. He eventually found an excuse to leave Zahn, but he carried the guilt of her sorrow and his dishonest motives with him for decades. Dreiser eventually came to associate this personal experience with a type of sensational crime that he believed characterized American life. It consisted of a murder in which the motive is not personal hatred but the desire of a man to escape from a romantic entanglement in order to marry another woman who brings with her upper-class position and wealth.

In California Dreiser began experimenting with this theme, and by 1922 he had written twenty chapters of a novel. Soon after, however, he decided that they amounted to a false start. He then turned to his notes on the Chester Gillette murder of Grace Brown in 1906, an upstate New York case that had been covered extensively in the newspapers. The Gillette-Brown trial rekindled his imagination, and he decided he needed to return to New York for purposes of research and inspiration. The story took hold of him again, and he isolated himself for nearly a year in a Brooklyn apartment, where Helen Richardson joined him until he finished the book in 1925. A huge manuscript, it was cut nearly in half by editors at Horace Liveright before it was published in two volumes as *An American Tragedy* (1925).

Although the novel was a critical and commercial success, in fact Dreiser's only bestseller, he was not yet finished battling the censors. In 1927 the Watch and Ward Society of Boston banned distribution of the novel, and a sale of the book led to a trial and an appeal that dragged on in the courts for years. This, however, was an isolated instance. Dreiser seemed finally to have won over even his former critics, and many were applauding the work as the Great American Novel. Dreiser soon sold the movie rights to the book, the first version of which appeared in 1931, followed in 1951 by a popular remake titled *A Place in the Sun*. For the first time, Dreiser could afford to live something of the high life he had yearned for since his youth. He moved into the fashionable Rodin Studios apartments at 200 West Fifty-seventh Street, across from Carnegie Hall. There he held open-house gatherings on Thursday evenings at which he entertained famous and talented celebrities. In addition, he built a country home at Mount Kisco, New York, which he called "Iroki" (Japanese for "beauty").

Dreiser's fights for freedom of expression found new outlets in the last two decades of his life. Although he had always prided himself on being "radically American," he had in the past championed the rights of socialists, anarchists, and other radical groups who criticized American capitalist values. In 1927 he visited Russia at the invitation of the Soviet government for the celebration of the tenth anniversary of the October Revolution. He accepted on condition that he be allowed to extend his stay and tour the Soviet Union to see what he called the "real, unofficial Russia." He arrived as an American "individualist," eager to question the reality of an ostensibly humane economy that claimed to have abolished social hierarchies. He left far from convinced of the new experiment, but when he returned to America in 1928 to find the first breadlines since 1910, he was outraged and began to compare the efforts of the Russians with what he felt was the neglect of American capitalists.

The personal significance the Russian program eventually came to have for Dreiser appeared in a muted way in the first newspaper articles he wrote after returning to America in early 1928. He speculated in the *New York World* that in the new Russia it might "be possible to remove that dreadful sense of social misery in one direction or another which has so afflicted me in my life in America ever since I have been old enough to know what social misery is." This aspect of his feelings about Russia emerged more powerfully in the 1930s, a decade in which Dreiser was one of many whose idealization of the Soviet Union was stimulated by the economic breakdown and social malaise of the depression years.

Dreiser wrote little fiction in the 1930s. Instead he devoted his energies and writing to political activities. He fought for the release of imprisoned labor leader Tom Mooney, and he played an active role in the social reform program of the League of American Writers. In 1931 he became chairman of the National Committee for the Defense of Political Prisoners, for which he organized a committee to investigate the allegations of abuses against the striking miners in Kentucky's Harlan coal mines. Dreiser and other members of his committee, including John Dos Passos, were indicted for criminal syndicalism. His introduction to *Harlan Miners Speak* (1932) expresses his outrage at the deplorable living and working conditions of the miners whose testimony he heard.

Dreiser attempted to collect his thoughts and research on the social problems of the day in *Tragic America*. This large volume of more than four hundred pages is a polemic against the organizations that Dreiser felt were responsible for the lack of economic equity in American society. Gathering a large amount of raw data, he focused his attack on large corporations, the banks and railroads, organized religion, the school system, and the leisure class in the United States. He tried also to publicize these ideas as associate editor of *American Spectator*, a new literary magazine whose other editors included Eugene O'Neill and George Jean Nathan. Dreiser withdrew after a year, protesting that the magazine was too literary and not concerned enough with the important issues of the day.

Before he left the journal, he became embroiled in a public debate with author Hutchins Hapgood on the nature of what Hapgood felt were anti-Semitic remarks Dreiser and the other editors made in an "Editorial Conference (with Wine)" article in May 1933. Always contentious, Dreiser responded angrily with a combination of Zionist and anti-Semitic remarks that haunted him for the rest of his days. He believed, he said, that the Jews should establish a national homeland and that they should otherwise assimilate completely into American life. In listing the unassimilated characteristics of American Jews, he used ugly ethnic stereotypes that convinced many that he was either anti-Semitic or, at the very least, totally insensitive to the events occurring in Europe at the time. Although he retracted his extreme language, he never could redeem himself completely.

Besides politics, Dreiser's other passion in the 1930s was a scientific-philosophical study for which he collected data from various sources. He visited scientists in their laboratories; he read in physics, biology, chemistry, and philosophy; he discussed the organization of matter with such kindred spirits as John Cowper Powys and George Douglas; he employed research assistants to collect notes and clippings on findings that fit into the categories he was developing in his philosophy; and he began to organize these materials into essays with titles such as "The Myth of Individuality," "Good and Evil," and "You—The Phantom." Dreiser died before completing the book he tentatively called "The Formula Called Man." Although the text he left behind suggests his book would not have revolutionized modern philosophy, this work is an important key to understanding Dreiser's thought in the last decades of his life. A selection of these essays and notes, titled *Notes on Life*, was edited by Marguerite Tjader and John McAleer in 1977.

Late in 1938 Dreiser left New York to live permanently in California with Helen Richardson. His last years were spent promoting his political views, working on his philosophical tract, and finishing *The Bulwark* and *The Stoic*. With the approach of war in Europe and the possibility of American involvement, Dreiser continued his political activism. In 1938 he attended an international peace conference in Paris and visited Spain to speak to supporters of the Spanish Civil War. He returned to meet with President Franklin D. Roosevelt and urged him to aid the Spanish Loyalists and the poor citizens who were victims of the war. In 1939 Dreiser traveled to Washington, D.C., and New York to lecture for the Committee for Soviet Friendship and American Peace Mobilization. He published pamphlets at his own expense and gave speeches on the radio and at public rallies. In 1941 he published *America Is Worth Saving*, which argued against support for the British and urged that America not involve itself in another world war.

The accolades from the literary establishment that he had sought most of his life came to him late. In 1944 he traveled for the last time to New York to receive the Award of Merit from the American Academy of Arts and Letters. When he returned he married his longtime companion Helen Richardson. (His first wife had died in 1942; both marriages were childless.) There were other signs of recognition. A movie was produced called *My Gal Sal*, which was based loosely on Dreiser's story of his songwriter brother Paul. The aging writer laughed at the portrait of himself in the film, a scene showing young Theodore in Indiana breaking into tears over some minor incident.

In July 1945, five months before his death, Dreiser made his last dramatic gesture of public protest by joining the Communist party. In the public statement he issued at the time, he tried to sum up his reasons for his decision: "Belief in the greatness and dignity of Man has been the guiding principle of my life and work. The logic of my life and work leads me therefore to apply for membership in the Communist Party." While this did nothing to increase his popularity, he was at the time of his death generally recognized as the greatest naturalist in American literary history—and among the best novelists in world literature. And his many battles with censors and publishers gained him a legendary reputation as an advocate of freedom of expression. These judgments have withstood the test of time.

His strength clearly ebbing, Dreiser died in Hollywood before completing the last chapter of *The Stoic*, which was published later with an appendix by Helen Dreiser that outlined the novelist's plans for the ending.

• The Dreiser papers are housed in the Special Collections Department of the Van Pelt Library at the University of Pennsylvania. The Dreiser collection contains 503 boxes and includes manuscripts of published and unpublished writings; notes; diaries; magazines edited by Dreiser; biographical documents of all kinds, including photographs, letters, family memorabilia, scrapbooks, postcards, personal possessions, business contracts, and correspondence; newspaper clippings covering Dreiser's career; and microfilms of materials housed in other collections. The most exhaustive bibliography is Donald Pizer et al., *Theodore Dreiser: A Primary Bibliography and Reference Guide*, 2d ed. (1991). Personal memoirs written by those who knew Dreiser include Helen Dreiser, *My Life with Dreiser* (1951); Vera Dreiser, *My Uncle Theodore* (1976); Dorothy Dudley, *Forgotten Frontiers: Dreiser and the Land of the Free* (1932); Clara Clark Jaeger, *Philadelphia Rebel* (1988); Ruth Kennell, *Theodore Dreiser and the Soviet Union* (1969); Marguerite Tjader, *Theodore Dreiser: A New Dimension* (1965); and Yvette Eastman, *Dearest Wilding: A Memoir, with Love Letters from Theodore Dreiser* (1995). Dreiser's personal diaries are collected in Thomas P. Riggio, ed., *Theodore Dreiser: American Diaries, 1902–1926* (1982), and Thomas P. Riggio and James L. W. West III, eds., *Dreiser's Russian Diary* (1996). The first scholarly biography by an author who also knew Dreiser is Robert H. Elias, *Theodore Dreiser: Apostle of Nature* (1949). The most detailed biography is the two-volume work by Richard Lingeman, *Theodore Dreiser: At the Gates of the City, 1871–1907* (1986) and *Theodore Dreiser: An American Journey, 1908–1945* (1990). W. A. Swanberg's informative *Dreiser* (1965) takes a generally negative view of Dreiser's personal and political life. There are two important collections of letters: Robert H. Elias, ed., *Letters of Theodore Dreiser* (3 vols., 1959), and Thomas P. Riggio, ed., *The Correspondence of Theodore Dreiser and H. L. Mencken, 1907–1945* (2 vols., 1986). Jack Salzman, *Theodore Dreiser: The Critical Reception* (1972), collects the published reviews of all of Dreiser's books. Dreiser's writing is the subject of numerous critical studies, but Ellen Moers, *Two Dreisers* (1969), is outstanding for its combination of biography, historical context, and critical analysis. For more than a dec-

ade, the University of Pennsylvania's Dreiser Edition has been publishing authoritative editions of the uncensored manuscripts of Dreiser's works, including novels, diaries, and travel books, as well as previously uncollected documents, such as Dreiser's letters and his journalism of the 1890s.

THOMAS P. RIGGIO

DRESEL, Otto (20 Dec. 1826–26 July 1890), pianist, teacher, and composer, was born in Geisenheim, Germany, the son of Johann Dietrich Dresel and Luise Ephardt, liberal and literate parents who raised him in an intellectual environment. Dresel studied with Moritz Hauptmann at Leipzig; he also had the friendship and guidance of Ferdinand Hiller in Cologne and of Felix Mendelssohn in Leipzig. He visited New York City in 1848, played in a series of concerts there in 1849, and was the first pianist in the chamber music concerts begun by Theodore Eisfeld in 1851. After a brief return to Germany in 1851, Dresel settled in Boston in 1852 and for more than fifteen years held his place as one of that city's most prominent pianists. In his later years he made several visits to Germany to keep abreast of new activities in its musical centers.

A man of impetuous temperament and unswerving faith in his own musical convictions, Dresel was thought to be too outspoken and often contradictory in his declarations about music. Contemporary criticisms indicate that he was an uneven pianist. An obituary in *The Folio* (Sept. 1890) describes Dresel as a pianist who lacked sufficient technique "to cope successfully with the works of the more modern writers for the piano, but nevertheless his playing was imbued with fine musical feeling, and was remarkably good in point of delivery, to the extent of his peculiar ability." But William Foster Apthorp, the renowned Boston music critic, greatly admired Dresel's playing:

As a pianist, Dresel was one of the most inspiring players I ever listened to. . . . For true genius at white heat, yet controlled by the finest artistic sense of measure, I have never heard his best playing surpassed by any of the greatest pianists. . . . He had an incisiveness and brilliancy of tone, a vigour of accent that carried everything before them. . . . Like [Louis Moreau] Gottschalk, he had the peculiar power of producing a brilliant, ringing quality of tone even in the softest pianissimos. (pp. 267–68)

As a pianist Dresel set a high value on the emotional aspects of music, both the performer's personal emotions and the emotional temperament of the composer; however, that did not mean a sentimental interpretation, nor did he allow himself great rhythmic freedom. Although the romantic side of his nature was as fully developed as that of any of his contemporaries, counterposing that romanticism was an equally well-developed spirit of classicism. He revered Bach and would hardly allow that anything worthwhile had been written since Beethoven. A conservative, cultured musician with high musical standards, he did much to broaden the taste of American audiences, especially those in Boston. His recitals always included fine classical music (according to Robert Franz, Dresel played "Bach, Handel, Mozart and Beethoven under classics: Schubert, Mendelssohn, Chopin and, Schumann under more modern composers"). Dresel also gave Boston audiences chamber music concerts similar to those of Eisfeld in New York, and he introduced his audiences to the songs of Robert Franz by performing them, with singer August Kreismann, at his concerts and by including them on his choral programs.

Perhaps Dresel's greatest legacy was his work in promoting the music of Bach and Handel. In his day the American public knew the Handel oratorios but seemed uninterested in hearing more of his work. There was almost no public interest in Bach. Dresel's efforts to promote Bach and Handel in America were at first largely ignored. It may have been that his vehement, often tactless tirades against the music of Berlioz, Liszt, Wagner, Raff, Rubinstein, Goldmark, Brahms, and others of the newer schools made the public distrust him. But in Dresel's later years his Bach Club became an important and beneficial influence. This group of twenty-four to thirty handpicked singers met weekly at Dresel's home during the winter months to practice choral works by Bach and Handel. Dresel trained and directed the group and also played the piano accompaniment; one of Boston's many fine organists provided further tonal accompaniment on the small pipe organ built into Dresel's music room. The high-strung, impetuous Dresel proved to be a most tactful choral director. Apthorp writes that at rehearsals he coaxed his chorus to overcome difficulties and that singers felt they sang their very best with him. Friends and music lovers invited to one of "the rare and charming little soirées" of the Bach Club became enthralled with the music of Bach and Handel, and their infectious enthusiasm created more interest in the works of these two composers.

Dresel's own compositions are now largely forgotten. Shortly after he settled in Boston, his setting of Tennyson's *Sweet and Low* won first prize in a song contest. He made a musical setting (soprano and orchestra) of Longfellow's *The Lost Child* to commemorate the fiftieth birthday of the great naturalist Louis Agassiz. He also composed *Army Hymn*, set for soloists, chorus, and orchestra, to a poem by Oliver Wendell Holmes. His other compositions include a piano trio, a quartet for piano and strings, some piano music, and one small book of songs, mostly reprints of songs that had originally appeared years earlier, published in 1892. Dresel collaborated with his longtime friend Robert Franz in writing accompaniments for vocal scores by Bach and Handel. His piano transcriptions—for example, the six *Two-Part Songs* by Mendelssohn arranged for solo piano—are equal to the best of his nineteenth-century contemporaries. His four-hand arrangements of Beethoven's symphonies are among the best ever published. He also arranged and published four sets of Handel arias. He died at his summer home in Beverly, Massachusetts.

• *Dwight's Journal of Music* gives a good survey of Dresel's activities. A chapter titled "Two Modern Classicists" in William F. Apthorp, *Musicians and Music-Lovers* (1894; repr. 1972), is devoted to Dresel and his friend Robert Franz. The *American Art Journal*, 6 Sept. 1890, reproduces testimonial letters by Robert Franz and Sebastian Schlesinger.

JOHN GILLESPIE

DRESSER, Louise Kerlin (5 Oct. 1882–24 Apr. 1965), actress, was born in Evansville, Indiana, the daughter of William Kerlin, a railroad engineer, and Ida (maiden name unknown). Her father died when Louise was thirteen; his death forced her to quit school and help support the family. Offered a singing engagement in Boston, she headed east, thinking the offer had been made by a legitimate theater. She arrived in Boston to find a burlesque house. Needing the money and with no other offers, she took the job. After gaining some experience, she moved from burlesque to vaudeville and toured the vaudeville houses from 1900 to 1905 as a singer.

In 1902 Louise Kerlin toured the country on the regular stage as the character Ernie in *California*. While in Chicago in 1905, she met songwriter Paul Dresser and asked him to write a special orchestration for her. As a youngster Dresser had been rescued by her father and in gratitude tried to help her find a part in his company. In response to her request, Dresser wrote "My Gal Sal" for her, and it became her greatest hit. Rumors later circulated that Dresser had adopted Louise, but these were never confirmed, and he died the next year. From that time on she used the name Louise Dresser.

Dresser made her debut in musical comedy at the age of twenty-three as Gertrude Gibson in Lew Fields's *About Town* (1906), which opened in August at the Herald Square Theatre in New York. While in New York she married another member of the cast, Jack Norworth, soon after the show opened. Norworth's weakness for other actresses, however, destroyed the marriage after two years. In 1908 Dresser married another actor/singer, Jack Gardner. The couple remained married until his death in 1950, but they had no children.

After *About Town*, Dresser played Millie Mostyn in *The Girl behind the Counter* (1907) at the Herald Square Theatre. Her big break came in 1909 when she landed a role in Charles Frohman's *Girls of Gottenburg*. This role established Dresser as the foremost musical comedienne on Broadway. Over the next ten years she starred in more than twenty productions on Broadway and around the country. She appeared as Daphne Dusseldorf in *The Golden Widow* (tour, 1909), Mrs. Burton in *A Matinee Idol* at Daly's Theatre in New York (opened Apr. 1910), Leonora Longacre in *Broadway to Paris* at the Winter Garden Theatre in New York (opened Nov. 1912), Ruth Snyder in *Potash and Perlmutter* at George M. Cohan's Theatre (opened Aug. 1913), and Cordelia in *Cordelia Blossom* at the Gaiety, New York (opened Aug. 1914). She was also Patsy Pygmalion in Cohan's *Hello Broadway!* at the Astor Theatre, New York (opened Dec. 1914); Ruth Perlmutter in *Abe and Mawrus* at the Republic Theatre, New York (opened Oct. 1915); Dolly Barbizon in Jerome Kern's *Have a Heart* at the Liberty Theatre (Jan. 1917), and Aggie Jinks in Kern's *Rock-a-Bye Baby* at the Astor Theatre (May 1918). Throughout these years Dresser occasionally appeared in vaudeville and spent part of 1918 touring a singing act with her husband. Dresser had an easygoing stage presence that endeared her to audiences. Often cast in stage roles that highlighted her beauty and comedic skills, Dresser had learned to play the part perfectly. Her lighthearted and unpretentious style suited the roles of her youth.

After 1918 Dresser's career seemed to have reached its peak and started to decline as she worked infrequently for the next few years. In 1922 she decided to try motion pictures and headed to California. Her first film was *Enter Madame* in 1922, and from 1922 to 1935 Dresser appeared in more than fifty films. Most notable are *Prodigal Daughters* (1923); *The City That Never Sleeps* (1924); as Catherine the Great in *The Eagle* (1925), with Rudolf Valentino; *The Goose Woman* (1925), which won her rave reviews as the drunken ex-star; *The Third Degree* and *Mr. Wu* (1927); *Mother Knows Best* (1928), 20th Century–Fox's first talking picture; *A Ship Comes In* (1928); *Lightnin'* (1930); and *State Fair* (1933), with Will Rogers. Her final film was *The Maid of Salem* (1937). In the film the youthful blonde characters no longer fit Dresser, and she began to display an incredible talent as a character actress. Her portrayal of the degraded opera star in *The Goose Woman*, for example, allowed a range of acting not often seen in her stage roles. *Variety* called her performance "nothing less than brilliant and unquestionably the peak of Miss Dresser's screen career to date" (2 Aug. 1925). During the first presentation of the Academy Awards (1927–1928), Dresser received a "Citation of Merit" and was nominated as best actress for her portrayal of the immigrant mother in *A Ship Comes In*. Dresser retired from acting at the age of fifty-five. During her retirement, Dresser lived at the Motion Picture Country House and Hospital and supported it by appearing at benefits and fundraisers. She died in Woodland Hills, California.

Known as a beautiful musical comedienne while a young actress on Broadway, Dresser became known as a talented character actress in film. Described variously as "the girl with the pleasing contralto voice" and "the female Lon Chaney" (*Pittsburgh Post*, 15 Aug. 1926), Dresser's versatility was fully recognized. Critic Richard Watts, Jr., listed Dresser among his ten best actresses of 1926. As a stage actress Dresser played roles that required beauty, comic timing, and usually a song or two. In film Dresser became known for her roles as the loving mother or the patient wife and in character parts such as Catherine the Great (*The Eagle*, 1925); Calamity Jane (*Caught*, 1931); or Empress Elizabeth (*The Scarlet Empress*, 1934). Dresser's popularity with audiences in her later years helped secure the motion picture industry, and her versatility as an actress helped to highlight its potential.

• Clippings and publicity photos concerning Dresser's career can be found in the Billy Rose Theatre Collection at the New York Public Library for the Performing Arts, Lincoln Center. Complete listings of her performances are in *Who Was Who in the Theatre* (1978) and *Who Was Who on Screen* (1983). Dresser gave numerous interviews during her career, including *Green Book*, Oct. 1912 and Jan. 1916; *Cosmopolitan*, June 1914; and *Motion Picture*, Aug. 1926, Nov. 1929, and Oct. 1933. Obituaries are in the *New York Times*, 25 Apr. 1965, and *Time*, 30 Apr. 1965.

MELISSA VICKERY-BAREFORD

DRESSER, Paul (21 or 22 Apr. 1857 or 1858–30 Jan. 1906), songwriter, was born John Paul Dreiser, Jr., in Terre Haute, Indiana, the son of John Paul Dreiser, a farmer, and Sarah M. Schänäb, and among his siblings was the celebrated American novelist Theodore Dreiser. Young Paul learned to play the guitar and piano as a child and, against his family's wishes, ran away with a traveling show at age sixteen, changing his name to Dresser. As Theodore Dreiser remembered his older brother's departure, "He had left without any explanation as to where he was going, tired of or irritated by the routine of a home which for any genuine opportunity it offered him might as well never have existed."

Around 1885 Dresser joined the Billy Rose Minstrels, for whom he composed sentimental songs and served as both end man and middle man. At various times he worked with other minstrel companies and in vaudeville. Dresser wrote five plays, including a farce called *A Green Goods Man*, which he acted in himself, although none of these found much success. He wrote more than 160 songs and is remembered less for his genial performing than for the songs themselves. Dresser performed frequently as a blackface minstrel and also without the minstrel accoutrements at such legendary theaters as Tony Pastor's, Miner's Bowery, and Niblo's Garden in the early days of his career. He relished this heyday of Broadway, and as Dreiser remembered, "the limelight district was his home." In the vaudeville and minstrel off-season (where, as Dreiser proclaimed, Dresser "shone like a star when only one is in the sky"), Dresser worked on writing songs influenced by the atmosphere of the New York theatrical world. Dreiser believed that had his brother received a formal musical education, "he might have composed operas and symphonies." Instead, Dresser wrote some of the most enduringly popular songs of the late nineteenth century.

Dresser's earliest published songs, "The Letter That Never Came" (1886) and "The Outcast Unknown" (1887), helped him find a position with the Willis Woodward Company, song publishers. His "The Pardon Came Too Late" was a modest success in 1891, and three years later Dresser was one of the founders of the George T. Worth Company, a music publishing firm, which became known as Howley, Haviland, and Dresser in 1901. His publishing company was kept afloat mostly on the strength of Dresser's nostalgic ballads, including his 1895 hit, "Just Tell Them That You Saw Me." Dreiser was present for the composition of this song, and as he recalled in the 1927 edition of Dresser's collected songs, it was inspired by

an actual encounter with a girl whose life had seemingly if not actually gone to wreck on the shore of love. He came into the office of his publishing house one gray November Sunday afternoon and, going into a small room in which was a piano, he began improvising, repeating over and over a certain strain which was evidently in his mind. A little while later he came out and said: "Listen to this, will you, Thee [Dreiser]?" He played and sang the first verse and chorus. In the middle of the latter, so moved was he by the sentiment of it, his voice broke and he had to stop. Tears stood in his eyes and he wiped them away.

Many of his more characteristically sad love songs were suggested by his brief, failed marriage to burlesque performer May Howard during his early career; they had no children. Dresser later became professionally and personally associated with a vaudevillian, Louise Kerlin, who became his protégé. She took Dresser's name, and as Louise Dresser she became a highly successful stage performer and, later, made a mark in motion pictures, from silent films through early talkies. Her popular stage act consisted of many of Dresser's songs.

Dresser's most enduring song, "On the Banks of the Wabash" (1897), eventually became the state song of Indiana. Its nostalgic longing for the bucolic splendor of Indiana may have seemed strange to his family, who all recalled that he left Indiana as soon as he could. Dresser's lyrics provide a classic sampling of the type of song at which he excelled:

Oh, the moonlight's fair tonight along the Wabash,
From the fields there comes the breath of new mown
    hay.
Thro' the sycamores the candle lights are gleaming,
On the banks of the Wabash, far away.
Many years have passed since I strolled by the river,
Arm in arm with my sweetheart, Mary, by my side.
It was there I tried to tell her that I loved her,
It was there I begged of her to be my bride.
Long years have passed since I strolled thro' the church-
    yard,
She's sleeping there, my angel Mary dear.
I loved her but she thought I didn't mean it,
Still I'd give my future were she only here.

This song's popularity inspired several others of a similar mood by Dresser, including "A Dream of My Boyhood Days" (1896), "Way Down in Old Indiana" (1901), and "In Dear Old Illinois" (1902). None of these attained the success of "On the Banks of the Wabash," although all were popular.

Edward B. Marks, one of the most prominent Tin Pan Alley song publishers, recalled that Dresser "usually wrote his songs on an organ at one of the Broadway hotels where he lived." Many of the songs in his

huge output are largely forgotten today, but his best songs, such as "On the Banks of the Wabash" and "My Gal Sal" (1905), endure. They feature what Theodore Dreiser described as his brother's "tender" poetic spirit, as the lyrics to "My Gal Sal" suggest:

They called her frivolous Sal,
A peculiar sort of a gal,
With a heart that was mellow,
An all 'round good fellow,
Was my old pal;
Your troubles, sorrows and care,
She was always willing to share,
A wild sort of devil,
But dead on the level,
Was my gal Sal.

At their best, Dresser's songs, like "My Gal Sal," are simple and melodic evocations of the wistful longings of ordinary lovers and evoke something of the spirit of the music of the nineteenth-century's greatest songwriter, Stephen Foster. Other outstanding Dresser songs include "I Wish That You Were Here Tonight" (1896), "If You See My Sweetheart" (1897), "Sweet Savannah" (1898), "The Blue and the Gray" (1900), and "Where Are the Friends of Other Days?" (1903).

After the turn of the century, Dresser's sentimental songs became less popular than they had been as the ragtime era came into vogue. Despite the commercial success of his last song, "My Gal Sal," Dresser's publishing company folded in 1905. This misfortune undoubtedly hastened his sudden death in the New York home of a sister, where he had lived during his final years. A prolific spender, it was reported at the time of Dresser's death that he had made and spent several fortunes during his lifetime. He enjoyed the company of many women, liked a good cigar and a glass of whiskey, and was apparently a "soft touch" for the "ne'er-do-wells" of Broadway.

Despite the inevitable changes of musical tastes, Theodore Dreiser saw to it that his brother was not forgotten. He aided in the publication of Dresser's best-known songs and wrote reminiscences of his brother's era. Dreiser also scripted a 1942 screen biography of Dresser, *My Gal Sal*, filmed under the direction of Irving Cummings as a big-budget technicolor musical by 20th Century–Fox. Victor Mature played Dresser, and Rita Hayworth (dubbed by Nan Wynn) was Sally Elliott, a fictional love interest made up of bits of several women in Dresser's life. The highly fictional plot was typical of 1940s Hollywood musicals, but the movie provided an opportunity for audiences to hear Dresser's songs performed in glossy production numbers. The title song, which was also heard in the first feature-length sound motion picture, *The Jazz Singer* (1927), and in comedian Jackie Gleason's "Joe the Bartender" sketches on television, remains a perennial favorite with barbershop quartets. Its sweetly nostalgic longing for a lost love vividly evokes the era of the Gay Nineties. Dresser's persona evoked the era as well, as Dreiser recalled many years later: "I still think of him as on Broadway between Twenty-ninth and Forty-second streets, the spring and summer time at hand, the doors of the grills and bars of the hotels open, the rout of actors and actresses ambling to and fro, his own delicious presence dressed in his best, his 'funny' stories, his songs being ground out by the hand organs, his friends extending their hands, clapping him on the shoulder, cackling over the latest idle yarn."

• For information on Dresser, see Theodore Dreiser, "My Brother Paul," in *Twelve Men* (1919); V. Dreiser, *My Uncle Theodore* (1976); Paul Dresser, *The Songs of Paul Dresser* (1927); David Ewen, *The Life and Death of Tin Pan Alley* (1964); I. Goldberg, *Tin Pan Alley: A Chronicle of the American Popular Music Racket* (1930, 1961); C. Hamm, *Yesterdays: Popular Song in America* (1979); R. D. Kinkle, *The Complete Encyclopedia of Popular Music and Jazz, 1900–1950* (1974); A. R. Markle, "Some Light on Paul Dresser," *Terre Haute Tribune and Terre Haute Star*, 14 Apr. 1940; E. B. Marks, *They All Sang: From Tony Pastor to Rudy Vallee* (1934); and Deane L. Root, "Paul Dresser," *New Grove Dictionary of American Music*, ed. H. Wiley Hitchcock and Stanley Sadie, vol. 1 (1986). An obituary is in the *New York Times*, 31 Jan. 1906.

JAMES FISHER

DRESSLER, Marie (9 Nov. 1871?–28 July 1934), stage and screen actress, was born in Leila von Koerber in Cobourg, Ontario, Canada, the daughter of Alexander Rudolph von Koerber, a music teacher, and Anne Henderson. Her year of birth has also been reported as 1869 and 1870. Dressler's mother came from a wealthy family; her father, Dressler's grandfather, founded a chain of department stores in Ontario and also bred horses. Anne Henderson had to work because her father refused to support her as long as she stayed married to von Koerber, and von Koerber's temper often prevented him from maintaining pupils.

As a child Dressler appeared in the theatrical presentations her mother directed in the various Canadian and American towns in which the family lived. She quickly discovered that she had a talent for making people laugh, and at the age of fourteen she left home to join a traveling stock theater company. That move ended her formal education, which had been sporadic in any case because the von Koerbers moved frequently. She also changed her name at this point, taking her stage name from an aunt, since, as she noted in her autobiography *My Own Story*, her father said she would "never drag the name of von Koerber through the mud by showing off behind the footlights."

After playing countless roles in the Nevada Company, Dressler took a job in the chorus of the Grau Grand Opera Company and soon moved on to the Deshon Opera Company, followed by the George Baker Opera Company, with whom she stayed for three years. Having spent so much time on the road, Dressler settled for a time in Chicago, Illinois, to join the runs first of *Little Robinson Crusoe* and then of *The Tar and the Tartar*. In the role of the Tartar, Dressler went back on the road, and when the play closed she was off to New York City.

Dressler's New York debut came in 1892 in a play called *The Robber of the Rhine*, which was written by Maurice Barrymore, father of the famous acting trio of Lionel, Ethel, and John. It was the senior Barrymore who encouraged Dressler to stick to comedy. She continued until 1893 in various short runs and even sang songs to make money. Then fortune struck with her role of the Duchess in the comic operetta *Princess Nicotine* alongside stage great Lillian Russell. The production was a success and was followed by *Giroflé-Girofla* the next year, also with Russell, and then *Lady Slavey* in 1896, which affirmed Dressler's success on the New York stage. She then had a four-year run as Flo Honeydew in *Lady Slavey*. During this time Dressler became acquainted with some of the most prominent figures of New York society, many of whom she maintained friendships with long after her second success in Hollywood.

Until the early 1920s Dressler divided her time between the Broadway stage and vaudeville, both in the United States and in London. Most notable was her performance in the 1910 production of *Tillie's Nightmare* and a subsequent tour a few years later. This was the play in which she introduced the signature tune "Heaven Will Protect the Working Girl." This play alone made Dressler a wealthy actress, and she wrote in *My Own Story* that her role as Tillie was her greatest stage success. She ultimately played the role for five years. She even repeated the role opposite Charlie Chaplin in her first film, *Tillie's Punctured Romance* (1914).

Dressler's career soon took a turn for the worse, however. In 1916, while under contract to Ziegfeld-Dillingham, Dressler was cut from the cast of their new show. Not far from fifty years old, she was deemed too old to make audiences laugh. At first she viewed this as a temporary setback, never believing that it would be more than a decade before she would again find steady work. She divided her time between Europe and America and pursued other projects such as participating in the battle, particularly in 1919, for stage actors' rights and fair wages. She helped found the Chorus Equity Association and was also a member of the Actors' Equity Association and the Academy of Motion Picture Arts and Sciences. During World War I she campaigned for Liberty Loans, making 149 speeches in less than a month to fund the Allied cause. As she grew more desperate for work, Dressler even considered opening an American hotel and restaurant in Paris or the possibility of selling real estate in Florida.

It was not until 1926 that Dressler returned to performing, this time in film. It was a minor part in *The Joy Girl*, but it led her to being cast as Ma Callahan in the comedy *The Callahans and the Murphys* in 1927. Although Dressler spent the next three years waiting for roles, accepting a succession of small character parts, her work was noted, and in 1930 she received her "big break" in *Anna Christie*. At last Dressler was a film star.

Although Dressler's film career spanned only seven years, it garnered her great success and professional acclaim. She took the Academy Award for best actress in 1931 for her portrayal of Min, the waterfront innkeeper, in *Min and Bill*. She was sixty years old.

Although best known for her comic roles in films like *Tugboat Annie* and *Dinner at Eight*, Dressler also did well in dramatic parts. As Old Marthy, she "stole" the film from Greta Garbo in *Anna Christie*; likewise in 1932 she was nominated for best actress for her performance as the title character in *Emma*. Her final role in a feature film was that of Abby in *The Late Christopher Bean* in 1933.

Dressler's fame was even greater the second time around. In addition to retaining her New York society friends, Dressler was loved by the public, her peers, and even political luminaries. President Franklin D. Roosevelt and his wife were among the first to sign greetings for Dressler's gala sixty-fourth birthday celebration in 1933. She even won a gold medal that same year as the most popular film actress in the British Empire.

In 1900 Dressler married George Hoppert, who died not long afterward. In 1914 she began living with her manager of several years, James H. Dalton, and the two called each other husband and wife. In fact, a 1921 article in the *New York Times* revealed that Dalton was still married to his first wife. Dalton and Dressler had planned to wed, contingent on Dalton getting a divorce, but Dalton died in 1921 before they could marry. Dressler had no children. She died in Santa Barbara, California.

Upon Dressler's death testimonials from other greats of the silent and early sound eras of American film poured in. Actor Lionel Barrymore said Dressler was "a trouper to the end." Silent star Harold Lloyd called her "the greatest comedienne of this generation, she made age a beautiful thing on the screen," and actor Edward G. Robinson said, "Her great comeback into public favor at her age should prove an inspiration to all who today may be faced with the same despair that once assailed her." She was one of twenty-three individuals chosen from a slate of 166 nominees elected as the first inductees to New York City's Theater Hall of Fame and Museum in 1972. The actress, who noted in her autobiography that in her first career on the stage, "because I was the biggest woman in the [theatre] company, I usually played royalty," and who during her second success in film was "an ugly old woman," actually died at the height of her popularity. Dressler, a shy, large, and "homely" Canadian woman, became the highest paid actress at Metro-Goldwyn-Mayer studios and remained the toast of America long after many younger beauties had lost their appeal.

• In addition to *My Own Story*, published posthumously in 1934, Dressler wrote another autobiography, *The Life Story of an Ugly Duckling* (1924). In these two books she offers a picture of her relatively unhappy home life and the trials of her early stage career before she began to earn $2,500 per week as a stage actress. Dressler's work is put in the context of motion picture history of the period in Richard Griffith, *The Movie Stars* (1970), including her position as one of the top performers of the 1930s, even though she died long before the decade ended. Her work in film is summarized in *International Dictionary of Films and Filmmakers*, vol. 3: *Actors and Actresses* (1990), which also notes some further sources on Dressler, such as Alfred Harding's *The Revolt of the Actors* (1929) and Daniel Blum's *Great Stars of the American Stage* (1952). Obituaries are in the *New York Times*, 29 July 1934, and *Variety*, 31 July 1934.

MARIANNE FEDUNKIW STEVENS

DREW, Charles Richard (3 June 1904–1 Apr. 1950), blood plasma scientist, surgeon, and teacher, was born in Washington, D.C., the son of Richard Thomas Drew, a carpet-layer, and Nora Rosella Burrell. Drew adored his hard-working parents and was determined from an early age to emulate them. Drew's parents surrounded their children with the many opportunities available in Washington's growing middle-class black community: excellent segregated schools, solid church and social affiliations, and their own strong example. Drew's father was the sole black member of his union and served as its financial secretary.

Drew graduated from Paul Lawrence Dunbar High School in 1922 and received a medal for best all-around athletic performance; he also won a scholarship to Amherst College. At Amherst he was a star in football and track, earning honorable mention as an All-American halfback in the eastern division, receiving the Howard Hill Mossman Trophy for bringing the greatest athletic honor to Amherst during his four years there, and taking a national high hurdles championship. A painful brush with discrimination displayed Drew's lifelong response to it: after Drew was denied the captaincy of the football team because he was black, he ended the controversy by quietly refusing to dispute the choice of a white player. His approach to racial prejudice, as he explained in a letter years later, was to knock down "at least one or two bricks" of the "rather high-walled prison of the 'Negro problem' by virtue of some worthwhile contribution" (Love, p. 175). Throughout his life Drew, whether as a pioneer or as a team leader, helped others scale hurdles so they too could serve society.

While recuperating from a leg injury, Drew decided to pursue a career in medicine. He worked for two years as an athletic director and biology and chemistry instructor at Morgan College (now Morgan State University), a black college in Baltimore, Maryland, to earn money for medical school. There were few openings for black medical students at this time, but Drew was finally admitted to McGill University Medical School in Montreal, Canada. Despite severe financial constraints, he graduated in 1933 with an M.D.C.M (doctor of medicine and master of surgery) degree, second in his class of 137. He was vice president of Alpha Omega Alpha, the medical honor society, and won both the annual prize in neuroanatomy and the J. Francis Williams Prize in Medicine on the basis of a competitive examination. Drew completed a year of internship and a year of residency in internal medicine at Montreal General Hospital. He hoped to pursue training as a surgery resident at a prestigious U.S. medical institution, but almost no clinical opportunities were available to African-American doctors at this time. Drew decided to return to Washington, taking a job as an instructor in pathology at Howard University Medical School during 1935–1936.

Howard's medical school was then being transformed from a mostly white-run institution to a black-led one, through the efforts of Numa P. G. Adams, dean of the medical school, and the charismatic Mordecai Johnson, Howard's first black president. Adams nominated Drew to receive a two-year fellowship at Columbia University's medical school.

No black resident had ever been trained at Presbyterian Hospital when Drew arrived at Columbia in the fall of 1938, but Drew so impressed Allen O. Whipple, director of the surgical residency program, that he received this training unofficially, regularly making rounds with Whipple. In the meantime, Drew pursued a doctor of science degree in medicine, doing extensive research on blood-banking, a field still in its infancy, under the guidance of John Scudder, who was engaged in studies relating to fluid balance, blood chemistry, and blood transfusion. With Scudder, Drew set up Presbyterian Hospital's first blood bank. After two years he produced his doctoral thesis, "Banked Blood: A Study in Blood Preservation" (1940), which pulled together existing scientific research on the subject. He became the first African American to receive the doctor of science degree, in 1940. In 1939 Drew had married Minnie Lenore Robbins, a home economics professor at Spelman College. They had four children.

Drew returned to Howard in 1940 as an assistant professor in surgery. In September of that year, however, he was called back to New York City to serve as medical director of the Blood for Britain Project, a hastily organized operation to prepare and ship liquid plasma to wounded British soldiers. He confronted the challenge of separating liquid plasma from whole blood on a much larger scale than it had ever been done before and shipping it overseas in a way that would ensure its stability and sterility. His success in this led to his being chosen in early 1941 to serve as medical director of a three-month American Red Cross pilot project involving the mass production of dried plasma. Once again Drew acted swiftly and effectively, aware that the model he was helping to create would be critical to a successful national blood collection program. Red Cross historians agree that Drew's work in this pilot program and the technical expertise he amassed were pivotal to the national blood collection program, a major life-saving factor during the war.

Soon after being certified as a diplomate of the American Board of Surgery, Drew returned to Howard in April 1941. In October he took over as chairman of Howard's Department of Surgery and became chief surgeon at Freedmen's Hospital, commencing what he viewed as his real life's work, the building of Howard's surgical residency program and the training of a team of top-notch black surgeons.

In December 1941 the United States entered the war, and the American Red Cross expanded its national blood collection program. It announced that it would exclude black donors, and then, in response to widespread protest, it adopted a policy of segregating the blood of black donors. Drew spoke out against this policy, pointing out that there was no medical or scientific reason to segregate blood supplies by race. (The Red Cross officially ended its segregation of blood in 1950.) His stance catapulted him into the national limelight: the irony of his being a blood expert and potentially facing exclusion or segregation himself was dramatized by both the black and white press and highlighted when he received the National Association for the Advancement of Colored People's Spingarn Medal in 1944.

A demanding yet unusually caring teacher, Drew stayed in touch with his students long after they left Howard. Between 1941 and 1950 he trained more than half the black surgeons certified by the American Board of Surgery (eight in all), and fourteen more surgeons certified after 1950 received part of their training from him. In 1942 he became the first black surgeon appointed an examiner for the American Board of Surgery. Other responsibilities and honors followed: in 1943 he was appointed a member of the American-Soviet Committee on Science, and in 1946 he was elected vice president of the American-Soviet Medical Society. From 1944 to 1946 he served as chief of staff, and from 1946 to 1948 as medical director of Freedmen's Hospital. In 1946 he was named a fellow of the U.S. chapter of the International College of Surgeons; in 1949 he was appointed surgical consultant to the surgeon general and was sent to Europe to inspect military medical facilities.

Throughout this period Drew was struggling to open doors for his young black residents, who still were barred from practicing at most white medical institutions as well as from joining the American Medical Association (AMA) and the American College of Surgeons (ACOG). Throughout the 1940s he waged a relentless campaign through letters and political contacts to try to open up the AMA and the ACOG to black physicians; he himself joined neither.

While driving to a medical conference in Alabama, Drew died as the result of an auto accident in North Carolina. His traumatic, untimely death sparked a false rumor that grew into a historical legend during the Civil Rights Movement era, alleging that Drew bled to death because he was turned away from a whites-only hospital. Drew's well-publicized protest of the segregated blood policy, combined with the hospital's refusals of many black patients during the era of segregation, undoubtedly laid the foundation for the legend that dramatized the medical deprivation Drew spent his life battling. Drew was a great American man of medicine by any measure; his extraordinary personality was best summed up by one of his oldest friends,

Ben Davis: "I can never forget him: his extraordinary nobleness of character, his honesty, his integrity and fearlessness" (Hepburn, p. 28).

• The Charles R. Drew Papers are located in the Moorland-Spingarn Research Center of Howard University. There are two scholarly biographies: Spencie Love, *One Blood: The Death and Resurrection of Charles R. Drew* (1996), and Charles E. Wynes, *Charles Richard Drew: The Man and the Myth* (1988). On Drew's work as a teacher, see Hamilton Bims, "Charles Drew's 'Other' Medical Revolution," *Ebony*, Feb. 1974, pp. 88–96; R. Frank Jones, "The Surgical Resident Training Program at Freedmen's Hospital," *Journal of the National Medical Association* 52, no. 3 (May 1960): 187–93; and W. Montague Cobb, "Numa P. G. Adams, 1885–1940," *Journal of the National Medical Association* 43, no. 1 (Jan. 1951): 43–52. See also the memoir by Drew's wife, Lenore Robbins Drew, "Unforgettable Charlie Drew," *Reader's Digest*, Mar. 1978, pp. 135–40. On Drew's life and legend, see Asa Yancey, Sr., "U.S. Postage Stamp in Honor of Charles R. Drew, M.D., MDSc.," *Journal of the National Medical Association* 74, no. 6 (1982): 561–65; and Calvin C. Sampson, "Dispelling the Myth Surrounding Drew's Death," *Journal of the National Medical Association* 76, no. 4 (1984): 415–18. The latter consists primarily of an eyewitness account of Drew's death. Valuable obituaries include W. Montague Cobb, "Charles Richard Drew, M.D., 1904–1950," *Journal of the National Medical Association* 42, no. 4 (July 1950): 239–46; Paul B. Cornely, "Charles R. Drew (1904–1950): An Appreciation," *Phylon* 11, no. 2 (1950): 176–77; David Hepburn, "The Life of Dr. Charles R. Drew," *Our World* (July 1950): 23–29; and C. Waldo Scott, "Biography of a Surgeon," *The Crisis* (Oct. 1951): 501–7, 555.

SPENCIE LOVE

DREW, Daniel (29 July 1797–18 Sept. 1879), financier, was born in Carmel, New York, the son of Gilbert Drew and Catherine Muckelworth, farmers. After brief, uneventful service in the War of 1812, Drew began his business career buying cattle and sheep from small farmers in New York, New England, and as far west as Illinois for New York City butchers. He quickly acquired a reputation for sharp dealing, and the term "watered stock" may have come from his fraudulent practice of denying cattle water and then feeding them salt to cause over-drinking just before their sale by weight.

"Uncle Dan" Drew married Roxana Mead in Carmel in 1820; they had one son. By 1829 he prospered in the livestock trade with his business in Manhattan, and by 1834 he invested his profits in a steamboat fleet on Long Island Sound and the Hudson River, where he was often in unscrupulous competition with Commodore Cornelius Vanderbilt. The growing demand for efficient transportation between Albany and New York City and improvements in steam power and ship design rapidly increased Drew's fortune.

In 1844 he abandoned these livestock and shipping ventures to open a Wall Street banking and brokerage firm, Drew, Robinson & Company. Drew specialized in railroad stocks and broke new ground in sharp speculation. By the 1857 panic he became a director of the Erie Railroad and amassed a fortune by secret manipulation (usually as a bear) of its stock on Wall Street. Like other robber barons, Drew saw the Civil War as another opportunity to reap profits at the public's expense, sometimes in association with Boss William M. Tweed and the Tammany machine.

In 1866 he joined the "Barnum of Wall Street" James Fisk and the notorious Jay Gould in a spectacular and unscrupulous struggle with Cornelius Vanderbilt for control of the Erie Railroad. As treasurer of the railroad, Drew issued 50,000 newly printed shares of fraudulent or "watered" stock that bilked the public in the "Erie War." To avoid arrest in New York, the three coconspirators retreated to Taylor's Hotel in Jersey City, which they fortified and converted into the Erie headquarters. They dumped Erie Railroad shares on the stock market after Gould bribed judges and state legislators in Albany to legalize this watered stock. Although they defeated Vanderbilt by 1868, this public scandal led to demands for regulation of railroads and securities, but little was changed.

Drew, Fisk, and Gould reaped further profits by bank and stock manipulations until Fisk and Gould lost heavily in their unsuccessful attempt to corner the gold market in the Black Friday Panic on 24 September 1869. The next year they betrayed Drew by driving down the value of his Erie holdings. Drew lost a million and a half dollars, and his reputation, which was never sound, suffered from his association with Fisk and Gould, as well as from newspaper and public criticism of steamship and railroad accidents on lines that he managed. He lost most of his fortune in the panic of 1873 and declared bankruptcy in 1876. Thereafter he lived modestly in Brewster, New York, and in Manhattan with his son William Henry Drew, a broken, semiliterate old rascal.

Although a cutthroat Wall Street tycoon, Drew was also quite pious, and like many self-made Gilded Age "robber barons" he contributed generously to the Methodist church. He founded the Drew Seminary for Young Ladies in his hometown, Carmel, and in 1866 he founded the Drew Theological Seminary (now Drew University) in Madison, New Jersey. Drew was best remembered for infamous business practices and ruthless competition, but when he died in obscurity in New York City his estate was worth less than $500.

Even in death Daniel Drew remained controversial. In 1905 Bouck White, an anticapitalist Congregational minister, announced that he had found Drew's memoirs in a trunk in an attic. White published *The Book of Daniel Drew* in 1910, but the purported memoirs disappeared. Because Drew had little formal education and was not known to keep a diary or private papers, White's book is considered a fraud that the Drew family denounced. Nonetheless, this historical novel is a clever recreation of Drew's legendary career as a Victorian tycoon in the era of unrestrained American capitalism.

• Good sources on Drew's life and times include Clifford Browder, *The Money Game in Old New York: Daniel Drew* and His Times (1986), Maury Klein, *The Life and Legend of Jay Gould* (1986), William A. Swanberg, *Jim Fisk* (1959), and Bouck White, *The Book of Daniel Drew* (1910).

PETER C. HOLLORAN

DREW, Howard Porter (28 June 1890–19 Feb. 1957), track and field athlete, was born in Lexington, Virginia, the son of David Henry Drew and May E. Mackey. At age twenty-one, after working for several years in a railroad depot, he entered high school in Springfield, Massachusetts. By the time Drew had entered high school, however, he ranked high among the nation's best sprinters. In 1910 and 1911 he won both the 100- and 220-yard dashes at the junior Amateur Athletic Union (AAU) track and field championships. Drew's best times as a junior were 10.0 seconds for 100 yards and 21.8 seconds for 220 yards.

In 1912 Drew competed in the senior AAU track and field championships and captured the 100-yard dash in 10 seconds flat. In the 1912 U.S. Olympic trials, the Springfield High School sophomore defeated the nation's top collegiate sprinter, Ralph Craig of the University of Michigan, in the 100 meters. After winning two qualifying heats of the 100 meters in the 1912 Olympics at Stockholm, Sweden, Drew pulled a muscle in the semifinal and was unable to compete in the final, won by Craig.

Although never achieving Olympic success, Drew enjoyed an outstanding track career, winning national championships and setting world records at several distances from 50 to 220 yards. After the 1912 Olympic Games, he set indoor world records of 5.4 seconds for 50 yards, 6.4 seconds for 60 yards, 7.2 seconds for 70 yards, and 10.2 seconds for 100 meters. In 1913 Drew defended his AAU senior title in the 100-yard dash and won the 220-yard dash as well. That same year he set world records of 7.6 seconds for 75 yards, 9.2 seconds for 90 yards, 11.6 seconds for 120 yards, 12.8 seconds for 130 yards, and 21.2 seconds for 220 yards. In 1914 he equaled the world record of 9.6 seconds in the 100-yard dash.

In addition to his track successes, Drew in 1913 graduated from Springfield High School and married Ethel Hawkins; they had two children. He then attended Lincoln University in Pennsylvania for one year before transferring to the University of Southern California (USC) in Los Angeles, where he graduated in 1916. At USC, he competed on the track team, served as the assistant manager of athletics, and edited sports for the college newspaper. In 1916 Drew entered Drake University in Des Moines, Iowa, and in 1920 he graduated with a law degree. That same year, at the age of 30, Drew attempted, but failed, to qualify for the U.S. Olympic team.

A member of the Connecticut and Ohio bar associations, Drew in 1943 became the first African American to become the assistant clerk of the city court of Hartford, Connecticut. He died in West Haven, Connecticut, after a protracted illness.

Drew was the first of a long line of African-American sprinters to earn the title of "world's fastest human." His performances astounded sportswriters and led Michael Murphy, the track coach of the U.S. Olympic Team and the University of Pennsylvania, to comment that he had never "seen any sprinter with such wonderful leg action, his legs fly back and forth just like pistons." Murphy, as well as other track and field coaches, thought that Drew might have had the quickest start of any sprinter of that time. Charles Paddock, the 1920 Olympic gold medalist in the 100 meters, remembered Drew as being "the smoothest piece of running machinery the world had ever seen." His record of 9.6 seconds in the 100-yard dash stood until 1929, when Eddie Tolan lowered it to 9.5 seconds. His record of 21.2 seconds in the 220-yard dash stood until 1921, when Paddock lowered it to 20.8 seconds.

• For references to Drew, see Arthur R. Ashe, Jr., *A Hard Road to Glory: A History of the African-American Athlete, 1619–1918* (1988); Frank G. Menke, *The Encyclopedia of Sports*, 4th rev. ed. (1969); David Wallechinsky, *The Complete Book of the Olympic Games*, rev. ed. (1988); and Roberto L. Quercetani, *A World History of Track and Field Athletics* (1964). An obituary is in the *New York Times*, 22 Feb. 1957.

ADAM R. HORNBUCKLE

DREW, John (3 Sept. 1827–21 May 1862), actor, was born in Dublin, Ireland. The names of his parents have been lost, but they were most likely theater people themselves, and his father apparently made his living as a piano maker. Sometime before Drew's tenth year the family came to the United States and settled in Buffalo, New York. Despite his theatrical heritage, Drew initially chose to go to sea on either a whaling ship or a merchant ship (reports differ). Whichever the case, he wasn't pleased with a life at sea and jumped ship near Liverpool, England, to join a theater. He returned to the United States and appeared in New York City at the Richmond Hill Theatre in 1842, but he wasn't successful until 1845, when he played Dr. O'Toole in *The Irish Tutor* at the Bowery Theatre. It was there that he began playing Irish comic roles, which remained his specialty for the rest of his career.

In 1850 Drew married the actress Louisa Lane, with whom he had three children, and they toured in Chicago, Buffalo, and New York City for a couple of years in the company of actors such as Joseph Jefferson and Lester Wallack (both of whom they performed with at Niblo's Garden in New York). In 1851 they went to Philadelphia and joined the Chestnut Street Theatre company and later the Arch Street Theatre company.

Drew took over the management of the Arch Street Theatre in 1853 with actor-manager William Wheatley, and he remained in that position for two years. It was at the Arch Street that Drew and his brother Frank made famous their interpretations of the Dromio twins in *The Comedy of Errors*. Contemporary observers claimed that not even company members could tell the two apart when they wanted to deceive. Drew left the management in 1855 and traveled with his wife for several years, presenting his Irish characters at several theaters, including Jefferson's in Richmond, Virginia.

After a short tour to England and Ireland in 1857 with his mother-in-law, also an actress, Drew joined Louisa at the Walnut Street Theatre in Philadelphia, at which she was quite successful. In 1858 he left her once again to go on tour to California, England, and Australia. He did quite well on this tour, especially at the American Theatre in San Francisco and in Melbourne, Australia, where his engagement was proclaimed "brilliant." He continued to expand his repertoire, adding more comic roles, but it was still his Irish characters that drew audiences.

By the time Drew returned to Philadelphia in early 1862, Louisa Drew had become the sole manager of the Arch Street Theatre. The theater was then under great financial strain, and Drew's well-attended appearances helped it through a difficult season. He played there for one hundred nights, presenting favorite plays and characters such as *London Assurance* and his Irish Emigrant. Drew died in Philadelphia a few days after the end of his run. According to Louisa Drew's autobiography, Drew died after a short illness, but at least one other source lists the cause of death as a fall.

Drew's acting style was natural and generous. He never formally studied acting and indeed thought that he had no need to. He was encouraged in this attitude by critics and actor friends, most especially Jefferson, who said that at his best Drew produced "simple, bold, and unconventional effects that invariably command[ed] recognition from an audience." His wife, however, felt that with more intensive practice he could have been a great actor, but he was not of her practical mind. The critics' and public's opinion of his acting was based almost completely on his presentation of his Irish characters, and Jefferson was not the only one to believe that there was no Irish comedian equal to Drew at the time. Although best known for his Irish characters such as Handy Andy and the Emigrant, Drew was capable of presenting a variety of comic roles, and he was praised for both his versatility and his generosity on stage.

Drew had a relatively short career—about twenty years—and achieved most of his limited fame through his tour appearances. Considered a pleasant actor to work with and a practical joker, Drew was extremely well liked by contemporary audiences and his fellow actors. He is probably best known today, however, not for his theatrical achievements but as the founding father of one of America's most famous theater families. His daughter Georgiana married into the Barrymore family, thereby starting the Drew-Barrymore legacy.

• Several playbills and photographs, as well as one unidentified article, are in the biography files at the Harry Ransom Humanities Research Center in Austin, Tex. Anecdotal stories appear in Joseph Whitton, *Wags of the Stage* (1902). *The Autobiography of Joseph Jefferson* (1890) and *Autobiographical Sketch of Mrs. John Drew* (1899) contain commentary on Drew's history and acting style. Montrose Moses, *Famous Actor Families in America* (1906), is also of use, as is *My Years on the Stage* (1921) by John Drew, Jr.

SUSAN KATTWINKEL

DREW, John (13 Nov. 1853–9 July 1927), actor, was born in Philadelphia, Pennsylvania, the son of John Drew and Louisa Lane, actors. Born into a theatrical family that could count many generations on the stage (perhaps back to the Shakespearean era on his maternal side), he became the prototype of the "matinee idol" of the American theater in the early twentieth century. His first schooling was at a military boarding school in Bucks County, Pennsylvania, which proved not to his liking, and he was allowed to return home to complete his education at the Episcopal Academy, a day school in Philadelphia.

His future career never in doubt, he first appeared as an actor with his mother's company on 22 March 1873 as Mr. Plumper in *Cool as a Cucumber* at the Arch Street Theatre. Louisa Lane Drew had taken over the management of the Philadelphia theater in 1861 and shaped it into one of the finest acting ensembles in the United States, second only to Wallack's in New York, with which it had arranged to receive first choice of all the plays Lester Wallack bought from English playwrights. (John Drew, Sr., died in 1862 from injuries sustained in a fall.) Also in the company was Mrs. Drew's young daughter Georgiana, (Georgiana Emma Drew Barrymore), who was later to marry Maurice Barrymore and perpetuate, at least for a few more generations, the dynasty of performers from the Drew line; their children were Ethel Barrymore, John Barrymore, and Lionel Barrymore.

After playing with the Arch Street company for two seasons, John Drew caught the eye of Augustin Daly of New York, who was evolving into one of the most influential managers of the American theater of his time. In January 1875 Drew moved to New York to join Daly's company, at the Fifth Avenue Theatre. He made his debut on 17 February 1875 in *The Big Bonanza*. For the next few years, he played parts large and small opposite such leading ladies as Fanny Davenport, Clara Morris, Adelaide Neilson, and his sister, Georgie Drew. Another member of the company was the actor James Lewis, with whom Drew formed a close and lifelong friendship. At Daly's he had the good fortune to act the part of Rosencrantz in support of Edwin Booth's Hamlet. When Daly lost control of the Fifth Avenue Theatre, Drew followed him over to Booth's Theatre to play in the perennial production of *Rip Van Winkle* starring Joseph Jefferson (1829–1905). He returned briefly to the Arch Street Theatre to play with his mother in *The School for Scandal*, then joined his brother-in-law Maurice Barrymore on a barnstorming tour of the country. In 1880, John Drew married the actress Josephine Baker. They had one child, Louise, who eventually followed in her parents' footsteps.

When Daly formed another company in a theater on Broadway (between Twenty-ninth and Thirtieth streets—considered far uptown and out of the way at the time), Drew was invited to become a member of the troupe. In 1880 the production of *Our First Families* brought together Drew, Ada Rehan, James Lewis, and the veteran Mrs. Annie Gilbert (Anne Hartley

Gilbert), who eventually constituted "The Big Four." Known for ensemble acting of the highest order, the troupe became "firmly entrenched in the public's favor." Whenever he could, Daly cast the four in his productions, sometimes going to such lengths as changing the gender of the characters to be played. The company at Daly's Theatre became so renowned that the manager braved London and continental audiences with four tours from 1884 to 1888. The company also toured the United States, becoming an American theatrical institution. Daly's repertory of plays included light comedies, farces, and old English comedies but was not heavily weighted toward Shakespeare and the classics. In them, Drew established himself as a proficient and attractive comedian who delivered his lines with apparent effortlessness. His cool and practiced stage demeanor always belied the kind of talent, experience, and preparation that went into the roles. One of his major successes, however, was in Shakespeare's *Taming of the Shrew*. His Petruchio and Rehan's Katherine became legendary performances of the era. His other Shakespearean roles were in *Twelfth Night*, *As You Like It*, *Richard II*, and *Love's Labour's Lost*, but his true métier was in light comedies on contemporary themes.

On New Year's Eve 1888 Drew joined Edwin Booth and an assemblage of his contemporary peers in founding The Players, a club for men of the theater and other professions. He was to become its third president, an office that he relished and in which he served honorably and long. Although he enjoyed great security and satisfaction and had achieved fame as a member of Daly's company, Drew became restive with the manager's policy that no one of his actors enjoy greater status over another. He was also unhappy with what he considered the meager salary that Daly paid him. In 1892 he was approached by the up-and-coming Charles Frohman, one of a new breed of producers who presented single productions in succession without the need of a permanent base (a theater), a company of performers, and a repertory of plays. Frohman offered him a contract at a great deal more money than he had ever made (reputed to be $500 per week). Drew quit Daly and under Frohman's management was on his way to stardom. Drew remained with Frohman until the latter's death on the SS *Lusitania* in 1915.

Drew's debut with Frohman, on 3 October 1892, was in *The Masked Ball*, adapted from the French by Clyde Fitch, and included a fresh young actress named Maude Adams. As he had been paired with Fanny Davenport and Ada Rehan, Drew found himself with a new leading lady in Adams for four seasons. In 1896 Ethel Barrymore, Drew's niece, made her first New York appearance in a small part in *Rosemary*, a production that starred her uncle and was an enduring favorite. John Drew became so popular as a Frohman star that his first appearance after Labor Day in one of the producer's presentations at the Empire Theatre signaled the beginning of each new season on Broadway. Unfortunately, many of the plays in which he appeared had no afterlife and have been forgotten. Others were simply vehicles for displaying his artistic talents. In real life he became the prototype of the roles he played, which came to be described as "John Drew parts." A strong-featured man of medium height and military bearing, he was always handsomely attired on stage and off and achieved a special celebrity as the best-dressed man in America. He was articulate, charming, and popular with his peers. In 1919, although he had had close relations with the Frohman organization, he supported the actors' strike and even appeared at the strike headquarters to cement his solidarity with his fellow actors. With the fortune he made as a star, he bought an estate in Easthampton, on Long Island, New York, where he spent his summers and hosted his many friends from the theater and other professions. He even had the dubious honor of having a five-cent cigar named for him.

In his last years on the stage, Drew appeared in *The Catbird*, produced by Arthur Hopkins, in 1920, and in Somerset Maugham's *The Circle* in 1921, but he largely confined his stage activities to the all-star productions mounted annually by the Players Club. For them he appeared in *The School for Scandal*, *Trelawney of the "Wells"*, and *Henry IV, Part One*. In 1923, the fiftieth anniversary of his debut on the stage, he was saluted at a dinner given for him at the Hotel Biltmore in New York, which was attended not only by his fellow actors, but also by bankers, lawyers, businessmen, critics, and journalists. Among those paying tribute to him were Judge Learned Hand, the artist Charles Dana Gibson, the actor Henry Miller (1860–1926), and the playwright Augustus Thomas. He announced his retirement in the summer of 1926 but was prevailed upon to make another appearance in *Trelawney*, which was then taken on tour. He became ill on 31 May 1927 in Vancouver and was hospitalized in San Francisco. His illness, diagnosed variously as poisoning from infected teeth, arthritis, and rheumatic fever, was severe enough to keep him in a hospital bed, where he died. At his bedside were his daughter Louise, her husband, the actor Jack Devereaux, and his nephew John Barrymore. His wife had predeceased him in 1918.

His death merited front-page notice in the *New York Times*. Called "the first gentleman of the theatre" by the actress Margaret Anglin, Drew was also eulogized by Otis Skinner as representing "the dignity and art of the theatre at its best." His niece Ethel Barrymore averred that he had never received the recognition as an actor that he deserved because of the seeming effortlessness of his style, and his nephew John Barrymore considered him the greatest actor of his time. At a time when the theater was in transition, John Drew successfully made the changeover from repertory companies to star-centered productions, just as he gracefully evolved from dashing young leading man to older character actor. In his era, John Drew probably had no peer.

• See John Drew's autobiography, *My Years on the Stage* (1922); also, Peggy Wood, *A Splendid Gypsy* (1928); Edward A. Dithmar, *John Drew* (1900); Montrose J. Moses, *Famous Actor-Families in America* (1906); James Kotsilibas-Davis, *Great Times, Good Times: The Odyssey of Maurice Barrymore* (1977); Margot Peters, *The House of Barrymore* (1990); and his obituary in the *New York Times*, 10 July 1927.

MARY C. HENDERSON

DREW, Louisa Lane (10 Jan. 1820–31 Aug. 1897), actress and theater manager, was born in London, England, the daughter of Thomas Frederick Lane and Eliza Trenter (or Trentner), both actors. On stage from infancy, she played numerous children's parts in regional repertory companies throughout England not only with her parents but also with traveling stars. Her father died when Louisa was five, and two years later she and her mother emigrated to the United States, arriving in New York City on 7 June 1827 after four weeks at sea. She made her American debut at Philadelphia's Walnut Street Theatre on 26 September 1827 as the Duke of York in Junius Brutus Booth's production of *Richard III*.

Louisa Lane and her mother, "a sweet singer of ballads" (autobiography, p. 5), acted with eastern repertory companies until her mother married the actor-manager John Kinlock. Capitalizing on the vogue for "infant prodigies," the Kinlocks brought Louisa out as a child star. She played Richard III and other adult roles, but she specialized in protean parts in such plays as *Winning a Husband* (seven characters), *72 Picadilly* (five characters), and *Actress of All Work* (six characters). In November 1830 the family sailed for Jamaica as part of an acting company Kinlock had organized with a New York manager named Jones. Their ship was wrecked on San Domingo, marooning the company for six weeks, after which they made their way to Kingston and began a successful tour. John Kinlock and his youngest child died of yellow fever on the island. Though stricken, Mrs. Kinlock survived the disease, and she and her family (the Kinlocks had two daughters, Georgia [or Georgiana] and Adine, who may have made this ill-fated trip) returned to the United States, where in 1832 Mrs. Kinlock and Louisa resumed their acting careers.

Now twelve, Louisa Lane moved into adult parts in her age range in bills of two to four pieces changed nightly. She acted in Albany, Boston, Providence, New York, Philadelphia, Louisville, Cincinnati, St. Louis, Natchez, New Orleans, Charleston, Washington, Baltimore, and smaller cities in between. She and her mother were jointly paid $16 a week, the sole income for their family of four. In 1835 Louisa Lane played the utility part of Maria in Richard Brinsley Sheridan's *The School for Scandal* and some three years later achieved a recognized position as leading lady and a salary of $20 per week. In 1836 Louisa Lane married Henry Blaine Hunt, whom she described as "a very good singer, a nice actor, and a very handsome man of forty." As Mrs. Hunt, she toured extensively with her husband and family as a stock actress throughout the South, Midwest, and East. She acted with the major stars and for the leading managers of the time, including Edwin Forrest, Junius Brutus Booth, Ellen Tree, James H. Hackett, Sol Smith, Francis C. Wemyss, James H. Caldwell, James F. Murdoch, William Macready, and Charles Kean. She performed in opera, operetta, and ballet and acted (as was then voguish) the male parts of Romeo and Antony, but she was best known and most admired as a comic actress.

The Hunts divorced in 1847, and in June 1848 Louisa Lane married George Mossop, a supporting player and a specialist in Irish roles. Mossop died following a short illness, and Louisa Lane continued to act under his name until April 1851, when her July 1850 marriage to her third and final husband, John Drew, (1827–1862), was revealed. Born in Dublin, John Drew was a noted actor of Irish parts and a partner with William Wheatley in the management of the Arch Street Theatre in Philadelphia for two seasons (1853 to 1855). He left management for starring engagements in Europe and Australia, while Mrs. Drew acted in the United States. Her husband returned to tour as a star in America and died in Philadelphia at the age of thirty-four, after a brief illness.

In the course of their marriage, Mrs. John Drew (as Louisa Lane was thereafter known) and her husband had three children: Louisa Eliza Drew Mendum; John Wheatley Sheridan Drew (1853–1927), a famous actor of drawing-room comedy and for many years one of Augustin Daly's "big four" stars; and Georgiana Emma Drew Barrymore, who had a successful though brief acting career and was the mother of the stage and screen actors Lionel Barrymore, Ethel Barrymore, and John Barrymore. In addition, when her half sister Georgiana Kinlock Stephens died in 1864 (after an unremarkable acting career), Louisa Lane Drew adopted her young daughter, Adine Stephens. Mrs. Drew also adopted Sidney Drew White, described by her as the orphaned son of relations of her husband's, who had considerable success in vaudeville and films under the name Sidney Drew.

In 1861 Louisa Lane Drew assumed the management of what became known as "Mrs. John Drew's Arch Street Theatre" in Philadelphia, whose lease she retained until 1892. She acted leading roles with the company in addition to managing it, the first season undertaking forty-two different ones, and averaging fifty to eighty parts a season in a mostly comic repertory. After an initial struggle to meet the weekly payroll, Mrs. Drew established herself sufficiently to prompt the stockholders to remodel the theater. "For about eight years," she reports in her autobiography (p. 114), "fortune favored me," and a well-managed and skilled company alternated with visiting stars through successful seasons of old and new favorites. Mrs. Drew established a play exchange with Wallack's stock company in New York, which at this time the Arch Street rivaled in excellence, to keep her repertory abreast of current hits. In 1872 and 1873, she brought out her daughter Georgiana and son John as actors, just as the nature of repertory companies in America began to change. Following national trends, the number of visiting stars and combination companies at her theater increased, while the quality of resident players gradually declined. After several seasons of pick-up companies, Mrs. Drew surrendered to the new system and, from 1879, operated the Arch Street solely as a road house for touring combinations.

In 1880 Mrs. Drew began a series of star tours as Mrs. Malaprop to Joseph Jefferson's (1829–1905) Bob Acres in a customized version of *The Rivals*. She hired managers to run the Arch Street Theatre in her absence while she continued to hold its lease and returned to the theater from time to time in starring engagements. Her Lady Teazle in *The School for Scandal* was still praised in 1885, though she was then sixty-five years old. The tours with Jefferson ceased upon his "retirement" in 1892, after eleven seasons and over 19,000 miles. That year, receipts at the Arch Street were so poor that Mrs. Drew gave up the theater's lease. With the period of her greatest achievement as stock actress, manager, and star behind her, the 72-year-old Mrs. Drew moved to New York and resumed touring under the management of Sidney Drew and Charles Frohman. The tours were not successful, and about 1894 she took up residence with her son John Drew in Larchmont, New York, writing her autobiography and "varying the scene by occasionally acting in Philadelphia, Boston, Saratoga, and New York" (p. 133). She died at Larchmont.

Countless actors who worked for and with Louisa Lane Drew attested to her skill as an actress. To a flawless voice, a striking (rather than beautiful) face, a good figure, and graceful, impressive carriage, Mrs. Drew added vivacity and a comic inventiveness and timing prompting American critic William Winter to describe her Mrs. Malaprop as "incomparable" and British actor Sir Henry Irving to say, "She was, in her line, the finest actress I have ever seen." Witty and engaging, dignified but unpretentious, Mrs. Drew was plainspoken for a woman of her day, and her expectations as a company manager were exacting. Perhaps unparalleled among her contemporaries in management, she trained the young stock actors at the Arch Street Theatre in varied aspects of their art, and many of them credited their subsequent successes to her teaching and example. Her revivals of the comic classics—Goldsmith, Sheridan, and Shakespeare—were particularly prized; indeed, critic and historian Thomas Allston Brown recorded that her contemporaries called her "the best stage director ever seen." Mrs. Drew's meticulous attention to the staging of plays at the Arch Street brought her productions to the first rank in the United States. Frank Stull, who worked for her in the 1860s, when her company was most successful, considered her "better than any man in the country" as a theatrical manager. In the face of relentless work, constant competition, changing theatrical conditions, personal tragedies, and a large number of family dependents, Louisa Lane Drew sustained an excellent regard as an actress and manager throughout a long and productive career.

• The Robinson Locke Scrapbooks in the Theatre Collection of the New York Public Library, Lincoln Center, contain clippings about Mrs. Drew. The most detailed biographies of her are her own *Autobiographical Sketch of Mrs. John Drew* (1899) and Dorothy E. Stolp's "Mrs. John Drew, American Actress and Manager, 1820–1897" (Ph.D. diss., Louisiana State Univ., 1952). Stage-related biographies and reminiscences discussing her include Lester Wallack, *Memories of Fifty Years* (1889); Joseph Jefferson, *The Autobiography of Joseph Jefferson* (1897); Clara Morris, *Life on the Stage* (1901) and "The Dressing Room Reception Where I First Met Ellen Terry and Mrs. John Drew," *McClure's*, Dec. 1903, pp. 204–11; A. Frank Stull, "Where Famous Actors Learned Their Art," *Lippincott's Monthly Magazine*, Mar. 1905, pp. 373–79; Otis Skinner, *Footlights and Spotlights* (1923); John Drew, *My Years on the Stage* (1921); Lionel Barrymore, *We Barrymores* (1951); Ethel Barrymore, *Memories* (1955); and Gene Fowler, *Goodnight Sweet Prince*, about John Barrymore (1944). Mrs. Drew is included as a historical subject in T. Allston Brown's entry in F. E. McKay and Charles E. L. Wingate, *Famous American Actors of To-day* (1896), and in Montrose J. Moses, *Famous Actor Families* (1906). Her training of actors is considered in Rosemarie K. Bank, "Louisa Lane Drew at the Arch Street Theatre: Repertory and Actor Training in Nineteenth-Century Philadelphia," *Theatre Studies* 24/25 (1977–1978/1978–1979): 37–46. Obituaries are in the *New York Times*, 1 Sept. 1897, and the *New York Dramatic Mirror*, 11 Sept. 1897.

ROSEMARIE K. BANK

DREW, Richard Gurley (22 June 1899–14 Dec. 1980), inventor, was born in St. Paul, Minnesota, the son of Edward Albert Drew, a clothing salesman, and Maude Shumway. He worked his way through a year of engineering courses at the University of Minnesota by playing the banjo in a dance band, but he dropped out when his father died in order to help support his mother and three siblings. He continued playing the banjo, took a daytime job, and studied mechanical engineering through International Correspondence Schools. In 1921 he found work with the St. Paul–based Minnesota Mining and Manufacturing Company (later known as 3M) as a laboratory technician in the glue bond coated abrasives laboratory. At the time the company manufactured only sandpaper and other abrasive products, and in 1923 Drew was assigned to deliver prototypical samples of waterproof sandpaper to local auto body shops for testing. In the process, he found out that what body repairmen really wanted, in order to produce the new, highly popular, two-tone finish, was a reliable way to mask one color of paint while spray painting a second color. None of the available techniques—water-activated gummed tape, newspapers glued on with paste, or cloth-backed surgical tape—provided consistent protection for a lacquer finish. After witnessing a particularly disastrous masking attempt, Drew impetuously promised to solve the problem.

His superiors at 3M were impressed with Drew's pluck and set him to work finding a solution. For the next two years he experimented with a variety of backings and adhesives in an effort to develop a product that could be anchored by finger pressure and would adhere to a lacquer finish without peeling off the paint or leaving a sticky residue. It also had to stretch flat around curved surfaces without tearing, not stick to itself while rolled up, be impervious to the solvents in automotive paint, and endure indefinite storage under varying conditions of heat and humidity without losing these properties. Finally, in 1925 he combined a crimped, towel-type paper with a rubber-based adhesive to create a tape that satisfied these criteria. Marketed as Scotch Brand Masking Tape, it was an instant hit. Its success allowed 3M to diversify its product line and led to the creation of the 3M Tape Group, which eventually developed more than 600 different types of industrial tape.

In 1926 Drew transferred to 3M's new tape laboratory, where he adapted masking tape for other industrial applications. Three years later, while trying to develop a product that could provide a waterproof seal for wrapped insulation, he first experimented with cellophane as a backing for tape. This brittle, transparent, moisture-proof packaging material, put on the market two years earlier by Du Pont, was becoming the wrapping of choice for confectioners, bakers, and meat packers; unfortunately, no aesthetically acceptable means of sealing packages wrapped in cellophane existed, nor could they be sealed in a way that kept out moisture. Drew applied the rubber-based adhesive he had developed for masking tape to a strip of cellophane and achieved a satisfactory waterproof seal. However, cellophane proved to be an exceptionally difficult material from which to make tape; it curled when it got too hot, it split when coated with adhesive by machine, it could not be coated evenly with adhesive, and the yellowish tint of the adhesive spoiled the appearance of the wrapped package. for almost a year Drew and his staff struggled to develop new processes and equipment so that cellophane tape could be manufactured profitably. In 1930 they produced the first roll of what became known as Scotch tape. This new product was an even bigger success than masking tape. Businesses used it to seal all sorts of packages. Introduced at the beginning of the Great Depression, it was enthusiastically received by people who used it to repair household items they could no longer afford to replace. In time, cellophane tape was put to thousands of uses its inventor had never envisioned.

In 1943 Drew became the technical director of 3M's products fabrication laboratory, a position he held until his retirement in 1962. He was responsible for creating new products and in the process filed thirty U.S. patents in his name. After retiring, he served 3M as a consultant until 1967; he then moved to Santa Barbara, California, where he died.

Drew made up for his lack of formal engineering training with an easygoing determination and inquisitiveness. He put no faith in holders of advanced degrees, preferring instead to work with high school graduates who lacked the technical sophistication to realize that what they were trying to accomplish was

impossible. In 1935 he had married Lorna Cassin; they had one child. Following her death, he married Margaret Page in 1957. In 1977 he was inducted into the Minnesota Inventors Hall of Fame. In 1982 3M renamed its creativity awards program recognizing high school juniors from Minnesota and Wisconsin in his honor.

Drew's inventions spawned a billion-dollar tape industry and helped to transform 3M into a diversified industrial giant. Virtually everyone who has lived in the United States during the past fifty years has used his inventions.

• Drew's papers are located in the archives of the 3M Corporation, St. Paul, Minn. Biographical sketches of Drew include Susan Feyder, "Scotch Brand Tape: A 'Free Spirit's' Invention," *St. Paul Pioneer Press*, 5 Oct. 1975; "Stick-up Man," *Saturday Evening Post*, 11 Dec. 1948, p. 45; and 3M Technical Liaison Department, *Richard Drew, the Inventor* (1996). Obituaries are in the *St. Paul Pioneer Press*, 16 Dec. 1980, and the *New York Times*, 17 Dec. 1980.

CHARLES W. CAREY, JR.

DREXEL, Anthony Joseph (13 Sept. 1826–30 June 1893), investment banker and philanthropist, was born in Philadelphia, Pennsylvania, the son of Francis Martin Drexel, an investor, and Catherine Hookey. Under the supervision of his father, young Tony Drexel was brought up in Philadelphia, where he was richly educated in art, music, and languages.

In 1839, at age thirteen, Drexel began to work as a clerk in the investment business of his father, then in operation for two years. Drexel was rigorously trained for investment banking; he was entrusted with major responsibility, traveling while still only a boy to New Orleans to deliver a large deposit of gold. During the early 1840s Drexel served as a currency broker, buying and selling domestic bills of exchange; he also extended short-term loans to Philadelphia merchants. During the Mexican War Drexel enhanced the reputation of the firm, selling for the federal government ten- and twenty-year Treasury bonds with coupons of 6 percent.

In 1847 Tony Drexel, then age twenty-one, was made a partner in the firm of Drexel and Company. That same year he married Ellen Rozet, the daughter of a Philadelphia merchant; they had seven children.

After the death of his father in 1863, Drexel provided the family's investment firm with capable, prudent management. The improvements in national banking, the increase of public debts on the national and state levels, and the demand for railroad and industrial securities enabled Drexel to enlarge the firm's operations during the post–Civil War era. Drexel did business with the San Francisco firm of Sather and Church and opened in 1868 an office in Paris under John H. Harjes. He engaged in business activities with Andrew Carnegie and with other leaders of the new American industrial class, developed large accounts in London and in Paris, and displayed great skill in the specialized field of foreign exchange. In July 1871 Drexel decided to merge with J. P. Morgan and to establish the firm of Drexel, Morgan, and Company. Drexel, who helped to keep the new firm solvent during the panic of 1873, built new headquarters that year in New York at 23 Wall Street; primarily, however, he directed the business activities of its Philadelphia office.

During the 1870s and 1880s Drexel, along with J. P. Morgan, emerged to a position of prominence in the world of American finance. He worked with Morgan to refund debt from the Civil War, participating between 1874 and 1879 in syndicates with the Seligmans, the Barings, and N. M. Rothschild to sell Treasury bonds with 4 percent and 4½ percent coupons, which were offered to replace those called bonds with 6 percent coupons. Having befriended Thomas A. Scott of the Pennsylvania Railroad and leaders of other lines, Drexel also became involved with the financing of American railroads. Through private placement in 1875, he sold Pennsylvania Railroad bonds with a coupon of 6 percent to established clients in Philadelphia and London. That same year Drexel played a major role in a bond offering for the Pittsburgh and Connelsville Railroad.

In 1885 his older brother Francis died, and that same year the Philadelphia office was moved to its new location at Fifth and Chestnut Streets. During this time Drexel sold bonds for the Schuylkill River and East Side Railroad. With the faltering of some carriers during the last years of the 1880s, he helped to reorganize and to fund the Philadelphia and Reading Railroad in 1886 and the Pittsburgh and Western Railroad the next year. Drexel also sold securities for electrical companies; in 1889 he offered shares of Thomas Edison's General Electric Company and those of the Philadelphia Electric Company.

Drexel contributed in other ways to late nineteenth-century Philadelphia. The owner of a large amount of real estate in the Philadelphia vicinity, Drexel accrued great profits from the rents of apartments and houses to city workers, but he also attempted to ameliorate their living conditions. With his close friend Philadelphia publisher George W. Childs, he was a partner of the *Public Ledger*; with Childs he also established the Childs-Drexel Home for Aged Printers in Colorado Springs, Colorado.

Drexel was a benevolent man, making large donations to museums, hospitals, and Protestant and Catholic churches in Philadelphia. Moreover, he was a staunch advocate of industrial education and established in the city a college that offered programs in technology and in business and that admitted students without regard for their religion, ethnic background, or gender. With gifts from its founder in the amount of approximately $3 million, the Drexel Institute opened in 1892 and featured scholarships, courses with minimal tuition, night classes, and special events such as concerts and public lectures.

As a proponent of civic improvement, Drexel belonged to the Reform Club of Philadelphia. He was also a Republican and affiliated with the Union League; on several occasions he entertained his friend President Ulysses S. Grant there. Drexel refused Grant's offer to serve as secretary of the Treasury but was one of the pallbearers at the president's funeral. While attempting to improve his health in Carlsbad, Germany, Drexel died.

The career of Drexel is associated with several major legacies. Through diligence and hard work, he became a symbol of the success of American finance capitalism. Yet this private man was greatly committed to public causes. Like other members of the nineteenth-century American aristocracy, Drexel provided needed assistance to the urban masses through his philanthropy.

• Significant business letters of Drexel are housed in the Pierpont Morgan Library in New York and in the Morgan, Grenfell and Company Archives in London. Short but older accounts of Drexel's career include an article by George W. Childs in *Harper's Weekly* (15 July 1893); W. W. Spooner, *Historic Families of America* (n.d.); and E. P. Oberholtzer, *Philadelphia: A History of the City and Its People*, vol. 2 (n.d.). A more recent account of Drexel's career and of his involvement in investment banking prior to 1871 is Fritz Redlich, *The Molding of American Banking: Men and Ideas*, vol. 2 (1951). Vincent P. Carosso, *The Morgans: Private International Bankers, 1854–1913* (1987), meticulously examines the leadership role of this Philadelphia financier in the Drexel and Morgan firm. Other explanations about Drexel's contributions to this firm are offered in Alfred D. Chandler, *The Visible Hand: The Managerial Revolution in American Business* (1977); E. Digby Baltzell, *Puritan Boston and Quaker Philadelphia: Two Protestant Ethics and the Spirit of Class Authority and Leadership* (1979); and Ron Chernow, *The House of Morgan: An American Dynasty and the Rise of Modern Finance* (1990). For Drexel's participation in the Union League and his ties to President Grant, consult Maxwell Whiteman, *Gentlemen in Crisis: The First Century of the Union League of Philadelphia, 1862–1962* (1975), and William S. McFeely, *Grant: A Biography* (1987). An obituary is in the *New York Times*, 1 July 1893.

WILLIAM WEISBERGER

DREXEL, Francis Martin (7 Apr. 1792–5 June 1863), investment banker and painter, was born in Dornbirn, Austria, the son of Franz Joseph Drexel, a merchant, and Magdalen Willhelm. Drexel's father sent him to Milan in 1803 to attend school; he took courses in Italian and in the fine arts and began his career as a painter. As a result of problems in his father's business and the eruption of the Napoleonic Wars, in 1806 Drexel returned to Dornbirn to assist his father. Drexel, who was not drafted into the Hapsburg army, two years later continued his studies, first in France and then in Switzerland. He also painted portraits, decorated coaches, and drew pictorial signs. After spending time in Dornbirn between 1815 and 1817, the adventurous Drexel, who was disenchanted with the economic and political conditions in Austria, decided to leave Europe. In 1817 he sailed from Amsterdam on the *John of Baltimore* and arrived in Philadelphia on 28 July of that year.

Between 1818 and 1836 Drexel became a prominent painter in Philadelphia and abroad. In 1818 he began to teach courses in drawing in a Catholic school directed by a Mr. Bazely. Between 1818 and 1825 Drexel gave exhibits of his portraits in the Pennsylvania Academy of the Fine Arts. In 1821 he married Catherine Hookey; they had three sons and three daughters. As a result of a dispute in 1825 with Bernard Gallagher, his brother-in-law, Drexel found that his painting business began to decline. In May 1826 he left for South America without his family. During a four-year trip, he visited Ecuador, Peru, Bolivia, Chile, and Argentina. He painted portraits of Simón Bolívar and other Latin American leaders; he also purchased and sold curios and engaged in currency trading. This business trip enabled him to make about $22,600. He returned to Philadelphia in 1830 and remained there for about five years. In 1835 he took a trip to Mexico City to promote his portrait business. He returned to Philadelphia in early 1837, having acquired valuable business experience through his many travels.

Between 1837 and 1840 Drexel began to develop a lucrative business as a financier. Realizing that markets for currencies and securities would suffer from the expiration of the charter of the Second Bank of the United States in 1836 and from the Panic of 1837, he decided to give up his career in art and enter the world of banking; for about nine months in 1837 he operated a currency trading brokerage in Louisville, Kentucky. He then returned to Philadelphia and in January 1838 opened F. M. Drexel, Exchange Broker, at 34 South Third Street. In 1839 he began to train his two oldest sons, Francis A. and Anthony J., for the business and became a successful currency broker by buying and selling the paper money of the nation's many state-chartered banks.

For the next twenty-three years, Drexel cautiously expanded the firm's services. He traded domestic and foreign bills of exchange, accepted deposits, and extended short-term loans to Philadelphia merchants. His firm acquired prominence, for between 1846 and 1847 it sold U.S. treasury bonds with a 6 percent coupon to help finance the Mexican War. Before the end of this war, in 1847, he formed a partnership, named Drexel and Company, with his two oldest sons. During the gold rush, he went to San Francisco and in 1849 established Drexel, Sather, and Church, a profitable firm that bought and sold both gold and securities. He returned to Philadelphia in 1857, where he spent the last years of his life. He died in Philadelphia after returning from a business errand in Pottstown, Pennsylvania, when he was thrown under the wheels of a train.

Drexel in several ways contributed to American history. His stature as a portrait painter enabled him to become part of the early nineteenth century Philadelphia cultural aristocracy; his interests in the fine arts, in literature, and in music, which were imparted to his children, well reveal that he was a man of gentility. He also helped to foster the development of finance capitalism. His investment firm assisted in the economic development and the industrial transformation of nineteenth-century America.

• Select business letters of Drexel, his unpublished autobiography, "Life and Travels of Francis M. Drexel," and his "Journal of a Trip to South America," are housed in the Pierpont Morgan Library in New York. There are some secondary sources and primary materials relating to Drexel's career. Terse accounts of his life are found in W. W. Spooner, *Historic Families of America* (n.d.), p. 190; Ellis Paxton Oberholtzer, *Philadelphia: A History of the City and Its People*, vol. 3 (n.d.); E. Digby Baltzell, *Puritan Boston and Quaker Philadelphia: Two Protestant Ethics and the Spirit of Class Authority and Leadership* (1979); and Russel F. Weigley, ed., *Philadelphia: A 300-Year History* (1982). For interpretations of Drexel's career as a portrait painter and about his gentility, consult Marie Elisabeth Letterhouse, *The Francis A. Drexel Family* (1939), and James Creese, *A. J. Drexel (1826–1893) and His "Industrial University"* (1949). The role of Drexel in investment banking is examined in Edward Hopkinson, Jr., *"Drexel and Company": Over a Century of History* (1952); and Vincent P. Carosso, *The Morgans: Private International Bankers, 1854–1913* (1987).

WILLIAM WEISBERGER

DREXEL, Katharine (26 Nov. 1858–3 Mar. 1955), philanthropist and mother superior, was born in Philadelphia, Pennsylvania, the daughter of Francis Anthony Drexel, a wealthy banker, and Hannah Jane Langstroth. When Drexel was an infant her mother died. In 1860, sixteen months after her mother's death, her father married Emma Bouvier, who thereafter raised Katharine and her two sisters. Drexel lived in luxury, receiving the benefits of private tutoring in her home and the ease that immense wealth could bring in the second half of the nineteenth century. As a young woman she traveled extensively with her parents in the United States and in Europe. In 1883 her stepmother, who was known for her generous aid to Philadelphia's poor, died. Two years later her father died, leaving his daughters an inheritance of more than $14 million that he had put in a trust fund for them and was to be distributed to various Philadelphia charities after they died.

In 1885, shortly after their father's death, the sisters received two visitors who were to have a significant impact on their lives, especially on Katharine Drexel's: Bishop Martin Marty, O.S.B., who was the former abbot of St. Meinrad's Abbey (Ind.), a missionary to the Sioux, and vicar apostolic of Dakota territory, and Joseph Stephan, director of the newly erected Bureau of Catholic Indian Missions. Marty and Stephan sought funds to assist Catholic missionary and educational work among the Indians in the United States; they planted the idea that the Drexel wealth could be put to good use by applying it to the Indian missions.

In 1886 and 1887 the Drexel sisters took their third trip to Europe to restore their health. While in Rome during January 1887 Katharine Drexel met Pope Leo XIII who, after hearing her concerns about Native and African Americans, challenged her to become a missionary to them.

Drexel returned to the United States in the spring of 1887, and in the fall of that year she took a trip to survey Catholic Indian missions in South Dakota (including St. Francis in Rosebud and Holy Rosary, where she met Chief Red Cloud), North Dakota, and Minnesota. The trip made her concretely aware of the Indians' and missionaries' needs. Other trips to Indian missions in the next two years convinced her that she must do something more than contribute money.

Throughout the late 1880s Drexel had been in regular correspondence with Bishop James O'Connor of Omaha, the former rector of St. Charles Seminary at Overbrook, Pennsylvania, and an old family friend. Repeatedly he suggested that Drexel found an order of women religious explicitly devoted to the needs of Native and African Americans. By 1889 she decided that she had a call to religious life and that she would establish such an order.

Since Drexel needed to be introduced to religious life herself before she could start her own religious community, she entered the novitiate of the Sisters of Mercy in Pittsburgh on 6 May 1889. In 1891, after she completed her novitiate, she established a new religious community devoted to the Eucharist and to Native and African Americans. With the help of Archbishop Patrick John Ryan of Philadelphia, who replaced O'Connor after his death as her confidant, Drexel called the new order the "Sisters of the Blessed Sacrament for Indians and Colored People" and in 1892 built a motherhouse for the order at Cornwells Heights, Pennsylvania, nineteen miles outside of Philadelphia. On 12 February 1891 Drexel was professed as the first Sister of the Blessed Sacrament; by the end of the year there were twenty-eight novices in the new congregation.

On 13 June 1894, after a brief period of organization, Drexel sent four sisters to open St. Catherine's School in Santa Fe, New Mexico, the first of many institutions the new congregation built with money she had inherited. In subsequent years she surveyed numerous sites for building projects and supervised the planning and construction of new convents and schools throughout Indian territory in Arizona, Washington, the Dakotas, Montana, and Wisconsin, and in twenty-six Catholic dioceses across the country. She established schools and convents for African Americans in Virginia, Ohio, New York, Massachusetts, Pennsylvania, Illinois, Tennessee, and Louisiana. Perhaps her most important and lasting work among African Americans was the establishment in 1925 of Xavier University in New Orleans, the first and only Catholic university explicitly for African Americans. She intended that the school provide education for African-American Catholic teachers to serve in the elementary and secondary schools and for an elite African-American Catholic professional class so that they might have an impact on the society in which they lived.

During her sixty-four years as a member of the new religious order, Drexel distributed more than $12 million of her wealth, building schools, convents, hospitals, and social agencies and supplying teaching staff for the schools and nursing sisters for the hospitals. She contributed support to the Bureau of Catholic Indian Missions, John Lafarge's Catholic Interracial Council in New York, African-American parishes throughout the country, the National Association for the Advancement of Colored People, and the 1930s campaign for antilynching legislation in the South.

Drexel's years of fervid activity and strenuous physical strain eventually caught up with her. In 1935 she suffered a heart attack that forced her into retirement in 1937, when she gave up the leadership of her order. As a resident in her motherhouse for the remaining eighteen years of her life, she became a contemplative devotee of the Eucharist and an exemplar of diligence in meditation and prayer. When she died at the Cornwells Heights motherhouse, she left a legacy of fifty-one convents in twenty-one states, forty-nine elementary and twelve high schools, one national university, three houses of social service, and more than 500 sisters who served these institutions.

• Drexel's personal papers and voluminous correspondence are located in the archives of the order's motherhouse at Cornwells Heights, Pa. The most accurate and best documented biography is Consuela Marie Duffy, *Katharine Drexel: A Biography* (1966). Katharine Burton, *The Golden Door: The Life of Katharine Drexel* (1957), is also useful but has a number of inaccuracies. Obituaries are in the *New York Times* and Philadelphia's *Catholic Standard and Times*, both 4 Mar. 1955.

PATRICK W. CAREY

DREYFUS, Camille Edouard (11 Nov. 1878–27 Sept. 1956), industrial chemist and entrepreneur, was born in Basel, Switzerland, the son of Abraham Dreyfus, a banker, and Henrietta Wahl. Camille and his younger brother, Henri (later Americanized to Henry), both received their education at the University of Basel, being awarded their Ph.D.s in chemistry in 1902 and 1905, respectively. Camille also pursued postgraduate study at the Sorbonne in Paris until 1906. After working several years in Basel to gain industrial experience, Camille and his brother established a chemical laboratory in their home town. Seeking a product that the public would readily buy, they developed a synthetic indigo. Although they made some money in this venture, it quickly became clear that synthetic indigo did not have a sufficient market. Consequently the Dreyfus brothers focused their attention on celluloid, which at that time was produced only in a flammable form. They recognized that a large potential market existed for nonflammable celluloid, if it could be developed. They focused on cellulose acetate and were shortly producing one to two tons per day. Half of their output went to the motion picture industry for film, with the other half going into the production of toilet articles.

In 1914, after the outbreak of World War I in Europe, the British government invited the Dreyfus brothers to erect a plant in England for the production of their nonflammable cellulose acetate to replace the then-current flammable nitrocellulose "dope" used to coat the canvas-covered wings of military aircraft. In 1916 British Cellulose and Chemical Manufacturing Company was formally established with Camille and

Henry as joint managers. The following year the United States, through the invitation of Secretary of War Newton D. Baker, asked Dreyfus to establish a similar plant. Thus, the American Cellulose and Chemical Manufacturing Company was incorporated in 1918, but before the new plant in Cumberland, Maryland, could be finished, the war ended, leaving Dreyfus with 800 acres of land, a half-built brick edifice, and no military market.

Dreyfus returned to England where he and his brother Henry went to work in the laboratory to perfect a commercial process for manufacturing a cellulose acetate fiber, on which they had begun work before the war, in the hope that it would gain them entry into the synthetic yarn market. They had to invent new machinery and redesign existing textile equipment to overcome problems in the spinning, weaving, and knitting of the synthetic fiber. They also discovered that the new yarn would not hold traditional dyes and had to turn to the Basel dyers Clavel and Lindenmeyer for the development of a new line of dyes suitable for the acetate. A side benefit of the dyeing experiments that would later prove of great economic benefit was the discovery of the cross-dyeing technique. Through experimentation it emerged that a material woven partly of acetate thread and partly of a conventional thread took acetate and traditional dyes differentially, thereby enabling the talented dyer to create two-colored effects after weaving or knitting, which was cheaper than dyeing the yarns separately beforehand.

The Dreyfuses' British company, British Celanese, was producing yarn as early as 1920, but it was not until very late 1924 that Camille was able to complete the Cumberland plant and begin commercial production of the acetate fiber. He had, however, already imported a million pounds of the British-produced yarn, which he sold under the trade name "Celanese." This was perhaps Camille's most insightful marketing technique, for it craftily placed the new fiber, in terms of both quality and price, between silk, for which it sought to substitute, and other "rayons," from which it sought to distinguish itself. Although other rayon producers resisted Dreyfus's attempt to distinguish his acetate from that produced by the then-common viscose process, the new product, which did not shrink or stretch as its moisture content changed, quickly found favor with the public. By 1927 the company was producing 3.5 million pounds of yarn and had become the country's third-largest producer after American Viscose and Du Pont, both of which produced primarily viscose rayon. At this time the company's name was changed to Celanese Corporation of America with Camille continuing as president, while his brother Henry presided over British Celanese.

In 1931 Dreyfus married Jean Tennyson, a radio singer; they had no children. Although the depression and falling prices cut into Celanese's profits, the company continued to expand during the 1930s. Under Dreyfus's leadership, Celanese developed a series of new acetate products including a permanent, washable and dry-cleanable moiré finish that simulated watered silk and the first synthetic ninon, high-count satin, and sharkskin materials. By 1940 Celanese held more than 230 patents related primarily to cellulose acetate. After the war the company also moved into the viscose rayon field.

The Celanese Corporation under Dreyfus's leadership continued to explore the plastics-related possibilities of cellulose acetate, and in 1927 the corporation acquired a controlling interest in Celluloid Corporation, the first American plastics company and owner of the Celluloid trademark. The company continued to produce materials such as films, toiletry articles, and basic plastic sheets, tubes, and rods. Dreyfus also developed a new product, Protectoid, designed to compete directly with Du Pont's Cellophane. Because cellulose acetate did not shrink or stretch as much as the viscose-based Cellophane, it had advantages in certain applications, especially as a transparent packaging material. In 1941 Celluloid Corporation was merged into Celanese and operated as the Plastics Division. During World War II, Celanese developed and produced plastics for the war effort and shortly thereafter introduced a particularly tough yet brilliant plastic, Forticel, a compound of cellulose and propionic acid. Other plastic trademark products included Lumarith, Vimlite, Celcon, and Lumapane.

As early as 1932 Celanese began experimenting with the production of chemicals, especially acetic acid, necessary to the manufacture of its product line. During World War II Celanese participated in the War Production Board's chemical program and began construction of a major plant in Bishop, Texas. The new plant, which was not finished until after the war, was designed to produce chemicals from natural gas, and in addition to the acetic acid, its products eventually included acetic anhydride, formaldehyde, methanol, propyl alcohol, and trioxane. The new plant enabled Celanese to more fully integrate its textile and plastics operations.

Thus, in 1945, when Dreyfus was elected chairman of the board, Celanese was well established with a strong three-sided foundation consisting of textiles, plastics, and chemicals on which to base postwar expansion. Dreyfus would remain as executive head of the corporation, as well as chairman, until his death in New York City. At that time he was also president of the affiliates Celanese Mexicana and Canadian Celanese and managing director of British Celanese.

Camille Dreyfus was of a fiery temperament, often given to outbursts, and frequently at odds with the rest of the industry with which he was ready to do battle over any affront, perceived or real. However, he was an excellent chemist and an exceptional promoter, who was able to create a market niche for his cellulose acetate products, thereby establishing Celanese as a profitable pioneer in the field. Dreyfus was a hardworking yet dapper individual given to wearing pince-nez and purple Celanese shirts. A member of a number of professional organizations, including the American Association for the Advancement of Science, the American Chemical Society, the Society of

Chemical Industry, and the Chemists Club of New York, Dreyfus was the recipient in 1940 of the Modern Pioneer Award from the National Association of Manufacturers. He was also a trustee of the Pestalozzi Foundation and founder and president of the Camille and Henry Dreyfus Foundation.

• No Dreyfus papers or biography are available; however, Williams Haynes, *American Chemical Industry*, vols. 3–6 (1945–1954), and an essay titled "Swiss Family Dreyfus," *Fortune*, Oct. 1933, pp. 50–55, 139–45, offer insights into Dreyfus's personality as well as a corporate history of Celanese. An obituary is in the *New York Times*, 28 Sept. 1956.

STEPHEN H. CUTCLIFFE

DREYFUS, Max (1 Apr. 1874–12 May 1964), music publisher, songwriter, and arranger, was born in Kuppenheim, near Baden, Germany, the son of Elias Dreyfus and Amelia Esther Hertz, farmers. As a child, he studied piano in Baden. In 1888, at age fourteen, Dreyfus emigrated to the United States hoping to find opportunities as a pianist and a composer. He had little luck, so he began to take jobs as a music arranger and worked for several songwriters, including Paul Dresser, composer of "On the Banks of the Wabash."

Dreyfus continued to try to publish his own compositions. When he interviewed at the song-publishing firm, Witmark's, Inc., they were uninterested in his compositions but hired him in 1895 for his arranging and piano-playing skills. In 1897 he married Victoria Drill; they did not have children. An astute businessman, Dreyfus had saved enough money by 1901 to buy a 25 percent share in Harms, Inc., another music-publishing firm. A few years later Dreyfus met composer Jerome Kern, who brought some of his music to Harms hoping to have it published. Dreyfus hired Kern as a song plugger before steering him to producer Sam S. Shubert, who hired Kern to write "Howd You Like to Spoon With Me?" for the Broadway musical *The Earl and the Girl* (1905). This began Kern's career as one of Broadway's finest and most successful composers. In this era Dreyfus himself also wrote a hit song, a popular tune called "Cupid's Garden" (c. 1900), but he published it under the name of Max Eugene because he believed that he could not become a first-rate composer.

In 1914 Dreyfus helped found the American Society of Composers, Authors, and Publishers (ASCAP). Dreyfus hired George Gershwin in 1917, when Gershwin was working as a rehearsal pianist. Dreyfus assigned him as an accompanist to vaudevillian Nora Bayes and began publishing Gershwin's music. Under the leadership of Dreyfus, Harms, Inc., published every piece of music Gershwin wrote after 1917. The relationship between Gershwin and Dreyfus is depicted in Warner Bros.' highly fictional screen biography of Gershwin, *Rhapsody in Blue* (1945). The small, soft-spoken Dreyfus was undoubtedly surprised to see himself portrayed on screen by the heavyset and gravelly voiced character actor Charles Coburn. His only known criticism of the movie was to ask a friend, "Did you ever see me wear a top hat?" In *Rhapsody in Blue*, the Dreyfus character is seen persuading Al Jolson (who appeared as himself) to introduce Gershwin's song, "Swanee," in the Broadway musical *Sinbad* (1918). This scene never occurred in real life, but this popular film helped to make Dreyfus, who was well known in music and theater circles, a familiar name to the American public.

In the mid-1920s Dreyfus first published music by Richard Rodgers, with whom he had a long professional association despite the fact that he did not like Rodgers's music at first. Rodgers noted in his autobiography, *Musical Stages*, that he found that with Dreyfus, "you couldn't tell by looking at him whether he liked something. He was not very enthusiastic, but his work was. He said nobody could tell if a song would become a hit but that it might become one if you worked to sell it. He knew how and where to promote a song."

In 1929 Dreyfus sold Harms to Warner Bros. for a figure reported between $8-$10 million. Warner Bros. hired Dreyfus as a consultant, but he disliked that role and took over Chappell & Co., Inc., in 1935 in London and expanded it significantly. He continued, as he had with Harms, to publish a significant part of the best American songwriters. Much later, the Harms catalog was sold to orchestra leader Lawrence Welk by Dreyfus's brother, Louis.

More importantly, by publishing Gershwin's music, along with songs and show scores by other American musical theater luminaries and Tin Pan Alley writers, Harms and later Chappell (along with its London partner, Chappell & Co., Ltd., which was run by Dreyfus's younger brother, Louis, significantly effected the development of American music. The era from World War I until the early 1960s was a golden age of American popular music, and Dreyfus published an inordinately large portion of the gold, including numerous works by Rodgers and Hammerstein, Sigmund Romberg, Cole Porter, Vincent Youmans, Otto Harbach, Kurt Weill, Lerner and Loewe, Harold Rome, and Jule Styne.

Although Dreyfus was an extremely self-effacing man, he was one of the most powerful figures in his profession. Irving Caesar, who wrote the lyrics to Gershwin's "Swanee" and numerous other songs in the Harms catalog, echoed Rodgers's view when he recalled in an interview for Edward Jablonski and Lawrence D. Stewart's *The Gershwin Years* that Dreyfus, "was the only publisher I knew who was a musician. He encouraged you. You could tell by his treatment rather than by his words what he thought of you." Others noted that Dreyfus could get as much enjoyment out of reading a score as he could from hearing it.

With his wife at his side, Dreyfus died at his 700-acre estate, "Madrey Farm," near Brewster, New York. Dreyfus died only days after the four-story building that housed Chappell & Sons in London was razed by fire, destroying original manuscripts by Irving Berlin, Cole Porter, Noël Coward, Ivor Novello, and Rodgers and Hammerstein.

• Musical scores that Dreyfus published early in his career are *The Lady with the Auburn Hair* (1899) and *Just a Lock of Hair for Mother* (1900). Carlene Mair, *The Chappell Story, 1811–1961* (1961), and Great Britain Monopolies and Mergers Commission, *Warner Communications, Inc., and Enterprises Belonging to Chappell & Co., Inc.* (1988), are useful sources on Chappell & Co. For additional information on Dreyfus, see Merle Armitage, *George Gershwin: Man and Legend* (1958); Gerald Bordman, *Jerome Kern: His Life and Music* (1980); David Ewen, *George Gershwin: His Journey to Greatness* (1970, 1986); Hugh Fordin, *Getting to Know Him: A Biography of Oscar Hammerstein II* (1977); Michael Freedland, *Jerome Kern: A Biography* (1978); William G. Hyland, *The Song Is Ended: Songwriters and American Music, 1900–1950* (1995); Edward Jablonski and Lawrence D. Stewart, *The Gershwin Years* (1973); Joan Peyser, *The Memory of All That: The Life of George Gershwin* (1993); Richard Rodgers, *Musical Stages* (1975); Charles Schwartz, *Cole Porter: A Biography* (1977); and Charles Schwartz, *Gershwin. His Life and Music* (1973). An obituary is in the *New York Times*, 16 May 1964.

JAMES FISHER

DREYFUSS, Henry (2 Mar. 1904–5 Oct. 1972), industrial designer, was born in New York City, the son of Louis Dreyfuss, a supplier of theatrical props and costumes, and Elsie Gorge. Dreyfuss attended New York City's Ethical Culture High School, from which he graduated in 1922. At Ethical Culture, Dreyfuss absorbed a seriousness of purpose and a set of progressive and reformist ideals that remained with him for the rest of his life. In 1924 Dreyfuss apprenticed himself to designer Norman Bel Geddes, assisting him with the sets for *The Miracle*. The following year Dreyfuss struck out on his own as a freelance stage designer. During the later 1920s he was closely associated with New York's Strand Theater and with the Roseland Ballrooms, where he acted as a consultant on all aspects of scenic, costume, and lighting design. Freelance stage design work from this period included the sets for *Hold Everything*, *The Last Mile*, *The Cat and the Fiddle*, and *Paths of Glory*. Success on these productions led to an affiliation with the RKO vaudeville chain for which he redesigned a number of theaters, including those in Denver, Colorado, and Davenport, Iowa.

In 1927 Macy's department store invited Dreyfuss to improve the appearance of a group of products with an aim to increasing their salability. In a characteristic gesture, Dreyfuss resigned this position after only two days when he discovered that Macy's sought not a fundamental redesign of its products, but simply a cosmetic makeover. In 1929 Dreyfuss established an independent industrial design consulting office. One of his first employees was Doris Marks, who became his wife (in 1930); she was also his business manager and collaborator. The couple had three children. Initially clients were scarce, but Dreyfuss worked hard to convince manufacturers that improved product design translated not only into better function but into increased sales as well. In 1930 he secured a commission from the Bell Telephone Laboratories to work directly with company engineers on the design of a new telephone that would be both attractive and functional. Dreyfuss's model 300 desk phone was introduced in 1937 and remained the national standard until 1949, when it was replaced by the Dreyfuss-designed model 500. The design of the model 500 accommodated both the technical requirements of Bell engineers and, because of its sculptured and comfortable handset, the preferences of customers. The result was a visually integrated and functional desk phone that was produced for more than twenty years. The designer's Trimline phone was introduced in 1964.

Bell Telephone was the first of a series of important clients including General Electric (refrigerator, 1934), Hoover (upright vacuum cleaner, 1935), Sears Roebuck (washing machine, 1933), and the John Deere Company. Other major Dreyfuss designs include the Mercury train (1936) and the 20th-Century Limited (1938) for the New York Central Railroad; airplane interiors for Lockheed (the Super Constellation and Electra), Pan Am, and American Airlines; and from 1944 a huge commission to redesign the entire fleet of the American Export Lines, including the S. S. Constitution and S. S. Independence. Dreyfuss also carried out product design commissions for Polaroid (model 100 folding camera, 1961); American Thermos, Minneapolis Honeywell, Westclock, Royal Typewriter, and Addressograph. The Hotel Statler (1941), Western Union (1936), U.S. War Department (1942), Socony-Vacuum Touring Service Bureau (1936), and Hilton Hotels were among his interior design clients. In 1939 Dreyfuss collaborated with architect Wallace K. Harrison on *Democracity*, a model urban environment, based on utopian ideas borrowed from Le Corbusier and others, inside the Perisphere at the center of the New York World's Fair.

Dreyfuss's relationship with the John Deere Company, which began in 1936 and lasted until his death, was in many ways typical. At Deere Dreyfuss involved himself not just in the design of individual products but with overall corporate identity. He redesigned trademarks, graphics, and packaging, collaborated with engineers to improve manufacturing processes, advised on the acquisition of works for the corporate art collection, and was a major influence on Deere's decision to commission Eero Saarinen to design the company's landmark headquarters building.

In the course of his career Dreyfuss became known as "a designer's designer" and was repeatedly honored by his colleagues. He received the American Design Institute Award in 1943 and gold medals from the Architectural League of New York in 1951 and 1954, as well as numerous other honors, including the presidency of the American Society of Industrial Design. In 1952 Dreyfuss was appointed professor of engineering at the California Institute of Technology and subsequently divided his time between New York City and Pasadena, California. Because of a long-standing agreement to live or die together, Dreyfuss and his wife, who was diagnosed with inoperable liver cancer in 1972, took their own lives by carbon monoxide poisoning in Pasadena.

Along with Bel Geddes, Walter Dorwin Teague, Donald Deskey, and Raymond Loewy, Dreyfuss was one of a small group of individuals who invented the profession of modern industrial design in New York City during the early 1930s. In contrast to the flamboyant and theatrical style of his design contemporaries, Dreyfuss was low-key and systematic in his personality and work. Throughout his career he retained a dedication to the needs of the user, a belief in the primacy of function over style. For Dreyfuss, machines were valuable only for the human service they performed. He concocted no grand schemes to remake the world; instead, he dedicated himself to improving individual products one by one, making things simpler, more logical, and easier to use. Dreyfuss was suspicious of what he saw as the cold, mechanical, and doctrinaire quality of much European modernism. "Good modern design," he wrote, "does not have to be 'modernistic.'" Streamlining in his view should be viewed as "cleanlining." In his 1952 *Industrial Design: A Progress Report* Dreyfuss summed up the criteria he used to evaluate the success of a design: convenience of use and safety, ease of maintenance, cost of manufacture, sales appeal, and appearance. Dreyfuss felt that the designer had succeeded "if people are made safer, more comfortable, more desirous of purchase, more efficient—or just plain happier by contact with the product."

• The Cooper-Hewitt Museum in New York houses the Dreyfuss archive, which has also been published on microfiche. His autobiography is *Designing for People* (1967). Dreyfuss also wrote *Industrial Design: A Pictorial Accounting, 1929–1957* (1957), *The Measure of Man: Human Factors in Design* (1960; 2d ed., 1967), and, with Doris Marks Dreyfuss, *Symbol Sourcebook: An Authoritative Guide to International Graphic Symbols* (1972). An important recent study is Russell Flinchum, *Henry Dreyfuss, Industrial Designer: The Man in the Brown Suit* (1997). Dreyfuss figures prominently in leading studies of industrial design such as Jeffrey Meikle, *Twentieth Century Limited: Industrial Design in America, 1925–39* (1979); Donald Bush, *The Streamlined Decade* (1975); Arthur J. Pulos, *American Design Ethic: A History of Industrial Design to 1940* (1983) and *The American Design Adventure, 1940–1975* (1988); and John Heskett, *Industrial Design* (1980). Two exhibition catalogs, Kathryn Hiesinger and George Marcus, eds., *Design Since 1945* (1983), and Richard Guy Wilson et al., eds., *The Machine Age in America, 1918–1941* (1986), are valuable for context and comparative material. Michael Kimmelman, "Last of the Heroes: This Man Should Redesign American Industry," *Connoisseur* 216 (Aug. 1986): 36–41, is a useful source, as is the collection of remembrances that appeared in *Industrial Design* 20 (Mar. 1973) shortly after Dreyfuss's death.

WILLIAM J. HENNESSEY

DRINKER, Cecil Kent (17 Mar. 1887–14 Apr. 1956), physician and industrial health expert, was born in Philadelphia, Pennsylvania, the son of Henry Sturgis Drinker, an engineer, lawyer, and president of Lehigh University, and Aimee Ernesta Beaux. He earned a B.S. from Haverford College in 1908 and an M.D. from the University of Pennsylvania in 1913. He then spent a year as research assistant for Alfred Newton Richards at the University of Pennsylvania, where he helped Richards devise an apparatus to supply blood to the kidneys. He began his residency at Peter Bent Brigham Hospital in Boston, Massachusetts, after his wife received her M.D. from Women's Medical College of Pennsylvania in 1914. He had married Katherine Livingston Rotan in 1910. They had two children, and she pursued a career that, like his, spanned the fields of industrial hygiene, public health, and physiology.

Drinker joined the physiology department at the Johns Hopkins University in 1915, then accepted an appointment the following year as instructor in the Harvard Medical School physiology department. He remained associated with Harvard for the rest of his career. In 1917–1918 he acted as head of the physiology department, standing in for a colleague who was involved in First World War–related work. In 1918 he worked closely with William B. Cannon to lobby for a position in physiology in Harvard's newly established industrial physiology department. Like Cannon, and also Cannon's teacher Henry P. Bowditch, who was Harvard's first physiology professor, Drinker aimed to advance the interests of physiology in a clinical direction. Promoted in rapid succession to assistant professor in 1918 and associate in 1919, Drinker achieved the rank of professor of applied physiology in 1924. Meanwhile, he served in 1921 on the committee that planned the curriculum and departmental organization for Harvard's new school of public health. The following year he functioned as acting head of physiology there. In 1930 he spent a year as acting dean of the School of Public Health, then in 1935 was appointed dean. During the 1920s and 1930s, he divided his energy between applied research and administration at the School of Public Health and basic research in physiology at the medical school.

As a result of his medical background and early clinical experience, Drinker committed his research interests to applied science. He is perhaps most well known for helping to develop, with his brother Philip, the Drinker tank respirator or "iron lung." First used on a polio patient in 1928, the iron lung performed the function of the muscles that control breathing by alternating pressure on the patient's chest, which forced air into and out of the lungs. With this device, which remained the standard treatment for polio into the 1950s, patients could be kept alive. Drinker's research on pulmonary function, lymphatic circulation in the lungs, and oxygen toxicity led to work during World War II on high-altitude oxygen masks used by army and navy bombers. The U.S. Navy took further advantage of Drinker's expertise in these areas by sending research physicians to work with him on oxygen poisoning and decompression sickness. This collaboration resulted in the development of decompression equipment for divers and submarine personnel. Another area in which Drinker applied theoretical knowledge to practical effect was industrial health. Occupational health became established as a significant field of public health in the decade after 1910 and Drinker integrated physiology into the study of several occupational diseases. In 1925 he demonstrated that gasoline containing tetraethyl lead, an anti-knock additive, formed a public health hazard. Later he and colleagues conducted health surveys of employees in a number of industries, documenting poisoning from radium, manganese, and carbon monoxide.

In 1919 Drinker helped found the *Journal of Industrial Hygiene*, the first English-language journal in that field. He served as managing editor from 1919 to 1932 and as associate editor from then until 1948. Between 1912 and 1950, he authored more than 250 articles, textbooks, books, and reports. He introduced the Drinker respirator, or iron lung, in a 1929 article in *American Medical Association* titled "The Use of a New Apparatus for the Prolonged Administration of Artificial Respiration," written with P. McKhann. His articles on asphyxia and resuscitation were widely read. His most comprehensive contribution about the lymph system, *Lymphatics, Lymph, and Lymphoid Tissue* (1941), was coauthored with Joseph M. Yoffey. Among other major works he wrote *Pulmonary Edema and Inflammation* (1945) and *The Clinical Physiology of the Lungs* (1954), as well as a book on the history of colonial medicine in Philadelphia: *Not So Long Ago* (1937).

In addition to his position at Harvard, Drinker held numerous other posts and also served as a medical consultant to industry and the military. From 1922 to 1924 he was visiting physician at Boston City Hospital. He spent a sabbatical leave in 1926–1927 in Copenhagen, Denmark, working with August Krogh, whose work on respiration and circulation had recently earned him a Nobel Prize. His consulting work for industry encompassed the areas of industrial poisoning and methods of artificial respiration. He worked, for example, for the Brooklyn Edison Company in the late 1920s, training artificial respiration and rescue squads. From 1943 to 1946 he sat on the Massachusetts Public Health Council and in 1944 served in the U.S. Public Health Service. During his career, he was a member of the American Society for Clinical Investigations, Association of American Physicians, American Physiological Society (treasurer in 1924), Public Health Association, and Royal Danish Academy. Drinker retired from the deanship of Harvard's School of Medicine in 1942 for health reasons. He retired from Harvard in 1948 and moved to Falmouth, Massachusetts, but spent a year as lecturer in physiology at Cornell Medical College in New York City. From that year until 1954, he was a consulting physiologist to the Naval Medical Research Institute in Bethesda, Maryland. He died in Falmouth.

• Drinker's papers, as well as faculty records that cover his tenure at Harvard, are housed at Harvard University Archives. Other archival materials are located at the Countway Library of Medicine in Boston. Secondary sources that address Drinker's personal life and work include Catherine Drinker Bowen, *Family Portrait* (1970); Jean Alonzo Curran, *Founders of the Harvard School of Public Health* (1970); Henry K. Beecher and Mark D. Altschule, *Medicine at Harvard* (1977); and Gerald L. Geison, ed., *Physiology in the American Context, 1850–1940* (1987). Obituaries are in the *New York Times*, 16 Apr. 1956; *Journal of the American Medical Association* (16 June 1956); *Transactions of the Association of American Physicians* (1956); and *AMA Archives of Industrial Health* (Jan. 1957).

HELEN M. ROZWADOWSKI

DRINKER, Elizabeth (27 Feb. 1735–24 Nov. 1807), diarist, was born in Philadelphia, Pennsylvania, the daughter of William Sandwith, a merchant, and Sarah Jervis. Elizabeth Sandwith grew up in relative comfort as an upper-class Quaker child in a city where members of the Society of Friends still influenced cultural and political life. Better educated than most women of her time, she received instruction from Anthony Benezet, the noted Quaker educator and abolitionist. Orphaned at the age of twenty-one, she and her sister lived with friends until 1761, when she married Henry Drinker, a young Quaker merchant with whom she had five surviving children. Throughout her life she lived in Philadelphia, where she raised her children, maintained her household, and entertained a steady stream of visitors, many of whom were Philadelphia's leading citizens. Although a pious Quaker, Drinker never assumed leadership among the Society of Friends, nor was she especially notable during her lifetime. Nonetheless, she was a careful observer of her own world. It is through Drinker's personal account of her day-by-day life that we know her today.

Drinker began her diary in 1758 and continued to make regular entries for the next forty-nine years. Volumes for two missing years, 1787–1788, cannot be found; Henry Biddle claimed they once existed (Biddle, *Extracts* [1889]). Her early diary entries seldom seem inspired; typical examples include "Stay'd at home all Day" (16 Dec. 1758) and "HD. [Henry Drinker] return'd this Morning" (26 May 1763). Yet her diary, like Drinker herself, matured over time. Nearly three-quarters of the completed diary was written between 1793 and 1807, with these later entries reflecting a wider range of interests and concerns, made all the more possible with the completion of her child-rearing years. (She gave birth to her youngest child at age forty-seven.) Still, the diary remained primarily a place to record the daily events of her household and her family. "When I began this year, I intended the book for memorandams, nor is it any thing else . . . as what I write answers no other purpose than to help the memory" (31 Dec. 1799). It is from the mundane entries of ordinary life that we glimpse Drinker's world—the constant struggle with pain and illness, experienced personally and among children and other kin; the steady flow of friends and family that extended her world beyond the confines of her North Front Street home; the regular rhythm of household production that continued, with the assistance of her sister, who lived with them, and several servants, throughout her life.

Despite such continuities, Drinker spent much of her adult life trying to reconcile unwelcome challenges to social and cultural norms brought about by the Revolution and its aftermath. She felt the impact of the Revolution most forcibly in September 1777 when Henry Drinker and nineteen other male Friends were arrested by patriots and banished to Virginia for refusing to sign Pennsylvania's loyalty oath. During her husband's absence, Drinker, a committed pacifist, reluctantly agreed to quarter a British officer. In March 1778, worried about reports of illness and death among the banished Friends, Drinker and three other Quaker women carried a petition signed by eighteen women pleading for the release of the prisoners. Leaving their households for nearly a month while negotiating for their husbands' release, the petitioners traveled across American lines, first to Valley Forge for an unsuccessful audience with General George Washington; and then to Lancaster, the temporary seat of the Supreme Executive Council of Pennsylvania, where they continued to press for the prisoners' release. Although it is unclear to what extent the eventual decision for release was based on the women's petition or on other political pressures, by the end of April they returned to Philadelphia with their newly-freed husbands.

In postrevolutionary Philadelphia, Drinker's life continued to center on family and friends. Sympathetic to the Federalist cause yet avowedly apolitical, Drinker increasingly spent her time reading and writing in her diary as her children matured and began to leave home. Her reading list for the year 1802, for instance, cites sixty-four works reflecting a wide range of intellectual interests. Her diary entries, too, expanded in length and scope during this time. Frequent, often lengthy diary entries during the recurring yellow fever outbreaks of the 1790s, for instance, provide valuable glimpses into the grim, alienating atmosphere of a plague-infested eighteenth-century city. "The woman that dy'd opposite Sniders was bury'd yesterday, they say, that nobody would assist, and her husband was under the necessity of putting her in the Coffin and that into the Hearse, then a Man took her to the Grave" (24 Sept. 1793).

As the concerns of family extended into a third generation, Drinker maintained close relationships with her adult children and with Friends of advancing age, many of whom she nursed or consulted with during illness or injury. Despite dissension in the ranks of the Society of Friends whose political and social influence had been waning since the mid-eighteenth century, Drinker remained a Friend in good standing, although she seldom attended meeting in her later years. She died in Philadelphia while still mourning the death, only two months earlier, of her daughter Sally Downing. In her obituary, Drinker was remembered as "a lady whose sweetness of disposition, and singular propriety of conduct, endeared her through life to all who had the happiness of knowing her" (*Poulson's American Daily Advertiser*, 2 Dec. 1807).

Drinker's life was not representative of most late eighteenth-century Americans. As a member of an elite Quaker family, as a literate woman, and as a diarist, Drinker benefited from greater opportunities than most women of her time. Her historical significance is not a result of achievements widely acclaimed by any of her contemporaries, but in the remarkable document she left to later generations. Drinker's diary has long been regarded by historians as an important source for the study of the social history of revolutionary Philadelphia and the Yellow Fever epidemics of the 1790s. In more recent years it has come to be regarded as an invaluable repository of a wide range of evidence on women's experience, including health and caregiving, family relationships, religious activities, political consciousness, the impact of literacy, and the unfolding of the life cycle. The very fact of the diary's size and duration, spanning nearly half a century, testifies to its uniqueness as an eighteenth-century American woman's diary. The surviving document, almost entirely intact and very legible, establishes Drinker's place in the social, political, and cultural history of eighteenth-century America.

• Drinker's 33-volume diary manuscript along with the Drinker-Sandwith Papers, are at the Historical Society of Pennsylvania in Philadelphia. For many years the only published source of the diary was in Henry D. Biddle, ed., *Extracts from the Journal of Elizabeth Drinker* (1889). In 1991 Elaine Forman Crane and her associates at Northeastern University Press edited the complete diary, including explanatory annotations and a lengthy biographical directory, published as *The Diary of Elizabeth Drinker* (3 vols., 1991). In addition, Crane's *The Diary of Elizabeth Drinker: The Life Cycle of an Eighteenth Century Woman* (1994) provides the best biographical portrait of Drinker and serves as an excellent source for further information.

TERRI L. PREMO

DRINKER, Sophie Lewis Hutchinson (24 Aug. 1888–6 Sept. 1967), feminist and amateur historian, was born in Haverford, Pennsylvania, the daughter of Sydney Pemberton Hutchinson, a business executive, and Amy Lewis. As a dedicated student of history in later life, she took pride in the fact that the Hutchinson family had played a prominent role in the Philadelphia area since colonial times. While not conspicuously wealthy, the family was socially prominent and considered to represent "blue blood." Drinker's education was completed at St. Timothy's School in Catonsville, Maryland, from which she graduated in 1906; she enjoyed her school years, and her historical studies there provided inspiration for her later work as a historian of women.

Drinker's relatively casual interest in music, hitherto limited to the piano lessons conventionally given to all young girls of her social class, was much stimulated when she met Henry S. Drinker, a young Philadelphia lawyer and dedicated amateur musician and musicologist. After a courtship marked by concert attendance and four-hands piano playing, they married in 1911 and established a household that eventually became nationally known for its engagement in amateur musical activities. The Drinkers developed a family "philosophy of music-making" according to which their five children were given daily music lessons and participated in weekly family singing; as part of the regimen, the house was frequented by a steady stream of musicians who came to play chamber music. Sophie participated enthusiastically in these pursuits, in addition to an array of outside philanthropic and civic activities including Sheltering Arms (a home for unwed mothers), the Community Chest, and the League of Women Voters.

In 1928 the Drinkers built a new home in Merion with a large music room, and they began what would be a thirty-year tradition of "singing parties" to which friends and acquaintances were invited, sometimes more than a hundred at a time, to play and sing Bach cantatas and other choral repertory. About 250 such parties were held over a thirty-year period, involving more than three thousand people.

Drinker's work as a historian of women in music was sparked by this family absorption, specifically by her experience with a women's chorus, The Montgomery Singers, which she joined in 1930. Appalled by the poor quality of music available for women's voices and struck by the fact that none of the chorus's repertory was composed by women, she set out to discover why women had become so marginal in the tradition of Western music. Despite her lack of formal education and armed only with curiosity, determination, and the assistance of many scholars to whom she wrote for advice and assistance, over a twenty-year period she researched the entire history of women's relationship to music on a global scale.

Drinker's book, *Music and Women: The Story of Women in Their Relation to Music* (1948; repr. 1977), was the first—and for some thirty years the only—attempt to address the history of women in music. The book makes clear that in the course of its preparation Drinker had come to a feminist consciousness unlikely for one of her background of wealth, insulation from contemporary social thought, and conservative politics. In it she anticipates several important insights of later feminist scholarship, for instance, the clear understanding that appropriate gender behavior is not "natural" but conditioned by societal expectations. Drinker concluded that women's disconnection from musical expression was a significant spiritual handicap and symptomatic of a deeper disorder in social relations between men and women. Women's unrest in contemporary society, she wrote in her memoir, "is caused by a divine discontent, a craving for self-development which they are denied by their subjection to men."

In addition to *Music and Women*, her best-known work, Drinker authored several other publications, most in the form of magazine articles, on musical topics from choral singing to family music-making to St. Cecilia as patroness of music. Later her attention turned to women in colonial America, inspired by her interest in her forebears and her membership in the Colonial Dames of America, which sponsored some of her work. Among the products of that research are a

biography of Hannah Penn (*Hannah Penn and the Proprietorship of Pennsylvania* [1958]) and a bibliography, coedited with Eugenie Leonard, of writings on colonial women (*The American Woman in Colonial and Revolutionary Times, 1656–1800* [1962]).

Sophie Drinker died in Philadelphia, at the home of her daughter Ernesta Ballard, in the midst of work on a book about laws pertaining to colonial women.

During a period of largely quiescent feminism in the United States, between the successful completion of the suffrage campaign in 1920 and the first stirrings of academic feminism in the late 1960s, Drinker's work occupies a unique position. Neither the discipline of music history nor that of women's history was in a state of development that encouraged acknowledgment of her research results at the time of their publication, but *Music and Women* has subsequently been "rediscovered" by musicians and musicologists to good effect. Although Drinker's writings are dated now and betray her lack of professional preparation, they remain extremely interesting, methodologically provocative, and insightful.

• There are three principal repositories of Sophie Drinker's papers: personal and scholarly papers, including her memoir, are in the Schlesinger Library, Radcliffe College; research notes and working papers for *Music and Women* are in the Sophia Smith Collection, Smith College, and in the Van Pelt Library, University of Pennsylvania. All of Drinker's published writings may be found among her papers at the Schlesinger Library, along with a number of unpublished lectures and a significant article entitled "Goddesses," commissioned by the *Encyclopedia Britannica* but never published.

On Drinker's importance to feminist musicians, see Jeannie G. Pool, "The Legacy of Sophie Drinker," *Paid My Dues* 3 (1979): 28–29, 40–41. On the impact of the Drinkers' singing parties, see Nora Waln, "The Sunday after Korea," *Atlantic Monthly*, May 1951. The Drinker family as a whole, in Harry and Sophie's generation, is the topic of a collective biography by Harry's sister Catherine Drinker Bowen, *Family Portrait* (1979).

Various aspects of the intellectual and social context of Drinker's musical writing are discussed in Ruth A. Solie, "Sophie Drinker's History," in *Disciplining Music: Musicology and Its Canons*, ed. Katherine Bergeron and Philip V. Bohlman (1992); "Women's History and Music History: The Feminist Historiography of Sophie Drinker," *Journal of Women's History* 5 (1993): 8–31; and "Culture, Feminism, and the Sacred: Sophie Drinker's Musical Activism," in *Cultivating Music in America: Women Patrons and Activists since 1850*, ed. Ralph P. Locke and Cyrilla Barr (1995). Obituaries are in the *Philadelphia Inquirer*, 8 Sept. 1967, and the *New York Times*, 10 Sept. 1967.

RUTH A. SOLIE

DRISCOLL, Clara (2 Apr. 1881–17 July 1945), businesswoman and philanthropist, was born in St. Mary's, Texas, the daughter of Robert Driscoll, Sr., a cattleman and land buyer, and Julia Fox. Born into privilege, Driscoll was reared on a ranch near Corpus Christi, Texas. She attended private schools in San Antonio, Texas, New York City, and France. In addition to intellectual training, Driscoll also learned ranching skills: "By her own admission she was equally skilled behind a revolver or a rifle, was born and bred to the saddle, proficient with a lariat. In fact, she was capable of doing almost anything her father's ranch hands could do except bulldog a steer" (Turner, p. 14).

Driscoll married Henry Hulme Sevier in July 1906. Living first in New York City and then Austin, Texas, Driscoll moved to Corpus Christi after the death of her brother in 1929 to administer the family estate. When Sevier was named ambassador to Chile in 1933, she accompanied him. Upon their return to the United States in 1935, Driscoll petitioned for divorce. The process was completed in July 1937, and she retook the Driscoll name in 1938.

As Democratic committeewoman from Texas (1928–1944), Driscoll engaged in national-level party politics, quadrennially donating $25,000 to the Democratic party. Her most noteworthy involvement was her failed attempt to have Vice President John Nance Garner nominated as the 1940 presidential candidate. Convinced that Franklin Delano Roosevelt would not, and should not, run for a third term, Driscoll supported Garner. Then, as international tensions heightened, sentiment against a third term eroded and Roosevelt was nominated.

Driscoll's business abilities were impressive. After inheriting the family estate, she multiplied its holdings as president of the Driscoll Properties Co. and Kingsville Produce and Milling Co., president and owner of Corpus Christi Bank and Trust Co., and director and largest stockholder of Corpus Christi National Bank. She was recognized as "one of the most astute businesswomen in the nation" (Turner, p. 66).

Driscoll is best known for saving the Alamo from commercial encroachment. However, this aspect of her history is complicated. While Driscoll did provide the funds to forestall commercial purchase of the property surrounding the Alamo chapel, she misunderstood the property's historical significance. Nor did she initiate the Alamo campaign; it was initiated by Adina De Zavala.

De Zavala began the fight for the Alamo in 1892, extracting a verbal promise from the Hugo-Schmeltzer interests not to sell their property surrounding the Alamo without giving the Daughters of the Republic of Texas (DRT) the opportunity to purchase it. Driscoll's first involvement came in 1900, when she wrote a letter on 29 April to the *San Antonio Express* condemning the deterioration of the missions. In 1903, as the option to buy was running out, De Zavala met Driscoll. They visited Charles Hugo, and Driscoll provided money for a thirty-day option. Driscoll later provided additional funds to extend the option so that the DRT could raise $75,000 to buy the property. Throughout 1903–1904, the De Zavala chapter of the DRT raised only $7,187.98 of the $25,000 for the first down payment, at which point Driscoll provided the remaining $17,812.02.

The Alamo mission originally encompassed many buildings, including the chapel (the edifice most asso-

ciated with the Alamo) and the Long Barrack (originally the convent), where the bulk of the bloodiest fighting occurred. Although the state already owned the chapel, it did not own the surrounding properties on which stood the Hugo-Schmeltzer building, whose bottom two floors' outer wall was part of the Long Barrack. After Driscoll's purchase of the Hugo-Schmeltzer building for the DRT, De Zavala wanted to restore the barracks. However, Driscoll believed the Hugo-Schmeltzer building was an entirely new construction and should be demolished so that "the Alamo should stand out free and clear. All the unsightly obstructions that hide it away should be torn down and the space utilized for a park" (*San Antonio Express*, 29 Apr. 1900).

This difference of opinion led to fights for control of the state DRT and court battles over who was the Alamo's custodian. In 1908, after rumors that the Hugo-Schmeltzer building was to be rented, De Zavala barricaded herself within and challenged Driscoll's custodial control. The courts found in favor of Driscoll's faction, and they took control on 10 March 1910. The De Zavala chapter remained active, despite being declared illegitimate, and continued to demand recognition of the Long Barrack.

In 1911 Governor Oscar B. Colquitt initiated restoration of the Alamo grounds. At an informational meeting, the DRT requested that the Hugo-Schmeltzer building be demolished. De Zavala produced numerous histories and an unpublished plat arguing for the restoration of the Long Barrack. After this meeting, the DRT decided that the governor's restoration plan constituted interference and opposed it. In response, Colquitt, on 4 March 1912, removed the Alamo from the custody of the DRT, claiming it had done nothing to improve it in six years. As part of his restoration plan, he removed all of the Hugo-Schmeltzer building except for the outer two-story walls of the Long Barrack. However, lack of funds prevented rebuilding the second story. While the governor was out of state, the lieutenant governor allowed San Antonio authorities to tear down the second story.

Despite her problematic generosity concerning the Alamo, Driscoll's other philanthropy is noteworthy. She transferred the deed of Laguna Gloria, her Austin home, to the Texas Fine Arts Association, which opened it as an exhibition art gallery in 1944. In her will, she created the Clara Driscoll Foundation to oversee the building and maintenance of the Children's Hospital in Corpus Christi.

Driscoll died in the Driscoll Hotel in Corpus Christi, Texas. After lying in state in the Alamo chapel, she was interred in the family mausoleum in San Antonio. At her death, *Time*'s obituary, titled "Empress Clara," opened, "Even for Texas a woman like Clara Driscoll was something."

• The main collections of Driscoll's papers are housed in the library of the Daughters of the Republic of Texas on the Alamo grounds in San Antonio, Texas, and in the vast and largely uncataloged Driscoll archives administered by members of the Clara Driscoll Foundation in the Bank and Trust Tower in Corpus Christi, Texas. Driscoll published many plays and books, including *The Girl of La Gloria* (1905), *Mexicana* (1905), and *In the Shadow of the Alamo* (1906). A comprehensive biography is Martha Anne Turner, *Clara Driscoll: An American Tradition* (1979); however, this biography functions more as an encomium than a critical assessment of Driscoll's life and includes a misleading description of the struggle to restore the Alamo. Two interesting analyses that strive for historical accuracy concerning the Driscoll–De Zavala battle are Holly Breachley Brear, *Inherit the Alamo* (1995), and L. Robert Ables, "The Second Battle for the Alamo," *Southwestern Historical Quarterly* 70, no. 3 (Jan. 1967): 372–413. Ables's article is heavily detailed and all historical claims are carefully referenced. Pompeo Coppini, who knew both of the women, provides an account of Driscoll's and De Zavala's co-operation and conflict in his autobiography, *From Dawn to Sunset* (1949). Obituaries appear in the *New York Times*, 19 July 1945, the *Corpus Christi Caller*, 18 July 1945, and *Time*, 30 July 1945.

CATHERINE HELEN PALCZEWSKI

DRISCOLL, Paddy (11 Jan. 1895–29 June 1968), professional athlete and coach, was born John Leo Driscoll in Evanston, Illinois, the son of Timothy Driscoll, a mason for the Milwaukee Railroad, and Elizabeth Mahoney. Of small stature, the 5'11", 150-pound Driscoll began his formal football career relatively late, as a junior at Evanston High School. In 1914 Driscoll matriculated at Northwestern University in his hometown, where he starred as a halfback and team captain. Northwestern nearly won the league championship in 1916, as Driscoll led the Wildcats and was named to the All–Western Conference team.

During the summers Driscoll earned extra money utilizing his athletic talents for several semipro baseball teams. In 1917 he lost his college eligibility by playing baseball professionally with the Chicago Cubs. Later that year Driscoll joined the U.S. Navy and played football on the remarkable Great Lakes Naval Training Station team that included George Halas and several other future professional stars. Great Lakes defeated the Mare Island Marines of California in the 1919 Rose Bowl game. Walter Camp, considered the "father of American football," declared Driscoll's performance the greatest he had ever seen by a quarterback.

In 1920, while Driscoll was playing for the Racine Cardinals, a Chicago semipro team, his 40-yard touchdown run against the better-known Chicago Tigers ensured not only a victory but allegedly the territorial and subsequent franchise rights to the city in the new American Professional Football League. Driscoll enjoyed a sterling career with the Cardinals from 1919 to 1925, earning $300 per game. The term "triple threat," purportedly coined to describe his prowess on the football field, proved to be insufficient. Driscoll could run, pass, catch, and kick from the single-wing formation. Both his punts and dropkicks displayed a deadly accuracy. In 1922 the Bears, who had moved to Chicago from downstate Decatur, offered Driscoll a partnership in the franchise if he would switch teams. The officers of the renamed National Football League

(NFL) intervened, however, to prevent such tampering.

The following year Driscoll scored 27 points against the Rochester team and led the NFL in scoring with 78 points, including 10 field goals. In 1925 he dropkicked a field goal of 50 yards, tying the NFL record, and led the Cardinals to a league championship. On Thanksgiving Day Driscoll upstaged the great Red Grange, who made his pro debut with the rival Chicago Bears. Thousands of fans were dismayed that Grange was unable to return Driscoll's 23 punts during the game.

In 1926 financially strapped Chris O'Brien, owner of the Cardinals, was forced to sell Driscoll to the Bears for $3,000. Driscoll soon proved his worth by leading the NFL in scoring with 86 points. Driscoll utilized such talents to augment his salary in the off-season. He continued to play baseball in Chicago's semipro city league and basketball for Paddy Carr's Big Five team. From 1924 to 1937 he served as athletic director and coach at St. Mel's High School in Chicago and as a Catholic League football official. In 1925 his basketball team at St. Mel's won the National Catholic Interscholastic Basketball championship.

In 1928 Driscoll married Mary McCarthy, with whom he had one son. He retired from pro football a year later. Driscoll served as head football coach at Marquette University from 1937 until joining the Chicago Bears staff as an assistant in 1940. A 1942 hip operation caused Driscoll to employ a cane; nevertheless, when George Halas went into temporary retirement in 1956–1957, Driscoll assumed the role of Bears head coach. He led the Bears to the 1956 western division title with a 9–2–1 record before losing, 47–7, in the memorable championship game in which the New York Giants cunningly employed gym shoes to their advantage on a frozen field. After a 5–8 record the following year, Halas returned to the sidelines. Driscoll assumed an administrative position in the Bears organization and served in it until his death.

After his wife died in 1960, Driscoll lived his remaining years with his son in Park Ridge, Illinois. He died in Chicago. Driscoll had already been honored with induction into the Pro Football Hall of Fame in 1965. Both the Pro Football Hall of Fame and the *Pro Football Digest* selected him to their all-1920s team, while contemporary sportswriters continually voted him to the unofficial all-star teams of the era.

• The *Chicago American*, 23 Dec. 1956, details Driscoll's triumph as the Chicago Bears head coach. Honors are listed in Bob Carroll, "The 1920s in Retrospect," *Coffin Corner* 8 (Sept.-Oct. 1985): 3–4, and in the *Chicago Bears Media Guide* (1992). *Bulldogs on Sunday*, a serial publication of the Pro Football Researchers Association, provides narrative game-by-game accounts and commentary of Driscoll's games during the 1920s. Biographical information was provided by Driscoll's sister, Mary Driscoll, in a telephone interview (14 June 1993). Biographical sketches appear in Denis J. Harrington, *The Pro Football Hall of Fame* (1991); William S. Jarrett, *Timetables of Sports History: Football* (1989); and David J. Porter, ed., *Biographical Dictionary of American Sports: Football* (1987). Obituaries are in the *Chicago Tribune*, 30 June 1968 and 3 July 1968.

GERALD R. GEMS

DROMGOOLE, Will Allen (25 Oct. 1860–1 Sept. 1934), writer and journalist, was born William Allen Dromgoole in Murfreesboro, Tennessee, the daughter of John Easter Dromgoole and Rebecca Mildred Blanch. Descended from locally prominent families in Virginia, the Dromgooles moved to Tennessee shortly before their daughter's birth. Dromgoole graduated from Clarksville Female Academy in Tennessee in 1876 and continued her studies at the Boston School of Expression. Throughout this period the Dromgoole family retreated regularly to a summer cottage in the foothills of the Cumberland Mountains. There Dromgoole, who early in life shortened her name to "Will," first considered becoming a writer.

Dromgoole did not seriously pursue a literary career until the mid-1880s, when the financial hardships faced by her family led her to writing as a money-making venture that she supplemented by working as an engrossing clerk for the Tennessee state legislature. Dromgoole sold her first story, "Columbus Tucker's Discontent," to *Youth's Companion* in 1886, receiving second prize in that magazine's literary contest. In the same year she published her first book, *The Sunny Side of the Cumberland*, a semiautobiographical account of a holiday taken by a group of young people to the Cumberland Mountains. In the people and the dialect of East Tennessee, Dromgoole discovered the subject matter and the writing style that characterize a substantial portion of her work. By the early 1890s she was a regular contributor to Atlanta's literary magazine, *The Sunny South*, as well as to periodicals with a national circulation. The social reformer Benjamin Orange Flower (1858–1918), editor of *Arena Magazine*, significantly advanced Dromgoole's career, publishing most of the stories that later appeared in her two collections, *The Heart of Old Hickory* (1895) and *Cinch* (1898).

The decade between 1890 and 1900 was Dromgoole's most prolific. In addition to her short story collections, she published two novels, *A Moonshiner's Son* and *The Valley Path*, both in 1898, and seven books for children. Dromgoole herself saw the 1890 publication of "Fiddling His Way to Fame" as the turning point of her career, remarking after that story's appearance, "I suddenly found myself famous, and since then I have had more orders for work than I have been able to fill." In 1904 Flower identified Dromgoole's predominant fictional theme as "the sweet, true, simple and sincere life of the Common People" and estimated that her stories "have been more widely used by public readers and elocutionists on the platform than the sketches of any other contemporaneous short story writer" ("A Daughter of Tennessee," pp. 94, 89). Dromgoole was a popular lecturer and reader of her own work well into the twentieth century.

The characters populating Dromgoole's stories and novels are those typically associated with local color: mountaineers and African-American figures rendered in the plantation tradition. Periodically, she used figures from real life as thinly veiled models for her fictional creations. "The Heart of Old Hickory," for instance, features Democratic statesman Robert Love Taylor (1850–1912) who, in Dromgoole's fiction and in life, defeated his brother Alfred for the governorship of Tennessee. Dromgoole engages in political mythmaking in such tales, clearly linking Taylor to a more famous advocate of the farmer class, Andrew Jackson: "the heart of old Hickory was there, in [Taylor's] own bosom, throbbing and alive with the burden of humanity."

Although Flower identifies in Dromgoole's fiction a penchant for writing about the "gloomy side of life," the tone of some of her finest fiction is decidedly humorous. "Who Broke Up De Meet'n?" is a comic account of a church gathering that culminates in the congregation singing "Granny, will yo' dog bite" as the meeting dissolves into chaos. The combination of humor and violence in the scene recalls the antebellum genre of southwestern humor and suggests more stylistic variety in Dromgoole's work than discussions of her as a conventional local colorist allow. Similarly, in "A Wonderful Experience Meeting," black characters comically recount the trances and visions that have brought them into direct contact with God. Old Jordan tells of a heaven that transforms black people into white people and white people into black—"'dey des' swops places'"—while Mose visits a heaven in which all people look alike, sharing the same woodpile and sitting at the same table. After the rollicking comedy that propels this tale, Dromgoole poses this serious question at the story's conclusion: "who shall say that the dusky worshippers, interpreting according to their light, had not experienced a foretaste of the 'great joy' promised to *all* men?"

Dromgoole's protagonists are largely men, yet observations she made outside of her fiction suggest a feminist perspective. In January 1895, for instance, she wrote an essay for a symposium published in *Arena* called "The Shame of America." After praising efforts by the Woman's Christian Temperance Union (WCTU) to raise the age of sexual consent for women, Dromgoole continues, "The day has gone by when women may be silenced by the old 'You don't know.' The man who hopes to silence her must invent some stronger quietus than that. Because she *does* know; she has informed and is still informing herself, upon all the great questions of the day." Dromgoole's active involvement in public life suggests her intolerance for traditional gender restrictions. In 1904 she joined the staff of the *Nashville Banner*, writing a regular column called "Song and Story," which included selections of her own poetry and prose. During her thirty years on the *Banner* staff, Dromgoole contributed an unprecedented 7,500 poems and 5,000 columns to its pages. With the onset of World War I, she divided her time between journalism and work as a warrant officer in the U.S. Naval Reserves, where her activities included delivering recruitment speeches. Following the war she was selected poet laureate of the Tennessee Federation of Women's Clubs, and in 1930 she became poet laureate of the Poetry Society of the South.

Although the prominence of her works has ebbed with time, when Dromgoole died, she could claim both regional and national status. She is buried in Murfreesboro.

• The bulk of Dromgoole's papers is at the University of Tennessee Library in Knoxville. An examination of Dromgoole's life is Kathy June Lyday-Lee, "Selected Mountain Literature of Will Allen Dromgoole" (Ph.D. diss., Univ. of Tennessee, 1983). Lyday-Lee offers a critical introduction to Dromgoole's work and reprints ten of her stories, excerpts from her columns, and the full text of Dromgoole's generalized and unflattering nonfiction essays about the Melungeon people of East Tennessee, which have recently drawn fire from scholars such as N. Brent Kennedy in his study, *The Melungeons: The Resurrection of a Proud People* (1994). For contemporary assessments of Dromgoole, see B. O. Flower, "A Southern Woman of Genius and Her Work," *Arena* 14 (Nov. 1895): 506–9, and Flower, "A Daughter of Tennessee," *Arena* 31 (Jan. 1904): 84–94, as well as M. L. Littleton, "In the Footsteps of Will Allen Dromgoole," *Arena* 32 (Sept. 1904): 293–95.

KATHRYN B. MCKEE

DR. SEUSS. *See* Geisel, Theodor Seuss.

DRUMGOOLE, John Christopher (15 Aug. 1816–28 Mar. 1888), founder of Catholic orphanages in New York City, was born in Granard, County Longford, Ireland, the son of John Drumgoole and Bridget (maiden name unknown). His father died when John was six years old, and his mother emigrated to the United States in 1823. John joined her in New York the following year.

Drumgoole worked at a variety of jobs to support his mother. In 1844 he became sexton of St. Mary's Church in Manhattan, where he remained until 1865. There he organized several youth clubs and taught catechism, and he became aware of the growing number of homeless children in the city. He vowed to do something to alleviate the problem. He aspired to the priesthood, but his poverty and lack of formal education, as well as his age, made this a dubious prospect. Undeterred, he attended classes at St. John's College and later at St. Francis Xavier College. In 1850 he opened a small religious bookstore near St. Mary's to earn money for his fees and to support his mother. In 1865, at the age of forty-nine, he entered the seminary of Our Lady of the Angels at Suspension Bridge, New York, near Niagara Falls, and was ordained to the priesthood in 1869 in Buffalo, New York. His first appointment was to St. Mary's, the church he had served so long as sexton.

In 1870 the local conference of the St. Vincent de Paul Society converted a warehouse on Warren Street in Manhattan into St. Vincent's Home for Homeless Boys of All Occupations, serving primarily newspaper and shoeshine boys. Drumgoole was appointed chaplain of the home, and he soon became superintendent of the operation. Under his direction the number of residents increased rapidly. The home offered night courses in reading, writing, and arithmetic, but Drumgoole placed special emphasis on the religious training of the children. He strove to see that Catholic children were not forced into non-Catholic institutions or homes. To support his work he hosted a Great Charity Bazaar in 1875 that netted close to $10,000. In addition, he established the St. Joseph's Union, which was to be a "union of small contributors" who each contributed twenty-five cents a year to support the home. In July 1877 the union began publishing monthly the *Homeless Child and Messenger of the St. Joseph's Union,* edited by Drumgoole, which reported on the activities and needs of the home.

In 1878 Drumgoole purchased four lots and built an eight-story home for the children, the Mission of the Immaculate Virgin for the Protection of Homeless and Destitute Children (opened in 1881). In 1882, to assist with his work, he brought the Sisters of St. Francis from Philadelphia to staff the home. That same year he purchased a large farm on Staten Island, which he named Mount Loretto. Here he established a vocational school to provide children with the opportunity to learn a trade. In 1886 he added a "Female Department" to Mount Loretto. The number of children under his care continued to grow, reaching as many as 2,000. His work earned him the title "Father of Homeless Children." He died in New York City.

• Further information is available through the Archives of the Archdiocese of New York, Yonkers. Though rather simplistic, the best biography is Katherine Burton, *Children's Shepherd: The Story of John Christopher Drumgoole* (1954).

JEFFREY M. BURNS

DRUMMOND, Roscoe (13 Jan. 1902–30 Sept. 1983), journalist, was born James Roscoe Drummond in Theresa, New York, the son of John Henry Drummond, a pharmacist, and Georgia Estella Peppers. He was raised in Syracuse, New York, where he attended Central High School and edited the school magazine, the *Recorder.* In 1920 he entered Syracuse University, majoring in journalism. While in college he worked part-time for the *Syracuse Journal* and was the editor of the *Daily Orange,* the university newspaper. A lifelong Christian Scientist, he inquired about possible employment with the *Christian Science Monitor* while at a journalism fraternity convention in Boston during his senior year. He learned that the *Monitor* did not require seasoned journalists for employment but "would rather take you—before you've been 'mistrained' elsewhere" (Marx, p. 13). When he graduated from college in 1924, he went to work for the *Monitor.* In 1926 he married Charlotte Bruner; they had one son.

Drummond held a series of positions with the *Monitor* that steadily increased his standing at the paper. He began as a reporter and then moved up to assistant city editor, assistant to the executive editor, and chief editorial writer. In 1930 he moved to London and became the European editorial manager of the *Monitor*. In 1934 he went back to Boston and assumed the position of executive editor. Before his appointment as executive editor, the *Monitor* formed a committee known as the "fact-finding mission" to help improve the long-range journalistic quality of the paper. Drummond's first task as executive editor was to implement the results of the fact-finding mission—to increase the size and quality of staff in order to allow for more hardhitting news stories, and to create a weekly magazine section. He served as executive editor until 1940.

Drummond was then appointed chief of the Washington bureau, a position he held until 1953. As chief of the Washington bureau he supervised four other *Monitor* correspondents and began writing his column "State of the Nation." Drummond's column reflected his moderate political philosophy, what he described as "liberal conservative" belief; he endorsed U.S. entry into World War II, and he supported the domestic policies of the Roosevelt, Truman, and Eisenhower administration. His writing followed the *Monitor*'s interpretive style over more traditional spot news reporting. Drummond strove to reduce the complex policy and political questions of the day in his column to readily understood terms. This approach allowed his columns to explain "yesterday's fact to today's news to produce tomorrow's meaning" (Kluger, p. 503).

From 1949 to 1951 Drummond took a leave of absence from the *Monitor* to serve as European director of information for the Marshall Plan, the U.S. program for the rehabilitation of Europe. In 1952 Drummond served as head of a Senate advisory committee investigating the manner in which government agencies handled the news. The panel found that government agencies were not forthright. Drummond is credited with coining the phrase "creeping censorship."

In 1953 Drummond left the *Monitor* and became head of the Washington bureau of the *New York Herald Tribune*. The move to the *Herald Tribune* coincided with the period in Drummond's career in which he was the most influential and received the most public acclaim. At one point 150 newspapers carried his column three times a week; it was variously titled "State of the Nation" or "Washington." President Dwight Eisenhower was a faithful reader of Drummond's column and occasionally invited him to dinner at the White House.

Drummond's friendship with Eisenhower began while Drummond worked for the Marshall Plan. On his return to the United States, Drummond's first column for the *Monitor* predicted that Eisenhower would seek the presidency. Drummond had access to key Republican leaders in and out of the administration. In a column early in the Eisenhower administration, Drummond argued that Republican leaders in Congress should support the White House and not attack the president as they had during the previous twenty years of Democratic ascendancy in the White House. Eisenhower clipped the column and sent it to Drummond with the note "How right you are." Drummond also supported the Cold War containment policy and expressed criticism of Senator Joe McCarthy and his methods.

In 1955 Drummond gave up his role as managing editor of the Washington bureau for the *New York Herald Tribune* and concentrated exclusively on writing his column. To Drummond "the judgment and insight a correspondent brings to the news is ninety per cent of what makes him an effective or distinguished correspondent" (Marx, p. 13). His access to top Washington policymakers made him one of the most popular columnists.

In 1960 Drummond and Gaston Coblentz wrote *Duel at the Brink: John Foster Dulles' Command of American Power*, a study that contradicted contemporary popular opinion by suggesting that Dulles was a less-than-commanding secretary of state for President Eisenhower. They concluded that Eisenhower and Dulles maintained an equal and fond regard for one another but that the president was not subordinate to Dulles's wishes.

Drummond was popular with his colleagues and well respected in the Washington press corps. He often took part in the annual Gridiron Press Club dinner and was a president of the organization.

Drummond's column continued in popularity into the 1960s. However, the *New York Herald Tribune* continued in its slow decline and closed in 1966. Drummond earlier had urged the publishers to change the focus of news coverage and recreate the paper as a daily newsmagazine, similar to the *Christian Science Monitor*. His wife Charlotte died in 1977. He then married Carol Cramer. After the *Herald Tribune* closed, his column was syndicated by the Los Angeles Times Syndicate until 1981. Drummond stopped writing his column in 1981 when he was severely injured in an automobile accident. While recuperating, he wrote occasional commentary for the *Monitor* and at the time of his death was working on his memoirs. He died in a Christian Science nursing home in Princeton, New Jersey.

• Drummond's papers are at Syracuse University, and an oral history of Drummond can be found at the Dwight D. Eisenhower Library in Abilene, Kans. Among the useful secondary literature are Erwin D. Canham, *Commitment to Freedom: The Story of the Christian Science Monitor* (1958); Richard Kluger, *The Paper: The Life and Death of the New York Herald Tribune* (1986); "Drummond in *Herald Tribune* D.C. Post," *Editor & Publisher*, 19 Sept. 1953, p. 13; and an interview by Herbert L. Marx, Jr., "Washington Dateline," *Senior Scholastic*, 9 Feb. 1948, p. 13. For obituaries see the *New York Times*, 1 Oct. 1983; *Washington Post*, 1 Oct. 1983; *Los Angeles Times*, 1 Oct. 1983; and the *Christian Science Monitor*, 5 Oct. 1983.

MARK E. YOUNG

DRURY, Victor S. (24 Feb. 1825–21 Jan. 1918), labor leader and political radical, was born in France. Little is known of his life before he participated in the overthrow of Louis-Philippe in 1848, except that he was a fresco painter. Drury was a delegate to the (First) International Working Men's Association in 1864, where he witnessed debates between Karl Marx and anarchist followers of Auguste Blanqui and Pierre-Joseph Proudhon. In 1867 Drury emigrated to New York City and organized French-speaking sections of the International. He contributed articles to the radical journals *Socialiste* and *Bulletin de l'union républicane.* He was in New York for the 1872 meeting of the International.

Drury's reflections on the Paris Commune (1871) and debates within the International led him to reevaluate doctrinaire Marxism, especially the assumption that trade unions were the vanguard of revolution. In 1876 Drury wrote a series of articles for the *Socialist,* later published as a book, *The Polity of Labor,* that demonstrated a shift toward the ideals of utopian socialist Charles Fourier and Albert Brisbane and toward the anti–trade union socialism of Ferdinand Lassalle. Like the former, Drury espoused cooperative production as an alternative to capitalism, and like Lassalle, he rejected trade unionism as the vehicle of political change.

By the 1880s Drury was an anarchist committed to the overthrow of the state. He was active in New York City's Social Revolutionary Club, and he escorted German revolutionary theorist Johann Most during his 1883 U.S. tour. Drury formed nearly two dozen anarchist clubs in New York City and numerous others across North America. In 1883 he coauthored the Pittsburgh Manifesto, an anarchist document that split the American radical community into a Marxist camp advocating revolutionary trade unionism and the anarchist "Black International" espousing immediate violence to hasten capitalism's demise.

Drury's conversion to anarchism coincided with the spread of the Knights of Labor (KOL) into New York City. He joined the Knights in the late 1870s and in 1882 cofounded District Assembly 49, the umbrella organization that oversaw many of the city's KOL assemblies. He led the coalition of Knights, radicals, and labor reformers that planned the 5 September 1882 parade acknowledged as America's first Labor Day celebration. Drury was also the architect of secret "Spread the Light" clubs, designed to educate workers about the Knights of Labor and political theory. These gatherings recruited new KOL members but also alarmed more conservative Knights. From 1882 to 1890 there were few challenges to KOL leadership that did not involve Drury.

Drury opposed the KOL's cautious leader, Terence Powderly. Within New York City, Drury allied himself with Lassallean anti–trade unionists and with Knights angered by an 1881 decision to abandon secrecy and alter the Order's rituals. By mid-1882 Drury headed the Home Club, an oath-bound inner circle within District 49 dedicated to controlling the Knights. At KOL conventions in 1883, 1884, and 1885, Drury led factions that lobbied for the return of ritual secrecy and for the replacement of craft-centered trade locals within the KOL with mixed assemblies of all laborers, the latter thought to be a better embodiment of revolutionary class consciousness. These efforts failed, but the Home Club gathered support. An explosion of new and undisciplined members following the KOL's dramatic strike victory over Jay Gould's Southwest Railway system in 1885 gave Drury the opportunity he sought. At a June 1886 special assembly, Home Club supporters captured control of the KOL's executive board, although they lacked sufficient votes to depose Powderly. For two years the Home Club dominated KOL affairs.

The peak of Drury's powers came at the 1886 convention held in Richmond, Virginia, in which a resolution passed demanding that trade unionists quit either the Knights or the international unions in which they held dual membership. Drury also protested southern Jim Crow assumptions on behalf of Frank Ferrell, an African-American Knight denied a room in the segregated hotel housing other delegates. Drury and his followers roomed with black families in the city. Later, Drury accompanied Ferrell to a play at a previously segregated theater. Under Drury's leadership, District 49 also organized two Chinese assemblies in defiance of the Order's ban on Chinese members. He was feted by the black community for his work on behalf of people of color.

The Home Club hoped that strikes would precipitate revolution and thus led the Order in numerous strikes in 1886 and 1887, despite the Order's official antistrike stance. Most of these were lost, and membership declined. Further, the Home Club's hostility toward trade unions led more Knights to quit the Order for the American Federation of Labor, an exclusively trade union association. Since 1884, anti–trade union policies within District 49 had led to clashes with the Cigar Makers' International Union (CMIU). As many cigarmakers also held KOL membership, District Assembly 49's squabbles with the CMIU over wage rates, jurisdictions, and craft union ideology resonated throughout the KOL and led many unionists to abandon the Knights, including CMIU official Samuel Gompers, a cofounder of the American Federation of Labor. Drury proved incapable of stanching anti–Home Club backlash within the Knights that sapped membership.

In late 1887 pro-Powderly forces within the Knights curtailed the Home Club's power. Drury was suspended briefly and resurfaced within a splinter group, the Provisional Order of the Knights of Labor, many of whose members were angry with Powderly for not supporting eight anarchists thought unjustly convicted of throwing a lethal bomb in Chicago's Haymarket Square in May 1886. Drury regrouped the Home Club as "The Class" and regained control of District 49 in late 1887. When Drury was again suspended in 1888, he helped form the Founders' Order of the Knights of Labor, a group led by four of the KOL's original members. It accomplished little beyond hastening the flow of members out of the Knights.

After Drury's expulsion, Daniel De Leon eventually took control of District 49. De Leon's Marxism clashed with Drury's anarchism, thus Drury was not reinstated until 1895, the year De Leon and the Knights parted company. By then, Drury was elderly and the Knights of Labor a weak organization of fewer than 70,000 members.

Drury devoted his remaining years to reflection, poetry, writing, and the political education of Leonora O'Reilly, a future leader of the Women's Trade Union League whom he first met in 1886. For the last nine years of his life, Drury resided with O'Reilly and her mother in Brooklyn. Drury's late writings show a return to cooperationist ideals as well as a strain of Christian socialism. He died at the O'Reilly home in Brooklyn.

One of the era's most active and influential anarchist theorists, Drury proved himself to be a superb organizer capable of building power coalitions. His career illustrates the diversity of Gilded Age radical thought and the ways in which ideologies were formed, mutated, and abandoned to fit changing exigencies. In the end, Drury proved to be a better agitator than administrator. His ill-conceived clashes with trade unionists ruptured the Knights of Labor, hastened its demise, and contributed to the rise of the American Federation of Labor.

• The details of Drury's life are hard to come by, due to his love of secrecy and the radical nature of his politics. Drury appears as a brief entry in *Dictionnaire biographique du mouvement ouvrier français* (1968), and the few personal papers that remain are found in the *Papers of the Women's Trade Union League and Its Principal Leaders* in the section dealing with Leonora O'Reilly (Radcliffe College, Special Collections). Drury's activities are also discussed in the *Papers of Terence V. Powderly* (University Microfilms) and in the *Joseph Labadie Collection* (University of Michigan Special Collections). Reprints of Drury's *The Polity of Labor* are available. Details of Drury's activities within the Knights of Labor appear in Robert E. Weir, "Tilting at Windmills: The Knights Joust among Themselves," *Labor History* (Winter 1993). There is a short profile of Drury in the *Knights of Labor* (Lynn, Mass.), 17 July 1886. He is also mentioned in Paul Avrich, *The Haymarket Tragedy* (1984); Philip S. Foner, *American Socialism and Black Americans: From the Age of Jackson to World War II* (1977); and Norman Ware, *The Labor Movement in the United States, 1860–1895* (1929).

ROBERT E. WEIR

DRYDEN, Hugh Latimer (2 July 1898–2 Dec. 1965), physicist, was born in Pocomoke City, Maryland, the son of Samuel Isaac Dryden, a schoolteacher, and Zenovia Hill Culver. In 1907 the practicing Methodist family moved to Baltimore City, where Dryden's father worked as a streetcar conductor for the rest of his life. In 1910 young Dryden saw an airplane for the first time, and, in his recollection, this prompted him to focus his life on aeronautics. He attended the Johns Hopkins University, receiving his B.A. with honors in 1916 and his M.A. in physics two years later.

On the recommendation of Johns Hopkins physicist Joseph Ames, Dryden then joined the National Bureau of Standards in Washington, D.C., in June 1918, starting as inspector of gauges. He soon transferred to the newly created wind-tunnel unit and used his evenings to conduct experiments for his dissertation, which considered experiments on the drag and distribution of air flowing around circular cylinders. This enabled Dryden to receive his Ph.D. in physics and mathematics in 1919 and later carry on with the study of turbulence in airflow. In January 1920 Dryden married Mary Libbie Travers; they had four children, one of whom died in infancy.

From 1920 to 1947 Dryden worked at the National Bureau of Standards, first as chief of the Aerodynamics Section (until 1934), then as chief of the Mechanics and Sound Division (until 1946), and finally as associate director of the bureau. To most who knew him or studied his work, these twenty-seven years constituted his period of active research. As both a scientist and an engineer, Dryden worked parallel tracks in studying physical problems and proposing applications for his solutions. The turbulence and boundary-layer research he began with his dissertation was expanded, for example, by investigations of wind pressures on chimneys and skyscrapers. This helped establish the basis for rational engineering design of structures subjected to wind loads.

Dryden and his collaborators (who included Arnold M. Kuethe, Leslie J. Briggs, and Walther Hill) also used the facilities available to them, in particular the wind tunnel, to prove certain hypotheses, such as Ludwig Prandtl's 1907 theoretical equations of laminar flow within a boundary layer and, later on, the theory of Tollmien and Schlichting on the stability of the laminar boundary layer. Extending his investigation of aeronautics, Dryden worked on determining aerodynamic behavior of airfoil sections at high speeds. The reason for this work was to understand the effect of high propeller tip velocities, which appeared when aircraft increased power and speed. Commissioned by the National Advisory Committee for Aeronautics (NACA), it provided propeller designers with valuable data on compressibility at high speeds. It also afforded Dryden one of the first observations of the "transonic drag rise," a phenomenon encountered when an object approaches the speed of sound.

During World War II Dryden headed "an unusual group" at the Navy Bureau of Ordnance Experimental Unit. This group developed and perfected the BAT. This was the first successfully used American guided missile, which was used as a radar homing device. Dryden also investigated extensively the aerodynamics of aircraft bombs in order to devise the most effective fin stabilizers for cylindrical explosives. He proposed a standardized form of bomb geometry that remained in use until new requirements appeared as airplanes began to approach the speed of sound. Furthermore, Dryden served as deputy scientific director of the Army Air Force's Scientific Advisory Group headed by Theodore von Kármán. This group, "in uniform with simulated rank," followed General Henry H. Arnold to Europe to study scientific and technical advances achieved there during the war. It was during that trip that Dryden first met with rocket scientist

Wernher von Braun, with whom he would later work in the American space program.

Soon after his return to the United States, Dryden's activities as a researcher ended as he assumed the mantel of director of research at NACA in 1947, eventually heading the agency two years later. Although he did occasionally write paper summaries on subjects related to his fields of interest, Dryden was climbing the management ladder. From his Washington, D.C., office he led some 8,000 people by the time NACA was replaced by NASA in 1958. Under his leadership, notable experimental aircraft were developed to study the problems of high altitude and high speed flight. The list ranges from the Bell X-1, which broke the speed of sound, to the X-15, which flew suborbital experimental missions at six times that speed. As a scientific manager, Dryden promoted the path that he himself had followed, emphasizing the need for contact between the research and engineering fields. His formula, "the selection of some common advanced technical development as the goal of both groups," was to become a kind of blueprint for NASA.

The launching of the world's first artificial satellite, the Russian Sputnik I, prompted the White House to draft legislation that would establish an agency directed at exploring space. Dryden helped prepare the document, yet when NASA was formed out of NACA, he became deputy administrator of the new office, rather than its head, possibly because he antagonized some politicians when he insisted on a safe space program (in which the existing booster rocket problems were eliminated) before a space race with the Soviet Union could begin. A Democrat, Dryden faced some of his toughest critics in the Kennedy administration's Wiesner Committee, which evaluated NASA's goals. Dryden nevertheless weathered the attack successfully, thanks to the very integrity that had cost him the NASA administrator's seat. Dryden's multiple World War II activities, which ranged from membership in the National Defense Research Committee to work for the Navy Bureau of Ordnance Experimental Unit, had brought him into regular contact with the military bureaucracy. The experience was crucial to his role at NASA, in which he constantly had to deal with a mix of civilian and military representatives, each with different agendas and goals. He continued on as an able administrator and, on the side, as a licensed Methodist preacher at Calvary Methodist Church in Washington, D.C., until his death from cancer in Bethesda, Maryland.

"The airplane and I grew up together," said Dryden once, while reminiscing to friends. His career did indeed parallel as well as push forward many trends in the development of aeronautics in the United States. His human qualities, conditioned in part by his deep religious convictions, provided the aerospace community with an able thinker capable of balancing priorities according to circumstances, while rarely losing sight of the human dimension of technological progress.

• Dryden's papers are at the Eisenhower Library of the Johns Hopkins University. The National Air and Space Museum of the Smithsonian Institution also has a biographical file that contains a series of clippings. Richard K. Smith, *The Hugh L. Dryden Papers, 1898–1965* (1974), is a valuable source. Two good reviews of Dryden's life are Jerome C. Hunsacker and Robert Seamans, Jr., *Hugh Latimer Dryden, 1898–1965* (1969), and Raymond L. Bisplinghoff, "Hugh Latimer Dryden," *Applied Mechanics Review* 19, no. 1 (1966): 1–5. Alex Roland, *Model Research* (1985), contains extensive explanations of several of Dryden's projects. See also *Pioneering in Aeronautics: Recipients of the Daniel Guggenheim Medal, 1929–1952* (1952): 131–35, and *Current Biography Yearbook* (1959), pp. 99–100, which provides an interesting evaluation of Dryden as he was beginning his tenure at NASA.

GUILLAUME DE SYON

DRYDEN, John Fairfield (7 Aug. 1839–24 Nov. 1911), life insurance pioneer, was born in Temple Mills near Farmington, Maine, the son of John Dryden and Elizabeth Butterfield, farmers. After attending grammar school and high school in Worcester, Massachusetts, he entered Yale College in 1861. Although he excelled in his studies, poor health forced him to withdraw during his senior year. In 1864 he married Cynthia Fairchild, with whom he had two children.

Perhaps it was his physical limitations that prompted the ambitious Dryden to enter the emerging life insurance business. By the early 1870s Dryden had helped to launch the Prudential Friendly Society, based in Newark, New Jersey, a firm that in 1878 became the Prudential Insurance Company of America. The bright and imaginative Dryden contributed the concept of industrial life insurance to the American marketplace. Patterned after a British plan, industrial life insurance required the weekly payment of premiums, averaging only a dime, that were collected by a door-to-door caller. Usually the amount of the policy was small, the face value averaging about $150, and coverage commonly required no medical examination. Shortly after Dryden's Prudential offered this "working-class" protection, other firms entered the field, including one that would soon be its arch-rival, Metropolitan Life Insurance Company. Because working-class insurance tended to lapse frequently for nonpayment, companies like Prudential and Metropolitan built huge cash reserves. And their financial strength increased further since policyholders often were not entitled to either dividends or cash-surrender payments. Still, industrial insurance filled a social need. As industrialization and urbanization accelerated after the 1870s and more Americans became dependent upon the wage system, some form of financial protection for survivors became necessary. Coverage meant that the policyholder might receive a proper burial and that heirs would have some money to make their personal loss less painful financially. Dryden sensed this need and became a millionaire.

Wishing to strengthen his power at Prudential (he assumed the presidency in 1881), Dryden and intimate associates ("the Group") early in the century used an allied financial firm, Fidelity Trust Company of Newark, to guarantee their control over Prudential's burgeoning assets. The two companies held blocks of each other's securities, and the Group used Fidelity's monies for wide-ranging investments. Although regulatory pressure soon forced Fidelity to reduce its position in Prudential, financial ties remained. Dryden later reflected why he pushed for this relationship: "The company [Prudential] has been my own life's work, and I have pride in it." He could have added that the Fidelity arrangement meant handsome profits for its principal investors, including himself.

When William J. Sewell, a conservative Republican U.S. senator from New Jersey, died in 1901, the business-oriented state legislature elected Dryden on 29 January 1902 to fill the unexpired term. Good-government forces alleged that Dryden received considerable financial help from business interests. They charged, for example, that a major local railroad, the Erie, had sent a lobbyist to Trenton to promote Dryden's candidacy; lawmakers reportedly received "sums of $2,500 and $10,000 to vote for Mr. Dryden." Dryden denied charges of impropriety and refused to endorse the rising Progressive movement. He immediately entered the orbit of the conservative "Stalwart" faction of the Republican party. A champion of the Panama Canal and federal supervision of life insurance (he feared state radicalism that erupted in the wake of a sensational New York State probe of life insurance in 1905), Dryden, in the words of muckraker Lincoln Steffens, "was the chief visible representative of the system." Dryden sought reelection in 1907. He won the endorsement of Republican party voters, but opponents, including progressive lawmakers, fought his bid. Discouraged with the political deadlock and his failing health, Dryden withdrew from the contest. Nevertheless, he remained active in insurance matters until his death.

John Dryden was a doting husband and father. A man without much humor (students at Yale called him "Old Sobersides"), he was a stately individual. Dryden was not a churchgoer; he enjoyed instead his membership in several exclusive social clubs in New York City and books from his extensive library.

• The best account of John Dryden's life is found in a popular study of the great life insurance corporation he created, Earl Chapin May and Will Oursler, *The Prudential: A Study of Human Security* (1950). Also of value are Morton Keller's *The Life Insurance Enterprise, 1885–1910* (1963), and H. Roger Grant's *Insurance Reform: Consumer Action in the Progressive Era* (1979). An obituary of Dryden is in the *New York Times*, 25 Nov. 1911.

H. ROGER GRANT

DUANE, James (6 Feb. 1733–1 Feb. 1797), jurist and statesman, was born in New York City, the son of Anthony Duane, a merchant, and his second wife Althea Kettletas, a marriage that united two prosperous merchant families until Duane's mother died when he was three years old. He received a classical education from the catechist of Trinity Church and proceeded without university schooling to a clerkship in the law office of James Alexander, beginning in 1747. He was admitted to the bar in August 1754. Duane quickly developed a prominent reputation for his defense of Trinity Church against the claims of the heirs of Anneke Jans to property on which the church stood and for his defense of the colonial courts against Crown interference in the reopening of the *Forsey v. Cunningham* case, decided in 1763, in which Duane argued that the governor should not have the right to determine the merits of cases appealed from the provincial supreme court. In October 1759 Duane married Mary Livingston, the oldest daughter of the Livingston Manor proprietor, Colonel Robert Livingston.

By the final colonial decades, Duane was embroiled in land disputes on the frontier. After inheriting about 1,500 acres of land in Schenectady County from his father in 1747, he proceeded to accumulate approximately equal amounts from each of two brothers upon their death and to purchase yet another roughly 1,500 acres from a third brother as well as hundreds of acres from speculators in the Mohawk Valley. By 1765 Duane had begun to recruit settlers to Duanesburg, the township on his great tract, from surrounding colonies. His actions were undoubtedly spurred by the king's decision that the Vermont territory was part of the jurisdiction of colonial New York. Indeed, Duane proceeded to purchase an additional 64,000 acres of Vermont lands, under the assumption that his claims would be protected by New York and imperial authorities. Over the final colonial years, however, the government of New Hampshire and the many colonists migrating from New England into the territory contested New York's jurisdiction. Violence erupted on numerous occasions as the Green Mountain Boys, under Ethan Allen's leadership, sought safe and legally secure settlement for hundreds of farmers in the area. Duane led New York proprietors' efforts over the 1770s to influence Crown decisions about the Vermont territory, to organize the division of New York counties to provide additional sheriffs and courts to defend speculators' interests, and to lobby the Crown for jurisdictional changes that would favor colonial New York. In the final settlement, Duane forfeited substantial landholdings.

Early in the revolutionary crisis, Duane made his mark as a moderate Whig. Although he opposed Crown taxation in 1765–1766, he also opposed violence by the Sons of Liberty against the Stamp Act. In 1768 he defended James Jauncey, a candidate for the provincial assembly and future Tory, from charges of corruption made by radical Whigs. By 1774 Duane had staked out a moderate position in the patriot camp; in May he was appointed to the Committee of Correspondence in New York, and in the next months he was elected to the First Continental Congress. There he supported the Galloway Plan of Union, on the grounds that Parliament still had an absolute right to tax colonists and that the colonies were so disunited that they would prove incapable of self-government. Although he signed the Association Agreement that committed the colonists to nonimportation and non-consumption in October 1774, he worked to have it modified in subsequent months. As New York's assembly retreated to Poughkeepsie, Duane agreed to serve in its Revolutionary Convention of 1775, its Committee of Sixty (formed to uphold the association), and its Committee of One Hundred. Duane moved his family from New York City to Livingston Manor just before the Declaration of Independence, a document he opposed because of its timing and wording, was signed. During the Revolution, he served as a delegate to the Continental Congress almost continuously from 1774 to 1781, contributing his time to committees for supplying and financing the Revolution. For the new state of New York, Duane served as Indian commissioner, advised the state government about settling the persistent challenges of Vermonters to New York's boundary claims, and drafted measures to both emit moderate sums of paper money and tax it out of circulation.

Duane returned to New York City after the evacuation in 1783 to find many of his city properties destroyed by fire or neglected. He served as state senator from 1782 to the end of 1789 and in 1784 was appointed mayor of the city, a post he held for almost six years. Presiding over the mayor's court in 1784, Duane was uniquely positioned to influence the outcome in *Rutgers v. Waddington*, the case that set the 1777 state constitution's affirmation of common law heritage against the 1783 New York Trespass Act's denial to military authorities of the use of private property during the Revolution. In 1784 Elizabeth Rutgers sued Joseph Waddington, a supply agent for British merchants who occupied her property during the occupation of New York City, for back rent. Duane argued that since the state law had not expressly repealed constitutional provisions, the latter could be used to construe state actions in the interests of equity, in this case, in favor of Waddington, from the time he gave up acting as a private citizen and assumed the duties of supplier for the British government. Although attacked for favoritism toward the British and for excessive judicial interference in the state's efforts to reconstruct the city, Duane had in fact delivered a more moderate judgment than Alexander Hamilton's defense of Waddington; Hamilton had declared the state statute in violation of the common law and the international peace treaty of 1783.

In 1788 Duane sat at the Poughkeepsie ratification convention as a strong advocate of the Constitution. In 1789 he was appointed as the first federal judge of the New York district. He held that office until March 1794 when he retired from public life and settled in Schenectady, where he died.

• The greatest amount of documentary evidence about Duane's life is in manuscript diaries, ledgers, and correspondence of Duane and his contemporaries, held by the New-York Historical Society. Some important information about land claims has been reprinted in the New-York Historical Society, *Collections*, vols. 2 and 3 (1870, 1871). The best full-length biography of Duane is Edward P. Alexander, *A Revolutionary Conservative, James Duane of New York* (1938); val-

uable information about the northern land controversies may be gleaned from Michael Bellesiles, *Revolutionary Outlaws: Ethan Allen and the Struggle for Independence on the Early American Frontier* (1993).

CATHY MATSON

DUANE, Margaret Hartman Markoe Bache (7 Nov. 1770–28 May 1836), editor and printer, was born on St. Croix, the daughter of Francis Markoe and Elizabeth Hartman, Danish immigrant sugar planters. She lived on St. Croix on her parents' plantation until her father's death, probably in the late 1770s, when she moved to Philadelphia with her mother. They lived, for a time, with Margaret's uncle, Abraham Markoe, a wealthy Philadelphia merchant who had constructed a large mansion in the heart of the city.

When Margaret was ten, her life-style changed when her mother married a Philadelphia physician, Adam Kuhn, who was not in the same social or economic circle as the Markoe family. Margaret underwent yet another transformation when she was courted by Benjamin Franklin Bache in the spring of 1788. Frightened by Bache's quick progression from courtship to "professed love" and feeling pressured to announce an engagement, she accompanied her ill mother to St. Croix in 1789. After her mother's death, Margaret returned to the United States in the summer of 1790 and moved to Somerset, New Jersey, in April 1791. She reestablished her relationship with Bache, and despite objections from his father that she was not wealthy enough to support a journalist, the two married in 1791 and had four sons from 1792 to 1798. Shortly before their marriage, the couple learned that Margaret's inheritance would be significantly less than they had imagined because of her cousin's financial mismanagement of her family's fortune and her mother's family estate on St. Croix, "Clifton Hill."

The newlyweds worked on the *General Advertiser*, a newspaper that Bache had established with his inheritance from his grandfather, Benjamin Franklin, a year before the two married. Although scorned by her former friends for marrying a journalist and a Republican, Margaret raised their children and assisted her husband in the publication of the newspaper. After they changed the name of the paper to the *Aurora*, she played a more active role in its publication, which was by then the leading newspaper critical of the administration of President George Washington. In 1795, with her husband touring in New England to sell copies of the Jay Treaty in an effort to encourage public hostility toward the treaty, she supervised the publication of the *Aurora*, maintaining the paper's stance against the ratification of the treaty. Throughout the 1790s she and her husband opposed the policies of the Federalist administrations of Washington and John Adams, supported the candidacy and the ideas of Thomas Jefferson, and were among the primary targets of the Sedition Act of 1798.

In September 1798, with her husband under arrest for seditious libel, with their newspaper in dire financial straits, and while pregnant with their fourth child,

Margaret was forced to run the *Aurora* and to nurse her husband. Bache contracted yellow fever during the epidemic that ravaged the capital city, and the disease eventually claimed his life. Despite advice from her family in St. Croix, she remained with her dying husband and ran their newspaper in the almost deserted city. She published his obituary within hours of his death and withstood heavy criticism for doing so from Federalist editors and politicians.

Although many other printers believed that she would not continue to publish the *Aurora* and thus stopped sending her their newspapers, with the help of one of the assistants of the *Aurora*, William Duane, she printed the paper and vowed that it would "be continued with inflexible fidelity to the principles upon which it was founded and reared up"—the support of Republican candidates and policies. Facing serious financial difficulties, she accepted the financial assistance of her stepfather, Dr. Kuhn, and other leading Republicans, but she refused their offer to purchase the newspaper in 1799. The Federalist press, especially William Cobbett (alias "Peter Porcupine"), attacked her and her newspaper and so highly regarded its importance and that of "Mother Bache" to the Republican cause that there were many rumors in 1798–1799 that the Federalists were trying to purchase the newspaper in an effort to silence her.

In 1800 she married Duane, who was by then the editor of the *Aurora*. The second marriage for both produced six children. Together they defended their newspaper and themselves from Federalist journalists and mobs unhappy with the *Aurora*'s editorials and polemics. During one altercation, Margaret Duane concealed a butcher knife under her apron when an angry mob attempted to storm the offices of the newspaper. She was very capable of defending herself, as years later, when her husband was touring South America, Duane, awakened by an intruder, captured the man and led him to the local authorities.

Although her second husband continued to be involved in the *Aurora* and in other newspapers until the 1830s, Duane did not. She worked part-time with her husband in a bookstore that he owned in Washington, D.C., but resided in Philadelphia until her death in that city. As one of a handful of women who operated a newspaper during the early republic, Duane demonstrates that women could and did have a role in politics in the Federalist era. The newspaper that she and her husbands operated was very significant in the rise of Jefferson and the Republican party.

• A collection of Margaret Bache Duane's papers, mainly letters to and from Benjamin Franklin Bache, is housed at the American Philosophical Society in Philadelphia. The papers from the Markoe family are at the Historical Society of Pennsylvania. A useful genealogical essay is Frank Leach, "Old Philadelphia Families," *North American*, 22 Sept. 1907, pp. 6–7. For background information on her courtship with Bache and her role on the *Aurora*, see James Tagg, *Benjamin Franklin Bache and the Philadelphia* Aurora (1991). See also Bernard Faÿ, *The Two Franklins: Fathers of American Democracy* (1933), and Jeffery Smith, *Franklin and Bache: Envision-*

ing the Enlightened Republic (1990). A summary of her marriage to William Duane can be found in Allen Clark, *William Duane* (1905). An obituary is in the (Philadelphia) *United States Gazette*, 30 May 1836.

MARK AUGUSTUS SMITH

DUANE, William (17 May 1760–24 Nov. 1835), newspaper publisher and politician, was born near Lake Champlain in modern-day Vermont, the son of John Duane and Anastasia Sarsfield, Irish-immigrant farmers. The elder Duane died in 1765, and the family returned to the village of Clonmel in Ireland when William was about eleven. He received schooling with Franciscan friars, and his mother apparently wanted him to become a priest. However, believing that the Church helped make people passive and therefore abusable by the rich, political elite, he embraced secularism. That action strained relations with his mother. The two broke completely in 1779 when Duane married Catharine Corcoran, a nineteen-year-old Protestant. They had three children. After apprenticing in the printing trade for two years, Duane moved his family to London where he probably worked as a parliamentary reporter for the *General Advertiser*. Having sent his wife and children to Clonmel, he sailed to India as an East India Company employee and arrived there in 1787. Duane spent almost a decade in India, principally as editor and co-owner of the Calcutta *Bengal Journal* and then, from late 1791, as owner and publisher of the Calcutta *World*, a paper he founded with borrowed money. Arbitrarily imprisoned on a slander charge in 1791, he was expelled from India in 1795 both because he had praised the French Revolution as an agent of change for a more republican and egalitarian world and because he had published complaints voiced by East India Company Army soldiers against their employer.

During a brief stint in London editing a radical paper that reflected the London Corresponding Society's ideal of universal suffrage and support for revolutionary France, Duane again faced government efforts to muzzle his press. Aided by a friend who paid the passage, Duane took his family to the United States in 1796. Settling in Philadelphia, they were, Duane lamented, "wretchedly poor and friendless." His entrée to a position with the *Aurora*, the leading Democratic-Republican newspaper, came from his famous—many said infamous—1796 essay, "A Letter to George Washington." Duane criticized George Washington's performance as president and questioned his commitment to the Revolution's social goals by saying that one would seek "in vain" for examples of Washington's championing "establishments or institutions calculated to secure the perpetuity of freedom on the strong basis of education and moral equality." Responding to Washington's blast at political parties, Duane stoutly defended free association for political purposes and stressed that the people, not governments, should determine what constituted proper civil liberties. The essay, which thereafter colored how people viewed Duane, evinced his enduring political philosophy: one must actively strive to create social and political equality.

By spring 1798, Duane, who had been working at various newspaper jobs, was unemployed. Within months his life was transformed: his wife died of cholera, and Benjamin Franklin Bache, the publisher of the *Aurora* who had hired Duane in the summer, was felled by yellow fever. In November Duane began editing the *Aurora* for Margaret Bache. They married in 1800 and eventually had five children.

In 1799 Federalists tried to use the Sedition Act to silence Duane when he printed stories about British influence in the American government. Duane forced them to halt the effort by producing a letter from President John Adams (1735–1826) that supported the truth of his charge. Federalists, and many moderate Republicans, detested Duane's Irish heritage as well as his radicalism. Duane was naturalized in 1802. Duane, who became the principal leader of Pennsylvania's Irish immigrants, helped forge them and Germans into a powerful ethnic political alliance that functioned smoothly until 1809.

Duane claimed in 1811 that the *Aurora* had the largest circulation of any American newspaper, and analysts of all persuasions agreed that, into the War of 1812, it remained the nation's most influential Republican paper. In the Republican party's turbulent internal battles, Duane aligned himself with those who stressed the need to champion both democracy and ordinary working people. For example, Duane maintained that all Pennsylvania officials, including judges, should periodically have to face the electorate so that they could be judged "upon the true principle of democracy—*utility to the people*" (*Experience*, p. 7).

He admired Thomas Jefferson and staunchly supported his policies, especially the determined opposition to British abuses that led to the War of 1812. Jefferson's urging helped convince Duane to back James Madison (1751–1836) in 1812, but he broke with Madison in part because of what Duane considered shabby treatment for his military efforts. Appointed a lieutenant colonel in 1808 during the national emergency, Duane served in that capacity until July 1810 and then became adjutant general for the Fourth Military District in March 1813. His *A Hand Book for Infantry* (1813) was selected as the army's basic infantry manual. It was discontinued in late 1814, however, and another manual Duane had produced got shunted aside. Moreover, disputes about his expenditures as adjutant general festered until 1824.

Duane blended economic nationalism with a commitment to stop powerful economic forces from gouging the public. He backed a high tariff to protect American manufacturing and advocated government spending for internal improvements, but he distrusted optimistic and expansive banking schemes. Charging that the Bank of the United States aided the few at the expense of the many and was, therefore, totally antithetical to the Revolution's true ideals, he vigorously challenged rechartering it. Duane eventually called for a national finance system using public lands as the basis of credit with the profits going to the public. From 1817 on, he supported a hard money policy.

Duane did not embrace the buoyant optimism of the Era of Good Feelings. Increasingly, the *Aurora* became a voice for dissenting political opinions as Duane emphasized the dangers of wild economic speculation, especially in banking, and denounced selecting candidates by the caucus system. In 1820 the paper ventured into the political wilderness when, in essays written by Stephen Simpson, it attacked the Missouri Compromise and asserted that reelecting James Monroe would merely benefit slaveholders. From 1818 until he sold the paper in 1822, Duane, who taught himself Spanish, focused his own writing on championing Latin American independence movements. In the process he unflinchingly applauded Andrew Jackson's 1818 strike against the Spanish in Florida and in so doing won Jackson's friendship.

Duane's finances were always precarious. He did not receive patronage support commensurate with the importance of the *Aurora*, and he was not a good businessman. Even in good times he depended upon loans and loan guarantees to keep the *Aurora* afloat. In the fall of 1822, faced with grave economic difficulties and given the opportunity to travel to South America, Duane sold the *Aurora*. He went on a triumphal visit to South America that included traveling well over 1,000 miles by mule. He returned to Philadelphia in 1823, and the income from a book describing his trip helped augment his small income as an alderman, a post he had received in 1822. His finances improved somewhat in 1829 when he was appointed a clerk to the state Supreme Court. On 4 July 1834 he resurrected the by-then-defunct *Aurora* as a biweekly to support President Andrew Jackson and his attack on the Second Bank of the United States. The paper, which at most had a circulation of 350, appeared sporadically until the spring of 1835. Duane died that fall at his Philadelphia home.

William Duane, who in 1816 made the *Aurora*'s motto "Principles and not Men," prided himself on his independence and on not printing scurrilous personal invective. Nevertheless, he took feuds personally and stridently challenged not only conservative Federalists but moderate Republicans as well. He would attack any who seemed to him more concerned with advancing themselves than with helping to achieve equality. Duane endured a wide range of criticism and attacks. In May 1799 about thirty men beat him unconscious for writing critically about their actions in repressing the Fries's Rebellion against the 1798 federal direct tax. Duane could have escaped the beating by divulging his source of information, but, as he did throughout his journalistic career, he courageously refused to name his source. Opponents regularly hauled the publisher into legal battles on various libel charges. Although he suffered a thirty-day imprisonment in 1801, Duane typically won these contests or avoided final judgment.

Considering Duane's American career, Jefferson perceptively observed that the publisher was "honest, and well intentioned, but over zealous." Indeed, said Jefferson, Duane was "very intolerant" but also "sincerely republican" (Phillips, pp. 1, 139). For Duane and the *Aurora* he published, true republicanism meant supporting democracy rooted in the ideal of political equality.

• Although some personal papers are in collections of the American Philosophical Society, the Historical Society of Pennsylvania, the New York Public Library, and the Library of Congress, no major collection of Duane papers exists. Items housed in the Library of Congress have appeared in "Letters of William Duane," *Proceedings of the Massachusetts Historical Society*, 2d ser., 20 (1907): 257–394. The Phillips work cited below lists Duane's various publications; among the more important or noted, in addition to items cited above, are *Politics for American Farmers* (1807), *Experience the Test of Government* (1807), *An Epitome of the Arts and Sciences . . . Adapted to the Use of Schools* (1811), *The Two Americas, Great Britain, and the Holy Alliance* (1824), and *A Visit to Colombia* (1826). On the nature and significance of the London Corresponding Society, see E. P. Thompson, *The Making of the English Working Class* (1963). Duane figures prominently in political biographies such as G. S. Rowe, *Thomas McKean: The Shaping of an American Republicanism* (1978), and in general studies such as Sanford W. Higginbotham, *The Keystone in the Democratic Arch: Pennsylvania Politics, 1800–1816* (1952); Donald H. Stewart, *The Opposition Press of the Federalist Period* (1969); and John C. Miller, *Crisis in Freedom: The Alien and Sedition Acts* (1952). James Tagg, *Benjamin Franklin Bache and the Philadelphia Aurora* (1991), is especially helpful on Margaret Hartman Markoe Bache Duane and on Duane's earliest period with the *Aurora*. William Duane II, *A Biographical Memoir of William J. Duane* (1868), offers important information, and Allan C. Clark, "William Duane," *Records of the Columbia Historical Society* 9 (1906): 14–62, is still valuable on Duane's activities in America. The one full biography is Kim T. Phillips's solid and essential study, "William Duane, Revolutionary Editor" (Ph.D. diss., Univ. of Calif., Berkeley, 1968).

JOHN K. ALEXANDER

DUANE, William (17 Feb. 1872–7 Mar. 1935), physicist, was born in Philadelphia, Pennsylvania, the son of Charles W. Duane, an Episcopalian minister, and Emma Cushman Lincoln. He was descended from Benjamin Franklin. Duane received the A.B. from both the University of Pennsylvania (1892) and Harvard University (1893) and the A.M. from Harvard (1895) after serving as assistant in physics from 1893 to 1895. He then used a Harvard Tyndall fellowship to study in Germany. Duane worked under Emil Warburg and Max Planck in Berlin and with Walther Nernst at Göttingen. For his dissertation he investigated thermoelectricity with cells containing electrolytic solutions, finding evidence for new forces and suggesting modifications of Nernst's and Planck's analyses. For this work the University of Berlin awarded him the Ph.D. in 1897. The next year he took a position at the University of Colorado as professor of physics, where he would remain until 1907. In 1899 he married Caroline Elise Ravenel; they had four children.

Duane showed mechanical aptitude at an early age, which he applied to his experimental researches. At Harvard he collaborated with Professor John Trowbridge on a paper that examined the velocity of electric waves in wires. He continued to work on problems in electricity and magnetism in Germany and after his return to the United States. While at Colorado he was awarded a patent for a device to send multiple telegraph messages over the same wire. During 1904–1905 he studied with Pierre Curie in Paris and Sir Joseph John Thomson in Cambridge. Curie was sufficiently impressed by Duane to request a fellowship for him from Andrew Carnegie. In 1906 Carnegie created a scholarship fund for the Curie laboratory, and Duane returned to Paris in 1907 as one of the first grantees. He worked in Marie Curie's laboratory for about five years, publishing approximately twenty papers on radioactivity.

Duane investigated the ionization produced by radioactivity and its relationships to decay rate, charge, and energy of the rays. He then undertook the difficult measurements of the heat evolved by various radioactive substances, the results of which he published in four articles in *Le Radium* in 1909 and 1910. He tried five experimental methods before settling on a differential gas calorimeter that he invented for the purpose. He also employed a thermostat that he had developed in 1900. Duane studied the path of alpha rays and the secondary radiation they produced. To circumvent the fatigue caused by counting large numbers of alpha particles, he invented a photographic method to register their arrival (*Le Radium* 7 [1910]: 196–98). With fellow researcher Jan Danysz he determined the charge carried by alpha and beta particles, the electronic charge, and a value for the then-contested half-life of radium (*Le Radium* 9 [1912]: 417–21).

In 1913 Duane returned to Harvard to fill a vacancy created by the retirement of Trowbridge, his former professor. His position as assistant professor of physics was combined with an appointment as research fellow in physics for the new Harvard Cancer Commission. Duane applied his experience in radioactivity to designing and constructing "radio-active lamps" for use in the treatment of cancer (*Physical Review* 5 [1915]: 311–14). His work on determining X-ray dosages benefited from his earlier researches on ionization. In 1917 Harvard appointed him to what was probably the first U.S. professorship in bio-physics.

Duane had inherited an unusually powerful voltage source from Trowbridge, and improved X-ray tubes had recently become available. This equipment enabled him to pursue researches that soon brought him worldwide renown. Investigating the relation between X-ray frequencies and the energy of the cathode rays (electrons) that produced them, he found these quantities were related by the factor h, Planck's constant. Duane and his student Franklin L. Hunt determined that electrons driven by a fixed voltage from Trowbridge's battery gave rise to X-rays of varying penetrating power (*Physical Review* 6 [1915]: 166–72). Not all types of rays were possible, however; their emission ceased abruptly at a definite wavelength (or frequency), which depended only upon the voltage used. The maximum frequency of the X-rays that the electron beams could generate equaled the energy of the beams divided by Planck's constant h, or $Ve = hv$, an application of the quantum theory anticipated by continental theorists but unfamiliar to Americans. Now experimentally confirmed, this relation became known as the Duane-Hunt law, which Duane used to calculate the most accurate values of Planck's constant then available.

Duane and his students studied the characteristic X-rays emitted by various elements as well as the reflection of X-rays in crystals. By deriving Bragg's law for reflection in crystals from quantum theory, Duane helped to reconcile quantum theory with the wave theory of radiation (*Proceedings of the National Academy of Sciences* 11 [1923]: 158–64; *Physical Review* 25 [1925]: 881).

During the 1920s Duane became involved in a controversy with Arthur Compton on the scattering of X-rays. At that time Duane had delegated experimental work to his students, since his duties directing the roentgenology laboratory at the Harvard Medical School occupied most of his time. Duane and his students were unable to reproduce Compton's results and claimed that they had found a different effect. The intensity and width of their X-ray beam probably were not suited for eliciting Compton's findings. Errors caused by scattered radiation and an impurity in a target further complicated their results. When Duane realized that experimental errors had kept him from observing what came to be known as the Compton effect, he graciously retracted and went on to make very accurate measurements of the effect. Although this episode harmed Duane's scientific reputation, he was admired for his forthright admission of error. Duane continued to study X-rays until poor health brought his work to a halt. He retired in 1934.

For his researches Duane was awarded the John Scott Medal from the Board of Directors of City Trusts of Philadelphia in 1922, the 1923 Leonard Prize of the American Roentgen Ray Society, and the 1923 Comstock Prize of the National Academy of Sciences. Duane was a Fellow of the AAAS (vice president, Section B, 1927–1928); a member of the National Academy of Sciences (chairman of the Division of Physical Sciences, 1922–1923), Phi Beta Kappa, and Sigma Xi; and active in many other organizations, such as the American Academy of Arts and Sciences, the American Physical, Philosophical, Radiological, and Roentgen Ray Societies, the American Society for Cancer Research (president, 1923), the (Paris) Société de Physique (councilor, 1920–1923), and the Society of the Descendants of the Signers of the Declaration of Independence.

Modest yet quietly confident, Duane was liked and respected by his colleagues. A lover of music, he was an able pianist and organist. For relaxation he enjoyed games of bridge whist with his friends. He died at home in Devon, Pennsylvania.

• Duane's correspondence is scattered among a number of U.S. and foreign institutions, most notably the National Academy of Sciences. Several letters from Duane to A. Sommerfeld and to Neils Bohr are in the Archive for History of Quantum Physics. Letters to Duane from Pierre Curie, Marie Curie, Sir Joseph John Thomson, Ernest Rutherford, Max Planck, and Karl T. Compton and a testimonial from Planck are at the Neils Bohr Library of the American Institute of Physics.

Duane's dissertation research was published in *Annalen der Physik und Chemie* 65 (1898): 374–402. Biographical articles are Percy W. Bridgman, National Academy of Sciences, *Biographical Memoirs* 18 (1938): 23–41, which includes a bibliography of Duane's publications; and G. W. Pierce, Bridgman, and F. H. Crawford, "Minute of the Life and Services of William Duane, Professor of Bio-Physics, *Emeritus*," *Harvard University Gazette* (May 1935). The controversy between Duane and Compton, as well as the scientific background for this period in physics, are detailed in Roger Stuewer, *The Compton Effect: Turning Point in Physics* (1975). See also Bruce R. Wheaton, *The Tiger and the Shark* (1983). Obituaries are in *Proceedings of the American Academy of Arts and Sciences* 70 (1936): 528; *Journal of the Optical Society of America* 26 (1936): 75; *British Journal of Radiology* 8 (1935): 226; and the *New York Times*, 8 Mar. 1935.

MARJORIE C. MALLEY

DUBBS, Joseph Henry (5 Oct. 1838–1 Apr. 1910), clergyman, educator, and historian, was born of Swiss-American parentage in rural North Whitehall Township, Lehigh County, Pennsylvania, the son of Joseph S. Dubbs, a German Reformed pastor, and Eleanor Lerch. In his mid-teenage years he enrolled at Franklin and Marshall College in Lancaster, Pennsylvania, graduating in 1856. In 1859 Dubbs completed his ministerial training at the Theological Seminary of the Reformed Church at Mercersburg, which was then guided by the scholar and churchman Philip Schaff, who is generally regarded as the outstanding North American church historian and ecumenist of the later nineteenth century. A synodical report of the time lists "J. Henry Dubbs" as one of the "young gentlemen" who were "connected with the seminary."

Following graduation from Mercersburg, Dubbs assisted his father in the North Whitehall Township parish for one year. He began his independent pastoral work in the nearby Zion's Reformed Church in Allentown, Pennsylvania, remaining there until 1863. In that year he married Mary Louisa Wilson and became pastor of the Trinity Reformed Parish in Pottstown, Pennsylvania. From 1871 to 1875 he served the Christ Reformed Church in Philadelphia as minister. In all of these posts he was popular and respected by his parishioners for his eloquence and theological acumen.

In 1873 Franklin and Marshall College received a legacy from the estate of Lewis Audenried, who admired and respected Dubbs, to endow and establish the Audenried Professorship of History and Archaeology, conditional upon the appointment of Dubbs to the post "to occupy the chair thereof so long as he may desire and be able to fulfill its duties." The board of the college accepted these conditions and Dubbs began his teaching duties in the fall session of 1875. This began a very happy relationship, with Dubbs remaining at the college as a respected and beloved teacher for some thirty-five years. As a professor he was much admired for his enthusiasm, wide-ranging erudition, engaging anecdotes, and personal interest in his students. He served twice as acting president of the institution, in 1904 and 1907, and was secretary of the faculty for fifteen years.

Dubbs was also known for his historical research and writing, concentrating on the history of his own denomination, the German Reformed church. Among his titles devoted to this theme were the *Historic Manual of the Reformed Church in the United States* (1888), which went through three editions; *Why Am I Reformed?* (1889); and *The Reformed Church in Pennsylvania* (1902). Because of his wide-ranging knowledge he was asked to contribute the section on the German Reformed church in the American Church History Series (1895).

Among Dubbs's many other publications was the book *Leaders of the Reformation* (1898) and a narrative history of the college he served for many years, *History of Franklin and Marshall College* (1903). He also published a book of poetry, *Home Ballads and Metrical Versions* (1888), and a partial autobiography serialized in a college periodical, *College Student* (1907–1909). His interests extended into folklore, art, genealogy, and musicology (especially of the Reformed church and the Ephrata Cloister).

Dubbs published articles on these themes, largely historical in nature, in journals such as the *Reformed Quarterly Review*, the *Pennsylvania German*, the *Pennsylvania Magazine of History and Biography*, *Papers and Addresses of the Lancaster County Historical Society*, the *Mercersburg Review*, *Der Deutsche Pionier*, and *Notes and Queries*. Dubbs also contributed articles to encyclopedias.

In addition to his pastoral and academic duties, Dubbs was active in denominational affairs. H. M. J. Klein's *The History of the Eastern Synod of the Reformed Church in the United States* (1943) mentions his name in many places. He served the synod as secretary (1867) and as president (1893), preaching the opening sermon of the synod in 1894. From 1882 to 1886 he edited a denominational journal, the *Guardian*, and from 1894 to 1895 he was one of the editors of the *Reformed Church Messenger*.

He was elected a corresponding member of the Ethnographic Institute of France in 1878, a fellow of the Royal Historical Society in 1895, and president of the Pennsylvania German Society for 1901–1902. He was an excellent example of the well educated, earnestly involved clergyman traditionally admired in the Reformed communion. By all accounts he was an effective, sincere, and engaged pastor and educator. An indication of the regard in which he was held by his students is that upon his death in Lancaster, after the college president presented a public eulogy, the entire student body marched in class formation as an honorary escort to the college chapel.

• Several appreciative assessments appeared after Dubbs's death, including George W. Richards, "Joseph Henry Dubbs," *German American Annals*, n.s., 8 (1910): 94–96; John S. Stahr, "The Rev. Joseph Henry Dubbs, D.D., LL.D.: An Appreciation," *Pennsylvania-German* 11 (1910): 420–22; [G. T. Ettinger], "Rev. Joseph Henry Dubbs, D.D., LL.D.," *Pennsylvania-German Society Proceedings and Addresses* 20 (1911): 48–50. Daniel G. Glass et al., eds., *History of the Classics of Lancaster of the Eastern Synod of the Reformed Church in the United States, 1852–1940* (1942), refers to his work. Dubbs's educational work is honored in H. M. J. Klein, *History of Franklin and Marshall College, 1787–1948* (1952). See also the entry in *Who Was Who in America* (1943). A brief biography and some reference to his publications are found in Homer T. Rosenberger, *The Pennsylvania Germans, 1891–1965* (1966). Obituaries are in the *Lancaster Daily New Era*, 1 Apr. 1910; the *Reformed Church Messenger*, 7 Apr. 1910; and the *Reformed Church Review* 14 (Oct. 1910): 545–53.

DONALD F. DURNBAUGH

DUBIN, Al (10 June 1891–11 Feb. 1945), popular lyricist, was born Alexander Dubin in Zurich, Switzerland, the son of Simon Dubin, a medical student who later became a gynecologist, and Minna (maiden name unknown), a chemist. In 1896 the family moved to Philadelphia, where Dubin was educated. At age eighteen, having already published two song lyrics, Dubin left high school. He was expelled from a preparatory school just before his twentieth birthday, having developed fondnesses for music, women, food, and intoxication.

Dubin's first significant collaborator was composer Joseph Burke, with whom he wrote the moderately popular "Oh, You Mister Moon" in 1911. In 1912 he moved to New York City, where he specialized in writing English lyrics to already established German, Italian, and Spanish songs.

After two short-lived hits, Dubin joined the army and saw active duty in France in 1917–1918. Returning, he married Helen McClay in 1919; they had two children. They were remarried in 1921 because McClay's annulment had not come through at the time of their first marriage. Working with various composers, Dubin enjoyed journeyman success with songs such as "Sundown Brings Back Memories of You" for the *Greenwich Village Follies of 1921* and "Chattachoochee" (1923). He also published a book, *The Art of Songwriting*, in 1925.

Dubin apparently sold to Edgar Leslie the melancholy lyric for "Among My Souvenirs" (1925), which later became a standard. For the second American *Charlot's Revue* (1926), Dubin collaborated with Billy Rose and Joe Meyer on his first credited standard, the sprightly, optimistic "A Cup of Coffee, a Sandwich and You." Working with Jimmy McHugh and Irving Mills, Dubin created his second standard, "The Lonesomest Gal in Town." Dubin also wrote lyrics for two uneventful 1927 Broadway shows, *White Lights* and *Take the Air*, working with Fred Coots and with Con Conrad and Silver, respectively.

In the rush for musical talent that followed the advent of talking motion pictures, Warner Brothers bought music publishers Witmark, Remick and Harms and all their contracts, including Dubin's and Burke's. In Hollywood, the team turned out scores, interpolations, and incidental music for seven 1928 and 1929 Warners films, including *Gold Diggers of Broadway* (1929). From that film came "Tip-Toe through the Tulips," a typical Burke-Dubin effort, its lyric mimicking the melody's mincing movement. As the apparent limitations imposed on movement by early sound recording became obvious, film musicals' popularity declined. The Burke-Dubin partnership continued until 1932 and included "Dancing with Tears in My Eyes" (1930) and "For You," which gained popularity only in 1948. In 1932, however, Burke was fired, and Dubin began collaborating with composer Harry Warren.

After an inauspicious beginning, Dubin and Warren produced the score for *Forty-Second Street* (1932), a film that shares, along with *Flying Down to Rio* (1933), the reputation of launching the second, greatest wave of film musicals. All five songs from *Forty-Second Street*, choreographed with amazing visual variety by Busby Berkeley, were hits. The huge Dubin (eventually over 300 pounds) was described by Warren as "a warm, friendly man who knew how to have a good time," and he often created images based upon his own indulgences, including "Where the underworld can meet the elite" (Forty-Second Street"); "You go home and get your scanties, I'll go home and get my panties" ("Shuffle Off to Buffalo"); and "Ev'ry kiss, ev'ry hug, seems to act just like a drug" ("You're Getting to Be a Habit with Me").

In the resulting, highly competitive world of 1930s musical films, the Dubin-Warren team remained a hit at the box office for five years. *Gold Diggers of 1933* brought the rousingly upbeat "We're In the Money," its lyrics incorporating Keynesian economics ("Lend it, spend it, send it rolling along") as well as a dramatic song of social protest based upon a Franklin D. Roosevelt speech, "Remember My Forgotten Man." Warren gave Dubin credit for the ideas for most of these songs, and Dubin became expert at writing about the dreams of the depression generation. As his biographer and daughter Patricia McGuire wrote, "Whether those dreams would ever come true really didn't matter . . . they needed a dream to cope with a rough reality. . . . A nation in crisis had become the songwriter's golden opportunity."

Musicals rolled off the Hollywood assembly lines. Improved recording techniques and the depression-driven demand for escapist entertainment had revived the genre. In 1933 the Dubin-Warren team turned out *Roman Scandals*. In the same year, while working on the score for *Footlight Parade*, Dubin made the first of several lengthy and often unexplained personal disappearances. In 1934 the Academy of Motion Picture Arts and Sciences created an award for best song. Within five full 1934 scores, Dubin and Warren produced the schmaltzy "The Boulevard of Broken Dreams" for *Moulin Rouge*, the innocent "I Only Have Eyes for You" and the show biz anthem "Dames" from

Dames, and the nonchalant "I'll String Along with You" from *Twenty Million Sweethearts*.

These films showcased Dubin's versatility and Warren's sweetly lilting tunes, which often translated easily into jazz performance. Their 1935 hits included "About a Quarter of Nine" and the wickedly satirical "She's a Latin from Manhattan" from *Go into Your Dance*; the saucy "Lulu's Back in Town" from *Broadway Gondolier*; "Don't Give Up the Ship" from *Shipmates Forever*," a march so stirring it was subsequently adopted by the U.S. Naval Academy; and the melodramatic "Lullaby of Broadway," the Academy Award–winning song for 1935, from *Gold Diggers of 1935*.

In 1936 followed the florid "I'll Sing You a Thousand Love Songs" from *Cain and Mabel* and another depression wish-fulfiller, "With Plenty of Money and You" from *Gold Diggers of 1937*. Among the five Dubin-Warren hit parade songs of 1937, a year in which Dubin was frequently ill, were "September in the Rain" from *Melody for Two* and the jaunty "Remember Me?," an Academy-nominated song, from *Mr. Dodd Takes the Air*.

After *Gold Diggers in Paris* (1938), Warners added Johnny Mercer to the Dubin-Warren team for *Garden of the Moon* (1938). The only song from the film that made any splash was its novelty "The Girl Friend of the Whirling Dervish," which owed most to Mercer's wisecracking influence. Dubin, who generally believed that he was a failure if one of his songs failed, decided to return to New York.

There, in 1939, Dubin's loveliest lyric—"You're the ghost of a romance in June, going astray, fading too soon"—graced a forgotten Victor Herbert melody as "Indian Summer." Dubin collaborated with composer Jimmy McHugh on two shows for knockabout comics Ole Olsen and Chic Johnson, *Streets of Paris* (1939), which included "South American Way," and *Keep Off the Grass* (1940), which included "Clear Out of This World."

Returning to Hollywood, Dubin supplied kaleidoscopic lyrics for "Along the Santa Fe Trail" from *The Santa Fe Trail* (1940). Back at Warners with a drug clause in his contract, Dubin collaborated with James Monaco on *Stage Door Canteen* (1943), whose unmemorable "We Mustn't Say Goodbye" was nominated for an Academy Award. In 1943 Dubin, who was never divorced, was also briefly married to Edwina Perrin. Called by his biographer a man "who wanted to prove he could corner any market," Dubin apparently supplied the idea and title for "Feudin' and Fightin'" (1944), a pseudo-backwoods song from the Broadway show *Laffing Room Only*. Nevertheless, Burton Lane received sole credit for the hit.

Dubin died in New York City. His death, technically from pneumonia, was hastened by barbiturate poisoning. He was named to the Songwriters Hall of Fame in 1971. In 1980 *42nd Street*, its score a compilation of Dubin-Warren songs from 1930s Warners films, opened on Broadway and remained an international success throughout the decade.

• Dubin's personal papers remain in Los Angeles with Patricia Dubin McGuire. For a biography of Dubin, see Patricia Dubin McGuire, *Lullaby of Broadway: A Biography of Al Dubin* (1985). Among books on the film musical, Miles Kreuger, *The American Musical Film* (1972), and Clive Hirschhorn, *The Hollywood Musical* (1981), are particularly good.

JAMES ROSS MOORE

DUBINSKY, David (22 Feb. 1892–17 Sept. 1982), labor union official, was born David Dubnievski in Brest Litovsk, Poland (now Brest, Belarus), the son of Bezalel Dubnievski, a bakery owner, and Shaine Wishingrad. The family moved to Lodz, Poland, where Dubinsky attended primary school. At the age of eleven he left school and became a baker's apprentice. Four years later he advanced to master baker and joined the socialist General Jewish Workers Union, known as the Bund. Over the next several years, he was jailed and exiled to Siberia for his union activities.

At the end of a two-year trek eastward through Russia, Dubinsky escaped from his police convoy in Chelyabinsk, Siberia. After six months in hiding, he made his way back to Lodz and resumed working as a baker under an assumed name in 1911. The same year, he and his brother Chaim were smuggled into Germany and then Belgium, where they boarded a steamship for New York City.

Dubinsky started work as an apprentice machine sewer in a knee pants shop in Brooklyn. Soon he began working as a cloak cutter and was admitted to Local 10 of the International Ladies' Garment Workers Union (ILGWU) in July 1911. In the 1910s Dubinsky worked as a cutter, served as an active member of Local 10, and gained experience as a speaker on soap boxes in Manhattan's Lower East Side. Soon after his arrival in America he had joined the Socialist party, which was then a prominent political force in the ILGWU. In 1914 he married Emma Goldberg, a Lithuanian garment worker and ILGWU member; they had one daughter.

Dubinsky helped organize a successful general strike of cloakmakers in 1916 and began to rise in union ranks. By 1920 he had risen to the presidency of the local. The following year he was elected as the vice president and a member of the General Executive Board of the ILGWU at the national convention in Cleveland.

In the 1920s the ILGWU experienced both a decline in membership and bitter internal fighting between Communist insurgents and the union's anti-Communist officers, including Dubinsky. By the end of the decade, however, the Communist faction was largely defeated and the union regained some of its power within the garment industry. Dubinsky coordinated a successful strike in 1929 and the following year led another successful strike, this one by 30,000 dressmakers that resulted in a long-term, citywide contract and a swelling of the union's membership. In 1929, largely as an acknowledgment of his rise to de facto leadership, Dubinsky was elected secretary-treasurer at the ILGWU's national convention in Cleveland. In 1932

the ailing union president Benjamin Schlesinger died, and Dubinsky was named as his successor by the General Executive Board. He remained the president of the union, with only sporadic opposition, until 1966.

The Great Depression dealt a heavy blow to the ILGWU's power in the garment industry. By 1932 the membership had shrunk and the union's treasury was nearly bankrupt. Dubinsky joined a number of national union leaders in looking to the federal government for support. In 1933, after the passage of the National Industrial Recovery Act (which guaranteed the right to union recognition), Dubinsky led an organizing drive that vastly increased union membership and funds. By 1935 the ILGWU had 200,000 members and assets of $850,000. Throughout the 1930s Dubinsky served as one of the leading labor supporters of President Franklin D. Roosevelt and the New Deal. During the 1936 election, he and Amalgamated Clothing Workers leader Sidney Hillman resigned from the Socialist party to establish the American Labor Party (ALP), which supported Roosevelt.

In part because of the tremendous growth of the ILGWU, in 1934 Dubinsky was rewarded with an appointment to the Executive Council of the American Federation of Labor (AFL). The following year he served as an AFL delegate to the International Labor Conference convention in Geneva, Switzerland.

In 1935 Dubinsky joined United Mine Workers leader John L. Lewis and Hillman to form the Committee for Industrial Organization (CIO). In 1936 the AFL Executive Council suspended all unions, including the ILGWU, that were affiliated with the CIO. In protest, Dubinsky resigned as vice president of the AFL and helped build the CIO with Lewis and Hillman. Relations between Dubinsky and Lewis soured, however, as Dubinsky sought reconciliation with the AFL and Lewis remained hostile to the older federation. In 1938 Dubinsky led the ILGWU out of the CIO, and it remained independent of both labor federations until 1940, when the union reaffiliated with the AFL. Later that year Dubinsky assailed Lewis's endorsement of Republican presidential candidate Wendell Willkie as a "betrayal of the father of the New Deal."

During World War II, Dubinsky presided over the growth of the ILGWU and strengthened its alliance with the federal government. The ILGWU's membership grew steadily through the war years, and from 1941 to 1945 the union and its affiliates bought more than $185 million in war bonds. The ALP proved more problematic. By 1943 the Communist party had gained control of much of the ALP, and in 1944 Dubinsky led an anti-Communist faction out of the party that established itself as the Liberal party. The New York–based Liberal party generally endorsed Democrats in municipal, state, and national elections, helping to reelect Roosevelt in 1944 and a great number of liberal candidates throughout Dubinsky's lifetime.

In the postwar period, Dubinsky turned his attention increasingly to international affairs. He was readmitted to the AFL Executive Board in 1945, and at the

1946 national convention he urged the creation of an International Labor Relations Department, which came to function as a major instrument of American anti-Communist foreign policy. As a leading AFL proponent of the Cold War, Dubinsky declared in 1950 that the ILGWU had for decades "been fighting that war, both cold and hot, against the Communist attempt to grab American trade unions and to use them for forcing on the American people a Moscow-type of dictatorship. . . . Unless the free labor movement is in the forefront of the fight, the cold war can never be won by the democracies." During the postwar period, the ILGWU contributed millions of dollars to foreign anti-Communist unions, including Italian and French garment worker unions and Histadrut, the Israeli labor federation.

The ILGWU continued to grow, reaching a membership of 425,000 by 1950, when it represented more than 85 percent of the women's wear industry in the United States and Canada. Under Dubinsky's leadership, the union also created substantial health care, housing, and educational services for members and established itself as a major force in New York and national politics.

In 1952 the AFL Executive Council appointed Dubinsky to its new antiracketeering subcommittee. Dubinsky was a particularly active member of the committee, calling for greater vigilance among union members in protecting union pension and welfare funds from plunder by corrupt union officials. Soon after the merger of the AFL and CIO in 1955, Dubinsky was named to the new organization's Committee on Ethical Practices. With Dubinsky as one of its leading members, the committee in 1957 recommended that the International Brotherhood of Teamsters be expelled from the federation for a host of abuses that had been exposed by a Senate select committee. The Teamsters were removed from the federation later that year.

In the late 1950s and 1960s, Dubinsky became less active in the ILGWU while serving more frequently as a national "labor statesman" on the AFL Executive Council. In 1966 he retired as president of the ILGWU and was replaced by Louis Stulberg. In the last years of his life he administered the union's retirees service program, continued to serve on the AFL Executive Council, and remained active in New York politics through the Liberal party. Dubinsky died in Manhattan.

Dubinsky was one of the most important American labor leaders of the twentieth century. His influence extended well beyond the affairs of the ILGWU. He was for more than three decades a major figure in the national leadership of the AFL and was one of the founders of the CIO. His influence in politics was vast, and his support was vital for local and national candidates in New York. Dubinsky also helped extend the American labor movement outside its national borders during the Cold War, when the AFL-CIO played a major role in American foreign policy.

• Dubinsky's autobiography, *David Dubinsky: A Life with Labor* (1977), does not follow a chronological narrative and is skimpy on his postwar career, but it does contain a number of illuminating personal anecdotes. Max D. Danish, *The World of David Dubinsky* (1957), is more useful but it was written nine years before Dubinsky retired from the ILGWU presidency. See also Gus Tyler, *Look for the Union Label: A History of the International Ladies' Garment Workers' Union* (1995). An obituary is in the *New York Times*, 18 Sept. 1982.

THADDEUS RUSSELL

DUBOIS, Eugene Floyd (4 June 1882–12 Feb. 1959), physiologist and physician, was born in West New Brighton, Staten Island, New York, the son of Eugene DuBois, a broker, and Anna Greenleaf Brooks. Between the ages of eight and fifteen, DuBois attended the Staten Island Academy; he then spent two years at the Milton Academy in Milton, Massachusetts. During the summer of 1898, while his family vacationed at Mastic, Long Island, DuBois and his brother Arthur served as orderlies for two weeks at the Army Hospital at Montauk Point, near Camp Wyckoff. There they aided in the care of soldiers from the Cuban campaign of the Spanish-American War, who were recovering from dysentery and typhoid fever. Despite the peril to his health, DuBois enjoyed this work and from that time never considered anything but medicine as a career.

In 1899 DuBois entered Harvard College, where he was skeptical of the quality of the education he received, since he had practically no contact with professors, only teaching assistants, and his instructors were not as qualified as those at his boarding school. DuBois decided to educate himself and graduated cum laude with an A.B. at the end of his junior year. In 1902 he entered the Columbia College of Physicians and Surgeons and graduated in 1906 after spending four years listening to what he regarded as rather boring lectures and receiving poor instruction. In the six months between graduating and beginning his internship, DuBois went to Berlin, Gremany, to work in the pathology laboratory of Friedrich Henke at the Charlottenburger Hospital. On his return to the United States, he served a two-year internship (1907–1909) at the Presbyterian Hospital in New York City.

Upon finishing his internship, DuBois was offered an assistantship in pathology at the Presbyterian Hospital, but to prepare for this work he decided to return to Europe for further studies. Originally, he planned to spend a year at the Pasteur Institute in Paris in the study of bacteriology, but just before leaving he met John Howland, a professor of pediatrics at New York University. Howland convinced him that the best opportunities were in the study of human metabolism and advised him to go to Berlin. In Berlin, DuBois worked in the Kraus laboratory under Theodor Brugsh at the Charité Hospital. DuBois and his American friend Borden Veeder of the Pennsylvania Medical School initiated studies on the total energy requirement in diabetes. They used a Pettenkofer-Voit metabolism chamber to measure the carbon dioxide excretion of diabetes patients. At the Kraus laboratory

DuBois met colleague Graham Lusk, to whom he would owe much of his future success. Little would have resulted from DuBois and Veeder's paper on diabetes ("The Total Energy Requirement in Diabetes Mellitus," *Archives of Internal Medicine* 5 [1910]: 37–46) if Lusk had not recalculated and rewritten the paper sent to him for analysis.

In June 1910 DuBois married Rebeckah Rutter of Irvington, New York; the couple had four children. Also in 1910 he became an instructor at Cornell Medical College in New York City in applied pharmacology. In 1911 he returned to Columbia Presbyterian Hospital to finish his training in pathology but soon realized he could not accomplish his goal to study metabolism in pathology and consequently accepted a job in the metabolic laboratory of Graham Lusk at Bellevue Hospital. DuBois became one of the United States's most distinguished metabolic physiologists as a result of the training he received from Lusk.

A member of the board of the Russell Sage Institute of Pathology, Lusk persuaded the institute to support metabolic research at Bellevue Hospital. With the money granted, Lusk constructed a respiration calorimeter near a small metabolism ward at Bellevue Hospital's Cornell Medical Division. In 1913 DuBois was named the medical director of this study, a position he held until 1950. The study was moved to New York Hospital in 1932. With G. F. Soderstrom, who kept this complicated machine functioning, DuBois mastered the use of the calorimeter and was able to measure directly the heat generated by a subject and compare this value with that calculated from oxygen consumed and carbon dioxide exhaled. DuBois found the two methods gave essentially the same results, indicating that the simpler method based on oxygen uptake and CO_2 production could be used for reliable metabolic studies.

DuBois worked with his cousin Delafield DuBois, a capable mathematician, to devise a method for accurately measuring surface area. They derived the formula for calculating body surface area from a person's height and weight. This formula allowed metabolic data to be presented in terms of relation to body-surface area. An important finding resulting from these procedures was that metabolism is related to body surface except during active states and in certain diseases. When DuBois moved his laboratory to Cornell, he became interested in the relationship between fever and metabolism. He found the metabolic rate roughly followed (Jacobus Hendricus) Van't Hoff's law: each three-degree increase in temperature raised metabolism 30 to 60 percent. This work led to studies on heat radiation from the skin. In this series of studies, DuBois found that as much heat was lost through cold skin as through hot skin. He also showed, with J. D. Hardy, that vasoconstriction can convert the subcutaneous tissue into an insulating layer that could manage the loss of heat. Between 1916 and 1918 DuBois also created a curve for determining the changes in basal metabolism as a person ages.

DuBois entered the U.S. Navy a few days before World War I started. He was assigned to the Navy Bureau of Medicine, where his duties concerned gas warfare training, aviation medicine, deep-sea diving, and submarine ventilation. For bravery in maintaining the ventilation in a submarine that had been in a collision, he was awarded the Navy Cross for heroism. From his discharge in 1919 until 1930, DuBois was associate professor of medicine at Cornell, and from 1930 to 1941 he was professor of medicine. DuBois spent 1928–1929 in the laboratory of Friedrich von Müller in Munich working on metabolism in thyroid disease. Offered the chairmanship of physiology at Cornell in 1941, he realized he could direct more time to research in a basic science department and accepted the appointment. In World War II he entered the navy as a captain and again carried out high-altitude and deep sea-diving experiments.

DuBois was a member of many professional organizations, including the National Academy of Sciences, and served as president of both the Association of American Physicians (1939) and the American Institute of Nutrition (1936). He lectured frequently and published regularly in journals such as the *Archives of Internal Medicine* and the *Journal of Nutrition*. In 1954 DuBois had a cerebral hemorrhage, which limited his activities. However, it did not retard his active mind, and with the capabilities left to him he continued to contribute to science until his death at his home in New York City.

• Some of DuBois's papers are in the Archives of Cornell Medical School in New York City. Among DuBois's works not already mentioned in the text are *Basal Metabolism in Health and Disease* (1924) and *Fever and the Regulation of Body Temperature* (1948). Biographical accounts include Joseph C. Aub, "Eugene Floyd DuBois (June 4, 1882–February 12, 1959)," National Academy of Sciences, *Biographical Memoirs* 36 (1962): 125–45; J. Howard Means, "Eugene Floyd DuBois (1882–1959)," *Transactions of the Association of American Physicians* 72 (1959): 23–28; David B. Dill, "Eugene F. DuBois, Environmental Physiologist," *Science* 130 (1959): 1746–47; "Eugene F. DuBois (1882–1959): Clinical Physiologist," *Journal of the American Medical Association* 202 (1967): 138–39; and Alexander Forbes, "Eugene Floyd DuBois (1882–1959)," *Year Book of the American Philosophical Society* (1959): 122–27. See also "Medical Research in New York," *Bulletin of the New York Academy of Medicine* 64 (1988): 269–71. An obituary is in the *New York Times*, 13 Feb. 1959.

DAVID Y. COOPER

DUBOIS, John (24 Aug. 1764–20 Dec. 1842), Catholic bishop and educator, was born in Paris, France. Nothing is known of his parents. He received his education at the Collège of Louis le Grand, the Seminary of St. Magloire, and the Sorbonne. He was ordained a priest by the archbishop of Paris on 22 September 1787 and was assigned as a curate to the large parish of Saint Sulpice, where he also served as chaplain to a mental institution and a group of nuns. With the help of the marquis de Lafayette, in 1791 Dubois fled from the French Revolution and found temporary refuge in

Virginia, where he served as an itinerant priest for the small Catholic communities in Norfolk and Richmond.

In 1794 Bishop John Carroll of Baltimore appointed Dubois pastor of a parish in Frederick, Maryland, with responsibility for a small number of Catholics scattered over a wide area of Maryland and Virginia. In 1808 Dubois moved the site of the parish to Emmitsburg, Maryland, where he also founded a preparatory seminary. To supplement the small number of seminarians, lay students were also admitted to the institution, which has continued in existence as Mount St. Mary's College and Seminary, the third oldest Catholic college in the United States. The original facilities consisted of primitive wooden buildings, which Dubois replaced with a stone building in 1826. The number of students grew from seven in 1808 to sixty in 1812. In 1808 Dubois himself joined the Society of Saint Sulpice, a small French religious community devoted exclusively to the operation of seminaries.

In addition to his duties as pastor and educator, Dubois also became associated with Mother Elizabeth Ann Seton, founder of the American Sisters of Charity, who settled in Emmitsburg with her companions in June 1809. Dubois served as spiritual director to the women and later became the ecclesiastical superior of their new religious community when the rule of the American Sisters of Charity was approved by Rome in 1815.

In 1826 Dubois unexpectedly began a new career when he was appointed the third bishop of New York. He received episcopal ordination from Archbishop Ambrose Maréchal in Baltimore on 29 October 1826, and he was installed as bishop of New York on 4 November 1826. Dubois's diocese included all of New York state and the northern half of New Jersey with a Catholic population that he estimated to be approximately 175,000. To care for this large population, he had only about fifteen priests and nine churches. In 1828 and again in 1829 he toured much of his diocese, in the latter year alone traveling 3,000 miles.

These were not the only problems that Bishop Dubois faced. In several of his churches, notably St. Patrick's Cathedral and St. Peter's Church in New York City, Dubois had serious difficulties with assertive lay trustees who held legal title to church properties and who, on occasion, even withheld his salary. Lay trusteeism was a common phenomenon at that time in the American Catholic church, but it was exacerbated in New York by Dubois's lack of financial and administrative acumen. Another contributing factor was the makeup of New York City's Catholic population; it consisted mainly of poor immigrants, most of whom were Irish with a substantial minority of Germans and only a few French. Many Irish Catholics, who would have preferred the appointment as bishop of Father John Power, the popular Irish-born pastor of St. Peter's Church, manifested a personal resentment of their French-born bishop. In his first pastoral letter, Dubois addressed the issue, asking: "Who are those who object to our foreign birth? Are they not in the same sense foreigners themselves?" New York's only Catholic newspaper, the *Truth Teller*, controlled by two Irish-born priests, refused to print Dubois's letter.

Dubois's financial problems were further aggravated by the panic of 1837, which precipitated a depression that lasted until 1843. Dubois's years in New York also coincided with the development of the anti-Catholic and anti-foreign movement known as nativism, a movement that was particularly strong in New York because the city was the port of entry for so many immigrants. In January 1831 the New York Protestant Association was formed; among its positions was the belief that the Catholic church was a corrupt institution that promoted superstition. The association also discouraged its members from reading the Bible and threatened the American system of separation of church and state. In 1836 one of the most popular anti-Catholic books was published in New York City, Maria Monk's *Awful Disclosures of the Hotel Dieu Nunnery of Montreal*, a scurrilous and wholly fictitious exposé of convent life.

Dubois was able nonetheless to make some modest additions to the facilities of the diocese. He established the first German national parish in New York City (St. Nicholas, 1833), built orphan asylums in Brooklyn and Utica, and added a half-dozen parochial schools and two "select academies" for girls. His great ambition was to build his own seminary, which he constructed at considerable expense in Nyack, New York, between 1833 and 1837, but it was destroyed by fire as it neared completion.

In 1837 the aging Dubois requested and received a coadjutor in the person of John Hughes, a Philadelphia priest whom Dubois had once temporarily barred from admission to the seminary in Emmitsburg because of his unsatisfactory educational background. In August 1839, after Dubois had suffered several strokes, Hughes was appointed administrator of the diocese, to the chagrin of Dubois, who lived uneasily in the same house with Hughes until his death in New York City three years later.

• Most of Dubois's surviving papers are in the Archives of Mount St. Mary's College and Seminary, Emmitsburg, Md., and in the Archives of the Archdiocese of New York. The best short account of Dubois's career in New York is Florence D. Cohalan, *A Popular History of the Archdiocese of New York* (1983), pp. 39–53. A good popular biography is Richard Shaw, *John Dubois: Founding Father* (1983). See also Charles G. Herbermann, "The Rt. Rev. John Dubois," *Historical Records and Studies* 1 (1899): 278–355.

THOMAS J. SHELLEY

DU BOIS, W. E. B. (23 Feb. 1868–27 Aug. 1963), African-American activist, historian, and sociologist, was born William Edward Burghardt Du Bois in Great Barrington, Massachusetts, the son of Mary Silvina Burghardt, a domestic worker, and Alfred Du Bois, a barber and itinerant laborer. In later life Du Bois made a close study of his family origins, weaving them rhetorically and conceptually—if not always accurately—into almost everything he wrote. Born in Haiti and descended from Bahamian mulatto slaves, Alfred Du Bois enlisted during the Civil War as a private in a New York regiment of the Union army but appears to have deserted shortly afterward. He also deserted the family less than two years after his son's birth, leaving him to be reared by his mother and the extended Burghardt kin. Long resident in New England, the Burghardts descended from a freedman of Dutch slave origin who had fought briefly in the American Revolution. Under the care of his mother and her relatives, young Will Du Bois spent his entire childhood in that small western Massachusetts town, where probably fewer than two-score of the 4,000 inhabitants were African American. He received a classical, college preparatory education in Great Barrington's racially integrated high school, from whence, in June 1884, he became the first African-American graduate. A precocious youth, Du Bois not only excelled in his high school studies but contributed numerous articles to two regional newspapers, the Springfield *Republican* and the black-owned New York *Globe*, then edited by T. Thomas Fortune.

In high school Du Bois came under the influence of and received mentorship from the principal, Frank Hosmer, who encouraged his extensive reading and solicited scholarship aid from local worthies that enabled Du Bois to enroll at Fisk University in September 1885, six months after his mother's death. One of the best of the southern colleges for newly freed slaves founded after the Civil War, Fisk offered a continuation of his classical education and the strong influence of teachers who were heirs to New England and Western Reserve (Ohio) abolitionism. It also offered the northern-reared Du Bois an introduction to southern American racism and African-American culture. His later writings and thought were strongly marked, for example, by his experiences teaching school in the hills of eastern Tennessee during the summers of 1886 and 1887.

In 1888 Du Bois enrolled at Harvard as a junior. He received a B.A. cum laude, in 1890, an M.A. in 1891, and a Ph.D. in 1895. Du Bois was strongly influenced by the new historical work of German-trained Albert Bushnell Hart and the philosophical lectures of William James, both of whom became friends and professional mentors. Other intellectual influences came with his studies and travels between 1892 and 1894 in Germany, where he was enrolled at the Friedrich-Wilhelm III Universität (then commonly referred to as the University of Berlin but renamed the Humboldt University after World War II). Because of the expiration of the Slater Fund fellowship that supported his stay in Germany, Du Bois could not meet the residency requirements that would have enabled him formally to stand for the degree in economics, despite his completion of the required doctoral thesis (on the history of southern U.S. agriculture) during his tenure. Returning to the United States in the summer of 1894, Du Bois taught classics and modern languages for two years at Wilberforce University in Ohio. While there,

he met Nina Gomer, a student at the college, whom he married in 1896 at her home in Cedar Rapids, Iowa. The couple had two children. By the end of his first year at Wilberforce, Du Bois had completed his Harvard doctoral thesis, "The Suppression of the African Slave Trade to the United States of America, 1638–1870," which was published in 1896 as the inaugural volume of the Harvard Historical Studies series.

Although he had written his Berlin thesis in economic history, received his Harvard doctorate in history, and taught languages and literature at Wilberforce, Du Bois made some of his most important early intellectual contributions to the emerging field of sociology. In 1896 he was invited by the University of Pennsylvania to conduct a study of the seventh ward in Philadelphia. There, after an estimated 835 hours of door-to-door interviews in 2,500 households, Du Bois completed the monumental study, *The Philadelphia Negro* (1899). The Philadelphia study was both highly empirical and hortatory, a combination that prefigured much of the politically engaged scholarship that Du Bois pursued in the years that followed and that reflected the two main strands of his intellectual engagement during this formative period: the scientific study of the so-called Negro Problem and the appropriate political responses to it. While completing his fieldwork in Philadelphia, Du Bois delivered to the Academy of Political and Social Science in November 1896 an address, "The Study of the Negro Problem," methodological manifesto on the purposes and appropriate methods for scholarly examination of the condition of black people. In March 1897, addressing the newly founded American Negro Academy in Washington, D.C., he outlined for his black intellectual colleagues, in "The Conservation of the Races," both a historical sociology and theory of race as a concept and a call to action in defense of African-American culture and identity. During the following July and August he undertook for the U.S. Bureau of Labor the first of several studies of southern African-American households, which was published as a bureau bulletin the following year under the title *The Negroes of Farmville, Virginia: A Social Study*. During that same summer, *Atlantic Monthly* published the essay "The Strivings of the Negro People," a slightly revised version of which later opened *The Souls of Black Folk* (1903).

Together these works frame Du Bois's evolving conceptualization of, methodological approach to, and political values and commitments regarding the problem of race in America. His conceptions were historical and global, his methodology empirical and intuitive, his values and commitments involving both mobilization of an elite vanguard to address the issues of racism and the conscious cultivation of the values to be drawn from African-American folk culture.

After the completion of the Philadelphia study in December 1897, Du Bois began the first of two long tenures at Atlanta University, where he taught sociology and directed empirical studies—modeled loosely on his Philadelphia and Farmville work—of the social and economic conditions and cultural and institutional lives of southern African Americans. During this first tenure at Atlanta he also wrote two more books, *The Souls of Black Folk*, a collection of poignant essays on race, labor, and culture, and *John Brown* (1909), an impassioned interpretation of the life and martyrdom of the militant abolitionist. He also edited two short-lived magazines, *Moon* (1905–1906) and *Horizon* (1907–1910), which represented his earliest efforts to establish journals of intellectual and political opinion for a black readership.

With the publication of *Souls of Black Folk*, Du Bois emerged as the most prominent spokesperson for the opposition to Booker T. Washington's policy of political conservatism and racial accommodation. Ironically, Du Bois had kept a prudent distance from Washington's opponents and had made few overt statements in opposition to the so-called Wizard of Tuskegee. In fact, his career had involved a number of near-misses whereby he himself might have ended up teaching at Tuskegee. Having applied to Washington for a job shortly after returning from Berlin, he had to decline Tuskegee's superior monetary offer because he had already accepted a position at Wilberforce. On a number of other occasions Washington—sometimes prodded by Albert Bushnell Hart—sought to recruit Du Bois to join him at Tuskegee, a courtship he continued at least until the summer of 1903, when Du Bois taught summer school at Tuskegee. Early in his career, moreover, Du Bois's views bore a superficial similarity to Washington's. In fact, he had praised Washington's 1895 "Atlanta Compromise" speech, which proposed to southern white elites a compromise wherein blacks would forswear political and civil rights in exchange for economic opportunities. Like many elite blacks at the time, Du Bois was not averse to some form of franchise restriction, so long as it was based on educational qualifications and applied equally to white and black. Du Bois had been charged with overseeing the African American Council's efforts to encourage black economic enterprise and worked with Washington's partisans in that effort. By his own account his overt rupture with Washington was sparked by the growing evidence of a conspiracy, emanating from Tuskegee, to dictate speech and opinion in all of black America and to crush any opposition to Washington's leadership. After the collapse of efforts to compromise their differences through a series of meetings in 1904, Du Bois joined William Monroe Trotter and other Washington opponents to form the Niagara Movement, an organization militantly advocating full civil and political rights for African Americans.

Although it enjoyed some success in articulating an alternative vision of how black Americans should respond to the growing segregation and racial violence of the early twentieth century, the Niagara Movement was fatally hampered by lack of funds and the overt and covert opposition of Washington and his allies. Indeed, the vision and program of the movement were fully realized only with the founding of a new biracial organization, the National Association for the Advancement of Colored People (NAACP). The NAACP grew out of the agitation and a 1909 conference called to protest the deteriorating status of and escalating violence against black Americans. Racial rioting in August 1908 in Springfield, Illinois, the home of Abraham Lincoln, sparked widespread protest among blacks and liberal whites appalled at the apparent spread of southern violence and lynch law into northern cities. Although its officers made some initial efforts to maintain a détente with Booker T. Washington, the NAACP represented a clear opposition to his policy of accommodation and political quietism. It launched legal suits, legislative lobbying, and propaganda campaigns that embodied uncompromising, militant attacks on lynching, Jim Crow, and disfranchisement. In 1910 Du Bois left Atlanta to join the NAACP as an officer, its only black board member, and to edit its monthly magazine, the *Crisis*.

As editor of the *Crisis* Du Bois finally established the journal of opinion that had so long eluded him, one that could serve as a platform from which to reach a larger audience among African Americans and one that united the multiple strands of his life's work. In its monthly issues he rallied black support for NAACP policies and programs and excoriated white opposition to equal rights. But he also opened the journal to discussions of diverse subjects related to race relations and black cultural and social life, from black religion to new poetic works. The journal's cover displayed a rich visual imagery embodying the sheer diversity and breadth of the black presence in America. Thus the journal constituted, simultaneously, a forum for multiple expressions of and the coherent representation and enactment of black intellectual and cultural life. A mirror for and to black America, it inspired a black intelligentsia and its public.

From his vantage as an officer of the NAACP, Du Bois also furthered another compelling intellectual and political interest, Pan-Africanism. He had attended the first conference on the global condition of peoples of African descent in London in 1900. Six other gatherings followed between 1911 and 1945, including the First Universal Races Congress in London in 1911, and Pan-African congresses held in Paris in 1919; London, Brussels, and Paris in 1921; London and Lisbon in 1923; New York City in 1927; and in Manchester, England, in 1945. Each conference focused in some fashion on the fate of African colonies in the postwar world, but the political agendas of the earliest meetings were often compromised by the ideological and political entanglements of the elite delegates chosen to represent the African colonies. Jamaican black nationalist Marcus Garvey enjoyed greater success in mobilizing a mass base for his version of Pan-Africanism and posed a substantial ideological and political challenge to Du Bois. Deeply suspicious of Garvey's extravagance and flamboyance, Du Bois condemned his scheme to collect funds from African Americans to establish a shipping line that would aid their "return" to Africa, his militant advocacy of racial separatism, and his seeming alliance with the Ku Klux Klan. Although he played no role in the efforts to have

Garvey jailed and eventually deported for mail fraud, Du Bois was not sorry to see him go. (In 1945, however, Du Bois joined Garvey's widow, Amy Jacques Garvey, and George Padmore to sponsor the Manchester Pan-African conference that demanded African independence.)

The rupture in world history that was World War I and the vast social and political transformations of the decade that followed were reflected in Du Bois's thought and program in other ways as well. During the war he had written "Close Ranks," a controversial editorial in the *Crisis* (July 1918), which urged African Americans to set aside their grievances for the moment and concentrate their energies on the war effort. In fact, Du Bois and the NAACP fought for officer training and equal treatment for black troops throughout the war, led a silent protest march down Fifth Avenue in 1917 against racism, and in 1919 launched an investigation into charges of discrimination against black troops in Europe. Meanwhile, the unprecedented scope and brutality of the war itself stimulated changes in Du Bois's evolving analyses of racial issues and phenomena. *Darkwater: Voices within the Veil* (1920) reflects many of these themes, including the role of African colonization and the fundamental role of the international recruitment and subjugation of labor in causing the war and in shaping its aftermath. His visit to Liberia in 1923 and the Soviet Union in 1926, his subsequent study of Marxism, his growing awareness of Freud, and the challenges posed by the Great Depression all brought him to question the NAACP's largely legalistic and propagandistic approach to fighting racism. In the early 1930s Du Bois opened the pages of the *Crisis* to wide-ranging discussions of the utility of Marxian thought and of racially-based economic cooperatives and other institutions in the fight against race prejudice. This led to increasing antagonism between him and his colleagues at the NAACP, especially executive director Walter White, and to his resignation in June 1934.

Du Bois accepted an appointment as chair of the sociology department at Atlanta University, where he had already been teaching as a visiting professor during the winter of 1934. There he founded and edited a new scholarly journal, *Phylon*, from 1940 to 1944. There, too, he published his most important historical work, *Black Reconstruction in America: An Essay toward a History of the Part Which Black Folk Played in the Attempt to Reconstruct Democracy in America, 1860–1880* (1935), and *Dusk of Dawn: An Essay toward an Autobiography of a Race Concept* (1940), his most engaging and poignant autobiographical essay since *Souls of Black Folk*. During this period Du Bois continued to be an active lecturer and an interlocutor with young scholars and activists; he also deepened his studies of Marxism and traveled abroad. He sought unsuccessfully to enlist the aid of the Phelps-Stokes Fund in launching his long-dreamed-of project to prepare an encyclopedia of black peoples in Africa and the diaspora. By 1944, however, Du Bois had lost an invaluable supporter and friend with the death of John

Hope, the president of Atlanta University, leaving him vulnerable to dismissal following sharp disagreements with Hope's successor.

Far from acceding to a peaceful retirement, however, in 1944 Du Bois (now seventy-six years old) accepted an invitation to return to the NAACP to serve in the newly created post of director of special research. Although the organization was still under the staff direction of Du Bois's former antagonist, Walter White, the 1930s depression and World War II had induced some modifications in the programs and tactics of the NAACP, perhaps in response to challenges raised by Du Bois and other younger critics. It had begun to address the problems of labor as well as legal discrimination, and even the court strategy was becoming much more aggressive and economically targeted. In hiring Du Bois, the board appears to have anticipated that other shifts in its approach would be necessary in the coming postwar era. Clearly it was Du Bois's understanding that his return portended continued study of and agitation around the implications of the coming postwar settlement as it might affect black peoples in Africa and the diaspora, and that claims for the representation of African and African-American interests in that settlement were to be pressed. He represented the NAACP in 1945 as a consultant to the U.S. delegation at the founding conference of the United Nations in San Francisco. In 1947 he prepared and presented to that organization *An Appeal to the World*, a 94-page, militant protest against American racism as an international violation of human rights. During this period and in support of these activities he wrote two more books, *Color and Democracy: Colonies and Peace* (1945) and *The World and Africa: An Inquiry into the Part Which Africa Has Played in World History* (1947), each of which addressed some aspect of European and American responsibilities for justice in the colonial world.

As ever, Du Bois learned from and was responsive to the events and developments of his time. Conflicts with the U.S. delegation to the United Nations (which included Eleanor Roosevelt, who was also a member of the NAACP board) and disillusionment with the evolving role of America as a postwar world power reinforced his growing radicalism and refusal to be confined to a safe domestic agenda. He became a supporter of the leftist Southern Negro Youth Congress at a time of rising hysteria about Communism and the onset of the Cold War. In 1948 he was an active supporter of the Progressive party and Henry Wallace's presidential bid. All of this put him at odds with Walter White and the NAACP board, who were drawn increasingly into collusion with the Truman administration and into fierce opposition to any leftist associations. In 1948, after an inconclusive argument over assigning responsibility for a leak to the *New York Times* of a Du Bois memorandum critical of the organization and its policies, he was forced out of the NAACP for a second time.

After leaving the NAACP, Du Bois joined the Council on African Affairs, where he chaired the Africa Aid Committee and was active in supporting the early struggle of the African National Congress of South Africa against apartheid. The council had been organized in London in the late 1930s by Max Yergan and Paul Robeson to push decolonization and to educate the general public about that issue. In the postwar period it, too, became tainted by charges of Communist domination and lost many former supporters (including Yergan and Ralph Bunche); it dissolved altogether in 1955. Having linked the causes of decolonialization and antiracism to the fate of peace in a nuclear-armed world, Du Bois helped organize the Cultural and Scientific Conference for World Peace in March 1949, was active in organizing its meetings in Paris and Mexico City later that year, and attended its Moscow conference that August. Subsequently this group founded the Peace Information Center in 1950, and Du Bois was chosen to chair its Advisory Council. The center endorsed and promoted the Stockholm Peace Appeal, which called for banning atomic weapons, declaring their use a crime against humanity and demanding international controls. During this year Du Bois, who actively opposed the Korean War and Truman's foreign policy more generally, accepted the nomination of New York's Progressive party to run for the U.S. Senate on the platform "Peace and Civil Rights." Although he lost, his vote total ran considerably ahead of the other candidates on the Progressive ticket.

During the campaign, on 25 August 1950, the officers of the Peace Information Center were directed to register as "agents of a foreign principal" under terms of the Foreign Agents Registration Act of 1938. Their distribution of the Stockholm Appeal, alleged to be a Soviet-inspired manifesto, was the grounds for these charges, although the so-called foreign principal was never specifically identified in the subsequent indictment. Although the center disbanded on 12 October 1950, indictments against its officers, including Du Bois, were handed down on 9 February 1951. Du Bois's lawyers won a crucial postponement of the trial until the following 18 November 1951, by which time national and international opposition to the trial had been mobilized. Given the good fortune of a weak case and a fair judge, Du Bois and his colleagues were acquitted. Meanwhile, following the death of his wife Nina in July 1950, Du Bois married Shirley Graham, the daughter of an old friend, in 1951. Although the union bore no children, David, Shirley's son from an earlier marriage, took Du Bois's surname.

After the trial, Du Bois continued to be active in the American Peace Crusade and received the International Peace Prize from the World Council of Peace in 1953. With Shirley, a militant leftist activist in her own right, he was drawn more deeply into leftist and Communist party intellectual and social circles during the 1950s. He was an unrepentant supporter of and apologist for Josef Stalin, arguing that though Stalin's methods might have been cruel, they were necessitated by unprincipled and implacable opposition from the West and by U.S. efforts to undermine the regime.

He was also convinced that American news reports about Stalin and the Soviet bloc were unreliable at best and sheer propaganda or falsehoods at worst. His views do not appear to have been altered by the Soviets' own exposure and condemnation of Stalin after 1956.

From February 1952 to 1958 both W. E. B. and Shirley were denied passports to travel abroad. Thus he could not accept the many invitations to speak abroad or participate in international affairs, including most notably the 1957 independence celebrations of Ghana, the first of the newly independent African nations. When these restrictions were lifted in 1958, the couple traveled to the Soviet Union, Eastern Europe, and China. While in Moscow, Du Bois was warmly received by Nikita Khrushchev, whom he strongly urged to promote the study of African civilization in Russia, a proposal that eventually led to the establishment in 1962 of the Institute for the Study of Africa. While there, he also received the Lenin Peace Prize.

But continued Cold War tensions and their potential impact on his ability to travel and remain active in the future led Du Bois to look favorably on an invitation in May 1961 from Kwame Nkrumah and the Ghana Academy of Sciences to move to Ghana and undertake direction of the preparation of an "Encyclopedia Africana," a project much like one he had long contemplated. Indeed, his passport had been rescinded again after his return from China (travel to that country was barred at the time), and it was only restored after intense lobbying by the Ghanaian government. Before leaving the United States for Ghana on 7 October 1961, Du Bois officially joined the American Communist party, declaring in his 1 October 1961 letter of application that it and socialism were the only viable hope for black liberation and world peace. His desire to travel and work freely also prompted his decision two years later to become a citizen of Ghana.

In some sense these actions brought full circle some of the key issues that had animated Du Bois's life. Having organized his life's work around the comprehensive, empirically grounded study of what had once been called the Negro Problem, he ended his years laboring on an interdisciplinary and global publication that might have been the culmination and symbol of that ambition: to document the experience and historical contributions of African peoples in the world. Having witnessed the formal détente among European powers by which the African continent was colonized in the late nineteenth century, he lived to taste the fruits of the struggle to decolonize it in the late twentieth century and to become a citizen of the first new African nation. Having posed at the end of the nineteenth century the problem of black identity in the diaspora, he appeared to resolve the question in his own life by returning to Africa. Undoubtedly the most important modern African-American intellectual, Du Bois virtually invented modern African-American letters and gave form to the consciousness animating the work of practically all other modern African-American intellectuals to follow. He authored seventeen books, including five novels; founded and edited four different journals; and pursued two full-time careers: scholar and political organizer. But more than that, he reshaped how the experience of America and African America could be thought; he made us know both the complexity of who black Americans have been and are, and why it matters; and he left Americans—black and white—a legacy of intellectual tools, a language with which they might analyze their present and imagine a future.

From late 1961 to 1963 Du Bois lived a full life in Accra, the Ghanaian capital, working on the encyclopedia, taking long drives in the afternoon, and entertaining its political elite and the small colony of African Americans during the evenings at the comfortable home the government had provided him. Du Bois died the day before his American compatriots assembled for the March on Washington for Jobs and Freedom. It was a conjuncture more than rich with historical symbolism. It was the beginning of the end of the era of segregation that had shaped so much of Du Bois's life, but it was also the beginning of a new era when "the Negro Problem" could not be confined to separable terrains of the political, economic, domestic, or international, or to simple solutions such as integration of separatism, rights or consciousness. The life and work of Du Bois had anticipated and pointed toward this necessary synthesis of diverse terrains and solutions. On 29 August 1963 Du Bois was interred in a state funeral outside Castle Osu, formerly a holding pen for the slave cargoes bound for America.

• Du Bois's papers are at the University of Massachusetts, Amherst. His papers are also available on microfilm. His published writings are compiled in *The Complete Published Works of W. E. B. Du Bois*, and ed. Herbert Aptheker (1982). Useful secondary sources include David Levering Lewis, *W. E. B. Du Bois: Biography of a Race, 1868–1919* (1993); Gerald Horne, *Black and Red: W. E. B. Du Bois and the Afro-American Response to the Cold War, 1944–1963* (1986); Manning Marable, *W. E. B. Du Bois: Black Radical Democrat* (1986); and Arnold Rampersad, *The Art and Imagination of W. E. B. Du Bois* (1976). An obituary is in the *New York Times*, 28 Aug. 1963.

THOMAS C. HOLT

DU BOIS, William Ewing (15 Dec. 1810–14 July 1881), U.S. Mint official and numismatist, was born at Doylestown, Pennsylvania, the son of the Reverend Uriah Du Bois, a Presbyterian clergyman and school principal, and Martha Patterson, the daughter of Robert Patterson, the director of the U.S. Mint from 1806 to 1824. Du Bois studied at the Union Academy of Doylestown, where his father was principal, and later at John Gummere's school in Burlington, New Jersey. Becoming a lawyer in his early twenties, Du Bois published in April 1832 a lengthy transcript of a recent celebrated trial. Lucretia Chapman, who had allegedly murdered her husband, William Chapman, by putting arsenic in his chicken soup, had twelve days later married her lodger Lino Amalia Espos y Mina. Chapman had claimed that her husband had died of cholera; and the jury had found her not guilty.

Although Du Bois was admitted to the Pennsylvania bar in September 1832, a bronchial infection injured his voice, and he soon gave up his practice. In later life he often preferred writing out answers to questions, rather than engaging in oral conversation. Through his grandfather Robert Patterson, Du Bois became clerk in 1833 in the office of the director of the U.S. Mint in Philadelphia. In 1835 he was transferred to the Assay Department, where he worked under the department head, Assayer of the Mint Jacob Rees Eckfeldt. The next year Du Bois became assistant assayer, and in 1840 he married Eckfeldt's sister Susanna; they had two sons and a daughter. In September 1872 Du Bois succeeded Eckfeldt as chief assayer and remained head of the department until his death.

Run by several interrelated families, the U.S. Mint in Philadelphia was rife with nepotism and corruption, in which Du Bois became deeply involved. In 1834 when the State Department wished to present the Sultan of Muscat with the denominations of all U.S. coins, it was found that during 1804—the last year that silver dollars had been coined—silver dollars were dated 1803. By retroactively making dies and striking off 1804 dollars in 1834, the mint created a fabulous rarity. The mint then enhanced its coin collection by trading this rarity with collectors for unusual specimens. Mint officials sold other newly minted 1804 silver dollars with phony pedigrees, sometimes through Philadelphia auction houses and sometimes in Europe. But they did not stop there. They restruck coins in proof and created imaginary pattern coins that purported to show the evolution of a coin's design. Many of these phony specimens were accompanied by letters from Du Bois attesting to their genuineness. Also Du Bois and his Assay Department, whose job it was to uphold standards, were implicated in debasing gold for coinage. Franklin Peale, the mint's chief coiner, had refused to part the silver from gold when the aggregate amount of silver was less than five dollars, and in the late 1840s the U.S. Mint in New Orleans began using this unseparated, debased gold for coinage. Despite the seriousness of this corruption, no action was taken by either the courts or the Treasury Department.

In 1842 *A Manual of the Gold and Silver Coins of All Nations*, written by Du Bois, appeared with the name of Jacob Eckfeldt listed before his own. It was one of the first books to have illustrations produced by Joseph Saxton's medal-ruling machine (one of these illustrations was the first picture of an 1804 silver dollar). Essentially a cambist, or money changer's manual, the book is riddled with errors. Augustus B. Sage, a founder of the American Numismatic Society, later called it "the poor Mint Book of Eckfeldt and Du Bois, that received so dreadful a drubbing." Du Bois also produced, again listing Eckfeldt's name before his own, *New Varieties of Gold and Silver Coins* (1850), which went through several editions and remains a useful source for many California gold rush private issues. In 1869 Du Bois published two essays in the *Banker's Magazine and Statistical Register*: "Propositions for a Revised System of Weight" (3d ser., 4, no. 3 [Sept. 1869]: 161–76) and "A Restoration of the Silver Coinage." The latter essay proposed the reintroduction of silver (which had stopped circulating during the Civil War) by reducing the weight of silver coins. The mint struck patterns of these low-weight silver coins, calling them "standard silver," for demonstration purposes.

In 1838 Du Bois convinced the mint to begin a collection of coins, which is now part of the National Numismatic Collection in the Smithsonian Institution. Many coins were obtained from the bullion deposits brought to the mint; others were purchased with funds authorized by Congress (initially $1,000, followed by yearly $300 appropriations at a time when Greek and Roman coins could sometimes be purchased for sixty cents). Another advantage in building the mint's collection was that the mint could illegally create artificial rarities (patterns, proofs, 1804 silver dollars) to swap for coveted coins. In 1846 Du Bois published a catalog of the mint's collection, *Pledges of History*, and in 1860 an updated catalog—also basically the work of Du Bois—was published under the name of James Ross Snowden, then director of the mint. In addition to his numismatic publications, Du Bois published genealogical histories of the Du Bois and Patterson families.

Du Bois, who died in Philadelphia, was a member of the Numismatic and Antiquarian Society of Philadelphia and after 1844 of the American Philosophical Society. In 1868 he was elected an honorary member of the American Numismatic Society. He contributed to the *American Journal of Numismatics* and was a close friend of Joseph J. Mickley, the first major American coin collector. In his publications Du Bois comes across as an assiduous worker, who sometimes appears shockingly ignorant of both numismatics and the history of the U.S. Mint. Although he was a pioneer of numismatics in the United States, his participation in the corruption of the mint has left Du Bois with a reputation as a crook and a major falsifier of numismatic fact.

• A copy of his rare *Trial of Lucretia Chapman . . .* (1832) is at the New York Public Library. Howard L. Adelson, *The American Numismatic Society 1858–1958* (1958), contains little about Du Bois but does reproduce a photograph. Newer studies on the history of early U.S. coins that reappraise Du Bois's work are Eric P. Newman and Kenneth Bressett, *The Fantastic 1804 Dollar* (1962), which disentangles the 1804 dollar story and was the first work to reveal to a wider audience the depth of corruption at the mint; and Don Taxay, *The U.S. Mint and Coinage: An Illustrated History from 1776 to the Present* (1966), especially chap. 14, "A Workshop for Their Gain." Two encyclopedias by Walter Breen cover the early mint, including details of the various fraudulent coins: *Encyclopedia of U.S. and Colonial Proof Coins 1722–1989* (1989) and *Complete Encyclopedia of United States and Colonial Coins* (1988). Laudatory obituaries by two of Du Bois's relatives are, by his cousin Robert Patterson, "An Obituary Notice of William E. Du Bois," *Proceedings of the American Philosophical Society* 20 (Jan.–June 1882): 102–7; and, by his son Patterson Du Bois, in the *American Journal of Numismatics* 16 (Oct. 1881): 44–46.

JOHN M. KLEEBERG

DUBOS, René Jules (20 Feb. 1901–20 Feb. 1982), microbiologist and author, was born in Saint Brice, France, a farming community north of Paris, the son of Georges Andre Dubos, a butcher, and Adeline De Bloedt. Dubos's parents soon moved farther into the countryside to the tiny village of Henonville, where René attended a one-room school until the family moved to Paris in 1914. The family's economic uncertainties worsened when his father died after serving in World War I. During his childhood Dubos suffered from episodes of rheumatic fever, which led to the cardiac damage common before antibiotics. These severe illnesses, together with extremely poor eyesight, restricted his youthful activities and had a permanent impact on his life.

Despite academic success at the Collège Chaptal, from which he graduated in 1919, Dubos had no occupation in mind when he took a competitive examination and was admitted to the Institut National Agronomique the same year. After graduation his ability to review technical articles in several languages, rather than his scientific preparation, qualified Dubos for a position in Rome as associate editor of the *Journal of International Agricultural Intelligence*, a League of Nations publication. A chance reading of an article by Serge Winogradsky, a Russian soil microbiologist who had emigrated to Paris and the Pasteur Institute after the Russian Revolution, inspired Dubos's interest in bacteriology. Winogradsky took issue with the reigning scientific practice in which pure cultures of specific bacteria were studied under restricted laboratory conditions, favoring a technique that simulated the natural environment so that microorganisms were studied in competition with other bacteria and soil components.

Still unsettled in 1924, Dubos determined to indulge his desire to visit the United States. He accepted a proposal to study with Selman A. Waksman in his laboratory at the New Jersey Agricultural Station, and in 1927 he was awarded a doctorate in bacteriology from Rutgers University.

Dubos's mature scientific work reproduced the problems that initially attracted him to bacteriology and were central to his doctoral research. Although he began his training in bacteriology at a time when investigation of the chemical bases of biological activity was central to advanced research, this was not a strength of the graduate program at Rutgers. Waksman was a soil microbiologist and directed Dubos to a research project that employed ordinary soil to determine empirically which bacteria could decompose cellulose fibers. Waksman was neither skilled in nor committed to biochemical methods, but he schooled Dubos in the ecological contexts of biological processes, introducing him to technical approaches from which he learned the general rule that microorganisms are capable of decomposing anything produced in nature. Dubos extrapolated from this maxim the corollary that many microorganisms have specialized properties that play important roles in the emergence and suppression of other organisms. The obstacles he encountered in his first research apparently encouraged Dubos to formulate the exploratory strategies that shaped his later laboratory investigations, as well as the ecological principles he later identified with the interplay of human health and microorganisms, social conditions and the ecosystem.

After he received his doctorate Dubos proposed to the physician-immunologist Oswald T. Avery that he adapt the lessons of his work on bacterial decomposition of cellulose to Avery's apparently dead-end search for an agent that could decompose the polysaccharide capsule shielding the pneumococcus from the human body's defense mechanisms. Dubos proposed that since polysaccharides were ordinarily decomposed in soil, he would tailor a culture medium derived from soil that lacked the carbohydrate component of the pneumococcus polysaccharide capsule. He believed he could then identify a carbohydrate-dependent organism that would decompose the polysaccharide capsule. He did this work on a fellowship at the Rockefeller Institute for Medical Research, the Organization with which he was identified for the rest of his life. Once Dubos isolated the organism through this clever technique, he cultivated it in pure culture and finally extracted and purified the active element to test its efficacy in animals. No one was treated for pneumonia with this product, however, because of the concurrent development of sulfa drugs.

In 1934 Dubos married Marie-Louise Bonnet, who died in 1942 from tuberculosis. In 1946 he married Jean Porter, who also suffered from tuberculosis but survived. He had no children in either marriage.

Over the next twenty-five years Dubos helped make medical knowledge and practice more scientific. Insistently he invoked strategies derived from his work on pneumonia to develop investigations ranging from a successful test of kidney function to a disappointing search for a vulnerable component of the tubercle bacillus that would make tuberculosis susceptible to treatment. His professional and popular reputation increased when he extracted an antibacterial substance from the organism *Bacillus brevis* that appeared capable of destroying a number of species associated with common infections. Dubos soon discovered that this substance, tyrothricin, was actually composed of two distinct materials. One destroyed pathogenic organisms only in laboratory cultures and, more seriously, was toxic to the infected animal. The other, gramicidin, was bacteriostatic, that is, it inhibited the growth of some bacteria and was useful in the treatment of local, external infections. In 1941 Dubos's scientific accomplishments were acknowledged when he was made a full member of the Rockefeller Institute and elected to the National Academy of Sciences.

Dubos, now well established, turned his energy to assessing his discipline broadly. The French school-boy's reverence for Louis Pasteur ripened into a classic biography, *Louis Pasteur: Free Lance of Science* (1950; repr. 1986). Dubos's admiration for Oswald Avery's aesthetic trust in pure reason and powerful investigative insight molded Dubos's ambition without dampening his enthusiasm. Dubos wrote of the early 1940s as a time when reading in bacteriology and immunology, more than laboratory work, prepared him to challenge the narrow perspective he felt too often dominated science. He urged not that science be less technical but that it be more philosophic. Bigger questions should be addressed and more broadly significant conclusions offered. In the same spirit, he called attention to important gaps in scientific progress. For instance, he reviewed current knowledge of antibacterial agents in an article titled simply "Microbiology" and advised, "It may be profitable to keep in mind that susceptible bacterial species often give rise by 'training' to variants endowed with great resistance to these agents" (*Annual Review of Biochemistry* 11 [1942]: 673). He later reflected that he had willingly been "a sort of loud speaker," reorienting investigations of infection and immunity.

Although many mid-twentieth-century Americans were eager for news of science, few scientists were able to interest lay readers. Dubos had an opportunity to do so while holding a research professorship at the Harvard Medical School; he was invited to give a series of lectures in winter 1944 at Boston's Lowell Institute, a public forum that attracted civic leaders and intellectuals. Dubos reviewed current knowledge of bacterial metabolism and chemistry and explained how new investigations of bacterial variability and mutation could reconfigure scientific conceptions of pathology. The presence of laymen in the audience encouraged him to present technical material in historical context and philosophic terms. It was time, he said, to realize the limitations of public health and medical practices dependent on identification and destruction of the bacterial agent specific to each infection, and to learn how to take advantage of new knowledge about bacterial activity in general. He elaborated this message when the lectures were published as *The Bacterial Cell in Its Relation to Problems of Virulence, Immunity and Chemotherapy* (1945), a book intended for the scientific community.

In *The Bacterial Cell* Dubos identified assumptions that constrained exploration of the structural and biochemical variability of bacteria and highlighted opportunities for research at the cellular level. Without this shift to determining the mechanisms of bacterial life, Dubos believed epidemiology would remain "to a large extent a mere statistical statement of mysterious events; the pathology of infectious diseases a purely descriptive science; immunity and chemotherapy a set of empirical procedures." He adopted a tone unusual in scientific monographs, expressing his position as a generalist as well as his conviction that the "ultimate understanding of the natural history of infectious diseases, and the rational development of methods for their control, depend on this knowledge" (p. 17). Dubos's first book extended his influence both within and outside the scientific community. *The Bacterial Cell* long remained a source of wisdom for microbiologists, prefiguring the direction of a revolution in biomedical sciences that eventually came to distress Dubos himself.

Dubos returned to the Rockefeller Institute in 1944 to do research focusing on the tubercle bacillus. This allowed him, for the first time in his professional career, to make rewarding contacts with doctors and patients. Dubos and his wife Jean wrote a history of tuberculosis, *The White Plague: Tuberculosis, Man and Society* (1952; repr. 1986), which rejected the popular romantic association of artistic temperament with tuberculosis and explained the historic impact of poverty on the epidemiology of what they called this "social disease." While they celebrated the role of bacteriology in consolidating tubercular pathology, they challenged expectations that the contagion could be controlled through antibiotics if medicine neglected the conditions in which tuberculosis was bred. In this pioneering history of a disease intimately connected to both his personal and scientific experience, themes originating in Dubos's investigations of single organisms converged with an old project—the contrast between the abundant determinants affecting biological systems in nature and the limited variables in laboratory experiments.

Over the next thirty years Dubos produced a stream of publications elaborating this theme and addressing both popular fantasies of science and issues of importance to his colleagues. In *Mirage of Health: Utopias, Progress, and Biological Change* (1959) he contributed a balanced, popular volume to a series in which leading intellectuals addressed the social and moral shortcomings of scientific and technical knowledge. Dubos received the Pulitzer Prize for *So Human an Animal* (1968), an optimistic formulation of his ecological perspective that offered a modest correction to the contemporary sentimental naturalism that sometimes dismayed him.

Dubos was made professor emeritus at Rockefeller University in 1971 and gave up the editorship of the *Journal of Experimental Medicine*, which he had held since 1946. His intellectual resources and his social conscience remained powerful, as did his public influence. Much of his time and energy was spent meeting requests to participate in forums, particularly where environmental activists and intellectuals met. Nonetheless, Dubos reserved time for another book, *The Professor, the Institute, and DNA* (1976), a biography of Oswald Avery that pulled together the most important influences in Dubos's professional life. He died in New York City.

Dubos's early life and education in France were reflected in his command of historical narrative as well as in personal characteristics. He maintained connections with scientific colleagues in France, and his work on the polysaccharide capsule of pneumonia, defining the phenomenon known as adaptive enzyme forma-

tion, led three French scientists of the next generation to research that won them the Nobel Prize.

Nonetheless, Dubos became an American citizen, and his scientific career and reputation were significantly influenced by distinctively American circumstances. He arrived in America with meager resources and casual connections yet acquired credentials leading to a permanent appointment in the most distinguished biomedical research center in the United States. There, however, his laboratory and theoretical work was constrained by institutional barriers, and his willingness to reach over those boundaries was not always advantageous for him or compatible with the ethos of science. Dubos earned the respect of his professional contemporaries but was not recognized for his scientific achievements; he was pleased to regard his approach to scientific problems as unorthodox. Nonetheless, to many educated Americans Dubos represented scientific wisdom and authority. He was popularly perceived as a working scientist who spoke clearly about the development of scientific knowledge, a responsible spokesman for the scientific establishment who shared the public's anxieties without pandering to gloom. Dubos recognized these qualities in himself and accounted for them in his explications of science and scientific responsibility.

• Dubos's manuscripts are in the Rockefeller University Archives at the Rockefeller Archive Center, Pocantico, N.Y. The transcript of a series of interviews with Dubos conducted by Saul Benison in 1956, a unique source of information and insight on Dubos's life and scientific work, is at the Columbia University Oral Research Office, Butler Library, Columbia University. A segment of the transcript was published by Benison, "Rene Dubos and the Capsular Polysaccharide of Pneumococcus," *Bulletin of the History of Medicine* 50 (1976): 459–77. A useful biographical note, written for the posthumous award of the Medal of the New York Academy of Medicine, is James G. Hirsch, *Bulletin of the New York Academy of Medicine* 58 (1982): 590–97. The notice by Hirsch and Carol L. Moberg, National Academy of Sciences, *Biographical Memoirs* 58 (1989): 132–61, includes a list of most of Dubos's publications. Also of interest is Carol L. Moberg, "Rene Dubos: A Harbinger of Microbial Resistance to Antibiotics," *Microbial Drug Resistance*, 2 (1996): 287–97.

BARBARA GUTMANN ROSENKRANTZ

DUBOSE, William Porcher (11 Apr. 1836–18 Aug. 1918), theologian, was born near Winnsboro, South Carolina, the son of Theodore Marion DuBose and Jane Porcher, planters. DuBose grew up in the aristocracy of the antebellum South. After attending Mount Sion Institute in Winnsboro, he went to the Citadel (the Military College of South Carolina), from which he was graduated as the ranking cadet officer in 1855. DuBose next attended the University of Virginia, where he received an M.A. in 1859. Then he entered the Episcopal diocesan seminary, established a year earlier, in Camden, South Carolina, to prepare for ordination. With the outbreak of the Civil War in the spring of 1861, DuBose left the seminary for service in the Confederate Army. In April 1863 he married Anne Barnwell Peronneau, and in December of that year was ordained to the diaconate of the Episcopal church. During the remainder of the war DuBose served as a military chaplain.

After the surrender of the Confederacy in April 1865, DuBose returned home "to find it a picture of the most utter desolation" (*Turning Points*, p. 39). In the fall of 1865 DuBose began to minister at St. John's Church, Winnsboro, and St. Stephen's Chapel at Ridgeway, a mission. He was ordained to the priesthood while serving in Winnsboro (according to DuBose, in the fall of 1865; according to some records, on 9 Sept. 1866). From 1868 to 1871 DuBose served as rector of Trinity Church, Abbeville, South Carolina. In 1871 he moved with his family to the University of the South at Sewanee, Tennessee, where he served as chaplain (until 1883), professor of ethics and New Testament exegesis and, after 1894, as dean of the theology department until his retirement in 1908. He was known as "the Sage of Sewanee" to generations of students who found him a wise, approachable man as well as a challenging intellect and a major force in the life of the university. DuBose's first wife died in 1873, and in 1878 he married Louisa Yerger. He had two daughters and a son by his first wife.

DuBose achieved wide recognition as a Christian theologian through the books he published beginning in 1892. William Sanday, Lady Margaret Professor of Divinity at Oxford, wrote in 1907 that DuBose was "the wisest Anglican writer" on the philosophy of the Christian religion (Armentrout, *A DuBose Reader*, p. xxii, reprints the full quote and source). DuBose may be classified as a "liberal catholic modernist." The area of DuBose's specialty was the theology of salvation (soteriology). The focus of DuBose's soteriology was the process of God's incarnation in Christ, the Church, the sacraments, and Christian life. DuBose viewed both God's move humanward and humanity's move Godward in Christ, the Church, the sacraments, and Christian living as a process in which humans realize in their lives and world the reality of the divine life actualized in Christ. On the human side the process of salvation requires real growth and sacrifice to overcome sin, disobedience, and death in order to actualize reconciliation, redemption, and resurrection. DuBose strongly opposed any theology that lessened the reality of the salvation process, and he was critical of vicarious theories of atonement that viewed Christ working in place of humanity rather than in and through humanity. At a gathering for his seventy-fifth birthday he remarked, "God does not want to put away our sin by magic" (*Turning Points*, p. 89).

DuBose sought to base his theology on the facts of human nature as disclosed by philosophy and science. For example, he was an advocate of historical criticism and evolution, which had a central place in his soteriology. In this sense DuBose was a modernist. Yet he sought to interpret the facts of human nature within the Christian tradition. In this sense he was orthodox and catholic in the widest sense. In DuBose's theology the facts and the tradition are held together by the dynamic element of process—a Christian cosmic process that includes all of life in God. In this sense he was what would later be called a process theologian. DuBose's method of exposition reflected his dynamic, process perspective. Characteristically he examined the topics he considered in his soteriology on each of three levels (the spiritual, the moral, and the natural or physical). This three-level method of exposition conveys depth perspective, dynamism, and even contingency, but it lacks the precision and finality of a more linear, systematic exposition.

The major influences on DuBose's theology were Christian scriptures, Aristotle, the early church councils, the German Protestant theologian Isaak A. Dorner (1809–1884), the "Lux Mundi" studies by Anglican theologians at Oxford University (1889), and DuBose's personal spiritual odyssey. During the last years of his life DuBose was involved in the establishment of an international ecumenical journal, the *Constructive Quarterly,* and was working on a large manuscript, "From Aristotle to Christ," when he died at Sewanee. DuBose's influence as a theologian has been mainly in Anglican circles in England rather than in his native United States. Fifty-two years after his death DuBose was added to the liturgical calendar of the Episcopal church for commemoration on 18 August.

• A fire destroyed many of DuBose's papers shortly after his death. The surviving papers are in the DuBose Collection, University of the South Archives, Sewanee, Tenn. Two important manuscripts are DuBose's "Reminiscences," compiled by his son, William Haskell Dubose (Southern Historical Collection, University of North Carolina, Chapel Hill, 1946), and "From Aristotle to Christ," comp. Alberry Charles Cannon, Jr. (1963). DuBose's major publications are *The Soteriology of the New Testament* (1892), *The Ecumenical Councils* (1896), *The Gospel in the Gospels* (1906), *The Gospel According to St. Paul* (1907), *High Priesthood and Sacrifice: An Exposition of the Epistle to the Hebrews* (1908), *The Reason of Life* (1911), and *Turning Points in my Life* (1912). DuBose's articles in the *Constructive Quarterly* are reprinted in *Unity in the Faith,* ed. W. Norman Pittenger (1957). Recent studies of DuBose include Ralph E. Luker, *A Southern Tradition in Theology and Social Criticism 1830–1930* (1984); Dennis Dean Kezar, "Many Sons to the Father's Glory" (Ph.D. diss., New College, Oxford, 1974); Charles S. Foss, "In Current Coin: A Study of the Theology of William Porcher DuBose" (Ph.D. diss., Graduate Theological Union, 1989); *A DuBose Reader,* ed. Donald S. Armentrout (1984). Dr. Armentrout's anthology and Dr. Foss's dissertation contain extensive bibliographies. For an attempt to reconstruct DuBose's personal spiritual odyssey, see *William Porcher DuBose: Selected Writings,* ed. Jon Alexander (1988), pp. 13–27.

JON ALEXANDER

DUBOURG, Louis William Valentine (probably 10 Jan. 1766–12 Dec. 1833), archbishop and educator, was born Louis-Guillaume-Valentin DuBourg at Cap Français, Santo Domingo, the son of Marguerite Armand de Vogluzan and Pierre DuBourg, chevalier de la Loubère et Saint-Christaud, Sieur de Rochemont. Pierre was a licensed sea captain who prospered from wholesale trade and plantations. From the age of two, William was raised by his maternal grandparents in Bordeaux, where he excelled at the local Royal College of Guyenne. He then studied in Paris at the Seminary of Saint Sulpice and the Sorbonne. On 20 March 1790, less than a year after the fall of the Bastille, DuBourg was ordained a Catholic priest by Antoine-Eléonore-Léon Leclerc de Juigné, archbishop of Paris, and he was urged to direct his talents toward education.

DuBourg was absent on 15 August 1792, when a mob massacred all but one instructor in the school he headed at Issy in the suburbs of Paris. A cleric from an aristocratic family, he was doubly at risk in revolutionary France. He went to Orense, Spain, mastered Spanish, but was dissatisfied with the laws restricting his teaching and religious ministry. He arrived in Baltimore, Maryland, on 14 December 1794 and joined the Society of Saint Sulpice on 9 March 1795. He began classes for West Indian youths and ministered to emigrants from the revolutions in France and Santo Domingo who were doubling the Catholic population of the United States. A commanding presence and a polished orator, DuBourg moved easily on all levels of society and became a popular speaker in English, French, and Spanish. In September 1795, nine months after DuBourg's arrival in Maryland, Bishop John Carroll named him third president of Georgetown College. DuBourg believed that schools should be cosmopolitan, open to all, and supported by patrons; therefore, he tried to recruit benefactors and an international student body. He dined with George Washington's family at "Mount Vernon." DuBourg left Georgetown at Christmas in 1798.

After heading a short-lived college in Havana, Cuba, DuBourg founded St. Mary's College in Baltimore in 1803 and served as president until 1812. He obtained the school's university charter in 1805. With the remains of his patrimony, he helped the Reverend John Dubois found Mount St. Mary's College at Emmitsburg, Maryland, in 1808. DuBourg invited Elizabeth Bayley Seton to Baltimore to open a primary school, considered the origin of the parochial school system in the United States. In 1809 he advised her on the establishment of St. Joseph's College at Emmitsburg and was her mentor as she founded an American branch of the Sisters of Charity.

Built in 1806–1808, the chapel of St. Mary's Seminary and College in Baltimore, called "Mr. DuBourg's chapel" by Seton, was the first important Gothic revival religious structure in the United States and was designated a national historic landmark in 1971. This was the first architectural work of Maximilian Godefroy, hired by DuBourg to teach design at the college, and it was frequently imitated. Although he was not at once enthusiastic, DuBourg expedited the building's completion by raising funds; consulting with Benjamin H. Latrobe, an architect of the U.S. Capitol; and borrowing Latrobe's Italian casters, plasterers, and artists to finish the interior.

In 1803 the Louisiana Purchase had more than doubled the size of the United States, and in 1812 DuBourg became apostolic administrator of the diocese of New Orleans, or the "Province of Louisiana." This largest ecclesiastical jurisdiction in the Western world ran from the Gulf of Mexico through the Illinois Territory and embraced the Floridas. During the 1814 battle of New Orleans, DuBourg urged the divided city to support the American cause, and on 23 January 1815 the victory celebration included, at General Andrew Jackson's request, a solemn Te Deum. Jackson was greeted, eulogized, and led into New Orleans's St. Louis Cathedral by DuBourg.

Nominated by Pope Pius VII for the bishopric of Louisiana and the Floridas, DuBourg was elevated to the episcopacy in Rome on 24 September 1815. He remained in Europe for two years, seeking personnel and support. In St. Louis, Missouri, he began construction of the first cathedral in that city. Philippine Duchesne and her companions arrived from France, the first members of the Society of the Sacred Heart in the United States. Their school for girls at St. Charles, Missouri, was the first free school west of the Mississippi. DuBourg's academy for young men, opened in 1820, grew into St. Louis University. In 1823 Secretary of War John C. Calhoun encouraged him to recruit Flemish Jesuits from Maryland and facilitated government aid for opening a school for Native American boys. Peter J. Verhaegen became the first president of St. Louis University. Pierre Jean DeSmet, the university's first treasurer, became a popular missionary among Native Americans of the Northwest. DuBourg resigned his bishopric on 26 June 1826, the year the Louisiana jurisdiction was split between New Orleans and the new diocese of St. Louis.

Returning to France on 3 July 1826, his rights and rank restored, DuBourg was named bishop of Montauban on 2 October 1826. He swore the oath of loyalty before King Charles X on 13 November. DuBourg improved diocesan education and increased scholarships, and he was installed as archbishop of Besançon on 10 October 1833. He died in Besançon two months later.

DuBourg's few publications consist of advertisements for and pamphlets answering objections to his schools, liturgical and theological instructions, and such historical records as *Notice sur l'état de la mission de la Louisiane* (1822). His correspondence is informative. A suggestion that Baltimore's Betsy Patterson, an imperial princess as wife of Jerome Bonaparte, "might perhaps think it suitable to her new dignity to pay for the honor of protecting the Sisters of Charity," shows his disdain for Napoleonic titles and support for a noblesse oblige that included patronage.

During DuBourg's thirty-one years in the United States, critics found him a Don Quixote, eager for great deeds but inattentive to difficulties and careless of debts. Some two centuries later, the results of his efforts are ample proof that this enterprising founding father of American Catholic education made shrewd investments with sparse resources.

• The principal archives are those of the dioceses in which DuBourg served and of the Baltimore Sulpicians. Annabelle M. Melville, *Louis William DuBourg: Bishop of Louisiana and the Floridas, Bishop of Montauban, and Archbishop of Besançon*

(2 vols., 1986), contains a comprehensive bibliography. See also William B. Faherty, "The Personality and Influence of Louis William Valentine DuBourg: Bishop of 'Louisiana and the Floridas' (1776–1833)," in *Frenchmen and French Ways in the Mississippi Valley*, ed. John Francis McDermott (1969).

FRANCIS F. BURCH

DUBUCLET, Antoine (1810–18 Dec. 1887), politician, was born in Iberville Parish, Louisiana, the son of Antoine Dubuclet, Sr., a plantation owner, and Rosie Belly. The Dubuclets were members of the *gens de couleur libre*, the class of free blacks permitted certain social and legal rights not typically accorded blacks in the antebellum South. Dubuclet's father owned slaves and a share of a plantation. After his father's death in 1828, Dubuclet remained on the plantation, while his mother and siblings moved to New Orleans. He learned the family business and prospered, owning more than one hundred slaves and an estate valued at $94,700 in 1864. His substantial holdings made Dubuclet the wealthiest of Louisiana's free blacks, and he was more successful than many white planters.

Dubuclet's fortunes suffered during the Civil War, a time of economic chaos in Louisiana. The demise of slavery meant the end of ready and inexpensive labor, a blow to the plantation economy. The sugar industry, a major source of Dubuclet's wealth, was nearly ruined. Production on his plantation fell dramatically and never returned to prewar levels.

The war also brought social change. The state constitutional convention of 1864 rejected universal male suffrage and ignored President Abraham Lincoln's request that wealthy free blacks be allowed to vote. Black opposition to the new constitution coalesced immediately, and blacks and whites formed numerous political organizations dedicated to black civil rights. In late 1865 Dubuclet served on the central committee of the Republican party, the party that supported many of the objectives of the black organizations. Dissatisfaction at the national level with southern postwar politics resulted in the Reconstruction Act of 1867, which allowed black males at least twenty-one years old to vote. Approximately half the delegates to the state constitutional convention of 1867–1868 were black. The convention produced a constitution that ended the repressive Black Codes and included a bill of rights, thus marking a new era in Louisiana politics.

Dubuclet did not serve as a delegate to the constitutional convention, but his rise to political prominence indicates that he supported the new constitution and held the confidence of blacks and moderate whites. He received the Republican party's nomination for state treasurer on 14 January 1868, but he opposed an attempt to nominate a black governor, siding with moderates, who argued that such a move would precipitate violence. The final party ticket included carpetbagger Henry C. Warmoth for governor and former slave Oscar J. Dunn for lieutenant governor. Black support for the Republican ticket ensured electoral victory, and in the elections held on 16–17 April 1868, Louisiana voters ratified the new constitution and elected the Re-

publicans to office. On 29 June 1868 Dubuclet took office as state treasurer.

As state treasurer, Dubuclet managed a financial system near collapse. Wartime devastation, property confiscation, title disputes, and the transition from slavery to free labor had ruined Louisiana's economy. Taxes during the wartime years were in arrears, and assessed taxable property value had declined by nearly 50 percent, from $470 million to $250 million. Instead of cutting spending in response to the loss of revenue, the state government increased expenditures, and Louisiana was bankrupt. Dubuclet recommended reduced appropriations and reform of the state's methods of revenue collection, but the legislature ignored him. One practice he objected to was that of accepting warrants for tax payments. Because the state lacked cash, it issued warrants, which served as pay for state legislators. In order to give the warrants value, the state took them in lieu of cash for payment of taxes. Warrants fluctuated in value, were often altered, and complicated bookkeeping. The legislature again ignored his suggestions, and Dubuclet turned his attention from reform to management of the treasury.

In addition to economic decline and legislative irresponsibility, corruption assailed Louisiana's financial health, reaching the highest public offices and draining the state of badly needed funds. Dubuclet resisted the temptation to enrich himself and opposed corruption. In 1869 a state commission consisting of Dubuclet, Governor Warmoth, and two state legislators was formed to sell bonds for levee repair. When the other commission members decided to retain a portion of the bond sales for themselves, Dubuclet protested. In Dubuclet's absence the other commission members voted to pocket some of the funds despite the treasurer's objections. Dubuclet learned of their deception and initiated court proceedings, which earned him the praise of the conservative press in New Orleans.

Dubuclet was reelected to a four-year term of office in 1870 by the considerable margin of 25,000 votes. The political and social turmoil of Reconstruction worsened during the new decade, and despite Dubuclet's capable management, the state's finances remained a shambles. He supported an 1874 fiscal reform measure offered by house member Theophile T. Allain. The measure passed the legislature, but the final appropriations bill for that year rendered Allain's efforts futile. Angered by the failure of reform, several prominent black politicians, including Dubuclet, issued an "Address of the Colored Men to the People of Louisiana," which was distributed as an extra in the *Louisianian* on 8 October 1874 and reprinted in other newspapers. The statement denounced the charge that black political participation was ruining the state and argued that black politicians were being intentionally excluded from Republican party operations. Although Dubuclet's annual reports as treasurer remained silent on reform issues, his signature on the document illustrates his support for the reform movement and his concern over the role of blacks in Louisiana government.

Dubuclet's ability earned him respect from unusual quarters. In September 1874 militant whites attempted to gain control of the state government, occupying the state house and placing their own men in state offices. However, they allowed Dubuclet to continue his work unmolested and apologized to him when he was mistakenly refused entry into his office. The coup failed after five days. Later that year voters again returned Dubuclet to office, but this term was marred by political conflict. In 1876 a house committee controlled by Democrats accused him of stealing $200,000. The charge was politically motivated, and Dubuclet was exonerated. An investigation of the treasurer's office in 1878 revealed only minor technical irregularities, and both Democrats and Republicans agreed that Dubuclet had faithfully discharged his duties. He did not seek reelection in 1878.

Dubuclet married twice. During the 1830s he married Claire Pollard; they had nine children before she died in 1852. In the 1860s he married Mary Ann Walsh; they had three children. After retiring from office in 1879, Dubuclet returned to Iberville Parish, where he lived with Felicite Roy. He sold his plantation to his son Francois and lived on a small homestead. Financial difficulties reduced the value of his property to $1,130. He died in Iberville Parish.

Some historical assessments have charged that African-American leadership during Reconstruction was marked by ineptitude and corruption. Revisionist historians have cited Dubuclet and similar politicians as proof that black leaders were often men of ability and integrity who faced difficult problems with skill and dedication.

• No collection of Dubuclet's personal papers exists. The most extensive account of his career is Charles Vincent, "Aspects of the Family and Public Life of Antoine Dubuclet: Louisiana's Black State Treasurer," *Journal of Negro History* 66 (Spring 1981): 26–36. Vincent discusses the larger issue of African-American politicians in his *Black Legislators in Louisiana during Reconstruction* (1976). Eric Foner offers a brief profile of Dubuclet in *Freedom's Lawmakers: A Directory of Black Officeholders during Reconstruction* (1993). Both H. E. Sterkx, *The Free Negro in Antebellum Louisiana* (1972), and Joe Gray Taylor, *Louisiana Reconstructed, 1863–1877* (1974), contain information concerning Dubuclet. An obituary is in the *New Orleans Daily Picayune*, 21 Dec. 1887.

THOMAS CLARKIN